1997-1998
FILM COMPOSERS GUIDE

Fourth Edition

COMPILED AND EDITED BY VINCENT JACQUET-FRANCILLON

lone eagle

FILM COMPOSERS GUIDE
Fourth Edition

LONE EAGLE PUBLISHING COMPANY, LLC™
2337 Roscomare Road, Suite Nine
Los Angeles, CA 90077-1851
310-471-8066 • FAX 310-471-4969
http://www.loneeagle.com

Printed in the United States of America

First Edition by Steven C. Smith
Cover design by Heidi Frieder
Logo Art by Liz and Frank Ridenour

This book was entirely typeset using a Power Macintosh 7500,
New Gen Turbo Printer, Microsoft Word and Adobe Pagemaker.

Printed by McNaughton & Gunn, Saline, Michigan 48176
Printed entirely on recycled paper.

ISBN: 0-943728-93-2
ISSN 1055 081X

LONE EAGLE PUBLISHING STAFF

JOAN V. SINGLETON, RALPH S. SINGLETON
Publishers

JEFF BLACK
Vice President, Sales & Marketing

BLAKE BUSBY
Production Manager

MERCEDES VAN HUIZUM
Accounting Manager

JEFFREY WINGELL
Customer Service

PAULA DISANTE
Researcher

LUIS BACALOV

JOHN BARRY

ELMER BERNSTEIN

KATE BUSH

STEWART COPELAND

DANNY ELFMAN

NICK GLENNIE-SMITH

THE KRAFT-BENJAMIN AGENCY

JERRY GOLDSMITH

WOJCIECH KILAR

THE ZOMBA GROUP OF COMPANIES in concert with SEGUE MUSIC is proud to announce a fresh, new approach to film and television composer management – ZOMBA SCREEN MUSIC.

Imagine a company dedicated to real career development where the culture provides a nurturing environment for composers and those who hire them. For quality and service, please contact:
DAVID MAY, Film Division
STEVEN CAGAN, Television Division
TRY US ON!

zomba screen music
A COMPOSER MANAGEMENT COMPANY
9000 SUNSET BLVD., STE. 300, W. HOLLYWOOD, CA 90069
TEL: (310) 246-0777 FAX: (310) 246-9231

LONDON OFFICE: 011-44-181-459-8899

Dreamhire
Equipment Rental

Battery Studios

Zomba Screen Music

Zomba Music Clearance

FirstCom Music

Segue Music

Zomba Music Services

CONTENTS

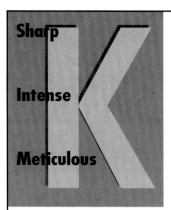

LETTER FROM THE PUBLISHER

Vincent has done an exceptional job of updating this year's edition. You will find many transactional credits in here—films and composers that were set at press time. As Vincent states in his introduction, some of these may change. But we feel this is the only way we can bring you the most current information without using a crystal ball.

For those of you who have not checked out our new website, *Eagle i* (http://www.loneeagle.com/eaglei/index.html) please do so. You will find not only all of Vincent's information from Film Composers, but also the information from all our other directories together in one large relational database that is "mouse-click" easy to use. We update that continuously, so when new job assignments come along, you will see them in *Eagle i* first. It's free to try for the first month. We expect to have audio clips in the near future so you can not only see the credits of your favorite composer, but also hear some of the score as well.

Keep listening to the movies, and let us know what you think of this edition and what you want in future editions.

Joan Singleton
Publisher

INTRODUCTION

In 1996's Third Edition of the *Film Composers Guide* we promised to regularly update our guide, *your* guide. A year later, thanks to the efforts of everyone at Lone Eagle Publishing, you now have in your hands the Fourth Edition of the *Film Composers Guide*.

For this edition, we updated, corrected and added credits, contact information, releasing information—once again, thanks to all those who responded by telling me about a film that was missed in the Third Edition. Some of the most recent credits are *anticipated* credits submitted by the composers or their agents. This helps us to be as up-to-date as possible. Be aware, however, that last minute changes are always possible. For instance: Alan Silvestri did not end up scoring *Mission: Impossible*, Danny Elfman did.

Thanks are due to the many composers and agencies that cooperated in the preparation of this book: Michael McGehee at BMI; Nancy Knutsen and Kim Dankner at ASCAP; all the film music agencies who always responded with diligence and friendliness and especially to all the composers, their spouses and staff who took time to either submit their credits and or submit themselves to lengthy interrogations over the phone. I would like to address a special thanks to Jon Burlingame, Hiro Wada, Yann Merluzeau, Edouard Dubois, Kyle Rennick, Nicolas Saada, Bob Townson and to Yancy. Recognition should also be given to the great people at Lone Eagle Publishing, especially Joan Singleton, Bethann Wetzel, Jordan Posell, Blake Busby and Jeff Black for their help and understanding throughout the project.

Let us know what you think of this edition of the *Film Composers Guide*. We are always striving to improve our publication and love to hear from you because, after all is said and done, we did it for you. I hope it will provide you with the information you want for enjoyment or work.

Vincent J. Francillon

KEY TO ABBREVIATIONS

(AF)　　= ANIMATED FEATURE denotes an animated theatrical feature

(ATF)　 = ANIMATED TELEFEATURE denotes an animated feature broadcast on television

(CMS)　= CABLE MINISERIES denotes a miniseries first shown on cable

(CTD)　 = CABLE DOCUMENTARY denotes a documentary made for cable

(CTF)　 = CABLE TELEFEATURE denotes a film made for cable television

(D)　　 = DOCUMENTARY denotes older documentaries which are included for historical reasons

(FD)　　= FEATURE DOCUMENTARY denotes a documentary first shown in a

(MS)　　= MINISERIES denotes a film more than four hours in length made for television and broadcast sequentially

(TD)　　= TELEVISION DOCUMENTARY denotes a documentary made for television

(TF)　　= TELEFEATURE denotes a film made for broadcast television theatrical run

All other titles are features made for theatrical release.

Note: All programs listed are at least one hour in length.

KEY TO SYMBOLS

*　　after a name in the main listing denotes a member of the Society of Composers and Lyricists

†　　after a composer's name in the index denotes deceased

★　　after a film title denotes an Academy Award Nomination

★★　after a film title denotes an Academy Award Winner

☆　　after a television film title denotes an Emmy Award Nominee

☆☆　after a television film title denotes an Emmy Award Winner

HOW TO USE THIS BOOK

Film Composers Guide provides an easy-to-use, accurate and up-to-date reference to film composers working in this country. Although designed mainly to be used by film production companies looking to hire composers, *Film Composers* has also found a strong audience among lovers of film music as well as researchers.

Among its features are:

• An alphabetical listing of composers by name with a chronological listing of their credits showing releasing company and date of release.

• Contact information, when available, as well as any union, guild and/or society information.

• A cross-referenced index of film titles in alphabetical order followed by the name of the composer. This will be especially helpful when you remember liking the music for a film, but do not remember who wrote it.

• Academy and Emmy Award winners and nominees among the composers listed in the book.

• A section on "Notable Composers of the Past," showing the careers of selected composers since the beginnings of sound.

Some explanation about the listings:

COMPOSERS: We strive to list every composer working in this country whose work meets our length requirements (see Film Criteria). If a composer is not listed, it may be because he or she has worked exclusively on television episodes or other programs that did not meet our length requirements. If this is not the case, please let us know so that we may include that composer in Eagle i, our online database, as well as in the next edition.

Because of the length requirement, large parts of some composer's careers who working consistently on television series will be ignored in spite of their quality. Inclusion in the "Notable Composers of the Past" section is based on the importance of the composer and the availability of reliable information on their careers (believe it or not, some of it is all but impossible to find).

As with the Second Edition, we have attempted to provide accurate, concise listings for the work of film composers—the individuals most responsible for what is commonly (if not always accurately) called "background music" or "dramatic underscore." For instance, in the case of musicals, we only list the composer of the background score. This would explain why Alan Menken's contribution to *Newsies* is ignored in favor of J. A. C. Redford's score. And although you may leave *Casablanca* humming "As Time Goes By," it was Max Steiner who wrote the film's original score, which incorporated the 1931 tune. Steiner receives sole credit here.

Generally we follow a film's official credits in the listings. There are a few exceptions. For example, John Barry did not officially receive credit for his contribution to the first Bond film, *Dr. No.* However considering his long association with the James Bond series, it seemed unfair to ignore this contribution. Similarly, we have avoided listing film scores that were never used, again with a few important exceptions that always noted (e.g., Bernard Herrmann's discarded score for *Torn Curtain*—the film that ended that composer's long relationship with Hitchcock). As for additional scores—those scores that are generally added after another cut of the movie has been made and are becoming more and more common—all credited additional scores are listed as well as some uncredited ones which could be legitimately documented.

Winners and nominees of Academy and Emmy awards are noted in the main listing sections ("Listing" as well as "Notable Composers"), as well as in the "Index of Film Titles." There is also a special section listing Academy Awards winners and nominees by year from 1955 and Emmy Awards winners and nominees since 1991.

In addition to their scoring duties, composers have occasionally appeared *onscreen* as well—not just typecast as intense conductors (Max Steiner in *The Half-Naked Truth*, Bernard Herrmann in *The Man Who Knew Too Much*) but also in more challenging roles (Jerry Goldsmith as the angry yoghurt shop customer in *Gremlins II*). As tacit encouragement of this nontraditional casting, we will note these appearances wherever possible.

FILM CRITERIA: Film credits listed through 1997, with anticipated major releases of 1998. We continue to discover additional credits by composers working in foreign countries—usually in the wee hours—on cable channels or local television stations. We add those credits as we discover them and welcome any information on those we might have missed.

Features: A running time of 60 minutes or longer (with some exceptions for older films.)

Telefeatures: On commercial television, an air time of 90 minutes to 4-1/2 hours. (Without commercials, a 90 minute television program runs approximately 72 minutes—the length of a short feature—and a

4-1/2 hour "miniseries" is about 3 hours and 45 minutes, the length of such long features as *Gone With The Wind* and *Heaven's Gate*.) We have included a few two-hour episodes from television series. These shows were shown as a two-hour entity and very often find a second life as cable, video or late-night movies, making their inclusion worthwhile.

Television Miniseries: On commercial television, an air time of 4-1/2 hours or longer; 4 hours or more on noncommercial television.

Documentaries: Whether for television or theatres, with a running time of 60 minutes or longer.

TITLES: American release titles are used with alternate titles following in italics. In case of films from English-speaking foreign countries, a title in italics usually represents the original title in that country if different from its American release title or, if the film has only been released under its original title, the English translation is listed as provided by the trade magazines. Alternate titles are also quite common especially for lesser known titles on the video market and are listed when available. Films that were not distributed in the United States—commonly found for foreign composers who worked only part time in the U.S.—are listed under their original title.

DISTRIBUTORS AND PRODUCTION COMPANIES: Original American distributors of feature films are listed. Telefeatures and miniseries are identified with the names of their production companies, usually several. Foreign films not distributed in the United States only mention the country of origin, unless the distributor or production company is a recognizable major name, such as the BBC.

YEAR OF RELEASE: It is the year of first release in the United States. In the case of foreign films, the original year of release is provided wherever possible. The reader may find other years listed in other directories as sometimes films are completed in a given year and wait for a few years for distribution. (*The Dark Half* scored by Christopher Young comes to mind among recent films.)

★ ★ ★

FILM COMPOSERS

INDEX OF FILM COMPOSERS

Note: This index is a *name-only* reference when searching for a Film Composer's name
from the Listing Section of this directory. Credits follow in the Listing Section.
★ = denotes Society of Composers and Lyricists

A

Michael Abene
Absolute Music
AC/DC
Lara Ackerlund
Jack Ackerman
John Adams
Tracy Adams
Barry Adamson
Stuart Adamson
John Addison
Larry Adler
Mark Adler*
Africa
Dian Agp
Alfonso Agullo
Wayne Alabardo
Bob Alcivar*
Scott Aldrich
Edesio Alejandro
Lorin Alexander*
Van Alexander
Eric Allaman*
Cameron Allan
David Allen
Richard Allen
Woody Allen
    (Allen Stewart Konigsberg)
Byron Allred
Allan Alper
Ron Altbach
Gerald Alters
John Altman
Ed Alton*
Minette Alton
Joey Altruda
Dave Alvin
David Amram
Anastasia
Benny Andersen
Laurie Anderson
Pete Anderson
Dwight Andrews
Gerard Anfosso
Scott Angley
Paul Antonelli
Philip Appleby
Ana Araiz
Neil Argo
Sebastian Argol
Eddie Arkin*
Martin Armiger
Michael Armstrong
David Arnold
Malcolm Arnold
Peter Arnow
Bruce Arnston
Leon Aronson
Jorge Arriagada
Eduard Artemyev
Bent Aserud
Gela Sawall Ashcroft
Jay Asher

Gil Askey
Edwin Astley
Paul Aston
Chet Atkins
Murray Attaway
Mark Austin
John Author
Pepe Avila
David A. Axelrod
Heidi Aydt
Roy Ayers
Pedro Aznar

B

Fryderyck Babinski
Bruce Babcock*
Luis Bacalov
Burt Bacharach
Pierre Bachelet
Michael Bacon
Angelo Badalamenti
Wally Badarou
Don Bagley
Louis Bague
Tom Bahler
Rachid Bahri
Pete Baikie
Achmad Bakaev
Buddy Baker*
    (Norman Dale Baker)
Fred Baker
Michael Conway Baker*
Alexander Balanescu
Richard H. Band*
Fran Banish
Anthony Banks
Brian Banks
Don Banks
Didier Barbelivien
Billy Barber
John Barber
Lesley Barber
Stephen Barber
Joseph Barbera
Gato Barbieri
James H. Barden
Nik Bariluk
Khaled Barkat
John Barnes
Charles P. Barnett*
Marc Barreca
George Barrie
Bebe Barron
De Wayne Barron
Louis Barron
Daemion Barry
Jeff Barry
John Barry
Lionel Bart
Alec Bartch
Steve Bartek
Dee Barton

Richard Baskin
Boris Basourov
Ulrich Bassenge
Kevin Bassinson*
George Bassman
Mike Batt
Franco Battiato
Arlene Battishil
Irwin Bazelon
Nigel Beaham-Powell
David Beal
Jeff Beal
John Beal*
Mike Bearden
Christopher Beck
Jeff Beck
Joe Beck
Frank W. Becker
Michael Becker
Danny Beckerman
Stephen Bedell
Michael Been
Daniel Bell
David Bell*
Thom Bell
Wayne Bell
Andrew Belling
Richard Bellis*
Roger Bellon*
Marco Beltrami
Vassal Benford
Michael Benghiat
James Bennett
Richard Rodney Bennett
David Benoit
Jean-Marie Benoit
Ray Benson
Robby Benson
    (Robby Segal)
Erik Berchot
Tony Berg
David Bergeaud
Cary Berger
Jake Berger
Tal Bergman
John D. Berkman
Berlin Game
James Bernard
Charles Bernstein*
Elmer Bernstein*
Peter Bernstein
Steve Bernstein*
Sanh Berti
Peter Best
Harry Betts
Amin Bhatia*
Vanraj Bhatia
Nick Bicat
Arnie Bieber
Rene Marc Bini
Nathan Birnbaum
Johnny Bishop
Casare Bixio
Kjetil Bjerkerstrand
Karen Black

Stanley Black
Wendy Blackstone
Ruben Blades
Howard Blake
Ronnie Blakley
Terence Blanchard
Larry Blank*
George Blondheim
Lisa Bloom
Kath Bloom
William Bloom
The Blue Hawaiians
Chris Boardman*
Jerry Bock
Roland Bocquet
The Bo Deans
Michael Boddicker*
Todd Boekelheide
Ed Bogas
Geir Bohren
William Bolcom
Martin D. Bolin
Bill Boll
Paul Boll
Claude Bolling
Roger Bolton
Bernardo Bonazzi
Leland Bond
Michael Bondert
Ray Bonneville
Al Borgoni
John Boshoff
Rick Boston
Simon Boswell
Perry Botkin
Chris Botti
Lili Boulanger
Jean Bouchety
Hubert Bougis
Jean-Paul Bourelly
Roger Bourland
Dennis Bovell
Richard Bowden
Richard Bowers*
Paul Bowles
Euel Box*
Michael Boyd
Robert Boyle
Owen Bradley
Ernst Bradner
Billy Bragg
Ken Brahmstedt
Steven Bramson*
Christian Brandauer
Carl Brandt
Fred Brathwaite
Creed Bratton
David Bravo
Goran Bregovic
Ferdi Brengen
Danny Brenner
Torsten Breuer
Alan Brewer
Peter Brewis
Leslie Briccuse

F
I
L
M

C
O
M
P
O
S
E
R
S

Tony Britten
Richard Bronskill*
Michael Brook
Joseph Brooks
Malcolm Brooks
Philip Brophy
Bruce Broughton*
Charles Brown
Earl Brown, Jr.
Greg Brown
Larry Brown*
Larry H. Brown
Tom Bruner
Robert F. Brunner
George Bruns
Stephen Bruton
Joanne Bruzdowicz
Benedikt Brydern*
Chico Buarque
Alexander Bubenheim
Bill Buckingham
Paul Buckmaster
Jimmy Buffett
Peter Buffett
Velton Ray Bunch*
Eric Burdon
Geoffrey Burgon
Chris Burke
Ralph Burns
George Burt
Carter Burwell*
Gerald Busby
Cobb Bussinger
Artie Butler
Buzzov-En
Billy Byers
Donald Byrd
Joseph Byrd
David Byrne

C

John Cacavas*
John Cafferty
Steven Cagan
Robert Cairns
Piro Cako
Jorge Calandrelli
Michael Calasso
John Cale
Charles Calello
Christopher Cameron
John Cameron
Michel Camilo
David Campbell
David Richard Campbell
James Campbell
Tom Canning
Michael Cannon
Larry Cansler
John Capek
Tom Capek
Claudio Cappani
Al Capps
Michael Carlos
Walter Carlos
   (See Wendy Carlos)
Wendy Carlos
   (Walter Carlos)
Larry Carlton
Ralph Carmichael
Danny Caron
John Carpenter
Fiorenzo Carpi
David Carradine

Nicholas Carras
Joseph Carrier
Berthold Carriere
Baikida Carroll
Rob Carroll
Benny Carter
Bill Carter
Ron Carter
Tristram Cary
Johnny Cash
Jose Luis Castineira de Dios
Dory Caynni
Matthieu Chabrol
Jean-Noel Chaleat
Frankie Chan
Carlo Jean Paul Chanez
Gary Chang*
Philippe Chany
John Charles*
Tom Chase*
Philippe Chatiliez
Jay Chattaway*
Vladimir Chekassine
Johnny Chen
Paul Chihara
Billy Childs
David Chilton
Jack Chipman
Elliot Chiprut
Edmundk.Choi
Kyung-Suk Chong
Chris Christian
David Chu
Danny Chung
Suzanne E. Ciani
Cinemascore
Stelvio Cipriani
Chuck Cirino*
Clannad
Eric Clapton
Stanley Clarke
Alf Clausen*
Paul Clemente
Richard Clements
Jimmy Cliff
John Clifford
Matt Clifford
George Clinton
George S. Clinton
Elia Cmiral*
Coati Mundi
Bob Cobert
Ted Cochran
John Coda
David Allan Coe
Harvey R. Cohen*
Jeff Cohen
Stephen Cohn*
John Colby
Ray Colcord*
Judd Cole
Lionel Cole
Cy Coleman
Graeme Coleman
Jim Coleman
Lisa Coleman
   (See Wendy & Lisa)
Patrick Coleman
Michael Colina
Judy Collero
Buddy Collette
Michel Colombier
Frank Comstock
Sergio Conforti
Cong Su
Joseph Conlan*
Bill Connor

Rick Conrad
Paolo Conte
Bill Conti*
Michael Convertino
Ry Cooder
Eric Cook
Jack Cookerly
Cole Coonce
Ray Cooper
Stewart Copeland*
Normand Corbeil
Carlo Mario Cordio
Maria Cordio
John Corigliano
Bill Cosby
Vladimir Cosma
Don Costa
Bruno Coulais
Cameron Coulter
Phil Coulter
Alexander Courage
Jean Cousineau
The Cowboy Junkies
Andy Cox
Richard Cox
Leo Crandall
Louis Crelier
Bob Crewe
Carlo Crivelli
Jim Crosby
Andrae Crouch
Patricia Cullen
David Cunningham
Bill Cuomo
Douglas J. Cuomo
Mike Curb
Lee Curreri
Hoyt Curtin
Miriam Cutler*

D

Lucio Dalla
Zhang Dalong
Quentin Damamme
Terry Dame
John D'Andrea*
Oswald D'Andrea
John Dankworth
Jeff Danna
Mychael Danna
Carl Dante
Peter D'Argenzio
Mason Daring*
Peter Dasent
Oliver Dassault
Shaun Davey
Martin Davich*
Alun Davies
Dave Davies
Peter Maxwell Davies
Ray Davies
Victor Davies
Aaron Davis
Bob Davis
Carl Davis
Carol Davis
David Davis
Don Davis
John E. Davis
Mark Davis
Rocky Davis
   (Byron McKay Davis)
Peter Davison*
Simon Davison

Alberto de Almar
Guido de Angelis
Maurizio de Angelis
Lex de Azevedo
Joseph S. de Beasi
Greg de Belles
Dick DeBenedictis*
Mario de Benito
John Debney*
Darrell Deck
Marc David Decker
Robert Decker
Christopher Dedrick
Christophe Defays
Olivier Defays
Luchi Dejesus
Matthew Delgado
   (Kevin Gilbert)
Joe Delia
Gaye Delorme
Jean Delorme
Al Delory
Paco de Lucia
Milton Delugg
Bob de Marco
Christopher de Marco
Eric Demarsan
Francesco de Masi
Gary Demichele
Edison Denisov
Rushmore de Nooyer
Frank Denson
Luis de Pablo
Delia Derbyshire
Aian Dermarderosian
Frederico de Robertis
Joel Derouin
Paul de Senneville
Manuel de Sica
Roberto de Simone
Alexandre Desplat
Leonid Desyatnikov
Mauro J. de Trizio
Steve Deutsch
Devo
Frank Devol
Barry Devorzon
Frederic Devreese
De Wolfe
John William Dexter
Von Dexter
A. S. Diamond
David Diamond
Neil Diamond
Manu Dibango
Andrew Dickson
John D. Dickson
Vince Dicola
Loek Dikker
Dan Dipaola
James Dipasqualle *
Antonio Dipofi
Andrew Dixon
Nana Djanelidz
Ray Dobbins
Craig Doerge
Brendan Dolan
Thomas Dolby
Klaus Doldinger
Francois Dompierre
Pino Donaggio
   (Giuseppe Donaggio)
Marc Donahue
James Donnellan
Henrik Otto Donner
Donovan
Steve Dorff

Joel Dorn
Michael Doucet
Terry Dougherty
Eliot Douglas
Johnny Douglas
Julia Downes
Patrick Doyle
Darryl Dragon
Dennis Dragon
Elizabeth Drake
Kamen Dranduski
Robert Drasnin *
Dennis Dreith*
Michael Dress
George Dreyfus
Tom Dube
Anne Dudley
Antoine Duhamel
David Dundas
George Duning *
Paul Dunlap
James Patrick Dunne
Murphy Dunne
John Duprez
Gordon Durity
David Duvall
Bob Dylan
    (Robert Zimmerman)
Arie Dzierlatka

E

Rich Eames
David Earl
Earwax
    (John Di Stefano,
    Kolonica McQuestin, Ear3)
Brian Easdale
Clint Eastwood
Bernard Ebbinghouse
Nicolas Economou
Brian Eddolls
Randy Edelman
Dave Edmonds
Greg Edmonson
Bernard Edwards
Kenny Edwards
Steve Edwards *
Seamus Egan
Cliff Eidelman *
Richard Einhorn
Inaki Eizagirre
Danny Elfman
Jonathan Elias
John Elizalde
Kirk Elliot
Don Elliott
Jack Elliott *
Richard Elliott
Ruth Ellenellsworth
Jeff Elmassian
Howard Warrenelmer
Kahil Elzabar
Keith Emerson
Stephen Endelman*
Matthew Ender
Jon A. English
Paul English
Charles Engstrom
Brian Eno
Roger Eno
Mickey Erbe
Sebastien Erms
Jim Ervin
Lee Erwin

Jack Eskew
David Essex
Pascal Esteve
Bob Esty
Melissa Etheridge
Alan Ett
Eurythmics
Greg Evigan

F

Donald Fagen
Jeff Fair
Gary Falcone
Harold Faltermeyer
Mo Fan
David Fanshawe
Ustad Zia Fariduddin
Jim Farmer
Braun Farnon
Dennis Farnon
Robert Farnon
Robert Farrar
Christopher Farrell*
Barry Fasman
Larry Fast
Ricky Fataar
Louis Febre
Jesse Federick
Don Felder
Richard Feldman
Eric Fenby
Guo Feng
Rick Fenn
George Fenton
Allyn Ferguson
David Ferguson
Jay Ferguson
Russell Ferrante
Paul Ferris
Brad Fiedel*
Ernie Fields
Mike Figgis
David Findlay
Richard Fiocca
Irwin Fisch
Guenther Fischer
Lubos Fiser
Peter Fish
Fishbone
Clare Fisher
Robert Morgan Fisher
Toby Fitch
Frank Fitzpatrick*
Robert Fitzsimmons
Vic Flick
Bob Floke
Dan Foliart*
Robert Folk
Russell Forante
Roy Forbes
Mitchel Forman
Greg Forrest
Keith Forsey
Ivano Fossati
Peter Howard Fosso
David Foster*
Jean-Pierre Fouquey
Charles Fox
R. Donovan Fox
Alun Francis
Simon Franglen
David Michael Frank*
Christopher Franke
Serge Franklin

Michael Franks
Carlos Franzetti
Dave Fraser
Ian Fraser*
Jill Fraser
Jesse Frederick
Marc Fredericks
Ian Freebairn-Smith
Daniel Freiberg
Gerald Fried
Gary William Friedman
Marco Frisena
Matthew Fritz
John Frizzell*
Fabio Frizzi
Edgar Froese
    (See Also Tangerine Dream)
Dominic Frontiere
Mitchell Froom
Gary Fry
Naoyuki Fujii
Jun Fukamachi
Parmer Fuller*
Lewis Furey
Magne Furuholmen

G

Reeves Gabrels
Peter Gabriel
Tedra Gabriel
Henry Gaffney
Andre Gagnon
Frederico Gaitorno
Jack Gale
John Gale
Scott Gale
Michael Galinsky
Philo Gallo
Phil Galston
Douglas Gamley
Peter Carl Ganderup
Liang Gang
Gang Of Four
Jan Garbarek
Gerardo Garcia
Roel A. Garcia
Russell Garcia
Stu Gardner
Jason Garfield
Adam Gargoni
Robert Garrett
Snuff Garrett
Mike Garson
Mort Garson
Brian Gascoigne
Roberto Gatto
Christian Gaubert
Claude Gaudette
Algirdas Gavrichenko
Frankie Gaye
Ralph Geddes
Kay Gee
Ron Geesin
Harry Geller
Lynne Geller
Rosalind George
Sergio George
Tryan George
Irving Gertz
Stephen Geyer
Barry Gibb
Maurice Gibb
Michael Gibbs
Richard Gibbs

David Gibney
Alex Gibson
David Gibson
Michael Gibson
Philip Giffin
Herschel Burke Gilbert
Alan Gill
Kevin Gillis
Richard Gillis
Iris Gillon
Paul Gilman
Paul Gilreath
Jon Gilutin
Egberto Gismonti
Claudio Gizzi
Jan Glaesel
Paul Glass
Philip Glass
Albert Glasser
Patrick Gleeson*
Nick Glennie-Smith
Goblin
Bill Goddard
Heiner Goebbels
Ernest Gold*
Barry Goldberg
Billy Goldenberg
Mark Goldenberg
Elliot Goldenthal
Peter Goldfoot
Bobby Goldsboro
Jerry Goldsmith*
Joel Goldsmith*
Jonathan Goldsmith
Gil Goldstein
Steven Goldstein*
William Goldstein*
Vinny Golia
Igor Goloviev
Benny Golson
John Gonzalez
Joseph Julian Gonzales
Howard Goodall
Jerry Goodman
Jim Goodman
Tommy Goodman
Gordon Goodwin*
Jim Goodwin
Ron Goodwin
Yuri Gorbachow
Paul Christian Gordon
Michael Gore*
Adam Gorgoni
Al Gorgoni
Alain Gorraguer
Martin Gotfrit
Orlando Gough
Morton Gould
Gerald Gouriet
John Goux
Mark Governor*
Patrick Gowers
Paul Grabowsky
Cedric Gradus-Samson
Ralph Graf
David Graham
Francis Grandmont
Ron Grant*
Stephane Grappelli
John Gray
Stephen Graziano
Don Great
D'Angio Greco
Bernard Green
Richard Greene
Richard Gregoire
Steve Gregoropoulos

FILM COMPOSERS

Harry Gregson-Williams
Ralph Grierson*
Mario Grigoriv
David Grisman
David Grohl
Shlomo Gronich
Andrew Gross*
Charles Gross*
Greg Gross
Guy Gross
Jim Gross
Larry Grossman
Dave Grusin
Jay Gruska*
Zhang Guangtian
Barrie Guard
Charles Guard
Sofia Gubaidulina
Anthony Guefen
Andrea Guerra
Juan Luis Guerra
Albert Guinovart
Nicholas Gunn
Christopher Gunning
Guru
Jonas Gwangwa
Adam Gyettel

H

Jurre Haanstra
Earle Hagen
Stephen Hague
Philippe Haim
Francis Haines
Chris Hajian
Ardell Hake*
Ken Hale
Jim Halfpenny*
Ronald Halicki
Tom T. Hall
Dick Halligan
Chico Hamilton
The Hamiltons
Marvin Hamlisch
Jan Hammer
Herbie Hancock
Craig Handy
Kentaro Haneda
Bruce Hanifan*
William Hanna
Jonathan Hannah
Petr Hapka
John Wesley Harding
Hagood Hardy
John Hardy
John Harle
Jeff B. Harmon
Joe Harnell*
Udi Harpaz
Scott Harper
Anthony Harris
Arthur Harris
Johnny Harris*
Max Harris
George Harrison
John Harrison
Ken Harrison*
Joey Harrow
James Hart
Mark Hart*
Richard Hartley
Paul Hartzop
Richard Harvey
Shane Harvey

Bo Harwood
Jimmie Haskell*
George Hatzinassios
Haunted Garage
Brent Havens
Richie Havens
Greg Hawkes
Alan Hawkshaw
Peter Haycock
Roy Hay
Todd Hayen*
Isaac Hayes
Jack Hayes
Red Hays
Richard Hazard
Christopher Hedge
Neal Hefti
Tom Heil
Fred Hellerman
Jim Helms
Louis Fredric Hemsey
David Hentschel
Hans Werner Henze
Larry Herbstritt
Ardy Hernandez
Marie-Claude Herry
Philippe Hersant
Paul Hertzog
David Alex Hess
Nigel Hess
Mike Hewer
Jerry Hey
John Hicks
Hidden Faces
   (See Frank Fitzpatrick)
Richard Hieronymous
John Hill
Richard Hill
Frances Hime
Peter Himmelman
Rupert Hine
Wilbert Hirsch
Joel Hirschhorn
David Hirshfelder
Jo Hisaishi
Gene Hobson
Brian Hodgson
Michael Hoenig
Gary Hoey
Bernard Hoffer
Paul Hoffert
Kurt Hoffman
Joakim Holbeck
Mark Holden
Lee Holdridge*
Deborah Holland
Nicky Holland
Richard Holmes
Rupert Holmes
Derek Holt
Nigel Holton
Junior Homrich
Shinsuke Honda
Toshiyuki Honda
Les Hooper
Nellee Hooper
Tobe Hooper
Dana Hoover
Anthony Hopkins
Antony Hopkins*
Kenyon Hopkins
Nicky Hopkins
Sarah Hopkins
Michael Hoppe
Stephen Horelick
James Horner
Joseph Horovitz

Richard Horowitz
Tim Horrigan
Vladimir Horunzhy*
Phillip Houghton
James Newton Howard*
Ken Howard
Rik Howard
Alan Howarth
Peter Howell
Chiang Hsiao-Wen
Mezoum H'Sine
An-Lu Huang
Eugene Huddleston
Jack Hues
Steven Hufsteter
Cooper Hughes
David A. Hughes
Klive And Nigel Humberstone
Tony Humecke
Craig Hundley
   (Craig Huxley)
Hundred Pound Head
Alberta Hunter
Kirk Hunter
Steve Hunter
Michael Hurd
Zakir Hussain
Brenda Hutchinson
Chen Hwai-En
Lucia Hwong
Christopher Hyans-Hart
Dick Hyman*

I

Akira Ifukube
Alberto Iglesias
Shinchiro Ikebe
Angel Illaramendi
The Imagineers
Jerrold Immel*
Paul Inder
Neil Innes
Tassos Ioannides
Robert E. Irving III
Ashley Irwin*
Pat Irwin
Reno Isaac
Bjorn Isfalt
Mark Isham*
Peter Ivers

J

David A. Jackson
Joe Jackson
Julian Jacobson
Denny Jaeger
Ethan James
Terrence James
Chaz Jankel
Enzo Jannacci
Alaric Jans
Pierre Jansen
Werner Janssen
Joseph Jarman
Jean-Michel Jarre
Maurice Jarre
Keith Jarrett
Herman Jeffreys
Zoltan Jeney
Tom Jenkins
Waylon Jennings

Merrill B. Jensen
Peter Jermyn
Zhao Jiping
Eddie Jobson
David Johansen
Carl Johnson*
J.J. Johnson
Jeffrey Johnson
Laurie Johnson
Scott Johnson
Steven Johnson
Adrian Johnston
Freddy Johnston
Jim Johnston
Phillip Johnston*
Richard Johnston
Alain Jomy
Darryl Jones
John Paul Jones
Kenneth V. Jones
Mick Jones
Quincy Jones*
Quincy Jones III
Ralph Jones
Ron Jones
Tony Jones
Trevor Jones
Glenn Jordan
Nicolas Jorelle
Julian Joseph
Wilfred Josephs
Paul Jost
Laurence Juber
Philip Judd
Tom Judson
Larry Juris
Bill Justis
Susan Justin*

K

Alfi Kabiljo
Jan Kaczmarek*
Eric Kadesky
Ustad Sultan Kahn
Michael Kamen
Jun Kamiyama
Vladimir Kamorov
John Kander
Artie Kane
Noam Kaniel
Igo Kantor
Sol Kaplan
Dana Kaproff*
Helena Karaindrou
   Eleni Karaindrou
Eddie Karam
Fred Karger
Fred Karlin*
Fred Karns
Laura Karpman*
Ardashes Kartalian
Al Kasha
Manu Katcke
Peter Kater
Fred Katz
Martin Katz
Steve Katz
Emilio Kauderer*
Gene Kauer
Frank Kavelin
Kenji Kawai
Eui Kawamura
Mashahiro Kawasaki
Fred Kaz

Brian Keane
John Keane
John E. Keane
John M. Keane
Shane Keister
Salif Keita
Roger Kellaway
Rickey Keller
Julianne Kelley
Victoria Kelly
Arthur Kempel*
Rolfe Kent
Randy Kerber
Robert Kessler
Khaled
William Kidd*
Robert Kikuchi-Yngojo
Wojciech Kilar
Bruce Kimmel
Kevin Kiner
Carol King
Denis King
Gershon Kingsley
Basil Kirchin
Barry Kirsch
Osamu Kitajima
Kitaro
David Kitay
Larry Klein
Tamara Kline
Kevin Klinger
Harold Kloser
Jan Klusak
Jurgen Knieper
Mark Knopfler
Akira Kobayachi
Buz Kohan
Margo Kolar
David Kole
Cristian Kolonovits
Tetsuya Komuro
Brian Koonin
Anders Koppel
Al Kooper
Stefanos Korkolis
Reijiro Koroku
Mark Korven
Andrzej Korzynski
Leo Kottke
Mark Koval*
Robert Kraft
William Kraft
Bernard Krause
Raoul Kraushaar
Amanda Kravat
Gabor Kristof
Greg Krochta
Tim Krog
Zane Kronje
David Krystal
Ted Kuhn
Christian Kunert
Russ Kunkel
David Kurtz
John Kusiac
Milan Kymlicka

L

John La Barbera
Douglas Lackey
Yves Laferriere
Francis Lai
Robert Lake
Frank Laloggia

Alan Lamb
Dennis Lambert
Jerry Lambert
Phillip Lambro
John Lanchbery
James Lane
Rob Lane
John Lang
Jim Lang
K.D.Lang
Michael Lang*
Bruce Langhorne
Michael Lanning
Henri Lanoe
Daniel Lanois
Charlotte Lansberg
David Lanz
Yves Lapierre
Antton Larrauri
Tito Larriva
Glen A. Larson
Richard Lasalle
Jeff Lass
Bob Last
Jim Latham*
Tats Lau
Ken Lauber
Bobby Laurel
Tom Lavin
David Lawrence
Elliot Lawrence
Stephen Lawrence
Maury Laws
Julian Laxton
L'azur
Antonio Lee
Bill Lee
David Lee
Gerald Lee
Pervis Lee
Carol Lees
Dick Le Fort
James Legg
Mark Leggett
Michel Legrand*
Jed Leiber
Mitch Leigh
Peter Leinheiser
Robin Lemesurier
Battista Lena
Christopher Lennertz*
Nicholas Lens
Jack Lenz
Jean-Francois Leon
Michael Leonard
Patrick Leonard*
Raymond Leppard
Cory Lerios*
Michael Levanios III
Sylvester Levay
Eric Levi
Geoff Levin
Stewart Levin*
Keith Levine
Walter Levinsky
Ross Levinson*
Jay Levy
Lou Levy
Shuki Levy
Gordon Lewis
Herschell Gordon Lewis
Michael J. Lewis
Paul H. Lewis
W. Michael Lewis
Webster Lewis
Blake Leyh
Daniel Licht

Richard Lieb
Martin Liebman
Jimmy Lifton
Hal Lindes
Mark Lindsay
Mort Lindsey
Steve Lindsey
David Lindup
Dam Linh
Peter Link
Wang Liping
Larry Lipkis
Alan Lisk
Zdenek Liska
John Lissauer
Russ Little
Brynmor Llewellyn-Jones
Charles Lloyd
Michael Lloyd
Lowell Lo
Los Lobos
Robert Lockhart
Didier Lockwood
Robert Lockwood
Malcom Lockyer
Joseph Lo Duca
Frank Loef
Nils Lofgren
Gary Logan
Richard Logan
Markus Lonardoni
Frank London
David Long
Tao Long
Paul Loomis
William Loos
Jeff Lorber
Bruno Louchouarn*
Diane Louie
Stepan Lousikyan
Mundell Lowe
Jesse Loya
Jeremy Lubbock
Ken Luber
Mark Lundquist
John Lunn
Donal Lunny
Michal Lurenc
Evan Lurie
John Lurie
Danny Lux
Shelby Lynne
Richard Lyons

M

Tony Macauley
Egisto Macchi
Geoff MacCormack
Galt MacDermott
Teo Macero
John Madara
Mader
Madredeus
Taj Mahal
Vincent Mai
Stefano Mainetti
Mauro Malavasi
Manuel Malou
Nikos Mamangakis
Bob Mamet
Norman Mamey
Mark Mancina
Johnny Mandel
Tommy Mandel

Harry Manfredini*
Hridaynath Mangeshkar
Chuck Mangione
Tony Mangurian
Barry Manilow
Barry Mann
Hummie Mann*
Franco Mannino
Ernie Mannix*
David Mansfield
Keith Mansfield
Eddie Lawrence Manson
Marita Manuel
Chris Many*
Jim Manzie
Nestor Marconi
Marc Marder
Susan Marder
Petre Margineanu
Mitch Margo
Stuart Margolin
Anthony Marinelli
Rick Marotta
Branford Marsalis
Delfeayo Marsalis
Wynton Marsalis
Ingram Marshall
Jack Marshall
Julian Marshall
Phil Marshall
George Martin
George Porter Martin
Peter Martin
Simon Michael Martin
Cliff Martinez
Mel Marvin
Richard Marvin*
Bill Marx
Davide Masarati
J Mascis
Janos Masik
Harvey W. Mason
Molly Mason
Nick Mason
Roger Mason
John Massari
George Massenburg
Michael Masser
Alejandro Masso
Eric Masunaga
Greg Mathieson
Jim Matison
Sasha Matson
Teizo Matsumara
David M. Matthews
Peter Matz*
Dylan Maulucci
Billy May
Daniel May
Scott May
Curtis Mayfield
Lincoln Mayorga
Lyle Mays
John McCabe
Jon McCallum
Paul McCallum
Valentine McCallum
Dennis McCarthy*
John McCarthy*
Linda McCartney
Paul McCartney
Michael McCarty
Matthew McCauley
Tim McCauley
Paul McCollough
Albritton McClain
Diane McCloughlin

F
I
L
M

C
O
M
P
O
S
E
R
S

Kristen McCord
Stephen McCurdy
Garry McDonald
Maureen McElheron
John McEuen
Anne McGarrigle
Kate McGarrigle
Don McGlashan
David McHugh
Tom McIntosh
Frank McKelvey
Mark McKenzie
Stephen McKeon
Rod McKuen
Malcolm McLaren
Don McLean
Gerard McMahon
Bob McNaughton
Joel McNeely*
Andy McNeill
Bill McRae*
James McVay*
Abigail Mead
Gary Meals
Paddy Meegan
Gil Melle
Laszlo Melis
Peter Rodgers Melnick*
Michael Melvoin*
Wendy Melvoin
   (See Wendy & Lisa)
E. D. Menasche
Bingen Mendizabal
Jaime Mendoza-Nava
Alan Menken*
Joey Mennonna
Dale Menten
Wim Mertens
Pat Metheny
Bill Meyers
Lanny Meyers
Randall Meyers
Valery Miagkih
Yuri Miamin
Franco Micalizzi
George Michalski
Harry Middlebrooks
Charlie Midnight
Cynthia Millar*
Bruce Miller*
Dominic Miller
Frankie Miller
Marcus Miller
Randy Miller
Mario Millo
John Mills-Cockell
Dan Milner
David Milroy
Michael Minard
David Mindel
Chen Ming-Chang
Charles Mingus
Ben Mink
Carlos Miranda
Sheldon Mirowitz*
Nan Mishkin
   (See Nan Schwartz-Mishkin)
Paul Misraki
Richard G. Mitchell
Robert Mitchell
Bob Mithoff*
Fumio Miyashita
Vic Mizzy
Mark Moffiatt
Fred Mollin
Paddy Moloney
Francis Monkman

Osvaldo Montes
Ronnie Montrose
Doug Moody
Guy Moon
Hal Mooney
Dudley Moore
Thurston Moore
Jacques Morali
Mike Moran
Patrick Moraz
Howard Morgan
John W. Morgan*
Kuroudo Mori
Ken-Ichiro Morioka
Angela Morley*
   (Wally Stott)
Giorgio Moroder
Ennio Morricone
John Morris*
Van Morrison
Charles Morrow
Jonathan Morse
   (Fuzzbee Morse)
Thomas Morse*
Arthur Morton
Mark Mothersbaugh
Tony Mottola
William Motzig
Rob Mounsey
Oliver Mtukudzi
James Mtume
Dominic Muldowney
Gerry Mulligan
Murray Munro
Judy Munsen
Michael Martin Murphey
Walter Murphy
William Murphy
Sean Murray
Alfredo Muschietto
Jennie Muskett
John Musser
Jean Musy
Bill Myers
Lenny Myers
Peter Myers
Fred Myrow

N

Angelique Nachon
Jean-Claude Nachon
Sean Naidoo
Mark Nakamura
Yuriko Nakamura
Giuseppe Napoli
Andy Narrell
Nash The Slash
Louis Natale
Ray Nathanson
Bruce Nazarian
Chris Neal
Litto Nebbia
Roger Neill
Bill Nelson
Steve Nelson
Willie Nelson
John Neschling
Michael Nesmith
Ethan Neuburg
Robert Neufeld
Wolfgang Neumann
Ira Newborn
David Newman
Randy Newman

Thomas Newman
David Nichtern
Ian Christian Nickus
Bruno Nicolai
Lennie Niehaus*
Jose Nieto
Stefan Nilsson
Jack Nitzche*
Matt Noble
Naz Nomad
Eric Nordgren
Arne Nordheim
John E. Nordstrom II
Per Norgaard
Monty Norman
Craig Northey
Julian Nott
Mohamed Nouh
Paul Novotny
Gary Numan
Giovanni Nuti
Michael Nyman
Sally Nyoto
Laura Nyro

O

Arlon Ober
Gene Ober*
Sebastian Oberg
Daniel O'Brien*
Oscar Cardozo Ocampo
Greg O'Connor*
Bruce Odland
Ohnay Oguz
Mary Margaret O'Hara
Patrick O'Hearn
Jimmy Oihid
Shinnosuka Okawa
John O'Kennedy
Alan Oldfield
Mike Oldfield
Terry Oldfield
Jay Oliver
Stephen Oliver
Tommy Oliver
Oscar O'Lochlainn
Keith Olsen
Albert Lloyd Olson*
William Olvis*
Russell O'Malley
Michael Omer
William Orbit
Cyril Ornadel
Malcolm Orrall
Frank Ortega
Luis Perico Ortiz
Riz Ortolani
Geoffrey Oryema
Daniel Osborn
Jason Osborn
Michiru Oshima
John Ottman
Vyecheslav Ovchinnikov

P

Paata
Johnny Pacheco
Gene Page
Jimmy Page
Scott Page-Pagter

Andy Paley
David Palmer
Nick Palmer
Gerulf Pannach
Aleksandr Pantychin
Daniele Paris
Simon Park
Alan Parker
Jim Parker
John Parker*
Van Dyke Parks
Starr Parodi
Stephen Parsons
Arvo Part
Johnny Pate
Cameron Patrick
Rick Patterson
John Pattison
Robbie Patton
Peter Pau
Algirdas Paulavichus
Charles Pavlosky
Glenn Paxton
Bill Payne
Don Peake*
Kevin Peak
Gunnar Moller Pedersen
Bob Pegg
Michel Pelletier
Samm Pena
Leon Pendarvis
The Penguin Cafe Orchestra
Danilo Perez
Coleridge-Taylor Perkinson
Haim Permont
Freddie Perren
Marc Perrone
Alexander Peskanov
Mark Peskanov
Joel C. Peskin
Randolph Peters
Oscar Peterson
Randy Petersen
Jean-Claude Petit
Laurent Petitgand
Laurent Petitgirard
Andrey Petrovic
Charlton Pettus
Tom Petty
Ahmad Pezhman
Barrington Pheloung
Herb Philhofer
Art Philipps
John Phillips
Mary Phillips
Stu Phillips
Astor Piazzola
Piero Piccioni
Michael Piccirillo
Nik Pickard
Rebecca Pidgeon
Franco Piersanti
Tom Pierson
Scooter Pietsch
Nicholas Pike*
Herb Pilhofer
Chuck Pinnell
Nicola Piovani
Pixies
Gianfranco Plenizio
Amotz Plessner*
Terry Plumeri
Basil Poledouris*
Tibar Polgar
Dave Pollecutt
Peter Ponger
Temistocle Popa

'97-'98
FILM
COMPOSERS
INDEX

Carole Pope
Popol Vuh
Steve Porcaro
Greg Poree
Michel Portal
Rachel Portman
Mike Post
Steve Postel
Alby Potts
Yarol Poupaud
Andrew Powell
Reg Powell
Dennis M. Pratt
Pray For Rain
Zbigniew Preisner
Graham Preskett
Gabor Presser
Don Preston
Jan Preston
Craig Preuss
Andre Previn
Alan Price
George S. Price
Jim Price
Stephen Price
Frank Primata
Robert Prince
Jean Prodromides
Sacha Puttnam

Q

Queen
Hamlet Lima Quintana

R

Peer Raben
Trevor Rabin
Harry Rabinowitz
Robert O. Ragland
Nick Raine
Tony Rains
David Raksin*
Ron Ramin*
Sid Ramin
Ariel Ramirez
Kennard Ramsey
Willis Alan Ramsey
Robert Randles
Rareview
Ken Rarick
Raf Ravenscroft
Eddie Raynor
Chris Rea
Robert Reale
Coby Recht
Iris Recht
Leon Redbone
Red Clay Ramblers
J.A.C. Redford*
Joshua Redman
Jerry Reed
Les Reed
Patrick C. Regan
Justin Reinhardt
Niki Reiser
Gary Remal-Malkin
    (Gary Remal)
Robert Renfrow
Adi Rennert
Ruth Rennie
Johnny Reno

Joe Renzetti*
Graeme Revell
Gian Reverberi
John Reynolds
The Rh Factor
Ken Richmond
David Rickets
Ned Rifle
Laurin Rinder
Tony Ripparetti*
Paul Riser
Lee Ritenour
Walter Rizzati
Tom Rizzo
David Robbins
Richard Robbins
Jim Roberge
Guy Robert
Max Robert
Andy Roberts
Bruce Roberts
B.A. Robertson
Bill Robertson
Eric N. Robertson
Harry Robertson
Robbie Robertson
Earl Robinson
Harry Robinson
J. Peter Robinson*
Larry Robinson
Pete Robinson
Peter Manning Robinson
Nile Rodgers
Scott Roewe*
Kenny Rogers,Jr
Simon Rogers
Michael Rokatyn
George Romanis
Joe Romano
Alain Romans
Richard Romanus
Jeff Rona
Jean-Louis Roques
Andrew Rose
Earl Rose*
Allan K. Rosen
Joel Rosenbaum
Brett Rosenberg
Leonard Rosenman*
Laurence Rosenthal
William Ross*
Miles Roston
Peter Francis Rotter
Glen Roven*
Hahn Rowe
Adam Rowland
Bruce Rowland
Lance Rubin
Michel Rubini
Arthur B. Rubinstein*
Donald Rubinstein
John Rubinstein
Keith Rubinstein
Steve Rucker*
Pete Rugolo
Todd Rundgren
Patrice Rushen*
Bella Russell
Julian Dylan Russell
Ray Russell
Willy Russell
Nicholas Russell-Pavier
David Russo
Gus Russo
William Russo
Carlo Rustichelli
Michael Rutherford

S

Haim Saban
Craig Safan
Sidney Sager
Michael Sahl
Buffy Sainte-Marie
Ryuichi Sakamoto
Gary Sales
Barry Salmon
Bennett Salvay
Leonard Salzedo
Caleb Sampson
Jonathan Sampson
Jeremy Sams
David Sanborn
Rick Sandler
Peter Sandloff
Mark Sandman
Arturo Sandoval
Pengbian Sang
Anton Sanko
Neftali Santiago
Carlos Santos
Michel Sanvoisin
Andrea Saparoff
Philippe Sarde
John Sargent
Sarah Sarhandi
Jerzy Satanowski
Masaru Sato
Somei Satoh
Eddie Sauter
Jordi Savall
Tom Saviano
Carlo Savina
Phil Sawyer
Frank Schaap
Walter Scharf*
Glenn Schellenberg
Anton Scherpenzeel
Peter Schickele
Donn Schiff
Steve Schiff
Lalo Schifrin*
Zander Schloss
Norbert J. Schneider
Charly Schoppner
Barry Schrader
Greg Schultz
Klaus Schulze
Richard Schumann
Gerard Schurmann
Isaac Schwarts
David Schwartz*
Nan Schwartz-Mishkin*
    (Nan Mishkin)
Stephen Schwartz
Garry Schyman*
Duane Sciaqua
Danny Sciarra
Ilona Sckacz
The Score Warriors
Gary Scott
Gary Stevan Scott
John Scott*
Tom Scott
Billy Scream
Earl Scruggs
Peter Sculthorpe
Jay Seagrave
Malcolm Seagrave
Walter Sear
John Sebastian
Don Sebesky
Jerry Segal

Misha Segal
Bernardo Segall
Matyas Seiber
Leon Seith
Ilona Sekacz
Timur Selcuk
Wladimir Selinsky
Gyorgy Selmeczi
Dov Seltzer
Caiphus Semenya
Jay Semko
Jean-Marie Senia
Frank Serafine
John Sereda
Renato Serio
Eric Serra
Philippe Servain
Patrick Seymour
Francis Seyrig
Shadowy Men On A Shadowy
Planet
Marc Shaiman*
Ravi Shankar
Ray Shanklin
Alex Shapiro*
Ted Shapiro
Theodore Shapiro
Shark
Jamshied Sharifi
Thom Sharp*
Avery Sharpe
Jennifer Sharpe
Edward Shearmur
Jonathan Sheffer
Bert A. Shefter*
Steve Shehan
Mark Shekter
Ernie Sheldon
Ward Shelley
Kirby Shelstad
Thomas Z. Shepard
Jamie Sheriff
Bobby Sherman
Garry Sherman
Joe Sherman
Mike Shields
Yashuaki Shimizu
David Shire*
Sheldon Shkolnik
Hank Shoklee And The Bomb
Squad
Howard Shore*
Richard Shores*
Paul Shorick
Phyllis Shotwell
Lawrence Shragge*
Mark Shreeve
Michael Shrieve
Watazumido Shuoo
Tony Silbert
Carlos Siliotto
Gregory Sill
Sheila Silver
Jeffrey Silverman
Stanley Silverman
Alan Silvestri*
Carly Simon
Lucy Simon
Marty Simon*
Paul Simon
Saimon Simonet
Michael Simpson
Byung Ha Sin
Scott Singer
Sion
Michael Skloff
Peter Skoumal

Wendy & Lisa
  *(Wendy Melvoin
  & Lisa Coleman)*
Rick Wentworth
Fred Werner
Jocelyn West
Paul Westerberg
Michael Wetherwax
John Wetton
Jim Wetzel
David Wheatley
Jack W. Wheaton
Harold Wheeler
Bill Whelen
Christopher Whiffen
David Whitaker
Kenn Whitaker
Daniel J. White
John Clifford White
Lenny White
Maurice White
Norman Whitfield
Michael Whitmore
Stacy Widelitz
Sonia Wieder-Atherton
Chuck Wilde*
Rolf Wilhelm
Scott Wilk
George Wilkins
Rick Wilkins
Marc Wilkinson
Frank Will
David C. Williams
H. Shep Williams
Jack Eric Williams
John Williams*
Patrick Williams*
Paul Williams*
Malcolm Williamson
Hal Wilner
Andrew Wilson
Nancy Wilson
Sam Winans
Chris Winfield
Debbie Wiseman
Jill Wisoff
Alain Wisniak
Leslie Winston
Erling Wold
Peter Wolf
Larry Wolff
Michael Wolff
David Wolinski
Hawk Wolinski
Stevie Wonder
  (Steveland Morris)
James Wong
Art Wood
Guy Woolfenden
Tom Worrall
Bernie Worrell
Jody Taylor Worth
Link Wray
Clive Wright
Gary Wright
Bill Wyman
Dan Wyman

Y

Motofumi Yamagushi
Shoji Yamashiro
Stomu Yamashita
Yanni
Yoshikazu Yano
Gabriel Yared
Yarol
Yello
Dwight Yoakam
Christopher Young*
Danny Young
Neil Young
Patrick Young
Russell Young
Joji Yuasa
Norio Yuasa
Liu Yuan
Richard Yuen
Jimmy Yuill
Atuhalpa Yupanqui
Wendall J. Yuponce

Z

Aleksei Zalivalov
Marilyn S. Zalkan
Allan Zavod
Paul J. Zaza
John Zeane
Denny Zeitlin
Guy Zerafa
Wen Zhongjia
Al Zima
Hans Zimmer*
Don Zimmers
Carl Zittrer
John Zorn

X

Stavros Xarchakos
Chen Xiangyu
Qu Xiaosong

A

MICHAEL ABENE
Contact: BMI - Los Angeles, 310-659-9109

GOODBYE NEW YORK   Castle Hill Productions, 1985, U.S.-Israeli

ABSOLUTE MUSIC
Contact: BMI - Los Angeles, 310-659-9109

CHANGING OUR MINDS: THE STORY OF DR. EVELYN HOOKER
(FD)   Intrepid Prods., 1992

AC/DC
Contact: APRA - Australia, 011-61-2-922-6422

MAXIMUM OVERDRIVE   DEG, 1986

LARA ACKERLUND
IL CAPITANO   co-composer with Sebastian Oberg, 1991, Swedish

JACK ACKERMAN
Contact: ASCAP - Los Angeles, 213-883-1000

FACES   Continental, 1968

JOHN ADAMS
Contact: ASCAP - Los Angeles, 213-883-1000

THE CABINET OF DOCTOR RAMIREZ   Mediascope, 1991,
U.S.-German

TRACY ADAMS
DEATH & TAXES (FD)   1993

BARRY ADAMSON
Contact: Ocean Park Music Group - Los Angeles, 310-315-5266
Affiliation: PRS - London, England, 011-44-1-580-5544

DELUSION   Cineville, 1991
GAS, FOOD AND LODGING   additional music, I.R.S., 1992

STUART ADAMSON
Contact: PRS - London, England, 011-44-1-580-5544

RESTLESS NATIVES   Thorn/EMI, 1985, British

JOHN ADDISON
b. March 16, 1920 - Surrey, England
Contact: ASCAP - Los Angeles, 213-883-1000

THE OUTSIDER *THE GUINEA PIG*   Pathe, 1948, British
SEVEN DAYS TO NOON   Mayer-Kingsley, 1950, British
POOL OF LONDON   Universal, 1951, British
THE LIGHT TOUCH   MGM, 1951
HIGH TREASON   Rank, 1952, British
THE HOUR OF 13   MGM, 1952, British
THE MAN BETWEEN   United Artists, 1953, British
THE BLACK KNIGHT   Columbia, 1954, British
TOUCH AND GO   Rank, 1954, British
THAT LADY   20th Century Fox, 1954, British
THE COCKLESHELL HEROES   Columbia, 1956, British
REACH FOR THE SKY   Rank, 1956, British
PRIVATE'S PROGRESS   DCA, 1956, British
THE SHIRALEE   MGM, 1957, British
LUCKY JIM   Kingsley International, 1957, British
THREE MEN IN A BOAT   DCA, 1958, British
LOOK BACK IN ANGER   Warner Bros., 1958, British
I WAS MONTY'S DOUBLE   NTA Pictures, 1958, British
MAN IN A COCKED HAT   *CARLTON BROWN OF THE F.O.*   Show
Corporation, 1960, British
SCHOOL FOR SCOUNDRELS   Warner Bros., 1960, British
THE ENTERTAINER   Continental, 1960, British
A TASTE OF HONEY   Continental, 1962, British
THE LONELINESS OF THE LONG DISTANCE RUNNER
Continental, 1962, British
TOM JONES ★★   Lopert, 1963, British
THE GIRL WITH GREEN EYES   United Artists, 1964, British
THE LOVED ONE   MGM, 1965
THE UNCLE   Lennart, 1966, British
GUNS AT BATASI   20th Century Fox, 1964, British-U.S.
THE AMOROUS ADVENTURES OF MOLL FLANDERS
Paramount, 1965, British
A FINE MADNESS   Warner Bros., 1966
TIME LOST AND TIME REMEMBERED   *I WAS HAPPY HERE*
Continental, 1966, British
TORN CURTAIN   Universal, 1966
THE HONEY POT   United Artists, 1967, British-U.S.-Italian
SMASHING TIME   Paramount, 1967, British
THE CHARGE OF THE LIGHT BRIGADE   United Artists, 1968,
British
BROTHERLY LOVE   *COUNTRY DANCE*   MGM, 1970, British
START THE REVOLUTION WITHOUT ME   Warner Bros., 1970,
British
CRY OF THE PENGUINS   *MR. FORBUSH AND THE PENGUINS*
EMI, 1971, British
SLEUTH ★   20th Century Fox, 1972, British
DEAD CERT   United Artists, 1973, British
LUTHER   American Film Theatre, 1974
THE SEVEN PER CENT SOLUTION   Universal, 1976
SWASHBUCKLER   Universal, 1976
RIDE A WILD PONY   Walt Disney Productions, 1976
A BRIDGE TOO FAR   United Artists, 1977, British
JOSEPH ANDREWS   Paramount, 1977, British
PEARL (TF)   Silliphant-Konigsberg Productions/Warner Bros. TV,
1978
BLACK BEAUTY (MS)   Universal TV, 1978
THE BASTARD (TF)   Universal TV, 1978
LIKE NORMAL PEOPLE (TF)   Christiana Productions, 20th
Century Fox TV, 1979
REX STOUT'S NERO WOLFE (TF)   Emmett Lavery, Jr.
Productions/Paramount TV, 1979
LOVE'S SAVAGE FURY (TF)   Aaron Spelling Productions, 1979
THE FRENCH ATLANTIC AFFAIR (TF)   1979
CENTENNIAL (MS)   Universal TV, 1980
HIGH POINT   1980, Canadian
MISTRESS OF PARADISE (TF)   Lorimar Productions, 1981
THE PILOT   Summit Features, 1981
I WAS A MAIL ORDER BRIDE (TF)   Jaffe Productions/Tuxedo
Limited Productions/MGM TV, 1982
CHARLES AND DIANA: A ROYAL LOVE STORY (TF)   St. Lorraine
Productions, 1982
ELEANOR, FIRST LADY OF THE WORLD (TF)   Murbill
Productions/Embassy TV, 1982
ELLIS ISLAND (MS)   1984
GRACE QUIGLEY   Cannon, 1984
AGATHA CHRISTIE'S 'THIRTEEN AT DINNER' (TF)   Warner Bros.
TV, 1985
CODE NAME: EMERALD   MGM/UA, 1985
SOMETHING IN COMMON (TF)   New World TV/Freyda Rothstein
Productions/Littke-Grossbart Productions, 1986
AGATHA CHRISTIE'S 'DEAD MAN'S FOLLY' (TF)   Warner Bros.
TV, 1986, U.S.-British
BRIDE OF BOOGEDY (TF)   Walt Disney TV, 1987
STRANGE VOICES (TF)   Forrest Hills Productions/Dacks-Geller
Productions/TLC, 1987
BERYL MARKHAM: A SHADOW ON THE SUN (TF)   Tamara
Asseyev Productions/New World TV, 1988
THE PHANTOM OF THE OPERA (TF) ☆   Saban-Scherick
Productions, 1990

LARRY ADLER
Contact: BMI - Los Angeles, 310-659-9109

GENEVIEVE ★   Universal, 1954, British
A CRY FROM THE STREETS   Tudor, 1959, British
THE HELLIONS   Columbia, 1962, British
THE HOOK   MGM, 1963

THE GREAT CHASE   Continental, 1963
A HIGH WIND IN JAMAICA   20th Century-Fox, 1965, British
KING AND COUNTRY   Allied Artists, 1965, British

MARK ADLER*
Agent: Zomba Screen Music - West Hollywood, 310-246-0777
Affiliation: BMI - Los Angeles, 310-659-9109

BREAK OF DAWN   Cinewest, 1988
EAT A BOWL OF TEA   Columbia, 1989
LIFE IS CHEAP   Far East Stars, 1989
SUPER CHIEF (FD)   Direct Cinema Limited, 1990
THE LOST FLEET OF GUADALCANAL (TD)   National
   Geographic/TBS/NHK/Central TV, 1993
COMING OUT UNDER FIRE (FD)   Deep Focus, 1994
VICTORY   Miramax, 1996
PICTURE BRIDE   Miramax, 1996
SLAM DUNK ERNEST   Buena Vista, 1996

AFRICA
JASON'S LYRIC   co-composer with Matt Noble, Gramercy, 1994

DIAN AGP
THE BATTLE OF JAYAKARTA   Rapi Films, 1997

ALFONSO AGULLO
Contact: SGAE - Spain, 011-34-1-319-2100

MONSTER ISLAND   Fort Films, 1981, U.S.-Spanish

WAYNE ALABARDO
TOGETHER ALONE   Frameline, 1992

BOB ALCIVAR*
Contact: BMI - Los Angeles, 310-659-9109

BUTTERFLIES ARE FREE   Columbia, 1972
THE CRAZY WORLD OF JULIUS VROODER   20th Century-Fox,
   1974
OLLY, OLLY, OXEN FREE   Sanrio, 1978
FOREVER LIKE THE ROSE (AF)   Hanna-Barbera Prods., 1978
ONE FROM THE HEART   additional music, Columbia, 1982
HYSTERICAL   co-composer with Robert O. Ragland, Embassy,
   1983
THAT SECRET SUNDAY (TF)   CBS Entertainment, 1986
NAKED LIE (TF)   Shadowplay Films/Phoenix Entertainment Group,
   1989
ROXANNE: THE PRIZE PULITZER (TF)   Qintex Entertainment,
   1989
BLIND WITNESS (TF)   King-Phoenix Entertainment/Victoria
   Principal Productions, 1989
SPARKS: THE PRICE OF PASSION (TF)   Shadowplay
   Films/Victoria Principal Productions/King Phoenix Entertainment,
   1990
DEADLY MEDICINE (TF)   Steve Krantz Prods., 1991
WEB OF DECEPTION (TF)   Morgan Hill/Hearst, 1994

SCOTT ALDRICH
GO FISH   co-composer with Brendan Dolan and Jennifer Sharpe,
   Samuel Goldwyn, 1994

EDESIO ALEJANDRO
ADORABLE LIES   co-composer with Gerardo Garcia, 1992, Cuban

LORIN ALEXANDER*
DEATH DANCERS   V.L.P., 1993

VAN ALEXANDER
Contact: ASCAP - Los Angeles, 213-883-1000

THE ATOMIC KID   Republic, 1954
THE TWINKLE IN GOD'S EYE   Republic, 1955
JAGUAR   Republic, 1956
WHEN GANGLAND STRIKES   Republic, 1956
BABY FACE NELSON   Allied Artists, 1957
ANDY HARDY COMES HOME   MGM, 1958

THE BIG OPERATOR   MGM, 1959
GIRLS TOWN   *INNOCENT AND THE DAMNED*   MGM, 1959
PLATINUM HIGH SCHOOL   *TROUBLE AT 16*   MGM, 1960
THE PRIVATE LIVES OF ADAM AND EVE   Universal, 1960
SAFE AT HOME!   Columbia, 1962
13 FRIGHTENED GIRLS   Columbia, 1963
STRAIT-JACKET   Columbia, 1964
I SAW WHAT YOU DID   Universal, 1965
A TIME FOR KILLING   Columbia, 1967

ERIC ALLAMAN*
Contact: BMI - Los Angeles, 310-659-9109

THE BATTLESHIP POTEMKIN   composer of new score for 1925
   silent film, Deutche Kinemathek
DOWN TWISTED   Cannon, 1987
ANGEL III: THE FINAL CHAPTER   New World, 1988
MIRACLE BEACH   Motion Picture Corporation of America, 1992
HITS!   Walron Films Ltd./LLC/Symphony Pictures, 1994

CAMERON ALLAN
Contact: ASCAP - Los Angeles, 213-883-1000

SUMMER OF SECRETS   Greater Union Film Distribution, 1976,
   Australian
THE NIGHT THE PROWLER   International Harmony, 1978,
   Australian
STIR   Hoyts Distribution, 1980, Australian
HEATWAVE   New Line, 1982, Australia
MIDNITE SPARES   Roadshow Australia, 1983, Australian
GOING SANE   Sea Change Films, 1986, Australian
THE GOOD WIFE   Atlantic Releasing Corporation, 1986,
   Australian
THE CLEAN MACHINE (TF)   Kennedy-Miller, 1988, Australian
KOJAK (TF)   Universal TV, 1989
THE NUTTY NUT   Connexion American Media, 1992
MEN DON'T TELL (TF)   Daniel H. Blatt Prods./Nancy Bein
   Prods./Lorimar TV, 1993
JFK: RECKLESS YOUTH (TF)   Polone Co./Hearst, 1993
JERICHO FEVER (CTF)   Sankan Prods./Wilshire Court, 1993

DAVID ALLEN
THE HARVEST   co-composer with Rick Boston, Curb
   Musifilm/Mike Curb and Lester Korn, 1993
HOUSE PARTY 3   New Line, 1994

RICHARD ALLEN
THIN ICE   additional music, 1995, British

WOODY ALLEN
(Allen Stewart Konigsberg)
b. December 1, 1935 - Brooklyn, New York
Contact: ASCAP - Los Angeles, 213-883-1000

SLEEPER   United Artists, 1973

BYRON ALLRED
Contact: ASCAP - Los Angeles, 213-883-1000

DON'T ANSWER THE PHONE!   Crown International, 1980

ALLAN ALPER
Contact: BMI - Los Angeles, 310-659-9109

ON ANY SUNDAY II (FD)   International Film Marketing, 1981

RON ALTBACH
Contact: ASCAP - Los Angeles, 213-883-1000

ALMOST SUMMER   co-composer with Charles Lloyd, Universal,
   1978

GERALD ALTERS
Contact: ASCAP - Los Angeles, 213-883-1000

YOUR PLACE OR MINE (TF)   Finnegan Associates/Poolhouse
   Productions, 1983

JOHN ALTMAN
Agent: Cathy Schleussner - Encino, 818-905-7475
Affiliation: PRS - London, England, 011-44-1-580-5544

HEAR MY SONG   Miramax, 1991
DEVLIN (CTF)   Viacom, 1992
BAD BEHAVIOR   1993, British
THE LONG ROAD (TD)   1993, British
SELECTED EXITS (TF)   1993, British
BHAJI ON THE BEACH   co-composer with Craig Preuss, 1993,
   British
FUNNY BONES   Buena Vista, 1995
BEAUTIFUL THING   1996
PRONTO (CTF)   Stohedge Films, 1997
GARDEN OF REDEMPTION (CTF)   Paramount, 1997

ED ALTON*
b. May 29, 1955 - Hartford, Connecticut
Contact: 5752 Murietta Ave., Van Nuys, CA 91401, 818-994-4809
Affiliation: ASCAP - Los Angeles, 213-883-1000

MY DEMON LOVER   additional music, New Line Cinema, 1987
THE SHOW FORMERLY KNOWN AS THE MARTIN SHORT SHOW
   (TF)   Dolshor Prods./NBC, 1995

MINETTE ALTON
CHILDREN OF DIVORCE (TF)   co-composer with Raoul Kraushaar,
   Christiana Productions/Marble Arch Productions, 1980

JOEY ALTRUDA
Contact: BMI - Los Angeles, 310-659-9109

REBEL HIGHWAY: SHAKE, RATTLE AND ROCK (CTF)   Drive-In
   Classics, 1994

DAVE ALVIN
Contact: BMI - Los Angeles, 310-659-9109

BORDER RADIO   co-composer, Coyote Films, 1987

DAVID AMRAM
b. 1933
Contact: BMI - Los Angeles, 310-659-9109

ECHO OF AN ERA   1957
PULL MY DAISY   G-String Productions, 1959
SPLENDOR IN THE GRASS   Warner Bros., 1961
THE YOUNG SAVAGES   United Artists, 1961
THE MANCHURIAN CANDIDATE   United Artists, 1962
WE ARE YOUNG   1967
THE ARRANGEMENT   Warner Bros., 1969

ANASTASIA
BEFORE THE RAIN   1994, British-French-Macedonian

BENNY ANDERSEN
b. Sweden
Contact: ASCAP - Los Angeles, 213-883-1000

WHEN SVANTE DISAPPEARED   Dagmar Distribution, 1976,
   Danish

LAURIE ANDERSON
Contact: BMI - Los Angeles, 310-659-9109

SOMETHING WILD   co-composer with John Cale, Orion, 1986
SWIMMING TO CAMBODIA   Cinecom, 1987
SPALDING GRAY'S MONSTER IN A BOX   Fine Line, 1991, British

PETE ANDERSON
Contact: ASCAP - Los Angeles, 213-883-1000

CHASERS   co-composer with Dwight Yoakam, Warner, 1994

DWIGHT ANDREWS
THE PIANO LESSON (TF)   co-composer with Stephen James
   Taylor, Signboard Hill, 1995

GERARD ANFOSSO
Contact: SACEM - France, 011-33-1-4715-4715

VOYAGE TO GRAND TARTARIE   LE VOYAGE EN GRANDE
   TARTARIE   New Line Cinema, 1973, French
COUSIN, COUSINE   Libra, 1975, French
THE BLUE COUNTRY   LE PAYS BLEU   Quartet, 1977, French
IT'S A LONG TIME THAT I'VE LOVED YOU   SOUPCON
   Durham/Pike, 1979, French

SCOTT ANGLEY
Contact: ASCAP - Los Angeles, 213-883-1000

CLERKS   View Askew, 1994

PAUL ANTONELLI
Contact: ASCAP - Los Angeles, 213-883-1000

AVENGING ANGEL   co-composer with David Wheatley, Weitraub
   Productions, 1985
PRINCESS ACADEMY   co-composer with David Wheatley,
   Weintraub Productions, 1987, U.S.-French-Yugoslav
THE WOMEN'S CLUB   co-composer with David Wheatley,
   Weintraub-Cloverleaf/Scorsese Productions, 1987
CHINA O'BRIEN   co-composer with David Wheatley, Golden
   Harvest, 1989, U.S.-Hong Kong
OUT OF THE DARK   co-composer with David Wheatley, New Line
   Cinema, 1989

PHILIP APPLEBY

D.W. GRIFFITH: FATHER OF FILM (TD)   co-composer with Carl
   Davis and Nic Raine, WNET/Thames TV, 1993

ANA ARAIZ
THE GIRL IN THE WATERMELON   Mommy & Daddy Prods., 1994

NEIL ARGO
Agent: SMC Artists - Studio City, 818-505-9600

HUSH   Frameline Prods., 1988
THE ANDY DEVINE STORY   Film Buff Prods., 1989
THE LAUREATE   Robert Jacobson Films, 1990
MY INDIAN SUMMER (TF)   Big Daddy Prods., 1995
MAN IN A BAR   Plummer Prods., 1997

SEBASTIAN ARGOL
YOL   Triumph/Columbia, 1982, Turkish-Swiss-West German

EDDIE ARKIN*
Contact: BMI - Los Angeles, 310-659-9109

HARDBODIES 2   co-composer with Jay Levy, CineTel Films, 1986
MODERN GIRLS   co-composer with Jay Levy, Atlantic Releasing
   Corporation, 1986
PRETTY SMART   co-composer with Jay Levy, New World, 1987

MARTIN ARMIGER
Contact: APRA - Australia, 011-61-2-922-6422

YOUNG EINSTEIN   co-composer with William Motzig and Tommy
   Tycho, Warner Bros., 1988, Australian
SWEETIE   Avenue Pictures, 1990, Australian

MICHAEL ARMSTRONG
SILENT NIGHT, DEADLY NIGHT PART II   Silent Night Releasing
   Corp./Ascot Entertainment Group, 1987

DAVID ARNOLD

Agent: Vangelos Management - Encino, 818-380-1919
Affiliation: PRS - London, England, 011-44-1-580-5544

THE YOUNG AMERICANS   Gramercy, 1993
STARGATE   MGM, 1994
LAST OF THE DOGMEN   Savoy, 1995
INDEPENDENCE DAY   20th Century Fox, 1996
TOMORROW NEVER DIES   MGM-UA, 1997
GODZILLA   1998

MALCOLM ARNOLD

b. October 21, 1921 - Northampton, England
Contact: PRS - London, England, 011-44-1-580-5544

AVALANCHE PATROL (FD)   1947, British
CHARTING THE SEAS (FD)   1948, British
BADGER'S GREEN   1948, British
EVW'S (FD)   1949, British
THE FORBIDDEN STREET   *BRITTANIA MEWS*   20th
   Century-Fox, 1949
EYE WITNESS   *YOUR WITNESS*   Eagle Lion, 1950, British
HOME TO DANGER   Eros, 1951, British
NO HIGHWAY IN THE SKY   *NO HIGHWAY*   20th Century-Fox,
   1951, British
BREAKING THE SOUND BARRIER   *THE SOUND BARRIER*
   United Artists, 1952, British
STOLEN FACE   Exclusive Films, 1952, U.S.-British
WINGS OF DANGER   *DEAD ON COURSE*   Exclusive Films,
   1952, British
THE RINGER   British Lion, 1952, British
IT STARTED IN PARADISE   Astor, 1952, British
CURTAIN UP   General Film Distributors, 1952, British
HOME AT SEVEN   *MURDER ON MONDAY*   1952, British
FOUR-SIDED TRIANGLE   Exclusive Films, 1953, British
THE HOLLY AND THE IVY   British Lion, 1953, British
THE CAPTAIN'S PARADISE   British Lion, 1953, British
BREAK TO FREEDOM   *ALBERT R.N.*   United Artists, 1953,
   British
DEVIL ON HORSEBACK   British Lion, 1953, British
TWIST OF FATE   *THE BEAUTIFUL STRANGER*   United Artists,
   1954, British
YOU KNOW WHAT SAILORS ARE   United Artists, 1954, British
THE SEA SHALL NOT HAVE THEM   United Artists, 1954, British
THE SLEEPING TIGER   Astor, 1954, British
HOBSON'S CHOICE   United Artists, 1954, British
A PRIZE OF GOLD   Columbia, 1954
THE CONSTANT HUSBAND   British Lion, 1955, British
THE DEEP, BLUE SEA   20th Century-Fox, 1955, British
A WOMAN FOR JOE   Rank Film Distributors, 1955, British
THE NIGHT MY NUMBER CAME UP   General Film Distributors,
   1955, British
I AM A CAMERA   British Lion, 1955, British
MAN OF AFRICA   Group 3/Eden, 1956
PORT AFRIQUE   Columbia, 1956, British
HELL IN KOREA   *A HILL IN KOREA*   British Lion, 1956, British
TRAPEZE   United Artists, 1956
1984   Columbia, 1956, British
PORTRAIT IN SMOKE   Columbia, 1956
VALUE FOR MONEY   Rank, 1957, British
BELLES OF ST. TRINIAN'S   British Lion, 1957, British
THE BRIDGE ON THE RIVER KWAI ★★   Columbia, 1957, British
ISLAND IN THE SUN   20th Century-Fox, 1957
WICKED AS THEY COME   Columbia, 1957, British
BLUE MURDER AT ST. TRINIAN'S   British Lion, 1958, British
DUNKIRK   MGM, 1958, British
THE INN OF THE SIXTH HAPPINESS   20th Century-Fox, 1958,
   British
THE KEY   Columbia, 1958, British
THE ROOTS OF HEAVEN   20th Century-Fox, 1958
SOLOMON AND SHEBA   United Artists, 1959
BOY AND THE BRIDGE   Columbia, 1959
SUDDENLY LAST SUMMER   co-composer with Buxton Orr,
   Columbia, 1960
THE ANGRY SILENCE   Valiant, 1960, British
TUNES OF GLORY   Lopert, 1960, British
PURE HELL OF ST. TRINIANS   British Lion/Continental, 1961,
   British
OPERATION SNAFU   American International, 1961, British
NO LOVE FOR JOHNNIE   Embassy, 1961, British
WHISTLE DOWN THE WIND   Pathe-America, 1962, British

LISA   *THE INSPECTOR*   20th Century-Fox, 1962
THE LION   20th Century-Fox, 1962, British
NINE HOURS TO RAMA   20th Century-Fox, 1963, British-U.S.
TAMAHINE   MGM, 1964, British
THE CHALK GARDEN   Universal, 1964, British
THE THIN RED LINE   Allied Artists, 1964
THE HEROES OF TELEMARK   Columbia, 1965, British
THE GREAT ST. TRINIAN'S TRAIN ROBBERY   British Lion, 1966,
   British
GYPSY GIRL   *SKY WEST AND CROOKED*   Rank/Continental,
   1966, British
AFRICA - TEXAS STYLE!   Paramount, 1967, British-U.S.
THE RECKONING   Columbia, 1969, British
DAVID COPPERFIELD (TF)   Omnibus Productions/Sagittarius
   Productions, 1970, British-U.S.

PETER ARNOW

Contact: ASCAP - Los Angeles, 213-883-1047

TORN APART   Castle Hill, 1990

BRUCE ARNSTSON

Contact: BMI - Los Angeles, 310-659-9109

ERNEST GOES TO JAIL   co-composer with Kirby Shelstad, Buena
   Vista, 1990
ERNEST SCARED STUPID   co-composer with Kirby Shelstad,
   Touchstone, 1991
ERNEST RIDES AGAIN   co-composer with Kirby Shelstad,
   Emshell, 1993

LEON ARONSON

Contact: SOCAN - Toronto, 416-445-8700

EDDIE AND THE CRUISERS II: EDDIE LIVES   co-composer with
   Marty Simon and Kenny Vance, Scotti Bros. Pictures/Aurora Film
   Partners, 1989

JORGE ARRIAGADA

IT'S ALL TRUE (FD)   Paramount, 1993, French-U.S.

EDUARD ARTEMYEV

Contact: BMI - Los Angeles, 310-659-9109

AT HOME AMONG STRANGERS   1974, Soviet
A SLAVE OF LOVE   Cinema 5, 1976, Soviet
PLATANOV   1977, Soviet
SOLARIS   Mosfilm, 1972, Soviet
STALKER   New Yorker/Media Transactions Corporation, 1979,
   Soviet
SIBERIADE   IFEX Film, 1979, Soviet
HOMER AND EDDIE   King's Road Entertainment, 1989
URGA   1991, French-Russian
THE INNER CIRCLE   Columbia, 1991
DOUBLE JEOPARDY (CTF)   Boxleitner-Bernstein/CBS
   Entertainment, 1992
ANNA 6-18   1994, Russian-French
BURNT BY THE SUN   *OUTOMLIONNYE SOLNTSEM*   Studio
   Trite/Camera One, 1994, Russian-French

BENT ASERUD

Contact: ASCAP - Los Angeles, 213-883-1047

FRIDA - STRAIGHT FROM THE HEART   *FRIDA- MED HJERTET I
   HANDEN*   co-composer with Geir Bohren, 1992, Norwegian

GELA SAWALL ASHCROFT

Contact: BMI - Los Angeles, 310-659-9109

THE LONG RIDE HOME   Rising Star, 1996

JAY ASHER

Contact: BMI - Los Angeles, 310-659-9109

FUGITIVE NIGHTS: DANGER IN THE DESERT (TF)   TriStar TV,
   1993

B

GIL ASKEY
Contact: BMI - Los Angeles, 310-659-9109

DUMMY (TF) The Konigsberg Company/Warner Bros. TV, 1979

EDWIN ASTLEY
Contact: PRS - London, England, 011-44-1-580-5544

TO PARIS, WITH LOVE General Film Distributors, 1955, British
THE CASE OF THE MUKKINESE BATTLEHORN 1956, British
KILL HER GENTLY 1957, British
WISHING WELL INN 1958, British
IN THE WAKE OF A STRANGER 1958, British
THE GIANT BEHEMOTH 1959, British
THE MOUSE THAT ROARED Columbia, 1959, British
WOMAN EATER 1959, British
THE DAY THEY ROBBED THE BANK OF ENGLAND MGM, 1960, British
PASSPORT TO CHINA VISA TO CANTON Columbia, 1961, British
A MATTER OF WHO Herts Lion, 1962, British
THE PHANTOM OF THE OPERA Universal, 1962, British
DIGBY, THE BIGGEST DOG IN THE WORLD Cinerama Releasing Corporation, 1974, British

PAUL ASTON
JOEY BREAKER Skouras, 1993

CHET ATKINS
Contact: BMI - Los Angeles, 310-659-9109

STROSZEK co-composer with Sonny Terry, New Yorker, 1977, West German

MURRAY ATTAWAY
Contact: BMI - Los Angeles, 310-659-9109

MIDNIGHT EDITION Shapiro Glickenhaus, 1994

MARK AUSTIN
Contact: BMI - Los Angeles, 310-659-9109

ABSENT WITHOUT LEAVE co-composer with Don McGlashan and David Long, 1993, New Zealand

JOHN AUTHOR
SHADOW OF THE DRAGON co-composer with Michael Benghiat, Hatch Entertainment, 1994

PEPE AVILA
MY FAMILY MI FAMILIA co-composer with Mark McKenzie, New Line, 1995

DAVID A. AXELROD
Contact: BMI - Los Angeles, 310-659-9109

CANNONBALL New World, 1976

HEIDI AYDT
DER OLYMPISCHE SOMMER THE OLYMPIC SUMMER (FD) co-composer with Frank Will, 1993, German

ROY AYERS
Contact: ASCAP - Los Angeles, 213-883-1000

COFFY American International, 1973

PEDRO AZNAR
Contact: BMI - Los Angeles, 310-659-9109

MAN FACING SOUTHEAST FilmDallas, 1987, Argentine
LAST IMAGES OF THE SHIPWRECK Enrique Marti, Films Cinequanon SRL, 1989, Argentine-Spanish

FRYDERYCK BABINSKI
GLUCHY TELEFON CROSSED LINES 1991, Polish

BRUCE BABCOCK*
Contact: BMI - Los Angeles, 310-659-9109

MATLOCK: THE HUNTING PARTY (TF) Dean Hargrove Prods./Fred Silverman Co.Viacom, 1989
MOMENT OF TRUTH: WHY MY DAUGHTER ? (TF) O'Hara-Horowitz Prods., 1993
MATLOCK: THE FORTUNE (TF) Dean Hargrove Prods./Fred Silverman Co.Viacom, 1993
MOMENT OF TRUTH: A CHILD TOO MANY? (TF) O'Hara-Horowitz Prods., 1993
MOMENT OF TRUTH: STALKING BACK (TF) O'Hara-Horowitz Prods., 1993
MEN WHO HATE WOMEN AND THE WOMEN WHO LOVE THEM (TF) O'Hara-Horowitz, 1994
MATLOCK: THE HEIST (TF) Dean Hargrove Prods./Fred Silverman Co.Viacom, 1995

LUIS BACALOV
b. Spain
Agent: The Kraft-Benjamin Agency - Beverly Hills, 310-247-0123
Affiliation: SIAE - Italy, 011-39-6-59-901

LA BANDA DEL BUCO 1960, Italian
VINO, WHISKY E ACQUA SALATA co-composer, 1962, Italian
I DUE DELLA LEGIONE Ultra Film, 1962, Italian
THE EMPTY CANVAS LA NOIA Embassy, 1964, Italian
DONDE TU ESTES 1964, Spanish-Italian
THE GOSPEL ACCORDING TO ST. MATTHEW ★ Continental, 1965, Italian
LA CONGIUNTURA Fair Film/Les Films Concordia, 1965, Italian-French
EXTRA CONJUGALE composer of "La Roccia" segment, 1965, Italian
LET'S TALK ABOUT MEN QUESTA VOLTA PARLIAMO DI UOMINI Allied Artists, 1965, Italian
ALTISSIMA PRESSIONE co-composer with Ennio Morricone, 1965, Italian
THRILLING co-composer with Ennio Morricone, 1965, Italian
DJANGO BRC, 1966, Italian
BALLATA DA UN MILIARDO 1966, Italian
A MATTER OF HONOR 1966, Italian
MI VEDRAI TORNARE co-composer, 1966, Italian
SE NON AVESSI PIU TE co-composer, 1966, Italian
LA STREGA IN AMORE Arco Film, 1966, Italian
SUGAR COLT 1966, Italian
PER AMORE...PER MAGIA 1967, Italian
A CIASCUNO IL SUO WE STILL KILL THE OLD WAY 1967, Italian
THE GREATEST KIDNAPPING IN THE WEST 1967, Italian
LO SCATENATO CATCH AS CATCH CAN 1967, Italian
QUESTI FANTASMI GHOSTS ITALIAN STYLE 1967, Italian
A QUALISIASI PREZZO VATICAN STORY 1968, Italian
LA BAMBOLONA BABY DOLL 1968, Italian
LA PECORA NERA THE BLACK SHEEP 1968, Italian
I PROTAGONISTI 1968, Italian
REBUS 1968, Italian
BULLET FOR THE GENERAL QUIEN SABE? Avco Embassy, 1968, Italian-Spanish
TUTTO PER TUTTO co-composer with Marcello Giombini, 1968, Italian
LA MORTE SULL' ALTA COLLINA 1969, Italian
I QUATTRO DEL PATER NOSTER 1969, Italian
IL PREZZO DEL POTERE THE PRICE OF POWER 1969, Italian
L'AMICA Fair Film, 1969, Italian
CUORI SOLITARI LONELY HEARTS 1970, Italian
L'ORO DEI BRAVADOS 1970, Italian

LA VITTIMA DESIGNATA   1971, Italian
LA SUPERTESTIMONE   1971, Italian
LA GRANDE SCROFA NERA   1971, Italian
LO CHIAMAVANO KING   1971, Italian
ROMA BENE   1971, Italian
THE SUMMERTIME KILLER   co-composer with Sergio Bardotti,
   1971, Italian
BEATI E RICCHI   1972, Italian
SI PUO FARE, AMIGO   *CAN BE DONE, AMIGO*   1972, Italian
IL GRANDE DUELLO   *THE GRAND DUEL*   1972, Italian
MILANO CALIBRO 9   1972, Italian
MONTA IN SELLA, FIGLIO DI...!   1972, Italian
LO CHIAMAVANO MEZZOGIORNO   *THE MAN CALLED NOON*
   1972, Italian
L'ULTIMA CHANCE   1973, Italian
LA ROSA ROSSA   *THE RED ROSE*   1973, Italian
PARTIRONO PRETI, TORNARONO...CURATI   1973, Italian
IL BOSS   1973, Italian
LA SEDUZIONE   *SEDUCTION*   Gemini, 1973, Italian
IN LOVE WITH SEX   EFC, 1973, French-Italian-Canadian
LA POLIZIA E AL SERVIZIO DEL CITTADINO?   1973, Italian
IL POLIZIOTTO E MARCIO   1974, Italian
SISTEMO L'AMERICA E TORNO   *I FIX AMERICA AND RETURN*
   1974, Italian
L'UOMO CHE SFIDO L'ORGANIZZAZIONE   1975, Italian
GLI ESECUTORI   *STREET PEOPLE*   1975, Italian
IL LUNGO VIAGGIO (TF)   1975, Italian
COLPO IN CANNA   1975, Italian
COLPITA DA IMPROVVISO BENESSERE   1975, Italian
LA CITTA SCONVOLTA: CACCIA SPIETATA AI RAPITORI   1975,
   Italian
GRAZIE TANTE E ARRIVEDERCI   1976, Italian
GLI AMICI DI NICK HEZARD   1976, Italian
IL CONTO E CHIUSO   *THE LAST ROUND*   1976, Italian
I PADRONI DELLA CITTA   1976, Italian
I PROSSENETI   1976, Italian
UN ANNO DI SCUOLA   1976, Italian
DIAMANTI SPORCHI DI SANGUE   1977, Italian
IL BALORDO (TF)   1978, Italian
IMPROVVISO   1979, Italian
LE MAESTRO (TF)   1979, Italian
THE GREEN JACKET   CEP, 1979, Italian
LE ROSE DI DANZICA   1979, Italian
VACANZE PER UN MASSACRO   1979, Italian
TEN TO SURVIVE (AF)   co-composer, 1979, Italian
LA RAGAZZA DI VIA MILLE LIRE   1980, Italian
CITY OF WOMEN   New Yorker, 1980, Italian-French
LE JEUNE MARIE   AMLF, 1982, French-Italian
ENTRE NOUS   *COUP DE FOUDRE*   United Artists Classics, 1983,
   French
L'ART D'AIMER   Parafrance, 1983, French-Italian
LE JUGE   1983, French
UN AMOUR INTERDIT   1983, French
UN CASO DI INCOSCIENZA (TF)   1983, Italian
UNA STRANA PASSIONE   1984, Italian-French
LE TRANSFUGE   1985, French-Italian
THE POSTMAN   *IL POSTINO* ★★   Miramax, 1995,
   Italian-French-Belgian
B. MONKEY   1997
POLISH WEDDING   1997

BURT BACHARACH
b. May 12, 1929 - Kansas City, Missouri
Contact: ASCAP - Los Angeles, 213-883-1000

WHAT'S NEW PUSSYCAT?   United Artists, 1965, British
AFTER THE FOX   United Artists, 1966, Italian-U.S.-British
CASINO ROYALE   Columbia, 1967, British
BUTCH CASSIDY AND THE SUNDANCE KID ★★   20th
   Century-Fox, 1969
LOST HORIZON   Columbia, 1972
TOGETHER?   1979, Italian
ARTHUR   Warner Bros., 1981
NIGHT SHIFT   The Ladd Company/Warner Bros., 1982
ARTHUR 2 - ON THE ROCKS   Warner Bros., 1988

PIERRE BACHELET
b. France
Contact: SACEM - France, 011-33-1-4715-4715

EMMANUELLE   Columbia, 1974, French
COUP DE TETE   *HOTHEAD*   Quartet, 1980, French
BLACK AND WHITE IN COLOR   *LA VICTOIRE EN CHANTANT*
   Allied Artists, 1978, French-Ivory Coast-Swiss
UN HOMME A MA TAILLE   1983, French
GWENDOLINE   Samuel Goldwyn Company, 1984, French
EMMANUELLE 5   AAA, 1987, French

MICHAEL BACON
Contact: BMI - Los Angeles, 310-659-9109

LBJ (TD)   KERA/David Grubin Prods., 1991
THE KENNEDYS (TD)   WGBH/Thames TV, 1992
THE AMERICAN EXPERIENCE: FDR (TD)   David Grubin
   Prods./WGBH-Boston, 1994
THE WINDSORS: A ROYAL FAMILY (TD)   WGBH-Boston/Brook
   Ass., 1994
DRIVING PASSION: AMERICA'S LOVE AFFAIR WITH THE CAR
   (CTD)   Turner, 1995
LOSING CHASE   1996

ANGELO BADALAMENTI
Agent: Film Music Associates - Hollywood, 213-463-1070
Affiliation: ASCAP - Los Angeles, 213-883-1000

GORDON'S WAR   20th Century Fox, 1973
LAW AND DISORDER   Columbia, 1974
ACROSS THE GREAT DIVIDE   Pacific International, 1976
BLUE VELVET   DEG, 1986
NIGHTMARE ON ELM STREET III: DREAM WARRIORS   New Line
   Cinema, 1987
TOUGH GUYS DON'T DANCE   Cannon, 1987
WEEDS   DEG, 1987
WAIT UNTIL SPRING, BANDINI   Orion Classics, 1989,
   Belgian-French-Italian-U.S.
COUSINS   Paramount, 1989
NATIONAL LAMPOON'S CHRISTMAS VACATION   Warner Bros.,
   1989
TWIN PEAKS (TF)   Lynch-Frost Productions/Propoganda Films, 1990
THE COMFORT OF STRANGERS   Elle Productions, 1990
WILD AT HEART   Samuel Goldwyn Co., 1990
TWIN PEAKS: FIRE WALK WITH ME   New Line, 1992
HOTEL ROOM (CTF)   Asymmetrical/Propaganda, 1993
NAKED IN NEW YORK   Fine Line, 1993
WITCH HUNT (CTF)   Pacific Western Prods., 1994
THE CITY OF LOST CHILDREN   *LA CITE DES ENFANTS
   PERDUS*   Sony Classics, 1995, French-Spanish-German
LOST HIGHWAY   October Films, 1997

WALLY BADAROU
Contact: SACEM - France, 011-33-1-4715-4715

COUNTRY MAN   1982
GOOD TO GO   Island Pictures, 1986
THE LUNATIC   Triton, 1992

DON BAGLEY
Contact: ASCAP - Los Angeles, 213-883-1000

MAMA'S DIRTY GIRLS   1974
THE STUDENT BODY   1975
YOUNG LADY CHATTERLEY   adaptation, PRO International,
   1977

LOUIS BAGUE
LA PALOMA BLANCA   *THE WHITE DOVE*   1991, Spanish

TOM BAHLER
Agent: BMI - Los Angeles, 310-659-9109

MARY, MARY, BLOODY MARY   1975
FAST FORWARD   Columbia, 1985
U.S. MARSHALS: WACO & RHINEHART (TF)   co-composer,
   Touchstone Films, 1987

COLD FEET Avenue, 1989
THE OBJECT OF BEAUTY Avenue, 1991, U.S.-British
IN THE EYES OF A STRANGER (TF) Power Pictures/Avenue
  Entertainment/Hearst Entertainment, 1992
GORDY Miramax, 1995

RACHID BAHRI
BAB EL-OUED CITY 1994, French-Algerian-German-Swiss

PETE BAIKIE
THIN ICE additional music, 1995, British

ACHMAD BAKAEV
KOSH BA KOSH *ODDS AND EVENS* 1993,
  Tadjik-Japanese-Swiss

BUDDY BAKER*
(Norman Dale Baker)
b. January 1, 1918 - Springfield, Missouri
Contact: ASCAP - Los Angeles, 213-883-1047

SUMMER MAGIC Buena Vista, 1963
THE MISADVENTURES OF MERLIN JONES Buena Vista, 1964
A TIGER WALKS Buena Vista, 1964
THE MONKEY'S UNCLE Buena Vista, 1964
THE GNOME-MOBILE Buena Vista, 1967
MILLION DOLLAR DUCK Buena Vista, 1971
NAPOLEON AND SAMANTHA ★ Buena Vista, 1972
SUPERDAD Buena Vista, 1974
THE BEARS AND I Buena Vista, 1974
THE APPLE DUMPLING GANG Buena Vista, 1975
NO DEPOSIT, NO RETURN Buena Vista, 1976
THE SHAGGY D.A. Buena Vista, 1976
TREASURE OF MATECUMBE Buena Vista, 1976
HOT LEAD AND COLD FEET Buena Vista, 1978
THE APPLE DUMPLING GANG RIDES AGAIN Buena Vista, 1979
THE DEVIL AND MAX DEVLIN co-composer with Marvin Hamlisch,
  Buena Vista, 1981
THE FOX AND THE HOUND (AF) Buena Vista, 1981
THE PUPPETOON MOVIE (FD) Expanded Entertainment, 1987

FRED BAKER
Contact: SESAC - New York, 212-586-3450

WHITE TRASH Fred Baker, 1992

MICHAEL CONWAY BAKER*
b. Canada
Contact: SOCAN - Toronto, 416-445-8700

SILENCE OF THE NORTH Universal, 1981, Canadian
DESERTERS Exile Productions, 1983, Canadian
THE GREY FOX United Artists Classics, 1983, Canadian
ONE MAGIC CHRISTMAS Buena Vista, 1985, U.S.-Canadian
LOYALTIES Norstar Releasing, 1986, Canadian-British
OVERNIGHT Lauron Productions, 1986, Canadian
ANYTHING TO SURVIVE (TF) ATL Productions/B.C. Films, 1990
THE PORTRAIT Raincoast, 1992

ALEXANDER BALANESCU
ANGELS AND INSECTS Samuel Goldwyn, 1995

RICHARD H. BAND*
Contact: BMI - Los Angeles, 310-659-9109

LASERBLAST co-composer with Joel Goldsmith, Irwin Yablans,
  1978
THE DAY TIME ENDED Compass International, 1979
DR. HECKLE AND MR. HYPE Cannon, 1980
PARASITE Embassy, 1982
THE HOUSE ON SORORITY ROW Artists Releasing
  Corporation/Film Ventures International, 1983
TIME WALKER New World, 1983
METALSTORM: THE DESTRUCTION OF JARED SYN Universal,
  1983
MUTANT *NIGHT SHADOWS* Artists Releasing Corporation/Film
  Ventures International, 1984

GHOULIES co-composer with Shirley Walker, Empire Pictures,
  1985
THE DUNGEONMASTER co-composer with Shirley Walker,
  Empire Pictures, 1985
THE ALCHEMIST Empire Pictures, 1985
H.P. LOVECRAFT'S REANIMATOR *REANIMATOR* Empire
  Pictures, 1985
ELIMINATORS Empire Pictures, 1986
TERRORVISION Empire Pictures, 1986
GHOST WARRIOR *SWORDKILL* Empire Pictures, 1986
FROM BEYOND Empire Pictures, 1986
TROLL Empire Pictures, 1986
ZONE TROOPERS Empire Pictures, 1986
THE CALLER Empire Pictures, 1987
DOLLS Empire Pictures, 1987
PRISON co-composer with Christopher L. Stone, Empire Pictures,
  1988
PUPPET MASTER Full Moon, 1989
BRIDE OF RE-ANIMATOR Empire Pictures, 1990
BRIDE OF THE RE-ANIMATOR 50th Street, 1991
THE PIT AND THE PENDULUM Full Moon, 1991
THE RESURRECTED Scotti Bros., 1992

FRAN BANISH
AT GROUND ZERO (FD) Proletariat Pictures/Roadfilm, 1994

ANTHONY BANKS
Contact: Soundtrack Music Management - London,
  011-44-81-876-2533
Affiliation: ASCAP - Los Angeles, 213-883-1047

THE SHOUT co-composer with Rupert Hine and Michael
  Rutherford, Films Inc., 1979, British
THE WICKED LADY MGM/UA/Cannon, 1983, British
QUICKSILVER Columbia, 1986

BRIAN BANKS
Contact: BMI - Los Angeles, 310-659-9109

EPILOGUE OF DOOM co-composer with Anthony Marinelli,
  Odette Productions, 1984
RIGGED co-composer with Anthony Marinelli, CineStar, 1985
NICE GIRLS DON'T EXPLODE co-composer with Anthony
  Marinelli, New World, 1987
PINOCCHIO AND THE EMPEROR OF THE NIGHT (AF)
  co-composer with Anthony Marinelli, New World, 1987
YOUNG GUNS co-composer with Anthony Marinelli, 20th Century
  Fox, 1988
SPOONER (TF) co-composer with Anthony Marinelli, Walt Disney
  Productions, 1989
INTERNAL AFFAIRS co-composer with Mike Figgis and Anthony
  Marinelli, Paramount, 1990
GRAVEYARD SHIFT co-composer with Anthony Marinelli,
  Paramount, 1990

DON BANKS
b. 1923 - Australia
Contact: APRA - Australia, 011-61-2-922-6422

NIGHT CREATURES *CAPTAIN CLEGG* 1962, British
NIGHTMARE Universal, 1964, British
THE EVIL OF FRANKENSTEIN Universal, 1964, British
HYSTERIA MGM, 1965, British
DIE, MONSTER, DIE! American International, 1965, U.S.-British
RASPUTIN - THE MAD MONK *I KILLED RASPUTIN* 20th
  Century-Fox, 1966, British-French-Italian
THE REPTILE 1966, British
THE MUMMY'S SHROUD 20th Century-Fox, 1967, British
THE FROZEN DEAD Warner Bros., 1967, British
TORTURE GARDEN co-composer with James Bernard, Columbia,
  1968, British

DIDIER BARBELIVIEN
LES MISERABLES co-composer with Francis Lai, Philippe Servain,
  Erik Berchot and Michel Legrand, Warner Bros., 1995, French

BILLY BARBER
MYSTERY SCIENCE THEATER 3000: THE MOVIE 1996

JOHN BARBER
Contact: ASCAP - Los Angeles, 213-883-1047

THE INCREDIBLE TWO-HEADED TRANSPLANT   American
    International, 1971
PINOCCHIO   EUE, 1971

LESLEY BARBER
Agent: CAA - Beverly Hills, 310-288-4545

TURNING APRIL   1996, Canadian-Australian

STEPHEN BARBER
Contact: ASCAP - Los Angeles, 213-883-1047

GALAXIES ARE COLLIDING   SC Entertainment, 1992

JOSEPH BARBERA
Contact: BMI - Los Angeles, 310-659-9109

I YABBA-DABBA DO! (ATF)   co-composer with John Debney, Hoyt
    Curtin and William Hanna, H-B Prods., 1993
JONNY'S GOLDEN QUEST (ATF)   co-composer of theme only with
    William Hanna and Hoyt Curtin,
    Hanna-Barbera/USA/Fil-Cartoons, 1993

GATO BARBIERI
Contact: BMI - Los Angeles, 310-659-9109

BEFORE THE REVOLUTION   co-composer with Ennio Morricone,
    New Yorker, 1964, Italian
NOTES FOR AN AFRICAN ORESTES   1970, Italian
LAST TANGO IN PARIS   United Artists, 1973, Italian-French
THE PIG'S WAR   1975, Argentine
FIREPOWER   AFD, 1979, British
STRANGER'S KISS   Orion Classics, 1983
DIARIO DI UN VIZIO   *DIARY OF A MANIAC*   1993, Italian

JAMES H. BARDEN
Contact: ASCAP - Los Angeles, 213-883-1047

THE JUDAS PROJECT   RS Entertainment, 1993

NIK BARILUK
AMERICA'S WAR ON POVERTY (TD)   co-composer with Brian
    Keane, Blackside Inc., 1995

KHALED BARKAT
YOUCEF, OU LA LEGENDE DU SEPTIEME DORMANT   *YOUCEF,*
    OR THE LEGEND OF THE SEVENTH SLEEPER   1993,
    Algerian-French

JOHN BARNES
Contact: ASCAP - Los Angeles, 213-883-1047

DAUGHTERS OF THE DUST   American Playhouse, 1991
BEBE'S KIDS (AF)   1992, Paramount
BETTER OFF DEAD (CTF)   Heller-Steinem/Viacom, 1992
CB4   Universal, 1993
COSMIC SLOP: SPACE TRADERS (CTF)   co-composer with
    George Clinton and Bernard Worrell, Hudlin Bros. Prods./HBO,
    1994
DON'T BE A MENACE TO SOUTH CENTRAL WHILE DRINKING
    YOUR JUICE IN THE HOOD   Mriamax, 1996

CHARLES P. BARNETT*
Contact: BMI - Los Angeles, 310-659-9109

HELL SQUAD   Cannon, 1986
BUSTED UP   Shapiro Entertainment, 1987
HEADLESS BODY IN A TOPLESS BAR   Curb, 1995

MARC BARRECA
THE ENQUIRERS   1992

GEORGE BARRIE
Contact: ASCAP - Los Angeles, 213-883-1000

FINGERS   Brut Productions, 1978

BEBE BARRON
Contact: BMI - Los Angeles, 310-659-9109

FORBIDDEN PLANET   co-composer with Louis Barron, MGM,
    1956
THE VERY EDGE OF THE NIGHT   co-composer with Louis Barron,
    1959
SPACEBOY   co-composer with Louis Barron, 1972

DE WAYNE BARRON
BEACH BEVERLY HILLS   Trident, 1993

LOUIS BARRON
FORBIDDEN PLANET   co-composer with Bebe Barron, MGM,
    1956
THE VERY EDGE OF THE NIGHT   co-composer with Bebe Barron,
    1959
SPACEBOY   co-composer with Bebe Barron, 1972

DAEMION BARRY
Contact: Soundtrack Music Management - London,
    011-44-71-581-0330

THICKER THAN WATER (TF)   co-composer with Julian Wastall,
    BBC/A&E, 1994, British

JEFF BARRY
Contact: BMI - Los Angeles, 310-659-9109

THE IDOLMAKER   United Artists, 1980
SPIKER   Seymour Borde & Associates, 1986
YOUR MOTHER WEARS COMBAT BOOTS (TF)   co-composer
    with Barry Fasman, NBC Productions, 1989

JOHN BARRY
b. 1933 - York, England
Agent: The Kraft-Benjamin Agency - Beverly Hills, 310-247-0123
Affiliation: BMI - Los Angeles, 310-659-9109

WILD FOR KICKS   *BEAT GIRL*   Renown, 1959, British
NEVER LET GO   Rank, 1960, British
DR. NO   uncredited composer of theme, United Artists, 1962,
    British
MIX ME A PERSON   1962, British
THEY ALL DIED LAUGHING   *A JOLLY BAD FELLOW*
    Continental, 1963, British
THE L-SHAPED ROOM   Columbia, 1963, British
FROM RUSSIA WITH LOVE   United Artists, 1963, British
THE AMOROUS MR. PRAWN   British Lion, 1964, British
MAN IN THE MIDDLE   20th Century-Fox, 1964, British-U.S.
ZULU   Embassy, 1964, British
SEANCE ON A WET AFTERNOON   Artixo, 1964, British
GOLDFINGER   United Artists, 1964, British
FOUR IN THE MORNING   West One, 1965, British
THE IPCRESS FILE   Universal, 1965, British
KING RAT   Columbia, 1965, British
THE KNACK...AND HOW TO GET IT   Lopert, 1965, British
MISTER MOSES   United Artists, 1965, British
THUNDERBALL   United Artists, 1965, British
BORN FREE ★★   Columbia, 1966, British
THE QUILLER MEMORANDUM   Paramount, 1966, British
THE CHASE   Columbia, 1966
THE WRONG BOX   Columbia, 1966, British
DUTCHMAN   Continental, 1967, British
THE WHISPERERS   United Artists, 1967, British
YOU ONLY LIVE TWICE   United Artists, 1967, British
PETULIA   Warner Bros., 1968, U.S.-British
BOOM!   Universal, 1968, British-U.S.
DEADFALL   also appears as conductor, 20th Century-Fox, 1968,
    British
THE LION IN WINTER ★★   Avco Embassy, 1968, British
THE APPOINTMENT   MGM, 1969

ON HER MAJESTY'S SECRET SERVICE   United Artists, 1969,
    British
MIDNIGHT COWBOY   United Artists, 1969
MONTE WALSH   National General, 1970
WALKABOUT   20th Century Fox, 1971, British-Australian
THE LAST VALLEY   Cinerama Releasing Corporation, 1971,
    British
MURPHY'S WAR   theme only, Universal, 1971
DIAMONDS ARE FOREVER   United Artists, 1971
MARY, QUEEN OF SCOTS ★   Universal, 1971, British
THEY MIGHT BE GIANTS   Universal, 1971
ALICE'S ADVENTURES IN WONDERLAND   American National
    Enterprises, 1972, British
THE PUBLIC EYE   Universal, 1972
A DOLL'S HOUSE   Tomorrow Entertainment, 1973, British-French
THE GLASS MENAGERIE (TF)   Talent Associates, 1973
THE MAN WITH THE GOLDEN GUN   United Artists, 1974, British
THE DOVE   Paramount, 1974
THE TAMARIND SEED   Avco Embassy, 1974
LOVE AMONG THE RUINS (TF)   ABC Circle Films, 1975
THE DAY OF THE LOCUST   Paramount, 1975
ELEANOR AND FRANKLIN (TF)   Talent Associates, 1976
ROBIN AND MARIAN   Columbia, 1976, British
KING KONG   Paramount, 1976
ELEANOR AND FRANKLIN: THE WHITE HOUSE YEARS (TF) ☆
    Talent Associates, 1977
THE WAR BETWEEN THE TATES (TF)   Talent Associates, 1977
THE GATHERING (TF)   Hanna-Barbera Productions, 1977
YOUNG JOE, THE FORGOTTEN KENNEDY (TF)   ABC Circle
    Films, 1977
THE DEEP   Columbia, 1977
THE WHITE BUFFALO   United Artists, 1977
FIRST LOVE   Paramount, 1977
THE BETSY   Allied Artists, 1978
THE CORN IS GREEN (TF)   Warner Bros. TV, 1979
GAME OF DEATH   Columbia, 1979, U.S.-Hong Kong
HANOVER STREET   Columbia, 1979
STARCRASH   New World, 1979, Italian
MOONRAKER   United Artists, 1979, British-French
WILLA (TF)   GJL Productions/Dove, Inc., 1979
THE BLACK HOLE   Buena Vista, 1979
RAISE THE TITANIC   AFD, 1980, British-U.S.
NIGHT GAMES   Avco Embassy, 1980
TOUCHED BY LOVE   Columbia, 1980
SOMEWHERE IN TIME   Universal, 1980
INSIDE MOVES   AFD, 1980
MURDER BY PHONE   *BELLS*   New World, 1980, Canadian
THE LEGEND OF THE LONE RANGER   Universal/AFD, 1981
BODY HEAT   The Ladd Company/Warner Bros., 1981
FRANCES   Universal, 1982
HAMMETT   Orion/Warner Bros., 1982
SVENGALI (TF)   Robert Halmi Productions, 1983
THE GOLDEN SEAL   co-composer with Dana Kaproff, Samuel
    Goldwyn Company, 1983
HIGH ROAD TO CHINA   Warner Bros., 1983, U.S.-Yugoslavian
OCTOPUSSY   MGM/UA, 1983, British
MIKE'S MURDER   Universal, 1984
UNTIL SEPTEMBER   MGM/UA, 1984
THE COTTON CLUB   Orion, 1984
A VIEW TO A KILL   MGM/UA, 1985, British
JAGGED EDGE   Columbia, 1985
OUT OF AFRICA ★★   Universal, 1985
HOWARD THE DUCK   co-composer with Sylvester Levay,
    Universal, 1986
PEGGY SUE GOT MARRIED   Tri-Star, 1986
HEARTS OF FIRE   Lorimar, 1987, U.S.-British
THE LIVING DAYLIGHTS   MGM/UA, 1987, British
A KILLING AFFAIR   Hemdale, 1988
MASQUERADE   MGM/UA, 1988
DANCES WITH WOLVES ★★   Orion, 1990
CHAPLIN ★   TriStar, 1992
RUBY CAIRO   Miramax, 1993
INDECENT PROPOSAL   Paramount, 1993
MY LIFE   Columbia, 1993
THE SPECIALIST   Warner Bros., 1994
THE SCARLET LETTER   Buena Vista, 1995
CRY THE BELOVED COUNTRY   Miramax, 1995
ACROSS THE SEA OF TIME   1995
THE HORSE WHISPERER   1997
AMY FOSTER   1997

LIONEL BART
b. 1930
Contact: PRS - London, England, 011-44-1-580-5544

BLACK BEAUTY   Paramount, 1971, British-West German-Spanish

ALEC BARTCH
THE HANGED MAN   Lot 49, 1993

STEVE BARTEK
Agent: Film Music Associates - Hollywood, 213-463-1070
Affiliation: BMI - Los Angeles, 310-659-9109

GUILTY AS CHARGED   I.R.S., 1991
PAST MIDNIGHT (CTF)   Cinetel, 1992
CABIN BOY   Buena Vista, 1994
COLD BLOODED   Polygram/Propaganda/MPCA, 1995
NATIONAL LAMPOON'S SENIOR TRIP   New Line, 1995,
    Canadian

DEE BARTON
Contact: ASCAP - Los Angeles, 213-883-1000

PLAY MISTY FOR ME   Universal, 1971
HIGH PLAINS DRIFTER   Universal, 1972
THUNDERBOLT AND LIGHTFOOT   United Artists, 1974

RICHARD BASKIN
Contact: ASCAP - Los Angeles, 213-883-1000

CONGRATULATIONS, IT'S A BOY! (TF)   co-composer with Basil
    Poledouris, Aaron Spelling Productions, 1971
NASHVILLE   Paramount, 1976
BUFFALO BILL AND THE INDIANS or SITTING BULL'S HISTORY
    LESSON   United Artists, 1976
WELCOME TO L.A.   United Artists/Lions Gate, 1976
JAMES AT 15 (TF)   20th Century-Fox TV, 1977
HONEYSUCKLE ROSE   Warner Bros., 1980
UFORIA   Universal, 1984

BORIS BASOUROV
RYABA, MY CHICKEN   *KOUROTCHKA RIABA/RIABA MA
    POULE*   1994, Russian-French

ULRICH BASSENGE
DIE MACHT DER BILER: LENI RIEFENSTAHL   *THE POWER OF
    THE IMAGE: LENI RIEFENSTAHL* (FD)   co-composer with
    Wolfgang Neumann, 1993, German-British-French

KEVIN BASSINSON*
Contact: ASCAP - Los Angeles, 213-883-1000

CYBORG   Cannon, 1989

GEORGE BASSMAN
b. 1914
Contact: ASCAP - Los Angeles, 213-883-1000

A DAMNSEL IN DISTRESS   adaptation, RKO Radio, 1937
A DAY AT THE RACES   MGM, 1937
EVERYBODY SING   MGM, 1938
BABES IN ARMS   MGM, 1939
TOO MANY GIRLS   adaptation, RKO Radio, 1940
TWO GIRLS ON BROADWAY   MGM, 1940
GO WEST   MGM, 1940
LADY BE GOOD   MGM, 1941
THE BIG STORE   MGM, 1941
BABES ON BROADWAY   MGM, 1941
PANAMA HATTIE   MGM, 1942
FOR ME AND MY GAL   MGM, 1942
CABIN IN THE SKY   adaptation, MGM, 1943
BEST FOOT FORWARD   adaptation, MGM, 1943
YOUNG IDEAS   MGM, 1943
WHISTLING IN BROOKLYN   MGM, 1943
THE CANTERVILLE GHOST   MGM, 1944
MAIN STREET AFTER DARK   MGM, 1945
THE CLOCK   MGM, 1945

ABBOTT & COSTELLO IN HOLLYWOOD   MGM, 1945
A LETTER FOR EVIE   MGM, 1946
THE POSTMAN ALWAYS RINGS TWICE   MGM, 1946
TWO SMART PEOPLE   MGM, 1946
LITTLE MISTER JIM   MGM, 1947
THE ROMANCE OF ROSY RIDGE   MGM, 1947
THE ARNELO AFFAIR   MGM, 1947
JAPAN AND THE WORLD TODAY (FD)   U.S. Government, 1950
THE JOE LOUIS STORY   United Artists, 1953
LOUISIANA TERRITORY   RKO Radio, 1953
CANYON CROSSROADS   United Artists, 1955
MIDDLE OF THE NIGHT   Columbia, 1959
RIDE THE HIGH COUNTRY   MGM, 1962
MAIL ORDER BRIDE   MGM, 1963

MIKE BATT
Contact: ASCAP - Los Angeles, 213-883-1000

WATERSHIP DOWN (AF)   theme only, Avco Embassy, 1978,
    British
WOMBLING FREE   1978, British
CARAVANS   Universal, 1979, U.S.-Iranian
DIGITAL DREAMS   Ripple Productions Ltd., 1983

FRANCO BATTIATO
Contact: SIAE - Italy, 011-39-6-59-901

AN INFAMOUS LIFE   Artisti Associati International, 1990,
    Italian-French-West German

ARLENE BATTISHIL
DEVOTION   Northern Arts, 1995

IRWIN BAZELON
Contact: ASCAP - Los Angeles, 213-883-1000

WILMA (TF)   Cappy Productions, 1977

NIGEL BEAHAM-POWELL
Contact: PRS - London, England, 011-44-1-580-5544

ISLAND INVADERS: OTHER WORLDS (TD)   co-composer with
    Bella Russell, WNET/BBC TV, 1993

DAVID BEAL
Contact: ASCAP - Los Angeles, 213-883-1000

THE TAKE (CTF)   co-composer with Michael Shrieve, Cine-Nevada
    Inc./MCA TV, 1990

JEFF BEAL
Agent: Ocean Park Music Group - Los Angeles, 310-315-5266
Affiliation: BMI - Los Angeles, 310-659-9109

LOOKIN' ITALIAN   Vision Quest, 1994

JOHN BEAL*
Agent: Marks Management - Tarzana, 818-776-8787
Contact: Gary Dohner - Los Angeles, 310-859-6559
Affiliation: ASCAP - Los Angeles, 213-883-1000

ZERO TO SIXTY   First Artists, 1977
SKATETOWN U.S.A.   additional music, Rastar, 1978
THE DEATH OF OCEAN PARK (TF)   additional music, John Furia
    Prods., 1979
THE MAN WITH BOGART'S FACE   additional music, 20th Century
    Fox, 1980
DEFIANCE   additional music, American International, 1980
THE FUNHOUSE   Universal, 1981
ROAR   additional music, Filmways, 1981
LOOKIN' TO GET OUT   additional music, 1982
TERROR IN THE AISLES   Universal, 1984
THE STONE BOY   additional music, 20th Century Fox, 1984
UNDER THE VOLCANO   additional music, Universal, 1984
KILLER PARTY   MGM/UA, 1986
FROM A WHISPER TO A SCREAM   additional music, TMS, 1987

MIKE BEARDEN
DROP SQUAD   Gramercy, 1994

CHRISTOPHER BECK
Agent: Carol Faith Agency - Beverly Hills, 310-274-0776

HOSTILE INTENT   Le Monde, 1997

JEFF BECK
Contact: PRS - London, England, 011-44-1-580-5544

FRANKIE'S HOUSE (MS)   co-composed with Jed Leiber, Anglia,
    1993, British
BLUE CHIPS   co-composed with Jed Leiber and Nile Rodgers,
    Paramount, 1994
LITTLE BIG LEAGUE   additional music, Columbia, 1994

JOE BECK
Contact: ASCAP - Los Angeles, 213-883-1000

GOODBYE, NORMA JEAN   Filmways, 1976, U.S.-Australian

FRANK W. BECKER
Contact: ASCAP - Los Angeles, 213-883-1000

TERMINAL BLISS   Distant Horizon, 1990

MICHAEL BECKER
SOLITAIRE   Highway One, 1992, Canadian

DANNY BECKERMAN
Contact: APRA - Australia, 011-61-2-922-6422

FORTRESS (CTF)   Crawford Productions/HBO Premiere Films,
    1985, Australian

STEPHEN BEDELL
JERSEY GIRL (TF)   co-composer with Misha Segal, Electric
    Pictures/Interscope, 1993

MICHAEL BEEN
Contact: ASCAP - Los Angeles, 213-883-1000

LIGHT SLEEPER   Seven Arts, 1992

DANIEL BELL
Contact: STIM - Sweden, 011-41-1-482-6666

FANNY AND ALEXANDER   Embassy, 1983,
    Swedish-French-West German

DAVID BELL*
Agent: Gorfaine-Schwartz - Los Angeles, 213-969-1011
Affiliation: BMI - Los Angeles, 310-659-9109

KILLING AT HELL'S GATE (TF)   CBS Entertainment, 1981
FINAL JUSTICE   Arista, 1985
THE RETURN OF THE SHAGGY DOG (TF)   Walt Disney TV, 1987
EQUAL JUSTICE (TF)   co-composer of theme with Susan Marder,
    The Thomas Carter Co./Orion TV, 1990
THE TAKE (CTF)   co-composer with Susan Marder, Cine-Nevada
    Inc./MCA-TV, 1990
LUCKY DAY (TF)   Hearst, 1991
STRANGER AT MY DOOR (TF)   Dry Canyon One, 1991
MEMPHIS (CTF)   Propaganda, 1992
STORMY WEATHERS (TF)   Haft-Nasatir/River Siren/Tri-Star TV,
    1992
THERE GOES THE NEIGHBORHOOD   Paramount, 1992
NED BLESSING: THE STORY OF HIS LIFE AND TIMES: RETURN
    TO PLUM CREEK (TF)   Wittliff-Pangaea Prods./Hearst
    Entertainment/CBS Entertainment Prods., 1993
JOHN JAKES' HEAVEN AND HELL: NORTH AND SOUTH PART 3
    (MS)   Wolper Organization/ABC Prods., 1994
SIN AND REDEMPTION (TF)   Stonehenge Prods./Viacom, 1994
CONVICT COWBOY (CTF)   MGM Worldwide Television/Showtime,
    1995

THOM BELL

Contact: BMI - Los Angeles, 310-659-9109

THE FISH THAT SAVED PITTSBURGH   United Artists, 1979

WAYNE BELL

THE TEXAS CHAINSAW MASSACRE   co-composer with Tobe
   Hooper, Bryanston, 1974
EATEN ALIVE   *DEATH TRAP*   Virgo International, 1977
LAST NIGHT AT THE ALAMO   co-composer with Chuck Pinnell,
   Alamo Films, 1983

ANDREW BELLING

Contact: BMI - Los Angeles, 310-659-9109

DELIVER US FROM EVIL (TF)   Playboy Productions, 1973
A SUMMER WITHOUT BOYS (TF)   Playboy Productions, 1973
THE KILLING KIND   Media Trend, 1974
WIZARDS (AF)   20th Century Fox, 1977
END OF THE WORLD   Yablans Films, 1977
CRASH!   *AKAZA, GOD OF VENGEANCE*   Group 1, 1977
CINDERELLA   Group 1, 1977
DRACULA'S DOG   *ZOLTAN, HOUND OF DRACULA*   Crown
   International, 1978
FAIRY TALES   Yablans Films, 1978
THE DEERSLAYER (TF)   co-composer with Bob Summers, Schick
   Sunn Classics Productions, 1978
THIRTY DANGEROUS SECONDS   Independent Productions
STARCHASER: THE LEGEND OF ORIN (AF)   Atlantic Releasing
   Corporation, 1985

RICHARD BELLIS*

Agent: Zomba Screen Music - West Hollywood, 310-246-0777
Affiliation: ASCAP - Los Angeles, 213-883-1000

BLACK MARKET BABY (TF)   co-composer with George Wilkins,
   Brut Productions, 1977
BREAKING UP IS HARD TO DO (TF)   source music only,
   Green-Epstein Productions/Columbia TV, 1979
A SHINING SEASON (TF)   Green-Epstein Productions/T-M
   Productions/Columbia TV, 1979
FALLEN ANGEL (TF)   Green-Epstein Productions/Columbia TV,
   1981
THE OTHER VICTIM (TF)   Shpetner Company, 1981
MONEY ON THE SIDE (TF)   Green-Epstein Productions/Hal
   Landers Productions/Columbia TV, 1982
SHATTERED INNOCENCE (TF)   Green-Epstein
   Productions/Lorimar TV, 1987
ADDICTED TO HIS LOVE (TF)   Green-Epstein
   Productions/Columbia TV, 1988
STEPHEN KING'S "IT"   *IT* (MS) ☆☆   Green-Epstein, 1990
THE HAUNTED (TF)   Bodhan Zachary/FNM Films, 1991
DOUBLE CROSSED (CTF) ☆   Green/Epstein, 1991
A MOTHER'S JUSTICE (TF)   Green/Epstein/Longbow
   Prods./Lorimar TV, 1991
NIGHTMARE IN COLUMBIA COUNTY (TF)   Landsburg Co., 1991
BLINDMAN'S BLUFF (CTF)   Wilshire Court, 1992
TO GRANDMOTHER'S HOUSE WE GO (TF)   Green-Epstein, 1992
A KILLER AMONG FRIENDS (TF)   Green-Epstein, 1992
WITHOUT A KISS GOODBYE (TF)   Green-Epstein, 1993
NO CHILD OF MINE (TF)   Green-Epstein/Warner Bros. TV, 1993
DOUBLE, DOUBLE, TOIL AND TROUBLE (TF) ☆
   Green-Epstein/Warner Bros. TV, 1993
THE SPIDER AND THE FLY (CTF)   Haft-Nasatir
   Co./Heartstar/Wilshire Court, 1994
THE DISAPPEARANCE OF VONNIE (TF)   Morrow-Heus
   Prods./TriStar TV, 1994
HOW THE WEST WAS FUN (TF)   Dualstar Prods./Green-Epstein
   Prods./Kicking Horse Prods./Warner Bros. TV, 1994
THE SISTER-IN-LAW (CTF)   CNM Entertainment/Wilshire Court,
   1995
KIDZ IN THE WOOD (TF)   Green-Epstein, 1995
WHERE'S THE MONEY, NOREEN? (CTF)   Wilshire Court, 1996
THE LEGEND OF RUBY SILVER (TF)   Green-Epstein, 1996

ROGER BELLON*

Contact: Derek Power Company - Los Angeles, 310-472-4647
Affiliation: ASCAP - Los Angeles, 213-883-1000

THE SHIEK   new score for 1926 silent film
THE PRINCESS ACADEMY   Empire Pictures, 1987
THE UNHOLY   Vestron, 1988
WAXWORK   Vestron, 1988
DARK HORSE   Carolco/Live/Republic, 1991
SOCIAL SUICIDE   Star, 1991
UNFORGIVEABLE (TF)   Grossbart-Barnett, 1996

MARCO BELTRAMI

Agent: Air-Edel - Los Angeles, 310-914-5000

SCREAM   Miramax-Dimension, 1996

VASSAL BENFORD

Contact: ASCAP - Los Angeles, 213-883-1000

CLASS ACT   Warner Bros., 1992
HOUSE PARTY 2   New Line, 1991

MICHAEL BENGHIAT

Contact: ASCAP - Los Angeles, 213-883-1000

SHADOW OF THE DRAGON   co-composer with John Author,
   Hatch Entertainment, 1994
DEVOTION (CTF)   CPV, 1995

JAMES BENNETT

POISON   Zeitgeist, 1991
SWOON   Fine Line, 1992

RICHARD RODNEY BENNETT

b. March 29, 1936 - Broadstairs, England
Contact: PRS - London, England, 011-44-1-580-5544

INTERPOL   *PICKUP ALLEY*   Columbia, 1957, British
INDISCREET   Warner Bros., 1958, British
THE MAN INSIDE   Columbia, 1958, British
MENACE IN THE NIGHT   United Artists, 1958, British
THE SAFECRACKER   MGM, 1958, British
CHANCE MEETING   *BLIND DATE*   Paramount, 1959, British
THE ANGRY HILLS   MGM, 1959
THE DEVIL'S DISCIPLE   United Artists, 1959, British
THE MAN WHO COULD CHEAT DEATH   Paramount, 1959,
   British
THE MARK   Continental, 1961, British
SATAN NEVER SLEEPS   20th Century Fox, 1962, U.S.-British
ONLY TWO CAN PLAY   British Lion, 1961, British
THE WRONG ARM OF THE LAW   Continental, 1963, British
HEAVENS ABOVE   British Lion, 1963, British
BILLY LIAR   Continental, 1963, British
ONE WAY PENDULUM   United Artists, 1964
THE NANNY   20th Century Fox, 1965, British
THE DEVIL'S OWN   *THE WITCHES*   1966, British
FAR FROM THE MADDING CROWD ★   MGM, 1967, British
BILLION DOLLAR BRAIN   United Artists, 1967, British
SECRET CEREMONY   Universal, 1968, British-U.S.
THE BUTTERCUP CHAIN   Warner Bros., 1970, British
FIGURES IN A LANDSCAPE   National General, 1971, British
NICHOLAS AND ALEXANDRA ★   Columbia, 1971, British
LADY CAROLINE LAMB   United Artists, 1973, British
VOICES   Hemdale, 1973, British
OF JEWELS AND GOLD   1973
MURDER ON THE ORIENT EXPRESS ★   Paramount, 1974,
   British
PERMISSION TO KILL   Warner Bros., 1975, British
SHERLOCK HOLMES IN NEW YORK (TF)   20th Century-Fox TV,
   1976
L'IMPRECATEUR   *THE ACCUSER*   Parafrance, 1977, French
EQUUS   United Artists, 1977, British
THE BRINK'S JOB   Universal, 1978
YANKS   Universal, 1979, British
RETURN OF THE SOLDIER   European Classics, 1982, British
AGATHA CHRISTIE'S 'MURDER WITH MIRRORS' (TF) ☆   Hajeno
   Productions/Warner Bros. TV, 1985

TENDER IS THE NIGHT (MS)   Showtime/BBC/Seven Network, 1985, U.S.-British-Australian
THE EBONY TOWER (TF)   Granada TV, 1987, British
POOR LITTLE RICH GIRL: THE BARBARA HUTTON STORY (MS)   Lester Persky Productions/ITC Productions, 1987
THE ATTIC: THE HIDING OF ANN FRANK (TF)   Telecom Entertainment, 1987
ENCHANTED APRIL   Miramax, 1991
FOUR WEDDINGS AND A FUNERAL   Gramercy, 1994

DAVID BENOIT

Agent: Vangelos Management - Encino, 818-380-1919
Affiliation: BMI - Los Angeles, 310-659-9109

CAPTIVE HEARTS   MGM/UA, 1987, Canadian
DON'T PAVE MAIN STREET: CARMEL'S HERITAGE (FD)   Julian Ludwig Prods., 1994
THE STARS FELL ON HENRIETTA   Warner Bros., 1995
A CHRISTMAS TREE (TF)   Walt Disney TV, 1996

JEAN-MARIE BENOIT

DING ET DONG: LE FILM *DING AND DONG: THE FILM*   co-composer with Yves Lapierre, Max, 1991, Canadian
KING OF THE AIRWAVES *LOUIS 19, LE ROI DES ONDES*   1994, Canadian-French

RAY BENSON

Contact: BMI - Los Angeles, 310-659-9109

NEVER LEAVE NEVADA   Cabriolet, 1991
WILD TEXAS WIND (TF)   Sandollar, 1991

ROBBY BENSON

(Robby Segal)
b. January 21, 1956 - Dallas, Texas
Agent: The Rothman Agency - Beverly Hills, 310-281-3585
Affiliation: ASCAP - Los Angeles, 213-883-1000

WALK PROUD   Universal, 1979
DIE LAUGHING   co-composer with Craig Safan and Jerry Segal, Orion, 1980

ERIK BERCHOT

LES MISERABLES   co-composer with Francis Lai, Philippe Servain, Michel Legrand and Didier Barbelivien, Warner Bros., 1995, French

TONY BERG

Contact: BMI - Los Angeles, 310-659-9109

HIGH SCHOOL U.S.A. (TF)   co-composer with Miles Goodman, Hill-Mandelker Productions, 1983
ATTACK ON FEAR (TF)   Tomorrow Entertainment, 1984
SPACE (MS)   co-composer with Miles Goodman, Stonehenge Productions/Paramount TV, 1985
AMERICA 3000   Cannon, 1986
WELCOME TO 18   American Distribution Group, 1986

DAVID BERGEAUD

Agent: Zomba Screen Music - West Hollywood, 310-246-0777
Affiliation: ASCAP - Los Angeles, 213-883-1000

TWICE DEAD   Concorde, 1989
AILEEN WUORNOS: THE SELLING OF A SERIAL KILLER (FD)   1992, British
VANISHING SON (TF)   Universal-MCA TV, 1994
EARTH 2 (TF)   Amblin TV/Universal TV, 1994
DONOR UNKNOWN (TF)   Universal TV, 1995
HEIDI FLEISS, HOLLYWOOD MADAME (TF)   Lafayette, 1995
PSYCHO SUSHI   Nath Productions, 1996
PRINCE VALIANT   Paramount, 1997

CARY BERGER

Contact: BMI - Los Angeles, 310-659-9109

SUTURE   Kino-Korsakoff, 1993

JAKE BERGER

Contact: BMI - Los Angeles, 310-659-9109

THE GREAT UNPLEASANTNESS   co-composer with Buzzov-en and Pervis Lee, Crescent Pictures, 1993

TAL BERGMAN

WEDDING BELL BLUES   co-composer with Paul Christian Gordon, Curb, 1997

JOHN D. BERKMAN

LOIS GIBBS AND LOVE CANAL (TF)   Moonlight Productions/Filmways Productions, 1982

BERLIN GAME

DOWN TWISTED   Cannon, 1987
ANGEL III: THE FINAL CHAPTER   New World, 1988

JAMES BERNARD

b. September 20, 1925 - London, England
Agent: PRS - London, England, 011-44-1-580-5544

THE CREEPING UNKNOWN *THE QUARTERMASS EXPERIMENT*   United Artists, 1955, British
X THE UNKNOWN   Warner Bros., 1956, British
THE CURSE OF FRANKENSTEIN   Warner Bros., 1957, British
THE DOOR IN THE WALL   1957, British
ENEMY FROM SPACE *QUARTERMASS II*   United Artists, 1957, British
ACROSS THE BRIDGE   Rank, 1958, British
HORROR OF DRACULA *DRACULA*   Universal, 1958, British
THE HOUND OF THE BASKERVILLES   United Artists, 1959, British
THE STRANGLERS OF BOMBAY   Columbia, 1959, British
THESE ARE THE DAMNED *THE DAMNED*   Columbia, 1961, British
THE TERROR OF THE TONGS   Columbia, 1961, British
THE KISS OF THE VAMPIRE   Universal, 1963, British
THE GORGON   Columbia, 1964, British
SHE   MGM, 1965, British
DRACULA - PRINCE OF DARKNESS   20th Century-Fox, 1967, British
THE PLAGUE OF THE ZOMBIES   Warner/Pathe, 1966, British
FRANKENSTEIN CREATED WOMAN   20th Century-Fox, 1967, British
TORTURE GARDEN   co-composer with Don Banks, Columbia, 1968, British
THE DEVIL'S BRIDE *THE DEVIL RIDES OUT*   20th Century-Fox, 1968, British
DRACULA HAS RISEN FROM THE GRAVE   Warner Bros., 1969, British
FRANKENSTEIN MUST BE DESTROYED!   Warner Bros., 1970, British
TASTE THE BLOOD OF DRACULA   Warner Bros., 1970, British
THE SCARS OF DRACULA   American Continental, 1971, British
FRANKENSTEIN AND THE MONSTER FROM HELL   Paramount, 1974, British
THE 7 BROTHERS MEET DRACULA *THE LEGEND OF THE SEVEN GOLDEN VAMPIRES*   Dynamite Entertainment, 1979, British

CHARLES BERNSTEIN*

b. Minneapolis, Minnesota
Agent: Film Music Associates - Hollywood, 213-463-1070
Affiliation: ASCAP - Los Angeles, 213-883-1000

CZECHOSLOVAKIA (FD)   USIA, 1969
HEX   20th Century-Fox, 1973
INVASION OF THE BEE GIRLS   Centaur, 1973
WHITE LIGHTNING   United Artists, 1973
THAT MAN BOLT   Universal, 1973
MR. MAJESTYK   United Artists, 1974
A SHADOW IN THE STREETS (TF)   Playboy Productions, 1975
TRACKDOWN   United Artists, 1976
GATOR   United Artists, 1976
A SMALL TOWN IN TEXAS   American International, 1976
LOOK WHAT'S HAPPENED TO ROSEMARY'S BABY (TF)   Paramount TV, 1976
NIGHTMARE IN BADHAM COUNTY (TF)   ABC Circle Films, 1976

OUTLAW BLUES   Warner Bros., 1977
ESCAPE FROM BOGEN COUNTY (TF)   Paramount TV, 1977
VIVA KNIEVEL!   Warner Bros., 1977
WILD AND WOOLY (TF)   Aaron Spelling Productions, 1978
THADDEUS ROSE AND EDDIE (TF)   CBS, Inc., 1978
KATIE: PORTRAIT OF A CENTERFOLD (TF)   Moonlight
   Productions/Warner Bros. TV, 1978
ARE YOU IN THE HOUSE ALONE? (TF)   Charles Fries
   Productions, 1978
STEEL COWBOY (TF)   Roger Gimbel Productions/EMI TV, 1978
THE WINDS OF KITTY HAWK (TF)   Charles Fries Productions,
   1978
FAST LANE BLUES (TF)   Viacom/Blinn-Thorp, 1978
COPS AND ROBIN (TF)   Paramount TV, 1978
LOVE AT FIRST BITE   American International, 1979
WOMEN AT WEST POINT (TF)   Green-Epstein Productions/Alan
   Sacks Productions, 1979
THE HOUSE ON GARIBALDI STREET (TF)   Charles Fries
   Productions, 1979
FOOLIN' AROUND   Columbia, 1980
COAST TO COAST   Paramount, 1980
THE HUNTER   composer of foreign version, additional music for
   U.S. version, Paramount, 1980
BOGIE: THE LAST HERO (TF)   Charles Fries Productions, 1980
SCRUPLES (MS)   Lou-Step Productions/Warner Bros. TV, 1981
THE ENTITY   20th Century Fox, 1982
INDEPENDENCE DAY   Warner Bros., 1983
SADAT (MS)   Blatt-Singer Productions/Columbia TV, 1983
CUJO   Warner Bros., 1983
DADDY'S DEAD DARLING   THE PIGS/DADDY'S GIRL   Aquarius,
   1984
A NIGHTMARE ON ELM STREET   New Line Cinema, 1984
SECRET WEAPONS (TF)   Goodman-Rosen Productions/ITC
   Productions, 1985
MALICE IN WONDERLAND (TF)   ITC Productions, 1985
GENERATION (TF)   Embassy TV, 1985
COVENANT (TF)   Michael Filerman Productions/20th Century Fox
   TV, 1985
THE LONG HOT SUMMER (MS)   Leonard Hill Productions, 1985
CHASE (TF)   CBS Entertainment, 1985
APRIL FOOL'S DAY   Paramount, 1986
DEADLY FRIEND   Warner Bros., 1986
ROCKABYE (TF)   Roger Gimbel Productions/Peregrine
   Entertainment/Bertinelli Poructions, 1986
THE LAST FLING (TF)   Leonard Hill Films, 1987
THE ALLNIGHTER   Universal, 1987
GHOST OF A CHANCE (TF)   Stuart-Phoenix Productions/Thunder
   Bird Road Productions/Lorimar-Telepictures Productions, 1987
THE MAN WHO BROKE 1,000 CHAINS (CTF)   HBO
   Pictures/Journey Entertainment, 1987
DUDES   Cineworld, 1987
A WHISPER KILLS (TF)   Sandy Hook Productions/Steve Tisch
   Company/Phoenix Entertainment Group, 1988
DESPERATE FOR LOVE (TF)   Vishudda Productions/Lorimar TV,
   1989
LOVE AND BETRAYAL (TF)   Gross-Weston Productions/ITC, 1989
TOO YOUNG TO DIE? (TF)   Von Zerneck-Sertner Films, 1990
CAROLINE? (TF)   Barry and Enright Productions, 1990
FALL FROM GRACE (TF)   NBC Productions, 1990
THE LOVE SHE SOUGHT (TF)   Orion TV/Andrew J. Fenady
   Productions, 1990
THE LAST ELEPHANT (TF)   RHI/Qunitex, 1990
A LIFE TO REMEMBER: ROSE KENNEDY (TD)   American Film
   Foundation, 1990
SHE SAID NO (TF)   Steve White, 1990
DRUG WARS: THE CAMARENA STORY (MS)   Michael Mann
   Prods., 1990
LOVE, LIES AND MURDER (MS)   Republic, 1991
PAYOFF (CTF)   Viacom Pictures/Aurora, 1991
GUILTY UNTIL PROVEN INNOCENT (TF)   Cosgrove-Meurer,
   1991
YES, VIRGINIA, THERE IS A SANTA CLAUS (TF)   Andrew J.
   Fenady/Quinta/Paradigm, 1991
DRUG WARS II: THE COCAINE CARTEL (MS)   Michael Mann
   Prods., 1992
TRIAL: THE PRICE OF PASSION (TF)   Sokolow/TriStar TV, 1992
SOMEBODY'S DAUGHTER (TF)   Karen Danaher-dorr
   Prods./Republic Pictures TV, 1992
THE SEA WOLF (CTF) ☆   Bob Banner/Primedia/Andrew J. Fenady,
   1993
EXCESSIVE FORCE   New Line, 1993
FINAL APPEAL (TF)   Republic TV, 1993

BETWEEN LOVE AND HATE (TF)   Cosgrove-Meurer Prods./WIN,
   1993
MY NAME IS KATE (TF)   a.k.a. Prods./Queen Prods./Donna Mills
   Prods./ABC Prods., 1994
WES CRAVEN'S NEW NIGHTMARE   series original theme only,
   New Line, 1994
OUT OF ANNIE'S PAST (CTF)   Karen Moore Prods./Point of View
   Prods./MTE, 1995
MAYA LIN: A STRONG CLEAR VISION (FD)   Sanders & Mock,
   1995
SOPHIE AND THE MOONHANGER (CTF)   Lifetime, 1995
RUMPELSTILTSKIN   Spelling, 1996

ELMER BERNSTEIN*
b. April 4, 1922 - New York, New York
Agent: The Kraft-Benjamin Agency - Beverly Hills, 310-247-0123
Affiliation: Contact: ASCAP - Los Angeles, 213-883-1000

SATURDAY'S HERO   Columbia, 1951
BOOTS MALONE   Columbia, 1952
BATTLES OF CHIEF PONTIAC   Realart, 1952
SUDDEN FEAR   RKO Radio, 1952
NEVER WAVE AT A WAC   RKO Radio, 1953
ROBOT MONSTER   Astor, 1953
CAT WOMEN OF THE MOON   Astor, 1954
MISS ROBIN CRUSOE   20th Century Fox, 1954
MAKE HASTE TO LIVE   Republic, 1954
SILENT RAIDERS   Lippert, 1954
THE ETERNAL SEA   Republic, 1955
IT'S A DOG'S LIFE   MGM, 1955
THE VIEW FROM POMPEY'S HEAD   20th Century Fox, 1955
THE MAN WITH THE GOLDEN ARM ★   United Artists, 1955
THE TEN COMMANDMENTS   Paramount, 1956
STORM FEAR   United Artists, 1956
DRANGO   United Artists, 1957
MEN IN WAR   United Artists, 1957
FEAR STRIKES OUT   Paramount, 1957
SWEET SMELL OF SUCCESS   United Artists, 1957
THE TIN STAR   Paramount, 1957
SADDLE THE WIND   MGM, 1957
DESIRE UNDER THE ELMS   Paramount, 1958
ANNA LUCASTA   United Artists, 1958
GOD'S LITTLE ACRE   United Artists, 1958
KINGS GO FORTH   United Artists, 1958
THE BUCCANEER   Paramount, 1959
THE RACE FOR SPACE (FD)   U.S. Government, 1959
THE STORY ON PAGE ONE   20th Century Fox, 1959
SOME CAME RUNNING   MGM, 1959
THE MIRACLE   Warner Bros., 1959
THE RAT RACE   Paramount, 1960
FROM THE TERRACE   20th Century Fox, 1960
THE MAGNIFICENT SEVEN   United Artists, 1960
THE MAKING OF THE PRESIDENT (TD) ☆☆   David Wolper
   Productions, 1960
BY LOVE POSSESSED   United Artists, 1961
THE YOUNG DOCTORS   United Artists, 1961
THE COMANCHEROS   20th Century-Fox, 1961
SUMMER AND SMOKE ★   Paramount, 1961
WALK ON THE WILD SIDE   Columbia, 1962
BIRDMAN OF ALCATRAZ   United Artists, 1962
TO KILL A MOCKINGBIRD ★   Universal, 1962
A GIRL NAMED TAMIKO   Paramount, 1962
THE GREAT ESCAPE   United Artists, 1963
HUD   Paramount, 1963
RAMPAGE   Warner Bros., 1963
THE CARETAKERS   United Artists, 1963
KINGS OF THE SUN   United Artists, 1963
THE CARPETBAGGERS   Paramount, 1964
LOVE WITH THE PROPER STRANGER   Paramount, 1964
THE WORLD OF HENRY ORIENT   United Artists, 1964
BABY, THE RAIN MUST FALL   Columbia, 1965
THE HALLELUJAH TRAIL   United Artists, 1965
SEVEN WOMEN   MGM, 1965
THE SONS OF KATIE ELDER   Paramount, 1965
THE REWARD   20th Century-Fox, 1965
FOUR DAYS IN NOVEMBER (FD)   United Artists, 1965
THE SILENCERS   Columbia, 1966
RETURN OF THE SEVEN ★   United Artists, 1966
HAWAII ★   United Artists, 1966
CAST A GIANT SHADOW   United Artists, 1966
THOROUGHLY MODERN MILLIE ★★   Universal, 1967

THE SCALPHUNTERS United Artists, 1968
I LOVE YOU, ALICE B. TOKLAS Warner Bros., 1968
WHERE'S JACK? Paramount, 1969, British
TRUE GRIT Paramount, 1969
THE GYPSY MOTHS MGM, 1969
MIDAS RUN Cinerama Releasing Corporation, 1969
GUNS OF THE MAGNIFICENT SEVEN United Artists, 1969
THE BRIDGE AT REMAGEN United Artists, 1969
WALK IN THE SPRING RAIN Columbia, 1970
THE LIBERATION OF L.B. JONES Columbia, 1970
CANNON FOR CORDOBA United Artists, 1970
BIG JAKE National General, 1971
SEE NO EVIL Columbia, 1971, British
DOCTORS' WIVES Columbia, 1971
OWEN MARSHALL, COUNSELOR AT LAW (TF) Universal TV, 1971
THE AMAZING MR. BLUNDEN Goldstone, 1972, British
THE ROOKIES (TF) Aaron Spelling Productions/ABC Circle Films, 1972
THE MAGNIFICENT SEVEN RIDE! United Artists, 1972
CAHILL, U.S. MARSHALL Warner Bros., 1973
DEADLY HONEYMOON NIGHTMARE HONEYMOON MGM, 1974
McQ Warner Bros., 1974
GOLD Allied Artists, 1974, British
MEN OF THE DRAGON (TF) Wolper Productions, 1974
THE TRIAL OF BILLY JACK Taylor-Laughlin, 1974
MR. QUILP Avco Embassy, 1975, British
ELLERY QUEEN (TF) Universal TV, 1975
REPORT TO THE COMMISSIONER United Artists, 1975
THE INCREDIBLE SARAH Reader's Digest, 1976, British
FROM NOON TILL THREE also cameo as piano player, United Artists, 1976
THE SHOOTIST Paramount, 1976
CAPTAINS AND THE KINGS (MS) ☆ Universal TV, 1976
SERPICO: THE DEADLY GAME (TF) Dino De Laurentiis Productions/Paramount TV, 1976
THE 3,000 MILE CHASE Public Arts Productions/Universal TV, 1977
SLAP SHOT Universal, 1977
BILLY JACK GOES TO WASHINGTON Taylor-Laughlin, 1978
NATIONAL LAMPOON'S ANIMAL HOUSE Universal, 1978
LITTLE WOMEN (TF) Universal TV, 1978
CHARLESTON (TF) Robert Stigwood Productions/RSO, Inc., 1979
BLOODBROTHERS Warner Bros., 1979
MEATBALLS Paramount, 1979
ZULU DAWN American Cinema, 1979, British
THE CHISHOLMS (MS) adaptation, Alan Landsburg Productions, 1979
THE GREAT SANTINI THE ACE Orion/Warner Bros., 1980
SATURN 3 AFD, 1980
AIRPLANE! Paramount, 1980
GUYANA TRAGEDY: THE STORY OF JIM JONES (TF) The Konigsberg Company, 1980
MOVIOLA: THIS YEAR'S BLONDE (MS) David S. Wolper-Stan Margulies Productions/Warner Bros. TV, 1980
TODAY'S F.B.I. (TF) David Gerber Company, 1981
STRIPES Columbia, 1981
GOING APE! Paramount, 1981
HEAVY METAL (AF) Columbia, 1981, Canadian
AN AMERICAN WEREWOLF IN LONDON Universal, 1981
HONKY TONK FREEWAY co-composer with George Martin, Universal/AFD, 1981
GENOCIDE (FD) Simon Wiesenthal Center, 1982
THE CHOSEN 20th Century Fox International Classics, 1982
FIVE DAYS ONE SUMMER The Ladd Company/Warner Bros., 1982, British
SPACEHUNTER: ADVENTURES IN THE FORBIDDEN ZONE Columbia, 1983, Canadian-U.S.
TRADING PLACES ★ adaptation, Paramount, 1983
CLASS Orion, 1983
BOLERO additional music, Cannon, 1984
PRINCE JACK Castle Hill Productions, 1984
GHOSTBUSTERS Columbia, 1984
MARY WARD 1985
THE BLACK CAULDRON (AF) Buena Vista, 1985
SPIES LIKE US Warner Bros., 1985
GULAG (CTF) Lorimar Productions/HBO Premiere Films, 1985
LEGAL EAGLES Universal, 1986
THREE AMIGOS! Orion, 1986
AMAZING GRACE AND CHUCK Tri-Star, 1987
LEONARD PART 6 Columbia, 1987

A NIGHT IN THE LIFE OF JIMMY REARDON foreign version only, 20th Century Fox, 1988
FUNNY FARM Warner Bros., 1988
THE GOOD MOTHER Buena Vista, 1988
DA FilmDallas, 1988
SLIPSTREAM Entertainment Film, 1989, British
MY LEFT FOOT Miramax, 1989, British-Irish
THE GRIFTERS Miramax, 1990
OSCAR Buena Vista, 1991
A RAGE IN HARLEM Miramax, 1991
RAMBLING ROSE Seven Arts, 1991
CAPE FEAR Universal, 1991, Adaptation of Bernard Herrmann's music
THE BABE Universal, 1992
MAD DOG AND GLORY Universal, 1993
THE CEMETERY CLUB Buena Vista, 1993
LOST IN YONKERS Columbia, 1993
THE AGE OF INNOCENCE ★ Columbia, 1993
THE GOOD SON 20th Century Fox, 1993
SEARCH AND DESTROY October Films, 1995
ROOMMATES Buena Vista, 1995
DEVIL IN A BLUE DRESS TriStar, 1995
CANADIAN BACON co-composer with Peter Bernstein, Gramercy, 1995
BULLETPROOF Universal, 1996
HOODLUM MGM-UA, 1997
BUDDY 1997

PETER BERNSTEIN

Agent: Gorfaine-Schwartz - Los Angeles, 213-969-1011
Affiliation: BMI - Los Angeles, 310-659-9109

THE HOUSE THAT CRIED MURDER THE BRIDE Golden Gate/Unisphere, 1974, Canadian
SILENT RAGE Columbia, 1982
NATIONAL LAMPOON'S CLASS REUNION 20th Century Fox, 1983
SURF II Arista, 1983
HOT DOG...THE MOVIE MGM/UA, 1984
BOLERO Cannon, 1984
SUMMER FANTASY (TF) Moonlight Productions II, 1984
THE EWOK ADVENTURE (TF) Lucasfilm Ltd./Korty Films, 1984
MY SCIENCE PROJECT Buena Vista, 1985
THE RAPE OF RICHARD BECK (TF) Robert Papazian Productions/Henerson-Hirsch Productions, 1985
KICKS 1985
EWOKS: THE BATTLE FOR ENDOR (TF) Lucasfilm Ltd., 1985
ALFRED HITCHCOCK PRESENTS (TF) Universal TV, 1985
HAMBURGER...THE MOTION PICTURE FM Entertainment, 1986
MIRACLES Orion, 1986
CLUB MED (TF) Lorimar Productions, 1986
THE RICHEST CAT IN THE WORLD (TF) Les Alexander Productions/Walt Disney TV, 1986
LITTLE SPIES (TF) Walt Disney TV, 1986
21 JUMP STREET (TF) Steven J. Cannell Prods., 1987
MORGAN STEWART'S COMING HOME New Century/Vista, 1987
THE ALAMO: 13 DAYS TO GLORY (TF) Briggle, Hennessy, Carrothers Productions/The Finnegan Company/Fries Entertainment, 1987
REMOTE CONTROL Vista Organization, 1988
HEARTBEAT (TF) Aaron Spelling Productions, 1988
NIGHTBREAKER (CTF) Turner Network TV, 1989
DREAM DATE (TF) Robert Kosberg Productions/Saban International, 1989
N.Y.P.D. MOUNTED (TF) Patrick Hasburgh Prods./Orion TV, 1991
FIFTY/FIFTY Cannon, 1993
TROUBLESHOOTERS: TRAPPED BENEATH THE EARTH (TF) Ginkgo Prods./Walter Mirisch, 1993
ISLAND CITY (TF) Lee Rich Co./MDT Prods., 1994
MY BREAST (TF) Diane Kerew Prods./Polone/Hearst, 1994
ED McBAIN'S 57TH PRECINCT (TF) Diana Kerew Prods./Hearst, 1995
SHE STOOD ALONE: THE TAILHOOK SCANDAL (TF) Harry Winer Prods./Symphony Prods./ABC, 1995
CANADIAN BACON co-composer with Elmer Bernstein, Gramercy, 1995

STEVE BERNSTEIN*

Contact: BMI - Los Angeles, 310-659-9109

BEFORE & AFTER Little Deer, 1985

SANH BERTI
Contact: BMI - Los Angeles, 310-659-9109

CATTLE ANNIE AND LITTLE BRITCHES   co-composer with Tom
   Slocum, Universal, 1981

PETER BEST
Contact: APRA - Australia, 011-61-2-922-6422

THE MORE THINGS CHANGE   Hoyts, 1986, Australian
"CROCODILE" DUNDEE   Paramount, 1986, Australian
THE HARP IN THE SOUTH (MS)   Quantum Films, 1987,
   Australian
HIGH TIDE   Tri-Star, 1987, Australian
CROCODILE DUNDEE II   Paramount, 1988, Australian
MURIEL'S WEDDING   Miramax, 1994, Australian
COUNTRY LIFE   1994, Australian

HARRY BETTS
Contact: BMI - Los Angeles, 310-659-9109

WINTER A-GO-GO   Columbia, 1965
THE BIG MOUTH   Columbia, 1967
THE FANTASTIC PLASTIC MACHINE   1969
A TIME FOR DYING   Etoile, 1971
HOT, HARD AND MEAN   American International, 1972
GOODNIGHT MY LOVE (TF)   ABC Circle Films, 1972
BLACK MAMA, WHITE MAMA   American International, 1973,
   U.S.-Filipino
LITTLE CIGARS   American International, 1973
CHEECH & CHONG'S NICE DREAMS   Columbia, 1981
RICHARD PRYOR LIVE ON THE SUNSET STRIP   Columbia, 1982

AMIN BHATIA*
Agent: Robert Light - Los Angeles, 213-651-1777
Affiliation: BMI - Los Angeles, 310-659-9109

STORM   Cannon, 1986
IRON EAGLE II   Tri-Star, 1988, Canadian-Israeli
ORDEAL IN THE ARCTIC (TF)   Citadel/Alliance, 1993,
   U.S.-Canadian
JUST ONE OF THE GIRLS (TF)   co-composer with Vincent Mai,
   Entertainment Securities/Saban Neal and Gary Prods., 1993
BLACK ICE (CTF)   Saban/Prism/Entertainment Securities, 1993
A STRANGER IN THE MIRROR (TF)   Sidney Sheldon
   Prods./Paragon/Spelling TV, 1993

VANRAJ BHATIA
SURAJ KA SATVAN GHODA   *SEVEN HORSE OF THE SUN*
   1994, Indian

NICK BICAT
Contact: PRS - London, England, 011-44-1-580-5544

OLIVER TWIST (TF)   Claridge Group Ltd./Grafton, 1982, British
THE SCARLET PIMPERNEL (TF)   London Films, 1982, British
TO CATCH A KING (CTF)   Entertainment Partners/Gaylord
   Production Co./HBO Premiere Films, 1984
LACE (MS)   Lorimar Productions, 1984
A CHRISTMAS CAROL (TF)   Entertainment Partners, 1984
LACE II (TF)   Lorimar Productions, 1985
WETHERBY   MGM/UA Classics, 1985, British
IF TOMORROW COMES (TF)   CBS Entertainment Productions,
   1986
STEALING HEAVEN   FilmDallas, 1988, British-Yugoslavian
STRAPLESS   Granada Film, 1989, British
FRAMED (TF)   Anglia/A&E/Tesauro, 1993
THE HAWK   BBC, 1993, British
THE PASSION OF DARKLY NOON   1995, German

ARNIE BIEBER
SMOKE   1993

RENE MARC BINI
GROSSE FATIGUE   *DEAD TIRED*   Miramax Zoë, 1995, French

NATHAN BIRNBAUM
Contact: BMI - Los Angeles, 310-659-9109

CHAIN OF DESIRE   1992, Anant Singh and Distant horizon

JOHNNY BISHOP
Contact: BMI - Los Angeles, 310-659-9109

THE GODS MUST BE CRAZY   TLC Films/20th Century Fox, 1979,
   Botswana

CASARE BIXIO
b. Italy
Contact: SIAE - Italy, 011-39-6-59-901

THE DIVINE NYMPH   1979, Italian

KJETIL BJERKERSTRAND
CROSS MY HEART AND HOPE TO DIE   *TI KNIVER I HJERTET*
   co-composer with Magne Furuholmen, 1995, Norwegian

KAREN BLACK
b. July 1, 1942 - Park Ridge, Illinois
Contact: ASCAP - Los Angeles, 213-883-1000

CAN SHE BAKE A CHERRY PIE?   Castle Hill Productions/Quartet
   Films, 1983

STANLEY BLACK
b. 1913 - London, England
Contact: PRS - London, England, 011-44-1-580-5544

THE FATAL NIGHT   1948, British
SHADOW OF THE PAST   1950, British
TONIGHT'S THE NIGHT   Allied Artists, 1954
THE CRAWLING EYE   1958, British
JACK THE RIPPER   British version only, Paramount, 1960
MANIA   *THE FIENDISH GHOULS*   1960, British
HOUSE OF MYSTERY   1961, British
MANIAC   Columbia, 1963, British
WAR GODS OF THE DEEP   *THE CITY UNDER THE SEA*
   American International, 1965, British-U.S.

WENDY BLACKSTONE
Agent: CAA - Beverly Hills, 310-288-4545
Affiliation: ASCAP - Los Angeles, 213-883-1000

EL SALVADOR: ANOTHER VIETNAM (FD)   Catalyst Productions,
   1982
EDDIE MACON'S RUN   Universal, 1983
THE GOOD FIGHT (FD)   1983
FIVE A.M.   N. Tanis Company, 1985
ARE WE WINNING, MOMMY? AMERICA & THE COLD WAR (FD)
   CineInformation/Canadian Film Board, 1985
A STITCH FOR TIME (FD)   1987
KING JAMES VERSION   Joseph E. Taylor/Vitascope Inc., 1988
THE LODZ GHETTO (FD)   1989
DANCE OF HOPE (FD)   1989
THE REFRIGERATOR   1989
STOOD UP (TF)   ABC-TV, 1990
BLOWBACK   Northern Arts, 1991
THE BOY WHO CRIED BITCH   1991
EMMA AND ELVIS   Northern Arts Entertainment, 1992
ONLY YOU   Pro Filmworks, 1992
DUTCH MASTER   Miramax, 1993
UPPER ROOM   American Playhouse, 1993
ANGEL OF DESIRE   MCEG-Sterling, 1993
HALLELUJAH (TF)   Rhinoceros Prods., 1993
EROTIC TALES   composer of one segment, 1994, German
SOMEONE SHE KNOWS (TF)   Thomas Carter Co./Warner Bros.
   TV, 1994

RUBEN BLADES
Contact: ASCAP - Los Angeles, 213-883-1000

Q&A   Tri-Star, 1990

HOWARD BLAKE
Agent: PRS - London, England, 011-44-1-580-5544

AN ELEPHANT CALLED SLOWLY   American Continental, 1971,
   British
THE RAINBOW BOYS   1973, Canadian
STRONGER THAN THE SUN (TF)   BBC, 1977, British
THE DUELLISTS   Paramount, 1978, British
THE ODD JOB   Columbia, 1978, British
THE RIDDLE OF THE SANDS   Satori, 1979, British
S.O.S. TITANIC (TF)   Roger Gimbel Productions/EMI TV/Argonaut
   Films Ltd., 1979, U.S.-British
FLASH GORDON   co-composer with Queen, Universal, 1980,
   British
AMITYVILLE II: THE POSSESSION   Orion, 1982
AMITYVILLE 3-D   Orion, 1983
THE LORDS OF DISCIPLINE   Paramount, 1983
THE CANTERVILLE GHOST (TF)   Pound Ridge Productions/Inter-
   Hemisphere Productions/HTV/Columbia TV, 1986, U.S.-British
A MONTH IN THE COUNTRY   Orion Classics, 1987, British

RONNIE BLAKLEY
b. 1946 - Caldwell, Idaho
Contact: ASCAP - Los Angeles, 213-883-1000

LIGHTNING OVER WATER   *NICK'S MOVIE*   Pari Films, 1980,
   West German-Swiss-U.S.
I PLAYED IT FOR YOU (FD)   Ronee Blakley Productions, 1985

TERENCE BLANCHARD
Agent: Gorfaine-Schwarz - Los Angeles, 213-969-1011
Affiliation: BMI - Los Angeles, 310-659-9109

JUNGLE FEVER   Universal, 1991
MALCOLM X   Warner Bros., 1992
SUGAR HILL   20th Century Fox, 1993
THE INKWELL   Buena Vista, 1994
ASSAULT AT WEST POINT (CTF)   Ultra Ent./Mosaic Group, 1994
CROOKLYN   Universal, 1994
TRIAL BY JURY   Warner Bros., 1994
THE PROMISED LAND (TD)   Discovery Prods./BBC-TV, 1995
CLOCKERS   Universal, 1995
GET ON THE BUS   1996

LARRY BLANK*
b. July 15, 1952 - Brooklyn, NY
Agent: HEI - Pacific Palisades, 310-573-1309
Affiliation: ASCAP - Los Angeles, 213-883-1000

TAXI DANCERS   co-composer with Jeffrey Silverman, Trident,
   1993

GEORGE BLONDHEIM
Contact: SOCAN - Toronto, 416-445-8700

MARILYN & ME (TF)   World International Network/Samuels Film,
   1991
CHRISTMAS ON DIVISION STREET (TF)
   Guber-Peters/Morrow-Heus/WIC/Columbia TV, 1991
GATE II   Triumph, 1992
WHALE MUSIC   Alliance, 1994, Canadian
PROBABLE CAUSE (CTF)   Wilmont Prods., 1994
THE WAR BETWEEN US (CTF)   Atlantis-Troika/CBC/Telefilm
   Canada/British Columbia Film/Rogers Telefun, 1995, Canadian
A DREAM IS A WISH YOUR HEART MAKES: THE ANNETTE
   FUNICELLO STORY (TF)   Once Upon a Time Films/Savoy
   TV/Cactus Pictures/Fireworks Entertainment, 1995

LISA BLOOM
Agent: Marks Management - Tarzana, 818-776-8787
Affiliation: ASCAP - Los Angeles, 213-883-1000

PHOENIX   Triad, 1995

KATH BLOOM
Contact: BMI - Los Angeles, 310-659-9109

A LITTLE STIFF   Just Above The Ground, 1991

WILLIAM BLOOM
Contact: ASCAP - Los Angeles, 213-883-1000

THE SEARCH FOR ONE-EYE JIMMY   1996

THE BLUE HAWAIIANS
RED MEAT   Treehouse Films, 1997

CHRIS BOARDMAN*
Agent: Vangelos Management - Encino, 818-380-1919
Affiliation: BMI - Los Angeles, 310-659-9109

THE COLOR PURPLE ★   co-composer, Warner Bros., 1985
THE HIJACKING OF THE ACHILLE LAURO (TF) ☆   Tamara
   Asseyev Productions/New World TV/Spectacor Films, 1989
JOHNNY RYAN (TF) ☆   Dan Curtis TV Productions/MGM/UA/NBC
   Productions, 1990
PRIME TARGET (TF)   MGM TV, 1991
ELVIS AND THE COLONEL: THE UNTOLD STORY (TF)   Ultra
   Entertainment, 1993
BEYOND SUSPICION (TF)   Patricia K. Meyer Prods./von
   Zerneck-Sertner Films, 1993
BROKEN PROMISES: TAKING EMILY BACK (TF)   Larry
   Thompson Ent./RHI, 1993
ULTIMATE BETRAYAL (TF)   Polonga Prods./Hearst, 1994
A FRIEND TO DIE FOR (TF)   Steve White Prods, 1994
TERROR IN THE SHADOWS (TF)   Freyda Rothstein Prods./Lois
   Luger Prods./Hearst, 1995
THE PAUL FLEISS STORY (TF)   1996
TALES FROM THE CRYPT PRESENTS BORDELLO OF BLOOD
   Universal, 1996

JERRY BOCK
Contact: BMI - Los Angeles, 310-659-9109

A STRANGER AMONG US   Buena Vista, 1992

ROLAND BOCQUET
b. France
Contact: SACEM - France, 011-33-1-4715-4715

LA BALANCE   1982, Spectrafilm, French

THE BO DEANS
DESERT WINDS   co-composer with the Cowboy Junkies, Desert
   Wind Prods., 1995

MICHAEL BODDICKER*
Contact: BMI - Los Angeles, 310-659-9109

GET CRAZY   Embassy, 1983
THE ADVENTURES OF BUCKAROO BANZAI: ACROSS THE 8TH
   DIMENSION   20th Century Fox, 1984
WHITE WATER SUMMER   Columbia, 1987
THE ADVENTURES OF MILO & OTIS   *THE ADVENTURES OF
   CHATRAN*   composer of U.S. version, Columbia, 1989,
   Japanese
STARFIRE   *SOLAR CRISIS*   additional music, 1991
FX 2 - THE DEADLY ART OF ILLUSION   additional music, Orion,
   1991
FREEJACK   additional music, Morgan Creek, 1991
BULLETPROOF   additional music, Universal, 1996

TODD BOEKELHEIDE
Contact: ASCAP - Los Angeles, 213-883-1000

DIM SUM: A LITTLE BIT OF HEART   Orion Classics, 1985
CONTRARY WARRIORS (FD)   Rattlesnake Prods., 1985
DEAR AMERICA: LETTERS HOME FROM VIETNAM (FD)   Taurus
   Entertainment, 1987
THE BLOOD OF HEROES   New Line Cinema, 1990
HEARTS OF DARKNESS: A FILMMAKER'S APOCALYPSE (CTD)
   ZM/Zoetrope, 1991
EARTH AND THE AMERICAN DREAM (FD)   Couturie/BBC, 1993
SHIMMER   American Playhouse, 1993

NINA TAKES A LOVER   Sharona Prods., 1994
LOYALTY AND BETRAYAL: THE STORY OF THE AMERICAN
   MOB (TD)   Pilleggi-Couturie Prods./Quest Prods., 1994

ED BOGAS

Contact: BMI - Los Angeles, 310-659-9109

BLACK GIRL   Cinerama Releasing Corporation, 1972
FRITZ THE CAT (AF)   American International, 1972
HEAVY TRAFFIC (AF)   American International, 1973
RACE FOR YOUR LIFE, CHARLIE BROWN (AF)   Paramount,
   1977
WHO ARE THE DE BOLTS? ...AND WHERE DID THEY GET 19
   KIDS? (FD)   Pyramid Films, 1977
LOVE AND THE MIDNIGHT AUTO SUPPLY   Producers Capitol
   Corporation, 1978
BON VOYAGE, CHARLIE BROWN (AND DON'T COME BACK)
   Paramount, 1980
A CHRISTMAS WITHOUT SNOW (TF)   Korty Films/Frank
   Konigsberg Productions, 1980
STREET MUSIC   co-composer, Specialty Films, 1983
THE HEART OF HEALING (TD)   Independent
   Communications/Institute of Noetic Sciences/TBS Prods., 1993

GEIR BOHREN

FRIDA - STRAIGHT FROM THE HEART   *FRIDA- MED HJERTET I
   HANDEN*   co-composer with Bent Aserud, 1992, Norwegian

WILLIAM BOLCOM

b. 1938 - Seattle, Washington
Contact: BMI - Los Angeles, 310-659-9109

HESTER STREET   Midwest Film Productions, 1975

MARTIN D. BOLIN

FORCED TO KILL   PM, 1993

BILL BOLL

THE LOW LIFE   Zuckerman/Heminway, 1995

PAUL BOLL

REBEL HIGHWAY: ROADRACERS (CTF)   co-composer with
   Johnny Reno, Drive-In Classics, 1994

CLAUDE BOLLING

b. April 10, 1930 - Cannes, France
Contact: SACEM - France, 011-33-1-4715-4715

AUTOUR D'UNE TROMPETTE (FD)   1952, French
BONJOUR CINEMA   co-composer with Sidney Bechet and
   Christian Chevallier, 1955, French
CETTE NUIT-LA   1958, French
L'HOMME A FEMMES   *MEN AND WOMEN*   1960, French
ON FRIDAY AT ELEVEN   British Lion, 1961, West German-British
THE HANDS OF ORLAC   Columbia, 1962, British-French
THE DAY AND THE HOUR   MGM, 1962, French-Italian
VIVRE LA NUIT   1967, French
CADET L'EAU DOUCE   1969, French
LE MUR DE L'ATLANTIQUE   1969, French
LA CROISIERE DU NAVIGATOR   1969, French
BORSALINO   Paramount, 1970, French-Italian
QUI?   1970, French
LA MANDARINE   1971, French
CATCH ME A SPY   Rank, 1971, British
DOUCEMENT LES BASSES!   CIC, 1971, French
LUCKY LUKE   1971, French
LE SOLITAIRE   *THE LONER*   1973, French
LE MAGNIFIQUE   *THE MAGNIFICENT ONE*   Cine III, 1973,
   French
J'AI MON VOYAGE   1973, French
BORSALINO AND CO.   Medusa, 1974, French-Italian
DEUX GRANDES FILLES DANS UN PYJAMA   1974, French
DIS-MOI QUE TU M'AIMES   *TELL ME YOU LOVE ME*   1974,
   French
DITES-LE AVEC DES FLEURS   *SAY IT WITH FLOWERS*   1974,
   French
FLIC STORY   Adel Productions/Lira Films/Mondial, 1975, French
LE GITAN   1975, French

IL FAUT VIVRE DANGEREUSEMENT   *ONE MUST LIVE
   DANGEROUSLY*   1975, French
L'ORDINATEUR DES POMPES FUNEBRES   1976, French
LES PASSAGERS   *THE PASSENGERS*   1976, French
L'ANNEE SAINTE   *SAINT ANNE*   1976, French
LE MILLE-PATTES FAIT DES CLAQUETTES   1977, French
SILVER BEARS   Columbia, 1978
UN PAPILLON SUR L'EPAULE   Action Films, 1978, French
L'HOROSCOPE   1978, French
LA BALLADE DES DALTON   *THE BALLAD OF THE DALTONS*
   1978, French
CALIFORNIA SUITE   Columbia, 1978
THE ANGRY MAN   1979, French
THE AWAKENING   Orion/Warner Bros., 1980
WILLIE & PHIL   20th Century-Fox, 1980
JIGSAW   1980, French
LOUISIANA (CTF)   ICC/Antenne-2/Superchannel/CTV/Societe de
   Development de L'Industrie Cinematographique Canadienne,
   1983, Canadian-French
LE LEOPARD   1983, French
LE BRACONNIER DE DIEU   Les Artistes Associes, 1983, French
BAY BOY   Orion, 1984, Canadian
ON NE MEURT QUE DEUX FOIS   UGC, 1985, French
LA RUMBA   Hachette Premiere/UIP, 1987, French

ROGER BOLTON

Contact: PRS - London, England, 011-44-1-580-5544

TO DIE FOR   British, 1994

BERNARDO BONAZZI

Contact: SACEM - France, 011-33-1-4715-4715

WOMEN ON THE VERGE OF A NERVOUS BREAKDOWN   Orion
   Classics, 1988, Spanish

LELAND BOND

JUST WRITE   Curb, 1997

MICHAEL BONDERT

GREEN ON THURSDAYS (FD)   co-composer with Leo Crandall,
   Red Branch, 1993

RAY BONNEVILLE

THE MYTH OF THE MALE ORGASM   co-composer with Michel
   Pelletier, Telescene, 1993, Canadian

AL BORGONI

SIMPLE JUSTICE (TF)   co-composer with Steve Tyrell,
   WGBH/WNET/KCET, 1993

JOHN BOSHOFF

Contact: SAMRO

THE GODS MUST BE CRAZY   TLC Films/20th Century-Fox, 1979,
   Botswana

RICK BOSTON

Contact: BMI - Los Angeles, 310-659-9109

THE HARVEST   co-composer with Dave Allen, Curb Musifilm/Mike
   Curb and Lester Korn, 1993

SIMON BOSWELL

Agent: Vangelos Management - Encino, 818-380-1919
Affiliation: PRS - London, England, 011-44-1-580-5544

PHENOMENA   *CREEPERS*   1984, Italian
DEMONS 2   1987, Italian
DANGEROUS OBSESSION   Curb Esquire Films, 1990
SANTA SANGRE   Expanded Entertainment, 1990
HARDWARE   Miramax, 1990
MORTAL SINS   Silver Chariots, 1991
YOUNG SOUL REBELS   1991, British
THE TURN OF THE SCREW   1992, British-French
DUST DEVIL: THE FINAL CUT   Miramax, 1993, British
LOVE MATTERS (CTF)   Chanticleer, 1993

PICCOLO GRANDE AMORE   1993, Italian
SHALLOW GRAVE   Gramercy, 1994, British
JACK AND SARAH   1994, British
SECOND BEST   Warner Bros., 1994, British-U.S.
THE HUMAN TOUCH (CTF)   MTE, 1994
LORD OF ILLUSIONS   MGM-UA, 1995
HACKERS   MGM-UA, 1995
JACK AND SARAH   1996
AMERICAN PERFECT   Gramercy, 1997
COUSIN BETTE   Fox-Searchlight, 1997
PHOTOGRAPHING FAIRIES   Polygram, 1997

PERRY BOTKIN
Contact: BMI - Los Angeles, 310-659-9109

R.P.M.   Columbia, 1970
BLESS THE BEASTS AND CHILDREN   Columbia, 1971
THEY ONLY KILL THEIR MASTERS   MGM, 1972
SKYJACKED   MGM, 1972
LADY ICE   National General, 1973
YOUR THREE MINUTES ARE UP   Cinerama Releasing
    Corporation, 1973
GOIN' SOUTH   co-composer with Van Dyke Parks, Paramount,
    1978
PLEASURE COVE (TF)   Lou Shaw Productions/David Gerber
    Productions/Columbia Pictures TV, 1979
THE GOLDEN MOMENT: AN OLYMPIC LOVE STORY (TF)   Don
    Ohlmeyer Productions/Telepictures Corporation, 1980
TARZAN THE APE MAN   co-composer with Barry DeVorzon,
    MGM/United Artists, 1981
DANCE OF THE DWARFS   Dove Inc., 1983
SILENT NIGHT, DEADLY NIGHT   Tri-Star, 1984
WEEKEND WARRIORS   The Movie Store, 1986
ORDINARY HEROES   Crow Productions/Ira Barmak Productions,
    1986
SIDNEY SHELDON'S WINDMILL OF THE GODS   *WINDMILL OF
THE GODS* (TF)   Dove Productions/ITC Productions, 1988
SIDNEY SHELDON'S THE SANDS OF TIME (TF)   co-composer
    with Alberto de Almar, Dove Audio/Jadran Films/Tribune
    Entertainment, 1992

CHRIS BOTTI
CAUGHT   1996

LILI BOULANGER
Contact: SACEM - France, 011-33-1-4715-4715

BEATRICE   *LA PASSION BEATRICE*   co-composer with Ron
    Carter, Samuel Goldwyn Company, 1987, French-Italian

JEAN BOUCHETY
Contact: SACEM - France, 011-33-1-4715-4715

THE GAME IS OVER   *LA CUREE*   Royal Films International, 1966,
    French-Italian

HUBERT BOUGIS
Contact: SACEM - France, 011-33-1-4715-4715

SWEET REVENGE   The Movie Group, 1990, U.S.-French

JEAN-PAUL BOURELLY
ALMA'S RAINBOW   Paradise Plum, 1994

ROGER BOURLAND
Contact: BMI - Los Angeles, 310-659-9109

THE WOLF AT THE DOOR   *OVIRI*   International Film Marketing,
    1986, Danish-French
THE TROUBLE WITH DICK   FilmDallas, 1987
NIGHT LIFE   Wild Night Productions, 1989

DENNIS BOVELL
Contact: PRS - London, England, 011-44-1-580-5544

BABYLON   National Film, 1980, British

RICHARD BOWDEN
THE SWEET CREEK COUNTY WAR   Key International, 1979

RICHARD BOWERS*
Contact: ASCAP - Los Angeles, 213-883-1000

CANDLES IN THE DARK (CTF)   Taska
    Films/Kushner-Locke/Family Prods., 1993

PAUL BOWLES
b. 1910 - New York
Contact: ASCAP - Los Angeles, 213-883-1000

SIVA   Central Films, 1933
INNOCENT ISLAND   Harry Durham, 1934
VENUS AND ADONIS   Harry Durham, 1934
145 WEST 21   Rudolph Burckhardt, 1936
SEEING THE WORLD: A VISIT TO NEW YORK   Rudolph
    Burckhardt, 1936
AMERICA'S DISINHERITED   Sharecropper Committee, 1937
HOW TO BECOME A CITIZEN OF THE UNITED STATES (FD)
    Rudolph Burckhardt, 1938
CHELSEA THROUGH THE MAGNIFYING GLASS   Rudolph
    Burckhardt, 1938
THE SEX LIFE OF THE COMMON FILM   Rudolph Burckhardt,
    1938
FILM MADE TO MUSIC WRITTEN BY PAUL BOWLES   Rudolph
    Burckhardt, 1939
ROOTS IN THE EARTH (FD)   Department of Agriculture, 1940
THE CONGO (FD)   Belgian Government, 1944
DREAMS THAT MONEY CAN BUY   co-composer, Films
    International of America, 1948
THE GLASS MENAGERIE   theme only, Cineplex Odeon, 1987

EUEL BOX*
Contact: ASCAP - Los Angeles, 213-883-1000

BENJI   Mulberry Square, 1974
HAWMPS   Mulberry Square, 1976
FOR THE LOVE OF BENJI   Mulberry Square, 1978
THE DOUBLE McGUFFIN   Mulberry Square, 1979
BENJI, THE HUNTED   Buena Vista, 1987

MICHAEL BOYD
Contact: ASCAP - Los Angeles, 213-883-1000

BREAKIN'   co-composer with Gary Remal, MGM/UA/Cannon,
    1984

ROBERT BOYLE
Contact: ASCAP - Los Angeles, 213-883-1000

ANNE DEVLIN   Aeon Films, 1984, Irish

OWEN BRADLEY
Contact: BMI - Los Angeles, 310-659-9109

COAL MINER'S DAUGHTER   Universal, 1980

ERNST BRADNER
BLOOD AND HONOR: YOUTH UNDER HITLER (MS)   Daniel
    Wilson Productions/SWF/Taurus Films, 1982

BILLY BRAGG
Contact: PRS - London, England, 011-44-1-580-5544

SAFE   1993, British
WALKING AND TALKING   1996

KEN BRAHMSTEDT
ASWANG   Young American Films/Purple Onion Pords., 1994

STEVEN BRAMSON*
Contact: Gorfaine-Schwartz - Los Angeles, 213-969-1011
Affiliation: ASCAP - Los Angeles, 213-883-1000

LOVE CAN BE MURDER (TF)   Konigsberg-Sanitsky, 1992
THE CRUDE OASIS   Miramax, 1995

CHRISTIAN BRANDAUER
MARIO AND THE MAGICIAN   *MARIO UND DER ZAUBERER*
   Miramax, 1994, Canadian-French-British

CARL BRANDT
Contact: ASCAP - Los Angeles, 213-883-1000

LITTLE MO (TF)   co-composer with Billy May, Mark VII
   Ltd./Worldvision Enterprises, 1978

FRED BRATHWAITE
WILD STYLE   co-composer with Chris Stein, Wild Style, 1983

CREED BRATTON
Contact: BMI - Los Angeles, 310-659-9109

DANGEROUS COMPANY (TF)   The Dangerous
   Company/Finnegan Associates, 1982

DAVID BRAVO
Contact: ASCAP - Los Angeles, 213-883-1000

FEDERAL HILL   Eagle Beach, 1994

GORAN BREGOVIC
Contact: SACEM - France, 011-33-1-4715-4715

THE LITTLE ONE   *MALA*   1992, Yugoslav
TOXIC AFFAIR   1993, French
LA NUIT SACREE   *THE SACRED NIGHT*   1993, French
QUEEN MARGOT   *LA REINE MARGOT*   Miramax, 1994, French
ARIZONA DREAM   Kit Parker Films, 1995, French
UNDERGROUND   1995, French-German-Hungarian

FERDI BRENGEN
THE ROAD TO MECCA   co-composer with Nik Pickard, Distant
   Horizon/Videovision, 1992

DANNY BRENNER
SPARE ME   Film Crash, 1993

TORSTEN BREUER
MAYBE...MAYBE NOT   1996

ALAN BREWER
Contact: BMI - Los Angeles, 310-659-9109

TOKYO POP   Skouras, 1988

PETER BREWIS
Contact: PRS - London, England, 011-44-1-580-5544

MORONS FROM OUTER SPACE   Thorn/EMI, 1985, British
THE TALL GUY   Vestron, 1989, British

LESLIE BRICCUSE
b. January 29, 1931 - London, England
Contact: BMI - Los Angeles, 310-659-9109

DR. DOOLITTLE ★   20th Century Fox, 1967
GOODBYE, MR. CHIPS ★   adaptation, MGM, 1969, British
SCROOGE ★   National General, 1970, British
WILLIE WONKA AND THE CHOCOLATE FACTORY ★
   Paramount, 1971, British
BABES IN TOYLAND (TF)   The Finnegan-Pinchuk Company/Orion
   TV/Bavaria Atelier GMBH, 1986

TONY BRITTEN
Contact: PRS - London, England, 011-44-1-580-5544

THE PIRATE MOVIE   co-composer, 1982, Austalian
JOYRIDERS   Granada Film Prods., 1989, British

RICHARD BRONSKILL*
Contact: BMI - Los Angeles, 310-659-9109

THE PERFECT BRIDE (CTF)   Perfect Bride Inc., 1991

MICHAEL BROOK
ALBINO ALLIGATOR   Miramax, 1997

JOSEPH BROOKS
Contact: ASCAP - Los Angeles, 213-883-1000

THE LORDS OF FLATBUSH   Columbia, 1974
YOU LIGHT UP MY LIFE   Columbia, 1977
IF EVER I SEE YOU AGAIN   Columbia, 1978
HEADIN' FOR BROADWAY   20th Century-Fox, 1980
INVITATION TO THE WEDDING   New Realm, 1983, British

MALCOLM BROOKS
MOON SHOT (CTD)   co-composer with Ed Van Fleet and
   Rushmore De Nooyer, TBS Prods., 1994

PHILIP BROPHY
BODY MELT   Dumb Films, 1993, Australian

BRUCE BROUGHTON*
b. 1945 - Los Angeles, California
Agent: Vangelos Management - Encino, 818-380-1919
Affiliation: ASCAP - Los Angeles, 213-883-1000

HOW THE WEST WAS WON (MS)   co-composer, MGM TV, 1977
PARADISE CONNECTION (TF)   Woodruff Productions/QM
   Productions, 1979
THE RETURN OF FRANK CANNON (TF)   QM Productions, 1980
DESPERATE VOYAGE (TF)   Barry Weitz Films/Jack Wizan TV
   Productions, 1980
THE GIRL, THE GOLD WATCH AND DYNAMITE (TF)
   Fellows-Keegan Company/Paramount TV, 1981
KILLJOY (TF) ☆   Lorimar Productions, 1981
DESPERATE LIVES (TF)   Fellows-Keegan Company/Lorimar
   Pictures, 1982
ONE SHOE MAKES IT MURDER (TF)   Fellows-Keegan
   Company/Lorimar Productions, 1982
THE BLUE AND THE GRAY (MS) ☆   Larry White-Lou Reda
   Productions/Columbia TV, 1982
TWO MARRIAGES (TF)   Lorimar Productions/Raven's Claw
   Productions, 1983
COWBOY (TF)   Bercovici-St. Johns Productions/MGM TV, 1983
M.A.D.D.: MOTHERS AGAINST DRUNK DRIVERS (TF)   Universal
   TV, 1983
THE ICE PIRATES   MGM/UA, 1983
THIS GIRL FOR HIRE (TF)   Barney Rosenzweig Productions/Orion
   TV, 1983
THE MASTER OF BALLANTRAE (TF)   Larry White-Hugh Benson
   Productions/HTV/Columbia TV, 1984, U.S.-British
THE PRODIGAL   World Wide, 1984
THE COWBOY AND THE BALLERINA (TF)   Cowboy Productions,
   1984
PASSIONS (TF)   Carson Production Group/Wizan TV Enterprises,
   1984
THE FIRST OLYMPICS - ATHENS 1896 (MS) ☆☆   Larry
   White-Gary Allison Productions/Columbia TV, 1984
SILVERADO ★   Columbia, 1985
STORMIN' HOME (TF)   CBS Entertainment, 1985
YOUNG SHERLOCK HOLMES   Paramount, 1985
SWEET LIBERTY   Universal, 1986
THE BOY WHO COULD FLY   20th Century Fox, 1986
SQUARE DANCE   Island Pictures, 1986
THE THANKSGIVING PROMISE (TF)   Mark H. Ovitz
   Productions/Walt Disney TV, 1986
GEORGE WASHINGTON: THE FORGING OF A NATION (TF)
   David Gerber Company/MGM TV, 1986
HARRY AND THE HENDERSONS   Universal, 1987

THE MONSTER SQUAD   Tri-Star, 1987
BIG SHOTS   20th Century Fox, 1987
CROSS MY HEART   Universal, 1987
THE PRESIDIO   Paramount, 1988
THE RESCUE   Buena Vista, 1988
MOONWALKER   Warner Bros., 1988
LAST RITES   MGM/UA, 1988
JACKNIFE   Kings Road, 1989
SORRY, WRONG NUMBER (CTF)   1989
ERNEST HEMINGWAY'S THE OLD MAN AND THE SEA (TF) ☆
   Stroke Enterprises/Green Pond Productions/Yorkshire TV, 1990
BETSY'S WEDDING   Buena Vista, 1990
THE RESCUERS DOWN UNDER (AF)   Buena Vista, 1990
NARROW MARGIN   Carolco, 1991
THE LAST HALLOWEEN (TF)   Hanna-Barbera Prods., 1991
ALL I WANT FOR CHRISTMAS   Paramount, 1991
O PIONEERS (TF) ☆☆   Craig Anderson Prods./Lorimar/Prairie
   Films, 1992
HONEY, I BLEW UP THE KID   Buena Vista, 1992
STAY TUNED   Warner Bros., 1992
HOMEWARD BOUND: THE INCREDIBLE JOURNEY   Buena Vista,
   1993
SO I MARRIED AN AXE MURDERER   TriStar, 1993
FOR LOVE OR MONEY   Universal, 1993
TOMBSTONE   Buena Vista, 1993
HOLY MATRIMONY   Buena Vista, 1994
BABY'S DAY OUT   20th Century Fox, 1994
MIRACLE ON 34TH STREET   20th Century Fox, 1994
JAG (TF)   Belisarius Prods./Paramount/NBC, 1995
ACTS OF LOVE   1995
HOMEWARD BOUND II: LOST IN SAN FRANCISCO   Buena Vista,
   1996
HOUSE ARREST   MGM/UA, 1996
INFINITY   First Look, 1996
CARRIED AWAY   Fine Line, 1996
THE SHADOW CONSPIRACY   Buena Vista, 1997

CHARLES BROWN
JOHNS   co-composer with Danny Caron, First Look, 1997

EARL BROWN, JR.
Contact: ASCAP - Los Angeles, 213-883-1000

AMERICATHON   United Artists, 1979

GREG BROWN
Contact: ASCAP - Los Angeles, 213-883-1000

ZADAR! COW FROM HELL   Stone Peach, 1989

LARRY BROWN*
Contact: BMI - Los Angeles, 310-659-9109

RIO DIABLO (TF)   Kenny Rogers Prods./RHI/World Intl. Network,
   1993
MACSHAYNE: WINNER TAKES ALL (TF)   co-composer with Edgar
   Struble, Kenny Rogers, Jr. and Bob DeMarco, Larry Levinson
   Prods./Kenny Rogers Prods., 1994
GAMBLER V: PLAYING FOR KEEPS (TF)   co-composer with
   Edgar Struble, Kenny Rogers Prods./WIN/RHI, 1994
THE WOMEN OF SPRING BREAK (TF)   Ron Gilbert
   Ass./Hill-Fields Entertainment, 1995

LARRY H. BROWN
TRIPLECROSS (CTF)   co-composer with Daniel Stein,
   Weintraub-Kuhn Prods./Showtime, 1995

TOM BRUNER
Contact: ASCAP - Los Angeles, 213-883-1000

SCHOOL SPIRIT   Concorde/Cinema Group, 1985

ROBERT F. BRUNNER
Contact: ASCAP - Los Angeles, 213-883-1000

THAT DARN CAT   Buena Vista, 1965
LT. ROBIN CRUSOE, U.S.N.   Buena Vista, 1966
MONKEYS, GO HOME!   Buena Vista, 1967

BLACKBEARD'S GHOST   Buena Vista, 1968
NEVER A DULL MOMENT   Buena Vista, 1968
THE COMPUTER WORE TENNIS SHOES   Buena Vista, 1969
SMITH!   Buena Vista, 1969
THE BOATNIKS   Buena Vista, 1970
THE BAREFOOT EXECUTIVE   Buena Vista, 1971
THE WILD COUNTRY   Buena Vista, 1971
THE BISCUIT EATER   Buena Vista, 1972
NOW YOU SEE HIM, NOW YOU DON'T   Buena Vista, 1972
THE SNOWBALL EXPRESS   Buena Vista, 1972
THE CASTAWAY COWBOY   Buena Vista, 1974
THE STRONGEST MAN IN THE WORLD   Buena Vista, 1975
GUS   Buena Vista, 1976
THE NORTH AVENUE IRREGULARS   Buena Vista, 1979
AMY   Buena Vista, 1981

GEORGE BRUNS
b. July 3, 1914 - Sandy, Oregon
Contact: ASCAP - Los Angeles, 213-883-1000

DAVY CROCKETT, KING OF THE WILD FRONTIER   Buena Vista,
   1955
DAVY CROCKETT AND THE RIVER PIRATES   Buena Vista, 1956
WESTWARD HO, THE WAGONS   Buena Vista, 1956
JOHNNY TREMAIN   Buena Vista, 1957
SLEEPING BEAUTY (AF) ★   adaptation, Buena Vista, 1959
ONE HUNDRED AND ONE DALMATIONS (AF)   Buena Vista, 1960
THE ABSENT-MINDED PROFESSOR   Buena Vista, 1960
BABES IN TOYLAND ★   adaptation, Buena Vista, 1961
SON OF FLUBBER   Buena Vista, 1963
THE SWORD IN THE STONE (AF) ★   Buena Vista, 1963
THE MAN FROM BUTTON WILLOW (AF)   co-composer with Dale
   Robertson and Mel Hank, 1965
THE FIGHTING PRINCE OF DONEGAL   Buena Vista, 1966
FOLLOW ME, BOYS!   Buena Vista, 1966
THE ADVENTURES OF BULLWHIP GRIFFIN   Buena Vista, 1967
THE JUNGLE BOOK (AF)   Buena Vista, 1967
ISLAND OF THE LOST   1967
DARING GAME   Paramount, 1968
THE HORSE IN THE GRAY FLANNEL SUIT   Buena Vista, 1968
THE LOVE BUG   Buena Vista, 1969
THE ARISTOCATS (AF)   Buena Vista, 1970
ROBIN HOOD (AF)   Buena Vista, 1973
HERBIE RIDES AGAIN   Buena Vista, 1974

STEPHEN BRUTON
Contact: BMI - Los Angeles, 310-659-9109

PICTURE THIS - THE TIMES OF PETER BOGDANOVICH IN
   ARCHER CITY, TEXAS (DF)   Kino-Eye American, 1991

JOANNE BRUZDOWICZ
Contact: SACEM - France, 011-33-1-4715-4715

JACQUOT DE NANTES (DF)   1991, French

BENEDIKT BRYDERN*
THE TIN SOLDIER (CTF)   Crystal Sky Comms./Showtime, 1995
RHYME & REASON   Miramax, 1997

CHICO BUARQUE
Contact: SACEM - France, 011-33-1-4715-4715

DONA FLOR AND HER TWO HUSBANDS   New Yorker, 1977,
   Brazilian

ALEXANDER BUBENHEIM
NIGHT TRAIN TO VENICE   1993, German

BILL BUCKINGHAM
HARMONY CATS   co-composer with Graeme Coleman, Alan
   Morinis and Richard Davis, 1993, Canadian

PAUL BUCKMASTER
Agent: Vangelos Management - Encino, 818-380-1919
Affiliation: ASCAP - Los Angeles, 213-883-1000

THE SPY WHO LOVED ME   additional music, United Artists, 1977
DIVING IN   co-composer with Guy Moon, Maurer/Shaw, 1991
CAPTIVE (TF)   co-composer with Steve Tyrell, Capital
   Cities-ABC/Bonny Dore/Ten-Four, 1991
12 MONKEYS   Universal, 1995
THE LAST WORD   Universal, 1995
ONCE UPON A TIME WHEN WE WERE COLORED   co-composer
   with Lionel Cole, 1996
MURDER IN MIND   Lakeshore Entertainment, 1997
THE MAKER   Mad Chance Prods., 1997
MOST WANTED   New Line, 1997

JIMMY BUFFETT
Contact: BMI - Los Angeles, 310-659-9109

RANCHO DELUXE   United Artists, 1975

PETER BUFFETT
DANCES WITH WOLVES   firedance music, Orion, 1990
500 NATIONS (TD)   Tig Prods./RCS/Majestic, 1995

VELTON RAY BUNCH*
Agent: Gorfaine-Schwartz - Los Angeles, 213-969-1011
Affiliation: BMI - Los Angeles, 310-659-9109

PALACE GUARD (TF)   co-composer with Mike Post, Stephen J.
   Cannell, 1991
QUANTUM LEAP: LEE HARVEY OSWALD - LEAPING ON A
   STRING (TF) ☆   Bellisarius/Universal TV, 1992
WORKING STIFFS   1993
WALKER, TEXAS RANGER: THE REUNION (TF)   Top Kick
   Prods./Columbia TV/Ruddy & Greig Prods./CBS TV Ent., 1994
CROWFOOT (TF)   Bellisarius, 1995
PROWLER (TF)   Bakula Prods./Warner Bros. TV, 1995

ERIC BURDON
Contact: BMI - Los Angeles, 310-659-9109

COMEBACK   Rocco Film, 1982, West German

GEOFFREY BURGON
Agent: PRS - London, England, 011-44-1-580-5544

LIFE OF BRIAN   Orion, 1979, British
TINKER, TAYLOR, SOLDIER, SPY (MS)   1980, British
THE DOGS OF WAR   United Artists, 1980
BRIDESHEAD REVISITED (MS)   Granada TV/WNET-13/NDR
   Hamburg, 1982, British-U.S.-West German
TURTLE DIARY   Samuel Goldwyn Company, 1985, British
BLEAK HOUSE (MS)   BBC, 1985, British
ROBIN HOOD (TF)   20th Century Fox/Working Title, 1991
A FOREIGN FIELD   1993, British
MARTIN CHUZZLEWIT (MS)   BBC/Pebble Mill/WGBH Boston,
   1995, British

CHRIS BURKE
Contact: BMI - Los Angeles, 310-659-9109

SPLATTER UNIVERSITY   Troma, 1984

RALPH BURNS
b. June 29, 1922 - Newton, Massachusetts
Contact: ASCAP - Los Angeles, 213-883-1000

CABARET ★★   Allied Artists, 1972
LENNY   United Artists, 1974
PIAF   AMLF, 1974
LUCKY LADY   20th Century Fox, 1977
NEW YORK, NEW YORK   United Artists, 1977
MOVIE MOVIE   Warner Brothers, 1978
ALL THAT JAZZ ★★   adaptation, 20th Century Fox, 1979
MAKE ME AN OFFER (TF)   ABC Circle Films, 1980
URBAN COWBOY   Paramount, 1980

FIRST FAMILY   adaptation, Warner Bros., 1980
GOLDEN GATE (TF)   Lin Bolen Productions/Warner Bros. TV,
   1981
SIDE SHOW (TF)   Krofft Entertainment, 1981
PENNIES FROM HEAVEN   co-composer with Marvin Hamlisch,
   MGM/United Artists, 1981
ANNIE ★   adaptation, Columbia, 1982
KISS ME GOODBYE   20th Century Fox, 1982
MY FAVORITE YEAR   MGM/UA, 1982
STAR 80   The Ladd Company/Warner Bros., 1983
NATIONAL LAMPOON'S VACATION   Warner Bros., 1983
PHANTOM OF THE OPERA (TF)   Robert Halmi Inc., 1983
THE MUPPETS TAKE MANHATTAN   Tri-Star, 1984
ERNIE KOVACS - BETWEEN THE LAUGHTER (TF)   ABC Circle
   Films, 1984
PERFECT   Columbia, 1985
A CHORUS LINE   Columbia, 1985
MOVING VIOLATIONS   20th Century-Fox, 1985
PENALTY PHASE (TF)   Tamara Asseyev Productions/New World
   TV, 1986
THE CHRISTMAS STAR (TF)   Lake Walloon Productions/Catalina
   Productions. Group/ Walt Disney TV, 1986
IN THE MOOD   Lorimar, 1987
AFTER THE PROMISE (TF)   Tamara Asseyev Productions/New
   World TV, 1987
BERT RIGBY, YOU'RE A FOOL   Warner Bros., 1989
SWEET BIRD OF YOUTH (TF)   1989
ALL DOGS GO TO HEAVEN (AF)   MGM/UA, 1989, British
THE JOSEPHINE BAKER STORY (CTF)   additional music, HBO
   Pictures/Anglia TV/John Kemeny/RH Entertainment, 1991

GEORGE BURT
Contact: ASCAP - Los Angeles, 213-883-1000

SECRET HONOR   Sandcastle 5, 1984
FOOL FOR LOVE   Cannon, 1985

CARTER BURWELL*
Agent: CAA - Beverly Hills, 310-288-4545
Affiliation: ASCAP - Los Angeles, 213-883-1000

BLOOD SIMPLE   Circle Releasing Corporation, 1984
PSYCHO III   Universal, 1986
RAISING ARIZONA   20th Century Fox, 1987
PASS THE AMMO   New Century/Vista, 1988
IT TAKES TWO   MGM/UA, 1988
BEAT   Vestron, 1988
CHECKING OUT   Warner Bros., 1989
MILLER'S CROSSING   1990
BARTON FINK   20th Century Fox, 1991
DOC HOLLYWOOD   Warner Bros., 1991
SCORCHERS   Nova, 1991
BUFFY THE VAMPIRE SLAYER   20th Century Fox, 1992
STORYVILLE   20th Century Fox, 1992
WATERLAND   Fine Line, 1992
AND THE BAND PLAYED ON (CTF)   HBO Pictures, 1993
KALIFORNIA   Gramercy, 1993
THIS BOY'S LIFE   Warner Bros., 1993
A DANGEROUS WOMAN   1993
WAYNE'S WORLD 2   Paramount, 1993
THE HUDSUCKER PROXY   Warner Bros., 1994
IT COULD HAPPEN TO YOU   TriStar, 1994
AIRHEADS   20th Century Fox, 1994
BAD COMPANY   Buena Vista, 1995
ROB ROY   MGM/UA, 1995
A GOOFY MOVIE (AF)   Buena Vista, 1995
FARGO   Gramercy, 1996
FEAR   1996
JOE'S APARTMENT   Warner Bros., 1996
THE CELLULOID CLOSET   1996
THE CHAMBER   Universal, 1996
PICTURE PERFECT   20th Century Fox, 1997

GERALD BUSBY
Contact: ASCAP - Los Angeles, 213-883-1000

THREE WOMEN   20th Century-Fox, 1977

COBB BUSSINGER

Contact: ASCAP - Los Angeles, 213-883-1000

I DON'T BUY KISSES ANYMORE   Skouras, 1992

ARTIE BUTLER

Contact: ASCAP - Los Angeles, 213-883-1000

THE LOVE MACHINE   Columbia, 1971
WHAT'S UP, DOC?   Warner Bros., 1972
THE HARRAD EXPERIMENT   Cinerama Releasing Corporation,
   1973
WONDER WOMAN (TF)   Warner Bros. TV, 1974
FOR PETE'S SAKE   Columbia, 1974
AT LONG LAST LOVE   adaptation, 20th Century Fox, 1975
RAFFERTY AND THE GOLD DUST TWINS   Warner Bros., 1975
IT'S SHOWTIME   United Artists, 1976
OPERATION PETTICOAT (TF)   Heyday Productions/Universal TV,
   1977
THE RESCUERS (AF)   Buena Vista, 1978
SEXTETTE   Crown International, 1978
SULTAN AND THE ROCK STAR (TF)   Walt Disney Productions,
   1978
ANGEL ON MY SHOULDER (TF)   Mace Neufeld
   Productions/Barney Rosenzweig Productions/Beowulf
   Productions, 1980
SIZZLE (TF)   Aaron Spelling Productions, 1981
AMERICAN DREAM (TF)   Mace Neufeld Productions/Viacom, 1981
SHE'S IN THE ARMY NOW (TF)   ABC Circle Films, 1981
GREASE 2   Paramount, 1982
O'HARA'S WIFE   Davis-Panzer Productions, 1982
THE MAKING OF A MALE MODEL (TF)   Aaron Spelling
   Productions, 1983
THE OTHER WOMAN (TF)   CBS Entertainment, 1983
LAST OF THE GREAT SURVIVORS (TF)   CBS Entertainment,
   1984
COPACABANA (TF)   Dick Clark Cinema Productions/Stiletto Ltd.,
   1985
CLASSIFIED LOVE (TF)   CBS Entertainment, 1986

BUZZOV-EN

THE GREAT UNPLEASANTNESS   co-composer with Jake Berger
   and Pervis Lee, Crescent Pictures, 1993

BILLY BYERS

Contact: BMI - Los Angeles, 310-659-9109

HAUSER'S MEMORY (TF)   Universal TV, 1970
THE BORROWERS (TF)   co-composer with Rod McKuen, Walt
   DeFaria Productions/20th Century-Fox TV, 1973
MOONCHILD   co-composer with Patrick Williams, Filmmakers
   Ltd./American Films Ltd., 1974

DONALD BYRD

Contact: BMI - Los Angeles, 310-659-9109

CORNBREAD, EARL AND ME   American International, 1975

JOSEPH BYRD

HEALTH   20th Century-Fox, 1980

DAVID BYRNE

b. Dumbarton, Scotland
Contact: ASCAP - Los Angeles, 213-883-1000

TRUE STORIES   Warner Bros., 1986
DEAD END KIDS (FD)   co-composer with Philip Glass, Mabou
   Mines, 1986
THE LAST EMPEROR ★★   co-composer with Cong Su and Ryuichi
   Sakamoto, Columbia, 1987, British-Chinese

C

JOHN CACAVAS*

b. South Dakota
Agent: Film Music Associates - Hollywood, 213-463-1070
Affiliation: ASCAP - Los Angeles, 213-883-1000

PANCHO VILLA   Scotia, 1972, Spanish
HORROR EXPRESS   1972, Spanish-British
BLADE   Green/Pintoff, 1973
COUNT DRACULA AND HIS VAMPIRE BRIDE   SATANIC RITES
   OF DRACULA   Warner Bros., 1973
REDNECK   International Amusements, 1975, British-Italian
SHE CRIED "MURDER" (TF)   Universal TV, 1973
LINDA (TF)   Universal TV, 1973
THE ELEVATOR (TF)   Universal TV, 1974
AIRPORT 1975   Universal, 1974
FRIENDLY PERSUASION (TF)   International TV Productions/Allied
   Artists, 1975
KATE McSHANE (TF)   Paramount TV, 1975
MURDER AT THE WORLD SERIES (TF)   ABC Circle Films, 1977
SST - DEATH FLIGHT (TF)   ABC Circle Films, 1977
AIRPORT '77   Universal, 1977
RELENTLESS (TF)   CBS, Inc., 1977
SUPERDOME (TF)   ABC Circle Films, 1978
BJ & THE BEAR   Universal TV, 1978
THE TIME MACHINE (TF)   Sunn Classic Productions, 1978
HUMAN FEELINGS (TF)   Crestview Productions/Worldvision, 1978
HANGAR 18   Sunn Classic, 1980
ONCE UPON A SPY (TF)   David Gerber Company/Columbia TV,
   1980
SEPARATE WAYS   Crown International, 1981
HELLINGER'S LAW (TF)   Universal TV, 1981
NO PLACE TO HIDE (TF)   Metromedia Producers Corporation,
   1981
THE GANGSTER CHRONICLES (TF)   Universal TV, 1981
TODAY'S FBI (TF)   David Gerber Company, 1981
CHILD BRIDE OF SHORT CREEK (TF)   Lawrence Schiller-Paul
   Monash Productions, 1981
THE NEIGHBORHOOD (TF)   David Gerber Company/Columbia TV,
   1982
THE EXECUTIONER'S SONG (TF)   Film Communications Inc.,
   1982
CRY FOR THE STRANGERS (TF)   David Gerber Company/MGM
   TV, 1982
MORTUARY   Artists Releasing Corporation/Film Ventures
   International, 1983
A TIME TO DIE   Almi Films, 1983
STILL THE BEAVER   Bud Austin Productions/Universal TV, 1983
WOMEN OF SAN QUENTIN (TF)   David Gerber
   Company/MGM-UA TV, 1983
HER LIFE AS A MAN (TF)   LS Entertainment, 1984
THEY'RE PLAYING WITH FIRE   New World, 1984
JESSIE (TF)   Lindsay Wagner Productions/MGM-UA TV. 1984
LADY BLUE (TF)   David Gerber Productions Productions/MGM-UA
   TV, 1985
A DEATH IN CALIFORNIA (TF)   Mace Neufeld Productions/Lorimar
   Productions, 1985
JENNY'S WAR (TF)   Louis Rudolph Productions/HTV/Columbia TV,
   1985, U.S.-British
A TIME TO TRIUMPH (TF)   Billos-Kauffman Productions/Phoenix
   Entertainment Group, 1986
THE DIRTY DOZEN: THE DEADLY MISSION (TF)   MGM-UA
   TV/Jadran Film, 1987, U.S.-Yugoslavian
POLICE STORY II: THE FREEWAY KILLINGS (TF)   David Gerber
   Productions/MGM-UA TV/Columbia TV, 1987
THE DIRTY DOZEN: THE FATAL MISSION (TF)   MGM-UA TV,
   1988
BODY OF EVIDENCE (TF)   CBS Entertainment, 1988
MARGARET-BOURKE WHITE (CTF)   TNT Inc./Project VII/Central
   TV, 1989
COLOMBO GOES TO THE GUILLOTINE (TF)   Universal TV, 1989
MURDER IN PARADISE (TF)   Bill McCutchen
   Productions/Columbia Pictures TV, 1990

COLUMBO: CAUTION MURDER CAN BE HAZARDOUS TO YOUR HEALTH (TF)   Universal TV, 1991
THE RETURN OF IRONSIDE (TF)   Riven Rock Prods./Windy City Prods., 1993

JOHN CAFFERTY

Contact: BMI - Los Angeles, 310-659-9109

EDDIE AND THE CRUISERS   Embassy, 1983

STEVEN CAGAN

Contact: ASCAP - Los Angeles, 213-883-1000

THE CAT AND THE CANARY   Quartet, 1978, British

ROBERT CAIRNS

I'LL LOVE YOU FOREVER...TONIGHT   Headliner, 1993

PIRO CAKO

LOIN DES BARBARES   *FAR FROM BARBARY*   1993, French-Italian-Belgian

JORGE CALANDRELLI

b. Argentina
Contact: ASCAP - Los Angeles, 213-883-1000

SOLA   1976, Argentinian
THE COLOR PURPLE ★   co-composer, Warner Bros., 1985
THE TOWN BULLY (TF)   Dick Clark Productions, 1988
I'LL BE HOME FOR CHRISTMAS (TF)   NBC Productions, 1988

MICHAEL CALASSO

CHUNKING EXPRESS   co-composer with Frankie Chan and Roel A. Garcia, 1996

JOHN CALE

Contact: ASCAP - Los Angeles, 213-466-7681

SOMETHING WILD   co-composer with Laurie Anderson, Orion, 1986
PRIMARY MOTIVE   Blossom Pictures, 1992
BASQUIAT   Miramax, 1996
I SHOT ANDY WARHOL   1996

CHARLES CALELLO

Contact: ASCAP - Los Angeles, 213-883-1000

THE LONELY LADY   Universal, 1983

CHRISTOPHER CAMERON

Contact: ASCAP - Los Angeles, 213-883-1000

GOD'S WILL   Power and Light Production, 1989

JOHN CAMERON

Contact: PRS - London, England, 011-44-1-580-5544

THINK DIRTY   *EVERY HOME SHOULD HAVE ONE*   1970, British
KES   United Artists, 1970, British
THE RISE AND RISE OF MICHAEL RIMMER   Warner Bros., 1970, British
THE RULING CLASS   Avco Embassy, 1972, British
CHARLEY-ONE-EYE   Paramount, 1973, British
NIGHT WATCH   Avco Embassy, 1973, British
A TOUCH OF CLASS ★   Avco Embassy, 1973, British
SCALAWAG   Paramount, 1973, U.S.-Italian
SEX PLAY   1974
MOMENTS   Warner/Columbia, 1974, British
MADE   International Co-Productions, 1975, British
OUT OF SEASON   *WINTER RATES*   Athenaeum, 1975, British
WHIFFS   20th Century-Fox, 1975
THE GREAT SCOUT AND CATHOUSE THURSDAY   American International, 1976
I WILL, I WILL...FOR NOW   20th Century-Fox, 1976
SPECTRE (TF)   Norway Productions/20th Century-Fox TV, 1977
NASTY HABITS   Brut Productions, 1977, British

THE THIEF OF BAGHDAD (TF)   Palm Productions, 1978
THE BERMUDA TRIANGLE   Sunn Classic, 1979
LOST AND FOUND   Columbia, 1979
SUNBURN   Paramount, 1979, U.S.-British
THE MIRROR CRACK'D   AFD, 1980, British
WHO?   Lorimar, 1982, British-West German
WITNESS FOR THE PROSECUTION (TF)   Norman Rosemont Productions/United Artists TV, 1982
THE JIGSAW MAN   United Film Distribution, 1984, British
THE SECRET GARDEN (TF)   Norman Rosemont Productions, 1987
JACK THE RIPPER (TF)   Euston Films/Thames TV/Hill-O'Connor Entertainment/Lorimar TV, 1988, British-U.S.
JEKYLL & HYDE (TF)   David Wickes TV/LWT/King Phoenix Entertainment, 1990
FRANKENSTEIN (CTF)   David Wickes Prods., 1993

MICHEL CAMILO

TWO MUCH   Buena Vista, 1996

DAVID CAMPBELL

Contact: ASCAP - Los Angeles, 213-883-1000

ALL THE RIGHT MOVES   20th Century Fox, 1983
NIGHT OF THE COMET   Atlantic Releasing Corporation, 1984

DAVID RICHARD CAMPBELL

MIRAGE   Roadhouse/Tigertail Flicks/Shonderosa, 1995

JAMES CAMPBELL

b. October 15, 1946 - Laguna Beach, California
Contact: BMI - Los Angeles, 310-659-9109

DRACULA'S WIDOW   DEG, 1988
ELVIRA, MISTRESS OF THE DARK   New World, 1988

TOM CANNING

Agent: The Artists Group - Los Angeles, 213-552-1100
Affiliation: BMI - Los Angeles, 310-659-9109

FALLING WATER   1986
THE HENRY SOLUTION   1988
THE KISS   Tri-Star, 1988, U.S.-Canadian

MICHAEL CANNON

Contact: BMI - Los Angeles, 310-659-9109

TORCHLIGHT   Film Ventures, 1984

LARRY CANSLER

Contact: ASCAP - Los Angeles, 213-883-1000

KENNY ROGERS AS THE GAMBLER (TF)   Kragen & Co., 1980
COWARD OF THE COUNTY (TF)   Kraco Productions, 1981
SEPTEMBER GUN (TF)   QM Productions, 1983
KENNY ROGERS AS THE GAMBLER - THE ADVENTURE CONTINUES (TF)   Lion Share Productions, 1983
SMOKEY & THE BANDIT - PART 3   Universal, 1983
SONGWRITER   Tri-Star, 1984
KENNY ROGERS AS THE GAMBLER III: THE LEGEND CONTINUES (TF)   Lion Share Productions, 1987

JOHN CAPEK

Contact: SOCAN - Toronto, 416-445-8700

EXCHANGE LIFEGUARDS   Beyond Films, 1993, Australian

TOM CAPEK

Contact: BMI - Los Angeles, 310-659-9109

THE LIFE AND TIMES OF ALLEN GINSBERG (FD)   Cannon, 1993

CLAUDIO CAPPANI

SPARROW   co-composer with Alessio Vlad, 1993, Italian

AL CAPPS
Contact: BMI - Los Angeles, 310-659-9109

TRIBES (TF)   20th Century-Fox TV/Marvin Schwartz Productions, 1970
TWICE IN A LIFETIME (TF)   Martin Rackin Productions, 1974
STROKER ACE   Universal, 1983
RUNNING HOT   New Line Cinema, 1984
CANNONBALL RUN II   Warner Bros., 1984

MICHAEL CARLOS
Contact: APRA - Australia, 011-61-2-922-6422

STORM BOY   South Australian Film Corp., 1976, Australian
BLUE FIN   Roadshow Distributors, 1978, Australian
LONG WEEKEND   1978, Australian

WALTER CARLOS
(See Wendy Carlos)

WENDY CARLOS
(Walter Carlos)
Contact: BMI - Los Angeles, 310-659-9109

A CLOCKWORK ORANGE   Warner Bros., 1971, British
THE SHINING   Warner Bros., 1980, British
TRON   Buena Vista, 1982

LARRY CARLTON
Contact: ASCAP - Los Angeles, 213-883-1000

AGAINST ALL ODDS   co-composer with Michel Colombier, Columbia, 1984
DEADLINE (TF)   1989

RALPH CARMICHAEL
Contact: ASCAP - Los Angeles, 213-883-1000

JONI   World Wide Pictures, 1980

DANNY CARON
JOHNS   co-composer with Charles Brown, First Look, 1997

JOHN CARPENTER
b. January 16, 1948 - Carthage, New York
Contact: ASCAP - Los Angeles, 213-883-1000

DARK STAR   Jack H. Harris Enterprises, 1974
ASSAULT ON PRECINCT 13   Turtle Releasing Corporation, 1976
HALLOWEEN   Compass International, 1978
THE FOG   Avco Embassy, 1981
ESCAPE FROM NEW YORK   co-composer with Alan Howarth, Avco Embassy, 1981
HALLOWEEN II   co-composer with Alan Howarth, Universal, 1981
HALLOWEEN III: SEASON OF THE WITCH   co-composer with Alan Howarth, Universal, 1982
CHRISTINE   co-composer with Alan Howarth, Columbia, 1983
BIG TROUBLE IN LITTLE CHINA   20th Century Fox, 1986
PRINCE OF DARKNESS   co-composer with Alan Howarth, Universal, 1987
THEY LIVE   co-composer with Alan Howarth, Universal, 1988
BODY BAGS (CTF)   co-composer with Jim Lang, 187 Corp., 1993
IN THE MOUTH OF MADNESS   co-composer with Jim Lang, New Line, 1995
VILLAGE OF THE DAMNED   co-composer with Dave Davies, Universal, 1995
ESCAPE FROM L.A.   co-composer with Shirley Walker, 1996

FIORENZO CARPI
b. 1918 - Milan, Italy
Contact: SIAE - Italy, 011-39-6-59-901

ZAZIE   *ZAZIE DANS LE METRO*   Astor, 1960, French
LEONI AL SOLE   1961, Italian
PARIGI O CARA   1962, Italian
A VERY PRIVATE AFFAIR   MGM, 1962, French-Italian
INCOMPRESO   1966, Italian

ITALIAN SECRET SERVICE   1968, Italian
INFANZIA, VOCAZIONE E PRIME ESPERIENZE DI GIACOMO CASANOVA - VENEZIANO   1969, Italian
I BAMBINI E NOI (TF)   1970, Italian
EQUINOZIO   San Diego, 1971, Italian
LA VACANZA   Lion Film, 1972, Italian
LE AVVENTURE DI PINNOCHIO   RAI/ORTF/Bavaria Film, 1972, Italian-French-West German
MIO DIO, COME SONO CADUTA IN BASSO!   Dean Film, 1974, Italian
LA CHAIR DE L'ORCHIDEE   1974, French
NON SI SCRIVE SUI MURI A MILANO   1975, Italian
VIETNAM SCENE DEL DOPOGUERRA   1975, Italian
SALON KITTY   American International, 1976, Italian

DAVID CARRADINE
b. December 8, 1936 - Hollywood, California

AMERICANA   co-composer with Craig Hundley, Crown International, 1981

NICHOLAS CARRAS
Contact: ASCAP - Los Angeles, 213-883-1000

THE DOLL SQUAD   *SEDUCE AND DESTROY*   1973
10 VIOLENT WOMEN   New American Films, 1984
OMEGA SYNDROME   co-composer with Jack Cookerly, New World, 1987

JOSEPH CARRIER
THE DEAN OF THIN AIR (TF)   co-composer with Joseph S. De Beasi, PBS, 1983

BERTHOLD CARRIERE
Contact: SOCAN - Toronto, 416-445-8700

LITTLE GLORIA...HAPPY AT LAST (TF)   Edgar J. Scherick Associates/Metromedia Producers Corporation, 1982, U.S.-Canadian-British

BAIKIDA CARROLL
DISCOVERING WOMEN (TD)   composer of segment, 1995

ROB CARROLL
MUSTARD BATH   9Y6S, 1993, Canadian

BENNY CARTER
b. August 7, 1907 - New York, New York
Contact: ASCAP - Los Angeles, 213-883-1000

THE HANGED MAN (TF)   Universal TV, 1964
A MAN CALLED ADAM   Embassy, 1966
FAME IS THE NAME OF THE GAME (TF)   Universal TV, 1966
BUCK AND THE PREACHER   Columbia, 1972
MANHUNTER (TF)   QM Productions, 1974
LOUIS ARMSTRONG - CHICAGO STYLE (TF)   Charles Fries Productions/Stonehenge Productions, 1976

BILL CARTER
DENISE CALLS UP   co-composer with Ruth Ellen Ellsworth, 1996

RON CARTER
Contact: BMI - Los Angeles, 310-659-9109

A GATHERING OF OLD MEN (TF)   Consolidated Productions/Jennie & Company/Zenith Productions, 1987
BEATRICE   *LA PASSION BEATRICE*   co-composer with Lili Boulanger, Samuel Goldwyn Co., 1987, French-Italian

TRISTRAM CARY
Contact: PRS - London, England, 011-44-1-580-5544

THE LADYKILLERS   Continental, 1956, British
TIME WITHOUT PITY   Astor, 1956, British
TOWN ON TRIAL   Columbia, 1957, British
THE BOY WHO STOLE A MILLION   Paramount, 1960, British

A LECTURE ON MAN   1962, British
A BOY TEN FEET TALL   *SAMMY GOING SOUTH*   Paramount, 1963, British
FIVE MILLION YEARS TO EARTH   *QUARTERMASS AND THE PIT*   20th Century-Fox, 1968, British
A TWIST OF SAND   United Artists, 1968, British
BLOOD FROM THE MUMMY'S TOMB   American International, 1971, British

JOHNNY CASH

b. February 26, 1932 - Kingsland, Arizona
Contact: ASCAP - Los Angeles, 213-883-1000

THE PRIDE OF JESSE HALLAM (TF)   The Konigsberg Company, 1981

JOSE LUIS CASTINEIRA DE DIOS

EVA PERON   1997, Argentine

DORY CAYNNI

Agent: Lesley Lotto - Woodland Hills, 818-884-2209
Contact: ASCAP - Los Angeles, 213-883-1000

TATI A GAROTA

MATTHIEU CHABROL

Contact: SACEM - France, 011-33-1-4715-4715

LES FANTOMES DU CHAPELIER   Gaumont, 1982, French
POULET AU VINAIGRE   MK2 Diffusion, 1985, French
INSPECTOR LAVARDIN   MK Diffusion, 1986, French
UNE AFFAIRE DE FEMMES   MK2, 1988, French
QUIET DAYS IN CLICKY   Pathe-Europa, 1990, French
BETTY   1992, French
LA CEREMONIE   1996, French

JEAN-NOEL CHALEAT

A GIFT FROM HEAVEN   Hatchwell-Lucarelli Prods., 1994

FRANKIE CHAN

CHUNKING EXPRESS   co-composer with Roel A. Garcia and Michael Calasso, 1996

CARLO JEAN PAUL CHANEZ

ALMOST HOLLYWOOD   Crown, 1994

GARY CHANG*

Agent: Cathy Schleussner - Encino, 818-905-7475
Affiliation: BMI - Los Angeles, 310-659-9109

THE BREAKFAST CLUB   additional music, Universal, 1985
3:15   Cannon, 1986
52 PICK-UP   Cannon, 1986
FIREWALKER   Cannon, 1986
STICKY FINGERS   Spectrafilm, 1988
DEAD-BANG   Warner Bros., 1989
MIAMI BLUES   Orion, 1989
SHOCK TO THE SYSTEM   Corsair, 1990
THE HOUSE OF USHER   co-composer with George S. Clinton, 21st Century, 1991
THE PERFECT WEAPON   Paramount, 1991
MURDER IN NEW HAMPSHIRE: THE PAMELA SMART STORY (TF)   New Hampshire Prods./Robert Greenwald, 1992
IN THE LINE OF DUTY: SIEGE AT MARION (TF)   Patchett Kaufman Entertainment, 1992
THE NIGHTMAN (TF)   Avnet-Kerner Prods., 1992
UNDER SIEGE   Warner Bros., 1992
SHADOW OF A STRANGER (TF)   Doris Keating Prods./NBC Prods., 1992
SNIPER   TriStar, 1993
THE LAST HIT (CTF)   Garson Studios/MTE, 1993
A FAMILY TORN APART (TF)   Red City Prods./Robert Halmi Inc., 1993
DEEP RED (CTF)   DBA Ent./MCA TV, 1994
AGAINST THE WALL (CTF)   Producers Entertainment Group, 1994
THE BURNING SEASON (CTF)   HBO Pictures, 1994

NOWHERE TO HIDE (TF)   Stan Rogow Prods./Paramount Network TV, 1994
FATHERLAND (CTF)   HBO Pictures, 1994
THE AVENGING ANGEL (CTF)   Esparza-Katz Prods./Curtis-Lowe Prods./First Corps Endeavors, 1995
THE WALKING DEAD   Savoy, 1995
ORIGINAL SINS (TF)   Sarabande Prods./Courage Prods., 1995
ANDERSONVILLE (CTF)   TNT, 1995
THE SUBSTITUTE   Live, 1996
THE ISLAND OF DOCTOR MOREAU   New Line, 1996
THE LIMBIC REGION (CTF)   MGM TV, 1996
TWISTED DESIRE (TF)   Polone-Winer, 1996
TWILIGHT MAN (TF)   MTA TV, 1996
MURDER LIVE ! (TF)   Von Zerneck-Sertner, 1997
THE COLONY   Columbia, 1997

PHILIPPE CHANY

Contact: SACEM - France, 011-33-1-4715-4715

THE CITY OF FEAR   French, 1994

JOHN CHARLES*

Contact: ASCAP - Los Angeles, 213-883-1000

UTU   1983, New Zealand
THE QUIET EARTH   Skouras Pictures, 1985, New Zealand
A SOLDIER'S TALE   Atlantic Releasing Corporation, 1988, New Zealand
THE SOUND AND THE SILENCE (CTF)   Screen Star/Atlantis/South Pacific/Kelcom, 1993
BREAD AND ROSES   1993, New Zealand

TOM CHASE*

Contact: ASCAP - Los Angeles, 213-883-1000

SCARED TO DEATH   co-composer with Ardell Hake, Lone Star Pictures, 1982
CREATURE   *TITAN FIND*   co-composer with Steve Rucker, Cardinal Releasing, 1985
FEEL THE HEAT   co-composer with Steve Rucker, Trans World Entertainment, 1987
ALIEN PREDATOR   co-composer with Steve Rucker, Trans World Entertainment, 1987
AND GOD CREATED WOMAN   co-composer with Steve Rucker, Vestron, 1988
976-EVIL   co-composer with Steve Rucker, New Line Cinema, 1988
SYNGENOR   co-composer with Steve Rucker, Syngenor Production Co., 1990
LITTLE NEMO: ADVENTURES IN SLUMBERLAND (AF)   co-composer with Steve Rucker, Hemdale, 1992, Japanese

PHILIPPE CHATILIEZ

NORD   *NORTH*   1991, French

JAY CHATTAWAY*

Agent: Zomba Screen Music - West Hollywood, 310-246-0777
Affiliation: ASCAP - Los Angeles, 213-883-1000

FIREPOWER   1979, British
MANIAC   Analysis, 1981
VIGILANTE   *STREET GANG*   Artists Releasing Corporation/Film Ventures International, 1983
THE LAST FIGHT   Marvin Films, 1983
THE BIG SCORE   Almi Distribution, 1983
HOME FREE ALL   Almi Classics, 1983
MISSING IN ACTION   Cannon, 1984
WALKING THE EDGE   Empire Pictures, 1985
THE ROSEBUD BEACH HOTEL   Almi Pictures, 1985
INVASION, U.S.A.   Cannon, 1985
STEPHEN KING'S SILVER BULLET   Paramount, 1985
HARD CHOICES   Lorimar, 1986
VERY CLOSE QUARTERS   Cable Star Ltd./Viacom, 1986
MANIAC COP   Shapiro Entertainment, 1987
BRADDOCK: MISSING IN ACTION III   Cannon, 1988
JAKARTA!   Troma, 1988, U.S.-Indonesian
RED SCORPION   Shapiro Glinkenhaus Entertainment, 1989
RELENTLESS   New Line Cinema, 1989
FAR OUT MAN   CineTel Films, 1989

BARR SINISTER   Intermedia, 1990
MANIAC COP 2   Movie House/Fadd, 1990
THE AMBULANCE   Esparza-Katz Productions, 1990
RICH GIRL   Studio Three/Film West, 1991
STAR TREK: VOYAGER: THE CARETAKER (TF)   Paramount TV, 1995
30 YEARS OF NATIONAL GEOGRAPHIC SPECIALS (TD)   National Geographic Society, 1995

VLADIMIR CHEKASSINE
Contact: RAIS - Russia, 011-7-95-203-3260

TAXI BLUES   MK2 Diffusion, 1990, Soviet-French
C'EST ARRIVE CHEZ NOUS   *MAN BITES DOG*   1992, Belgian

JOHNNY CHEN
RED ROSE WHITE ROSE   *HONG MEIGUI BAI MEGUI*   1995, Hong-Kong-Taiwanese

PAUL CHIHARA
b. July 9, 1938 - Seattle, Washington
Contact: ASCAP - Los Angeles, 213-883-1000

DEATH RACE 2000   New World, 1975
FAREWELL TO MANZANAR (TF)   Korty Films/Universal TV, 1976
SWEET REVENGE   *DANDY, THE ALL AMERICAN GIRL*   MGM/United Artists, 1976
THE KEEGANS (TF)   Universal TV, 1976
I NEVER PROMISED YOU A ROSE GARDEN   New World, 1977
THE BAD NEWS BEARS GO TO JAPAN   Paramount, 1978
NIGHT CRIES (TF)   Charles Fries Productions, 1978
DEATH MOON (TF)   Roger Gimbel Productions/EMI TV, 1978
A FIRE IN THE SKY (TF)   Bill Driskell Productions, 1978
DR. STRANGE (TF)   Universal TV, 1978
BETRAYAL (TF)   Roger Gimbel Productions/EMI TV, 1978
THE DARKER SIDE OF TERROR (TF)   Shaner-Ramrus Productions/Bob Banner Associates, 1979
MIND OVER MURDER (TF)   Paramount TV, 1979
ACT OF VIOLENCE (TF)   Emmet Lavery, Jr. Productions/Paramount TV, 1979
BRAVE NEW WORLD (TF)   Universal TV, 1980
THE CHILDREN OF AN LAC (TF)   Charles Fries Productions, 1980
THE PROMISE OF LOVE (TF)   Pierre Cossette Productions, 1980
PRINCE OF THE CITY   Orion/Warner Bros., 1981
THE LEGEND OF WALKS FAR WOMAN (TF)   Roger Gimbel Productions/EMI TV/Racquel Welch Productions/Lee Levinson Productions, 1982
THE RULES OF MARRIAGE (TF)   Entheos Unlimited Productions/Brownstone Productions/20th Century Fox TV, 1982
MISS ALL-AMERICAN BEAUTY (TF)   Marian Rees Associates, 1982
DIVORCE WARS: A LOVE STORY (TF)   Wrye-Kenigsberg Films/Warner Bros. TV, 1982
THE SURVIVORS   Columbia, 1983
JANE DOE (TF)   ITC, 1983
THE HAUNTING PASSION (TF)   BSR Productions/ITC, 1983
MANIMAL (TF)   Glen A. Larson Productions/20th Century-Fox TV, 1983
COVER UP (TF)   Glen A. Larson Productions/20th Century Fox TV, 1984
CRACKERS   Universal, 1984
IMPULSE   20th Century Fox, 1984
WITH INTENT TO KILL (TF)   London Productions, 1984
VICTIMS FOR VICTIMS (TF)   Daniel L. Paulson-Loehr Spivey Productions/Orion TV, 1984
MACGRUDER AND LOUD (TF)   Aaron Spelling Productions, 1985
NOON WINE (TF)   Noon Wine Company, 1985
THE BAD SEED (TF)   Hajeno Productions/Warner Bros. TV, 1985
A BUNNY'S TALE (TF)   Stan Margulies Company/ABC Circle Films, 1985
PICKING UP THE PIECES (TF)   CBS Entertainment, 1985
RIGHT TO KILL? (TV)   Wrye-Konigsberg Productions/Taper Media Enterprises/Telepictures Productions, 1985
TOUGHLOVE (TF)   Fries Entertainment, 1985
CRIME OF INNOCENCE (TF)   Ohlmeyer Communications Company, 1985
THE MORNING AFTER   20th Century Fox, 1986
A DEADLY BUSINESS (TF)   Thebaut-Frey Productions/Taft Entertainment TV, 1986
JACKALS   *AMERICAN JUSTICE*   The Movie Store, 1986

THE LAST DAYS OF FRANK AND JESSE JAMES (TF)   Joseph Cates Productions, 1986
RESTING PLACE (TF)   Marian Rees Associates, 1986
A CASE OF DEADLY FORCE (TF)   Telecom Entertainment, 1986
WHEN THE BOUGH BREAKS (TF)   Taft Entertainment TV/TDF Productions, 1986
ROANOAK (TF)   South Carolina ETV Network/First Contact Films/National Video Corporation, 1986
A WALK ON THE MOON   Skouras Productions, 1987
THE KILLING TIME   New World, 1987
THE KING OF LOVE (TF)   Sarabande Productions/MGM-UA TV, 1987
WE ARE THE CHILDREN (TF)   Paulist Pictures/Dan Fauci-Ted Danson Productions/The Furia Organization, 1987
BABY GIRL SCOTT (TF)   Poison Company Productions/The Finnegan-Pinchuk Company, 1987
DOTTIE (TF)   Dottie Films Inc., 1987
ALMOST PARTNERS (TF)   South Carolina Educational TV Network, 1987
HAUNTED BY HER PAST (TF)   Norton Wright Productions/ITC Productions, 1987
CROSSING DELANCEY   Warner Bros., 1988
CHINA BEACH (TF)   Sacret Inc. Productions/Warner Bros. TV, 1988
JAMES CLAVELL'S NOBLE HOUSE   *NOBLE HOUSE* (MS)   Noble House Productions Ltd./De Laurentiis Entertainment Group, 1988
SHOOTER (TF)   UBU Productions/Paramount TV, 1988
KING OF THE OLYPMICS (TF)   Harmony Gold/Rete Europa/SFP Productions, 1988, U.S.-Italian
KILLER INSTINCT (TF)   Millar-Bromberg Productions/ITC, 1988
BRIDESMAIDS (TF)   Motown Productions/Qintex Entertainment/Deaune Productions, 1989
DARK HOLIDAY (TF)   Peter Nelson/Lou Antonio Productions/The Finnegan-Pinchuk Co./Orion TV, 1989
PENN AND TELLER GET KILLED   Warner Bros., 1989
ROCK HUDSON (TF)   Konigsberg-Sanitsky Co., 1990
FAMILY OF SPIES (MS)   King Phoenix Entertainment, 1990
QUICKSAND: NO ESCAPE (CTF)   Finnegan-Pinchuk/MCA, 1992

BILLY CHILDS
Contact: ASCAP - Los Angeles, 213-883-1000

IN SEARCH OF OUR FATHERS (FD)   Conjure Films, 1992
MY FORGOTTEN MAN   co-composer with Anthony Marinelli, Boulevard Films, 1993

DAVID CHILTON
LOOK ME IN THE EYE   co-composer with Nicholas Russell-Pavier, Skreba-Creon, 1994, British

JACK CHIPMAN
Contact: BMI - Los Angeles, 310-659-9109

BEHIND ENEMY LINES (TF)   co-composer with Steve Lindsey, MTM Enterprises/TVS, 1985

ELLIOT CHIPRUT
Contact: ASCAP - Los Angeles, 213-883-1000

THE G.I. EXECUTIONER   *WIT'S END*   co-composer with Jason Garfield, Troma, 1985

EDMUNDK.CHOI
Agent: Marks Management - Tarzana, 818-776-8787
Contact: BMI - New York, 212-586-2000

PRAYING WITH ANGER   Crescent Moon, 1992
WIDE AWAKE   Miramax, 1997

KYUNG-SUK CHONG
HOW TO TOP MY WIFE   *MANURA CHUGIGI*   Morning Calm, 1995, Korean

CHRIS CHRISTIAN
Contact: ASCAP - Los Angeles, 213-883-1000

DAKOTA   Miramax, 1988

DAVID CHU
Contact: ASCAP - Los Angeles, 213-883-1000

LOVE YA TOMORROW   Atlas Entertainment, 1991

DANNY CHUNG
Contact: ASCAP - Los Angeles, 213-883-1000

HAK MAU   *BLACK CAT*   1992, Hong Kong

SUZANNE E. CIANI
Contact: ASCAP - Los Angeles, 213-883-1000

THE INCREDIBLE SHRINKING WOMAN   Universal, 1981
MOTHER TERESA (FD)   Petrie Productions, 1986

CINEMASCORE
RAW DEAL   DEG, 1986

STELVIO CIPRIANI
b. Italy
Contact: SIAE - Italy, 011-39-6-59-901

EL PRECIO DE UN HOMBRE   *THE STRANGER RETURNS*   1966, Italian
OPERAZIONE SAN PIETRO   Ultra Film, 1967, Italian
LUANA LA FIGLIA DELLA FORESTA VERGINE   1968, Italian
WOMAN LAUGHS LAST   1969, Italian
THE ANONYMOUS VENETIAN   1970, Italian
INTIMITA PROIBITA DI UNA GIOVANE SPOSA   1970, Italian
LA BELVA   1970, Italian
A CUORE FREDDO   1971, Italian
IL DIAVOLO A SETTE FACCIE   1971, Italian
L'IGUANA DALLA LINGUA DI FUOCO   1971, Italian
SE TI INCONTRO TI AMMAZZO   1971, Italian
LA MORTE CAMMINA CON I TACCHI ALTI   1971, Italian
TESTA T'AMMAZZO, CROCE...SEI MORTO...MI CHIAMANO ALLELUJA   1971, Italian
ESTRATTO DAGLI ARCHIVI SEGRETI DELLA POLIZIA DI UNA CAPITALE EUROPA   *FROM THE POLICE, WITH THANKS*   1972, Italian
IL WEST TI VA STRETTO AMICO...E ARRIVATO ALLEJUA   1972, Italian
ECOLOGIA DEL DELITTO   1972, Italian
LA POLIZIA RINGRAZIA   1972, Italian
L'ASSASSINO E AL TELEFONO   1972, Italian
EL MAS FABULOSO GOLF DEL FAR WEST   1972, Italian
METTI LO DIAVOLO TUO NE LO MIO INFERNO   1972, Italian
RACCONTI PROIBITI...DI NIENTE VESTITI   1972, Italian
UCCIDERE IN SILENZIO   1972, Italian
IL MIO CORPO CON RABBIA   1972, Italian
LA NOTTE DELL'ULTIMO GIORNO   1973, Italian
CONTINUAVAMO A METTERE LO DIAVOLO NE LO INFERNO   1973, Italian
LEVA LO DIAVOLO TUO DAL CONVENTO   1973, Italian
TRE PER UNA GRANDE RAPINA   1974, Italian
LA MANO SPIETATA DELLA LEGGE   1974, Italian
DUE CUORI, UNA CAPPELLA   1974, Italian
PROCESSO PER DIRETTISSIMA   1974, Italian
BLONDY   1975, Italian
MARK IL POLIZIOTTO   1975, Italian
IL MEDAGLIONE INSANGUINATO   1975, Italian
PECCATO SENZA MALIZIA   1975, Italian
FRANKENSTEIN—ITALIAN STYLE   1976, Italian
MARK COLPISCE ANCORA   1976, Italian
GLI ANGELI DALLE MANI BENDATE   1976, Italian
TENTACLES   American International, 1977, Italian
TAKE ALL OF ME   Group 1, 1978
SOLAMENTE NERO   1978, Italian
SCORTICATELI VIVI   1978, Italian
UN POLIZIOTTO SCOMODO   *CONVOY BUSTERS*   1978, Italian
PICCOLE LABBRA   1978, Italian
PROVINZIA VIOLENTA   1978, Italian
DISCRETAMENTE UNA SERA D'ESTATE   1978, Italian
IL FIUME DEL GRANDE CAIMANO   *THE GREAT ALLIGATOR*   1979, Italian
MATERNALE   Rai-Radiotelvision Italiana, 1978, Italian
LIBIDINE   1979, Italian
UN OMBRA NELL'OMBRA   1979, Italian

PENSIONE AMORE SERVIZIO COMPLETE   *DER SEXBOMBER*   1979, Italian
SBIRRO, LA TUA LEGGE E LENTA...LA MIA NO!   1979, Italian
LA VEDOVA DEL TRULLO   1979, Italian
VUDU BABY   1979, Italian-Spanish
BERSAGLIO ALTEZZA UOMO   1979, Italian
DE CRIADA A SIGNORA   1979, Italian
CONCORDE AFFAIR '79   1979, French-Italian
LA SUPPLENTE VA IN CITTA   1979, Italian
TWO IN THE STARS   1980, Italian
CITY OF THE WALKING DEAD   *NIGHTMARE CITY*   21st Century, 1980, Italian
AVVOLTOI SULLA CITTA   1980, Italian
TRES MUJERES DE NOW   1980, Spanish-Italian
POLIZIOTTO SOLITUDINE E RABBIA   1980, Italian
VERTIGO EN LA PISTA   1980, Italian-Spanish
JOURNAL D'UNE MAISON DE CORRECTION   1980, French-Italian
EL PODEROSO INFLUJO DE LA LUNA   1980, Spanish-Italian
PORNO, SITUACION LIMITE   1980, Spanish-Italian
IL GIARDINO DELL'EDEN   1980, Italian
TIMIDO Y SALVAJE   1980, Italian
UN LENTESIMO DI SECONDO   1980, Italian
L'ULTIMA VOLTA INSIEME   1981, Italian
MAFIA, UNA LEGGE CHE NON PERDONA   1981, Italian
IL FALCO E LA COLOMBA   1981, Italian
L'ULTIMO HAREM   1981, Italian
SWEET SINS   *BONA COME IL PANO*   1981, Italian
LA MAESTRA DI SCI   1981, Italian
PIERINO IL FICHISSIMO   1981, Italian
ANGKOR-CAMBODIA EXPRESS   Monarex Hollywood, 1981, Thai-Italian
LA VOCE   1982, Italian
LOS LIOS DE STEFANIA   1982, Italian
PIRANHA II - THE SPAWNING   Saturn International, 1983, Italian-U.S.
IL SOMMERGIBILE PIU PAZZO DEL MONDO   1983, Italian
UN POVERE RICCO   1983, Italian
LA CASA DEL TAPPETO GIALLO   Gaumont, 1983, Italian
UN TENERO TRAMONTO   1984, Italian
LA CLASSE   1984, Italian
RAGE   Tiber International, 1984, Italian-Spanish
RAGE OF HONOR   Trans World Entertainment, 1987

CHUCK CIRINO*
Contact: Back-O-Beyond Music - Van Nuys, 818-376-8618
Affiliation: BMI - Los Angeles, 310-659-9109

DEATHSTALKER II   New World, 1983, U.S.-Argentine
CHOPPING MALL   Concorde/Cinema Group, 1986
BIG BAD MAMA II   Concorde, 1987
TERROR SQUAD   MCEG, 1987
DEATH HOUSE   Death House Prods., 1987
NOT OF THIS EARTH   Concorde, 1988
DEADLY STRANGER   MCEG, 1988
TRANSYLVANIA TWIST   New Horizon/Concorde, 1988
BEVERLY HILLS VAMP   AIP, 1988
ALIENATOR   AIP, 1988
THE RETURN OF SWAMP THING   Lightyear Entertainment, 1989
A MAN CALLED SARGE   Cannon, 1989
THE HAUNTING FEAR   AIP, 1989
W.B. BLUE AND THE BEAN   Movie Group, 1989
MOB BOSS   AIP, 1989
SOLDIER'S FORTUNE   Republic, 1989
GYPSY ANGELS   Coconut Grove, 1990
THE CHANNELER   Magnum, 1990
THE HAUNTING OF MORELLA   co-composer with Fredrick Teetsel, 1990
TEENAGE EXORCIST   Austin Enterprises, 1990
EVILTOONS   AIP, 1990
TOWER OF TERROR   New Horizon/Concorde, 1990
NIGHTIE NIGHTMARE   New Horizon/Concorde, 1990
SORORITY HOUSE MASSACRE III   Concorde/New Horizons, 1991
LITTLE DEVILS   AIP, 1991
976-EVIL PART II   Cinetel, 1991
THE ALIEN WITHIN   AIP, 1991
MUNCHIE   New Horizon/Concorde, 1991
INNER SANCTUM   ANA Prods., 1991
HARD TO DIE   Concorde/New Horizons, 1991
ANGEL EYES   AIP, 1992

SINS OF DESIRE   Cinetel, 1992
BODY CHEMISTRY III   Concorde/New Horizons, 1993
POSSESSED BY THE NIGHT   Vision International, 1993
DINOSAUR ISLAND   Wyn-Ray Media, 1993
GHOULIES IV   Cinetel, 1993
INNER SANCTUM II   Vision International, 1993
MUNCHIE II   Concorde/New Horizons, 1993

CLANNAD

ROBIN HOOD AND THE SORCERER (CTF)   Goldcrest/HTV, 1984

ERIC CLAPTON

b. March 30, 1945 - Surrey, England
Agent: CAA - Los Angeles, 310-288-4545
Affiliation: PRS - London, England, 011-44-1-580-5544

EDGE OF DARKNESS (MS)   co-composer with Michael Kamen,
   BBC/Lionheart Television International, 1986, British
LETHAL WEAPON   co-composer with Michael Kamen and David
   Sanborn, Warner Bros., 1987
HOMEBOY   co-composer with Michael Kamen, Redbury Ltd./Elliott
   Kastner Productions, 1988
LETHAL WEAPON II   co-composer with Michael Kamen and David
   Sanborn, Warner Bros., 1989
COMMUNION   theme only, New Line Cinema, 1989
RUSH   MGM, 1991
LETHAL WEAPON 3   co-composer with Michael Kamen and David
   Sanborn, Warner Bros., 1992

STANLEY CLARKE

Agent: Film Music Associates - Hollywood, 213-463-1070
Affiliation: BMI - Los Angeles, 310-659-9109

OUT ON THE EDGE (TF)   Rick Dawn Enterprises/The Steve Tisch
   Co./King Phoenix Entertainment, 1989
THE COURT-MARTIAL OF JACKIE ROBINSON (CTF)   von
   Zerneck-Sertner/TNT, 1990
THE KID WHO LOVED CHRISTMAS (TF)   Eddie Murphy
   TV/Paramount TV, 1990
BOOK OF LOVE   New Line, 1991
THE FIVE HEARTBEATS   20th Century Fox, 1991
BOYZ N THE HOOD   Columbia, 1991
COOL AS ICE   Universal, 1991
LOVE KILLS (TF)   O.T.P.L. Prods., 1991
PASSENGER 57   Warner Bros., 1992
FINAL SHOT: THE HANK GATHERS STORY (TF)
   McGillen/Enright/Tribune, 1992
RELENTLESS: MIND OF A KILLER (TF)   Universal TV, 1993
WATCH IT   Skouras, 1993
WHAT'S LOVE GOT TO DO WITH IT   Buena Vista, 1993
POETIC JUSTICE   Columbia, 1993
ROYCE (CTF)   Gerber/ITC Prods./Showtime, 1994
LITTLE BIG LEAGUE   Columbia, 1994
HIGHER LEARNING   Columbia, 1995
PANTHER   Gramercy, 1995
THE SHOW   Rysher, 1995
WHITE MAN'S BURDEN   1995
ROAD TO GALVESTON (CTF)   Wilshire Court, 1995
EDDIE   Buena Vista, 1996
DANGEROUS GROUND   New Line, 1997
B.A.P.S.   New Line, 1997

ALF CLAUSEN*

Agent: Film Music Associates - Hollywood, 213-463-1070
Affiliation: ASCAP - Los Angeles, 213-883-1000

WEIRD SCIENCE   additional music, Universal, 1986
STRANDED (TF)   Tim Flack Productions/Columbia TV, 1986
AGATHA CHRISTIE'S 'MURDER IN THREE ACTS' (TF)   Warner
   Bros. TV, 1986
FERRIS BUELLER'S DAY OFF   additional music, Paramount,
   1986
DRAGNET   additional music, Universal, 1987
NUMBER ONE WITH A BULLET   Cannon, 1987
DOUBLE AGENT (TF)   Walt Disney TV, 1987
MY FIRST LOVE (TF)   The Avnet-Kerner Company, 1988
POLICE STORY: WATCH COMMANDER (TF)   Columbia Pictures
   TV, 1988

SHE KNOWS TOO MUCH (TF)   The Fred Silverman
   Company/Finnegan-Pinchuk Productions/MGM TV, 1989
CHRISTINE CROMWELL: IN VINO VERITAS (TF)   co-composer
   with Lee Holdridge, Wolf Film Productions/Universal TV, 1990
CHRISTINE CROMWELL: EASY COME, EASY GO (TF)   Wolf Film
   Productions/Universal TV, 1990
CHRISTINE CROMWELL: ONLY THE GOOD DIE YOUNG (TF)
   co-composer with Lee Holdridge, Wolf Film Productions/Universal
   TV, 1990
THE SIMPSONS HALLOWEEN SPECIAL (ATF) ☆   Gracie
   Films/20th Century Fox TV, 1993

PAUL CLEMENTE

CALIGULA   Analysis Film Releasing, 1979, Italian-U.S.

RICHARD CLEMENTS

YOU'LL NEVER SEE ME AGAIN (TF)   Universal TV, 1973
HOUSTON, WE'VE GOT A PROBLEM (TF)   Universal TV, 1974
THE INVISIBLE MAN (TF)   Universal TV, 1975
PEEPER   20th Century-Fox, 1975
STRANGE NEW WORLD (TF)   co-composer with Elliot Kaplan,
   Warner Bros. TV, 1975

JIMMY CLIFF

Contact: BMI - Los Angeles, 310-659-9109

THE HARDER THEY COME   New World, 1973, Jamaican
BONGO MAN   Arsenal Kino Tubingen, 1982, Jamaican

JOHN CLIFFORD

WHO KILLED THE BABY JESUS   Douglas Broghi, 1992

MATT CLIFFORD

THE RETURN OF THE LIVING DEAD   Orion, 1985

GEORGE CLINTON

COSMIC SLOP: SPACE TRADERS (CTF)   co-composer with John
   Barnes and Bernard Worrell, Hudlin Bros. Prods./HBO, 1994

GEORGE S. CLINTON

Agent: Seth Kaplan Entertainment - Los Angeles, 213-525-3477
Affiliation: ASCAP - Los Angeles, 213-883-1000

CHEECH & CHONG STILL SMOKIN'   Paramount, 1983
THE BOYS NEXT DOOR   New World, 1985
AMERICAN NINJA   Cannon, 1985
THE CORSICAN BROTHERS (TF)   Rosemont Productions, 1985,
   British-U.S.
AVENGING FORCE   Cannon, 1986
WILD THING   Atlantic Releasing Corp., 1987
TOO MUCH   Cannon, 1987
THE LION OF AFRICA (CTF)   HBO Pictures/Lois Luger
   Productions, 1987
PLATOON LEADER   Cannon, 1988
GOTHAM (CTF)   Phoenix Entertainment/Keith Addis and
   Associates Productions, 1988
AMERICAN NINJA 3: BLOOD HUNT   Cannon, 1989
THE HOUSE OF USHER   co-composer with Gary Chang, 21st
   Century, 1991
HIGHLANDER 2: THE QUICKENING   additional music, Interscope,
   1991
TILL DEATH DO US PART (TF)   Saban/Scherick, 1992
WILD ORCHID II: TWO SHADES OF BLUE   Triumph, 1992
RED SHOE DIARIES (CTF)   Saunders-King, 1992
CRUEL DOUBTS (TF)   Susan Baerwald Prods./NBC Prods., 1992
THROUGH THE EYES OF A KILLER (TF)   Pacific/Morgan
   Hill/Wilshire Court, 1992
BOUNDS OF LOVE (TF)   Hearst, 1993
LAKE CONSEQUENCE (CTF)   10dB, 1993
A KISS TO DIE FOR (TF)   Polone Co./Hearst, 1993
BETRAYED BY LOVE (TF)   Greengrass Prods./Edgar Scherick &
   Associates, 1994
MOTHER'S BOY   Miramax-Dimension, 1994
ONE OF HER OWN (TF)   Grossbart-Barnett Prods./ABC TV, 1994
AMELIA EARHART: THE FINAL FLIGHT (CTF)   Avenue Pictures,
   1994
SEDUCED BY EVIL (CTF)   CNM Entertainment/Cinestage
   Prods./Wilshire Court, 1994

FATAL VOWS: THE ALEXANDRA O'HARA STORY (TF)   Roaring Fork/Karen Danaher-Dorr Prods./Republic/Spelling Ent., 1994
BRAINSCAN   Triumph, 1994
TAD (CTF)   Chris-Rose Prods./Family Prods., 1995
MORTAL KOMBAT   New Line, 1995
DELTA OF VENUS (CTF)   New Line/Alliance/Evzen Kolar Prods., 1995
BEVERLY HILLS NINJA   TriStar, 1997
THE LAST DAYS OF FRANKIE THE FLY   Millenium Pictures, 1997
RESCUE ME   Warner Bros., 1997
AUSTIN POWERS: INTERNATIONAL MAN OF MYSTERY   New Line, 1997
BUSINESS FOR PLEASURE   Spectacor, 1997

ELIA CMIRAL*
Agent: Seth Kaplan Entertainment - Los Angeles, 213-525-3477
Affiliation: STIM - Sweden, 011-46-8-783-8800

APARTMENT ZERO   Summit Company Ltd., 1988, British-Argentine
SOMEBODY IS WAITING   1997

COATI MUNDI
Contact: ASCAP - Los Angeles, 213-883-1000

SPIKE OF BENSONHURST   FilmDallas, 1988

BOB COBERT
b. 1926
Agent: Robert Light - Los Angeles, 213-651-1777
Affiliation: BMI - Los Angeles, 310-659-9109

LADYBUG, LADYBUG   United Artists, 1963
HOUSE OF DARK SHADOWS   MGM, 1970
NIGHT OF DARK SHADOWS   MGM, 1971
FRANKENSTEIN (TF)   Dan Curtis Productions, 1973
THE PICTURE OF DORIAN GRAY (TF)   Dan Curtis Productions, 1973
THE NIGHT STRANGLER (TF)   ABC Circle Films, 1973
THE NORLISS TAPES (TF)   Metromedia Producers Corporation, 1973
SCREAM OF THE WOLF (TF)   Metromedia Producers Corporation, 1974
DRACULA (TF)   Universal TV/Dan Curtis Productions, 1974
MELVIN PURVIS: G-MAN (TF)   American International TV, 1974
THE GREAT ICE RIP-OFF (TF)   ABC Circle Films, 1974
TURN OF THE SCREW (TF)   Dan Curtis Productions, 1974
TRILOGY OF TERROR (TF)   ABC Circle Films, 1975
THE KANSAS CITY MASSACRE (TF)   ABC Circle Films, 1975
BURNT OFFERINGS   United Artists, 1976
SCALPEL   *FALSE FACE*   United International, 1976
CURSE OF THE BLACK WIDOW (TF)   Dan Curtis Productions/ABC Circle Films, 1977
THE LAST RIDE OF THE DALTON GANG (TF)   NBC Productions/Dan Curtis Productions, 1979
MRS. R'S DAUGHTER (TF)   NBC Productions/Dan Curtis Productions, 1979
THE SCARLET PIMPERNEL (TF)   London Films Ltd., 1982, British
THE LAST NINJA (TF)   Paramount TV, 1983
THE WINDS OF WAR (MS)   Paramount TV/Dan Curtis Productions, 1983
BONANZA: THE NEXT GENERATION (TF)   Gaylord Production Company/LBS Communications/Bonanza Ventures, 1988
WAR AND REMEMBRANCE (MS) ☆   Dan Curtis Productions/ABC Circle Films, 1989
DARK SHADOWS (MS)   Dan Curtis TV/MGM-UA TV, 1991
INTRUDERS (TF)   Osiris Films/Dan Curtis Prods./CBS Entertainment, 1992
ME AND THE KID   Orion, 1993

TED COCHRAN
Contact: ASCAP - Los Angeles, 213-883-1000

CAT CHASER   Vestron, 1989

JOHN CODA
Contact: BMI - Los Angeles, 310-659-9109

RED SUN RISING, 1993

DAVID ALLAN COE
Contact: BMI - Los Angeles, 310-659-9109

STAGECOACH (TF)   co-composer with Willie Nelson, Raymond Katz Productions/Heritage Entertainment, 1986

HARVEY R. COHEN*
Agent: SMC Artists - Studio City, 818-505-9600
Affiliation: BMI - Los Angeles, 310-659-9109

GHOST TOWN   Trans World Entertainment, 1988
BABE RUTH (TF)   1991
AMORE   LDC Films, 1993

JEFF COHEN
TOMBES DU CIEL   *FALLEN FROM HEAVEN/IN TRANSIT*   1993, French

STEPHEN COHN*
Agent: Paul Kohner - Los Angeles, 310-550-1060
Affiliation: ASCAP - Los Angeles, 213-883-1000

NICKEL & DIME   August Entertainment, 1992

JOHN COLBY
Contact: BMI - Los Angeles, 310-659-9109

HUEY LONG (FD)   RKB/Florentine Films, 1985

RAY COLCORD*
Agent: Vangelos Management - Encino, 818-380-1919
Affiliation: ASCAP - Los Angeles, 213-883-1000

THE DEVONSHIRE TERROR   MPM, 1983
OFF YOUR ROCKER   Hal Roach Films, 1986
JURY DUTY (TF)   Steve White Productions/Spectacor, 1990
THE SLEEPING CAR   Vidmark Entertainment, 1990
THE PAPER BRIGADE (TF)   Leucadia Films, 1995
AMITYVILLE DOLLHOUSE   Spectacor Films, 1996
DEVIL'S FOOD (TF)   Jaffe/Braunstein Films, Ltd., 1996
WISH UPON A STAR   Leucadia Films, 1997
HEARTWOOD   Cotler Bros. Films, 1997

JUDD COLE
Contact: BMI - Los Angeles, 310-659-9109

LAST LIGHT (CTF)   1993 Showtime, 1993

LIONEL COLE
ONCE UPON A TIME WHEN WE WERE COLORED   co-composer with Paul Buckmaster, 1996

CY COLEMAN
b. June 14, 1929 - New York, New York
Contact: ASCAP - Los Angeles, 213-883-1000

FATHER GOOSE   Universal, 1964
THE TROUBLEMAKER   Janus, 1964
THE ART OF LOVE   Universal, 1965
SWEET CHARITY ★   adaptation, Universal, 1969
GARBO TALKS   MGM/UA, 1984
POWER   20th Century Fox, 1986
FAMILY BUSINESS   Tri-Star, 1989

GRAEME COLEMAN
Contact: SOCAN - Toronto, 416-445-8700

CHAINDANCE   Festival Films, 1992
NORTH OF PITTSBURGH   Cinephile, 1992
DANGEROUS DESIRE   Saban, 1993
HARMONY CATS   co-composer with Bill Buckingham, Alan Morinis-Richard Davis, 1993, Canadian
KILLER   Keystone/Worldvision, 1994
BULLETPROOF HEART   Keystone, 1995

JIM COLEMAN
THE UNBELIEVABLE TRUTH   Action Features, 1989

LISA COLEMAN
(see Wendy & Lisa)

PATRICK COLEMAN
Contact: SOCAN - Toronto, 416-445-8700

BLUE MONKEY   co-composer with Paul Novotny, Spectrafilm, 1987, Canadian

MICHAEL COLINA
Contact: ASCAP - Los Angeles, 213-883-1000

FINNEGAN BEGIN AGAIN (CTF)   co-composer with David Sanborn, HBO Premiere Films/Zenith Productions/Jennie & Co. Film Productions, 1985, U.S.-British

JUDY COLLERO
TREACHEROUS BEAUTIES (TF)   Alliance/CBS/CTV/UFA, 1994

BUDDY COLLETTE
Contact: ASCAP - Los Angeles, 213-883-1000

TRAUMA   Parade, 1962
TODAY IS FOR THE CHAMPIONSHIP (FD)   Breakthrough Racing, 1980

MICHEL COLOMBIER
b. 1939 - France
Agent: Cathy Schleussner - Encino, 818-905-7475
Affiliation: ASCAP - Los Angeles, 213-883-1000

L'ARME A GAUCHE   1965, French
UN MONDE NOUVEAU   *A NEW WORLD*   1966, French-Italian
COLOSSUS: THE FORBIN PROJECT   Universal, 1970
THE OTHER MAN (TF)   Universal TV, 1970
LES ASSASSINS DE L'ORDRE   1971, French
UN FLIC   *DIRTY MONEY*   Warner Bros., 1972, French-Italian
L'HERITIER   *THE INHERITOR*   EMI, 1973, French-Italian
LE HASARD ET LA VIOLENCE   *CHANCE AND VIOLENCE*   1974, French
PAUL AND MICHELLE   Paramount, 1974, British-French
L'ALPAGUEUR   1975, French
LES 11,000 VERGES   1975, French
THE PREDATOR   1976, French
THE GUINEA PIG COUPLE   1977, French
TESTIMONY OF TWO MEN   composer of parts 1 and 3, Universal TV/Operation Prime Time, 1977
THE RHINEMANN EXCHANGE (MS)   Universal TV, 1977
11TH VICTIM (TF)   Marty Katz Productions/Paramount Pictures TV, 1979
STEEL   *LOOK DOWN AND DIE*   World Northal, 1980
UNE CHAMBRE EN VILLE   1982, French
AGAINST ALL ODDS   co-composer with Larry Carlton, Columbia, 1984
PURPLE RAIN   Warner Bros., 1984
WHITE NIGHTS   Columbia, 1985
THE MONEY PIT   Universal, 1986
RUTHLESS PEOPLE   Buena Vista, 1986
THE GOLDEN CHILD   Paramount, 1986
FLORIDA STRAITS (CTF)   HBO Premiere Films/Robert Cooper Productions, 1986
DOUBLE SWITCH (TF)   Walt Disney TV, 1987
DESPERADO (TF)   Walter Mirisch Productions/Universal TV, 1987
SURRENDER   Warner Bros., 1987
MIDNIGHT CABARET   1987
THE RETURN OF DESPERADO (TF)   Walter Mirisch Productions/Universal TV, 1988
THE COUCH TRIP   Orion, 1988
COP   Atlantic Releasing Corporation, 1988
DESPERADO: AVALANCHE AT DEVIL'S RIDGE (TF)   Walter Mirisch Productions/Universal TV, 1988
SATISFACTION   20th Century Fox, 1988
THE WIZARD OF LONELINESS   Skouras, 1988
OUT COLD   Hemdale, 1989
LOVERBOY   Tri-Star, 1989
WHO'S HARRY CRUMB?   Tri-Star, 1989
BACKTRACK   Vestron, 1990
IMPULSE   Warner Bros., 1990

BURIED ALIVE (CTF)   Niki Marvin Productions/MCA Entertainment, 1990
SUDIE & SIMPSON (CTF)   1990
FATAL EXPOSURE (CTF)   G.C. Group/Wilshire Court, 1991
TAGGET (CTF)   Mirisch/Tagget Prods., 1991
NEW JACK CITY   Warner Bros., 1991
THE DARK WIND   Seven Arts, 1991
STRICTLY BUSINESS   Warner Bros., 1991
FEVER (CTF)   Saban-Scherick, 1991
STRAYS (CTF)   Niki Marvin Productions/MTE Entertainment, 1991
DEEP COVER   New Line, 1992
DIRTY WORK (CTF)   Wilshire Court/Pacific, 1992
DIARY OF A HIT MAN   Vision International, 1992
FOLKS !   20th Century Fox, 1992
FADE TO BLACK (CTF)   Francine LeFrak/Wilshire Court, 1993
POSSE   Gramercy, 1993
DAYBREAK (CTF)   Foundation/HBO, 1993
THE PROGRAM   Buena Vista, 1993
OUT OF DARKNESS (TF)   Andrew Adelson Co./Anaid Films/ABC Prods., 1994
MAJOR LEAGUE II   Warner Bros., 1994
BARB WIRE   Gramercy, 1996
FOXFIRE   Rysher, 1996
MARY AND TIM (TF)   Hallmark Entertainment, 1996
BURIED ALIVE II (CTF)   Universal TV, 1997
MUDER IN MY MIND (TF)   CBS TV, 1997
MEET WALLY SPARKS   Trimark, 1997

FRANK COMSTOCK
Contact: ASCAP - Los Angeles, 213-883-1000

THE LAST TIME I SAW ARCHIE   United Artists, 1961
THE D.A.: MURDER ONE (TF)   Mark VII Ltd./Universal TV/Jack Webb Productions, 1969
THE D.A.: CONSPIRACY TO KILL (TF)   Mark VII Ltd./Universal TV/Jack Webb Productions, 1971
THE NIGHT THAT PANICKED AMERICA (TF)   The Culzean Corporation/Paramount Pictures TV, 1975

SERGIO CONFORTI
STEFANO QUANTESTORIE   1993, Italian

CONG SU
b. China

THE LAST EMPEROR ★★   co-composer with David Byrne and Ryuichi Sakamoto, Columbia, 1987, British-Chinese

JOSEPH CONLAN*
Agent: Carol Faith Agency - Beverly Hills - 310-274-0776
Affiliation: BMI - Los Angeles, 310-659-9109

KILL SQUAD   Summa Vista Pictures, 1982
THE CONCRETE JUNGLE   Pentagon, 1982
THE RENEGADES (TF)   co-composer with Barry De Vorzon, Lawrence Gordon Productions/Paramount Pictures TV, 1982
CHAINED HEAT   Jensen Farley Pictures, 1983
SCREAM   *THE OUTING*   Cal-Com Releasing, 1983
V: THE FINAL BATTLE (TF)   co-composer of part one with Barry De Vorzon, Blatt-Singer Productions/Warner Bros. TV, 1984
KOJAK: THE BELARUS FILE (TF)   co-composer with Barry DeVorzon, Universal TV, 1985
STICK   co-composer with Barry DeVorzon, Universal, 1985
THE HIGH PRICE OF PASSION (TF)   Edgar J. Scherick Associates/Taft Entertainment, 1986
HOT PURSUIT   Indie, 1987
THE STEPFORD CHILDREN (TF)   Edgar Scherick, 1987
THE WRONG GUYS   New World, 1988
NICK KNIGHT (TF)   Barry Weitz Films/Robirdle Pictures/New World TV, 1989
MEMORIES OF MURDER (CTF)   Lifetime Television/Houston Lady Co./Viacom, 1990
THE BRIDE IN BLACK (TF)   New World TV, 1990
BLACKMAIL (CTF)   Pacific/Barry Weitz Films/Wilshire Court Prods., 1991
MORTAL SINS (CTF) ☆   Blake Edwards TV/Barry Weitz Films, 1992
MARYLIN & BOBBY: HER FINAL AFFAIR (CTF)   Barry Weitz Films/Auerbach Co./Reitalia Prods., 1993

RETURN TO TWO MOON JUNCTION   Trimark, 1993
MENENDEZ: A KILLING IN BEVERLY HILLS (TF)   Frederick S.
   Pierce Co., 1994
DON'T TALK TO STRANGERS (CTF)   Pacific Motion Pictures/Barry
   Weitz Films/MTE, 1994
SIMON & SIMON: IN TROUBLE AGAIN (TF)   Windy City
   Prods./MTE, 1995
GRAMPS (TF)   Fred Silverman Co./Viacom, 1995
DEADLY WHISPERS (TF)   Hill-Fields/ACI, 1995
CIRCUMSTANCES UNKNOWN (CTF)   Shooting Star/Wilshire
   Court, 1995

BILL CONNOR

Contact: BMI - Los Angeles, 310-659-9109

THE VISION (TF)   BBC-TV, 1988, British

RICK CONRAD

Contact: BMI - Los Angeles, 310-659-9109

THE DRIFTER   Concorde, 1988
CRIME ZONE   Concorde, 1989
THE TERROR WITHIN   Concorde, 1989
AMITYVILLE: THE EVIL ESCAPES (TF)   Steve White
   Productions/Spectacor, 1989
WATCHERS II   Concorde, 1990
THE HIT LIST (CTF)   Westwind Prods., 1993

PAOLO CONTE

Contact: SIAE - Italy, 011-39-6-59-901

SOTTO...SOTTO   Triumph/Columbia, 1984, Italian

BILL CONTI*

b. April 13, 1942 - Providence, Rhode Island
Agent: Vangelos Management - Encino, 818-380-1919
Affiliation: ASCAP - Los Angeles, 213-883-1000

JULIETTE DE SADE   *MADEMOISELLE DE SADE E I SUOVI VIZI*
   1967, Italian
CANDIDATE PER UN ASSASSINO   1969, Italian-Spanish
LIQUID SUBWAY   1972, Italian
BLUME IN LOVE   Warner Bros., 1973
HARRY AND TONTO   20th Century Fox, 1974
PACIFIC CHALLENGE (FD)   Concord Films, 1975
NEXT STOP, GREENWICH VILLAGE   20th Century Fox, 1976
ROCKY   United Artists, 1976
SMASH-UP ON INTERSTATE 5 (TF)   Filmways, 1976
CITIZENS BAND   *HANDLE WITH CARE*   Paramount, 1977
IN THE MATTER OF KAREN ANN QUINLAN (TF)   Warren V. Bush
   Productions, 1977
A SENSITIVE, PASSIONATE MAN (TF)   Factor-Newland
   Production Corporation, 1977
KILL ME IF YOU CAN (TF)   Columbia TV, 1977
AN UNMARRIED WOMAN   20th Century Fox, 1978
SLOW DANCING IN THE BIG CITY   United Artists, 1978
F.I.S.T.   United Artists, 1978
FIVE DAYS FROM HOME   Universal, 1978
THE BIG FIX   Universal, 1978
PARADISE ALLEY   Universal, 1978
HAROLD ROBBINS' THE PIRATE (TF)   Howard W. Koch
   Productions/Warner Bros. TV, 1978
RING OF PASSION (TF)   20th Century Fox, 1978
UNCLE JOE SHANNON   United Artists, 1979
ROCKY II   United Artists, 1979
DREAMER   20th Century Fox, 1979
A MAN, A WOMAN, AND A BANK   Avco Embassy, 1979,
   Canadian
STUNT SEVEN (TF)   Martin Poll Productions, 1979
GOLDENGIRL   Avco Embassy, 1979
THE SEDUCTION OF JOE TYNAN   Universal, 1979
THE FORMULA   MGM/United Artists, 1980
GLORIA   Columbia, 1980
PRIVATE BENJAMIN   Warner Bros., 1980
CARBON COPY   Avco Embassy, 1981
VICTORY   Paramount, 1981
FOR YOUR EYES ONLY   United Artists, 1981, British
I, THE JURY   20th Century Fox, 1982
ROCKY III   MGM/UA, 1982

NEIGHBORS   Columbia, 1982
SPLIT IMAGE   Orion, 1982
FARRELL FOR THE PEOPLE (TF)   InterMedia Entertainment/TAL
   Productions/MGM-UA TV, 1982
THAT CHAMPIONSHIP SEASON   Cannon, 1982
BAD BOYS   Universal/AFD, 1983
THE RIGHT STUFF ★★   The Ladd Company/Warner Bros., 1983
THE TERRY FOX STORY (CTF)   HBO Premiere Films/Robert
   Cooper Films II, 1983, Canadian
UNFAITHFULLY YOURS   20th Century Fox, 1984
MASS APPEAL   Universal, 1984
THE KARATE KID   Columbia, 1984
THE BEAR   Embassy, 1984
THE COOLANGATTA GOLD   Film Gallery, 1984, Australian
NOMADS   Atlantic Releasing Corporation, 1985
GOTCHA!   Universal, 1985
BEER   Orion, 1985
NORTH AND SOUTH (MS) ☆   Wolper Productions/Warner Bros.
   TV, 1985
BIG TROUBLE   Columbia, 1986
F/X   Orion, 1986
THE KARATE KID II   Columbia, 1986
NORTH AND SOUTH, BOOK II (MS)   Wolper Productions/Robert A.
   Papazian Productions/Warner Bros. TV, 1986
HAPPY NEW YEAR   Columbia, 1987
THE BOSS'S WIFE   Tri-Star, 1987
MASTERS OF THE UNIVERSE   Cannon, 1987
BABY BOOM   MGM/UA, 1987
A PRAYER FOR THE DYING   Samuel Goldwyn Company, 1987,
   British
NAPOLEON & JOSEPHINE: A LOVE STORY (MS)   David L.
   Wolper Productions/Warner Bros. TV, 1987
BROADCAST NEWS   20th Century Fox, 1987
I LOVE N.Y.   Manhattan Films, 1988
FOR KEEPS   Tri-Star, 1988
A NIGHT IN THE LIFE OF JIMMY REARDON   composer of U.S.
   version, Island Pictures/20th Century Fox, 1988
BETRAYED   MGM/UA, 1988
COHEN & TATE   Hemdale, 1988
THE BIG BLUE   composer of U.S. version, Columbia/WEG, 1988,
   French
LEAN ON ME   Warner Bros., 1989
MURDERERS AMONG US: THE SIMON WISENTHAL STORY
   (CTF)   HBO Pictures/Robert Cooper Productions/TVS Films,
   1989, U.S.-Canadian-British
KARATE KID III   Columbia, 1989
LOCK UP   Tri-Star, 1989
BIONIC SHOWDOWN (TF)   Universal, 1989
THE FOURTH WAR   Cannon, 1990
BACKSTREET DREAMS   *BACKSTREET STRAYS*   Vidmark, 1990
ROCKY V   MGM/UA, 1990
A CAPTIVE IN THE LAND   Gloria, 1991, U.S.-U.S.S.R.
UNDER COVER (TF)   Sacret/Paint Rock/Warner TV, 1991
NECESSARY ROUGHNESS   Paramount, 1991
YEAR OF THE GUN   Triumph, 1991
BY THE SWORD   Movie Group, 1991
DYNASTY: THE REUNION (TF)   theme only, Richard and Esther
   Shapiro Prods./Aaron Spelling Prods., 1991
NAILS (CTF)   Viacom, 1992
BLOOD IN BLOOD OUT   Buena Vista, 1993
THE ADVENTURES OF HUCK FINN   Buena Vista, 1993
ROOKIE OF THE YEAR   20th Century Fox, 1993
8 SECONDS   New Line, 1994
THE NEXT KARATE KID   Columbia, 1994
THE SCOUT   20th Century Fox, 1994
BUSHWACKED   1995
ENTERTAINING ANGELS   co-composer with Ashley Irwin, 1996
SPY HARD   Buena Vista, 1996

MICHAEL CONVERTINO

Agent: CAA - Beverly Hills, 310-288-4545
Affiliation: BMI - Los Angeles, 310-659-9109

HOLLYWOOD VICE   co-composer with Keith Levine,
   Concorde/Cinema Group, 1986
CHILDREN OF A LESSER GOD ★   Paramount, 1986
THE HIDDEN   New Line Cinema, 1987
MISTRESS (TF)   Jaffe/Lansing Productions/Republic, 1987
BULL DURHAM   Orion, 1988
QUEEN OF HEARTS   Cinecom, 1989, British

SHATTERED DREAMS (TF)   Roger Gimbel Productions/Carolco
    TV, 1990
THE END OF INNOCENCE   Skouras, 1991
THE DOCTOR   Buena Vista, 1991
THE WATERDANCE   Samuel Goldwyn, 1992
ASPEN EXTREME   Buena Vista, 1993
BODIES, REST, AND MOTION   Fine Line, 1993
A HOME OF OUR OWN   Gramercy, 1993
WRESTLING ERNEST HEMINGWAY   Warner Bros., 1993
GUARDING TESS   TriStar, 1994
THE SANTA CLAUSE   Buena Vista, 1994
MILK MONEY   Paramount, 1994
THINGS TO DO IN DENVER WHEN YOU'RE DEAD   Miramax,
    1995
BED OF ROSES   New Line, 1996
MOTHER NIGHT   Fine Line, 1996
JUNGLE2JUNGLE   Buena Vista, 1997

RY COODER
Contact: BMI - Los Angeles, 310-659-9109

THE LONG RIDERS   United Artists, 1980
SOUTHERN COMFORT   20th Century Fox, 1981
THE BORDER   Universal, 1983
PARIS, TEXAS   TLC Films/20th Century Fox, 1984, West
    German-French
STREETS OF FIRE   Universal, 1984
ALAMO BAY   Tri-Star, 1985
BREWSTER'S MILLIONS   Universal, 1985
BLUE CITY   Paramount, 1986
CROSSROADS   Columbia, 1986
TALES FROM THE CRYPT (CTF)   co-composer, Tales from the
    Crypt Holdings, 1989
JOHNNY HANDSOME   Tri-Star, 1989
TRESPASS   Universal, 1992
GERONIMO: AN AMERICAN LEGEND   Columbia, 1993
LAST MAN STANDING   New Line, 1996

ERIC COOK
Contact: APRA - Australia, 011-61-2-922-6422

BREAKER MORANT   New World/Quartet, 1980, Australian

JACK COOKERLY
Contact: BMI - Los Angeles, 310-659-9109

OMEGA SYNDROME   co-composer with Nicholas Carras, New
    World, 1987

COLE COONCE
THE LIVING END   Strand/Desperate Pictures, 1992

RAY COOPER
Contact: PRS - London, England, 011-44-1-580-5544

SCRUBBERS   co-composer with Michael Hurd, Orion Classics,
    1983, British
SHOOT FOR THE SUN (TF)   co-composer with Michael Kamen,
    BBC-TV, 1986, British

STEWART COPELAND*
Agent: The Kraft-Benjamin Agency - Beverly Hills, 310-247-0123
Manager: Derek Power Company - Los Angeles, 310-472-4647
Affiliation: BMI - Los Angeles, 310-659-9109

RUMBLE FISH   Universal, 1983
OUT OF BOUNDS   Columbia, 1986
WALL STREET   20th Century Fox, 1987
TALK RADIO   Universal, 1988
SHE'S HAVING A BABY   Paramount, 1988
SEE NO EVIL, HEAR NO EVIL   Tri-Star, 1989
HIDDEN AGENDA   Hemdale, 1990, British
THE FIRST POWER   Orion, 1990
TAKING CARE OF BUSINESS   1990
MEN AT WORK   Triumph, 1990
RIFF RAFF   1991
HIGHLANDER 2: THE QUICKENING   Interscope, 1991

FUGITIVE AMONG US (TF)   Andrew Adelson Co./ABC Prods.,
    1992
AFTERBURN (CTF)   Steve Tisch Co., 1992
BABYLON 5 (TF)   Rattlesnake Prods./Synthetic World/Warner
    Bros., 1993
WIDE SARGASSO SEA   Fine Line, 1993, Australian
AIRBORNE   Warner Bros., 1993
RAINING STONES   1993, U.K.
BANK ROBBER   IRS, 1993
FRESH   Miramax, 1994, U.S.-French
DECADENCE   1994, British-German
RAPA NUI   Warner Bros., 1994
SURVIVING THE GAME   New Line, 1994
SILENT FALL   Warner Bros., 1994
TYSON (CTF)   co-composer with Judd Miller and Michael
    Thompson, HBO Pictures, 1995
WHITE DWARF (TF)   RHI Ent./Elemental Films/American Zoetrope,
    1995
COSI   1995
BOYS   Buena Vista, 1996
THE LEOPARD SON   1996
THE PALLBEARER   Miramax, 1996
GRIDLOCK'D   Gramercy, 1997
LITTLE BOY BLUE   1997
FOUR DAYS IN SEPTEMBER   1997
BIG RED   1997

NORMAND CORBEIL
PRINCES IN EXILE (TF)   Cinepix/Canada National Film
    Board/CBC, 1991
KIDS OF THE ROUND TABLE   Malofilm, 1995, Canadian
SCREAMERS   Triumph, 1996

CARLO MARIO CORDIO
Contact: SIAE - Italy, 011-39-6-59-901

SONNY BOY   Triumph, 1990

MARIA CORDIO
ATOR   Comworld Pictures, 1983

JOHN CORIGLIANO
b. February 16, 1938
Agent: Gorfaine-Schwartz - Los Angeles, 213-969-1011
Affiliation: ASCAP - Los Angeles, 213-883-1000

ALTERED STATES   Warner Bros., 1980
REVOLUTION   Warner Bros., 1985

BILL COSBY
Contact: BMI - Los Angeles, 310-659-9109

THE COSBY MYSTERIES (TF)   co-composer with Craig Handy and
    Charles Mingus, SAH Ent./Columbia Pictures TV/NBC Prods.,
    1994

VLADIMIR COSMA
b. 1940 - Bucharest, Romania
Contact: ASCAP - Los Angeles, 213-883-1000

VERY HAPPY ALEXANDER   ALEXANDER   Cinema 5, 1968,
    French
LES PRISONNIERS DE LA LIBERTE   1968, French
ILS ALLAIENT DANS LES CHAMPS   1968, French
MALDONNE   1968, French
CLEREMBARD   1969, French
LE DISTRAIT   THE DAYDREAMER   1970, French
CAFEN DE NULLE PART   1970, French
TERESA   1970, French
CHALEURS   1971, French
LES MALHEURS D'ALFRED   1971, French
LES ZOZOS   1972, French
THE TALL BLOND MAN WITH ONE BLACK SHOE   Cinema 5,
    1972, French
LA RAISON DU PLUS FOU   1972, French
LE DINGUE   1972, French
NEITHER BY DAY NOR BY NIGHT   1972, Israeli

LES EXPERIENCES EROTIQUES DE FRANKENSTEIN   1972,
  French
LA VIEREE SUPERBE   1973, French
LA DERNIERE BOURREE A PARIS   1973, French
PLEURE PAS LA BOUCHE PLEINE   *DON'T CRY WITH YOUR
  MOUTH FULL*   1973, French
LES GRANDS SENTIMENTS FONT LES BONS GUEULETONS
  BIG SENTIMENTS MAKE FOR GOOD SPORTS   1973, French
SALUT L'ARTISTE   Exxel, 1973, French
L'AFFAIRE CRAZY CAPO   1973, French
LA GUEULE DE L'EMPLOI   1973, French
THE MAD ADVENTURES OF 'RABBI' JACOB   20th Century-Fox,
  1974, French-Italian
LUCKY PIERRE   *LA MOUTARDE ME MONTE AU NEZ*   1974,
  French
LE JOURNAL INTIME D'UNE NYMPHOMANE   co-composer,
  1974, French
LA RIVALE   *MY HUSBAND, HIS MISTRESS AND I*   1974, French
RETURN OF THE TALL BLONDE MAN WITH ONE BLACK SHOE
  Lanir Releasing, 1974, French
DUPONT-LAJOIE   *RAPE OF INNOCENCE*   1974, French
LE CHAUD LAPIN   1974, French
HUGHES LE LOUP (TF)   1974, French
CATHERINE ET CIE   1975, French
THE PINK TELEPHONE   *LE TELEPHONE ROSE*   SJ International,
  1975, French
LA COURSE A L'ECHALOTE   *WILD GOOSE CHASE*   1975,
  French
LA SURPRISE DU CHEF   1975, French
LES OEUFS BROUILLES   1975, French
DRACULA AND SON   1976, French
PARDON MON AFFAIRE   *AN ELEPHANT CA TROMPE
  ENORMEMENT*   First Artists, 1976, French
L'AILE OU LA CUISSE   1976, French
THE TOY   *LE JOUET*   Show Biz Company, 1976, French
A CHACUN SON ENFER   1976, French
L'ENFER DES AUTRES   1976, French
LES FELINES   Key Films, 1976, French
PARDON MON AFFAIRE, TOO!   *NOUS IRONS TOUS AU
  PARADIS*   First Artists, 1977, French
L'ANIMAL   *THE ANIMAL*   1977, French
LA ZIZANIE   1978, French
LA RAISON D'ETAT   *STATE REASONS*   1978, French
ANNE (TF)   1978, French
JE SUIS TIMIDE...MAIS JE ME SOIGNE   1978, French
CONFIDENCES POUR CONFIDENCES   1978, French
LE CONNETABLE DE BOURBON (TF)   1978, French
ILS SONT GRANDS CES PETITS!   1978, French
LA SERVANTE (TF)   1978, French
HISTOIRE DE VOYOUS: LES MARLOUPINS (TF)   1978, French
LE BAISER AU LEPREUX (TF)   1978, French
CAUSE TOUJOURS, TU M'INTERESSES   1978, French
COURAGE FUYONS   *COURAGE - LET'S RUN!*   Gaumont, 1979,
  French
LA DEROBADE   *THE GETAWAY*   1979, French
C'EST PAS MOI, C'EST LUI!   1979, French
MEDECINS DE NUIT: HENRI GILLOT, RETRAITE (TF)   1979,
  French
MEDECINS DE NUIT: LEGITIME DEFENSE (TF)   1979, French
LA BELLE VIE (TF)   1979, French
LES MAITRES SONNEURS (TF)   1979, French
HISTOIRES INSOLITES: LA STRATEGIE DU SERPENT (TF)   1979,
  French
LE BAR DU TELEPHONE   1980, French
LA FEMME-ENFANT   1980, French
LE COUP DU PARAPLUIE   1980, French
LAAT DE DOCKTER MAAR SCHUIVEN!   1980, Dutch
INSPECTEUR LA BAVURE   1980, French
LA BOUM   1980, French
CELLES QU'ON N'A PAS EUES   1980, French
MEDECINS DE NUIT: L'USINE CA STEL (TF)   1980, French
MEDECINS DE NUIT: LA DECAPOTABLE (TF)   1980, French
PURQUOI PAS NOUS?   1980, French
STUMME LIEBE   *MUTE LOVE*   1980, French-West German
MEDECINS DE NUIT: UN PLAT CUISINE (TF)   1980, French
MEDECINS DE NUIT: AMALGINE (TF)   1980, French
MEDECINS DE NUIT: LA PENSION MICHEL (TF)   1980, French
MEDECINS DE NUIT: L'ENTREPOT (TF)   1980, French
L'ANNEE PROCHAINE, SI TOUT VA BIEN   1981, French
LA DOUBLE VIE DE THEOPHRASTE LONGUET (TF)   1981,
  French
UNE AFFAIRE D'HOMMES   1981, French

DIVA   United Artists Classics, 1982, French
LA CHEVRE   1982, French
L'AS DES AS   *ACE OF ACES*   Gaumont/Cerito Rene Chateau,
  1982, French-West German
LA BOUM II   Gaumont, 1983, French
LE BAL   Almi Classics, 1983, French-Italian-Algerian
LES COMPRES   AAA, 1983, French
L'ETINCELLE   1983, French
LE PRIX DU DANGER   UGC, 1983, French
TOUT LE MONDE PEUT SE TROMPER   S.N. Prodis, 1983,
  French
BANZAI   AMLF, 1983, French
RETENEZ MOIL...OU JE FAIS UN MALHEUR   *TO CATCH A COP*
  Gaumont, 1984, French
P'TIT CON   *LITTLE JERK*   Gaumont, 1984, French
MISTRAL'S DAUGHTER (MS)   Steve Krantz Productions/R.T.L.
  Productions/Antenne-2, 1984, U.S.-French
JUST THE WAY YOU ARE   MGM/UA, 1984
LE JUMEAU   *THE TWIN*   AAA, 1984, French
ASTERIX VS. CAESAR (AF)   Gaumont, 1985, French
LES FUGITIFS   Gaumont, 1986, French
THE NIGHTMARE YEARS (CMS)   Consolidated Productions, 1989
JUDITH KRANTZ'S TILL WE MEET AGAIN (MS)   Steve Krantz
  Productions/Yorkshire TV, 1989
LA GLOIRE DE MON PERE   *MY FATHER'S GLORY*   1991,
  French
LE CHATEAU DE MA MERE   *MY MOTHER'S CASTLE*   1991,
  French
THE FAVOUR, THE WATCH, AND THE VERY BIG FISH   1991,
  French/British
LA TOTALE!   *THE JACKPOT!*   1992, French
LE BAL DES CASSE-PIEDS   co-composer with Marie-Claude
  Herry, 1992, French
LA SOIF DE L'OR   *THE THIRST FOR GOLD*   1993, France

DON COSTA
Contact: ASCAP - Los Angeles, 213-883-1000

ROUGH NIGHT IN JERICHO   Universal, 1967
THE IMPOSSIBLE YEARS   MGM, 1968
MADIGAN   Universal, 1968
THE SOUL OF NIGGER CHARLEY   Paramount, 1973
LOOSE CHANGE (MS)   Universal TV, 1978
THE GREAT BRAIN   Osmond Distribution Company, 1978

BRUNO COULAIS
LES EQUILIBRISTES   1992, French
LE FILS DU REQUIN   *THE SON OF THE SHARK*   1993,
  French-Belgian-Luxemburger
SIMEON   1993, Martinique-French
VIEILLE CANAILLE   1993, French
WAATI   co-composer with Dave Pollecutt, 1995,
  Malian-French-Burkina Fasso
MICROCOSMOS (FD)   1996

CAMERON COULTER
LOVE AND HAPPINESS   Terminal Bliss Pictures, 1995

PHIL COULTER
Contact: PRS - London, England, 011-44-1-580-5544

THE WATER BABIES   Pethurst International/Film Polski, 1978,
  British-Polish

ALEXANDER COURAGE
Contact: BMI - Los Angeles, 310-659-9109

HOT ROD RUMBLE   Allied Artists, 1957
SIERRA STRANGER   Allied Artists, 1957
UNDERSEA GIRL   Allied Artists, 1957
HANDLE WITH CARE   MGM, 1958
THE LEFT-HANDED GUN   Warner Bros., 1958
DAY OF THE OUTLAW   United Artists, 1959
TOKYO AFTER DARK   Paramount, 1959
MOTHER'S DAY ON WALTONS MOUNTAIN (TF)   Amanda
  Productions/Lorimar, 1982
A WEDDING ON WALTONS MOUNTAIN (TF)   Amanda
  Productions/Lorimar Productions, 1982

A DAY FOR THANKS ON WALTONS MOUNTAIN (TF)   Amanda Productions/Lorimar Productions, 1982
SUPERMAN IV: THE QUEST FOR PEACE   adaptation, Warner Bros., 1987
A WALTON THANKSGIVING REUNION (TF)   Lee Rich Co./Amanda Prods./Warner Bros TV, 1993

JEAN COUSINEAU
Contact: SOCAN - Toronto, 416-445-8700

LES BEAUX SOUVENIRS   *FOND MEMORIES*   National Film Board of Canada, 1982, Canadian

THE COWBOY JUNKIES
DESERT WINDS   co-composer with the Bo Deans, Desert Wind Prods., 1995

ANDY COX
Contact: PRS - London, England, 011-44-1-580-5544

TIN MEN   co-composer with David Steele, Buena Vista, 1987

RICHARD COX
Contact: BMI - Los Angeles, 310-659-9109

SLUMBER PARTY MASSACRE II   Concorde/New Horizons, 1987
THE AMERICAN SCREAM   Genesis Home Video, 1988
BACK TO BACK   Motion Picture Corporation of America, 1989
INSIDE MONKEY ZETTERLAND   co-composer with Jeff Elmassian, Coast Entertainment, 1992
CORRINA, CORRINA   based on themes by Thomas Newman, New Line, 1994

LEO CRANDALL
GREEN ON THURSDAYS (FD)   co-composer with Michael Bondert, Red Branch, 1993

LOUIS CRELIER
ASHAKARA   co-composer with Sally Nyoto, 1993 Togolese

BOB CREWE
Contact: BMI - Los Angeles, 310-659-9109

BARBARELLA   co-composer with Charles Fox, Paramount, 1968, Italian-French

CARLO CRIVELLI
Contact: SIAE - Italy, 011-39-6-59-901

DEVIL IN THE FLESH   Istuto Luce/Italnoleggio, 1986, Italian-French
LA RIBELLE   *THE REBEL*   1993, Italian

JIM CROSBY
Contact: BMI - Los Angeles, 310-659-9109

BOY MEETS GIRL   co-composer with Geoff Southall, Kino Eye, 1994, British

ANDRAE CROUCH
Contact: ASCAP - Los Angeles, 213-883-1000

THE COLOR PURPLE ★   co-composer, Warner Bros., 1985

PATRICIA CULLEN
Contact: SOCAN - Toronto, 416-445-8700

AFTER THE AXE (FD)   Canadian
ROME-O AND JULIE 8 IN OUTER SPACE (ATF)   Canadian
ROCK & RULE (AF)   MGM/UA, 1983, Canadian
UPS AND DOWNS   co-composer, JAD International, 1983, Canadian
UNFINISHED BUSINESS   Zebra Films/National Film Board of Canada/CBC, 1984, Canadian
THE CARE BEARS MOVIE (AF)   Samuel Goldwyn Company, 1985, Canadian

CARE BEARS MOVIE II: A NEW GENERATION (AF)   Columbia, 1986, Canadian

DAVID CUNNINGHAM
Contact: ASCAP - Los Angeles, 213-883-1000

END OF THE LINE   *TERMINUS*   Hemdale, 1987, French-West German
NAKED MAKING LUNCH (FD)   Lucinda/LWT, 1992

BILL CUOMO
Contact: BMI - Los Angeles, 310-659-9109

THAT WAS THEN...THIS IS NOW   co-composer with Keith Olsen, Paramount, 1985

DOUGLAS J. CUOMO
Agent: Gorfaine-Schwartz - Los Angeles, 213-969-1011

HAND GUN   Workin' Man, 1993

MIKE CURB
b. December 24, 1944 - Savannah, Georgia
Contact: BMI - Los Angeles, 310-659-9109

THE WILD ANGELS   American International, 1966
THE GLORY STOMPERS   American International, 1967
DEVIL'S ANGELS   American International, 1967
BORN LOSERS   American International, 1967
THE BIG BOUNCE   Warner Bros., 1969
BLACK WATER GOLD (TF)   co-composer with Jerry Steiner, Metromedia Producers Corporation/CTV, 1970

LEE CURRERI
Agent: Gorfaine-Schwartz - Los Angeles, 213-969-1011
Affiliation: ASCAP - Los Angeles, 213-883-1000

BILL: ON HIS OWN (TF)   Alan Landsburg Productions, 1983

HOYT CURTIN
b. Los Angeles, California
Contact: Anihanbar Publishing - Los Angeles, 213-851-5000
Affiliation: BMI - Los Angeles, 310-659-9109

THE MESA OF LOST WOMEN   1952
SHOOTOUT IN A ONE-DOG TOWN (TF)   Hanna-Barbera Productions, 1974
KISS MEETS THE PHANTOM OF THE PARK (TF)   Hanna-Barbera Productions/KISS Productions, 1978
C.H.O.M.P.S.   American International, 1979
HEIDI'S SONG (AF)   Paramount, 1982
GOBOTS: BATTLE OF THE ROCK LORDS (AF)   Clubhouse/Atlantic Releasing Corporation, 1986
I YABBA-DABBA DO! (TF)   co-composer with John Debney, William Hanna and Joseph Barbera, H-B Prods., 1993
JONNY'S GOLDEN QUEST (ATF)   co-composer of theme only with William Hanna and Joseph Barbera, Hanna-Barbera/USA/Fil-Cartoons, 1993

MIRIAM CUTLER*
Contact: Miriam Cutler Productions - Los Angeles, 213-664-1807
Affiliation: BMI - Los Angeles, 310-659-9109

GETTING LUCKY   Vista Street Entertainment, 1990
TIME BARBARIANS   Vista Street Entertainment, 1990
WITCHCRAFT PART II: THE TEMPTRESS   Vista Street Entertainment, 1990
BODY PARTS   Vista Street Entertainment, 1991
UNDER CRYSTAL LAKE   American Entertainment Circle, 1991
WITCHCRAFT III: KISS OF DEATH   Vista Street Entertainment, 1991
CAUSE OF DEATH   Vista Street Entertainment, 1991
ALIEN INTRUDER   PM Entertainment, 1992
PUSHED TO THE LIMIT   Stepping Out Productions, 1992
WITCHCRAFT IV: THE VIRGIN HEART   Vista Street Entertainment, 1992
EYES OF THE SERPENT   Vista Street Entertainment, 1992

WITCHCRAFT V: DANCE WITH THE DEVIL   Vista Street
   Entertainment, 1993
BEYOND FEAR   Stepping Out Productions, 1993
MARRIED PEOPLE, SINGLE SEX   Miklen Entertainment, 1993
WITCHCRAFT VI: THE DEVIL'S MISTRESS   Vista Street
   Entertainment, 1994
FLEXING WITH MONTY   Quarter Moon Films, 1994
STREET OF RAGE   Stepping Out Productions, 1994
NIGHTFIRE   Miklen Entertainment, 1994
GIRL CRAZY   Charlie Horse Prods., 1994
REVENGE OF THE CALENDAR GIRLS   HMS Partnership, 1995
SALEM'S GHOST   Vista Street Entertainment, 1995
WITCHCRAFT VII: JUDGEMENT HOUR, Vista Street
   Entertainment, 1995

D

LUCIO DALLA
b. Italy
Contact: SIAE - Italy, 011-39-6-59-901

MARIO PUZO'S THE FORTUNE PILGRIM (MS)   co-composer with
   Mauro Malavasi, Carlo & Alex Ponti Productions/Reteitalia S.P.A.,
   1988, Italian

ZHANG DALONG
WU KUI   *THE WOODEN MAN'S BRIDE*   1994, Taiwanese

QUENTIN DAMAMME
THE KING OF PARIS   *LE ROI DE PARIS*   1995, French-British

TERRY DAME
THE INCREDIBLY TRUE ADVENTURE OF TWO GIRLS IN LOVE
   Fine Line, 1995

JOHN D'ANDREA*
Agent: Gorfaine-Schwartz - Los Angeles, 213-969-1011
Affiliation: ASCAP - Los Angeles, 213-883-1000

LOVE'S DARK RIDE (TF)   co-composer with Michael Lloyd, Mark
   VII/Worldvision Enterprises, 1978
STRANGER IN OUR HOUSE (TF)   co-composer with Michael
   Lloyd, InterPlanetary Pictures Productions/Finnegan Associates,
   1978
GRAMBLING'S WHITE TIGER (TF)   co-composer with Michael
   Lloyd, Inter Planetary Productions/Jenner/Wallach Productions,
   1981
SAVAGE STREETS   co-composer with Michael Lloyd, MPM, 1984
BODY SLAM   co-composer with Michael Lloyd, DEG, 1987
SWIMSUIT (TF)   co-composer with Michael Lloyd, Musifilm
   Productions/American First Run Studios, 1989
CHILD'S PLAY 3   co-composer with Cory Lerios, Universal, 1991
BAYWATCH: NIGHTMARE BAY (TF)   co-composer with Cory
   Lerios, The Baywatch Production Co./All American TV/Tower
   12/LBS, 1991
THE ENTERTAINERS (TF)   co-composer with Cory Lerios, Robert
   Greenwald Prods., 1991
THE GREY KNIGHT   co-composer with Cory Lerios, Motion Picture
   Corp. of America, 1993
BOILING POINT   co-composer with Cory Lerios, Warner Bros.,
   1993
THE TOWER (TF)   co-composer with Cory Lerios, Catalina/FNM
   Films, 1993
BAYWATCH: RACE AGAINST TIME (TF)   co-composer with Cory
   Lerios, The Baywatch Production Company, 1993
THUNDER IN PARADISE (TF)   co-composer with Cory Lerios,
   Berk-Schwartz-Bonnan Prods./Rysher/Trimark, 1994
DEADLY VOWS (TF)   co-composer with Cory Lerios, Carla Singer
   Prods./WIN, 1994

OSWALD D'ANDREA
Contact: SACEM - France, 011-33-1-4715-4715

LA VIE ET RIEN D'AUTRE   UGC, 1989, French

JOHN DANKWORTH
b. 1927 - London, England
Contact: PRS - London, England, 011-44-1-580-5544

WE ARE THE LAMBETH BOYS   Rank, 1958, British
THE CONCRETE JUNGLE   *THE CRIMINAL*   Fanfare, 1960,
   British
SATURDAY NIGHT AND SUNDAY MORNING   Continental, 1961,
   British
THE SERVANT   Landau, 1964, British
MORGAN!   *MORGAN: A SUITABLE CASE FOR TREATMENT*
   Cinema 5, 1966, British
MODESTY BLAISE   20th Century-Fox, 1966, British
SANDS OF THE KALAHARI   Paramount, 1965, British
DARLING   Embassy, 1965, British
THE IDOL   Embassy, 1966, British
FATHOM   20th Century-Fox, 1967
ACCIDENT   Cinema 5, 1967, British
THE LAST SAFARI   Paramount, 1967, British
RETURN FROM THE ASHES   United Artists, 1965, British-U.S.
SALT AND PEPPER   United Artists, 1968, British
THE MAGUS   20th Century-Fox, 1968, British
THE LAST GRENADE   Cinerama Releasing Corporation, 1970,
   British
PERFECT FRIDAY   Chevron, 1970, British
10 RILLINGTON PLACE   Columbia, 1971, British
LOSER TAKE ALL   Miramax Films, 1989, British

JEFF DANNA
Agent: Vangelos Management - Encino, 818-380-1919
Affiliation: SOCAN - Toronto, 416-445-8700

COLD COMFORT   Norstar Ent./Ray Sagar Prod., 1990, Canadian

MYCHAEL DANNA
Agent: Vangelos Management - Encino, 818-380-1919

HUSH LITTLE BABY (CTF)   USA Pictures/ Power Pictures/Hearst,
   1994
EXOTICA   Alliance/ARP, 1994
DANCE ME OUTSIDE   Cineplex-Odeon, 1994, Canadian
KAMA SUTRA   Rasa Films, 1997
LILIES   Triptych Media, 1997
THE ICE STORM   20th Century Fox, 1997

CARL DANTE
b. July 15, 1950 - Detroit, Michigan
Home: 818-901-0030
In Europe: 011-49-40-66-88-5411
Affiliation: BMI - Los Angeles, 310-659-9109

KIEZ   United Artists, 1983
IMPRESSIONS OF MONET   Zeitlos Films, 1983, West German
THE FREE RETURN   NDR Fernsehen, 1984, West German
2006   Filminvest, 1986
MIDNIGHT DREAMS   Filminvest, 1986
SUMMER CAMP   Filminvest, 1986
THE DANGEROUS TYPE   Sony Corp., 1987
SLAVE GIRLS FROM BEYOND INFINITY   Urban Classics, 1987
STORIES FROM LOBOS CREEK   Home Vision, 1988
CELLAR DWELLER   Empire Pictures, 1988
CANNIBAL WOMEN IN THE AVOCADO JUNGLE OF DEATH
   Paramount, 1989
901: AFTER 45 YEARS OF WORKING   Home Vision, 1990

PETER D'ARGENZIO
IL TUFFO   *THE DIVE*   co-composer with Mario Tronco, 1993,
   Italian

MASON DARING*
Agent: Cathy Schleussner - Encino, 818-905-7475
Affiliation: ASCAP - Los Angeles, 213-883-1000

RETURN OF THE SECAUCUS SEVEN   Libra/Specialty Films,
   1980
LIANNA   United Artists Classics, 1983
THE BROTHER FROM ANOTHER PLANET   Cinecom, 1984
KEY EXCHANGE   TLC Films/20th Century Fox, 1985
OSA   1985
MATEWAN   Cinecom, 1987
JENNY'S SONG (TF)   Westinghouse Broadcasting, 1988
DAY ONE (TF)   Aaron Spelling Productions/Paragon Motion
   Pictures, 1988
EIGHT MEN OUT   Orion, 1988
THE LASERMAN   Peter Wang Films/Hong Kong Film Workshop,
   1988
MURDER IN MISSISSIPPI (TF)   David L. Wolper Productions,
   1990
LITTLE VEGAS   I.R.S., 1990
CITY OF HOPE   Esperanza, 1991
WILD HEARTS CAN'T BE BROKEN   Buena Vista, 1991
DOGFIGHT   Warner Bros., 1991
FATHERS & SONS   Addis-Wechsler, 1992
OFF AND RUNNING   Rank/Aaron Russo, 1992
PASSION FISH   Atchafalaya, 1992
THE ERNEST GREEN STORY (CTF)   Emmalyn Enterprises, 1993
STOLEN BABIES (CTF)   ABC Video Enterprises/Sanders-Moses
   Prods., 1993
BON APPETIT MAMA   ITC, 1993
THE LAST OUTLAW (CTF)   Davis Entertainment, 1993
THE SECRET OF ROAN INISH   Jones Entertainment Group, 1994
ON PROMISED LAND (CTF)   Anosazi Prods./Walt Disney Co.,
   1994
GETTING OUT (TF)   Dorothea G. Petrie Prods./Signboard Hill/RHI,
   1994
YOUNG AT HEART (TF)   TSProductions/Warner Bros. TV, 1995
THE OLD CURIOSITY SHOP (CTF)   Curiosity Prods., 1995
LONE STAR   Sony Classics, 1996
PREFONTAINE   Buena Vista, 1997

PETER DASENT
BRAINDEAD   1992, New Zealand
HEAVENLY CREATURES   Miramax, 1994, New Zealand

OLIVER DASSAULT
b. France
Contact: SACEM - France, 011-33-1-4715-4715

UNE FILLE COUSUE DE FIL BLANC   A STRAITLACED GIRL
   Parafrance, 1977, French
LOVE IN QUESTION   1978, French
THE HEROINES OF EVIL   1979, French

SHAUN DAVEY
TWELFTH NIGHT   1996

MARTIN DAVICH*
Agent: Gorfaine-Schwartz - Los Angeles, 213-969-1011

TIES THAT BIND: THE WILLIAM COIT STORY (TF)   Citadel, 1995

ALUN DAVIES
THE DARK   co-composer with Guy Zerafa, Norstar, 1993

DAVE DAVIES
VILLAGE OF THE DAMNED   co-composer with John Carpenter,
   Universal, 1995

PETER MAXWELL DAVIES
b. 1934 - Salford, England
Contact: PRS - London, England, 011-44-1-580-5544

THE DEVILS   Warner Bros., 1971, British
THE BOY FRIEND   MGM, 1971, British

RAY DAVIES
b. England
Contact: PRS - London, England, 011-44-1-580-5544

PERCY   MGM, 1971, British

VICTOR DAVIES
Contact: BMI - Los Angeles, 310-659-9109

THE NUTCRACKER PRINCE (AF)   Warner Bros., 1990, Canadian
FOR THE MOMENT   John Aaron Features II, 1994

AARON DAVIS
Contact: SOCAN - Toronto, 416-445-8700

STREETS   Concorde, 1990
TALK 16 (DF)   Films Transit, 1991
POISON IVY   New Line, 1992
A TOWN TORN APART (TF)   Paragon/World Intl. Network/David W.
   Rintels, 1992
ANATOMY OF LOVE (TD)   co-composer with John Lang, TBS
   Prods./Primedia Prods., 1995

BOB DAVIS
VEGAS IN SPACE   Philip R. Ford, 1992

CARL DAVIS
b. 1936 - Brooklyn, New York
Agent: Gorfaine-Schwartz - Los angeles, 213-969-1011
Affiliation: PRS - London, England, 011-44-1-580-5544

THE OTHER WORLD OF WINSTON CHURCHILL   1967, British
THE BOFORS GUN   Universal, 1968, British
THE ONLY WAY OKTOBER DAGE   1970,
   Dutch-Panamanian-U.S.
PRAISE MARX AND PASS THE AMMUNITION   1970, British
UP POMPEII   MGM, 1971, British
THE SNOW GOOSE (TF) ☆   NBC, 1971
UP THE CHASTITY BELT   1971
I MONSTER   Cannon, 1972, British
WHAT BECAME OF JACK AND JILL?   co-composer, 1972, British
RENTADICK   1972, British
THE LOVERS   British Lion, 1972, British
THE NATIONAL HEALTH   1972, British
CATHOLICS (TF)   Sidney Glazier Productions, 1973
WHAT'S NEXT?   Kingsgate Films, 1974, British
MAN FRIDAY   Avco Embassy, 1975, British
THE NAKED CIVIL SERVANT (TF)   Thames TV, 1976, British
THE SAILOR'S RETURN   Euston Films Ltd., 1978
BIRTH OF THE BEATLES (TF)   Dick Clark Productions, 1979,
   British-U.S.
NAPOLEON   new score for 1927 silent film, 1980
THE FRENCH LIEUTENANT'S WOMAN   United Artists, 1981,
   British
THE CROWD   new score for 1928 silent film, 1981
OPPENHEIMER (MS)   BBC-TV/WGBH-Boston, 1982, British-U.S.
PRAYING MANTIS   Portman Productions/Channel Four, 1982,
   British
SHOW PEOPLE   new score for 1928 silent film, 1982
FLESH AND THE DEVIL   new score for 1927 silent film, 1982
CHAMPIONS   Embassy, 1983, British
THE AEODROME (TF)   BBC, 1983, British
THE WEATHER IN THE STREETS (TF)   Rediffusion
   Films/BBC/Britannia TV, 1983, British
WINSTON CHURCHILL: THE WILDERNESS YEARS (MS)
   Southern Pictures Productions, 1983, British
GEORGE STEVENS: A FILMMAKER'S JOURNEY (FD)   Castle Hill
   Productions, 1984
SAKHAROV (CTF)   HBO Premiere Films/Titus Productions, 1984,
   U.S.-British
THE FAR PAVILLIONS (CMS)   Geoff Reeve &
   Associates/Goldcrest, 1984, British
THE THIEF OF BAGHDAD   new score for 1924 silent film, 1985
KING DAVID   Paramount, 1985, U.S.-British
SILAS MARNER (TF)   BBC, 1985, British
MURROW (CTF)   HBO Premiere Films/Titus Productions/TVS Ltd.
   Productions, 1986, U.S.-British
HOTEL DULAC (TF)   Channel Four, 1986, British
THE BIG PARADE   new score for silent film

INTOLERANCE   new score for silent film
GREED   new score for silent film
THE GENERAL   new score for silent film
THE WIND   new score for silent film
BEN HUR   new score for silent film
SCANDAL   Miramax Films, 1989, British
THE RAINBOW   Vestron, 1989, British
THE GIRL IN THE SWING   Millimeter Films, 1989, British-U.S.
THE SECRET LIFE OF IAN FLEMING (CTF)   Saban/Scherick
  Productions, 1990
CROSSING TO FREEDOM (TF)   Procter & Gamble/Stan
  Margulies/Granada TV, 1990, U.S.-British
FRANKENSTEIN UNBOUND   20th Century Fox, 1990
SEPARATE BUT EQUAL (TF)   New Liberty Prods./Republic, 1991
THE CRUCIFER OF BLOOD (CTF)   Turner/Agamemnon
  Films/British Lion, 1991
ASHENDEN (CTF)   Kelso Films/A&E/BBC, 1992
VOYAGE, 1993
A YEAR IN PROVENCE (MS)   BBC/A&E, 1993
D.W. GRIFFITH: FATHER OF FILM (TD)   co-composer with Nic
  Raine and Philip Appleby, WNET/Thames TV, 1993
CLIVE JAMES' FAME IN THE 20TH CENTURY (TD)
  BBC-TV/WQED, 1993
WIDOWS PEAK   Fine Line, 1994
GENGIS COHN (TF)   BBC-TV/A&E, 1994, British-U.S.
THE RETURN OF THE NATIVE (TF)   Craig Anderson
  Prods./Signboard Hill, 1994
ANNE FRANK REMEMBERED (FD)   Sony Classics, 1996

CAROL DAVIS

Contact: BMI - Los Angeles, 310-659-9109

VOYAGE (CTF)   Davis TV/Quinta, 1993

DAVID DAVIS

Contact: ASCAP - Los Angeles, 213-883-1000

H.O.T.S.   Derio Productions, 1979

DON DAVIS

Agent: Gorfaine-Schwartz - Los Angeles, 213-969-1011
Affiliation: BMI - Los Angeles, 310-659-9109

HYPERSPACE   Regency Entertainment, 1986
A STONING AT FULHAM COUNTY (TF)   The Landsburg Company,
  1988
BLUEGRASS (TF)   co-composer with Mark Snow, The Landsburg
  Company, 1988
QUIET VICTORY: THE CHARLIE WEDEMEYER STORY (TF)   The
  Landsburg Company, 1988
HOME FIRES BURNING (TF)   Marian Rees Associates, 1989
BLACKOUT   Magnum Entertainment, 1989
RUNNING AGAINST TIME (CTF)   Finnegan-Pinchuk Prods., 1990
LIES BEFORE KISSES (TF) ☆   Grossbart-Barnett/Spectacor, 1991
A LITTLE PIECE OF HEAVEN (TF) ☆   Grossbart-Barnett, 1991
NOTORIOUS (CTF)   ABC Entertainment, 1992
WOMAN WITH A PAST (TF)   World International
  Networks/Greystone/Art Harris/Neal and Gary/von
  Zerneck-Sertner, 1992
MURDER OF INNOCENCE (TF)   Samuels Film/Polone/Hearst,
  1993
IN THE BEST OF FAMILIES: MARRIAGE, PRIDE AND MADNESS
  (TF)   Ambroco Media/Dan Wigutow Prods., 1994
LEAVE OF ABSENCE (TF)   Grossbart-Barnett/NBC, 1994
SEAQUEST DSV: 2ND SEASON PREMIERE (TF)   Amblin
  TV/Universal TV, 1994
WHEN A MAN LOVES A WOMAN   additional music, Buena Vista,
  1994
BOUND   1996

JOHN E. DAVIS

Contact: ASCAP - Los Angeles, 213-883-1000

BREACH OF CONTRACT   Atlantic Releasing Corporation, 1984
BLOOD SPORT (TF)   Spelling-Goldberg Productions/Columbia TV,
  1986

MARK DAVIS

Contact: BMI - Los Angeles, 310-659-9109

WHICH WAY IS UP?   co-composer with Paul Riser, Universal,
  1977
CHEECH AND CHONG'S NEXT MOVIE   Universal, 1980
BUSTIN' LOOSE   Universal, 1980
CRASH COURSE (TF)   Fries Entertainment, 1988
CLASS CRUISE (TF)   Portoangelo Productions, 1989

ROCKY DAVIS

(Byron McKay Davis)
b. July 22, 1951 - Chicago, Illinois
Contact: ASCAP - Los Angeles, 213-883-1000

LA VIDA   Jeffrey Penichet, 1976
IN MacARTHUR PARK   Bruce R. Schwartz, 1977
THE CONCRETE JUNGLE (TF)   additional music, Pentagon, 1982
PAYBACK TIME   UNINHIBITED   co-composer with Joel C. Peskin,
  Antigua Films, 1993

PETER DAVISON*

Contact: BMI - Los Angeles, 310-659-9109

SHELLEY DUVALL'S FAERIE TALE THEATRE (CTF)   Platypus
  Prods./Think Prods., 1984
THE AUDITION   Lifflander Prods., 1986
EARTH ISLAND - PACIFIC CHRONICLES (TD)   Sierra Club, 1986
THE SECRET OF THE LENS   Harmony Gold Prods., 1989

SIMON DAVISON

BLUE JUICE   1995, British

ALBERTO DE ALMAR

SIDNEY SHELDON'S THE SANDS OF TIME (TF)   co-composer
  with Perry Botkin, Dove Audio/Jadran Films/Tribune
  Entertainment, 1992

GUIDO De ANGELIS

Contact: SIAE - Italy, 011-39-6-59-901

RUN RUN JOE   co-composer with Maurizio De Angelis, 1974,
  Italian-French-Spanish-West German
KILLER FISH   co-composer with Maurizio De Angelis, Associated
  Film Distribution, 1979
GREAT WHITE   co-composer with Morton Stevens, Film Ventures
  International, 1982

MAURIZIO De ANGELIS

Contact: SIAE - Italy, 011-39-6-59-901

RUN RUN JOE   co-composer with Guido De Angelis, 1974,
  Italian-French-Spanish-West German
KILLER FISH   co-composer with Guido De Angelis, Associated
  Film Distribution, 1979
GREAT WHITE   co-composer with Guido and Maurizio De Angelis,
  Film Ventures International, 1982

LEX DE AZEVEDO

Agent: The Kordek Agency - Burbank, 818-559-4248
Affiliation: ASCAP - Los Angeles, 213-883-1000

WHERE THE RED FERN GROWS   Doty-Dayton, 1974
THE SWAN PRINCESS (AF)   New Line, 1994

JOSEPH S. DE BEASI

Contact: ASCAP - Los Angeles, 213-883-1000

THE DEAN OF THIN AIR (TF)   co-composer with Joseph Carrier,
  PBS, 1983
CONFESSIONS OF A SUBURBAN GIRL   1992, British
BLESSING   Starr Valley Films, 1994

GREG DE BELLES

Contact: BMI - Los Angeles, 310-659-9109

KINJITE *FORBIDDEN GAMES* Cannon, 1989
LONGTIME COMPANION Samuel Goldwyn Company, 1990
LAMBADA Warner Bros., 1990
MEN AT WORK co-composer with Stewart Copeland, Triumph
   Releasing Corporation, 1990
SHE SAYS SHE'S INNOCENT (TF) Robert Greenwald Prods.,
   1991
LITTLE SISTER InterStar Releasing, 1992

DICK DeBENEDICTIS*

b. 1937
Agent: Film Music Associates - Hollywood, 213-463-1070
Affiliation: ASCAP - Los Angeles, 213-883-1000

THE COUPLE TAKES A WIFE Universal TV, 1972
THE GREATEST GIFT (TF) Universal TV, 1974
THIS IS THE WEST THAT WAS (TF) Public Arts
   Productions/Universal TV, 1974
THE BIG RIPOFF (TF) Universal TV, 1975
THE MANCHU EAGLE MURDER CAPER MYSTERY United
   Artists, 1975
DEADLY TRIANGLE (TF) Barry Weitz Productions/Columbia
   Pictures TV, 1975
THE RETURN OF THE WORLD'S GREATEST DETECTIVE (TF)
   Universal TV, 1976
HOW THE WEST WAS WON (MS) co-composer, MGM TV, 1977
CRISIS IN SUN VALLEY (TF) Barry Weitz Films/Columbia Pictures
   TV, 1978
ZIGFELD: THE MAN AND HIS WOMEN (TF) ☆ Frankovich
   Productions/Columbia TV, 1978
DESPERATE WOMEN (TF) Lorimar Productions, 1978
MURDER BY NATURAL CAUSES (TF) Levinson-Link Productions,
   1979
THE EARTHLING 1980, Australian
PERRY MASON RETURNS (TF) Intermedia
   Productions/Strathmore Productions/Viacom Productions, 1985
PERRY MASON: THE CASE OF THE NOTORIOUS NUN (TF)
   Intermedia Productions/Viacom Productions, 1985
DIARY OF A PERFECT MURDER (TF) Viacom
   Productions/InterMedia Entertainment/Strathmore Productions,
   1986
PERRY MASON: THE CASE OF THE SHOOTING STAR (TF)
   Intermedia Entertainment Company/Strathmore
   Productions/Viacom, 1986
PERRY MASON: THE CASE OF THE MURDERED MADAM (TF)
   The Fred Silverman Company/Strathmore Productions/Viacom,
   1987
PERRY MASON: THE CASE OF THE LOST LOVE (TF) The Fred
   Silverman Company/Strathmore Productions/Viacom Productions,
   1987
PERRY MASON: THE CASE OF THE SCANDALOUS SECRETS
   (TF) The Fred Silverman Company/Strathmore
   Productions/Viacom, 1987
PERRY MASON: THE CASE OF THE SINISTER SPIRIT (TF) The
   Fred Silverman Company/Strathmore Productions/Viacom
   Productions, 1987
FATAL CONFESSION: A FATHER DOWLING MYSTERY (TF)
   co-composer with Artie Kane, Fred Silverman
   Company/Strathmore Productions/Viacom Productions, 1987
IN THE HEAT OF THE NIGHT (TF) The Fred Silverman
   Company/Jadda Productions/MGM/UA TV, 1988
PERRY MASON: THE CASE OF THE LADY OF THE LAKE (TF)
   The Fred Silverman Company/Strathmore Productions/Viacom,
   1988
PERRY MASON: THE CASE OF THE AVENGING ACE (TF) ☆
   The Fred Silverman Company/Strathmore Productions/Viacom,
   1988
PERRY MASON: THE CASE OF THE LETHAL LESSON (TF) The
   Fred Silverman Company/Dean Hargrove Productions/Viacom,
   1989
PERRY MASON: THE CASE OF THE MUSICAL MURDERER (TF)
   The Fred Silverman Company/Dean Hargrove
   Productions/Viacom, 1989
JAKE AND THE FATMAN (TF) The Fred Silverman Company/Dean
   Hargrove Productions/Viacom, 1989
PERRY MASON: THE CASE OF THE ALL-STAR ASSASSIN (TF)
   The Fred Silverman Company/Dean Hargrove
   Productions/Viacom, 1989

PERRY MASON: THE CASE OF THE FINAL CURTAIN (TF) The
   Fred Silverman Company/Dean Hargrove Productions/Viacom,
   1990
PERRY MASON: THE CASE OF THE DESPERATE DECEPTION
   (TF) The Fred Silverman Company/Dean Hargrove
   Productions/Viacom, 1990
PERRY MASON: THE CASE OF THE RUTHLESS REPORTER
   (TF) Dean Hargrove/Fred Silverman/Viacom, 1991
PERRY MASON: THE CASE OF THE GLASS COFFIN (TF) Dean
   Hargrove/Fred Silverman/Viacom, 1991
PERRY MASON: THE CASE OF THE FATAL FASHION (TF) Dean
   Hargrove/Fred Silverman/Viacom, 1991
MATLOCK: THE WITNESS KILLINGS (TF) Dean Hargrove/Fred
   Silverman/Viacom, 1991
PERRY MASON: THE CASE OF THE FATAL FRAMING (TF) Dean
   Hargrove Prods/Fred Silverman Co./Viacom, 1992
THE HOUSE ON SYCAMORE STREET (TF) Fred Silverman
   Co./Dean Hargrove Prods./Viacom, 1992
PERRY MASON: THE CASE OF THE RECKLESS ROMEO (TF)
   Fred Silverman Co./Dean Hargrove Prods./Viacom, 1992
COLUMBO: A BIRD IN THE HAND (TF) Universal TV, 1992
A TWIST OF THE KNIFE (TF) Dean Hargrove Prods./Fred
   Silverman Co./Viacom, 1993
PERRY MASON: THE CASE OF THE SKIN DEEP SCANDAL (TF)
   Fred Silverman Co./Dean Hargrove Prods./Viacom, 1993
MATLOCK: THE FINAL DAYS (TF) theme only, Dean Hargrove
   Prods./Fred Silverman Co./Viacom, 1993
PERRY MASON: THE CASE OF THE KILLER KISS (TF) Dean
   Hargrove Prods./Fred Silverman Co./Viacom, 1994
RAY ALEXANDER: A TASTE FOR JUSTICE (TF) Logo
   Entertainment/Viacom, 1994
MATLOCK: THE IDOL (TF) theme only, Dean Hargrove
   Prods./Fred Silverman Co./Viacom, 1994

MARIO DE BENITO

LA VIA LACTEA *THE MILKY WAY* 1993,
   Spanish-German-French

JOHN DEBNEY*

Agent: Gorfaine-Schwartz - Los Angeles, 213-969-1011
Affiliation: ASCAP - Los Angeles, 213-883-1000

THE WILD PAIR *DEVIL'S ODDS* Trans World Entertainment,
   1987
NOT SINCE CASANOVA Filmworks/MCEG, 1988
SEVEN HOURS TO JUDGMENT Trans World Entertainment,
   1988
THE FURTHER ADVENTURES OF TENNESSEE BUCK Trans
   World Entertainment, 1988
TRENCHCOAT IN PARADISE (TF) Ogiens/Kate Co., 1989
THE EYES OF THE PANTHER (CTF) Think Entertainment, 1989
JETSONS: THE MOVIE (AF) Universal, 1990
FACE OF FEAR (TF) Lee Rich Productions/Warner Bros. TV, 1990
INTO THE BADLANDS (TF) Ogiens-Kane Prods., 1991
A SEDUCTION IN TRAVIS COUNTY (TF) David Braun
   Productions/Co-Star Entertainment/Zev Braun Pictures/New World
   TV, 1991
STILL NOT QUITE HUMAN (CTF) Resnick-Margellos Prods., 1992
SUNSTROKE (CTF) Wilshire Court, 1992
I YABBA-DABBA DO! (ATF) co-composer with Hoyt Curtin, William
   Hanna and Joseph Barbera, H-B Prods., 1993
JONNY'S GOLDEN QUEST (ATF)
   Hanna-Barbera/USA/Fil-Cartoons, 1993
CLASS OF '61 (TF) Amblin TV, Universal TV, 1993
HOCUS POCUS Buena Vista, 1993
PREYING MANTIS (CTF) Fast Track Films/Wilshire Court Prods.,
   1993
SEA QUEST: DSV (TF) Amblin TV, 1993
FOR LOVE AND GLORY (TF) Gerber Co./CBS, 1993
HOLLYROCK-A-BYE BABY (ATF) Hanna-Barbera Prods.
   Animation/Wang Film Prod. Co., 1993
GUNMEN Dimension/Miramax, 1994
WHITE FANG 2: MYTH OF THE WHITE WOLF Buena Vista, 1994
LITTLE GIANTS Warner Bros., 1994
HOUSE GUEST Buena Vista, 1995
IN PURSUIT OF HONOR (CTF) Marian Rees Associates/Village
   Roadshow/HBO Pictures, 1995
CUTTHROAT ISLAND MGM-UA, 1995
CARPOOL Warner Bros., 1996
GETTING AWAY WITH MURDER Savoy, 1996
THE RELIC Paramount, 1997

DARRELL DECK
RETURN TO BOGGY CREEK 777 Distributors, 1977

MARC DAVID DECKER
Contact: BMI - Los Angeles, 310-659-9109

BIKINI ISLAND 1991
THE DARK BACKWARD Elwes/Wyman/Talmadge/L.A. Bridge,
    1991

ROBERT DECKER
SHOCK'EM DEAD Noma, 1991

CHRISTOPHER DEDRICK
Contact: SOCAN - Toronto, 416-445-8700

GLORY! GLORY! (CTF) Atlantis Films Ltd./Orion TV, 1989
THE RACE TO FREEDOM: THE UNDERGROUND RAILROAD
    (CTF) Atlantis/United Image Ent./Family Channel/BET/CTV,
    1994
MILLION DOLLAR BABIES (TF) Bernard Zuckerman
    Prods./Cinar/CBC/CBS Ent./Telefilm Canada/Ontario Film
    Development Corp., 1994, U.S.-Canadian

CHRISTOPHE DEFAYS
LA CAVALE DES FOUS *LOONIES AT LARGE* co-composer with
    Olivier Defays. 1993, French

OLIVIER DEFAYS
Contact: SACEM - France, 011-33-1-4715-4715

LA CAVALE DES FOUS *LOONIES AT LARGE* co-composer with
    Christophe Defays, 1993, French

LUCHI DeJESUS
Contact: ASCAP - Los Angeles, 213-883-1000

THE CALIFORNIA KID (TF) Universal TV, 1974
SWEET HOSTAGE (TF) Brut Productions, 1975

MATTHEW DELGADO
(Kevin Gilbert)
Contact: ASCAP - Los Angeles, 213-883-1000

P.S.I. LUV U (TF) CBS Entertainment/Glen Larson Prods., 1991

JOE DELIA
Agent: Film Music Associates - Hollywood, 213-463-1070
Affiliation: BMI - Los Angeles, 310-659-9109

DRILLER KILLER Rochelle Films, 1979
CHINA GIRL Vestron, 1987
FREEWAY New World, 1988
KING OF NEW YORK Reteitalia/Scena Films, 1990, Italian-U.S.
BAD LIEUTENANT Odyssey, 1992
SNAKE EYES Mario & Vittorio Cecchi Gori, 1993
BODY SNATCHERS Warner Bros., 1993
DANGEROUS GAME Cecchi Gori Group, 1994
THE ENEMY WITHIN (CTF) HBO Pictures/Vincent Pictures, 1994
THE ADDICTION October, 1995
DRUNKS Drunks Prods., 1995
THE FUNERAL October, 1996

GAYE DELORME
Contact: SOCAN - Toronto, 416-445-8700

THINGS ARE TOUGH ALL OVER Columbia, 1982

JEAN DELORME
PUDDING CHOMEUR Aska Film, 1997, Canadian

AL DeLORY
Contact: BMI - Los Angeles, 310-659-9109

PIONEER WOMAN (TF) Filmways, 1973
THE DEVIL'S RAIN Bryanston, 1975, U.S.-Mexican
MAD BULL (TF) Steckler Productions/Filmways, 1977
RODEO GIRL (TF) Steckler Productions/Marble Arch Productions,
    1980

PACO DE LUCIA
Contact: SGAE - Spain, 011-34-1-319-2100

CARMEN Orion Classics, 1983, Spanish
THE HIT Island Alive, 1984, British
MANOUSHE: THE LEGEND OF GYPSY LOVE 1993, Brazilian

MILTON DeLUGG
Contact: ASCAP - Los Angeles, 213-883-1000

SANTA CLAUS CONQUERS THE MARTIANS Embassy, 1964
GULLIVER'S TRAVELS BEYOND THE MOON (AF) co-composer
    with Anne DeLugg, U.S. version only, 1966, Japanese
THE GONG SHOW MOVIE Universal, 1980

BOB DE MARCO
MACSHAYNE: WINNER TAKES ALL (TF) co-composer with Edgar
    Struble, Larry Brown and Kenny Rogers, Jr., Larry Levinson
    Prods./Kenny Rogers Prods., 1994
GAMBLER V: PLAYING FOR KEEPS (TF) additional music,
    Kenny Rogers Prods./WIN/RHI, 1994
RIDERS IN THE STORM co-composer with Ken Rogers,
    Filmhaus, 1995

CHRISTOPHER DE MARCO
Contact: ASCAP - Los Angeles, 213-883-1000

TROMA'S WAR Troma, 1988

ERIC DEMARSAN
Contact: SACEM - France, 011-33-1-4715-4715

TARGET OF SUSPICION (CTF) Ellipse Programme/Barry Weitz
    Films, 1994

FRANCESCO DE MASI
b. 1930 - Rome, Italy
Contact: SIAE - Italy, 011-39-6-59-901

TI-KOYO E IL SUO PESCECANE 1962, Italian
MACISTE IL GLADIATORE PIU FORTE DEL MONDO 1962,
    Italian
LO SCEICCO ROSSO 1962, Italian
MACISTE L'EROE PIU GRANDE DEL MONDO 1963, Italian
GLI SCHIAVI PIU FORTI DEL MONDO 1964, Italian
IL LEONE DI TEBE 1964, Italian
ARIZONA COLT 1966, Italian
F.B.I. OPERAZIONE VIPERA GIALLA 1966, Italian
LA MORTE VIENE DA MANILA 1966, Italian
LA LAMA NEL CORPO 1966, Italian
RINGO IL VOLTO DELLA VENDETTA 1966, Italian
SETTE DOLLARI SUL ROSSO 1966, Italian
SETTE CONTRO TUTTI 1966, Italian
KOMMISSAR X, DREI GRUNE HUNDE 1967, Italian
087 MISION APOCALIPSIS 1967, Italian
QUINDICI FORCHE PER UN ASSASSINO 1968, Italian
AMMAZZALI TUTTI E TORNA SOLO 1968, Italian
QUELLA SPORCA STORIA DEL WEST 1968, Italian
OSTIA 1969, Italian
EL LARGO DIA DEL AGUILA 1969, Italian
CONCERTO PER PISTOLA SOLISTA 1970, Italian
QUEL MALEDETTO GIORNO DELLA RESA DEI CONTI 1971,
    Italian
LA ORGIA DE LOS MUERTOS 1971, Italian
F.B.I. OPERAZIONE PAKISTAN 1972, Italian
BAWDY TALES United Artists, 1973, Italian-French
THE ARENA New World, 1974
LA TECNICA E IL RITO 1975, Italian
PRIVATE VICES, PUBLIC VIRTUES 1976, Italian

COUNTERFEIT COMMANDOS *INGLORIOUS BASTARDS*
    Aquarius, 1978, Italian
LONE WOLF McQUADE   Orion, 1983
THUNDER WARRIOR *THUNDER*   Trans World Entertainment,
    1983
RUSH   Cinema Shares International, 1984, Italian
THE MANHUNT   Samuel Goldwyn Company, 1985, Italian
ESCAPE FROM THE BRONX   New Line Cinema, 1985, Italian
FORMULA FOR MURDER   Fulvia International, 1986, Italian

GARY DEMICHELE
BIG NIGHT   Samuel Goldwyn, 1996

EDISON DENISOV
Contact: SACEM - France, 011-33-1-4715-4715

OCHENJ VERNAJA ZHENA   *A VERY FAITHFUL WIFE*   1993,
    Russian

RUSHMORE DE NOOYER
MOON SHOT (CTD)   co-composer with Ed Van Fleet and Malcolm
    Brooks, TBS Prods., 1994

FRANK DENSON
Contact: BMI - Los Angeles, 310-659-9109

BAKER'S HAWK   Doty-Dayton, 1976
RABBIT TEST   Avco Embassy, 1978
OH HEAVENLY DOG   20th Century Fox, 1980
SUNSET LIMOUSINE (TF)   Witzend Productions/ITC Productions,
    1983
BLOSSOM IN PARIS (TF)   Witt-Thomas Prods./Touchstone TV,
    1993

LUIS De PABLO
b. Spain
Contact: SGAE - Spain, 011-34-1-319-2100

THE CHALLENGES   1970, Spanish
GOYA   1971, Spanish
ANNA AND THE WOLVES   1973, Spanish
THE SPIRIT OF THE BEEHIVE   Janus, 1973, Spanish
DON RAMIRO   1973, Spanish
PASCUAL DUARTE   1976, Spanish
TO AN UNKNOWN GOD   1977, Spanish
THE CARROT QUEEN   1978, Spanish
WHAT MAX SAID   1978, Spanish

DELIA DERBYSHIRE
Contact: PRS - London, England, 011-44-1-580-5544

THE LEGEND OF HELL HOUSE   co-composer with Brian Hodgson,
    20th Century-Fox, 1973, British

ALAN DERMARDEROSIAN
Contact: ASCAP - Los Angeles, 213-883-1000

A HOLLYWOOD STORY   Double Helix, 1989
IMPROPER CONDUCT   Everest Pictures, 1994
IRRESISTIBLE IMPULSE   Everest Pictures, 1995

FREDERICO DE ROBERTIS
SUD *SOUTH*   1993, Italian
S.P.Q.R.: 2,000 AND A HALF YEARS AGO   *S.P.Q.R. 2.000 E 1/2
    ANNI FA*   1995, Italian

JOEL DEROUIN
Contact: BMI - Los Angeles, 310-659-9109

THE HITMAN   Cannon, 1991

PAUL De SENNEVILLE
b. France
Contact: SACEM - France, 011-33-1-4715-4715

CELESTINE, MAID AT YOUR SERVICE   co-composer with Oliver
    Touissaint, 1974, French
IRRECONCILABLE DIFFERENCES   co-composer with Oliver
    Touissaint, Warner Bros., 1984

MANUEL DE SICA
b. Italy
Contact: SIAE - Italy, 011-39-6-59-901

A PLACE FOR LOVERS   *AMANTI*   MGM, 1968, Italian-French
IO E DIO   1970, Italian
LE COPPIE   "Il Leone" segment, 1971, Italian
THE GARDEN OF THE FINZI-CONTINIS   Cinema 5, 1971,
    Italian-West German
COSE DI COSA NOSTRA   1971, Italian
IO NON VEDO, TU NON PARLI, LUI NON SENTE   Italian, 1971
CAMORRA   1972, Italian
LO CHIAMEREMO ANDREA   1972, Italian
L'ETA DI COSIMO (TF)   1973, Italian T.V.
A BRIEF VACATION   Allied Artists, 1973, Italian
IL VIAGGIO *THE VOYAGE*   United Artists, 1974, Italian
IL CASO RAOUL   Iskra Cinematografica, 1975, Italian
LA MADAMA   1975, Italian
OCCHIO ALLA VEDOVA!   1975, Italian
QUEL MOVIMENTO CHE MI PACE   1975, Italian
CAGLIOSTRO   1975, Italian
FOLIES BOURGEOISES   FFCM, 1976, French-Italian-West
    German
SETTE SCIALLI DI SETA GIALLA   Italian
VADO A VIVERE DA SOLO   Italian
LUI E PEGGIO DI ME   Italian
CARO PAPA   Dean Film/AMLF/Prospect Film, 1979,
    Italian-French-Canadian
SONO FOTOGENICO   Dean Film/Marceau Cocinor, 1980,
    Italian-French
SUNDAY LOVERS   MGM/United Artists, 1980,
    U.S.-British-French-Italian
IL MATRIMONIO DI CATERINA (TF)   1982, Italian
IL MOMENTO DELL'AVVENTURA   SACIS, 1983, Italian
VACANZE IN AMERICA   C.G. Silver Film, 1984, Italian
BYE BYE BABY   Seymour Borde & Associates, 1989, Italian-U.S.
DELLAMORTE DELLAMORE   1994, Italian-French-German
CEMETARY MAN   1996

ROBERTO DE SIMONE
Contact: SIAE - Italy, 011-39-6-59-901

HOW WONDERFUL TO DIE ASSASSINATED   1975, Italian
THE END OF THE WORLD IN OUR USUAL BED IN A NIGHT FULL
    OF RAIN   Warner Bros., 1978, Italian-U.S.

ALEXANDRE DESPLAT
A LAPSE OF MEMORY   1991, French-Canadian
AU NOM DU PERE ET DU FILS   1991, French
SEXE FAIBLE   1992, French
LE TRONC   1993, French
THE HOUR OF THE PIG   Miramax, 1993, French-British
REGARDE LES HOMMES TOMBER   1994, French
MARIE-LOUISE OU LA PERMISSION   1995, French
HALCYON DAYS *LES PECHERS MORTELS*   1995, French
LES MILLES   1995, French
LUCKY PUNCH   1996
UN HEROS   1996, French

LEONID DESYATNIKOV
PRISONER OF THE MOUNTAINS   Orion Classics, 1997

MAURO J. DE TRIZIO
UNDYING LOVE   co-composer with Danny Sciarra, Slaughtered
    Lamb, 1991

STEVE DEUTSCH

Contact: PRS - London, England, 011-44-1-580-5544

RAV'E' - DANCING TO A DIFFERENT BEAT   Smart Egg, 1993
HARD TIMES (TF)   BBC-TV/WGBH Boston, 1995, British-U.S.

DEVO

Contact: BMI - Los Angeles, 310-659-9109

HUMAN HIGHWAY   co-composer with Neil Young, Shakey
   Pictures, 1982

FRANK DEVOL

b. 1925
Contact: ASCAP - Los Angeles, 213-883-1000

WORLD FOR RANSOM   Allied Artists, 1954
KISS ME DEADLY   United Artists, 1955
THE BIG KNIFE   United Artists, 1955
PARIS FOLLIES OF 1956   *FRESH FROM PARIS*   Allied Artists,
   1955
ATTACK!   United Artists, 1956
PARDNERS   Paramount, 1956
JOHNNY TROUBLE   Warner Bros., 1957
THE RIDE BACK   United Artists, 1957
PILLOW TALK ★   Universal, 1959
MURDER, INC.   20th Century-Fox, 1960
LOVER, COME BACK   Universal, 1962
BOY'S NIGHT OUT   MGM, 1962
WHATEVER HAPPENED TO BABY JANE?   Warner Bros., 1962
FOR LOVE OR MONEY   Universal, 1963
McLINTOCK!   United Artists, 1963
THE THRILL OF IT ALL   Universal, 1963
UNDER THE YUM-YUM TREE   Columbia, 1963
THE WHEELER DEALERS   MGM, 1963
GOOD NEIGHBOR SAM   Columbia, 1964
SEND ME NO FLOWERS   Universal, 1964
HUSH...HUSH SWEET CHARLOTTE ★   20th Century-Fox, 1964
CAT BALLOU   Columbia, 1965
THE FLIGHT OF THE PHOENIX   20th Century-Fox, 1966
THE GLASS BOTTOM BOAT   MGM, 1966
TEXAS ACROSS THE RIVER   Universal, 1966
CAPRICE   20th Century-Fox, 1967
THE DIRTY DOZEN   MGM, 1967
GUESS WHO'S COMING TO DINNER ★   Columbia, 1967
THE HAPPENING   Columbia, 1967
THE LEGEND OF LYLAH CLARE   MGM, 1968
WHAT'S SO BAD ABOUT FEELING GOOD?   Universal, 1968
KRAKATOA, EAST OF JAVA   Cinerama Releasing Corporation,
   1969
THE RELUCTANT HEROES (TF)   Aaron Spelling Productions,
   1971
ULZANA'S RAID   Universal, 1972
FEMALE ARTILLERY (TF)   Universal TV, 1973
EMPEROR OF THE NORTH POLE   *EMPEROR OF THE NORTH*
   20th Century-Fox, 1973
KEY WEST (TF)   Warner Bros. TV, 1973
THE LONGEST YARD   Paramount, 1974
DOC SAVAGE, THE MAN OF BRONZE   Warner Bros., 1975
HUSTLE   Paramount, 1975
HEY, I'M ALIVE! (TF)   Charles Fries Productions/Worldvision
   Enterprises, 1975
PANACHE (TF)   Warner Bros. TV, 1976
HERBIE GOES TO MONTE CARLO   Buena Vista, 1977
THE CHOIRBOYS   Universal, 1977
THE MILLIONAIRE (TF)   Don Fedderson Productions, 1978
THE FRISCO KID   Warner Bros., 1979
THE GHOSTS OF BUXLEY HALL (TF)   Walt Disney Productions,
   1980
...ALL THE MARBLES   MGM/United Artists, 1981
THE WILD WOMEN OF CHASTITY GULCH (TF)   co-composer with
   Tom Worrall, Aaron Spelling Productions, 1982

BARRY DEVORZON

Contact: BMI - Los Angeles, 310-659-9109

DILLINGER   American International, 1973
HARD TIMES   Columbia, 1975
BOBBIE JO AND THE OUTLAW   American International, 1976
DOG AND CAT (TF)   Largo Productions, 1977

ROLLING THUNDER   American International, 1977
SKI LIFT TO DEATH (TF)   The Jozak Company/Paramount Pictures
   TV, 1978
LACY AND THE MISSISSIPPI QUEEN (TF)   Lawrence Gordon
   Productions/Paramount Pictures TV, 1978
THE WARRIORS   Paramount, 1979
STUNTS UNLIMITED (TF)   Lawrence Gordon
   Productions/Paramount Pictures TV, 1980
THE NINTH CONFIGURATION   Warner Bros., 1980
REWARD (TF)   Jerry Adler Productions/Espirit Enterprises/Lorimar
   Productions, 1980
THE COMEBACK KID (TF)   ABC Circle Films, 1980
XANADU   Universal, 1980
LOOKER   The Ladd Company/Warner Bros., 1981
TATTOO   20th Century-Fox, 1981
THE CHILDREN NOBODY WANTED (TF)   Blatt-Singer
   Productions/Warner Bros. TV, 1981
TARZAN, THE APE MAN   co-composer with Perry Botkin,
   MGM/UA, 1981
THE RENEGADES (TF)   co-composer with Joseph Conlan,
   Lawrence Gordon Productions/Paramount Pictures TV, 1982
JEKYLL AND HYDE...TOGETHER AGAIN   Paramount, 1982
INTIMATE STRANGERS (TF)   Nederlander TV and Film
   Productions/Telepictures Productions, 1983
V: THE FINAL BATTLE (TF)   co-composer of part one with Joseph
   Conlan, Blatt-Singer Productions/Warner Bros. TV, 1984
KOJAK: THE BELARUS FILE (TF)   co-composer with Joseph
   Conlan, Universal TV, 1985
STICK   co-composer with Joseph Conlan, Universal, 1985
NIGHT OF THE CREEPS   Tri-Star, 1986
EXORCIST III   20th Century-Fox, 1990

FREDERIC DEVREESE

Contact: SABAM - Brussels, Belgium, 011-32-2-230-2660

L'HOMME AU CRANE RASE   1966, French
UN SOIR UN TRAIN   1969, French
RENDEZ-VOUS A BRAY   1971, French
BELLE   1973, French
DU BOUT DES LEVRES   *ON THE TIP OF THE TONGUE*   Elan
   Films, 1976, Belgian
BENVENUTA   UGC, 1983, Belgian-French

DE WOLFE

Contact: BMI - Los Angeles, 310-659-9109

ON THE GAME   Eagle, 1973, British
THE HOT GIRLS   New Realm, 1974, British
MONTY PYTHON AND THE HOLY GRAIL   co-composer with Neil
   Innes, Cinema 5, 1974, British
JABBERWOCKY   Cinema 5, 1977, British

JOHN WILLIAM DEXTER

Contact: SOCAN - Toronto, 416-445-8700

DREAM A LITTLE DREAM   Vestron, 1989

VON DEXTER

Contact: BMI - Los Angeles, 310-659-9109

THE TINGLER   Columbia, 1959
HOUSE ON HAUNTED HILL   Allied Artists, 1959
13 GHOSTS   Columbia, 1960
MR. SARDONICUS   Columbia, 1961

A. S. DIAMOND

THE FANTASTIC LIFE OF D.C. COLLINS (TF)   co-composer with
   Dennis Dreith and Mitch Margo, Zephyr
   Productions/Guillaume-Margo Productions, 1984
THE GODDESS OF LOVE (TF)   co-composer with Mitch Margo and
   Dennis Dreith, Phil Margo Enterprises/New World TV/Phoenix
   Entertainment Group, 1988

DAVID DIAMOND
b. 1915 - Rochester, New York

A PLACE TO LIVE (D)   Philadelphia Housing Association, 1941
DREAMS THAT MONEY CAN BUY   co-composer, Films
   International of America, 1948
STRANGE VICTORY (D)   Target, 1948
ANNA LUCASTA   Columbia, 1949

NEIL DIAMOND
Affiliation: SESAC - New York, 212-586-3450

JONATHAN LIVINGSTON SEAGULL   co-composer with Lee
   Holdridge, Paramount, 1973
THE JAZZ SINGER   composer of song score (underscore by
   Leonard Rosenman), AFD, 1980
SWITCHING CHANNELS   co-composer of theme with Michel
   Legrand, Columbia, 1988

MANU DIBANGO
Contact: SACEM - France, 011-33-1-4715-4715

FORTY DEUCE   Island, 1982

ANDREW DICKSON
SOMEONE ELSE'S AMERICA   1995, French-U.K.-German
SECRETS AND LIES   1996

JOHN D. DICKSON
Contact: ASCAP - Los Angeles, 213-883-1000

COOL WORLD   additional music, Paramount, 1992

VINCE DiCOLA
Contact: ASCAP - Los Angeles, 213-883-1000

STAYIN' ALIVE   Paramount, 1983
ROCKY IV   MGM/UA, 1985
THE TRANSFORMERS - THE MOVIE (AF)   DEG, 1986

LOEK DIKKER
b. 1944 - Amsterdam, Holland
Agent: Seth Kaplan Entertainment - Los Angeles, 213-525-3477
Affiliation: BUMA - Holland, 011-31/20-540-7911

THE 4TH MAN   Spectrafilm, 1983, Dutch
SLOW BURN (CTF)   Joel Schumacher Prods./Universal Pay TV,
   1986
PASCALI'S ISLAND   Avenue Pictures, 1988, British-U.S.
BODY PARTS   Paramount, 1991
TELLING LIES IN AMERICA   Telling Lies Productions, 1997

DAN DIPAOLA
Contact: Splash Productions - New York, 212-695-3665

JACK'S BACK   Palisades Entertainment, 1988
SUFFERING BASTARDS   AIP, 1990

JAMES DIPASQUALLE *
Agent: Gorfaine-Schwartz - Los Angeles, 213-969-1011
Affiliation: ASCAP - Los Angeles, 213-883-1000

SHOWDOWN   Universal, 1973
SENIOR YEAR (TF)   Universal TV, 1974
FORCE FIVE (TF)   Universal TV, 1975
THE JERICHO MILE (TF)   composer of theatrical version, ABC
   Circle Films, 1976
SARAH T. - PORTRAIT OF A TEENAGE ALCOHOLIC (TF)
   Universal TV, 1975
MALLORY: CIRCUMSTANTIAL EVIDENCE (TF)   Universal
   TV/Crescendo Productions/R.B. Productions, 1976
THE CRITICAL LIST (TF)   MTM Productions, 1978
FAST BREAK   co-composer with David Shire, Columbia, 1979
THE CONTENDER (TF)   Universal TV, 1980
ESCAPE (TF)   Henry Jaffe Enterprises, 1980
ADVICE TO THE LOVELORN (TF) ☆   Universal TV, 1981

MCCLAIN'S LAW (TF)   Eric Bercovici Productions/Epipsychidion,
   1982
FANTASIES (TF)   Mandy Productions, 1982
TWO OF A KIND (TF) ☆☆   Lorimar Productions, 1982
LISTEN TO YOUR HEART (TF)   CBS Entertainment, 1983
TRAUMA CENTER (TF)   Glen A. Larson Productions/Jeremac
   Productions/20th Century-Fox TV, 1983
AGATHA CHRISTIE'S 'SPARKLING CYANIDE' (TF)   Stan
   Margulies Productions/Warner Bros. TV, 1983
QUARTERBACK PRINCESS (TF)   CBS Entertainment, 1983
THE RED-LIGHT STING (TF)   J.E. Productions/Universal TV, 1984
LOVE LIVES ON (TF) ☆☆   Script-Song Prods./ABC Circle Films,
   1985
ARMED AND DANGEROUS   Columbia, 1986
YOUNG AGAIN (TF)   Sharmhill Productions/Walt Disney
   Productions, 1986, U.S.-Canadian
ONE CRAZY SUMMER   Warner Bros., 1986
RAD   Tri-Star, 1986
A STRANGER WAITS (TF)   Bruce Lansbury Productions/Edgar
   Lansbury Productions/Lewisfilm Ltd./New Century TV Productions,
   1987
BROKEN ANGEL (TF)   The Stan Margulies Company/MGM-UA TV,
   1988
THE SHELL SEEKERS (TF) ☆   Marian Rees Associates/Central
   TV, 1989
STOLEN: ONE HUSBAND (TF)   King Phoenix Entertainment, 1990
COLUMBO: AGENDA FOR MURDER (TF)   Universal TV, 1990
THE KILLING MIND (CTF) ☆   Hearst, 1991
RUNAWAY FATHER (TF)   Polone Co./Bonaparte Prods./Lee
   Levinson Prods./Hearst, 1991
IN THE BEST INTEREST OF THE CHILDREN (TF)   NBC Prods.,
   1992
SEDUCTION: THREE TALES FROM THE INNER SANCTUM (TF)
   Carroll Newman Prods./Victoria Principal Prods./Polone
   Co./Hearst Entertainment, 1992
GETTING UP AND GOING HOME (CTF)   Carroll Newman/Polone
   Co./Hearst, 1992
1994 BAKER STREET: SHERLOCK HOLMES RETURNS (TF)
   Paragon/Kenneth Johnson, 1993
UNTAMED LOVE (CTF)   Cathy Lee Crosby Prods./Carroll Newman
   Prods./Hearst, 1994
SEE JANE RUN (TF)   Avenue Pictures/Hearst, 1995
NEVER SAY NEVER: THE DEIDRE HALL STORY (TF)   Stan
   Margulies Co./Panache/TriStar TV, 1995

ANTONIO DIPOFI
CONDANNATO A NOZZE   *CONDEMNED TO WED*   1993, Italian
BONUS MALUS   1993, Italian

ANDREW DIXON
Contact: PRS - London, England, 011-44-1-580-5544

MEANTIME   1983, British
HIGH HOPES   Skouras Pictures, 1988, British
NAKED   1993, British

NANA DJANELIDZ
b. U.S.S.R.
Contact: RAIS - Russia, 011-7-95-203-3260

REPENTANCE   Cannon, 1984, Soviet, originally made for
   television

RAY DOBBINS
HAPPILY EVER AFTER: FAIRY TALES FOR EVERY CHILD
   (ATF)   co-composer, Two Oceans/Confetti/Hyperion, 1995

CRAIG DOERGE
Contact: ASCAP - Los Angeles, 213-883-1000

RICH KIDS   United Artists, 1979

BRENDAN DOLAN
GO FISH   co-composer with Jennifer Sharpe and Scott Aldrich,
   Samuel Goldwyn, 1994

THOMAS DOLBY

Contact: ASCAP - Los Angeles, 213-883-1000

FEVER PITCH   MGM/UA, 1985
GOTHIC   Vestron, 1987

KLAUS DOLDINGER

Contact: ASCAP - Los Angeles, 213-883-1000

DAS BOOT   *THE BOAT*   Triumph/Columbia, 1981, West German
DIE WILDEN FUENZIGER   1983, West German
LOVE IS FOREVER   *COMEBACK* (TF)   Michael Landon-Hall
   Bartlett Films/NBC-TV/20th Century-Fox TV, 1983
THE NEVERENDING STORY   co-composer with Giorgio Moroder,
   Warner Bros., 1984, West German
A FATHER'S REVENGE (TF)   Shadowplay/Rosco
   Productions/Phoenix Entertainment Group, 1987
ME AND HIM   Columbia, 1989, West German
SALT ON OUR SKIN   1993, German-French-Canadian

FRANCOIS DOMPIERRE

b. France
Contact: SACEM - France, 011-33-1-4715-4715

THE BLOOD OF OTHERS (CTF)   HBO Premiere Films/ICC/Filmex
   Productions, 1984, Canadian-French
DANIELLE STEEL'S VANISHED (TF)   Cramer Co./NBC Prods., 1995

PINO DONAGGIO

(Giuseppe Donaggio)
b. November 24, 1941 - Burano, Italy
Agent: The Ryan Company - Sherman Oaks, 818-981-4111
Affiliation: SIAE - Italy, 011-39-6-59-901

DON'T LOOK NOW   Paramount, 1974, British-Italian
CORRUPTION IN THE HALLS OF JUSTICE   Italnoleggio, 1975,
   Italian
UN SUSURRO NEL BUIO   1976, Italian
CARRIE   United Artists, 1976
HAUNTS   *THE VEIL*   Intercontinental, 1977
NERO VENEZIANO   *DAMNED IN VENICE/VENETIAN BLACK*
   1978, Italian
CHINA 9, LIBERTY 37   Titanus, 1978, Italian
PIRANHA   New World, 1978
TOURIST TRAP   Compass International, 1979
SENZA BUCCIA   *WITHOUT SKIN*   1979, Italian
HOME MOVIES   United Artists Classics, 1980
BEYOND EVIL   IFI-Scope III, 1980
DRESSED TO KILL   Filmways, 1980
LA VITA INTERIORE   1980, Italian
THE BLACK CAT   Selenia Cinematografica, 1980, Italian
THE HOWLING   Avco Embassy, 1981
THE FAN   Paramount, 1981
BLOW OUT   Filmways, 1981
A VENEZIA, CARNEVALE, UN AMORE   1981, Italian
MORTE IN VATICANO   1982, Italian
THE SECRET BEYOND THE DOOR   Gaumont, 1982, Italian
TEX   Buena Vista, 1982
DON CAMILLO   1983, Italian
VIA DEGLI SPECCHI   *STREET OF MIRRORS*   1983, Italian
HERCULES   Cannon, 1983
HERCULES II   Cannon, 1983, Italian
OVER THE BROOKLYN BRIDGE   *MY DARLING SHIKSA*
   MGM/UA/Cannon, 1984
BODY DOUBLE   Columbia, 1984
ORDEAL BY INNOCENCE   Cannon, 1984, British
DEJA VU   Cannon, 1985, British
THE ASSISI UNDERGROUND   Cannon, 1985
THE BERLIN AFFAIR   Cannon, 1985, Italian-West German
THE FIFTH MISSILE (TF)   Bercovici-St. Johns
   Productions/MGM-UA TV, 1986
CRAWLSPACE   Empire Pictures, 1986
HOTEL COLONIAL   Orion, 1987, U.S.-Italian
DANCERS   Cannon, 1987
THE BARBARIANS   Cannon, 1987
CATACOMBS   Empire Pictures, 1988
APPOINTMENT WITH DEATH   Cannon, 1988
ZELLY AND ME   Columbia, 1988
KANSAS   Trans World Entertainment, 1988
PHANTOM OF DEATH   Globe Films, 1989, Italian

NIGHT GAME   Trans World Entertainment, 1989
MERIDIAN   Full Moon Entertainment, 1990
TCHIN-TCHIN   1991, Italian
INDIO 2: THE REVOLT   1991, Italian
RAISING CAIN   Universal, 1992
DOVE SIETE? IO SONO QUI   *WHERE ARE YOU? I AM HERE*
   1993, Italian
GIOVANNI FALCONE   1993, Italian
OBLIVION   R.S. Entertainment, 1994
UN EROE BORGHESE   1995, Italian-French

MARC DONAHUE

Contact: BMI - Los Angeles, 310-659-9109

OPPOSING FORCE   *HELL CAMP*   Orion, 1986
MURPHY'S LAW   Cannon, 1986

JAMES DONNELLAN

Contact: BMI - Los Angeles, 310-659-9109

FATAL CHARM (CTF)   Jonathan D. Krane/Bruce Cohn Curtis,
   1992

HENRIK OTTO DONNER

DOLLY AND HER LOVER   1992, Finnish

DONOVAN

Contact: PRS - London, England, 011-44-1-580-5544

THE PIED PIPER   Paramount, 1972, British-West German

STEVE DORFF

Agent: Gorfaine-Schwartz - Los Angeles, 213-969-1011
Affiliation: BMI - Los Angeles, 310-659-9109

EVERY WHICH WAY BUT LOOSE   Warner Bros., 1978
BRONCO BILLY   Warner Bros., 1980
HONKY TONK FREEWAY   Universal/AFD, 1981
HONKYTONK MAN   Warner Bros., 1982
WALTZ ACROSS TEXAS   Atlantic Releasing Corporation, 1983
CANNONBALL RUN II   Warner Bros., 1984
STICK   Universal, 1985
RUSTLERS' RHAPSODY   Paramount, 1985
THE DEFIANT ONES (TF)   MGM-UA TV, 1986
CONVICTED (TF)   Larry A. Thompson Productions, 1986
MANHUNT FOR CLAUDE DALLAS (TF)   London Films, Inc., 1986
BACK TO THE BEACH   Paramount, 1987
THE QUICK AND THE DEAD (CTF)   HBO Pictures/Joseph Cates
   Company, 1987
INFIDELITY (TF)   Mark-Jett Productions/ABC Circle Films, 1987
MY BEST FRIEND IS A VAMPIRE   Kings Road, 1988
TOO YOUNG THE HERO (TF)   Rick-Dawn Productions/Pierre
   Cossette Productions/The Landsburg Company, 1988
KISS SHOT (TF)   Lonson Productions/Whoop Inc., 1989
THE RETURN OF SAM McCLOUD (TF)   Michael Sloan
   Productions/Universal TV, 1989
PINK CADILLAC   Warner Bros., 1989
B.L. STRYKER: PLATES (TF)   Blue Period Productions/TWS
   Productions/Universal TV, 1990
COLUMBO AND THE MURDER OF A ROCK STAR (TF)   Universal
   TV, 1991
BABE RUTH (TF)   A Lyttle Production, 1991
COLUMBO: DEATH HITS THE JACKPOT (TF)   Universal TV, 1991
IN THE NICK OF TIME (TF)   Spectacor/Walt Disney Television,
   1991
CHROME SOLDIERS (CTF)   Wilshire Court Prods., 1992
PURE COUNTRY   Warner Bros., 1992
POISONED BY LOVE: THE KERN COUNTY MURDERS (TF)
   Morgan Hill/Hearst, 1993

JOEL DORN

BOARDWALK   Atlantic Releasing Corporation, 1979

MICHAEL DOUCET

Contact: BMI - Los Angeles, 310-659-9109

BELIZAIRE THE CAJUN   Skouras Pictures, 1986
I WENT TO THE DANCE (FD)   Brazos Films/Flower Films, 1989

TERRY DOUGHERTY
Contact: PRS - London, England, 011-44-1-580-5544

LONG SHOT   Mithras Films, 1978, British

ELIOT DOUGLAS
THE BORDER OF TONG   co-composer with Paul Shorick, CPG,
    1991

JOHNNY DOUGLAS
Contact: PRS - London, England, 011-44-1-580-5544

CRACK IN THE WORLD   Paramount, 1965, British
THE BRIDES OF FU MANCHU   7 Arts, 1966, British

JULIA DOWNES
Contact: PRS - London, England, 011-44-1-580-5544

A MAN FOR ALL SEASONS (CTF)   Agamemnon Films, 1988

PATRICK DOYLE
b. Scotland
Agent: Air-Edel - Los Angeles, 310-914-5000
Affiliation: ASCAP - Los Angeles, 213-883-1000

HENRY V   Samuel Goldwyn Company, 1989, British
DEAD AGAIN   Paramount, 1991
INDOCHINE   INDOCHINA   Sony Classics, 1992, French
MUCH ADO ABOUT NOTHING   Samuel Goldwyn, 1993,
    British-U.S.
NEEDFUL THINGS   Columbia/Castle Rock/New Line, 1993
CARLITO'S WAY   Universal, 1993
EXIT TO EDEN   Savoy, 1994
MARY SHELLEY'S FRANKENSTEIN   TriStar, 1994
UNE FEMME FRANCAISE   A FRENCH WOMAN   1995, French
A LITTLE PRINCESS ★   Warner Bros., 1995
MRS. WINTERBOURNE   TriStar, 1996
HAMLET ★   1996

DARRYL DRAGON
Contact: BMI - Los Angeles, 310-659-9109

SANDSTONE   co-composer with Dennis Dragon, Henderson Films,
    1977

DENNIS DRAGON
Contact: BMI - Los Angeles, 310-659-9109

GO FOR IT   World Entertainment, 1976
SANDSTONE   co-composer with Darryl Dragon, Henderson Films,
    1977

ELIZABETH DRAKE
Contact: BMI - Los Angeles, 310-659-9109

BREATHING UNDER WATER   1992, Australian

KAMEN DRANDUSKI
HEALER   1994

ROBERT DRASNIN *
Contact: BMI - Los Angeles, 310-659-9109

PICTURE MOMMY DEAD   Embassy, 1966
RIDE IN THE WHIRLWIND   American International, 1966
DAUGHTER OF THE MIND (TF)   20th Century-Fox, 1969
THE KREMLIN LETTER   20th Century-Fox, 1970
CROWHAVEN FARM (TF)   Aaron Spelling Productions, 1970
THE OLD MAN WHO CRIED WOLF (TF)   Aaron Spelling
    Productions, 1970
DR. COOK'S GARDEN (TF)   Paramount TV, 1970
DESPERATE MISSION (TF)   20 Century-Fox TV, 1971
A TATTERED WEB (TF)   Metromedia Productions, 1971
CANNON (TF)   QM Productions, 1971
MURDER ONCE REMOVED (TF)   Metromedia Productions, 1971
LONGSTREET (TF)   Paramount TV, 1971

A TASTE OF EVIL (TF)   Aaron Spelling Productions, 1971
THEY CALL IT MURDER (TF)   20th Century-Fox TV, 1971
NIGHT OF TERROR (TF)   Paramount TV, 1972
JIGSAW   MAN ON THE MOVE (TF)   Universal TV, 1972
THE HEIST (TF)   Paramount TV, 1972
CRISIS IN MID-AIR (TF)   CBS Entertainment, 1979
ILLUSIONS (TF)   CBS Entertainment, 1983
HOBSON'S CHOICE (TF)   CBS Entertainment, 1983
BURNING RAGE (TF)   Gilbert Cates Productions, 1984
LOVE, MARY (TF)   CBS Entertainment, 1985
WHO IS JULIA? (TF)   CBS Entertainment, 1986
SECRET WITNESS (TF)   Just Greene Productions/CBS
    Entertainment Productions, 1988

DENNIS DREITH*
Contact: ASCAP - Los Angeles, 213-883-1000

THE FANTASTIC LIFE OF D.C. COLLINS (TF)   co-composer with
    A.S. Diamond and Mitch Margo, Zephyr
    Productions/Guillaume-Margo Productions, 1984
THE GODDESS OF LOVE (TF)   co-composer with Mitch Margo and
    A.S. Diamond, Phil Margo Enterprises/New World TV/Phoenix
    Entertainment Group, 1988
THE PUNISHER   New World International, 1990

MICHAEL DRESS
Contact: PRS - London, England, 011-44-1-580-5544

THE MIND OF MR. SOAMES   Columbia, 1970, British
THE HOUSE THAT DRIPPED BLOOD   Cinerama Releasing
    Corporation, 1971, British

GEORGE DREYFUS
Contact: APRA - Australia, 011-61-2-922-6422

LET THE BALOON GO   1976, Australian
BREAK OF DAY   1976, Australian
DIMBOOLA   1976, Australian
TENDER MERCIES   Universal/AFD, 1983
THE FRINGE DWELLERS   1986, Australian

TOM DUBE
Contact: ASCAP - Los Angeles, 213-883-1000

HUGH HEFNER: ONCE UPON A TIME (FD)   additional music,
    IRS, 1992

ANNE DUDLEY
Agent: Air-Edel - Los Angeles, 310-914-5000
Affiliation: PRS - London, England, 011-44-1-580-5544

DISORDERLIES   co-composer with Art of Noise, Warner Bros.,
    1987
HIDING OUT   DEG, 1987
BUSTER   Hemdale, 1988, British
SILENCE LIKE GLASS   Bavaria/Lisa/Roxy, 1989, West German
THE MIGHTY QUINN   MGM/UA, 1989
SAY ANYTHING   20th Century-Fox, 1989
THE MISADVENTURES OF MR. WILT   Samuel Goldwyn, 1990,
    British
THE CRYING GAME   Miramax, 1992, British
ANNA LEE: DUPE   Carnival Films, 1994, British
FELIDAE   1994, German

ANTOINE DUHAMEL
b. July 30, 1925 - France
Contact: SACEM - France, 011-33-1-4715-4715

GALA   1962, French
LIBERTE DE LA NUIT   1962, French
MEDITERRANEE   1963, French
LE PUITS ET LE PENDULE   1963, French
UN AMOUR DE GUERRE   1964, French
EVARISTE GALOIS   1964, French
LE GRAIN DE SABLE   1964, French
LE VOLEUR DE TIBIDABO   1964, French
TINTIN ET LES ORANGES BLEUES   1964, French
BELPHEGOR (TF)   1965, French

PIERROT LE FOU   Pathe Contemporary, 1965, French
LES MIETTES   1965, French
FUGUE   1966, French
LA LONGUE MARCHE   1966, French
ROGER LA HONTE   1966, French
POUR LE MISTRAL   1966, French
LE GRAND DADAIS   1967, French
UN HOMME A ABATTRE   1967, French
LE FRANCISCAIN DE BOURGES   1967, French
WEEKEND   Grove Press, 1968, French-Italian
STOLEN KISSES   Lopert, 1969, French
MISSISSIPPI MERMAID   United Artists, 1970, French-Italian
THE WILD CHILD   United Artists, 1970, French-Italian
BED AND BOARD   *DOMICILE CONJUGAL*   Columbia, 1971,
   French
LE MISTRAL   1972, French
M. COMME MATHIEU   1973, French
LA COUPE A DIX FRANCS   *THE TWO DOLLAR HAIRCUT*
   co-composer with Anthony Braxton, 1974, French
LET JOY REIGN SUPREME   *QUE LA FETE COMMENCE...*
   adaptation, SJ International, 1975, French
L'ACROBATE   1975, French
LA QUESTION   1977, French
AU PLAISIR DE DIEU (TF)   1977, French
LA BARRICADE DU POINT DU JOUR   1977, French
LA CHANSON DE ROLAND   1978, French
BIT BETWEEN THE TEETH   1979, French
FELICITE   1979, French
MAIS OU ET DONC ORNICAR   1979, French
RETURN TO THE BELOVED   1979, French
DEATH WATCH   *LA MORT EN DIRECT*   Quartet, 1980,
   French-West German-British-U.S.
TWISTED OBSESSION   Iberoamericana, 1990
DADDY NOSTALGIE   Clea Productions, 1990, French
RIDICULE   1996, French

DAVID DUNDAS

Contact: PRS - London, England, 011-44-1-580-5544

WITHNAIL AND I   Cineplex Odeon, 1987, British
HOW TO GET AHEAD IN ADVERTISING   co-composer with Rick
   Wentworth, Warner Bros., 1989, British
SLEEPERS (MS)   co-composer with Rick Wentworth, Cinema
   Verity, 1991
FREDDIE AS F.R.0.7. (AF)   co-composer with Rick Wentworth,
   Miramax, 1992

GEORGE DUNING *

b. 1919 - Richmond, Virginia
Contact: ASCAP - Los Angeles, 213-883-1000

THE DEVIL'S MASK   co-composer with Irving Gertz, Columbia,
   1946
MYSTERIOUS INTRUDER   Columbia, 1946
JOHNNY O'CLOCK   Columbia, 1947
THE GUILT OF JANET AMES   Columbia, 1947
THE CORPSE CAME C.O.D.   Columbia, 1947
DOWN TO EARTH   co-composer with Heinz Roemheld, Columbia,
   1947
HER HUSBAND'S AFFAIRS   Columbia, 1947
I LOVE TROUBLE   Columbia, 1948
TO THE ENDS OF THE EARTH   Columbia, 1948
THE UNTAMED BREED   Columbia, 1948
THE RETURN OF OCTOBER   Columbia, 1948
THE GALLANT BLADE   Columbia, 1948
THE MAN FROM COLORADO   Columbia, 1948
SHOCKPROOF   Columbia, 1949
THE DARK PAST   Columbia, 1949
SLIGHTLY FRENCH   Columbia, 1949
THE UNDERCOVER MAN   Columbia, 1949
LUST FOR GOLD   Columbia, 1949
JOHNNY ALLEGRO   Columbia, 1949
THE DOOLINS OF OKLAHOMA   co-composer with Paul Sawtell,
   Columbia, 1949
JOLSON SINGS AGAIN ★   Columbia, 1949
AND BABY MAKES THREE   Columbia, 1949
CARGO TO CAPETOWN   Columbia, 1950
NO SAD SONGS FOR ME ★   Columbia, 1950
CONVICTED   Columbia, 1950
THE PETTY GIRL   Columbia, 1950
BETWEEN MIDNIGHT AND DAWN   Columbia, 1950

HARRIET CRAIG   Columbia, 1950
THE FLYING MISSILE   Columbia, 1951
LORNA DOONE   Columbia, 1951
TWO OF A KIND   Columbia, 1951
THE LADY AND THE BANDIT   Columbia, 1951
THE MOB   Columbia, 1951
THE BAREFOOT MAILMAN   Columbia, 1951
THE FAMILY SECRET   Columbia, 1951
MAN IN THE SADDLE   Columbia, 1951
SCANDAL SHEET   Columbia, 1952
SOUND OFF   Columbia, 1952
PAULA   Columbia, 1952
CAPTAIN PIRATE   Columbia, 1952
ASSIGNMENT—PARIS   Columbia, 1952
LAST OF THE COMMANCES   Columbia, 1953
ALL ASHORE   Columbia, 1953
SALOME   Columbia, 1953
FROM HERE TO ETERNITY ★   Columbia, 1953
PICNIC ★   Columbia, 1955
THE EDDY DUCHIN STORY ★   Columbia, 1956
HOUSEBOAT   Paramount, 1958
BELL, BOOK AND CANDLE   Columbia, 1958
COWBOY   Columbia, 1958
1001 ARABIAN NIGHTS (AF)   Columbia, 1959
THE DEVIL AT 4 O'CLOCK   Columbia, 1961
MY BLOOD RUNS COLD   Warner Bros., 1965
ANY WEDNESDAY   Warner Bros., 1966
THEN CAME BRONSON (TF)   MGM TV, 1969
QUARANTINED (TF)   Paramount Pictures TV, 1970
BUT I DON'T WANT TO GET MARRIED! (TF)   Aaron Spelling
   Productions, 1970
YUMA (TF)   Aaron Spelling Productions, 1971
BLACK NOON (TF)   Fenady Associates/Screen Gems, 1971
CLIMB AN ANGRY MOUNTAIN (TF)   Herbert F. Solow
   Productions/Warner Bros. TV, 1972
A GREAT AMERICAN TRAGEDY (TF)   Metromedia Producers
   Corporation/J. Lee Thompson/Ronald Shedlo Productions, 1972
THE WOMAN HUNTER (TF)   Bing Crosby Productions/Jerome L.
   Epstein Productions, 1972
HONOR THY FATHER (TF)   Metromedia Producers
   Corporation/Halcyon Productions, 1973
ARNOLD   Cinerama Releasing Corporation, 1973
TERROR IN THE WAX MUSEUM   Cinerama Releasing
   Corporation, 1974
THE ABDUCTION OF SAINT ANNE (TF)   QM Productions, 1975
THE TOP OF THE HILL (TF)   Fellows-Keegan Co./Paramount
   Pictures TV, 1980
THE DREAM MERCHANTS (TF)   Columbia TV, 1980
THE MAN WITH BOGART'S FACE   20th Century-Fox, 1980
GOLIATH AWAITS (TF)   Larry White Productions/Hugh Benson
   Productions/Columbia TV, 1981

PAUL DUNLAP

Contact: ASCAP - Los Angeles, 213-883-1000

THE BARON OF ARIZONA   Lippert, 1950
HI-JACKED   Lippert, 1950
THE STEEL HELMET   Lippert, 1950
CRY DANGER   RKO Radio, 1951
LITTLE BIG HORN   Lippert, 1951
JOURNEY INTO LIGHT   20th Century-Fox, 1951
THE LOST CONTINENT   Lippert, 1951
BREAKDOWN   Realart, 1952
PARK ROW   United Artists, 1952
HELLGATE   Lippert, 1952
BIG JIM McLAIN   Warner Bros., 1952
THE SAN FRANCISCO STORY   Warner Bros., 1952
COMBAT SQUAD   Columbia, 1953
FORT VENGEANCE   Allied Artists, 1953
JACK SLADE   Allied Artists, 1953
THE ROYAL AFRICAN RIFLES   Allied Artists, 1953
DUFFY OF SAN QUENTIN   Warner Bros., 1953
DRAGONFLY SQUADRON   Allied Artists, 1954
FANGS OF THE WILD   Lippert, 1954
LOOPHOLE   Allied Artists, 1954
RETURN FROM THE SEA   Allied Artists, 1954
SHIELD FOR MURDER   United Artists, 1954
TARGET EARTH!   Allied Artists, 1954
BLACK TUESDAY   United Artists, 1955
BIG HOUSE, U.S.A.   United Artists, 1955
DESERT SANDS   United Artists, 1955

FINGERMAN   Allied Artists, 1955
FORT YUMA   United Artists, 1955
GHOST TOWN   United Artists, 1955
THE RETURN OF JACK SLADE   Allied Artists, 1955
ROBBER'S ROOST   United Artists, 1955
SHACK OUT ON 101   Allied Artists, 1955
STRANGER ON HORSEBACK   United Artists, 1955
THE BRASS LEGEND   United Artists, 1956
THE BROKEN STAR   United Artists, 1956
THE COME-ON   Allied Artists, 1956
CRIME AGAINST JOE   United Artists, 1956
THE CRUEL TOWER   Allied Artists, 1956
DANCE WITH ME, HENRY   United Artists, 1956
EMERGENCY HOSPITAL   United Artists, 1956
MAGNIFICENT ROUGHNECKS   Allied Artists, 1956
STAGECOACH TO FURY   20th Century-Fox, 1956
STRANGE INTRUDER   Allied Artists, 1956
THREE BAD SISTERS   United Artists, 1956
WALK THE DARK STREET   Associated Artists, 1956
APACHE WARRIOR   20th Century-Fox, 1957
CRIME OF PASSION   United Artists, 1957
DRAGON WELLS MASSACRE   Allied Artists, 1957
I WAS A TEENAGE WEREWOLF   American International, 1957
I WAS A TEENAGE FRANKENSTEIN   American International, 1957
THE QUIET GUN   20th Century-Fox, 1957
BLOOD OF DRACULA   American International, 1957
LURE OF THE SWAMP   20th Century-Fox, 1957
YOUNG AND DANGEROUS   20th Century-Fox, 1957
OREGON PASSAGE   Allied Artists, 1957
PORTLAND EXPOSE   Allied Artists, 1957
ROCKABILLY BABY   20th Century-Fox, 1957
UNDER FIRE   20th Century-Fox, 1957
GOD IS MY PARTNER   20th Century-Fox, 1957
FRANKENSTEIN - 1970   Allied Artists, 1958
FRONTIER GUN   20th Century-Fox, 1958
GANG WAR   20th Century-Fox, 1958
GUN FEVER   United Artists, 1958
TOUGHEST GUN IN TOMBSTONE   United Artists, 1958
WOLF LARSEN   Allied Artists, 1958
HOW TO MAKE A MONSTER   American International, 1958
THE FOUR SKULLS OF JONATHAN DRAKE   United Artists, 1959
HERE COME THE JETS   20th Century-Fox, 1959
LONE TEXAN   20th Century-Fox, 1959
THE OREGON TRAIL   20th Century-Fox, 1959
THE REBEL SET   Allied Artists, 1959
THE ROOKIE   20th Century-Fox, 1959
GUNFIGHTERS OF ABILENE   United Artists, 1960
THE PURPLE GANG   Allied Artists, 1960
TWELVE HOURS TO KILL   20th Century-Fox, 1960
WALK LIKE A DRAGON   Paramount, 1960
THE ANGRY RED PLANET   American International, 1960
SEVEN WOMEN FROM HELL   20th Century-Fox, 1961
THE THREE STOOGES MEET HERCULES   Columbia, 1962
THE THREE STOOGES IN ORBIT   Columbia, 1962
BLACK ZOO   Allied Artists, 1963
SHOCK CORRIDOR   Allied Artists, 1963
THE THREE STOOGES GO ROUND THE WORLD IN A DAZE   Columbia, 1963
THE NAKED KISS   Allied Artists, 1964
STAGE TO THUNDER ROCK   Paramount, 1964
VOICE OF THE HURRICANE   RAM, 1964
THE OUTLAWS IS COMING!   Columbia, 1965
YOUNG FURY   Paramount, 1965
CASTLE OF EVIL   United Pictures, 1966
CYBORG 2087   Features, 1966
DESTINATION INNER SPACE   Magna, 1966
PANIC IN THE CITY   United Pictures, 1967
THE DESTRUCTORS   United Pictures, 1968
THE MONEY JUNGLE   United Pictures, 1968

JAMES PATRICK DUNNE
Agent: Carol Faith Agency - Beverly Hills, 310-274-0776

DEAR GOD   co-composer with Jeremy Lubbock, Paramount, 1996

MURPHY DUNNE
Contact: BMI - Los Angeles, 310-659-9109

OUTSIDE CHANCE (TF)   co-composer with Lou Levy, New World Productions/Miller-Begun Productions, 1978
LOOSE SHOES   COMING ATTRACTIONS   Atlantic Films, 1981

JOHN DUPREZ
Agent: Air-Edel - Los Angeles, 310-914-5000
Affiliation: PRS - London, England, 011-44-1-580-5544

MONTY PYTHON AT THE HOLLYWOOD BOWL   Columbia, 1982, British
BULLSHOT!   Island Alive, 1983, British
MONTY PYTHON'S THE MEANING OF LIFE   Universal, 1983, British
A PRIVATE FUNCTION   Island Alive, 1984, British
OXFORD BLUES   MGM/UA, 1984, British
SHE'LL BE WEARING PINK PAJAMAS   Film Four International, 1985, British
ONCE BITTEN   Samuel Goldwyn Company, 1985
LOVE WITH A PERFECT STRANGER (CTF)   Yorkshire Television/Atlantic Video Ventures, 1986, British
PERSONAL SERVICES   Vestron, 1987, British
A FISH CALLED WANDA   MGM/UA, 1988
U.H.F.   Orion, 1989
A CHORUS OF DISAPPROVAL   Orion, 1989, British
TEENAGE MUTANT NINJA TURTLES   New Line Cinema, 1990
TEENAGE MUTANT NINJA TURTLES II: THE SECRET OF THE OOZE   New Line, 1991
BULLSEYE!   21st Century, 1991
MYSTERY DATE   Orion, 1991
CARRY ON COLUMBUS   1992, British
TEENAGE MUTANT NINJA TURTLES III: THE TURTLES ARE BACK...IN TIME   New Line, 1993
A GOOD MAN IN AFRICA   Gramercy, 1994

GORDON DURITY
THE BURNING SEASON   Astral Communications, 1993, Canadian

DAVID DUVALL
Contact: BMI - Los Angeles, 310-659-9109

DEATH: THE TRIP OF A LIFETIME (TD)   1993

BOB DYLAN
(Robert Zimmerman)
b. May 24, 1941
Affiliation: SESAC - New York, 212-586-3450

PAT GARRETT AND BILLY THE KID   MGM, 1973

ARIE DZIERLATKA
L'HOMME QUI A PERDU SON OMBRE   THE MAN WHO LOST HIS SHADOW   1991, Spanish-Swiss-French
LE JOURNAL DE LADY M   THE DIARY OF LADY M   1993, Swiss-Belgian-Spanish-French

E

RICH EAMES
Contact: BMI - Los Angeles, 310-659-9109

SAVED BY THE BELL - HAWAIIAN STYLE (TF)   co-composer with
Scott Gale, Peter Engel Prods./NBC, 1992

DAVID EARL
Contact: PRS - London, England, 011-44-1-580-5544

KIPPERBANG   *P'TANG YANG, KIPPERBANG*   MGM/UA Classics,
1983, British

EARWAX
(John Di Stefano, Kolonica McQuestin, Ear3)

VIRTUAL LOVE   HOTwire Prods., 1993

BRIAN EASDALE
b. 1909 - Manchester, England
Contact: PRS - London, England, 011-44-1-580-5544

MEN IN DANGER   1939, British
SPRING OFFENSIVE   1940, British
BLACK NARCISSUS   Universal, 1947, British
THE RED SHOES ★★   Eagle-Lion, 1948, British
THE SMALL BACK ROOM   *HOUR OF GLORY*   Snader
Productions, 1948, British
THE WILD HEART   *GONE TO EARTH*   RKO Radio, 1950, British
OUTCAST OF THE ISLANDS   United Artists, 1951, British
THE GREEN SCARF   1955, British
PURSUIT OF THE GRAF SPEE   *THE BATTLE OF THE RIVER
PLATE*   Rank, 1956, British
PEEPING TOM   Astor, 1960, British

CLINT EASTWOOD
Contact: ASCAP - Los Angeles, 213-883-1000

UNFORGIVEN   theme only, Universal, 1992
A PERFECT WORLD   theme only, Warner Bros., 1993

BERNARD EBBINGHOUSE
Contact: PRS - London, England, 011-44-1-580-5544

PRUDENCE AND THE PILL   20th Century-Fox, 1968, British
MUMSY, NANNY, SONNY AND GIRLY   *GIRLY*   Cinerama
Releasing Corporation, 1970, British
TALES THAT WITNESS MADNESS   Paramount, 1973, British

NICOLAS ECONOMOU
Contact: GEMA - Germany, 011-49-89-480-03610

ROSA LUXEMBOURG   New Yorker, 1986, West German

BRIAN EDDOLLS
Contact: ASCAP - Los Angeles, 213-883-1000

THE FEUD   Castle Hill, 1990

RANDY EDELMAN
Agent: Gorfaine-Schwartz - Los Angeles, 213-969-1011
Affiliation: BMI - Los Angeles, 310-659-9109

OUTSIDE IN   Harold Robbins International, 1972
SNATCHED (TF)   Spelling-Goldberg Productions/ABC Circle Films,
1973
EXECUTIVE ACTION   National General, 1973
BLOOD SPORT (TF)   Danny Thomas Productions, 1973

RYAN'S FOUR (TF)   Fair Dinkum Inc./Groverton
Productions/Paramount TV, 1983
WHEN YOUR LOVER LEAVES (TF)   Major H Productions, 1983
A DOCTOR'S STORY (TF)   Embassy TV, 1984
SCANDAL SHEET (TF)   Fair Dinkum Productions, 1985
THE CHIPMUNK ADVENTURE (AF)   Samuel Goldwyn Company,
1987
DENNIS THE MENACE (TF)   DIC Enterprises Productions, 1987
FEDS   Warner Bros., 1988
TWINS   co-composer with Georges Delerue, Universal, 1988
TROOP BEVERLY HILLS   Columbia, 1989
GHOSTBUSTERS II   Columbia, 1989
QUICK CHANGE   Warner Bros., 1990
COME SEE THE PARADISE   20th Century-Fox, 1990
KINDERGARTEN COP   Universal, 1990
DROP DEAD FRED   New Line, 1991
V.I. WARSHAWSKI   Buena Vista, 1991
SHOUT   Universal, 1991
TAKING BACK MY LIFE (TF)   Elliot Fredgen/Lyttle-Heshty/Warner
Bros. TV, 1992
BEETHOVEN   Universal, 1992
THE LAST OF THE MOHICANS   co-composer with Trevor Jones,
20th Century Fox, 1992
MY COUSIN VINNY   20th Century Fox, 1992
THE DISTINGUISHED GENTLEMAN   Buena Vista, 1992
DRAGON: THE BRUCE LEE STORY   Universal, 1993
THE ADVENTURES OF BRISCO COUNTY JR. (TF)   Boam/Cuse
Prods., 1993
GETTYSBURG   New Line, 1993
BEETHOVEN'S 2nd   Universal, 1993
GREEDY   Universal, 1994
ANGELS IN THE OUTFIELD   Buena Vista, 1994
THE MASK   New Line, 1994
PONTIAC MOON   Paramount, 1994
BILLY MADISON   Universal, 1995
CITIZEN X (CTF)   Asylum Films/Citadel/HBO Pictures, 1995
THE INDIAN IN THE CUPBOARD   Paramount, 1995
WHILE YOU WERE SLEEPING   Buena Vista, 1995
TALL TALE: THE UNBELIEVABLE ADVENTURES OF PECOS
BILL   Buena Vista, 1995
THE BIG GREEN   Buena Vista, 1995
DOWN PERISCOPE   20th Century Fox, 1996
THE QUEST   Universal, 1996
DIABOLIQUE   Warner Bros., 1996
DRAGONHEART   Universal, 1996
DAYLIGHT   Universal, 1996
SELENA   Warner Bros., 1997
ANACONDA   Columbia, 1997

DAVE EDMONDS
Contact: PRS - London, England, 011-44-1-580-5544

PORKY'S REVENGE   20th Century Fox, 1985

GREG EDMONSON
Contact: BMI - Los Angeles, 310-659-9109

SCIENCE-FICTION: A JOURNEY INTO THE UNKNOWN (TD)
Museum of Television & Radio/SGP, 1994
LAST LIVES   Promark, 1997

BERNARD EDWARDS
Contact: ASCAP - Los Angeles, 213-883-1000

SOUP FOR ONE   co-composer with Nile Rodgers, Warner Bros.,
1982

KENNY EDWARDS
WILDFLOWER (CTF)   co-composer with Jon Gilutin, Freed-Laufer
Prods./Polone Co./Hearst, 1991
SECRET SINS OF THE FATHER (TF)   co-composer with Jon
Gilutin, Ultra Ent./Dick Clark Film Group, 1994

STEVE EDWARDS *

Agent: SMC Artists - Studio City, 818-505-9600
Affiliation: ASCAP - Los Angeles, 213-883-1000

THE BADGE (CTF)   1991
MIDNIGHT FEAR   New World, 1991
THE MINISTER'S WIFE   Homesick Pictures, 1992
SAVED   Lionheart Films, 1993
SHOWDOWN   Imperial Entertainment, 1993
THE TRIP   Homesick Pictures, 1994
PROJECT SHADOWCHASER II   EGM Films, 1994
WITHOUT MERCY   Rapi Films, 1994
ILLEGAL IN BLUE   Stu Segall Productions, 1994
SHATTERED IMAGE   Arjay Productions, 1994
PROJECT SHADOWCHASER III   Escee Films, 1995
CONSPIRACY OF FEAR   Bosi Films, 1995
BLOODSPORT II   DEM Productions, 1995
BLOSSOM TIME   Possomtown Pictures, 1996
BLOODSPORT III   DEM Productions, 1996
MAN WITH A GUN   October Films, 1996
TRUE VENGEANCE   FM Entertainment, 1996
HEAVEN OR VEGAS   Storm Entertainment/Cineville, 1997
TNT   Interlight Pictures, 1997

SEAMUS EGAN

THE BROTHERS McMULLEN   20th Century Fox Searchlight, 1995

CLIFF EIDELMAN *

Agent: CAA - Beverly Hills, 310-288-4545
Affiliation: ASCAP - Los Angeles, 213-883-1000

SILENT NIGHT   TAT, 1988, West German
DEAD MAN OUT (CTF)   HBO Showcase/Robert Cooper
   Entertainment/Granada TV, 1988, U.S.-Canadian-British
TO DIE FOR   Skouras Pictures, 1989
THE FINAL DAYS (TF)   The Samuels Film Co., 1989
ANIMAL BEHAVIOR   Millimeter Films, 1989
TRIUMPH OF THE SPIRIT   Triumph Releasing Corporation, 1989
STRIKE IT RICH   co-composer with Shirley Walker, Millimeter
   Films, 1990
CRAZY PEOPLE   Paramount, 1990
SON OF DARKNESS: TO DIE FOR II   theme only, Trimark, 1991
DELIRIOUS   MGM, 1991
BACKFIELD IN MOTION (TF)   Think/Avnet-Kerner, 1991
CHRISTOPHER COLUMBUS: THE DISCOVERY   Warner Bros.,
   1992
STAR TREK VI: THE UNDISCOVERED COUNTRY   Paramount,
   1992
LEAP OF FAITH   Paramount, 1992
UNTAMED HEART   1992
THE METEOR MAN   MGM, 1993
MY GIRL 2   Columbia, 1994
A SIMPLE TWIST OF FATE   Buena Vista, 1994
NOW AND THEN   New Line, 1995
IF THESE WALLS COULD TALK (CTF)   Moving Pictures, 1996
THE BEAUTICIAN AND THE BEAST   Paramount, 1997

RICHARD EINHORN

Contact: ASCAP - Los Angeles, 213-883-1000

SHOCK WAVES   DEATH CORPS.   Joseph Brenner Associates,
   1977
DON'T GO IN THE HOUSE   Film Ventures International, 1980
EYES OF A STRANGER   Warner Bros., 1981
THE PROWLER   Sandhurst Corporation, 1981
NIGHTMARE AT SHADOW WOODS   FCG, 1987
DEAD OF WINTER   MGM/UA, 1987
SISTER, SISTER   New World, 1987
CLOSET LAND   Universal, 1991
DARROW (TF)   KCET/Heuss-Stept Prods., 1991
DISCOVERING WOMEN (TD)   theme only, 1995
JOAN OF ARC   new live score to the 1927 film, 1995
NOBODY'S GIRLS (TF)   Maryland Public Television, 1995

INAKI EIZAGIRRE

LOS ANOS OSCUROS   URTE ILUNAK/THE DARK DAYS   1993,
   Spanish

DANNY ELFMAN

Agent: The Kraft-Benjamin Agency - Beverly Hills, 310-247-0123
Affiliation: BMI - Los Angeles, 310-659-9109

FORBIDDEN ZONE   Samuel Goldwyn Co., 1980
PEE WEE'S BIG ADVENTURE   Warner Bros., 1985
BACK TO SCHOOL   Orion, 1986
WISDOM   20th Century Fox, 1987
SUMMER SCHOOL   Paramount, 1987
HOT TO TROT   Warner Bros., 1988
BIG TOP PEE WEE   Paramount, 1988
BEETLEJUICE   The Geffen Company/Warner Bros., 1988
MIDNIGHT RUN   Universal, 1988
SCROOGED   Paramount, 1988
BATMAN   Warner Bros., 1989
NIGHTBREED   20th Century Fox, 1990
DARKMAN   Universal, 1990
DICK TRACY   Buena Vista, 1990
EDWARD SCISSORHANDS   20th Century-Fox, 1990
PURE LUCK   theme only, Universal, 1991
ARTICLE 99   Orion, 1992
BATMAN RETURNS   Warner Bros., 1992
ARMY OF DARKNESS: EVIL DEAD 3   theme only, Universal,
   1992
SOMMERSBY   Warner Bros., 1993
THE NIGHTMARE BEFORE CHRISTMAS (AF)
   Buena Vista, 1993
BLACK BEAUTY   Warner Bros., 1994
DOLORES CLAIBORNE   Columbia, 1995
DEAD PRESIDENTS   Buena Vista, 1995
TO DIE FOR   Columbia, 1995
MISSION: IMPOSSIBLE   Paramount, 1996
THE FRIGHTENERS   Universal, 1996
EXTREME MEASURES   1996
MARS ATTACKS!   1996
MEN IN BLACK   1997

JONATHAN ELIAS

Contact: ASCAP - Los Angeles, 213-883-1000

CHILDREN OF THE CORN   New World, 1984
ALMOST YOU   20th Century-Fox, 1984
TUFF TURF   New World, 1985
KEY EXCHANGE   TLC Films/20th Century Fox, 1985
VAMP   New World, 1986
TWO MOON JUNCTION   Lorimar, 1988
SHAKEDOWN   Universal, 1988
PARENTS   Vestron, 1989
FAR FROM HOME   Vestron, 1989
RUDE AWAKENING   Orion, 1989
HOWARD BEACH: MAKING THE CASE FOR MURDER (TF)
   Patchett-Kaufman Entertainment Productions/WIN, 1989
THE HEART OF JUSTICE (CTF)   TNT Screenworks, 1993
MORNING GLORY   Academy, 1993
LEPRECHAUN 2   Trimark, 1994

JOHN ELIZALDE

Contact: ASCAP - Los Angeles, 213-883-1000

THE CITY (TF)   QM Productions, 1977
DEATH RAY 2000 (TF)   Woodruff Productions/QM Productions,
   1981

KIRK ELLIOT

Contact: GEMA - Germany, 011-49-89-480-03610

SMALL PLEASURES   co-composer with An-Lun Huang Wondrous
   Light, 1993

DON ELLIOTT

Contact: BMI - Los Angeles, 310-659-9109

THE HAPPY HOOKER   Cannon, 1975

JACK ELLIOTT *

Agent: Gorfaine-Schwartz - Los Angeles, 213-969-1011
Affiliation: BMI - Los Angeles, 310-659-9109

THE COMIC   Columbia, 1969
WHERE'S POPPA?   United Artists, 1970
THE FEMINIST AND THE FUZZ (TF)   co-composer with Allyn
   Ferguson, Screen Gems/Columbia Pictures TV, 1971
T.R. BASKIN   Paramount, 1971
GET TO KNOW YOUR RABBIT   Warner Bros., 1972
EVERY MAN NEEDS ONE (TF)   co-composer with Allyn Ferguson,
   Spelling-Goldberg Productions/ABC Circle Films, 1972
PLAYMATES (TF)   co-composer with Allyn Ferguson, ABC Circle
   Films, 1972
THE BAIT (TF)   co-composer with Allyn Ferguson,
   Spelling-Goldberg Productions/ABC Circle Films, 1973
THE MAN WITHOUT A COUNTRY (TF)   co-composer with Allyn
   Ferguson, Norman Rosemont Productions, 1973
JARRETT (TF)   co-composer with Allyn Ferguson, Screen
   Gems/Columbia Pictures TV, 1973
BIRDS OF PREY (TF)   co-composer with Allyn Ferguson,
   Tomorrow Entertainment Inc., 1973
HIJACK! (TF)   co-composer with Allyn Ferguson, Spelling-Goldberg
   Productions, 1973
WHAT ARE BEST FRIENDS FOR? (TF)   co-composer with Allyn
   Ferguson, ABC Circle Films, 1973
GET CHRISTIE LOVE! (TF)   co-composer with Allyn Ferguson,
   David L. Wolper Productions, 1974
THE GIRL WHO CAME GIFT-WRAPPED (TF)   co-composer with
   Allyn Ferguson, Spelling-Goldberg Productions, 1974
ONLY WITH MARRIED MEN (TF)   co-composer with Allyn
   Ferguson, Spelling-Goldberg Productions, 1974
THE RED BADGE OF COURAGE (TF)   Norman Rosemont
   Productions/20th Century-Fox TV, 1974
ROLL, FREDDY, ROLL! (TF)   co-composer with Allyn Ferguson,
   ABC Circle Films, 1974
CHARLIE'S ANGELS (TF)   co-composer with Allyn Ferguson,
   Spelling-Goldberg Productions, 1976
DANGER IN PARADISE (TF)   co-composer with Allyn Ferguson,
   Filmways, 1977
THE MAGNIFICENT MAGICAL MAGNET OF SANTA MESA (TF)
   co-composer with Allyn Ferguson, David Gerber
   Productions/Columbia Pictures TV, 1977
DELTA COUNTY U.S.A. (TF)   co-composer with Allyn Ferguson,
   Leonard Goldberg Company/Paramount Pictures TV, 1977
OH, GOD!   Warner Bros., 1978
A GUIDE FOR THE MARRIED WOMAN (TF)   co-composer with
   Allyn Ferguson, 20th Century-Fox TV, 1978
SANCTUARY OF FEAR (TF)   co-composer with Allyn Ferguson,
   Marble Arch Productions, 1979
JUST YOU AND ME, KID   Columbia, 1979
THE JERK   Universal, 1979
THE SOLITARY MAN (TF)   John Conboy Productions, 1979
DON'T LOOK BACK (TF)   TBA Productions/Satie
   Productions/TRISEME, 1981
THE DAY THE BUBBLE BURST (TF)   Tamara Productions/20th
   Century-Fox TV/The Production Company, 1982
COMPUTERSIDE (TF)   co-composer with Allyn Ferguson, The
   Culzean Corporation/Paramount Pictures TV, 1982
FOUND MONEY (TF)   Cypress Point Productions/Warner Bros. TV,
   1983
SENTIMENTAL JOURNEY (TF)   Lucille Ball
   Productions/Smith-Richmond Productions/20th Century Fox TV,
   1984
SPIES, LIES AND NAKED THIES (TF)   Robert Halmi Productions,
   1988
SIBLING RIVALRY   Columbia, 1990

RICHARD ELLIOTT

Contact: BMI - Los Angeles, 310-659-9109

COVERUP: BEHIND THE IRAN CONTRA AFFAIR (FD)
   Empowerment Project, 1988
TEEN WITCH   Trans World Entertainment, 1989

RUTH ELLENELLSWORTH

DENISE CALLS UP   co-composer with Bill Carter, 1996

JEFF ELMASSIAN

Contact: BMI - Los Angeles, 310-659-9109

INSIDE MONKEY ZETTERLAND   co-composer with Rick Cox,
   Coast Entertainment, 1992

HOWARD WARRENELMER

b. October 10, 1963 in Seattle, WA
Contact: Tony Marando - New York, 212-645-7045

TIME FRAMES   Amidei Productions, 1988

KAHIL ELZABAR

HOW U LIKE ME NOW   co-composer with Chuck Webb,
   Shapiro-Glickenhaus, 1993

KEITH EMERSON

Agent: MCEG - Santa Monica, 310-315-7800
Affiliation: PRS - London, England, 011-44-1-580-5544

INFERNO   20th Century Fox, 1980
NIGHTHAWKS   Universal, 1981
BEST REVENGE   Lorimar Distribution International, 1983,
   Canadian
MURDEROCK, UCCIDE A PASSO DI DANZA   Scena Film, 1984,
   Italian

STEPHEN ENDELMAN*

Agent: Gorfaine-Schwartz - Los Angeles, 213-969-1011
Affiliation: ASCAP - Los Angeles, 213-883-1000

HOUSEHOLD SAINTS   Fine Line, 1993
A BRONX TALE   Savoy, 1993
IMAGINARY CRIMES   Warner Bros., 1994
POSTCARDS FROM AMERICA   Islet/Channel Four, 1994
THE DESPERATE TRAIL   Turner, 1994
THE ENGLISHMAN WHO WENT UP A HILL BUT CAME DOWN A
   MOUNTAIN   Miramax, 1995, British
THE DESPERATE TRAIL (CTF)   Motion Picture Corp. of
   America/Turner Network Television, 1995
ED   Universal, 1996
FLIRTING WITH DISASTER   Miramax, 1996
COSI   Miramax, 1997

MATTHEW ENDER

Contact: BMI - Los Angeles, 310-659-9109

STREETWALKIN'   co-composer with Doug Timm, Concorde, 1985
BREAKFAST OF ALIENS   co-composer with Haunted Garage, Eric
   Parkinson and Hemdale, 1993

JON A. ENGLISH

FRAMEUP   Complex, 1993

PAUL ENGLISH

THE MAN WITH THE PERFECT SWING   Hovis Films, 1995

CHARLES ENGSTROM

A FLASH OF GREEN   Spectrafilm, 1984
RUBY IN PARADISE   1993

BRIAN ENO

b. 1948
Agent: CAA - Beverly Hills, 310-288-4545
Affiliation: PRS - London, England, 011-44-1-580-5544

LAND OF THE MINOTAUR   THE DEVIL'S MEN   co-composer with
   Harold Budd, 1976, U.S.-British
EGON SCHIELE - EXCESS AND PUNISHMENT   Gamma Film,
   1981, West German
DUNE   additional music, Universal, 1984
FOR ALL MANKIND (FD)   Apollo Associates, 1989
GLITTERBUG   1994, British
SLING BLADE   Miramax, 1996

FILM COMPOSERS

ROGER ENO
Agent: Music for Films - London, 011-44-71-278-4288
Affiliation: PRS - London, England, 011-44-1-580-5544

WARM SUMMER RAIN   Trans World Entertainment, 1989

MICKEY ERBE
Contact: SOCAN - Toronto, 416-445-8700

THE WOMEN OF WINDSOR (TF)   co-composer with Marybeth
    Solomon, Sharmhill/Samuels/World International Network, 1992
TRIAL AND ERROR (CTF)   co-composer with Marybeth Solomon,
    Alliance/USA, 1993
SHATTERED TRUST: THE SHARI KARNEY STORY (TF)
    co-composer with Marybeth Solomon, Heartstar
    Prods./Spectacor/Michael Jaffe Films, 1993
I KNOW MY SON IS ALIVE (TF)   co-composer with Marybeth
    Solomon, Alexander-Enright & Associates/WIN, 1994
TO SAVE THE CHILDREN (TF)   co-composer with Marybeth
    Solomon, Children's Films/Westcom Ent./Kushner-Locke, 1994
AGAINST HER WILL: THE CARRIE BULK STORY (CTF)
    co-composer with Marybeth Solomon, Janet Faust Krusi
    Prods./Viacom, 1994
FRIENDS AT LAST (TF)   co-composer with Maribeth Solomon,
    Procter & Gamble/Tele Vest/Atlantis/Stewart
    Pictures/Columbia-TriStar TV, 1995
LADY KILLER (TF)   co-composer with Maribeth Solomon,
    Kushner-Locke/CBS Entertainment, 1995
DANCING IN THE DARK (CTF)   co-composer with Maribeth
    Solomon, Power Pictures-Dream City Films/Hearst, 1995

SEBASTIEN ERMS
CONTE D'HIVER   *A WINTER'S TALE*   1992, French
L'ARBRE, LE MAIRE ET LA MEDIATHEQUE   *THE TREE, THE
    MAYOR AND THE MEDIATHEQUE*   1993, French

JIM ERVIN
ACAPULCO H.E.A.T. (TF)   co-composer with Michael Lloyd and
    Tommy Oliver, Keller & Keller/Balenciaga/All-American, 1993
LET IT BE ME   arranger, Rysher, 1997

LEE ERWIN
Contact: ASCAP - Los Angeles, 213-883-1000

THE MAN WITHOUT A WORLD   co-composer with Charles
    Morrow, Milestone, 1992

JACK ESKEW
Contact: ASCAP - Los Angeles, 213-883-1000

SUPERCARRIER (TF)   co-composer with Bill Conti, Real Tinsel
    Productions/Fries Entertainment, 1987

DAVID ESSEX
Contact: PRS - London, England, 011-44-1-580-5544

SILVER DREAM RACER   Rank, 1980, British

PASCAL ESTEVE
THE SCENT OF YVONNE   *LE PARFUM D'YVONNE*   1994,
    French

BOB ESTY
Contact: BMI - Los Angeles, 310-659-9109

ROLLER BOOGIE   United Artists, 1980
YOU CAN'T HURRY LOVE   Lightning Pictures, 1988

MELISSA ETHERIDGE
IT WAS A WONDERFUL LIFE (FD)   Cinewomen, 1993

ALAN ETT
Contact: BMI - Los Angeles, 310-659-9109

ANGEL III: THE FINAL CHAPTER   additional music, New World,
    1988

EURYTHMICS
Contact: PRS - London, England, 011-44-1-580-5544

1984   co-composers with Dominic Muldowney, Atlantic Releasing
    Corporation, 1984, British

GREG EVIGAN
Contact: BMI - Los Angeles, 310-659-9109

PRIVATE ROAD   *NO TRESPASSING*   Trans World Entertainment,
    1987

DONALD FAGEN
Contact: ASCAP - Los Angeles, 213-883-1000

BRIGHT LIGHTS, BIG CITY   MGM/UA, 1988

JEFF FAIR
SHAME II: THE SECRET (CTF)   co-composer with Starr Parodi,
    Viacom/Lifetime TV, 1995

GARY FALCONE
Contact: BMI - Los Angeles, 310-659-9109

NINJA TURF   co-composer with Charles Pavlosky and Chris Stone,
    Ascot Entertainment Group, 1986

HAROLD FALTERMEYER
Contact: ASCAP - Los Angeles, 213-883-1000

THIEF OF HEARTS   Paramount, 1984
BEVERLY HILLS COP   Paramount, 1984
FLETCH   Universal, 1985
TOP GUN   Paramount, 1986
FIRE AND ICE   co-composer, Concorde, 1987
FATAL BEAUTY   MGM/UA, 1987
BEVERLY HILLS COP II   Paramount, 1987
THE RUNNING MAN   Tri-Star, 1987
FLETCH LIVES   Universal, 1989
TANGO & CASH   Warner Bros., 1989
KUFFS   Universal, 1992

MO FAN
GE LAO YE ZI   *OLD MAN GE*   1993, Chinese

DAVID FANSHAWE
Contact: PRS - London, England, 011-44-1-580-5544

THREE MEN IN A BOAT (TF)   BBC, 1975, British
REQUIEM FOR A VILLAGE (FD)   British Film Institute, 1976
HERE ARE LADIES (FD)   Arthur Cantor Films, 1983, Irish
DIRTY WEEKEND   1993, British

USTAD ZIA FARIDUDDIN
EROTIC TALES   composer of one segment, 1994, German

JIM FARMER
Contact: ASCAP - Los Angeles, 213-883-1000

JOHNNY SUEDE   Mainstream, 1991
LIVING IN OBLIVION   JDI & Lemon Sky Prods., 1995

BRAUN FARNON
Contact: SOCAN - Toronto, 416-445-8700

XTRO II   co-composer with Robert Smart, 1991

DENNIS FARNON
ARRIVEDERCI, BABY! *DROP DEAD, DARLING*   Paramount,
   1966, British

ROBERT FARNON
Contact: PRS - London, England, 011-44-1-580-5544

JUST WILLIAM'S LUCK   United Artists, 1947, British
CAPTAIN HORATIO HORNBLOWER   Warner Bros., 1951, British
GENTLEMEN MARRY BRUNETTES   United Artists, 1955
LET'S MAKE UP *LILACS IN THE SPRING*   Republic, 1954,
   British
THE LITTLE HUT   MGM, 1957, British
THE SHERIFF OF FRACTURED JAW   20th Century-Fox, 1959,
   British
EXPRESSO BONGO   co-composer with Norrie Paramor,
   Continental, 1960, British
THE ROAD TO HONG KONG   United Artists, 1962
THE TRUTH ABOUT SPRING   Universal, 1965, British-U.S.
SHALAKO   Dimitri De Grunwald, 1968
COLDITZ (TF)   British
A MAN CALLED INTREPID (MS)   Lorimar Productions/Astral
   Bellevue Pathe/CTV Network, 1979, British-Canadian
MARY AND JOSEPH: A STORY OF FAITH (TF)   Astral
   Films/Lorimar Productions, 1979

ROBERT FARRAR
DON'T LOOK IN THE BASEMENT   Hallmark, 1973

CHRISTOPHER FARRELL*
Contact: BMI - Los Angeles, 310-659-9109

DOUBLE THREAT   Pyramid, 1992
MARDI GRAS FOR THE DEVIL   Pyramid, 1993
WARLORD 3000   Cinema Studio Corporation, 1993

BARRY FASMAN
Contact: ASCAP - Los Angeles, 213-883-1000

DEAD RINGER   co-composer with Dana Walden, Stock Grange
   Productions, 1988
MY MOM'S A WEREWOLF   co-composer with Dana Walden,
   Crown International, 1988
THE IMMORTALIZER   co-composer with Dana Walden, Filmwest
   Productions, 1989
WHISPERS   co-composer with Dana Walden, Distant Horizon,
   1989
YOUR MOTHER WEARS COMBAT BOOTS (TF)   co-composer
   with Jeff Barry, NBC Productions, 1989
HELLGATE   co-composer with Dana Walden, New World, 1989
RICH GIRL   co-composer with Dana Walden, Filmwest
   Productions, 1989
STREET HUNTER   co-composer with Dana Walden, 21st Century,
   1989
NIGHT CLUB   co-composer with Dana Walden, Crown
   International, 1990

LARRY FAST
Contact: ASCAP - Los Angeles, 213-883-1000

JUPITER MENACE   1982

RICKY FATAAR
Contact: APRA - Australia, 011-61-2-922-6422

HIGH TIDE   co-composer with Mark Moffiatt, Hemdale, 1987,
   Australian

LOUIS FEBRE
Agent: Gorfaine-Schwartz - Los Angeles, 213-969-1011
Affiliation: BMI - Los Angeles, 310-659-9109

A TIME TO DIE   PM Entertainment, 1991
C.I.A. II: TARGET ALEXA   PM, 1993
L.A. WARS   American Cinema, 1993
LAST MAN STANDING   PM Entertainment, 1995

JESSE FEDERICK
Contact: ASCAP - Los Angeles, 213-883-1000

ALOHA SUMMER   Spectrafilm, 1988

DON FELDER
Contact: ASCAP - Los Angeles, 213-883-1000

FLESHBURN   additional music, Crown International, 1984
BLUE De VILLE (TF)   B & E Enterprises Ltd./NBC Productions,
   1986

RICHARD FELDMAN
BOCA   co-composer with Midge Ure and Adam Gargoni, 1994,
   U.S.-Brazilian

ERIC FENBY
b. 1906 - Scarborough, England
Contact: PRS - London, England, 011-44-1-580-5544

JAMAICA INN   Paramount, 1939, British

GUO FENG
DAIHAO 'MEIZHOUBAO'   *CODE NAME 'COUGAR' /OPERATION
'COUGAR'/MEIZHOUBAO XINGDONG*   1988, Chinese

RICK FENN
Contact: PRS - London, England, 011-44-1-580-5544

WHITE OF THE EYE   co-composer with Nick Mason, Palisades
   Entertainment, 1988

GEORGE FENTON
Agent: The Ryan Company - Sherman Oaks, 818-981-4111
Affiliation: PRS - London, England, 011-44-1-580-5544

HUSSY   Watchgrove Ltd., 1980, British
PAROLE (TF)   Parole Production Company/Robert Stigwood
   Organization, 1982
GANDHI ★   co-composer with Ravi Shankar, Columbia, 1982,
   British-Indian
RUNNERS   Goldcrest Films & TV, 1983, British
AN ENGLISHMAN ABROAD (TF)   BBC, 1983, British
SAIGON - YEAR OF THE CAT (TF)   Thames TV, 1983, British
THE COMPANY OF WOLVES   Cannon, 1984, British
THE JEWEL IN THE CROWN (MS)   Granada TV, 1984, British
CLOCKWISE   Universal, 1986, British
LOVING WALTER (TF)   Central TV Productions, 1986, British
EAST OF IPSWITCH (TF)   BBC, 1986, British
WHITE OF THE EYE   Palisades Entertainment, 1987, British
84 CHARING CROSS ROAD   Columbia, 1987, British
CRY FREEDOM ★   co-composer with Jonas Gwangwa, Universal,
   1987, British-U.S.
HIGH SPIRITS   Tri-Star, 1988, British
THE DRESSMAKER   Euro-American, 1988, British
A HANDFUL OF DUST   New Line Cinema, 1988, British
WHITE MISCHIEF   Columbia, 1987, British
DANGEROUS LIASONS ★   Warner Bros., 1988
WE'RE NO ANGELS   Paramount, 1989
MEMPHIS BELLE   Warner Bros., 1990
WHITE PALACE   Universal, 1990
THE TRIALS OF LIFE (TD)   BBC/Australian Broadcasting Co./TBS,
   1991
THE FISHER KING ★   TriStar, 1991
FINAL ANALYSIS   Warner Bros., 1992
HERO   Columbia, 1992
GROUNHOG DAY   Columbia, 1993
BORN YESTERDAY   Buena Vista, 1993

SHADOWLANDS   Savoy, 1993
CHINA MOON   Orion, 1994
LADYBIRD LADYBIRD   1994, British
CHINA: BEYOND THE CLOUDS (TD)   River Film Prods./Channel 4
   TV/Canal Plus, 1994
THE MADNESS OF KING GEORGE   adaptations, Samuel
   Goldwyn, 1994, British
MIXED NUTS   TriStar, 1994
LAND AND FREEDOM   1995, British-Spanish-German
THE FALL OF SAIGON (CTD)   Barraclough Carey, 1995
MARIETTE IN ECSTASY   Savoy, 1995
MARY REILLY   TriStar, 1996
HEAVEN'S PRISONERS   Savoy, 1996
MULTIPLICITY   Columbia, 1996
THE CRUCIBLE   20th Century Fox, 1996
IN LOVE AND WAR   New Line, 1996

ALLYN FERGUSON

b. October 18, 1924 - San Jose, California
Agent: Carol Faith Agency - Beverly Hills, 310-274-0776
Affiliation: BMI - Los Angeles, 310-659-9109

THE FEMINIST AND THE FUZZ (TF)   co-composer with Jack Elliot,
   Screen Gems/Columbia TV, 1971
SUPPORT YOUR LOCAL GUNFIGHTER   United Artists, 1971
EVERY MAN NEEDS ONE (TF)   co-composer with Jack Elliot,
   Spelling-Goldberg Productions/ABC Circle Films, 1972
PLAYMATES (TF)   co-composer with Jack Elliot, ABC Circle Films,
   1972
JARRETT (TF)   co-composer with Jack Elliot, Screen
   Gems/Columbia TV, 1973
THE BAIT (TF)   co-composer with Jack Elliot, Spelling-Goldberg
   Productions/ABC Circle Films, 1973
THE MAN WITHOUT A COUNTRY (TF)   co-composer with Jack
   Elliot, Norman Rosemont Productions, 1973
BIRDS OF PREY (TF)   co-composer with Jack Elliot, Tomorrow
   Entertainment Inc., 1973
HIJACK! (TF)   co-composer with Jack Elliot, Spelling-Goldberg
   Productions, 1973
WHAT ARE BEST FRIENDS FOR? (TF)   co-composer with Jack
   Elliot, ABC Circle Films, 1973
GET CHRISTIE LOVE! (TF)   co-composer with Jack Elliot, David L.
   Wolper Productions, 1974
THE GIRL WHO CAME GIFT-WRAPPED (TF)   co-composer with
   Jack Elliot, Spelling-Goldberg Productions, 1974
ONLY WITH MARRIED MEN (TF)   co-composer with Jack Elliot,
   Spelling-Goldberg Productions, 1974
RED FLAG: THE ULTIMATE GAME (TF)   Marble Arch Productions,
   1974
ROLL, FREDDY, ROLL! (TF)   co-composer with Jack Elliot, ABC
   Circle Films, 1974
THE COUNT OF MONTE CRISTO (TF)   Norman Rosemont
   Productions/ITC, 1975, U.S.-British
CHARLIE'S ANGELS (TF)   co-composer with Jack Elliot,
   Spelling-Goldberg Productions, 1976
CAPTAINS COURAGEOUS (TF)   Norman Rosemont Productions,
   1977
DANGER IN PARADISE (TF)   co-composer with Jack Elliot,
   Filmways, 1977
THE MAGNIFICENT MAGICAL MAGNET OF SANTA MESA (TF)
   co-composer with Jack Elliot, David Gerber Productions/Columbia
   Pictures TV, 1977
DELTA COUNTY U.S.A. (TF)   co-composer with Jack Elliot,
   Leonard Goldberg Productions/Paramount Pictures TV, 1977
THE MAN IN THE IRON MASK (TF)   Norman Rosemont
   Productions/ITC, 1977, U.S.-British
THE FOUR FEATHERS (TF)   Norman Rosemont
   Productions/Trident Films Ltd., 1978, U.S.-British
LES MISERABLES (TF)   Norman Rosemont Productions/ITV
   Entertainment, 1978
A GUIDE FOR THE MARRIED WOMAN (TF)   co-composer with
   Jack Elliot, 20th Century-Fox TV, 1978
SANCTUARY OF FEAR (TF)   co-composer with Jack Elliot, Marble
   Arch Productions, 1979
AVALANCHE EXPRESS   20th Century-Fox, 1979
ALL QUIET ON THE WESTERN FRONT (TF)   Norman Rosemont
   Productions/Marble Arch Productions, 1979
LITTLE LORD FAUNTLEROY (TF)   Norman Rosemont Productions,
   1980, U.S.-British
A TALE OF TWO CITIES (TF)   Norman Rosemont
   Productions/Marble Arch Productions, 1980, U.S.-British

THE GOSSIP COLUMNIST (TF)   Universal TV, 1980
CRY OF THE INNOCENT (TF)   Tara Productions, 1980
BEULAH LAND (TF)   David Gerber Company/Columbia TV, 1980
PLEASURE PALACE (TF)   Norman Rosemont Productions/Marble
   Arch Productions, 1980
TERROR AMONG US (TF)   David Gerber Productions, 1981
THE RED FLAG: THE ULTIMATE GAME (TF)   Marble Arch
   Productions, 1981
PETER AND PAUL (TF)   Universal TV/Procter & Gamble
   Productions, 1981
ELVIS AND THE BEAUTY QUEEN (TF)   David Gerber
   Company/Columbia TV, 1981
IVANHOE (TF) ☆   Rosemont Productions, 1982, British-U.S.
COMPUTERSIDE (TF)   co-composer with Jack Elliot, The Culzean
   Corporation/Paramount Pictures TV, 1982
MASTER OF THE GAME (MS) ☆   Rosemont Productions, 1984
CAMILLE (TF) ☆☆   Rosemont Productions, 1984, U.S.-British
ROMANCE ON THE ORIENT EXPRESS (TF)   Frank von Zerneck
   Productions/Yorkshire TV, 1985, U.S.-British
THE CORSICAN BROTHERS (TF)   Rosemont Productions, 1985,
   British-U.S.
THE LAST DAYS OF PATTON (TF) ☆   Entertainment Partners,
   1986
THE CHRISTMAS GIFT (TF)   Rosemont Productions/Sunn Classic
   Pictures, 1986
ANGEL IN GREEN (TF)   Aligre Productions/Taft Hardy Group,
   1987, U.S.-New Zealand
STONE FOX (TF)   co-composer with Peter Matz, Hanna-Barbera
   Productions/Allarcom Ltd./Taft Entertainment TV, 1987,
   U.S.-Canadian
THE WOMAN HE LOVED (TF)   The Larry Thompson
   Organization/HTV/New World TV, 1988, U.S.-British
APRIL MORNING (TF) ☆   Robert Halmi, Inc./Samuel Goldwyn TV,
   1988
PANCHO BARNES (TF) ☆   Blue Andre Productions/Orion TV,
   1988
IRONCLADS (CTF)   Rosemont, 1991
SHADOW OF A DOUBT (TF)   Rosemont, 1991
FERGIE AND ANDREW: BEHIND THE PALACE DOORS (TF)
   Rosemont, 1992
LOVE, HONOR & OBEY: THE LAST MAFIA MARRIAGE (TF)   CBS,
   1993

DAVID FERGUSON

Agent: Music For Films - London 011-44-71-278-4288

TAILSPIN: BEHIND THE KOREAN AIRLINE TRAGEDY (CTF)
   Darlow Smithson Productions/HBO, 1989
DEAD AHEAD: THE EXXON VALDEZ DISASTER (CTF)   HBO
   Showcase/BBC, 1992
CRACKER: TO BE A SOMEBODY (CTF)   Granada TV/A&E, 1995,
   British-U.S.
A DARK ADAPTED EYE (TF)   BBC, 1995, British

JAY FERGUSON

Agent: Vangelos Management - Encino, 818-380-1919
Affiliation: BMI - Los Angeles, 310-659-9109

DEATH OF AN ANGEL   20th Century-Fox, 1985
THE PATRIOT   Crown International, 1986
QUIET COOL   New Line Cinema, 1986
BEST SELLER   Orion, 1987
PULSE   Columbia, 1988
JOHNNY BE GOOD   Orion, 1988
BAD DREAMS   20th Century Fox, 1988
LICENSE TO DRIVE   20th Century Fox, 1988
AMERICAN BUILT   Midwood Productions, 1989
GLEAMING THE CUBE   20th Century Fox, 1989
A NIGHTMARE ON ELM STREET 5: THE DREAM CHILD   New
   Line Cinema, 1989
RACE FOR GLORY   New Century/Vista, 1989
PARKER KANE (TF)   Orion TV, 1990
NERVOUS TICKS   I.R.S., 1992
MELROSE PLACE (TF)   Darren Star Prods./Spelling, 1992
GOING TO EXTREMES (TF)   Brand-Falsey, 1992
DOUBLE DRAGON   Gramercy, 1994
TREMORS II: AFTERSHOCK   Universal, 1996
DRIVEN   Paramount, 1996

RUSSELL FERRANTE

Contact: BMI - Los Angeles, 310-659-9109

WIRED TO KILL   American Distribution Group, 1986

PAUL FERRIS

Contact: PRS - London, England, 011-44-1-580-5544

THE SORCERERS   1967, British
THE CONQUEROR WORM   *THE WITCHFINDER GENERAL*
   American International, 1968, British
THE VAMPIRE BEAST CRAVES BLOOD   1969, British
THE CREEPING FLESH   Columbia, 1973, British
THE TERROR OF SHEBA   *PERSECUTION*   Blueberry Hill, 1974,
   British

BRAD FIEDEL*

Agent: Gorfaine-Schwartz - Los Angeles, 213-969-1011
Affiliation: ASCAP - Los Angeles, 213-883-1000

APPLE PIE   Aumont Productions, 1975
DEADLY HERO   co-composer with Tommy Mandel, Avco
   Embassy, 1976
LOOKING UP   Levitt-Pickman, 1977
MAYFLOWER: THE PILGRIM'S ADVENTURE (TF)   Syzygy
   Productions, 1979
HARDHAT AND LEGS (TF)   Syzygy Productions, 1980
THE DAY THE WOMEN GOT EVEN (TF)   Otto Salamon
   Productions/PKO Television Ltd., 1980
PLAYING FOR TIME (TF)   Syzygy Productions, 1980
THE BUNKER (TF)   Time-Life Productions/SFP France/Antenne-2,
   1981, U.S.-French
PEOPLE VS. JEAN HARRIS (TF)   PKO TV Ltd., 1981
JUST BEFORE DAWN   Picturmedia Limited, 1981
NIGHT SCHOOL   *TERROR EYES*   Paramount, 1981
DREAM HOUSE (TF)   Hill-Mandelker Productions/Time-Life
   Productions, 1981
HIT AND RUN   Comworld, 1982
MAE WEST (TF)   Hill-Mandelker Productions, 1982
DREAMS DON'T DIE (TF)   Hill-Mandelker Productions, 1982
BORN BEAUTIFUL (TF)   Procter & Gamble Productions/Telecom
   Entertainment, 1982
MURDER IN COWETA COUNTY (TF)   Telecom
   Entertainment/International Picture Show Company, 1983
COCAINE: ONE MAN'S SEDUCTION (TF)   Charles Fries
   Productions/David Goldsmith Productions, 1983
RIGHT OF WAY (CTF)   HBO Premiere Films, Schaefer-Karpf
   Productions/Post-Newsweek Video, 1983
JACOBO TIMERMAN: PRISONER WITHOUT A NAME, CELL
   WITHOUT A NUMBER   Chrysalis-Yellen Productions, 1983
GIRLS OF THE WHITE ORCHID   *DEATH RIDE TO OSAKA* (TF)
   Hill-Mandelker Productions, 1983
HEART OF STEEL (TF)   Beowulf Productions, 1983
WHEN SHE SAYS NO (TF)   I&C Productions, 1984
MY MOTHER'S SECRET LIFE (TF)   Furia-Oringer Productions/ABC
   Circle Films, 1984
ANATOMY OF AN ILLNESS (TF)   Hamner Productions/Jerry
   Gershwin Productions/CBS Entertainment, 1984
CALENDAR GIRL MURDERS (TF)   Tisch-Avnet Productions, 1984
EYES OF FIRE   Elysian Pictures, 1984
THE TERMINATOR   Orion, 1984
THE BARON AND THE KID (TF)   Telecom Entertainment, 1984
THE THREE WISHES OF BILLY GRIER (TF)   I&C Productions,
   1984
CHILDREN IN THE CROSSFIRE (TF)   Schaefer-Karpf
   Productions/Prendergast-Brittcadia Productions, 1984
DEADLY MESSAGES (TF)   Columbia Pictures TV, 1985
FRATERNITY VACATION   New World, 1985
COMPROMISING POSITIONS   Paramount, 1985
BRAKER (TF)   Blatt-Singer Productions/Centerpoint
   Productions/MGM/UA TV, 1985
FRIGHT NIGHT   Columbia, 1985
INTO THIN AIR (TF)   Major H Productions/Tony Ganz Productions,
   1985
THE MIDNIGHT HOUR (TF)   ABC Circle Films, 1985
UNDER SIEGE (TF)   Ohlmeyer Communications Co./Telepictures
   Productions, 1986
SECOND SERVE (TF)   Linda Yellen
   Productions/Lorimar-Telepictures, 1986
DESERT BLOOM   Columbia, 1986

A FIGHTING CHOICE (TF)   Walt Disney Pictures, 1986
BROTHERHOOD OF JUSTICE (TF)   Guber-Peters Entertainment
   Co. Productions/Phoenix Entertainment Group, 1986
NORTHSTAR (TF)   Daniel Grodnick Productions/Warner Bros. TV,
   1986
POPEYE DOYLE (TF)   December 3rd Productions/20th
   Century-Fox TV, 1986
LET'S GET HARRY   Trl-Star, 1986
OF PURE BLOOD (TF)   K-M Productions/Joseph Sargent
   Productions/Warner Bros. TV, 1986
SUNDAY DRIVE (TF)   Wizan TV Enterprises/Walt Disney TV, 1986
THE BIG EASY   Columbia, 1987
THE LAST INNOCENT MAN (CTF)   HBO Pictures/Maurice Singer
   Productions, 1987
BLUFFING IT (TF)   Don Ohlmeyer Productions, 1987
NOWHERE TO HIDE   New Century/Vista, 1987, U.S.-Canadian
RIGHT TO DIE (TF)   Ohlmeyer Communications, 1987
WEEKEND WAR (TF)   Pompian/Columbia Pictures TV, 1988
HOSTAGE (TF)   CBS Entertainment, 1988
THE SERPENT AND THE RAINBOW   Universal, 1988
HOT PAINT (TF)   Catalina Production Group, 1988
THE ACCUSED   Paramount, 1988
FRIGHT NIGHT PART 2   New Century/Vista, 1989
TRUE BELIEVER   Columbia, 1989
COLD SASSY TREE (CTF)   Faye Dunaway Productions/Ohlmeyer
   Productions, 1989
PERFECT WITNESS (CTF)   HBO Pictures/Granger Productions,
   1989
IMMEDIATE FAMILY   Columbia, 1989
BLUE STEEL   MGM/UA, 1990
PLYMOUTH (TF)   Touchstone TV/RAI-Uno/Zlotoff Inc., 1991
BLOOD TIES (TF)   Shapiro Entertainment, 1991
TERMINATOR 2: JUDGEMENT DAY   Tri-Star, 1991
GLADIATOR   Columbia, 1992
STRAIGHT TALK   Buena Vista, 1992
TEAMSTER BOSS: THE JACKIE PRESSER STORY (CTF)
   HBO/Abby Mann Prods., 1992
REASONABLE DOUBTS: FOREVER MY LOVE (TF)   theme only,
   Lorimar, 1992
THE REAL McCOY   Universal, 1993
STRIKING DISTANCE   Columbia, 1993
BLINK   New Line, 1994
TRUE LIES   20th Century Fox, 1994
JOHNNY MNEMONIC   TriStar, 1995, Canadian

ERNIE FIELDS

Contact: BMI - Los Angeles, 310-659-9109

DISCO GODFATHER   1980

MIKE FIGGIS

Contact: PRS - London, England, 011-44-1-580-5544

STORMY MONDAY   Atlantic Releasing Corporation, 1988, British
INTERNAL AFFAIRS   co-composer with Anthony Marinelli and
   Brian Banks, Paramount, 1990
LIEBESTRAUM   MGM-UA, 1991
LEAVING LAS VEGAS   MGM-UA, 1995

DAVID FINDLAY
DEAD INNOCENT   Blackwatch Communications, 1997
CAPTIVE   Blackwatch Communications, 1997

RICHARD FIOCCA
BEFORE YOUR EYES: A HEART FOR OLIVIA (TD)   CBS News,
   1995
ONE SURVIVOR REMEMBERS (TD)   HBO, 1995

IRWIN FISCH

Contact: ASCAP - Los Angeles, 213-883-1000

SPEARFIELD'S DAUGHTER (MS)   Robert Halmi, Inc/Channel
   Seven, 1986, U.S.-Australian

GUENTHER FISCHER

Contact: GEMA - Germany, 011-49-89-480-03610

THE FLIGHT   1978, East German

OTTOKAR, THE WORLD REFORMER   1978, East German
JUST A GIGOLO   United Artists Classics, 1979, West German
DER AUFENTHALT   DEFA, East German
MAERKISCHE FORSCHUNGEN   DEFA, 1983, East German
DER STEINERNE FLUSS   *THE STONE RIVER*   1983, West German
DER KINOERZAEHLER   *THE MOVIE TELLER*   1993, German

LUBOS FISER
Contact: OSA - Tr. Cs. Armady 20, 160-56 Prague 6-Bubene, Czechoslovakia

LABYRINTH   1992, German

PETER FISH
Contact: ASCAP - Los Angeles, 213-883-1000

PAINTING THE TOWN (FD)   Padded Cell, 1992
WIGSTOCK: THE MOVIE (FD)   co-composer with Robert Reale, Samuel Goldwyn, 1995

FISHBONE
TAPEHEADS   DEG, 1988

CLARE FISHER
Contact: BMI - Los Angeles, 310-659-9109

UNDER THE CHERRY MOON   Warner Bros., 1986

ROBERT MORGAN FISHER
PHILOSOPHY IN THE BEDROOM   Filmhaus, 1995

TOBY FITCH
HOTEL OKLAHOMA   European American, 1991

FRANK FITZPATRICK*
Agent: The Kordek Agency - Bunbank, 818-559-4248
Affiliation: ASCAP - Los Angeles, 213-883-1000

MARTIANS GO HOME   co-composer of end title with Allan Zavod, Orion, 1989
HER ALIBI   co-composer of end title with Georges Delerue, Warner Bros., 1990
NUNS ON THE RUN   20th Century Fox, 1990
HIGHWAY TO HELL   Hemdale, 1992
BREAKING THE RULES   song score (instrumental score by David Kitay), Miramax, 1992
FRIDAY   New Line, 1995
UNDER THE HULA MOON   Trident, 1996

ROBERT FITZSIMMONS
PEARL HARBOR - SURPRISE AND REMEMBERANCE (TD)   Tom Johnson, Lance Bird and John Crowley, 1991

VIC FLICK
Contact: ASCAP - Los Angeles, 213-883-1000

HULLABALOO OVER GEORGIE AND BONNIE'S PICTURES   Corinth, 1979

BOB FLOKE
STITCHES   International Film Marketing, 1985

DAN FOLIART*
Agent: Film Music Associates - Hollywood, 213-463-1070
Affiliation: ASCAP - Los Angeles, 213-883-1000

THE ONLY WAY HOME   Regional, 1972
RETURN TO GREEN ACRES (TF)   Jaygoe Productions/Orion TV, 1990
NOT OUR SON (TF)   Multimedia, 1995

ROBERT FOLK
Agent: Vangelos Management - Encino, 818-380-1919
Affiliation: ASCAP - Los Angeles, 213-883-1000

SAVAGE HARVEST   20th Century-Fox, 1981
THE SLAYER   21st Century Distribution, 1982
PURPLE HEARTS   The Ladd Company/Warner Bros., 1984
BACHELOR PARTY   20th Century Fox, 1984
POLICE ACADEMY   The Ladd Company/Warner Bros., 1984
THUNDER ALLEY   Cannon, 1985
POLICE ACADEMY 2: THEIR FIRST ASSIGNMENT   Warner Bros., 1985
PRINCE OF BEL-AIR (TF)   Leonard Hill Films, 1986
STEWARDESS SCHOOL   Columbia, 1986
POLICE ACADEMY 3: BACK IN TRAINING   Warner Bros., 1986
ODD JOBS   Tri-Star, 1986
COMBAT HIGH (TF)   Frank & Julie Films/Frank Von Zerneck Productions/Lynch-Biller Productions, 1986
THE ROOM UPSTAIRS (TF)   Marian Rees Associates/The Alexander Group Productions, 1987
CAN'T BUY ME LOVE   Buena Vista, 1987
POLICE ACADEMY 4: CITIZENS ON PATROL   Warner Bros., 1987
HIGH MOUNTAIN RANGERS (TF)   Shane Productions, 1987
MILES FROM HOME   Cinecom, 1988
POLICE ACADEMY 5: ASSIGNMENT MIAMI BEACH   Warner Bros., 1988
GLORY DAYS (TF)   A. Shane Company/Sibling Rivalries, 1988
POLICE ACADEMY 6: CITY UNDER SIEGE   Warner Bros., 1989
WICKED STEPMOTHER   MGM/UA, 1989
JESSE HAWKS (TF)   A. Shane Co., 1989
A CLIMATE FOR KILLING   Propaganda, 1990
TREMORS   Universal, 1990
HONEYMOON ACADEMY   Triumph, 1990
HAPPY TOGETHER   Borde Releasing Corporation, 1990
THE NEVERENDING STORY II: THE NEXT CHAPTER   Warner Bros., 1990
A ROW OF CROWS   Propaganda, 1991
TOY SOLDIERS   Tri-Star, 1991
BEASTMASTER 2: THROUGH THE PORTAL OF TIME   New Line, 1991
ROCK-A-DOODLE (AF)   Samuel Golwyn, 1992
NATIONAL LAMPOON'S LOADED WEAPON 1   New Line, 1993
SHADOW HUNTER (CTF)   Republic/Sandstorm, 1993
SWORN TO VENGEANCE (TF)   A. Shane Co./RHI Entertainment, 1993
STATE OF EMERGENCY (CTF)   Chestnut Hill Prods., 1994
SEARCH AND RESCUE (TF)   Black Sheep Prods./NBC, 1994
POLICE ACADEMY: MISSION TO MOSCOW   Warner Bros., 1994
IN THE ARMY NOW   Buena Vista, 1994
A TROLL IN CENTRAL PARK (AF)   Warner Bros., 1994
TRAPPED IN PARADISE   20th Century Fox, 1994
MAXIMUM RISK   Columbia, 1996
LAWMOWER MAN 2: BEYOND CYBERSPACE   New Line, 1996
THEODORE REX   New Line, 1996
NOTHING TO LOSE   Buena Vista, 1997
BOOTY CALL   1997

RUSSELL FORANTE
WIRED TO KILL   American Distribution Group, 1986

ROY FORBES
BLOCKADE (FD)   Canada Wild Prods., 1993, Canadian

MITCHEL FORMAN
Contact: ASCAP - Los Angeles, 213-883-1000

JEZEBEL'S KISS   Shapiro-Glickenhaus, 1990

GREG FORREST
Contact: BMI - Los Angeles, 310-659-9109

CRYSTAL EYES   1981

KEITH FORSEY
Contact: ASCAP - Los Angeles, 213-883-1000

THE BREAKFAST CLUB   1984, Universal

IVANO FOSSATI

Contact: SIAE - Italy, 011-39-6-59-901

THE BULL IL TORO 1994, Italian

PETER HOWARD FOSSO

Contact: BMI - Los Angeles, 310-659-9109

SHIRTLESS SOUL Bergersen Films, 1992

DAVID FOSTER*

Contact: BMI - Los Angeles, 310-659-9109

ST. ELMO'S FIRE Columbia, 1985
THE SECRET OF MY SUCCESS Universal, 1987
STEALING HOME Warner Bros., 1988
FRESH HORSES co-composer with Patrick Williams,
 Columbia/WEG, 1988
LISTEN TO ME Columbia, 1989
IF LOOKS COULD KILL Warner Bros., 1991
ONE GOOD COP co-composer with William Ross, Hollywood,
 1991
GOLDEN FIDDLES (MS) co-composer with William Ross, 1991
THE BODYGUARD cameo as Oscar conductor, Warner Bros.,
 1992

JEAN-PIERRE FOUQUEY

LOUIS, ENFANT ROI LOUIS THE CHILD KING 1993, French

CHARLES FOX

Agent: Marks Management - Tarzana, 818-776-8787
Contact: BMI - Los Angeles, 310-659-9109

THE INCIDENT 20th Century Fox, 1967
BARBARELLA co-composer with Bob Crewe, Paramount, 1968,
 Italian-French
GOODBYE COLUMBUS Paramount, 1969
PUFNSTUFF Universal, 1970
STAR-SPANGLED GIRL Paramount, 1971
A SEPARATE PEACE Paramount, 1972
THE LAST AMERICAN HERO 20th Century Fox, 1973
DYING ROOM ONLY (TF) Lorimar Productions, 1973
THE LAUGHING POLICEMAN 20th Century Fox, 1973
ALOHA MEANS GOODBYE Universal TV, 1974
THE STRANGER WITHIN (TF) Lorimar Productions, 1974
THE DROWNING POOL co-composer with Michael Small, Warner
 Bros., 1975
THE OTHER SIDE OF THE MOUNTAIN Universal, 1975
BUG Paramount, 1975
THE DUCHESS AND THE DIRTWATER FOX 20th Century Fox,
 1976
TWO-MINUTE WARNING Universal, 1976
ONE ON ONE Warner Bros., 1977
FOUL PLAY Paramount, 1978
RAINBOW (TF) Ten-Four Productions, 1978
OUR WINNING SEASON American International, 1978
BETTER LATE THAN NEVER (TF) Ten-Four Productions, 1979
THE LAST MARRIED COUPLE IN AMERICA Universal, 1980
LITTLE DARLINGS Paramount, 1980
WHY WOULD I LIE? MGM/United Artists, 1980
OH GOD! BOOK II Warner Bros., 1980
NINE TO FIVE 20th Century Fox, 1980
ZAPPED! Embassy, 1982
SIX PACK 20th Century Fox, 1982
LOVE CHILD The Ladd Company/Warner Bros., 1982
TRENCHCOAT Buena Vista, 1983
STRANGE BREW MGM/UA, 1983, Canadian
DOIN' TIME The Ladd Company/Warner Bros., 1984
FAMILY SECRETS (TF) Katz-Gallin Prods./Half-Pint
 Prods./Karoger Prods., 1984
NATIONAL LAMPOON'S EUROPEAN VACATION Warner Bros.,
 1985
A SUMMER TO REMEMBER (TF) Inter Planetary Productions,
 1985
BETRAYED BY INNOCENCE (TF) Inter Planetary Pictures/CBS
 Entertainment, 1986
THE LONGSHOT Orion, 1986
UNNATURAL CAUSES (TF) Blue Andre Productions/ITC
 Productions, 1986
PARENT TRAP II (TF) The Landsburg Company/Walt Disney TV,
 1987
CHRISTMAS COMES TO WILLOW CREEK (TF) Blue Andre
 Productions/ITC Productions, 1987
IT HAD TO BE YOU Panther Filmworks, 1988
BABY M (TF) ABC Circle Films, 1988
LOVE AT STAKE BURNIN' LOVE Tri-Star, 1988
SHORT CIRCUIT II Tri-Star, 1988
GOING TO THE CHAPEL (TF) Furia
 Organization/Finnegan-Pinchuk Company, 1988
THE GODS MUST BE CRAZY II WEG/Columbia, 1989, South
 African
TARZAN IN MANHATTAN (TF) American First Run Productions,
 1989
RICH MEN, SINGLE WOMEN (TF) Aaron Spelling Productions,
 1990
A FAMILY FOR JOE (TF) Grosso-Jacobson Productions/NBC
 Productions, 1990
VOICES WITHIN: THE LIVES OF TRUDDI CHASE (TF) Itzbinzo
 Long Productions/P.A. Productions/New World TV, 1990
HELD HOSTAGE: THE SIS AND JERRY LEVIN STORY (TF)
 Paragon/Carol Polakoff Prods., 1991
ABSOLUTE STRANGERS (TF) The Absolute Strangers Co./Gilbert
 Cates Prods., 1991
CRASH LANDING: THE RESCUE OF FLIGHT 232 (TF) Dorothea
 G. Petrie/Helios/Bob Banner/Gary L. Pudney Co., 1992
CHRISTMAS IN CONNECTICUT (CTF) Once Upon A Time Films,
 1992
IN MY DAUGHTER'S NAME (TF) Cates-Doty Prods., 1992
WOMAN ON THE LEDGE (TF) Louis Rudolph Films/Fenton
 Ent./Fries Ent., 1993
THE ODD COUPLE (TF) Howard W. Koch Prods./Paramount TV,
 1993
GORDY Robson Entertainment, 1993
THE BROKEN CHAIN (CTF) Von Zerneck-Sertner, 1993
CONFESSIONS: TWO FACES OF EVIL (TF) Cates-Doty Prods.,
 1994
INNOCENT VICTOMS (TF) Kushner-Locke/Cates-Doty, 1996

R. DONOVAN FOX

THE GEORGIA PEACHES (TF) New World Pictures, 1980

ALUN FRANCIS

Contact: PRS - London, England, 011-44-1-580-5544

GIRO CITY Silvarealm, 1982, British

SIMON FRANGLEN

Contact: PRS - London, England, 011-44-1-580-5544

BORN TO RUN (TF) Fox West Pictures, 1993

DAVID MICHAEL FRANK*

Agent: Jeff Kaufman - Studio City, 818-506-6013
Affiliation: BMI - Los Angeles, 310-659-9109

A DIFFERENT STORY Avco Embassy, 1978
THE KID FROM LEFT FIELD (TF) Gary Coleman
 Productions/Deena Silver-Kramer's Movie Company, 1979
AN INNOCENT LOVE (TF) Steve Binder Productions, 1982
MAID IN AMERICA (TF) Georgian Boy Productions/CBS
 Entertainment, 1982
THE INVISIBLE WOMAN (TF) Universal TV, 1983
CODE OF SILENCE Orion, 1985
GLADIATOR (TF) Walker Brothers Productions/New World TV,
 1986
THE CHECK IS IN THE MAIL Ascot Entertainment Group, 1986
OFF THE MARK Fries Entertainment, 1987
ABOVE THE LAW Warner Bros., 1988
HERO AND THE TERROR Cannon, 1988
CALL ME Vestron, 1988
I'M GONNA GET YOU SUCKA MGM/UA, 1988
ONE MAN FORCE Shaprio Glickenhaus, 1989
FALSE WITNESS (TF) Valente-Kritzer-EPI Productions/New World
 TV, 1989
DIVE Warner Bros., 1990
HARD TO KILL Warner Bros., 1990
CHIPS, THE WAR DOG (CTF) 1990
OUT FOR JUSTICE Warner Bros., 1991

SHOWDOWN IN LITTLE TOKYO   Warner Bros., 1991
SUBURBAN COMMANDO   New Line, 1991
THE FIFTH CORNER (TF)   John
   Herzfeld/Adelson-Baumgartner/TriStar, 1992
EXCLUSIVE (TF)   Hamel-Somers/Freyda Rothstein/Hearst, 1992
FROM THE FILES OF JOSEPH WAMBAUGH: A JURY OF ONE
   (TF)   Grossbart-Barnett/TriStar TV, 1992
CASUALTIES OF LOVE: THE LONG ISLAND LOLITA STORY (TF)
   Diane Sokolow Prods./TriStar TV, 1992
POISON IVY   New Line, 1992
BLINDSIDED (CTF)   MTE/Alan Barnette Prods, 1993
BEST OF THE BEST II   20th Century Fox, 1993
STREET KNIGHT   Cannon, 1993
BLACK WIDOW MURDERS: THE BLANCHE TAYLOR MOORE
   STORY (TF)   Andrea Baynes/Finnegan-Pinchuk/Lorimar TV,
   1993
EXTREME JUSTICE (CTF)   Trimark, 1993
LINDA (CTF)   Linda Prods./Wilshire Court, 1993
A MATTER OF JUSTICE (TF)   Ron Gilbert Associates/Hill-Fields
   Entertainment, 1993
TEKWAR (TF)   Atlantis Films/Western Int'l Communications/Lemly
   Prods./Universal City Studios, 1994
TEKLAB (TF)   Atlantis Films/Western Int'l Communications/Lemly
   Prods./Universal City Studios, 1994
TEKLORDS (TF)   Atlantis Films/Western Int'l
   Communications/Lemly Prods./Universal City Studios, 1994
CHILDREN OF THE DARK (TF)   Steve Krantz Prods./Multimedia,
   1994
DANCING WITH DANGER (CTF)   Fast Track Films/Wilshire
   Court/USA Network, 1994
BITTER VENGEANCE (CTF)   Fast Track Films/Wilshire Court,
   1994
THE MASK   additional music, New Line, 1994
LOVE AND BETRAYAL: THE MIA FARROW STORY (TF)   Fox
   Circle Prods., 1995
PROBLEM CHILD 3: JUNIOR IN LOVE (TF)   Telven Prods./Robert
   Simonds Co., 1995
THE BABY-SITTERS CLUB   Columbia, 1995
WHEN THE DARK MAN CALLS (CTF)   Power Pictures/Wilshire
   Court, 1995
ANNIE: A ROYAL ADVENTURE (TF)   Rastar/TriStar TV, 1995

CHRISTOPHER FRANKE
Agent: Gorfaine-Schwartz - Los Angeles, 213-969-1011
Affiliation: BMI - Los Angeles, 310-659-9109

SORCERER   co-composer as part of Tangerine Dream,
   Universal/Paramount, 1977
THIEF   co-composer as part of Tangerine Dream, United Artists,
   1981
IDENTIFICATION OF A WOMAN   co-composer as part of
   Tangerine Dream, Iter Film/Gaumont, 1982, Italian-French
THE SOLDIER   co-composer as part of Tangerine Dream,
   Embassy, 1982
RISKY BUSINESS   co-composer as part of Tangerine Dream, The
   Geffen Company/Warner Bros., 1983
THE KEEP   co-composer as part of Tangerine Dream, Paramount,
   1983
WAVELENGTH   co-composer as part of Tangerine Dream, New
   World, 1983
HEARTBREAKERS   co-composer as part of Tangerine Dream,
   Orion, 1984
FLASHPOINT   co-composer as part of Tangerine Dream, Tri-Star,
   1984
FIRESTARTER   co-composer as part of Tangerine Dream,
   Universal, 1984
FORBIDDEN (CTF)   co-composer as part of Tangerine Dream,
   HBO Premiere Films/Mark Forstater Productions/Clasart/Anthea
   Productions, 1985, U.S.-British-West German
VISION QUEST   co-composer as part of Tangerine Dream, Warner
   Bros., 1985
STREET HAWK (TF)   co-composer as part of Tangerine Dream,
   Limekiln and Templar Productions/Universal TV, 1985
THE PARK IS MINE (CTF)   co-composer as part of Tangerine
   Dream, Astral Film Enterprises/HBO, 1985
LEGEND   co-composer as part of Tangerine Dream, U.S. version
   only, Universal, 1986
NEAR DARK   co-composer as part of Tangerine Dream, DEG,
   1987
THREE O'CLOCK HIGH   co-composer as part of Tangerine Dream,
   Universal, 1987

SHY PEOPLE   co-composer as part of Tangerine Dream, Cannon,
   1987
TONIGHT'S THE NIGHT (CTF)   *SINGLE MAN*   co-composer as
   part of Tangerine Dream, Phoenix Entertainment Group, 1987
CANYON DREAMS   co-composer as part of Tangerine Dream,
   Miramar, 1987
DEADLY CARE (TF)   co-composer as part of Tangerine Dream,
   Universal TV, 1987
MCBAIN   Shapiro Glickenhaus, 1991
EYE OF THE STORM   Strongmaster Productions, 1991
DRIVING ME CRAZY   Motion Picture Corporation of America, 1991
SHE WOKE UP (TF)   Empty Chair AProductions, 1992
UNIVERSAL SOLDIER   TriStar, 1992
RAVEN (TF)   Invader Prods./Columbia TV, 1992
THE TOMMYKNOCKERS (TF)   Konigsberg-Sanitsky, 1993
ANGEL FALLS (TF)   Konigsberg-Sanitsky, 1993
THE YARN PRINCESS (TF)   Konisberg-Sanistsky, 1994
EXQUISITE TENDERNESS   Capella, 1994
BEYOND BETRAYAL (TF)   Daniel H. Blatt Prods./Warner Bros. TV,
   1994
M.A.N.T.I.S. (TF)   Universal TV, 1994
NIGHT OF THE RUNNING MAN   American World Pictures, 1995
IN THE LINE OF DUTY: KIDNAPPED (TF)   Patchett-Kaufman/WIN,
   1995
SOLO   Triumph, 1996

SERGE FRANKLIN
Contact: SACEM - France, 011-33-1-4715-4715

THE SIROCCO BLOW   *LE COUP DE SIROCCO*   1979, French
LE GRAND CARNAVAL   Gaumont, 1983, French
HOLD-UP   AMLF-Cerito, 1985, French
THE SAINT: THE BRAZILIAN CONNECTION (TF)   Saint
   Productions/London Weekend Television, 1989, British
A TALE OF TWO CITIES (TF)   Granada TV/Antenne 2, 1989,
   British-French

MICHAEL FRANKS
Contact: BMI - Los Angeles, 310-659-9109

ZANDY'S BRIDE   Warner Bros., 1974
BORN TO KILL   New World, 1975

CARLOS FRANZETTI
Contact: BMI - Los Angeles, 310-659-9109

THE MAMBO KINGS   co-composer with Robert Kraft, Warner
   Bros., 1992

DAVE FRASER
Contact: APRA - Australia, 011-61-2-922-6422

WILD HORSES   Endeavour, 1983, Australian
THE LOST TRIBE   Meridian Films/Film Investment Corporation of
   New Zealand/New Zealand Film Commission, 1983, New
   Zealand

IAN FRASER*
Contact: ASCAP - Los Angeles, 213-883-1000

TORN BETWEEN TWO LOVERS (TF)   Alan Landsburg
   Productions, 1979
HOPSCOTCH   Avco Embassy, 1980
ZORRO, THE GAY BLADE   20th Century-Fox, 1981
FIRST MONDAY IN OCTOBER   adaptation, Paramount, 1981
LIFE OF THE PARTY: THE STORY OF BEATRICE (TF)
   Welch-Welch Productions/Columbia Pictures TV, 1982

JILL FRASER
Contact: ASCAP - Los Angeles, 213-883-1000

PERSONAL BEST   co-composer with Jack Nitzche, The Geffen
   Company/Warner Bros., 1982
CUTTING CLASS   Republic, 1989

'97-'98
**FILM
COMPOSERS**
LISTING

**F
I
L
M

C
O
M
P
O
S
E
R
S**

JESSE FREDERICK
Contact: ASCAP - Los Angeles, 213-883-1000

ALOHA SUMMER   co-composer with Bennett Salvay, Spectrafilm, 1988

MARC FREDERICKS
Contact: ASCAP - Los Angeles, 213-883-1000

THE RED MANTLE   1973, Finnish
SEEDS OF EVIL   *THE GARDENER*   KKI Films, 1981

IAN FREEBAIRN-SMITH
Contact: ASCAP - Los Angeles, 213-883-1000

THE STRAWBERRY STATEMENT   MGM, 1970
DEADLY LESSONS (TF)   Leonard Goldberg Company, 1983
MAGNUM, pi (TF)   Glen Larson/Bellisarius/Universal TV, 1985

DANIEL FREIBERG
Contact: BMI - Los Angeles, 310-659-9109

8-A (FD)   P.M. Films, 1993, U.S.-Cuban

GERALD FRIED
b. February 13, 1928 - New York, New York
Contact: ASCAP - Los Angeles, 213-883-1000

FEAR AND DESIRE   Joseph Burstyn, Inc., 1954
BLOOD MONEY   1954
KILLER'S KISS   United Artists, 1955
THE KILLING   United Artists, 1956
BAYOU   United Artists, 1957
THE VAMPIRE   *MARK OF THE VAMPIRE*   United Artists, 1957
PATHS OF GLORY   United Artists, 1957
TROOPER HOOK   United Artists, 1957
DINO   Allied Artists, 1957
I BURY THE LIVING   United Artists, 1958
CRY BABY KILLER   Allied Artists, 1958
THE RETURN OF DRACULA   *THE CURSE OF DRACULA*   United Artists, 1958
THE FLAME BARRIER   United Artists, 1958
CURSE OF THE FACELESS MAN   United Artists, 1958
THE LOST MISSILE   United Artists, 1958
TERROR IN A TEXAS TOWN   United Artists, 1958
MACHINE GUN KELLY   American International, 1958
TIMBUKTU   United Artists, 1959
I, MOBSTER   20th Century Fox, 1959
CAST A LONG SHADOW   United Artists, 1959
A COLD WIND IN AUGUST   Lopert, 1961
TWENTY PLUS TWO   Allied Artists, 1961
THE SECOND TIME AROUND   20th Century Fox, 1961
THE CABINET OF DR. CALIGARI   20th Century Fox, 1962
ONE POTATO, TWO POTATO   Cinema 5, 1964
ONE SPY TOO MANY   MGM, 1966
THE KILLING OF SISTER GEORGE   Cinerama Releasing Corporation, 1968
WHAT EVER HAPPENED TO AUNT ALICE?   Cinerama Releasing Corporation, 1968
TOO LATE THE HERO   Cinerama Releasing Corporation, 1970
THE GRISSOM GANG   Cinerama Releasing Corporation, 1971
THE BABY   Scotia International, 1973, British
BIRDS DO IT, BEES DO IT ★   Columbia, 1975
I WILL FIGHT NO MORE FOREVER (FD)   Wolper Productions, 1975
SURVIVE!   Paramount, 1975
VIGILANTE FORCE   United Artists, 1976
FRANCIS GARY POWERS: THE TRUE STORY OF THE U-2 SPY INCIDENT (TF)   Charles Fries Productions, 1976
ROOTS (MS) ☆☆   co-composer with Quincy Jones, Wolper Productions, 1977
SEX AND THE MARRIED WOMAN (TF)   Universal TV, 1977
THE SPELL (TF)   Charles Fries Productions, 1977
TESTIMONY OF TWO MEN (MS)   Universal TV, 1977
CRUISE INTO TERROR (TF)   Aaron Spelling Productions, 1978
MANEATERS ARE LOOSE! (TF)   Mona Productions/Finnegan Associates, 1978
THE BEASTS ARE ON THE STREETS (TF)   Hanna-Barbera Productions, 1978

RESCUE FROM GILLIGAN'S ISLAND (TF)   Sherwood Schwartz, 1978
THE IMMIGRANTS (TF)   Universal TV, 1978
THE TWO-FIVE (TF)   Universal TV, 1978
THE SEEKERS (TF)   Universal TV, 1978
ROOTS: THE NEXT GENERATION (MS)   Wolper Productions, 1979
THE INCREDIBLE JOURNEY OF DOCTOR MEG LAUREL (TF)   Columbia TV, 1979
THE BELL JAR   Avco Embassy, 1979
SON RISE: A MIRACLE OF LOVE (TF)   Rothman-Wohl Productions/Filmways, 1979
THE REBELS (MS)   Universal TV, 1979
BREAKING UP IS HARD TO DO (TF)   Green-Epstein Productions/Columbia TV, 1979
THE CASTAWAYS OF GILLIGAN'S ISLAND (TF)   Sherwood Schwartz Productions, 1979
DISASTER ON THE COASTLINER (TF)   Moonlight Productions/Filmways, 1979
THE CHISHOLMS (MS)   Alan Landsburg Productions, 1979
ROOTS: THE NEXT GENERATIONS (MS)   Wolper Productions, 1979
THE ORDEAL OF DR. MUDD (TF)   BSR Productions/Marble Arch Productions, 1980
MOVIOLA: THE SILENT LOVERS (MS) ☆   David L. Wolper-Stan Margulies Productions/Warner Bros. TV, 1980
FLAMINGO ROAD (TF)   MF Productions/Lorimar Productions, 1980
THE WILD AND THE FREE (TF)   BSR Productions/Marble Arch Productions, 1980
CONDOMINIUM (TF)   Universal TV, 1980
THE HARLEM GLOBETROTTERS ON GILLIGAN'S ISLAND (TF)   Sherwood Schwartz Productions, 1981
MURDER IS EASY (TF)   David L. Wolper-Stan Margulies Productions/Warner Bros. TV, 1982
FOR US, THE LIVING (TF)   Charles Fries Productions, 1983
THE RETURN OF THE MAN FROM U.N.C.L.E. (TF)   Martin Sloan Productions/Viacom Productions, 1983
KILLER IN THE FAMILY (TF)   Stan Margulies Productions/Sunn Classic Pictures, 1983
THE MYSTIC WARRIOR (MS) ☆   David S. Wolper-Stan Margulies Productions/Warner Bros. TV, 1984
EMBASSY (TF)   Stan Margulies Company/ABC Circle Films, 1985
NAPOLEON AND JOSEPHINE: A LOVE STORY (TF) ☆   David L. Wolper Productions/Warner Bros. TV, 1987
ROOTS: THE GIFT (TF)   Wolper Productions/Warner Bros. TV, 1988
DROP-OUT MOTHER (TF)   Fries Entertainment/Comco Productions, 1988

GARY WILLIAM FRIEDMAN
Contact: BMI - Los Angeles, 310-659-9109

FORE PLAY   Cinema National, 1975
SURVIVAL RUN   Spiegel-Bergman, 1980
FULL MOON HIGH   Filmways, 1981
MY TWO LOVES (TF)   Alvin Cooperman Productions/Taft Entertainment TV, 1986
NIGHT OF COURAGE (TF)   Titus Productions/The Eugene O'Neill Memorial Theater Center, 1987
WHO GETS THE FRIENDS? (TF)   CBS Entertainment, 1988
LIBERACE (TF)   The Liberace Foundation for the Performing and Creative Arts/Dick Clark Productions/Republic Pictures, 1988
BUMP IN THE NIGHT (TF)   Craig Anderson Prods./rhi, 1991

MARCO FRISENA
ABRAHAM (CTF)   Turner Pictures, 1994
JACOB (CTF)   LUBE Prods./LUX/Betafilm/RAI Uno/Turner Pictures, 1995

MATTHEW FRITZ
LOSER   co-composer with Joey Harrow, LTM, 1991

JOHN FRIZZELL*
Agent: Gorfaine-Schwartz - Los Angeles, 213-969-1011
Affiliation: BMI - Los Angeles, 310-659-9109

OPPOSITE CORNERS   Opposite Corners Prods., 1995
RED RIBBON BLUES   Red Ribbon Prods., 1995
UNDERTOW (CTF)   Weintraub-Kuhn, 1995
KEYS (TF)   ABC Prods., 1995
WHOSE DAUGHTER IS SHE? (TF)   1995
THE EMPTY MIRROR   1995
SHATTERED (TF)   1995
IT WAS HIM OR US (TF)   1995
BLOODHOUNDS (CTF)   1995
THE RICH MAN'S WIFE   Buena Vista, 1996
CRIME OF THE CENTURY (CTF)   1996
BEAVIS AND BUTTHEAD DO AMERICA (AF)   Paramount, 1996
DANTE'S PEAK   Universal, 1997
ALIEN: RESURRECTION   20th Century Fox, 1997

FABIO FRIZZI
b. Italy
Contact: SIAE - Italy, 011-39-6-59-901

HOT DREAMS   AMORE LIBERO   1974, Italian
DRACULA IN THE PROVINCES   co-composer, 1975
ZOMBI 2   ZOMBIE FLESH EATERS   co-composer with Giorgio
   Tucci, Variety Film, 1979, Italian
PAURA NELLA CITTA' DEI MORTI VIVENTI   Dania Film/Medusa
   Distribuzione/National Cinematografica, 1980, Italian
...E TU VIVRAI NEL TERRORE! L'ALDILA'   Fulvia Film, 1980,
   Italian
MANHATTAN BABY   Fulvia Film, 1982, Italian
THE GATES OF HELL   MPM, 1983, Italian
SUPERFANTAGENIO   ALADDIN   Cannon, 1987, Italian

EDGAR FROESE
(See Also Tangerine Dream)
Contact: GEMA - Germany, 011-49-89-480-03610

KAMIKAZE 1989   1982

DOMINIC FRONTIERE
b. June 17, 1931 - New Haven, Connecticut
Contact: BMI - Los Angeles, 310-659-9109

ONE FOOT IN HELL   20th Century-Fox, 1960
SEVEN THIEVES   20th Century-Fox, 1960
INCUBUS   1961
HERO'S ISLAND   United Artists, 1962
BILLIE   United Artists, 1965
HANG 'EM HIGH   United Artists, 1968
THE IMMORTAL (TF)   Paramount TV, 1969
LOST FLIGHT (TF)   Universal TV, 1969
NUMBER ONE   United Artists, 1969
POPI   United Artists, 1969
THE LOVE WAR (TF)   Aaron Spelling Productions, 1970
BARQUERO   United Artists, 1970
CHISUM   Warner Bros., 1970
THE SHERIFF (TF)   Screen Gems/Columbia Pictures TV, 1971
ON ANY SUNDAY (FD)   Tigon, 1971
REVENGE (TF)   Mark Carliner Productions, 1972
HAUNTS OF THE VERY RICH (TF)   ABC Circle Films, 1972
HAMMERSMITH IS OUT   Cinerama Releasing Corporation, 1972
THE TRAIN ROBBERS   Warner Bros., 1973
CLEOPATRA JONES   Warner Bros., 1973
FREEBIE AND THE BEAN   Warner Bros., 1974
FER DE LANCE   Leslie Stevens Productions, 1974
THE MARK OF ZORRO (TF)   Thompson-Paul Productions/20th
   Century-Fox TV, 1974
VELVET (TF)   Aaron Spelling Productions, 1974
WHO IS THE BLACK DAHLIA? (TF)   Douglas S. Cramer
   Productions, 1975
BRANNIGAN   United Artists, 1975, British
CLEOPATRA JONES AND THE CASINO OF GOLD   Warner Bros.,
   1975
YOUNG PIONEERS (TF)   Lorimar TV, 1976
GUMBALL RALLY   Warner Bros., 1976
PIPE DREAMS   Avco Embassy, 1976
YESTERDAY'S CHILD (TF)   Paramount TV, 1977

WASHINGTON: BEHIND CLOSED DOORS (MS)   Paramount TV,
   1977
PERFECT GENTLEMEN (TF)   Paramount TV, 1978
VEGAS (TF)   Aaron Spelling Productions, 1978
MY OLD MAN (TF)   Zeitman-McNichol-Halmi Productions, 1979
DEFIANCE   American International, 1980
THE STUNT MAN   20th Century-Fox, 1980
ROAR   Filmways Australasian, 1981
MODERN PROBLEMS   20th Century-Fox, 1981
DON'T GO TO SLEEP (TF)   Aaron Spelling Productions/Warner
   Bros. TV, 1982
SHOOTING STARS (TF)   Aaron Spelling Productions, 1983
DARK MIRROR (TF)   Aaron Spelling Productions, 1984
VELVET (TF)   Aaron Spelling Productions, 1984
THE AVIATOR   MGM/UA, 1985
HARRY'S HONG KONG (TF)   Aaron Spelling Productions, 1987
DANIELLE STEEL'S 'PALOMINO' (TF)   Cramer Co./NBC Prods.,
   1991
COLOR OF NIGHT   Buena Vista, 1994

MITCHELL FROOM
Contact: ASCAP - Los Angeles, 213-883-1000

CAFE FLESH   1983
SLAM DANCE   Island Pictures, 1987

GARY FRY
Contact: ASCAP - Los Angeles, 213-883-1000

CEASE FIRE   Cineworld, 1985

NAOYUKI FUJII
KYOSO TANJO   MANY HAPPY RETURNS   1993, Japanese

JUN FUKAMACHI
b. Japan
Contact: JASRAC - Tokyo, Japan, 011-81-3-502-6551

HINOTORI   co-composer with Michel Legrand, Toho, 1980,
   Japanese

PARMER FULLER*
b. 1949 - San Francisco, California
Contact: ASCAP - Los Angeles, 213-883-1000

SATURDAY THE 14TH   New World, 1981
WHITE GHOST   Trans World Entertainment, 1987
SATURDAY THE 14TH STRIKES BACK   Concorde, 1988
SPIRIT OF THE EAGLE   Queen's Cross Productions, 1989
TIMETRACKERS   Concorde, 1989
MORTAL PASSIONS   Gibraltar Releasing Organization, 1989
NIGHT VISITOR   NEVER CRY DEVIL   MGM/UA, 1989
SPACE CASE   Lunar Bynne, 1990
FEMME FATALE   Crawford-Lane, 1990
ULTERIOR MOTIVES   DEN Music/Ian-Page, 1990

LEWIS FUREY
Contact: SACEM - France, 011-33-1-4715-4715

FANTASTICA   Les Productions du Verseau/El Productions, 1980,
   Canadian-French
AGENCY   Taft International, 1980, Canadian
AMERICAN DREAMER   Warner Bros., 1984
THE PEANUT BUTTER SOLUTION   New World, 1985, Canadian

MAGNE FURUHOLMEN
Contact: PRS - London, England, 011-44-1-580-5544

CROSS MY HEART AND HOPE TO DIE   TI KNIVER I HJERTET
   co-composer with Kjetil Bjerkerstrand, 1995, Norwegian

G

REEVES GABRELS
Contact: ASCAP - Los Angeles, 213-883-1000

HUGH HEFNER: ONCE UPON A TIME (FD)   additional music,
    IRS, 1992
DISCOVERING WOMEN (TD)   composer of segment, 1995

PETER GABRIEL
b. 1950
Contact: BMI - Los Angeles, 310-659-9109

BIRDY   Tri-Star, 1984
THE LAST TEMPTATION OF CHRIST   Universal, 1988

TEDRA GABRIEL
REFORM SCHOOL GIRLS   New World, 1986

HENRY GAFFNEY
Contact: BMI - Los Angeles, 310-659-9109

SIDEWALK STORIES   Island Pictures, 1989

ANDRE GAGNON
Contact: SOCAN - Toronto, 416-445-8700

RUNNING   Columbia, 1979, Canadian-U.S.
PHOBIA   Paramount, 1980, Canadian

FREDERICO GAITORNO
JERICO   1991, Venezuela

JACK GALE
Contact: BMI - Los Angeles, 310-659-9109

THE LUCKIEST MAN IN THE WORLD   co-composer with Warren
    Vache, Co-Star Entertainment, 1989

JOHN GALE
Contact: ASCAP - Los Angeles, 213-883-1000

DR. PHIBES RISES AGAIN   American International, 1972, British

SCOTT GALE
Contact: ASCAP - Los Angeles, 213-883-1000

SAVED BY THE BELL - HAWAIIAN STYLE (TF)   co-composer with
    Rich Eames, Peter Engel Prods./NBC, 1992

MICHAEL GALINSKY
HALF-COCKED   Bullhorn, 1995

PHILO GALLO
THE REDEEMER...SON OF SATAN!   co-composer with Clem
    Vicari, 1978
MOTHER'S DAY   co-composer with Clem Vicari, United Film
    Distribution, 1980

PHIL GALSTON
Contact: ASCAP - Los Angeles, 213-883-1000

THE JERK, TOO (TF)   co-composer with John Sebastian, Share
    Productions/Universal TV, 1984

DOUGLAS GAMLEY
b. 1924
Contact: PRS - London, England, 011-44-1-580-5544

ONE WISH TOO MANY   1956, British
THE ADMIRABLE CRICHTON   *PARADISE LAGOON*   Columbia,
    1957, British
ANOTHER TIME, ANOTHER PLACE   Paramount, 1958
tom thumb   co-composer with Ken Jones, MGM, 1958
GIDEON OF SCOTLAND YARD   *GIDEON'S DAY*   Columbia,
    1958, British
TARZAN'S GREATEST ADVENTURE   Paramount, 1959,
    British-U.S.
WEB OF EVIDENCE   *BEYOND THIS PLACE*   Allied Artists, 1959,
    British
HORROR HOTEL   *CITY OF THE DEAD*   Trans-World, 1960,
    British
THE HORROR OF IT ALL   20th Century-Fox, 1964, British
THE RETURN OF MR. MOTO   20th Century-Fox, 1965
SPRING AND PORT WINE   EMI, 1970, British
TALES FROM THE CRYPT   Cinerama Releasing Corporation,
    1972, British
ASYLUM   Cinerama Releasing Corporation, 1972, British
THE VAULT OF HORROR   *TALES FROM THE CRYPT II*
    Cinerama Releasing Corporation, 1973, British
AND NOW THE SCREAMING STARTS   Cinerama Releasing
    Corporation, 1973, British
FROM BEYOND THE GRAVE   *THE CREATURES*   Howard Mahler
    Films, 1973, British
MADHOUSE   American International, 1974, British
THE BEAST MUST DIE   Cinerama Releasing Corporation, 1974,
    British
THE LAND THAT TIME FORGOT   American International, 1975,
    British
THE MONSTER CLUB   ITC, 1981, British

PETER CARL GANDERUP
MARILYN MONROE: LIFE AFTER DEATH (FD)
    Freedman/Greene, 1994

LIANG GANG
DA SA BA   *AFTER SEPARATION*   1993, Chinese

GANG OF FOUR
DELINQUENT   Big Bad Prods., 1995

JAN GARBAREK
Contact: TONO - Norway, 011-47-2-17-0500

SHUTTLECOCK   1991, British/French

GERARDO GARCIA
Contact: ASCAP - Los Angeles, 213-883-1000

ADORABLE LIES   co-composer with Edesio Alejandro, 1992,
    Cuban

ROEL A. GARCIA
CHUNKING EXPRESS   co-composer with Frankie Chan and
    Michael Calasso, 1996

RUSSELL GARCIA
b. 1916
Contact: ASCAP - Los Angeles, 213-883-1000

RADAR SECRET SERVICE   co-composer with Richard Hazard,
    1949
THE TIME MACHINE   MGM, 1960, British
ATLANTIS, THE LOST CONTINENT   MGM, 1961
THE PAD (AND HOW TO USE IT)   Universal, 1966
THREE GUNS FOR TEXAS   Universal, 1968

STU GARDNER
Contact: BMI - Los Angeles, 310-659-9109

THE KLANSMAN   co-composer with Dale O. Warren, Paramount, 1974
TOP SECRET (TF)   co-composer with Teo Macero, Jemmin, Inc./Sheldon Leonard Productions, 1978

JASON GARFIELD
Contact: BMI - Los Angeles, 310-659-9109

THE G.I. EXECUTIONER   *WIT'S END*   co-composer with Elliot Chiprut, Troma, 1985

ADAM GARGONI
BOCA   co-composer with Richard Feldman and Midge Ure, 1994, U.S.-Brazilian

ROBERT GARRETT
PRIME TARGET   Hero, 1991
THE ABYSS SPECIAL EDITION   additional music, 20th Century Fox, 1993

SNUFF GARRETT
Contact: BMI - Los Angeles, 310-659-9109

BRONCO BILLY   Warner Bros., 1980
SMOKEY AND THE BANDIT II   Universal, 1980
THE CANNONBALL RUN   20th Century-Fox, 1981
ANY WHICH WAY YOU CAN   Warner Bros., 1981

MIKE GARSON
Agent: Andi Howard - Los Angeles, 213-278-6483
Affiliation: BMI - Los Angeles, 310-659-9109

A YEAR IN THE LIFE (MS)   Universal TV, 1986
TIME FLIES WHEN YOU'RE ALIVE (CTF)   HBO Showcase/Kings Road Entertainment, 1989
LIFE ON THE EDGE   Festival Entertainment, 1992
CRIMINAL BEHAVIOR (TF)   Preston Stephen Fischer Co./Tolivar Prods./World International Network, 1992

MORT GARSON
Contact: ASCAP - Los Angeles, 213-883-1000

BEWARE! THE BLOB   *SON OF BLOB*   Jack H. Harris Enterprises, 1972
BLACK EYE   Warner Bros., 1974

BRIAN GASCOIGNE
Agent: Air-Edel - London, 011-44-71-486-6466
Affiliation: PRS - London, England, 011-44-1-580-5544

UNDER MILK WOOD   Altura, 1973, British
PHASE IV   Paramount, 1974
THE ARCHER AND THE SORCERESS   1983
THE EMERALD FOREST   co-composer with Junior Homrich, Embassy, 1985, British

ROBERTO GATTO
VERSO SERA   *BY NIGHTFALL*   co-composer with Battista Lena, 1991, Italian

CHRISTIAN GAUBERT
Contact: SACEM - France, 011-33-1-4715-4715

THE LITTLE GIRL WHO LIVES DOWN THE LANE   American International, 1977, U.S.-Canadian-French
THE DEMON OF THE ISLE   AMLF, 1983, French

CLAUDE GAUDETTE
Agent: Shankman-DeBlasio-Melina - Los Angeles
Affiliation: ASCAP - Los Angeles, 213-883-1000

DEAD AS A DOORMAN   Just Spoke Prods., 1986
RAW DEAL   co-composer, DEG, 1986
AMERICAN ME   co-composer with Dennis Lambert, Universal, 1992
ILLICIT DREAMS   Midnight Kiss Prods., 1994
THE SKATEBOARD KID II   Amritraj Entertainment, 1994
GRID RUNNERS   *VIRTUAL COMBAT*   Amritraj Entertainment, 1995
THE IMMORTALS   End Prods., 1995

ALGIRDAS GAVRICHENKO
THE HOUSE BUILT ON SAND   Sovexportfilm, 1991

FRANKIE GAYE
Contact: ASCAP - Los Angeles, 213-883-1000

PENITENTIARY   Jerry Gross Organization, 1979

RALPH GEDDES
Contact: BMI - Los Angeles, 310-659-9109

THE LAND OF NO RETURN   International Picture Show, 1981

KAY GEE
SUNSET PARK   co-composer with Miles Goodman, TriStar, 1996

RON GEESIN
Contact: PRS - London, England, 011-44-1-580-5544

SWORD OF THE VALIANT   Cannon, 1984, British

HARRY GELLER
Contact: BMI - Los Angeles, 310-659-9109

LET'S SWITCH (TF)   Universal TV, 1975
DEAD MAN ON THE RUN (TF)   Sweeney-Finnegan Productions, 1975

LYNNE GELLER
DENISE CALLS UP   Davis/Skyline/Dark Matter, 1995

ROSALIND GEORGE
THE MOZART BIRD   Spellbound, 1993, Dutch

SERGIO GEORGE
Contact: ASCAP - Los Angeles, 213-883-1000

I LIKE IT LIKE THAT   Columbia, 1994

TRYAN GEORGE
RIFT   co-composer with Eric Masunaga, Off-Screen Prods., 1993

IRVING GERTZ
b. May 19, 1915 - Providence, Rhode Island
Contact: ASCAP - Los Angeles, 213-883-1000

THE DEVIL'S MASK   co-composer with George Duning, Columbia, 1946
DRAGNET   Screen Guild, 1947
BLONDE ICE   Film Classics, 1948
THE COUNTERFEITERS   20th Century-Fox, 1948
THE ADVENTURES OF GALLANT BESS   Eagle Lion, 1948
JUNGLE GODDESS   Screen Guild, 1948
PREJUDICE   New World/MPSC, 1949
DESTINATION MURDER   RKO Radio, 1950
EXPERIMENT ALCATRAZ   RKO Radio, 1950
SKIPALONG ROSENBLOOM   United Artists, 1951
TWO DOLLAR BETTOR   Realart, 1951
THE BANDITS OF CORSICA   United Artists, 1953
IT CAME FROM OUTER SPACE   co-composer, Universal, 1953

THE CREATURE WALKS AMONG US   co-composer, Universal, 1956
THE INCREDIBLE SHRINKING MAN   co-composer, Universal, 1957
LOVE SLAVES OF THE AMAZON   co-composer, Universal, 1957
THE MONOLITH MONSTER   co-composer, Universal, 1957
THE ALLIGATOR PEOPLE   20th Century-Fox, 1959
CURSE OF THE UNDEAD   Universal, 1959
THE LEECH WOMAN   Universal, 1960
THE WIZARD OF BAGHDAD   20th Century-Fox, 1960

STEPHEN GEYER
NO MAN'S LAND (TF)   co-composer of song with Mike Post, JADDA Productions/Warner Bros. TV, 1984

BARRY GIBB
Contact: BMI - Los Angeles, 310-659-9109

HAWKS Skouras Pictures, 1989

MAURICE GIBB
Contact: BMI - Los Angeles, 310-659-9109

A BREED APART Orion, 1984

MICHAEL GIBBS
b. Sept. 25, 1937 - Salisbury, S. Rhodesia
Agent: Film Music Associates - Hollywood, 213-463-1070
Affiliation: PRS - London, England, 011-44-1-580-5544

SECRETS   Lone Star, 1971, British
MADAME SIN (TF)   ITC, 1972, British
INTIMATE REFLECTIONS   1974, British
SECRETS   Lone Star, 1978
RIDING THE EDGE   Kodiak Films
HEAT   New Century/Vista, 1987
HOUSEKEEPING   Columbia, 1987
AMERICANROULETTE   Film Four International/British Screen/Mandemar Group, 1988, British
RIDING THE EDGE   Trans World Entertainment, 1989
BREAKING IN   Samuel Goldwyn Company, 1989
IRON AND SILK   Prestige, 1991
WHORE   Trimark, 1991
CLOSE MY EYES   1991, British
HARD-BOILED   1992, Hong-Kong
CENTURY   I.R.S., 1994, British
BEING HUMAN   Warner Bros., 1994

RICHARD GIBBS
Contact: BMI - Los Angeles, 310-659-9109

SWEET HEART'S DANCE   Tri-Star, 1988
A DEADLY SILENCE (TF)   Robert Greenwald Productions, 1989
SAY ANYTHING   20th Century-Fox, 1989
UPWORLD   Vestron, 1989
KILLING IN A SMALL TOWN (TF)   The IndieProd Co./Hearst Entertainment Productions, 1990
HOW TO MURDER A MILLIONAIRE (TF)   Robert Greenwald Films, 1990
DEADLOCK (CTF)   Spectacor, Frederick S. Pierce, 1991
BINGO   TriStar, 1991
THE GUN IN BETTY LOU'S HAND BAG   Buena Vista, 1992
LADYBUGS   Paramount, 1992
ONCE UPON A CRIME   MGM, 1992
PASSED AWAY   Buena Vista, 1992
THREE OF HEARTS   New Line, 1993
BARBARIANS AT THE GATE (CTF)   Columbia/HBO, 1993
AMOS AND ANDREW   Columbia, 1993
SON-IN-LAW   Hollywood, 1993
FATAL INSTINCT   MGM, 1993
THE CHASE   20th Century Fox, 1994
CLIFFORD   Orion, 1994
BLIND JUSTICE (CTF)   Heyman-Moritz Prods./HBO Pictures, 1994
THE CHASE   20th Century Fox, 1994
FIRST KID   Buena Vista, 1996
THAT DARN CAT   Buena Vista, 1997

DAVID GIBNEY
Contact: BMI - Los Angeles, 310-659-9109

SUPERSTITION   *THE WITCH* Almi Pictures, 1985

ALEX GIBSON
Contact: BMI - Los Angeles, 310-659-9109

THE WILD SIDE   New World, 1983
FROM HOLLYWOOD TO DEADWOOD   Island Pictures, 1989

DAVID GIBSON
SCHLOCK   Jack H. Harris Enterprises, 1973

MICHAEL GIBSON
ROSELAND   Cinema Shares, 1977

PHILIP GIFFIN
Contact: BMI - Los Angeles, 310-659-9109

MURDER 101 (CTF)   Alan Barnette Prods./MCA TV, 1991
RED WIND (CTF)   Alan Barnette Prods., 1991
WHITE LIE (CTF)   USA, 1991
DEAD IN THE WATER (CTF)   Kevin Bright/MTE, 1991
LADYKILLER (TF)   MTE, 1992
DEADLY RELATIONS (TF)   O.T.M.L. Prods./Wilshire Court, 1993
THE COMPUTER WORE TENNIS SHOES (TF)   ZM Prods./Walt Disney TV, 1995

HERSCHEL BURKE GILBERT
b. 1918 - Milwaukee, Wisconsin
Contact: ASCAP - Los Angeles, 213-883-1000

MR. DISTRICT ATTORNEY   Columbia, 1947
OPEN SECRET   Eagle Lion, 1948
AN OLD-FASHIONED GIRL   Eagle Lion, 1948
SHAMROCK HILL   Eagle Lion, 1949
THERE'S A GIRL IN MY HEART   Allied Artists, 1949
THE JACKIE ROBINSON STORY   Eagle Lion, 1950
THREE HUSBANDS   United Artists, 1950
THE SCARF   United Artists, 1951
THE MAGIC FACE   Columbia, 1951
THE HIGHWAYMAN   Allied Artists, 1951
WITHOUT WARNING   United Artists, 1952
KID MONK BARONI   Realart, 1952
MODELS, INC.   Mutual, 1952
THE RING   United Artists, 1952
THE THIEF ★   United Artists, 1952
NO TIME FOR FLOWERS   RKO Radio, 1952
THE MOON IS BLUE   United Artists, 1953
SABRE JET   United Artists, 1953
VICE SQUAD   United Artists, 1953
RIOT IN CELL BLOCK 11   Allied Artists, 1954
CARMEN JONES ★   adaptation, 20th Century-Fox, 1954
WITNESS TO MURDER   United Artists, 1954
THE NAKED DAWN   Universal, 1955
WHILE THE CITY SLEEPS   RKO Radio, 1956
THE BOLD AND THE BRAVE   RKO Radio, 1956
BEYOND A REASONABLE DOUBT   RKO Radio, 1956
COMANCHE   Universal, 1956
THE NAKED HILLS   Allied Artists, 1956
NIGHTMARE   United Artists, 1956
NO PLACE TO HIDE   Allied Artists, 1956
SLAUGHTER ON TENTH AVENUE   Universal, 1957
CRIME AND PUNISHMENT, USA   Allied Artists, 1959
SAM WHISKEY   United Artists, 1969
I DISMEMBER MAMA   *POOR ALBERT AND LITTLE ANNIE* Valiant International, 1972

ALAN GILL
Agent: Marks Management - Tarzana, 818-776-8787
Contact: ASCAP - Los Angeles, 213-883-1000

BLONDE FIST   Glinwood, 1991, British

KEVIN GILLIS

Contact: SOCAN - Toronto, 416-445-8700

ROBOCOP: THE SERIES (TF)   co-composer with Jon Stroll,
     Skyvision Ent./RoBoCop Prods./Rysher, 1994

RICHARD GILLIS

Contact: ASCAP - Los Angeles, 213-883-1000

DEMONOID   American Panorama, 1981

IRIS GILLON

Contact: ASCAP - Los Angeles, 213-883-1000

FAST FOOD   Fries Entertainment, 1989

PAUL GILMAN

Contact: BMI - Los Angeles, 310-659-9109

BEST OF THE BEST Taurus Entertainment, 1989

PAUL GILREATH

Contact: ASCAP - Los Angeles, 213-883-1000

NO RETREAT NO SURRENDER   New World, 1986

JON GILUTIN

WILDFLOWER (CTF)   co-composer with Ken Edwards,
     Freed-Laufer Prods./Polone Co./Hearst, 1991
SECRET SINS OF THE FATHER (TF)   co-composer with Kenny
     Edwards, Ultra Ent./Dick Clark Film Group, 1994

EGBERTO GISMONTI

Contact: SUISA - Switzerland, 011-41-1-485-6666

AMAZONIA: VOICES FROM THE RAIN FOREST (FD)   Amazonia,
     1991

CLAUDIO GIZZI

Contact: SIAE - Italy, 011-39-6-59-901

WHAT?   Avco Embassy, 1973, Italian-French-West German
ANDY WARHOL'S FRANKENSTEIN   FLESH FOR
     FRANKENSTEIN   Bryanston, 1974, Italian-French
ANDY WARHOL'S DRACULA   BLOOD FOR DRACULA
     Bryanston, 1974, Italian-French

JAN GLAESEL

DET FORSOMTE FORAR   THE STOLEN SPRING   1993, Danish

PAUL GLASS

b. 1910
Contact: ASCAP - Los Angeles, 213-883-1000

THE ABDUCTORS   20th Century-Fox, 1957
LADY IN A CAGE   United Artists, 1964
BUNNY LAKE IS MISSING   Columbia, 1965, British
SOLE SURVIVOR (TF)   Cinema Center 100, 1970
FIVE DESPERATE WOMEN (TF)   Aaron Spelling Productions,
     1971
SANDCASTLES (TF)   Metromedia Productions, 1972
OVERLORD   1975, British
TO THE DEVIL A DAUGHTER   EMI, 1976, British

PHILIP GLASS

b. 1937 - Baltimore, Maryland
Contact: ASCAP - Los Angeles, 213-883-1000

MARK DI SUVERO, SCULPTOR (FD)   1977
KOYAANISQATSI   Island Alive/New Cinema, 1983
MISHIMA: A LIFE IN FOUR CHAPTERS   Warner Bros., 1985,
     Japanese-U.S.
DEAD END KIDS (FD)   co-composer with David Byrne, Mabou
     Mines, 1986
HAMBURGER HILL   Paramount, 1987

POWAQQATSI   Cannon, 1988
THE THIN BLUE LINE (FD)   Miramax Films, 1988
A BRIEF HISTORY OF TIME (FD)   1992, British-U.S.
CANDYMAN   TriStar, 1992
CANDYMAN: FAREWELL TO THE FLESH   Gramercy, 1995
THE SECRET AGENT   1996

ALBERT GLASSER

b. January 25, 1916 - Chicago, Illinois
Contact: ASCAP - Los Angeles, 213-883-1000

CALL OF THE JUNGLE   Monogram, 1944
THE CONTENDER   Producers Releasing Corp., 1944
THE MONSTER MAKER   Producers Releasing Corp., 1944
THE CISCO KID IN OLD NEW MEXICO   Producers Releasing
     Corp., 1945
THE CISCO KID RETURNS   Producers Releasing Corp., 1945
THE KID SISTER   Producers Releasing Corp., 1945
ABILENE TOWN   United Artists, 1946
GAS HOUSE KIDS IN HOLLYWOOD   Producers Releasing Corp.,
     1947
BORDER FEUD   Producers Releasing Corp., 1947
KILLER AT LARGE   co-composer with Alvin Levin, Producers
     Releasing Corp., 1947
GAS HOUSE KIDS GO WEST   Producers Releasing Corp., 1947
LAW OF THE LASH   Producers Releasing Corp., 1947
PHILO VANCE RETURNS   Producers Releasing Corp., 1947
WHERE THE NORTH BEGINS   Screen Guild, 1947
HE TRAIL OF THE MOUNTIES   Screen Guild, 1948
ASSIGNED TO DANGER   Eagle Lion, 1948
BEHIND LOCKED DOORS   Eagle Lion, 1948
THE COBRA STRIKES   Eagle Lion, 1948
IN THIS CORNER   Eagle Lion, 1948
LAST OF THE WILD HORSES   Lippert, 1948
THE RETURN OF WILDFIRE   Lippert, 1948
THE WHITE PHANTOM   1948
URUBU   United Artists, 1948
THE VALIANT HOMBRE   United Artists, 1948
THE GAY AMIGO   United Artists, 1949
THE DARING CABALLERO   United Artists, 1949
APACHE CHIEF   Lippert, 1949
I SHOT JESSE JAMES   Lippert, 1949
OMOO-OMOO, THE SHARK GOD   Screen Guild, 1949
GRAND CANYON   Lippert, 1949
SATAN'S CRADLE   United Artists, 1949
THE TREASURE OF MONTE CRISTO   Lippert, 1949
TOUGH ASSIGNMENT   Lippert, 1949
HOLLYWOOD VARIETIES   Lippert, 1950
THE GIRL FROM SAN LORENZO   United Artists, 1950
WESTERN PACIFIC AGENT   Lippert, 1950
EVERYBODY'S DANCIN'   Lippert, 1950
GUNFIRE   Lippert, 1950
TRAIN TO TOMBSTONE   Lippert, 1950
I SHOT BILLY THE KID   Lippert, 1950
THE RETURN OF JESSE JAMES   Lippert, 1950
BORDER RANGERS   Lippert, 1950
BANDIT QUEEN   Lippert, 1950
TRAIN TO TOMBSTONE   Lippert, 1950
THREE DESPERATE MEN   Lippert, 1951
TOKYO FILE 212   RKO Radio, 1951
THE BUSHWACKERS   Realart, 1951
OKLAHOMA TERRITORY   United Artists, 1951
GEISHA GIRL   Realart, 1952
INVASION U.S.A.   Columbia, 1952
THE NEANDERTHAL MAN   United Artists, 1952
PORT SINISTER   RKO Radio, 1953
CAPTAIN JOHN SMITH AND POCAHONTAS   United Artists, 1953
PARIS MODEL   Columbia, 1953
PROBLEM GIRLS   Columbia, 1953
MAN OF CONFLICT   Atlas, 1953
DRAGON'S GOLD   United Artists, 1954
TOP BANANA   United Artists, 1954
THE GIANT OF DEVIL'S CRAG   GIANT FROM THE UNKNOWN
     Astor, 1955
MURDER IS MY BEAT   Allied Artists, 1955
TOP OF THE WORLD   United Artists, 1955
THE BOSS   United Artists, 1956
HUK   United Artists, 1956
PLEASE MURDER ME   DCA, 1956
THE INDESTRUCTIBLE MAN   Allied Artists, 1956
BEGINNING OF THE END   Republic, 1957

BAILOUT AT 43,000   United Artists, 1957
THE BIG CAPER   United Artists, 1957
CYCLOPS   American International, 1957
THE BUCKSKIN LADY   United Artists, 1957
THE SAGA OF THE VIKING WOMEN AND THEIR VOYAGE TO
   THE WATERS OF THE GREAT SEA SERPENT   American
   International, 1957
THE AMAZING COLOSSAL MAN   American International, 1957
DESTINATION 60,000   Allied Artists, 1957
FOUR BOYS AND A GUN   United Artists, 1957
THE HIRED GUN   MGM, 1957
MOTORCYCLE GANG   American International, 1957
STREET OF SINNERS   United Artists, 1957
VALERIE   United Artists, 1957
TEENAGE BAD-GIRL   DCA, 1957
MONSTER FROM GREEN HELL   DCA, 1957
GIRL IN THE WOODS   Republic, 1958
HIGH SCHOOL CONFIDENTIAL   YOUNG HELLIONS   MGM, 1958
THE MUGGER   United Artists, 1958
SNOWFIRE   Allied Artists, 1958
WHEN HELL BROKE LOOSE   Paramount, 1958
ATTACK OF THE PUPPET PEOPLE   American International, 1958
THE SPIDER   American International, 1958
TEENAGE CAVEMAN   American International, 1958
WAR OF THE COLOSSAL BEAST   American International, 1958
THE BEAT GENERATION   THIS REBEL AGE   MGM, 1959
NIGHT OF THE QUARTER MOON   FLESH AND FLAME   MGM,
   1959
OKLAHOMA TERRITORY   United Artists, 1960
TORMENTED   Allied Artists, 1960
THE HIGH POWERED-RIFLE   20th Century-Fox, 1960
THE BOY AND THE PIRATES   United Artists, 1960
20,000 EYES   20th Century-Fox, 1961
AIR PATROL   20th Century-Fox, 1962
CONFESSIONS OF AN OPIUM EATER   SOULS FOR SALE/EVILS
   OF CHINATOWN   Allied Artists, 1962
THE UNBELIEVABLE   1966
THE CREMATORS   New World, 1972

PATRICK GLEESON*

Contact: BMI - Los Angeles, 310-659-9109

THE PLAGUE DOGS (AF)   Nepenthe Productions, 1982, British
THE ZOO GANG   New World, 1985
THE CHILDREN OF TIMES SQUARE (TF)   Gross-Weston
   Productions/Fries Entertainment, 1986
STACKING   Spectrafilm, 1987
IN SELF DEFENSE (TF)   Leonard Hill Films, 1987
THE BEDROOM WINDOW   co-composer with Michael Shrieve,
   DEG, 1987
DEADLY ILLUSION   CineTel Films, 1987
PERFECT PEOPLE (TF)   Robert Greenwald Productions, 1988
EDEN: FORBIDDEN INTERLUDES (CTF)   Pacific Rim, 1993

NICK GLENNIE-SMITH

Agent: The Kraft-Benjamin Agency - Beverly Hills, 310 247-0123

POINT OF NO RETURN   additional music, Warner Bros., 1993
DROP ZONE   additional music, Paramount 1994
THE ROCK   co-composer with Hans Zimmer and Harry
   Gregson-Williams, Buena Vista, 1996
TWO IF BY SEA   co-composer with Paddy Moloney, Warner Bros.,
   1996

GOBLIN

Contact: SIAE - Italy, 011-39-6-59-901

PROFUNDO ROSSO   Howard Mahler Films, 1976, Italian
SUSPIRIA   International Classics, 1977, Italian
DAWN OF THE DEAD   United Film Distribution, 1979
PATRICK   composers of Italian version only, Cinema Shares
   International, 1979, Australian
ALIEN CONTAMINATION   Cannon, 1980, Italian
NIGHT OF THE ZOMBIES   Motion Picture Marketing, 1980,
   Spanish-Italian
BURIED ALIVE   Aquarius Releasing, 1981, Italian
CREEPERS   PHENOMENA   New Line Cinema, 1985, Italian

BILL GODDARD

SODBUSTERS (CTF)   Atlantis Films/Bond Street Prods., 1994

HEINER GOEBBELS

Contact: GEMA - Germany, 011-49-89-480-03610

LUDWIG 1881   1993, Swiss-German

ERNEST GOLD*

b. July 13, 1921 - Vienna, Austria
Contact: ASCAP - Los Angeles, 213-883-1000

THE GIRL OF THE LIMBERLOST   Columbia, 1945
SMOOTH AS SILK   Universal, 1946
THE FALCON'S ALIBI   RKO Radio, 1946
G.I. WAR BRIDES   Republic, 1947
LIGHTHOUSE   Producers Releasing Corp., 1947
WYOMING   co-composer with Nathan Scott, Republic, 1947
EXPOSED   Republic, 1947
OLD LOS ANGELES   Republic, 1948
UNKNOWN WORLD   Lippert, 1951
JENNIFER   Allied Artists, 1953
MAN CRAZY   20th Century-Fox, 1953
KARAMOJA (FD)   Hallmark, 1954
THE OTHER WOMAN   20th Century-Fox, 1954
THE NAKED STREET   United Artists, 1955
UNIDENTIFIED FLYING OBJECTS (FD)   United Artists, 1956
EDGE OF HELL   Universal, 1956
RUNNING TARGET   United Artists, 1956
AFFAIR IN HAVANA   Allied Artists, 1957
MAN ON THE PROWL   United Artists, 1957
TOO MUCH TOO SOON   Warner Bros., 1958
WINK OF AN EYE   United Artists, 1958
TARZAN'S FIGHT FOR LIFE   MGM, 1958
THE DEFIANT ONES   United Artists, 1958
THE SCREAMING SKULL   American International, 1958
THE YOUNG PHILADELPHIANS   Warner Bros., 1959
THE BATTLE OF THE CORAL SEA   Columbia, 1959
ON THE BEACH ★   United Artists, 1959
INHERIT THE WIND   United Artists, 1960
EXODUS ★★   United Artists, 1960
A FEVER IN THE BLOOD   Warner Bros., 1961
THE LAST SUNSET   Universal, 1961
JUDGMENT AT NUREMBERG   United Artists, 1961
PRESSURE POINT   United Artists, 1962
A CHILD IS WAITING   United Artists, 1963
IT'S A MAD, MAD, MAD, MAD WORLD ★   United Artists, 1963
SHIP OF FOOLS   Columbia, 1965
THE SECRET OF SANTA VITTORIA ★   United Artists, 1969
FOOTSTEPS (TF)   Metromedia Producers Corporation/Stonehenge
   Productions, 1972
THE SMALL MIRACLE (TF)   FCB Productions/Alan Landsburg
   Productions, 1973
BETRAYAL (TF)   Metromedia Producers Corporation, 1974
THE WILD McCULLOCHS   American International, 1975
FUN WITH DICK AND JANE   Columbia, 1977
CROSS OF IRON   Avco Embassy, 1977, British-West German
GOOD LUCK, MISS WYCKOFF   Bel Air/Gradison, 1979
THE RUNNER STUMBLES   20th Century-Fox, 1979
LETTERS FROM FRANK (TF)   Paramount Pictures Television,
   1979
MARCIANO (TF)   ABC Circle Films, 1979
TOM HORN   Warner Bros., 1980
SAFARI 3000   United Artists, 1982
WALLENBERG: A HERO'S STORY (TF)   Dick Berg-Stonehenge
   Productions/Paramount TV, 1985
DREAMS OF GOLD: THE MEL FISHER STORY (TF)   Inter
   Planetary Productions, 1986
GORE VIDAL'S LINCOLN (MS)   Chris-Rose
   Productions/Finnegan-Pinchuk Company, 1988

BARRY GOLDBERG

Contact: BMI - Los Angeles, 310-659-9109

THE TRIP   American International, 1967
THRASHIN'   Fries Entertainment, 1986
THE SPIRIT (TF)   von Zerneck-Samuels Productions/Warner Bros.
   TV, 1987
THREE FOR THE ROAD   New Century/Vista, 1987
POWWOW HIGHWAY   Warner Bros., 1989, U.S.-British

BEVERLY HILLS BRATS   Taurus Entertainment, 1989
FLASHBACK   Paramount, 1990
HOMETOWN BOY MAKES GOOD (CTF)   HBO, 1990
CAPTAIN AMERICA   21st Century, 1992
RETURN OF THE LIVING DEAD   Trimark, 1993

BILLY GOLDENBERG
b. February 10, 1936 - New York, New York
Contact: BMI - Los Angeles, 310-659-9109

CHANGE OF HABIT   Universal, 1968
THE GRASSHOPPER   National General, 1969
FEAR NO EVIL (TF)   Universal TV, 1969
SILENT NIGHT, LONELY NIGHT (TF)   Universal TV, 1969
NIGHT GALLERY (TF)   Universal TV, 1969
RED SKY AT MORNING   Universal, 1971
THE HARNESS (TF)   Universal TV, 1971
THE NEON CEILING (TF)   Universal TV, 1971
DUEL (TF)   Universal TV, 1971
UP THE SANDBOX   National General, 1972
PLAY IT AGAIN, SAM   Paramount, 1972
TRUMAN CAPOTE'S THE GLASS HOUSE   THE GLASS HOUSE
    (TF)   Tomorrow Entertainment, 1972
THE LAST OF SHEILA   Warner Bros., 1973
A BRAND NEW LIFE (TF) ☆   Tomorrow Entertainment, 1973
BUSTING   United Artists, 1974
THE MIGRANTS (TF) ☆   CBS, Inc., 1974
REFLECTIONS OF MURDER (TF)   ABC Circle Films, 1974
THE LEGEND OF LIZZIE BORDEN (TF)   Paramount TV, 1975
QUEEN OF THE STARDUST BALLROOM (TF) ☆   Tomorrow
    Entertainment, 1975
GEMINI MAN (TF)   Universal TV, 1976
DARK VICTORY (TF) ☆   Universal TV, 1976
THE LINDBERGH KIDNAPPING CASE (TF)   Columbia TV, 1976
HELTER SKELTER (TF) ☆   Lorimar Productions, 1976
JAMES DEAN (TF)   The Jozak Company, 1976
THE DOMINO PRINCIPLE   Avco Embassy, 1977
MARY JANE HARPER CRIED LAST NIGHT (TF)   Paramount TV,
    1977
KING (MS) ☆☆   Abby Mann Productions/Filmways, 1978
A QUESTION OF LOVE (TF)   Viacom, 1978
SCAVENGER HUNT   20th Century-Fox, 1979
FLESH AND BLOOD (TF)   The Jozak Company/Cypress Point
    Productions/Paramount TV, 1979
THE FAMILY MAN (TF)   Time-Life Productions, 1979
THE CRACKER FACTORY (TF)   Roger Gimbel Productions/EMI
    TV, 1979
THE MIRACLE WORKER (TF)   Katz-Gallin Productions/Half-Pint
    Productions, 1979
THE LOVE TAPES (TF)   Christiana Productions/MGM TV, 1980
ALL GOD'S CHILDREN (TF)   Blinn-Thorpe Productions/Viacom,
    1980
THE DIARY OF ANNE FRANK (TF)   Katz-Gallin/Half-Pint
    Productions/20th Century-Fox TV, 1980
A PERFECT MATCH (TF)   Lorimar Productions, 1980
FATHER FIGURE (TF)   Finnegan Associates/Time-Life
    Productions, 1980
THE WOMEN'S ROOM (TF)   Philip Mandelker Productions/Warner
    Bros. TV, 1980
HAYWIRE (TF)   Pando Productions/Warner Bros. TV, 1980
SIDNEY SCHORR (TF)   Hajeno Productions/Warner Bros. TV,
    1981
DIAL M FOR MURDER (TF)   Freyda Rothstein Productions/Time
    Life TV, 1981
CRISIS AT CENTRAL HIGH (TF)   Time-Life Productions, 1981
CALLIE & SON (TF)   Rosilyn Heller Productions/Hemdale
    Presentations/City Films/Motown Pictures Co., 1981
THE BEST LITTLE GIRL IN THE WORLD (TF)   Aaron Spelling
    Productions, 1981
THE ORDEAL OF BILL CARNEY (TF)   Belle Company/Comworld
    Productions, 1981
JACQUELINE BOUVIER KENNEDY (TF) ☆   ABC Circle Films,
    1981
REHEARSAL FOR MURDER (TF)   Levinson-Link
    Productions/Robert Papazian Productions, 1982
MASSARATI AND THE BRAIN (TF)   Aaron Spelling Productions,
    1982
THE GIFT OF LIFE (TF)   CBS Entertainment, 1982
A QUESTION OF HONOR (TF)   Roger Gimbel Prods./Sonny
    Grosso Prods./EMI-TV, 1982

MARION ROSE WHITE (TF)   Gerald Abram Productions/Cypress
    Point Productions, 1982
COUNTRY GOLD (TF)   CBS Entertainment, 1982
BARE ESSENCE (TF)   Warner Bros. TV, 1982
REUBEN, REUBEN   20th Century-Fox International Classics, 1983
SIDNEY SHELDON'S RAGE OF ANGELS   RAGE OF ANGELS (TF)
    ☆☆   Furia-Oringer Productions/NBC Productions, 1983
INTIMATE AGONY (TF)   Henperson-Hirsch Productions/Robert
    Papazian Productions, 1983
WILL THERE REALLY BE A MORNING? (TF)   Jaffe-Blakely
    Films/Sama Productions/Orion TV, 1983
DEMPSEY (TF)   Charles Fries Productions, 1983
PROTOTYPE (TF)   Levinson-Link Productions/Robert Papazian
    Productions, 1983
HAPPY (TF)   Bacchus Films Inc., 1983
MEMORIAL DAY (TF)   Charles Fries Productions, 1983
THE AWAKENING OF CANDRA (TF)   Michael Klein Productions,
    1983
CONFESSIONS OF A MARRIED MAN (TF)   Gloria Monty
    Productions/Comworld, 1983
ANOTHER WOMAN'S CHILD (TF)   CBS Entertainment, 1983
WHY ME? (TF)   Lorimar Productions, 1984
SENTIMENTAL JOURNEY (TF)   Lucille Ball
    Productions/Smith-Richmond Productions/20th Century Fox TV,
    1984
SCORNED AND SWINDLED (TF)   Cypress Point Productions,
    1984
HIS MISTRESS (TF)   David L. Wolper Productions/Warner Bros.
    TV, 1984
THE SUN ALSO RISES (TF)   Furia-Oringer Productions/20th
    Century Fox TV, 1984
FOR LOVE OR MONEY (TF)   Robert Papazian
    Productions/Henerson-Hirsch Productions, 1984
THE ATLANTA CHILD MURDERS (TF)   Mann-Rafshoon
    Productions/Finnegan Associates, 1985
KANE & ABEL (MS)   Schrekinger Communications/Embassy TV,
    1985
OBSESSED WITH A MARRIED WOMAN (TF)   Sidaris-Camhe
    Productions/The Feldman-Meeker Company, 1985
LOVE ON THE RUN (TF)   NBC Productions, 1985
LOVE IS NEVER SILENT (TF)   Marian Rees Associates, 1985
THE RIGHT OF THE PEOPLE (TF)   Big Name Films/Fries
    Entertainment, 1986
DRESS GRAY (TS)   Frank von Zerneck Productions/Warner Bros.
    TV, 1986
RAGE OF ANGELS: THE STORY CONTINUES (MS)   NBC
    Productions, 1986
JOHNNIE MAE GIBSON: FBI (TF)   Fool's Cap Productions, 1986
THERE MUST BE A PONY (TF)   R.J. Productions/Columbia TV,
    1986
SADIE AND SON (TF)   Norton Wright Productions/Kenny Rogers
    Organization/ITC Productions, 1987
NUTCRACKER: MONEY, MADNESS AND MURDER (MS) ☆
    Green Arrow Productions/Warner Bros. TV, 1987
LITTLE GIRL LOST (TF)   Marian Rees Associates, 1988
THE RICHEST MAN IN THE WORLD: THE ARISTOTLE ONASSIS
    STORY (TF)   The Konigsberg-Sanitsky Company, 1988
18 AGAIN   New World, 1988
AROUND THE WORLD IN 80 DAYS (MS)   Harmony
    Gold/ReteEuropa/Valente-Baerwald Productions, 1989
PEOPLE LIKE US (TF) ☆   CM Two Productions/ITC, 1990
CHERNOBYL: THE FINAL WARNING (CTF)   Carolco-Gimger
    Prods./USSR Film Service, 1991
ONE SPECIAL VICTORY (TF)   Port Street Films/NBC Prods., 1991
MILES FROM NOWHERE (TF)   Sokolow Co./New World Television,
    1992
MISS ROSE WHITE (TF)   Marian Reese Associates/Lorimar TV,
    1992
MISS AMERICA: BEHIND THE CROWN (TF)   Katz-Rush
    Entertainment, 1992
A HOUSE OF SECRETS AND LIES (TF)   Elliot
    Friedgen/Chris-Rose, 1992
THE MAN UPSTAIRS (TF)   Burt Reynolds Prods., 1992
SILENT CRIES (TF)   Sokolow/Yorkshire TV/TriStar TV, 1993
DANIELLE STEEL'S MESSAGE FROM NAM (TF)   Cramer
    Co./NBC Prods., 1993
A BURNING PASSION: THE MARGARET MITCHELL STORY
    (TF)   Renee Valente Prods./NBC Prods., 1994
SOMEONE ELSE'S CHILD (TF)   Greengrass Prods./de Passe Ent.,
    1994

MARK GOLDENBERG

Contact: BMI - Los Angeles, 310-659-9109

SILENT RAGE   additional music, Columbia, 1982
NATIONAL LAMPOON'S CLASS REUNION   additional music, 20th
    Century Fox, 1983
TEEN WOLF TOO   Atlantic Releasing Corporation, 1987

ELLIOT GOLDENTHAL

Agent: Gorfaine-Schwartz - Los Angeles, 213-969-1011
Affiliation: ASCAP - Los Angeles, 213-883-1000

PET SEMETARY   Paramount, 1989
DRUGSTORE COWBOY   Avenue Pictures, 1989
GRAND ISLE   Kelly McGillis/Turner Pictures, 1991
ALIEN³   20th Century Fox, 1992
FOOL'S FIRE   American   Playhouse, 1992
DEMOLITION MAN   Warner Bros., 1993
GOLDEN GATE   Samuel Goldwyn, 1994
ROSWELL (CTF)   Citadel/Viacom/Showtime Entertainment, 1994
INTERVIEW WITH THE VAMPIRE ★   Warner Bros./Geffen, 1994
COBB   Warner Bros., 1994
BATMAN FOREVER   Warner Bros., 1995
HEAT   Warner Bros., 1995
MICHAEL COLLINS ★   Warner Bros., 1996
A TIME TO KILL   Warner Bros., 1996
BATMAN AND ROBIN   Warner Bros., 1997

PETER GOLDFOOT

JUDGMENT IN BERLIN   New Line Cinema, 1988

BOBBY GOLDSBORO

Contact: BMI - Los Angeles, 310-659-9109

THE MAN FROM LEFT FIELD (TF)   Burt Reynolds Prods., 1993

JERRY GOLDSMITH*

b. 1929 - Los Angeles, California
Agent: The Kraft-Benjamin Agency - Beverly Hills, 310-247-0123
Affiliation: BMI - Los Angeles, 310-659-9109

BLACK PATCH   Warner Bros., 1957
CITY OF FEAR   Columbia, 1959
FACE OF A FUGITIVE   Columbia, 1959
STUDS LONIGAN   United Artists, 1960
THE PEOPLE NEXT DOOR (TF)   1961
THE CRIMEBUSTER   MGM, 1961
LONELY ARE THE BRAVE   Universal, 1962
THE SPIRAL ROAD   Universal, 1962
THE STRIPPER   20th Century-Fox, 1962
FREUD ★   Universal, 1963
THE LIST OF ADRIAN MESSENGER   Universal, 1963
A GATHERING OF EAGLES   Universal, 1963
LILIES OF THE FIELD   United Artists, 1963
TAKE HER, SHE'S MINE   20th Century-Fox, 1963
THE PRIZE   MGM, 1963
SEVEN DAYS IN MAY   Paramount, 1964
SHOCK TREATMENT   20th Century-Fox, 1964
FATE IS THE HUNTER   20th Century-Fox, 1964
RIO CONCHOS   20th Century-Fox, 1964
IN HARM'S WAY   Paramount, 1964
THE SATAN BUG   United Artists, 1965
VON RYAN'S EXPRESS   20th Century-Fox, 1965
MORITURI   THE SABOTEUR, CODE NAME "MORITURI"   20th
    Century-Fox, 1965
A PATCH OF BLUE ★   MGM, 1965
THE AGONY AND THE ECSTASY   composer of prologue music,
    20th Century-Fox, 1965
OUR MAN FLINT   20th Century-Fox, 1966
TO TRAP A SPY   MGM, 1966
THE TROUBLE WITH ANGELS   Columbia, 1966
STAGECOACH   20th Century-Fox, 1966
THE BLUE MAX   20th Century-Fox, 1966, British-U.S.
SECONDS   Paramount, 1966
THE SAND PEBBLES ★   20th Century-Fox, 1966
IN LIKE FLINT   20th Century-Fox, 1967
THE FLIM FLAM MAN   20th Century-Fox, 1967
HOUR OF THE GUN   United Artists, 1967
WARNING SHOT   Paramount, 1967

SEBASTIAN   Paramount, 1968, British
PLANET OF THE APES ★   20th Century-Fox, 1968
THE DETECTIVE   20th Century-Fox, 1968
BANDOLERO!   20th Century-Fox, 1968
THE ILLUSTRATED MAN   Warner Bros., 1969
100 RIFLES   20th Century-Fox, 1969
THE CHAIRMAN   20th Century-Fox, 1969, British
JUSTINE   20th Century-Fox, 1969
PATTON ★   20th Century-Fox, 1970
THE BALLAD OF CABLE HOGUE   Warner Bros., 1970
TORA! TORA! TORA!   20th Century-Fox, 1970, U.S.-Japanese
THE TRAVELING EXECUTIONER   MGM, 1970
BROTHERHOOD OF THE BELL (TF)   Cinema Center 100, 1970
RIO LOBO   National General, 1970
THE MEPHISTO WALTZ   20th Century-Fox, 1971
DO NOT FOLD, SPINDLE OR MUTILATE (TF)   Lee Rich
    Productions, 1971
ESCAPE FROM THE PLANET OF THE APES   20th Century-Fox,
    1971
THE LAST RUN   MGM, 1971
THE CABLE CAR MURDER (TF)   Warner Bros. TV, 1971
WILD ROVERS   MGM, 1971
THE HOMECOMING (TF)   Lorimar Productions, 1971
THE CULPEPPER CATTLE CO.   original score by Tom Scott,
    includes tracked music by Jerry Goldsmith, 20th Century-Fox,
    1972
THE MAN   Paramount, 1972
CRAWLSPACE (TF)   Titus Productions, 1972
THE OTHER   20th Century-Fox, 1972
PURSUIT (TF)   ABC Circle Films, 1972
SHAMUS   Columbia, 1973
ACE ELI AND RODGER OF THE SKIES   20th Century-Fox, 1973
ONE LITTLE INDIAN   Buena Vista, 1973
HAWKINS ON MURDER (TF)   Arena-Leda Productions/MGM TV,
    1973
THE DON IS DEAD   Universal, 1973
THE RED PONY (TF) ☆   Universal TV/Omnibus Productions, 1973
POLICE STORY (TF)   Screen Gems/Columbia TV, 1973
THE GOING UP OF DAVID LEV (TF)   1973
PAPILLON ★   Allied Artists, 1973
TAKE A HARD RIDE   20th Century-Fox, 1974
A TREE GROWS IN BROOKYLN (TF)   Norman Rosemont
    Productions/20th Century-Fox TV, 1974
S.P.Y.S.   U.S. version only, 20th Century-Fox, 1974, British-U.S.
WINTER KILL (TF)   Andy Griffith Enterprises/MGM Television,
    1974
INDICT AND CONVICT (TF)   1974
CHINATOWN ★   Paramount, 1974
QB VII (MS) ☆☆   Screen Gems/Columbia TV/The Douglas Cramer
    Company, 1974
THE REINCARNATION OF PETER PROUD   American
    International, 1975
BREAKOUT   Columbia, 1975
THE WIND AND THE LION ★   MGM/United Artists, 1975
A GIRL NAMED SOONER (TF)   Frederick Brogger Associates/20th
    Century-Fox TV, 1975
THE TERRORISTS   RANSOM   20th Century-Fox, 1975, British
TAKE A HARD RIDE   20th Century Fox, 1975
MEDICAL STORY (TF)   theme only, 1975
BABE (TF) ☆☆   MGM TV, 1975
LOGAN'S RUN   MGM/United Artists, 1976
THE LAST HARD MEN   20th Century-Fox, 1976
BREAKHEART PASS   United Artists, 1976
THE OMEN ★★   20th Century-Fox, 1976
THE CASSANDRA CROSSING   Avco Embassy, 1977,
    British-Italian-West German
HIGH VELOCITY   1977
TWILIGHT'S LAST GLEAMING   Allied Artists, 1977, U.S.-West
    German
ISLANDS IN THE STREAM   Paramount, 1977
MacARTHUR   Universal, 1977
CONTRACT ON CHERRY STREET (TF)   Columbia TV, 1977
SIX CHARACTERS IN SEARCH OF AN AUTHOR (TF)   1977
DAMNATION ALLEY   20th Century-Fox, 1977
COMA   MGM/United Artists, 1978
CAPRICORN ONE   20th Century-Fox, 1978
DAMIEN: OMEN II   20th Century-Fox, 1978
THE SWARM   Warner Bros., 1978
MAGIC   20th Century-Fox, 1978
THE BOYS FROM BRAZIL ★   20th Century-Fox, 1978
THE GREAT TRAIN ROBBERY   United Artists, 1979, British
ALIEN   20th Century-Fox, 1979, U.S.-British

GO

F
I
L
M

C
O
M
P
O
S
E
R
S

PLAYERS   Paramount, 1979
STAR TREK: THE MOTION PICTURE ★   Paramount, 1979
CABOBLANCO   Avco Embassy, 1981
THE SALAMANDER   ITC, 1981, British-Italian-U.S.
THE FINAL CONFLICT   20th Century-Fox, 1981
OUTLAND   The Ladd Company/Warner Bros., 1981
MASADA (MS) ☆☆   composer of Parts 1 and 2, Arnon Milchan
    Productions/Universal TV, 1981
RAGGEDY MAN   Universal, 1981
INCHON   MGM/UA, 1982, South Korean-U.S.
THE CHALLENGE   Embassy, 1982
THE SECRET OF NIMH (AF)   MGM/UA, 1982
NIGHT CROSSING   Buena Vista, 1982
POLTERGEIST ★   MGM/UA, 1982
FIRST BLOOD   Orion, 1982, Canadian
TWILIGHT ZONE: THE MOVIE   Warner Bros., 1983
PSYCHO II   Universal, 1983
UNDER FIRE ★   Orion, 1983
THE RETURN OF THE MAN FROM U.N.C.L.E. (TF)   theme from
    the TV show re-used, Martin Sloan Productions/Viacom
    Productions, 1983
GREMLINS   also cameo as phone booth user, Warner Bros., 1984
SUPERGIRL   Warner Bros., 1984, British-U.S.
THE LONELY GUY   Universal, 1984
BABY - SECRET OF THE LOST LEGEND   Buena Vista, 1985
RUNAWAY   Tri-Star, 1984
LEGEND   composer of European version, Universal, 1986, British
EXPLORERS   Paramount, 1985
RAMBO: FIRST BLOOD PART II   Tri-Star, 1985
KING SOLOMON'S MINES   Cannon, 1985
LINK   Thorn EMI/Cannon, 1986, U.S.-British
POLTERGEIST II: THE OTHER SIDE   MGM/UA, 1986
HOOSIERS ★   Orion, 1986
EXTREME PREJUDICE   Tri-Star, 1987
INNERSPACE   Warner Bros., 1987
LIONHEART   Orion, 1987
RENT-A-COP   Kings Road Productions, 1988
RAMBO III   Tri-Star, 1988
CRIMINAL LAW   Hemdale, 1988
WARLOCK   New World, 1989
THE 'BURBS   Universal, 1989
LEVIATHAN   MGM/UA, 1989, U.S.-Italian
STAR TREK V: THE FINAL FRONTIER   Paramount, 1989
TOTAL RECALL   Tri-Star, 1990
GREMLINS 2: THE NEW BATCH   also cameo as yoghurt shop
    customer, Warner Bros., 1990
THE RUSSIA HOUSE   Pathe, 1990
NOT WITHOUT MY DAUGHTER   MGM, 1991
SLEEPING WITH THE ENEMY   20th Century Fox, 1991
BROTHERHOOD OF THE GUN (TF)   theme only, 1991
BASIC INSTINCT ★   TriStar, 1992
MEDICINE MAN   Buena Vista, 1992
Mr. BASEBALL   Universal, 1992
MOM AND DAD SAVE THE WORLD   Warner Bros., 1992
FOREVER YOUNG   Warner Bros., 1992
LOVE FIELD   Orion, 1992
HOLLISTER (TF)   theme only, 1993
MATINEE   Universal, 1993
THE VANISHING   20th Century Fox, 1993
DENNIS THE MENACE   Warner Bros., 1993
MALICE   Columbia, 1993
RUDY   TriStar, 1993
SIX DEGREES OF SEPARATION   MGM, 1993
ANGIE   Buena Vista, 1994
BAD GIRLS   20th Century Fox, 1994
THE SHADOW   Universal, 1994
THE RIVER WILD   Universal, 1994
STAR TREK: VOYAGER: THE CARETAKER (TF) ☆☆   theme
    only, Paramount TV, 1995
I.Q.   Paramount, 1994
CONGO   Paramount, 1995
FIRST KNIGHT   Columbia, 1995
CITY HALL   Columbia, 1995
POWDER   1995
EXECUTIVE DECISION   Warner Bros., 1996
CHAIN REACTION   20th Century Fox, 1996
THE GHOST AND THE DARKNESS   Paramount, 1996
STAR TREK: FIRST CONTACT   Paramount, 1996
FIERCE CREATURES   Universal, 1997
DEEP RISING   1997
BOOKWORM   1997
L.A. CONFIDENTIAL   1997

JOEL GOLDSMITH*
Agent: Vangelos Management - Encino, 818-380-1919
Affiliation: BMI - Los Angeles, 310-659-9109

LASERBLAST   co-composer with Richard Band, Irwin Yablans,
    1978
A TASTE OF SIN   FACES OF FEAR   Ambassador Pictures, 1981
THE MAN WITH TWO BRAINS   Warner Bros., 1983
CRYSTAL HEART   New World, 1987
BANZAI RUNNER   Montage Films, 1987
WATCHERS   Universal, 1988
RICKY I   Tapeworm, 1988
NO SAFE HAVEN   Overseas Filmgroup, 1989
JOBMAN   Blue Rock Films, 1990
INSTANT KARMA   MGM, 1990
BLUE DESERT   Neo, 1991
BROTHERHOOD OF THE GUN (TF)   1991
A WOMAN, HER MEN, AND HER FUTON   Interpersonal, 1992
THE UNTOUCHABLES (TF)   Christopher Crowe Prods./Paramount
    TV, 1993
MAN'S BEST FRIEND   New Line, 1993
HAWKEYE (TF)   Stephen J. Cannell Prods., 1994
ONE GOOD TURN   Zeta Entertainment, 1995
STAR TREK: FIRST CONTACT   additional music, Paramount,
    1996
SHILOH   Overseas Film Group, 1997
KULL THE CONQUEROR   Universal, 1997

JONATHAN GOLDSMITH
Contact: SOCAN - Toronto, 416-445-8700

VISITING HOURS   20th Century-Fox, 1982, Canadian
PALAIS ROYALE   Spectrafilm, 1988, Canadian
HEADS (CTF)   Showtime
    Ent./Atlantis/Credo/Sojourn/Tudor-Evenmore/Davis Ent. TV, 1994
AVALANCHE (TF)   Atlantis/Propaganda/CTV TV Net, 1994
FALLING FOR YOU (TF)   Falling For You prods./BBS Prods., 1995
KISSINGER AND NIXON (CTF)   Paragon, 1995
DAED SILENCE (CTF)   Alliance/HBO Pictures, 1996

GIL GOLDSTEIN
Contact: ASCAP - Los Angeles, 213-883-1000

RECKLESS DISREGARD (CTF)   Telecom Entertainment/Polar Film
    Corporation/Fremantle of Canada Ltd., 1985, U.S.-Canadian
RADIO INSIDE (CTF)   MGM-UA/Showtime Entertainment, 1994

STEVEN GOLDSTEIN*
Agent: William Morris - Beverly Hills, 310-859-4000
Affiliation: BMI - Los Angeles, 310-659-9109

MGM: WHEN THE LION ROARS (TD)   Joni Levin Point Blank
    Prods., 1992
IN SEARCH OF DR. SEUSS (CTF)   Point Blank, 1994

WILLIAM GOLDSTEIN*
Contact: BMI - Los Angeles, 310-659-9109

THE STOOLIE   Jama, 1972
THE BINGO LONG TRAVELING ALL STARS AND MOTOR KINGS
    Universal, 1976
NORMAN...IS THAT YOU?   MGM/United Artists, 1976
DOOMSDAY 2000   Savadove Productions, 1977
TERROR OUT OF THE SKY (TF)   Alan Landsburg Productions,
    1978
THE WHITE LIONS   Alan Landsburg Productions, 1979
JENNIFER: A WOMAN'S STORY (TF)   Marble Arch Productions,
    1979
THE ALIENS ARE COMING (TF)   Woodruff Productions/QM
    Productions, 1980
MARILYN: THE UNTOLD STORY (TF)   Lawrence Schiller
    Productions, 1980
MANBEAST (TF)   Alan Landsburg Productions, 1981
FORCE: FIVE   American Cinema, 1981
AN EYE FOR AN EYE   Avco Embassy, 1981
A LONG WAY HOME (TF)   Alan Landsburg Productions, 1981
FORCED VENGEANCE   MGM/United Artists, 1982
REMEMBRANCE OF LOVE (TF)   Doris Quinlan
    Productions/Comworld Productions, 1982

HAPPY ENDINGS (TF)   Motown Productions, 1983
UP THE CREEK   Orion, 1983
GETTING PHYSICAL (TF)   CBS Entertainment, 1984
THE TOUGHEST MAN IN THE WORLD (TF)   Guber-Peters
     Productions/Centerpoint Productions, 1984
REARVIEW MIRROR (TF)   Simon-Asher Entertainment/Sunn
     Classic Pictures, 1984
LOTS OF LUCK (CTF)   Tomorrow Entertainment, 1985
BAD GUYS   Interpictures, 1986
SAVING GRACE   Columbia, 1986
LIBERTY (TF)   Robert Greenwald Productions, 1986
HERO IN THE FAMILY (TF)   Barry & Enright Productions/Alexander
     Productions/Walt Disney Productions, 1986
ON FIRE (TF)   Robert Greenwald Productions, 1987
BLOOD VOWS: THE STORY OF A MAFIA WIFE (TF)   Louis
     Rudolph Films/Fries Entertainment, 1987
SIX AGAINST THE ROCK (TF)   Schaefer-Karpf-Epstein
     Productions/Gaylord Production Company, 1987
HELLO AGAIN   Buena Vista, 1987
THE THREE KINGS (TF)   Aaron Spelling Productions, 1987
THE FAVORITE   Kings Road, 1989, U.S.-French
SHOCKER   Universal, 1989
CROSS OF FIRE (TF)   Leonard Hill Films, 1989
THE QUARREL   Apple & Honey, 1992
DANIELLE STEEL'S ZOYA (TF)   Cramer Co./NBC Prods., 1995

VINNY GOLIA
Contact: BMI - Los Angeles, 310-659-9109

BLOOD AND CONCRETE   I.R.S., 1991
NO SECRETS   I.R.S., 1991
TROUBLE BOUND   ITC, 1993

IGOR GOLOVIEV
UNKNOWN ISRAEL (FD)   1991, Soviet/Israeli

BENNY GOLSON
Contact: BMI - Los Angeles, 310-659-9109

THE SOPHISTICATED GENTS (TF)   Daniel Wilson Productions,
     1981
ED'S NEXT MOVE   Curb, 1996

JOHN GONZALEZ
Contact: BMI - Los Angeles, 310-659-9109

THE LAST RIDERS   PM, 1991
FINAL IMPACT   PM Entertainment, 1992
ICE   PM, 1993
HOLOGRAM MAN   PM Entertainment, 1995

JOSEPH JULIAN GONZALES
Affiliation: BMI - Los Angeles, 310-659-9109

LA PASTORELLA (TF)   Richard Soto Prods./El Teatro
     Campasino/WNET/Channel Four, 1991
FOR THE LOVE OF MY CHILD: THE ANISSA AYALA STORY (TF)
     Viacom/Stonehenge, 1993
THE CISCO KID (CTF)   Esparza-Katz Prods./Goodman
     Rosen/Turner Pictures, 1994
CURDLED   Miramax, 1996

HOWARD GOODALL
Affiliation: PRS - London, England, 011-44-1-580-5544

THE BORROWERS (CTF)   Working Title TV/BBC-TV/Turner
     Network TV/BBC's Children Intl./Children's Film Foundation/De
     Faria Co., 1993

JERRY GOODMAN
Contact: BMI - Los Angeles, 310-659-9109

THE SEARCH FOR SIGNS OF INTELLIGENT LIFE IN THE
     UNIVERSE   Orion Classics, 1991

JIM GOODMAN
Contact: ASCAP - Los Angeles, 213-883-1000

THE ICE RUNNER   additional music, Borde Film, 1993

TOMMY GOODMAN
Contact: ASCAP - Los Angeles, 213-883-1000

MY LITTLE PONY - THE MOVIE (AF)   DEG, 1986

GORDON GOODWIN*
Contact: ASCAP - Los Angeles, 213-883-1000

ATTACK OF THE KILLER TOMATOES   co-composer with Paul
     Sundfor, NAI Entertainment, 1979

JIM GOODWIN
Contact: BMI - Los Angeles, 310-659-9109

APEX   Republic, 1994

RON GOODWIN
b. 1929 - Plymouth, England
Agent: Robert Light - Los Angeles, 213-651-1777
Affiliation: PRS - London, England, 011-44-1-580-5544

WHIRLPOOL   Continental, 1959, British
THE WITNESS   Anglo-Amalgam, 1959, British
I'M ALL RIGHT JACK   Columbia, 1960, British
IN THE NICK   Columbia, 1960, British
VILLAGE OF THE DAMNED   MGM, 1960, British
THE TRIALS OF OSCAR WILDE   Kingsley International, 1960,
     British
THE MAN WITH THE GREEN CARNATION
     Warwick-Viceroy/Kingsley,   1960
THE MAN AT THE CARLTON TOWER   Anglo-Amalgam, 1961,
     British
THE CLUE OF THE NEW PIN   Merton Park, 1961, British
PARTNERS IN CRIME   Allied Artists, 1961, British
INVASION QUARTET   MGM, 1961, British
MURDER, SHE SAID   MGM, 1962, British
POSTMAN'S KNOCK   MGM, 1962, British
VILLAGE OF DAUGHTERS   MGM, 1962
THE DAY OF THE TRIFFIDS   Allied Artists, 1963, British
I THANK A FOOL   MGM, 1962
KILL OR CURE   MGM, 1962, British
FOLLOW THE BOYS   MGM, 1963
SWORD OF LANCELOT   *LANCELOT AND GUINEVERE*
     Universal, 1963, British
MURDER AT THE GALLOP   MGM, 1963, British
THE CRACKSMAN   Warner Bros./Pathe, 1963, British
LADIES WHO DO   Fanfare/Continental, 1963, British
OF HUMAN BONDAGE   MGM, 1964, British
CHILDREN OF THE DAMNED   MGM, 1964, British
633 SQUADRON   United Artists, 1964, British
MURDER AHOY!   MGM, 1964, British
GO KART GO!   Fanfare/CFF, 1964
JOHNNY NOBODY   Victory-Medallion, 1965, British
MURDER MOST FOUL   MGM, 1965, British
A HOME OF YOUR OWN   Dormer/British Lion, 1965, British
THOSE MAGNIFICENT MEN IN THEIR FLYING MACHINES   20th
     Century-Fox, 1965, British
OPERATION CROSSBOW   MGM, 1965, British-Italian
THE ALPHABET MURDERS   *THE A.B.C. MURDERS*   MGM, 1966,
     British
THE EARLY BIRD   Rank, 1966, British
THAT RIVIERA TOUCH   Continental, 1966, British
THE TRAP   Rank, 1966, British
MISTER TEN PERCENT   Associated British, 1966
WHAT HAPPENED AT CAMPO GRANDE?   *THE MAGNIFICENT
     TWO*   Alan Enterprises, 1967, British
MRS. BROWN, YOU'VE GOT A LOVELY DAUGHTER   MGM,
     1968, British
SUBMARINE X-1   United Artists, 1969, British
DECLINE AND FALL OF A BIRD WATCHER   20th Century-Fox,
     1969, British
WHERE EAGLES DARE   MGM, 1969, British
THOSE DARING YOUNG MEN IN THEIR JAUNTY JALOPIES
     Paramount, 1969, British-Italian-French

BATTLE OF BRITAIN   United Artists, 1969, British
THE EXECUTIONER   Columbia, 1970, British
THE SELFISH GIANT (AF)   Readers Digest, 1971
GAWAIN AND THE GREEN KNIGHT   United Artists, 1972, British
FRENZY   Universal, 1972, British
DIAMOND ON WHEELS   Buena Vista, 1972, U.S.-British
THE LITTLE MERMAID (AF)   Readers Digest, 1973
THE HAPPY PRINCE (AF)   Readers Digest, 1974
DEADLY STRANGERS   Fox-Rank, 1974, British
ONE OF OUR DINOSAURS IS MISSING   Buena Vista, 1975,
   U.S.-British
SPANISH FLY   EMI, 1975, British
RIDE A WILD PONY   *BORN TO RUN*   Buena Vista, 1976,
   U.S.-Australian
BEAUTY AND THE BEAST (TF)   Palms Films Ltd., 1976, British
THE LITTLEST HORSE THIEVES   *ESCAPE FROM THE DARK*
   Buena Vista, 1977, U.S.-British
CANDLESHOE   Buena Vista, 1977, U.S.-British
FORCE 10 FROM NAVARONE   American International, 1978
UNIDENTIFIED FLYING ODDBALL   Buena Vista, 1979
CLASH OF LOYALTIES   Jorephani, 1983
VALHALLA (AF)   Swan Productions, 1985, Danish

YURI GORBACHOW
BLAST'EM   1992, Canadian

PAUL CHRISTIAN GORDON
WEDDING BELL BLUES   co-composer with Tal Bergman, Curb,
   1997

MICHAEL GORE*
Agent: Cathy Schleussner - Encino, 818-905-7475
Affiliation: BMI - Los Angeles, 310-659-9109

FAME ★★   MGM/United Artists, 1980
TERMS OF ENDEARMENT ★   Paramount, 1983
PRETTY IN PINK   Paramount, 1986
BOYFRIEND SCHOOL   Hemdale, 1990
DEFENDING YOUR LIFE   Warner Bros., 1991
THE BUTCHER'S WIFE   Paramount, 1991
MR. WONDERFUL   Warner Bros., 1993

ADAM GORGONI
Contact: BMI - Los Angeles, 310-659-9109

THE TOLLBOOTH   1996

AL GORGONI
Contact: BMI - Los Angeles, 310-659-9109

I NEVER SANG FOR MY FATHER   co-composer with Barry Mann,
   Columbia, 1970

ALAIN GORRAGUER
b. France
Contact: SACEM - France, 011-33-1-4715-4715

LE CORBUSIER   1956, French
LE PIEGE   co-composer with Maurice Le Roux, 1957, French
LE BEL AGE   1958, French
J'IRAI CRACHER SUR VOS TOMBES   1959, French
BLAGUE DANS LE COIN   1963, French
PARIS-SECRET   1965, French
THAT MAN GEORGE!   *L'HOMME DE MARRAKECH*   Allied Artists,
   1966, French-Italian-Spanish
UN CHOIX D'ASSASSINS   1967, French
SUR UN ARBRE PERCHE   1971, French
L'AFFAIRE DOMINICI   1972, French
LA PLANETE SAUVAGE   1972, French
THE FANTASTIC PLANET (AF)   Hemdale, 1973, French
THE SILENT ONE   co-composer with Jacques Datin, 1973,
   French-Italian
URSULE ET GRELU   1973, French
AU-DELA DE LA PEUR   1975, French

MARTIN GOTFRIT
Contact: SOCAN - Toronto, 416-445-8700

LEY LINES (FD)   Noema Prods., 1993, Canadian

ORLANDO GOUGH
TOP GIRLS (TF)   1992, British

MORTON GOULD
b. 1913 - Richmond Hill, New York
Contact: ASCAP - Los Angeles, 213-883-1000

DELIGHTFULLY DANGEROUS   United Artists, 1945
WINDJAMMER   1958
F. SCOTT FIZTGERALD IN HOLLYWOOD (TF)   Titus Productions,
   1976
HOLOCAUST (MS) ☆   Titus Productions, 1978

GERALD GOURIET
Contact: BMI - Los Angeles, 310-659-9109

MADAME SOUSATZKA   Universal, 1988, British
NUNS ON THE RUN   composer of British version, 1989, British
GRAND TOUR (CTF)   HBO Pictures, 1989
SEEDS OF TRAGEDY (TF)   Sanford-Pillsbury Prods./FNM Films,
   1991
DEATH DREAMS (CTF)   Ultra/Dick Clark Film Group/Roni
   Weisberg Prods., 1991
HOLD ME, THRILL ME, KISS ME   1992
A QUESTION OF ATTRIBUTION   1992, British
DOUBLE EDGE (TF)   Konigsberg-Sanitsky Co., 1992
DISASTER IN TIME (CTF)   Wildstreet Pictures, 1992
MAD AT THE MOON (CTF)   Michael
   Jaffe/Spectacor/Elwes-Kastenbaum, 1992
CHILD OF RAGE (TF)   Gilliam Prods./C.M. Two Prods./Republic
   Pictures, 1992
OVEREXPOSED (TF)   LOMO Prods., 1992
RUBDOWN (CTF)   Wilshire Court/Fast Track Films, 1993
THE SUBSTITUTE (CTF)   Pacific Motion Pictures/Wilshire Court,
   1993
THEY (CTF)   Bridget Terry Prods./Viacom, 1993
TO DANCE WITH THE WHITE DOG (TF)   Patricia Clifford
   Prods./Signboard Hill Prods., 1993
THE PHILADELPHIA EXPERIMENT 2   Trimark, 1993
THE ONLY WAY OUT (TF)   Berger Queen Prods./Adam
   Prods./ABC Prods., 1993
MEN OF WAR   Dimension/Miramax, 1994
THE INNOCENT   Miramax, 1995, British-German

JOHN GOUX
Contact: BMI - Los Angeles, 310-659-9109

ALFRED HITCHCOCK PRESENTS (TF)   co-composer, Universal
   TV, 1985

MARK GOVERNOR*
Agent: The Kordek Agency - Bunbank, 818-559-4248
Affiliation: ASCAP - Los Angeles, 213-883-1000

SURF II   IFM, 1983
PARADISE MOTEL   Saturn, 1984
LAND OF DOOM   Manson/Maris, 1985
THE DESTROYERS   Concorde, 1986
BEACH BALLS   Concorde, 1988
HOLLYWOOD BOULEVARD II   Concorde, 1989
MASQUE OF THE RED DEATH   Concorde, 1989
OVEREXPOSED   Concorde, 1990
PET SEMETARY TWO   Paramount, 1992

PATRICK GOWERS
b. May 5, 1936 - London, England
Agent: Nigel Britton, Lemon Unna & Durbridge Ltd., 24 Pottery Lane,
   Holland Park, London W11 4LZ, 01/727-1346 or 01/229-9216
Affiliation: PRS - London, England, 011-44-1-580-5544

GIVE GOD A CHANCE ON SUNDAYS   Asafilms, 1970, British
THE VIRGIN AND THE GYPSY   Chevron, 1970, British
A BIGGER SPLASH   Lagoon Associates, 1975, British

CHILDREN OF RAGE   LSF, 1975, U.S.-Israeli
STEVIE   First Artists, 1978, British
SMILEY'S PEOPLE (MS)   BBC/Paramount TV, 1982, British
MY COUSIN RACHEL (TF)   BBC, 1983, British
ANNA KARENINA (TF)   Rastar Productions/Colgems Productions,
   1985
SORRELL AND SON (TF)   Yorkshire Television, 1986, British
WHOOPS APOCALYPSE   ITC Entertainment, 1986, British
THE SIGN OF FOUR (TF)   Grenada, 1988, British
THE HOUND OF THE BASKERVILLES (TF)   Grenada, 1988,
   British

PAUL GRABOWSKY
Contact: APRA - Australia, 011-61-2-922-6422

THE LAST DAYS OF CHEZ NOUS   1992, Australian
EXILE   Beyond Films, 1994, Australian

CEDRIC GRADUS-SAMSON
MANDELA AND DE KLERK (CTF)   Showtime/Hallmark, 1997

RALPH GRAF
LANGER GANG *PASSAGES*   Wild Okapi Film, 1993 German

DAVID GRAHAM
Contact: PRS - London, England, 011-44-1-580-5544

COMRADES   co-composer with Hans Werner Henze, British Film
   Institute, 1986, British

FRANCIS GRANDMONT
KANEHSATAKE: 270 YEARS OF RESISTANCE (FD)   co-composer
   with Claude Vendette, National Film Board of Canada, 1993,
   Canadian

RON GRANT*
Agent: Gorfaine-Schwartz - Los Angeles, 213-969-1011
Affiliation: ASCAP - Los Angeles, 213-883-1000

THE KID FROM NOT-SO-BIG   William Crain Productions, 1982
"SAY YES"   Cinetel, 1986

STEPHANE GRAPPELLI
b. 1908 - Paris, France
Contact: SACEM - France, 011-33-1-4715-4715

GOING PLACES *LES VALSEUSES*   Cinema 5, 1974, French
MAY FOOLS   Orion, 1990, French

JOHN GRAY
METAMORPHOSIS: THE ALIEN FACTOR   International, 1991

STEPHEN GRAZIANO
Agent: Vangelos Management - Encino, 818-380-1919
Affiliation: BMI - Los Angeles, 310-659-9109
SCAM (CTF)   Viacom, 1993
PAST TENSE (CTF)   Arnold Kopelson Prods./Showtime Ent., 1994
JOHN GRISHAM'S THE CLIENT (TF)   Michael Filerman
   Prods./Judith Paige Mitchell Prods./New Regency/Warner Bros.
   TV, 1995
RUBY JEAN & JOE   1996
CONTAGIOUS (TF)   Wilshire Court, 1996
ESCAPE FROM ATLANTIS (TF)   Universal TV, 1997

DON GREAT
Contact: BMI - Los Angeles, 310-659-9109

ANGEL III: THE FINAL CHAPTER   additional music, New World,
   1988

D'ANGIO GRECO
IO SPERIAMO CHE ME LA CAVO *ME LET'S HOPE I MAKE IT*
   Miramax, 1993, Italian

BERNARD GREEN
Contact: ASCAP - Los Angeles, 213-883-1000

BLIND GODDESS   1948
THE FAT MAN   Universal, 1951
EVERYTHING'S DUCKY   Columbia, 1961
ZOTZ!   Columbia, 1962
ALL THE WAY HOME   Paramount, 1963
MGM'S BIG PARADE OF COMEDY   MGM, 1964
THE BRASS BOTTLE   Universal, 1964
HARVEY MIDDLEMAN, FIREMAN   Columbia, 1965

RICHARD GREENE
Contact: BMI - Los Angeles, 310-659-9109

GETTING EVEN   Quantum Films, 1981

RICHARD GREGOIRE
PERFECTLY NORMAL   Four Seasons, 1991, Canadian
BACK AT HOME WITH CLAUDE   1992, Canadian

STEVE GREGOROPOULOS
NAKED JANE   Anamorph, 1995

HARRY GREGSON-WILLIAMS
Agent: Gorfaine-Schwartz - Los Angeles, 213-969-1011

WHITE ANGEL   1993, British
THE ROCK   co-composer with Nick Glennie-Smith and Hans
   Zimmer, Buena Vista, 1996

RALPH GRIERSON*
Contact: BMI - Los Angeles, 310-659-9109

TO FIND MY SON (TF)   Green-Epstein Productions/Columbia
   Pictures TV, 1980
RED EARTH, WHITE EARTH (TF)   Chris/Rose Productions, 1989

MARIO GRIGORIV
THIS WON'T HURT A BIT!   Dendy, 1993, Australian

DAVID GRISMAN
Contact: BMI - Los Angeles, 310-659-9109

BIG MAD MAMA   New World, 1974
CAPONE   20th Century-Fox, 1975
EAT MY DUST   New World, 1976
KING OF THE GYPSIES   Paramount, 1978

DAVID GROHL
TOUCH   MGM-UA, 1997

SHLOMO GRONICH
OVER THE OCEAN   1992, Israeli

ANDREW GROSS*
Agent: Vangelos Management - Encino, 818-380-1919
Affiliation: BMI - Los Angeles, 310-659-9109

ANGEL'S TIDE   Mont Peru Prods., 1994
BIO-DOME   MGM-UA, 1996
OVERNIGHT DELIVERY   New Line, 1997
EIGHT HEADS IN A DUFFEL BAG   MPCA/Orion, 1997

CHARLES GROSS*
Agent: Gorfaine-Schwartz - Los Angeles, 213-969-1011
Affiliation: ASCAP - Los Angeles, 213-883-1000

THE GROUP   United Artists, 1965
TEACHER, TEACHER   NBC, 1969
VALDEZ IS COMING   United Artists, 1971
BROCK'S LAST CASE (TF)   Talent Associates/Universal TV, 1973
NICKY'S WORLD (TF)   Tomorrow Entertainment, 1974
THE TENTH LEVEL (TF)   CBS, Inc., 1976
THE GARDENER'S SON (TF)   RIP/Filmhaus, 1977

THE DAIN CURSE (MS)   Martin Poll Productions, 1978
SIEGE (TF)   Titus Productions, 1978
HEARTLAND   Levitt-Pickman, 1979
YOU CAN'T GO HOME AGAIN (TF)   CBS Entertainment, 1979
NO OTHER LOVE (TF)   Tisch-Avnet Productions, 1979
A PRIVATE BATTLE (TF)   Procter & Gamble ProductionsRobert
   Halmi, Inc., 1980
A RUMOR OF WAR (TF)   Charles Fries Productions, 1980
WHEN THE CIRCUS CAME TO TOWN (TF)   Entheos Unlimited
   Productions/Meteor Films, 1981
PRIME SUSPECT (TF)   Tisch-Avnet Television, 1982
SOMETHING SO RIGHT (TF)   List-Estrin Productions/Tisch-Avnet
   Television, 1982
MY BODY, MY CHILD (TF)   Titus Productions, 1982
CHINA ROSE (TF)   Robert Halmi, Inc., 1983
SESSIONS (TF)   Roger Gimbel Productions/EMI TV/Sarabande
   Productions, 1983
COOK & PEARY: THE RACE TO THE POLE (TF)   Robert Halmi
   Productions/ITT Productions, 1983
COUNTRY   Buena Vista, 1984
BRADY'S ESCAPE   Satori Entertainment, 1984, U.S.-Hungarian
TERRIBLE JOE MORAN (TF)   Robert Halmi, Inc., 1984
THE BURNING BED (TF)   Tisch-Avnet Productions, 1984
NAIROBI AFFAIR (TF)   Robert Halmi, Inc., 1984
THE NIGHT THEY SAVED CHRISTMAS (TF)   Robert Halmi, Inc.,
   1984
SWEET DREAMS   Tri-Star, 1985
ARTHUR THE KING (TF)   Martin Poll Productions/Comworld
   Productions/Jadran Film, 1985, U.S.-Yugoslavian
IZZY AND MOE (TF)   Robert Halmi, Inc., 1985
THREE SOVEREIGNS FOR SARAH (TF)   Night Owl Productions,
   1985
CHOICES (TF)   Robert Halmi, Inc., 1986
BETWEEN TWO WOMEN (TF)   The Jon Avnet Company, 1986
VENGEANCE: THE STORY OF TONY CIMO (TF)   Nederlander TV
   and Film Productions/Robirdie Pictures, 1986
BARNUM (TF)   Robert Halmi, Inc./Filmline International, 1986,
   U.S.-Canadian
TRAPPED IN SILENCE (TF)   Reader's Digest Productions, 1986
THE MURDERS IN THE RUE MORGUE (TF)   Robert Halmi,
   Inc./International Film Productions, 1986
BROKEN VOWS (TF)   Brademan-Self Productions/Robert Halmi,
   Inc., 1987
AT MOTHER'S REQUEST (TF)   Vista Organization Ltd., 1987
IN LOVE AND WAR (TF)   Carol Schreder Productions/Tisch-Avnet
   Productions, 1987
APPRENTICE TO MURDER   New World, 1988, Canadian
PUNCHLINE   Columbia, 1988
OPEN ADMISSIONS (TF)   The Mount Company/Viacom
   Productions, 1988
SIDE BY SIDE (TF)   Avnet-Kerner Productions, 1988
LEAP OF FAITH (TF)   Hart, Thomas & Berlin Productions, 1988
THIRD DEGREE BURN (CTF)   HBO Pictures/MTM
   Enterprises/Paramount Pictures, 1989
TURNER AND HOOCH   Buena Vista, 1989
NO PLACE LIKE HOME (TF)   Feury-Grant Productions/Orion TV,
   1989
AIR AMERICA   TriStar, 1990
EYES OF A WITNESS (TF)   RHI, 1991
ANOTHER YOU   Tri-Star, 1991
LETHAL INNOCENCE (TF)   Entertainment Group/Turtleback, 1991
IN THE SHADOW OF A KILLER (TF)   NBC Prods., 1992
PASSPORT TO MURDER (TF)   FTM Prods., 1993
GOOD KING WENCESLAS (CTF)   1994
A FAMILY THING   MGM-UA, 1996

GREG GROSS
Contact: ASCAP - Los Angeles, 213-883-1000

BUFORD'S BEACH BUNNIES   Axis, 1992

GUY GROSS
Contact: APRA - Australia, 011-61-2-922-6422

THE ADVENTURES OF PRISCILLA, QUEEN OF THE DESERT
   Gramercy, 1994, Australian

JIM GROSS
A DIFFERENT AFFAIR (TF)   Rogers/Samuels Productions, 1987

LARRY GROSSMAN
Contact: BMI - Los Angeles, 310-659-9109

SUSPICION (TF)   Hemisphere Productions/HTV, 1988

DAVE GRUSIN
b. June 26, 1934 - Denver, Colorado
Agent: Gorfaine-Schwartz - Los Angeles, 213-969-1011
Affiliation: BMI - Los Angeles, 310-659-9109

THE SCORPIO LETTERS (TF)   MGM TV, 1967
DIVORCE AMERICAN STYLE   Columbia, 1967
WATERHOLE #3   Paramount, 1967
THE GRADUATE   Avco Embassy, 1967
CANDY   Cinerama Releasing Corporation, 1968,
   U.S.-Italian-French
THE HEART IS A LONELY HUNTER   Warner Bros., 1968
PRESCRIPTION: MURDER (TF)   Universal, 1968
TELL THEM WILLIE BOY WAS HERE   Universal, 1969
GENERATION   Avco Embassy, 1969
WINNING   Universal, 1969
THE MAD ROOM   Columbia, 1969
HALLS OF ANGER   United Artists, 1970
THE INTRUDERS (TF)   Universal TV, 1970
SARGE: THE BADGE OR THE CROSS (TF)   Universal TV,
   1971
THE DEADLY DREAM (TF)   Universal TV, 1971
A HOWLING IN THE WOODS (TF)   Universal TV, 1971
THE FORGOTTEN MAN (TF)   Grauman Productions, 1971
FUZZ   United Artists, 1972
THE GREAT NORTHFIELD, MINNESOTA RAID   Universal,
   1972
THE FAMILY RICO (TF)   CBS Entertainment, 1972
THE FRIENDS OF EDDIE COYLE   Paramount, 1973
THE MIDNIGHT MAN   Universal, 1974
THE NICKEL RIDE   20th Century-Fox, 1974
THE TRIAL OF CHAPLAIN JENSEN (TF)   Monash-Preissman
   Productions/20th Century-Fox TV, 1975
W.W. AND THE DIXIE DANCEKINGS   20th Century-Fox, 1975
THE YAKUZA   Warner Bros., 1975
3 DAYS OF THE CONDOR   Paramount, 1975
ERIC (TF)   Lorimar Productions, 1975
MURDER BY DEATH   Columbia, 1976
THE FRONT   Columbia, 1976
MR. BILLION   20th Century-Fox, 1976
BOBBY DEERFIELD   Columbia, 1977
FIRE SALE   20th Century-Fox, 1977
THE GOODBYE GIRL   Warner Bros., 1977
HEAVEN CAN WAIT ★   Paramount, 1978
THE CHAMP ★   MGM/United Artists, 1979
...AND JUSTICE FOR ALL   Columbia, 1979
THE ELECTRIC HORSEMAN   Columbia, 1979
MY BODYGUARD   20th Century-Fox, 1980
ABSENCE OF MALICE   Columbia, 1981
REDS   Paramount, 1981
ON GOLDEN POND ★   Universal/AFD, 1981
AUTHOR! AUTHOR!   20th Century-Fox, 1982
TOOTSIE   Columbia, 1982
RACING WITH THE MOON   Paramount, 1984
SCANDALOUS   Orion, 1984
THE POPE OF GREENWICH VILLAGE   MGM/UA, 1984
THE LITTLE DRUMMER GIRL   Warner Bros., 1984
FALLING IN LOVE   Paramount, 1984
GOONIES   Warner Bros., 1985
LUCAS   20th Century Fox, 1986
ISHTAR   Columbia, 1987
THE MILAGRO BEANFIELD WAR ★★   Universal, 1988
CLARA'S HEART   Warner Bros., 1988
TEQUILA SUNRISE   Warner Bros., 1988
A DRY WHITE SEASON   MGM/UA, 1989, U.S.-British
THE FABULOUS BAKER BOYS ★   20th Century Fox, 1989
THE BONFIRE OF THE VANITIES   Warner Bros., 1990
HAVANA ★   Universal, 1990
FOR THE BOYS   20th Century Fox, 1991
THE FIRM ★   Paramount, 1993
THE CURE   Universal, 1995
MULHOLLAND FALLS   MGM-UA, 1995
SELENA   Warner Bros., 1997

JAY GRUSKA*
b. April 23, 1952
Agent: Gorfaine-Schwartz - Los Angeles, 213-969-1011
Affiliation: ASCAP - Los Angeles, 213-883-1000

THE PRINCIPAL   Tri-Star, 1987
THERE WERE TIMES, DEAR (TF)   Lilac Productions, 1987
SHADOW DANCING   Shapiro Glickenhaus Entertainment, 1988,
   Canadian
TRAXX   DEG, 1988
SING   Tri-Star, 1989
WHEELS OF TERROR (CTF)   Once Upon a Time
   Productions/Wilshire Court Productions, 1990
BABY OF THE BRIDE (TF)   Baby Productions/Leonard Hill Films,
   1991
ANOTHER PAIR OF ACES: THREE OF A KIND (TF)   co-composer
   with Shelby Lynne, Pedernales/Once Upon A Time Films, 1991
CHILD OF DARKNESS, CHILD OF LIGHT (TF)   Wilshire Court/G.C.
   Group, 1991
MO' MONEY   Columbia, 1992
WITHOUT WARNING: TERROR IN THE TOWERS (TF)
   Melnicker/Wilshire Court, 1993
LOIS & CLARK: THE NEW ADVENTURES OF SUPERMAN (TF)
   Roundelay/Warner Bros. TV, 1993
DYING TO REMEMBER (CTF)   Cardera-Schenck, 1993
A TIME TO HEAL (TF)   based on Jay Gruska's life, Susan
   Baerwald Prods./NBC Prods., 1994
SAVED BY THE BELL (TF)   Peter Engel Prods./NBC Prods., 1994
TRAPPED IN SPACE (CTF)   CNM Ent./Village Roadshow
   Pictures/Wilshire Court, 1995

ZHANG GUANGTIAN
SHANGHAI TRIAD   *YAO A YAO YAO DAO WAIPO QIAO*   Sony
   Classics, 1995, Chinese-French

BARRIE GUARD
Contact: PRS - London, England, 011-44-1-580-5544

THE TOXIC AVENGER, PART II   Troma, 1989

CHARLES GUARD
THE MAN FROM THE PRU (TF)   1991, British

SOFIA GUBAIDULINA
Contact: GEMA - Germany, 011-49-89-480-03610

DE DOMEINEN DITVOORST   *THE DITVOORST DOMAIN*   1993,
   Dutch

ANTHONY GUEFEN
Contact: ASCAP - Los Angeles, 213-883-1000

DEADLY EYES   THE RATS   Warner Bros., 1983, Canadian
ASSASSIN (TF)   Sankan Productions, 1986

ANDREA GUERRA
JOURNEY OF LOVE   *VIAGGIO D'AMORE*   Centaur, 1991, Italian

JUAN LUIS GUERRA
Contact: BMI - Los Angeles, 310-659-9109

AMERICAS (TD)   WGBH/Central Television, 1993

ALBERT GUINOVART
EL LARGO INVIERNO   *THE LONG WINTER*   1992, Spanish

NICHOLAS GUNN
Contact: ASCAP - Los Angeles, 213-883-1000

TUESDAY NEVER COMES... V.L.P., 1993

CHRISTOPHER GUNNING
Contact: PRS - London, England, 011-44-1-580-5544

GOODBYE GEMINI   Cinerama Releasing Corporation, 1970,
   British
HANDS OF THE RIPPER   Universal, 1972, British
MAN ABOUT THE HOUSE   EMI, 1974, British
GET CHARLIE TULLY   TBS Distributing Corporation, 1976, British
WHEN THE WHALES CAME   20th Century Fox, 1989, British
UNDER SUSPICION   Columbia, 1991

GURU
GIRLS TOWN   1996

JONAS GWANGWA
Contact: BMI - Los Angeles, 310-659-9109

CRY FREEDOM ★   additional music, Universal, 1987, British-U.S.

ADAM GYETTEL
JACK (TD)   CBS Entertainment Prods., 1993

H

JURRE HAANSTRA
Affiliation: BUMA - Holland, 011-31/20-540-7911

LITTLE BLOND DEATH   *DE KLEINE BLONDE DOOD*
   co-composer with Toots Thielemans, 1994, Netherlands

EARLE HAGEN
Contact: BMI - Los Angeles, 310-659-9109

THE MONK (TF)   Thomas-Spelling Productions, 1969
HAVING BABIES (TF)   The Jozak Company, 1976
KILLER ON BOARD (TF)   Lorimar Productions, 1977
TRUE GRIT (A FURTHER ADVENTURE) (TF)   Parmaount Pictures
   TV, 1978
MURDER IN MUSIC CITY (TF)   Frankel Films/Gank Inc., 1979
EBONY, IVORY AND JADE (TF)   Frankel Films, 1979
THE HUSTLER OF MUSCLE BEACH (TF)   Furia-Oringer
   Productions, 1980
STAND BY YOUR MAN (TF)   Robert Papazian
   Productions/Guber-Peters Productions, 1981
MUGGABLE MARY: STREET COP (TF)   CBS Entertainment, 1982
MICKEY SPILLANE'S MIKE HAMMER: MURDER ME, MURDER
   YOU (TF)   Jay Bernstein Productions/Columbia Pictures
   Television, 1983
I TAKE THESE MEN (TF)   Lillian Gallo Productions/United Artists
   TV, 1983
MICKEY SPILLANE'S MIKE HAMMER: MORE THAN MURDER
   (TF)   Jay Bernstein/Columbia, 1984
NORTH BEACH AND RAWHIDE (TF)   CBS Entertainment
   Productions, 1985
RETURN TO MAYBERRY (TF)   Viacom Productions/Strathmore
   Productions, 1986
THE RETURN OF MICKEY SPILLANE'S MIKE HAMMER (TF)
   Columbia Pictures TV/Jay Bernstein Productions, 1986
I SPY RETURNS (TF)   theme only, SAH Ent./Sheldon Leonard
   Ent.,/Citadel, 1994

STEPHEN HAGUE
Contact: ASCAP - Los Angeles, 213-883-1000

SOME KIND OF WONDERFUL   co-composer with John Musser,
   Paramount, 1987

PHILIPPE HAIM
L'APPAT   *FRESH BAIT*   1995, French

FRANCIS HAINES
Contact: PRS - London, England, 011-44-1-580-5544

SPLIT SECOND   co-composer with Stephen Parsons, InterStar, 1992, British

CHRIS HAJIAN
NOTHING TO LOSE   Cubb Prods./Visland, 1995

ARDELL HAKE*
Contact: ASCAP - Los Angeles, 213-883-1000

SCARED TO DEATH   co-composer with Tom Chase, Lone Star Pictures, 1982

KEN HALE
THE NORMAL LIFE   co-composer with Bob McNaughton, 1996

JIM HALFPENNY*
Contact: BMI - Los Angeles, 310-659-9109

BIKINI SUMMER 2, 1992
MAGIC KID 2   PM, 1993
THE POWER WITHIN   PM Entertainment, 1995

RONALD HALICKI
Contact: BMI - Los Angeles, 310-659-9109

GONE IN 60 SECONDS   H.B. Halicki International, 1974

TOM T. HALL
Contact: BMI - Los Angeles, 310-659-9109

DEADHEAD MILES   Paramount, 1971

DICK HALLIGAN
Contact: BMI - Los Angeles, 310-659-9109

THE OWL AND THE PUSSYCAT   Columbia, 1970
GO TELL THE SPARTANS   Avco Embassy, 1978
ZUMA BEACH (TF)   Edgar J. Scherick Associates/Bruce Cohn Curtis Films/Warner Bros. TV, 1978
DIRT   American Cinema Releasing, 1979
A FORCE OF ONE   American Cinema Releasing, 1979
THE OCTAGON   American Cinema, 1980
CHEAPER TO KEEP HER   American Cinema, 1980
FEAR CITY   Chevy Chase Distribution, 1985

CHICO HAMILTON
b. 1921
Contact: BMI - Los Angeles, 310-659-9109

REPULSION   Royal Films International, 1965, British
THE CONFESSOR   1973
MR. RICCO   United Artists, 1975
COONSKIN   Bryanston Pictures, 1975
DIE SONNENGOTTIN   *THE SUN GODDESS*   1993, German

THE HAMILTONS
RUSH WEEK   Noble, 1991

MARVIN HAMLISCH
b. June 2, 1944 - New York, New York
Agent: Gorfaine-Schwartz - Los Angeles, 213-969-1011
Affiliation: ASCAP - Los Angeles, 213-883-1000

THE SWIMMER   Columbia, 1968
TAKE THE MONEY AND RUN   Cinerama Releasing Corporation, 1969
THE APRIL FOOLS   National General, 1969
MOVE   20th Century-Fox, 1970
FLAP   *THE LAST WARRIOR*   Warner Bros., 1970
BANANAS   United Artists, 1971
SOMETHING BIG   National General, 1971
KOTCH   Cinerama Releasing Corporation, 1971
FAT CITY   Columbia, 1972

THE WAR BETWEEN MEN AND WOMEN   National General, 1972
THE WORLD'S GREATEST ATHLETE   Buena Vista, 1973
SAVE THE TIGER   Paramount, 1973
THE WAY WE WERE ★★   Columbia, 1973
THE STING ★★   partial adaptation, Universal, 1973
THE PRISONER OF SECOND AVENUE   Warner Bros., 1975
THE ENTERTAINER (TF)   RSO Films, 1976
THE SPY WHO LOVED ME ★   United Artists, 1977, British-U.S.
SAME TIME NEXT YEAR   Universal, 1979
ICE CASTLES   Columbia, 1979
STARTING OVER   Paramount, 1979
ORDINARY PEOPLE   adaptation, Paramount, 1980
NEIL SIMON'S SEEMS LIKE OLD TIMES   *SEEMS LIKE OLD TIMES*   Columbia, 1980
THE DEVIL AND MAX DEVLIN   co-composer with Buddy Baker, Buena Vista, 1981
PENNIES FROM HEAVEN   MGM/UA, 1981
I OUGHT TO BE IN PICTURES   20th Century-Fox, 1982
SOPHIE'S CHOICE ★   Universal/AFD, 1982
ROMANTIC COMEDY   MGM/UA, 1983
A STREETCAR NAMED DESIRE (TF)   Keith Barish Productions, 1984
D.A.R.Y.L.   Paramount, 1985
THE TWO MRS. GRENVILLES (TF)   Lorimar-Telepictures, 1987
RETURN OF THE SIX MILLION DOLLAR MAN & THE BIONIC WOMAN (TF)   Michael Sloan Productions/Universal TV, 1987
WHEN THE TIME COMES (TF)   Jaffe-Lansing Productions/Republic Pictures, 1987
THREE MEN AND A BABY   Buena Vista, 1987
LITTLE NIKITA   Columbia, 1988
DAVID (TF)   Tough Boys Inc./Donald March Productions/ITC Entertainment Group, 1988
THE JANUARY MAN   MGM/UA, 1989
THE EXPERTS   Paramount, 1989
FRANKIE AND JOHNNY   Paramount, 1991
SWITCHED AT BIRTH (TF)   O'Hara-Horowitz Prods./Morrow-Heus Prods./Guber-Peters/Columbia TV, 1991
SEASONS OF THE HEART (TF)   Joseph Feury Prods./RHI, 1994
OPEN SEASON   Frozen Rope Prods., 1995
THE MIRROR HAS TWO FACES   TriStar, 1996

JAN HAMMER
Contact: ASCAP - Los Angeles, 213-883-1000

A NIGHT IN HEAVEN   20th Century-Fox, 1983
GIMME AN F   20th Century Fox, 1984
MIAMI VICE (TF)   The Michael Mann Company/Universal TV, 1984
TWO FATHER'S JUSTICE (TF)   A Shane Co. Productions, 1985
SECRET ADMIRER   Orion, 1985
CHARLEY HANNAH (TF)   A Shane Co. Productions/Telepictures Productions, 1986
CLINTON AND NADINE (CTF)   HBO Pictures/ITC, 1988
CAPITOL NEWS (TF)   MTM, 1989
CURIOSITY KILLS (CTF)   Universal/Davis Entertainment, 1990
KNIGHT RIDER 2000 (TF)   Desperado Films, 1991
THE TAKING OF BEVERLY HILLS   Columbia, 1991
I COME IN PEACE   Triumph, 1991
K-9000 (TF)   De Souza Prods./Fries Ent., 1991
IN THE KINGDOM OF THE BLIND, THE MAN WITH ONE EYE IS KING   1995
BEASMASTER 3 (CTF)   1996
COPORATE LADDER   Orion, 1997

HERBIE HANCOCK
b. 1940
Contact: BMI - Los Angeles, 310-659-9109

BLOWUP   Premier, 1966, British-Italian
THE SPOOK WHO SAT BY THE DOOR   United Artists, 1973
DEATH WISH   Paramount, 1974
A SOLDIER'S STORY   Columbia, 1984
JO JO DANCER, YOUR LIFE IS CALLING   Columbia, 1986
ROUND MIDNIGHT ★★   Warner Bros., 1986, U.S.-French
THE GEORGE McKENNA STORY (TF)   The Landsburg Company, 1986
ACTION JACKSON   co-composer with Michael Kamen, Lorimar, 1988
COLORS   Orion, 1988
HARLEM NIGHTS   Paramount, 1989
LIVIN' LARGE   Samuel Goldwyn, 1991

CRAIG HANDY

THE COSBY MYSTERIES (TF)   co-composer with Bill Cosby and Charles Mingus, SAH Ent./Columbia Pictures TV/NBC Prods., 1994

KENTARO HANEDA

b. Japanese
Contact: JASRAC - Tokyo, Japan, 011-81-3-502-6551

SENGOKU JIEITAL *TIME SLIP*   Toei, 1981, Japanese

BRUCE HANIFAN*

Contact: BMI - Los Angeles, 310-659-9109

GUARDIAN ANGEL   PM, 1993

WILLIAM HANNA

Contact: BMI - Los Angeles, 310-659-9109

I YABBA-DABBA DO! (TF)   co-composer with John Debney, Hoyt Curtin and Joseph Barbera, H-B Prods., 1993
JONNY'S GOLDEN QUEST (ATF)   co-composer of theme only with Joseph Barbera and Hoyt Curtin, Hanna-Barbera/USA/Fil-Cartoons, 1993

JONATHAN HANNAH

ROOMMATES   Platinum Pictures, 1982

PETR HAPKA

Contact: OSA - Tr. Cs. Armady 20, 160-56 Prague 6-Bubene, Czechoslovakia

THE NINTH HEART   Ceskoslovensky Filmexport, 1980, Czech

JOHN WESLEY HARDING

Contact: PRS - London, England, 011-44-1-580-5544

THE PAINT JOB   Second Son, 1992

HAGOOD HARDY

b. Canada
Contact: SOCAN - Toronto, 416-445-8700

SECOND WIND   Health and Entertainment Corporation of America, 1976, Canadian
TELL ME MY NAME (TF)   co-composer with Mickey Erbe, Talent Associates Ltd., 1977
HOME TO STAY (TF)   Time-Life Productions, 1978
ANATOMY OF A SEDUCTION (TF)   Moonlight Productions/Filmways, 1979
AN AMERICANCHRISTMAS CAROL (TF)   Scherick/Chase/Slan Productions/Smith-Hemion Productions/Scrooge Productions, 1979
PORTRAIT OF AN ESCORT (TF)   Moonlight Productions/Filmways, 1980
KLONDIKE FEVER   1980
DIRTY TRICKS Avco Embassy, 1981, Canadian
FORBIDDEN LOVE (TF)   Gross-Weston Productions, 1982
THE WILD PONY (TF)   Sullivan Films, Inc., 1982, Canadian
RONA JAFFE'S MAZES AND MONSTERS (TF)   McDermott Productions/Procter & Gamble Productions, 1982
THIS CHILD IS MINE (TF)   Beth Polson Productions/Finnegan Associates/Telepictures Productions, 1985
THE CANADIANS (MS)   Cineworld, Canadian
ANNE OF GREEN GABLES (MS)   Anne of Green Gables Productions/PBS WonderWorks/CBS/60 Film Productions/ZDF/City TV/Telefilm Canada, 1985, Canadian-U.S.-West German
ANNE OF AVONLEA: THE CONTINUING STORY OF ANNE OF GREEN GABLES (MS)   Sullivan Films/CBC/The Disney Channel/PBS WonderWorks/Telefilm Canada, 1987, Canadian-U.S.
LIBERACE: BEHIND THE MUSIC (TF)   Canadian International Studios/Kushner-Locke Productions, 1988, U.S.-Canadian
PASSION AND PARADISE (TF)   Picturebase International/Primedia Productions/Leonard Hill Films, 1989, U.S.-Canadian
AVONLEA (CTF)   The Disney Channel/Sullivan Films, 1990

JOHN HARDY

STREETLIFE   1995, British

JOHN HARLE

BUTTERFLY KISS   1995, British

JEFF B. HARMON

ISLE OF LESBOS   Duce Films, 1997

JOE HARNELL*

b. August 2, 1924 - New York, New York
Contact: ASCAP - Los Angeles, 213-883-1000

THE INCREDIBLE HULK (TF)   Universal TV, 1977
THE RETURN OF THE INCREDIBLE HULK (TF)   Universal TV, 1977
THE MURDER THAT WOULDN'T DIE (TF)   co-composer with Glen A. Larson, Glen A. Larson Productions/Universal TV, 1980
SENIOR TRIP (TF)   Kenneth Johnson Productions, 1981
V (TF) ☆   Kenneth Johnson Productions/Warner Bros. TV, 1983
HOT PURSUIT (TF)   Kenneth Johnson Productions/NBC Productions, 1984
THE LIBERATORS (TF)   Kenneth Johnson Productions/Walt Disney TV, 1987

UDI HARPAZ

Agent: Zomba Screen Music - West Hollywood, 310-246-0777
Affiliation: BMI - Los Angeles, 310-659-9109

THE LAST HORROR FILM *FANATIC*   Twin Continental, 1982
THE MAN WHO WASN'T THERE   additional music, Paramount, 1983
NINJA III: THE DOMINATION   Cannon, 1984
THE LAST HORROR FILM   Shere Productions, 1984
THE ANNIHILATOR (TF)   Universal TV, 1986
RUNNING SCARED   additional music, MGM, 1986
THE WHOOPEE BOYS   additional music, Paramount, 1986
HOLLYWOOD SHUFFLE   co-composer with Patrice Rushen, Samuel Goldwyn Company, 1987
UNCLE TOM'S CABIN (CTF)   additional music, Showtime, 1987
NAKED TARGET   Frade Prods., 1992
SHADOW OF OBSESSION (TF)   Saban, 1994

SCOTT HARPER

Agent: Carol Faith Agency - Beverly Hills, 310-274-0776
Contact: BMI - Los Angeles, 310-659-9109

ROSEANNE: AN UNAUTHORIZED BIOGRAPHY (TF)   DDF Films, 1994

ANTHONY HARRIS

Contact: ASCAP - Los Angeles, 213-883-1000

THE KILLING OF A CHINESE BOOKIE   Faces Distribution, 1976
COACH   Crown International, 1978

ARTHUR HARRIS

Contact: BMI - Los Angeles, 310-659-9109

BRONTE   Charlotte Ltd. Partnership/Radio Telefis Eireann, 1983, U.S.-Irish

JOHNNY HARRIS*

Contact: BMI - Los Angeles, 310-659-9109

MAN IN THE WILDERNESS   Warner Bros., 1971
THE INITIATION OF SARAH (TF)   Charles Fries Productions/Stonehenge Productions, 1978
THE EVIL   New World, 1978
THE LAST SONG (TF)   Ron Samuels Productions/Motown Productions, 1980
BORN TO BE SOLD (TF)   Ron Samuels Productions, 1981
HOTLINE (TF)   Ron Samuels Productions/Wrather Entertainment International, 1982
CAN YOU FEEL ME DANCING? (TF)   Robert Greenwald Productions, 1986
NECESSITY (TF)   Barry-Enright Productions/Alexander Prods., 1988

MAID FOR EACH OTHER (TF)   Alexander-Enright &
Associates/Hearst, 1992
LIES AND LULLABIES (TF)   Susan Dey
Prods./Alexander-Enright/Hearst. 1993
FAMILY PICTURES (TF)   Alexander-Enright & Associates/Hearst,
1993
I SPY RETURNS (TF)   SAH Ent./Sheldon Leonard Ent,/Citadel,
1994
THICKER THAN BLOOD: THE LARRY McLINDEN STORY (TF)
Alexander-Enright & Associates, 1994

MAX HARRIS

Contact: PRS - London, England, 011-44-1-580-5544

DREAMCHILD   additional music, Universal, 1985, British

GEORGE HARRISON

b. February 25, 1943 - Wavertree, England
Contact: PRS - London, England, 011-44-1-580-5544

SHANGHAI SURPRISE   co-composer with Michael Kamen,
MGM/UA, 1986, British-U.S.

JOHN HARRISON

CREEPSHOW   Warner Bros., 1982
DAY OF THE DEAD   United Film Distribution, 1985
TALES OF THE DARKSIDE: THE MOVIE   co-composer,
Paramount, 1990

KEN HARRISON*

Agent: Film Music Associates - Hollywood, 213-463-1070
Affiliation: ASCAP - Los Angeles, 213-883-1000

WAIT TILL YOUR MOTHER GETS HOME (TF)   Blue-Greene
Productions/NBC Productions, 1983
MEATBALLS PART II   Tri-Star, 1984
HOLLYWOOD BEAT (TF)   Aaron Spelling Productions, 1985
DARK MANSIONS (TF)   Aaron Spelling Productions, 1986
A NIGHTMARE ON ELM STREET III: DREAM WARRIORS
additional music, New Line, 1987
HEARTBEAT (TF)   Aaron Spelling Productions, 1988
JAILBIRDS (TF)   Spelling, 1991
I STILL DREAM OF JEANNIE (TF)   Jeannie Ent./Carla Singer
Prods./Bar-Gene TV, 1991
THE FORGET ME NOT MURDERS (TF)   Janek Prods./Pendick
Ent./Spelling TV, 1994
MacGYVER: LOST TREASURE OF ATLANTIS (TF)   Gekko
Films/Winkler-Rich Prods./Paramount Network TV, 1994
MacGYVER: TRAIL TO DOOMSDAY (TF)   Gekkofilm/Winkler-Rich
Prods./Paramount Network TV, 1994
A SILENT BETRAYAL (TF)   Pendick Enterprises/Spelling TV, 1994
THE SHAMROCK CONSPIRACY (TF)   Crescendo Prods./Michael
Gleason Prods./Paramount TV, 1995
LEGEND (TF)   Gekko Film Corp./Mike & Bill Prods./UPN, 1995

JOEY HARROW

LOSER   co-composer with Matthew Fritz, LTM, 1991

JAMES HART

Contact: BMI - Los Angeles, 310-659-9109

GHOST FEVER   Miramax, 1987

MARK HART

LIFE AMONG THE CANNIBALS   Trident, 1997

RICHARD HARTLEY

Agent: Film Music Associates - Hollywood, 213-463-1070
Affiliation: PRS - London, England, 011-44-1-580-5544

GALILEO   co-composer with Hanns Eisler, American Film Theatre,
1975
THE ROMANTIC ENGLISHWOMAN   New World, 1975, British
THE ROCKY HORROR PICTURE SHOW   20th Century-Fox, 1975,
British
ACES HIGH   Cinema Shares International, 1977, British

THE LADY VANISHES   Rank, 1979, British
BAD TIMING/A SENSUAL OBSESSION   World Northal, 1980,
British
SHOCK TREATMENT   20th Century-Fox, 1981, British
LA TRUITE   THE TROUT   Gaumont, 1982, French
BAD BLOOD   Southern Pictures/New Zealand Film Commission,
1983, New Zealand
KENNEDY (MS)   Central Independent Television Productions/Alan
Landsburg Productions, 1983, British-U.S.
SHEENA   Columbia, 1984
HITLER'S S.S.: PORTRAIT IN EVIL (TF)   Colason Limited
Productions/Edgar J. Scherick Associates, 1985, British-U.S.
BLUE MONEY (TF)   London Weekend Television, 1985, British
PARKER   Virgin Films, 1985, British
THE McGUFFIN (TF)   BBC, 1985, British
DANCE WITH A STRANGER   Samuel Goldwyn Company, 1985,
British
THE GOOD FATHER   Skouras Pictures, 1986, British
NAZI HUNTER: THE BEATE KLARSFELD STORY (TF)   William
Kayden Productions/Orion TV/Silver Chalice/Revcom/George
Walker TV/TF1/SFP, 1986, U.S.-British-French
THE IMPOSSIBLE SPY (CTF)   HBO Showcase/BBC/Quartet
International/IMGC, 1987, British-Israeli
MANDELA (CTF)   Titus Productions/Polymuse Inc./TVS Ltd., 1987,
U.S.-British
TUMBLEDOWN (TF)   BBC, 1988, British
SOURSWEET   Skouras Pictures, 1988, British
CONSUMING PASSIONS   Samuel Goldwyn Company, 1988,
British
THE FOUR MINUTE MILE (TF)   Oscar-Sullivan Productions/Centre
Films, 1988, Australian
THE TREE OF HANDS   Greenpoint/Granada/British Screen, 1989,
British
DEALERS   Samuel Goldwyn Company, 1989, British
SHE'S BEEN AWAY   BBC Films, 1989, British
ADAM BEDE (TF)   BBC/WGBH, 1992, British
SUDDENLY LAST SUMMER (TF)   1993, British
THE SECRET RAPTURE   1993, British
THE RECTOR'S WIFE (TF)   Talisman Films, 1994, British
PRINCESS CARABOO   TriStar, 1994
AN AWFULLY BIG ADVENTURE   Fine Line, 1995
ROUGH MAGIC   Savoy, 1995, British-French
STEALING BEAUTY   1996
THE VAN   20th Century Fox, 1997

PAUL HARTZOP

KICKBOXER   Pathe Entertainment, 1989

RICHARD HARVEY

Contact: PRS - London, England, 011-44-1-580-5544

THE MARTIAN CHRONICLES (TF)   co-composer with Stanley
Myers, Charles Fries Productions/Stonehenge Productions, 1980
DEATH OF AN EXPERT WITNESS (MS)   Anglia TV, 1982, British
BEYOND THE LIMIT   THE HONORARY CONSUL   additional
music, Paramount, 1983, British
HOUSE OF THE LONG SHADOWS   MGM/UA/Cannon, 1983,
British
STEAMING   New World, 1984, British
WINTER FLIGHT   Cinecom, 1984, British, originally made for
television
THE ASSAM GARDEN   The Moving Picture Company, 1985,
British
PING PONG   Samuel Goldwyn Company, 1985, British
DEFENSE OF THE REALM   Hemdale, 1985, British
DIRTY DOZEN: THE NEXT MISSION (TF)   MGM-UA TV, 1985
HALF MOON STREET   20th Century Fox, 1986, British
FIRST AMONG EQUALS (MS)   Grenada, 1987, British
INSIDE STORY (MS)   Anglia International, 1988, British
GAME, SET AND MATCH (MS)   Grenada, 1989, British
A SMALL DANCE (TF)   1991, British
THE SHAPE OF THE WORLD (TD)   Grenada/WNET, 1991
THE MARCH (CTF)   BBC TV/One World, 1991
HOSTAGES (CTF)   HBO/Granada, 1993, U.S.-British
DOOMSDAY GUN (CTF)   Griffin Prods./HBO Showcase, 1994
DOCTOR FINLAY (TF)   Scottish TV, 1994, British

SHANE HARVEY

CLEARCUT   Alliance, 1991, Canadian

BO HARWOOD

Contact: ASCAP - Los Angeles, 213-883-1000

A WOMAN UNDER THE INFLUENCE   Faces International, 1974
THE KILLING OF A CHINESE BOOKIE   Faces International, 1976
OPENING NIGHT   Faces International, 1978
HAPPY BIRTHDAY TO ME   co-composer with Lance Rubin,
    Columbia, 1981
UPS & DOWNS   Astral Films, 1983, Canadian
LOVE STREAMS   Cannon, 1984

JIMMIE HASKELL*

b. Brooklyn, New York
Agent: Andi Howard - Los Angeles, 310-278-6483
Affiliation: ASCAP - Los Angeles, 213-883-1000

LOVE IN A GOLDFISH BOWL   Paramount, 1961
THE GUN HAWK   Allied Artists, 1963
BLACK SPURS   Paramount, 1965
I'LL TAKE SWEDEN   United Artists, 1965
LOVE AND KISSES   co-composer with William Loose, Universal,
    1965
TOWN TAMER   Paramount, 1965
WILD ON THE BEACH   20th Century-Fox, 1965
WACO   Paramount, 1966
APACHE UPRISING   Paramount, 1966
JOHNNY RENO   Paramount, 1966
RED TOMAHAWK   Paramount, 1967
FORT UTAH   Paramount, 1967
HOSTILE GUNS   Paramount, 1967
BUCKSKIN   Paramount, 1967
ARIZONA BUSHWACKERS   Paramount, 1967
THE WICKED DREAMS OF PAULA SCHULTZ   United Artists,
    1968
DAGMAR'S HOT PANTS, INC.   1971
WALLS OF FIRE   1971, U.S.-Mexican
ZACHARIAH   Cinerama Releasing Corporation, 1971
THE HONKERS   United Artists, 1972
NIGHT OF THE LEPUS   MGM, 1972
OUTRAGE! (TF)   ABC Circle Films, 1973
DIRTY MARY CRAZY LARRY   20th Century-Fox, 1974
LIPSTICK   co-composer with Michel Polnareff, Paramount, 1976
DEATH GAME   Levitt-Pickman, 1977
JOYRIDE   American International, 1977
JUST A LITTLE INCONVENIENCE (TF)   Universal TV, 1977
SEE HOW SHE RUNS (TF) ☆☆   CLN Productions, 1978
A CHRISTMAS TO REMEMBER (TF)   George Englund Enterprises,
    1978
DALLAS COWBOY CHEERLEADERS (TF)   Aubrey-Hamner
    Productions, 1979
SILENT VICTORY: THE KITTY O'NEIL STORY (TF)   The
    Channing-Debin-Locke Company, 1979
THE SEEDING OF SARAH BURNS (TF)   Michael Klein
    Productions/Papazian Productions, 1979
THE JERICHO MILE (TF)   ABC Circle Films, 1979
THE CHILD STEALER (TF)   The Production Company/Columbia
    TV, 1979
BEFORE AND AFTER (TF)   The Konigsberg Company, 1979
MIRROR, MIRROR (TF)   Christiana Productions, 1979
GOLDIE AND THE BOXER (TF)   Orenthal Productions/Columbia
    Pictures TV, 1979
WHEN HELL WAS IN SESSION (TF)   Aubrey-Hamner Productions,
    1979
THE STREETS OF L.A. (TF)   George Englund Productions, 1979
THE $5.20 AN HOUR DREAM (TF)   Thomas-Sagal
    Productions/Finnegan Associates/Big Deal, 1980
DALLAS COWBOY CHEERLEADERS II (TF)   Aubrey-Hamner
    Productions, 1980
A CRY FOR LOVE (TF)   Charles Fries Productions/Alan Sacks
    Productions, 1980
FOR THE LOVE OF IT (TF)   Charles Fries Productions/Neila
    Productions, 1980
THE JAYNE MANSFIELD STORY (TF)   Alan Landsburg
    Productions, 1980
MARK, I LOVE YOU (TF)   The Aubrey Company, 1980
GOLDIE AND THE BOXER GO HOLLYWOOD (TF)   Orenthal
    Productions/Columbia Pictures TV, 1980
A GUN IN THE HOUSE (TF)   The Channing-Debin-Locke
    Company, 1981
THE STAR MAKER (TF)   The Channing-Debin-Locke
    Company/Carson Productions, 1981

LEAVE 'EM LAUGHING (TF)   Julian Fowles Productions/Charles
    Fries Productions, 1981
HARD COUNTRY   co-composer with Michael Martin Murphey,
    Universal/AFD, 1981
TWIRL (TF)   Charles Fries Productions/Atrium Productions, 1981
PORTRAIT OF A SHOWGIRL (TF)   Hamner Productions, 1982
DIXIE: CHANGING HABITS (TF)   George Englund Productions,
    1983
CARPOOL (TF)   Charles Fries Productions, 1983
JEALOUSY (TF)   co-composer with Gil Melle, Charles Fries
    Productions/Alan Sacks Productions, 1984
THE VEGAS STRIP WARS (TF)   George Englund Productions,
    1984
TERRORIST ON TRIAL: THE UNITED STATES VS. SALIM AJAMI
    (TF)   George Englund Productions/Robert Papazian Productions,
    1988
BRING ME THE HEAD OF DOBIE GILLIS (TF)   20th Century Fox
    TV, 1988
SHE'S BACK   Vestron, 1989
JAKE SPANNER, PRIVATE EYE (TF)   Andrew J. Fenady
    Productions/Scotti-Vinnedge TV, 1989

GEORGE HATZINASSIOS

b. Greece
Contact: SACEM - France, 011-33-1-4715-4715

JUPITER'S THIGH   ON A VOLE LA CRUISSE DE JUPITER
    Quartet/Films Inc., 1980, French
SWEET BUNCH   GLYKIA SYMMORIA   1983, Greek
SHIRLEY VALENTINE   co-composer with Willy Russell,
    Paramount, 1989

HAUNTED GARAGE

BREAKFAST OF ALIENS   co-composer with Mathew Ender, Eric
    Parkinson and Hemdale, 1993

BRENT HAVENS

Contact: ASCAP - Los Angeles, 213-883-1000

THE PISTOL: THE BIRTH OF A LEGEND   Premier, 1991

RICHIE HAVENS

Contact: ASCAP - Los Angeles, 213-883-1000

BROTHER MINISTER: THE ASSASSINATION OF MALCOLM X
    (FD)   X-Ceptional Prods., 1994

GREG HAWKES

Contact: ASCAP - Los Angeles, 213-883-1000

ANNA   Vestron, 1987

ALAN HAWKSHAW

Contact: PRS - London, England, 011-44-1-580-5544

MAGIC MOMENTS (CTF)   Arena Films/Atlantic
    Videoventures/Yorkshire TV, 1989, U.S.-British

PETER HAYCOCK

Contact: ASCAP - Los Angeles, 213-883-1000

ONE FALSE MOVE   co-composer with Derek Holt, I.R.S., 1991

ROY HAY

GOODBYE AMERICA   Quantum entertainment, 1997

TODD HAYEN*

Agent: Carol Faith Agency - Beverly HIlls, 310-274-0776
Affiliation: BMI - Los Angeles, 310-659-9109

THE DEVIL'S GIFT   Zenith International, 1984
AEROBICIDE   Maverick Films, 1986
THROUGH THE LOOKING GLASS (AF)   Jambre Productions, 1987
TIME BURST   Action International Pictures, 1988
A SINFUL LIFE   New Line Cinema, 1989
NEXT OF KIN   additional music, Warner Bros., 1989
THE SHOOTERS   Action International Pictures, 1990

ISAAC HAYES
b. August 20, 1942 - Covington, Kentucky
Contact: BMI - Los Angeles, 310-659-9109

SHAFT★   MGM, 1971
SHAFT'S BIG SCORE   co-composer with Gordon Parks, MGM, 1972
THREE TOUGH GUYS   Paramount, 1974, Italian-U.S.
TRUCK TURNER   American International, 1974

JACK HAYES
Contact: ASCAP - Los Angeles, 213-883-1000

FAST FORWARD   co-composer with Tom Scott, Columbia, 1985
THE COLOR PURPLE ★   co-composer, Warner Bros., 1985

RED HAYS
MY LIFE'S IN TURNAROUND   Islet, 1993

RICHARD HAZARD
b. 1921
Contact: BMI - Los Angeles, 310-659-9109

SOME CALL IT LOVING   Cine Globe, 1973
THE UNDERGROUND MAN (TF)   Aries Films/Paramount Pictures TV, 1974
LAW AND ORDER (TF)   P A Productions/Paramount Pictures TV, 1976
NICKELODEON   Columbia, 1976
HEROES   co-composer with Jack Nitzsche, Universal, 1977
WITH THIS RING (TF)   co-composer with George Aliceson Tipton, The Jozak Company/Paramount Pictures TV, 1978
ALL NIGHT LONG   co-composer with Ira Newborn, Universal, 1981
BETWEEN TWO BROTHERS (TF)   Turman-Foster Company Productions/Finnegan Associates, 1982
AIRPLANE II: THE SEQUEL   Paramount, 1982

CHRISTOPHER HEDGE
LAND OF MILK & HONEY   1995

NEAL HEFTI
b. October 29, 1922 - Hastings, Nebraska
Contact: BMI - Los Angeles, 310-659-9109

SEX AND THE SINGLE GIRL   Warner Bros., 1965
HOW TO MURDER YOUR WIFE   United Artists, 1965
BOEING BOEING   Paramount, 1965
HARLOW   Paramount, 1965
SYNANON   Columbia, 1965
LORD LOVE A DUCK   United Artists, 1966
DUEL AT DIABLO   United Artists, 1966
BAREFOOT IN THE PARK   Paramount, 1966
OH DAD, POOR DAD, MAMA'S HUNG YOU IN THE CLOSET AND I'M FEELIN' SO SAD   Paramount, 1967
THE ODD COUPLE   Paramount, 1968
P.J.   Universal, 1968
LAST OF THE RED HOT LOVERS   Paramount, 1972
THE 500-POUND JERK (TF)   David L. Wolper Productions, 1973
CONSPIRACY OF TERROR (TF)   Lorimar Productions, 1975
WON TON TON, THE DOG WHO SAVED HOLLYWOOD   Paramount, 1976
THE ODD COUPLE (TF)   theme only, Howard W. Koch Prods/Paramount TV, 1993

TOM HEIL
THE BUDDY FACTOR   Cineville, 1994

FRED HELLERMAN
Contact: ASCAP - Los Angeles, 213-883-1000

LOVIN' MOLLY   Columbia, 1974

JIM HELMS
Contact: ASCAP - Los Angeles, 213-883-1000

ACE OF SPADES   HowCo International, 1969
THE LOVING TOUCH   Wakeford/Orloff, 1969
GLORY BOY   additional music, Cinerama, 1969
THE LOW PRICE OF FAME   Carvell Productions, 1970
HOW DO I LOVE THEE?   ABC Films, 1970
HIS WIFE'S HABIT   HowCo International, 1971
KEEP OFF MY GRASS   Alan Yasni, 1971
ANGEL UNCHAINED   American International, 1972
THE E BOX   P&C Productions, 1972
KUNG FU (TF)   Warner Bros. TV, 1972
THE UFO CHRONICLES   Ocean Park, 1973
DEATH AMONG FRIENDS (TF)   The Douglas Cramer Company/Warner Bros. TV, 1975
NIGHT CREATURE   Dimension Pictures, 1979

LOUIS FREDRIC HEMSEY
Contact: ASCAP - Los Angeles, 213-883-1000

BORNEO (TD)   1986

DAVID HENTSCHEL
Contact: PRS - London, England, 011-44-1-580-5544

OPERATION DAYBREAK   Warner Bros., 1976
SEVEN NIGHTS IN JAPAN   Paramount, 1976, British-French
THE SQUEEZE   Warner Bros., 1977
EDUCATING RITA   Columbia, 1983, British

HANS WERNER HENZE
Contact: GEMA - Germany, 011-49-89-480-03610

MURIEL   Lopert, 1963, French-Italian
YOUNG TORLESS   Kanawha, 1966, West German-French
THE LOST HONOR OF KATHARINA BLUM   New World, 1975, West German
GOOD FOR NOTHING   1978, French
SWANN IN LOVE   Orion Classics, 1984, French-West German
L'AMOUR A MORT   Roissy Film, 1984, French
COMRADES   co-composer with David Graham, British Film Institute, 1986, British

LARRY HERBSTRITT
BANDIT: BEAUTY AND THE BANDIT (TF)   Yahi Prods./IPS Prods., 1994

ANDY HERNANDEZ
Contact: ASCAP - Los Angeles, 213-883-1000

MIXED BLOOD   Sara Films, 1984, U.S.-French

MARIE-CLAUDE HERRY
LE BAL DES CASSE-PIEDS   co-composer with Vladimir Cosma, 1992, French

PHILIPPE HERSANT
Contact: SACEM - France, 011-33-1-4715-4715

LETTRE POUR L...   *LETTER FOR L...*   1993, French

PAUL HERTZOG
Agent: Artists Group - Los Angeles, 310-552-1100
Affiliation: BMI - Los Angeles, 310-659-9109

MY CHAUFFEUR   Crown International, 1985
BLOODSPORT   Cannon, 1988
DANGEROUS LOVE   Concorde, 1988
KICKBOXER   Kings Road, 1989
STREET JUSTICE   co-composer with Jamii Szmadzinski, Street Justice Productions, 1989

DAVID ALEX HESS
LAST HOUSE ON THE LEFT   Hallmark Releasing Corporation, 1973

NIGEL HESS

Agent: Air-Edel - Los Angeles, 310-914-5000
Affiliation: PRS - London, England, 011-44-1-580-5544

A WOMAN OF SUBSTANCE (MS) Artemis Productions/Portman
   Productions, 1984
REUNION AT FAIRBOROUGH (CTF) HBO Premiere Films/Alan
   Wagner Productions/Alan King Productions/Columbia TV, 1985
DECEPTIONS (TF) Louis Rudolph Productions/Consolidated
   Productions/Columbia TV, 1985, U.S.-British
THE DOG IT WAS THAT DIED (TF) Granada TV, 1988, British
SUMMER'S LEASE (TF) 1991, British

MIKE HEWER

KNUCKLEBALL 1995, U.S.-British

JERRY HEY

Contact: BMI - Los Angeles, 310-659-9109

THE COLOR PURPLE ★ co-composer, Warner Bros., 1985

JOHN HICKS

HARLEM DIARY: NINE VOICES OF RESILIENCE (FD) Gabriel
   Films, 1995

HIDDEN FACES

(see Frank Fitzpatrick)

RICHARD HIERONYMOUS

Contact: ASCAP - Los Angeles, 213-883-1000

THE FOREST *TERROR IN THE FOREST* co-composer with Alan
   Oldfield, Fury Film Distribution Ltd., 1983
INVISIBLE STRANGLER co-composer with Alan Oldfield,
   Seymour Borde & Associates, 1984

JOHN HILL

THE POMPATUS OF LOVE 1996

RICHARD HILL

Contact: BMI - Los Angeles, 310-659-9109

BAFFLED! (TF) Arena Productions/ITC, 1973

FRANCES HIME

Contact: SBAT

DONA FLOR AND HER TWO HUSBANDS New Yorker, 1977,
   Brazilian
LOVE LESSON Embra, 1978, Brazilian

PETER HIMMELMAN

Agent: Seth Kaplan Entertainment - Los Angeles, 213-525-3477
Affiliation: ASCAP - Los Angeles, 213-883-1000

CROSSING THE BRIDGE Buena Vista, 1992
THE SOULER OPPOSITE Buffalo Jump Productions, 1997

RUPERT HINE

Contact: PRS - London, England, 011-44-1-580-5544

THE SHOUT co-composer with Anthony Banks and Michael
   Rutherford, Films Inc., 1979, British
BETTER OFF DEAD Warner Bros., 1985

WILBERT HIRSCH

MUTE WITNESS Sony Classics, 1995, British

JOEL HIRSCHHORN

Contact: BMI - Los Angeles, 310-659-9109

WHO KILLED TEDDY BEAR? co-composer with Al Kasha, Magna,
   1965
FAT SPY co-composer with Al Kasha, Magna, 1966

TRAPPED BENEATH THE SEA (TF) co-composer with Al Kasha,
   ABC Circle Films, 1974
CHINA CRY co-composer with Al Kasha, Penland, 1990
THE CLOSER co-composer with Al Kasha, Ion, 1991
THE GIANT OF THUNDER MOUNTAIN co-composer with Al
   Kasha, New Generation, 1991
RESCUE ME co-composer with Al Kasha and David Waters,
   Cannon, 1993

DAVID HIRSHFELDER

Agent: Air-Edel - Los Angeles, 310-914-5000
Affiliation: APRA - Australia, 011-61-2-922-6422

STRICTLY BALLROOM 1992, Australian
SHINE ★ Fine Line, 1996, Australian

JO HISAISHI

MY NEIGHBOR TOTORO (AF) Troma, 1993, Japanese

GENE HOBSON

Contact: ASCAP - Los Angeles, 213-883-1000

STUDENT BODIES Paramount, 1981
LITTLE SECRETS Cinecam, 1991

BRIAN HODGSON

Contact: PRS - London, England, 011-44-1-580-5544

THE LEGEND OF HELL HOUSE co-composer with Delia
   Derbyshire, 20th Century-Fox, 1973, British

MICHAEL HOENIG

Agent: Gorfaine-Schwartz - Los Angeles, 213-969-1011
Affiliation: ASCAP - Los Angeles, 213-883-1000

DEADLY ENCOUNTER (TF) co-composer with Fred Karlin, Roger
   Gimbel Productions/EMI TV/Promises Productions, 1982
SILENT WITNESS (TF) Robert Greenwald Productions, 1985
SHATTERED SPIRITS (TF) Sheen-Greenblatt Productions/Robert
   Greenwald Productions, 1986
THE WRAITH New Century/Vista, 1986
THE GATE co-composer with J. Peter Robinson, New
   Century/Vista, 1987, Canadian
THE BLOB Tri-Star, 1988
CLASS OF 1999 Vestron, 1989
I, MADMAN Trans World Entertainment, 1989
BEYOND CONTROL: THE AMY FISHER STORY (TF) Andrew
   Adelson Co./ABC Prods., 1992
VISIONS OF MURDER (TF) Bar-Gene Prods./Freyda Rothstein
   Prods./Hearst, 1993
EYES OF TERROR (TF) Bar-Gene Prods./Freyda Rothstein
   Prods./Hearst, 1994
SEARCH FOR GRACE (TF) CBS Entertainment Prods., 1994

GARY HOEY

Contact: ASCAP - Los Angeles, 213-883-1000

THE ENDLESS SUMMER II co-composer with Phil Marshall, New
   Line, 1994

BERNARD HOFFER

Contact: ASCAP - Los Angeles, 213-883-1000

THE IVORY APE (TF) co-composer with Maury Laws,
   Rankin-Bass Productions, 1980
THE SINS OF DORIAN GRAY (TF) Rankin-Bass Productions,
   1983

PAUL HOFFERT

Contact: SOCAN - Toronto, 416-445-8700

FLICK 1970, Canadian
DR. FRANKENSTEIN ON CAMPUS co-composer with Skip
   Prokop, 1970
THE GROUNDSTAR CONSPIRACY Universal, 1972,
   U.S.-Canadian
SUNDAY IN THE COUNTRY American International, 1973, British

OUTRAGEOUS!   Cinema 5, 1977, Canadian
HIGH-BALLIN'   American International, 1978
THE THIRD WALKER   1978
THE SHAPE OF THINGS TO COME   Film Ventures International, 1979, Canadian
WILD HORSE HANK   Film Consortium of Canada, 1979, Canadian
DOUBLE NEGATIVE   Quadrant Films, 1980
MR. PATMAN   Film Consortium, 1980, Canadian
CIRCLE OF TWO   World Northal, 1981, Canadian
PARADISE   Embassy, 1982
HOOVER VS. THE KENNEDYS: THE SECOND CIVIL WAR (MS)   Sunrise Films/Selznick-Glickman Productions, 1987
CATWALK (TF)   Franklin-Waterman-Marvellous TV/Lewis B. Chester/King St. Entertainment, 1992

KURT HOFFMAN

LITTLE NOISES   co-composer with Fritz Van Orden, Monument, 1991

JOAKIM HOLBECK

EUROPA   ZENTROPA   1991, German
SMUKKE DRENG   PRETTY BOY   1993, Danish
BREAKING THE WAVES   1996
NIGHTWATCH   Miramax, 1997

MARK HOLDEN*

Contact: ASCAP - Los Angeles, 213-883-1000

THE RIGHT WAY   co-composer with Jay Oliver, 1996

LEE HOLDRIDGE*

b. 1944
Agent: Jeff Kaufman - Studio City, 818-506-6013
Affiliation: ASCAP - Los Angeles, 213-883-1000

JONATHAN LIVINGSTON SEAGULL   co-composer with Neil Diamond, Paramount, 1973
JEREMY   United Artists, 1973
SKYWAY TO DEATH (TF)   Universal TV, 1974
NOTHING BY CHANCE   Hugh Downs/Richard Bach, 1974
MAHOGANY   co-composer with Michael Masser and Gil Askey, Paramount, 1975
WINTERHAWK   Howco International, 1976
MUSTANG COUNTRY   Universal, 1976
GOIN' HOME   Chris Prentiss, 1976
FOREVER YOUNG, FOREVER FREE   E'LOLLIPOP   Universal, 1976, British
PINE CANYON IS BURNING (TF)   Universal TV, 1977
THE GREATEST   co-composer with Michael Masser, Columbia, 1977
ALASKA: AN AMERICANCHILD (FD)   1977
SUNSHINE CHRISTMAS (TF)   Universal TV, 1977
THE PACK   Warner Bros., 1977
TO KILL A COP (TF)   David Gerber Company/Columbia TV, 1978
HAVING BABIES III (TF)   The Jozak Company/Paramount TV, 1978
LIKE MOM, LIKE ME (TF)   CBS Entertainment, 1978
THE OTHER SIDE OF THE MOUNTAIN - PART 2   Universal, 1978
MOMENT BY MOMENT   Universal, 1978
FRENCH POSTCARDS   Paramount, 1978
VALENTINE (TF)   Malloy-Philips Productions/Edward S. Feldman Company, 1979
TILT   Warner Bros., 1979
OLIVER'S STORY   co-composer with Francis Lai, Paramount, 1979
IF THINGS WERE DIFFERENT (TF)   Bob Banner Associates, 1980
MOTHER AND DAUGHTER - THE LOVING WAR (TF)   Edgar J. Scherick Associates, 1980
SKYWARD (TF)   Major H-Anson Productions, 1980
AMERICAN POP (AF)   Paramount, 1981
JOHN STEINBECK'S EAST OF EDEN   EAST OF EDEN (MS)   Mace Neufeld Productions, 1981
300 MILES FOR STEPHANIE (TF)   Edward S. Feldman Company/Yellow Ribbon Productions/PKO, 1981
FREEDOM (TF)   Hill-Mandelker Films, 1981
THE DAY THE LOVING STOPPED (TF)   Monash-Zeitman Productions, 1981
FLY AWAY HOME (TF)   An Lac Productions/Warner Bros. TV, 1981

FOR LADIES ONLY (TF)   The Catalina Production Group/Viacom, 1981
THE BEASTMASTER   MGM/UA, 1982
THOU SHALT NOT KILL (TF)   Edgar J. Scherick Associates/Warner Bros. TV, 1982
THIS IS KATE BENNETT (TF)   Lorimar, 1982
IN LOVE WITH AN OLDER WOMAN (TF)   Pound Ridge Productions/Charles Fries Productions, 1982
MR. MOM   20th Century-Fox, 1983
AGATHA CHRISTIE'S 'A CARIBBEAN MYSTERY' (TF)   Stan Margulies Productions/Warner Bros. TV, 1983
THURSDAY'S CHILD (TF)   The Catalina Production Group/Viacom, 1983
LEGS (TF)   The Catalina Production Group/Radio City Music Hall Productions/Comworld Productions, 1983
RUNNING OUT (TF)   CBS Entertainment, 1983
I WANT TO LIVE (TF)   United Artists Corporation, 1983
FIRST AFFAIR (TF)   CBS Entertainment, 1983
LOVE IS FOREVER   COMEBACK (TF)   theme only, Michael Landon-Hall Bartlett Films/NBC-TV/20th Century-Fox TV, 1983
SPLASH   Buena Vista, 1984
MICKI & MAUDE   Columbia, 1984
HE'S FIRED, SHE'S HIRED (TF)   CBS, 1984
SHATTERED VOWS (TF)   Bertinelli-Pequod Productions, 1984
MOONLIGHTING (TF)   Picturemaker Productions/ABC Circle Films, 1985
LETTING GO (TF)   Adam Productions/ITC Productions, 1985
SYLVESTER   Columbia, 1985
16 DAYS TO GLORY (FD)   Paramount, 1985
TRANSYLVANIA 6-5000   New World, 1985
THE OTHER LOVER (TF)   Larry Thompson Productions/Columbia TV, 1985
MAFIA PRINCESS (TF)   Jack Farren Productions/Group W Productions, 1985
THE MEN'S CLUB   Atlantic Releasing Corporation, 1986
MIRACLE OF THE HEART: A BOY'S TOWN STORY (TF)   Larry White Productions/Columbia TV, 1986
PLEASURES (TF)   Catalina Productions Group/Columbia TV, 1986
WALK LIKE A MAN   MGM/UA, 1987
I'LL TAKE MANHATTAN (MS)   Steve Krantz Productions, 1987
YOUNG HARRY HOUDINI (TF)   Walt Disney TV, 1987
A TIGER'S TALE   Atlantic Releasing Corporation, 1987
BORN IN EAST L.A.   Universal, 1987
DESPERATE (TF)   Toots Productions/Warner Bros. TV, 1987
EIGHT IS ENOUGH: A FAMILY REUNION (TF)   Lorimar TV, 1987
HIGHER GROUND (TF)   Green-Epstein Productions/Columbia TV, 1988
FATAL JUDGMENT (TF)   Jack Farren Productions/Group W Productions, 1988
BIG BUSINESS   Buena Vista, 1988
A FRIENDSHIP IN VIENNA (CTF)   Finnegan-Pinchuk Productions, 1988
THE TENTH MAN (TF)   Rosemont Productions/William Self Productions, 1988, U.S.-British
A MOTHER'S COURAGE: THE MARY THOMAS STORY (TF)   Interscope Communications/Chet Walker Enterprises/Walt Disney TV, 1989
DO YOU KNOW THE MUFFIN MAN? (TF) ☆   Avnet-Kerner Co., 1989
OLD GRINGO   Columbia, 1989
CHRISTINE CROMWELL (TF)   Wolf Film Productions/Universal TV, 1989
INCIDENT AT DARK RIVER (TF)   Farrell-Minoff Productions/Turner Network TV, 1989
BACK TO HANNIBAL: THE RETURN OF TOM SAWYER AND HUCKLEBERRY FINN (CTF)   Gay-Jay Productions/The Disney Channel/WonderWorks, 1990
DAUGHTER OF THE STREETS (TF)   Adam Productions/20th Century Fox Film Corp., 1990
CHRISTINE CROMWELL: IN VINO VERITAS (TF)   co-composer with Alf Clausen, Wolf Film Productions/Universal TV, 1990
CHRISTINE CROMWELL: ONLY THE GOOD DIE YOUNG (TF)   co-composer with Alf Clausen, Wolf Film Productions/Universal TV, 1990
FACE OF A STRANGER (TF)   Linda Gottlieb Productions/Viacom, 1991
THE STORY LADY (TF)   Michael Filerman Prods./NBC Prods., 1991
LUCY & DESI: BEFORE THE LAUGHTER (TF)   Larry Thompson Entertainment, 1991
THE SUMMER MY FATHER GREW UP (TF)   Robert Shapiro TV, 1991

DANIELLE STEEL'S 'CHANGES' (TF)   Cramer Co./NBC Prods., 1991
THE PERFECT TRIBUTE (TF)   Dorothea Petrie/Procter & Gamble/World International Network, 1991
MRS. LAMBERT REMEMBERS LOVE (TF)   RHI, 1991
PASTIME   *ONE CUP OF COFFEE*   Bullpen/Open Road, 1991
FINDING THE WAY HOME (TF)   Peter K. Duchow Enterprises, 1991
THE RETURN OF ELIOT NESS (TF)   Michael Filerman Prods., 1991
ONE AGAINST THE WIND (TF)   Karen Mack/Republic, 1991
IN THE ARMS OF A KILLER (TF)   RLC/Monarch, 1992
DAYO (TF)   Steve White Prods., 1992
OBSESSED (TF)   Peter K. Duchow/World International Network, 1992
DEALY MATRIMONY (TF)   Steve Krantz Prods./Multimedia TV, 1992
KILLER RULES (TF)   Lee Rich Co./Warner Bros. TV, 1993
CALL OF THE WILD (TF) ☆   RHI Entertainment, 1993
JUDITH KRANTZ'S TORCH SONG (TF)   Steve Krantz Prods., 1993
HEIDI (CTF)   Harmony Gold/Bill McCutchen Prods./Silvio Berlusconi Communications/Disney Channel, 1993
DANIELLE STEEL'S STAR (TF)   Schoolfield Prods., 1993
JACK REED: BADGE OF HONOR (TF)   Steve Krantz Prods/Multimedia, 1993
ROBIN COOK'S HARMFUL INTENT (TF)   Rosemont Productions, 1993
ROOMMATES (TF)   Pacific Motion Pictures/Michael Filerman Prods., 1994
THE WHIPPING BOY (CTF)   Gemini Films/Jones Ent./Disney Channel, 1994
DANIELLE STEEL'S A PERFECT STRANGER (TF)   Cramer Co./NBC Prods., 1994
JACK REED: A SEARCH FOR JUSTICE (TF)   Kushner-Locke/Steve Krantz Prods., 1994
DANIELLE STEEL'S FAMILY ALBUM (TF)   Cramer Co>/NBC Prods., 1994
JAMES A. MICHENER'S TEXAS (MS)   Spelling TV, 1994
FREEFALL (CTF)   Nu World Prods., 1994
A MOTHER'S GIFT (TF)   RHI/TeleVest, 1995
BUFFALO GIRLS (TF) ☆   dePasse Ent./Cabin Fever/CBS Ent., 1995
THE TUSKEGEE AIRMEN (CTF)   Price Entertainment Prods., 1995

DEBORAH HOLLAND
Contact: ASCAP - Los Angeles, 213-883-1000

CIRCUITRY MAN   Skouras, 1989
GENUINE RISK   I.R.S. Media, 1990
DECEMBER   I.R.S. Media, 1991
THE FROG PRINCE   Zygomat Pictures, 1992

NICKY HOLLAND
Contact: ASCAP - Los Angeles, 213-883-1000

THE GREAT OUTDOORS   Universal, 1988
SHE'S HAVING A BABY   Paramount, 1988

RICHARD HOLMES
Contact: BMI - Los Angeles, 310-659-9109

A PERFECT HERO (MS)   ITV, 1992, British

RUPERT HOLMES
b. 1947
Contact: ASCAP - Los Angeles, 213-883-1000

THE ANIMALS   1971
A.W.O.L.   BFB, 1972
MEMORIES WITHIN MISS AGGIE   1974
DEATH PLAY   New Line Cinema, 1976
A STAR IS BORN   co-composer, Warner Bros., 1976
NO SMALL AFFAIR   Columbia, 1984

DEREK HOLT
ONE FALSE MOVE   co-composer with Peter Haycock, I.R.S., 1991

NIGEL HOLTON
Agent: Artists Group - Los Angeles, 310-552-1100
Affiliation: BMI - Los Angeles, 310-659-9109

SOUTH OF RENO   co-composer with Clive Wright, Open Road Productions/Pendulum Productions, 1987
GEMINI, THE TWIN STARS   1988, Swiss-U.S.
GRANDMOTHER'S HOUSE   Omega Pictures, 1988
WELCOME TO YOUR LIFE MICHAEL ANGELO   Last Laugh, 1990
BLOODFIST II   Concord-New Horizons, 1990
BODY CHEMISTRY II - VOICE OF A STRANGER   1991
KISS ME A KILLER   Califilm, 1991
BLOODFIST III: FORCED TO FIGHT   Concorde, 1991
TO SLEEP WITH A VAMPIRE   Concorde-New Horizons, 1992
QUAKE   Concorde-New Horizons, 1992
KILLER INSTINCT   Concorde-New Horizons, 1992
TWOGETHER   Twogether Limited, 1992
CARNOSAUR   Concorde-New Horizons, 1993

JUNIOR HOMRICH
Contact: ASCAP - Los Angeles, 213-883-1000

THE EMERALD FOREST   co-composer with Brian Gascoine, Embassy, 1985, British
STREETS OF JUSTICE (TF)   Universal TV, 1985
GHOSTS CAN'T DO IT   Trans World Entertainment, 1989

SHINSUKE HONDA
KOI TO TASOGARE   *BREAKABLE*   1994, Japanese

TOSHIYUKI HONDA
b. Japan
Contact: JASRAC - Tokyo, Japan, 011-81-3-502-6551

A TAXING WOMAN   Toho, 1987, Japanese
THE LAST DANCE   *DAIBYONIN*   1995, Japanese

LES HOOPER
Contact: BMI - Los Angeles, 310-659-9109

BACK IN THE U.S.S.R.   1992, 20th Century Fox

NELLEE HOOPER
WILLIAM SHAKESPEARE'S ROMEO + JULIET   1996

TOBE HOOPER
b. 1943 - Austin, Texas
Contact: BMI - Los Angeles, 310-659-9109

THE TEXAS CHAINSAW MASSACRE   co-composer with Wayne Bell, Bryanston, 1974
THE TEXAS CHAINSAW MASSACRE PART 2   co-composer with Jerry Lambert, Cannon, 1986

DANA HOOVER
TRIBULATION 99: ALIEN ANOMALIES UNDER AMERICA (FD)   Ohter Cinema, 1992

ANTHONY HOPKINS
AUGUST   Samuel Goldwyn, 1996

ANTONY HOPKINS
b. 1921 - London, England
Contact: PRS - London, England, 011-44-1-580-5544

IT'S HARD TO BE GOOD   1946, British
VICE VERSA   General Film Distributors, 1948, British
VOTE FOR HUGGETT   General Film Distributors, 1949, British
DECAMERON NIGHTS   RKO Radio, 1953, British-U.S.
JOHNNY ON THE RUN   Associated British Film Distributors/Children's Film Foundation, 1953, British
THE PICKWICK PAPERS   1954, British
THE ANGEL WHO PAWNED HER HARP   1954, British
CHILD'S PLAY   1954, British
BILLY BUDD   Allied Artists, 1962, British

KENYON HOPKINS

b. 1932
Contact: BMI - Los Angeles, 310-659-9109

BABY DOLL   Warner Bros., 1956
THE STRANGE ONE   *END AS A MAN*   Columbia, 1957
TWELVE ANGRY MEN   United Artists, 1957
THE FUGITIVE KIND   United Artists, 1957
WILD RIVER   20th Century-Fox, 1960
WILD IN THE COUNTRY   20th Century-Fox, 1961
THE YELLOW CANARY   20th Century-Fox, 1963
LILITH   Columbia, 1964
MISTER BUDDWING   MGM, 1966
THIS PROPERTY IS CONDEMNED   Paramount, 1966
DOCTOR, YOU'VE GOT TO BE KIDDING   MGM, 1967
THE BORGIA STICK (TF)   Universal TV, 1967
A LOVELY WAY TO DIE   Universal, 1968
DOWNHILL RACER   Paramount, 1969
THE FIRST TIME United Artists, 1969
THE TREE   Guenette, 1969

NICKY HOPKINS

Contact: ASCAP - Los Angeles, 213-883-1000

LAST SONG   1993, Japanese

SARAH HOPKINS

Contact: APRA - Australia, 011-61-2-922-6422

SCREAM OF STONE   co-composer with Ingram Marshall, Alan
   Lamb and Atahualpa Yupanqui, Saxer/Lange/Sadler, 1991

MICHAEL HOPPE

Contact: ASCAP - Los Angeles, 213-883-1000

MISUNDERSTOOD   MGM/UA, 1984
EYES OF THE WIND   1986

STEPHEN HORELICK

Contact: ASCAP - Los Angeles, 213-883-1000

MADMAN   Jensen Farley Pictures, 1982

JAMES HORNER

b. 1953 - Los Angeles, California
Agent: Gorfaine-Schwartz - Los Angeles, 213-969-1011
Affiliation: ASCAP - Los Angeles, 213-883-1000

UP FROM THE DEPTHS   New World, 1979
THE LADY IN RED   New World, 1979
BATTLE BEYOND THE STARS   New World, 1979
ANGEL DUSTED (TF)   NRW Features, 1980
HUMANOIDS FROM THE DEEP   New World, 1980
A FEW DAYS IN WEASEL CREEK (TF)   Hummingbird
   Productions/Warner Bros., 1981
DEADLY BLESSING   United Artists, 1981
THE HAND   Orion/Warner Bros., 1981
WOLFEN   Orion/Warner Bros., 1981
THE PURSUIT OF D.B. COOPER   Universal, 1981
RASCALS AND ROBBERS—THE SECRET ADVENTURES OF TOM
   SAWYER AND HUCK FINN (TF)   CBS Entertainment, 1982
A PIANO FOR MRS. CIMINO (TF)   Roger Gimbel Productions/EMI
   TV, 1982
STAR TREK II: THE WRATH OF KHAN   Paramount, 1982
48 HOURS   Paramount, 1982
BETWEEN FRIENDS (CTF)   HBO Premiere Films/Marian Rees
   Associates/Robert Cooper Films III/List-Estrin Productions, 1983,
   U.S.-Canadian
BRAINSTORM   MGM/UA, 1983
SOMETHING WICKED THIS WAY COMES   Buena Vista, 1983
KRULL   Columbia, 1983, U.S.-British
UNCOMMON VALOR   Paramount, 1983
TESTAMENT   Paramount, 1983
THE DRESSER   Columbia, 1983, British
GORKY PARK   Orion, 1983
THE STONE BOY   TLC Films/20th Century Fox, 1984
STAR TREK III: THE SEARCH FOR SPOCK   Paramount, 1984
SURVIVING (TF)   Telepictures Corporation, 1985
HEAVEN HELP US   Tri-Star, 1985

VOLUNTEERS   Tri-Star, 1985
COCOON   20th Century Fox, 1985
THE JOURNEY OF NATTY GANN   Buena Vista, 1985
COMMANDO   20th Century Fox, 1985
OFF BEAT   Buena Vista, 1986
ALIENS ★   20th Century Fox, 1986
THE NAME OF THE ROSE   20th Century Fox, 1986, West
   German-Italian-French
WHERE THE RIVER RUNS BLACK   MGM/UA, 1986
AN AMERICANTAIL (AF)   Universal, 1986
P.K. AND THE KID   Castle Hill Productions, 1987, made in 1982
PROJECT X   20th Century Fox, 1987
BATTERIES NOT INCLUDED   Universal, 1987
WILLOW   MGM/UA, 1988
RED HEAT   Tri-Star, 1988
VIBES   Columbia, 1988
THE LAND BEFORE TIME (AF)   Universal, 1988
COCOON: THE RETURN   20th Century Fox, 1988
FIELD OF DREAMS ★   Universal, 1989
HONEY, I SHRUNK THE KIDS   Buena Vista, 1989
IN COUNTRY   Warner Bros., 1989
DAD   Universal, 1989
GLORY   Tri-Star, 1989
I LOVE YOU TO DEATH   Warner Bros., 1990
ANOTHER 48 HOURS   Paramount, 1990
ONCE AROUND   Universal, 1991
MY HEROES HAVE ALWAYS BEEN COWBOYS   Samuel
   Goldwyn, 1991
CLASS ACTION   20th Century Fox, 1991
THE ROCKETEER   Buena Vista, 1991
AN AMERICAN TAIL: FIEVEL GOES WEST (AF)   Universal, 1991
PATRIOT GAMES   Paramount, 1992
SNEAKERS   Universal, 1992
THUNDERHEART   TriStar, 1992
UNLAWFUL ENTRY   20th Century Fox, 1992
HOUSE OF CARDS   Miramax, 1993
JACK THE BEAR   20th Century Fox, 1993
SWING KIDS   Hollywood, 1993
A FAR OFF PLACE   Buena Vista, 1993
ONCE UPON A FOREST (AF)   20th Century Fox, 1993
SEARCHING FOR BOBBY FISHER   Paramount, 1993
THE MAN WITHOUT A FACE   Warner Bros., 1993
BOPHA!   Paramount, 1993
WE'RE BACK! A DINOSAUR'S STORY (AF)   Universal, 1993
THE PELICAN BRIEF   Warner Bros., 1993
THE PAGEMASTER   Turner Pictures, 1994
CLEAR AND PRESENT DANGER   Paramount, 1994
THE PAGEMASTER (AF)   20th Century Fox, 1994
LEGENDS OF THE FALL   TriStar, 1994
BRAVEHEART ★   Paramount, 1995
CASPER   Universal, 1995
APOLLO 13 ★   Universal, 1995
JUMANJI   TriStar, 1995
BALTO (AF)   Universal, 1995
COURAGE UNDER FIRE   20th Century Fox, 1996
THE SPITFIRE GRILL   Columbia, 1996
TO GILLIAN ON HER 37TH BIRTHDAY   Triumph, 1996
RANSOM   Buena Vista, 1996
DOUBLE ZONE   1997
TITANIC   1997

JOSEPH HOROVITZ

b. 1926 - Vienna, Austria
Contact: BMI - Los Angeles, 310-659-9109

TARZAN'S THREE CHALLENGES   MGM, 1963, British

RICHARD HOROWITZ

Contact: BMI - Los Angeles, 310-659-9109

THE SHELTERING SKY   original north african music, Warner
   Bros., 1990
L'ATLANTIDE   1992, French-Italian
GENGHIS KHAN   1993, British-Italian
LAKOTA WOMAN: SIEGE AT WOUNDED KNEE (CTF)   Fonda
   Films, 1994
BROKEN TRUST (CTF)   Fonda-Bonfiglio Films/TNT, 1995

TIM HORRIGAN

Contact: BMI - Los Angeles, 310-659-9109

LAST CALL AT MAUD'S (FD)   The Maud's Project, 1993

VLADIMIR HORUNZHY*

b. September 19, 1949 - Kirovgrad, U.S.S.R.
Agent: SMC Artists - Studio City, 818-505-9600
Affiliation: ASCAP - Los Angeles, 213-883-1000

FUNNY COMPANY (AF)   Kiev Studio, 1972, Soviet
ANOTHER LIFE   DocuStudio, Kiev, 1974, Soviet
ROYAL REGATTA   Dovzsenco Films, 1976, Soviet
UNSUNG SONG   Dovzsenco Films, 1977, Soviet
ROAD TO VICTORY   Mosfilm, 1978, Soviet
SILENT KILLER (TD)   CBS, 1984
FINE GOLD   Overseas Film Group, 1988
A MAN OF PASSION   Noble Entertainment, 1988
ELVES   Windstar Studios, 1989
THE FORBIDDEN DANCE   21st Century, 1990
FIREHEAD   Pyramid, 1990
WARPED   Kassel Prods., 1990
HIGH STRUNG   Grey Cat Films, 1991
THE STRANGER WITHIN (TF)   Goodman-Rosen Prods., 1991
BLINK OF AN EYE   Trimark, 1992
MIRACLE IN THE WILDERNESS (CTF)   Ruddy & Morgan, 1991
SPANISH ROSE   Trimark, 1993
BEYOND FORGIVENESS   Trimark, 1994
STEPHEN KING'S THE LANGOLIERS THE LANGOLIERS (TF)
   Laurel-King Prods., 1995
ORIGINAL GANGSTAS   Orion, 1996
LORD PROTECTOR   Alpine Pictures, 1996

PHILLIP HOUGHTON

Contact: APRA - Australia, 011-61-2-922-6422

THE CUSTODIAN   1993, Australian

JAMES NEWTON HOWARD*

Agent: Gorfaine-Schwartz - Los Angeles, 213-969-1011
Affiliation: ASCAP - Los Angeles, 213-883-1000

HEAD OFFICE   Tri-Star, 1986
WILDCATS   co-composer with Hawk Wolinski, Warner Bros., 1986
NEVER TOO YOUNG TO DIE   Paul Releasing, 1986
8 MILLION WAYS TO DIE   Tri-Star, 1986
NOBODY'S FOOL   Island Pictures, 1986
TOUGH GUYS   Buena Vista, 1986
CAMPUS MAN   Paramount, 1987
PROMISED LAND   Vestron, 1987
FIVE CORNERS   Cineplex Odeon, 1987
RUSSKIES   New Century/Vista, 1987
OFF LIMITS   20th Century Fox, 1988
SOME GIRLS   MGM/UA, 1988
EVERYBODY'S ALL AMERICAN Warner Bros., 1988
GO TOWARD THE LIGHT (TF)   Corapeake Productions, 1988
TAP   Tri-Star, 1989
MAJOR LEAGUE   Paramount, 1989
THE PACKAGE   Orion, 1989
THE IMAGE (CTF)   Citadel Entertainment/HBO, 1990
COUPE DE VILLE   Universal, 1990
PRETTY WOMAN   Buena Vista, 1990
FLATLINERS   Columbia, 1990
MARKED FOR DEATH   20th Century Fox, 1990
THREE MEN AND A LITTLE LADY   Buena Vista, 1990
SOMEBODY HAS TO SHOOT THE PICTURE (CTF)   HBO, 1990
KING RALPH   Universal, 1991
GUILTY BY SUSPICION   Warner Bros., 1991
REVEALING EVIDENCE (TF)   T.W.S. Productions/Universal TV,
   1991
DYING YOUNG   20th Century Fox, 1991
THE MAN IN THE MOON   MGM, 1991
GRAND CANYON   20th Century Fox, 1991
MY GIRL   Columbia, 1991
THE PRINCE OF TIDES ★   Columbia, 1991
AMERICANHEART   Avenue Pictures, 1992
DIGGSTOWN   MGM, 1992
A PRIVATE MATTER (CTF)   HBO Pictures/Longbow/Mirage, 1992
2000 MALIBU ROAD (TF)   Spelling TV/Fisher Ent./CGD Prods.,
   1992

GLENGARRY GLEN ROSS   New Line, 1992
NIGHT AND THE CITY   20th Century Fox, 1992
ALIVE   Buena Vista, 1993
FALLING DOWN   Warner Bros., 1993
DAVE   Warner Bros., 1993
THE FUGITIVE ★   Warner Bros., 1993
THE SAINT OF FORT WASHINGTON   Warner Bros., 1993
WYATT EARP   Warner Bros., 1994
MAJOR LEAGUE II   additional music, Warner Bros., 1994
ER (TF)   Constant C Prods./Amblin TV, 1994
JUNIOR   Universal, 1994
JUST CAUSE   Warner Bros., 1995
OUTBREAK   Warner Bros., 1995
FRENCH KISS   20th Century Fox, 1995
WATERWORLD   Universal, 1995
RESTORATION   Miramax, 1996
EYE FOR AN EYE   Paramount, 1996
THE JUROR   Columbia, 1996
PRIMAL FEAR   Paramount, 1996
THE TRIGGER EFFECT   Universal, 1996
THE RICH MAN'S WIFE   theme only, Buena Vista, 1996
SPACE JAM   Warner Bros., 1996
ONE FINE DAY   20th Century Fox, 1996
DANTE'S PEAK   theme only, Universal, 1997
MY BEST FRIEND'S WEDDING   TriStar, 1997

KEN HOWARD

Contact: ASCAP - Los Angeles, 213-883-1000

FOREIGN BODY   Orion, 1986

RIK HOWARD

Contact: Andi Howard - Los Angeles, 213-278-6483
Affiliation: BMI - Los Angeles, 310-659-9109

BOYS WILL BE BOYS (TF)   co-composer with Bob Wirth,
SECOND CHANCE (TF)   co-composer with Bob Wirth,

ALAN HOWARTH

Affiliation: ASCAP - Los Angeles, 213-883-1000

ESCAPE FROM NEW YORK   co-composer with John Carpenter,
   Avco Embassy, 1981
HALLOWEEN II   co-composer with John Carpenter, Universal,
   1981
HALLOWEEN III: SEASON OF THE WITCH   co-composer with
   John Carpenter, Universal, 1982
CHRISTINE   co-composer with John Carpenter, Columbia, 1983
THE LOST EMPIRE   JGM Enterprises, 1984
RETRIBUTION   United Film Distribution, 1987
PRINCE OF DARKNESS   co-composer with John Carpenter,
   Universal, 1987
HALLOWEEN 4: THE RETURN OF MICHAEL MYERS   Galaxy
   International, 1988
THEY LIVE   co-composer with John Carpenter, Universal, 1988
HALLOWEEN 5: THE REVENGE OF MICHAEL MYERS   Galaxy
   International, 1989
HALLOWEEN: THE CURSE OF MICHAEL MYERS   Dimension,
   1995

PETER HOWELL

Contact: PRS - London, England, 011-44-1-580-5544

YURI NOSENKO, KGB (CTF)   BBC TV/Primetime TV Ltd., 1986,
   British

CHIANG HSIAO-WEN

GOOD MEN, GOOD WOMEN HAO NAN HAO NU   co-composer
   with Chen Hwai-en, 1995, Japanese-Taiwanese

MEZOUM H'SINE

TOUCHIA SONG OF ALGERIAN WOMEN   1993,
   Alegerian-French

AN-LU HUANG

SMALL PLEASURES   co-composer with Kirk Elliot, Wondrous
   Light, 1993

EUGENE HUDDLESTON
WORLD AND TIME ENOUGH   1 in 10 Films, 1994

JACK HUES
Contact: PRS - London, England, 011-44-1-580-5544

THE GUARDIAN   Universal, 1990

STEVEN HUFSTETER
Contact: ASCAP - Los Angeles, 213-883-1000

REPO MAN   co-composer with Tito Larriva, Universal, 1984
UNHOOK THE STARS   Miramax, 1995

COOPER HUGHES
C.H.U.D.   New World, 1984

DAVID A. HUGHES
BEYOND BEDLAM   1994, British

KLIVE AND NIGEL HUMBERSTONE
AN AMBUSH OF GHOSTS   Stress Fiesta, 1993

TONY HUMECKE*
THE FEMININE TOUCH   Miracon Pictures, 1995

CRAIG HUNDLEY
(Craig Huxley)
Contact: ASCAP - Los Angeles, 213-883-1000

DISAPPEARANCE   1977, Canadian
ALLIGATOR   Group 1, 1980
ROADIE   United Artists, 1980
SCHIZOID   *MURDER BY MAIL*   Cannon, 1980
THE ACORN PEOPLE (TF)   Rollins-Joffe-Morra-Breszner
   Productions/NBC Entertainment, 1981
AMERICANA   co-composer with David Carradine, Crown
   International, 1981
BOOGEYMAN II   New West Films, 1983
PROGRAMMED TO KILL   Trans World Entertainment, 1987

HUNDRED POUND HEAD
BOYS LIFE   composer of segment, Strand, 1995

ALBERTA HUNTER
Contact: ASCAP - Los Angeles, 213-883-1000

REMEMBER MY NAME   Columbia/Lagoon Associates, 1979

KIRK HUNTER
Contact: ASCAP - Los Angeles, 213-883-1000

FINAL APPROACH   Trimark, 1991

STEVE HUNTER
Contact: BMI - Los Angeles, 310-659-9109

THE INVISIBLE KID   Taurus Entertainment, 1988
MEATBALLS 4   Moviestore, 1992

MICHAEL HURD
Contact: PRS - London, England, 011-44-1-580-5544

SCRUBBERS   co-composer with Ray Cooper, Orion Classics,
   1983, British

ZAKIR HUSSAIN
Contact: ASCAP - Los Angeles, 213-883-1000

HIFAZAAT   *IN CUSTODY*   co-composer with Ustad Sultan Khan,
   Merchant Ivory, 1993, British

BRENDA HUTCHINSON
LIQUID SKY   co-composer with Slava Tsukerman and Clive Smith,
   Cinevista, 1982

CHEN HWAI-EN
GOOD MEN, GOOD WOMEN   *HAO NAN HAO NU*   co-composer
   with Chiang Hsiao-wen, 1995, Japanese-Taiwanese

LUCIA HWONG
Contact: ASCAP - Los Angeles, 213-883-1000

YEAR OF THE DRAGON   title theme only, MGM/UA, 1985
FORBIDDEN NIGHTS (TF)   Tristine Rainer Productions/Warner
   Bros., 1990

CHRISTOPHER HYANS-HART
HELL HIGH   co-composer with Rich Macar, MGM Enterprises,
   1989

DICK HYMAN*
b. 1927
Agent: Jeff Kaufman - Studio City, 818-506-6013
Affiliation: ASCAP - Los Angeles, 213-883-1000

SCOTT JOPLIN   adaptation, Universal, 1977
THE DEADLIEST SEASON (TF)   Titus Productions, 1977
THE LAST TENANT (TF)   Titus Productions, 1978
THE HENDERSON MONSTER (TF)   Titus Productions, 1980
KING CRAB (TF)   Titus Productions, 1980
ZELIG   Orion/Warner Bros., 1983
BROADWAY DANNY ROSE   Orion, 1983
THE PURPLE ROSE OF CAIRO   Orion, 1985
JOHNNY BULL (TF)   Titus Productions/Eugene O'Neill Memorial
   Theatre Center, 1986
RADIO DAYS   Orion, 1987
LEADER OF THE BAND   New Century/Vista, 1987
MOONSTRUCK   MGM/UA, 1987
ASK ME AGAIN (TF)   DBR Films Ltd./American Playhouse, 1989
WOMEN & MEN 2 (CTF)   arranger of one segment, David
   Brown/HOB Showcase, 1991
ALAN & NAOMI   Triton, 1992

I

AKIRA IFUKUBE
b. 1914 - Hokkaido, Japan
Contact: JASRAC - Tokyo, Japan, 011-81-3-502-6551

THE QUIET DUEL   Daiei, 1949, Japanese
CHILDREN OF HIROSHIMA   *CHILDREN OF THE ATOM BOMB*
   1952, Japanese
THE SAGA OF ANATAHAN   *ANA-TA-HAN*   1953, Japanese
GODZILLA, KING OF THE MONSTERS   *GOJIRA*   Embassy,
   1954, Japanese-U.S.
DOWNTOWN   1955, Japanese
HIROSHIMA   1955, Japanese
THE BURMESE HARP   *HARP OF BURMA*   Brandon, 1956,
   Japanese
RODAN   DCA, 1957, Japanese
SECRET SCROLLS   Toho, 1957, Japanese
VARAN THE UNBELIEVABLE   Crown International, 1958,
   Japanese-U.S.
THE MYSTERIANS   Columbia, 1959, Japanese
THE THREE TREASURES   1960, Japanese
BATTLE IN OUTER SPACE   Columbia, 1960, Japanese
DAREDEVIL IN THE CASTLE   1961, Japanese
CHUSHINGURA   Toho, 1962, Japanese
THE WHALE GOD   1962, Japanese
BUDDHA   1963, Japanese

KING KONG VS. GODZILLA   composer of Japanese version only, Universal, 1963, Japanese
THE LITTLE PRINCE AND THE EIGHT-HEADED DRAGON (AF)   1963, Japanese
GODZILLA VS. THE THING   *GODZILLA VS. MOTHRA*   American   International, 1964, Japanese
FRANKENSTEIN CONQUERS THE WORLD   American International, 1964, Japanese
ATTRAGON   American International, 1965, Japanese
DAGORA, THE SPACE MONSTER   Toho, 1965, Japanese
KIGANJO NO BOKEN   *ADVENTURES OF TAKLA MAKAN*   1965, Japanese
GHIDRAH, THE THREE-HEADED MONSTER   Continental, 1966, Japanese
MAJIN, THE HIDEOUS IDOL   1966, Japanese
WAR OF THE GARGANTUAS   1966, U.S.-Japanese
MONSTER ZERO   1966, Japanese
RETURN OF GIANT MAJIN   1967, Japanese
MAJIN STRIKES AGAIN   1967, Japanese
KAIDEN YUKUJORO   *SNOW GHOST*   1968, Japanese
KING KONG ESCAPES   Universal, 1968, Japanese
DESTROY ALL MONSTERS   American International, 1969, Japanese
LATITUDE ZERO   National General, 1970, Japanese
YOG - MONSTER FROM SPACE   American International, 1971, Japanese
THE HUMAN REVOLUTION   1974
BOKYO   Toho, 1975, Japanese
REVENGE OF MECHA-GODZILLA   *TERROR OF MECHA-GODZILLA/TERROR OF GODZILLA*   1977, Japanese
LOVE AND FAITH: LADY OGIN   1979, Japanese

ALBERTO IGLESIAS

DISPARA!   *SHOOT!*   1993, Spanish-Italian
THE FLOWER OF MY SECRET   1996

SHINCHIRO IKEBE

b. Japan
Contact: JASRAC - Tokyo, Japan, 011-81-3-502-6551

KAGEMUSHA: THE SHADOW WARRIOR   20th Century-Fox, 1980, Japanese
VENGEANCE IS MINE   Shochiku Co. Ltd., 1980, Japanese
OKINAWAN BOYS   1983, Japanese
THE BALLAD OF NARAYAMA   Kino International/Janus, 1983, Japanese
MacARTHUR'S CHILDREN (FD)   Orion Classics, 1985, Japanese
ZEGEN   Toei, 1987, Japanese
AKIRA KUROSAWA'S DREAMS   Warner Bros., 1990, Japanese
RHAPSODY IN AUGUST   Orion Classics, 1991, Japanese
MADADAYO   *NOT YET*   1993, Japanese

ANGEL ILLARAMENDI

EL ALIENTO DEL DIABLO   *THE DEVIL'S BREATH*   1993, Spanish

THE IMAGINEERS

TWO BROTHERS, A GIRL AND A GUN   co-composer with Mike Shields, Black Market, 1993, Canadian

JERROLD IMMEL*

Contact: ASCAP - Los Angeles, 213-883-1000

THE HOUSE ON SKULL MOUNTAIN   20th Century-Fox, 1974
THE MACAHANS (TF)   Albert S. Ruddy Productions/MGM TV, 1976
REVENGE FOR A RAPE (TF)   Albert S. Ruddy Productions, 1976
HOW THE WEST WAS WON (MS)   co-composer, MGM TV, 1977
SOURDOUGH   Film Saturation Inc., 1977
NOWHERE TO HIDE (TF)   MTM Enterprises, 1978
GO WEST, YOUNG GIRL! (TF)   Bennett-Katleman Productions/Columbia Pictures TV, 1978
MATILDA   American International, 1978
THE SACKETTS (TF)   Douglas Netter Enterprises/M.B. Scott Productions/Shalako Enterprises, 1979
THE LEGEND OF THE GOLDEN GUN (TF)   Bennett-Katleman Productions/Columbia Pictures TV, 1979
WILD TIMES (TF)   Metromedia Producers Corporation/Rattlesnake Productions, 1980

POWER (TF)   David Gerber Productions/Columbia Pictures TV, 1980
ROUGHNECKS (TF)   Metromedia Producers Corporation/Rattlesnake Productions, 1980
ALCATRAZ: THE WHOLE SHOCKING STORY (TF)   Pierre Cossette Enterprises, 1980
THE OKLAHOMA CITY DOLLS (TF)   IKE Productions/Columbia Pictures TV, 1981
DEATH HUNT   20th Century-Fox, 1981
SILENCE OF THE NORTH   adaptation, Universal, 1981, Canadian
MEGAFORCE   20th Century-Fox, 1982
THE SHADOW RIDERS (TF)   Pegasus Group Ltd./Columbia Pictures TV, 1982
TRAVIS McGEE (TF)   Hajeno Productions/Warner Bros. TV, 1983
THE OUTLAWS (TF)   Limekiln and Templar Productions/Universal TV, 1984
PEYTON PLACE: THE NEXT GENERATION (TF)   Michael Filerman Productions/20th Century-Fox TV, 1985
MIDAS VALLEY (TF)   Edward S. Feldman Productions/Warner Bros. TV, 1985
DALLAS: THE EARLY YEARS (TF)   Roundelay Productions/Lorimar-Telepictures, 1986
PROGRAMMED TO KILL   co-composer with Craig Huxley, Trans World Entertainment, 1987
GUNSMOKE: RETURN TO DODGE (TF)   CBS Entertainment, 1987
NORMAN ROCKWELL'S BREAKING HOME TIES (TF)   John Wilder Productions/Telecom Entertainment, 1987
PARADISE (TF)   Roundelay Productions/Lorimar TV, 1988
WALKER, TEXAS RANGER: FLASHBACK (TF)   Ruddy & Grief Prods./Columbia Pictures TV/CBS-TV Ent., 1995

PAUL INDER

THE GIRL WITH THE HUNGRY EYES   co-composer with Oscar O'Lochlainn, Merton Shapiro/Cassian Elwes, 1995

NEIL INNES

Contact: PRS - London, England, 011-44-1-580-5544

MONTY PYTHON AND THE HOLY GRAIL   co-composer with De Wolfe, Cinema 5, 1974, British
ERIC THE VIKING   Orion, 1989, British

TASSOS IOANNIDES

Contact: APRA - Australia, 011-61-2-922-6422

THE SILVER BRUMBY   Skouras, 1994

ROBERT E. IRVING III

Contact: BMI - Los Angeles, 310-659-9109

STREET SMART   Cannon, 1987

ASHLEY IRWIN*

ENTERTAINING ANGELS   co-composer with Bill Conti, 1996

PAT IRWIN

Agent: Vangelos Management - Encino, 818-380-1919
Affiliation: ASCAP - New York, 212-621-6000

I TALK TO ANIMALS (FD)   Peter Friedman Productions, 1990
MY NEW GUN   A New Gun, 1992
HEADING HOME   On Board Prods., 1995
SUDDEN MANHATTAN   1997
ARRESTING GENA   Good Machine, 1997
COLIN FITZ   Babyshark Films, 1997

RENO ISAAC

L'OMBRE DU DOUTE   1993, French

BJORN ISFALT

Contact: STIM - Sweden, 011-46-8-783-8800

KADISBELLAN   *THE SLINGSHOT*   1993, Swedish
WHAT'S EATING GILBERT GRAPE   co-composer with Alan Parker, Paramount, 1993
HOUSE OF ANGELS: THE SECOND SUMMER   *ANGLAGARD: ANDRA SOMMAREN*   1995, Swedish

MARK ISHAM*

Agent: CAA - Beverly Hills, 310-288-4545
Affiliation: ASCAP - Los Angeles, 213-883-1000

NEVER CRY WOLF   Buena Vista, 1983
MRS. SOFFEL   MGM/UA, 1984
THE TIMES OF HARVEY MILK (FD)   Teleculture, 1984
TROUBLE IN MIND   Alive Films, 1985
THE HITCHER   Tri-Star, 1986
MADE IN HEAVEN   Lorimar, 1987
THE MODERNS   Alive Films, 1988
THE BEAST   Columbia, 1988
EVERYBODY WINS   Orion, 1990
LOVE AT LARGE   Orion, 1990
REVERSAL OF FORTUNE   Warner Bros., 1990
MORTAL THOUGHTS   Columbia, 1991
CROOKED HEARTS   MGM, 1991
POINT BREAK   20th Century Fox, 1991
LITTLE MAN TATE   Orion, 1991
BILLY BATHGATE   Buena Vista, 1991
COOL WORLD   Paramount, 1992
A MIDNIGHT CLEAR   InterStar, 1992
OF MICE AND MEN   MGM, 1992
THE PUBLIC EYE   Universal, 1992
A RIVER RUNS THROUGH IT ★   Columbia, 1992
SKETCH ARTIST (CTF)   Motion Picture Corp. of America, 1992
NOWHERE TO RUN   Columbia, 1993
FIRE IN THE SKY   Paramount, 1993
MADE IN AMERICA   Warner Bros., 1993
SHORT CUTS   Fine Line, 1993
ROMEO IS BLEEDING   Gramercy, 1994
THE GETAWAY   Universal, 1994
MRS. PARKER AND THE VICIOUS CIRCLE   Fine Line/Miramax, 1994
THE BROWNING VERSION   Paramount, 1994
QUIZ SHOW   Buena Vista, 1994
TIMECOP   Universal, 1994
NELL   20th Century Fox, 1994
SAFE PASSAGE   New Line, 1994
MIAMI RHAPSODY   Buena Vista, 1995
LOSING ISAIAH   Paramount, 1995
FLY AWAY HOME   Columbia, 1996
LAST DANCE   Buena Vista, 1996
EZ STREETS (TF)   Paul Haggis Prods., 1996
NIGHT FALLS ON MANHATTAN   Paramount, 1997
FACE OFF   Paramount, 1997

PETER IVERS

Contact: BMI - Los Angeles, 310-659-9109

GRAND THEFT AUTO   New World, 1977
ERASERHEAD   Libra, 1977

J

DAVID A. JACKSON

Contact: ASCAP - Los Angeles, 213-883-1000

COLD STEEL   Cinetel, 1987
CYCLONE   Cinetel, 1987

JOE JACKSON

Agent: CAA - Beverly Hills, 310-288-4545
Affiliation: PRS - London, England, 011-44-1-580-5544

MIKE'S MURDER   additional music, The Ladd Company/Warner Bros., 1984
PRIVATE EYE (TF)   Yerkovich Productions/Universal TV, 1987
TUCKER   Paramount, 1988
QUEEN'S LOGIC   Seven Arts, 1991
THREE OF HEARTS   New Line, 1993

JULIAN JACOBSON

Contact: PRS - London, England, 011-44-1-580-5544

WE THINK THE WORLD OF YOU   Cinecom, 1988, British

DENNY JAEGER

Contact: BMI - Los Angeles, 310-659-9109

THE HUNGER   co-composer with Michel Rubini, MGM/UA, 1983, British
WHAT WAITS BELOW   co-composer with Michel Rubini, Blossom Pictures, 1984

ETHAN JAMES

Contact: BMI - Los Angeles, 310-659-9109

THE BLUE IGUANA   Paramount, 1988
DEADLY INTENT   Fries Entertainment, 1988

TERRENCE JAMES

Contact: ASCAP - Los Angeles, 213-883-1000

FREDDOM ROAD (TF)   co-composer with Coleridge-Taylor Perkinson, Zev Braun TV/Freedom Road Films, 1979

CHAZ JANKEL

Agent: The Ryan Company - Sherman Oaks, 818-981-4111
Affiliation: BMI - Los Angeles, 310-659-9109

MAKING MR. RIGHT   Orion, 1987
D.O.A.   Buena Vista, 1988
KILLING DAD (TF)   1989
THE RACHEL PAPERS   MGM/UA, 1989, U.S.-British
WAR PARTY   Hemdale, 1989
TALES FROM THE DARKSIDE: THE MOVIE   co-composer, Paramount, 1990
K2   U.S. Version only   Miramax, 1992

ENZO JANNACCI

b. Italy
Contact: SIAE - Italy, 011-39-6-59-901

COME HOME AND MEET MY WIFE   1974, Italian
SEVEN BEAUTIES   *PASQUALINO SETTEBELLEZZE*   Cinema 5, 1976, Italian
STORMTROOPERS   1977, Italian
SAXAPHONE   1978, Italian

ALARIC JANS

Contact: ASCAP - Los Angeles, 213-883-1000

HOUSE OF GAMES   Orion, 1987
THINGS CHANGE   Columbia, 1988
HOMICIDE   Triumph, 1991
THE WATER ENGINE (CTF)   Brandman Prods./Amblin, 1992

PIERRE JANSEN

b. February 28, 1930 - Roubaix, France
Contact: SACEM - France, 011-33-1-4715-4715

LES BONNES FEMMES   Robert Hakim, 1960, French-Italian
LES GODELUREAUX   Cocinor-Marceau, 1961, French-Italian
SEVEN DEADLY SINS   composer of Chabrol segment, Embassy, 1962, French-Italian
OPHELIA   New Line Cinema, 1962, French-Italian
LANDRU   Embassy, 1963, French-Italian
LES PLUS BELLES ESCROQUERIES DU MONDE   composer of Chabrol segment, 1964, French-Italian-Japanese
LE TIGRE AIME LA CHAIR FRAICHE   Gaumont, 1964, French-Italian
MARIE-CHANTAL CONTRE LE DOCTEUR KHA   SNC, 1965, French-Italian-Moroccan
LA 317 ÈME SECTION   1965, French
LA LIGNE DE DEMARCATION   CCFC, 1966, French
THE CHAMPAGNE MURDERS   *LE SCANDALE*   Universal, 1967, French

LA ROUTE DE CORINTHE CCFC, 1967, French-Italian-West German
OBJECTIF 500 MILLIONS 1967, French
LES BICHES VGC, 1968, French-Italian
LA FEMME INFIDELE Allied Artists, 1968, French-Italian
LE SAUVEUR 1969, French
THIS MAN MUST DIE *QUE LA BETE MEURE* Allied Artists, 1969, French-Italian
LE BOUCHER Cinerama Releasing Corporation, 1969, French-Italian
LA RUPTURE New Line Cinema, 1970, French-Italian-Belgian
JUST BEFORE NIGHTFALL *JUSTE AVANT LA NUIT* Libra, 1971, French-Italian
TEN DAYS' WONDER *LA DECADE PRODIGIEUSE* Levitt-Pickman, 1971, French
HIGH HEELS *DOCTEUR POPAUL* Les Films La Boetie, 1972, French-Italian
WEDDING IN BLOOD *LES NOCES ROUGES* New Line Cinema, 1973, French-Italian
THE NADA GANG *NADA* New Line Cinema, 1974, French-Italian
DIRTY HANDS *LES INNOCENTS AUX MAIN SALES* New Line Cinema, 1975, French-Italian-West German
NUIT D'OR *GOLDEN NIGHTS* 1976, French
ALICE OU LA DERNIERE FUGUE *ALICE OR THE LAST ESCAPADE* Filmel/PHPG, 1977, French
LA DENTELLIERE *THE LACEMAKER* New Yorker, 1977, Swiss-French
LES LIENS DE SANG Filmcorp, 1978, Canadian-French
VIOLETTE *VIOLETTE NOZIERE* New Yorker, 1978, French
L'ETAT SAUVAGE 1978, French
LE CHEVAL D'ORGEUIL Planfilm, 1980, French

WERNER JANSSEN

b. June 1, 1900 - New York, New York
Contact: ASCAP - Los Angeles, 213-883-1000

THE GENERAL DIED AT DAWN Paramount, 1936
BLOCKADE ★ Warner Bros., 1938
ETERNALLY YOURS ★ United Artists, 1939
WINTER CARNIVAL Warner Bros., 1939
LIGHTS OUT IN EUROPE (FD) 1939
THE HOUSE ACROSS THE BAY United Artists, 1940
SLIGHTLY HONORABLE United Artists, 1940
GUEST IN THE HOUSE ★ United Artists, 1944
CAPTAIN KIDD ★ United Artists, 1945
THE SOUTHERNER ★ United Artists, 1945
A NIGHT IN CASABLANCA United Artists, 1946
RUTHLESS Eagle Lion, 1948
UNCLE VANYA 1958

JOSEPH JARMAN

Contact: ASCAP - Los Angeles, 213-883-1000

FIRES IN THE MIRROR (TF) co-composer with Tony Mangurian, American Playhouse, 1993

JEAN-MICHEL JARRE

LES GRANGES BRULEES 1972, French
LA MALADIE DE HAMBOURG 1978, French-German

MAURICE JARRE

b. September 13, 1924 - Lyons, France
Agent: Paul Kohner - Los Angeles - 310-550-1060
Affiliation: SACEM - France, 011-33-1-4715-4715

HOTEL DES INVALIDES 1951, French
LE VOYAGE D'ABDALLAH 1952, French
L'UNIVERS DU TRIO 1954, French
LE THEATRE NATIONAL POPULAIRE (DF) 1956, French
SUR LE PONT D'AVIGNON (FD) 1956, French
TOUTE LA MEMOIRE DU MONDE (FD) 1956, French
BRAVO ALFA (FD) 1956, French
LE GRAND SILENCE 1956, French
LA GENERATION DU DESERT 1957, French
LE BEL INDIFFERENT 1958, French
LE GRAND OEUVRE 1958, French
DONNE MOI LA MAIN 1958, French
VOUS N'AVEZ RIEN A DECLARER? theme, 1958, French

CHRONIQUE PROVINCIALE 1958, French
LA BETE A L'AFFUT 1958, French
LES DRAGUEURS 1958, French
LA TETE CONTRE LES MURS 1958, French
LE VEL'-D'HIV (FD) 1959, French
LES ETOILES DU MIDI 1959, French
LE TAPIS VOLANT 1959, French
LA CORDE RAIDE 1959, French
MALRIF, AIGLE ROYAL 1959, French
LE MAIN CHAUDE 1959, French
CRACK IN THE MIRROR 20th Century-Fox, 1959
RECOURS EN GRACE 1960, French
THE BIG GAMBLE 20th Century-Fox, 1960
THE HORROR CHAMBER OF DR. FAUSTUS *LES YEUX SANS VISAGE* Lopert, 1960, French-Italian
LE PRESIDENT 1961, French
PLEINS FEUX SUR L'ASSASSIN 1961, French
THE WITNESSES *LE TEMPS DU GHETTO* 1961, French
THE OLIVE TREES OF JUSTICE *LES OLIVIERS DE LA JUSTICE* 1961, French
LE TEMPS DU GHETTO (FD) 1961, French
LE SOLEIL DANS L'OEIL 1961, French
LES MYSTERES DE PARIS (MS) 1961, French
LES AMOURS CELEBRES 1961, French
LE PUITS AUX TROIS VERITES 1961, French
THERESE DESQUEYROUX 1962, French
SUNDAYS AND CYBELE *CYBELE OU LES DIMANCHES DE VILLE d'AVRAY* ★ Davis-Royal, 1962, French
THE LONGEST DAY 20th Century-Fox, 1962
LES TRAVESTIS DU DIABLE 1962, French
TON OMBRE EST LA MIENNE 1962, French
L'OISEAU DE PARADIS 1962, French
LAWRENCE OF ARABIA ★★ Columbia, 1962, British
MOURIR A MADRID *TO DIE IN MADRID* (FD) 1963, French
MORT, OU EST TA VICTOIRE? 1963, French
LES ANIMAUX (FD) 1963, French
PRESENCE D'ALBERT CAMUS (FD) 1963
UN ROI SANS DIVERTISSEMENT 1963, French
POUR L'ESPAGNE (FD) 1963, French
JUDEX 1963, French
BEHOLD A PALE HORSE Columbia, 1963
WEEKEND A ZUYDCOOTE 1964, French
LE DERNIER MATIN DE... (MS) 1964, French
THE TRAIN United Artists, 1964, U.S.-French-Italian
ENCORE PARIS (FD) 1964, French
THE COLLECTOR Columbia, 1965, U.S.-British
DOCTOR ZHIVAGO ★★ MGM, 1965, British
IS PARIS BURNING? Paramount, 1966, French-U.S.
THE PROFESSIONALS Columbia, 1966
GRAND PRIX MGM, 1966
GAMBIT Universal, 1966
THE NIGHT OF THE GENERALS Columbia, 1966, British-French
VILLA RIDES! Paramount, 1968
5 CARD STUD Paramount, 1968
THE FIXER MGM, 1968, British
ISADORA *THE LOVES OF ISADORA* Universal, 1968, British
THE EXTRAORDINARY SEAMAN MGM, 1968
THE DAMNED *LA CADUTA DEGLI DEI/GOTTERDAMERUNG* Warner Bros., 1968, Italian-West German
TOPAZ Universal, 1968
THE ONLY GAME IN TOWN 20th Century-Fox, 1969
EL CONDOR National General, 1970
RYAN'S DAUGHTER MGM, 1970, British
PLAZA SUITE Paramount, 1970
A SEASON IN HELL 1971, Italian
RED SUN National General, 1971, French-Italian-Spanish
POPE JOAN Columbia, 1972, British
THE EFFECT OF GAMMA RAYS ON MAN-IN-THE-MOON MARIGOLDS 20th Century-Fox, 1972
THE LIFE AND TIMES OF JUDGE ROY BEAN National General, 1972
THE MACKINTOSH MAN Warner Bros., 1973, U.S.-British
ASH WEDNESDAY Paramount, 1973
LIFE SIZE *GRANDEUR NATURE* 1974, French
THE ISLAND AT THE TOP OF THE WORLD Buena Vista, 1974
MANDINGO Paramount, 1974
GREAT EXPECTATIONS Transcontinental Film Productions, 1975, British
POSSE Paramount, 1975
MR. SYCAMORE Film Venture, 1975
THE MAN WHO WOULD BE KING Allied Artists, 1975, British
THE SILENCE (TF) Palomar Productions, 1975

SHOUT AT THE DEVIL   American International, 1976, British
THE LAST TYCOON   Paramount, 1976
MOHAMMED, MESSENGER OF GOD   *THE MESSAGE* ★   Tarik Ben Amar, 1976, Lebanese-British
MARCH OR DIE   Columbia, 1977, British
JESUS OF NAZARETH (MS)   Sir Lew Grade Productions/ITC, 1977, British-Italian
CROSSED SWORDS   *THE PRINCE AND THE PAUPER*   Warner Bros., 1977, British
LORENZACCIO (TF)   1977, French
TWO SOLITUDES   New World-Mutual, 1977, Canadian
ISHI: THE LAST OF HIS TRIBE (TF)   Edward & Mildred Lewis Productions, 1978
THE USERS (TF)   Aaron Spelling Productions, 1978
ONE OF A KIND (TF)   1978
MON ROYAUME POUR UN CHEVAL   1978, French
MORNING BECOMES ELECTRA (MS)   1978
THE MAGICIAN OF LUBLIN   Cannon, 1978, Israeli-West German-U.S.
WINTER KILLS   Avco Embassy, 1979
THE TIN DRUM   Argos Films, 1979, West German-French
THE AMERICAN SUCCESS COMPANY   *SUCCESS*   Columbia, 1979, West German-U.S.
THE BLACK MARBLE   Avco Embassy, 1979
THE LAST FLIGHT OF NOAH'S ARK   Buena Vista, 1980
SHOGUN (MS)   Paramount TV/NBC Entertainment, 1980, U.S.-Japanese
RESURRECTION   Universal, 1980
ENOLA GAY (TF)   The Productions Company/Viacom, 1980
LION OF THE DESERT   United Film Distribution, 1980, Libyan-British
CHUCHU AND THE PHILLY FLASH (TF)   1981
TAPS   20th Century-Fox, 1981
DON'T CRY, IT'S ONLY THUNDER   Sanrio, 1981, U.S.-Japanese
CIRCLE OF DECEIT   *DIE FALSCHUNG*   United Artists Classics, 1981, West German-French
VENDREDI OU LA VIE SAUVAGE (TF)   1981, French
COMING OUT OF THE ICE (TF)   The Konigsberg Company, 1982
FIREFOX   Warner Bros., 1982
PICASSO: A PAINTER'S DIARY (FD)   1982
YOUNG DOCTORS IN LOVE   20th Century-Fox, 1982
THE YEAR OF LIVING DANGEROUSLY   MGM/UA, 1982, Australian
FOR THOSE I LOVED   20th Century-Fox, 1983, Canadian-French
THE SKY'S NO LIMIT (TF)   Palance-Levy Productions, 1983
SAMSON AND DELILAH (TF)   Catalina Production Group/Comworld Productions, 1983
DREAMSCAPE   20th Century Fox, 1983
TOP SECRET!   Paramount, 1984
A PASSAGE TO INDIA ★★   Columbia, 1984, British
WITNESS ★   Paramount, 1984
THE BRIDE   Columbia, 1985, British
MAD MAX BEYOND THUNDERDOME   Warner Bros., 1985, Australian
ENEMY MINE   20th Century Fox, 1985
SOLARBABIES   MGM/UA, 1986
TAI-PAN   DEG, 1986
APOLOGY (CTF)   Roger Gimbel Productions/Peregrine Entertainment Ltd./ASAP Productions/HBO Pictures, 1986
THE MOSQUITO COAST   Warner Bros., 1986
GABY - A TRUE STORY   Tri-Star, 1987, U.S.-Mexican
NO WAY OUT   Orion, 1987
JULIA AND JULIA   Cinecom, 1987, Italian
FATAL ATTRACTION   Paramount, 1987
WILDFIRE   Zupnick Enterprises/Jody Ann Productions, 1987
THE MURDER OF MARY PHAGAN (MS)   George Stevens Jr. Productions/Century Tower Productions, 1988
LE PALANQUIN DES LARMES   1988, French
DISTANT THUNDER   Paramount, 1988
GORILLAS IN THE MIST ★   Universal, 1988
MOON OVER PARADOR   Universal, 1988, U.S.-Brazilian
CHANCES ARE   Tri-Star, 1989
DEAD POETS SOCIETY   Buena Vista, 1989
PRANCER   Orion, 1989
ENEMIES, A LOVE STORY   20th Century Fox, 1989
GHOST ★   Paramount, 1990
AFTER DARK, MY SWEET   Avenue Pictures, 1990
JACOB'S LADDER   Tri-Star, 1990
ALMOST AN ANGEL   Paramount, 1990
ONLY THE LONELY   20th Century Fox, 1991
FIRES WITHIN   Pathe/MGM, 1991
SOLAR CRISIS   *STARFIRE*   1991, U.S.-Japanese

THE SETTING SUN   *TOKYO BLACKOUT*   1991, Japanese
SCHOOL TIES   Paramount, 1992
SHADOW OF THE WOLF   Triumph, 1993
FEARLESS   Warner Bros. 1993
Mr. JONES   Columbia, 1993
A WALK IN THE CLOUDS   20th Century Fox, 1995
SUNCHASER   Warner Bros., 1996

KEITH JARRETT
b. 1945
Contact: BMI - Los Angeles, 310-659-9109

SORCERER   additional music, Universal/Paramount, 1977
MY HEART IS RED   1977, French
THE EIGHTH DAY   1979, Swedish

HERMAN JEFFREYS
KILLPOINT   co-composer with Daryl Stevenett, Crown International, 1984

ZOLTAN JENEY
VIGYAZOK   *THE WATCHERS*   1993, Hungarian

TOM JENKINS
GOOD-BYE, CRUEL WORLD   Sharp Features, 1982

WAYLON JENNINGS
b. June 15, 1937 - Littlefield, Texas
Contact: BMI - Los Angeles, 310-659-9109

MACKINTOSH & T.J.   Penland Productions, 1975

MERRILL B. JENSEN
Contact: ASCAP - Los Angeles, 213-883-1000

TAKE DOWN   Buena Vista, 1979
WINDWALKER   Pacific International, 1980
HARRY'S WAR   Taft International, 1981

PETER JERMYN
b. Canada
Contact: SOCAN - Toronto, 416-445-8700

ESCAPE FROM IRAN: THE CANADIAN CAPER (TF)   Canamedia Productions, 1981, Canadian

ZHAO JIPING
Contact: ASCAP - Los Angeles, 213-883-1000

RAISE THE RED LANTERN   *DAHONG DENGLONG GAOGAO GUA*   Orion Classics, 1991, China-Hong Kong-Taiwan
THE STORY OF QIU JU   *QIU JU DA GUANSI*   1992, China-Hong Kong
FAREWELL TO MY CONCUBINE   *BAWANG BIE JI*   Miramax, 1993, Hong Kong
PAODA SHUANG DENG   *RED FIRECRACKER, GREEN FIRECRACKER*   1994, Hong Kong
TO LIVE   Samuel Goldwyn, 1994, Chinese

EDDIE JOBSON
Agent: Gorfaine-Schwartz - Los Angeles, 213-969-1011

VIPER (TF)   Pet Fly Prods./Paramount Network TV, 1994

DAVID JOHANSEN
MR. NANNY   co-composer with Brian Koonin, New Line, 1993

CARL JOHNSON*
Agent: Air-Edel - Los Angeles, 310-914-5000
Affiliation: BMI - Los Angeles, 310-659-9109

GARGOYLES, THE MOVIE: THE HEROES AWAKEN (ATF)   Disney TV, 1995

J.J. JOHNSON

Contact: BMI - Los Angeles, 310-659-9109

ACROSS 110TH STREET   United Artists, 1972
MAN AND BOY   Levitt-Pickman, 1972
TOP OF THE HEAP   Fanfare, 1972
CLEOPATRA JONES   Warner Bros., 1973
WILLIE DYNAMITE   Universal, 1974
STREET KILLING (TF)   ABC Circle Films, 1976

JEFFREY JOHNSON

Contact: BMI - Los Angeles, 310-659-9109

A MILLION TO JUAN   co-composer with Steven Johnson and
    Samm Pena, Samuel Goldwyn, 1994

LAURIE JOHNSON

b. 1927 - Hampstead, England
Contact: PRS - London, England, 011-44-1-580-5544

I AIM AT THE STARS   Columbia, 1960, U.S.-West German
DR. STRANGELOVE OR: HOW I LEARNED TO STOP WORRYING
    AND LOVE THE BOMB   Columbia, 1964, British
FIRST MEN IN THE MOON   Columbia, 1964, British
YOU MUST BE JOKING!   Columbia, 1965, British
HOT MILLIONS   MGM, 1968, British
MR. JERICHO (TF)   ITC, 1970, British
THE BELSTONE FOX   *FREE SPIRIT*   Cine III, 1973, British
CAPTAIN KRONOS: VAMPIRE HUNTER   Paramount, 1974,
    British
THE MAIDS   American Film Theatre, 1975, British
HEDDA   Brut Productions, 1975, British
IT SHOULDN'T HAPPEN TO A VET   EMI, 1976, British
IT LIVES AGAIN   *IT'S ALIVE II*   adaptation of Bernard Herrmann
    score for "It's Alive", Warner Bros., 1978
A HAZARD OF HEARTS (TF)   The Grade Company/Gainsborough
    Pictures, 1987, British
THE LADY AND THE HIGHWAYMAN (TF)   Lord Grade
    Productions/Gainsborough Pictures, 1989, British
A GHOST IN MONTE CARLO (CTF)   TNT/The Grade Co., 1990,
    U.S.-British
DUEL OF HEARTS (CTF)   TNT/The Grade Co./Gainsborough
    Pictures, 1992, U.S.-British

SCOTT JOHNSON

PATTY HEARST   Zenith Group/Atlantic Entertainment, 1988

STEVEN JOHNSON

Contact: BMI - Los Angeles, 310-659-9109

A MILLION TO JUAN   co-composer with Jeffrey Johnson and
    Samm Pena, Samuel Goldwyn, 1994

ADRIAN JOHNSTON

JUDE   1996

FREDDY JOHNSTON

KINGPIN   MGM-UA, 1996

JIM JOHNSTON

NO HOLDS BARRED   New Line Cinema, 1989

PHILLIP JOHNSTON*

Contact: BMI - Los Angeles, 310-659-9109

THE MUSIC OF CHANCE   I.R.S., 1993
UMBRELLAS (FD)   Maysles Films, 1994
FAITHFUL   Gramercy, 1996

RICHARD JOHNSTON

Contact: SOCAN - Toronto, 416-445-8700

TERROR IN THE AISLES   additional music, Universal, 1984

ALAIN JOMY

b. France
Contact: SACEM - France, 011-33-1-4715-4715

LA MEILLEURE FACON DE MARCHER   1975, French
DITES-LUI QUE JE L'AIME   1977, French
L'EFFRONTEE   *THE HUSSY*   UGC, 1985, French
THE LITTLE THIEF   AMLF, 1989, French

DARRYL JONES

LOVE JONES   New Line, 1997

JOHN PAUL JONES

Contact: ASCAP - Los Angeles, 213-883-1000

SCREAM FOR HELP   Lorimar, 1984
RISK   Northern Arts, 1994

KENNETH V. JONES

Contact: PRS - London, England, 011-44-1-580-5544

HOW TO MURDER A RICH UNCLE   Columbia, 1957, British
TANK FORCE   Columbia, 1958, British
INTENT TO KILL   20th Century-Fox, 1958, British
INDISCREET   Warner Bros., 1958, British
ROOM 43   1958, British
TOM THUMB   co-composer with David Gamley, MGM, 1958
THE HORSE'S MOUTH   United Artists, 1958, British
TEN SECONDS TO HELL   United Artists, 1959, British
TARZAN THE MAGNIFICENT   Paramount, 1960, British
OSCAR WILDE   Films Around the World, 1960, British
JAZZ BOAT   Columbia, 1960, British
TWO-WAY STRETCH   Showcorporation, 1960, British
HORROR HOTEL   *THE CITY OF THE DEAD*   Trans-World, 1960,
    British
THE GREEN HELMET   MGM, 1961, British
NEARLY A NASTY ACCIDENT   Universal, 1961, British
TARZAN GOES TO INDIA   MGM, 1962, British-U.S.-Swiss
OPERATION SNATCH   Continental, 1962, British
THE BRAIN   *VENGEANCE*   Garrick, 1962, British-West German
DR. CRIPPEN   Warner Bros., 1964, British
THE TOMB OF LIGEIA   American International, 1965
MAROC 7
THE PROJECTED MAN   1967, British
BATTLE BENEATH THE EARTH   1968, British
TOWER OF HELL   1971, British
WHO SLEW AUNTIE ROO?   American International, 1971, British
HORROR ON SNAPE ISLAND   *BEYOND THE FOG*   Fanfare,
    1972, British
PROFESSOR POPPER'S PROBLEMS   1974

MICK JONES

Contact: PRS - London, England, 011-44-1-580-5544

RUDE BOY   co-composer with Joe Strummer, Atlantic Releasing
    Corporation, 1980
AMONGST FRIENDS   Islet, 1993

QUINCY JONES*

b. March 14, 1933 - Chicago, Illinois
Contact: ASCAP - Los Angeles, 213-466-7681

BOY IN THE TREE   1961
THE PAWNBROKER   Landau/Allied Artists, 1965
THE SLENDER THREAD   Paramount, 1965
WALK, DON'T RUN   Columbia, 1966
ENTER LAUGHING   Columbia, 1967
IRONSIDE (TF)   Harbour Productions/Universal TV, 1967
IN COLD BLOOD   Columbia, 1967
IN THE HEAT OF THE NIGHT ★   United Artists, 1967
THE DEADLY AFFAIR   Columbia, 1967, British
THE COUNTERFEIT KILLER   Universal, 1968
A DANDY IN ASPIC   Columbia, 1968, British
FOR LOVE OF IVY   Cinerama Releasing Corporation, 1968
THE HELL WITH HEROES   Universal, 1968
SPLIT SECOND TO AN EPITAPH (TF)   Universal TV, 1968
THE SPLIT   MGM, 1968
THE ITALIAN JOB   Paramount, 1969, British
BOB & CAROL & TED & ALICE   Columbia, 1969

CACTUS FLOWER   Columbia, 1969
JOHN AND MARY   20th Century-Fox, 1969
MACKENNA'S GOLD   Columbia, 1969
THE LOST MAN   Universal, 1969
LAST OF THE MOBILE HOT-SHOTS   Warner Bros., 1970
THEY CALL ME MISTER TIBBS!   United Artists, 1970
THE ANDERSON TAPES   Columbia, 1971
$ DOLLARS   Columbia, 1971
BROTHER JOHN   Columbia, 1971
HONKY   Jack H. Harris Enterprises, 1971
KILLER BY NIGHT (TF)   Cinema Center 100, 1972
MAN AND BOY   Levitt-Pickman, 1972
THE GETAWAY   National General, 1972
THE HOT ROCK   20th Century-Fox, 1972
THE NEW CENTURIONS   Columbia, 1972
ROOTS (MS) ☆☆   co-composer with Gerald Fried, Wolper
   Productions, 1977
THE WIZ ★   adaptation, Universal, 1978
THE COLOR PURPLE ★   co-composer, Warner Bros., 1985
THE RETURN OF IRONSIDE (TF)   original series theme, Riven
   Rock Prods./Windy City Prods., 1993

QUINCY JONES III
Agent: Lesley Lotto - Woodland Hills, 818-884-2209
Contact: ASCAP - Los Angeles, 213-883-1000

MENACE II SOCIETY   co-composed with Theodor Miller, New
   Line, 1993
JASON'S LYRIC   theme only, co-composed with Theodor Miller,
   Gramercy, 1994

RALPH JONES
THE SLUMBER PARTY MASSACRE   Santa Fe, 1982
MY LOVE LETTERS   New World, 1983

RON JONES
Agent: Robert Light - Los Angeles, 213-651-1777
Affiliation: BMI - Los Angeles, 310-659-9109

NAKED VENGEANCE   Concorde/Cinema Group, 1986
KIDNAPPED   Virgin Vision, 1987

TONY JONES
HOMEWORK   co-composer Jim Wetzel, Jensen Farley Pictures,
   1982

TREVOR JONES
b. South Africa
Agent: Zomba Screen Music - West Hollywood, 310-246-0777
Affiliation: PRS - London, England, 011-44-1-580-5544

THE BENEFICIARY   National Film School, 1980, British
BROTHERS AND SISTERS   British Film Institute, 1980, British
EXCALIBUR   Orion/Warner Bros., 1981, British-Irish
THE SENDER   Paramount, 1982, U.S.-British
THE DARK CRYSTAL   Universal/AFD, 1982, British
THOSE GLORY, GLORY DAYS   Cinecom, 1983, British, originally
   made for television
NATE AND HAYES   SAVAGE ISLANDS   Paramount, 1983, New
   Zealand
AND PIGS MUST FLY (TF)   S4C, 1984, Welsh
THE LAST DAYS OF POMPEII (MS)   David Gerber
   Company/Columbia TV/Centerpoint Films/RAI, 1984,
   U.S.-British-Italian
DOCTOR FISCHER OF GENEVA (TF)   Consolidated
   Productions/BBC, 1985, British
THE LAST PLACE ON EARTH (MS)   Central
   Productions/Renegade Films, 1985, British
RUNAWAY TRAIN   Cannon, 1985
LABYRINTH   Tri-Star, 1986, British
ANGEL HEART   Tri-Star, 1987
DOMINICK AND EUGENE   Orion, 1988
JUST ASK FOR DIAMOND   Kings Road, 1988, British
SWEET LIES   Island Pictures, 1988, U.S.-French
MISSISSIPPI BURNING   Orion, 1988
SEA OF LOVE   Universal, 1989
MURDER BY MOONLIGHT (TF)   Tamara Asseyev
   Productions/London Weekend TV/Viacom, 1989, U.S.-British
DEFENSELESS   New Visions, 1990

BAD INFLUENCE   Triumph Releasing Corporation, 1990
BY DAWN'S EARLY LIGHT (CTF)   HBO/Paravision International,
   1990
ARACHNOPHOBIA   Buena Vista, 1990
TRUE COLORS   Paramount, 1991
BLAME IT ON THE BELLBOY   1992, Buena Vista
CRISSCROSS   MGM, 1992
FREEJACK   Warner Bros., 1992
THE LAST OF THE MOHICANS   co-composer with Randy
   Edelman, 20th Century Fox, 1992
CLIFFHANGER   TriStar, 1993
HIDEAWAY   TriStar, 1995
KISS OF DEATH   20th Century Fox, 1995
RICHARD III   MGM-UA, 1996
LAWN DOGS   Rank, 1997
GULLIVER'S TRAVELS (TF)   Henson Prods., 1996
LOCKNESS   Gramercy, 1996
TALK OF ANGELS   Miramax, 1996
BRASSED OFF   Miramax, 1996
FOR ROSEANNA   FineLine, 1996
G.I. JANE   Buena Vista, 1997
DESPERATE MEASURES   TriStar, 1997

GLENN JORDAN
Contact: ASCAP - Los Angeles, 213-883-1000

MEET THE HOLLOWHEADS   Moviestore Entertainment, 1989

NICOLAS JORELLE
FANFAN   1993, French

JULIAN JOSEPH
TALE OF A VAMPIRE   1992, Japanese-British

WILFRED JOSEPHS
Agent: Air-Edel Associates - London, 011-44-71-486-6466
Affiliation: PRS - London, England, 011-44-1-580-5544

CASH ON DEMAND   Columbia, 1962, British
DIE! DIE! MY DARLING   FANATIC   Columbia, 1965, British
THE DEADLY BEES   Paramount, 1967, British
MY SIDE OF THE MOUNTAIN   Paramount, 1969
DARK PLACES   Cinerama Releasing Corporation, 1974, British
SWALLOWS AND AMAZONS   LDS, 1974, British
ROBINSON CRUSOE (TF)   BBC/NBC TV, 1974, British
ALL CREATURES GREAT AND SMALL (TF)   Talent Associates
   Ltd./EMI, 1975
CALLAN   Cinema National, 1975, British
THE UNCANNY   1977, British-Canadian
A MARRIED MAN (TF)   LWT Productions/Lionhearted Productions,
   1984, British
POPE JOHN PAUL II (TF)   Cooperman-DePaul Productions/Taft
   International Pictures, 1984
MARTIN'S DAY   MGM/UA, 1985
MATA HARI   Cannon, 1985

PAUL JOST
Contact: ASCAP - Los Angeles, 213-883-1000

LAST RITES   DRACULA'S LAST RITES   co-composer with George
   Small, Cannon, 1980

LAURENCE JUBER
Contact: ASCAP - Los Angeles, 213-883-1000

WORLD GONE WILD   Lorimar, 1988
A VERY BRADY CHRISTMAS (TF)   The Sherwood Schwartz
   Co./Paramount Network TV, 1988
THE BRADYS (TF)   Brady Productions, Paramount TV, 1990

PHILIP JUDD
Contact: APRA - Australia, 011-61-2-922-6422

RIKKY AND PETE   co-composer with Eddie Raynor, MGM/UA,
   1988, Australian
HERCULES RETURNS   1993, Australian

TOM JUDSON

METROPOLITAN   co-composer with Mark Suozzo, New Line, 1990
REVOLUTION!   Dream Bird, 1991
GRIEF   Grief Prods., 1993
BOYS LIFE   composer of segment, Strand, 1995

LARRY JURIS

Contact: ASCAP - Los Angeles, 213-883-1000

THE REJUVENATOR   SVS Films, 1988

BILL JUSTIS

Contact: ASCAP - Los Angeles, 213-883-1000

SMOKEY AND THE BANDIT   co-composer with Jerry Reed and Dick Feller, Universal, 1977
HOOPER   Warner Bros., 1978
THE VILLAIN   Columbia, 1979

SUSAN JUSTIN*

Contact: ASCAP - Los Angeles, 213-883-1000

FORBIDDEN WORLD   New World, 1982
THE FINAL TERROR   Aquarius, 1984
GRUNT! THE WRESTLING MOVIE   New World, 1985

K

ALFI KABILJO

b. Yugoslavia
Contact: SOKOJ - Yugoslavia

FALL OF ITALY   Yugoslavian
THE MISS   Yugoslavian
DEPS   1974, Yugoslavian
GET IT MAN   Yugoslavian
ACCUSED   Yugoslavian
THE DREAM ROSE   Yugoslavian
ANNO DOMINI 1573   1976, Yugoslavian
FLYERS OF THE OPEN SKIES   1977, Yugoslavian
OCCUPATION IN 26 PICTURES   1978, Yugoslavian
THE JOURNALIST   1979, Yugoslavian
SLOW MOTION   1979, Yugoslavian
THE PEASANT UPRISING   Yugoslavian
CHRONICLE OF A CRIME   Yugoslavian
THE AFTERNOON OF A PEASANT   Yugoslavian
TRAVEL TO THE PLACE OF THE ACCIDENT   Yugoslavian
PROMISED LAND   Yugoslavian
HONEYMOON   1983, Yugoslavian
NIGHT AFTER DEATH   1983, Yugoslavian
THE AMBASSADOR   MGM-UA/Cannon, 1984
GYMKATA   MGM/UA, 1985
THE GIRL IN THE PICTURE   Samuel Goldwyn Company, 1986, British
SKY BANDITS   Galaxy International, 1986, British
SLEEP WELL, MY LOVE   Planbourg Films, 1987
FEAR   CineTel Films, 1988

JAN KACZMAREK*

Agent: Beth Rickman Agency
Affiliation: ASCAP - Los Angeles, 213-883-1000

EMPTY CRADLE (TF)   Bein-Mills, 1993

ERIC KADESKY

MEN WITH GUNS   Norstar, 1996

USTAD SULTAN KAHN

HIFAZAAT   IN CUSTODY   co-composer with Zakir Hussain, Merchant Ivory, 1993, British

MICHAEL KAMEN

b. 1948 - New York, New York
Agent: Gorfaine-Schwartz - Los Angeles, 213-969-1011
Affiliation: BMI - Los Angeles, 310-659-9109

THE NEXT MAN   Allied Artists, 1976
LIZA'S PIONEER DIARY (TF)   Nell Cox Films, 1976
BETWEEN THE LINES   Midwest Film Productions, 1977
STUNTS   New Line Cinema, 1977
S*H*E (TF)   Martin Bregman Productions, 1980
POLYESTER   co-composer with Chris Stein, New Line Cinema, 1981
VENOM   Paramount, 1982, British
PINK FLOYD - THE WALL   MGM/UA, 1982, British
ANGELO, MY LOVE   Cinecom, 1983
THE DEAD ZONE   Paramount, 1983, Canadian
BRAZIL   Universal, 1985, British
LIFEFORCE   additional music, Tri-Star, 1985
EDGE OF DARKNESS (MS)   co-composer with Eric Clapton, BBC/Lionheart Television International, 1986, British
HIGHLANDER   20th Century Fox, 1986, British-U.S.
MONA LISA   Island Pictures, 1986, British
SHANGHAI SURPRISE   co-composer with George Harrison, MGM/UA, 1986, British-U.S.
SHOOT FOR THE SUN (TF)   co-composer with Ray Cooper, BBC-TV, 1986, British
RITA, SUE AND BOB, TOO   Orion Classics, 1987, British
LETHAL WEAPON   co-composer with Eric Clapton and David Sanborn, Warner Bros., 1987
ADVENTURES IN BABYSITTING   Buena Vista, 1987
SOMEONE TO WATCH OVER ME   Columbia, 1987
SUSPECT   Tri-Star, 1987
ACTION JACKSON   Lorimar, 1988
DIE HARD   20th Century Fox, 1988
THE RAGGEDY RAWNEY   HandMade Films, 1988, British
CRUSOE   Island Pictures, 1988, U.S.-British
FOR QUEEN AND COUNTRY   Atlantic Releasing, 1988, British
HOMEBOY   co-composer with Eric Clapton, Redbury Ltd./Elliott Kastner Productions, 1988
THE ADVENTURES OF BARON MUNCHAUSEN   Columbia, 1989, British
ROOFTOPS   co-composer with Dave A. Stewart, New Century/Vista, 1989
ROADHOUSE   MGM/UA, 1989
RENEGADES   Universal, 1989
LICENSE TO KILL   MGM/UA, 1989, British
LETHAL WEAPON 2   co-composer with Eric Clapton and David Sanborn, Warner Bros., 1989
THE KRAYS   Rank, 1990, British
DIE HARD II   20th Century Fox, 1990
NOTHING BUT TROUBLE   Warner Bros., 1991
HUDSON HAWK   co-composer with Robert Kraft, Tri-Star, 1991
ROBIN HOOD: PRINCE OF THIEVES   Warner Bros., 1991
COMPANY BUSINESS   MGM, 1991
LET HIM HAVE IT   co-composer with Edward Shearmur, 1991, British
THE LAST BOY SCOUT   Warner Bros., 1991
LETHAL WEAPON 3   co-composer with Eric Clapton and David Sanborn, Warner Bros., 1992
SHINING THROUGH   20th Century Fox, 1992
BLUE ICE (CTF)   M&M/HBO, 1992, British
SPLITTING HEIRS   Universal, 1993
THE LAST ACTION HERO   Columbia, 1993
WILDER NAPALM   TriStar, 1993
THE THREE MUSKETEERS   Buena Vista, 1993
CIRCLE OF FRIENDS   Savoy, 1995
DON JUAN DE MARCO   New Line, 1995
DIE HARD WITH A VENGEANCE   20th Century Fox, 1995
THE FIRST HUNDRED YEARS (CTD)   Silver Pictures, 1995
MR. HOLLAND'S OPUS   Buena Vista, 1995
JACK   Buena Vista, 1996
101 DALMATIANS   Buena Vista, 1996
INVENTING THE ABBOTTS   20th Century Fox, 1997

JUN KAMIYAMA

ROUGH SKETCH OF A SPIRAL (FD)   co-composer with Yoshikazu
   Yano, 1991, Japanese

VLADIMIR KAMOROV

HELLFIRE (CTF)   co-composer with Bruno Louchouarn, New
   Horizons, 1995

JOHN KANDER

b. March 18, 1927 - Kansas City, Missouri
Contact: BMI - Los Angeles, 310-659-9109

SOMETHING FOR EVERYONE   National General, 1970, British
KRAMER VS. KRAMER   Columbia, 1979
STILL OF THE NIGHT   MGM/UA, 1982
BLUE SKIES AGAIN   Warner Bros., 1983
AN EARLY FROST (TF) ☆   NBC Productions, 1985
I WANT TO GO HOME   MK2, 1989, French
BREATHING LESSONS (TF)   Signboard Hill Prods., 1994

ARTIE KANE

Contact: BMI - Los Angeles, 310-659-9109

THE BAT PEOPLE *IT LIVES BY NIGHT*   American International,
   1974
THE NEW LOVE BOAT (TF)   additional music, Aaron Spelling
   Productions, 1977
LOOKING FOR MR. GOODBAR   Paramount, 1977
EYES OF LAURA MARS   Columbia, 1978
DEVIL DOG: THE HOUND OF HELL (TF)
   Zeitman-Landers-Roberts Productions, 1978
A QUESTION OF GUILT (TF)   Lorimar Productions, 1978
YOUNG LOVE, FIRST LOVE (TF)   Lorimar Productions, 1979
MURDER CAN HURT YOU! (TF)   Aaron Spelling Productions, 1980
NIGHT OF THE JUGGLER   Columbia, 1980
WRONG IS RIGHT   Columbia, 1982
MILLION DOLLAR INFIELD (TF)   CBS Entertainment, 1982
CONCRETE BEAT (TF)   Picturemaker Productions/Viacom, 1984
LONG TIME GONE (TF)   Picturemaker Productions/ABC Circle
   Films, 1986
FATAL CONFESSION: A FATHER DOWLING MYSTERY (TF)
   co-composer with Dick DeBenedictis, Fred Silverman
   Company/Strathmore Productions/Viacom, 1987
THE RED SPIDER (TF)   CBS Entertainment, 1988
TERROR ON HIGHWAY 91 (TF)   Katy Film Productions, 1989
MAN AGAINST THE MOB: THE CHINATOWN MURDERS (TF)
   von Zerneck-Sertner Productions, 1989
GUNSMOKE II: TO THE LAST MAN (TF)   CBS Enterprises, 1991
GUNSMOKE: THE LONG RIDE (TF)   CBS, 1993
MATLOCK: THE FINAL DAYS (TF)   Viacom, 1993
GUNSMOKE: ONE MAN'S JUSTICE (TF)   CBS Entertainment
   Prods., 1994
MATLOCK: THE IDOL (TF)   Dean Hargrove Prods./Fred Silverman
   Co./Viacom, 1994

NOAM KANIEL

Contact: SACEM - France, 011-33-1-4715-4715

ROUND TRIP TO HEAVEN   co-composer with Shuki Levy,
   Saban/Prism, 1991

IGO KANTOR

Contact: BMI - Los Angeles, 310-659-9109

GOOD MORNING...AND GOODBYE   Eve, 1967
RUSS MEYER'S VIXEN   Eve, 1968
CHERRY, HARRY AND RACQUEL   Eve, 1969
THE PROJECTIONIST   Maron Films Limited, 1971
THE COMEBACK TRAIL   Dynamite Entertainment/Rearguard
   Productions, 1971
SCORCHY   American International, 1976

SOL KAPLAN

b. 1913 - New York

TALES OF MANHATTAN   20th Century-Fox, 1942
UNEXPECTED RICHES   MGM, 1942
APACHE TRAIL   MGM, 1943

HOLLOW TRIUMPH   Eagle Lion, 1948
REIGN OF TERROR   Eagle Lion, 1949
DOWN MEMORY LANE   Eagle Lion, 1949
TRAPPED   Eagle Lion, 1949
PORT OF NEW YORK   Eagle Lion, 1949
711 OCEAN DRIVE   Columbia, 1950
MISTER 880   20th Century-Fox, 1951
HALLS OF MONTEZUMA   20th Century-Fox, 1951
I'D CLIMB THE HIGHEST MOUNTAIN   20th Century-Fox, 1951
I CAN GET IT FOR YOU WHOLESALE   20th Century-Fox, 1951
RAWHIDE   20th Century-Fox, 1951
HOUSE ON TELEGRAPH HILL   20th Century-Fox, 1951
THE SECRET OF CONVICT LAKE   20th Century-Fox, 1951
ALICE IN WONDERLAND   1951
RED SKIES OF MONTANA   20th Century-Fox, 1952
RETURN OF THE TEXAN   20th Century-Fox, 1952
KANGAROO   20th Century-Fox, 1952
DIPLOMATIC COURIER   20th Century-Fox, 1952
WAY OF A GAUCHO   20th Century-Fox, 1952
SOMETHING FOR THE BIRDS   20th Century-Fox, 1952
NIAGRA   20th Century-Fox, 1953
TREASURE OF THE GOLDEN CONDOR   20th Century-Fox, 1953
SALT OF THE EARTH   Independent Productions, 1954
THE BURGLAR   Columbia, 1956
HAPPY ANNIVERSARY   United Artists, 1959
GIRL OF THE NIGHT   Warner Bros., 1960
THE VICTORS   Columbia, 1963
THE GUNS OF AUGUST (FD)   Universal, 1964
THE YOUNG LOVERS   MGM, 1964
THE SPY WHO CAME IN FROM THE COLD   Paramount, 1965,
   British
JUDITH   Paramount, 1965, U.S.-British-Israeli
WINCHESTER '73 (TF)   Universal TV, 1967
NEW YORK CITY—THE MOST   1968
SHADOW ON THE LAND (TF)   Screen Gems/Columbia Pictures
   TV, 1968
EXPLOSION   1969, Canadian
LIVING FREE   Columbia, 1972, British
LIES MY FATHER TOLD ME   Columbia, 1975, Canadian
OVER THE EDGE   Orion/Warner Bros., 1979
THE GOLDEN GATE MURDERS (TF)   Universal TV, 1979

DANA KAPROFF*

b. April 24, 1954 - Los Angeles, California
Agent: Vangelos Management - Encino, 818-380-1919
Affiliation: ASCAP - Los Angeles, 213-883-1000

ONCE AN EAGLE (MS)   Universal TV, 1976
EMPIRE OF THE ANTS   American International, 1977
EXO-MAN (TF)   Universal TV, 1977
SPIDER-MAN (TF)   Charles Fries Productions, 1977
THE LAST OF THE GOOD GUYS (TF)   Columbia TV, 1978
THE LATE GREAT PLANET EARTH (FD)   Robert Amram
   Productions, 1979
WHEN A STRANGER CALLS   Columbia, 1979
THE ULTIMATE IMPOSTER (TF)   Universal TV, 1979
BELLE STARR (TF)   Entheos Unlimited Productions/Hanna-Barbera
   Productions, 1980
THE BIG RED ONE   United Artists, 1980
SCARED STRAIGHT! ANOTHER STORY (TF)   Golden West TV,
   1980
INMATES: A LOVE STORY (TF)   Henerson-Hirsch
   Productions/Finnegan Associates, 1981
BERLIN TUNNEL 21 (TF)   Cypress Point Productions/Filmways,
   1981
DEATH VALLEY   Universal, 1982
PANDEMONIUM   MGM/UA, 1982
THE GOLDEN SEAL   co-composer with John Barry, Samuel
   Goldwyn Company, 1983
SECOND SIGHT: A LOVE STORY (TF)   Entheos Unlimited
   Productions/T.T.C. Enterprises, 1984
CHILLER (TF)   Polar Film Corporation/J.D. Feigleson Productions,
   1985
BETWEEN THE DARKNESS AND THE DAWN (TF)   Doris Quinlan
   Productions/Warner Bros. TV, 1985
A WINNER NEVER QUITS (TF)   Blatt-Singer Productions/Columbia
   TV, 1985
A SMOKY MOUNTAIN CHRISTMAS (TF)   Sandollar Productions,
   1986
FIREFIGHTER (TF)   Forest Hills Productions/Embassy TV, 1986
DOCTORS WILDE (TF)   Columbia TV, 1987

THE STICK   Distant Horizon International, 1987,   South African
DOIN' TIME ON PLANET EARTH   Cannon, 1988
I SAW WHAT YOU DID (TF)   Universal TV, 1988
GLITZ (TF)   Robert Cooper Films, 1988
THE PEOPLE ACROSS THE LAKE (TF)   Bill McCutchen
    Productions/Columbia TV, 1988
FULL EXPOSURE: THE SEX TAPES SCANDAL (TF)   von
    Zemeck-Sertner Films, 1989
THE CHINA LAKE MURDERS (CTF)   Papazian-Hirsch
    Entertainment/MCA TV, 1990
SILENT MOTIVE (CTF)   Farrell-Minoff/Viacom, 1991
MY SON JOHNNY (TF)   Capital Cities-ABC/Citadel/Carla Singer
    Prods., 1991
DUPLICATES (CTF)   Sankan Prods./Wilshire Court, 1992
CALENDAR GIRL, COP, KILLER?: THE BAMBI BEMBENECK
    STORY (TF)   von Zerneck-Sertner Films, 1992
JACKIE COLLINS' LADY BOSS (TF)   Puma/von Zerneck-Sertner,
    1992
TAINTED BLOOD (CTF)   Fast Track Films/Wilshire Court, 1993
WHEN A STRANGER CALLS BACK (CTF)
    Krost-Chapin/Producers Entertainment Group/MTE, 1993
TERROR IN THE NIGHT (TF)   Landsburg Co./Cinematique/CBS
    Ent. Prods., 1994
DEAD AIR (CTF)   Alan Barnette Prods./Viacom, 1994
CAGNEY & LACEY: THE RETURN (TF)   The Rozenzweig Co., 1994
A FAMILY DIVIDED (TF)   Citadel, 1995
A CASE FOR LIFE (TF)   ABC/Mirish Corp., 1995
THE STEPFORD HUSBANDS (TF)   Edgar Scherick Associates,
    1996
STOLEN WOMEN (TF)   CBS Prods., 1996
DYING TO BE PERFECT (TF)   Citadel, 1996
CHRISTMAS IN MY HOMETOWN (TF)   Jaffe-Braunstein, 1996
BORN INTO EXILE (TF)   NBC Prods., 1997
BLUE HEAVEN (TF)   Paramount TV, 1997

HELENA KARAINDROU
ELENI KARAINDROU
TO METEORO VIMA TO PELARGOU   *THE SUSPENDED STEP OF
    THE STORK*   1991, Greek-French-Swiss-Italian
ULYSSES' GAZE   *TO VLEMMA TOU ODYSSEA*   1995,
    Greek-French-Italian

EDDIE KARAM
Contact: SOCAN - Toronto, 416-445-8700

TULIPS   Avco-Embassy, 1981, Canadian

FRED KARGER
Contact: ASCAP - Los Angeles, 213-883-1000

NECROMANCY   American International, 1972
CHATTER-BOX   American International, 1977

FRED KARLIN*
b. June 16, 1936 - Chicago, Illinois
Contact: ASCAP - Los Angeles, 213-883-1000

UP THE DOWN STAIRCASE   Warner Bros., Warner Bros., 1967
YOURS, MINE AND OURS   United Artists, 1968
THE STALKING MOON   National General, 1969
THE STERILE CUCKOO   Paramount, 1969
LOVERS AND OTHER STRANGERS   Cinerama Releasing
    Corporation, 1970
THE BABY MAKER   National General, 1970
MARRIAGE OF A YOUNG STOCKBROKER   20th Century-Fox, 1971
MR. & MRS. BO JO JONES (TF)   20th Century-Fox TV, 1971
BELIEVE IN ME   MGM, 1971
THE LITTLE ARK   National General, 1972
EVERY LITTLE CROOK AND NANNY   MGM, 1972
WESTWORLD   MGM, 1973
THE MAN WHO COULD TALK TO KIDS (TF)   Tomorrow
    Entertainment, 1973
CHOSEN SURVIVORS   Columbia, 1974
MIXED COMPANY   United Artists, 1974
IT COULDN'T HAPPEN TO A NICER GUY (TF)   The Jozak
    Company, 1974
BAD RONALD (TF)   Lorimar Productions, 1974
THE GRAVY TRAIN   *THE DION BROTHERS*   Columbia, 1974
BORN INNOCENT (TF)   Tomorrow Entertainment, 1974

THE AUTOBIOGRAPHY OF MISS JANE PITTMAN (TF) ☆☆
    Tomorrow Entertainment, 1974
PUNCH AND JODY (TF)   Metromedia Producers
    Corporation/Stonehenge Productions, 1974
THE SPIKES GANG   United Artists, 1974
THE TAKE   Columbia, 1974
DEATH BE NOT PROUD (TF)   Good Housekeeping
    Productions/Westfall Productions, 1975
BABY BLUE MARINE   Columbia, 1976
LEADBELLY   Paramount, 1976
WOMAN OF THE YEAR (TF)   MGM TV, 1976
DAWN: PORTRAIT OF A TEENAGE RUNAWAY (TF)   Douglas S.
    Cramer Productions, 1976
WANTED: THE SUNDANCE WOMAN (TF)   20th Century-Fox TV,
    1976
FUTUREWORLD   American International, 1976
JOE PANTHER   Artists Creation & Associates, 1976
THE DEATH OF RICHIE (TF)   Henry Jaffe Enterprises/NBC TV,
    1977
ALEXANDER: THE OTHER SIDE OF DAWN (TF)   Douglas Cramer
    Productions, 1977
LUCAN (TF)   MGM TV, 1977
THE TRIAL OF LEE HARVEY OSWALD (TF)   Charles Fries
    Productions, 1977
BILLY: PORTRAIT OF A STREET KID (TF)   Mark Carliner
    Productions, 1977
THE HOSTAGE HEART (TF)   Andrew J. Fenady Associates/MGM
    TV, 1977
HAVING BABIES II (TF)   The Jozak Company, 1977
THE MAN FROM ATLANTIS (TF)   Solow Production Company,
    1977
THE MAN FROM ATLANTIS: DEATH SCOUTS (TF)   Solow
    Production Company, 1977
THE MAN FROM ATLANTIS: KILLER SPORES (TF)   Solow
    Production Company, 1977
THE MAN FROM ATLANTIS IV (TF)   Solow Production Company,
    1977
GREASED LIGHTNING   Warner Bros., 1977
MINSTREL MAN (TF) ☆   Roger Gimbel Productions/EMI TV, 1977
GREEN EYES (TF)   ABC TV, 1977
THE GIRL CALLED HATTER FOX (TF)   EMI TV, 1977
DEADMAN'S CURVE (TF)   Roger Gimbel Productions/EMI TV,
    1978
KISS MEETS THE PHANTOM OF THE PARK (TF)   Hanna-Barbera
    Productions/KISS Productions, 1978
FOREVER (TF)   Roger Gimbel Productions/EMI TV, 1978
ROLL OF THUNDER, HEAR MY CRY (TF)   Tomorrow
    Entertainment, 1978
LEAVE YESTERDAY BEHIND (TF)   ABC Circle Films, 1978
JUST ME & YOU (TF)   Roger Gimbel Productions/EMI, 1978
BUD AND LOU (TF)   Bob Banner Associates, 1978
MORE THAN FRIENDS (TF)   Reiner-Mishkin Productions/Columbia
    TV, 1978
LADY OF THE HOUSE (TF)   Metromedia Productions, 1978
WHO'LL SAVE OUR CHILDREN? (TF)   Time-Life Productions,
    1978
LONG JOURNEY BACK (TF)   Lorimar Productions, 1978
MEAN DOG BLUES   American International, 1978
THE AWAKENING LAND (MS) ☆   Bensen-Kuhn-Sagal
    Productions/Warner Bros. TV, 1978
THIS MAN STANDS ALONE (TF)   Roger Gimbel Productions/EMI
    TV/Abby Mann Productions, 1979
SAMURAI (TF)   Danny Thomas Productions/Universal TV, 1979
VAMPIRE (TF)   MTM Enterprises, 1979
...AND YOUR NAME IS JONAH (TF)   Charles Fries Productions,
    1979
TRANSPLANT (TF)   Time-Life Productions, 1979
AND BABY MAKES SIX (TF)   Alan Landsburg Productions, 1979
STRANGERS: THE STORY OF A MOTHER AND A DAUGHTER
    (TF)   Chris-Rose Productions, 1979
WALKING THROUGH THE FIRE (TF)   Time-Life Films, 1979
SEX AND THE SINGLE PARENT (TF)   Time-Life Productions,
    1979
TOPPER (TF)   Cosmo Productions/Robert A. Papazian
    Productions, 1979
CALIFORNIA DREAMING   American International, 1979
RAVAGERS   Columbia, 1979
BLIND AMBITION (MS)   Parts 3 and 4, Time-Life Productions,
    1979
IKE (MS)   ABC Circle Films, 1979
RAISING DAISY ROTHCHILD   *THE LAST GIRAFFE*   Westfall
    Productions, 1979

ONCE UPON A FAMILY (TF)   Universal TV, 1980
THE SECRET WAR OF JACKIE'S GIRLS (TF)   Public Arts
   Productions/Penthouse Productions/Universal TV, 1980
MARRIAGE IS ALIVE AND WELL (TF)   Lorimar Productions, 1980
A TIME FOR MIRACLES (TF)   ABC Circle Films, 1980
LOVING COUPLES   20th Century-Fox, 1980
THE PLUTONIUM INCIDENT (TF)   Time-Life Productions, 1980
FIGHTING BACK: THE STORY OF ROCKY BLIER (TF)   MTM
   Enterprises, 1980
HOMEWORD BOUND (TF) ☆   Tisch-Avnet Productions, 1980
CLOUD DANCER   Blossom, 1980
MY KIDNAPPER, MY LOVE (TF)   Roger Gimbel Productions/EMI
   TV, 1980
MOM, THE WOLFMAN AND ME (TF)   Time-Life Productions, 1981
THORNWELL (TF)   MTM Enterprises, 1981
JACQUELINE SUSANN'S VALLEY OF THE DOLLS 1981 (MS)
   20th Century-Fox TV, 1981
WE'RE FIGHTING BACK (TF)   Highgate Pictures, 1981
BROKEN PROMISE (TF)   EMI TV, 1981
THE FIVE OF ME (TF)   Jack Farren Productions/Factor-Newland
   Production Corporation, 1981
BITTER HARVEST (TF)   Charles Fries Productions, 1981
THE MARVA COLLINS STORY (TF)   NRW Productions, 1981
NOT IN FRONT OF THE CHILDREN (TF)   Tamtco Productions/The
   Edward S. Feldman Company, 1982
MISSING CHILDREN: A MOTHER'S STORY (TF)   Kayden-Gleason
   Productions, 1982
INSIDE THE THIRD REICH (MS)   ABC Circle Films, 1982
DEADLY ENCOUNTER (TF)   co-composer with Michael Hoenig,
   Roger Gimbel Productions/EMI TV/Promises Productions, 1982
THE FIRST TIME (TF)   Moonlight Productions/Orion TV
   Productions, 1982
IN DEFENSE OF KIDS (TF)   MTM Enterprises, 1983
ONE COOKS, THE OTHER DOESN'T (TF)   Kaleidoscope Films
   Ltd./Lorimar Productions, 1983
BABY SISTER (TF)   Moonlight Productions II, 1983
NIGHT PARTNERS (TF)   Moonlight Productions II, 1983
POLICEWOMAN CENTERFOLD (TF)   Moonlight Productions, 1983
THE GIFT OF LOVE: A CHRISTMAS STORY (TF)   Telecom
   Entertainment/Amanda Productions, 1983
CALAMITY JANE (TF)   CBS Entertainment, 1983
KIDS DON'T TELL (TF)   Chris-Rose Productions/Viacom
   Productions, 1985
ROBERT KENNEDY AND HIS TIMES (MS)   Chris-Rose
   Productions/Columbia TV, 1985
HOSTAGE FLIGHT (TF)   Frank von Zerneck Films, 1985
OFF THE RACK (TF)   1985
DREAM WEST (MS)   Sunn Classic Pictures, 1986
INTIMATE STRANGERS (TF)   Nederlander TV & Film
   Productions/Telepictures Productions, 1986
VASECTOMY: A DELICATE MATTER   Seymour Borde &
   Associates, 1986
A PLACE TO CALL HOME (TF)   Big Deal Productions/Crawford
   Productions/Embassy TV, 1987, U.S.-Australian
CELEBRATION FAMILY (TF)   Frank von Zerneck Films, 1987
THE FACTS OF LIFE DOWN UNDER (TF)   Embassy
   Communications, 1987
LADY MOBSTER (TF)   Danjul Films/Frank von Zerneck
   Productions, 1988
WHAT PRICE VICTORY (TF)   Wolper Productions/Warner Bros.
   TV, 1988
MOVING TARGET (TF)   Lewis B. Chesler Productions/Bateman
   Company Productions/Finnegan-Pinchuk Company/MGM-UA TV,
   1988
DADAH IS DEATH (MS)   Steve Krantz Productions/Roadshow,
   Coote & Carroll Productions/Samuel Goldwyn TV, 1988,
   U.S.-Australian
BRIDGE TO SILENCE (TF) ☆   Fries Entertainment, 1989
FEAR STALK (TF)   Donald March Productions/ITC, 1989
HER WICKED, WICKED WAYS (TF)   ITC Productions, 1989
STRAWBERRY ROAD   Primat Music Group, 1990, Japanese
MURDER C.O.D. (TF)   Kushner-Locke/NBC, 1990
THE LAST PROSTITUTE (CTF)   Wilshire Court/BBK
   Productions/Carmen Culver Films, 1991
SURVIVE THE SAVAGE SEA (TF) ☆   von Zerneck-Sertner Films,
   1992
THE SECRET (TF)   RHI Entertainment, 1992
DESPERATE RESCUE: THE CATHY MAHONE STORY (TF)
   Gimbel-Adelson/Multimedia/World Intl. Network, 1993
LABOR OF LOVE: THE ARLETTE SCHWEITZER STORY (TF)
   Lauren Film/KLM, 1993

FRED KARNS
Contact: BMI - Los Angeles, 310-659-9109

FAMILY BUSINESS (TF)   Screenscope Inc./South Carolina
   Educational TV Network, 1983
THE IMAGEMAKER   Castle Hill Prods., 1986
VOLGA, THE SOUL OF RUSSIA (TD)   National Geographic TV,
   1993

LAURA KARPMAN*
Agent: Cathy Schleussner - Encino, 818-905-7475
Affiliation: BMI - Los Angeles, 310-659-9109

MY BROTHER'S WIFE (TF)   Adam Productions/Robert Greenwald
   Productions, 1989
THE SITTER (TF)   FNM Films, 1991
THE BROKEN CORD (TF)   Carmen Culver Films/Alan Barnette
   Prods./Universal, 1992
DOING TIME ON MAPLE DRIVE (TF)   FNM Films, 1992
A CHILD LOST FOREVER (TF)   ERB Productions/TriStar TV, 1992
BASED ON AN UNTRUE STORY (TF)   Westgate Prods., 1993
A MOTHER'S REVENGE (TF)   Carla Singer/World Intl. Pictures,
   1993
MOMENT OF TRUTH: TO WALK AGAIN (TF)   O'Hara-Horowitz
   Prods., 1994
MOMENT OF TRUTH: BROKEN PLEDGES (TF)   O'Hara-Horowitz
   Prods., 1994
A CENTURY OF WOMEN (CMS)   Vu Productions, 1994
MOMENT OF TRUTH: A MOTHER'S DECEPTION (TF)
   O'Hara-Horowitz, 1994
A WOMAN OF INDEPENDENT MEANS (MS)   Fogwood
   Films/Robert Greenwald Prods., 1995
ABANDONED AND DECEIVED (TF)   Crystal Beach/TriStar TV, 1995
SEX AND THE SILVER SCREEN (CMS)   ZM Prods., 1995
IF SOMEONE HAD KNOWN (TF)   Landsburg Co., 1995
LOVER'S KNOT   Two Pauls Prods., 1996
BLUE RODEO (TF)   Warner Bros. TV, 1996
A STRANGER TO LOVE (TF)   Longbow Prods., 1996
A PROMISE TO CAROLINE (TF)   The Kaufman Company/Citadel,
   1996

ARDASHES KARTALIAN
DEADLINE IN SEVEN DAYS   *ZHAMGEDEH YOT OR*   1992,
   Armenian

AL KASHA
b. January 22, 1937 - New York, New York
Contact: ASCAP - Los Angeles, 213-883-1000

WHO KILLED TEDDY BEAR?   co-composer with Joel Hirschhorn,
   Magna, 1965
FAT SPY   co-composer with Joel Hirschhorn, Magna, 1966
TRAPPED BENEATH THE SEA (TF)   co-composer with Joel
   Hirschhorn, ABC Circle Films, 1974
SOMEONE I TOUCHED (TF)   Charles Fries
   Productions/Stonehenge Productions, 1975
CHINA CRY   co-composer with Joel Hirshhorn, Penland, 1990
THE CLOSER   co-composer with Joel Hischhorn, Ion, 1991
THE GIANT OF THUNDER MOUNTAIN   co-composer with Joel
   Hirschhorn, New Generation, 1991
RESCUE ME   co-composer with Joel Hirschhorn and David Waters,
   Cannon, 1993

MANU KATCKE
AN INDIAN IN THE CITY   *UN INDIEN DANS LA VILLE*
   co-composer with Geoffrey Oryema and Tonton David, Buena
   Vista, 1996, French

PETER KATER
HOW THE WEST WAS LOST (TD)   9K*USA/Discovery Prods.,
   1995

FRED KATZ
b. 1919 - Brooklyn, New York
Contact: ASCAP - Los Angeles, 213-883-1000

A BUCKET OF BLOOD   American International, 1959
THE WASP WOMAN   American International, 1959

MARTIN KATZ
CHANGING GEARS   Santelmo International, 1997

STEVE KATZ
Contact: BMI - Los Angeles, 310-659-9109

HOME REMEDY   Kino International, 1988

EMILIO KAUDERER*
Contact: BMI - Los Angeles, 310-659-9109

LOPEZ'S SONS   Aries, Argentine
LA DISCOTECA DEL AMOR   Aries Films, 1980, Argentine
HOLIDAY LOVE   Aries Films/Microfon, Argentine
TIEMPO DE REVANCHA   Aries Films, 1981, Argentine
SWEET MONEY   Aries Films, Argentine
ULTIMOS DIAS DE LA VICTIMA   Aries Films, 1982, Argentine
SEARCH FOR THE LOST DIAMOND   Microfon, Argentine
GRAY OF ABSENCE   Argencine, Argentine
IN DANGEROUS COMPANY   Manson International, 1988
FISTFIGHTER   Taurus Entertainment, 1989
SLASH DANCE   Glencoe Entertainment, 1989
LOVE $ GREED   Oneira, 1991
JULIA HAS TWO LOVERS   South Gate, 1991
THE ICE RUNNER   Borde Film, 1993

GENE KAUER
Contact: ASCAP - Los Angeles, 213-883-1000

THE ADVENTURES OF THE WILDERNESS FAMILY   co-composer
   with Douglas Lackey, Pacific International, 1976
ACROSS THE GREAT DIVIDE   co-composer with Douglas Lackey,
   Pacific International, 1976
FURTHER ADVENTURES OF THE WILDERNESS FAMILY
   co-composer with Douglas Lackey, Pacific International, 1978

FRANK KAVELIN
LAST TRAIN OUT   co-composer with Daniel O'Brien, Renegade,
   1992

KENJI KAWAI
GHOST IN THE SHELL   1996

EUI KAWAMURA
BLACK JACK (AF)   1997, Japanese

MASHAHIRO KAWASAKI
THE PAINTED DESERT   Kazuyoshi Okuyama, 1993

FRED KAZ
Contact: BMI - Los Angeles, 310-659-9109

THE MONITORS   Commonwealth United, 1969
LITTLE MURDERS   20th Century-Fox, 1970

BRIAN KEANE
Contact: ASCAP - Los Angeles, 213-883-1000

THE DONNER PARTY (FD)   Steeplechase Films/WGBH &
   WNET/13, 1992
THE GREAT DEPRESSION (TD)   1993
THE VERNON JOHNS STORY (TF)   Laurel Ent./Tribune, 1994
AMERICA'S WAR ON POVERTY (TD)   co-composer with Nik
   Bariluk, Blackside Inc., 1995
THE WAY WEST (TD)   Steeplechase Films/Channel Four TV, 1995

JOHN KEANE
SMALL FACES   1995, British

JOHN E. KEANE
Agent: Artists Group - Los Angeles, 310-552-1100
Affiliation: BMI - Los Angeles, 310-659-9109

NANOU   Umbrella Films/Arion, 1986, British-French
THE KITCHEN TOTO   Cannon, 1988

A VERY BRITISH COUP (TF)   Skreba Films, 1988, British
CHATTAHOOCHEE   Hemdale, 1989, British
HARD PROMISES   additional music, Columbia, 1991
THE LAST OF HIS TRIBE (CTF)   River City Prods., 1992
KEEP THE CHANGE (CTF)   Steve Tisch Co./High Horse Films,
   1992
DESPERATE CHOICES: TO SAVE MY CHILD (TF)   Andrew
   Adelson/ABC Prods., 1992
SEX, LOVE AND COLD HARD CASH (CTF)   Citadel/MTE, 1993
TALES OF THE CITY (MS)   Working Title/Propaganda, 1994

JOHN M. KEANE
ONE WOMAN'S COURAGE (TF)   Bonnie Raskin Prods./NBC
   Prods., 1994
A VOW TO KILL (CTF)   Power Pictures/Wilshire Court, 1995

SHANE KEISTER
Contact: BMI - Los Angeles, 310-659-9109

ERNEST GOES TO CAMP   Buena Vista, 1987

SALIF KEITA
Contact: PRS - London, England, 011-44-1-580-5544

L'ENFANT LION *SIRGA*   1993, French

ROGER KELLAWAY
Contact: BMI - Los Angeles, 310-659-9109

PAPER LION   United Artists, 1968
THE PSYCHIATRIST: GOD BLESS THE CHILDREN (TF)
   Universal TV/Arena Productions, 1970
WHO FEARS THE DEVIL *THE LEGEND OF HILLBILLY JOHN*
   Jack H. Harris Enterprises, 1974
LEGACY   Kino International, 1976
THE MOUSE AND HIS CHILD (AF)   Sanrio, 1977
SHARON: PORTRAIT OF A MISTRESS (TF)   Moonlight
   Productions/Paramount Pictures TV, 1977
THE MAFU CAGE   Clouds Production, 1979
THE DARK   Film Ventures, 1979
SILENT SCREAM   American Cinema, 1980
SATAN'S MISTRESS   MPM, 1982

RICKEY KELLER
Contact: BMI - Los Angeles, 310-659-9109

GETTING IT ON   Comworld, 1983

JULIANNE KELLEY
SWINGERS   co-composer with Justin Reinhardt, 1996

VICTORIA KELLY
THE UGLY   Essential Prods., 1997, New Zealand

ARTHUR KEMPEL*
Contact: BMI - Los Angeles, 310-659-9109

GRADUATION DAY   IFI-Scope III, 1981
THE WOMAN WHO WILLED A MIRACLE (TF)   Dick Clark
   Prods./ABC, 1982
WACKO   Jensen Farley, 1983
LONDON AND DAVIS IN NEW YORK (TF)   Columbia/CBS, 1984
FLESHBURN   Crown International, 1984
THE HIT MAN (TF)   Scherick-Cardea/Christopher Morgan Co./ABC
   Circle Films, 1991
DOUBLE IMPACT   Columbia, 1991
CRY IN THE WILD (TF)   Wonderworks, 1991
FIRE IN THE DARK (TF) ☆   Kushner-Locke/Don Gregory and
   Bernie Kahn, 1991
WINDRUNNER   Leucadia, 1993
SENSATION (TF)   MDP, 1994
CHEYENNE WARRIOR   Concorde/New Horizons, 1994
MAX IS MISSING (CTF)   Showtime, 1995
RIDERS OF THE PURPLE SAGE (TF)   TNT, 1996
ADDRESS UNKNOWN   Leucadia, 1996
THE ARRIVAL   Live, 1996
BEHIND ENEMY LINES   Orion, 1997

ROLFE KENT

Agent: Zomba Screen Music - Los Angeles, 310-246-1593
Affiliation: ASCAP - Los Angeles, 213-883-1000

BARNEY BARNABY   Abzurd, 1995
CITIZEN RUTH   Miramax, 1996
FINAL COMBINATION   Propaganda, 1996
MERCY   Propaganda, 1996
THE ROYALE (CTF)   A&E, 1996

RANDY KERBER

Contact: BMI - Los Angeles, 310-659-9109

THE COLOR PURPLE ★   co-composer, Warner Bros., 1985
DATE WITH AN ANGEL   DEG, 1987

ROBERT KESSLER

Contact: BMI - Los Angeles, 310-659-9109

BUM RAP   co-composer with Ethan Neuburg, Millenium, 1988

KHALED

UN DEUX TROIS SOLEIL   *1,2,3, SUN*   1993, French

WILLIAM KIDD*

Agent: Film Music Associates - Hollywood, 213-463-1070
Affiliation: ASCAP - Los Angeles, 213-883-1000

RING OF STEEL   Shapiro Glickenhaus, 1993

ROBERT KIKUCHI-YNGOJO

CHAN IS MISSING   New Yorker, 1982

WOJCIECH KILAR

b. Poland
Agent: The Kraft-Benjamin Agency - Beverly Hills, 310-247-0123
Affiliation: ZAIKS - Poland, 011-48-22-2 75 77

VAMPIRE UPIOR   1968, Polish
LOKIS   1970, Polish
THE BEAR   1970, Polish
THE TASTE OF THE BLACK EARTH   1970, Polish
THE STAR OF THE SEASON   1971, Polish
PEARL IN THE CROWN   1972, Polish
THE WICKET GATE   1974, Polish
LAND OF PROMISE   1975, Polish
QUARTERLY BALANCE-TAKING   1975
CAMOUFLAGE   Libra, 1977, Polish
LEPER   1977, Polish
THE SPIRAL   1978, Polish
DAVID   Kino International, 1979, 1979, West German
THE KING AND THE MOCKINGBIRD   Gaumont, 1980, French
FROM A FAR COUNTRY   *POPE JOHN PAUL II* (TF)   Trans World
   Film/ITC/RAI/Film Polski, 1981, British-Italian-Polish
IMPERATIV   Telefilm Saar, 1982, West German
LE POUVOIR DU MAL   Films Moliere, 1985, French-Italian
WHEREVER YOU ARE   Mark Forstater Productions/Gerhard
   Schmidt Filmproduktion/Film Polski, 1988, British-West
   German-Polish
THE TURNING TABLE (AF)   Neuf de Coeur, 1988, French
KORCZAK   Filmstudio Perspektywa, 1990, Polish
BRAM STOKER'S DRACULA   Columbia, 1992
DEATH AND THE MAIDEN   Fine Line, 1994
PORTRAIT OF A LADY   Gramercy, 1996

BRUCE KIMMEL

b. December 8, 1947 - Los Angeles, California
Contact: ASCAP - Los Angeles, 213-883-1000

THE ALL-AMERICAN WOMAN   Conde Enterprises, 1974
THE FIRST NUDIE MUSICAL   Paramount, 1976
THE RATINGS GAME (CTF)   additional music, Imagination-New
   Street Productions, 1984
PRIME SUSPECT   S.V.S., 1989

KEVIN KINER

Agent: Vangelos Management - Encino, 818-380-1919
Affiliation: BMI - Los Angeles, 310-659-9109

KISS AND BE KILLED   Monarch, 1991
LEPRECHAUN   Trimark, 1993
FREAKED   20th Century Fox, 1993
THE STRANGER   King's Road Ent., 1993
SAVATE   MDP Worldwide, 1994
FORCE ON FORCE   New Line, 1994
INVADER   Showcase Entertainment, 1995
JOHNNY AND CLYDE   MPCA/Viacom, 1995
SAFE HOUSE   Viacom, 1997
THE PEST   TriStar, 1997

CAROL KING

Contact: BMI - Los Angeles, 310-659-9109

MURPHY'S ROMANCE   Columbia, 1985

DENIS KING

Contact: PRS - London, England, 011-44-1-580-5544

PRIVATES ON PARADE   Orion Classics, 1983, British

GERSHON KINGSLEY

Contact: ASCAP - Los Angeles, 213-883-1000

SILENT NIGHT, BLOODY NIGHT   Cannon, 1974
DEATHHOUSE   Cannon, 1981

BASIL KIRCHIN

Contact: PRS - London, England, 011-44-1-580-5544

THE SHUTTERED ROOM   Warner Bros., 1966, British
ASSIGNMENT K   Columbia, 1968, British
NEGATIVES   Continental, 1968, British
THE STRANGE AFFAIR   Paramount, 1968, British
I START COUNTING   United Artists, 1969, British
THE ABOMINABLE DR. PHIBES   American International, 1971,
   British
THE MUTATIONS   Columbia, 1974, British

BARRY KIRSCH

PRISONER OF HONOR (CTF)   HBO, 1991

OSAMU KITAJIMA

Contact: BMI - Los Angeles, 310-659-9109

CAPTIVE HEARTS   MGM/UA, 1987

KITARO

Agent: Film Music Associates - Hollywood, 213-463-1070
Affiliation: JASRAC - Tokyo, Japan, 011-81-3-502-6551

QUEEN MILLENIA (AF)   1982
CATCH YOUR DREAMS   1983, West German
SAMUEL LOUNT   Moonshine Prods., 1985, Canadian
HEAVEN AND EARTH   Warner Bros., 1993

DAVID KITAY

Contact: Cray Artist Management - Los Angeles, 310-788-8484
Affiliation: BMI - Los Angeles, 310-659-9109

UNDER THE BOARDWALK   New World, 1988
LOOK WHO'S TALKING   Tri-Star, 1989
SKETCHES   MCEG, 1990
BORIS AND NATASHA (CTF)   MCEG, 1990
LOOK WHO'S TALKING TOO   Tri-Star, 1990
NUNS ON THE RUN   20th Century Fox, 1990, British
PROBLEM CHILD 2   Universal Pictures, 1991
BREAKING THE RULES   Miramax, 1992
ROOSTERS (TF)   released theatrically in 1995 by IRS,
   KCET/WMG, 1993
TACK'S CHICKS   Trimark, 1993
MOMMY MARKET   Trimark, 1993
SURF NINJAS   New Line, 1993

TRADING MOM   Trimark, 1994
FATHER AND SCOUT (TF)   New Line Prods., 1994
SOLOMON & SHEBA (CTF)   Dino De Laurentiis Communications, 1995
JURY DUTY   TriStar, 1995
CLUELESS   Paramount, 1995
THE STONED AGE   Trimark, 1995

LARRY KLEIN
GRACE OF MY HEART   Gramercy, 1996

TAMARA KLINE
Contact: ASCAP - Los Angeles, 213-883-1000

THE CLEARING   Kodiak, 1991, U.S.-Soviet

KEVIN KLINGER
Contact: BMI - Los Angeles, 310-659-9109

HARD TICKET TO HAWAII   co-composer with Gary Stockdale, Malibu Bay Films, 1987
ARIZONA HEAT   co-composer with Gary Stockdale, Spectrum Entertainment, 1988
PICASSO TRIGGER   co-composer with Gary Stockdale, Malibu Bay Films, 1988
AFTERSHOCK   Bonaire Films, 1989
NECROMANCER   co-composer with Gary Stockdale and Bob Mamet, Bonaire Films, 1989
EARTH ANGEL (TF)   Ron Gilbert Prods./Leonard Hill Films, 1991

HAROLD KLOSER
FATAL DECEPTION: MRS. LEE HARVEY OSWALD (TF)   David L. Wolper Prods./Bernard Sofronsky/Warner Bros. TV, 1993
THE O.J. SIMPSON STORY (TF)   National Studios, 1995

JAN KLUSAK
Contact: OSA - Czach Republic, 011-42-2-312-12-41-8

THE BEGGAR'S OPERA   1991, Czechoslovakia

JURGEN KNIEPER
Contact: GEMA - Germany, 011-49-89-480-03610

THE SCARLET LETTER   Bauer International, 1973, West German-Spanish
THE WRONG MOVE   New Yorker, 1975, West German
DIE ANGST DES TORMAN   West German
OUTPUT   West German
EIEDRIEBE   West German
LIEB VATTERLAND MAGS   West German
THE AMERICAN FRIEND   New Yorker, 1977, West German-French
DERBY FIEBER USA   West German
KALTE HEIMAT   COLD HOMELAND   Triangel Film, 1979, West German
ARABISCHE NACHTE   West German
DEUTSCHLAND, BLEICHE   West German
ALLES IN EIMER   West German
CHRISTIANE F.   additional music, 20th Century-Fox, 1981, West German
KAUBERGERG   West German
DABBEL TRABBEL   West German
MENSCHEN AUS GLASS   West German
THE STATE OF THINGS   Gray City, 1982, U.S.-West German-Portugese
EDITH'S DIARY   1983, West German
DER KLEINE BRUDER   THE LITTLE BROTHER   1983, West German
FLUGEL UND FESSELN   West German
EINMAL KU'DAMM UND Z   West German
THE RIVER'S EDGE   Island Pictures, 1986
DES TEUFELS PARADIES   West German
WINGS OF DESIRE   DER HIMMEL UBER BERLIN   Orion Classics, 1987, West German-French
GETEILTE LIEBE   MANEUVERS   Helma Sanders-Brahms/Metropolis Films, 1988, West German
PAINT IT BLACK   co-composer with Shirley Walker, Vestron, 1989
END OF THE NIGHT   In Absentia, 1990

EXPOSURE   Miramax, 1991
MADREGILDA   1993, Spanish
THE PROMISE   DAS VERSPRECHEN   Fine Line, 1995, German
LISBON STORY   co-composer with Madredeus, 1995, German

MARK KNOPFLER
Contact: PRS - London, England, 011-44-1-580-5544

LOCAL HERO   Warner Bros., 1983, British-Scottish
CAL   Warner Bros., 1984, Irish
COMFORT AND JOY   Universal, 1984, British-Scottish
THE PRINCESS BRIDE   20th Century Fox, 1987
LAST EXIT TO BROOKLYN   Cinecom, 1990

AKIRA KOBAYACHI
SKINLESS NIGHT   1991, Japanese

BUZ KOHAN
Contact: ASCAP - Los Angeles, 213-883-1000

THE NEW ADVENTURES OF HEIDI (TF)   Pierre Cossette Enterprises, 1978

MARGO KOLAR
SUFLOOR   THE PROMPTER   1993, Estonian

DAVID KOLE
Contact: ASCAP - Los Angeles, 213-883-1000

THE KAREN CARPENTER STORY (TF)   Weintraub Entertainment Group, 1989
CHALLENGER (TF)   The Indie Production Company/King Phoenix Entertainment/George Englund Productions, 1990

CRISTIAN KOLONOVITS
TAFELSPITZ   1993, German

TETSUYA KOMURO
HEAVEN & EARTH   Triton, 1991, Japanese

BRIAN KOONIN
MR. NANNY   co-composer with David Johansen, New Line, 1993

ANDERS KOPPEL
Contact: KODA - Denmark, 011-45-31-68-38-00

A JUST WAR? (FD)   1992, Swedish

AL KOOPER
AGAINST THEIR WILL: WOMEN IN PRISON (TF)   Their Own Prods./Jaffe-Braunstein Films/ABC, 1994

STEFANOS KORKOLIS
PANO KATO KE PLAGIOS   UP, DOWN AND SIDEWAYS   1993, Greek

REIJIRO KOROKU
b. Japan
Contact: JASRAC - Tokyo, Japan, 011-81-3-502-6551

GODZILLA 1985   New World, 1985

MARK KORVEN
Contact: SOCAN - Toronto, 416-445-8700

I'VE HEARD THE MERMAIDS SINGING   Miramax, 1987
SAM & ME   Sunrise, 1991, Canadian

ANDRZEJ KORZYNSKI
b. Poland
Contact: ZAIKS - Poland, 011-48-22-2 75 77

THE THIRD PART OF THE NIGHT   1971, Polish
SALVATION   1973, Polish

TAKE IT EASY   1974, Polish
DOCTOR JUDYM   1976, Polish
MAN OF MARBLE   New Yorker, 1977, Polish
JOERG RATGEB, PAINTER   1978, Polish
MAN OF IRON   United Artists Classics, 1981, Polish
POSSESSION   Gaumont, 1981, French-West German

LEO KOTTKE
DAYS OF HEAVEN   additional music, Paramount, 1978
LITTLE TREASURE   Tri-Star, 1985
FAT GUY GOES NUTZOID   Troma, 1987

MARK KOVAL*
Agent: Carol Faith Agency - Beverly Hills, 310-274-0776
Affiliation: BMI - Los Angeles, 310-659-9109

THE RELUCTANT VAMPIRE   Waymar, 1992

ROBERT KRAFT
Contact: BMI - Los Angeles, 310-659-9109

SEVEN MINUTES IN HEAVEN   Warner Bros., 1986
HUDSON HAWK   co-composer with Michael Kamen, Tri-Star,
   1991
THE MAMBO KINGS   co-composer with Carlos Franzetti, Warner
   Bros., 1992

WILLIAM KRAFT
b. Chicago, Illinois
Contact: ASCAP - Los Angeles, 213-883-1000

PSYCHIC KILLER   Avco Embassy, 1975
AVALANCHE   New World, 1978
BILL (TF)   Alan Landsburg Productions, 1981
FIRE AND ICE (AF)   20th Century Fox, 1983

BERNARD KRAUSE
Contact: BMI - Los Angeles, 310-659-9109

DARK CIRCLE (FD)   co-composer with Gary Remal, Independent
   Documentary Group, 1983

RAOUL KRAUSHAAR
b. 1908 - Paris
Contact: ASCAP - Los Angeles, 213-883-1000

(The following is an incomplete list of Mr. Kraushaar's credits.)

PREHISTORIC WOMEN   co-composer with Mort Glickman, United
   Artists, 1950
BRIDE OF THE GORILLA   co-composer with Mort Glickman,
   Realart, 1951
UNTAMED WOMEN   co-composer with Mort Glickman, United
   Artists, 1952
INVADERS FROM MARS   co-composer with Mort Glickman, 20th
   Century-Fox, 1953
THE GOLDEN MISTRESS   United Artists, 1954
BACK FROM THE DEAD   co-composer with Dave Kahn, 20th
   Century-Fox, 1957
THE UNKNOWN TERROR   co-composer with Dave Kahn, 20th
   Century-Fox, 1957
THE 30-FOOT BRIDE OF CANDY ROCK   Columbia, 1959
JESSE JAMES MEETS FRANKENSTEIN'S DAUGHTER   1966
CHILDREN OF DIVORCE (TF)   co-composer with Minette Alton,
   Christiana Productions/Marble Arch Productions, 1980

AMANDA KRAVAT
IF LUCY FELL   co-composer with Charlton Pettus, TriStar, 1996
FALL   Capella, 1997

GABOR KRISTOF
Contact: GEMA - Germany, 011-49-89-480-03610

LE CRI DU LEZARD   1991, French/Swiss

GREG KROCHTA
Contact: BMI - Los Angeles, 310-659-9109

PERFECT PROFILE   Magnum Entertainment, 1991

TIM KROG
Contact: BMI - Los Angeles, 310-659-9109

THE BOOGEY MAN   Jerry Gross Organization, 1980
BOOGEYMAN II   1983

ZANE KRONJE
SCHWEITZER   Sugar Entertainment, 1990

DAVID KRYSTAL
Contact: SOCAN - Toronto, 416-445-8700

BUYING TIME   MGM/UA, 1989

TED KUHN
Contact: BMI - Los Angeles, 310-659-9109

CHILDREN OF FATE: DEATH IN A SICILIAN FAMILY (FD)
   co-composer with John La Barbera, Young-Friedson, 1993

CHRISTIAN KUNERT
Contact: SACEM - France, 011-33-1-4715-4715

SINGING THE BLUES IN RED *FATHERLAND*   co-composer with
   Gerulf Pannach, Angelika Films, 1986, British-West
   German-French

RUSS KUNKEL
Contact: BMI - Los Angeles, 310-659-9109

CERTAIN FURY   co-composer with Bill Payne and George
   Massenburg, New World, 1985, Canadian
SMOOTH TALK   co-composer with Bill Payne and George
   Massenburg, Spectrafilm, 1985

DAVID KURTZ
Contact: ASCAP - Los Angeles, 213-883-1000

BLADE IN HONG KONG (TF)   Becker Enterprises Productions,
   1985
THE LAST ELECTRIC KNIGHT (TF)   Walt Disney Productions,
   1986
IMPURE THOUGHTS ASA Communications, 1986
HUNK   Crown International, 1987
THE WOMAN WHO SINNED (TF)   WIN/Samuels Film, 1991
JOURNEY TO THE CENTER OF THE EARTH (TF)   High Prods.,
   1993
ALIEN NATION: DARK HORIZONS (TF)   Foxstar/Kenneth Johnson
   Prods., 1994

JOHN KUSIAC
Contact: ASCAP - Los Angeles, 213-883-1000

THE SECRET OF LIFE (TD)   co-composer with Caleb Sampson,
   WGBH/BBC, 1993

MILAN KYMLICKA
Agent: Robert Light - Los Angeles, 213-651-1777
Affiliation: SOCAN - Toronto, 416-445-8700

BABAR: THE MOVIE   New Line Cinema, 1989
PSYCHIC (CTF)   Trimark, 1992
DEADBOLT (TF)   Allegro Films/Image, 1993
MARGARET'S MUSEUM   1995, Canadian-British

L

JOHN LA BARBERA
Contact: ASCAP - Los Angeles, 213-883-1000

CHILDREN OF FATE: DEATH IN A SICILIAN FAMILY (FD)
co-composer with Ted Kuhn, Young-Friedson, 1993

DOUGLAS LACKEY
Contact: ASCAP - Los Angeles, 213-883-1000

THE ADVENTURES OF THE WILDERNESS FAMILY   co-composer
with Gene Kauer, Pacific International, 1976
ACROSS THE GREAT DIVIDE   co-composer with Gene Kauer,
Pacific International, 1976
FURTHER ADVENTURES OF THE WILDERNESS FAMILY
co-composer with Gene Kauer, Pacific International, 1978

YVES LAFERRIERE
Contact: SOCAN - Toronto, 416-445-8700

JESUS OF MONTREAL   *JESUS OF MONTREAL*   Max Films
International, 1989, Canadian-French
LE SEXE DES ETOILES   *THE SEX OF THE STARS*   1993,
Canadian

FRANCIS LAI
b. 1932 - Nice, France
Agent: Film Music Associates - Hollywood, 213-463-1070
Affiliation: SACEM - France, 011-33-1-4715-4715

CIRCLE OF LOVE   *LA RONDE*   Continental, 1964, French
A MAN AND A WOMAN   *UN HOMME ET UNE FEMME* ★★   Allied
Artists, 1966, French
THE BOBO   Warner Bros., 1967, British
LIVE FOR LIFE   United Artists, 1967, French
THE ACTION MAN   *LE SOLEIL DES VOYOUS*   H.K. Film
Distribution, 1967, French
I'LL NEVER FORGET WHAT'S 'IS NAME   Regional, 1968, British
LIFE LOVE DEATH   Lopert, 1969, French
THREE INTO TWO WON'T GO   Universal, 1969, British
HOUSE OF THE CARDS   Universal, 1969
MAYERLING   MGM, 1969, British-French
HANNIBAL BROOKS   United Artists, 1969, British
THE GAMES   20th Century-Fox, 1970, British
HELLO - GOODBYE   20th Century-Fox, 1970
LE PETIT MATIN   1970, French
LOVE IS A FUNNY THING   *UN HOMME QUI ME PLAIT*   United
Artists, 1970, French-Italian
RIDER IN THE RAIN   Avco Embassy, 1970, French-Italian
LOVE STORY ★★   Paramount, 1970
BERLIN AFFAIR (TF)   Universal TV, 1970
DU SOLEIL PLEIN LES YEUX   1970, French
SMIC, SMAC, SMOC   GSF, 1971, French
THE CROOK   United Artists, 1971, French
...AND HOPE TO DIE   *LA COURSE DU LIEVRE A TRAVERS LES
CHAMPS*   20th Century-Fox, 1972, French
MONEY MONEY MONEY   *L'AVENTURE C'EST L'AVENTURE*
GSF, 1972, French
LE PETIT POUCET   *TOM THUMB*   1972, French
LA LOUVE SOLITAIRE   French
LA LECON PARTICULIERE   French
L'ODEUR DES FAUVES   French
DANS LA POUSSIERE DU SOLEIL   French
LES PETROLEUSES   French
UN HOMME LIBRE   *A FREE MAN*   1973, French
HAPPY NEW YEAR   *LA BONNE ANNEE*   Avco Embassy, 1973,
French-Italian
LES HOMMES   Cocinor, 1973, French-Italian
PAR LE SANG DES AUTRES   1973, French
UN AMOUR DE PLUIE   1973, French
VISIT TO A CHIEF'S SON   United Artists, 1974

LA BABY-SITTER   Titanus, 1975, Italian-French-Monacan
CAT AND MOUSE   Quartet, 1975, French
CHILD UNDER A LEAF   Cinema National, 1975, Canadian
MARIAGE   1975, French
AND NOW MY LOVE   *TOUTE UNE VIE*   Avco Embassy, 1975,
French-Italian
EMMANUELLE II   1975, French
SECOND CHANCE   *SI C'ETAIT A REFAIRE*   United Artists
Classics, 1976, French
LE CORPS DE MON ENNEMI   AMLF, 1976, French
THE GOOD AND THE BAD   Paramount, 1976, French
BILITIS   Topar, 1976, French
ANOTHER MAN, ANOTHER CHANCE   United Artists, 1977,
U.S.-French
ANIMA PERSA   Dean Film/Les Productions Fox Europe, 1977,
Italian-French
WIDOWS' NEST   Navarro Prods., 1977, U.S.-Spanish
ROBERT ET ROBERT   Quartet, 1978, French
INTERNATIONAL VELVET   MGM/United Artists, 1978, British
OLIVER'S STORY   co-composer with Lee Holdridge, Paramount,
1979
LES RINGARDS   1978, French
PASSION FLOWER HOTEL   1978, West German
A NOUS DEUX   AMLF, 1979, French-Canadian
LES BORSALINI   French-Italian
INDIAN SUMMER   French
SEA KILLER   Italian
BEYOND THE REEF   Universal, 1981
BOLERO   *LES UNS ET LES AUTRES/WITHIN MEMORY*
co-composer with Michel Legrand, Double 13/Sharp Features,
1982, French
EDITH AND MARCEL   Miramax, 1983, French
SALUT LA PUCE   Naja Film, 1983, French
CANICULE   *DOG DAY*   UGC, 1984, French
LES RIPOUX   AMLF, 1984, French
MADAME CLAUDE 2   1985, French
HERE COMES SANTA CLAUS   *J'AI RECONTRE LE PERE NOEL*
New World, 1985, French
MARIE   MGM/UA, 1985
SINS (MS)   New World TV/The Greif-Dore Company/Collins-Holm
Productions, 1986
A MAN AND A WOMAN: 20 YEARS LATER   Warner Bros., 1986,
French
BANDITS   *ATTENTION BANDITS*   Grange Communications/Jerry
Winters, 1987, French
DARK EYES   Island Pictures, 1987, Italian-French
BERNADETTE   Cannon, 1988, French
LES PYRAMIDES BLEUES   Sofracima/FR3 Films/Mexico Inc.,
French
ITINERAIRE D'UN ENFANT GATE   Films 13/Cerito Films/TFI Films,
1989, French
KEYS TO FREEDOM   RPB Pictures/Queen's Cross Productions,
1989, U.S.-Malaysian
MY NEW PARTNER 2   AMLF, 1990, French
LA BELLE HISTOIRE   *THE BEAUTIFUL STORY*   co-composer
with Philippe Servain, 1992, French
TOUT CA...POUR CA!   *ALL THAT...FOR THIS?!*   co-composer with
Philippe Servain, 1993, French
LES MISERABLES   co-composer with Philippe Servain, Erik
Berchot, Michel Legrand and Didier Barbelivien, Warner Bros.,
1995, French

ROBERT LAKE
THE YOUNG POISONER'S HANDBOOK   co-composer with Frank
Strubel, Mass-Sam Taylor, 1995, British-German

FRANK LaLOGGIA
Business: LaLaoggia Productions - Los Angeles, 213-462-3055
Affiliation: ASCAP - Los Angeles, 213-883-1000

FEAR NO EVIL   co-composer with David Spear, Avco Embassy,
1981
THE LADY IN WHITE   New Century Vista, 1988

ALAN LAMB
SCREAM OF STONE   co-composer with Ingram Marshall, Sarah
Hopkins and Atahualpa Yupanqui, Saxer/Lange/Sadler, 1991

DENNIS LAMBERT
Contact: BMI - Los Angeles, 310-659-9109

AMERICAN ME   co-composer with Claude Gaudette, Universal, 1992

JERRY LAMBERT
Contact: BMI - Los Angeles, 310-659-9109

THE TEXAS CHAINSAW MASSACRE PART 2   co-composer with Tobe Hooper, Cannon, 1986

PHILLIP LAMBRO
Contact: ASCAP - Los Angeles, 213-883-1000

AND NOW MIGUEL   Paramount, 1966
LIVE A LITTLE, STEAL A LOT   *MURPH THE SURF/YOU CAN'T STEAL LOVE*   American International, 1975

JOHN LANCHBERY
b. 1923 - London, England
Contact: PRS - London, England, 011-44-1-580-5544

THE TURNING POINT   20th Century-Fox, 1977
NIJINSKY   Paramount, 1980
EVIL UNDER THE SUN   adaptation, Universal/AFD, 1982, British

JAMES LANE
HOUSEWIFE FROM HELL   Crown, 1993

ROB LANE
THE YOUNG POISONER'S HANDBOOK   co-composer with Frank Strobel, 1996

JOHN LANG
ANATOMY OF LOVE (TD)   co-composer with Aaron Davis, TBS Prods./Primedia Prods., 1995

JIM LANG
Contact: ASCAP - Los Angeles, 213-883-1000

BODY BAGS (CTF)   co-composer with John Carpenter, 187 Corp., 1993
IN THE MOUTH OF MADNESS   co-composer with John Carpenter, New Line, 1995

k.d.lang
Contact: SOCAN - Toronto, 416-445-8700

EVEN COWGIRLS GET THE BLUES   co-composer with Ben Mink, Fine Line, 1993

MICHAEL LANG*
Contact: ASCAP - Los Angeles, 213-883-1000

HOLLYWOOD HARRY   Shapiro Entertainment, 1985

BRUCE LANGHORNE
Contact: BMI - Los Angeles, 310-659-9109

IDAHO TRANSFER   Cinemation, 1975
FIGHTING MAD   20th Century-Fox, 1976
STAY HUNGRY   co-composer with Byron Berline, United Artists, 1976
OUTLAW BLUES   co-composer with Charles Fox, Warner Bros., 1977
JIMMY B. & ANDRE (TF)   Georgian Bay Productions, 1980
MELVIN AND HOWARD   Universal, 1980
WORD OF HONOR (TF)   Georgian Bay Productions, 1981
NIGHT WARNING   Comworld, 1983
HOLLYWOOD DREAMING   co-composer, American Twist/Boulevard Productions, 1986
ANNIE'S GARDEN   Cubr, 1994

MICHAEL LANNING
Contact: ASCAP - Los Angeles, 213-883-1000

THUNDER IN PARADISE (TF)   co-composer of theme with Cory Lerios, Berk-Schwartz-Bonnan Prods./Rysher/Trimark, 1994

HENRI LANOE
b. France
Contact: SACEM - France, 011-33-1-4715-4715

LA RIVIERE DU HIBOU   1961, French
AU COEUR DE LA VIE   1962, French
LA BELLE VIE   1963, French
THE THIEF OF PARIS   *LE VOLEUR*   Lopert, 1967, French-Italian
NE JOUEZ PAS AVEC LES MARTIENS   1967, French

DANIEL LANOIS
Manager: Melanie Ciccone - Los Angeles, 213-660-0091

CAMILLA   composer of worldwide version, Miramax, 1994, Canadian-British
SLING BLADE   Miramax, 1996

CHARLOTTE LANSBERG
Contact: ASCAP - Los Angeles, 213-883-1000

HUGH HEFNER: ONCE UPON A TIME (FD)   IRS, 1992

DAVID LANZ
Contact: BMI - Los Angeles, 310-659-9109

TO CROSS THE RUBICON   co-composer with Paul Speer, Lensman, 1991

YVES LAPIERRE
Contact: SOCAN - Toronto, 416-445-8700

DING ET DONG: LE FILM   *DING AND DONG: THE FILM*   co-composer with Jean-Marie Benoit, Max, 1991, Canadian

ANTTON LARRAURI
LA MONJA ALFEREZ   1992, Spanish

TITO LARRIVA
Contact: BMI - Los Angeles, 310-659-9109

REPO MAN   co-composer with Steven Hufsteter, Universal, 1984
HAPPILY EVER AFTER: FAIRY TALES FOR EVERY CHILD (ATF)   co-composer, Two Oceans/Confetti/Hyperion, 1995

GLEN A. LARSON
Contact: BMI - Los Angeles, 310-659-9109

BATTLESTAR GALACTICA (TF)   co-composer of theme with Stu Phillips, Glen A. Larson Productions/Universal TV, 1978
BUCK ROGERS   theme only, Universal, 1979
THE MURDER THAT WOULDN'T DIE (TF)   co-composer with Joe Harnell, Glen A. Larson Productions/Universal TV, 1980
P.S.I. LUV U (TF)   co-composer of theme with Matthew Delgado, CBS Entertainment/Glen Larson Prods., 1991

RICHARD LaSALLE
Contact: BMI - Los Angeles, 310-659-9109

SPEED CRAZY   Allied Artists, 1959
THE BIG NIGHT   Paramount, 1960
THE BOY WHO CAUGHT A CROOK   United Artists, 1961
THE FLIGHT THAT DISAPPEARED   United Artists, 1961
SECRET OF DEEP HARBOR   United Artists, 1961
SNIPER'S RIDGE   20th Century-Fox, 1961
WHEN THE CLOCK STRIKES   United Artists, 1961
YOU HAVE TO RUN FAST   United Artists, 1961
DEADLY DUO   United Artists, 1962
BROKEN LAND   20th Century-Fox, 1962
THE FIREBRAND   20th Century-Fox, 1962
GUN STREET   United Artists, 1962

HANDS OF A STRANGER   Allied Artists, 1962
INCIDENT IN AN ALLEY   United Artists, 1962
SAINTLY SINNERS   United Artists, 1962
THE DAY MARS INVADED EARTH   20th Century-Fox, 1962
POLICE NURSE   20th Century-Fox, 1963
DIARY OF A MADMAN   United Artists, 1963
TWICE-TOLD TALES   United Artists, 1963
APACHE RIFLES   20th Century-Fox, 1964
BLOOD ON THE ARROW   Allied Artists, 1964
THE TIME TRAVELERS   American International, 1964
THE QUICK GUN   Columbia, 1964
A YANK IN VIET-NAM   *YEAR OF THE TIGER*   Allied Artists, 1964
FORT COURAGEOUS   20th Century-Fox, 1965
ARIZONA RAIDERS   Columbia, 1965
WAR PARTY   20th Century-Fox, 1965
CONVICT STAGE   20th Century-Fox, 1965
AMBUSH BAY   United Artists, 1966
BOY, DID I GET THE WRONG NUMBER!   United Artists, 1966
CITY BENEATH THE SEA (TF)   20th Century-Fox TV/Motion
   Pictures International/Kent Productions, 1971
DAUGHTERS OF SATAN   United Artists, 1972
SUPERBEAST   United Artists, 1972
DOCTOR DEATH, SEEKER OF SOULS   20th Century-Fox, 1973
ALICE DOESN'T LIVE HERE ANYMORE   Warner Bros., 1974
SWISS FAMILY ROBINSON (TF)   Irwin Allen Productions/20th
   Century-Fox TV, 1975
ADVENTURES OF THE QUEEN (TF)   Irwin Allen Productions/20th
   Century-Fox TV, 1975
FLOOD (TF)   Irwin Allen Productions/Warner Bros. TV, 1976
FIRE! (TF)   Irwin Allen Productions/Warner Bros. TV, 1977
HANGING BY A THREAD (TF)   Irwin Allen Productions/Warner
   Bros. TV, 1979
KEN MURRAY SHOOTING STARS   Royal Oak, 1979
THE MEMORY OF EVA RYKER (TF)   Irwin Allen Productions,
   1980
CODE RED (TF)   Irwin Allen Productions/Columbia Pictures TV,
   1981
THE NIGHT THE BRIDGE FELL DOWN (TF)   Irwin Allen
   Productions/Warner Bros. Television, 1983
CAVE-IN! (TF)   Irwin Allen Productions/Warner Bros. Television,
   1983

JEFF LASS
Contact: BMI - Los Angeles, 310-659-9109

THE KILLING ZONE   PM, 1991
UNBECOMING AGE   Ringelvision, 1992

BOB LAST
THE LONG DAY CLOSES   co-composer with Robert Lockhart,
   1992, British
ORLANDO   1992, British

JIM LATHAM*
THE HUMAN QUEST (TD)   KCET/Science & Society Prods., 1995

TATS LAU
Contact: CASH - Kowloon, 011-852-3-722-5225

YOU SENG   *TEMPTATION OF A MONK*   1993, Hong Kong

KEN LAUBER
Contact: ASCAP - Los Angeles, 213-883-1000

SCRATCH HARRY   1969
BRAND X   1970
CRY PANIC (TF)   Spelling-Goldberg Productions, 1974
THINGS IN THEIR SEASON (TF)   Tomorrow Entertainment, 1974
THE HATFIELDS AND THE MCCOYS (TF)   Charles Fries
   Productions, 1975
JOURNEY FROM DARKNESS (TF)   Bob Banner Associates, 1975
RETURNING HOME (TF)   Samuel Goldwyn Productions/Lorimar
   Productions, 1975
HEARTS OF THE WEST   United Artists, 1975
THE CHICKEN CHRONICLES   Avco Embassy, 1977
STUDS LONIGAN (MS)   Lorimar Productions, 1979
WANDA NEVADA   United Artists, 1979
HEAD OVER HEELS   *CHILLY SCENES OF WINTER*   United
   Artists, 1979

THE LITTLE DRAGONS   Aurora, 1980
KENT STATE (TF)   Inter Planetary Productions/Osmond TV
   Productions, 1981

BOBBY LAUREL
Contact: ASCAP - Los Angeles, 213-883-1000

THE ROSARY MURDERS   co-composer with Don Sebesky,
   Samuel Goldwyn Company, 1987

TOM LAVIN
Contact: SOCAN - Toronto, 416-445-8700

OUT OF THE BLUE   Discovery Films, 1980, Canadian

DAVID LAWRENCE
Agent: Gorfaine-Schwartz - Los Angeles, 213-969-1011

SLEEP WITH ME   MGM, 1994
CAMP NOWHERE   Buena Vista, 1994

ELLIOT LAWRENCE
Contact: ASCAP - Los Angeles, 213-883-1000

YOUR MONEY OR YOUR WIFE (TF)   Brentwood Productions,
   1972
NETWORK   United Artists, 1976
THE CRADLE WILL FALL (TF)   Cates Films Inc./Procter & Gamble
   Productions, 1983

STEPHEN LAWRENCE
Contact: ASCAP - Los Angeles, 213-883-1000

JENNIFER ON MY MIND   United Artists, 1971
BANG THE DRUM SLOWLY   Paramount, 1973
HURRY UP OR I'LL BE THIRTY   Avco Embassy, 1973
DRAGONFLY   American International, 1976
ALICE, SWEET ALICE   *COMMUNION/HOLY TERROR*   Allied
   Artists, 1977
IT HAPPENED ONE CHRISTMAS (TF)   Daisy
   Productions/Universal TV, 1977
SOONER OR LATER (TF)   Laughing Willow Company, 1979
TRACKDOWN: FINDING THE GOODBAR KILLER (TF)
   Grosso-Jacobson Productions/Centerpoint Productions, 1983
MEET THE MUNCEYS (TF)   Walt Disney TV, 1988

MAURY LAWS
Contact: ASCAP - Los Angeles, 213-883-1000

THE DAYDREAMER   Embassy, 1966
MAD MONSTER PARTY (AF)   Embassy, 1967
THE LAST DINOUSAUR (TF)   Rankin-Bass Productions, 1977,
   U.S.-Japanese
THE HOBBIT (ATF)   Rankin-Bass Productions, 1977
THE BERMUDA DEPTHS (TF)   Rankin-Bass Productions, 1978
THE RETURN OF THE KING (ATF)   Rankin-Bass Productions,
   1979
THE IVORY APE (TF)   co-composer with Bernard Hoffer,
   Rankin-Bass Productions, 1980
THE BUSHIDO BLADE   Aquarius, 1982, U.S.-Japanese

JULIAN LAXTON
Contact: SAMRO - South Africa, 011-27-11-725-1425

PURGATORY   New Star Entertainment, 1989
RISING STORM   Gibraltar Releasing, 1989

L'AZUR
STREET WARS   Jamaa Fanaka, 1992

ANTONIO LEE
A CONFUCIAN CONFUSION   *DULI SHIDAI*   1994, Taiwanese

BILL LEE

Contact: BMI - Los Angeles, 310-659-9109

JOE'S BED-STUY BARBERSHOP: WE CUT HEADS   First Run
   Features, 1983
SHE'S GOTTA HAVE IT   Island Pictures, 1986
SCHOOL DAZE   Columbia, 1988
DO THE RIGHT THING   Universal, 1989
MO' BETTER BLUES   Universal, 1990

DAVID LEE

THE MASQUE OF THE RED DEATH   American International,
   1964, British-U.S.

GERALD LEE

Contact: ASCAP - Los Angeles, 213-883-1000

SATAN'S CHEERLEADERS   World Amusement, 1977

PERVIS LEE

Contact: BMI - Los Angeles, 310-659-9109

THE GREAT UNPLEASANTNESS   co-composer with Jake Berger
   and Buzzov-en, Crescent Pictures, 1993

CAROL LEES

Contact: BMI - Los Angeles, 310-659-9109

THE LAST WORD   Samuel Goldwyn Company, 1979

DICK LE FORT

RUGGED GOLD (CTF)   co-composer with Eric N. Robertson,
   Alliance/Gibson Group/Family Channel, 1994

JAMES LEGG

b. 1962
Contact: BMI - Los Angeles, 310-659-9109

SKIN ART   ITC, 1993
LIVING PROOF: HIV AND THE PURSUIT OF HAPPINESS (FD)
   co-composer with Mark Suozzo, First Run, 1993
WOUNDED HEART (CTF)   USA/Boardwalk/Hallmark/Stu Segall
   Prods., 1995

MARK LEGGETT

Contact: ASCAP - Los Angeles, 213-883-1000

SMALL KILL   Rayfield Co. II, 1992

MICHEL LEGRAND*

b. 1932 - Paris, France
Agent: Zomba Screen Music - West Hollywood, 310-246-0777
Affiliation: SACEM - France, 011-33-1-4715-4715

BEAU FIXE   1953, French
LES AMANTS DU TAGE   1954, French
L'AMERICAIN SE DETEND (TF)   1958, French
L'AMERIQUE INSOLITE (FD)   1960, French
TERRAIN VAGUE   co-composer with Francis Lemarque, 1960,
   French
LE COEUR BATTANT   1960, French
LOLA   Films Around the World, 1961, French
UN COEUR GROS COMME CA (FD)   co-composer with Georges
   Delerue, 1961, French
A WOMAN IS A WOMAN   Pathe Contemporary, 1961, French
CLEO FROM 5 TO 7   CLEO DE 5 A 7   Zenith, 1962, French
SEVEN CAPITAL SINS   co-composer, Embassy, 1962,
   French-Italian
RETOUR A NEW YORK (FD)   1962, French
EVA   Times, 1962, French-Italian
MY LIFE TO LIVE   Pathe Contemporary, 1962, French
L'AMERIQUE LUNAIRE (FD)   1962, French
HISTOIRE D'UN PETIT GARCON DEVENU GRAND   1962, French
ILLUMINATIONS (FD)   1963, French
LE GRAND ESCROC   1963, French
L'EMPIRE DE LA NUIT   1963, French
BAY OF THE ANGELS   Pathe Contemporary, 1964, French

THE UMBRELLAS OF CHERBOURG   LES PARAPLUIES DE
   CHERBOURG ★   Landau, 1964, French-West German
UNE RAVISSANTE IDIOTE   1964, French
BAND OF OUTSIDERS   Royal Films International, 1964, French
LES AMOUREUX DU "FRANCE" (FD)   1964, French
LA DOUCEUR DU VILLAGE (FD)   1964, French
LA VIE DE CHATEAU   1965, French
QUAND PASSENT LES FAISANS   1965, French
MONNAIRE DE SINGE   1965, French
L'AN 2000   1966, French
TENDRE VOYOU   1966, French
QUI ETES-VOUS POLLY MAGGOO?   1966, French
L'OR ET LE PLUMB   GOLD AND LEAD   1966, French
SWEET NOVEMBER   Warner Bros., 1967
THE YOUNG GIRLS OF ROCHEFORT   LES DEMOISELLES DE
   ROCHEFORT ★   Warner Bros., 1968, French
A MATTER OF INNOCENCE   PRETTY POLLY   Universal, 1968,
   British
THE THOMAS CROWN AFFAIR ★   United Artists, 1968
LA PISCINE   1968, French
PLAY DIRTY   United Artists, 1968, British
ICE STATION ZEBRA   MGM, 1968
HOW TO SAVE A MARRIAGE AND RUIN YOUR LIFE   Columbia,
   1968
CASTLE KEEP   Columbia, 1969
THE HAPPY ENDING   United Artists, 1969
THE PICASSO SUMMER   Warner Bros., 1969
THE LADY IN THE CAR WITH GLASSES AND A GUN   Columbia,
   1970, French-U.S.
LE MANS   National General, 1970
PIECES OF DREAMS   United Artists, 1970
THE MAGIC GARDEN OF STANLEY SWEETHEART   MGM, 1970
DONKY SKIN   PEAU D'ANE   Janus, 1971, French
THE GO-BETWEEN   Columbia, 1971, British
WUTHERING HEIGHTS   American International, 1971, British
SUMMER OF '42 ★★   Warner Bros., 1971
BRIAN'S SONG (TF) ☆   Screen Gems/Columbia TV, 1971
LADY SINGS THE BLUES   Paramount, 1972
ONE IS A LONELY NUMBER   MGM, 1972
PORTNOY'S COMPLAINT   Warner Bros., 1972
THE ADVENTURES OF DON QUIXOTE (TF)   Universal TV/BBC,
   1973, U.S.-British
COPS AND ROBBERS   United Artists, 1973
THE IMPOSSIBLE OBJECT   Valoria, 1973, French-Italian
40 CARATS   Columbia, 1973
BREEZY   Universal, 1973
THE OUTSIDE MAN   UN HOMME EST MORT   United Artists,
   1973, French-Italian
LE GANG DES OTAGES   Gaumont, 1973, French
L'EVENEMENT LE PLUS IMPORTANT DEPUIS QUE L'HOMME A
   MARCHE SUR LA LUNE   Lira Films/Roas Productions, 1973,
   French-Italian
THE THREE MUSKETEERS   THE QUEEN'S DIAMONDS   20th
   Century-Fox, 1974, British
IT'S GOOD TO BE ALIVE (TF)   Metromedia Producers
   Corporation/Larry Harmon Pictures Corporation, 1974
F FOR FAKE   Specialty Films, 1974, French-Iranian-West German
OUR TIME   Warner Bros., 1974
CAGE WITHOUT A KEY (TF)   Columbia TV, 1975
SHEILA LEVINE IS DEAD AND LIVING IN NEW YORK
   Paramount, 1975
LE SAUVAGE   1975, French
ODE TO BILLY JOE   Warner Bros., 1976
GABLE AND LOMBARD   Universal, 1976
LE VOYAGE DE NOCES   1976, French
LA FLUTE A SIX SCHTROUMPFS   1976, French
THE OTHER SIDE OF MIDNIGHT   20th Century-Fox, 1977
GULLIVER'S TRAVELS   EMI, 1977, British-Belgian
LES ROUTES DU SUD   Parafrance, 1978, French
LES FABULEUSES AVENTURES DU LEGENDAIRE BARON
   MICHAUSEN (AF)   1979, French
THE HUNTER   U.S. version only, Paramount, 1980
FALLING IN LOVE AGAIN   International Picture Show Company,
   1980
THE MOUNTAIN MEN   Columbia, 1980
HINOTORI   co-composer with Jun Fukamachi, Toho, 1980,
   Japanese
YOUR TICKET IS NO LONGER VALID   RSL
   Productions/Ambassador, 1981, Canadian
ATLANTIC CITY   Paramount, 1981, Canadian-French
A WOMAN CALLED GOLDA (TF) ☆   Harve Bennett
   Productions/Paramount TV, 1982

BEST FRIENDS   Warner Bros., 1982
THE GIFT   Samuel Goldwyn Company, 1982, French-Italian
NEVER SAY NEVER AGAIN   Warner Bros., 1983
YENTL ★★   MGM/UA, 1983
A LOVE IN GERMANY   Triumph/Columbia, 1983, West
   German-French
LE REVANCHE DES HUMANOIDES (AF)   Planfilm, 1983, French
THE SMURFS AND THE MAGIC FLUTE (AF)   Atlantic Releasing,
   1984, Belgian-French
SECRET PLACES   TLC Films/20th Century-Fox, 1984, British
THE JESSE OWENS STORY (TF)   Harve Bennett
   Productions/Paramount TV, 1984
PAROLES ET MUSIQUES   A.A.A., 1984, French
PROMISES TO KEEP (TF)   Sandra Harmon
   Productions/Green-Epstein Productions/Telepictures, 1985
PARTIR REVENIR   UGC, 1985, French
PARKING   A.M. Films, 1985, French
SINS (MS)   additional music, New World TV/The Greif-Dore
   Company/Collins-Holm Productions, 1986
CROSSINGS (MS)   Aaron Spelling Productions, 1986
AS SUMMERS DIE (CTF)   HBO Premiere Films/Chris-Rose
   Productions/Baldwin/Aldrich Productions/Lorimar-Telepictures
   Productions, 1986
CASANOVA (TF)   Konigsberg-Sanitsky Productions/Reteitalia,
   1987
TROIS PLACES POUR LE 26   1988, French
SWITCHING CHANNELS   Columbia, 1988
NOT A PENNY MORE, NOT A PENNY LESS (CTF)
   BBC/Paramount TV Ltd./Revcom, 1990, U.S.-British
THE PICKLE   Columbia, 1993
READY TO WEAR   *PRET-A-PORTER*   Miramax, 1994
LES MISERABLES   co-composer with Francis Lai, Philippe Servain,
   Erik Berchot, Didier Barbelivien, Warner Bros., 1995, French

JED LEIBER
Contact: ASCAP - Los Angeles, 213-883-1000

LOVE POTION #9   20th Century Fox, 1992
FRANKIE'S HOUSE (MS)   co-composer with Jeff Beck, Anglia,
   1993, British
BLUE CHIPS   co-composer with Jeff Beck and Nile Rodgers,
   Paramount, 1994

MITCH LEIGH
Contact: ASCAP - Los Angeles, 213-883-1000

ONCE IN PARIS...   Atlantic Releasing Corporation, 1978

PETER LEINHEISER
THE REAL THING   L.A.C.L.P., 1997

ROBIN LEMESURIER
Contact: ASCAP - Los Angeles, 213-883-1000

INSIDE THE GOLDMINE   Cineville, 1994

BATTISTA LENA
VERSO SERA   *BY NIGHTFALL*   co-composer with Roberto Gatto,
   1991, Italian

CHRISTOPHER LENNERTZ*
Agent: Gorfaine-Schwartz - Los Angeles, 213-969-1011

SUSPECT DEVICE (CTF)   New Horizons-Hillwood Entertainment,
   1995

NICHOLAS LENS
b. November 14, 1957 - Ypres, Belgium
Contact: Brussels - Belgium, 32-02-242-6773

CRUEL HORIZON   Skyline Films, 1989, Belgian

JACK LENZ
Contact: The Einstein Brothers Music Inc.
Affiliation: SOCAN - Toronto, 416-445-8700

DUE SOUTH (TF)   co-composer with John McCarthy and Jay
   Semko, Alliance/CTV, 1994, Canadian

JEAN-FRANCOIS LEON
b. France
Contact: SACEM - France, 011-33-1-4715-4715

LES LONGS MANTEAUX   Fechner-Gaumont, 1986, French

MICHAEL LEONARD
BILLION DOLLAR HOBO   International Picture Show Company,
   1978
THEY WENT THAT-A-WAY AND THAT-A-WAY   International
   Picture Show Company, 1978

PATRICK LEONARD*
Agent: Gorfaine-Schwartz - Los Angeles, 213-969-1011
Affiliation: ASCAP - Los Angeles, 213-883-1000

AT CLOSE RANGE   Orion, 1986
NOTHING IN COMMON   Tri-Star, 1986
HEART CONDITION   New Line Cinema, 1990
TIMEBOMB   MGM/UA, 1992
WITH HONORS   Warner Bros., 1994

RAYMOND LEPPARD
b. 1927
Contact: PRS - London, England, 011-44-1-580-5544

LORD OF THE FLIES   Continental, 1963, British
PENALTY PHASE (TF)   Tamara Asseyev Productions/New World
   TV, 1986

CORY LERIOS*
Agent: Gorfaine-Schwartz - Los Angeles, 213-969-1011
Affiliation: ASCAP - Los Angeles, 213-883-1000

ONE CRAZY SUMMER   Warner Bros., 1986
NIGHT ANGEL   Fries Entertainment, 1990
CHILD'S PLAY 3   co-composer with John D'Andrea, Universal,
   1991
BAYWATCH: NIGHTMARE BAY (TF)   co-composer with John
   D'Andrea, The Baywatch Production Co./All American TV/Tower
   12/LBS, 1991
THE ENTERTAINERS (TF)   co-composer with John D'Andrea,
   Robert Greenwald Prods., 1991
THE GREY KNIGHT   co-composer with John D'Andrea, Motion
   Picture Corp. of America, 1993
BOILING POINT   co-composer with John D'Andrea, Warner Bros.,
   1993
THE TOWER (TF)   co-composer with John D'Andrea,
   Catalina/FNM Films, 1993
BAYWATCH: RACE AGAINST TIME (TF)   co-composer with John
   D'Andrea, The Baywatch Production Company, 1993
THUNDER IN PARADISE (TF)   co-composer with John D'Andrea,
   co-composer of theme with Michael Lanning,
   Berk-Schwartz-Bonnan Prods./Rysher/Trimark, 1994
DEADLY VOWS (TF)   co-composer with John D'Andrea, Carla
   Singer Prods./WIN

MICHAEL LEVANIOS III
Contact: ASCAP - Los Angeles, 213-883-1000

UNCLE SCAM   New World, 1981

SYLVESTER LEVAY
Contact: ASCAP - Los Angeles, 213-883-1000

TIME BOMB (TF)   Barry Weitz Films/Universal TV, 1984
INVITATION TO HELL (TF)   Moonlight Productions II, 1984
WET GOLD (TF)   Telepictures Productions, 1984
WHERE THE BOYS ARE '84   Tri-Star, 1984
AIRWOLF (TF)   Belisarius Productions/Universal TV, 1984

A TOUCH OF SCANDAL (TF)   Doris M. Keating Productions/Columbia TV, 1984
SINS OF THE FATHER (TF)   Fries Entertainment, 1985
CREATOR   Universal, 1985
COBRA   Warner Bros., 1986
INTIMATE ENCOUNTERS (TF)   Larry A. Thompson Productions/Donna Mills Productions/Columbia TV, 1986
CHOKE CANYON   United Film Distribution, 1986
THE ANNIHILATOR (TF)   Universal TV, 1986
HOWARD THE DUCK   co-composer with John Barry, Universal, 1986
WHERE ARE THE CHILDREN?   Columbia, 1986
TOUCH & GO   Tri-Star, 1986
THE ABDUCTION OF KARI SWENSON (TF)   NBC Productions, 1987
MANNEQUIN   20th Century Fox, 1987
WEREWOLF (TF)   Lycanthrope Productions/Tri-Star TV, 1987
BURGLAR   Warner Bros., 1987
THREE O'CLOCK HIGH   additional music, Universal, 1987
PROBE (TF)   MCA TV Ltd., 1988
THE TRACKER (CTF)   HBO Pictures/Lance Hool Productions, 1988
SOMETHING IS OUT THERE (TF)   Columbia TV, 1988
THE COVER GIRL AND THE COP (TF)   Barry-Enright Productions/Alexander Productions, 1988
POLICE STORY: GLADIATOR SCHOOL (TF)   Columbia Pictures TV, 1988
MANHUNT: SEARCH FOR THE NIGHT STALKER (TF)   Leonard Hill Films, 1989
COURAGE MOUNTAIN   Triumph Releasing Corporation, 1989, U.S.-French
THE LAKER GIRLS (TF)   Viacom Productions/Finnegan-Pinchuk Co./Valente-Hamilton Productions, 1990
SNOW KILL (CTF)   Wilshire Court Productions, 1990
NAVY SEALS   Orion, 1990
FALSE ARREST (TF)   Ron Gilbert/Leonard Hill Films, 1991
CRY IN THE WILD: THE TAKING OF PEGGY ANN (TF)   Ron Gilbert Associates/Leonard Hill Films, 1991
STONE COLD   Columbia, 1991
HOT SHOTS   20th Century Fox, 1991
FALSE ARREST (TF)   Ron Gilbert Associates/Leonard Hill Films, 1991
THE HEROES OF DESERT STORM (TF)   1991
IN THE DEEP WOODS (TF)   Frederic Golchan Prods./Leonard Hill Films, 1992
DEAD BEFORE DAWN (TF)   Joel Fields Prods./Leonard Hill Films, 1993
I CAN MAKE YOU LOVE ME: THE STALKING OF LAURA BLACK (TF)   Joel Fields/Frank Abatemarco/Leonard Hill, 1993
DONATO AND DAUGHTER (TF)   Multimedia Motion Pictures, 1993

ERIC LEVI

THE VISITORS   *LES VISITEURS*   Miramax, 1996, French

GEOFF LEVIN

Contact: ASCAP - Los Angeles, 213-883-1000

HEART   co-composer with Chris Many, New World, 1987
PERSONAL CHOICE   co-composer with Chris Smart, Moviestore Entertainment, 1989
THE PRICE SHE PAID (TF)   co-composer with Chris Many, Producers Entertainment Group/Sandy Hook/World International Network, 1992

STEWART LEVIN*

Agent: Marks Management - Tarzana, 818-776-8787
Affiliation: BMI - Los Angeles, 310-659-9109

HOMEFRONT: S.N.A.F.U. (TF)   Lorimar TV, 1991
STAY THE NIGHT (TF)   New World TV/Stan Margulies, 1992
PICKET FENCES (TF)   20th TV, 1992
A MESSAGE FROM HOLLY (TF)   Corapeake/Polson/Procter & Gamble, 1992
PAST THE BLEACHERS (TF)   Signboard Hill, 1995

KEITH LEVINE

HOLLYWOOD VICE   co-composer with Michael Convertino, Concorde/Cinema Group, 1986

WALTER LEVINSKY

Contact: ASCAP - Los Angeles, 213-883-1000

BREAKING UP (TF)   Time-Life Productions/Talent Associates Ltd., 1978
LINCOLN (TF)   additional music, Kunhardt Prods., 1992

ROSS LEVINSON*

Contact: ASCAP - Los Angeles, 213-883-1000

MIDNIGHT CALLER: LIFE WITHOUT POSSIBILITY (TF)   Lorimar TV, 1991
MURDER WITHOUT MOTIVE: THE EDMUND PERRY STORY (TF)   Leonard Hill Films, 1992
REASONABLE DOUBTS: FOREVER MY LOVE (TF)   Lorimar, 1992

JAY LEVY

Contact: BMI - Los Angeles, 310-659-9109

HARDBODIES 2   co-composer with Ed Arkin, CineTel Films, 1986
MODERN GIRLS   co-composer with Ed Arkin, Atlantic Releasing Corporation, 1986
THUNDER RUN   Cannon, 1986
PRETTY SMART   New World, 1987
LADY AVENGER   Marco Colombo, 1989

LOU LEVY

Contact: PRS - London, England, 011-44-1-580-5544

OUTSIDE CHANCE (TF)   co-composer with Murphy Dunne, New World Pictures/Miller-Begun TV, 1978

SHUKI LEVY

Contact: BMI - Los Angeles, 310-659-9109

DAWN OF THE MUMMY   Harmony Gold Ltd., 1981
LE SECRET DES SELENITES (AF)   co-composer, 1983, French
HERE COME THE LITTLES (AF)   Atlantic Releasing, 1985
RAINBOW BRITE AND THE STAR STEALER (AF)   co-composer with Haim Saban, Warner Bros., 1985
BAY COVEN (TF)   Guber-Peters Entertainment/Phoenix Entertainment Group, 1987
ROUND TRIP TO HEAVEN   co-composer with Noam Kaniel, Saban/Prism, 1991
PREY OF THE CHAMELEON (TF)   Saban/Prism, 1992
REVENGE ON THE HIGHWAY (TF)   Arvin Kaufman Prods./Saban, 1992
UNDER INVESTIGATION   New Line, 1993
IN THE SHADOWS, SOMEONE IS WATCHING (TF)   Arvin Kaufman/Saban, 1993
HONOR THY FATHER AND MOTHER: THE TRUE STORY OF THE MENENDEZ MURDERS (TF)   Saban Entertainment, 1994
BLINDFOLD: ACTS OF OBSESSION (CTF)   Libra Pictures, 1994

GORDON LEWIS

HAPPILY EVER AFTER: FAIRY TALES FOR EVERY CHILD (ATF)   co-composer, Two Oceans/Confetti/Hyperion, 1995

HERSCHELL GORDON LEWIS

Contact: BMI - Los Angeles, 310-659-9109

BLOOD FEAST   Box Office Spectaculars, 1963
2000 MANIACS   co-composer with Larry Wellington, Box Office Spectaculars, 1964
SHE-DEVILS ON WHEELS   1968
THE GORE-GORE GIRLS   *BLOOD ORGY*   Lewis Motion Picture Enterprises, 1972

MICHAEL J. LEWIS

Contact: ASCAP - Los Angeles, 213-883-1000

THE MAN WHO HAUNTED HIMSELF   Levitt-Pickman, 1970, British
UNMAN, WITTERING & ZIGO   Paramount, 1971, British
THEATRE OF BLOOD   United Artists, 1973, British
II HARROWHOUSE   20th Century-Fox, 1974, British

92 IN THE SHADE   United Artists, 1975
RUSSIAN ROULETTE   Avco Embassy, 1975
THE MEDUSA TOUCH   Warner Bros., 1978, British
THE STICK UP   *MUD*   Trident-Barber, 1978, British
THE PASSAGE   United Artists, 1979
THE LEGACY   Universal, 1979
ffolkes   *NORTH SEAS HIJACK*   Universal, 1980, British
THE UNSEEN   World Northal, 1981
SPHINX   Orion/Warner Bros., 1981
YES, GIORGIO   MGM/UA, 1982
THE NAKED FACE   Cannon, 1985
THE ROSE AND THE JACKAL (CTF)   Steve White
    Productions/PWD Productions/Spectator Films/TNT, 1990
SHE STOOD ALONE (TF)   Mighty Fortress Prods./Walt Disney TV,
    1991

PAUL H. LEWIS
THE DARK ANGEL (TF)   1991, U.K.-New Zealand

W. MICHAEL LEWIS
Contact: ASCAP - Los Angeles, 213-883-1000

ENTER THE NINJA   co-composer with Laurin Rinder, Cannon,
    1981
FIRECRACKER   co-composer with Laurin Rinder, New World,
    1981, U.S.-Filipino
SHOGUN ASSASSIN   co-composer with Laurin Rinder, New
    World, 1981, Japanese-U.S.
HOT BUBBLEGUM   *LEMON POPSICLE III*   co-composer with
    Laurin Rinder, Noah Films, 1981, Israeli
NEW YEAR'S EVIL   co-composer with Laurin Rinder, Cannon, 1981
THE KILLING OF AMERICA (FD)   co-composer with Mark Lindsay,
    Filmlink Corp., 1982, U.S.-Japanese
THE KULIES   co-composer with Laurin Rinder, Global
THE BALLAD OF GREGORIO CORTEZ   co-composer with Laurin
    Rinder, Embassy, 1983
REVENGE OF THE NINJA   additional music, MGM/UA/Cannon,
    1983
NINJA III—THE DOMINATION   co-composer with Laurin Rinder,
    Cannon, 1984
BAD MANNERS   *GROWING PAINS*   co-composer with Laurin
    Rinder, New World, 1984
HOT CHILD IN THE CITY   co-composer with Laurin Rinder,
    Mediacom Filmworks, 1987

WEBSTER LEWIS
Contact: BMI - Los Angeles, 310-659-9109

THE HEARSE   Crown International, 1980
BODY AND SOUL   Cannon, 1981
MY TUTOR   Crown International, 1983
GO TELL IT ON THE MOUNTAIN (TF)   Learning in Focus, 1984

BLAKE LEYH
Contact: 213-663-1696
Affiliation: BMI - Los Angeles, 310-659-9109

STAR TIME   Alexander Cassini, 1992
2nd COUSIN, ONCE REMOVED   Shorney/McColpin, 1992
ODILE & YVETTE AT THE EDGE OF THE WORLD   Bam
    Productions, 1993
THE SERPENT'S TALE   1993, Turkish
AMERICAN CYBORG: STEEL WARRIOR   Cannon, 1994
NEW EDEN (CTF)   Davis Ent./MTE, 1995

DANIEL LICHT
Agent: Ocean Park Music Group - Los Angeles, 310-315-5266
Affiliation: BMI - Los Angeles, 310-659-9109

CHILDREN OF THE NIGHT   Fangoria, 1990
WHERE ARE WE: OUR TRIP THROUGH AMERICA (FD)   Telling
    Pictures, 1992
CHILDREN OF THE CORN II: THE FINAL SACRIFICE   Dimension,
    1993
ACTING ON IMPULSE (CTF)   Spectacor, 1993
ZOOMAN (CTF)   Manheim/Logo Prods., 1995
BAD MOON   1996
HELLRAISER: BLOODLINE   1996
STEPHEN KING'S THINNER   Paramount, 1996

RICHARD LIEB
Contact: ASCAP - Los Angeles, 213-883-1000

LINCOLN (TF)   additional music, Kunhardt Prods., 1992

MARTIN LIEBMAN
LET'S KILL ALL THE LAWYERS   Lighten Up Films, 1992

JIMMY LIFTON
RAVEN DANCE   Orphan, 1993

HAL LINDES
Agent: William Morris - Beverly Hills, 310-859-4000
Affiliation: PRS - London, England, 011-44-1-580-5544

JOYRIDERS   Granada Films, 1989, British
DROWNING IN THE SHALLOW END (TF)   BBC, 1990, British
BORN KICKING (TF)   BBC, 1992, British
CORIOLIS EFFECT   Secondary Modern, 1993
THE SECRETS OF LAKE SUCCESS (MS)   Cramer Co./NBC
    Prods., 1993
BERMUDA GRACE (TF)   Catalyst Prods., 1994
DON'T DO IT   Trans Atlantic, 1995
THE GREAT KANDINSKY (TF)   BBC, 1995, U.S.-British
THE INFILTRATOR (CTF)   HBO Showcase/Francine LeFrak
    Prods./Carnival, 1995
KISS AND TELL (TF)   LWT, 1996, British

MARK LINDSAY
Contact: BMI - Los Angeles, 310-659-9109

THE KILLING OF AMERICA   co-composer with W. Michael Lewis,
    Filmlink Corp., 1982, U.S.-Japanese

MORT LINDSEY
Contact: ASCAP - Los Angeles, 213-883-1000

40 POUNDS OF TROUBLE   Universal, 1962
I COULD GO ON SINGING   United Artists, 1963, British
STOLEN HOURS   United Artists, 1963
THE BEST MAN   United Artists, 1964
REAL LIFE   Paramount, 1979

STEVE LINDSEY
BEHIND ENEMY LINES (TF)   co-composer with Jack Chipman,
    MTM Enterprises/TVS, 1985

DAVID LINDUP
Contact: PRS - London, England, 011-44-1-580-5544

THE SPIRAL STAIRCASE   Warner Bros., 1975, British

DAM LINH
PAGE BLANCHE   1991, Cambodian-Swiss

PETER LINK
Contact: ASCAP - Los Angeles, 213-883-1000

NIGHTMARE (TF)   Mark Carliner Productions/CBS Entertainment,
    1974

WANG LIPING
XIANG HUN NU   *THE WOMEN FROM THE LAKE OF SCENTED
    SOULS*   1993, China

LARRY LIPKIS
Contact: BMI - Los Angeles, 310-659-9109

THE JUNIPER TREE   Keene/Moyroud, 1991, U.S.-Icelandic

ALAN LISK
Contact: PRS - London, England, 011-44-1-580-5544

CODENAME: KYRIL (TF)   Incito Productions/HTV, 1989, British

ZDENEK LISKA

b. Czechoslovakia
Contact: OSA - Tr. Cs. Armady 20, 160-56 Prague 6-Bubene,
Czechoslovakia

POKLAD NA PTACIM OSTROVE *THE TREASURE OF BIRD
ISLAND* (AF) 1952, Czech
PAN PROKOUK PRITEL ZVIRATEK (AF) 1953, Czech
FLICEK THE BALL *THE NAUGHTY BALL* 1956, Czech
THE FABULOUS WORLD OF JULES VERNE 1958, Czech
DEN ODPLATY *THE DAY OF RECKONING* (AF) 1960, Czech
WHERE THE DEVIL CANNOT GO 1960, Czech
THE FABULOUS BARON MUNCHAUSEN 1961, Czech
THE SHOP ON MAIN STREET *THE SHOP ON HIGH STREET*
1965, Czech
VRAZDA PO CESKY *MURDER, CZECH STYLE* 1966, Czech
BYT *THE FLAT* 1968, Czech
THE VALLEY OF THE BEES 1968, Czech
MARKETA LAZAROVA 1969, Czech
OVOCE STROMJ RAJSHYCH JIME 1970, Czech
PRIPAD PRO ZACINAJICHO KATA *A CASE FOR A YOUNG
HANGMAN* 1970, Czech
WE'LL EAT THE FRUIT OF PARADISE 1970, Czech
ADRIFT 1971, Czech
JUMPING OVER PUDDLES AGAIN 1971, Czech
THE TRICKY GAME OF LOVE 1971, Czech
QUITE GOOD CHAPS 1972
DAYS OF BETRAYAL 1974
PAVLINKA 1974
WHO LEAVES IN THE RAIN 1976
THE LITTLE MERMAID 1977
SMOKE IN THE POTATO FIELDS 1977
SHADOWS OF A HOT SUMMER 1978

JOHN LISSAUER

MANAGUA Everest Entertainment, 1997

RUSS LITTLE

Contact: SOCAN - Toronto, 416-445-8700

TOO OUTRAGEOUS! Spectrafilm, 1987

BRYNMOR LLEWELLYN-JONES

GORILLA BATHES AT NOON 1993, German-Yugoslav

CHARLES LLOYD

Contact: BMI - Los Angeles, 310-659-9109

ALMOST SUMMER co-composer with Ron Altbach, Universal,
1978

MICHAEL LLOYD

Contact: ASCAP - Los Angeles, 213-883-1000

THE POM POM GIRLS Crown International, 1976
LOVE'S DARK RIDE (TF) co-composer with John D'Andrea, Mark
VII Ltd./Worldvision Enterprises, 1978
STRANGER IN OUR HOUSE (TF) co-composer with John
D'Andrea, Inter Planetary Pictures/Finnegan Associates, 1978
GRAMBLING'S WHITE TIGER (TF) co-composer with John
D'Andrea, Inter Planetary Productions/Jenner/Wallach
Productions, 1981
THE BEACH GIRLS Crown International, 1982
TOUGH ENOUGH co-composer with Steve Wax, 20th
Century-Fox, 1983
SAVAGE STREETS co-composer with John D'Andrea, MPM,
1984
BODY SLAM co-composer with John D'Andrea, DEG, 1987
THE GARBAGE PAIL KIDS MOVIE Atlantic Entertainment Group,
1987
SWIMSUIT (TF) co-composer with John D'Andrea, Musifilm
Productions/American First Run Studios, 1989
ACAPULCO H.E.A.T. (TF) co-composer with Tommy Oliver and
Jim Ervin, Keller & Keller/Balenciaga/All-American, 1993

LOWELL LO

Contact: CASH - Kowloon, 011-852-3-722-5225

FONG SAI-YUK TSUKTSAP *FONG SAI-YUK II* 1993, Hong Kong
92 HAK MUIGWAI DUI HAK MUIGWAI *92 LEGENDARY LA ROSE
NOIRE* 1993, Hong Kong

LOS LOBOS

Contact: BMI - Los Angeles, 310-659-9109

THE WRONG MAN (CTF) Beattie-Chesser, 1993
DESPERADO Columbia, 1995
FEELING MINNESOTA New Line, 1996

ROBERT LOCKHART

Contact: PRS - London, England, 011-44-1-580-5544

THE LONG DAY CLOSES co-composer with Bob Last, 1992,
British
THE EXECUTION PROTOCOL (FD) 1992, British
THE NEON BIBLE arrangements, Miramax, 1995, U.S.-British

DIDIER LOCKWOOD

Contact: SACEM - France, 011-33-1-4715-4715

LUNE FROIDE *COLD MOON* 1991, French

ROBERT LOCKWOOD

COLD COMFORT FARM 1996

MALCOM LOCKYER

Contact: PRS - London, England, 011-44-1-580-5544

THE LITTLE ONES Columbia, 1965, British
TEN LITTLE INDIANS 1965, British
BANG BANG, YOU'RE DEAD! *OUR MAN IN MARRAKESH*
American International, 1966, British
DEADLIER THAN THE MALE Universal, 1966, British
ISLAND OF TERROR Universal, 1966, British
THE VENGEANCE OF FU-MANCHU Warner Bros., 1968, British

JOSEPH LO DUCA

Contact: ASCAP - Los Angeles, 213-883-1000

THE EVIL DEAD New Line Cinema, 1983
THE XYZ MURDERS Embassy International, 1985
THOU SHALT NOT KILL Troma, 1985
CRIMEWAVE additional music, Renaissance, 1985
THE CARRIER Swan Productions, 1986
EVIL DEAD 2 Rosebud Releasing Corporation, 1987
MOONTRAP Shapiro Glickenhaus, 1989
LUNATICS: A LOVE STORY Renaissance II, 1991
ARMY OF DARKNESS: EVIL DEAD 3 Universal, 1992
DYING TO LOVE YOU (TF) Longbow Productions/World
International Network, 1993
RIVER OF RAGE: THE TAKING OF MAGGIE KEENE (TF) David
C. Thomas, 1993
NECROMICON Davis Film, 1993
HERCULES AND THE AMAZON WOMEN (TF) Renaissance
Pictures, 1994
A CHILD'S CRY FOR HELP (TF) RHI/Ronald J. Kahn Prods., 1994

FRANK LOEF

JUSTIZ *JUSTICE* 1993, German-Swiss

NILS LOFGREN

EVERY BREATH Motion Picture Corp. of America, 1993

GARY LOGAN

Contact: ASCAP - Los Angeles, 213-883-1000

THE HUMAN FACTOR co-composer with Richard Logan,
MGM/UA, 1979

RICHARD LOGAN

THE HUMAN FACTOR   co-composer with Gary Logan, MGM/UA,
   1979

MARKUS LONARDONI

HAPPY BIRTHDAY, TURKE!   co-composer with Peer Raben,
   Senator Films, 1992, German

FRANK LONDON

EVERYTHING RELATIVE   1996

DAVID LONG

ABSENT WITHOUT LEAVE   co-composer with Don McGlashan and
   Mark Austin, 1993, New Zealand

TAO LONG

SHUANG-QI-ZHEN DAOKE   *THE SWORDSMAN IN
   DOUBLE-FLAG TOWN*   1991, Chinese

PAUL LOOMIS

Contact: ASCAP - Los Angeles, 213-883-1000

THE PASSAGE   Manson International, 1988
RIVERBEND   Intercontinental Releasing, 1989

WILLIAM LOOS

THE MAN WHO SAW TOMORROW   co-composer with Jack TIllar,
   Warner Bros., 1981
HELEN KELLER - THE MIRACLE CONTINUES (TF)   co-composer
   of theme song with Jack Tillar, Castle Combe Productions/20th
   Century Fox TV, 1984, US-British

JEFF LORBER

Contact: ASCAP - Los Angeles, 213-883-1000

SIDE OUT   Tri-Star, 1990

BRUNO LOUCHOUARN*

Contact: Music to your Eyes - Santa Monica, 310-450-4630
Affiliation: BMI - Los Angeles. 310-659-9190

COVER UP   Live, 1991
INNOCENT OBSESSION   Belle Avery Prods., 1992
NO GOODBYES   Sam Yeung Prods., 1995
HELLFIRE (CTF)   co-composer with Vladimir Kamorov, New
   Horizons, 1995

DIANE LOUIE

Contact: BMI - Los Angeles, 310-659-9109

LATINO   Cinecom, 1985
HAPPILY EVER AFTER: FAIRY TALES FOR EVERY CHILD
   (ATF)   co-composer, Two Oceans/Confetti/Hyperion, 1995

STEPAN LOUSIKYAN

KORSVATS DRAKHT   *THE LOST PARADISE*   1992, Armenian

MUNDELL LOWE

Contact: ASCAP - Los Angeles, 213-883-1000

EVERYTHING YOU WANTED TO KNOW ABOUT SEX (BUT WERE
   AFRAID TO ASK)   United Artists, 1972
ATTACK ON TERROR: THE FBI VERSUS THE KU KLUX KLAN
   (TF)   QM Productions/Warner Bros. TV, 1975
SIDEWINDER 1   Avco Embassy, 1977
THE GIRL IN THE EMPTY GRAVE (TF)   Manteo Enterprises/MGM
   TV, 1977
TARANTULAS: THE DEADLY CARGO (TF)   Alan Landsburg
   Productions, 1977
DEADLY GAME (TF)   Manteo Enterprises/MGM TV, 1977

JESSE LOYA

Contact: BMI - Los Angeles, 310-659-9109

LIFE IS NICE   AFI USA Independent Showcase, 1991

JEREMY LUBBOCK

Agent: Air-Edel - Los Angeles, 310-914-5000
Affiliation: BMI - Los Angeles, 310-659-9109

THE COLOR PURPLE ★   co-composer, Warner Bros., 1985
ANY MAN'S DEATH   INI Entertainment, 1990
DEAR GOD   co-composer with James Patrick Dunne, Paramount,
   1996

KEN LUBER

WORLD GONE WILD   Lorimar, 1988

MARK LUNDQUIST

Contact: BMI - Los Angeles, 310-659-9109

THE LINGUINI INCIDENT   additional music, Academy
   Entertainment, 1992

JOHN LUNN

THE CORMORANT (CTF)   Holmes Associates, 1995, British

DONAL LUNNY

b. Ireland
Contact: PRS - London, England, 011-44-1-580-5544

EAT THE PEACH   Skouras Pictures, 1986, Irish
THE RETURN (TF)   Spectre Productions, 1988, Irish

MICHAL LURENC

BLOOD & WINE   Fox Searchlight, 1997

EVAN LURIE

Contact: BMI - Los Angeles, 310-659-9109

JOHNNY STECCHINO   1991, Italian
THE NIGHT WE NEVER MET   Miramax, 1993
THE MONSTER   1996
TREES LOUNGE   Live, 1996
LAYIN' LOW   Curb, 1997

JOHN LURIE

Agent: Jeff Kaufman - Studio City, 818-506-6013
Affiliation: BMI - Los Angeles, 310-659-9109

SUBWAY RIDERS   co-composer, Hep Pictures, 1981
PERMANENT VACATION   co-composer, Gray City Inc., 1982
STRANGER THAN PARADISE   Samuel Goldwyn Company, 1984
VARIETY   Horizon Films, 1985
DOWN BY LAW   Island Pictures, 1986
POLICE STORY: MONSTER MANOR (TF)   Columbia Pictures TV,
   1988
MYSTERY TRAIN   Orion Classics, 1989
BLUE IN THE FACE   Miramax, 1995
GET SHORTY   MGM-UA, 1995
MANNY AND LO   Miramax, 1996
BOX OF MOONLIGHT   Trimark, 1996
EXCESS BAGGAGE   Columbia, 1997

DANNY LUX

Agent: Carol Faith Agency - Beverly Hills, 310-274-0776
Contact: BMI - Los Angeles, 310-659-9109

SILK STALKINGS: NATURAL SELECTION (TF)   Stu Segall
   Prods./Steven J. Cannell, 1994

SHELBY LYNNE

Contact: BMI - Los Angeles, 310-659-9109

ANOTHER PAIR OF ACES: THREE OF A KIND (TF)   co-composer
   with Jay Gruska, Pedernales/Once Upon A Time Films, 1991

RICHARD LYONS

Contact: BMI - Los Angeles, 310-659-9109

DO OR DIE   Malibu Bay Films, 1991
HARD HUNTED   Malibu Bay Films, 1992

M

TONY MACAULEY

Contact: PRS - London, England, 011-44-1-580-5544

THE BEAST IN THE CELLAR   1971, British
IT'S NOT THE SIZE THAT COUNTS   *PERCY'S PROGRESS*
   Joseph Brenner Associates, 1974, British
MIDDLE AGE CRAZY   20th Century-Fox, 1980, Canadian

EGISTO MACCHI

Contact: SIAE - Italy, 011-39-6-59-901

MUSSOLINI: THE DECLINE AND FALL OF IL DUCE (CTF)   HBO
   Premiere Films/RAI/Antenne-2/Beta Film/TVE/RTSI, 1985,
   U.S.-Italian-French-West German
THE ROSE GARDEN   21st Century, 1989, West German-U.S.

GEOFF MacCORMACK

Contact: PRS - London, England, 011-44-1-580-5544

WILD ORCHID   Triumph Releasing Corporation, 1990

GALT MACDERMOTT

Contact: SOCAN - Toronto, 416-445-8700

MISTRESS   J&M, 1992

TEO MACERO

Contact: BMI - Los Angeles, 310-659-9109

TOP SECRET (TF)   co-composer with Stu Gardner, Jemmin
   Productions/Sheldon Leonard Productions, 1978
SERGEANT MATLOVICH VS. THE U.S. AIR FORCE (TF)
   Tomorrow Entertainment, 1978
FRIDAY THE 13TH...THE ORPHAN   World Northal, 1979,
   Japanese
VIRUS   Haruki Kadokawa, 1980, Japanese
THE TED KENNEDY JR. STORY (TF)   Entertainment Partners,
   1986
A SPECIAL FRIENDSHIP (TF)   Entertainment Partners, 1987

JOHN MADARA

Contact: BMI - Los Angeles, 310-659-9109

HEY, GOOD LOOKIN'   co-composer with Ric Sandler, Warner
   Bros., 1982

MADER

Agent: CAA - Beverly Hills, 310-288-4545
Management: Derek Power Company - Los Angeles, 310-472-4647
Affiliation: GEMA - Germany, 011-49-30-214-54-0

IN THE SOUP   Jim Stark, 1992
HSI YEN   *THE WEDDING BANQUET*   1993, Taiwanese
TALLINN PIMEDUSES   *DARKNESS IN TALLINN*   FilmZolfo, 1993,
   Finnish-U.S.
EAT DRINK MAN WOMAN   Samuel Goldwyn, 1994, Taiwanese
SOMEBODY TO LOVE   Lumiere Pictures, 1994
COMFORTABLY NUMB   The Shooting Gallery, 1995
LETTING GO (CTF)   Maysles Film, 1996
CLOCKWATCHERS   John Flock Prods., 1997

MADREDEUS

LISBON STORY   co-composer with Jurgen Knieper, 1995,
   German

TAJ MAHAL

Contact: BMI - Los Angeles, 310-659-9109

ZEBRAHEAD   Oliver Stone, 1992

VINCENT MAI

JUST ONE OF THE GIRLS (TF)   co-composer with Amin Bhatia,
   Entertainment Securities/Saban Neal and Gary Prods., 1993

STEFANO MAINETTI

Agent: Robert Light - Los Angeles, 213-651-1777

VENDETTA II: THE NEW MAFIA (TF)   Titanus/Silvio Berlusconi
   Ent./Tribune, 1993

MAURO MALAVASI

b. Italy
Contact: SIAE - Italy, 011-39-6-59-901

MARIO PUZO'S THE FORTUNATE PILGRIM (MS)   co-composer
   with Mauro Malavasi, Carlo & Alex Ponti Productions/Reteitalia
   S.P.A., 1988, Italian

MANUEL MALOU

BUSHWACKED   *GAZON MAUDIT*   1995, French
FRENCH TWIST   Miramax Zoe, 1996

NIKOS MAMANGAKIS

Contact: GEMA - Germany, 011-49-30-214-54-0

KASPAR HAUSER   1993, German
PHANOUROPITTA   *SAINT PHANOURIOS' PIE*   1993, Greek

BOB MAMET

Contact: ASCAP - Los Angeles, 213-883-1000

NECROMANCER   co-composer with Gary Stockdale and Kevin
   Klinger, Bonnaire Films, 1989

NORMAN MAMEY

Contact: BMI - Los Angeles, 310-659-9109

MALEDICTION   Henry Plott Productions, 1989
SATAN'S PRINCESS   Sun Heat, 1991
ROUND NUMBERS   Filumthropix, 1992

MARK MANCINA

Agent: Gorfaine-Schwartz - Los Angeles, 213-969-1011
Affiliation: BMI - Los Angeles, 310-659-9109

WHERE SLEEPING DOGS LIE   co-composer with Hans Zimmer,
   August Entertainment, 1992
LIFEPOD (TF)   RHI/Trilogy, 1993
TRUE ROMANCE   additional music, Warner Bros., 1993
MONKEY TROUBLE   New Line, 1994
SPEED   20th Century Fox, 1994
MAN OF THE HOUSE   Buena Vista, 1995
THE OUTER LIMITS: SANDKINGS (CTF)   co-composer with John
   Van Tongeren, Trilogy, Atlantis, 1995
BAD BOYS   Columbia, 1995
ASSASSINS   Warner Bros., 1995
MONEY TRAIN   Columbia, 1995
MOLL FLANDERS   MGM-UA, 1996
TWISTER   Warner Bros., 1996
SPEED 2   20th Century Fox, 1997

JOHNNY MANDEL

b. November 23, 1935 - New York, New York
Agent: Carol Faith Agency - Beverly Hills, 310-274-0776
Affiliation: ASCAP - Los Angeles, 213-883-1000

I WANT TO LIVE!   United Artists, 1958
THE THIRD VOICE   20th Century Fox, 1959
DRUMS OF AFRICA   MGM, 1963
THE AMERICANIZATION OF EMILY   MGM, 1964
THE SANDPIPER   MGM, 1965

THE RUSSIANS ARE COMING THE RUSSIANS ARE COMING
United Artists, 1966
HARPER   Warner Bros., 1966
AN AMERICAN DREAM   Warner Bros., 1966
POINT BLANK   MGM, 1967
PRETTY POISON   20th Century-Fox, 1968
HEAVEN WITH A GUN   MGM, 1969
THAT COLD DAY IN THE PARK   Commonwealth United, 1969,
Canadian-U.S.
SOME KIND OF A NUT   United Artists, 1969
M*A*S*H   20th Century-Fox, 1970
THE MAN WHO HAD POWER OVER WOMEN   Avco Embassy,
1971, British
A NEW LEAF   Paramount, 1971
CACTUS MOLLY AND LAWLESS JOHN   Malibu Productions, 1971
THE TRACKERS (TF)   Aaron Spelling Productions, 1971
JOURNEY THROUGH ROSEBUD   GSF, 1972
SUMMER WISHES, WINTER DREAMS   Columbia, 1973
THE LAST DETAIL   Columbia, 1973
"W"   Cinerama Releasing Corporation, 1974, British
THE TURNING POINT OF JIM MALLOY (TF)   David Gerber
Productions/Columbia Pictures TV, 1975
ESCAPE TO WITCH MOUNTAIN   Buena Vista, 1975
THE SAILOR WHO FELL FROM GRACE WITH THE SEA   Avco
Embassy, 1976, British
FREAKY FRIDAY   Buena Vista, 1976
AGATHA   Warner Bros., 1979, British
BEING THERE   United Artists, 1979
THE BALTIMORE BULLET   Avco Embassy, 1980
CADDYSHACK   Orion/Warner Bros., 1980
EVITA PERON (TF)   Hartwest Productions/Zephyr Productions, 1981
DEATHTRAP   Warner Bros., 1982
SOUP FOR ONE   additional music, Warner Bros., 1982
LOOKIN' TO GET OUT   Paramount, 1982
THE VERDICT   20th Century-Fox, 1982
STAYING ALIVE   Paramount, 1983
A LETTER TO THREE WIVES (TF) ☆   20th Century Fox TV, 1985
CHRISTMAS EVE (TF)   NBC Productions, 1986
BRENDA STARR   New World, 1987
LBJ: THE EARLY YEARS (TF) ☆   Louis Rudolph Films/Fries
Entertainment, 1987
ASSAULT AND MATRIMONY (TF)   Michael Filerman
Productions/NBC Productions, 1987
FOXFIRE (TF) ☆   Marian Rees Associates, 1987
THE GREAT ESCAPE II: THE UNTOLD STORY (TF)   Spectacor
Films/Michael Jaffe Films, 1988
SINGLE MEN, MARRIED WOMEN (TF)   Michele Lee
Productions/CBS Entertainment, 1989

TOMMY MANDEL
DEADLY HERO   co-composer with Brad Fiedel, Avco Embassy, 1976

HARRY MANFREDINI*
Contact: BMI - Los Angeles, 310-659-9109

HERE COME THE TIGERS   American International, 1978
THE KIRLIAN WITNESS   1978
NIGHT FLOWERS   Willow Production Co., 1979
THE CHILDREN   1980
FRIDAY THE 13TH   Paramount, 1980
FRIDAY THE 13TH PART 2   Paramount, 1981
FRIDAY THE 13TH PART 3   Paramount, 1982
SWAMP THING   Avco Embassy, 1982
SPRING BREAK   Columbia, 1983
THE RETURNING   Willow Films, 1983
THE LAST PICNIC   1983
FRIDAY THE 13TH - THE FINAL CHAPTER   Paramount, 1984
FRIDAY THE 13TH PART V - A NEW BEGINNING   Paramount,
1985
THE HILLS HAVE EYES PART II   Castle Prods., 1985, British-U.S.
HOUSE   New World, 1986
FRIDAY THE 13TH PART VI: JASON LIVES   Paramount, 1986
HOUSE II: THE SECOND STORY   New World, 1987
FRIDAY THE 13TH PART VII - THE NEW BLOOD   co-composer
with Fred Mollin, Paramount, 1988
DOUBLE REVENGE   Smart Egg Releasing, 1988
THE HORROR SHOW   MGM/UA, 1989
DEEP STAR SIX   Tri-Star, 1989
CAMERON'S CLOSET   SVS Films, 1989
DOUBLE REVENGE   Smart Egg Pictures, 1990
MY BOYFRIEND'S BACK   Touchstone, 1993

JASON GOES TO HELL: THE FINAL FRIDAY   New Line, 1993
ACES: IRON EAGLE III   New Line, 1992
CRIES UNHEARD: THE DONNA VARLICH STORY (TF)   Carla
Singer Prods, 1994
FOLLOW YOUR HEART   DMG Entertainment, 1997

HRIDAYNATH MANGESHKAR
MAYA MEMSAAB   MAYA: THE ENCHANTING ILLUSION   1993,
Indian

CHUCK MANGIONE
b. November 29, 1940 - Rochester, New York
Contact: BMI - Los Angeles, 310-659-9109

THE CHILDREN OF SANCHEZ   Lone Star, 1978, U.S.-Mexican

TONY MANGURIAN
Contact: BMI - Los Angeles, 310-659-9109

FIRES IN THE MIRROR (TF)   co-composer with Joseph Jarman,
American Playhouse, 1993

BARRY MANILOW
HANS CHRISTIAN ANDERSEN'S THUMBELINA   co-composer with
William Ross, Warner Bros., 1994

BARRY MANN
Contact: BMI - Los Angeles, 310-659-9109

I NEVER SANG FOR MY FATHER   co-composer with Al Gorgoni,
Columbia, 1970

HUMMIE MANN*
b. 1955 - Montreal, Canada
Agent: Zomba Screen Music - West Hollywood, 310-246-0777
Affiliation: ASCAP - Los Angeles, 213-883-1000

STOOGEMANIA   Atlantic Releasing Corporation, 1985
IN GOLD WE TRUST   Little Bear Films, 1990
YEAR OF THE COMET   Columbia, 1992
BENEFIT OF THE DOUBT   Miramax, 1993
ROBIN HOOD: MEN IN TIGHTS   20th Century Fox, 1993
REBEL HIGHWAY: MOTORCYCLE GANG (CTF)   Drive-In
Classics, 1994
REBEL HIGHWAY: CONFESSIONS OF A SORORITY GIRL
(CTF)   Drive-In Classics, 1994
REBEL HIGHWAY: RUNAWAY DAUGHTERS (CTF)   Drive-In
Classics, 1994
REBEL HIGHWAY: GIRLS IN PRISON (CTF)   Drive-In Classics,
1994
REBEL HIGHWAY: DRAGSTRIP GIRL (CTF)   Drive-In Classics,
1994
REBEL HIGHWAY: JAILBREAKERS (CTF)   Drive-In Classics,
1994
REBEL HIGHWAY: COOL AND THE CRAZY (CTF)   Drive-In
Classics, 1994
REBEL HIGHWAY: REFORM SCHOOL GIRLS (CTF)   Drive-In
Classics, 1994
FALL TIME   Live Ent., 1995
LANGUAGE OF THE HEART (CTF)   Showtime, 1995
LIGHTNING (CTF)   Showtime, 1995
SOIR BLEU (CTF)   Showtime, 1995
ARMED RESPONSE (CTF)   Showtime, 1995
DRACULA: DEAD AND LOVING IT   Columbia, 1995
STICKS AND STONES   Goldbar, 1995
IN COLD BLOOD (TF)   Hallmark, 1996
FIRST DO NO HARM   Jaffe-Brainstein, 1996
THE RESCUERS (CTF)   Paramount TV, 1997
THE SECOND CIVIL WAR (CTF)   HBO Pictures, 1997

FRANCO MANNINO
b. 1924 - Palermo, Italy
Contact: SIAE - Italy, 011-39-6-59-901

DOMANI E UN ALTRO GIORNO   1951, Italian
BELLISSIMA   Italian Films Export, 1951, Italian
CINEMA D'ALTRI TEMPI   1953, Italian
LA PROVINCIALE   1953, Italian

IL SOLE NEGLI OCCHI   1953, Italian
AI MARGINI DELLA METROPOLI   1953, Italian
BEAT THE DEVIL   co-composer with Lambert Williamson, United
   Artists, 1954, British
VESTIRE GLI INUDI   1954, Italian
I VAMPIRI   1956, Italian
MORGAN THE PIRATE   MGM, 1961, Italian
SEVEN SEAS TO CALAIS   IL DOMINATORE DEI SETTE MARI
   MGM, 1962, Italian
GOLD FOR THE CAESARS   Colorama, 1962, Italian-French
MADEMOISELLE DE MAUPIN   Jolly Film/Consortium Pathe/Tecisa,
   1965, Italian-French-Spanish
LOVE IN FOUR DIMENSIONS   1965, Italian
DEATH IN VENICE   adaptation, Warner Bros., 1971, Italian-French
LUDWIG   adaptation, MGM, 1972, Italian-French-West German
IDENTIKIT   1974, Italian
CONVERSATION PIECE   GRUPPO DI FAMIGLIAIN UNO
   INTERNO   New Line Cinema, 1975, Italian-French
UN CUORE SEMPLICE   1976, Italian
THE INNOCENT   1976, Italian
A SIMPLE HEART   1978, Italian

ERNIE MANNIX*

TONY AND TINA'S WEDDING   Castle Rock, 1992
MEN LIE   Lexington Pictures, 1994

DAVID MANSFIELD

Agent: CAA - Beverly Hills, 310-288-4545
Affiliation: BMI - Los Angeles, 310-659-9109

HEAVEN'S GATE   United Artists, 1980
YEAR OF THE DRAGON   MGM/UA, 1985
CLUB PARADISE   co-composer with Van Dyke Parks, Warner
   Bros., 1986
THE SICILIAN   20th Century Fox, 1987
INTO THE HOMELAND (CTF)   Kevin McCormick/Anna Hamilton
   Phelan Productions, 1987
FRESH HORSES   Columbia/WEG, 1988
MISS FIRECRACKER   Firecracker Co. Productions/Corsair
   Pictures, 1989
DESPERATE HOURS   MGM/UA, 1990
LATE FOR DINNER   Columbia, 1991
ME AND VERONICA   True One/True Pictures, 1992
THE BALLAD OF LITTLE JOE   Fine Line, 1993
DAVID'S MOTHER (TF)   Morgan Hill Films/Hearst, 1994
A DANGEROUS AFFAIR (TF)   Stalking Prods./Greengrass Prods.,
   1994

KEITH MANSFIELD

Contact: PRS - London, England, 011-44-1-580-5544

FIST OF FEAR TOUCH OF DEATH   Aquarius, 1980

EDDIE LAWRENCE MANSON

b. May 9, 1925 - New York, New York
Contact: ASCAP - Los Angeles, 213-883-1000

THE LITTLE FUGITIVE   1953
LOVERS AND LOLLIPOPS   1956
DAY OF THE PAINTER   1960
THREE BITES OF THE APPLE   1967
A LOVE AFFAIR: THE ELEANOR AND LOU GEHRIG STORY (TF)
   Charles Fries Productions/Stonehenge Productions, 1978
CRASH (TF)   Charles Fries Productions, 1978
TIGER TOWN (CTF)   Thompson Street Pictures, 1983
EYE ON THE SPARROW (TF)   Sarabande Productions/Republic
   Pictures, 1987

MARITA MANUEL

THE FIRING LINE   Silver Screen, 1991, Filipino

CHRIS MANY*

Contact: ASCAP - Los Angeles, 213-883-1000

HEART   co-composer with Geoff Levin, New World, 1987
THE PRICE SHE PAID (TF)   co-composer with Geoff Levin,
   Producers Entertainment Group/Sandy Hook/World International
   Network, 1992

JIM MANZIE

Agent: Robert Light - Los Angeles, 213-651-1777
Affiliation: APRA - Australia, 011-61-2-922-6422

PUBERTY BLUES   Universal Classics, 1982, Australian
RUNNING FROM THE GUNS   1987, Australian
THE OFFSPRING   FROM A WHISPER TO A SCREAM   TMS
   Pictures, 1987
STEPFATHER II   co-composer with Pat Regan, Millimeter Films,
   1989
LEATHERFACE: THE TEXAS CHAINSAW MASSACRE III
   co-composer with Pat Regan, New Line Cinema, 1990
TALES FROM THE DARKSIDE: THE MOVIE   co-composer,
   Paramount, 1990
THE SERVANTS OF TWILIGHT   DEAN R. KOONTZ'S SERVANTS
   OF TWILIGHT (CTF)   Trimark/Gibraltar, 1991
SWEET POISON (CTF)   Smart Money Prods./MTE, 1991
NIGHT OF THE DEMONS 2   Republic, 1994

NESTOR MARCONI

Contact: SADAIC - Argentina, 011-54-1-40-4867/8

UN MURO DE SILENCIO   A WALL OF SILENCE   1993, Argentine

MARC MARDER

Contact: SACEM - France, 011-33-1-4715-4715

SIDEWALK STORIES   Island Pictures, 1989
TRUE IDENTITY   Buena Vista, 1991

SUSAN MARDER

Contact: ASCAP - Los Angeles, 213-883-1000

THE TAKE (CTF)   co-composer with David Bell, Cine-Nevada
   Inc./MCA-TV, 1990

PETRE MARGINEANU

THE SENATOR'S SNAILS   SENATORUL MELCILOR   1995,
   Rumanian

MITCH MARGO

Contact: ASCAP - Los Angeles, 213-883-1000

THE GODDESS OF LOVE (TF)   co-composer with Dennis Dreith
   and A.S. Diamond, Phil Margo Enterprises/New World
   TV/Phoenix Entertainment Group, 1988

STUART MARGOLIN

b. January 31 - Davenport, Iowa
Home: Box 478, Ganges, Salt Spring Island, British Columbia VOS
   1E0, Canada, 604-537-4224
Affiliation: BMI - Los Angeles, 310-659-9109

THE LONG SUMMER OF GEORGE ADAMS (TF)   co-composer,
   Cherokee Productions/Warner Bros. TV, 1982
THE GLITTER DOME (CTF)   HBO Premiere Films/Telepictures
   Corporation/Trincomali Film Productions, 1984

ANTHONY MARINELLI

Agent: Film Music Associates - Hollywood, 213-463-1070
Affiliation: BMI - Los Angeles, 310-659-9109

EPILOGUE OF DOOM   co-composer with Brian Banks, Odette
   Productions, 1984
RIGGED   co-composer with Brian Banks, CineStar, 1985
NICE GIRLS DON'T EXPLODE   co-composer with Brian Banks,
   New World, 1987
PINOCCHIO AND THE EMPEROR OF THE NIGHT (AF)
   co-composer with Brian Banks, New World, 1987
YOUNG GUNS   co-composer with Brian Banks, 20th Century Fox,
   1988
SPOONER (TF)   co-composer with Brian Banks, Walt Disney
   Productions, 1989
INTERNAL AFFAIRS   co-composer with Mike Figgis and Brian
   Banks, Paramount, 1990
GRAVEYARD SHIFT   co-composer with Brian Banks, Paramount,
   1990

ANGEL STREET (TF)   John Wells & Friends/Warner Bros. TV, 1992
THE SANDMAN (TF)   Finnegan-Pinchuk/NBC Prods., 1993
THERE WAS A LITTLE BOY (TF)   Craig Anderson Prods./Lorimar TV, 1993
MY FORGOTTEN MAN   co-composer with Billy Childs, Boulevard Films, 1993
HOUSE OF SECRETS (TF)   Steve Krantz Prods./Multimedia, 1993
BABY BROKERS (TF)   Steinhardt Baer Pictures/BBK Prods./Columbia Pictures TV, 1994
THE INNOCENT (TF)   Todman-Simon/Grammnet Prods./Warner Bros. TV, 1994
2 DAYS IN THE VALLEY   MGM-UA, 1996

RICK MAROTTA
Contact: ASCAP - Los Angeles, 213-883-1000

THE COVER GIRL MURDERS (CTF)   River Enterprises/Wilshire Court, 1993

BRANFORD MARSALIS
Contact: ASCAP - Los Angeles, 213-883-1000

BLACK TO THE PROMISED LAND (FD)   Blues Prods., 1992
TO MY DAUGHTER WITH LOVE (TF)   Disney Family Classics/Steve White Prods., 1994

DELFEAYO MARSALIS
Contact: BMI - Los Angeles, 310-659-9109

112TH & CENTRAL: THROUGH THE EYES OF THE CHILDREN (FD)   Flatfields, 1993

WYNTON MARSALIS
Agent: CAA - Beverly Hills, 310-288-4545
Affiliation: ASCAP - Los Angeles, 213-883-1000

SHANNON'S DEAL (TF)   Stan Rogaw Productions/NBC Productions, 1989
TUNE IN TOMORROW   1990

INGRAM MARSHALL
Contact: BMI - Los Angeles, 310-659-9109

SCREAM OF STONE   co-composer with Alan Lamb, Sarah Hopkins and Atahualpa Yupanqui, Saxer/Lange/Sadler, 1991

JACK MARSHALL
Contact: BMI - Los Angeles, 310-659-9109

THE MISSOURI TRAVELER   Buena Vista, 1958
THE RABBIT TRAP   United Artists, 1959
TAKE A GIANT STEP   United Artists, 1959
MY DOG BUDDY   Columbia, 1960
MUNSTER, GO HOME   Universal, 1966
TAMMY AND THE MILLIONAIRE   Universal, 1967
KONA COAST   Warner Bros., 1968
STAY AWAY, JOE   MGM, 1968
SOMETHING FOR A LONELY MAN (TF)   Universal TV, 1968

JULIAN MARSHALL
Contact: PRS - London, England, 011-44-1-580-5544

OLD ENOUGH   Orion Classics, 1984

PHIL MARSHALL
Agent: Film Music Associates - Hollywood, 213-463-1070
Affiliation: BMI - Los Angeles, 310-659-9109

PRIME RISK   Almi Pictures, 1985
THE LAST OF PHILIP BANTER   Tesauro, 1986, Spanish-Swiss
STUDENT EXCHANGE (TF)   Disney/ABC, 1987
FULL MOON IN BLUE WATER   Trans World Entertainment, 1988
ILLEGALLY YOURS   MGM/UA, 1988
TEXASVILLE   adaptations, Nelson, 1990
FLYING BLIND (TF)   NBC Productions, 1990
RUN   Hollywood, 1991

NOISES OFF   adaptations, Buena Vista, 1992
REVOLVER (TF)   Victoria Prods./Noel Films/Catalunya Prods./Columbia, 1992
THE ENDLESS SUMMER II   co-composer with Gary Hoey, New Line, 1994
KICKING & SCREAMING   Trimark, 1995

GEORGE MARTIN
b. 1926
Agent: Air-Edel - Los Angeles, 310-914-5000
Affiliation: PRS - London, England, 011-44-1-580-5544

A HARD DAY'S NIGHT ★   adaptation, United Artists, 1964, British
YELLOW SUBMARINE   United Artists, 1968, British
PULP   United Artists, 1972, British
LIVE AND LET DIE   United Artists, 1973, British
THE OPTIMISTS   THE OPTIMISTS OF NINE ELMS   Paramount, 1973, British
HONKY TONK FREEWAY   co-composer with Elmer Bernstein, Universal/AFD, 1981

GEORGE PORTER MARTIN
Contact: BMI - Los Angeles, 310-659-9109

THE WHITE GIRL   Tony Brown Productions, 1990

PETER MARTIN
Contact: PRS - London, England, 011-44-1-580-5544

HOPE AND GLORY   Columbia, 1987, British

SIMON MICHAEL MARTIN
Contact: ASCAP - Los Angeles, 213-883-1000

HEARTACHES   Rising Star, 1981, Canadian

CLIFF MARTINEZ
b. February 2, 1954 - New York, New York
Contact: BMI - Los Angeles, 310-659-9109

SEX, LIES AND VIDEOTAPE   Outlaw Productions, 1989
PUMP UP THE VOLUME   New Line, 1990
KAFKA   Miramax, 1991
BLACK MAGIC (CTF)   Point of View Prods./MCA TV, 1992
KING OF THE HILL   Gramercy, 1993
THE UNDERNEATH   Gramercy, 1995
SCHIZOPOLIS   1997
GRAY'S ANATOMY   1997
THE SECOND WIFE   1997

MEL MARVIN
COOPERSTOWN (CTF)   Turner/Amblin TV, 1993

RICHARD MARVIN*
Agent: Seth Kaplan Entertainment - Los Angeles, 213-525-3477
Affiliation: BMI - Los Angeles, 310-659-9109

FLIGHT OF THE BLACK ANGEL (CTF)   Hess-Kallbers, 1991
3 NINJAS   Buena Vista, 1992
WHEN LOVE KILLS: THE SEDUCTION OF JOHN HEARN (TF)   Harvey Kahn Prods./Alexander Enright & Associates/McGillen Entertainment, 1993
3 NINJAS KICK BACK   TriStar, 1994
SEPARATED BY MURDER (TF)   Larry Thompson Ent./CBS, 1994
GALGAMETH   Sheen Communications, 1997
THE LAST RESORT   Dayton Productions, 1997
DEAD MEN CAN'T DANCE   Live, 1997

BILL MARX
Contact: ASCAP - Los Angeles, 213-883-1000

WALK THE ANGRY BEACH   1961
COUNT YORGA, VAMPIRE   American International, 1970
THE RETURN OF COUNT YORGA   American International, 1971
THE DEATHMASTER   American International, 1972
THE FOLKS AT RED WOLF INN   TERROR HOUSE   Scope III, 1972

SCREAM, BLACULA, SCREAM   American International, 1973
JOHNNY VIK   1973
ACT OF VENGEANCE   American International, 1974

DAVIDE MASARATI
VELENO   POISON   1993, Italian

J MASCIS
Contact: BMI - Los Angeles, 310-659-9109

GAS, FOOD AND LODGING   I.R.S., 1992

JANOS MASIK
Contact: ARTISJUS - Budapest, 011-36-1-176-222

GYEREKGYILKOSS GOK   *CHILD MURDERS*   1993, Hungarian

HARVEY W. MASON
Contact: ASCAP - Los Angeles, 213-883-1000

ONLY THE STRONG   20th Century Fox, 1993

MOLLY MASON
Contact: BMI - Los Angeles, 310-659-9109

BROTHER'S KEEPER (FD)   co-composer with Jay Ungar,
   American Playhouse Theatrical Films, 1992

NICK MASON
Contact: PRS - London, England, 011-44-1-580-5544

WHITE OF THE EYE   co-composer with Rick Fenn, Palisades
   Entertainment, 1988

ROGER MASON
Contact: APRA - Australia, 011-61-2-922-6422

LOVE CRIMES   additional music only, Millimeter, 1992

JOHN MASSARI
Contact: ASCAP - Los Angeles, 213-883-1000

KILLER KLOWNS FROM OUTER SPACE   Trans World
   Entertainment, 1988
STEEL & LACE   Fries, 1990
SNAKE EATER III ...HIS LAW   Cinepix, 1992
THE MAKING OF...AND GOD SPOKE   Brookwood, 1993

GEORGE MASSENBURG
Contact: SOCAN - Toronto, 416-445-8700

CERTAIN FURY   co-composer with Bill Payne and Russ Kunkel,
   New World, 1985, Canadian
SMOOTH TALK   co-composer with Bill Payne and Russ Kunkel,
   Spectrafilm, 1985

MICHAEL MASSER
Contact: ASCAP - Los Angeles, 213-883-1000

MAHOGANY   co-composer with Gil Askey and Lee Holdridge,
   Paramount, 1975
THE GREATEST   co-composer with Lee Holdridge, Columbia,
   1977

ALEJANDRO MASSO
Contact: SGAE - Spain, 011-34-1-319-2100

THE WITCHING HOUR   Serva Films, 1985, Spanish

ERIC MASUNAGA
RIFT   co-composer with Tryan George, Off-Screen Prods., 1993

GREG MATHIESON
Contact: ASCAP - Los Angeles, 213-883-1000

AMERICAN FLYERS   co-composer with Lee Ritenour, Warner
   Bros., 1985

JIM MATISON
THE LISA THEORY   Farallon Pictures/Colossal Pictures, 1994

SASHA MATSON
Contact: BMI - Los Angeles, 310-659-9109

DADDY'S BOYS   Concorde, 1988
LOBSTER MAN FROM MARS   Electric Pictures, 1989
RED SURF   Arrowhead Entertainment, 1990

TEIZO MATSUMARA
Contact: JASRAC

MY SONS   *MUSUKO*   1992, Japanese

DAVID M. MATTHEWS
Contact: ASCAP - Los Angeles, 213-883-1000

THE FIGHTERS   1974
STONY ISLAND   World-Northal, 1978
VALHALLA   Arclight Film, 1992

PETER MATZ*
b. November 6, 1928 - Pittsburgh, Pennsylvania
Contact: BMI - Los Angeles, 310-659-9109

BYE BYE BRAVERMAN   Warner Bros., 1968
MARLOWE   MGM, 1969
RIVALS   *SINGLE PARENT*   Avco Embassy, 1972
EMERGENCY! (TF)   Mark VII Ltd./Universal TV, 1972
I HEARD THE OWL CALL MY NAME (TF)   Tomorrow
   Entertainment, 1973
LARRY (TF)   Tomorrow Entertainment, 1974
FUNNY LADY ★   adaptation, Columbia, 1975
IN THIS HOUSE OF BREDE (TF)   Tomorrow Entertainment, 1975
THE DARK SIDE OF INNOCENCE (TF)   Warner Bros. TV, 1976
JUST AN OLD SWEET SONG (TF)   MTM Enterprises, 1976
THE CALL OF THE WILD (TF)   Charles Fries Productions, 1976
THE GREAT HOUDINIS (TF)   ABC Circle Films, 1976
TERRACES (TF)   Charles Fries Productions/Worldvision, 1977
THE LAST HURRAH (TF)   O'Connor-Becker Productions/Columbia
   TV, 1977
SPECIAL OLYMPICS (TF)   Roger Gimbel Productions/EMI TV,
   1978
ONE IN A MILLION: THE RON LeFLORE STORY (TF)   Roger
   Gimbel Productions/EMI TV, 1978
HAPPILY EVER AFTER (TF)   Tri-Media II, Inc./Hamel-Somers
   Entertainment, 1978
THE GRASS IS ALWAYS GREENER OVER THE SEPTIC TANK
   (TF)   Joe Hamilton Productions, 1978
FIRST YOU CRY (TF) ☆   MTM Enterprises, 1978
LOVE FOR RENT (TF)   Warren V. Bush Productions, 1979
CAN YOU HEAR THE LAUGHTER? THE STORY OF FREDDIE
   PRINZE (TF)   Roger Gimbel Productions/EMI TV, 1979
I KNOW WHY THE CAGED BIRD SINGS (TF)   Tomorrow
   Entertainment, 1979
THE TENTH MONTH (TF)   Joe Hamilton Productions, 1979
THE PRIZE FIGHTER   New World, 1979
THE MAN IN THE SANTA CLAUS SUIT (TF)   Dick Clark
   Productions, 1979
VALENTINE MAGIC ON LOVE ISLAND (TF)   Dick Clark
   Productions/PKO Television/Osmond TV Productions, 1980
THE PRIVATE EYES   New World, 1980
WHITE MAMA (TF)   Tomorrow Entertainment, 1980
FUN AND GAMES (TF)   Kanin-Gallo Productions/Warner Bros. TV,
   1980
DAMIEN: THE LEPER PRIEST (TF) ☆   Tomorrow Entertainment,
   1980
CRAZY TIMES (TF)   Kayden-Gleason Productions/George Reeves
   Productions/Warner Bros. TV, 1981
THE KILLING OF RANDY WEBSTER (TF)   Roger Gimbel
   Productions/EMI TV, 1981

TAKE YOUR BEST SHOT (TF)   Levinson-Link Productions/Robert
    Papazian Productions, 1982
DROP-OUT FATHER (TF) ☆   CBS Entertainment, 1982
LUST IN THE DUST   New World, 1985
MRS. DELAFIELD WANTS TO MARRY (TF)   Schaefer-Karpf
    Productions/Gaylord Production Company, 1986
STONE FOX (TF)   co-composer with Allyn Ferguson,
    Hanna-Barbera Productions/Allarcom Ltd./Taft Entertainment TV,
    1987, U.S.-Canadian
MERCY OR MURDER? (TF)   John J. McMahon
    Productions/MGM-UA TV, 1987
LAURA LANSING SLEPT HERE (TF)   Schaefer-Karpf-Eckstein
    Productions/Gaylord Production Company, 1988
TORCH SONG TRILOGY   adaptation, New Line Cinema, 1988
WHEN WE WERE YOUNG (TF)   Richard & Esther Shapiro
    Entertainment, 1989
THE GUMSHOE KID   Skouras Pictures, 1989
THE 10 MILLION DOLLAR GETAWAY (CTF)   Alan Cooperman
    Productions/Wilshire Court, 1991
STEPPING OUT   Paramount, 1991
THIS CAN'T BE LOVE (TF)   Davis Ent./Pacific Motion Picture/WIN,
    1994

DYLAN MAULUCCI

ARE THEY STILL SHOOTING?   It Takes Two, 1993

BILLY MAY

b. November 10, 1916 - Pittsburgh, Pennsylvania
Contact: BMI - Los Angeles, 310-659-9109

THE FUZZY PINK NIGHTGOWN   United Artists, 1957
SERGEANTS 3   United Artists, 1962
JOHNNY COOL   United Artists, 1963
THE PLEASURE SEEKERS   20th Century-Fox, 1964
TONY ROME   20th Century-Fox, 1967
THE SECRET LIFE OF AN AMERICAN WIFE   20th Century-Fox,
    1968
THE BALLAD OF ANDY CROCKER (TF)   Thomas-Spelling
    Productions, 1969
THE PIGEON (TF)   Thomas-Spelling Productions, 1969
THE FRONT PAGE   Universal, 1974
THE SPECIALISTS (TF)   Mark VII Ltd./Universal TV, 1975
TAIL GUNNER JOE (TF)   Universal TV, 1977
LITTLE MO (TF)   co-composer with Carl Brandt, Mark VII
    Ltd./Worldvision Enterprises, 1978
RETURN OF THE BEVERLY HILLBILLIES (TF)   The Energy
    Venture, 1981

DANIEL MAY

Contact: BMI - Los Angeles, 310-659-9109

ZOMBIE HIGH   Cinema Group, 1987
SEVERANCE   Fox/Lorber Films, 1989
DEAD SPACE   Califilm, 1991
PIZZA MAN   Megalomania, 1991

SCOTT MAY

MEET THE PARENTS   C.E.M., 1992

CURTIS MAYFIELD

b. June 3, 1942 - Chicago, Illinois
Contact: BMI - Los Angeles, 310-659-9109

SUPERFLY   Warner Bros., 1972
CLAUDINE   20th Century-Fox, 1974
LET'S DO IT AGAIN   Warner Bros., 1975
SPARKLE   Warner Bros., 1976
A PIECE OF THE ACTION   Warner Bros., 1977
SHORT EYES   *SLAMMER*   The Film League, 1977
THE RETURN OF SUPERFLY   Triton, 1990

LINCOLN MAYORGA

Contact: ASCAP - Los Angeles, 213-883-1000

NICKEL MOUNTAIN   Ziv International, 1985

LYLE MAYS

Contact: BMI - Los Angeles, 310-659-9109

THE SEARCH FOR SOLUTIONS (FD)   co-composer with Pat
    Metheny, Playback Associates, 1979
THE FALCON AND THE SNOWMAN   co-composer with Pat
    Metheny, Orion, 1985
MUSTANG: THE HIDDEN KINGDOM (TD)   Intrepid
    Films/Discovery, 1994

JOHN McCABE

Contact: PRS - London, England, 011-44-1-580-5544

FEAR IN THE NIGHT   International Co-Productions, 1972, British

JON McCALLUM

Contact: BMI - Los Angeles, 310-659-9109

PROJECT ELIMINATOR   South Gate, 1991
THE LEGEND OF WOLF MOUNTAIN   Hemdale, 1993
YOUNG GOODMAN BROWN   50th Street, 1993

PAUL McCALLUM

Contact: BMI - Los Angeles, 310-659-9109

DEATH WISH 4: THE CRACKDOWN   co-composer with Valentine
    McCallum and John Bisharat, Cannon, 1988

VALENTINE McCALLUM

Contact: BMI - Los Angeles, 310-659-9109

MURPHY'S LAW   co-composer with Marc Donahue, Cannon, 1986
ASSASSINATION   co-composer with Robert O. Ragland, Cannon,
    1987
DEATH WISH 4: THE CRACKDOWN   co-composer with Paul
    McCallum and John Bisharat, Cannon, 1988

DENNIS McCARTHY*

Agent: Vangelos Management - Encino, 818-380-1919
Affiliation: ASCAP - Los Angeles, 213-883-1000

PRAY TV (TF)   ABC Circle Films, 1982
THE KID WITH THE 200 I.Q. (TF)   Guillaume-Margo
    Productions/Zephyr Productions, 1983
OFF THE WALL   Jensen Farley Pictures, 1983
V: THE FINAL BATTLE (MS)   composer of parts 2 and 3,
    Blatt-Singer Productions/Warner Bros. TV, 1984
PLAYING WITH FIRE (TF)   Zephyr Productions/New World
    Pictures, 1985
HOUSTON: THE LEGEND OF TEXAS (TF)   Taft Entertainment
    TV/J.D. Feigelson Productions, 1986
DADDY (TF)   Doug Cramer, 1987
HOUSTON KNIGHTS (TF)   Jay Bernstein Productions/Columbia
    Pictures TV, 1987
SWORN TO SILENCE (TF)   Daniel H. Blatt-Robert Singer
    Productions, 1987
STAR TREK: THE NEXT GENERATION: ENCOUNTER AT FAR
    POINT (TF)   Paramount TV, 1987
THE LOVE BOAT: A VALENTINE VOYAGE (TF)   Aaron Spelling
    Productions/Douglas S. Cramer Co., 1990
LEONA HELMSLEY: THE QUEEN OF MEAN (TF)   1990
DANIELLE STEEL'S 'PALOMINO' (TF)   Cramer Co./NBS Prods.,
    1991
OVERKILL: THE AILEEN WUORNOS STORY (TF)   Republic/C.M.
    Two, 1992
STAR TREK: DEEP SPACE NINE: EMISSARY (TF)   Paramount
    TV, 1993
STAYING AFLOAT (TF)   Ruddy Morgan Organization/TriStar TV,
    1993
TONYA & NANCY: THE INSIDE STORY (TF)   Brian Pike
    Prods./NBC Prods., 1994
ARMED & INNOCENT (TF)   Gillian Prods./Republic, 1994
STAR TREK: THE NEXT GENERATION: ALL GOOD THINGS (TF)
    ☆   Paramount TV, 1994
STAR TREK: GENERATIONS   Paramount, 1994
SLIDERS (TF)   Cinevu Films/St. Clare Ent./MCA TV/Fox, 1995
DEADLY GAMES (TF)   Shaken Not Stirred Prods./Rumbleseat
    Prods./Viacom, 1995
INFLAMMABLE (TF)   Savoy TV, 1995

FIGHT FOR THIRTEEN (TF)   Hearst, 1995
THE COLONY (TF)   Universal TV, 1995
IN THE NAME OF LOVE: A TEXAS TRAGEDY (TF)   1995
THE ERICA FRENCH STORY (CTF)   Lifetime, 1996
BED OF LIES (TF)   NBC Prods., 1996
LOVE'S DEADLY TRIANGLE: THE TEXAS CADET MURDER (TF)
   Steve White Prods., 1996
McHALE'S NAVY   Universal, 1997
LETTERS FROM A KILLER   Columbia, 1998

JOHN McCARTHY*

Contact: PRS - London, England, 011-44-1-580-5544

EVEN COWGIRLS GET THE BLUES   co-composer with Ben Mink,
   Fine Line, 1993
LOVE AND HUMAN REMAINS   1993, Canadian
PARIS, FRANCE   Alliance, 1993, Canadian
DUE SOUTH (TF)   co-composer with Jack Lenz and Jay Semko,
   Alliance/CTV, 1994, Canadian
SOUL SURVIVOR   1995, Canadian
THE POSSESSION OF MICHAEL D. (TF)
   Atlantis/Flashner-Gernon/CTV, 1995, Canadian
RELUCTANT ANGEL   Blackwatch Communications, 1997
THE HOST   ASP Prods., 1997

LINDA McCARTNEY

Contact: ASCAP - Los Angeles, 213-883-1000

LIVE AND LET DIE   co-composer of theme with Paul McCartney,
   United Artists, 1973, British

PAUL McCARTNEY

b. June 18, 1942 - Liverpool, England
Contact: PRS - London, England, 011-44-1-580-5544

THE FAMILY WAY   Warner Bros., 1967, British
LIVE AND LET DIE   co-composer of theme with Linda McCartney,
   United Artists, 1973, British
GIVE MY REGARDS TO BROAD STREET   song score, 20th
   Century Fox, 1984, British

MICHAEL McCARTY

Contact: ASCAP - Los Angeles, 213-883-1000

DANGEROUSLY CLOSE   Cannon, 1986

MATTHEW McCAULEY

Contact: ASCAP - Los Angeles, 213-883-1000

BETWEEN FRIENDS   Eudon Productions, 1973, Canadian
SUDDEN FURY   Filmscan, 1975, Canadian
CITY ON FIRE!   Avco Embassy, 1979, Canadian
RIEL   CBC/Green River Productions, 1979, Canadian
MIDDLE AGE CRAZY   20th Century-Fox, 1980, Canadian-U.S.
IN THE CUSTODY OF STRANGERS (TF)   Moonlight
   Productions/Filmways, 1982
THE LAST UNICORN (AF)   Jensen Farley Pictures, 1982
A MATTER OF SEX (CTD)   Willmar 8 Productions/Orion TV, 1984
OBSESSIVE LOVE (TF)   Onza Inc./Moonlight Productions, 1984
THE UNDERGRADS (CTF)   Sharmhill Productions/The Disney
   Channel, 1985, U.S.-Canadian
MANY HAPPY RETURNS (TF)   Alan M. Levin & Steven H. Stern
   Films, 1986, U.S.-Canadian
THUNDER RUN   Cannon, 1986
STATE PARK   ITC, 1987, Canadian
THE ADVENTURES OF SINBAD (TF)   Atlantis, 1996

TIM McCAULEY

Contact: SOCAN - Toronto, 416-445-8700

LOVE   Velvet Films, 1982, Canadian
SCREWBALLS   New World, 1983

PAUL McCOLLOUGH

Contact: ASCAP - Los Angeles, 213-883-1000

NIGHT OF THE LIVING DEAD   Columbia, 1990

ALBRITTON McCLAIN

DILEMMA   Cinequannon, 1997

DIANE McCLOUGHLIN

FEED THEM TO THE CANNIBALS! (FD)   1993, Australian

KRISTEN McCORD

Contact: BMI - Los Angeles, 310-659-9109

GLAMAZON: A DIFFERENT KIND OF GIRL (FD)   Maria
   Demopoulos, 1993

STEPHEN McCURDY

Contact: APRA - Australia, 011-61-2-922-6422

SHAKER RUN   Challenge Film Corporation, 1985, New Zealand

GARRY McDONALD

Agent: Robert Light - Los Angeles, 213-651-1777
Affiliation: APRA - Australia, 011-61-2-922-6422

TIME TRAX (TF)   co-composer with Laurie Stone, Gary Nardino
   Prods./Lorimar TV, 1993
THE FLOOD: WHO WILL SAVE OUR CHILDREN? (TF)
   co-composer with Laurie Stone, Wolper Organization/Warner
   Bros. TV, 1993
OFFICIAL DENIAL (CTF)   co-composer with Laurie Stone, Wilshire
   Court, 1993

MAUREEN McELHERON

Contact: ASCAP - Los Angeles, 213-883-1000

THE TUNE (AF)   1992

JOHN McEUEN

Contact: ASCAP - Los Angeles, 213-883-1000

MAN OUTSIDE   Virgin Vision, 1988
THE WILD WEST   Warner Bros., 1993
THE GOOD OLD BOYS (CTF)   Edgar J. Scherick Prods./Firebrand
   Prods./Javelina Films, 1995

ANNE McGARRIGLE

Contact: ASCAP - Los Angeles, 213-883-1000

DEUX ACTRICES   TWO CAN PLAY   co-composer with Kate
   McGarrigle, Max Films, 1993, Canadian

KATE McGARRIGLE

Contact: ASCAP - Los Angeles, 213-883-1000

DEUX ACTRICES   TWO CAN PLAY   co-composer with Anne
   McGarrigle, Max Films, 1993, Canadian

DON McGLASHAN

Contact: APRA - Australia, 011-61-2-922-6422

ABSENT WITHOUT LEAVE   co-composer with David Long and
   Mark Austin, 1993, New Zealand

DAVID McHUGH

Agent: Seth Kaplan Entertainment - Los Angeles, 213-525-3477
Affiliation: ASCAP - Los Angeles, 213-883-1000

NOBODY'S PERFEKT   Columbia, 1981
GO FOR THE GOLD   Go for the Gold Productions, 1984
MOSCOW ON THE HUDSON   Columbia, 1984
PUMPING IRON II: THE WOMEN (FD)   Cinecom, 1985
ONE MORE SATURDAY NIGHT   Columbia, 1986
SOMETHING SPECIAL   WILLY MILLY/I WAS A TEENAGE BOY
   Cinema Group, 1986
WELCOME HOME, BOBBY (TF)   Titus Productions, 1986
A YEAR IN THE LIFE (MS)   Universal TV, 1986
JOCKS   Crown International, 1987
MR. NORTH   Heritage Entertainment, 1988
MYSTIC PIZZA   Samuel Goldwyn Company, 1988

THREE FUGITIVES   Buena Vista, 1989
THE DREAM TEAM   Universal, 1989
MONTANA (CTF)   HBO Productions/Zoetrope Studios/Roger
   Gimbel Productions, 1990
DADDY'S DYIN'...WHO'S GOT THE WILL?   MGM/UA, 1990
DILLINGER (TF)   David L. Wolper/Bernard Sofronski, 1991
MANNEQUIN TWO: ON THE MOVE   20th Century Fox, 1991
LONELY HEARTS   Live, 1991
LIES OF THE TWINS (CTF)   Ricochet Prods., 1991
FINAL VERDICT (CTF)   Foxboro Ent., 1991
CHANCE OF A LIFETIME (TF)   Lynn Roth Prods., 1991
OVER THE HILL   1992, Australian
SHAME (CTF)   Dalrymple Prods./Steinhardt Baer Pictures/Viacom,
   1992
JUST MY IMAGINATION (TF)   Andrea Baynes Prods./Lorimar TV,
   1992
DESPERATE JOURNEY: THE ALLISON WILCOX STORY (TF)
   D'Antoni Prods./Viacom, 1993
DARK REFLECTIONS (TF)   Stillwater Prods./WIN/Fox West
   Pictures, 1994
A PASSION FOR JUSTICE: THE HAZEL BRANNON SMITH
   STORY (TF)   David Brooks
   Prods./Catfish/Saban-Sherick/Procter & Gamble Prods., 1994
JUSTICE IN A SMALL TOWN (TF)   Hill-Field Prods., 1994
EROTIC TALES   co-composer, 1994, German
TRADE OFF (CTF)   Showtime Entertainment/Viacom, 1995
CHANGING HABITS   Teagarden Pictures, 1997

TOM McINTOSH

Contact: BMI - Los Angeles, 310-659-9109

SLITHER   MGM, 1973
A HERO AIN'T NOTHIN' BUT A SANDWICH   New World, 1977

FRANK McKELVEY

BOGGY CREEK II   Howco International, 1985

MARK McKENZIE

Agent: Marks Management - Woodland Hills, 818-587-5656
Affiliation: BMI - Los Angeles, 310-659-9109

SON OF DARKNESS: TO DIE FOR II   Trimark, 1991
WARLOCK: THE ARMAGEDDON   Trimark, 1993
MY FAMILY   MI FAMILIA   co-composer with Pepe Avila, New Line,
   1995
FRANK AND JESSE (CTF)   Trimark/Cassian Elwes/Elliott Kastner,
   1995
DR. JEKYLL AND MS. HYDE   Savoy, 1995

STEPHEN McKEON

KOREA   1995, Irish

ROD McKUEN

b. April 29, 1933 - Oakland, California
Contact: ASCAP - Los Angeles, 213-883-1000

JOANNA   20th Century-Fox, 1968, British
A BOY NAMED CHARLIE BROWN (AF)   National General, 1968
THE PRIME OF MISS JEAN BRODIE   20th Century-Fox, 1969,
   British
COME TO YOUR SENSES   1971
SCANDALOUS JOHN   Buena Vista, 1971
THE BORROWERS (TF)   co-composer with Billy Byers, Walt
   DeFaria Productions/20th Century-Fox TV, 1973
LISA, BRIGHT AND DARK (TF)   Bob Banner Associates, 1973
EMILY   1976, British

MALCOLM McLAREN

Agent: CAA - Beverly Hills, 310-288-4545

LIVE NUDE GIRLS   Republic, 1995

DON McLEAN

Contact: BMI - Los Angeles, 310-659-9109

FRATERNITY ROW   Paramount, 1977

GERARD McMAHON

Contact: ASCAP - Los Angeles, 213-883-1000

DEFIANCE   co-composer with Basil Poledouris, American
   International, 1980

BOB McNAUGHTON

THE NORMAL LIFE   co-composer with Ken Hale, 1996

JOEL McNEELY*

Agent: The Kraft-Benjamin Agency - Beverly Hills, 310-247-0123
Affiliation: ASCAP - Los Angeles, 213-883-1000

YOU TALKIN' TO ME   MGM/UA, 1987
SPLASH, TOO (TF)   Mark H. Ovitz Productions/Walt Disney TV,
   1988
DAVY CROCKETT: RAINBOW IN THE THUNDER (TF)   Echo Cove
   Productions/Walt Disney TV, 1988
APPEARANCES (TF)   Echo Cove Productions/Touchstone TV,
   1990
FRANKENSTEIN: THE COLLEGE YEARS (TF)   Sprit Prods/FNM
   Films, 1991
SAMANTHA   1991
LADY AGAINST THE ODDS (TF)   Robert Greenwald Prods., 1992
THE YOUNG INDIANA JONES CHRONICLES: INDIANA JONES
   AND THE MYSTERY OF THE BLUES (TF)
   Lucasfilm/Paramount TV, 1993
IRON WILL   Buena Vista, 1994
SQUANTO: A WARRIOR'S TALE   Buena Vista, 1994
TERMINAL VELOCITY   Buena Vista, 1994
THE RADIOLAND MURDERS   Universal, 1994
FLIPPER   Universal, 1996
SUPERCOP   Dimension, 1996
VEGAS VACATION   Warner Bros., 1997

ANDY McNEILL

PROJECT: GENESIS   Prism, 1993

BILL McRAE*

Contact: BMI - Los Angeles, 310-659-9109

MASTERGATE (CTF)   Showtime, 1992

JAMES McVAY*

Agent: Carol Faith Agency - Beverly Hills, 310-274-0776
Affiliation: ASCAP - Los Angeles, 213-883-1000

A TRIUMPH OF THE HEART: THE RICKY BELL STORY (TF)
   Procter & Gamble/Landsburg Co., 1991
THE DIAMOND FLEECE (CTF)   Landsburg/Astral Film/Moving
   Image, 1992
A MOTHER'S RIGHT: THE ELIZABETH MORGAN STORY (TF)
   Landsburg, 1992
CHARLES AND DIANA: UNHAPPILY EVER AFTER (TF)
   Konigsberg-Sanitsky, 1992
GREGORY K (TF)   Spectacor/Michael Jaffe, 1993
NOT IN MY FAMILY (TF)   Robert Greenwald Films, 1993
BABYMAKER: THE CECIL JACOBSON STORY (TF)
   Jaffe-Braunstein Films/Heartstar Prods., 1994
CRIES FROM THE HEART (TF)   Wild Rice
   Prods./Grossbart-Barnett-Iezman Ent., 1994
DANGEROUS INTENTIONS (TF)   Kaufman Co./Wildcare
   Prods./Kushner-Locke, 1995
BETWEEN LOVE AND HONOR (TF)   Grossbart Barnett Prods.,
   1995
FREAKY FRIDAY (TF)   ZM Prods./Walt Disney TV, 1995

ABIGAIL MEAD

Contact: PRS - London, England, 011-44-1-580-5544

FULL METAL JACKET   Warner Bros., 1987

GARY MEALS

PHAT BEACH   co-composer with Paul Stewart, 1996

PADDY MEEGAN

Contact: PRS - London, England, 011-44-1-580-5544

DANNY BOY *ANGEL* Triumph/Columbia, 1983, Irish

GIL MELLE

b. December 31, 1935 - Jersey City, New Jersey
Contact: BMI - Los Angeles, 310-659-9109

MY SWEET CHARLIE (TF) Bob Banner Associates/Universal TV, 1970
THE ANDROMEDA STRAIN Universal, 1971
THE ORGANIZATION United Artists, 1971
IF TOMORROW COMES (TF) Aaron Spelling Productions/American Broadcasting Company, 1971
THE ASTRONAUT (TF) Universal TV, 1972
YOU'LL LIKE MY MOTHER Universal, 1972
BONE Jack H. Harris Enterprises, 1972
THE VICTIM (TF) Universal TV, 1972
LIEUTENANT SCHUSTER'S WIFE (TF) Universal TV, 1972
THE JUDGE AND JAKE WYLER (TF) Universal TV, 1972
A COLD NIGHT'S DEATH (TF) ABC Circle Films, 1973
TENAFLY (TF) Universal TV, 1973
SAVAGE (TF) Universal TV, 1973
PARTNERS IN CRIME (TF) Fairmont/Foxcroft Productions/Universal TV, 1973
THE SIX-MILLION DOLLAR MAN (TF) Universal TV, 1973
TRAPPED (TF) Universal TV, 1973
THE PRESIDENT'S PLANE IS MISSING (TF) ABC Circle Films, 1973
FRANKENSTEIN: THE TRUE STORY (TF) Universal TV, 1973
THE QUESTOR TAPES (TF) Universal TV, 1974
HITCHHIKE! (TF) Universal TV, 1974
THE LAST ANGRY MAN (TF) The Jozak Company/Screen Gems/Columbia Pictures TV, 1974
KILLDOZER (TF) Universal TV, 1974
THE SAVAGE IS LOOSE Campbell Devon, 1974
THE MISSING ARE DEADLY (TF) Lawrence Gordon Productions, 1975
A CRY FOR HELP (TF) Fairmont-Foxcroft Productions/Universal TV, 1975
THE IMPOSTER (TF) Warner Bros. TV, 1975
CRIME CLUB (TF) Universal TV, 1975
DEATH SCREAM (TF) RSO Films, 1975
JAMES MICHENER'S DYNASTY (TF) David Paradine TV, 1976
THE ULTIMATE WARRIOR Warner Bros., 1976
PERILOUS VOYAGE (TF) Universal TV, 1976
EMBRYO Cine Artists, 1976
THE SENTINEL Universal, 1977
STARSHIP INVASIONS Warner Bros., 1977, Canadian
GOLD OF THE AMAZON WOMEN (TF) MI-KA Productions Inc., 1979
ATTICA (TF) ABC Circle Films, 1980
BORDERLINE ITC, 1980
THE CURSE OF KING TUT'S TOMB (TF) Stromberg-Kerby Productions/Columbia TV/HTV West, 1980
RAPE AND MARRIAGE—THE RIDEOUT CASE (TF) Dick Berg/Stonehenge Productions/Lorimar Productions, 1980
BLOOD BEACH Jerry Gross Organization, 1981
THE INTRUDER WITHIN (TF) Furia-Oringer Productions, 1981
THE LAST CHASE Crown International, 1981, Canadian
WORLD WAR III (TF) Finnegan Associates/David Greene Productions, 1982
THROUGH NAKED EYES (TF) Charles Fries Productions, 1983
JEALOUSY (TF) co-composer with Jimmie Haskell, Charles Fries Productions/Alan Sacks Productions, 1984
FLIGHT 90: DISASTER ON THE POTOMAC (TF) Sheldon Pinchuk Productions/Finnegan Associates, 1984
BEST KEPT SECRETS (TF) ABC Circle Films, 1984
SWEET REVENGE (TF) David Greene Productions/Robert Papazian Productions, 1984
FATAL VISION (TF) NBC Entertainment, 1984
STARCROSSED (TF) Fries Entertainment, 1985
WHEN DREAMS COME TRUE (TF) I&C Productions, 1985
HOT TARGET Crown International, 1985, New Zealand
KILLER IN THE MIRROR (TF) Litke-Grossbart Productions/Warner Bros. TV, 1986
THE DELIBERATE STRANGER (TF) Stuart Phoenix Productions/Lorimar-Telepictures, 1986
RESTLESS Endeavour Productions, 1986, Australian

CIRCLE OF VIOLENCE: A FAMILY DRAMA (TF) Sheldon Pinchuk Productions/Rafshoon Communications Inc./Finnegan Associates/Telepictures Productions, 1986
STILLWATCH (TF) Zev Braun Pictures/Potomac Productions/Interscope Communications, 1987
THE TAKING OF FLIGHT 847: THE ULI DERICKSON STORY (TF) Columbia TV, 1988
FROM THE DEAD OF NIGHT (TF) Shadowplay Films/Phoenix Entertainment Group, 1989
THE CASE OF THE HILLSIDE STRANGLER (TF) Kenwood Productions/Fries Entertainment, 1989
SO PROUDLY WE HAIL (TF) Lionel Chetwynd Productions/CBS Entertainment, 1990
FIRE! TRAPPED ON THE 37TH FLOOR (TF) Papazian-Hirsch/Republic, 1991
NIGHT OWL (CTF) Morgan Hill Films and Hearst Entertainment Inc., 1993

LASZLO MELIS

SENKIFOLDJE *WHY WASN'T HE THERE?* 1993, Hungarian

PETER RODGERS MELNICK*

Agent: Film Music Associates - Hollywood, 213-463-1070
Affiliation: ASCAP - Los Angeles, 213-883-1000

ROXANNE additional music, Columbia, 1987
GET SMART, AGAIN! (TF) IndieProd Productions/Phoenix Entertainment Group, 1989
L.A. STORY Tri-Star, 1991
CONVICTS MCEG, 1991
BAD ATTITUDES (TF) FNM Films, 1991
RUNNING MATES (CTF) Marvin Worth Prods., 1992
ONLY YOU Seven Arts, 1992
12:01 (TF) Fox West Pictures/New Line TV/Chanticleer Films, 1993
ARCTIC BLUE 1993
INDICTMENT: THE McMARTIN TRIAL (CTF) Ixlan Prods./Abby Mann Prods./Breakheart Films, 1995

MICHAEL MELVOIN*

Contact: ASCAP - Los Angeles, 213-883-1000

MONGO'S BACK IN TOWN (TF) Bob Banner Associates, 1971
THE LAST SURVIVORS (TF) Bob Banner Associates, 1975
ASPEN (MS) co-composer with Tom Scott, Universal TV, 1977
ASHANTI Columbia, 1979, Swiss-U.S.
THE MAIN EVENT Warner Bros., 1979
PICKING UP THE PIECES Saratoga Films, 1981
KING OF THE MOUNTAIN Universal, 1981
RETURN OF THE REBELS (TF) Moonlight Productions/Filmways, 1981
ARMED AND DANGEROUS Columbia, 1986
THE BIG TOWN Columbia, 1987
SHARING RICHARD (TF) Houston Motion Picture Entertainment/CBS Entertainment, 1988
BLIND FEAR Lance Entertainment/Allegro Films, 1989

WENDY MELVOIN

(see Wendy & Lisa)

E. D. MENASCHE

PARALLEL SONS Black Brook Films, 1995

BINGEN MENDIZABAL

MI HERMANO DEL ALMA *MY SOUL BROTHER* 1993, Spanish
LA MADRE MUERTA *THE DEAD MOTHER* 1993, Spanish

JAIME MENDOZA-NAVA

BOOTLEGGERS Howco International, 1974
PSYCHO FROM TEXAS New American Films, 1974
TEARS OF HAPPINESS 1974
THE TOWN THAT DREADED SUNDOWN American International, 1977
GRAYEAGLE American International, 1977
THE BOYS IN COMPANY C Columbia, 1978
THE NORSEMAN American International, 1978
THE EVICTORS American International, 1979
MAUSOLEUM MPM, 1983

ALAN MENKEN*
Agent: The Shukat Company - New York, 212-582-7614
Affiliation: BMI - Los Angeles, 310-659-9109

THE LITTLE MERMAID (AF) ★★   Buena Vista, 1989
BEAUTY AND THE BEAST (AF) ★★   Buena Vista, 1991
ALADDIN (AF) ★★   Buena Vista, 1992
LINCOLN (TF)   Kunhardt Prods., 1992
LIFE WITH MICKEY   Buena Vista, 1993
POCAHONTAS (AF) ★★   Buena Vista, 1995
THE HUNCHBACK OF NOTRE DAME (AF) ★   Buena Vista, 1996
HERCULES (AF)   Buena Vista, 1997

JOEY MENNONNA
Contact: ASCAP - Los Angeles, 213-883-1000

BAD BLOOD   Platinum Pictures, 1989

DALE MENTEN
Contact: BMI - Los Angeles, 310-659-9109

LIFEGUARD   Paramount, 1976
THE KEYS (TF)   Riven Rock Prods./Universal TV, 1992

WIM MERTENS
BETWEEN THE DEVIL AND THE DEEP BLUE SEA   1995,
   Belgian-French-British

PAT METHENY
Contact: BMI - Los Angeles, 310-659-9109

THE SEARCH FOR SOLUTIONS (FD)   co-composer with Lyle
   Mays, Playback Associates, 1979
TWICE IN A LIFETIME   The Yorkin Company, 1985
THE FALCON AND THE SNOWMAN   co-composer with Lyle Mays,
   Orion, 1985
LEMON SKY   American Playhouse, 1987

BILL MEYERS
Contact: ASCAP - Los Angeles, 213-883-1000

ARMED AND DANGEROUS   Columbia, 1986

LANNY MEYERS
Contact: ASCAP - Los Angeles, 213-883-1000

THE FIRST TIME   New Line Cinema, 1983
BEIRUT: THE LAST HOME MOVIE (FD)   Zohe Film, 1987

RANDALL MEYERS
SECONDLOJTNANTEN   *THE SECOND LIEUTENANT*   1993,
   Norwegian

VALERY MIAGKIH
NA TEBIA UPOVAYU   *IN THEE I TRUST*   1993, Russian

YURI MIAMIN
OKNO V PARIZH   *WINDOW TO PARIS*   co-composer with Aleksei
   Zalivalov, Sony Classics, 1994, Russian-French

FRANCO MICALIZZI
b. Italy
Contact: SIAE - Italy, 011-39-6-59-901

LO CHIAMAVANO TRINITA   1970, Italian
BEYOND THE DOOR   1974, U.S.-Italian
IL FOGLIO DELLA SEPOLTA VIVA   1974, Italian
L'ULTIMA NEVE DI PRIMAVERA   1974, Italian
IL PIATTO PIANGE   1974, Italian
ALLA MIA CARA MAMMA NEL GIORNO DEL SUO
   COMPLEANNO   1974, Italian
L'ALBERO DALLE FOGLIE ROSA   1974, Italian
BIANCHI CAVALLI D'AGOSTO   1975, Italian
GIOVANNINO   1975, Italian
IL GIUSTIZIERE SFIDA LA CITTA   1975, Italian
TRE SUPERMEN CONTRO LE AMAZZONI   1975, Italian

LAURE   1975, Italian
LEZIONI PRIVATE   1975, Italian
SYNDICATE SADISTS   Summit Associates Ltd., 1975, Italian
IL CINICO, L'INFAME, IL VIOLENTO   1976, Italian
GENOVA A MANO ARMATA   1976, Italian
ITALIA A MANO ARMATA   1976, Italian
NAPOLI VIOLENTA   1976, Italian
THE LAST HUNTER   *HUNTER OF THE APOCALYPSE*   World
   Northal, 1980, Italian
FOREVER EMMANUELLE   Movies for Cable, 1982, Italian-French
THE CURSE   Trans World Entertainment, 1987

GEORGE MICHALSKI
Contact: ASCAP - Los Angeles, 213-883-1000

KANDYLAND   New World, 1988

HARRY MIDDLEBROOKS
Contact: BMI - Los Angeles, 310-659-9109

GUS BROWN AND MIDNIGHT BREWSTER (TF)   Kaledonia
   Productions/SCOMI, 1985

CHARLIE MIDNIGHT
HAPPILY EVER AFTER: FAIRY TALES FOR EVERY CHILD
   (ATF)   co-composer, Two Oceans/Confetti/Hyperion, 1995

CYNTHIA MILLAR*
Agent: The Kraft-Benjamin Agency - Beverly Hills, 310-247-0123
Contact: ASCAP - Los Angeles, 213-883-1000

CRAZY IN LOVE (CTF)   Ohlmeyer Communications/Karen
   Danaher-Dorr Prods., 1992
THE PORTRAIT (CTF)   Atticus/Robert Greenwald, 1993
FOREIGN AFFAIRS (CTF)   Stagescreen Prods./Interscope
   Communications, 1993
THE RUN OF THE COUNTRY   Columbia, 1995
THREE WISHES   Savoy, 1995

BRUCE MILLER*
Agent: Film Music Associates - Hollywood, 213-463-1070
Affiliation: BMI - Los Angeles, 310-659-9109

MOTHER OF THE BRIDE (TF)   Baby/Leonard Hill, 1993
BONANZA: THE RETURN (TF)   Legend Entertainment/NBC Prods.,
   1993

DOMINIC MILLER
Contact: PRS - London, England, 011-44-1-580-5544

WILD WEST   1992, British

FRANKIE MILLER
ACT OF VENGEANCE (CTF)   Telepic Canada Corporation
   Productions/Frank Koenigsberg Productions/Lorimar-Telepictures
   Productions, 1986

JUDD MILLER
TYSON (CTF)   co-composer with Stewart Copeland and Michael
   Thompson, HBO Pictures, 1995

MARCUS MILLER
Contact: ASCAP - Los Angeles, 213-883-1000

SIESTA   co-composer with Miles Davis, Lorimar, 1987, British
HOUSE PARTY   co-composer with Lenny White, New Line
   Cinema, 1990
BOOMERANG   1992, Paramount
ABOVE THE RIM   New Line, 1994
A LOW DOWN DIRTY SHAME   Buena Vista, 1994
THE GREAT WHITE HYPE   20th Century Fox, 1996

RANDY MILLER
Agent: Film Music Associates - Hollywood, 213-463-1070
Affiliation: BMI - Los Angeles, 310-659-9109

DR. HACKENSTEIN   Vista Street Productions, 1988
WITCHCRAFT   Film Mirage, 1988, Italian

AND YOU THOUGHT YOUR PARENTS WERE WEIRD   Trimark, 1991
BLACK MAGIC WOMAN   Trimark, 1991
HELLRAISER III: HELL ON EARTH   partially based on themes by Chris Young from Hellraiser, Dimension Pictures, 1992
INTO THE SUN   Trimark, 1992
A CASE FOR MURDER (CTF)   Bodega Bay Prods./MTE, 1993

THEODOR MILLER
Contact: ASCAP - Los Angeles, 213-883-1000

MENACE II SOCIETY   co-composed with Quincy Jones III, New Line, 1993
JASON'S LYRIC   co-composed with Quincy Jones III, Gramercy, 1994

MARIO MILLO
Contact: APRA - Australia, 011-61-2-922-6422

THE LIGHTHORSEMAN   Cinecom International, 1988
WRANGLER   Hemdale, 1993
BRIDES OF CHRIST (MS)   1993, Australian

JOHN MILLS-COCKELL
Contact: SOCAN - Toronto, 416-445-8700

TERROR TRAIN   20th Century-Fox, 1980, Canadian
HUMONGOUS   Avco Embassy, 1982, Canadian

DAN MILNER
Contact: BMI - Los Angeles, 310-659-9109

HAPPY HOUR   TMS Pictures, 1987

DAVID MILROY
EXILE AND KINGDOM (FD)   Snakewood Films, 1993, Australian

MICHAEL MINARD
Contact: ASCAP - Los Angeles, 213-883-1000

SPECIAL EFFECTS   New Line Cinema, 1985
DEAD ON THE MONEY (CTF)   Perfect Circle Corp./Voyager/Indieprod, 1991

DAVID MINDEL
Contact: PRS - London, England, 011-44-1-580-5544

REAL LIFE   Bedford, 1984, British

CHEN MING-CHANG
HSIMENG JENSHENG   THE PUPPETMASTER   1993, Taiwan

CHARLES MINGUS
Contact: BMI - Los Angeles, 310-659-9109

THE COSBY MYSTERIES (TF)   co-composer with Bill Cosby and Craig Handy, SAH Entertainment/Columbia Pictures TV/NBC Prods., 1994

BEN MINK
Contact: SOCAN - Toronto, 416-445-8700

EVEN COWGIRLS GET THE BLUES   co-composer with k.d. lang, Fine Line, 1993

CARLOS MIRANDA
THE HOUSE OF BERNARDA ALBA (TF)   1991, British

SHELDON MIROWITZ*
Agent: Jeff Kaufman - Studio City, 818-506-6013
Affiliation: ASCAP - Los Angeles, 213-883-1000

COLUMBUS AND THE AGE OF DISCOVERY (TD)   WGBH/BBC TV/NHK/RAI/RTD/NDR/TVE/SEQS, 1991
AMERICA AND THE HOLOCAUST: DECEIT AND INDIFFERENCE (TD)   American Experience, 1994
APOLLO 13: TO THE EDGE AND BACK (TD)   WGBH Boston/TV Asahi/Central TV, 1994

NAN MISHKIN
(See Nan Schwartz-Mishkin)

PAUL MISRAKI
b. 1908 - Constantinople
Contact: SACEM - France, 011-33-1-4715-4715

CLAUDINE A L'ECOLE   1936, French
TOUT VA TRES BIEN MADAME LA MARQUISE   1936, French
PRINCE BOUBOULE   1938, French
CHERI-BIBI   1938, French
LE CHANTEUR DE MINUIT   1938, French
J'ETAIS UNE AVENTURIERE   1938, French
FEUX DE JOIE   1938, French
RETOUR A L'AUBE   1939, French
TOURBILLONS DE PARIS   1939, French
BATTEMENTS DE COEUR   1939, French
STELLA   1943
SIETE MUJERES   1943
LA PETITE FEMME DU MOULIN ROUGE   1943, French
PASSEPORT POUR RIO   1944, French
ECLIPSE DE SOL   1944, French
HEARTBEAT   RKO Radio, 1946, French
LA FOIRE AUX CHIMERES   1946, French
SI JEUNESSE SAVAIT   1947, French
MADEMOISELLE S'AMUSE   1948, French
MANON   1949, French
NOUS IRONS A PARIS   1949, French
TOUS LE CHEMINS MENENT A ROME   1949, French
MANEGES   1949, French
LE ROSIER DE MADAME HUSSON   1950, French
KNOCK   1950, French
NOUS IRONS A MONTE-CARLO   1950, French
PIGALLE SAINT-GERMAIN-DES-PRES   1950, French
UTOPIA   ATOLL K   1950, French
UNE HISTOIRE D'AMOUR   1951, French
LES MAINS SALES   1951, French
LE GARCON SAUVAGE   1951, French
COIFFEUR POUR DAMES   1952, French
LA JEUNE FOLLE   1952, French
ELLE ET MOI   1952, French
LE TROU NORMAND   1952, French
THE MOMENT OF TRUTH   Arlan Pictures, 1952, French
LES ORGUEILLEUX   1953, French
LA ROUTE NAPOLEON   1953, French
ALI-BABA ET LES 40 VOLEURS   1954, French
MR. ARKADIN   CONFIDENTIAL REPORT   Warner Bros., 1955, Spanish-Swiss
OBSESSION   Gibe Films, 1954, French-Italian
LES FEMMES S'EN BALANCENT   1954, French
FORTUNE CARREE   1954, French
OASIS   1954, French
LA REINE MARGOT   1954, French
LE FIL A LA PATTE   co-composer with Rene Cloerec, 1954, French
ESCALE A ORLY   1955, French
CHIENS PERDUS SANS COLLIER   1955, French
LA MEILLEURE PART   1955, French
LE COUTURIER DE CES DAMES   1956, French
AND GOD CREATED WOMAN   Kingsley International, 1956, French
EN EFFEUILLANT LA MARGUERITE   1956, French
DEATH IN THE GARDEN   Bauer International, 1956, French-Mexican
LA CHATELAINE DU LIBAN   1956, French
SOUS LE CIEL DE PROVENCE   1956, French
MEFIEZ-VOUS FILLETTES   1957, French
A PIED A CHEVAL ET EN VOITURE   1957, French
QUAND LA FEMME S'EN MELE   1957, French
LES FANATIQUES   1957, French

INSPECTOR MAIGRET   *MAIGRET TEND UN PIEGE*   Lopert,
   1958, French-Italian
SANS FAMILE   1958, French
A DOG, A MOUSE AND A SPUTNIK   1958, French
UN DROLE DE DIMANCHE   1958, French
MONTPARNASSE 19   1958, French
THE COUSINS   Films Around the World, 1959, French
FAIBLES FEMMES   1959, French
LE CHEMINS DES ECOLIERS   1959, French
LEDA   *WEB OF PASSION/A DOUBLE TOUR*   Times, 1959, French
COMMENT QU'ELLE EST   1960, French
LE CAID   1960, French
LOVE AND THE FRENCHWOMAN   Kingsley International, 1960,
   French
LES BONNES FEMMES   Robert Hakim, 1960, French-Italian
LES 3 MOUSQUETAIRES   1961, French
LE RENDEZ-VOUS   1961, French
LENNY POUR LES DAMES   1962, French
LE DOULOUS   1962, French
LE CHEVALIER DE PARDAILLAN   1962, French
HARDI PARDAILLAN   1963, French
L'ASSASSIN CONNAIT LA MUSIQUE   1963, French
A TOI DE FAIRE MIGNONNE   1963, French
LA MARJOLAINE   1965, French
ALPHAVILLE   Pathe Contemporary, 1965, French
DIS-MOI QUI TU ES   1965, French
CARTES SUR TABLE   1966, French
SEVEN HOMMES ET UNE GARCE   1966, French
A MURDER IS A MURDER   1972, French
LES VOLETS CLOS   1972, French
JULIETTE ET JULIETTE   1973, French
LA MAIN A COUPER   1974, French
LE CHASSEUR DE CHEZ MAXIM   1975, French
LE MAESTRO   1975, French
LA PART DU FEU   1977, French
SUCH A LOVELY TOWN...   1979, French
STRESS   1985, French

RICHARD G. MITCHELL

Contact: PRS - London, England, 011-44-1-580-5544

BORN AMERICAN   Concorde, 1986, Finnish-U.S.
THE BRIDGE   1991, British

ROBERT MITCHELL

ONE NATION UNDER GOD (FD)   3Z/Hourglass, 1993

BOB MITHOFF*

b. El Paso, Texas
Contact: ASCAP - Los Angeles, 213-883-1000
e-mail: bobmithoff@earthlink.net

CITY (TF)   CBS/MTM, 1990
WORKING TRASH (TF)   Fox, 1990
DRAGONFIGHT (CTF)   Warner/HBO, 1991
CLASS OF NUKE 'EM HIGH PART II: SUBHUMANOID
   MELTDOWN   Troma, 1991
LANDSLIDE (CTF)   HBO, 1992
CYBORG SOLDIER   New Line Cinema, 1993
DEAD GIVEAWAY   Curb Entertainment, 1995
NEW YORK COP   Columbia TriStar, 1996

FUMIO MIYASHITA

Contact: BMI - Los Angeles, 310-659-9109

TENKAWA DENSETSU SASUJIN JIKEN   *NOH MASK MURDERS*
   1991, Japanese

VIC MIZZY

b. 1922 - Brooklyn, New York
Contact: ASCAP - Los Angeles, 213-883-1000

THE NIGHT WALKER   Universal, 1965
A VERY SPECIAL FAVOR   Universal, 1965
THE GHOST AND MR. CHICKEN   Universal, 1966
THE BUSY BODY   Paramount, 1967
THE CAPER OF THE GOLDEN BULLS   Embassy, 1967

THE RELUCTANT ASTRONAUT   Universal, 1967
DON'T MAKE WAVES   MGM, 1967
THE SPIRIT IS WILLING   Paramount, 1967
THE PERILS OF PAULINE   Universal, 1967
DID YOU HEAR THE ONE ABOUT THE TRAVELING
   SALESLADY?   Universal, 1968
THE SHAKIEST GUN IN THE WEST   Universal, 1968
HOW TO FRAME A FIGG   Universal, 1971
THE DEADLY HUNT (TF)   Four Star International, 1971
A VERY MISSING PERSON (TF)   Universal TV, 1972
GETTING AWAY FROM IT ALL (TF)   Palomar Productions, 1972
HURRICANE (TF)   Montagne Productions/Metromedia Producers
   Corporation, 1974
TERROR ON THE 40TH FLOOR (TF)   Montagne
   Productions/Metromedia Producers Corporation, 1974
THE MILLION DOLLAR RIP-OFF (TF)   Charles Fries
   Productions/Montagne Productions, 1976
THE MUNSTERS' REVENGE (TF)   Universal TV, 1981

MARK MOFFIATT

Contact: APRA - Australia, 011-61-2-922-6422

HIGH TIDE   co-composer with Ricky Fataar, Hemdale, 1987,
   Australian

FRED MOLLIN

Agent: Film Music Associates - Hollywood, 213-463-1070
Affiliation: SOCAN - Toronto, 416-445-8700

LUNCH WAGON   *LUNCH WAGON GRILS/COME 'N GET IT*
   Seymour Borde & Associates, 1980
FAMILY REUNION (TF)   CBC TV, 1981, Canadian
SPRING FEVER   Comworld, 1983, Canadian
HOCKEY NIGHT (TF)   Martin Paul/CBC, 1984, Canadian
FRIDAY THE 13TH, PART VII - THE NEW BLOOD   co-composer
   with Harry Manfredini, Paramount, 1988
FRIDAY THE 13TH, PART VIII - JASON TAKES MANHATTAN
   Paramount, 1989
WHISPERS   ITC/Cinepix, 1990, Canadian
AMY FISHER: MY STORY (TF)   KLM/Spectacor/Michael Jaffe
   Films, 1992
FOREVER KNIGHT: DARK KNIGHT (TF)
   Paragon/Tele-Munchen/Tri-Star TV, 1991
SURVIVE THE NIGHT (CTF)   Heartstar/Once Upon A
   Time/USA/RAI/Spector, 1993
LIAR, LIAR (TF)   CBC Prods., 1993, Canadian

PADDY MOLONEY

TWO IF BY SEA   co-composer with Nick Glennie-Smith, Warner
   Bros., 1996

FRANCIS MONKMAN

Contact: PRS - London, England, 011-44-1-580-5544

THE LONG GOOD FRIDAY   Embassy, 1982, British

OSVALDO MONTES

AMIGOMIO   1993, Argentine-German
THE LIFEFORCE EXPERIMENT (CTF)   Filmline
   International/Screen Partners/USA Pictures, 1994

RONNIE MONTROSE

Contact: BMI - Los Angeles, 310-659-9109

BORN TO SKI (FD)   1992, Warren Miller Entertainment

DOUG MOODY

Contact: BMI - Los Angeles, 310-659-9109

DU BEAT-E-O   H-Z-H Presentation, 1984

GUY MOON

Contact: BMI - Los Angeles, 310-659-9109

DIVING IN   co-composer with Paul Buckmaster, Maurer/Shaw, 1991
THE BRADY BUNCH MOVIE   Paramount, 1995
A VERY BRADY SEQUEL   Paramount, 1996

HAL MOONEY

Contact: ASCAP - Los Angeles, 213-883-1000

THE LONGEST NIGHT (TF)   Universal TV, 1972
TOM SAWYER (TF)   Hal Roach Productions/Universal TV, 1973
RUNAWAY! (TF)   Universal TV, 1973
MY DARLING DAUGHTERS' ANNIVERSARY (TF)   Groverton Productions/Universal TV, 1973
THE CHADWICK FAMILY (TF)   Universal TV, 1974
THE TRIBE (TF)   Universal TV, 1974
THE STORYTELLER (TF)   co-composer with David Shire, Fairmount/Foxcroft Productions/Universal TV, 1977

DUDLEY MOORE

b. April 19, 1935 - London, England
Contact: ASCAP - Los Angeles, 213-883-1000

BEDAZZLED   20th Century-Fox, 1967, British
30 IS A DANGEROUS AGE, CYNTHIA   Columbia, 1968, British
INADMISSABLE EVIDENCE   Paramount, 1968, British
STAIRCASE   20th Century-Fox, 1969, British
THE HOUND OF THE BASKERVILLES   Atlantic Releasing Corporation, 1979, British
DEREK AND CLIVE GET THE HORN   Peter Cook Productions, 1981, British
SIX WEEKS   Universal, 1982

THURSTON MOORE

HEAVY   CFP Distribution, 1995

JACQUES MORALI

Contact: SACEM - France, 011-33-1-4715-4715

CRAZY HORSE PARIS—FRANCE   SNC, 1977, French
I'VE GOT YOU, YOU'VE GOT ME BY THE HAIRS OF MY CHINNY CHIN CHIN   1979, French
CAN'T STOP THE MUSIC   AFD, 1980

MIKE MORAN

Contact: PRS - London, England, 011-44-1-580-5544

TIME BANDITS   Avco Embassy, 1981, British
THE MISSIONARY   Columbia, 1982, British
WATER   Atlantic Releasing Corporation, 1984, British

PATRICK MORAZ

Contact: SUISA - Zurich, Switzerland, 011-41-1-482-6666

THE STEPFATHER   New Century/Vista, 1987

HOWARD MORGAN

Contact: ASCAP - Los Angeles, 213-883-1000

MERCENARY FIGHTERS   Cannon, 1988

JOHN W. MORGAN*

b. October 21, 1946 - Los Angeles, California
Contact: Tarzana, 818-344-0930
Affiliation: BMI - Los Angeles, 310-659-9109

THE AFTERMATH   Prism Entertainment, 1982
FLICKS   United Film Distribution Co., 1987
BACK FROM THE PAST   additional music, 1990
EVIL NIGHT   Nautilus Film Co., 1990

KUROUDO MORI

b. Japan
Contact: JASRAC - Tokyo, Japan, 011-81-3-502-6551

MUDDY RIVER   Japan Film Center, 1981, Japanese

KEN-ICHIRO MORIOKA

b. Japan
Contact: JASRAC - Tokyo, Japan, 011-81-3-502-6551

MESSAGE FROM SPACE (AF)   United Artists, 1978, Japanese

ANGELA MORLEY*

(Wally Stott)
Contact: ASCAP - Los Angeles, 213-883-1000

THE LOOKING GLASS WAR   Columbia, 1970, British
CAPTAIN NEMO AND THE UNDERWATER CITY   MGM, 1970, British
WHEN EIGHT BELLS TOLL   Cinerama Releasing Corporation, 1971, British
THE LITTLE PRINCE   Paramount, 1974, British
THE SLIPPER AND THE ROSE: THE STORY OF CINDERELLA ★ adaptation, Universal, 1976, Brtiish
WATERSHIP DOWN (AF)   Avco Embassy, 1978, British
LA COLINA DEI COMALI   1979, Italian
FRIENDSHIPS, SECRETS AND LIES (TF)   Wittman-Riche Productions/Warner Bros. TV, 1979
MADAME X (TF)   Levenback-Riche Productions/Universal TV, 1981
SUMMER GIRL (TF)   Bruce Lansbury Productions/Roberta Haynes Productions/Finnegan Associates, 1983
TWO MARRIAGES (TF)   Lorimar Productions/Raven's Claw Productions, 1983
THREESOME (TF)   CBS Entertainment, 1984

GIORGIO MORODER

b. April 26, 1940 - Ortisei, Italy
Agent: Film Music Associates - Hollywood, 213-463-1070
Affiliation: ASCAP - Los Angeles, 213-883-1000

MIDNIGHT EXPRESS ★★   Columbia, 1978, British
FOXES   Paramount, 1980
AMERICAN GIGOLO   Paramount, 1980
CAT PEOPLE   Universal, 1982
D.C. CAB   Universal, 1983
FLASHDANCE   Paramount, 1983
METROPOLIS   new score for 1926 silent, 1983
SCARFACE   Universal, 1983
THE NEVERENDING STORY   co-composer with Klaus Doldinger, Warner Bros., 1984, West German
ELECTRIC DREAMS   MGM/UA, 1984
OVER THE TOP   Cannon, 1987
FAIR GAME   1988
LET IT RIDE   Paramount, 1989

ENNIO MORRICONE

b. October 11, 1928 - Rome, Italy
Agent: Gorfaine-Schwartz - Los Angeles, 213-969-1011
Affiliation: SIAE - Italy, 011-39-6-59-901

THE FASCIST   1961, Italian
CRAZY DESIRE   LA VOGLIE MATTA   1962, Italian
DICIOTTENNI AL SOLE   1962, Italian
I MOTORIZATTI   1962, Italian
LA CUCCAGNA   A GIRL...AND A MILLION   1963, Italian
THE HOURS OF LOVE   LE ORE DELL'AMORE   1963, Italian
IL SUCCESSO   1963, Italian
I BASILISCHI   1963, Italian
LE MONASCHINE   THE LITTLE NUNS   1963, French
GRINGO   DUELLO NEL TEXAS/GUNFIGHT AT RED SANDS   1963, Italian
I MANIACI   1964, Italian
I MALAMONDO   1964, Italian
IN GINOCCHIO DA TE   1964, Italian
BEFORE THE REVOLUTION   co-composer with Gato Barbieri, New Yorker, 1964, Italian
I MARZIANI HANNO 12 MANI   1964, Italian
I DUE EVASI DI SING SING   1964, Italian

LE PISTOLE NON DISCUTUNO   1964, Italian
A FISTFUL OF DOLLARS   United Artists, 1964,
   Italian-Spanish-West German
NON SON DEGNO DI TE   1965, Italian
UNA PISTOLA PER RINGO   1965, Italian
ALTISSIMA PRESSIONE   co-composer with Luis Bacalov, 1965,
   Italian
I PUGNI IN TASCA   1965, Italian
SLALOM   1965, Italian
NIGHTMARE CASTLE   AMANTI D'OLTRE TOMBA   1965, Italian
FOR A FEW DOLLARS MORE   United Artists, 1965,
   Italian-Spanish-West German
IL RITORNO DI RINGO   1965, Italian
MENAGE ALL'ITALIANA   1965, Italian
SETTE PISTOLE PER I MACGREGOR   1965, Italian
EL GRECO   1966, Italian
SE NON AVESSI PIU TE   1966, Italian
IDOLI CONTROLUCE   1966, Italian
MI VEDRAI TORNARE   1966, Italian
TOO SOON TO DIE   SVEGLIATI E UCCIDI   1966, Italian
ADULTERIO ALL'ITALIANA   1966, Italian
THE HAWKS AND THE SPARROWS   UCCELLACI E UCCELLINI
   1966, Italian
NAVAJO JOE   UN DOLLARO A TESTA   1966, Italian
UN UOMO A META   1966, Italian
THE HILLS RUN RED   I FIUME DI DOLLARI   1966, Italian
THE HELLBENDERS   I CRUDELI   1966, Italian
RIFIFI IM BEIRUT   1966, Italian
THE BIG GUNDOWN   LA RESA DEI CONTI   1966, Italian
THE GOOD, THE BAD AND THE UGLY   United Artists, 1966,
   Italian
THE BATTLE OF ALGIERS   Rizzoli, 1967, Italian-Algerian
COME IMPARI AD AMARE LE DONNE   1967, Italian
UP THE MACGREGORS   SETTE DONNE PER I MACGREGOR
   1967, Italian
THE WITCHES   co-composer with Pierro Piccioni, Lopert, 1967,
   Italian-French
OPERATION KID BROTHER   co-composer with Bruno Nicolai,
   1967, Italian
THE GIRL AND THE GENERAL   LA RAGAZZA E IL GENERALE
   1967, Italian
GRAND SLAM   AD OGNI COSTO   1967, Italian
DEATH RIDES A HORSE   DA UOMO A UOMO   1967, Italian
CHINA IS NEAR   LA CINE E VICINA   1967, Italian
MATCHLESS   1967, Italian
DANGER: DIABOLIK   DIABOLIK   1967, Italian
THE ROVER   L'AVVENTURIERO   1967, Italian
HAREM   1967, Italian
ARABELLA   Cram Film, 1967, Italian
ESCALATION   1967, Italian
FACCIA A FACCIA   1967, Italian
THE DIRTY HEROES   DALLE ARDENNE ALL'INFERNO
   co-composer with Bruno Nicolai, 1968, Italian
GUNS FOR SAN SEBASTIAN   1968, Italian
COME PLAY WITH ME   GRAZIE ZIA   1968, Italian
A FINE PAIR   RUBA AL PROSSIMO TUO   1968, Italian
FRAULEIN DOKTOR   1968, West German
GALILEO   1968
THEOREM   TEOREMA   1968, Italian
COMANDEMENTI PER UN GANGSTER   1968, Italian
LISTEN, LET'S MAKE LOVE   1968, Italian
THAT SPLENDID NOVEMBER   1968, Italian
E PER TETTO UN CIELO DI STELLE   1968, Italian
IL GRANDE SILENZIO   1968, Italian
PARTNER   1968
ROME LIKE CHICAGO   co-composer with Bruno Nicolai, 1968,
   Italian
MACHINE GUN McCAIN   GLI INTOCCABILI   1968, Italian
A QUIET PLACE IN THE COUNTRY   1968, Italian
VERGOGNA SCHIFOSI   1968, Italian
MOTHER'S HEART   CUORE DI MAMMA   1968, Italian
TEPEPA   1968, Italian
EAT IT   MANGIALA   1968, Italian
H-2-S   1968, Italian
ECCE HOMO   1968, Italian
SENZA SAPERE NIENTE DI LEI   1968, Italian
THE MERCENARY   co-composer with Bruno Nicolai, 1969, Italian
THE AWFUL STORY OF THE NUN OF MONZA   1969, Italian
ONCE UPON A TIME IN THE WEST   Paramount, 1969,
   Italian-U.S.
METTI UNA SERA A CENA   LOVE CIRCLE   1969, Italian
LA STAGIONE DEI SENSI   1969, Italian

SAI COSA FACEVA STALIN ALLE DONNE?   1969, Italian
UNA BREVE STAGIONE   1969, Italian
THE YEAR OF THE CANNIBALS   I CANNIBALI   American
   International, 1969, Italian
UCCIDETE IL VITELLO GRASSO E ARROSTITELO   1969, Italian
L'ASSOLUTO NATURALE   SHE AND HE   1969, Italian
LA NOTTE DEI SERPENTI   1969, Italian
GOTT MIT UNS   THE LAST FIVE DAYS OF PEACE   1969, Italian
THE SICILLIAN CLAN   20th Century-Fox, 1970, Italian
THE FIVE MAN ARMY   UN ESERCITO DI 5 UOMIN   MGM, 1970,
   Italian
TWO MULES FOR SISTER SARAH   Universal, 1970,
   U.S.-Mexican
BURN!   QUEIMADA!   United Artists, 1970, Italian-French
INVESTIGATION OF A CITIZEN ABOVE SUSPICION   Columbia,
   1970, Italian
METELLO   1970, Italian
THE BIRD WITH THE CRYSTAL PLUMAGE   UMC, 1970,
   Italian-West German
LUI PER LEI   1970, Italian
LA MOGLIE PIU BELLA   1970, Italian
VERUSCHKA, POESIA DI UNA DONNA   1970, Italian
HORNET'S NEST   United Artists, 1970
QUANDO LE DONNE AVEVANO LA CODA   WHEN WOMEN HAD
   TAILS   1970, Italian
CITTA VIOLENTA   THE FAMILY   1970, Italian
VAMOS A MATAR, COMPANEROS   1970, Italian
GIOCHI PARTICOLARI   1970, Italian
FORZA G   WINGED DEVILS   1970, Italian
LE FOTO PROIBITE DI UNA SIGNORA PER BENE   1970, Italian
TRE NEL MILLE   1970, French
LA CALIFFA   1970, Italian
THE RED TENT   Paramount, 1971, Italian-Russian
CAT O'NINE TAILS   National General, 1971, Italian-West
   German-French
MADDALENA   1971, Italian
SACCO AND VANZETTI   1971, Italian
IL DECAMERONE   1971, Italian
OCEANO   1971, Italian
GLI OCCHI FEDDI DELLA PAURA   1971, Italian
GIORNATA NERA PER L'ARIETE   1971, Italian
ADDIO, FRATELLO CRUDELE   'TIS A PITY SHE'S A WHORE
   1971, Italian
LA CLASE OPERAIA VA IN PARADISO   LULU THE TOOL   1971,
   Italian
SANS MOBILE APPARENT   1971, Italian
INCONTRO   1971, Italian
LE CASSE   THE BURGLARS   1971, Italian
LA CORTA NOTTE DELLE BAMBOLE DI VETRO   1971, Italian
LA TARANTOLA DAL VENTRO NERO   THE BLACK BELLY OF
   THE TARANTULA   1971, Italian
L'ISTRUTTORIA E' CHIUSA: DIMENTICHI   co-composer with
   Walter Branchi, 1971, Italian
IMPUTAZIONE DI OMICIDIO PER UNO STUDENTE   1971, Italian
QUATTRO MOSCHE DI VELLUTO GRIGIO   FOUR FLIES ON
   GREY VELVET   1971, Italian
IL DIAVOLO NEL CERVELLO   1971, Italian
LA VIOLENZA: QUNITO POTERE   1971, Italian
QUANDO LE DONNE PERSERO LA CODA   WHEN WOMEN LOST
   THEIR TAILS   co-composer with Bruno Nicolai, 1971, Italian
...CORREVA L'ANNO DI GRAZIE 1870   1972, Italian
I BAMBINI CI CHIEDONO PERCHE   1972, Italian
QUESTA SPECIE D'AMORE   1972, Italian
COSA AVETE FATTO A SOLANGE?   1972, Italian
MIO CARO ASSASSINO   1972, Italian
ANCHE SE VOLESSI LAVORARE, CHE COSA FACCIO?   1972,
   Italian
CHI L'HA VISTA MORIRE?   1972, Italian
THE CANTERBURY TALES   United Artists, 1972, Italian
IL MAESTRO E MARGHERITA   1972, Italian
LES DEUX SAISONS DE LA VIE   1972, Italian
BARBABLU   BLUEBEARD   1972, Hungarian
L'ATTENTAT   THE FRENCH CONSPIRACY   1972, French
LA VITA, A VOLTE, E MOLTO DURO NEL WEST, VERO
   PROVVIDENZA?   1972, Italian
SBATTI IL MONSTRO IN PRIMA PAGINA   1972, Italian
LA COSA BUFFA   1972, Italian
LA BANDA J & S: CRONACA CRIMINALE DEL FAR WEST
   SONNY AND JED   1972, Italian
UN UOMO DA RISPETTARE   THE MASTER TOUCH/HEARTS
   AND MINDS/A MAN TO RESPECT   1972, Italian
CHE C'ENTRIAMO NOI CON LA RIVOLUZIONE?   1972, Italian

DUCK! YOU SUCKER *GIU LA TESTA/FISTFUL OF DYNAMITE*
United Artists, 1972, Italian-U.S.
QUANDO L'AMORE E SENSUALITA   Gemini, 1972, Italian
D'AMORE SI MUORE   1973, Italian
THE SERPENT   *NIGHT FLIGHT TO MOSCOW*   Avco Embassy,
1973, French-Italian-West German
FORSE UN FIORE   theme only, 1973, Italian
REVOLVER   *BLOOD IN THE STREETS*   1973
CRESCETE E MOLTIPLICATEVI   1973, Italian
VIA RASELLA   *MASSACRE IN ROME*   1973, Italian
LA PROPRIETA NON PIU UN FURTO   1973, Italian
SPOGLIATI, PROTESTA, UCCIDI   1973, Italian
L'ULTIMO UOMO DI SARA   1973, Italian
SEPOLTA VIVA   1973, Italian
GIORDANO BRUNO   1973, Italian
CI RISIAMO, VERO PROVVIDENZA?   co-composer with Bruno
Nicolai, 1973, Italian
SESSO IN CONFESSIONALE   1973, Italian
VAARWEL   *THE ROMANTIC AGONY*   1974, Dutch
MY NAME IS NOBODY   1974, Italian-French-West German
THE TEMPTER   Euro International, 1974, British-Italian
THE LAST DAYS OF MUSSOLINI   *MUSSOLINI: ULTIMO ATTO*
Paramount, 1974, Italian
SPASMO   1974, Italian
THE DEATH DEALER   *MILANO ODIA: LA POLIZIA NON PUO*
SPARARE   1974, Italian
LE TRIO INFERNAL   1974, French
LA CUGINA   1974
LE SECRET   1974, French
L'ANTICRISTO   1974
MACCIE SOLARI   1974, Italian
LA FAILLE   1974, French
LAST STOP ON THE NIGHT TRAIN   *L'ULTIMO TRENO DELLA*
NOTTE   1974, Italian
THE MASTER TOUCH   Warner Bros., 1974, Italian
LA GRANDE BOURGEOISE   1974, French-Italian
ALLONSANFAN   Cinematographic Cooperative, 1975, Italian
DRAMA OF THE RICH   *FATTI DI GENTE PERBENE*   PAC, 1975,
Italian-French
LIBERA, AMORE MIO   *LIBERA, MY LOVE*   Italnoleggio, 1975,
Italian
THE DEVIL IS A WOMAN   *IL SORRISO DEL GRANDE*
TENTATORE   1975, British-Italian
THE NIGHT CALLER   *PEUR SUR LA VILLE*   1975, French
STORIE DI VITA E MALAVITA   1975, Italian
LEONOR   1975
DOWN THE ANCIENT STAIRS   *PER LE ANTICHE SCALE*   1975,
Italian
END OF THE GAME   *DER RICHTER UND SEIN HENKER*   20th
Century-Fox, 1975, German-Italian
THE HUMAN FACTOR   Bryanston, 1975
ATTENTI AL BUFFONE   1975, Italian
DIVINA CREATURA   1975
GENTE DI RISPETTO   1975
LABBRA DI LURIDO BLU   1975, Italian
SALO OR THE 120 DAYS OF SODOM   United Artists, 1975,
Italian
LA DONNA DELLA DOMENICA   1975, Italian
MOSES (MS)   ITC/RAI, 1975, British-Italian
UN GENIO, DUE COMPARI, UN POLLO   Titanus, 1976, Italian
SAN BABILA ORE 20: UN DELITTO INUTILE   1976, Italian
L'EREDITA FERRAMONTI   1976
UNA VITA VENDUTA   1976
L'AGNESE VA A MORIRE   1976, Italian
BLOOD IN THE STREETS   Independent-International, 1976,
Italian-French-West German
SUNDAY WOMAN   20th Century-Fox, 1976, Italian-French
EREDITA FERRAMONTI   1976, Italian
L'UOMO E LA MAGIA (TF)   1976, Italian
THE THRUSTER   1976, Belgian
IL GATTO   1977
PARTNER   1977
IL MOSTRO   1977
THE DESERT OF THE TARTARS   *IL DESIERTO DEI TARTARI*
Gaumont, 1977, French-Italian-Iranian
IL PREFETTO DI FERRO   1977, Italian
1900   *NOVECENTO*   Paramount, 1977, Italian
EXORCIST II: THE HERETIC   Warner Bros., 1977
ORCA   Paramount, 1977
RENE LA CANNE   *RENE THE CANE*   AMLF, 1977, French
PEDRO PERAMO   1977, Mexican
HOLOCAUST 2000   1977, British-Italian

CORLEONE   1978
L'IMMORALISTA   1978
DAYS OF HEAVEN ★   Paramount, 1978
THE HUMANOID   1978
THE TEMPTER   Avco Embassy, 1978, Italian
LA CAGE AUX FOLLES   1978, French-Italian
TRAVELS WITH ANITA   1979
SIDNEY SHELDON'S BLOODLINE   Paramount, 1979
LUNA   20th Century-Fox, 1979, Italian-U.S.
LA MANI SPORCHE   1979
IL PRATO   1979
IL BANAITO DAGLI OCCHI AZZURRI   1980
LA BANQUIERE   1980, French
LA DAME AUX CAMELIAS   1980, French
PROFESSIONE FIGLIO   1980
STARK SYSTEM   1980
WINDOWS   United Artists, 1980
MILANO ODIA: LA POLIZIA NON PUO' SPARARE   Joseph
Brenner, 1980, Italian
THE ISLAND   Universal, 1980
TODO MODO   Nu-Image, 1980, Italian
LA CAGE AUX FOLLES II   United Artists, 1981, French-Italian
LOVERS AND LIARS   Levitt-Pickman, 1981
OCCHIO ALLA PENNA   1981
BUTTERFLY   Analysis, 1981
SO FINE   Warner Bros., 1981
WHITE DOG   Paramount, 1982
MARCO POLO (MS)   RAI/Franco Cristaldi Productions/Vincenzo
Labella Productions, 1982, Italian
THE THING   Universal, 1982
THE LINK   1982
TREASURE OF THE FOUR CROWNS   Cannon, 1983,
U.S.-Spanish
THE SCARLET AND THE BLACK (TF)   Bill McCutchen
Productions/ITC Productions/RAI, 1983
LE MARGINAL   *THE OUTSIDER*   Gaumont, 1983, Italian
NANA   Cannon, 1983, Italian
A TIME TO DIE   *SEVEN GRAVES FOR ROGAN*   additional music,
Almi Films, 1983
HUNDRA   1983
SAHARA   MGM/UA, 1983
LA CHIAVE   *THE KEY*   San Francisco Films, 1983, Italian
LE RUFFIAN   AMLF, 1983, French
ORDER OF DEATH   1983, Italian
ONCE UPON A TIME IN AMERICA   The Ladd Company/Warner
Bros., 1984, U.S.-Italian-Canadian
RED SONJA   MGM/UA, 1985
LA GABBIA   1985
LA CAGE AUX FOLLES 3   Warner Bros./Columbia, 1985, French
C.A.T. SQUAD (TF)   NBC Productions/Filmline International, 1986
THE MISSION ★   Warner Bros., 1986, British
MOSCA ADDIO   Istituto Luce/Italnoleggio, 1987, Italian
THE UNTOUCHABLES ★   Paramount, 1987
RAMPAGE   DEG, 1987
SECRET OF THE SAHARA   1987
MAMBA   Eidoscope/Reteitalia, 1988, Italian
C.A.T. SQUAD: PYTHON WOLF (TF)   NBC Productions, 1988
A TIME OF DESTINY   Columbia, 1988
FRANTIC   Warner Bros., 1988
CASUALTIES OF WAR   Columbia, 1989
FAT MAN AND LITTLE BOY   Paramount, 1989
TEMPO DI UCCIDERE   *THE SHORT CUT*   Titanus, 1989,
Italian-French
CINEMA PARADISO   Miramax, 1989, Italian
ENDLESS GAME (CTF)   Showtime/Telso International/Roteitalia,
1990
TO FORGET PALERMO   Penta, 1990, Italian
THE ACHILLE LAURO AFFAIR (TF)   Mike Robe Productions, 1990
EVERYBODY'S FINE   Miramax, 1990, Italian-French
TIE ME UP! TIE ME DOWN!   Miramax, 1990, Spanish
STATE OF GRACE   1990
HAMLET   Warner Bros., 1990
LA PIOVRA 5 (TF)   1990, Italian
LA DOMENICA SPECIALMENTE   *ESPECIALLY ON SUNDAY*
1991, Italian/French/Belgian
PIAZZA DI SPAGNA   1991
BUGSY ★   TriStar, 1991
CITY OF JOY   TriStar, 1992
IN THE LINE OF FIRE   Columbia, 1993
IL LUNGO SILENZIO   *THE LONG SILENCE*   1993,
Italian-French-German
LA SCORTA   *THE BODYGUARDS*   1993, Italian

SERGIO LEONE'S COLT (MS)   1993, Italian
A PURE FORMALITY   *UNA PURA FORMALITA*   Sony Classics,
   1994, Italian-French
LOVE AFFAIR   Warner Bros., 1994
WOLF   Columbia, 1994
ABRAHAM (CTF)   theme only, Turner Pictures, 1994
DISCLOSURE   Warner Bros., 1994
LA NOTTE E IL MOMENTO   1995
THE STAR MAKER   1996
LOLITA   1997

JOHN MORRIS*

b. October 18, 1926 - Elizabeth, New Jersey
Contact: ASCAP - Los Angeles, 213-883-1000

THE PRODUCERS   Avco Embassy, 1968
THE TWELVE CHAIRS   UMC, 1970
THE GAMBLERS   20th Century-Fox, 1969
BLAZING SADDLES   Warner Bros., 1973
THE BANK SHOT   United Artists, 1974
YOUNG FRANKENSTEIN   20th Century-Fox, 1974
THE ADVENTURE OF SHERLOCK HOLMES' SMARTER
   BROTHER   20th Century-Fox, 1975
SILENT MOVIE   20th Century-Fox, 1976
THE LAST REMAKE OF BEAU GESTE   Universal, 1977
THE WORLD'S GREATEST LOVER   20th Century-Fox, 1977
HIGH ANXIETY   20th Century-Fox, 1977
THE IN-LAWS   Columbia, 1979
IN GOD WE TRUST   Universal, 1980
THE MATING SEASON (TF)   Highgate Pictures, 1980
THE ELEPHANT MAN ★   Paramount, 1980, British-U.S.
THE HISTORY OF THE WORLD, PART 1   20th Century-Fox, 1981
SPLENDOR IN THE GRASS (TF)   Katz-Gallin Productions/Half-Pint
   Productions/Warner Bros. TV, 1981
THE ELECTRIC GRANDMOTHER (TF)   Highgate Pictures, 1982
YELLOWBEARD   Orion, 1983, British
TABLE FOR FIVE   co-composer with Miles Goodman, Warner
   Bros., 1983
TO BE OR NOT TO BE   20th Century-Fox, 1983
GHOST DANCING (TF)   Herbert Brodkin Productions/The Eugene
   O'Neill Memorial Theatre Center/Titus Productions, 1983
JOHNNY DANGEROUSLY   20th Century Fox, 1984
THE WOMAN IN RED   Orion, 1984
THE DOCTOR AND THE DEVILS   20th Century Fox, 1985, British
CLUE   Paramount, 1985
HAUNTED HONEYMOON   Orion, 1986
FRESNO (MS)   MTM Productions, 1986
DIRTY DANCING   Vestron, 1987
SPACEBALLS   MGM/UA, 1987
IRONWEED   Tri-Star, 1987
THE LITTLE MATCH GIRL (TF)   NBC Productions, 1987
THE WASH   Skouras Pictures, 1988
FAVORITE SON (MS)   NBC Productions, 1988
SECOND SIGHT   Warner Bros., 1989
STELLA   Buena Vista, 1990
THE LAST TO GO (TF)   Freyda Rothstein/Interscope, 1991
CAROLINA SKELETONS (TF)   Kushner-Locke, 1991
LIFE STINKS   MGM, 1991
WORLD WAR II: WHEN LIONS ROARED (TF)   WWII Co./Gideon
   Prods., 1994
SCARLETT (TF)   RHI/Beta Film/Silvio Berlusconi Comm./TF1,
   1994

VAN MORRISON

b. 1945
Contact: BMI - Los Angeles, 310-659-9109

SLIPSTREAM   co-composer, 1974, Canadian
LAMB   Limehouse/Flickers/Channel Four, 1985, British

CHARLES MORROW

Contact: ASCAP - Los Angeles, 213-883-1000

THE MAN WITHOUT A WORLD   co-composer with Lee Erwin,
   Milestone, 1992

JONATHAN MORSE

(Fuzzbee Morse)
Contact: BMI - Los Angeles, 310-659-9109

DOLLS   Empire Pictures, 1987
EVOLUTION (FD)   Elan Vital Production
GHOULIES II   Empire Pictures, 1988

THOMAS MORSE*

Contact: BMI - Los Angeles, 310-659-9109

RHINOSKIN: THE MAKING OF A MOVIE STAR (FD)   co-composer
   with Ian Christian Nickus, Hapwood, 1994

ARTHUR MORTON

Contact: BMI - Los Angeles, 310-659-9109

NIGHT LIFE OF THE GODS   Universal, 1935
PRINCESS O'HARA   Universal, 1935
PICK A STAR   co-composer with T. Marvin Hatley, MGM, 1937
RIDING ON AIR   RKO Radio, 1937
FIT FOR A KING   RKO Radio, 1937
THE DAY THE BOOKIES WEPT   RKO Radio, 1939
TURNABOUT   United Artists, 1940
MILLIE'S DAUGHTER   Columbia, 1947
IT HAD TO BE YOU   co-composer with Heinz Roemheld,
   Columbia, 1947
THE THIRTEENTH HOUR   Columbia, 1947
THE WALKING HILLS   Columbia, 1949
THE NEVADAN   Columbia, 1950
FATHER IS A BACHELOR   Columbia, 1950
ROGUES OF SHERWOOD FOREST   co-composer with Heinz
   Roemheld, Columbia, 1950
NEVER TRUST A GAMBLER   Columbia, 1951
THE HARLEM GLOBETROTTERS   Columbia, 1951
MEDICAL STORY (TF)   David Gerber Productions/Columbia
   Pictures TV, 1975

MARK MOTHERSBAUGH

Agent: Vangelos Management - Encino, 818-380-1919
Affiliation: BMI - Los Angeles, 310-659-9109

HUMAN HIGHWAY   co-composer with Neil Young (as a member of
   Devo), Shakey Pictures, 1982
TAPEHEADS   Avenue Pictures, 1988
SOUTH BEACH (TF)   Wolf Films/Universal, 1993
SECOND CHANCES (TF)   Latham-Lechowick Prods., 1993
IT'S PAT   Buena Vista, 1994
THE NEW AGE   Warner Bros., 1994
FLESH SUITCASE   Valiant Films, 1995
THE LAST SUPPER   Sony Classics, 1996
BOTTLE ROCKET   Columbia, 1996
HAPPY GILMORE   Universal, 1996
THE BIG SQUEEZE   1996
BEST MEN   Orion, 1997
MEN   Gramercy, 1997
MR. MAGOO   Buena Vista, 1997
NO BEST MAN   Orion, 1997

TONY MOTTOLA

Contact: ASCAP - Los Angeles, 213-883-1000

RUNNING ON EMPTY   Warner Bros., 1988

WILLIAM MOTZIG

Contact: ASCAP - Los Angeles, 213-883-1000

NEWSFRONT   1978, Australian
THE RETURN OF CAPTAIN INVINCIBLE   *LEGEND IN
   LEOTARDS*   New World, 1983, Australian
SILVER CITY   1984, Australian
THE COCA COLA KID   Cinecom/Film Gallery, 1985, Australian
THE FIRST KANGAROOS (TF)   Roadshow/Channel 4, 1987,
   Australian
ECHOES OF PARADISE   *SHADOWS OF THE PEACOCK*   Castle
   Hill Productions/Quartet Films, 1987, Australian
YOUNG EINSTEIN   co-composer with Martin Arminger and Tommy
   Tycho, Warner Bros., 1989, Australian

ROB MOUNSEY
Contact: ASCAP - Los Angeles, 213-883-1000

BRIGHT LIGHTS, BIG CITY   additional music, MGM/UA, 1988
WORKING GIRL   additional music, 20th Century Fox, 1988
TAKEN AWAY (TF)   Hart, Thomas & Berlin Productions, 1989
DANGEROUS PASSION (TF)   Stormy Weathers Production/Davis
    Entertainment, 1990

OLIVER MTUKUDZI
NERIA   KJM3, 1993, Zimbabwe

JAMES MTUME
Contact: BMI - Los Angeles, 310-659-9109

NATIVE SON   Cinecom, 1986

DOMINIC MULDOWNEY
Contact: PRS - London, England, 011-44-1-580-5544

BETRAYAL   20th Century-Fox International Classics, 1983, British
THE PLOUGHMAN'S LUNCH   Samuel Goldwyn Company, 1983,
    British
LOOSE CONNECTIONS   co-composer with Andy Roberts, Orion
    Classics, 1983, British
LAUGHTER HOUSE (TF)   Film Four International, 1984, British
1984   co-composer with Eurythmics, Atlantic Releasing
    Corporation, 1984, British
TALES FROM HOLLYWOOD (TF)   BBC-TV/American Playhouse,
    1992, British-U.S.

GERRY MULLIGAN
I'M NOT RAPPAPORT   1996

MURRAY MUNRO
Contact: PRS - London, England, 011-44-1-580-5544

PRIVATE INVESTIGATIONS   MGM/UA, 1987

JUDY MUNSEN
Contact: BMI - Los Angeles, 310-659-9109

STREET MUSIC   co-composer with Ed Bogas, Specialty Films,
    1983

MICHAEL MARTIN MURPHEY
Contact: BMI - Los Angeles, 310-659-9109

HARD COUNTRY   co-composer with Jimmie Haskell,
    Universal/AFD, 1981

WALTER MURPHY
Agent: Air-Edel - Los Angeles, 310-914-5000
Affiliation: BMI - Los Angeles, 310-659-9109

THE SAVAGE BEES (TF)   Landsburg-Kirshner Productions/NBC,
    1976
THE NIGHT THEY TOOK MISS BEAUTIFUL (TF)   Don Kirshner
    Productions/LaRose Productions, 1977
RAW FORCE   American Panorama, 1982
TRICKS OF THE TRADE (TF)   Leonard Hill Films, 1988
THE LADY FORGETS (TF)   Leonard Hill Films, 1989

WILLIAM MURPHY
BOUND AND GAGGED, A LOVE STORY   G.E.L./Cinescope, 1993

SEAN MURRAY
Contact: BMI - Los Angeles, 310-659-9109

SCORPION   Crown International, 1986

ALFREDO MUSCHIETTO
DONNE IN UN GIORNO DI FESTA   *WOMEN ON A HOLIDAY*
    1993, Italian

JENNIE MUSKETT
Contact: PRS - London, England, 011-44-1-580-5544

SPIRITS OF THE RAINFOREST (TD)   Discovery Prods., 1993

JOHN MUSSER
Contact: BMI - Los Angeles, 310-659-9109

SOME KIND OF WONDERFUL   co-composer with Stephen Hague,
    Paramount, 1987

JEAN MUSY
Contact: SACEM - France, 011-33-1-4715-4715

CLAIRE DE FEMME   Atlantic Releasing Corporation, 1979,
    French-Italian-West German
CHANEL SOLITAIRE   United Film Distribution, 1981,
    French-British
TANYA'S ISLAND   International Film Exchange/Fred Baker Films,
    1981, Canadian
LA PALOMBIERE   *THE BIRD WATCH*   Gaumont, 1983, French
PRENDS TON PASSE-MONTAGNE ON VA A LA PLAGE!   UGC,
    1983, French
ITINERAIRE BIS   *SIDEROADS*   1983, French

BILL MYERS
Contact: BMI - Los Angeles, 310-659-9109

ALL'S FAIR   Moviestore Entertainment, 1989

LENNY MYERS
BAR GIRLS   Lavender Hill Mob, 1994

PETER MYERS
Agent: Film Music Associates - Hollywood, 213-463-1070
Affiliation: ASCAP - Los Angeles, 213-883-1000

STUNT SEVEN (TF)   additional music, Martin Poll Productions,
    1979
STARK (TF)   CBS Entertainment, 1985
DEATH OF AN ANGEL   20th Century Fox, 1985
STARK: MIRROR IMAGE (TF)   CBS Entertainment, 1986
DYNASTY: THE REUNION (TF)   Richard and Esther Shapiro
    Prods./Aaron Spelling Prods., 1991
TRADE WINDS (TF)   Cramer Co./NBC Prods., 1993

FRED MYROW
Contact: ASCAP - Los Angeles, 213-883-1000

LEO THE LAST   United Artists, 1970, British
IN SEARCH OF AMERICA (TF)   Four Star International, 1971
THE STEAGLE   Avco Embassy, 1971
SOYLENT GREEN   co-composer with Gerald Fried, MGM, 1972
SCARECROW   Warner Bros., 1973
A REFLECTION OF FEAR   Columbia, 1973, British
LOLLY-MADONNA XXX   MGM, 1973
MESSAGE TO MY DAUGHTER (TF)   Charles Fries
    Productions/Metromedia Producers Corporation, 1973
PRAY FOR THE WILDCATS (TF)   ABC Circle Films, 1974
JIM, THE WORLD'S GREATEST   Universal, 1976
BLUE ANGELS   1976
KENNY & COMPANY   20th Century-Fox, 1976
THE SECRET LIFE OF JOHN CHAPMAN (TF)   The Jozak
    Company, 1976
PHANTASM   co-composer with Malcolm Seagrave, Avco Embassy,
    1979
ON THE NICKEL   Rose's Park, 1980
HOUR OF THE ASSASSIN   Concorde, 1987, U.S.-Peruvian
PHANTASM II   Universal, 1988
JOURNEY TO SPIRIT ISLAND   Pal Prods.-Seven Wonders
    Entertainment, 1988
RUBIN AND ED   Working Title, 1991

N

ANGELIQUE NACHON
ALBERTO EXPRESS   co-composer with Jean-Claude Nachon, 1990, French
TANGO   co-composer with Jean-Claude Nachon, 1993, French

JEAN-CLAUDE NACHON
ALBERTO EXPRESS   co-composer with Angelique Nachon, 1990, French
TANGO   co-composer with Angelique Nachon, 1993, French

SEAN NAIDOO
TOUGHGUY   Green Tea/Net City, 1995

MARK NAKAMURA
PROVOCATEUR   co-composer with Richard Uglow, Capella, 1997

YURIKO NAKAMURA
b. Japan
Contact: JASRAC - Tokyo, Japan, 011-81-3-502-6551

SUMMER VACATION: 1999   New Yorker, 1989, Japanese

GIUSEPPE NAPOLI
MANILA PALOMA BLANCA   1993, Italian

ANDY NARRELL
Contact: BMI - Los Angeles, 310-659-9109

SIGNAL 7   Myron-Taylor Productions, 1986

NASH THE SLASH
Contact: SOCAN - Toronto, 416-445-8700

HIGHWAY 61   Shadow Shows, 1991, Canadian

LOUIS NATALE
Agent: Film Music Associates - Hollywood, 213-463-1070
Affiliation: SOCAN - Toronto, 416-445-8700

COWBOYS DON'T CRY   Cineplex Odeon, 1988, Canadian
LAST TRAIN HOME (CTF)   Atlantis Films/Great North Productions/CBC, 1990, Canadian-U.S.
THE GIRL FROM MARS (CTF)   Northstar/Family Channel/South Pacific, 1991
DEADLY BETRAYAL: THE BRUCE CURTIS STORY (TF)   Atlantis Films/Citadel, 1992, Canadian
PARTNERS 'N LOVE (CTF)   Atlantis/Barry Jossen Prods./Family Channel, 1992
ADRIFT (TF)   Atlantis/WIC, 1993
SNOWBOUND: THE JIM AND JENNIFER STOLPA STORY (TF)   Pacific Motion Pictures (Stolpa) Prods./Jaffe-Braunstein Films, 1994

RAY NATHANSON
HAPPILY EVER AFTER: FAIRY TALES FOR EVERY CHILD (ATF)   co-composer, Two Oceans/Confetti/Hyperion, 1995

BRUCE NAZARIAN
Contact: ASCAP - Los Angeles, 213-883-1000

DON'T TELL MOM THE BABYSITTER'S DEAD   additional music, Warner Bros., 1991

CHRIS NEAL
b. Australia
Contact: APRA - Australia, 011-61-2-922-6422

BUDDIES   1983, Australian
REBEL   Vestron, 1985, Australian
SHORT CHANGED   Greater Union, 1986, Australian
BULLSEYE   Cinema Group, 1987, Australian
GROUND ZERO   Avenue Pictures, 1987, Australian
THE SHIRALEE (MS)   SAFC Productions, 1988, Australian
GRIEVOUS BODILY HARM   International Film Management, 1988, Australian
EMERALD CITY   Greater Union, 1989, Australian
CELIA   Hoyts, 1989, Australian
TROUBLE IN PARADISE (TF)   Qintex Entertainment, 1989, U.S.-Australian
TURTLE BEACH   Warner Bros., 1992
THE NOSTRADAMUS KID   1993, Australian
JACK BE NIMBLE   1993, New Zealand

LITTO NEBBIA
Contact: SADAIC - Argentina, 011-54-1-40-4867/8

MATAR AL ABUELTO   *KILLING GRANDDAD*   1993, Argentine

ROGER NEILL
Agent: Zomba Screen Music - West Hollywood, 310-246-0777
Affiliation: BMI - Los Angeles, 310-659-9109

AN AMERICAN SUMMER   Boss Entertainment Group, 1989
SAVAGE   Mahogany Pictures, 1995
MERCENARY   Mahogany Pictures, 1996
BLOOD MONEY (CTF)   Concorde/New Horizons, 1996
THE OUTSIDER   Mahogany Pictures, 1996
TRUE BLUE   Mahogany Pictures, 1997
THE SEA WOLF   Concorde, 1997
URBAN JUSTICE (CTF)   Concorde/New Horizons, 1996
RULES OF ENGAGEMENT   Mahogany Pictures, 1997

BILL NELSON
Contact: PRS - London, England, 011-44-1-580-5544

DREAM DEMON   Spectrafilm, 1988, British

STEVE NELSON
Contact: ASCAP - Los Angeles, 213-883-1000

LAST RESORT   co-composer with Thom Sharp, Concorde, 1986

WILLIE NELSON
b. April 30, 1933 - Abbott, Texas
Contact: BMI - Los Angeles, 310-659-9109

HONEYSUCKLE ROSE   co-composer with Richard Baskin, Warner Bros., 1980
STAGECOACH (TF)   co-composer with David Allan Coe, Raymond Katz Productions/Heritage Entertainment, 1986

JOHN NESCHLING
Contact: SICAM - Brazil, 011-55-11-223-8555

LUCIO FLAVIO   Unifilm/Embrafilme, 1978, Brazilian
KISS OF THE SPIDER WOMAN   Island Alive/Film Dallas, 1985, Brazillian-U.S.

MICHAEL NESMITH
Contact: BMI - Los Angeles, 310-659-9109

TIMERIDER   Jensen Farley Pictures, 1983

ETHAN NEUBURG
Contact: ASCAP - Los Angeles, 213-883-1000

BUM RAP   co-composer with Robert Kessler, Millennium, 1988

ROBERT NEUFELD
CREATURES OF LIGHT   1992, British

WOLFGANG NEUMANN
DIE MACHT DER BILER: LENI RIEFENSTAHL   *THE POWER OF THE IMAGE: LENI RIEFENSTAHL* (FD)   co-composer with Ulrich Bassenge, 1993, German-British-French

IRA NEWBORN
Agent: Vangelos Management - Encino, 818-380-1919
Affiliation: ASCAP - Los Angeles, 213-883-1000

THE BLUES BROTHERS   Universal, 1980
ALL NIGHT LONG   co-composer with Richard Hazard, Universal, 1981
SIXTEEN CANDLES   Universal, 1984
INTO THE NIGHT   Universal, 1985
WEIRD SCIENCE   Universal, 1985
FERRIS BUELLER'S DAY OFF   Paramount, 1986
WISE GUYS   MGM/UA, 1986
DRAGNET   Universal, 1987
AMAZON WOMEN ON THE MOON   Universal, 1987
PLANES, TRAINS AND AUTOMOBILES   Paramount, 1987
CADDYSHACK II   Warner Bros., 1988
THE NAKED GUN: FROM THE FILES OF POLICE SQUAD!   Paramount, 1988
UNCLE BUCK   Universal, 1989
CAST THE FIRST STONE (TF)   Mench Productions/Columbia Pictures TV, 1989
SHORT TIME   20th Century-Fox, 1990
MY BLUE HEAVEN   Warner Bros., 1990
THE NAKED GUN 2 1/2: THE SMELL OF FEAR   Paramount, 1991
BRAIN DONORS   Paramount, 1992
INNOCENT BLOOD   Warner Bros., 1992
THE OPPOSITE SEX AND HOW TO LIVE WITH THEM   Miramax, 1993
ACE VENTURA, PET DETECTIVE   Warner Bros., 1994
NAKED GUN 33 1/3: THE FINAL INSULT   Paramount, 1994
THE JERKY BOYS   Buena Vista, 1995
MALLRATS   Gramercy, 1995
THE LATE SHIFT (CTF)   HBO/Northern Lights, 1996
HIGH SCHOOL HIGH   TriStar, 1996
GHOST IN THE MACHINE   Davis Entertainment Classics, 1997

DAVID NEWMAN
b. 1954
Agent: The Kraft-Benjamin Agency - Beverly Hills, 310-247-0123
Affiliation: BMI - Los Angeles, 310-659-9109

CRITTERS   New Line Cinema, 1985
VENDETTA   Concorde, 1986
THE KINDRED   FM Entertainment, 1987
THE BRAVE LITTLE TOASTER (TF)   Hyperion-Kushner-Locke Productions, 1987
MALONE   Orion, 1987
MY DEMON LOVER   New Line Cinema, 1987
THROW MOMMA FROM THE TRAIN   Orion, 1987
PASS THE AMMO   Vista Films, 1988
HEATHERS   New World, 1989
BILL & TED'S EXCELLENT ADVENTURE   Orion, 1989
DISORGANIZED CRIME   Buena Vista, 1989
LITTLE MONSTERS   Vestron, 1989
THE WAR OF THE ROSES   20th Century Fox, 1989
GROSS ANATOMY   Touchstone, 1989
MADHOUSE   Orion, 1990
FIRE BIRDS   Buena Visa, 1990
THE FRESHMAN   Tri-Star, 1990
MR. DESTINY   Buena Vista, 1990
MEET THE APPLEGATES   New World, 1991
THE MARRYING MAN   Buena Vista, 1991
DON'T TELL MOM THE BABYSITTER'S DEAD   Warner Bros., 1991
BILL AND TED'S BOGUS JOURNEY   Orion, 1991
ROVER DANGERFIELD (AF)   Warner Bros., 1991
TALENT FOR THE GAME   Paramount, 1991
PARADISE   Buena Vista, 1991
OTHER PEOPLE'S MONEY   Warner Bros., 1991
HONEYMOON IN VEGAS   Buena Vista, 1992
THE RUNESTONE   Hyperion/Signature, 1992
THE MIGHTY DUCKS   Buena Vista, 1992

THAT NIGHT   Warner Bros., 1992
HOFFA   20th Century Fox, 1992
THE SANDLOT   20th Century Fox, 1993
CONEHEADS   Paramount, 1993
UNDERCOVER BLUES   MGM, 1993
THE AIR UP THERE   Buena Vista, 1994
MY FATHER THE HERO   Buena Vista, 1994
THE COWBOY WAY   Universal, 1994
THE FLINTSTONES   Universal, 1994
I LOVE TROUBLE   Buena Vista, 1994
BOYS ON THE SIDE   Warner Bros., 1995
TOMMY BOY   Paramount, 1995
OPERATION DUMBO DROP   Buena Vista, 1995
BIG BULLY   Warner Bros., 1996
THE PHANTOM   Paramount, 1996
THE NUTTY PROFESSOR   Universal, 1996
MATILDA   TriStar, 1996
JINGLE ALL THE WAY   20th Century Fox, 1996
OUT TO SEA   Fox, 1997

RANDY NEWMAN
b. November 28, 1943 - Los Angeles, California
Agent: Gorfaine-Schwartz - Los Angeles, 213-969-1011
Affiliation: ASCAP - Los Angeles, 213-883-1000

COLD TURKEY   United Artists, 1971
RAGTIME ★   Paramount, 1981
THE NATURAL ★   Tri-Star, 1984
PARENTHOOD   Universal, 1989
AVALON   Columbia, 1990
AWAKENINGS   Columbia, 1990
THE PAPER   Universal, 1994
MAVERICK   Warner Bros., 1994
TOY STORY (AF) ★   Buena Vista, 1995
JAMES AND THE GIANT PEACH (AF) ★   Buena Vista, 1996
MICHAEL   New Line, 1996

THOMAS NEWMAN
Agent: Gorfaine-Schwartz - Los Angeles, 213-969-1011
Affiliation: BMI - Los Angeles, 310-659-9109

GRANDVIEW, U.S.A.   Warner Bros., 1984
THE SEDUCTION OF GINA (TF)   Bertinelli-Jaffee Productions, 1984
RECKLESS   MGM/UA, 1984
REVENGE OF THE NERDS   20th Century Fox, 1984
GIRLS JUST WANT TO HAVE FUN   New World, 1985
DESPERATELY SEEKING SUSAN   Orion, 1985
THE MAN WITH ONE RED SHOE   20th Century Fox, 1985
REAL GENIUS   Tri-Star, 1985
GUNG HO   Paramount, 1986
JUMPIN' JACK FLASH   20th Century Fox, 1986
QUICKSILVER   additional music, Columbia, 1986
LIGHT OF DAY   Tri-Star, 1987
THE LOST BOYS   Warner Bros., 1987
LESS THAN ZERO   20th Century Fox, 1987
THE GREAT OUTDOORS   Universal, 1988
THE PRINCE OF PENNSYLVANIA   New Line Cinema, 1988
COOKIE   Warner Bros., 1989
MEN DON'T LEAVE   The Geffen Company/Warner Bros., 1990
NAKED TANGO   Sugarloaf/Gotan, 1990
WELCOME HOME, ROXY CARMICHAEL   Paramount, 1990
HEAT WAVE (CTF)   Avnet-Kenner/Propaganda, 1991
CAREER OPPORTUNITIES   Universal, 1991
DECEIVED   Touchstone, 1991
THE RAPTURE   Fine Line, 1991
FRIED GREEN TOMATOES   Universal, 1991
THOSE SECRETS (TF)   Sarabande Prods., 1992
THE LINGUINI INCIDENT   Academy Entertainment, 1992
THE PLAYER   Fine Line, 1992
WHISPERS IN THE DARK   Paramount, 1992
CITIZEN COHN (CTF)   Spring Creek Prods./Breakheart Films/Viacom, 1992
SCENT OF A WOMAN   Universal, 1992
FLESH AND BONE   Paramount, 1993
JOSH AND S.A.M.   1993
THREESOME   TriStar, 1994
THE FAVOR   Orion, 1994
CORRINA, CORRINA   themes only, New Line, 1994
THE WAR   Universal, 1994
THE SHAWSHANK REDEMPTION ★   Columbia, 1994

LITTLE WOMEN ★   Columbia, 1994
HOW TO MAKE AN AMERICAN QUILT   Universal, 1995
UNSTRUNG HEROES ★   Buena Vista, 1995
UP CLOSE AND PERSONAL   Buena Vista, 1996
PHENOMENON   Buena Vista, 1996
AMERICAN BUFFALO   Samuel Goldwyn, 1996
THE PEOPLE VS. LARRY FLYNT   Columbia, 1996

DAVID NICHTERN

Contact: BMI - Los Angeles, 310-659-9109

WHITE LINE FEVER   Columbia, 1975
THE BIG PICTURE   Columbia, 1989
THE SPIRIT OF '76   Columbia, 1990

IAN CHRISTIAN NICKUS

RHINOSKIN: THE MAKING OF A MOVIE STAR (FD)   co-composer
with Thomas Morse, Hapwood, 1994

BRUNO NICOLAI

b. 1926 - Italy
Contact: SIAE - Italy, 011-39-6-59-901

MONDO CANE #2   co-composer with Nino Olivieri, 1963, Italian
IL PELO NEL MONDO   co-composer with Nino Olivieri, 1963,
Italian
VITA DI MICHELANGELO (TF)   1964, Italian
10,000 DOLLARI PER RINGO   1965, Italian
MISSIONE SPECIALE LADY CHAPLIN   1966, Italian
EL CISCO   1966, Italian
DA BERLINO L'APOCALISSE   1966, Italian-West German
99 WOMEN   1966, Italian
THE CHRISTMAS THAT ALMOST WASN'T   1966, Italian-U.S.
ROMEO AND JULIET   adaptation, 1966, Italian
DJANGO SPARA PER PRIMO   1966, Italian
AGENTE SPECIALE - OPERAZIONE RE MIDA   1966, Italian
KISS KISS BANG BANG   1966, Spanish
LUCKY EL INTREPIDO   1967, Italian
OPERATION KID BROTHER   O.K. CONNERY   co-composer with
Ennio Morricone, 1967, Italian
I GIORNI DELLA VIOLENZA   1967, Italian
THE DITY HEROES   DALLE ARDENNE ALL'INFERNO
co-composer with Ennio Morricone, 1968, Italian
RUN MAN RUN!   1968, Italian
FLASHBACK   1968
JUSTINE OVVERO LE DISAVVENTURE DELLA VIRTU   1968,
Italian
GIUGNO '44, SBARCHEREMO IN NORMANDIA   1968, Italian
LA BATTAGLIA DEL DESERTO   1968, Italian
ROME LIKE CHICAGO   co-composer with Ennio Morricone, 1968,
Italian
RINGO, DOVE VAI?   1968, Italian
GENTLEMAN JO...UCCIDI   1968, Italian
THE MERCENARY   co-composer with Ennio Morricone, 1969,
Italian
THE INSATIADLES   FEMMINE INSAZIABILI   1969, Italian
LA SFIDA DI MACKENNA   1969, Italian
LOVE BIRDS   1969, Italian
THE LAST MERCENARY   1969, Italian
LAND RAIDERS   1969, Italian
ZENABEL   1969, Italian
EUGENIE...THE STORY OF HER JOURNEY INTO PERVERSION
MARQUIS DE SADE   1969, Italian
REBUS (TF)   1969, Italian
LES CAUCHEMARS NAISSENT LA NUIT   1970, Italian
GEMINUS (TF)   1970, Italian
COUNT DRACULA   NIGHTS OF DRACULA   1970, Spanish
SEX CHARADE   1970, Italian
X312 FLUG ZUR HOLLE   co-composer with Wolf Hartmayer, 1970,
West German
PAOLO E FRANCESCA   1970, Italian
DIO IN CIELO, ARIZONA IN TERRA   1970, Italian
ADIOS, SABATA   1970, Italian
AMERICA...COSI NUDA, COSI VIOLENTA   1970, Italian
I DUE MAGHI DEL PALLONE   1970, Italian
ROBIN HOOD, L'INVINCIBILE ARCIERE   1970, Italian
ARIZONA SI SCATENO...E LI FECE FUORI TUTTI   1970, Italian
BUON FUNERALE, AMIGOS...PAGE SARTANA   1970, Italian
DUE BIANCHI NELL 'AFRICA NERA   1970, Italian
UNA NUVOLA DI POLVERE   1970, Italian

UN UOMO CHIAMATO APOCALISSE JOE   1970, Italian
ANDA MUCHACHO, SPARA!   1971, Italian
LA CODA DELLO SCORPIONE   1971, Italian
GLI FUMAVANO LE COLT   1971, Italian
IL SOLE SOTTO TERRA   1971, Italian
LO CHIAMAVANO SPIRITO SANTO   1971, Italian
LOS BUITRES CARAVAN TU FOSA   1971, Spanish
CHRISTINA PRINCESSE DE L'EROTISME   co-composer with
Jesus Franco, 1971, Italian-French
DRACULA CONTRA EL DR. FRANKENSTEIN   co-composer with
Daniel J. White, 1971, Italian-West German
EL CRISTO DEL OCEANO   CHRIST OF THE OCEAN   1971,
Italian
ROBINSON UND SEINE WILDEN SKLAVINNEN   co-composer with
Daniel J. White, 1971, West German
LA PREDA E L'AVVOLTOIO   1972, Italian
QUANDO LE DONNE PERSERO LA CODA   co-composer with
Ennio Morricone, 1972, Italian
UNE JOURNEE BIEN REMPLIE   1972, French-Italian
COSI SIA   1972, Italian
DOMANI PASSERO A SALUTARE LA TUA VEDOVA...PAROLIA DI
EPIDEMIA!   1972, Italian
IL TUO VIZIO E UNA STANZA CHIUSA E SOLO IO NE HO LA
CHIAVE   EXCITE ME   1972, Italian
L'ALPIN L'E SEMPRE QUEL   1972, French-Italian
LOS AMANTES DE LA ISLA DEL DIABLO   1972, Spanish
UN CAPITAN DE QUINCE ANOS   co-composer with Daniel J.
White, 1972, Spanish
QUEL GRAN PEZZO DELL'UBALDA, TUTTA NUDA E TUTTA
CALDA   1972, Italian
LA DAMA ROSSA UCCIDE SETTE VOLTE   1972, Italian
NIGHT OF THE BLOOD MONSTER   THRONE OF FIRE   1972,
Italian
PERCHE QUELLE STRANE GOCCI DE SANGUE SIL CORPE DE
JENNIFER?   WHAT ARE THOSE STRANGE DROPS OF
BLOOD ON THE BODY OF JENNIFER?   1972, Italian
TUTTI I COLORI DEL BUIO   ALL THE COLORS OF
DARKNESS/THEY'RE COMING TO GET YOU   1972, Italian
DEFENSE DE SAVOIR   1973, French-Italian
IL MIO NOME E SHANGHAI JOE   1973, Italian
LE CHEMIN SOLITAIRE   1973, French-Italian
CI RISIAMO, VERO PROVVIDENZA?   co-composer with Ennio
Morricone, 1973, Italian
LO CHIAMAVANO "TRESETTE"   1973, Italian
L'ONORATO FAMIGLIA UCCIDERE E COSA NOSTRA   1973,
Italian
ELEANORA (TF)   1973, Italian
THE NIGHT EVELYN CAME OUT OF THE GRAVE   1973, Italian
L'ANTICRISTO   ANTICHRIST/THE TEMPTER   co-composer with
Ennio Morricone, 1974, Italian
DON GIOVANNI IN SICILIA (TF)   1974, Italian
I FIGLI CHIEDONE PERCHE   1974, Italian
ALLORA IL TRENO   1974, Italian
TEN LITTLE INDIANS   Talia Films, 1975,
Italian-French-Spanish-German
GATTI ROSSI IN UN LABIRINTO DI VETRO   1975, Italian
L'UOMO DELLA STRADA FA GIUSTIZIA   1975, Italian
LA FURIE DU DESIR   1975, French
I MIEI AMICI (TF)   1976, Italian
IL MAESTRO DI VIOLINO   1976, Italian
DUE MAGNUM 38 PER UNA CITTA DI CAROGNE   1976, Italian
LEZIONI DI VIOLONCELLO   1976, Italian
LUCA, BAMBINO MIO   1977, Italian
OLTRE LA NOTTE   1977, Italian
EYEBALL   1978, Italian
IL CAPPOTTO DI ASTRAKAN   1980, Italian
GOODBYE MARY (TF)   1980, Italian
CAMMINA CAMMINA   Gaumont, 1983, Italian

LENNIE NIEHAUS*

Agent: Robert Light - Los Angeles, 213-651-1777
Affiliation: BMI - Los Angeles, 310-659-9109

TIGHTROPE   Warner Bros., 1984
CITY HEAT   Warner Bros., 1984
SESAME STREET PRESENTS: FOLLOW THAT BIRD
co-composer with Van Dyke Parks, Warner Bros., 1985
PALE RIDER   Warner Bros., 1985
NEVER TOO YOUNG TO DIE   Paul Releasing 1986
RATBOY   Warner Bros., 1986
HEARTBREAK RIDGE   Warner Bros., 1986

EMANON   Paul Releasing 1987
THE CHILD SAVER (TF)   Michael Filerman Productions/NBC
   Productions, 1988
BIRD   Warner Bros., 1988
HOT MEN   1989
WHITE HUNTER, BLACK HEART   Warner Bros., 1990
THE ROOKIE   Warner Bros., 1990
UNFORGIVEN   Universal, 1992
A PERFECT WORLD   Warner Bros., 1993
LUSH LIFE (CTF) ☆☆   Showtime, 1993
THE BRIDGES OF MADISON COUNTY   Warner Bros., 1995
ABSOLUTE POWER   Warner Bros., 1997

JOSE NIETO
b. Madrid, 1942
Contact: SGAE - Spain, 011-34-1-319-2100

INTRUSO   INTRUDER   1993, Spanish
EL AMANTE BILINGE   THE BILINGUAL LOVER   1993, Spanish
GUANTANAMERA   1995, Spanish
OF LOVE AND SHADOWS   Miramax, 1996

STEFAN NILSSON
Contact: STIM - Sweden, 011-46-8-783-8800

PELLE THE CONQUEROR   Miramax Films, 1988,
   Danish-Swedish
DEN GODA VILJEAN   THE BEST INTENTIONS   1992, Swedish

JACK NITZCHE*
b. 1937 - Chicago, Illinois
Agent: CAA - Beverly Hills, 310-288-4545
Affiliation: ASCAP - Los Angeles, 213-883-1000

THE T.A.M.I. SHOW   1964
VILLAGE OF THE GIANTS   Embassy, 1965
PERFORMANCE   Warner Bros., 1970, British
GREASER'S PALACE   Greaser's Palace, 1972
THE EXORCIST   co-composer, Warner Bros., 1973
ONE FLEW OVER THE CUCKOO'S NEST ★   United Artists, 1976
HEROES   co-composer with Richard Hazard, Universal, 1977
BLUE COLLAR   Universal, 1978
HARDCORE   Columbia, 1979
WHEN YOU COMIN' BACK, RED RYDER?   Columbia, 1979
HEART BEAT   Orion/Warner Bros., 1980
CRUISING   United Artists, 1980
CUTTER'S WAY   CUTTER AND BONE   United Artists Classics,
   1981
CANNERY ROW   MGM/UA, 1982
PERSONAL BEST   co-composer with Jill Fraser, The Geffen
   Company/Warner Bros., 1982
AN OFFICER AND A GENTLEMAN ★   Paramount, 1982
BREATHLESS   Orion, 1983
WITHOUT A TRACE   20th Century-Fox, 1983
THE RAZOR'S EDGE   Columbia, 1984
STARMAN   Columbia, 1984
WINDY CITY   Warner Bros., 1984
STRIPPER   co-composer with Buffy Sainte-Marie, 20th Century
   Fox, 1985
JEWEL OF THE NILE   20th Century-Fox, 1985
9-1/2 WEEKS   MGM/UA, 1986
STAND BY ME   Columbia, 1986
THE WHOOPEE BOYS   Paramount, 1986
STREETS OF GOLD   20th Century Fox, 1986
THE SEVENTH SIGN   Tri-Star, 1988
REVENGE   Columbia, 1989
NEXT OF KIN   Warner Bros., 1989
THE HOT SPOT   Orion, 1990
REVENGE   Columbia, 1990
THE LAST OF THE FINEST   Orion, 1990
MERMAIDS   Orion, 1990
THE INDIAN RUNNER   Mount, 1991
MIDDLE AGES (TF)   Stan Rogow Prods./Paramount TV, 1992
BLUE SKY   Orion, 1994

MATT NOBLE
Contact: BMI - Los Angeles, 310-659-9109

JASON'S LYRIC   co-composer with Afrika, Gramercy, 1994

NAZ NOMAD
GIVE DADDY THE KNIFE   1984

ERIC NORDGREN
b. 1913 - Sweden
Contact: STIM - Sweden, 011-46-8-783-8800

KVINNA UTAN ANSIKTE   1947, Swedish
EVA   1948, Swedish
THREE STRANGE LOVES   THIRST   Janus, 1949, Swedish
DIVORCE   1951, Swedish
THIS CAN'T HAPPEN HERE   Svensk Filmindustri, 1951, Swedish
ILLICIT INTERLUDE   SOMMARLEK   Janus, 1951, Swedish
SECRETS OF WOMEN   Janus, 1952, Swedish
MONIKA   Janus, 1953, Swedish
SMILES OF A SUMMER NIGHT   Janus, 1955, Swedish
LAST PAIR OUT   1956, Swedish
THE SEVENTH SEAL   Janus, 1957, Swedish
WILD STRAWBERRIES   Janus, 1957, Swedish
THE MAGICIAN   Janus, 1958, Swedish
FACE OF FIRE   Allied Artists, 1959
THE VIRGIN SPRING   Janus, 1960, Swedish
PLEASURE GARDEN   1961, Swedish
ALL THESE WOMEN   Janus, 1964, Swedish
THE ISLAND   1966, Swedish

ARNE NORDHEIM
Contact: TONO - Norway, 011-47-2-17-0500

STELLA POLARIS   1993, Norwegian

JOHN E. NORDSTROM II
Agent: Gorfaine-Schwartz - Los Angeles, 213-969-1011
Affiliation: ASCAP - Los Angeles, 213-883-1000

TOO SOON FOR JEFF (TF)   ABC Prods., 1996
RAVAGER   Republic, 1997

PER NORGAARD
Contact: TONO - Norway, 011-47-2-17-0500

PRINCE OF JUTLAND   1994, French-British-Danish-German

MONTY NORMAN
Contact: PRS - London, England, 011-44-1-580-5544

HOUSE OF FRIGHT   THE TWO FACES OF DR. JEKYLL
   co-composer with David Heneker, American International, 1960,
   British
DR. NO   United Artists, 1962, British

CRAIG NORTHEY
KIDS IN THE HALL: BRAIN CANDY   1996

JULIAN NOTT
Contact: PRS - London, England, 011-44-1-580-5544
Agent: Zomba Screen Music - West Hollywood, 310-246-0777

A MAN OF NO IMPORTANCE   Sony Classics, 1994, British

MOHAMED NOUH
MARCEDES   MERCEDES   1993, Egyptian-French

PAUL NOVOTNY
Contact: SOCAN - Toronto, 416-445-8700

BLUE MONKEY   co-composer with Patrick Coleman, Spectrafilm,
   1987, Canadian

GARY NUMAN
Contact: PRS - London, England, 011-44-1-580-5544

THE UNBORN   co-composer with Michael R. Smith, Califilm, 1991

GIOVANNI NUTI
OCCHIOPINOCCHIO   1995, Italian

MICHAEL NYMAN
Contact: PRS - London, England, 011-44-1-580-5544

THE DRAUGHTSMAN'S CONTRACT   United Artists Classics,
   1982, British
NELLY'S VERSION   Mithras Films, 1983, British
THE COLD ROOM (TD)   Jethro Films/Mark Forstater Productions,
   1984, British
A ZED AND TWO NOUGHTS   Skouras Pictures, 1985,
   British-Dutch
DROWNING BY NUMBERS   Galaxy International, 1988, British
THE COOK, THE THIEF, HIS WIFE & HER LOVER   Recorded
   Releasing, 1989, British
PROSPERO'S BOOKS   Miramax, 1991, U.K.-France
THE PIANO   Miramax, 1993, Australian
MESMER   Mayfair, 1994, Canadian-British-German
CARRINGTON   Gramercy, 1995, British-French
GATTACA   1997

SALLY NYOTO
ASHAKARA   co-composer with Louis Crelier, 1993 Togolese

LAURA NYRO
Contact: BMI - Los Angeles, 310-659-9109

BROKEN RAINBOW (FD)   Earthworks, 1985

ARLON OBER
Contact: BMI - Los Angeles, 310-659-9109

ILLUSIONS OF A LADY   1974
THROUGH THE LOOKING GLASS   Mature Pictures, 1976
THE INCREDIBLE MELTING MAN   American International, 1977
X-RAY HOSPITAL MASSACRE   Cannon, 1981
HAPPY BIRTHDAY   *BLOODY BIRTHDAY/CREEPS*   1980
EATING RAOUL   20th Century Fox International Classics, 1982
NIGHTBEAST   co-composer, 1982
CRIMEWAVE   *BROKEN HEARTS AND NOSES*   Columbia, 1985
IN THE SHADOW OF KILIMANJARO   Scotti Brothers, 1986

GENE OBER*
ALL'S FAIR IN LOVE & WAR   Star Land, 1996

SEBASTIAN OBERG
IL CAPITANO   co-composer with Lara Ackerlund, 1991, Swedish

DANIEL O'BRIEN*
LAST TRAIN OUT   co-composer with Frank Kavelin, Renegade,
   1992

OSCAR CARDOZO OCAMPO
b. Argentina
Contact: SADAIC - Argentina, 011-54-1-40-4867/8

THERE WILL BE NO MORE SORROWS NOR OBLIVION   Aries,
   1983, Argentine
LOS FIERECILLOS SE DIVIERTEN   Aries, 1983, Argentine
DEATHSTALKER   New World, 1984

GREG O'CONNOR*
Agent: Vangelos Management - Encino, 818-380-1919
Affiliation: BMI - Los Angeles, 310-659-9109

REALITY BITES   additional music, Universal, 1994
TIMECOP   source music, Universal, 1994
MONA MUST DIE   Jones & Reiker, 1994, U.S.-German
SHAKESPEARE IN THE PARK   SIP Productions, 1994

BRUCE ODLAND
Contact: BMI - Los Angeles, 310-659-9109

TOP OF THE WORLD   Denver Center, 1993

OHNAY OGUZ
DONERSEN ISLIK CAL   *WHISTLE IF YOU COME BACK*   1993,
   Turkish
ZIKKIMIN KOKU   *BULLSHIT*   1993, Turkish

MARY MARGARET O'HARA
Contact: SOCAN - Toronto, 416-445-8700

THE EVENTS LEADING UP TO MY DEATH   Flat Rock Films,
   1992, Canadian

PATRICK O'HEARN
Agent: Marks Management - Tarzana, 818-776-8787
Affiliation: BMI - Los Angeles, 310-659-9109

HEAVEN IS A PLAYGROUND   New Line, 1991
WHITE SANDS   Warner Bros., 1992
SILENT TONGUE   Belbo Films/Alive Films, 1993
FATHER HOOD   Buena Vista, 1993
AS GOOD AS DEAD (CTF)   Larco Prods./CNM Ent./Wilshire Court,
   1995

JIMMY OIHID
BYE BYE   co-composer with Steve Shehan, 1996

SHINNOSUKA OKAWA
b. Japan
Contact: JASRAC - Tokyo, Japan, 011-81-3-502-6551

THE MAKIOKA SISTERS   RS/58, 1983, Japanese

JOHN O'KENNEDY
Contact: ASCAP - Los Angeles, 213-883-1000

STRIPPED TO KILL   Concorde, 1987

ALAN OLDFIELD
Contact: ASCAP - Los Angeles, 213-883-1000

THE FOREST   *TERROR IN THE FOREST*   co-composer with
   Richard Hieronymous, Fury Film Distribution Ltd., 1983
INVISIBLE STRANGLER   co-composer with Richard Hieronymous,
   Seymour Borde & Associates, 1984

MIKE OLDFIELD
b. 1953
Contact: PRS - London, England, 011-44-1-580-5544

CHARLOTTE   1975
THE SPACE MOVIE (FD)   International Harmony, 1980, British
THE KILLING FIELDS   Warner Bros., 1984, British

TERRY OLDFIELD
Contact: PRS - London, England, 011-44-1-580-5544

THE NATURE OF SEX (TD)   Genesis Film
   Prods/13-WNET/Channel Four, 1993

JAY OLIVER
THE RIGHT WAY   co-composer with Mark Holden, 1996

STEPHEN OLIVER
Contact: BMI - Los Angeles, 310-659-9109

LADY JANE   Paramount, 1986, British

TOMMY OLIVER
ACAPULCO H.E.A.T. (TF)   co-composer with Michael Lloyd and Jim Ervin, Keller & Keller/Balenciaga/All-American, 1993

OSCAR O'LOCHLAINN
THE GIRL WITH THE HUNGRY EYES   co-composer with Paul Inder, Merton Shapiro/Cassian Elwes, 1995

KEITH OLSEN
Contact: ASCAP - Los Angeles, 213-883-1000

THAT WAS THEN...THIS IS NOW   co-composer with Bill Cuomo, Paramount, 1985

ALBERT LLOYD OLSON*
Contact: BMI - Los Angeles, 310-659-9109

THE TRIP   American International, 1967

WILLIAM OLVIS*
Agent: Marks Management - Tarzana, 818-776-8787
Contact: ASCAP - Los Angeles, 213-883-1000

NIGHTINGALES (TF)   Aaron Spelling Productions, 1988
EVIL IN CLEAR RIVER (TF)   The Steve Tisch Company/Lionel Chetwynd Productions/Phoenix Entertainment Group, 1988
BABYCAKES (TF)   The Konigsburg-Sanitsky Co., 1989
FINISH LINE (CTF)   Guber-Peters Entertainment Productions/Phoenix Entertainment Group, 1989
DREAM STREET (TF)   Bedford Falls Co./Finnegan Pinchuk/MGM/UA, 1989
KILL ME AGAIN   MGM/UA, 1990
PAIR OF ACES (TF)   Pedernales Films/Once Upon a Time Films Ltd., 1990
EL DIABLO (CTF)   Wizan-Black Film Productions, 1990
FRAMED (CTF)   HBO Pictures, 1990
29th STREET   20th Century Fox, 1991
FOURTH STORY (CTF)   Viacom, 1991
IN SICKNESS AND IN HEALTH (TF)   Konigsberg-Sanitsky Prods., 1992
THE COMRADES OF SUMMER (CTF)   HBO Pictures/Grossbart-Barnett, 1992
THE WOMAN WHO LOVED ELVIS (TF)   Wapello County Prods./Grossbart-Barnett Prods., 1993
RED ROCK WEST   Polygram, 1993
DR. QUINN MEDICINE WOMAN-'94 PILOT (TF)   Sullivan Co./CBC Ent., 1994
A PART OF THE FAMILY (CTF)   Interscope Communications, 1994
DR. QUINN MEDICINE WOMAN: LADIES NIGHT (TF)   Sullivan Co./CBS Entertainment, 1994

RUSSELL O'MALLEY
UP FROM THE DEPTHS   New World, 1979

MICHAEL OMER
LITTLE LORD FAUNTLEROY (CTF)   BBC, 1995

WILLIAM ORBIT
Contact: PRS - London, England, 011-44-1-580-5544

YOUNGBLOOD   MGM/UA, 1986
HOTSHOT   International Film Marketing, 1987

CYRIL ORNADEL
Contact: PRS - London, England, 011-44-1-580-5544

BRIEF ENCOUNTER (TF)   Carlo Ponti Productions/Cecil Clarke Productions, 1974, British

MALCOLM ORRALL
Contact: ASCAP - Los Angeles, 213-883-1000

DUNE WARRIORS   Califilm, 1991

FRANK ORTEGA
Contact: ASCAP - Los Angeles, 213-883-1000

ROSIE: THE ROSEMARY CLOONEY STORY (TF)   Charles Fries Productions/Alan Sacks Productions, 1982

LUIS PERICO ORTIZ
Contact: BMI - Los Angeles, 310-659-9109

MONDO NEW YORK   co-composer with Johnny Pacheco, Fourth and Broadway Films/Island Pictures, 1988

RIZ ORTOLANI
b. 1926 - Pesaro, Italy
Contact: SIAE - Italy, 011-39-6-59-901

MONDO CANE   co-composer with Nino Oliviero, 1962, Italian
THE EASY LIFE   IL SORPASSO   Embassy, 1962, Italian
LA DONNA NEL MONDO   1963, Italian
LE VERGINE DI NUREMBERG   Atlantica Cinematografica, 1964, Italian
THE SEVENTH DAWN   United Artists, 1964, U.S.-British
LE ORE NUDE   1964, Italian
AFRICA ADDIO   1965, Italian
THE YELLOW ROLLS-ROYCE   MGM, 1965, British
THE GLORY GUYS   United Artists, 1965
MAYA   MGM, 1966
TIFFANY MEMORANDUM   1966, British
WOMAN TIMES SEVEN   Avco Embassy, 1967, French-Italian-U.S.
REQUIESCANT   Castoro Film, 1967, Italian
THE VIOLENT FOUR   BANDITI A MILANO   Paramount, 1968, Italian
SEQUESTRO DI PERSONA   1968, Italian
ANZIO   Columbia, 1968, Italian
LES AMOURS DE LADY HAMILTON   1968, French-Italian
AL DI LA DELLA LEGGE   1968, Italian
THE BLISS OF MRS. BLOSSOM   Paramount, 1969, British
PERVERSION STORY   1969, Italian
O CANGACEIRO   1969, Italian
BORA BORA   1969, Italian
LA CATTURA   1969, Italian
THE ADVENTURES OF GIRARD   United Artists, 1969, British-Swiss
LA PRIMA NOTTA DEL DOTTOR DANIELI, INDUSTRIALE, COL COMPLESSO DEL...GIOCATTOLO   1970, Italian
L'INVASION   1970, French-Italian
THE HUNTING PARTY   United Artists, 1970
CONFESSIONS OF A POLICE CAPTAIN   CONFESSIONE DI UN COMMISSARIO   1970, Italian
THE STATUE   Cinerama Releasing Corporation, 1971, British
ADDIO ZIO TOM   1971, Italian
IL MERLO MASCHIO   1971, Italian
FRATELLO SOLE, SORELLA LUNA   co-composer with Donovan, 1972, Italian
GLI EROI   THE HEROES   1972, Italian-French-Spanish
UNA RAGIONE PER VIVERE E UNA PER MORIRE   1972, Italian-French-Spanish-West German
GIROLIMONI - IL MOSTRO DI ROMA   Dino De Laurentiis Cinematografica, 1972, Italian
THE VALACHI PAPERS   JOE VILACHI: I SEGRETI DI COSA NOSTRA   Columbia, 1972, Italian-French
E GUERRIERE DAL SENO NUDA   THE AMAZONS   EMI, 1973, Italian-French
TERESA LA LADRA   1973, Italian
BISTURI, MAFIA BIANCA   1973, Italian
LE MATAF   1973, French-Italian
GLI EROI   1973, Italian
DIO, SEI UN PADRETERNO!   1973, Italian
MONDO CANDIDO   1975, Italian
LA FACCIA VIOLENTA DI NEW YORK   1975, Italian
PASSI DI MORTE PERDUTI NEL BUIO   1976, Italian
SUBMISSION   SCANDALO   Joseph Brenner Associates, 1977, Italian
BRUTES AND SAVAGES   1978, Italian

DOUBLE MURDER   1978, Italian
FIRST LOVE   1978
THE GIRL IN YELLOW PAJAMAS   1978, Italian
THE RETURN OF CASANOVA   1978, Italian
TIGERS IN LIPSTICK   *WILD BEDS/HIJINKS*   Castle Hill, 1978, Italian
UN DRAMMA BORGHESE   *MIMI*   1979, Italian
THE 5TH MUSKETEER   Columbia, 1979
FROM HELL TO VICTORY   1979, French-Italian-Spanish
CANNIBAL HOLOCAUST   Trans Continental Film, 1979, Italian
HOUSE ON THE EDGE OF THE PARK   Bedford Entertainment, 1979, Italian
UNA GITA SCOLASTICA   *A SCHOOL OUTING*   1983, Italian
1919   1983, Spanish
LA RAGAZZA DI TRIESTE   1983, Italian
CHRISTOPHER COLUMBUS (MS)   RAI/Clesi Cinematografica Productions/Antenne 2/Bavaria Atelier/Lorimar Productions, 1985, Italian-West German-U.S.-French
A SEASON OF GIANTS (CTF)   TNT/RAI-1/Tiber, 1991, U.S.-Italian
MAGNIFICAT   1993, Italian

GEOFFREY ORYEMA
Contact: SACEM - France, 011-33-1-4715-4715

AN INDIAN IN THE CITY   *UN INDIEN DANS LA VILLE*   co-composer with Manu Katke and Tonton David, Buena Vista, 1996, French

DANIEL OSBORN
SMILE   United Artists, 1975

JASON OSBORN
Contact: PRS - London, England, 011-44-1-580-5544

HIGH SEASON   Hemdale, 1987, British

MICHIRU OSHIMA
WINDS OF GOD   1993, Japanese

JOHN OTTMAN
Agent: The Kraft-Benjamin Agency - Beverly Hills, 310-247-0123
Affiliation: BMI - Los Angeles, 310-659-9109

PUBLIC ACCESS   Cinemabeam, 1993
THE USUAL SUSPECTS   Gramercy, 1995
THE CABLE GUY   Columbia, 1996
SNOW WHITE IN THE DARK FOREST   1997
APT PUPIL   1997
INCOGNITO   1997

VYECHESLAV OVCHINNIKOV
b. 1937 - U.S.S.R.
Contact: RAIS - Russia, 011-7-95-203-3260

THE ROLLER AND THE VIOLIN   Mosfilm, 1961, Soviet
MY NAME IS IVAN   Shore International, 1962, Soviet
THE FIRST TEACHER   Mosfilm/Kirghizfilm, 1965, Soviet
ASYA'S HAPPINESS   Mosfilm, 1967, Soviet
WAR AND PEACE   Continental, 1968, Soviet
ANDREI RUBLEV   Columbia, 1968, Soviet
A NEST OF GENTRY   Corinth, 1969, Soviet
ARSENAL   new score for 1929 silent film, 1971, Soviet
OPERATION LIBERTY   1973, Soviet
THEY FOUGHT FOR THEIR MOTHERLAND   Mosfilm, 1974, Soviet
THE STEPPE   IFEX Film/Sovexport film, 1977, Soviet

P

PAATA
UNDERTOW   Capstone, 1991

JOHNNY PACHECO
Contact: BMI - Los Angeles, 310-659-9109

MONDO NEW YORK   co-composer with Luis Perico Ortiz, Fourth and Broadway Films/Island Pictures, 1988

GENE PAGE
Contact: ASCAP - Los Angeles, 213-883-1000

BREWSTER McCLOUD   MGM, 1970
BLACULA   American International, 1972

JIMMY PAGE
Contact: PRS - London, England, 011-44-1-580-5544

DEATH WISH II   Filmways, 1982
DEATH WISH 3   Cannon, 1985

SCOTT PAGE-PAGTER
Contact: ASCAP - Los Angeles, 213-883-1000

BONNIE AND CLYDE: THE TRUE STORY (TF)   co-composer with John Valentino, Hoffman-Israel/FNM Films, 1992

ANDY PALEY
Contact: ASCAP - Los Angeles, 213-883-1000

SHELF LIFE   1993

DAVID PALMER
Contact: PRS - London, England, 011-44-1-580-5544

THE ROYAL ROMANCE OF CHARLES AND DIANA (TF)   Chrysalis-Yellen Productions, 1982

NICK PALMER
Contact: APRA - Australia, 011-61-2-922-6422

SACRED SEX (FD)   1992, Australian

GERULF PANNACH
Contact: SACEM - France, 011-33-1-4715-4715

SINGING THE BLUES IN RED   *FATHERLAND*   co-composer with Christian Kunert, Angelika Films, 1986, British-West German-French

ALEKSANDR PANTYCHIN
GET THEE OUT   1991, Soviet
TE Y MENYA ODNA   *YOU ARE MY ONE AND ONLY*   1993, Russian

DANIELE PARIS
b. 1921
Contact: SIAE - Italy, 011-39-6-59-901

EVERY DAY EXCEPT CHRISTMAS   1957, British
LA STORIA DEL TERZO REICH (TD)   1971, Italian
STORIA DELLA BOMBA ATOMICA (TD)   1971, Italian
MILAREPA   Lotar Film, 1974, Italian
THE NIGHT PORTER   Avco Embassy, 1974, Italian
BEYOND GOOD AND EVIL   United Artists, 1977, Italian-French-West German

SIMON PARK

Contact: PRS - London, England, 011-44-1-580-5544

NUTCRACKER   Jezshaw Film, 1982, British

ALAN PARKER

Contact: BMI - Los Angeles, 310-659-9109

JAWS 3-D   Universal, 1983
DEMPSEY AND MAKEPEACE (TF)   LWT, 1986, British
AMERICAN GOTHIC   Vestron, 1988
OUT OF TIME   Motion Picture International, 1989
VOICE OF THE HEART (TF)   Portman Productions/HTV, 1990
TO BE THE BEST (MS)   Gemmy Prods., 1992
WILD JUSTICE (MS)   Reitalia/Tribune/Taurus, 1993
WHAT'S EATING GILBERT GRAPE   co-composer with Bjorn Isfalt,
   Paramount, 1993

JIM PARKER

Contact: PRS - London, England, 011-44-1-580-5544

TIME AFTER TIME   BBC-TV, 1985, British
DEADLINE (TF)   BBC Enterprises, 1988, British
THE HOUSE OF ELIOTT (CTF)   BBC Enterprises/A&E, 1992,
   British
BODY AND SOUL (MS)   1994, British

JOHN PARKER*

Contact: ASCAP - Los Angeles, 213-883-1000

LAUREL AND HARDY'S LAUGHING '20s   MGM, 1965
THE FURTHER PERILS OF LAUREL AND HARDY   MGM, 1968
DARKER THAN AMBER   National General, 1970
CUTTER'S TRAIL (TF)   CBS Studio Center, 1970
HUNGRY WIVES   Jack H. Harris Enterprises, 1973
THE MAN WHO DIED TWICE (TF)   Cinema Center, 1973
STRANGE HOMECOMING (TF)   Alpine Productions/Worldvision,
   1974
THE SECRET NIGHT CALLER (TF)   Charles Fries Productions/
   Penthouse Productions, 1975
LAW OF THE LAND (TF)   QM Productions, 1976
IN THE GLITTER PALACE (TF)   The Writer's Company/Columbia
   TV, 1977
SECRETS OF THREE HUNGRY WIVES (TF)   Penthouse
   Productions, 1978
THE GIRLS IN THE OFFICE (TF)   ABC Circle Films, 1979
THE GREAT CASH GIVEAWAY GETAWAY (TF)   Penthouse
   Productions/Cine Guarantors, 1980
DALLAS: CONUNDRUM (TF)   Lorimar TV, 1991

VAN DYKE PARKS

Agent: Vangelos Management - Encino, 818-380-1919
Affiliation: BMI - Los Angeles, 310-659-9109

GOIN' SOUTH   co-composer with Perry Botkin, Paramount, 1978
POPEYE   Paramount, 1980
SESAME STREET PRESENTS: FOLLOW THAT BIRD
   co-composer, Warner Bros., 1985
CLUB PARADISE   co-composer with David Mansfield, Warner
   Bros., 1986
RENTED LIPS   New Century Vista, 1988
CASUAL SEX?   Universal, 1988
THE TWO JAKES   also appears as prosecutor, Paramount, 1990
OUT ON A LIMB   Universal, 1992
NEXT DOOR (CTF)   Nederlander Television & Film Prods./Tudor
   Ent./TriStar TV, 1994
ONE CHRISTMAS (TF)   Davis Entertainment, 1994
WILD BILL   MGM-UA, 1995
THE SUMMER OF BEN TYLER (TF)   Hallmark Hall of Fame, 1996
BASTARD OUT OF CAROLINA   Turner Pictures, 1996
PRIVATE PARTS   Paramount, 1997

STARR PARODI

SHAME II: THE SECRET (CTF)   co-composer with Jeff Fair,
   Viacom/Lifetime TV, 1995

STEPHEN PARSONS

Contact: PRS - London, England, 011-44-1-580-5544

HOWLING II...YOUR SISTER IS A WEREWOLF   Thorn-EMI, 1985,
   British
RECRUITS   Concorde, 1986
SOCCER SHOOTOUT (FD)   Overseas, 1991
SPLIT SECOND   co-composer with Francis Haines, InterStar,
   1992, British

ARVO PART

Contact: GEMA - Germany, 011-49-89-480-03610

RACHEL RIVER   Taurus Entertainment, 1987

JOHNNY PATE

Contact: BMI - Los Angeles, 310-659-9109

SHAFT IN AFRICA   MGM, 1973
BROTHER ON THE RUN   1974
SATAN'S TRIANGLE (TF)   Danny Thomas Productions, 1975
BUCKTOWN   American International, 1975
DR. BLACK, MR. HYDE   Dimension, 1976
THE WATTS MONSTER   Dimension, 1979

CAMERON PATRICK

Contact: Patrick McCann Music - Redondo Beach, 310-374-7036
Affiliation: BMI - Los Angeles, 310-659-9109

THE MAGICAL WORLD OF CHUCK JONES (FD)   Warner Bros.,
   1992
PETER AND THE WOLF (TF)   Industrial FX, 1995

RICK PATTERSON

Contact: SOCAN - Toronto, 416-445-8700

YOUNG GIANTS   Entertainment Enterprises, 1983

JOHN PATTISON

SMOKING/NO SMOKING   1993, French

ROBBIE PATTON

Contact: ASCAP - Los Angeles, 213-883-1000

THE HUMAN SHIELD   Cannon, 1992

PETER PAU

FEIYING GAIWAK   ARMOUR OF GOD II: OPERATION CONDOR
   1992, Hong Kong

ALGIRDAS PAULAVICHUS

THE HOUSE BUILT ON SAND   1991, U.S.S.R.

CHARLES PAVLOSKY

Contact: BMI - Los Angeles, 310-659-9109

NINJA TURF   co-composer with Gary Falcone and Chris Stone,
   Ascot Entertainment Group, 1986

GLENN PAXTON

Contact: ASCAP - Los Angeles, 213-883-1000

THE CLONE MASTER (TF)   Mel Ferber Productions/Paramount
   Pictures TV, 1978
THE TWO WORLDS OF JENNIE LOGAN (TF)   Joe Wizan TV
   Productions/Charles Fries Productions, 1979
DARK NIGHT OF THE SCARECROW (TF)   Wizan Productions,
   1981
ISABEL'S CHOICE (TF)   Stuart Miller Productions/Pantheon
   Television, 1981
VITAL SIGNS (TF)   CBS Entertainment, 1986
DREAM BREAKERS (TF)   CBS Entertainment, 1989

BILL PAYNE

CERTAIN FURY   co-composer with Russ Kunkel and George
    Massenburg, New World, 1985, Canadian
SMOOTH TALK   co-composer with Russ Kunkel and George
    Massenburg, Spectrafilm, 1985

KEVIN PEAK

Contact: APRA - Australia, 011-61-2-922-6422

BATTLETRUCK   *WARLORDS OF THE 21ST CENTURY*   New
    World, 1982, U.S.-New Zealand
WINDRIDER   Hoyts, 1986, Australian

DON PEAKE*

Contact: BMI - Los Angeles, 310-659-9109

HAROLD LLOYD: SAFETY LAST   New score for 1923 silent,
    Time-Life Films, 1974
HAROLD LLOYD: WHY WORRY?   New score for 1923 silent,
    Time-Life Films
HAROLD LLOYD: THE FRESHMAN   New score for 1925 silent,
    Time-Life Films
HAROLD LLOYD: HOT WATER   New score for 1924 silent,
    Time-Life Films
THE LEGEND OF BIGFOOT   Palladium Productions, 1975
BAD GEORGIA ROAD   Dimension, 1976
MOVING VIOLATION   20th Century-Fox, 1976
BLACK OAK CONSPIRACY   New World, 1977
THE HILLS HAVE EYES   Vanguard, 1977
BATTERED (TF)   Henry Jaffe Enterprises, 1978
WALK PROUD   Universal, 1979
FLATBED ANNIE AND SWEETIE PIE: LADY TRUCKERS (TF)
    Moonlight Productions/Filmways, 1979
FAST FRIENDS (TF)   Columbia TV, 1979
DELUSION   New Line Cinema, 1981
I, DESIRE (TF)   Green-Epstein Productions/Columbia TV, 1982
THE HOUSE WHERE DEATH LIVES   New American, 1984
CODE OF VENGEANCE (TF)   Universal TV, 1985
DALTON: CODE OF VENGEANCE II (TF)   Universal TV, 1986
MODERN LOVE   Skouras Pictures, 1990
THE PEOPLE UNDER THE STAIRS   Universal, 1991

GUNNAR MOLLER PEDERSEN

Contact: KODA - Denmark, 011-45-31-68-38-00

KAERLIGHEDENS SMERTE   *PAIN OF LOVE*   1993,
    Danish-Swedish

BOB PEGG

Contact: PRS - London, England, 011-44-1-580-5544

BLACK JACK   Kestrel Films, 1979, British

MICHEL PELLETIER

Contact: SOCAN - Toronto, 416-445-8700

THE MYTH OF THE MALE ORGASM   co-composer with Ray
    Bonneville, Telescene, 1993, Canadian

SAMM PENA

A MILLION TO JUAN   co-composer with Steven Johnson and
    Jeffrey Johnson, Samuel Goldwyn, 1994

LEON PENDARVIS

Contact: BMI - Los Angeles, 310-659-9109

AMERICA   ASA Communications, 1986

THE PENGUIN CAFE ORCHESTRA

Contact: BMI - Los Angeles, 310-659-9109

MALCOLM   Vestron, 1986, Australian

DANILO PEREZ

Contact: BMI - Los Angeles, 310-659-9109

THE WINTER IN LISBON   additional music, Castle Hill, 1992,
    Spanish/French/Portuguese

COLERIDGE-TAYLOR PERKINSON

Contact: ASCAP - Los Angeles, 213-883-1000

IF HE HOLLERS, LET HIM GO   Cinerama Releasing Corporation,
    1968
THE McMASTERS   Chevron, 1970
TOGETHER FOR DAYS   Olas, 1973
A WARM DECEMBER   National General, 1973
AMAZING GRACE   United Artists, 1974
THOMASINE AND BUSHROD   Columbia, 1974
TIIE EDUCATION OF SONNY CARSON   Paramount, 1974
LOVE IS NOT ENOUGH (TF)   Universal TV, 1978
A WOMAN CALLED MOSES (TF)   Henry Jaffe Enterprises/IKE
    Productions, 1978
FREEDOM ROAD (TF)   co-composer with Terrence James, Zev
    Braun TV/Freedom Road Films, 1979

HAIM PERMONT

GOLEM BAMA'AGAL   *BLIND MAN'S BLUFF*   1993, Israeli

FREDDIE PERREN

Contact: ASCAP - Los Angeles, 213-883-1000

HELL UP IN HARLEM   co-composer with Fonce Mizell, American
    International, 1973
COOLEY HIGH   American International, 1975

MARC PERRONE

LA TRACE   co-composer with Nicola Piovani, Fox-Hachette, 1984,
    French-Swiss

ALEXANDER PESKANOV

Contact: RAIS - Russia, 011-7-95-203-3260

HE KNOWS YOU'RE ALONE   co-composer with Mark Peskanov,
    MGM/United Artists, 1980

MARK PESKANOV

Contact: RAIS - Russia, 011-7-95-203-3260

HE KNOWS YOU'RE ALONE   co-composer with Alexander
    Peskanov, MGM/United Artists, 1980

JOEL C. PESKIN

PAYBACK TIME   *UNINHIBITED*   co-composer with Rocky Davis,
    Antigua Films, 1993

RANDOLPH PETERS

Contact: SOCAN - Toronto, 416-445-8700

CURSE OF THE VIKING GRAVE (CTF)   Muddy River Films/Atlantic
    Films/South Pacific Pictures/CanWest, 1992

OSCAR PETERSON

b. August 15, 1925 - Montreal, Canada
Contact: BMI - Los Angeles, 310-659-9109

THE SILENT PARTNER   EMC Film/Aurora, 1979, Canadian

RANDY PETERSEN

Contact: BMI - Los Angeles, 310-659-9109

THE ZOO GANG   New World, 1985

JEAN-CLAUDE PETIT
b. France
Agent: Jeff Kaufman - Studio City, 818-506-6013
Affiliation: SACEM - France, 011-33-1-4715-4715

TUSK   Yank Films-Films 21, 1980, French
VIVE LA SOCIALE!   Fox-Hachette, 1983, French
TRANCHES DE VIE   1984, French
PAS DE VIEUX OS (TF)   1984, French
L'ADDITION   *THE CAGED HEART*   New World, 1985, French
TRISTESSE ET BEAUTE   1985, French
BILLY-ZE-KICK   1985, French
L'HOMME DES BATEAUX SUR LA VILLE   1985, French
LE CAVIAR ROUGE   1986, French
L'INCONNUE DE VIENNE (TF)   1986, French
JEAN DE FLORETTE   Orion Classics, 1987, French
MANON OF THE SPRING   *MANON DES SOURCES*   Orion
   Classics, 1987, French
TANT QU'IL Y AURA DES FEMMES   1987, French
FUCKING FERNAND   1987, French
LE FILS CARDINAUD (TF)   1987, French
L'ILE (TF)   1987, French
VENT DE PANIQUE   1988, French
SAVANNAH   1988, French
LE DESERTEUR (TF)   1988, French
LES CIGOGNES N'EN FONT QU'A LEUR TETE   1989, French
DEUX   1989, French
THE RETURN OF THE MUSKETEERS   Universal, 1989, British
BILLE EN TETE   1989, French
LA GRANDE DUNE (TF)   1990, French
CYRANO DE BERGERAC   Orion Classic, 1990, French
URANUS   Prestige, 1991, French
ALL OUT   *DE PLEIN FOUET*   1991, French
LE COLLIER PERDU DE LA COLOMBE   1991, French
TOUCH AND DIE (TF)   1991, French
RUE DU BAC   1991, French
TOUJOURS SEULS   1991, French
MAYRIG   1991, French
588, RUE PARADIS   1992, French
THE PLAYBOYS   Samuel Goldwyn, 1992, U.S.-Irish
QUAND LA RAISON DORT   1992, French
LE ZEBRE   1992, French
SCARLET AND BLACK   originally filmed for television, Miramax,
   1993, British
LE CHATEAU DES OLIVIERS (TF)   1993, French
BONJOUR LA FAMILLE (TF)   1993, French
LADY CHATTERLEY   Global Arts/London Films/BBC, 1993, British
FOREIGN STUDENT   Universal, 1994, French
NOBODY'S CHILDREN (CTF)   Winkler-Daniel Prods./Quinta, 1994
THE HORSEMAN ON THE ROOF   *LE HUSSARD SUR LE TOIT*
   1995, French

LAURENT PETITGAND
Contact: SACEM - France, 011-33-1-4715-4715

IN WEITER FERNE, SO NAH!   *FARAWAY, SO CLOSE!*   Sony
   Classics, 1993, German

LAURENT PETITGIRARD
Contact: SACEM - France, 011-33-1-4715-4715

ROSEBUD   United Artists, 1975

ANDREY PETROVIC
b. U.S.S.R.
Contact: RAIS - Russia, 011-7-95-203-3260

THE BLUE BIRD   20th Century-Fox, 1976, U.S.-Soviet

CHARLTON PETTUS
IF LUCY FELL   co-composer with Amanda Kravat, TriStar, 1996

TOM PETTY
SHE'S THE ONE   20th Century Fox, 1996

AHMAD PEZHMAN
HONARPISHEH   *THE ACTOR*   1993, Iranian

BARRINGTON PHELOUNG
Contact: PRS - London, England, 011-44-1-580-5544

PORTRAIT OF A MARRIAGE (MS)   1992, British
SHOPPING   Film Four International, 1994, British
POWER PLAYS (TF)   Oxford TV/KCET/ITEL/Channel 4, 1994,
   U.S.-British
NOSTRADAMUS   Orion Classics, 1994
THE CINDER PATH (TF)   1995, British
THE MANGLER   New Line, 1995
SHOPPING   1996

HERB PHILHOFER
ON THE EDGE   Skouras Pictures, 1985

ART PHILIPPS
Contact: BMI - Los Angeles, 310-659-9109

THE LUCKY STAR   Pickman Films, 1980, Canadian

JOHN PHILLIPS
Contact: PRS - London, England, 011-44-1-580-5544

MYRA BRECKENRIDGE   20th Century-Fox, 1971
THE MAN WHO FELL TO EARTH   Cinema 5, 1976, British

MARY PHILLIPS
Contact: ASCAP - Los Angeles, 213-883-1000

CARAVAGGIO   co-composer with Simon Fisher Turner, British Film
   Institute, 1986, British

STU PHILLIPS
Contact: BMI - Los Angeles, 310-659-9109

MAD DOG COLL   Columbia, 1961
THE MAN FROM THE DINER'S CLUB   Columbia, 1963
RIDE THE WILD SURF   Columbia, 1964
DEAD HEAT ON A MERRY-GO-ROUND   Columbia, 1966
HELL'S ANGELS ON WHEELS   American International, 1967
THE NAME OF THE GAME IS TO KILL   *THE FEMALE TRAP*
   Fanfare, 1968
ANGELS FROM HELL   American International, 1968
RUN, ANGEL, RUN!   Fanfare, 1969
THE APPOINTMENT   MGM, 1969
2000 YEARS LATER   Warner Bros., 1969
THE GAY DECEIVERS   Fanfare, 1969
FOLLOW ME!   Cinerama, 1969
THE LOSERS   Fanfare, 1970
BEYOND THE VALLEY OF THE DOLLS   20th Century-Fox, 1970
SIMON, KING OF THE WITCHES   Fanfare, 1971
THE SEVEN MINUTES   20th Century-Fox, 1971
JUD   Duque Films, 1971
HOW TO SEDUCE A WOMAN   Cinerama, 1974
MACON COUNTY LINE   American International, 1974
SWITCH (TF)   Glen Larson Productions/Universal TV, 1975
THE MEAL   *DEADLY ENCOUNTER*   Ambassador Releasing,
   1975
BENNY AND BARNEY: LAS VEGAS UNDERCOVER (TF)   Glen A.
   Larson Productions/Universal TV, 1977
EVENING IN BYZANTIUM (TF)   Universal TV, 1978
BATTLESTAR GALACTICA (TF)   Glen A. Larson
   Productions/Universal TV, 1978
FAST CHARLIE, THE MOONBEAM RIDER   *FAST CHARLIE AND
   THE MOONBEAM*   Universal, 1979
BUCK ROGERS   Universal, 1979
WAIKIKI (TF)   Aaron Spelling Productions, 1980
MIDNIGHT LACE (TF)   Four R. Productions/Universal TV, 1981
ROOSTER (TF)   Glen A. Larson Productions/Tugboat
   Productions/20th Century-Fox TV, 1982
TERROR AT ALCATRAZ (TF)   Glen A. Larson
   Productions/Universal TV, 1982
IN LIKE FLYNN (TF)   Glen A. Larson Productions/20th Century-Fox
   TV, 1985
THE HIGHWAYMAN (TF)   Glen A. Larson Productions/20th Century
   Fox TV, 1987
THE ROAD RAIDERS (TF)   New East Entertainment/Universal TV,
   1989

ASTOR PIAZZOLA

Contact: SIAE - Italy, 011-39-6-59-901

ARMAGUEDON   1977, French
HENRY IV   Orion Classics, 1984, Italian
SUR   1986, French-Argentine

PIERO PICCIONI

b. 1921 - Turin, Italy
Contact: SIAE - Italy, 011-39-6-59-901

SAMPAN BOY   1950, Italian
IL MONDO LE CONDANNA   1952, Italian
LA SPIAGGIA   1954, Italian
LA DONNA CHE VENNE DEL MARE   1956, Italian
POOR BUT BEAUTIFUL   Trans-Lux, 1956, Italian-French
GUENDALINA   Carlo Ponti/Les Films Marceau, 1957,
   Italian-French
BELLE, MA POVERE   Titanus, 1957, Italian
LA FINESTRA SUL LUNA PARK   Noria Film, 1957, Italian
IL SEGRETO DELLA SIERRA DORADA   1957, Italian
TEMPEST   Paramount, 1958, Italian-French-Yugoslavian
LA BALLERINA ED IL BUON DIO   1958, Italian
I RAGAZZI DEL PARIOLI   1958, Italian
AVVENTURA A CAPRI   1958, Italian
I TARTASSATI   1958, Italian
LA NOTTE BRAVA   ON ANY STREET/BAD GIRLS DON'T CRY
   Ajace Film/Franco London Film, 1959, Italian-French
RUN WITH THE DEVIL   VIA MARGUTTA   1959, Italian
RACCONTI D'ESTATE   1959, Italian
I DOLCI INGANNI   1959, Italian
L'IMPIEGATO   1959, Italian
I MAGLIARI   Vides/Titanus, 1959, Italian
NATA DI MARZO   1959, Italian
ADUA E LE COMPAGNE   1960, Italian
IL BELL'ANTONIO   Cino Del Duca/Arco Film/Lyre
   Cinematographique, 1960, Italian-French
FROM A ROMAN BALCONY   LA GIORNATA BALORDA/LOVE IS A
   DAY'S WORK/PICKUP IN ROME   Continental, 1960,
   Italian-French
LA VIACCIA   adaptation, Embassy, 1960, Italian
IL GOBBO   Dino De Laurentiis Cinematografica, 1960, Italian
L'ASSASSINO   THE LADY KILLER OF ROME   Manson, 1961,
   Italian-French
SENILITA   Zebra Film/Aera Film, 1961, Italian-French
SALVATORE GIULIANO   CCM Films, 1962, Italian-French
ANNI RUGGENTI   1962, Italian
CONGO VIVO   1962, Italian
THE SLAVE   IL FIGLIO DI SPARTACUS   1962, Italian
LA MANI SULLA CITTA   Galatea Film, 1963, Italian
L'ATTICO   1963, Italian
CHI LAVORA E'PERDUTO   IN CAPO AL MONDO   Zebra
   Film/Franco London Film, 1963, Italian-French
LA PARMIGIANA   1963, Italian
IL TERRORISTA   22 Dicembre/Galatea, 1964, Italian
LA FUGA   1964, Italian
THE TENTH VICTIM   Embassy, 1965, Italian
THE MOMENT OF TRUTH   Rizzoli, 1965, Italian-Spanish
CACCIA ALLA VOLPE   1966, Italian
MATCHLESS   United Artists, 1966, Italian
THE STRANGER   Paramount, 1967, Italian-French-Algerian
THE WITCHES   Lopert, 1967, Italian-French
IL MEDICO DELLA MUTUA   1968, Italian
CAPRICCIO ALL'ITALIANA   De Laurentiis, 1968, Italian
SARTANA   1968
PAS DE ROSES POUR OSS 117   1968, Italian
TO'E MORTA LA NONNA   Vides, 1969, Italian
UOMINI CONTRO   Prima Cinematografica/Jadran Film, 1970,
   Italian-Yugoslavian
LA CONTESTAZIONE GENERALE   1970, Italian
BELLO, ONESTO, EMIGRATO AUSTRALIA SPOSEREBBE
   COMPAESANA ILLIBATA   1970, Italian
ER PIU, STORIA D'AMORE E DI COLTELLO   1970, Italian
THE LIGHT AT THE EDGE OF THE WORLD   National General,
   1971, U.S.-Spanish
THE SEDUCTION OF MIMI   MIMI METALLURGICO FERITO
   NELL'ONORE   New Line Cinema, 1972, Italian
LE MOINE   THE MONK   Rank, 1972, French-Italian-West German
LO SCOPIONE SCIENTIFICO   De Laurentiis, 1972, Italian
LE MONACHE DI SANT' ARCANGELO   Miracle, 1973,
   Italian-French

THE MATTEI AFFAIR   Paramount, 1973, Italian
POLVERE DI STELLE   Capitolina Produzioni Cinematografiche,
   1973, Italian
LUCKY LUCIANO   Avco Embassy, 1974, Italian
ALL SCREWED UP   TUTTO A POSTO, NIENTE IN ORDINE   New
   Line Cinema, 1974, Italian
APPASSIONATA   1974, Italian
IL DIO SOTTO LA PELLE   1974, Italian
SWEPT AWAY BY AN UNUSUAL DESTINY IN THE BLUE SEA OF
   AUGUST   Cinema 5, 1974, Italian
CHI DICE DONNA DICE...DONNA   1975, Italian
CUORE DI CANE   Italnoleggio, 1975, Italian
FRATELLO MARE   1975, Italian
CADAVERI ECCELENTI   United Artists, 1976, Italian-French
IL COMUNE SENSO DEL PUDORE   Rizzoli Film, 1976, Italian
I VIZI MORBOSI DI UNA GOVERNANTE   1976, Italian
QUELLE STRANE OCCASIONI   Cineriz, 1977, Italian
STRANGE EVENTS   1977, Italian
THE WITNESS   1978, Italian
DOVE VAI IN VACANZA?   co-composer, Rizzoli, 1978, Italian
THE HYPOCHONDRIAC   1979, Italian
EBOLI   CHRIST STOPPED AT EBOLI   Franklin Media, 1980,
   Italian-French
IL MALATO IMMAGINARIO   1980, Italian
FIGHTING BACK   Paramount, 1982

MICHAEL PICCIRILLO

Contact: BMI - Los Angeles, 310-659-9109

CRACK HOUSE   Cannon, 1989

NIK PICKARD

THE ROAD TO MECCA   co-composer with Ferdi Brengen, Distant
   Horizon/Videovision, 1992

REBECCA PIDGEON

OLEANNA   Samuel Goldwyn, 1994

FRANCO PIERSANTI

Contact: SIAE - Italy, 011-39-6-59-901

ON MY OWN   1992
IL LADRO DI BAMBINI   THE STOLEN CHILDREN   1992,
   Italian-French
IL SEGRETO DEL BOSCH VECCHIO   THE SECRET OF THE OLD
   WOODS   1993, Italian
MILLE BOLLE BLU   1993, Italian
VRIJEME ZA...   A TIME FOR...   1994, Croatian-Italian
LAMERICA   1994, Italian-French

TOM PIERSON

Contact: BMI - Los Angeles, 310-659-9109

QUINTET   20th Century-Fox, 1979

SCOOTER PIETSCH

THE SECRET WORLD OF DREAMS (TD)   Nash Prods./DBA Ent.,
   1995

NICHOLAS PIKE*

Agent: Cathy Schleussner - Encino, 818-905-7475
Affiliation: ASCAP - Los Angeles, 213-883-1000

GRAVEYARD SHIFT   Shapiro/Virgin, 1986, Canadian
CRITTERS 2: THE MAIN COURSE   New Line Cinema, 1988
TALES FROM THE CRYPT (CTF)   co-composer, Tales from the
   Crypt Holdings, 1989
CHUD II: BUD THE CHUD   Vestron, 1989
CAPTAIN RON   Buena Vista, 1992
SLEEPWALKERS   Columbia, 1992
THE SECRET PASSION OF ROBERT CLAYTON (CTF)   Producers
   Entertainment Group/Wilshire Court Prods., 1992
ATTACK OF THE 50 ft. WOMAN (CTF)   HBO Pictures/Warner Bros.
   TV, 1993
BLANK CHECK   Buena Vista, 1994
IN THE SHADOW OF EVIL (TF)   D.W. Prods./CBS Entertainment,
   1995

THE SURROGATE (TF)   Moore-Weiss Prods./Stephen J. Cannell
   Prods., 1995
THE SHINING (TF)   Warner Bros. TV, 1997

HERB PILHOFER
Contact: ASCAP - Los Angeles, 213-883-1000

HOME FIRES BURNING   William P. O'Boyle, 1992

CHUCK PINNELL
LAST NIGHT AT THE ALAMO   co-composer with Wayne Bell,
   Alamo Films, 1983
DOC'S FULL SERVICE   co-composer with John Sargent, Brazos
   Films, 1994

NICOLA PIOVANI
b. 1946 - Italy
Contact: SIAE - Italy, 011-39-6-59-901

NEL NOME DEL PADRE   1970, Italian
LA REGAZZA DI LATTA   1970, Italian
DANIELE E MARIA   1972, Italian
N.P. IL SEGRETO   1972, Italian
SBATTI IL MOSTRO IN PRIMA PAGINA   1972, Italian
LA VITA IN GIOCO   1973, Italian
THE REBEL NUN FLAVIA LA MONACA MUSULMANA   1974,
   Italian
L'INVENZIONE DI MOREL   1974, Italian
IL PROFUMO DELLA SIGNORA IN NERO   1974, Italian
LE ORME   1975, Italian
VERMISAT   1975, Italian
VICTORY MARCH   Summit Features, 1976, Italian-French
MORIRE A ROMA   1976, Italian
IL GABBIANO (TF)   RAI, 1976, Italian
HYENA'S SUN ACH CHAMS WADHDHIBA/LE SOLEIL DES
   HYENES   1977, Dutch-Algerian-British
GLI ULTIMI TRE GIORNI   1977, Italian
NEL PIU ALTO DEI CIELI   1977, Italian
SALTO NEL VUOTO   1980, Italian
VACANZE IN VAL TREBBIA   1980, Italian
IL MINESTRONE   1981, Italian
HET MEISJE MET HET RODE HAAR   1981, Dutch
IL MARCHESE DEL GRILLO   1981, Italian
THE NIGHT OF THE SHOOTING STARS LA NOTTE DI SAN
   LORENZO   United Artists Classics, 1981, Italian
LA VELA INCANTATA   1982, Italian
GIL OCCHI, LA BOCCA THE EYES, THE MOUTH   Gaumont,
   1982, Italian-French
DE SCHORPIOEN   1983, Dutch
LA TRACE   co-composer with Marc Perrone, Fox-Hachette, 1984,
   French-Swiss
GINGER AND FRED   MGM/UA, 1986, Italian-French-West
   German
DEVIL IN THE FLESH   Istituto Luce/Italnoleggio, 1986,
   Italian-French
GOOD MORNING, BABYLON   Vestron, 1987, Italian-French-U.S.
MANIFESTO   Cannon, 1989
THE VOICE OF THE MOON   Penta Distribuzione, 1990, Italian
HORS LA VIE   1991, French-Italian-Belgian
UTZ   1992, British/Italian/German
FIORILE   1993, Italian-French-German
HUEVOS DE ORO GOLDEN BALLS   1993, Spanish
A MONTH BY THE LAKE   Miramax, 1995

PIXIES
ALBERT SOUFFRE ALBERT SUFFERS   1992, French

GIANFRANCO PLENIZIO
b. Italy
Contact: SIAE - Italy, 011-39-6-59-901

BELLA DI GIORNO, MOGLIE DI NOTTE   1971, Italian
I LEONI DI SAN PETERSBURG   1972, Italian
NO...SONO VERGINE   1973, Italian
AH SI? E IO LO DICO A ZZZORO!   1975, Italian
LIBERI, ARMATI, PERICOLOSI   1976, Italian
MASOCH   Difilm, 1980, Italian
AND THE SHIP SAILS ON   Triumph/Columbia, 1983,
   Italian-French

AMOTZ PLESSNER*
Contact: BMI - Los Angeles, 310-659-9109

RAVE REVIEW   Wildebeest Co., 1994

TERRY PLUMERI
Contact: BMI - Los Angeles, 310-659-9109

ANGEL TOWN   Taurus Entertainment Company, 1990
BODY CHEMISTRY   Concorde, 1990
THE RAIN KILLER   Concorde, 1990
CRACKDOWN   Concorde, 1991
STEPHEN KING'S 'SOMETIME THEY COME BACK' (TF)   Come
   Back Prods., 1991
UNCAGED   Califilm, 1991
HIT THE DUTCHMAN   21st Century, 1992, U.S.-Russian
MAD DOG COLL   21st Century, 1992, U.S.-Russian
DEATH WISH V: THE FACE OF DEATH   Trimark, 1994
BREACH OF CONDUCT (CTF)   Finnegan-Pinchuk/MTE, 1994

BASIL POLEDOURIS*
b. 1945
Agent: The Kraft-Benjamin Agency - Beverly Hills, 310-247-0123
Affiliation: BMI - Los Angeles, 310-659-9109

CONGRATULATIONS, IT'S A BOY! (TF)   co-composer with Richard
   Baskin, Aaron Spelling Productions, 1971
EXTREME CLOSE-UP   National General, 1973
TINTORERA - THE SILENT DEATH   1977, British-Mexican
BIG WEDNESDAY   Warner Bros., 1978
DOLPHIN (FD)   Michael Wiese Film Productions, 1979
90028   1979
DEFIANCE   co-composer with Gerard McMahon, American
   International, 1980
THE BLUE LAGOON   Columbia, 1980
THE HOUSE OF GOD   (H.O.G.)   United Artists, 1981
A WHALE FOR THE KILLING (TF)   Play Productions/Beowulf
   Productions, 1981
FIRE ON THE MOUNTAIN (TF)   Bonnard Productions, 1982
CONAN THE BARBARIAN   Universal, 1982
SUMMER LOVERS   Filmways, 1982
AMAZONS (TF)   ABC Circle Films, 1984
CONAN THE DESTROYER   Universal, 1984
SINGLE BARS, SINGLE WOMEN (TF)   Carsey Werner
   Productions/Sunn Classic Pictures, 1984
MAKING THE GRADE   MGM/UA/Cannon, 1984
RED DAWN   MGM/UA, 1984
PROTOCOL   Warner Bros., 1984
ALFRED HITCHCOCK PRESENTS (TF)   co-composer, Universal
   TV, 1985
FLESH + BLOOD   Orion, 1985, U.S.-Dutch
MISFITS OF SCIENCE (TF)   Universal, 1985
IRON EAGLE   Tri-Star, 1986
CHERRY 2000   Orion, 1986
AMERIKA (MS)   ABC Circle Films, 1987
ISLAND SONS (TF)   Universal TV, 1987
ROBOCOP   Orion, 1987
NO MAN'S LAND   Orion, 1987
SPELLBINDER WITCHING HOUR   MGM/UA, 1988
INTRIGUE (TF)   Crew Neck Productions/Linnea
   Productions/Columbia Pictures TV, 1988
SPLIT DECISIONS   New Century/Vista, 1988
FAREWELL TO THE KING   Orion, 1989
LONESOME DOVE (MS) ☆☆   Motown Productions/Pangaea/Qintex
   Entertainment, Inc., 1989
WIRED   The Wired Joint Venture, 1989
WHY ME?   Trans World Entertainment, 1989
L.A. TAKEDOWN (TF)   additional music, AJAR/Mories Film
   Productions, 1989
THE HUNT FOR RED OCTOBER   Paramount, 1990
QUIGLEY DOWN UNDER   MGM/UA, 1990
FLIGHT OF THE INTRUDER   Paramount, 1991
WHITE FANG   Buena Vista, 1991
RETURN TO THE BLUE LAGOON   Columbia, 1991
HARLEY DAVIDSON AND THE MARLBORO MAN   MGM, 1991
WIND   TriStar, 1992
NED BLESSING (TF)   Wittliff-Pangaea/Hearst, 1992
ROBOCOP 3   Orion, 1993
HOT SHOT, PART DEUX!   20th Century Fox, 1993
FREE WILLY   Warner Bros., 1993

ON DEADLY GROUND   Warner Bros., 1994
SERIAL MOM   Savoy, 1994
ROBOCOP: THE SERIES (TF)   theme only, Skyvision
   Ent./RoBoCop Prods./Rysher, 1994
LASSIE   Paramount, 1994
THE JUNGLE BOOK   *RUDYARD KIPLING'S JUNGLE BOOK*
   Buena Vista, 1994
UNDER SIEGE 2: DARK TERRITORY   Warner Bros., 1995
FREE WILLY 2: THE ADVENTURE HOME   Warner Bros., 1995
IT'S MY PARTY   1996
CELTIC PRIDE   Buena Vista, 1996
THE WAR AT HOME   1996
STARSHIP TROOPERS   1997
GOING WEST   1997
BREAKDOWN   1997

TIBAR POLGAR

Contact: SOCAN - Toronto, 416-445-8700

IN PRAISE OF OLDER WOMEN   Avco Embassy, 1978, Canadian

DAVE POLLECUTT

WAATI   co-composer with Bruno Coulais, 1995,
   Malian-French-Burkina Fasso

PETER PONGER

DEATH OF A SCHOOLBOY   1991, Austrian

TEMISTOCLE POPA

TRAHIR   *BETRAYAL*   1993, French-Romanian-Swiss-Spanish

CAROLE POPE

Contact: SOCAN - Toronto, 416-445-8700

THE SILENCER   Crown, 1992

POPOL VUH

Contact: GEMA - Germany, 011-49-89-480-03610

AGUIRRE, THE WRATH OF GOD   New Yorker, 1973, West
   German-Mexican-Peruvian
HEART OF GLASS   New Yorker, 1976, West German
NOSFERATU THE VAMPYRE   20th Century-Fox, 1979, West
   German-French-U.S.
FITZCARRALDO   New World, 1982, West German
COBRA VERDE   DEG, 1988, West German

STEVE PORCARO

Agent: Gorfaine-Schwartz - Los Angeles, 213-969-1011
Affiliation: ASCAP - Los Angeles, 213-883-1000

METRO   Buena Vista, 1997

GREG POREE

Contact: BMI - Los Angeles, 310-659-9109

AND THE CHILDREN SHALL LEAD (TF)   Rainbow TV Workshop,
   1985

MICHEL PORTAL

b. 1935 - Bayonne, France
Contact: SACEM - France, 011-33-1-4715-4715

CINEMATOGRAPHIE   co-composer, 1966, French
LE VIOL   *A QUESTION OF RAPE*   1967, French
GROMAIRE (FD)   1967, French
SOLEIL DE PIERRE   1967, French
HAXAN WITCHCRAFT THROUGH THE AGES   1968, French
HOA-BINH   1969, French
FEU FIRE   1970, French
ALECHINSKY D'APRES NATURE   1970, French
FRANCE SOCIETE ANONYME   1973, French
LA CECILIA   1974, French
LES CONQUISTADORS   1975, French
SERAIL   1975, French
FOR CLEMENCE   1977, French
THE ADOPTION   1978, French

LES CAVALIERS DE L'ORAGE   1983, French-Yugoslavian
BALLES PERDUES   *STRAY BULLETS*   Films Galatee, 1983,
   French
SORCERESS   *LA MOINE ET LA SORCIERE*   European Classics,
   1987, French-U.S.

RACHEL PORTMAN

Agent: The Kraft-Benjamin Agency - Beverly Hills, 310-247-0123
Affiliation: PRS - London, England, 011-44-1-580-5544 and BMI -
   Los Angeles, 310-659-9109

SHARMA AND BEYOND   Cinecom International, 1986, British
YOUNG CHARLIE CHAPLIN (TF)   Thames TV
   Productions/WonderWorks, 1989, British-U.S.
ANTONIA AND JANE   Miramax, 1991, British
LIFE IS SWEET   1991, British
WHERE ANGELS FEAR TO TREAD   1991, British
THE CLONING OF JOANNA MAY (CTF)   Granada/A&E, 1992
REBECCA'S DAUGHTERS   1992, German/British
ELIZABETH R: A YEAR IN THE LIFE OF THE QUEEN (TD)
   BBC/Lionheart, 1992, British
USED PEOPLE   20th Century Fox, 1992
ETHAN FROME   Miramax, 1993
BENNY AND JOON   MGM, 1993
FRIENDS   1993, U.K.-French
THE JOY LUCK CLUB   Buena Vista, 1993
SIRENS   Miramax, 1994, Australian-British
ONLY YOU   TriStar, 1994
THE ROAD TO WELLVILLE   Columbia, 1994
WAR OF THE BUTTONS   Warner Bors., 1995, British-French
A PYROMANIAC'S LOVE STORY   Buena Vista, 1995
SMOKE   Miramax, 1995
TO WONG FOO, THANKS FOR EVERYTHING! JULIE NEWMAR
   Universal, 1995
THE ADVENTURES OF PINOCCHIO   New Line, 1996
EMMA ★   Miramax, 1996
PALOOKAVILLE   1996
MARVIN'S ROOM   Miramax, 1996
VENICE   1997
HOME FRIES   1997

MIKE POST

Agent: Gorfaine-Schwartz - Los Angeles, 213-969-1011
Affiliation: BMI - Los Angeles, 310-659-9109

TWO ON A BENCH (TF)   co-composer with Pete Carpenter,
   Universal TV, 1971
GIDGET GETS MARRIED (TF)   co-composer with Pete Carpenter,
   Screen Gems/Columbia Pictures TV, 1972
THE ROCKFORD FILES (TF)   co-composer with Pete Carpenter,
   Cherokee Productions/Roy Huggins Productions/Universal TV, 1974
THE MORNING AFTER (TF)   co-composer with Pete Carpenter,
   Wolper Productions, 1974
LOCUSTS (TF)   co-composer with Pete Carpenter, Carson
   Productions/Paramount Pictures TV, 1974
THE INVASION OF JOHNSON COUNTY (TF)   co-composer with
   Pete Carpenter, Roy Huggins Productions/Universal TV, 1976
SCOTT FREE (TF)   co-composer with Pete Carpenter, Cherokee
   Productions/Universal TV, 1976
RICHIE BROCKELMAN: MISSING 24 HOURS (TF)   co-composer
   with Pete Carpenter, Universal TV, 1976
BAA BAA BLACK SHEEP (TF)   co-composer with Pete Carpenter,
   Universal TV, 1976
CHARLIE COBB: NICE NIGHT FOR A HANGING (TF)
   co-composer with Pete Carpenter, Fairmount/Foxcroft
   Productions/Universal TV, 1977
DR. SCORPION (TF)   co-composer with Pete Carpenter, Universal
   TV, 1978
RABBIT TEST   co-composer with Pete Carpenter, Avco Embassy,
   1978
CAPTAIN AMERICA (TF)   co-composer with Pete Carpenter,
   Universal TV, 1979
THE NIGHT RIDER (TF)   co-composer with Pete Carpenter,
   Stephen J. Cannell Productions/Universal TV, 1979
CAPTAIN AMERICA II (TF)   co-composer with Pete Carpenter,
   Universal TV, 1979
SCOUT'S HONOR (TF)   Zephyr Productions, 1980
TENSPEED AND BROWNSHOE (TF)   co-composer with Pete
   Carpenter, Stephen J. Cannell Prods., 1980
COACH OF THE YEAR (TF)   co-composer with Pete Carpenter,
   Shane Company Productions/NBC Entertainment, 1980

DEEP IN THE HEART   HANDGUN   Warner Bros., 1981
WILL, G. GORDON LIDDY (TF)   co-composer with Pete Carpenter,
     Shayne Company Productions, 1982
ADAM (TF)   Alan Landsburg Productions, 1983
RUNNING BRAVE   Buena Vista, 1983, Canadian
HARD KNOX (TF)   co-composer with Pete Carpenter, Shane
     Company Productions, 1984
NO MAN'S LAND (TF)   co-composer with Pete Carpenter, JADDA
     Productions/Warner Bros. TV, 1984
RIPTIDE (TF)   co-composer with Pete Carpenter, Stephen J.
     Cannell Prods., 1984
HADLEY'S REBELLION   American Film Distributors, 1984
RHINESTONE   adaptation, 20th Century Fox, 1984
THE RIVER RAT   Paramount, 1984
HUNTER (TF)   co-composer with Pete Carpenter, Stephen J.
     Cannell Prods., 1984
HEART OF A CHAMPION: THE RAY MANCINI STORY (TF)   Rare
     Titles Productions/Robert Papazian Productions, 1985
BROTHERS-IN-LAW (TF)   co-composer with Pete Carpenter,
     Stephen J. Cannell Productions, 1985
STINGRAY (TF)   co-composer with Pete Carpenter, Stephen J.
     Cannell Productions, 1985
THE LAST PRECINCT (TF)   co-composer with Pete Carpenter,
     Stephen J. Cannell Productions, 1986
ADAM: HIS SONG CONTINUES (TF)   Alan Landsburg Productions,
     1986
L.A. LAW (TF)   20th Century Fox TV, 1986
DESTINATION: AMERICA (TF)   Stephen J. Cannell Productions,
     1987
WISEGUY (TF)   Stephen J. Cannell Productions, 1987
J.J. STARBUCK (TF)   Stephen J. Cannell Productions, 1987
THE RYAN WHITE STORY (TF)   The Landsburg Co., 1989
B.L. STRYKER: THE DANCER'S TOUCH (TF)   Blue Period
     Productions/TWS Productions/Universal TV, 1989
B.L. STRYKER: BLIND CHESS (TF)   Blue Period Productions/TWS
     Prods./Universal TV, 1989
QUANTUM LEAP (TF)   Belisarius Productions/Universal TV, 1989
UNSPEAKABLE ACTS (TF)   Alan Landsburg Productions, 1990
WITHOUT HER CONSENT (TF)   Raymond Katz Enterprises/Half
     Pint Productions/Carla Singer Productions, 1990
THE 100 LIVES OF BLACK JACK SAVAGE (TF)   Stephen J.
     Cannell/Walt Disney TV, 1991
THE GREAT PRETENDER (TF)   Stephen J. Cannell, 1991
PALACE GUARD (TF)   co-composer with Velton Ray Bunch,
     composer of theme, Stephen J. Cannell, 1991
THE HAT SQUAD (TF)   Stephen J. Cannell, 1992
SILK STALKINGS: NATURAL SELECTION (TF)   theme only,
     Stephen J. Cannell, 1994
THE ROCKFORD FILES: I STILL LOVE L.A. (TF)   MGB
     Prods./Universal TV, 1994
JAKE LASSITER: JUSTICE ON THE BAYOU (TF)   Ron Gilbert
     Associates/Big Prods./Spanish Trail, 1995
MURDER ONE: FINAL VERDICT (TF)   Steven Bochco Prods., 1997

STEVE POSTEL
Contact: BMI - Los Angeles, 310-659-9109

JUMPIN' AT THE BONEYARD   20th Century Fox, 1991

ALBY POTTS
Contact: BMI - Los Angeles, 310-659-9109

SEASON CHANGE   Jaguar Pictures, 1994

YAROL POUPAUD
TRAVOLTA ET MOI   *TRAVOLTA AND ME*   1993, French

ANDREW POWELL
Contact: PRS - London, England, 011-44-1-580-5544

LADYHAWKE   Warner Bros., 1985
ROCKET GIBRALTAR   Columbia, 1988

REG POWELL
Contact: ASCAP - Los Angeles, 213-883-1000

CALIFORNIA CASANOVA   co-composer with Sam Winans,
     Academy, 1991
ALASKA   Columbia, 1996

DENNIS M. PRATT
Contact: 417-335-3581

UPHILL ALL THE WAY   New World, 1985

PRAY FOR RAIN
Agent: William Morris - Beverly Hills, 310-859-4000
Affiliation: BMI - Los Angeles, 310-659-9109

STRAIGHT TO HELL   1987
TRUST ME   1989
ZANDALEE   1991
ROADSIDE PROPHETS   Fine Line, 1992
LOVE, CHEAT AND STEAL (CTF)   Showtime, 1993
FLOUNDERING   Front Films, 1994
CAR 54, WHERE ARE YOU?   co-composer with Bernie Worrell,
     Orion, 1994
WHITE MILE (CTF)   Stonehenge, 1994
A BOY CALLED HATE   Skouras, 1995

ZBIGNIEW PREISNER
Agent: Vangelos Management - Encino, 818-380-1919
Affiliation: SACEM - France, 011-33-1-4715-4715

AT PLAY IN THE FIELDS OF THE LORD   1991, Universal
OLIVIER, OLIVIER   Sony Classics, 1992, French
LA DOUBLE VIE DE VERONIQUE   *THE DOUBLE LIFE OF
     VERONIKA*   Miramax, 1991, French-Polish
DAMAGE   New Line, 1992
THE SECRET GARDEN   Warner Bros., 1993
TROIS COULEURS: BLEU   *THREE COLORS: BLUE*   Miramax,
     1993, French
TROIS COULEURS: BLANC   *THREE COLORS: WHITE*   Miramax,
     1994, French-Swiss-Polish
MOUVEMENTS DU DESIR   *DESIRE IN MOTION*
     Alliance-Vivafilm, 1994, Canadian-Swiss
TROIS COULEURS: ROUGE   *THREE COLORS: RED*   Miramax,
     1994, French-Swiss-Polish
WHEN A MAN LOVES A WOMAN   Buena Vista, 1994
FEAST OF JULY   Buena Vista, 1995

GRAHAM PRESKETT
SOMETHING TO TALK ABOUT   co-composer with Hans Zimmer,
     Warner Bros., 1995

GABOR PRESSER
Contact: PRS - London, England, 011-44-1-580-5544

FELALOM   *BRATS*   1992, Hungarian

DON PRESTON
Contact: BMI - Los Angeles, 310-659-9109

ANDROID   Island Alive/New Realm, 1982
THE BEING   Embassy, 1983
NIGHT PATROL   New World, 1984
SILENT WITNESS (TF)   Robert Greenwald Productions, 1985
EYE OF THE TIGER   Scotti Brothers, 1986
BLOOD DINER   Vestron, 1987
THE UNDERACHIEVERS   Vestron, 1987
TIPS   Paragon Arts, 1987

JAN PRESTON
Contact: APRA - Australia, 011-61-2-922-6422

ILLUSTRIOUS ENERGY   Mirage Entertainment, 1988, New
     Zealand

CRAIG PREUSS
Contact: PRS - London, England, 011-44-1-580-5544

BHAJI ON THE BEACH   co-composer with John Altman, 1993,
     British

ANDRE PREVIN
b. April 6, 1929 - Berlin, Germany
Contact: ASCAP - Los Angeles, 213-883-1000

THE SUN COMES UP   MGM, 1949
SCENE OF THE CRIME   MGM, 1949
BORDER INCIDENT   MGM, 1949
CHALLENGE TO LASSIE   MGM, 1949
TENSION   MGM, 1949
SHADOW ON THE WALL   MGM, 1950
THE OUTRIDERS   MGM, 1950
THREE LITTLE WORDS ★   adaptation, MGM, 1950
DIAL 1119   MGM, 1950
KIM   MGM, 1950
CAUSE FOR ALARM   MGM, 1951
SMALL TOWN GIRL   MGM, 1953
THE GIRL WHO HAD EVERYTHING   MGM, 1953
KISS ME KATE ★   adaptation, MGM, 1953
GIVE A GIRL A BREAK   MGM, 1953
BAD DAY AT BLACK ROCK   MGM, 1955
IT'S ALWAYS FAIR WEATHER   MGM, 1955
KISMET   adaptation, MGM, 1955
THE CATERED AFFAIR   MGM, 1956
THE FASTEST GUN ALIVE   MGM, 1956
HOT SUMMER NIGHT   MGM, 1957
DESIGNING WOMAN   MGM, 1957
SILK STOCKINGS   adaptation, MGM, 1957
HOUSE OF NUMBERS   Columbia, 1957
GIGI ★★   adaptation, MGM, 1958
PORGY AND BESS ★★   adaptation, Columbia, 1959
WHO WAS THAT LADY?   Columbia, 1960
THE SUBTERRANEANS   MGM, 1960
BELLS ARE RINGING ★   adaptation, MGM, 1960
ELMER GANTRY ★   United Artists, 1960
ALL IN A NIGHT'S WORK   Paramount, 1961
ONE, TWO, THREE   United Artists, 1961
THE FOUR HORSEMEN OF THE APOCALYPSE   MGM, 1962
LONG DAY'S JOURNEY INTO NIGHT   Embassy, 1962
TWO FOR THE SEESAW   United Artists, 1962
IRMA LA DOUCE ★★   United Artists, 1963
DEAD RINGER   Warner Bros., 1964
MY FAIR LADY ★★   adaptation, Warner Bros., 1964
GOODBYE CHARLIE   20th Century-Fox, 1964
KISS ME, STUPID   Lopert, 1964
INSIDE DAISY CLOVER   Warner Bros., 1965
THE FORTUNE COOKIE   United Artists, 1966
ROLLERBALL   also supervision, United Artists, 1975

ALAN PRICE
b. 1942
Contact: PRS - London, England, 011-44-1-580-5544

OH, LUCKY MAN!   Warner Bros., 1973, British
ALFIE DARLING   OH! ALFIE   EMI Films, 1975, British
BRITTANIA HOSPITAL   United Artists Classics, 1982, British
THE WHALES OF AUGUST   Alive Films, 1987

GEORGE S. PRICE
Contact: BMI - Los Angeles, 310-659-9109

GUYANA, CULT OF THE DAMNED   co-composer with Nelson
   Riddle and Robert Summers, Universal, 1980

JIM PRICE
HANGFIRE   Motion Picture Corp. of America, 1991

STEPHEN PRICE
DEADLY CURRENTS (FD)   Associated Producers, 1991,
   Canadian

FRANK PRIMATA
MAUSOLEUM   MPM, 1983

ROBERT PRINCE
Contact: ASCAP - Los Angeles, 213-883-1000

A LITTLE GAME (TF)   Universal TV, 1971
WHAT'S A NICE GIRL LIKE YOU...? (TF)   Universal TV, 1971

GARGOYLES (TF)   Tomorrow Entertainment, 1972
COOL MILLION (TF)   Universal TV, 1972
SCREAM, PRETTY PEGGY (TF)   Universal TV, 1973
A CRY IN THE WILDERNESS (TF)   Universal TV, 1974
WHERE HAVE ALL THE PEOPLE GONE? (TF)   Metromedia
   Producers Corporation/The Jozak Company, 1974
THE STRANGE AND DEADLY OCCURRENCE (TF)   Metromedia
   Productions, 1974
BIG ROSE (TF)   20th Century-Fox TV, 1974
NEWMAN'S LAW   Universal, 1974
THE STRANGE AND DEADLU OCCURRENCE (TF)   Metromedia
   Producers Corporation/Alpine Productions, 1974
WHERE HAVE ALL THE PEOPLE GONE? (TF)   Metromedia
   Productions, 1974
THE DEAD DON'T DIE (TF)   Douglas S. Cramer Productions, 1975
J.D.'S REVENGE   American International, 1976
SQUIRM   American International, 1976
THE FANTASTIC JOURNEY (TF)   Bruce Lansbury/Columbia TV,
   1977
SNOWBEAST (TF)   Douglas Cramer Productions, 1977
HAPPINESS IS A WARM CLUE   THE RETURN OF CHARLIE
   CHAN (TF)   Charlie Chan Company/Universal TV, 1979
THE GATHERING, PART II (TF)   Hanna-Barbera Productions,
   1979
THE SEDUCTION OF MISS LEONA (TF)   Edgar J. Scherick
   Associates, 1980
THE VIOLATION OF SARAH McDAVID (TF)   CBS Entertainment,
   1981

JEAN PRODROMIDES
b. July 3, 1927 - Neuilly-sur-Seine, France
Contact: SACEM - France, 011-33-1-4715-4715

L'HOMME DANS LA MUIERE   1952, French
GENEVIEVE A GAGNE SON PARI   1953, French
DANS L'OMBRE DES COMBATS   1954, French
UN JARDIN PUBLIC   1955, French
COURTE TETE   1955, French
LES BIENS DE CE MONDE   1957, French
ARCHIMEDE LE CLOCHARD   1958, French
LE VOYAGE EN BALLON   1958, French
MAIGRET ET L'AFFAIRE SAINT-FIACRE   1959, French
LE BARON DE L'ECLUSE   1959, French
BLOOD AND ROSES   ET MOURIR DE PLAISIR   Paramount,
   1960, Italian
LES PERSES   1961, French
SPIRITS OF THE DEAD   composer of "Metzengerstein" segment,
   American International, 1967, Italian-French
SOUS LE SIGNE DU TAUREAU   1968, French
24 HEURES DE LA VIE D'UNE FEMME   1968, French
THE EDUCATION IN LOVE OF VALENTIN   1975, French
DANTON   Triumph/Columbia, 1983, French-Polish

SACHA PUTTNAM
THE CONFESSIONAL   LE CONFESSIONAL   1995,
   Canadian-British-French

QUEEN
Contact: PRS - London, England, 011-44-1-580-5544

FLASH GORDON   co-composers with Howard Blake, Universal,
   1980, British
HIGHLANDER   additional music/song score, instrumental score by
   Michael Kamen, 20th Century Fox, 1986, British-U.S.

HAMLET LIMA QUINTANA
EL SUR   THE SOUTH   co-composer with Ariel Ramirez, 1992,
   Spanish

R

PEER RABEN

Contact: GEMA - Germany, 011-49-89-480-03610

GODS OF PESTILENCE 1970, West German
THE AMERICAN SOLDIER New Yorker, 1970, West German
RECRUITS IN INGOLSTADT 1971, West German
WHITY 1971, West German
CHETAN, INDIAN BOY 1973, West German
THE TENDERNESS OF WOLVES 1973, West German
ICE-AGE 1975, West German
MIGHT MAKES RIGHT 1975, West German
CHINESE ROULETTE New Yorker, 1976, West German
FEAR OF FEAR 1976, West German
GAME PASS 1976, West German
SATAN'S BREW New Yorker, 1976, West German
VIOLANTA 1976, West German
DESPAIR New Line Cinema, 1978, West German
FIFTY-FIFTY 1978, West German
THE THIRD GENERATION 1979, West German
LILI MARLEEN Luggi Waldleitner, 1981, West German
VERONIKA VOSS Laura Film, 1982, West German
QUERELLE Triumph/Columbia, 1982, West German-French
THE WIZARD OF BABYLON (FD) Planet, 1982, West German
THE SWING 1983, West German
GLUT EMBERS 1983, Swiss-West German
LES TRICHEURS Films du Galatee, 1983, French-West German
GRENZENLOS *OPEN ENDS* 1983, West German
A WOMAN FLAMBEE 1983, West German
NOTHING LEFT TO LOVE 1983, West German
SINS OF THE FATHERS (CTF) Bavaria Atelier
   GmbH/Taurus-Film/RAI/RETE, 1988, West German
HAPPY BIRTHDAY, TURKE! co-composer with Markus Lonardoni,
   Senator Films, 1992, German

TREVOR RABIN

THE GLIMMER MAN Warner Bros., 1996

HARRY RABINOWITZ

Contact: PRS - London, England, 011-44-1-580-5544

REILLY - ACE OF SPIES (MS) Euston Films Ltd., 1984, British

ROBERT O. RAGLAND

b. July 3, 1931 - Chicago, Illinois
Contact: ASCAP - Los Angeles, 213-883-1000

THE THING WITH TWO HEADS American International, 1972
THE TOUCH OF SATAN Embassy, 1973
ABBY American International, 1974
RETURN TO MACON COUNTY American International, 1975
SEVEN ALONE Doty-Dayton, 1975
SHARK'S TREASURE United Artists, 1975
GRIZZLY Film Ventures International, 1976
MANSION OF THE DOOMED 1977
JAGUAR LIVES! American International, 1979
DEADLY GAMES Monterey Films, 1979
ONLY ONCE IN A LIFETIME 1979
MOUNTAIN FAMILY ROBINSON Pacific International, 1979
HIGH ICE (TF) ESJ Productions, 1980
THE GLOVE BLOOD MAD Pro International, 1981
Q United Film Distribution, 1982
10 TO MIDNIGHT Cannon, 1983
BRAIN WAVES Motion Picture Marketing, 1983
A TIME TO DIE *SEVEN GRAVES FOR ROGAN* Almi Films, 1983
LOVELY BUT DEADLY Juniper Releasing Co., 1983
HYSTERICAL co-composer with Robert Alcivar, Embassy, 1983
THE GUARDIAN (CTF) HBO Premiere Films/Robert Cooper
   Productions/Stanely Chase Productions, 1984, U.S.-Canadian
THE SUPERNATURALS Republic Entertainment/Sandy Howard
   Productions, 1985
PRETTYKILL Spectrafilm, 1987

ASSASSINATION co-composer with Valentine McCallum, Cannon,
   1987
NIGHTSTICK Production Distribution Co., 1987
MESSENGER OF DEATH Cannon, 1988
THE FEAR Devin Intl., 1995
THE RAFFLE Devin Int'l, 1995
TOO FAST TOO YOUNG U.S. Filmcorp, 1996
SHADOWCHASER IV Nu Image, 1996
WARHEAD Nu Image, 1996
TOP OF THE WORLD Nu Image, 1997
PLATO'S RUN Nu Image, 1997

NICK RAINE

D.W. GRIFFITH: FATHER OF FILM (TD) co-composer with Carl
   Davis and Philip Appleby, WNET/Thames TV, 1993

TONY RAINS

AN INVASION OF PRIVACY (TF) Dick Berg-Stonehenge
   Productions/Embassy TV, 1983

DAVID RAKSIN*

b. August 4, 1912 - Philadelphia, Pennsylvania
Agent: Robert Light - Los Angeles, 213-651-1777
Affiliation: ASCAP - Los Angeles, 213-883-1000

MARRY THE GIRL Warner Bros., 1937
MIDNIGHT COURT co-composer, Warner Bros., 1937
MARKED WOMAN co-composer, Warner Bros., 1937
52ND STREET co-composer, 1937
DON'T PULL YOUR PUNCHES co-composer, 1937
THE MIGHTY TREVE Universal, 1937
LET THEM LIVE 1937
AS GOOD AS MARRIED 1937
SHE'S DANGEROUS Universal, 1937
SAN QUENTIN Warner Bros., 1937
WINGS OVER HONOLULU Universal, 1937
THE KID COMES BACK co-composer, Warner Bros., 1938
FRONTIER MARSHAL co-composer, 20th Century-Fox, 1939
THE ADVENTURES OF SHERLOCK HOLMES co-composer, 20th
   Century-Fox, 1939
HOLLYWOOD CAVALCADE co-composer, 20th Century-Fox, 1939
MR. MOTO'S LAST WARNING co-composer, 20th Century-Fox,
   1939
STANLEY AND LIVINGSTONE co-composer, 20th Century-Fox,
   1939
SUEZ co-composer, 20th Century-Fox, 1939
STORM WARNING 1940
DEAD MEN TELL 20th Century-Fox, 1940
THE MEN IN HER LIFE Columbia, 1941
RIDE ON, VAQUERO co-composer, 20th Century-Fox, 1941
DR. RENAULT'S SECRET co-composer, 20th Century-Fox, 1942
JUST OFF BROADWAY co-composer, 20th Century-Fox, 1942
THE MAN WHO WOULDN'T DIE 20th Century-Fox, 1942
THE MAGNICIENT DOPE 20th Century-Fox, 1942
MANILA CALLING co-composer, 20th Century-Fox, 1942
THE UNDYING MONSTER 20th Century-Fox, 1942
WHISPERING GHOSTS co-composer, 20th Century-Fox, 1942
WHO IS HOPE SCHUYLER? co-composer, 20th Century-Fox,
   1942
CITY WITHOUT MEN Columbia, 1943
SOMETHING TO SHOUT ABOUT adaptation, Columbia, 1943
LAURA 20th Century-Fox, 1944
TAMPICO 20th Century-Fox, 1944
ATTACK IN THE PACIFIC (FD) U.S. Navy, 1945
DON JUAN QUILLIGAN 20th Century-Fox, 1945
FALLEN ANGEL 20th Century-Fox, 1945
WHERE DO WE GO FROM HERE? 20th Century-Fox, 1945
SMOKY 20th Century-Fox, 1946
THE SHOCKING MISS PILGRIM adaptation, 20th Century-Fox,
   1947
FOREVER AMBER ★ 20th Century-Fox, 1947
DAISY KENYON 20th Century-Fox, 1947
THE HOMESTRETCH 20th Century-Fox, 1947
THE SECRET LIFE OF WALTER MITTY RKO Radio, 1947
APARTMENT FOR PEGGY 20th Century-Fox, 1948
FURY AT FURNACE CREEK 20th Century-Fox, 1948
FORCE OF EVIL MGM, 1948
WHIRLPOOL 20th Century-Fox, 1950
GROUNDS FOR MARRIAGE co-composer with Bronislau Kaper,
   MGM, 1950
A LADY WITHOUT PASSPORT MGM, 1950

THE MAGNIFICENT YANKEE   MGM, 1950
THE NEXT VOICE YOU HEAR   MGM, 1950
THE REFORMER AND THE REDHEAD   MGM, 1950
RIGHT CROSS   MGM, 1950
ACROSS THE WIDE MISSOURI   MGM, 1951
KIND LADY   MGM, 1951
THE MAN WITH A CLOAK   MGM, 1951
IT'S A BIG COUNTRY   co-composer, MGM, 1952
THE BAD AND THE BEAUTIFUL   MGM, 1952
CARRIE   Paramount, 1952
BLOODHOUNDS OF BROADWAY   20th Century-Fox, 1952
THE GIRL IN WHITE   MGM, 1952
PAT AND MIKE   MGM, 1952
LIFE WITH FATHER (TF)   CBS TV, 1954
APACHE   United Artists, 1954
SUDDENLY   United Artists, 1954
THE BIG COMBO   Allied Artists, 1955
BIGGER THAN LIFE   20th Century-Fox, 1956
HILDA CRANE   20th Century-Fox, 1956
JUBAL   Columbia, 1956
SEVEN WONDERS OF THE WORLD   co-composer, Stanley
    Warner Cinema Corporation, 1956
GUNSIGHT RIDGE   United Artists, 1957
MAN ON FIRE   MGM, 1957
UNTIL THEY SAIL   MGM, 1957
THE VINTAGE   MGM, 1957
TWILIGHT FOR THE GODS   Universal, 1958
SEPARATE TABLES ★   United Artists, 1958
AL CAPONE   Allied Artists, 1959
PAY OR DIE   Allied Artists, 1960
FATHER OF THE BRIDE (TF)   MGM TV, 1960
TOO LATE BLUES   Paramount, 1962
TWO WEEKS IN ANOTHER TOWN   MGM, 1962
NIGHT TIDE   Universal, 1963
INVITATION TO A GUNFIGHTER   United Artists, 1964
THE PATSY   Paramount, 1964
LOVE HAS MANY FACES   Columbia, 1965
SYLVIA   Paramount, 1965
THE REDEEMER   Empire, 1966
A BIG HAND FOR THE LITTLE LADY   Warner Bros., 1966
WILL PENNY   Paramount, 1968
THE OVER-THE-HILL GANG RIDES AGAIN (TF)   Thomas-Spelling
    Productions, 1970
WHAT'S THE MATTER WITH HELEN?   United Artists, 1971
GLASS HOUSES   Columbia, 1972
THE GHOST OF FLIGHT 401 (TF)   Paramount TV, 1978
THE SUICIDE'S WIFE (TF)   Factor-Newland Production
    Corporation, 1979
THE DAY AFTER (TF)   ABC Circle Films, 1983
LADY IN A CORNER (TF)   Fries Entertainment, 1989

RON RAMIN*
Agent: Film Music Associates - Hollywood, 213-463-1070
Affiliation: BMI - Los Angeles, 310-659-9109

STRANGER ON MY LAND (TF)   Edgar J. Scherick Associates/Taft
    Entertainment TV, 1988
FROG (TF)   Platypus Productions, 1988
THE DIAMOND TRAP (TF)   Jay Bernstein Productions/Columbia
    TV, 1988
MICKEY SPILLANE'S MIKE HAMMER: MURDER TAKES ALL (TF)
    Jay Bernstein Productions/Columbia Pictures TV, 1989
SIDNEY SHELDON'S MEMORIES OF MIDNIGHT (TF)   Dove
    Audio/WIN/Tribune, 1991
THEY'VE TAKEN OUR CHILDREN: THE CROWCHILLA
    KIDNAPPING (TF)   Rom Gilbert/Joel Fields/Leonard Hill, 1993
CHRISTY (TF) ☆   1994
THE BIRDS II: LAND'S END (CTF)   Rosemont/MTE-Universal,
    1994
BIONIC EVER AFTER (TF)   Michael Sloan Prods./Gallant
    Ent./MTE, 1994
COME WITH ME: A MICKEY SPILLANE's MIKE HAMMER MYSTERY
    (TF)   Caroline Films Prods./CBS Entertainment Prods., 1994
DARE TO LOVE (TF)   WildRice Prods./CBS Ent., 1995

SID RAMIN
Contact: ASCAP - Los Angeles, 213-883-1000

SIDNEY SHELDON'S MEMORIES OF MIDNIGHT (TF)   theme only,
    Dove Audio/WIN/Tribune, 1991

ARIEL RAMIREZ
Contact: SADAIC - Argentina, 011-54-1-40-4867/8

EL SUR *THE SOUTH*   co-composer with Hamlet Lima Quintana,
    1992, Spanish

KENNARD RAMSEY
Contact: ASCAP - Los Angeles, 213-883-1000

THE HEAVENLY KID   Orion, 1985
UNCLE TOM'S CABIN (CTF)   Edgar J. Scherick Productions/Taft
    Entertainment TV, 1987

WILLIS ALAN RAMSEY
Contact: ASCAP - Los Angeles, 213-883-1000

SECOND-HAND HEARTS   Lorimar, 1980

ROBERT RANDLES
Contact: BMI - Los Angeles, 310-659-9109

NOBODY'S PERFECT   Moviestore Entertainment, 1989
RUBY CAIRO   ethnic music only, Miramax, 1993

RAREVIEW
HOT PURSUIT   Paramount, 1987

KEN RARICK
Contact: BMI - Los Angeles, 310-659-9109

IN THE HEAT OF PASSION   co-composer with Art Wood,
    Concorde, 1992

RAF RAVENSCROFT
DOUBLE X: THE NAME OF THE GAME   1992, British

EDDIE RAYNOR
Contact: APRA - Australia, 011-61-2-922-6422

RIKKY AND PETE   co-composer with Phil Judd, MGM/UA, 1988,
    Australian

CHRIS REA
Contact: PRS - London, England, 011-44-1-580-5544

CROSS COUNTRY   New World, 1983

ROBERT REALE
Contact: ASCAP - Los Angeles, 213-883-1000

WIGSTOCK: THE MOVIE (FD)   co-composer with Peter Fish,
    Samuel Goldwyn, 1995

COBY RECHT
Contact: ASCAP - Los Angeles, 213-883-1000

THE APPLE   co-composer with Iris Recht, Cannon, 1980,
    U.S.-West German

IRIS RECHT
Contact: SACEM - France, 011-33-1-4715-4715

THE APPLE   co-composer with Coby Recht, Cannon, 1980,
    U.S.-West German

LEON REDBONE
Contact: BMI - Los Angeles, 310-659-9109

EVERYBODY WINS   additional music, Orion, 1990

RED CLAY RAMBLERS
FAR NORTH   Alive Films, 1988

J.A.C. REDFORD*

Agent: Gorfaine-Schwartz - Los Angeles, 213-969-1011
Affiliation: ASCAP - Los Angeles, 213-883-1000

STINGRAY   Avco Embassy, 1978
THE LONG SUMMER OF GEORGE ADAMS (TF)   co-composer,
   Warner Bros. TV, 1982
HONEYBOY (TF)   Fan Fares Inc. Productions/Estrada Productions,
   1982
HAPPY ENDINGS (TF)   Blinn-Thorpe Productions, 1983
HELEN KELLER - THE MIRACLE CONTINUES (TF)   Castle Combe
   Productions/20th Century-Fox TV, 1984, U.S.-British
THE TRIP TO BOUNTIFUL   Island Pictures/Film Dallas, 1985
GOING FOR THE GOLD: THE BILL JOHNSON STORY (TF)   ITC
   Productions/Sullivan-Carter Interests/Goodman-Rosen
   Productions, 1985
THE KFY TO REBECCA (TF)   Taft Entertainment TV/Castle Combe
   Productions, 1985, U.S.-British
EXTREMITIES   Atlantic Releasing Corporation, 1986
CRY FROM THE MOUNTAIN   World Wide, 1986
ALEX: THE LIFE OF A CHILD (TF)   Mandy Productions, 1986
EASY PREY (TF)   New World TV/Rene Malo Productions, 1986,
   U.S.-Canadian
INDEPENDENCE (TF)   Sunn Classic Pictures, 1987
THE LONG JOURNEY HOME (TF)   Andrea Baynes
   Productions/Grail Productions/Lorimar-Telepictures, 1987
OLIVER & CO. (AF)   Buena Vista, 1988
SAVE THE DOG (CTF)   The Disney Channel, 1988
BREAKING POINT (CTF)   Avnet/Kerner Co., 1989
A SON'S PROMISE (TF)   Marian Rees Associates, 1990
STOP AT NOTHING (CTF)   Chair/ABC, 1991
CONAGHER (CTF)   Imagine TV, 1991
NEWSIES   Buena Vista, 1992
KISS OF A KILLER (TF)   Andrew Adelson Co./John Conboy
   Prods./ABC Prods., 1993
FOR THEIR OWN GOOD (TF)   Avnet-Kerner Co., 1993
D2: THE MIGHTY DUCKS   Buena Vista, 1994
ONE MORE MOUNTAIN (TF)   Marian Rees Associates/Walt Disney
   TV, 1994
AND THEN THERE WAS ONE (TF)   Freyda Rothstein
   Prods./Hearst, 1994
IS THERE LIFE OUT THERE? (TF)   Marian Rees
   Associates/Starstruck Ent., 1994
BYE BYE, LOVE   20th Century Fox, 1995
HEAVYWEIGHTS   Buena Vista, 1995
NAOMI & WYNONNA: LOVE CAN BUILD A BRIDGE (TF)
   Avnet-Kerner Co., 1995
D3: THE MIGHTY DUCKS   Buena Vista, 1996

JOSHUA REDMAN

VANYA ON 42nd STREET   Sony Classics, 1994

JERRY REED

b. March 20, 1937
Contact: BMI - Los Angeles, 310-659-9109

SMOKEY AND THE BANDIT   Universal, 1977

LES REED

Contact: PRS - London, England, 011-44-1-580-5544

THE GIRL ON A MOTORCYCLE   *NAKED UNDER LEATHER*
   Claridge, 1968, British-French
LES BICYCLETTES DE BELSIZE   1969, British-French
THE BUSHBABY   MGM, 1970
ONE MORE TIME   United Artists, 1970
CREEPSHOW 2   New World, 1987

PATRICK C. REGAN

Contact: ASCAP - Los Angeles, 213-883-1000

STEPFATHER II   co-composer with Jim Manzie, Millimeter Films,
   1989
LEATHERFACE: THE TEXAS CHAINSAW MASSACRE III
   co-composer with Jim Manzie, New Line Cinema, 1990
TALES FROM THE DARKSIDE: THE MOVIE   co-composer,
   Paramount, 1990
STEPFATHER III (CTF)   ITC Entertainment Group, 1992

JUSTIN REINHARDT

SWINGERS   co-composer with Julianne Kelley, 1996

NIKI REISER

I WAS ON MARS   1992, Germany
NOBODY LOVES ME   *KEINER LIEBT MICH*   German, 1995

GARY REMAL-MALKIN
(Gary Remal)

Contact: ASCAP - Los Angeles, 213-883-1000

DARK CIRCLE (FD)   co-composer with Bernard Krause,
   Independent Documentary Group, 1982
BREAKIN'   co-composer with Michael Boyd, MGM/UA, 1984
MARIA'S LOVERS   MGM/UA/Cannon, 1984

ROBERT RENFROW

FUTURE-KILL   International Film Marketing, 1985

ADI RENNERT

REAL TIME   1991, Israeli
TIME FOR CHEERIES   1991, Israeli

RUTH RENNIE

Contact: PRS - London, England, 011-44-1-580-5544

WHEN THE WHALES CAME   additional music, 20th Century Fox,
   1989, British

JOHNNY RENO

REBEL HIGHWAY: ROADRACERS (CTF)   co-composer with Paul
   Boll, Drive-In Classics, 1994

JOE RENZETTI*

Contact: BMI - Los Angeles, 310-659-9109

THE BUDDY HOLLY STORY ★★   Columbia, 1978
COTTON CANDY (TF)   Major H Productions, 1978
ELVIS (TF)   Dick Clark Productions, 1979
DIARY OF A HITCHHIKER (TF)   The Shpetner Company, 1979
MARATHON (TF)   Alan Landsburg Productions, 1980
FATSO   20th Century-Fox, 1980
THE EXTERMINATOR   Avco Embassy, 1980
DEAD AND BURIED   Avco Embassy, 1981
UNDER THE RAINBOW   Orion/Warner Bros., 1981
THROUGH THE MAGIC PYRAMID (TF)   Major H Productions,
   1981
MYSTERIOUS TWO (TF)   Alan Landsburg Productions, 1982
WANTED: DEAD OR ALIVE   New World, 1987
CHILD'S PLAY   MGM/UA, 1988
POLTERGEIST 3   MGM/UA, 1988
LISA   United Artists, 1989
BASKET CASE 2   Shapiro-Glickenhaus Entertainment, 1990
FRANKENHOOKER   Shapiro-Glickenhaus Entertainment, 1990
MURDEROUS VISION (CTF)   Gary Sherman Prods./Wilshire Court,
   1991
BASKET CASE 3: THE PROGENY   Shapiro Glickenhaus, 1992
MISSING PERSONS (TF)   Stephen J. Cannell, 1993

GRAEME REVELL

Agent: The Kraft-Benjamin Agency - Beverly Hills, 310-247-0123
Affiliation: APRA - Australia, 011-61-2-922-6422

DEAD CALM   Warner Bros., 1989, Australian
SPONTANEOUS COMBUSTION   Taurus Entertainment, 1990
CHILD'S PLAY 2   Universal, 1990
UNTIL THE END OF THE WORLD   Warner Bros., 1991,
   German-French-Australian
THE HAND THAT ROCKS THE CRADLE   Buena Vista, 1991
LOVE CRIMES   Millimeter, 1992
TRACES OF RED   Samuel Goldwyn, 1992
BODY OF EVIDENCE   MGM/UA, 1993
HEAR NO EVIL   20th Century Fox, 1993
THE CRUSH   Warner Bros., 1993
HARD TARGET   Universal, 1993
BOXING HELENA   Main Line, 1993
GHOST IN THE MACHINE   20th Century Fox, 1993

THE CROW   Miramax-Dimension, 1994
S.F.W.   Gramercy, 1994
NO ESCAPE   Savoy, 1994
STREET FIGHTER   Universal, 1994
THE BASKETBALL DIARIES   New Line, 1995
TANK GIRL   MGM-UA, 1995
MIGHTY MORPHIN POWER RANGERS THE MOVIE   20th Century
    Fox, 1995
STRANGE DAYS   20th Century Fox, 1995
DOWN CAME A BLACKBIRD (CTF)   Viacom/Chanticleer, 1995
FROM DUSK TILL DAWN   Miramax-Dimension, 1996
RACE THE SUN   TriStar, 1996
THE CRAFT   Columbia, 1996
FLED   MGM-UA, 1996
THE CROW: CITY OF ANGELS   1996
KILLER: A JOURNAL OF MURDER   1996
THE SAINT   Paramount, 1997
SPAWN   1997

GIAN REVERBERI
Contact: SIAE - Italy, 011-39-6-59-901

NOT QUITE PARADISE   *NOT QUITE JERUSALEM*   New World,
    1985, British

JOHN REYNOLDS
FRANK & OLLIE   1996

THE RH FACTOR
FOREVER   Triax/DDM, 1992

KEN RICHMOND
Contact: ASCAP - Los Angeles, 213-883-1000

IT HAPPENED AT LAKEWOOD MANOR (TF)   Alan Landsburg
    Productions, 1977

DAVID RICKETS
ECHO PARK   Atlantic Releasing Corporation, 1985, U.S.-Austrian

NED RIFLE
Contact: ASCAP - Los Angeles, 213-883-1000

SIMPLE MEN   Fine Line, 1992
AMATEUR   co-composer with Jeffrey Taylor, 1994, U.S.-French
FLIRT   co-composer with Jeff Taylor, 1996

LAURIN RINDER
Contact: BMI - Los Angeles, 310-659-9109

ENTER THE NINJA   co-composer with W. Michael Lewis, Cannon,
    1981
FIRECRACKER   co-composer with W. Michael Lewis, New World,
    1981, U.S.-Filipino
SHOGUN ASSASSIN   co-composer with W. Michael Lewis, New
    World, 1981, Japanese-U.S.
HOT BUBBLEGUM   *LEMON POPSICLE III*   co-composer with W.
    Michael Lewis, Noah Films, 1981, Israeli
NEW YEAR'S EVIL   co-composer with W. Michael Lewis, Cannon,
    1981
THE KILLING OF AMERICA   co-composer with W. Michael Lewis,
    Toho, 1982, Japanese
THE KULIES   co-composer with W. Michael Lewis, Global
THE BALLAD OF GREGORIO CORTEZ   co-composer with W.
    Michael Lewis, Embassy, 1983
REVENGE OF THE NINJA   additional music, MGM/UA/Cannon,
    1983
NINJA III—THE DOMINATION   co-composer with W. Michael
    Lewis, Cannon, 1984
BAD MANNERS   *GROWING PAINS*   co-composer with W. Michael
    Lewis, New World, 1984
HOT CHILD IN THE CITY   co-composer with W. Michael Lewis,
    Mediacom Filmworks, 1987

TONY RIPPARETTI*
Agent: Robert Light - Los Angeles, 213-651-1777
Affiliation: ASCAP - Los Angeles, 213-883-1000

RADIOACTIVE DREAMS   DEG, 1987
SAY YES   Cinetel Films, 1987
PLEASURE PLANET   Empire Films, 1988
COMMANDO SQUAD   Cinetel Films, 1988
ALIEN FROM L.A.   Cannon, 1989
DECEIT   21st Century, 1990
KICKBOXER II: THE ROAD BACK   KINGS ROAD, 1991
BLOODMATCH   21st Century, 1992
DOLLMAN   Full Moon, 1992
KNIGHTS   Kings Road, 1993
ARCADE   Full Moon, 1993
DOLLMAN VS. DEMONIC TOYS   Full Moon, 1993
BRAIN SMASHER...A LOVE STORY   Kings Road, 1993
KICKBOXER IV: THE AGRESSOR   Kings Road, 1994
TAMMY AND THE TEENAGE T-REX   Imperial Ent., 1994
SPIT FIRE   Trimark, 1994
HEAT SEEKER   Trimark, 1994
NEMESIS III: TIME LAPSE   Imperial Ent., 1995
NEMESIS IV: ANGEL CRY   Imperial Ent., 1995
FAST MONEY   Stu Segall Productions, 1996
ADRENALIN: FEAR THE RUSH   1996
BLAST   Toga Prods., 1996
OMEGA DOOM   Filmwerks, 1996
MEAN GUNS   Filmwerks, 1997

PAUL RISER
Contact: BMI - Los Angeles, 310-659-9109

WHICH WAY IS UP?   co-composer with Mark Davis, Universal,
    1977

LEE RITENOUR
Contact: ASCAP - Los Angeles, 213-883-1000

AMERICAN FLYERS   co-composer with Greg Mathieson, Warner
    Bros., 1985
ROCK'N'ROLL MOM (TF)   Walt Disney TV, 1988

WALTER RIZZATI
Contact: SIAE - Italy, 011-39-6-59-901

THE HOUSE BY THE CEMETARY   Almi Pictures, 1981, Italian
1990: THE BRONX   United Film Distribution, 1983, Italian

TOM RIZZO
Agent: Carol Faith Agency - Beverly Hills, 310-274-0776
Affiliation: ASCAP - Los Angeles, 213-883-1000

LOVE AT STAKE   Hemdale, 1987

DAVID ROBBINS
Agent: The Kordek Agency - Bunbank, 818-559-4248
Affiliation: ASCAP - Los Angeles, 213-883-1000

TOO MUCH SUN   New Line, 1990
TED AND VENUS   Double Helix, 1991
BOB ROBERTS   Paramount/Miramax, 1992
TWENTY BUCKS   Big Tomorrow Productions, 1993
DEAD MAN WALKING   Gramercy, 1995

RICHARD ROBBINS
Agent: CAA - Beverly Hills, 310-288-4545
Affiliation: PRS - London, England, 011-44-1-580-5544

THE EUROPEANS   Levitt-Pickman, 1979, British
JANE AUSTEN IN MANHATTAN   Contemporary, 1980
QUARTET   New World, 1981, British-French
HEAT AND DUST   Universal Classics, 1983, British
THE BOSTONIANS   Almi Pictures, 1984
A ROOM WITH A VIEW   Cinecom, 1986, British
MY LITTLE GIRL   Hemdale, 1986
SWEET LORRAINE   Angelika Films, 1987
MAURICE   Cinecom, 1987, British

F
I
L
M

C
O
M
P
O
S
E
R
S

THE PERFECT MURDER   Merchant Ivory Productions, 1988,
   British-Indian
SLAVES OF NEW YORK   Tri-Star, 1989
BAIL JUMPER   Angelika Films, 1990
MR. AND MRS. BRIDGE   Miramax, 1990
THE BALLAD OF THE SAD CAFE   Angelika, 1991, U.S.-British
HOWARDS END ★   Orion Classics, 1992
THE REMAINS OF THE DAY ★   Columbia, 1993
JEFFERSON IN PARIS   Buena Vista, 1995
THE PROPRIETOR   1996
SURVIVING PICASSO   Warner Bros., 1996

JIM ROBERGE
Contact: ASCAP - Los Angeles, 213-883-1000

JOEY   Satori Entertainment, 1985

GUY ROBERT
b. France
Contact: SACEM - France, 011-33-1-4715-4715

PERCEVAL LE GALLOIS   Gaumont, 1978, French

MAX ROBERT
Contact: BMI - Los Angeles, 310-659-9109

RUMPELSTILTSKIN   Cannon, 1987

ANDY ROBERTS
Contact: PRS - London, England, 011-44-1-580-5544

LOOSE CONNECTIONS   co-composer with Dominic Muldowney,
   Orion Classics, 1983, British
PRIEST   1994, British
MAD LOVE   Buena Vista, 1995

BRUCE ROBERTS
Contact: BMI - Los Angeles, 310-659-9109

JINXED   co-composer with Miles Goodman, MGM/UA, 1982

B.A. ROBERTSON
Contact: PRS - London, England, 011-44-1-580-5544

GOSPEL ACCORDING TO VIC   JUST ANOTHER MIRACLE
   Skouras Pictures, 1986, British

BILL ROBERTSON
THE EVENTS LEADING UP TO MY DEATH   additional Music, Flat
   Rock Films, 1992

ERIC N. ROBERTSON
Contact: SOCAN - Toronto, 416-445-8700

SPASMS   Producers Distribution Company, 1983, Canadian
SPECIAL PEOPLE (TF)   Joe Cates Productions, 1986
HOME IS WHERE THE HART IS   Atlantic Entertainment Group,
   1987
MILLENNIUM   20th Century Fox, 1989
RUGGED GOLD (CTF)   co-composer with Dick Le Fort,
   Alliance/Gibson Group/Family Channel, 1994

HARRY ROBERTSON
b. Scotland
Contact: PRS - London, England, 011-44-1-580-5544

THE OBLONG BOX   American International, 1969, British
THE VAMPIRE LOVERS   American International, 1970, British
LUST FOR A VAMPIRE   American Continental, 1971, British
THE JOHNSTOWN MONSTER   Sebastian Films, Ltd., 1971,
   British
FRIGHT   1971, British
TWINS OF EVIL   Universal, 1972, British
COUNTESS DRACULA   20th Century-Fox, 1972, British
DEMONS OF THE MIND   MGM-EMI, 1972, British
THE HOUSE IN NIGHTMARE PARK   MGM-EMI, 1973, British
THE GHOUL   Rank, 1974, British

LEGEND OF THE WEREWOLF   Tyburn, 1975, British
HAWK THE SLAYER   ITC, 1980, British
PRISONER OF THE LOST UNIVERSE (CTF)   Marcel-Robertson
   Productions/United Media Finance, 1983

ROBBIE ROBERTSON
Agent: CAA - Beverly Hills, 310-288-4545
Affiliation: ASCAP - Los Angeles, 213-883-1000

THE KING OF COMEDY   20th Century-Fox, 1983
THE COLOR OF MONEY   Buena Vista, 1986
JIMMY HOLLYWOOD   Paramount, 1994
THE NATIVE AMERICANS (TD)   Turner Broadcasting, 1994

EARL ROBINSON
MAYBE HE'LL COME HOME IN THE SPRING (TF)   Metromedia
   Producers Corporation, 1971
THE GREAT MAN'S WHISKERS (TF)   Universal TV, 1973
HUCKLEBERRY FINN (TF)   ABC Circle Films, 1975

HARRY ROBINSON
Contact: BMI - Los Angeles, 310-659-9109

THERE GOES THE BRIDE   Vanguard Releasing, 1980

J. PETER ROBINSON*
Agent: Film Music Associates - Hollywood, 213-463-1070
Management: Derek Power Company - Los Angeles, 310-472-4647
Affiliation: ASCAP - Los Angeles, 213-883-1000

DEADLY ENCOUNTER (TF)   Roger Gimbel Productions/EMI TV,
   1982
KATE'S SECRET (TF)   Andrea Baynes Productions/Columbia TV,
   1986
THE WRAITH   New Century/Vista, 1986
J. EDGAR HOOVER (CTF)   RLC Productions/Finnegan Co., 1987
THE BELIVERS   Orion, 1987
THE GATE   co-composer with Michael Hoenig, New Century/Vista,
   1987, Canadian
BATES MOTEL (TF)   Universal TV, 1987
RETURN OF THE LIVING DEAD PART II   Lorimar, 1988
COCKTAIL   Buena Vista, 1988
DESERT RATS (TF)   Universal TV, 1988
THE KISS   Tri-Star, 1988, U.S.-Canadian
BLIND FURY   Tri-Star, 1989
THE GIFTED ONE (TF)   Richard Rothstein Productions/NBC
   Productions, 1989
THE WIZARD   Universal, 1989
CADILLAC MAN   Orion, 1990
DEADLY INTENTIONS...AGAIN ? (TF)   Green-Epstein/Lorimar TV,
   1991
HELL HATH NO FURY (TF)   Bar-Gene Prods./Finnegan-Pinchuk,
   1991
LIGHTNING FIELD (CTF)   Mark Gordon Co./Christopher
   Meledandri, 1991
ARE YOU LONESOME TONIGHT ? (CTF)   OTML Prods./Mahoney
   Co./Wilshire Court, 1992
ENCINO MAN   Buena Vista, 1992
WAYNE'S WORLD   Paramount, 1992
THE PRESIDENT'S CHILD (TF)   Lauren Films, 1992
THE NIGHT MY PARENTS RAN AWAY (TF)   Fox West
   Pictures/New Line TV/Chanticleer, 1993
WES CRAVEN'S NEW NIGHTMARE   New Line, 1994
HIGHLANDER III: THE SORCERER   Miramax, 1994,
   Canadian-French-British
RUMBLE IN THE BRONX   New Line, 1996
JACKIE CHAN'S FIRST STRIKE   New Line, 1997
FIRESTORM   20th Century Fox, 1997

LARRY ROBINSON
Contact: ASCAP - Los Angeles, 213-883-1000

FEAR OF A BLACK HAT   Oakwood, 1993

PETE ROBINSON
Contact: ASCAP - Los Angeles, 213-883-1000

RADIOACTIVE DREAMS   DEG, 1986
PIN   New World, 1989, Canadian

PETER MANNING ROBINSON
Agent: Seth Kaplan Entertainment - Los Angeles, 213-525-3477
Affiliation: BMI - Los Angeles, 310-659-9109

THE PENTHOUSE (TF)   Greene-White Productions/Spectacor
   Films, 1989
SMALL SACRIFICES (TF)   Louis Rudolph Silms/Motown/Allarcom
   Ltd./Fries Entertainment, 1989
IN THE BEST INTEREST OF THE CHILD (TF)   Papazian-Hirsch
   Entertainment, 1990
WHAT EVER HAPPENED TO BABY JANE? (TF)   Steve
   White/Aldrich Group/Spectacor, 1991
AND THE SEA WILL TELL (TF)   Green-Epstein/Columbia TV, 1991
NIGHT OF THE HUNTER (TF)   Diana Keren
   Prods./Konigsberg-Sanitsky, 1991
AND THEN SHE WAS GONE (TF)   Steve White Prods., 1991
HONOR THY MOTHER (TF)   Universal/MCA TV/Point of View,
   1992
DANGER ISLAND (TF)   von Zerneck-Sertner/NBC Prods., 1992
DARKNESS BEFORE DAWN (TF)   Diana Kerew Prods./Polone,
   1993
A FAMILY OF STRANGERS (TF)   Alliance, 1993
WOMAN ON THE RUN: THE LAWRENCIA BEMBENEK STORY
   (TF)   Alliance/CanWest/NBC, 1993
OTHER WOMEN'S CHILDREN (CTF)   Crescent Entertainment,
   1993
BEYOND OBSESSION (TF)   Pacific Motion Pictures/Western Intl.
   Comm./Green-Epstein/Warner Bros. TV, 1994
LONG SHADOWS (TF)   NHK/KCET/KCTS, 1994
GREEN DOLPHIN BEAT (TF)   Robert Ward Prods./Spelling TV,
   1994
THE BEANS OF EGYPT, MAINE   Live, 1994
FROSTFIRE   CBC, 1994
DEADLOCKED: ESCAPE FROM ZONE 14   *DEADLOCK II* (TF)
   Pacific/Spectacor/Jaffe-Braunstein/Signboard Hill, 1995
THE MADDENING   IRS Media, 1995
FAMILY OF COPS (TF)   Alliance, 1995
SOMETIMES THEY COME BACK...AGAIN   Trimark, 1996
A SEASON IN PURGATORY (TF)   Spelling TV, 1996
PRINCESS IN LOVE (TF)   Kushner-Locke, 1996
ONCE YOU MEET A STRANGER (TF)   Warner Bros. TV, 1996
EVERY WOMAN'S DREAM (TF)   Kushner-Locke, 1996
ECHOES (TF)   Kushner-Locke, 1996
KEEPING THE PROMISE (TF)   Marion Rees/Atlantis, 1996
TO FACE HER PAST (TF)   Citadel, 1996
SPREE (CTF)   MGM-TV, 1997
FAMILY OF COPS 2   Alliance, 1997
THE STEPSISTER (CTF)   Wilshire Court, 1997
HIT ME   Slough Pond Prods., 1997

NILE RODGERS
Contact: BMI - Los Angeles, 310-659-9109

SOUP FOR ONE   co-composer with Bernard Edwards, Warner
   Bros., 1982
ALPHABET CITY   Atlantic Releasing, 1984
WHITE HOT   *CRACK IN THE MIRROR*   Triax Entertainment
   Group, 1988
COMING TO AMERICA   Universal, 1988
EARTH GIRLS ARE EASY   Vestron, 1989
BLUE CHIPS   co-composer with Jeff Beck and Jed Lieber,
   Paramount, 1994
BEVERLY HILLS COP III   Paramount, 1994

SCOTT ROEWE*
Contact: BMI - Los Angeles, 310-659-9109

VIPER   Fries Distribution, 1988
TRUE BLOOD   Fries Entertainment, 1989
MINISTRY OF VENGEANCE   Concorde, 1989

KENNY ROGERS,JR
Contact: ASCAP - Los Angeles, 213-883-1000

MAC SHAYNE: WINNER TAKES ALL (TF)   co-composer with
   Edgar Struble, Larry Brown and Bob De Marco, Larry Levinson
   Prods./Kenny Rogers Prods., 1994
GAMBLER V: PLAYING FOR KEEPS (TF)   additional music,
   Kenny Rogers Prods./WIN/RHI, 1994
RIDERS IN THE STORM   co-composer with Bob Demarco,
   Filmhaus, 1995

SIMON ROGERS
Contact: PRS - London, England, 011-44-1-580-5544

DADDY (TF)   Robert Greenwald Productions, 1987

MICHAEL ROKATYN
ANGELA   Tree Farm Pictures, 1995

GEORGE ROMANIS
Contact: BMI - Los Angeles, 310-659-9109

U.M.C. (TF)   MGM TV, 1969
CRIME CLUB (TF)   CBS Entertainment, 1973
MANEATER (TF)   Universal TV, 1973
LIVE AGAIN, DIE AGAIN (TF)   Universal TV, 1974
THE FAMILY NOBODY WANTED (TF)   Groverton
   Productions/Universal TV, 1975
SHARK KILL (TF)   D'Antoni-Weitz Productions, 1976
NEVER CON A KILLER (TF)   Larry White Productions/Columbia
   Pictures TV, 1977
SHE'S DRESSED TO KILL (TF)   Grant-Case-McGrath
   Enterprises/Barry Weitz Films, 1979
REUNION (TF)   Barry Weitz Films, 1980
THE MONKEY MISSION (TF)   Mickey Productions/Filmways, 1981
THE BIG BLACK PILL (TF)   Filmways/Micky Productions/NBC
   Entertainment, 1981
OF MICE AND MEN (TF)   Of Mice and Men Productions, 1981
KENTUCKY WOMAN (TF)   Walter Doniger Productions/20th
   Century-Fox TV, 1983
MURDER 1, DANCER 0 (TF)   Mickey Productions/Filmways, 1983

JOE ROMANO
Contact: BMI - Los Angeles, 310-659-9109

WHEN THE PARTY'S OVER   WPTO, 1992
STRAPPED (CTF)   Osiris Films/HBO Showcase, 1993

ALAIN ROMANS
b. France
Contact: SACEM - France, 011-33-1-4715-4715

MR. HULOT'S HOLIDAY   *LES VACANCES DE MR. HULOT*
   G-B-D International, 1953, French
MY UNCLE, MR. HULOT   *MON ONCLE*   Continental, 1956,
   French
FADILA   1961

RICHARD ROMANUS
SITTING DUCKS   Speciality Films, 1980

JEFF RONA
Agent: Gorfaine-Schwartz - Los Angeles, 213-969-1011

ASSASSINS   additional music, Warner Bros., 1995
WHITE SQUALL   Buena Vista, 1996

JEAN-LOUIS ROQUES
Contact: SACEM - France, 011-33-1-4715-4715

GERMINAL   1993, French

ANDREW ROSE
CAMPFIRE TALES   Vault/Kunert-Manes Productions, 1997
PLAN B   Curb, 1997

EARL ROSE*
Affiliation: ASCAP - Los Angeles, 213-883-1000

THIN ICE (TF)   CBS Entertainment, 1981
MAD DOG TIME   1996

ALLAN K. ROSEN
SHAMEFUL SECRETS (TF)   Steve White Films/ABC, 1993

JOEL ROSENBAUM
Contact: ASCAP - Los Angeles, 213-883-1000

PSYCHO GIRLS   Cannon, 1985, Canadian
THE COLOR PURPLE ★   co-composer, Warner Bros., 1985
BILLY GALVIN   Vestron, 1986
THE OUTING   THE LAMP   TMS Pictures, 1987
WACO AND RINEHART (TF)   Touchstone Films I V, 1987
FATHER DOWLING: THE MISSING BODY MYSTERY (TF)   The
    Fred Silverman Company/Dean Hargrove Productions/Viacom,
    1989

BRETT ROSENBERG
HOTEL DE LOVE   Live, 1997

LEONARD ROSENMAN*
b. Sept. 7, 1924 - Brooklyn, New York
Contact: ASCAP - Los Angeles, 213-883-1000

EAST OF EDEN   Warner Bros., 1955
THE COBWEB   MGM, 1955
REBEL WITHOUT A CAUSE   Warner Bros., 1955
BOMBERS B-52   Warner Bros., 1957
EDGE OF THE CITY   MGM, 1957
THE YOUNG STRANGER   Universal, 1957
LAFAYETTE ESCADRILLE   Warner Bros., 1958
THE HIDDEN WORLD (FD)   Small World, 1958
PORK CHOP HILL   United Artists, 1959
THE SAVAGE EYE   Trans-Lux, 1959
THE RISE AND FALL OF LEGS DIAMOND   Warner Bros., 1960
THE BRAMBLE BUSH   Warner Bros., 1960
THE CROWDED SKY   Warner Bros., 1960
THE PLUNDERERS   Allied Artists, 1960
THE OUTSIDER   Universal, 1961
HELL IS FOR HEROES   Paramount, 1962
CONVICTS FOUR   Allied Artists, 1962
THE CHAPMAN REPORT   Warner Bros., 1962
FANTASTIC VOYAGE   20th Century-Fox, 1966
A COVENANT WITH DEATH   Warner Bros., 1966
STRANGER ON THE RUN (TF)   Universal TV, 1967
SHADOW OVER ELVERON (TF)   Universal TV, 1968
COUNTDOWN   Warner Bros., 1968
HELLFIGHTERS   Universal, 1969
ANY SECOND NOW (TF)   Public Arts Productions/Universal TV,
    1969
MARCUS WELBY, M.D. (TF)   Universal TV, 1969
A MAN CALLED HORSE   National General, 1970
BENEATH THE PLANET OF THE APES   20th Century-Fox, 1970
BANYON (TF)   Warner Bros. TV, 1971
VANISHED (TF)   Universsal TV, 1971
SKIPPER   National General, 1971
IN BROAD DAYLIGHT (TF)   Aaron Spelling Productions, 1971
THE BRAVOS (TF)   Groverton Productions/Universal TV, 1972
BATTLE FOR THE PLANET OF THE APES   20th Century-Fox,
    1973
THE CAT CREATURE (TF)   Screen Gems/Columbia TV, 1973
THE PHANTOM OF HOLLYWOOD (TF)   MGM TV, 1974
NAKIA (TF)   David Gerber Productions/Screen Gems/Columbia
    Pictures TV, 1974
JUDGE DEE AND THE MONASTERY MURDERS (TF)   ABC Circle
    Films, 1974
BARRY LYNDON ★★   adaptation, Warner Bros., 1975, British
SKY HEIST (TF)   A J Fenady Associates/Warner Bros. TV, 1975
RACE WITH THE DEVIL   20th Century-Fox, 1975
BIRCH INTERVAL   Gamma III, 1976
BOUND FOR GLORY ★★   adaptation, United Artists, 1976
LANIGAN'S RABBI (TF)   Hayday Productions/Universal TV, 1976
KINGSTON: THE POWER PLAY (TF)   Groverton
    Productions/Universal TV, 1976
SYBIL (TF) ☆☆   Lorimar Productions, 1976

THE CAR   Universal, 1977
THE POSSESSED (TF)   Warner Bros. TV, 1977
9/30/55 SEPTEMBER 30, 1955   Universal, 1977
MARY WHITE (TF)   Radnitz-Mattel Productions, 1977
AN ENEMY OF THE PEOPLE   Warner Bros., 1978
THE LORD OF THE RINGS (AF)   United Artists, 1978
FRIENDLY FIRE (TF) ☆☆   Marble Arch Productions, 1979
PROPHECY   Paramount, 1979
PROMISES IN THE DARK   Orion, 1979
NERO WOLFE (TF)   Emmet Lavery Jr. Productions/Paramount
    Pictures TV, 1979
CITY IN FEAR (TF)   Trans World International, 1980
HIDE IN PLAIN SIGHT   United Artists, 1980
THE JAZZ SINGER   AFD, 1980
MURDER IN TEXAS (TF)   Dick Clark Productions/Billy Hale Films,
    1981
MAKING LOVE   20th Century-Fox, 1981
THE WALL (TF)   Cinetex International/Time-Life Productions, 1982
CROSS CREEK ★   Universal/AFD, 1983
MISS LONELYHEARTS   H. Jay Holman Productions/American Film
    Institute, 1983
CELEBRITY (MS)   NBC Productions, 1984
THE RETURN OF MARCUS WELBY, M.D. (TF)   Marstar
    Productions/Universal TV, 1984
HEARTSOUNDS (TF)   Embassy TV, 1984
HEART OF THE STAG   New World, 1984, New Zealand
FIRST STEPS (TF)   CBS Entertainment, 1985
SYLVIA   MGM/UA Classics, 1985, New Zealand
STAR TREK IV: THE VOYAGE HOME ★   Paramount, 1986
PROMISED A MIRACLE (TF)   Dick Clark Productions/Republic
    Pictures Roni Weisberg Productions, 1988
WHERE PIGEONS GO TO DIE (TF)   Michael Landon
    Productions/World International Network, 1990
ROBOCOP 2   Orion, 1990
AFTERMATH: A TEST OF LOVE (TF)   Interscope, 1991
AMBITION   Miramax, 1991
KEEPER OF THE CITY (CTF)   Viacom, 1992
THE FACE ON THE MILK CARTON (TF)   Dorothea G. Petrie
    Prods./Family Prods., 1995

LAURENCE ROSENTHAL
b. November 4, 1926 - Detroit, Michigan
Agent: Air-Edel - Los Angeles, 310-914-5000
Affiliation: ASCAP - Los Angeles, 213-883-1000

YELLOWNECK   Republic, 1955
NAKED IN THE SUN   Allied Artists, 1957
A RAISIN IN THE SUN   Columbia, 1961
DARK ODYSSEY   Era, 1961
THE MIRACLE WORKER   United Artists, 1962
REQUIEM FOR A HEAVYWEIGHT   Columbia, 1962
BECKET ★   Paramount, 1964
HOTEL PARADISO   MGM, 1966, British
THE COMEDIANS   MGM, 1967
THREE   United Artists, 1969
HOW AWFUL ABOUT ALLAN (TF)   Aaron Spelling Productions,
    1970
THE HOUSE THAT WOULD NOT DIE (TF)   Aaron Spelling
    Productions, 1970
NIGHT CHASE (TF)   Cinema Center 100, 1970
THE LAST CHILD (TF)   Aaron Spelling Productions, 1971
A GUNFIGHT   Paramount, 1971
THE AFRICAN ELEPHANT   KING ELEPHANT (FD)   1972
MAN OF LA MANCHA ★   adaptation, United Artists, 1972
HEC RAMSEY (TF)   Universal TV/Mark VII Ltd., 1972
CALL TO DANGER (TF)   Paramount Pictures TV, 1973
THE DEVIL'S DAUGHTER (TF)   Paramount Pictures Television,
    1973
SATAN'S SCHOOL FOR GIRLS (TF)   Spelling-Goldberg
    Productions, 1973
DEATH SENTENCE (TF)   Spelling-Goldberg Productions, 1974
THE LOG OF THE BLACK PEARL (TF)   Mark VII Ltd./Universal TV,
    1975
THE WILD PARTY   American International, 1975
ROOSTER COGBURN   Universal, 1975
YOUNG PIONEERS (TF)   ABC Circle Films, 1976
THE RETURN OF A MAN CALLED HORSE   United Artists, 1976
21 HOURS AT MUNICH (TF)   Moonlight Productions/Filmways
    Pictures, 1976
YOUNG PIONEERS' CHRISTMAS (TF)   ABC Circle Films, 1976

THE AMAZING HOWARD HUGHES (TF)   Roger Gimbel
    Productions/EMI TV, 1977
MURDER IN PEYTON PLACE (TF)   20th Century-Fox TV, 1977
THE ISLAND OF DR. MOREAU   American International, 1977
FANTASY ISLAND (TF)   Spelling-Goldberg Productions, 1977
LOGAN'S RUN (TF)   Goff-Roberts-Steiner Productions/MGM TV,
    1977
WHO'LL STOP THE RAIN   United Artists, 1978
BRASS TARGET   MGM/United Artists, 1978
AND I ALONE SURVIVED (TF)   Jerry Leider/OJL Productions,
    1978
MEETINGS WITH REMARKABLE MEN   Libra, 1979, British
METEOR   American International, 1979
ORPHAN TRAIN (TF)   EMI TV, 1979
THE DAY CHRIST DIED (TF)   Martin Manulis Productions/20th
    Century-Fox TV, 1980
F.D.R.—THE LAST YEAR (TF)   Titus Productions, 1980
RAGE (TF)   Diane Silver Productions/Charles Fries Productions,
    1980
REVENGE OF THE STEPFORD WIVES (TF)   Edgar J. Scherick
    Productions, 1980
CLASH OF THE TITANS   MGM/United Artists, 1981, British
THE LETTER (TF) ☆ partial adaptation, Hajeno Productions/Warner
    Bros. TV, 1982
WHO WILL LOVE MY CHILDREN? (TF) ☆ ABC Circle Films, 1983
HEART LIKE A WHEEL   20th Century-Fox, 1983
EASY MONEY   Orion, 1983
LICENSE TO KILL (TF)   Marian Rees Associates/D. Petrie
    Productions, 1984
THE LOST HONOR OF KATHERINE BECK (TF)   Open Road
    Productions, 1984
GEORGE WASHINGTON (MS)   David Gerber Productions/MGM
    Television, 1984
CONSENTING ADULT (TF)   Starger Company/Lawrence-Aghayan
    Productions, 1985
EVERGREEN (MS)   Edgar J. Scherick Associates/Metromedia
    Producers Corporation, 1985
BLACKOUT (CTF)   HBO Premiere Films/Roger Gimbel
    Productions/Peregrine Entertainment Ltd./Lee Buck
    Industries/Alexander Smith & Parks, 1985, U.S.-Canadian
MUSSOLINI: THE UNTOLD STORY (MS)   Trian Productions, 1985
PETER THE GREAT (MS) ☆☆ PTG Productions/NBC Productions,
    1986
STRANGER IN MY BED (TF)   Taft Entertainment TV/Edgar J.
    Sherick Productions, 1986
ON WINGS OF EAGLES (MS)   Edgar J. Scherick Productions/Taft
    Entertainment TV, 1986
ANASTASIA: THE MYSTERY OF ANNA (TF) ☆☆ Telecom
    Entertainment/Consolidated Productions/Reteitalia, 1986,
    U.S.-Italian
FIGHT FOR LIFE (TF)   Fries Entertainment, 1987
DOWNPAYMENT ON MURDER (TF)   Adam Productions/20th
    Century Fox TV, 1987
PROUD MEN (TF)   Cowboy Productions/Agamemnon Films
    Productions/von Zerneck-Samuels Productions, 1987
FREEDOM FIGHTER (TF)   HTV/Columbia TV/Embassy TV, 1988,
    U.S.-British
TO HEAL A NATION (TF)   Lionel Chetwynd Productions/Orion
    TV/von Zerneck-Samuels Productions, 1988
MY FATHER, MY SON (TF)   Fred Weintraub Productions/John J.
    McMahon Productions, 1988
STREET OF DREAMS (TF)   Bill Stratton-Myrtos
    Productions/Phoenix Entertainment Group, 1988
THE BOURNE IDENTITY (TF) ☆☆ Alan Shayne
    Productions/Warner Bros. TV, 1988
BLACKOUT   Ambient Light Entertainment, 1988
IN THE LINE OF DUTY: THE FBI MURDERS (TF)   Telecom
    Entertainment/World International Network, 1988
TWIST OF FATE (TF)   Henry Plitt-Larry White
    Productions/HTV/Columbia TV, 1989, British-U.S.
BROTHERHOOD OF THE ROSE (TF)   NBC Productions, 1989
MY NAME IS BILL W. (TF)   Garner/Duchow Productions, 1989
GORE VIDAL'S BILLY THE KID (CTF)   von Zerneck-Sertner
    Productions, 1989
BLIND FAITH (TF)   NBC Productions, 1990
THE INCIDENT (TF)   Qintex Entertainment, 1990
THE KISSING PLACE (CTF)   Cynthia A. Cherbak
    Production/Wilshire Court Productions, 1990
GRASS ROOTS (TF)   Team Cherokee/JBS Prods., 1992
THE YOUNG INDIANA JONES CHRONICLES (TF)
    Lucasfilm/Paramount, 1992

THE FIRE NEXT TIME (TF)   RHI Entertainment/Kirch Group, 1993
YOUNG INDIANA JONES & THE HOLLYWOOD FOLLIES (CTF)
    Lucasfilm/Amblin/Paramount TV, 1994

WILLIAM ROSS*
Agent: Vangelos Management - Encino, 818-380-1919
Affiliation: BMI - Los Angeles, 310-659-9109

ONE GOOD COP   co-composer with David Foster, Hollywood,
    1991
GOLDEN FIDDLES (MS)   co-composer with David Foster, 1991
LOOK WHO'S TALKING NOW   TriStar, 1993
COPS AND ROBBERSONS   TriStar, 1994
HANS CHRISTIAN ANDERSEN'S THUMBELINA   co-composer with
    Barry Manilow, Warner Bros., 1994
LITTLE RASCALS   Universal, 1994
THE AMAZING PANDA ADVENTURE   Warner Bros., 1995
BLACK SHEEP   Paramount, 1996
TIN CUP   Warner Bros., 1996
THE EVENING STAR   Paramount, 1996
MY FELLOW AMERICANS   Warner Bros., 1996
A SMILE LIKE YOURS   Paramount, 1997

MILES ROSTON
Contact: BMI - Los Angeles, 310-659-9109

MR. WRITE   Shapiro Glickenhaus, 1994

PETER FRANCIS ROTTER
Contact: BMI - Los Angeles, 310-659-9109

DEAD SILENCE...the movie   Curb/Esquire Films, 1989

GLEN ROVEN*
Contact: ASCAP - Los Angeles, 213-883-1000

LIFE IN THE FOOD CHAIN   Katzfilms, 1992

HAHN ROWE
Contact: BMI - Los Angeles, 310-659-9109

CLEAN, SHAVEN   DSM III Films, 1993

ADAM ROWLAND
Contact: ASCAP - Los Angeles, 213-883-1000

FAST GETAWAY   additional music, New Line, 1991

BRUCE ROWLAND
b. Australia
Contact: APRA - Australia, 011-61-2-922-6422

FREE ENTERPRISE   Burrowes Film Group, Australian
THE MAN FROM SNOWY RIVER   20th Century-Fox, 1982,
    Australian
COOL CHANGE   Hoyts, 1986, Australian
NOW AND FOREVER   Klevand Productions, 1983, Australian
PHAR LAP   20th Century-Fox, 1983, Australian
ALL THE RIVERS RUN (CMS)   Crawford Productions/Nine
    Network, 1984, Australian
REBEL   Vestron, 1985, Australian
COOL CHANGE   Hoyts, 1986, Australian
LES PATTERSON SAVES THE WORLD   Hoyts Distribution, 1987,
    Australian
BIGFOOT (TF)   Walt Disney TV, 1987
RUNNING FROM THE GUNS   1987, Australian
ANZACS: THE WAR DOWN UNDER (MS)   Orbis
    Communications/Hal Roach Studios, 1987, Australian
THE CHRISTMAS VISITOR   BUSHFIRE MOON (CTF)
    Entertainment Media/The Disney Channel/WonderWorks, 1987,
    Australian-U.S.
BACKSTAGE   Hoyts, Australian, 1988
RETURN TO SNOWY RIVER   Buena Vista, 1988, Australian
DANGER DOWN UNDER (TF)   Weintraub Entertainment
    Group/Hoyts Productions Ltd., 1988, U.S.-Australian
CHEETAH   Buena Vista, 1989
ALL THE RIVERS RUN II (CTF)   Crawford Productions/HBO, 1989

GUNSMOKE: THE LAST APACHE (TF)   CBS Entertainment
   Productions/Galatea Productions, 1990
WHICH WAY HOME (CTF)   McElroy & McElroy/TV New Zealand,
   1991
FAST GETAWAY   New Line, 1991
GROSS MISCONDUCT   1993, Australian
LIGHTNING JACK   Savoy, 1994
ANDRE   Paramount, 1994
THE NORTH STAR   Warner Bros., 1996
ZEUS AND ROXANNE   MGM-UA, 1997

LANCE RUBIN

Contact: BMI - Los Angeles, 310-659-9109

LEO AND LOREE   United Artists, 1980
MOTEL HELL   United Artists, 1980
HAPPY BIRTHDAY TO ME   co-composer with Bo Harwood,
   Columbia, 1981, Canadian
MODERN ROMANCE   Columbia, 1981
HEAR NO EVIL (TF)   Paul Pompian Productions/MGM TV, 1982
THE INCREDIBLE HULK RETURNS (TF)   B&B Productions/New
   World TV, 1988
THE TRIAL OF THE INCREDIBLE HULK (TF)   Bixby-Brandon
   Productions/New World TV, 1989
THE DEATH OF THE INCREDIBLE HULK (TF)   Bixby-Brandon
   Productions/New World TV, 1990
HEXED   Columbia, 1993

MICHEL RUBINI

Contact: BMI - Los Angeles, 310-659-9109

RACQUET   Cal-Am Artists, 1979
THE HUNGER   co-composer with Denny Jaeger, MGM/UA, 1983,
   British
WHAT WAITS BELOW   co-composer with Denny Jaeger, Blossom
   Pictures, 1984
THE NEW KIDS   Columbia, 1985
BAND OF THE HAND   Tri-Star, 1986
ABDUCTED   InterPictures, 1986, Canadian
MANHUNTER   DEG, 1986
HANDS OF A STRANGER (TF)   Taft Entertainment TV, 1987
MOVING TARGET (TF)   Lewis B. Chesler Productions/Bateman
   Company Productions/Finnegan-Pinchuk Company/MGM-UA TV,
   1988
UNHOLY MATRIMONY (TF)   Edgar J. Scherick Associates/Taft
   Entertainment TV, 1988
TOO GOOD TO BE TRUE (TF)   Newland-Raynor Productions,
   1988
CROSSING THE MOB (TF)   Bateman Company
   Productions/Interscope Communications, 1988
THE EDGE (CTF)   Lewis B. Chesler Productions/The Christopher
   Morgan Co./MGM-UA, 1989
THE HAUNTING OF SARAH HARDY (CTF)   USA Network, 1989
TWIST OF FATE   Condor, 1991
STRANGER IN THE FAMILY (TF)   Polongo Pictures/Hearst, 1991
THE FEAR INSIDE (CTF)   Viacom, 1992
NEMESIS   Imperial Entertainment, 1993
RIDE WITH THE WIND (TF)   Family Tree Prods./Peter Frankovich
   Prods./Hearst, 1994
BLOODKNOT (CTF)   Chesler Perlmutter Prods./Showtime, 1995

ARTHUR B. RUBINSTEIN*

Agent: Vangelos Management - Encino, 818-380-1919
Contact: BMI - Los Angeles, 310-659-9109

THE PRINCE OF CENTRAL PARK (TF)   Lorimar Productions,
   1977
THE GREAT BANK HOAX *SHENANIGANS*   Warner Bros., 1978
PORTRAIT OF A STRIPPER (TF)   Moonlight Productions/Filmways,
   1979
AUNT MARY (TF)   Henry Jaffe Enterprises, 1979
THE GREAT AMERICAN TRAFFIC JAM *GRIDLOCK* (TF)
   Ten-Four Productions, 1980
PORTRAIT OF A REBEL: MARGARET SANGER (TF)   Marvin
   Minoff Productions/David Paradine TV, 1980
ON THE RIGHT TRACK   20th Century-Fox, 1981
THE PHOENIX (TF)   Mark Carliner Productions, 1981
RIVKIN, BOUNTY HUNTER (TF)   Chiarascurio
   Productions/Ten-Four Productions, 1981
WHOSE LIFE IS IT ANYWAY?   MGM/United Artists, 1981

NOT JUST ANOTHER AFFAIR (TF)   Ten-Four Productions, 1982
FAKE OUT   Analysis, 1982
SKEEZER (TF)   Margie-Lee Enterprises/The Blue Marble
   Company/Marble Arch Productions, 1982
DEAL OF THE CENTURY   Warner Bros., 1983
BLUE THUNDER   Columbia, 1983
WARGAMES   MGM/UA, 1983
IT CAME UPON THE MIDNIGHT CLEAR (TF)   Schenck-Cardea
   Productions/Columbia TV/LBS Communications, 1984
SINS OF THE PAST (TF)   Sinpast Entertainment Company
   Productions, 1984
THE PARADE (TF)   Hill-Mandelker Productions, 1984
THE CARTIER AFFAIR (TF)   Hill-Mandelker Productions, 1984
LOST IN AMERICA   The Geffen Company/Warner Bros., 1985
MURDER IN SPACE (CTF)   Robert Cooper/Zenith Productions,
   1985
DOUBLETAKE (TF)   Titus Productions, 1985
DOING LIFE (TF)   Castillian Productions/Phoenix Entertainment
   Group, 1986
HYPER SAPIEN   Taliafilm II, 1986
THE BEST OF TIMES   Universal, 1986
LOVE AMONG THIEVES (TF)   Robert A. Papazian Productions,
   1987
STAKEOUT   Buena Vista, 1987
ROSES ARE FOR THE RICH (TF)   Phoenix Entertainment Group,
   1987
THE BETTY FORD STORY (TF)   David L. Wolper
   Productions/Warner Bros. TV, 1987
ONCE UPON A TEXAS TRAIN (TF)   CBS Entertainment, 1988
DEFENSE PLAY   Trans World Entertainment, 1988
INHERIT THE WIND (TF)   Vincent Pictures Productions/David
   Greene-Robert Papazian Productions, 1988
INTERNAL AFFAIRS (TF)   Titus Productions, 1988
WHERE THE HELL'S THAT GOLD?!! (TF)   Willie Nelson
   Productions/Brigade Productions/Konigsberg-Sanitsky Company,
   1988
NIGHTMARE AT BITTER CREEK (TF)   Swanton
   Films/Guber-Peters Entertainment/Phoenix Entertainment Group,
   1988
INDISCREET (TF)   Karen Mack Productions/HTV/Republic Pictures,
   1988, U.S.-British
AGATHA CHRISTIE'S THE MAN IN THE BROWN SUIT (TF)   Alan
   Shayne Productions/Warner Bros. TV, 1989
UNCONQUERED (TF)   Alexandra Film Productions, 1989
GIDEON OLIVER: SLEEP WELL, PROFESSOR OLIVER (TF)   Wolf
   Films/Crescendo Productions/Universal TV, 1989
BAYWATCH: PANIC AT MALIBU PIER (TF)   GTG
   Entertainment/NBC, 1989
GUTS AND GLORY: THE RISE AND FALL OF OLIVER NORTH
   (TF)   Mike Robe Productions/Papazian-Hirsch Entertainment,
   1989
LINE OF FIRE: THE MORRIS DEES STORY (TF)   BoJames
   Entertainment/Papazian-Hirsch, 1991
THE HARD WAY   Universal, 1991
CRAZY FROM THE HEART (CTF)   De Mann
   Entertainment/Papazian-Hirsch, 1991
FATAL FRIENDSHIP (TF)   Papazian-Hirsch, 1991
DANIELLE STEEL'S SECRETS (TF)   Cramer Co./NBC Prods.,
   1992
WHEN NO ONE WOULD LISTEN (TF)   Bruce Sallan Prods., 1992
DEEP TROUBLE (CTF)   Papazian-Hirsch/Ellipse, 1993
ANOTHER STAKEOUT   Buena Vista, 1993
CAUGHT IN THE ACT (CTF)   Davis Entertainment
   TV/Meltzer-Viviano Prods./MTE Prods., 1993
HART TO HART RETURNS (TF)   Papazian-Hirsch/Robert Wagner
   Prods./Columbia TV, 1993
DOUBLE JEOPARDY: THE KILLING OF GINA MARIE (TF)
   Wilshire Court, 1996
RUBY RING (TF)   1997, Scottish
THE PRINCESS STALLION (TF)   1997, Scottish

DONALD RUBINSTEIN

Agent: The Artists Group, Ltd. - Los Angeles, 310-552-1100
Affiliation: ASCAP - Los Angeles, 213-883-1000

MARTIN   Libra, 1978
KNIGHTRIDERS   United Film Distribution, 1981
TALES FROM THE DARKSIDE: THE MOVIE   co-composer,
   Paramount, 1990

JOHN RUBINSTEIN

b. December 8, 1946
Contact: ASCAP - Los Angeles, 213-883-1000

KID BLUE   co-composer with Tim McIntire, 20th Century-Fox, 1973
ALL TOGETHER NOW (TF)   RSO Films, 1975
STALK THE WILD CHILD (TF)   Charles Fries Productions, 1976
THE KILLER INSIDE ME   co-composer with Tim McIntire, Warner Bros., 1976
STICKING TOGETHER (TF)   Blinn-Thorpe Productions/Viacom Productions, 1978
THE NEW MAVERICK (TF)   Cherokee Productions/Warner Bros. TV, 1978
CHAMPIONS: A LOVE STORY (TF)   Warner Bros. TV, 1979
TO RACE THE WIND (TF)   Walter Grauman Productions, 1980
AMBER WAVES (TF)   Time-Life Productions, 1980
JOHNNY BELINDA (TF)   Dick Berg/Stonehenge Productions/Lorimar Productions, 1982
SECRETS OF A MOTHER AND DAUGHTER (TF)   The Shpetner Company/Sunrise Productions, 1983
CHOICES OF THE HEART (TF)   Katz-Gallin Associates/Half-Pint Productions/Metromedia Producers Corporation/NBC Entertainment, 1983
THE DOLLMAKER (TF)   Finnegan Associates/IPC Films/Dollmaker Productions, 1984
CITY KILLER (TF)   Stan Shpetner Productions, 1984
CONSPIRACY OF LOVE (TF)   New World TV, 1987
CHINA BEACH (TF)   Sacret Inc./Warner Bros. TV, 1988
A WALTON WEDDING (TF)   Lee Rich Co./Amanda Prods./Warner Bros. TV, 1995

KEITH RUBINSTEIN

Contact: ASCAP - Los Angeles, 213-883-1000

VICE SQUAD   Avco Embassy, 1982

STEVE RUCKER*

Contact: ASCAP - Los Angeles, 213-883-1000

CREATURE   TITAN FIND   co-composer with Tom Chase, Cardinal Releasing, 1985
FEEL THE HEAT   co-composer with Tom Chase, Trans World Entertainment, 1987
ALIEN PREDATOR   co-composer with Tom Chase, Trans World Entertainment, 1987
AND GOD CREATED WOMAN   co-composer with Tom Chase, Vestron, 1988
976-EVIL   co-composer with Tom Chase, New Line Cinema, 1988
BULLETPROOF   co-composer with Tom Chase, Cinetel, 1988
SYNGENOR   co-composer with Tom Chase, Syngenor Production Co., 1990
LITTLE NEMO: ADVENTURES IN SLUMBERLAND (AF)   co-composer with Thomas Chase, Hemdale, 1992, Japanese

PETE RUGOLO

b. December 25, 1915 - Sicily, Italy
Contact: BMI - Los Angeles, 310-659-9109

JACK THE RIPPER   composer of U.S. version, 1960
THE OUTSIDER (TF)   Public Arts Productions/Universal TV, 1967
THE SWEET RIDE   20th Century-Fox, 1968
THE SOUND OF ANGER (TF)   Public Arts Productions/Universal TV, 1968
THE WHOLE WORLD IS WATCHING (TF)   Public Arts Productions/Universal TV, 1969
THE LONELY PROFESSION (TF)   Universal TV/Public Arts Productions, 1969
THE YOUNG COUNTRY (TF)   Public Arts Productions/Universal TV, 1970
THE CHALLENGERS (TF) ☆☆   Universal TV, 1970
DO YOU TAKE THIS STRANGER? (TF) ☆   Universal TV/Public Arts Productions, 1971
SAM HILL: WHO KILLED THE MYSTERIOUS MR. FOSTER? (TF)   Public Arts Productions/Universal TV, 1971
THE DEATH OF ME YET (TF)   Aaron Spelling Productions, 1971
HOW TO STEAL AN AIRPLANE (TF)   Universal TV, 1972
SET THIS TOWN ON FIRE (TF)   Public Arts Productions/Universal TV, 1973
TOMA (TF)   Universal TV, 1973

THE LETTERS   Spelling-Goldberg Productions/ABC Circle Films, 1973
DRIVE HARD, DRIVE FAST (TF)   Public Arts Productions/Universal TV, 1973
LETTERS FROM THREE LOVERS   Spelling-Goldberg Productions, 1973
THE STORY OF PRETTY BOY FLOYD (TF)   Public Arts Productions/Universal TV, 1974
DEATH CRUISE (TF)   Spelling-Goldberg Productions, 1974
LAST HOURS BEFORE MORNING (TF)   Charles Fries Productions/MGM Television, 1975
DEATH STALK (TF)   Herman Rush Associates/David L. Wolper Productions, 1975
FOXTROT   THE OTHER SIDE OF PARADISE   New World, 1976, Mexican-Swiss
THE SAN PEDRO BUMS (TF)   Aaron Spelling Productions, 1977
THE JORDAN CHANCE (TF)   Universal TV, 1978
THE LAST CONVERTIBLE (MS) ☆   Roy Huggins Productions/Universal TV, 1979
CHU CHU AND THE PHILLY FLASH   20th Century-Fox, 1981
FOR LOVERS ONLY (TF)   Henerson-Hirsch Productions/Caesar Palace Productions, 1982

TODD RUNDGREN

b. 1948
Contact: BMI - Los Angeles, 310-659-9109

UNDER COVER   Cannon, 1987
DUMB AND DUMBER   New Line, 1994

PATRICE RUSHEN*

Agent: Zomba Screen Music - West Hollywood, 310-246-0777
Affiliation: ASCAP - Los Angeles, 213-883-1000

HOLLYWOOD SHUFFLE   co-composer with Udi Harpaz, Samuel Goldwyn Co., 1987

BELLA RUSSELL

Contact: PRS - London, England, 011-44-1-580-5544

ISLAND INVADERS: OTHER WORLDS (TD)   co-composer with Nigel Beaham-Powell, WNET/BBC TV, 1993

JULIAN DYLAN RUSSELL

BALLOT MEASURE 9 (FD)   Oregon Tape Project, 1995

RAY RUSSELL

Contact: PRS - London, England, 011-44-1-580-5544

THAT SUMMER!   Columbia, 1979, British

WILLY RUSSELL

Contact: PRS - London, England, 011-44-1-580-5544

MR. LOVE (TF)   Enigma/Goldcrest Films & TV, 1986, British
SHIRLEY VALENTINE   co-composer with George Hatzinassios, Paramount, 1989

NICHOLAS RUSSELL-PAVIER

Contact: PRS - London, England, 011-44-1-580-5544

SECRET FRIENDS   1991, British
LOOK ME IN THE EYE   co-composer with David Chilton, Skreba-Creon, 1994, British

DAVID RUSSO

Contact: BMI - Los Angeles, 310-659-9109

SPACED INVADERS   Buena Vista, 1990
ANGUS   New Line, 1995
SOULMATES   Curb, 1997

GUS RUSSO

Contact: ASCAP - Los Angeles, 213-883-1000

BASKET CASE   Analysis, 1982

WILLIAM RUSSO

Contact: ASCAP - Los Angeles, 213-883-1000

THE COSMIC EYE (AF) 1985

CARLO RUSTICHELLI

b. December 24, 1916 - Emilia, Italy
Contact: SIAE - Italy, 011-39-6-59-901

GLI ULTIMI FILIBUSTIERI co-composer, 1941, Italian
IL FIGLIO DEL CORSARO NERO co-composer, 1941, Italian
GRAN PREMIO 1943, Italian
GIOVENTU PERDUTA *LOST YOUTH* 1947, Italian
IN NOME DELLA LEGGE 1948, Italian
THE WHITE LINE *CUORI SENZA FRONTIERE* 1949, Italian
TOTO CERCA CASA ATA, 1949, Italian
BARRIERA A SETTENTRIONE 1949, Italian
CINTURA DI CASTITA 1949, Italian
PERSIANE CHIUSE 1950, Italian
ATTO DI ACCUSA 1950, Italian
IL CAMINO DELLA SPERANZA 1950, Italian
CAVALCATA DI MEZZO SECOLO 1950, Italian
IL LEONE DI AMALFI 1950, Italian
DOMANI E UN ALTRO GIORNO co-composer, 1950, Italian
I FALSARI 1950, Italian
LA CITTA SI DIFENDE *FOUR WAYS OUT* 1951, Italian
LORENZACCIO 1951, Italian
IL BILVIO 1951, Italian
REVENGE OF THE PIRATES *LA VENDETTA DEL CORSARO*
    1951, Italian
IL BRIGANTE DI TACCA DEL LUPO 1951, Italian
PERSIANE CHIUSE Rovere Film, 1951, Italian
LA CIECA DI SORRENTO 1952, Italian
TI HO SEMPRE AMATO 1952, Italian
PRIGIONIERA DELLA TORRE DI FUOCO 1952, Italian
LA PRESIDENTESSA 1952, Italian
TOTO E LE DONNE 1952, Italian
HIS TWO LOVES *PUCCINI* adaptation, 1952, Italian
PERDONAMI! 1952, Italian
BLACK 13 1953, British
CAPTAIN FANTASMA, IL TESORO DELLE INDIE 1953, Italian
LA NEMICA 1953, Italian
LA FIGLIA DEL DIAVOLO 1953, Italian
CANZONI, CANZONI, CANZONI 1953, Italian
GELOSIA 1953, Italian
GRAN VARIETA 1953, Italian
L'OMBRA 1954, Italian
PIETA PER CHI CADE 1955, Italian
DISPERATO ADDIO 1955, Italian
WILD LOVE *GLI INNAMORATI* Jacovoni, 1955, Italian
LA VENA D'ORO Athena Cinematografica, 1955, Italian
THE RAILROAD MAN *IL FERROVIERE* Continental, 1956, Italian
GUARDIA, GUARDIA SCELTA, BRIGADIERE E MARESCIALLO
    Imperial Film, 1956, Italian
SINFONIA D'AMORE adaptation, 1956, Italian
IL TESORO DI ROMMEL 1956, Italian
LAZZARELLA 1957, Italian
THE TAILOR'S MAID *PADRI E FIGLI* Trans-Lux, 1957, Italian
LA MINA 1957, Italian
MARISA LA CIVETTA Ponti/Balcazar, 1957, Italian-Spanish
DINANZI A NOI IL CIELO 1957, Italian
L'UOMO DI PAGLIA 1957, Italian
SAMIR E IL MARE 1958, Italian
TOTO E MARCELLINO 1958, Italian
THE DAY THE SKY EXPLODED *LA MORTE VIENE DALLO
    SPAZIO* 1958, Italian
ANNIBALE 1958, Italian
LE SECRET DU CHEVALIER D'EON 1959, French-Italian
ARRANGIATEVI Cineriz, 1959, Italian
NON SIAMO DUE EVASI 1959, Italian-French
THE FACTS OF MURDER *UN MALEDETTO IMBROGLIO* Seven
    Arts, 1959, Italian
LOVE THE ITALIAN WAY *FEMMINE DI LUSSO* 1959, Italian
ESTERINA 1959, Italian
UN UOMO FACILE co-composer, 1959, Italian
LA NOTTE DEL GRANDE ASSALTO 1959, Italian
I GIGANTI DELLA TESSAGLIA 1959, Italian
KAPO 1959, Italian
L'UOMO DAI CALZONI CORTI 1960, Italian
OLIMPIADI DEI MARITI 1960, Italian
LETTO A TRE PIAZZE 1960, Italian

A NOI PIACE FREDDO 1960, Italian
ROBIN HOOD AND THE PIRATES 1960, Italian
CATERINA SFORZA 1960, Italian
THE MINOTAUR *TESEO CONTRO IL MINOTAURO*
UN AMORE A ROMA CEI Incom/Fair Film/Laetitia Film/Les Films
    Cocinor/Alpha Film, 1960, Italian-French-West German
LA VENERE DEI PIRATI 1960, Italian
LA LUNGA NOTTE DEL '43 1960, Italian
IL LADRO DI BAGDAD 1960, Italian
JOURNEY BENEATH THE DESERT *ANTINEA - L'AMANTE DELLA
    CITTA SEPOLTA* Embassy, 1961, Italian-French
ACCATONE! adaptation, Brandon, 1961, Italian
UN GIORNO DA LEONI 1961, Italian
IL COLPO SEGRETO DI D'ARTAGNAN 1961, Italian
GIORNO PER GIORNO DISPERATAMENTE 1961, Italian
QUEEN OF THE NILE *NEFERTITE, REGINA DEL NILO* 1961,
    Italian
DIVORCE ITALIAN STYLE Embassy, 1961, Italian
TIRO AL PICCIONE 1961, Italian
THE BLACK PIRATE 1961, Italian
PSYCOSISSIMO 1961, Italian
ROMULUS AND THE SABINES *IL RATTO DELLE SABINE* 1961,
    Italian
SWORD OF THE CONQUEROR *ROSMUNDA E ALBOINO* 1961,
    Italian
IL COMMISSARIO 1962, Italian
MAMMA ROMA adaptation, 1962, Italian
I MISCHETTIERI DEL MARE 1962, Italian
PASTACIATTA NEL DESERTO 1962, Italian
PELLA VIVA 1962, Italian
VENERE CREOLA co-composer, 1962, Italian
LA TIGRE DEI SETTE MARI 1962, Italian
I TROMBONI DI FRAI DIAVOLO 1962, Italian
AGOSTINO Baltea Film, 1962, Italian
LA BELLEZZA D'IPPOLITA 1962, Italian
MY SON THE HERO *ARRIVANO I TITANI* 1962, Italian
ROGOPAG co-composer, 1962, Italian
THE EYE OF THE NEEDLE *LA SMANIA ADOSSO* 1962, Italian
ARTURO'S ISLAND MGM, 1962, Italian
LE QUATTRO GIORNATE DI NAPOLI 1962, Italian
TRIUMPH OF THE SON OF HERCULES *IL TRIONFO DI
    MACISTE* 1963, Italian
FINCHE DURA LA TEMPESTA 1963, Italian
THE ORGANIZER *I COMPAGNI* Continental, 1963,
    Italian-French-Yugoslavian
ATLAS AGAINST THE TSAR *MACISTE ALLA CORTE DELLO
    ZAR* 1963, Italian
IL BOIA DI VENEZIA 1963, Italian
MARE MATTO 1963, Italian
CONQUEST OF MYCENE *ERCOLE CONTRO MOLOCH* 1963,
    Italian
CORIOLANO, EROE SENZA PATRIA 1963, Italian
LA FASDIZIOSA 1963, Italian
I GIGANTI DI ROMA 1963, Italian
SEDUCED AND ABANDONED Continental, 1964, Italian-French
GLI IMBROGLIANI Produzione D.S./Tecisa Film, 1963,
    Italian-Spanish
TERROR OF THE STEPPE *I PREDONI DELLA STEPPA* 1963,
    Italian
BEBO'S GIRL Continental, 1963, Italian-French
IL TERRORE DEI MANTELLI ROSSI 1963, Italian
LOS DINAMITEROS 1963, Italian
ADULTERO LUI...ADULTERO LEI 1963, Italian
TOTO E CLEOPATRA 1963, Italian
LA MANE SUL FUCILE 1963, Italian
IL CRIMINALE 1963, Italian
GLI ULTIMI 1963, Italian
TOTO CONTRO IL PIRATA NERO 1963, Italian
WHAT! *LA FRUSTA E IL CORPO* 1963, Italian
LA CARICA DEL 7 CAVALLEGGERI 1964, Italian
THE WARM LIFE *LA CALDA VITA* 1964, Italian
THE CAVERN *SETTE CONTRO LA MORTE* 1964, Italian
I PROMESSI SPOSI 1964, Italian
SEDOTTI E BIDONATI 1964, Italian
IL LEONE DI SAN MARCO 1964, Italian
L'ANTIMIRACOLO 1964, Italian
LOS MANGANTES 1964, Spanish-Italian
AMORI PERICOLOSI co-composer, 1964, Italian
LA DONNA E UNA COSA MERAVIGLIOSA 1964, Italian
BAFFALO BILL, L'EROE DEL FAR WEST 1964, Italian
SANDOKAN FIGHTS BACK 1964, Italian

BLOOD AND BLACK LACE *SEI DONNE PER L'ASSASSINO*
1964, Italian
GLI EROI DI FORT WORTH 1964, Italian
SANDOKAN CONTRO IL LEOPARDO DI SARAWAK 1964, Italian
DESERT RAIDERS *IL DOMINATORE DEL DESERTO* 1964,
Italian
TRE NOTTI D'AMORE co-composer, 1964, Italian
I LUNGHI CAPELLI DELLA MORTE 1964, Italian
HERCULES OF THE DESERT *LA VALLE DELL'ECO TONANTE*
1964, Italian
GENOVEVA DE BRABANTE 1965, Italian
LETTI SBAGLIATI 1965, Italian
L'AVVENTURIERO DELLA TORTUGA 1965, Italian
IL FIGLIO DI CLEOPATRA 1965, Italian
LIBIDO 1965, Italian
MADE IN ITALY co-composer, 1965, Italian
ON A VOLE LA JOCONDE 1965, Italian
THE MYSTERY OF THUG ISLAND 1965, Italian
I CAVALIERI DELLA VENDETTA 1965, Italian
LE NOTTE DEL DESPERADO 1965, Italian
LE STAGIONI DEL NOSTRO AMORE 1965, Italian
FORT ALESIA 1965, Italian
THE BIRDS, THE BEES AND THE ITALIANS *SIGNORE E
SIGNORI* Claridge, 1966, Italian
FOR LOVE AND GOLD *L'ARMATA BRANCALEONE* Fair Film,
1966, Italian
MONDO SOMMERSO 1966, Italian
IO, IO, IO E GLI ALTRI 1966, Italian
KILL, BABY, KILL *OPERAZIONE PAURA* 1966, Italian
LA GRANDE NOTTE DI RINGO 1966, Itlaian
KILL OR BE KILLED *UCCIDI E MUORI* 1966, Italian
DELITTO QUASI PERFETTO 1966, Italian
THE CLIMAX *L'IMMORALE* Lopert, 1967, Italian-French
I DUE VIGILI 1967, Italian
ASSICURASI VERGINE 1967, Italian
I DIAMANTI CHE NESSUNO VOLEVA ROBARE 1967, Italian
A MINUTE TO PRAY, A SECOND TO DIE 1967, Italian
IL PADRE DI FAMIGLIA 1967, Italian
L'UOMO, L'ORGIGLIO, LA VENDETTA 1967, Italian
COLPO DOPPIO DEL CAMALEONTE D'ORO 1967, Italian
DIO PERDONA, IO NO 1967, Italian
UN TRENO PER DURANGO 1967, Italian
THE SECRET WAR OF HARRY FRIGG Universal, 1968
HEROES A LA FUERZA 1968, Italian
BATTAGLIE SUI MARI 1968, Italian
DUE PISTOLE E UN VIGLIACCIO 1968, Italian
THE RUTHLESS FOUR *EVERY MAN FOR HIMSELF/SAM
COOPER'S GOLD* 1968, Italian-West German
SERAFINO Royal Films International, 1968, Italian-French
L'ISOLA 1968, Italian
VADO, VERO E SPARO 1968, Italian
MEGLIO VEDOVA 1968, Italian
LA BATTAGLIA DI EL ALAMEIN 1968, Italian
DAI NEMICI MI GUARDO IO 1968, Italian
I 7 FRATELLI CERVI 1968, Italian
ACE HIGH *I QUATTRO DELL'AVE MARIA* 1969, Italian
GLI INTERMIERI DELLA MUTUA 1969, Italian
LA PORTA DEL CANNONE 1969, Italian
STUNTMAN 1969, Italian
CRIMINAL SYMPHONY 1969, Italian
SCACCO INTERNAZIONALE 1969, Italian
IL TERRIBILE ISPETTORE 1969, Italian
CERTO, CERTISSIMI, ANZI...PROBABILE 1969, Italian
IL RAGAZZO CHE SORRIDE 1969, Italian
PROBABILITA ZERO 1969, Italian
PER UN PUGNO DI DIAMANTI 1969, Italian
UN ESTATE IN QUATTRO 1969, Italian
A DOPPIA FACCIA 1969, Italian
IL PISTOLERO SEGNATO DA DIO 1969, Italian
SATYRICON 1969, Italian
LA COLLINA DEGLI STIVALI 1970, Italian
BASTARDO! VAMOS A MATAR 1970, Italian
SATYRICOSISSIMO 1970, Italian
E VENNE IL GIORNO DEI LIMONI NERI 1970, Italian
UNA SPADA PER BRANDO 1970, Italian
NINI TIRABUSCIO, LA DONNA CHE INVENTO LA MOSSA 1970,
Italian
TILL DIVORCE DO YOU PART *LE CASTAGNE SONO BUONO*
1970, Italian
ROSOLINO PATERNO, SOLDATO 1970, Italian
ER PIU, STORIA D'AMORE E DI COLTELLO 1970, Italian
MA CHI T'HA DATE LA PATENTE? 1970, Italian

BUBU' BRC, 1970, Italian
BRANCALEONE ALLE CROCIATE Fair Film, 1970, Italian
IL SERGENTE KLEMS 1971, Italian
DETENUTO IN ATTESA DI GIUDIZIO 1971, Italian
LA BETIA, OVVERO IN AMORE PER OGNI GAUDENZA 1971,
Italian
ARMIAMOCI E PARTITE! 1971, Italian
BELLA, RICCA, LIEVE DIFETTO FISICO, CERCA, ANIMA
GEMELLA 1972, Italian
DON CAMILLO E I GIOVANI D'OGGI 1972, Italian
IN NOME DEL POPOLO ITALIANO Apollo International Film,
1972, Italian
BOCCACCIO 1972, Italian
CAUSA DI DIVORZIO 1972, Italian
CALL OF THE WILD Constantin, 1972, West German-Spanish
AVANTI! United Artists, 1972, U.S.-Italian
ALFREDO ALFREDO Paramount, 1973, Italian
THE RAMAZZE IN FUORI GIOCO 1973, Italian
UNA MATTA MATTA CORSA IN RUSSIA 1973, Italian
LE FUHRER EN FOLIE 1973, French
IL FIGLIOCCIO DEL PADRINO 1973, Italian
MILANO ROVENTE 1973, Italian
LA MANO NERA 1973, Italian
VOGLIAMO I COLONELLI Dean Film, 1973, Italian
MORDI E FUGGE C.C. Champion/Les Films Concordia, 1973,
Italian-French
L'EMIGRANTE 1973, Italian
MING, RAGAZZI! 1973, Italian
TUTTI PER UNO, BOTTE PER TUTTI 1973, Italian
UN UOMO, UNA CITTA 1974, Italian
ZANNA BIANCA 1974, Italian
IL RITORNO DI ZANNA BIANCA 1974, Italian
DELITTO D'AMORE Documento Film, 1974, Italian
PERMETTO SIGNORA CHE AMI VOSTRA FIGLIA? 1974, Italian
IL GATTO MAMMONE 1975, Italian
ZANNA BIANCA ALLA RISCOSSA 1975, Italian
GIUBBE ROSSE 1975, Italian
M TUTTI W NOI 1975, Italian
FIGHT TO THE DEATH *METRALLETA STEIN* co-composer,
1975, Italian
MY FRIENDS Allied Artists, 1975, Italian
LES RANGERS DEFIENT LES KARATEKAS 1975, French
SALVO D'ACQUISTO 1975, French
UNE FEMME A SA FENETRE 1976, French
LE GANG Warner-Columbia, 1977, French
L'HOMME PRESSE AMLF, 1977, French
LE BEAUJOLAIS NOUVEAU EST ARRIVE 1978, French
ASSASSINIO SUL TEVERE 1980, Italian
AMICI MIEII II Sacis, 1982, Italian
CLARETTA AND BEN Aquarius Films, 1983, Italian-French
HEADS OR TAILS co-composer with Paolo Rustichelli, CIDIF,
1983, Italian

MICHAEL RUTHERFORD

Contact: PRS - London, England, 011-44-1-580-5544

THE SHOUT co-composer with Rupert Hine and Anthony Banks,
Films Inc., 1979, British

S

HAIM SABAN

Contact: BMI - Los Angeles, 310-659-9109

RAINBOW BRITE AND THE STAR STEALER (AF)   co-composer
   with Shuki Levy, Warner Bros., 1985

CRAIG SAFAN

Agent: Air-Edel - Los Angeles, 310-914-5000
Affiliation: ASCAP - Los Angeles, 213-883-1000

THE CALIFORNIA REICH (FD)   City Life Films, 1975
THE GREAT TEXAS DYNAMITE CHASE   New World, 1976
THE GREAT SMOKEY ROADBLOCK *THE LAST OF THE
   COWBOYS* Dimension, 1976
THE BAD NEWS BEARS IN BREAKING TRAINING   Paramount,
   1977
ACAPULCO GOLD   R.C. Riddell, 1978
GETTING MARRIED (TF)   Paramount TV, 1978
CORVETTE SUMMER   MGM/United Artists, 1978
GOOD GUYS WEAR BLACK   American Cinema, 1979
THE SURVIVAL OF DANA (TF)   Roger Gimbel Productions/Marc
   Trabulus Enterprises/EMI TV, 1979
ROLLER BOOGIE   United Artists, 1979
DIE LAUGHING   co-composer with Robby Benson and Jerry Segal,
   Orion, 1980
FADE TO BLACK   American Cinema, 1980
THIEF   additional music, United Artists, 1981
T.A.G.: THE ASSASSINATION GAME   New World, 1982
NIGHTMARES   Universal, 1983
ANGEL   New World, 1984
THE LAST STARFIGHTER   Universal, 1984
THE IMPOSTER (TF)   Gloria Monty Productions/Comworld
   Productions, 1984
WARNING SIGN   20th Century Fox, 1985
ALFRED HITCHCOCK PRESENTS (TF)   co-composer, Universal
   TV, 1985
THE LEGEND OF BILLIE JEAN   Tri-Star, 1985
MIRRORS (TF)   Leonard Hill Films, 1985
REMO WILLIAMS: THE ADVENTURE BEGINS...   Orion, 1985
MIRRORS (TF)   Leonard Hill Films, 1985
HELP WANTED: KIDS (TF)   Stan Rogow Productions, 1986
I-MAN (TF)   Mark H. Ovitz Productions/Walt Disney TV, 1986
SAMARITAN (TF)   Levine-Robins Productions/Fries Entertainment,
   1986
COURAGE (TF)   Highgate Pictures/New World TV, 1986
TIMESTALKERS (TF)   Fries Entertainment/Newland-Raynor
   Productions, 1987
LADY BEWARE   Scotti Brothers, 1987
THE STRANGER   Columbia, 1987, U.S.-Argentine
NIGHTMARE ON ELM STREET PART 4: THE DREAM MASTER
   New Line Cinema, 1988
ALMOST GROWN (TF)   Universal TV/Atlantis Films, 1988
SUPERCARRIER (TF)   Fries Entertainment/Richard Hayward-Real
   Tinsel Productions, 1988
SHOOTDOWN (TF)   Leonard Hill Films, 1988
STAND AND DELIVER   Warner Bros., 1988
THE COMEBACK (TF)   CBS Entertainment, 1989
THE REVENGE OF AL CAPONE (TF)   Unity Productions/River City,
   1989
ENID IS SLEEPING   Vestron, 1990
SON OF THE MORNING STAR (TF)   Republic, 1991
LONG ROAD HOME (TF)   Rosemont, 1991
AN INCONVENIENT WOMAN (MS)   ABC Prods., 1991
MISSION OF THE SHARK (TF)   Richard Maynard Prods./Fries
   Entertainment, 1991
THE BURDEN OF PROOF (TF)   Mike Robe Prods/Capital
   Cities/ABC, 1992
TERROR ON TRACK 9 (TF)   Richard Crenna Prods./Spelling, 1992
JUDGEMENT DAY: THE JOHN LIST STORY (TF)   Republic, 1993
MIRACLE CHILD (TF)   Steve White Prods., 1993

PROPHET OF EVIL: THE ERVIL LeBARON STORY (TF)   Dream
   City Films/Hearst, 1993
CHEERS: ONE FOR THE ROAD (TF)   Charles-Burrows-Charles
   Prods./Paramount, 1993
RIO SHANNON (TF)   Sacret Inc./Warner Bros. TV, 1993
MONEY FOR NOTHING   Buena Vista, 1993
THE CONVICTION OF KITTY DODDS (TF)   Republic, 1993
ROSEANNE AND TOM: BEHIND THE SCENES (TF)   Brian Pike
   Prods./NBC Prods., 1994
WITHOUT WARNING (TF)   Wolper Organization/Warner Bros. TV,
   1994
WHERE ARE MY CHILDREN? (TF)   MDT Prods./Andrea Baynes
   Prods./Warner Bros. TV, 1994
WITHOUT CONSENT (TF)   Once Upon A Time Films/Blue Paddle
   Prods., 1994
MAJOR PAYNE   Universal, 1995
MR. WRONG   Buena Vista, 1996

SIDNEY SAGER

Contact: PRS - London, England, 011-44-1-580-5544

THE BEST OF FRIENDS (TF)   1992, British

MICHAEL SAHL

Contact: ASCAP - Los Angeles, 213-883-1000

BLOODSUCKING FREAKS   Troma, 1982
ROY COHN/JACK SMITH   Icon & Idiom Prods., 1994

BUFFY SAINTE-MARIE

Contact: ASCAP - Los Angeles, 213-883-1000

STRIPPER (FD)   co-composer with Jack Nitzsche, 20th Century
   Fox, 1985

RYUICHI SAKAMOTO

b. Japan
Agent: CAA - Beverly Hills, 310-288-4545
Affiliation: ASCAP - Los Angeles, 213-883-1000

MERRY CHRISTMAS, MR. LAWRENCE   Universal, 1983,
   British-Japanese
THE LAST EMPEROR ★★   co-composer with David Byrne and
   Cong Su, Columbia, 1987, British-Chinese
THE HANDMAID'S TALE   Cinecom, 1990
THE SHELTERING SKY   Warner Bros., 1990
TACONES LEJANOS *HIGH HEELS* Miramax, 1991, Spanish
EMILY BRONTE'S WUTHERING HEIGHTS *WUTHERING
   HEIGHTS* Paramount, 1992
WILD PALMS (MS)   Ixtlan/Greengrass, 1993
LITTLE BUDDHA   Miramax, 1993
WINGS OF HONNEAMISE: ROYAL SPACE FORCE (AF)   1995,
   Japanese

GARY SALES

Contact: ASCAP - Los Angeles, 213-883-1000

MADMAN   co-composer with Stephen Horelick, Jensen Farley
   Pictures, 1982

BARRY SALMON

Contact: BMI - Los Angeles, 310-659-9109

SILENT MADNESS   Almi Pictures, 1984

BENNETT SALVAY

Agent: Gorfaine-Schwartz - Los Angeles, 213-969-1011
Affiliation: BMI - Los Angeles, 310-659-9109

ALOHA SUMMER   co-composer with Jesse Frederick, Spectrafilm,
   1988
BURNING BRIDGES (TF)   co-composer with W.G. Snuffy Walden,
   Andrea Baynes Productions/Lorimar TV, 1990
I'LL FLY AWAY - THEN AND NOW (TF)   co-composer with W. G.
   Snuffy Walden, Brand-Falsey/Lorimar TV, 1993
SANDTRAP   PM Entertainment, 1997

LEONARD SALZEDO
b. 1921 - London
Contact: PRS - London, England, 011-44-1-580-5544

SHADOW OF FEAR *BEFORE I WAKE* 1956, British
THE REVENGE OF FRANKENSTEIN Columbia, 1958, British
THE STEEL BAYONET United Artists, 1958, British

CALEB SAMPSON
Contact: BMI - Los Angeles, 310-659-9109

THE SECRET OF LIFE (TD) co-composer with John Kusiak, WGBH/BBC, 1993

JONATHAN SAMPSON
Contact: BMI - Los Angeles, 310-659-9109

JO-JO AT THE GATE OF LIONS Nana Films, 1992
WADECK'S MOTHER'S FRIEND'S SON Accordion, 1992

JEREMY SAMS
PERSUASION Sony Classics, 1995, British

DAVID SANBORN
b. 1945
Contact: BMI - Los Angeles, 310-659-9109

FINNEGAN BEGIN AGAIN (CTF) co-composer with Michael Colina, HBO Premiere Films/Zenith Productions/Jennie & Co. Film Productions, 1985, U.S.-British
LETHAL WEAPON co-composer with Michael Kamen and Eric Clapton, Warner Bros., 1987
LETHAL WEAPON 2 co-composer with Michael Kamen and Eric Clapton, Warner Bros., 1989
LETHAL WEAPON 3 co-composer with Michael Kamen and Eric Clapton, Warner Bros., 1992

RICK SANDLER
Contact: ASCAP - Los Angeles, 213-883-1000

HEY, GOOD LOOKIN' co-composer with John Madara, Warner Bros., 1982

PETER SANDLOFF
Contact: GEMA - Germany, 011-49-89-480-03610

MAEDCHEN IN UNIFORM 1965, West German
MICHAEL KOHLHAAS Horst Film, 1979, West German

MARK SANDMAN
Contact: BMI - Los Angeles, 310-659-9109

SPANKING THE MONKEY song score, Fine Line, 1994

ARTURO SANDOVAL
THE PEREZ FAMILY composer of traditional music Samuel Goldwyn, 1995

PENGBIAN SANG
NUEBA YOL 1996

ANTON SANKO
Contact: ASCAP - Los Angeles, 213-883-1000

WOMEN & MEN 2 (CTF) co-composer of one segment with Suzanne Vega, composer of another segment, David Brown/HBO Showcase, 1991
COUSIN BOBBY Tesauro, 1992
ONE FOOT ON A BANANA PEEL, THE OTHER FOOT IN THE GRAVE: SECRETS FROM THE DOLLY MADISON ROOM (FD) Clinica Estetico/Joanne Howard, 1994
PARTY GIRL First Look, 1995
GIRL IN THE CADILLAC Steinhardt Baer Pictures, 1995
LIVE NUDE GIRLS Republic, 1995

NEFTALI SANTIAGO
Contact: ASCAP - Los Angeles, 213-883-1000

DIRECT HIT PM, 1993

CARLOS SANTOS
Contact: ASCAP - Los Angeles, 213-883-1000

JETLAG Wieland Schulz-Keil/Figaro Films, 1981, U.S.-Spanish

MICHEL SANVOISIN
Contact: SACEM - France, 011-33-1-4715-4715

A DANGEROUS MAN: LAWRENCE AFTER ARABIA (TF) Enigma TV/Sands Films/WNET, 1992
AS YOU LIKE IT Buena Vista, 1992, British

ANDREA SAPAROFF
Contact: ASCAP - Los Angeles, 213-883-1000

NO MAN IS AN ISLAND Dana Productions
THE JOY OF ACHIEVEMENT Dana Productions
THE JOYS OF COMMUNICATION Dana Productions
AMERICA'S PEOPLE Dana Productions
HOME ALONE Hi-Tops Productions
A SIMPLE MATTER OF JUSTICE PS Films
APPOINTMENT WITH FEAR Galaxy International, 1985
DEADLY PRESENCE Trancas International
THE UFO REPORT: SIGHTINGS (TD) Winkler-Daniels Prods., 1991

PHILIPPE SARDE
b. June 21, 1945 - Neuilly-sur-Seine, France
Agent: Vangelos Management - Encino, 818-380-1919
Affiliation: SACEM - France, 011-33-1-4715-4715

LES CHOSES DE LA VIE *THE THINGS OF LIFE* Columbia, 1970, French
SORTIE DE SECOURS 1970, French
LA LIBERTE EN CROUPE 1970, French
MAX ET LES FERRAILLEURS CFDC, 1971, French
LE CHAT 1971, French
LA VEUVE COUDERC 1972, French
LIZA Horizon, 1972, French-Italian
LE FILS 1972, French
HELLE Cocinor, 1972, French
LE DROIT D'AIMER 1972, French
CESAR AND ROSALIE Cinema 5, 1972, French-Italian-West German
LA GRANDE BOUFFE ABKCO, 1973, French-Italian
LE TRAIN 1973, French
TOUCHE PAS A LA FEMME BLANCHE! *HANDS OFF WHITE WOMEN* CFDC, 1974, French
LES CORPS CELESTES Les Productions Carle-Lamy, 1973, Canadian
LA VALISE 1973, French
LE MARIAGE A LA MODE 1973, French
CHARLIE ET SES DEUX NENETTES 1973, French
THE CLOCKMAKER OF ST. PAUL Joseph Green Pictures, 1974, French
DOROTHEA 1974, French
LA RACE DES SEIGNEURS 1974, French
DEUX HOMMES DANS LA VILLE 1974, French
LES SEINS DE GLACE 1974, French
VINCENT, FRANCOIS, PAUL AND THE OTHERS Joseph Green Pictures, 1974, French-Italian
SOUVENIRS D'EN FRANCE adaptation, 1974, French
LANCELOT OF THE LAKE New Yorker, 1975, French-Italian
UN DIVORCE HEUREUX CFDC, 1975, French-Danish
LA CAGE 1975, French
PAS DE PROBLEME *NO PROBLEM* 1975, French
FOLLE A TUER 1975, French
UN SAC DE BILLES 1975, French
LES GALETTES DE PONT-AVEN adaptation, 1975, French
THE FRENCH DETECTIVE 1975, French
THE JUDGE AND THE ASSASSIN Libra, 1976, French
THE LAST WOMAN Columbia, 1976, Italian-French
ADIEU, POULET 1976, French
ON AURA TOUT VU 1976, French

SEPT MORTS SUR ORDONNANCE   1976, French
THE TENANT   Paramount, 1976, French-U.S.
MARIE POUPEE   1976, French
BAROCCO   1976, French
MADO   Joseph Green Pictures, 1976, French
LE JUGE FAYARD DIT LE SHERIFF   CCFC, 1977, French
VIOLETTE ET FRANCOIS   1977, French
LE DIABLE PROBABLEMENT   Gaumont, 1977, French
UN TAXI MAUVE   *THE PURPLE TAXI*   Parafrance Films, 1977,
   French-Italian-Irish
COMME LA LUNE...   1977, Italian
DES ENFANTS GATES   *SPOILED CHILDREN*   Gaumont, 1977,
   French
LE CRABE-TAMBOUR   1977, French
MADAME ROSA   *LA VIE DEVANT SOI*   Atlantic Releasing
   Corporation, 1978, French
BYE BYE MONKEY   Gaumont, 1978, Italian-French
ILS SONT FOUS CES SORCIERS!   1978, French
PASSE MONTAGNE   1978, French
LE SUCRE   1978, French
LA CLE SUR LA PORTE   *THE KEY IS IN THE DOOR*   1978,
   French
L'ADOLESCENTE   1978, French
A SIMPLE STORY   Quartet, 1979, French
THE BRONTE SISTERS   Gaumont, 1979, French
LE TOUBIB   1979, French
FLIC OU VOYOU   1979, French
TESS ★   Columbia, 1979, French-British
CHIEDO ASILO   *MY ASYLUM*   1979
LA FEMME-FLIC   1980, French
BUFFET FROID   *COLD CUTS*   adaptation, 1980, French
I SENT A LETTER TO MY LOVE   *CHERE INCONNUE*   Atlantic
   Releasing Corporation, 1980, French
LE GUIGNOLO   1980, French
BEAU PERE   New Line Cinema, 1981, French
GHOST STORY   Universal, 1981
CHOICE OF ARMS   1981, French
COUP DE TORCHON   *CLEAN SLATE*   Biograph/Quartet/Films
   Inc./The Frank Moreno Company, 1982
L'ETOILE DU NORD   *THE NORTH STAR*   Parafrance, 1982,
   French
A STRANGE AFFAIR   Parafrance, 1982, French
QUEST FOR FIRE   20th Century-Fox, 1982, Canadian-French
LOVESICK   The Ladd Company/Warner Bros., 1983
J'AI ESPOUSE UN OMBRE   AMLF, 1983, French
ATTENTION, UME FEMME PEUT EN CACHER UNE AUTRE
   Gaumont, 1983, French
GARCON   Sara Film/Renn Productions, 1983, French
FIRST DESIRES   AMLF, 1983, French
A FRIEND OF VINCENT   AMLF, 1983, French
STELLA   Fox-Hachette, 1983, French
FORT SAGANNE   A.A.A., 1984, French
SUNDAY IN THE COUNTRY   MGM/UA Classics, 1984, French
JOSHUA, THEN AND NOW   20th Century Fox, 1985, Canadian
RENDEZVOUS   UGC, 1985, French
HAREM   Sara Films, 1985, French
DEVIL IN THE FLESH   World Film Alliance, 1986, Australian
MON BEAU-FRERE A TUE MA SOEUR   World Marketing, 1986,
   French
THE SCENE OF THE CRIME   AMLF, 1986, French
THE MANHATTAN PROJECT   20th Century Fox, 1986
PIRATES   Cannon, 1986, French-Tunisian
EVERY TIME WE SAY GOODBYE   Tri-Star, 1987, Israeli
LES MOIS D'AVRIL SONT MEURTRIERS   Sara/CDF, 1987,
   French
A FEW DAYS WITH ME   Galaxy International, 1988, French
LOST ANGELS   Orion, 1989
REUNION   Les Films Ariane-FR3 Films, 1989, French
THE BEAR   Tri-Star, 1989, French
THE MUSIC BOX   Tri-Star, 1989
LA BAULE-LES PINS   UGC, 1990, French
LORD OF THE FLIES   Columbia, 1990
EVE OF DESTRUCTION   Orion, 1991
J'EMBRASSE PAS   *I DON'T KISS*   1991, French
L.627   1992, French
LA VOIX   *THE VOICE*   1992, French
LA PETITE APOCALYPSE   *THE LITTLE APOCALYPSE*   1993,
   French-Italian-Polish
MY FAVORITE SEASON   *MA SAISON PREFEREE*   1993, French
UNCOVERED   1994, British-Spanish
THE DAUGHTER OF D'ARTAGNAN   *LA FILLE DE D'ARTAGNAN*
   1994, French

LES VOLEURS   1996, French
MA SAISON PREFEREE   1996, French
NELLY ET MONSIEUR ARNAUD   1996, French

JOHN SARGENT
Contact: BMI - Los Angeles, 310-659-9109

DOC'S FULL SERVICE   co-composer with Chuck Pinnell, Brazos
   Films, 1994

SARAH SARHANDI
LONDON KILLS ME   co-composer with Mark Springer, Fine Line,
   1991, British

JERZY SATANOWSKI
KOLEJNOSC UCZUC   *SEQUENCES OF FEELING*   1993, Polish

MASARU SATO
b. 1928 - Hokkaido, Japan
Contact: JASRAC - Tokyo, Japan, 011-81-3-502-6551

JUVENILE PASSIONS   co-composer with Toru Takemitsu, 1956,
   Japanese
RECORD OF A LIVING BEING   co-composer with Fumio
   Hayasaka, 1956, Japanese
THE LOWER DEPTHS   Brandon, 1957, Japanese
THRONE OF BLOOD   *THE CASTLE OF THE SPIDER'S WEB*
   Brandon, 1957, Japanese
HALF HUMAN   DCA, 1957, Japanese
THE HIDDEN FORTRESS   *THREE BAD MEN IN A HIDDEN
   FORTRESS*   Toho, 1958, Japanese
GIGANTIS THE FIRE MONSTER   1959, Japanese
THE H-MAN   Columbia, 1959, Japanese
THE BAD SLEEP WELL   Toho, 1960, Japanese
YOJIMBO   Seneca International, 1961, Japanese
SANJURO   Toho, 1962, Japanese
HIGH AND LOW   East West Classics, 1963, Japanese
THE LOST WORLD OF SINBAD   1964
RED BEARD   Toho, 1965, Japanese
THE EMPEROR AND THE GENERAL   *THE LONGEST DAY IN
   JAPAN*   Toho, 1967, Japanese
THREE SISTERS   1967, Japanese
SATSUJINYO JUDAI   *THE AGE OF ASSASSINS*   1967, Japanese
THE SWORD OF DOOM   Toho, 1967, Japanese
GODZILLA VS. THE SEA MONSTER   *EBIRAH, HORROR OF THE
   DEEP*   1968, Japanese
KILL!   1968, Japanese
PORTRAIT OF CHICKO   1968, Japanese
SON OF GODZILLA   1969, Japanese
SAMURAI BANNERS   1969, Japanese
RED LION   1969, Japanese
OUTLAWS   1970, Japanese
KAZOKU   1971, Japanese
THE BATTLE OF OKINAWA   1971, Japanese
SAPPORO WINTER OLYMPICS   1972, Japanese
THE WOLVES   1972, Japanese
SUBMERSION OF JAPAN   *TIDAL WAVE*   1973, Japanese
MAN AND WAR, PART III   1974, Japanese
GODZILLA VS. MECHA-GODZILLA   *GODZILLA VS. BIONIC
   MONSTER/GODZILLA VS. COSMIC MONSTER*   1976,
   Japanese
A PORTRAIT OF SHUNKIN   1977, Japanese
THE YELLOW HANDKERCHIEF OF HAPPINESS   1978, Japanese
U.F.O. BLUE CHRISTMAS   *BLOOD TYPE BLUE*   1979
THE GLACIER FOX (FD)   Sanrio Film, 1979
OH! THE NOMUGI PASS   1979, Japanese
TOWARD THE TERRA   1980, Japanese
SENSEI   *THE TEACHER*   Daiei, 1983, Japanese
IREZUMI: SPIRIT OF TATTOO   Daiei, 1983, Japanese
SHOGUN'S SHADOW   Toei, 1989, Japanese

SOMEI SATOH
Contact: JASRAC - Tokyo, Japan, 011-81-3-502-6551

TO LIV(E)   Riverdrive, 1992

EDDIE SAUTER

Contact: ASCAP - Los Angeles, 213-883-1000

MICKEY ONE   Columbia, 1965
BEGGERMAN, THIEF (TF)   Universal TV, 1979

JORDI SAVALL

Contact: PRS - London, England, 011-44-1-580-5544

JEANNE LA PUCELLE   *JOAN THE MAID*   1994, French

TOM SAVIANO

Agent: Andi Howard - Los Angeles, 213-278-6483
Affiliation: BMI - Los Angeles, 310-659-9109

DEFIANCE   American International, 1980

CARLO SAVINA

b. 1919 - Turin, Italy
Contact: SIAE - Italy, 011-39-6-59-901

ERODE IL GRANDE   1958, Italian
EUROPA DI NOTTE   1959, Italian
IL MORALISTA   1959, Italian
IL PRINCIPE FUSTO   1960, Italian
LA RAGAZZA SOTTO IL LENZUOLO   1961, Italian
L'IRA DI ACHILLE   1962, Italian
LIOLA   1964, Italian
SFIDA AL RE DI CASTIGLIA   1964, Italian
LE SPIE UCCIDONO A BEIRUT   1965, Italian
GLI AMANTI LATINI   1965, Italian
FURIA A MARRAKESCH   1966, Italian
L'UOME CHE RIDE   1966, Italian
JOHNNY ORO   1966, Italian
A 077 SFIDA AL KILLERS   Aenit/Flora/Regina, 1967, Italian
PROCESSO A STALIN...?   1967, Italian
JOE L'IMPLACABILE   Seven/Hispamer, 1967, Italian-Spanish
JOKO INVOCA DIO E MUORI   1968, Italian
SIMON BOLIVAR   1969, Italian
HYPNOS   1969, Italian
EHI AMIGO SEI MORTO   1970, Italian
E LO CHIAMARONO SPIRITO SANTO   1971, Italian
LE CALDE NOTTE DI DON GIOVANNI   1971, Italian
FINALMENTE...LE MILLE E UNA NOTTE   Pink Medusa, 1972, Italian
UN ANIMAL CHIAMATO UOMO   1972, Italian
TRINITA E SARTANA: FIGLI DI...   1972, Italian
JESSE E LESTER DUE FRATELLI IN UN POSTO CHIAMATO TRINITA   1972, Italian
INGRID SULLA STRADA   1973, Italian
MING, RAGAZZI!   1973, Italian
MR. HERCULES AGAINST KARATE   *MR. HERCULES AGAINST KUNG FU*   United Artists, 1973, Italian
MANONE IL LADRONE   Laser Film, 1974, Italian
CARNALITA   1974, Italian
LA PROFANAZIONE   1974, Italian
L'ASSASSINO HA RISERVATO 9 POLTRONE   1974, Italian
LA DOVE NON BATTE IL SOLE   1975, Italian
LA BOLOGNESE   1975, Italian
LA NUORA GIOVANE   1975, Italian
LA NIPOTE   1975, Italian
LA NIPOTE DEL PRETE   1975, Italian
ORDINE FIRMATO IN BIANCO   1975, Italian
IL VIZIO HA LE CALZE NERE   1975, Italian
UNA VERGINE IN FAMIGLIA   1975, Italian
L'INGENUA   1975, Italian
ULTIME GRIDA DALLA SAVANA (FD)   1975, Italian
CALORE IN PROVINCIA   1975, Italian
CARI MOSTRI DEL MARE   1976, Italian
COMIN' AT YA! Filmways, 1981, Italian-U.S.
THE HUNTERS OF THE GOLDEN COBRA   *THE RAIDERS OF THE GOLDEN COBRA*   World Northal, 1982, Italian

PHIL SAWYER

Contact: BMI - Los Angeles, 310-659-9109

TWENTY-ONE   Anglo International, 1991

FRANK SCHAAP

WARREN OATES: ACROSS THE BORDER (FD)   1993

WALTER SCHARF*

b. August 1, 1910 - New York, New York
Contact: ASCAP - Los Angeles, 213-883-1000

MERCY ISLAND ★   co-composer with Cy Feuer, Republic, 1941
JOHNNY DOUGHBOY ★   adaptation, Republic, 1942
CHATTERBOX   Republic, 1943
HIT PARADE OF 1943 ★   Republic, 1943
NOBODY'S DARLING   Republic, 1943
SECRETS OF THE UNDERGROUND   Republic, 1943
HANDS ACROSS THE BORDER   Republic, 1943
SHANTYTOWN   Republic, 1943
SLEEPY LAGOON   Republic, 1943
SOMEONE TO REMEMBER   Republic, 1943
IN OLD OKLAHOMA ★   Republic, 1943
THUMBS UP   Republic, 1943
ATLANTIC CITY   Republic, 1944
THE FIGHTING SEABEES ★   Republic, 1944
THE COWBOY AND THE SENORITA   Republic, 1944
CASANOVA IN BURLESQUE   Republic, 1944
BRAZIL ★   Republic, 1944
LAKE PLACID SERENADE   Republic, 1944
THE LADY AND THE MONSTER   Republic, 1944
STORM OVER LISBON   Republic, 1944
THE CHEATERS   Republic, 1945
DAKOTA   Republic, 1945
EARL CARROLL'S VANITIES   Repubic, 1945
I'VE ALWAYS LOVED YOU   Republic, 1946
THE SAXON CHARM   United Artists, 1948
THE COUNTESS OF MONTE CRISTO   United Artists, 1948
ARE YOU WITH IT?   Universal, 1948
RED CANYON   United Artists, 1948
CITY ACROSS THE RIVER   Universal, 1949
TAKE ONE FALSE STEP   Universal, 1949
YES SIR, THAT'S MY BABY   Universal, 1949
ABANDONED   Universal, 1949
SOUTH SEA SINNER   Universal, 1950
BUCCANNEER'S GIRL   Universal, 1950
CURTAIN CALL AT CACTUS CREEK   Universal, 1950
SIERRA   Universal, 1950
SPY HUNT   Universal, 1950
DEPORTED   Universal, 1950
TWO TICKETS TO BROADWAY   RKO Radio, 1951
HANS CHRISTIAN ANDERSON   adaptation, RKO Radio, 1952
THE FRENCH LINE   RKO Radio, 1953
LIVING IT UP   Paramount, 1954
THREE RING CIRCUS   Paramount, 1954
ARTISTS AND MODELS   Paramount, 1955
YOU'RE NEVER TOO YOUNG   Paramount, 1955
THE BIRDS AND THE BEES   Paramount, 1956
HOLLYWOOD OR BUST   Paramount, 1956
THREE FOR JAMIE DAWN   Allied Artists, 1956
TIMETABLE   United Artists, 1956
THREE VIOLENT PEOPLE   Paramount, 1957
THE JOKER IS WILD   *ALL THE WAY*   Paramount, 1957
LOVING YOU   Paramount, 1957
THE SAD SACK   Paramount, 1957
ROCK-A-BYE BABY   Paramount, 1958
KING CREOLE   Paramount, 1958
THE GEISHA BOY   Paramount, 1958
DON'T GIVE UP THE SHIP   Paramount, 1959
THE BELLBOY   Paramount, 1960
CINDERFELLA   Paramount, 1960
THE LADIES' MAN   Paramount, 1961
POCKETFUL OF MIRACLES   United Artists, 1961
THE ERRAND BOY   Paramount, 1962
HAROLD LLOYD'S WORLD OF COMEDY   Continental, 1962
IT'S ONLY MONEY   Paramount, 1962
MY SIX LOVES   Paramount, 1963
THE NUTTY PROFESSOR   Paramount, 1963
HONEYMOON HOTEL   MGM, 1964
WHERE LOVE HAS GONE   Paramount, 1964
TICKLE ME   Allied Artists, 1965
FUNNY GIRL ★   adaptation, Columbia, 1968
PENDULUM   Columbia, 1969
THE CHEYENNE SOCIAL CLUB   National General, 1970
BEN   Cinerama Releasing Corporation, 1972
WALKING TALL   Cinerama Releasing Corporation, 1973

PART 2, WALKING TALL   American International, 1975
FINAL CHAPTER—WALKING TALL   American International, 1977
GASP!   Avala Films, 1977, Yugoslavian
WHEN EVERY DAY WAS THE FOURTH OF JULY (TF)   Dan Curtis
    Productions, 1978
A REAL AMERICAN HERO (TF)   Bing Crosby Productions, 1978
THE TRIANGLE FACTORY FIRE SCANDAL (TF)   Alan Landsburg
    Productions/Don Kirshner Productions, 1979
SALVAGE (TF)   Bennett-Katleman Productions/Columbia Pictures
    TV, 1979
FROM HERE TO ETERNITY (MS)   Bennett-Katleman
    Productions/Columbia Pictures TV, 1979
BLIND AMBITION (MS)   Time-Life Productions Inc., 1979
MOVIOLA: THE SCARLETT O'HARA WAR (TF)   David
    Wolper-Stan Margulies Productions/Warner Bros. TV, 1980
THE LONG DAYS OF SUMMER (TF)   Dan Curtis Productions,
    1980
THIS IS ELVIS (FD)   Warner Bros., 1981
MIDNIGHT OFFERINGS (TF)   Stephen J. Cannell Productions,
    1981
TWILIGHT TIME   MGM/UA, 1983, U.S.-Yugoslavian
K I M   S C H A R N B E R G
LIES OF THE HEART: THE STORY OF LAURIE KELLOGG (TF)
    MDT Prods./Daniel H. Blatt Prods/Warner Bros. TV, 1994

GLENN SCHELLENBERG

ZERO PATIENCE   Zero Patience Prods., 1993, Canadian

ANTON SCHERPENZEEL

b. Denmark
Contact: BUMA - Holland, 011-31-20-540-7911

SPETTERS   Samuel Goldwyn Company, 1980, Dutch

PETER SCHICKELE

b. 1935 - Ames, Iowa
Contact: ASCAP - Los Angeles, 213-466-7681

FUNNYMAN   New Yorker, 1967
SILENT RUNNING   Universal, 1972
OH CALCUTTA!   co-composer, Tigon, 1972

DONN SCHIFF

Contact: ASCAP - Los Angeles, 213-883-1000

LIVE: FROM DEATH ROW (TF)   D.R. Prods./Charles Mopic Co.,
    1992
THE PORNOGRAPHER   Charlie MoPic, 1994

STEVE SCHIFF

Contact: BMI - Los Angeles, 310-659-9109

LENA'S HOLIDAY   Crown, 1991

LALO SCHIFRIN*

b. 1932 - Buenos Aires, Argentina
Contact: BMI - Los Angeles, 310-659-9109

EL JEFE   1957, Argentine
JOY HOUSE   LES FELINS   MGM, 1964, French
RHINO!   MGM, 1964
SEE HOW THEY RUN (TF)   Universal TV, 1964
ONCE A THIEF   MGM, 1965
THE CINCINATTI KID   MGM, 1965
GONE WITH THE WAVE (FD)   1965
DARK INTRUDER   Universal, 1965
THE LIQUIDATOR   MGM, 1966, British
I DEAL IN DANGER   20th Century-Fox, 1966
THE DOOMSDAY FLIGHT (TF)   Universal TV, 1966
BLINDFOLD   Universal, 1966
WAY...WAY OUT!   20th Century-Fox, 1966
HOW I SPENT MY SUMMER VACATION (TF)   Universal TV, 1967
MURDERERS' ROW   Columbia, 1967
SULLIVAN'S EMPIRE   Universal, 1967
THE PRESIDENT'S ANALYST   Paramount, 1967
WHO'S MINDING THE MINT?   Columbia, 1967
COOL HAND LUKE ★   Warner Bros., 1967
THE VENETIAN AFFAIR   MGM, 1967

THE FOX ★   Claridge, 1968
WHERE ANGELS GO...TROUBLE FOLLOWS!   Columbia, 1968
SOL MADRID   MGM, 1968
THE BROTHERHOOD   Paramount, 1968
BULLITT   Warner Bros., 1968
COOGAN'S BLUFF   Universal, 1968
HELL IN THE PACIFIC   Cinerama Releasing Corporation, 1968
U.M.C. (TF)   MGM TV, 1969
CHE!   20th Century-Fox, 1969
EYE OF THE CAT   Universal, 1969
THE YOUNG LAWYERS (TF)   Paramount Pictures TV, 1969
PUSSYCAT, PUSSYCAT, I LOVE YOU   United Artists, 1970,
    British
IMAGO   Emerson, 1970
THE MASK OF SHEBA (TF)   MGM TV, 1970
KELLY'S HEROES   MGM, 1970, U.S.-Yugoslavian
THE AQUARIANS (TF)   Universal TV, 1970
WUSA   Paramount, 1970
I LOVE MY WIFE   Universal, 1970
MRS. POLIFAX: - SPY   United Artists, 1971
THE BEGUILED   Universal, 1971
ESCAPE (TF)   Paramount TV, 1971
PRETTY MAIDS ALL IN A ROW   MGM, 1971
THX-1138   Warner Bros., 1971
THE CHRISTIAN LICORICE STORE   National General, 1971
THE HELLSTROM CHRONICLE (FD)   Cinema 5, 1971
EARTH II (TF)   MGM TV, 1971
DIRTY HARRY   Warner Bros., 1971
HUNTER (TF)   CBS Entertainment, 1971
WELCOME HOME, JOHNNY BRISTOL (TF)   Cinema Center, 1972
THE WRATH OF GOD   MGM, 1972
RAGE   Warner Bros., 1972
JOE KIDD   Universal, 1972
PRIME CUT   National General, 1972
CHARLIE VARRICK   Universal, 1973
ENTER THE DRAGON   Warner Bros., 1973, U.S.-Hong Kong
HARRY IN YOUR POCKET   United Artists, 1973
HIT!   Paramount, 1973
MAGNUM FORCE   Warner Bros., 1973
THE NEPTUNE FACTOR   20th Century-Fox, 1973
NIGHT GAMES (TF)   Paramount TV, 1974
MAN ON A SWING   Paramount, 1974
GOLDEN NEEDLES   American International, 1974
THE FOUR MUSKETEERS   MILADY'S REVENGE   20th
    Century-Fox, 1975, British
STARSKY AND HUTCH (TF)   Spelling-Goldberg Productions, 1975
DELANCEY STREET: THE CRISIS WITHIN (TF)   Paramount TV,
    1975
THE MASTER GUNFIGHTER   Taylor-Laughlin, 1975
GUILTY OR INNOCENT: THE SAM SHEPPARD MURDER CASE
    (TF)   Universal TV, 1975
FOSTER AND LAURIE (TF)   Charles Fries Productions, 1975
SKY RIDERS   20th Century-Fox, 1976
ST. IVES   Warner Bros., 1976
SPECIAL DELIVERY   American International, 1976
BRENDA STARR (TF)   Wolper Productions, 1976
VOYAGE OF THE DAMNED ★   Avco Embassy, 1976, British
THE EAGLE HAS LANDED   Columbia, 1977, British
DAY OF THE ANIMALS   Film Ventures, 1977
ROLLERCOASTER   Universal, 1977
GOOD AGAINST EVIL (TF)   Frankel-Bolen Productions/20th
    Century-Fox TV, 1977
TELEFON   MGM/United Artists, 1977
THE MANITOU   Avco Embassy, 1978
THE PRESIDENT'S MISTRESS (TF)   Stephen Friedman/Kings
    Road Productions, 1978
NUNZIO   Universal, 1978
RETURN FROM WITCH MOUNTAIN   Buena Vista, 1978
THE CAT FROM OUTER SPACE   Buena Vista, 1978
THE NATIVITY (TF)   D'Angelo-Bullock-Allen Productions/20th
    Century-Fox TV, 1978
LOVE AND BULLETS   AFD, 1979
INSTITUTE FOR REVENGE (TF)   Gold-Driskill
    Productions/Columbia TV, 1979
ESCAPE TO ATHENA   AFD, 1979, British
BOULEVARD NIGHTS   Warner Bros., 1979
THE CONCORDE - AIRPORT '79   Universal, 1979
THE AMITYVILLE HORROR ★   American International, 1979
SERIAL   Paramount, 1980
WHEN TIME RAN OUT   Warner Bros., 1980
THE NUDE BOMB   Universal, 1980
BRUBAKER   20th Century-Fox, 1980

THE BIG BRAWL   Warner Bros., 1980
THE COMPETITION ★   Columbia, 1980
LOOPHOLE   MGM/United Artists, 1981, British
THE CHICAGO STORY (TF)   Eric Bercovici Productions/MGM TV, 1981
CAVEMAN   United Artists, 1981
LA PELLE   1981, Italian
BUDDY BUDDY   MGM/United Artists, 1981
THE SEDUCTION   Avco Embassy, 1981
VICTIMS (TF)   Hajeno Productions/Warner Bros. TV, 1982
THE CLASS OF 1984   United Film Distribution, 1982, Canadian
LAS VIERNES DE LA ETERNIDAD   1982, Argentine
FAST-WALKING   Pickman Films, 1982
A STRANGER IS WATCHING   MGM/United Artists, 1982
FALCON'S GOLD (CTF)   Paul Heller Productions/Schulz Productions/Sonesta Productions/Intrepid Productions, 1982
STARFLIGHT: THE PLANE THAT COULDN'T LAND (TF)   Orgolini-Nelson Productions, 1983
DOCTOR DETROIT   Universal, 1983
THE STING II ★   adaptation, Universal, 1983
SUDDEN IMPACT   Warner Bros., 1983
THE OSTERMAN WEEKEND   20th Century-Fox, 1983
RITA HAYWORTH: THE LOVE GODDESS (TF)   The Susskind Company, 1983
PRINCESS DAISY (TF)   Steve Krantz Productions/NBC Entertainment, 1983
TANK   Universal, 1984
SPRAGGUE (TF)   MG Productions/Lorimar Productions, 1984
THE NEW KIDS   Columbia, 1985
A.D. (TF)   Procter & Gamble Productions/International Film Productions, 1985
HOLLYWOOD WIVES (MS)   Aaron Spelling Productions, 1985
PRIVATE SESSIONS (TF)   Raven's Claw Productions/Seltzer-Gimbel Productions/Comworld Productions, 1985
THE MEAN SEASON   Orion, 1985
BAD MEDICINE   20th Century Fox, 1985
COMMAND 5 (TF)   Paramount Pictures TV, 1985
BRIDGE ACROSS TIME   TERROR AT LONDON BRIDGE/ARIZONA RIPPER (TF)   Fries Entertainment, 1985
KUNG FU: THE MOVIE (TF)   Lou-Step Productions/Warner Bros. TV, 1986
TRIPLECROSS (TF)   Tisch-Avnet Productions/ABC Circle Films, 1986
THE LADIES CLUB   New Line Cinema, 1986
BEVERLY HILLS MADAM (TF)   BLS Productions/Orion TV Productions, 1986
BLACK MOON RISING   New World, 1986
OUT ON A LIMB (TF)   Stan Margulies Co./ABC Circle Films, 1987
THE FOURTH PROTOCOL   Lorimar, 1987, British
EARTH*STAR VOYAGER (TF)   Walt Disney TV/Marstar Productions, 1988
SHAKEDOWN ON THE SUNSET STRIP (TF)   CBS Entertainment, 1988
THE SILENCE AT BETHANY   Keener Productions/American Playhouse Theatrical Films, 1988
THE DEAD POOL   Warner Bros., 1988
LITTLE SWEETHEART   Columbia, 1988, U.S.-British
BERLIN BLUES   1988, Spanish
FRIDAYS OF ETERNITY   Aires, 1989
ORIGINAL SIN (TF)   The Larry Thompson Organization/New World TV, 1989
THE NEON EMPIRE (CTF)   Fries Entertainment, 1989
LITTLE WHITE LIES (TF)   Larry A. Thompson Organization/New World TV, 1989
FX 2 - THE DEADLY ART OF ILLUSION   Orion, 1991
A WOMAN NAMED JACKIE (TF)   Lester Persky Prods., 1991
THE BEVERLY HILLBILLIES   20th Century Fox, 1993

ZANDER SCHLOSS

HIGHWAY PATROLMAN   EL PATRULLERO   Cable HOgue/Marubeni, 1992, Mexican

NORBERT J. SCHNEIDER

STALINGRAD   1992, German
BROTHER OF SLEEP   co-composer with Hubert von Goisern, 1996

CHARLY SCHOPPNER

VIA APPIA   Strand, 1992, German

BARRY SCHRADER

GALAXY OF TERROR   MINDWARP: AN INFINITY OF TERROR/PLANET OF HORRORS   New World, 1981

GREG SCHULTZ

Contact: APRA - Australia, 011-61-2-922-6422

FRAN   Harron Films, 1985, Australian

KLAUS SCHULZE

BARRACUDA   THE LUCIFER PROJECT   1978

RICHARD SCHUMANN

EDES EMMA, DRAGA BOBE - VAZLATOK, AKTOK   SWEET EMMA, DEAR BOBE - SKETCHES, NUDES   1992, Hungarian

GERARD SCHURMANN

b. January 19, 1928 - Dutch East Indies
Contact: Carolyn Nott - Los Angeles, 213-850-0744
Affiliation: ASCAP - Los Angeles, 213-883-1000

BUT NOT IN VAIN   1948, British-Dutch
THE THIRD KEY   THE LONG ARM   Ealing, 1956, British
DECISION AGAINST TIME   THE MAN IN THE SKY   MGM, 1956, British
THE RUTHLESS ONE   1957, British
THE CAMP ON BLOOD ISLAND   Columbia, 1958, British
THE NUMBER SEVEN   British Lion, 1959, British
THE HEADLESS GHOST   American International, 1959
THE TWO-HEADED SPY   Columbia, 1959
HORRORS OF THE BLACK MUSEUM   American International, 1959, British
THE DESPERATE MAN   1959, British
CONE OF SILENCE   Bryanston, 1960, British
THE LIVING EARTH (FD)   Buena Vista, 1961
PAYROLL   1961, British
KONGA   American International, 1961, British
DR. SYN, ALIAS THE SCARECROW   Buena Vista, 1962, originally made for television
DAY IN DAY OUT   1965, British
THE BEDFORD INCIDENT   Columbia, 1965
ATTACK ON THE IRON COAST   United Artists, 1968, U.S.-British
THE LOST CONTINENT   Warner Bros., 1968
CLARETTA   Trans World, 1984, Italian

ISAAC SCHWARTS

YOUNG CATHERINE (CTF)   Primedia/Lenfilm, 1991

DAVID SCHWARTZ*

Contact: BMI - Los Angeles, 310-659-9109

DEADMAN'S REVENGE (CTF)   MTE/Finnegan-Pinchuk/USA Network, 1994
MAGIC IN THE WATER   TriStar, 1995

NAN SCHWARTZ-MISHKIN*
(Nan Mishkin)

Contact: ASCAP - Los Angeles, 213-883-1000

HOME (TF)   Leonard Goldberg Productions, 1986
UNDER THE INFLUENCE (TF) ☆   CBS Entertainment, 1986
SHE WAS MARKED FOR MURDER (TF)   Jack Grossbart Productions, 1988
TURN BACK THE CLOCK (TF)   Michael Filerman Productions/Republic/NBC Productions, 1989
DEADLY DESIRE (CTF)   Skylark Films, 1991
WRITER'S BLOCK (TF)   Talent Court, 1991
COMPLEX OF FEAR (TF)   Cosgrove-Meurer/World International Network, 1993
CAGNEY AND LACEY: TOGETHER AGAIN (TF)   Rosenzweig Co./CBS, 1995

STEPHEN SCHWARTZ

Contact: ASCAP - Los Angeles, 213-466-7681

ECHOES   Continental, 1983

GARRY SCHYMAN*

Agent: Carol Faith Agency - Beverly Hills, 310-274-0776
Affiliation: ASCAP - Los Angeles, 213-883-1000

ASSASSIN (TF) co-composer, Sankan Productions, 1986
NEVER TOO YOUNG TO DIE Paul Releasing, 1986
PENITENTIARY III Cannon, 1987
HIT LIST New Line Cinema, 1989
JUDGMENT Juvie Productions, 1989
REVENGE OF THE NERDS III: THE NEXT GENERATION (TF)
    FNM Films/Zacharias and Buhai, 1992
REVENGE OF THE NERDS IV: NERDS IN LOVE (TF)
    Zacharial-Buhai Prods./Fox West Pictures, 1994
ROBIN COOKS 'MORTAL FEAR' (TF) Von Zerneck-Sertner Films,
    1994
DEADLY INVASION: THE KILLER BEE NIGHTMARE (TF) St.
    Francis of Assisi Pictures/WIN/Von Zerneck Films, 1995
ROBIN COOK'S VIRUS (TF) Von Zerneck-Sertner, 1995

DUANE SCIAQUA

Contact: ASCAP - Los Angeles, 213-466-7681

EVIL SPIRITS Prism, 1991

DANNY SCIARRA

UNDYING LOVE co-composer with Mauro DeTrizio, Slaughtered
    Lamb, 1991

ILONA SCKACZ

BACK HOME (CTF) TVS Films/Verronmead Productions/Citadel,
    1990, British-U.S.

THE SCORE WARRIORS

DUNE WARRIORS Califilm, 1991

GARY SCOTT

b. Los Angeles, California
Contact: BMI - Los Angeles, 310-659-9109

FINAL EXAM MPM, 1981
DEADLY FORCE Embassy, 1983
ROADHOUSE 66 Atlantic Releasing, 1984
THE FULFILLMENT OF MARY GRAY (TF) Mary Gray Inc./Lee
    Caplin Productions/Indian Neck Entertainment, 1989
DECEPTIONS (CTF) Republic Pictures, 1990

GARY STEVAN SCOTT

3 NINJAS KNUCKLE UP TriStar, 1995
SAVANNAH (TF) Spelling TV, 1996

JOHN SCOTT*

b. November 1, 1930 - Bristol, England
Contact: ASCAP - Los Angeles, 213-883-1000

A STUDY IN TERROR Columbia, 1965, British
CARNABY, M.D. *DOCTOR IN CLOVER* Continental, 1966,
    British
THE LONG DUEL Paramount, 1967, British
THE 1,000 EYES OF SU-MURU 1967, Japanese
COP-OUT *STRANGER IN THE HOUSE* Rank, 1967, British
THOSE FANTASTIC FLYING FOOLS *BLAST OFF/JULES
    VERNE'S ROCKET TO THE MOON* American International,
    1967, British
BERSERK! Columbia, 1968, British
AMSTERDAM AFFAIR Lippert, 1968, British
SOPHIE'S PLACE *CROOKS AND CORONETS* Warner Bros.,
    1969, British
THE VIOLENT ENEMY 1969, British
TROG Warner Bros., 1970, British
LOLA *TWINKY* American International, 1970, British-Italian
CONQUISTA 1971
GIRL STROKE BOY London Screen Distributors, 1971, British
OUTBACK *WAKE IN FRIGHT* United Artists, 1971, Australian
BILLY TWO HATS United Artists, 1972, British
DOOMWATCH Avco Embassy, 1972, British
WILD DOG IN AMERICA (TD)☆☆ 1972
THE JERUSALEM FILE MGM, 1972, U.S.-Israeli

ANTONY AND CLEOPATRA Rank, 1973, British-Spanish-Swiss
ENGLAND MADE ME Cine Globe, 1973, British
CRAZE Warner Bros., 1974, British
S*P*Y*S European version only, 20th Century-Fox, 1974,
    British-U.S.
SYMPTOMS *THE BLOOD VIRGIN* 1974
HENNESSY American International, 1975, British
THAT LUCKY TOUCH Allied Artists, 1975, British
SATAN'S SLAVE 1976
THE PEOPLE THAT TIME FORGOT American International, 1977,
    British
THE QUINNS (TF) Daniel Wilson Productions, 1977
NORTH DALLAS FORTY Paramount, 1979
THE HOSTAGE TOWER (TF) Jerry Leider Productions, 1980
THE FINAL COUNTDOWN United Artists, 1980
HORROR PLANET *INSEMINOID* Almi Films, 1982, British
YOR, THE HUNTER FROM THE FUTURE co-composer,
    Columbia, 1983, Italian-Turkish-U.S.
GREYSTOKE: THE LEGEND OF TARZAN, LORD OF THE APES
    Warner Bros., 1984, British-U.S.
THE SHOOTING PARTY European Classics, 1984, British
WET GOLD (TF) Telepictures Corporation, 1984
BLOOD ROYAL (TF) Goldcrest Films, British
MOUNTBATTEN: THE LAST VICEROY (MS) George Walker TV
    Productions, 1986, British
HAREM (TS) Highgate Pictures, 1986
KING KONG LIVES DEG, 1986
THE WHISTLE BLOWER Hemdale, 1987
MAN ON FIRE Tri-Star, 1987, Italian-French
THE DECEIVERS Cinecom, 1988
SHOOT TO KILL Buena Vista, 1988
WINTER PEOPLE Columbia, 1989
RED KING, WHITE KNIGHT (CTF) John Kemeny Citdale
    Entertainment/Zenith, 1989
DOG TAGS Cinevest Entertainment Group, 1990
BECOMING COLETTE Intercontinental, 1992
RUBY Triumph, 1992
FAR FROM HOME: THE ADVENTURES OF YELLOW DOG 20th
    Century Fox, 1995

TOM SCOTT

b. 1948
Agent: Air-Edel - Los Angeles, 310-914-5000
Affiliation: BMI - Los Angeles, 310-659-9109

THE CULPEPPER CATTLE CO. 20th Century-Fox, 1972
CONQUEST OF THE PLANET OF THE APES 20th Century-Fox,
    1972
TROUBLE COMES TO TOWN (TF) ABC Circle Films, 1973
THE GIRLS OF HUNTINGTON HOUSE (TF) Lorimar Productions,
    1973
FIREHOUSE (TF) Metromedia Producers Corporation/Stonehenge
    Productions, 1973
CLASS OF '63 (TF) Metromedia Productions/Stonehenge
    Productions, 1973
THE NINE LIVES OF FRITZ THE CAT (AF) American International,
    1974
SIDECAR RACERS Universal, 1975, Australian
TWIN DETECTIVES (TF) Charles Fries Productions, 1976
ASPEN (MS) co-composer with Michael Melvoin, Universal TV,
    1977
THE COMPANY COMEDY (TF) Malloy-Adler Productions/MGM
    TV, 1978
AMERICATHON United Artists, 1979
STIR CRAZY Columbia, 1980
OUR FAMILY BUSINESS (TF) Lorimar Productions, 1981
HANKY PANKY Columbia, 1982
CLASS additional music, Orion, 1983
GOING BERSERK Universal, 1983, Canadian
HARD TO HOLD Universal, 1984
FAST FORWARD co-composer with Jack Hayes, Columbia, 1985
THE SURE THING Embassy, 1985
JUST ONE OF THE GUYS Columbia, 1985
FAMILY TIES VACATION (TF) UBU Productions/Paramount
    Pictures TV, 1985
BADGE OF THE ASSASSIN (TF) Daniel H. Blatt/Robert Singer
    Productions, 1985
SOUL MAN New World, 1986
THE LEFTOVERS (TF) Walt Disney TV, 1986
NOT QUITE HUMAN (CTF) Sharmhill Productions/Walt Disney TV,
    1987

A FATHER'S HOMECOMING (TF)   NBC Productions, 1988
RUN TILL YOU FALL (TF)   CBS Entertainment, 1988
IT'S NOTHING PERSONAL (TF)   Lee Rich/Bruce
   Sallan/Papazian-Hirsch, 1993
PERCY AND THUNDER (CTF)   co-composer with Grover
   Washington, Jr., TNT/Amblin TV/Brandman Prod., 1993

BILLY SCREAM
Contact: ASCAP - Los Angeles, 213-883-1000

MARK TWAIN (AF)   Atlantic Releasing Corporation, 1985

EARL SCRUGGS
Contact: BMI - Los Angeles, 310-659-9109

WHERE THE LILLIES BLOOM   United Artists, 1974

PETER SCULTHORPE
Contact: APRA - Australia, 011-61-2-922-6422

BURKE & WILLIS   Hemdale, 1985, Australian

JAY SEAGRAVE
THE CENSUS TAKER   Argentum Prods., 1984

MALCOLM SEAGRAVE
Contact: ASCAP - Los Angeles, 213-883-1000

PHANTASM   co-composer with Fred Myrow, Avco Embassy, 1979

WALTER SEAR
Contact: ASCAP - Los Angeles, 213-883-1000

DR. BUTCHER, M.D.   Aquarius, 1982, Italian
THE ORACLE   co-composer, Reeltime Distributing, 1987
LURKERS   Concorde, 1988

JOHN SEBASTIAN
Agent: BMI - Los Angeles, 310-659-9109

THE JERK, TOO (TF)   co-composer with Phil Galston, Share
   Productions/Universal TV, 1984
THE CARE BEARS MOVIE (AF)   Samuel Goldwyn Company, 1985

DON SEBESKY
Contact: ASCAP - Los Angeles, 213-883-1000

F. SCOTT FITZGERALD AND "THE LAST OF THE BELLES" (TF)
   Titus Productions, 1974
HOW TO PICK UP GIRLS! (TF)   King-Hitzig Productions, 1978
HOLLOW IMAGE (TF)   Titus Productions, 1979
THE ROSARY MURDERS   co-composer with Bobby Laurel,
   Samuel Goldwyn Company, 1987

JERRY SEGAL
Contact: BMI - Los Angeles, 310-659-9109

DIE LAUGHING   co-composer with Robby Benson and Craig Safan,
   Orion, 1980

MISHA SEGAL
Agent: Zomba Screen Music - West Hollywood, 310-246-0777
Affiliation: BMI - Los Angeles, 310-659-9109

TWO HEARTBEATS   1972, Israeli
THE FACTS OF LIFE GOES TO PARIS (TF)   Embassy TV, 1982
BERRY GORDY'S THE LAST DRAGON   THE LAST DRAGON
   Tri-Star, 1985
LETHAL   KGB—THE SECRET WAR   Cinema Group, 1985
KNIGHTS OF THE CITY   New World, 1986
UNSETTLED LAND   ONCE WE WERE DREAMERS   Hemdale,
   1987, U.S.-Israeli
LENA: MY 100 CHILDREN (TF)   Robert Greenwald Productions,
   1987
THE NEW ADVENTURES OF PIPPI LONGSTALKING   Columbia,
   1988

THE PHANTOM OF THE OPERA   21st Century, 1989
WITH MURDER IN MIND (TF)   Helios Prods./Bob Banner
   Associates, 1992
BODY LANGUAGE (CTF)   Mi Sammy/Wilshire Court, 1992
FIRESTORM: 72 HOURS IN OAKLAND (TF)   Gross-Weston/Capital
   Cities-ABC/Cannell Entertainment, 1993
JERSEY GIRL (TF)   co-composer with Stephen Bedell, Electric
   Pictures/Interscope, 1993

BERNARDO SEGALL
Contact: ASCAP - Los Angeles, 213-883-1000

THE GREAT ST. LOUIS BANK ROBBERY   United Artists, 1959
THE LUCK OF GINGER COFFEY   Continental, 1964, Canadian
HALLUCINATION GENERATION   1966
CUSTER OF THE WEST   Cinerama Releasing Corporation, 1968,
   U.S.-Spanish
LOVING   Columbia, 1970
NIGHT SLAVES (TF)   Bing Crosby Productions, 1970
THE JESUS TRIP   EMCO, 1971
MOON OF THE WOLF (TF)   Filmways, 1972
THE GIRL MOST LIKELY TO... (TF)   ABC Circle Films, 1973
HOMEBODIES   Avco Embassy, 1974
TURNOVER SMITH (TF)   Wellington Productions, 1980

MATYAS SEIBER
Contact: PRS - London, England, 011-44-1-580-5544

THE MAGIC CANVAS (AF)   1949, British
THE FAKE   adaptation, 1953
THE DIAMOND WIZARD   1954
ANIMAL FARM (AF)   1954, British
THE OWL AND THE PUSSYCAT (FD)   1954
A TOWN LIKE ALICE   RAPE OF MALAYA   1956, British
THE SHIRALEE   1956, British
CHASE A CROOKED SHADOW   Warner Bros., 1958, British
THE MARK OF THE HAWK   1958, British
ROBBERY UNDER ARMS   1958, British
MALAGA   MOMENT OF DANGER   Warner Bros., 1959

LEON SEITH
OH HEAVENLY DOG   20th Century-Fox, 1980

ILONA SEKACZ
Contact: PRS - London, England, 011-44-1-580-5544

INTIMATE CONTACT (CTF)   Zenith Productions/Central TV, 1987,
   British
COUNTESS ALICE (TF)   BBC-TV, 1993, British
ANTONIA'S LINE   1996

TIMUR SELCUK
MAVI SURGUN   THE BLUE EXILE   1993, Turkish-German

WLADIMIR SELINSKY
Contact: ASCAP - Los Angeles, 213-883-1000

GOODBYE RAGGEDY ANN (TF)   Metromedia Producers
   Corporation, 1971
SOMETHING EVIL (TF)   Belford Productions/CBS International,
   1972
MILES TO GO BEFORE I SLEEP (TF)   Roger Gimbel
   Productions/Tomorrow Entertainment, 1975
FAMILY REUNION (TF)   Creative Projects/Columbia Pictures TV,
   1981

GYORGY SELMECZI
Contact: ARTISJUS - Budapest, 011-36-1-176-222

THE LONG SHADOW   Prolitera, 1992, U.S./Hungarian/Israeli

DOV SELTZER
Contact: ACUM - Tel Aviv, Israel, Telex: 922-342471

THE DREAM BOAT   1964, Israeli
THE SIMHON FAMILY   1964, Israeli
EIGHT FOLLOWING ONE   1965, Israeli

FORTUNA   American International, 1966, French-Israeli
TRUNK TO CAIRO   American International, 1967, Israeli-West
   German
ERVINKA   1967, Israeli
THREE DAYS AND A CHILD   1967, Israeli
TEVIA AND HIS SEVEN DAUGHTERS   1968, Israeli
MY LOVE IN JERUSALEM   1969, Israeli
EAGLES ATTACK AT DAWN   1970, Israeli-Italian
HIGHWAY QUEEN   Golan-Globus, 1971, Israeli
SALOMONICO   1972, Israeli
ESCAPE TO THE SUN   Cinevision, 1972, Israeli-West
   German-French
I LOVE YOU, ROSA   1972, Israeli
THE GREAT TELEPHONE ROBBERY   1973, Israeli
KAZABLAN   MGM, 1973, Israeli
MY FATHER   1975, Israeli
MOSES (MS)   additional music, ITC/RAI, 1975,
   British-Italian
THE RABBI AND THE SHIKSE   1976, Israeli
OPERATION THUNDERBOLT   *ENTEBBE: OPERATION
   THUNDERBOLT*   Menahem Golan Prods., 1977, Israeli
MILLIONAIRE IN TROUBLE   1978, Israeli
KUNI LEMI IN TEL AVIV   1978, Israeli
URANIUM CONSPIRACY   Golan-Globus, 1979, Italian
THE 7 MAGNIFICIENT GLADIATORS   1983
FORCED WITNESS   Cannon, 1984, Israeli
THE AMBASSADOR   MGM-UA/Cannon, 1984
MASTER LEON   1985, Isreali
BUBA   1986
HAME'AHEV   *THE LOVER*   Cannon, 1986
SINBAD THE SAILOR   1987, Italian
HANNA'S WAR   Cannon, 1988
THIEVES IN THE NIGHT (MS)   1988, German
A BIT OF LUCK   1992, Israeli
NIGHTMARE   Cannon, 1993, U.S.-Israeli
MUMMY   1993

CAIPHUS SEMENYA
Contact: BMI - Los Angeles, 310-659-9109

THE COLOR PURPLE ★   co-composer, Warner Bros., 1985

JAY SEMKO
DUE SOUTH (TF)   co-composer with Jack Lenz and John
   McCarthy, Alliance/CTV, 1994, Canadian

JEAN-MARIE SENIA
Contact: SACEM - France, 011-33-1-4715-4715

L'HONNEUR DE LA TRIBU   *THE HONOR OF THE TRIBE*   1993,
   Algerian-French

FRANK SERAFINE
Contact: ASCAP - Los Angeles, 213-883-1000

NIGHTFALL   Concorde, 1988

JOHN SEREDA
Contact: SOCAN - Toronto, 416-445-8700

THE LOTUS EATERS   Malofilm, 1993, Canadian

RENATO SERIO
Contact: SIAE - Italy, 011-39-6-59-901

ALONE IN THE DARK   New Line Cinema, 1982
SILHOUETTES   Primi Piani Enterprises, 1982

ERIC SERRA
Contact: SACEM - France, 011-33-1-4715-4715

LE DERNIER COMBAT   Gaumont/Les Films du Loup/Constantin
   Alexandrof Productions, 1983, French
SUBWAY   Island Pictures, 1985, French
THE BIG BLUE   composer of European version, Columbia/WEG,
   1988, French
LA FEMME NIKITA   1990, French-Italian
ATLANTIS   1992, French

THE PROFESSIONAL   *LEON*   Columbia, 1994, French
GOLDENEYE   MGM-UA, 1995
THE FIFTH ELEMENT   Columbia, 1997

PHILIPPE SERVAIN
LA BELLE HISTOIRE   *THE BEAUTIFUL STORY*   co-composer
   with Francis Lai, 1992, French
TOUT CA...POUR CA!   *ALL THAT...FOR THIS?!*   co-composer with
   Francis Lai, 1993, French
LES MISERABLES   co-composer with Francis Lai, Erik Berchot,
   Michel Legrand and Didier Barbelivien, Warner Bros., 1995,
   French

PATRICK SEYMOUR
Contact: PRS - London, England, 011-44-1-580-5544

CHANTILLY LACE (CTF)   Showtime, 1993
PARALLEL LIVES (CTF)   Showtime Ent., 1994

FRANCIS SEYRIG
Contact: SACEM - France, 011-33-1-4715-4715

LAST YEAR AT MARIENBAD   Astor, 1961, French-Italian
THE TRIAL OF JOAN OF ARC   Pathe Contemporary, 1962,
   French
MARIE SOLEIL   1964, French

SHADOWY MEN ON A SHADOWY PLANET
DOUBLE HAPPINESS   First Generation/New Views, 1994,
   Canadian

MARC SHAIMAN*
Agent: The Kraft-Benjamin Agency - Beverly Hills, 310-247-0123
Affiliation: ASCAP - Los Angeles, 213-883-1000

WHEN HARRY MET SALLY...   adaptation, Columbia, 1989
MISERY   Columbia, 1990
SCENES FROM A MALL   Touchstone, 1991
CITY SLICKERS   Columbia, 1991
THE ADDAMS FAMILY   Paramount, 1991
SISTER ACT   Buena Vista, 1992
Mr. SATURDAY NIGHT   Universal, 1992
A FEW GOOD MEN   Columbia,1992
SLEEPLESS IN SEATTLE   TriStar, 1993
HEARTS AND SOULS   Universal, 1993
ADDAMS FAMILY VALUES   Paramount, 1993
SISTER ACT 2: BACK IN THE HABIT   adaptation, Buena Vista,
   1993
CITY SLICKERS II: THE LEGEND OF CURLY'S GOLD   Columbia,
   1994
NORTH   Columbia, 1994
THAT'S ENTERTAINMENT III   additional music and arrangements,
   MGM, 1994
SPEECHLESS   MGM, 1994
STUART SAVES HIS FAMILY   Paramount, 1995
FORGET PARIS   Columbia, 1995
AN AMERICAN PRESIDENT ★   1995
BOGUS   Warner Bros., 1996
THE FIRST WIVES CLUB ★   Paramount, 1996
MOTHER   Paramount, 1996
GHOSTS OF THE MISSISSIPPI   1996
IN AND OUT   1997
GEORGE OF THE JUNGLE   1997

RAVI SHANKAR
b. 1920 - Varanasi, Uttar Pradesh, India
Contact: ASCAP - Los Angeles, 213-883-1000

PANTHER PANCHALI   1956, Indian
APARAJITO   1958, Indian
THE WORLD OF APU   1959, Indian
CHAPPAQUA   Hunter, 1966, Indian
CHARLY   Cinerama Releasing Corporation, 1968
RAGA   1971, Indian
GANDHI   co-composer with George Fenton, Columbia, 1982,
   British-Indian
GENESIS   Scarabee Films, 1986, Indian-French-Belgian-Swiss

RAY SHANKLIN

Contact: BMI - Los Angeles, 310-659-9109

BLACK GIRL   Cinerama Releasing Corporation, 1972
FRITZ THE CAT (AF)   co-composer with Ed Bogas, American International, 1972
HEAVY TRAFFIC (AF)   co-composer with Ed Bogas, American International, 1973

ALEX SHAPIRO*

Contact: ASCAP - Los Angeles, 213-883-1000

HORSES AND CHAMPIONS   Augusta Grace Prods., 1995
THE LAST JOB   Northern Drive PRods., 1995
STRANGE FRUIT   1995

TED SHAPIRO

Contact: ASCAP - Los Angeles, 213-883-1000

BLOODEATERS   Parker National, 1980

THEODORE SHAPIRO

Agent: Cathy Schleussner - Encino, 818-905-7475
Contact: BMI - Los Angeles, 310-659-9109

HURRICANE   MGM-UA, 1997

SHARK

I SHOT A MAN IN RENO   Trans Atlantic, 1995

JAMSHIED SHARIFI

HARRIET THE SPY   Paramoun t, 1996

THOM SHARP*

Contact: ASCAP - Los Angeles, 213-883-1000

LAST RESORT   co-composer with Steve Nelson, Concorde, 1986

AVERY SHARPE

AN UNREMARKABLE LIFE   Continental Film Group, 1989

JENNIFER SHARPE

Contact: BMI - Los Angeles, 310-659-9109

GO FISH   co-composer with Brendan Dolan and Scott Aldrich, Can I Watch Pictures/KUPI, 1994

EDWARD SHEARMUR

Contact: PRS - London, England, 011-44-1-580-5544

LET HIM HAVE IT   co-composer with Michael Kamen, 1991, British
THE CEMENT GARDEN   1993, German-British-French
TALES FROM THE CRYPT PRESENTS DEMON KNIGHT   Universal, 1995

JONATHAN SHEFFER

Contact: BMI - Los Angeles, 310-659-9109

ON VALENTINE'S DAY   Angelika Films, 1986
VIETNAM WAR STORY (CTF)   Nexus Productions, 1987
IN A SHALLOW GRAVE   Skouras Pictures, 1988
LIKEWISE   Cinema Group, 1988
BLOODHOUNDS OF BROADWAY   Columbia, 1989
DINNER AT EIGHT (CTF)   Think Entertainment/Turner Network TV, 1989
INTIMATE STRANGERS   SouthGate, 1991
PURE LUCK   Universal, 1991
OMEN IV: THE AWAKENING (TF)   FNM Films, 1991

BERT A. SHEFTER*

b. 1904 - Russia
Contact: ASCAP - Los Angeles, 213-883-1000

ONE TOO MANY   co-composer with Nelly Coletti, 1950
HOLIDAY RHYTHM   Lippert, 1950
DANGER ZONE   Lippert, 1951
LEAVE IT TO THE MARINES   Lippert, 1951
PIER 23   Lippert, 1951
ROARING CITY   Lippert, 1951
SKY HIGH   Lippert, 1951
NO ESCAPE   United Artists, 1953
SCANDAL, INC.   co-composer with Paul Sawtell, Republic, 1956
THE DESPERADOES ARE IN TOWN   co-composer with Paul Sawtell, 20th Century-Fox, 1956
THE DEERSLAYER   co-composer with Paul Sawtell, 20th Century-Fox, 1957
GHOST DIVER   co-composer with Paul Sawtell, 20th Century-Fox, 1957
GUN DUEL IN DURANGO   co-composer with Paul Sawtell, United Artists, 1957
HELL SHIP MUTINY   co-composer with Paul Sawtell, Republic, 1957
THE BLACK SCORPION   co-composer with Paul Sawtell and Jack Cookerly, Warner Bros., 1957
SHE DEVIL   co-composer with Paul Sawtell, 20th Century-Fox, 1957
KRONOS   co-composer with Paul Sawtell, 20th Century-Fox, 1957
MONKEY ON MY BACK   co-composer with Paul Sawtell, United Artists, 1957
AMBUSH AT CIMARRON PASS   co-composer with Paul Sawtell, 20th Century-Fox, 1958
THE FLY   co-composer with Paul Sawtell, 20th Century-Fox, 1958
CATTLE EMPIRE   co-composer with Paul Sawtell, 20th Century-Fox, 1958
HONG KONG CONFIDENTIAL   co-composer with Paul Sawtell, United Artists, 1958
IT! THE TERROR FROM BEYOND SPACE   co-composer with Paul Sawtell, United Artists, 1958
MACHETE   co-composer with Paul Sawtell, United Artists, 1958
SIERRA BARON   co-composer with Paul Sawtell, 20th Century-Fox, 1958
VILLA!   co-composer with Paul Sawtell, 20th Century-Fox, 1958
THE COSMIC MAN   co-composer with Paul Sawtell, Allied Artists, 1959
COUNTERPLOT   co-composer with Paul Sawtell, United Artists, 1959
THE MIRACLE OF THE HILLS   co-composer with Paul Sawtell, 20th Century-Fox, 1959
THE SAD HORSE   co-composer with Paul Sawtell, 20th Century-Fox, 1959
VICE RAID   co-composer with Paul Sawtell, United Artists, 1959
RETURN OF THE FLY   co-composer with Paul Sawtell, 20th Century-Fox, 1959
A DOG OF FLANDERS   co-composer with Paul Sawtell, 20th Century-Fox, 1959
THE BIG CIRCUS   co-composer with Paul Sawtell, Allied Artists, 1959
A DOG'S BEST FRIEND   co-composer with Paul Sawtell, United Artists, 1960
THE LOST WORLD   co-composer, 20th Century-Fox, 1960
TESS OF THE STORM COUNTRY   co-composer with Paul Sawtell, 20th Century-Fox, 1960
THREE CAME TO KILL   United Artists, 1960
FIVE GUNS TO TOMBSTONE   co-composer with Paul Sawtell, United Artists, 1960
FRONTIER UPRISING   co-composer with Paul Sawtell, United Artists, 1961
VOYAGE TO THE BOTTOM OF THE SEA   co-composer with Paul Sawtell, 20th Century-Fox, 1961
THE LONG ROPE   co-composer with Paul Sawtell, 20th Century-Fox, 1961
PIRATES OF TORTUGA   co-composer with Paul Sawtell, 20th Century-Fox, 1961
JACK THE GIANT KILLER   co-composer with Paul Sawtell, United Artists, 1962
THUNDER ISLAND   co-composer with Paul Sawtell, 20th Century-Fox, 1963
THE LAST MAN ON EARTH   co-composer with Paul Sawtell, 1964, U.S.-Italian
THE CURSE OF THE FLY   20th Century-Fox, 1965
MOTOR PSYCHO   co-composer with Paul Sawtell, Eve, 1965
THE BUBBLE   FANTASTIC INVASION OF THE PLANET EARTH   co-composer with Paul Sawtell, Oboler Films, 1967
THE LAST SHOT YOU HEAR   20th Century-Fox, 1969, British
THE CHRISTINE JORGENSEN STORY   co-composer with Paul Sawtell, United Artists, 1970

STEVE SHEHAN
BYE BYE   co-composer with Jimmy Oihid, 1996

MARK SHEKTER
Contact: SOCAN - Toronto, 416-445-8700

B.S. I LOVE YOU   20th Century-Fox, 1971

ERNIE SHELDON
Contact: ASCAP - Los Angeles, 213-883-1000

HARD TRAVELING   New World, 1986

WARD SHELLEY
IGNATZ& LOTTE   Big Stick & Swagger, 1995

KIRBY SHELSTAD
Contact: BMI - Los Angeles, 310-659-9109

ERNEST GOES TO JAIL   co-composer with Bruce Arnstson,
   Buena Vista, 1990
ERNEST SCARED STUPID   co-composer with Bruce Arnston,
   Touchstone, 1991
ERNEST RIDES AGAIN   co-composer with Bruce Arnston,
   Emshell, 1993

THOMAS Z. SHEPARD
Contact: BMI - Los Angeles, 310-659-9109

SUCH GOOD FRIENDS   Paramount, 1971

JAMIE SHERIFF
SLUMBER PARTY MASSACRE 3   Concorde, 1991

BOBBY SHERMAN
Contact: BMI - Los Angeles, 310-659-9109

THE DAY THE EARTH MOVED (TF)   ABC Circle Films, 1974

GARRY SHERMAN
Contact: ASCAP - Los Angeles, 213-883-1000

ALICE'S RESTAURANT   United Artists, 1969
BEEN DOWN SO LONG IT LOOKS LIKE UP TO ME   Paramount,
   1971
THE HEARTBREAK KID   20th Century-Fox, 1972
PARADES   Cinerama Releasing Corporation, 1972
JOHNNY, WE HARDLY KNEW YE (TF)   Talent Associates/Jamel
   Productions, 1977
THE KID FROM NOWHERE (TF)   Cates-Bridges Company, 1982
CHILD'S CRY (TF)   Shoot the Moon Enterprises/Phoenix
   Entertainment Group, 1986
WHATEVER IT TAKES   Aquarius Films, 1986

JOE SHERMAN
Contact: ASCAP - Los Angeles, 213-883-1000

BRASS (TF)   Carnan Productions/Jaygee Productions/Orion TV,
   1985

MIKE SHIELDS
Contact: SOCAN - Toronto, 416-445-8700

TWO BROTHERS, A GIRL AND A GUN   co-composer with The
   Imagineers, Black Market, 1993, Canadian

YASHUAKI SHIMIZU
Contact: JASRAC - Tokyo, Japan, 011-81-3-502-6551

SHADOW OF CHINA   New Line, 1991, Japanese-American

DAVID SHIRE*
b. July 3, 1937 - Buffalo, New York
Agent: Gorfaine-Schwartz - Los Angeles, 213-969-1011
Affiliation: BMI - Los Angeles, 310-659-9109

HARPY (TF)   Cinema Center 100, 1970
McCLOUD: WHO KILLED MISS U.S.A.? (TF)   Universal TV, 1970
MARRIAGE: YEAR ONE (TF)   Universal TV, 1971
THE IMPATIENT HEART (TF)   Universal TV, 1971
ONE MORE TRAIN TO ROB   Universal, 1971
THE PRIEST KILLER (TF)   Universal TV, 1971
SUMMERTREE   Columbia, 1971
SKIN GAME   Warner Bros., 1971
DRIVE, HE SAID   Columbia, 1971
SEE THE MAN RUN (TF)   Universal TV, 1971
TO FIND A MAN   THE BOY NEXT DOOR/SEX AND THE
   TEENAGER   Columbia, 1972
ISN'T IT SHOCKING? (TF)   ABC Circle Films, 1973
STEELYARD BLUES   adaptation, Warner Bros., 1973
TWO PEOPLE   Universal, 1973
SHOWDOWN   Universal, 1973
CLASS OF '44   Warner Bros., 1973
KILLER BEES (TF)   RSO Films, 1974
SIDEKICKS (TF)   Warner Bros. TV, 1974
THE TRIBE (TF)   Universal TV, 1974
TELL ME WHERE IT HURTS (TF)   Tomorrow Entertainment, 1974
THE CONVERSATION   Paramount, 1974
LUCAS TANNER (TF)   Universal TV, 1974
THE HEALERS (TF)   Warner Bros. TV, 1974
THE TAKING OF PELHAM 1-2-3   United Artists, 1974
THE GODCHILD (TF)   MGM TV, 1974
WINNER TAKE ALL (TF)   The Jozak Company, 1975
THE FORTUNE   adaptation, Columbia, 1975
FAREWELL, MY LOVELY   Avco Embassy, 1975
THE HINDENBURG   Universal, 1975
OREGON TRAIL (TF)   Universal TV, 1976
ALL THE PRESIDENT'S MEN   Warner Bros., 1976
McNAUGHTON'S DAUGHTER (TF)   Universal TV, 1976
AMELIA EARHART (TF)   Universal TV, 1976
THE BIG BUS   Paramount, 1976
HARRY AND WALTER GO TO NEW YORK   Columbia, 1976
SOMETHING FOR JOEY (TF)   MTM Productions, 1977
THE GREATEST THING THAT ALMOST HAPPENED (TF)   Charles
   Fries Productions, 1977
SATURDAY NIGHT FEVER   Paramount, 1977
RAID ON ENTEBBE (TF) ☆   Edgar J. Scherick Associates/20th
   Century-Fox TV, 1977
THE STORYTELLER (TF)   co-composer with Hal Mooney,
   Universal TV, 1977
STRAIGHT TIME   Warner Bros., 1978
DADDY, I DON'T LIKE IT LIKE THIS (TF)   CBS Entertainment,
   1978
THE DEFECTION OF SIMAS KUDIRKA (TF) ☆   The Jozak
   Company/Paramount TV, 1978
THE PROMISE   Universal, 1979
OLD BOYFRIENDS   Avco Embassy, 1979
FAST BREAK   co-composer with James Di Pasquale, Columbia,
   1979
NORMA RAE   20th Century-Fox, 1979
NEIL SIMON'S ONLY WHEN I LAUGH   Columbia, 1981
THE NIGHT THE LIGHTS WENT OUT IN GEORGIA   Avco
   Embassy, 1981
PATERNITY   Paramount, 1981
THE WORLD ACCORDING TO GARP   Warner Bros., 1982
MAX DUGAN RETURNS   20th Century-Fox, 1983
OH, GOD! YOU DEVIL   Warner Bros., 1984
2010   MGM/UA, 1984
DO YOU REMEMBER LOVE (TF) ☆   Dave Bell Productions, 1985
RETURN TO OZ   Buena Vista, 1985
TIME FLYER (TF)   Three Blind Mice Productions, 1986
SHORT CIRCUIT   Tri-Star, 1986
PROMISE (TF)   Garner-Duchow Productions/Warner Bros. TV,
   1986
'NIGHT, MOTHER   Universal, 1986
BACKFIRE   New Century/Vista, 1987
CONVICTED: A MOTHER'S STORY (TF)   NBC Productions, 1987
MAYFLOWER MADAM (TF)   Robert Halmi Inc., 1987
JOSEPH WAMBAUGH'S ECHOES IN THE DARKNESS   ECHOES
   IN THE DARKNESS (MS)   Litke-Grossbart Productions/New
   World TV, 1987
VICE VERSA   Columbia, 1988

MONKEY SHINES   Orion, 1988
JESSE (TF)   Turman-Foster Company/Jordan Productions/Republic
   Pictures, 1988
GOD BLESS THE CHILD (TF)   Indieprod Company/Phoenix
   Entertainment Group, 1988
THE WOMEN OF BREWSTER PLACE (MS)   Phoenix
   Entertainment Group, 1989
I KNOW MY FIRST NAME IS STEVEN (TF)   Lorimar/NBC
   Productions, 1989
THE KENNEDYS OF MASSACHUSETTS (MS) ☆   Edgar J.
   Scherick Associates/Orion TV, 1990
SARAH PLAIN AND TALL (TF)   Self Help Prods./Trillium, 1991
THE BOYS (TF)   William Link Prods./Papazian-Hirsch, 1991
PARIS TROUT (CTF)   Viacom/Konigsberg-Sanitsky, 1991
LAST WISH (TF)   Grossbart-Barnett, 1992
BED OF LIES (TF)   David L. Wolper, 1992
SOMETHING TO LIVE FOR: THE ALISON GERTZ STORY (TF)
   Grossbart-Barnett, 1992
BED & BREAKFAST   Hemdale, 1992
THE HABITATION OF DRAGONS (CTF)   Brandman/Amblin TV,
   1992
NIGHTMARE IN THE DAYLIGHT (TF)
   Smith-Richmond/Saban-Sherick, 1992
FOUR EYES AND SIX-GUNS (CTF)   Firebrand/Saban-Sherick,
   1992
SKYLARK (TF)   Self/Trillium, 1993
DANIELLE STEEL'S HEARTBEAT (TF)   Cramer Co./NBC Prods.,
   1993
BLOODLINES: MURDER IN THE FAMILY (TF)
   Stonehenge/Lorimar TV, 1993
BARBARA TAYLOR BRADFORD'S REMEMBER (TF)   List-Estrin
   Prods./H.R. Prods/NBC Prods., 1993
JANE'S HOUSE (TF)   Michael Phillips Prods./Spelling TV, 1993
DANIELLE STEEL'S ONCE IN A LIFETIME (TF)   Cramer Co./NBC
   Prods., 1994
LILY IN WINTER (CTF)   Walter Mirisch Prods./MTE/USA, 1994
REUNION (TF)   Hart, Thomas & Berlin Prods./RHI, 1994
A FATHER FOR CHARLIE (TF)   Jacobs-Gardner Prods./Lo Co
   Entertainment/Finnegan-Pinchuk, 1994
SERVING IN SILENCE: THE MARGARETHE CAMMERMEYER
   STORY (TF)   Barwood Films/Storyline Prods./Trillium
   Prods./TriStar TV, 1995
THE HEIDI CHRONICLES (CTF)   Turner, 1995
MY BROTHER'S KEEPER (TF)   Holiday Prods./RHI, 1995
MY ANTONIA (CTF)   Gideon Prods./Fast Track Films/Wilshire
   Court, 1995
TALKING WITH (TF)   Thirteen-WNET, 1995
THE MAN WHO WOULDN'T DIE (TF)   Alan Barnette
   Prods./Universal TV, 1995
TECUMSEH: THE LAST WARRIOR (CTF)   Daniel H. Blatt
   Prods./American Zoetrope, 1995

SHELDON SHKOLNIK
Contact: ASCAP - Los Angeles, 213-883-1000

TELL ME A RIDDLE   Filmways, 1980

HANK SHOKLEE AND THE BOMB SQUAD
Contact: BMI - Los Angeles, 310-659-9109

JUICE   Paramount, 1992

HOWARD SHORE*
b. Canada
Agent: Gorfaine-Schwartz - Los Angeles, 213-969-1011
Contact: ASCAP - Los Angeles, 213-883-1000

I MISS YOU, HUGS AND KISSES   1978, Canadian
THE BROOD   New World, 1979, Canadian
SCANNERS   Avco Embassy, 1981, Canadian
VIDEODROME   Universal, 1983, Canadian
PLACES IN THE HEART   Tri-Star, 1984
AFTER HOURS   The Geffen Company/Warner Bros., 1985
BELIZAIRE THE CAJUN   Skouras Pictures, 1986
FIRE WITH FIRE   Paramount, 1986
THE FLY   20th Century Fox, 1986, U.S.-Canadian
HEAVEN (FD)   Island Pictures, 1987
NADINE   Tri-Star, 1987
MOVING   Warner Bros., 1988

BIG   20th Century Fox, 1988
DEAD RINGERS   20th Century Fox, 1988, Canadian
AN INNOCENT MAN   Buena Vista, 1989
SHE DEVIL   Orion, 1989
QUICK CHANGE   additional music, Warner Bros., 1990
THE SILENCE OF THE LAMBS   Orion, 1991
A KISS BEFORE DYING   Universal, 1991
NAKED LUNCH   20th Century Fox, 1991, Canadian/British
PRELUDE TO A KISS   20th Century Fox, 1992
SINGLE WHITE FEMALE   Columbia, 1992
GUILTY AS SIN   Buena Vista, 1993
SLIVER   Paramount, 1993
M. BUTTERFLY   Warner Bros., 1993
MRS. DOUBTFIRE   20th Century Fox, 1993
PHILADELPHIA   TriStar, 1993
THE CLIENT   Warner Bros., 1994
ED WOOD   Buena Vista, 1994
NOBODY'S FOOL   Paramount, 1994
MOONLIGHT & VALENTINO   Gramercy, 1995
SEVEN   New Line, 1995
WHITE MAN'S BURDEN   1995
STRIPTEASE   1995
BEFORE AND AFTER   Buena Vista, 1996
THE TRUTH ABOUT CATS AND DOGS   20th Century Fox, 1996
THAT THING YOU DO!   20th Century Fox, 1996
LOOKING FOR RICHARD   20th Century Fox, 1996
STRIPTEASE   Columbia, 1996
CRASH   Fine Line, 1997, Canadian
THE GAME   1997

RICHARD SHORES*
Contact: ASCAP - Los Angeles, 213-883-1000

LOOK IN ANY WINDOW   Allied Artists, 1961
TOMBOY AND THE CHAMP   Universal, 1961
THE LAST CHALLENGE   MGM, 1967
THE HELICOPTER SPIES   MGM, 1968
A MATTER OF WIFE...AND DEATH (TF)   Robert M. Weitman
   Productions/Columbia Pictures TV, 1976
THE QUEST (TF)   David Gerber Productions/Columbia Pictures TV,
   1976
A KILLING AFFAIR (TF)   David Gerber Productions/Columbia
   Pictures TV, 1977
COVER GIRLS (TF)   David Gerber Productions/Columbia Pictures
   TV, 1977
THE COURAGE AND THE PASSION (TF)   David Gerber
   Productions/Columbia Pictures TV, 1978
THE BILLION DOLLAR THREAT (TF)   David Gerber
   Productions/Columbia Pictures TV, 1979

PAUL SHORICK
THE BORDER OF TONG   co-composer with Eliot Douglas, CPG,
   1991

PHYLLIS SHOTWELL
CALIFORNIA SPLIT   Columbia, 1974

LAWRENCE SHRAGGE*
b. April 29, 1954, Montreal, Quebec
Agent: Gorfaine-Schwartz - Los Angeles, 213-969-1011
Affiliation: BMI - Los Angeles, 310-659-9109

DANCE FOR MODERN TIMES   Mossanen, 1988, Canadian
PALAIS ROYALE   Metaphor, 1989, Canadian
BROWN BREAD SANDWICHES   Leader Media Productions, 1989,
   Canadian
BEAUTIFUL DREAMERS   Cinexus, 1990, Canadian
ONE NIGHT ONLY   RSL, Canadian
FIREBIRD 2015   2002 INC, Canadian
STREET JUSTICE: LEGACY (TF)   Stephen J. Cannell, 1991
WHOSE CHILD IS THIS? THE WAR FOR BABY JESSICA (TF)
   Sofronski Productions/ABC, 1993
FOR THE LOVE OF AARON (TF)   Patterdale Prods./The Storyteller
   Group/Marian Rees Associates, 1994
SPOILS OF WAR (TF)   Evolution Entertainment/Signboard Hill/RHI,
   1994
REDWOOD CURTAIN (TF)   Hallmark Hall of Fame, 1995
SECRETS (TF)   Dorothea G. Petrie Prods./Signboard Hill/Robert
   Halmi Ent., 1995

THE RANGER, THE COOK AND A HOLE IN THE SKY (TF)
   Signboard Hill, 1995
THE WRONG GUY   Handmade, 1997

MARK SHREEVE
Contact: PRS - London, England, 011-44-1-580-5544

TURNAROUND   Major/Rose Productions, 1987
BUY AND CELL   Trans World Entertainment, 1989
HONOR BOUND   MGM/UA, 1989, U.S.-French

MICHAEL SHRIEVE
Contact: BMI - Los Angeles, 310-659-9109

THE CHILDREN OF TIMES SQUARE (TF)   Gross-Weston
   Productions/Fries Entertainment, 1986
THE BEDROOM WINDOW   co-composer with Patrick Gleeson,
   DEG, 1987
THE TAKE (CTF)   co-composer with David Beal, Cine-Nevada
   Inc./MCA-TV, 1990

WATAZUMIDO SHUOO
THE SACRIFICE   Orion Classics, 1986, Swedish-French

TONY SILBERT
Contact: ASCAP - Los Angeles, 213-883-1000

VERMONT IS FOR LOVERS   Zeitgeist, 1992

CARLOS SILIOTTO
FLUKE   MGM-UA, 1995

GREGORY SILL
Contact: ASCAP - Los Angeles, 213-883-1000

FOR THE VERY FIRST TIME (TF)   Michael Zinberg/Lorimar TV,
   1991

SHEILA SILVER
DEAD FUNNY   Avondale Pictures/Movie Screen Entertainment,
   1995

JEFFREY SILVERMAN
b. April 21, 1953 - Long Beach, CA
Contact: ASCAP - Los Angeles, 213-883-1000

AND ONCE UPON A TIME   *FANTASIES*   Joseph Brenner
   Associates, 1973
TAXI DANCERS   co-composer with Larry Blank, Trident, 1993

STANLEY SILVERMAN
Contact: BMI - Los Angeles, 310-659-9109

SIMON   Orion, 1980
EYEWITNESS   20th Century-Fox, 1981
I'M DANCING AS FAST AS I CAN   Paramount, 1982

ALAN SILVESTRI*
Agent: Gorfaine-Schwartz - Los Angeles, 213-969-1011
Affiliation: BMI - Los Angeles, 310-659-9109

THE MACK   Cinema Releasing Corporation, 1973
LAS VEGAS LADY   Crown International, 1976
THE AMAZING DOBERMANS   Golden, 1976
PAR OU TES RENTRE...ON TA PAS VU SORTIR   Carthago Films,
   1984, French
ROMANCING THE STONE   20th Century Fox, 1984
FANDANGO   Warner Bros., 1985
STEPHEN KING'S CAT'S EYE   *CAT'S EYE*   MGM/UA, 1985
BACK TO THE FUTURE   Universal, 1985
SUMMER RENTAL   Paramount, 1985
DELTA FORCE   Cannon, 1986
AMERICAN ANTHEM   Columbia, 1986
CLAN OF THE CAVE BEAR   Warner Bros., 1986
FLIGHT OF THE NAVIGATOR   Buena Vista, 1986
NO MERCY   Tri-Star, 1987

CRITICAL CONDITION   Paramount, 1987
OUTRAGEOUS FORTUNE   Buena Vista, 1987
PREDATOR   20th Century Fox, 1987
OVERBOARD   MGM/UA, 1987
MAC AND ME   Orion, 1988
WHO FRAMED ROGER RABBIT?   Buena Vista, 1988
MY STEPMOTHER IS AN ALIEN   Columbia/WEG, 1988
SHE'S OUT OF CONTROL   Columbia/WEG, 1989
THE ABYSS   20th Century Fox, 1989
TALES FROM THE CRYPT (CTF)   co-composer, Tales from the
   Crypt Holdings, 1989
BACK TO THE FUTURE 2   Universal, 1989
DOWNTOWN   20th Century-Fox, 1990
BACK TO THE FUTURE 3   Universal, 1990
YOUNG GUNS II   20th Century-Fox, 1990
PREDATOR 2   20th Century Fox, 1990
SOAPDISH   Paramount, 1991
DUTCH   20th Century Fox, 1991
RICOCHET   Warner Bros., 1991
SHATTERED   MGM-Pathe, 1991
FATHER OF THE BRIDE   Buena Vista, 1991
DEATH BECOMES HER   Universal, 1992
FERNGULLY...THE LAST RAINFOREST   20th Century Fox, 1992
STOP! OR MY MOM WILL SHOOT   Universal, 1992
THE BODYGUARD   Warner Bros., 1992
COP AND A HALF   Universal, 1993
SIDEKICKS   Triumph, 1993
SUPER MARIO BROS.   Buena Vista, 1993
JUDGMENT NIGHT   Universal, 1993
GRUMPY OLD MEN   Warner Bros., 1993
CLEAN SLATE   MGM, 1994
FORREST GUMP ★   Paramount, 1994
BLOWN AWAY   MGM, 1994
RICHIE RICH   Warner Bros., 1994
THE QUICK AND THE DEAD   TriStar, 1995
THE PEREZ FAMILY   Samuel Goldwyn, 1995
JUDGE DREDD   Buena Vista, 1995
FATHER OF THE BRIDE PART II   Buena Vista, 1995
ERASER   Warner Bros., 1996
THE LONG KISS GOODNIGHT   New Line, 1996
SGT. BILKO   Universal, 1996
FOOLS RUSH IN   1997
VOLACNO   Fox, 1997
TARZAN: THE ANIMATED MOVIE (AF)   Buena Vista, 1997

CARLY SIMON
b. June 25, 1945
Contact: ASCAP - Los Angeles, 213-883-1000

HEARTBURN   Paramount, 1986
POSTCARDS FROM THE EDGE   1990
THIS IS MY LIFE   20th Century Fox, 1992

LUCY SIMON
Contact: ASCAP - Los Angeles, 213-883-1000

THE POSITIVELY TRUE ADVENTURES OF THE ALLEGED TEXAS
   CHEERLEADER-MURDERING MOM (CTF)   Frederick S. Pierce
   Co./Sudden Entertainment, 1993

MARTY SIMON*
Contact: ASCAP - Los Angeles, 213-883-1000

EDDIE AND THE CRUISERS II: EDDIE LIVES   co-composer with
   Leon Aronson and Kenny Vance, Scotti Bros. Pictures/Aurora
   Film Partners, 1989
GEORGE'S ISLAND   New Line, 1991, Canadian
SCANNERS II: THE NEW WORLD ORDER   Triton, 1991,
   Canadian
SCANNERS III: THE TAKEOVER   1992, Canadian
QUIET KILLER (TF)   Sunrise Films/Saban-Scherick, 1992

PAUL SIMON
b. November 8, 1942 - Newark, New Jersey
Contact: BMI - Los Angeles, 310-659-9109

ONE TRICK PONY   Warner Bros., 1980

SAIMON SIMONET

Contact: PRS - London, England, 011-44-1-580-5544

JARDINES COLGANTES *HANGING GARDENS* 1993, Spanish

MICHAEL SIMPSON

Contact: ASCAP - Los Angeles, 213-883-1000

HOT ROD (TF) ABC Circle Films, 1979

BYUNG HA SIN

WHITE BADGE Morning Calm, 1994, Korean

SCOTT SINGER

Contact: ASCAP - Los Angeles, 213-883-1000

NAKED OBSESSION Concorde, 1991
MIDNIGHT CONFESSIONS Kravis-Shustak, 1993

SION

ELEPHANT SONG 1995, Japanese

MICHAEL SKLOFF

Agent: Gorfaine-Schwartz - Los Angeles, 213-969-1011
Affiliation: ASCAP - Los Angeles, 213-883-1000

DREAM ON: AND BIMBO WAS HIS NAME-O (CTF) Theme only,
    Kevin Bright Prods./St. Clare/MTE, 1992

PETER SKOUMAL

Contact: OSA - Prague, Czech Republic, 011-42-2-312-12-41-8

THE FLYING SNEAKER 1992, Czech/Canadian

ROD SLANE

Contact: BMI - Los Angeles, 310-659-9109

ALL-AMERICAN MURDER 1992, Prism

IVOR SLANEY

Contact: PRS - London, England, 011-44-1-580-5544

TERROR Crown International, 1979, British

DAN SLIDER*

Contact: BMI - Los Angeles, 310-659-9109

KID NINJAS Reel Movies
FORCE OF THE NINJA Reel Movies
UNINVITED Amazing Movies, 1988
DEMONWARP Vidmark, 1988
SKINHEADS Amazing Movies, 1989
LITTLE NINJAS AND THE SACRED TREASURE Comet, 1991
FOR THE LOVE OF NANCY (TF) Vin Di Bona Prods./ABC TV
    Network, 1994

TOM SLOCUM

Contact: BMI - Los Angeles, 310-659-9109

CATTLE ANNIE AND LITTLE BRITCHES co-composer with Sanh
    Berti, Universal, 1981

GEORGE SMALL

Contact: ASCAP - Los Angeles, 213-883-1000

LAST RITES *DRACULA'S LAST RITES* co-composer with Paul
    Jost, Cannon, 1980

MICHAEL SMALL

b. 1939
Agent: Marks Management - Woodland Hills, 818-587-5656
Affiliation: BMI - Los Angeles, 310-659-9109

OUT OF IT United Artists, 1969
PUZZLE OF A DOWNFALL CHILD Universal, 1970
JENNY Cinerama Releasing Corporation, 1970
THE REVOLUTIONARY United Artists, 1970
THE SPORTING CLUB Avco Embassy, 1971
KLUTE Warner Bros., 1971
CHILD'S PLAY Paramount, 1972
DEALING: OR THE BERKELEY-TO-BOSTON FORTY-BRICK
    LOST-BAG BLUES Warner Bros., 1972
LOVE AND PAIN AND THE WHOLE DAMNED THING Columbia,
    1973, British-U.S.
THE PARALLAX VIEW Paramount, 1974
THE DROWNING POOL co-composer with Charles Fox, Warner
    Bros., 1975
THE STEPFORD WIVES Columbia, 1975
NIGHT MOVES Warner Bros., 1975
MARATHON MAN Paramount, 1976
PUMPING IRON (FD) Cinema 5. 1977
AUDREY ROSE United Artists, 1977
GIRLFRIENDS Warner Bros., 1978
THE DRIVER 20th Century-Fox, 1978
COMES A HORSEMAN United Artists, 1978
GOING IN STYLE Warner Bros., 1979
THE BOY WHO DRANK TOO MUCH (TF) MTM Enterprises Inc.,
    1980
THOSE LIPS, THOSE EYES United Artists, 1980
THE LATHE OF HEAVEN (TF) 1980
THE POSTMAN ALWAYS RINGS TWICE Paramount, 1981
CONTINENTAL DIVIDE Universal, 1981
ROLLOVER Orion/Warner Bros., 1981
THE STAR CHAMBER 20th Century-Fox, 1983
CHIEFS (MS) Highgate Pictures, 1983
KIDCO 20th Century-Fox, 1984
FIRSTBORN Paramount, 1984
TARGET Warner Bros., 1985
DREAM LOVER MGM/UA, 1986
NOBODY'S CHILD (TF) Joseph Feury Productions/Gaylord
    Production Company, 1986
BRIGHTON BEACH MEMOIRS Universal, 1986
BLACK WIDOW 20th Century Fox, 1987
ORPHANS Lorimar, 1987
JAWS THE REVENGE Universal 1987
1969 Atlantic Releasing Corporation, 1988
AMERICAN DREAM (FD) Miramax, 1989
SEE YOU IN THE MORNING Warner Bros., 1989
MOUNTAINS OF THE MOON Tri-Star, 1990
MOBSTERS Universal, 1991
CONSENTING ADULTS Buena Vista, 1992
QUEEN (MS) Wolper Organization/Bernard Sofronski Prods, 1993
WAGONS EAST! TriStar, 1994

JACK SMALLEY*

Contact: BMI - Los Angeles, 310-659-9109

TOURIST (TF) Castle Combe Productions/20th Century-Fox TV,
    1980

SCOTT SMALLEY

Contact: 818-784-9182

THE UNSINKABLE SHECKY The Landmark Organization, 1989
MARTIAL MARSHALL The Landmark Organization, 1989
DISTURBED Live/Odyssey, 1990

CHRIS SMART

Contact: BMI - Los Angeles, 310-659-9109

PERSONAL CHOICE co-composer with Geoff Levin, Moviestore
    Entertainment, 1989

ED SMART

HANK AARON: CHASING THE DREAM (CTF)
    Tollin-Robbins/Television Production Partners/Mundy Lane/TBS
    Prods., 1995

ROBERT SMART

Contact: SOCAN - Toronto, 416-445-8700

XTRO II co-composer with Braun Farnon, 1991

BRUCE SMEATON

b. Australia
Contact: APRA - Australia, 011-61-2-922-6422

THE CARS THAT EAT PEOPLE *THE CARS THAT ATE PARIS*
   New Line Cinema, 1974, Australian
PICNIC AT HANGING ROCK   Atlantic Releasing Corporation,
   1975, Australian
THE GREAT MacARTHY   1975, Australian
THE DEVIL'S PLAYGROUND   Entertainment Marketing, 1976,
   Australian
ELIZA FRASER   Hexagon Productions, 1976, Australian
THE TRESPASSERS   Vega Film Productions, 1976, Australian
SUMMERFIELD   1977, Australian
THE CHANT OF JIMMIE BLACKSMITH   New Yorker, 1978,
   Australian
THE LAST OF THE KNUCKLEMEN   Hexagon, 1978, Australian
CIRCLE OF IRON *THE SILENT FLUTE* Avco Embassy, 1979
GRENDEL, GRENDEL, GRENDEL (AF)   Victorian Film Corp.,
   1980, Australian
DOUBLE DEAL   Samuel Goldwyn Company, 1981, Australian
BARBAROSA   Universal/AFD, 1982, West German
THE WINDS OF JARRAH   1983, Australian
UNDERCOVER   Filmco, 1983, Australian
THE NAKED COUNTRY   Naked Country Productions, 1984,
   Australian
ICEMAN   Universal, 1984
PLENTY   20th Century-Fox, 1985, British
ELENI   Warner Bros., 1985
ROXANNE   Columbia, 1987
A CRY IN THE DARK   Warner Bros., 1988, Australian

NICHOLAS SMILEY

BUFFALO JUMP   1992, Machipongo Inlet Films

ARTHUR SMITH

Contact: BMI - Los Angeles, 310-659-9109

LADY GREY   co-composer with Clay Smith, Maverick Pictures,
   1980

BRADLEY SMITH

Agent: Zomba Screen Music - West Hollywood, 310-246-0777
Affiliation: BMI - Los Angeles, 310-659-9109

SUMMERTIME SWITCH (TF)   Louis Randolph Family Films/Victor
   TV, 1994

CLAY SMITH

Contact: BMI - Los Angeles, 310-659-9109

SEABO   co-composer, 1977
LADY GREY   co-composer with Arthur Smith, Maverick Pictures,
   1980

CLIVE SMITH

Contact: PRS - London, England, 011-44-1-580-5544

LIQUID SKY   co-composer with Slava Tsukerman and Brenda
   Hutchinson, Cinevista, 1982

JOSEPH SMITH*

RICH GIRL   additional music, Studio Three, 1991

MAURICIO SMITH

Contact: BMI - Los Angeles, 310-659-9109

CROSSOVER DREAMS   Crossover Films, 1985

MICHAEL R. SMITH

THE UNBORN   co-composer with Gary Numan, Califilm, 1991
MOONDANCE   Mozumdar, 1992

SCOTT THOMAS SMITH

THE NOVEMBER MEN   Arrow, 1993

NEIL SMOLAR

Agent: Jeff Kaufman - Studio City, 818-506-6013
Affiliation: SOCAN - Toronto, 416-445-8700

THE BOYS OF ST. VINCENT   1993, Canadian

MARK SNOW*

Agent: Gorfaine-Schwartz - Los Angeles, 213-969-1011
Affiliation: ASCAP - Los Angeles, 213-883-1000

THE BOY IN THE PLASTIC BUBBLE (TF)   Spelling-Goldberg
   Productions, 1976
BIG BOB JOHNSON AND HIS FANTASTIC SPEED CIRCUS (TF)
   Playboy Productions/Paramount TV, 1978
OVERBOARD (TF)   Factor-Newland Production Corporation, 1978
THE RETURN OF THE MOD SQUAD (TF)   co-composer with
   Shorty Rogers, Thomas-Spelling Productions, 1979
SOMETHING SHORT OF PARADISE   American International,
   1979
ANGEL CITY (TF)   Factor-Newland Productions, 1980
CASINO (TF)   Aaron Spelling Productions/Metromedia Producers
   Corporation, 1980
CAGNEY AND LACEY (TF)   Mace Neufeld Productions/Filmways,
   1981
HIGH RISK   American Cinema, 1981
GAMES MOTHER NEVER TAUGHT YOU (TF)   CBS
   Entertainment, 1982
PAPER DOLLS (TF)   Leonard Goldberg Productions, 1982
TWO KINDS OF LOVE (TF)   CBS Entertainment, 1983
PACKIN' IT IN (TF)   Roger Gimbel Productions/Thorn EMI
   TV/Jones-Reiker Ink Corporation, 1983
THE WINTER OF OUR DISCONTENT (TF)   Lorimar Productions,
   1983
MALIBU (TF)   Hamner Productions/Columbia TV, 1983
SECRETS OF A MARRIED MAN (TF)   ITC Productions, 1984
A GOOD SPORT (TF)   Ralph Waite Productions/Warner Bros. TV,
   1984
SOMETHING ABOUT AMELIA (TF) ☆   Leonard Goldberg
   Productions, 1984
CHALLENGE OF A LIFETIME (TF)   20th Century-Fox TV, 1985
INTERNATIONAL AIRPORT (TF)   Aaron Spelling Productions,
   1985
CALIFORNIA GIRLS (TF)   ABC Circle Films, 1985
THE LADY FROM YESTERDAY (TF)   Barry Weitz Films/Comworld
   Productions, 1985
I DREAM OF JEANNIE...15 YEARS LATER (TF)   Can't Sing Can't
   Dance Production/Columbia Pictures TV, 1985
BEVERLY HILLS COWGIRL BLUES (TF)   Leonard Goldberg
   Company, 1985
NOT MY KID (TF)   Beth Polson Productions/Finnegan Associates,
   1985
ACCEPTABLE RISKS (TF)   ABC Circle Films, 1986
JAKE SPEED   New World, 1986
MURDER BY THE BOOK (TF)   TVS Ltd./Benton Evans
   Productions, 1986, British
ONE POLICE PLAZA (TF)   CBS Entertainment, 1986
ONE TERRIFIC GUY (TF)   CBS Entertainment, 1986
THE GIRL WHO SPELLED FREEDOM (TF)   Knopf-Simons
   Productions/ITC Productions/Walt Disney Productions, 1986
NEWS AT ELEVEN (TF)   Turman-Foster Productions/Finnegan
   Associates, 1986
BLOOD AND ORCHIDS (MS)   Lorimar Productions, 1986
DOWN THE LONG HILLS (TF)   The Finnegan Company/Walt
   Disney TV, 1986
WARM HEARTS, COLD FEET (TF)   Lorimar-Telepictures, 1987
PALS (TF)   Robert Halmi, Inc., 1987
STILL CRAZY LIKE A FOX (TF)   Schenck-Cardea
   Productions/Columbia TV, 1987
CRACKED UP (TF)   Aaron Spelling Productions, 1987
ROMAN HOLIDAY (TF)   Jerry Ludwig Enterprises/Paramount TV,
   1987
VIETNAM WAR STORIES (CTF)   Nexus Productions, 1987
MURDER ORDAINED (MS)   Zev Braun Productions/Interscope
   Communications, 1987
KIDS LIKE THESE (TF)   Taft Entertainment TV/Nexus Productions,
   1987
THE FATHER CLEMENTS STORY (TF)   Zev Braun
   Productions/Interscope Communications, 1987
A HOBO'S CHRISTMAS (TF)   Joe Byrnne-Falrose
   Productions/Phoenix Entertainment, 1987

AARON'S WAY: THE HARVEST (TF)   Blinn-Thorpe
    Productions/Lorimar Telepictures, 1988
BLUEGRASS (TF)   co-composer with Don Davis, The Landsburg
    Company, 1988
THE IN-CROWD   Orion, 1988
ALONE IN THE NEON JUNGLE (TF)   Robert Halmi Inc., 1988
SCANDAL IN A SMALL TOWN (TF)   Carliner-Rappoport
    Productions, 1988
ERNEST SAVES CHRISTMAS   Buena Vista, 1988
THOSE SHE LEFT BEHIND (TF)   NBC Productions, 1989
EVERYBODY'S BABY: THE RESCUE OF JESSIE McCLURE (TF)
    Interscope, 1989
STUCK WITH EACH OTHER (TF)   Nexus Productions, 1989
SETTLE THE SCORE (TF)   Steve Sohmer Productions/ITC, 1989
MIRACLE LANDING (TF)   CBS Entertainment, 1990
CHILD IN THE NIGHT (TF)   Mike Robe Productions, 1990
ARCHIE: TO RIVERDALE AND BACK AGAIN (TF)   Patchett
    Kaufman Entertainment/DIC, 1990
THE GIRL WHO CAME BETWEEN (TF)   Saban/Scherick
    Productions/Saban International, 1990
DEAD RECKONING (CTF)   Houston Lady Productions, 1990
THE GAMBLER RETURNS: THE LUCK OF THE DRAW (TF)
    Kenny Rogers Productions, 1991
THE RAPE OF DR. WILLIS (TF)   Interprod, 1991
WHITE HOT: THE MYSTERIOUS MURDER OF THELMA TODD
    (TF)   Sandy Hook Prods./Neufeld-Keating Prods./von
    Zerneck-Sertner, 1991
IN THE LINE OF DUTY: MANHUNT IN THE DAKOTAS (TF)
    Patchett-Kaufman, 1991
THE MARLA HANSON STORY (TF)   Citadel, 1991
LIVING A LIE (TF)   Bernhardt-Freistat/Cannell, 1991
WIFE, MOTHER MURDERER (TF)   Wilshire Court, 1991
BATTLING FOR BABY (TF)   Von Zerneck-Sertner, 1992
A WOMAN SCORNED (TF)   Patchett-Kaufman, 1992
HIGHWAY HEARTBREAKER (TF)   Gross-Weston/Cannell
    Entertainment, 1992
DELIVER THEM FROM EVIL: THE TAKING OF ALTA VIEW (TF)
    Citadel Pictures, 1992
DOLLY DEAREST   Trimark, 1992
A TASTE FOR KILLING (CTF)   Bodega Bay/MCA TV, 1992
THE DANGER OF LOVE (TF)   Lois Luger Prods/Citadel Pictures,
    1992
IN THE LINE OF DUTY: STREET WAR (TF)   Patchett-Kaufman,
    1992
AN AMERICAN STORY (TF) ☆   Signboard Hill/RHI Entertainment,
    1992
THE DISAPPEARANCE OF NORA (TF)   Citadel, 1993
THE MAN WITH THREE WIVES (TF)   CBS Entertainment/Arnold
    Shapiro Prods., 1993
FATHER AND SON: DANGEROUS RELATIONS (TF)
    Kushner-Locke/Logo/Gregory-Kahn, 1993
BORN TOO SOON (TF)   Adam Prods., 1993
IN THE LINE OF DUTY: AMBUSH IN WACO (TF)
    Patchett-Kaufman/World Intl Network, 1993
THE LAST P.O.W.?: THE BOBBY GARWOOD STORY (TF)   EMR
    Prods./Nexus/Fries, 1993
PRECIOUS VICTIMS (TF)   Laurel Prods., 1993
SCATTERED DREAMS: THE KATHRYN MESSENGER STORY
    (TF)   Robert Greenwald Prods., 1993
MURDER BETWEEN FRIENDS (TF)   Gimbel-Adelson Co./Anaid
    Films/ABC Prods., 1994
A PLACE FOR ANNIE (TF)   Gross-Weston Prods./Signboard
    Hill/Cannell Entertainment, 1994
MOMENT OF TRUTH: CRADLE OF CONSPIRACY (TF)
    O'Hara-Horowitz Prods./NBC Prods., 1994
OLDEST LIVING CONFEDERATE WIDOW TELLS ALL (TF) ☆
    Konigsberg-Sanitsky/RHI, 1994
HEART OF A CHILD (TF)   O'Hara-Horowitz Prods., 1994
THE SUBSTITUTE WIFE (TF)   Frederick S. Pierce Co., 1994
WITNESS FOR THE EXECUTION (TF)   Frederick S. Pierce Co.,
    1994
PLAYMAKER   Odyssey, 1994
DEAD BADGE   Odyssey, 1994
MOMENT OF TRUTH: CAUGHT IN THE CROSSFIRE (TF)
    O'Hara-Horowitz, 1994
SHADOWS OF DESIRE (TF)   Konigsberg Co., 1994
FOLLOWING HER HEART (TF)   Atlantis/Roni Weisberg
    Prods./Ann-Margret Prods., 1994
TEXAS JUSTICE (TF)   Patchett-Kaufman Ent./WIN/Nancy Hardin,
    1995
CHILDREN OF THE DUST (TF)   Konigsberg Co., 1995
BORN TO BE WILD   Warner Bros., 1995

SEDUCED AND BETRAYED (TF)   von Zerneck-Sertner, 1995
MOMENT OF TRUTH: THE OTHER MOTHER (TF)
    O'Hara-Horowitz Prods., 1995
THE UNSPOKEN TRUTH (TF)   Peter Frankovich Prods./Hearst,
    1995
NOWHERE MAN (TF)   Touchstone TV, 1995
NIGHT SINS (TF)   Michele Brustin Prods./Scripps-Howard
    Entertainment, 1997

STEPHEN SNYDER

Contact: ASCAP - Los Angeles, 213-883-1000

VICTOR'S BIG SCORE   Mushikuki, 1992

CURT SOBEL*

Contact: BMI - Los Angeles, 310-659-9109

THE FLAMINGO KID   arranger, 20th Century Fox, 1984
LA BAMBA   additional music, Columbia, 1987
CROSS MY HEART   additional music, Universal, 1987
BRIGHT LIGHTS, BIG CITY   additional music, MGM/UA, 1988
ALIEN NATION   20th Century Fox, 1988
BACKTRACK   *CATCHFIRE*   Vestron, 1990
DEFENSELESS   Seven Arts, 1991
CAST A DEADLY SPELL (CTF)   Pacific Western, 1992
TREACHEROUS CROSSING (TF)   O.T.M.L./Wilshire Court, 1992
BETRAYAL OF TRUST (TF)   Cosgrove-Meurer, 1993
RACE AGAINST THE DARK (TF)   Cosgrove-Meurer, 1993
NURSES ON THE LINE: THE CRASH OF FLIGHT 7 (TF)
    Cosgrove-Meurer, 1993
BETRAYAL OF TRUST (TF)   Cosgrove-Meurer Prods., 1994

JOHAN SODERQVIST

LIKE IT NEVER WAS BEFORE   *PENSIONAT OSKAR*   1995,
    Swedish

LOU SOLA

MOVING THE MOUNTAIN   1994, British

STEVE SOLES

Agent: Seth Kaplan Entertainment - Los Angeles, 213-525-3477

DESTINY TURNS ON THE RADIO   Savoy, 1995

IAN SOLOMON

THE GOOD FASCIST   Living Pictures, 1992, South African

DARREN SOLOMON

HOSTILE INTENT   Amsell Entertainment, 1997
ABSOLUTE AGGRESSION   Amsell Entertainment, 1997

MARYBETH SOLOMON

Contact: SOCAN - Toronto, 416-445-8700

THE WOMEN OF WINDSOR (TF)   co-composer with Mickey Erbe,
    Sharmhill/Samuels/World International Network, 1992
TRIAL AND ERROR (CTF)   co-composer with Mickey Erbe,
    Alliance/USA, 1993
SHATTERED TRUST: THE SHARI KARNEY STORY (TF)
    co-composer with Mickey Erbe, Heartstar
    Prods./Spectacor/Michael Jaffe Films, 1993
TO SAVE THE CHILDREN (TF)   co-composer with Mickey Erbe,
    Children's Films/Westcom Ent./Kushner-Locke, 1994
I KNOW MY SON IS ALIVE (TF)   co-composer with Mickey Erbe,
    Alexander-Enright & Associates/WIN, 1994
AGAINST HER WILL: THE CARRIE BUCK STORY (TF)
    co-composer with Mickey Erbe, Janet Faust Krusi Prods./Viacom,
    1994
FRIENDS AT LAST (TF)   co-composer with Mickey Erbe, Procter &
    Gamble/Tele Vest/Atlantis/Stewart Pictures/Columbia-TriStar TV,
    1995
LADY KILLER (TF)   co-composer with Mickey Erbe,
    Kushner-Locke/CBS Entertainment, 1995
DANCING IN THE DARK (CTF)   co-composer with Mickey Erbe,
    Power Pictures-Dream City Films/Hearst, 1995

STEPHEN SONDHEIM
b. March 22, 1930 - New York, New York
Contact: ASCAP - Los Angeles, 213-883-1000

STAVISKY   Cinemation, 1974, French
REDS   theme only, Paramount, 1981

SONIC YOUTH
SUBURBIA   Sony Classics, 1997

KIM SOO-CHUL
THE TAEBAEK MOUNTAINS   *TAEBAEK SANMAEK*   1995, South
   Korean

LUDOVICO SORRET
WHAT HAPPENED WAS   Good Machine, 1994
THE WIFE   Ciby 2000, 1995

MOHAMMED SOUDANI
AU NOM DU CHRIST   *IN THE NAME OF CHRIST*   1993, Ivory
   Coast-Swiss

ONDREJ SOUKUP
KOLYA   Miramax, 1997

MOMO WANDEL SOUMAH
L'ENFANT NOIR   1995, France-Guinea

TIM SOUSTER
Contact: PRS - London, England, 011-44-1-580-5544

THE GREEN MAN (TF)   BBC TV/A&E, 1991

GEOFF SOUTHAL
BOY MEETS GIRL   co-composer with Jim Crosby, Kino Eye, 1994,
   British

SONNY SOUTHON
Contact: PRS - London, England, 011-44-1-580-5544

THE PLEASURE PRINCIPLE   1991, British

DAVID SPEAR
Contact: ASCAP - Los Angeles, 213-883-1000

FEAR NO EVIL   co-composer with Frank LaLoggia, Avco Embassy,
   1981
SPACESHIP   *THE CREATURE WASN'T NICE*   Almi Cinema 5,
   1982
EXTERMINATOR 2   Cannon, 1984
THE RAT!NGS GAME (TF)   Imagination-New Street Prods., 1984
NO RETREAT, NO SURRENDER   New World, 1986, Hong Kong
MORTUARY ACADEMY   Landmark Releasing, 1987
ARAB AND JEW   Rob Gardner Productions
NO RETREAT, NO SURRENDER II   Shapiro Glickenhaus
   Entertainment, 1989

CHRIS SPEDDING
Contact: PRS - London, England, 011-44-1-580-5544

HOLLYWOOD VICE SQUAD   Concorde/Cinema Group, 1986

PAUL SPEER
Contact: BMI - Los Angeles, 310-659-9109

TO CROSS THE RUBICON   co-composer with David Lanz,
   Lensman, 1991

JOHN SPENCE
Contact: PRS - London, England, 011-44-1-580-5544

PANIC IN ECHO PARK (TF)   Edgar J. Scherick Associates, 1977
THE AMAZING SPIDERMAN (TF)   Charles Fries Productions/Dan
   Goodman Productions, 1977

ROGER HAMILTON SPOTTS
Contact: ASCAP - Los Angeles, 213-883-1000

THE IMPORTANCE OF BEING EARNEST   Eclectic Concepts/Paco
   Global, 1991

ROBERT SPRAYBERRY
Contact: BMI - Los Angeles, 310-659-9109

QUICK   Academy/Promark, 1993
A PASSION TO KILL   A-Pix, 1994

MARK SPRINGER
Contact: BMI - Los Angeles, 310-659-9109

LONDON KILLS ME   co-composer with Sarah Sarhandi, Fine Line,
   1991, British

ATILIO STAMPONE
Contact: SADAIC - Argentina, 011-54-1-40-4867/8

TANGO BAR   Beco Films/Zaga Films, 1988,
   Puerto-Rican-Argentine

VIVIAN STANSHALL
Contact: PRS - London, England, 011-44-1-580-5544

SIR HENRY AT RAWLINSON END   Charisma Films, 1980, British

MICHAEL STEARNS
Contact: BMI - Los Angeles, 310-659-9109

BARAKA (FD)   1992, Magidson Films

DAVID STEELE
TIN MEN   co-composer with Andy Cox, Buena Vista, 1987

ANDREW STEIN
Contact: BMI - Los Angeles, 310-659-9109

HOLLYWOOD BOULEVARD   New World, 1976
THUNDER AND LIGHTNING   American International, 1977
DEATHSPORT   New World, 1978
NATIONAL LAMPOON'S MOVIE MADNESS   United Artists, 1981

CHRIS STEIN
Contact: ASCAP - Los Angeles, 213-883-1000

UNION CITY   Kinesis, 1980
POLYESTER   co-composer with Michael Kamen, New Line
   Cinema, 1981
WILD STYLE   co-composer with Fred Brathwaite, Wild Style, 1983

DANIEL STEIN
TRIPLECROSS (CTF)   co-composer with Larry H. Brown,
   Weintraub-Kuhn Prods./Showtime, 1995

HERMAN STEIN
b. 1915 - Philadelphia, Pennsylvania
Contact: ASCAP - Los Angeles, 213-883-1000

BACK AT THE FRONT   co-composer with Henry Mancini,
   Universal, 1952
THE DUEL AT SILVER CREEK   co-composer, Universal, 1952
FRANCIS GOES TO WEST POINT   co-composer, Universal, 1952
HAS ANYBODY SEEN MY GAL?   co-composer, Universal, 1952
HERE COME THE NELSONS   co-composer, Universal, 1952
HORIZONS WEST   co-composer, Universal, 1952
JUST ACROSS THE STREET   co-composer, Universal, 1952
THE LAWLESS BREED   co-composer, Universal, 1952
MEET ME AT THE FAIR   co-composer, Universal, 1952
THE RAIDERS   co-composer, Universal, 1952
THE REDHEAD FROM WYOMING   co-composer, Universal, 1952
SON OF ALI BABA   co-composer, Universal, 1952
ABBOTT & COSTELLO GO TO MARS   co-composer, Universal,
   1953

ABBOTT & COSTELLO MEET DR. JEKYLL & MR. HYDE
    co-composer, Universal, 1953
ALL I DESIRE   co-composer, Universal, 1953
CITY BENEATH THE SEA   co-composer, Universal, 1953
COLUMN SOUTH   co-composer, Universal, 1953
EAST OF SUMATRA   co-composer, Universal, 1953
FRANCIS COVERS THE BIG TOWN   co-composer, Universal, 1953
GIRLS IN THE NIGHT   co-composer, Universal, 1953
THE GLASS WEB   co-composer, Universal, 1953
THE GOLDEN BLADE   co-composer, Universal, 1953
THE GREAT SIOUX UPRISING   co-composer, Universal, 1953
GUNSMOKE   co-composer, Universal, 1953
IT CAME FROM OUTER SPACE   co-composer with Irving Gertz
    and Henry Mancini, Universal, 1953
THE LONE HAND   co-composer, Universal, 1953
TAKE ME TO TOWN   co-composer, Universal, 1953
TUMBLEWEED   co-composer, Universal, 1953
THE VEILS OF BAGDAD   co-composer, Universal, 1953
WAR ARROW   co-composer, Universal, 1953
BENGAL BRIGADE   co-composer, Universal, 1954
BLACK HORSE CANYON   co-composer, Universal, 1954
THE BLACK SHIELD OF FALWORTH   co-composer, Universal,
    1954
BORDER RIVER   co-composer, Universal, 1954
THE CREATURE FROM THE BLACK LAGOON   co-composer,
    Universal, 1954
DESTRY   co-composer, Universal, 1954
DRUMS ACROSS THE RIVER   co-composer, Universal, 1954
FIREMAN SAVE MY CHILD   co-composer, Universal, 1954
FOUR GUNS TO THE BORDER   co-composer, Universal, 1954
THE GLENN MILLER STORY   co-composer, Universal, 1954
JOHNNY DARK   co-composer, Universal, 1954
MA AND PA KETTLE AT HOME   co-composer, Universal, 1954
NAKED ALIBI   co-composer, Universal, 1954
PLAYGIRL   co-composer, Universal, 1954
RAILS INTO LARAMIE   co-composer, Universal, 1954
RIDE CLEAR OF DIABLO   co-composer, Universal, 1954
SASKATCHEWAN   co-composer, Universal, 1954
SIGN OF THE PAGAN   co-composer, Universal, 1954
SO THIS IS PARIS   co-composer with Henry Mancini, Universal,
    1954
TANGANYIKA   co-composer, Universal, 1954
YELLOW MOUNTAIN   co-composer, Universal, 1954
ABBOTT & COSTELLO MEET THE KEYSTONE COPS
    co-composer, Universal, 1955
CAPTAIN LIGHTFOOT   co-composer, Universal, 1955
THE FAR COUNTRY   co-composer, Universal, 1955
FEMALE ON THE BEACH   co-composer, Universal, 1955
KISS OF FIRE   co-composer, Universal, 1955
MA AND PA KETTLE AT WAIKIKI   co-composer, Universal, 1955
MAN WITHOUT A STAR   co-composer, Universal, 1955
THE PRIVATE WAR OF MAJOR BENSON   co-composer,
    Universal, 1955
THE PURPLE MASK   co-composer, Universal, 1955
REVENGE OF THE CREATURE   main title only, Universal, 1955
SIX BRIDGES TO CROSS   co-composer, Universal, 1955
THE SPOILERS   co-composer, Universal, 1955
TARANTULA   co-composer, Universal, 1955
THIS ISLAND EARTH   co-composer with Henry Mancini and Hans
    J. Salter, Universal, 1955
BACKLASH   Universal, 1956
THE CREATURE WALKS AMONG US   co-composer, Universal,
    1956
A DAY OF FURY   co-composer, Universal, 1956
EVERYTHING BUT THE TRUTH   co-composer, Universal, 1956
FOUR GIRLS IN TOWN   co-composer, Universal, 1956
FRANCIS IN THE HAUNTED HOUSE   Universal, 1956
THE GREAT MAN   co-composer, Universal, 1956
I'VE LIVED BEFORE   co-composer with Don Roseland and Ray
    Cormier, Universal, 1956
THE KETTLES IN THE OZARKS   co-composer, Universal, 1956
THE MOLE PEOPLE   co-composer, Universal, 1956
THERE'S ALWAYS TOMORROW   co-composer, Universal, 1956
THE TOY TIGER   co-composer, Universal, 1956
THE UNGUARDED MOMENT   co-composer, Universal, 1956
WALK THE PROUD LAND   co-composer, Universal, 1956
THE INCREDIBLE SHRINKING MAN   co-composer, Universal,
    1957
ISTANBUL   co-composer, Universal, 1957
JOE DAKOTA   co-composer, Universal, 1957
THE LAND UNKNOWN   co-composer, Universal, 1957
LOVE SLAVES OF THE AMAZON   co-composer, Universal, 1957

MAN IN THE SHADOW   co-composer, Universal, 1957
MISTER CORY   co-composer, Universal, 1957
THE MONOLITH MOSTERS   co-composer, Universal, 1957
THE NIGHT RUNNER   co-composer, Universal, 1957
QUANTEZ   Universal, 1957
SLIM CARTER   Universal, 1957
THE LADY TAKES A FLYER   co-composer, Universal, 1958
LAST OF THE FAST GUNS   *THE WESTERN STORY*
    co-composer with Hans J. Salter, Universal, 1958
MONEY, WOMEN & GUNS   co-composer, Universal, 1958
THE SAGA OF HEMP BROWN   Universal, 1958
THIS IS RUSSIA (FD)   co-composer, Universal, 1958
NO NAME ON THE BULLET   co-composer with Irving Gertz,
    Universal, 1959
THE INTRUDER   *I HATE YOUR GUTS!/SHAME*   Pathe American,
    1961

FRED STEINER*

b. February 24, 1923 - New York, New York
Contact: ASCAP - Los Angeles, 213-883-1000

RUN FOR THE SUN   United Artists, 1956, British
MAN FROM DEL RIO   United Artists, 1956
TIME LIMIT   United Artists, 1957
THE COLOSSUS OF NEW YORK   uncredited co-composer with
    Nathan Van Cleave, Paramount, 1958
ROBINSON CRUSOE ON MARS   uncredited co-composer with
    Nathan Van Cleave, Paramount, 1964
FIRST TO FIGHT   Warner Bros., 1967
THE ST. VALENTINE'S DAY MASSACRE   20th Century-Fox, 1967
WAKE ME WHEN THE WAR IS OVER (TF)   Thomas-Spelling
    Productions, 1969
CARTER'S ARMY (TF)   Thomas-Spelling Productions, 1970
RIVER OF GOLD (TF)   Aaron Spelling Productions, 1971
FAMILY FLIGHT (TF)   Silverton Productions/Universal TV, 1972
HEC RAMSEY (TF)   Mark VII Ltd./Universal TV, 1972
HEATWAVE! (TF)   Universal TV, 1974
NIGHT TERROR (TF)   Charles Fries Productions, 1977
THE SEA GYPSIES   Warner Bros., 1978
BLOOD FEUD (TF)   20th Century-Fox TV/Glickman-Selznick
    Productions, 1983
THE COLOR PURPLE ★   co-composer, Warner Bros., 1985

JIM STEINMAN

Contact: BMI - Los Angeles, 310-659-9109

A SMALL CIRCLE OF FRIENDS   United Artists, 1980

JAMES WESLEY STEMPLE*

b. July 3, 1955 - Arlington, Virginia
Contact: BMI - Los Angeles, 310-659-9109

THE LAST RIDE (CTF)   Fitzgerald/Hartley Films, 1988
DAMNED RIVER   MGM/UA, 1989

JAKE STERN

Contact: ASCAP - Los Angeles, 213-883-1000

FEEDBACK   Feedback Company, 1979

STEVEN M. STERN*

SWEET NOTHING   Concrete Films, 1995

DARYL STEVENETT

Contact: BMI - Los Angeles, 310-659-9109

KILLPOINT   co-composer with Herman Jeffreys, Crown
    International, 1984

DAVID A. STEWART

Agent: Gorfaine-Schwartz - Los Angeles, 213-969-1011
Affiliation: PRS - London, England, 011-44-1-580-5544

ROOFTOPS   co-composer with Michael Kamen, New
    Century/Vista, 1989
THE REF   Buena Vista, 1994
SHOWGIRLS   MGM-UA, 1995
BEAUTIFUL GIRLS   Miramax, 1996

F
I
L
M

C
O
M
P
O
S
E
R
S

PAUL STEWART
PHAT BEACH   co-composer with Gary Meals, 1996

STING
(Gordon Matthew Summer)
Contact: PRS - London, England, 011-44-1-580-5544

BRIMSTONE AND TREACLE   United Artists Classics, 1982,
   British

HARRY STINSON
Contact: BMI - Los Angeles, 310-659-9109

XXX'S & OOO'S(TF)   co-composer with Bill Watson, John
   Wilder-Nightwatch Prods/Brandon Tartikoff-Moving Target Prods.,
   1994

JON ST. JAMES
Contact: BMI - Los Angeles, 310-659-9109

CAVE GIRL   Crown International, 1985

GARY STOCKDALE*
Contact: BMI - Los Angeles, 310-659-9109

HARD TICKET TO HAWAII   co-composer with Kevin Klinger,
   Malibu Bay Films, 1986
ARIZONA HEAT   co-composer with Kevin Klinger, Overseas Film
   Group, 1986
PICASSO TRIGGER   co-composer with Kevin Klinger, Malibu Bay
   Films, 1987
DANCE OF THE DAMNED   Concorde, 1989
STRIPPED TO KILL 2   Concorde, 1989
NECROMANCER   co-composer with Kevin Klinger and Bob Mamet,
   Bonnaire Films, 1989
SAVAGE BEACH (TF)   Malibu Bay Films, 1989
DEMONSTONE   Fries, 1990

MARCUS STOCKHAUSEN
Contact: GEMA - Germany, 011-49-89-480-03610

PETRIFIED GARDEN   co-composer with Simon Stockhausen,
   1993, French-German

SIMON STOCKHAUSEN
Contact: GEMA - Germany, 011-49-89-480-03610

PETRIFIED GARDEN   co-composer with Marcus Stockhausen,
   1993, French-German

CHRISTOPHER L. STONE*
Contact: ASCAP - Los Angeles, 213-883-1000

NEVER PUT IT IN WRITING   Allied Artists, 1964, British
THE SECRET OF MY SUCCESS   MGM, 1965, British
THE TREASURE OF JAMAICA REEF   MGM, 1974
MONEY TO BURN   Victoria Films
GONE WITH THE WEST   International Cinefilm, 1975
CHOICES   Choices Company, 1981, Canadian
COVERGIRL   New World, 1984, Canadian
NADIA (TF)   Dave Bell Productions/Tribune Entertainment
   Company/Jadran Film, 1984, U.S.-Yugoslavian
SWORD OF HEAVEN   Trans World Entertainment, 1985
NINJA TURF   co-composer with Charles Pavlosky and Gary
   Falcone, Ascot Entertainment Group, 1986
TERRORVISION   Empire Pictures, 1986
THE NAKED CAGE   Cannon, 1986
PRISON   co-composer with Richard Band, Empire Pictures, 1988
FELIX THE CAT (AF)   New World, 1989
ANGELS: THE MYSTERIOUS MESSENGERS (TD)   American
   Artists Prods./Greystone Comm., 1994
ANCIENT PROPHECIES (TD)   Coast-to-Coast Prods./Greystone
   PRods., 1994
THE AMERICAN REVOLUTION (TD)   Greystone/A&E, 1994
THE STUPIDS   New Line, 1996

HOWARD STONE
Contact: ASCAP - Los Angeles, 213-466-7681

SIGNS OF LIFE   Avenue Pictures, 1989

LAURIE STONE
Agent: Robert Light - Los Angeles, 213-651-1777

TIME TRAX (TF)   co-composer with Garry McDonald, Gary Nardino
   Prods./Lorimar TV, 1993
THE FLOOD: WHO WILL SAVE OUR CHILDREN? (TF)
   co-composer with Garry McDonald, Wolper Organization/Warner
   Bros. TV, 1993
OFFICIAL DENIAL (CTF)   co-composer with Garry McDonald,
   Wilshire Court, 1993

RICHARD STONE*
Agent: The Ryan Company - Sherman Oaks, 818-981-4111
Affiliation: BMI - Los Angeles, 310-659-9109

NORTH SHORE   Universal, 1987
SUMMER HEAT   Atlantic Releasing Corporation, 1987
LONGARM (TF)   Universal TV, 1988
NEVER ON TUESDAY   Cinema Group, 1988
ELVIS AND ME (TF)   Navarone Productions/New World TV, 1988
PUMPKINHEAD   MGM/UA, 1988
HIROSHIMA MAIDEN (TF)   Arnold Shapiro Productions, 1988
SUNDOWN   Vestron, 1989
VIETNAM TEXAS   Trans World Entertainment, 1990
VICTIM OF LOVE (TF)   Nevermore, 1991
IN A CHILD'S NAME (TF)   New World TV, 1991

KEVIN STONEY
THE LONGEST HATRED (TD)   Nucleus Prods., 1993

MICHAEL STOREY
Contact: PRS - London, England, 011-44-1-580-5544

ANOTHER COUNTRY   Orion Classics, 1984, British
COMING UP ROSES   *RHOSYN A RHITH*   Red Rooster, 1986,
   British
A PERFECT SPY (MS)   BBC, 1987, British

DAVID STORRS
P.O.W. THE ESCAPE   Cannon, 1986
INVADERS FROM MARS   co-composer with Christopher Young,
   Cannon, 1986

WALLY STOTT
(See Angela Morley)

TED STOVALL
Contact: BMI - Los Angeles, 310-659-9109

THE BOY WHO CRIED WEREWOLF   Universal, 1973

FRANK STRANGIO
Contact: APRA - Australia, 011-61-2-922-6422

THE BLUE LIGHTNING (TF)   Alan Sloan Productions/The Seven
   Network/Coote-Carroll Australia/Roadshow, 1986,
   U.S.-Australian

JOHN STRAUSS
Contact: ASCAP - Los Angeles, 213-466-7681

MIKEY AND NICKY   Paramount, 1976
IMPROMPTU   arrangements, Hemdale, 1991

BARBRA STREISAND
b. April 24, 1942 - New York, New York
Contact: ASCAP - Los Angeles, 213-883-1000

NUTS   Universal, 1987

FRANK STROBEL
THE YOUNG POISONER'S HANDBOOK   co-composer with Frank Strobel, 1996

JOHN STROLL
ROBOCOP: THE SERIES (TF)   co-composer with Kevin Gillis, Skyvision Ent./RoBoCop Prods./Rysher, 1994

WILLIAM T. STROMBERG
b. May 23, 1964 - Oceanside, California
Contact: 818-345-3279
Affiliation: BMI - Los Angeles, 310-659-9109

ORDER OF THE EAGLE   AIP, 1989
BACK FROM THE PAST   AIP, 1990
WOODEN NICKELS   1990
EDGE OF HONOR   Wind River, 1991
SILENT VICTIM   21st Century, 1993

CHARLES STROUSE
b. 1929
Contact: ASCAP - Los Angeles, 213-883-1000

BONNIE AND CLYDE   Warner Bros., 1967
THE NIGHT THEY RAIDED MINSKY'S   United Artists, 1968
THERE WAS A CROOKED MAN   Warner Bros., 1970
JUST TELL ME WHAT YOU WANT   Columbia, 1980
CHALLENGE TO AMERICA WITH HEDRICK SMITH (TD)   Hedrick Smith Prods./WETA, 1994

FRANK STRUBEL
THE YOUNG POISONER'S HANDBOOK   co-composer with Robert Lake, Mass-Sam Taylor, 1995, British-German

EDGAR STRUBLE
Contact: ASCAP - Los Angeles, 213-466-7681

MAC SHAYNE: WINNER TAKES ALL (TF)   co-composer with Larry Brown, Kenny Rogers, Jr and Bob De Marco, Larry Levinson Prods./Kenny Rogers Prods., 1994
GAMBLER V: PLAYING FOR KEEPS (TF)   co-composer with Larry Brown, Kenny Rogers Prods./WIN/RHI, 1994
BIG DREAMS & BROKEN HEARTS: THE DOTTIE WEST STORY (TF)   Ken Kragen Prods./Michelle Lee Prods./CBS, 1995

JOE STRUMMER
Contact: PRS - London, England, 011-44-1-580-5544

RUDE BOY   co-composer with Mick Jones, Atlantic Releasing Corporation, 1980
WALKER   Universal, 1987
PERMANENT RECORD   Paramount, 1988
WHEN PIGS FLY   1993, Dutch-Japanese-German-US
GROSSE POINT BLANK   Buena Vista, 1997

JEFF STURGES
Contact: ASCAP - Los Angeles, 213-883-1000

HELLHOLE   Arkoff International Pictures, 1985
WALKER, TEXAS RANGER: ONE RIOT, ONE RANGER (TF)   Cannon TV, 1993

JERRY STYNE
SKI FEVER   co-composer with Guy Hemric, Allied Artists, 1969
CYCLE SAVAGES   Trans American, 1970
THE MAGIC GARDEN OF STANLEY SWEETHEART   MGM, 1970
CORKY   MGM, 1972
THE GENESIS CHILDREN   1972
BLACK JACK   WILD IN THE SKY   1972
JENNIFER   American International, 1978

L. SUBRAMANIAM
Contact: BMI - Los Angeles, 310-659-9109

MISSISSIPPI MASALA   Cinecom, 1991

MAURI SUMEN
TUHLAAJAPOIKA   THE PRODIGAL SON   1993, Finnish

ANDY SUMMERS
Contact: PRS - London, England, 011-44-1-580-5544

DOWN AND OUT IN BEVERLY HILLS   Buena Vista, 1986
OUT OF TIME (TF)   Columbia TV, 1988
END OF THE LINE   Orion Classics, 1988
WEEKEND AT BERNIE'S   20th Century Fox, 1989
MOTORAMA   Planet Productions, 1993

ROBERT SUMMERS
Contact: ASCAP - Los Angeles, 213-883-1000

GUARDIAN OF THE WILDERNESS   Sunn Classic, 1977
THE LINCOLN CONSPIRACY   Sunn Classic, 1977
SIXTH AND MAIN   National Cinema, 1977
THE INCREDIBLE ROCKY MOUNTAIN RACE (TF)   Schick Sunn Classics Productions, 1977
THE LAST OF THE MOHICANS (TF)   Schick Sunn Classics Productions, 1977
BEYOND AND BACK   Sunn Classic, 1978
DONNER PASS: THE ROAD TO SURVIVAL (TF)   Schick Sunn Classics Productions, 1978
THE DEERSLAYER (TF)   co-composer with Andrew Belling, Schick Sunn Classics Productions, 1978
BEYOND DEATH'S DOOR   Sunn Classic, 1979
IN SEARCH OF HISTORIC JESUS   Sunn Classic, 1980
GUYANA, CULT OF THE DAMNED   co-composer with Nelson Riddle and George S. Price, Universal, 1980
THE LEGEND OF SLEEPY HOLLOW (TF)   Schick Sunn Classics Productions/Taft International Pictures, 1980
THE ADVENTURES OF NELLIE BLY (TF)   Schick Sunn Classics Productions/Taft International Pictures, 1981
THE ADVENTURES OF HUCKLEBERRY FINN (TF)   Schick Sunn Classics Productions/Taft International Pictures, 1981
THE BOOGENS   Jensen Farley Pictures, 1981
THE CAPTURE OF GRIZZLY ADAMS (TF)   Schick Sunn Classics Productions/Taft International Pictures, 1982
THE FALL OF THE HOUSE OF USHER (TF)   Schick Sunn Classics Productions/Taft International Pictures, 1982
ONE DARK NIGHT   Comworld, 1983
UNCOMMON VALOR (TF)   Brademan-Self Productions/Sunn Classic, 1983
THE ANNIHILATORS   New World, 1986
THE BIKINI SHOP   THE MALIBU BIKINI SHOP   International Film Marketing, 1986
MURDER BY NUMBERS   Burnhill, 1990
FRAME-UP II: THE COVER-UP   Promark Entertainment Group, 1992

WILL SUMNER
Contact: BMI - Los Angeles, 310-659-9100

THE PERSONALS   New World, 1982

PAUL SUNDFOR
ATTACK OF THE KILLER TOMATOES   co-composer with Gordon Goodwin, 1979

MARK SUOZZO
Contact: BMI - Los Angeles, 310-659-9109

METROPOLITAN   adaptation/co-composer with Tom Judson, New Line, 1990
THANK YOU AND GOODNIGHT (FD)   Aries, 1992
LIVING PROOF: HIV AND THE PURSUIT OF HAPPINESS (FD)   co-composer with James Legg, First Run, 1993
BARCELONA   Fine Line, 1994

RON SURES
THE SILENCER   additional music, Crown, 1992
MAN IN A UNIFORM   co-composer with The Tragically Hip, IRS, 1994

ANTON SUTEU

AN UNFORGETTABLE SUMMER   *UNE ETE INOUBLIABLE*   1994,
   French-Romanian

JIM SUTHERLAND
Contact: BMI - Los Angeles, 310-659-9109

AS AN EILEAN   *FROM THE ISLAND*   1993, British

KEN SUTHERLAND
Contact: ASCAP - Los Angeles, 213-883-1000

SAVANNAH SMILES   Embassy, 1982
DARK BEFORE DAWN   PSM Entertainment, 1989

SAEKO SUZUKI
NO LIFE KING   New Century, 1991

ELIZABETH SWADOS
Contact: BMI - Los Angeles, 310-659-9109

TOO FAR TO GO (TF)   Sea Cliff Productions/Polytel Films, 1979
OHMS (TF)   Grant-Case-McGrath Enterprises, 1980
FOUR FRIENDS   Filmways, 1982
SEIZE THE DAY (TF)   Learning in Focus, 1986
A YEAR IN THE LIFE (MS)   Falsey/Austin Street
   Productions/Universal TV, 1986
FAMILY SINS (TF)   London Films, 1987

SWANS
TWO SMALL BODIES   1993, German

JIRI SWOBODA
Contact: BMI - Los Angeles, 310-659-9109

OBECNA SKOLA   *THE ELEMENTARY SCHOOL*   1992, Czech

STANISLAS SYREWICZ
(Stanilas)
Contact: ASCAP - Los Angeles, 213-883-1000

BEWITCHED EYES   1980, French
LE PART DU CHOSE   1983, French
L'AMOUR BRAQUE   1985, French
THE HOLCROFT COVENANT   Universal, 1985
BIGGLES   Compact Yellowbill/Tambarle, 1986, British
THE FANTASIST   ITC, 1986, Irish
THE LAIR OF THE WHITE WORM   Vestron, 1988, British
STALIN (CTF)   HBO, 1992

T

TAJ MAHAL
Contact: BMI - Los Angeles, 310-659-9109

SOUNDER   20th Century-Fox, 1972
PART 2, SOUNDER   Gamma III, 1976
BROTHERS   Warner Bros., 1977

BILLY TALBOT
HELL'S KITCHEN   Kushner-Locke, 1997

FREDERIC TALGORN
b. July 2, 1961 - Toulouse, France
Agent: Film Music Associates - Hollywood, 213-463-1070
Affiliation: ASCAP - Los Angeles, 213-883-1000

EDGE OF SANITY   August Entertainment, 1989, British
BURIED ALIVE   The Movie Group, 1989, British
STRANGLEHOLD: DELTA FORCE II   Cannon, 1989
ROBOTJOX   Trans World Entertainment, 1990
LE BRASIER   1990, French
THE TEMP   Paramount, 1992
FORTRESS   Dimension, 1993
ACROSS CHINA WITH THE YELLOW RIVER (CTD)   Cousteau
   Society, Turner, 1996
THE STORY OF MONTY THE MAD RAT (AF)   Warner Bros., 1997

TANGERINE DREAM
Contact: ASCAP - Los Angeles, 213-883-1000

SORCERER   Universal/Paramount, 1977
KNEUSS   1978, West German-Swiss
THIEF   United Artists, 1981
IDENTIFICATION OF A WOMAN   Iter Film/Gaumont, 1982,
   Italian-French
THE SOLDIER   Embassy, 1982
RISKY BUSINESS   The Geffen Company/Warner Bros., 1983
THE KEEP   Paramount, 1983
WAVELENGTH   New World, 1983
HEARTBREAKERS   Orion, 1984
FLASHPOINT   Tri-Star, 1984
TRIBES   Queensland Pictures
FIRESTARTER   Universal, 1984
FORBIDDEN (CTF)   HBO Premiere Films/Mark Forstater
   Productions/Clasart/Anthea Productions, 1985, U.S.-British-West
   German
VISION QUEST   Warner Bros., 1985
STREET HAWK (TF)   Limekiln and Templar Productions/Universal
   TV, 1985
THE PARK IS MINE (CTF)   Astral Film Enterprises/HBO Premiere
   Films, 1985
LEGEND   U.S. version only, Universal, 1986
TONIGHT'S THE NIGHT (CTF)   *SINGLE MAN*   Phoenix
   Entertainment Group, 1987
CANYON DREAMS   Miramar, 1987
DEADLY CARE (TF)   Universal TV, 1987
NEAR DARK   DEG, 1987
THREE O'CLOCK HIGH   Universal, 1987
KAMIKAZE   Gaumont, 1987, French
SHY PEOPLE   Cannon, 1987
DEAD SOLID PERFECT (CTF)   HBO Pictures/David Merrick
   Productions, 1988
MIRACLE MILE   Hemdale, 1988
CATCH ME IF YOU CAN   MCEG, 1989
RAINBOW   ITC, 1990
HIGHWAY TO HELL   Additional Music, Hemdale, 1992
THE SWITCH (TF)   Avnet-Kerner/Companionway, 1993

KENSAKU TANAGAWA
FUSA   1993, Japanese

GRAHAM TARDIF
Contact: APRA - Australia, 011-61-2-922-6422

BAD BOY BUBBY   1993, Australian-Italian

JOHN ANDREW TARTAGLIA
Contact: ASCAP - Los Angeles, 213-883-1000

POWDERKEG (TF)   Filmways/Rodphi Productions, 1971
THE ADVENTURES OF NICK CARTER (TF)   Universal TV, 1972
THE BARBARY COAST (TF)   Paramount Pictures TV, 1975
THE ISLANDER (TF)   Glen A. Larson Productions/Universal TV,
   1978
GRACE KELLY (TF)   Takota Productions/Embassy TV, 1983

DUANE TATRO*
Contact: Miller Agency - Santa Clarita, 805-255-7286
Affiliation: BMI - Los Angeles, 310-659-9109

THE HOUSE ON GREENAPPLE ROAD (TF)   QM Productions,
   1970
KEEFER (TF)   David Gerber Productions/Columbia Pictures TV,
   1978

MICHAEL TAVERA*
Agent: Gorfaine-Schwartz - Los Angeles, 213-969-1011
Affiliation: BMI - Los Angeles, 310-659-9109

LUCKY STIFF   New Line, 1988
FROZEN ASSETS   Paramount/Skouras, 1992
DYING TO BELONG (TF)   Jean Abounader Prods./Hallmark/Von
   Zerneck-Sertner, 1997

JEFFREY TAYLOR
AMATEUR   co-composer with Ned Rifle, 1994, U.S.-French
FLIRT   co-composer with Ned Rifle, 1996

JOE TAYLOR
STEPHEN KING'S 'GOLDEN YEARS' (TF)   Laurel, 1991

JOHN TAYLOR
Contact: PRS - London, England, 011-44-1-580-5544

MI VIDA LOCA   Sony Classics, 1993

STEPHEN JAMES TAYLOR
Agent: Film Music Associates - Hollywood, 213-463-1070
Affiliation: BMI - Los Angeles, 310-659-9109

TO SLEEP WITH ANGER   Samuel Goldwyn, 1990
THE GIVING   Three Cats, 1991
BROTHER FUTURE (TF)   Laneauville/Morris, 1991
THE GLASS SHIELD   1994
THE PIANO LESSON (TF)   co-composer with Dwight Andrews,
   Signboard Hill, 1995
HAPPILY EVER AFTER: FAIRY TALES FOR EVERY CHILD
   (ATF)   co-composer, Two Oceans/Confetti/Hyperion, 1995

FREDRICK TEETSEL
Contact: ASCAP - Los Angeles, 213-883-1000

THE HAUNTING OF MORELLA   co-composer with Chuck Cirino,
   1990

MANUEL TEJADA
BITTER SUGAR   1996

BOB TELSON
Contact: BMI - Los Angeles, 310-659-9109

BAGDAD CAFE   *OUT OF ROSENHEIM*   Island Pictures, 1987,
   West German-U.S.
ROSALIE GOES SHOPPING   Futura Filmverlag/Pelemele Film,
   1989, West German-U.S.
SALMONBERRIES   1991, German
YOUNGER & YOUNGER   co-composer with Hans Zimmer, Vine,
   1993

ROD TEMPERTON
Contact: ASCAP - Los Angeles, 213-883-1000

THE COLOR PURPLE ★   co-composer, Warner Bros., 1985
RUNNING SCARED   MGM/UA, 1986

GERMINAL TENAS
Contact: SACEM - France, 011-33-1-4715-4715

JUSTINIEN TROUVE, OU LE BATARD DE DIEU   *JUSTINIEN
   TROUVE, OR GOD'S BASTARD*   Gaumont Buena Vista
   International, 1993, French

NICOLAS TENBROEK
AMERICAN NINJA IV: THE ANNIHILATION Cannon, 1991
WHO'S THE MAN   co-composer with Michael Wolff, New Line,
   1993

DENNIS TENNEY
Contact: BMI - Los Angeles, 310-659-9109

WITCHBOARD   Cinema Group, 1986
NIGHT OF THE DEMONS   International Film Marketing, 1988

RICHARD TERMINI
Contact: ASCAP - Los Angeles, 213-883-1000

MAC   co-composer with Vin Tese, Tenenbaum/Goodman, 1992

SONNY TERRY
Contact: BMI - Los Angeles, 310-659-9109

STROSZEK   co-composer with Chet Atkins, New Yorker, 1977,
   West German

AVET TERTERIAN
Contact: VAAP

RETURN TO THE PROMISED LAND   *VERATARTS AVEDYATS
   YERGIR*   1992, Armenian
THE WIND OF EMPTINESS   *KAMIN OUNAYNOUTIAN*   1992,
   Armenian

VIN TESE
Contact: ASCAP - Los Angeles, 213-883-1000

MAC   co-composer with Richard Termini, Tenenbaum/Goodman,
   1992

JOHN TESH*
Contact: BMI - Los Angeles, 310-659-9109

LIMIT UP   MCEG, 1990

MIKIS THEODORAKIS
b. 1925 - Khios, Greece
Contact: SACEM - France, 011-33-1-4715-4715

EVA   1953, Greek
NIGHT AMBUSH   *ILL MET BY MOONLIGHT*   Rank, 1957, British
HONEYMOON   RKO Radio, 1958, Spanish
THE SHADOW OF THE CAT   1961, British
THE LOVERS OF TERUEL   co-composer, 1962, French
ELECTRA   Lopert, 1962, Greek
PHAEDRA   Lopert, 1962, Greek-U.S.-French
FIVE MILES TO MIDNIGHT   United Artists, 1963,
   U.S.-French-Italian
ZORBA THE GREEK   International Classics, 1964, Greek
THE ISLAND OF APHRODITE   1966, Greek
THE DAY THE FISH CAME OUT   20th Century-Fox, 1967,
   British-Greek
Z   Cinema 5, 1969, French-Algerian
THE TROJAN WOMEN   Cinerama Releasing Corporation, 1971,
   U.S.-Greek
BIRIBI   1971, French
STATE OF SIEGE   Cinema 6, 1973, French
SERPICO   Paramount, 1973
SUTJESKA   1973, Yugoslavian
THE STORY OF JACOB AND JOSEPH (TF)   Milberg Theatrical
   Productions/Columbia Pictures TV, 1974
HELL RIVER   1974
PARTISANS   1974, Yugoslavian
LETTERS FROM MARUSIA   Azteca Films, 1975, Mexican
IPHIGENIA   Cinema 5, 1977, Greek
EASY ROAD   co-composer with George Thoedorakis, 1979, Greek

THE THIRD EAR BAND
MACBETH   Columbia, 1971, British

TOOTS THIELEMANS
Contact: BMI - Los Angeles, 310-659-9109

LITTLE BLOND DEATH *DE KLEINE BLONDE DOOD*
co-composer with Jurre Haanstra, 1994, Netherlands

IAN THOMAS
Contact: SOCAN - Toronto, 416-445-8700

OH, WHAT A NIGHT   Norstar, 1992
GHOST MOM (TF)   A Power Picture Corp./Richard Crystal
Co./Hearst, 1993
HOSTAGE FOR A DAY (TF)   Frostback/Once Upon A Time
Films/Fox West/Western Int'l Comm., 1994
FALLING FROM THE SKY! FLIGHT 174 (TF)   Pacific/Hill-Fields,
1995

PETER THOMAS
Contact: GEMA - Germany, 011-49-89-480-03610

THE INDIAN SCARF   1963, West German
STOP TRAIN 349   1964, West German-French
THE LAST OF THE MOHICANS   1965, West German
THE SHOT FROM A VIOLIN CASE   1965, West German
UNCLE TOM'S CABIN   1965, West German
THE BLOOD DEMON   1967, West German
JACK OF DIAMONDS   MGM, 1967, U.S.-West German
WINNETOU AND HIS FRIEND, OLD FIREHAND   1967, West
German
THE SNAKE PIT AND THE PENDULUM   1967
THE TRYGON FACTOR   1967, British
INTIMATE DESIRES OF WOMEN   Gemini, 1968, West German
DEADLY SHOTS ON BROADWAY   1969, West German
TO HELL WITH SCHOOL   1969, West German
DIE WEIBCHEN   *THE FEMALES*   1970, West German
GENTLEMEN IN WHITE VESTS   1970, West German
MEMORIES OF THE FUTURE   1970, West German
THE DEAD ONE IN THE THAMES RIVER   1971, West German
OUR WILLI IS THE BEST   1972, West German
SOHO GORILLA   1972, West German
HAND OF POWER   1972, West German
THE STUFF THAT DREAMS ARE MADE OF   1972, West German
CHARIOTS OF THE GODS (FD)   1973, West German
TEMPTATIONS IN THE SUMMER WIND   1973, West German
BOTTSCHEFT DER GOETTER   *MYSTERIES OF THE GODS*
1976, West German
ONCE UPON A TIME   *MARIA D'ORO UND BELLO BLUE* (AF)
G.G. Communications, 1976, Italian-West German
BREAKTHROUGH   *SERGEANT STEINER*   Maverick Pictures
International, 1978, West German

ANDY THOMPSON
Contact: SOCAN - Toronto, 416-445-8700

INTO THE FIRE   Moviestore Entertainment, 1988, Canadian

MICHAEL THOMPSON
TYSON (CTF)   co-composer with Stewart Copeland and Judd Miller,
HBO Pictures, 1995

KEN THORNE
Agent: Jeff Kaufman - Studio City, 818-506-6013
Affiliation: ASCAP - Los Angeles, 213-883-1000

HELP   United Artists, 1965, British
A FUNNY THING HAPPENED ON THE WAY TO THE FORUM ★★
United Artists, 1966, British
HOW I WON THE WAR   United Artists, 1967, British
INSPECTOR CLOUSEAU   United Artists, 1968, British
HEAD   Columbia, 1968
THE TOUCHABLES   20th Century-Fox, 1968, British
THE BED SITTING ROOM   United Artists, 1969, British
SINFUL DAVEY   United Artists, 1969, British
A TALENT FOR LOVING   The Mirisch Company, 1969
THE MAGIC CHRISTIAN   Commonwealth United, 1970, British
HANNIE CAULDER   Paramount, 1971, British
MURPHY'S WAR   Paramount, 1971, British
JUGGERNAUT   United Artists, 1974, British
ROYAL FLASH   20th Century-Fox, 1976, British

ASSAULT ON AGATHON   Nine Network, 1976
THE RITZ   Warner Bros., 1976
POWER PLAY   Magnum International Pictures/Cowry Film
Productions, 1978, Canadian-British
ARABIAN ADVENTURE   AFD, 1979, British
THE OUTSIDER   Paramount, 1980, U.S.-Irish
SUPERMAN II   re-uses themes by John Williams, Warner Bros.,
1981, U.S.-British
WOLF LAKE   *THE HONOR GUARD*   Filmcorp Distribution, 1981,
Canadian
THE HOUSE WHERE EVIL DWELLS   MGM/UA, 1982,
U.S.-Japanese
THE HUNCHBACK OF NOTRE DAME (TF)   Norman Rosemont
Productions/Columbia TV, 1982, U.S.-British
SUPERMAN III   re-uses themes by John Williams, Warner Bros.,
1983, U.S.-British
WHITE WATER REBELS (TF)   CBS Entertainment, 1983
THE EVIL THAT MEN DO   Tri-Star, 1984
LASSITER   Warner Bros., 1984
FINDERS KEEPERS   Warner Bros., 1984
THE PROTECTOR   Warner Bros., 1985, U.S.-Hong Kong
MY WICKED, WICKED WAYS: THE LEGEND OF ERROL FLYNN
(TF)   CBS Entertainment, 1985
LOST IN LONDON (TF)   Emmanuel Lewis Entertainment
Enterprises/D'Angelo Productions/Group W. Productions, 1985
THE TROUBLE WITH SPIES   DEG, 1987
THE RETURN OF SHERLOCK HOLMES (TF)   CBS Entertainment,
1987, British
IF IT'S TUESDAY, IT STILL MUST BE BELGIUM (TF)
Eisenstock & Mintz Productions, 1987
GREAT EXPECTATIONS (CTF)   The Disney Channel/Harlech
TV/Primetime TV, 1989, U.S.-British
BEJEWELLED (CTF)   TVS/PWD, 1991
LETHAL EXPOSURE (TF)   Allan B.
Schwartz/Papazian-Hirsch/Ellipse, 1993
DIANA: HER TRUE STORY (TF)   Martin Poll Prods., 1993
RETURN TO LONESOME DOVE (MS)   RHI/de Passe
Entertainment/Nightwatch Prods., 1993
A SEASON OF HOPE (TF)   Getting Out Prods./Signboard Hill,
1995
LIZ: THE ELIZABETH TAYLOR STORY (TF)   Lester Persky Prods.,
1995

BRIAN TIBBS
Contact: BMI - Los Angeles, 310-659-9109

COMBINATION PLATTER   Arrow Releasing, 1993

TON THAT TIET
MUI DU DU XANH   *THE SCENT OF THE GREEN PAPAYA*   1993,
French
CYCLO   1996

ANSSI TIKANMAKI
THE LAST BORDER   1993, Finnish

JUHA TIKKA
b. Finland
Contact: TEOSTO - Finland, 358-0-692-2511

TALVISOTA   National-Filmi Oy, 1989, Finnish

JACK TILLAR
Contact: BMI - Los Angeles, 310-659-9109

THE MAN WHO SAW TOMORROW   co-composer with William
Loose, Warner Bros., 1981

COLIN TIMMS
Contact: APRA - Australia, 011-61-2-922-6422

AUSTRALIAN DREAM   Ronin Films, 1987, Australian

KEITH TIPPET
Contact: PRS - London, England, 011-44-1-580-5544

THE SUPERGRASS   Hemdale, 1985, British

SIR MICHAEL TIPPETT
b. 1905 - London, England
Contact: PRS - London, England, 011-44-1-580-5544

AKENFIELD (FD)   Angle Films, 1975, British

GEORGE ALICESON TIPTON
Contact: ASCAP - Los Angeles, 213-883-1000

NO PLACE TO RUN (TF)   Spelling-Goldberg Productions/ABC
   Circle Films, 1972
HOME FOR THE HOLIDAYS (TF)   Spelling-Goldberg
   Productions/ABC Circle Films, 1972
THE AFFAIR (TF)   Spelling-Goldberg Productions, 1973
THE STRANGER WHO LOOKS LIKE ME (TF)   Lillian Gallo
   Productions/Filmways, 1974
THE GUN AND THE PULPIT (TF)   Cine Television/Danny Thomas
   Productions, 1974
REMEMBER WHEN (TF)   Danny Thomas Productions/The Raisin
   Company, 1974
BADLANDS   Warner Bros., 1974
PHANTOM OF THE PARADISE ★   co-composer with Paul
   Williams, 20th Century-Fox, 1974
HIT LADY (TF)   Spelling-Goldberg Productions, 1974
GRIFFIN AND PHOENIX (TF)   ABC Circle Films, 1976
I WANT TO KEEP MY BABY! (TF)   CBS Entertainment, 1976
SECRETS (TF)   The Jozak Company, 1977
RED ALERT (TF)   The Jozak Company/Paramount Pictures TV,
   1977
MULLIGAN'S STEW (TF)   Christiana Productions/Paramount
   Pictures TV, 1977
THREE ON A DATE (TF)   ABC Circle Films, 1978
WITH THIS RING (TF)   co-composer with Richard Hazard, The
   Jozak Company/Paramount Pictures TV, 1978
CHRISTMAS LILLIES OF THE FIELD (TF)   Rainbow
   Productions/Osmond Television Productions, 1979
SEIZURE: THE STORY OF KATHY MORRIS (TF)   The Jozak
   Company, 1980
TROUBLE IN HIGH TIMBER COUNTRY (TF)   Witt-Thomas
   Productions/Warner Bros. TV, 1980
SIDE BY SIDE: THE TRUE STORY OF THE OSMOND FAMILY
   (TF)   Osmond TV Productions/Comworld Productions, 1982
THE DEMON MURDER CASE (TF)   Dick Clark Productions/Len
   Steckler Productions, 1983

WAGNER TISO
Contact: AMAR - Brazil, 011-5-21-286-4017

ENCONTROS IMPERFEITOS   *LIGHT TRAP*   1993, Portuguese

PYOTR TODOROVSKY
ANKOR, ESCHYO ANKOR!   *ENCORE, ONCE MORE ENCORE!*
   1993, Russian

GERRY TOLAND
Contact: APRA - Australia, 011-61-2-922-6422

THE PLUMBER   Barbary Coast, 1978, Australian, originally made
   for television

TOMANDANDI
KILLING ZOE   Samuel Hadida, 1994

ISAO TOMITA
b. Japan
Contact: JASRAC - Tokyo, Japan, 011-81-3-502-6551

THE HEAVENS AND THE EARTH   1969, Japanese
THE STORY OF THE TAIRA FAMILY   1972, Japanese
KATSU TAIHEIKI   1974, Japanese
CATASTROPHE 1999   New World, 1977
DEMON POND   Shochiku, 1980, Japanese

ED TOMNEY
Contact: ASCAP - Los Angeles, 213-883-1000

NIGHT OF THE WARRIOR   Trimark, 1991
LIQUID DREAMS   Fox/Elwes, 1991
GUNCRAZY   Zeta Entertainment, 1992
WHEN THE BOUGH BREAKS   Prism, 1993
SAFE   Sony Classics, 1995

TONTON DAVID
AN INDIAN IN THE CITY   *UN INDIEN DANS LA VILLE*
   co-composer with Manu Katke and Geoffrey Oryema, Buena
   Vista, 1996, French

GERARD TORIKIAN
THE PATRIOTS   *LES PATRIOTES*   1994, French

TIM TORRANCE
Contact: BMI - Los Angeles, 310-659-9109

MUTANT ON THE BOUNTY   Skouras Pictures, 1989

TOTO
Contact: ASCAP - Los Angeles, 213-883-1000

DUNE   Universal, 1984

OLIVER TOUISSAINT
b. France
Contact: SACEM - France, 011-33-1-4715-4715

MAID FOR PLEASURE   co-composer with Bernard Gerard, 1974,
   French
CELESTINE, MAID AT YOUR SERVICE   co-composer with Paul de
   Senneville, 1974, French
IRRECONCILABLE DIFFERENCES   co-composer with Paul De
   Senneville, Warner Bros., 1984

COLIN TOWNS
Agent: Film Music Associates - Hollywood, 213-463-1070
Affiliation: PRS - London, England, 011-44-1-580-5544

THE HAUNTING OF JULIA   *FULL CIRCLE*   Discovery Films,
   1977, British-Canadian
SLAYGROUND   Universal/AFD, 1983, British
SHADEY   Skouras Pictures, 1986, British
KNIGHTS AND EMERALDS   Warner Bros., 1986, British
BORN OF FIRE   Film Four International
BELLMAN AND TRUE   Island Pictures, 1987, British
RAWHEAD REX   Empire Pictures, 1987, British
THE FEAR (MS)   Euston Films, 1988, British
CHASE   Zenith Films
VAMPIRE'S KISS   Hemdale, 1988
THE WOLVES OF WILLOUGHBY CHASE   Atlantic Releasing
   Corporation, 1989, British
GETTING IT RIGHT   MCEG, 1989, U.S.-British
DAUGHTER OF DARKNESS (TF)   King Phoenix Entertainment,
   1990
FELLOW TRAVELLER (CTF)   1990
HANDS OF A MURDERER (TF)   Storke/Fuisz
   Productions/Yorkshire TV, 1990, U.S.-British
CURACAO (CTF)   Jones Programming/Circling Curacao, 1993
THE PUPPET MASTERS   Buena Vista, 1994
CADFAEL: THE LEPER OF ST. GILES (TF)   British Central Films
   Prods., 1995
THE WIND IN THE WILLOWS   GoodTimes, 1996, British
CAPTIVES   Miramax, 1996, British

GEOFFREY LEIGH TOZER
Contact: BMI - Los Angeles, 310-659-9109

9 1/2 NINJAS   Cassian Elwes, 1991

THE TRAGICALLY HIP
MAN IN A UNIFORM   co-composer with Ron Sures, IRS, 1994

FIACHRA TRENCH
Agent: Air-Edel - Los Angeles, 310-914-5000
Affiliation: PRS - London, England, 011-44-1-580-5544

WHITE FANG   additional music, Buena Vista, 1991
MOONDANCE   1996

DOMENIC TROIANO
Contact: BMI - Los Angeles, 310-659-9109

THE GUNFIGHTERS (TF)   Grosso-Jacobson Productions/Alliance
    Entertainment/Tribune Entertainment, 1987, U.S.-Canadian
TRUE BLUE (CTF)   Grosso-Jacobson Productions/NBC
    Productions, 1989
THE SWORDSMAN   SC Entertainment, 1992

MARIO TRONCO
IL TUFFO   *THE DIVE*   co-composer with Peter D'Argenzio, 1993,
    Italian

ERNEST TROOST*
Agent: Zomba Screen Music - West Hollywood, 310-246-0777
Affiliation: BMI - Los Angeles, 310-659-9109

MUNCHIES   Concorde, 1987
SWEET REVENGE   Concorde, 1987
DEAD HEAT   New World, 1988
NIGHT VISITORS   Continental, 1988
TIGER WARSAW   Sony Pictures, 1988
MOM   Transworld, 1990
TREMORS   Universal, 1990
FOLLOW THE RIVER (TF)   Signboard Hill, 1995
THE CANTERVILLE GHOST (TF)   Signboard Hill, 1995
CALM AT SUNSET (TF)   Hallmark, 1996
PERVERSIONS OF SCIENCE (TF)   HBO, 1997

ROGER TROUTMAN
HATE   New Line, 1996

ARMANDO TROVAJOLI
b. 1917 - Rome, Italy
Contact: SIAE - Italy, 011-39-6-59-901

LA TRATTA DELLE BIANCHE   *GIRLS MARKED FOR DANGER*
    1952, Italian
LE INFIDELI   1952, Italian
DUE NOTTI CON CLEOPATRA   *TWO NIGHTS WITH
    CLEOPATRA*   1953, Italian
UN GIORNO IN PRETURA   *A DAY IN COURT*   1954, Italian
QUESTA E LA VITA   *OF LIFE AND LOVE*   co-composer with Carlo
    Innocenzi, 1954, Italian
LA DONNA DEL FIUME   *THE WOMAN OF THE RIVER*
    co-composer with Angelo Francesco Lavagnino, 1954, Italian
LE DICIOTENNI   1956, Italian
IL COCCO DI MAMMA   1957, Italian
CAMPINE   1957, Italian
POVERI MILIONARI   1958, Italian
IL VEDOVO   1959, Italian
A QUALCUNO PIACE CALVO   1959, Italian
VACANZE D'INVERNO   1959, Italian
NOSTALGIE ROMANE   1959, Italian
LA NOTTE DEI TEDDY-BOYS   1959, Italian
TEMPI DURI PER I VAMPIRI   1959, Italian
IL CARRO ARMATO DELL' 8 SETTEMBRE   1959, Italian
UN MILITARE E MEZZO   1960, Italian
TU CHE NE DICI?   1960, Italian
LA CENTO CHILOMETRI   1960, Italian
QUESTO AMORE AL CONFINI DEL MONDO   1960, Italian
I PIACERE DEL SABATO NOTTE   *CALL-GIRLS OF ROME*   1960,
    Italian
I PIACERE DELLO SCAPOLO   1960, Italian
IL CORAZZIERE   1960, Italian
LE PILLOLE DI ERCOLE   *THE HERCULES PILLS*   1960, Italian
LA CIOCIARA   *TWO WOMEN*   1960, Italian
ANONIMA COCOTTES   *THE CALL-GIRL BUSINESS*   1960,
    Italian
CHIAMATA 22-22 TENENTE SHERIDAN   1960, Italian
THE GRAND OLYMPICS   co-composer with Angelo Francesco
    Lavagnino, 1960

A PORTE CHIUSE   Fair Film/Cinematografica Rire/Societe
    Generale de Cinematographie/Ultra Film/Lyre Film/Roxy Film,
    1960, Italian-French-West German
BLOOD OF THE WARRIORS   *LA SCHIAVA DI ROMA*   1960,
    Italian
ATOM AGE VAMPIRE   *SEDDOK, L'EREDE DI SATANA*   1961,
    Italian
TOTO, PEPPINO E LA DOLCE VITA   1961, Italian
THE PLANETS AGAINST US   *I PIANETI CONTRO DI NOI*   1961,
    Italian
HERCULES IN THE HAUNTED WORLD   *ERCOLE AL CENTRO
    DELLA TERRA*   1961, Italian
GLI ATTENDENTI   1961, Italian
TOGNAZZI E LA MINORENNE   1961, Italian
LA RAGAZZA DI MILLE MESI   1961, Italian
MOLEMEN VS. THE SON OF HERCULES   1961, Italian
THE MAGIC WORLD OF TOPO GIGIO (AF)   1961, Italian
IL MANTENUTO   *HIS WOMEN*   1961, Italian
PUGNI, PUPE E MARINAI   1961, Italian
WEREWOLF IN A GIRLS' DORMITORY   *LUCANTROPUS*   1961,
    Italian
HERCULES AND THE CAPTIVE WOMEN   co-composer with Gino
    Marinuzzi, 1961, Italian
WARRIORS FIVE   *LA GUERRA CONTINUA*   1962, Italian
RUGANTINO   co-composer with Gianfranco Plenizio, 1962, Italian
UNA DOMENICA D'ESTATE   1962, Italian
BOCCACCIO '70   composer of "The Raffle" segment, Embassy,
    1962, Italian
TOTO DI NOTTE   1962, Italian
IL MIO AMICO BENITO   1962, Italian
OGGI A BERLINO   1962, Italian
DIECI ITALIANI PER UN TEDESCO   1962, Italian
I QUATTRO MONACI   1962, Italian
ALONE AGAINST ROME   *SOLO CONTRO ROMA*   1962, Italian
TOTO E PEPPINO DIVISI A BERLINO   1962, Italian
THE GIANT OF METROPOLIS   1962, Italian
IL GIOVEDI   1962, Italian
LA VISITA   1963, Italian
IL MONACA DI MONZA   1963, Italian
IN ITALIA SI CHIAMA AMORE   1963, Italian
TOTO SEXY   1963, Italian
IL FORNARETTO DI VENEZIA   1963, Italian
GLI ONOREVOLI   1963, Italian
OPIATE '67   *I MOSTRI*   1963, Italian
YESTERDAY, TODAY AND TOMORROW   Embassy, 1963,
    Italian-French
IL VUOTO   1963, Italian
ASSASSINO MADE IN ITALY   1963, Italian
ITALIANI BRAVA GENTE   1963, Italian
I TABU (FD)   co-composer with Francesco Lavagnino, 1963, Italian
I TERRIBILI SETTE   1964, Italian
I CAGASOTTO   1964, Italian
HIGH INFIDELITY   Magna, 1964, Italian-French
IL GAUCHO   Fair Film/Clemente Lococo, 1964, Italian-Argentinian
LA MIA SIGNORA   1964, Italian
THE MAGNIFICENT CUCKOLD   co-composer with Roman Vlad,
    1964, Italian
MARRIAGE ITALIAN STYLE   Embassy, 1964, Italian-French
LA BELLE FAMIGLIE   1964, Italian
THE DOLLS   *LE BAMBOLE*   1964, Italian
ENGAGEMENT ITALIANO   *LA RAGAZZA IN PRESTITO*   1964,
    Italian
LA CONGIUNTURA   1965, Italian
OGGI, DOMANI, DOPODOMANI   co-composer, 1965, Italian
CASANOVA '70   co-composer with Franco Bassi, Embassy, 1965,
    Italian-French
SEVEN GOLDEN MEN   *SETTE UOMINI D'ORO*   1965, Italian
I COMPLESSI   Documento Film/SPCE, 1965, Italian-French
GUGLIELMO IL DENTONE   1965, Italian
I LUNGHI GIORNI DELLA VENDETTA   co-composer with Ennio
    Morricone, 1965, Italian
THE DEVIL IN LOVE   *L'ARCODIAVOLO*   1966, Italian
UNA STORIA DI NOTTE   1966, Italian
LE SPIE AMANO I FIORI   co-composer with Francesco Lavagnino,
    1966, Italian
IL PANE AMARO   co-composer with Francesco Lavagnino, 1966,
    Italian
AMERICA - PAESE DI DIO (FD)   co-composer with Francesco
    Lavagnino, 1966, Italian
THE QUEENS   *LE FATE*   Royal Films International, 1966,
    Italian-French
MAIGRET A PIGALLE   1966, Italian

ADULTERIO ALL'ITALIANA 1966, Italian
SIGNOR DYANMITE 1966, Italian
TREASURE OF SAN GENNARO *OPERAZIONE SAN GENNARO*
  Paramount, 1966, Italian-French-West German
THE 7 GOLDEN MEN STRIKE AGAIN 1966, Italian
I NOSTRI MARITI Documento Film, 1966, Italian
IL PROFETA MR. KINKY 1967, Italian
ACID *DELIRIO DEI SENSI* co-composer with Francesco
  Lavagnino, 1967, Italian
DON GIOVANNI IN SICILIA 1967, Italian
DROP DEAD, MY LOVE 1967, Italian
ANYONE CAN PLAY *LE DOLCE SIGNORE* 1967, Italian
WITH BATED BREATH *COL CUORE IN GOLA* 1967, Italian
RAPPORTE FULLER BASE STOCCOLMA 1967, Italian
7 VOLTE 7 1967, Italian
OMICIDIO PER APPUNTAMENTO 1967, Italian
TORTURE ME, BUT KILL ME WITH KISSES 1968, Italian
FAUSTINA 1968, Italian
NELL'ANNO DEL SIGNORE 1968, Italian
THE LIBERTINE *LA MATRIARCA* 1968, Italian
L'URLO DEI GIGANTI 1968, Italian
RIUSCIRANNO I NOSTRI EROI A TROVARE L'AMICO
  MISTERIOSAMENTE SCOMPARSO IN AFRICA? Documento
  Film, 1968, Italian
LOVEMAKER - L'UOMO PER FARE L'AMORE 1969, Italian
WHERE ARE YOU GOING ALL NAKED? 1969, Italian
IL COMMISSARIO PEPE Dean Film, 1969, Italian
VEDO NUDO Dean Film/Jupiter Generale Cinematografica, 1969,
  Italian
LA FAMIGLIA BENVENUTI (TF) 1969, Italian
IL GIOVANE NORMALE Dean Film/Italnoleggio, 1969, Italian
MAY MORNING 1969, Italian
QUELLA CHIARA NOTTE D'OTTOBRE 1970, Italian
THE PRIEST'S WIFE Warner Bros., 1970, Italian-French
THE MOTIVE WAS JEALOUSY 1970, Italian
THE SWINGING CONFESSORS *IL PRETE SPOSATO* 1970,
  Italian
NOI DONNE SIAMO FATTI COSI Apollo International Film, 1971,
  Italian
LA CONTROFIGURA 1971, Italian
EXCUSE ME, MY NAME IS ROCCO PAPALEO Rumson, 1971,
  Italian
HOMO EROTICUS 1971, Italian
IL VICHINGO VENUTO DAL SUD 1971, Italian
STANZA 17-17: PALAZZO DEL TASSE-UFFICIO DELLA
  IMPOSTE 1971, Italian
THE ITALIAN CONNECTION *LA MALA ORDINA* 1972, Italian
L'UCCELLO MIGRATORE 1972, Italian
SONO STATO IO 1973, Italian
AMORE E GIMNISTICA 1973, Italian
THE SENSUOUS SICILIAN *PAOLO IL CALDO* 1973, Italian
LA VIA DEI BABBUINI 1974, Italian
THERE IS NO. 13 1974, Italian
UN AMOUR COMME LE NOTRE 1974, Italian
HOW, WHEN AND WITH WHOM Warner Bros., 1974, Italian
SESSO MATTO 1974, Italian
DI MAMMA NON CE N'E UNA SOLA 1974, Italian
WE ALL LOVED EACH OTHER SO MUCH Cinema 5, 1975,
  Italian
LA MOGLIE VERGINE 1975, Italian
DUCK IN ORANGE SAUCE 1975, Italian
TELEFONI BIANCHI Dean Film, 1975, Italian
SCENT OF A WOMAN 20th Century-Fox, 1976, Italian
STRANGE SHADOWS IN AN EMPTY ROOM 1976, Italian
BASTE CHE NON SI SAPPIA IN GIRO 1976, Italian
PRIMA NOTTE DI NOZZE 1976, Italian
LUNA DI MIELE IN TRE 1976, Italian
BRUTTI SPORCHI E CATTIVI 1976, Italian
DIMMI CHE FAI TUTTO PER ME 1976, Italian
LA BANCA DI MONATE 1976, Italian
CATTIVI PENSIERI 1976, Italian
IL MARITO IN COLLEGIO 1976, Italian
E UNA BANCA RAPINAMMO PER FATAL CAMBINAZION
  co-composer with Renato Serio, 1976, Italian
THE BISHOP'S ROOM 1976, Italian
A SPECIAL DAY Cinema 5, 1977, Italian
RENATA 1977, Italian
LA PIU BELLA SERATA DELLA MIA VITA 1977, Italian
IN NOME DEL PAPA RE 1977, Italian
WIFEMISTRESS *MOGLIAMENTE* 1977, Italian
I NUOVI MOSTRI 1977, Italian
VIVA ITALIA! *I NUOVI MOSTRI* Cinema 6, 1978, Italian

DOTTORE JEKYLL E GENTILE SIGNORA co-composer with
  Renato Serio, 1978, Italian
DAS FUENFTE GEBOT 1979, West German
AMORE MIEI 1979, Italian
LA TERRAZZA United Artists, 1980, Italian-French
LA VITA E BELLA 1980, Italian
ARRIVANO I BERSAGLIERI 1980, Italian
PASSIONE D'AMORE 1980, Italian
PORQUE NO HACEMOS EL AMOR 1981, Italian-Spanish
A PIEDI NUDI NEL PARCO 1981, Italian
IL PARAMEDICO 1982, Italian
VIULENTEMENTE MIA 1982, Italian
IL MONDO NUOVO 1982, Italian
GRAND HOTEL EXCELSIOR 1982, Italian
LA BALLADE DE MAMLOUK 1982, Tunisian-Czech
PLUS BEAU QUE MOI TU MEURS 1983, French-Italian
IL CONTE TACCHIA Gaumont, 1983, Italian
MYSTERE Titanus, 1983, Italian
MACARONI Paramount, 1985, Italian

MARTIN TRUM
PARANOIA L.E.D. Pictures & Dan Purjes, 1997

TIM TRUMAN*
Agent: Film Music Associates - Hollywood, 213-463-1070
Affiliation: ASCAP - Los Angeles, 213-883-1000

L.A. TAKEDOWN (TF) AJAR/Mories Film Productions, 1989
DEAD SILENCE (TF) FNM Films, 1991
SOUTH CENTRAL Warner Bros., 1992
THE ROUND TABLE (TF) Spelling TV, 1992
IN THE COMPANY OF DARKNESS (TF) Windy City, 1992
MODELS, INC. (TF) Spelling TV, 1994
SKETCH ARTIST II: HANDS THAT SEE (CTF) Motion Picture
  Corporation of America, 1995
EXECUTIVE POWER Usonia Pictures, 1997
RETROACTIVE Orion, 1997

MARC TSCHANTZ
FUN Neo Modern Ent./Damian Lee Prods., 1994

SULKHAN TSINTSADZE
Contact: RAIS - Russia, 011-7-95-203-3260

DRAGON LORD Golden Harvest, 1982, Hong Kong

TOSHI TSUCHITORI
Contact: ASCAP - Los Angeles, 213-883-1000

THE MAHABHARATA (MS) 1991, U.K.-U.S.-French

SLAVA TSUKERMAN
LIQUID SKY co-composer with Brenda Hutchinson and Clive
  Smith, Clnevista, 1982

GIORGIO TUCCI
b. Italy
Contact: SIAE - Italy, 011-39-6-59-901

ZOMBI 2 *ZOMBIE FLESH EATERS* co-composer with Fabbio
  Frizzi, Variety Film, 1979, Italian

COLIN TULLY
Contact: PRS - London, England, 011-44-1-580-5544

THAT SINKING FEELING Samuel Goldwyn Company, 1979,
  Scottish
GREGORY'S GIRL Samuel Goldwyn Company, 1982, British

JONATHAN TUNICK*
Agent: Film Music Associates - Hollywood, 213-463-1070
Affiliation: ASCAP - Los Angeles, 213-883-1000

A LITTLE NIGHT MUSIC ★★ adaptation, New World, 1978,
  Austrian-U.S.
FLYING HIGH (TF) Mark Carliner Productions, 1978
RENDEZVOUS HOTEL (TF) Mark Carliner Productions, 1979

SWAN SONG (TF)   Renee Valente Productions/Topanga Services
   Ltd./20th Century-Fox, 1980
THE JILTING OF GRANNY WEATHERALL (TF)   Learning in
   Focus/American Short Story, 1980
BLINDED BY THE LIGHT (TF)   Time-Life Films, 1980
ENDLESS LOVE   Universal, 1981
FORT APACHE THE BRONX   20th Century-Fox, 1981
I AM THE CHEESE   Libra Cinema 5, 1983
CONCEALED ENEMIES (TF) ☆   WGBH-Boston/Goldcrest Films
   and Television/Comworld Productions, 1984, U.S.-British
BROTHERLY LOVE (TF)   CBS Entertainment, 1985
THE B.R.A.T. PATROL (TF)   Mark H. Ovitz Productions/Walt Disney
   Productions, 1986
YOU RUINED MY LIFE (TF)   Lantana-Kosberg Productions/Mark H.
   Ovitz Productions/Walt Disney TV, 1987
THE LAST GOOD TIME   Samuel Goldwyn, 1995
THE BIRDCAGE   MGM-UA, 1996

GREGG TURNER
Contact: BMI - Los Angeles, 310-659-9109

RAW NERVE   Pyramid/AIP, 1991
CENTER OF THE WEB   Pyramid, 1992

SIMON FISHER TURNER
Contact: PRS - London, England, 011-44-1-580-5544

CARAVAGGIO   co-composer with Mary Phillips, British Film
   Institute, 1986, British
THE GARDEN   1991, British
EDWARD II   1991, British
BLUE   1993, British
NADJA   October, 1995
LOADED   1996

JONATHAN TURRIN
A NEW LIFE   Paramount, 1988

TOMMY TYCHO
Contact: APRA - Australia, 011-61-2-922-6422

YOUNG EINSTEIN   co-composer with Martin Armiger and William
   Motzig, Warner Bros., 1988, Australian
RECKLESS KELLY   Warner Bros., 1993, Australian

CHRISTOPHER TYNG
Agent: Vangelos Management - Encino, 818-380-1919
Affiliation: BMI - Los Angeles, 310-659-9109

NATIONAL LAMPOON'S ATTACK OF THE 5'2" WOMEN (CTF)
   Imagination Prods., 1994
CADILLAC RANCH   Sony Classics, 1994
BRING ME THE HEAD OF MAVIS DAVIS   Goldcrest, 1995
THE ASSOCIATE   Buena Vista, 1996
KAZAAM   Buena Vista, 1996

STEVE TYRELL
Contact: BMI - Los Angeles, 310-659-9109

MIDNIGHT CROSSING   Vestron, 1988
POUND PUPPIES AND THE LEGEND OF BIG PAW (AF)   Tri-Star,
   1988
PINK LIGHTNING (TF)   FNM Films, 1991
CAPTIVE (TF)   co-composer with Paul Buckmaster, Capital
   Cities-ABC/Bonny Dore/Ten-Four, 1991
T BONE N WEASEL (CTF)   TNT, 1992
SIMPLE JUSTICE (TF)   co-composer with Al Borgoni,
   WGBH/WNET/KCET, 1993
FAMILY PRAYERS   Arrow, 1993

NERIDA TYSON-CHEW
Agent: Zomba Screen Music - West Hollywood, 310-246-0777

HOTEL SORRENTO   Bayside Picvvtures, 1994, Australian
BRILLIANT LIES   Bayside Pictures, 1995, Australian
THE LAST BULLET (TF)   1995, Japanese, Australian
UNDER THE LIGHTHOUSE DANCING   1996, Australian

RICHARD UGLOW
PROVOCATEUR   co-composer with Mark Nakamura, Capella,
   1997

IAN UNDERWOOD
Contact: ASCAP - Los Angeles, 213-883-1000

THE ARCHER—FUGITIVE FROM THE EMPIRE   *FUGITIVE FROM
   THE EMPIRE* (TF)   Mad-Dog Productions/Universal TV, 1981

JAY UNGAR
Contact: BMI - Los Angeles, 310-659-9109

BROTHER'S KEEPER (FD)   1992, American Playhouse Theatrical
   Films   co-coposer with Molly Mason

MARKUS URCHS
Contact: GEMA - Germany, 011-49-89-480-03610

THE LAST YEAR OF CHILDHOOD   1979, West German

MIDGE URE
Agent: Air-Edel - Los Angeles, 310-914-5000
Affiliation: PRS - London, England, 011-44-1-580-5544

BOCA   co-composer with Richard Feldman and Adam Gorgoni,
   1994, U.S.-Brazilian

TEO USUELLI
b. 1920 - Milan, Italy
Contact: SIAE - Italy, 011-39-6-59-901

DONNE E SOLDATI   1952, Italian
ITALIA K2   1955, Italian
MICHELE STROGOFF   1956, Italian
UN GIORNO IN EUROPA (FD)   1958, Italian
MADRI PERICOLOSE   1960, Italian
THE CONJUGAL BED   *UNA STORIA MODERNA - L'APE REGINA*
   Embassy, 1963, Italian-French
I PATRIARCHI DELLA BIBBIA   *THE PATRIARCHS OF THE BIBLE*
   co-composer with Gino Marinuzzi, Italian, 1963
THE APE WOMAN   Embassy, 1964, Italian
SAUL E DAVID   1965, Italian
PARANOIA   1966, Italian
THE MAN WITH THE BALLOONS   Sigma III, 1968, French-Italian
DILLINGER E MORTO   Pegaso Film, 1969, Italian
THE SEED OF MAN   SRL, 1970, Italian
L'UDIENZA   Vides, 1971, Italian
TROIS MILLIARDS SANS ASCENSEUR   1972, Italian
R.S.I.: LA REPUBBLICA DI MUSSOLINI (FD)   1976, Italian
IL VOLCO DI PESCA   1976, Italian

RYUDO UZAKI
b. Japan
Contact: JASRAC - Tokyo, Japan, 011-81-3-502-6551

DOUBLE SUICIDE OF SONEZAKI   1978, Japanese
GOODBYE, FLICKMANIA   Nippon Herald, 1979, Japanese

V

WARREN VACHE
Contact: ASCAP - Los Angeles, 213-883-1000

THE LUCKIEST MAN IN THE WORLD   co-composer with Jack
    Gale, Co-Star Entertainment, 1989

STEVE VAI
Contact: ASCAP - Los Angeles, 213-883-1000

PCU   20th Century Fox, 1994

JOHN VALENTINO
BONNIE AND CLYDE: THE TRUE STORY (TF)   co-composer with
    John Valentino, Hoffman-Israel/FNM Films, 1992

JEAN-LOUIS VALERO
Contact: SACEM - France, 011-33-1-4715-4715

PAULINE AT THE BEACH   Orion Classics, 1983, French
SUMMER   *LE RAYON VERT*   Orion Classics, 1986, French

CELSO VALLI
b. Italy
Contact: SIAE - Italy, 011-39-6-59-901

BLOOD TIES (CTF)   RAI Channel One/Racing Pictures/Viacom
    International, 1986, Italian-U.S.

BERINGTON VAN CAMPEN
Contact: ASCAP - Los Angeles, 213-883-1000

IN DANGEROUS COMPANY   Manson International, 1988

CLAIRE VAN CAMPEN
THIN ICE   1995, British

KENNY VANCE
Contact: ASCAP - Los Angeles, 213-883-1000

HAIRSPRAY   New Line Cinema, 1988
EDDIE AND THE CRUISERS II: EDDIE LIVES   co-composer with
    Marty Simon and Leon Aronson, Embassy, 1989
HEART OF DIXIE   Orion, 1989
HARD PROMISES   Columbia, 1991
A MURDEROUS AFFAIR: THE CAROLYN WARMUS STORY (TF)
    Steve White Films/Spectacor, 1992

PIERRE VAN DORMAEL
Contact: SABAM - Brussels, Belgium, 011-32-2-230-2660

TOTO LE HEROS   1991, Belgian-French-German
THE EIGHTH DAY   Gramercy, 1997

ED VAN FLEET
MOON SHOT (CTD)   co-composer with Rushmore De Nooyer and
    Malcolm Brooks, TBS Prods., 1994

VANGELIS
(Evangelos Papathinassou)
b. Greece
Contact: SACEM - France, 011-33-1-4715-4715

L'APOCALYPSE DES ANIMAUX   1970
CHARIOTS OF FIRE ★★   The Ladd Company/Warner Bros., 1981,
    British
BLADE RUNNER   The Ladd Company/Warner Bros., 1982

MISSING   Universal, 1982
ANTARTICA   TLC Films, 1984, Japanese
THE BOUNTY   Orion, 1984, British
FRANCESCO   Istituto Luce/Italnoleggio, 1989, West
    German-Italian
BITTER MOON   1992, French-British
THE PLAGUE   1992, French-Argentine
1492: CONQUEST OF PARADISE   Paramount, 1992,
    British-French-Spanish

ROSS VANNELLI
Contact: BMI - Los Angeles, 310-659-9109

BORN TO RACE   MGM/UA, 1988

FRITZ VAN ORDEN
Contact: BMI - Los Angeles, 310-659-9109

LITTLE NOISES   co-composer with Kurt Hoffman, Monument,
    1991

MELVIN VAN PEEBLES
b. 1932 - Chicago, Illinois
Home: 353 West 56th Street - Apt. 10F, New York, NY 10019,
    212-489-6570
Affiliation: ASCAP - Los Angeles, 213-883-1000

WATERMELON MAN   Columbia, 1970
EROTIC TALES   co-composer, 1994, German

LAURENS VAN ROOYEN
b. Denmark
Contact: KODA - Denmark, 011-45-31-68-38-00

REMBRANDT: FECIT 1668   1978, Dutch
MYSTERIES   1979, Dutch
DEAR BOYS   Sigma Films, 1980, Dutch
A WOMAN LIKE EVE   Sigma Films, 1980, Dutch
FLIGHT OF THE RAINBIRD   Dutch

DAVID VAN TIEGHEM
Contact: ASCAP - Los Angeles, 213-883-1000

WORKING GIRLS   Miramax Films, 1987
MY FATHER IS COMING   Tara, 1991, German

JOHN VAN TONGEREN*
Agent: Gorfaine-Schwartz - Los Angeles, 213-969-1011

DAYS OF THUNDER   additional music, Paramount, 1990
TRUE ROMANCE   additional music, Warner Bros., 1993
SPEED   additional music, 20th Century Fox, 1994
RNAISSANCE MAN   additional music, Buena Vista, 1994
DROP ZONE   additional music, Paramount, 1994
MAN OF THE HOUSE   additional music, Buena Vista, 1995
THE OUTER LIMITS: SANDKINGS (CTF)   co-composer with Mark
    Mancina, Trilogy, Atlantis, 1995
FAIR GAME   additional music, Warner Bros., 1995
ASSASSINS   additional music, Warner Bros., 1995
MONEY TRAIN   additional music, Columbia, 1995

ANTONIO PINHO VARGAS
AQUI NA TERRA   *HERE ON EARTH*   1993, Portuguese

VAROUJE
Contact: SOCAN - Toronto, 416-445-8700

TALONS OF THE EAGLE   Shapiro Glickenhaus, 1993
OPERATION GOLDEN PHOENIX   Le Monde Entertainment, 1994
CRISIS   Film One-Tri Media, 1997
EXPECT TO DIE   Film One, 1997

VA

'97-'98
FILM
COMPOSERS
LISTING

F
I
L
M

C
O
M
P
O
S
E
R
S

NANA VASCONCELOS
Contact: SACEM - France, 011-33-1-4715-4715

AMAZON   1992, Cabriolet Films
BECAUSE WHY   Aska Film, 1993, Canadian
TOGRERO: A FILM THAT WAS NEVER MADE (FD)   1994,
   Finnish-German-Brazilian

PAOLO VASILE
b. Italy
Contact: SIAE - Italy, 011-39-6-59-901

THE SQUEEZE   *THE RIP-OFF*   Maverick International, 1976,
   Italian-U.S.

DIDIER VASSEUR
Contact: SACEM - France, 011-33-1-4715-4715

SWEET REVENGE (CTF)   Turner Pictures/Chrysalide
   Films/Canal/The Movie Group, 1990
STROKE OF MIDNIGHT   Chrysalide/Movie Group/Canal Plus,
   1991
A BUSINESS AFFAIR   Capella, 1994,
   French-British-German-Spanish

SUZANNE VEGA
Contact: ASCAP - Los Angeles, 213-883-1000

WOMEN & MEN 2 (CTF)   co-composer of one segment with Anton
   Sanko, David Brown/HBO Showcase, 1991

CLAUDE VENDETTE
Contact: SOCAN - Toronto, 416-445-8700

KANEHSATAKE: 270 YEARS OF RESISTANCE (FD)   co-composer
   with Francis Grandmont, National Film Board of Canada, 1993,
   Canadian

MAURICIO VENEGAS
Contact: ASCAP - Los Angeles, 213-883-1000

LADYBIRD LADYBIRD   additional music, British, 1994

GIOVANNI VENOSTA
UN'ANIMA DIVISA IN DUE   *A SOUL SPLIT IN TWO*   1993,
   Italian-French

JAMES VERBOORT
Contact: BMI - Los Angeles, 310-659-9109

THE FIRE THIS TIME (FD)   Blacktop Films, 1994

TOM VERLAINE
Contact: PRS - London, England, 011-44-1-580-5544

LOVE AND A .45   Trimark, 1994

CLEM VICARI
THE REDEEMER...SON OF SATAN!   co-composer with Phil Gallo,
   1978
MOTHER'S DAY   co-composer with Phil Gallo, United Film
   Distribution, 1980

MICHAEL VICKERS
Contact: BMI - Los Angeles, 310-659-9109

DRACULA TODAY   *DRACULA A.D. 1972*   Warner Bros., 1972,
   British
THE SEX THIEF   1974, British
AT THE EARTH'S CORE   American International, 1976, British
WARRIORS OF ATLANTIS   EMI, 1978, British

TOMMY VIG
Contact: ASCAP - Los Angeles, 213-883-1000

SWEET SIXTEEN   CI Films, 1981
THE KID WITH THE BROKEN HALO (TF)   Satellite Productions,
   1982
THEY CALL ME BRUCE?   *A FISTFUL OF CHOPSTICKS*   Artists
   Releasing Corporation/Film Ventures International, 1982

STAN VINCENT
Contact: BMI - Los Angeles, 310-659-9109

FOREPLAY   Cinema National Corporation, 1975

JOSEPH VITARELLI
Agent: CAA - Los Angeles, 310-288-4545
Affiliation: BMI - Los Angeles, 310-659-9109

BIG MAN ON CAMPUS   *BMOC*   Vestron, 1989
HOW I GOT INTO COLLEGE   20th Century Fox, 1989
PAPAKOLEA-A STORY OF HAWAIIAN LAND   1993
THE LAST SEDUCTION (CTF)   also released theatrically, ITC,
   1994
UNDER SUSPICION (TF)   Lakeside Prods./Warner Bros. TV, 1994
TALL, DARK AND DEADLY (CTF)   Fast Track Films/Wilshire Court,
   1995
NOTHING BUT THE TRUTH (TF)   Once Upon A Time Films, 1995
SUBSTANCE OF FIRE   1996

JOSE MARIA VITIER
FRESA Y CHOCOLATE   *STRAWBERRY AND CHOCOLATE*
   1994, Cuban-Mexican-Spanish

JOAN VIVES
HO SAP EL MINISTRE?   *DOES THE MINISTER KNOW?*   1992,
   Spanish-Catalonian

ALESSIO VLAD
Contact: SIAE - Italy, 011-39-6-59-901

SPARROW   co-composer with Claudio Cappani, 1993, Italian

HUBERT VON GOISERN
BROTHER OF SLEEP   co-composer with Norbert J. Schneider,
   1996

GYORGY VUKAN
Contact: ARTISJUS - Budapest, Hungary, Telex: 861-226527

HANUSSEN   Studio Objektiv/CCC Filmkunst/Hungarofilm/MOKEP,
   1988, Hungarian-West German

ALEXANDER VUSTIN
ANNA KARAMAZOVA   1991, French-Soviet

BOB WAHLER
A DIFFERENT STORY   Avco Embassy, 1978

WU WAI-LAP
THE EAST IS RED   *SWORDSMAN III*   1993, Hong Kong

ROBERT WAIT
MOM & DAD SAVE THE WORLD   additional music, Warner Bros.,
   1994

TOM WAITS

b. 1949
Contact: ASCAP - Los Angeles, 213-883-1000

ONE FROM THE HEART ★   Columbia, 1982
STREETWISE (FD)   Angelika Films, 1985
NIGHT ON EARTH   JVC, 1991

RICK WAKEMAN

b. 1949
Contact: PRS - London, England, 011-44-1-580-5544

LISZTOMANIA   Warner Bros., 1975, British
WHITE ROCK (FD)   Shueisha Publishing Co., 1977
THE BURNING   Orion, 1982
G'OLE (FD)   IVECO, 1983, British
SHE   American National Enterprises, 1983, Italian
CRIMES OF PASSION   New World, 1984
CREEPSHOW II   additional music, New World, 1987

NATHAN WAKS

Contact: APRA - Australia, 011-61-2-922-6422

MY BRILLIANT CAREER   Analysis, 1980, Australian

DANA WALDEN

Contact: BMI - Los Angeles, 310-659-9109

DEAD RINGER   co-composer with Barry Fasman, Stock Grange
   Productions, 1988
MY MOM'S A WEREWOLF   co-composer with Barry Fasman,
   Crown International, 1988
THE IMMORTALIZER   co-composer with Barry Fasman, Filmwest
   Productions, 1989
WHISPERS   co-composer with Barry Fasman, Distant Horizon,
   1989
HELLGATE   co-composer with Barry Fasman, New World, 1989
RICH GIRL   co-composer with Barry Fasman, Filmwest
   Productions, 1989
STREET HUNTER   co-composer with Barry Fasman, 21st Century,
   1989
NIGHT CLUB   co-composer with Barry Fasman, Crown
   International, 1990
THE BABY DOLL MURDERS   Trident, 1993

W.G. SNUFFY WALDEN

Agent: Gorfaine-Schwartz - Los Angeles, 213-969-1011
Affiliation: BMI - Los Angeles, 310-659-9109

WINNIE (TF)   All Girls Productions/NBC Productions, 1988
ROE VS. WADE (TF)   The Manheim Co./NBC Productions, 1989
BURNING BRIDGES (TF)   co-composer with Bennett Salvay,
   Andrea Baynes Productions/Lorimar TV, 1990
THE CHASE (TF)   Steve White Prods./Spectacor, 1991
SHOOT FIRST: A COP'S VENGEANCE (TF)   Harvey Khan
   Prods./Interscope, 1991
I'LL FLY AWAY (TF)   Falakey/Austin Street/Lorimar TV, 1991
LEAVING NORMAL   Universal, 1992
WILD CARD (CTF)   Davis Entertainment/MCA TV, 1992
THE GOOD FIGHT (CTF)   Freyda Rothstein/Hearst, 1992
A PLACE TO BE LOVED (TF)   Polson Co./Corapeake
   Prods./Procter & Gamble Prods., 1993
I'LL FLY AWAY - THEN AND NOW (TF)   co-composer with Bennett
   Salvay, Brand-Falsey/Lorimar TV, 1993
THE STAND (MS) ☆   Laurel/Greengrass Prods., 1994
RISE AND WALK: THE DENNIS BYRD STORY (TF)   Fox West
   Pictures, 1994
HOMAGE (TF)   Skyline Entertainment, 1994

JACK WALDMAN

Contact: BMI - Los Angeles, 310-659-9109

A MARRIAGE   Cinecom, 1983

SHIRLEY WALKER*

Agent: Vangelos Management - Encino, 818-380-1919
Affiliation: BMI - Los Angeles, 310-659-9109

BLUE MOON   Winfield Films
THE BLACK STALLION   additional music, United Artists, 1979
TOUCHED   Lorimar Productions/Wildwoods Partners, 1983
THE VIOLATED   The Violated Co., 1984
GHOULIES   co-composer with Richard H. Band, Empire Pictures,
   1985
THE DUNGEONMASTER   co-composer with Richard H. Band,
   Empire Pictures, 1985
THE END OF AUGUST   Quartett Films
PAINT IT BLACK   co-composer with Jurgen Knieper, Vestron,
   1989
STRIKE IT RICH   co-composer with Cliff Eidelman, Millimeter
   Films, 1990
CHICAGO JOE AND THE SHOWGIRL   co-composer with Hans
   Zimmer, 1990, British
NIGHTBREED   additional music, 20th Century Fox, 1990
WHITE FANG   additional music, Buena Vista, 1991
MEMOIRS OF AN INVISIBLE MAN   Warner Bros., 1992
MAJORITY RULE (CTF)   Ultra/Citadel, 1992
BATMAN: MASK OF THE PHANTASM (AF)   Warner Bros., 1993
THE ADVENTURES OF CAPTAIN ZOOM IN OUTER SPACE
   (CTF)   Telvan Prods./MCA TV/Starz!, 1995
SPACE: ABOVE AND BEYOND (TF)   20th Century Fox TV/Hard
   Eight Pictures/Village Roadshow, 1995
THE LOVE BUG   Buena Vista, 1996
ESCAPE FROM L.A.   co-composer with John Carpenter   1996
ASTEROID (TF)   Davis Entertainment, 1997
TURBULENCE   MGM-UA, 1997

SIMON WALKER

Contact: APRA - Australia, 011-61-2-922-6422

FOR THE TERM OF HIS NATURAL LIFE (MS)   1982, Australian
THE WILD DUCK   RKR Releasing, 1983, Australian

BENNIE WALLACE

Agent: The Kordek Agency - Bunbank, 818-559-4248
Affiliation: BMI - Los Angeles, 310-659-9109

BLAZE   Buena Vista, 1989
WHITE MEN CAN'T JUMP   20th Century Fox, 1992
BETTY BOOP (AF)   MGM, 1994
MIDNIGHT RUN-AROUND (TF)   Toto Prods./Viacom, 1994

ROB WALLACE

Contact: BMI - Los Angeles, 310-659-9109

KILL AND GO HIDE   *THE CHILD*   Boxoffice International, 1977

KARL WALLINGER

REALITY BITES   Universal, 1994

DEAN WALRAFF

Contact: Raff Music - Shadow Hills, 818-353-8652

CASTING AGENCY   DB USA, 1991
LUKAS' CHILD   DB USA, 1992
SOUNDS OF SILENCE   Artist's View, 1992

ROBERT J. WALSH

Contact: BMI - Los Angeles, 310-659-9109

THE GALACTIC CONNECTION   Barrich Corporation, 1979
THE LOONEY, LOONEY, LOONEY BUGS BUNNY MOVIE (AF)
   Warner Bros., 1981
BLOOD SONG   Allstate Films, 1981
REVENGE OF THE SHOGUN WOMEN   21st Century, 1982,
   Taiwanese
BUGS BUNNY'S 3RD MOVIE: 1001 RABBIT TALES (AF)   Warner
   Bros., 1982
NOMAD RIDERS   Windjammer Productions, 1982
THE DAFFY DUCK MOVIE: FANTASTIC ISLAND (AF)   Warner
   Bros., 1982
HEARTBREAKER   Monarex/Emerson Film Enterprises, 1983

LOVE YA FLORENCE NIGHTINGALE   TPL Productions, 1983
THE WITCHING   Associated Entertainment, 1983
YOUNG WARRIORS   Cannon, 1983
REVENGE OF THE NINJA   MGM/UA/Cannon, 1983
MY LITTLE PONY - THE MOVIE (AF)   DEG, 1986
BLOOD MONEY   Shapiro Entertainment, 1987
OVERKILL   Manson International, 1987
DIGGIN' UP BUSINESS   Curb Esquire Films, 1990

JULIAN WALSTALL
THE LOST LANGUAGE OF CRANES   1991, British

CASTLE & DOUG WALTER
Contact: ASCAP - Los Angeles, 213-883-1000

DESIRE & HELL AT SUNSET MOTEL   Two Moon Releasing, 1992

JEFF WALTON
Contact: Four Score Productions - Houston, 713-956-9069
Affiliation: BMI - Los Angeles, 310-659-9109

FATAL JUSTICE   Trident, 1993
CYBERZONE   1995

NATHAN WANG
b. August 8, 1956
Contact: North Light Sound, 213-467-8513
Affiliation: BMI - Los Angeles, 310-659-9109

SPELLCASTER   Empire Pictures, 1987
SCREWBALL HOTEL   Maurice Smith Productions/Avatar Film,
   1988, Canadian
NATURAL CAUSES   Pacific Rim, 1994

WANG CHUNG
Contact: PRS - London, England, 011-44-1-580-5544

TO LIVE AND DIE IN L.A.   MGM/UA, 1985

KEN WANNBERG
Contact: BMI - Los Angeles, 310-659-9109

THE TENDER WARRIOR   Safari, 1971
THE PEACE KILLERS   1971
WELCOME HOME, SOLDIER BOYS   music supervisor, 20th
   Century-Fox, 1972
THE GREAT AMERICAN BEAUTY CONTEST (TF)   ABC Circle
   Films, 1973
THE FOUR DEUCES   Avco Embassy, 1974
LEPKE   Warner Bros., 1975
BITTERSWEET LOVE   Avco Embassy, 1976
THE LATE SHOW   Warner Bros., 1977
SILENT PARTNER   arranger, 1979, Canadian
THE CHANGELING   arranger, AFD, 1980, Canadian
TRIBUTE   20th Century-Fox, 1980, U.S.-Canadian
THE AMATEUR   20th Century-Fox, 1982, Canadian
MOTHER LODE   Agamemnon Films, 1982, Canadian
LOSIN' IT   Embassy, 1983, Canadian-U.S.
OF UNKNOWN ORIGIN   Warner Bros., 1983, Canadian
BLAME IT ON RIO   20th Century Fox, 1984
THE PHILADELPHIA EXPERIMENT   New World, 1984
DRAW! (CTF)   HBO Premiere Films/Astral Film Productions/Bryna
   Company, 1984, U.S.-Canadian
VANISHING ACT (TF)   Robert Cooper Productions/Levinson-Link
   Productions, 1986
MILES TO GO... (TF)   Keating-Shostak Productions, 1986,
   U.S.-Canadian
RED RIVER (TF)   Catalina Production Group/MGM-UA TV, 1988
FATAL MEMORIES (TF)   Green's Point/WIC/MGM-UA TV, 1992

WAR
Contact: ASCAP - Los Angeles, 213-883-1000

THE RIVER BIGER   Cine Artists Pictures, 1976
YOUNGBLOOD   American International, 1978

STEPHEN WARBECK
Contact: PRS - London, England, 011-44-1-580-5544

PRIME SUSPECT (TF)   1992, British
THE CHANGELLING (CTF)   BBC TV, 1994, British
O MARY THIS LONDON   Samuel Goldwyn, 1994, British

BILL WARE
HAPPILY EVER AFTER: FAIRY TALES FOR EVERY CHILD
   (ATF)   co-composer, Two Oceans/Confetti/Hyperion, 1995

DALE O. WARREN
Contact: BMI - Los Angeles, 310-659-9109

THE KLANSMAN   co-composer with Stu Gardner, Paramount,
   1974

MERVYN WARREN
Agent: Vangelos Management - Encino, 818-380-1919

SISTER ACT 2: BACK IN THE HABIT   additional music, Buena
   Vista, 1993
THE WHARF RAT (CTF)   Showtime, 1995
STEEL   Warner Bros., 1997
THE KISS   Universal, 1998

RICHARD LEWIS WARREN
Contact: ASCAP - Los Angeles, 213-883-1000

CARLY'S WEB (TF)   MTM Enterprises, 1987

DON WAS
Contact: ASCAP - Los Angeles, 213-883-1000

BACKBEAT   Gramercy, 1994
RHYTHM COUNTRY & BLUES (TD)   Thirteen-WNET/Perery
   Films/MCA Music Ent. Group, 1994

GROVER WASHINGTON, JR.
Contact: ASCAP - Los Angeles, 213-883-1000

PERCY AND THUNDER (CTF)   co-composer with Tom Scott,
   TNT/Amblin TV/Brandman Prod., 1993

JULIAN WASTALL
Contact: PRS - London, England, 011-44-1-580-5544

THICKER THAN WATER (TF)   co-composer with Daemion Barry,
   BBC/A&E, 1994, British

CHUMEI WATANABE
b. Japan
Contact: JASRAC - Tokyo, Japan, 011-81-3-502-6551

SUPER-GIANT 2   *SPACEMEN AGAINST THE VAMPIRES FROM
   SPACE*   1956, Japanese
THE NIGHT OF THE SEAGULL   1970, Japanese
EIJANAIKA   Shochiku, 1981, Japanese

DAVID WATERS
Contact: BMI - Los Angeles, 310-659-9109

RESCUE ME   co-composer with Al Kasha and Joel Hirschhorn,
   Cannon, 1993

MARY WATHING
FREEDOM ON MY MIND (FD)   Clarity Films, 1994

BILL WATSON
Contact: BMI - Los Angeles, 310-659-9109

XXX'S & OOO'S(TF)   co-composer with Harry Stinson, John
   Wilder-Nightwatch Prods/Brandon Tartikoff-Moving Target Prods.,
   1994

MARK WATTERS*
Agent: Air-Edel - Los Angeles, 310-914-5000

THE RETURN OF JAFAR (AF)   Buena Vista, 1994
THE PEBBLE AND THE PENGUIN (AF)   MGM-UA, 1995
ALL DOGS GO TO HEAVEN 2 (AF)   MGM-UA, 1996

WAVEMAKER
Contact: ASCAP - Los Angeles, 213-883-1000

THE TEMPEST   Boyd's Co., 1979, British

STEVE WAX
TOUGH ENOUGH   co-composer with Michael Lloyd, 20th
   Century-Fox, 1983

SAM WAYMON
Contact: BMI - Los Angeles, 310-659-9109

GANJA AND HESS   Kelly-Jordan, 1973
JUST CRAZY ABOUT HORSES (FD)   Fred Baker Films, 1979

JEFF WAYNE
Contact: PRS - London, England, 011-44-1-580-5544

McVICAR   Crown International, 1981, British

CHUCK WEBB
Contact: ASCAP - Los Angeles, 213-883-1000

HOW U LIKE ME NOW   co-composer with Kahil El Zabar,
   Shapiro-Glickenhaus, 1993

JIMMY WEBB
Contact: ASCAP - Los Angeles, 213-883-1000

THE NAKED APE   Universal, 1973
VOICES   United Artists, 1979
THE LAST UNICORN (AF)   Jensen Farley Pictures, 1982
THE HANOI HILTON   Cannon, 1987

ROGER WEBB
Contact: PRS - London, England, 011-44-1-580-5544

THE GODSEND   Cannon, 1980
DEATH OF A CENTERFOLD: THE DOROTHY STRATTEN STORY
   (TF)   Wilcox Productions/MGM TV, 1981
THE BOY IN BLUE   20th Century Fox, 1986, Canadian

ANDREW LLOYD WEBBER
b. England
Contact: PRS - London, England, 011-44-1-580-5544

GUMSHOE   Columbia, 1971, British
THE ODESSA FILE   Columbia, 1974, British-West German

STEPHEN WEBBER
Contact: BMI - Los Angeles, 310-659-9109

KNOWING LISA   Imagining Things Enterprises, 1992

JULIUS WECHTER
Contact: ASCAP - Los Angeles, 213-883-1000

MIDNIGHT MADNESS   Buena Vista, 1980

KONSTANTIN WECKER
SCHTONK   1992, German

JOHN WEISMAN
Contact: ASCAP - Los Angeles, 213-883-1000

LOOKING FOR MIRACLES (CTF)   Sullivan Films, 1989

JOSEPH WEISS
Contact: ASCAP - Los Angeles, 213-883-1000

GIDEON'S TRUMPET (TF)   Gideon Productions/Worldvision
   Enterprises, 1980

ED WELCH
Contact: BMI - Los Angeles, 310-659-9109

STAND UP, VIRGIN SOLDIERS   Warner Bros., 1977, British
THE 39 STEPS   International Picture Show Company, 1978,
   British
THE SHILLINGBURY BLOWERS   ...AND THE BAND PLAYED ON
   Inner Circle, 1980, British
DANGEROUS DAVIES - THE LAST DETECTIVE   ITC/Inner
   Circle/Maidenhead Films, 1980, British
THE BOYS IN BLUE   MAM Ltd./Apollo Leisure Group, 1983,
   British

KEN WELCH
Contact: BMI - Los Angeles, 310-659-9109

MOVERS & SHAKERS   co-composer with Mitzie Welch, MGM/UA,
   1985

MITZIE WELCH
Contact: ASCAP - Los Angeles, 213-883-1000

MOVERS & SHAKERS   co-composer with Ken Welch, MGM/UA,
   1985

LARRY WELLINGTON
Contact: BMI - Los Angeles, 310-659-9109

2000 MANIACS   co-composer with Herschell Gordon Lewis, Box
   Office Spectaculars, 1964
HOW TO MAKE A DOLL   1967
A TASTE OF BLOOD   THE SECRET OF DR. ALUCARD   Creative
   Film Enterprises, 1967
THE WIZARD OF GORE   Mayflower Pictures, 1970

JOHN WELSMAN
Contact: SOCAN - Toronto, 416-445-8700

LANTERN HILL (TF)   Lantern Hill/Disney
   Channel/CBC/WonderWorks/CPB/Telefilm Canada, 1991

WENDY & LISA
(Wendy Melvoin & Lisa Coleman)
Agent: CAA - Beverly Hills, 310-288-4545
Affiliation: ASCAP - Los Angeles, 213-883-1000

DANGEROUS MINDS   Buena Vista, 1995

RICK WENTWORTH
Agent: Air-Edel - Los Angeles, 310-914-5000
Affiliation: PRS - London, England, 011-44-1-580-5544

HOW TO GET AHEAD IN ADVERTISING   co-composer with David
   Dundas, Warner Bros., 1989, British
SLEEPERS (MS)   co-composer with David Dundas, Cinema Verity,
   1991
FREDDIE AS F.R.0.7. (AF)   co-composer with David Dundas,
   Miramax, 1992

FRED WERNER
Contact: ASCAP - Los Angeles, 213-883-1000

HUCKLEBERRY FINN   United Artists, 1974
MOONSHINE COUNTY EXPRESS   New World, 1977
THE DEATH OF OCEAN VIEW PARK (TF)   Furia-Oringer
   Productions/Playboy Productions, 1979
A SMALL KILLING (TF)   Orgolini-Nelson Productions/Motown
   Productions, 1981

JOCELYN WEST
TWO NUDES BATHING   1995, British

PAUL WESTERBERG
Contact: ASCAP - Los Angeles, 213-883-1000

SINGLES   Warner Bros., 1992

MICHAEL WETHERWAX
Contact: ASCAP - Los Angeles, 213-883-1000

CAGE   New Century/Vista, 1989
MIDNIGHT   SVS, 1989

JOHN WETTON
CHASING THE DEER   British, 1995

JIM WETZEL
HOMEWORK   co-composer with Tony Jones, Jensen Farley
    Pictures, 1982

DAVID WHEATLEY
Contact: ASCAP - Los Angeles, 213-883-1000

TOUGH ENOUGH   co-composer with Michael Lloyd, 20th
    Century-Fox, 1983
AVENGING ANGEL   co-composer with Paul Antonelli, Weitraub
    Productions, 1985
PRINCESS ACADEMY   co-composer with Paul Antonelli,
    Weintraub Productions, 1987, U.S.-French-Yugoslav
MANY CLASSIC MOMENTS   Da Capo Films
THE WOMEN'S CLUB   co-composer with Paul Antonelli,
    Weintraub-Cloverleaf/Scorsese Productions, 1987
CHINA O'BRIEN   co-composer with Paul Antonelli, Golden Harvest,
    1989, U.S.-Hong Kong
OUT OF THE DARK   co-composer with Paul Antonelli, New Line
    Cinema, 1989
SPEED ZONE   Orion, 1989

JACK W. WHEATON
PENITENTIARY II   MGM/UA, 1982

HAROLD WHEELER
Contact: ASCAP - Los Angeles, 213-883-1000

BENNY'S PLACE (TF)   Titus Productions, 1982
STRAIGHT OUT OF BROOKLYN   American Playhouse, 1991
STOMPIN' AT THE SAVOY (TF)   Richard Maynard Prods./Gallant
    Entertainment/Universal TV, 1992
THE JACKSONS - AN AMERICAN DREAM (MS)   Stan
    Margulies/de Passe/Motown/Polygram/KJ Films, 1992
YOU MUST REMEMBER THIS (TF)   Longride/QED West/Limbo,
    1992
LAUREL AVENUE (CTF)   HBO Independent Prods., 1993
THERE ARE NO CHILDREN HERE (TF)   Do We/Harpo
    Prods./LOMO Prods., 1993
TEARS AND LAUGHTER: THE JOAN AND MELISSA RIVERS
    STORY (TF)   Davis Ent., 1994
SILENT WITNESS: WHAT A CHILD SAW (CTF)   USA Pictures,
    1994

BILL WHELEN
SOME MOTHER'S SON   1996

CHRISTOPHER WHIFFEN
Contact: BMI - Los Angeles, 310-659-9109

INEVITABLE GRACE   Silverstar, 1994

DAVID WHITAKER
Contact: PRS - London, England, 011-44-1-580-5544

HAMMERHEAD   Columbia, 1968, British
DON'T RAISE THE BRIDGE - LOWER THE RIVER   Columbia,
    1968, British
RUN WILD, RUN FREE   Columbia, 1969, British

SCREAM AND SCREAM AGAIN   American International, 1970,
    British
THE DEATH WHEELERS   *PSYCHOMANIA*   Scotia International,
    1971, British
DR. JEKYLL AND SISTER HYDE   American International, 1972,
    British
VAMPIRE CIRCUS   Rank, 1972, British
OLD DRACULA   *VAMPIRA*   American International, 1975, British
DOMINIQUE   Sword and Sworcery Productions, 1979, British
THE SWORD AND THE SORCERER   Group 1, 1982

KENN WHITAKER
Contact: BMI - Los Angeles, 310-659-9109

STRAPPED (CTF)   additional music, Osiris Films/HBO Showcase,
    1993

DANIEL J. WHITE
DON QUIJOTE DE ORSON WELLES   *DON QUIXOTE OF ORSON
    WELLES*   1992, Spanish

JOHN CLIFFORD WHITE
Contact: APRA - Australia, 011-61-2-922-6422

METAL SKIN   1994, Australian
ANGEL BABY   1996

LENNY WHITE
Contact: BMI - Los Angeles, 310-659-9109

HOUSE PARTY   co-composer with Marcus Miller, New Line
    Cinema, 1990

MAURICE WHITE
Contact: ASCAP - Los Angeles, 213-883-1000

THAT'S THE WAY OF THE WORLD   United Artists, 1975

NORMAN WHITFIELD
Contact: BMI - Los Angeles, 310-659-9109

CAR WASH   Universal, 1976

MICHAEL WHITMORE
BELOW 30/ABOVE 10,000   damaged Californians, 1994

STACY WIDELITZ
Agent: William Morris - Beverly Hills, 310-859-4000
Affiliation: BMI - Los Angeles, 310-659-9109

RETURN TO HORROR HIGH   New World, 1987
STRANDED   New Line Cinema, 1987
DARK TOWER   Spectrafilm, 1987, Canadian
PHANTOM OF THE MALL   Fries Distribution, 1989
PRAYER OF THE ROLLERBOYS   Gaga, 1991
EYE OF THE STALKER (TF)   O'Hara-Horowitz, 1995

SONIA WIEDER-ATHERTON
LA CRISE   *CRISIS-GO-'ROUND*   1992, French

CHUCK WILDE*
Contact: BMI - Los Angeles, 310-659-9109

THE PANAMA DECEPTION (FD)   Empowerment Project, 1992

ROLF WILHELM
b. Germany
Contact: GEMA - Germany, 011-49-89-480-03610

THE REVOLT OF GUNNER ASCH   1955, West German
SIEGFRIED   *WHOM THE GODS WISH TO DESTROY/DIE
    NIBELUNGEN*   1967, West German
HURRAH! THE SCHOOL IS BURNING   1970, West German
LUDWIG ON THE LOOKOUT FOR A WIFE   1970, West German
WE CHOP THE TEACHERS INTO MINCE MEAT   1970, West
    German

THE SERPENT'S EGG   Paramount, 1978, West German-U.S.
FROM THE LIFE OF THE MARIONETTES   Universal/AFD, 1980,
   West German

SCOTT WILK
Contact: ASCAP - Los Angeles, 213-883-1000

PLAIN CLOTHES   Paramount, 1988

GEORGE WILKINS
Contact: ASCAP - Los Angeles, 213-883-1000

BLACK MARKET BABY (TF)   co-composer with Richard Bellis, Brut
   Productions, 1977

RICK WILKINS
Contact: BMI - Los Angeles, 310-659-9109

THE CHANGELING   AFD, 1980, Canadian

MARC WILKINSON
Contact: PRS - London, England, 011-44-1-580-5544

IF...   Paramount, 1969, British
THE ROYAL HUNT OF THE SUN   National General, 1969, British
BLOOD ON SATAN'S CLAW   SATAN'S SKIN   Cannon, 1971,
   British
EAGLE IN A CAGE   National General, 1971, British-Yugoslavian
THE DARWIN ADVENTURE   20th Century-Fox, 1972, British
THE MAN AND THE SNAKE   1972
THE RETURN   1973
THE HIRELING   Columbia, 1973, British
THE MANGO TREE   1977, Australian
THE QUARTERMASS CONCLUSION   co-composer with Nic
   Rowley, Euston Films Ltd., 1979, British
EAGLE'S WING   International Picture Show, 1979, British
THE FIENDISH PLOT OF DR. FU MANCHU   Orion/Warner Bros.,
   1980, British
ENIGMA   Embassy, 1983
KIM (TF)   London Films, 1984

FRANK WILL
DER OLYMPISCHE SOMMER   THE OLYMPIC SUMMER (FD)
   co-composer with Heidi Aydt, 1993, German

DAVID C. WILLIAMS
Agent: Film Music Associates - Hollywood, 213-463-1070

DELIRIUM   Maris Entertainment, 1980
HARMONY   Anvil Productions, 1981
FREE RIDE   Galaxy International, 1986
TERROR SQUAD   The Matterhorn Group, 1987
BEFORE GOD   Quest Productions, 1987
SIDE ROADS   Side Roads Productions, 1988
DEADLY INNOCENCE   Universal, 1988
AFTER SCHOOL   Moviestore Entertainment, 1988
THE PROPHECY   Dimension, 1995

H. SHEP WILLIAMS
LILLIAN   1993

JACK ERIC WILLIAMS
Contact: ASCAP - Los Angeles, 213-883-1000

NIGHTMARE   21st Century, 1981

JOHN WILLIAMS*
b. 1932 - Long Island, New York
Agent: Gorfaine-Schwartz - Los Angeles, 213-969-1011
Affiliation: BMI - Los Angeles, 310-659-9109

DADDY-O   AIP, 1959
I PASSED FOR WHITE   Allied Artists, 1960
BECAUSE THEY'RE YOUNG   Columbia, 1960
THE SECRET WAYS   Universal, 1961
BACHELOR FLAT   20th Century-Fox, 1962
DIAMOND HEAD   Columbia, 1963

GIDGET GOES TO ROME   Columbia, 1963
NONE BUT THE BRAVE   Warner Bros., 1964, U.S.-Japanese
THE KILLERS   Universal, 1964, originally filmed for television
JOHN GOLDFARB, PLEASE COME HOME   20th Century-Fox,
   1965
HOW TO STEAL A MILLION   Columbia, 1966
NOT WITH MY WIFE, YOU DON'T!   Warner Bros., 1966
THE PLAINSMAN   Universal, 1966
PENELOPE   MGM, 1966
THE RARE BREED   Universal, 1966
A GUIDE FOR THE MARRIED MAN   20th Century-Fox, 1967
FITZWILLY   United Artists, 1967
VALLEY OF THE DOLLS ★   adaptation, 20th Century-Fox, 1967
SERGEANT RYKER   THE CASE AGAINST PAUL RYKER
   Universal, 1968, originally filmed for television in 1963
HEIDI (TF) ☆☆   Omnibus-Biography Productions, 1968
DADDY'S GONE A-HUNTING   National General, 1969
THE REIVERS ★   National General, 1969
GOODBYE, MR. CHIPS ★   adaptation, MGM, 1969, British
THE STORY OF A WOMAN   1970, Italian
JANE EYRE (TF) ☆☆   Omnibus Productions/Sagittarius
   Productions, 1971, British-U.S.
FIDDLER ON THE ROOF ★★   adaptation, United Artists, 1971
THE SCREAMING WOMAN (TF)   Universal TV, 1972
THE COWBOYS   Warner Bros., 1972
THE POSEIDON ADVENTURE ★   20th Century-Fox, 1972
PETE N'TILLIE   Universal, 1972
IMAGES ★   Columbia, 1972, Irish
THE MAN WHO LOVED CAT DANCING   MGM, 1973
TOM SAWYER ★   adaptation, United Artists, 1973
THE PAPER CHASE   20th Century-Fox, 1973
THE LONG GOODBYE   United Artists, 1973
CINDERELLA LIBERTY ★   20th Century-Fox, 1974
THE TOWERING INFERNO ★   20th Century-Fox, 1974
EARTHQUAKE   Universal, 1974
THE SUGARLAND EXPRESS   Universal, 1974
CONRACK   20th Century-Fox, 1974
CALIFORNIA SPLIT   Columbia, 1974
THE EIGER SANCTION   Universal, 1975
JAWS ★★   Universal, 1975
THE MISSOURI BREAKS   United Artists, 1976
FAMILY PLOT   Universal, 1976
MIDWAY   Universal, 1976
BLACK SUNDAY   Universal, 1976
STAR WARS ★★   20th Century-Fox, 1977
CLOSE ENCOUNTERS OF THE THIRD KIND ★   Columbia, 1977
SUPERMAN ★   Warner Bros., 1978, U.S.-British
JAWS 2   Universal, 1978
THE FURY   20th Century-Fox, 1978
DRACULA   Universal, 1979
1941   Universal/Columbia, 1979
THE EMPIRE STRIKES BACK ★   20th Century-Fox, 1980
RAIDERS OF THE LOST ARK ★   Paramount, 1981
HEARTBEEPS   Universal, 1981
E.T. THE EXTRA-TERRESTRIAL ★★   Universal, 1982
MONSIGNOR   20th Century-Fox, 1982
THE RETURN OF THE JEDI ★   20th Century-Fox, 1983
INDIANA JONES AND THE TEMPLE OF DOOM ★   Paramount,
   1984
THE RIVER ★   Universal, 1984
SPACECAMP   20th Century Fox, 1986
THE WITCHES OF EASTWICK ★   Warner Bros., 1987
EMPIRE OF THE SUN ★   Warner Bros., 1987
THE ACCIDENTAL TOURIST ★   Warner Bros., 1988
INDIANA JONES AND THE LAST CRUSADE ★   Paramount, 1989
ALWAYS   Universal, 1989
BORN ON THE FOURTH OF JULY ★   Universal, 1989
STANLEY AND IRIS   MGM/UA, 1990
PRESUMED INNOCENT   Warner Bros., 1990
HOME ALONE ★   20th Century Fox, 1990
HOOK   TriStar, 1991
JFK ★   Warner Bros., 1991
FAR AND AWAY   Universal, 1992
HOME ALONE 2: LOST IN NEW YORK   20th Century Fox, 1992
JURASSIC PARK   Universal, 1993
SCHINDLER'S LIST ★★   Universal, 1993
SABRINA ★   Paramount, 1995
NIXON ★   Buena Vista, 1995
SLEEPERS ★   Warner Bros., 1996
ROSEWOOD   Warner Bros., 1997
THE LOST WORLD   Universal, 1997

PATRICK WILLIAMS*

b. April 23, 1939 - Bonne Terre, Missouri
Agent: Gorfaine-Schwartz - Los Angeles, 213-969-1011
Affiliation: BMI - Los Angeles, 310-659-9109

HOW SWEET IT IS! Buena Vista, 1968
DON'T DRINK THE WATER Avco Embassy, 1969
A NICE GIRL LIKE ME Avco Embassy, 1969, British
PIGEONS THE SIDELONG GLANCES OF A PIGEON KICKER
   MGM, 1970
SAN FRANCISCO INTERNATIONAL (TF) Universal TV, 1970
MACHO CALLAHAN Avco Embassy, 1970
INCIDENT IN SAN FRANCISCO (TF) QM Productions/American
   Broadcasting Company, 1971
TRAVIS LOGAN, D.A. (TF) QM Productions, 1971
THE FAILING OF RAYMOND (TF) Universal TV, 1971
LOCK, STOCK AND BARREL (TF) Universal TV, 1971
TERROR IN THE SKY (TF) Paramount Pictures TV, 1971
HARDCASE (TF) Hanna-Barbera Productions, 1972
EVEL KNIEVEL Fanfare, 1972
THE STREETS OF SAN FRANCISCO (TF) QM
   Productions/Warner Bros. TV, 1972
SHORT WALK TO DAYLIGHT (TF) Universal TV, 1972
THE MAGICIAN (TF) B&B Productions/Paramount Pictures TV,
   1973
HITCHED (TF) Universal TV, 1973
SSSSSSS Universal, 1973
ORDEAL INFERNO (TF) 20th Century-Fox TV, 1973
MRS. SUNDANCE (TF) 20th Century-Fox TV, 1974
MURDER OR MERCY (TF) QM Productions, 1974
MOONCHILD co-composer with Billy Byers, Filmmakers
   Ltd./American Films Ltd., 1974
HARRAD SUMMER Cinerama Releasing Corporation, 1974
FRAMED Paramount, 1974
STOWAWAY TO THE MOON (TF) 20th Century-Fox TV, 1975
CROSSFIRE (TF) QM Productions, 1975
HEX 1975
THE LIVES OF JENNY DOLAN (TF) Ross Hunter
   Productions/Paramount Pictures TV, 1975
MOST WANTED (TF) QM Productions, 1976
STONESTREET: WHO KILLED THE CENTERFOLD MODEL? (TF)
   Universal TV, 1977
THE MAN WITH THE POWER (TF) Universal TV, 1977
THE ONE AND ONLY Paramount, 1978
THE CHEAP DETECTIVE Columbia, 1978
CASEY'S SHADOW Columbia, 1978
BREAKING AWAY ★ adaptation, 20th Century-Fox, 1979
BUTCH AND SUNDANCE: THE EARLY DAYS 20th Century-Fox,
   1979
HOT STUFF Columbia, 1979
CUBA United Artists, 1979
CHARLIE CHAN AND THE CURSE OF THE DRAGON QUEEN
   American Cinema, 1980
WHOLLY MOSES Columbia, 1980
HERO AT LARGE MGM/United Artists, 1980
USED CARS Columbia, 1980
IT'S MY TURN Columbia, 1980
HOW TO BEAT THE HIGH COST OF LIVING American
   International, 1980
THE MIRACLE OF KATHY MILLER (TF) Rothman-Wohl
   Productions/Universal TV, 1981
THE PRINCESS AND THE CABBIE (TF) ☆☆ Freyda Rothstein
   Productions/Time-Life Productions, 1981
TOMORROW'S CHILD (TF) 20th Century-Fox TV, 1982
SOME KIND OF HERO Paramount, 1982
THE BEST LITTLE WHOREHOUSE IN TEXAS adaptation,
   Universal, 1982
MOONLIGHT (TF) Universal TV, 1982
THE TOY Columbia, 1982
SWING SHIFT Warner Bros., 1983
THE FIGHTER (TF) Martin Manulis Productions/The Catalina
   Production Group, 1983
MARVIN AND TIGE LIKE FATHER AND SON 20th Century-Fox
   International Classics, 1983
THE BUDDY SYSTEM 20th Century Fox, 1984
BEST DEFENSE Paramount, 1984
ALL OF ME Universal, 1984
THE SLUGGER'S WIFE Columbia, 1985
SEDUCED (TF) ☆ Catalina Production Group/Comworld
   Productions, 1985
JUST BETWEEN FRIENDS Orion, 1986

VIOLETS ARE BLUE Columbia, 1986
OCEANS OF FIRE (TF) Catalina Production Group, 1986
KOJAK: THE PRICE OF JUSTICE (TF) Universal TV, 1987
LAGUNA HEAT (CTF) HBO Pictures/Jay Weston Productions,
   1987
FRESH HORSES co-composer with David Foster, Columbia/WEG,
   1988
DOUBLE STANDARD (TF) Louis Randolph Productions/Fenton
   Entertainment Group/Fries Entertainment, 1988
MAYBE BABY (TF) Perry Lafferty Productions/von
   Zerneck-Samuels Productions, 1988
WORTH WINNING 20th Century Fox, 1989
COLUMBO: MURDER - SELF-PORTRAIT (TF) Universal TV, 1989
LOVE AND LIES (TF) Fredya Rothstein Productions, 1990
CRY BABY Universal, 1990
IN THE SPIRIT Castle Hill, 1990
DECORATION DAY (TF) ☆ 1990
THE WHEREABOUTS OF JENNY (TF) Katie Face
   Prods./Columbia TV, 1991
IN BROAD DAYLIGHT (TF) Force Ten/New World TV, 1991
DAUGHTERS OF PRIVILEGE (TF) NBC Prods., 1991
KEEPING SECRETS (TF) Freyda
   Rothstein-Hamel-Somers/Finnegan-Pinchuk, 1991
BACK TO THE STREETS OF SAN FRANCISCO (TF) Aaron
   Spelling, 1992
GRAVE SECRETS: THE LEGACY OF HILLTOP DRIVE (TF)
   Freyda Rothstein/Hearst, 1992
NO TIME TO DIE (TF) Universal TV, 1992
LEGACY OF LIES (CTF) BAL/MTE, 1992
BIG GIRLS DON'T CRY...THEY GET EVEN 1992, New Line
THE CUTTING EDGE MGM, 1992
DANIELLE STEEL'S JEWELS (TF) ☆☆ List-Estrin/RCS Video/NBC
   Prods., 1992
BLIND SPOT (TF) Signboard Hill/RHI Entertainment, 1993
MURDER IN THE HEARTLAND (TF) O'Hara-Horowitz Prods.,
   1993
ZELDA (CTF) Turner Pictures/ZDF/ORF/SRG, 1993
GERONIMO (CTF) ☆ Yorktown Prods./von Zerneck-Sertner Films,
   1993
MERCY MISSION: THE RESCUE OF FLIGHT 771 (TF)
   RHI/Anasazi Prods., 1993
GETTING GOTTI (TF) Kushner-Locke, 1994
THE CORPSE HAD A FAMILIAR FACE (TF) Von
   Zerneck-Sertner/Touchstone TV, 1994
THE TWILIGHT ZONE: ROD SERLIN'S LOST CLASSICS (TF)
   O'Hara-Horowitz Prods., 1994
THE GIFT OF LOVE (TF) Marian Rees Associates/Family Prods.,
   1994
TAKE ME HOME AGAIN (TF) Von Zerneck-Sertner/Patricia K.
   Meyer Prods./ACI, 1994
BECAUSE MOMMY WORKS (TF) Newport-Balboa Prods./spring
   Creek Prods./Warner Bros. TV, 1994
KINGFISH: A STORY OF HUEY P. LONG (CTF) Chris-Rose
   Prods., 1995
BETRAYED: A STORY OF THREE WOMEN (TF) Freyda
   Rothstein Prods./Hearst, 1995
TOM CLANCY'S OP CENTER OP CENTER (TF) MT3
   Services/New World, 1995
DEADLINE FOR MURDER: FROM THE FILES OF EDNA
   BUCHANAN (TF) Von Zerneck-Sertner/Touchstone TV, 1995
JOURNEY (TF) Hallmark Hall of Fame Prods., 1995
THE GRASS HARP Fine Line, 1996

PAUL WILLIAMS*

b. September 19, 1940 - Omaha, Nebraska
Contact: ASCAP - Los Angeles, 213-883-1000

PHANTOM OF THE PARADISE ★ co-composer with George
   Aliceson Tipton, 20th Century-Fox, 1974
BUGSY MALONE ★ Paramount, 1976, British
A STAR IS BORN co-composer, Warner Bros., 1976
FLIGHT TO HOLOCAUST (TF) Aycee Productions/First Artists
   Production Company, 1977
THE END United Artists, 1978
THE MUPPET MOVIE ★ co-composer with Kenny Ascher, AFD,
   1979

MALCOLM WILLIAMSON
b. 1931 - Mosmon Bay, Australia
Contact: PRS - London, England, 011-44-1-580-5544

THE BRIDES OF DRACULA   Universal, 1960, British
THE HORROR OF FRANKENSTEIN   Levitt-Pickman, 1970, British
CRESCENDO   Warner Bros., 1972, British
NOTHING BUT THE NIGHT   Cinema Systems, 1975, British
WATERSHIP DOWN (AF)   co-composer, Avco Embassy, 1978,
   British

HAL WILNER
THEREMIN: AN ELECTRONIC ODYSSEY (FD)   Kaga Bay, 1994

ANDREW WILSON
Contact: APRA - Australia, 011-61-2-922-6422

CHAIN REACTION   1980, Australian

NANCY WILSON
JERRY MAGUIRE   TriStar, 1996

SAM WINANS
Contact: BMI - Los Angeles, 310-659-9109

PARTY LINE   SVS Films, 1988
CALIFORNIA CASANOVA   co-composer with Reg Powell,
   Academy, 1993

CHRIS WINFIELD
FEELIN' SCREWY   Raedon Entertainment, 1991

DEBBIE WISEMAN
Contact: PRS - London, England, 011-44-1-580-5544

TOM & VIV   Miramax, 1994, British-U.S.
HAUNTED   October Films, 1995, British

JILL WISOFF
WELCOME TO THE DOLLHOUSE   Sony Classics, 1996

ALAIN WISNIAK
Contact: SACEM - France, 011-33-1-4715-4715

FEMME PUBLIQUE   1984, French

LESLIE WINSTON
Contact: BMI - Los Angeles, 310-659-9109

MASALA   Strand, 1993, Canadian

ERLING WOLD
Contact: BMI - Los Angeles, 310-659-9109

THE BED YOU SLEPT IN   Complex, 1993

PETER WOLF
Contact: ASCAP - Los Angeles, 213-883-1000

WEEKEND AT BERNIE'S II   Artimm, 1993
THE NEVERENDING STORY III   Warner Bros., 1994, German

LARRY WOLFF
Contact: BMI - Los Angeles, 310-659-9109

CAGED HEARTS   PM Entertainment, 1995

MICHAEL WOLFF
Contact: BMI - Los Angeles, 310-659-9109

WHO'S THE MAN   co-composer with Nicolas Tenbroek, New Line,
   1993

DAVID WOLINSKI
Contact: ASCAP - Los Angeles, 213-883-1000

SEASON OF FEAR   MGM/UA, 1989

HAWK WOLINSKI
WILDCATS   co-composer with James Newton Howard, Warner
   Bros., 1986

STEVIE WONDER
(Steveland Morris)
Contact: ASCAP - Los Angeles, 213-883-1000

THE SECRET LIFE OF PLANTS (FD)   Paramount, 1978

JAMES WONG
CHUNG ON TSOU *CRIME STORY*   1993, Hong Kong

ART WOOD
Contact: BMI - Los Angeles, 310-659-9109

IN THE HEAT OF PASSION   co-composer with Ken Rarick,
   Concorde, 1992

GUY WOOLFENDEN
Contact: PRS - London, England, 011-44-1-580-5544

SECRETS   Samuel Goldwyn Company, 1983, British
A DOLL'S HOUSE (TF)   BBC-TV, 1993, British

TOM WORRALL
Contact: ASCAP - Los Angeles, 213-883-1000

THE WILD WOMEN OF CHASTITY GULCH (TF)   co-composer with
   Frank De Vol, Aaron Spelling Productions, 1982

BERNIE WORRELL
Contact: ASCAP - Los Angeles, 213-883-1000

CAR 54, WHERE ARE YOU?   co-composer with Pray For Rain,
   Orion, 1994
COSMIC SLOP: SPACE TRADERS (CTF)   co-composer with John
   Barnes and George Clinton, Hudlin Bros. Prods./HBO, 1994

JODY TAYLOR WORTH
Contact: ASCAP - Los Angeles, 213-883-1000

UP THE ACADEMY   Warner Bros., 1980

LINK WRAY
Contact: KODA - Denmark, 011-45-31-68-38-00

JOHNNY SUEDE   additional music, Mainstream, 1991

CLIVE WRIGHT
Contact: BMI - Los Angeles, 310-659-9109

SOUTH TO RENO   co-composer with Nigel Holton, Open Road
   Productions/Pendulum Productions, 1987

GARY WRIGHT
Contact: ASCAP - Los Angeles, 213-466-7681

BENJAMIN   1973, West German
ENDANGERED SPECIES   MGM/UA, 1982

BILL WYMAN
Contact: PRS - London, England, 011-44-1-580-5544

GREEN ICE   ITC Films, 1981, British

DAN WYMAN
Contact: ASCAP - Los Angeles, 213-883-1000

WITHOUT WARNING   Filmways, 1980
THE RETURN   *THE ALIEN'S RETURN*   1981
HELL NIGHT   Compass International, 1981
THE LAWNMOWER MAN   New Line, 1992

STAVROS XARCHAKOS
b. Greece
Contact: AEPI - Athens, Greece, 011-30-1-821-9512

RED LANTERNS   1964, Greek
THE STONE   1965, Greek
THE HOT MONTH OF AUGUST   1966, Greek
SIGNS OF LIFE   1968, Greek
GIRLS IN THE SUN   1968, Greek
LYCISTRATA   1972, Greek
REBETICO   1983, Greek
SWEET COUNTRY   Cinema Group, 1987

CHEN XIANGYU
POSTMAN   *YOUCHAI*   1995, Chinese

QU XIAOSONG
BIAN ZHOUI BIAN CHANG   *LIFE ON A STRING*   Serene, 1991,
   German-British-Chinese

MOTOFUMI YAMAGUSHI
THE HUNTED   Universal, 1995

SHOJI YAMASHIRO
Contact: JASRAC - Tokyo, Japan, 011-81-3-502-6551

AKIRA (AF)   Streamline Pictures, 1990, Japanese

STOMU YAMASHITA
Contact: PRS - London, England, 011-44-1-580-5544

ONE BY ONE   *EAST WIND*   1974
ART OF KILLING   1978, Japanese
THE MAN WHO FELL TO EARTH   Cinema 5, 1976, British
THE TEMPEST   Columbia, 1982

YANNI
Contact: ASCAP - Los Angeles, 213-883-1000

HEART OF MIDNIGHT   Samuel Goldwyn Company, 1988
STEAL OF THE SKY (CTF)   Yorma Ben-Ami/Paramount, 1988
FRANK NITTI: THE ENFORCER (TF)   Leonard Hill Films, 1988

YOSHIKAZU YANO
ROUGH SKETCH OF A SPIRAL (FD)   co-composer with Jun
   Kamiyama, 1991, Japanese

GABRIEL YARED
Agent: Gorfaine-Schwartz - Los Angeles, 213-969-1011
Affiliation: SACEM - France, 011-33-1-4715-4715

MISS O'GYNIE AND THE FLOWER MAN   1974, Belgian
EVERY MAN FOR HIMSELF   *SAUVE QUI PEUT LA VIE*   New
   Yorker/Zoetrope, 1980, Swiss-French
MALEVIL   UGC, 1981, French-West German
INVITATION AU VOYAGE   Mel Difussion/Filmalpha, 1982,
   French-Italian
INTERDIT AUX MOINS DE 13 ANS   1982, French
THE MOON AND THE GUTTER   *LA LUNE DANS LE CANIVEAU*
   Triumph/Columbia, 1983, French-Italian
LUCIE SUR SEINE   Nicole Jouve Interama, 1983, French
HANNA K.   Universal Classics, 1983, French
LA JAVA DES OMBRES   *SHADOW DANCE*   1983, French
SARAH   UGC, 1983, French
AL HOUROB AL SAGHIRA   *LITTLE WARS   LES PETITES*
   GUERRES   1983, Lebanese
LA SCARLATINE   UGC, 1984, French
DANGEROUS MOVES   *LA DIAGONALE DU FOU*   Arthur Cohn
   Productions, 1984, Swiss
DREAM ONE   *NEMO*   NEF, 1984, British
TIR A VUE   1984, French
LE TELEPHONE SONNE TOUJOURS DEUX FOIS   1985, French
ADIEU, BONAPARTE   AMLF, 1985, French-Egyptian
SCOUT TOUJOURS   1985, French
ZONE ROUGE   *RED ZONE*   AAA/Revcom Films, 1986, French
FLAGRANT DESIR   *A CERTAIN DESIRE*   UGC, 1986, French
BETTY BLUE   *37.2 LE MATIN*   Alive Films, 1986, French
DESORDRE   Forum Distribution, 1986, French
L'EAU ET LES HOMMES (FD)   1986, French
BEYOND THERAPY   New World, 1987
AGENT TROUBLE   1987, French
GANDAHAR (AF)   1987, French
LE TESTAMENT D'UN POETE JUIF ASSASSINE   1988, French
LES SAISONS DU PLAISIR   1988, French
L'HOMME VOILE   1988, French
CLEAN AND SOBER   Warner Bros., 1988
UNE NUIT A L'ASSEMBLEE NATIONALE   1988, French
LA ROMANA   1988, Italian
CAMILLE CLAUDEL   Orion Classics, 1988, French
ROMERO   Four Seasons Entertainment, 1989
TENNESSEE NIGHTS   *TENNESSEE WALTZ*   Condor
   Prods./Allianz Films/Intermedia/WDR, 1989, Swiss-French
LES 1001 NUITS   1990, French-Italian
VINCENT & THEO   Hemdale, 1990, British-French
TATIE DANIELLE   Prestige, 1990, French
THE KING'S WHORE   *JEANNE, LA PUTAIN DU ROI*   J&M
   Entertainment, 1990, French-Italian-U.S.
THE LOVER   *L'AMANT*   MGM, 1992, French-British
I.P.5: L'ILE AUX PACHIDERMES   *I.P.5: THE ISLAND OF*
   PACHYDERMS   1992, French
L'ARCHE ET LES DELUGES   1992, French
LA FILLE DE L'AIR   1992, French
MAP OF THE HUMAN HEART   Miramax, 1992,
   British-Australian-French-Canadian
L'INSTINCT DE L'ANGE   1993, French
PROFIL BAS   1993, French
LES MARMOTTES   1993, French
DES FEUX MAL ETEINTS   1994, French
FORTITUDE (TF)   1994
THE ENGLISH PATIENT ★   Miramax, 1996
THE BICYCLE   August Entertainment, 1997

YAROL
U.S. GO HOME (TF)   1994, French

YELLO
THE ADVENTURES OF FORD FAIRLANE   20th Century-Fox,
   1990

DWIGHT YOAKAM
Contact: BMI - Los Angeles, 310-659-9109

CHASERS   co-composer with Pete Anderson, Warner Bros., 1994

CHRISTOPHER YOUNG*
Agent: The Kraft-Benjamin Agency - Beverly Hills, 310-247-0123
Affiliation: BMI - Los Angeles, 310-659-9109

THE DORM THAT DRIPPED BLOOD *DEATH DORM/PRANKS*
   New Image, 1982
ROBBIE   Award Films, 1982
THE POWER   Artists Releasing Corporation/Film Ventures
   International, 1983
SAVAGE HUNGER *OASIS* Shapiro Entertainment, 1984
HIGHPOINT   New World, 1984
WHEELS OF FIRE *DESERT WARRIOR* Concorde/New Horizons,
   1984, U.S.-Filipino
AVENGING ANGEL   New World, 1984
DEF-CON 4   New World, 1985, Canadian
WIZARDS OF THE LOST KINGDOM   Concorde/Cinema Group,
   1985, U.S.-Argentine
BARBARIAN QUEEN   Concorde/Cinema Group, 1985,
   U.S.-Argentine
NIGHTMARE ON ELM STREET, PART 2: FREDDY'S REVENGE
   New Line Cinema, 1985
GODZILLA 1985   additional music, New World, 1985
TORMENT   New World, 1986
GETTING EVEN   American Distribution Group, 1986
INVADERS FROM MARS   co-composer with David Storrs, Cannon,
   1986
TRICK OR TREAT   DEG, 1986
AMERICAN HARVEST (TF)   Ruth-Stratton Productions/The
   Finnegan Company, 1987
HELLRAISER   New World, 1987, British
FLOWERS IN THE ATTIC   New World, 1987
THE TELEPHONE   New World, 1987
BAT-21   Tri-Star, 1988
HAUNTED SUMMER   Cannon, 1988
HELLBOUND: HELLRAISER II   New World, 1988, British-U.S.
THE FLY II   20th Century Fox, 1989, U.S.-Canadian
HIDER IN THE HOUSE   Vestron, 1989
LAST FLIGHT OUT (TF) ☆   The Mannheim Co./Co-Star
   Entertainment/NBC Productions, 1990
MAX AND HELEN (CTF)   Turner Pictures, 1990
BRIGHT ANGEL   Hemdale, 1991
THE FIVE HEARTBEATS   additional music, 20th Century Fox,
   1991
THE VAGRANT   MGM/Pathe, 1992
THE DARK HALF   Orion, 1992
RAPID FIRE   20th Century Fox, 1992
JENNIFER EIGHT   Paramount, 1992
SLIVER   additional music, Paramount, 1993
DREAM LOVER   Gramercy, 1994
MURDER IN THE FIRST   Warner Bros., 1994
JUDICIAL CONSENT (CTF)   Rysher/Prelude, 1995
TALES FROM THE HOOD   Savoy, 1995
SPECIES   MGM-UA, 1995
VIRTUOSITY   Paramount, 1995
COPYCAT   Warner Bros., 1995
UNFORGETTABLE   MGM-UA, 1996
HEAD ABOVE WATER   Fine Line, 1996
NORMA JEAN AND MARILYN (CTF)   HBO, 1996
SET IT OFF   New Line, 1996
MURDER AT 1600   Warner Bros., 1997
THE FLOOD   Paramount, 1997
KILRONAN   TriStar, 1997
WATCH THAT MAN   Warner Bros., 1997

DANNY YOUNG
Contact: BMI - Los Angeles, 310-659-9109

RUSSIAN TERMINATOR   Kimmy Christensen and Finn Madsen,
   1991

NEIL YOUNG
b. November 12, 1945 - Toronto, Canada
Contact: ASCAP - Los Angeles, 213-883-1000

JOURNEY THROUGH THE PAST   1973
WHERE THE BUFFALO ROAM   Universal, 1980
HUMAN HIGHWAY   co-composer with Devo, Shakey Pictures,
   1982
DEAD MAN   Miramax, 1995

PATRICK YOUNG
Contact: ASCAP - Los Angeles, 213-883-1000

STEVIE   First Artists, 1978, British

RUSSELL YOUNG
Contact: ASCAP - Los Angeles, 213-883-1000

RUN OF THE HOUSE   Zoo, 1992

JOJI YUASA
Contact: JASRAC - Tokyo, Japan, 011-81-3-502-6551

MY CRASY LIFE   Allan/Marks, 1992

NORIO YUASA
b. Japan
Contact: JASRAC - Tokyo, Japan, 011-81-3-502-6551

ISLAND OF THE EVIL SPIRITS   Kadokawa/Toei, 1981, Japanese

LIU YUAN
CONSUMING SUN   Dali International, 1993, Chinese-U.S.

RICHARD YUEN
Contact: CASH - Kowloon, 011-852-3-722-5225

SWORDSMAN II   1992, Hong Kong
JIANG-HU   1993

JIMMY YUILL
A MIDWINTER'S TALE   Sony Classics, 1996

ATUHALPA YUPANQUI
Contact: SADAIC - Argentina, 011-54-1-40-4867/8

SCREAM OF STONE   co-composer with Ingram Marshall, Alan
   Lamb and Sarah Hopkins, Saxer/Lange/Sadler, 1991

WENDALL J. YUPONCE
BOYS LIFE   composer of one segment, Strand, 1995

Z

ALEKSEI ZALIVALOV
OKNO V PARIZH *WINDOW TO PARIS* co-composer with Yuri
   Miamin, Sony Classics, 1994, Russian-French

MARILYN S. ZALKAN
A.R.M. AROUND MOSCOW (FD)   Finley-Stoeltje, 1994

ALLAN ZAVOD
b. Australia
Contact: BMI - Los Angeles, 310-659-9109

DEATH OF A SOLDIER   Scotti Brothers, 1986, Australian
THE BIG HURT   Valhalla Films, 1986, Australian
THE RIGHT HAND MAN   FilmDallas, 1987, Australian
THE HOWLING III *THE MARSUPIALS: THE HOWLING III* Square
   Pictures, 1987, Australian
THE TIME GUARDIAN   Hemdale, 1987, Australian
SEBASTIAN AND THE SPARROW   Kino Films, 1988
COMMUNION   New Line Cinema, 1989
MARTIANS GO HOME   Taurus Entertainment Co., 1989
ART DECO DETECTIVE   Trident, 1994

PAUL J. ZAZA

Contact: SOCAN - Toronto, 416-445-8700

TITLE SHOT   1979, Canadian
MURDER BY DECREE   co-composer with Carl Zittrer, Avco
   Embassy, 1979, Canadian-British
PROM NIGHT   co-composer with Carl Zittrer, Avco Embassy,
   1980, Canadian
THE KIDNAPPING OF THE PRESIDENT   Crown International,
   1980, Canadian
GAS   Paramount, 1981
MY BLOODY VALENTINE   Paramount, 1981, Canadian
PORKY'S   co-composer with Carl Zittrer, 20th Century-Fox, 1981,
   U.S.-Canadian
MELANIE   Embassy, 1982, Canadian
CURTAINS   Jensen Farley Pictures, 1983, Canadian
A CHRISTMAS STORY   co-composer with Carl Zittrer, MGM/UA,
   1983, Canadian
TURK 182   20th Century Fox, 1985
BREAKING ALL THE RULES   New World, 1985, Canadian
ISAAC LITTLEFEATHERS   Lauron Productions, 1985, Canadian
THE VINDICATOR   *FRANKENSTEIN '88*   20th Century Fox, 1985,
   Canadian
BULLIES   Universal, 1986, Canadian
THE PINK CHIQUITAS   Shapiro Entertainment, 1986, Canadian
FROM THE HIP   DEG, 1987
MEATBALLS III   Movie Store, 1987
FORD: THE MAN AND THE MACHINE (TF)   Lantana
   Productions/Robert Halmi, Inc., 1987
LOOSE CANNONS   Tri-Star, 1990
POPCORN   Studio Three, 1991
TO CATCH A KILLER (TF)   Schrekinger-Kinberg Prods/Creative
   Entertainment Group/Tribune Entertainment, 1992
LIAR'S EDGE (CTF)   Showtime/New Line/Peter Simpson/Norstar,
   1992
ARTHUR MILLER'S THE AMERICAN CLOCK (TF)   Amblin
   Entertainment and Michael Brandman Prods., 1993
SPENSER: CEREMONY (CTF)   Norstar/Boardwalk/Ultra/ABC
   Video, 1993
SPENSES: PALE KINGS AND PRINCES (CTF)
   Norstar/Boardwalk/Ultra/ABC Video, 1994
COLD SWEAT (CTF)   Norstar Ent., 1994
DERBY (TF)   Atlantis/All American TV, 1995
A BROOKLYN STATE OF MIND   Norstar, 1996
THE EX (CTF)   American World Pictures/Cinepix, 1996,
   US-Canada
STAG   Cinepix, 1997

JOHN ZEANE
SMALL FACES   1996

DENNY ZEITLIN

Contact: BMI - Los Angeles, 310-659-9109

INVASION OF THE BODY SNATCHERS   United Artists, 1978

GUY ZERAFA

Contact: SOCAN - Toronto, 416-445-8700

THE DARK   co-composer with Alun Davies, Norstar, 1993
SHADOWBUILDER   Imperial, 1997

WEN ZHONGJIA
ZA ZUI ZI   *CHATTERBOX*   1993, Chinese

AL ZIMA

Contact: ASCAP - Los Angeles, 213-883-1000

SOUTH BRONX HEROES   Continental, 1985

HANS ZIMMER*

Agent: Gorfaine-Schwartz - Los Angeles, 213-969-1011
Affiliation: PRS - London, England, 011-44-1-580-5544/BMI - Los
   Angeles, 310-659-9109

MOONLIGHTING   co-composer with Stanley Myers, Universal
   Classics, 1982, British
HISTOIRE D'O No. 2   co-composer with Stanley Myers, 1983

SUCCESS IS THE BEST REVENGE   co-composer with Stanley
   Myers, Triumph/Columbia, 1984, British
EUREKA   co-composer with Stanley Myers, MGM/UA Classics,
   1984, British
BLIND DATE   co-composer with Stanley Myers, New Line Cinema,
   1984, British-Greek
INSIGNIFICANCE   co-composer with Stanley Myers, Island Alive,
   1985, British
THE LIGHTSHIP   co-composer with Stanley Myers, Castle Hill
   Productions, 1985, U.S.-West German
DREAMCHILD   co-composer with Stanley Myers, Universal, 1985,
   British
WILD HORSES (TF)   co-composer with Stanley Myers, Wild
   Horses Productions/Telepictures Productions, 1985
MY BEAUTIFUL LAUNDRETTE (TF)   co-composer with Stanley
   Myers, Orion Classics, 1985, British
CASTAWAY   co-composer with Stanley Myers, Cannon, 1986,
   British
THE ZERO BOYS   co-composer with Stanley Myers, Omega
   Pictures, 1986
THE WIND   co-composer with Stanley Myers, Omega Pictures,
   1987
DOUBLE EXPOSURE   co-composer with Stanley Myers, United
   Film Distribution Co., 1987
THE NATURE OF THE BEAST   co-composer with Stanley Myers,
   Rosso Productions, 1988, British
A WORLD APART   Atlantic Releasing Corporation, 1988, British
BURNING SECRET   Vestron, 1988, U.S.-British-West German
ELPHIDA   Working Title Films, 1988, British
WONDERLAND   *THE FRUIT MACHINE*   Vestron, 1988, British
PAPERHOUSE   Vestron, 1988, British
THE PRISONER OF RIO   Multi Media AG/Samba Corporation,
   1988, Swiss
VARDO   Working Title Films, 1988, British
RAIN MAN ★   MGM/UA, 1988
TWISTER   Vestron, 1989, British
S.P.O.O.K.S.   Vestron, 1989
DIAMOND SKULLS   Film Four International/British Screen/Working
   Title, 1989, British
BLACK RAIN   Paramount, 1989
DRIVING MISS DAISY   Warner Bros., 1989
FOOLS OF FORTUNE   New Line Cinema, 1990, British
BIRD ON A WIRE   Universal, 1990
CHICAGO JOE AND THE SHOWGIRL   co-composer with Shirley
   Walker, 1990, British
DAYS OF THUNDER   Paramount, 1990
PACIFIC HEIGHTS   20th Century-Fox, 1990
GREEN CARD   Buena Vista, 1990
BACKDRAFT   Universal, 1991
THELMA AND LOUISE   Pathe, 1991
REGARDING HENRY   Paramount, 1991
K2   Worldwide version only British, 1992
MILLENIUM (MS)   Biniman Prods./Adrian Malone
   Prods./KCET/BBC, 1992
A LEAGUE OF THEIR OWN   Columbia, 1992
THE POWER OF ONE   Warner Bros., 1992
RADIO FLYER   Columbia, 1992
WHERE SLEEPING DOGS LIE   co-composer with Mark Mancina,
   August Entertainment, 1992
SNIPER   additional music, TriStar, 1993
YOUNGER & YOUNGER   co-composer with Bob Telson, Vine,
   1993
POINT OF NO RETURN   Warner Bros., 1993
LIFEPOD (TF)   theme only co-composed with Marc Mancina,
   RHI/Trilogy, 1993
TRUE ROMANCE   Warner Bros., 1993
CALENDAR GIRL   Columbia, 1993
COOL RUNNING   Buena Vista, 1993
THE HOUSE OF THE SPIRITS   Miramax, 1993,
   German-Danish-Portuguese-U.S.
I'LL DO ANYTHING   Columbia, 1994
RENAISSANCE MAN   Buena Vista, 1994
THE LION KING (AF) ★★   Buena Vista, 1994
DROP ZONE   Paramount, 1994
CRIMSON TIDE   Buena Vista, 1995
BEYOND RANGOON   Columbia, 1995
NINE MONTHS   20th Century Fox, 1995
SOMETHING TO TALK ABOUT   co-composer with Graham
   Preskett, Warner Bros., 1995
TWO DEATHS   BBC Films, 1995
BROKEN ARROW   20th Century Fox, 1996
MUPPET TREASURE ISLAND   Buena Vista, 1996

THE ROCK   co-composer with Nick Glennie-Smith and Harry
   Gregson-Williams, Buena Vista, 1996
THE FAN   TriStar, 1996
THE WHOLE WIDE WORLD   1996
THE PREACHER'S WIFE ★   Buena Vista, 1996
SMILLA'S SENSE OF SNOW   20th Century Fox, 1997
THE PEACEMAKER   DreamWorks SKG, 1997

DON ZIMMERS

Contact: BMI - Los Angeles, 310-659-9109

SCREAMS OF A WINTER NIGHT   Dimension Pictures, 1979

CARL ZITTRER

Contact: SOCAN - Toronto, 416-445-8700

CHILDREN SHOULDN'T PLAY WITH DEAD THINGS   Gemini Film,
   1972, Canadian
BLOOD ORGY OF THE SHE DEVILS   Gemini Films, 1973
DERANGED   American International, 1974
DEATH DREAM   *DEAD OF NIGHT/THE NIGHT ANDY CAME
   HOME*   Europix International, 1974, Canadian
BLACK CHRISTMAS   *SILENT NIGHT, EVIL NIGHT/STRANGER IN
   THE HOUSE*   Warner Bros., 1975, Canadian
MURDER BY DECREE   co-composer with Paul Zaza, Avco
   Embassy, 1979, Canadian-British
PROM NIGHT   co-composer wih Paul Zaza, Avco Embassy, 1980,
   Canadian
PORKY'S   co-composer with Paul Zaza, 20th Century-Fox, 1981,
   U.S.-Canadian
PORKY'S II: THE NEXT DAY   20th Century-Fox, 1983,
   U.S.-Canadian
A CHRISTMAS STORY   co-composer with Paul Zaza, MGM/UA,
   1983, Canadian

JOHN ZORN

Contact: BMI - Los Angeles, 310-659-9109

THIEVES QUARTET   Headline Entertainment, 1994

★ ★ ★

NOTABLE COMPOSERS
OF THE PAST

IN MEMORIAM

LES BAXTER

MICHAEL CRUZ

WILLIE DIXON

MILES GOODMAN

MANOS HADJIDAKIS

IRWIN KOSTAL

MICHAEL J. LINN

HENRY MANCINI

RICHARD MARKOWITZ

BRIAN MAY

DAVID MUNROW

MARTY PAICH

CHRISTOPHER PALMER

SHORTY ROGERS

MILTON ROSEN

MIKLOS ROZSA

HANS J . SALTER

JULE STYNE

TORU TAKEMITSU

INDEX OF NOTABLE FILM COMPOSERS

Note: This index is a *name-only* reference when searching for a Notable Film Composer's name from the Notable Listing Section of this directory. Credits follow in the Notable Listing Section.

A

Richard Addinsell
Jeff Alexander
Vic tor Allix
William Alwyn
Daniele Amfitheatrof
George Antheil
Georges Auric
William Axt

B

Mischa Bakaleinikoff
R. H. Bassett
Hubert Bath
Sir Arnold Bax
Les Baxter
Giuseppe Becce
Arthur Benjamin
Robert Russell Bennett
Lord Berners
   (Gerald Hugh Tyrwhitt-Wilson)
Leonard Bernstein
Sir Arthur Bliss
Marc Blitzstein
Joseph Carl Breil
Benjamin Britten
Nicholas Brodzsky
David Broekman
Roy Budd
David Buttolph

C

John Cage
Pete Carpenter
Mario Castelnuovo - Tedesco
Frances Chagrin
   Alexander Paucker
Charles Chaplin
Frank Churchill
Alessandro Cicognini
Anthony Collins

Ray Cook
Aaron Copland
Carmine Coppola
Frank Cordell
Sir Noel Coward
Michael Cruz
Sidney Cutner

D

Miles Davis
Georges Delerue
Paul Dessau
Adolph Deutsch
Willie Dixon
Robert Emmett Dolan
Carmen Dragon

E

Hanns Eisler
Carli D. Elinor
Duke Ellington
   (Edward Kennedy)
Don Ellis
Lehman Engel
Leo Erdody
Hans Erdmann

F

Jerry Fielding
Benjamin Frankel
Hugo Friedhofer

G

Serge Gainsbourg
Georges Garvarentz
Paul Giovanni
Jackie Gleason
Mort Glickman

Lud Gluskin
Walter Goehr
Miles Goodman
Ron Grainer
Percy Grainger
Allan Gray
Barry Gray
John Green
John Greenwood
Ferde Grofe
   (Ferdinand Rudolf Von Grofe)
Louis Gruenberg

H

Manos Hadjidakis
Richard Hageman
Karl Hajos
Leigh Harline
W. Franke Harling
Roy Harris
T. Marvin Hatley
Fumio Hayasaka
Charles Henderson
Victor Herbert
Bernard Herrmann
Werner R. Heymann
Paul Hindemith
Gustav Hinrichs
Frederick Hollander
   (Friedrich Hollander)
Arthur Honegger
Gottfried Huppertz

I

Jacques Ibert
John Ireland

J

Paul Jabara
Gordon Jenkins

K

Dmitri Kabalevsky
Bronislau Kaper
Elliot Kaplan
Anton Karas
Bernhard Kaun
Aram Khachaturian
Christopher Komeda
   (Krzysztof T. Komeda)
Erich Wolfgang Korngold
Joseph Kosma
Irwin Kostal
Sigmund Krumgold
Gail Kubik

L

William Lava
Angelo Francesco Lavagnino
John Leipold
Oscar Levant
Louis Levy
Michael J. Linn
William Loose
Leighton Lucas
Elisabeth Luytens

M

Michel Magne
Henry Mancini
Richard Markowitz
Brian May
Doug Maynard
Edmund Meisel
Michel Michelet
Darius Milhaud
Cyril J. Mockridge
Thelonious Monk
Lucien Moraweck
Jerome Moross

N
O
T
A
B
L
E

C
O
M
P
O
S
E
R
S

O
F

T
H
E

P
A
S
T

David Munrow
Lyn Murray
(Lionel Breeze)
Stanley Myers

N

Oliver Nelson
Alfred Newman
Emil Newman
Lionel Newman
Alex North

P

Marty Paich
(Martin Louis Paich)
Christopher Palmer
Clifton Parker
Lothar Perl
Edward Plumb
Charles Previn
Sergei Prokofiev

R

Joe Raposo
Karol Rathaus
Alan Rawsthorne
Satyajit Ray
Franz Reizenstein
Nelson Riddle
Richard Rodgers
Milan Roder
Heinz Roemheld
Eric Rogers
Shorty Rogers
Sigmund Romberg
David Rose
Milton Rosen
Nino Rota
Miklos Rozsa

S

Camille Saint-Saens
Philip Sainton
Conrad Salinger
Hans J. Salter
Paul Sawtell
Victor Schertzinger
Walter Schumann
Humphrey Searle
Andrea Setaro
Nathaniel Shilkret

Dmitri Shostakovitch
Leo Shuken
Elie Siegmeister
Louis Silvers
Frank Skinner
Paul J. Smith
Mischa Spoliansky
Ronald Stein
Max Steiner
Leith Stevens
Morton Stevens
William Grant Still
Herbert Stothart
Jule Styne
Jules Stein
Harry Sukman

T

Toru Takemitsu
Alexandre Tansman
Deems Taylor
Virgil Thomson
Doug Timm
Dimitri Tiomkin
Ernst Toch

V

Nathan Van Cleave
Rogier Van Otterloo
Georges Van Parys
Clifford Vaughan
Ralph Vaughan Williams
Heitor Villa-Lobos

W

Oliver Wallace
Sir William Walton
Edward Ward
Franz Waxman
Roy Webb
Kurt Weill
Jean Wiener
Meredith Willson
Mortimer Wilson

Y

Victor Young

Z

John S. Zamecnik
Frank Zappa
Wolfgang Zeller

A

RICHARD ADDINSELL
b. January 13, 1904 - London, England
d. November 15, 1977 - Chelsea, England

AMATEUR GENTLEMAN   co-composer
    with Walter Goehr, United Artists, 1936,
    British
DARK JOURNEY   1937, British
FAREWELL AGAIN   1937, British
FIRE OVER ENGLAND   1937, British
THE BEACHCOMBER   *VESSEL OF
    WRATH*   1937, British
SOUTH RIDING   1938, British
GOODBYE MR. CHIPS   MGM, 1939
THE LION HAS WINGS   United Artists,
    1939, British
GASLIGHT   *ANGEL STREET*   1939,
    British
BRITAIN AT BAY   1940, British
CONTRABAND   *BLACKOUT*
    Anglo-American, 1940, British
THIS ENGLAND   1940, British
CAMOUFLAGE   1940, British
SPECIAL DISPATCH   1940, British
MEN OF THE LIGHTSHIP   1940, British
THE GREEN BELT   1941, British
LOVE ON THE DOLE   1941, British
SUICIDE SQUADRON   *DANGEROUS
    MOONLIGHT*   RKO Radio, 1941,
    British
THE BIG BLOCKADE   1942, British
THE SIEGE OF TOBRUK   1942, British
THE DAY WILL DAWN   1942, British
THE AVENGERS   1942, British
WE SAIL AT MIDNIGHT   1943, British
A.T.S.   1943, British
THE NEW LOT   1943, British
BLITHE SPIRIT   United Artists, 1945,
    British
A DIARY FOR TIMOTHY   1945, British
ONE WOMAN'S STORY   *THE
    PASSIONATE FRIENDS*   Universal,
    1949, British
UNDER CAPRICORN   Warner Bros.,
    1949, British-U.S.
THE BLACK ROSE   20th Century-Fox,
    1950, British-U.S.
RING AROUND THE MOON   1950, British
TOM BROWN'S SCHOOLDAYS   United
    Artists, 1951, British
A CHRISTMAS CAROL   *SCROOGE*
    United Artists, 1951, British
HIGHLY DANGEROUS   Lippert, 1951,
    British
ENCORE   1952, British
SEA DEVILS   RKO Radio, 1953
BEAU BRUMMEL   MGM, 1954
OUT OF THE CLOUDS   Rank, 1954,
    British
THE PRINCE AND THE SHOWGIRL
    Warner Bros., 1957, U.S.-British
A TALE OF TWO CITIES   Rank, 1958,
    British
LOSS OF INNOCENCE   *THE
    GREENGAGE SUMMER*   Columbia,
    1961, British
MACBETH   British Lion, 1961, British
THE ROMAN SPRING OF MRS. STONE
    Warner Bros., 1961
WALTZ OF THE TOREADORS
    Continental, 1962, British

THE WAR LOVER   Columbia, 1962,
    British
LIFE AT THE TOP   Columbia, 1965,
    British

JEFF ALEXANDER
b. 1910 - Seattle, Washington
d. December 23, 1989 - Seattle, Washington

WESTWARD THE WOMEN   MGM, 1952
AFFAIRS OF DOBIE GILLIS   MGM, 1953
ESCAPE FROM FORT BRAVO   MGM,
    1953
REMAINS TO BE SEEN   MGM, 1953
PRISONER OF WAR   MGM, 1954
ROGUE COP   MGM, 1954
THE TENDER TRAP   MGM, 1955
THE GREAT AMERICAN PASTIME   MGM,
    1956
RANSOM   MGM, 1956
SLANDER   MGM, 1956
THESE WILDER YEARS   MGM, 1956
GUN GLORY   MGM, 1957
JAILHOUSE ROCK   MGM, 1957
THE WINGS OF EAGLES   MGM, 1957
THE HIGH COST OF LOVING   MGM,
    1958
PARTY GIRL   MGM, 1958
THE SHEEPMAN   MGM, 1958
THE MATING GAME   MGM, 1959
ASK ANY GIRL   MGM, 1959
IT STARTED WITH A KISS   MGM, 1959
THE GAZEBO   MGM, 1959
ALL THE FINE YOUNG CANNIBALS
    MGM, 1960
THE GEORGE RAFT STORY   Allied
    Artists, 1961
KID GALAHAD   United Artists, 1962
THE ROUNDERS   MGM, 1965
DOUBLE TROUBLE   MGM, 1967
DAY OF THE EVIL GUN   MGM, 1968
SPEEDWAY   MGM, 1968
SUPPORT YOUR LOCAL SHERIFF!
    MGM, 1969
DIRTY DINGUS MAGEE   MGM, 1970
THE DAUGHTERS OF JOSHUA CABE
    (TF)   Spelling-Goldberg Productions,
    1972
THE SEX SYMBOL (TF)   The Douglas
    Cramer Company/Columbia Pictures TV,
    1974
THE DAUGHTERS OF JOSHUA CABE
    RETURN (TF)   Spelling-Goldberg
    Productions, 1975
THE NEW DAUGHTERS OF JOSHUA
    CABE (TF)   Spelling-Goldberg
    Productions, 1976
KATE BLISS AND THE TICKER TAPE KID
    (TF)   Aaron Spelling Productions, 1978
THE WILD WILD WEST REVISITED (TF)
    CBS Entertainment, 1979
MORE WILD WILD WEST (TF)   CBS
    Entertainment, 1980

VICTOR ALLIX
THE PASSION OF JOAN OF ARC   M.J.
    Gourland, 1928, French

WILLIAM ALWYN
b. November 7, 1905 - Northampton,
    England
d. September 12, 1985 - Southwold, England

THE REMARKABLE MR. KIPPS   *KIPPS*
    20th Century-Fox, 1941, British
THE YOUNG MR. PITT   20th Century-Fox,
    1942, British
DESERT VICTORY   1943, British
THE WAY AHEAD   *THE IMMORTAL
    BATTALION*   20th Century-Fox, 1944,
    British

NOTORIOUS GENTLEMAN   *THE RAKE'S
    PROGRESS*   1945, British
THE TRUE GLORY (FD)   Columbia, 1945,
    British
GREEN FOR DANGER   1946, British
ODD MAN OUT   General Film Distributors,
    1947, British
CAPTAIN BOYCOTT   1947, British
THE WINSLOW BOY   British Lion Film
    Corporation, 1947, British
THE OCTOBER MAN   Eagle Lion, 1947,
    British
TAKE MY LIFE   Eagle Lion, 1947, British
I SEE A DARK STRANGER   1947, British
THE FALLEN IDOL   Selznick Releasing,
    1948, British
SO EVIL MY LOVE   co-composer with
    Victor Young, Paramount, 1948
OPERATION DISASTER   *MORNING
    DEPARTURE*   Universal, 1950, British
MADELINE   Universal, 1950, British
THE ROCKING HORSE WINNER   1950,
    British
THE MUDLARK   20th Century-Fox, 1950
STATE SECRET   1950, British
THE GOLDEN SALAMANDER   Eagle Lion,
    1951, British
I'LL NEVER FORGET YOU   *THE HOUSE
    IN THE SQUARE*   20th Century-Fox,
    1951, British
THE MAGNET   1951, British
THE MAGIC BOX   Rank, 1951, British
THE CRIMSON PIRATE   Warner Bros.,
    1952, U.S.-British
NO RESTING PLACE   1952
THE PROMOTER   *THE CARD*   Universal,
    1952, British
CRASH OF SILENCE   *MANDY*   Universal,
    1952, British
THE MASTER OF BALLANTRAE   Warner
    Bros., 1953, British
THE MALTA STORY   Universal, 1953,
    British
MAN WITH A MILLION   *THE MILLION
    POUND NOTE*   United Artists, 1954,
    British
A PERSONAL AFFAIR   United Artists,
    1954, British
THE CONSTANT HUSBAND   1954, British
BEDEVILLED   MGM, 1955
LAND OF FURY   1955, British
SVENGALI   MGM, 1955, British
THE SHIP THAT DIED OF SHAME   *P.T.
    RAIDERS*   Continental, 1955, British
SAFARI   Columbia, 1956
ZARAK   Columbia, 1956, British
THE BLACK TENT   Rank, 1956, British
SEA WIFE   20th Century-Fox, 1957,
    British
THE SMALLEST SHOW ON EARTH
    Times Film Corporation, 1957, British
SMILEY   1957, Australian
STOWAWAY GIRL   *MANUELA*
    Paramount, 1957, British
CARVE HER NAME WITH PRIDE   Lopert,
    1958, British
I ACCUSE!   MGM, 1958, British
A NIGHT TO REMEMBER   Rank, 1958,
    British
SHE PLAYED WITH FIRE   Columbia,
    1958, British
THE SILENT ENEMY   Universal, 1958,
    British
SHAKE HANDS WITH THE DEVIL   United
    Artists, 1959, British
THIRD MAN ON THE MOUNTAIN   Buena
    Vista, 1959, U.S.-British
SWISS FAMILY ROBINSON   Buena Vista,
    1960
THE NAKED EDGE   United Artists, 1961

BURN WITCH BURN *NIGHT OF THE EAGLE* American International, 1962, British
IN SEARCH OF THE CASTAWAYS Buena Vista, 1962, British-U.S.
WALK IN THE SHADOW *LIFE FOR RUTH* Continental, 1962, British
THE RUNNING MAN Columbia, 1963, British

DANIELE AMFITHEATROF

b. 1901 - St. Petersburg, Russia
d. June 7, 1983 - Rome, Italy

LA SIGNORA DI TUTTI 1934, Italian
FAST AND FURIOUS MGM, 1939
THE MAN FROM DAKOTA co-composer with David Snell, MGM, 1940
AND ONE WAS BEAUTIFUL MGM, 1940
KEEPING COMPANY MGM, 1940
THE GET-AWAY MGM, 1941
JOE SMITH, AMERICAN MGM, 1942
CALLING DR. GILLESPIE MGM, 1942
DR. GILLESPIE'S NEW ASSISTANT MGM, 1942
ANDY HARDY'S DOUBLE LIFE MGM, 1942
NORTHWEST RANGERS co-composer with David Snell, MGM, 1943
A STRANGER IN TOWN co-composer with Nathaniel Shilkret, MGM, 1943
AERIAL GUNNER Paramount, 1943
HIGH EXPLOSIVE Paramount, 1943
HARRIGAN'S KID MGM, 1943
DR. GILLESPIE'S CRIMINAL CASE MGM, 1943
LASSIE COME HOME MGM, 1943
LOST ANGEL MGM, 1943
CRY HAVOC MGM, 1943
DAYS OF GLORY RKO Radio, 1944
I'LL BE SEEING YOU RKO Radio, 1944
GUEST WIFE ★ United Artists, 1945
MISS SUSIE SLAGLE'S Paramount, 1946
THE VIRGINIAN Paramount, 1946
SUSPENSE Monogram, 1946
O.S.S. Paramount, 1946
SONG OF THE SOUTH ★ co-composer with Paul Smith, RKO Radio, 1946
TEMPTATION Universal, 1946
THE BEGINNING OR THE END MGM, 1947
IVY Universal, 1947
SINGAPORE Universal, 1947
THE LOST MOMENT Universal, 1947
THE SENATOR WAS INDISCREET Universal, 1947
LETTER FROM AN UNKNOWN WOMAN Universal, 1948
ANOTHER PART OF THE FOREST Universal, 1948
ROGUE'S REGIMENT Universal, 1948
YOU GOTTA STAY HAPPY Universal, 1948
AN ACT OF MURDER Universal, 1948
THE FAN 20th Century-Fox, 1948
SAND 20th Century-Fox, 1949
HOUSE OF STRANGERS 20th Century-Fox, 1949
BACKFIRE Warner Bros., 1950
UNDER MY SKIN 20th Century-Fox, 1950
THE CAPTURE RKO Radio, 1950
THE DAMNED DON'T CRY Warner Bros., 1950
DEVIL'S DOORWAY MGM, 1950
COPPER CANYON Paramount, 1950
STORM WARNING Warner Bros., 1951
BIRD OF PARADISE 20th Century-Fox, 1951
THE PAINTED HILLS MGM, 1951
GOODBYE MY FANCY Warner Bros., 1951

ANGELS IN THE OUTFIELD MGM, 1951
TOMORROW IS ANOTHER DAY Warner Bros., 1951
THE DESERT FOX 20th Century-Fox, 1951
DEVIL'S CANYON RKO Radio, 1953
SALOME co-composer with George Duning, Columbia, 1953
THE BIG HEAT Columbia, 1953
SCANDAL AT SCOURIE MGM, 1953
DAY OF TRIUMPH 1954
HUMAN DESIRE Columbia, 1954
THE NAKED JUNGLE Paramount, 1954
TRIAL MGM, 1955
THE LAST HUNT MGM, 1956
THE MOUNTAIN Paramount, 1956
THE UNHOLY WIFE Universal, 1957
FRAULEIN 20th Century-Fox, 1958
FROM HELL TO TEXAS 20th Century-Fox, 1958
SPANISH AFFAIR Paramount, 1958, Spanish
EDGE OF ETERNITY Columbia, 1959
HELLER IN PINK TIGHTS Paramount, 1960
MAJOR DUNDEE Columbia, 1965

GEORGE ANTHEIL

b. June 8, 1900 - Trenton, New Jersey
d. 1959 - New York

BALLET MECHANIQUE 1924, French
ONCE IN A BLUE MOON Paramount, 1935
THE SCOUNDREL Paramount, 1935
THE PLAINSMAN Paramount, 1937
MAKE WAY FOR TOMORROW Paramount, 1937
THE BUCCANEER Paramount, 1938
ANGELS OVER BROADWAY Columbia, 1940
SPECTER OF THE ROSE Republic, 1946
PLAINSMAN AND THE LADY Republic, 1946
THAT BRENNAN GIRL Republic, 1946
REPEAT PERFORMANCE Eagle Lion, 1947
KNOCK ON ANY DOOR Columbia, 1949
WE WERE STRANGERS Columbia, 1949
THE FIGHTING KENTUCKIAN Republic, 1949
TOKYO JOE Columbia, 1949
HOUSE BY THE RIVER Republic, 1950
IN A LONELY PLACE Columbia, 1950
SIROCCO Columbia, 1951
THE SNIPER Columbia, 1952
ACTORS AND SIN United Artists, 1952
THE JUGGLER Columbia, 1953
DEMENTIA Parker, 1953
HUNTERS OF THE DEEP (FD) DCA, 1954
NOT AS A STRANGER United Artists, 1955
THE YOUNG DON'T CRY Columbia, 1957
THE PRIDE AND THE PASSION United Artists, 1957

GEORGES AURIC

b. February 15, 1899 - Lodeve, France
d. 1983

THE BLOOD OF A POET Brandon, 1930, French
A NOUS LA LIBERTE 1931, French
LAC AUX DAMES 1934, French
LES MYSTERES DE PARIS 1935, French
L'AFFAIRE LAFARGE 1936, French
SOUS LES YEUX D'OCCIDENT 1936, French
GRIBOUILLE *HEART OF PARIS* 1937, French

ORAGE 1937, French
ENTREE DES ARTISTES *THE CURTAIN RISES* 1938, French
L'ALIBI 1938, French
L'ENFER DU JEU 1939, French
L'ETERNEL RETOUR *THE ETERNAL RETURN* 1943, French
LE BOSSU 1944, French
LA BELLE AVENTURE *TWILIGHT* 1945, French
DEAD OF NIGHT Universal, 1945, British
CAESAR AND CLEOPATRA United Artists, 1945, British
LA PART DE L'OMBRE 1945, French
BEAUTY AND THE BEAST Lopert, 1946, French
RUY BLAS 1947, French
LES JEUX SONT FAITS *THE CHIPS ARE DOWN* 1947, French
HUE AND CRY Fine Arts, 1947, British
IT ALWAYS RAINS ON SUNDAY General Film Distributors, 1947, British
CORRIDOR OF MIRRORS Universal, 1948, British
L'AIGLE A DEUX TETES *EAGLE WITH TWO HEADS* 1948, French
ANOTHER SHORE 1948
BLIND DESIRE 1948
LES PARENTS TERRIBLES 1948, French
THE QUEEN OF SPADES 1948, British
LA SYMPHONIE PASTORALE 1948, French
AUX YEUX DU SOUVENIR 1949, French
PASSPORT TO PIMLICO 1949, British
THE SPIDER AND THE FLY General Film Distributors, 1949, British
ORPHEE *ORPHEUS* Discina International, 1950, French
MAYA 1950
LES AMANTS DE BRAS-MORT 1950, French
NEZ DE CUIR 1951, French
CAROLINE CHERIE 1951, French
THE LAVENDER HILL MOB Universal, 1951, British
THE GALLOPING MAJOR 1951, British
LA PUTAIN RESPECTUEUSE *THE RESPECTFUL PROSTITUTE* 1952, French
DAUGHTER OF THE SANDS 1952
MOULIN ROUGE United Artists, 1952, British
L'ESCLAVE 1953, French
ROMAN HOLIDAY Paramount, 1953
THE TITFIELD THUNDERBOLT Universal, 1953, British
LA FETE A HENRIETTE *HOLIDAY FOR HENRIETTE* 1953, French
THE WAGES OF FEAR DCA, 1953, French
RIFIFI Pathe, 1954, French
THE DIVIDED HEART Republic, 1954, British
THE GOOD DIE YOUNG United Artists, 1954, British
FATHER BROWN *THE DETECTIVE* Columbia, 1954, British
THE BESPOKE OVERCOAT 1955
FLESH AND DESIRE 1955, French
LOLA MONTES *THE SINS OF LOLA MONTES* Brandon, 1955, French-West German
ABDULLAH'S HAREM 20th Century-Fox, 1956, Egyptian
GERVAISE Continental, 1956, French
THE MYSTERY OF PICASSO (FD) Samuel Goldwyn Company, 1956, French
LES HUSSARDS 1956, French
THE HUNCHBACK OF NOTRE DAME *NOTRE DAME DE PARIS* RKO Radio, 1956, French

THE CRUCIBLE   1957, French-East
   German
HEAVEN KNOWS, MR. ALLISON   20th
   Century-Fox, 1957
THE STORY OF ESTHER COSTELLO
   Columbia, 1957
WALK INTO HELL   1957, Australian
DANGEROUS EXILE   Rank, 1957, British
LES ESPIONS   1957, French
THE NIGHT HEAVEN FELL   *LES
   BIJOUTIERS DU CLAIR DE LUNE*
   Kingsley International, 1957,
   French-Italian
LES AVENTURES DE TILL L'ESPIEGLE
   1957, French
BONJOUR TRISTESSE   Columbia, 1958
CELUI QUI DOIT MOURIR   *HE WHO MUST
   DIE*   1958, French
NEXT TO NO TIME!   1958, British
THE JOURNEY   MGM, 1959
S.O.S. PACIFIC   Universal, 1960, British
LE TESTAMENT D'ORPHEE   1960,
   French
BRIDGE TO THE SUN   MGM, 1961,
   U.S.-French
GOODBYE AGAIN   *AIMEZ-VOUS
   BRAHMS?*   United Artists, 1961,
   French-U.S.
THE INNOCENTS   20th Century-Fox,
   1961, British
LA RENDEZ-VOUS DE MINUIT   1962,
   French
LA CHAMBRE ARDENTE   *THE BURNING
   COURT*   1962, French
THE MIND BENDERS   American
   International, 1963, British
DON'T LOOK NOW...WE'RE BEING SHOT
   AT   *LA GRANDE VADROUILLE*
   Cinepix, 1966, French-British
THE POPPY IS ALSO A FLOWER   Comet,
   1966, European
THERESE AND ISABELLE   Audubon,
   1968, West German-U.S.
THE CHRISTMAS TREE   Continental,
   1969, French-Italian

WILLIAM AXT
b. 1882
d. February 13, 1959 - Ukiah, California

THE BIG PARADE   co-composer with
   David Mendoza, MGM, 1925
BEN-HUR   co-composer with David
   Mendoza, MGM, 1926
DON JUAN   co-composer with David
   Mendoza, MGM, 1926
THE FIRE BRIGADE   MGM, 1926
MARE NOSTRUM   MGM, 1926
THE SCARLET LETTER   MGM, 1926
ANNIE LAURIE   MGM, 1927
CAMILLE   MGM, 1927
SLIDE, KELLY SLIDE   MGM, 1927
WHITE SHADOWS OF THE SOUTH
   SEAS   co-composer with David
   Mendoza, MGM, 1928
OUR DANCING DAUGHTERS
   co-composer with David Mendoza, MGM,
   1928
THE TRAIL OF '98   co-composer with
   David Mendoza, MGM, 1929
THUNDER   MGM, 1929
THE SINGLE STANDARD   MGM, 1929
OUR MODERN MAIDENS   MGM, 1929
SPEEDWAY   MGM, 1929
THE KISS   MGM, 1929
POLLY OF THE CIRCUS   MGM, 1932
SEA SPIDERS   MGM, 1932
THE WET PARADE   MGM, 1932
WASHINGTON MASQUERADE   MGM,
   1932
SMILIN' THROUGH   MGM, 1932

THE SECRET OF MADAME BLANCHE
   MGM, 1933
GABRIEL OVER THE WHITE HOUSE
   MGM, 1933
REUNION IN VIENNA   MGM, 1933
MIDNIGHT MARY   MGM, 1933
STORM AT DAYBREAK   MGM, 1933
PENTHOUSE   MGM, 1933
BROADWAY TO HOLLYWOOD   MGM,
   1933
DINNER AT EIGHT   MGM, 1933
ESKIMO   MGM, 1933
YOU CAN'T BUY EVERYTHING   MGM,
   1934
THIS SIDE OF HEAVEN   MGM, 1934
LAZY RIVER   MGM, 1934
MEN IN WHITE   MGM, 1934
MANHATTAN MELODRAMA   MGM, 1934
SADIE McKEE   MGM, 1934
THE THIN MAN   MGM, 1934
OPERATOR 13   MGM, 1934
THE GIRL FROM MISSOURI   MGM, 1934
STRAIGHT IS THE WAY   MGM, 1934
HIDE-OUT   MGM, 1934
A WICKED WOMAN   MGM, 1934
FORSAKING ALL OTHERS   MGM, 1934
THE MURDER MAN   MGM, 1935
WOMAN WANTED   MGM, 1935
PURSUIT   MGM, 1935
O'SHAUGHNESSY'S BOY   MGM, 1935
IT'S IN THE AIR   MGM, 1935
RENDEZVOUS   MGM, 1935
THE PERFECT GENTLEMAN   MGM, 1935
DAVID COPPERFIELD   co-composer with
   Herbert Stothart, MGM, 1935
THE LAST OF THE PAGANS   MGM, 1935
WHIPSAW   MGM, 1935
THREE LIVE GHOSTS   MGM, 1936
TOUGH GUY   MGM, 1936
THE PERFECT SET-UP   MGM, 1936
THE GARDEN MURDER CASE   MGM,
   1936
THE THREE GODFATHERS   MGM, 1936
PETTICOAT FEVER   MGM, 1936
THE UNGUARDED HOUR   MGM, 1936
THREE WISE GUYS   MGM, 1936
WE WENT TO COLLEGE   MGM, 1936
SUZY   MGM, 1936
PICCADILLY JIM   MGM, 1936
OLD HUTCH   MGM, 1936
LIBELED LADY   MGM, 1936
ALL-AMERICAN CHUMP   MGM, 1936
MAD HOLIDAY   MGM, 1936
UNDER COVER OF NIGHT   MGM, 1937
THE LAST OF MRS. CHEYNEY   MGM,
   1937
ESPIONAGE   MGM, 1937
SONG OF THE CITY   MGM, 1937
PARNELL   MGM, 1937
BETWEEN TWO WOMEN   MGM, 1937
LONDON BY NIGHT   MGM, 1937
BIG CITY   MGM, 1937
THOROUGHBREDS DON'T CRY   MGM,
   1937
BEG, BORROW OR STEAL   MGM, 1937
BAD MAN OF BRIMSTONE   MGM, 1937
FRIEND INDEED   MGM, 1938
EVERYBODY SING   MGM, 1938
THE FIRST HUNDRED YEARS   MGM,
   1938
YELLOW JACK   MGM, 1938
WOMAN AGAINST WOMAN   MGM, 1938
FAST COMPANY   MGM, 1938
RICH MAN, POOR GIRL   MGM, 1938
THREE LOVES HAS NANCY   MGM, 1938
LISTEN, DARLING   MGM, 1938
SPRING MADNESS   MGM, 1938
PYGMALION   additional music for U.S.
   version, MGM, 1938, British
THE GIRL DOWNSTAIRS   MGM, 1939
STAND UP AND FIGHT   MGM, 1939
WITHIN THE LAW   MGM, 1939

SERGEANT MADDEN   MGM, 1939
THE KID FROM TEXAS   MGM, 1939
TELL NO TALES   MGM, 1939

B

MISCHA BAKALEINIKOFF
b. Russia
d. 1960

*(The following is an incomplete list of Mr.
Bakaleinikoff's credits.)*

CRY OF THE WEREWOLF   Columbia,
   1944
MY NAME IS JULIA ROSS   Columbia,
   1945
BLONDIE KNOWS BEST   Columbia, 1946
BARBARY PIRATE   Columbia, 1949
LAST OF THE BUCCANEERS   Columbia,
   1950
THE MAGIC CARPET   Columbia, 1951
SMUGGLER'S GOLD   Columbia, 1951
WHIRLWIND   Columbia, 1951
OKINAWA   Columbia, 1952
HANGMAN'S KNOT   Columbia, 1952
THE PATHFINDER   Columbia, 1952
VOODOO TIGER   Columbia, 1952
THE BIG HEAT   Columbia, 1953
THE 49TH MAN   Columbia, 1953
KILLER APE   Columbia, 1953
GUN FURY   Columbia, 1953
THE STRANGER WORE A GUN
   Columbia, 1953
MISSION OVER KOREA   Columbia, 1953
PRINCE OF PIRATES   Columbia, 1953
BAD FOR EACH OTHER   Columbia, 1954
THE BAMBOO PRISON   Columbia, 1954
BATTLE OF ROGUE RIVER   Columbia,
   1954
THE IRON GLOVE   Columbia, 1954
CELL 2455, DEATH ROW   Columbia, 1955
CREATURE WITH THE ATOM BRAIN
   Columbia, 1955
THE CROOKED WEB   Columbia, 1955
DEVIL GODDESS   Columbia, 1955
DUEL ON THE MISSISSIPPI   Columbia,
   1955
INSIDE DETROIT   Columbia, 1955
IT CAME FROM BENEATH THE SEA
   Columbia, 1955
EARTH VS. THE FLYING SAUCERS
   Columbia, 1956
THE FLYING FONTAINES   Columbia,
   1956
THE WEREWOLF   Columbia, 1956
SEVENTH CAVALRY   Columbia, 1956
THE 27TH DAY   Columbia, 1956
HELLCATS OF THE NAVY   Columbia,
   1957
NO TIME TO BE YOUNG   Columbia, 1957
THE PHANTOM STAGECOACH
   Columbia, 1957
THE TIJUANA STORY   Columbia, 1957
20 MILLION MILES TO EARTH   Columbia,
   1957
ZOMBIES OF MORA-TAU   Columbia,
   1957
THE CASE AGAINST BROOKLYN
   Columbia, 1958
CRASH LANDING   Columbia, 1958

HAVE ROCKET, WILL TRAVEL   Columbia, 1959
COMANCHE STATION   Columbia, 1960
THE ENEMY GENERAL   Columbia, 1960

R. H. BASSETT

WHAT PRICE GLORY?   Fox, 1926
SEVENTH HEAVEN   Fox, 1927
TRANSATLANTIC   Fox, 1931
SHERLOCK HOLMES   Fox, 1932
DANTE'S INFERNO   MGM, 1935
THE PRISONER OF SHARK ISLAND   20th Century-Fox, 1936
SINS OF MAN   20th Century-Fox, 1936

HUBERT BATH

b. England
d. April 24, 1945 - Middlesex, England

KITTY   British International, 1929, British
BLACKMAIL   British International Pictures, 1929, British
THE THIRTY-NINE STEPS   Gaumont-British, 1935, British
RHODES OF AFRICA   1936, British
NINE DAYS A QUEEN   TUDOR ROSE   Gaumont, 1936, British
SILENT BARRIERS   1937, British
A YANK AT OXFORD   MGM, 1938
MILLIONS LIKE US   1943, British
LOVE STORY   1944, British

SIR ARNOLD BAX

b. November 8, 1883 - Streatham, England
d. October 3, 1953 - Cork, Ireland

MALTA, G.C. (D)   1942, British
OLIVER TWIST   United Artists, 1948, British
JOURNEY INTO HISTORY (D)   British Transport Films, 1951, British

LES BAXTER

b. March 14, 1922 - Mexia, Texas
d. Jan. 15, 1996 - Newport Beach, CA

TANGA TIKA   1953
THE YELLOW TOMAHAWK   United Artists, 1954
THE KEY MAN   United Artists, 1955
WETBACKS   1955
THE BLACK SLEEP   United Artists, 1956
HOT BLOOD   Columbia, 1956
HOT CARS   United Artists, 1956
QUINCANNON, FRONTIER SCOUT   United Artists, 1956
REBEL IN TOWN   United Artists, 1956
A WOMAN'S DEVOTION   Republic, 1956
BOP GIRL   BOP GIRL GOES CALYPSO   United Artists, 1957
THE VICIOUS BREED   1957
VOODOO ISLAND   United Artists, 1957
PHARAOH'S CURSE   United Artists, 1957
HELL BOUND   United Artists, 1957
THE DALTON GIRLS   United Artists, 1957
THE INVISIBLE BOY   MGM, 1957
JUNGLE HEAT   United Artists, 1957
OUTLAW'S SON   United Artists, 1957
THE STORM RIDER   20th Century-Fox, 1957
TOMAHAWK TRAIL   United Artists, 1957
UNTAMED YOUTH   United Artists, 1957
WAR DRUMS   United Artists, 1957
REVOLT AT FORT LARAMIE   United Artists, 1957
THE GIRL IN BLACK STOCKINGS   United Artists, 1958
THE BRIDE AND THE BEAST   QUEEN OF THE GORILLAS   Allied Artists, 1958

ESCAPE FROM RED ROCK   20th Century-Fox, 1958
FORT BOWIE   United Artists, 1958
THE LONE RANGER AND THE LOST CITY OF GOLD   United Artists, 1958
MACABRE   Allied Artists, 1958
MONIKA   re-scoring of 1953 Ingmar Bergman film, 1959
GOLIATH AND THE BARBARIANS   composer of U.S. version only, American International, 1959
LA CIUDAD SAGRADA   1959, Mexican
GOLIATH AND THE DRAGON   composer of U.S. version only, American International, 1960
ALAKAZAM THE GREAT   composer of U.S. version only, American International, 1960
HOUSE OF USHER   FALL OF THE HOUSE OF USHER   American International, 1960
BLACK SUNDAY   composer of U.S. version only, American International, 1960, Italian
MASTER OF THE WORLD   American International, 1961
LISETTE   1961
GUNS OF THE BLACK WITCH   American International, 1961
THE PIT AND THE PENDULUM   American International, 1961
SAMSON AND THE 7 MIRACLES OF THE WORLD   composer of U.S. version only, American International, 1961
REPTILICUS   composer of U.S. version only, American International, 1961
ERIC THE CONQUEROR   GLI INVASORI/FURY OF THE VIKINGS   American International, 1961, Italian-French
MARCO POLO   American International, 1961, Italian-French
WARRIORS FIVE   American International, 1962, Italian
TALES OF TERROR   American International, 1962
DAUGHTER OF THE SUN GOD   American International, 1962
LOST BATTALION   American International, 1962, Filipino-U.S.
SAMSON AND THE SEVEN MIRACLES OF THE WORLD   American International, 1962
A HOUSE OF SAND   American International, 1962
GOLIATH AND THE VAMPIRES   VAMPIRES   composer of title music for U.S. release, American International, 1962
SAMSON AND THE SLAVE QUEEN   American International, 1962
WHITE SLAVE SHIP   American International, 1962, Italian
PANIC IN THE YEAR ZERO   American International, 1962
THE RAVEN   American International, 1963
EVIL EYE   LA RAGAZZA CHE SAPEVE TROPPO   American International, 1963, Italian
BEACH PARTY   American International, 1963
THE COMEDY OF TERRORS   American International, 1963
OPERATION BIKINI   American International, 1963
BATTLE BEYOND THE SUN   American International, 1963
"X" - THE MAN WITH X-RAY EYES   American International, 1963
THE YOUNG RACERS   American International, 1963

MUSCLE BEACH PARTY   American International, 1963
BLACK SABBATH   I TRE VOLTI DELLA PAURA   composer of U.S. version only, American International, 1963, U.S.-French-Italian
PAJAMA PARTY   American International, 1964
BEACH BLANKET BINGO   American International, 1965
A BOY TEN FEET TALL   Paramount, 1965
DR. GOLDFOOT AND THE BIKINI MACHINE   American International, 1965
HOW TO STUFF A WILD BIKINI   American International, 1965
SERGEANT DEADHEAD   SERGEANT DEADHEAD, THE ASTRONAUT   American International, 1965
DR. GOLDFOOT AND THE GIRL BOMBS   LE SPIE VENGONO DAL SEMIFREDDO   American International, 1966, U.S.-Italian
GHOST IN THE INVISIBLE BIKINI   American International, 1966
FIREBALL 500   American International, 1966
SADISMO   American International, 1967
TERROR IN THE JUNGLE   co-composer with Stan Hoffman, 1967
THE GLASS SPHINX   composer of U.S. version only, 1967, American International, Italian-Spanish
THE YOUNG REBEL   CERVANTES   American International, 1968, Italian-Spanish-French
THE MINI-SKIRT MOB   American International, 1968
THE YOUNG ANIMALS   American International, 1968
ALL THE LOVING COUPLES   U-M, 1968
BORA BORA   1968, French-Italian
TARGET: HARRY   HOW TO MAKE IT   ABC Pictures International, 1968
WILD IN THE STREETS   American International, 1968
FLAREUP   MGM, 1969
HELL'S BELLES   American International, 1969
THE DUNWICH HORROR   American International, 1970
EL OGRO   THE OGRE   1970
CRY OF THE BANSHEE   American International, 1970, British
THE BIG DOLL HOUSE   New World, 1971
FROGS   American International, 1972
THE DEVIL AND LEROY BASSETT   1972
BARON BLOOD   GLI ORRORI DEL CASTELLO DE NORIMBERGA   composer of U.S. version only, American International, 1972, Italian-West German
BLOOD SABBATH   YGALAH   1972
I ESCAPED FROM DEVIL'S ISLAND   United Artists, 1973
SAVAGE SISTERS   American International, 1974, U.S.-Filipino
SWITCHBLADE SISTERS   THE JEZEBELS/PLAYGIRL GANG   Centaur, 1975
BORN AGAIN   Avco Embassy, 1978
THE BEAST WITHIN   United Artists, 1982

GIUSEPPE BECCE

b. 1881 - Padua, Italy

DER MUDE TOD   DESTINY   1921, German
TARTUFFE   1926, German
DER GUNSTLING VON SCHONBRUNN   1929, German
DER SOHN DER WEISSEN BERGE   1930, German

DAS BLAUE LICHT   1932, German
DER REBELL   1932, German
EXTASE   1932, German
PEER GYNT   1933, German
HAN WESTMAR   1933, German
DER VERLORENE SOHN   1934, German
HUNDERT TAGE   1935, German
DER EWIGE TRAUM   1935, German
DER LAUFER VON MARATHON   1935, German
DER KAISER VON KALIFORNIEN   1936, German
CONDOTTIERI   1937, German
DER BERG RUFT   1937, German
MADAME BOVARY   1937, German
DU BIST MEIN GLUCK   1937, German
LIEBESBRIEFE AUS DEM ENGADIN   1938, German
FRAU IM STROM   1939, German
DER FEUERTEUFEL   1940, German
LA CENA DELLA BEFFE   1941, Italian
VIEL LARM UM NICHTS   1942, German
EIN ABENTEUER AM THUNERSEE   1942, German
TIEFLAND   1945, German
DAS SCHWEIGEN IM WALDE   1955, German
DER JAGER VON FALL   1957, German
DER SCHAFER VON TRUTKBERG   1958, German

ARTHUR BENJAMIN
b. 1893 - Sydney, Australia
d. 1960 - London, England

THE MAN WHO KNEW TOO MUCH   Gaumont-British, 1934, British
THE SCARLET PIMPERNEL   1934, British
THE TURN OF THE TIDE   1935, British
THE CLAIRVOYANT   1936, British
UNDER THE RED ROBE   20th Century-Fox, 1937, British
WINGS OF THE MORNING   1937, British
THE RETURN OF THE SCARLET PIMPERNEL   1938, British
THE CUMBERLAND STORY   1947, British
AN IDEAL HUSBAND   20th Century-Fox, 1947, British
STEPS OF THE BALLET   1948, British
THE CONQUEST OF EVEREST   1953, British
UNTERNEHMEN XARIFA   1954
ABOVE US THE WAVES   Republic, 1955, British
THE MAN WHO KNEW TOO MUCH   new main title and "Storm Clouds" cantata from 1934 version, Paramount, 1956
FIRE DOWN BELOW   Columbia, 1957
THE NAKED EARTH   20th Century-Fox, 1959

ROBERT RUSSELL BENNETT
b. 1894 - Kansas City
d. August 18, 1981 - New York

FUGITIVES FOR A NIGHT   RKO Radio, 1938
ANNABEL TAKES A TOUR   RKO Radio, 1938
PACIFIC LINER ★   RKO Radio, 1938
CAREER   RKO Radio, 1939
FIFTH AVENUE GIRL   RKO Radio, 1939

LORD BERNERS
(Gerald Hugh Tyrwhitt-Wilson)
b. 1883 - Shropshire, England
d. 1950 - Berks, England

HALFWAY HOUSE   Ealing, 1944, British
NICHOLAS NICKLEBY   1946, British

LEONARD BERNSTEIN
b. August 25, 1918 - Lawrence, Massachusetts

ON THE WATERFRONT ★   Columbia, 1954

SIR ARTHUR BLISS
b. 1891 - London, England
d. 1975 - London, England

THINGS TO COME   United Artists, 1936, British
CONQUEST OF THE AIR   1938, British
MEN OF TWO WORLDS   1946, British
CHRISTOPHER COLUMBUS   1949, British
WELCOME TO THE QUEEN (FD)   1954, British

MARC BLITZSTEIN
b. 1905 - Philadelphia, Pennsylvania
d. 1964 - Martinique, France

SURF AND SEAWEED   Ralph Steiner, 1931
CHESAPEAKE BAY RETRIEVER   Pedigreed Pictures, 1936
THE SPANISH EARTH   Contemporary Historians, 1937
VALLEY TOWN   Willard Van Dyke, 1940
NATIVE LAND   Frontier Films, 1942
NIGHT SHIFT   O.W.I., 1942

JOSEPH CARL BREIL
b. 1870 - Pittsburgh, Pennsylvania
d. January 24, 1926 - Los Angeles, California

QUEEN ELIZABETH   Paramount, 1912
CABIRIA   1913
THE PRISONER OF ZENDA   1913
THE BIRTH OF A NATION   Mutual, 1915
DOUBLE TROUBLE   1915
THE LILY AND THE ROSE   1915
THE MARTYRS OF THE ALAMO   1915
LOS PENITENTES   1915
INTOLERANCE   Triangle, 1916
THE WOOD NYMPH   1916
THE DRAMATIC LIFE OF ABRAHAM LINCOLN   1923
THE WHITE ROSE   United Artists, 1923
AMERICA   United Artists, 1924

BENJAMIN BRITTEN
b. November 22, 1913 - Lowestoft, England
d. December 4, 1976 - Aldeburgh, England

COAL FACE   1935, British
THE CALENDAR OF THE YEAR   1936, British
NIGHT MAIL   1936, British
THE SAVING OF BILL BLEWETT   1936, British
LINE TO THE TSCHIERVA HUT   1937, British
LOVE FROM A STRANGER   United Artists, 1937, British
THE TOCHER (FD)   1938, British
VILLAGE HARVEST (FD)   1938, British
INSTRUMENTS OF THE ORCHESTRA   1946, British

NICHOLAS BRODZSKY
b. 1905 - Odessa, Russia
d. December 25, 1958 - Hollywood, California

FRENCH WITHOUT TEARS   Paramount, 1940, British

A VOICE IN THE NIGHT   FREEDOM RADIO   Columbia, 1941, British
THE DEMI-PARADISE   ADVENTURE FOR TWO   General Film Distributors, 1943, British
THE WAY TO THE STARS   JOHNNY IN THE CLOUDS   United Artists, 1945, British
CARNIVAL   1946, British
BEWARE OF PITY   1946, British
WHILE THE SUN SHINES   Pathe, 1947, British
A MAN ABOUT THE HOUSE   1947, British
HER MAN GILBEY   1948, British
THE TOAST OF NEW ORLEANS   MGM, 1950
RICH, YOUNG AND PRETTY   MGM, 1951
THE STUDENT PRINCE   MGM, 1954
THE OPPOSITE SEX   MGM, 1956
LET'S BE HAPPY   Allied Artists, 1957, British

DAVID BROEKMAN
b. 1902 - Holland
d. April 1, 1958 - New York

MISSISSIPPI GAMBLER   Universal, 1929
TONIGHT AT TWELVE   Universal, 1929
THE PHANTOM OF THE OPERA   additional music for 1930 release, Universal, 1925
OUTSIDE THE LAW   Universal, 1930
ALL QUIET ON THE WESTERN FRONT   Universal, 1930
THE OLD DARK HOUSE   main title only, Universal, 1932
GIMME MY QUARTERBACK   Educational, 1934

ROY BUDD
d. August 7, 1993 - London

SOLDIER BLUE   Avco Embassy, 1970
FLIGHT OF THE DOVES   Columbia, 1971, British
ZEPPELIN   1971
GET CARTER   MGM, 1971, British
KIDNAPPED   American International, 1971, British
CATLOW   MGM, 1971, U.S.-Spanish
THE MAGNIFICENT SEVEN DEADLY SINS   1971, British
SOMETHING TO HIDE   SHATTERED   1972, British
EXTREMES (FD)   co-composer, 1972, British
THE CAREY TREATMENT   MGM, 1972
FEAR IS A KEY   Paramount, 1972, British
THE STONE KILLER   Columbia, 1973
THE DESTRUCTORS   THE MARSEILLES CONTRACT   American International, 1974, British-French
THE INTERNECINE PROJECT   Allied Artists, 1974, British
THE BLACK WINDMILL   Universal, 1974, British
DIAMONDS   Avco Embassy, 1975, U.S.-Israeli-Swiss
PAPER TIGER   Joseph E. Levine Presents, 1976, British
SINBAD AND THE EYE OF THE TIGER   Columbia, 1977, British
WELCOME TO BLOOD CITY   EMI, 1977, British
TOMORROW NEVER COMES   1977, British
FOXBAT   1978
THE WILD GEESE   Allied Artists, 1979, British
THE MISSING LINK   1980, French
MAMMA DRACULA   1980, French-Belgian

THE SEA WOLVES   Paramount, 1981,
 British
THE FINAL OPTION   *WHO DARES WINS*
 MGM/UA, 1982, British
WILD GEESE II   Universal, 1985, British
FIELD OF HONOR   Cannon, 1986,
 U.S.-Dutch
THE BIG BANG (AF)   20th Century Fox,
 1987, Belgian-French
THE PHANTOM OF THE OPERA   new
 score for the 1925 silent film, 1993

DAVID BUTTOLPH
b. August 3, 1902 - New York, New York

THIS IS THE LIFE   co-composer, 20th
 Century-Fox, 1935
NAVY WIFE   co-composer, 20th
 Century-Fox, 1935
SHOW THEM NO MERCY   co-composer,
 20th Century-Fox, 1935
EVERYBODY'S OLD MAN   co-composer,
 20th Century-Fox, 1936
LOVE IS NEWS   co-composer, 20th
 Century-Fox, 1937
NANCY STEELS IS MISSING
 co-composer, 20th Century-Fox, 1937
FIFTY ROADS TO TOWN   co-composer,
 20th Century-Fox, 1937
YOU CAN'T HAVE EVERYTHING
 co-composer, 20th Century-Fox, 1937
DANGER! LOVE AT WORK   co-composer,
 20th Century-Fox, 1937
SECOND HONEYMOON   20th
 Century-Fox, 1937
JOSETTE   co-composer, 20th
 Century-Fox, 1938
THE THREE MUSKETEERS   co-composer,
 20th Century-Fox, 1939
HUSBAND, WIFE AND FRIEND
 co-composer, 20th Century-Fox, 1939
THE GORILLA   co-composer, 20th
 Century-Fox, 1939
HOTEL FOR WOMEN   co-composer, 20th
 Century-Fox, 1939
BARRICADE   co-composer, 20th
 Century-Fox, 1939
STANLEY AND LIVINGSTONE
 co-composer, 20th Century-Fox, 1939
HOLLYWOOD CAVALCADE   20th
 Century-Fox, 1939
THE ADVENTURES OF SHERLOCK
 HOLMES   co-composer, 20th
 Century-Fox, 1939
BARRICADE   co-composer, 20th
 Century-Fox, 1939
HE MARRIED HIS WIFE   co-composer,
 20th Century-Fox, 1940
STAR DUST   co-composer, 20th
 Century-Fox, 1940
I WAS AN ADVENTURESS   co-composer,
 20th Century-Fox, 1940
FOUR SONS   co-composer, 20th
 Century-Fox, 1940
THE MAN I MARRIED   co-composer, 20th
 Century-Fox, 1940
THE RETURN OF FRANK JAMES
 co-composer, 20th Century-Fox, 1940
CHAD HANNA   20th Century-Fox, 1940
WESTERN UNION   co-composer, 20th
 Century-Fox, 1941
TOBACCO ROAD   co-composer, 20th
 Century-Fox, 1941
CONFIRM OR DENY   co-composer, 20th
 Century-Fox, 1941
SWAMP WATER   20th Century-Fox, 1941
BAHAMA PASSAGE   Paramount, 1941
LADY FOR A NIGHT   Republic, 1942
MY FAVORITE BLONDE   Paramount,
 1942
THIS GUN FOR HIRE   Paramount, 1942

MOONTIDE   co-composer with Cyril J.
 Mockridge, 20th Century-Fox, 1942
IN OLD CALIFORNIA   Republic, 1942
WAKE ISLAND   Paramount, 1942
MANILA CALLING   co-composer with Cyril
 J. Mockridge and David Raksin, 20th
 Century-Fox, 1942
THUNDER BIRDS   20th Century-Fox, 1942
STREET OF CHANCE   Paramount, 1942
THE IMMORTAL SERGEANT   20th
 Century-Fox, 1943
CRASH DIVE   20th Century-Fox, 1943
BOMBER'S MOON   20th Century-Fox,
 1943
CORVETTE K-225   Universal, 1943
GUADALCANAL DIARY   20th Century-Fox,
 1943
BUFFALO BILL   20th Century-Fox, 1944
THE HITLER GANG   Paramount, 1944
TILL WE MEET AGAIN   Paramount, 1944
IN THE MEANTIME, DARLING   20th
 Century-Fox, 1944
THE FIGHTING LADY (FD)   20th
 Century-Fox, 1944
CIRCUMSTANTIAL EVIDENCE   20th
 Century-Fox, 1945
THE BULLFIGHTERS   20th Century-Fox,
 1945
NOB HILL   20th Century-Fox, 1945
WITHIN THESE WALLS   20th Century-Fox,
 1945
JUNIOR MISS   20th Century-Fox, 1945
THE CARIBBEAN MYSTERY   20th
 Century-Fox, 1945
THE HOUSE ON 92ND STREET   20th
 Century-Fox, 1945
THE SPIDER   20th Century-Fox, 1945
SHOCK   20th Century-Fox, 1946
JOHNNY COMES FLYING HOME   20th
 Century-Fox, 1946
SOMEWHERE IN THE NIGHT   20th
 Century-Fox, 1946
STRANGE TRIANGLE   20th Century-Fox,
 1946
IT SHOULDN'T HAPPEN TO A DOG   20th
 Century-Fox, 1946
HOME SWEET HOMICIDE   20th
 Century-Fox, 1946
13 RUE MADELINE   20th Century-Fox,
 1947
BOOMERANG   20th Century-Fox, 1947
THE BRASHER DOUBLOON   20th
 Century-Fox, 1947
MOSS ROSE   20th Century-Fox, 1947
KISS OF DEATH   20th Century-Fox, 1947
THE FOXES OF HARROW   20th
 Century-Fox, 1947
BILL AND COO   Republic, 1947
TO THE VICTOR   Warner Bros., 1948
SMART GIRLS DON'T TALK   Warner
 Bros., 1948
JUNE BRIDE   Warner Bros., 1948
ONE SUNDAY AFTERNOON   Warner
 Bros., 1948
ROPE   Warner Bros., 1948
JOHN LOVES MARY   Warner Bros., 1949
COLORADO TERRITORY   Warner Bros.,
 1949
THE GIRL FROM JONES BEACH   Warner
 Bros., 1949
ONE LAST FLING   Warner Bros., 1949
ROSEANNA McCOY   RKO Radio, 1949
THE STORY OF SEABISCUIT   Warner
 Bros., 1949
MONTANA   Warner Bros., 1950
CHAIN LIGHTNING   Warner Bros., 1950
RETURN OF THE FRONTIERSMAN
 Warner Bros., 1950
PRETTY BABY   Warner Bros., 1950
THREE SECRETS   Warner Bros., 1950
THE DAUGHTER OF ROSIE O'GRADY
 Warner Bros., 1950

THE ENFORCER   Warner Bros., 1951
THE REDHEAD AND THE COWBOY
 Paramount, 1951
FIGHTING COAST GUARD   Republic,
 1951
ALONG THE GREAT DIVIDE   Warner
 Bros., 1951
FORT WORTH   Warner Bros., 1951
SUBMARINE COMMAND   Paramount,
 1951
TEN TALL MEN   Columbia, 1951
THE SELLOUT   MGM, 1951
LONE STAR   MGM, 1952
THIS WOMAN IS DANGEROUS   Warner
 Bros., 1952
TALK ABOUT A STRANGER   MGM, 1952
CARSON CITY   Warner Bros., 1952
THE WINNING TEAM   Warner Bros., 1952
MY MAN AND I   MGM, 1952
THE MAN BEHIND THE GUN   Warner
 Bros., 1953
HOUSE OF WAX   Warner Bros., 1953
SOUTH SEA WOMAN   Warner Bros., 1953
THUNDER OVER THE PLAINS   Warner
 Bros., 1953
THE SYSTEM   Warner Bros., 1953
THE BEAST FROM 20,000 FATHOMS
 Warner Bros., 1953
RIDING SHOTGUN   Warner Bros., 1954
THE CITY IS DARK   Warner Bros., 1954
THE BOUNTY HUNTER   Warner Bros.,
 1954
PHANTOM OF THE RUE MORGUE
 Warner Bros., 1954
SECRET OF THE INCAS   Warner Bros.,
 1954
I DIE A THOUSAND TIMES   Warner Bros.,
 1955
JUMP INTO HELL   Warner Bros., 1955
TARGET ZERO   Warner Bros., 1955
THE LONE RANGER   Warner Bros., 1956
A CRY IN THE NIGHT   Warner Bros., 1956
THE BURNING HILLS   Warner Bros., 1956
SANTIAGO   Warner Bros., 1956
THE STEEL JUNGLE   Warner Bros., 1956
THE BIG LAND   Warner Bros., 1957
THE D.I.   Warner Bros., 1957
THE DEEP SIX   Warner Bros., 1958
ONIONHEAD   Warner Bros., 1958
THE HORSE SOLDIERS   United Artists,
 1959
WESTBOUND   Warner Bros., 1959
GUNS OF THE TIMBERLAND   Warner
 Bros., 1960
PT-109   co-composer with William Lava,
 Warner Bros., 1963
THE MAN FROM GALVESTON   Warner
 Bros., 1964

C

JOHN CAGE
b. 1912 - Los Angeles, California
d. August, 1993

HORROR DREAM   Peterson
DREAMS THAT MONEY CAN BUY
 co-composer, Films International of
 America, 1948
WORKS OF CALDER   Herbert Matter,
 1950

PETE CARPENTER
d. October 18, 1987

TWO ON A BENCH (TF)   co-composer with
Mike Post, Universal TV, 1971
GIDGET GETS MARRIED (TF)
co-composer with Mike Post, Screen
Gems/Columbia Pictures TV, 1972
THE ROCKFORD FILES (TF)   co-composer
with Mike Post, Cherokee
Productions/Roy Huggins
Productions/Universal TV, 1974
THE MORNING AFTER (TF)   co-composer
with Mike Post, David L. Wolper
Productions, 1974
LOCUSTS (TF)   co-composer with Mike
Post, Carson Productions/Paramount
Pictures TV, 1974
THE INVASION OF JOHNSON COUNTY
(TF)   co-composer with Mike Post, Roy
Huggins Productions/Universal TV, 1976
SCOTT FREE (TF)   co-composer with Mike
Post, Cherokee Productions/Universal
TV, 1976
RICHIE BROCKELMAN: MISSING 24
HOURS (TF)   co-composer with Mike
Post, Universal TV, 1976
BAA BAA BLACK SHEEP (TF)
co-composer with Mike Post, Universal
TV, 1976
CHARLIE COBB: NICE NIGHT FOR A
HANGING (TF)   co-composer with Mike
Post, Fairmount/Foxcroft
Productions/Universal TV, 1977
DR. SCORPION (TF)   co-composer with
Mike Post, Stephen J. Cannell
Productions/Universal TV, 1978
RABBIT TEST   co-composer with Mike
Post, Avco Embassy, 1978
CAPTAIN AMERICA (TF)   co-composer
with Mike Post, Universal TV, 1979
THE NIGHT RIDER (TF)   co-composer with
Mike Post, Stephen J. Cannell
Productions/Universal TV, 1979
STONE (TF)   co-composer with Mike Post,
Stephen J. Cannell/Universal TV, 1979
CAPTAIN AMERICA II (TF)   co-composer
with Mike Post, Universal TV, 1979
TENSPEED AND BROWNSHOE (TF)
co-composer with Mike Post, Stephen J.
Cannell Prods., 1980
COACH OF THE YEAR (TF)   co-composer
with Mike Post, Shane Company
Productions/NBC Entertainment, 1980
WILL, G. GORDON LIDDY (TF)
co-composer with Mike Post, Shayne
Company Productions, 1982
HARD KNOX (TF)   co-composer with Mike
Post, Shane Company Productions,
1984
THE ROUSTERS (TF)   Stephen J. Cannell
Productions, 1983
NO MAN'S LAND (TF)   co-composer with
Mike Post, JADDA Productions/Warner
Bros. TV, 1984
RIPTIDE (TF)   co-composer with Mike Post,
Stephen J. Cannell Prods., 1984
HUNTER (TF)   co-composer with Mike
Post, Stephen J. Cannell, 1984
BROTHERS-IN-LAW (TF)   co-composer
with Mike Post, Stephen J. Cannell
Productions, 1985
STINGRAY (TF)   co-composer with Mike
Post, Stephen J. Cannell Productions,
1985
THE LAST PRECINCT (TF)   co-composer
with Mike Post, Stephen J. Cannell
Productions, 1986

MARIO CASTELNUOVO - TEDESCO
b. 1895 - Florence
d. 1968 - Los Angeles, California

THE RETURN OF THE VAMPIRE
Columbia, 1943
TWO-MAN SUBMARINE   Columbia, 1944
THE BLACK PARACHUTE   Columbia,
1944
SHE'S A SOLDIER, TOO   Columbia, 1944
I LOVE A MYSTERY   Columbia, 1945
THE CRIME DOCTOR'S COURAGE
Columbia, 1945
AND THEN THERE WAS NONE   20th
Century-Fox, 1945
PRISON SHIP   Columbia, 1945
THE PICTURE OF DORIAN GRAY
uncredited co-composer with Herbert
Stothart, MGM, 1945
NIGHT EDITOR   Columbia, 1946
DANGEROUS BUSINESS   Columbia,
1946
TIME OUT OF MIND   co-composer with
Miklos Rozsa, Universal, 1947
THE LOVES OF CARMEN   Columbia,
1948
MASK OF THE AVENGER   Columbia,
1951
THE BRIGAND   Columbia, 1952
THE LONG WAIT   United Artists, 1954

FRANCES CHAGRIN
Alexander Paucker
b. 1905 - Bucharest, Hungary
d. 1972 - London, England

LAST HOLIDAY   1950, British
AN INSPECTOR CALLS   Associated
Artists, 1954, British
THE MONSTER OF HIGHGATE PONDS
1966, British

CHARLES CHAPLIN
b. April 16, 1889 - Walworth, England
d. 1977 - Switzerland

SHOULDER ARMS   United Artists, 1918
THE KID   United Artists, 1921
THE PILGRIM   United Artists, 1923
THE GOLD RUSH   arranged by Carli D.
Elinor, United Artists, 1925
THE CIRCUS   United Artists, 1928
CITY LIGHTS   arranged by Arthur
Johnston, United Artists, 1931
MODERN TIMES   arranged by David
Raksin, United Artists, 1936
THE GREAT DICTATOR ★   arranged by
Meredith Willson, United Artists, 1940
MONSIEUR VERDOUX   arranged by
Rudolph Schrager, United Artists, 1947
LIMELIGHT ★★   arranged by Ray Rasch,
United Artists, 1952
A KING IN NEW YORK   Archway, 1957,
British
THE COUNTESS FROM HONG KONG
Universal, 1967, British

FRANK CHURCHILL
d. 1941

SNOW WHITE AND THE SEVEN DWARFS
(AF) ★   co-composer with Leigh Harline
and Paul Smith, RKO Radio, 1938
THE RELUCTANT DRAGON (AF)   RKO
Radio, 1941
DUMBO ★★   co-composer with Oliver
Wallace, RKO Radio, 1941
BAMBI ★   co-composer with Edward
Plumb, RKO Radio, 1942

ALESSANDRO CICOGNINI
b. January 25, 1906 - Pescara, Italy

NAPOLI D'ALTRI TEMPI   1937, Italian
ETTORE FIERAMOSCA   1938, Italian
NAPOLI CHE NON MUORE   1938, Italian
UN'AVVENTURA DI SALVATORE ROSA
1939, Italian
UNA ROMANTICA AVVENTURA   1940,
Italian
PRIMO AMORE   1941, Italian
LA CORONDA DI FERRO   1941, Italian
QUATTRO PASSI NELLE NUVOLE   1942,
Italian
DUE LETTERE ANONIME   1945, Italian
I MISERABILI   *LES MISERABLES*   1948,
Italian
THE BICYCLE THIEF   *LADRI DI
BICICLETTE*   Mayer-Burstyn, 1949,
Italian
PRIMA COMMUNIONE   1949, Italian
DOMANI E TROPPO TARDI   1950, Italian
THE THIEF OF VENICE   1950, Italian
MIRACLE IN MILAN   *MIRACOLO A
MILANO*   Joseph Burstyn, 1951, Italian
ALTRI TEMPI   1951, Italian
GUARDIE E LADRI   1951, Italian
THE LITTLE WORLD OF DON CAMILLO
Italian Films Export, 1951, French
UMBERTO D.   Harrison Pictures, 1952,
Italian
BUONGIORNO, ELEFANTE   1952, Italian
INDISCRETION OF AN AMERICAN WIFE
STAZIONE TERMINI   Columbia, 1953,
U.S.-Italian
THE RETURN OF DON CAMILLO   1953,
French-Italian
MOGLIE PER UNA NOTTE   1953, Italian
BREAD, LOVE AND DREAMS   *PANE,
AMORE E FANTASIA*   Italian Film
Export, 1953, Italian
ULISSE   *ULYSSES*   1954, Italian
FRISKY   *PANE, AMORE E GELOSIA*
DCA, 1954, Italian
GOLD OF NAPLES   *L'ORO DI NAPOLI*
DCA, 1955, Italian
SUMMERTIME   *SUMMER MADNESS*
United Artists, 1955, British
SCANDAL IN SORRENTO   *PANE, AMORE
E...*   DCA, 1955, Italian
THE ROOF   *IL TETTO*   Trans-Lux, 1956,
Italian
ANNA DE BROOKLYN   1958, Italian
VACANZE A ISCHIA   1958, Italian
THE BLACK ORCHID   Paramount, 1959
IL GIUDIZIO UNIVERSALE   1960, Italian
A BREATH OF SCANDAL   Paramount,
1960
IT STARTED IN NAPLES   Paramount,
1960
DON CAMILLO MONSIGNORE MA NON
TROPPO   1961
THE PIGEON THAT TOOK ROME
Paramount, 1962
IL COMPAGNO DON CAMILLO   Rizzoli
Film/Francoriz/Omnia Film, 1965,
Italian-West German

ANTHONY COLLINS
b. 1903 - Hastings, England
d. 1963 - Los Angeles, California

VICTORIA THE GREAT   RKO Radio, 1937
THE RAT   RKO Radio, 1938
SIXTY GLORIOUS YEARS   RKO Radio,
1938
A ROYAL DIVORCE   Paramount, 1938
NURSE EDITH CAVELL ★   RKO Radio,
1939
ALLEGHENY UPRISING   RKO Radio,
1939

CO

'97-'98
FILM
COMPOSERS
LISTING

N O T A B L E   C O M P O S E R S   O F   T H E   P A S T

213

SWISS FAMILY ROBINSON   RKO Radio, 1940
IRENE ★   adaptation, RKO Radio, 1940
TOM BROWN'S SCHOOLDAYS   RKO Radio, 1940
NO, NO, NANETTE   adaptation, RKO Radio, 1940
SUNNY ★   RKO Radio, 1941
UNEXPECTED UNCLE   RKO Radio, 1941
FOREVER AND A DAY   RKO Radio, 1943
THE DESTROYER   Columbia, 1943
A YANK IN LONDON   20th Century-Fox, 1946
PICCADILLY INCIDENT   Pathe, 1946, British
THE FABULOUS TEXAN   Republic, 1947
THE COURTNEY AFFAIR   *THE COURTNEYS OF CURZON STREET* British Lion, 1947, British
ODETTE   British Lion, 1950, British
THE LADY WITH THE LAMP   British Lion, 1951, British
MACAO   RKO Radio, 1952
TRENT'S LAST CASE   British Lion, 1952, British
THE ADVENTURES OF ROBINSON CRUSOE   United Artists, 1952, Mexican
LAUGHING ANNE   Republic, 1953, British

RAY COOK
b. 1937 - Australia
d. March 20, 1989 - London, England

CAREFUL HE MIGHT HEAR YOU   TLC Films/20th Century Fox, 1983, Australian

AARON COPLAND
b. November 14, 1900 - Brooklyn, N.Y.

THE CITY (D)   Civic Films, 1939
OF MICE AND MEN ★   United Artists, 1939
OUR TOWN ★   United Artists, 1940
THE NORTH STAR   *ARMORED ATTACK* ★   RKO Radio, 1943
THE CUMMINGTON STORY (D)   U.S. Government, 1945
THE RED PONY   Republic, 1949
THE HEIRESS ★★   Paramount, 1949
SOMETHING WILD   United Artists, 1961

(Note: "Love and Money" [Paramount, 1982] uses existing Copland music, utilized with input from the composer.)

CARMINE COPPOLA
d. April 1991- Los Angeles

TONIGHT FOR SURE   Premier Pictures, 1961
THE PEOPLE (TF)   Metromedia Productions/American Zoetrope, 1972
THE GODFATHER, PART II ★★   co-composer with Nino Rota, Paramount, 1974
THE LAST DAY (TF)   C Lyles Productions/Paramount Pictures TV, 1975
APOCALYPSE NOW   United Artists, 1979
THE BLACK STALLION   United Artists, 1979
NAPOLEON   composer of new score for 1927 silent film, Zoetrope, 1980
THE OUTSIDERS   Warner Bros., 1983
GARDENS OF STONE   Tri-Star, 1987
TUCKER   additional music, Paramount, 1988

NEW YORK STORIES   composer of "Life with Zoe" segment, also cameo as street flutist, Buena Vista, 1989
THE GODFATHER PART III   also cameo as conductor, Paramount, 1990

FRANK CORDELL
d. July 6, 1980 - Sussex, England

THE CAPTAIN'S TABLE   20th Century-Fox, 1960
FLIGHT FROM ASHIYA   United Artists, 1964
NEVER PUT IT IN WRITING   Allied Artists, 1964, British
KHARTOUM   United Artists, 1966, British
RING OF BRIGHT WATER   Cinerama Releasing Corporation, 1969, British
MOSQUITO SQUADRON   United Artists, 1970, British
CROMWELL★   Columbia, 1970, British
DIRTY KNIGHT'S WORK   *TRIAL BY COMBAT/A CHOICE OF WEAPONS* Gamma III, 1976, British
DEMON   *GOD TOLD ME TO*   New World, 1977

SIR NOEL COWARD
b. December 16, 1899 - Teddington, England
d. 1973 - Blue Harbor, Jamaica

IN WHICH WE SERVE   Universal, 1942, British
THE ASTONISHED HEART   GFD, 1950, British

MICHAEL CRUZ
d. May 31, 1994 - Los Angeles, California

BASIC TRAINING   The Movie Store, 1985

SIDNEY CUTNER
d. September 20, 1971 - Hollywood, California

HOLIDAY   Columbia, 1938
CITY STREETS   Columbia, 1938
THE LADY OBJECTS   Columbia, 1938
FLIGHT TO FAME   Columbia, 1938
HOMICIDE BUREAU   Columbia, 1939
MUSIC IN MY HEART   Columbia, 1940
THE LONE WOLF STRIKES   Columbia, 1940
THE LONE WOLF MEETS A LADY   Columbia, 1940
HIS GIRL FRIDAY   Columbia, 1940
THE LONE WOLF KEEPS A DATE   Columbia, 1940
THE FACE BEHIND THE MASK   Columbia, 1941
THE LONE WOLF TAKES A CHANCE   Columbia, 1941
TEXAS   Columbia, 1941
HOLD BACK TOMORROW   Universal, 1955
GUNSMOKE IN TUCSON   Allied Artists, 1958

D

MILES DAVIS
b. 1926 - Alton, Illinois
d. Sept 28, 1991

FRANTIC   *ASCENSEUR POUR L'ECHAFAUD* Times, 1957, French
STREET SMART   Cannon, 1987
SIESTA   co-composer with Marcus Miller, Lorimar, 1987, British

GEORGES DELERUE
b. March 12, 1925 - Roubaix, France
d. March 20, 1992 - Los Angeles, CA

LE CHAPEAU DE PAILLE D'ITALIE   new score for 1927 silent film, 1952, French
LES DEUX TIMIDES   new score for 1928 silent film, 1952, French
MARCHE FRANCAISE   1956, French
DES HOMMES...UNE DOCTRINE   1959, French
LE BEL AGE   co-composer with Alain Goraguer, 1959, French
HIROSHIMA, MON AMOUR   co-composer with Giovanni Fusco, Zenith, 1959, French
MERCI NATERCIA   1959, French
MARCHE OU CREVE   1959, French
THE BIG RISK   United Artists, 1960, French-Italian
UNE FILLE POUR L'ETE   1960, French
LES JEUX DE L'AMOUR   1960, French
LE VILLAGE AU MILIEU DES BRUMES   1960, French
PAR-DESSUS LE MUR   1960, French
LA MORTE SAISON DES AMOUR   1960, French
SHOOT THE PIANO PLAYER   *TIREZ SUR LE PIANISTE*   Astor, 1960, French
UNE AUSSI LONGUE ABSENCE   1960, French
LA FRANCAISE ET L'AMOUR   composer of "La Femme Seule" segment, 1960, French
ARRETEZ LES TAMBOURS   1960, French
LE RECREATION   *PLAYTIME*   1960, French
THE PASSION OF SLOW FIRE   *LA MORT DE BELLE*   Trans-Lux, 1961, French
THE JOKER   Lopert, 1961, French
THE FIVE DAY LOVER   Kingsley International, 1961, French- Italian
JULES AND JIM   Janus, 1961, French
EN PLEIN CIRAGE   1961, French
LE PETIT GARCON DE L'ASCENSEUR   1961, French
LE DENONCIATION   1961, French
UN COEUR GROS COMME CA (FD)   co-composer with Michel Legrand, 1961, French
RIFIFI IN TOKYO   MGM, 1961, French-Italian
L'AFFAIRE NINA B   1962, French-West German
CRIME DOES NOT PAY   Embassy, 1962, French-Italian
CARTOUCHE   Embassy, 1962, French-Italian
LE BONHEUR EST POUR DEMAIN   1962, French

L'ABOMINABLE GOMME DES DOUANES 1962, French
JUSQU'AU BOUT DU MONDE 1962, French
L'IMMORTELLE co-composer with Tashim Kavacioglu, 1962, French
LE MONTE-CHARGE 1962, French
LOVE AT TWENTY co-composer, Embassy, 1962, French-Italian-Japanese-Polish-West German
L'AINE DES FERCHAUX 1962, French
VACANCES PORTUGAISES 1963, French
MURIEL additional music, Lopert, 1963, French-Italian
L'HONORABLE STANISLAS, AGENT SECRET 1963, French
DES PISSENLITS PAR LA RACINE 1963, French
DU GRABUGE CHEZ LES VEUVES 1963, French
CHAIR DE POULE HIGHWAY PICKUP 1963, French-Italian
LE JOURNAL D'UN FOU 1963, French
NUNCA PASA NADA 1963, Spanish
HITLER...CONNAIS PAS 1963, French
L'AUTRE FEMME 1963, French
GREED IN THE SUN 1963
FRENCH DRESSING Warner-Pathe, 1963, British
CONTEMPT LE MEPRIS Embassy, 1964, French-Italian
THE SOFT SKIN Cinema 5, 1964, French
THAT MAN FROM RIO L'HOMME DE RIO Lopert, 1964, French-Italian
L'INSOUMIS 1964, French
LE GROS COUP 1964, French
L'AMOUR A LA CHAINE 1964, French
LUCKY JO 1964
THE PUMPKIN EATER Royal International, 1964, British
L'AGE INGRAT 1964, French
LOS PIANOS MECANICOS THE UNINHIBITED 1964, Spanish
MATA-HARI AGENT H21 1964, French
KILLER SPY 1965
LE BESTIAIRE D'AMOUR (FD) 1965, French
VIVA MARIA! United Artists, 1965, French-Italian
PLEINS FEUX SUR STANISLAS 1965, French
RAPTURE International Classics, 1965, British-French
MONA, L'ETOILE SANS NOM 1965, French
THE SUCKER Royal Films International, 1966, French-Italian
UN MONSIEUR DE COMPAGNIE MALE COMPANION International Classics, 1966, French-Italian
UP TO HIS EARS LES TRIBULATIONS D'UN CHINOIS EN CHINE Lopert, 1966, French-Italian
LOUIS DECOIN 1966, French
IT BEGAN IN BRIGHTON 1966, British
DERRIERE LA FENETRE 1966, French
UNE ALCHIMIE 1966, French
LE TEMPS REDONNE 1966, French
A MAN FOR ALL SEASONS Columbia, 1966, British
JEUDI ON CHANTERA COMME DIMANCHE 1966, French
MONSIEUR ROBERT HOUDIN (TF) 1966, French
LE DIMANCHE DE LA VIE 1967, French
THE KING OF HEARTS Lopert, 1967, French-Italian
THE 25TH HOUR MGM, 1967, French-Italian-Yugoslavian

OUR MOTHER'S HOUSE MGM, 1967, British
LES CRACKS 1967, French
LA PETITE VERTU 1967, French
LE SECRET DE WILHELM STORITZ (TF) 1967, French
UN COEUR QUI SE BRISE (TF) 1967, French
OSCAR co-composer with Jean Marion, 1968, French
THE TWO OF US LE VIEL HOMME ET L'ENFANT Cinema 5, 1968, French
INTERLUDE Columbia, 1968, British
THE HIGH COMMISSIONER NOBODY RUNS FOREVER Cinerama Releasing Corporation, 1968, British
THE DEVIL BY THE TAIL Lopert, 1969, French-Italian
THE BRAIN Paramount, 1969, French-Italian
LES GOMMES 1969, French
LE JEU DE LA PUCE 1969, French
HEUREUX QUI COMME ULYSSE 1969, French
HIBERNATUS 1969, French
A WALK WITH LOVE AND DEATH 20th Century-Fox, 1969, British
ANNE OF A THOUSAND DAYS ★ Universal, 1969, British
PROMISE AT DAWN Avco Embassy, 1970, French-U.S.
GIVE HER THE MOON LES CAPRICES DE MARIE United Artists, 1970, French-Italian
WOMEN IN LOVE United Artists, 1970, British
COUNTDOWN COMPTES A REBOURS 1970, French
YVETTE 1970, French
SULTAN A VENDRE (TF) 1970, French
UN OTAGE (TF) Also cameo as "Alfred," 1970, French
MIRA 1971, Dutch
THE CONFORMIST Paramount, 1971, Italian-French-West German
THE HORSEMEN Columbia, 1971
LES AVEUX LES PLUS DOUX MGM, 1971, French
L'INGENU 1971, French
MALPERTUIS: HISTOIRE D'UNE MAISON MAUDITE 1971, French
SOMEWHERE, SOMEONE QUELQUE PART, QUELQU'UN 1971, French
CHERE LOUISE Warner-Columbia, 1972, French-Italian
TWO ENGLISH GIRLS LES DEUX ANGLAISES ET LE CONTINENT also cameo as a businessman, Janus, 1972, French
SUCH A GORGEOUS KID LIKE ME Columbia, 1973, French
THE DAY OF THE JACKAL Universal, 1973, British-French
ANGELA LOVE COMES QUIETLY 1973, Dutch
DAY FOR NIGHT LA NUIT AMERICAINE Warner Bros., 1973, French-Italian
THE DAY OF THE DOLPHIN ★ Avco Embassy, 1973
LA FEMME DE JEAN JOHN'S WIFE 1973, French
DAN CANDY'S LAW ALIEN THUNDER 1973, Canadian
THE SLAP LA GIFLE 1974, French
PLUS AMER QUE LA MORT (TF) 1974, French
L'IMPORTANT C'EST D'AIMER 1974, French
OUBLIE-MOI MANDOLINE 1975, French
INCORRIGIBLE EDP, 1975, French
JAMAIS PLUS TOUJOURS 1975, French
MILADY (TF) 1975, French

COMME UN BOOMERANG 1976, French
LE GRAND ESCOGRIFFE 1976, French
LE JEU DU SOLITAIRE 1976, French
THE CASE AGAINST FERRO POLICE PYTHON 357 1976, French
FEMMES FATALES CALMOS New Line Cinema, 1976, French
JULIE-POT-DE-COLLE Prodis, 1977, French
JULIA ★ 20th Century-Fox, 1977
LE POINT DE MIRE Warner-Columbia, 1977, French
TENDRE POULET 1977, French
VA VOIR MAMAN...PAPA TRAVAILLE 1977, French
LA PETITE FILLE EN VELOURS BLEU 1977, French
LE NAUFRAGE DE MONTE CRISTO (TF) 1977, French
GET OUT YOUR HANDKERCHIEFS New Line Cinema, 1978, French
DEAR DETECTIVE 1978, French
LE CAVALEUR 1978, French
PIERROT MON AMI (TF) 1978, French
POURQUOI PATRICIA (TF) 1978, French
LES JEUDIS D'ADRIENNE (TF) 1978, French
LE MECREANT (TF) 1979, French
LUNDI (TF) 1979, French
LOVE ON THE RUN New World, 1979, French
A LITTLE ROMANCE ★★ Orion/Warner Bros., 1979, U.S.-French
AN ALMOST PERFECT AFFAIR Paramount, 1979
MIJN VRIENDE 1979, Dutch
LE CADRAN SOLAIRE (TF) 1979, French
SIMONE DE BEAUVOIR 1979, French
PREMIER VOYAGE 1979, French
MESSIEURS DE VOUOUS: LE CONCIERGE REVIENT DE SUITE (TF) 1980, French
LA FOLLE DE CHAILLOT (TF) 1980, French
THE LAST METRO United Artists Classics, 1980, French
RICHARD'S THINGS New World, 1981, British
RICH AND FAMOUS MGM/United Artists, 1981
LA PASSANTE 1981, French
GARDE A VUE UNDER SUSPICION 1981, French
BROKEN ENGLISH Lorimar, 1981
TRUE CONFESSIONS United Artists, 1981
THE WOMAN NEXT DOOR United Artists Classics, 1981
DOCUMENTEUR: AN EMOTION PICTURE (FD) Cine-Tamaris, 1981
LA VIE CONTINUE Triumph/Columbia, 1982, French
L'AFRICAIN Renn Productions, 1982, French
A LITTLE SEX Universal, 1982
PARTNERS Paramount, 1982
THE ESCAPE ARTIST Orion/Warner Bros., 1982
LIBERTY BELLE Gaumont, 1983, French
EXPOSED MGM/UA, 1983
MAN, WOMAN AND CHILD Paramount, 1983
THE BLACK STALLION RETURNS MGM/UA, 1983
CONFIDENTIALLY YOURS VIVEMENT DIMANCHE Spectrafilm, 1983, French
SILKWOOD 20th Century-Fox, 1983
L'ETE MEURTRIER ONE DEADLY SUMMER SNV, 1983, French
FEMMES DE PERSONNE 1983, French
LES MORFALOUS AAA, 1984, French
LE BON PLAISIR MK2, 1984, French

LOVE THY NEIGHBOR (TF)   Patricia
Nardo Productions/20th Century Fox TV,
1984
SILENCE OF THE HEART (TF)   David A.
Simons Productions/Tisch-Avnet
Productions, 1984
AURORA (TF)   Roger Gimbel
Productions/The Peregrine Producers
Group/Sacis, 1984, U.S.-Italian
AGNES OF GOD★   Columbia, 1985
ARCH OF TRIUMPH (TF)   Newland-Raynor
Productions/HTV, 1985, U.S.-British
THE EXECUTION (TF)   Newland-Raynor
Productions/Comworld Productions, 1985
AMOS (TF)   The Bryna Company/Vincent
Pictures, 1985
DEADLY INTENTIONS (TF)   Green-Epstein
Productions, 1985
STONE PILLOW (TF)   Schaefer-Karpf
Productions/Gaylord Productions, 1985
A TIME TO LIVE (TF)   Blue Andre
Productions/ITC Productions, 1985
MAXIE   Orion, 1985
CASANOVA   new score for silent film,
Cinema '89, 1985
SIN OF INNOCENCE (TF)   Renee Valente
Productions/Jeremac Productions/20th
Century Fox TV, 1986
CONSEIL DE FAMILLE   European
Classics, 1986, French
SALVADOR   Hemdale, 1986
LA DESCENTE AUX ENFERS   1986,
French
SWORD OF GIDEON (CTF)   Alliance
Entertainment/Les Films Ariane/HBO
Premiere Films/CTV/Telefilm
Canada/Rogers
Cablesystems/Radio-Canada, 1986,
Canadian-French
CRIMES OF THE HEART   DEG, 1986
PLATOON   Hemdale, 1986
WOMEN OF VALOR (TF)   Inter Planetary
Productions/Jeni Productions, 1986
MAID TO ORDER   New Century/Vista,
1987
THE PICK-UP ARTIST   20th Century-Fox,
1987
HER SECRET LIFE (TF)   Phoenix
Entertainment Group, 1987
THE LONELY PASSION OF JUDITH
HEARNE   Island Films, 1987, British
ESCAPE FROM SOBIBOR (TF)
Rule-Starger Productions/Zenith
Productions, 1987, U.S.-British
QUEENIE (MS)   von Zerneck-Samuels
Productions/Highgate Pictures, 1987
A MAN IN LOVE   Cinecom, 1987, French
CHOUANS   UGC, 1988, French
A SUMMER STORY   Atlantic Releasing
Corporation, 1988, British
THE HOUSE ON CARROLL STREET
Orion, 1988
BILOXI BLUES   Universal, 1988
MEMORIES OF ME   MGM/UA, 1988
TO KILL A PRIEST   Columbia, 1988,
U.S.-French
HEARTBREAK HOTEL   Buena Vista, 1988
TWINS   co-composer with Randy Edelman,
Universal, 1988
BEACHES   Buena Vista, 1988
PARIS BY NIGHT   Cineplex Odeon, 1988,
British
HER ALIBI   Warner Bros., 1989
STEEL MAGNOLIAS   Columbia/Tri-Star,
1989
THE FRENCH REVOLUTION   Films
Ariane/Films A2/Laura Films/Antea, 1989,
French
JOE VS. THE VOLCANO   Warner Bros.,
1990
SHOW OF FORCE   Paramount, 1990
CADENCE   New Line, 1990

THE JOSEPHINE BAKER STORY (CTF)
HBO Pictures/Anglia TV/John Kemeny/RH
Entertainment, 1991
WITHOUT WARNING: THE JAMES BRADY
STORY (CTF)   Enigma TV, 1991
BLACK ROBE   Samuel Goldwyn, 1991,
Canadian-Australian
CURLY SUE   Warner Bros., 1991
DIEN BIEN PHU   1992, French
MAN TROUBLE   20th Century Fox, 1992
MEMENTO MORI   1992, British
RICH IN LOVE   MGM, 1992

PAUL DESSAU

b. 1894 - Germany
d. June 28, 1979 - East Berlin, East Germany

HOUSE OF FRANKENSTEIN
co-composer, Universal, 1944
HOUSE OF DRACULA   co-composer,
Universal, 1945

ADOLPH DEUTSCH

b. October 20, 1897 - London, England
d. January 1, 1980

MR. DODD TAKES THE AIR   Warner Bros.,
1937
THEY WON'T FORGET   Warner Bros.,
1937
THE GREAT GARRICK   Warner Bros.,
1937
SUBMARINE D-1   Warner Bros., 1937
SWING YOUR LADY   Warner Bros., 1938
RACKET BUSTERS   Warner Bros., 1938
VALLEY OF THE GIANTS   co-composer
with Hugo Friedhofer, Warner Bros.,
1938
BROADWAY MUSKETEERS   Warner
Bros., 1938
FOUR'S A CROWD   Warner Bros., 1938
HEART OF THE NORTH   Warner Bros.,
1938
OFF THE RECORD   Warner Bros., 1939
THE KID FROM KOKOMO   Warner Bros.,
1939
INDIANAPOLIS SPEEDWAY   Warner
Bros., 1939
ANGELS WASH THEIR FACES   Warner
Bros., 1939
ESPIONAGE AGENT   Warner Bros., 1939
THE FIGHTING 69TH   Warner Bros., 1940
CASTLE ON THE HUDSON   Warner Bros.,
1940
THREE CHEERS FOR THE IRISH   Warner
Bros., 1940
SATURDAY'S CHILDREN   Warner Bros.,
1940
TORRID ZONE   Warner Bros., 1940
THEY DRIVE BY NIGHT   Warner Bros.,
1940
FLOWING GOLD   Warner Bros., 1940
TUGBOAT ANNIE SAILS AGAIN   Warner
Bros., 1940
EAST OF THE RIVER   Warner Bros., 1940
HIGH SIERRA   Warner Bros., 1941
THE GREAT MR. NOBODY   Warner Bros.,
1941
SINGAPORE WOMAN   Warner Bros.,
1941
UNDERGROUND   Warner Bros., 1941
KISSES FOR BREAKFAST   Warner Bros.,
1941
MANPOWER   Warner Bros., 1941
THE MALTESE FALCON   Warner Bros.,
1941
ALL THROUGH THE NIGHT   Warner Bros.,
1941
LARCENY, INC.   Warner Bros., 1942
JUKE GIRL   Warner Bros., 1942
THE BIG SHOT   Warner Bros., 1942

ACROSS THE PACIFIC   Warner Bros.,
1942
YOU CAN'T ESCAPE FOREVER   Warner
Bros., 1942
GEORGE WASHINGTON SLEPT HERE
Warner Bros., 1942
LUCKY JORDAN   Paramount, 1942
ACTION IN THE NORTH ATLANTIC
Warner Bros., 1943
NORTHERN PURSUIT   Warner Bros.,
1943
UNCERTAIN GLORY   Warner Bros., 1944
THE MASK OF DIMITRIOS   Warner Bros.,
1944
THE DOUGHGIRLS   Warner Bros., 1944
ESCAPE IN THE DESERT   Warner Bros.,
1945
DANGER SIGNAL   Warner Bros., 1945
THREE STRANGERS   Warner Bros., 1946
SHADOW OF A WOMAN   Warner Bros.,
1946
NOBODY LIVES FOREVER   Warner Bros.,
1945
RAMROD   United Artists, 1947
BLAZE OF NOON   Paramount, 1947
JULIA MISBEHAVES   MGM, 1948
WHISPERING SMITH   Paramount, 1949
LITTLE WOMEN   MGM, 1949
THE STRATTON STORY   MGM, 1949
INTRUDER IN THE DUST   MGM, 1949
STARS IN MY CROWN   MGM, 1950
THE BIG HANGOVER   MGM, 1950
TAKE ME OUT TO THE BALL GAME
MGM, 1949
ANNIE GET YOUR GUN ★★   adaptation,
MGM, 1950
FATHER OF THE BRIDE   MGM, 1950
MRS. O'MALLEY AND MR. MALONE
MGM, 1950
THE YELLOW CAB MAN   MGM, 1950
SOLDIERS THREE   MGM, 1951
SHOW BOAT ★   adaptation, MGM, 1951
THE BAND WAGON ★   adaptation, MGM,
1953
TORCH SONG   MGM, 1953
SEVEN BRIDES FOR SEVEN BROTHERS
★★   adaptation, MGM, 1954
THE LONG, LONG TRAILER   MGM, 1954
INTERRUPTED MELODY   MGM, 1955
OKLAHOMA! ★★   adaptation, 20th
Century-Fox, 1955
THE RACK   MGM, 1956
TEA AND SYMPATHY   MGM, 1956
FUNNY FACE   adaptation, Paramount,
1957
LES GIRLS   MGM, 1957
THE MATCHMAKER   Paramount, 1958
SOME LIKE IT HOT   United Artists, 1959
THE APARTMENT   United Artists, 1960
GO NAKED INTO THE WORLD   MGM,
1961

WILLIE DIXON

GINGER ALE AFTERNOON   NeoPictures
Ltd., 1989

ROBERT EMMETT DOLAN

b. 1906 - Hartford, Connecticut
d. September 25, 1972 - Westwood,
California

BIRTH OF THE BLUES ★   adaptation,
Paramount, 1941
ARE HUSBANDS NECESSARY?
Paramount, 1942
THE MAJOR AND THE MINOR
Paramount, 1942
ONCE UPON A HONEYMOON
Paramount, 1942
HOLIDAY INN ★   adaptation, Paramount,
1942

STAR SPANGLED RHYTHM ★
Paramount, 1943
HAPPY GO LUCKY   Paramount, 1943
DIXIE   Paramount, 1943
GOING MY WAY   Paramount, 1944
HERE COME THE WAVES   Paramount,
1944
STANDING ROOM ONLY   Paramount,
1944
LADY IN THE DARK ★   adaptation,
Paramount, 1944
I LOVE A SOLDIER   Paramount, 1944
SALTY O'ROURKE   Paramount, 1945
BRING ON THE GIRLS   Paramount, 1945
MURDER, HE SAYS   Paramount, 1945
INCENDIARY BLONDE ★   Paramount,
1945
THE BELLS OF ST. MARY'S ★   RKO
Radio, 1945
DUFFY'S TAVERN   Paramount, 1945
THE STORK CLUB   Paramount, 1945
BLUE SKIES ★   adaptation, Paramount,
1946
MONSIEUR BEAUCAIRE   Paramount,
1946
CROSS MY HEART   Paramount, 1947
MY FAVORITE BRUNETTE   Paramount,
1947
THE ROAD TO RIO ★   superivision,
Paramount, 1947
WELCOME STRANGER   Paramount, 1947
THE TROUBLE WITH WOMEN
Paramount, 1947
THE PERILS OF PAULINE   Paramount,
1947
DEATH RUTH   Paramount, 1947
SAIGON   Paramount, 1948
MR. PEABODY AND THE MERMAID
Universal, 1948
GOOD SAM   RKO Radio, 1948
MY OWN TRUE LOVE   Paramount, 1948
SORROWFUL JONES   Paramount, 1949
THE GREAT GATSBY   Paramount, 1949
TOP O' THE MORNING   supervision,
Paramount, 1949
LET'S DANCE   supervision, Paramount,
1950
AARON SLICK FROM PUMPKIN CRICK
Paramount, 1952
MY SON JOHN   Paramount, 1952
THE THREE FACES OF EVE   20th
Century-Fox, 1957
THE MAN WHO UNDERSTOOD WOMEN
20th Century-Fox, 1959

CARMEN DRAGON
d. March 28, 1984

COVER GIRL ★★   adaptation, Columbia,
1943
MR. WINKLE GOES TO WAR   Columbia,
1944
YOUNG WIDOW   United Artists, 1946
THE STRANGE WOMAN   United Artists,
1946
DISHONORED LADY   United Artists, 1947
OUT OF THE BLUE   Eagle Lion, 1947
THE TIME OF YOUR LIFE   United Artists,
1948
KISS TOMORROW GOODBYE   Warner
Bros., 1950
NIGHT INTO MORNING   MGM, 1951
THE LAW AND THE LADY   MGM, 1951
THE PEOPLE AGAINST O'HARA   MGM,
1951
WHEN IN ROME   MGM, 1952
AT GUNPOINT   Allied Artists, 1955
INVASION OF THE BODY SNATCHERS
Allied Artists, 1956

HANNS EISLER
b. July 6, 1898 - Leipzig, Germany
d. 1962 - Berlin, West Germany

OPUS 3   1928, German
NO MAN'S LAND   1930
WAR IS HELL   1930
KUHLE WAMPE   1931
A SONG ABOUT HEROES   1932, French
ABDUL THE DAMNED   1934, French
LE GRAND JEU   1934, French
NEW EARTH   1934
THE 400 MILLION   1939
PETE ROLEUM AND HIS COUSINS
co-composer with Oscar Levant, 1939
SOIL (FD)   Department of Agriculture, 1939
WHITE FLOOD   Frontier Films, 1940
RAIN   Joris Ivens, 1940
THE FORGOTTEN VILLAGE (FD)   1941
HANGMEN ALSO DIE ★   United Artists,
1943
NONE BUT THE LONELY HEART ★   RKO
Radio, 1944
JEALOUSY   Republic, 1945
THE SPANISH MAIN   RKO Radio, 1945
DEADLINE AT DAWN   RKO Radio, 1946
A SCANDAL IN PARIS   United Artists,
1946
THE WOMAN ON THE BEACH   RKO
Radio, 1947
SO WELL REMEMBERED   RKO Radio,
1948
RAT DER GOTTER   1951, German
BEL AMI   1955, French
NIGHT AND FOG   1955
SCHICKSAL AM LENKRAD   1956
MAITRE PUNTILA ET SON VALET MATTI
1956, French
THE CRUCIBLE   1957, French-East
German
LES ARRIVISTES   1960, French

CARLI D. ELINOR
THE BIRTH OF A NATION   Mutual, 1915
[Note: Two scores were written for this
film; the other is by Joseph Carl Breil.]

DUKE ELLINGTON
(Edward Kennedy)
b. April 29, 1899 - Washington, D.C.
d. May 24, 1974 - New York

JONAS   1957, German
ANATOMY OF A MURDER   Columbia,
1959
PARIS BLUES ★   United Artists, 1961
ASSAULT ON A QUEEN   Paramount,
1966
RACING WORLD   1968
CHANGE OF MIND   Cinerama Releasing
Corporation, 1969

DON ELLIS
b. 1934
d. December 17, 1978

MOON ZERO TWO   Warner Bros., 1970,
British
THE FRENCH CONNECTION   20th
Century-Fox, 1971

KANSAS CITY BOMBER   MGM, 1972
THE SEVEN UPS   20th Century-Fox, 1973
IN TANDEM (TF)   D'Antoni-Weitz TV
Productions, 1974
THE FRENCH CONNECTION II   20th
Century-Fox, 1975
THE DEADLY TOWER (TF)   MGM TV,
1975
RUBY   Dimension, 1977
NATURAL ENEMIES   Cinema 5, 1979

LEHMAN ENGEL
b. 1910 - Jackson, Mississippi
d. August 29, 1982 - New York, New York

THE FLEET THAT CAME TO STAY
Paramount, 1946
ROOGIE'S RUMP   1954

LEO ERDODY
d. April 5, 1949 - Los Angeles, California

BABY FACE MORGAN   Producers
Releasing Corp., 1942
TOMORROW WE LIVE   Producers
Releasing Corp., 1942
CITY OF SILENT MEN   Producers
Releasing Corp., 1942
PRISONER OF JAPAN   Producers
Releasing Corp., 1942
DEAD MEN WALK   Producers Releasing
Corp., 1943
QUEEN OF BROADWAY   Producers
Releasing Corp., 1942
CORREGIDOR   Producers Releasing
Corp., 1943
MY SON, THE HERO   Producers Releasing
Corp., 1943
WILD HORSE RUSTLERS   Producers
Releasing Corp., 1943
GIRLS IN CHAINS   Producers Releasing
Corp., 1943
ISLE OF FORGOTTEN SINS   MONSOON
Producers Releasing Corp., 1943
FUGITIVE OF THE PLAINS   Producers
Releasing Corp., 1943
BLUEBEARD   Producers Releasing Corp.,
1944
MINSTREL MAN ★   co-composer with
Ferde Grofe, Producers Releasing Corp.,
1944
STRANGE ILLUSION   OUT OF THE
NIGHT   Producers Releasing Corp.,
1945
APOLOGY FOR MURDER   Producers
Releasing Corp., 1945
WHITE PONGO   Producers Releasing
Corp., 1945
DETOUR   Producers Releasing Corp.,
1945
THE FLYING SERPENT   Producers
Releasing Corp., 1946
I RING DOORBELLS   Producers Releasing
Corp., 1946
MURDER IS MY BUSINESS   Producers
Releasing Corp., 1946
LARCENY IN HER HEART   Producers
Releasing Corp., 1946
BLONDE FOR A DAY   Producers
Releasing Corp., 1946
GAS HOUSE KIDS   Producers Releasing
Corp., 1946
THE RETURN OF RIN TIN TIN   Eagle Lion,
1947
BLONDE SAVAGE   Eagle Lion, 1947
MONEY MADNESS   Film Classics, 1948
LADY AT MIDNIGHT   Eagle Lion, 1948
MIRACULOUS JOURNEY   Film Classics,
1948

HANS ERDMANN

b. Germany

NOSFERATU THE VAMPIRE
*NOSFERATU - EINE SYMPHONIE DES
GRAUENS* Film Arts Guild, 1922,
German
THE TESTAMENT DES DR. MABUSE
Janus, 1933, German

F

JERRY FIELDING

b. June 17, 1922 - Pittsburgh, Pennsylvania
d. February 17, 1980

ADVISE AND CONSENT Columbia, 1962
THE NUN AND THE SERGEANT United
Artists, 1962
FOR THOSE WHO THINK YOUNG United
Artists, 1964
McHALE'S NAVY Universal, 1964
McHALE'S NAVY JOINS THE AIR FORCE
Universal, 1965
THE CRAZY WORLD OF LAUREL &
HARDY MGM, 1967
THE WILD BUNCH ★ Warner Bros., 1969
HUNTERS ARE FOR KILLING (TF)
Cinema Center 100, 1970
SUPPOSE THEY GAVE A WAR AND
NOBODY CAME? Cinerama Releasing
Corporation, 1970
LAWMAN United Artists, 1971
JOHNNY GOT HIS GUN Cinemation,
1971
ELLERY QUEEN: DON'T LOOK BEHIND
YOU (TF) Universal TV, 1971
ONCE UPON A DEAD MAN (TF) Universal
TV, 1971
STRAW DOGS ★ Cinerama Releasing
Corporation, 1971, British
CHATO'S LAND United Artists, 1972
THE NIGHTCOMERS Avco Embassy,
1972, British
THE MECHANIC United Artists, 1972
A WAR OF CHILDREN (TF) Tomorrow
Entertainment, 1972
THE SNOOP SISTERS *FEMALE
INSTINCT* (TF) Universal TV, 1972
JUNIOR BONNER Cinerama Releasing
Corporation, 1973
SCORPIO United Artists, 1973
THE DEADLY TRACKERS Warner Bros.,
1973
SHIRTS/SKINS (TF) MGM TV, 1973
UNWED FATHER (TF) David L. Wolper
Productions, 1974
THE OUTFIT MGM, 1974
HONKY-TONK (TF) Douglas Heyes
Productions/MGM TV, 1974
THE SUPER COPS MGM, 1974
THE GAMBLER Paramount, 1974
BRING ME THE HEAD OF ALFREDO
GARCIA United Artists, 1974
HUSTLING (TF) Filmways/Lillian Gallo
Productions, 1975
THE BLACK BIRD Columbia, 1975
MATT HELM (TF) Meadway
Productions/Columbia Pictures TV, 1975
ONE OF OUR OWN (TF) Universal TV,
1975
THE KILLER ELITE United Artists, 1975

THE BAD NEWS BEARS adaptation,
Paramount, 1976
THE OUTLAW JOSEY WALES ★ Warner
Bros., 1976
THE ENFORCER Warner Bros., 1976
LITTLE LADIES OF THE NIGHT (TF)
Spelling-Goldberg Productions, 1977
THE GAUNTLET Warner Bros., 1977
DEMON SEED MGM/United Artists, 1977
SEMI-TOUGH United Artists, 1978
GREY LADY DOWN Universal, 1978
THE BIG SLEEP United Artists, 1978,
British
LOVEY: A CIRCLE OF CHILDREN, PART II
(TF) Time-Life Productions, 1978
MR. HORN (TF) Lorimar Productions,
1979
ESCAPE FROM ALCATRAZ Paramount,
1979
BEYOND THE POSEIDON ADVENTURE
Warner Bros., 1979
HIGH MIDNIGHT (TF) ☆☆ The Mirisch
Corporation/Universal TV, 1979
BELOW THE BELT Atlantic Releasing,
1980
FUNERAL HOME 1981, Canadian

BENJAMIN FRANKEL

b. 1906 - London, England
d. 1973 - London, England

THE SEVENTH VEIL Universal, 1945,
British
DEAR MURDERER 1947, British
MINE OWN EXECUTIONER 1947, British
DULCIMER STREET *LONDON BELONGS
TO ME* 1948, British
PORTRAIT FROM LIFE *THE GIRL IN THE
PAINTING* Universal, 1948, British
SLEEPING CAR TO TRIESTE 1948,
British
THE AMAZING MR. BEECHAM 1948,
British
THE GAY LADY *TROTTIE TRUE* Eagle
Lion, 1949, British
SALT TO THE DEVIL 1949, British
SO LONG AT THE FAIR GFD, 1950,
British
THE CLOUDED YELLOW General Film
Distributors, 1950, British
HOTEL SAHARA United Artists, 1951,
British
THE LONG DARK HALL 1951, British
ISLAND RESCUE *APPOINTMENT WITH
VENUS* Universal, 1951, British
THE IMPORTANCE OF BEING ERNEST
Universal, 1952, British
THE MAN IN THE WHITE SUIT Rank,
1952, British
THE FINAL TEST 1953, British
PROJECT M-7 *THE NET* Universal,
1953, British
MAD ABOUT MEN General Film
Distributors, 1954, British
ALWAYS A BRIDE 1954, British
FIRE OVER AFRICA Columbia, 1954
CHANCE MEETING 1955, British
THE END OF THE AFFAIR Columbia,
1955
FOOTSTEPS IN THE FOG Columbia,
1955
THE MAN WHO LOVED REDHEADS
United Artists, 1955, British
THE PRISONER Columbia, 1955, British
A KID FOR TWO FARTHINGS Lopert,
1956, British
THE IRON PETTICOAT MGM, 1956,
British
SIMON AND LAURA 1956, British
STORM OVER THE NILE Columbia,
1956, British

TEARS FOR SIMON *LOST* Republic,
1956, British
ORDERS TO KILL United Motion Picture
Organization, 1958, British
HAPPY IS THE BRIDE Kassler, 1959,
British
LIBEL MGM, 1959, British
SURPRISE PACKAGE Columbia, 1960
THE CURSE OF THE WEREWOLF
Universal, 1961, British
SEASON OF PASSION United Artists,
1961, British
GUNS OF DARKNESS Warner Bros.,
1962, British
THE OLD DARK HOUSE Columbia, 1963,
British-U.S.
NIGHT OF THE IGUANA MGM, 1964
BATTLE OF THE BULGE Warner Bros.,
1965

HUGO FRIEDHOFER

b. May 3, 1902 - San Francisco, California
d. May 17, 1981 - Los Angeles, California

JUST IMAGINE Fox, 1930
SHERLOCK HOLMES co-composer with
R.H. Bassett, Fox, 1932
MY LIPS BETRAY Fox, 1933
THE ADVENTURES OF MARCO POLO
United Artists, 1938
VALLEY OF THE GIANTS co-composer
with Adolph Deutsch, Warner Bros.,
1938
TOPPER TAKES A TRIP co-composer with
Edward Powell, MGM, 1939
CHINA GIRL 20th Century-Fox, 1943
CHETNIKS! 20th Century-Fox, 1943
THEY CAME TO BLOW UP AMERICA
20th Century-Fox, 1943
PARIS AFTER DARK 20th Century-Fox,
1943
THE LODGER 20th Century-Fox, 1944
LIFEBOAT 20th Century-Fox, 1944
ROGER TOUHY, GANGSTER 20th
Century-Fox, 1944
HOME IN INDIANA 20th Century-Fox,
1944
WING AND A PRAYER 20th Century-Fox,
1944
BREWSTER'S MILLIONS United Artists,
1945
GETTING GERTIE'S GARTER United
Artists, 1945
THE WOMAN IN THE WINDOW ★ RKO
Radio, 1945
THE BANDIT OF SHERWOOD FOREST
Columbia, 1946
GILDA Columbia, 1946
SO DARK THE NIGHT Columbia, 1946
THE BEST YEARS OF OUR LIVES ★★
RKO Radio, 1946
BODY AND SOUL United Artists, 1947
WILD HARVEST Paramount, 1947
THE BISHOP'S WIFE ★ RKO Radio, 1947
THE SWORDSMAN Columbia, 1947
A SONG IS BORN RKO Radio, 1948
THE ADVENTURES OF CASANOVA
Eagle Lion, 1948
BLACK BART Universal, 1948
SEALED VERDICT Paramount, 1948
JOAN OF ARC ★ RKO Radio, 1948
ENCHANTMENT RKO Radio, 1948
BRIDE OF VENGEANCE Paramount,
1949
ROSEANNA McCOY RKO Radio, 1949
GUILTY OF TREASON Eagle Lion, 1950
THREE CAME HOME 20th Century-Fox,
1950
CAPTAIN CAREY, U.S.A. Paramount,
1950
NO MAN OF HER OWN Paramount, 1950

BROKEN ARROW   20th Century-Fox, 1950
EDGE OF DOOM   RKO Radio, 1950
TWO FLAGS WEST   20th Century-Fox, 1950
THE SOUND OF FURY   United Artists, 1951
QUEEN FOR A DAY   United Artists, 1951
ACE IN THE HOLE   Paramount, 1951
RANCHO NOTORIOUS   RKO Radio, 1952
THE MARRYING KIND   Columbia, 1952
THE OUTCASTS OF POKER FLAT   20th Century-Fox, 1952
LYDIA BAILEY   20th Century-Fox, 1952
JUST FOR YOU   Paramount, 1952
ABOVE AND BEYOND ★   MGM, 1952
FACE TO FACE   RKO Radio, 1952
THUNDER IN THE EAST   Paramount, 1953
ISLAND IN THE SKY   Warner Bros., 1953
HONDO   Warner Bros., 1953
VERA CRUZ   United Artists, 1954
WHITE FEATHER   20th Century-Fox, 1955
VIOLENT SATURDAY   20th Century-Fox, 1955
SOLDIER OF FORTUNE   20th Century-Fox, 1955
SEVEN CITIES OF GOLD   20th Century-Fox, 1955
THE RAINS OF RANCHIPUR   20th Century-Fox, 1955
THE HARDER THEY FALL   Columbia, 1956
THE REVOLT OF MAMIE STOVER   20th Century-Fox, 1956
BETWEEN HEAVEN AND HELL ★   20th Century-Fox, 1956
OH, MEN! OH, WOMEN!   20th Century-Fox, 1957
BOY ON A DOLPHIN ★   20th Century-Fox, 1957
AN AFFAIR TO REMEMBER ★   20th Century-Fox, 1957
THE SUN ALSO RISES   20th Century-Fox, 1957
THE YOUNG LIONS ★   20th Century-Fox, 1958
THE BRAVADOS   20th Century-Fox, 1958
THE BARBARIAN AND THE GEISHA   20th Century-Fox, 1958
IN LOVE AND WAR   20th Century-Fox, 1958
WOMAN OBSESSED   20th Century-Fox, 1959
THIS EARTH IS MINE   Universal, 1959
THE BLUE ANGEL   20th Century-Fox, 1959
NEVER SO FEW   MGM, 1959
ONE-EYED JACKS   Paramount, 1960
HOMICIDAL   Columbia, 1961
GERONIMO   United Artists, 1962
BEAUTY AND THE BEAST   United Artists, 1962
THE SECRET INVASION   United Artists, 1964
THE OVER-THE-HILL GANG (TF)   Thomas-Spelling Productions, 1969
VON RICHTOFEN AND BROWN   United Artists, 1971
PRIVATE PARTS   MGM, 1972

G

SERGE GAINSBOURG
b. Paris, France
d. March 2, 1991 - Paris, France

L'EAU A LA BOUCHE   1960, French
COMMENT TROUVEZ-VOUS MA SOEUR?   1964, French
SI J'ETAIS UN ESPION   1966, French
MANON 70   1966, French
L'HORIZON   1967, French
LE JARDINIER D'ARGENTEUIL   1967, French
L'INCONNU DE SHANDIGOR   1967, French
LA PACHA   1968, French
PARIS N'EXISTE PAS   1968, French
MISTER FREEDOM   1969, French
LES CHEMINS DE KATMANDOU   1969, French
LA HORSE   1969, French
CANNABIS   1970, French
TROP JOLIES POUR ETRE HONNETES   1972, French
PROJECTION PRIVEE   1972, French
LE SEX SHOP   Peppercorn-Wormser, 1973, French
JE T'AIME MOI NON PLUS   1975, French
GOODBYE EMMANUELLE   1977, French
THE FRENCH WOMAN   *MADAME CLAUDE*   Monarch, 1979, French
EQUATOR   Gaumont, 1983, French
MENAGE   *TENUE DE SOIREE*   Cinecom, 1986, French

GEORGES GARVARENTZ
b. France
d. 1991

UN TAXI POUR TOBROUK   1961, French
LES BONNES CAUSES   1963, French
COMMENT REUSSIR EN AMOUR   1963, French
LE RAT D'AMERIQUE   1964, French
PARIS AU MOIS D'AOUT   1966, French
LE GRAND DADAIS   1966, French
L'HOMME QUI VALAIT DES MILLIARDS   1967, French
UN MILLIARD DANS UN BILLARD   1967, French
TRIPLE CROSS   1967, French-British
THEY CAME TO ROB LAS VEGAS   *SUDARIO DI SABBIA*   1968, Spanish-French-Italian
THE SOUTHERN STAR   Columbia, 1969, French-British
LE TATOUE   1969, French
L'INVITEE   1969, French
LE TEMPS DES LOUPS   1969, French
UN BEAU MONSTRE   *A LOVELY MONSTER*   1970, French
L'INTRUS   1971, French
LES GALETS D'ETRETAT   *PEBBLES OF ETRETAT*   1972, French
CAROLINE CHERIE   1973, French
KILLER FORCE   American International, 1975
THE KILLER WHO WOULDN'T DIE (TF)   Paramount Pictures TV, 1976
THE GOLDEN LADY   Target International, 1979, British
LA LUMIERE DES JUSTES   1979, French

TRIUMPHS OF A MAN CALLED HORSE   Jensen Farley Pictures, 1984
TOO SCARED TO SCREAM   The Movie Store, 1985
A STATE OF EMERGENCY   Norkat Co., 1986
QUICKER THAN THE EYE   Condor, 1989, Swiss
PETAIN   1991, French
WHISPERS OF WHITE   Lone Star Pictures, 1992

PAUL GIOVANNI
d. June 17, 1990

THE WICKER MAN   Warner Bros., 1975, British

JACKIE GLEASON
b. February 26, 1916 - New York, New York
d. June 24, 1987 - Los Angeles, California

IZZY AND MOE (TF)   Robert Halmi Productions, 1985

MORT GLICKMAN
d. 1953

(In addition to the titles below, Mr. Glickman scored dozens of low-budget films, mostly westerns, for Republic.)

PREHISTORIC WOMEN   uncredited co-composer with Rene Kraushaar, United Artists, 1950
BRIDE OF THE GORILLA   uncredited co-composer with Rene Kraushaar, Realart, 1951
UNTAMED WOMEN   uncredited co-composer with Rene Kraushaar, United Artists, 1952
INVADERS FROM MARS   uncredited co-composer with Rene Kraushaar, 20th Century-Fox, 1953

LUD GLUSKIN
d. 1989

THE HOUSEKEEPER'S DAUGHTER   United Artists, 1939
THE MAN IN THE IRON MASK ★   co-composer with Lucien Moraweck, United Artists, 1939
ABROAD WITH TWO YANKS   United Artists, 1944
HIGH CONQUEST   Monogram, 1947
MICHAEL O'HALLORAN   Monogram, 1948
MIRACLE IN HARLEM   Screen Guild, 1948
MASSACRE RIVER   Allied Artists, 1949
BOY FROM INDIANA   Eagle Lion, 1950

WALTER GOEHR
d. December 4, 1960 - Sheffield, England

AMATEUR GENTLEMAN   co-composer with Richard Addinsell, United Artists, 1936, British
GREAT EXPECTATIONS   Universal, 1947, British
STOP PRESS GIRL   1949, British
LUCKY NICK CAIN   20th Century-Fox, 1951
BETRAYED   MGM, 1954

MILES GOODMAN
d. 1996

SLUMBER PARTY '57   Cannon, 1976
A LAST CRY FOR HELP (TF)   Myrt-Hal Productions/Viacom Productions, 1979

SKATETOWN, U.S.A.   Columbia, 1979
LOOKIN' TO GET OUT   Paramount, 1982
JINXED   co-composer with Bruce Roberts, MGM/UA, 1982
HAVING IT ALL (TF)   Hill-Mandelker Productions, 1982
THE FACE OF RAGE (TF)   Hal Sitowitz Productions/Viacom, 1983
THE MAN WHO WASN'T THERE   Paramount, 1983
HIGH SCHOOL U.S.A. (TF)   co-composer with Tony Berg, Hill-Mandelker Productions, 1983
TABLE FOR FIVE   co-composer with John Morris, Warner Bros., 1983
AN UNCOMMON LOVE (TF)   Beechwood Productions/Lorimar, 1983
FOOTLOOSE   Paramount, 1984
A REASON TO LIVE (TF)   Rastar Productions/Robert Papazian Productions, 1985
POISON IVY (TF)   NBC Entertainment, 1985
SPACE (MS)   co-composer with Tony Berg, Stonehenge Productions/Paramount Pictures TV, 1985
TEEN WOLF   Atlantic Releasing Corporation, 1985
CHILDREN OF THE NIGHT (TF)   Robert Guenette Productions, 1985
THOMPSON'S LAST RUN (TF)   Cypress Point Productions, 1986
PASSION FLOWER (TF)   Doris Keating Productions/Columbia Pictures TV, 1986
BLIND JUSTICE (TF)   CBS Entertainment Productions, 1986
ABOUT LAST NIGHT...   Tri-Star, 1986
AMERICANGEISHA (TF)   Interscope Communications/Stonehenge Productions, 1986
LITTLE SHOP OF HORRORS   The Geffen Company/Warner Bros., 1986
LA BAMBA   co-composer with Carlos Santana, Columbia, 1987
REAL MEN   MGM/UA, 1987
THE SQUEEZE   Tri-Star, 1987
LIKE FATHER LIKE SON   Tri-Star, 1987
DIRTY ROTTEN SCOUNDRELS   Orion, 1988
OUTBACK BOUND (TF)   Andrew Gottlieb Productions/CBS Entertainment, 1988
K-9   Universal, 1989
THE TRAVELLING MAN (CTF)   Irvin Kershner Films, 1989
STAYING TOGETHER   Hemdale, 1989
MONEY, POWER, MURDER (TF)   Skids Productions/CBS Entertainment, 1989
OPPORTUNITY KNOCKS   Universal, 1990
FUNNY ABOUT LOVE   Paramount, 1990
VITAL SIGNS   20th Century-Fox, 1990
PROBLEM CHILD   Universal, 1990
HE SAID, SHE SAID   Paramount, 1991
WHAT ABOUT BOB?   Buena Vista, 1991
THE SUPER   20th Century Fox, 1991
FOR RICHER, FOR POORER (CTF)   Citadel Entertainment, 1992
HOUSESITTER   Universal, 1992
INDECENCY (TF)   Wind Dancer/Touchstone TV, 1992
THE MUPPET CHRISTMAS CAROL   Buena Vista, 1992
INDIAN SUMMER   Buena Vista, 1993
SISTER ACT 2: BACK IN THE HABIT   Buena Vista, 1993
GETTING EVEN WITH DAD   MGM, 1994
BLANKMAN   Columbia, 1994
DUNSTON CHECKS IN   20th Century Fox, 1996
LARGER THAN LIFE   MGM-UA, 1996
SUNSET PARK   co-composer with Kay Gee, TriStar, 1996

RON GRAINER
b. 1922 - Australia
d. February 21, 1981

A KIND OF LOVING   Continental, 1962, British
THE MOUSE ON THE MOON   United Artists, 1963, British
STATION SIX-SAHARA   Allied Artists, 1963, British-West German
THE GUEST   THE CARETAKER   Janus, 1963, British
THE FINEST HOURS   1964, British
THE MOONSPINNERS   Buena Vista, 1964
NIGHT MUST FALL   Embassy, 1964, British
NOTHING BUT THE BEST   Royal Films International, 1964, British
THE TIGER MAKES OUT   Columbia, 1967
TO SIR WITH LOVE   Columbia, 1967, British
ONLY WHEN I LARF   Paramount, 1968, British
THE ASSASSINATION BUREAU   Paramount, 1969, British
BEFORE WINTER COMES   Columbia, 1969, British
DESTINY OF A SPY (TF)   Universal TV, 1969
LOCK UP YOUR DAUGHTERS   1969
IN SEARCH OF GREGORY   Universal, 1970, British
HOFFMAN   Levitt-Pickman, 1971, British
THE OMEGA MAN   Warner Bros., 1971
THIEF (TF)   Stonehenge Productions/Metromedia Producers Corporation, 1971
YELLOW DOG   1973
AND NO ONE COULD SAVE HER (TF)   Associated London Films, 1973
MOUSEY   CAT AND MOUSE (TF)   Universal TV/Associated British Films, 1974, U.S.-British
THE BAWDY ADVENTURES OF TOM JONES   Universal, 1976, British
THE DEVIL WITHIN HER   I DON'T WANT TO BE BORN   American International, 1976, British

PERCY GRAINGER
b. 1882 - Brighton, Victoria
d. 1961 - White Plains, New York

FLYING FEET   1929

ALLAN GRAY
b. 1904

EMIL AND THE DETECTIVES   1931, German
BERLIN ALEXANDER PLATZ   1931, German
DIE GRAFFIN VON MONTE-CRISTO   1931, German
F.P.I. ANTWORTET NICHT   1932, German
SANS LENDEMAIN   1939, French
THE LIFE AND DEATH OF COLONEL BLIMP   COLONEL BLIMP   GFO, 1943, British
A CANTERBURY TALE   Eagle-Lion, 1944, British
I KNOW WHERE I'M GOING   Universal, 1945, British
STAIRWAY TO HEAVEN   A MATTER OF LIFE AND DEATH   Universal, 1946, British
THIS MAN IS MINE   1946, British
MR. PERRIN AND MR. TRAILL   1948, British
MADNESS OF THE HEART   1949, British
THE RELUCTANT WIDOW   1951, British

NO PLACE FOR JENNIFER   1951, British
THE OBSESSED   1951
HER PANELLED DOOR   1951, British
THE AFRICAN QUEEN   United Artists, 1951
OUTPOST IN MALAYA   THE PLANTER'S WIFE   United Artists, 1952, British
TWILIGHT WOMEN   Lippert, 1953
THE GENIE   1953
SOLANG 'ES HUBSCHE MADCHEN GIBT   1955, West German

BARRY GRAY

THUNDERBIRDS ARE GO   1966
THUNDERBIRDS SIX   1968
JOURNEY TO THE FAR SIDE OF THE SUN   DOPPLEGANGER   Universal, 1969, British
THUNDERBIRDS TO THE RESCUE   1980
REVENGE OF THE MYSTERIONS FROM MARS   1981

JOHN GREEN
b. October 10, 1908 - New York, New York
d. 1989 - Los Angeles, California

(Mr. Green was arranger, music director or supervisor for dozens of films in the 1940s and 1950s. This list is limited to scores composed or adapted by Mr. Green.)

SECRETS OF A SECRETARY   Paramount, 1931
MY SIN   Paramount, 1931
WAYWARD   Paramount, 1931
THE WISER SEX   Paramount, 1931
BROADWAY RHYTHM   MGM, 1944
BATHING BEAUTY   MGM, 1944
WEEKEND AT THE WALDORF   MGM, 1945
THE SAILOR TAKES A WIFE   MGM, 1945
EASY TO WED   MGM, 1946
FIESTA ★   adaptation, MGM, 1947
IT HAPPENED IN BROOKLYN   MGM, 1947
SOMETHING IN THE WIND   Universal, 1947
EASTER PARADE ★★   adaptation, MGM, 1948
UP IN CENTRAL PARK   Universal, 1948
THE INSPECTOR GENERAL   Warner Bros., 1949
SUMMER STOCK   MGM, 1950
ROYAL WEDDING   MGM, 1951
THE GREAT CARUSO ★   MGM, 1951
AN AMERICAN IN PARIS ★★   adaptation, MGM, 1951
TOO YOUNG TO KISS   MGM, 1951
BECAUSE YOU'RE MINE   MGM, 1952
BRIGADOON   adaptation, MGM, 1954
RHAPSODY   MGM, 1954
HIGH SOCIETY ★   adaptation, MGM, 1956
MEET ME IN LAS VEGAS ★   adaptation, MGM, 1956
RAINTREE COUNTY ★   MGM, 1957
PEPE ★   Columbia, 1960
WEST SIDE STORY ★   adaptation, United Artists, 1961
BYE BYE BIRDIE ★   adaptation, Columbia, 1963
TWILIGHT OF HONOR   MGM, 1963
ALVAREZ KELLY   Columbia, 1966
JOHNNY TIGER   Universal, 1966
OLIVER! ★★   adaptation, Columbia, 1968, British
THEY SHOOT HORSES, DON'T THEY? ★   Cinerama Releasing Corporation, 1969

JOHN GREENWOOD
b. 1889

THE CONSTANT NYMPH   co-composer
    with Eugene Goossens, 1933, British
MAN OF ARAN (FD)   Gaumont-British,
    1934, British
ELEPHANT BOY   United Artists, 1937,
    British
THE DRUM   United Artists, 1938, British
PIMPERNEL SMITH   MISTER V
    Anglo-American, 1941, British
NINE MEN   1943, British
HUNGRY HILL   Universal, 1947, British
FRIEDA   Universal, 1947, British
THE LAST DAYS OF DOLWYN   WOMAN
    OF DOLWYN   1948, British
TRIO   Paramount, 1950, British
EUREKA STOCKADE   1950, British
FAMILY PORTRAIT   1950, British
ANOTHER MAN'S POISON   United Artists,
    1952, British
THE GENTLE GUNMAN   Universal, 1952,
    British
WICKED WIFE   Allied Artists, 1955, British

FERDE GROFE
(Ferdinand Rudolf von Grofe)
b. 1892 - New York
d. 1972 - Santa Monica, California

KING OF JAZZ   Universal, 1930
DIAMOND JIM   co-composer with Franz
    Waxman, Universal, 1935
MINSTREL MAN ★   co-composer with Leo
    Erdody, Producers Releasing Corp.,
    1944
ROCKETSHIP X-M   Lippert, 1950

LOUIS GRUENBERG
b. 1884 - Brest-Litovsk, Russia
d. June 6, 1964 - Los Angeles, California

THE FIGHT FOR LIFE ★   Columbia, 1940
SO ENDS OUR NIGHT ★   United Artists,
    1941
COMMANDOS STRIKE AT DAWN ★
    Columbia, 1943
AN AMERICAN ROMANCE   MGM, 1944
COUNTER-ATTACK   Columbia, 1945
THE GANGSTER   Allied Artists, 1947
ARCH OF TRIUMPH   United Artists, 1948
SMART WOMAN   Allied Artists, 1948
ALL THE KING'S MEN   Columbia, 1949
QUICKSAND   United Artists, 1950

MANOS HADJIDAKIS
b. October 1925 - Xanthi, Greece
d. June 15, 1994 - Los Angeles

STELLA   Milas Films, 1955, Greek
BED OF GRASS   1957, Greek
NEVER ON SUNDAY   Lopert, 1960,
    Greek
IT HAPPENED IN ATHENS   20th
    Century-Fox, 1962
THE 300 SPARTANS   20th Century-Fox,
    1962

ALIKI   Funos-Aquarius, 1963, West
    German-U.S.
AMERICA, AMERICA   Warner Bros., 1963
TOPKAPI   United Artists, 1964
GREECE, LAND OF DREAMS   1965
BLUE   Paramount, 1968, British
THE MARLET'S TALE   1970
THE PEDESTRIAN   Cinerama Releasing
    Corporation, 1974, West
    German-Swiss-Israeli
SWEET MOVIE   Biograph, 1975,
    French-Canadian-West German
HONEYMOON   1979

RICHARD HAGEMAN
d. March 6, 1966

IF I WERE KING ★   Paramount, 1938
HOTEL IMPERIAL   Paramount, 1939
STAGECOACH ★★   co-composer, United
    Artists, 1939
RULERS OF THE SEA   Paramount, 1939
THE HOWARDS OF VIRGINIA ★
    Columbia, 1940
THE LONG VOYAGE HOME ★   United
    Artists, 1940
THIS WOMAN IS MINE ★   Universal, 1941
PARIS CALLING   Universal, 1942
THE SHANGHAI GESTURE ★   United
    Artists, 1942
ANGEL AND THE BADMAN   Republic,
    1947
THE FUGITIVE   RKO Radio, 1947
FORT APACHE   RKO Radio, 1948
MOURNING BECOMES ELECTRA   RKO
    Radio, 1947
THREE GODFATHERS   MGM, 1948
SHE WORE A YELLOW RIBBON   RKO
    Radio, 1949
WAGON MASTER   RKO Radio, 1950

KARL HAJOS
b. 1889 - Budapest, Hungary
d. 1950 - Los Angeles, California

LOVES OF AN ACTRESS   Paramount,
    1928
BEGGARS OF LIFE   Paramount, 1928
MOROCCO   Paramount, 1930
SUPERNATURAL   co-composer,
    Paramount, 1933
FOUR FRIGHTENED PEOPLE
    Paramount, 1934
MANHATTAN MOON   Universal, 1935
WEREWOLF OF LONDON   Universal,
    1935
TWO WISE MAIDS   Republic, 1937
HITLER'S HANGMAN   MGM, 1943
THE SULTAN'S DAUGHTER   Monogram,
    1943
CHARLIE CHAN IN THE SECRET
    SERVICE   Monogram, 1944
SUMMER STORM ★   United Artists, 1944
THE MAN WHO WALKED ALONE ★
    Producers Releasing Corp., 1945
THE PHANTOM OF 42ND STREET
    Producers Releasing Corp., 1945
THE MISSING CORPSE   Producers
    Releasing Corp., 1945
DANGEROUS INTRUDER   Producers
    Releasing Corp., 1945
SHADOW OF TERROR   Producers
    Releasing Corp., 1945
FOG ISLAND   Universal, 1945
THE MASK OF DIIJON   Producers
    Releasing Corp., 1946
QUEEN OF BURLESQUE   Producers
    Releasing Corp., 1946
SECRETS OF A SORORITY GIRL
    Producers Releasing Corp., 1946

DOWN MISSOURI WAY   Producers
    Releasing Corp., 1946
DRIFTIN' RIVER   Producers Releasing
    Corp., 1946
STARS OVER TEXAS   Producers
    Releasing Corp., 1946
WILD WEST   Producers Releasing Corp.,
    1946
TUMBLEWEED TRAIL   Producers
    Releasing Corp., 1946
APPOINTMENT WITH MURDER
    Producers Releasing Corp., 1948
SEARCH FOR DANGER   Film Classics,
    1949
THE LOVABLE CHEAT   Film Classics,
    1949
KILL OR BE KILLED   Eagle Lion, 1950
IT'S A SMALL WORLD   Eagle Lion, 1950

LEIGH HARLINE
b. March 26, 1907 - Salt Lake City, Utah
d. 1969

SNOW WHITE AND THE SEVEN DWARFS
    (AF) ★   co-composer with Frank
    Churchill and Paul Smith, RKO Radio,
    1938
BEWARE, SPOOKS!   main and end title,
    1939
PINOCCHIO (AF) ★★   co-composer with
    Paul Smith, RKO Radio, 1940
BLONDIE ON A BUDGET   Columbia, 1940
BLONDIE HAS SERVANT TROUBLE
    Columbia, 1940
SO YOU WON'T TALK   Columbia, 1940
BLONDIE PLAYS CUPID   Columbia, 1940
MR. BUG GOES TO TOWN   HOPPITY
    GOES TO TOWN (AF)   Paramount,
    1941
THE LADY HAS PLANS   co-composer with
    Leo Shuken, Paramount, 1942
WHISPERING GHOSTS   co-composer,
    20th Century-Fox, 1942
THE PRIDE OF THE YANKEES ★   RKO
    Radio, 1942
CAREFUL, SOFT SHOULDER   20th
    Century-Fox, 1942
YOU WERE NEVER LOVELIER ★
    Columbia, 1942
THEY GOT ME COVERED   RKO Radio,
    1943
MARGIN FOR ERROR   20th Century-Fox,
    1943
THE MORE THE MERRIER   Columbia,
    1943
THE SKY'S THE LIMIT ★   RKO Radio,
    1943
JOHNNY COME LATELY ★   United Artists,
    1943
GOVERNMENT GIRL   RKO Radio, 1943
TENDER COMRADE   RKO Radio, 1944
FOLLOW THE BOYS   co-composer with
    Oliver Wallace and Frank Skinner,
    Universal, 1944
A NIGHT OF ADVENTURE   RKO Radio,
    1944
HEAVENLY DAYS   RKO Radio, 1944
MUSIC IN MANHATTAN   RKO Radio,
    1944
WHAT A BLONDE   RKO Radio, 1945
HAVING WONDERFUL CRIME   RKO
    Radio, 1945
CHINA SKY   RKO Radio, 1945
THE BRIGHTON STRANGLER
    co-composer, RKO Radio, 1945
GEORGE WHITE'S SCANDALS   RKO
    Radio, 1945
JOHNNY ANGEL   RKO Radio, 1945
MAMA LOVES PAPA   RKO Radio, 1945
FIRST YANK INTO TOKYO   RKO Radio,
    1945

ISLE OF THE DEAD   RKO Radio, 1945
MAN ALIVE   RKO Radio, 1945
ROAD TO UTOPIA   Paramount, 1946
FROM THIS DAY FORWARD   RKO Radio, 1946
THE TRUTH ABOUT MURDER   RKO Radio, 1946
TILL THE END OF TIME   RKO Radio, 1946
CRACK-UP   RKO Radio, 1946
CHILD OF DIVORCE   RKO Radio, 1946
LADY LUCK   RKO Radio, 1946
NOCTURNE   RKO Radio, 1946
THE FARMER'S DAUGHTER   RKO Radio, 1947
A LIKELY STORY   RKO Radio, 1947
HONEYMOON   RKO Radio, 1947
THE BACHELOR AND THE BOBBY-SOXER   RKO Radio, 1947
TYCOON   RKO Radio, 1947
THE MIRACLE OF THE BELLS   RKO Radio, 1948
MR. BLANDINGS BUILDS HIS DREAM HOUSE   RKO Radio, 1948
THE VELVET TOUCH   RKO Radio, 1948
EVERY GIRL SHOULD BE MARRIED   RKO Radio, 1948
THE BOY WITH GREEN HAIR   RKO Radio, 1948
IT HAPPENS EVERY SPRING   20th Century-Fox, 1949
THE JUDGE STEPS OUT   RKO Radio, 1949
THE BIG STEAL   RKO Radio, 1949
THEY LIVE BY NIGHT   RKO Radio, 1949
THE WOMAN ON PIER 13   RKO Radio, 1950
PERFECT STRANGERS   Warner Bros., 1950
MY FRIEND IRMA GOES WEST   Paramount, 1950
THE HAPPY YEARS   MGM, 1950
UNION STATION   Paramount, 1950
THE COMPANY SHE KEEPS   RKO Radio, 1950
CALL ME MISTER   20th Century-Fox, 1951
THE GUY WHO CAME BACK   20th Century-Fox, 1951
THAT'S MY BOY   Paramount, 1951
HIS KIND OF WOMAN   RKO Radio, 1951
ON THE LOOSE   RKO Radio, 1951
BEHAVE YOURSELF   RKO Radio, 1951
DOUBLE DYNAMITE   RKO Radio, 1951
I WANT YOU   RKO Radio, 1951
PICK-UP ON SOUTH STREET   20th Century-Fox, 1951
THE LAS VEGAS STORY   RKO Radio, 1952
MONKEY BUSINESS   20th Century-Fox, 1952
MY WIFE'S BEST FRIEND   20th Century-Fox, 1952
MY PAL GUS   20th Century-Fox, 1952
TAXI   20th Century-Fox, 1953
THE DESERT RATS   20th Century-Fox, 1953
VICKI   20th Century-Fox, 1953
BLACK WIDOW   20th Century-Fox, 1954
BROKEN LANCE   20th Century-Fox, 1954
MONEY FROM HOME   Paramount, 1954
SUSAN SLEPT HERE   RKO Radio, 1954
THE GIRL IN THE RED VELVET SWING   20th Century-Fox, 1955
GOOD MORNING, MISS DOVE   20th Century-Fox, 1955
THE LAST FRONTIER   Columbia, 1956
THE BOTTOM OF THE BOTTLE   20th Century-Fox, 1956
GREAT DAY IN THE MORNING   RKO Radio, 1956

TEEN-AGE REBEL   20th Century-Fox, 1956
23 PACES TO BAKER STREET   20th Century-Fox, 1956, British-U.S.
THE ENEMY BELOW   20th Century-Fox, 1957
NO DOWN PAYMENT   20th Century-Fox, 1957
THE TRUE STORY OF JESSE JAMES   20th Century-Fox, 1957
THE WAYWARD BUS   20th Century-Fox, 1957
MAN OF THE WEST   United Artists, 1958
TEN NORTH FREDERICK   20th Century-Fox, 1958
THE REMARKABLE MR. PENNYPACKER   20th Century-Fox, 1958
HOLIDAY FOR LOVERS   20th Century-Fox, 1959
THESE THOUSAND HILLS   20th Century-Fox, 1959
WARLOCK   20th Century-Fox, 1959
THE FACTS OF LIFE   United Artists, 1960
VISIT TO A SMALL PLANET   Paramount, 1960
THE HONEYMOON MACHINE   MGM, 1961
THE WONDERFUL WORLD OF THE BROTHERS GRIMM ★   MGM/Cinerama, 1962
THE SEVEN FACES OF DR. LAO   MGM, 1964
STRANGE BEDFELLOWS   Universal, 1965

W. FRANKE HARLING

b. 1887
d. November 22, 1958 - Sierra Madre, California

HONEY   Paramount, 1930
MONTE CARLO   Paramount, 1930
THE RIGHT TO LOVE   Paramount, 1930
RANGO   Paramount, 1931
SHANGHAI EXPRESS   Paramount, 1932
BROKEN LULLABY   Paramount, 1932
FIREMAN, SAVE MY CHILD   Warner Bros., 1932
THE EXPERT   Warner Bros., 1932
PLAY GIRL   Warner Bros., 1932
ONE HOUR WITH YOU   co-composer, Paramount, 1932
THE MIRACLE MAN   Paramount, 1932
THIS IS THE NIGHT   Paramount, 1932
THE RICH ARE ALWAYS WITH US   Warner Bros., 1932
TWO SECONDS   Warner Bros., 1932
STREET OF WOMEN   Warner Bros., 1932
WEEK-END MARRIAGE   Warner Bros., 1932
WINNER TAKE ALL   Warner Bros., 1932
TROUBLE IN PARADISE   Paramount, 1932
ONE WAY PASSAGE   theme only, Warner Bros., 1932
MEN ARE SUCH FOOLS   RKO Radio, 1932
MADAME BUTTERFLY   Paramount, 1932
THE BITTER TEA OF GENERAL YEN   Columbia, 1933
DESTINATION UNKNOWN   Universal, 1933
A KISS BEFORE THE MIRROR   Universal, 1933
CRADLE SONG   Paramount, 1933
A MAN'S CASTLE   Columbia, 1933
BY CANDLELIGHT   Universal, 1933
ONE MORE RIVER   Universal, 1933
THE SCARLETT EMPRESS   co-composer with John Leipold, Paramount, 1934

THE CHURCH MOUSE   Warner Bros., 1934
SO RED THE ROSE   Paramount, 1935
I MARRIED A DOCTOR   Warner Bros., 1936
THE GOLDEN ARROW   Warner Bros., 1936
CHINA CLIPPER   Warner Bros., 1936
MOUNTAIN JUSTICE   Warner Bros., 1937
SOULS AT SEA ★   co-composer with Milan Roder, 1937
MEN WITH WINGS   co-composer with Gerard Carbonara, Paramount, 1938
STAGECOACH ★★   co-composer, United Artists, 1939
ADAM HAD FOUR SONS   Columbia, 1941
PENNY SERENADE   Columbia, 1941
ADVENTURE IN WASHINGTON   Columbia, 1941
THE LADY IS WILLING   Columbia, 1942
I ESCAPED FROM THE GESTAPO   Monogram, 1943
SOLDIERS OF THE SOIL   Du Pont, 1943
THREE RUSSIAN GIRLS ★   United Artists, 1944
JOHNNY DOESN'T LIVE HERE ANYMORE   King Bros./Mon., 1944
WHEN THE LIGHTS GO ON AGAIN   Producers Releasing Corp., 1944
RED WAGON   American Film Center, 1945
THE BACHELOR'S DAUGHTERS   United Artists, 1946

ROY HARRIS

b. 1898 - Lincoln County, Nebraska
d. October 1, 1979 - Santa Monica, California

ONE-TENTH OF A NATION (FD)   Rockefeller, 1940

T. MARVIN HATLEY

d. August 26, 1986

KELLY THE SECOND   MGM, 1936
MISTER CINDERELLA   MGM, 1936
GENERAL SPANKY   MGM, 1936
WAY OUT WEST ★   MGM, 1937
NOBODY'S BABY   MGM, 1937
PICK A STAR   MGM, 1937
TOPPER   MGM, 1937
MERRILY WE LIVE   MGM, 1938
SWISS MISS   MGM, 1933
BLOCKHEADS ★   MGM, 1938
THERE GOES MY HEART ★   United Artists, 1938
ZENOBIA   United Artists, 1939
CAPTAIN FURY   United Artists, 1939
A CHUMP AT OXFORD   United Artists, 1940
SAPS AT SEA   United Artists, 1940

FUMIO HAYASAKA

b. August 19, 1914 - Sendai, Japan
d. 1955 - Japan

DRUNKEN ANGEL   Toho, 1948, Japanese
RASHOMON   RKO Radio, 1950, Japanese
THE PICTURE OF MADAME YUKI   1950, Japanese
WOMAN OF MUSAHINO   1951, Japanese
IKIRU   Brandon, 1952, Japanese
UGETSU   Harrison Pictures, 1953, Japanese
SANSHO THE BAILIFF   1954, Japanese
SEVEN SAMURAI   Landmark Releasing, 1954, Japanese

TALES OF THE TAIRA CLAN 1955,
Japanese
I LIVE IN FEAR Brandon, 1955, Japanese
YANG KWEI FEI 1955, Japanese

CHARLES HENDERSON
b. 1907 - Boston, Massachusetts
d. March 7, 1970 - Laguna Beach, California

BLACK FRIDAY co-composer, Universal,
1940
HORROR ISLAND co-composer,
Universal, 1941
THE BLACK CAT co-composer, Universal,
1941
THE MAD GHOUL co-composer,
Universal, 1943
HOUSE OF DRACULA co-composer,
Universal, 1945
STATE FAIR ★ adaptation, 20th
Century-Fox, 1945

VICTOR HERBERT
b. 1859 - Dublin, Ireland
d. 1924 - New York

THE FALL OF A NATION National Films,
1916

BERNARD HERRMANN
b. June 30, 1911 - New York, New York
d. December 24, 1975 - Los Angeles,
California

CITIZEN KANE ★ RKO Radio, 1941
ALL THAT MONEY CAN BUY THE DEVIL
AND DANIEL WEBSTER ★★ RKO
Radio, 1941
THE MAGNIFICENT AMBERSONS RKO
Radio, 1942
JANE EYRE 20th Century-Fox, 1943
HANGOVER SQUARE 20th Century-Fox,
1945
ANNA AND THE KING OF SIAM ★ 20th
Century-Fox, 1946
THE GHOST AND MRS. MUIR 20th
Century-Fox, 1947
PORTRAIT OF JENNIE composer of
Jennie's theme, Selznick, 1948
THE DAY THE EARTH STOOD STILL 20th
Century-Fox, 1951
ON DANGEROUS GROUND RKO Radio,
1952
THE SNOWS OF KILIMANJARO 20th
Century-Fox, 1952
FIVE FINGERS 20th Century-Fox, 1952
WHITE WITCH DOCTOR 20th
Century-Fox, 1953
BENEATH THE TWELVE-MILE REEF 20th
Century-Fox, 1953
KING OF THE KHYBER RIFLES 20th
Century-Fox, 1954
GARDEN OF EVIL 20th Century-Fox,
1954
THE EGYPTIAN co-composer with Alfred
Newman, 20th Century-Fox, 1954
PRINCE OF PLAYERS 20th Century-Fox,
1954
THE TROUBLE WITH HARRY Paramount,
1955
THE KENTUCKIAN Paramount, 1955
THE MAN WHO KNEW TOO MUCH also
appears as conductor in Albert Hall
sequence, Paramount, 1956
THE MAN IN THE GRAY FLANNEL SUIT
20th Century-Fox, 1956
THE WRONG MAN Warner Bros., 1956
WILLIAMSBURG: THE STORY OF A
PATRIOT Paramount, 1956
A HATFUL OF RAIN 20th Century-Fox,
1957

VERTIGO Paramount, 1958
THE NAKED AND THE DEAD Warner
Bros., 1958
THE SEVENTH VOYAGE OF SINBAD
Columbia, 1958
NORTH BY NORTHWEST MGM, 1959
BLUE DENIM 20th Century-Fox, 1959
JOURNEY TO THE CENTER OF THE
EARTH 20th Century-Fox, 1959
PSYCHO Paramount, 1960
THE THREE WORLDS OF GULLIVER
Columbia, 1960
MYSTERIOUS ISLAND Columbia, 1961
TENDER IS THE NIGHT 20th Century-Fox,
1962
CAPE FEAR Universal, 1962
JASON AND THE ARGONAUTS
Columbia, 1963
THE BIRDS sound-consultant only,
Universal, 1963
MARNIE Universal, 1964
JOY IN THE MORNING MGM, 1965
TORN CURTAIN score not used,
Universal, 1965
FAHRENHEIT 451 Universal, 1966,
British
COMPANIONS IN NIGHTMARE (TF)
Universal, 1968
THE BRIDE WORE BLACK Lopert, 1968,
French-Italian
TWISTED NERVE National General,
1969, British
THE NIGHT DIGGER MGM, 1971, British
THE BATTLE OF NERETVA American
International, 1971,
Yugoslavian-U.S.-Italian-German
ENDLESS NIGHT Rank, 1971, British
SISTERS American International, 1973
IT'S ALIVE Warner Bros., 1974
OBSESSION ★ Columbia, 1976
TAXI DRIVER ★ Columbia, 1976

*(Several films use "tracked" [pre-existing]
music by Herrmann, including
"Obsessions" [1969] and "The Hound of
the Baskervilles" [1972]. Scores for "It
Lives Again" (1978) and "It's Alive III:
Island of the Alive" (1987) are based on
Herrmann's score for "It's Alive." The new
version of "Cape Fear" (1991) is based on
Herrmann's score to the original.)*

WERNER R. HEYMANN
b. Germany

THE SPY 1927
MELODIE DES HERZENS 1929, German
LIEBESWALZER 1929, German
DER SIEGER 1931, German
DER BALL 1931, German
EIN BLONDER TRAUM 1932, German
ICH BEI TAG, DU BEI NACHT 1932,
German
LA PETITE SAUVAGE 1933, German
ADORABLE Fox, 1933
CARAVAN Fox, 1934
THE KING AND THE CHORUS GIRL
Warner Bros., 1937
BLUEBEARD'S EIGHTH WIFE
co-composer with Frederick Hollander,
Paramount, 1938
NINOTCHKA MGM, 1939
THE EARL OF CHICAGO MGM, 1940
THE SHOP AROUND THE CORNER
MGM, 1940
PRIMROSE PATH RKO Radio, 1940
ONE MILLION B.C. ★ United Artists, 1940
HE STAYED FOR BREAKFAST Columbia,
1940
THIS THING CALLED LOVE Columbia,
1941

TOPPER RETURNS United Artists, 1941
THAT UNCERTAIN FEELING ★ United
Artists, 1941
MY LIFE WITH CAROLINE RKO Radio,
1941
BEDTIME STORY Columbia, 1941
TO BE OR NOT TO BE ★ United Artists,
1942
THE WIFE TAKES A FLYER Columbia,
1942
THEY ALL KISSED THE BRIDE Columbia,
1942
FLIGHT LIEUTENANT Columbia, 1942
A NIGHT TO REMEMBER Columbia,
1942
APPOINTMENT IN BERLIN Columbia,
1943
KNICKERBOCKER HOLIDAY ★ adaptation,
United Artists, 1944
HAIL THE CONQUERING HERO
Paramount, 1944
MADEMOISELLE FIFI RKO Radio, 1944
OUR HEARTS WERE YOUNG AND GAY
Paramount, 1944
MY PAL, WOLF RKO Radio, 1944
THREE IS A FAMILY United Artists, 1944
TOGETHER AGAIN Columbia, 1944
IT'S IN THE BAG United Artists, 1945
KISS AND TELL Columbia, 1945
LOST HONEYMOON Eagle Lion, 1947
THE SIN OF HAROLD DIDDLEBOCK MAD
WEDNESDAY RKO Radio, 1947
ALWAYS TOGETHER Warner Bros., 1948
THE MATING OF MILLIE Columbia, 1948
LET'S LIVE A LITTLE Eagle Lion, 1948
A KISS FOR CORLISS United Artists,
1949
TELL IT TO THE JUDGE Columbia, 1949
A WOMAN OF DISTINCTION Columbia,
1949
EMERGENCY WEDDING Columbia, 1950
HEIDELBERGER ROMANZE 1951, West
German
ALRAUNE 1952, West German
EIN HAUS VOLL LIEBE 1952, West
German
DER KONGRESS TANZT 1955, West
German

PAUL HINDEMITH
b. 1895 - Hanau, Germany
d. 1963 - Frankfurt, West Germany

VORMITTAGSPUK 1928, German

GUSTAV HINRICHS
b. 1850 - Germany

THE PHANTOM OF THE OPERA
Universal, 1925

FREDERICK HOLLANDER
(Friedrich Hollander)
b. October 18, 1896 - London, England
d. 1976

THE BLUE ANGEL UFA, 1930, German
I AM SUZANNE Fox, 1934
SHANGHAI Paramount, 1935
DESIRE Paramount, 1936
TILL WE MEET AGAIN Paramount, 1936
VALIANT IS THE WORD FOR CARRIE
Paramount, 1936
JOHN MEADE'S WOMAN Paramount,
1937
TRUE CONFESSION Paramount, 1937
BLUEBEARD'S EIGHTH WIFE
co-composer with Werner R. Heymann,
Paramount, 1938
MIDNIGHT Paramount, 1939

N
O
T
A
B
L
E

C
O
M
P
O
S
E
R
S

O
F

T
H
E

P
A
S
T

INVITATION TO HAPPINESS   Paramount,
1939
DISPUTED PASSAGE   Paramount, 1939
REMEMBER THE NIGHT   Paramount,
1940
TOO MANY HUSBANDS   Columbia, 1940
THE DOCTOR TAKES A WIFE   Columbia,
1940
TYPHOON   Paramount, 1940
THE BISCUIT EATER   Paramount, 1940
SAFARI   Paramount, 1940
THE GREAT McGINTY   Paramount, 1940
RANGERS OF FORTUNE   Paramount,
1940
SOUTH OF SUEZ   Warner Bros., 1940
VICTORY   Paramount, 1941
LIFE WITH HENRY   Paramount, 1941
THERE'S MAGIC IN MUSIC   Paramount,
1941
FOOTSTEPS IN THE DARK   Warner Bros.,
1941
MILLION DOLLAR BABY   Warner Bros.,
1941
HERE COMES MR. JORDAN   Columbia,
1941
YOU BELONG TO ME   Columbia, 1942
THE MAN WHO CAME TO DINNER
Warner Bros., 1942
WINGS FOR THE EAGLE   Warner Bros.,
1942
TALK OF THE TOWN ★   Columbia, 1942
BACKGROUND TO DANGER   Warner
Bros., 1943
PRINCESS O'ROURKE   Warner Bros.,
1943
ONCE UPON A TIME   Columbia, 1944
THE AFFAIRS OF SUSAN   Paramount,
1945
PILLOW TO POST   Warner Bros., 1945
CONFLICT   Warner Bros., 1945
CHRISTMAS IN CONNECTICUT   Warner
Bros., 1945
CINDERELLA JONES   Warner Bros., 1946
THE BRIDE WORE BOOTS   Paramount,
1946
JANIE GETS MARRIED   Warner Bros.,
1946
TWO GUYS FROM MILWAUKEE   Warner
Bros., 1946
NEVER SAY GOODBYE   Warner Bros.,
1946
THE VERDICT   Warner Bros., 1946
THE TIME, THE PLACE AND THE GIRL
Warner Bros., 1946
THE PERFECT MARRIAGE   Paramount,
1947
THAT WAY WITH WOMEN   Warner Bros.,
1947
STALLION ROAD   Warner Bros., 1947
THE RED STALLION   Eagle Lion, 1947
BERLIN EXPRESS   RKO Radio, 1948
WALLFLOWER   Warner Bros., 1948
A FOREIGN AFFAIR   Paramount, 1948
A WOMAN'S SECRET   RKO Radio, 1949
CAUGHT   MGM, 1949
ADVENTURE IN BALTIMORE   RKO Radio,
1949
STRANGE BARGAIN   RKO Radio, 1949
BRIDE FOR SALE   RKO Radio, 1949
A DANGEROUS PROFESSION   RKO
Radio, 1949
BORN TO BE BAD   RKO Radio, 1950
WALK SOFTLY, STRANGER   RKO Radio,
1950
NEVER A DULL MOMENT   RKO Radio,
1950
BORN YESTERDAY   Columbia, 1950
MY FORBIDDEN PAST   RKO Radio, 1951
DARLING, HOW COULD YOU?
Paramount, 1951
THE FIRST TIME   Columbia, 1952

ANDROCLES AND THE LION   RKO Radio,
1952
THE 5,000 FINGERS OF DR. T ★
co-composer with Heinz Roemheld and
Hans J. Salter, Columbia, 1953
IT SHOULD HAPPEN TO YOU   Columbia,
1954
PHFFFT   Columbia, 1954
SABRINA   Paramount, 1954
WE'RE NO ANGELS   Paramount, 1955
DAS SPUKSCHLOSS IN SPESSART   *THE
SPOOK CASTLE IN SPESSART*   1960,
West German

ARTHUR HONEGGER
b. March 10, 1892 - Le Havre, France
d. 1955 - Paris, France

LA ROUE   1922, French
FAIT DIVERS   1924, French
NAPOLEON   1926, French
L'IDEE   1926, French
PACIFIC 231   1931
LES MISERABLES   1934
CRIME AND PUNISHMENT   1935
L'EQUIPAGE   *FLIGHT INTO DARKNESS*
1935, French
MADEMOISELLE DOCTEUR   1935,
French
NITCHEVO   1936, French
MAYERLING   1936, French
REGAIN   1937, French
LA CITADELLE DU SILENCE   co-composer
with Darius Milhaud, 1937, French
THE WOMAN I LOVE   RKO Radio, 1937
PYGMALION   MGM, 1938, British
JE T'ATTENDRAI   1939, French
CAVALCADE d'AMOUR   co-composer with
Darius Milhaud, 1939, French
LE CAPITAINE FRACASSE   1942, French
SECRETS   1942, French
UN SEUL AMOUR   1943, French
UN AMI VIENDRA CE SOIR   1945, French
UN REVENANT   1946, French
STORM OVER TIBET   Columbia, 1951
JOAN OF ARC AT THE STAKE   1954,
French

GOTTFRIED HUPPERTZ
b. Germany

DIE NIBELUNGEN   UFA, 1924, German
METROPOLIS   UFA, 1926, German

I

JACQUES IBERT
b. August 15, 1890 - Paris, France
d. 1962 - Paris, France

UN CHAPEAU DE PAILLE D'ITALIE   *THE
ITALIAN STRAW HAT*   1927, French
LES CINQ GENTLEMAN MAUDITS   1930,
French
S.O.S. FOCH   1931, French
LES DEUX ORPHELINES   1932, French
DON QUIXOTE   1933, British
JUSTIN DE MARSEILLES   co-composer,
1935, French
GOLGOTHA   1935, French
MATERNITE   1935, French
KOENIGSMARK   1935, French

LE COUPABLE   1936, French
PARIS   1936, French
ANNE-MARIE   1936, French
COURRIER SUD   co-composer with
Maurice Thiriet, 1936, French
L'HOMME DE NULLE PART   1936, French
LA MAISON DU MALTAIS   1937, French
LE PERE LEBONNARD   1937, French
ANGELICA   1938, French
LE HEROS DE LA MARNE   1938, French
LE PATRIOTE   1938, French
THERESE MARTIN   1938, French
LE COMEDIE DU BONHEUR   1939,
French
LA CHARRETTE FANTOME   1939, French
FELICIE NANTEUIL   1942, French
LES PETITES DU QUAI AUX FLEURS
1943, French
LE PERE SERGE   1945, French
PANIC   Tricolore, 1946, French
MACBETH   Republic, 1948
EQUILIBRE   1952, French
MARIANNE OF MY YOUTH   United Motion
Picture Organization, 1955, French

JOHN IRELAND
b. 1879 - Bowden, England
d. 1962 - Sussex, England

THE OVERLANDERS   1946,
Australian-British

J

PAUL JABARA
b. 1948 - Brooklyn, NY
d. September 29, 1992 - Los Angeles, CA

CHANEL SOLITAIRE   United Film
Distribution, 1981, French-British

GORDON JENKINS
b. May 12, 1910 - Webster Groves, Missouri
d. May 1, 1984 - Los Angeles, California

STRANGE HOLIDAY   Producers Releasing
Corporation, 1946
BWANA DEVIL   United Artists, 1953
THE FIRST DEADLY SIN   Filmways
Pictures, 1980

K

DMITRI KABALEVSKY
b. 1904 - St. Petersburg, Russia
d. 1987 - Moscow, U.S.S.R.

AEROGRAD   *FRONTIER*   1936, Soviet
SHORS   1939, Soviet
ACADEMICIAN IVAN PAVLOV   1949,
Soviet
IVAN PAVLOV   1950, Soviet
FLAMES ON THE VOLGA   1950, Soviet

THE GADFLY   1955, Soviet
THE SISTERS   1957, Soviet
1918   1958, Soviet
BLEAK MORNING   1959, Soviet

BRONISLAU KAPER
b. February 5, 1902 - Warsaw, Poland
d. 1983

DIE LUSTIGEN MUSIKANTEN   1930,
    German
ALRAUNE   *DAUGHTER OF EVIL*   1930,
    German
DIE GROSSE ATTRAKTION   1931,
    German
MELODIE DER LIEBE   1932, German
EIN LIED FUR DICH   1933, German
MADAME WUNSCHT KEINE KINDER
    1933, German
I TAKE THIS WOMAN   MGM, 1940
THE MORTAL STORM   MGM, 1940
THE CAPTAIN IS A LADY   MGM, 1940
WE WHO ARE YOUNG   MGM, 1940
DULCY   MGM, 1940
COMRADE X   MGM, 1940
BLONDE INSPIRATION   MGM, 1941
RAGE IN HEAVEN   MGM, 1941
A WOMAN'S FACE   MGM, 1941
I'LL WAIT FOR YOU   MGM, 1941
BARNACLE BILL   MGM, 1941
WHISTLING IN THE DARK   MGM, 1941
DR. KILDARE'S WEDDING DAY   MGM,
    1941
WHEN LADIES MEET   MGM, 1941
THE CHOCOLATE SOLDIER ★
    adaptation, MGM, 1941
H.M. PULHAM, ESQUIRE   MGM, 1941
JOHNNY EAGER   MGM, 1941
TWO-FACED WOMAN   MGM, 1942
WE WERE DANCING   MGM, 1942
FINGERS AT THE WINDOW   MGM, 1942
CROSSROADS   MGM, 1942
THE AFFAIRS OF MARTHA   MGM, 1942
SOMEWHERE I'LL FIND YOU   MGM,
    1942
A YANK AT EATON   MGM, 1942
WHITE CARGO   MGM, 1942
KEEPER OF THE FLAME   MGM, 1942
SLIGHTLY DANGEROUS   MGM, 1943
ABOVE SUSPICION   MGM, 1943
BATAAN   MGM, 1943
THE CROSS OF LORRAINE   MGM, 1943
THE HEAVENLY BODY   MGM, 1944
GASLIGHT   MGM, 1944
MARRIAGE IS A PRIVATE AFFAIR   MGM,
    1944
MRS. PARKINGTON   MGM, 1945
WITHOUT LOVE   MGM, 1945
BEWITCHED   MGM, 1945
OUR VINES HAVE TENDER GRAPES
    MGM, 1945
THREE WISE FOOLS   MGM, 1946
THE STRANGER   RKO Radio, 1946
COURAGE OF LASSIE   MGM, 1946
THE SECRET HEART   MGM, 1946
CYNTHIA   MGM, 1947
SONG OF LOVE   MGM, 1947
GREEN DOLPHIN STREET   MGM, 1947
HIGH WALL   MGM, 1948
B.F.'S DAUGHTER   MGM, 1948
HOMECOMING   MGM, 1948
THE SECRET LAND (FD)   MGM, 1948
ACT OF VIOLENCE   MGM, 1948
THE SECRET GARDEN   MGM, 1949
THE GREAT SINNER   MGM, 1949
THAT FORSYTE WOMAN   MGM, 1949
MALAYA   MGM, 1949
KEY TO THE CITY   MGM, 1950
THE SKIPPER SURPRISED HIS WIFE
    MGM, 1950
A LIFE OF HER OWN   MGM, 1950

TO PLEASE A LADY   MGM, 1950
GROUNDS FOR MARRIAGE   MGM, 1950
THREE GUYS NAMED MIKE   MGM, 1951
MR. IMPERIUM   MGM, 1951
THE RED BADGE OF COURAGE   MGM,
    1951
TOO YOUNG TO KISS   MGM, 1951
IT'S A BIG COUNTRY   MGM, 1951
SHADOW IN THE SKY   MGM, 1951
INVITATION, 1952
THE WILD NORTH   MGM, 1952
THE NAKED SPUR   MGM, 1953
LILI ★★   MGM, 1953
RIDE, VAQUERO!   MGM, 1953
THE ACTRESS   MGM, 1953
SAADIA   MGM, 1953
THEM!   Warner Bros., 1954
HER TWELVE MEN   MGM, 1954
THE GLASS SLIPPER   MGM, 1955
THE PRODIGAL   MGM, 1955
QUENTIN DURWARD   MGM, 1955
FOREVER, DARLING   MGM, 1955
THE SWAN   MGM, 1956
THE POWER AND THE PRIZE   MGM,
    1956
SOMEBODY UP THERE LIKES ME   MGM,
    1956
THE BARRETTS OF WIMPOLE STREET
    MGM, 1957
JET PILOT   RKO Radio, 1957
DON'T GO NEAR THE WATER   MGM,
    1957
THE BROTHERS KARAMAZOV   MGM,
    1957
AUNTIE MAME   Warner Bros., 1958
THE SCAPEGOAT   MGM, 1958
GREEN MANSIONS   MGM, 1959
HOME FROM THE HILL   MGM, 1959
THE ANGEL WORE RED   MGM, 1960
BUTTERFIELD 8   MGM, 1960
TWO LOVES   MGM, 1961
ADA   MGM, 1961
MUTINY ON THE BOUNTY ★   MGM, 1962
KISSES FOR MY PRESIDENT   Warner
    Bros., 1964
LORD JIM   Columbia, 1965
TOBRUK   Universal, 1967
THE WAY WEST   United Artists, 1967
COUNTERPOINT   Universal, 1968
A FLEA IN HER EAR   20th Century-Fox,
    1968

ELLIOT KAPLAN
b. Boston, Massachusetts

THE PLAYGROUND   General, 1965
THE SQUARE ROOT OF ZERO   1965
FINNEGANS WAKE   Evergreen Films,
    1965
CRY BLOOD, APACHE   Golden Eagle
    International, 1970
STRANGE NEW WORLD (TF)
    co-composer with Richard Clements,
    Warner Bros. TV, 1975
MAN ON THE OUTSIDE (TF)   Universal
    TV, 1975
YOU LIE SO DEEP, MY LOVE (TF)
    Universal TV, 1975
BRIDGER (TF)   Universal TV, 1976
THE FOOD OF THE GODS   American
    International, 1976
A MARRIED MAN (TF)   London Weekend
    TV Productions/Lionhearted Productions,
    1984

ANTON KARAS
d. January 10, 1985

THE THIRD MAN   Selznick Releasing,
    1949, British

BERNHARD KAUN
b. 1899 - Germany
d. January 3, 1980

HEAVEN ON EARTH   Universal, 1931
FRANKENSTEIN   Universal, 1931
DR. X   Warner Bros., 1932
ONE WAY PASSAGE   Warner Bros., 1932
THE MYSTERY OF THE WAX MUSEUM
    Warner Bros., 1933
20,000 YEARS IN SING SING   Warner
    Bros., 1933
DEATH TAKES A HOLIDAY   additional
    music, Paramount, 1934
RETURN OF THE TERROR   Warner Bros.,
    1934
THE STORY OF LOUIS PASTEUR   Warner
    Bros., 1936
THE WALKING DEAD   Warner Bros., 1936
THE INVISIBLE MENACE   Warner Bros.,
    1937
THE RETURN OF DR. X   Warner Bros.,
    1939
THE BODY DISAPPEARS   additional
    music, 1941
THE SMILING GHOST   co-composer with
    William Lava, 1941
SPECIAL DELIVERY   *VON HIMMEL
    GEFALLEN*   Columbia, 1955, West
    German-U.S.

ARAM KHACHATURIAN
b. 1903 - Tbilisi, Russia
d. May 2, 1978 - Moscow, U.S.S.R.

PEPO   1935, Soviet
SALAVAT YULAYEV   1941, Soviet
GIRL NO. 217   1944, Soviet
THE RUSSIAN QUESTION   1948, Soviet
THE BATTLE OF STALINGRAD   1949,
    Soviet
ADMIRAL USHAKOV   1953, Soviet
ATTACK FROM THE SEA   1953, Soviet
SALTANAT   1955, Soviet
OTHELLO   1955, Soviet

CHRISTOPHER KOMEDA
(Krzysztof T. Komeda)
b. April 27, 1937 - Poland
d. April 23, 1969 - Los Angeles, California

THE GLASS MOUNTAIN   1960
INNOCENT SORCERERS   1960
SEE YOU TOMORROW   1960
THE FAT AND THE LEAN   1961
KNIFE IN THE WATER   Kanawha, 1962,
    Polish
AMBULANCE   1962
MAMMALS   1962
OPENING TOMORROW   1962
EPILOGUE   1963
NEW CLOTHES   1963
THE BEAUTIFUL SWINDLERS   *LES PLUS
    BELLES ESCROQUERIES DU MONDE*
    composer of Polanski segment, Jack Ellis
    Films, 1964,
    French-Italian-Japanese-Dutch
CATS   *KATTORNA*   1964
THE PENGUIN   1965
BARRIER   Film Polski, 1966, Polish
LE DEPART   Pathe Contemporary, 1966,
    Belgian
HUNGER   1966
CUL-DE-SAC   Sigma III, 1966, British
PEOPLE MEET AND SWEET MUSIC FILLS
    THE AIR   1967
THE FEARLESS VAMPIRE KILLERS, OR
    PARDON ME BUT YOUR TEETH ARE IN
    MY NECK   *DANCE OF THE
    VAMPIRES*   MGM, 1967, British

ROSEMARY'S BABY   Paramount, 1968
RIOT   Paramount, 1969

ERICH WOLFGANG KORNGOLD
b. May 29, 1897 - Brno, Czechoslovakia
d. 1957 - Los Angeles, California

A MIDSUMMER NIGHT'S DREAM
    adaptation, Warner Bros., 1935
CAPTAIN BLOOD   Warner Bros., 1935
GIVE US THE NIGHT   Paramount, 1936
THE GREEN PASTURES   Warner Bros.,
    1936
ANTHONY ADVERSE ★★   Warner Bros.,
    1936
THE PRINCE AND THE PAUPER   Warner
    Bros., 1937
ANOTHER DAWN   Warner Bros., 1937
THE ADVENTURES OF ROBIN HOOD
    ★★ Warner Bros., 1938
JUAREZ   Warner Bros., 1939
THE PRIVATE LIVES OF ELIZABETH AND
    ESSEX ★   Warner Bros., 1939
THE SEA HAWK ★   Warner Bros., 1940
THE SEA WOLF   Warner Bros., 1941
KINGS ROW   Warner Bros., 1942
THE CONSTANT NYMPH   Warner Bros.,
    1943
BETWEEN TWO WORLDS   Warner Bros.,
    1944
DEVOTION   Warner Bros., 1946
OF HUMAN BONDAGE   Warner Bros.,
    1946
DECEPTION   Warner Bros., 1946
ESCAPE ME NEVER   Warner Bros., 1947
MAGIC FIRE   adaptation, Republic, 1956

JOSEPH KOSMA
b. 1905 - Budapest, Hungary
d. 1969 - Paris, France

JENNY   co-composer with Lionel Cazaux,
    1936, French
A DAY IN THE COUNTRY   UN PARTIE DE
    CAMPAGNE   1936, French
GRAND ILLUSION   World Pictures, 1937,
    French
LA BETE HUMAINE   THE HUMAN
    BEAST   1938, French
LA MARSEILLAISE   1938, French
THE RULES OF THE GAME   Janus, 1939,
    French
THE DEVIL'S ENVOYS   LES VISITEURS
    DU SOIR   1942, French
ADIEU LEONARD   1943, French
CHILDREN OF PARADISE   Tricolore,
    1944, French
LES PORTES DE LA NUIT   1945, French
AUBERVILLIERS   1945, French
L'HOMME   1945, French
LES CHOUANS   1946, French
VOYAGE SURPRISE   1946, French
PETRUS   1946, French
L'ARCHE DE NOE   1946, French
L'AMOUR AUTOUR DE LA MAISON   1946,
    French
MONSIEUR LUDOVIC   1946, French
BETHSABEE   1947, French
LE PETIT SOLDAT   1947, French
LA DAME D'ONZE HEURES   1947, French
LE PARADIS DES PILOTES PERDUS
    1947, French
L'ECOLE BUISSONNIERE   1947, French
BAGARRES   1948, French
D'HOMMES A HOMMES   1948, French
LES AMANTS DE VERONE   1948, French
HANS LE MARIN   1948, French
LE SANG DES BETES   1948, French
AU GRAND BALCON   1949, French
VENDETTA EN CAMARGUE   1949,
    French

LA MARIE DU PORT   1949, French
LA GRAND RENDEZ-VOUS   1949, French
LA BELLE QUE VOILA   1949, French
LA CIGALE ET LA FOURMI   1949, French
LE LOUP ET L'AGNEAU   1949, French
SOUVENIRS PERDUS   1950, French
TROIS TELEGRAMMES   1950, French
SANS LAISSER D'ADRESSE   1950,
    French
OMBRE ET LUMIERE   1950, French
CAPTAIN BLACK JACK   United Artists,
    1950, French-British-Spanish
DESORDRES   1950, French
JULIETTE OU LA CLE DES SONGES
    1951, French
UN GRAN PATRON   1951, French
THE GREEN GLOVE   LE GANTELET
    VERT   United Artists, 1952
LA BERGERE ET LE RAMONEUR   1952,
    French
LE RIDEAU ROUGE   1952, French
AGENCE MATRIMONIALE   1952, French
LES FRUITS SAUVAGES   1953, French
FRANCOIS LE RHINOCEROS   1953,
    French
HUIS CLOS   1954, French
LES EVADES   1954, French
LES CHIFFONNIERS d'EMMAUS   1954,
    French
LE PORT DU DESIR   1954, French
LE VILLAGE MAGIQUE   1954, French
LOUIS LUMIERE   1954, French
INNOCENTS IN PARIS   1955, British
MONSIEUR LA CAILLE   1955, French
DES GENS SANS IMPORTANCE   1955,
    French
L'AMANT DE LADY CHATTERLEY   1955,
    French
MA JEANNETTE ET MES COPAINS   1955,
    French
MERMOZ   1955, French
CELA S'APPELLE L'AURORE   1956,
    French-Italian
PARIS DOES STRANGE THINGS   ELENA
    ET LES HOMMES   Warner Bros., 1956,
    French
CALLE MAYOR   1956, French
JE REVIENDRAI A KANDARA   1956,
    French
LE LONG DES TROTTOIRS   1956, French
L'INSPECTEUR AIME LA BAGARRE
    1956, French
LES LOUVES   1956, French
THE CASE OF DR. LAURENT   1957,
    French
TAMANGO   Valiant, 1957, French
DEMONIAQUE   1958, French
THE DOCTOR'S DILEMMA   1958, French
THE LOVEMAKER   1958, French
THE WILD FRUIT   1958, French
PICNIC ON THE GRASS   Kingsley-Union,
    1959, French
LE HUITIEME JOUR   1959, French
LOVE AND THE FRENCHWOMAN
    Kingsley International, 1960, French
LE PAVE DE PARIS   1961, French
LE TESTAMENT DU DR. CORDELIER
    (TF)   1961, French
LA PUPEE   1962, French
THE ELUSIVE CORPORAL   LE CAPORAL
    EPINGLE   Pathe Contemporary, 1962,
    French
IN THE FRENCH STYLE   Columbia, 1963,
    French-U.S.
THE MAGNIFICENT SUMMER   1963,
    French
THANK HEAVEN FOR SMALL FAVORS
    1965, French
BITTER FRUIT   1967, French
THE LITTLE THEATRE OF JEAN RENOIR
    (TF)   Phoenix Films, 1969,
    French-Italian-West German

IRWIN KOSTAL
b. October 1, 1911 - Chicago, Illinois
d. November 23, 1994 - Studio City,
California

WEST SIDE STORY ★★   adaptation,
    United Artists, 1961
MARY POPPINS ★   adaptation, Buena
    Vista, 1964
THE SOUND OF MUSIC ★★   adaptation,
    20th Century-Fox, 1965
BEDKNOBS AND BROOMSTICKS ★
    adaptation, Buena Vista, 1971
THE BLUE BIRD   20th Century-Fox, 1976,
    U.S.-Soviet
PETE'S DRAGON ★   adaptation, Buena
    Vista, 1977

SIGMUND KRUMGOLD
DEATH TAKES A HOLIDAY   co-composer,
    Paramount, 1934
WE'RE NOT DRESSING   co-composer,
    Paramount, 1934
SHE LOVES ME NOT   co-composer,
    Paramount, 1934
COLLEGE RHYTHM   co-composer,
    Paramount, 1934
MISSISSIPPI   co-composer, Paramount,
    1935
STOLEN HARMONY   co-composer,
    Paramount, 1935
PARIS IN SPRING   Paramount, 1935
THE BIG BROADCAST OF 1936
    co-composer, Paramount, 1935
UNION PACIFIC   co-composer,
    Paramount, 1939

GAIL KUBIK
b. 1914 - S. Coffeyville, Oklahoma
d. July 20, 1984 - Covina, California

MEN AND SHIPS (FD)   U.S. Maritime
    Commission, 1940
THE WORLD AT WAR (FD)   O.W.I., 1942
PARATROOPS (FD)   O.W.I., 1942
MANPOWER (FD)   O.W.I., 1942
DOVER (FD)   O.W.I., 1942
COLLEGES AT WAR (FD)   O.W.I., 1942
EARTHQUAKERS (FD)   A.A.F., 1943
THE MEMPHIS BELLE (FD)   A.A.F., 1943
AIR PATTERN—PACIFIC (FD)   A.A.F.,
    1944
THUNDERBOLT (FD)   A.A.F., 1945
C-MAN   Film Classics, 1949
THE MINER'S DAUGHTER (AS)
    Columbia, 1950
GERALD McBOING BOING (AS)
    Columbia, 1950
TWO GALS AND A GUY   United Artists,
    1951
THE DESPERATE HOURS   Paramount,
    1955
I THANK A FOOL   MGM, 1962, British

L

WILLIAM LAVA

b. March 18, 1911 - Minnesota
d. February 20, 1971

HAWK OF THE WILDERNESS   serial,
   Republic, 1938
SANTA FE STAMPEDE   Republic, 1938
RED RIVER RANGE   Republic, 1938
DAREDEVILS OF THE RED CIRCLE
   serial, Republic, 1939
THE NIGHT RAIDERS   Republic, 1939
DICK TRACY'S G-MEN   serial, Republic,
   1939
THREE TEXAS STEERS   Republic, 1939
WYOMING OUTLAW   Republic, 1939
NEW FRONTIER   Republic, 1939
THE LONE RANGER RIDES AGAIN   serial,
   Republic, 1939
THE KANSAS TERRORS   Republic, 1939
COWBOYS FROM TEXAS   Republic, 1939
ZORRO'S FIGHTING LEGION   serial,
   Republic, 1939
THE COURAGEOUS DR. CHRISTIAN
   RKO Radio, 1940
THE SMILING GHOST   co-composer with
   Bernhard Kraun, 1941
THE MYSTERIOUS DOCTOR
   co-composer with Howard Jackson, 1943
THE INVISIBLE MAN'S REVENGE
   co-composer with Hans J. Salter, Eric
   Zeisl, Universal, 1944
JUNGLE CAPTIVE   co-composer,
   Universal, 1944
HOUSE OF DRACULA   co-composer,
   Universal, 1945
SHE-WOLF OF LONDON   Universal, 1946
MOONRISE   Republic, 1948
THE BIG PUNCH   Warner Bros., 1948
EMBRACEABLE YOU   Warner Bros., 1948
FLAXI MARTIN   Warner Bros., 1949
HOMICIDE   Warner Bros., 1949
THE YOUNGER BROTHERS   Warner
   Bros., 1949
THE HOUSE ACROSS THE STREET
   Warner Bros., 1949
BARRICADE   Warner Bros., 1950
COLT .45   Warner Bros., 1950
THIS SIDE OF THE LAW   Warner Bros.,
   1950
THE GREAT JEWEL ROBBER   Warner
   Bros., 1950
BREAKTHROUGH   Warner Bros., 1950
HIGHWAY 301   Warner Bros., 1951
INSIDE THE WALLS OF FOLSOM
   PRISON   Warner Bros., 1951
THE TANKS ARE COMING   Warner Bros.,
   1951
RETREAT, HELL!   Warner Bros., 1952
CATTLE TOWN   Warner Bros., 1952
PHANTOM FROM SPACE   1952
TOBOR THE GREAT   co-composer with
   Howard Jackson, Republic, 1954
REVENGE OF THE CREATURE
   co-composer, Universal, 1955
THE LITTLEST OUTLAW   Buena Vista,
   1955
THE DEADLY MANTIS   Universal, 1957
HELL BENT FOR LEATHER   Universal,
   1960
SEVEN WAYS FROM SUNDOWN
   co-composer, Universal, 1960

THE SIGN OF ZORRO   Buena Vista, 1960
PT-109   co-composer with David Buttolph,
   Warner Bros., 1963
WALL OF NOISE   Warner Bros., 1963
THE TATTOOED POLICE HORSE   Buena
   Vista, 1964
CHAMBER OF HORRORS   Warner Bros.,
   1966
ASSIGNMENT TO KILL   Warner Bros.,
   1968
CHUBASCO   Warner Bros., 1968
IN ENEMY COUNTRY   Universal, 1968
THE GOOD GUYS AND THE BAD GUYS
   Warner Bros., 1969
O'HARA, UNITED STATES TREASURY:
   OPERATION COBRA (TF)   co-composer
   with Ray Heindorf, Mark VII
   Ltd./Universal TV, 1971
DRACULA VS. FRANKENSTEIN   *BLOOD
   OF FRANKENSTEIN*
   Independent-International, 1971

ANGELO FRANCESCO
LAVAGNINO

b. 1909 - Italy
d. September, 1987

STRANO APPUNTAMENTO   *STRANGE
   APPOINTMENT*   1950, Italian
OTHELLO   co-composer with Alberto
   Barberis, United Artists, 1952,
   U.S.-Italian
JUNGLE SPELL   *MAGIA VERDE* (FD)
   1953, Italian
MAMBO   co-composer with Nino Rota,
   Paramount, 1954, U.S.-Italian
SINS OF CASANOVA   1954, Italian
LA DONNA DEL FIUME   *THE WOMAN OF
   THE RIVER*   co-composer with Armando
   Trovajoli, 1954, Italian
RICE GIRL   *LA RISAIA*   1955, Italian
THE MILLER'S BEAUTIFUL WIFE   *LA
   BELLA MUGNAIA*   1955, Italian
THE LAST PARADISE (FD)   1956, Italian
NERO'S WEEKEND   *MIO FIGLIO
   NERONE*   1956, Italian
LEGEND OF THE LOST   United Artists,
   1957
IL CIELO BRUCIA   co-composer with
   Francesco De Masi, 1957, Italian
CALYPSO (FD)   1958, Italian
BEHIND THE GREAT WALL   *LA
   MURAGLIA CINESE* (FD)   1958, Italian
THE NAKED MAJA   United Artists, 1959
MESSALINA   1959, Italian
POLICARPO   1959, Italian
CHE GIOIA VIVERE   1960, Italian
CONSPIRACY OF HEARTS   Paramount,
   1960, British
ESTHER AND THE KING   co-composer
   with Roberto Nicolosi, 1960, Italian
FIVE BRANDED WOMEN   1960, Italian
THE GRAND OLYMPICS (FD)
   co-composer with Armando Trovajoli,
   1960
THE LAST DAYS OF POMPEII   United
   Artists, 1960, Italian
THE SAVAGE INNOCENTS   Paramount,
   1960, Italian
HERCULES AGAINST ROME   1960,
   Italian
THE NIGHT THEY KILLED RASPUTIN
   L'ULTIMO ZAR   1960, Italian
NUDE ODYSSEY   1961, Italian
THE WARRIOR EMPRESS   1961, Italian
THE COLOSSUS OF RHODES   1961,
   Italian
GORGO   MGM, 1961, British
THE REVOLT OF THE SLAVES   1961,
   Italian
ULYSSES AGAINST THE SONS OF
   HERCULES   1961, Italian

THE WONDERS OF ALADDIN   MGM,
   1961, Italian-U.S.
THE CORSICAN BROTHERS   1961,
   Italian
GOLIATH AND THE VAMPIRES   Italian
   version only, 1961, Italian
DAMON AND PYTHIAS   1962, Italian
MARCO POLO   1962, Italian
THE SIEGE OF SYRACUSE   Paramount,
   1962, Italian
MADAME   1962, French-Italian
COMMANDO   *MARCIA O CREPA*   1963,
   Italian
SAMSON & THE SLAVE QUEEN
   composer of Italian version only, 1963,
   Italian
SAMSON CONTRO I PARATI   *SAMSON
   VS. THE PIRATES*   1963, Italian
AGENT 8 3/4   *HOT ENOUGH FOR JUNE*
   Continental, 1963, British
DARK PURPOSE   *L'INTRIGO*   1964,
   Italian
THE CASTLE OF THE LIVING DEAD
   1964, Italian-French
HERCULES AND THE TYRANTS OF
   BABYLON   1964, Italian
GLI INVINCIBILI TRE   *THE INVINCIBLE
   THREE*   1964, Italian
TOTO DE ARABIA   1964, Italian
THE HERO OF ROME   1964, Italian
L'INVINCIBILE CAVALIERE
   MASCHERATO   1964, French-Italian
McGUIRE GO HOME   *THE HIGH BRIGHT
   SUN*   1964, British-Italian
GUNMEN OF THE RIO GRANDE   1965,
   Italian
I TABU #2 (FD)   1965, Italian
I PREDONI DEL SAHARA   1965, Italian
IL MISTERO DELL'ISOLA MALEDETTA
   1965, Italian
IL CASTELLO DEI MORTI VIVI   1965,
   Italian
JOHNNY WEST IL MANCINO   1965,
   Italian
HERCULES, SAMSON & ULYSSES   1965,
   Italian
SEVEN HOURS OF GUNFIRE   1965,
   Italian
SNOW DEVILS   1965, Italian
SALADINO   1966, Italian
CHIMES AT MIDNIGHT   *FALSTAFF*
   Peppercorn-Wormser, 1966,
   Spanish-Swiss
WILD WILD PLANET   *I CRIMINALI DELLA
   GELASSIA*   MGM, 1966, Italian
WAR BETWEEN THE PLANETS
   MISSIONE PIANETA ERRANTE
   Fanfare, 1966, Italian
GUNGALA, LA VIRGINE DELLS GIUNGLA
   *GUNGALA, THE VIRGIN OF THE
   JUNGLE*   1967, Italian
ACID   co-composer with Armando Trovajoli,
   1967, Italian
OGGI A ME, DOMANI A TE   1968, Italian
SCUSI, LEI CONOSCE IL SESSO?
   co-composer with Piero Umiliani, 1968,
   Italian
REQUIEM PER UN GRINGO   1968, Italian
STORY OF A GIRL ALONE   1969, Spanish
GLI SPECIALISTI   1969, French-Italian
QUALCOSA STRISCIA NEL BUIO
   *SOMETHING IS CREEPING IN THE
   DARK*   1970, Italian
ZORRO, MARCHESE DI NAVARRE   1971,
   Italian
QUEENS OF EVIL   *IL DELITTO DEL
   DIAVOLO*   1971, Italian
AFRICA NUDA, AFRICA VIOLENTA (FD)
   1973, Italian
NAKED MAGIC   *SHOCKING CANNIBALS*
   Fury Films, 1974, Italian
L'ITALIA IN PIGIAMA   1976, Italian

JOHN LEIPOLD

STAGECOACH ★★ co-composer, United
Artists, 1939
DISPUTED PASSAGE co-composer,
Paramount, 1939
THE FLYING DEUCES co-composer,
RKO Radio, 1939
UNION PACIFIC co-composer,
Paramount, 1939
THE PARSON OF PANAMINT Paramount,
1941
SHUT MY BIG MOUTH Columbia, 1942
TWO YANKS IN TRINIDAD Columbia,
1942
THE DARING YOUNG MAN Columbia,
1943
THE DESPERADOES Columbia, 1943
GOOD LUCK, MR. YATES Columbia,
1943
NINE GIRLS Columbia, 1944

OSCAR LEVANT

b. December 27, 1906 - Pittsburgh,
Pennsylvania
d. 1972 - Beverly Hills, California

CRIME WITHOUT PASSION co-composer
with Frank Tours, Paramount, 1934
CHARLIE CHAN AT THE OPERA opera
sequence, 20th Century-Fox, 1937
NOTHING SACRED United Artists, 1937
MADE FOR EACH OTHER United Artists,
1939
PETE ROLEUM AND HIS COUSINS
co-composer with Hans Eisler, 1939

LOUIS LEVY

b. 1893
d. August 18, 1957

EVENSONG 1934, British
ALIAS BULLDOG DRUMMOND 1935,
British
MR. HOBO 1935, British
TRANSATLANTIC TUNNEL 1935, British
EAST MEETS WEST 1936, British
IT'S LOVE AGAIN co-composer, 1936,
British
NINE DAYS A QUEEN 1936, British
THE PASSING OF THE THIRD FLOOR
BACK 1936, British
THE SECRET AGENT Gaumont-British,
1936, British
SEVEN SINNERS 1936, British
SABOTAGE A WOMAN ALONE
Gaumont-British, 1936, British
HEAD OVER HEELS IN LOVE 1937,
British
YOUNG AND INNOCENT THE GIRL WAS
YOUNG Gaumont-British, 1937, British
MAN OF AFFAIRS 1937, British
THE CITADEL MGM, 1938
NIGHT TRAIN NIGHT TRAIN TO
MUNICH MGM, 1940, British
HAUNTED HONEYMOON MGM, 1941,
British
THE HASTY HEART Warner Bros., 1949
WOMAN IN A DRESSING GOWN Warner
Bros., 1957, British

MICHAEL J. LINN

d. March 23, 1995 - Los Angeles, California

BREAKIN' 2: ELECTRIC BOOGALOO
Tri-Star/Cannon, 1984
TRIAL BY TERROR 1985
AMERICAN NINJA II Cannon, 1985
RAPPIN' Cannon, 1985
DUET FOR ONE Cannon, 1986

SURVIVAL GAME Trans World
Entertainment, 1987
ALLAN QUARTERMAIN AND THE LOST
CITY OF GOLD Cannon, 1987
ILLICIT BEHAVIOR (CTF)
Prism/Promark/Asok Amritraj Prods.,
1992
SNAPDRAGON Prism, 1993

WILLIAM LOOSE

LOVE AND KISSES co-composer with
Jimmie Haskell, Universal, 1965
NAVAJO RUN co-composer with Emil
Cadkin, American International, 1966,
Italian-Spanish
TARZAN AND THE GREAT RIVER
Paramount, 1967
TARZAN AND THE JUNGLE BOY
Paramount, 1968
THE BIG BIRD CAGE co-composer with
William Castleman, 1972
THE EROTIC ADVENTURES OF ZORRO
co-composer with Betty Allen, 1972,
French-West German
THE WONDER OF IT ALL 1973
DEVIL TIMES FIVE PEOPLE TOYS/THE
HORRIBLE HOUSE ON THE HILL 1974
SWEET SUZY! BLACKSNAKE
co-composer with Al Teeter, Signal 166,
1975
RUSS MEYER'S UP! RM Films, 1976
MYSTERIOUS ISLAND OF BEAUTIFUL
WOMEN (TF) co-composer with Jack
Tillar, Alan Landsburg Productions, 1979
THE MAN WHO SAW TOMORROW
co-composer with Jack Tillar, Warner
Bros., 1981

LEIGHTON LUCAS

b. 1903 - London, England
d. 1982 - London, England

TARGET FOR TONIGHT 1941, British
STAGE FRIGHT Warner Bros., 1950
THE WEAK AND THE WICKED Allied
Artists, 1954, British
THE DAM BUSTERS Warner Bros., 1955,
British
BATTLE HELL YANGTSE INCIDENT
DCA, 1957, British
DESERT ATTACK ICE COLD IN ALEX
20th Century-Fox, 1958, British
THE SON OF ROBIN HOOD 20th
Century-Fox, 1959, British

ELISABETH LUYTENS

b. 1906 - London, England
d. 1983 - London, England

A STRING OF BEADS 1947, British
THE BOY KUMASENU 1951, British
EL DORADO 1951, British
WORLD WITHOUT END 1953, British
THE MALPAS MYSTERY
Anglo-Amalgamated, 1960, British
PARANOIAC Universal, 1964, British
THE EARTH DIES SCREAMING 20th
Century-Fox, 1964, British
WHY BOTHER TO KNOCK? 1964, British
DR. TERROR'S HOUSE OF HORRORS
Paramount, 1965, British
THE SKULL Paramount, 1965, British
SPACEFLIGHT IC-1 1965, British
THE PSYCHOPATH Paramount, 1966,
British
THEATRE OF DEATH BLOOD FIEND
1967, British
THE TERRORNAUTS 1967, British
MIJN HACHTEN MET SUSAN OLGA
ALBERT JULIE PIET & SANDRA 1975,
Dutch

M

MICHEL MAGNE

b. 1930 - Lisieux, France
d. 1985 - France

LE PAIN VIVANT 1954, French
LES PIQUE-ASSIETTES 1959, French
LES LIVREURS 1960, French
UN SINGE EN HIVER 1961, French
LES BRICOLEURS 1961, French
LOVE ON A PILLOW LE REPOS DU
GUERRIER Royal Films International,
1962, French-Italian
GIGOT ★ 20th Century-Fox, 1962
LE VICE ET LA VERTU 1962, French
ANY NUMBER CAN WIN MELODIE EN
SOUS-SOL MGM, 1963, French
GERMINAL 1963, French
LES GRANDS CHEMINS 1963, French
LES TONTONS FLINGLEURS 1963,
French
LE MONOCLE RIT JAUNE 1963, French
LA MARQUISE DES ANGES 1963,
French
CIRCLE OF LOVE LA RONDE
Continental, 1964, French
FANTOMAS 1964, French
MARVEILLEUSE ANGELIQUE 1964,
French
PAR UN BEAU MATIN D'ETE 1964,
French
SYMPHONY FOR A MASSACRE 7 Arts,
1965, French-Italian
LE JOURNAL D'UNE FEMME EN BLANC
1965, French
GALIA 1965, French
THE SLEEPING CAR MURDERS 7 Arts,
1966, French
LES BONS VIVANTS 1966, French
ANGELIQUE ET LE ROI 1966, French
LE NOUVEAU JOURNAL D'UNE FEMME
EN BLANC 1966, French
AVEC LA PEAU AUTRES 1967, French
TWO WEEKS IN SEPTEMBER A COEUR
JOIE Paramount, 1967, French
BELLE DE JOUR Allied Artists, 1967,
French-Italian
FLEUR D'OSEILLE 1968, French
ANGELIQUE ET LE SULTAN 1969,
French
LA ROUTE DE SALINA 1970, French
MANON 70 1970, French
UN FEMME EN BLANC SE REVOLTE
1970, French
COLD SWEAT DE LA PART DES
COPAINS Emerson, 1970, French
CRAN D'ARRET 1971, French
TOUT LE MONDE IL EST BEAU... 1973,
French
MS. DON JUAN DON JUAN ETAIT UNE
FEMME Scotia American, 1973,
French
MOI Y'EN A VOULOIR DES SOUS 1973,
French
UN ANGE AU PARADIS 1973, French
LES CHINOIS A PARIS 1974, French
LE COMPLOT CIC, 1975, French
NEA NEA - A YOUNG EMMANUELLE
Libra, 1976, French
SURPRISE PARTY co-composer,
Uranium Films, 1982, French

L'INDIC *THE INFORMER* GEF/CCFC, 1983, French
S.A.S. A SAN SALVADOR *S.A.S. - TERMINATE WITH EXTREME PREJUDICE* UGC, 1983, West German-French
EMMANUELLE 4 AAA/Sedpa, 1984, French
REVEILLON CHEZ BOB 1984, French

HENRY MANCINI

b. April 16, 1924 - Cleveland, Ohio
d. June 14, 1994 - Los Angeles, California

BACK FROM THE FRONT co-composer with Herman Stein, Universal, 1952
HAS ANYBODY SEEN MY GAL? co-composer, Universal, 1952
HORIZONS WEST co-composer, Universal, 1952
LOST IN ALASKA co-composer, Universal, 1952
MEET ME AT THE FAIR co-composer, Universal, 1952
THE RAIDERS co-composer, Universal, 1952
ALL I DESIRE co-composer, Universal, 1953
CITY BENEATH THE SEA co-composer, Universal, 1953
COLUMN SOUTH co-composer, Universal, 1953
IT CAME FROM OUTER SPACE co-composer, Universal, 1953
EAST OF SUMATRA co-composer, Universal, 1953
GIRLS IN THE NIGHT co-composer, Universal, 1953
THE GOLDEN BLADE co-composer, Universal, 1953
THE GREAT SIOUX UPRISING co-composer, Universal, 1953
GUNSMOKE co-composer, Universal, 1953
WALKING MY BABY BACK HOME Universal, 1953
IT HAPPENS EVERY THURSDAY Universal, 1953
LAW AND ORDER co-composer, Universal, 1953
THE LONE HAND co-composer, Universal, 1953
TAKE ME TO TOWN co-composer, Universal, 1953
TUMBLEWEED co-composer, Universal, 1953
THE VEILS OF BAGDAD co-composer, Universal, 1953
THE WORLD'S MOST BEAUTIFUL GIRLS Universal, 1953
THE CREATURE FROM THE BLACK LAGOON co-composer, 1954
FIREMAN SAVE MY CHILD co-composer, Universal, 1954
FOUR GUNS TO THE BORDER co-composer, Universal, 1954
THIS ISLAND EARTH co-composer, Universal, 1954
THE GLENN MILLER STORY ★ co-composer, Universal, 1954
JOHNNY DARK co-composer, Universal, 1954
MA AND PA KETTLE AT HOME co-composer, Universal, 1954
SO THIS IS PARIS co-composer with Herman Stein, Universal, 1954
TANGANYIKA co-composer, Universal, 1954
YELLOW MOUNTAIN co-composer, Universal, 1954

ABBOTT & COSTELLO MEET THE KEYSTONE COPS co-composer, Universal, 1955
THE FAR COUNTRY co-composer, Universal, 1955
THE PRIVATE WAR OF MAJOR BENSON co-composer, Universal, 1955
THE SPOILERS co-composer, Universal, 1955
THE SECOND GREATEST SEX Universal, 1955
THE BENNY GOODMAN STORY Universal, 1955
AIN'T MISBEHAVIN' Universal, 1955
THE CREATURE WALKS AMONG US co-composer, Universal, 1956
A DAY OF FURY co-composer, Universal, 1956
EVERYTHING BUT THE TRUTH co-composer, Universal, 1956
FRANCIS IN THE HAUNTED HOUSE Universal, 1956
THE GREAT MAN co-composer, Universal, 1956
ROCK PRETTY BABY Universal, 1956
THE TOY TIGER co-composer, Universal, 1956
THE UNGUARDED MOMENT co-composer, Universal, 1956
JOE DAKOTA co-composer, Universal, 1957
THE KETTLES ON OLD MACDONALD'S FARM co-composer, Universal, 1957
THE LAND UNKNOWN co-composer, Universal, 1957
MISTER CORY co-composer, Universal, 1957
THE MONOLITH MONSTERS co-composer, Universal, 1957
THE NIGHT RUNNER co-composer, Universal, 1957
MAN AFRAID Universal, 1957
DAMN CITIZEN co-composer, Universal, 1958
SUMMER LOVE Universal, 1958
FLOOD TIME Universal, 1958
THE THING THAT COULDN'T DIE co-composer, Universal, 1958
VOICE IN THE MIRROR Universal, 1958
TOUCH OF EVIL Universal, 1958
NEVER STEAL ANYTHING SMALL Universal, 1959
HIGH TIME 20th Century-Fox, 1960
THE GREAT IMPOSTOR 1960
BREAKFAST AT TIFFANY'S ★★ Paramount, 1961
BACHELOR IN PARADISE MGM, 1961
HATARI! Paramount, 1962
EXPERIMENT IN TERROR Warner Bros., 1962
DAYS OF WINE AND ROSES Warner Bros., 1962
MR. HOBBS TAKES A VACATION 20th Century-Fox, 1962
SOLDIER IN THE RAIN Allied Artists, 1963
THE PINK PANTHER ★ United Artists, 1964
CHARADE Universal, 1964
MAN'S FAVORITE SPORT? Universal, 1964
A SHOT IN THE DARK United Artists, 1964
DEAR HEART Warner Bros., 1964
THE GREAT RACE Warner Bros., 1965
ARABESQUE Universal, 1966, British-U.S.
MOMENT TO MOMENT Universal, 1966
WHAT DID YOU DO IN THE WAR, DADDY? United Artists, 1966
TWO FOR THE ROAD 20th Century-Fox, 1967, British-U.S.

WAIT UNTIL DARK Warner Bros., 1967
GUNN Warner Bros., 1967
THE PARTY United Artists, 1968
GAILY, GAILY United Artists, 1969
ME, NATALIE Cinema Center, 1969
SUNFLOWER ★ Avco Embassy, 1969, Italian-French
DARLING LILI Paramount, 1970
THE HAWAIIANS United Artists, 1970
THE MOLLY MAGUIRES Paramount, 1970
SOMETIMES A GREAT NOTION *NEVER GIVE AN INCH* Universal, 1971
THE NIGHT VISITOR UMC, 1971
THE THIEF WHO CAME TO DINNER Warner Bros., 1972
VISIONS OF EIGHT Cinema 5, 1973
OKLAHOMA CRUDE Columbia, 1973
THE GIRL FROM PETROVKA Universal, 1974
THAT'S ENTERTAINMENT! (FD) MGM/United Artists, 1974
99 & 44/100% DEAD 20th Century-Fox, 1974
THE WHITE DAWN Paramount, 1974
RETURN OF THE PINK PANTHER United Artists, 1975, British
THE BLUE NIGHT (TF) Lorimar Productions, 1975
THE GREAT WALDO PEPPER Universal, 1975
JACQUELINE SUSANN'S ONCE IS NOT ENOUGH *ONCE IS NOT ENOUGH* Paramount, 1975
SILVER STREAK 20th Century-Fox, 1976
THE PINK PANTHER STRIKES AGAIN United Artists, 1976, British
W.C. FIELDS AND ME Universal, 1976
ALEX & THE GYPSY 20th Century-Fox, 1976
ANGELA Embassy Home Entertainment, 1976, Canadian
ARTHUR HAILEY'S 'THE MONEY-CHANGERS' (MS) Ross Hunter Productions/Paramount Pictures TV, 1976
REVENGE OF THE PINK PANTHER United Artists, 1978, British
SUDDENLY, LOVE (TF) Ross Hunter Productions, 1978
A FAMILY UPSIDE DOWN (TF) Ross Hunter-Jacques Mapes Film/Paramount TV, 1978
HOUSE CALLS Universal, 1978
WHO IS KILLING THE GREAT CHEFS OF EUROPE? Warner Bros., 1978
THE PRISONER OF ZENDA Universal, 1979
THE BEST PLACE TO BE (TF) Ross Hunter Productions, 1979
NIGHTWING Columbia, 1979
10 ★ Orion/Warner Bros., 1979
LITTLE MISS MARKER Universal, 1980
THE SHADOW BOX (TF) The Shadow Box Film Company, 1980
A CHANGE OF SEASONS 20th Century-Fox, 1980
BACK ROADS Warner Bros., 1981
S.O.B. Paramount, 1981
CONDORMAN Buena Vista, 1981
MOMMIE DEAREST Paramount, 1981
VICTOR/VICTORIA ★★ MGM/United Artists, 1982
TRAIL OF THE PINK PANTHER MGM/UA, 1982
SECOND THOUGHTS Universal, 1983
BETTER LATE THAN NEVER Warner Bros., 1983, British
CURSE OF THE PINK PANTHER MGM/UA, 1983

THE THORN BIRDS (MS) ☆ David L. Wolper-Stan Margulies Productions/Edward Lewis Productions/Warner Bros. TV, 1983
THE MAN WHO LOVED WOMEN Columbia, 1983
HARRY & SON Orion, 1984
THAT'S DANCING! (FD) MGM/UA, 1985
LIFEFORCE Tri-Star, 1985, British
SANTA CLAUS: THE MOVIE Tri-Star, 1985, U.S.-British
THE GREAT MOUSE DETECTIVE Buena Vista, 1986
A FINE MESS Columbia, 1986
THAT'S LIFE! Columbia, 1986
BLIND DATE Tri-Star, 1987
THE GLASS MENAGERIE Cineplex Odeon, 1987
SUNSET Tri-Star, 1988
WITHOUT A CLUE Orion, 1988
JUSTIN CASE (TF) The Blake Edwards Company/Walt Disney TV, 1988
PHYSICAL EVIDENCE Columbia, 1989
PETER GUNN (TF) The Blake Edwards Co./New World TV, 1989
SKIN DEEP 20th Century Fox, 1989
WELCOME HOME Columbia, 1989
FEAR (CTF) Vestron, 1990
GHOST DAD Universal, 1990
NEVER FORGET (CTF) Nimoy-Radnitz, 1991
SWITCH Warner Bros., 1991
MARRIED TO IT Orion, 1991
TOM AND JERRY: THE MOVIE (AF) Turner Pictures, 1992
SON OF THE PINK PANTHER MGM, 1993

RICHARD MARKOWITZ

b. 1926
d. Dec 6, 1994 - Los Angeles, CA

STAKE-OUT ON DOPE STREET Warner Bros., 1958
THE HOT ANGEL Paramount, 1958
THE YOUNG CAPTIVES Paramount, 1959
OPERATION DAMES American International, 1959
ROAD RACERS American International, 1960
THE HOODLUM PRIEST United Artists, 1961
THE MAGIC SWORD United Artists, 1962
CRY OF BATTLE Allied Artists, 1963
A FACE IN THE RAIN Embassy, 1963
ONE MAN'S WAY Columbia, 1964
BUS RILEY'S BACK IN TOWN Universal, 1965
THE WILD SEED Universal, 1965
SCALPLOCK (TF) Columbia Pictures TV, 1966
THE SHOOTING American International, 1966
RIDE BEYOND VENGEANCE Columbia, 1966
A BLACK VEIL FOR LISA Commonwealth United, 1969, Italian-West German
WEEKEND OF TERROR (TF) Paramount TV, 1970
CRY FOR ME, BILLY COUNT YOUR BULLETS/FACE TO THE WIND/APACHE MASSACRE/THE LONG TOMORROW Brut Productions, 1972
THE VOYAGE OF THE YES (TF) Bing Crosby Productions, 1973
THE STRANGER (TF) Bing Crosby Productions, 1973
THE HANGED MAN (TF) Fenady Associates/Bing Crosby Productions, 1974

PANIC ON THE 5:22 (TF) QM Productions, 1974
THE GIRL ON THE LATE, LATE SHOW (TF) Screen Gems/Columbia TV, 1974
WINNER TAKE ALL (TF) The Jozak Company, 1975
THE RETURN OF JOE FORRESTER (TF) David Gerber Productions/Columbia Pictures TV, 1975
BRINK'S: THE GREAT ROBBERY (TF) QM Productions/Warner Bros. TV, 1976
KISS ME...KILL ME (TF) The Writers Company/Columbia Pictures TV, 1976
MAYDAY AT 40,000 FEET (TF) Andrew J. Fenady Associates/Warner Bros. TV, 1976
WASHINGTON, BEHIND CLOSED DOORS (MS) composer of Parts 4 and 6 only, Paramount TV, 1977
DOCTORS' PRIVATE LIVES (TF) David Gerber Company/Columbia TV, 1978
STANDING TALL (TF) QM Productions, 1978
HUNTERS OF THE REEF (TF) Writers Company Productions/Paramount TV, 1978
THE BOSS' SON The Boss' Son Prods., 1978
DEATH CAR ON THE FREEWAY (TF) Shpetner Productions, 1979
THE NEIGHBORHOOD (TF) David Gerber Company/Columbia TV, 1982
CIRCLE OF POWER MYSTIQUE/BRAINWASH/THE NAKED WEEKEND QUI Productions, 1983
A MASTERPIECE OF MURDER (TF) 20th Century Fox TV, 1986
THE LAW & HARRY MCGRAW (TF) Universal TV, 1987

BRIAN MAY

b. Australia
d. 1997

THE TRUE STORY OF ESKIMO NELL DICK DOWN UNDER Quest Films/Filmways Australasian Distributors, 1975, Australian
NO ROOM TO RUN (TF) Australian Broadcasting Commission/Trans-Atlantic Enterprises, 1977, Australian
BARNABY AND ME Trans-Atlantic Enterprises, 1978
PATRICK Cinema Shares International, 1979, Australian
THE DAY AFTER HALLOWEEN SNAPSHOT Group 1, 1979, Australian
THIRST 1979, Australian
MAD MAX American International, 1979, Australian
HARLEQUIN New Image, 1980, Australian
THE LAST OUTLAW (MS) Network Seven/Pegasus Productions, 1980, Australian
NIGHTMARES Australian
THE SURVIVOR Hemdale, 1981, Australian
DEADLINE Australian
GALLIPOLI Paramount, 1981, Australian
ROAD GAMES Avco Embassy, 1981
DANGEROUS SUMMER Filmco Ltd., 1982, Australian
TREASURE OF THE YANKEE ZEPHYR RACE TO THE YANKEE ZEPHYR Artists Releasing Corporation/Film Ventures International, 1984, New Zealand-British
THE KILLING OF ANGEL STREET Forest Home Films, 1981, Australian
BREAKFAST IN PARIS 1982, Australian

THE ROAD WARRIOR MAD MAX II Warner Bros., 1982, Australian
TURKEY SHOOT Second FGH Film Consortium, 1982, Australian
KITTY & THE BAGMAN Quartet/Films Incorporated, 1982, Australian
RETURN TO EDEN (MS) McElroy & McElroy/Hanna-Barbera Australia Productions, 1983, Australian
A SLICE OF LIFE Australian
VOYEUR Australian
CLOAK & DAGGER Universal, 1984
MISSING IN ACTION II: THE BEGINNING Cannon, 1984
FROG DREAMING Middle Reef Productions, 1985
THE LAST FRONTIER (TF) McElroy & McElroy Productions, 1986, Australian
SKY PIRATES John Lamond Motion Pictures, 1986, Australian
DEATH BEFORE DISHONOR New World, 1987
STEEL DAWN Vestron, 1987
A DANGEROUS LIFE (CTF) HBO/McElroy & McElroy/FilmAccord Corporation/Australian Broadcasting Corporation/Zenith Productions, 1988, U.S.-Australian
DARLING OF THE GODS (MS) 1989, Australian-U.K.
BLOOD MOON 1989, Australian
DEAD SLEEP 1990, Australian
HURRICANE SMITH 1990, Australian
FREDDY'S DEAD: THE FINAL NIGHTMARE New Line, 1991
DR. GIGGLES Universal, 1992
BLIND SIDE (CTF) Chestnut Hill Prods./HBO, 1993

DOUG MAYNARD

d. November 29

PATTI ROCKS FilmDallas, 1987

EDMUND MEISEL

d. 1930

THE BATTLESHIP POTEMKIN POTEMKIN Amkino, 1925, Soviet
BERLIN—SYMPHONY OF A GREAT CITY 1927
OCTOBER TEN DAYS THAT SHOOK THE WORLD Amkino, 1928,

MICHEL MICHELET

b. June 27, 1899 - Kiev, Russia

THE END OF THE WORLD 1930, French
LE MONT SAINT-MICHEL 1934, French
LES YEUX NOIRS 1935, French
NOSTALGIE 1935, French
LES BATELIERS DE LA VOLGA 1935, French
SOUS LA TERREUR 1935, French
FORFAITURE 1936, French
LE MENSONGE DE NINA PETROVNA 1937, French
ALERTE EN MEDITERRANEE 1938, French
LE DERNIER TOURNANT 1939, French
VOICE IN THE WIND United Artists, 1944
THE HAIRY APE ★ United Artists, 1944
UP IN MABEL'S ROOM United Artists, 1944
MUSIC FOR MILLIONS MGM, 1944
THE DIARY OF A CHAMBERMAID United Artists, 1946
THE CHASE United Artists, 1946
LURED PERSONAL COLUMN Universal, 1947
SIREN OF ATLANTIS United Artists, 1948

IMPACT   United Artists, 1949
OUTPOST IN MOROCCO   United Artists, 1949
THE MAN ON THE EIFFEL TOWER   RKO Radio, 1949
ONCE A THIEF   United Artists, 1950
DOUBLE DEAL   RKO Radio, 1950
M   Columbia, 1951
TARZAN'S PERIL   RKO Radio, 1951
FORT ALGIERS   United Artists, 1953
UN MISSIONNAIRE   1955, French
LE SECRET DE SOEUR ANGELE   1955, French
LA VENERE DI CHERONEA   1957, French
DER TIGER VON ESCHNAPUR   *JOURNEY TO THE LOST CITY*   American International, 1959, West German-French-Italian
DAS INDISCHE GRABMAL   *JOURNEY TO THE LOST CITY*   American International, 1959, West German-French-Italian
GODDESS OF LOVE   1960, Italian
CAPTAIN SINDBAD   MGM, 1963
THE CHALLENGE OF GREATNESS   1976

DARIUS MILHAUD
b. September 4, 1892 - Aix-en-Provence, France
d. 1974 - Geneva, Switzerland

L'INHUMAINE   1925, French
ACTUALITIES   1928, French
LA PETITE LILI   1929, French
HALLO EVERYBODY   1933, French
L'HIPPOCAMPE   1934, French
TARTARIN DE TARASCON   1934, French
MADAME BOVARY   C.I.D., 1934, French
THE SEA HORSE   1934, French
THE BELOVED VAGABOND   1934, British
GRANDS FEUX   1937, French
LA CITADELLE DU SILENCE   co-composer with Arthur Honegger, 1937, French
A LA CONQUETE DU CIEL   1937, French
MOLLENARD   *HATRED*   1938, French
LA TRAGEDIE IMPERIALE   1938, French
LES OTAGES   1938, French
GULF STREAM   1939, French
CAVALCADE d'AMOUR   co-composer with Arthur Honegger, 1939, French
L'ESPOIR   1939, French
THE ISLANDERS   1939, British
THE PRIVATE AFFAIRS OF BEL AMI   United Artists, 1947
DREAMS THAT MONEY CAN BUY   co-composer, Films International of America, 1948
LIFE BEGINS TOMORROW   *LA VIE COMMENCE DEMAIN*   1950, French
ILS ETAIENT TOUS DES VOLONTAIRES (FD)   1954, French
CELLE QUI N'ETAIT PLUS   co-composer with Pierre Henry, 1957, French

CYRIL J. MOCKRIDGE
b. August 6, 1896 - London, England
d. January 18, 1979

THE ADVENTURES OF SHERLOCK HOLMES   co-composer, 20th Century-Fox, 1939
WHISPERING GHOSTS   co-composer, 20th Century-Fox, 1942
THE UNDYING MONSTER   co-composer, 20th Century-Fox, 1942
MOONTIDE   co-composer with David Buttolph, 20th Century-Fox, 1942
MANILA CALLING   co-composer with David Buttolph and David Raksin, 20th Century-Fox, 1942

THE MAN IN THE TRUNK   20th Century-Fox, 1942
THE MEANEST MAN IN THE WORLD   20th Century-Fox, 1943
OVER MY DEAD BODY   20th Century-Fox, 1943
TONIGHT WE RAID CALAIS   20th Century-Fox, 1943
THE OX-BOW INCIDENT   20th Century-Fox, 1943
HOLY MATRIMONY   20th Century-Fox, 1943
HAPPY LAND   20th Century-Fox, 1943
THE SULLIVANS   20th Century-Fox, 1944
THE EVE OF ST. MARK   20th Century-Fox, 1944
LADIES OF WASHINGTON   20th Century-Fox, 1944
THE BIG NOISE   20th Century-Fox, 1944
THUNDERHEAD—SON OF FLICKA   20th Century-Fox, 1945
MOLLY AND ME   20th Century-Fox, 1945
CAPTAIN EDDIE   20th Century-Fox, 1945
COLONEL EFFINGHAM'S RAID   20th Century-Fox, 1946
SENTIMENTAL JOURNEY   20th Century-Fox, 1946
THE DARK CORNER   20th Century-Fox, 1946
CLUNY BROWN   20th Century-Fox, 1946
CLAUDIA AND DAVID   20th Century-Fox, 1946
MY DARLING CLEMENTINE   20th Century-Fox, 1946
WAKE UP AND DREAM   20th Century-Fox, 1946
THE LATE GEORGE APLEY   20th Century-Fox, 1947
MIRACLE ON 34TH STREET   20th Century-Fox, 1947
NIGHTMARE ALLEY   20th Century-Fox, 1947
THUNDER IN THE VALLEY   20th Century-Fox, 1947
SCUDDA HOO! SCUDDA HAY!   20th Century-Fox, 1948
GREEN GRASS OF WYOMING   20th Century-Fox, 1948
DEEP WATERS   20th Century-Fox, 1948
THE WALLS OF JERICHO   20th Century-Fox, 1948
LUCK OF THE IRISH   20th Century-Fox, 1948
ROAD HOUSE   20th Century-Fox, 1948
THAT WONDERFUL URGE   20th Century-Fox, 1949
THE BEAUTIFUL BLONDE FROM BASHFUL BEND   20th Century-Fox, 1949
SLATTERY'S HURRICANE   20th Century-Fox, 1949
COME TO THE STABLE   20th Century-Fox, 1949
I WAS A MALE WAR BRIDE   20th Century-Fox, 1949
FATHER WAS A FULLBACK   20th Century-Fox, 1949
MOTHER DIDN'T TELL ME   20th Century-Fox, 1950
CHEAPER BY THE DOZEN   20th Century-Fox, 1950
A TICKET TO TOMAHAWK   20th Century-Fox, 1950
LOVE THAT BRUTE   20th Century-Fox, 1950
WHERE THE SIDEWALK ENDS   20th Century-Fox, 1950
STELLA   20th Century-Fox, 1950
AMERICAN GUERRILLA IN THE PHILIPPINES   20th Century-Fox, 1950
YOU'RE IN THE NAVY NOW   20th Century-Fox, 1951

FOLLOW THE SUN   20th Century-Fox, 1951
HALF ANGEL   20th Century-Fox, 1951
AS YOUNG AS YOU FEEL   20th Century-Fox, 1951
THE FROGMEN   20th Century-Fox, 1951
MR. BELVEDERE RINGS THE BELL   20th Century-Fox, 1951
LOVE NEST   20th Century-Fox, 1951
LET'S MAKE IT LEGAL   20th Century-Fox, 1951
ELOPEMENT   20th Century-Fox, 1951
THE MODEL AND THE MARRIAGE BROKER   20th Century-Fox, 1952
DEADLINE U.S.A.   20th Century-Fox, 1952
BELLES ON THEIR TOES   20th Century-Fox, 1952
WE'RE NOT MARRIED   20th Century-Fox, 1952
DREAMBOAT   20th Century-Fox, 1952
NIGHT WITHOUT SLEEP   20th Century-Fox, 1952
MISTER SCOUTMASTER   20th Century-Fox, 1953
HOW TO MARRY A MILLIONAIRE   20th Century-Fox, 1953
NIGHT PEOPLE   20th Century-Fox, 1954
WOMAN'S WORLD   20th Century-Fox, 1954
RIVER OF NO RETURN   20th Century-Fox, 1954
THE LIEUTENANT WORE SKIRTS   20th Century-Fox, 1956
DESK SET   20th Century-Fox, 1957
OH, MEN! OH, WOMEN!   20th Century-Fox, 1957
WILL SUCCESS SPOIL ROCK HUNTER?   20th Century-Fox, 1957
THE GIFT OF LOVE   20th Century-Fox, 1958
I MARRIED A WOMAN   Universal, 1958
RALLY 'ROUND THE FLAG, BOYS!   20th Century-Fox, 1958
HOUND-DOG MAN   20th Century-Fox, 1959
A PRIVATE'S AFFAIR   20th Century-Fox, 1959
THUNDER IN THE SUN   Paramount, 1959
TALL STORY   Warner Bros., 1960
WAKE ME WHEN IT'S OVER   20th Century-Fox, 1960
ALL HANDS ON DECK   20th Century-Fox, 1961
THE MAN WHO SHOT LIBERTY VALANCE   Paramount, 1962
DONOVAN'S REEF   Paramount, 1963

THELONIOUS MONK
d. February 17, 1982 - Englewood, New Jersey

LES LIASONS DANGEREUSES   co-composer with Jack Murray, Astor, 1959, French-Italian

LUCIEN MORAWECK
d. October 20, 1973

THE MAN IN THE IRON MASK ★   co-composer with Lud Gluskin, United Artists, 1939
THE LADY IN QUESTION   Columbia, 1940
DREAMING OUT LOUD   RKO Radio, 1940
INTERNATIONAL LADY   United Artists, 1941
FRIENDLY ENEMIES   United Artists, 1942
AVALANCHE   Producers Releasing Corp., 1946
STRANGE VOYAGE   Monogram, 1946
THE RETURN OF MONTE CRISTO   Small/Col., 1946

HIGH CONQUEST   co-composer with Rene Garriguenc and Lyn Murray, Monogram, 1947
16 FATHOMS DEEP   co-composer with Rene Garriguenc, Lake/Mon., 1948
MASSACRE RIVER   co-composer with John Leipold, Allied Artists, 1949
NEW MEXICO   co-composer with Rene Garriguenc, United Artists, 1951

JEROME MOROSS

b. August 1, 1913 - Brooklyn, New York
d. July 25, 1983 - Miami, Florida

CLOSE-UP   Eagle Lion, 1948
WHEN I GROW UP   United Artists, 1951
CAPTIVE CITY   United Artists, 1952
HANS CHRISTIAN ANDERSEN   ballet music only, RKO Radio, 1952
SEVEN WONDERS OF THE WORLD   co-composer with David Raksin and Sol Kaplan, Cinerama, 1956
THE SHARKFIGHTERS   United Artists, 1956
THE PROUD REBEL   Buena Vista, 1958
THE BIG COUNTRY ★   United Artists, 1958
THE JAYHAWKERS   Paramount, 1959
THE MOUNTAIN ROAD   Columbia, 1960
THE ADVENTURES OF HUCKLEBERRY FINN   MGM, 1960
FIVE FINGER EXERCISE   Columbia, 1962
THE CARDINAL   Columbia, 1963
THE WAR LORD   Universal, 1965
RACHEL RACHEL   Warner Bros., 1968
VALLEY OF THE GWANGI   Warner Bros., 1969
HAIL, HERO!   National General, 1969

DAVID MUNROW

THE DEVILS   additional music only, Warner Bros., 1971, British
ZARDOZ   20th Century Fox, 1974, British

LYN MURRAY

(Lionel Breeze)
b. December 6, 1909 - London, England
d. May 20, 1989 - Los Angeles, California

HIGH CONQUEST   co-composer with Rene Garriguenc and Lucien Moraweck, Monogram, 1947
THE PROWLER   United Artists, 1951
THE BIG NIGHT   United Artists, 1951
THE RETURN OF GILBERT & SULLIVAN   United Artists, 1951
SON OF PALEFACE   Paramount, 1952
THE GIRLS OF PLEASURE ISLAND   Paramount, 1952
HERE COME THE GIRLS   Paramount, 1953
CASANOVA'S BIG NIGHT   Paramount, 1954
THE BRIDGES AT TOKO-RI   Paramount, 1955
TO CATCH A THIEF   Paramount, 1955
D-DAY, THE SIXTH OF JUNE   20th Century-Fox, 1956
ON THE THRESHHOLD OF SPACE   20th Century-Fox, 1956
SNOW WHITE AND THE THREE STOOGES   Columbia, 1961
ESCAPE FROM ZAHRAIN   Paramount, 1962
PERIOD OF ADJUSTMENT   MGM, 1962
COME FLY WITH ME   MGM, 1963
WIVES AND LOVERS   Paramount, 1963
SIGNPOST TO MURDER   MGM, 1965

PROMISE HER ANYTHING   Paramount, 1966
ROSIE!   Universal, 1967
ESCAPE TO MINDANAO (TF)   Universal TV, 1968
NOW YOU SEE IT, NOW YOU DON'T (TF)   Universal TV, 1968
THE SMUGGLERS (TF)   Universal TV, 1968
DRAGNET (TF)   Mark VII Ltd./Universal TV, 1969
STRATEGY OF TERROR   IN DARKNESS WAITING   Universal, 1969, originally made for television
COCKEYED COWBOYS OF CALICO COUNTY   Universal, 1970
LOVE, HATE, LOVE (TF)   Aaron Spelling Productions, 1971
MAGIC CARPET (TF)   Westwood Productions/Universal TV, 1972
DON'T PUSH, I'LL CHARGE WHEN I'M READY (TF)   Universal TV, 1977, filmed in 1969

STANLEY MYERS

b. 1939
d. November 9, 1993

KALEIDOSCOPE   Warner Bros., 1966, British
ULYSSES   Continental, 1967
NO WAY TO TREAT A LADY   Paramount, 1968
OTLEY   Columbia, 1969, British
TWO GENTLEMEN SHARING   American International, 1969, British
AGE OF CONSENT   Columbia, 1970, Australian
TROPIC OF CANCER   Paramount, 1970
THE WALKING STICK   MGM, 1970, British
A SEVERED HEAD   Columbia, 1971, British
LONG AGO TOMORROW   THE RAGING MOON   Cinema 5, 1971, British
SUMMER LIGHTNING   1972, West German
SITTING TARGET   MGM, 1972, British
KING, QUEEN, KNAVE   Avco Embassy, 1972, West German-British
X, Y, ZEE   ZEE & CO.   Columbia, 1972, British
DIVORCE HIS/DIVORCE HERS (TF)   World Films Services, 1973
LITTLE MALCOLM AND HIS STRUGGLE AGAINST THE EUNUCHS   Multicetera Investments, 1974, British
FRIGHTMARE   Miracle, 1974, British
THE APPRENTICESHIP OF DUDLEY KRAVITZ   Paramount, 1974, Canadian
HOUSE OF WHIPCORD   Miracle, 1974, British
THE WILBY CONSPIRACY   United Artists, 1975, British
CARAVAN TO VACCARES   Bryanston, 1976, British-French
COUP DE GRACE   Cinema 5, 1976, West German
THE COMEBACK   THE DAY THE SCREAMING STOPPED   Enterprise, 1978, British
THE GREEK TYCOON   Universal, 1978
THE CLASS OF MISS MacMICHAELS   Brut Prods., 1978, British
THE DEER HUNTER   Universal, 1978
SUMMER OF MY GERMAN SOLDIER (TF)   Highgate Productions, 1978
A PORTRAIT OF THE ARTIST AS A YOUNG MAN   Howard Mahler Films, 1979

THE CLASS OF MISS MacMICHAEL   Brut Productions, 1979, British
ABSOLUTION   Trans World Entertainment, 1979, British
YESTERDAY'S HERO   EMI, 1979, British
THE WATCHER IN THE WOODS   Buena Vista, 1980, British
THE MARTIAN CHRONICLES (TF)   Charles Fries Productions/Stonehenge Productions, 1980
THE GENTLEMAN BANDIT (TF)   Highgate Pictures, 1981
LADY CHATTERLEY'S LOVER   Cannon, 1982, French-British
THE INCUBUS   Artists Releasing Corporation/Film Ventures International, 1982, Canadian
MOONLIGHTING   co-composer with Hans Zimmer, Universal Classics, 1982, British
HISTOIRE D'O No. 2   co-composer with Hans Zimmer, 1983
BEYOND THE LIMIT   THE HONORARY CONSUL   Paramount, 1983, British
BLIND DATE   co-composer with Hans Zimmer, New Line Cinema, 1984, British-Greek
SUCCESS IS THE BEST REVENGE   co-composer with Hans Zimmer, Triumph/Columbia, 1984, British
EUREKA   co-composer with Hans Zimmer, MGM/UA Classics, 1984, British
THE ZANY ADVENTURES OF ROBIN HOOD (TF)   Bobka Productions/Charles Fries Entertainment, 1984
BLACK ARROW (TF)   Harry Towers Productions/Pan-Atlantic Pictures Productions, 1985
THE CHAIN   Rank, 1985, British
THE LIGHTSHIP   co-composer with Hans Zimmer, Castle Hill Productions, 1985, U.S.-West German
FLORENCE NIGHTENGALE (TF)   Cypress Point Productions, 1985
INSIGNIFICANCE   co-composer with Hans Zimmer, Island Alive, 1985, British
THE RUSSIAN SOLDIER (TF)   BBC, 1985, British
CONDUCT UNBECOMING   Allied Artists, 1985, British
DREAMCHILD   co-composer with Hans Zimmer, Universal, 1985, British
WILD HORSES (TF)   co-composer with Hans Zimmer, Wild Horses Productions/Telepictures Productions, 1985
MY BEAUTIFUL LAUNDRETTE (TF)   co-composer with Hans Zimmer, Orion Classics, 1985, British
THE ZERO BOYS   co-composer with Hans Zimmer, Omega Pictures, 1986
SEPARATE VACATIONS   RSL Entertainment, 1986, Canadian
CASTAWAY   co-composer with Hans Zimmer, Cannon, 1986, British
STRONG MEDICINE (TF)   Telepictures Productions/TVS Ltd. Productions, 1986, U.S.-British
MONTE CARLO (TF)   New World TV/Phoenix Entertainment Group/Collins-Holm Productions/Highgate Pictures, 1986
RAINY DAY WOMEN (TF)   BBC, 1986, British
THE WIND   co-composer with Hans Zimmer, Omega Pictures, 1987
PACK OF LIES (TF)   Robert Halmi Inc., 1987
THE SECOND VICTORY   Filmworld Distributors, 1987, Australian-British
PRICK UP YOUR EARS   Samuel Goldwyn Company, 1987, British

SAMMIE & ROSIE GET LAID   Cinecom, 1987, British
WISH YOU WERE HERE   Atlantic Releasing Corporation, 1987, British
SCOOP (TF)   London Weekend TV, 1987, British
DOUBLE EXPOSURE   co-composer with Hans Zimmer, United Film Distribution Co., 1987
THE NATURE OF THE BEAST   co-composer with Hans Zimmer, Rosso Productions, 1988, British
TAFFIN   MGM/UA, 1988, U.S.-Irish
STARS AND BARS   Columbia, 1988
TRADING HEARTS   Cineworld, 1988
BAJA OKLAHOMA (CTF)   HBO Pictures/Rastar Productions, 1988
TIDY ENDINGS (CTF)   HBO Showcase/Sandollar Productions, 1988
THE MOST DANGEROUS MAN IN THE WORLD (TF)   BBC/Iberoamericana/Celtic Films, 1988, British
STONES FOR IBARRA (TF)   Titus Productions, 1988
TRACK 29   Island Pictures, 1988
THE BOOST   Hemdale, 1988
DANNY: CHAMPION OF THE WORLD (CTF)   Portobello Productions/British Screen/Thames TV/The Disney Channel/WonderWorks/Children's Film & Television Foundation, 1989, British-U.S.
SCENES FROM THE CLASS STRUGGLE IN BEVERLY HILLS   Cinecom, 1989
LADDER OF SWORDS   Film Four International, 1989
A MONTH OF SUNDAYS (CTF)   HBO Showcase, 1989
AGE-OLD FRIENDS (CTF)   Granger Productions/HBO Showcase, 1989
THE WITCHES   Warner Bros., 1990, British
TORRENTS OF SPRING   Millimeter, 1990, Italian
VOYAGER   Capella, 1991
IRON MAZE   Edward R. Pressman/Oliver Stone, 1991
CLAUDE   JJ Films, 1992
SARAFINA!   Miramax, 1992
COLD HEAVEN   Hemdale, 1992
MRS. 'ARRIS GOES TO PARIS (TF)   Accent Films/Novo Films/Corymore Prods., 1992
TRUSTING BEATRICE   Castle Hill, 1992
THE SUMMER HOUSE   Samuel Goldwyn, 1993
HEART OF DARKNESS (CTF)   Chris-Rose Prods./Turner Pictures, 1994

N

OLIVER NELSON
b. June 4, 1932 - Saint Louis, Missouri
d. October 28, 1975 - Los Angeles, California

DEATH OF A GUNFIGHTER   Universal, 1967
ISTANBUL EXPRESS (TF)   Universal TV, 1968
DIAL HOT LINE (TF)   Universal TV, 1970
SKULLDUGGERY   Universal, 1970
ZIGZAG   Universal, 1970

CUTTER (TF)   Universal TV, 1972
CHASE (TF)   CBS Entertainment, 1973
LAST TANGO IN PARIS   arranger, United Artists, 1973, Italian-French
INSIDE JOB   1973
MONEY TO BURN (TF)   Silverton Productions/Universal TV, 1973

ALFRED NEWMAN
b. March 17, 1901 - New Haven, Connecticut
d. February, 1970

THE DEVIL TO PAY   United Artists, 1931
REACHING FOR THE MOON   United Artists, 1931
KIKI   United Artists, 1931
INDISCREET   United Artists, 1931
STREET SCENE   United Artists, 1931
THE UNHOLY GARDEN   United Artists, 1931
THE AGE FOR LOVE   United Artists, 1931
CORSAIR   United Artists, 1931
AROUND THE WORLD IN EIGHTY MINUTES   United Artists, 1931
TONIGHT OR NEVER   United Artists, 1931
ARROWSMITH   United Artists, 1931
COCK OF THE AIR   United Artists, 1932
THE GREEKS HAD A WORD FOR THEM   United Artists, 1932
SKY DEVILS   United Artists, 1932
MR. ROBINSON CRUSOE   United Artists, 1932
RAIN   United Artists, 1932
CYNARA   United Artists, 1932
SECRETS   United Artists, 1933
I COVER THE WATERFRONT   United Artists, 1933
THE MASQUERADER   United Artists, 1933
THE BOWERY   United Artists, 1933
BLOOD MONEY   United Artists, 1933
ADVICE TO THE LOVELORN   United Artists, 1933
GALLANT LADY   United Artists, 1934
LOOKING FOR TROUBLE   United Artists, 1934
NANA   United Artists, 1934
THE HOUSE OF ROTHSCHILD   United Artists, 1934
BORN TO BE BAD   United Artists, 1934
THE AFFAIRS OF CELLINI   United Artists, 1934
THE LAST GENTLEMAN   United Artists, 1934
BULLDOG DRUMMOND STRIKES BACK   United Artists, 1934
THE CAT'S PAW   20th Century-Fox, 1934
OUR DAILY BREAD   United Artists, 1934
WE LIVE AGAIN   United Artists, 1934
THE COUNT OF MONTE CRISTO   United Artists, 1934
THE MIGHTY BARNUM   United Artists, 1935
CLIVE OF INDIA   United Artists, 1935
THE WEDDING NIGHT   United Artists, 1935
LES MISERABLES   United Artists, 1935
CARDINAL RICHELIEU   United Artists, 1935
THE CALL OF THE WILD   United Artists, 1935
THE DARK ANGEL   United Artists, 1935
BARBARY COAST   United Artists, 1935
THE MELODY LINGERS ON   United Artists, 1935
SPLENDOR   United Artists, 1935
THESE THREE   United Artists, 1936
RAMONA   20th Century-Fox, 1936
DODSWORTH   United Artists, 1936
COME AND GET IT   United Artists, 1936
BELOVED ENEMY   United Artists, 1937

YOU ONLY LIVE ONCE   United Artists, 1937
HISTORY IS MADE AT NIGHT   United Artists, 1937
WOMAN CHASES MAN   United Artists, 1937
SLAVE SHIP   20th Century-Fox, 1937
WEE WILLIE WINKIE   20th Century-Fox, 1937
STELLA DALLAS   United Artists, 1937
DEAD END   United Artists, 1937
THE PRISONER OF ZENDA ★   United Artists, 1937
THE HURRICANE★   United Artists, 1938
ALEXANDER'S RAGTIME BAND ★★   adaptation, 20th Century-Fox, 1938
THE COWBOY AND THE LADY ★   United Artists, 1938
TRADE WINDS   United Artists, 1938
GUNGA DIN   RKO Radio, 1939
WUTHERING HEIGHTS ★   United Artists, 1939
YOUNG MR. LINCOLN   20th Century-Fox, 1939
BEAU GESTE   Paramount, 1939
THE RAINS CAME ★   20th Century-Fox, 1939
THE REAL GLORY   United Artists, 1939
THEY SHALL HAVE MUSIC ★   United Artists, 1939
DRUMS ALONG THE MOHAWK   20th Century-Fox, 1939
THE HUNCHBACK OF NOTRE DAME ★   RKO Radio, 1939
THE BLUE BIRD   20th Century-Fox, 1940
THE GRAPES OF WRATH   20th Century-Fox, 1940
VIGIL IN THE NIGHT   RKO Radio, 1940
LITTLE OLD NEW YORK   20th Century-Fox, 1940
EARTHBOUND   20th Century-Fox, 1940
FOREIGN CORRESPONDENT   United Artists, 1940
BRIGHAM YOUNG   20th Century-Fox, 1940
THEY KNEW WHAT THEY WANTED   RKO Radio, 1940
THE MARK OF ZORRO ★   20th Century-Fox, 1940
HUDSON'S BAY   20th Century-Fox, 1940
THAT NIGHT IN RIO   20th Century-Fox, 1941
BLOOD AND SAND   20th Century-Fox, 1941
A YANK IN THE R.A.F.   20th Century-Fox, 1941
BALL OF FIRE ★   United Artists, 1941
HOW GREEN WAS MY VALLEY ★   20th Century-Fox, 1941
SON OF FURY   20th Century-Fox, 1942
ROXIE HART   20th Century-Fox, 1942
TO THE SHORES OF TRIPOLI   20th Century-Fox, 1942
THIS ABOVE ALL   20th Century-Fox, 1942
THE PIED PIPER   20th Century-Fox, 1942
GIRL TROUBLE   20th Century-Fox, 1942
THE BLACK SWAN ★   20th Century-Fox, 1942
LIFE BEGINS AT EIGHT-THIRTY   20th Century-Fox, 1942
THE MOON IS DOWN   20th Century-Fox, 1943
MY FRIEND FLICKA   20th Century-Fox, 1943
HEAVEN CAN WAIT   20th Century-Fox, 1943
CLAUDIA   20th Century-Fox, 1943
THE SONG OF BERNADETTE ★★   20th Century-Fox, 1943
THE PURPLE HEART   20th Century-Fox, 1944
WILSON ★   20th Century-Fox, 1944

SUNDAY DINNER FOR A SOLDIER   20th
Century-Fox, 1944
THE KEYS OF THE KINGDOM ★   20th
Century-Fox, 1944
A TREE GROWS IN BROOKLYN   20th
Century-Fox, 1945
STATE FAIR ★   adaptation, 20th
Century-Fox, 1945
A ROYAL SCANDAL   20th Century-Fox,
1945
A BELL FOR ADANO   20th Century-Fox,
1945
LEAVE HER TO HEAVEN   20th
Century-Fox, 1945
DRAGONWYCK   20th Century-Fox, 1946
CENTENNIAL SUMMER ★   20th
Century-Fox, 1946
MARGIE   20th Century-Fox, 1946
THE RAZOR'S EDGE   20th Century-Fox,
1946
GENTLEMAN'S AGREEMENT   20th
Century-Fox, 1947
CAPTAIN FROM CASTILE ★   20th
Century-Fox, 1947
MOTHER WORE TIGHTS ★★   adaptation,
20th Century-Fox, 1947
CALL NORTHSIDE 777   20th Century-Fox,
1948
SITTING PRETTY   20th Century-Fox, 1948
THE WALLS OF JERICHO   20th
Century-Fox, 1948
CRY OF THE CITY   20th Century-Fox,
1948
THE SNAKE PIT ★   20th Century-Fox,
1948
YELLOW SKY   20th Century-Fox, 1948
WHEN MY BABY SMILES AT ME ★
adaptation, 20th Century-Fox, 1948
CHICKEN EVERY SUNDAY   20th
Century-Fox, 1949
A LETTER TO THREE WIVES   20th
Century-Fox, 1949
DOWN TO THE SEA IN SHIPS   20th
Century-Fox, 1949
MOTHER IS A FRESHMAN   20th
Century-Fox, 1949
MR. BELVEDERE GOES TO COLLEGE
20th Century-Fox, 1949
YOU'RE IN EVERYTHING   20th
Century-Fox, 1949
PINKY   20th Century-Fox, 1949
PRINCE OF FOXES   20th Century-Fox,
1949
TWELVE O'CLOCK HIGH   20th
Century-Fox, 1949
WHEN WILLIE COMES MARCHING
HOME   20th Century-Fox, 1950
THE BIG LIFT   20th Century-Fox, 1950
THE GUNFIGHTER   20th Century-Fox,
1950
PANIC IN THE STREETS   20th
Century-Fox, 1950
NO WAY OUT   20th Century-Fox, 1950
ALL ABOUT EVE★   20th Century-Fox,
1950
FOR HEAVEN'S SAKE   20th Century-Fox,
1950
FOURTEEN HOURS   20th Century-Fox,
1951
TAKE CARE OF MY LITTLE GIRL   20th
Century-Fox, 1951
DAVID AND BATHSHEBA ★   20th
Century-Fox, 1951
ON THE RIVIERA ★   20th Century-Fox,
1951
WITH A SONG IN MY HEART ★★   20th
Century-Fox, 1952
WAIT 'TILL THE SUN SHINES, NELLIE
20th Century-Fox, 1952
WHAT PRICE GLORY?   20th Century-Fox,
1952

O. HENRY'S FULL HOUSE   20th
Century-Fox, 1952
STARS AND STRIPES FOREVER   20th
Century-Fox, 1952
TONIGHT WE SING   20th Century-Fox,
1953
CALL ME MADAM ★★   adaptation, 20th
Century-Fox, 1953
THE PRESIDENT'S LADY   20th
Century-Fox, 1953
THE ROBE   20th Century-Fox, 1953
HELL AND HIGH WATER   20th
Century-Fox, 1954
THE EGYPTIAN   co-composer with Bernard
Herrmann, 20th Century-Fox, 1954
THERE'S NO BUSINESS LIKE SHOW
BUSINESS ★   20th Century-Fox, 1954
A MAN CALLED PETER   20th Century-Fox,
1955
THE SEVEN YEAR ITCH   20th
Century-Fox, 1955
LOVE IS A MANY SPLENDORED THING
★★ 20th Century-Fox, 1955
ANASTASIA ★   20th Century-Fox, 1956
A CERTAIN SMILE   20th Century-Fox,
1958
THE DIARY OF ANNE FRANK ★   20th
Century-Fox, 1959
THE BEST OF EVERYTHING   20th
Century-Fox, 1959
THE PLEASURE OF HIS COMPANY
Paramount, 1961
THE COUNTERFEIT TRAITOR
Paramount, 1962
HOW THE WEST WAS WON ★   MGM,
1962
THE GREATEST STORY EVER TOLD ★
United Artists, 1965
NEVADA SMITH   Paramount, 1966
FIRECREEK   Warner Bros., 1968
AIRPORT ★   Universal, 1970

EMIL NEWMAN

d. August 30, 1984 - Woodland Hills,
California

REUNION   MGM, 1936
RISE AND SHINE   20th Century-Fox, 1941
TALL, DARK AND HANDSOME   20th
Century-Fox, 1941
BERLIN CORRESPONDENT   20th
Century-Fox, 1941
SUN VALLEY SERENADE ★   adaptation,
20th Century-Fox, 1941
THE LOVES OF EDGAR ALLAN POE   20th
Century-Fox, 1942
THE MAGNIFICENT DOPE   co-composer,
20th Century-Fox, 1942
THE MAN WHO WOULDN'T DIE   20th
Century-Fox, 1942
TIME TO KILL   20th Century-Fox, 1942
DIXIE DUGAN   20th Century-Fox, 1943
TONIGHT WE RAID CALAIS   20th
Century-Fox, 1943
PIN-UP GIRL   20th Century-Fox, 1944
BEDSIDE MANNER   20th Century-Fox,
1945
NOB HILL   20th Century-Fox, 1945
BEHIND GREEN LIGHTS   20th
Century-Fox, 1946
RENDEZVOUS 24   20th Century-Fox,
1946
TEXAS, BROOKLYN AND HEAVEN
United Artists, 1948
GUILTY OF TREASON   Eagle Lion, 1949
CRY DANGER   co-composer with Paul
Dunlap, RKO Radio, 1951
THE LADY SAYS NO   United Artists, 1951
BIG JIM McLAIN   Warner Bros., 1952
THE CAPTIVE CITY   United Artists, 1952

JAPANESE WAR BRIDE   20th
Century-Fox, 1952
JUST FOR YOU   Paramount, 1952
THE SAN FRANCISCO STORY   Warner
Bros., 1952
RANCHO NOTORIOUS   RKO Radio, 1952
ISLAND IN THE SKY   Warner Bros., 1953
THE STEEL LADY   United Artists, 1953
WAR PAINT   United Artists, 1953
99 RIVER STREET   United Artists, 1953
BEACHHEAD   co-composer with Arthur
Lange, United Artists, 1954
THE MAD MAGICIAN   co-composer with
Arthur Lange, Columbia, 1954
RING OF FEAR   co-composer with Arthur
Lange, Warner Bros., 1954
SOUTHWEST PASSAGE   co-composer
with Arthur Lange, United Artists, 1954
THE NAKED STREET   United Artists, 1955
CHICAGO CONFIDENTIAL   United Artists,
1957
THE IRON SHERIFF   United Artists, 1957
DEATH IN SMALL DOSES   Allied Artists,
1957
UNWED MOTHER   Allied Artists, 1958
RIOT IN JUVENILE PRISON   United
Artists, 1959
THE GREAT SIOUX MASSACRE
Columbia, 1965

LIONEL NEWMAN

b. January 4, 1916
d. February 3, 1989 - Los Angeles, California

THE STREET WITH NO NAME   20th
Century-Fox, 1948
I'LL GET BY ★   adaptation, 20th
Century-Fox, 1950
CHEAPER BY THE DOZEN   20th
Century-Fox, 1950
THE JACKPOT   20th Century-Fox, 1950
MISTER 880   20th Century-Fox, 1950
MOTHER DIDN'T TELL ME   20th
Century-Fox, 1950
WHERE THE SIDEWALK ENDS   20th
Century-Fox, 1950
THE FROGMEN   20th Century-Fox, 1951
DEADLINE - U.S.A.   MGM, 1952
DIPLOMATIC COURIER   20th Century-Fox,
1952
DON'T BOTHER TO KNOCK   20th
Century-Fox, 1952
LYDIA BAILEY   20th Century-Fox, 1952
MONKEY BUSINESS   20th Century-Fox,
1952
THE OUTCASTS OF POKER FLAT   20th
Century-Fox, 1952
RED SKIES OF MONTANA   20th
Century-Fox, 1952
RETURN OF THE TEXAN   20th
Century-Fox, 1952
WE'RE NOT MARRIED   20th Century-Fox,
1952
BLUEPRINT FOR MURDER   20th Century
Fox, 1953
DANGEROUS CROSSING   20th
Century-Fox, 1953
THE FARMER TAKES A WIFE   20th
Century-Fox, 1953
THE KID FROM LEFT FIELD   20th
Century-Fox, 1953
GORILLA AT LARGE   20th Century-Fox,
1954
THE ROCKET MAN   20th Century-Fox,
1954
THERE'S NO BUSINESS LIKE SHOW
BUSINESS ★   20th Century-Fox, 1954
HOUSE OF BAMBOO   20th Century-Fox,
1955
HOW TO BE VERY, VERY POPULAR   20th
Century-Fox, 1955

VIOLENT SATURDAY   20th Century-Fox, 1955

THE KILLER IS LOOSE   United Artists, 1956

THE BEST THINGS IN LIFE ARE FREE ★ adaptation, 20th Century-Fox, 1956

THE LAST WAGON   20th Century-Fox, 1956

LOVE ME TENDER   20th Century-Fox, 1956

THE PROUD ONES   20th Century-Fox, 1956

BERNADINE   20th Century-Fox, 1957

KISS THEM FOR ME   20th Century-Fox, 1957

MARDI GRAS   20th Century-Fox, 1958

THE BRAVADOS   20th Century-Fox, 1958

COMPULSION   20th Century-Fox, 1959

SAY ONE FOR ME ★   20th Century-Fox, 1959

LET'S MAKE LOVE ★   20th Century-Fox, 1960

NORTH TO ALASKA   20th Century-Fox, 1960

MOVE OVER, DARLING   20th Century-Fox, 1963

THE PLEASURE SEEKERS ★   20th Century-Fox, 1964

HELLO, DOLLY! ★   adaptation, 20th Century-Fox, 1969

THE GREAT WHITE HOPE   20th Century-Fox, 1970

FIREBALL FORWARD (TF)   20th Century-Fox, 1972

WHEN MICHAEL CALLS (TF)   Palomar Productions/20th Century-Fox TV, 1972

THE SALZBURG CONNECTION   20th Century-Fox, 1972

ALEX NORTH
b. December 4, 1910 - Chester, Pennsylvania
d. September 8, 1991 - Pacific Palisades, California

[In 1986, Mr. North was the first composer to receive an honorary Academy Award for his lifetime achievement.]

A STREETCAR NAMED DESIRE ★ Warner Bros., 1951

THE 13TH LETTER   20th Century-Fox, 1951

DEATH OF A SALESMAN ★   Columbia, 1951

VIVA ZAPATA! ★   20th Century-Fox, 1952

LES MISERABLES   20th Century Fox, 1952

PONY SOLDIER   20th Century-Fox, 1952

THE MEMBER OF THE WEDDING   Columbia, 1953

GO, MAN, GO   United Artists, 1954

DESIREE   20th Century Fox, 1954

DADDY LONG LEGS   ballet music only, 20th Century-Fox, 1955

THE RACERS   20th Century-Fox, 1955

UNCHAINED   Warner Bros., 1955

MAN WITH THE GUN   United Artists, 1955

I'LL CRY TOMORROW   MGM, 1956

THE ROSE TATTOO ★   Paramount, 1955

THE BAD SEED   Warner Bros., 1956

THE RAINMAKER ★   Paramount, 1956

FOUR GIRLS IN TOWN   Universal, 1956

THE KING AND FOUR QUEENS   United Artists, 1956

THE BACHELOR PARTY   United Artists, 1957

THE LONG, HOT SUMMER   MGM, 1958

STAGE STRUCK   RKO Radio, 1958

HOT SPELL   Paramount, 1958

SOUTH SEAS ADVENTURE   Cinerama Releasing Corporation, 1958

THE SOUND AND THE FURY   20th Century Fox, 1959

THE WONDERFUL COUNTRY   United Artists, 1959

SPARTACUS ★   Universal, 1960

THE CHILDREN'S HOUR   United Artists, 1961

SANCTUARY   20th Century Fox, 1961

THE MISFITS   United Artists, 1961

ALL FALL DOWN   MGM, 1962

CLEOPATRA ★   20th Century Fox, 1963

THE OUTRAGE   MGM, 1964

CHEYENNE AUTUMN   Warner Bros., 1964

THE AGONY AND THE ECSTASY ★   20th Century Fox, 1965

WHO'S AFRAID OF VIRGINIA WOOLF? ★ Warner Bros., 1966

AFRICA (FD)   ABC, 1967

THE DEVIL'S BRIGADE   United Artists, 1968

THE SHOES OF THE FISHERMAN ★ MGM, 1968

HARD CONTRACT   20th Century Fox, 1969

A DREAM OF KINGS   National General, 1969

WILLARD   Cinerama Releasing Corporation, 1971

REBEL JESUS   1972

POCKET MONEY   National General, 1972

ONCE UPON A SCOUNDREL   Image International, 1974, U.S.-Mexican

SHANKS ★   Paramount, 1974

LOST IN THE STARS   American Film Theatre, 1974

JOURNEY INTO FEAR   Stirling Gold, 1975, Canadian

BITE THE BULLET ★   Columbia, 1975

RICH MAN, POOR MAN (MS) ☆☆ Universal TV, 1976

THE PASSOVER PLOT   Atlas, 1976, U.S.-Israeli

THE WORD (MS) ☆   Charles Fries Productions/Stonehenge Productions, 1978

SOMEBODY KILLED HER HUSBAND   Columbia, 1978

WISE BLOOD   New Line Cinema, 1979

CARNY   United Artists, 1980

DRAGONSLAYER ★   Paramount, 1981, U.S.-British

SISTER, SISTER (TF)   20th Century-Fox TV, 1982

UNDER THE VOLCANO ★   Universal, 1984

PRIZZI'S HONOR   20th Century Fox, 1985

DEATH OF A SALESMAN (TF) ☆   Roxbury and Punch Productions, 1985

THE DEAD   Vestron, 1987

GOOD MORNING VIETNAM   Buena Vista, 1987

THE PENITENT   New Century Vista, 1988

THE LAST BUTTERFLY   co-composer, 1990

MARTY PAICH
(Martin Louis Paich)
b. January 23, 1925 - Oakland, California
d. August 12, 1995 - Santa Ynez, California

HEY THERE, IT'S YOGI BEAR (AF) Hanna-Barbera, 1964

THE SWINGER   Paramount, 1966

CHANGES   Cinerama Releasing Corporation, 1969

DUNE   additional music, Universal, 1984

CHRISTOPHER PALMER
b. England
d. Jan 22, 1995 - London, England

VALMONT   Orion, 1989

CLIFTON PARKER
d. September 2, 1989 - Bucks, England

This is a partial list of the composer's credits.

YELLOW CANARY   RKO Radio, 1943, British

BLANCHE FURY   1948

TREASURE ISLAND   RKO-Radio, 1950, U.S.-British

HELL BELOW ZERO   MGM, 1954, British

TARZAN AND THE LOST SAFARI   MGM, 1957, British-U.S.

CURSE OF THE DEMON   *NIGHT OF THE DEMON*   Columbia, 1957, British

HARRY BLACK AND THE TIGER   20th Century Fox, 1958, British

SINK THE BISMARK!   20th Century Fox, 1960, British

SCREAM OF FEAR   *TASTE OF FEAR* Columbia, 1961, British

DAMN THE DEFIANT!   *HMS DEFIANT* Columbia, 1962, British

LOTHAR PERL
b. Germany
d. April 28, 1975 - New York

THIS LAND IS MINE   RKO Radio, 1943

EDWARD PLUMB
b. 1907 - Streator, Illinois
d. April, 1958

BAMBI (AF) ★   co-composer with Frank Churchill, RKO Radio, 1942

SALUDOS AMIGOS ★   co-composer with Paul J. Smith, RKO Radio, 1943

VICTORY THROUGH AIR POWER co-composer with Paul J. Smith and Oliver Wallace, United Artists, 1943

THE THREE CABALLEROS (AF) ★ co-composer, RKO Radio, 1944

THE PHANTOM SPEAKS   Republic, 1945

THE WOMAN WHO CAME BACK   Republic, 1945

QUEBEC   co-composer with Van Cleave, Paramount, 1951

CHARLES PREVIN
b. 1888 - Brooklyn, New York
d. September 22, 1973 - Hollywood,
California

THE MAGNIFICENT BRUTE   Universal,
1936
TWO IN A CROWD   Universal, 1936
THREE SMART GIRLS   Universal, 1937
WHEN LOVE IS YOUNG   Universal, 1937
WINGS OVER HONOLULU   Universal,
1937
MAD ABOUT MUSIC ★   co-composer with
Frank Skinner, Universal, 1938
MIDNIGHT INTRUDER   Universal, 1938
RIO   Universal, 1939
TOWER OF LONDON   Universal, 1939
THE BANK DICK   Universal, 1940
IT'S A DATE   Universal, 1940
SEVEN SINNERS   Universal, 1940
THE INVISIBLE WOMAN   Universal, 1940
BLACK FRIDAY   co-composer, Universal,
1940
MODEL WIFE   Universal, 1941
THE WOLF MAN   co-composer, Universal,
1941
HORROR ISLAND   co-composer,
Universal, 1941
NICE GIRL?   Universal, 1941
THE BLACK CAT   co-composer, Universal,
1941
HOLD THAT GHOST   co-composer,
Universal, 1941
DRUMS OF THE CONGO   co-composer,
Universal, 1941
BUCK PRIVATES ★   adaptation,
Universal, 1941
MAN-MADE MONSTER   co-composer,
Universal, 1941
INVISIBLE AGENT   co-composer,
Universal, 1942
THE MUMMY'S TOMB   co-composer,
Universal, 1942
FRANKENSTEIN MEETS THE WOLF
MAN   co-composer, Universal, 1943
SON OF DRACULA   co-composer,
Universal, 1943
THE MAD GHOUL   co-composer,
Universal, 1943
HOUSE OF FRANKENSTEIN
co-composer, Universal, 1944
JUNGLE CAPTIVE   co-composer,
Universal, 1944
THE MUMMY'S GHOST   co-composer,
Universal, 1944
SONG OF THE OPEN ROAD ★   Universal,
1944
HOUSE OF DRACULA   co-composer,
Universal, 1945

SERGEI PROKOFIEV
b. April 23, 1891 - Sontsovka, Russia
d. March 5, 1953 - Moscow, U.S.S.R.

LIEUTENANT KIJE   1934, Soviet
ALEXANDER NEVSKY   Amkino, 1938,
Soviet
KOTOVSKY   1943, Soviet
LERMONTOV   1944, Soviet
IVAN THE TERRIBLE, PART I   Artkino,
1945, Soviet
IVAN THE TERRIBLE, PART II   Artkino,
1946, Soviet

R

JOE RAPOSO
b. February 8, 1937 - Far River,
Massachusetts
d. February 4, 1989 - Bronxville, New York

THE POSSESSION OF JOEL DELANEY
Paramount, 1972
SAVAGES   Angelika, 1972
RAGGEDY ANN AND ANDY (AF)   20th
Century-Fox, 1977
THE GREAT MUPPET CAPER
Universal/AFD, 1981, British

KAROL RATHAUS
b. 1895 - Tarnopol, Poland
d. 1954 - New York

THE BROTHERS KARAMAZOV   1931,
German
THE DICTATOR   *THE LOVE AFFAIR OF A
DICTATOR/LOVES OF A DICTATOR*
1935, British
LET US LIVE   Columbia, 1939
JAGUAS (D)   Viking Fund, 1942
HISTADRUTH (D)   Palestine Labor Union,
1945

ALAN RAWSTHORNE
b. 1905 - Haslingden, England
d. 1971 - Cambridge, England

BURMA VICTORY (FD)   Army Film Init,
1945, British
THE CAPTIVE HEART   Universal, 1946,
British
SARABAND   *SARABAND FOR DEAD
LOVERS*   Eagle Lion, 1948, British
THE DANCING FLEECE   1950, British
WATERS OF TIME   1951, British
PANDORA AND THE FLYING
DUTCHMAN   MGM, 1951, British
IVORY HUNTER   *WHERE NO VULTURES
FLY*   1951, British
THE CRUEL SEA   1953, British
WEST OF ZANZIBAR   1954, British
THE DRAWINGS OF LEONARDO DA
VINCI   1954, British
LEASE OF LIFE   1954, British
THE MAN WHO NEVER WAS   20th
Century-Fox, 1956, British
FLOODS OF FEAR   Universal, 1958,
British

SATYAJIT RAY
b. May 2, 1921 - Calcutta, India
d. 1992

KANCHENJUNGHA   Harrison, 1962,
Indian
NAYAK   1966, Indian
SHAKESPEARE WALLAH   Continental,
1966, Indian
DAYS AND NIGHTS IN THE FOREST
Pathe Contemporary, 1970, Indian
THE ADVERSARY   Audio Brandon, 1971,
Indian
SIMABADDHA   1972, Indian
DISTANT THUNDER   Cinema 5, 1973,
Indian
THE GOLDEN FORTRESS   1975, Indian

THE CHESS PLAYERS   Creative, 1977,
Indian
THE ELEPHANT GOD   R.D. Bansal &
Company, 1979, Indian
PHATIK AND THE JUGGLER   1983,
Indian
THE HOME AND THE WORLD   European
Classics, 1984, Indian
AGANTUK   *THE STRANGER*   1991,
Indian

FRANZ REIZENSTEIN
b. 1911 - Nuremberg, Germany
d. 1968 - London, England

THE MUMMY   Universal, 1959, British
CIRCUS OF HORRORS   American
International, 1960, British

NELSON RIDDLE
b. 1921 - Hackensack, New Jersey
d. 1985

JOHNNY CONCHO   United Artists, 1956
LISBON   Republic, 1956
A HOLE IN THE HEAD   United Artists,
1959
LI'L ABNER ★   adaptation, Paramount,
1959
CAN-CAN ★   adaptation, 20th
Century-Fox, 1960
LOLITA   co-composer with Bob Harris,
MGM, 1962, British
COME BLOW YOUR HORN   Paramount,
1963
FOUR FOR TEXAS   Warner Bros., 1963
PARIS WHEN IT SIZZLES   Paramount,
1964
ROBIN AND THE SEVEN HOODS ★
Warner Bros., 1964
WHAT A WAY TO GO!   20th Century-Fox,
1964
HARLOW   co-composer with Al Ham,
Magna, 1965
MARRIAGE ON THE ROCKS   Warner
Bros., 1965
A RAGE TO LIVE   United Artists, 1965
RED LINE 7000   Paramount, 1965
BATMAN   20th Century-Fox, 1966
ONE SPY TOO MANY   MGM, 1966
EL DORADO   Paramount, 1967
HOW TO SUCCEED IN BUSINESS
WITHOUT REALLY TRYING
adaptation, United Artists, 1967
PAINT YOUR WAGON ★   adaptation,
Paramount, 1969
THE GREAT BANK ROBBERY   Warner
Bros., 1969
THE MALTESE BIPPY   MGM, 1969
HELL'S BLOODY DEVILS   *THE
FAKERS/SMASHING THE CRIME
SYNDICATE*   Independent-International,
1970
EMERGENCY! (TF)   Mark VII Ltd./Universal
TV, 1972
THE BLUE KNIGHT (TF)   Lorimar
Productions, 1973
THE GREAT GATSBY ★★   Paramount,
1974
THE RUNAWAY BARGE (TF)   Lorimar
Productions, 1975
PROMISE HIM ANYTHING... (TF)   ABC
Circle Films, 1975
MOBILE TWO (TF)   Mark VII Ltd./Universal
TV, 1975
AMERICA AT THE MOVIES (FD)
American Film Institute, 1976
THAT'S ENTERTAINMENT, PART 2
MGM/United Artists, 1976
HOW TO BREAK UP A HAPPY DIVORCE
(TF)   Charles Fries Productions, 1976

SEVENTH AVENUE (MS)   Universal TV,
1977
A CIRCLE OF CHILDREN (TF)   Edgar J.
Scherick Associates/20th Century-Fox TV,
1977
HARPER VALLEY PTA   April Fools, 1978
GOIN' COCOANUTS   Osmond Distribution,
1978
GUYANA, CULT OF THE DAMNED
co-composer with Robert Summers and
George S. Price, Universal, 1980
ROUGH CUT   adaptation, Paramount,
1980
MICKEY SPILLANE'S MARGIN FOR
MURDER (TF)   Hamner Productions,
1981
HELP WANTED: MALE (TF)
Brademan-Self Productions/QM
Productions, 1982

RICHARD RODGERS
b. June 28, 1902 - New York, New York
d. December 30, 1979 - New York

LOVE ME TONIGHT   Paramount, 1932

MILAN RODER
b. 1878
d. 1956

SILVER DOLLAR   Warner Bros., 1932
SUPERNATURAL   co-composer with Karl
Hajos and Howard Jackson, Paramount,
1933
DEATH TAKES A HOLIDAY   co-composer
with John Leipold and Bernhard Kaun,
Paramount, 1934
THE LAST OF THE PAGANS   MGM, 1935
THE LIVES OF A BENGAL LANCER
Paramount, 1935
ALL THE KING'S HORSES   Paramount,
1935
THE LAST OUTPOST   Paramount, 1935
TOO MANY PARENTS   Paramount, 1936
EASY LIVING   Paramount, 1937
EXCLUSIVE   Paramount, 1937
SOULS AT SEA ★   co-composer with W.
Franke Harling, Paramount, 1937
BULLDOG DRUMMOND IN AFRICA
Paramount, 1938
NEVER SAY DIE   Paramount, 1939

HEINZ ROEMHELD
b. 1901 - Milwaukee
d. February 11, 1985

THE HUNCHBACK OF NOTRE DAME
co-composer of score for 1931 reissue
with Sam Perry, Universal, 1923
GOLDEN HARVEST   Paramount, 1933
THE INVISIBLE MAN   Universal, 1933
THE BLACK CAT   Universal, 1934
IMITATION OF LIFE   Universal, 1934
THE MAN WHO RECLAIMED HIS HEAD
Universal, 1934
KLIOU   THE TIGER   RKO Radio, 1935
MARY BURNS, FUGITIVE   Paramount,
1935
DRACULA'S DAUGHTER   Universal, 1936
THREE SMART GIRLS   Universal, 1936
STAND-IN   United Artists, 1937
I MET MY LOVE AGAIN   United Artists,
1938
FOUR'S A CROWD   Warner Bros., 1938
COMET OVER BROADWAY   Warner Bros.,
1938
NANCY DREW, REPORTER   Warner
Bros., 1939
YOU CAN'T GET AWAY WITH MURDER
Warner Bros., 1939
INVISIBLE STRIPES   Warner Bros., 1939

A CHILD IS BORN   Warner Bros., 1940
BROTHER RAT AND BABY   Warner Bros.,
1940
BRITISH INTELLIGENCE   Warner Bros.,
1940
BROTHER ORCHID   Warner Bros., 1940
THE MAN WHO TALKED TOO MUCH
Warner Bros., 1940
MY LOVE CAME BACK   Warner Bros.,
1940
NO TIME FOR COMEDY   Warner Bros.,
1940
LADY WITH RED HAIR   Warner Bros.,
1940
FOUR MOTHERS   Warner Bros., 1941
HONEYMOON FOR THREE   Warner Bros.,
1941
FLIGHT FROM DESTINY   Warner Bros.,
1941
THE STRAWBERRY BLONDE ★   Warner
Bros., 1941
THE WAGONS ROLL AT NIGHT   Warner
Bros., 1941
AFFECTIONATELY YOURS   Warner Bros.,
1941
BLUES IN THE NIGHT   Warner Bros.,
1941
ALWAYS IN MY HEART   Warner Bros.,
1942
THE MALE ANIMAL   Warner Bros., 1942
GENTLEMAN JIM   Warner Bros., 1942
YANKEE DOODLE DANDY ★★
adaptation, Warner Bros., 1942
THE MUMMY'S TOMB   co-composer,
Universal, 1942
THE HARD WAY   Warner Bros., 1943
THE DESERT SONG   adaptation, Warner
Bros., 1944
SHINE ON, HARVEST MOON   Warner
Bros., 1944
MAKE YOUR OWN BED   Warner Bros.,
1944
JANIE   Warner Bros., 1944
TOO YOUNG TO KNOW   Warner Bros.,
1945
O.S.S.   co-composer with Daniele
Amfitheatrof, Paramount, 1946
MR. ACE   United Artists, 1947
CURLEY   United Artists, 1947
THE FABULOUS JOE   United Artists, 1947
HEAVEN ONLY KNOWS   United Artists,
1947
DOWN TO EARTH   co-composer with
George Duning, Columbia, 1947
CHRISTMAS EVE   United Artists, 1947
THE FLAME   Republic, 1947
IT HAD TO BE YOU   co-composer with
Arthur Morton, Columbia, 1947
HERE COMES TROUBLE   United Artists,
1948
WHO KILLED DOC ROBBIN?   United
Artists, 1948
THE LADY FROM SHANGHAI   Columbia,
1948
I, JANE DOE   Republic, 1948
ON OUR MERRY WAY   United Artists,
1948
THE FULLER BRUSH MAN   Columbia,
1948
THE GIRL FROM MANHATTAN   United
Artists, 1948
STATION WEST   RKO Radio, 1948
MY DEAR SECRETARY   United Artists,
1948
THE LUCKY STIFF   United Artists, 1949
MR. SOFT TOUCH   Columbia, 1949
MISS GRANT TAKES RICHMOND
Columbia, 1949
KILL THE UMPIRE   Columbia, 1950
THE GOOD HUMOR MAN   Columbia,
1950

ROGUES OF SHERWOOD FOREST
Columbia, 1950
THE FULLER BRUSH GIRL   Columbia,
1950
VALENTINO   Columbia, 1951
CHICAGO CALLING   United Artists, 1952
THE BIG TREES   Warner Bros., 1952
JACK AND THE BEANSTALK   Warner
Bros., 1952
THREE FOR BEDROOM C   Warner Bros.,
1952
RUBY GENTRY   20th Century-Fox, 1953
THE 5,000 FINGERS OF DR. T
co-composer with Hans Salter and
Frederick Hollander, Columbia, 1953
THE MOONLIGHTER   Warner Bros., 1953
HELL'S HORIZON   Columbia, 1955
THE SQUARE JUNGLE   Universal, 1956
THERE'S ALWAYS TOMORROW
Universal, 1956
THE CREATURE WALKS AMONG US
co-composer, Universal, 1956
THE MOLE PEOPLE   co-composer with
Hans Salter and Herman Stein,
Universal, 1956
THE LAND UNKNOWN   co-composer,
Universal, 1957
THE MONSTER THAT CHALLENGED THE
WORLD   United Artists, 1957
THE TALL T   Columbia, 1957
DECISION AT SUNDOWN   Columbia,
1958
RIDE LONESOME   Columbia, 1959
LAD: A DOG   Warner Bros., 1961

ERIC ROGERS
b. England
d. April 8, 1981 - Buckinghamshire, England

THE SWINGIN' MAIDEN   THE IRON
MAIDEN   Columbia, 1962, British
CARRY ON SPYING   Governor, 1964,
British
CARRY ON CLEO   Governor, 1964,
British
CARRY ON COWBOY
Anglo-Amalgamated/Warner-Pathe,
1966, British
CARRY ON SCREAMING
Anglo-Amalgamated/Warner-Pathe,
1966, British
DON'T LOSE YOUR HEAD   1967, British
FOLLOW THAT CAMEL   Schoenfeld Film
Distributing, 1967, British
CARRY ON DOCTOR   Rank, 1968, British
CARRY ON...UP THE KHYBER   Rank,
1969, British
CARRY ON CAMPING   Rank, 1969,
British
CARRY ON UP THE JUNGLE   Rank,
1970, British
CARRY ON AGAIN, DOCTOR   Rank,
1970, British
DOCTOR IN TROUBLE   Rank, 1970,
British
IN THE DEVIL'S GARDEN   ASSAULT
Hemisphere, 1971, British
QUEST FOR LOVE   Rank, 1971, British
CARRY ON DICK   Rank, 1974, British
CARRY ON EMMANUELLE   Rank, 1978,
British

SHORTY ROGERS
d. Nov 7, 1994

GIDGET GROWS UP (TF)   Screen
Gems/Columbia Pictures TV, 1969
BREAKOUT (TF)   Universal TV, 1970
THE RETURN OF THE MOD SQUAD (TF)
co-composer with Mark Snow,
Thomas-Spelling Productions, 1979

SIGMUND ROMBERG

b. 1887 - Szeged, Hungary
d. 1951 - New York

FOOLISH WIVES   Universal, 1922

DAVID ROSE

b. June 24, 1910 - London, England
d. August 23, 1990 - Los Angeles, California

THE PRINCESS AND THE PIRATE ★
   RKO Radio, 1944
WINGED VICTORY   20th Century-Fox,
   1944
THE WHIPPED   United Artists, 1950
THE UNDERWORLD STORY   United
   Artists, 1950
RICH, YOUNG AND PRETTY   MGM, 1951
TEXAS CARNIVAL   MGM, 1951
JUST THIS ONCE   MGM, 1952
YOUNG MAN WITH IDEAS   MGM, 1952
EVERYTHING I HAVE IS YOURS   MGM,
   1952
THE CLOWN   MGM, 1953
CONFIDENTIALLY YOURS   MGM, 1953
BRIGHT ROAD   MGM, 1953
JUPITER'S DARLING   MGM, 1955
PUBLIC PIGEON NO. ONE   Universal,
   1957
OPERATION PETTICOAT   Universal, 1959
PLEASE DON'T EAT THE DAISIES   MGM,
   1960
THIS REBEL BREED   Warner Bros., 1960
QUICK, BEFORE IT MELTS   MGM, 1965
NEVER TOO LATE   Warner Bros., 1965
HOMBRE   20th Century-Fox, 1967
ALONG CAME A SPIDER (TF)   20th
   Century-Fox TV, 1970
THE DEVIL AND MISS SARAH (TF)
   Universal TV, 1971
THE BIRDMEN (TF)   Universal TV, 1971
A DREAM FOR CHRISTMAS (TF)   Lorimar
   Productions, 1973
LITTLE HOUSE ON THE PRAIRIE (TF)
   NBC Entertainment, 1974
THE LONELIEST RUNNER (TF)   NBC TV,
   1976
RANSOM FOR ALICE! (TF)   Universal TV,
   1977
KILLING STONE (TF)   Universal TV, 1978
SUDDENLY, LOVE (TF)   Ross Hunter
   Productions, 1978
LITTLE HOUSE: LOOK BACK TO
   YESTERDAY (TF)   NBC Productions/Ed
   Friendly Productions, 1983
SAM'S ROSE   Invictus Entertainment,
   1984
LITTLE HOUSE: THE LAST FAREWELL
   (TF)   Ed Friendly Productions/NBC
   Entertainment, 1984
LITTLE HOUSE: BLESS ALL THE DEAR
   CHILDREN (TF)   NBC Productions/Ed
   Friendly Productions, 1984

MILTON ROSEN

b. 1906 - Yonkers, NY
d. Dec 28, 1994 - Kailua, HI

ENTER ARSENE LUPIN   Universal, 1944
SUDAN   Universal, 1945
SWING OUT, SISTER   Universal, 1945
ON STAGE EVERYBODY   co-composer,
   Universal, 1945
SHADY LADY   Universal, 1945
MEN IN HER DIARY   Universal, 1945
TANGIER   Universal, 1945
THE SPIDER WOMAN STRIKES BACK
   co-composer, Universal, 1946
DRESSED TO KILL   co-composer,
   Universal, 1946

CUBAN PETE   co-composer, Universal,
   1946
SLIGHTLY SCANDALOUS   co-composer,
   Universal, 1946
RUSTLER'S ROUND-UP   co-composer,
   Universal, 1946
THE TIME OF THEIR LIVES   Universal,
   1946
LAWLESS BREED   co-composer,
   Universal, 1946
WHITE TIE AND TAILS   Universal, 1946
SLAVE GIRL   Universal, 1947
PIRATES OF MONTEREY   Universal,
   1947
ABRAHAM AND ISAAC   Churchcraft, 1948
DANIEL IN THE LION'S DEN   Churchcraft,
   1948
OF SUCH IS THE KINGDOM   Churchcraft,
   1948
THE RAISING OF LAZARUS   Churchcraft,
   1948
BOB AND SALLY   Social Guidance, 1948
THE CHALLENGE   20th Century-Fox,
   1948
13 LEAD SOLDIERS   20th Century-Fox,
   1948
THE CREEPER   20th Century-Fox, 1948
THE MILKMAN   Universal, 1950
SON OF ALI BABA   co-composer with
   Herman Stein, Universal, 1951
CITY BENEATH THE SEA   co-composer
   with Herman Stein and Henry Mancini,
   Universal, 1952
FRANCIS GOES TO WEST POINT
   co-composer with Herman Stein and
   Frank Skinner, Universal, 1952
EVERYTHING BUT THE TRUTH
   Universal, 1956
OUTSIDE THE LAW   Universal, 1956
DEATH RACE (TF)   Silverton
   Productions/Universal TV, 1973

NINO ROTA

b. December 31, 1911 - Milan, Italy
d. April 10, 1979 - Rome, Italy

TRENO POPOLARE   1933, Italian
GIORNO DI NOZZE   1942, Italian
IL BIRICHINO DI PAPA   1942, Italian
ZAZA   1943, Italian
THE ARROW   LA FRECCIA NEL FIANCO
   1943, Italian
LA DONNA DELLA MONTAGNA   1943,
   Italian
HIS YOUNG WIFE   LE MISERIE DEL
   SIGNOR TRAVET   1945, Italian
SOTTO IL SOLE DI ROMA   1946, Italian
ROMA, CITTA LIBERA   1946, Italian
ALBERGO LUNA, CAMERA 34   1946,
   Italian
MIO FIGLIO PROFESSORE   1946, Italian
UN AMERICANO IN VAZANZA
   co-composer with Giovanni d'Anzi, 1946,
   Italian
VIVERE IN PACE   1947, Italian
AMANTI SENZA AMORE   1947, Italian
DANIELE CORTIS   1947, Italian
FLESH WILL SURRENDER   IL DELITTO DI
   GIOVANNI EPISCOPO   1947, Italian
SPRINGTIME IN ITALY   E PRIMAVERA
   1947, Italian
COME PERSI LA GUERRA   1947, Italian
ARRIVEDERCI PAPA   1948, Italian
SENZA PIETA   1948, Italian
FUGA IN FRANCIA   1948, Italian
CAMPANE A MARTELLO   1948, Italian
SOTTO IL SOLE DI ROMA   1948, Italian
L'EROE DELLA STRADA   1948, Italian
PROIBITO RUBARE   Lux Film, 1948,
   Italian

THE PIRATES OF CAPRI   CAPTAIN
   SIROCCO   Film Classics, 1949, Italian
THE GLASS MOUNTAIN   1949, British
THE HIDDEN ROOM   OBSESSION
   British Lion, 1949, British
COME SCOPERSI L'AMERICA   1949,
   Italian
DUE MOGLI SONO TROPPE   1950, Italian
NAPOLI MILIONARIA   1950, Italian
A DOG'S LIFE   VITA DA CANI   ATA,
   1950, Italian
E PIU FACILE CHE UN CAMELLO...   1950,
   Italian
VALLEY OF THE EAGLES   1951
FILUMENA MARTURANO   1951, Italian
ANNA   Italian Films Export, 1951, Italian
DONNE E BRIGANTI   1951, Italian
ERA LUI...SI! SI!   1951, Italian
PEPPINO E VIOLETTA   1951, Italian
TOTO E IL RE DI ROMA   1951, Italian
IL MONELLO DELLA STRADA   STREET
   URCHIN   1951, Italian
THE WHITE SHIEK   Pathe Contemporary,
   1952, Italian
SOMETHING MONEY CAN'T BUY   1952,
   Italian
JOLANDA, LA FIGLIA DEL CORSARO
   NERO   1952, Italian
LA REGINA DI SABA   1952, Italian
DUE SOLDI DI SPERANZA   1952, Italian
LA MANO DEL STRANIERO   1952, Italian
MARITO E MOGLIE   1952, Italian
LE MERAVIGLIOSE AVVENTURE DI
   GUERRIN MESCHINO   1952, Italian
HELL RAIDERS OF THE DEEP   1952,
   Italian
THE ASSASSIN   VENETIAN BIRD   1952,
   Italian
SCAMPOLO 53'   1953, Italian
I VITELLONI   API Productions, 1953,
   Italian
ANNI DIFICILI   1953, Italian
RISCATTO   1953, Italian
NOI DUE SOLI   1953, Italian
LUXURY GIRLS   FANCIULLE DI LUSSO
   1953, Italian
STAR OF INDIA   1953
MUSODURO   1954, Italian
MAMBO   co-composer with Francesco
   Lavagnino, Paramount, 1954,
   U.S.-Italian
LA STRADA   Trans-Lux, 1954, Italian
LA VERGINE MODERNA   1954, Italian
LE DUE ORFANELLE   1954, Italian
PROIBITO   Documento
   Film/UGC/Cormoran Film, 1954, Italian
ENNEMI PUBLIC #1   co-composer with
   Raymond Legrand, 1954, Italian
CENTO ANNI D'AMORE   co-composer,
   1954, Italian
LOVES OF THREE QUEENS   HELEN OF
   TROY—THE FACE THAT LAUNCHED A
   THOUSAND SHIPS   1954, Italian
LA DOMENICA DELLA BUONA GENTE
   1954, Italian
LA GRANDE SPERANZA   1954, Italian
VIA PADOVA, 46   1954, Italian
FRIENDS FOR LIFE   AMICI PER LA
   PELLE   1955, Italian
THE SWINDLE   IL BIDONE   Astor, 1955,
   Italian
LA BELLA DI ROMA   Lux Film, 1955,
   Italian
UN EROE DEI BOSTRI TEMPI   1955,
   Italian
THE MOST WONDERFUL MOMENT
   1956, Italian
CITTA DI NOTTE   1956, Italian
WAR AND PEACE   Paramount, 1956,
   Italian
NIGHTS OF CABIRIA   Lopert, 1957,
   Italian

THE HOUSE OF INTRIGUE   1957, Italian
ITALIA PICCOLA   1957, Italian
WHITE NIGHTS   *LE NOTTI BIANCHE*
   United Motion Picture Organization,
   1957, Italian-French
IL MEDICO E LO STREGONE   1957,
   Italian
FORTUNELLA   1957, Italian
THIS ANGRY AGE   Columbia, 1958,
   Italian-French
GLI ITALIANI SONO MATTI   1958, Italian
THE LAW IS THE LAW   *LA LOI C'EST LA
   LOI*   1958, French
THE GREAT WAR   United Artists, 1959,
   Italian
UN ETTARO DI CIELO   1959, Italian
LA DOLCE VITA   Astor, 1960, Italian
UNDER TEN FLAGS   *SOTTO DIECI
   BANDIERE*   1960, U.S.-Italian
PURPLE NOON   Times, 1960,
   French-Italian
PHANTOM LOVERS   *FANTASMI A
   ROMA*   1960, Italian
ROCCO AND HIS BROTHERS   Astor,
   1960, Italian-French
ITALIAN BRIGANDS   *IL BRIGANTE*   1961,
   Italian
THE RELUCTANT SAINT   Davis-Royal,
   1962, Italian-U.S.
THE BEST OF ENEMIES   *IL DUE NEMICI*
   Columbia, 1962, Italian-British
MAFIOSO   1962, Italian
BOCCACCIO '70   composer of Fellini and
   Visconti segments, Embassy, 1962,
   Italian
ARTURO'S ISLAND   MGM, 1962, Italian
8-1/2   Embassy, 1963, Italian
THE LEOPARD   20th Century-Fox, 1963,
   Italian-French
IL MAESTRO DI VIGEVANO   1963, Italian
JULIET OF THE SPIRITS   Rizzoli, 1965,
   Italian-French-West German
SHOOT LOUD...LOUDER, I DON'T
   UNDERSTAND   1966, Italian
THE TAMING OF THE SHREW   Columbia,
   1967, Italian-British
KISS THE OTHER SHEIK   *OGGI, DOMANI
   E DOPODAMANI*   1968, Italian-French
ROMEO AND JULIET   Paramount, 1968,
   Italian-British
SPIRITS OF THE DEAD   *HISTOIRES
   EXTRAORDINAIRES*   composer of
   "Toby Dammit" segment, American
   International, 1969, French-Italian
FELLINI SATYRICON   United Artists,
   1970, Italian-French
THE CLOWNS   Levitt-Pickman, 1971,
   Italian-French-West German, originally
   made for television
WATERLOO   Paramount, 1971,
   Italian-Soviet
FELLINI'S ROMA   United Artists, 1972,
   Italian-French
THE GODFATHER   Paramount, 1972
LOVE AND ANARCHY   *FILM D'AMORE E
   D'ANARCHIA*   co-composer with Carlo
   Savina, Peppercorn-Wormser, 1973,
   Italian
SUNSET, SUNRISE   1973, Italian
AMARCORD   New World, 1974, Italian
THE ABDICATION   Warner Bros., 1974,
   British
THE GODFATHER, PART II ★★
   co-composer with Carmine Coppola,
   Paramount, 1974
BOY FROM THE SUBURBS   *RAGAZZO DI
   BORGATA*   co-composer with Carlo
   Savina, Italneggio, 1976, Italian
CARO MICHELE   Cineriz, 1976, Italian
CASANOVA   *IL CASANOVA DI FEDERICO
   FELLINI*   Universal, 1976, Italian

DEATH ON THE NILE   Paramount, 1978,
   British
HURRICANE   Paramount, 1979
ORCHESTRA REHEARSAL   New Yorker,
   1979, Italian-West German, originally
   made for television

MIKLOS ROZSA
b. April 18, 1907 - Budapest, Hungary
d. July 1995 - Los Angeles, California

KNIGHT WITHOUT ARMOUR   United
   Artists, 1937, British
THUNDER IN THE CITY   Columbia, 1937,
   British
THE SQUEAKER   *MURDER ON DIAMOND
   ROAD*   United Artists, 1937, British
THE GREEK COCKATOO   *FOUR DARK
   HOURS*   New World, 1937, British
THE DIVORCE OF LADY X   United Artists,
   1938, British
THE FOUR FEATHERS   United Artists,
   1939, British
THE SPY IN BLACK   *U BOAT 29*
   Columbia, 1939, British
TEN DAYS IN PARIS   Columbia, 1939,
   British
THE THIEF OF BAGHDAD ★   United
   Artists, 1940, British
THAT HAMILTON WOMAN   *LADY
   HAMILTON*   United Artists, 1941,
   British
LYDIA ★   United Artists, 1941
SUNDOWN ★   United Artists, 1941
NEW WINE   adaptation, United Artists,
   1941
JUNGLE BOOK ★   United Artists, 1942,
   British
JACARE   United Artists, 1942
FIVE GRAVES TO CAIRO   Paramount,
   1943
SO PROUDLY WE HAIL!   Paramount,
   1943
SAHARA   Columbia, 1943
WOMAN OF THE TOWN ★   United Artists,
   1943
THE HOUR BEFORE THE DAWN
   Paramount, 1944
DOUBLE INDEMNITY ★   Paramount, 1944
DARK WATERS   United Artists, 1944
THE MAN IN HALF MOON STREET
   Paramount, 1944
A SONG TO REMEMBER ★   adaptation,
   Columbia, 1945
BLOOD ON THE SUN   United Artists, 1945
THE LOST WEEKEND ★   Paramount,
   1945
LADY ON A TRAIN   Universal, 1945
SPELLBOUND ★★   United Artists, 1945
BECAUSE OF HIM   Universal, 1946
THE STRANGE LOVE OF MARTHA
   IVERS   Paramount, 1946
THE KILLERS ★   Universal, 1946
THE RED HOUSE   United Artists, 1947
SONG OF SCHEHERAZADE   adaptation,
   Universal, 1947
THE MACOMBER AFFAIR   United Artists,
   1947
TIME OUT OF MIND   Universal, 1947
DESERT FURY   Paramount, 1947
BRUTE FORCE   Universal, 1947
THE OTHER LOVE   United Artists, 1947
A WOMAN'S VENGEANCE   Universal,
   1947
A DOUBLE LIFE ★★   Universal, 1947
SECRET BEYOND THE DOOR   Universal,
   1948
THE NAKED CITY   Universal, 1948
KISS THE BLOOD OFF MY HANDS
   Universal, 1948
COMMAND DECISION   MGM, 1948

CRISS CROSS   Universal, 1949
THE BRIBE   MGM, 1949
MADAME BOVARY   MGM, 1949
THE RED DANUBE   MGM, 1949
EAST SIDE, WEST SIDE   MGM, 1949
ADAM'S RIB   MGM, 1949
THE MINIVER STORY   adaptation, MGM,
   1950
THE ASPHALT JUNGLE   MGM, 1950
CRISIS   MGM, 1950
THE LIGHT TOUCH   MGM, 1951
QUO VADIS ★   MGM, 1951
IVANHOE ★   MGM, 1952
PLYMOUTH ADVENTURE   MGM, 1952
JULIUS CAESAR ★   MGM, 1953
THE STORY OF THREE LOVES   MGM,
   1953
YOUNG BESS   MGM, 1953
ALL THE BROTHERS WERE VALIANT
   MGM, 1953
KNIGHTS OF THE ROUND TABLE   MGM,
   1953
MEN OF THE FIGHTING LADY   MGM,
   1954
VALLEY OF THE KINGS   MGM, 1954
CREST OF THE WAVE   *GREEN FIRE*
   MGM, 1954, British
MOONFLEET   MGM, 1955
THE KING'S THIEF   MGM, 1955
DIANE   MGM, 1956
TRIBUTE TO A BAD MAN   MGM, 1956
BHOWANI JUNCTION   MGM, 1956,
   U.S.-British
LUST FOR LIFE   MGM, 1956
SOMETHING OF VALUE   MGM, 1957
THE SEVENTH SIN   MGM, 1957
TIP ON A DEAD JOCKEY   MGM, 1957
A TIME TO LOVE AND A TIME TO DIE
   Universal, 1958
THE WORLD, THE FLESH AND THE
   DEVIL   MGM, 1959
BEN HUR ★★   MGM, 1959
KING OF KINGS   MGM, 1961
EL CID ★   Allied Artists, 1961
SODOM AND GOMORRAH   20th
   Century-Fox, 1962, Italian-French-U.S.
THE V.I.P.'S   MGM, 1963, British
THE POWER   MGM, 1968
THE GREEN BERETS   Warner Bros.,
   1968
THE PRIVATE LIFE OF SHERLOCK
   HOLMES   also cameo as ballet
   conductor, United Artists, 1970,
   U.S.-British
THE GOLDEN VOYAGE OF SINBAD
   Columbia, 1974, British
PROVIDENCE   Cinema 5, 1977,
   French-Swiss
THE SECRET FILES OF J. EDGAR
   HOOVER   American International, 1978
FEDORA   United Artists, 1979, West
   German-French
LAST EMBRACE   United Artists, 1979
TIME AFTER TIME   Warner Bros., 1979
EYE OF THE NEEDLE   United Artists,
   1981, U.S.-British
DEAD MEN DON'T WEAR PLAID
   Universal, 1982

CAMILLE SAINT-SAENS

b. 1835 - Paris, France
d. 1921 - Algiers

THE ASSASSINATION OF THE DUC DE
   GUISE   Le Film d'Art, 1908, French

PHILIP SAINTON

b. England
d. 1967

MOBY DICK   United Artists, 1956, British

CONRAD SALINGER

d. June 18, 1962 - Hollywood, California

THE UNKNOWN MAN   MGM, 1951
CARBINE WILLIAMS   MGM, 1952
WASHINGTON STORY   MGM, 1952
THE PRISONER OF ZENDA   adaptation of
   1937 score by Alfred Newman, MGM,
   1952
DREAM WIFE   MGM, 1953
THE LAST TIME I SAW PARIS   MGM,
   1954
TENNESSEE CHAMP   MGM, 1954
THE SCARLET COAT   MGM, 1955
GABY   MGM, 1956
LONELYHEARTS   United Artists, 1958

HANS J. SALTER

b. Jan 14, 1896 - Vienna, Austria
d. Jul 23, 1994 - Los Angeles, California

*(Between the late 1930s and 1950s
Mr. Salter contributed music to over
150 films for Universal, almost all
of them in collaboration.)*

YOUNG FUGITIVE   Universal, 1938
BIG GUY   Universal, 1939
CALL A MESSENGER   Universal, 1939
THE GREAT COMMANDMENT   Universal,
   1939
ALIAS THE DEACON   Universal, 1940
BLACK DIAMONDS   Universal, 1940
BLACK FRIDAY   Universal, 1940
THE DEVIL'S PIPELINE   Universal, 1940
ENEMY AGENT   Universal, 1940
FIRST LOVE   Universal, 1940
FRAMED   Universal, 1940
GIVE US WINGS   Universal, 1940
I CAN'T GIVE YOU ANYTHING BUT LOVE,
   BABY   Universal, 1940
I'M NOBODY'S SWEETHEART NOW
   Universal, 1940
THE INVISIBLE MAN RETURNS
   Universal, 1940
SEVEN SINNERS   co-composer with Frank
   Skinner, Universal, 1940
LAW AND ORDER   Universal, 1940
THE LEATHER PUSHERS   Universal,
   1940
LOVE, HONOR AND OH, BABY!
   Universal, 1940
MARGIE   Universal, 1940
MEET THE WILDCAT   Universal, 1940
MIRACLE ON MAIN STREET   Universal,
   1940
THE MUMMY'S HAND   Universal, 1940

PRIVATE AFFAIRS   Universal, 1940
SANDY GETS HER MAN   Universal, 1940
SEVEN SINNERS   Universal, 1940
SKI PATROL   Universal, 1940
SLIGHTLY TEMPTED   Universal, 1940
SOUTH TO KARANGA   Universal, 1940
SPRING PARADE   Universal, 1940
TRAIL OF THE VIGILANTES   Universal,
   1940
YOU'RE NOT SO TOUGH   Universal, 1940
ZANZIBAR   Universal, 1940
ARIZONA CYCLONE   Universal, 1941
BACHELOR DADDY   Universal, 1941
BADLANDS OF DAKOTA   Universal, 1941
THE BLACK CAT   Universal, 1941
BURMA CONVOY   Universal, 1941
A DANGEROUS GAME   Universal, 1941
DARK STREETS OF CAIRO   Universal,
   1941
DOUBLE DATE   Universal, 1941
THE WOLF MAN   Universal, 1941
FLYING CADETS   Universal, 1941
HELLO SUCKER   Universal, 1941
HIT THE ROAD   Universal, 1941
HOLD THAT GHOST   Universal, 1941
HORROR ISLAND   Universal, 1941
IT STARTED WITH EVE   Universal, 1941
LUCKY DEVILS   Universal, 1941
MAN-MADE MONSTER   Universal, 1941
THE MAN WHO LOST HIMSELF
   Universal, 1941
MEET THE CHUMP   Universal, 1941
MEN OF THE TIMBERLAND   Universal,
   1941
MR. DYNAMITE   Universal, 1941
MOB TOWN   Universal, 1941
MODEL WIFE   Universal, 1941
MUTINY IN THE ARCTIC   Universal, 1941
RAIDERS OF THE DESERT   Universal,
   1941
ROAD AGENT   Universal, 1941
SAN FRANCISCO DOCKS   Universal,
   1941
SEALED LIPS   Universal, 1941
TIGHT SHOES   Universal, 1941
WHERE DID YOU GET THAT GIRL?
   Universal, 1941
DESTINATION UNKNOWN   Universal,
   1942
FRISCO LIL   Universal, 1942
HALF WAY TO SHANGHAI   Universal,
   1942
THE INVISIBLE AGENT   Universal, 1942
THE MAD DOCTOR OF MARKET
   STREET   Universal, 1942
MADAME SPY   Universal, 1942
THE OLD CHISHOLM TRAIL   Universal,
   1942
PITTSBURGH   Universal, 1942
SHERLOCK HOLMES AND THE SECRET
   WEAPON   Universal, 1942
WHO DONE IT?   Universal, 1942
BOMBAY CLIPPER   Universal, 1942
DANGER IN THE PACIFIC   Universal,
   1942
DEEP IN THE HEART OF TEXAS
   Universal, 1942
DRUMS OF THE CONGO   Universal, 1942
FIGHTING BILL FARGO   Universal, 1942
THE GHOST OF FRANKENSTEIN
   Universal, 1942
LITTLE JOE, THE WRANGLER   Universal,
   1942
THE MUMMY'S TOMB   Universal, 1942
THE MYSTERY OF MARIE ROGET
   Universal, 1942
NIGHT MONSTER   Universal, 1942
NORTH TO THE KLONDIKE   Universal,
   1942
PITTSBURGH   Universal, 1942
THE SILVER BULLET   Universal, 1942
SIN TOWN   Universal, 1942

THE SPOILERS   Universal, 1942
STAGECOACH BUCKAROO   Universal,
   1942
THE STRANGE CASE OF DR. RX
   Universal, 1942
THERE'S ONE BORN EVERY MINUTE
   Universal, 1942
TIMBER   Universal, 1942
TOP SERGEANT   Universal, 1942
TOUGH AS THEY COME   Universal, 1942
TREAT 'EM ROUGH   Universal, 1942
YOU'RE TELLING ME   Universal, 1942
THE AMAZING MRS. HOLIDAY ★
   co-composer with Frank Skinner,
   Universal, 1943
ARIZONA TRAIL   Universal, 1943
CALLING DR. DEATH   Universal, 1943
EYES OF THE UNDERWORLD   Universal,
   1943
FRONTIER BADMEN   Universal, 1943
BOSS OF HANGTOWN MESA   Universal,
   1943
CAPTIVE WILD WOMAN   Universal, 1943
CHEYENNE ROUNDUP   Universal, 1943
COWBOY IN MANHATTAN   Universal,
   1943
FRANKENSTEIN MEETS THE WOLFMAN
   Universal, 1943
GET GOING   Universal, 1943
HIS BUTLER'S SISTER   Universal, 1943
HI YA, CHUM   Universal, 1943
HI'YA, SAILOR   Universal, 1943
KEEP 'EM SLUGGING   Universal, 1943
LONE STAR TRAIL   Universal, 1943
THE MAD GHOUL   Universal, 1943
MUG TOWN   Universal, 1943
NEVER A DULL MOMENT   Universal,
   1943
RAIDERS OF SAN JOAQUIN   Universal,
   1943
SHERLOCK HOLMES FACES DEATH
   Universal, 1943
SON OF DRACULA   Universal, 1943
THE STRANGE DEATH OF ADOLPH
   HITLER   Universal, 1943
TENTING TONIGHT ON THE OLD CAMP
   GROUND   Universal, 1943
ALLERGIC TO LOVE   Universal, 1944
BOSS OF BOOMTOWN   Universal, 1944
CAN'T HELP SINGING   Universal, 1944
CHRISTMAS HOLIDAY ★   Universal, 1944
HAT CHECK HONEY   Universal, 1944
THE HOUSE OF FEAR   Universal, 1944
HI, GOOD LOOKIN'   Universal, 1944
HOUSE OF FRANKENSTEIN   Universal,
   1944
THE INVISIBLE MAN'S REVENGE
   Universal, 1944
JUNGLE CAPTIVE   Universal, 1944
SHERLOCK HOLMES AND THE SPIDER
   WOMAN   Universal, 1944
JUNGLE WOMAN   Universal, 1944
THE MERRY MONAHANS ★   Universal,
   1944
MARSHAL OF GUNSMOKE   Universal,
   1944
THE MUMMY'S GHOST   Universal, 1944
PARDON MY RHYTHM   Universal, 1944
THE PEARL OF DEATH   Universal, 1944
SAN DIEGO, I LOVE YOU   Universal, 1944
THE SCARLET CLAW   Universal, 1944
TWILIGHT ON THE PRAIRIE   Universal,
   1944
WEIRD WOMAN   Universal, 1944
HOUSE OF DRACULA   Universal, 1945
EASY TO LOOK AT   Universal, 1945
THE FROZEN GHOST   Universal, 1945
PURSUIT TO ALGIERS   Universal, 1945
THE STRANGE AFFAIR OF UNCLE
   HARRY   Universal, 1945
THE WOMAN IN GREEN   Universal, 1945
I'LL TELL THE WORLD   Universal, 1945

PATRICK THE GREAT   Universal, 1945
THE RIVER GANG   Universal, 1945
SCARLET STREET   Universal, 1945
SEE MY LAWYER   Universal, 1945
THAT NIGHT WITH YOU   Universal, 1945
THAT'S THE SPIRIT   Universal, 1945
THIS LOVE OF OURS ★   Universal, 1945
THE BRUTE MAN   Universal, 1946
DRESSED TO KILL   Universal, 1946
GUNG HO!   Universal, 1946
THE MAGNIFICENT DOLL   Universal, 1946
THE DARK HOUSE   Universal, 1946
HER ADVENTUROUS NIGHT   Universal, 1946
TERROR BY NIGHT   Universal, 1946
HOUSE OF HORRORS   Universal, 1946
LITTLE MISS BIG   Universal, 1946
LOVER COME BACK   Universal, 1946
SO GOES MY LOVE   Universal, 1946
THE MICHIGAN KID   Universal, 1947
THAT'S MY MAN   Universal, 1947
THE WEB   Universal, 1947
LOVE FROM A STRANGER   Universal, 1947
THE SIGN OF THE RAM   Universal, 1948
MAN-EATER OF KUMAON   Universal, 1948
DON'T TRUST YOUR HUSBAND   Universal, 1948
AN INNOCENT AFFAIR   Universal, 1948
COVER-UP   Universal, 1949
THE RECKLESS MOMENT   Universal, 1949
BORDERLINE   Universal, 1950
PLEASE BELIEVE ME   Universal, 1950
THE KILLER THAT STALKED NEW YORK   Universal, 1950
FRENCHIE   Universal, 1950
WOMAN FROM HEADQUARTERS   Universal, 1950
FINDERS KEEPERS   Universal, 1951
ABBOTT AND COSTELLO MEET THE INVISIBLE MAN   Universal, 1951
THE PRINCE WHO WAS A THIEF   Universal, 1951
THUNDER ON THE HILL   Universal, 1951
TOMAHAWK   Universal, 1951
APACHE DRUMS   Universal, 1951
YOU CAN NEVER TELL   Universal, 1951
THE GOLDEN HORDE   Universal, 1951
AGAINST ALL FLAGS   Universal, 1952
THE BLACK CASTLE   Universal, 1952
THE BATTLE OF APACHE PASS   Universal, 1952
BEND OF THE RIVER   Universal, 1952
THE DUEL AT SILVER CREEK   Universal, 1952
FLESH AND FURY   Universal, 1952
UNTAMED FRONTIER   Universal, 1952
ABBOTT AND COSTELLO MEET DR. JEYKLL AND MR. HYDE   Universal, 1953
THE 5,000 FINGERS OF DR. T   co-composer with Frederick Hollander and Heinz Roemheld, Columbia, 1953
BENGAL BRIDE   Universal, 1954
BLACK HORSE CANYON   co-composer with Frank Skinner, Universal, 1954
THE BLACK SHIELD OF FALWORTH   Universal, 1954
THE CREATURE FROM THE BLACK LAGOON   co-composer, Universal, 1954
THE FAR COUNTRY   Universal, 1954
FOUR GUNS TO THE BORDER   co-composer with Frank Skinner, Universal, 1954
JOHNNY DARK   Universal, 1954
NAKED ALIBI   Universal, 1954
SASKATCHEWAN   Universal, 1954
SIGN OF THE PAGAN   Universal, 1954

TANGANYIKA   Universal, 1954
YANKEE PASHA   Universal, 1954
THE HUMAN JUNGLE   Universal, 1954
ABBOTT AND COSTELLO MEET THE MUMMY   Universal, 1955
CAPTAIN LIGHTFOOT   Universal, 1955
MAN WITHOUT A STAR   Universal, 1955
THIS ISLAND EARTH   Universal, 1955
THE FAR HORIZONS   Universal, 1955
WICHITA   Universal, 1955
LADY GODIVA   Universal, 1956
AUTUMN LEAVES   Universal, 1956
HOLD BACK THE NIGHT   Universal, 1956
THE MOLE PEOPLE   Universal, 1956
NAVY WIFE   Universal, 1956
THE RAW EDGE   Universal, 1956
THE RAWHIDE YEARS   Universal, 1956
WALK THE PROUD LAND   Universal, 1956
RED SUNDOWN   Universal, 1956
THE OKLAHOMAN   Universal, 1957
THE INCREDIBLE SHRINKING MAN   Universal, 1957
JOE DAKOTA   Universal, 1957
THE LAND UNKNOWN   Universal, 1957
THE MAN IN THE SHADOW   Universal, 1957
THE MIDNIGHT STORY   Universal, 1957
THE TALL STRANGER   Universal, 1957
THREE BRAVE MEN   Universal, 1957
DAY OF THE BAD MAN   Universal, 1958
THE FEMALE ANIMAL   Universal, 1958
APPOINTMENT WITH A SHADOW   Universal, 1958
SUMMER LOVE   Universal, 1958
RAW WIND IN EDEN   Universal, 1958
THE GUNFIGHT AT DODGE CITY   Universal, 1959
MAN IN THE NET   Universal, 1959
THE WILD AND THE INNOCENT   Universal, 1959
COME SEPTEMBER   Universal, 1961
FOLLOW THAT DREAM   Universal, 1962
HITLER   Universal, 1962
IF A MAN ANSWERS   Universal, 1962
SHOWDOWN   Universal, 1963
BEDTIME STORY   Universal, 1964
THE WAR LORD   Universal, 1965
BEAU GESTE   Universal, 1966
GUNPOINT   Universal, 1966
I KNEW HER WELL   Universal, 1966
INCIDENT AT PHANTOM HILL   Universal, 1966
RETURN OF THE GUNFIGHTER (TF)   King Brothers/MGM TV, 1967

PAUL SAWTELL
b. 1906 - Poland
d. August 1, 1971

(The following is an incomplete list of Mr. Sawtell's credits.)

LEGION OF THE LAWLESS   RKO Radio, 1940
MEXICAN SPITFIRE   RKO Radio, 1940
NO HANDS ON THE CLOCK   Paramount, 1941
RED RIVER RIDING HOOD   RKO Radio, 1942
THE GREAT GILDERSLEEVE   RKO Radio, 1943
CALLING DR. DEATH   RKO Radio, 1943
THE SCARLET CLAW   Universal, 1944
GILDERSLEEVE'S GHOST   RKO Radio, 1944
MR. WINKLE GOES TO WAR   co-composer with Carmen Dragon, Columbia, 1944
THE PEARL OF DEATH   co-composer with Hans J. Salter, Universal, 1944

DEAD MAN'S EYES   Universal, 1944
JUNGLE CAPTIVE   co-composer, Universal, 1944
JUNGLE WOMAN   co-composer with Hans J. Salter, Universal, 1944
THE MUMMY'S CURSE   co-composer, Universal, 1945
THE HOUSE OF FEAR   Universal, 1945
THE POWER OF THE WHISTLER   Columbia, 1945
CRIME DOCTOR'S WARNING   Columbia, 1945
GENIUS AT WORK   co-composer with Roy Webb, RKO Radio, 1946
TARZAN AND THE LEOPARD WOMAN   RKO Radio, 1946
THE CAT CREEPS   Universal, 1946
DICK TRACY MEETS GRUESOME   RKO Radio, 1947
THE BLACK ARROW   Columbia, 1948
THE DOOLINS OF OKLAHOMA   co-composer with George Duning, Columbia, 1949
DAVY CROCKETT, INDIAN SCOUT   United Artists, 1950
THE WHIP HAND   RKO, 1951
THE SON OF DR. JEKYLL   Columbia, 1951
TARZAN'S SAVAGE FURY   RKO Radio, 1952
TARZAN AND THE SHE-DEVIL   RKO Radio, 1953
ABBOTT & COSTELLO MEET DR. JEKYLL AND MR. HYDE   co-composer, Universal, 1953
CAPTAIN KIDD AND THE SLAVE GIRL   United Artists, 1954
RETURN TO TREASURE ISLAND   United Artists, 1954
THE LIVING SWAMP   20th Century-Fox, 1955
SCANDAL, INC.   co-composer with Bert A. Shefter, Republic, 1956
THE DEERSLAYER   co-composer with Bert A. Shefter, 20th Century-Fox, 1957
THE BLACK SCORPION   co-composer with Bert A. Shefter and Jack Cookerly, Warner Bros., 1957
SHE DEVIL   co-composer with Bert A. Shefter, 20th Century-Fox, 1957
KRONOS   co-composer with Bert A. Shefter, 20th Century-Fox, 1957
THE FLY   co-composer with Bert A. Shefter, 20th Century-Fox, 1958
IT! THE TERROR FROM BEYOND SPACE   co-composer with Bert A. Shefter, United Artists, 1958
THE COSMIC MAN   co-composer with Bert A. Shefter, Allied Artists, 1959
RETURN OF THE FLY   co-composer with Bert A. Shefter, 20th Century-Fox, 1959
A DOG OF FLANDERS   co-composer with Bert A. Shefter, 20th Century-Fox, 1959
GIGANTIS THE FIRE MONSTER   co-composer of U.S. version only, 1959, Japanese
THE BIG CIRCUS   co-composer with Bert A. Shefter, Allied Artists, 1959
THE LOST WORLD   co-composer, 20th Century-Fox, 1960
VOYAGE TO THE BOTTOM OF THE SEA   co-composer with Bert A. Shefter, 20th Century-Fox, 1961
MISTY   20th Century-Fox, 1961
JACK THE GIANT KILLER   co-composer with Bert A. Shefter, United Artists, 1962
FIVE WEEKS IN A BALLOON   20th Century-Fox, 1962
THUNDER ISLAND   co-composer with Bert A. Shefter, 20th Century-Fox, 1963
ISLAND OF THE BLUE DOLPHINS   Universal, 1964

THE LAST MAN ON EARTH   co-composer
with Bert A. Shefter, 1964, U.S.-Italian
MOTOR PSYCHO   co-composer with Bert
A. Shefter, Eve, 1965
FASTER, PUSSYCAT, KILL! KILL!   Eve,
1965
THE BUBBLE   *FANTASTIC INVASION OF
THE PLANET EARTH*   co-composer with
Bert A. Shefter, Oboler Films, 1967
THE CHRISTINE JORGENSEN STORY
co-composer with Bert A. Shefter, United
Artists, 1970

VICTOR SCHERTZINGER
b. April 8, 1880 - Mahanoy City,
Pennsylvania
d. 1941

BETWEEN MEN   co-composer, Triangle,
1915
D'ARTAGNAN   co-composer, Triangle,
1915
THE GOLDEN CLAW   co-composer,
Triangle, 1915
THE WINGED IDOL   co-composer,
Triangle, 1915
THE EDGE OF THE ABYSS   Triangle,
1916
THE BECKONING FLAME   Triangle, 1916
THE CONQUEROR   Triangle, 1916
PEGGY   Triangle, 1916
CIVILIZATION   Ince, 1916
THE PRINCESS OF THE DARK   Ince,
1917
ROBIN HOOD   United Artists, 1922
BELOVED   co-composer with Howard
Jackson, Universal, 1934
ONE NIGHT OF LOVE ★   co-composer
with Gus Kahn, Columbia, 1937
SOMETHING TO SING ABOUT ★   Grand
National, 1937

WALTER SCHUMANN
d. August 21, 1958 - Minneapolis

THE NIGHT OF THE HUNTER   United
Artists, 1955

HUMPHREY SEARLE
b. 1915 - Oxford, England
d. May 12, 1982 - London, England

BEYOND MOMBASA   Columbia, 1956,
British-U.S.
THE ABOMINABLE SNOWMAN OF THE
HIMALAYAS   *ABOMINABLE
SNOWMAN*   uncredited, 20th
Century-Fox, 1957, British
ACTION OF THE TIGER   MGM, 1957,
British
LAW AND DISORDER   Continental, 1958,
British
LEFT, RIGHT AND CENTER   1961, British
THE HAUNTING   MGM, 1963, British-U.S.

ANDREA SETARO
b. November 11, 1886 - Philadelphia,
Pennsylvania

BOLERO   co-composer, Paramount, 1934
THE OLD-FASHIONED WAY
co-composer, Paramount, 1934
BELLE OF THE NINETIES   co-composer,
Paramount, 1934
GOIN' TO TOWN   co-composer,
Paramount, 1935
COLLEGE SCANDAL   co-composer,
Paramount, 1935

NATHANIEL SHILKRET
b. 1895

BATTLE OF THE SEXES   United Artists,
1928
LILAC TIME   First National, 1928
THE BIG GAME   RKO Radio, 1936
MARY OF SCOTLAND   RKO Radio, 1936
THE SMARTEST GIRL IN TOWN   RKO
Radio, 1936
THE LAST OF THE MOHICANS   United
Artists, 1936
THAT GIRL FROM PARIS   RKO Radio,
1936
WALKING ON AIR   RKO Radio, 1936
WINTERSET★   RKO Radio, 1936
THE SOLDIER AND THE LADY   RKO
Radio, 1937
BORDER CAFE   RKO Radio, 1937
THE TOAST OF NEW YORK   RKO Radio,
1937
...ONE THIRD OF A NATION...   Paramount,
1939
FRANK BUCK'S JUNGLE CAVALCADE
RKO Radio, 1941
STOLEN PARADISE   RKO Radio, 1941
A STRANGER IN TOWN   co-composer with
Daniele Amfitheatrof, MGM, 1943
AIR RAD WARDENS   MGM, 1943
BLONDE FEVER   MGM, 1944
NOTHING BUT TROUBLE   MGM, 1944
THREE MEN IN WHITE   MGM, 1944
SHE WENT TO THE RACES   MGM, 1945
THIS MAN'S NAVY   MGM, 1945
BOY'S RANCH   MGM, 1946
FAITHFUL IN MY FASHION   MGM, 1946
THE HOODLUM SAINT   MGM, 1946

DMITRI SHOSTAKOVITCH
b. September 25, 1906 - St. Petersburg,
Russia
d. 1975 - U.S.S.R.

THE NEW BABYLON   1929, Soviet
ALONE   1930, Soviet
GOLDEN MOUNTAINS   1931, Soviet
HAMLET   1931, Soviet
COUNTERPLAN   1932, Soviet
THE YOUTH OF MAXIM   1934, Soviet
GIRL FRIENDS   1936, Soviet
THE RETURN OF MAXIM GORKY   1936,
Soviet
A GREAT CITIZEN   1938, Soviet
THE MAN WITH A GUN   1938, Soviet
VOLOCHAYEVSK DAYS   1938, Soviet
THE VYBORG SIDE   1939, Soviet
THE BATTLE FOR SIBERIA   1940, Soviet
ZOYA   1944, Soviet
THE FALL OF BERLIN   1945, Soviet
PLAIN PEOPLE   1945, Soviet
MICHURIN   1947, Soviet
PIROGOV   1947, Soviet
YOUNG GUARD   1947, Soviet
FIVE DAYS AND FIVE NIGHTS   1948,
Soviet
MEETING ON THE ELBA   1949, Soviet
THE UNFORGETTABLE YEAR—1919
1952, Soviet
THE FIRST ECHELON   1956, Soviet
KHOVANSHCHINA ★   Artkino, 1961,
Soviet
THE CONDEMNED OF ALTONA   1963,
Soviet
HAMLET   United Artists, 1964, Soviet
KING LEAR   Artkino, 1971, Soviet

NATHANIEL SHILKRET

LEO SHUKEN
b. December 8, 1906 - Los Angeles,
California
d. July 24, 1976 - Santa Monica, California

WAIKIKI WEDDING   Paramount, 1937
EVERY DAY'S A HOLIDAY   Paramount,
1938
ARTISTS AND MODELS ABROAD
Paramount, 1938
PARIS HONEYMOON   Paramount, 1939
CAFE SOCIETY   Paramount, 1939
STAGECOACH ★★   co-composer, United
Artists, 1939
THE LADY FROM KENTUCKY   United
Artists, 1939
THE FLYING DEUCES   co-composer,
RKO Radio, 1939
ADVENTURE IN DIAMONDS   Paramount,
1940
THE LADY EVE   Paramount, 1941
WEST POINT WIDOW   Paramount, 1941
OUR WIFE   Columbia, 1941
NEW YORK TOWN   Paramount, 1941
SULLIVAN'S TRAVELS   co-composer with
Charles Bradshaw, Paramount, 1941
THE LADY HAS PLANS   co-composer with
Leigh Harline, Paramount, 1942
MEET THE STEWARTS   Columbia, 1942
HENRY ALDRICH, EDITOR   Paramount,
1942
THE GOOD FELLOWS   Paramount, 1943
THE MIRACLE OF MORGAN'S CREEK
co-composer with Charles Bradshaw,
Paramount, 1944
THE FABULOUS DORSEYS   United
Artists, 1947
THOSE REDHEADS FROM SEATTLE
Paramount, 1953

ELIE SIEGMEISTER
b. 1909 - New York

THEY CAME TO CORDURA Columbia,
1959

LOUIS SILVERS
d. March 26, 1954 - Hollywood, California

WAY DOWN EAST   United Artists, 1920
DREAM STREET   Griffith, 1921
ISN'T LIFE WONDERFUL?   co-composer,
United Artists, 1924
THE JAZZ SINGER   Warner Bros., 1927
NOAH'S ARK   Warner Bros., 1929
DANCING LADY   MGM, 1933
ONE NIGHT OF LOVE   Columbia, 1934
LOVE ME FOREVER   Columbia, 1935
CAPTAIN JANUARY   20th Century-Fox,
1936
DIMPLES   20th Century-Fox, 1936
LADIES IN LOVE   20th Century-Fox, 1936
A MESSAGE TO GARCIA   20th
Century-Fox, 1936
POOR LITTLE RICH GIRL   20th
Century-Fox, 1936
PRIVATE NUMBER   20th Century-Fox,
1936
PROFESSIONAL SOLDIER   20th
Century-Fox, 1936
ROAD TO GLORY   20th Century-Fox,
1936
TO MARY, WITH LOVE   20th Century-Fox,
1936
UNDER TWO FLAGS   20th Century-Fox,
1936
CAFE METROPOLE   20th Century-Fox,
1937
LLOYDS OF LONDON   20th Century-Fox,
1937

SEVENTH HEAVEN   20th Century-Fox, 1937

STOWAWAY   20th Century-Fox, 1937

FOUR MEN AND A PRAYER   20th Century-Fox, 1937

IN OLD CHICAGO ★   20th Century-Fox, 1938

KENTUCKY   20th Century-Fox, 1938

KENTUCKY MOONSHINE   20th Century-Fox, 1938

SUEZ ★   20th Century-Fox, 1938

HOLLYWOOD CAVALCADE   co-composer, 20th Century-Fox, 1939

SECOND FIDDLE   20th Century-Fox, 1939

SUSANNAH OF THE MOUNTIES   20th Century-Fox, 1939

SWANEE RIVER ★   adaptation, 20th Century-Fox, 1939

FRANK SKINNER

b. 1897 - Meredosia, Illinois
d. 1968 - Los Angeles, California

MAD ABOUT MUSIC ★   co-composer with Charles Previn, Universal, 1938

SON OF FRANKENSTEIN   co-composer with Hans J. Salter and Charles Previn, Universal, 1939

THE SUN NEVER SETS   Universal, 1939

CHARLIE McCARTHY, DETECTIVE   Universal, 1939

DESTRY RIDES AGAIN   Universal, 1939

TOWER OF LONDON   Universal, 1939

THE INVISIBLE MAN RETURNS   co-composer with Hans J. Salter, Universal, 1940

MY LITTLE CHICKADEE   Universal, 1940

THE HOUSE OF THE SEVEN GABLES ★   Universal, 1940

HIRED WIFE   Universal, 1940

WHEN THE DALTONS RODE   Universal, 1940

BLACK FRIDAY   co-composer, Universal, 1940

THE MUMMY'S HAND   co-composer with Hans J. Salter, Universal, 1940

SEVEN SINNERS   co-composer with Hans J. Salter, Universal, 1940

BACK STREET ★   Universal, 1941

THE LADY FROM CHEYENNE   Universal, 1941

THE FLAME OF NEW ORLEANS   Universal, 1941

NEVER GIVE A SUCKER AN EVEN BREAK   Universal, 1941

APPOINTMENT FOR LOVE   Universal, 1941

KEEP 'EM FLYING   Universal, 1941

HELZAPOPPIN   Universal, 1941

THE WOLF MAN   co-composer with Hans J. Salter, Universal, 1941

HORROR ISLAND   co-composer, Universal, 1941

THE BLACK CAT   co-composer, Universal, 1941

HOLD THAT GHOST   co-composer, Universal, 1941

MAN-MADE MONSTER   co-composer with Hans J. Salter and Charles Henderson, Universal, 1941

JAIL HOUSE BLUES   Universal, 1942

RIDE 'EM COWBOY   Universal, 1942

SABOTEUR   Universal, 1942

BROADWAY   Universal, 1942

LADY IN A JAM   Universal, 1942

EAGLE SQUADRON   Universal, 1942

SHERLOCK HOLMES AND THE VOICE OF TERROR   Universal

WHO DONE IT?   Universal, 1942

PITTSBURGH   co-composer with Hans J. Salter, Universal, 1942

ARABIAN NIGHTS ★   Universal, 1942

SHERLOCK HOLMES AND THE SECRET WEAPON   Universal, 1943

THE AMAZING MRS. HOLLIDAY ★   co-composer with Hans J. Salter, Universal, 1943

WHITE SAVAGE   Universal, 1943

SHERLOCK HOLMES IN WASHINGTON   Universal, 1943

TWO TICKETS IN LONDON   Universal, 1943

HERS TO HOLD   Universal, 1943

WE'VE NEVER BEEN LICKED   Universal, 1943

FIRED WIFE   Universal, 1943

GUNG HO!   Universal, 1943

FRANKENSTEIN MEETS THE WOLF MAN   co-composer with Hans J. Salter and Charles Previn, Universal, 1943

SON OF DRACULA   co-composer with Hans J. Salter and Charles Previn, Universal, 1943

THE MAD GHOUL   co-composer, Universal, 1943

CALLING DR. DEATH   co-composer with Hans J. Salter and Paul Sawtell, Universal, 1943

HI, BEAUTIFUL   Universal, 1944

HOUSE OF FRANKENSTEIN   co-composer, Universal, 1944

DESTINY   co-composer with Alexander Tansman, Universal, 1944

THE MUMMY'S GHOST   co-composer with Hans J. Salter and Charles Previn, Universal, 1944

FOLLOW THE BOYS   co-composer with Leigh Harline and Oliver Wallace, Universal, 1944

THE SUSPECT   Universal, 1945

UNDER WESTERN SKIES   co-composer, Universal, 1945

BLONDE RANSOM   co-composer, Universal, 1945

STRANGE CONFESSION   co-composer, Universal, 1945

THE DALTONS RIDE AGAIN   co-composer, Universal, 1945

PILLOW OF DEATH   co-composer, Universal, 1945

FRONTIER GAL   Universal, 1945

IDEA GIRL   co-composer, Universal, 1946

NIGHT IN PARADISE   Universal, 1946

THE RUNAROUND   Universal, 1946

WHITE SAVAGE   co-composer, Universal, 1946

CANYON PASSAGE   Universal, 1946

BLACK ANGEL   Universal, 1946

THE DARK MIRROR   co-composer with Dimitri Tiomkin, 1946

SWELL GUY   Universal, 1947

I'LL BE YOURS   Universal, 1947

THE EGG AND I   Universal, 1947

RIDE THE PINK HORSE   Universal, 1947

THE EXILE   Universal, 1947

SMASH-UP, THE STORY OF A WOMAN   Universal, 1947

THE NAKED CITY   co-composer with Miklos Rozsa, Universal, 1948

HAZARD   Paramount, 1948

ABBOTT AND COSTELLO MEET FRANKENSTEIN   Universal, 1948

TAP ROOTS   Universal, 1948

FOR THE LOVE OF MARY   Universal, 1948

THE FIGHTING O'FLYNN   Universal, 1949

FAMILY HONEYMOON   Universal, 1949

THE LIFE OF RILEY   Universal, 1949

TULSA   Eagle Lion, 1949

THE LADY GAMBLES   Universal, 1949

THE GAL WHO TOOK THE WEST   Universal, 1949

SWORD IN THE DESERT   Universal, 1949

FREE FOR ALL   Universal, 1949

WOMAN IN HIDING   Universal, 1950

FRANCIS   Universal, 1950

ONE-WAY STREET   Universal, 1950

COMANCHE TERRITORY   Universal, 1950

THE DESERT HAWK   Universal, 1950

LOUISA   Universal, 1950

THE SLEEPING CITY   Universal, 1950

HARVEY   Universal, 1950

BEDTIME FOR BONZO   Universal, 1951

DOUBLE CROSSBONES   Universal, 1951

KATIE DID IT   Universal, 1951

FRANCIS GOES TO THE RACES   Universal, 1951

MARK OF THE RENEGADE   Universal, 1951

BRIGHT VICTORY   Universal, 1951

THE LADY PAYS OFF   Universal, 1951

THE RAGING TIDE   Universal, 1951

WEEKEND WITH FATHER   Universal, 1951

NO ROOM FOR THE GROOM   Universal, 1952

SALLY AND SAINT ANNE   Universal, 1952

THE WORLD IN HIS ARMS   Universal, 1952

BONZO GOES TO COLLEGE   Universal, 1952

BECAUSE OF YOU   Universal, 1952

IT GROWS ON TREES   Universal, 1952

MISSISSIPPI GAMBLER   Universal, 1953

THE MAN FROM THE ALAMO   Universal, 1953

THUNDER BAY   Universal, 1953

WINGS OF THE HAWK   Universal, 1953

BACK TO GOD'S COUNTRY   Universal, 1953

DESERT LEGION   Universal, 1953

FORBIDDEN   Universal, 1953

TAZA, SON OF COCHISE   Universal, 1954

MAGNIFICENT OBSESSION   Universal, 1954

SIGN OF THE PAGAN   Universal, 1954

FOUR GUNS TO THE BORDER   co-composer with Hans Salter, 1954

BLACK HORSE CANYON   co-composer with Hans Salter, Universal, 1954

CHIEF CRAZY HORSE   Universal, 1955

FOXFIRE   Universal, 1955

THE SHRIKE   Universal, 1955

ONE DESIRE   Universal, 1955

ALL THAT HEAVEN ALLOWS   Universal, 1956

FRANCIS IN THE HAUNTED HOUSE   Universal, 1956

AWAY ALL BOATS   Universal, 1956

NEVER SAY GOODBYE   Universal, 1956

THE RAWHIDE YEARS   Universal, 1956

STAR IN THE DUST   Universal, 1956

WRITTEN ON THE WIND   Universal, 1957

BATTLE HYMN   Universal, 1957

INTERLUDE   Universal, 1957

MAN OF A THOUSAND FACES   Universal, 1957

MY MAN GODFREY   Universal, 1957

THE TATTERED DRESS   Universal, 1957

THE TARNISHED ANGELS   Universal, 1958

THIS HAPPY FEELING   Universal, 1958

KATHY O'   Universal, 1958

THE SNOW QUEEN (AF)   composer of U.S. version only, Universal, 1959

THE PERFECT FURLOUGH   Universal, 1959

IMITATION OF LIFE   Universal, 1959

MIDNIGHT LACE   Universal, 1960

PORTRAIT IN BLACK   Universal, 1960

BACK STREET   Universal, 1961

CAPTAIN NEWMAN M. D.   Universal, 1963

TAMMY AND THE DOCTOR   Universal, 1963
THE UGLY AMERICAN   Universal, 1963
BULLET FOR A BADMAN   Universal, 1964
SHENANDOAH   Universal, 1965
THE SWORD OF ALI BABA   Universal, 1965
THE APPALOOSA   Universal, 1966
MADAME X   Universal, 1966
RIDE TO HANGMAN'S TREE   Universal, 1967

PAUL J. SMITH
b. October 30, 1906 - Calumet, Michigan
d. January 25, 1985

SNOW WHITE AND THE SEVEN DWARFS (AF) ★   co-composer with Frank Churchill and Leigh Harline, RKO Radio, 1938
PINOCCHIO (AF) ★★   co-composer with Leigh Harline, RKO Radio, 1940
SALUDOS AMIGOS ★   co-composer with Edward Plumb, RKO Radio, 1943
VICTORY THROUGH AIR POWER ★   co-composer with Edward Plumb and Oliver Wallace, United Artists, 1943
THE THREE CABALLEROS (AF) ★   co-composer, RKO Radio, 1944
SONG OF THE SOUTH ★   co-composer with Daniele Amfitheatrof, RKO Radio, 1946
FUN AND FANCY FREE   co-composer with Eliot Daniel and Oliver Wallace, RKO Radio, 1947
THE STRANGE MRS. CRANE   Eagle Lion, 1948
SO DEAR TO MY HEART   RKO Radio, 1948
CINDERELLA (AF) ★   co-composer with Oliver Wallace, RKO Radio, 1950
BEAVER VALLEY   RKO Radio, 1950
NATURE'S HALF ACRE   RKO Radio, 1951
THE OLYMPIC ELK   RKO Radio, 1952
WATER BIRDS   RKO Radio, 1952
20,000 LEAGUES UNDER THE SEA   Buena Vista, 1954
PERRI ★   Buena Vista, 1957
THE SHAGGY DOG   Buena Vista, 1959
MOON PILOT   Buena Vista, 1962
THE THREE LIVES OF THOMASINA   Buena Vista, 1963

MISCHA SPOLIANSKY
d. June 29, 1985

THE GHOST GOES WEST   1936, British
THE MAN WHO COULD WORK MIRACLES   1937, British

RONALD STEIN
b. April 12, 1930 - St. Louis, Missouri
d. August 15, 1988

THE APACHE WOMAN   American International, 1955
THE DAY THE WORLD ENDED   American International, 1956
THE PHANTOM FROM 10,000 LEAGUES 1956
THE OKLAHOMA WOMAN   American International, 1956
THE GUNSLINGER   ARC, 1956
GIRLS IN PRISON   American International, 1956
IT CONQUERED THE WORLD   American International, 1956
THE SHE CREATURE   American International, 1956
FLESH AND THE SPUR   American International, 1957

SHE GODS OF SHARK REEF   American International, 1957
NOT OF THIS EARTH   Allied Artists, 1957
THE UNDEAD   American International, 1957
THUNDER OVER HAWAII   *NAKED PARADISE*   American International, 1957
RUNAWAY DAUGHTERS   American International, 1957
ATTACK OF THE CRAB MONSTERS   Allied Artists, 1957
DRAGSTRIP GIRL   American International, 1957
INVASION OF THE SAUCER-MEN   American International, 1957
REFORM SCHOOL GIRL   American International, 1957
ROCK ALL NIGHT   American International, 1957
SORORITY GIRL   American International, 1957
JET ATTACK   American International, 1958
SUICIDE BATTALION   American International, 1958
THE ATTACK OF THE 50 FOOT WOMAN   American International, 1958
THE BONNIE PARKER STORY   American International, 1958
HOT ROD GANG   American International, 1958
HIGH SCHOOL HELLCATS   American International, 1958
THE LITTLEST HOBO   Allied Artists, 1958
THE DEVIL'S PARTNER   Filmgroup, 1959
PARATROOP COMMAND   American International, 1959
TANK COMMANDOS   American International, 1959
THE VIOLENT EVIL   1959
THE DEVIL'S PARTNER   Filmgroup, 1959
DIAL 111 - JUVENILE SQUAD   1959
THE LEGEND OF TOM DOOLEY   Columbia, 1959
DIARY OF A HIGH SCHOOL BRIDE   American International, 1959
GHOST OF DRAGSTRIP HOLLOW   American International, 1959
TOO SOON TO LOVE   Universal, 1960
RAYMIE   Allied Artists, 1960
THE THREAT   Warner Bros., 1960
THE LAST WOMAN ON EARTH   Filmgroup, 1960
DINOSAURUS!   Universal, 1960
STAKEOUT   1960
ATLAS   Filmgroup, 1961
JUST BETWEEN US   1961
THE PREMATURE BURIAL   American International, 1962
THE BASHFUL ELEPHANT   Allied Artists, 1962
THE UNDERWATER CITY   Columbia, 1962
OF LOVE AND DESIRE   20th Century-Fox, 1963
DEMENTIA 13   American International, 1963
THE TERROR   American International, 1963
DIME WITH A HALO   MGM, 1963
THE HAUNTED PALACE   American International, 1963
THE YOUNG AND THE BRAVE   MGM, 1963
WAR HERO   *WAR IS HELL*   Allied Artists, 1963
THE BASHFUL BIKINI   1964
MY SOUL RUNS NAKED   *RAT FINK/WILD AND WILLING*   Genesis, 1964
SPIDER BABY   *THE LIVER EATERS/CANNIBAL ORGY*   1965

THE BOUNTY KILLER   Embassy, 1965
REQUIEM FOR A GUNFIGHTER   Embassy, 1965
PORTRAIT IN TERROR   American International, 1966
PSYCH-OUT   American International, 1968
TARGETS   co-composer, Paramount, 1968
THE RAIN PEOPLE   Warner Bros., 1969
GETTING STRAIGHT   Columbia, 1970
THE PRISONER   1973
FRANKENSTEIN'S GREAT AUNT TILLIE   1984
RASCAL DAZZLE   1985

MAX STEINER
b. May 10, 1888 - Vienna, Austria
d. 1971

RIO RITA   RKO Radio, 1929
DIXIANA   RKO Radio, 1930
HALF SHOT AT SUNRISE   RKO Radio, 1930
CHECK AND DOUBLE CHECK   RKO Radio, 1930
BEAU IDEAL   RKO Radio, 1930
CIMARRON   RKO Radio, 1931
KEPT HUSBANDS   RKO Radio, 1931
CRACKED NUTS   RKO Radio, 1931
YOUNG DONOVAN'S KID   RKO Radio, 1931
TRANSGRESSION   RKO Radio, 1931
THE PUBLIC DEFENDER   RKO Radio, 1931
TRAVELING HUSBANDS   RKO Radio, 1931
THE RUNAROUND   RKO Radio, 1931
THE GAY DIPLOMAT   RKO Radio, 1931
FANNY FOLEY HERSELF   RKO Radio, 1931
CONSOLATION MARRIAGE   RKO Radio, 1931
WAY BACK HOME   RKO Radio, 1931
ARE THESE OUR CHILDREN?   RKO Radio, 1931
SECRET SERVICE   RKO Radio, 1931
MEN OF CHANCE   RKO Radio, 1932
GIRL OF THE RIO   RKO Radio, 1932
LADIES OF THE JURY   RKO Radio, 1932
THE LOST SQUADRON   RKO Radio, 1932
YOUNG BRIDE   RKO Radio, 1932
SYMPHONY OF SIX MILLION   RKO Radio, 1932
STATE'S ATTORNEY   RKO Radio, 1932
WESTWARD PASSAGE   RKO Radio, 1932
IS MY FACE RED?   RKO Radio, 1932
WHAT PRICE HOLLYWOOD   RKO Radio, 1932
ROAR OF THE DRAGON   RKO Radio, 1932
BIRD OF PARADISE   RKO Radio, 1932
THE MOST DANGEROUS GAME   RKO Radio, 1932
A BILL OF DIVORCEMENT   RKO Radio, 1932
THIRTEEN WOMEN   RKO Radio, 1932
THE PHANTOM OF CRESTWOOD   RKO Radio, 1932
LITTLE ORPHAN ANNIE   RKO Radio, 1932
RENEGADES OF THE WEST   RKO Radio, 1932
SECRETS OF THE FRENCH POLICE   RKO Radio, 1932
THE CONQUERORS   RKO Radio, 1932
THE SPORT PARADE   RKO Radio, 1932
ROCKABYE   RKO Radio, 1932
THE HALF NAKED TRUTH   also cameo as conductor, RKO Radio, 1932

PENGUIN POOL MURDER   RKO Radio, 1932

THE ANIMAL KINGDOM   RKO Radio, 1932

THE MONKEY'S PAW   RKO Radio, 1932

NO OTHER WOMAN   RKO Radio, 1933

THE CHEYENNE KID   RKO Radio, 1933

LUCKY DEVILS   RKO Radio, 1933

THE GREAT JASPER   RKO Radio, 1933

TOPAZE   RKO Radio, 1933

OUR BETTERS   RKO Radio, 1933

KING KONG   RKO Radio, 1933

CHRISTOPHER STRONG   RKO Radio, 1933

SWEEPINGS   RKO Radio, 1933

DIPLOMANIACS   RKO Radio, 1933

THE SILVER CORD   RKO Radio, 1933

SON OF THE BORDER   RKO Radio, 1933

EMERGENCY CALL   RKO Radio, 1933

PROFESSIONAL SWEETHEART   RKO Radio, 1933

FLYING DEVILS   RKO Radio, 1933

MELODY CRUISE   RKO Radio, 1933

BED OF ROSES   RKO Radio, 1933

DOUBLE HARNESS   RKO Radio, 1933

HEADLINE SHOOTER   RKO Radio, 1933

BEFORE DAWN   RKO Radio, 1933

NO MARRIAGE TIES   RKO Radio, 1933

MORNING GLORY   RKO Radio, 1933

BLIND ADVENTURE   RKO Radio, 1933

ONE MAN'S JOURNEY   RKO Radio, 1933

RAFTER ROMANCE   RKO Radio, 1933

MIDSHIPMAN JACK   RKO Radio, 1933

ANN VICKERS   RKO Radio, 1933

ACE OF ACES   RKO Radio, 1933

CHANCE AT HEAVEN   RKO Radio, 1933

AFTER TONIGHT   RKO Radio, 1933

LITTLE WOMEN   RKO Radio, 1933

THE RIGHT TO ROMANCE   RKO Radio, 1933

AGGIE APPLEBY   RKO Radio, 1933

IF I WERE FREE   RKO Radio, 1933

THE SON OF KONG   RKO Radio, 1933

FLYING DOWN TO RIO   RKO Radio, 1933

MAN OF TWO WORLDS   RKO Radio, 1934

THE MEANEST GAL IN TOWN   RKO Radio, 1934

LONG LOST FATHER   RKO Radio, 1934

TWO ALONE   RKO Radio, 1934

THE LOST PATROL★   RKO Radio, 1934

KEEP 'EM ROLLING   RKO Radio, 1934

SPITFIRE   RKO Radio, 1934

SUCCESS AT ANY PRICE   RKO Radio, 1934

THIS MAN IS MINE   RKO Radio, 1934

SING AND LIKE IT   RKO Radio, 1934

THE CRIME DOCTOR   RKO Radio, 1934

FINISHING SCHOOL   RKO Radio, 1934

STRICTLY DYNAMITE   RKO Radio, 1934

WHERE SINNERS MEET   RKO Radio, 1934

STINGAREE   RKO Radio, 1934

MURDER ON THE BLACKBOARD   RKO Radio, 1934

THE LIFE OF VERGIE MINTERS   RKO Radio, 1934

LET'S TRY AGAIN   RKO Radio, 1934

OF HUMAN BONDAGE   RKO Radio, 1934

WE'RE RICH AGAIN   RKO Radio, 1934

HIS GREATEST GAMBLE   RKO Radio, 1934

HAT, COAT AND GLOVE   RKO Radio, 1934

BACHELOR BAIT   RKO Radio, 1934

THEIR BIG MOMENT   RKO Radio, 1934

DOWN TO THEIR LAST YACHT   RKO Radio, 1934

THE FOUNTAIN   RKO Radio, 1934

THE AGE OF INNOCENCE   RKO Radio, 1934

THE RICHEST GIRL IN THE WORLD   RKO Radio, 1934

THE GAY DIVORCEE   RKO Radio, 1934

DANGEROUS CORNER   RKO Radio, 1934

GRIDIRON FLASH   RKO Radio, 1934

WEDNESDAY'S CHILD   RKO Radio, 1934

KENTUCKY KERNELS   RKO Radio, 1934

BY YOUR LEAVE   RKO Radio, 1934

ANNE OF GREEN GABLES   RKO Radio, 1934

THE LITTLE MINISTER   RKO Radio, 1934

ROMANCE IN MANHATTAN   RKO Radio, 1935

ENCHANTED APRIL   RKO Radio, 1935

ROBERTA   RKO Radio, 1935

LADDIE   RKO Radio, 1935

STAR OF MIDNIGHT   RKO Radio, 1935

THE INFORMER ★★   RKO Radio, 1935

BREAK OF HEARTS   RKO Radio, 1935

SHE   RKO Radio, 1935

ALICE ADAMS   RKO Radio, 1935

TOP HAT   RKO Radio, 1935

THE THREE MUSKETEERS   RKO Radio, 1935

I DREAM TOO MUCH   RKO Radio, 1935

FOLLOW THE FLEET   RKO Radio, 1936

TWO IN REVOLT   RKO Radio, 1936

M'LISS   RKO Radio, 1936

LITTLE LORD FAUNTLEROY   United Artists, 1936

THE CHARGE OF THE LIGHT BRIGADE ★   Warner Bros., 1936

THE GARDEN OF ALLAH ★   United Artists, 1936

GOD'S COUNTRY AND THE WOMAN   Warner Bros., 1936

GREEN LIGHT   Warner Bros., 1937

SLIM   Warner Bros., 1937

KID GALAHAD   Warner Bros., 1937

A STAR IS BORN   United Artists, 1937

THE LIFE OF EMILE ZOLA ★   Warner Bros., 1937

THAT CERTAIN WOMAN   Warner Bros., 1937

FIRST LADY   Warner Bros., 1937

SUBMARINE D-I   Warner Bros., 1937

TOVARICH   Warner Bros., 1937

GOLD IS WHERE YOU FIND IT   Warner Bros., 1938

JEZEBEL ★   Warner Bros., 1938

THE ADVENTURES OF TOM SAWYER   Warner Bros., 1938

CRIME SCHOOL   Warner Bros., 1938

WHITE BANNERS   Warner Bros., 1938

THE AMAZING DR. CLITTERHOUSE   Warner Bros., 1938

FOUR DAUGHTERS   Warner Bros., 1938

THE SISTERS   Warner Bros., 1938

ANGELS WITH DIRTY FACES   Warner Bros., 1938

THE DAWN PATROL   Warner Bros., 1938

THEY MADE ME A CRIMINAL   Warner Bros., 1939

THE OKLAHOMA KID   Warner Bros., 1939

DODGE CITY   Warner Bros., 1939

CONFESSIONS OF A NAZI SPY   Warner Bros., 1939

DAUGHTERS COURAGEOUS   Warner Bros., 1939

EACH DAWN I DIE   Warner Bros., 1939

THE OLD MAID   Warner Bros., 1939

DARK VICTORY ★   Warner Bros., 1939

DUST BE MY DESTINY   Warner Bros., 1939

INTERMEZZO   United Artists, 1939

WE ARE NOT ALONE   Warner Bros., 1939

GONE WITH THE WIND ★   MGM, 1939

FOUR WIVES   Warner Bros., 1940

DR. ERLICH'S MAGIC BULLET   Warner Bros., 1940

VIRGINIA CITY   Warner Bros., 1940

ALL THIS AND HEAVEN TOO   Warner Bros., 1940

CITY FOR CONQUEST   Warner Bros., 1940

A DISPATCH FROM REUTER'S   Warner Bros., 1940

THE LETTER ★   Warner Bros., 1940

SANTA FE TRAIL   Warner Bros., 1940

THE GREAT LIE   Warner Bros., 1941

SHINING VICTORY   Warner Bros., 1941

THE BRIDE CAME C.O.D.   Warner Bros., 1941

DIVE BOMBER   Warner Bros., 1941

SERGEANT YORK ★   Warner Bros., 1941

ONE FOOT IN HEAVEN   Warner Bros., 1941

THEY DIED WITH THEIR BOOTS ON   Warner Bros., 1942

CAPTAINS OF THE CLOUDS   Warner Bros., 1942

IN THIS OUR LIFE   Warner Bros., 1942

THE GAY SISTERS   Warner Bros., 1942

DESPERATE JOURNEY   Warner Bros., 1942

NOW, VOYAGER ★★   Warner Bros., 1942

CASABLANCA ★   Warner Bros., 1943

MISSION TO MOSCOW   Warner Bros., 1943

WATCH ON THE RHINE   Warner Bros., 1943

THIS IS THE ARMY   Warner Bros., 1943

PASSAGE TO MARSEILLE   Warner Bros., 1944

THE ADVENTURES OF MARK TWAIN ★   Warner Bros., 1944

SINCE YOU WENT AWAY ★★   United Artists, 1944

ARSENIC AND OLD LACE   Warner Bros., 1944

THE CONSPIRATORS   Warner Bros., 1944

ROUGHLY SPEAKING   Warner Bros., 1945

THE CORN IS GREEN   Warner Bros., 1945

RHAPSODY IN BLUE ★   adaptation, Warner Bros., 1945

MILDRED PIERCE   Warner Bros., 1945

TOMORROW IS FOREVER   RKO Radio, 1946

SAN ANTONIO   Warner Bros., 1946

MY REPUTATION   Warner Bros., 1946

SARATOGA TRUNK   Warner Bros., 1946

ONE MORE TOMORROW   Warner Bros., 1946

A STOLEN LIFE   Warner Bros., 1946

THE BIG SLEEP   Warner Bros., 1946

NIGHT AND DAY ★   adaptation, Warner Bros., 1946

CLOAK AND DAGGER   Warner Bros., 1946

THE MAN I LOVE   Warner Bros., 1947

THE BEAST WITH FIVE FINGERS   Warner Bros., 1947

PURSUED   Warner Bros., 1947

LOVE AND LEARN   Warner Bros., 1947

MY WILD IRISH ROSE ★   adaptation, Warner Bros., 1947

CHEYENNE   Warner Bros., 1947

THE UNFAITHFUL   Warner Bros., 1947

DEEP VALLEY   Warner Bros., 1947

LIFE WITH FATHER ★   Warner Bros., 1947

THE VOICE OF THE TURTLE   Warner Bros., 1947

THE TREASURE OF THE SIERRA MADRE   Warner Bros., 1948

MY GIRL TISA   Warner Bros., 1948

WINTER MEETING   Warner Bros., 1948

THE WOMAN IN WHITE   Warner Bros., 1948

SILVER RIVER   Warner Bros., 1948

KEY LARGO   Warner Bros., 1948
JOHNNY BELINDA ★   Warner Bros., 1948
FIGHTER SQUADRON   Warner Bros., 1948
THE DECISION OF CHRISTOPHER BLAKE   Warner Bros., 1948
A KISS IN THE DARK   Warner Bros., 1949
ADVENTURES OF DON JUAN   Warner Bros., 1949
SOUTH OF ST. LOUIS   Warner Bros., 1949
FLAMINGO ROAD   Warner Bros., 1949
THE FOUNTAINHEAD   Warner Bros., 1949
WITHOUT HONOR   United Artists, 1949
BEYOND THE FORREST ★   Warner Bros., 1949
WHITE HEAT   Warner Bros., 1949
MRS. MIKE   United Artists, 1949
THE LADY TAKES A SAILOR   Warner Bros., 1949
CAGED   Warner Bros., 1950
THE FLAME AND THE ARROW ★   Warner Bros., 1950
THE GLASS MENAGERIE   Warner Bros., 1950
ROCKY MOUNTAIN   Warner Bros., 1950
SUGARFOOT   Warner Bros., 1950
DALLAS   Warner Bros., 1950
OPERATION PACIFIC   Warner Bros., 1951
LIGHTNING STRIKES TWICE   Warner Bros., 1951
RATON PASS   Warner Bros., 1951
I WAS A COMMUNIST FOR THE F.B.I.   Warner Bros., 1951
ON MOONLIGHT BAY   Warner Bros., 1951
JIM THORPE—ALL AMERICAN   Warner Bros., 1951
FORCE OF ARMS   Warner Bros., 1951
CLOSE TO MY HEART   Warner Bros., 1951
DISTANT DRUMS   Warner Bros., 1951
ROOM FOR ONE MORE   Warner Bros., 1952
THE LION AND THE HORSE   Warner Bros., 1952
MARA MARU   Warner Bros., 1952
THE MIRACLE OF OUR LADY OF FATIMA ★   Warner Bros., 1952
SPRINGFIELD RIFLE   Warner Bros., 1952
THE IRON MISTRESS   Warner Bros., 1952
THIS IS CINERAMA   Cinerama, 1952
THE JAZZ SINGER ★   Warner Bros., 1953
TROUBLE ALONG THE WAY   Warner Bros., 1953
BY THE LIGHT OF THE SILVERY MOON   Warner Bros., 1953
THE DESERT SONG   Warner Bros., 1953
THE CHARGE AT FEATHER RIVER   Warner Bros., 1953
SO THIS IS LOVE   Warner Bros., 1953
SO BIG   Warner Bros., 1953
THE BOY FROM OKLAHOMA   Warner Bros., 1954
THE CAINE MUTINY ★   Columbia, 1954
KING RICHARD AND THE CRUSADERS   Warner Bros., 1954
THE VIOLENT MEN   Columbia, 1954
BATTLE CRY ★   Warner Bros., 1955
THE LAST COMMAND   Republic, 1955
THE McCONNELL STORY   Warner Bros., 1955
ILLEGAL   Warner Bros., 1955
COME NEXT SPRING   Republic, 1956
HELL ON FRISCO BAY   Warner Bros., 1956
HELEN OF TROY   Warner Bros., 1956
THE SEARCHERS   Warner Bros., 1956
BANDIDO   Warner Bros., 1956

DEATH OF A SCOUNDREL   RKO Radio, 1956
CHINA GATE   co-composer with Victor Young, 20th Century-Fox, 1957
BAND OF ANGELS   Warner Bros., 1957
ESCAPADE IN JAPAN   Universal, 1957
ALL MINE TO GIVE   THE DAY THEY GAVE BABIES AWAY   Universal, 1958
FORT DOBBS   Warner Bros., 1958
DARBY'S RANGERS   Warner Bros., 1958
MARJORIE MORNINGSTAR   Warner Bros., 1958
THE HANGING TREE   Warner Bros., 1959
JOHN PAUL JONES   Warner Bros., 1959
THE FBI STORY   Warner Bros., 1959
A SUMMER PLACE   Warner Bros., 1959
CASH McCALL   Warner Bros., 1960
ICE PALACE   Warner Bros., 1960
THE DARK AT THE TOP OF THE STAIRS   Warner Bros., 1960
THE SINS OF RACHEL CADE   Warner Bros., 1961
PORTRAIT OF A MOBSTER   Warner Bros., 1961
PARRISH   Warner Bros., 1961
SUSAN SLADE   Warner Bros., 1961
A MAJORITY OF ONE   Warner Bros., 1961
ROME ADVENTURE   Warner Bros., 1962
SPENCER'S MOUNTAIN   Warner Bros., 1963
A DISTANT TRUMPET   Warner Bros., 1964
FBI CODE 98   Warner Bros., 1964
YOUNGBLOOD HAWKE   Warner Bros., 1964
THOSE CALLOWAYS   Buena Vista, 1965
TWO ON A GUILLOTINE   Warner Bros., 1965

LEITH STEVENS

b. 1909 - Mount Moriah, Missouri
d. 1970

SYNCOPATION   RKO Radio, 1942
NIGHT SONG   RKO Radio, 1947
BLACK BART   Universal, 1948
ALL MY SONS   Universal, 1948
FEUDIN', FUSSIN' AND A'FIGHTIN'   Universal, 1948
LARCENY   Universal, 1948
NOT WANTED   Film Classics, 1949
NEVER FEAR   Eagle Lion, 1950
THE GREAT RUPERT   Eagle Lion, 1950
DESTINATION MOON   Eagle Lion, 1950
THE SUN SETS AT DAWN   Eagle Lion, 1951
NO QUESTIONS ASKED   MGM, 1951
WHEN WORLDS COLLIDE   Paramount, 1951
STORM OVER TIBET   additional music, Columbia, 1951
NAVAJO (FD)   Lippert, 1952
THE ATOMIC CITY   Paramount, 1952
BEWARE, MY LOVELY   RKO Radio, 1952
EIGHT IRON MEN   Columbia, 1952
THE GLASS WALL   Columbia, 1953
THE HITCHHIKER   RKO Radio, 1953
SCARED STIFF   Paramount, 1953
WAR OF THE WORLDS   Paramount, 1953
THE BIGAMIST   Filmmakers, 1953
THE BOB MATHIAS STORY   Allied Artists, 1954
PRIVATE HELL 36   RKO Radio, 1954
THE WILD ONE   Columbia, 1954
THE TREASURE OF PANCHO VILLA   RKO Radio, 1955
CRASHOUT   Filmmakers, 1955
MAD AT THE WORLD   Filmmakers, 1955
JULIE   MGM, 1956

GREAT DAY IN THE MORNING   RKO Radio, 1956
WORLD WITHOUT END   Allied Artists, 1956
THE SCARLET HOUR   Paramount, 1956
THE CARELESS YEARS   United Artists, 1957
THE GARMENT JUNGLE   Columbia, 1957
EIGHTEEN AND ANXIOUS   Republic, 1957
THE GREEN-EYED BLONDE   Warner Bros., 1957
LIZZIE   MGM, 1957
RIDE OUT FOR REVENGE   United Artists, 1957
THE JAMES DEAN STORY   Warner Bros., 1957
BULLWHIP   Allied Artists, 1958
THE GUN RUNNERS   United Artists, 1958
COP HATER   United Artists, 1958
SEVEN GUNS TO MESA   Allied Artists, 1958
VIOLENT ROAD   Warner Bros., 1958
THE GENE KRUPA STORY   Columbia, 1959
BUT NOT FOR ME   Paramount, 1959
THE FIVE PENNIES ★   Paramount, 1959
HELL TO ETERNITY   Allied Artists, 1960
MAN TRAP   Paramount, 1961
ON THE DOUBLE   Paramount, 1961
THE INTERNS   Columbia, 1962
IT HAPPENED AT THE WORLD'S FAIR   MGM, 1963
A NEW KIND OF LOVE ★   Paramount, 1963
THE NIGHT OF THE GRIZZLY   Paramount, 1966
SMOKY   20th Century-Fox, 1966
CHUKA   Paramount, 1967
THE SILENT GUN (TF)   Paramount Pictures TV, 1969
ASSAULT ON THE WAYNE (TF)   Paramount Pictures TV, 1971

MORTON STEVENS

b. 1929 - New Jersey
d. Nov. 11, 1991 - Encino, CA

WILD AND WONDERFUL   Universal, 1964
HAWAII FIVE-O (TF) ☆   Leonard Freeman Productions/CBS Entertainment, 1968
A DEATH OF INNOCENCE (TF)   Mark Carliner Productions, 1971
THE FACE OF FEAR (TF)   QM Productions, 1971
SHE WAITS (TF)   Metromedia Productions, 1972
DEADLY HARVEST (TF)   CBS Entertainment, 1972
THE STRANGERS IN 7A (TF)   Palomar Pictures International, 1972
VISIONS... (TF)   CBS Entertainment, 1972
HORROR AT 37,000 FEET (TF)   CBS Entertainment, 1973
GUESS WHO'S SLEEPING IN MY BED? (TF)   ABC Circle Films, 1973
POOR DEVIL (TF)   Paramount TV, 1973
COFFEE, TEA OR ME? (TF)   CBS, Inc., 1973
JURY OF ONE   1974, French-Italian
THE DISAPPEARANCE OF FLIGHT 412 (TF)   Cine Films/Cinemobile Productions, 1974
BANJO HACKETT: ROAMIN' FREE (TF)   Bruce Lansbury Productions/Columbia TV, 1976
THE TIME TRAVELERS (TF)   Irwin Allen Productions/20th Century-Fox TV, 1976
THE STRANGE POSSESSION OF MRS. OLIVER (TF)   The Shpetner Company, 1977

PETER LUNDY AND THE MEDICINE HAT
   STALLION (TF)   Ed Friendly
   Productions, 1977
CODE NAME: DIAMOND HEAD (TF)   QM
   Productions, 1977
ARTHUR HAILEY'S WHEELS (MS) ☆
   Universal TV, 1978
WOMEN IN WHITE (MS)   NBC, 1979
MANDRAKE (TF)   Universal TV, 1979
THE FLAME IS LOVE (TF)   Ed Friendly
   Productions/Friendly-O'Herlihy Ltd., 1979
BACKSTAIRS AT THE WHITE HOUSE
   (MS)   Ed Friendly Productions, 1979
UNDERCOVER WITH THE KKK
   FREEDOM RIDERS (TF)   Columbia TV,
   1979
DETOUR TO TERROR (TF)   Orenthal
   Productions/Playboy
   Productions/Columbia TV, 1980
M STATION: HAWAII (TF)   Lord and Lady
   Enterprises, 1980
FUGITIVE FAMILY (TF)   Aubrey-Hamner
   Productions, 1980
HARDLY WORKING   20th Century-Fox,
   1981
THE MILLION DOLLAR FACE (TF)
   Nephi-Hamner Productions, 1981
THE MANIONS OF AMERICA (MS)   Roger
   Gimbel Productions/EMI TV/Argonaut
   Films Ltd., 1981
MASADA (MS) ☆   composer of Parts 3 and
   4, Arnon Milchan Productions/Universal
   TV, 1981
GREAT WHITE   co-composer with Guido &
   Maurizio De Angelis, Film Ventures
   International, 1982
MEMORIES NEVER DIE (TF)   Groverton
   Productions/Scholastic
   Productions/Universal TV, 1982
I MARRIED WYATT EARP (TF)   Osmond
   TV Productions/Comworld Productions,
   1983
COCAINE AND BLUE EYES (TF)   Orenthal
   Productions/Columbia TV, 1983
SMORGASBORD   Warner Bros., 1983
SLAPSTICK OF ANOTHER KIND
   SLAPSTICK   Entertainment Releasing
   Corporation/International Film Marketing,
   1983
THE LADIES (TF)   NBC, 1987, filmed in
   1983
ALICE IN WONDERLAND (TF)   Irwin Allen
   Productions/Procter & Gamble
   Productions/Columbia TV, 1985
OUTRAGE! (TF)   Irwin Allen
   Productions/Columbia TV, 1986
THEY STILL CALL ME BRUCE   Shapiro
   Entertainment, 1987
ACT OF PIRACY   The Movie Group, 1988

WILLIAM GRANT STILL

b. 1895 - Woodville, Miss.
d. December 3, 1978 - Los Angeles,
   California

LADY OF SECRETS   Columbia, 1936
THEODORA GOES WILD   Columbia, 1936
PENNIES FROM HEAVEN   Columbia,
   1936

HERBERT STOTHART

b. September 11, 1885 - Milwaukee,
   Wisconsin
d. February 1, 1949

DEVIL MAY CARE   MGM, 1930
MONTANA MOON   MGM, 1930
THE ROGUE SONG   MGM, 1930
IN GAY MADRID   MGM, 1930
THE FLORADORA GIRL   MGM, 1930
CALL OF THE FLESH   MGM, 1930

MADAM SATAN   MGM, 1930
A LADY'S MORALS   MGM, 1930
NEW MOON   MGM, 1931
THE PRODIGAL   MGM, 1931
THE SQUAW MAN   MGM, 1931
THE CUBAN LOVE SONG   MGM, 1931
THE SON-DAUGHTER   MGM, 1932
RASPUTIN AND THE EMPRESS   MGM,
   1932
THE WHITE SISTER   MGM, 1933
THE BARBARIAN   MGM, 1933
PEG O' MY HEART   MGM, 1933
TURN BACK THE CLOCK   MGM, 1933
NIGHT FLIGHT   MGM, 1933
GOING HOLLYWOOD   MGM, 1933
QUEEN CHRISTINA   MGM, 1934
THE CAT AND THE FIDDLE   MGM, 1934
RIPTIDE   MGM, 1934
LAUGHING BOY   MGM, 1934
VIVA VILLA!   MGM, 1934
TREASURE ISLAND   MGM, 1934
CHAINED   MGM, 1934
THE BARRETTS OF WIMPOLE STREET
   MGM, 1934
WHAT EVERY WOMAN KNOWS   MGM,
   1934
THE MERRY WIDOW   adaptation, MGM,
   1934
THE PAINTED VEIL   MGM, 1934
BIOGRAPHY OF A BACHELOR GIRL
   MGM, 1935
THE NIGHT IS YOUNG   MGM, 1935
DAVID COPPERFIELD   MGM, 1935
SEQUOIA   MGM, 1935
VANESSA, HER LOVE STORY   MGM,
   1935
NAUGHTY MARIETTA   adaptation, MGM,
   1935
CHINA SEAS   MGM, 1935
ANNA KARENINA   MGM, 1935
MUTINY ON THE BOUNTY ★   MGM, 1935
A NIGHT AT THE OPERA   MGM, 1935
AH, WILDERNESS!   MGM, 1935
A TALE OF TWO CITIES   MGM, 1935
ROSE MARIE   adaptation, MGM, 1936
WIFE VS. SECRETARY   co-composer with
   Edward Ward, MGM, 1936
MOONLIGHT MURDER   co-composer with
   Edward Ward, MGM, 1936
SMALL TOWN GIRL   co-composer with
   Edward Ward, MGM, 1936
THE ROBIN HOOD OF EL DORADO
   MGM, 1936
SAN FRANCISCO   MGM, 1936
THE GORGEOUS HUSSY   MGM, 1936
THE DEVIL IS A SISSY   MGM, 1936
AFTER THE THIN MAN   co-composer with
   Edward Ward, MGM, 1936
ROMEO AND JULIET   MGM, 1936
CAMILLE   MGM, 1937
MAYTIME ★   adaptation, MGM, 1937
THE GOOD EARTH   MGM, 1937
CONQUEST   MGM, 1937
THE FIREFLY   MGM, 1937
ROSALIE   MGM, 1937
OF HUMAN HEARTS   MGM, 1938
THE GIRL OF THE GOLDEN WEST   MGM,
   1938
MARIE ANTOINETTE ★   MGM, 1938
SWEETHEARTS ★   MGM, 1938
IDIOT'S DELIGHT   MGM, 1939
BROADWAY SERENADE   MGM, 1939
THE WIZARD OF OZ ★★   adaptation,
   MGM, 1939
BALALAIKA   MGM, 1939
NORTHWEST PASSAGE   MGM, 1940
EDISON, THE MAN   MGM, 1940
WATERLOO BRIDGE ★   MGM, 1940
SUSAN AND GOD   MGM, 1940
NEW MOON   adaptation, MGM, 1940
PRIDE AND PREJUDICE   MGM, 1940
BITTER SWEET   adaptation, MGM, 1940

COME LIVE WITH ME   MGM, 1941
ANDY HARDY'S PRIVATE SECRETARY
   MGM, 1941
MEN OF BOYS TOWN   MGM, 1941
ZIEGFELD GIRL   MGM, 1941
THEY MET IN BOMBAY   MGM, 1941
BLOSSOMS IN THE DUST   MGM, 1941
SMILIN' THROUGH   MGM, 1941
THE CHOCOLATE SOLDIER ★
   adaptation, MGM, 1941
RIO RITA   adaptation, MGM, 1942
I MARRIED AN ANGEL   MGM, 1942
MRS. MINIVER   MGM, 1942
CAIRO   MGM, 1942
RANDOM HARVEST ★   MGM, 1942
TENNESSEE JOHNSON   MGM, 1943
THREE HEARTS FOR JULIA   MGM, 1943
THE HUMAN COMEDY   MGM, 1943
THOUSANDS CHEER ★   MGM, 1944
MADAME CURIE ★   MGM, 1944
SONG OF RUSSIA   MGM, 1944
A GUY NAMED JOE   MGM, 1944
THE WHITE CLIFFS OF DOVER   MGM,
   1944
DRAGON SEED   MGM, 1944
KISMET ★   MGM, 1944
THIRTY SECONDS OVER TOKYO   MGM,
   1945
NATIONAL VELVET   MGM, 1945
THE PICTURE OF DORIAN GRAY
   co-composer with Mario
   Castelnuovo-Tedesco, MGM, 1945
THE VALLEY OF DECISION ★   MGM,
   1945
SON OF LASSIE   MGM, 1945
THEY WERE EXPENDABLE   MGM, 1945
ADVENTURE   MGM, 1946
THE GREEN YEARS   MGM, 1946
UNDERCURRENT   MGM, 1946
THE SEA OF GRASS   MGM, 1947
THE YEARLING   based on music by Delius,
   MGM, 1947
HIGH BARBAREE   MGM, 1947
THE UNFINISHED DANCE   MGM, 1947
DESIRE ME   MGM, 1947
IF WINTER COMES   MGM, 1948
THREE DARING DAUGHTERS   MGM,
   1948
THE THREE MUSKETEERS   based on
   music by Tchaikovsky, MGM, 1948
HILLS OF HOME   MGM, 1948
BIG JACK   MGM, 1949

JULE STYNE

Jules Stein
b. December 31, 1905 - London, England

THIEVES   Paramount, 1977

HARRY SUKMAN

b. 1912
d. December 4, 1984 - Palm Springs,
   California

GOG   United Artists, 1954
RIDERS TO THE STARS   United Artists,
   1954
BATTLE TAXI   United Artists, 1955
A BULLET FOR JOEY   United Artists, 1955
THE PHENIX CITY STORY   Allied Artists,
   1955
SCREAMING EAGLES   Allied Artists, 1956
FORTY GUNS   20th Century-Fox, 1957
FURY AT SUNDOWN   United Artists, 1957
SABU AND THE MAGIC RING   Allied
   Artists, 1957
OUTCASTS OF THE CITY   Republic, 1958
UNDERWATER WARRIOR   MGM, 1958
VERBOTEN!   Columbia, 1958
THE HANGMAN   Paramount, 1959
THE CRIMSON KIMONO   Columbia, 1959

SONG WITHOUT END   adaptation,
   Columbia, 1960
UNDERWORLD, U.S.A.   Columbia, 1961
A THUNDER OF DRUMS   MGM, 1961
FANNY   Warner Bros., 1961
BELLE SOMERS   Columbia, 1962
MADISON AVENUE   20th Century-Fox,
   1962
AROUND THE WORLD UNDER THE SEA
   MGM, 1966
THE SINGING NUN   MGM, 1966
THE NAKED RUNNER   Warner Bros.,
   1967
WELCOME TO HARD TIMES   MGM, 1967
IF HE HOLLERS, LET HIM GO   Cinerama
   Releasing Corporation, 1968
THE PRIVATE NAVY OF SGT.
   O'FARRELL   United Artists, 1968
MISTER KINGSTREET'S WAR   H.R.S.
   Films, 1971
GENESIS II (TF)   Warner Bros. TV, 1973
THE FAMILY KOVAK (TF)   Playboy
   Productions, 1974
PLANET EARTH (TF)   Warner Bros. TV,
   1974
BEYOND THE BERMUDA TRIANGLE (TF)
   Playboy Productions, 1975
SOMEONE IS WATCHING ME (TF)
   Warner Bros. TV, 1978
SALEM'S LOT (TF) ☆   Warner Bros. TV,
   1979

T

TORU TAKEMITSU

b. October 8, 1930 - Manchuria

JUVENILE PASSIONS   co-composer with
   Masaru Sato, 1958, Japanese
JOSE TORRES (FD)   1959, Japanese
BAD BOYS   1960, Japanese
A FULL LIFE   1962, Japanese
THE PITFALL   1962, Japanese
THE INHERITANCE   Shochiku, 1962,
   Japanese
TEARS IN THE LION'S MANE   1962,
   Japanese
PALE FLOWER   Shochiku, 1963,
   Japanese
HARAKIRI SEPPUKU   Shochiku, 1963,
   Japanese
TWIN SISTERS OF KYOTO   1963,
   Japanese
A MARVELOUS KID   1963, Japanese
ALONE IN THE PACIFIC   1963, Japanese
WOMAN OF THE DUNES   1964,
   Japanese
OUR HAPPINESS BEFORE   1964,
   Japanese
THE ASSASSIN   1964, Japanese
THE FEMALE BODY   1964, Japanese
THE CAR THIEF   1964, Japanese
KWAIDAN   Continental, 1964, Japanese
THE WHITE DAWN   1964, Japanese
WITH BEAURTY AND SORROW   1965,
   Japanese
BWANA TOSHI   1965, Japanese
SAMURAI SPY   1965, Japanese
LAST JUDGEMENT   1965, Japanese
BEAST ALLEY   1965, Japanese
PUNISHMENT ISLAND   1965, Japanese
ILLUSION ISLAND   1965, Japanese

MINATOMO YOSHITSUNE   1966,
   Japanese
THE KII RIVER   1966, Japanese
THE FACE OF ANOTHER   1966,
   Japanese
LONGING   1966, Japanese
IZU DANCER   1967, Japanese
CLOUDS AT SUNSET
   Hyogensha/Shochiku, 1967, Japanese
REBELLION SAMURAI REBELLION
   Toho, 1967, Japanese
BELLOWING CLOUD   1967, Japanese
RUINED MAP   1968, Japanese
HYMN TO A TIRED MAN   1968, Japanese
KYO (FD)   1968, Japanese
DOUBLE SUICIDE   Toho, 1969, Japanese
DODES'KA'DEN   Janus, 1970, Japanese
CLICKETY-CLACK   1970, Japanese
SUN'S HUNTER   1970, Japanese
HE DIED AFTER THE WAR   1971,
   Japanese
SILENCE   Toho, 1971, Japanese
INN OF EVIL   Toho, 1971, Japanese
THE CEREMONY   1971, Japanese
DEAR SUMMER SISTER   1972, Japanese
A SILENCE   1972, Japanese
SUMMER SOLDIERS   1972, Japanese
THE PETRIFIED FOREST
   Hyogensha/Toho, 1973, Japanese
TIME WITHIN MEMORY   1973, Japanese
HIMIKO   Hyogensha/ATG, 1974,
   Japanese
HAPPINESS   1974, Japanese
KASEKI   Haiyuza Films, 1975, Japanese
SHIAWASE   1975, Japanese
UNDER THE BLOSSOMING CHERRY
   TREES   1975, Japanese
THE FOSSILS   1975, Japanese
INCANDESCENT FLAME   1977, Japanese
PHANTOM LOVE   1978, Japanese
BANISHED ORIN   Toho, 1978, Japanese
GLOWING AUTUMN   1978, Japanese
THE LOUVRE MUSEUM (TD)   1979,
   Japanese
EMPIRE OF PASSION CORRIDA OF
   LOVE   Barbary Coast, 1980, Japanese
TOKYO TRIALS   1983, Japanese
RAN   Orion Classics, 1985,
   Japanese-French
FIRE FESTIVAL   1985, Japanese
THE EMPTY TABLE   1985, Japanese
A.K. (FD)   1985, Japanese
GONZA THE SPEARMAN   1986,
   Japanese
ARASHI GA OKA ONIMARU   Toho, 1988,
   Japanese-Swiss
RIKYU   1989, Japanese
BLACK RAIN   Toei, 1989, Japanese
GO-HIME   1992, Japanese
RISING SUN   20th Century Fox, 1993
SHARAKU   1995, Japanese

ALEXANDRE TANSMAN

b. 1897 - Lodz, Poland
d. November 15, 1986

POIL DE CAROTTE   1932, French
FLESH AND FANTASY   Universal, 1943
DESTINY   co-composer with Frank Skinner,
   Universal, 1944
PARIS—UNDERGROUND ★   United
   Artists, 1945
SISTER KENNY   RKO Radio, 1946

DEEMS TAYLOR

b. 1885 - New York
d. 1966 - New York

JANICE MEREDITH   MGM, 1924

VIRGIL THOMSON

b. November 25, 1896 - Kansas City,
   Missouri
d. 1989

THE PLOW THAT BROKE THE PLAINS
   (D)   U.S. Government, 1936
THE SPANISH EARTH (D)   Contemporary
   Historians, 1937
THE RIVER (D)   U.S. Government, 1937
TUESDAY IN NOVEMBER (D)   U.S.
   Government, 1945
LOUISIANA STORY (D)   Lopert, 1948
THE GODDESS   Columbia, 1958
POWER AMONG MEN (D)   United Nations,
   1959
VOYAGE TO AMERICA (D)   N.Y. World's
   Fair, 1964

DOUG TIMM

d. July 29, 1989

MISSION HILL   Atlantic Releasing
   Corporation, 1983
TERROR IN THE AISLES   additional music,
   Universal, 1984
STREETWALKIN'   co-composer with
   Matthew Ender, Concorde, 1985
FORTUNE DANE (TF)   Stormy Weathers
   Productions/The Movie Company
   Enterprises/The Rosenzweig Company,
   1986
U.S. MARSHALS: WACO & RHINEHART
   (TF)   co-composer, Touchstone Films,
   1987
WINNERS TAKE ALL   Apollo Pictures,
   1987
THE MAN WHO FELL TO EARTH (TF)
   David Gerber Productions/MGM TV,
   1987
NIGHTFLYERS   New Century/Vista, 1987
DIRTY DOZEN: DANKO'S DOZEN (TF)
   MGM-UA TV/Jadran Films/TV Espanola,
   1988, U.S.-Yugoslavian

DIMITRI TIOMKIN

b. May 10, 1894 - near St. Petersburg,
   Russia
d. November 11, 1979 - London, England

DEVIL MAY CARE   ballet music only,
   MGM, 1930
LORD BYRON OF BROADWAY   ballet
   music only, MGM, 1930
THE ROGUE SONG   ballet music only,
   MGM, 1930
OUR BLUSHING BRIDES   ballet music
   only, MGM, 1930
RESURRECTION   Universal, 1931
BROADWAY TO HOLLYWOOD   ballet
   only, Universal, 1933
ALICE IN WONDERLAND   Paramount,
   1933
NAUGHTY MARIETTA   ballet only, MGM,
   1935
CASINO MURDER CASE   MGM, 1935
MAD LOVE   MGM, 1935
I LIVE MY LIFE   MGM, 1935
MR. DEEDS GOES TO TOWN   Columbia,
   1936
LOST HORIZON ★   Columbia, 1937
THE ROAD BACK   Universal, 1937
SPAWN OF THE NORTH   Paramount,
   1938
YOU CAN'T TAKE IT WITH YOU
   Columbia, 1938
THE GREAT WALTZ   MGM, 1938
ONLY ANGELS HAVE WINGS   Columbia,
   1939
MR. SMITH GOES TO WASHINGTON ★
   Columbia, 1939

LUCKY PARTNERS   RKO Radio, 1940
THE WESTERNER   United Artists, 1940
MEET JOHN DOE   Warner Bros., 1941
FORCED LANDING   Paramount, 1941
SCATTERGOOD MEETS BROADWAY
   RKO Radio, 1941
FLYING BLIND   Paramount, 1941
THE CORSICAN BROTHERS ★   United
   Artists, 1942
GENTLEMAN AFTER DARK   United
   Artists, 1942
TWIN BEDS   United Artists, 1942
THE MOON AND SIXPENCE ★   United
   Artists, 1942
SHADOW OF A DOUBT   Universal, 1943
THE UNKNOWN GUEST   Monogram, 1943
THE IMPOSTER   Universal, 1944
THE BRIDGE OF SAN LUIS REY ★   United
   Artists, 1944
LADIES COURAGEOUS   Universal, 1944
WHEN STRANGERS MARRY   Monogram,
   1944
FOREVER YOURS   Monogram, 1944
DILLINGER   Monogram, 1945
CHINA'S LITTLE DEVILS   Monogram,
   1945
PARDON MY PAST   Columbia, 1945
WHISTLE STOP   United Artists, 1946
BLACK BEAUTY   20th Century-Fox, 1946
ANGEL ON MY SHOULDER   United Artists,
   1946
THE DARK MIRROR   co-composer with
   Frank Skinner, Universal, 1946
DUEL IN THE SUN   Selznick Releasing,
   1946
IT'S A WONDERFUL LIFE   RKO Radio,
   1946
THE LONG NIGHT   RKO Radio, 1947
TARZAN AND THE MERMAIDS   RKO
   Radio, 1948
THE DUDE GOES WEST   Allied Artists,
   1948
SO THIS IS NEW YORK   United Artists,
   1948
RED RIVER   United Artists, 1948
PORTRAIT OF JENNIE   adaptation of
   Debussy, Selznick, 1948
CANADIAN PACIFIC   20th Century-Fox,
   1949
CHAMPION ★   United Artists, 1949
HOME OF THE BRAVE   United Artists,
   1949
RED LIGHT   United Artists, 1949
D.O.A.   United Artists, 1949
DAKOTA LIL   20th Century-Fox, 1950
GUILTY BYSTANDER   Film Classics, 1950
CHAMPAGNE FOR CAESAR   United
   Artists, 1950
THE MEN   United Artists, 1950
CYRANO DE BERGERAC   United Artists,
   1950
MR. UNIVERSE   United Artists, 1951
THE THING   RKO Radio, 1951
STRANGERS ON A TRAIN   Warner Bros.,
   1951
PEKING EXPRESS   Paramount, 1951
THE WELL   United Artists, 1951
DRUMS IN THE DEEP SOUTH   RKO
   Radio, 1951
BUGLES IN THE AFTERNOON   Warner
   Bros., 1952
MUTINY   United Artists, 1952
MY SIX CONVICTS   Columbia, 1952
LADY IN THE IRON MASK   20th
   Century-Fox, 1952
THE HAPPY TIME   Columbia, 1952
THE BIG SKY   RKO Radio, 1952
HIGH NOON ★★   United Artists, 1952
THE FOUR POSTER   Columbia, 1952
THE STEEL TRAP   20th Century-Fox,
   1952
ANGEL FACE   RKO Radio, 1953

JEOPARDY   MGM, 1953
I CONFESS   Warner Bros., 1953
RETURN TO PARADISE   United Artists,
   1953
BLOWING WILD   Warner Bros., 1953
TAKE THE HIGH GROUND   MGM, 1953
CEASE FIRE!   Paramount, 1953
HIS MAJESTY O'KEEFE   Warner Bros.,
   1953
THE COMMAND   Warner Bros., 1954
DIAL M FOR MURDER   Warner Bros.,
   1954
THE HIGH AND THE MIGHTY ★★   Warner
   Bros., 1954
A BULLET IS WAITING   Columbia, 1954
THE ADVENTURES OF HAJJI BABA   20th
   Century-Fox, 1954
STRANGE LADY IN TOWN   Warner Bros.,
   1955
LAND OF THE PHARAOHS   Warner Bros.,
   1955
THE COURT-MARTIAL OF BILLY
   MITCHELL   Warner Bros., 1955
FRIENDLY PERSUASION   Allied Artists,
   1956
TENSION AT TABLE ROCK   RKO Radio,
   1956
GIANT ★   Warner Bros., 1956
GUNFIGHT AT THE O.K. CORRAL
   Paramount, 1957
NIGHT PASSAGE   Universal, 1957
SEARCH FOR PARADISE   Cinerama
   Releasing Corporation, 1957
WILD IS THE WIND   Paramount, 1957
THE OLD MAN AND THE SEA ★★   Warner
   Bros., 1958
THE YOUNG LAND   Columbia, 1959
RIO BRAVO   Warner Bros., 1959
LAST TRAIN FROM GUN HILL
   Paramount, 1959
THE UNFORGIVEN   United Artists, 1960
THE ALAMO ★   United Artists, 1960
THE SUNDOWNERS   Warner Bros., 1960
THE GUNS OF NAVARONE ★   Columbia,
   1961
TOWN WITHOUT PITY   United Artists,
   1961
WITHOUT EACH OTHER   Allen Klein,
   1962
55 DAYS AT PEKING ★   Allied Artists,
   1963
THE FALL OF THE ROMAN EMPIRE ★
   Paramount, 1964
CIRCUS WORLD   Paramount, 1964
36 HOURS   MGM, 1964
THE WAR WAGON   Universal, 1967
GREAT CATHERINE   Warner Bros., 1968,
   British
TCHAIKOVSKY ★   adaptation, Mosfilm,
   1971, Soviet

ERNST TOCH
b. 1887 - Vienna, Austria
d. 1964 - Santa Monica, California

CATHERINE THE GREAT   United Artists,
   1934
THE PRIVATE LIFE OF DON JUAN   United
   Artists, 1934
LITTLE FRIEND   Gaumont-British, 1934
PETER IBBETSON ★   Paramount, 1935
OUTCAST   Paramount, 1937
ON SUCH A NIGHT   Paramount, 1937
THE CAT AND THE CANARY   Paramount,
   1939
DR. CYCLOPS   co-composer, Paramount,
   1940
GHOST BREAKERS   Paramount, 1940
LADIES IN RETIREMENT ★   Columbia,
   1941

FIRST COMES COURAGE   Columbia,
   1943
NONE SHALL ESCAPE   Columbia, 1944
ADDRESS UNKNOWN   Columbia, 1944
THE UNSEEN   Paramount, 1945

NATHAN VAN CLEAVE
b. 1910
d. July 2, 1970 - Hollywood, California

THE SAINTED SISTERS   Paramount,
   1948
DEAR WIFE   co-composer, Paramount,
   1949
FANCY PANTS   Paramount, 1950
MOLLY   Paramount, 1951
QUEBEC   co-composer, Paramount, 1951
DEAR BRAT   Paramount, 1951
RHUBARB   Paramount, 1951
OFF LIMITS   Paramount, 1953
CONQUEST OF SPACE   Paramount, 1955
LUCY GALLANT   Paramount, 1955
THE DEVIL'S HAIRPIN   Paramount, 1957
THE LONELY MAN   Paramount, 1957
THE COLOSSUS OF NEW YORK
   co-composer with Fred Steiner,
   Paramount, 1958
THE SPACE CHILDREN   Paramount, 1958
THAT KIND OF WOMAN   Paramount,
   1959
BLUEPRINT FOR ROBBERY   Paramount,
   1961
ROBINSON CRUSOE ON MARS
   co-composer with Fred Steiner,
   Paramount, 1964
PROJECT X   Paramount, 1968

ROGIER VAN OTTERLOO
b. Netherlands

TURKISH DELIGHT   Cinemation, 1973,
   Dutch
KEETJE TIPPEL   1975, Dutch
SOLDIER OF ORANGE   Rank, 1979,
   Dutch
GRIJPSTRA & DE GLER   Verenigade
   Nederland Filmcompagnie, 1983, Dutch

GEORGES VAN PARYS
b. 1902 - Paris, France
d. 1971 - Paris, France

LA FEMME ET LE PANTIN   1929, French
UN SOIR DE RAFLE   co-composer, 1931,
   French
LE MILLION   1931, French
MADEMOISELLE JOSETTE MA FEMME
   1933, French
CETTE VIELLE CANAILLE   1933, French
JEUNESSE   1934, French
L'OR DANS LA RUE   co-composer, 1934,
   French
QUELLE DROLE DE GOSSE   co-composer
   with Jean Lenoir, 1934, French
LES BEUX JOURS   1935, French
LA ROUTE HEUREUSE   1935, French
PRENDS LA ROUTE   1936, French
UN MAUVAIS GARCON   1936, French
ABUS DE CONFIANCE   1937, French
L'ENTRAINEUSE   1938, French

CIRCONSTANCES ATTENUANTES   1939,
    French
PREMIER BAL   1941, French
LA MAISON DES SEPT JEUNES FILLES
    1941, French
LE BIENFAITEUR   1942, French
CAPRICES   1942, French
MARIE-MARTINE   1943, French
L'HOMME DE LONDRES   1943, French
LE COUPLE IDEAL   1945, French
SILENCE EST D'OR   1947, French
LA VIE EN ROSE   1947, French
L'ARMOIRE VOLANTE   1948, French
PARIS AU PRINTEMPS   1948, French
JEAN DE LA LUNE   1948, French
UNE FEMME PAR JOUR   1948, French
HISTOIRES EXTRAORDINAIRES   1949,
    French
MONSEIGNEUR   1949, French
LADY PANAME   1949, French
UN CERTAIN MONSIEUR   1949, French
LE 84 PREND DES VACANCES   1949,
    French
LES ANCIENS DE SAINT-LOUP   1950,
    French
LA VIE DRAMATIQUE DE MAURICE
    UTRILLO   1950, French
LE PASSE-MURAILLE   1950, French
REMAKE   1950, French
DEUX SOUS DE VIOLETTES   1951,
    French
L'AFFAIRE MANET   1951, French
LA MAISON BONNADIEU   1951, French
CASQUE D'OR   1951, French
TROIS FEMMES   co-composer with Louis
    Beydts, 1951, French
FANFAN LA TULIPE   co-composer with
    Maurice Thiriet, 1951, French
ADORABLES CREATURES   1952, French
LE GRAND MELIES   *THE GREAT
    MELIES*   1952, French
DORTOIR DES GRANDES   1952, French
RECONTRES SUR LE RHIN   1952,
    French
AVANT LE DELUGE   1953, French
ON TRIAL   *L'AFFAIRE MAURIZIUS*
    co-composer, New Realm, 1953,
    French-Italian
VIRGILE   1953, French
FLESH AND THE WOMAN   *LE GRAND
    JEU*   Dominant Pictures, 1954,
    French-Italian
ESCALIER DE SERVICE   1954, French
SECRETS D'ALCOVE   1954, French
THE SHEEP HAS FIVE LEGS   United
    Motion Picture Organization, 1954,
    French
A NOUS DEUX PARIS   1954, French
MADAME DU BARRY   1954, French
PAPA, MAMA, THE MAID AND I   1954,
    French
NANA   1954, French
FRENCH CAN-CAN   *ONLY THE FRENCH
    CAN*   United Motion Picture
    Organization, 1954, French
LES GRANDES MANOEUVRES   1955,
    French
PARIS LA NUIT   1955, French
L'ARCHITECTE MAUDIT   1955, French
DIABOLIQUE   United Motion Picture
    Organization, 1955, French
LES TRUANDS   1956, French
C'EST ARRIVE A ADEN   1956, French
THE MAN IN THE RAINCOAT   Kingsley
    International, 1956, French-Italian
COMME EN CHEVEU SUR LA SOUPE
    1957, French
FILOUS ET COMPAGNIE   1957, French
LE GORILLE VOUS SALUE BIEN   1958,
    French
NINA   1958, French
GUINGUETTE   1958, French

RUE DES PRAIRIES   1959, French
THE MILLIONAIRESS   20th Century-Fox,
    1960, British
ALL THE GOLD IN THE WORLD   1961,
    French
I LIKE MONEY   1962, British

CLIFFORD VAUGHAN
b. 1893 - New Jersey
d. November 23, 1987 - Arcadia, California

THE RAVEN   Universal, 1935
WHITE BONDAGE   1937

RALPH VAUGHAN WILLIAMS
b. 1872 - Gloustershire, England
d. 1958 - London, England

THE FORTY-NINTH PARALLEL   *THE
    INVADERS* Columbia, 1941, British
COASTAL COMMAND   1942, British
THE PEOPLE'S LAND   1942, British
THE FLEMISH FARM   1943, British
STRICKEN PENINSULA   1944, British
THE LOVES OF JOANNA GODDEN   1946,
    British
SCOTT OF THE ANTARCTIC   1948,
    British
DIM LITTLE ISLAND   1949, British

HEITOR VILLA-LOBOS
b. 1887 - Rio de Janeiro, Brazil
d. 1959 - Rio de Janeiro, Brazil

GREEN MANSIONS   MGM, 1959
JOAO   1972, Dutch

OLIVER WALLACE
b. 1887 - London, England
d. 1963

MURDER BY TELEVISION   1935
DUMBO (AF) ★★   co-composer with Frank
    Churchill, RKO Radio, 1941
VICTORY   *THROUGH AIR POWER* ★
    co-composer, 1943, United Artists
FOLLOW THE BOYS   co-composer with
    Leigh Harline and Frank Skinner,
    Universal, 1944
FUN AND FANCY FREE   co-composer,
    RKO Radio, 1947
THE ADVENTURES OF ICHABOD AND MR.
    TOAD (AF)   RKO Radio, 1949
CINDERELLA (AF) ★   co-composer with
    Paul J. Smith, RKO Radio, 1950
SEAL ISLAND   RKO Radio, 1950
ALICE IN WONDERLAND (AF) ★   RKO
    Radio, 1951
PETER PAN (AF)   RKO Radio, 1953
LADY AND THE TRAMP (AF)   Buena Vista,
    1955
SAMOA   Buena Vista, 1956
OLD YELLER   Buena Vista, 1957
TONKA   Buena Vista, 1958
WHITE WILDERNESS ★   Buena Vista,
    1958
DARBY O'GILL AND THE LITTLE
    PEOPLE   Buena Vista, 1959
JUNGLE CAT   Buena Vista, 1960

TEN WHO DARED   Buena Vista, 1960
NIKKI, WILD DOG OF THE NORTH   Buena
    Vista, 1961
BIG RED   Buena Vista, 1962
THE LEGEND OF LOBO   Buena Vista,
    1962
THE INCREDIBLE JOURNEY   Buena Vista,
    1963
SAVAGE SAM   Buena Vista, 1963

SIR WILLIAM WALTON
b. March 29, 1902 - Oldham, England
d. March 8, 1983 - Ischia

ESCAPE ME NEVER   United Artists, 1935,
    British
AS YOU LIKE IT   20th Century-Fox, 1936,
    British
STOLEN LIFE   Paramount, 1939, British
MAJOR BARBARA   United Artists, 1941,
    British
THE FOREMAN WENT TO FRANCE
    1941, British
SPITFIRE   *THE FIRST OF THE FEW*
    RKO Radio, 1942, British
NEXT OF KIN   1942, British
HENRY V ★   Rank, 1945, British
HAMLET ★   Universal, 1946, British
RICHARD III   Lopert, 1956, British
BATTLE OF BRITAIN   score unused except
    for "Battle in Air" sequence, United
    Artists, 1969, British
THREE SISTERS   American Film Theatre,
    1970, British

EDWARD WARD
d. September 26, 1971 - Hollywood,
    California

PARIS   Warner Bros., 1929
SHOW OF SHOWS   Warner Bros., 1929
WEDDING RINGS   Warner Bros., 1930
SONG OF THE FLAME   Warner Bros.,
    1930
BRIDE OF THE REGIMENT   Warner Bros.,
    1930
KISMET   Warner Bros., 1931
HYPNOTIZED   World Wide, 1932
I LIKE IT THAT WAY   Universal, 1934
EMBARRASSING MOMENTS   Universal,
    1934
ROMANCE IN THE RAIN   Universal, 1934
GIFT OF GAB   Universal, 1934
GREAT EXPECTATIONS   Universal, 1934
CHEATING CHEATERS   Universal, 1934
GIRL O' MY DREAMS   Monogram, 1934
THE MYSTERY OF EDWIN DROOD
    Universal, 1935
TIMES SQUARE LADY   MGM, 1935
RECKLESS   MGM, 1935
AGE OF INDISCRETION   MGM, 1935
PUBLIC HERO NO. 1   MGM, 1935
NO MORE LADIES   MGM, 1935
HERE COMES THE BAND   MGM, 1935
THE BISHOP MISBEHAVES   MGM, 1935
KIND LADY   MGM, 1935
RIFF RAFF   MGM, 1936
EXCLUSIVE STORY   MGM, 1936
WIFE VS. SECRETARY   co-composer with
    Herbert Stothart, MGM, 1936
MOONLIGHT MURDER   co-composer with
    Herbert Stothart, MGM, 1936
SMALL TOWN GIRL   co-composer with
    Herbert Stothart, MGM, 1936
SPEED   MGM, 1936
WOMEN ARE TROUBLE   MGM, 1936
SWORN ENEMY   MGM, 1936
THE LONGEST NIGHT   MGM, 1936
SINNER TAKE ALL   MGM, 1936
AFTER THE THIN MAN   co-composer with
    Herbert Stothart, MGM, 1936

MAN OF THE PEOPLE   MGM, 1937
MAMA STEPS OUT   MGM, 1937
THE GOOD OLD SOAK   MGM, 1937
NIGHT MUST FALL   MGM, 1937
SARATOGA   MGM, 1937
BAD GUY   MGM, 1937
THE WOMEN MEN MARRY   MGM, 1937
DOUBLE WEDDING   MGM, 1937
LIVE, LOVE AND LEARN   MGM, 1937
THE LAST GANGSTER   MGM, 1937
NAVY BLUE AND GOLD   MGM, 1937
LOVE IS A HEADACHE   MGM, 1938
MANNEQUIN   MGM, 1938
PARADISE FOR THREE   MGM, 1938
A YANK AT OXFORD   co-composer with
    Hubert Bath, MGM, 1938
HOLD THAT KISS   MGM, 1938
THE TOY WIFE   MGM, 1938
LORD JEFF   MGM, 1938
THE SHOPWORN ANGEL   MGM, 1938
THE CROWN ROARS   MGM, 1938
BOYS TOWN   MGM, 1938
MEET THE MAYOR   Times Exchange,
    1938
VACATION FROM LOVE   MGM, 1938
STABLEMATES   MGM, 1938
SOCIETY LAWYER   MGM, 1939
IT'S A WONDERFUL WORLD   MGM, 1939
6,000 ENEMIES   MGM, 1939
MAISIE   MGM, 1939
STRONGER THAN DESIRE   co-composer
    with David Snell, MGM, 1939
THEY ALL COME OUT   co-composer with
    David Snell, MGM, 1939
ANDY HARDY GETS SPRING FEVER
    co-composer with David Snell, MGM,
    1939
THESE GLAMOUR GIRLS   co-composer
    with David Snell, MGM, 1939
THE WOMEN   co-composer with David
    Snell, MGM, 1939
BLACKMAIL   co-composer with David
    Snell, MGM, 1939
THUNDER AFLOAT   co-composer with
    David Snell, MGM, 1939
DANCING CO-ED   co-composer with David
    Snell, MGM, 1939
BAD LITTLE ANGEL   MGM, 1939
REMEMBER?   MGM, 1939
ANOTHER THIN MAN   MGM, 1939
JOE AND ETHEL TURP CALL ON THE
    PRESIDENT   co-composer with David
    Snell, MGM, 1939
NICK CARTER, MASTER DETECTIVE
    MGM, 1939
CONGO MAISIE   MGM, 1940
YOUNG TOM EDISON   MGM, 1940
MY SON, MY SON   United Artists, 1940
SOUTH OF PAGO PAGO   United Artists,
    1940
DANCE, GIRL, DANCE   RKO Radio, 1940
KIT CARSON   United Artists, 1940
THE SON OF MONTE CRISTO   United
    Artists, 1941
MR. AND MRS. SMITH   RKO Radio, 1941
CHEERS FOR MISS BISHOP ★   United
    Artists, 1941
TANKS A MILLION ★   United Artists, 1941
NIAGRA FALLS   United Artists, 1941
ALL-AMERICAN CO-ED ★   United Artists,
    1941
MISS POLLY   United Artists, 1941
HAY FOOT   United Artists, 1942
BROOKLYN ORCHID   United Artists, 1942
DUDES ARE PRETTY PEOPLE   United
    Artists, 1942
ABOUT FACE   United Artists, 1942
FLYING WITH MUSIC ★   United Artists,
    1942
MEN OF TEXAS   Universal, 1942
THE DEVIL WITH HITLER   United Artists,
    1942

THE McGUERINS FROM BROOKLYN
    United Artists, 1942
CALABOOSE   United Artists, 1943
FALL IN   United Artists, 1943
TAXI, MISTER   United Artists, 1943
PRAIRIE CHICKENS   United Artists, 1943
YANKS AHOY   United Artists, 1943
THAT NATZY NUISANCE   United Artists,
    1943
PHANTOM OF THE OPERA ★   Universal,
    1943
MOONLIGHT IN VERMONT   Universal,
    1943
ALI BABA AND THE FORTY THIEVES
    Universal, 1944
HER PRIMITIVE MAN   Universal, 1944
COBRA WOMAN   Universal, 1944
GHOST CATCHERS   Universal, 1944
GYPSY WILDCAT   Universal, 1944
THE CLIMAX   Universal, 1944
BOWERY TO BROADWAY   Universal,
    1944
FRISCO SAL   Universal, 1945
SONG OF THE SARONG   Universal, 1945
SALOME, WHERE SHE DANCED
    Universal, 1945
IT HAPPENED ON FIFTH AVENUE   Allied
    Artists, 1947
COPACABANA   United Artists, 1947
THE BABE RUTH STORY   Allied Artists,
    1948

FRANZ WAXMAN

b. December 24, 1906 - Konigshutte,
    Germany
d. February 24, 1967 - Los Angeles,
    California

LILLIOM   Fox-Europa, 1934, French
THE BRIDE OF FRANKENSTEIN
    Universal, 1935
DIAMOND JIM   co-composer with Ferde
    Grofe, Universal, 1935
THE AFFAIR OF SUSAN   Universal, 1935
HIS NIGHT OUT   Universal, 1935
THREE KIDS AND A QUEEN   Universal,
    1935
REMEMBER LAST NIGHT?   Universal,
    1935
EAST OF JAVA   Universal, 1935
THE GREAT IMPERSONATION   Universal,
    1935
MAGNIFICENT OBSESSION   Universal,
    1935
THE INVISIBLE RAY   Universal, 1936
NEXT TIME WE LOVE   Universal, 1936
DON'T GET PERSONAL   Universal, 1936
LOVE BEFORE BREAKFAST   Universal,
    1936
SUTTER'S GOLD   Universal, 1936
ABSOLUTE QUIET   MGM, 1936
TROUBLE FOR TWO   MGM, 1936
FURY   MGM, 1936
THE DEVIL-DOLL   MGM, 1936
HIS BROTHER'S WIFE   MGM, 1936
LOVE ON THE RUN   MGM, 1936
PERSONAL PROPERTY   MGM, 1937
CAPTAINS COURAGEOUS   MGM, 1937
THE EMPEROR'S CANDLESTICKS   MGM,
    1937
THE BRIDE WORE RED   MGM, 1937
MAN-PROOF   MGM, 1938
ARSENE LUPIN RETURNS   MGM, 1938
TEST PILOT   MGM, 1938
PORT OF SEVEN SEAS   MGM, 1938
THREE COMRADES   MGM, 1938
TOO HOT TO HANDLE   MGM, 1938
THE SHINING HOUR   MGM, 1938
THE YOUNG IN HEART ★   Selznick
    International, 1938
DRAMATIC SCHOOL   MGM, 1938

A CHRISTMAS CAROL   MGM, 1938
HONOLULU   MGM, 1939
HUCKLEBERRY FINN   MGM, 1939
ON BORROWED TIME   MGM, 1939
LADY OF THE TROPICS   MGM, 1939
STRANGE CARGO   MGM, 1940
FLORIAN   MGM, 1940
REBECCA ★   United Artists, 1940
SPORTING BLOOD   MGM, 1940
BOOM TOWN   MGM, 1940
I LOVE YOU AGAIN   MGM, 1940
ESCAPE   MGM, 1940
THE PHILADELPHIA STORY   MGM, 1940
FLIGHT COMMAND   MGM, 1940
THE BAD MAN   MGM, 1941
DR. JEKYLL AND MR. HYDE ★   MGM,
    1941
UNFINISHED BUSINESS   MGM, 1941
THE FEMININE TOUCH   MGM, 1941
HONKY TONK   MGM, 1941
KATHLEEN   MGM, 1941
SUSPICION ★   RKO Radio, 1941
DESIGN FOR SCANDAL   MGM, 1941
WOMAN OF THE YEAR   MGM, 1942
TORTILLA FLAT   MGM, 1942
HER CARDBOARD LOVER   MGM, 1942
SEVEN SWEETHEARTS   MGM, 1942
JOURNEY FOR MARGARET   MGM, 1942
REUNION IN FRANCE   MGM, 1942
AIR FORCE   Warner Bros., 1943
EDGE OF DARKNESS   Warner Bros.,
    1943
OLD ACQUAINTANCE   Warner Bros.,
    1943
DESTINATION TOKYO   Warner Bros.,
    1943
IN OUR TIME   Warner Bros., 1944
MR. SKEFFINGTON   Warner Bros., 1944
THE VERY THOUGHT OF YOU   Warner
    Bros., 1944
TO HAVE AND HAVE NOT   Warner Bros.,
    1944
OBJECTIVE, BURMA! ★   Warner Bros.,
    1945
HOTEL BERLIN   Warner Bros., 1945
GOD IS MY CO-PILOT   Warner Bros.,
    1945
THE HORN BLOWS AT MIDNIGHT
    Warner Bros., 1945
PRIDE OF THE MARINES   Warner Bros.,
    1945
CONFIDENTIAL AGENT   Warner Bros.,
    1945
HER KIND OF MAN   Warner Bros., 1946
HUMORESQUE ★   Warner Bros., 1946
NORA PRENTISS   Warner Bros., 1947
THE TWO MRS. CARROLLS   Warner
    Bros., 1947
POSSESSED   Warner Bros., 1947
CRY WOLF   Warner Bros., 1947
DARK PASSAGE   Warner Bros., 1947
THE UNSUSPECTED   Warner Bros., 1947
THAT HAGEN GIRL   Warner Bros., 1947
THE PARADINE CASE   Selznick
    Releasing, 1947
SORRY, WRONG NUMBER   Paramount,
    1948
NO MINOR VICES   MGM, 1948
WHIPLASH   Warner Bros., 1948
ALIAS NICK BEAL   Paramount, 1949
ROPE OF SAND   Paramount, 1949
NIGHT UNTO NIGHT   Warner Bros., 1949
TASK FORCE   Warner Bros., 1949
JOHNNY HOLIDAY   United Artists, 1949
NIGHT AND THE CITY   20th Century-Fox,
    1950
THE FURIES   Paramount, 1950
SUNSET BOULEVARD ★★   Paramount,
    1950
DARK CITY   Paramount, 1950
ONLY THE VALIANT   Warner Bros., 1951

HE RAN ALL THE WAY   United Artists, 1951
A PLACE IN THE SUN ★★   Paramount, 1951
ANNE OF THE INDIES   20th Century-Fox, 1951
THE BLUE VEIL   RKO Radio, 1951
RED MOUNTAIN   Paramount, 1951
DECISION BEFORE DAWN   20th Century-Fox, 1951
PHONE CALL FROM A STRANGER   20th Century-Fox, 1952
LURE OF THE WILDERNESS   20th Century-Fox, 1952
MY COUSIN RACHEL   20th Century-Fox, 1952
COME BACK, LITTLE SHEBA   Paramount, 1952
MAN ON A TIGHTROPE   20th Century-Fox, 1953
STALAG 17   Paramount, 1953
I, THE JURY   United Artists, 1953
A LION IS IN THE STREETS   Warner Bros., 1953
BOTANY BAY   Paramount, 1953
PRINCE VALIANT   20th Century-Fox, 1954
ELEPHANT WALK   Paramount, 1954
DEMETRIUS AND THE GLADIATORS   20th Century-Fox, 1954
REAR WINDOW   Paramount, 1954
THIS IS MY LOVE   RKO Radio, 1954
THE SILVER CHALICE ★   Warner Bros., 1954
UNTAMED   20th Century-Fox, 1955
MISTER ROBERTS   Warner Bros., 1955
THE VIRGIN QUEEN   20th Century-Fox, 1955
THE INDIAN FIGHTER   United Artists, 1955
MIRACLE IN THE RAIN   Warner Bros., 1956
CRIME IN THE STREETS   Allied Artists, 1956
BACK FROM ETERNITY   RKO Radio, 1956
THE SPIRIT OF ST. LOUIS   Warner Bros., 1957
LOVE IN THE AFTERNOON   Allied Artists, 1957
PEYTON PLACE   20th Century-Fox, 1957
SAYONARA   Warner Bros., 1957
RUN SILENT, RUN DEEP   United Artists, 1958
HOME BEFORE DARK   Warner Bros., 1958
COUNT YOUR BLESSINGS   MGM, 1959
THE NUN'S STORY ★   Warner Bros., 1959
CAREER   Paramount, 1959
BELOVED INFIDEL   20th Century-Fox, 1959
THE STORY OF RUTH   20th Century-Fox, 1960
SUNRISE AT CAMPOBELLO   Warner Bros., 1960
CIMARRON   MGM, 1960
RETURN TO PEYTON PLACE   20th Century-Fox, 1961
KING OF THE ROARING '20's—THE STORY OF ARNOLD ROTHSTEIN   Allied Artists, 1961
MY GEISHA   Paramount, 1962
HEMINGWAY'S ADVENTURES OF A YOUNG MAN   20th Century-Fox, 1962
TARAS BULBA ★   United Artists, 1962
LOST COMMAND   Columbia, 1966
THE LONGEST HUNDRED MILES (TF)   Universal TV, 1967

ROY WEBB

b. 1888 - New York, New York
d. 1982

PROFESSIONAL SWEETHEART   RKO Radio, 1933
COCKEYED CAVALIERS   RKO Radio, 1934
KENTUCKY KERNELS   RKO Radio, 1934
LIGHTNING STRIKES TWICE   RKO Radio, 1934
ENCHANTED APRIL   RKO Radio, 1935
CAPTAIN HURRICANE   RKO Radio, 1935
LADDIE   RKO Radio, 1935
STRANGERS ALL   RKO Radio, 1935
THE NITWITS   RKO Radio, 1935
THE ARIZONIAN   RKO Radio, 1935
BECKY SHARP   RKO Radio, 1935
OLD MAN RHYTHM   RKO Radio, 1935
THE LAST DAYS OF POMPEII   RKO Radio, 1935
THE RAINMAKERS   RKO Radio, 1935
ANOTHER FACE   RKO Radio, 1935
WE'RE ONLY HUMAN   RKO Radio, 1935
SYLVIA SCARLETT   RKO Radio, 1936
THE LADY CONSENTS   RKO Radio, 1936
MUSS 'EM UP   RKO Radio, 1936
SILLY BILLIES   RKO Radio, 1936
MURDER ON A BRIDLE PATH   RKO Radio, 1936
THE WITNESS CHAIR   RKO Radio, 1936
SPECIAL INVESTIGATOR   RKO Radio, 1936
THE EX-MRS. BRADFORD   RKO Radio, 1936
BUNKER BEAN   RKO Radio, 1936
THE BRIDE WALKS OUT   RKO Radio, 1936
SECOND WIFE   RKO Radio, 1936
THE LAST OF THE MOHICANS   United Artists, 1936
MUMMY'S BOYS   RKO Radio, 1936
THE PLOUGH AND THE STARS   RKO Radio, 1937
RACING LADY   RKO Radio, 1937
SEA DEVILS   RKO Radio, 1937
QUALITY STREET ★   RKO Radio, 1937
THE OUTCASTS OF POKER FLAT   RKO Radio, 1937
MEET THE MISSUS   RKO Radio, 1937
NEW FACES OF 1937   RKO Radio, 1937
ON AGAIN—OFF AGAIN   RKO Radio, 1937
THE LIFE OF THE PARTY   RKO Radio, 1937
FORTY NAUGHTY GIRLS   RKO Radio, 1937
STAGE DOOR   RKO Radio, 1937
HIGH FLYERS   RKO Radio, 1937
BRINGING UP BABY   RKO Radio, 1938
NIGHT SPOT   RKO Radio, 1938
CONDEMNED WOMEN   RKO Radio, 1938
GO CHASE YOURSELF   RKO Radio, 1938
VIVACIOUS LADY   RKO Radio, 1938
GUN LAW   RKO Radio, 1938
BLOND CHEAT   RKO Radio, 1938
BORDER G-MAN   RKO Radio, 1938
HAVING WONDERFUL TIME   RKO Radio, 1938
CRIME RING   RKO Radio, 1938
SKY GIANT   RKO Radio, 1938
I'M FROM THE CITY   RKO Radio, 1938
PAINTED DESERT   RKO Radio, 1938
THE AFFAIRS OF ANNABEL   RKO Radio, 1938
THE RENEGADE RANGER   RKO Radio, 1938
ROOM SERVICE   RKO Radio, 1938
MR. DOODLE KICKS OFF   RKO Radio, 1938

A MAN TO REMEMBER   RKO Radio, 1938
THE MAD MISS MANTON   RKO Radio, 1938
LAWLESS VALLEY   RKO Radio, 1938
THE LAW WEST OF TOMBSTONE   RKO Radio, 1938
NEXT TIME I MARRY   RKO Radio, 1938
THE GREAT MAN VOTES   RKO Radio, 1939
ARIZONA LEGION   RKO Radio, 1939
TWELVE CROWDED HOURS   RKO Radio, 1939
THE SAINT STRIKES BACK   RKO Radio, 1939
THE FLYING IRISHMAN   RKO Radio, 1939
TROUBLE IN SUNDOWN   RKO Radio, 1939
LOVE AFFAIR   RKO Radio, 1939
THEY MADE HER A SPY   RKO Radio, 1939
FIXER DUGAN   RKO Radio, 1939
THE ROOKIE COP   RKO Radio, 1939
SORORITY HOUSE   RKO Radio, 1939
PANAMA LADY   RKO Radio, 1939
RACKETEERS OF THE RANGE   RKO Radio, 1939
THE GIRL FROM MEXICO   RKO Radio, 1939
THE GIRL AND THE GAMBLER   RKO Radio, 1939
FIVE CAME BACK   RKO Radio, 1939
TIMBER STAMPEDE   RKO Radio, 1939
BACHELOR MOTHER   RKO Radio, 1939
BAD LANDS   RKO Radio, 1939
IN NAME ONLY   RKO Radio, 1939
THE FIGHTING GRINGO   RKO Radio, 1939
FULL CONFESSION   RKO Radio, 1939
THREE SONS   RKO Radio, 1939
SUED FOR LIBEL   RKO Radio, 1939
RENO   RKO Radio, 1939
TWO THOROUGHBREDS   RKO Radio, 1939
MARRIED AND IN LOVE   RKO Radio, 1940
THE SAINT'S DOUBLE TROUBLE   RKO Radio, 1940
THE MARINES FLY HIGH   RKO Radio, 1940
ABE LINCOLN IN ILLINOIS   RKO Radio, 1940
CURTAIN CALL   RKO Radio, 1940
MY FAVORITE WIFE ★   RKO Radio, 1940
YOU CAN'T FOOL YOUR WIFE   RKO Radio, 1940
A BILL OF DIVORCEMENT   RKO Radio, 1940
THE SAINT TAKES OVER   RKO Radio, 1940
ANNE OF WINDY POPLARS   RKO Radio, 1940
CROSS COUNTRY ROMANCE   RKO Radio, 1940
MILLIONAIRES IN PRISON   RKO Radio, 1940
ONE CROWDED NIGHT   RKO Radio, 1940
THE STRANGER ON THE THIRD FLOOR   RKO Radio, 1940
I'M STILL ALIVE   RKO Radio, 1940
LADDIE   RKO Radio, 1940
MEXICAN SPITFIRE OUT WEST   RKO Radio, 1940
YOU'LL FIND OUT   RKO Radio, 1940
KITTY FOYLE   RKO Radio, 1941
LITTLE MEN   RKO Radio, 1941
LET'S MAKE MUSIC   RKO Radio, 1941
THE SAINT IN PALM SPRINGS   RKO Radio, 1941
A GIRL, A GUY AND A GOB   RKO Radio, 1941

THE DEVIL AND MISS JONES   RKO Radio, 1941
HURRY, CHARLIE, HURRY   RKO Radio, 1941
TOM, DICK AND HARRY   RKO Radio, 1941
PARACHUTE BATTALION   RKO Radio, 1941
FATHER TAKES A WIFE   RKO Radio, 1941
LOOK WHO'S LAUGHING   RKO Radio, 1941
WEEKEND FOR THREE   RKO Radio, 1941
PLAYMATES   RKO Radio, 1941
OBLIGING YOUNG LADY   RKO Radio, 1942
JOAN OF PARIS ★   RKO Radio, 1942
THE TUTTLES OF TAHITI   RKO Radio, 1942
MY FAVORITE SPY   RKO Radio, 1942
THE MAGNIFICENT AMBERSONS   additional music, RKO Radio, 1942
POWDER TOWN   RKO Radio, 1942
MEXICAN SPITFIRE SEES A GHOST   RKO Radio, 1942
THE BIG STREET   RKO Radio, 1942
MEXICAN SPITFIRE'S ELEPHANT   RKO Radio, 1942
HERE WE GO AGAIN   RKO Radio, 1942
HIGHWAYS BY NIGHT   RKO Radio, 1942
THE NAVY COMES THROUGH   RKO Radio, 1942
I MARRIED A WITCH ★   United Artists, 1942
THE FALCON'S BROTHER   RKO Radio, 1942
SEVEN DAYS' LEAVE   RKO Radio, 1942
ARMY SURGEON   RKO Radio, 1942
CAT PEOPLE   RKO Radio, 1942
SEVEN MILES FROM ALCATRAZ   RKO Radio, 1943
JOURNEY INTO FEAR   RKO Radio, 1943
HITLER'S CHILDREN   RKO Radio, 1943
FLIGHT FOR FREEDOM   RKO Radio, 1943
LADIES' DAY   RKO Radio, 1943
I WALKED WITH A ZOMBIE   RKO Radio, 1943
THE FALCON STRIKES BACK   RKO Radio, 1943
BOMBARDIER   RKO Radio, 1943
MR. LUCKY   RKO Radio, 1943
THE LEOPARD MAN   RKO Radio, 1943
PETTICOAT LARCENY   RKO Radio, 1943
THE FALCON IN DANGER   RKO Radio, 1943
BEHIND THE RISING SUN   RKO Radio, 1943
A LADY TAKES A CHANCE   RKO Radio, 1943
THE FALLEN SPARROW ★   RKO Radio, 1943
THE SEVENTH VICTIM   RKO Radio, 1943
GANGWAY FOR TOMORROW   RKO Radio, 1943
THE IRON MAJOR   RKO Radio, 1943
THE GHOST SHIP   RKO Radio, 1943
PASSPORT TO DESTINY   RKO Radio, 1944
CURSE OF THE CAT PEOPLE   RKO Radio, 1944
ACTION IN ARABIA   RKO Radio, 1944
THE FALCON OUT WEST   RKO Radio, 1944
MARINE RAIDERS   RKO Radio, 1944
BRIDE BY MISTAKE   RKO Radio, 1944
THE SEVENTH CROSS   MGM, 1944
RAINBOW ISLAND   Paramount, 1944
TALL IN THE SADDLE   RKO Radio, 1944
THE MASTER RACE   RKO Radio, 1944
MURDER, MY SWEET   RKO Radio, 1944

EXPERIMENT PERILOUS   RKO Radio, 1945
THE ENCHANTED COTTAGE ★   RKO Radio, 1945
BETRAYAL FROM THE EAST   RKO Radio, 1945
THOSE ENDEARING YOUNG CHARMS   RKO Radio, 1945
ZOMBIES ON BROADWAY   RKO Radio, 1945
THE BODY SNATCHER   RKO Radio, 1945
BACK TO BATAAN   RKO Radio, 1945
TWO O'CLOCK COURAGE   RKO Radio, 1945
LOVE, HONOR AND GOODBYE   Republic, 1945
CORNERED   RKO Radio, 1945
DICK TRACY   RKO Radio, 1945
THE SPIRAL STAIRCASE   RKO Radio, 1945
BADMAN'S TERRITORY   RKO Radio, 1946
BEDLAM   RKO Radio, 1946
THE WELL GROOMED BRIDE   Paramount, 1946
WITHOUT RESERVATIONS   RKO Radio, 1946
NOTORIOUS   RKO Radio, 1946
EASY COME, EASY GO   Paramount, 1947
THE LOCKET   RKO Radio, 1947
SINBAD THE SAILOR   RKO Radio, 1947
THEY WON'T BELIEVE ME   RKO Radio, 1947
CROSSFIRE   RKO Radio, 1947
RIFFRAFF   RKO Radio, 1947
MAGIC TOWN   RKO Radio, 1947
OUT OF THE PAST   RKO Radio, 1947
CASS TIMBERLANE   MGM, 1948
I REMEMBER MAMA   RKO Radio, 1948
FIGHTING FATHER DUNNE   RKO Radio, 1948
RACE STREET   RKO Radio, 1948
RACHEL AND THE STRANGER   RKO Radio, 1948
BLOOD ON THE MOON   RKO Radio, 1948
BAD MEN OF TOMBSTONE   Allied Artists, 1949
THE WINDOW   RKO Radio, 1949
ROUGHSHOD   RKO Radio, 1949
MIGHTY JOE YOUNG   RKO Radio, 1949
EASY LIVING   RKO Radio, 1949
MY FRIEND IRMA   Paramount, 1949
HOLIDAY AFFAIR   RKO Radio, 1949
THE SECRET FURY   RKO Radio, 1950
THE WHITE TOWER   RKO Radio, 1950
WHERE DANGER LIVES   RKO Radio, 1950
VENDETTA   RKO Radio, 1950
BRANDED   Paramount, 1951
GAMBLING HOUSE   RKO Radio, 1951
SEALED CARGO   RKO Radio, 1951
HARD, FAST AND BEAUTIFUL   RKO Radio, 1951
FLYING LEATHERNECKS   RKO Radio, 1951
FIXED BAYONETS!   20th Century-Fox, 1951
A GIRL IN EVERY PORT   RKO Radio, 1952
AT SWORD'S POINT   RKO Radio, 1952
CLASH BY NIGHT   RKO Radio, 1952
THE LUSTY MEN   RKO Radio, 1952
OPERATION SECRET   Warner Bros., 1952
SECOND CHANCE   RKO Radio, 1953
SHE COULDN'T SAY NO   RKO Radio, 1953
HOUDINI   Paramount, 1953
DANGEROUS MISSION   RKO Radio, 1954
TRACK OF THE CAT   Warner Bros., 1954

BENGAZI   RKO Radio, 1955
THE AMERICANO   Columbia, 1955
BLOOD ALLEY   Warner Bros., 1955
MARTY   United Artists, 1955
THE SEA CHASE   Warner Bros., 1955
UNDERWATER!   RKO Radio, 1955
THE GIRL HE LEFT BEHIND   Warner Bros., 1956
THE FIRST TEXAN   Allied Artists, 1956
OUR MISS BROOKS   Warner Bros., 1956
THE RIVER CHANGES   Warner Bros., 1956
SHOOT-OUT AT MEDICINE BEND   Warner Bros., 1957
TOP SECRET AFFAIR   Warner Bros., 1957
TEACHER'S PET   Paramount, 1958

KURT WEILL
b. March 2, 1900 - Dessau, Germany
d. April 3, 1950 - New York

YOU AND ME   Paramount, 1938

JEAN WIENER
b. March 19, 1896 - Paris, France
d. June 8, 1982 - Paris France

KNOCK   1932, French
L'HOMME A L'HISPANO   *THE MAN FROM SPAIN*   1932, French
THE GREAT GLASS BLOWER   1933, French
L'AVENTURIER   1934, French
LA PAQUEBOT "TENACITY"   1934, French
MARIA CHAPDELAINE   1934, French
LES AFFAIRES PUBLIQUES   Arc Films, 1934, French
LA CATHEDRALE DES MORTES   1935, French
LA BANDERA   1935, French
LE CLOWN BUX   co-composer with Roger Desormieres, 1935, French
THE CRIME OF MONSIEUR LANGE   co-composer with Joseph Kosma, Brandon, 1936, French
L'HOMME DU JOUR   1936, French
LES BAS-FONDS   *THE LOWER DEPTHS*   1936, French
ROSE   1936, French
LA LETTRE   1938, French
NUITS DE FEU   1939, French
DERRIERE LA FACADE   1939, French
LES PASSAGERS DE LA GRANDE OUISE   1939, French
UNTEL, PERE ET FILS   *HEART OF A NATION*   1940, French
LA VOYAGEUR DE LA TOUSSAINT   1942, French
SUITE FRANCAISE   1943, French
LE PERE GORIOT   1944, French
LE VOLEUR DE PARATONNERRES   1944, French
LA FILLE AUX YEUX GRIS   1945, French
LE CAPITAN   1945, French
PATRIE   1946, French
CONTRE-ENQUETE   1946, French
POUR UNE NUIT D'AMOUR   1946, French
MACADAM   1946, French
LES FRERES BOUQUINQUANT   1947, French
LE DIABLE SOUFFLE   1947, French
LA CARCASSE ET LE TORD-COU   1947, French
L'ESCADRON BLANC   1948, French
LE POINT DU JOUR   1948, French
ZANZABELLE A PARIS   1948, French
RENDEZ-VOUS DE JUILLET   1949, French

LE PARFUM DE LA DAME EN NOIR   1949, French
MAITRE APRES DIEU   1950, French
UN SOURIRE DANS LA TEMPETE   1950, French
SOUS LE CIEL DE PARIS   *UNDER THE PARIS SKY*   Discina International, 1951, French
LE CHEMIN DE l'ETOILE   1953, French
LE COMTE DE MONTE-CRISTO   1953, French
LA RAFLE EST POUR CE SOIR   1953, French
TOUCHEZ PAS AU GRISBI   1953, French
LES POUSSIERES   1954, French
FUTURES VEDETTES   1954, French
DEADLIER THAN THE MALE   *VOICI LE TEMPS DES ASSASSINS*   Continental, 1955, French
LA VIE EST BELLE   1956, French
LA GARCONNE   1956, French
MOTRE-DAME, CATHEDRALE DE PARIS   1957, French
POT-BOUILLE   *THE HOUSE OF LOVERS*   Continental, 1957, French
A WOMAN LIKE SATAN   *THE FEMALE/LA FEMME ET LA PANTIN*   Lopert, 1958, French-Italian
PANTALASKAS   1959, French
ILS ONT TUE JAURES   1962, French
LADY L   MGM, 1965, U.S.-Italian-French
AU HASARD, BALTHAZAR   Cinema Ventures, 1966, French
LES FILOUS   1966, French
MOUCHETTE   1967, French
LA REVOLUTION D'OCTOBRE   1968, French
DIEU A CHOISI PARIS   1968, French
LA FAUTE DE L'ABBE MOURET   1970, French

MEREDITH WILLSON
b. 1902 - Mason City, Iowa
d. June 15, 1984 - Santa Monica, California

THE LITTLE FOXES ★   RKO Radio, 1941

MORTIMER WILSON
d. January 27, 1932 - New York

THE THIEF OF BAGDAD   United Artists, 1924

VICTOR YOUNG
b. August 8, 1900 - Chicago, Illinois
d. 1956 - Los Angeles, California

CHAMPAGNE WALTZ   Paramount, 1937
MAID OF SALEM   Paramount, 1937
SWING HIGH, SWING LOW   Paramount, 1937
VOGUES   *VOGUES OF 1938*   United Artists, 1937
EBB TIDE   Paramount, 1937
WELLS FARGO   Paramount, 1937
ARMY GIRL ★   Republic, 1938
BREAKING THE ICE ★   RKO Radio, 1938
PECK'S BAD BOY WITH THE CIRCUS   RKO Radio, 1938
FLIRTING WITH FATE   MGM, 1938

FISHERMAN'S WHARF   RKO Radio, 1939
MAN OF CONQUEST ★   Republic, 1939
HERITAGE OF THE DESERT   Paramount, 1939
WAY DOWN SOUTH ★   RKO Radio, 1939
GOLDEN BOY ★   Columbia, 1939
RANGE WAR   Paramount, 1939
OUR NEIGHBORS—THE CARTERS   Paramount, 1939
THE NIGHT OF NIGHTS   Paramount, 1939
THE LLANO KID   Paramount, 1939
GULLIVER'S TRAVELS ★   Paramount, 1939
THE LIGHT THAT FAILED   Paramount, 1939
RAFFLES   United Artists, 1940
DARK COMMAND   Republic, 1940
BUCK BENNY RIDES AGAIN   Paramount, 1940
THE WAY OF ALL FLESH   Paramount, 1940
THREE FACES WEST   Republic, 1940
UNTAMED   Paramount, 1940
I WANT A DIVORCE   Paramount, 1940
MOON OVER BURMA   Paramount, 1940
ARISE, MY LOVE ★   Paramount, 1940
THREE MEN FROM TEXAS   Paramount, 1940
NORTHWEST MOUNTED POLICE ★   Paramount, 1940
ARIZONA ★   Columbia, 1940
THE MAD DOCTOR   Paramount, 1940
VIRGINIA   Paramount, 1941
REACHING FOR THE SUN   Paramount, 1941
CAUGHT IN THE DRAFT   Paramount, 1941
I WANTED WINGS   Paramount, 1941
ALOMA OF THE SOUTH SEAS   Paramount, 1941
HOLD BACK THE DAWN ★   Paramount, 1941
SKYLARK   Paramount, 1941
THE REMARKABLE ANDREW   Paramount, 1942
REAP THE WILD WIND   Paramount, 1942
THE GREAT MAN'S LADY   Paramount, 1942
BEYOND THE BLUE HORIZON   Paramount, 1942
TAKE A LETTER, DARLING ★   Paramount, 1942
THE FOREST RANGERS   Paramount, 1942
MRS. WIGGS OF THE CABBAGE PATCH   Paramount, 1942
FLYING TIGERS ★   Republic, 1942
THE GLASS KEY   Paramount, 1942
THE PALM BEACH STORY   Paramount, 1942
SILVER QUEEN ★   United Artists, 1942
THE OUTLAW   United Artists, 1943
BUCKSKIN FRONTIER   United Artists, 1943
THE CRYSTAL BALL   United Artists, 1943
YOUNG AND WILLING   United Artists, 1943
CHINA   Paramount, 1943
FOR WHOM THE BELL TOLLS ★   Paramount, 1943
HOSTAGES   Paramount, 1943
TRUE TO LIFE   Paramount, 1943
NO TIME FOR LOVE   Paramount, 1943
THE UNINVITED   Paramount, 1944
THE STORY OF DR. WASSELL   Paramount, 1944
THE GREAT MOMENT   Paramount, 1944
FRENCHMAN'S CREEK   Paramount, 1944
MINISTRY OF FEAR   Paramount, 1944
PRACTICALLY YOURS   Paramount, 1944

AND NOW TOMORROW   Paramount, 1944
A MEDAL FOR BENNY   Paramount, 1945
THE GREAT JOHN L.   United Artists, 1945
YOU CAME ALONG   Paramount, 1945
KITTY   Paramount, 1945
LOVE LETTERS ★   Paramount, 1945
MASQUERADE IN MEXICO   Paramount, 1945
HOLD THAT BLONDE   Paramount, 1945
THE BLUE DAHLIA   Paramount, 1946
THE SEARCHING WIND   Paramount, 1946
OUR HEARTS WERE GROWING UP   Paramount, 1946
TO EACH HIS OWN   Paramount, 1946
TWO YEARS BEFORE THE MAST   Paramount, 1946
SUDDENLY, IT'S SPRING   Paramount, 1947
CALIFORNIA   Paramount, 1947
THE IMPERFECT LADY   Paramount, 1947
CALCUTTA   Paramount, 1947
THE TROUBLE WITH WOMEN   Paramount, 1947
I WALK ALONE   Paramount, 1947
UNCONQUERED   Paramount, 1947
GOLDEN EARRINGS   Paramount, 1947
STATE OF THE UNION   MGM, 1948
THE BIG CLOCK   Paramount, 1948
THE EMPEROR WALTZ ★   Paramount, 1948
DREAM GIRL   Paramount, 1948
SO EVIL MY LOVE   co-composer with William Alwyn, Paramount, 1948
BEYOND GLORY   Paramount, 1948
THE NIGHT HAS A THOUSAND EYES   Paramount, 1948
MISS TATLOCK'S MILLIONS   Paramount, 1948
THE PALEFACE   Paramount, 1948
THE ACCUSED   Paramount, 1948
A CONNECTICUT YANKEE IN KING ARTHUR'S COURT   Paramount, 1949
STREETS OF LAREDO   Paramount, 1949
THE FILE ON THELMA JORDAN   *THELMA JORDAN*   Paramount, 1949
SONG OF SURRENDER   Paramount, 1949
CHICAGO DEADLINE   Paramount, 1949
SANDS OF IWO JIMA   Republic, 1949
GUN CRAZY   *DEADLY IS THE FEMALE*   United Artists, 1949
MY FOOLISH HEART   RKO Radio, 1949
SAMSON AND DELILAH ★   Paramount, 1949
OUR VERY OWN   RKO Radio, 1950
PAID IN FULL   Paramount, 1950
BRIGHT LEAF   Warner Bros., 1950
THE FIREBALL   20th Century-Fox, 1950
RIO GRANDE   Republic, 1950
SEPTEMBER AFFAIR   Paramount, 1950
BELLE LE GRAND   Republic, 1951
PAYMENT ON DEMAND   RKO Radio, 1951
THE BULLFIGHTER AND THE LADY   Republic, 1951
THE LEMON DROP KID   Paramount, 1951
APPOINTMENT WITH DANGER   Paramount, 1951
HONEYCHILE   Republic, 1951
A MILLIONAIRE FOR CHRISTY   20th Century-Fox, 1951
THE WILD BLUE YONDER   Republic, 1951
MY FAVORITE SPY   Paramount, 1951
THE QUIET MAN   Republic, 1952
ANYTHING CAN HAPPEN   Paramount, 1952
SOMETHING TO LIVE FOR   Paramount, 1952

'97-'98
FILM
COMPOSERS
LISTING

Z

THE GREATEST SHOW ON EARTH
Paramount, 1952
SCARAMOUCHE MGM, 1952
THE STORY OF WILL ROGERS Warner
Bros., 1952
ONE MINUTE TO ZERO RKO Radio,
1952
THUNDERBIRDS Republic, 1952
BLACKBEARD, THE PIRATE RKO Radio,
1952
THE STAR 20th Century-Fox, 1952
FAIR WIND TO JAVA Republic, 1953
A PERILOUS JOURNEY Republic, 1953
THE SUN SHINES BRIGHT Republic,
1953
SHANE Paramount, 1953
LITTLE BOY LOST Paramount, 1953
FOREVER FEMALE Paramount, 1953
TROUBLE IN THE GLEN Republic, 1953,
British
FLIGHT NURSE Republic, 1954
JUBILEE TRAIL Republic, 1954
JOHNNY GUITAR Republic, 1954
THREE COINS IN THE FOUNTAIN 20th
Century-Fox, 1954
ABOUT MRS. LESLIE Paramount, 1954
DRUM BEAT Warner Bros., 1954
THE COUNTRY GIRL Paramount, 1954
TIMBERJACK Republic, 1955
STRATEGIC AIR COMMAND Paramount,
1955
SON OF SINBAD RKO Radio, 1955
A MAN ALONE Republic, 1955
THE LEFT HAND OF GOD 20th
Century-Fox, 1955
THE TALL MEN 20th Century-Fox, 1955
THE CONQUEROR RKO Radio, 1956
THE MAVERICK QUEEN Republic, 1956
THE VAGABOND KING Paramount, 1956
THE PROUD AND PROFANE Paramount,
1956
AROUND THE WORLD IN 80 DAYS ★★
United Artists, 1956
THE BRAVE ONE RKO Radio, 1956
THE BUSTER KEATON STORY
Paramount 1957
OMAR KHAYYAM Paramount, 1957
RUN OF THE ARROW co-composer with
Max Steiner, RKO Radio, 1957

JOHN S. ZAMECNIK

d. June 13, 1953 - Los Angeles, California

OLD IRONSIDES Paramount, 1926
WINGS Paramount, 1927
ABIE'S IRISH ROSE Paramount, 1928
THE WEDDING MARCH Paramount, 1928
BETRAYAL Paramount, 1929
REDSKIN Paramount, 1929

FRANK ZAPPA

b. December 21, 1940 - Baltimore, Maryland
d. 1993

200 MOTELS United Artists, 1971, British
BABY SNAKES Intercontinental
Absurdities, 1979

WOLFGANG ZELLER

b. Germany
d. 1967 - West Germany

ADVENTURES OF PRINCE ACHMED
1926, German
WELTMELODIE 1929, German
VAMPYR VAMPYR OU L'ETRANGE
AVENTURE DE DAVID GRAY 1932,
French-German
L'ATLANTIDE LOST ATLANTIS 1932,
French-German
WAJAN SON OF A WITCH 1934,
German
DIE UNJEIMLICHEN WUNSCHE THE
UNHOLY WITCH 1939, German
MARRIAGE IN THE SHADOWS 1947
SERENGETI SHALL NOT DIE 1960

★ ★ ★

INDEX BY FILM TITLE

INDEX BY FILM TITLE

This is an index of film titles from the Listing Sections of this directory.
† = denotes a deceased composer

$ DOLLARS Columbia, 1971
QUINCY JONES

THE $5.20 AN HOUR DREAM (TF) Thomas-Sagal Productions/Finnegan Associates/Big Deal, 1980
JIMMIE HASKELL

2 DAYS IN THE VALLEY MGM-UA, 1996
ANTHONY MARINELLI

2ND COUSIN, ONCE REMOVED Shorney/McColpin, 1992
BLAKE LEYH

3:15 Cannon, 1986
GARY CHANG

3 DAYS OF THE CONDOR Paramount, 1975
DAVE GRUSIN

3 NINJAS Buena Vista, 1992
RICHARD MARVIN

3 NINJAS KICK BACK TriStar, 1994
RICHARD MARVIN

3 NINJAS KNUCKLE UP TriStar, 1995
GARY STEVAN SCOTT

THE 4TH MAN Spectrafilm, 1983
LOEK DIKKER

5 CARD STUD Paramount, 1968
MAURICE JARRE

THE 5TH MUSKETEER Columbia, 1979
RIZ ORTOLANI

7 VOLTE 7 1967
ARMANDO TROVAJOLI

THE 7 BROTHERS MEET DRACULA *THE LEGEND OF THE SEVEN GOLDEN VAMPIRES* Dynamite Entertainment, 1979
JAMES BERNARD

THE 7 GOLDEN MEN STRIKE AGAIN 1966
ARMANDO TROVAJOLI

THE 7 MAGNIFICIENT GLADIATORS 1983
DOV SELTZER

8-1/2 Embassy, 1963
NINO ROTA†

8-A (FD) P.M. Films, 1993
DANIEL FREIBERG

8 MILLION WAYS TO DIE Tri-Star, 1986
JAMES NEWTON HOWARD

8 SECONDS New Line, 1994
BILL CONTI

9 1/2 NINJAS Cassian Elwes, 1991
GEOFFREY LEIGH TOZER

9-1/2 WEEKS MGM/UA, 1986
JACK NITZCHE

9/30/55 *SEPTEMBER 30, 1955* Universal, 1977
LEONARD ROSENMAN

10 Orion/Warner Bros., 1979
HENRY MANCINI† ★

THE 10 MILLION DOLLAR GETAWAY (CTF) Alan Cooperman Productions/Wilshire Court, 1991
PETER MATZ

10 RILLINGTON PLACE Columbia, 1971
JOHN DANKWORTH

10 TO MIDNIGHT Cannon, 1983
ROBERT O. RAGLAND

10 VIOLENT WOMEN New American Films, 1984
NICHOLAS CARRAS

11TH VICTIM (TF) Marty Katz Productions/Paramount Pictures TV, 1979
MICHEL COLOMBIER

12:01 (TF) Fox West Pictures/New Line TV/Chanticleer Films, 1993
PETER RODGERS MELNICK

12 MONKEYS Universal, 1995
PAUL BUCKMASTER

13 FRIGHTENED GIRLS Columbia, 1963
VAN ALEXANDER

13 GHOSTS Columbia, 1960
VON DEXTE

13 LEAD SOLDIERS 20th Century-Fox, 1948
MILTON ROSEN†

13 RUE MADELINE 20th Century-Fox, 1947
DAVID BUTTOLPH†

THE 13TH LETTER 20th Century-Fox, 1951
ALEX NORTH†

16 DAYS TO GLORY (FD) Paramount, 1985
LEE HOLDRIDGE

16 FATHOMS DEEP Lake/Mon., 1948
RENE GARRIGUENC†
LUCIEN MORAWECK†

18 AGAIN New World, 1988
BILLY GOLDENBERG

20 MILLION MILES TO EARTH Columbia, 1957
MISCHA BAKALEINIKOFF†

21 HOURS AT MUNICH (TF) Moonlight Productions/Filmways Pictures, 1976
LAURENCE ROSENTHAL

21 JUMP STREET (TF) Steven J. Cannell Prods., 1987
PETER BERNSTEIN

23 PACES TO BAKER STREET 20th Century-Fox, 1956
LEIGH HARLINE†

24 HEURES DE LA VIE D'UNE FEMME 1968
JEAN PRODROMIDES

THE 25TH HOUR MGM, 1967
GEORGES DELERUE†

THE 27TH DAY Columbia, 1956
MISCHA BAKALEINIKOFF†

29th STREET 20th Century Fox, 1991
WILLIAM OLVIS

30 IS A DANGEROUS AGE, CYNTHIA Columbia, 1968
DUDLEY MOORE

30 YEARS OF NATIONAL GEOGRAPHIC SPECIALS (TD) National Geographic Society, 1995
JAY CHATTAWAY

THE 30-FOOT BRIDE OF CANDY ROCK Columbia, 1959
RAOUL KRAUSHAAR

36 HOURS MGM, 1964
DIMITRI TIOMKIN†

THE 39 STEPS International Picture Show Company, 1978
ED WELCH

40 CARATS Columbia, 1973
MICHEL LEGRAND

40 POUNDS OF TROUBLE Universal, 1962
MORT LINDSEY

48 HOURS Paramount, 1982
JAMES HORNER

THE 49TH MAN Columbia, 1953
MISCHA BAKALEINIKOFF†

52 PICK-UP Cannon, 1986
GARY CHANG

52ND STREET 1937
DAVID RAKSIN

55 DAYS AT PEKING Allied Artists, 1963
DIMITRI TIOMKIN† ★

A 077 SFIDA AL KILLERS Aenii/Flora/Regina, 1967
CARLO SAVINA

84 CHARING CROSS ROAD Columbia, 1987
GEORGE FENTON

087 MISION APOCALIPSIS 1967
FRANCESCO DE MASI

92 HAK MUIGWAI DUI HAK MUIGWAI *92 LEGENDARY LA ROSE NOIRE* 1993
LOWELL

92 IN THE SHADE United Artists, 1975
MICHAEL J. LEWIS

99 & 44/100% DEAD 20th Century-Fox, 1974
HENRY MANCINI†

99 RIVER STREET United Artists, 1953
EMIL NEWMAN†

99 WOMEN 1966
BRUNO NICOLAI

THE 100 LIVES OF BLACK JACK SAVAGE (TF) Stephen J. Cannell/Walt Disney TV, 1991
MIKE POST

100 RIFLES 20th Century-Fox, 1969
JERRY GOLDSMITH

101 DALMATIANS Buena Vista, 1996
MICHAEL KAMEN

112TH & CENTRAL: THROUGH THE EYES OF THE CHILDREN (FD) Flatfields, 1993
DELFEAYO MARSALIS

145 WEST 21 Rudolph Burckhardt, 1936
PAUL BOWLES

200 MOTELS United Artists, 1971
FRANK ZAPPA†

300 MILES FOR STEPHANIE (TF) Edward S. Feldman Company/Yellow Ribbon Productions/PKO, 1981
LEE HOLDRIDGE

THE 300 SPARTANS 20th Century-Fox, 1962
MANOS HADJIDAKIS†

THE 400 MILLION 1939
HANNS EISLER†

500 NATIONS (TD) Tig Prods./RCS/Majestic, 1995
PETER BUFFETT

THE 500-POUND JERK (TF) David L. Wolper Productions, 1973
NEAL HEFTI

588, RUE PARADIS 1992
JEAN-CLAUDE PETIT

633 SQUADRON United Artists, 1964
RON GOODWIN

711 OCEAN DRIVE Columbia, 1950
SOL KAPLAN

901: AFTER 45 YEARS OF WORKING Home Vision, 1990
CARL DANTE

976-EVIL New Line Cinema, 1988
TOM CHASE
STEVE RUCKER

976-EVIL PART II Cinetel, 1991
CHUCK CIRINO

THE 1,000 EYES OF SU-MURU 1967
JOHN SCOTT

10,000 DOLLARI PER RINGO 1965
BRUNO NICOLAI

1001 ARABIAN NIGHTS (AF) Columbia, 1959;1001 ARA
GEORGE DUNIN

1492: CONQUEST OF PARADISE Paramount, 1992
VANGELIS

1900 *NOVECENTO* Paramount, 1977
ENNIO MORRICONE

1918 1958
DMITRI KABALEVSKY†

1919 1983
RIZ ORTOLANI

1941 Universal/Columbia, 1979
JOHN WILLIAMS

1969 Atlantic Releasing Corporation, 1988
MICHAEL SMALL

1984 Atlantic Releasing Corporation, 1984
EURYTHMICS
DOMINIC MULDOWNEY

1990: THE BRONX United Film Distribution, 1983
WALTER RIZZATI

1994 BAKER STREET: SHERLOCK HOLMES RETURNS (TF) Paragon/Kenneth Johnson, 1993
JAMES DIPASQUAL

20,000 YEARS IN SING SING Warner Bros., 193320000 YEA
BERNHARD KAUN†

2000 MALIBU ROAD (TF) Spelling TV/Fisher Ent./CGD Prods., 1992
JAMES NEWTON HOWARD

2000 MANIACS Box Office Spectaculars, 1964
HERSCHELL GORDON LEWIS
LARRY WELLINGTON

2000 YEARS LATER Warner Bros., 1969
STU PHILLIPS

2006 Filminvest, 1986
CARL DANTE

2010 MGM/UA, 1984
DAVID SHIRE

THE 3,000 MILE CHASE Public Arts Productions/Universal TV, 1977
ELMER BERNSTEIN

THE 5,000 FINGERS OF DR. T Columbia, 1953
FREDERICK HOLLANDER† ★
HEINZ ROEMHELD†
HANS J. SALTER†

6,000 ENEMIES MGM, 1939
EDWARD WARD†

90028 1979
BASIL POLEDOURIS

20,000 EYES 20th Century-Fox, 1961
ALBERT GLASSER

20,000 LEAGUES UNDER THE SEA Buena Vista, 1954
PAUL J. SMITH†

A

AARON SLICK FROM PUMPKIN CRICK Paramount, 1952
ROBERT EMMETT DOLAN†

AARON'S WAY: THE HARVEST (TF) Blinn-Thorpe Productions/Lorimar Telepictures, 1988
MARK SNOW

ABANDONED Universal, 1949
WALTER SCHARF

ABANDONED AND DECEIVED (TF) Crystal Beach/TriStar TV, 1995
LAURA KARPMAN

ABBOTT & COSTELLO GO TO MARS Universal, 1953
HERMAN STEIN

ABBOTT & COSTELLO IN HOLLYWOOD MGM, 1945
GEORGE BASSMAN

ABBOTT & COSTELLO MEET DR. JEKYLL AND MR. HYDE Universal, 1953
PAUL SAWTELL†
HERMAN STEIN

ABBOTT & COSTELLO MEET THE KEYSTONE COPS Universal, 1955
HENRY MANCINI†
HERMAN STEIN

ABBOTT AND COSTELLO MEET DR. JEYKLL AND MR. HYDE Universal, 1953
HANS J. SALTER†

ABBOTT AND COSTELLO MEET FRANKENSTEIN Universal, 1948
FRANK SKINNER†

ABBOTT AND COSTELLO MEET THE INVISIBLE MAN Universal, 1951
HANS J. SALTER†

ABBOTT AND COSTELLO MEET THE MUMMY Universal, 1955
HANS J. SALTER†

ABBY American International, 1974
ROBERT O. RAGLAND

THE ABDICATION Warner Bros., 1974
NINO ROTA†

ABDUCTED InterPictures, 1986
MICHEL RUBINI

THE ABDUCTION OF KARI SWENSON (TF) NBC Productions, 1987
SYLVESTER LEVAY

THE ABDUCTION OF SAINT ANNE (TF) QM Productions, 1975
GEORGE DUNING

THE ABDUCTORS 20th Century-Fox, 1957
PAUL GLASS

ABDUL THE DAMNED 1934
HANNS EISLER†

ABDULLAH'S HAREM 20th Century-Fox, 1956
GEORGES AURIC†

ABE LINCOLN IN ILLINOIS RKO Radio, 1940
ROY WEBB†

ABIE'S IRISH ROSE Paramount, 1928
JOHN S. ZAMECNIK†

ABILENE TOWN United Artists, 1946
ALBERT GLASSER

THE ABOMINABLE DR. PHIBES American International, 1971
BASIL KIRCHIN

THE ABOMINABLE SNOWMAN OF THE HIMALAYAS *ABOMINABLE SNOWMAN* uncredited, 20th Century-Fox, 1957
HUMPHREY SEARLE†

ABOMINABLE SNOWMAN uncredited, 20th Century-Fox, 1957
HUMPHREY SEARLE†

ABOUT FACE United Artists, 1942
EDWARD WARD†

ABOUT LAST NIGHT... Tri-Star, 1986
MILES GOODMAN†

ABOUT MRS. LESLIE Paramount, 1954
VICTOR YOUNG†

AFTER HOURS The Geffen Company/Warner Bros., 1985
HOWARD SHORE

AFTER SCHOOL Moviestore Entertainment, 1988
DAVID C. WILLIAMS

AFTER SEPARATION 1993
LIANG GANG

AFTER THE AXE (FD) Canadian
PATRICIA CULLEN

AFTER THE FOX United Artists, 1966
BURT BACHARACH

AFTER THE PROMISE (TF) Tamara Asseyev
Productions/New World TV, 1987
RALPH BURNS

AFTER THE THIN MAN MGM, 1936
HERBERT STOTHART†
EDWARD WARD†

AFTER TONIGHT RKO Radio, 1933
MAX STEINER†

AFTERBURN (CTF) Steve Tisch Co., 1992
STEWART COPELAND

THE AFTERMATH Prism Entertainment, 1982
JOHN W. MORGAN

AFTERMATH: A TEST OF LOVE (TF) Interscope, 1991
LEONARD ROSENMAN

THE AFTERNOON OF A PEASANT Yugoslavian
ALFI KABILJO

AFTERSHOCK Bonaire Films, 1989
KEVIN KLINGER

AGAINST ALL FLAGS Universal, 1952
HANS J. SALTER†

AGAINST ALL ODDS Columbia, 1984
LARRY CARLTON
MICHEL COLOMBIER

AGAINST HER WILL: THE CARRIE BULK STORY (CTF) Janet Faust Krusi Prods./Viacom, 1994
MICKEY ERBE
MARYBETH SOLOMON

AGAINST THE WALL (CTF) Producers
Entertainment Group, 1994
GARY CHANG

AGAINST THEIR WILL: WOMEN IN PRISON (TF) Their Own Prods./Jaffe-Braunstein Films/ABC, 1994
AL KOOPER

AGANTUK *THE STRANGER* 1991
SATYAJIT RAY†

AGATHA Warner Bros., 1979
JOHNNY MANDEL

AGATHA CHRISTIE'S 'A CARIBBEAN MYSTERY' (TF) Stan Margulies Productions/Warner Bros. TV, 1983
LEE HOLDRIDGE

AGATHA CHRISTIE'S 'DEAD MAN'S FOLLY' (TF) Warner Bros. TV, 1986
JOHN ADDISON

AGATHA CHRISTIE'S 'MURDER IN THREE ACTS' (TF) Warner Bros. TV, 1986
ALF CLAUSEN

AGATHA CHRISTIE'S 'MURDER WITH MIRRORS' (TF) Hajeno Productions/Warner Bros. TV, 1985
RICHARD RODNEY BENNETT ☆

AGATHA CHRISTIE'S 'SPARKLING CYANIDE' (TF) Stan Margulies Productions/Warner Bros. TV, 1983
JAMES DIPASQUALE

AGATHA CHRISTIE'S 'THIRTEEN AT DINNER' (TF) Warner Bros. TV, 1985
JOHN ADDISON

AGATHA CHRISTIE'S THE MAN IN THE BROWN SUIT (TF) Alan Shayne Productions/Warner Bros. TV, 1989
ARTHUR B. RUBINSTEIN

THE AGE FOR LOVE United Artists, 1931
ALFRED NEWMAN†

THE AGE OF ASSASSINS 1967
MASARU SATO

AGE OF CONSENT Columbia, 1970
STANLEY MYERS†

AGE OF INDISCRETION MGM, 1935
EDWARD WARD†

THE AGE OF INNOCENCE Columbia, 1993
ELMER BERNSTEIN ★

THE AGE OF INNOCENCE RKO Radio, 1934
MAX STEINER†

AGENCE MATRIMONIALE 1952
JOSEPH KOSMA†

AGENCY Taft International, 1980
LEWIS FUREY

AGENT 8 3/4 *HOT ENOUGH FOR JUNE* Continental, 1963
ANGELO FRANCESCO LAVAGNINO†

AGENT TROUBLE 1987
GABRIEL YARED

AGENTE SPEZIALE - OPERAZIONE RE MIDA 1966
BRUNO NICOLAI

AGE-OLD FRIENDS (CTF) Granger Productions/HBO Showcase, 1989
STANLEY MYERS†

AGGIE APPLEBY RKO Radio, 1933
MAX STEINER†

AGNES OF GOD Columbia, 1985
GEORGES DELERUE† ★

THE AGONY AND THE ECSTASY 20th Century Fox, 1965
ALEX NORTH† ★

THE AGONY AND THE ECSTASY 20th Century-Fox, 1965
JERRY GOLDSMITH

AGOSTINO Baltea Film, 1962
CARLO RUSTICHELLI

AGUIRRE, THE WRATH OF GOD New Yorker, 1973
POPOL VUH

AH SI? E IO LO DICO A ZZZORO! 1975
GIANFRANCO PLENIZIO

AH, WILDERNESS! MGM, 1935
HERBERT STOTHART†

AI MARGINI DELLA METROPOLI 1953
FRANCO MANNINO

AILEEN WUORNOS: THE SELLING OF A SERIAL KILLER (FD) 1992
DAVID BERGEAUD

AIMEZ-VOUS BRAHMS? United Artists, 1961
GEORGES AURIC†

AIN'T MISBEHAVIN' Universal, 1955
HENRY MANCINI†

AIR AMERICA TriStar, 1990
CHARLES GROSS

AIR FORCE Warner Bros., 1943
FRANZ WAXMAN†

AIR PATROL 20th Century-Fox, 1962
ALBERT GLASSER

AIR PATTERN—PACIFIC (FD) A.A.F., 1944
GAIL KUBIK†

AIR RAID WARDENS MGM, 1943
NATHANIEL SHILKRET†

THE AIR UP THERE Buena Vista, 1994
DAVID NEWMAN

AIRBORNE Warner Bros., 1993
STEWART COPELAND

AIRHEADS 20th Century Fox, 1994
CARTER BURWELL

AIRPLANE II: THE SEQUEL Paramount, 1982
RICHARD HAZARD

AIRPLANE! Paramount, 1980
ELMER BERNSTEIN

AIRPORT Universal, 1970
ALFRED NEWMAN† ★

AIRPORT '77 Universal, 1977
JOHN CACAVAS

AIRPORT 1975 Universal, 1974
JOHN CACAVAS

AIRWOLF (TF) Belisarius Productions/Universal TV, 1984
SYLVESTER LEVAY

A.K. (FD) 1985
TORU TAKEMITSU†

AKENFIELD (FD) Angle Films, 1975
SIR MICHAEL TIPPETT

AKIRA (AF) Streamline Pictures, 1990
SHOJI YAMASHIRO

AKIRA KUROSAWA'S DREAMS Warner Bros., 1990
SHINCHIRO IKEBE

AL CAPONE Allied Artists, 1959
DAVID RAKSIN

AL DI LA DELLA LEGGE 1968
RIZ ORTOLANI

AL HOUROB AL SAGHIRA *LITTLE WARS LES PETITES GUERRES* 1983
GABRIEL YARED

ALADDIN Cannon, 1987
FABIO FRIZZI

ALADDIN (AF) Buena Vista, 1992
ALAN MENKEN ★★

ALAKAZAM THE GREAT American International, 1960
LES BAXTER†

THE ALAMO United Artists, 1960
DIMITRI TIOMKIN† ★

ALAMO BAY Tri-Star, 1985
RY COODER

THE ALAMO: 13 DAYS TO GLORY (TF) Briggle, Hennessy, Carrothers Productions/The Finnegan Company/Fries Entertainment, 1987
PETER BERNSTEIN

ALAN & NAOMI Triton, 1992
DICK HYMAN

ALASKA Columbia, 1996
REG POWELL

ALASKA: AN AMERICANCHILD (FD) 1977
LEE HOLDRIDGE

ALBERGO LUNA, CAMERA 34 1946
NINO ROTA†

ALBERT R.N. United Artists, 1953
MALCOLM ARNOLD

ALBERT SOUFFRE *ALBERT SUFFERS* 1992
PIXIES

ALBERT SUFFERS 1992
PIXIES

ALBERTO EXPRESS 1990
ANGELIQUE NACHON
JEAN-CLAUDE NACHON

ALBINO ALLIGATOR Miramax, 1997
MICHAEL BROOK

ALCATRAZ: THE WHOLE SHOCKING STORY (TF) Pierre Cossette Enterprises, 1980
JERROLD IMMEL

THE ALCHEMIST Empire Pictures, 1985
RICHARD H. BAND

ALECHINSKY D'APRES NATURE 1970
MICHEL PORTAL

ALERTE EN MEDITERRANEE 1938
MICHEL MICHELET†

ALEX & THE GYPSY 20th Century-Fox, 1976
HENRY MANCINI†

ALEX: THE LIFE OF A CHILD (TF) Mandy Productions, 1986
J.A.C. REDFORD

ALEXANDER Cinema 5, 1968
VLADIMIR COSMA

ALEXANDER NEVSKY Amkino, 1938
SERGEI PROKOFIEV†

ALEXANDER'S RAGTIME BAND 20th Century-Fox, 1938
ALFRED NEWMAN† ★★

ALEXANDER: THE OTHER SIDE OF DAWN (TF) Douglas Cramer Productions, 1977
FRED KARLIN

ALFIE DARLING *OH! ALFIE* EMI Films, 1975
ALAN PRICE

ALFRED HITCHCOCK PRESENTS (TF) Universal TV, 1985
PETER BERNSTEIN
JOHN GOUX
BASIL POLEDOURIS
CRAIG SAFAN

ALFREDO ALFREDO Paramount, 1973
CARLO RUSTICHELLI

ALI BABA AND THE FORTY THIEVES Universal, 1944
EDWARD WARD†

ALIAS BULLDOG DRUMMOND 1935
LOUIS LEVY†

ALIAS NICK BEAL Paramount, 1949
FRANZ WAXMAN†

ALIAS THE DEACON Universal, 1940
HANS J. SALTER†

ALI-BABA ET LES 40 VOLEURS 1954
PAUL MISRAKI

ALICE ADAMS RKO Radio, 1935
MAX STEINER†

ALICE DOESN'T LIVE HERE ANYMORE Warner Bros., 1974
RICHARD LASALLE

ALICE IN WONDERLAND 1951
SOL KAPLAN

ALICE IN WONDERLAND Paramount, 1933
DIMITRI TIOMKIN†

ALICE IN WONDERLAND (AF) RKO Radio, 1951
OLIVER WALLACE† ★

ALICE IN WONDERLAND (TF) Irwin Allen Productions/Procter & Gamble Productions/Columbia TV, 1985
MORTON STEVENS†

ALICE OR THE LAST ESCAPADE Filmel/PHPG, 1977
PIERRE JANSEN

ALICE OU LA DERNIERE FUGUE *ALICE OR THE LAST ESCAPADE* Filmel/PHPG, 1977
PIERRE JANSEN

ALICE'S ADVENTURES IN WONDERLAND American National Enterprises, 1972
JOHN BARRY

ALICE'S RESTAURANT United Artists, 1969
GARRY SHERMAN

ALICE, SWEET ALICE *COMMUNION/HOLY TERROR* Allied Artists, 1977
STEPHEN LAWRENCE

ALIEN 20th Century-Fox, 1979
JERRY GOLDSMITH

ALIEN CONTAMINATION Cannon, 1980
GOBLIN

ALIEN FROM L.A. Cannon, 1989
TONY RIPPARETTI

ALIEN INTRUDER PM Entertainment, 1992
MIRIAM CUTLER

ALIEN NATION 20th Century Fox, 1988
CURT SOBEL

ALIEN NATION: DARK HORIZONS (TF) Foxstar/Kenneth Johnson Prods., 1994
DAVID KURTZ

ALIEN PREDATOR Trans World Entertainment, 1987
TOM CHASE
STEVE RUCKER

ALIEN THUNDER 1973
GEORGES DELERUE†

THE ALIEN WITHIN AIP, 1991
CHUCK CIRINO

THE ALIEN'S RETURN 1981
DAN WYMAN

ALIEN³ 20th Century Fox, 1992
ELLIOT GOLDENTHAL

ALIEN: RESURRECTION 20th Century Fox, 1997
JOHN FRIZZELL

ALIENATOR AIP, 1988
CHUCK CIRINO

ALIENS 20th Century Fox, 1986
JAMES HORNER ★

THE ALIENS ARE COMING (TF) Woodruff Productions/QM Productions, 1980
WILLIAM GOLDSTEIN

ALIKI Funos-Aquarius, 1963
MANOS HADJIDAKIS†

ALIVE Buena Vista, 1993
JAMES NEWTON HOWARD

ALL ABOUT EVE 20th Century-Fox, 1950
ALFRED NEWMAN† ★

ALL ASHORE Columbia, 1953
GEORGE DUNING

ALL CREATURES GREAT AND SMALL (TF) Talent Associates Ltd./EMI, 1975
WILFRED JOSEPHS

ALL DOGS GO TO HEAVEN (AF) MGM/UA, 1989
RALPH BURNS

ALL DOGS GO TO HEAVEN 2 (AF) MGM-UA, 1996
MARK WATTERS

ALL FALL DOWN MGM, 1962
ALEX NORTH†

ALL GOD'S CHILDREN (TF) Blinn-Thorpe Productions/Viacom, 1980
BILLY GOLDENBERG

ALL HANDS ON DECK 20th Century-Fox, 1961
CYRIL J. MOCKRIDGE†

ALL I DESIRE Universal, 1953
HENRY MANCINI†
HERMAN STEIN

ALL I WANT FOR CHRISTMAS Paramount, 1991
BRUCE BROUGHTON

ALL IN A NIGHT'S WORK Paramount, 1961
ANDRE PREVIN

ALL MINE TO GIVE *THE DAY THEY GAVE BABIES AWAY* Universal, 1958
MAX STEINER†

ALL MY SONS Universal, 1948
LEITH STEVENS†

ALL NIGHT LONG Universal, 1981
RICHARD HAZARD
IRA NEWBORN

ALL OF ME Universal, 1984
PATRICK WILLIAMS

ALL OUT *DE PLEIN FOUET* 1991
JEAN-CLAUDE PETIT

ALL QUIET ON THE WESTERN FRONT Universal, 1930
DAVID BROEKMAN†

ALL QUIET ON THE WESTERN FRONT (TF) Norman Rosemont Productions/Marble Arch Productions, 1979
ALLYN FERGUSON

ALL SCREWED UP *TUTTO A POSTO, NIENTE IN ORDINE* New Line Cinema, 1974
PIERO PICCIONI

ALL THAT HEAVEN ALLOWS Universal, 1956
FRANK SKINNER†

ALL THAT JAZZ 20th Century Fox, 1979
RALPH BURNS ★★

ALL THAT MONEY CAN BUY *THE DEVIL AND DANIEL WEBSTER* RKO Radio, 1941
BERNARD HERRMANN† ★★

ALL THE COLORS OF DARKNESS/THEY'RE COMING TO GET YOU 1972
BRUNO NICOLAI

ALL THE FINE YOUNG CANNIBALS MGM, 1960
JEFF ALEXANDER†

ALL THE GOLD IN THE WORLD 1961
GEORGES VAN PARYS†

ALL THE KING'S HORSES Paramount, 1935
MILAN RODER†

ALL THE KING'S MEN Columbia, 1949
LOUIS GRUENBERG†

ALL THE LOVING COUPLES U-M, 1968
LES BAXTER†

...ALL THE MARBLES MGM/United Artists, 1981
FRANK DEVOL

ALL THE PRESIDENT'S MEN Warner Bros., 1976
DAVID SHIRE

ALL THE RIGHT MOVES 20th Century Fox, 1983
DAVID CAMPBELL

ALL THE RIVERS RUN (CMS) Crawford Productions/Nine Network, 1984
BRUCE ROWLAND

ALL THE RIVERS RUN II (CTF) Crawford Productions/HBO, 1989
BRUCE ROWLAND

ALL THE WAY Paramount, 1957
WALTER SCHARF

ALL THE WAY HOME Paramount, 1963
BERNARD GREEN

F
I
L
M

T
I
T
L
E
S

ALL THESE WOMEN   Janus, 1964
ERIC NORDGREN

ALL THIS AND HEAVEN TOO   Warner Bros., 1940
MAX STEINER†

ALL THROUGH THE NIGHT   Warner Bros., 1941
ADOLPH DEUTSCH†

ALL TOGETHER NOW (TF)   RSO Films, 1975
JOHN RUBINSTEIN

ALL'S FAIR   Moviestore Entertainment, 1989
BILL MYERS

ALL'S FAIR IN LOVE & WAR   Star Land, 1996
GENE OBER

**ALLA MIA CARA MAMMA NEL GIORNO DEL SUO
COMPLEANNO**   1974
FRANCO MICALIZZI

THE ALL-AMERICAN WOMAN   Conde Enterprises,
1974
BRUCE KIMMEL

ALL-AMERICAN CHUMP   MGM, 1936
WILLIAM AXT†

ALL-AMERICAN CO-ED   United Artists, 1941
EDWARD WARD† ★

ALL-AMERICAN MURDER   1992
ROD SLANE

**ALLAN QUARTERMAIN AND THE LOST CITY OF
GOLD**   Cannon, 1987
MICHAEL J. LINN†

ALLEGHENY UPRISING   RKO Radio, 1939
ANTHONY COLLINS†

ALLERGIC TO LOVE   Universal, 1944
HANS J. SALTER†

ALLES IN EIMER   West German
JURGEN KNIEPER

THE ALLIGATOR PEOPLE   20th Century-Fox, 1959
IRVING GERTZ

ALLIGATOR   Group 1, 1980
CRAIG HUNDLEY

THE ALLNIGHTER   Universal, 1987
CHARLES BERNSTEIN

ALLONSANFAN   Cinematographic Cooperative, 1975
ENNIO MORRICONE

ALLORA IL TRENO   1974
BRUNO NICOLAI

ALMA'S RAINBOW   Paradise Plum, 1994
JEAN-PAUL BOURELLY

ALMOST AN ANGEL   Paramount, 1990
MAURICE JARRE

ALMOST GROWN (TF)   Universal TV/Atlantis Films,
1988
CRAIG SAFAN

ALMOST HOLLYWOOD   Crown, 1994
CARLO JEAN PAUL CHANEZ

ALMOST PARTNERS (TF)   South Carolina
Educational TV Network, 1987
PAUL CHIHARA

AN ALMOST PERFECT AFFAIR   Paramount, 1979
GEORGES DELERUE†

ALMOST SUMMER   Universal, 1978
RON ALTBACH
CHARLES LLOYD

ALMOST YOU   20th Century-Fox, 1984
JONATHAN ELIAS

ALOHA MEANS GOODBYE (TF)   Universal TV,
1974
CHARLES FOX

ALOHA SUMMER   Spectrafilm, 1988
JESSE FREDERICK
BENNETT SALVAY

ALOMA OF THE SOUTH SEAS   Paramount, 1941
VICTOR YOUNG†

ALONE   1930
DMITRI SHOSTAKOVITCH†

ALONE AGAINST ROME   *SOLO CONTRO
ROMA*   1962
ARMANDO TROVAJOLI

ALONE IN THE DARK   New Line Cinema, 1982
RENATO SERIO

ALONE IN THE NEON JUNGLE (TF)   Robert Halmi
Inc., 1988
MARK SNOW

ALONE IN THE PACIFIC   1963
TORU TAKEMITSU†

ALONG CAME A SPIDER (TF)   20th Century-Fox TV,
1970
DAVID ROSE†

ALONG THE GREAT DIVIDE   Warner Bros., 1951
DAVID BUTTOLPH†

ALPHABET CITY   Atlantic Releasing, 1984
NILE RODGERS

THE ALPHABET MURDERS   *THE A.B.C.
MURDERS*   MGM, 1966
RON GOODWIN

ALPHAVILLE   Pathe Contemporary, 1965
PAUL MISRAKI

ALRAUNE   1952
WERNER R. HEYMANN†

ALRAUNE   *DAUGHTER OF EVIL*   1930
BRONISLAU KAPER†

ALTERED STATES   Warner Bros., 1980
JOHN CORIGLIANO

ALTISSIMA PRESSIONE   1965
LUIS BACALOV
ENNIO MORRICONE

ALTRI TEMPI   1951
ALESSANDRO CICOGNINI†

ALVAREZ KELLY   Columbia, 1966
JOHN GREEN†

ALWAYS   Universal, 1989
JOHN WILLIAMS

ALWAYS A BRIDE   1954
BENJAMIN FRANKEL†

ALWAYS IN MY HEART   Warner Bros., 1942
HEINZ ROEMHELD†

ALWAYS TOGETHER   Warner Bros., 1948
WERNER R. HEYMANN†

AMANTI   MGM, 1968
MANUEL DE SICA

AMANTI D'OLTRE TOMBA   1965
ENNIO MORRICONE

AMANTI SENZA AMORE   1947
NINO ROTA†

AMARCORD   New World, 1974
NINO ROTA†

THE AMATEUR   20th Century-Fox, 1982
KEN WANNBERG

AMATEUR   1994
NED RIFLE
JEFFREY TAYLOR

AMATEUR GENTLEMAN   United Artists, 1936
RICHARD ADDINSELL†
WALTER GOEHR†

THE AMAZING COLOSSAL MAN   American
International, 1957
ALBERT GLASSER

THE AMAZING DOBERMANS   Golden, 1976
ALAN SILVESTRI

THE AMAZING DR. CLITTERHOUSE   Warner Bros.,
1938
MAX STEINER†

AMAZING GRACE   United Artists, 1974
COLERIDGE-TAYLOR PERKINSON

AMAZING GRACE AND CHUCK   Tri-Star, 1987
ELMER BERNSTEIN

THE AMAZING HOWARD HUGHES (TF)   Roger
Gimbel Productions/EMI TV, 1977
LAURENCE ROSENTHAL

THE AMAZING MR. BEECHAM   1948
BENJAMIN FRANKEL†

THE AMAZING MR. BLUNDEN   Goldstone, 1972
ELMER BERNSTEIN

THE AMAZING MRS. HOLLIDAY   Universal, 1943
HANS J. SALTER† ★
FRANK SKINNER† ★

THE AMAZING PANDA ADVENTURE   Warner
Bros., 1995
WILLIAM ROSS

THE AMAZING SPIDERMAN (TF)   Charles Fries
Productions/Dan Goodman Productions, 1977
JOHN SPENCE

AMAZON   1992
NANA VASCONCELOS

AMAZON WOMEN ON THE MOON   Universal,
1987
IRA NEWBORN

**AMAZONIA: VOICES FROM THE RAIN FOREST
(FD)**   Amazonia, 1991
EGBERTO GISMONTI

THE AMAZONS   EMI, 1973
RIZ ORTOLANI

AMAZONS (TF)   ABC Circle Films, 1984
BASIL POLEDOURIS

THE AMBASSADOR   MGM-UA/Cannon, 1984
ALFI KABILJO
DOV SELTZER

AMBER WAVES (TF)   Time-Life Productions, 1980
JOHN RUBINSTEIN

AMBITION   Miramax, 1991
LEONARD ROSENMAN

THE AMBULANCE   Esparza-Katz Productions, 1990
JAY CHATTAWAY

AMBULANCE   1962
CHRISTOPHER KOMEDA†

AMBUSH AT CIMARRON PASS   20th Century-Fox,
1958
PAUL SAWTELL
BERT A. SHEFTER

AMBUSH BAY   United Artists, 1966
RICHARD LASALLE

AN AMBUSH OF GHOSTS   Stress Fiesta, 1993
KLIVE AND NIGEL HUMBERSTONE

AMELIA EARHART (TF)   Universal TV, 1976
DAVID SHIRE

AMELIA EARHART: THE FINAL FLIGHT (CTF)
Avenue Pictures, 1994
GEORGE S. CLINTON

AMERICA   ASA Communications, 1986
LEON PENDARVIS

AMERICA   United Artists, 1924
JOSEPH CARL BREIL†

AMERICA - PAESE DI DIO (FD)   1966
FRANCESCO LAVAGNINO
ARMANDO TROVAJOLI

AMERICA 3000   Cannon, 1986
TONY BERG

**AMERICA AND THE HOLOCAUST: DECEIT AND
INDIFFERENCE (TD)**   American Experience, 1994
SHELDON MIROWITZ

AMERICA AT THE MOVIES (FD)   American Film
Institute, 1976
NELSON RIDDLE†

AMERICA'S DISINHERITED   Sharecropper
Committee, 1937
PAUL BOWLES

AMERICA'S PEOPLE   Dana Productions
ANDREA SAPAROFF

AMERICA'S WAR ON POVERTY (TD)   Blackside
Inc., 1995
NIK BARILUK
BRIAN KEANE

AMERICA, AMERICA   Warner Bros., 1963
MANOS HADJIDAKIS†

AMERICA...COSI NUDA, COSI VIOLENTA   1970
BRUNO NICOLAI

AMERICAN ANTHEM   Columbia, 1986
ALAN SILVESTRI

AMERICAN BUFFALO   Samuel Goldwyn, 1996
THOMAS NEWMAN

AMERICAN BUILT   Midwood Productions, 1989
JAY FERGUSON

AMERICAN CYBORG: STEEL WARRIOR   Cannon,
1994
BLAKE LEYH

AN AMERICAN DREAM   Warner Bros., 1966
JOHNNY MANDEL

AMERICAN DREAM (FD)   Miramax, 1989
MICHAEL SMALL

AMERICAN DREAM (TF)   Mace Neufeld
Productions/Viacom, 1981
ARTIE BUTLER

AMERICAN DREAMER   Warner Bros., 1984
LEWIS FUREY

THE AMERICAN EXPERIENCE: FDR (TD)   David
Grubin Prods./WGBH-Boston, 1994
MICHAEL BACON

THE AMERICAN FRIEND   New Yorker, 1977
JURGEN KNIEPER

AMERICAN FLYERS   Warner Bros., 1985
GREG MATHIESON
LEE RITENOUR

AMERICAN GIGOLO   Paramount, 1980
GIORGIO MORODER

AMERICAN GOTHIC   Vestron, 1988
ALAN PARKER

AMERICAN GUERRILLA IN THE PHILIPPINES
20th Century-Fox, 1950
CYRIL J. MOCKRIDGE†

AMERICAN HARVEST (TF)   Ruth-Stratton
Productions/The Finnegan Company, 1987
CHRISTOPHER YOUNG

AN AMERICAN IN PARIS   MGM, 1951
JOHN GREEN† ★★

AMERICAN ME   Universal, 1992
CLAUDE GAUDETTE
DENNIS LAMBERT

AMERICAN NINJA   Cannon, 1985
GEORGE S. CLINTON

AMERICAN NINJA II   Cannon, 1985
MICHAEL J. LINN†

AMERICAN NINJA 3: BLOOD HUNT   Cannon,
1989
GEORGE S. CLINTON

AMERICAN NINJA IV: THE ANNIHILATION
Cannon, 1991
NICOLAS TENBROEK

AN AMERICAN PRESIDENT   1995
MARC SHAIMAN ★

AMERICAN PERFECT   Gramercy, 1997
SIMON BOSWELL

AMERICAN POP (AF)   Paramount, 1981
LEE HOLDRIDGE

AN AMERICAN ROMANCE   MGM, 1944
LOUIS GRUENBERG†

THE AMERICAN REVOLUTION (TD)   Greystone/
A&E, 1994
CHRISTOPHER L. STONE

AN AMERICAN STORY (TF)   Signboard Hill/RHI
Entertainment, 1992
MARK SNOW ☆

AN AMERICAN SUMMER   Bass Entertainment
Group, 1989
ROGER NEILL

THE AMERICAN SCREAM   Genesis Home Video,
1988
RICHARD COX

THE AMERICAN SOLDIER   New Yorker, 1970
PEER RABEN

THE AMERICAN SUCCESS COMPANY   *SUCCESS*
Columbia, 1979
MAURICE JARRE

AN AMERICAN TAIL: FIEVEL GOES WEST (AF)
Universal, 1991
JAMES HORNER

AN AMERICAN WEREWOLF IN LONDON
Universal, 1981
ELMER BERNSTEIN

AMERICANA   Crown International, 1981
DAVID CARRADINE
CRAIG HUNDLEY

AN AMERICANCHRISTMAS CAROL (TF)
Scherick/Chase/Slan Productions/Smith-Hemion
Productions/Scrooge Productions, 1979
HAGOOD HARDY

AMERICANGEISHA (TF)   Interscope
Communications/Stonehenge Productions, 1986
MILES GOODMAN†

AMERICANHEART   Avenue Pictures, 1992
JAMES NEWTON HOWARD

THE AMERICANIZATION OF EMILY   MGM, 1964
JOHNNY MANDEL

THE AMERICANO   Columbia, 1955
ROY WEBB†

AMERICANROULETTE   Film Four International/
British Screen/Mandemar Group, 1988
MICHAEL GIBBS

AN AMERICANTAIL (AF)   Universal, 1986
JAMES HORNER

AMERICAS (TD)   WGBH/Central Television, 1993
JUAN LUIS GUERRA

AMERICATHON   United Artists, 1979
EARL BROWN, JR
TOM SCOTT

AMERIKA (MS)   ABC Circle Films, 1987
BASIL POLEDOURIS

AMICI MIEII II   Sacis, 1982
CARLO RUSTICHELLI

AMICI PER LA PELLE   1955
NINO ROTA†

AMIGOMIO   1993
OSVALDO MONTES

THE AMITYVILLE HORROR   American International,
1979
LALO SCHIFRIN ★

AMITYVILLE 3-D   Orion, 1983
HOWARD BLAKE

AMITYVILLE DOLLHOUSE   Spectacor Films, 1996
RAY COLCORD

AMITYVILLE II: THE POSSESSION   Orion, 1982
HOWARD BLAKE

AMITYVILLE: THE EVIL ESCAPES (TF)   Steve White
Productions/Spectacor, 1989
RICK CONRAD

AMMAZZALI TUTTI E TORNA SOLO   1968
FRANCESCO DE MASI

AMONGST FRIENDS   Islet, 1993
MICK JONES

AMORE   LDC Films, 1993
HARVEY R. COHEN

AMORE E GIMNISTICA   1973
ARMANDO TROVAJOLI

AMORE LIBERO   1974
FABIO FRIZZI

AMORE MIEI   1979
ARMANDO TROVAJOLI

AMORI PERICOLOSI   1964
CARLO RUSTICHELLI

**THE AMOROUS ADVENTURES OF MOLL
FLANDERS**   Paramount, 1965
JOHN ADDISON

THE AMOROUS MR. PRAWN   British Lion, 1964
JOHN BARRY

AMOS (TF)   The Bryna Company/Vincent Pictures,
1985
GEORGES DELERUE†

AMOS AND ANDREW   Columbia, 1993
RICHARD GIBBS

AMSTERDAM AFFAIR   Lippert, 1968
JOHN SCOTT

AMY   Buena Vista, 1981
ROBERT F. BRUNNER

AMY FISHER: MY STORY (TF)   KLM/Spectacor/
Michael Jaffe Films, 1992
FRED MOLLIN

AMY FOSTER   1997
JOHN BARRY

ANACONDA   Columbia, 1997
RANDY EDELMAN

ANASTASIA   20th Century-Fox, 1956
ALFRED NEWMAN† ★

ANASTASIA: THE MYSTERY OF ANNA (TF)
Telecom Entertainment/Consolidated Productions/
Reteitalia, 1986
LAURENCE ROSENTHAL II

ANA-TA-HAN   1953
AKIRA IFUKUBE

ANATOMY OF A MURDER   Columbia, 1959
DUKE ELLINGTON†

ANATOMY OF A SEDUCTION (TF)   Moonlight
Productions/Filmways, 1979
HAGOOD HARDY

ANATOMY OF AN ILLNESS (TF)   Hamner
Productions/Jerry Gershwin Productions/CBS
Entertainment, 1984
BRAD FIEDEL

ANATOMY OF LOVE (TD)   TBS Prods./Primedia
Prods., 1995
AARON DAVIS
JOHN LANG

ANCHE SE VOLESSI LAVORARE, CHE COSA FACCIO? 1972
ENNIO MORRICONE

ANCIENT PROPHECIES (TD) Coast-to Coast Prods./Greystone PRods., 1994
CHRISTOPHER L. STONE

AND BABY MAKES SIX (TF) Alan Landsburg Productions, 1979
FRED KARLIN

AND BABY MAKES THREE Columbia, 1949
GEORGE DUNING

AND GOD CREATED WOMAN Kingsley International, 1956
PAUL MISRAKI

AND GOD CREATED WOMAN Vestron, 1988
TOM CHASE
STEVE RUCKER

...AND HOPE TO DIE *LA COURSE DU LIEVRE A TRAVERS LES CHAMPS* 20th Century-Fox, 1972
FRANCIS LAI

AND I ALONE SURVIVED (TF) Jerry Leider/OJL Productions, 1978
LAURENCE ROSENTHAL

...AND JUSTICE FOR ALL Columbia, 1979
DAVE GRUSIN

AND NO ONE COULD SAVE HER (TF) Associated London Films, 1973
RON GRAINER†

AND NOW MIGUEL Paramount, 1966
PHILLIP LAMBRO

AND NOW MY LOVE *TOUTE UNE VIE* Avco Embassy, 1975
FRANCIS LAI

AND NOW THE SCREAMING STARTS Cinerama Releasing Corporation, 1973
DOUGLAS GAMLEY

AND NOW TOMORROW Paramount, 1944
VICTOR YOUNG†

AND ONCE UPON A TIME *FANTASIES* Joseph Brenner Associates, 1973
JEFFREY SILVERMAN

AND ONE WAS BEAUTIFUL MGM, 1940
DANIELE AMFITHEATROF†

AND PIGS MUST FLY (TF) S4C, 1984
TREVOR JONES

AND THE BAND PLAYED ON (CTF) HBO Pictures, 1993
CARTER BURWELL

AND THE CHILDREN SHALL LEAD (TF) Rainbow TV Workshop, 1985
GREG POREE

AND THE SEA WILL TELL (TF) Green-Epstein/Columbia TV, 1991
PETER MANNING ROBINSON

AND THE SHIP SAILS ON Triumph/Columbia, 1983
GIANFRANCO PLENIZIO

AND THEN SHE WAS GONE (TF) Steve White Prods., 1991
PETER MANNING ROBINSON

AND THEN THERE WAS NONE 20th Century-Fox, 1945
MARIO†

AND THEN THERE WAS ONE (TF) Freyda Rothstein Prods./Hearst, 1994
J.A.C. REDFORD

AND YOU THOUGHT YOUR PARENTS WERE WEIRD Trimark, 1991
RANDY MILLER

...AND YOUR NAME IS JONAH (TF) Charles Fries Productions, 1979
FRED KARLIN

ANDA MUCHACHO, SPARA! 1971
BRUNO NICOLAI

THE ANDERSON TAPES Columbia, 1971
QUINCY JONES

ANDERSONVILLE (CTF) TNT, 1995
GARY CHANG

ANDRE Paramount, 1994
BRUCE ROWLAND

ANDREI RUBLEV Columbia, 1968
VYECHESLAV OVCHINNIKOV

ANDROCLES AND THE LION RKO Radio, 1952
FREDERICK HOLLANDER†

ANDROID Island Alive/New Realm, 1982
DON PRESTON

THE ANDROMEDA STRAIN Universal, 1971
GIL MELLE

THE ANDY DEVINE STORY Film Buff Prods., 1989
NEIL ARGO

ANDY HARDY COMES HOME MGM, 1958
VAN ALEXANDER

ANDY HARDY GETS SPRING FEVER MGM, 1939
DAVID SNELL
EDWARD WARD†

ANDY HARDY'S DOUBLE LIFE MGM, 1942
DANIELE AMFITHEATROF†

ANDY HARDY'S PRIVATE SECRETARY MGM, 1941
HERBERT STOTHART†

ANDY WARHOL'S DRACULA *BLOOD FOR DRACULA* Bryanston, 1974
CLAUDIO GIZZI

ANDY WARHOL'S FRANKENSTEIN *FLESH FOR FRANKENSTEIN* Bryanston, 1974
CLAUDIO GIZZI

ANGEL New World, 1984
CRAIG SAFAN

ANGEL Triumph/Columbia, 1983
PADDY MEEGAN

ANGEL AND THE BADMAN Republic, 1947
RICHARD HAGEMAN†

ANGEL BABY 1996
JOHN CLIFFORD WHITE

ANGEL CITY (TF) Factor-Newland Productions, 1980
MARK SNOW

ANGEL DUSTED (TF) NRW Features, 1980
JAMES HORNER

ANGEL EYES AIP, 1992
CHUCK CIRINO

ANGEL FACE RKO Radio, 1953
DIMITRI TIOMKIN†

ANGEL FALLS (TF) Konigsberg-Sanitsky, 1993
CHRISTOPHER FRANKE

ANGEL HEART Tri-Star, 1987
TREVOR JONES

ANGEL III: THE FINAL CHAPTER New World, 1988
ERIC ALLAMAN
ALAN ETT
BERLIN GAME
DON GREAT

ANGEL IN GREEN (TF) Aligre Productions/Taft Hardy Group, 1987
ALLYN FERGUSON

ANGEL OF DESIRE MCEG-Sterling, 1993
WENDY BLACKSTONE

ANGEL ON MY SHOULDER United Artists, 1946
DIMITRI TIOMKIN†

ANGEL ON MY SHOULDER (TF) Mace Neufeld Productions/Barney Rosenzweig Productions/Beowulf Productions, 1980
ARTIE BUTLER

ANGEL STREET 1939
RICHARD ADDINSELL†

ANGEL STREET (TF) John Wells & Friends/Warner Bros. TV, 1992
ANTHONY MARINELLI

ANGEL TOWN Taurus Entertainment Company, 1990
TERRY PLUMERI

ANGEL UNCHAINED American International, 1972
JIM HELMS

THE ANGEL WHO PAWNED HER HARP 1954
ANTONY HOPKINS

THE ANGEL WORE RED MGM, 1960
BRONISLAU KAPER†

ANGEL'S TIDE Mont Peru Prods., 1994
ANDREW GROSS

ANGELA Embassy Home Entertainment, 1976
HENRY MANCINI†

ANGELA Tree Farm Pictures, 1995
MICHAEL ROKATYN

ANGELA *LOVE COMES QUIETLY* 1973
GEORGES DELERUE†

ANGELICA 1938
JACQUES IBERT†

ANGELIQUE ET LE ROI 1966
MICHEL MAGNE†

ANGELIQUE ET LE SULTAN 1969
MICHEL MAGNE†

ANGELO, MY LOVE Cinecom, 1983
MICHAEL KAMEN

ANGELS AND INSECTS Samuel Goldwyn, 1995
ALEXANDER BALANESCU

ANGELS FROM HELL American International, 1968
STU PHILLIPS

ANGELS IN THE OUTFIELD Buena Vista, 1994
RANDY EDELMAN

ANGELS IN THE OUTFIELD MGM, 1951
DANIELE AMFITHEATROF†

ANGELS OVER BROADWAY Columbia, 1940
GEORGE ANTHEIL†

ANGELS WASH THEIR FACES Warner Bros., 1939
ADOLPH DEUTSCH†

ANGELS WITH DIRTY FACES Warner Bros., 1938
MAX STEINER†

ANGELS: THE MYSTERIOUS MESSENGERS (TD) American Artists Prods./Greystone Comm., 1994
CHRISTOPHER L. STONE

ANGIE Buena Vista, 1994
JERRY GOLDSMITH

ANGKOR-CAMBODIA EXPRESS Monarex Hollywood, 1981
STELVIO CIPRIANI

ANGLAGARD: ANDRA SOMMAREN 1995
BJORN ISFALT

THE ANGRY HILLS MGM, 1959
RICHARD RODNEY BENNETT

THE ANGRY MAN 1979
CLAUDE BOLLING

THE ANGRY RED PLANET American International, 1960
PAUL DUNLAP

THE ANGRY SILENCE Valiant, 1960
MALCOLM ARNOLD

ANGUS New Line, 1995
DAVID RUSSO

ANIMA PERSA Dean Film/Les Productions Fox Europe, 1977
FRANCIS LAI

THE ANIMAL 1977
VLADIMIR COSMA

ANIMAL BEHAVIOR Millimeter Films, 1989
CLIFF EIDELMAN

ANIMAL FARM (AF) 1954
MATYAS SEIBER

THE ANIMAL KINGDOM RKO Radio, 1932
MAX STEINER†

THE ANIMALS 1971
RUPERT HOLMES

ANKOR, ESCHYO ANKOR! *ENCORE, ONCE MORE ENCORE!* 1993
PYOTR TODOROVSKY

ANN VICKERS RKO Radio, 1933
MAX STEINER†

ANNA Italian Films Export, 1951
NINO ROTA†

ANNA Vestron, 1987
GREG HAWKES

ANNA 6-18 1994
EDUARD ARTEMYEV

ANNA AND THE KING OF SIAM 20th Century-Fox, 1946
BERNARD HERRMANN† ★

ANNA AND THE WOLVES 1973
LUIS DE PABLO

ANNA DE BROOKLYN 1958
ALESSANDRO CICOGNINI†

ANNA KARAMAZOVA 1991
ALEXANDER VUSTIN

ANNA KARENINA MGM, 1935
HERBERT STOTHART†

ANNA KARENINA (TF) Rastar Productions/Colgems Productions, 1985
PATRICK GOWERS

ANNA LEE: DUPE Carnival Films, 1994
ANNE DUDLEY

ANNA LUCASTA Columbia, 1949
DAVID DIAMOND

ANNA LUCASTA United Artists, 1958
ELMER BERNSTEIN

ANNABEL TAKES A TOUR RKO Radio, 1938
ROBERT RUSSELL BENNETT†

ANNE (TF) 1978
VLADIMIR COSMA

ANNE DEVLIN Aeon Films, 1984
ROBERT BOYLE

ANNE FRANK REMEMBERED (FD) Sony Classics, 1996
CARL DAVIS

ANNE OF A THOUSAND DAYS Universal, 1969
GEORGES DELERUE† ★

ANNE OF AVONLEA: THE CONTINUING STORY OF ANNE OF GREEN GABLES (MS) Sullivan Films/CBC/The Disney Channel/PBS WonderWorks/Telefilm Canada, 1987
HAGOOD HARDY

ANNE OF GREEN GABLES RKO Radio, 1934
MAX STEINER†

ANNE OF GREEN GABLES (MS) Anne of Green Gables Productions/PBS WonderWorks/CBS/60 Film Productions/ZDF/City TV/Telefilm Canada, 1985
HAGOOD HARDY

ANNE OF THE INDIES 20th Century-Fox, 1951
FRANZ WAXMAN†

ANNE OF WINDY POPLARS RKO Radio, 1940
ROY WEBB†

ANNE-MARIE 1936
JACQUES IBERT†

ANNI DIFICILI 1953
NINO ROTA†

ANNI RUGGENTI 1962
PIERO PICCIONI

ANNIBALE 1958
CARLO RUSTICHELLI

ANNIE Columbia, 1982
RALPH BURNS ★

ANNIE GET YOUR GUN MGM, 1950
ADOLPH DEUTSCH† ★★

ANNIE LAURIE MGM, 1927
WILLIAM AXT†

ANNIE: A ROYAL ADVENTURE (TF) Rastar/TriStar TV, 1995
DAVID MICHAEL FRANK

ANNIE'S GARDEN Curb, 1994
BRUCE LANGHORNE

THE ANNIHILATOR (TF) Universal TV, 1986
UDI HARPAZ
SYLVESTER LEVAY

THE ANNIHILATORS New World, 1986
ROBERT SUMMERS

ANNO DOMINI 1573 1976
ALFI KABILJO

ANONIMA COCOTTES *THE CALL-GIRL BUSINESS* 1960
ARMANDO TROVAJOLI

THE ANONYMOUS VENETIAN 1970
STELVIO CIPRIANI

ANOTHER 48 HOURS Paramount, 1990
JAMES HORNER

ANOTHER COUNTRY Orion Classics, 1984
MICHAEL STOREY

ANOTHER DAWN Warner Bros., 1937
ERICH WOLFGANG KORNGOLD†

ANOTHER FACE RKO Radio, 1935
ROY WEBB†

ANOTHER LIFE DocuStudio, Kiev, 1974
VLADIMIR HORUNZHY

ANOTHER MAN'S POISON United Artists, 1952
JOHN GREENWOOD†

ANOTHER MAN, ANOTHER CHANCE United Artists, 1977
FRANCIS LAI

ANOTHER PAIR OF ACES: THREE OF A KIND (TF) Pedernales/Once Upon A Time Films, 1991
JAY GRUSKA
SHELBY LYNNE

ANOTHER PART OF THE FOREST Universal, 1948
DANIELE AMFITHEATROF†

ANOTHER SHORE 1948
GEORGES AURIC†

ANOTHER STAKEOUT Buena Vista, 1993
ARTHUR B. RUBINSTEIN

ANOTHER THIN MAN MGM, 1939
EDWARD WARD†

ANOTHER TIME, ANOTHER PLACE Paramount, 1958
DOUGLAS GAMLEY

ANOTHER WOMAN'S CHILD (TF) CBS Entertainment, 1983
BILLY GOLDENBERG

ANOTHER YOU Tri-Star, 1991
CHARLES GROSS

ANTARTICA TLC Films, 1984
VANGELIS

ANTHONY ADVERSE Warner Bros., 1936
ERICH WOLFGANG KORNGOLD† ★★

ANTICHRIST/THE TEMPTER 1974
ENNIO MORRICONE
BRUNO NICOLAI

ANTINEA - L'AMANTE DELLA CITTA SEPOLTA Embassy, 1961
CARLO RUSTICHELLI

ANTONIA AND JANE Miramax, 1991
RACHEL PORTMAN

ANTONIA'S LINE 1996
ILONA SEKACZ

ANTONY AND CLEOPATRA Rank, 1973
JOHN SCOTT

ANY MAN'S DEATH INI Entertainment, 1990
JEREMY LUBBOCK

ANY NUMBER CAN WIN *MELODIE EN SOUS-SOL* MGM, 1963
MICHEL MAGNE†

ANY SECOND NOW (TF) Public Arts Productions/Universal TV, 1969
LEONARD ROSENMAN

ANY WEDNESDAY Warner Bros., 1966
GEORGE DUNING

ANY WHICH WAY YOU CAN Warner Bros., 1981
SNUFF GARRETT

ANYONE CAN PLAY *LE DOLCE SIGNORE* 1967
ARMANDO TROVAJOLI

ANYTHING CAN HAPPEN Paramount, 1952
VICTOR YOUNG†

ANYTHING TO SURVIVE (TF) ATL Productions/B.C. Films, 1990
MICHAEL CONWAY BAKER

ANZACS: THE WAR DOWN UNDER (MS) Orbis Communications/Hal Roach Studios, 1987
BRUCE ROWLAND

ANZIO Columbia, 1968
RIZ ORTOLANI

APACHE United Artists, 1954
DAVID RAKSIN

APACHE CHIEF Lippert, 1949
ALBERT GLASSER

APACHE DRUMS Universal, 1951
HANS J. SALTER†

APACHE RIFLES 20th Century-Fox, 1964
RICHARD LASALLE

APACHE TRAIL MGM, 1943
SOL KAPLAN

APACHE UPRISING Paramount, 1966
JIMMIE HASKELL

APACHE WARRIOR 20th Century-Fox, 1957
PAUL DUNLAP

THE APACHE WOMAN American International, 1955
RONALD STEIN†

APARAJITO 1958
RAVI SHANKAR

THE APARTMENT United Artists, 1960
ADOLPH DEUTSCH†

APARTMENT FOR PEGGY 20th Century-Fox, 1948
DAVID RAKSIN

APARTMENT ZERO Summit Company Ltd., 1988
ELIA CMIRAL

THE APE WOMAN Embassy, 1964
TEO USUELLI

APEX Republic, 1994
JIM GOODWIN

APOCALYPSE NOW United Artists, 1979
CARMINE COPPOLA†★

APOLLO 13 Universal, 1995
JAMES HORNER ★

APOLLO 13: TO THE EDGE AND BACK (TD)
WGBH Boston/TV Asahi/Central TV, 1994
SHELDON MIROWITZ

APOLOGY (CTF) Roger Gimbel Productions/
Peregrine Entertainment Ltd./ASAP Productions/HBO
Pictures, 1986
MAURICE JARRE

APOLOGY FOR MURDER Producers Releasing
Corp., 1945
LEO ERDODY†

THE APPALOOSA Universal, 1966
FRANK SKINNER†

APPASSIONATA 1974
PIERO PICCIONI

APPEARANCES (TF) Echo Cove Productions/
Touchstone TV, 1990
JOEL McNEELY

THE APPLE Cannon, 1980
COBY RECHT
IRIS RECHT

THE APPLE DUMPLING GANG Buena Vista, 1975
BUDDY BAKER

THE APPLE DUMPLING GANG RIDES AGAIN
Buena Vista, 1979
BUDDY BAKER

APPLE PIE Aumont Productions, 1975
BRAD FIEDEL

THE APPOINTMENT MGM, 1969
JOHN BARRY
STU PHILLIPS

APPOINTMENT FOR LOVE Universal, 1941
FRANK SKINNER†

APPOINTMENT IN BERLIN Columbia, 1943
WERNER R. HEYMANN†

APPOINTMENT WITH A SHADOW Universal,
1958
HANS J. SALTER†

APPOINTMENT WITH DANGER Paramount, 1951
VICTOR YOUNG†

APPOINTMENT WITH DEATH Cannon, 1988
PINO DONAGGIO

APPOINTMENT WITH FEAR Galaxy International,
1985
ANDREA SAPAROFF

APPOINTMENT WITH MURDER Producers
Releasing Corp., 1948
KARL HAJOS†

APPOINTMENT WITH VENUS Universal, 1951
BENJAMIN FRANKEL†

THE APPRENTICESHIP OF DUDLEY KRAVITZ
Paramount, 1974
STANLEY MYERS†

APPRENTICE TO MURDER New World, 1988
CHARLES GROSS

THE APRIL FOOLS National General, 1969
MARVIN HAMLISCH

APRIL FOOL'S DAY Paramount, 1986
CHARLES BERNSTEIN

APRIL MORNING (TF) Robert Halmi, Inc./Samuel
Goldwyn TV, 1988
ALLYN FERGUSON ☆

APT PUPIL 1997
JOHN OTTMAN

THE AQUARIANS (TF) Universal TV, 1970
LALO SCHIFRIN

AQUI NA TERRA HERE ON EARTH 1993
ANTONIO PINHO VARGAS

ARAB AND JEW Rob Gardner Productions
DAVID SPEAR

ARABELLA Cram Film, 1967
ENNIO MORRICONE

ARABESQUE Universal, 1966
HENRY MANCINI†

ARABIAN ADVENTURE AFD, 1979
KEN THORNE

ARABIAN NIGHTS Universal, 1942
FRANK SKINNER†★

ARABISCHE NACHTE West German
JURGEN KNIEPER

ARACHNOPHOBIA Buena Vista, 1990
TREVOR JONES

ARASHI GA OKA ONIMARU Toho, 1988
TORU TAKEMITSU†

ARCADE Full Moon, 1993
TONY RIPPARETTI

ARCH OF TRIUMPH United Artists, 1948
LOUIS GRUENBERG†

ARCH OF TRIUMPH (TF) Newland-Raynor
Productions/HTV, 1985
GEORGES DELERUE†

THE ARCHER AND THE SORCERESS 1983
BRIAN GASCOIGNE

THE ARCHER—FUGITIVE FROM THE EMPIRE
FUGITIVE FROM THE EMPIRE (TF) Mad-Dog
Productions/Universal TV, 1981
IAN UNDERWOOD

ARCHIE: TO RIVERDALE AND BACK AGAIN (TF)
Patchett Kaufman Entertainment/DIC, 1990
MARK SNOW

ARCHIMEDE LE CLOCHARD 1958
JEAN PRODROMIDES

ARCTIC BLUE 1993
PETER RODGERS MELNICK

ARE HUSBANDS NECESSARY? Paramount, 1942
ROBERT EMMETT DOLAN†

ARE THESE OUR CHILDREN? RKO Radio, 1931
MAX STEINER†

ARE THEY STILL SHOOTING? It Takes Two, 1993
DYLAN MAULUCCI

ARE WE WINNING, MOMMY? AMERICA & THE
COLD WAR (FD) CineInformation/Canadian Film
Board, 1985
WENDY BLACKSTONE

ARE YOU IN THE HOUSE ALONE? (TF) Charles
Fries Productions, 1978
CHARLES BERNSTEIN

ARE YOU LONESOME TONIGHT ? (CTF) OTML
Prods./Mahoney Co./Wilshire Court, 1992
J. PETER ROBINSON

ARE YOU WITH IT? Universal, 1948
WALTER SCHARF

THE ARENA New World, 1974
FRANCESCO DE MASI

ARISE, MY LOVE Paramount, 1940
VICTOR YOUNG†★

THE ARISTOCATS (AF) Buena Vista, 1970
GEORGE BRUNS

ARIZONA Columbia, 1940
VICTOR YOUNG†★

ARIZONA BUSHWACKERS Paramount, 1967
JIMMIE HASKELL

ARIZONA COLT 1966
FRANCESCO DE MASI

ARIZONA CYCLONE Universal, 1941
HANS J. SALTER†

ARIZONA DREAM Kit Parker Films, 1995
GORAN BREGOVIC

ARIZONA HEAT Spectrum Entertainment/Overseas
Film Group, 1988
KEVIN KLINGER
GARY STOCKDALE

ARIZONA LEGION RKO Radio, 1939
ROY WEBB†

ARIZONA RAIDERS Columbia, 1965
RICHARD LASALLE

ARIZONA SI SCATENO...E LI FECE FUORI TUTTI
1970
BRUNO NICOLAI

ARIZONA TRAIL Universal, 1943
HANS J. SALTER†

THE ARIZONIAN RKO Radio, 1935
ROY WEBB†

A.R.M. AROUND MOSCOW (FD) Finley-Stoeltje,
1994
MARILYN S. ZALKAN

ARMAGUEDON 1977
ASTOR PIAZZOLA

ARMED & INNOCENT (TF) Gillian Prods./Republic,
1994
DENNIS MCCARTHY

ARMED AND DANGEROUS Columbia, 1986
JAMES DIPASQUALE
MICHAEL MELVOIN
BILL MEYERS

ARMED RESPONSE (CTF) Showtime, 1995
HUMMIE MANN

ARMIAMOCI E PARTITE! 1971
CARLO RUSTICHELLI

ARMORED ATTACK RKO Radio, 1943
AARON COPLAND†★

ARMOUR OF GOD II: OPERATION CONDOR
1992
PETER PAU

ARMY GIRL Republic, 1938
VICTOR YOUNG†★

ARMY OF DARKNESS: EVIL DEAD 3 Universal,
1992
JOSEPH LO DUCA
DANNY ELFMAN

ARMY SURGEON RKO Radio, 1942
ROY WEBB†

THE ARNELO AFFAIR MGM, 1947
GEORGE BASSMAN

ARNOLD Cinerama Releasing Corporation, 1973
GEORGE DUNING

AROUND THE WORLD IN 80 DAYS United Artists,
1956
VICTOR YOUNG†★★

AROUND THE WORLD IN 80 DAYS (MS)
Harmony Gold/ReteEuropa/Valente-Baerwald
Productions, 1989
BILLY GOLDENBERG

AROUND THE WORLD IN EIGHTY MINUTES
United Artists, 1931
ALFRED NEWMAN†

AROUND THE WORLD UNDER THE SEA MGM,
1966
HARRY SUKMAN†

THE ARRANGEMENT Warner Bros., 1969
DAVID AMRAM

ARRANGIATEVI Cineriz, 1959
CARLO RUSTICHELLI

ARRESTING GENA Good Machine, 1997
PAT IRWIN

ARRETEZ LES TAMBOURS 1960
GEORGES DELERUE†

THE ARRIVAL Live, 1996
ARTHUR KEMPEL

ARRIVANO I BERSAGLIERI 1980
ARMANDO TROVAJOLI

ARRIVANO I TITANI 1962
CARLO RUSTICHELLI

ARRIVEDERCI PAPA 1948
NINO ROTA†

ARRIVEDERCI, BABY! DROP DEAD, DARLING
Paramount, 1966
DENNIS FARNON

THE ARROW LA FRECCIA NEL FIANCO 1943
NINO ROTA†

ARROWSMITH United Artists, 1931
ALFRED NEWMAN†

ARSENAL 1971
VYECHESLAV OVCHINNIKOV

ARSENE LUPIN RETURNS MGM, 1938
FRANZ WAXMAN†

ARSENIC AND OLD LACE Warner Bros., 1944
MAX STEINER†

ART DECO DETECTIVE Trident, 1994
ALLAN ZAVOD

ART OF KILLING 1978
STOMU YAMASHITA

THE ART OF LOVE Universal, 1965
CY COLEMAN

ARTHUR Warner Bros., 1981
BURT BACHARACH

ARTHUR 2 - ON THE ROCKS Warner Bros., 1988
BURT BACHARACH

ARTHUR HAILEY'S 'THE MONEY-CHANGERS'
(MS) Ross Hunter Productions/Paramount Pictures
TV, 1976
HENRY MANCINI†

ARTHUR HAILEY'S WHEELS (MS) Universal TV,
1978
MORTON STEVENS ☆†

ARTHUR MILLER'S THE AMERICAN CLOCK (TF)
Amblin Entertainment and Michael Brandman Prods.,
1993
PAUL J. ZAZA

ARTHUR THE KING (TF) Martin Poll Productions/
Comworld Productions/Jadran Film, 1985
CHARLES GROSS

ARTICLE 99 Orion, 1992
DANNY ELFMAN

ARTISTS AND MODELS Paramount, 1955
WALTER SCHARF

ARTISTS AND MODELS ABROAD Paramount,
1938
LEO SHUKEN†

ARTURO'S ISLAND MGM, 1962
NINO ROTA†

ARTURO'S ISLAND MGM, 1962
CARLO RUSTICHELLI

AS AN EILEAN FROM THE ISLAND 1993
JIM SUTHERLAND

AS GOOD AS DEAD (CTF) Larco Prods./CNM Ent./
Wilshire Court, 1995
PATRICK O'HEARN

AS GOOD AS MARRIED 1937
DAVID RAKSIN

AS SUMMERS DIE (CTF) HBO Premiere Films/
Chris-Rose Productions/Baldwin/Aldrich Productions/
Lorimar-Telepictures Productions, 1986
MICHEL LEGRAND

AS YOU LIKE IT 20th Century-Fox, 1936
SIR WILLIAM WALTON†

AS YOU LIKE IT Buena Vista, 1992
MICHEL SANVOISIN

AS YOUNG AS YOU FEEL 20th Century-Fox, 1951
CYRIL J. MOCKRIDGE†

ASCENSEUR POUR L'ECHAFAUD Times, 1957
MILES DAVIS†

ASH WEDNESDAY Paramount, 1973
MAURICE JARRE

ASHAKARA 1993 Togolese
LOUIS CRELIER
SALLY NYOTO

ASHANTI Columbia, 1979
MICHAEL MELVOIN

ASHENDEN (CTF) Kelso Films/A&E/BBC, 1992
CARL DAVIS

ASK ANY GIRL MGM, 1959
JEFF ALEXANDER†

ASK ME AGAIN (TF) DBR Films Ltd./
AmericanPlayhouse, 1989
DICK HYMAN

ASPEN (MS) Universal TV, 1977
MICHAEL MELVOIN
TOM SCOTT

ASPEN EXTREME Buena Vista, 1993
MICHAEL CONVERTINO

THE ASPHALT JUNGLE MGM, 1950
MIKLOS ROZSA†

THE ASSAM GARDEN The Moving Picture Company,
1985
RICHARD HARVEY

THE ASSASSIN VENETIAN BIRD 1952
NINO ROTA†

THE ASSASSIN 1964
TORU TAKEMITSU†

ASSASSIN (TF) Sankan Productions, 1986
ANTHONY GUEFEN
GARRY SCHYMAN

THE ASSASSINATION BUREAU Paramount,
1969
RON GRAINER†

THE ASSASSINATION OF THE DUC DE GUISE Le
Film d'Art, 1908
CAMILLE SAINT-SAENS†

ASSASSINATION Cannon, 1987
VALENTINE MCCALLUM
ROBERT O. RAGLAND

ASSASSINIO SUL TEVERE 1980
CARLO RUSTICHELLI

ASSASSINO MADE IN ITALY 1963
ARMANDO TROVAJOLI

ASSASSINS Warner Bros., 1995
MARK MANCINA
JEFF RONA
JOHN VAN TONGEREN

ASSAULT Hemisphere, 1971
ERIC ROGERS†

ASSAULT AND MATRIMONY (TF) Michael
Filerman Productions/NBC Productions, 1987
JOHNNY MANDEL

ASSAULT AT WEST POINT (CTF) Ultra Ent./Mosaic
Group, 1994
TERENCE BLANCHARD

ASSAULT ON A QUEEN Paramount, 1966
DUKE ELLINGTON†

ASSAULT ON AGATHON Nine Network, 1976
KEN THORNE

ASSAULT ON PRECINCT 13 Turtle Releasing
Corporation, 1976
JOHN CARPENTER

ASSAULT ON THE WAYNE (TF) Paramount
Pictures TV, 1971
LEITH STEVENS†

ASSICURASI VERGINE 1967
CARLO RUSTICHELLI

ASSIGNED TO DANGER Eagle Lion, 1948
ALBERT GLASSER

ASSIGNMENT K Columbia, 1968
BASIL KIRCHIN

ASSIGNMENT TO KILL Warner Bros., 1968
WILLIAM LAVA†

ASSIGNMENT—PARIS Columbia, 1952
GEORGE DUNING

THE ASSISI UNDERGROUND Cannon, 1985
PINO DONAGGIO

THE ASSOCIATE Buena Vista, 1996
CHRISTOPHER TYNG

ASTERIX VS. CAESAR (AF) Gaumont, 1985
VLADIMIR COSMA

ASTEROID (TF) Davis Entertainment, 1997
SHIRLEY WALKER

THE ASTONISHED HEART GFD, 1950
SIR NOEL COWARD†

THE ASTRONAUT (TF) Universal TV, 1972
GIL MELLE

ASWANG Young American Films/Purple Onion
Pords., 1994
KEN BRAHMSTEDT

ASYA'S HAPPINESS Mosfilm, 1967
VYECHESLAV OVCHINNIKOV

ASYLUM Cinerama Releasing Corporation, 1972
DOUGLAS GAMLEY

AT CLOSE RANGE Orion, 1986
PATRICK LEONARD

AT GROUND ZERO (FD) Proletariat Pictures/
Roadfilm, 1994
FRAN BANISH

AT GUNPOINT Allied Artists, 1955
CARMEN DRAGON†

AT HOME AMONG STRANGERS 1974
EDUARD ARTEMYEV

AT LONG LAST LOVE 20th Century Fox, 1975
ARTIE BUTLER

AT MOTHER'S REQUEST (TF) Vista Organization
Ltd., 1987
CHARLES GROSS

AT PLAY IN THE FIELDS OF THE LORD 1991
ZBIGNIEW PREISNER

AT SWORD'S POINT RKO Radio, 1952
ROY WEBB†

AT THE EARTH'S CORE American International, 1976
MICHAEL VICKERS

THE ATLANTA CHILD MURDERS (TF) Mann-Rafshoon Productions/Finnegan Associates, 1985
BILLY GOLDENBERG

ATLANTIC CITY Paramount, 1981
MICHEL LEGRAND

ATLANTIC CITY Republic, 1944
WALTER SCHARF

ATLANTIS 1992
ERIC SERRA

ATLANTIS, THE LOST CONTINENT MGM, 1961
RUSSELL GARCIA

ATLAS Filmgroup, 1961
RONALD STEIN†

ATLAS AGAINST THE TSAR MACISTE ALLA CORTE DELLO ZAR 1963
CARLO RUSTICHELLI

ATOLL K 1950
PAUL MISRAKI

ATOM AGE VAMPIRE SEDDOK, L'EREDE DI SATANA 1961
ARMANDO TROVAJOLI

THE ATOMIC CITY Paramount, 1952
LEITH STEVENS†

THE ATOMIC KID Republic, 1954
VAN ALEXANDER

ATOR Comworld Pictures, 1983
MARIA CORDIO

A.T.S. 1943
RICHARD ADDINSELL†

ATTACK FROM THE SEA 1953
ARAM KHACHATURIAN†

ATTACK IN THE PACIFIC (FD) U.S. Navy, 1945
DAVID RAKSIN

THE ATTACK OF THE 50 FOOT WOMAN American International, 1958
RONALD STEIN†

ATTACK OF THE 50 ft. WOMAN (CTF) HBO Pictures/Warner Bros. TV, 1993
NICHOLAS PIKE

ATTACK OF THE CRAB MONSTERS Allied Artists, 1957
RONALD STEIN†

ATTACK OF THE KILLER TOMATOES NAI Entertainment, 1979
GORDON GOODWIN
PAUL SUNDFOR

ATTACK OF THE PUPPET PEOPLE American International, 1958
ALBERT GLASSER

ATTACK ON FEAR (TF) Tomorrow Entertainment, 1984
TONY BERG

ATTACK ON TERROR: THE FBI VERSUS THE KU KLUX KLAN (TF) QM Productions/Warner Bros. TV, 1975
MUNDELL LOWE

ATTACK ON THE IRON COAST United Artists, 1968
GERARD SCHURMANN

ATTACK! United Artists, 1956
FRANK DEVOL

ATTENTI AL BUFFONE 1975
ENNIO MORRICONE

ATTENTION BANDITS Grange Communications/Jerry Winters, 1987
FRANCIS LAI

ATTENTION, UNE FEMME PEUT EN CACHER UNE AUTRE Gaumont, 1983
PHILIPPE SARDE

THE ATTIC: THE HIDING OF ANN FRANK (TF) Telecom Entertainment, 1987
RICHARD RODNEY BENNETT

ATTICA (TF) ABC Circle Films, 1980
GIL MELLE

ATTO DI ACCUSA 1950
CARLO RUSTICHELLI

ATTRAGON American International, 1965
AKIRA IFUKUBE

AU COEUR DE LA VIE 1962
HENRI LANOE

AU GRAND BALCON 1949
JOSEPH KOSMA†

AU HASARD, BALTHAZAR Cinema Ventures, 1966
JEAN WIENER†

AU NOM DU CHRIST IN THE NAME OF CHRIST 1993
MOHAMMED SOUDANI

AU NOM DU PERE ET DU FILS 1991
ALEXANDRE DESPLAT

AU PLAISIR DE DIEU (TF) 1977
ANTOINE DUHAMEL

AUBERVILLIERS 1945
JOSEPH KOSMA†

AU-DELA DE LA PEUR 1975
ALAIN GORRAGUER

THE AUDITION Lifflander Prods., 1986
PETER DAVISON

AUDREY ROSE United Artists, 1977
MICHAEL SMALL

AUF BIEGEN UND BRECH West German
JURGEN KNIEPER

AUGUST Samuel Goldwyn, 1996
ANTHONY HOPKINS

AUNT MARY (TF) Henry Jaffe Enterprises, 1979
ARTHUR B. RUBINSTEIN

AUNTIE MAME Warner Bros., 1958
BRONISLAU KAPER†

AURORA (TF) Roger Gimbel Productions/The Peregrine Producers Group/Sacis, 1984
GEORGES DELERUE†

AUSTIN POWERS: INTERNATIONAL MAN OF MYSTERY New Line, 1997
GEORGE S. CLINTON

AUSTRALIAN DREAM Ronin Films, 1987
COLIN TIMMS

AUTHOR! AUTHOR! 20th Century-Fox, 1982
DAVE GRUSIN

THE AUTOBIOGRAPHY OF MISS JANE PITTMAN (TF) Tomorrow Entertainment, 1974
FRED KARLIN II

AUTOUR D'UNE TROMPETTE (FD) 1952
CLAUDE BOLLING

AUTUMN LEAVES Universal, 1956
HANS J. SALTER†

AUX YEUX DU SOUVENIR 1949
GEORGES AURIC†

AVALANCHE New World, 1978
WILLIAM KRAFT

AVALANCHE Producers Releasing Corp., 1946
LUCIEN MORAWECK†

AVALANCHE (TF) Atlantis/Propaganda/CTV TV Net, 1994
JONATHAN GOLDSMITH

AVALANCHE EXPRESS 20th Century-Fox, 1979
ALLYN FERGUSON

AVALANCHE PATROL (FD) 1947
MALCOLM ARNOLD

AVALON Columbia, 1990
RANDY NEWMAN

AVANT LE DELUGE 1953
GEORGES VAN PARYS†

AVANTI! United Artists, 1972
CARLO RUSTICHELLI

AVEC LA PEAU AUTRES 1967
MICHEL MAGNE†

THE AVENGERS 1942
RICHARD ADDINSELL†

THE AVENGING ANGEL (CTF) Esparza-Katz Prods./Curtis-Lowe Prods./First Corps Endeavors, 1995
GARY CHANG

AVENGING ANGEL New World, 1984
CHRISTOPHER YOUNG

AVENGING ANGEL Weintraub Productions, 1985
PAUL ANTONELLI
DAVID WHEATLEY

AVENGING FORCE Cannon, 1986
GEORGE S. CLINTON

THE AVIATOR MGM/UA, 1985
DOMINIC FRONTIERE

AVONLEA (CTF) The Disney Channel/Sullivan Films, 1990
HAGOOD HARDY

AVVENTURA A CAPRI 1958
PIERO PICCIONI

AVVOLTOI SULLA CITTA 1980
STELVIO CIPRIANI

THE AWAKENING LAND (MS) Bensen-Kuhn-Sagal Productions/Warner Bros. TV, 1978
FRED KARLIN ☆

THE AWAKENING OF CANDRA (TF) Michael Klein Productions, 1983
BILLY GOLDENBERG

THE AWAKENING Orion/Warner Bros., 1980
CLAUDE BOLLING

AWAKENINGS Columbia, 1990
RANDY NEWMAN

AWAY ALL BOATS Universal, 1956
FRANK SKINNER†

THE AWFUL STORY OF THE NUN OF MONZA 1969
ENNIO MORRICONE

AN AWFULLY BIG ADVENTURE Fine Line, 1995
RICHARD HARTLEY

A.W.O.L. BFB, 1972
RUPERT HOLMES

B

BAA BAA BLACK SHEEP (TF) Universal TV, 1976
PETE CARPENTER
PETE CARPENTER†
MIKE POST

BAB EL-OUED CITY 1994
RACHID BAHRI

BABAR: THE MOVIE New Line Cinema, 1989
MILAN KYMLICKA

THE BABE Universal, 1992
ELMER BERNSTEIN

BABE (TF) MGM TV, 1975
JERRY GOLDSMITH ☆☆

THE BABE RUTH STORY Allied Artists, 1948
EDWARD WARD†

BABE RUTH (TF) A Lyttle Production, 1991
HARVEY R. COHEN
STEVE DORFF

BABES IN ARMS MGM, 1939
GEORGE BASSMAN

BABES IN TOYLAND Buena Vista, 1961
GEORGE BRUNS

BABES IN TOYLAND (TF) The Finnegan-Pinchuk Company/Orion TV/Bavaria Atelier GMBH, 1986
LESLIE BRICUSSE

BABES ON BROADWAY MGM, 1941
GEORGE BASSMAN

THE BABY Scotia International, 1973
GERALD FRIED

BABY - SECRET OF THE LOST LEGEND Buena Vista, 1985
JERRY GOLDSMITH

BABY BLUE MARINE Columbia, 1976
FRED KARLIN

BABY BOOM MGM/UA, 1987
BILL CONTI

BABY BROKERS (TF) Steinhardt Baer Pictures/BBK Prods./Columbia Pictures TV, 1994
ANTHONY MARINELLI

THE BABY DOLL MURDERS Trident, 1993
DANA WALDEN

BABY DOLL 1968
LUIS BACALOV

BABY DOLL Warner Bros., 1956
KENYON HOPKINS

BABY FACE MORGAN Producers Releasing Corp., 1942
LEO ERDODY†

BABY FACE NELSON Allied Artists, 1957
VAN ALEXANDER

BABY GIRL SCOTT (TF) Poison Company Productions/The Finnegan-Pinchuk Company, 1987
PAUL CHIHARA

BABY M (TF) ABC Circle Films, 1988
CHARLES FOX

THE BABY MAKER National General, 1970
FRED KARLIN

BABY OF THE BRIDE (TF) Baby Productions/Leonard Hill Films, 1991
JAY GRUSKA

BABY SISTER (TF) Moonlight Productions II, 1983
FRED KARLIN

BABY SNAKES Intercontinental Absurdities, 1979
FRANK ZAPPA†

BABY'S DAY OUT 20th Century Fox, 1994
BRUCE BROUGHTON

BABY, THE RAIN MUST FALL Columbia, 1965
ELMER BERNSTEIN

BABYCAKES (TF) The Konigsburg-Sanitsky Co., 1989
WILLIAM OLVIS

BABYLON National Film, 1980
DENNIS BOVELL

BABYLON 5 (TF) Rattlesnake Prods./Synthetic World/Warner Bros., 1993
STEWART COPELAND

BABYMAKER: THE CECIL JACOBSON STORY (TF) Jaffe-Braunstein Films/Heartstar Prods., 1994
JAMES MCVAY

THE BABY-SITTERS CLUB Columbia, 1995
DAVID MICHAEL FRANK

THE BACHELOR AND THE BOBBY-SOXER RKO Radio, 1947
LEIGH HARLINE†

BACHELOR BAIT RKO Radio, 1934
MAX STEINER†

BACHELOR DADDY Universal, 1941
HANS J. SALTER†

BACHELOR FLAT 20th Century-Fox, 1962
JOHN WILLIAMS

BACHELOR IN PARADISE MGM, 1961
HENRY MANCINI†

BACHELOR MOTHER RKO Radio, 1939
ROY WEBB†

THE BACHELOR PARTY United Artists, 1957
ALEX NORTH†

BACHELOR PARTY 20th Century Fox, 1984
ROBERT FOLK

THE BACHELOR'S DAUGHTERS United Artists, 1946
W. FRANKE HARLING†

BACK AT HOME WITH CLAUDE 1992
RICHARD GREGOIRE

BACK AT THE FRONT Universal, 1952
HERMAN STEIN

BACK FROM ETERNITY RKO Radio, 1956
FRANZ WAXMAN†

BACK FROM THE DEAD 20th Century-Fox, 1957
RAOUL KRAUSHAAR

BACK FROM THE FRONT Universal, 1952
HENRY MANCINI†

BACK FROM THE PAST AIP, 1990
JOHN W. MORGAN
WILLIAM T. STROMBERG

BACK HOME (CTF) TVS Films/Verronmead Productions/Citadel, 1990
ILONA SCKACZ

BACK IN THE U.S.S.R. 1992
LES HOOPER

BACK ROADS Warner Bros., 1981
HENRY MANCINI†

BACK STREET Universal, 1941
FRANK SKINNER† ★

BACK STREET Universal, 1961
FRANK SKINNER†

BACK TO BACK Motion Picture Corporation of America, 1989
RICHARD COX

BACK TO BATAAN RKO Radio, 1945
ROY WEBB†

BACK TO GOD'S COUNTRY Universal, 1953
FRANK SKINNER†

BACK TO HANNIBAL: THE RETURN OF TOM SAWYER AND HUCKLEBERRY FINN (CTF) Gay-Jay Productions/The Disney Channel/WonderWorks, 1990
LEE HOLDRIDGE

BACK TO SCHOOL Orion, 1986
DANNY ELFMAN

BACK TO THE BEACH Paramount, 1987
STEVE DORFF

BACK TO THE FUTURE Universal, 1985
ALAN SILVESTRI

BACK TO THE FUTURE 2 Universal, 1989
ALAN SILVESTRI

BACK TO THE FUTURE 3 Universal, 1990
ALAN SILVESTRI

BACK TO THE STREETS OF SAN FRANCISCO (TF) Aaron Spelling, 1992
PATRICK WILLIAMS

BACKBEAT Gramercy, 1994
DON WAS

BACKDRAFT Universal, 1991
HANS ZIMMER

BACKFIELD IN MOTION (TF) Think/Avnet-Kerner, 1991
CLIFF EIDELMAN

BACKFIRE New Century/Vista, 1987
DAVID SHIRE

BACKFIRE Warner Bros., 1950
DANIELE AMFITHEATROF†

BACKGROUND TO DANGER Warner Bros., 1943
FREDERICK HOLLANDER†

BACKLASH Universal, 1956
HERMAN STEIN

BACKSTAGE Hoyts, Australian, 1988
BRUCE ROWLAND

BACKSTAIRS AT THE WHITE HOUSE (MS) Ed Friendly Productions, 1979
MORTON STEVENS†

BACKSTREET DREAMS BACKSTREET STRAYS Vidmark, 1990
BILL CONTI

BACKSTREET STRAYS Vidmark, 1990
BILL CONTI

BACKTRACK CATCHFIRE Vestron, 1990
MICHEL COLOMBIER
CURT SOBEL

THE BAD AND THE BEAUTIFUL MGM, 1952
DAVID RAKSIN

BAD ATTITUDES (TF) FNM Films, 1991
PETER RODGERS MELNICK

BAD BEHAVIOR 1993
JOHN ALTMAN

BAD BLOOD Platinum Pictures, 1989
JOEY MENNONNA

BAD BLOOD Southern Pictures/New Zealand Film Commission, 1983
RICHARD HARTLEY

BAD BOY BUBBY 1993
GRAHAM TARDIF

BAD BOYS 1960
TORU TAKEMITSU†

BAD BOYS Columbia, 1995
MARK MANCINA

BAD BOYS Universal/AFD, 1983
BILL CONTI

BAD COMPANY Buena Vista, 1995
CARTER BURWELL

BAD DAY AT BLACK ROCK MGM, 1955
ANDRE PREVIN

BAD DREAMS 20th Century Fox, 1988
JAY FERGUSON

BAD FOR EACH OTHER Columbia, 1954
MISCHA BAKALEINIKOFF†

BAD GEORGIA ROAD Dimension, 1976
DON PEAKE

BAD GIRLS 20th Century Fox, 1994
JERRY GOLDSMITH

BAD GUY MGM, 1937
EDWARD WARD†

BAD GUYS Interpictures, 1986
WILLIAM GOLDSTEIN

BAD INFLUENCE Triumph Releasing Corporation,
1990
TREVOR JONES

BAD LANDS RKO Radio, 1939
ROY WEBB†

BAD LIEUTENANT Odyssey, 1992
JOE DELIA

BAD LITTLE ANGEL MGM, 1939
EDWARD WARD†

THE BAD MAN MGM, 1941
FRANZ WAXMAN†

BAD MAN OF BRIMSTONE MGM, 1937
WILLIAM AXT†

BAD MANNERS *GROWING PAINS* New World,
1984
W. MICHAEL LEWIS
LAURIN RINDER

BAD MEDICINE 20th Century Fox, 1985
LALO SCHIFRIN

BAD MEN OF TOMBSTONE Allied Artists, 1949
ROY WEBB†

BAD MOON 1996
DANIEL LICHT

THE BAD NEWS BEARS Paramount, 1976
JERRY FIELDING†

THE BAD NEWS BEARS GO TO JAPAN
Paramount, 1978
PAUL CHIHARA

**THE BAD NEWS BEARS IN BREAKING
TRAINING** Paramount, 1977
CRAIG SAFAN

BAD RONALD (TF) Lorimar Productions, 1974
FRED KARLIN

THE BAD SEED Warner Bros., 1956
ALEX NORTH†

THE BAD SEED (TF) Hajeno Productions/Warner
Bros. TV, 1985
PAUL CHIHARA

THE BAD SLEEP WELL Toho, 1960
MASARU SATO

BAD TIMING/A SENSUAL OBSESSION World
Northal, 1980
RICHARD HARTLEY

THE BADGE (CTF) 1991
STEVE EDWARDS

BADGE OF THE ASSASSIN (TF) Daniel H. Blatt/
Robert Singer Productions, 1985
TOM SCOTT

BADGER'S GREEN 1948
MALCOLM ARNOLD

BADLANDS Warner Bros., 1974
GEORGE ALICESON TIPTON

BADLANDS OF DAKOTA Universal, 1941
HANS J. SALTER†

BADMAN'S TERRITORY RKO Radio, 1946
ROY WEBB†

BAFFALO BILL, L'EROE DEL FAR WEST 1964
CARLO RUSTICHELLI

BAFFLED! (TF) Arena Productions/ITC, 1973
RICHARD HILL

BAGARRES 1948
JOSEPH KOSMA†

BAGDAD CAFE *OUT OF ROSENHEIM* Island
Pictures, 1987
BOB TELSON

BAIL JUMPER Angelika Films, 1990
RICHARD ROBBINS

BAILOUT AT 43,000 United Artists, 1957
ALBERT GLASSER

THE BAIT (TF) Spelling-Goldberg Productions/ABC
Circle Films, 1973
ALLYN FERGUSON
JACK ELLIOTT

BAJA OKLAHOMA (CTF) HBO Pictures/Rastar
Productions, 1988
STANLEY MYERS†

BAKER'S HAWK Doty-Dayton, 1976
FRANK DENSON

BALALAIKA MGM, 1939
HERBERT STOTHART†

BALL OF FIRE United Artists, 1941
ALFRED NEWMAN† ★

THE BALLAD OF ANDY CROCKER (TF)
Thomas-Spelling Productions, 1969
BILLY MAY

THE BALLAD OF CABLE HOGUE Warner Bros.,
1970
JERRY GOLDSMITH

THE BALLAD OF GREGORIO CORTEZ Embassy,
1983
W. MICHAEL LEWIS
LAURIN RINDER

THE BALLAD OF LITTLE JOE Fine Line, 1993
DAVID MANSFIELD

THE BALLAD OF NARAYAMA Kino International/
Janus, 1983
SHINCHIRO IKEBE

THE BALLAD OF THE DALTONS 1978
CLAUDE BOLLING

THE BALLAD OF THE SAD CAFE Angelika, 1991
RICHARD ROBBINS

BALLATA DA UN MILIARDO 1966
LUIS BACALOV

BALLES PERDUES *STRAY BULLETS* Films
Galatee, 1983
MICHEL PORTAL

BALLET MECHANIQUE 1924
GEORGE ANTHEIL†

BALLOT MEASURE 9 (FD) Oregon Tape Project,
1995
JULIAN DYLAN RUSSELL

THE BALTIMORE BULLET Avco Embassy, 1980
JOHNNY MANDEL

BALTO (AF) Universal, 1995
JAMES HORNER

BAMBI (AF) RKO Radio, 1942
FRANK CHURCHILL† ★
EDWARD PLUMB† ★

THE BAMBOO PRISON Columbia, 1954
MISCHA BAKALEINIKOFF†

BANANAS United Artists, 1971
MARVIN HAMLISCH

BAND OF ANGELS Warner Bros., 1957
MAX STEINER†

BAND OF OUTSIDERS Royal Films International,
1964
MICHEL LEGRAND

BAND OF THE HAND Tri-Star, 1986
MICHEL RUBINI

THE BAND WAGON MGM, 1953
ADOLPH DEUTSCH† ★

BANDIDO Warner Bros., 1956
MAX STEINER†

THE BANDIT OF SHERWOOD FOREST Columbia,
1946
HUGO FRIEDHOFER†

BANDIT QUEEN Lippert, 1950
ALBERT GLASSER

BANDIT: BEAUTY AND THE BANDIT (TF) Yahi
Prods./IPS Prods., 1994
LARRY HERBSTRITT

BANDITI A MILANO Paramount, 1968
RIZ ORTOLANI

BANDITS *ATTENTION BANDITS* Grange
Communications/Jerry Winters, 1987
FRANCIS LAI

THE BANDITS OF CORSICA United Artists, 1953
IRVING GERTZ

BANDOLERO! 20th Century-Fox, 1968
JERRY GOLDSMITH

BANG BANG, YOU'RE DEAD! *OUR MAN IN
MARRAKESH* American International, 1966
MALCOM LOCKYER

BANG THE DRUM SLOWLY Paramount, 1973
STEPHEN LAWRENCE

BANISHED *ORIN* Toho, 1978
TORU TAKEMITSU†

BANJO HACKETT: ROAMIN' FREE (TF) Bruce
Lansbury Productions/Columbia TV, 1976
MORTON STEVENS†

THE BANK DICK Universal, 1940
CHARLES PREVIN†

BANK ROBBER IRS, 1993
STEWART COPELAND

THE BANK SHOT United Artists, 1974
JOHN MORRIS

BANYON (TF) Warner Bros. TV, 1971
LEONARD ROSENMAN

BANZAI AMLF, 1983
VLADIMIR COSMA

BANZAI RUNNER Montage Films, 1987
JOEL GOLDSMITH

B.A.P.S. NewLine, 1997
STANLEY CLARKE

BAR GIRLS Lavender Hill Mob, 1994
LENNY MYERS

BARAKA (FD) Magidson Films, 1992
MICHAEL STEARNS

BARB WIRE Gramercy, 1996
MICHEL COLOMBIER

BARBABLU *BLUEBEARD* 1972
ENNIO MORRICONE

**BARBARA TAYLOR BRADFORD'S REMEMBER
(TF)** List-Estrin Prods./H.R. Prods/NBC Prods.,
1993
DAVID SHIRE

BARBARELLA Paramount, 1968
BOB CREWE
CHARLES FOX

THE BARBARIAN AND THE GEISHA 20th
Century-Fox, 1958
HUGO FRIEDHOFER†

THE BARBARIAN MGM, 1933
HERBERT STOTHART†

BARBARIAN QUEEN Concorde/Cinema Group,
1985
CHRISTOPHER YOUNG

THE BARBARIANS Cannon, 1987
PINO DONAGGIO

BARBARIANS AT THE GATE (CTF) Columbia/HBO,
1993
RICHARD GIBBS

BARBAROSA Universal/AFD, 1982
BRUCE SMEATON

THE BARBARY COAST (TF) Paramount Pictures TV,
1975
JOHN ANDREW TARTAGLIA

BARBARY COAST United Artists, 1935
ALFRED NEWMAN†

BARBARY PIRATE Columbia, 1949
MISCHA BAKALEINIKOFF†

BARCELONA Fine Line, 1994
MARK SUOZZO

BARE ESSENCE (TF) Warner Bros. TV, 1982
BILLY GOLDENBERG

THE BAREFOOT EXECUTIVE Buena Vista, 1971
ROBERT F. BRUNNER

BAREFOOT IN THE PARK Paramount, 1966
NEAL HEFTI

THE BAREFOOT MAILMAN Columbia, 1951
GEORGE DUNING

BARNABY AND ME Trans-Atlantic Enterprises, 1978
BRIAN MAY†

BARNACLE BILL MGM, 1941
BRONISLAU KAPER†

BARNEY BARNABY Abzurd, 1995
ROLFE KENT

BARNUM (TF) Robert Halmi, Inc./Filmline
International, 1986
CHARLES GROSS

BAROCCO 1976
PHILIPPE SARDE

THE BARON AND THE KID (TF) Telecom
Entertainment, 1984
BRAD FIEDEL

BARON BLOOD *GLI ORRORI DEL CASTELLO DE
NORIMBERGA* American International, 1972
LES BAXTER†

THE BARON OF ARIZONA Lippert, 1950
PAUL DUNLAP

BARQUERO United Artists, 1970
DOMINIC FRONTIERE

BARR SINISTER Intermedia, 1990
JAY CHATTAWAY

BARRACUDA *THE LUCIFER PROJECT* 1978
KLAUS SCHULZE

THE BARRETTS OF WIMPOLE STREET MGM,
1934
HERBERT STOTHART†

THE BARRETTS OF WIMPOLE STREET MGM,
1957
BRONISLAU KAPER†

BARRICADE 20th Century-Fox, 1939
DAVID BUTTOLPH†

BARRICADE Warner Bros., 1950
WILLIAM LAVA†

BARRIER Film Polski, 1966
CHRISTOPHER KOMEDA†

BARRIERA A SETTENTRIONE 1949
CARLO RUSTICHELLI

BARRY LYNDON Warner Bros., 1975
LEONARD ROSENMAN ★★

BARTON FINK 20th Century Fox, 1991
CARTER BURWELL

BASED ON AN UNTRUE STORY (TF) Westgate
Prods., 1993
LAURA KARPMAN

THE BASHFUL BIKINI 1964
RONALD STEIN†

THE BASHFUL ELEPHANT Allied Artists, 1962
RONALD STEIN†

BASIC INSTINCT TriStar, 1992
JERRY GOLDSMITH ★

BASIC TRAINING The Movie Store, 1985
MICHAEL CRUZ*

BASKET CASE Analysis, 1982
GUS RUSSO

BASKET CASE 2 Shapiro-Glickenhaus Entertainment,
1990
JOE RENZETTI

BASKET CASE 3: THE PROGENY Shapiro
Glickenhaus, 1992
JOE RENZETTI

THE BASKETBALL DIARIES New Line, 1995
GRAEME REVELL

BASQUIAT Miramax, 1996
JOHN CALE

THE BASTARD (TF) Universal TV, 1978
JOHN ADDISON

BASTARD OUT OF CAROLINA Turner Pictures,
1996
VAN DYKE PARKS

BASTARDO! VAMOS A MATAR 1970
CARLO RUSTICHELLI

BASTE CHE NON SI SAPPIA IN GIRO 1976
ARMANDO TROVAJOLI

THE BAT PEOPLE *IT LIVES BY NIGHT* American
International, 1974
ARTIE KANE

BAT-21 Tri-Star, 1988
CHRISTOPHER YOUNG

BATAAN MGM, 1943
BRONISLAU KAPER†

BATES MOTEL (TF) Universal TV, 1987
J. PETER ROBINSON

BATHING BEAUTY MGM, 1944
JOHN GREEN†

BATMAN 20th Century-Fox, 1966
NELSON RIDDLE†

BATMAN Warner Bros., 1989
DANNY ELFMAN

BATMAN AND ROBIN Warner Bros., 1997
ELLIOT GOLDENTHAL

BATMAN FOREVER Warner Bros., 1995
ELLIOT GOLDENTHAL

BATMAN RETURNS Warner Bros., 1992
DANNY ELFMAN

BATMAN: MASK OF THE PHANTASM (AF)
Warner Bros., 1993
SHIRLEY WALKER

BATTAGLIE SUI MARI 1968
CARLO RUSTICHELLI

BATTEMENTS DE COEUR 1939
PAUL MISRAKI

BATTERED (TF) Henry Jaffe Enterprises, 1978
DON PEAKE

BATTERIES NOT INCLUDED Universal, 1987
JAMES HORNER

BATTLE BENEATH THE EARTH 1968
KENNETH V. JONES

BATTLE BEYOND THE STARS New World, 1979
JAMES HORNER

BATTLE BEYOND THE SUN American International,
1963
LES BAXTER†

BATTLE CRY Warner Bros., 1955
MAX STEINER† ★

THE BATTLE FOR SIBERIA 1940
DMITRI SHOSTAKOVITCH†

BATTLE FOR THE PLANET OF THE APES 20th
Century-Fox, 1973
LEONARD ROSENMAN

BATTLE HELL *YANGTSE INCIDENT* DCA, 1957
LEIGHTON LUCAS†

BATTLE HYMN Universal, 1957
FRANK SKINNER†

BATTLE IN OUTER SPACE Columbia, 1960
AKIRA IFUKUBE

THE BATTLE OF ALGIERS Rizzoli, 1967
ENNIO MORRICONE

THE BATTLE OF APACHE PASS Universal, 1952
HANS J. SALTER†

THE BATTLE OF JAYAKARTA Rapi Films, 1997
DIAN AGP

THE BATTLE OF NERETVA American International,
1971
BERNARD HERRMANN†

THE BATTLE OF OKINAWA 1971
MASARU SATO

THE BATTLE OF STALINGRAD 1949
ARAM KHACHATURIAN†

THE BATTLE OF THE CORAL SEA Columbia, 1959
ERNEST GOLD

THE BATTLE OF THE RIVER PLATE Rank, 1956
BRIAN EASDALE

BATTLE OF BRITAIN United Artists, 1969
RON GOODWIN
SIR WILLIAM WALTON†

BATTLE OF ROGUE RIVER Columbia, 1954
MISCHA BAKALEINIKOFF†

BATTLE OF THE BULGE Warner Bros., 1965
BENJAMIN FRANKEL†

BATTLE OF THE SEXES United Artists, 1928
NATHANIEL SHILKRET†

BATTLE TAXI United Artists, 1955
HARRY SUKMAN†

BATTLES OF CHIEF PONTIAC Realart, 1952
ELMER BERNSTEIN

THE BATTLESHIP POTEMKIN Deutche Kinemathek
ERIC ALLAMAN

THE BATTLESHIP POTEMKIN *POTEMKIN*
Amkino, 1925
EDMUND MEISEL†

BATTLESTAR GALACTICA (TF) Glen A. Larson
Productions/Universal TV, 1978
GLEN A. LARSON
STU PHILLIPS

BATTLETRUCK *WARLORDS OF THE 21ST CENTURY* New World, 1982
KEVIN PEAK

BATTLING FOR BABY (TF) Von Zerneck-Sertner, 1992
MARK SNOW

BAWANG BIE JI Miramax, 1993
ZHAO JIPING

THE BAWDY ADVENTURES OF TOM JONES Universal, 1976
RON GRAINER†

BAWDY TALES United Artists, 1973
FRANCESCO DE MASI

BAY BOY Orion, 1984
CLAUDE BOLLING

BAY COVEN (TF) Guber-Peters Entertainment/ Phoenix Entertainment Group, 1987
SHUKI LEVY

BAY OF THE ANGELS Pathe Contemporary, 1964
MICHEL LEGRAND

BAYOU United Artists, 1957
GERALD FRIED

BAYWATCH: NIGHTMARE BAY (TF) The Baywatch Production Co./All American TV/Tower 12/LBS, 1991
JOHN D'ANDREA
CORY LERIOS

BAYWATCH: PANIC AT MALIBU PIER (TF) GTG Entertainment/NBC, 1989
ARTHUR B. RUBINSTEIN

BAYWATCH: RACE AGAINST TIME (TF) The Baywatch Production Company, 1993
JOHN D'ANDREA
CORY LERIOS

BEACH BALLS Concorde, 1988
MARK GOVERNOR

BEACH BEVERLY HILLS Trident, 1993
DE WAYNE BARRON

BEACH BLANKET BINGO American International, 1965
LES BAXTER†

THE BEACH GIRLS Crown International, 1982
MICHAEL LLOYD

BEACH PARTY American International, 1963
LES BAXTER†

THE BEACHCOMBER *VESSEL OF WRATH* 1937
RICHARD ADDINSELL†

BEACHES Buena Vista, 1988
GEORGES DELERUE†

BEACHHEAD United Artists, 1954
EMIL NEWMAN†

THE BEANS OF EGYPT, MAINE Live, 1994
PETER MANNING ROBINSON

THE BEAR 1970
WOJCIECH KILAR

THE BEAR Embassy, 1984
BILL CONTI

THE BEAR Tri-Star, 1989
PHILIPPE SARDE

THE BEARS AND I Buena Vista, 1974
BUDDY BAKER

BEASMASTER 3 (CTF) 1996
JAN HAMMER

THE BEAST Columbia, 1988
MARK ISHAM

BEAST ALLEY 1965
TORU TAKEMITSU†

THE BEAST FROM 20,000 FATHOMS Warner Bros., 1953
DAVID BUTTOLPH†

THE BEAST IN THE CELLAR 1971
TONY MACAULEY

THE BEAST MUST DIE Cinerama Releasing Corporation, 1974
DOUGLAS GAMLEY

THE BEAST WITH FIVE FINGERS Warner Bros., 1947
MAX STEINER†

THE BEAST WITHIN United Artists, 1982
LES BAXTER†

THE BEASTMASTER MGM/UA, 1982
LEE HOLDRIDGE

BEASTMASTER 2: THROUGH THE PORTAL OF TIME New Line, 1991
ROBERT FOLK

THE BEASTS ARE ON THE STREETS (TF) Hanna-Barbera Productions, 1978
GERALD FRIED

BEAT Vestron, 1988
CARTER BURWELL

THE BEAT GENERATION *THIS REBEL AGE* MGM, 1959
ALBERT GLASSER

BEAT GIRL Renown, 1959
JOHN BARRY

BEAT THE DEVIL United Artists, 1954
FRANCO MANNINO

BEATI E RICCHI 1972
LUIS BACALOV

BEATRICE *LA PASSION BEATRICE* Samuel Goldwyn Co., 1987
LILI BOULAɴGER
RON CARTER

BEAU BRUMMEL MGM, 1954
RICHARD ADDINSELL†

BEAU FIXE 1953
MICHEL LEGRAND

BEAU GESTE Paramount, 1939
ALFRED NEWMAN†

BEAU GESTE Universal, 1966
HANS J. SALTER†

BEAU IDEAL RKO Radio, 1930
MAX STEINER†

BEAU PERE New Line Cinema, 1981
PHILIPPE SARDE

THE BEAUTICIAN AND THE BEAST Paramount, 1997
CLIFF EIDELMAN

THE BEAUTIFUL BLONDE FROM BASHFUL BEND 20th Century-Fox, 1949
CYRIL J. MOCKRIDGE†

THE BEAUTIFUL STORY 1992
FRANCIS LAI
PHILIPPE SERVAIN

THE BEAUTIFUL STRANGER United Artists, 1954
MALCOLM ARNOLD

THE BEAUTIFUL SWINDLERS *LES PLUS BELLES ESCROQUERIES DU MONDE* Jack Ellis Films, 1964
CHRISTOPHER KOMEDA†

BEAUTIFUL DREAMERS Cinexus, 1990
LAWRENCE SHRAGGE

BEAUTIFUL GIRLS Miramax, 1996
DAVID A. STEWART

BEAUTIFUL THING 1996
JOHN ALTMAN

BEAUTY AND THE BEAST Lopert, 1946
GEORGES AURIC†

BEAUTY AND THE BEAST United Artists, 1962
HUGO FRIEDHOFER†

BEAUTY AND THE BEAST (AF) Buena Vista, 1991
ALAN MENKEN ★★

BEAUTY AND THE BEAST (TF) Palms Films Ltd., 1976
RON GOODWIN

BEAVER VALLEY RKO Radio, 1950
PAUL J. SMITH†

BEAVIS AND BUTTHEAD DO AMERICA (AF) Paramount, 1996
JOHN FRIZZELL

BEBE'S KIDS (AF) 1992
JOHN BARNES

BEBO'S GIRL Continental, 1963
CARLO RUSTICHELLI

BECAUSE MOMMY WORKS (TF) Newport-Balboa Prods./spring Creek Prods./Warner Bros. TV, 1994
PATRICK WILLIAMS

BECAUSE OF HIM Universal, 1946
MIKLOS ROZSA†

BECAUSE OF YOU Universal, 1952
FRANK SKINNER†

BECAUSE THEY'RE YOUNG Columbia, 1960
JOHN WILLIAMS

BECAUSE WHY Aska Film, 1993
NANA VASCONCELOS

BECAUSE YOU'RE MINE MGM, 1952
JOHN GREEN†

BECKET Paramount, 1964
LAURENCE ROSENTHAL ★

THE BECKONING FLAME Triangle, 1916
VICTOR SCHERTZINGER†

BECKY SHARP RKO Radio, 1935
ROY WEBB†

BECOMING COLETTE Intercontinental, 1992
JOHN SCOTT

BED & BREAKFAST Hemdale, 1992
DAVID SHIRE

BED AND BOARD *DOMICILE CONJUGAL* Columbia, 1971
ANTOINE DUHAMEL

BED OF GRASS 1957
MANOS HADJIDAKIS†

BED OF LIES (TF) David L. Wolper, 1992
DAVID SHIRE

BED OF LIES (TF) NBC Prods., 1996
DENNIS MCCARTHY

BED OF ROSES New Line, 1996
MICHAEL CONVERTINO

BED OF ROSES RKO Radio, 1933
MAX STEINER†

THE BED SITTING ROOM United Artists, 1969
KEN THORNE

THE BED YOU SLEPT IN Complex, 1993
ERLING WOLD

BEDAZZLED 20th Century-Fox, 1967
DUDLEY MOORE

BEDEVILLED MGM, 1955
WILLIAM ALWYN†

THE BEDFORD INCIDENT Columbia, 1965
GERARD SCHURMANN

BEDKNOBS AND BROOMSTICKS Buena Vista, 1971
IRWIN KOSTAL† ★

BEDLAM RKO Radio, 1946
ROY WEBB†

THE BEDROOM WINDOW DEG, 1987
PATRICK GLEESON
MICHAEL SHRIEVE

BEDSIDE MANNER 20th Century-Fox, 1945
EMIL NEWMAN†

BEDTIME FOR BONZO Universal, 1951
FRANK SKINNER†

BEDTIME STORY Columbia, 1941
WERNER R. HEYMANN†

BEDTIME STORY Universal, 1964
HANS J. SALTER†

BEEN DOWN SO LONG IT LOOKS LIKE UP TO ME Paramount, 1971
GARRY SHERMAN

BEER Orion, 1985
BILL CONTI

BEETHOVEN Universal, 1992
RANDY EDELMAN

BEETHOVEN'S 2nd Universal, 1993
RANDY EDELMAN

BEETLEJUICE The Geffen Company/Warner Bros., 1988
DANNY ELFMAN

BEFORE & AFTER Little Deer, 1985
STEVE BERNSTEIN

BEFORE AND AFTER Buena Vista, 1996
HOWARD SHORE

BEFORE AND AFTER (TF) The Konigsberg Company, 1979
JIMMIE HASKELL

BEFORE DAWN RKO Radio, 1933
MAX STEINER†

BEFORE GOD Quest Productions, 1987
DAVID C. WILLIAMS

BEFORE I WAKE 1956
LEONARD SALZEDO

BEFORE THE RAIN 1994
ANASTASIA

BEFORE THE REVOLUTION New Yorker, 1964
GATO BARBIERI
ENNIO MORRICONE

BEFORE WINTER COMES Columbia, 1969
RON GRAINER†

BEFORE YOUR EYES: A HEART FOR OLIVIA (TD) CBS News, 1995
RICHARD FIOCCA

BEG, BORROW OR STEAL MGM, 1937
WILLIAM AXT†

THE BEGGAR'S OPERA 1991
JAN KLUSAK

BEGGARS OF LIFE Paramount, 1928
KARL HAJOS†

BEGGERMAN, THIEF (TF) Universal TV, 1979
EDDIE SAUTER

THE BEGINNING OR THE END MGM, 1947
DANIELE AMFITHEATROF†

BEGINNING OF THE END Republic, 1957
ALBERT GLASSER

THE BEGUILED Universal, 1971
LALO SCHIFRIN

BEHAVE YOURSELF RKO Radio, 1951
LEIGH HARLINE†

BEHIND ENEMY LINES Orion, 1997
ARTHUR KEMPEL

BEHIND ENEMY LINES (TF) MTM Enterprises/TVS, 1985
JACK CHIPMAN
STEVE LINDSEY

BEHIND GREEN LIGHTS 20th Century Fox, 1946
EMIL NEWMAN†

BEHIND LOCKED DOORS Eagle Lion, 1948
ALBERT GLASSER

BEHIND THE GREAT WALL *LA MURAGLIA CINESE* (FD) 1958
ANGELO FRANCESCO LAVAGNINO†

BEHIND THE RISING SUN RKO Radio, 1943
ROY WEBB†

BEHOLD A PALE HORSE Columbia, 1963
MAURICE JARRE

THE BEING Embassy, 1983
DON PRESTON

BEING HUMAN Warner Bros., 1994
MICHAEL GIBBS

BEING THERE United Artists, 1979
JOHNNY MANDEL

BEIRUT: THE LAST HOME MOVIE (FD) Zohe Film, 1987
LANNY MEYERS

BEJEWELLED (CTF) TVS/PWD, 1991
KEN THORNE

BEL AMI 1955
HANNS EISLER†

BELIEVE IN ME MGM, 1971
FRED KARLIN

THE BELIVERS Orion, 1987
J. PETER ROBINSON

BELIZAIRE THE CAJUN Skouras Pictures, 1986
MICHAEL DOUCET
HOWARD SHORE

A BELL FOR ADANO 20th Century-Fox, 1945
ALFRED NEWMAN†

THE BELL JAR Avco Embassy, 1979
GERALD FRIED

BELL, BOOK AND CANDLE Columbia, 1958
GEORGE DUNING

BELLA DI GIORNO, MOGLIE DI NOTTE 1971
GIANFRANCO PLENIZIO

BELLA, RICCA, LIEVE DIFETTO FISICO, CERCA, ANIMA GEMELLA 1972
CARLO RUSTICHELLI

THE BELLBOY Paramount, 1960
WALTER SCHARF

BELLE 1973
FREDERIC DEVREESE

BELLE DE JOUR Allied Artists, 1967
MICHEL MAGNE†

BELLE LE GRAND Republic, 1951
VICTOR YOUNG†

BELLE OF THE NINETIES Paramount, 1934
ANDREA SETARO†

BELLE SOMERS Columbia, 1962
HARRY SUKMAN†

BELLE STARR (TF) Entheos Unlimited Productions/ Hanna-Barbera Productions, 1980
DANA KAPROFF

BELLE, MA POVERE Titanus, 1957
PIERO PICCIONI

BELLES OF ST. TRINIAN'S British Lion, 1957
MALCOLM ARNOLD

BELLES ON THEIR TOES 20th Century-Fox, 1952
CYRIL J. MOCKRIDGE†

BELLISSIMA Italian Films Export, 1951
FRANCO MANNINO

BELLMAN AND TRUE Island Pictures, 1987
COLIN TOWNS

BELLO, ONESTO, EMIGRATO AUSTRALIA SPOSEREBBE COMPAESANA ILLIBATA 1970
PIERO PICCIONI

BELLOWING CLOUD 1967
TORU TAKEMITSU†

BELLS New World, 1980
JOHN BARRY

BELLS ARE RINGING MGM, 1960
ANDRE PREVIN ★

THE BELLS OF ST. MARY'S RKO Radio, 1945
ROBERT EMMETT DOLAN† ★

BELOVED Universal, 1934
VICTOR SCHERTZINGER†

BELOVED ENEMY United Artists, 1937
ALFRED NEWMAN†

BELOVED INFIDEL 20th Century-Fox, 1959
FRANZ WAXMAN†

THE BELOVED VAGABOND 1934
DARIUS MILHAUD†

BELOW 30/ABOVE 10,000 damaged Californians, 1994
MICHAEL WHITMORE

BELOW THE BELT Atlantic Releasing, 1980
JERRY FIELDING†

BELPHEGOR (TF) 1965
ANTOINE DUHAMEL

THE BELSTONE FOX *FREE SPIRIT* Cine III, 1973
LAURIE JOHNSON

BEN Cinerama Releasing Corporation, 1972
WALTER SCHARF

BEN HUR
CARL DAVIS

BEN HUR MGM, 1959
MIKLOS ROZSA† ★★

BEND OF THE RIVER Universal, 1952
HANS J. SALTER†

BENEATH THE PLANET OF THE APES 20th Century-Fox, 1970
LEONARD ROSENMAN

BENEATH THE TWELVE-MILE REEF 20th Century-Fox, 1953
BERNARD HERRMANN†

THE BENEFICIARY National Film School, 1980
TREVOR JONES

BENEFIT OF THE DOUBT Miramax, 1993
HUMMIE MANN

BENGAL BRIDE Universal, 1954
HANS J. SALTER†

BENGAL BRIGADE Universal, 1954
HERMAN STEIN

BENGAZI RKO Radio, 1955
ROY WEBB†

BEN-HUR MGM, 1926
WILLIAM AXT†

BENJAMIN 1973
GARY WRIGHT

BENJI Mulberry Square, 1974
EUEL BOX

BENJI, THE HUNTED Buena Vista, 1987
EUEL BOX

THE BLACK SWAN   20th Century-Fox, 1942
ALFRED NEWMAN† ★

THE BLACK TENT   Rank, 1956
WILLIAM ALWYN†

BLACK TO THE PROMISED LAND (FD)   Blues Prods., 1992
BRANFORD MARSALIS

BLACK TUESDAY   United Artists, 1955
PAUL DUNLAP

A BLACK VEIL FOR LISA   Commonwealth United, 1969
RICHARD MARKOWITZ†

BLACK WATER GOLD (TF)   Metromedia Producers Corporation/CTV, 1970
MIKE CURB

BLACK WIDOW   20th Century Fox, 1987
MICHAEL SMALL

BLACK WIDOW   20th Century-Fox, 1954
LEIGH HARLINE†

BLACK WIDOW MURDERS: THE BLANCHE TAYLOR MOORE STORY (TF)   Andrea Baynes/Finnegan-Pinchuk/Lorimar TV, 1993
DAVID MICHAEL FRANK

THE BLACK WINDMILL   Universal, 1974
ROY BUDD†

BLACK ZOO   Allied Artists, 1963
PAUL DUNLAP

BLACKBEARD'S GHOST   Buena Vista, 1968
ROBERT F. BRUNNER

BLACKBEARD, THE PIRATE   RKO Radio, 1952
VICTOR YOUNG†

BLACKMAIL   British International Pictures, 1929
HUBERT BATH†

BLACKMAIL   MGM, 1939
EDWARD WARD†

BLACKMAIL (CTF)   Pacific/Barry Weitz Films/Wilshire Court Prods., 1991
JOSEPH CONLAN

BLACKOUT   Ambient Light Entertainment, 1988
LAURENCE ROSENTHAL

BLACKOUT   Anglo-American, 1940
RICHARD ADDINSELL†

BLACKOUT   Magnum Entertainment, 1989
DON DAVIS

BLACKOUT (CTF)   HBO Premiere Films/Roger Gimbel Productions/Peregrine Entertainment Ltd./Lee Buck Industries/Alexander Smith & Parks, 1985
LAURENCE ROSENTHAL

BLACULA   American International, 1972
GENE PAGE

BLADE   Green/Pintoff, 1973
JOHN CACAVAS

BLADE IN HONG KONG (TF)   Becker Enterprises Productions, 1985
DAVID KURTZ

BLADE RUNNER   The Ladd Company/Warner Bros., 1982
VANGELIS

BLAGUE DANS LE COIN   1963
ALAIN GORRAGUER

BLAME IT ON RIO   20th Century Fox, 1984
KEN WANNBERG

BLAME IT ON THE BELLBOY   1992
TREVOR JONES

BLANCHE FURY   1948
CLIFTON PARKER†

BLANK CHECK   Buena Vista, 1994
NICHOLAS PIKE

BLANKMAN   Columbia, 1994
MILES GOODMAN†

BLAST   Toga Prods., 1996
TONY RIPPARETTI

BLAST OFF/JULES VERNE'S ROCKET TO THE MOON   American International, 1967
JOHN SCOTT

BLAST'EM   1992
YURI GORBACHOW

BLAZE   Buena Vista, 1989
BENNIE WALLACE

BLAZE OF NOON   Paramount, 1947
ADOLPH DEUTSCH†

BLAZING SADDLES   Warner Bros., 1973
JOHN MORRIS

BLEAK HOUSE (MS)   BBC, 1985
GEOFFREY BURGON

BLEAK MORNING   1959
DMITRI KABALEVSKY†

BLESS THE BEASTS AND CHILDREN   Columbia, 1971
PERRY BOTKIN

BLESSING   Starr Valley Films, 1994
JOSEPH S. DE BEASI

BLIND ADVENTURE   RKO Radio, 1933
MAX STEINER†

BLIND AMBITION (MS)   Parts 3 and 4, Time-Life Productions, 1979
FRED KARLIN

BLIND AMBITION (MS)   Time-Life Productions Inc., 1979
WALTER SCHARF

BLIND DATE   New Line Cinema, 1984
STANLEY MYERS†
HANS ZIMMER

BLIND DATE   Paramount, 1959
RICHARD RODNEY BENNETT

BLIND DATE   Tri-Star, 1987
HENRY MANCINI†

BLIND DESIRE   1948
GEORGES AURIC†

BLIND FAITH (TF)   NBC Productions, 1990
LAURENCE ROSENTHAL

BLIND FEAR   Lance Entertainment/Allegro Films, 1989
MICHAEL MELVOIN

BLIND FURY   Tri-Star, 1989
J. PETER ROBINSON

BLIND GODDESS   1948
BERNARD GREEN

BLIND JUSTICE (CTF)   Heyman-Moritz Prods./HBO Pictures, 1994
RICHARD GIBBS

BLIND JUSTICE (TF)   CBS Entertainment Productions, 1986
MILES GOODMAN†

BLIND MAN'S BLUFF   1993
HAIM PERMONT

BLIND SIDE (CTF)   Chestnut Hill Prods./HBO, 1993
BRIAN MAY†

BLIND SPOT (TF)   Signboard Hill/RHI Entertainment, 1993
PATRICK WILLIAMS

BLIND WITNESS (TF)   King-Phoenix Entertainment/Victoria Principal Productions, 1989
BOB ALCIVAR

BLINDED BY THE LIGHT (TF)   Time-Life Films, 1980
JONATHAN TUNICK

BLINDFOLD   Universal, 1966
LALO SCHIFRIN

BLINDFOLD: ACTS OF OBSESSION (CTF)   Libra Pictures, 1994
SHUKI LEVY

BLINDMAN'S BLUFF (CTF)   Wilshire Court, 1992
RICHARD BELLIS

BLINDSIDED (CTF)   MTE/Alan Barnette Prods, 1993
DAVID MICHAEL FRANK

BLINK   New Line, 1994
BRAD FIEDEL

BLINK OF AN EYE   Trimark, 1992
VLADIMIR HORUNZHY

THE BLISS OF MRS. BLOSSOM   Paramount, 1969
RIZ ORTOLANI

BLITHE SPIRIT   United Artists, 1945
RICHARD ADDINSELL†

THE BLOB   Tri-Star, 1988
MICHAEL HOENIG

BLOCKADE   Warner Bros., 1938
WERNER JANSSEN ★

BLOCKADE (FD)   Canada Wild Prods., 1993
ROY FORBES

BLOCKHEADS   MGM, 1938
T. MARVIN HATLEY† ★

BLOND CHEAT   RKO Radio, 1938
ROY WEBB†

BLONDE FEVER   MGM, 1944
NATHANIEL SHILKRET†

BLONDE FIST   Glinwood, 1991
ALAN GILL

BLONDE FOR A DAY   Producers Releasing Corp., 1946
LEO ERDODY†

BLONDE ICE   Film Classics, 1948
IRVING GERTZ

BLONDE INSPIRATION   MGM, 1941
BRONISLAU KAPER†

BLONDE RANSOM   Universal, 1945
FRANK SKINNER†

BLONDE SAVAGE   Eagle Lion, 1947
LEO ERDODY†

BLONDIE HAS SERVANT TROUBLE   Columbia, 1940
LEIGH HARLINE†

BLONDIE KNOWS BEST   Columbia, 1946
MISCHA BAKALEINIKOFF†

BLONDIE ON A BUDGET   Columbia, 1940
LEIGH HARLINE†

BLONDIE PLAYS CUPID   Columbia, 1940
LEIGH HARLINE†

BLONDY   1975
STELVIO CIPRIANI

BLOOD & WINE   Fox Searchlight, 1997
MICHAL LURENC

BLOOD ALLEY   Warner Bros., 1955
ROY WEBB†

BLOOD AND BLACK LACE   SEI DONNE PER L'ASSASSINO   1964
CARLO RUSTICHELLI

BLOOD AND CONCRETE   I.R.S., 1991
VINNY GOLIA

BLOOD AND HONOR: YOUTH UNDER HITLER (MS)   Daniel Wilson Productions/SWF/Taurus Films, 1982
ERNST BRADNER

BLOOD AND ORCHIDS (MS)   Lorimar Productions, 1986
MARK SNOW

BLOOD AND ROSES   ET MOURIR DE PLAISIR   Paramount, 1960
JEAN PRODROMIDES

BLOOD AND SAND   20th Century-Fox, 1941
ALFRED NEWMAN†

BLOOD BEACH   Jerry Gross Organization, 1981
GIL MELLE

THE BLOOD DEMON   1967
PETER THOMAS

BLOOD DINER   Vestron, 1987
DON PRESTON

BLOOD FEAST   Box Office Spectaculars, 1963
HERSCHELL GORDON LEWIS

BLOOD FEUD (TF)   20th Century-Fox TV/Glickman-Selznick Productions, 1983
FRED STEINER

BLOOD FIEND   1967
ELISABETH LUYTENS†

BLOOD FOR DRACULA   Bryanston, 1974
CLAUDIO GIZZI

BLOOD FROM THE MUMMY'S TOMB   American International, 1971
TRISTRAM CARY

BLOOD IN BLOOD OUT   Buena Vista, 1993
BILL CONTI

BLOOD IN THE STREETS   1973
ENNIO MORRICONE

BLOOD IN THE STREETS   Independent-International, 1976
ENNIO MORRICONE

BLOOD MAD   Pro International, 1981
ROBERT O. RAGLAND

BLOOD MONEY   1954
GERALD FRIED

BLOOD MONEY   Shapiro Entertainment, 1987
ROBERT J. WALSH

BLOOD MONEY   United Artists, 1933
ALFRED NEWMAN†

BLOOD MONEY (CTF)   Concorde/New Horizons, 1996
ROGER NEILL

BLOOD MOON   1989
BRIAN MAY†

THE BLOOD OF A POET   Brandon, 1930
GEORGES AURIC†

BLOOD OF DRACULA   American International, 1957
PAUL DUNLAP

BLOOD OF FRANKENSTEIN   Independent-International, 1971
WILLIAM LAVA†

THE BLOOD OF HEROES   New Line Cinema, 1990
TODD BOEKELHEIDE

THE BLOOD OF OTHERS (CTF)   HBO Premiere Films/ICC/Filmex Productions, 1984
FRANCOIS DOMPIERRE

BLOOD OF THE WARRIORS   LA SCHIAVA DI ROMA   1960
ARMANDO TROVAJOLI

BLOOD ON SATAN'S CLAW   SATAN'S SKIN   Cannon, 1971
MARC WILKINSON

BLOOD ON THE ARROW   Allied Artists, 1964
RICHARD LASALLE

BLOOD ON THE MOON   RKO Radio, 1948
ROY WEBB†

BLOOD ON THE SUN   United Artists, 1945
MIKLOS ROZSA†

BLOOD ORGY   Lewis Motion Picture Enterprises, 1972
HERSCHELL GORDON LEWIS

BLOOD ORGY OF THE SHE DEVILS   Gemini Films, 1973
CARL ZITTRER

BLOOD ROYAL (TF)   Goldcrest Films, British
JOHN SCOTT

BLOOD SABBATH   YGALAH   1972
LES BAXTER†

BLOOD SIMPLE   Circle Releasing Corporation, 1984
CARTER BURWELL

BLOOD SONG   Allstate Films, 1981
ROBERT J. WALSH

BLOOD SPORT (TF)   Danny Thomas Productions, 1973
RANDY EDELMAN

BLOOD SPORT (TF)   Spelling-Goldberg Productions/Columbia TV, 1986
JOHN E. DAVIS

BLOOD TIES (CTF)   RAI Channel One/Racing Pictures/Viacom International, 1986
CELSO VALLI

BLOOD TIES (TF)   Shapiro Entertainment, 1991
BRAD FIEDEL

BLOOD TYPE BLUE   1979
MASARU SATO

THE BLOOD VIRGIN   1974
JOHN SCOTT

BLOOD VOWS: THE STORY OF A MAFIA WIFE (TF)   Louis Rudolph Films/Fries Entertainment, 1987
WILLIAM GOLDSTEIN

BLOODBROTHERS   Warner Bros., 1979
ELMER BERNSTEIN

BLOODEATERS   Parker National, 1980
TED SHAPIRO

BLOODFIST II   Concord-New Horizons, 1990
NIGEL HOLTON

BLOODFIST III: FORCED TO FIGHT   Concorde, 1991
NIGEL HOLTON

BLOODHOUNDS (CTF)   1995
JOHN FRIZZELL

BLOODHOUNDS OF BROADWAY   20th Century-Fox, 1952
DAVID RAKSIN

BLOODHOUNDS OF BROADWAY   Columbia, 1989
JONATHAN SHEFFER

BLOODKNOT (CTF)   Chesler Perlmutter Prods./Showtime, 1995
MICHEL RUBINI

BLOODLINES: MURDER IN THE FAMILY (TF)   Stonehenge/Lorimar TV, 1993
DAVID SHIRE

BLOODMATCH   21st Century, 1992
TONY RIPPARETTI

BLOODSPORT   Cannon, 1988
PAUL HERTZOG

BLOODSPORT II   DEM Productions, 1995
STEVE EDWARDS

BLOODSPORT III   DEM Productions, 1996
STEVE EDWARDS

BLOODSUCKING FREAKS   Troma, 1982
MICHAEL SAHL

BLOODY BIRTHDAY/CREEPS   1980
ARLON OBER

BLOSSOM IN PARIS (TF)   Witt-Thomas Prods./Touchstone TV, 1993
FRANK DENSON

BLOSSOM TIME   Possomtown Pictures, 1996
STEVE EDWARDS

BLOSSOMS IN THE DUST   MGM, 1941
HERBERT STOTHART†

BLOW OUT   Filmways, 1981
PINO DONAGGIO

BLOWBACK   Northern Arts, 1991
WENDY BLACKSTONE

BLOWING WILD   Warner Bros., 1953
DIMITRI TIOMKIN†

BLOWN AWAY   MGM, 1994
ALAN SILVESTRI

BLOWUP   Premier, 1966
HERBIE HANCOCK

BLUE   1993
SIMON FISHER TURNER

BLUE   Paramount, 1968
MANOS HADJIDAKIS†

THE BLUE AND THE GRAY (MS)   Larry White-Lou Reda Productions/Columbia TV, 1982
BRUCE BROUGHTON ☆

THE BLUE ANGEL   20th Century-Fox, 1959
HUGO FRIEDHOFER†

THE BLUE ANGEL   UFA, 1930
FREDERICK HOLLANDER†

BLUE ANGELS   1976
FRED MYROW

THE BLUE BIRD   20th Century-Fox, 1940
ALFRED NEWMAN†

THE BLUE BIRD   20th Century-Fox, 1976
IRWIN KOSTAL†
ANDREY PETROVIC

BLUE CHIPS   Paramount, 1994
JEFF BECK
JED LEIBER
NILE RODGERS

BLUE CITY   Paramount, 1986
RY COODER

BLUE COLLAR   Universal, 1978
JACK NITZCHE

THE BLUE COUNTRY   LE PAYS BLEU   Quartet, 1977
GERARD ANFOSSO

THE BLUE DAHLIA   Paramount, 1946
VICTOR YOUNG†

BLUE De VILLE (TF)   B & E Enterprises Ltd./NBC Productions, 1986
DON FELDER

BLUE DENIM   20th Century-Fox, 1959
BERNARD HERRMANN†

BLUE DESERT   Neo, 1991
JOEL GOLDSMITH

THE BLUE EXILE   1993
TIMUR SELCUK

BLUE FIN   Roadshow Distributors, 1978
MICHAEL CARLOS

BLUE HEAVEN (TF) Paramount TV, 1997
DANA KAPROFF

BLUE ICE (CTF) M&M/HBO, 1992
MICHAEL KAMEN

THE BLUE IGUANA Paramount, 1988
ETHAN JAMES

BLUE IN THE FACE Miramax, 1995
JOHN LURIE

BLUE JUICE 1995
SIMON DAVISON

THE BLUE KNIGHT (TF) Lorimar Productions, 1973
NELSON RIDDLE†

THE BLUE LAGOON Columbia, 1980
BASIL POLEDOURIS

THE BLUE LIGHTNING (TF) Alan Sloan Productions/
The Seven Network/Coote-Carroll Australia/
Roadshow, 1986
FRANK STRANGIO

THE BLUE MAX 20th Century-Fox, 1966
JERRY GOLDSMITH

BLUE MONEY (TF) London Weekend Television,
1985
RICHARD HARTLEY

BLUE MONKEY Spectrafilm, 1987
PATRICK COLEMAN
PAUL NOVOTNY

BLUE MOON Winfield Films
SHIRLEY WALKER

BLUE MURDER AT ST. TRINIAN'S British Lion,
1958
MALCOLM ARNOLD

THE BLUE NIGHT (TF) Lorimar Productions, 1975
HENRY MANCINI†

BLUE RODEO (TF) Warner Bros. TV, 1996
LAURA KARPMAN

BLUE SKIES Paramount, 1946
ROBERT EMMETT DOLAN† ★

BLUE SKIES AGAIN Warner Bros., 1983
JOHN KANDER

BLUE SKY Orion, 1994
JACK NITZCHE

BLUE STEEL MGM/UA, 1990
BRAD FIEDEL

BLUE THUNDER Columbia, 1983
ARTHUR B. RUBINSTEIN

THE BLUE VEIL RKO Radio, 1951
FRANZ WAXMAN†

BLUE VELVET DEG, 1986
ANGELO BADALAMENTI

BLUEBEARD 1972
ENNIO MORRICONE

BLUEBEARD Producers Releasing Corp., 1944
LEO ERDODY†

BLUEBEARD'S EIGHTH WIFE Paramount, 1938
WERNER R. HEYMANN†
FREDERICK HOLLANDER†

BLUEGRASS (TF) The Landsburg Company, 1988
DON DAVIS
MARK SNOW

BLUEPRINT FOR MURDER 20th Century Fox,
1953
LIONEL NEWMAN†

BLUEPRINT FOR ROBBERY Paramount, 1961
NATHAN VAN CLEAVE†

THE BLUES BROTHERS Universal, 1980
IRA NEWBORN

BLUES IN THE NIGHT Warner Bros., 1941
HEINZ ROEMHELD†

BLUFFING IT (TF) Don Ohlmeyer Productions, 1987
BRAD FIEDEL

BLUME IN LOVE Warner Bros., 1973
BILL CONTI

BMOC Vestron, 1989
JOSEPH VITARELLI

BOARDWALK Atlantic Releasing Corporation, 1979
JOEL DORN

THE BOAT Triumph/Columbia, 1981
KLAUS DOLDINGER

THE BOATNIKS Buena Vista, 1970
ROBERT F. BRUNNER

BOB & CAROL & TED & ALICE Columbia, 1969
QUINCY JONES

BOB AND SALLY Social Guidance, 1948
MILTON ROSEN†

THE BOB MATHIAS STORY Allied Artists, 1954
LEITH STEVENS†

BOB ROBERTS Paramount/Miramax, 1992
DAVID ROBBINS

BOBBIE JO AND THE OUTLAW American
International, 1976
BARRY DEVORZON

BOBBY DEERFIELD Columbia, 1977
DAVE GRUSIN

THE BOBO Warner Bros., 1967
FRANCIS LAI

BOCA 1994
RICHARD FELDMAN
ADAM GARGONI
MIDGE URE

BOCCACCIO 1972
CARLO RUSTICHELLI

BOCCACCIO '70 Embassy, 1962
NINO ROTA†

BODIES, REST, AND MOTION Fine Line, 1993
MICHAEL CONVERTINO

BODY AND SOUL Cannon, 1981
WEBSTER LEWIS

BODY AND SOUL United Artists, 1947
HUGO FRIEDHOFER†

BODY AND SOUL (MS) 1994
JIM PARKER

BODY BAGS (CTF) 187 Corp., 1993
JOHN CARPENTER
JIM LANG

BODY CHEMISTRY Concorde, 1990
TERRY PLUMERI

BODY CHEMISTRY II - VOICE OF A STRANGER
1991
NIGEL HOLTON

BODY CHEMISTRY III Concorde/New Horizons,
1993
CHUCK CIRINO

THE BODY DISAPPEARS 1941
BERNHARD KAUN†

BODY DOUBLE Columbia, 1984
PINO DONAGGIO

BODY HEAT The Ladd Company/Warner Bros., 1981
JOHN BARRY

BODY LANGUAGE (CTF) Mi Sammy/Wilshire Court,
1992
MISHA SEGAL

BODY MELT Dumb Films, 1993
PHILIP BROPHY

BODY OF EVIDENCE MGM/UA, 1993
GRAEME REVELL

BODY OF EVIDENCE (TF) CBS Entertainment, 1988
JOHN CACAVAS

BODY PARTS Paramount, 1991
LOEK DIKKER

BODY PARTS Vista Street Entertainment, 1991
MIRIAM CUTLER

BODY SLAM DEG, 1987
JOHN D'ANDREA
MICHAEL LLOYD

THE BODY SNATCHER RKO Radio, 1945
ROY WEBB†

BODY SNATCHERS Warner Bros., 1993
JOE DELIA

THE BODYGUARD Warner Bros., 1992
DAVID FOSTER
ALAN SILVESTRI

THE BODYGUARDS 1993
ENNIO MORRICONE

BOEING BOEING Paramount, 1965
NEAL HEFTI

THE BOFORS GUN Universal, 1968
CARL DAVIS

BOGGY CREEK II Howco International, 1985
FRANK MCKELVEY

BOGIE: THE LAST HERO (TF) Charles Fries
Productions, 1980
CHARLES BERNSTEIN

BOGUS Warner Bros., 1996
MARC SHAIMAN

BOILING POINT Warner Bros., 1993
JOHN D'ANDREA
CORY LERIOS

BOKYO Toho, 1975
AKIRA IFUKUBE

THE BOLD AND THE BRAVE RKO Radio, 1956
HERSCHEL BURKE GILBERT

BOLERO Cannon, 1984
ELMER BERNSTEIN
PETER BERNSTEIN

BOLERO Paramount, 1934
ANDREA SETARO†

BOLERO LES UNS ET LES AUTRES/WITHIN
MEMORY Double 13/Sharp Features, 1982
FRANCIS LAI

BOMBARDIER RKO Radio, 1943
ROY WEBB†

BOMBAY CLIPPER Universal, 1942
HANS J. SALTER†

BOMBER'S MOON 20th Century-Fox, 1943
DAVID BUTTOLPH†

BOMBERS B-52 Warner Bros., 1957
LEONARD ROSENMAN

BON APPETIT MAMA ITC, 1993
MASON DARING

BON VOYAGE, CHARLIE BROWN (AND DON'T
COME BACK) Paramount, 1980
ED BOGAS

BONA COME IL PANO 1981
STELVIO CIPRIANI

BONANZA: THE NEXT GENERATION (TF)
Gaylord Production Company/LBS Communications/
Bonanza Ventures, 1988
BOB COBERT

BONANZA: THE RETURN (TF) Legend
Entertainment/NBC Prods., 1993
BRUCE MILLER

BONE Jack H. Harris Enterprises, 1972
GIL MELLE

THE BONFIRE OF THE VANITIES Warner Bros.,
1990
DAVE GRUSIN

BONGO MAN Arsenal Kino Tubingen, 1982
JIMMY CLIFF

BONJOUR CINEMA 1955
CLAUDE BOLLING

BONJOUR LA FAMILLE (TF) 1993
JEAN-CLAUDE PETIT

BONJOUR TRISTESSE Columbia, 1958
GEORGES AURIC†

BONNIE AND CLYDE Warner Bros., 1967
CHARLES STROUSE

BONNIE AND CLYDE: THE TRUE STORY (TF)
Hoffman-Israel/FNM Films, 1992
SCOTT PAGE-PAGTER
JOHN VALENTINO

THE BONNIE PARKER STORY American
International, 1958
RONALD STEIN†

BONUS MALUS 1993
ANTONIO DIPOFI

BONZO GOES TO COLLEGE Universal, 1952
FRANK SKINNER†

THE BOOGENS Jensen Farley Pictures, 1981
ROBERT SUMMERS

THE BOOGEY MAN Jerry Gross Organization, 1980
TIM KROG

BOOGEYMAN II New West Films, 1983
CRAIG HUNDLEY
TIM KROG

BOOK OF LOVE New Line, 1991
STANLEY CLARKE

BOOKWORM 1997
JERRY GOLDSMITH

BOOM TOWN MGM, 1940
FRANZ WAXMAN†

BOOM! Universal, 1968
JOHN BARRY

BOOMERANG 1992
MARCUS MILLER

BOOMERANG 20th Century-Fox, 1947
DAVID BUTTOLPH†

THE BOOST Hemdale, 1988
STANLEY MYERS†

BOOTLEGGERS Howco International, 1974
JAIME MENDOZA-NAVA

BOOTS MALONE Columbia, 1952
ELMER BERNSTEIN

BOOTY CALL 1997
ROBERT FOLK

BOP GIRL BOP GIRL GOES CALYPSO United
Artists, 1957
LES BAXTER†

BOP GIRL GOES CALYPSO United Artists, 1957
LES BAXTER†

BOPHA! Paramount, 1993
JAMES HORNER

BORA BORA 1969
LES BAXTER†
RIZ ORTOLANI

THE BORDER Universal, 1983
RY COODER

BORDER CAFE RKO Radio, 1937
NATHANIEL SHILKRET†

BORDER FEUD Producers Releasing Corp., 1947
ALBERT GLASSER

BORDER G-MAN RKO Radio, 1938
ROY WEBB†

BORDER INCIDENT MGM, 1949
ANDRE PREVIN

THE BORDER OF TONG CPG, 1991
ELIOT DOUGLAS
PAUL SHORICK

BORDER RADIO Coyote Films, 1987
DAVE ALVIN

BORDER RANGERS Lippert, 1950
ALBERT GLASSER

BORDER RIVER Universal, 1954
HERMAN STEIN

BORDERLINE ITC, 1980
GIL MELLE

BORDERLINE Universal, 1950
HANS J. SALTER†

THE BORGIA STICK (TF) Universal TV, 1967
KENYON HOPKINS

BORIS AND NATASHA (CTF) MCEG, 1990
DAVID KITAY

BORN AGAIN Avco Embassy, 1978
LES BAXTER†

BORN AMERICAN Concorde, 1986
RICHARD G. MITCHELL

BORN BEAUTIFUL (TF) Procter & Gamble
Productions/Telecom Entertainment, 1982
BRAD FIEDEL

BORN FREE Columbia, 1966
JOHN BARRY ★★

BORN IN EAST L.A. Universal, 1987
LEE HOLDRIDGE

BORN INNOCENT (TF) Tomorrow Entertainment,
1974
FRED KARLIN

BORN INTO EXILE (TF) NBC Prods., 1997
DANA KAPROFF

BORN KICKING (TF) BBC, 1992
HAL LINDES

BORN LOSERS American International, 1967
MIKE CURB

BORN OF FIRE Film Four International
COLIN TOWNS

BORN ON THE FOURTH OF JULY Universal, 1989
JOHN WILLIAMS ★

BORN TO BE BAD RKO Radio, 1950
FREDERICK HOLLANDER†

BORN TO BE BAD United Artists, 1934
ALFRED NEWMAN†

BORN TO BE SOLD (TF) Ron Samuels Productions,
1981
JOHNNY HARRIS

BORN TO BE WILD Warner Bros., 1995
MARK SNOW

BORN TO KILL New World, 1975
MICHAEL FRANKS

BORN TO RACE MGM/UA, 1988
ROSS VANNELLI

BORN TO RUN Buena Vista, 1976
RON GOODWIN

BORN TO RUN (TF) Fox West Pictures, 1993
SIMON FRANGLEN

BORN TO SKI (FD) 1992
RONNIE MONTROSE

BORN TOO SOON (TF) Adam Prods., 1993
MARK SNOW

BORN YESTERDAY Buena Vista, 1993
GEORGE FENTON

BORN YESTERDAY Columbia, 1950
FREDERICK HOLLANDER†

BORNEO (TD) 1986
LOUIS FREDRIC HEMSEY

THE BORROWERS (CTF) Working Title TV/BBC-TV/
Turner Network TV/BBC's Children Intl./Children's
Film Foundation/De Faria Co., 1993
HOWARD GOODALL

THE BORROWERS (TF) Walt DeFaria Productions/
20th Century-Fox TV, 1973
BILLY BYERS
ROD MCKUEN

BORSALINO Paramount, 1970
CLAUDE BOLLING

BORSALINO AND CO. Medusa, 1974
CLAUDE BOLLING

THE BOSS United Artists, 1956
ALBERT GLASSER

BOSS OF BOOMTOWN Universal, 1944
HANS J. SALTER†

BOSS OF HANGTOWN MESA Universal, 1943
HANS J. SALTER†

THE BOSS' SON The Boss' Son Prods., 1978
RICHARD MARKOWITZ†

THE BOSS'S WIFE Tri-Star, 1987
BILL CONTI

THE BOSTONIANS Almi Pictures, 1984
RICHARD ROBBINS

BOTANY BAY Paramount, 1953
FRANZ WAXMAN†

BOTTLE ROCKET Columbia, 1996
MARK MOTHERSBAUGH

THE BOTTOM OF THE BOTTLE 20th Century-Fox,
1956
LEIGH HARLINE†

BOTTSCHEFF DER GOETTER MYSTERIES OF THE
GODS 1976
PETER THOMAS

BOULEVARD NIGHTS Warner Bros., 1979
LALO SCHIFRIN

BOUND 1996
DON DAVIS

BOUND AND GAGGED, A LOVE STORY G.E.L./
Cinescope, 1993
WILLIAM MURPHY

BOUND FOR GLORY United Artists, 1976
LEONARD ROSENMAN ★★

BOUNDS OF LOVE (TF) Hearst, 1993
GEORGE S. CLINTON

THE BOUNTY Orion, 1984
VANGELIS

THE BOUNTY HUNTER Warner Bros., 1954
DAVID BUTTOLPH†

THE BOUNTY KILLER Embassy, 1965
RONALD STEIN†

THE BOURNE IDENTITY (TF) Alan Shayne
Productions/Warner Bros. TV, 1988
LAURENCE ROSENTHAL ☆☆

THE BOWERY United Artists, 1933
ALFRED NEWMAN†

BOWERY TO BROADWAY Universal, 1944
EDWARD WARD†

BOX OF MOONLIGHT Trimark, 1996
JOHN LURIE

'97-'98
FILM
COMPOSERS
INDEX

FILM

TITLES

BOXING HELENA   Main Line, 1993
GRAEME REVELL

THE BOY AND THE PIRATES   United Artists, 1960
ALBERT GLASSER

BOY AND THE BRIDGE   Columbia, 1959
MALCOLM ARNOLD

A BOY CALLED HATE   Skouras, 1995
PRAY FOR RAIN

THE BOY FRIEND   MGM, 1971
PETER MAXWELL DAVIES

BOY FROM INDIANA   Eagle Lion, 1950
LUD GLUSKIN†

THE BOY FROM OKLAHOMA   Warner Bros., 1954
MAX STEINER†

BOY FROM THE SUBURBS   RAGAZZO DI
BORGATA   Italneggio, 1976
NINO ROTA†

THE BOY IN BLUE   20th Century Fox, 1986
ROGER WEBB

THE BOY IN THE PLASTIC BUBBLE (TF)
Spelling-Goldberg Productions, 1976
MARK SNOW

BOY IN THE TREE   1961
QUINCY JONES

THE BOY KUMASENU   1951
ELISABETH LUYTENS†

BOY MEETS GIRL   Kino Eye, 1994
JIM CROSBY
GEOFF SOUTHAL

A BOY NAMED CHARLIE BROWN (AF)   National
General, 1968
ROD MCKUEN

THE BOY NEXT DOOR/SEX AND THE
TEENAGER   Columbia, 1972
DAVID SHIRE

BOY ON A DOLPHIN   20th Century-Fox, 1957
HUGO FRIEDHOFER ★

A BOY TEN FEET TALL   Paramount, 1965
LES BAXTER†

A BOY TEN FEET TALL   SAMMY GOING SOUTH
Paramount, 1963
TRISTRAM CARY

THE BOY WHO CAUGHT A CROOK   United Artists,
1961
RICHARD LASALLE

THE BOY WHO COULD FLY   20th Century Fox,
1986
BRUCE BROUGHTON

THE BOY WHO CRIED BITCH   1991
WENDY BLACKSTONE

THE BOY WHO CRIED WEREWOLF   Universal,
1973
TED STOVALL

THE BOY WHO DRANK TOO MUCH (TF)   MTM
Enterprises Inc., 1980
MICHAEL SMALL

THE BOY WHO STOLE A MILLION   Paramount,
1960
TRISTRAM CARY

THE BOY WITH GREEN HAIR   RKO Radio, 1948
LEIGH HARLINE†

BOY'S NIGHT OUT   MGM, 1962
FRANK DEVOL

BOY'S RANCH   MGM, 1946
NATHANIEL SHILKRET†

BOY, DID I GET THE WRONG NUMBER!   United
Artists, 1966
RICHARD LASALLE

BOYFRIEND SCHOOL   Hemdale, 1990
MICHAEL GORE

BOYS   Buena Vista, 1996
STEWART COPELAND

THE BOYS (TF)   William Link Prods./Papazian-Hirsch,
1991
DAVID SHIRE

THE BOYS FROM BRAZIL   20th Century-Fox, 1978
JERRY GOLDSMITH ★

THE BOYS IN BLUE   MAM Ltd./Apollo Leisure Group,
1983
ED WELCH

THE BOYS IN COMPANY C   Columbia, 1978
JAIME MENDOZA-NAVA

BOYS LIFE   Strand, 1995
HUNDRED POUND HEAD
TOM JUDSON
WENDALL J. YUPONCE

THE BOYS NEXT DOOR   New World, 1985
GEORGE S. CLINTON

THE BOYS OF ST. VINCENT   1993
NEIL SMOLAR

BOYS ON THE SIDE   Warner Bros., 1995
DAVID NEWMAN

BOYS TOWN   MGM, 1938
EDWARD WARD†

BOYS WILL BE BOYS (TF)
RIK HOWARD

BOYZ N THE HOOD   Columbia, 1991
STANLEY CLARKE

BRADDOCK: MISSING IN ACTION III   Cannon,
1988
JAY CHATTAWAY

THE BRADY BUNCH MOVIE   Paramount, 1995
GUY MOON

BRADY'S ESCAPE   Satori Entertainment, 1984
CHARLES GROSS

THE BRADYS (TF)   Brady Productions, Paramount
TV, 1990
LAURENCE JUBER

THE BRAIN   Paramount, 1969
GEORGES DELERUE†

THE BRAIN   VENGEANCE   Garrick, 1962
KENNETH V. JONES

BRAIN DONORS   Paramount, 1992
IRA NEWBORN

BRAIN SMASHER...A LOVE STORY   Kings Road,
1993
TONY RIPPARETTI

BRAIN WAVES   Motion Picture Marketing, 1983
ROBERT O. RAGLAND

BRAINDEAD   1992
PETER DASENT

BRAINSCAN   Triumph, 1994
GEORGE S. CLINTON

BRAINSTORM   MGM/UA, 1983
JAMES HORNER

BRAKER (TF)   Blatt-Singer Productions/Centerpoint
Productions/MGM/UA TV, 1985
BRAD FIEDEL

BRAM STOKER'S DRACULA   Columbia, 1992
WOJCIECH KILAR

THE BRAMBLE BUSH   Warner Bros., 1960
LEONARD ROSENMAN

BRANCALEONE ALLE CROCIATE   Fair Film, 1970
CARLO RUSTICHELLI

A BRAND NEW LIFE (TF)   Tomorrow Entertainment,
1973
BILLY GOLDENBERG ☆

BRAND X   1970
KEN LAUBER

BRANDED   Paramount, 1951
ROY WEBB†

BRANNIGAN   United Artists, 1975
DOMINIC FRONTIERE

THE BRASHER DOUBLOON   20th Century-Fox,
1947
DAVID BUTTOLPH†

BRASS (TF)   Carnan Productions/Jaygee Productions/
Orion TV, 1985
JOE SHERMAN

THE BRASS BOTTLE   Universal, 1964
BERNARD GREEN

THE BRASS LEGEND   United Artists, 1956
PAUL DUNLAP

BRASS TARGET   MGM/United Artists, 1978
LAURENCE ROSENTHAL

BRASSED OFF   Miramax, 1996
TREVOR JONES

THE B.R.A.T. PATROL (TF)   Mark H. Ovitz
Productions/Walt Disney Productions, 1986
JONATHAN TUNICK

BRATS   1992
GABOR PRESSER

THE BRAVADOS   20th Century-Fox, 1958
HUGO FRIEDHOFER†
LIONEL NEWMAN†

THE BRAVE LITTLE TOASTER (TF)
Hyperion-Kushner-Locke Productions, 1987
DAVID NEWMAN

BRAVE NEW WORLD (TF)   Universal TV, 1980
PAUL CHIHARA

THE BRAVE ONE   RKO Radio, 1956
VICTOR YOUNG†

BRAVEHEART   Paramount, 1995
JAMES HORNER ★

BRAVO ALFA (FD)   1956
MAURICE JARRE

THE BRAVOS (TF)   Groverton Productions/Universal
TV, 1972
LEONARD ROSENMAN

BRAZIL   Republic, 1944
WALTER SCHARF ★

BRAZIL   Universal, 1985
MICHAEL KAMEN

BREACH OF CONDUCT (CTF)   Finnegan-Pinchuk/
MTE, 1994
TERRY PLUMERI

BREACH OF CONTRACT   Atlantic Releasing
Corporation, 1984
JOHN E. DAVIS

BREAD AND ROSES   1993
JOHN CHARLES

BREAD, LOVE AND DREAMS   PANE, AMORE E
FANTASIA   Italian Film Export, 1953
ALESSANDRO CICOGNINI†

BREAK OF DAWN   Cinewest, 1988
MARK ADLER

BREAK OF DAY   1976
GEORGE DREYFUS

BREAK OF HEARTS   RKO Radio, 1935
MAX STEINER†

BREAK TO FREEDOM   ALBERT R.N.   United
Artists, 1953
MALCOLM ARNOLD

BREAKABLE   1994
SHINSUKE HONDA

BREAKDOWN   1997
BASIL POLEDOURIS

BREAKDOWN   Realart, 1952
PAUL DUNLAP

BREAKER MORANT   New World/Quartet, 1980
ERIC COOK

THE BREAKFAST CLUB   Universal, 1985
GARY CHANG
KEITH FORSEY

BREAKFAST AT TIFFANY'S   Paramount, 1961
HENRY MANCINI† ★★

BREAKFAST IN PARIS   1982
BRIAN MAY†

BREAKFAST OF ALIENS   Eric Parkinson and
Hemdale, 1993
HAUNTED GARAGE
MATTHEW ENDER

BREAKHEART PASS   United Artists, 1976
JERRY GOLDSMITH

BREAKIN'   MGM/UA/Cannon, 1984
MICHAEL BOYD
GARY REMAL-MALKIN

BREAKIN' 2: ELECTRIC BOOGALOO   Tri-Star/
Cannon, 1984
MICHAEL J. LINN†

BREAKING ALL THE RULES   New World, 1985
PAUL J. ZAZA

BREAKING AWAY   20th Century-Fox, 1979
PATRICK WILLIAMS ★

BREAKING IN   Samuel Goldwyn Company, 1989
MICHAEL GIBBS

BREAKING POINT (CTF)   Avnet/Kerner Co., 1989
J.A.C. REDFORD

BREAKING THE ICE   RKO Radio, 1938
VICTOR YOUNG† ★

BREAKING THE RULES   Miramax, 1992
FRANK FITZPATRICK
DAVID KITAY

BREAKING THE SOUND BARRIER   THE SOUND
BARRIER   Lippert, 1952
MALCOLM ARNOLD

BREAKING THE WAVES   1996
JOAKIM HOLBECK

BREAKING UP (TF)   Time-Life Productions/Talent
Associates Ltd., 1978
WALTER LEVINSKY

BREAKING UP IS HARD TO DO (TF)
Green-Epstein Productions/Columbia TV, 1979
RICHARD BELLIS
GERALD FRIED

BREAKOUT   Columbia, 1975
JERRY GOLDSMITH

BREAKOUT (TF)   Universal TV, 1970
SHORTY ROGERS†

BREAKTHROUGH   Warner Bros., 1950
WILLIAM LAVA†

BREAKTHROUGH   SERGEANT STEINER   Maverick
Pictures International, 1978
PETER THOMAS

A BREATH OF SCANDAL   Paramount, 1960
ALESSANDRO CICOGNINI†

BREATHING LESSONS (TF)   Signboard Hill Prods.,
1994
JOHN KANDER

BREATHING UNDER WATER   1992
ELIZABETH DRAKE

BREATHLESS   Orion, 1983
JACK NITZCHE

A BREED APART   Orion, 1984
MAURICE GIBB

BREEZY   Universal, 1973
MICHEL LEGRAND

BRENDA STARR   New World, 1987
JOHNNY MANDEL

BRENDA STARR (TF)   Wolper Productions, 1976
LALO SCHIFRIN

BREWSTER McCLOUD   MGM, 1970
GENE PAGE

BREWSTER'S MILLIONS   United Artists, 1945
HUGO FRIEDHOFER†

BREWSTER'S MILLIONS   Universal, 1985
RY COODER

BRIAN'S SONG (TF)   Screen Gems/Columbia TV,
1971
MICHEL LEGRAND ☆

THE BRIBE   MGM, 1949
MIKLOS ROZSA†

THE BRIDE   Columbia, 1985
MAURICE JARRE

THE BRIDE   Golden Gate/Unisphere, 1974
PETER BERNSTEIN

THE BRIDE AND THE BEAST   QUEEN OF THE
GORILLAS   Allied Artists, 1958
LES BAXTER†

BRIDE BY MISTAKE   RKO Radio, 1944
ROY WEBB†

THE BRIDE CAME C.O.D.   Warner Bros., 1941
MAX STEINER†

BRIDE FOR SALE   RKO Radio, 1949
FREDERICK HOLLANDER†

THE BRIDE IN BLACK (TF)   New World TV, 1990
JOSEPH CONLAN

BRIDE OF BOOGEDY (TF)   Walt Disney TV, 1987
JOHN ADDISON

THE BRIDE OF FRANKENSTEIN   Universal, 1935
FRANZ WAXMAN†

BRIDE OF RE-ANIMATOR   Empire Pictures, 1990
RICHARD H. BAND

BRIDE OF THE GORILLA   Realart, 1951
MORT GLICKMAN†
RAOUL KRAUSHAAR

BRIDE OF THE RE-ANIMATOR   50th Street, 1991
RICHARD H. BAND

BRIDE OF THE REGIMENT   Warner Bros., 1930
EDWARD WARD†

BRIDE OF VENGEANCE   Paramount, 1949
HUGO FRIEDHOFER†

THE BRIDE WALKS OUT   RKO Radio, 1936
ROY WEBB†

THE BRIDE WORE BLACK   Lopert, 1968
BERNARD HERRMANN†

THE BRIDE WORE BOOTS   Paramount, 1946
FREDERICK HOLLANDER†

THE BRIDE WORE RED   MGM, 1937
FRANZ WAXMAN†

THE BRIDES OF DRACULA   Universal, 1960
MALCOLM WILLIAMSON

THE BRIDES OF FU MANCHU   7 Arts, 1966
JOHNNY DOUGLAS

BRIDES OF CHRIST (MS)   1993
MARIO MILLO

BRIDESHEAD REVISITED (MS)   Granada TV/
WNET-13/NDR Hamburg, 1982
GEOFFREY BURGON

BRIDESMAIDS (TF)   Motown Productions/Qintex
Entertainment/Deaune Productions, 1989
PAUL CHIHARA

THE BRIDGE   1991
RICHARD G. MITCHELL

BRIDGE ACROSS TIME   TERROR AT LONDON
BRIDGE/ARIZONA RIPPER (TF)   Fries
Entertainment, 1985
LALO SCHIFRIN

THE BRIDGE AT REMAGEN   United Artists, 1969
ELMER BERNSTEIN

THE BRIDGE OF SAN LUIS REY   United Artists,
1944
DIMITRI TIOMKIN† ★

THE BRIDGE ON THE RIVER KWAI   Columbia,
1957
MALCOLM ARNOLD ★★

BRIDGE TO SILENCE (TF)   Fries Entertainment,
1989
FRED KARLIN ☆

BRIDGE TO THE SUN   MGM, 1961
GEORGES AURIC†

A BRIDGE TOO FAR   United Artists, 1977
JOHN ADDISON

BRIDGER (TF)   Universal TV, 1976
ELLIOT KAPLAN†

THE BRIDGES AT TOKO-RI   Paramount, 1955
LYN MURRAY†

THE BRIDGES OF MADISON COUNTY   Warner
Bros., 1995
LENNIE NIEHAUS

BRIEF ENCOUNTER (TF)   Carlo Ponti Productions/
Cecil Clarke Productions, 1974
CYRIL ORNADEL

A BRIEF HISTORY OF TIME (FD)   1992
PHILIP GLASS

A BRIEF VACATION   Allied Artists, 1973
MANUEL DE SICA

BRIGADOON   MGM, 1954
JOHN GREEN†

THE BRIGAND   Columbia, 1952
MARIO †

BRIGHAM YOUNG   20th Century-Fox, 1940
ALFRED NEWMAN†

BRIGHT ANGEL   Hemdale, 1991
CHRISTOPHER YOUNG

BRIGHT LEAF   Warner Bros., 1950
VICTOR YOUNG†

BRIGHT LIGHTS, BIG CITY   MGM/UA, 1988
DONALD FAGEN
ROB MOUNSEY
CURT SOBEL

BRIGHT ROAD   MGM, 1953
DAVID ROSE†

BRIGHT VICTORY   Universal, 1951
FRANK SKINNER†

BRIGHTON BEACH MEMOIRS   Universal, 1986
MICHAEL SMALL

THE BRIGHTON STRANGLER   RKO Radio, 1945
LEIGH HARLINE†

BRILLIANT LIES   Bayside Pictures, 1995, Australian
NERIDA TYSON-CHEW

BRIMSTONE AND TREACLE United Artists Classics, 1982
STING

BRING ME THE HEAD OF ALFREDO GARCIA United Artists, 1974
JERRY FIELDING†

BRING ME THE HEAD OF DOBIE GILLIS (TF) 20th Century Fox TV, 1988
JIMMIE HASKELL

BRING ME THE HEAD OF MAVIS DAVIS Goldcrest, 1995
CHRISTOPHER TYNG

BRING ON THE GIRLS Paramount, 1945
ROBERT EMMETT DOLAN†

BRINGING UP BABY RKO Radio, 1938
ROY WEBB†

THE BRINK'S JOB Universal, 1978
RICHARD RODNEY BENNETT

BRINK'S: THE GREAT ROBBERY (TF) QM Productions/Warner Bros. TV, 1976
RICHARD MARKOWITZ†

BRITAIN AT BAY 1940
RICHARD ADDINSELL†

BRITISH INTELLIGENCE Warner Bros., 1940
HEINZ ROEMHELD†

BRITTANIA HOSPITAL United Artists Classics, 1982
ALAN PRICE

BRITTANIA MEWS 20th Century-Fox, 1949
MALCOLM ARNOLD

BROADCAST NEWS 20th Century Fox, 1987
BILL CONTI

BROADWAY Universal, 1942
FRANK SKINNER†

BROADWAY DANNY ROSE Orion, 1983
DICK HYMAN

BROADWAY MUSKETEERS Warner Bros., 1938
ADOLPH DEUTSCH†

BROADWAY RHYTHM MGM, 1944
JOHN GREEN†

BROADWAY SERENADE MGM, 1939
HERBERT STOTHART†

BROADWAY TO HOLLYWOOD MGM, 1933
WILLIAM AXT†

BROADWAY TO HOLLYWOOD Universal, 1933
DIMITRI TIOMKIN†

BROCK'S LAST CASE (TF) Talent Associates/Universal TV, 1973
CHARLES GROSS

BROKEN ANGEL (TF) The Stan Margulies Company/MGM-UA TV, 1988
JAMES DIPASQUALE

BROKEN ARROW 20th Century Fox, 1996
HANS ZIMMER

BROKEN ARROW 20th Century-Fox, 1950
HUGO FRIEDHOFER†

THE BROKEN CHAIN (CTF) Von Zerneck-Sertner, 1993
CHARLES FOX

THE BROKEN CORD (TF) Carmen Culver Films/Alan Barnette Prods./Universal, 1992
LAURA KARPMAN

BROKEN ENGLISH Lorimar, 1981
GEORGES DELERUE†

BROKEN HEARTS AND NOSES Columbia, 1985
ARLON OBER

BROKEN LANCE 20th Century-Fox, 1954
LEIGH HARLINE†

BROKEN LAND 20th Century-Fox, 1962
RICHARD LASALLE

BROKEN LULLABY Paramount, 1932
W. FRANKE HARLING†

BROKEN PROMISE (TF) EMI TV, 1981
FRED KARLIN

BROKEN PROMISES: TAKING EMILY BACK (TF) Larry Thompson Ent./RHI, 1993
CHRIS BOARDMAN

BROKEN RAINBOW (FD) Earthworks, 1985
LAURA NYRO

THE BROKEN STAR United Artists, 1956
PAUL DUNLAP

BROKEN TRUST (CTF) Fonda-Bonfiglio Films/TNT, 1995
RICHARD HOROWITZ

BROKEN VOWS (TF) Brademan-Self Productions/Robert Halmi, Inc., 1987
CHARLES GROSS

BRONCO BILLY Warner Bros., 1980
SNUFF GARRETT
STEVE DORFF

BRONTE Charlotte Ltd. Partnership/Radio Telefis Eireann, 1983
ARTHUR HARRIS

THE BRONTE SISTERS Gaumont, 1979
PHILIPPE SARDE

A BRONX TALE Savoy, 1993
STEPHEN ENDELMAN

THE BROOD New World, 1979
HOWARD SHORE

BROOKLYN ORCHID United Artists, 1942
EDWARD WARD†

A BROOKLYN STATE OF MIND Norstar, 1996
PAUL J. ZAZA

THE BROTHER FROM ANOTHER PLANET Cinecom, 1984
MASON DARING

BROTHER FUTURE (TF) Lanceuville/Morris, 1991
STEPHEN JAMES TAYLOR

BROTHER JOHN Columbia, 1971
QUINCY JONES

BROTHER MINISTER: THE ASSASSINATION OF MALCOLM X (FD) X-Ceptional Prods., 1994
RICHIE HAVENS

BROTHER OF SLEEP 1996
NORBERT J. SCHNEIDER
HUBERT VON GOISERN

BROTHER ON THE RUN 1974
JOHNNY PATE

BROTHER ORCHID Warner Bros., 1940
HEINZ ROEMHELD†

BROTHER RAT AND BABY Warner Bros., 1940
HEINZ ROEMHELD†

BROTHER'S KEEPER (FD) American Playhouse Theatrical Films, 1992
MOLLY MASON
JAY UNGAR

THE BROTHERHOOD Paramount, 1968
LALO SCHIFRIN

BROTHERHOOD OF JUSTICE (TF) Guber-Peters Entertainment Co. Productions/Phoenix Entertainment Group, 1986
BRAD FIEDEL

BROTHERHOOD OF THE BELL (TF) Cinema Center 100, 1970
JERRY GOLDSMITH

BROTHERHOOD OF THE GUN (TF) 1991
JERRY GOLDSMITH
JOEL GOLDSMITH

BROTHERHOOD OF THE ROSE (TF) NBC Productions, 1989
LAURENCE ROSENTHAL

BROTHERLY LOVE COUNTRY DANCE MGM, 1970
JOHN ADDISON

BROTHERLY LOVE (TF) CBS Entertainment, 1985
JONATHAN TUNICK

BROTHERS Warner Bros., 1977
TAJ MAHAL

BROTHERS AND SISTERS British Film Institute, 1980
TREVOR JONES

THE BROTHERS KARAMAZOV 1931
KAROL RATHAUS†

THE BROTHERS KARAMAZOV MGM, 1957
BRONISLAU KAPER†

THE BROTHERS McMULLEN 20th Century Fox Searchlight, 1995
SEAMUS EGAN

BROTHERS-IN-LAW (TF) Stephen J. Cannell Productions, 1985
PETE CARPENTER†
MIKE POST

BROWN BREAD SANDWICHES Leader Media Productions, 1989
LAWRENCE SHRAGGE

THE BROWNING VERSION Paramount, 1994
MARK ISHAM

BRUBAKER 20th Century-Fox, 1980
LALO SCHIFRIN

BRUTE FORCE Universal, 1947
MIKLOS ROZSA†

THE BRUTE MAN Universal, 1946
HANS J. SALTER†

BRUTES AND SAVAGES 1978
RIZ ORTOLANI

BRUTTI SPORCHI E CATTIVI 1976
ARMANDO TROVAJOLI

B.S. I LOVE YOU 20th Century-Fox, 1971
MARK SHEKTER

BUBA 1986
DOV SELTZER

THE BUBBLE FANTASTIC INVASION OF THE PLANET EARTH Obeler Films, 1967
PAUL SAWTELL†
BERT A. SHEFTER

BUBU' BRC, 1970
CARLO RUSTICHELLI

THE BUCCANEER Paramount, 1938
GEORGE ANTHEIL†

THE BUCCANEER Paramount, 1959
ELMER BERNSTEIN

BUCCANEER'S GIRL Universal, 1950
WALTER SCHARF

BUCK AND THE PREACHER Columbia, 1972
BENNY CARTER

BUCK BENNY RIDES AGAIN Paramount, 1940
VICTOR YOUNG†

BUCK PRIVATES Universal, 1941
CHARLES PREVIN† ★

BUCK ROGERS Universal, 1979
GLEN A. LARSON
STU PHILLIPS

A BUCKET OF BLOOD American International, 1959
FRED KATZ

BUCKSKIN Paramount, 1967
JIMMIE HASKELL

BUCKSKIN FRONTIER United Artists, 1943
VICTOR YOUNG†

THE BUCKSKIN LADY United Artists, 1957
ALBERT GLASSER

BUCKTOWN American International, 1975
JOHNNY PATE

BUD AND LOU (TF) Bob Banner Associates, 1978
FRED KARLIN

BUDDHA 1963
AKIRA IFUKUBE

BUDDIES 1983
CHRIS NEAL

BUDDY 1997
ELMER BERNSTEIN

BUDDY BUDDY MGM/United Artists, 1981
LALO SCHIFRIN

THE BUDDY FACTOR Cineville, 1994
TOM HEIL

THE BUDDY HOLLY STORY Columbia, 1978
JOE RENZETTI ★★

THE BUDDY SYSTEM 20th Century Fox, 1984
PATRICK WILLIAMS

BUFFALO BILL 20th Century-Fox, 1944
DAVID BUTTOLPH†

BUFFALO BILL AND THE INDIANS or SITTING BULL'S HISTORY LESSON United Artists, 1976
RICHARD BASKIN

BUFFALO GIRLS (TF) dePasse Ent./Cabin Fever/CBS Ent., 1995
LEE HOLDRIDGE ☆

BUFFALO JUMP 1992
NICHOLAS SMILEY

BUFFET FROID COLD CUTS 1980
PHILIPPE SARDE

BUFFY THE VAMPIRE SLAYER 20th Century Fox, 1992
CARTER BURWELL

BUFORD'S BEACH BUNNIES Axis, 1992
GREG GROSS

BUG Paramount, 1975
CHARLES FOX

BUGLES IN THE AFTERNOON Warner Bros., 1952
DIMITRI TIOMKIN†

BUGS BUNNY'S 3RD MOVIE: 1001 RABBIT TALES (AF) Warner Bros., 1982
ROBERT J. WALSH

BUGSY TriStar, 1991
ENNIO MORRICONE ★

BUGSY MALONE Paramount, 1976
PAUL WILLIAMS ★

THE BULL IL TORO 1994
IVANO FOSSATI

BULL DURHAM Orion, 1988
MICHAEL CONVERTINO

BULLDOG DRUMMOND IN AFRICA Paramount, 1938
MILAN RODER†

BULLDOG DRUMMOND STRIKES BACK United Artists, 1934
ALFRED NEWMAN†

A BULLET FOR JOEY United Artists, 1955
HARRY SUKMAN†

BULLET FOR A BADMAN Universal, 1964
FRANK SKINNER†

BULLET FOR THE GENERAL QUIEN SABE? Avco Embassy, 1968
LUIS BACALOV

A BULLET IS WAITING Columbia, 1954
DIMITRI TIOMKIN†

BULLETPROOF Cinetel, 1988
STEVE RUCKER

BULLETPROOF Universal, 1996
ELMER BERNSTEIN
MICHAEL BODDICKER

BULLETPROOF HEART Keystone, 1995
GRAEME COLEMAN

THE BULLFIGHTER AND THE LADY Republic, 1951
VICTOR YOUNG†

THE BULLFIGHTERS 20th Century-Fox, 1945
DAVID BUTTOLPH†

BULLIES Universal, 1986
PAUL J. ZAZA

BULLITT Warner Bros., 1968
LALO SCHIFRIN

BULLSEYE Cinema Group, 1987
CHRIS NEAL

BULLSEYE! 21st Century, 1991
JOHN DUPREZ

BULLSHIT 1993
OHNAY OGUZ

BULLSHOT! Island Alive, 1983
JOHN DUPREZ

BULLWHIP Allied Artists, 1958
LEITH STEVENS†

BUM RAP Millennium, 1988
ROBERT KESSLER
ETHAN NEUBURG

BUMP IN THE NIGHT (TF) Craig Anderson Prods./rhi, 1991
GARY WILLIAM FRIEDMAN

THE BUNKER (TF) Time-Life Productions/SFP France/Antenne-2, 1981
BRAD FIEDEL

BUNKER BEAN RKO Radio, 1936
ROY WEBB†

BUNNY LAKE IS MISSING Columbia, 1965
PAUL GLASS

A BUNNY'S TALE (TF) Stan Margulies Company/ABC Circle Films, 1985
PAUL CHIHARA

BUON FUNERALE, AMIGOS...PAGE SARTANA 1970
BRUNO NICOLAI

BUONGIORNO, ELEFANTE 1952
ALESSANDRO CICOGNINI†

THE 'BURBS Universal, 1989
JERRY GOLDSMITH

THE BURDEN OF PROOF (TF) Mike Robe Prods/Capital Cities/ABC, 1992
CRAIG SAFAN

THE BURGLAR Columbia, 1956
SOL KAPLAN

BURGLAR Warner Bros., 1987
SYLVESTER LEVAY

THE BURGLARS 1971
ENNIO MORRICONE

BURIED ALIVE Aquarius Releasing, 1981
GOBLIN

BURIED ALIVE The Movie Group, 1989
FREDERIC TALGORN

BURIED ALIVE (CTF) Niki Marvin Productions/MCA Entertainment, 1990
MICHEL COLOMBIER

BURIED ALIVE II (CTF) Universal TV, 1997
MICHEL COLOMBIER

BURKE & WILLS Hemdale, 1985
PETER SCULTHORPE

BURMA CONVOY Universal, 1941
HANS J. SALTER†

BURMA VICTORY (FD) Army Film Init., 1945
ALAN RAWSTHORNE†

THE BURMESE HARP HARP OF BURMA Brandon, 1956
AKIRA IFUKUBE

BURN WITCH BURN NIGHT OF THE EAGLE American International, 1962
WILLIAM ALWYN†

BURN! QUEIMADA! United Artists, 1970
ENNIO MORRICONE

BURNIN' LOVE Tri-Star, 1988
CHARLES FOX

THE BURNING Orion, 1982
RICK WAKEMAN

THE BURNING BED (TF) Tisch-Avnet Productions, 1984
CHARLES GROSS

BURNING BRIDGES (TF) Andrea Baynes Productions/Lorimar TV, 1990
BENNETT SALVAY
W.G. SNUFFY WALDEN

THE BURNING COURT 1962
GEORGES AURIC†

THE BURNING HILLS Warner Bros., 1956
DAVID BUTTOLPH†

A BURNING PASSION: THE MARGARET MITCHELL STORY (TF) Renee Valente Prods./NBC Prods., 1994
BILLY GOLDENBERG

BURNING RAGE (TF) Gilbert Cates Productions, 1984
ROBERT DRASNIN

THE BURNING SEASON Astral Communications, 1993
GORDON DURITY

THE BURNING SEASON (CTF) HBO Pictures, 1994
GARY CHANG

BURNING SECRET Vestron, 1988
HANS ZIMMER

BURNT BY THE SUN OUTOMLIONNYE SOLNTSEM Studio Trite/Camera One, 1994
EDUARD ARTEMYEV

BURNT OFFERINGS United Artists, 1976
BOB COBERT

BUS RILEY'S BACK IN TOWN Universal, 1965
RICHARD MARKOWITZ†

THE BUSHBABY MGM, 1970
LES REED

BUSHFIRE MOON (CTF) Entertainment Media/The Disney Channel/WonderWorks, 1987
BRUCE ROWLAND

THE BUSHIDO BLADE Aquarius, 1982
MAURY LAWS

BUSHWACKED 1995
BILL CONTI

BUSHWACKED GAZON MAUDIT 1995
MANUEL MALOU

THE BUSHWACKERS   Realart, 1951
ALBERT GLASSER

A BUSINESS AFFAIR   Capella, 1994
DIDIER VASSEUR

BUSINESS FOR PLEASURE   Spectacor, 1997
GEORGE S. CLINTON

BUSTED UP   Shapiro Entertainment, 1987
CHARLES P. BARNETT

BUSTER   Hemdale, 1988
ANNE DUDLEY

THE BUSTER KEATON STORY   Paramount 1957
VICTOR YOUNG†

BUSTIN' LOOSE   Universal, 1980
MARK DAVIS

BUSTING   United Artists, 1974
BILLY GOLDENBERG

THE BUSY BODY   Paramount, 1967
VIC MIZZY

BUT I DON'T WANT TO GET MARRIED! (TF)
Aaron Spelling Productions, 1970
GEORGE DUNING

BUT NOT FOR ME   Paramount, 1959
LEITH STEVENS†

BUT NOT IN VAIN   1948
GERARD SCHURMANN

BUTCH AND SUNDANCE: THE EARLY DAYS   20th
Century-Fox, 1979
PATRICK WILLIAMS

BUTCH CASSIDY AND THE SUNDANCE KID   20th
Century-Fox, 1969
BURT BACHARACH ★★

THE BUTCHER'S WIFE   Paramount, 1991
MICHAEL GORE

THE BUTTERCUP CHAIN   Warner Bros., 1970
RICHARD RODNEY BENNETT

BUTTERFIELD 8   MGM, 1960
BRONISLAU KAPER†

BUTTERFLIES ARE FREE   Columbia, 1972
BOB ALCIVAR

BUTTERFLY   Analysis, 1981
ENNIO MORRICONE

BUTTERFLY KISS   1995
JOHN HARLE

BUY AND CELL   Trans World Entertainment, 1989
MARK SHREEVE

BUYING TIME   MGM/UA, 1989
DAVID KRYSTAL

BWANA DEVIL   United Artists, 1953
GORDON JENKINS†

BWANA TOSHI   1965
TORU TAKEMITSU†

BY CANDLELIGHT   Universal, 1933
W. FRANKE HARLING†

BY DAWN'S EARLY LIGHT (CTF)   HBO/Paravision
International, 1990
TREVOR JONES

BY LOVE POSSESSED   United Artists, 1961
ELMER BERNSTEIN

BY NIGHTFALL   1991
ROBERTO GATTO
BATTISTA LENA

BY THE LIGHT OF THE SILVERY MOON   Warner
Bros., 1953
MAX STEINER†

BY THE SWORD   Movie Group, 1991
BILL CONTI

BY YOUR LEAVE   RKO Radio, 1934
MAX STEINER†

BYE BYE   1996
JIMMY OIHID
STEVE SHEHAN

BYE BYE BABY   Seymour Borde & Associates, 1989
MANUEL DE SICA

BYE BYE BIRDIE   Columbia, 1963
JOHN GREEN† ★

BYE BYE BRAVERMAN   Warner Bros., 1968
PETER MATZ

BYE BYE MONKEY   Gaumont, 1978
PHILIPPE SARDE

BYE BYE, LOVE   20th Century Fox, 1995
J.A.C. REDFORD

BYT   THE FLAT   1968
ZDENEK LISKA

C

CABARET   Allied Artists, 1972
RALPH BURNS ★★

CABIN BOY   Buena Vista, 1994
STEVE BARTEK

CABIN IN THE SKY   MGM, 1943
GEORGE BASSMAN

THE CABINET OF DOCTOR RAMIREZ   Mediascope,
1991
JOHN ADAMS

THE CABINET OF DR. CALIGARI   20th Century Fox,
1962
GERALD FRIED

CABIRIA   1913
JOSEPH CARL BREIL†

THE CABLE CAR MURDER (TF)   Warner Bros. TV,
1971
JERRY GOLDSMITH

THE CABLE GUY   Columbia, 1996
JOHN OTTMAN

CABOBLANCO   Avco Embassy, 1981
JERRY GOLDSMITH

CACCIA ALLA VOLPE   1966
PIERO PICCIONI

CACTUS FLOWER   Columbia, 1969
QUINCY JONES

CACTUS MOLLY AND LAWLESS JOHN   Malibu
Productions, 1971
JOHNNY MANDEL

CADAVERI ECCELENTI   United Artists, 1976
PIERO PICCIONI

CADDYSHACK   Orion/Warner Bros., 1980
JOHNNY MANDEL

CADDYSHACK II   Warner Bros., 1988
IRA NEWBORN

CADENCE   New Line, 1990
GEORGES DELERUE†

CADET L'EAU DOUCE   1969
CLAUDE BOLLING

CADFAEL: THE LEPER OF ST. GILES (TF)   British
Central Films Prods., 1995
COLIN TOWNS

CADILLAC MAN   Orion, 1990
J. PETER ROBINSON

CADILLAC RANCH   Sony Classics, 1994
CHRISTOPHER TYNG

CAESAR AND CLEOPATRA   United Artists, 1945
GEORGES AURIC†

CAFE FLESH   1983
MITCHELL FROOM

CAFE METROPOLE   20th Century-Fox, 1937
LOUIS SILVERS†

CAFE SOCIETY   Paramount, 1939
LEO SHUKEN†

CAFEN DE NULLE PART   1970
VLADIMIR COSMA

CAGE   New Century/Vista, 1989
MICHAEL WETHERWAX

CAGE WITHOUT A KEY (TF)   Columbia TV, 1975
MICHEL LEGRAND

CAGED   Warner Bros., 1950
MAX STEINER†

THE CAGED HEART   New World, 1985
JEAN-CLAUDE PETIT

CAGED HEARTS   PM Entertainment, 1995
LARRY WOLFF

CAGLIOSTRO   1975
MANUEL DE SICA

CAGNEY & LACEY: THE RETURN (TF)   The
Rozenzweig Co., 1994
DANA KAPROFF

CAGNEY AND LACEY (TF)   Mace Neufeld
Productions/Filmways, 1981
MARK SNOW

CAGNEY AND LACEY: TOGETHER AGAIN (TF)
Rosenzweig Co./CBS, 1995
NAN SCHWARTZ-MISHKIN

CAHILL, U.S. MARSHALL   Warner Bros., 1973
ELMER BERNSTEIN

THE CAINE MUTINY   Columbia, 1954
MAX STEINER† ★

CAIRO   MGM, 1942
HERBERT STOTHART†

CAL   Warner Bros., 1984
MARK KNOPFLER

CALABOOSE   United Artists, 1943
EDWARD WARD†

CALAMITY JANE (TF)   CBS Entertainment, 1983
FRED KARLIN

CALCUTTA   Paramount, 1947
VICTOR YOUNG†

CALENDAR GIRL   Columbia, 1993
HANS ZIMMER

CALENDAR GIRL MURDERS (TF)   Tisch-Avnet
Productions, 1984
BRAD FIEDEL

CALENDAR GIRL, COP, KILLER?: THE BAMBI
BEMBENECK STORY (TF)   von Zerneck-Sertner
Films, 1992
DANA KAPROFF

THE CALENDAR OF THE YEAR   1936
BENJAMIN BRITTEN†

THE CALIFORNIA KID (TF)   Universal TV, 1974
LUCHI DEJESUS

THE CALIFORNIA REICH (FD)   City Life Films, 1975
CRAIG SAFAN

CALIFORNIA   Paramount, 1947
VICTOR YOUNG†

CALIFORNIA CASANOVA   Academy, 1991
REG POWELL
SAM WINANS

CALIFORNIA DREAMING   American International,
1979
FRED KARLIN

CALIFORNIA GIRLS (TF)   ABC Circle Films, 1985
MARK SNOW

CALIFORNIA SPLIT   Columbia, 1974
PHYLLIS SHOTWELL
JOHN WILLIAMS

CALIFORNIA SUITE   Columbia, 1978
CLAUDE BOLLING

CALIGULA   Analysis Film Releasing, 1979
PAUL CLEMENTE

CALL A MESSENGER   Universal, 1939
HANS J. SALTER†

CALL ME   Vestron, 1988
DAVID MICHAEL FRANK

CALL ME MADAM   20th Century-Fox, 1953
ALFRED NEWMAN† ★★

CALL ME MISTER   20th Century-Fox, 1951
LEIGH HARLINE†

CALL NORTHSIDE 777   20th Century-Fox, 1948
ALFRED NEWMAN†

THE CALL OF THE WILD   United Artists, 1935
ALFRED NEWMAN†

THE CALL OF THE WILD (TF)   Charles Fries
Productions, 1976
PETER MATZ

CALL OF THE FLESH   MGM, 1930
HERBERT STOTHART†

CALL OF THE JUNGLE   Monogram, 1944
ALBERT GLASSER

CALL OF THE WILD   Constantin, 1972
CARLO RUSTICHELLI

CALL OF THE WILD (TF)   RHI Entertainment, 1993
LEE HOLDRIDGE ☆

CALL TO DANGER (TF)   Paramount Pictures TV,
1973
LAURENCE ROSENTHAL

CALLAN   Cinema National, 1975
WILFRED JOSEPHS

CALLE MAYOR   1956
JOSEPH KOSMA†

THE CALLER   Empire Pictures, 1987
RICHARD H. BAND

THE CALL-GIRL BUSINESS   1960
ARMANDO TROVAJOLI

CALL-GIRLS OF ROME   1960
ARMANDO TROVAJOLI

CALLIE & SON (TF)   Rosilyn Heller Productions/
Hemdale Presentations/City Films/Motown Pictures
Co., 1981
BILLY GOLDENBERG

CALLING DR. DEATH   RKO Radio, 1943
PAUL SAWTELL†

CALLING DR. DEATH   Universal, 1943
HANS J. SALTER†
FRANK SKINNER†

CALLING DR. GILLESPIE   MGM, 1942
DANIELE AMFITHEATROF†

CALM AT SUNSET (TF)   Hallmark, 1996
ERNEST TROOST

CALMOS   New Line Cinema, 1976
GEORGES DELERUE†

CALORE IN PROVINCIA   1975
CARLO SAVINA

CALYPSO (FD)   1958
ANGELO FRANCESCO LAVAGNINO†

CAMERON'S CLOSET   SVS Films, 1989
HARRY MANFREDINI

CAMILLA   Miramax, 1994
DANIEL LANOIS

CAMILLE   MGM, 1927
WILLIAM AXT†

CAMILLE   MGM, 1937
HERBERT STOTHART†

CAMILLE (TF)   Rosemont Productions, 1984
ALLYN FERGUSON ☆☆

CAMILLE CLAUDEL   Orion Classics, 1988
GABRIEL YARED

CAMMINA CAMMINA   Gaumont, 1983
BRUNO NICOLAI

CAMORRA   1972
MANUEL DE SICA

CAMOUFLAGE   1940
RICHARD ADDINSELL†

CAMOUFLAGE   Libra, 1977
WOJCIECH KILAR

CAMP NOWHERE   Buena Vista, 1994
DAVID LAWRENCE

THE CAMP ON BLOOD ISLAND   Columbia, 1958
GERARD SCHURMANN

CAMPANE A MARTELLO   1948
NINO ROTA†

CAMPFIRE TALES   Vault/Kunert-Manes Productions,
1997
ANDREW ROSE

CAMPINE   1957
ARMANDO TROVAJOLI

CAMPUS MAN   Paramount, 1987
JAMES NEWTON HOWARD

CAN BE DONE, AMIGO   1972
LUIS BACALOV

CAN SHE BAKE A CHERRY PIE?   Castle Hill
Productions/Quartet Films, 1983
KAREN BLACK

CAN YOU FEEL ME DANCING? (TF)   Robert
Greenwald Productions, 1986
JOHNNY HARRIS

CAN YOU HEAR THE LAUGHTER? THE STORY OF
FREDDIE PRINZE (TF)   Roger Gimbel
Productions/EMI TV, 1979
PETER MATZ

CAN'T BUY ME LOVE   Buena Vista, 1987
ROBERT FOLK

CAN'T HELP SINGING   Universal, 1944
HANS J. SALTER†

CAN'T STOP THE MUSIC   AFD, 1980
JACQUES MORALI

CANADIAN BACON   Gramercy, 1995
ELMER BERNSTEIN
PETER BERNSTEIN

CANADIAN PACIFIC   20th Century-Fox, 1949
DIMITRI TIOMKIN†

THE CANADIANS (MS)   Cineworld, Canadian
HAGOOD HARDY

CAN-CAN   20th Century-Fox, 1960
NELSON RIDDLE† ★

CANDIDATE PER UN ASSASSINO   1969
BILL CONTI

CANDLES IN THE DARK (CTF)   Taska Films/
Kushner-Locke/Family Prods., 1993
RICHARD BOWERS

CANDLESHOE   Buena Vista, 1977
RON GOODWIN

CANDY   Cinerama Releasing Corporation, 1968
DAVE GRUSIN

CANDYMAN   TriStar, 1992
PHILIP GLASS

CANDYMAN: FAREWELL TO THE FLESH
Gramercy, 1995
PHILIP GLASS

CANICULE   DOG DAY   UGC, 1984
FRANCIS LAI

CANNABIS   1970
SERGE GAINSBOURG†

CANNERY ROW   MGM/UA, 1982
JACK NITZCHE

CANNIBAL HOLOCAUST   Trans Continental Film,
1979
RIZ ORTOLANI

CANNIBAL WOMEN IN THE AVOCADO JUNGLE
OF DEATH   Paramount, 1989
CARL DANTE

CANNON (TF)   QM Productions, 1971
ROBERT DRASNIN

CANNON FOR CORDOBA   United Artists, 1970
ELMER BERNSTEIN

THE CANNONBALL RUN   20th Century-Fox, 1981
SNUFF GARRETT

CANNONBALL   New World, 1976
DAVID A. AXELROD

CANNONBALL RUN II   Warner Bros., 1984
AL CAPPS
STEVE DORFF

A CANTERBURY TALE   Eagle-Lion, 1944
ALLAN GRAY†

THE CANTERBURY TALES   United Artists, 1972
ENNIO MORRICONE

THE CANTERVILLE GHOST   MGM, 1944
GEORGE BASSMAN

THE CANTERVILLE GHOST (TF)   Pound Ridge
Productions/Inter- Hemisphere Productions/HTV/
Columbia TV, 1986
HOWARD BLAKE

THE CANTERVILLE GHOST (TF)   Signboard Hill,
1995
ERNEST TROOST

CANYON CROSSROADS   United Artists, 1955
GEORGE BASSMAN

CANYON DREAMS   Miramar, 1987
TANGERINE DREAM
CHRISTOPHER FRANKE

CANYON PASSAGE   Universal, 1946
FRANK SKINNER†

CANZONI, CANZONI, CANZONI   1953
CARLO RUSTICHELLI

CAPE FEAR   Universal, 1962
BERNARD HERRMANN†

CAPE FEAR   Universal, 1991
ELMER BERNSTEIN

THE CAPER OF THE GOLDEN BULLS   Embassy,
1967
VIC MIZZY

CAPITOL NEWS (TF)   MTM, 1989
JAN HAMMER

CAPONE   20th Century-Fox, 1975
DAVID GRISMAN

CAPRICCIO ALL'ITALIANA   De Laurentiis, 1968
PIERO PICCIONI

CAPRICE   20th Century-Fox, 1967
FRANK DEVOL

CAPRICES 1942
GEORGES VAN PARYS†

CAPRICORN ONE 20th Century-Fox, 1978
JERRY GOLDSMITH

CAPTAIN AMERICA 21st Century, 1992
BARRY GOLDBERG

CAPTAIN AMERICA (TF) Universal TV, 1979
PETE CARPENTER†
MIKE POST

CAPTAIN AMERICA II (TF) Universal TV, 1979
PETE CARPENTER†
MIKE POST

CAPTAIN BLACK JACK United Artists, 1950
JOSEPH KOSMA†

CAPTAIN BLOOD Warner Bros., 1935
ERICH WOLFGANG KORNGOLD†

CAPTAIN BOYCOTT 1947
WILLIAM ALWYN†

CAPTAIN CAREY, U.S.A. Paramount, 1950
HUGO FRIEDHOFER†

CAPTAIN CLEGG 1962
DON BANKS

CAPTAIN EDDIE 20th Century-Fox, 1945
CYRIL J. MOCKRIDGE†

CAPTAIN FANTASMA, IL TESORO DELLE INDIE
1953
CARLO RUSTICHELLI

CAPTAIN FROM CASTILE 20th Century-Fox, 1947
ALFRED NEWMAN† ★

CAPTAIN FURY United Artists, 1939
T. MARVIN HATLEY†

CAPTAIN HORATIO HORNBLOWER Warner Bros.,
1951
ROBERT FARNON

CAPTAIN HURRICANE RKO Radio, 1935
ROY WEBB†

THE CAPTAIN IS A LADY MGM, 1940
BRONISLAU KAPER†

CAPTAIN JANUARY 20th Century-Fox, 1936
LOUIS SILVERS†

CAPTAIN JOHN SMITH AND POCAHONTAS
United Artists, 1953
ALBERT GLASSER

CAPTAIN KIDD United Artists, 1945
WERNER JANSSEN ★

CAPTAIN KIDD AND THE SLAVE GIRL United
Artists, 1954
PAUL SAWTELL†

CAPTAIN KRONOS: VAMPIRE HUNTER
Paramount, 1974
LAURIE JOHNSON

CAPTAIN LIGHTFOOT Universal, 1955
HANS J. SALTER†
HERMAN STEIN

CAPTAIN NEMO AND THE UNDERWATER CITY
MGM, 1970
ANGELA MORLEY

CAPTAIN NEWMAN M. D. Universal, 1963
FRANK SKINNER†

CAPTAIN PIRATE Columbia, 1952
GEORGE DUNING

CAPTAIN RON Buena Vista, 1992
NICHOLAS PIKE

CAPTAIN SINDBAD MGM, 1963
MICHEL MICHELET†

CAPTAIN SIROCCO Film Classics, 1949
NINO ROTA†

THE CAPTAIN'S TABLE 20th Century-Fox, 1960
FRANK CORDELL†

THE CAPTAIN'S PARADISE British Lion, 1953
MALCOLM ARNOLD

CAPTAINS AND THE KINGS (MS) Universal TV,
1976
ELMER BERNSTEIN ☆

CAPTAINS COURAGEOUS MGM, 1937
FRANZ WAXMAN†

CAPTAINS COURAGEOUS (TF) Norman Rosemont
Productions, 1977
ALLYN FERGUSON

CAPTAINS OF THE CLOUDS Warner Bros., 1942
MAX STEINER†

CAPTIVE Blackwatch Communications, 1997
DAVID FINDLAY

CAPTIVE (TF) Capital Cities-ABC/Bonny Dore/
Ten-Four, 1991
PAUL BUCKMASTER
STEVE TYRELL

THE CAPTIVE CITY United Artists, 1952
EMIL NEWMAN†

CAPTIVE CITY United Artists, 1952
JEROME MOROSS†

THE CAPTIVE HEART Universal, 1946
ALAN RAWSTHORNE†

CAPTIVE HEARTS MGM/UA, 1987
DAVID BENOIT
OSAMU KITAJIMA

A CAPTIVE IN THE LAND Gloria, 1991
BILL CONTI

CAPTIVE WILD WOMAN Universal, 1943
HANS J. SALTER†

CAPTIVES Miramax, 1996
COLIN TOWNS

THE CAPTURE RKO Radio, 1950
DANIELE AMFITHEATROF†

THE CAPTURE OF GRIZZLY ADAMS (TF) Schick
Sunn Classics Productions/Taft International Pictures,
1982
ROBERT SUMMERS

THE CAR Universal, 1977
LEONARD ROSENMAN

CAR 54, WHERE ARE YOU? Orion, 1994
PRAY FOR RAIN
BERNIE WORRELL

THE CAR THIEF 1964
TORU TAKEMITSU†

CAR WASH Universal, 1976
NORMAN WHITFIELD

CARAVAGGIO British Film Institute, 1986
MARY PHILLIPS
SIMON FISHER TURNER

CARAVAN Fox, 1934
WERNER R. HEYMANN†

CARAVAN TO VACCARES Bryanston, 1976
STANLEY MYERS†

CARAVANS Universal, 1979
MIKE BATT

CARBINE WILLIAMS MGM, 1952
CONRAD SALINGER†

CARBON COPY Avco Embassy, 1981
BILL CONTI

THE CARD Universal, 1952
WILLIAM ALWYN†

THE CARDINAL Columbia, 1963
JEROME MOROSS†

CARDINAL RICHELIEU United Artists, 1935
ALFRED NEWMAN†

THE CARE BEARS MOVIE (AF) Samuel Goldwyn
Company, 1985
PATRICIA CULLEN
JOHN SEBASTIAN

CARE BEARS MOVIE II: A NEW GENERATION
(AF) Columbia, 1986
PATRICIA CULLEN

CAREER Paramount, 1959
FRANZ WAXMAN†

CAREER RKO Radio, 1939
ROBERT RUSSELL BENNETT†

CAREER OPPORTUNITIES Universal, 1991
THOMAS NEWMAN

CAREFUL HE MIGHT HEAR YOU TLC Films/20th
Century Fox, 1983
RAY COOK†

CAREFUL, SOFT SHOULDER 20th Century-Fox,
1942
LEIGH HARLINE†

THE CARELESS YEARS United Artists, 1957
LEITH STEVENS†

THE CARETAKER Janus, 1963
RON GRAINER†

THE CARETAKERS United Artists, 1963
ELMER BERNSTEIN

THE CAREY TREATMENT MGM, 1972
ROY BUDD†

CARGO TO CAPETOWN Columbia, 1950
GEORGE DUNING

CARI MOSTRI DEL MARE 1976
CARLO SAVINA

THE CARIBBEAN MYSTERY 20th Century-Fox,
1945
DAVID BUTTOLPH†

CARLITO'S WAY Universal, 1993
PATRICK DOYLE

CARLTON BROWN OF THE F.O. Show Corporation,
1960
JOHN ADDISON

CARLY'S WEB (TF) MTM Enterprises, 1987
RICHARD LEWIS WARREN

CARMEN Orion Classics, 1983
PACO DE LUCIA

CARMEN JONES 20th Century-Fox, 1954
HERSCHEL BURKE GILBERT ★

CARNABY, M.D. DOCTOR IN CLOVER
Continental, 1966
JOHN SCOTT

CARNALITA 1974
CARLO SAVINA

CARNIVAL 1946
NICHOLAS BRODZSKY†

CARNOSAUR Concorde-New Horizons, 1993
NIGEL HOLTON

CARNY United Artists, 1980
ALEX NORTH†

CARO MICHELE Cineriz, 1976
NINO ROTA†

CARO PAPA Dean Film/AMLF/Prospect Film, 1979
MANUEL DE SICA

CAROLINA SKELETONS (TF) Kushner-Locke, 1991
JOHN MORRIS

CAROLINE CHERIE 1951
GEORGES AURIC†

CAROLINE CHERIE 1973
GEORGES GARVARENTZ†

CAROLINE? (TF) Barry and Enright Productions,
1990
CHARLES BERNSTEIN

THE CARPETBAGGERS Paramount, 1964
ELMER BERNSTEIN

CARPOOL Warner Bros., 1996
JOHN DEBNEY

CARPOOL (TF) Charles Fries Productions, 1983
JIMMIE HASKELL

CARRIE Paramount, 1952
DAVID RAKSIN

CARRIE United Artists, 1976
PINO DONAGGIO

CARRIED AWAY Fine Line, 1996
BRUCE BROUGHTON

THE CARRIER Swan Productions, 1986
JOSEPH LO DUCA

CARRINGTON Gramercy, 1995
MICHAEL NYMAN

THE CARROT QUEEN 1978
LUIS DE PABLO

CARRY ON AGAIN, DOCTOR Rank, 1970
ERIC ROGERS†

CARRY ON CAMPING Rank, 1969
ERIC ROGERS†

CARRY ON CLEO Governor, 1964
ERIC ROGERS†

CARRY ON COLUMBUS 1992
JOHN DUPREZ

CARRY ON COWBOY Anglo-Amalgamated/
Warner-Pathe, 1966
ERIC ROGERS†

CARRY ON DICK Rank, 1974
ERIC ROGERS†

CARRY ON DOCTOR Rank, 1968
ERIC ROGERS†

CARRY ON EMMANUELLE Rank, 1978
ERIC ROGERS†

CARRY ON SCREAMING Anglo-Amalgamated/
Warner-Pathe, 1966
ERIC ROGERS†

CARRY ON SPYING Governor, 1964
ERIC ROGERS†

CARRY ON UP THE JUNGLE Rank, 1970
ERIC ROGERS†

CARRY ON...UP THE KHYBER Rank, 1969
ERIC ROGERS†

THE CARS THAT ATE PARIS New Line Cinema,
1974
BRUCE SMEATON

THE CARS THAT EAT PEOPLE THE CARS THAT
ATE PARIS New Line Cinema, 1974
BRUCE SMEATON

CARSON CITY Warner Bros., 1952
DAVID BUTTOLPH†

CARTER'S ARMY (TF) Thomas-Spelling Productions,
1970
FRED STEINER

CARTES SUR TABLE 1966
PAUL MISRAKI

THE CARTIER AFFAIR (TF) Hill-Mandelker
Productions, 1984
ARTHUR B. RUBINSTEIN

CARTOUCHE Embassy, 1962
GEORGES DELERUE†

CARVE HER NAME WITH PRIDE Lopert, 1958
WILLIAM ALWYN†

CASABLANCA Warner Bros., 1943
MAX STEINER† ★

CASANOVA Cinema '89, 1985
GEORGES DELERUE†

CASANOVA IL CASANOVA DI FEDERICO
FELLINI Universal, 1976
NINO ROTA†

CASANOVA '70 Embassy, 1965
ARMANDO TROVAJOLI

CASANOVA (TF) Konigsberg-Sanitsky Productions/
Reteitalia, 1987
MICHEL LEGRAND

CASANOVA IN BURLESQUE Republic, 1944
WALTER SCHARF

CASANOVA'S BIG NIGHT Paramount, 1954
LYN MURRAY†

THE CASE AGAINST BROOKLYN Columbia, 1958
MISCHA BAKALEINIKOFF†

THE CASE AGAINST FERRO POLICE PYTHON
357 1976
GEORGES DELERUE†

THE CASE AGAINST PAUL RYKER Universal,
1968
JOHN WILLIAMS

A CASE FOR A YOUNG HANGMAN 1970
ZDENEK LISKA

A CASE FOR LIFE (TF) ABC/Mirish Corp., 1995
DANA KAPROFF

A CASE FOR MURDER (CTF) Bodega Bay Prods./
MTE, 1993
RANDY MILLER

A CASE OF DEADLY FORCE (TF) Telecom
Entertainment, 1986
PAUL CHIHARA

THE CASE OF DR. LAURENT 1957
JOSEPH KOSMA†

THE CASE OF THE HILLSIDE STRANGLER (TF)
Kenwood Productions/Fries Entertainment, 1989
GIL MELLE

THE CASE OF THE MUKKINESE BATTLEHORN
1956
EDWIN ASTLEY

CASEY'S SHADOW Columbia, 1978
PATRICK WILLIAMS

CASH McCALL Warner Bros., 1960
MAX STEINER†

CASH ON DEMAND Columbia, 1962
WILFRED JOSEPHS

CASINO (TF) Aaron Spelling Productions/Metromedia
Producers Corporation, 1980
MARK SNOW

CASINO MURDER CASE MGM, 1935
DIMITRI TIOMKIN†

CASINO ROYALE Columbia, 1967
BURT BACHARACH

CASPER Universal, 1995
JAMES HORNER

CASQUE D'OR 1951
GEORGES VAN PARYS†

CASS TIMBERLANE MGM, 1948
ROY WEBB†

THE CASSANDRA CROSSING Avco Embassy, 1977
JERRY GOLDSMITH

CAST A DEADLY SPELL (CTF) Pacific Western,
1992
CURT SOBEL

CAST A GIANT SHADOW United Artists, 1966
ELMER BERNSTEIN

CAST A LONG SHADOW United Artists, 1959
GERALD FRIED

CAST THE FIRST STONE (TF) Mench Productions/
Columbia Pictures TV, 1989
IRA NEWBORN

CASTAWAY Cannon, 1986
STANLEY MYERS†
HANS ZIMMER

THE CASTAWAY COWBOY Buena Vista, 1974
ROBERT F. BRUNNER

THE CASTAWAYS OF GILLIGAN'S ISLAND (TF)
Sherwood Schwartz Productions, 1979
GERALD FRIED

CASTING AGENCY DB USA, 1991
DEAN WALRAFF

CASTLE KEEP Columbia, 1969
MICHEL LEGRAND

THE CASTLE OF THE LIVING DEAD 1964
ANGELO FRANCESCO LAVAGNINO†

THE CASTLE OF THE SPIDER'S WEB Brandon,
1957
MASARU SATO

CASTLE OF EVIL United Pictures, 1966
PAUL DUNLAP

CASTLE ON THE HUDSON Warner Bros., 1940
ADOLPH DEUTSCH†

CASUAL SEX? Universal, 1988
VAN DYKE PARKS

CASUALTIES OF LOVE: THE LONG ISLAND LOLITA
STORY (TF) Diane Sokolow Prods./TriStar TV,
1992
DAVID MICHAEL FRANK

CASUALTIES OF WAR Columbia, 1989
ENNIO MORRICONE

CAT AND MOUSE Quartet, 1975
FRANCIS LAI

CAT AND MOUSE (TF) Universal TV/Associated
British Films, 1974
RON GRAINER†

THE CAT AND THE CANARY Paramount, 1939
ERNST TOCH†

THE CAT AND THE CANARY Quartet, 1978
STEVEN CAGAN

THE CAT AND THE FIDDLE MGM, 1934
HERBERT STOTHART†

CAT BALLOU Columbia, 1965
FRANK DEVOL

CAT CHASER Vestron, 1989
TED COCHRAN

THE CAT CREATURE (TF) Screen Gems/Columbia
TV, 1973
LEONARD ROSENMAN

THE CAT CREEPS Universal, 1946
PAUL SAWTELL†

THE CAT FROM OUTER SPACE Buena Vista, 1978
LALO SCHIFRIN

CAT O'NINE TAILS National General, 1971
ENNIO MORRICONE

CAT PEOPLE RKO Radio, 1942
ROY WEBB†

CAT PEOPLE Universal, 1982
GIORGIO MORODER

C.A.T. SQUAD (TF) NBC Productions/Filmline International, 1986
ENNIO MORRICONE

C.A.T. SQUAD: PYTHON WOLF (TF) NBC Productions, 1988
ENNIO MORRICONE

CAT WOMEN OF THE MOON Astor, 1954
ELMER BERNSTEIN

CAT'S EYE MGM/UA, 1985
ALAN SILVESTRI

THE CAT'S PAW 20th Century-Fox, 1934
ALFRED NEWMAN†

CATACOMBS Empire Pictures, 1988
PINO DONAGGIO

CATASTROPHE 1999 New World, 1977
ISAO TOMITA

CATCH AS CATCH CAN 1967
LUIS BACALOV

CATCH ME A SPY Rank, 1971
CLAUDE BOLLING

CATCH ME IF YOU CAN MCEG, 1989
TANGERINE DREAM

CATCH YOUR DREAMS 1983
KITARO

CATCHFIRE Vestron, 1990
CURT SOBEL

THE CATERED AFFAIR MGM, 1956
ANDRE PREVIN

CATERINA SFORZA 1960
CARLO RUSTICHELLI

CATHERINE ET CIE 1975
VLADIMIR COSMA

CATHERINE THE GREAT United Artists, 1934
ERNST TOCH†

CATHOLICS (TF) Sidney Glazier Productions, 1973
CARL DAVIS

CATLOW MGM, 1971
ROY BUDD†

CATS *KATTORNA* 1964
CHRISTOPHER KOMEDA†

CATTIVI PENSIERI 1976
ARMANDO TROVAJOLI

CATTLE ANNIE AND LITTLE BRITCHES Universal, 1981
SANH BERTI
TOM SLOCUM

CATTLE EMPIRE 20th Century-Fox, 1958
BERT A. SHEFTER

CATTLE TOWN Warner Bros., 1952
WILLIAM LAVA†

CATWALK (TF) Franklin-Waterman-Marvellous TV/Lewis B. Chester/King St. Entertainment, 1992
PAUL HOFFERT

CAUGHT 1996
CHRIS BOTTI

CAUGHT MGM, 1949
FREDERICK HOLLANDER†

CAUGHT IN THE ACT (CTF) Davis Entertainment TV/Meltzer-Viviano Prods./MTE Prods., 1993
ARTHUR B. RUBINSTEIN

CAUGHT IN THE DRAFT Paramount, 1941
VICTOR YOUNG†

CAUSA DI DIVORZIO 1972
CARLO RUSTICHELLI

CAUSE FOR ALARM MGM, 1951
ANDRE PREVIN

CAUSE OF DEATH Vista Street Entertainment, 1991
MIRIAM CUTLER

CAUSE TOUJOURS, TU M'INTERESSES 1978
VLADIMIR COSMA

CAVALCADE d'AMOUR 1939
ARTHUR HONEGGER†
DARIUS MILHAUD†

CAVALCATA DI MEZZO SECOLO 1950
CARLO RUSTICHELLI

CAVE GIRL Crown International, 1985
JON ST. JAMES

CAVE-IN! (TF) Irwin Allen Productions/Warner Bros. Television, 1983
RICHARD LASALLE

CAVEMAN United Artists, 1981
LALO SCHIFRIN

THE CAVERN *SETTE CONTRO LA MORTE* 1964
CARLO RUSTICHELLI

CB4 Universal, 1993
JOHN BARNES

CEASE FIRE Cineworld, 1985
GARY FRY

CEASE FIRE! Paramount, 1953
DIMITRI TIOMKIN†

CELA S'APPELLE L'AURORE 1956
JOSEPH KOSMA†

CELEBRATION FAMILY (TF) Frank von Zerneck Films, 1987
FRED KARLIN

CELEBRITY (MS) NBC Productions, 1984
LEONARD ROSENMAN

CELESTINE, MAID AT YOUR SERVICE 1974
PAUL DE SENNEVILLE
OLIVER TOUISSANT

CELIA Hoyts, 1989
CHRIS NEAL

CELL 2455, DEATH ROW Columbia, 1955
MISCHA BAKALEINIKOFF†

CELLAR DWELLER Empire Pictures, 1988
CARL DANTE

CELLE QUI N'ETAIT PLUS 1957
DARIUS MILHAUD†

CELLES QU'ON N'A PAS EUES 1980
VLADIMIR COSMA

THE CELLULOID CLOSET 1996
CARTER BURWELL

CELTIC PRIDE Buena Vista, 1996
BASIL POLEDOURIS

CELUI QUI DOIT MOURIR *HE WHO MUST DIE* 1958
GEORGES AURIC†

THE CEMENT GARDEN 1993
EDWARD SHEARMUR

CEMETARY MAN 1996
MANUEL DE SICA

THE CEMETERY CLUB Buena Vista, 1993
ELMER BERNSTEIN

THE CENSUS TAKER Argentum Prods., 1984
JAY SEAGRAVE

CENTENNIAL (MS) Universal TV, 1980
JOHN ADDISON

CENTENNIAL SUMMER 20th Century-Fox, 1946
ALFRED NEWMAN† ★

CENTER OF THE WEB Pyramid, 1992
GREGG TURNER

CENTO ANNI D'AMORE 1954
NINO ROTA†

CENTURY I.R.S., 1994
MICHAEL GIBBS

A CENTURY OF WOMEN (CMS) Vu Productions, 1994
LAURA KARPMAN

THE CEREMONY 1971
TORU TAKEMITSU†

A CERTAIN DESIRE UGC, 1986
GABRIEL YARED

CERTAIN FURY New World, 1985
RUSS KUNKEL
GEORGE MASSENBURG
BILL PAYNE

A CERTAIN SMILE 20th Century-Fox, 1958
ALFRED NEWMAN†

CERTO, CERTISSIMI, ANZI...PROBABILE 1969
CARLO RUSTICHELLI

CERVANTES American International, 1968
LES BAXTER†

CESAR AND ROSALIE Cinema 5, 1972
PHILIPPE SARDE

C'EST ARRIVE A ADEN 1956
GEORGES VAN PARYS†

C'EST ARRIVE CHEZ NOUS *MAN BITES DOG* 1992
VLADIMIR CHEKASSINE

C'EST PAS MOI, C'EST LUI! 1979
VLADIMIR COSMA

CETTE NUIT-LA 1958
CLAUDE BOLLING

CETTE VIEILLE CANAILLE 1933
GEORGES VAN PARYS†

A CHACUN SON ENFER 1976
VLADIMIR COSMA

CHAD HANNA 20th Century-Fox, 1940
DAVID BUTTOLPH†

THE CHADWICK FAMILY (TF) Universal TV, 1974
HAL MOONEY

THE CHAIN Rank, 1985
STANLEY MYERS†

CHAIN LIGHTNING Warner Bros., 1950
DAVID BUTTOLPH†

CHAIN OF DESIRE 1992
NATHAN BIRNBAUM

CHAIN REACTION 1980
ANDREW WILSON

CHAIN REACTION 20th Century Fox, 1996
JERRY GOLDSMITH

CHAINDANCE Festival Films, 1992
GRAEME COLEMAN

CHAINED MGM, 1934
HERBERT STOTHART†

CHAINED HEAT Jensen Farley Pictures, 1983
JOSEPH CONLAN

CHAIR DE POULE *HIGHWAY PICKUP* 1963
GEORGES DELERUE†

THE CHAIRMAN 20th Century-Fox, 1969
JERRY GOLDSMITH

CHALEURS 1971
VLADIMIR COSMA

THE CHALK GARDEN Universal, 1964
MALCOLM ARNOLD

THE CHALLENGE OF GREATNESS 1976
MICHEL MICHELET†

THE CHALLENGE 20th Century-Fox, 1948
MILTON ROSEN†

THE CHALLENGE Embassy, 1982
JERRY GOLDSMITH

CHALLENGE OF A LIFETIME (TF) 20th Century-Fox TV, 1985
MARK SNOW

CHALLENGE TO AMERICA WITH HEDRICK SMITH (TD) Hedrick Smith Prods./WETA, 1994
CHARLES STROUSE

CHALLENGE TO LASSIE MGM, 1949
ANDRE PREVIN

THE CHALLENGERS (TF) Universal TV, 1970
PETE RUGOLO ☆☆

CHALLENGER (TF) The Indie Production Company/King Phoenix Entertainment/George Englund Productions, 1990
DAVID KOLE

THE CHALLENGES 1970
LUIS DE PABLO

THE CHAMBER Universal, 1996
CARTER BURWELL

CHAMBER OF HORRORS Warner Bros., 1966
WILLIAM LAVA†

THE CHAMP MGM/United Artists, 1979
DAVE GRUSIN ★★

THE CHAMPAGNE MURDERS *LE SCANDALE* Universal, 1967
PIERRE JANSEN

CHAMPAGNE FOR CAESAR United Artists, 1950
DIMITRI TIOMKIN†

CHAMPAGNE WALTZ Paramount, 1937
VICTOR YOUNG†

CHAMPION United Artists, 1949
DIMITRI TIOMKIN† ★

CHAMPIONS Embassy, 1983
CARL DAVIS

CHAMPIONS: A LOVE STORY (TF) Warner Bros. TV, 1979
JOHN RUBINSTEIN

CHAN IS MISSING New Yorker, 1982
ROBERT KIKUCHI-YNGOJO

CHANCE AND VIOLENCE 1974
MICHEL COLOMBIER

CHANCE AT HEAVEN RKO Radio, 1933
MAX STEINER†

CHANCE MEETING 1955
BENJAMIN FRANKEL†

CHANCE MEETING *BLIND DATE* Paramount, 1959
RICHARD RODNEY BENNETT

CHANCE OF A LIFETIME (TF) Lynn Roth Prods., 1991
DAVID MCHUGH

CHANCES ARE Tri-Star, 1989
MAURICE JARRE

CHANEL SOLITAIRE United Film Distribution, 1981
PAUL JABARA†
JEAN MUSY

A CHANGE OF SEASONS 20th Century-Fox, 1980
HENRY MANCINI†

CHANGE OF HABIT Universal, 1968
BILLY GOLDENBERG

CHANGE OF MIND Cinerama Releasing Corporation, 1969
DUKE ELLINGTON†

THE CHANGELING AFD, 1980
KEN WANNBERG
RICK WILKINS

THE CHANGELLING (CTF) BBC TV, 1994
STEPHEN WARBECK

CHANGES Cinerama Releasing Corporation, 1969
MARTY PAICH†

CHANGING GEARS Santelmo International, 1997
MARTIN KATZ

CHANGING HABITS Teagarden Pictures, 1997
DAVID MCHUGH

CHANGING OUR MINDS: THE STORY OF DR. EVELYN HOOKER (FD) Intrepid Prods., 1992
ABSOLUTE MUSIC

THE CHANNELER Magnum, 1990
CHUCK CIRINO

THE CHANT OF JIMMIE BLACKSMITH New Yorker, 1978
BRUCE SMEATON

CHANTILLY LACE (CTF) Showtime, 1993
PATRICK SEYMOUR

CHAPLIN TriStar, 1992
JOHN BARRY ★

THE CHAPMAN REPORT Warner Bros., 1962
LEONARD ROSENMAN

CHAPPAQUA Hunter, 1966
RAVI SHANKAR

CHARADE Universal, 1964
HENRY MANCINI†

THE CHARGE AT FEATHER RIVER Warner Bros., 1953
MAX STEINER†

THE CHARGE OF THE LIGHT BRIGADE United Artists, 1968
JOHN ADDISON

THE CHARGE OF THE LIGHT BRIGADE Warner Bros., 1936
MAX STEINER† ★

CHARIOTS OF FIRE The Ladd Company/Warner Bros., 1981
VANGELIS ★★

CHARIOTS OF THE GODS (FD) 1973
PETER THOMAS

CHARLES AND DIANA: A ROYAL LOVE STORY (TF) St. Lorraine Productions, 1982
JOHN ADDISON

CHARLES AND DIANA: UNHAPPILY EVER AFTER (TF) Konigsberg-Sanitsky, 1992
JAMES MCVAY

CHARLESTON (TF) Robert Stigwood Productions/RSO, Inc., 1979
ELMER BERNSTEIN

CHARLEY HANNAH (TF) A Shane Co. Productions/Telepictures Productions, 1986
JAN HAMMER

CHARLEY-ONE-EYE Paramount, 1973
JOHN CAMERON

CHARLIE CHAN AND THE CURSE OF THE DRAGON QUEEN American Cinema, 1980
PATRICK WILLIAMS

CHARLIE CHAN AT THE OPERA opera sequence, 20th Century-Fox, 1937
OSCAR LEVANT†

CHARLIE CHAN IN THE SECRET SERVICE Monogram, 1944
KARL HAJOS†

CHARLIE COBB: NICE NIGHT FOR A HANGING (TF) Fairmount/Foxcroft Productions/Universal TV, 1977
PETE CARPENTER†
MIKE POST

CHARLIE ET SES DEUX NENETTES 1973
PHILIPPE SARDE

CHARLIE McCARTHY, DETECTIVE Universal, 1939
FRANK SKINNER†

CHARLIE VARRICK Universal, 1973
LALO SCHIFRIN

CHARLIE'S ANGELS (TF) Spelling-Goldberg Productions, 1976
ALLYN FERGUSON
JACK ELLIOTT

CHARLOTTE 1975
MIKE OLDFIELD

CHARLY Cinerama Releasing Corporation, 1968
RAVI SHANKAR

CHARTING THE SEAS (FD) 1948
MALCOLM ARNOLD

THE CHASE 20th Century Fox, 1994
RICHARD GIBBS.

THE CHASE Columbia, 1966
JOHN BARRY

THE CHASE United Artists, 1946
MICHEL MICHELET†

CHASE Zenith Films
COLIN TOWNS

THE CHASE (TF) Steve White Prods./Spectacor, 1991
W.G. SNUFFY WALDEN

CHASE (TF) CBS Entertainment, 1973
OLIVER NELSON†

CHASE (TF) CBS Entertainment, 1985
CHARLES BERNSTEIN

CHASE A CROOKED SHADOW Warner Bros., 1958
MATYAS SEIBER†

CHASERS Warner Bros., 1994
PETE ANDERSON
DWIGHT YOAKAM

CHASING THE DEER British, 1995
JOHN WETTON

CHATO'S LAND United Artists, 1972
JERRY FIELDING†

CHATTAHOOCHEE Hemdale, 1989
JOHN E. KEANE

CHATTERBOX 1993
WEN ZHONGJIA

CHATTER-BOX American International, 1977
FRED KARGER

CHATTERBOX Republic, 1943
WALTER SCHARF

CHE C'ENTRIAMO NOI CON LA RIVOLUZIONE? 1972
ENNIO MORRICONE

CHE GIOIA VIVERE 1960
ANGELO FRANCESCO LAVAGNINO†

CHE! 20th Century-Fox, 1969
LALO SCHIFRIN

THE CHEAP DETECTIVE Columbia, 1978
PATRICK WILLIAMS

CHEAPER BY THE DOZEN 20th Century-Fox, 1950
CYRIL J. MOCKRIDGE†
LIONEL NEWMAN†

CHEAPER TO KEEP HER American Cinema, 1980
DICK HALLIGAN

THE CHEATERS Republic, 1945
WALTER SCHARF

CHEATING CHEATERS Universal, 1934
EDWARD WARD†

CHECK AND DOUBLE CHECK RKO Radio, 1930
MAX STEINER†

THE CHECK IS IN THE MAIL   Ascot Entertainment
Group, 1986
DAVID MICHAEL FRANK

CHECKING OUT   Warner Bros., 1989
CARTER BURWELL

CHEECH & CHONG STILL SMOKIN'   Paramount,
1983
GEORGE S. CLINTON

CHEECH & CHONG'S NICE DREAMS   Columbia,
1981
HARRY BETTS

CHEECH AND CHONG'S NEXT MOVIE   Universal,
1980
MARK DAVIS

CHEERS FOR MISS BISHOP   United Artists, 1941
EDWARD WARD† ★

CHEERS: ONE FOR THE ROAD (TF)
Charles-Burrows-Charles Prods./Paramount, 1993
CRAIG SAFAN

CHEETAH   Buena Vista, 1989
BRUCE ROWLAND

CHELSEA THROUGH THE MAGNIFYING GLASS
Rudolph Burckhardt, 1938
PAUL BOWLES

CHERE INCONNUE   Atlantic Releasing Corporation,
1980
PHILIPPE SARDE

CHERE LOUISE   Warner-Columbia, 1972
GEORGES DELERUE†

CHERI-BIBI   1938
PAUL MISRAKI

CHERNOBYL: THE FINAL WARNING (CTF)
Carolco-Gimger Prods./USSR Film Service, 1991
BILLY GOLDENBERG

CHERRY 2000   Orion, 1986
BASIL POLEDOURIS

CHERRY, HARRY AND RACQUEL   Eve, 1969
IGO KANTOR

CHESAPEAKE BAY RETRIEVER   Pedigreed Pictures,
1936
MARC BLITZSTEIN†

THE CHESS PLAYERS   Creative, 1977
SATYAJIT RAY†

CHETAN, INDIAN BOY   1973
PEER RABEN

CHETNIKS!   20th Century-Fox, 1943
HUGO FRIEDHOFER†

CHEYENNE   Warner Bros., 1947
MAX STEINER†

CHEYENNE AUTUMN   Warner Bros., 1964
ALEX NORTH†

THE CHEYENNE KID   RKO Radio, 1933
MAX STEINER†

CHEYENNE ROUNDUP   Universal, 1943
HANS J. SALTER†

THE CHEYENNE SOCIAL CLUB   National General,
1970
WALTER SCHARF

CHEYENNE WARRIOR   Concorde/New Horizons,
1994
ARTHUR KEMPEL

CHI DICE DONNA DICE...DONNA   1975
PIERO PICCIONI

CHI L'HA VISTA MORIRE?   1972
ENNIO MORRICONE

CHI LAVORA E'PERDUTO   IN CAPO AL
MONDO   Zebra Film/Franco London Film, 1963
PIERO PICCIONI

CHIAMATA 22-22 TENENTE SHERIDAN   1960
ARMANDO TROVAJOLI

CHICAGO CALLING   United Artists, 1952
HEINZ ROEMHELD†

CHICAGO CONFIDENTIAL   United Artists, 1957
EMIL NEWMAN†

CHICAGO DEADLINE   Paramount, 1949
VICTOR YOUNG†

CHICAGO JOE AND THE SHOWGIRL   1990
SHIRLEY WALKER
HANS ZIMMER

THE CHICAGO STORY (TF)   Eric Bercovici
Productions/MGM TV, 1981
LALO SCHIFRIN

THE CHICKEN CHRONICLES   Avco Embassy, 1977
KEN LAUBER

CHICKEN EVERY SUNDAY   20th Century-Fox,
1948
ALFRED NEWMAN†

CHIEDO ASILO   MY ASYLUM   1979
PHILIPPE SARDE

CHIEF CRAZY HORSE   Universal, 1955
FRANK SKINNER†

CHIEFS (MS)   Highgate Pictures, 1983
MICHAEL SMALL

CHIENS PERDUS SANS COLLIER   1955
PAUL MISRAKI

THE CHILD   Boxoffice International, 1977
ROB WALLACE

CHILD BRIDE OF SHORT CREEK (TF)   Lawrence
Schiller-Paul Monash Productions, 1981
JOHN CACAVAS

CHILD IN THE NIGHT (TF)   Mike Robe Productions,
1990
MARK SNOW

A CHILD IS BORN   Warner Bros., 1940
HEINZ ROEMHELD†

A CHILD IS WAITING   United Artists, 1963
ERNEST GOLD

A CHILD LOST FOREVER (TF)   ERB Productions/
TriStar TV, 1992
LAURA KARPMAN

CHILD MURDERS   1993
JANOS MASIK

CHILD OF DARKNESS, CHILD OF LIGHT (TF)
Wilshire Court/G.C. Group, 1991
JAY GRUSKA

CHILD OF DIVORCE   RKO Radio, 1946
LEIGH HARLINE†

CHILD OF RAGE (TF)   Gilliam Prods./C.M. Two
Prods./Republic Pictures, 1992
GERALD GOURIET

THE CHILD SAVER (TF)   Michael Filerman
Productions/NBC Productions, 1988
LENNIE NIEHAUS

THE CHILD STEALER (TF)   The Production Company/
Columbia TV, 1979
JIMMIE HASKELL

CHILD UNDER A LEAF   Cinema National, 1975
FRANCIS LAI

A CHILD'S CRY FOR HELP (TF)   RHI/Ronald J.
Kahn Prods., 1994
JOSEPH LO DUCA

CHILD'S CRY (TF)   Shoot the Moon Enterprises/
Phoenix Entertainment Group, 1986
GARRY SHERMAN

CHILD'S PLAY   1954
ANTONY HOPKINS

CHILD'S PLAY   MGM/UA, 1988
JOE RENZETTI

CHILD'S PLAY   Paramount, 1972
MICHAEL SMALL

CHILD'S PLAY 2   Universal, 1990
GRAEME REVELL

CHILD'S PLAY 3   Universal, 1991
JOHN D'ANDREA
CORY LERIOS

THE CHILDREN   1980
HARRY MANFREDINI

CHILDREN IN THE CROSSFIRE (TF)
Schaefer-Karpf Productions/Prendergast-Brittcadia
Productions, 1984
BRAD FIEDEL

THE CHILDREN NOBODY WANTED (TF)
Blatt-Singer Productions/Warner Bros. TV, 1981
BARRY DEVORZON

THE CHILDREN OF AN LAC (TF)   Charles Fries
Productions, 1980
PAUL CHIHARA

THE CHILDREN OF SANCHEZ   Lone Star, 1978
CHUCK MANGIONE

THE CHILDREN OF TIMES SQUARE (TF)
Gross-Weston Productions/Fries Entertainment, 1986
PATRICK GLEESON
MICHAEL SHRIEVE

CHILDREN OF A LESSER GOD   Paramount, 1986
MICHAEL CONVERTINO ★

CHILDREN OF DIVORCE (TF)   Christiana
Productions/Marble Arch Productions, 1980
MINETTE ALTON
RAOUL KRAUSHAAR

CHILDREN OF FATE: DEATH IN A SICILIAN
FAMILY (FD)   Young-Friedson, 1993
TED KUHN
JOHN LA BARBERA

CHILDREN OF HIROSHIMA   CHILDREN OF THE
ATOM BOMB   1952
AKIRA IFUKUBE

CHILDREN OF PARADISE   Tricolore, 1944
JOSEPH KOSMA†

CHILDREN OF RAGE   LSF, 1975
PATRICK GOWERS

CHILDREN OF THE ATOM BOMB   1952
AKIRA IFUKUBE

CHILDREN OF THE CORN   New World, 1984
JONATHAN ELIAS

CHILDREN OF THE CORN II: THE FINAL
SACRIFICE   Dimension, 1993
DANIEL LICHT

CHILDREN OF THE DAMNED   MGM, 1964
RON GOODWIN

CHILDREN OF THE DARK (TF)   Steve Krantz
Prods./Multimedia, 1994
DAVID MICHAEL FRANK

CHILDREN OF THE DUST (TF)   Konigsberg Co.,
1995
MARK SNOW

CHILDREN OF THE NIGHT   Fangoria, 1990
DANIEL LICHT

CHILDREN OF THE NIGHT (TF)   Robert Guenette
Productions, 1985
MILES GOODMAN†

CHILDREN SHOULDN'T PLAY WITH DEAD
THINGS   Gemini Film, 1972
CARL ZITTRER

THE CHILDREN'S HOUR   United Artists, 1961
ALEX NORTH†

CHILLER (TF)   Polar Film Corporation/J.D. Feigleson
Productions, 1985
DANA KAPROFF

CHILLY SCENES OF WINTER   United Artists, 1979
KEN LAUBER

CHIMES AT MIDNIGHT   FALSTAFF
Peppercorn-Wormser, 1966
ANGELO FRANCESCO LAVAGNINO†

CHINA   Paramount, 1943
VICTOR YOUNG†

CHINA 9, LIBERTY 37   Titanus, 1978
PINO DONAGGIO

CHINA BEACH (TF)   Sacret Inc. Productions/Warner
Bros. TV, 1988
PAUL CHIHARA
JOHN RUBINSTEIN

CHINA CLIPPER   Warner Bros., 1936
W. FRANKE HARLING†

CHINA CRY   Penland, 1990
JOEL HIRSCHHORN
AL KASHA

CHINA GATE   20th Century-Fox, 1957
MAX STEINER†

CHINA GIRL   20th Century-Fox, 1943
HUGO FRIEDHOFER†

CHINA GIRL   Vestron, 1987
JOE DELIA

CHINA IS NEAR   LA CINE E VICINA   1967
ENNIO MORRICONE

THE CHINA LAKE MURDERS (CTF)
Papazian-Hirsch Entertainment/MCA TV, 1990
DANA KAPROFF

CHINA MOON   Orion, 1994
GEORGE FENTON

CHINA O'BRIEN   Golden Harvest, 1989
PAUL ANTONELLI
DAVID WHEATLEY

CHINA ROSE (TF)   Robert Halmi, Inc., 1983
CHARLES GROSS

CHINA SEAS   MGM, 1935
HERBERT STOTHART†

CHINA SKY   RKO Radio, 1945
LEIGH HARLINE†

CHINA'S LITTLE DEVILS   Monogram, 1945
DIMITRI TIOMKIN†

CHINA: BEYOND THE CLOUDS (TD)   River Film
Prods./Channel 4 TV/Canal Plus, 1994
GEORGE FENTON

CHINATOWN   Paramount, 1974
JERRY GOLDSMITH ★

CHINESE ROULETTE   New Yorker, 1976
PEER RABEN

THE CHIPMUNK ADVENTURE (AF)   Samuel
Goldwyn Company, 1987
RANDY EDELMAN

THE CHIPS ARE DOWN   1947
GEORGES AURIC†

CHIPS, THE WAR DOG (CTF)   1990
DAVID MICHAEL FRANK

THE CHISHOLMS (MS)   Alan Landsburg Productions,
1979
ELMER BERNSTEIN
GERALD FRIED

CHISUM   Warner Bros., 1970
DOMINIC FRONTIERE

THE CHOCOLATE SOLDIER   MGM, 1941
BRONISLAU KAPER† ★
HERBERT STOTHART† ★

CHOICE OF ARMS   1981
PHILIPPE SARDE

CHOICES   Choices Company, 1981
CHRISTOPHER L. STONE

CHOICES (TF)   Robert Halmi, Inc., 1986
CHARLES GROSS

CHOICES OF THE HEART (TF)   Katz-Gallin
Associates/Half-Pint Productions/Metromedia
Producers Corporation/NBC Entertainment, 1983
JOHN RUBINSTEIN

THE CHOIRBOYS   Universal, 1977
FRANK DEVOL

CHOKE CANYON   United Film Distribution, 1986
SYLVESTER LEVAY

C.H.O.M.P.S.   American International, 1979
HOYT CURTIN

CHOPPING MALL   Concorde/Cinema Group, 1986
CHUCK CIRINO

A CHORUS LINE   Columbia, 1985
RALPH BURNS

A CHORUS OF DISAPPROVAL   Orion, 1989
JOHN DUPREZ

THE CHOSEN   20th Century Fox International Classics,
1982
ELMER BERNSTEIN

CHOSEN SURVIVORS   Columbia, 1974
FRED KARLIN

CHOUANS   UGC, 1988
GEORGES DELERUE†

CHRIST OF THE OCEAN   1971
BRUNO NICOLAI

CHRIST STOPPED AT EBOLI   Franklin Media, 1980
PIERO PICCIONI

THE CHRISTIAN LICORICE STORE   National
General, 1971
LALO SCHIFRIN

CHRISTIANE F.   20th Century-Fox, 1981
JURGEN KNIEPER

CHRISTINA PRINCESSE DE L'EROTISME   1971
BRUNO NICOLAI

THE CHRISTINE JORGENSEN STORY   United
Artists, 1970
PAUL SAWTELL†
BERT A. SHEFTER

CHRISTINE   Columbia, 1983
JOHN CARPENTER
ALAN HOWARTH

CHRISTINE CROMWELL (TF)   Wolf Film
Productions/Universal TV, 1989
LEE HOLDRIDGE

CHRISTINE CROMWELL: EASY COME, EASY GO
(TF)   Wolf Film Productions/Universal TV, 1990
ALF CLAUSEN

CHRISTINE CROMWELL: IN VINO VERITAS (TF)
Wolf Film Productions/Universal TV, 1990
ALF CLAUSEN
LEE HOLDRIDGE

CHRISTINE CROMWELL: ONLY THE GOOD DIE
YOUNG (TF)   Wolf Film Productions/Universal TV,
1990
ALF CLAUSEN
LEE HOLDRIDGE

A CHRISTMAS CAROL   MGM, 1938
FRANZ WAXMAN†

A CHRISTMAS CAROL   SCROOGE   United Artists,
1951
RICHARD ADDINSELL†

A CHRISTMAS CAROL (TF)   Entertainment Partners,
1984
NICK BICAT

A CHRISTMAS STORY   MGM/UA, 1983
PAUL J. ZAZA
CARL ZITTRER

A CHRISTMAS TO REMEMBER (TF)   George
Englund Enterprises, 1978
JIMMIE HASKELL

A CHRISTMAS TREE (TF)   Walt Disney TV, 1996
DAVID BENOIT

A CHRISTMAS WITHOUT SNOW (TF)   Korty
Films/Frank Konigsberg Productions, 1980
ED BOGAS

THE CHRISTMAS GIFT (TF)   Rosemont Productions/
Sunn Classic Pictures, 1986
ALLYN FERGUSON

THE CHRISTMAS STAR (TF)   Lake Walloon
Productions/Catalina Productions. Group/ Walt Disney
TV, 1986
RALPH BURNS

THE CHRISTMAS THAT ALMOST WASN'T   1966
BRUNO NICOLAI

THE CHRISTMAS TREE   Continental, 1969
GEORGES AURIC†

THE CHRISTMAS VISITOR   BUSHFIRE MOON
(CTF)   Entertainment Media/The Disney Channel/
WonderWorks, 1987
BRUCE ROWLAND

CHRISTMAS COMES TO WILLOW CREEK (TF)
Blue Andre Productions/ITC Productions, 1987
CHARLES FOX

CHRISTMAS EVE   United Artists, 1947
HEINZ ROEMHELD†

CHRISTMAS EVE (TF)   NBC Productions, 1986
JOHNNY MANDEL

CHRISTMAS HOLIDAY   Universal, 1944
HANS J. SALTER† ★

CHRISTMAS IN CONNECTICUT   Warner Bros.,
1945
FREDERICK HOLLANDER†

CHRISTMAS IN CONNECTICUT (CTF)   Once Upon A
Time Films, 1992
CHARLES FOX

CHRISTMAS IN MY HOMETOWN (TF)
Jaffe-Braunstein, 1996
DANA KAPROFF

CHRISTMAS LILLIES OF THE FIELD (TF)   Rainbow
Productions/Osmond Television Productions, 1979
GEORGE ALICESON TIPTON

CHRISTMAS ON DIVISION STREET (TF)
Guber-Peters/Morrow-Heus/WIC/Columbia TV, 1991
GEORGE BLONDHEIM

CHRISTOPHER COLUMBUS   1949
SIR ARTHUR BLISS†

CHRISTOPHER COLUMBUS (MS)   RAI/Clesi
Cinematografica Productions/Antenne 2/Bavaria
Atelier/Lorimar Productions, 1985
RIZ ORTOLANI

CHRISTOPHER COLUMBUS: THE DISCOVERY
Warner Bros., 1992
CLIFF EIDELMAN

CHRISTOPHER STRONG   RKO Radio, 1933
MAX STEINER†

CHRISTY (TF)   1994
RON RAMIN ☆

'97-'98
FILM
COMPOSERS
INDEX

FILM

TITLES

CHROME SOLDIERS (CTF) Wilshire Court Prods., 1992
STEVE DORFF

CHRONICLE OF A CRIME Yugoslavian
ALFI KABILJO

CHRONIQUE PROVINCIALE 1958
MAURICE JARRE

CHU CHU AND THE PHILLY FLASH 20th Century-Fox, 1981
PETE RUGOLO

CHUBASCO Warner Bros., 1968
WILLIAM LAVA†

CHUCHU AND THE PHILLY FLASH (TF) 1981
MAURICE JARRE

C.H.U.D. New World, 1984
COOPER HUGHES

CHUD II: BUD THE CHUD Vestron, 1989
NICHOLAS PIKE

CHUKA Paramount, 1967
LEITH STEVENS†

A CHUMP AT OXFORD United Artists, 1940
T. MARVIN HATLEY†

CHUNG ON TSOU *CRIME STORY* 1993
JAMES WONG

CHUNKING EXPRESS 1996
MICHAEL CALASSO
FRANKIE CHAN
ROEL A. GARCIA

THE CHURCH MOUSE Warner Bros., 1934
W. FRANKE HARLING†

CHUSHINGURA Toho, 1962
AKIRA IFUKUBE

CI RISIAMO, VERO PROVVIDENZA? 1973
ENNIO MORRICONE
BRUNO NICOLAI

C.I.A. II: TARGET ALEXA PM, 1993
LOUIS FEBRE

A CIASCUNO IL SUO *WE STILL KILL THE OLD WAY* 1967
LUIS BACALOV

CIMARRON MGM, 1960
FRANZ WAXMAN†

CIMARRON RKO Radio, 1931
MAX STEINER†

THE CINCINATTI KID MGM, 1965
LALO SCHIFRIN

THE CINDER PATH (TF) 1995
BARRINGTON PHELOUNG

CINDERELLA Group 1, 1977
ANDREW BELLING

CINDERELLA (AF) RKO Radio, 1950
PAUL J. SMITH† ★
OLIVER WALLACE† ★

CINDERELLA JONES Warner Bros., 1946
FREDERICK HOLLANDER†

CINDERELLA LIBERTY 20th Century-Fox, 1974
JOHN WILLIAMS ★

CINDERFELLA Paramount, 1960
WALTER SCHARF

CINEMA D'ALTRI TEMPI 1953
FRANCO MANNINO

CINEMA PARADISO Miramax, 1989
ENNIO MORRICONE

CINEMATOGRAPHIE 1966
MICHEL PORTAL

CINTURA DI CASTITA 1949
CARLO RUSTICHELLI

A CIRCLE OF CHILDREN (TF) Edgar J. Scherick Associates/20th Century-Fox TV, 1977
NELSON RIDDLE†

CIRCLE OF DECEIT *DIE FALSCHUNG* United Artists Classics, 1981
MAURICE JARRE

CIRCLE OF FRIENDS Savoy, 1995
MICHAEL KAMEN

CIRCLE OF IRON *THE SILENT FLUTE* Avco Embassy, 1979
BRUCE SMEATON

CIRCLE OF LOVE *LA RONDE* Continental, 1964
FRANCIS LAI
MICHEL MAGNE†

CIRCLE OF POWER *MYSTIQUE/BRAINWASH/THE NAKED WEEKEND* QUI Productions, 1983
RICHARD MARKOWITZ†

CIRCLE OF TWO World Northal, 1981
PAUL HOFFERT

CIRCLE OF VIOLENCE: A FAMILY DRAMA (TF) Sheldon Pinchuk Productions/Rafshoon Communications Inc./Finnegan Associates/Telepictures Productions, 1986
GIL MELLE

CIRCONSTANCES ATTENUANTES 1939
GEORGES VAN PARYS†

CIRCUITRY MAN Skouras, 1989
DEBORAH HOLLAND

CIRCUMSTANCES UNKNOWN (CTF) Shooting Star/Wilshire Court, 1995
JOSEPH CONLAN

CIRCUMSTANTIAL EVIDENCE 20th Century-Fox, 1945
DAVID BUTTOLPH†

THE CIRCUS United Artists, 1928
CHARLES CHAPLIN†

CIRCUS OF HORRORS American International, 1960
FRANZ REIZENSTEIN†

CIRCUS WORLD Paramount, 1964
DIMITRI TIOMKIN†

THE CISCO KID (CTF) Esparza-Katz Prods./Goodman Rosen/Turner Pictures, 1994
JOSEPH JULIAN GONZALES

THE CISCO KID IN OLD NEW MEXICO Producers Releasing Corp., 1945
ALBERT GLASSER

THE CISCO KID RETURNS Producers Releasing Corp., 1945
ALBERT GLASSER

THE CITADEL MGM, 1938
LOUIS LEVY†

CITIZEN COHN (CTF) Spring Creek Prods./Breakheart Films/Viacom, 1992
THOMAS NEWMAN

CITIZEN KANE RKO Radio, 1941
BERNARD HERRMANN† ★

CITIZEN RUTH Miramax, 1996
ROLFE KENT

CITIZEN X (CTF) Asylum Films/Citadel/HBO Pictures, 1995
RANDY EDELMAN

CITIZENS BAND *HANDLE WITH CARE* Paramount, 1977
BILL CONTI

CITTA DI NOTTE 1956
NINO ROTA†

CITTA VIOLENTA *THE FAMILY* 1970
ENNIO MORRICONE

CITY (TF) CBS/MTM, 1990
BOB MITHOFF

THE CITY (D) Civic Films, 1939
AARON COPLAND†

THE CITY (TF) QM Productions, 1977
JOHN ELIZALDE

CITY ACROSS THE RIVER Universal, 1949
WALTER SCHARF

CITY BENEATH THE SEA Universal, 1953
HENRY MANCINI†
MILTON ROSEN†
HERMAN STEIN

CITY BENEATH THE SEA (TF) 20th Century-Fox TV/Motion Pictures International/Kent Productions, 1971
RICHARD LASALLE

CITY FOR CONQUEST Warner Bros., 1940
MAX STEINER†

CITY HALL Columbia, 1995
JERRY GOLDSMITH

CITY HEAT Warner Bros., 1984
LENNIE NIEHAUS

CITY IN FEAR (TF) Trans World International, 1980
LEONARD ROSENMAN

THE CITY IS DARK Warner Bros., 1954
DAVID BUTTOLPH†

CITY KILLER (TF) Stan Shpetner Productions, 1984
JOHN RUBINSTEIN

CITY LIGHTS United Artists, 1931
CHARLES CHAPLIN†

THE CITY OF FEAR French, 1994
PHILIPPE CHANY

CITY OF FEAR Columbia, 1959
JERRY GOLDSMITH

CITY OF HOPE Esperanza, 1991
MASON DARING

CITY OF JOY TriStar, 1992
ENNIO MORRICONE

THE CITY OF LOST CHILDREN *LA CITE DES ENFANTS PERDUS* Sony Classics, 1995
ANGELO BADALAMENTI

CITY OF SILENT MEN Producers Releasing Corp., 1942
LEO ERDODY†

THE CITY OF THE DEAD Trans-World, 1960
KENNETH V. JONES

CITY OF THE DEAD Trans-World, 1960
DOUGLAS GAMLEY

CITY OF THE WALKING DEAD *NIGHTMARE CITY* 21st Century, 1980
STELVIO CIPRIANI

CITY OF WOMEN New Yorker, 1980
LUIS BACALOV

CITY ON FIRE! Avco Embassy, 1979
MATTHEW MCCAULEY

CITY SLICKERS Columbia, 1991
MARC SHAIMAN

CITY SLICKERS II: THE LEGEND OF CURLY'S GOLD Columbia, 1994
MARC SHAIMAN

CITY STREETS Columbia, 1938
SIDNEY CUTNER†

THE CITY UNDER THE SEA American International, 1965
STANLEY BLACK

CITY WITHOUT MEN Columbia, 1943
DAVID RAKSIN

CIVILIZATION Ince, 1916
VICTOR SCHERTZINGER†

CLAIRE DE FEMME Atlantic Releasing Corporation, 1979
JEAN MUSY

THE CLAIRVOYANT 1936
ARTHUR BENJAMIN†

CLAN OF THE CAVE BEAR Warner Bros., 1986
ALAN SILVESTRI

CLARA'S HEART Warner Bros., 1988
DAVE GRUSIN

CLARETTA Trans World, 1984
GERARD SCHURMANN

CLARETTA AND BEN Aquarius Films, 1983
CARLO RUSTICHELLI

CLASH BY NIGHT RKO Radio, 1952
ROY WEBB†

CLASH OF LOYALTIES Jorephani, 1983
RON GOODWIN

CLASH OF THE TITANS MGM/United Artists, 1981
LAURENCE ROSENTHAL

CLASS Orion, 1983
ELMER BERNSTEIN
TOM SCOTT

CLASS ACT Warner Bros., 1992
VASSAL BENFORD

CLASS ACTION 20th Century Fox, 1991
JAMES HORNER

CLASS CRUISE (TF) Portoangelo Productions, 1989
MARK DAVIS

CLASS OF '44 Warner Bros., 1973
DAVID SHIRE

CLASS OF '61 (TF) Amblin TV, Universal TV, 1993
JOHN DEBNEY

CLASS OF '63 (TF) Metromedia Productions/Stonehenge Productions, 1973
TOM SCOTT

THE CLASS OF 1984 United Film Distribution, 1982
LALO SCHIFRIN

CLASS OF 1999 Vestron, 1989
MICHAEL HOENIG

THE CLASS OF MISS MacMICHAEL Brut Productions, 1979
STANLEY MYERS†.

CLASS OF NUKE 'EM HIGH PART II: SUBHUMANOID MELTDOWN Troma, 1991
BOB MITHOFF

CLASSIFIED LOVE (TF) CBS Entertainment, 1986
ARTIE BUTLER

CLAUDE JJ Films, 1992
STANLEY MYERS†

CLAUDIA 20th Century-Fox, 1943
ALFRED NEWMAN†

CLAUDIA AND DAVID 20th Century-Fox, 1946
CYRIL J. MOCKRIDGE†

CLAUDINE 20th Century-Fox, 1974
CURTIS MAYFIELD

CLAUDINE A L'ECOLE 1936
PAUL MISRAKI

CLEAN AND SOBER Warner Bros., 1988
GABRIEL YARED

THE CLEAN MACHINE (TF) Kennedy-Miller, 1988
CAMERON ALLAN

CLEAN SLATE Biograph/Quartet/Films Inc./The Frank Moreno Company, 1982
PHILIPPE SARDE

CLEAN SLATE MGM, 1994
ALAN SILVESTRI

CLEAN, SHAVEN DSM III Films, 1993
HAHN ROWE

CLEAR AND PRESENT DANGER Paramount, 1994
JAMES HORNER

CLEARCUT Alliance, 1991
SHANE HARVEY

THE CLEARING Kodiak, 1991
TAMARA KLINE

CLEO FROM 5 TO 7 *CLEO DE 5 A 7* Zenith, 1962
MICHEL LEGRAND

CLEOPATRA 20th Century Fox, 1963
ALEX NORTH† ★

CLEOPATRA JONES Warner Bros., 1973
DOMINIC FRONTIERE
J.J. JOHNSON

CLEOPATRA JONES AND THE CASINO OF GOLD Warner Bros., 1975
DOMINIC FRONTIERE

CLEREMBARD 1969
VLADIMIR COSMA

CLERKS View Askew, 1994
SCOTT ANGLEY

CLICKETY-CLACK 1970
TORU TAKEMITSU†

THE CLIENT Warner Bros., 1994
HOWARD SHORE

CLIFFHANGER TriStar, 1993
TREVOR JONES

CLIFFORD Orion, 1994
RICHARD GIBBS

A CLIMATE FOR KILLING Propaganda, 1990
ROBERT FOLK

THE CLIMAX Universal, 1944
EDWARD WARD†

THE CLIMAX *L'IMMORALE* Lopert, 1967
CARLO RUSTICHELLI

CLIMB AN ANGRY MOUNTAIN (TF) Herbert F. Solow Productions/Warner Bros. TV, 1972
GEORGE DUNING

CLINTON AND NADINE (CTF) HBO Pictures/ITC, 1988
JAN HAMMER

CLIVE JAMES' FAME IN THE 20TH CENTURY (TD) BBC-TV/WQED, 1993
CARL DAVIS

CLIVE OF INDIA United Artists, 1935
ALFRED NEWMAN†

CLOAK & DAGGER Universal, 1984
BRIAN MAY†

CLOAK AND DAGGER Warner Bros., 1946
MAX STEINER†

THE CLOCK MGM, 1945
GEORGE BASSMAN

CLOCKERS Universal, 1995
TERENCE BLANCHARD

THE CLOCKMAKER OF ST. PAUL Joseph Green Pictures, 1974
PHILIPPE SARDE

CLOCKWATCHERS John Flock Prods., 1997
MADER

CLOCKWISE Universal, 1986
GEORGE FENTON

A CLOCKWORK ORANGE Warner Bros., 1971
WENDY CARLOS

THE CLONE MASTER (TF) Mel Ferber Productions/Paramount Pictures TV, 1978
GLENN PAXTON

THE CLONING OF JOANNA MAY (CTF) Granada/A&E, 1992
RACHEL PORTMAN

CLOSE ENCOUNTERS OF THE THIRD KIND Columbia, 1977
JOHN WILLIAMS ★

CLOSE MY EYES 1991
MICHAEL GIBBS

CLOSE TO MY HEART Warner Bros., 1951
MAX STEINER†

THE CLOSER Ion, 1991
JOEL HIRSCHHORN
AL KASHA

CLOSET LAND Universal, 1991
RICHARD EINHORN

CLOSE-UP Eagle Lion, 1948
JEROME MOROSS†

CLOUD DANCER Blossom, 1980
FRED KARLIN

THE CLOUDED YELLOW General Film Distributors, 1950
BENJAMIN FRANKEL†

CLOUDS AT SUNSET Hyogensha/Shochiku, 1967
TORU TAKEMITSU†

THE CLOWN MGM, 1953
DAVID ROSE†

THE CLOWNS Levitt-Pickman, 1971
NINO ROTA†

CLUB MED (TF) Lorimar Productions, 1986
PETER BERNSTEIN

CLUB PARADISE Warner Bros., 1986
DAVID MANSFIELD
VAN DYKE PARKS

CLUE Paramount, 1985
JOHN MORRIS

THE CLUE OF THE NEW PIN Merton Park, 1961
RON GOODWIN

CLUELESS Paramount, 1995
DAVID KITAY

CLUNY BROWN 20th Century-Fox, 1946
CYRIL J. MOCKRIDGE†

C-MAN Film Classics, 1949
GAIL KUBIK†

COACH Crown International, 1978
ANTHONY HARRIS

COACH OF THE YEAR (TF) Shane Company Productions/NBC Entertainment, 1980
PETE CARPENTER†
MIKE POST

COAL FACE 1935
BENJAMIN BRITTEN†

COAL MINER'S DAUGHTER Universal, 1980
OWEN BRADLEY

COAST TO COAST Paramount, 1980
CHARLES BERNSTEIN

COASTAL COMMAND 1942
RALPH VAUGHAN WILLIAMS†

COBB Warner Bros., 1994
ELLIOT GOLDENTHAL

COBRA Warner Bros., 1986
SYLVESTER LEVAY

THE COBRA STRIKES Eagle Lion, 1948
ALBERT GLASSER

COBRA VERDE DEG, 1988
POPOL VUH

COBRA WOMAN Universal, 1944
EDWARD WARD†

THE COBWEB MGM, 1955
LEONARD ROSENMAN

THE COCA COLA KID Cinecom/Film Gallery, 1985
WILLIAM MOTZIG

COCAINE AND BLUE EYES (TF) Orenthal
Productions/Columbia TV, 1983
MORTON STEVENS†

COCAINE: ONE MAN'S SEDUCTION (TF) Charles
Fries Productions/David Goldsmith Productions, 1983
BRAD FIEDEL

COCK OF THE AIR United Artists, 1932
ALFRED NEWMAN†

COCKEYED CAVALIERS RKO Radio, 1934
ROY WEBB†

COCKEYED COWBOYS OF CALICO COUNTY
Universal, 1970
LYN MURRAY†

THE COCKLESHELL HEROES Columbia, 1956
JOHN ADDISON

COCKTAIL Buena Vista, 1988
J. PETER ROBINSON

COCOON 20th Century Fox, 1985
JAMES HORNER

COCOON: THE RETURN 20th Century Fox, 1988
JAMES HORNER

CODE NAME: DIAMOND HEAD (TF) QM
Productions, 1977
MORTON STEVENS†

CODE NAME: EMERALD MGM/UA, 1985
JOHN ADDISON

CODE OF SILENCE Orion, 1985
DAVID MICHAEL FRANK

CODE OF VENGEANCE (TF) Universal TV, 1985
DON PEAKE

CODE RED (TF) Irwin Allen Productions/Columbia
Pictures TV, 1981
RICHARD LASALLE

CODENAME: KYRIL (TF) Incito Productions/HTV,
1989
ALAN LISK

A COEUR JOIE Paramount, 1967
MICHEL MAGNE†

COFFEE, TEA OR ME? (TF) CBS, Inc., 1973
MORTON STEVENS†

COFFY American International, 1973
ROY AYERS

COHEN & TATE Hemdale, 1988
BILL CONTI

COIFFEUR POUR DAMES 1952
PAUL MISRAKI

COL CUORE IN GOLA 1967
ARMANDO TROVAJOLI

COLD BLOODED Polygram/Propaganda/MPCA,
1995
STEVE BARTEK

COLD COMFORT Norstar Ent./Ray Sagar Prod.,
1990
JEFF DANNA

COLD COMFORT FARM 1996
ROBERT LOCKWOOD

COLD CUTS 1980
PHILIPPE SARDE

COLD FEET Avenue, 1989
TOM BAHLER

COLD HEAVEN Hemdale, 1992
STANLEY MYERS†

COLD HOMELAND Triangel Film, 1979
JURGEN KNIEPER

COLD MOON 1991
DIDIER LOCKWOOD

A COLD NIGHT'S DEATH (TF) ABC Circle Films,
1973
GIL MELLE

THE COLD ROOM (TD) Jethro Films/Mark Forstater
Productions, 1984
MICHAEL NYMAN

COLD SASSY TREE (CTF) Faye Dunaway
Productions/Ohlmeyer Productions, 1989
BRAD FIEDEL

COLD STEEL Cinetel, 1987
DAVID A. JACKSON

COLD SWEAT DE LA PART DES COPAINS
Emerson, 1970
MICHEL MAGNE†

COLD SWEAT (CTF) Norstar Ent., 1994
PAUL J. ZAZA

COLD TURKEY United Artists, 1971
RANDY NEWMAN

A COLD WIND IN AUGUST Lopert, 1961
GERALD FRIED

COLDITZ (TF) British
ROBERT FARNON

COLIN FITZ Babyshark Films, 1997
PAT IRWIN

THE COLLECTOR Columbia, 1965
MAURICE JARRE

COLLEGE RHYTHM Paramount, 1934
SIGMUND KRUMGOLD†

COLLEGE SCANDAL Paramount, 1935
ANDREA SETARO†

COLLEGES AT WAR (FD) O.W.I., 1942
GAIL KUBIK†

COLOMBO GOES TO THE GUILLOTINE (TF)
Universal TV, 1989
JOHN CACAVAS

COLONEL BLIMP GFO, 1943
ALLAN GRAY†

COLONEL EFFINGHAM'S RAID 20th Century-Fox,
1946
CYRIL J. MOCKRIDGE†

THE COLONY Columbia, 1997
GARY CHANG

THE COLONY (TF) Universal TV, 1995
DENNIS MCCARTHY

THE COLOR OF MONEY Buena Vista, 1986
ROBBIE ROBERTSON

COLOR OF NIGHT Buena Vista, 1994
DOMINIC FRONTIERE

THE COLOR PURPLE Warner Bros., 1985
CHRIS BOARDMAN ★
JORGE CALANDRELLI ★
ANDRAE CROUCH ★
JACK HAYES ★
JERRY HEY ★
QUINCY JONES ★
RANDY KERBER ★
JEREMY LUBBOCK ★
JOEL ROSENBAUM ★
CAIPHUS SEMENYA ★
FRED STEINER ★
ROD TEMPERTON ★

COLORADO TERRITORY Warner Bros., 1949
DAVID BUTTOLPH†

COLORS Orion, 1988
HERBIE HANCOCK

THE COLOSSUS OF NEW YORK Paramount, 1958
FRED STEINER
NATHAN VAN CLEAVE†

THE COLOSSUS OF RHODES 1961
ANGELO FRANCESCO LAVAGNINO†

COLOSSUS: THE FORBIN PROJECT Universal,
1970
MICHEL COLOMBIER

COLPITA DA IMPROVVISO BENESSERE 1975
LUIS BACALOV

COLPO DOPPIO DEL CAMALEONTE D'ORO 1967
CARLO RUSTICHELLI

COLPO IN CANNA 1975
LUIS BACALOV

COLT .45 Warner Bros., 1950
WILLIAM LAVA†

COLUMBO AND THE MURDER OF A ROCK STAR
(TF) Universal TV, 1991
STEVE DORFF

COLUMBO: A BIRD IN THE HAND (TF) Universal
TV, 1992
DICK DEBENEDICTIS

COLUMBO: AGENDA FOR MURDER (TF)
Universal TV, 1990
JAMES DIPASQUALLE

COLUMBO: CAUTION MURDER CAN BE
HAZARDOUS TO YOUR HEALTH (TF)
Universal TV, 1991
JOHN CACAVAS

COLUMBO: DEATH HITS THE JACKPOT (TF)
Universal TV, 1991
STEVE DORFF

COLUMBO: MURDER - SELF-PORTRAIT (TF)
Universal TV, 1989
PATRICK WILLIAMS

COLUMBUS AND THE AGE OF DISCOVERY (TD)
WGBH/BBC TV/NHK/RAI/RTD/NDR/TVE/SEQS, 1991
SHELDON MIROWITZ

COLUMN SOUTH Universal, 1953
HENRY MANCINI†
HERMAN STEIN

COMA MGM/United Artists, 1978
JERRY GOLDSMITH

COMANCHE Universal, 1956
HERSCHEL BURKE GILBERT

COMANCHE STATION Columbia, 1960
MISCHA BAKALEINIKOFF†

COMANCHE TERRITORY Universal, 1950
FRANK SKINNER†

THE COMANCHEROS 20th Century-Fox, 1961
ELMER BERNSTEIN

COMANDEMENTI PER UN GANGSTER 1968
ENNIO MORRICONE

COMBAT HIGH (TF) Frank & Julie Films/Frank Von
Zerneck Productions/Lynch-Biller Productions, 1986
ROBERT FOLK

COMBAT SQUAD Columbia, 1953
PAUL DUNLAP

COMBINATION PLATTER Arrow Releasing, 1993
BRIAN TIBBS

COME AND GET IT United Artists, 1936
ALFRED NEWMAN†

COME BACK, LITTLE SHEBA Paramount, 1952
FRANZ WAXMAN†

COME BLOW YOUR HORN Paramount, 1963
NELSON RIDDLE†

COME FLY WITH ME MGM, 1963
LYN MURRAY†

COME HOME AND MEET MY WIFE 1974
ENZO JANNACCI

COME IMPARAI AD AMARE LE DONNE 1967
ENNIO MORRICONE

COME LIVE WITH ME MGM, 1941
HERBERT STOTHART†

COME NEXT SPRING Republic, 1956
MAX STEINER†

COME PERSI LA GUERRA 1947
NINO ROTA†

COME PLAY WITH ME GRAZIE ZIA 1968
ENNIO MORRICONE

COME SCOPERSI L'AMERICA 1949
NINO ROTA†

COME SEE THE PARADISE 20th Century-Fox, 1990
RANDY EDELMAN

COME SEPTEMBER Universal, 1961
HANS J. SALTER†

COME TO THE STABLE 20th Century-Fox, 1949
CYRIL J. MOCKRIDGE†

COME TO YOUR SENSES 1971
ROD MCKUEN

COME WITH ME: A MICKEY SPILLANE's MIKE
HAMMER MYSTERY (TF) Caroline Films
Prods./CBS Entertainment Prods., 1994
RON RAMIN

THE COMEBACK THE DAY THE SCREAMING
STOPPED Enterprise, 1978
STANLEY MYERS†

COMEBACK Rocco Film, 1982
ERIC BURDON

COMEBACK (TF) Michael Landon-Hall Bartlett
Films/NBC-TV/20th Century-Fox TV, 1983
LEE HOLDRIDGE
KLAUS DOLDINGER

THE COMEBACK (TF) CBS Entertainment, 1989
CRAIG SAFAN

THE COMEBACK KID (TF) ABC Circle Films, 1980
BARRY DEVORZON

THE COMEBACK TRAIL Dynamite Entertainment/
Rearguard Productions, 1971
IGO KANTOR

THE COMEDIANS MGM, 1967
LAURENCE ROSENTHAL

THE COMEDY OF TERRORS American
International, 1963
LES BAXTER†

THE COME-ON Allied Artists, 1956
PAUL DUNLAP

COMES A HORSEMAN United Artists, 1978
MICHAEL SMALL

COMET OVER BROADWAY Warner Bros., 1938
HEINZ ROEMHELD†

COMFORT AND JOY Universal, 1984
MARK KNOPFLER

THE COMFORT OF STRANGERS Elle Productions,
1990
ANGELO BADALAMENTI

COMFORTABLY NUMB The Shooting Gallery, 1995
MADER

THE COMIC Columbia, 1969
JACK ELLIOTT

COMIN' AT YA! Filmways, 1981
CARLO SAVINA

COMING ATTRACTIONS Atlantic Films, 1981
MURPHY DUNNE

COMING OUT OF THE ICE (TF) The Konigsberg
Company, 1982
MAURICE JARRE

COMING OUT UNDER FIRE (FD) Deep Focus,
1994
MARK ADLER

COMING TO AMERICA Universal, 1988
NILE RODGERS

COMING UP ROSES RHOSYN A RHITH Red
Rooster, 1986
MICHAEL STOREY

THE COMMAND Warner Bros., 1954
DIMITRI TIOMKIN†

COMMAND 5 (TF) Paramount Pictures TV, 1985
LALO SCHIFRIN

COMMAND DECISION MGM, 1948
MIKLOS ROZSA†

COMMANDO 20th Century Fox, 1985
JAMES HORNER

COMMANDO MARCIA O CREPA 1963
ANGELO FRANCESCO LAVAGNINO†

COMMANDO SQUAD Cinetel Films, 1988
TONY RIPPARETTI

COMMANDOS STRIKE AT DAWN Columbia,
1943
LOUIS GRUENBERG† ★

COMME EN CHEVEU SUR LA SOUPE 1957
GEORGES VAN PARYS†

COMME LA LUNE... 1977
PHILIPPE SARDE

COMME UN BOOMERANG 1976
GEORGES DELERUE†

COMMENT QU'ELLE EST 1960
PAUL MISRAKI

COMMENT REUSSIR EN AMOUR 1963
GEORGES GARVARENTZ†

COMMENT TROUVEZ-VOUS MA SOEUR? 1964
SERGE GAINSBOURG†

COMMUNION New Line Cinema, 1989
ERIC CLAPTON
ALLAN ZAVOD

COMMUNION/HOLY TERROR Allied Artists, 1977
STEPHEN LAWRENCE

COMPANIONS IN NIGHTMARE (TF) Universal,
1968
BERNARD HERRMANN†

THE COMPANY COMEDY (TF) Malloy-Adler
Productions/MGM TV, 1978
TOM SCOTT

THE COMPANY OF WOLVES Cannon, 1984
GEORGE FENTON

THE COMPANY SHE KEEPS RKO Radio, 1950
LEIGH HARLINE†

THE COMPETITION Columbia, 1980
LALO SCHIFRIN

COMPLEX OF FEAR (TF) Cosgrove-Meurer/World
International Network, 1993
NAN SCHWARTZ-MISHKIN

COMPROMISING POSITIONS Paramount, 1985
BRAD FIEDEL

COMPTES A REBOURS 1970
GEORGES DELERUE†

COMPULSION 20th Century-Fox, 1959
LIONEL NEWMAN†

THE COMPUTER WORE TENNIS SHOES Buena
Vista, 1969
ROBERT F. BRUNNER

THE COMPUTER WORE TENNIS SHOES (TF) ZM
Prods./Walt Disney TV, 1995
PHILIP GIFFIN

COMPUTERSIDE (TF) The Culzean Corporation/
Paramount Pictures TV, 1982
ALLYN FERGUSON
JACK ELLIOTT

COMRADE X MGM, 1940
BRONISLAU KAPER†

COMRADES British Film Institute, 1986
DAVID GRAHAM
HANS WERNER HENZE

THE COMRADES OF SUMMER (CTF) HBO
Pictures/Grossbart-Barnett, 1992
WILLIAM OLVIS

CONAGHER (CTF) Imagine TV, 1991
J.A.C. REDFORD

CONAN THE BARBARIAN Universal, 1982
BASIL POLEDOURIS

CONAN THE DESTROYER Universal, 1984
BASIL POLEDOURIS

CONCEALED ENEMIES (TF) WGBH-Boston/Goldcrest
Films and Television/Comworld Productions, 1984
JONATHAN TUNICK ☆

CONCERTO PER PISTOLA SOLISTA 1970
FRANCESCO DE MASI

THE CONCORDE - AIRPORT '79 Universal, 1979
LALO SCHIFRIN

CONCORDE AFFAIR '79 1979
STELVIO CIPRIANI

CONCRETE BEAT (TF) Picturemaker Productions/
Viacom, 1984
ARTIE KANE

THE CONCRETE JUNGLE THE CRIMINAL
Fanfare, 1960
JOHN DANKWORTH

THE CONCRETE JUNGLE (TF) Pentagon, 1982
JOSEPH CONLAN
ROCKY DAVIS

CONDANNATO A NOZZE CONDEMNED TO
WED 1993
ANTONIO DIPOFI

THE CONDEMNED OF ALTONA 1963
DMITRI SHOSTAKOVITCH†

CONDEMNED TO WED 1993
ANTONIO DIPOFI

CONDEMNED WOMEN RKO Radio, 1938
ROY WEBB†

CONDOMINIUM (TF) Universal TV, 1980
GERALD FRIED

CONDORMAN Buena Vista, 1981
HENRY MANCINI†

CONDOTTIERI 1937
GIUSEPPE BECCE†

CONDUCT UNBECOMING Allied Artists, 1985
STANLEY MYERS†

CONE OF SILENCE Bryanston, 1960
GERARD SCHURMANN

CONEHEADS Paramount, 1993
DAVID NEWMAN

THE CONFESSIONAL LE CONFESSIONAL 1995
SACHA PUTTNAM

CONFESSIONE DI UN COMMISSARIO 1970
RIZ ORTOLANI

CONFESSIONS OF A MARRIED MAN (TF) Gloria Monty Productions/Comworld, 1983
BILLY GOLDENBERG

CONFESSIONS OF A NAZI SPY Warner Bros., 1939
MAX STEINER†

CONFESSIONS OF A POLICE CAPTAIN CONFESSIONE DI UN COMMISSARIO 1970
RIZ ORTOLANI

CONFESSIONS OF A SUBURBAN GIRL 1992
JOSEPH S. DE BEASI

CONFESSIONS OF AN OPIUM EATER SOULS FOR SALE/EVILS OF CHINATOWN Allied Artists, 1962
ALBERT GLASSER

CONFESSIONS: TWO FACES OF EVIL (TF) Cates-Doty Prods., 1994
CHARLES FOX

THE CONFESSOR 1973
CHICO HAMILTON

CONFIDENCES POUR CONFIDENCES 1978
VLADIMIR COSMA

CONFIDENTIAL AGENT Warner Bros., 1945
FRANZ WAXMAN†

CONFIDENTIAL REPORT Warner Bros., 1955
PAUL MISRAKI

CONFIDENTIALLY YOURS MGM, 1953
DAVID ROSE†

CONFIDENTIALLY YOURS VIVEMENT DIMANCHE Spectrafilm, 1983
GEORGES DELERUE†

CONFIRM OR DENY 20th Century-Fox, 1941
DAVID BUTTOLPH†

CONFLICT Warner Bros., 1945
FREDERICK HOLLANDER†

THE CONFORMIST Paramount, 1971
GEORGES DELERUE†

A CONFUCIAN CONFUSION DULI SHIDAI 1994
ANTONIO LEE

CONGO Paramount, 1995
JERRY GOLDSMITH

THE CONGO (FD) Belgian Government, 1944
PAUL BOWLES

CONGO MAISIE MGM, 1940
EDWARD WARD†

CONGO VIVO 1962
PIERO PICCIONI

CONGRATULATIONS, IT'S A BOY! (TF) Aaron Spelling Productions, 1971
RICHARD BASKIN
BASIL POLEDOURIS

THE CONJUGAL BED UNA STORIA MODERNA - L'APE REGINA Embassy, 1963
TEO USUELLI

A CONNECTICUT YANKEE IN KING ARTHUR'S COURT Paramount, 1949
VICTOR YOUNG†

THE CONQUEROR WORM THE WITCHFINDER GENERAL American International, 1968
PAUL FERRIS

THE CONQUEROR RKO Radio, 1956
VICTOR YOUNG†

THE CONQUEROR Triangle, 1916
VICTOR SCHERTZINGER†

THE CONQUERORS RKO Radio, 1932
MAX STEINER†

CONQUEST MGM, 1937
HERBERT STOTHART†

THE CONQUEST OF EVEREST 1953
ARTHUR BENJAMIN†

CONQUEST OF MYCENE ERCOLE CONTRO MOLOCH 1963
CARLO RUSTICHELLI

CONQUEST OF SPACE Paramount, 1955
NATHAN VAN CLEAVE†

CONQUEST OF THE AIR 1938
SIR ARTHUR BLISS†

CONQUEST OF THE PLANET OF THE APES 20th Century-Fox, 1972
TOM SCOTT

CONQUISTA 1971
JOHN SCOTT

CONRACK 20th Century-Fox, 1974
JOHN WILLIAMS

CONSEIL DE FAMILLE European Classics, 1986
GEORGES DELERUE†

CONSENTING ADULT (TF) Starger Company/ Lawrence-Aghayan Productions, 1985
LAURENCE ROSENTHAL

CONSENTING ADULTS Buena Vista, 1992
MICHAEL SMALL

CONSOLATION MARRIAGE RKO Radio, 1931
MAX STEINER†

CONSPIRACY OF FEAR Bosi Films, 1995
STEVE EDWARDS

CONSPIRACY OF HEARTS Paramount, 1960
ANGELO FRANCESCO LAVAGNINO†

CONSPIRACY OF LOVE (TF) New World TV, 1987
JOHN RUBINSTEIN

CONSPIRACY OF TERROR (TF) Lorimar Productions, 1975
NEAL HEFTI

THE CONSPIRATORS Warner Bros., 1944
MAX STEINER†

THE CONSTANT HUSBAND British Lion, 1955
WILLIAM ALWYN†
MALCOLM ARNOLD

THE CONSTANT NYMPH 1933
JOHN GREENWOOD†

THE CONSTANT NYMPH Warner Bros., 1943
ERICH WOLFGANG KORNGOLD†

CONSUMING PASSIONS Samuel Goldwyn Company, 1988
RICHARD HARTLEY

CONSUMING SUN Dali International, 1993
LIU YUAN

CONTAGIOUS (TF) Wilshire Court, 1996
STEPHEN GRAZIANO

CONTE D'HIVER A WINTER'S TALE 1992
SEBASTIEN ERMS

CONTEMPT LE MEPRIS Embassy, 1964
GEORGES DELERUE†

THE CONTENDER (TF) Universal TV, 1980
JAMES DIPASQUALLE

THE CONTENDER Producers Releasing Corp., 1944
ALBERT GLASSER

CONTINENTAL DIVIDE Universal, 1981
MICHAEL SMALL

CONTINUAVAMO A METTERE LO DIAVOLO NE LO INFERNO 1973
STELVIO CIPRIANI

CONTRABAND BLACKOUT Anglo-American, 1940
RICHARD ADDINSELL†

CONTRACT ON CHERRY STREET (TF) Columbia TV, 1977
JERRY GOLDSMITH

CONTRARY WARRIORS (FD) Rattlesnake Prods., 1985
TODD BOEKELHEIDE

CONTRE-ENQUETE 1946
JEAN WIENER†

THE CONVERSATION Paramount, 1974
DAVID SHIRE

CONVERSATION PIECE GRUPPO DI FAMIGLIAIN UNO INTERNO New Line Cinema, 1975
FRANCO MANNINO

CONVICT COWBOY (CTF) MGM Worldwide Television/Showtime, 1995
DAVID BELL

CONVICT STAGE 20th Century-Fox, 1965
RICHARD LASALLE

CONVICTED Columbia, 1950
GEORGE DUNING

CONVICTED (TF) Larry A. Thompson Productions, 1986
STEVE DORFF

CONVICTED: A MOTHER'S STORY (TF) NBC Productions, 1987
DAVID SHIRE

THE CONVICTION OF KITTY DODDS (TF) Republic, 1993
CRAIG SAFAN

CONVICTS MCEG, 1991
PETER RODGERS MELNICK

CONVICTS FOUR Allied Artists, 1962
LEONARD ROSENMAN

CONVOY BUSTERS 1978
STELVIO CIPRIANI

COOGAN'S BLUFF Universal, 1968
LALO SCHIFRIN

COOK & PEARY: THE RACE TO THE POLE (TF) Robert Halmi Productions/ITT Productions, 1983
CHARLES GROSS

THE COOK, THE THIEF, HIS WIFE & HER LOVER Recorded Releasing, 1989
MICHAEL NYMAN

COOKIE Warner Bros., 1989
THOMAS NEWMAN

COOL AS ICE Universal, 1991
STANLEY CLARKE

COOL CHANGE Hoyts, 1986
BRUCE ROWLAND

COOL HAND LUKE Warner Bros., 1967
LALO SCHIFRIN ★

COOL MILLION (TF) Universal TV, 1972
ROBERT PRINCE

COOL RUNNING Buena Vista, 1993
HANS ZIMMER

COOL WORLD Paramount, 1992
MARK ISHAM
JOHN D. DICKSON

THE COOLANGATTA GOLD Film Gallery, 1984
BILL CONTI

COOLEY HIGH American International, 1975
FREDDIE PERREN

COONSKIN Bryanston Pictures, 1975
CHICO HAMILTON

COOPERSTOWN (CTF) Turner/Amblin TV, 1993
MEL MARVIN

COP Atlantic Releasing Corporation, 1988
MICHEL COLOMBIER

COP AND A HALF Universal, 1993
ALAN SILVESTRI

COP HATER United Artists, 1958
LEITH STEVENS†

COPACABANA United Artists, 1947
EDWARD WARD†

COPACABANA (TF) Dick Clark Cinema Productions/ Stiletto Ltd., 1985
ARTIE BUTLER

COPORATE LADDER Orion, 1997
JAN HAMMER

COP-OUT STRANGER IN THE HOUSE Rank, 1967
JOHN SCOTT

COPPER CANYON Paramount, 1950
DANIELE AMFITHEATROF†

COPS AND ROBBERS United Artists, 1973
MICHEL LEGRAND

COPS AND ROBBERSONS TriStar, 1994
WILLIAM ROSS

COPS AND ROBIN (TF) Paramount TV, 1978
CHARLES BERNSTEIN

COPYCAT Warner Bros., 1995
CHRISTOPHER YOUNG

CORIOLANO, EROE SENZA PATRIA 1963
CARLO RUSTICHELLI

CORIOLIS EFFECT Secondary Modern, 1993
HAL LINDES

CORKY MGM, 1972
JERRY STYNE

CORLEONE 1978
ENNIO MORRICONE

THE CORMORANT (CTF) Holmes Associates, 1995
JOHN LUNN

THE CORN IS GREEN Warner Bros., 1945
MAX STEINER†

THE CORN IS GREEN (TF) Warner Bros. TV, 1979
JOHN BARRY

CORNBREAD, EARL AND ME American International, 1975
DONALD BYRD

CORNERED RKO Radio, 1945
ROY WEBB†

THE CORPSE CAME C.O.D. Columbia, 1947
GEORGE DUNING

THE CORPSE HAD A FAMILIAR FACE (TF) Von Zerneck-Sertner/Touchstone TV, 1994
PATRICK WILLIAMS

CORREGIDOR Producers Releasing Corp., 1943
LEO ERDODY†

...CORREVA L'ANNO DI GRAZIE 1870 1972
ENNIO MORRICONE

CORRIDA OF LOVE Barbary Coast, 1980
TORU TAKEMITSU†

CORRIDOR OF MIRRORS Universal, 1948
GEORGES AURIC†

CORRINA, CORRINA New Line, 1994
RICHARD COX
THOMAS NEWMAN

CORRUPTION IN THE HALLS OF JUSTICE Italnoleggio, 1975
PINO DONAGGIO

CORSAIR United Artists, 1931
ALFRED NEWMAN†

THE CORSICAN BROTHERS 1961
ANGELO FRANCESCO LAVAGNINO†

THE CORSICAN BROTHERS United Artists, 1942
DIMITRI TIOMKIN† ★

THE CORSICAN BROTHERS (TF) Rosemont Productions, 1985
GEORGE S. CLINTON
ALLYN FERGUSON

CORVETTE K-225 Universal, 1943
DAVID BUTTOLPH†

CORVETTE SUMMER MGM/United Artists, 1978
CRAIG SAFAN

COSA AVETE FATTO A SOLANGE? 1972
ENNIO MORRICONE

THE COSBY MYSTERIES (TF) SAH Entertainment/ Columbia Pictures TV/NBC Prods., 1994
BILL COSBY
CRAIG HANDY
CHARLES MINGUS

COSE DI COSA NOSTRA 1971
MANUEL DE SICA

COSI 1995
STEWART COPELAND

COSI Miramax, 1997
STEPHEN ENDELMAN

COSI SIA 1972
BRUNO NICOLAI

THE COSMIC EYE (AF) 1985
WILLIAM RUSSO

THE COSMIC MAN Allied Artists, 1959
PAUL SAWTELL†
BERT A. SHEFTER

COSMIC SLOP: SPACE TRADERS (CTF) Hudlin Bros. Prods./HBO, 1994
JOHN BARNES
GEORGE CLINTON
BERNIE WORRELL

COTTON CANDY (TF) Major Productions, 1978
JOE RENZETTI ★

THE COTTON CLUB Orion, 1984
JOHN BARRY

THE COUCH TRIP Orion, 1988
MICHEL COLOMBIER

COUNT DRACULA NIGHTS OF DRACULA 1970
BRUNO NICOLAI

COUNT DRACULA AND HIS VAMPIRE BRIDE SATANIC RITES OF DRACULA Warner Bros., 1973
JOHN CACAVAS

THE COUNT OF MONTE CRISTO United Artists, 1934
ALFRED NEWMAN†

THE COUNT OF MONTE CRISTO (TF) Norman Rosemont Productions/ITC, 1975
ALLYN FERGUSON

COUNT YORGA, VAMPIRE American International, 1970
BILL MARX

COUNT YOUR BLESSINGS MGM, 1959
FRANZ WAXMAN†

COUNT YOUR BULLETS/FACE TO THE WIND/ APACHE MASSACRE/THE LONG TOMORROW Brut Productions, 1972
RICHARD MARKOWITZ†

COUNTDOWN Warner Bros., 1968
LEONARD ROSENMAN

COUNTDOWN COMPTES A REBOURS 1970
GEORGES DELERUE†

COUNTER-ATTACK Columbia, 1945
LOUIS GRUENBERG†

THE COUNTERFEIT KILLER Universal, 1968
QUINCY JONES

THE COUNTERFEIT TRAITOR Paramount, 1962
ALFRED NEWMAN†

THE COUNTERFEITERS 20th Century-Fox, 1948
IRVING GERTZ

COUNTERFEIT COMMANDOS INGLORIOUS BASTARDS Aquarius, 1978
FRANCESCO DE MASI

COUNTERPLAN 1932
DMITRI SHOSTAKOVITCH†

COUNTERPLOT United Artists, 1959
BERT A. SHEFTER

COUNTERPOINT Universal, 1968
BRONISLAU KAPER†

COUNTESS ALICE (TF) BBC-TV, 1993
ILONA SEKACZ

COUNTESS DRACULA 20th Century-Fox, 1972
HARRY ROBERTSON

THE COUNTESS FROM HONG KONG Universal, 1967
CHARLES CHAPLIN†

THE COUNTESS OF MONTE CRISTO United Artists, 1948
WALTER SCHARF

COUNTRY Buena Vista, 1984
CHARLES GROSS

COUNTRY DANCE MGM, 1970
JOHN ADDISON

THE COUNTRY GIRL Paramount, 1954
VICTOR YOUNG†

COUNTRY GOLD (TF) CBS Entertainment, 1982
BILLY GOLDENBERG

COUNTRY LIFE 1994
PETER BEST

COUNTRY MAN 1982
WALLY BADAROU

COUP DE FOUDRE United Artists Classics, 1983
LUIS BACALOV

COUP DE GRACE Cinema 5, 1976
STANLEY MYERS†

COUP DE TETE HOTHEAD Quartet, 1980
PIERRE BACHELET

COUP DE TORCHON CLEAN SLATE Biograph/ Quartet/Films Inc./The Frank Moreno Company, 1982
PHILIPPE SARDE

COUPE DE VILLE Universal, 1990
JAMES NEWTON HOWARD

THE COUPLE TAKES A WIFE Universal TV, 1972
DICK DEBENEDICTIS

COURAGE - LET'S RUN! Gaumont, 1979
VLADIMIR COSMA

COURAGE (TF) Highgate Pictures/New World TV, 1986
CRAIG SAFAN

THE COURAGE AND THE PASSION (TF) David Gerber Productions/Columbia Pictures TV, 1978
RICHARD SHORES

COURAGE FUYONS COURAGE - LET'S RUN! Gaumont, 1979
VLADIMIR COSMA

COURAGE MOUNTAIN Triumph Releasing Corporation, 1989
SYLVESTER LEVAY

COURAGE OF LASSIE MGM, 1946
BRONISLAU KAPER†

COURAGE UNDER FIRE 20th Century Fox, 1996
JAMES HORNER

THE COURAGEOUS DR. CHRISTIAN   RKO Radio, 1940
WILLIAM LAVA†

COURRIER SUD   1936
JACQUES IBERT†

COURTE TETE   1955
JEAN PRODROMIDES

THE COURT-MARTIAL OF BILLY MITCHELL
Warner Bros., 1955
DIMITRI TIOMKIN†

THE COURT-MARTIAL OF JACKIE ROBINSON
(CTF)   von Zerneck-Sertner/TNT, 1990
STANLEY CLARKE

THE COURTNEY AFFAIR   THE COURTNEYS OF
CURZON STREET   British Lion, 1947
ANTHONY COLLINS†

THE COURTNEYS OF CURZON STREET   British
Lion, 1947
ANTHONY COLLINS†

COUSIN BETTE   Fox-Searchlight, 1997
SIMON BOSWELL

COUSIN BOBBY   Tesauro, 1992
ANTON SANKO

COUSIN, COUSINE   Libra, 1975
GERARD ANFOSSO

THE COUSINS   Films Around the World, 1959
PAUL MISRAKI

COUSINS   Paramount, 1989
ANGELO BADALAMENTI

COVENANT (TF)   Michael Filerman Productions/20th
Century Fox TV, 1985
CHARLES BERNSTEIN

A COVENANT WITH DEATH   Warner Bros., 1966
LEONARD ROSENMAN

THE COVER GIRL AND THE COP (TF)
Barry-Enright Productions/Alexander Productions, 1988
SYLVESTER LEVAY

THE COVER GIRL MURDERS (CTF)   River
Enterprises/Wilshire Court, 1993
RICK MAROTTA

COVER GIRL   Columbia, 1943
CARMEN DRAGON† ★★

COVER GIRLS (TF)   David Gerber Productions/
Columbia Pictures TV, 1977
RICHARD SHORES

COVER UP   Live, 1991
BRUNO LOUCHOUARN

COVER UP (TF)   Glen A. Larson Productions/20th
Century Fox TV, 1984
PAUL CHIHARA

COVERGIRL   New World, 1984
CHRISTOPHER L. STONE

COVER-UP   Universal, 1949
HANS J. SALTER†

COVERUP: BEHIND THE IRAN CONTRA AFFAIR
(FD)   Empowerment Project, 1988
RICHARD ELLIOTT

COWARD OF THE COUNTY (TF)   Kraco
Productions, 1981
LARRY CANSLER

COWBOY   Columbia, 1958
GEORGE DUNING

COWBOY (TF)   Bercovici-St. Johns Productions/MGM
TV, 1983
BRUCE BROUGHTON

THE COWBOY AND THE BALLERINA (TF)   Cowboy
Productions, 1984
BRUCE BROUGHTON

THE COWBOY AND THE LADY   United Artists, 1938
ALFRED NEWMAN† ★

THE COWBOY AND THE SENORITA   Republic, 1944
WALTER SCHARF

COWBOY IN MANHATTAN   Universal, 1943
HANS J. SALTER†

THE COWBOY WAY   Universal, 1994
DAVID NEWMAN

THE COWBOYS   Warner Bros., 1972
JOHN WILLIAMS

COWBOYS DON'T CRY   Cineplex Odeon, 1988
LOUIS NATALE

COWBOYS FROM TEXAS   Republic, 1939
WILLIAM LAVA†

CRACK HOUSE   Cannon, 1989
MICHAEL PICCIRILLO

CRACK IN THE MIRROR   20th Century-Fox, 1959
MAURICE JARRE

CRACK IN THE MIRROR   Triax Entertainment
Group, 1988
NILE RODGERS

CRACK IN THE WORLD   Paramount, 1965
JOHNNY DOUGLAS

CRACKDOWN   Concorde, 1991
TERRY PLUMERI

CRACKED NUTS   RKO Radio, 1931
MAX STEINER†

CRACKED UP (TF)   Aaron Spelling Productions, 1987
MARK SNOW

THE CRACKER FACTORY (TF)   Roger Gimbel
Productions/EMI TV, 1979
BILLY GOLDENBERG

CRACKER: TO BE A SOMEBODY (CTF)   Granada
TV/A&E, 1995
DAVID FERGUSON

CRACKERS   Universal, 1984
PAUL CHIHARA

THE CRACKSMAN   Warner Bros./Pathe, 1963
RON GOODWIN

CRACK-UP   RKO Radio, 1946
LEIGH HARLINE†

CRADLE SONG   Paramount, 1933
W. FRANKE HARLING†

THE CRADLE WILL FALL (TF)   Cates Films Inc./
Procter & Gamble Productions, 1983
ELLIOT LAWRENCE

THE CRAFT   Columbia, 1996
GRAEME REVELL

CRAN D'ARRET   1971
MICHEL MAGNE†

CRASH   Fine Line, 1997
HOWARD SHORE

CRASH (TF)   Charles Fries Productions, 1978
EDDIE LAWRENCE MANSON

CRASH COURSE (TF)   Fries Entertainment, 1988
MARK DAVIS

CRASH DIVE   20th Century-Fox, 1943
DAVID BUTTOLPH†

CRASH LANDING   Columbia, 1958
MISCHA BAKALEINIKOFF†

CRASH LANDING: THE RESCUE OF FLIGHT 232
(TF)   Dorothea G. Petrie/Helios/Bob Banner/Gary
L. Pudney Co., 1992
CHARLES FOX

CRASH OF SILENCE   MANDY   Universal, 1952
WILLIAM ALWYN†

CRASH! AKAZA, GOD OF VENGEANCE   Group
1, 1977
ANDREW BELLING

CRASHOUT   Filmmakers, 1955
LEITH STEVENS†

THE CRAWLING EYE   1958
STANLEY BLACK

CRAWLSPACE   Empire Pictures, 1986
PINO DONAGGIO

CRAWLSPACE (TF)   Titus Productions, 1972
JERRY GOLDSMITH

CRAZE   Warner Bros., 1974
JOHN SCOTT

CRAZY DESIRE   LA VOGLIE MATTA   1962
ENNIO MORRICONE

CRAZY FROM THE HEART (CTF)   De Mann
Entertainment/Papazian-Hirsch, 1991
ARTHUR B. RUBINSTEIN

CRAZY HORSE PARIS—FRANCE   SNC, 1977
JACQUES MORALI

CRAZY IN LOVE (CTF)   Ohlmeyer Communications/
Karen Danaher-Dorr Prods., 1992
CYNTHIA MILLAR

CRAZY PEOPLE   Paramount, 1990
CLIFF EIDELMAN

CRAZY TIMES (TF)   Kayden-Gleason Productions/
George Reeves Productions/Warner Bros. TV, 1981
PETER MATZ

THE CRAZY WORLD OF JULIUS VROODER   20th
Century-Fox, 1974
BOB ALCIVAR

THE CRAZY WORLD OF LAUREL & HARDY
MGM, 1967
JERRY FIELDING†

CREATOR   Universal, 1985
SYLVESTER LEVAY

CREATURE   TITAN FIND   Cardinal Releasing, 1985
TOM CHASE
STEVE RUCKER

THE CREATURE FROM THE BLACK LAGOON
Universal, 1954
HENRY MANCINI†
HANS J. SALTER†
HERMAN STEIN

THE CREATURE WALKS AMONG US   Universal, 1956
IRVING GERTZ
HENRY MANCINI†
HEINZ ROEMHELD†
HERMAN STEIN

THE CREATURE WASN'T NICE   Almi Cinema 5, 1982
DAVID SPEAR

CREATURE WITH THE ATOM BRAIN   Columbia, 1955
MISCHA BAKALEINIKOFF†

THE CREATURES   Howard Mahler Films, 1973
DOUGLAS GAMLEY

CREATURES OF LIGHT   1992
ROBERT NEUFELD

THE CREEPER   20th Century-Fox, 1948
MILTON ROSEN†

CREEPERS   1984
SIMON BOSWELL

CREEPERS   PHENOMENA   New Line Cinema, 1985
GOBLIN

THE CREEPING FLESH   Columbia, 1973
PAUL FERRIS

THE CREEPING UNKNOWN   THE QUARTERMASS
EXPERIMENT   United Artists, 1955
JAMES BERNARD

CREEPSHOW   Warner Bros., 1982
JOHN HARRISON

CREEPSHOW II   New World, 1987
LES REED
RICK WAKEMAN

THE CREMATORS   New World, 1972
ALBERT GLASSER

CRESCENDO   Warner Bros., 1972
MALCOLM WILLIAMSON

CRESCETTE E MOLTIPLICATEVI   1973
ENNIO MORRICONE

CREST OF THE WAVE   GREEN FIRE   MGM, 1954
MIKLOS ROZSA†

CRIES FROM THE HEART (TF)   Wild Rice Prods./
Grossbart-Barnett-Iezman Ent., 1994
JAMES McVAY

CRIES UNHEARD: THE DONNA VARLICH STORY
(TF)   Carla Singer Prods., 1994
HARRY MANFREDINI

CRIME AGAINST JOE   United Artists, 1956
PAUL DUNLAP

CRIME AND PUNISHMENT   1935
ARTHUR HONEGGER†

CRIME AND PUNISHMENT, USA   Allied Artists, 1959
HERSCHEL BURKE GILBERT

CRIME CLUB (TF)   CBS Entertainment, 1973
GEORGE ROMANIS

CRIME CLUB (TF)   Universal TV, 1975
GIL MELLE

THE CRIME DOCTOR   RKO Radio, 1934
MAX STEINER†

THE CRIME DOCTOR'S COURAGE   Columbia, 1945
MARIO †

CRIME DOCTOR'S WARNING   Columbia, 1945
PAUL SAWTELL†

CRIME DOES NOT PAY   Embassy, 1962
GEORGES DELERUE†

CRIME IN THE STREETS   Allied Artists, 1956
FRANZ WAXMAN†

CRIME OF INNOCENCE (TF)   Ohlmeyer
Communications Company, 1985
PAUL CHIHARA

THE CRIME OF MONSIEUR LANGE   Brandon, 1936
JEAN WIENER†

CRIME OF PASSION   United Artists, 1957
PAUL DUNLAP

CRIME OF THE CENTURY (CTF)   1996
JOHN FRIZZELL

CRIME RING   RKO Radio, 1938
ROY WEBB†

CRIME SCHOOL   Warner Bros., 1938
MAX STEINER†

CRIME STORY   1993
JAMES WONG

CRIME WITHOUT PASSION   Paramount, 1934
OSCAR LEVANT†

CRIME ZONE   Concorde, 1989
RICK CONRAD

THE CRIMEBUSTER   MGM, 1961
JERRY GOLDSMITH

CRIMES OF PASSION   New World, 1984
RICK WAKEMAN

CRIMES OF THE HEART   DEG, 1986
GEORGES DELERUE†

CRIMEWAVE   Renaissance, 1985
JOSEPH LO DUCA

CRIMEWAVE   BROKEN HEARTS AND NOSES
Columbia, 1985
ARLON OBER

THE CRIMINAL   Fanfare, 1960
JOHN DANKWORTH

CRIMINAL BEHAVIOR (TF)   Preston Stephen Fischer
Co./Tolivar Prods./World International Network, 1992
MIKE GARSON

CRIMINAL LAW   Hemdale, 1988
JERRY GOLDSMITH

CRIMINAL SYMPHONY   1969
CARLO RUSTICHELLI

THE CRIMSON KIMONO   Columbia, 1959
HARRY SUKMAN†

THE CRIMSON PIRATE   Warner Bros., 1952
WILLIAM ALWYN†

CRIMSON TIDE   Buena Vista, 1995
HANS ZIMMER

CRISIS   Film One-Tri Media, 1997
VAROUJE

CRISIS   MGM, 1950
MIKLOS ROZSA†

CRISIS AT CENTRAL HIGH (TF)   Time-Life
Productions, 1981
BILLY GOLDENBERG

CRISIS IN MID-AIR (TF)   CBS Entertainment, 1979
ROBERT DRASNIN

CRISIS IN SUN VALLEY (TF)   Barry Weitz Films/
Columbia Pictures TV, 1978
DICK DEBENEDICTIS

CRISIS-GO-'ROUND   1992
SONIA WIEDER-ATHERTON

CRISS CROSS   Universal, 1949
MIKLOS ROZSA†

CRISSCROSS   MGM, 1992
TREVOR JONES

CRITICAL CONDITION   Paramount, 1987
ALAN SILVESTRI

THE CRITICAL LIST (TF)   MTM Productions, 1978
JAMES DIPASQUALLE

CRITTERS   New Line Cinema, 1985
DAVID NEWMAN

CRITTERS 2: THE MAIN COURSE   New Line
Cinema, 1988
NICHOLAS PIKE

CROCODILE DUNDEE II   Paramount, 1988
PETER BEST

CROMWELL   Columbia, 1970
FRANK CORDELL† ★

THE CROOK   United Artists, 1971
FRANCIS LAI

CROOKED HEARTS   MGM, 1991
MARK ISHAM

THE CROOKED WEB   Columbia, 1955
MISCHA BAKALEINIKOFF†

CROOKLYN   Universal, 1994
TERENCE BLANCHARD

CROOKS AND CORONETS   Warner Bros., 1969
JOHN SCOTT

CROSS COUNTRY   New World, 1983
CHRIS REA

CROSS COUNTRY ROMANCE   RKO Radio, 1940
ROY WEBB†

CROSS CREEK   Universal/AFD, 1983
LEONARD ROSENMAN ★

CROSS MY HEART   Paramount, 1947
ROBERT EMMETT DOLAN†

CROSS MY HEART   Universal, 1987
BRUCE BROUGHTON
CURT SOBEL

CROSS MY HEART AND HOPE TO DIE   TI
KNIVER I HJERTET   1995
KJETIL BJERKERSTRAND
MAGNE FURUHOLMEN

CROSS OF FIRE (TF)   Leonard Hill Films, 1989
WILLIAM GOLDSTEIN

CROSS OF IRON   Avco Embassy, 1977
ERNEST GOLD

THE CROSS OF LORRAINE   MGM, 1943
BRONISLAU KAPER†

CROSSED LINES   1991
FRYDERYCK BABINSKI

CROSSED SWORDS   THE PRINCE AND THE
PAUPER   Warner Bros., 1977
MAURICE JARRE

CROSSFIRE   RKO Radio, 1947
ROY WEBB†

CROSSFIRE (TF)   QM Productions, 1975
PATRICK WILLIAMS

CROSSING DELANCEY   Warner Bros., 1988
PAUL CHIHARA

CROSSING THE BRIDGE   Buena Vista, 1992
PETER HIMMELMAN

CROSSING THE MOB (TF)   Bateman Company
Productions/Interscope Communications, 1988
MICHEL RUBINI

CROSSING TO FREEDOM (TF)   Procter & Gamble/
Stan Margulies/Granada TV, 1990
CARL DAVIS

CROSSINGS (MS)   Aaron Spelling Productions, 1986
MICHEL LEGRAND

CROSSOVER DREAMS   Crossover Films, 1985
MAURICIO SMITH

CROSSROADS   Columbia, 1986
RY COODER

CROSSROADS   MGM, 1942
BRONISLAU KAPER†

THE CROW   Miramax-Dimension, 1994
GRAEME REVELL

THE CROW: CITY OF ANGELS   1996
GRAEME REVELL

THE CROWD   1981
CARL DAVIS

THE CROWDED SKY   Warner Bros., 1960
LEONARD ROSENMAN

CROWFOOT (TF)   Bellisarius, 1995
VELTON RAY BUNCH

CROWHAVEN FARM (TF)   Aaron Spelling
Productions, 1970
ROBERT DRASNIN

THE CROWN ROARS   MGM, 1938
EDWARD WARD†

THE CRUCIBLE 1957
GEORGES AURIC†
HANNS EISLER†
THE CRUCIBLE 20th Century Fox, 1996
GEORGE FENTON
THE CRUCIFER OF BLOOD (CTF) Turner/
Agamemnon Films/British Lion, 1991
CARL DAVIS
THE CRUDE OASIS Miramax, 1995
STEVEN BRAMSON
CRUEL DOUBTS (TF) Susan Baerwald Prods./NBC
Prods., 1992
GEORGE S. CLINTON
CRUEL HORIZON Skyline Films, 1989
NICHOLAS LENS
THE CRUEL SEA 1953
ALAN RAWSTHORNE†
THE CRUEL TOWER Allied Artists, 1956
PAUL DUNLAP
CRUISE INTO TERROR (TF) Aaron Spelling
Productions, 1978
GERALD FRIED
CRUISING United Artists, 1980
JACK NITZCHE
THE CRUSH Warner Bros., 1993
GRAEME REVELL
CRUSOE Island Pictures, 1988
MICHAEL KAMEN
CRY BABY Universal, 1990
PATRICK WILLIAMS
CRY BABY KILLER Allied Artists, 1958
GERALD FRIED
CRY BLOOD, APACHE Golden Eagle International,
1970
ELLIOT KAPLAN†
CRY DANGER RKO Radio, 1951
EMIL NEWMAN†
PAUL DUNLAP
A CRY FOR HELP (TF) Fairmont-Foxcroft
Productions/Universal TV, 1975
GIL MELLE
A CRY FOR LOVE (TF) Charles Fries Productions/
Alan Sacks Productions, 1980
JIMMIE HASKELL
CRY FOR ME, BILLY COUNT YOUR BULLETS/
FACE TO THE WIND/APACHE MASSACRE/THE
LONG TOMORROW Brut Productions, 1972
RICHARD MARKOWITZ†
CRY FOR THE STRANGERS (TF) David Gerber
Company/MGM TV, 1982
JOHN CACAVAS
CRY FREEDOM Universal, 1987
GEORGE FENTON ★
JONAS GWANGWA ★
A CRY FROM THE STREETS Tudor, 1959
LARRY ADLER
CRY FROM THE MOUNTAIN World Wide, 1986
J.A.C. REDFORD
CRY HAVOC MGM, 1943
DANIELE AMFITHEATROF†
A CRY IN THE DARK Warner Bros., 1988
BRUCE SMEATON
A CRY IN THE NIGHT Warner Bros., 1956
DAVID BUTTOLPH†
A CRY IN THE WILDERNESS (TF) Universal TV,
1974
ROBERT PRINCE
CRY IN THE WILD (TF) Wonderworks, 1991
ARTHUR KEMPEL
CRY IN THE WILD: THE TAKING OF PEGGY ANN
(TF) Ron Gilbert Associates/Leonard Hill Films,
1991
SYLVESTER LEVAY
CRY OF BATTLE Allied Artists, 1963
RICHARD MARKOWITZ†
CRY OF THE BANSHEE American International,
1970
LES BAXTER†
CRY OF THE CITY 20th Century-Fox, 1948
ALFRED NEWMAN†
CRY OF THE INNOCENT (TF) Tara Productions,
1980
ALLYN FERGUSON
CRY OF THE PENGUINS MR. FORBUSH AND
THE PENGUINS EMI, 1971
JOHN ADDISON
CRY OF THE WEREWOLF Columbia, 1944
MISCHA BAKALEINIKOFF†
CRY PANIC (TF) Spelling-Goldberg Productions,
1974
KEN LAUBER
CRY THE BELOVED COUNTRY Miramax, 1995
JOHN BARRY
CRY WOLF Warner Bros., 1947
FRANZ WAXMAN†
THE CRYING GAME Miramax, 1992
ANNE DUDLEY
THE CRYSTAL BALL United Artists, 1943
VICTOR YOUNG†
CRYSTAL EYES 1981
GREG FORREST

CRYSTAL HEART New World, 1987
JOEL GOLDSMITH
CUBA United Artists, 1979
PATRICK WILLIAMS
THE CUBAN LOVE SONG MGM, 1931
HERBERT STOTHART†
CUBAN PETE Universal, 1946
MILTON ROSEN†
CUJO Warner Bros., 1983
CHARLES BERNSTEIN
CUL-DE-SAC Sigma III, 1966
CHRISTOPHER KOMEDA†
THE CULPEPPER CATTLE CO. 20th Century-Fox,
1972
JERRY GOLDSMITH
TOM SCOTT
THE CUMBERLAND STORY 1947
ARTHUR BENJAMIN†
THE CUMMINGTON STORY (D) U.S. Government,
1945
AARON COPLAND†
CUORE DI CANE Italnoleggio, 1975
PIERO PICCIONI
CUORE DI MAMMA 1968
ENNIO MORRICONE
A CUORE FREDDO 1971
STELVIO CIPRIANI
CUORI SENZA FRONTIERE 1949
CARLO RUSTICHELLI
CUORI SOLITARI LONELY HEARTS 1970
LUIS BACALOV
CURACAO (CTF) Jones Programming/Circling
Curacao, 1993
COLIN TOWNS
CURDLED Miramax, 1996
JOSEPH JULIAN GONZALES
THE CURE Universal, 1995
DAVE GRUSIN
CURIOSITY KILLS (CTF) Universal/Davis
Entertainment, 1990
JAN HAMMER
CURLEY United Artists, 1947
HEINZ ROEMHELD†
CURLY SUE Warner Bros., 1991
GEORGES DELERUE†
THE CURSE Trans World Entertainment, 1987
FRANCO MICALIZZI
THE CURSE OF DRACULA United Artists, 1958
GERALD FRIED
THE CURSE OF FRANKENSTEIN Warner Bros.,
1957
JAMES BERNARD
THE CURSE OF KING TUT'S TOMB (TF)
Stromberg-Kerby Productions/Columbia TV/HTV West,
1980
GIL MELLE
THE CURSE OF THE FLY 20th Century-Fox, 1965
BERT A. SHEFTER
CURSE OF THE WEREWOLF Universal, 1961
BENJAMIN FRANKEL†
CURSE OF THE BLACK WIDOW (TF) Dan Curtis
Productions/ABC Circle Films, 1977
BOB COBERT
CURSE OF THE CAT PEOPLE RKO Radio, 1944
ROY WEBB†
CURSE OF THE DEMON NIGHT OF THE
DEMON Columbia, 1957
CLIFTON PARKER†
CURSE OF THE FACELESS MAN United Artists,
1958
GERALD FRIED
CURSE OF THE PINK PANTHER MGM/UA, 1983
HENRY MANCINI†
CURSE OF THE UNDEAD Universal, 1959
IRVING GERTZ
CURSE OF THE VIKING GRAVE (CTF) Muddy
River Films/Atlantic Films/South Pacific Pictures/
CanWest, 1992
RANDOLPH PETERS
CURTAIN CALL RKO Radio, 1940
ROY WEBB†
CURTAIN CALL AT CACTUS CREEK Universal,
1950
WALTER SCHARF
THE CURTAIN RISES 1938
GEORGES AURIC†
CURTAIN UP General Film Distributors, 1952
MALCOLM ARNOLD
CURTAINS Jensen Farley Pictures, 1983
PAUL J. ZAZA
CUSTER OF THE WEST Cinerama Releasing
Corporation, 1968
BERNARDO SEGALL
THE CUSTODIAN 1993
PHILLIP HOUGHTON
CUTTER (TF) Universal TV, 1972
OLIVER NELSON†
CUTTER AND BONE United Artists Classics, 1981
JACK NITZCHE
CUTTER'S TRAIL (TF) CBS Studio Center, 1970
JOHN PARKER

CUTTER'S WAY CUTTER AND BONE United
Artists Classics, 1981
JACK NITZCHE
CUTTHROAT ISLAND MGM-UA, 1995
JOHN DEBNEY
CUTTING CLASS Republic, 1989
JILL FRASER
THE CUTTING EDGE MGM, 1992
PATRICK WILLIAMS
CYBELE OU LES DIMANCHES DE VILLE
d'AVRAY Davis-Royal, 1962
MAURICE JARRE ★
CYBERZONE 1995
JEFF WALTON
CYBORG Cannon, 1989
KEVIN BASSINSON
CYBORG 2087 Features, 1966
PAUL DUNLAP
CYCLE SAVAGES Trans American, 1970
JERRY STYNE
CYBORG SOLDIER New Line Cinema, 1993
BOB MITHOFF
CYCLO 1996
TON THAT TIET
CYCLONE Cinetel, 1987
DAVID A. JACKSON
CYCLOPS American International, 1957
ALBERT GLASSER
CYNARA United Artists, 1932
ALFRED NEWMAN†
CYNTHIA MGM, 1947
BRONISLAU KAPER†
CYRANO DE BERGERAC Orion Classic, 1990
JEAN-CLAUDE PETIT
CYRANO DE BERGERAC United Artists, 1950
DIMITRI TIOMKIN†
CZECHOSLOVAKIA (FD) USIA, 1969
CHARLES BERNSTEIN

D

D2: THE MIGHTY DUCKS Buena Vista, 1994
J.A.C. REDFORD
D3: THE MIGHTY DUCKS Buena Vista, 1996
J.A.C. REDFORD
DA FilmDallas, 1988
ELMER BERNSTEIN
DA BERLINO L'APOCALISSE 1966
BRUNO NICOLAI
THE D.A.: CONSPIRACY TO KILL (TF) Mark VII
Ltd./Universal TV/Jack Webb Productions, 1971
FRANK COMSTOCK
THE D.A.: MURDER ONE (TF) Mark VII Ltd./
Universal TV/Jack Webb Productions, 1969
FRANK COMSTOCK
DA SA BA AFTER SEPARATION 1993
LIANG GANG
DA UOMO A UOMO 1967
ENNIO MORRICONE
DABBEL TRABBEL West German
JURGEN KNIEPER
DAD Universal, 1989
JAMES HORNER
DADAH IS DEATH (MS) Steve Krantz Productions/
Roadshow, Coote & Carroll Productions/Samuel
Goldwyn TV, 1988
FRED KARLIN
DADDY (TF) Doug Cramer, 1991
DENNIS MCCARTHY
DADDY (TF) Robert Greenwald Productions, 1987
SIMON ROGERS
DADDY LONG LEGS 20th Century-Fox, 1955
ALEX NORTH†
DADDY NOSTALGIE Clea Productions, 1990
ANTOINE DUHAMEL
DADDY'S BOYS Concorde, 1988
SASHA MATSON
DADDY'S DEAD DARLING THE PIGS/DADDY'S
GIRL Aquarius, 1984
CHARLES BERNSTEIN
DADDY'S DYIN'...WHO'S GOT THE WILL?
MGM/UA, 1990
DAVID MCHUGH
DADDY'S GONE A-HUNTING National General,
1969
JOHN WILLIAMS
DADDY, I DON'T LIKE IT LIKE THIS (TF) CBS
Entertainment, 1978
DAVID SHIRE
DADDY-O AIP, 1959
JOHN WILLIAMS
DAED SILENCE (CTF) Alliance/HBO Pictures, 1996
JONATHAN GOLDSMITH
THE DAFFY DUCK MOVIE: FANTASTIC ISLAND
(AF) Warner Bros., 1982
ROBERT J. WALSH
DAGMAR'S HOT PANTS, INC. 1971
JIMMIE HASKELL

DAGORA, THE SPACE MONSTER Toho, 1965
AKIRA IFUKUBE
DAHONG DENGLONG GAOGAO GUA Orion
Classics, 1991
ZHAO JIPING
DAI NEMICI MI GUARDO IO 1968
CARLO RUSTICHELLI
DAIBYONIN 1995
TOSHIYUKI HONDA
DAIHAO 'MEIZHOUBAO' CODE NAME
'COUGAR' /OPERATION 'COUGAR'/
MEIZHOUBAO XINGDONG 1988, Chinese
GUO FENG
THE DAIN CURSE (MS) Martin Poll Productions,
1978
CHARLES GROSS
DAISY KENYON 20th Century-Fox, 1947
DAVID RAKSIN
DAKOTA Miramax, 1988
CHRIS CHRISTIAN
DAKOTA Republic, 1945
WALTER SCHARF
DAKOTA LIL 20th Century-Fox, 1950
DIMITRI TIOMKIN†
DALLAS Warner Bros., 1950
MAX STEINER†
DALLAS COWBOY CHEERLEADERS (TF)
Aubrey-Hamner Productions, 1979
JIMMIE HASKELL
DALLAS COWBOY CHEERLEADERS II (TF)
Aubrey-Hamner Productions, 1980
JIMMIE HASKELL
DALLAS: CONUNDRUM (TF) Lorimar TV, 1991
JOHN PARKER
DALLAS: THE EARLY YEARS (TF) Roundelay
Productions/Lorimar-Telepictures, 1986
JERROLD IMMEL
DALLE ARDENNE ALL'INFERNO 1968
ENNIO MORRICONE
BRUNO NICOLAI
THE DALTON GIRLS United Artists, 1957
LES BAXTER†
DALTON: CODE OF VENGEANCE II (TF) Universal
TV, 1986
DON PEAKE
THE DALTONS RIDE AGAIN Universal, 1945
FRANK SKINNER†
THE DAM BUSTERS Warner Bros., 1955
LEIGHTON LUCAS†
DAMAGE New Line, 1992
ZBIGNIEW PREISNER
DAMIEN: OMEN II 20th Century-Fox, 1978
JERRY GOLDSMITH
DAMIEN: THE LEPER PRIEST (TF) Tomorrow
Entertainment, 1980
PETER MATZ ☆
DAMN CITIZEN Universal, 1958
HENRY MANCINI†
DAMN THE DEFIANT! HMS DEFIANT Columbia,
1962
CLIFTON PARKER†
DAMNATION ALLEY 20th Century-Fox, 1977
JERRY GOLDSMITH
THE DAMNED Columbia, 1961
JAMES BERNARD
THE DAMNED LA CADUTA DEGLI DEI/
GOTTERDAMERUNG Warner Bros., 1968
MAURICE JARRE
THE DAMNED DON'T CRY Warner Bros., 1950
DANIELE AMFITHEATROF†
DAMNED IN VENICE/VENETIAN BLACK 1978
PINO DONAGGIO
DAMNED RIVER MGM/UA, 1989
JAMES WESLEY STEMPLE
A DAMNSEL IN DISTRESS RKO Radio, 1937
GEORGE BASSMAN
DAMON AND PYTHIAS 1962
ANGELO FRANCESCO LAVAGNINO†
D'AMORE SI MUORE 1973
ENNIO MORRICONE
DAN CANDY'S LAW ALIEN THUNDER 1973
GEORGES DELERUE†
DANCE FOR MODERN TIMES Mossanen, 1988
LAWRENCE SHRAGGE
DANCE ME OUTSIDE Cineplex-Odeon, 1994
MYCHAEL DANNA
DANCE OF HOPE (FD) 1989
WENDY BLACKSTONE
DANCE OF THE DAMNED Concorde, 1989
GARY STOCKDALE
DANCE OF THE DWARFS Dove Inc., 1983
PERRY BOTKIN
DANCE OF THE VAMPIRES MGM, 1967
CHRISTOPHER KOMEDA†
DANCE WITH A STRANGER Samuel Goldwyn
Company, 1985
RICHARD HARTLEY
DANCE WITH ME, HENRY United Artists, 1956
PAUL DUNLAP
DANCE, GIRL, DANCE RKO Radio, 1940
EDWARD WARD†

DANCERS Cannon, 1987
PINO DONAGGIO

DANCES WITH WOLVES Orion, 1990
JOHN BARRY ★★
PETER BUFFETT

DANCING CO-ED MGM, 1939
EDWARD WARD†

THE DANCING FLEECE 1950
ALAN RAWSTHORNE†

DANCING IN THE DARK (CTF) Power
Pictures-Dream City Films/Hearst, 1995
MICKEY ERBE
MARYBETH SOLOMON

DANCING LADY MGM, 1933
LOUIS SILVERS†

DANCING WITH DANGER (CTF) Fast Track Films/
Wilshire Court/USA Network, 1994
DAVID MICHAEL FRANK

A DANDY IN ASPIC Columbia, 1968
QUINCY JONES

DANDY, THE ALL AMERICAN GIRL MGM/United
Artists, 1976
PAUL CHIHARA

DANGER DOWN UNDER (TF) Weintraub
Entertainment Group/Hoyts Productions Ltd., 1988
BRUCE ROWLAND

DANGER IN PARADISE (TF) Filmways, 1977
ALLYN FERGUSON
JACK ELLIOTT

DANGER IN THE PACIFIC Universal, 1942
HANS J. SALTER†

DANGER ISLAND (TF) von Zerneck-Sertner/NBC
Prods., 1992
PETER MANNING ROBINSON

THE DANGER OF LOVE (TF) Lois Luger Prods/
Citadel Pictures, 1992
MARK SNOW

DANGER SIGNAL Warner Bros., 1945
ADOLPH DEUTSCH†

DANGER ZONE Lippert, 1951
BERT A. SHEFTER

DANGER! LOVE AT WORK 20th Century-Fox,
1937
DAVID BUTTOLPH†

DANGER: DIABOLIK DIABOLIK 1967
ENNIO MORRICONE

A DANGEROUS AFFAIR (TF) Stalking Prods./
Greengrass Prods., 1994
DAVID MANSFIELD

A DANGEROUS GAME Universal, 1941
HANS J. SALTER†

A DANGEROUS LIFE (CTF) HBO/McElroy &
McElroy/FilmAccord Corporation/Australian
Broadcasting Corporation/Zenith Productions, 1988
BRIAN MAY†

**A DANGEROUS MAN: LAWRENCE AFTER ARABIA
(TF)** Enigma TV/Sands Films/WNET, 1992
MICHEL SANVOISIN

A DANGEROUS PROFESSION RKO Radio, 1949
FREDERICK HOLLANDER†

A DANGEROUS WOMAN 1993
CARTER BURWELL

THE DANGEROUS TYPE Sony Corp., 1987
CARL DANTE

DANGEROUS BUSINESS Columbia, 1946
MARIO †

DANGEROUS COMPANY (TF) The Dangerous
Company/Finnegan Associates, 1982
CREED BRATTON

DANGEROUS CORNER RKO Radio, 1934
MAX STEINER†

DANGEROUS CROSSING 20th Century-Fox, 1953
LIONEL NEWMAN†

DANGEROUS DAVIES - THE LAST DETECTIVE
ITC/Inner Circle/Maidenhead Films, 1980
ED WELCH

DANGEROUS DESIRE Saban, 1993
GRAEME COLEMAN

DANGEROUS EXILE Rank, 1957
GEORGES AURIC†

DANGEROUS GAME Cecchi Gori Group, 1994
JOE DELIA

DANGEROUS GROUND New Line, 1997
STANLEY CLARKE

DANGEROUS INTENTIONS (TF) Kaufman Co./
Wildcare Prods./Kushner-Locke, 1995
JAMES MCVAY

DANGEROUS INTRUDER Producers Releasing Corp.,
1945
KARL HAJOS†

DANGEROUS LIASIONS Warner Bros., 1988
GEORGE FENTON ★

DANGEROUS LOVE Concorde, 1988
PAUL HERTZOG

DANGEROUS MINDS Buena Vista, 1995
WENDY & LISA

DANGEROUS MISSION RKO Radio, 1954
ROY WEBB†

DANGEROUS MOONLIGHT RKO Radio, 1941
RICHARD ADDINSELL†

DANGEROUS MOVES LA DIAGONALE DU FOU
Arthur Cohn Productions, 1984
GABRIEL YARED

DANGEROUS OBSESSION Curb Esquire Films,
1990
SIMON BOSWELL

DANGEROUS PASSION (TF) Stormy Weathers
Production/Davis Entertainment, 1990
ROB MOUNSEY

DANGEROUS SUMMER Filmco Ltd., 1982
BRIAN MAY†

DANGEROUSLY CLOSE Cannon, 1986
MICHAEL MCCARTY

DANIEL IN THE LION'S DEN Churchcraft, 1948
MILTON ROSEN†

DANIELE CORTIS 1947
NINO ROTA†

DANIELE E MARIA 1972
NICOLA PIOVANI

DANIELLE STEEL'S 'CHANGES' (TF) Cramer Co./
NBC Prods., 1991
LEE HOLDRIDGE

DANIELLE STEEL'S 'PALOMINO' (TF) Cramer Co./
NBC Prods., 1991
DOMINIC FRONTIERE

DANIELLE STEEL'S 'PALOMINO' (TF) Cramer Co./
NBS Prods., 1991
DENNIS MCCARTHY

DANIELLE STEEL'S A PERFECT STRANGER (TF)
Cramer Co./NBC Prods., 1994
LEE HOLDRIDGE

DANIELLE STEEL'S FAMILY ALBUM (TF) Cramer
Co>/NBC Prods., 1994
LEE HOLDRIDGE

DANIELLE STEEL'S HEARTBEAT (TF) Cramer Co./
NBC Prods., 1993
DAVID SHIRE

DANIELLE STEEL'S JEWELS (TF) List-Estrin/RCS
Video/NBC Prods., 1992
PATRICK WILLIAMS ☆☆

DANIELLE STEEL'S MESSAGE FROM NAM (TF)
Cramer Co./NBC Prods., 1993
BILLY GOLDENBERG

DANIELLE STEEL'S ONCE IN A LIFETIME (TF)
Cramer Co./NBC Prods., 1994
DAVID SHIRE

DANIELLE STEEL'S SECRETS (TF) Cramer Co./NBC
Prods., 1992
ARTHUR B. RUBINSTEIN

DANIELLE STEEL'S STAR (TF) Schoolfield Prods.,
1993
LEE HOLDRIDGE

DANIELLE STEEL'S VANISHED (TF) Cramer Co./
NBC Prods., 1995
FRANCOIS DOMPIERRE

DANIELLE STEEL'S ZOYA (TF) Cramer Co./NBC
Prods., 1995
WILLIAM GOLDSTEIN

DANNY BOY ANGEL Triumph/Columbia, 1983
PADDY MEEGAN

DANNY: CHAMPION OF THE WORLD (CTF)
Portobello Productions/British Screen/Thames TV/The
Disney Channel/WonderWorks/Children's Film &
Television Foundation, 1989
STANLEY MYERS†

DANS L'OMBRE DES COMBATS 1954
JEAN PRODROMIDES

DANS LA POUSSIERE DU SOLEIL French
FRANCIS LAI

DANTE'S INFERNO MGM, 1935
R. H. BASSETT†

DANTE'S PEAK Universal, 1997
JOHN FRIZZELL
JAMES NEWTON HOWARD

DANTON Triumph/Columbia, 1983
JEAN PRODROMIDES

DARBY O'GILL AND THE LITTLE PEOPLE Buena
Vista, 1959
OLIVER WALLACE†

DARBY'S RANGERS Warner Bros., 1958
MAX STEINER†

DARE TO LOVE (TF) WildRice Prods./CBS Ent.,
1995
RON RAMIN

DAREDEVIL IN THE CASTLE 1961
AKIRA IFUKUBE

DAREDEVILS OF THE RED CIRCLE serial, Republic,
1939
WILLIAM LAVA†

THE DARING CABALLERO United Artists, 1949
ALBERT GLASSER

DARING GAME Paramount, 1968
GEORGE BRUNS

THE DARING YOUNG MAN Columbia, 1943
JOHN LEIPOLD†

THE DARK Norstar, 1993
ALUN DAVIES
GUY ZERAFA

THE DARK Film Ventures, 1979
ROGER KELLAWAY

A DARK ADAPTED EYE (TF) BBC, 1995
DAVID FERGUSON

THE DARK ANGEL United Artists, 1935
ALFRED NEWMAN†

THE DARK ANGEL (TF) 1991
PAUL H. LEWIS

THE DARK AT THE TOP OF THE STAIRS Warner
Bros., 1960
MAX STEINER†

THE DARK BACKWARD Elwes/Wyman/Talmadge/
L.A. Bridge, 1991
MARC DAVID DECKER

DARK BEFORE DAWN PSM Entertainment, 1989
KEN SUTHERLAND

DARK CIRCLE (FD) Independent Documentary
Group, 1982
BERNARD KRAUSE
GARY REMAL-MALKIN

DARK CITY Paramount, 1950
FRANZ WAXMAN†

DARK COMMAND Republic, 1940
VICTOR YOUNG†

THE DARK CORNER 20th Century-Fox, 1946
CYRIL J. MOCKRIDGE†

THE DARK CRYSTAL Universal/AFD, 1982
TREVOR JONES

DARK EYES Island Pictures, 1987
FRANCIS LAI

THE DARK HALF Orion, 1992
CHRISTOPHER YOUNG

DARK HOLIDAY (TF) Peter Nelson/Lou Antonio
Productions/The Finnegan-Pinchuk Co./Orion TV,
1989
PAUL CHIHARA

DARK HORSE Carolco/Live/Republic, 1991
ROGER BELLON

THE DARK HOUSE Universal, 1946
HANS J. SALTER†

DARK INTRUDER Universal, 1965
LALO SCHIFRIN

DARK JOURNEY 1937
RICHARD ADDINSELL†

DARK MANSIONS (TF) Aaron Spelling Productions,
1986
KEN HARRISON

THE DARK MIRROR Universal, 1946
FRANK SKINNER†
DIMITRI TIOMKIN†

DARK MIRROR (TF) Aaron Spelling Productions,
1984
DOMINIC FRONTIERE

DARK NIGHT OF THE SCARECROW (TF) Wizan
Productions, 1981
GLENN PAXTON

DARK ODYSSEY Era, 1961
LAURENCE ROSENTHAL

DARK PASSAGE Warner Bros., 1947
FRANZ WAXMAN†

THE DARK PAST Columbia, 1949
GEORGE DUNING

DARK PLACES Cinerama Releasing Corporation,
1974
WILFRED JOSEPHS

DARK PURPOSE L'INTRIGO 1964
ANGELO FRANCESCO LAVAGNINO†

DARK REFLECTIONS (TF) Stillwater Prods./WIN/
Fox West Prods., 1994
DAVID MCHUGH

DARK SHADOWS (MS) Dan Curtis TV/MGM-UA TV,
1991
BOB COBERT

THE DARK SIDE OF INNOCENCE (TF) Warner
Bros. TV, 1976
PETER MATZ

DARK STAR Jack H. Harris Enterprises, 1974
JOHN CARPENTER

DARK STREETS OF CAIRO Universal, 1941
HANS J. SALTER†

DARK TOWER Spectrafilm, 1987
STACY WIDELITZ

DARK VICTORY Warner Bros., 1939
MAX STEINER† ★

DARK VICTORY (TF) Universal TV, 1976
BILLY GOLDENBERG ☆

DARK WATERS United Artists, 1944
MIKLOS ROZSA†

THE DARK WIND Seven Arts, 1991
MICHEL COLOMBIER

THE DARKER SIDE OF TERROR (TF)
Shaner-Ramrus Productions/Bob Banner Associates,
1979
PAUL CHIHARA

DARKER THAN AMBER National General, 1970
JOHN PARKER

DARKMAN Universal, 1990
DANNY ELFMAN

DARKNESS BEFORE DAWN (TF) Diana Kerew
Prods./Polone, 1993
PETER MANNING ROBINSON

DARKNESS IN TALLINN FilmZolfo, 1993
MADER

DARLING Embassy, 1965
JOHN DANKWORTH

DARLING LILI Paramount, 1970
HENRY MANCINI†

DARLING OF THE GODS (MS) 1989
BRIAN MAY†

DARLING, HOW COULD YOU? Paramount, 1951
FREDERICK HOLLANDER†

DARROW (TF) KCET/Heuss-Stept Prods., 1991
RICHARD EINHORN

D'ARTAGNAN Triangle, 1915
VICTOR SCHERTZINGER†

THE DARWIN ADVENTURE 20th Century-Fox,
1972
MARC WILKINSON

D.A.R.Y.L. Paramount, 1985
MARVIN HAMLISCH

DAS BLAUE LICHT 1932
GIUSEPPE BECCE†

DAS BOOT THE BOAT Triumph/Columbia, 1981
KLAUS DOLDINGER

**DAS INDISCHE GRABMAL JOURNEY TO THE
LOST CITY** American International, 1959
MICHEL MICHELET†

DAS SCHWEIGEN IM WALDE 1955
GIUSEPPE BECCE†

**DAS SPUKSCHLOSS IM SPESSART THE SPOOK
CASTLE IN SPESSART** 1960
FREDERICK HOLLANDER†

DAS VERSPRECHEN Fine Line, 1995
JURGEN KNIEPER

DATE WITH AN ANGEL DEG, 1987
RANDY KERBER

**THE DAUGHTER OF D'ARTAGNAN LA FILLE DE
D'ARTAGNAN** 1994
PHILIPPE SARDE

THE DAUGHTER OF ROSIE O'GRADY Warner
Bros., 1950
DAVID BUTTOLPH†

DAUGHTER OF DARKNESS (TF) King Phoenix
Entertainment, 1990
COLIN TOWNS

DAUGHTER OF EVIL 1930
BRONISLAU KAPER†

DAUGHTER OF THE MIND (TF) 20th Century-Fox,
1969
ROBERT DRASNIN

DAUGHTER OF THE SANDS 1952
GEORGES AURIC†

DAUGHTER OF THE STREETS (TF) Adam
Productions/20th Century Fox Film Corp., 1990
LEE HOLDRIDGE

DAUGHTER OF THE SUN GOD American
International, 1962
LES BAXTER†

THE DAUGHTERS OF JOSHUA CABE (TF)
Spelling-Goldberg Productions, 1972
JEFF ALEXANDER†

**THE DAUGHTERS OF JOSHUA CABE RETURN
(TF)** Spelling-Goldberg Productions, 1975
JEFF ALEXANDER†

DAUGHTERS COURAGEOUS Warner Bros., 1939
MAX STEINER†

DAUGHTERS OF PRIVILEGE (TF) NBC Prods.,
1991
PATRICK WILLIAMS

DAUGHTERS OF SATAN United Artists, 1972
RICHARD LASALLE

DAUGHTERS OF THE DUST American Playhouse,
1991
JOHN BARNES

DAVE Warner Bros., 1993
JAMES NEWTON HOWARD

DAVID Kino International, 1979
WOJCIECH KILAR

DAVID (TF) Tough Boys Inc./Donald March
Productions/ITC Entertainment Group, 1988
MARVIN HAMLISCH

DAVID AND BATHSHEBA 20th Century-Fox, 1951
ALFRED NEWMAN† ★

DAVID COPPERFIELD MGM, 1935
WILLIAM AXT†
HERBERT STOTHART†

DAVID COPPERFIELD (TF) Omnibus Productions/
Sagittarius Productions, 1970
MALCOLM ARNOLD

DAVID'S MOTHER (TF) Morgan Hill Films/Hearst,
1994
DAVID MANSFIELD

DAVY CROCKETT AND THE RIVER PIRATES
Buena Vista, 1956
GEORGE BRUNS

DAVY CROCKETT, INDIAN SCOUT United Artists,
1950
PAUL SAWTELL†

**DAVY CROCKETT, KING OF THE WILD
FRONTIER** Buena Vista, 1955
GEORGE BRUNS

**DAVY CROCKETT: RAINBOW IN THE THUNDER
(TF)** Echo Cove Productions/Walt Disney TV, 1988
JOEL MCNEELY

DAWN OF THE DEAD United Film Distribution, 1979
GOBLIN

DAWN OF THE MUMMY Harmony Gold Ltd., 1981
SHUKI LEVY

THE DAWN PATROL Warner Bros., 1938
MAX STEINER†

DAWN: PORTRAIT OF A TEENAGE RUNAWAY (TF) Douglas S. Cramer Productions, 1976
FRED KARLIN

THE DAY AFTER (TF) ABC Circle Films, 1983
DAVID RAKSIN

THE DAY AFTER HALLOWEEN *SNAPSHOT* Group 1, 1979
BRIAN MAY†

THE DAY AND THE HOUR MGM, 1962
CLAUDE BOLLING

A DAY AT THE RACES MGM, 1937
GEORGE BASSMAN

THE DAY CHRIST DIED (TF) Martin Manulis Productions/20th Century-Fox TV, 1980
LAURENCE ROSENTHAL

DAY FOR NIGHT *LA NUIT AMERICAINE* Warner Bros., 1973
GEORGES DELERUE†

A DAY FOR THANKS ON WALTONS MOUNTAIN (TF) Amanda Productions/Lorimar Productions, 1982
ALEXANDER COURAGE

A DAY IN COURT 1954
ARMANDO TROVAJOLI

DAY IN DAY OUT 1965
GERARD SCHURMANN

A DAY IN THE COUNTRY *UN PARTIE DE CAMPAGNE* 1936
JOSEPH KOSMA†

THE DAY MARS INVADED EARTH 20th Century-Fox, 1962
RICHARD LASALLE

A DAY OF FURY Universal, 1956
HENRY MANCINI†
HERMAN STEIN

THE DAY OF RECKONING (AF) 1960
ZDENEK LISKA

THE DAY OF THE DOLPHIN Avco Embassy, 1973
GEORGES DELERUE† ★

THE DAY OF THE JACKAL Universal, 1973
GEORGES DELERUE†

THE DAY OF THE LOCUST Paramount, 1975
JOHN BARRY

THE DAY OF THE TRIFFIDS Allied Artists, 1963
RON GOODWIN

DAY OF THE ANIMALS Film Ventures, 1977
LALO SCHIFRIN

DAY OF THE BAD MAN Universal, 1958
HANS J. SALTER†

DAY OF THE DEAD United Film Distribution, 1985
JOHN HARRISON

DAY OF THE EVIL GUN MGM, 1968
JEFF ALEXANDER†

DAY OF THE OUTLAW United Artists, 1959
ALEXANDER COURAGE

DAY OF THE PAINTER 1960
EDDIE LAWRENCE MANSON

DAY OF TRIUMPH 1954
DANIELE AMFITHEATROF†

DAY ONE (TF) Aaron Spelling Productions/Paragon Motion Pictures, 1988
MASON DARING

THE DAY THE BOOKIES WEPT RKO Radio, 1939
ARTHUR MORTON

THE DAY THE BUBBLE BURST (TF) Tamara Productions/20th Century-Fox TV/The Production Company, 1982
JACK ELLIOTT

THE DAY THE EARTH MOVED (TF) ABC Circle Films, 1974
BOBBY SHERMAN

THE DAY THE EARTH STOOD STILL 20th Century-Fox, 1951
BERNARD HERRMANN†

THE DAY THE FISH CAME OUT 20th Century-Fox, 1967
MIKIS THEODORAKIS

THE DAY THE LOVING STOPPED (TF) Monash-Zeitman Productions, 1981
LEE HOLDRIDGE

THE DAY THE SCREAMING STOPPED Enterprise, 1978
STANLEY MYERS†

THE DAY THE SKY EXPLODED *LA MORTE VIENE DALLO SPAZIO* 1958
CARLO RUSTICHELLI

THE DAY THE WOMEN GOT EVEN (TF) Otto Salomon Productions/PKO Television Ltd., 1980
BRAD FIEDEL

THE DAY THE WORLD ENDED American International, 1956
RONALD STEIN†

THE DAY THEY GAVE BABIES AWAY Universal, 1958
MAX STEINER†

THE DAY THEY ROBBED THE BANK OF ENGLAND MGM, 1960
EDWIN ASTLEY

THE DAY TIME ENDED Compass International, 1979
RICHARD H. BAND

THE DAY WILL DAWN 1942
RICHARD ADDINSELL†

DAYBREAK (CTF) Foundation/HBO, 1993
MICHEL COLOMBIER

THE DAYDREAMER 1970
VLADIMIR COSMA

THE DAYDREAMER Embassy, 1966
MAURY LAWS

DAYLIGHT Universal, 1996
RANDY EDELMAN

DAYO (TF) Steve White Prods., 1992
LEE HOLDRIDGE

DAYS AND NIGHTS IN THE FOREST Pathe Contemporary, 1970
SATYAJIT RAY†

DAYS OF BETRAYAL 1974
ZDENEK LISKA

DAYS OF GLORY RKO Radio, 1944
DANIELE AMFITHEATROF†

DAYS OF HEAVEN Paramount, 1978
LEO KOTTKE
ENNIO MORRICONE ★

DAYS OF THUNDER Paramount, 1990
JOHN VAN TONGEREN
HANS ZIMMER

DAYS OF WINE AND ROSES Warner Bros., 1962
HENRY MANCINI†

D.C. CAB Universal, 1983
GIORGIO MORODER

D-DAY, THE SIXTH OF JUNE 20th Century-Fox, 1956
LYN MURRAY†

DE CRIADA A SIGNORA 1979
STELVIO CIPRIANI

DE DOMEINEN DITVOORST *THE DITVOORST DOMAIN* 1993
SOFIA GUBAIDULINA

DE KLEINE BLONDE DOOD 1994
JURRE HAANSTRA
TOOTS THIELEMANS

DE LA PART DES COPAINS Emerson, 1970
MICHEL MAGNE†

DE PLEIN FOUET 1991
JEAN-CLAUDE PETIT

DE SCHORPIOEN 1983
NICOLA PIOVANI

THE DEAD Vestron, 1987
ALEX NORTH†

DEAD AGAIN Paramount, 1991
PATRICK DOYLE

DEAD AHEAD: THE EXXON VALDEZ DISASTER (CTF) HBO Showcase/BBC, 1992
DAVID FERGUSON

DEAD AIR (CTF) Alan Barnette Prods./Viacom, 1994
DANA KAPROFF

DEAD AND BURIED Avco Embassy, 1981
JOE RENZETTI

DEAD AS A DOORMAN Just Spoke Prods., 1986
CLAUDE GAUDETTE

DEAD BADGE Odyssey, 1994
MARK SNOW

DEAD BEFORE DAWN (TF) Joel Fields Prods./Leonard Hill Films, 1993
SYLVESTER LEVAY

DEAD CALM Warner Bros., 1989
GRAEME REVELL

DEAD CERT United Artists, 1973
JOHN ADDISON

THE DEAD DON'T DIE (TF) Douglas S. Cramer Productions, 1975
ROBERT PRINCE

DEAD END United Artists, 1937
ALFRED NEWMAN†

DEAD END KIDS (FD) Mabou Mines, 1986
DAVID BYRNE
PHILIP GLASS

DEAD FUNNY Avondale Pictures/Movie Screen Entertainment, 1995
SHEILA SILVER

DEAD GIVEAWAY Curb Entertainment, 1995
BOB MITHOFF

DEAD HEAT New World, 1988
ERNEST TROOST

DEAD HEAT ON A MERRY-GO-ROUND Columbia, 1966
STU PHILLIPS

DEAD IN THE WATER (CTF) Kevin Bright/MTE, 1991
PHILIP GIFFIN

DEAD INNOCENT Blackwatch Communications, 1997
DAVID FINDLAY

DEAD MAN Miramax, 1995
NEIL YOUNG

DEAD MAN ON THE RUN (TF) Sweeney-Finnegan Productions, 1975
HARRY GELLER

DEAD MAN OUT (CTF) HBO Showcase/Robert Cooper Entertainment/Granada TV, 1988
CLIFF EIDELMAN

DEAD MAN WALKING Gramercy, 1995
DAVID ROBBINS

DEAD MAN'S EYES Universal, 1944
PAUL SAWTELL†

DEAD MEN CAN'T DANCE Live, 1997
RICHARD MARVIN

DEAD MEN DON'T WEAR PLAID Universal, 1982
MIKLOS ROZSA†

DEAD MEN TELL 20th Century-Fox, 1940
DAVID RAKSIN

DEAD MEN WALK Producers Releasing Corp., 1943
LEO ERDODY†

THE DEAD MOTHER 1993
BINGEN MENDIZABAL

DEAD OF NIGHT Universal, 1945
GEORGES AURIC†

DEAD OF NIGHT/THE NIGHT ANDY CAME HOME Europix International, 1974
CARL ZITTRER

DEAD OF WINTER MGM/UA, 1987
RICHARD EINHORN

DEAD ON COURSE Exclusive Films, 1952
MALCOLM ARNOLD

DEAD ON THE MONEY (CTF) Perfect Circle Corp./Voyager/Indieprod, 1991
MICHAEL MINARD

THE DEAD ONE IN THE THAMES RIVER 1971
PETER THOMAS

DEAD POETS SOCIETY Buena Vista, 1989
MAURICE JARRE

THE DEAD POOL Warner Bros., 1988
LALO SCHIFRIN

DEAD PRESIDENTS Buena Vista, 1995
DANNY ELFMAN

DEAD RECKONING (CTF) Houston Lady Productions, 1990
MARK SNOW

DEAD RINGER Stock Grange Productions, 1988
BARRY FASMAN
DANA WALDEN

DEAD RINGER Warner Bros., 1964
ANDRE PREVIN

DEAD RINGERS 20th Century Fox, 1988
HOWARD SHORE

DEAD SILENCE (TF) FNM Films, 1991
TIM TRUMAN

DEAD SILENCE...the movie Curb/Esquire Films, 1989
PETER FRANCIS ROTTER

DEAD SLEEP 1990
BRIAN MAY†

DEAD SOLID PERFECT (CTF) HBO Pictures/David Merrick Productions, 1988
TANGERINE DREAM

DEAD SPACE Califilm, 1991
DANIEL MAY

DEAD TIRED Miramax Zoë, 1995
RENE MARC BINI

THE DEAD ZONE Paramount, 1983
MICHAEL KAMEN

DEAD-BANG Warner Bros., 1989
GARY CHANG

DEADBOLT (TF) Allegro Films/Image, 1993
MILAN KYMLICKA

DEADFALL also appears as conductor, 20th Century-Fox, 1968
JOHN BARRY

DEADHEAD MILES Paramount, 1971
TOM T. HALL

DEADLIER THAN THE MALE Universal, 1966
MALCOM LOCKYER

DEADLIER THAN THE MALE *VOICI LE TEMPS DES ASSASSINS* Continental, 1955
JEAN WIENER†

THE DEADLIEST SEASON (TF) Titus Productions, 1977
DICK HYMAN

DEADLINE Australian
BRIAN MAY†

DEADLINE - U.S.A. MGM, 1952
LIONEL NEWMAN†

DEADLINE (TF) 1989
LARRY CARLTON

DEADLINE (TF) BBC Enterprises, 1988
JIM PARKER

DEADLINE AT DAWN RKO Radio, 1946
HANNS EISLER†

DEADLINE FOR MURDER: FROM THE FILES OF EDNA BUCHANAN (TF) Von Zerneck-Sertner/Touchstone TV, 1995
PATRICK WILLIAMS

DEADLINE IN SEVEN DAYS *ZHAMGEDEH YOT OR* 1992
ARDASHES KARTALIAN

DEADLINE U.S.A. 20th Century-Fox, 1952
CYRIL J. MOCKRIDGE†

DEADLOCK (CTF) Spectacor, Frederick S. Pierce, 1991
RICHARD GIBBS

DEADLOCKED: ESCAPE FROM ZONE 14 *DEADLOCK II* (TF) Pacific/Spectacor/Jaffe-Braunstein/Signboard Hill, 1995
PETER MANNING ROBINSON

THE DEADLY AFFAIR Columbia, 1967
QUINCY JONES

THE DEADLY BEES Paramount, 1967
WILFRED JOSEPHS

DEADLY BETRAYAL: THE BRUCE CURTIS STORY (TF) Atlantis Films/Citadel, 1992
LOUIS NATALE

DEADLY BLESSING United Artists, 1981
JAMES HORNER

A DEADLY BUSINESS (TF) Thebaut-Frey Productions/Taft Entertainment TV, 1986
PAUL CHIHARA

DEADLY CARE (CTF) Universal TV, 1987
TANGERINE DREAM
CHRISTOPHER FRANKE

DEADLY CURRENTS (FD) Associated Producers, 1991
STEPHEN PRICE

DEADLY DESIRE (CTF) Skylark Films, 1991
NAN SCHWARTZ-MISHKIN

THE DEADLY DREAM (TF) Universal TV, 1971
DAVE GRUSIN

DEADLY DUO United Artists, 1962
RICHARD LASALLE

DEADLY ENCOUNTER Ambassador Releasing, 1975
STU PHILLIPS

DEADLY ENCOUNTER (TF) Roger Gimbel Productions/EMI TV/Promises Productions, 1982
MICHAEL HOENIG
FRED KARLIN
J. PETER ROBINSON

DEADLY EYES *THE RATS* Warner Bros., 1983
ANTHONY GUEFEN

DEADLY FORCE Embassy, 1983
GARY SCOTT

DEADLY FRIEND Warner Bros., 1986
CHARLES BERNSTEIN

DEADLY GAME (TF) Manteo Enterprises/MGM TV, 1977
MUNDELL LOWE

DEADLY GAMES Monterey Films, 1979
ROBERT O. RAGLAND

DEADLY GAMES (TF) Shaken Not Stirred Prods./Rumbleseat Prods./Viacom, 1995
DENNIS McCARTHY

DEADLY HARVEST (TF) CBS Entertainment, 1972
MORTON STEVENS†

DEADLY HERO Avco Embassy, 1976
BRAD FIEDEL
TOMMY MANDEL

DEADLY HONEYMOON *NIGHTMARE HONEYMOON* MGM, 1974
ELMER BERNSTEIN

THE DEADLY HUNT (TF) Four Star International, 1971
VIC MIZZY

DEADLY ILLUSION CineTel Films, 1987
PATRICK GLEESON

DEADLY INNOCENCE Universal, 1988
DAVID C. WILLIAMS

DEADLY INTENT Fries Entertainment, 1988
ETHAN JAMES

DEADLY INTENTIONS (TF) Green-Epstein Productions, 1985
GEORGES DELERUE†

DEADLY INTENTIONS...AGAIN ? (TF) Green-Epstein/Lorimar TV, 1991
J. PETER ROBINSON

DEADLY INVASION: THE KILLER BEE NIGHTMARE (TF) St. Francis of Assisi Pictures/WIN/Von Zerneck Films, 1995
GARRY SCHYMAN

DEADLY IS THE FEMALE United Artists, 1949
VICTOR YOUNG†

DEADLY LESSONS (TF) Leonard Goldberg Company, 1983
IAN FREEBAIRN-SMITH

THE DEADLY MANTIS Universal, 1957
WILLIAM LAVA†

DEADLY MEDICINE (TF) Steve Krantz Prods., 1991
BOB ALCIVAR

DEADLY MESSAGES (TF) Columbia Pictures TV, 1985
BRAD FIEDEL

DEADLY PRESENCE Trancas International
ANDREA SAPAROFF

DEADLY RELATIONS (TF) O.T.M.L. Prods./Wilshire Court, 1993
PHILIP GIFFIN

DEADLY SHOTS ON BROADWAY 1969
PETER THOMAS

A DEADLY SILENCE (TF) Robert Greenwald Productions, 1989
RICHARD GIBBS

DEADLY STRANGER MCEG, 1988
CHUCK CIRINO

DEADLY STRANGERS Fox-Rank, 1974
RON GOODWIN

THE DEADLY TOWER (TF) MGM TV, 1975
DON ELLIS†

THE DEADLY TRACKERS Warner Bros., 1973
JERRY FIELDING†

DEADLY TRIANGLE (TF) Barry Weitz Productions/
Columbia Pictures TV, 1975
DICK DEBENEDICTIS

DEADLY VOWS (TF) Carla Singer Prods./WIN,
1994
JOHN D'ANDREA
CORY LERIOS

DEADLY WHISPERS (TF) Hill-Fields/ACI, 1995
JOSEPH CONLAN

DEADMAN'S CURVE (TF) Roger Gimbel
Productions/EMI TV, 1978
FRED KARLIN

DEADMAN'S REVENGE (CTF) MTE/
Finnegan-Pinchuk/USA Network, 1994
DAVID SCHWARTZ

DEAL OF THE CENTURY Warner Bros., 1983
ARTHUR B. RUBINSTEIN

DEALERS Samuel Goldwyn Company, 1989
RICHARD HARTLEY

DEALING: OR THE BERKELEY-TO-BOSTON
FORTY-BRICK LOST-BAG BLUES Warner Bros.,
1972
MICHAEL SMALL

DEALY MATRIMONY (TF) Steve Krantz Prods./
Multimedia TV, 1992
LEE HOLDRIDGE

THE DEAN OF THIN AIR (TF) PBS, 1983
JOSEPH CARRIER
JOSEPH S. DE BEASI

DEAN R. KOONTZ'S SERVANTS OF TWILIGHT
(CTF) Trimark/Gibraltar, 1991
JIM MANZIE

DEAR AMERICA: LETTERS HOME FROM
VIETNAM (FD) Taurus Entertainment, 1987
TODD BOEKELHEIDE

DEAR BOYS Sigma Films, 1980
LAURENS VAN ROOYEN

DEAR BRAT Paramount, 1951
NATHAN VAN CLEAVE†

DEAR DETECTIVE 1978
GEORGES DELERUE†

DEAR GOD Paramount, 1996
JAMES PATRICK DUNNE
JEREMY LUBBOCK

DEAR HEART Warner Bros., 1964
HENRY MANCINI†

DEAR MURDERER 1947
BENJAMIN FRANKEL†

DEAR SUMMER SISTER 1972
TORU TAKEMITSU†

DEAR WIFE Paramount, 1949
NATHAN VAN CLEAVE†

DEATH & TAXES (FD) 1993
TRACY ADAMS

DEATH AMONG FRIENDS (TF) The Douglas Cramer
Company/Warner Bros. TV, 1975
JIM HELMS

DEATH AND THE MAIDEN Fine Line, 1994
WOJCIECH KILAR

DEATH BE NOT PROUD (TF) Good Housekeeping
Productions/Westfall Productions, 1975
FRED KARLIN

DEATH BECOMES HER Universal, 1992
ALAN SILVESTRI

DEATH BEFORE DISHONOR New World, 1987
BRIAN MAY†

DEATH CAR ON THE FREEWAY (TF) Shpetner
Productions, 1979
RICHARD MARKOWITZ†

DEATH CORPS. Joseph Brenner Associates, 1977
RICHARD EINHORN

DEATH CRUISE (TF) Spelling-Goldberg Productions,
1974
PETE RUGOLO

DEATH DANCERS V.I.P., 1993
LORIN ALEXANDER

THE DEATH DEALER MILANO ODIA: LA POLIZIA
NON PUO SPARARE 1974
ENNIO MORRICONE

DEATH DORM/PRANKS New Image, 1982
CHRISTOPHER YOUNG

DEATH DREAM DEAD OF NIGHT/THE NIGHT
ANDY CAME HOME Europix International, 1974
CARL ZITTRER

DEATH DREAMS (CTF) Ultra/Dick Clark Film
Group/Roni Weisberg Prods., 1991
GERALD GOURIET

DEATH GAME Levitt-Pickman, 1977
JIMMIE HASKELL

DEATH HOUSE Death House Prods., 1987
CHUCK CIRINO

DEATH HUNT 20th Century-Fox, 1981
JERROLD IMMEL

A DEATH IN CALIFORNIA (TF) Mace Neufeld
Productions/Lorimar Productions, 1985
JOHN CACAVAS

DEATH IN SMALL DOSES Allied Artists, 1957
EMIL NEWMAN†

DEATH IN THE GARDEN Bauer International, 1956
PAUL MISRAKI

DEATH IN VENICE Warner Bros., 1971
FRANCO MANNINO

DEATH MOON (TF) Roger Gimbel Productions/EMI
TV, 1978
PAUL CHIHARA

DEATH OF A CENTERFOLD: THE DOROTHY
STRATTEN STORY (TF) Wilcox Productions/MGM
TV, 1981
ROGER WEBB

DEATH OF A GUNFIGHTER Universal, 1967
OLIVER NELSON†

DEATH OF A SALESMAN Columbia, 1951
ALEX NORTH† ★

DEATH OF A SALESMAN (TF) Roxbury and Punch
Productions, 1985
ALEX NORTH† ☆

DEATH OF A SCHOOLBOY 1991
PETER PONGER

DEATH OF A SCOUNDREL RKO Radio, 1956
MAX STEINER†

DEATH OF A SOLDIER Scotti Brothers, 1986
ALLAN ZAVOD

DEATH OF AN ANGEL 20th Century Fox, 1985
PETER MYERS

DEATH OF AN ANGEL 20th Century-Fox, 1985
JAY FERGUSON

DEATH OF AN EXPERT WITNESS (MS) Anglia TV,
1982
RICHARD HARVEY

A DEATH OF INNOCENCE (TF) Mark Carliner
Productions, 1971
MORTON STEVENS†

THE DEATH OF ME YET (TF) Aaron Spelling
Productions, 1971
PETE RUGOLO

THE DEATH OF OCEAN PARK (TF) John Furia
Prods., 1979
JOHN BEAL

THE DEATH OF OCEAN VIEW PARK (TF)
Furia-Oringer Productions/Playboy Productions, 1979
FRED WERNER

THE DEATH OF RICHIE (TF) Henry Jaffe
Enterprises/NBC TV, 1977
FRED KARLIN

THE DEATH OF THE INCREDIBLE HULK (TF)
Bixby-Brandon Productions/New World TV, 1990
LANCE RUBIN

DEATH ON THE NILE Paramount, 1978
NINO ROTA†

DEATH PLAY New Line Cinema, 1976
RUPERT HOLMES

DEATH RACE (TF) Silverton Productions/Universal
TV, 1973
MILTON ROSEN†

DEATH RACE 2000 New World, 1975
PAUL CHIHARA

DEATH RAY 2000 (TF) Woodruff Productions/QM
Productions, 1981
JOHN ELIZALDE

DEATH RIDE TO OSAKA (TF) Hill-Mandelker
Productions, 1983
BRAD FIEDEL

DEATH RIDES A HORSE DA UOMO A UOMO
1967
ENNIO MORRICONE

DEATH RUTH Paramount, 1947
ROBERT EMMETT DOLAN†

DEATH SCREAM (TF) RSO Films, 1975
GIL MELLE

DEATH SENTENCE (TF) Spelling-Goldberg
Productions, 1974
LAURENCE ROSENTHAL

DEATH STALK (TF) Herman Rush Associates/David
L Wolper Productions, 1975
PETE RUGOLO

DEATH TAKES A HOLIDAY Paramount, 1934
BERNHARD KAUN†
SIGMUND KRUMGOLD†
MILAN RODER†

DEATH TRAP Virgo International, 1977
WAYNE BELL

DEATH VALLEY Universal, 1982
DANA KAPROFF

DEATH WATCH LA MORT EN DIRECT Quartet,
1980
ANTOINE DUHAMEL

THE DEATH WHEELERS PSYCHOMANIA Scotia
International, 1971
DAVID WHITAKER

DEATH WISH Paramount, 1974
HERBIE HANCOCK

DEATH WISH II Filmways, 1982
JIMMY PAGE

DEATH WISH 3 Cannon, 1985
JIMMY PAGE

DEATH WISH 4: THE CRACKDOWN Cannon,
1988
PAUL MCCALLUM
VALENTINE MCCALLUM

DEATH WISH V: THE FACE OF DEATH Trimark,
1994
TERRY PLUMERI

DEATH: THE TRIP OF A LIFETIME (TD) 1993
DAVID DUVALL

DEATHHOUSE Cannon, 1981
GERSHON KINGSLEY

THE DEATHMASTER American International, 1972
BILL MARX

DEATHSPORT New World, 1978
ANDREW STEIN

DEATHSTALKER New World, 1984
OSCAR CARDOZO OCAMPO

DEATHSTALKER II New World, 1983
CHUCK CIRINO

DEATHTRAP Warner Bros., 1982
JOHNNY MANDEL

DECADENCE 1994
STEWART COPELAND

DECAMERON NIGHTS RKO Radio, 1953
ANTONY HOPKINS

DECEIT 21st Century, 1990
TONY RIPPARETTI

DECEIVED Touchstone, 1991
THOMAS NEWMAN

THE DECEIVERS Cinecom, 1988
JOHN SCOTT

DECEMBER I.R.S. Media, 1991
DEBORAH HOLLAND

DECEPTION Warner Bros., 1946
ERICH WOLFGANG KORNGOLD†

DECEPTIONS (CTF) Republic Pictures, 1990
GARY SCOTT

DECEPTIONS (TF) Louis Rudolph Productions/
Consolidated Productions/Columbia TV, 1985
NIGEL HESS

DECISION AGAINST TIME THE MAN IN THE
SKY MGM, 1956
GERARD SCHURMANN

DECISION AT SUNDOWN Columbia, 1958
HEINZ ROEMHELD†

DECISION BEFORE DAWN 20th Century-Fox, 1951
FRANZ WAXMAN†

THE DECISION OF CHRISTOPHER BLAKE Warner
Bros., 1948
MAX STEINER†

DECLINE AND FALL OF A BIRD WATCHER 20th
Century-Fox, 1969
RON GOODWIN

DECORATION DAY (TF) 1990
PATRICK WILLIAMS ☆

THE DEEP Columbia, 1977
JOHN BARRY

DEEP COVER New Line, 1992
MICHEL COLOMBIER

DEEP IN THE HEART HANDGUN Warner Bros.,
1981
MIKE POST

DEEP IN THE HEART OF TEXAS Universal, 1942
HANS J. SALTER†

DEEP RED (CTF) DBA Ent./MCA TV, 1994
GARY CHANG

DEEP RISING 1998
JERRY GOLDSMITH

THE DEEP SIX Warner Bros., 1958
DAVID BUTTOLPH†

DEEP STAR SIX Tri-Star, 1989
HARRY MANFREDINI

DEEP TROUBLE (CTF) Papazian-Hirsch/Ellipse,
1993
ARTHUR B. RUBINSTEIN

DEEP VALLEY Warner Bros., 1947
MAX STEINER†

DEEP WATERS 20th Century-Fox, 1948
CYRIL J. MOCKRIDGE†

THE DEEP, BLUE SEA 20th Century-Fox, 1955
MALCOLM ARNOLD

THE DEER HUNTER Universal, 1978
STANLEY MYERS†

THE DEERSLAYER 20th Century-Fox, 1957
PAUL SAWTELL†
BERT A. SHEFTER

THE DEERSLAYER (TF) Schick Sunn Classics
Productions, 1978
ANDREW BELLING
ROBERT SUMMERS

DEF-CON 4 New World, 1985
CHRISTOPHER YOUNG

THE DEFECTION OF SIMAS KUDIRKA (TF) The
Jozak Company/Paramount TV, 1978
DAVID SHIRE ☆

DEFENDING YOUR LIFE Warner Bros., 1991
MICHAEL GORE

DEFENSE DE SAVOIR 1973
BRUNO NICOLAI

DEFENSE OF THE REALM Hemdale, 1985
RICHARD HARVEY

DEFENSE PLAY Trans World Entertainment, 1988
ARTHUR B. RUBINSTEIN

DEFENSELESS New Visions, 1990
TREVOR JONES

DEFENSELESS Seven Arts, 1991
CURT SOBEL

DEFIANCE American International, 1980
JOHN BEAL
DOMINIC FRONTIERE
GERARD MCMAHON
BASIL POLEDOURIS
TOM SAVIANO

THE DEFIANT ONES United Artists, 1958
ERNEST GOLD

THE DEFIANT ONES (TF) MGM-UA TV, 1986
STEVE DORFF

DEJA VU Cannon, 1985
PINO DONAGGIO

DELANCEY STREET: THE CRISIS WITHIN (TF)
Paramount TV, 1975
LALO SCHIFRIN

THE DELIBERATE STRANGER (TF) Stuart Phoenix
Productions/Lorimar-Telepictures, 1986
GIL MELLE

DELIGHTFULLY DANGEROUS United Artists, 1945
MORTON GOULD

DELINQUENT Big Bad Prods., 1995
GANG OF FOUR

DELIRIO DEI SENSI 1967
ARMANDO TROVAJOLI

DELIRIOUS MGM, 1991
CLIFF EIDELMAN

DELIRIUM Maris Entertainment, 1980
DAVID C. WILLIAMS

DELITTO D'AMORE Documento Film, 1974
CARLO RUSTICHELLI

DELITTO QUASI PERFETTO 1966
CARLO RUSTICHELLI

DELIVER THEM FROM EVIL: THE TAKING OF
ALTA VIEW (TF) Citadel Pictures, 1992
MARK SNOW

DELIVER US FROM EVIL (TF) Playboy Productions,
1973
ANDREW BELLING

DELLAMORTE DELLAMORE 1994
MANUEL DE SICA

DELTA COUNTY U.S.A. (TF) Leonard Goldberg
Productions/Paramount Pictures TV, 1977
ALLYN FERGUSON
JACK ELLIOTT

DELTA FORCE Cannon, 1986
ALAN SILVESTRI

DELTA OF VENUS (CTF) New Line/Alliance/Evzen
Kolar Prods., 1995
GEORGE S. CLINTON

DELUSION Cineville, 1991
BARRY ADAMSON

DELUSION New Line Cinema, 1981
DON PEAKE

DEMENTIA Parker, 1953
GEORGE ANTHEIL†

DEMENTIA 13 American International, 1963
RONALD STEIN†

DEMETRIUS AND THE GLADIATORS 20th
Century-Fox, 1954
FRANZ WAXMAN†

THE DEMI-PARADISE ADVENTURE FOR TWO
General Film Distributors, 1943
NICHOLAS BRODZSKY†

DEMOLITION MAN Warner Bros., 1993
ELLIOT GOLDENTHAL

DEMON GOD TOLD ME TO New World, 1977
FRANK CORDELL†

THE DEMON MURDER CASE (TF) Dick Clark
Productions/Len Steckler Productions, 1983
GEORGE ALICESON TIPTON

THE DEMON OF THE ISLE AMLF, 1983
CHRISTIAN GAUBERT

DEMON POND Shochiku, 1980
ISAO TOMITA

DEMON SEED MGM/United Artists, 1977
JERRY FIELDING†

DEMONIAQUE 1958
JOSEPH KOSMA†

DEMONOID American Panorama, 1981
RICHARD GILLIS

DEMONS 2 1987
SIMON BOSWELL

DEMONS OF THE MIND MGM-EMI, 1972
HARRY ROBERTSON

DEMONSTONE Fries, 1990
GARY STOCKDALE

DEMONWARP Vidmark, 1988
DAN SLIDER

DEMPSEY (TF) Charles Fries Productions, 1983
BILLY GOLDENBERG

DEMPSEY AND MAKEPEACE (TF) LWT, 1986
ALAN PARKER

DEN GODA VILJEAN THE BEST INTENTIONS
1992
STEFAN NILSSON

DEN ODPLATY *THE DAY OF RECKONING* (AF)
1960
ZDENEK LISKA

DENISE CALLS UP 1996
BILL CARTER
RUTH ELLENELLSWORTH

DENISE CALLS UP Davis/Skyline/Dark Matter,
1995
LYNNE GELLER

DENNIS THE MENACE Warner Bros., 1993
JERRY GOLDSMITH

DENNIS THE MENACE (TF) DIC Enterprises
Productions, 1987
RANDY EDELMAN

DEPORTED Universal, 1950
WALTER SCHARF

DEPS 1974
ALFI KABILJO

DER AUFENTHALT DEFA, East German
GUENTHER FISCHER

DER BALL 1931
WERNER R. HEYMANN†

DER BERG RUFT 1937
GIUSEPPE BECCE†

DER EWIGE TRAUM 1935
GIUSEPPE BECCE†

DER FEUERTEUFEL 1940
GIUSEPPE BECCE†

DER GUNSTLING VON SCHONBRUNN 1929
GIUSEPPE BECCE†

DER HIMMEL UBER BERLIN Orion Classics, 1987
JURGEN KNIEPER

DER JAGER VON FALL 1957
GIUSEPPE BECCE†

DER KAISER VON KALIFORNIEN 1936
GIUSEPPE BECCE†

DER KINOERZAEHLER *THE MOVIE TELLER*
1993
GUENTHER FISCHER

DER KLEINE BRUDER *THE LITTLE BROTHER*
1983
JURGEN KNIEPER

DER KONGRESS TANZT 1955
WERNER R. HEYMANN†

DER LAUFER VON MARATHON 1935
GIUSEPPE BECCE†

DER MUDE TOD *DESTINY* 1921
GIUSEPPE BECCE†

DER OLYMPISCHE SOMMER *THE OLYMPIC
SUMMER* (FD) 1993
HEIDI AYDT
FRANK WILL

DER REBELL 1932
GIUSEPPE BECCE†

DER RICHTER UND SEIN HENKER 20th
Century-Fox, 1975
ENNIO MORRICONE

DER SCHAFER VON TRUTKBERG 1958
GIUSEPPE BECCE†

DER SEXBOMBER 1979
STELVIO CIPRIANI

DER SIEGER 1931
WERNER R. HEYMANN†

DER SOHN DER WEISSEN BERGE 1930
GIUSEPPE BECCE†

DER STEINERNE FLUSS *THE STONE RIVER*
1983
GUENTHER FISCHER

DER TIGER VON ESCHNAPUR *JOURNEY TO THE
LOST CITY* American International, 1959
MICHEL MICHELET†

DER VERLORENE SOHN 1934
GIUSEPPE BECCE†

DERANGED American International, 1974
CARL ZITTRER

DERBY (TF) Atlantis/All American TV, 1995
PAUL J. ZAZA

DERBY FIEBER USA West German
JURGEN KNIEPER

DEREK AND CLIVE GET THE HORN Peter Cook
Productions, 1981
DUDLEY MOORE

DERRIERE LA FACADE 1939
JEAN WIENER†

DERRIERE LA FENETRE 1966
GEORGES DELERUE†

DES ENFANTS GATES *SPOILED CHILDREN*
Gaumont, 1977
PHILIPPE SARDE

DES FEUX MAL ETEINTS 1994
GABRIEL YARED

DES GENS SANS IMPORTANCE 1955
JOSEPH KOSMA†

DES HOMMES...UNE DOCTRINE 1959
GEORGES DELERUE†

DES PISSENLITS PAR LA RACINE 1963
GEORGES DELERUE†

DES TEUFELS PARADIES West German
JURGEN KNIEPER

DESERT ATTACK *ICE COLD IN ALEX* 20th
Century-Fox, 1958
LEIGHTON LUCAS†

DESERT BLOOM Columbia, 1986
BRAD FIEDEL

THE DESERT FOX 20th Century-Fox, 1951
DANIELE AMFITHEATROF†

DESERT FURY Paramount, 1947
MIKLOS ROZSA†

THE DESERT HAWK Universal, 1950
FRANK SKINNER†

DESERT LEGION Universal, 1953
FRANK SKINNER†

THE DESERT OF THE TARTARS *IL DESIERTO DEI
TARTARI* Gaumont, 1977
ENNIO MORRICONE

DESERT RAIDERS *IL DOMINATORE DEL
DESERTO* 1964
CARLO RUSTICHELLI

THE DESERT RATS 20th Century-Fox, 1953
LEIGH HARLINE†

DESERT RATS (TF) Universal TV, 1988
J. PETER ROBINSON

DESERT SANDS United Artists, 1955
PAUL DUNLAP

THE DESERT SONG Warner Bros., 1944
HEINZ ROEMHELD†

THE DESERT SONG Warner Bros., 1953
MAX STEINER†

DESERT VICTORY 1943
WILLIAM ALWYN†

DESERT WARRIOR Concorde/New Horizons, 1984
CHRISTOPHER YOUNG

DESERT WINDS Desert Wind Prods., 1995
THE BO DEANS
THE COWBOY JUNKIES

DESERTERS Exile Productions, 1983
MICHAEL CONWAY BAKER

DESIGN FOR SCANDAL MGM, 1941
FRANZ WAXMAN†

DESIGNING WOMAN MGM, 1957
ANDRE PREVIN

DESIRE Paramount, 1936
FREDERICK HOLLANDER†

DESIRE & HELL AT SUNSET MOTEL Two Moon
Releasing, 1992
CASTLE & DOUG WALTER

DESIRE IN MOTION Alliance-Vivafilm, 1994
ZBIGNIEW PREISNER

DESIRE ME MGM, 1947
HERBERT STOTHART†

DESIRE UNDER THE ELMS Paramount, 1958
ELMER BERNSTEIN

DESIREE 20th Century Fox, 1954
ALEX NORTH†

DESK SET 20th Century-Fox, 1957
CYRIL J. MOCKRIDGE†

DESORDRE Forum Distribution, 1986
GABRIEL YARED

DESORDRES 1950
JOSEPH KOSMA†

DESPAIR New Line Cinema, 1978
PEER RABEN

DESPERADO Columbia, 1995
LOS LOBOS

DESPERADO (TF) Walter Mirisch Productions/
Universal TV, 1987
MICHEL COLOMBIER

DESPERADO: AVALANCHE AT DEVIL'S RIDGE
(TF) Walter Mirisch Productions/Universal TV,
1988
MICHEL COLOMBIER

THE DESPERADOES Columbia, 1943
JOHN LEIPOLD†

THE DESPERADOES ARE IN TOWN 20th
Century-Fox, 1956
BERT A. SHEFTER

THE DESPERATE HOURS Paramount, 1955
GAIL KUBIK†

THE DESPERATE MAN 1959
GERARD SCHURMANN

THE DESPERATE TRAIL Turner, 1994
STEPHEN ENDELMAN

THE DESPERATE TRAIL (CTF) Motion Picture Corp.
of America/Turner Network Television, 1995
STEPHEN ENDELMAN

DESPERATE (TF) Toots Productions/Warner Bros. TV,
1987
LEE HOLDRIDGE

DESPERATE CHOICES: TO SAVE MY CHILD (TF)
Andrew Adelson/ABC Prods., 1992
JOHN E. KEANE

DESPERATE FOR LOVE (TF) Vishudda Productions/
Lorimar TV, 1989
CHARLES BERNSTEIN

DESPERATE HOURS MGM/UA, 1990
DAVID MANSFIELD

DESPERATE JOURNEY Warner Bros., 1942
MAX STEINER†

DESERT ATTACK column...

DESPERATE JOURNEY: THE ALLISON WILCOX
STORY (TF) D'Antoni Prods./Viacom, 1993
DAVID MCHUGH

DESPERATE LIVES (TF) Fellows-Keegan Company/
Lorimar Pictures, 1982
BRUCE BROUGHTON

DESPERATE MEASURES TriStar, 1997
TREVOR JONES

DESPERATE MISSION (TF) 20 Century-Fox TV,
1971
ROBERT DRASNIN

DESPERATE RESCUE: THE CATHY MAHONE
STORY (TF) Gimbel-Adelson/Multimedia/World
Intl. Network, 1993
FRED KARLIN

DESPERATE VOYAGE (TF) Barry Weitz Films/Jack
Wizan TV Productions, 1980
BRUCE BROUGHTON

DESPERATE WOMEN (TF) Lorimar Productions,
1978
DICK DEBENEDICTIS

DESPERATELY SEEKING SUSAN Orion, 1985
THOMAS NEWMAN

DESTINATION 60,000 Allied Artists, 1957
ALBERT GLASSER

DESTINATION INNER SPACE Magna, 1966
PAUL DUNLAP

DESTINATION MOON Eagle Lion, 1950
LEITH STEVENS†

DESTINATION MURDER RKO Radio, 1950
IRVING GERTZ

DESTINATION TOKYO Warner Bros., 1943
FRANZ WAXMAN†

DESTINATION UNKNOWN Universal, 1933
W. FRANKE HARLING†

DESTINATION UNKNOWN Universal, 1942
HANS J. SALTER†

DESTINATION: AMERICA (TF) Stephen J. Cannell
Productions, 1987
MIKE POST

DESTINY 1921
GIUSEPPE BECCE†

DESTINY Universal, 1944
FRANK SKINNER†
ALEXANDRE TANSMAN†

DESTINY OF A SPY (TF) Universal TV, 1969
RON GRAINER†

DESTINY TURNS ON THE RADIO Savoy, 1995
STEVE SOLES

DESTROY ALL MONSTERS American International,
1969
AKIRA IFUKUBE

THE DESTROYER Columbia, 1943
ANTHONY COLLINS†

THE DESTROYERS Concorde, 1986
MARK GOVERNOR

THE DESTRUCTORS United Pictures, 1968
PAUL DUNLAP

THE DESTRUCTORS *THE MARSEILLES
CONTRACT* American International, 1974
ROY BUDD†

DESTRY Universal, 1954
HERMAN STEIN

DESTRY RIDES AGAIN Universal, 1939
FRANK SKINNER†

DET FORSOMTE FORAR *THE STOLEN SPRING*
1993
JAN GLAESEL

THE DETECTIVE 20th Century-Fox, 1968
JERRY GOLDSMITH

THE DETECTIVE Columbia, 1954
GEORGES AURIC†

DETENUTO IN ATTESA DI GIUDIZIO 1971
CARLO RUSTICHELLI

DETOUR Producers Releasing Corp., 1945
LEO ERDODY†

DETOUR TO TERROR (TF) Orenthal Productions/
Playboy Productions/Columbia TV, 1980
MORTON STEVENS†

DEUTSCHLAND, BLEICHE West German
JURGEN KNIEPER

DEUX 1989
JEAN-CLAUDE PETIT

DEUX ACTRICES *TWO CAN PLAY* Max Films,
1993
ANNE MCGARRIGLE
KATE MCGARRIGLE

DEUX GRANDES FILLES DANS UN PYJAMA
1974
CLAUDE BOLLING

DEUX HOMMES DANS LA VILLE 1974
PHILIPPE SARDE

DEUX SOUS DE VIOLETTES 1951
GEORGES VAN PARYS†

THE DEVIL AND DANIEL WEBSTER RKO Radio,
1941
BERNARD HERRMANN† ★★

THE DEVIL AND LEROY BASSETT 1972
LES BAXTER†

THE DEVIL AND MAX DEVLIN Buena Vista, 1981
BUDDY BAKER
MARVIN HAMLISCH

THE DEVIL AND MISS JONES RKO Radio, 1941
ROY WEBB†

THE DEVIL AND MISS SARAH (TF) Universal TV,
1971
DAVID ROSE†

THE DEVIL AT 4 O'CLOCK Columbia, 1961
GEORGE DUNING

THE DEVIL BY THE TAIL Lopert, 1969
GEORGES DELERUE†

DEVIL DOG: THE HOUND OF HELL (TF)
Zeitman-Landers-Roberts Productions, 1978
ARTIE KANE

DEVIL GODDESS Columbia, 1955
MISCHA BAKALEINIKOFF†

DEVIL IN A BLUE DRESS TriStar, 1995
ELMER BERNSTEIN

THE DEVIL IN LOVE *L'ARCODIAVOLO* 1966
ARMANDO TROVAJOLI

DEVIL IN THE FLESH Istituto Luce/Italnoleggio,
1986
CARLO CRIVELLI
NICOLA PIOVANI

DEVIL IN THE FLESH World Film Alliance, 1986
PHILIPPE SARDE

THE DEVIL IS A SISSY MGM, 1936
HERBERT STOTHART†

THE DEVIL IS A WOMAN *IL SORRISO DEL
GRANDE TENTATORE* 1975
ENNIO MORRICONE

DEVIL MAY CARE MGM, 1930
HERBERT STOTHART†
DIMITRI TIOMKIN†

DEVIL ON HORSEBACK British Lion, 1953
MALCOLM ARNOLD

THE DEVIL RIDES OUT 20th Century-Fox, 1968
JAMES BERNARD

DEVIL TIMES FIVE *PEOPLE TOYS/THE
HORRIBLE HOUSE ON THE HILL* 1974
WILLIAM LOOSE†

THE DEVIL TO PAY United Artists, 1931
ALFRED NEWMAN†

THE DEVIL WITH HITLER United Artists, 1942
EDWARD WARD†

THE DEVIL WITHIN HER *I DON'T WANT TO BE
BORN* American International, 1976
RON GRAINER†

DEVIL'S ANGELS American International, 1967
MIKE CURB

THE DEVIL'S BRIGADE United Artists, 1968
ALEX NORTH†

THE DEVIL'S BREATH 1993
ANGEL ILLARRAMENDI

THE DEVIL'S BRIDE *THE DEVIL RIDES OUT*
20th Century-Fox, 1968
JAMES BERNARD

DEVIL'S CANYON RKO Radio, 1953
DANIELE AMFITHEATROF†

THE DEVIL'S DAUGHTER (TF) Paramount Pictures
Television, 1973
LAURENCE ROSENTHAL

THE DEVIL'S DISCIPLE United Artists, 1959
RICHARD RODNEY BENNETT

DEVIL'S DOORWAY MGM, 1950
DANIELE AMFITHEATROF†

THE DEVIL'S ENVOYS *LES VISITEURS DU
SOIR* 1942
JOSEPH KOSMA†

THE DEVIL'S GIFT Zenith International, 1984
TODD HAYEN

THE DEVIL'S HAIRPIN Paramount, 1957
NATHAN VAN CLEAVE†

THE DEVIL'S MASK Columbia, 1946
GEORGE DUNING
IRVING GERTZ

THE DEVIL'S MEN 1976
BRIAN ENO

DEVIL'S ODDS Trans World Entertainment, 1987
JOHN DEBNEY

THE DEVIL'S OWN *THE WITCHES* 1966
RICHARD RODNEY BENNETT

THE DEVIL'S PARTNER Filmgroup, 1959
RONALD STEIN†

THE DEVIL'S PIPELINE Universal, 1940
HANS J. SALTER†

THE DEVIL'S PLAYGROUND Entertainment
Marketing, 1976
BRUCE SMEATON

THE DEVIL'S RAIN Bryanston, 1975
AL DELORY

THE DEVIL-DOLL MGM, 1936
FRANZ WAXMAN†

THE DEVILS Warner Bros., 1971
PETER MAXWELL DAVIES
DAVID MUNROW†

DEVLIN (CTF) Viacom, 1992
JOHN ALTMAN

THE DEVONSHIRE TERROR MPM, 1983
RAY COLCORD

DEVOTION Northern Arts, 1995
ARLENE BATTISHIL

DO YOU TAKE THIS STRANGER? (TF)   Universal TV/Public Arts Productions, 1971
PETE RUGOLO ☆

D.O.A.   Buena Vista, 1988
CHAZ JANKEL

D.O.A.   United Artists, 1949
DIMITRI TIOMKIN†

DOC HOLLYWOOD   Warner Bros., 1991
CARTER BURWELL

DOC SAVAGE, THE MAN OF BRONZE   Warner Bros., 1975
FRANK DEVOL

DOC'S FULL SERVICE   Brazos Films, 1994
CHUCK PINNELL
JOHN SARGENT

DOCTEUR POPAUL   Les Films La Boetie, 1972
PIERRE JANSEN

THE DOCTOR   Buena Vista, 1991
MICHAEL CONVERTINO

THE DOCTOR AND THE DEVILS   20th Century Fox, 1985
JOHN MORRIS

DOCTOR DEATH, SEEKER OF SOULS   20th Century-Fox, 1973
RICHARD LASALLE

DOCTOR DETROIT   Universal, 1983
LALO SCHIFRIN

DOCTOR FINLAY (TF)   Scottish TV, 1994
RICHARD HARVEY

DOCTOR FISCHER OF GENEVA (TF)   Consolidated Productions/BBC, 1985
TREVOR JONES

DOCTOR IN TROUBLE   Rank, 1970
ERIC ROGERS†

DOCTOR JUDYM   1976
ANDRZEJ KORZYNSKI

THE DOCTOR TAKES A WIFE   Columbia, 1940
FREDERICK HOLLANDER†

DOCTOR ZHIVAGO   MGM, 1965
MAURICE JARRE ★★

THE DOCTOR'S DILEMMA   1958
JOSEPH KOSMA†

A DOCTOR'S STORY (TF)   Embassy TV, 1984
RANDY EDELMAN

DOCTOR, YOU'VE GOT TO BE KIDDING   MGM, 1967
KENYON HOPKINS

DOCTORS WILDE (TF)   Columbia TV, 1987
DANA KAPROFF

DOCTORS' PRIVATE LIVES (TF)   David Gerber Company/Columbia TV, 1978
RICHARD MARKOWITZ†

DOCTORS' WIVES   Columbia, 1971
ELMER BERNSTEIN

DOCUMENTEUR: AN EMOTION PICTURE (FD)   Cine-Tamaris, 1981
GEORGES DELERUE†

DODES'KA'DEN   Janus, 1970
TORU TAKEMITSU†

DODGE CITY   Warner Bros., 1939
MAX STEINER†

DODSWORTH   United Artists, 1936
ALFRED NEWMAN†

DOG AND CAT (TF)   Largo Productions, 1977
BARRY DEVORZON

DOG DAY   UGC, 1984
FRANCIS LAI

THE DOG IT WAS THAT DIED (TF)   Granada TV, 1988
NIGEL HESS

A DOG OF FLANDERS   20th Century-Fox, 1959
PAUL SAWTELL†
BERT A. SHEFTER

DOG TAGS   Cinevest Entertainment Group, 1990
JOHN SCOTT

A DOG'S BEST FRIEND   United Artists, 1960
BERT A. SHEFTER

A DOG'S LIFE   VITA DA CANI   ATA, 1950
NINO ROTA†

A DOG, A MOUSE AND A SPUTNIK   1958
PAUL MISRAKI

DOGFIGHT   Warner Bros., 1991
MASON DARING

THE DOGS OF WAR   United Artists, 1980
GEOFFREY BURGON

DOIN' TIME   The Ladd Company/Warner Bros., 1984
CHARLES FOX

DOIN' TIME ON PLANET EARTH   Cannon, 1988
DANA KAPROFF

DOING LIFE (TF)   Castillian Productions/Phoenix Entertainment Group, 1986
ARTHUR B. RUBINSTEIN

DOING TIME ON MAPLE DRIVE (TF)   FNM Films, 1992
LAURA KARPMAN

THE DOLL SQUAD   SEDUCE AND DESTROY   1973
NICHOLAS CARRAS

A DOLL'S HOUSE   Tomorrow Entertainment, 1973
JOHN BARRY

A DOLL'S HOUSE (TF)   BBC-TV, 1993
GUY WOOLFENDEN

THE DOLLMAKER (TF)   Finnegan Associates/IPC Films/Dollmaker Productions, 1984
JOHN RUBINSTEIN

DOLLMAN   Full Moon, 1992
TONY RIPPARETTI

DOLLMAN VS. DEMONIC TOYS   Full Moon, 1993
TONY RIPPARETTI

DOLLS   Empire Pictures, 1987
RICHARD H. BAND
JONATHAN MORSE

THE DOLLS   LE BAMBOLE   1964
ARMANDO TROVAJOLI

DOLLY AND HER LOVER   1992
HENRIK OTTO DONNER

DOLLY DEAREST   Trimark, 1992
MARK SNOW

DOLORES CLAIBORNE   Columbia, 1995
DANNY ELFMAN

DOLPHIN (FD)   Michael Wiese Film Productions, 1979
BASIL POLEDOURIS

DOMANI E TROPPO TARDI   1950
ALESSANDRO CICOGNINI†

DOMANI E UN ALTRO GIORNO   1951
FRANCO MANNINO
CARLO RUSTICHELLI

DOMANI PASSERO A SALUTARE LA TUA VEDOVA...PAROLIA DI EPIDEMIA!   1972
BRUNO NICOLAI

DOMICILE CONJUGAL   Columbia, 1971
ANTOINE DUHAMEL

DOMINICK AND EUGENE   Orion, 1988
TREVOR JONES

DOMINIQUE   Sword and Sworcery Productions, 1979
DAVID WHITAKER

THE DOMINO PRINCIPLE   Avco Embassy, 1977
BILLY GOLDENBERG

DON CAMILLO   1983
PINO DONAGGIO

DON CAMILLO E I GIOVANI D'OGGI   1972
CARLO RUSTICHELLI

DON CAMILLO MONSIGNORE MA NON TROPPO   1961
ALESSANDRO CICOGNINI†

DON GIOVANNI IN SICILIA   1967
ARMANDO TROVAJOLI

DON GIOVANNI IN SICILIA   1974
BRUNO NICOLAI

THE DON IS DEAD   Universal, 1973
JERRY GOLDSMITH

DON JUAN   MGM, 1926
WILLIAM AXT†

DON JUAN DE MARCO   New Line, 1995
MICHAEL KAMEN

DON JUAN ETAIT UNE FEMME   Scotia American, 1973
MICHEL MAGNE†

DON JUAN QUILLIGAN   20th Century-Fox, 1945
DAVID RAKSIN

DON KIRSCHNER'S ROCK CONCERT   1978
BOB MITHOFF

DON QUIJOTE DE ORSON WELLES   DON QUIXOTE OF ORSON WELLES   1992
DANIEL J. WHITE

DON QUIXOTE   1933
JACQUES IBERT†

DON QUIXOTE OF ORSON WELLES   1992
DANIEL J. WHITE

DON RAMIRO   1973
LUIS DE PABLO

DON'T ANSWER THE PHONE!   Crown International, 1980
BYRON ALLRED

DON'T BE A MENACE TO SOUTH CENTRAL WHILE DRINKING YOUR JUICE IN THE HOOD   Mriamax, 1996
JOHN BARNES

DON'T BOTHER TO KNOCK   20th Century-Fox, 1952
LIONEL NEWMAN†

DON'T CRY WITH YOUR MOUTH FULL   1973
VLADIMIR COSMA

DON'T CRY, IT'S ONLY THUNDER   Sanrio, 1981
MAURICE JARRE

DON'T DO IT   Trans Atlantic, 1995
HAL LINDES

DON'T DRINK THE WATER   Avco Embassy, 1969
PATRICK WILLIAMS

DON'T GET PERSONAL   Universal, 1936
FRANZ WAXMAN†

DON'T GIVE UP THE SHIP   Paramount, 1959
WALTER SCHARF

DON'T GO IN THE HOUSE   Film Ventures International, 1980
RICHARD EINHORN

DON'T GO NEAR THE WATER   MGM, 1957
BRONISLAU KAPER†

DON'T GO TO SLEEP (TF)   Aaron Spelling Productions/Warner Bros. TV, 1982
DOMINIC FRONTIERE

DON'T LOOK BACK (TF)   TBA Productions/Satie Productions/TRISEME, 1981
JACK ELLIOTT

DON'T LOOK IN THE BASEMENT   Hallmark, 1973
ROBERT FARRAR

DON'T LOOK NOW   Paramount, 1974
PINO DONAGGIO

DON'T LOOK NOW...WE'RE BEING SHOT AT   LA GRANDE VADROIULLE   Cinepix, 1966
GEORGES AURIC†

DON'T LOSE YOUR HEAD   1967
ERIC ROGERS†

DON'T MAKE WAVES   MGM, 1967
VIC MIZZY

DON'T PAVE MAIN STREET: CARMEL'S HERITAGE (FD)   Julian Ludwig Prods., 1994
DAVID BENOIT

DON'T PULL YOUR PUNCHES   1937
DAVID RAKSIN

DON'T PUSH, I'LL CHARGE WHEN I'M READY (TF)   Universal TV, 1977
LYN MURRAY†

DON'T RAISE THE BRIDGE - LOWER THE RIVER   Columbia, 1968
DAVID WHITAKER

DON'T TALK TO STRANGERS (CTF)   Pacific Motion Pictures/Barry Weitz Films/MTE, 1994
JOSEPH CONLAN

DON'T TELL MOM THE BABYSITTER'S DEAD   Warner Bros., 1991
BRUCE NAZARIAN
DAVID NEWMAN

DON'T TRUST YOUR HUSBAND   Universal, 1948
HANS J. SALTER†

DONA FLOR AND HER TWO HUSBANDS   New Yorker, 1977
CHICO BUARQUE
FRANCES HIME

DONATO AND DAUGHTER (TF)   Multimedia Motion Pictures, 1993
SYLVESTER LEVAY

DONDE TU ESTES   1964
LUIS BACALOV

DONERSEN ISLIK CAL   WHISTLE IF YOU COME BACK   1993
OHNAY OGUZ

DONKY SKIN   PEAU D'ANE   Janus, 1971
MICHEL LEGRAND

DONNE E BRIGANTI   1951
NINO ROTA†

DONNE E SOLDATI   1952
TEO USUELLI

DONNE IN UN GIORNO DI FESTA   WOMEN ON A HOLIDAY   1993
ALFREDO MUSCHIETTO

DONNE MOI LA MAIN   1958
MAURICE JARRE

THE DONNER PARTY (FD)   Steeplechase Films/WGBH & WNET/13, 1992
BRIAN KEANE

DONNER PASS: THE ROAD TO SURVIVAL (TF)   Schick Sunn Classics Productions, 1978
ROBERT SUMMERS

DONOR UNKNOWN (TF)   Universal TV, 1995
DAVID BERGEAUD

DONOVAN'S REEF   Paramount, 1963
CYRIL J. MOCKRIDGE†

THE DOOLINS OF OKLAHOMA   Columbia, 1949
GEORGE DUNING
PAUL SAWTELL†

DOOMSDAY 2000   Savadove Productions, 1977
WILLIAM GOLDSTEIN

THE DOOMSDAY FLIGHT (TF)   Universal TV, 1966
LALO SCHIFRIN

DOOMSDAY GUN (CTF)   Griffin Prods./HBO Showcase, 1994
RICHARD HARVEY

DOOMWATCH   Avco Embassy, 1972
JOHN SCOTT

THE DOOR IN THE WALL   1957
JAMES BERNARD

A DOPPIA FACCIA   1969
CARLO RUSTICHELLI

DOPPLEGANGER   Universal, 1969
BARRY GRAY†

THE DORM THAT DRIPPED BLOOD   DEATH DORM/PRANKS   New Image, 1982
CHRISTOPHER YOUNG

DOROTHEA   1974
PHILIPPE SARDE

DORTOIR DES GRANDES   1952
GEORGES VAN PARYS†

DOTTIE (TF)   Dottie Films Inc., 1987
PAUL CHIHARA

DOTTORE JEKYLL E GENTILE SIGNORA   1978
ARMANDO TROVAJOLI

DOUBLE AGENT (TF)   Walt Disney TV, 1987
ALF CLAUSEN

DOUBLE CROSSBONES   Universal, 1951
FRANK SKINNER†

DOUBLE CROSSED (CTF)   Green/Epstein, 1991
RICHARD BELLIS ☆

DOUBLE DATE   Universal, 1941
HANS J. SALTER†

DOUBLE DEAL   RKO Radio, 1950
MICHEL MICHELET†

DOUBLE DEAL   Samuel Goldwyn Company, 1981
BRUCE SMEATON

DOUBLE DRAGON   Gramercy, 1994
JAY FERGUSON

DOUBLE DYNAMITE   RKO Radio, 1951
LEIGH HARLINE†

DOUBLE EDGE (TF)   Konigsberg-Sanitsky Co., 1992
GERALD GOURIET

DOUBLE EXPOSURE   United Film Distribution Co., 1987
STANLEY MYERS†
HANS ZIMMER

DOUBLE HAPPINESS   First Generation/New Views, 1994
SHADOWY MEN ON A SHADOWY PLANET

DOUBLE HARNESS   RKO Radio, 1933
MAX STEINER†

DOUBLE IMPACT   Columbia, 1991
ARTHUR KEMPEL

DOUBLE INDEMNITY   Paramount, 1944
MIKLOS ROZSA† ★

DOUBLE JEOPARDY (CTF)   Boxleitner-Bernstein/CBS Entertainment, 1992
EDUARD ARTEMYEV

DOUBLE JEOPARDY: THE KILLING OF GINA MARIE (TF)   Wilshire Court, 1996
ARTHUR B. RUBINSTEIN

A DOUBLE LIFE   Universal, 1947
MIKLOS ROZSA† ★★

THE DOUBLE LIFE OF VERONIKA   Miramax, 1991
ZBIGNIEW PREISNER

THE DOUBLE McGUFFIN   Mulberry Square, 1979
EUEL BOX

DOUBLE MURDER   1978
RIZ ORTOLANI

DOUBLE NEGATIVE   Quadrant Films, 1980
PAUL HOFFERT

DOUBLE REVENGE   Smart Egg Releasing, 1988
HARRY MANFREDINI

DOUBLE STANDARD (TF)   Louis Randolph Productions/Fenton Entertainment Group/Fries Entertainment, 1988
PATRICK WILLIAMS

DOUBLE SUICIDE   Toho, 1969
TORU TAKEMITSU†

DOUBLE SUICIDE OF SONEZAKI   1978
RYUDO UZAKI

DOUBLE SWITCH (TF)   Walt Disney TV, 1987
MICHEL COLOMBIER

DOUBLE THREAT   Pyramid, 1992
CHRISTOPHER FARRELL

DOUBLE TROUBLE   1915
JOSEPH CARL BREIL†

DOUBLE TROUBLE   MGM, 1967
JEFF ALEXANDER†

DOUBLE WEDDING   MGM, 1937
EDWARD WARD†

DOUBLE X: THE NAME OF THE GAME   1992
RAF RAVENSCROFT

DOUBLE ZONE   1997
JAMES HORNER

DOUBLE, DOUBLE, TOIL AND TROUBLE (TF)   Green-Epstein/Warner Bros. TV, 1993
RICHARD BELLIS ☆

DOUBLETAKE (TF)   Titus Productions, 1985
ARTHUR B. RUBINSTEIN

DOUCEMENT LES BASSES!   CIC, 1971
CLAUDE BOLLING

THE DOUGHGIRLS   Warner Bros., 1944
ADOLPH DEUTSCH†

THE DOVE   Paramount, 1974
JOHN BARRY

DOVE SIETE? IO SONO QUI   WHERE ARE YOU? I AM HERE   1993
PINO DONAGGIO

DOVE VAI IN VACANZA?   Rizzoli, 1978
PIERO PICCIONI

DOVER (FD)   O.W.I., 1942
GAIL KUBIK†

DOWN AND OUT IN BEVERLY HILLS   Buena Vista, 1986
ANDY SUMMERS

DOWN BY LAW   Island Pictures, 1986
JOHN LURIE

DOWN CAME A BLACKBIRD (CTF)   Viacom/Chanticleer, 1995
GRAEME REVELL

DOWN MEMORY LANE   Eagle Lion, 1949
SOL KAPLAN

DOWN MISSOURI WAY   Producers Releasing Corp., 1946
KARL HAJOS†

DOWN PERISCOPE 20th Century Fox, 1996
RANDY EDELMAN

DOWN THE ANCIENT STAIRS *PER LE ANTICHE SCALE* 1975
ENNIO MORRICONE

DOWN THE LONG HILLS (TF) The Finnegan Company/Walt Disney TV, 1986
MARK SNOW

DOWN TO EARTH Columbia, 1947
GEORGE DUNING
HEINZ ROEMHELD†

DOWN TO THE SEA IN SHIPS 20th Century-Fox, 1949
ALFRED NEWMAN†

DOWN TO THEIR LAST YACHT RKO Radio, 1934
MAX STEINER†

DOWN TWISTED Cannon, 1987
ERIC ALLAMAN
BERLIN GAME

DOWNHILL RACER Paramount, 1969
KENYON HOPKINS

DOWNPAYMENT ON MURDER (TF) Adam Productions/20th Century Fox TV, 1987
LAURENCE ROSENTHAL

DOWNTOWN 1955
AKIRA IFUKUBE

DOWNTOWN 20th Century-Fox, 1990
ALAN SILVESTRI

DR. BLACK, MR. HYDE Dimension, 1976
JOHNNY PATE

DR. BUTCHER, M.D. Aquarius, 1982
WALTER SEAR

DR. COOK'S GARDEN (TF) Paramount TV, 1970
ROBERT DRASNIN

DR. CRIPPEN Warner Bros., 1964
KENNETH V. JONES

DR. CYCLOPS Paramount, 1940
ERNST TOCH†

DR. DOOLITTLE 20th Century Fox, 1967
LESLIE BRICCUSE ★

DR. ERLICH'S MAGIC BULLET Warner Bros., 1940
MAX STEINER†

DR. FRANKENSTEIN ON CAMPUS 1970
PAUL HOFFERT

DR. GIGGLES Universal, 1992
BRIAN MAY†

DR. GILLESPIE'S CRIMINAL CASE MGM, 1943
DANIELE AMFITHEATROF†

DR. GILLESPIE'S NEW ASSISTANT MGM, 1942
DANIELE AMFITHEATROF†

DR. GOLDFOOT AND THE BIKINI MACHINE American International, 1965
LES BAXTER†

DR. GOLDFOOT AND THE GIRL BOMBS *LE SPIE VENGONO DAL SEMIFREDDO* American International, 1966
LES BAXTER†

DR. HACKENSTEIN Vista Street Productions, 1988
RANDY MILLER

DR. HECKLE AND MR. HYPE Cannon, 1980
RICHARD H. BAND

DR. JEKYLL AND MR. HYDE MGM, 1941
FRANZ WAXMAN† ★

DR. JEKYLL AND MS. HYDE Savoy, 1995
MARK MCKENZIE

DR. JEKYLL AND SISTER HYDE American International, 1972
DAVID WHITAKER

DR. KILDARE'S WEDDING DAY MGM, 1941
BRONISLAU KAPER†

DR. NO United Artists, 1962
JOHN BARRY
MONTY NORMAN

DR. PHIBES RISES AGAIN American International, 1972
JOHN GALE

DR. QUINN MEDICINE WOMAN-'94 PILOT (TF) Sullivan Co./CBC Ent., 1994
WILLIAM OLVIS

DR. QUINN MEDICINE WOMAN: LADIES NIGHT (TF) Sullivan Co./CBS Entertainment, 1994
WILLIAM OLVIS

DR. RENAULT'S SECRET 20th Century-Fox, 1942
DAVID RAKSIN

DR. SCORPION (TF) Stephen J. Cannell Productions/Universal TV, 1978
PETE CARPENTER†
MIKE POST

DR. STRANGE (TF) Universal TV, 1978
PAUL CHIHARA

DR. STRANGELOVE OR: HOW I LEARNED TO STOP WORRYING AND LOVE THE BOMB Columbia, 1964
LAURIE JOHNSON

DR. SYN, ALIAS THE SCARECROW Buena Vista, 1962
GERARD SCHURMANN

DR. TERROR'S HOUSE OF HORRORS Paramount, 1965
ELISABETH LUYTENS†

DR. X Warner Bros., 1932
BERNHARD KAUN†

DRACULA Universal, 1958
JAMES BERNARD

DRACULA Universal, 1979
JOHN WILLIAMS

DRACULA - PRINCE OF DARKNESS 20th Century-Fox, 1967
JAMES BERNARD

DRACULA (TF) Universal TV/Dan Curtis Productions, 1974
BOB COBERT

DRACULA A.D. 1972 Warner Bros., 1972
MICHAEL VICKERS

DRACULA AND SON 1976
VLADIMIR COSMA

DRACULA CONTRA EL DR. FRANKENSTEIN 1971
BRUNO NICOLAI

DRACULA HAS RISEN FROM THE GRAVE Warner Bros., 1969
JAMES BERNARD

DRACULA IN THE PROVINCES 1975
FABIO FRIZZI

DRACULA TODAY *DRACULA A.D. 1972* Warner Bros., 1972
MICHAEL VICKERS

DRACULA VS. FRANKENSTEIN *BLOOD OF FRANKENSTEIN* Independent-International, 1971
WILLIAM LAVA†

DRACULA'S DAUGHTER Universal, 1936
HEINZ ROEMHELD†

DRACULA'S DOG *ZOLTAN, HOUND OF DRACULA* Crown International, 1978
ANDREW BELLING

DRACULA'S LAST RITES Cannon, 1980
PAUL JOST
GEORGE SMALL

DRACULA'S WIDOW DEG, 1988
JAMES CAMPBELL

DRACULA: DEAD AND LOVING IT Columbia, 1995
HUMMIE MANN

DRAGNET Screen Guild, 1947
IRVING GERTZ

DRAGNET Universal, 1987
ALF CLAUSEN
IRA NEWBORN

DRAGNET (TF) Mark VII Ltd./Universal TV, 1969
LYN MURRAY†

DRAGONFIGHT Warner/HBO, 1991
BOB MITHOFF

DRAGON LORD Golden Harvest, 1982
SULKHAN TSINTSADZE

DRAGON SEED MGM, 1944
HERBERT STOTHART†

DRAGON WELLS MASSACRE Allied Artists, 1957
PAUL DUNLAP

DRAGON'S GOLD United Artists, 1954
ALBERT GLASSER

DRAGON: THE BRUCE LEE STORY Universal, 1993
RANDY EDELMAN

DRAGONFLY American International, 1976
STEPHEN LAWRENCE

DRAGONFLY SQUADRON Allied Artists, 1954
PAUL DUNLAP

DRAGONHEART Universal, 1996
RANDY EDELMAN

DRAGONSLAYER Paramount, 1981
ALEX NORTH† ★

DRAGONWYCK 20th Century-Fox, 1946
ALFRED NEWMAN†

DRAGSTRIP GIRL American International, 1957
RONALD STEIN†

DRAMA OF THE RICH *FATTI DI GENTE PERBENE* PAC, 1975
ENNIO MORRICONE

THE DRAMATIC LIFE OF ABRAHAM LINCOLN 1923
JOSEPH CARL BREIL†

DRAMATIC SCHOOL MGM, 1938
FRANZ WAXMAN†

DRANGO United Artists, 1957
ELMER BERNSTEIN

THE DRAUGHTSMAN'S CONTRACT United Artists Classics, 1982
MICHAEL NYMAN

DRAW! (CTF) HBO Premiere Films/Astral Film Productions/Bryna Company, 1984
KEN WANNBERG

THE DRAWINGS OF LEONARDO DA VINCI 1954
ALAN RAWSTHORNE†

DREAM A LITTLE DREAM Vestron, 1989
JOHN WILLIAM DEXTER

THE DREAM BOAT 1964
DOV SELTZER

DREAM BREAKERS (TF) CBS Entertainment, 1989
GLENN PAXTON

DREAM DATE (TF) Robert Kosberg Productions/Saban International, 1989
PETER BERNSTEIN

DREAM DEMON Spectrafilm, 1988
BILL NELSON

A DREAM FOR CHRISTMAS (TF) Lorimar Productions, 1973
DAVID ROSE†

DREAM GIRL Paramount, 1948
VICTOR YOUNG†

DREAM HOUSE (TF) Hill-Mandelker Productions/Time-Life Productions, 1981
BRAD FIEDEL

A DREAM IS A WISH YOUR HEART MAKES: THE ANNETTE FUNICELLO STORY (TF) Once Upon a Time Films/Savoy TV/Cactus Pictures/Fireworks Entertainment, 1995
GEORGE BLONDHEIM

DREAM LOVER Gramercy, 1994
CHRISTOPHER YOUNG

DREAM LOVER MGM/UA, 1986
MICHAEL SMALL

THE DREAM MERCHANTS (TF) Columbia TV, 1980
GEORGE DUNING

A DREAM OF KINGS National General, 1969
ALEX NORTH†

DREAM ON: AND BIMBO WAS HIS NAME-O (CTF) Kevin Bright Prods./St. Clare/MTE, 1992
MICHAEL SKLOFF

DREAM ONE *NEMO* NEF, 1984
GABRIEL YARED

THE DREAM ROSE Yugoslavian
ALFI KABILJO

DREAM STREET Griffith, 1921
LOUIS SILVERS†

DREAM STREET (TF) Bedford Falls Co./Finnegan Pinchuk/MGM/UA, 1989
WILLIAM OLVIS

THE DREAM TEAM Universal, 1989
DAVID MCHUGH

DREAM WEST (MS) Sunn Classic Pictures, 1986
FRED KARLIN

DREAM WIFE MGM, 1953
CONRAD SALINGER†

DREAMBOAT 20th Century-Fox, 1952
CYRIL J. MOCKRIDGE†

DREAMCHILD Universal, 1985
MAX HARRIS
STANLEY MYERS†
HANS ZIMMER

DREAMER 20th Century Fox, 1979
BILL CONTI

DREAMING OUT LOUD RKO Radio, 1940
LUCIEN MORAWECK†

DREAMS DON'T DIE (TF) Hill-Mandelker Productions, 1982
BRAD FIEDEL

DREAMS OF GOLD: THE MEL FISHER STORY (TF) Inter Planetary Productions, 1986
ERNEST GOLD

DREAMS THAT MONEY CAN BUY Films International of America, 1948
PAUL BOWLES
JOHN CAGE†
DAVID DIAMOND
DARIUS MILHAUD†

DREAMSCAPE 20th Century Fox, 1983
MAURICE JARRE

DRESS GRAY (TS) Frank von Zerneck Productions/Warner Bros. TV, 1986
BILLY GOLDENBERG

DRESSED TO KILL Filmways, 1980
PINO DONAGGIO

DRESSED TO KILL Universal, 1946
MILTON ROSEN†
HANS J. SALTER†

THE DRESSER Columbia, 1983
JAMES HORNER

THE DRESSMAKER Euro-American, 1988
GEORGE FENTON

THE DRIFTER Concorde, 1988
RICK CONRAD

DRIFTIN' RIVER Producers Releasing Corp., 1946
KARL HAJOS†

DRILLER KILLER Rochelle Films, 1979
JOE DELIA

DRIVE HARD, DRIVE FAST (TF) Public Arts Productions/Universal TV, 1973
PETE RUGOLO

DRIVE, HE SAID Columbia, 1971
DAVID SHIRE

DRIVEN Paramount, 1996
JAY FERGUSON

THE DRIVER 20th Century-Fox, 1978
MICHAEL SMALL

DRIVING ME CRAZY Motion Picture Corporation of America, 1991
CHRISTOPHER FRANKE

DRIVING MISS DAISY Warner Bros., 1989
HANS ZIMMER

DRIVING PASSION: AMERICA'S LOVE AFFAIR WITH THE CAR (CTD) Turner, 1995
MICHAEL BACON

DROP DEAD FRED New Line, 1991
RANDY EDELMAN

DROP DEAD, MY LOVE 1967
ARMANDO TROVAJOLI

DROP SQUAD Gramercy, 1994
MIKE REARDEN

DROP ZONE Paramount, 1994
NICK GLENNIE-SMITH
JOHN VAN TONGEREN
HANS ZIMMER

DROP-OUT FATHER (TF) CBS Entertainment, 1982
PETER MATZ ☆

DROP-OUT MOTHER (TF) Fries Entertainment/Comco Productions, 1988
GERALD FRIED

DROWNING BY NUMBERS Galaxy International, 1988
MICHAEL NYMAN

DROWNING IN THE SHALLOW END (TF) BBC, 1990
HAL LINDES

THE DROWNING POOL Warner Bros., 1975
CHARLES FOX
MICHAEL SMALL

DRUG WARS II: THE COCAINE CARTEL (MS) Michael Mann Prods., 1992
CHARLES BERNSTEIN

DRUG WARS: THE CAMARENA STORY (MS) Michael Mann Prods., 1990
CHARLES BERNSTEIN

DRUGSTORE COWBOY Avenue Pictures, 1989
ELLIOT GOLDENTHAL

THE DRUM United Artists, 1938
JOHN GREENWOOD†

DRUM BEAT Warner Bros., 1954
VICTOR YOUNG†

DRUMS ACROSS THE RIVER Universal, 1954
HERMAN STEIN

DRUMS ALONG THE MOHAWK 20th Century-Fox, 1939
ALFRED NEWMAN†

DRUMS IN THE DEEP SOUTH RKO Radio, 1951
DIMITRI TIOMKIN†

DRUMS OF AFRICA MGM, 1963
JOHNNY MANDEL

DRUMS OF THE CONGO Universal, 1942
CHARLES PREVIN†
HANS J. SALTER†

DRUNKEN ANGEL Toho, 1948
FUMIO HAYASAKA†

DRUNKS Drunks Prods., 1995
JOE DELIA

A DRY WHITE SEASON MGM/UA, 1989
DAVE GRUSIN

DU BEAT-E-O H-Z-H Presentation, 1984
DOUG MOODY

DU BIST MEIN GLUCK 1937
GIUSEPPE BECCE†

DU BOUT DES LEVRES *ON THE TIP OF THE TONGUE* Elan Films, 1976
FREDERIC DEVREESE

DU GRABUGE CHEZ LES VEUVES 1963
GEORGES DELERUE†

DU SOLEIL PLEIN LES YEUX 1970
FRANCIS LAI

THE DUCHESS AND THE DIRTWATER FOX 20th Century Fox, 1976
CHARLES FOX

DUCK IN ORANGE SAUCE 1975
ARMANDO TROVAJOLI

DUCK! YOU SUCKER *GIU LA TESTA/FISTFUL OF DYNAMITE* United Artists, 1972
ENNIO MORRICONE

THE DUDE GOES WEST Allied Artists, 1948
DIMITRI TIOMKIN†

DUDES Cineworld, 1987
CHARLES BERNSTEIN

DUDES ARE PRETTY PEOPLE United Artists, 1942
EDWARD WARD†

DUE BIANCHI NELL 'AFRICA NERA 1970
BRUNO NICOLAI

DUE CUORI, UNA CAPPELLA 1974
STELVIO CIPRIANI

DUE LETTERE ANONIME 1945
ALESSANDRO CICOGNINI†

DUE MAGNUM 38 PER UNA CITTA DI CAROGNE 1976
BRUNO NICOLAI

DUE MOGLI SONO TROPPE 1950
NINO ROTA†

DUE NOTTI CON CLEOPATRA *TWO NIGHTS WITH CLEOPATRA* 1953
ARMANDO TROVAJOLI

DUE PISTOLE E UN VIGLIACCIO 1968
CARLO RUSTICHELLI

DUE SOLDI DI SPERANZA 1952
NINO ROTA†

DUE SOUTH (TF) Alliance/CTV, 1994
JACK LENZ
JOHN MCCARTHY
JAY SEMKO

DUEL (TF) Universal TV, 1971
BILLY GOLDENBERG

DUEL AT DIABLO United Artists, 1966
NEAL HEFTI

THE DUEL AT SILVER CREEK Universal, 1952
HANS J. SALTER†
HERMAN STEIN

DUEL IN THE SUN Selznick Releasing, 1946
DIMITRI TIOMKIN†

DUEL OF HEARTS (CTF) TNT/The Grade Co./
Gainsborough Pictures, 1992
LAURIE JOHNSON

DUEL ON THE MISSISSIPPI Columbia, 1955
MISCHA BAKALEINIKOFF†

THE DUELLISTS Paramount, 1978
HOWARD BLAKE

DUELLO NEL TEXAS/GUNFIGHT AT RED SANDS
1963
ENNIO MORRICONE

DUET FOR ONE Cannon, 1986
MICHAEL J. LINN†

DUFFY OF SAN QUENTIN Warner Bros., 1953
PAUL DUNLAP

DUFFY'S TAVERN Paramount, 1945
ROBERT EMMETT DOLAN†

DULCIMER STREET *LONDON BELONGS TO ME*
1948
BENJAMIN FRANKEL†

DULCY MGM, 1940
BRONISLAU KAPER†

DULI SHIDAI 1994
ANTONIO LEE

DUMB AND DUMBER New Line, 1994
TODD RUNDGREN

DUMBO (AF) RKO Radio, 1941
FRANK CHURCHILL† ★★
OLIVER WALLACE† ★★

DUMMY (TF) The Konigsberg Company/Warner
Bros. TV, 1979
GIL ASKEY

DUNE Universal, 1984
BRIAN ENO
MARTY PAICH†
TOTO

DUNE WARRIORS Califilm, 1991
MALCOLM ORRALL
THE SCORE WARRIORS

THE DUNGEONMASTER Empire Pictures, 1985
RICHARD H. BAND
SHIRLEY WALKER

DUNKIRK MGM, 1958
MALCOLM ARNOLD

DUNSTON CHECKS IN 20th Century Fox, 1996
MILES GOODMAN†

THE DUNWICH HORROR American International,
1970
LES BAXTER†

DUPLICATES (CTF) Sankan Prods./Wilshire Court,
1992
DANA KAPROFF

DUPONT-LAJOIE *RAPE OF INNOCENCE* 1974
VLADIMIR COSMA

DUST BE MY DESTINY Warner Bros., 1939
MAX STEINER†

DUST DEVIL: THE FINAL CUT Miramax, 1993
SIMON BOSWELL

DUTCH 20th Century Fox, 1991
ALAN SILVESTRI

DUTCH MASTER Miramax, 1993
WENDY BLACKSTONE

DUTCHMAN Continental, 1967
JOHN BARRY

D.W. GRIFFITH: FATHER OF FILM (TD) WNET/
Thames TV, 1993
PHILIP APPLEBY
CARL DAVIS
NICK RAINE

DYING ROOM ONLY (TF) Lorimar Productions,
1973
CHARLES FOX

DYING TO BE PERFECT (TF) Citadel, 1996
DANA KAPROFF

DYING TO BELONG (TF) Jean Abounader Prods./
Hallmark/Von Zerneck-Sertner, 1997
MICHAEL TAVERA

DYING TO LOVE YOU (TF) Longbow Productions/
World International Network, 1993
JOSEPH LO DUCA

DYING TO REMEMBER (CTF) Cardera-Schenck,
1993
JAY GRUSKA

DYING YOUNG 20th Century Fox, 1991
JAMES NEWTON HOWARD

DYNASTY: THE REUNION (TF) Richard and Esther
Shapiro Prods./Aaron Spelling Prods., 1991
BILL CONTI
PETER MYERS

E

THE E BOX P&C Productions, 1972
JIM HELMS

*E GUERRIERE DAL SENO NUDA THE
AMAZONS* EMI, 1973
RIZ ORTOLANI

E LO CHIAMARONO SPIRITO SANTO 1971
CARLO SAVINA

E PER TETTO UN CIELO DI STELLE 1968
ENNIO MORRICONE

E PIU FACILE CHE UN CAMELLO... 1950
NINO ROTA†

E PRIMAVERA 1947
NINO ROTA†

...E TU VIVRAI NEL TERRORE! L'ALDILA' Fulvia
Film, 1980
FABIO FRIZZI

*E UNA BANCA RAPINAMMO PER FATAL
CAMBINAZION* 1976
ARMANDO TROVAJOLI

E VENNE IL GIORNO DEI LIMONI NERI 1970
CARLO RUSTICHELLI

E'LOLLIPOP Universal, 1976
LEE HOLDRIDGE

EACH DAWN I DIE Warner Bros., 1939
MAX STEINER†

THE EAGLE HAS LANDED Columbia, 1977
LALO SCHIFRIN

EAGLE IN A CAGE National General, 1971
MARC WILKINSON

EAGLE SQUADRON Universal, 1942
FRANK SKINNER†

EAGLE WITH TWO HEADS 1948
GEORGES AURIC†

EAGLE'S WING International Picture Show, 1979
MARC WILKINSON

EAGLES ATTACK AT DAWN 1970
DOV SELTZER

EARL CARROLL'S VANITIES Republic, 1945
WALTER SCHARF

THE EARL OF CHICAGO MGM, 1940
WERNER R. HEYMANN†

THE EARLY BIRD Rank, 1966
RON GOODWIN

AN EARLY FROST (TF) NBC Productions, 1985
JOHN KANDER ☆

EARTH 2 (TF) Amblin TV/Universal TV, 1994
DAVID BERGEAUD

EARTH AND THE AMERICAN DREAM (FD)
Couturie/BBC, 1993
TODD BOEKELHEIDE

EARTH ANGEL (TF) Ron Gilbert Prods./Leonard Hill
Films, 1991
KEVIN KLINGER

THE EARTH DIES SCREAMING 20th Century-Fox,
1964
ELISABETH LUTYENS†

EARTH GIRLS ARE EASY Vestron, 1989
NILE RODGERS

EARTH II (TF) MGM TV, 1971
LALO SCHIFRIN

EARTH ISLAND - PACIFIC CHRONICLES (TD)
Sierra Club, 1986
PETER DAVISON

EARTH VS. THE FLYING SAUCERS Columbia,
1956
MISCHA BAKALEINIKOFF†

EARTHBOUND 20th Century-Fox, 1940
ALFRED NEWMAN†

THE EARTHLING 1980
DICK DEBENEDICTIS

EARTHQUAKE Universal, 1974
JOHN WILLIAMS

EARTHQUAKERS (FD) A.A.F., 1943
GAIL KUBIK†

EARTHSTAR VOYAGER (TF) Walt Disney TV/
Marstar Productions, 1988
LALO SCHIFRIN

THE EAST IS RED *SWORDSMAN III* 1993
WU WAI-LAP

EAST MEETS WEST 1936
LOUIS LEVY†

EAST OF EDEN Warner Bros., 1955
LEONARD ROSENMAN

EAST OF EDEN (MS) Mace Neufeld Productions,
1981
LEE HOLDRIDGE

EAST OF IPSWITCH (TF) BBC, 1986
GEORGE FENTON

EAST OF JAVA Universal, 1935
FRANZ WAXMAN†

EAST OF SUMATRA Universal, 1953
HENRY MANCINI†★
HERMAN STEIN

EAST OF THE RIVER Warner Bros., 1940
ADOLPH DEUTSCH†

EAST SIDE, WEST SIDE MGM, 1949
MIKLOS ROZSA†

EAST WIND 1974
STOMU YAMASHITA

EASTER PARADE MGM, 1948
JOHN GREEN† ★★

EASY COME, EASY GO Paramount, 1947
ROY WEBB†

THE EASY LIFE *IL SORPASSO* Embassy, 1962
RIZ ORTOLANI

EASY LIVING Paramount, 1937
MILAN RODER†

EASY LIVING RKO Radio, 1949
ROY WEBB†

EASY MONEY Orion, 1983
LAURENCE ROSENTHAL

EASY PREY (TF) New World TV/Rene Malo
Productions, 1986
J.A.C. REDFORD

EASY ROAD 1979
MIKIS THEODORAKIS

EASY TO LOOK AT Universal, 1945
HANS J. SALTER†

EASY TO WED MGM, 1946
JOHN GREEN†

EAT A BOWL OF TEA Columbia, 1989
MARK ADLER

EAT DRINK MAN WOMAN Samuel Goldwyn,
1994
MADER

EAT IT MANGIALA 1968
ENNIO MORRICONE

EAT MY DUST New World, 1976
DAVID GRISMAN

EAT THE PEACH Skouras Pictures, 1986
DONAL LUNNY

EATEN ALIVE *DEATH TRAP* Virgo International,
1977
WAYNE BELL

EATING RAOUL 20th Century Fox International
Classics, 1982
ARLON OBER

EBB TIDE Paramount, 1937
VICTOR YOUNG†

EBIRAH, HORROR OF THE DEEP 1968
MASARU SATO

EBOLI *CHRIST STOPPED AT EBOLI* Franklin
Media, 1980
PIERO PICCIONI

THE EBONY TOWER (TF) Granada TV, 1987
RICHARD RODNEY BENNETT

EBONY, IVORY AND JADE (TF) Frankel Films,
19/9
EARLE HAGEN

ECCE HOMO 1968
ENNIO MORRICONE

ECHO OF AN ERA 1957
DAVID AMRAM

ECHO PARK Atlantic Releasing Corporation, 1985
DAVID RICKETTS

ECHOES Continental, 1983
STEPHEN SCHWARTZ

ECHOES (TF) Kushner-Locke, 1996
PETER MANNING ROBINSON

ECHOES IN THE DARKNESS (MS) Litke-Grossbart
Productions/New World TV, 1987
DAVID SHIRE

ECHOES OF PARADISE *SHADOWS OF THE
PEACOCK* Castle Hill Productions/Quartet Films,
1987
WILLIAM MOTZIG

ECLIPSE DE SOL 1944
PAUL MISRAKI

ECOLOGIA DEL DELITTO 1972
STELVIO CIPRIANI

ED Universal, 1996
STEPHEN ENDELMAN

ED McBAIN'S 57TH PRECINCT (TF) Diana Kerew
Prods./Hearst, 1995
PETER BERNSTEIN

ED WOOD Buena Vista, 1994
HOWARD SHORE

ED'S NEXT MOVE Curb, 1996
BENNY GOLSON

EDDIE Buena Vista, 1996
STANLEY CLARKE

EDDIE AND THE CRUISERS Embassy, 1983
JOHN CAFFERTY

EDDIE AND THE CRUISERS II: EDDIE LIVES Scotti
Bros. Pictures/Aurora Film Partners, 1989
LEON ARONSON
MARTY SIMON
KENNY VANCE

EDDIE MACON'S RUN Universal, 1983
WENDY BLACKSTONE

THE EDDY DUCHIN STORY Columbia, 1956
GEORGE DUNING ★

EDEN: FORBIDDEN INTERLUDES (CTF) Pacific
Rim, 1993
PATRICK GLEESON

*EDES EMMA, DRAGA BOBE - VAZLATOK, AKTOK
SWEET EMMA, DEAR BOBE - SKETCHES,
NUDES* 1992
RICHARD SCHUMANN

THE EDGE (CTF) Lewis B. Chesler Productions/The
Christopher Morgan Co./MGM/UA, 1989
MICHEL RUBINI

EDGE OF DARKNESS Warner Bros., 1943
FRANZ WAXMAN†

EDGE OF DARKNESS (MS) BBC/Lionheart
Television International, 1986
ERIC CLAPTON
MICHAEL KAMEN

EDGE OF DOOM RKO Radio, 1950
HUGO FRIEDHOFER†

EDGE OF ETERNITY Columbia, 1959
DANIELE AMFITHEATROF†

EDGE OF HELL Universal, 1956
ERNEST GOLD

EDGE OF HONOR Wind River, 1991
WILLIAM T. STROMBERG

EDGE OF SANITY August Entertainment, 1989
FREDERIC TALGORN

THE EDGE OF THE ABYSS Triangle, 1916
VICTOR SCHERTZINGER†

EDGE OF THE CITY MGM, 1957
LEONARD ROSENMAN

EDISON, THE MAN MGM, 1940
HERBERT STOTHART†

EDITH AND MARCEL Miramax, 1983
FRANCIS LAI

EDITH'S DIARY 1983
JURGEN KNIEPER

EDUCATING RITA Columbia, 1983
DAVID HENTSCHEL

THE EDUCATION IN LOVE OF VALENTIN 1975
JEAN PRODROMIDES

THE EDUCATION OF SONNY CARSON
Paramount, 1974
COLERIDGE-TAYLOR PERKINSON

EDWARD II 1991
SIMON FISHER TURNER

EDWARD SCISSORHANDS 20th Century-Fox,
1990
DANNY ELFMAN

**THE EFFECT OF GAMMA RAYS ON
MAN-IN-THE-MOON MARIGOLDS** 20th
Century-Fox, 1972
MAURICE JARRE

THE EGG AND I Universal, 1947
FRANK SKINNER†

EGON SCHIELE - EXCESS AND PUNISHMENT
Gamma Film, 1981
BRIAN ENO

THE EGYPTIAN 20th Century-Fox, 1954
BERNARD HERRMANN†
ALFRED NEWMAN†

EHI AMIGO SEI MORTO 1970
CARLO SAVINA

EIEDRIEBE West German
JURGEN KNIEPER

THE EIGER SANCTION Universal, 1975
JOHN WILLIAMS

EIGHT FOLLOWING ONE 1965
DOV SELTZER

EIGHT HEADS IN A DUFFEL BAG MPCA/Orion,
1997
ANDREW GROSS

EIGHT IRON MEN Columbia, 1952
LEITH STEVENS†

EIGHT IS ENOUGH: A FAMILY REUNION (TF)
Lorimar TV, 1987
LEE HOLDRIDGE

EIGHT MEN OUT Orion, 1988
MASON DARING

EIGHTEEN AND ANXIOUS Republic, 1957
LEITH STEVENS†

THE EIGHTH DAY 1979
KEITH JARRETT

THE EIGHTH DAY Gramercy, 1997
PIERRE VAN DORMAEL

EIJANAIKA Shochiku, 1981
CHUMEI WATANABE

EIN ABENTEUER AM THUNERSEE 1942
GIUSEPPE BECCE†

EIN BLONDER TRAUM 1932
WERNER R. HEYMANN†

EIN HAUS VOLL LIEBE 1952
WERNER R. HEYMANN†

EIN LIED FUR DICH 1933
BRONISLAU KAPER†

EINMAL KU'DAMM UND Z West German
JURGEN KNIEPER

EL ALIENTO DEL DIABLO *THE DEVIL'S BREATH*
1993
ANGEL ILLARAMENDI

EL AMANTE BILINGE *THE BILINGUAL LOVER*
1993
JOSE NIETO

EL CID Allied Artists, 1961
MIKLOS ROZSA† ★

EL CISCO 1966
BRUNO NICOLAI

EL CONDOR National General, 1970
MAURICE JARRE

F
I
L
M

T
I
T
L
E
S

'97-'98
FILM
COMPOSERS
INDEX

F
I
L
M

T
I
T
L
E
S

EROTIC TALES 1994
WENDY BLACKSTONE
USTAD ZIA FARIDUDDIN
DAVID MCHUGH
MELVIN VAN PEEBLES

THE ERRAND BOY Paramount, 1962
WALTER SCHARF

ERVINKA 1967
DOV SELTZER

ESCALATION 1967
ENNIO MORRICONE

ESCALE A ORLY 1955
PAUL MISRAKI

ESCALIER DE SERVICE 1954
GEORGES VAN PARYS†

ESCAPADE IN JAPAN Universal, 1957
MAX STEINER†

ESCAPE MGM, 1940
FRANZ WAXMAN†

ESCAPE (TF) Henry Jaffe Enterprises, 1980
JAMES DIPASQUALLE

ESCAPE (TF) Paramount TV, 1971
LALO SCHIFRIN

THE ESCAPE ARTIST Orion/Warner Bros., 1982
GEORGES DELERUE†

ESCAPE FROM ALCATRAZ Paramount, 1979
JERRY FIELDING†

ESCAPE FROM ATLANTIS (TF) Universal TV, 1997
STEPHEN GRAZIANO

ESCAPE FROM BOGEN COUNTY (TF) Paramount TV, 1977
CHARLES BERNSTEIN

ESCAPE FROM FORT BRAVO MGM, 1953
JEFF ALEXANDER†

ESCAPE FROM IRAN: THE CANADIAN CAPER (TF) Canamedia Productions, 1981
PETER JERMYN

ESCAPE FROM L.A. 1996
JOHN CARPENTER
SHIRLEY WALKER

ESCAPE FROM NEW YORK Avco Embassy, 1981
JOHN CARPENTER
ALAN HOWARTH

ESCAPE FROM RED ROCK 20th Century-Fox, 1958
LES BAXTER†

ESCAPE FROM SOBIBOR (TF) Rule-Starger Productions/Zenith Productions, 1987
GEORGES DELERUE†

ESCAPE FROM THE BRONX New Line Cinema, 1985
FRANCESCO DE MASI

ESCAPE FROM THE DARK Buena Vista, 1977
RON GOODWIN

ESCAPE FROM THE PLANET OF THE APES 20th Century-Fox, 1971
JERRY GOLDSMITH

ESCAPE FROM ZAHRAIN Paramount, 1962
LYN MURRAY†

ESCAPE IN THE DESERT Warner Bros., 1945
ADOLPH DEUTSCH†

ESCAPE ME NEVER United Artists, 1935
SIR WILLIAM WALTON†

ESCAPE ME NEVER Warner Bros., 1947
ERICH WOLFGANG KORNGOLD†

ESCAPE TO ATHENA AFD, 1979
LALO SCHIFRIN

ESCAPE TO MINDANAO (TF) Universal TV, 1968
LYN MURRAY†

ESCAPE TO THE SUN Cinevision, 1972
DOV SELTZER

ESCAPE TO WITCH MOUNTAIN Buena Vista, 1975
JOHNNY MANDEL

ESKIMO MGM, 1933
WILLIAM AXT†

ESPECIALLY ON SUNDAY 1991
ENNIO MORRICONE

ESPIONAGE MGM, 1937
WILLIAM AXT†

ESPIONAGE AGENT Warner Bros., 1939
ADOLPH DEUTSCH†

ESTERINA 1959
CARLO RUSTICHELLI

ESTHER AND THE KING 1960
ANGELO FRANCESCO LAVAGNINO†

ESTRATTO DAGLI ARCHIVI SEGRETI DELLA POLIZIA DI UNA CAPITALE EUROPA *FROM THE POLICE, WITH THANKS* 1972
STELVIO CIPRIANI

ET MOURIR DE PLAISIR Paramount, 1960
JEAN PRODROMIDES

E.T. THE EXTRA-TERRESTRIAL Universal, 1982
JOHN WILLIAMS ★★

THE ETERNAL RETURN 1943
GEORGES AURIC†

THE ETERNAL SEA Republic, 1955
ELMER BERNSTEIN

ETERNALLY YOURS United Artists, 1939
WERNER JANSSEN ★

ETHAN FROME Miramax, 1993
RACHEL PORTMAN

ETTORE FIERAMOSCA 1938
ALESSANDRO CICOGNINI†

EUGENIE...THE STORY OF HER JOURNEY INTO PERVERSION *MARQUIS DE SADE* 1969
BRUNO NICOLAI

EUREKA MGM/UA Classics, 1984
STANLEY MYERS†
HANS ZIMMER

EUREKA STOCKADE 1950
JOHN GREENWOOD†

EUROPA *ZENTROPA* 1991
JOAKIM HOLBECK

EUROPA DI NOTTE 1959
CARLO SAVINA

THE EUROPEANS Levitt-Pickman, 1979
RICHARD ROBBINS

EVA 1948
ERIC NORDGREN

EVA 1953
MIKIS THEODORAKIS

EVA Times, 1962
MICHEL LEGRAND

EVA PERON JOSE LUIS CASTINEIRA DE DIOS

EVARISTE GALOIS 1964
ANTOINE DUHAMEL

EVE OF DESTRUCTION Orion, 1991
PHILIPPE SARDE

THE EVE OF ST. MARK 20th Century-Fox, 1944
CYRIL J. MOCKRIDGE†

EVEL KNIEVEL Fanfare, 1972
PATRICK WILLIAMS

EVEN COWGIRLS GET THE BLUES Fine Line, 1993
K.D.LANG
JOHN MCCARTHY
BEN MINK

EVENING IN BYZANTIUM (TF) Universal TV, 1978
STU PHILLIPS

THE EVENING STAR Paramount, 1996
WILLIAM ROSS

EVENSONG 1934
LOUIS LEVY†

THE EVENTS LEADING UP TO MY DEATH Flat Rock Films, 1992
MARY MARGARET O'HARA
BILL ROBERTSON

EVERGREEN (MS) Edgar J. Scherick Associates/Metromedia Producers Corporation, 1985
LAURENCE ROSENTHAL

EVERY BREATH Motion Picture Corp. of America, 1993
NILS LOFGREN

EVERY DAY EXCEPT CHRISTMAS 1957
DANIELE PARIS

EVERY DAY'S A HOLIDAY Paramount, 1938
LEO SHUKEN†

EVERY GIRL SHOULD BE MARRIED RKO Radio, 1948
LEIGH HARLINE†

EVERY HOME SHOULD HAVE ONE 1970
JOHN CAMERON

EVERY LITTLE CROOK AND NANNY MGM, 1972
FRED KARLIN

EVERY MAN FOR HIMSELF *SAUVE QUI PEUT LA VIE* New Yorker/Zoetrope, 1980
GABRIEL YARED

EVERY MAN FOR HIMSELF/SAM COOPER'S GOLD 1968
CARLO RUSTICHELLI

EVERY MAN NEEDS ONE (TF) Spelling-Goldberg Productions/ABC Circle Films, 1972
ALLYN FERGUSON
JACK ELLIOTT

EVERY TIME WE SAY GOODBYE Tri-Star, 1987
PHILIPPE SARDE

EVERY WHICH WAY BUT LOOSE Warner Bros., 1978
STEVE DORFF

EVERY WOMAN'S DREAM (TF) Kushner-Locke, 1996
PETER MANNING ROBINSON

EVERYBODY SING MGM, 1938
WILLIAM AXT†
GEORGE BASSMAN

EVERYBODY WINS Orion, 1990
MARK ISHAM
LEON REDBONE

EVERYBODY'S ALL AMERICAN Warner Bros., 1988
JAMES NEWTON HOWARD

EVERYBODY'S BABY: THE RESCUE OF JESSIE McCLURE (TF) Interscope, 1989
MARK SNOW

EVERYBODY'S DANCIN' Lippert, 1950
ALBERT GLASSER

EVERYBODY'S FINE Miramax, 1990
ENNIO MORRICONE

EVERYBODY'S OLD MAN 20th Century-Fox, 1936
DAVID BUTTOLPH†

EVERYTHING BUT THE TRUTH Universal, 1956
HENRY MANCINI†
MILTON ROSEN†
HERMAN STEIN

EVERYTHING I HAVE IS YOURS MGM, 1952
DAVID ROSE†

EVERYTHING RELATIVE 1996
FRANK LONDON

EVERYTHING YOU WANTED TO KNOW ABOUT SEX (BUT WERE AFRAID TO ASK) United Artists, 1972
MUNDELL LOWE

EVERYTHING'S DUCKY Columbia, 1961
BERNARD GREEN

THE EVICTORS American International, 1979
JAIME MENDOZA-NAVA

THE EVIL New World, 1978
JOHNNY HARRIS

THE EVIL DEAD New Line Cinema, 1983
JOSEPH LO DUCA

EVIL DEAD 2 Rosebud Releasing Corporation, 1987
JOSEPH LO DUCA

EVIL EYE *LA RAGAZZA CHE SAPEVE TROPPO* American International, 1963
LES BAXTER†

EVIL IN CLEAR RIVER (TF) The Steve Tisch Company/Lionel Chetwynd Productions/Phoenix Entertainment Group, 1988
WILLIAM OLVIS

EVIL NIGHT Nautilus Film Co., 1990
JOHN W. MORGAN

THE EVIL OF FRANKENSTEIN Universal, 1964
DON BANKS

EVIL SPIRITS Prism, 1991
DUANE SCIAQUA

THE EVIL THAT MEN DO Tri-Star, 1984
KEN THORNE

EVIL UNDER THE SUN Universal/AFD, 1982
JOHN LANCHBERY

EVILTOONS AIP, 1990
CHUCK CIRINO

EVITA PERON (TF) Hartwest Productions/Zephyr Productions, 1981
JOHNNY MANDEL

EVOLUTION (FD) Elan Vital Production
JONATHAN MORSE

EVW'S (FD) 1949
MALCOLM ARNOLD

THE EWOK ADVENTURE (TF) Lucasfilm Ltd./Korty Films, 1984
PETER BERNSTEIN

EWOKS: THE BATTLE FOR ENDOR (TF) Lucasfilm Ltd., 1985
PETER BERNSTEIN

THE EX (CTF) American World Pictures/Cinepix, 1996
PAUL J. ZAZA

EXCALIBUR Orion/Warner Bros., 1981
TREVOR JONES

EXCESS BAGGAGE COLUMBIA, 1997
JOHN LURIE

EXCESSIVE FORCE New Line, 1993
CHARLES BERNSTEIN

EXCHANGE LIFEGUARDS Beyond Films, 1993
JOHN CAPEK

EXCITE ME 1972
BRUNO NICOLAI

EXCLUSIVE Paramount, 1937
MILAN RODER†

EXCLUSIVE (TF) Hamel-Somers/Freyda Rothstein/Hearst, 1992
DAVID MICHAEL FRANK

EXCLUSIVE STORY MGM, 1936
EDWARD WARD†

EXCUSE ME, MY NAME IS ROCCO PAPALEO Rumson, 1971
ARMANDO TROVAJOLI

THE EXECUTION (TF) Newland-Raynor Productions/Comworld Productions, 1985
GEORGES DELERUE†

THE EXECUTION PROTOCOL (FD) 1992
ROBERT LOCKHART

THE EXECUTIONER Columbia, 1970
RON GOODWIN

THE EXECUTIONER'S SONG (TF) Film Communications Inc., 1982
JOHN CACAVAS

EXECUTIVE ACTION National General, 1973
RANDY EDELMAN

EXECUTIVE DECISION Warner Bros., 1996
JERRY GOLDSMITH

EXECUTIVE POWER Usonia Pictures, 1997
TIM TRUMAN

EXILE Beyond Films, 1994
PAUL GRABOWSKY

THE EXILE Universal, 1947
FRANK SKINNER†

EXILE AND KINGDOM (FD) Snakewood Films, 1993
DAVID MILROY

EXIT TO EDEN Savoy, 1994
PATRICK DOYLE

THE EX-MRS. BRADFORD RKO Radio, 1936
ROY WEBB†

EXODUS United Artists, 1960
ERNEST GOLD ★★

EXO-MAN (TF) Universal TV, 1977
DANA KAPROFF

THE EXORCIST Warner Bros., 1973
JACK NITZCHE

EXORCIST II: THE HERETIC Warner Bros., 1977
ENNIO MORRICONE

EXORCIST III 20th Century-Fox, 1990
BARRY DEVORZON

EXOTICA Alliance/ARP, 1994
MYCHAEL DANNA

EXPECT TO DIE Film One, 1997
VAROUJE

EXPERIMENT ALCATRAZ RKO Radio, 1950
IRVING GERTZ

EXPERIMENT IN TERROR Warner Bros., 1962
HENRY MANCINI†

EXPERIMENT PERILOUS RKO Radio, 1945
ROY WEBB†

THE EXPERT Warner Bros., 1932
W. FRANKE HARLING†

THE EXPERTS Paramount, 1989
MARVIN HAMLISCH

EXPLORERS Paramount, 1985
JERRY GOLDSMITH

EXPLOSION 1969
SOL KAPLAN

EXPOSED MGM/UA, 1983
GEORGES DELERUE†

EXPOSED Republic, 1947
ERNEST GOLD

EXPOSURE Miramax, 1991
JURGEN KNIEPER

EXPRESSO BONGO Continental, 1960
ROBERT FARNON

EXQUISITE TENDERNESS Capella, 1994
CHRISTOPHER FRANKE

EXTASE 1932
GIUSEPPE BECCE†

THE EXTERMINATOR Avco Embassy, 1980
JOE RENZETTI

EXTERMINATOR 2 Cannon, 1984
DAVID SPEAR

EXTRA CONJUGALE 1965
LUIS BACALOV

THE EXTRAORDINARY SEAMAN MGM, 1968
MAURICE JARRE

EXTREME CLOSE-UP National General, 1973
BASIL POLEDOURIS

EXTREME JUSTICE (CTF) Trimark, 1993
DAVID MICHAEL FRANK

EXTREME MEASURES 1996
DANNY ELFMAN

EXTREME PREJUDICE Tri-Star, 1987
JERRY GOLDSMITH

EXTREMES (FD) 1972
ROY BUDD†

EXTREMITIES Atlantic Releasing Corporation, 1986
J.A.C. REDFORD

AN EYE FOR AN EYE Avco Embassy, 1981
WILLIAM GOLDSTEIN

EYE FOR AN EYE Paramount, 1996
JAMES NEWTON HOWARD

THE EYE OF THE NEEDLE *LA SMANIA ADOSSO* 1962
CARLO RUSTICHELLI

EYE OF THE CAT Universal, 1969
LALO SCHIFRIN

EYE OF THE NEEDLE United Artists, 1981
MIKLOS ROZSA†

EYE OF THE STALKER (TF) O'Hara-Horowitz, 1995
STACY WIDELITZ

EYE OF THE STORM Strongmaster Productions, 1991
CHRISTOPHER FRANKE

EYE OF THE TIGER Scotti Brothers, 1986
DON PRESTON

EYE ON THE SPARROW (TF) Sarabande Productions/Republic Pictures, 1987
EDDIE LAWRENCE MANSON

EYE WITNESS *YOUR WITNESS* Eagle Lion, 1950
MALCOLM ARNOLD

EYEBALL 1978
BRUNO NICOLAI

EYES OF A STRANGER Warner Bros., 1981
RICHARD EINHORN

EYES OF A WITNESS (TF) RHI, 1991
CHARLES GROSS

EYES OF FIRE Elysian Pictures, 1984
BRAD FIEDEL

EYES OF LAURA MARS Columbia, 1978
ARTIE KANE

EYES OF TERROR (TF) Bar-Gene Prods./Freyda Rothstein Prods./Hearst, 1994
MICHAEL HOENIG

THE EYES OF THE PANTHER (CTF)   Think
Entertainment, 1989
JOHN DEBNEY

EYES OF THE SERPENT   Vista Street Entertainment,
1992
MIRIAM CUTLER

EYES OF THE UNDERWORLD   Universal, 1943
HANS J. SALTER†

EYES OF THE WIND   1986
MICHAEL HOPPE

THE EYES, THE MOUTH   Gaumont, 1982
NICOLA PIOVANI

EYEWITNESS   20th Century-Fox, 1981
STANLEY SILVERMAN

EZ STREETS (TF)   Paul Haggis Prods., 1996
MARK ISHAM

F

F FOR FAKE   Specialty Films, 1974
MICHEL LEGRAND

F. SCOTT FIZTGERALD IN HOLLYWOOD (TF)
Titus Productions, 1976
MORTON GOULD

THE FABULOUS BAKER BOYS   20th Century Fox,
1989
DAVE GRUSIN ★

THE FABULOUS BARON MUNCHAUSEN   1961
ZDENEK LISKA

THE FABULOUS DORSEYS   United Artists, 1947
LEO SHUKEN†

THE FABULOUS JOE   United Artists, 1947
HEINZ ROEMHELD†

THE FABULOUS TEXAN   Republic, 1947
ANTHONY COLLINS†

THE FABULOUS WORLD OF JULES VERNE   1958
ZDENEK LISKA

FACCIA A FACCIA   1967
ENNIO MORRICONE

THE FACE BEHIND THE MASK   Columbia, 1941
SIDNEY CUTNER†

A FACE IN THE RAIN   Embassy, 1963
RICHARD MARKOWITZ†

FACE OF A FUGITIVE   Columbia, 1959
JERRY GOLDSMITH

FACE OF A STRANGER (TF)   Linda Gottlieb
Productions/Viacom, 1991
LEE HOLDRIDGE

THE FACE OF ANOTHER   1966
TORU TAKEMITSU†

THE FACE OF FEAR (TF)   QM Productions, 1971
MORTON STEVENS†

FACE OF FEAR (TF)   Lee Rich Productions/Warner
Bros. TV, 1990
JOHN DEBNEY

FACE OF FIRE   Allied Artists, 1959
ERIC NORDGREN

THE FACE OF RAGE (TF)   Hal Sitowitz Productions/
Viacom, 1983
MILES GOODMAN†

FACE OFF   Paramount, 1997
MARK ISHAM

THE FACE ON THE MILK CARTON (TF)   Dorothea
G. Petrie Prods./Family Prods., 1995
LEONARD ROSENMAN

FACE TO FACE   RKO Radio, 1952
HUGO FRIEDHOFER†

FACES   Continental, 1968
JACK ACKERMAN

FACES OF FEAR   Ambassador Pictures, 1981
JOEL GOLDSMITH

THE FACTS OF LIFE   United Artists, 1960
LEIGH HARLINE†

THE FACTS OF LIFE DOWN UNDER (TF)   Embassy
Communications, 1987
FRED KARLIN

THE FACTS OF LIFE GOES TO PARIS (TF)
Embassy TV, 1982
MISHA SEGAL

THE FACTS OF MURDER   *UN MALEDETTO
IMBROGLIO*   Seven Arts, 1959
CARLO RUSTICHELLI

FADE TO BLACK   American Cinema, 1980
CRAIG SAFAN

FADE TO BLACK (CTF)   Francine LeFrak/Wilshire
Court, 1993
MICHEL COLOMBIER

FADILA   1961
ALAIN ROMANS

FAHRENHEIT 451   Universal, 1966
BERNARD HERRMANN†

FAIBLES FEMMES   1959
PAUL MISRAKI

THE FAILING OF RAYMOND (TF)   Universal TV,
1971
PATRICK WILLIAMS

FAIR GAME   1988
GIORGIO MORODER

FAIR GAME   Warner Bros., 1995
JOHN VAN TONGEREN

FAIR WIND TO JAVA   Republic, 1953
VICTOR YOUNG†

FAIRY TALES   Yablans Films, 1978
ANDREW BELLING

FAIT DIVERS   1924
ARTHUR HONEGGER†

FAITHFUL   Gramercy, 1996
PHILLIP JOHNSTON

FAITHFUL IN MY FASHION   MGM, 1946
NATHANIEL SHILKRET†

THE FAKE   1953
MATYAS SEIBER

FAKE OUT   Analysis, 1982
ARTHUR B. RUBINSTEIN

*THE FAKERS/SMASHING THE CRIME
SYNDICATE*   Independent-International, 1970
NELSON RIDDLE†

THE FALCON AND THE SNOWMAN   Orion, 1985
LYLE MAYS
PAT METHENY

THE FALCON IN DANGER   RKO Radio, 1943
ROY WEBB†

THE FALCON OUT WEST   RKO Radio, 1944
ROY WEBB†

THE FALCON STRIKES BACK   RKO Radio, 1943
ROY WEBB†

THE FALCON'S ALIBI   RKO Radio, 1946
ERNEST GOLD

THE FALCON'S BROTHER   RKO Radio, 1942
ROY WEBB†

FALCON'S GOLD (CTF)   Paul Heller Productions/
Schulz Productions/Sonesta Productions/Intrepid
Productions, 1982
LALO SCHIFRIN

FALL   Capella, 1997
AMANDA KRAVAT

FALL FROM GRACE (TF)   NBC Productions, 1990
CHARLES BERNSTEIN

FALL IN   United Artists, 1943
EDWARD WARD†

THE FALL OF A NATION   National Films, 1916
VICTOR HERBERT†

THE FALL OF BERLIN   1945
DMITRI SHOSTAKOVITCH†

FALL OF ITALY   Yugoslavian
ALFI KABILJO

THE FALL OF SAIGON (CTD)   Barraclough Carey,
1995
GEORGE FENTON

THE FALL OF THE HOUSE OF USHER (TF)   Schick
Sunn Classics Productions/Taft International Pictures,
1982
ROBERT SUMMERS

THE FALL OF THE ROMAN EMPIRE   Paramount,
1964
DIMITRI TIOMKIN† ★

FALL OF THE HOUSE OF USHER   American
International, 1960
LES BAXTER†

FALL TIME   Live Ent., 1995
HUMMIE MANN

FALLEN ANGEL   20th Century-Fox, 1945
DAVID RAKSIN

FALLEN ANGEL (TF)   Green-Epstein Productions/
Columbia TV, 1981
RICHARD BELLIS

FALLEN FROM HEAVEN/IN TRANSIT   1993
JEFF COHEN

THE FALLEN IDOL   Selznick Releasing, 1948
WILLIAM ALWYN†

THE FALLEN SPARROW   RKO Radio, 1943
ROY WEBB† ★

FALLING DOWN   Warner Bros., 1993
JAMES NEWTON HOWARD

FALLING FOR YOU (TF)   Falling For You prods./BBS
Prods., 1995
JONATHAN GOLDSMITH

FALLING FROM THE SKY! FLIGHT 174 (TF)
Pacific/Hill-Fields, 1995
IAN THOMAS

FALLING IN LOVE   Paramount, 1984
DAVE GRUSIN

FALLING IN LOVE AGAIN   International Picture
Show Company, 1980
MICHEL LEGRAND

FALLING WATER   1986
TOM CANNING

FALSE ARREST (TF)   Ron Gilbert Associates/Leonard
Hill Films, 1991
SYLVESTER LEVAY.

FALSE FACE   United International, 1976
BOB COBERT

FALSE WITNESS (TF)   Valente-Kritzer-EPI
Productions/New World TV, 1989
DAVID MICHAEL FRANK

FALSTAFF   Peppercorn-Wormser, 1966
ANGELO FRANCESCO LAVAGNINO†

FAME   MGM/United Artists, 1980
MICHAEL GORE ★★

FAME IS THE NAME OF THE GAME (TF)
Universal TV, 1966
BENNY CARTER

THE FAMILY   1970
ENNIO MORRICONE

FAMILY BUSINESS   Tri-Star, 1989
CY COLEMAN

FAMILY BUSINESS (TF)   Screenscope Inc./South
Carolina Educational TV Network, 1983
FRED KARNS

A FAMILY DIVIDED (TF)   Citadel, 1995
DANA KAPROFF

FAMILY FLIGHT (TF)   Silverton Productions/
Universal TV, 1972
FRED STEINER

A FAMILY FOR JOE (TF)   Grosso-Jacobson
Productions/NBC Productions, 1990
CHARLES FOX

FAMILY HONEYMOON   Universal, 1949
FRANK SKINNER†

THE FAMILY KOVAK (TF)   Playboy Productions,
1974
HARRY SUKMAN†

THE FAMILY MAN (TF)   Time-Life Productions,
1979
BILLY GOLDENBERG

THE FAMILY NOBODY WANTED (TF)   Groverton
Productions/Universal TV, 1975
GEORGE ROMANIS

A FAMILY OF STRANGERS (TF)   Alliance, 1993
PETER MANNING ROBINSON

FAMILY OF COPS (TF)   Alliance, 1995
PETER MANNING ROBINSON

FAMILY OF COPS 2   Alliance, 1997
PETER MANNING ROBINSON

FAMILY OF SPIES (MS)   King Phoenix
Entertainment, 1990
PAUL CHIHARA

FAMILY PICTURES (TF)   Alexander-Enright &
Associates/Hearst, 1993
JOHNNY HARRIS

FAMILY PLOT   Universal, 1976
JOHN WILLIAMS

FAMILY PORTRAIT   1950
JOHN GREENWOOD†

FAMILY PRAYERS   Arrow, 1993
STEVE TYRELL

FAMILY REUNION (TF)   CBC TV, 1981
FRED MOLLIN

FAMILY REUNION (TF)   Creative Projects/Columbia
Pictures TV, 1981
WLADIMIR SELINSKY

THE FAMILY RICO (TF)   CBS Entertainment, 1972
DAVE GRUSIN

THE FAMILY SECRET   Columbia, 1951
GEORGE DUNING

FAMILY SECRETS (TF)   Katz-Gallin Prods./Half-Pint
Prods./Karoger Prods., 1984
CHARLES FOX

FAMILY SINS (TF)   London Films, 1987
ELIZABETH SWADOS

A FAMILY THING   MGM-UA, 1996
CHARLES GROSS

FAMILY TIES VACATION (TF)   UBU Productions/
Paramount Pictures TV, 1985
TOM SCOTT

A FAMILY TORN APART (TF)   Red City Prods./
Robert Halmi Inc., 1993
GARY CHANG

A FAMILY UPSIDE DOWN (TF)   Ross
Hunter-Jacques Mapes Film/Paramount TV, 1978
HENRY MANCINI†

THE FAMILY WAY   Warner Bros., 1967
PAUL MCCARTNEY

THE FAN   20th Century-Fox, 1948
DANIELE AMFITHEATROF†

THE FAN   Paramount, 1981
PINO DONAGGIO

THE FAN   TriStar, 1996
HANS ZIMMER

FANATIC   Columbia, 1965
WILFRED JOSEPHS

FANATIC   Twin Continental, 1982
UDI HARPAZ

FANCIULLE DI LUSSO   1953
NINO ROTA†

FANCY PANTS   Paramount, 1950
NATHAN VAN CLEAVE†

FANDANGO   Warner Bros., 1985
ALAN SILVESTRI

FANFAN   1993
NICOLAS JORELLE

FANFAN LA TULIPE   1951
GEORGES VAN PARYS†

Fanfare, 1972
J.J. JOHNSON

FANGS OF THE WILD   Lippert, 1954
PAUL DUNLAP

FANNY   Warner Bros., 1961
HARRY SUKMAN†

FANNY AND ALEXANDER   Embassy, 1983
DANIEL BELL

FANNY FOLEY HERSELF   RKO Radio, 1931
MAX STEINER†

FANTASIES   Joseph Brenner Associates, 1973
JEFFREY SILVERMAN

FANTASIES (TF)   Mandy Productions, 1982
JAMES DIPASQUALE

THE FANTASIST   ITC, 1986
STANISLAS SYREWICZ

FANTASMI A ROMA   1960
NINO ROTA†

THE FANTASTIC JOURNEY (TF)   Bruce Lansbury/
Columbia TV, 1977
ROBERT PRINCE

THE FANTASTIC LIFE OF D.C. COLLINS (TF)
Zephyr Productions/Guillaume-Margo Productions,
1984
A. S. DIAMOND
DENNIS DREITH

THE FANTASTIC PLANET (AF)   Hemdale, 1973
ALAIN GORRAGUER

THE FANTASTIC PLASTIC MACHINE   1969
HARRY BETTS

FANTASTIC INVASION OF THE PLANET EARTH
Oboler Films, 1967
PAUL SAWTELL†
BERT A. SHEFTER

FANTASTIC VOYAGE   20th Century-Fox, 1966
LEONARD ROSENMAN

FANTASTICA   Les Productions du Verseau/El
Productions, 1980
LEWIS FUREY

FANTASY ISLAND (TF)   Spelling-Goldberg
Productions, 1977
LAURENCE ROSENTHAL

FANTOMAS   1964
MICHEL MAGNE†

FAR AND AWAY   Universal, 1992
JOHN WILLIAMS

THE FAR COUNTRY   Universal, 1955
HENRY MANCINI†
HANS J. SALTER†
HERMAN STEIN

FAR FROM BARBARY   1993
PIRO CAKO

FAR FROM HOME   Vestron, 1989
JONATHAN ELIAS

FAR FROM HOME: THE ADVENTURES OF
YELLOW DOG   20th Century Fox, 1995
JOHN SCOTT

FAR FROM THE MADDING CROWD   MGM, 1967
RICHARD RODNEY BENNETT ★

THE FAR HORIZONS   Universal, 1955
HANS J. SALTER†

FAR NORTH   Alive Films, 1988
RED CLAY RAMBLERS

A FAR OFF PLACE   Buena Vista, 1993
JAMES HORNER

FAR OUT MAN   CineTel Films, 1989
JAY CHATTAWAY

THE FAR PAVILLIONS (CMS)   Geoff Reeve &
Associates/Goldcrest, 1984
CARL DAVIS

FAREWELL AGAIN   1937
RICHARD ADDINSELL†

FAREWELL TO MANZANAR (TF)   Korty Films/
Universal TV, 1976
PAUL CHIHARA

FAREWELL TO MY CONCUBINE   *BAWANG BIE
JI*   Miramax, 1993
ZHAO JIPING

FAREWELL TO THE KING   Orion, 1989
BASIL POLEDOURIS

FAREWELL, MY LOVELY   Avco Embassy, 1975
DAVID SHIRE

FARGO   Gramercy, 1996
CARTER BURWELL

THE FARMER TAKES A WIFE   20th Century-Fox,
1953
LIONEL NEWMAN†

THE FARMER'S DAUGHTER   RKO Radio, 1947
LEIGH HARLINE†

FARRELL FOR THE PEOPLE (TF)   InterMedia
Entertainment/TAL Productions/MGM-UA TV, 1982
BILL CONTI

THE FASCIST   1961
ENNIO MORRICONE

FAST AND FURIOUS   MGM, 1939
DANIELE AMFITHEATROF†

FAST BREAK   Columbia, 1979
JAMES DIPASQUALE
DAVID SHIRE

FAST CHARLIE AND THE MOONBEAM   Universal,
1979
STU PHILLIPS

FAST CHARLIE, THE MOONBEAM RIDER   *FAST
CHARLIE AND THE MOONBEAM*   Universal,
1979
STU PHILLIPS

FAST COMPANY   MGM, 1938
WILLIAM AXT†

FAST FOOD   Fries Entertainment, 1989
IRIS GILLON

FAST FORWARD   Columbia, 1985
TOM BAHLER
JACK HAYES
TOM SCOTT

FAST FRIENDS (TF)   Columbia TV, 1979
DON PEAKE

FAST GETAWAY   New Line, 1991
ADAM ROWLAND
BRUCE ROWLAND

FAST LANE BLUES (TF)   Viacom/Blinn-Thorp, 1978
CHARLES BERNSTEIN

FAST MONEY   Stu Segall Productions, 1996
TONY RIPPARETTI

FASTER, PUSSYCAT, KILL! KILL!   Eve, 1965
PAUL SAWTELL†

THE FASTEST GUN ALIVE   MGM, 1956
ANDRE PREVIN

FAST-WALKING   Pickman Films, 1982
LALO SCHIFRIN

THE FAT AND THE LEAN   1961
CHRISTOPHER KOMEDA†

FAT CITY   Columbia, 1972
MARVIN HAMLISCH

FAT GUY GOES NUTZOID   Troma, 1987
LEO KOTTKE

THE FAT MAN   Universal, 1951
BERNARD GREEN

FAT MAN AND LITTLE BOY   Paramount, 1989
ENNIO MORRICONE

FAT SPY   Magna, 1966
JOEL HIRSCHHORN
AL KASHA

FATAL ATTRACTION   Paramount, 1987
MAURICE JARRE

FATAL BEAUTY   MGM/UA, 1987
HAROLD FALTERMEYER

FATAL CHARM (CTF)   Jonathan D. Krane/Bruce Cohn Curtis, 1992
JAMES DONNELLAN

FATAL CONFESSION: A FATHER DOWLING MYSTERY (TF)   Fred Silverman Company/Strathmore Productions/Viacom Productions, 1987
DICK DEBENEDICTIS
ARTIE KANE

FATAL DECEPTION: MRS. LEE HARVEY OSWALD (TF)   David L. Wolper Prods./Bernard Sofronsky/Warner Bros. TV, 1993
HAROLD KLOSER

FATAL EXPOSURE (CTF)   G.C. Group/Wilshire Court, 1991
MICHEL COLOMBIER

FATAL FRIENDSHIP (TF)   Papazian-Hirsch, 1991
ARTHUR B. RUBINSTEIN

FATAL INSTINCT   MGM, 1993
RICHARD GIBBS

FATAL JUDGMENT (TF)   Jack Farren Productions/Group W Productions, 1988
LEE HOLDRIDGE

FATAL JUSTICE   Trident, 1993
JEFF WALTON

FATAL MEMORIES (TF)   Green's Point/WIC/MGM-UA TV, 1992
KEN WANNBERG

THE FATAL NIGHT   1948
STANLEY BLACK

FATAL VISION (TF)   NBC Entertainment, 1984
GIL MELLE

FATAL VOWS: THE ALEXANDRA O'HARA STORY (TF)   Roaring Fork/Karen Danaher-Dorr Prods./Republic/Spelling Ent., 1994
GEORGE S. CLINTON

FATE IS THE HUNTER   20th Century-Fox, 1964
JERRY GOLDSMITH

FATHER AND SCOUT (TF)   New Line Prods., 1994
DAVID KITAY

FATHER AND SON: DANGEROUS RELATIONS (TF)   Kushner-Locke/Logo/Gregory-Kahn, 1993
MARK SNOW

FATHER BROWN   THE DETECTIVE   Columbia, 1954
GEORGES AURIC†

THE FATHER CLEMENTS STORY (TF)   Zev Braun Productions/Interscope Communications, 1987
MARK SNOW

FATHER DOWLING: THE MISSING BODY MYSTERY (TF)   The Fred Silverman Company/Dean Hargrove Productions/Viacom, 1989
JOEL ROSENBAUM

FATHER FIGURE (TF)   Finnegan Associates/Time-Life Productions, 1980
BILLY GOLDENBERG

A FATHER FOR CHARLIE (TF)   Jacobs-Gardner Prods./Lo Co Entertainment/Finnegan-Pinchuk, 1994
DAVID SHIRE

FATHER GOOSE   Universal, 1964
CY COLEMAN

FATHER HOOD   Buena Vista, 1993
PATRICK O'HEARN

FATHER IS A BACHELOR   Columbia, 1950
ARTHUR MORTON

FATHER OF THE BRIDE   Buena Vista, 1991
ALAN SILVESTRI

FATHER OF THE BRIDE   MGM, 1950
ADOLPH DEUTSCH†

FATHER OF THE BRIDE (TF)   MGM TV, 1960
DAVID RAKSIN

FATHER OF THE BRIDE PART II   Buena Vista, 1995
ALAN SILVESTRI

FATHER TAKES A WIFE   RKO Radio, 1941
ROY WEBB†

FATHER WAS A FULLBACK   20th Century-Fox, 1949
CYRIL J. MOCKRIDGE†

A FATHER'S HOMECOMING (TF)   NBC Productions, 1988
TOM SCOTT

A FATHER'S REVENGE (TF)   Shadowplay/Rosco Productions/Phoenix Entertainment Group, 1987
KLAUS DOLDINGER

FATHERLAND   Angelika Films, 1986
CHRISTIAN KUNERT
GERULF PANNACH

FATHERLAND (CTF)   HBO Pictures, 1994
GARY CHANG

FATHERS & SONS   Addis-Wechsler, 1992
MASON DARING

FATHOM   20th Century-Fox, 1967
JOHN DANKWORTH

FATSO   20th Century-Fox, 1980
JOE RENZETTI

FATTI DI GENTE PERBENE   PAC, 1975
ENNIO MORRICONE

FAUSTINA   1968
ARMANDO TROVAJOLI

THE FAVOR   Orion, 1994
THOMAS NEWMAN

THE FAVORITE   Kings Road, 1989
WILLIAM GOLDSTEIN

FAVORITE SON (MS)   NBC Productions, 1988
JOHN MORRIS

THE FAVOUR, THE WATCH, AND THE VERY BIG FISH   1991
VLADIMIR COSMA

FBI CODE 98   Warner Bros., 1964
MAX STEINER†

F.B.I. OPERAZIONE PAKISTAN   1972
FRANCESCO DE MASI

F.B.I. OPERAZIONE VIPERA GIALLA   1966
FRANCESCO DE MASI

THE FBI STORY   Warner Bros., 1959
MAX STEINER†

F.D.R.—THE LAST YEAR (TF)   Titus Productions, 1980
LAURENCE ROSENTHAL

FEAR   1996
CARTER BURWELL

FEAR   CineTel Films, 1988
ALFI KABILJO

THE FEAR   Devin Intl., 1995
ROBERT O. RAGLAND

THE FEAR (MS)   Euston Films, 1988
COLIN TOWNS

FEAR (CTF)   Vestron, 1990
HENRY MANCINI†

FEAR AND DESIRE   Joseph Burstyn, Inc., 1954
GERALD FRIED

FEAR CITY   Chevy Chase Distribution, 1985
DICK HALLIGAN

FEAR IN THE NIGHT   International Co-Productions, 1972
JOHN MCCABE

THE FEAR INSIDE (CTF)   Viacom, 1992
MICHEL RUBINI

FEAR IS A KEY   Paramount, 1972
ROY BUDD†

FEAR NO EVIL   Avco Embassy, 1981
FRANK LALOGGIA
DAVID SPEAR

FEAR NO EVIL (TF)   Universal TV, 1969
BILLY GOLDENBERG

FEAR OF A BLACK HAT   Oakwood, 1993
LARRY ROBINSON

FEAR OF FEAR   1976
PEER RABEN

FEAR STALK (TF)   Donald March Productions/ITC, 1989
FRED KARLIN

FEAR STRIKES OUT   Paramount, 1957
ELMER BERNSTEIN

FEARLESS   Warner Bros.1993
MAURICE JARRE

THE FEARLESS VAMPIRE KILLERS, OR PARDON ME BUT YOUR TEETH ARE IN MY NECK   DANCE OF THE VAMPIRES   MGM, 1967
CHRISTOPHER KOMEDA†

FEAST OF JULY   Buena Vista, 1995
ZBIGNIEW PREISNER

FEDERAL HILL   Eagle Beach, 1994
DAVID BRAVO

FEDORA   United Artists, 1979
MIKLOS ROZSA†

FEDS   Warner Bros., 1988
RANDY EDELMAN

FEED THEM TO THE CANNIBALS! (FD)   1993
DIANE MCCLOUGHLIN

FEEDBACK   Feedback Company, 1979
JAKE STERN

FEEL THE HEAT   Trans World Entertainment, 1987
TOM CHASE
STEVE RUCKER

FEELIN' SCREWY   Raedon Entertainment, 1991
CHRIS WINFIELD

FEELING MINNESOTA   New Line, 1996
LOS LOBOS

FEIYING GAIWAK   ARMOUR OF GOD II: OPERATION CONDOR   1992
PETER PAU

FELALOM   BRATS   1992
GABOR PRESSER

FELICIE NANTEUIL   1942
JACQUES IBERT†

FELICITE   1979
ANTOINE DUHAMEL

FELIDAE   1994
ANNE DUDLEY

FELIX THE CAT (AF)   New World, 1989
CHRISTOPHER L. STONE

FELLINI SATYRICON   United Artists, 1970
NINO ROTA†

FELLINI'S ROMA   United Artists, 1972
NINO ROTA†

FELLOW TRAVELLER (CTF)   1990
COLIN TOWNS

THE FEMALE ANIMAL   Universal, 1958
HANS J. SALTER†

FEMALE ARTILLERY (TF)   Universal TV, 1973
FRANK DEVOL

THE FEMALE BODY   1964
TORU TAKEMITSU†

FEMALE INSTINCT (TF)   Universal TV, 1972
JERRY FIELDING†

FEMALE ON THE BEACH   Universal, 1955
HERMAN STEIN

THE FEMALE TRAP   Fanfare, 1968
STU PHILLIPS

THE FEMALE/LA FEMME ET LA PANTIN   Lopert, 1958
JEAN WIENER†

THE FEMALES   1970
PETER THOMAS

THE FEMININE TOUCH   MGM, 1941
FRANZ WAXMAN†

THE FEMININE TOUCH   Miracon Pictures, 1995
TONY HUMECKE

THE FEMINIST AND THE FUZZ (TF)   Screen Gems/Columbia Pictures TV, 1971
ALLYN FERGUSON
JACK ELLIOTT

FEMME FATALE   Crawford-Lane, 1990
PARMER FULLER

FEMME PUBLIQUE   1984
ALAIN WISNIAK

FEMMES DE PERSONNE   1983
GEORGES DELERUE†

FEMMES FATALES   CALMOS   New Line Cinema, 1976
GEORGES DELERUE†

FEMMINE DI LUSSO   1959
CARLO RUSTICHELLI

FEMMINE INSAZIABILI   1969
BRUNO NICOLAI

FENDER BENDER 500 (ATF)   Hanna-Barbera/ABC, 1991
BOB MITHOFF

FER DE LANCE (TF)   Leslie Stevens Productions, 1974
DOMINIC FRONTIERE

FERGIE AND ANDREW: BEHIND THE PALACE DOORS (TF)   Rosemont, 1992
ALLYN FERGUSON

FERNGULLY...THE LAST RAINFOREST   20th Century Fox, 1992
ALAN SILVESTRI

FERRIS BUELLER'S DAY OFF   Paramount, 1986
ALF CLAUSEN

FERRIS BUELLER'S DAY OFF   Paramount, 1986
IRA NEWBORN

FEU   FIRE   1970
MICHEL PORTAL

THE FEUD   Castle Hill, 1990
BRIAN EDDOLLS

FEUDIN', FUSSIN' AND A'FIGHTIN'   Universal, 1948
LEITH STEVENS†

FEUX DE JOIE   1938
PAUL MISRAKI

FEVER (CTF)   Saban-Scherick, 1991
MICHEL COLOMBIER

A FEVER IN THE BLOOD   Warner Bros., 1961
ERNEST GOLD

FEVER PITCH   MGM/UA, 1985
THOMAS DOLBY

A FEW DAYS IN WEASEL CREEK (TF)   Hummingbird Productions/Warner Bros., 1981
JAMES HORNER

A FEW DAYS WITH ME   Galaxy International, 1988
PHILIPPE SARDE

A FEW GOOD MEN   Columbia,1992
MARC SHAIMAN

ffolkes   NORTH SEAS HIJACK   Universal, 1980
MICHAEL J. LEWIS

FIDDLER ON THE ROOF   United Artists, 1971
JOHN WILLIAMS ★★

FIELD OF DREAMS   Universal, 1989
JAMES HORNER ★

FIELD OF HONOR   Cannon, 1986
ROY BUDD†

THE FIENDISH GHOULS   1960
STANLEY BLACK

THE FIENDISH PLOT OF DR. FU MANCHU   Orion/Warner Bros., 1980
MARC WILKINSON

FIERCE CREATURES   Universal, 1997
JERRY GOLDSMITH

FIESTA   MGM, 1947
JOHN GREEN† ★

FIFTH AVENUE GIRL   RKO Radio, 1939
ROBERT RUSSELL BENNETT†

THE FIFTH CORNER (TF)   John Herzfeld/Adelson-Baumgartner/TriStar, 1992
DAVID MICHAEL FRANK

THE FIFTH ELEMENT   Columbia, 1997
ERIC SERRA

THE FIFTH MISSILE (TF)   Bercovici-St. Johns Productions/MGM-UA TV, 1986
PINO DONAGGIO

FIFTY ROADS TO TOWN   20th Century-Fox, 1937
DAVID BUTTOLPH†

FIFTY/FIFTY   Cannon, 1993
PETER BERNSTEIN

FIFTY-FIFTY   1978
PEER RABEN

THE FIGHT FOR LIFE   Columbia, 1940
LOUIS GRUENBERG† ★

FIGHT FOR LIFE (TF)   Fries Entertainment, 1987
LAURENCE ROSENTHAL

FIGHT FOR THIRTEEN (TF)   Hearst, 1995
DENNIS MCCARTHY

FIGHT TO THE DEATH   METRALLETA STEIN   1975
CARLO RUSTICHELLI

THE FIGHTER (TF)   Martin Manulis Productions/The Catalina Production Group, 1983
PATRICK WILLIAMS

FIGHTER SQUADRON   Warner Bros., 1948
MAX STEINER†

THE FIGHTERS   1974
DAVID M. MATTHEWS

THE FIGHTING 69TH   Warner Bros., 1940
ADOLPH DEUTSCH†

FIGHTING BACK   Paramount, 1982
PIERO PICCIONI

FIGHTING BACK: THE STORY OF ROCKY BLIER (TF)   MTM Enterprises, 1980
FRED KARLIN

FIGHTING BILL FARGO   Universal, 1942
HANS J. SALTER†

A FIGHTING CHOICE (TF)   Walt Disney Pictures, 1986
BRAD FIEDEL

FIGHTING COAST GUARD   Republic, 1951
DAVID BUTTOLPH†

FIGHTING FATHER DUNNE   RKO Radio, 1948
ROY WEBB†

THE FIGHTING GRINGO   RKO Radio, 1939
ROY WEBB†

THE FIGHTING KENTUCKIAN   Republic, 1949
GEORGE ANTHEIL†

THE FIGHTING LADY (FD)   20th Century-Fox, 1944
DAVID BUTTOLPH†

FIGHTING MAD   20th Century-Fox, 1976
BRUCE LANGHORNE

THE FIGHTING O'FLYNN   Universal, 1949
FRANK SKINNER†

THE FIGHTING PRINCE OF DONEGAL   Buena Vista, 1966
GEORGE BRUNS

THE FIGHTING SEABEES   Republic, 1944
WALTER SCHARF ★

FIGURES IN A LANDSCAPE   National General, 1971
RICHARD RODNEY BENNETT

THE FILE ON THELMA JORDAN   THELMA JORDAN   Paramount, 1949
VICTOR YOUNG†

FILM D'AMORE E D'ANARCHIA   Peppercorn-Wormser, 1973
NINO ROTA†

FILM MADE TO MUSIC WRITTEN BY PAUL BOWLES   Rudolph Burckhardt, 1939
PAUL BOWLES

FILOUS ET COMPAGNIE 1957
GEORGES VAN PARYS†

FILUMENA MARTURANO 1951
NINO ROTA†

FINAL ANALYSIS Warner Bros., 1992
GEORGE FENTON

FINAL APPEAL (TF) Republic TV, 1993
CHARLES BERNSTEIN

FINAL APPROACH Trimark, 1991
KIRK HUNTER

FINAL CHAPTER—WALKING TALL American
International, 1977
WALTER SCHARF

FINAL COMBINATION Propaganda, 1996
ROLFE KENT

THE FINAL CONFLICT 20th Century-Fox, 1981
JERRY GOLDSMITH

THE FINAL COUNTDOWN United Artists, 1980
JOHN SCOTT

THE FINAL DAYS (TF) The Samuels Film Co., 1989
CLIFF EIDELMAN

FINAL EXAM MPM, 1981
GARY SCOTT

FINAL IMPACT PM Entertainment, 1992
JOHN GONZALEZ

FINAL JUSTICE Arista, 1985
DAVID BELL

THE FINAL OPTION WHO DARES WINS MGM/
UA, 1982
ROY BUDD†

FINAL SHOT: THE HANK GATHERS STORY (TF)
McGillen/Enright/Tribune, 1992
STANLEY CLARKE

THE FINAL TERROR Aquarius, 1984
SUSAN JUSTIN

THE FINAL TEST 1953
BENJAMIN FRANKEL†

FINAL VERDICT (CTF) Foxboro Ent., 1991
DAVID MCHUGH

FINALMENTE...LE MILLE E UNA NOTTE Pink
Medusa, 1972
CARLO SAVINA

FINCHE DURA LA TEMPESTA 1963
CARLO RUSTICHELLI

FINDERS KEEPERS Universal, 1951
HANS J. SALTER†

FINDERS KEEPERS Warner Bros., 1984
KEN THORNE

FINDING THE WAY HOME (TF) Peter K. Duchow
Enterprises, 1991
LEE HOLDRIDGE

FINE GOLD Overseas Film Group, 1988
VLADIMIR HORUNZHY

A FINE MADNESS Warner Bros., 1966
JOHN ADDISON

A FINE MESS Columbia, 1986
HENRY MANCINI†

A FINE PAIR RUBA AL PROSSIMO TUO 1968
ENNIO MORRICONE

THE FINEST HOURS 1964
RON GRAINER†

FINGERMAN Allied Artists, 1955
PAUL DUNLAP

FINGERS Brut Productions, 1978
GEORGE BARRIE

FINGERS AT THE WINDOW MGM, 1942
BRONISLAU KAPER†

FINISH LINE (CTF) Guber-Peters Entertainment
Productions/Phoenix Entertainment Group, 1989
WILLIAM OLVIS

FINISHING SCHOOL RKO Radio, 1934
MAX STEINER†

FINNEGAN BEGIN AGAIN (CTF) HBO Premiere
Films/Zenith Productions/Jennie & Co. Film
Productions, 1985
MICHAEL COLINA
DAVID SANBORN

FINNEGANS WAKE Evergreen Films, 1965
ELLIOT KAPLAN†

FIORILE 1993
NICOLA PIOVANI

FIRE 1970
MICHEL PORTAL

FIRE AND ICE Concorde, 1987
HAROLD FALTERMEYER

FIRE AND ICE (AF) 20th Century Fox, 1983
WILLIAM KRAFT

FIRE BIRDS Buena Vista, 1990
DAVID NEWMAN

THE FIRE BRIGADE MGM, 1926
WILLIAM AXT†

FIRE DOWN BELOW Columbia, 1957
ARTHUR BENJAMIN†

FIRE FESTIVAL 1985
TORU TAKEMITSU†

A FIRE IN THE SKY (TF) Bill Driskell Productions,
1978
PAUL CHIHARA

FIRE IN THE DARK (TF) Kushner-Locke/Don
Gregory and Bernie Kahn, 1991
ARTHUR KEMPEL ☆

FIRE IN THE SKY Paramount, 1993
MARK ISHAM

THE FIRE NEXT TIME (TF) RHI Entertainment/Kirch
Group, 1993
LAURENCE ROSENTHAL

FIRE ON THE MOUNTAIN (TF) Bonnard
Productions, 1982
BASIL POLEDOURIS

FIRE OVER AFRICA Columbia, 1954
BENJAMIN FRANKEL†

FIRE OVER ENGLAND 1937
RICHARD ADDINSELL†

FIRE SALE 20th Century-Fox, 1977
DAVE GRUSIN

THE FIRE THIS TIME (FD) Blacktop Films, 1994
JAMES VERBOORT

FIRE WITH FIRE Paramount, 1986
HOWARD SHORE

FIRE! (TF) Irwin Allen Productions/Warner Bros. TV,
1977
RICHARD LASALLE

FIRE! TRAPPED ON THE 37TH FLOOR (TF)
Papazian-Hirsch/Republic, 1991
GIL MELLE

THE FIREBALL 20th Century-Fox, 1950
VICTOR YOUNG†

FIREBALL 500 American International, 1966
LES BAXTER†

FIREBALL FORWARD (TF) 20th Century-Fox, 1972
LIONEL NEWMAN†

FIREBIRD 2015 2002 INC, Canadian
LAWRENCE SHRAGGE

THE FIREBRAND 20th Century-Fox, 1962
RICHARD LASALLE

FIRECRACKER New World, 1981
W. MICHAEL LEWIS
LAURIN RINDER

FIRECREEK Warner Bros., 1968
ALFRED NEWMAN†

FIRED WIFE Universal, 1943
FRANK SKINNER†

FIREFIGHTER (TF) Forest Hills Productions/Embassy
TV, 1986
DANA KAPROFF

THE FIREFLY MGM, 1937
HERBERT STOTHART†

FIREFOX Warner Bros., 1982
MAURICE JARRE

FIREHEAD Pyramid, 1990
VLADIMIR HORUNZHY

FIREHOUSE (TF) Metromedia Producers Corporation/
Stonehenge Productions, 1973
TOM SCOTT

FIREMAN SAVE MY CHILD Universal, 1954
HENRY MANCINI†
HERMAN STEIN

FIREMAN, SAVE MY CHILD Warner Bros., 1932
W. FRANKE HARLING†

FIREPOWER 1979
JAY CHATTAWAY

FIREPOWER AFD, 1979
GATO BARBIERI

FIRES IN THE MIRROR (TF) American Playhouse,
1993
JOSEPH JARMAN
TONY MANGURIAN

FIRES WITHIN Pathe/MGM, 1991
MAURICE JARRE

FIRESTARTER Universal, 1984
TANGERINE DREAM
CHRISTOPHER FRANKE

FIRESTORM 20th Century Fox, 1997
J. PETER ROBINSON

FIRESTORM: 72 HOURS IN OAKLAND (TF)
Gross Weston/Capital Cities-ABC/Connell
Entertainment, 1993
MISHA SEGAL

FIREWALKER Cannon, 1986
GARY CHANG

THE FIRING LINE Silver Screen, 1991
MARITA MANUEL

THE FIRM Paramount, 1993
DAVE GRUSIN ★★

FIRST AFFAIR (TF) CBS Entertainment, 1983
LEE HOLDRIDGE

FIRST AMONG EQUALS (MS) Grenada, 1987
RICHARD HARVEY

FIRST BLOOD Orion, 1982
JERRY GOLDSMITH

FIRST COMES COURAGE Columbia, 1943
ERNST TOCH†

THE FIRST DEADLY SIN Filmways Pictures, 1980
GORDON JENKINS†

FIRST DESIRES AMLF, 1983
PHILIPPE SARDE

FIRST DO NO HARM Jaffe-Braunstein, 1996
HUMMIE MANN

THE FIRST ECHELON 1956
DMITRI SHOSTAKOVITCH†

FIRST FAMILY Warner Bros., 1980
RALPH BURNS

THE FIRST HUNDRED YEARS MGM, 1938
WILLIAM AXT†

THE FIRST HUNDRED YEARS (CTD) Silver
Pictures, 1995
MICHAEL KAMEN

THE FIRST KANGAROOS (TF) Roadshow/Channel
4, 1987
WILLIAM MOTZIG

FIRST KID Buena Vista, 1996
RICHARD GIBBS

FIRST KNIGHT Columbia, 1995
JERRY GOLDSMITH

FIRST LADY Warner Bros., 1937
MAX STEINER†

FIRST LOVE 1978
RIZ ORTOLANI

FIRST LOVE Paramount, 1977
JOHN BARRY

FIRST LOVE Universal, 1940
HANS J. SALTER†

FIRST MEN IN THE MOON Columbia, 1964
LAURIE JOHNSON

FIRST MONDAY IN OCTOBER Paramount, 1981
IAN FRASER

THE FIRST NUDIE MUSICAL Paramount, 1976
BRUCE KIMMEL

THE FIRST OF THE FEW RKO Radio, 1942
SIR WILLIAM WALTON†

THE FIRST OLYMPICS - ATHENS 1896 (MS)
Larry White-Gary Allison Productions/Columbia TV,
1984
BRUCE BROUGHTON ☆☆

THE FIRST POWER Orion, 1990
STEWART COPELAND

FIRST STEPS (TF) CBS Entertainment, 1985
LEONARD ROSENMAN

THE FIRST TEACHER Mosfilm/Kirghizfilm, 1965
VYECHESLAV OVCHINNIKOV

THE FIRST TEXAN Allied Artists, 1956
ROY WEBB†

THE FIRST TIME Columbia, 1952
FREDERICK HOLLANDER†

THE FIRST TIME New Line Cinema, 1983
LANNY MEYERS

THE FIRST TIME United Artists, 1969
KENYON HOPKINS

THE FIRST TIME (TF) Moonlight Productions/Orion
TV Productions, 1982
FRED KARLIN

FIRST TO FIGHT Warner Bros., 1967
FRED STEINER

THE FIRST WIVES CLUB Paramount, 1996
MARC SHAIMAN ★

FIRST YANK INTO TOKYO RKO Radio, 1945
LEIGH HARLINE†

FIRST YOU CRY (TF) MTM Enterprises, 1978
PETER MATZ ☆

FIRSTBORN Paramount, 1984
MICHAEL SMALL

A FISH CALLED WANDA MGM/UA, 1988
JOHN DUPREZ

THE FISH THAT SAVED PITTSBURGH United
Artists, 1979
THOM BELL

THE FISHER KING TriStar, 1991
GEORGE FENTON ★

FISHERMAN'S WHARF RKO Radio, 1939
VICTOR YOUNG†

F.I.S.T. United Artists, 1978
BILL CONTI

FIST OF FEAR TOUCH OF DEATH Aquarius, 1980
KEITH MANSFIELD

FISTFIGHTER Taurus Entertainment, 1989
EMILIO KAUDERER

A FISTFUL OF DOLLARS United Artists, 1964
ENNIO MORRICONE

FIT FOR A KING RKO Radio, 1937
ARTHUR MORTON

FITZCARRALDO New World, 1982
POPOL VUH

FITZWILLY United Artists, 1967
JOHN WILLIAMS

FIVE A.M. N. Tanis Company, 1985
WENDY BLACKSTONE

FIVE BRANDED WOMEN 1960
ANGELO FRANCESCO LAVAGNINO†

FIVE CAME BACK RKO Radio, 1939
ROY WEBB†

FIVE CORNERS Cineplex Odeon, 1987
JAMES NEWTON HOWARD

THE FIVE DAY LOVER Kingsley International, 1961
GEORGES DELERUE†

FIVE DAYS AND FIVE NIGHTS 1948
DMITRI SHOSTAKOVITCH†

FIVE DAYS FROM HOME Universal, 1978
BILL CONTI

FIVE DAYS ONE SUMMER The Ladd Company/
Warner Bros., 1982
ELMER BERNSTEIN

FIVE DESPERATE WOMEN (TF) Aaron Spelling
Productions, 1971
PAUL GLASS

FIVE FINGER EXERCISE Columbia, 1962
JEROME MOROSS†

FIVE FINGERS 20th Century-Fox, 1952
BERNARD HERRMANN†

FIVE GRAVES TO CAIRO Paramount, 1943
MIKLOS ROZSA†

FIVE GUNS TO TOMBSTONE United Artists, 1960
BERT A. SHEFTER

THE FIVE HEARTBEATS 20th Century Fox, 1991
STANLEY CLARKE
CHRISTOPHER YOUNG

THE FIVE MAN ARMY UN ESERCITO DI 5
UOMIN MGM, 1970
ENNIO MORRICONE

FIVE MILES TO MIDNIGHT United Artists, 1963
MIKIS THEODORAKIS

FIVE MILLION YEARS TO EARTH
QUATERMASS AND THE PIT 20th
Century-Fox, 1968
TRISTRAM CARY

THE FIVE OF ME (TF) Jack Farren Productions/
Factor-Newland Production Corporation, 1981
FRED KARLIN

THE FIVE PENNIES Paramount, 1959
LEITH STEVENS† ★

FIVE WEEKS IN A BALLOON 20th Century-Fox,
1962
PAUL SAWTELL†

FIXED BAYONETS! 20th Century-Fox, 1951
ROY WEBB†

THE FIXER MGM, 1968
MAURICE JARRE

FIXER DUGAN RKO Radio, 1939
ROY WEBB†

FLAGRANT DESIR A CERTAIN DESIRE UGC,
1986
GABRIEL YARED

THE FLAME Republic, 1947
HEINZ ROEMHELD†

THE FLAME AND THE ARROW Warner Bros.,
1950
MAX STEINER† ★

THE FLAME BARRIER United Artists, 1958
GERALD FRIED

THE FLAME IS LOVE (TF) Ed Friendly Productions/
Friendly-O'Herlihy Ltd., 1979
MORTON STEVENS†

THE FLAME OF NEW ORLEANS Universal, 1941
FRANK SKINNER†

FLAMES ON THE VOLGA 1950
DMITRI KABALEVSKY†

THE FLAMINGO KID 20th Century Fox, 1984
CURT SOBEL

FLAMINGO ROAD Warner Bros., 1949
MAX STEINER†

FLAMINGO ROAD (TF) MF Productions/Lorimar
Productions, 1980
GERALD FRIED

FLAP THE LAST WARRIOR Warner Bros., 1970
MARVIN HAMLISCH

FLARE UP MGM, 1969
LES BAXTER†

FLASH GORDON Universal, 1980
HOWARD BLAKE
QUEEN

A FLASH OF GREEN Spectrafilm, 1984
CHARLES ENGSTROM

FLASHBACK 1968
BRUNO NICOLAI

FLASHBACK Paramount, 1990
BARRY GOLDBERG

FLASHDANCE Paramount, 1983
GIORGIO MORODER

FLASHPOINT Tri-Star, 1984
TANGERINE DREAM
CHRISTOPHER FRANKE

THE FLAT 1968
ZDENEK LISKA

FLATBED ANNIE AND SWEETIE PIE: LADY
TRUCKERS (TF) Moonlight Productions/Filmways,
1979
DON PEAKE

FLATLINERS Columbia, 1990
JAMES NEWTON HOWARD

FLAXI MARTIN Warner Bros., 1949
WILLIAM LAVA†

A FLEA IN HER EAR 20th Century-Fox, 1968
BRONISLAU KAPER†

FLED MGM-UA, 1996
GRAEME REVELL

THE FLEET THAT CAME TO STAY Paramount,
1946
LEHMAN ENGEL†

THE FLEMISH FARM 1943
RALPH VAUGHAN WILLIAMS†

FLESH + BLOOD Orion, 1985
BASIL POLEDOURIS

FLESH AND BLOOD (TF) The Jozak Company/
Cypress Point Productions/Paramount TV, 1979
BILLY GOLDENBERG

FLESH AND BONE Paramount, 1993
THOMAS NEWMAN

FLESH AND DESIRE 1955
GEORGES AURIC†

FLESH AND FANTASY Universal, 1943
ALEXANDRE TANSMAN†

FLESH AND FLAME MGM, 1959
ALBERT GLASSER

FLESH AND FURY Universal, 1952
HANS J. SALTER†

FLESH AND THE DEVIL 1982
CARL DAVIS

FLESH AND THE SPUR American International,
1957
RONALD STEIN†

FLESH AND THE WOMAN *LE GRAND JEU*
Dominant Pictures, 1954
GEORGES VAN PARYS†

FLESH FOR FRANKENSTEIN Bryanston, 1974
CLAUDIO GIZZI

FLESH SUITCASE Valiant Films, 1995
MARK MOTHERSBAUGH

FLESH WILL SURRENDER *IL DELITTO DI
GIOVANNI EPISCOPO* 1947
NINO ROTA†

FLESHBURN Crown International, 1984
DON FELDER
ARTHUR KEMPEL

FLETCH Universal, 1985
HAROLD FALTERMEYER

FLETCH LIVES Universal, 1989
HAROLD FALTERMEYER

FLEUR D'OSEILLE 1968
MICHEL MAGNE†

FLEXING WITH MONTY Quarter Moon Films, 1994
MIRIAM CUTLER

FLIC OU VOYOU 1979
PHILIPPE SARDE

FLIC STORY Adel Productions/Lira Films/Mondial,
1975
CLAUDE BOLLING

FLICEK THE BALL *THE NAUGHTY BALL* (AF)
1956
ZDENEK LISKA

FLICK 1970
PAUL HOFFERT

FLICKS United Film Distribution Co., 1987
JOHN W. MORGAN

THE FLIGHT 1978
GUENTHER FISCHER

FLIGHT 90: DISASTER ON THE POTOMAC (TF)
Sheldon Pinchuk Productions/Finnegan Associates,
1984
GIL MELLE

FLIGHT COMMAND MGM, 1940
FRANZ WAXMAN†

FLIGHT FOR FREEDOM RKO Radio, 1943
ROY WEBB†

FLIGHT FROM ASHIYA United Artists, 1964
FRANK CORDELL†

FLIGHT FROM DESTINY Warner Bros., 1941
HEINZ ROEMHELD†

FLIGHT INTO DARKNESS 1935
ARTHUR HONEGGER†

FLIGHT LIEUTENANT Columbia, 1942
WERNER R. HEYMANN†

FLIGHT NURSE Republic, 1954
VICTOR YOUNG†

THE FLIGHT OF THE PHOENIX 20th Century-Fox,
1966
FRANK DEVOL

FLIGHT OF THE BLACK ANGEL (CTF)
Hess-Kallbers, 1991
RICHARD MARVIN

FLIGHT OF THE DOVES Columbia, 1971
ROY BUDD†

FLIGHT OF THE INTRUDER Paramount, 1991
BASIL POLEDOURIS

FLIGHT OF THE NAVIGATOR Buena Vista, 1986
ALAN SILVESTRI

FLIGHT OF THE RAINBIRD Dutch
LAURENS VAN ROOYEN

THE FLIGHT THAT DISAPPEARED United Artists,
1961
RICHARD LASALLE

FLIGHT TO FAME Columbia, 1938
SIDNEY CUTNER†

FLIGHT TO HOLOCAUST (TF) Aycee Productions/
First Artists Production Company, 1977
PAUL WILLIAMS

THE FLIM FLAM MAN 20th Century-Fox, 1967
JERRY GOLDSMITH

THE FLINTSTONES Universal, 1994
DAVID NEWMAN

FLIPPER Universal, 1996
JOEL MCNEELY

FLIRT 1996
NED RIFLE
JEFFREY TAYLOR

FLIRTING WITH DISASTER Miramax, 1996
STEPHEN ENDELMAN

FLIRTING WITH FATE MGM, 1938
VICTOR YOUNG†

THE FLOOD Paramount, 1997
CHRISTOPHER YOUNG

FLOOD (TF) Irwin Allen Productions/Warner Bros. TV,
1976
RICHARD LASALLE

FLOOD TIME Universal, 1958
HENRY MANCINI†

THE FLOOD: WHO WILL SAVE OUR CHILDREN?
(TF) Wolper Organization/Warner Bros. TV, 1993
GARRY MCDONALD
LAURIE STONE

FLOODS OF FEAR Universal, 1958
ALAN RAWSTHORNE†

THE FLORADORA GIRL MGM, 1930
HERBERT STOTHART†

FLORENCE NIGHTENGALE (TF) Cypress Point
Productions, 1985
STANLEY MYERS†

FLORIAN MGM, 1940
FRANZ WAXMAN†

FLORIDA STRAITS (CTF) HBO Premiere Films/
Robert Cooper Productions, 1986
MICHEL COLOMBIER

FLOUNDERING Front Films, 1994
PRAY FOR RAIN

THE FLOWER OF MY SECRET 1996
ALBERTO IGLESIAS

FLOWERS IN THE ATTIC New World, 1987
CHRISTOPHER YOUNG

FLOWING GOLD Warner Bros., 1940
ADOLPH DEUTSCH†

FLUGEL UND FESSELN West German
JURGEN KNIEPER

FLUKE MGM-UA, 1995
CARLOS SILIOTTO

THE FLY 20th Century Fox, 1986
HOWARD SHORE

THE FLY 20th Century-Fox, 1958
PAUL SAWTELL†
BERT A. SHEFTER

FLY AWAY HOME Columbia, 1996
MARK ISHAM

FLY AWAY HOME (TF) An Lac Productions/Warner
Bros. TV, 1981
LEE HOLDRIDGE

THE FLY II 20th Century Fox, 1989
CHRISTOPHER YOUNG

FLYERS OF THE OPEN SKIES 1977
ALFI KABILJO

FLYING BLIND Paramount, 1941
DIMITRI TIOMKIN†

FLYING BLIND (TF) NBC Productions, 1990
PHIL MARSHALL

FLYING CADETS Universal, 1941
HANS J. SALTER†

THE FLYING DEUCES RKO Radio, 1939
JOHN LEIPOLD†
LEO SHUKEN†

FLYING DEVILS RKO Radio, 1933
MAX STEINER†

FLYING DOWN TO RIO RKO Radio, 1933
MAX STEINER†

FLYING FEET 1929
PERCY GRAINGER†

THE FLYING FONTAINES Columbia, 1956
MISCHA BAKALEINIKOFF†

FLYING HIGH (TF) Mark Carliner Productions, 1978
JONATHAN TUNICK

THE FLYING IRISHMAN RKO Radio, 1939
ROY WEBB†

FLYING LEATHERNECKS RKO Radio, 1951
ROY WEBB†

THE FLYING MISSILE Columbia, 1951
GEORGE DUNING

THE FLYING SERPENT Producers Releasing Corp.,
1946
LEO ERDODY†

THE FLYING SNEAKER 1992
PETER SKOUMAL

FLYING TIGERS Republic, 1942
VICTOR YOUNG† ★

FLYING WITH MUSIC United Artists, 1942
EDWARD WARD† ★

THE FOG Avco Embassy, 1981
JOHN CARPENTER

FOG ISLAND Universal, 1945
KARL HAJOS†

FOLIES BOURGEOISES FFCM, 1976
MANUEL DE SICA

FOLKS ! 20th Century Fox, 1992
MICHEL COLOMBIER

THE FOLKS AT RED WOLF INN *TERROR
HOUSE* Scope III, 1972
BILL MARX

FOLLE A TUER 1975
PHILIPPE SARDE

FOLLOW ME! Cinerama, 1969
STU PHILLIPS

FOLLOW ME, BOYS! Buena Vista, 1966
GEORGE BRUNS

FOLLOW THAT CAMEL Schoenfeld Film Distributing,
1967
ERIC ROGERS†

FOLLOW THAT DREAM Universal, 1962
HANS J. SALTER†

FOLLOW THE BOYS MGM, 1963
RON GOODWIN

FOLLOW THE BOYS Universal, 1944
LEIGH HARLINE†
FRANK SKINNER†
OLIVER WALLACE†

FOLLOW THE FLEET RKO Radio, 1936
MAX STEINER†

FOLLOW THE RIVER (TF) Signboard Hill, 1995
ERNEST TROOST

FOLLOW THE SUN 20th Century-Fox, 1951
CYRIL J. MOCKRIDGE†

FOLLOW YOUR HEART DMG Entertainment, 1997
HARRY MANFREDINI

FOLLOWING HER HEART (TF) Atlantis/Roni
Weisberg Prods./Ann-Margret Prods., 1994
MARK SNOW

FOND MEMORIES National Film Board of Canada,
1982
JEAN COUSINEAU

FONG SAI-YUK II 1993
LOWELL

FONG SAI-YUK TSUKTSAP *FONG SAI-YUK II*
1993
LOWELL

THE FOOD OF THE GODS American International,
1976
ELLIOT KAPLAN†

FOOL FOR LOVE Cannon, 1985
GEORGE BURT

FOOL'S FIRE American Playhouse, 1992
ELLIOT GOLDENTHAL

FOOLIN' AROUND Columbia, 1980
CHARLES BERNSTEIN

FOOLISH WIVES Universal, 1922
SIGMUND ROMBERG†

FOOLS OF FORTUNE New Line Cinema, 1990
HANS ZIMMER

FOOLS RUSH IN 1997
ALAN SILVESTRI

FOOTLOOSE Paramount, 1984
MILES GOODMAN†

FOOTSTEPS (TF) Metromedia Producers
Corporation/Stonehenge Productions, 1972
ERNEST GOLD

FOOTSTEPS IN THE DARK Warner Bros., 1941
FREDERICK HOLLANDER†

FOOTSTEPS IN THE FOG Columbia, 1955
BENJAMIN FRANKEL†

FOR A FEW DOLLARS MORE United Artists, 1965
ENNIO MORRICONE

FOR ALL MANKIND (FD) Apollo Associates, 1989
BRIAN ENO

FOR CLEMENCE 1977
MICHEL PORTAL

FOR HEAVEN'S SAKE 20th Century-Fox, 1950
ALFRED NEWMAN†

FOR KEEPS Tri-Star, 1988
BILL CONTI

FOR LADIES ONLY (TF) The Catalina Production
Group/Viacom, 1981
LEE HOLDRIDGE

FOR LOVE AND GLORY (TF) Gerber Co./CBS,
1993
JOHN DEBNEY

FOR LOVE AND GOLD *L'ARMATA
BRANCALEONE* Fair Film, 1966
CARLO RUSTICHELLI

FOR LOVE OF IVY Cinerama Releasing Corporation,
1968
QUINCY JONES

FOR LOVE OR MONEY Universal, 1963
FRANK DEVOL

FOR LOVE OR MONEY Universal, 1993
BRUCE BROUGHTON

FOR LOVE OR MONEY (TF) Robert Papazian
Productions/Henerson-Hirsch Productions, 1984
BILLY GOLDENBERG

FOR LOVERS ONLY (TF) Henerson-Hirsch
Productions/Caesar Palace Productions, 1982
PETE RUGOLO

FOR ME AND MY GAL MGM, 1942
GEORGE BASSMAN

FOR PETE'S SAKE Columbia, 1974
ARTIE BUTLER

FOR QUEEN AND COUNTRY Atlantic Releasing,
1988
MICHAEL KAMEN

FOR ROSEANNA Fine Line, 1996
TREVOR JONES

FOR RICHER, FOR POORER (CTF) Citadel
Entertainment, 1992
MILES GOODMAN†

FOR THE BOYS 20th Century Fox, 1991
DAVE GRUSIN

FOR THE LOVE OF AARON (TF) Patterdale Prods./
The Storyteller Group/Marian Rees Associates, 1994
LAWRENCE SHRAGGE

FOR THE LOVE OF BENJI Mulberry Square, 1978
EUEL BOX

FOR THE LOVE OF IT (TF) Charles Fries
Productions/Neila Productions, 1980
JIMMIE HASKELL

FOR THE LOVE OF MARY Universal, 1948
FRANK SKINNER†

**FOR THE LOVE OF MY CHILD: THE ANISSA
AYALA STORY (TF)** Viacom/Stonehenge, 1993
JOSEPH JULIAN GONZALES

FOR THE LOVE OF NANCY (TF) Vin Di Bona
Prods./ABC TV Network, 1994
DAN SLIDER

FOR THE MOMENT John Aaron Features II, 1994
VICTOR DAVIES

FOR THE TERM OF HIS NATURAL LIFE (MS)
1982
SIMON WALKER

FOR THE VERY FIRST TIME (TF) Michael Zinberg/
Lorimar TV, 1991
GREGORY SILL

FOR THEIR OWN GOOD (TF) Avnet-Kerner Co.,
1993
J.A.C. REDFORD

FOR THOSE I LOVED 20th Century-Fox, 1983
MAURICE JARRE

FOR THOSE WHO THINK YOUNG United Artists,
1964
JERRY FIELDING†

FOR US, THE LIVING (TF) Charles Fries
Productions, 1983
GERALD FRIED

FOR WHOM THE BELL TOLLS Paramount, 1943
VICTOR YOUNG† ★

FOR YOUR EYES ONLY United Artists, 1981
BILL CONTI

THE FORBIDDEN DANCE 21st Century, 1990
VLADIMIR HORUNZHY

THE FORBIDDEN STREET *BRITTANIA MEWS*
20th Century-Fox, 1949
MALCOLM ARNOLD

FORBIDDEN Universal, 1953
FRANK SKINNER†

FORBIDDEN (CTF) HBO Premiere Films/Mark
Forstater Productions/Clasart/Anthea Productions,
1985
TANGERINE DREAM
CHRISTOPHER FRANKE

FORBIDDEN GAMES Cannon, 1989
GREG DE BELLES

FORBIDDEN LOVE (TF) Gross-Weston Productions,
1982
HAGOOD HARDY

FORBIDDEN NIGHTS (TF) Tristine Rainer
Productions/Warner Bros., 1990
LUCIA HWONG

FORBIDDEN PLANET MGM, 1956
BEBE BARRON
LOUIS BARRON

FORBIDDEN WORLD New World, 1982
SUSAN JUSTIN

FORBIDDEN ZONE Samuel Goldwyn Co., 1980
DANNY ELFMAN

FORCE 10 FROM NAVARONE American
International, 1978
RON GOODWIN

FORCE FIVE (TF) Universal TV, 1975
JAMES DIPASQUALLE

FORCE OF ARMS Warner Bros., 1951
MAX STEINER†

FORCE OF EVIL MGM, 1948
DAVID RAKSIN

A FORCE OF ONE American Cinema Releasing,
1979
DICK HALLIGAN

FORCE OF THE NINJA Reel Movies
DAN SLIDER

FORCE ON FORCE New Line, 1994
KEVIN KINER

FORCE: FIVE American Cinema, 1981
WILLIAM GOLDSTEIN

FORCED LANDING Paramount, 1941
DIMITRI TIOMKIN†

FORCED TO KILL PM, 1993
MARTIN D. BOLIN

FORCED VENGEANCE MGM/United Artists, 1982
WILLIAM GOLDSTEIN

FORCED WITNESS Cannon, 1984
DOV SELTZER

FORD: THE MAN AND THE MACHINE (TF)
Lantana Productions/Robert Halmi, Inc., 1987
PAUL J. ZAZA

FORE PLAY Cinema National, 1975
GARY WILLIAM FRIEDMAN

A FOREIGN AFFAIR Paramount, 1948
FREDERICK HOLLANDER†

FOREIGN AFFAIRS (CTF) Stagescreen Prods./
Interscope Communications, 1993
CYNTHIA MILLAR

FOREIGN BODY Orion, 1986
KEN HOWARD

FOREIGN CORRESPONDENT United Artists, 1940
ALFRED NEWMAN†

A FOREIGN FIELD 1993
GEOFFREY BURGON

FOREIGN STUDENT Universal, 1994
JEAN-CLAUDE PETIT

THE FOREMAN WENT TO FRANCE 1941
SIR WILLIAM WALTON†

FOREPLAY Cinema National Corporation, 1975
STAN VINCENT

THE FOREST TERROR IN THE FOREST Fury Film
Distribution Ltd., 1983
RICHARD HIERONYMOUS
ALAN OLDFIELD

THE FOREST RANGERS Paramount, 1942
VICTOR YOUNG†

FOREVER Triax/DDM, 1992
THE RH FACTOR

FOREVER (TF) Roger Gimbel Productions/EMI TV,
1978
FRED KARLIN

FOREVER AMBER 20th Century-Fox, 1947
DAVID RAKSIN ★

FOREVER AND A DAY RKO Radio, 1943
ANTHONY COLLINS†

FOREVER EMMANUELLE Movies for Cable, 1982
FRANCO MICALIZZI

FOREVER FEMALE Paramount, 1953
VICTOR YOUNG†

FOREVER KNIGHT: DARK KNIGHT (TF)
Paragon/Tele-Munchen/Tri-Star TV, 1991
FRED MOLLIN

FOREVER LIKE THE ROSE (AF) Hanna-Barbera
Prods., 1978
BOB ALCIVAR

FOREVER YOUNG Warner Bros., 1992
JERRY GOLDSMITH

FOREVER YOUNG, FOREVER FREE
E'LOLLIPOP Universal, 1976
LEE HOLDRIDGE

FOREVER YOURS Monogram, 1944
DIMITRI TIOMKIN†

FOREVER, DARLING MGM, 1955
BRONISLAU KAPER†

FORFAITURE 1936
MICHEL MICHELET†

THE FORGET ME NOT MURDERS (TF) Janek
Prods./Pendick Ent./Spelling TV, 1994
KEN HARRISON

FORGET PARIS Columbia, 1995
MARC SHAIMAN

THE FORGOTTEN MAN (TF) Grauman Productions,
1971
DAVE GRUSIN

THE FORGOTTEN VILLAGE (FD) 1941
HANNS EISLER†

THE FORMULA MGM/United Artists, 1980
BILL CONTI

FORMULA FOR MURDER Fulvia International,
1986
FRANCESCO DE MASI

FORREST GUMP Paramount, 1994
ALAN SILVESTRI ★

FORSAKING ALL OTHERS MGM, 1934
WILLIAM AXT†

FORSE UN FIORE 1973
ENNIO MORRICONE

FORT ALESIA 1965
CARLO RUSTICHELLI

FORT ALGIERS United Artists, 1953
MICHEL MICHELET†

FORT APACHE RKO Radio, 1948
RICHARD HAGEMAN†

FORT APACHE THE BRONX 20th Century-Fox,
1981
JONATHAN TUNICK

FORT BOWIE United Artists, 1958
LES BAXTER†

FORT COURAGEOUS 20th Century-Fox, 1965
RICHARD LASALLE

FORT DOBBS Warner Bros., 1958
MAX STEINER†

FORT SAGANNE A.A.A., 1984
PHILIPPE SARDE

FORT UTAH Paramount, 1967
JIMMIE HASKELL

FORT VENGEANCE Allied Artists, 1953
PAUL DUNLAP

FORT WORTH Warner Bros., 1951
DAVID BUTTOLPH†

FORT YUMA United Artists, 1955
PAUL DUNLAP

FORTITUDE (TF) 1994
GABRIEL YARED

FORTRESS Dimension, 1993
FREDERIC TALGORN

FORTRESS (CTF) Crawford Productions/HBO
Premiere Films, 1985
DANNY BECKERMAN

FORTUNA American International, 1966
DOV SELTZER

THE FORTUNE Columbia, 1975
DAVID SHIRE

FORTUNE CARREE 1954
PAUL MISRAKI

THE FORTUNE COOKIE United Artists, 1966
ANDRE PREVIN

FORTUNE DANE (TF) Stormy Weathers Productions/
The Movie Company Enterprises/The Rosenzweig
Company, 1986
DOUG TIMM

FORTUNELLA 1957
NINO ROTA†

FORTY DEUCE Island, 1982
MANU DIBANGO

FORTY GUNS 20th Century-Fox, 1957
HARRY SUKMAN†

FORTY NAUGHTY GIRLS RKO Radio, 1937
ROY WEBB†

THE FORTY-NINTH PARALLEL THE INVADERS
Columbia, 1941
RALPH VAUGHAN WILLIAMS†

FORZA G WINGED DEVILS 1970
ENNIO MORRICONE

THE FOSSILS 1975
TORU TAKEMITSU†

FOSTER AND LAURIE (TF) Charles Fries
Productions, 1975
LALO SCHIFRIN

FOUL PLAY Paramount, 1978
CHARLES FOX

FOUND MONEY (TF) Cypress Point Productions/
Warner Bros. TV, 1983
JACK ELLIOTT

THE FOUNTAIN RKO Radio, 1934
MAX STEINER†

THE FOUNTAINHEAD Warner Bros., 1949
MAX STEINER†

FOUR BOYS AND A GUN United Artists, 1957
ALBERT GLASSER

FOUR DARK HOURS New World, 1937
MIKLOS ROZSA†

FOUR DAUGHTERS Warner Bros., 1938
MAX STEINER†

FOUR DAYS IN NOVEMBER (FD) United Artists,
1965
ELMER BERNSTEIN

FOUR DAYS IN SEPTEMBER 1997
STEWART COPELAND

THE FOUR DEUCES Avco Embassy, 1974
KEN WANNBERG

FOUR EYES AND SIX-GUNS (CTF) Firebrand/
Saban-Sherick, 1992
DAVID SHIRE

THE FOUR FEATHERS United Artists, 1939
MIKLOS ROZSA†

THE FOUR FEATHERS (TF) Norman Rosemont
Productions/Trident Films Ltd., 1978
ALLYN FERGUSON

FOUR FLIES ON GREY VELVET 1971
ENNIO MORRICONE

FOUR FOR TEXAS Warner Bros., 1963
NELSON RIDDLE†

FOUR FRIENDS Filmways, 1982
ELIZABETH SWADOS

FOUR FRIGHTENED PEOPLE Paramount, 1934
KARL HAJOS†

FOUR GIRLS IN TOWN Universal, 1956
ALEX NORTH†
HERMAN STEIN

FOUR GUNS TO THE BORDER Universal, 1954
HENRY MANCINI†
HANS J. SALTER†
FRANK SKINNER†
HERMAN STEIN

THE FOUR HORSEMEN OF THE APOCALYPSE
MGM, 1962
ANDRE PREVIN

FOUR IN THE MORNING West One, 1965
JOHN BARRY

FOUR MEN AND A PRAYER 20th Century-Fox,
1937
LOUIS SILVERS†

THE FOUR MINUTE MILE (TF) Oscar-Sullivan
Productions/Centre Films, 1988
RICHARD HARTLEY

FOUR MOTHERS Warner Bros., 1941
HEINZ ROEMHELD†

THE FOUR MUSKETEERS MILADY'S REVENGE
20th Century-Fox, 1975
LALO SCHIFRIN

THE FOUR POSTER Columbia, 1952
DIMITRI TIOMKIN†

THE FOUR SKULLS OF JONATHAN DRAKE
United Artists, 1959
PAUL DUNLAP

FOUR SONS 20th Century-Fox, 1940
DAVID BUTTOLPH†

FOUR WAYS OUT 1951
CARLO RUSTICHELLI

FOUR WEDDINGS AND A FUNERAL Gramercy,
1994
RICHARD RODNEY BENNETT

FOUR WIVES Warner Bros., 1940
MAX STEINER†

FOUR'S A CROWD Warner Bros., 1938
ADOLPH DEUTSCH†
HEINZ ROEMHELD†

FOUR-SIDED TRIANGLE Exclusive Films, 1953
MALCOLM ARNOLD

FOURTEEN HOURS 20th Century-Fox, 1951
ALFRED NEWMAN†

THE FOURTH PROTOCOL Lorimar, 1987
LALO SCHIFRIN

FOURTH STORY (CTF) Viacom, 1991
WILLIAM OLVIS

THE FOURTH WAR Cannon, 1990
BILL CONTI

THE FOX Claridge, 1968
LALO SCHIFRIN ★★

THE FOX AND THE HOUND (AF) Buena Vista,
1981
BUDDY BAKER

FOXBAT 1978
ROY BUDD†

FOXES Paramount, 1980
GIORGIO MORODER

THE FOXES OF HARROW 20th Century-Fox, 1947
DAVID BUTTOLPH†

FOXFIRE Rysher, 1996
MICHEL COLOMBIER

FOXFIRE Universal, 1955
FRANK SKINNER†

FOXFIRE (TF) Marian Rees Associates, 1987
JOHNNY MANDEL ☆

FOXTROT THE OTHER SIDE OF PARADISE New
World, 1976
PETE RUGOLO

F.P.I. ANTWORTET NICHT 1932
ALLAN GRAY†

FRAMED Paramount, 1974
PATRICK WILLIAMS

FRAMED Universal, 1940
HANS J. SALTER†

FRAMED (CTF) HBO Pictures, 1990
WILLIAM OLVIS

FRAMED (TF) Anglia/A&E/Tesauro, 1993
NICK BICAT

FRAMEUP Complex, 1993
JON A. ENGLISH

FRAME-UP II: THE COVER-UP Promark
Entertainment Group, 1992
ROBERT SUMMERS

FRAN Harron Films, 1985
GREG SCHULTZ

FRANCE SOCIETE ANONYME 1973
MICHEL PORTAL

FRANCES Universal, 1982
JOHN BARRY

FRANCESCO Istituto Luce/Italnoleggio, 1989
VANGELIS

FRANCIS Universal, 1950
FRANK SKINNER†

FRANCIS COVERS THE BIG TOWN Universal,
1953
HERMAN STEIN

FRANCIS GARY POWERS: THE TRUE STORY OF
THE U-2 SPY INCIDENT (TF) Charles Fries
Productions, 1976
GERALD FRIED

FRANCIS GOES TO THE RACES Universal, 1951
FRANK SKINNER†

FRANCIS GOES TO WEST POINT Universal, 1952
MILTON ROSEN†
HERMAN STEIN

FRANCIS IN THE HAUNTED HOUSE Universal,
1956
HENRY MANCINI†
FRANK SKINNER†
HERMAN STEIN

FRANCOIS LE RHINOCEROS 1953
JOSEPH KOSMA†

FRANK & OLLIE 1996
JOHN REYNOLDS

FRANK AND JESSE (CTF) Trimark/Cassian Elwes/
Elliott Kastner, 1995
MARK MCKENZIE

FRANK BUCK'S JUNGLE CAVALCADE RKO Radio,
1941
NATHANIEL SHILKRET†

FRANK NITTI: THE ENFORCER (TF) Leonard Hill
Films, 1988
YANNI

FRANKENHOOKER Shapiro-Glickenhaus
Entertainment, 1990
JOE RENZETTI

FRANKENSTEIN Universal, 1931
BERNHARD KAUN†

FRANKENSTEIN - 1970 Allied Artists, 1958
PAUL DUNLAP

FRANKENSTEIN '88 20th Century Fox, 1985
PAUL J. ZAZA

FRANKENSTEIN (CTF) David Wickes Prods., 1993
JOHN CAMERON

FRANKENSTEIN (TF) Dan Curtis Productions, 1973
BOB COBERT

FRANKENSTEIN AND THE MONSTER FROM
HELL Paramount, 1974
JAMES BERNARD

FRANKENSTEIN CONQUERS THE WORLD
American International, 1964
AKIRA IFUKUBE

FRANKENSTEIN CREATED WOMAN 20th
Century-Fox, 1967
JAMES BERNARD

FRANKENSTEIN MEETS THE WOLF MAN
Universal, 1943
CHARLES PREVIN†
HANS J. SALTER†
FRANK SKINNER†

FRANKENSTEIN MUST BE DESTROYED! Warner
Bros., 1970
JAMES BERNARD

FRANKENSTEIN UNBOUND 20th Century Fox,
1990
CARL DAVIS

FRANKENSTEIN'S GREAT AUNT TILLIE 1984
RONALD STEIN†

FRANKENSTEIN: THE COLLEGE YEARS (TF) Sprit
Prods/FNM Films, 1991
JOEL MCNEELY

FRANKENSTEIN: THE TRUE STORY (TF) Universal
TV, 1973
GIL MELLE

FRANKENSTEIN—ITALIAN STYLE 1976
STELVIO CIPRIANI

FRANKIE AND JOHNNY Paramount, 1991
MARVIN HAMLISCH

FRANKIE'S HOUSE (MS) Anglia, 1993
JEFF BECK
JED LEIBER

FRANTIC Warner Bros., 1988
ENNIO MORRICONE

FRANTIC ASCENSEUR POUR L'ECHAFAUD
Times, 1957
MILES DAVIS†

FRATELLO MARE 1975
PIERO PICCIONI

FRATELLO SOLE, SORELLA LUNA 1972
RIZ ORTOLANI

FRATERNITY ROW Paramount, 1977
DON MCLEAN

FRATERNITY VACATION New World, 1985
BRAD FIEDEL

FRAU IM STROM 1939
GIUSEPPE BECCE†

FRAULEIN 20th Century-Fox, 1958
DANIELE AMFITHEATROF†

FRAULEIN DOKTOR 1968
ENNIO MORRICONE

FREAKED 20th Century Fox, 1993
KEVIN KINER

FREAKY FRIDAY Buena Vista, 1976
JOHNNY MANDEL

FREAKY FRIDAY (TF) ZM Prods./Walt Disney TV,
1995
JAMES MCVAY

FREDDIE AS F.R.O.7. (AF) Miramax, 1992
DAVID DUNDAS
RICK WENTWORTH

FREEDOM ROAD (TF) Zev Braun TV/Freedom Road
Films, 1979
TERRENCE JAMES

FREDDY'S DEAD: THE FINAL NIGHTMARE New
Line, 1991
BRIAN MAY†

FREE ENTERPRISE Burrowes Film Group, Australian
BRUCE ROWLAND

FREE FOR ALL Universal, 1949
FRANK SKINNER†

A FREE MAN 1973
FRANCIS LAI

THE FREE RETURN NDR Fernsehen, 1984
CARL DANTE

FREE RIDE Galaxy International, 1986
DAVID C. WILLIAMS

FREE SPIRIT Cine III, 1973
LAURIE JOHNSON

FREE WILLY Warner Bros., 1993
BASIL POLEDOURIS

FREE WILLY 2: THE ADVENTURE HOME Warner
Bros., 1995
BASIL POLEDOURIS

FREEBIE AND THE BEAN Warner Bros., 1974
DOMINIC FRONTIERE

FREEDOM (TF) Hill-Mandelker Films, 1981
LEE HOLDRIDGE

FREEDOM FIGHTER (TF) HTV/Columbia TV/
Embassy TV, 1988
LAURENCE ROSENTHAL

FREEDOM ON MY MIND (FD) Clarity Films, 1994
MARY WATHING

FREEDOM RADIO Columbia, 1941
NICHOLAS BRODZSKY†

FREEDOM RIDERS (TF) Columbia TV, 1979
MORTON STEVENS†

FREEDOM ROAD (TF) Zev Braun TV/Freedom Road
Films, 1979
COLERIDGE-TAYLOR PERKINSON

FREEFALL (CTF) Nu World Prods., 1994
LEE HOLDRIDGE

FREEJACK Warner Bros., 1992
MICHAEL BODDICKER
TREVOR JONES

FREEWAY New World, 1988
JOE DELIA

THE FRENCH ATLANTIC AFFAIR (TF) 1979
JOHN ADDISON

FRENCH CAN-CAN *ONLY THE FRENCH CAN*
United Motion Picture Organization, 1954
GEORGES VAN PARYS†

THE FRENCH CONNECTION 20th Century-Fox,
1971
DON ELLIS†

THE FRENCH CONNECTION II 20th Century-Fox,
1975
DON ELLIS†

THE FRENCH CONSPIRACY 1972
ENNIO MORRICONE

THE FRENCH DETECTIVE 1975
PHILIPPE SARDE

FRENCH DRESSING Warner-Pathe, 1963
GEORGES DELERUE†

FRENCH KISS 20th Century Fox, 1995
JAMES NEWTON HOWARD

THE FRENCH LIEUTENANT'S WOMAN United
Artists, 1981
CARL DAVIS

THE FRENCH LINE RKO Radio, 1953
WALTER SCHARF

FRENCH POSTCARDS Paramount, 1978
LEE HOLDRIDGE

THE FRENCH REVOLUTION Films Ariane/Films A2/
Laura Films/Antea, 1989
GEORGES DELERUE†

FRENCH TWIST Miramax Zoe, 1996
MANUEL MALOU

FRENCH WITHOUT TEARS Paramount, 1940
NICHOLAS BRODZSKY†

A FRENCH WOMAN 1995
PATRICK DOYLE

THE FRENCH WOMAN *MADAME CLAUDE*
Monarch, 1979
SERGE GAINSBOURG†

FRENCHIE Universal, 1950
HANS J. SALTER†

FRENCHMAN'S CREEK Paramount, 1944
VICTOR YOUNG†

FRENZY Universal, 1972
RON GOODWIN

FRESA Y CHOCOLATE *STRAWBERRY AND
CHOCOLATE* 1994
JOSE MARIA VITIER

FRESH Miramax, 1994
STEWART COPELAND

FRESH BAIT 1995
PHILIPPE HAIM

FRESH HORSES Columbia/WEG, 1988
DAVID FOSTER
DAVID MANSFIELD
PATRICK WILLIAMS

THE FRESHMAN Tri-Star, 1990
DAVID NEWMAN

FRESNO (MS) MTM Productions, 1986
JOHN MORRIS

FREUD Universal, 1963
JERRY GOLDSMITH ★

FRIDA - STRAIGHT FROM THE HEART *FRIDA-
MED HJERTET I HANDEN* 1992
BENT ASERUD
GEIR BOHREN

FRIDA- MED HJERTET I HANDEN 1992
BENT ASERUD
GEIR BOHREN

FRIDAY New Line, 1995
FRANK FITZPATRICK

FRIDAY THE 13TH Paramount, 1980
HARRY MANFREDINI

FRIDAY THE 13TH - THE FINAL CHAPTER
Paramount, 1984
HARRY MANFREDINI

FRIDAY THE 13TH PART 2 Paramount, 1981
HARRY MANFREDINI

FRIDAY THE 13TH PART 3 Paramount, 1982
HARRY MANFREDINI

**FRIDAY THE 13TH PART V - A NEW
BEGINNING** Paramount, 1985
HARRY MANFREDINI

FRIDAY THE 13TH PART VI: JASON LIVES
Paramount, 1986
HARRY MANFREDINI

**FRIDAY THE 13TH PART VII - THE NEW
BLOOD** Paramount, 1988
HARRY MANFREDINI

**FRIDAY THE 13TH, PART VII - THE NEW
BLOOD** Paramount, 1988
FRED MOLLIN

**FRIDAY THE 13TH, PART VIII - JASON TAKES
MANHATTAN** Paramount, 1989
FRED MOLLIN

FRIDAY THE 13TH...THE ORPHAN World Northal,
1979
TEO MACERO

FRIDAYS OF ETERNITY Aires, 1989
LALO SCHIFRIN

FRIED GREEN TOMATOES Universal, 1991
THOMAS NEWMAN

FRIEDA Universal, 1947
JOHN GREENWOOD†

FRIEND INDEED MGM, 1938
WILLIAM AXT†

A FRIEND OF VINCENT AMLF, 1983
PHILIPPE SARDE

A FRIEND TO DIE FOR (TF) Steve White Prods.,
1994
CHRIS BOARDMAN

FRIENDLY ENEMIES United Artists, 1942
LUCIEN MORAWECK†

FRIENDLY FIRE (TF) Marble Arch Productions, 1979
LEONARD ROSENMAN ☆☆

FRIENDLY PERSUASION Allied Artists, 1956
DIMITRI TIOMKIN†

FRIENDLY PERSUASION (TF) International TV
Productions/Allied Artists, 1975
JOHN CACAVAS

FRIENDS 1993
RACHEL PORTMAN

FRIENDS AT LAST (TF) Procter & Gamble/Tele
Vest/Atlantis/Stewart Pictures/Columbia-TriStar TV,
1995
MICKEY ERBE
MARYBETH SOLOMON

FRIENDS FOR LIFE *AMICI PER LA PELLE* 1955
NINO ROTA†

THE FRIENDS OF EDDIE COYLE Paramount, 1973
DAVE GRUSIN

A FRIENDSHIP IN VIENNA (CTF)
Finnegan-Pinchuk Productions, 1988
LEE HOLDRIDGE

FRIENDSHIPS, SECRETS AND LIES (TF)
Wittman-Riche Productions/Warner Bros. TV, 1979
ANGELA MORLEY

FRIGHT 1971
HARRY ROBERTSON

FRIGHT NIGHT Columbia, 1985
BRAD FIEDEL

FRIGHT NIGHT PART 2 New Century/Vista, 1989
BRAD FIEDEL

THE FRIGHTENERS Universal, 1996
DANNY ELFMAN

FRIGHTMARE Paramount, 1974
STANLEY MYERS†

THE FRINGE DWELLERS 1986
GEORGE DREYFUS

THE FRISCO KID Warner Bros., 1979
FRANK DEVOL

FRISCO LIL Universal, 1942
HANS J. SALTER†

FRISCO SAL Universal, 1945
EDWARD WARD†

FRISKY *PANE, AMORE E GELOSIA* DCA, 1954
ALESSANDRO CICOGNINI†

FRITZ THE CAT (AF) American International, 1972
ED BOGAS
RAY SHANKLIN

FROG (TF) Platypus Productions, 1988
RON RAMIN

FROG DREAMING Middle Reef Productions, 1985
BRIAN MAY†

THE FROG PRINCE Zygomat Pictures, 1992
DEBORAH HOLLAND

THE FROGMEN 20th Century-Fox, 1951
CYRIL J. MOCKRIDGE†
LIONEL NEWMAN†

FROGS American International, 1972
LES BAXTER†

FROM A FAR COUNTRY *POPE JOHN PAUL II*
(TF) Trans World Film/ITC/RAI/Film Polski, 1981
WOJCIECH KILAR

FROM A ROMAN BALCONY *LA GIORNATA
BALORDA/LOVE IS A DAY'S WORK/PICKUP
IN ROME* Continental, 1960
PIERO PICCIONI

FROM A WHISPER TO A SCREAM TMS Pictures,
1987
JIM MANZIE

FROM A WHISPER TO A SCREAM TMS, 1987
JOHN BEAL

FROM BEYOND Empire Pictures, 1986
RICHARD H. BAND

FROM BEYOND THE GRAVE *THE CREATURES*
Howard Mahler Films, 1973
DOUGLAS GAMLEY

FROM DUSK TILL DAWN Miramax-Dimension,
1996
GRAEME REVELL

FROM HELL TO TEXAS 20th Century-Fox, 1958
DANIELE AMFITHEATROF†

FROM HELL TO VICTORY 1979
RIZ ORTOLANI

FROM HERE TO ETERNITY Columbia, 1953
GEORGE DUNING

FROM HERE TO ETERNITY (MS)
Bennett-Katleman Productions/Columbia Pictures TV,
1979
WALTER SCHARF ★

FROM HOLLYWOOD TO DEADWOOD Island
Pictures, 1989
ALEX GIBSON

FROM NOON TILL THREE also cameo as piano
player, United Artists, 1976
ELMER BERNSTEIN

FROM RUSSIA WITH LOVE United Artists, 1963
JOHN BARRY

FROM THE DEAD OF NIGHT (TF) Shadowplay
Films/Phoenix Entertainment Group, 1989
GIL MELLE

**FROM THE FILES OF JOSEPH WAMBAUGH: A
JURY OF ONE (TF)** Grossbart-Barnett/TriStar TV,
1992
DAVID MICHAEL FRANK

FROM THE HIP DEG, 1987
PAUL J. ZAZA

FROM THE ISLAND 1993
JIM SUTHERLAND

FROM THE LIFE OF THE MARIONETTES
Universal/AFD, 1980
ROLF WILHELM

FROM THE POLICE, WITH THANKS 1972
STELVIO CIPRIANI

FROM THE TERRACE 20th Century Fox, 1960
ELMER BERNSTEIN

FROM THIS DAY FORWARD RKO Radio, 1946
LEIGH HARLINE†

THE FRONT Columbia, 1976
DAVE GRUSIN

THE FRONT PAGE Universal, 1974
BILLY MAY

FRONTIER 1936
DMITRI KABALEVSKY†

FRONTIER BADMEN Universal, 1943
HANS J. SALTER†

FRONTIER GAL Universal, 1945
FRANK SKINNER†

FRONTIER GUN 20th Century-Fox, 1958
PAUL DUNLAP

FRONTIER MARSHAL 20th Century-Fox, 1939
DAVID RAKSIN

FRONTIER UPRISING United Artists, 1961
BERT A. SHEFTER

FROSTFIRE CBC, 1994
PETER MANNING ROBINSON

FROZEN ASSETS Paramount/Skouras, 1992
MICHAEL TAVERA

THE FROZEN DEAD Warner Bros., 1967
DON BANKS

THE FROZEN GHOST Universal, 1945
HANS J. SALTER†

THE FRUIT MACHINE Vestron, 1988
HANS ZIMMER

FUCKING FERNAND 1987
JEAN-CLAUDE PETIT

FUGA IN FRANCIA 1948
NINO ROTA†

THE FUGITIVE Warner Bros., 1993
JAMES NEWTON HOWARD ★

THE FUGITIVE RKO Radio, 1947
RICHARD HAGEMAN†

FUGITIVE AMONG US (TF) Andrew Adelson Co./
ABC Prods., 1992
STEWART COPELAND

FUGITIVE FAMILY (TF) Aubrey-Hamner
Productions, 1980
MORTON STEVENS†

FUGITIVE FROM THE EMPIRE (TF) Mad-Dog
Productions/Universal TV, 1981
IAN UNDERWOOD

THE FUGITIVE KIND United Artists, 1957
KENYON HOPKINS

**FUGITIVE NIGHTS: DANGER IN THE DESERT
(TF)** TriStar TV, 1993
JAY ASHER

FUGITIVE OF THE PLAINS Producers Releasing
Corp., 1943
LEO ERDODY†

FUGITIVES FOR A NIGHT RKO Radio, 1938
ROBERT RUSSELL BENNETT†

FUGUE 1966
ANTOINE DUHAMEL

THE FULFILLMENT OF MARY GRAY (TF) Mary
Gray Inc./Lee Caplin Productions/Indian Neck
Entertainment, 1989
GARY SCOTT

FULL CIRCLE Discovery Films, 1977
COLIN TOWNS

FULL CONFESSION RKO Radio, 1939
ROY WEBB†

**FULL EXPOSURE: THE SEX TAPES SCANDAL
(TF)** von Zemeck-Sertner Films, 1989
DANA KAPROFF

A FULL LIFE 1962
TORU TAKEMITSU†

FULL METAL JACKET Warner Bros., 1987
ABIGAIL MEAD

FULL MOON HIGH Filmways, 1981
GARY WILLIAM FRIEDMAN

FULL MOON IN BLUE WATER Trans World
Entertainment, 1988
PHIL MARSHALL

THE FULLER BRUSH GIRL Columbia, 1950
HEINZ ROEMHELD†

THE FULLER BRUSH MAN Columbia, 1948
HEINZ ROEMHELD†

FUN Neo Modern Ent./Damian Lee Prods., 1994
MARC TSCHANTZ

FUN AND FANCY FREE RKO Radio, 1947
PAUL J. SMITH†
OLIVER WALLACE†

FUN AND GAMES (TF) Kanin-Gallo Productions/
Warner Bros. TV, 1980
PETER MATZ

FUN WITH DICK AND JANE Columbia, 1977
ERNEST GOLD

THE FUNERAL October, 1996
JOE DELIA

FUNERAL HOME 1981
JERRY FIELDING†

THE FUNHOUSE Universal, 1981
JOHN BEAL

FUNNY ABOUT LOVE Paramount, 1990
MILES GOODMAN†

FUNNY BONES Buena Vista, 1995
JOHN ALTMAN

FUNNY COMPANY (AF) Kiev Studio, 1972
VLADIMIR HORUNZHY

FUNNY FACE Paramount, 1957
ADOLPH DEUTSCH†

FUNNY FARM Warner Bros., 1988
ELMER BERNSTEIN

FUNNY GIRL Columbia, 1968
WALTER SCHARF ★

FUNNY LADY Columbia, 1975
PETER MATZ ★

**A FUNNY THING HAPPENED ON THE WAY TO
THE FORUM** United Artists, 1966
KEN THORNE ★★

FUNNYMAN New Yorker, 1967
PETER SCHICKELE

FURIA A MARRAKESCH 1966
CARLO SAVINA

THE FURIES Paramount, 1950
FRANZ WAXMAN†

**THE FURTHER ADVENTURES OF TENNESSEE
BUCK** Trans World Entertainment, 1988
JOHN DEBNEY

**FURTHER ADVENTURES OF THE WILDERNESS
FAMILY** Pacific International, 1978
GENE KAUER
DOUGLAS LACKEY

THE FURTHER PERILS OF LAUREL AND HARDY
MGM, 1968
JOHN PARKER

THE FURY 20th Century-Fox, 1978
JOHN WILLIAMS

FURY MGM, 1936
FRANZ WAXMAN†

FURY AT FURNACE CREEK 20th Century-Fox,
1948
DAVID RAKSIN

FURY AT SUNDOWN United Artists, 1957
HARRY SUKMAN†

FUSA 1993
KENSAKU TANAGAWA

FUTURE-KILL International Film Marketing, 1985
ROBERT RENFROW

FUTURES VEDETTES 1954
JEAN WIENER†

FUTUREWORLD American International, 1976
FRED KARLIN

FUZZ United Artists, 1972
DAVE GRUSIN

THE FUZZY PINK NIGHTGOWN United Artists,
1957
BILLY MAY

F/X Orion, 1986
BILL CONTI

FX 2 - THE DEADLY ART OF ILLUSION Orion,
1991
MICHAEL BODDICKER
LALO SCHIFRIN

G

GABLE AND LOMBARD Universal, 1976
MICHEL LEGRAND
GABRIEL OVER THE WHITE HOUSE MGM, 1933
WILLIAM AXT†
GABY MGM, 1956
CONRAD SALINGER†
GABY - A TRUE STORY Tri-Star, 1987
MAURICE JARRE
THE GADFLY 1955
DMITRI KABALEVSKY†
GAILY, GAILY United Artists, 1969
HENRY MANCINI†
THE GAL WHO TOOK THE WEST Universal, 1949
FRANK SKINNER†
GALA 1962
ANTOINE DUHAMEL
THE GALACTIC CONNECTION Barrich Corporation, 1979
ROBERT J. WALSH
GALAXIES ARE COLLIDING SC Entertainment, 1992
STEPHEN BARBER
GALAXY OF TERROR *MINDWARP: AN INFINITY OF TERROR/PLANET OF HORRORS* New World, 1981
BARRY SCHRADER
GALGAMETH Sheen Communications, 1997
RICHARD MARVIN
GALIA 1965
MICHEL MAGNE†
GALILEO 1968
ENNIO MORRICONE
GALILEO American Film Theatre, 1975
RICHARD HARTLEY
THE GALLANT BLADE Columbia, 1948
GEORGE DUNING
GALLANT LADY United Artists, 1934
ALFRED NEWMAN†
GALLIPOLI Paramount, 1981
BRIAN MAY†
THE GALLOPING MAJOR 1951
GEORGES AURIC†
GAMBIT Universal, 1966
MAURICE JARRE
THE GAMBLER Paramount, 1974
JERRY FIELDING†
THE GAMBLER RETURNS: THE LUCK OF THE DRAW (TF) Kenny Rogers Productions, 1991
MARK SNOW
GAMBLER V: PLAYING FOR KEEPS (TF) Kenny Rogers Prods./WIN/RHI, 1994
KENNY ROGERS,
LARRY BROWN
BOB DE MARCO
EDGAR STRUBLE
THE GAMBLERS 20th Century-Fox, 1969
JOHN MORRIS
GAMBLING HOUSE RKO Radio, 1951
ROY WEBB†
THE GAME 1997
HOWARD SHORE
THE GAME IS OVER *LA CUREE* Royal Films International, 1966
JEAN BOUCHETY
GAME OF DEATH Columbia, 1979
JOHN BARRY
GAME PASS 1976
PEER RABEN
GAME, SET AND MATCH (MS) Grenada, 1989
RICHARD HARVEY
THE GAMES 20th Century-Fox, 1970
FRANCIS LAI
GAMES MOTHER NEVER TAUGHT YOU (TF) CBS Entertainment, 1982
MARK SNOW
GANDAHAR (AF) 1987
GABRIEL YARED
GANDHI Columbia, 1982
GEORGE FENTON ★
RAVI SHANKAR
GANG WAR 20th Century-Fox, 1958
PAUL DUNLAP
THE GANGSTER Allied Artists, 1947
LOUIS GRUENBERG†
THE GANGSTER CHRONICLES (TF) Universal TV, 1981
JOHN CACAVAS
GANGWAY FOR TOMORROW RKO Radio, 1943
ROY WEBB†
GANJA AND HESS Kelly-Jordan, 1973
SAM WAYMON
THE GARBAGE PAIL KIDS MOVIE Atlantic Entertainment Group, 1987
MICHAEL LLOYD
GARBO TALKS MGM/UA, 1984
CY COLEMAN
GARCON Sara Film/Renn Productions, 1983
PHILIPPE SARDE

GARDE A VUE *UNDER SUSPICION* 1981
GEORGES DELERUE†
THE GARDEN 1991
SIMON FISHER TURNER
THE GARDEN MURDER CASE MGM, 1936
WILLIAM AXT†
THE GARDEN OF ALLAH United Artists, 1936
MAX STEINER† ★
THE GARDEN OF THE FINZI-CONTINIS Cinema 5, 1971
MANUEL DE SICA
GARDEN OF EVIL 20th Century-Fox, 1954
BERNARD HERRMANN†
GARDEN OF REDEMPTION (CTF) Paramount, 1997
JOHN ALTMAN
THE GARDENER KKI Films, 1981
MARC FREDERICKS
THE GARDENER'S SON (TF) RIP/Filmhaus, 1977
CHARLES GROSS
GARDENS OF STONE Tri-Star, 1987
CARMINE COPPOLA†
GARGOYLES (TF) Tomorrow Entertainment, 1972
ROBERT PRINCE
GARGOYLES, THE MOVIE: THE HEROES AWAKEN (ATF) Disney TV, 1995
CARL JOHNSON
THE GARMENT JUNGLE Columbia, 1957
LEITH STEVENS†
GAS Paramount, 1981
PAUL J. ZAZA
GAS HOUSE KIDS Producers Releasing Corp., 1946
LEO ERDODY†
GAS HOUSE KIDS GO WEST Producers Releasing Corp., 1947
ALBERT GLASSER
GAS HOUSE KIDS IN HOLLYWOOD Producers Releasing Corp., 1947
ALBERT GLASSER
GAS, FOOD AND LODGING I.R.S., 1992
BARRY ADAMSON
J MASCIS
GASLIGHT MGM, 1944
BRONISLAU KAPER†
GASLIGHT *ANGEL STREET* 1939
RICHARD ADDINSELL†
GASP! Avala Films, 1977
WALTER SCHARF
THE GATE New Century/Vista, 1987
MICHAEL HOENIG
J. PETER ROBINSON
GATE II Triumph, 1992
GEORGE BLONDHEIM
THE GATES OF HELL MPM, 1983
FABIO FRIZZI
A GATHERING OF EAGLES Universal, 1963
JERRY GOLDSMITH
A GATHERING OF OLD MEN (TF) Consolidated Productions/Jennie & Company/Zenith Productions, 1987
RON CARTER
THE GATHERING (TF) Hanna-Barbera Productions, 1977
JOHN BARRY
THE GATHERING, PART II (TF) Hanna-Barbera Productions, 1979
ROBERT PRINCE
GATOR United Artists, 1976
CHARLES BERNSTEIN
GATTACA 1997
MICHAEL NYMAN
GATTI ROSSI IN UN LABIRINTO DI VETRO 1975
BRUNO NICOLAI
THE GAUNTLET Warner Bros., 1977
JERRY FIELDING†
GAWAIN AND THE GREEN KNIGHT United Artists, 1972
RON GOODWIN
THE GAY AMIGO United Artists, 1949
ALBERT GLASSER
THE GAY DECEIVERS Fanfare, 1969
STU PHILLIPS
THE GAY DIPLOMAT RKO Radio, 1931
MAX STEINER†
THE GAY DIVORCEE RKO Radio, 1934
MAX STEINER†
THE GAY LADY *TROTTIE TRUE* Eagle Lion, 1949
BENJAMIN FRANKEL†
THE GAY SISTERS Warner Bros., 1942
MAX STEINER†
THE GAZEBO MGM, 1959
JEFF ALEXANDER†
GAZON MAUDIT 1995
MANUEL MALOU
GE LAO YE ZI *OLD MAN GE* 1993
MO FAN
THE GEISHA BOY Paramount, 1958
WALTER SCHARF
GEISHA GIRL Realart, 1952
ALBERT GLASSER

GELOSIA 1953
CARLO RUSTICHELLI
GEMINI MAN (TF) Universal TV, 1976
BILLY GOLDENBERG
GEMINI, THE TWIN STARS 1988
NIGEL HOLTON
GEMINUS (TF) 1970
BRUNO NICOLAI
THE GENE KRUPA STORY Columbia, 1959
LEITH STEVENS†
THE GENERAL
CARL DAVIS
THE GENERAL DIED AT DAWN Paramount, 1936
WERNER JANSSEN
GENERAL SPANKY MGM, 1936
T. MARVIN HATLEY†
GENERATION Avco Embassy, 1969
DAVE GRUSIN
GENERATION (TF) Embassy TV, 1985
CHARLES BERNSTEIN
GENESIS Scarabee Films, 1986
RAVI SHANKAR
THE GENESIS CHILDREN 1972
JERRY STYNE
GENESIS II (TF) Warner Bros. TV, 1973
HARRY SUKMAN†
GENEVIEVE Universal, 1954
LARRY ADLER ★
GENEVIEVE A GAGNE SON PARI 1953
JEAN PRODROMIDES
GENGHIS KHAN 1993
RICHARD HOROWITZ
GENGIS COHN BBC-TV/A&E, 1994
CARL DAVIS
THE GENIE 1953
ALLAN GRAY†
GENIUS AT WORK RKO Radio, 1946
PAUL SAWTELL†
GENOCIDE (FD) Simon Wiesenthal Center, 1982
ELMER BERNSTEIN
GENOVA A MANO ARMATA 1976
FRANCO MICALIZZI
GENOVEVA DE BRABANTE 1965
CARLO RUSTICHELLI
GENTE DI RISPETTO 1975
ENNIO MORRICONE
THE GENTLE GUNMAN Universal, 1952
JOHN GREENWOOD†
THE GENTLEMAN BANDIT (TF) Highgate Pictures, 1981
STANLEY MYERS†
GENTLEMAN AFTER DARK United Artists, 1942
DIMITRI TIOMKIN†
GENTLEMAN JIM Warner Bros., 1942
HEINZ ROEMHELD†
GENTLEMAN JO...UCCIDI 1968
BRUNO NICOLAI
GENTLEMAN'S AGREEMENT 20th Century-Fox, 1947
ALFRED NEWMAN†
GENTLEMEN IN WHITE VESTS 1970
PETER THOMAS
GENTLEMEN MARRY BRUNETTES United Artists, 1955
ROBERT FARNON
GENUINE RISK I.R.S. Media, 1990
DEBORAH HOLLAND
THE GEORGE McKENNA STORY (TF) The Landsburg Company, 1986
HERBIE HANCOCK
GEORGE OF THE JUNGLE 1997
MARC SHAIMAN
THE GEORGE RAFT STORY Allied Artists, 1961
JEFF ALEXANDER†
GEORGE STEVENS: A FILMMAKER'S JOURNEY (FD) Castle Hill Productions, 1984
CARL DAVIS
GEORGE WASHINGTON (MS) David Gerber Productions/MGM Television, 1984
LAURENCE ROSENTHAL
GEORGE WASHINGTON SLEPT HERE Warner Bros., 1942
ADOLPH DEUTSCH†
GEORGE WASHINGTON: THE FORGING OF A NATION (TF) David Gerber Company/MGM TV, 1986
BRUCE BROUGHTON
GEORGE WHITE'S SCANDALS RKO Radio, 1945
LEIGH HARLINE†
GEORGE'S ISLAND New Line, 1991
MARTY SIMON
THE GEORGIA PEACHES (TF) New World Pictures, 1980
R. DONOVAN FOX
GERALD McBOING BOING (AS) Columbia, 1950
GAIL KUBIK†
GERMINAL 1963
MICHEL MAGNE†
GERMINAL 1993
JEAN-LOUIS ROQUES

GERONIMO United Artists, 1962
HUGO FRIEDHOFER†
GERONIMO (CTF) Yorktown Prods./von Zerneck-Sertner Films, 1993
PATRICK WILLIAMS ☆
GERONIMO: AN AMERICAN LEGEND Columbia, 1993
RY COODER
GERVAISE Continental, 1956
GEORGES AURIC†
GET CARTER MGM, 1971
ROY BUDD†
GET CHARLIE TULLY TBS Distributing Corporation, 1976
CHRISTOPHER GUNNING
GET CHRISTIE LOVE! (TF) David L. Wolper Productions, 1974
ALLYN FERGUSON
JACK ELLIOTT
GET CRAZY Embassy, 1983
MICHAEL BODDICKER
GET GOING Universal, 1943
HANS J. SALTER†
GET IT MAN Yugoslavian
ALFI KABILJO
GET ON THE BUS 1996
TERENCE BLANCHARD
GET OUT YOUR HANDKERCHIEFS New Line Cinema, 1978
GEORGES DELERUE†
GET SHORTY MGM-UA, 1995
JOHN LURIE
GET SMART, AGAIN! (TF) IndieProd Productions/Phoenix Entertainment Group, 1989
PETER RODGERS MELNICK
GET THEE OUT 1991
ALEKSANDR PANTYCHIN
GET TO KNOW YOUR RABBIT Warner Bros., 1972
JACK ELLIOTT
THE GET-AWAY MGM, 1941
DANIELE AMFITHEATROF†
THE GETAWAY 1979
VLADIMIR COSMA
THE GETAWAY Universal, 1994
MARK ISHAM
THE GETAWAY National General, 1972
QUINCY JONES
GETEILTE LIEBE *MANEUVERS* Helma Sanders-Brahms/Metropolis Films, 1988
JURGEN KNIEPER
GETTING AWAY FROM IT ALL (TF) Palomar Productions, 1972
VIC MIZZY
GETTING AWAY WITH MURDER Savoy, 1996
JOHN DEBNEY
GETTING EVEN American Distribution Group, 1986
CHRISTOPHER YOUNG
GETTING EVEN Quantum Films, 1981
RICHARD GREENE
GETTING EVEN WITH DAD MGM, 1994
MILES GOODMAN†
GETTING GERTIE'S GARTER United Artists, 1945
HUGO FRIEDHOFER†
GETTING GOTTI (TF) Kushner-Locke, 1994
PATRICK WILLIAMS
GETTING IT ON Comworld, 1983
RICKEY KELLER
GETTING IT RIGHT MCEG, 1989
COLIN TOWNS
GETTING LUCKY Vista Street Entertainment, 1990
MIRIAM CUTLER
GETTING MARRIED (TF) Paramount TV, 1978
CRAIG SAFAN
GETTING OUT (TF) Dorothea G. Petrie Prods./Signboard Hill/RHI, 1994
MASON DARING
GETTING PHYSICAL (TF) CBS Entertainment, 1984
WILLIAM GOLDSTEIN
GETTING STRAIGHT Columbia, 1970
RONALD STEIN†
GETTING UP AND GOING HOME (CTF) Carroll Newman/Polone Co./Hearst, 1992
JAMES DIPASQUALLE
GETTYSBURG New Line, 1993
RANDY EDELMAN
GHIDRAH, THE THREE-HEADED MONSTER Continental, 1966
AKIRA IFUKUBE
GHOST Paramount, 1990
MAURICE JARRE ★
THE GHOST AND MR. CHICKEN Universal, 1966
VIC MIZZY
THE GHOST AND MRS. MUIR 20th Century-Fox, 1947
BERNARD HERRMANN†
THE GHOST AND THE DARKNESS Paramount, 1996
JERRY GOLDSMITH
GHOST BREAKERS Paramount, 1940
ERNST TOCH†

FILM TITLES

GL - GO

'97-'98
FILM
COMPOSERS
INDEX

FILM

TITLES

THE GLASS WALL Columbia, 1953
LEITH STEVENS†

THE GLASS WEB Universal, 1953
HERMAN STEIN

GLEAMING THE CUBE 20th Century Fox, 1989
JAY FERGUSON

GLENGARRY GLEN ROSS New Line, 1992
JAMES NEWTON HOWARD

THE GLENN MILLER STORY Universal, 1954
HENRY MANCINI† ★
HERMAN STEIN

GLI AMANTI LATINI 1965
CARLO SAVINA

GLI AMICI DI NICK HEZARD 1976
LUIS BACALOV

GLI ANGELI DALLE MANI BENDATE 1976
STELVIO CIPRIANI

GLI ATTENDENTI 1961
ARMANDO TROVAJOLI

GLI EROI 1973
RIZ ORTOLANI

GLI EROI THE HEROES 1972
RIZ ORTOLANI

GLI EROI DI FORT WORTH 1964
CARLO RUSTICHELLI

GLI ESECUTORI STREET PEOPLE 1975
LUIS BACALOV

GLI FUMAVANO LE COLT 1971
BRUNO NICOLAI

GLI IMBROGLIANI Produzione D.S./Tecisa Film,
1963
CARLO RUSTICHELLI

GLI INNAMORATI Jacovoni, 1955
CARLO RUSTICHELLI

GLI INTERMIERI DELLA MUTUA 1969
CARLO RUSTICHELLI

GLI INTOCCABILI 1968
ENNIO MORRICONE

GLI INVASORI/FURY OF THE VIKINGS American
International, 1961
LES BAXTER†

GLI INVINCIBILI TRE THE INVINCIBLE THREE
1964
ANGELO FRANCESCO LAVAGNINO†

GLI ITALIANI SONO MATTI 1958
NINO ROTA†

GLI OCCHI FEDDI DELLA PAURA 1971
ENNIO MORRICONE

GLI ONOREVOLI 1963
ARMANDO TROVAJOLI

GLI ORRORI DEL CASTELLO DE NORIMBERGA
American International, 1972
LES BAXTER†

GLI SCHIAVI PIU FORTI DEL MONDO 1964
FRANCESCO DE MASI

GLI SPECIALISTI 1969
ANGELO FRANCESCO LAVAGNINO†

GLI ULTIMI 1963
CARLO RUSTICHELLI

GLI ULTIMI FILIBUSTIERI 1941
CARLO RUSTICHELLI

GLI ULTIMI TRE GIORNI 1977
NICOLA PIOVANI

THE GLIMMER MAN Warner Bros., 1996
TREVOR RABIN

THE GLITTER DOME (CTF) HBO Premiere Films/
Telepictures Corporation/Trincomali Film Productions,
1984
STUART MARGOLIN

GLITTERBUG 1994
BRIAN ENO

GLITZ (TF) Robert Cooper Films, 1988
DANA KAPROFF

GLORIA Columbia, 1980
BILL CONTI

GLORY Tri-Star, 1989
JAMES HORNER

GLORY BOY Cinerama, 1969
JIM HELMS

GLORY DAYS (TF) A. Shane Company/Sibling
Rivalries, 1988
ROBERT FOLK

THE GLORY GUYS United Artists, 1965
RIZ ORTOLANI

THE GLORY STOMPERS American International,
1967
MIKE CURB

GLORY! GLORY! (CTF) Atlantis Films Ltd./Orion TV,
1989
CHRISTOPHER DEDRICK

THE GLOVE BLOOD MAD Pro International,
1981
ROBERT O. RAGLAND

GLOWING AUTUMN 1978
TORU TAKEMITSU†

GLUCHY TELEFON CROSSED LINES 1991
FRYDERYCK BABINSKI

GLUT EMBERS 1983
PEER RABEN

GLYKIA SYMMORIA 1983
GEORGE HATZINASSIOS

THE GNOME-MOBILE Buena Vista, 1967
BUDDY BAKER

GO CHASE YOURSELF RKO Radio, 1938
ROY WEBB†

GO FISH Can I Watch Pictures/KUPI, 1994
JENNIFER SHARPE

GO FISH Samuel Goldwyn, 1994
SCOTT ALDRICH
BRENDAN DOLAN

GO FOR IT World Entertainment, 1976
DENNIS DRAGON

GO FOR THE GOLD Go for the Gold Productions,
1984
DAVID MCHUGH

GO KART GO! Fanfare/CFF, 1964
RON GOODWIN

GO NAKED INTO THE WORLD MGM, 1961
ADOLPH DEUTSCH†

GO TELL IT ON THE MOUNTAIN (TF) Learning in
Focus, 1984
WEBSTER LEWIS

GO TELL THE SPARTANS Avco Embassy, 1978
DICK HALLIGAN

GO TOWARD THE LIGHT (TF) Corapeake
Productions, 1988
JAMES NEWTON HOWARD

GO WEST MGM, 1940
GEORGE BASSMAN

GO WEST, YOUNG GIRL! (TF) Bennett-Katleman
Productions/Columbia Pictures TV, 1978
JERROLD IMMEL

GO, MAN, GO United Artists, 1954
ALEX NORTH†

THE GO-BETWEEN Columbia, 1971
MICHEL LEGRAND

GOBOTS: BATTLE OF THE ROCK LORDS (AF)
Clubhouse/Atlantic Releasing Corporation, 1986
HOYT CURTIN

GOD BLESS THE CHILD (TF) Indieprod Company/
Phoenix Entertainment Group, 1988
DAVID SHIRE

GOD IS MY CO-PILOT Warner Bros., 1945
FRANZ WAXMAN†

GOD IS MY PARTNER 20th Century-Fox, 1957
PAUL DUNLAP

GOD TOLD ME TO New World, 1977
FRANK CORDELL†

GOD'S COUNTRY AND THE WOMAN Warner
Bros., 1936
MAX STEINER†

GOD'S LITTLE ACRE United Artists, 1958
ELMER BERNSTEIN

GOD'S WILL Power and Light Production, 1989
CHRISTOPHER CAMERON

THE GODCHILD (TF) MGM TV, 1974
DAVID SHIRE

THE GODDESS Columbia, 1958
VIRGIL THOMSON†

THE GODDESS OF LOVE (TF) Phil Margo
Enterprises/New World TV/Phoenix Entertainment
Group, 1988
A. S. DIAMOND
DENNIS DREITH
MITCH MARGO

GODDESS OF LOVE 1960
MICHEL MICHELET†

THE GODFATHER PART III also cameo as
conductor, Paramount, 1990
CARMINE COPPOLA†

THE GODFATHER Paramount, 1972
NINO ROTA†

THE GODFATHER, PART II Paramount, 1974
CARMINE COPPOLA† ★★
NINO ROTA† ★★

THE GODS MUST BE CRAZY TLC Films/20th
Century Fox, 1979
JOHNNY BISHOP

THE GODS MUST BE CRAZY TLC Films/20th
Century-Fox, 1979
JOHN BOSHOFF

THE GODS MUST BE CRAZY II WEG/Columbia,
1989
CHARLES FOX

GODS OF PESTILENCE 1970
PEER RABEN

THE GODSEND Cannon, 1980
ROGER WEBB

GODZILLA 1998
DAVID ARNOLD

GODZILLA 1985 New World, 1985
REIJIRO KOROKU
CHRISTOPHER YOUNG

GODZILLA VS. BIONIC MONSTER/GODZILLA VS.
COSMIC MONSTER 1976
MASARU SATO

GODZILLA VS. MECHA-GODZILLA GODZILLA
VS. BIONIC MONSTER/GODZILLA VS.
COSMIC MONSTER 1976
MASARU SATO

GODZILLA VS. MOTHRA American
International, 1964
AKIRA IFUKUBE

GODZILLA VS. THE SEA MONSTER EBIRAH,
HORROR OF THE DEEP 1968
MASARU SATO

GODZILLA VS. THE THING GODZILLA VS.
MOTHRA American International, 1964
AKIRA IFUKUBE

GODZILLA, KING OF THE MONSTERS GOJIRA
Embassy, 1954
AKIRA IFUKUBE

GOG United Artists, 1954
HARRY SUKMAN†

GO-HIME 1992
TORU TAKEMITSU†

GOIN' COCOANUTS Osmond Distribution, 1978
NELSON RIDDLE†

GOIN' HOME Chris Prentiss, 1976
LEE HOLDRIDGE

GOIN' SOUTH Paramount, 1978
PERRY BOTKIN
VAN DYKE PARKS

GOIN' TO TOWN Paramount, 1935
ANDREA SETARO†

GOING APE! Paramount, 1981
ELMER BERNSTEIN

GOING BERSERK Universal, 1983
TOM SCOTT

GOING FOR THE GOLD: THE BILL JOHNSON
STORY (TF) ITC Productions/Sullivan-Carter
Interests/Goodman-Rosen Productions, 1985
J.A.C. REDFORD

GOING HOLLYWOOD MGM, 1933
HERBERT STOTHART†

GOING IN STYLE Warner Bros., 1979
MICHAEL SMALL

GOING MY WAY Paramount, 1944
ROBERT EMMETT DOLAN†

GOING PLACES LES VALSEUSES Cinema 5,
1974
STEPHANE GRAPPELLI

GOING SANE Sea Change Films, 1986
CAMERON ALLAN

GOING TO EXTREMES (TF) Brand-Falsey, 1992
JAY FERGUSON

GOING TO THE CHAPEL (TF) Furia Organization/
Finnegan-Pinchuk Company, 1988
CHARLES FOX

THE GOING UP OF DAVID LEV (TF) 1973
JERRY GOLDSMITH

GOING WEST 1997
BASIL POLEDOURIS

GOJIRA Embassy, 1954
AKIRA IFUKUBE

GOLD Allied Artists, 1974
ELMER BERNSTEIN

GOLD AND LEAD 1966
MICHEL LEGRAND

GOLD FOR THE CAESARS Colorama, 1962
FRANCO MANNINO

GOLD IS WHERE YOU FIND IT Warner Bros.,
1938
MAX STEINER†

GOLD OF NAPLES L'ORO DI NAPOLI DCA,
1955
ALESSANDRO CICOGNINI†

GOLD OF THE AMAZON WOMEN (TF) MI-KA
Productions Inc., 1979
GIL MELLE

THE GOLD RUSH United Artists, 1925
CHARLES CHAPLIN†

THE GOLDEN ARROW Warner Bros., 1936
W. FRANKE HARLING†

GOLDEN BALLS 1993
NICOLA PIOVANI

THE GOLDEN BLADE Universal, 1953
HENRY MANCINI†
HERMAN STEIN

GOLDEN BOY Columbia, 1939
VICTOR YOUNG† ★

THE GOLDEN CHILD Paramount, 1986
MICHEL COLOMBIER

THE GOLDEN CLAW Triangle, 1915
VICTOR SCHERTZINGER†

GOLDEN EARRINGS Paramount, 1947
VICTOR YOUNG†

GOLDEN FIDDLES (MS) 1991
DAVID FOSTER
WILLIAM ROSS

THE GOLDEN FORTRESS 1975
SATYAJIT RAY†

THE GOLDEN GATE MURDERS (TF) Universal TV,
1979
SOL KAPLAN

GOLDEN GATE Samuel Goldwyn, 1994
ELLIOT GOLDENTHAL

GOLDEN GATE (TF) Lin Bolen Productions/Warner
Bros. TV, 1981
RALPH BURNS

GOLDEN HARVEST Paramount, 1933
HEINZ ROEMHELD†

THE GOLDEN HORDE Universal, 1951
HANS J. SALTER†

THE GOLDEN LADY Target International, 1979
GEORGES GARVARENTZ†

THE GOLDEN MISTRESS United Artists, 1954
RAOUL KRAUSHAAR

THE GOLDEN MOMENT: AN OLYMPIC LOVE
STORY (TF) Don Ohlmeyer Productions/
Telepictures Corporation, 1980
PERRY BOTKIN

GOLDEN MOUNTAINS 1931
DMITRI SHOSTAKOVITCH†

GOLDEN NEEDLES American International, 1974
LALO SCHIFRIN

GOLDEN NIGHTS 1976
PIERRE JANSEN

THE GOLDEN SALAMANDER Eagle Lion, 1951
WILLIAM ALWYN†

THE GOLDEN SEAL Samuel Goldwyn Company,
1983
JOHN BARRY
DANA KAPROFF

THE GOLDEN VOYAGE OF SINBAD Columbia,
1974
MIKLOS ROZSA†

GOLDENEYE MGM-UA, 1995
ERIC SERRA

GOLDENGIRL Avco Embassy, 1979
BILL CONTI

GOLDFINGER United Artists, 1964
JOHN BARRY

GOLDIE AND THE BOXER (TF) Orenthal
Productions/Columbia Pictures TV, 1979
JIMMIE HASKELL

GOLDIE AND THE BOXER GO HOLLYWOOD
(TF) Orenthal Productions/Columbia Pictures TV,
1981
JIMMIE HASKELL

G'OLE (FD) IVECO, 1983
RICK WAKEMAN

GOLEM BAMA'AGAL BLIND MAN'S BLUFF
1993
HAIM PERMONT

GOLGOTHA 1935
JACQUES IBERT†

GOLIATH AND THE BARBARIANS American
International, 1959
LES BAXTER†

GOLIATH AND THE DRAGON American
International, 1960
LES BAXTER†

GOLIATH AND THE VAMPIRES 1961
ANGELO FRANCESCO LAVAGNINO†

GOLIATH AND THE VAMPIRES VAMPIRES
American International, 1962
LES BAXTER†

GOLIATH AWAITS (TF) Larry White Productions/
Hugh Benson Productions/Columbia TV, 1981
GEORGE DUNING

GONE IN 60 SECONDS H.B. Halicki International,
1974
RONALD HALICKI

GONE TO EARTH RKO Radio, 1950
BRIAN EASDALE

GONE WITH THE WAVE (FD) 1965
LALO SCHIFRIN

GONE WITH THE WEST International Cinefilm,
1975
CHRISTOPHER L. STONE

GONE WITH THE WIND MGM, 1939
MAX STEINER† ★

THE GONG SHOW MOVIE Universal, 1980
MILTON DELUGG

GONZA THE SPEARMAN 1986
TORU TAKEMITSU†

GOOD AGAINST EVIL (TF) Frankel-Bolen
Productions/20th Century-Fox TV, 1977
LALO SCHIFRIN

THE GOOD AND THE BAD Paramount, 1976
FRANCIS LAI

THE GOOD DIE YOUNG United Artists, 1954
GEORGES AURIC†

THE GOOD EARTH MGM, 1937
HERBERT STOTHART†

THE GOOD FASCIST Living Pictures, 1992
IAN SOLOMON

THE GOOD FATHER Skouras Pictures, 1986
RICHARD HARTLEY

THE GOOD FELLOWS Paramount, 1943
LEO SHUKEN†

THE GOOD FIGHT (CTF) Freyda Rothstein/Hearst,
1992
W.G. SNUFFY WALDEN

THE GOOD FIGHT (FD) 1983
WENDY BLACKSTONE

GOOD FOR NOTHING 1978
HANS WERNER HENZE

THE GOOD GUYS AND THE BAD GUYS Warner
Bros., 1969
WILLIAM LAVA†

GOOD GUYS WEAR BLACK American Cinema,
1979
CRAIG SAFAN

'97-'98
FILM
COMPOSERS
INDEX

F
I
L
M

T
I
T
L
E
S

THE GOOD HUMOR MAN Columbia, 1950
HEINZ ROEMHELD†

GOOD KING WENCESLAS (CTF) 1994
CHARLES GROSS

GOOD LUCK, MISS WYCKOFF Bel Air/Gradison, 1979
ERNEST GOLD

GOOD LUCK, MR. YATES Columbia, 1943
JOHN LEIPOLD†

A GOOD MAN IN AFRICA Gramercy, 1994
JOHN DUPREZ

GOOD MEN, GOOD WOMEN HAO NAN HAO NU 1995
CHIANG HSIAO-WEN
CHEN HWAI-EN

GOOD MORNING VIETNAM Buena Vista, 1987
ALEX NORTH†

GOOD MORNING, BABYLON Vestron, 1987
NICOLA PIOVANI

GOOD MORNING, MISS DOVE 20th Century-Fox, 1955
LEIGH HARLINE†

GOOD MORNING...AND GOODBYE Eve, 1967
IGO KANTOR

THE GOOD MOTHER Buena Vista, 1988
ELMER BERNSTEIN

GOOD NEIGHBOR SAM Columbia, 1964
FRANK DEVOL

THE GOOD OLD BOYS (CTF) Edgar J. Scherick Prods./Fireband Prods./Javelina Films, 1995
JOHN MCEUEN

THE GOOD OLD SOAK MGM, 1937
EDWARD WARD†

GOOD SAM RKO Radio, 1948
ROBERT EMMETT DOLAN†

THE GOOD SON 20th Century Fox, 1993
ELMER BERNSTEIN

A GOOD SPORT (TF) Ralph Waite Productions/Warner Bros. TV, 1984
MARK SNOW

GOOD TO GO Island Pictures, 1986
WALLY BADAROU

THE GOOD WIFE Atlantic Releasing Corporation, 1986
CAMERON ALLAN

THE GOOD, THE BAD AND THE UGLY United Artists, 1966
ENNIO MORRICONE

GOODBYE AGAIN AIMEZ-VOUS BRAHMS? United Artists, 1961
GEORGES AURIC†

GOODBYE AMERICA Quantum entertainment, 1997
ROY HAY

GOODBYE CHARLIE 20th Century-Fox, 1964
ANDRE PREVIN

GOODBYE COLUMBUS Paramount, 1969
CHARLES FOX

GOODBYE EMMANUELLE 1977
SERGE GAINSBOURG†

GOODBYE GEMINI Cinerama Releasing Corporation, 1970
CHRISTOPHER GUNNING

THE GOODBYE GIRL Warner Bros., 1977
DAVE GRUSIN

GOODBYE MARY (TF) 1980
BRUNO NICOLAI

GOODBYE MR. CHIPS MGM, 1939
RICHARD ADDINSELL†

GOODBYE MY FANCY Warner Bros., 1951
DANIELE AMFITHEATROF†

GOODBYE NEW YORK Castle Hill Productions, 1985
MICHAEL ABENE

GOODBYE RAGGEDY ANN (TF) Metromedia Producers Corporation, 1971
WLADIMIR SELINSKY

GOOD-BYE, CRUEL WORLD Sharp Features, 1982
TOM JENKINS

GOODBYE, FLICKMANIA Nippon Herald, 1979
RYUDO UZAKI

GOODBYE, MR. CHIPS MGM, 1969
LESLIE BRICCUSE ★
JOHN WILLIAMS ★

GOODBYE, NORMA JEAN Filmways, 1976
JOE BECK

GOODNIGHT MY LOVE (TF) ABC Circle Films, 1972
HARRY BETTS

A GOOFY MOVIE (AF) Buena Vista, 1995
CARTER BURWELL

GOONIES Warner Bros., 1985
DAVE GRUSIN

GORDON'S WAR 20th Century Fox, 1973
ANGELO BADALAMENTI

GORDY Miramax, 1995
TOM BAHLER

GORDY Robson Entertainment, 1993
CHARLES FOX

GORE VIDAL'S BILLY THE KID (CTF) von Zerneck-Sertner Productions, 1989
LAURENCE ROSENTHAL

GORE VIDAL'S LINCOLN (MS) Chris-Rose Productions/Finnegan-Pinchuk Company, 1988
ERNEST GOLD

THE GORE-GORE GIRLS BLOOD ORGY Lewis Motion Picture Enterprises, 1972
HERSCHELL GORDON LEWIS

THE GORGEOUS HUSSY MGM, 1936
HERBERT STOTHART†

GORGO MGM, 1961
ANGELO FRANCESCO LAVAGNINO†

THE GORGON Columbia, 1964
JAMES BERNARD

THE GORILLA 20th Century-Fox, 1939
DAVID BUTTOLPH†

GORILLA AT LARGE 20th Century-Fox, 1954
LIONEL NEWMAN†

GORILLA BATHES AT NOON 1993
BRYNMOR LLEWELLYN-JONES

GORILLAS IN THE MIST Universal, 1988
MAURICE JARRE ★

GORKY PARK Orion, 1983
JAMES HORNER

THE GOSPEL ACCORDING TO ST. MATTHEW Continental, 1965
LUIS BACALOV ★

GOSPEL ACCORDING TO VIC JUST ANOTHER MIRACLE Skouras Pictures, 1986
B.A. ROBERTSON

THE GOSSIP COLUMNIST (TF) Universal TV, 1980
ALLYN FERGUSON

GOTCHA! Universal, 1985
BILL CONTI

GOTCHA! Universal/MCA T.V., 1992
BOB MITHOFF

GOTHAM (CTF) Phoenix Entertainment/Keith Addis and Associates Productions, 1988
GEORGE S. CLINTON

GOTHIC Vestron, 1987
THOMAS DOLBY

GOTT MIT UNS THE LAST FIVE DAYS OF PEACE 1969
ENNIO MORRICONE

GOVERNMENT GIRL RKO Radio, 1943
LEIGH HARLINE†

GOYA 1971
LUIS DE PABLO

GRACE KELLY (TF) Takota Productions/Embassy TV, 1983
JOHN ANDREW TARTAGLIA

GRACE OF MY HEART Gramercy, 1996
LARRY KLEIN

GRACE QUIGLEY Cannon, 1984
JOHN ADDISON

THE GRADUATE Avco Embassy, 1967
DAVE GRUSIN

GRADUATION DAY IFI-Scope III, 1981
ARTHUR KEMPEL

GRAMBLING'S WHITE TIGER (TF) Inter Planetary Productions/Jenner/Wallach Productions, 1981
JOHN D'ANDREA
MICHAEL LLOYD

GRAMPS (TF) Fred Silverman Co./Viacom, 1995
JOSEPH CONLAN

GRAN PREMIO 1943
CARLO RUSTICHELLI

GRAN VARIETA 1953
CARLO RUSTICHELLI

GRAND CANYON 20th Century Fox, 1991
JAMES NEWTON HOWARD

GRAND CANYON Lippert, 1949
ALBERT GLASSER

THE GRAND DUEL 1972
LUIS BACALOV

GRAND HOTEL EXCELSIOR 1982
ARMANDO TROVAJOLI

GRAND ILLUSION World Pictures, 1937
JOSEPH KOSMA†

GRAND ISLE Kelly McGillis/Turner Pictures, 1991
ELLIOT GOLDENTHAL

THE GRAND OLYMPICS 1960
ARMANDO TROVAJOLI

THE GRAND OLYMPICS (FD) 1960
ANGELO FRANCESCO LAVAGNINO†

GRAND PRIX MGM, 1966
MAURICE JARRE

GRAND SLAM AD OGNI COSTO 1967
ENNIO MORRICONE

GRAND THEFT AUTO New World, 1977
PETER IVERS

GRAND TOUR (CTF) HBO Pictures, 1989
GERALD GOURIET

GRANDEUR NATURE 1974
MAURICE JARRE

GRANDMOTHER'S HOUSE Omega Pictures, 1988
NIGEL HOLTON

GRANDS FEUX 1937
DARIUS MILHAUD†

GRANDVIEW, U.S.A. Warner Bros., 1984
THOMAS NEWMAN

THE GRAPES OF WRATH 20th Century-Fox, 1940
ALFRED NEWMAN†

THE GRASS HARP Fine Line, 1996
PATRICK WILLIAMS

THE GRASS IS ALWAYS GREENER OVER THE SEPTIC TANK (TF) Joe Hamilton Productions, 1978
PETER MATZ

GRASS ROOTS (TF) Team Cherokee/JBS Prods., 1992
LAURENCE ROSENTHAL

THE GRASSHOPPER National General, 1969
BILLY GOLDENBERG

GRAVE SECRETS: THE LEGACY OF HILLTOP DRIVE (TF) Freyda Rothstein/Hearst, 1992
PATRICK WILLIAMS

GRAVEYARD SHIFT Paramount, 1990
BRIAN BANKS
ANTHONY MARINELLI

GRAVEYARD SHIFT Shapiro/Virgin, 1986
NICHOLAS PIKE

THE GRAVY TRAIN THE DION BROTHERS Columbia, 1974
FRED KARLIN

GRAY OF ABSENCE Argencine, Argentine
EMILIO KAUDERER

GRAYEAGLE American International, 1977
JAIME MENDOZA-NAVA

GRAY'S ANATOMY 1997
CLIFF MARTINEZ

GRAZIE TANTE E ARRIVEDERCI 1976, Italian
LUIS BACALOV

GRAZIE ZIA 1968
ENNIO MORRICONE

GREASE 2 Paramount, 1982
ARTIE BUTLER

GREASED LIGHTNING Warner Bros., 1977
FRED KARLIN

GREASER'S PALACE Greaser's Palace, 1972
JACK NITZCHE

THE GREAT ALLIGATOR 1979
STELVIO CIPRIANI

A GREAT AMERICAN TRAGEDY (TF) Metromedia Producers Corporation/J. Lee Thompson/Ronald Shedlo Productions, 1972
GEORGE DUNING

THE GREAT AMERICAN BEAUTY CONTEST (TF) ABC Circle Films, 1973
KEN WANNBERG

THE GREAT AMERICAN PASTIME MGM, 1956
JEFF ALEXANDER†

THE GREAT AMERICAN TRAFFIC JAM GRIDLOCK (TF) Ten-Four Productions, 1980
ARTHUR B. RUBINSTEIN

THE GREAT BANK HOAX SHENANIGANS Warner Bros., 1978
ARTHUR B. RUBINSTEIN

THE GREAT BANK ROBBERY Warner Bros., 1969
NELSON RIDDLE†

THE GREAT BRAIN Osmond Distribution Company, 1978
DON COSTA

THE GREAT CARUSO MGM, 1951
JOHN GREEN† ★

THE GREAT CASH GIVEAWAY GETAWAY (TF) Penthouse Productions/Cine Guarantors, 1980
JOHN PARKER

GREAT CATHERINE Warner Bros., 1968
DIMITRI TIOMKIN†

THE GREAT CHASE Continental, 1963
LARRY ADLER

A GREAT CITIZEN 1938
DMITRI SHOSTAKOVITCH†

THE GREAT COMMANDMENT Universal, 1939
HANS J. SALTER†

GREAT DAY IN THE MORNING RKO Radio, 1956
LEIGH HARLINE†
LEITH STEVENS†

THE GREAT DEPRESSION (TD) 1993
BRIAN KEANE

THE GREAT DICTATOR United Artists, 1940
CHARLES CHAPLIN† ★

THE GREAT ESCAPE United Artists, 1963
ELMER BERNSTEIN

THE GREAT ESCAPE II: THE UNTOLD STORY (TF) Spectacor Films/Michael Jaffe Films, 1988
JOHNNY MANDEL

GREAT EXPECTATIONS Transcontinental Film Productions, 1975
MAURICE JARRE

GREAT EXPECTATIONS Universal, 1934
EDWARD WARD†

GREAT EXPECTATIONS Universal, 1947
WALTER GOEHR†

GREAT EXPECTATIONS (CTF) The Disney Channel/Harlech TV/Primetime TV, 1989
KEN THORNE

THE GREAT GARRICK Warner Bros., 1937
ADOLPH DEUTSCH†

THE GREAT GATSBY Paramount, 1949
ROBERT EMMETT DOLAN†

THE GREAT GATSBY Paramount, 1974
NELSON RIDDLE† ★★

THE GREAT GILDERSLEEVE RKO Radio, 1943
PAUL SAWTELL†

THE GREAT GLASS BLOWER 1933
JEAN WIENER†

THE GREAT HOUDINIS (TF) ABC Circle Films, 1976
PETER MATZ

THE GREAT ICE RIP-OFF (TF) ABC Circle Films, 1974
BOB COBERT

THE GREAT IMPERSONATION Universal, 1935
FRANZ WAXMAN†

THE GREAT IMPOSTOR 1960
HENRY MANCINI†

THE GREAT JASPER RKO Radio, 1933
MAX STEINER†

THE GREAT JEWEL ROBBER Warner Bros., 1950
WILLIAM LAVA†

THE GREAT JOHN L. United Artists, 1945
VICTOR YOUNG†

THE GREAT KANDINSKY (TF) BBC, 1995
HAL LINDES

THE GREAT LIE Warner Bros., 1941
MAX STEINER†

THE GREAT MacARTHY 1975
BRUCE SMEATON

THE GREAT MAN VOTES RKO Radio, 1939
ROY WEBB†

THE GREAT MAN Universal, 1956
HENRY MANCINI†
HERMAN STEIN

THE GREAT MAN'S LADY Paramount, 1942
VICTOR YOUNG†

THE GREAT MAN'S WHISKERS (TF) Universal TV, 1973
EARL ROBINSON

THE GREAT McGINTY Paramount, 1940
FREDERICK HOLLANDER†

THE GREAT MELIES 1952
GEORGES VAN PARYS†

THE GREAT MOMENT Paramount, 1944
VICTOR YOUNG†

THE GREAT MOUSE DETECTIVE Buena Vista, 1986
HENRY MANCINI†

THE GREAT MR. NOBODY Warner Bros., 1941
ADOLPH DEUTSCH†

THE GREAT MUPPET CAPER Universal/AFD, 1981
JOE RAPOSO†

THE GREAT NORTHFIELD, MINNESOTA RAID Universal, 1972
DAVE GRUSIN

THE GREAT OUTDOORS Universal, 1988
NICKY HOLLAND
THOMAS NEWMAN

THE GREAT PRETENDER (TF) Stephen J. Cannell, 1991
MIKE POST

THE GREAT RACE Warner Bros., 1965
HENRY MANCINI†

THE GREAT RUPERT Eagle Lion, 1950
LEITH STEVENS†

THE GREAT SANTINI THE ACE Orion/Warner Bros., 1980
ELMER BERNSTEIN

THE GREAT SCOUT AND CATHOUSE THURSDAY American International, 1976
JOHN CAMERON

THE GREAT SINNER MGM, 1949
BRONISLAU KAPER†

THE GREAT SIOUX MASSACRE Columbia, 1965
EMIL NEWMAN†

THE GREAT SIOUX UPRISING Universal, 1953
HENRY MANCINI†
HERMAN STEIN

THE GREAT SMOKEY ROADBLOCK THE LAST OF THE COWBOYS Dimension, 1976
CRAIG SAFAN

THE GREAT ST. LOUIS BANK ROBBERY United Artists, 1959
BERNARDO SEGALL

THE GREAT ST. TRINIAN'S TRAIN ROBBERY British Lion, 1966
MALCOLM ARNOLD

THE GREAT TELEPHONE ROBBERY 1973
DOV SELTZER

THE GREAT TEXAS DYNAMITE CHASE New World, 1976
CRAIG SAFAN

THE GREAT TRAIN ROBBERY United Artists, 1979
JERRY GOLDSMITH

THE GREAT UNPLEASANTNESS Crescent Pictures, 1993
JAKE BERGER
BUZZOV-EN
PERVIS LEE

THE GREAT WALDO PEPPER Universal, 1975
HENRY MANCINI†

THE GREAT WALTZ MGM, 1938
DIMITRI TIOMKIN†

THE GREAT WAR United Artists, 1959
NINO ROTA†

'97-'98
FILM
COMPOSERS
INDEX

THE GREAT WHITE HOPE 20th Century-Fox, 1970
LIONEL NEWMAN†

THE GREAT WHITE HYPE 20th Century Fox, 1996
MARCUS MILLER

GREAT WHITE Film Ventures International, 1982
GUIDO DE ANGELIS
MAURIZIO DE ANGELIS
MORTON STEVENS†

THE GREATEST Columbia, 1977
LEE HOLDRIDGE
MICHAEL MASSER

THE GREATEST GIFT (TF) Universal TV, 1974
DICK DEBENEDICTIS

THE GREATEST KIDNAPPING IN THE WEST
1967
LUIS BACALOV

THE GREATEST SHOW ON EARTH Paramount,
1952
VICTOR YOUNG†

THE GREATEST STORY EVER TOLD United Artists,
1965
ALFRED NEWMAN† ★

**THE GREATEST THING THAT ALMOST HAPPENED
(TF)** Charles Fries Productions, 1977
DAVID SHIRE

GREECE, LAND OF DREAMS 1965
MANOS HADJIDAKIS†

GREED
CARL DAVIS

GREED IN THE SUN 1963
GEORGES DELERUE†

GREEDY Universal, 1994
RANDY EDELMAN

THE GREEK COCKATOO *FOUR DARK HOURS*
New World, 1937
MIKLOS ROZSA†

THE GREEK TYCOON Universal, 1978
STANLEY MYERS†

THE GREEKS HAD A WORD FOR THEM United
Artists, 1932
ALFRED NEWMAN†

THE GREEN BELT 1941
RICHARD ADDINSELL†

THE GREEN BERETS Warner Bros., 1968
MIKLOS ROZSA†

GREEN CARD Buena Vista, 1990
HANS ZIMMER

GREEN DOLPHIN BEAT (TF) Robert Ward Prods./
Spelling TV, 1994
PETER MANNING ROBINSON

GREEN DOLPHIN STREET MGM, 1947
BRONISLAU KAPER†

GREEN EYES (TF) ABC TV, 1977
FRED KARLIN

GREEN FIRE MGM, 1954
MIKLOS ROZSA†

GREEN FOR DANGER 1946
WILLIAM ALWYN†

THE GREEN GLOVE *LE GANTELET VERT* United
Artists, 1952
JOSEPH KOSMA†

GREEN GRASS OF WYOMING 20th Century-Fox,
1948
CYRIL J. MOCKRIDGE†

THE GREEN HELMET MGM, 1961
KENNETH V. JONES

GREEN ICE ITC Films, 1981
BILL WYMAN

THE GREEN JACKET CEP, 1979
LUIS BACALOV

GREEN LIGHT Warner Bros., 1937
MAX STEINER†

THE GREEN MAN (TF) BBC TV/A&E, 1991
TIM SOUSTER

GREEN MANSIONS MGM, 1959
BRONISLAU KAPER†
HEITOR VILLA-LOBOS†

GREEN ON THURSDAYS (FD) Red Branch, 1993
MICHAEL BONDERT
LEO CRANDALL

THE GREEN PASTURES Warner Bros., 1936
ERICH WOLFGANG KORNGOLD†

THE GREEN SCARF 1955
BRIAN EASDALE

THE GREEN YEARS MGM, 1946
HERBERT STOTHART†

THE GREEN-EYED BLONDE Warner Bros., 1957
LEITH STEVENS†

THE GREENGAGE SUMMER Columbia, 1961
RICHARD ADDINSELL†

GREGORY K (TF) Spectacor/Michael Jaffe, 1993
JAMES MCVAY

GREGORY'S GIRL Samuel Goldwyn Company, 1982
COLIN TULLY

GREMLINS also cameo as phone booth user, Warner
Bros., 1984
JERRY GOLDSMITH

GREMLINS 2: THE NEW BATCH also cameo as
yoghurt shop customer, Warner Bros., 1990
JERRY GOLDSMITH

GRENDEL, GRENDEL, GRENDEL (AF) Victorian
Film Corp., 1980
BRUCE SMEATON

GRENZENLOS *OPEN ENDS* 1983
PEER RABEN

THE GREY FOX United Artists Classics, 1983
MICHAEL CONWAY BAKER

THE GREY KNIGHT Motion Picture Corp. of America,
1993
JOHN D'ANDREA
CORY LERIOS

GREY LADY DOWN Universal, 1978
JERRY FIELDING†

**GREYSTOKE: THE LEGEND OF TARZAN, LORD OF
THE APES** Warner Bros., 1984
JOHN SCOTT

GRIBOUILLE *HEART OF PARIS* 1937
GEORGES AURIC†

GRID RUNNERS *VIRTUAL COMBAT* Amritraj
Entertainment, 1995
CLAUDE GAUDETTE

GRIDIRON FLASH RKO Radio, 1934
MAX STEINER†

GRIDLOCK (TF) Ten-Four Productions, 1980
ARTHUR B. RUBINSTEIN

GRIDLOCK'D Gramercy, 1997
STEWART COPELAND

GRIEF Grief Prods., 1993
TOM JUDSON

GRIEVOUS BODILY HARM International Film
Management, 1988
CHRIS NEAL

GRIFFIN AND PHOENIX (TF) ABC Circle Films,
1976
GEORGE ALICESON TIPTON

THE GRIFTERS Miramax, 1990
ELMER BERNSTEIN

GRIJPSTRA & DE GIER Vereinigade Nederland
Filmcompagnie, 1983
ROGIER VAN OTTERLOO†

GRINGO *DUELLO NEL TEXAS/GUNFIGHT AT
RED SANDS* 1963
ENNIO MORRICONE

THE GRISSOM GANG Cinerama Releasing
Corporation, 1971
GERALD FRIED

GRIZZLY Film Ventures International, 1976
ROBERT O. RAGLAND

GROMAIRE (FD) 1967
MICHEL PORTAL

GROSS ANATOMY Touchstone, 1989
DAVID NEWMAN

GROSS MISCONDUCT 1993
BRUCE ROWLAND

GROSSE FATIGUE *DEAD TIRED* Miramax Zoë,
1995
RENE MARC BINI

GROSSE POINT BLANK Buena Vista, 1997
JOE STRUMMER

GROUND ZERO Avenue Pictures, 1987
CHRIS NEAL

GROUNDS FOR MARRIAGE MGM, 1950
BRONISLAU KAPER†
DAVID RAKSIN

THE GROUNDSTAR CONSPIRACY Universal,
1972
PAUL HOFFERT

GROUNHOG DAY Columbia, 1993
GEORGE FENTON

THE GROUP United Artists, 1965
CHARLES GROSS

GROWING PAINS New World, 1984
W. MICHAEL LEWIS
LAURIN RINDER

GRUMPY OLD MEN Warner Bros., 1993
ALAN SILVESTRI

GRUNT! THE WRESTLING MOVIE New World,
1985
SUSAN JUSTIN

GRUPPO DI FAMIGLIAIN UNO INTERNO New
Line Cinema, 1975
FRANCO MANNINO

GUADALCANAL DIARY 20th Century-Fox, 1943
DAVID BUTTOLPH†

GUANTANAMERA 1995
JOSE NIETO

**GUARDIA, GUARDIA SCELTA, BRIGADIERE E
MARESCIALLO** Imperial Film, 1956
CARLO RUSTICHELLI

THE GUARDIAN Universal, 1990
JACK HUES

THE GUARDIAN (CTF) HBO Premiere Films/Robert
Cooper Productions/Stanely Chase Productions, 1984
ROBERT O. RAGLAND

GUARDIAN ANGEL PM, 1993
BRUCE HANIFAN

GUARDIAN OF THE WILDERNESS Sunn Classic,
1977
ROBERT SUMMERS

GUARDIE E LADRI 1951
ALESSANDRO CICOGNINI†

GUARDING TESS TriStar, 1994
MICHAEL CONVERTINO

GUENDALINA Carlo Ponti/Les Films Marceau, 1957
PIERO PICCIONI ★

GUESS WHO'S COMING TO DINNER Columbia,
1967
FRANK DEVOL

GUESS WHO'S SLEEPING IN MY BED? (TF) ABC
Circle Films, 1973
MORTON STEVENS†

THE GUEST *THE CARETAKER* Janus, 1963
RON GRAINER†

GUEST IN THE HOUSE United Artists, 1944
WERNER JANSSEN ★

GUEST WIFE United Artists, 1945
DANIELE AMFITHEATROF† ★

GUGLIELMO IL DENTONE 1965
ARMANDO TROVAJOLI

A GUIDE FOR THE MARRIED MAN 20th
Century-Fox, 1967
JOHN WILLIAMS

A GUIDE FOR THE MARRIED WOMAN (TF) 20th
Century-Fox TV, 1978
ALLYN FERGUSON
JACK ELLIOTT

THE GUILT OF JANET AMES Columbia, 1947
GEORGE DUNING

GUILTY AS CHARGED I.R.S., 1991
STEVE BARTEK

GUILTY AS SIN Buena Vista, 1993
HOWARD SHORE

GUILTY BY SUSPICION Warner Bros., 1991
JAMES NEWTON HOWARD

GUILTY BYSTANDER Film Classics, 1950
DIMITRI TIOMKIN†

GUILTY OF TREASON Eagle Lion, 1949
HUGO FRIEDHOFER†
EMIL NEWMAN†

**GUILTY OR INNOCENT: THE SAM SHEPPARD
MURDER CASE (TF)** Universal TV, 1975
LALO SCHIFRIN

GUILTY UNTIL PROVEN INNOCENT (TF)
Cosgrove-Meurer, 1991
CHARLES BERNSTEIN

THE GUINEA PIG Pathe, 1948
JOHN ADDISON

THE GUINEA PIG COUPLE 1977
MICHEL COLOMBIER

GUINGUETTE 1958
GEORGES VAN PARYS†

GULAG (CTF) Lorimar Productions/HBO Premiere
Films, 1985
ELMER BERNSTEIN

GULF STREAM 1939
DARIUS MILHAUD†

GULLIVER'S TRAVELS EMI, 1977
MICHEL LEGRAND

GULLIVER'S TRAVELS Paramount, 1939
VICTOR YOUNG† ★

GULLIVER'S TRAVELS Henson Productions, 1996
TREVOR JONES

**GULLIVER'S TRAVELS BEYOND THE MOON
(AF)** 1966
MILTON DELUGG

GUMBALL RALLY Warner Bros., 1976
DOMINIC FRONTIERE

GUMSHOE Columbia, 1971
ANDREW LLOYD WEBBER

THE GUMSHOE KID Skouras Pictures, 1989
PETER MATZ

THE GUN AND THE PULPIT (TF) Cine Television/
Danny Thomas Productions, 1974
GEORGE ALICESON TIPTON

GUN CRAZY *DEADLY IS THE FEMALE* United
Artists, 1949
VICTOR YOUNG†

GUN DUEL IN DURANGO United Artists, 1957
BERT A. SHEFTER

GUN FEVER United Artists, 1958
PAUL DUNLAP

GUN FURY Columbia, 1953
MISCHA BAKALEINIKOFF†

GUN GLORY MGM, 1957
JEFF ALEXANDER†

THE GUN HAWK Allied Artists, 1963
JIMMIE HASKELL

THE GUN IN BETTY LOU'S HAND BAG Buena
Vista, 1992
RICHARD GIBBS

A GUN IN THE HOUSE (TF) The
Channing-Debin-Locke Company, 1981
JIMMIE HASKELL

GUN LAW RKO Radio, 1938
ROY WEBB†

THE GUN RUNNERS United Artists, 1958
LEITH STEVENS†

GUN STREET United Artists, 1962
RICHARD LASALLE

GUNCRAZY Zeta Entertainment, 1992
ED TOMNEY

A GUNFIGHT Paramount, 1971
LAURENCE ROSENTHAL

THE GUNFIGHT AT DODGE CITY Universal, 1959
HANS J. SALTER†

GUNFIGHT AT THE O.K. CORRAL Paramount,
1957
DIMITRI TIOMKIN†

THE GUNFIGHTER 20th Century-Fox, 1950
ALFRED NEWMAN†

THE GUNFIGHTERS (TF) Grosso-Jacobson
Productions/Alliance Entertainment/Tribune
Entertainment, 1987
DOMENIC TROIANO

GUNFIGHTERS OF ABILENE United Artists, 1960
PAUL DUNLAP

GUNFIRE Lippert, 1950
ALBERT GLASSER

GUNG HO Paramount, 1986
THOMAS NEWMAN

GUNG HO! Universal, 1943
HANS J. SALTER†
FRANK SKINNER†

GUNGA DIN RKO Radio, 1939
ALFRED NEWMAN†

GUNGALA, LA VIRGINE DELLS GIUNGLA
GUNGALA, THE VIRGIN OF THE JUNGLE
1967
ANGELO FRANCESCO LAVAGNINO†

GUNGALA, THE VIRGIN OF THE JUNGLE 1967
ANGELO FRANCESCO LAVAGNINO†

GUNMEN Dimension/Miramax, 1994
JOHN DEBNEY

GUNMEN OF THE RIO GRANDE 1965
ANGELO FRANCESCO LAVAGNINO†

GUNN Warner Bros., 1967
HENRY MANCINI†

GUNPOINT Universal, 1966
HANS J. SALTER†

GUNS AT BATASI 20th Century Fox, 1964
JOHN ADDISON

GUNS FOR SAN SEBASTIAN 1968
ENNIO MORRICONE

THE GUNS OF AUGUST (FD) Universal, 1964
SOL KAPLAN

GUNS OF DARKNESS Warner Bros., 1962
BENJAMIN FRANKEL†

THE GUNS OF NAVARONE Columbia, 1961
DIMITRI TIOMKIN† ★

GUNS OF THE BLACK WITCH American
International, 1961
LES BAXTER†

GUNS OF THE MAGNIFICENT SEVEN United
Artists, 1969
ELMER BERNSTEIN

GUNS OF THE TIMBERLAND Warner Bros., 1960
DAVID BUTTOLPH†

GUNSIGHT RIDGE United Artists, 1957
DAVID RAKSIN

THE GUNSLINGER ARC, 1956
RONALD STEIN†

GUNSMOKE Universal, 1953
HENRY MANCINI†
HERMAN STEIN

GUNSMOKE II: TO THE LAST MAN (TF) CBS
Enterprises, 1991
ARTIE KANE

GUNSMOKE IN TUCSON Allied Artists, 1958
SIDNEY CUTNER†

GUNSMOKE: ONE MAN'S JUSTICE (TF) CBS
Entertainment Prods., 1994
ARTIE KANE

GUNSMOKE: RETURN TO DODGE (TF) CBS
Entertainment, 1987
JERROLD IMMEL

GUNSMOKE: THE LAST APACHE (TF) CBS
Entertainment Productions/Galatea Productions,
1990
BRUCE ROWLAND

GUNSMOKE: THE LONG RIDE (TF) CBS, 1993
ARTIE KANE

GUS Buena Vista, 1976
ROBERT F. BRUNNER

GUS BROWN AND MIDNIGHT BREWSTER (TF)
Kaledonia Productions/SCOMI, 1985
HARRY MIDDLEBROOKS

**GUTS AND GLORY: THE RISE AND FALL OF
OLIVER NORTH (TF)** Mike Robe Productions/
Papazian-Hirsch Entertainment, 1989
ARTHUR B. RUBINSTEIN

A GUY NAMED JOE MGM, 1944
HERBERT STOTHART†

THE GUY WHO CAME BACK 20th Century-Fox,
1951
LEIGH HARLINE†

**GUYANA TRAGEDY: THE STORY OF JIM JONES
(TF)** The Konigsberg Company, 1980
ELMER BERNSTEIN

GUYANA, CULT OF THE DAMNED Universal,
1980
GEORGE S. PRICE
NELSON RIDDLE†
ROBERT SUMMERS

GWENDOLINE Samuel Goldwyn Company, 1984
PIERRE BACHELET

GYEREKGYILKOSS GOK *CHILD MURDERS*
1993
JANOS MASIK

GYMKATA MGM/UA, 1985
ALFI KABILJO

GYPSY ANGELS Coconut Grove, 1990
CHUCK CIRINO

GYPSY GIRL *SKY WEST AND CROOKED* Rank/
Continental, 1966
MALCOLM ARNOLD

THE GYPSY MOTHS MGM, 1969
ELMER BERNSTEIN

GYPSY WILDCAT Universal, 1944
EDWARD WARD†

H

H-2-S 1968
ENNIO MORRICONE

THE HABITATION OF DRAGONS (CTF)
Brandman/Amblin TV, 1992
DAVID SHIRE

HACKERS MGM-UA, 1995
SIMON BOSWELL

HADLEY'S REBELLION American Film Distributors,
1984
MIKE POST

HAIL THE CONQUERING HERO Paramount, 1944
WERNER R. HEYMANN†

HAIL, HERO! National General, 1969
JEROME MOROSS†

HAIRSPRAY New Line Cinema, 1988
KENNY VANCE

THE HAIRY APE United Artists, 1944
MICHEL MICHELET† ★

HAK MAU *BLACK CAT* 1992
DANNY CHUNG

HALCYON DAYS *LES PECHERS MORTELS* 1995
ALEXANDRE DESPLAT

HALF ANGEL 20th Century-Fox, 1951
CYRIL J. MOCKRIDGE†

HALF HUMAN DCA, 1957
MASARU SATO

HALF MOON STREET 20th Century Fox, 1986
RICHARD HARVEY

THE HALF NAKED TRUTH also cameo as conductor,
RKO Radio, 1932
MAX STEINER†

HALF SHOT AT SUNRISE RKO Radio, 1930
MAX STEINER†

HALF WAY TO SHANGHAI Universal, 1942
HANS J. SALTER†

HALF-COCKED Bullhorn, 1995
MICHAEL GALINSKY

HALFWAY HOUSE Ealing, 1944
LORD BERNERS†

THE HALLELUJAH TRAIL United Artists, 1965
ELMER BERNSTEIN

HALLELUJAH (TF) Rhinoceros Prods., 1993
WENDY BLACKSTONE

HALLO EVERYBODY 1933
DARIUS MILHAUD†

HALLOWEEN Compass International, 1978
JOHN CARPENTER

**HALLOWEEN 4: THE RETURN OF MICHAEL
MYERS** Galaxy International, 1988
ALAN HOWARTH

**HALLOWEEN 5: THE REVENGE OF MICHAEL
MYERS** Galaxy International, 1989
ALAN HOWARTH

HALLOWEEN II Universal, 1981
JOHN CARPENTER
ALAN HOWARTH

HALLOWEEN III: SEASON OF THE WITCH
Universal, 1982
JOHN CARPENTER
ALAN HOWARTH

HALLOWEEN: THE CURSE OF MICHAEL MYERS
Dimension, 1995
ALAN HOWARTH

HALLS OF ANGER United Artists, 1970
DAVE GRUSIN

HALLS OF MONTEZUMA 20th Century-Fox, 1951
SOL KAPLAN

HALLUCINATION GENERATION 1966
BERNARDO SEGALL

HAMBURGER HILL Paramount, 1987
PHILIP GLASS

HAMBURGER...THE MOTION PICTURE FM
Entertainment, 1986
PETER BERNSTEIN

HAME'AHEV *THE LOVER* Cannon, 1986
DOV SELTZER

HAMLET 1931
DMITRI SHOSTAKOVITCH†

HAMLET 1996
PATRICK DOYLE

HAMLET United Artists, 1964
DMITRI SHOSTAKOVITCH†

HAMLET Universal, 1946
SIR WILLIAM WALTON† ★

HAMLET Warner Bros., 1990
ENNIO MORRICONE ★

HAMMERHEAD Columbia, 1968
DAVID WHITAKER

HAMMERSMITH IS OUT Cinerama Releasing
Corporation, 1972
DOMINIC FRONTIERE

HAMMETT Orion/Warner Bros., 1982
JOHN BARRY

HAN WESTMAR 1933
GIUSEPPE BECCE†

THE HAND Orion/Warner Bros., 1981
JAMES HORNER

HAND GUN Workin' Man, 1993
DOUGLAS J. CUOMO

HAND OF POWER 1972
PETER THOMAS

THE HAND THAT ROCKS THE CRADLE Buena
Vista, 1991
GRAEME REVELL

A HANDFUL OF DUST New Line Cinema, 1988
GEORGE FENTON

HANDGUN Warner Bros., 1981
MIKE POST

HANDLE WITH CARE MGM, 1958
ALEXANDER COURAGE

HANDLE WITH CARE Paramount, 1977
BILL CONTI

THE HANDMAID'S TALE Cinecom, 1990
RYUICHI SAKAMOTO

HANDS ACROSS THE BORDER Republic, 1943
WALTER SCHARF

HANDS OF A MURDERER (TF) Storke/Fuisz
Productions/Yorkshire TV, 1990
COLIN TOWNS

HANDS OF A STRANGER Allied Artists, 1962
RICHARD LASALLE

HANDS OF A STRANGER (TF) Taft Entertainment
TV, 1987
MICHEL RUBINI

THE HANDS OF ORLAC Columbia, 1962
CLAUDE BOLLING

HANDS OF THE RIPPER Universal, 1972
CHRISTOPHER GUNNING

HANG 'EM HIGH United Artists, 1968
DOMINIC FRONTIERE

HANGAR 18 Sunn Classic, 1980
JOHN CACAVAS

THE HANGED MAN Lot 49, 1993
ALEC BARTCH

THE HANGED MAN (TF) Fenady Associates/Bing
Crosby Productions, 1974
RICHARD MARKOWITZ†

THE HANGED MAN (TF) Universal TV, 1964
BENNY CARTER

HANGFIRE Motion Picture Corp. of America, 1991
JIM PRICE

HANGING BY A THREAD (TF) Irwin Allen
Productions/Warner Bros. TV, 1979
RICHARD LASALLE

HANGING GARDENS 1993
SAIMON SIMONET

THE HANGING TREE Warner Bros., 1959
MAX STEINER†

THE HANGMAN Paramount, 1959
HARRY SUKMAN†

HANGMAN'S KNOT Columbia, 1952
MISCHA BAKALEINIKOFF†

HANGMEN ALSO DIE United Artists, 1943
HANNS EISLER† ★

HANGOVER SQUARE 20th Century-Fox, 1945
BERNARD HERRMANN†

HANK AARON: CHASING THE DREAM (CTF)
Tollin-Robbins/Television Production Partners/Mundy
Lane/TBS Prods., 1995
ED SMART

HANKY PANKY Columbia, 1982
TOM SCOTT

HANNA K. Universal Classics, 1983
GABRIEL YARED

HANNA'S WAR Cannon, 1988
DOV SELTZER

HANNIBAL BROOKS United Artists, 1969
FRANCIS LAI

HANNIE CAULDER Paramount, 1971
KEN THORNE

THE HANOI HILTON Cannon, 1987
JIMMY WEBB

HANOVER STREET Columbia, 1979
JOHN BARRY

HANS CHRISTIAN ANDERSEN RKO Radio, 1952
JEROME MOROSS†

HANS CHRISTIAN ANDERSEN'S THUMBELINA
Warner Bros., 1994
BARRY MANILOW
WILLIAM ROSS

HANS CHRISTIAN ANDERSON RKO Radio, 1952
WALTER SCHARF

HANS LE MARIN 1948
JOSEPH KOSMA†

HANUSSEN Studio Objektiv/CCC Filmkunst/
Hungarofilm/MOKEP, 1988
GYÖRGY VUKAN

HAO NAN HAO NU 1995
CHIANG HSIAO-WEN
CHEN HWAI-EN

THE HAPPENING Columbia, 1967
FRANK DEVOL

HAPPILY EVER AFTER (TF) Tri-Media II, Inc./
Hamel-Somers Entertainment, 1978
PETER MATZ

**HAPPILY EVER AFTER: FAIRY TALES FOR EVERY
CHILD (ATF)** Two Oceans/Confetti/Hyperion,
1995
TITO LARRIVA
GORDON LEWIS
DIANE LOUIE
CHARLIE MIDNIGHT
RAY NATHANSON
RAY DOBBINS
STEPHEN JAMES TAYLOR
BILL WARE

HAPPINESS 1974
TORU TAKEMITSU†

HAPPINESS IS A WARM CLUE *THE RETURN OF
CHARLIE CHAN (TF)* Charlie Chan Company/
Universal TV, 1979
ROBERT PRINCE

HAPPY (TF) Bacchus Films Inc., 1983
BILLY GOLDENBERG

HAPPY ANNIVERSARY United Artists, 1959
SOL KAPLAN

HAPPY BIRTHDAY *BLOODY BIRTHDAY/
CREEPS* 1980
ARLON OBER

HAPPY BIRTHDAY TO ME Columbia, 1981
BO HARWOOD
LANCE RUBIN

HAPPY BIRTHDAY, TURKE! Senator Films, 1992
MARKUS LONARDONI
PEER RABEN

THE HAPPY ENDING United Artists, 1969
MICHEL LEGRAND

HAPPY ENDINGS (TF) Blinn-Thorpe Productions,
1983
J.A.C. REDFORD

HAPPY ENDINGS (TF) Motown Productions, 1983
WILLIAM GOLDSTEIN

HAPPY GILMORE Universal, 1996
MARK MOTHERSBAUGH

HAPPY GO LUCKY Paramount, 1943
ROBERT EMMETT DOLAN†

THE HAPPY HOOKER Cannon, 1975
DON ELLIOTT

HAPPY HOUR TMS Pictures, 1987
DAN MILNER

HAPPY IS THE BRIDE Kassler, 1959
BENJAMIN FRANKEL†

HAPPY LAND 20th Century-Fox, 1943
CYRIL J. MOCKRIDGE†

HAPPY NEW YEAR Columbia, 1987
BILL CONTI

HAPPY NEW YEAR *LA BONNE ANNEE* Avco
Embassy, 1973
FRANCIS LAI

THE HAPPY PRINCE (AF) Readers Digest, 1974
RON GOODWIN

THE HAPPY TIME Columbia, 1952
DIMITRI TIOMKIN†

HAPPY TOGETHER Borde Releasing Corporation,
1990
ROBERT FOLK

THE HAPPY YEARS MGM, 1950
LEIGH HARLINE†

HARAKIRI *SEPPUKU* Shochiku, 1963
TORU TAKEMITSU†

HARD CHOICES Lorimar, 1986
JAY CHATTAWAY

HARD CONTRACT 20th Century Fox, 1969
ALEX NORTH†

HARD COUNTRY Universal/AFD, 1981
JIMMIE HASKELL
MICHAEL MARTIN MURPHEY

A HARD DAY'S NIGHT United Artists, 1964
GEORGE MARTIN ★

HARD KNOX (TF) Shane Company Productions,
1984
PETE CARPENTER†
MIKE POST

HARD PROMISES Columbia, 1991
JOHN E. KEANE
KENNY VANCE

HARD TARGET Universal, 1993
GRAEME REVELL

HARD TICKET TO HAWAII Malibu Bay Films, 1986
GARY STOCKDALE

HARD TICKET TO HAWAII Malibu Bay Films, 1987
KEVIN KLINGER

HARD TIMES Columbia, 1975
BARRY DEVORZON

HARD TIMES (TF) BBC-TV/WGBH Boston, 1995
STEVE DEUTSCH

HARD TO DIE Concorde/New Horizons, 1991
CHUCK CIRINO

HARD TO HOLD Universal, 1984
TOM SCOTT

HARD TO KILL Warner Bros., 1990
DAVID MICHAEL FRANK

HARD TRAVELING New World, 1986
ERNIE SHELDON

THE HARD WAY Universal, 1991
ARTHUR B. RUBINSTEIN

THE HARD WAY Warner Bros., 1943
HEINZ ROEMHELD†

HARD, FAST AND BEAUTIFUL RKO Radio, 1951
ROY WEBB†

HARDBODIES 2 CineTel Films, 1986
EDDIE ARKIN
JAY LEVY

HARD-BOILED 1992
MICHAEL GIBBS

HARDCASE (TF) Hanna-Barbera Productions, 1972
PATRICK WILLIAMS

HARDCORE Columbia, 1979
JACK NITZCHE

THE HARDER THEY COME New World, 1973
JIMMY CLIFF

THE HARDER THEY FALL Columbia, 1956
HUGO FRIEDHOFER†

HARDHAT AND LEGS (TF) Syzygy Productions,
1980
BRAD FIEDEL

HARDI PARDAILLAN 1963
PAUL MISRAKI

HARDLY WORKING 20th Century-Fox, 1981
MORTON STEVENS†

HARDWARE Miramax, 1990
SIMON BOSWELL

HAREM 1967
ENNIO MORRICONE

HAREM Sara Films, 1985
PHILIPPE SARDE

HAREM (TS) Highgate Pictures, 1986
JOHN SCOTT

**HARLEM DIARY: NINE VOICES OF RESILIENCE
(FD)** Gabriel Films, 1995
JOHN HICKS

THE HARLEM GLOBETROTTERS Columbia, 1951
ARTHUR MORTON

**THE HARLEM GLOBETROTTERS ON GILLIGAN'S
ISLAND (TF)** Sherwood Schwartz Productions,
1981
GERALD FRIED

HARLEM NIGHTS Paramount, 1989
HERBIE HANCOCK

HARLEQUIN New Image, 1980
BRIAN MAY†

**HARLEY DAVIDSON AND THE MARLBORO
MAN** MGM, 1991
BASIL POLEDOURIS

HARLOW Magna, 1965
NELSON RIDDLE†

HARLOW Paramount, 1965
NEAL HEFTI

HARMONY Anvil Productions, 1981
DAVID C. WILLIAMS

HARMONY CATS Alan Morinis-Richard Davis, 1993
BILL BUCKINGHAM
GRAEME COLEMAN

THE HARNESS (TF) Universal TV, 1971
BILLY GOLDENBERG

HAROLD LLOYD'S WORLD OF COMEDY
Continental, 1962
WALTER SCHARF

HAROLD LLOYD: WHY WORRY? Time-Life Films
DON PEAKE

HAROLD LLOYD: HOT WATER Time-Life Films
DON PEAKE

HAROLD LLOYD: SAFETY LAST Time-Life Films,
1974
DON PEAKE

HAROLD LLOYD: THE FRESHMAN Time-Life Films
DON PEAKE

HAROLD ROBBINS' THE PIRATE (TF) Howard W.
Koch Productions/Warner Bros. TV, 1978
BILL CONTI

THE HARP IN THE SOUTH (MS) Quantum Films,
1987
PETER BEST

HARP OF BURMA Brandon, 1956
AKIRA IFUKUBE

HARPER Warner Bros., 1966
JOHNNY MANDEL

HARPER VALLEY PTA April Fools, 1978
NELSON RIDDLE†

HARPY (TF) Cinema Center 100, 1970
DAVID SHIRE

HELD HOSTAGE: THE SIS AND JERRY LEVIN STORY (TF) Paragon/Carol Polakoff Prods., 1991
CHARLES FOX

HELEN KELLER - THE MIRACLE CONTINUES (TF) Castle Combe Productions/20th Century Fox TV, 1984
WILLIAM LOOS

HELEN KELLER - THE MIRACLE CONTINUES (TF) Castle Combe Productions/20th Century-Fox TV, 1984
J.A.C. REDFORD

HELEN OF TROY Warner Bros., 1956
MAX STEINER†

HELEN OF TROY—THE FACE THAT LAUNCHED A THOUSAND SHIPS 1954
NINO ROTA†

THE HELICOPTER SPIES MGM, 1968
RICHARD SHORES

HELL AND HIGH WATER 20th Century-Fox, 1954
ALFRED NEWMAN†

HELL BELOW ZERO MGM, 1954
CLIFTON PARKER†

HELL BENT FOR LEATHER Universal, 1960
WILLIAM LAVA†

HELL BOUND United Artists, 1957
LES BAXTER†

HELL CAMP Orion, 1986
MARC DONAHUE

HELL HATH NO FURY (TF) Bar-Gene Prods./Finnegan-Pinchuk, 1991
J. PETER ROBINSON

HELL HIGH MGM Enterprises, 1989
CHRISTOPHER HYANS-HART

HELL IN KOREA *A HILL IN KOREA* British Lion, 1956
MALCOLM ARNOLD

HELL IN THE PACIFIC Cinerama Releasing Corporation, 1968
LALO SCHIFRIN

HELL IS FOR HEROES Paramount, 1962
LEONARD ROSENMAN

HELL NIGHT Compass International, 1981
DAN WYMAN

HELL ON FRISCO BAY Warner Bros., 1956
MAX STEINER†

HELL RAIDERS OF THE DEEP 1952
NINO ROTA†

HELL RIVER 1974
MIKIS THEODORAKIS

HELL SHIP MUTINY Republic, 1957
BERT A. SHEFTER

HELL SQUAD Cannon, 1986
CHARLES P. BARNETT

HELL TO ETERNITY Allied Artists, 1960
LEITH STEVENS†

HELL UP IN HARLEM American International, 1973
FREDDIE PERREN

THE HELL WITH HEROES Universal, 1968
QUINCY JONES

HELL'S ANGELS ON WHEELS American International, 1967
STU PHILLIPS

HELL'S BELLES American International, 1969
LES BAXTER†

HELL'S BLOODY DEVILS *THE FAKERS/SMASHING THE CRIME SYNDICATE* Independent-International, 1970
NELSON RIDDLE†

HELL'S HORIZON Columbia, 1955
HEINZ ROEMHELD†

HELL'S KITCHEN Kushner-Locke, 1997
BILLY TALBOT

THE HELLBENDERS *I CRUDELLI* 1966
ENNIO MORRICONE

HELLBOUND: HELLRAISER II New World, 1988
CHRISTOPHER YOUNG

HELLCATS OF THE NAVY Columbia, 1957
MISCHA BAKALEINIKOFF†

HELLE Cocinor, 1972
PHILIPPE SARDE

HELLER IN PINK TIGHTS Paramount, 1960
DANIELE AMFITHEATROF†

HELLFIGHTERS Universal, 1969
LEONARD ROSENMAN

HELLFIRE (CTF) New Horizons, 1995
VLADIMIR KAMOROV
BRUNO LOUCHOUARN

HELLGATE Lippert, 1952
PAUL DUNLAP

HELLGATE New World, 1989
BARRY FASMAN
DANA WALDEN

HELLHOLE Arkoff International Pictures, 1985
JEFF STURGES

HELLINGER'S LAW (TF) Universal TV, 1981
JOHN CACAVAS

THE HELLIONS Columbia, 1962
LARRY ADLER

HELLO - GOODBYE 20th Century-Fox, 1970
FRANCIS LAI

HELLO AGAIN Buena Vista, 1987
WILLIAM GOLDSTEIN

HELLO SUCKER Universal, 1941
HANS J. SALTER†

HELLO, DOLLY! 20th Century-Fox, 1969
LIONEL NEWMAN† ★

HELLRAISER New World, 1987
CHRISTOPHER YOUNG

HELLRAISER III: HELL ON EARTH Dimension Pictures, 1992
RANDY MILLER

HELLRAISER: BLOODLINE 1996
DANIEL LICHT

THE HELLSTROM CHRONICLE (FD) Cinema 5, 1971
LALO SCHIFRIN

HELP United Artists, 1965
KEN THORNE

HELP WANTED: KIDS (TF) Stan Rogow Productions, 1986
CRAIG SAFAN

HELP WANTED: MALE (TF) Brademan-Self Productions/QM Productions, 1982
NELSON RIDDLE†

HELTER SKELTER (TF) Lorimar Productions, 1976
BILLY GOLDENBERG ☆

HELZAPOPPIN Universal, 1941
FRANK SKINNER†

HEMINGWAY'S ADVENTURES OF A YOUNG MAN 20th Century-Fox, 1962
FRANZ WAXMAN†

THE HENDERSON MONSTER (TF) Titus Productions, 1980
DICK HYMAN

HENNESSY American International, 1975
JOHN SCOTT

HENRY ALDRICH, EDITOR Paramount, 1942
LEO SHUKEN†

HENRY IV Orion Classics, 1984
ASTOR PIAZZOLA

THE HENRY SOLUTION 1988
TOM CANNING

HENRY V Rank, 1945
SIR WILLIAM WALTON† ★

HENRY V Samuel Goldwyn Company, 1989
PATRICK DOYLE

HER ADVENTUROUS NIGHT Universal, 1946
HANS J. SALTER†

HER ALIBI Warner Bros., 1989
GEORGES DELERUE†
FRANK FITZPATRICK

HER CARDBOARD LOVER MGM, 1942
FRANZ WAXMAN†

HER HUSBAND'S AFFAIRS Columbia, 1947
GEORGE DUNING

HER KIND OF MAN Warner Bros., 1946
FRANZ WAXMAN†

HER LIFE AS A MAN (TF) LS Entertainment, 1984
JOHN CACAVAS

HER MAN GILBEY 1948
NICHOLAS BRODZSKY†

HER PANELLED DOOR 1951
ALLAN GRAY†

HER PRIMITIVE MAN Universal, 1944
EDWARD WARD†

HER SECRET LIFE (TF) Phoenix Entertainment Group, 1987
GEORGES DELERUE†

HER TWELVE MEN MGM, 1954
BRONISLAU KAPER†

HER WICKED, WICKED WAYS (TF) ITC Productions, 1989
FRED KARLIN

HERBIE GOES TO MONTE CARLO Buena Vista, 1977
FRANK DEVOL

HERBIE RIDES AGAIN Buena Vista, 1974
GEORGE BRUNS

HERCULES Cannon, 1983
PINO DONAGGIO

HERCULES (AF) Buena Vista, 1997
ALAN MENKEN

HERCULES AGAINST ROME 1960
ANGELO FRANCESCO LAVAGNINO†

HERCULES AND THE AMAZON WOMEN (TF) Renaissance Pictures, 1994
JOSEPH LO DUCA

HERCULES AND THE CAPTIVE WOMEN 1961
ARMANDO TROVAJOLI

HERCULES AND THE TYRANTS OF BABYLON 1964
ANGELO FRANCESCO LAVAGNINO†

HERCULES II Cannon, 1983
PINO DONAGGIO

HERCULES IN THE HAUNTED WORLD *ERCOLE AL CENTRO DELLA TERRA* 1961
ARMANDO TROVAJOLI

HERCULES OF THE DESERT *LA VALLE DELL'ECO TONANTE* 1964
CARLO RUSTICHELLI

THE HERCULES PILLS 1960
ARMANDO TROVAJOLI

HERCULES RETURNS 1993
PHILIP JUDD

HERCULES, SAMSON & ULYSSES 1965
ANGELO FRANCESCO LAVAGNINO†

HERE ARE LADIES (FD) Arthur Cantor Films, 1983
DAVID FANSHAWE

HERE COME THE GIRLS Paramount, 1953
LYN MURRAY†

HERE COME THE JETS 20th Century-Fox, 1959
PAUL DUNLAP

HERE COME THE LITTLES (AF) Atlantic Releasing, 1985
SHUKI LEVY

HERE COME THE NELSONS Universal, 1952
HERMAN STEIN

HERE COME THE TIGERS American International, 1978
HARRY MANFREDINI

HERE COME THE WAVES Paramount, 1944
ROBERT EMMETT DOLAN†

HERE COMES MR. JORDAN Columbia, 1941
FREDERICK HOLLANDER†

HERE COMES SANTA CLAUS *J'AI RECONTRE LE PERE NOEL* New World, 1985
FRANCIS LAI

HERE COMES THE BAND MGM, 1935
EDWARD WARD†

HERE COMES TROUBLE United Artists, 1948
HEINZ ROEMHELD†

HERE ON EARTH 1993
ANTONIO PINHO VARGAS

HERE WE GO AGAIN RKO Radio, 1942
ROY WEBB†

HERITAGE OF THE DESERT Paramount, 1939
VICTOR YOUNG†

HERO Columbia, 1992
GEORGE FENTON

A HERO AIN'T NOTHIN' BUT A SANDWICH New World, 1977
TOM McINTOSH

HERO AND THE TERROR Cannon, 1988
DAVID MICHAEL FRANK

HERO AT LARGE MGM/United Artists, 1980
PATRICK WILLIAMS

HERO IN THE FAMILY (TF) Barry & Enright Productions/Alexander Productions/Walt Disney Productions, 1986
WILLIAM GOLDSTEIN

THE HERO OF ROME 1964
ANGELO FRANCESCO LAVAGNINO†

HERO'S ISLAND United Artists, 1962
DOMINIC FRONTIERE

THE HEROES 1972
RIZ ORTOLANI

HEROES Universal, 1977
RICHARD HAZARD
JACK NITZCHE

HEROES A LA FUERZA 1968
CARLO RUSTICHELLI

THE HEROES OF DESERT STORM (TF) 1991
SYLVESTER LEVAY

THE HEROES OF TELEMARK Columbia, 1965
MALCOLM ARNOLD

THE HEROINES OF EVIL 1979
OLIVER DASSAULT

HERS TO HOLD Universal, 1943
FRANK SKINNER†

HESTER STREET Midwest Film Productions, 1975
WILLIAM BOLCOM

HET MEISJE MET HET RODE HAAR 1981
NICOLA PIOVANI

HEUREUX QUI COMME ULYSSE 1969
GEORGES DELERUE†

HEX 1975
PATRICK WILLIAMS

HEX 20th Century-Fox, 1973
CHARLES BERNSTEIN

HEXED Columbia, 1993
LANCE RUBIN

HEY THERE, IT'S YOGI BEAR (AF) Hanna-Barbera, 1964
MARTY PAICH†

HEY, GOOD LOOKIN' Warner Bros., 1982
JOHN MADARA
RICK SANDLER

HEY, I'M ALIVE! (TF) Charles Fries Productions/Worldvision Enterprises, 1975
FRANK DEVOL

HI YA, CHUM Universal, 1943
HANS J. SALTER†

HI'YA, SAILOR Universal, 1943
HANS J. SALTER†

HI, BEAUTIFUL Universal, 1944
FRANK SKINNER†

HI, GOOD LOOKIN' Universal, 1944
HANS J. SALTER†

HIBERNATUS 1969
GEORGES DELERUE†

THE HIDDEN New Line Cinema, 1987
MICHAEL CONVERTINO

HIDDEN AGENDA Hemdale, 1990
STEWART COPELAND

THE HIDDEN FORTRESS *THREE BAD MEN IN A HIDDEN FORTRESS* Toho, 1958
MASARU SATO

THE HIDDEN ROOM *OBSESSION* British Lion, 1949
NINO ROTA†

THE HIDDEN WORLD (FD) Small World, 1958
LEONARD ROSENMAN

HIDE IN PLAIN SIGHT United Artists, 1980
LEONARD ROSENMAN

HIDEAWAY TriStar, 1995
TREVOR JONES

HIDE-OUT MGM, 1934
WILLIAM AXT†

HIDER IN THE HOUSE Vestron, 1989
CHRISTOPHER YOUNG

HIDING OUT DEG, 1987
ANNE DUDLEY

HIFAZAAT *IN CUSTODY* Merchant Ivory, 1993
ZAKIR HUSSAIN
USTAD SULTAN KAHN

HIGH AND LOW East West Classics, 1963
MASARU SATO

THE HIGH AND THE MIGHTY Warner Bros., 1954
DIMITRI TIOMKIN† ★★

HIGH ANXIETY 20th Century-Fox, 1977
JOHN MORRIS

HIGH BARBAREE MGM, 1947
HERBERT STOTHART†

THE HIGH BRIGHT SUN 1964
ANGELO FRANCESCO LAVAGNINO†

THE HIGH COMMISSIONER *NOBODY RUNS FOREVER* Cinerama Releasing Corporation, 1968
GEORGES DELERUE†

HIGH CONQUEST Monogram, 1947
LUD GLUSKIN†
LUCIEN MORAWECK†
LYN MURRAY†

THE HIGH COST OF LOVING MGM, 1958
JEFF ALEXANDER†

HIGH EXPLOSIVE Paramount, 1943
DANIELE AMFITHEATROF†

HIGH FLYERS RKO Radio, 1937
ROY WEBB†

HIGH HEELS Miramax, 1991
RYUICHI SAKAMOTO

HIGH HEELS *DOCTEUR POPAUL* Les Films La Boetie, 1972
PIERRE JANSEN

HIGH HOPES Skouras Pictures, 1988
ANDREW DIXON

HIGH ICE ESJ Productions, 1980
ROBERT O. RAGLAND

HIGH INFIDELITY Magna, 1964
ARMANDO TROVAJOLI

HIGH MIDNIGHT (TF) The Mirisch Corporation/Universal TV, 1979
JERRY FIELDING† ☆☆

HIGH MOUNTAIN RANGERS (TF) Shane Productions, 1987
ROBERT FOLK

HIGH NOON United Artists, 1952
DIMITRI TIOMKIN† ★★

HIGH PLAINS DRIFTER Universal, 1972
DEE BARTON

HIGH POINT 1980
JOHN ADDISON

THE HIGH POWERED-RIFLE 20th Century-Fox, 1960
ALBERT GLASSER

THE HIGH PRICE OF PASSION (TF) Edgar J. Scherick Associates/Taft Entertainment, 1986
JOSEPH CONLAN

HIGH RISK American Cinema, 1981
MARK SNOW

HIGH ROAD TO CHINA Warner Bros., 1983
JOHN BARRY

HIGH SCHOOL CONFIDENTIAL *YOUNG HELLIONS* MGM, 1958
ALBERT GLASSER

HIGH SCHOOL HELLCATS American International, 1958
RONALD STEIN†

HIGH SCHOOL HIGH TriStar, 1996
IRA NEWBORN

HIGH SCHOOL U.S.A. (TF) Hill-Mandelker Productions, 1983
TONY BERG
MILES GOODMAN†

HIGH SEASON Hemdale, 1987
JASON OSBORN

HIGH SIERRA Warner Bros., 1941
ADOLPH DEUTSCH†

HIGH SOCIETY MGM, 1956
JOHN GREEN† ★

HIGH SPIRITS Tri-Star, 1988
GEORGE FENTON

HIGH STRUNG Grey Cat Films, 1991
VLADIMIR HORUNZHY

HIGH TIDE Hemdale, 1987
RICKY FATAAR
MARK MOFFIATT

HIGH TIDE Tri-Star, 1987
PETER BEST

HIGH TIME 20th Century-Fox, 1960
HENRY MANCINI†

HIGH TREASON Rank, 1952
JOHN ADDISON

HIGH VELOCITY 1977
JERRY GOLDSMITH

HIGH WALL MGM, 1948
BRONISLAU KAPER†

A HIGH WIND IN JAMAICA 20th Century-Fox, 1965
LARRY ADLER

HIGH-BALLIN' American International, 1978
PAUL HOFFERT

HIGHER GROUND (TF) Green-Epstein Productions/Columbia TV, 1988
LEE HOLDRIDGE

HIGHER LEARNING Columbia, 1995
STANLEY CLARKE

HIGHLANDER 20th Century Fox, 1986
MICHAEL KAMEN
QUEEN

HIGHLANDER 2: THE QUICKENING Interscope, 1991
GEORGE S. CLINTON
STEWART COPELAND

HIGHLANDER III: THE SORCERER Miramax, 1994
J. PETER ROBINSON

HIGHLY DANGEROUS Lippert, 1951
RICHARD ADDINSELL†

HIGHPOINT New World, 1984
CHRISTOPHER YOUNG

HIGHWAY 301 Warner Bros., 1951
WILLIAM LAVA†

HIGHWAY 61 Shadow Shows, 1991
NASH THE SLASH

HIGHWAY HEARTBREAKER (TF) Gross-Weston/Cannell Entertainment, 1992
MARK SNOW

HIGHWAY PATROLMAN *EL PATRULLERO* Cable HOgue/Marubeni, 1992
ZANDER SCHLOSS

HIGHWAY PICKUP 1963
GEORGES DELERUE†

HIGHWAY QUEEN Golan-Globus, 1971
DOV SELTZER

HIGHWAY TO HELL Hemdale, 1992
TANGERINE DREAM
FRANK FITZPATRICK

THE HIGHWAYMAN Allied Artists, 1951
HERSCHEL BURKE GILBERT

THE HIGHWAYMAN (TF) Glen A. Larson Productions/20th Century Fox TV, 1987
STU PHILLIPS

HIGHWAYS BY NIGHT RKO Radio, 1942
ROY WEBB†

HIJACK! (TF) Spelling-Goldberg Productions, 1973
ALLYN FERGUSON
JACK ELLIOTT

HI-JACKED Lippert, 1950
PAUL DUNLAP

THE HIJACKING OF THE ACHILLE LAURO (TF) Tamara Asseyev Productions/New World TV/Spectacor Films, 1989
CHRIS BOARDMAN ☆

HILDA CRANE 20th Century-Fox, 1956
DAVID RAKSIN

A HILL IN KOREA British Lion, 1956
MALCOLM ARNOLD

THE HILLS HAVE EYES Vanguard, 1977
DON PEAKE

THE HILLS HAVE EYES PART II Castle Prods., 1985
HARRY MANFREDINI

HILLS OF HOME MGM, 1948
HERBERT STOTHART†

THE HILLS RUN RED *I FIUME DI DOLLARI* 1966
ENNIO MORRICONE

HIMIKO Hyogensha/ATG, 1974
TORU TAKEMITSU†

THE HINDENBURG Universal, 1975
DAVID SHIRE

HINOTORI Toho, 1980
JUN FUKAMACHI
MICHEL LEGRAND

THE HIRED GUN MGM, 1957
ALBERT GLASSER

HIRED WIFE Universal, 1940
FRANK SKINNER†

THE HIRELING Columbia, 1973
MARC WILKINSON

HIROSHIMA 1955
AKIRA IFUKUBE

HIROSHIMA MAIDEN (TF) Arnold Shapiro Productions, 1988
RICHARD STONE

HIROSHIMA, MON AMOUR Zenith, 1959
GEORGES DELERUE†

HIS BROTHER'S WIFE MGM, 1936
FRANZ WAXMAN†

HIS BUTLER'S SISTER Universal, 1943
HANS J. SALTER†

HIS GIRL FRIDAY Columbia, 1940
SIDNEY CUTNER†

HIS GREATEST GAMBLE RKO Radio, 1934
MAX STEINER†

HIS KIND OF WOMAN RKO Radio, 1951
LEIGH HARLINE†

HIS MAJESTY O'KEEFE Warner Bros., 1953
DIMITRI TIOMKIN†

HIS MISTRESS (TF) David L. Wolper Productions/Warner Bros. TV, 1984
BILLY GOLDENBERG

HIS NIGHT OUT Universal, 1935
FRANZ WAXMAN†

HIS TWO LOVES *PUCCINI* 1952
CARLO RUSTICHELLI

HIS WIFE'S HABIT HowCo International, 1971
JIM HELMS

HIS WOMEN 1961
ARMANDO TROVAJOLI

HIS YOUNG WIFE *LE MISERIE DEL SIGNOR TRAVET* 1945
NINO ROTA†

HISTADRUTH (D) Palestine Labor Union, 1945
KAROL RATHAUS†

HISTOIRE D'O No. 2 1983
STANLEY MYERS†

HISTOIRE D'O No. 2 1983
HANS ZIMMER

HISTOIRE D'UN PETIT GARCON DEVENU GRAND 1962
MICHEL LEGRAND

HISTOIRE DE VOYOUS: LES MARLOUPINS (TF) 1978
VLADIMIR COSMA

HISTOIRES EXTRAORDINAIRES American International, 1969
NINO ROTA†

HISTOIRES INSOLITES: LA STRATEGIE DU SERPENT (TF) 1979, French
VLADIMIR COSMA

HISTORIES EXTRAORDINAIRES 1949
GEORGES VAN PARYS†

HISTORY IS MADE AT NIGHT United Artists, 1937
ALFRED NEWMAN†

THE HISTORY OF THE WORLD, PART 1 20th Century-Fox, 1981
JOHN MORRIS

THE HIT Island Alive, 1984
PACO DE LUCIA

HIT AND RUN Comworld, 1982
BRAD FIEDEL

HIT LADY (TF) Spelling-Goldberg Productions, 1974
GEORGE ALICESON TIPTON

HIT LIST New Line Cinema, 1989
GARRY SCHYMAN

THE HIT LIST (CTF) Westwind Prods., 1993
RICK CONRAD

THE HIT MAN (TF) Scherick-Cardea/Christopher Morgan Co.,/ABC Circle Films, 1991
ARTHUR KEMPEL

HIT ME Slough Pond Prods., 1997
PETER MANNING ROBINSON

HIT PARADE OF 1943 Republic, 1943
WALTER SCHARF ★

HIT THE DUTCHMAN 21st Century, 1992
TERRY PLUMERI

HIT THE ROAD Universal, 1941
HANS J. SALTER†

HIT! Paramount, 1973
LALO SCHIFRIN

HITCHED (TF) Universal TV, 1973
PATRICK WILLIAMS

THE HITCHER Tri-Star, 1986
MARK ISHAM

HITCHHIKE! (TF) Universal TV, 1974
GIL MELLE

THE HITCHHIKER RKO Radio, 1953
LEITH STEVENS†

HITLER Universal, 1962
HANS J. SALTER†

THE HITLER GANG Paramount, 1944
DAVID BUTTOLPH†

HITLER'S CHILDREN RKO Radio, 1943
ROY WEBB†

HITLER'S HANGMAN MGM, 1943
KARL HAJOS†

HITLER'S S.S.: PORTRAIT IN EVIL (TF) Colason Limited Productions/Edgar J. Scherick Associates, 1985
RICHARD HARTLEY

HITLER...CONNAIS PAS 1963
GEORGES DELERUE†

THE HITMAN Cannon, 1991
JOEL DEROUIN

HITS! Walron Films Ltd./LLC/Symphony Pictures, 1994
ERIC ALLAMAN

H.M. PULHAM, ESQUIRE MGM, 1941
BRONISLAU KAPER†

THE H-MAN Columbia, 1959
MASARU SATO

HO SAP EL MINISTRE? *DOES THE MINISTER KNOW?* 1992
JOAN VIVES

HOA-BINH 1969
MICHEL PORTAL

THE HOBBIT (ATF) Rankin-Bass Productions, 1977
MAURY LAWS

A HOBO'S CHRISTMAS (TF) Joe Byrnne-Falrose Productions/Phoenix Entertainment, 1987
MARK SNOW

HOBSON'S CHOICE United Artists, 1954
MALCOLM ARNOLD

HOBSON'S CHOICE (TF) CBS Entertainment, 1983
ROBERT DRASNIN

HOCKEY NIGHT (TF) Martin Paul/CBC, 1984
FRED MOLLIN

HOCUS POCUS Buena Vista, 1993
JOHN DEBNEY

HOFFA 20th Century Fox, 1992
DAVID NEWMAN

HOFFMAN Levitt-Pickman, 1971
RON GRAINER†

THE HOLCROFT COVENANT Universal, 1985
STANISLAS SYREWICZ

HOLD BACK THE DAWN Paramount, 1941
VICTOR YOUNG† ★

HOLD BACK THE NIGHT Universal, 1956
HANS J. SALTER†

HOLD BACK TOMORROW Universal, 1955
SIDNEY CUTNER†

HOLD ME, THRILL ME, KISS ME 1992
GERALD GOURIET

HOLD THAT BLONDE Paramount, 1945
VICTOR YOUNG†

HOLD THAT GHOST Universal, 1941
CHARLES PREVIN†
HANS J. SALTER†
FRANK SKINNER†

HOLD THAT KISS MGM, 1938
EDWARD WARD†

HOLD-UP AMLF-Cerito, 1985
SERGE FRANKLIN

A HOLE IN THE HEAD United Artists, 1959
NELSON RIDDLE†

HOLIDAY Columbia, 1938
SIDNEY CUTNER†

HOLIDAY AFFAIR RKO Radio, 1949
ROY WEBB†

HOLIDAY FOR HENRIETTE 1953
GEORGES AURIC†

HOLIDAY FOR LOVERS 20th Century-Fox, 1959
LEIGH HARLINE†

HOLIDAY INN Paramount, 1942
ROBERT EMMETT DOLAN† ★

HOLIDAY LOVE Aries Films/Microfon, Argentine
EMILIO KAUDERER

HOLIDAY RHYTHM Lippert, 1950
BERT A. SHEFTER

HOLLISTER 1993
JERRY GOLDSMITH

HOLLOW IMAGE (TF) Titus Productions, 1979
DON SEBESKY

HOLLOW TRIUMPH Eagle Lion, 1948
SOL KAPLAN

THE HOLLY AND THE IVY British Lion, 1953
MALCOLM ARNOLD

HOLLYROCK-A-BYE BABY (ATF) Hanna-Barbera Prods. Animation/Wang Film Prod. Co., 1993
JOHN DEBNEY

A HOLLYWOOD STORY Double Helix, 1989
ALAN DERMARDEROSIAN

HOLLYWOOD BEAT (TF) Aaron Spelling Productions, 1985
KEN HARRISON

HOLLYWOOD BOULEVARD New World, 1976
ANDREW STEIN

HOLLYWOOD BOULEVARD II Concorde, 1989
MARK GOVERNOR

HOLLYWOOD CAVALCADE 20th Century-Fox, 1939
DAVID BUTTOLPH†
DAVID RAKSIN
LOUIS SILVERS†

HOLLYWOOD DREAMING American Twist/Boulevard Productions, 1986
BRUCE LANGHORNE

HOLLYWOOD HARRY Shapiro Entertainment, 1985
MICHAEL LANG

HOLLYWOOD OR BUST Paramount, 1956
WALTER SCHARF

HOLLYWOOD SHUFFLE Samuel Goldwyn Co., 1987
UDI HARPAZ
PATRICE RUSHEN

HOLLYWOOD VARIETIES Lippert, 1950
ALBERT GLASSER

HOLLYWOOD VICE Concorde/Cinema Group, 1986
MICHAEL CONVERTINO
KEITH LEVINE

HOLLYWOOD VICE SQUAD Concorde/Cinema Group, 1986
CHRIS SPEDDING

HOLLYWOOD WIVES (MS) Aaron Spelling Productions, 1985
LALO SCHIFRIN

HOLOCAUST (MS) Titus Productions, 1978
MORTON GOULD ☆

HOLOCAUST 2000 1977
ENNIO MORRICONE

HOLOGRAM MAN PM Entertainment, 1995
JOHN GONZALEZ

HOLY MATRIMONY 20th Century-Fox, 1943
CYRIL J. MOCKRIDGE†

HOLY MATRIMONY Buena Vista, 1994
BRUCE BROUGHTON

HOMAGE (TF) Skyline Entertainment, 1994
W.G. SNUFFY WALDEN

HOMBRE 20th Century-Fox, 1967
DAVID ROSE†

HOME (TF) Leonard Goldberg Productions, 1986
NAN SCHWARTZ-MISHKIN

HOME ALONE Hi-Tops Productions
ANDREA SAPAROFF

HOME ALONE 20th Century-Fox, 1990
JOHN WILLIAMS ★

HOME ALONE 2: LOST IN NEW YORK 20th Century Fox, 1992
JOHN WILLIAMS

THE HOME AND THE WORLD European Classics, 1984
SATYAJIT RAY†

HOME AT SEVEN *MURDER ON MONDAY* 1952
MALCOLM ARNOLD

HOME BEFORE DARK Warner Bros., 1958
FRANZ WAXMAN†

HOME FIRES BURNING William P. O'Boyle, 1992
HERB PILHOFER

HOME FIRES BURNING (TF) Marian Rees Associates, 1989
DON DAVIS

HOME FOR THE HOLIDAYS (TF) Spelling-Goldberg Productions/ABC Circle Films, 1972
GEORGE ALICESON TIPTON

HOME FREE ALL Almi Classics, 1983
JAY CHATTAWAY

HOME FRIES 1997
RACHEL PORTMAN

HOME FROM THE HILL MGM, 1959
BRONISLAU KAPER†

HOME IN INDIANA 20th Century-Fox, 1944
HUGO FRIEDHOFER†

HOME IS WHERE THE HART IS Atlantic Entertainment Group, 1987
ERIC N. ROBERTSON

HOME MOVIES United Artists Classics, 1980
PINO DONAGGIO

A HOME OF OUR OWN Gramercy, 1993
MICHAEL CONVERTINO

HOME OF THE BRAVE United Artists, 1949
DIMITRI TIOMKIN†

A HOME OF YOUR OWN Dormer/British Lion, 1965
RON GOODWIN

HOME REMEDY Kino International, 1988
STEVE KATZ

HOME SWEET HOMICIDE 20th Century-Fox, 1946
DAVID BUTTOLPH†

HOME TO DANGER Eros, 1951
MALCOLM ARNOLD

HOME TO STAY (TF) Time-Life Productions, 1978
HAGOOD HARDY

HOMEBODIES Avco Embassy, 1974
BERNARDO SEGALL

HOMEBOY Redbury Ltd./Elliott Kastner Productions, 1988
ERIC CLAPTON
MICHAEL KAMEN

THE HOMECOMING (TF) Lorimar Productions, 1971
JERRY GOLDSMITH

HOMECOMING MGM, 1948
BRONISLAU KAPER†

HOMEFRONT: S.N.A.F.U. (TF) Lorimar TV, 1991
STEWART LEVIN

HOMER AND EDDIE King's Road Entertainment, 1989
EDUARD ARTEMYEV

THE HOMESTRETCH 20th Century-Fox, 1947
DAVID RAKSIN

HOMETOWN BOY MAKES GOOD (CTF) HBO, 1990
BARRY GOLDBERG

HOMEWARD BOUND II: LOST IN SAN FRANCISCO Buena Vista, 1996
BRUCE BROUGHTON

HOMEWARD BOUND: THE INCREDIBLE
JOURNEY Buena Vista, 1993
BRUCE BROUGHTON

HOMEWORD BOUND (TF) Tisch-Avnet Productions,
1980
FRED KARLIN ☆

HOMEWORK Jensen Farley Pictures, 1982
TONY JONES
JIM WETZEL

HOMICIDAL Columbia, 1961
HUGO FRIEDHOFER†

HOMICIDE Triumph, 1991
ALARIC JANS

HOMICIDE Warner Bros., 1949
WILLIAM LAVA†

HOMICIDE BUREAU Columbia, 1939
SIDNEY CUTNER†

HOMO EROTICUS 1971
ARMANDO TROVAJOLI

HONARPISHEH THE ACTOR 1993
AHMAD PEZHMAN

HONDO Warner Bros., 1953
HUGO FRIEDHOFER†

HONEY Paramount, 1930
W. FRANKE HARLING†

THE HONEY POT United Artists, 1967
JOHN ADDISON

HONEY, I BLEW UP THE KID Buena Vista, 1992
BRUCE BROUGHTON

HONEY, I SHRUNK THE KIDS Buena Vista, 1989
JAMES HORNER

HONEYBOY (TF) Fan Fares Inc. Productions/Estrada
Productions, 1982
J.A.C. REDFORD

HONEYCHILE Republic, 1951
VICTOR YOUNG†

THE HONEYMOON MACHINE MGM, 1961
LEIGH HARLINE†

HONEYMOON 1979
MANOS HADJIDAKIS†

HONEYMOON 1983
ALFI KABILJO

HONEYMOON RKO Radio, 1947
LEIGH HARLINE†

HONEYMOON RKO Radio, 1958
MIKIS THEODORAKIS

HONEYMOON ACADEMY Triumph, 1990
ROBERT FOLK

HONEYMOON FOR THREE Warner Bros., 1941
HEINZ ROEMHELD†

HONEYMOON HOTEL MGM, 1964
WALTER SCHARF

HONEYMOON IN VEGAS Columbia, 1992
DAVID NEWMAN

HONEYSUCKLE ROSE Warner Bros., 1980
RICHARD BASKIN
WILLIE NELSON

HONG KONG CONFIDENTIAL United Artists, 1958
BERT A. SHEFTER

HONG MEIGUI BAI MEGUI 1995
JOHNNY CHEN

THE HONKERS United Artists, 1972
JIMMIE HASKELL

HONKY Jack H. Harris Enterprises, 1971
QUINCY JONES

HONKY TONK MGM, 1941
FRANZ WAXMAN†

HONKY TONK FREEWAY Universal/AFD, 1981
ELMER BERNSTEIN
GEORGE MARTIN
STEVE DORFF

HONKY-TONK (TF) Douglas Heyes Productions/
MGM TV, 1974
JERRY FIELDING†

HONKYTONK MAN Warner Bros., 1982
STEVE DORFF

HONOLULU MGM, 1939
FRANZ WAXMAN†

HONOR BOUND MGM/UA, 1989
MARK SHREEVE

THE HONOR GUARD Filmcorp Distribution, 1981
KEN THORNE

THE HONOR OF THE TRIBE 1993
JEAN-MARIE SENIA

HONOR THY FATHER (TF) Metromedia Producers
Corporation/Halcyon Productions, 1973
GEORGE DUNING

HONOR THY FATHER AND MOTHER: THE TRUE
STORY OF THE MENENDEZ MURDERS (TF)
Saban Entertainment, 1994
SHUKI LEVY

HONOR THY MOTHER (TF) Universal/MCA TV/
Point of View, 1992
PETER MANNING ROBINSON

THE HONORARY CONSUL Paramount, 1983
RICHARD HARVEY
STANLEY MYERS†

HOODLUM MGM-UA, 1997
ELMER BERNSTEIN

THE HOODLUM PRIEST United Artists, 1961
RICHARD MARKOWITZ†

THE HOODLUM SAINT MGM, 1946
NATHANIEL SHILKRET†

THE HOOK MGM, 1963
LARRY ADLER

HOOK TriStar, 1991
JOHN WILLIAMS

HOOPER Warner Bros., 1978
BILL JUSTIS

HOOSIERS Orion, 1986
JERRY GOLDSMITH ★

HOOVER VS. THE KENNEDYS: THE SECOND CIVIL
WAR (MS) Sunrise Films/Selznick-Glickman
Productions, 1987
PAUL HOFFERT

HOPE AND GLORY Columbia, 1987
PETER MARTIN

HOPPITY GOES TO TOWN (AF) Paramount, 1941
LEIGH HARLINE†

HOPSCOTCH Avco Embassy, 1980
IAN FRASER

HORIZONS WEST Universal, 1952
HENRY MANCINI†
HERMAN STEIN

THE HORN BLOWS AT MIDNIGHT Warner Bros.,
1945
FRANZ WAXMAN†

HORNET'S NEST United Artists, 1970
ENNIO MORRICONE

HORROR AT 37,000 FEET (TF) CBS Entertainment,
1973
MORTON STEVENS†

THE HORROR CHAMBER OF DR. FAUSTUS LES
YEUX SANS VISAGE Lopert, 1960
MAURICE JARRE

HORROR DREAM Peterson
JOHN CAGE†

HORROR EXPRESS 1972
JOHN CACAVAS

HORROR HOTEL CITY OF THE DEAD
Trans-World, 1960
DOUGLAS GAMLEY

HORROR HOTEL THE CITY OF THE DEAD
Trans-World, 1960
KENNETH V. JONES

HORROR ISLAND Universal, 1941
CHARLES HENDERSON†
CHARLES PREVIN†
HANS J. SALTER†
FRANK SKINNER†

THE HORROR OF FRANKENSTEIN Levitt-Pickman,
1970
MALCOLM WILLIAMSON

THE HORROR OF IT ALL 20th Century-Fox, 1964
DOUGLAS GAMLEY

HORROR OF DRACULA DRACULA Universal,
1958
JAMES BERNARD

HORROR ON SNAPE ISLAND BEYOND THE
FOG Fanfare, 1972
KENNETH V. JONES

HORROR PLANET INSEMINOID Almi Films,
1982
JOHN SCOTT

THE HORROR SHOW MGM/UA, 1989
HARRY MANFREDINI

HORRORS OF THE BLACK MUSEUM American
International, 1959
GERARD SCHURMANN

HORS LA VIE 1991
NICOLA PIOVANI

THE HORSE IN THE GRAY FLANNEL SUIT Buena
Vista, 1968
GEORGE BRUNS

THE HORSE SOLDIERS United Artists, 1959
DAVID BUTTOLPH†

THE HORSE WHISPERER 1997
JOHN BARRY

THE HORSE'S MOUTH United Artists, 1958
KENNETH V. JONES

THE HORSEMAN ON THE ROOF LE HUSSARD
SUR LE TOIT 1995
JEAN-CLAUDE PETIT

THE HORSEMEN Columbia, 1971
GEORGES DELERUE†

HORSES AND CHAMPIONS Augusta Grace Prods.,
1995
ALEX SHAPIRO

HOSPITAL MASSACRE Cannon, 1981
ARLON OBER

THE HOST ASP Prods., 1997
JOHN McCARTHY

HOSTAGE (TF) CBS Entertainment, 1988
BRAD FIEDEL

HOSTAGE FLIGHT (TF) Frank von Zerneck Films,
1985
FRED KARLIN

HOSTAGE FOR A DAY (TF) Frostback/Once Upon A
Time Films/Fox West/Western Int'l Comm., 1994
IAN THOMAS

THE HOSTAGE HEART (TF) Andrew J. Fenady
Associates/MGM TV, 1977
FRED KARLIN

THE HOSTAGE TOWER (TF) Jerry Leider
Productions, 1980
JOHN SCOTT

HOSTAGES Paramount, 1943
VICTOR YOUNG†

HOSTAGES (CTF) HBO/Granada, 1993
RICHARD HARVEY

HOSTILE GUNS Paramount, 1967
JIMMIE HASKELL

HOSTILE INTENT Amsell Entertainment, 1997
DARREN SOLOMON

HOSTILE INTENT Le Monde, 1997
CHRISTOPHER BECK

THE HOT ANGEL Paramount, 1958
RICHARD MARKOWITZ†

HOT BLOOD Columbia, 1956
LES BAXTER†

HOT BUBBLEGUM LEMON POPSICLE III Noah
Films, 1981
W. MICHAEL LEWIS
LAURIN RINDER

HOT CARS United Artists, 1956
LES BAXTER†

HOT CHILD IN THE CITY Mediacom Filmworks,
1987
W. MICHAEL LEWIS
LAURIN RINDER

HOT DOG...THE MOVIE MGM/UA, 1984
PETER BERNSTEIN

HOT DREAMS AMORE LIBERO 1974
FABIO FRIZZI

THE HOT GIRLS New Realm, 1974
DE WOLFE

HOT LEAD AND COLD FEET Buena Vista, 1978
BUDDY BAKER

HOT MEN 1989
LENNIE NIEHAUS

HOT MILLIONS MGM, 1968
LAURIE JOHNSON

THE HOT MONTH OF AUGUST 1966
STAVROS XARCHAKOS

HOT PAINT (TF) Catalina Production Group, 1988
BRAD FIEDEL

HOT PURSUIT Indie, 1987
JOSEPH CONLAN

HOT PURSUIT Paramount, 1987
RAREVIEW

HOT PURSUIT (TF) Kenneth Johnson Productions/
NBC Productions, 1984
JOE HARNELL

THE HOT ROCK 20th Century-Fox, 1972
QUINCY JONES

HOT ROD (TF) ABC Circle Films, 1979
MICHAEL SIMPSON

HOT ROD GANG American International, 1958
RONALD STEIN†

HOT ROD RUMBLE Allied Artists, 1957
ALEXANDER COURAGE

HOT SHOT, PART DEUX! 20th Century Fox, 1993
BASIL POLEDOURIS

HOT SHOTS 20th Century Fox, 1991
SYLVESTER LEVAY

HOT SPELL Paramount, 1958
ALEX NORTH†

THE HOT SPOT Orion, 1990
JACK NITZCHE

HOT STUFF Columbia, 1979
PATRICK WILLIAMS

HOT SUMMER NIGHT MGM, 1957
ANDRE PREVIN

HOT TARGET Crown International, 1985
GIL MELLE

HOT TO TROT Warner Bros., 1988
DANNY ELFMAN

HOT, HARD AND MEAN American International,
1972
HARRY BETTS

HOTEL BERLIN Warner Bros., 1945
FRANZ WAXMAN†

HOTEL COLONIAL Orion, 1987
PINO DONAGGIO

HOTEL DE LOVE Live, 1997
BRETT ROSENBERG

HOTEL DES INVALIDES 1951
MAURICE JARRE

HOTEL DULAC (TF) Channel Four, 1986
CARL DAVIS

HOTEL FOR WOMEN 20th Century-Fox, 1939
DAVID BUTTOLPH†

HOTEL IMPERIAL Paramount, 1939
RICHARD HAGEMAN†

HOTEL OKLAHOMA European American, 1991
TOBY FITCH

HOTEL PARADISO MGM, 1966
LAURENCE ROSENTHAL

HOTEL ROOM (CTF) Asymmetrical/Propaganda,
1993
ANGELO BADALAMENTI

HOTEL SAHARA United Artists, 1951
BENJAMIN FRANKEL†

HOTEL SORRENTO Bayside Pictures, 1994,
Australian
BENJAMIN FRANKEL†

HOTHEAD Quartet, 1980
PIERRE BACHELET

HOTLINE (TF) Ron Samuels Productions/Wrather
Entertainment International, 1982
JOHNNY HARRIS

H.O.T.S. Derio Productions, 1979
DAVID DAVIS

HOTSHOT International Film Marketing, 1987
WILLIAM ORBIT

HOUDINI Paramount, 1953
ROY WEBB†

THE HOUND OF THE BASKERVILLES Atlantic
Releasing Corporation, 1979
DUDLEY MOORE

THE HOUND OF THE BASKERVILLES United
Artists, 1959
JAMES BERNARD

THE HOUND OF THE BASKERVILLES (TF)
Grenada, 1982
PATRICK GOWERS

HOUND-DOG MAN 20th Century-Fox, 1959
CYRIL J. MOCKRIDGE†

THE HOUR BEFORE THE DAWN Paramount, 1944
MIKLOS ROZSA†

THE HOUR OF 13 MGM, 1952
JOHN ADDISON

HOUR OF GLORY Snader Productions, 1948
BRIAN EASDALE

THE HOUR OF THE PIG Miramax, 1993
ALEXANDRE DESPLAT

HOUR OF THE ASSASSIN Concorde, 1987
FRED MYROW

HOUR OF THE GUN United Artists, 1967
JERRY GOLDSMITH

THE HOURS OF LOVE LE ORE DELL'AMORE
1963
ENNIO MORRICONE

HOUSE New World, 1986
HARRY MANFREDINI

THE HOUSE BUILT ON SAND 1991
ALGIRDAS PAULAVICHUS

THE HOUSE ACROSS THE BAY United Artists,
1940
WERNER JANSSEN

THE HOUSE ACROSS THE STREET Warner Bros.,
1949
WILLIAM LAVA†

HOUSE ARREST MGM-UA, 1996
BRUCE BROUGHTON

THE HOUSE BUILT ON SAND Sovexportfilm, 1991
ALGIRDAS GAVRICHENKO

THE HOUSE BY THE CEMETERY Almi Pictures,
1981
WALTER RIZZATI

HOUSE BY THE RIVER Republic, 1950
GEORGE ANTHEIL†

HOUSE CALLS Universal, 1978
HENRY MANCINI†

HOUSE GUEST Buena Vista, 1995
JOHN DEBNEY

HOUSE II: THE SECOND STORY New World, 1987
HARRY MANFREDINI

THE HOUSE IN NIGHTMARE PARK MGM-EMI,
1973
HARRY ROBERTSON

THE HOUSE IN THE SQUARE 20th Century-Fox,
1951
WILLIAM ALWYN†

A HOUSE OF SECRETS AND LIES (TF) Elliot
Friedgen/Chris-Rose, 1992
BILLY GOLDENBERG

HOUSE OF ANGELS: THE SECOND SUMMER
ANGLAGARD: ANDRA SOMMAREN 1995
BJORN ISFALT

THE HOUSE OF BERNARDA ALBA (TF) 1991
CARLOS MIRANDA

HOUSE OF BAMBOO 20th Century-Fox, 1955
LIONEL NEWMAN†

HOUSE OF CARDS Miramax, 1993
JAMES HORNER

HOUSE OF DARK SHADOWS MGM, 1970
BOB COBERT

HOUSE OF DRACULA Universal, 1945
PAUL DESSAU†
CHARLES HENDERSON†
WILLIAM LAVA†
CHARLES PREVIN†
HANS J. SALTER†

THE HOUSE OF ELIOTT (CTF) BBC Enterprises/A&E,
1992
JIM PARKER

THE HOUSE OF FEAR Universal, 1945
HANS J. SALTER†
PAUL SAWTELL†

HOUSE OF FRANKENSTEIN Universal, 1944
PAUL DESSAU†
CHARLES PREVIN†
HANS J. SALTER†
FRANK SKINNER†

HOUSE OF FRIGHT *THE TWO FACES OF DR. JEKYLL* American International, 1960
MONTY NORMAN

THE HOUSE OF GOD *(H.O.G.)* United Artists, 1981
BASIL POLEDOURIS

HOUSE OF GAMES Orion, 1987
ALARIC JANS

HOUSE OF HORRORS Universal, 1946
HANS J. SALTER†

THE HOUSE OF INTRIGUE 1957
NINO ROTA†

THE HOUSE OF LOVERS Continental, 1957
JEAN WIENER†

HOUSE OF MYSTERY 1961
STANLEY BLACK

HOUSE OF NUMBERS Columbia, 1957
ANDRE PREVIN

THE HOUSE OF ROTHSCHILD United Artists, 1934
ALFRED NEWMAN†

A HOUSE OF SAND American International, 1962
LES BAXTER†

HOUSE OF SECRETS (TF) Steve Krantz Prods./Multimedia, 1993
ANTHONY MARINELLI

HOUSE OF STRANGERS 20th Century-Fox, 1949
DANIELE AMFITHEATROF†

THE HOUSE OF THE SEVEN GABLES Universal, 1940
FRANK SKINNER† ★

THE HOUSE OF THE SPIRITS Miramax, 1993
HANS ZIMMER

HOUSE OF THE CARDS Universal, 1969
FRANCIS LAI

HOUSE OF THE LONG SHADOWS MGM/UA/Cannon, 1983
RICHARD HARVEY

THE HOUSE OF USHER 21st Century, 1991
GARY CHANG
GEORGE S. CLINTON

HOUSE OF USHER *FALL OF THE HOUSE OF USHER* American International, 1960
LES BAXTER†

HOUSE OF WAX Warner Bros., 1953
DAVID BUTTOLPH†

HOUSE OF WHIPCORD Miracle, 1974
STANLEY MYERS†

THE HOUSE ON 92ND STREET 20th Century-Fox, 1945
DAVID BUTTOLPH†

THE HOUSE ON CARROLL STREET Orion, 1988
GEORGES DELERUE†

THE HOUSE ON GARIBALDI STREET (TF) Charles Fries Productions, 1979
CHARLES BERNSTEIN

THE HOUSE ON GREENAPPLE ROAD (TF) QM Productions, 1970
DUANE TATRO

HOUSE ON HAUNTED HILL Allied Artists, 1959
VON DEXTER

THE HOUSE ON SKULL MOUNTAIN 20th Century-Fox, 1974
JERROLD IMMEL

THE HOUSE ON SORORITY ROW Artists Releasing Corporation/Film Ventures International, 1983
RICHARD H. BAND

THE HOUSE ON SYCAMORE STREET (TF) Fred Silverman Co./Dean Hargrove Prods./Viacom, 1992
DICK DEBENEDICTIS

HOUSE ON TELEGRAPH HILL 20th Century-Fox, 1951
SOL KAPLAN

HOUSE ON THE EDGE OF THE PARK Bedford Entertainment, 1979
RIZ ORTOLANI

HOUSE PARTY New Line Cinema, 1990
MARCUS MILLER
LENNY WHITE

HOUSE PARTY 2 New Line, 1991
VASSAL BENFORD

HOUSE PARTY 3 New Line, 1994
DAVID ALLEN

THE HOUSE THAT CRIED MURDER *THE BRIDE* Golden Gate/Unisphere, 1974
PETER BERNSTEIN

THE HOUSE THAT DRIPPED BLOOD Cinerama Releasing Corporation, 1971
MICHAEL DRESS

THE HOUSE THAT WOULD NOT DIE (TF) Aaron Spelling Productions, 1970
LAURENCE ROSENTHAL

THE HOUSE WHERE DEATH LIVES New American, 1984
DON PEAKE

THE HOUSE WHERE EVIL DWELLS MGM/UA, 1982
KEN THORNE

HOUSEBOAT Paramount, 1958
GEORGE DUNING

HOUSEHOLD SAINTS Fine Line, 1993
STEPHEN ENDELMAN

THE HOUSEKEEPER'S DAUGHTER United Artists, 1939
LUD GLUSKIN†

HOUSEKEEPING Columbia, 1987
MICHAEL GIBBS

HOUSESITTER Universal, 1992
MILES GOODMAN†

HOUSEWIFE FROM HELL Crown, 1993
JAMES LANE

HOUSTON KNIGHTS (TF) Jay Bernstein Productions/Columbia Pictures TV, 1987
DENNIS MCCARTHY

HOUSTON, WE'VE GOT A PROBLEM (TF) Universal TV, 1974
RICHARD CLEMENTS

HOUSTON: THE LEGEND OF TEXAS (TF) Taft Entertainment TV/J.D. Feigelson Productions, 1986
DENNIS MCCARTHY

HOW AWFUL ABOUT ALLAN (TF) Aaron Spelling Productions, 1970
LAURENCE ROSENTHAL

HOW DO I LOVE THEE? ABC Films, 1970
JIM HELMS

HOW GREEN WAS MY VALLEY 20th Century-Fox, 1941
ALFRED NEWMAN† ★

HOW I GOT INTO COLLEGE 20th Century Fox, 1989
JOSEPH VITARELLI

HOW I SPENT MY SUMMER VACATION (TF) Universal TV, 1967
LALO SCHIFRIN

HOW I WON THE WAR United Artists, 1967
KEN THORNE

HOW SWEET IT IS! Buena Vista, 1968
PATRICK WILLIAMS

HOW THE WEST WAS FUN (TF) Dualstar Prods./Green-Epstein Prods./Kicking Horse Prods./Warner Bros. TV, 1994
RICHARD BELLIS

HOW THE WEST WAS LOST (TD) 9KUSA/Discovery Prods., 1995
PETER KATER

HOW THE WEST WAS WON MGM, 1962
ALFRED NEWMAN† ★

HOW THE WEST WAS WON (MS) MGM TV, 1977
BRUCE BROUGHTON
DICK DEBENEDICTIS
JERROLD IMMEL

HOW TO BE VERY, VERY POPULAR 20th Century-Fox, 1955
LIONEL NEWMAN†

HOW TO BEAT THE HIGH COST OF LIVING American International, 1980
PATRICK WILLIAMS

HOW TO BECOME A CITIZEN OF THE UNITED STATES (FD) Rudolph Burckhardt, 1938
PAUL BOWLES

HOW TO BREAK UP A HAPPY DIVORCE (TF) Charles Fries Productions, 1976
NELSON RIDDLE†

HOW TO FRAME A FIGG Universal, 1971
VIC MIZZY

HOW TO GET AHEAD IN ADVERTISING Warner Bros., 1989
DAVID DUNDAS
RICK WENTWORTH

HOW TO MAKE A DOLL 1967
LARRY WELLINGTON

HOW TO MAKE A MONSTER American International, 1958
PAUL DUNLAP

HOW TO MAKE AN AMERICAN QUILT Universal, 1995
THOMAS NEWMAN

HOW TO MAKE IT ABC Pictures International, 1968
LES BAXTER†

HOW TO MARRY A MILLIONAIRE 20th Century-Fox, 1953
CYRIL J. MOCKRIDGE†

HOW TO MURDER A MILLIONAIRE (TF) Robert Greenwald Films, 1990
RICHARD GIBBS

HOW TO MURDER A RICH UNCLE Columbia, 1957
KENNETH V. JONES

HOW TO MURDER YOUR WIFE United Artists, 1965
NEAL HEFTI

HOW TO PICK UP GIRLS! (TF) King-Hitzig Productions, 1978
DON SEBESKY

HOW TO SAVE A MARRIAGE AND RUIN YOUR LIFE Columbia, 1968
MICHEL LEGRAND

HOW TO SEDUCE A WOMAN Cinerama, 1974
STU PHILLIPS

HOW TO STEAL A MILLION Columbia, 1966
JOHN WILLIAMS

HOW TO STEAL AN AIRPLANE (TF) Universal TV, 1972
PETE RUGOLO

HOW TO STUFF A WILD BIKINI American International, 1965
LES BAXTER†

HOW TO SUCCEED IN BUSINESS WITHOUT REALLY TRYING United Artists, 1967
NELSON RIDDLE†

HOW TO TOP MY WIFE *MANURA CHUGIGI* Morning Calm, 1995
KYUNG-SUK CHONG

HOW U LIKE ME NOW Shapiro-Glickenhaus, 1993
KAHIL ELZABAR
CHUCK WEBB

HOW WONDERFUL TO DIE ASSASSINATED 1975
ROBERTO DE SIMONE

HOW, WHEN AND WITH WHOM Warner Bros., 1974
ARMANDO TROVAJOLI

HOWARD BEACH: MAKING THE CASE FOR MURDER (TF) Patchett-Kaufman Entertainment Productions/WIN, 1989
JONATHAN ELIAS

HOWARD THE DUCK Universal, 1986
JOHN BARRY
SYLVESTER LEVAY

HOWARDS END Orion Classics, 1992
RICHARD ROBBINS ★

THE HOWARDS OF VIRGINIA Columbia, 1940
RICHARD HAGEMAN† ★

THE HOWLING Avco Embassy, 1981
PINO DONAGGIO

THE HOWLING III *THE MARSUPIALS: THE HOWLING III* Square Pictures, 1987
ALLAN ZAVOD

HOWLING II...YOUR SISTER IS A WEREWOLF Thorn-EMI, 1985
STEPHEN PARSONS

A HOWLING IN THE WOODS (TF) Universal TV, 1971
DAVE GRUSIN

H.P. LOVECRAFT'S REANIMATOR *REANIMATOR* Empire Pictures, 1985
RICHARD H. BAND

HSI YEN *THE WEDDING BANQUET* 1993
MADER

HSIMENG JENSHENG *THE PUPPETMASTER* 1993
CHEN MING-CHANG

HUCKLEBERRY FINN MGM, 1939
FRANZ WAXMAN†

HUCKLEBERRY FINN United Artists, 1974
FRED WERNER

HUCKLEBERRY FINN (TF) ABC Circle Films, 1975
EARL ROBINSON

HUD Paramount, 1963
ELMER BERNSTEIN

HUDSON HAWK Tri-Star, 1991
MICHAEL KAMEN
ROBERT KRAFT

HUDSON'S BAY 20th Century-Fox, 1940
ALFRED NEWMAN†

THE HUDSUCKER PROXY Warner Bros., 1994
CARTER BURWELL

HUE AND CRY Fine Arts, 1947
GEORGES AURIC†

HUEVOS DE ORO *GOLDEN BALLS* 1993
NICOLA PIOVANI

HUEY LONG (FD) RKB/Florentine Films, 1985
JOHN COLBY

HUGH HEFNER: ONCE UPON A TIME (FD) IRS, 1992
REEVES GABRELS
CHARLOTTE LANSBERG
TOM DUBE

HUGHES LE LOUP (TF) 1974
VLADIMIR COSMA

HUIS CLOS 1954
JOSEPH KOSMA†

HUK United Artists, 1956
ALBERT GLASSER

HULLABALOO OVER GEORGIE AND BONNIE'S PICTURES Corinth, 1979
VIC FLICK

THE HUMAN BEAST 1938
JOSEPH KOSMA†

THE HUMAN COMEDY MGM, 1943
HERBERT STOTHART†

HUMAN DESIRE Columbia, 1954
DANIELE AMFITHEATROF†

THE HUMAN FACTOR Bryanston, 1975
ENNIO MORRICONE

THE HUMAN FACTOR MGM/UA, 1979
GARY LOGAN
RICHARD LOGAN

HUMAN FEELINGS (TF) Crestview Productions/Worldvision, 1978
JOHN CACAVAS

HUMAN HIGHWAY Shakey Pictures, 1982
DEVO
MARK MOTHERSBAUGH
NEIL YOUNG

THE HUMAN JUNGLE Universal, 1954
HANS J. SALTER†

THE HUMAN QUEST (TD) KCET/Science & Society Prods., 1995
JIM LATHAM

THE HUMAN REVOLUTION 1974
AKIRA IFUKUBE

THE HUMAN SHIELD Cannon, 1992
ROBBIE PATTON

THE HUMAN TOUCH (CTF) MTE, 1994
SIMON BOSWELL

THE HUMANOID 1978
ENNIO MORRICONE

HUMANOIDS FROM THE DEEP New World, 1980
JAMES HORNER

HUMONGOUS Avco Embassy, 1982
JOHN MILLS-COCKELL

HUMORESQUE Warner Bros., 1946
FRANZ WAXMAN† ★

THE HUNCHBACK OF NOTRE DAME RKO Radio, 1939
ALFRED NEWMAN† ★

THE HUNCHBACK OF NOTRE DAME Universal, 1923
HEINZ ROEMHELD†

THE HUNCHBACK OF NOTRE DAME *NOTRE DAME DE PARIS* RKO Radio, 1956
GEORGES AURIC†

THE HUNCHBACK OF NOTRE DAME (AF) Buena Vista, 1996
ALAN MENKEN ★

THE HUNCHBACK OF NOTRE DAME (TF) Norman Rosemont Productions/Columbia TV, 1982
KEN THORNE

HUNDERT TAGE 1935
GIUSEPPE BECCE†

HUNDRA 1983
ENNIO MORRICONE

THE HUNGER MGM/UA, 1983
DENNY JAEGER
MICHEL RUBINI

HUNGER 1966
CHRISTOPHER KOMEDA†

HUNGRY HILL Universal, 1947
JOHN GREENWOOD†

HUNGRY WIVES Jack H. Harris Enterprises, 1973
JOHN PARKER

HUNK Crown International, 1987
DAVID KURTZ

THE HUNT FOR RED OCTOBER Paramount, 1990
BASIL POLEDOURIS

THE HUNTED Universal, 1995
MOTOFUMI YAMAGUSHI

HUNTED Malibu Bay Films, 1992
RICHARD LYONS

THE HUNTER Paramount, 1980
CHARLES BERNSTEIN
MICHEL LEGRAND

HUNTER (TF) CBS Entertainment, 1971
LALO SCHIFRIN

HUNTER (TF) Stephen J. Cannell Prods., 1984
MIKE POST

HUNTER (TF) Stephen J. Cannell, 1984
PETE CARPENTER†

HUNTER OF THE APOCALYPSE World Northal, 1980
FRANCO MICALIZZI

HUNTERS ARE FOR KILLING (TF) Cinema Center 100, 1970
JERRY FIELDING†

THE HUNTERS OF THE GOLDEN COBRA *THE RAIDERS OF THE GOLDEN COBRA* World Northal, 1982
CARLO SAVINA

HUNTERS OF THE DEEP (FD) DCA, 1954
GEORGE ANTHEIL†

HUNTERS OF THE REEF (TF) Writers Company Productions/Paramount TV, 1978
RICHARD MARKOWITZ†

THE HUNTING PARTY United Artists, 1970
RIZ ORTOLANI

HURRAH! THE SCHOOL IS BURNING 1970
ROLF WILHELM

THE HURRICANE United Artists, 1938
ALFRED NEWMAN† ★

HURRICANE MGM-UA, 1997
THEODORE SHAPIRO

HURRICANE Paramount, 1979
NINO ROTA†

HURRICANE (TF) Montagne Productions/Metromedia Producers Corporation, 1974
VIC MIZZY

HURRICANE SMITH 1990
BRIAN MAY†

HURRY UP OR I'LL BE THIRTY Avco Embassy, 1973
STEPHEN LAWRENCE

HURRY, CHARLIE, HURRY RKO Radio, 1941
ROY WEBB†

HUSBAND, WIFE AND FRIEND 20th Century-Fox, 1939
DAVID BUTTOLPH†

HUSH Frameline Prods., 1988
NEIL ARGO

FILM TITLES

HUSH LITTLE BABY (CTF) USA Pictures/ Power Pictures/Hearst, 1994
MYCHAEL DANNA ★

HUSH...HUSH SWEET CHARLOTTE 20th Century-Fox, 1964
FRANK DEVOL

THE HUSSY UGC, 1985
ALAIN JOMY

HUSSY Watchgrove Ltd., 1980
GEORGE FENTON

HUSTLE Paramount, 1975
FRANK DEVOL

THE HUSTLER OF MUSCLE BEACH (TF) Furia-Oringer Productions, 1980
EARLE HAGEN

HUSTLING (TF) Filmways/Lillian Gallo Productions, 1975
JERRY FIELDING†

HYENA'S SUN *ACH CHAMS WADHDHIBA/LE SOLEIL DES HYENES* 1977
NICOLA PIOVANI

HYMN TO A TIRED MAN 1968
TORU TAKEMITSU†

HYPER SAPIEN Taliafilm II, 1986
ARTHUR B. RUBINSTEIN

HYPERSPACE Regency Entertainment, 1986
DON DAVIS

HYPNOS 1969
CARLO SAVINA

HYPNOTIZED World Wide, 1932
EDWARD WARD†

THE HYPOCHONDRIAC 1979
PIERO PICCIONI

HYSTERIA MGM, 1965
DON BANKS

HYSTERICAL Embassy, 1983
BOB ALCIVAR
ROBERT O. RAGLAND

I

I 7 FRATELLI CERVI 1968
CARLO RUSTICHELLI

I ACCUSE! MGM, 1958
WILLIAM ALWYN†

I AIM AT THE STARS Columbia, 1960
LAURIE JOHNSON

I AM A CAMERA British Lion, 1955
MALCOLM ARNOLD

I AM SUZANNE Fox, 1934
FREDERICK HOLLANDER†

I AM THE CHEESE Libra Cinema 5, 1983
JONATHAN TUNICK

I BAMBINI CI CHIEDONO PERCHE 1972
ENNIO MORRICONE

I BAMBINI E NOI (TF) 1970
FIORENZO CARPI

I BASILISCHI 1963
ENNIO MORRICONE

I BURY THE LIVING United Artists, 1958
GERALD FRIED

I CAGASOTTO 1964
ARMANDO TROVAJOLI

I CAN GET IT FOR YOU WHOLESALE 20th Century-Fox, 1951
SOL KAPLAN

I CAN MAKE YOU LOVE ME: THE STALKING OF LAURA BLACK (TF) Joel Fields/Frank Abatemarco/Leonard Hill, 1993
SYLVESTER LEVAY

I CAN'T GIVE YOU ANYTHING BUT LOVE, BABY Universal, 1940
HANS J. SALTER†

I CANNIBALI American International, 1969
ENNIO MORRICONE

I CAVALIERI DELLA VENDETTA 1965
CARLO RUSTICHELLI

I COME IN PEACE Triumph, 1991
JAN HAMMER

I COMPAGNI Continental, 1963
CARLO RUSTICHELLI

I COMPLESSI Documento Film/SPCE, 1965
ARMANDO TROVAJOLI

I CONFESS Warner Bros., 1953
DIMITRI TIOMKIN†

I COULD GO ON SINGING United Artists, 1963
MORT LINDSEY

I COVER THE WATERFRONT United Artists, 1933
ALFRED NEWMAN†

I CRIMINALI DELLA GELASSIA MGM, 1966
ANGELO FRANCESCO LAVAGNINO†

I CRUDELLI 1966
ENNIO MORRICONE

I DEAL IN DANGER 20th Century-Fox, 1966
LALO SCHIFRIN

I, DESIRE (TF) Green-Epstein Productions/Columbia TV, 1982
DON PEAKE

I DIAMANTI CHE NESSUNO VOLEVA ROBARE 1967
CARLO RUSTICHELLI

I DIE A THOUSAND TIMES Warner Bros., 1955
DAVID BUTTOLPH†

I DISMEMBER MAMA *POOR ALBERT AND LITTLE ANNIE* Valiant International, 1972
HERSCHEL BURKE GILBERT

I DOLCI INGANNI 1959
PIERO PICCIONI

I DON'T BUY KISSES ANYMORE Skouras, 1992
COBB BUSSINGER

I DON'T KISS 1991
PHILIPPE SARDE

I DON'T WANT TO BE BORN American International, 1976
RON GRAINER†

I DREAM OF JEANNIE...15 YEARS LATER (TF) Can't Sing Can't Dance Production/Columbia Pictures TV, 1985
MARK SNOW

I DREAM TOO MUCH RKO Radio, 1935
MAX STEINER†

I DUE DELLA LEGIONE Ultra Film, 1962
LUIS BACALOV

I DUE EVASI DI SING SING 1964
ENNIO MORRICONE

I DUE MAGHI DEL PALLONE 1970
BRUNO NICOLAI

I DUE VIGILI 1967
CARLO RUSTICHELLI

I ESCAPED FROM DEVIL'S ISLAND United Artists, 1973
LES BAXTER†

I ESCAPED FROM THE GESTAPO Monogram, 1943
W. FRANKE HARLING†

I FALSARI 1950
CARLO RUSTICHELLI

I FIGLI CHIEDONO PERCHE 1974
BRUNO NICOLAI

I FIUME DI DOLLARI 1966
ENNIO MORRICONE

I FIX AMERICA AND RETURN 1974
LUIS BACALOV

I GIGANTI DELLA TESSAGLIA 1959
CARLO RUSTICHELLI

I GIGANTI DI ROMA 1963
CARLO RUSTICHELLI

I GIORNI DELLA VIOLENZA 1967
BRUNO NICOLAI

I HATE YOUR GUTS!/SHAME Pathe American, 1961
HERMAN STEIN

I HEARD THE OWL CALL MY NAME (TF) Tomorrow Entertainment, 1973
PETER MATZ

I, JANE DOE Republic, 1948
HEINZ ROEMHELD†

I KILLED RASPUTIN 20th Century-Fox, 1966
DON BANKS

I KNEW HER WELL Universal, 1966
HANS J. SALTER†

I KNOW MY FIRST NAME IS STEVEN (TF) Lorimar/NBC Productions, 1989
DAVID SHIRE

I KNOW MY SON IS ALIVE (TF) Alexander-Enright & Associates/WIN, 1994
MICKEY ERBE
MARYBETH SOLOMON

I KNOW WHERE I'M GOING Universal, 1945
ALLAN GRAY†

I KNOW WHY THE CAGED BIRD SINGS (TF) Tomorrow Entertainment, 1979
PETER MATZ

I LEONI DI SAN PETERSBURG 1972
GIANFRANCO PLENIZIO

I LIKE IT LIKE THAT Columbia, 1994
SERGIO GEORGE

I LIKE IT THAT WAY Universal, 1934
EDWARD WARD†

I LIKE MONEY 1962
GEORGES VAN PARYS†

I LIVE IN FEAR Brandon, 1955
FUMIO HAYASAKA†

I LIVE MY LIFE MGM, 1935
DIMITRI TIOMKIN†

I LOVE A MYSTERY Columbia, 1945
MARIO †

I LOVE A SOLDIER Paramount, 1944
ROBERT EMMETT DOLAN†

I LOVE MY WIFE Universal, 1970
LALO SCHIFRIN

I LOVE N.Y. Manhattan Films, 1988
BILL CONTI

I LOVE TROUBLE Buena Vista, 1994
DAVID NEWMAN

I LOVE TROUBLE Columbia, 1948
GEORGE DUNING

I LOVE YOU AGAIN MGM, 1940
FRANZ WAXMAN†

I LOVE YOU TO DEATH Warner Bros., 1990
JAMES HORNER

I LOVE YOU, ALICE B. TOKLAS Warner Bros., 1968
ELMER BERNSTEIN

I LOVE YOU, ROSA 1972
DOV SELTZER

I LUNGHI CAPELLI DELLA MORTE 1964
CARLO RUSTICHELLI

I LUNGHI GIORNI DELLA VENDETTA 1965
ARMANDO TROVAJOLI

I, MADMAN Trans World Entertainment, 1989
MICHAEL HOENIG

I MAGLIARI Vides/Titanus, 1959
PIERO PICCIONI

I MALAMONDO 1964
ENNIO MORRICONE

I MANIACI 1964
ENNIO MORRICONE

I MARRIED A DOCTOR Warner Bros., 1936
W. FRANKE HARLING†

I MARRIED A WITCH United Artists, 1942
ROY WEBB† ★

I MARRIED A WOMAN Universal, 1958
CYRIL J. MOCKRIDGE†

I MARRIED AN ANGEL MGM, 1942
HERBERT STOTHART†

I MARRIED WYATT EARP (TF) Osmond TV Productions/Comworld Productions, 1983
MORTON STEVENS†

I MARZIANI HANNO 12 MANI 1964
ENNIO MORRICONE

I MET MY LOVE AGAIN United Artists, 1938
HEINZ ROEMHELD†

I MIEI AMICI (TF) 1976
BRUNO NICOLAI

I MISCHETTIERI DEL MARE 1962
CARLO RUSTICHELLI

I MISERABILI *LES MISERABLES* 1948
ALESSANDRO CICOGNINI†

I MISS YOU, HUGS AND KISSES 1978
HOWARD SHORE

I, MOBSTER 20th Century Fox, 1959
GERALD FRIED

I MONSTER Cannon, 1972
CARL DAVIS

I MOTORIZZATI 1962
ENNIO MORRICONE

I NEVER PROMISED YOU A ROSE GARDEN New World, 1977
PAUL CHIHARA

I NEVER SANG FOR MY FATHER Columbia, 1970
AL GORGONI
BARRY MANN

I NOSTRI MARITI Documento Film, 1966
ARMANDO TROVAJOLI

I NUOVI MOSTRI 1977
ARMANDO TROVAJOLI

I OUGHT TO BE IN PICTURES 20th Century-Fox, 1982
MARVIN HAMLISCH

I PADRONI DELLA CITTA 1976
LUIS BACALOV

I PASSED FOR WHITE Allied Artists, 1960
JOHN WILLIAMS

I PATRIARCHI DELLA BIBBIA *THE PATRIARCHS OF THE BIBLE* Italian, 1963
TEO USUELLI

I PIACERE DEL SABATO NOTTE *CALL-GIRLS OF ROME* 1960
ARMANDO TROVAJOLI

I PIACERE DELLO SCAPOLO 1960
ARMANDO TROVAJOLI

I PIANETI CONTRO DI NOI 1961
ARMANDO TROVAJOLI

I PLAYED IT FOR YOU (FD) Ronee Blakley Productions, 1985
RONNIE BLAKLEY

I PREDONI DEL SAHARA 1965
ANGELO FRANCESCO LAVAGNINO†

I PREDONI DELLA STEPPA 1963
CARLO RUSTICHELLI

I PROMESSI SPOSI 1964
CARLO RUSTICHELLI

I PROSSENETI 1976
LUIS BACALOV

I PROTAGONISTI 1968
LUIS BACALOV

I PUGNI IN TASCA 1965
ENNIO MORRICONE

I QUATTRO DEL PATER NOSTER 1969
LUIS BACALOV

I QUATTRO DELL'AVE MARIA 1969
CARLO RUSTICHELLI

I QUATTRO MONACI 1962
ARMANDO TROVAJOLI

I RAGAZZI DEL PARIOLI 1958
PIERO PICCIONI

I REMEMBER MAMA RKO Radio, 1948
ROY WEBB†

I RING DOORBELLS Producers Releasing Corp., 1946
LEO ERDODY†

I SAW WHAT YOU DID Universal, 1965
VAN ALEXANDER

I SAW WHAT YOU DID (TF) Universal TV, 1988
DANA KAPROFF

I SEE A DARK STRANGER 1947
WILLIAM ALWYN†

I SENT A LETTER TO MY LOVE *CHERE INCONNUE* Atlantic Releasing Corporation, 1980
PHILIPPE SARDE

I SHOT A MAN IN RENO Trans Atlantic, 1995
SHARK

I SHOT ANDY WARHOL 1996
JOHN CALE

I SHOT BILLY THE KID Lippert, 1950
ALBERT GLASSER

I SHOT JESSE JAMES Lippert, 1949
ALBERT GLASSER

I SPY RETURNS (TF) SAH Ent./Sheldon Leonard Ent./Citadel, 1994
EARLE HAGEN
JOHNNY HARRIS

I START COUNTING United Artists, 1969
BASIL KIRCHIN

I STILL DREAM OF JEANNIE (TF) Jeannie Ent./Carla Singer Prods./Bar-Gene TV, 1991
KEN HARRISON

I TABU #2 (FD) 1965
ANGELO FRANCESCO LAVAGNINO†

I TABU (FD) 1965
ARMANDO TROVAJOLI

I TAKE THESE MEN (TF) Lillian Gallo Productions/United Artists TV, 1983
EARLE HAGEN

I TAKE THIS WOMAN MGM, 1940
BRONISLAU KAPER†

I TALK TO ANIMALS (FD) Peter Friedman Productions, 1990
PAT IRWIN

I TARTASSATI 1958
PIERO PICCIONI

I TERRIBILI SETTE 1964
ARMANDO TROVAJOLI

I THANK A FOOL MGM, 1962
RON GOODWIN
GAIL KUBIK†

I, THE JURY 20th Century Fox, 1982
BILL CONTI

I, THE JURY United Artists, 1953
FRANZ WAXMAN†

I TRE VOLTI DELLA PAURA American International, 1963
LES BAXTER†

I TROMBONI DI FRAI DIAVOLO 1962
CARLO RUSTICHELLI

I VAMPIRI 1956
FRANCO MANNINO

I VITELLONI API Productions, 1953
NINO ROTA†

I VIZI MORBOSI DI UNA GOVERNANTE 1976
PIERO PICCIONI

I WALK ALONE Paramount, 1947
VICTOR YOUNG†

I WALKED WITH A ZOMBIE RKO Radio, 1943
ROY WEBB†

I WANT A DIVORCE Paramount, 1940
VICTOR YOUNG†

I WANT TO GO HOME MK2, 1989
JOHN KANDER

I WANT TO KEEP MY BABY! (TF) CBS Entertainment, 1976
GEORGE ALICESON TIPTON

I WANT TO LIVE (TF) United Artists Corporation, 1983
LEE HOLDRIDGE

I WANT TO LIVE! United Artists, 1958
JOHNNY MANDEL

I WANT YOU RKO Radio, 1951
LEIGH HARLINE†

I WANTED WINGS Paramount, 1941
VICTOR YOUNG†

I WAS A COMMUNIST FOR THE F.B.I. Warner Bros., 1951
MAX STEINER†

I WAS A MAIL ORDER BRIDE (TF) Jaffe Productions/Tuxedo Limited Productions/MGM TV, 1982
JOHN ADDISON

I WAS A MALE WAR BRIDE 20th Century-Fox, 1949
CYRIL J. MOCKRIDGE†

I WAS A TEENAGE FRANKENSTEIN American International, 1957
PAUL DUNLAP

I WAS A TEENAGE WEREWOLF American International, 1957
PAUL DUNLAP

I WAS AN ADVENTURESS 20th Century-Fox, 1940
DAVID BUTTOLPH†

I WAS HAPPY HERE Continental, 1966
JOHN ADDISON

I WAS MONTY'S DOUBLE NTA Pictures, 1958
JOHN ADDISON

I WAS ON MARS 1992
NIKI REISER

I WENT TO THE DANCE (FD) Brazos Films/Flower Films, 1989
MICHAEL DOUCET

I WILL FIGHT NO MORE FOREVER (FD) Wolper Productions, 1975
GERALD FRIED

I WILL, I WILL...FOR NOW 20th Century-Fox, 1976
JOHN CAMERON

I YABBA-DABBA DO! (ATF) William Hanna, Joseph Barbera and Hoyt Curtin, H-B Prods., 1993
JOSEPH BARBERA
HOYT CURTIN
JOHN DEBNEY
WILLIAM HANNA

ICE PM, 1993
JOHN GONZALEZ

ICE CASTLES Columbia, 1979
MARVIN HAMLISCH

ICE COLD IN ALEX 20th Century-Fox, 1958
LEIGHTON LUCAS†

ICE PALACE Warner Bros., 1960
MAX STEINER†

THE ICE PIRATES MGM/UA, 1983
BRUCE BROUGHTON

THE ICE RUNNER Borde Film, 1993
JIM GOODMAN
EMILIO KAUDERER

ICE STATION ZEBRA MGM, 1968
MICHEL LEGRAND

THE ICE STORM 20th Century Fox, 1997
MYCHAEL DANNA

ICE-AGE 1975
PEER RABEN

ICEMAN Universal, 1984
BRUCE SMEATON

ICH BEI TAG, DU BEI NACHT 1932
WERNER R. HEYMANN†

I'D CLIMB THE HIGHEST MOUNTAIN 20th Century-Fox, 1951
SOL KAPLAN

IDAHO TRANSFER Cinemation, 1975
BRUCE LANGHORNE

IDEA GIRL Universal, 1946
FRANK SKINNER†

AN IDEAL HUSBAND 20th Century-Fox, 1947
ARTHUR BENJAMIN†

IDENTIFICATION OF A WOMAN Iter Film/Gaumont, 1982
TANGERINE DREAM
CHRISTOPHER FRANKE

IDENTIKIT 1974
FRANCO MANNINO

IDIOT'S DELIGHT MGM, 1939
HERBERT STOTHART†

THE IDOL Embassy, 1966
JOHN DANKWORTH

IDOLI CONTROLUCE 1966
ENNIO MORRICONE

THE IDOLMAKER United Artists, 1980
JEFF BARRY

IF A MAN ANSWERS Universal, 1962
HANS J. SALTER†

IF EVER I SEE YOU AGAIN Columbia, 1978
JOSEPH BROOKS

IF HE HOLLERS, LET HIM GO Cinerama Releasing Corporation, 1968
COLERIDGE-TAYLOR PERKINSON
HARRY SUKMAN†

IF I WERE FREE RKO Radio, 1933
MAX STEINER†

IF I WERE KING Paramount, 1938
RICHARD HAGEMAN† ★

IF IT'S TUESDAY, IT STILL MUST BE BELGIUM (TF) Eisenstock & Mintz Productions, 1987
KEN THORNE

IF LOOKS COULD KILL Warner Bros., 1991
DAVID FOSTER

IF LUCY FELL TriStar, 1996
AMANDA KRAVAT
CHARLTON PETTUS

IF SOMEONE HAD KNOWN (TF) Landsburg Co., 1995
LAURA KARPMAN

IF THESE WALLS COULD TALK (CTF) Moving Pictures, 1996
CLIFF EIDELMAN

IF THINGS WERE DIFFERENT (TF) Bob Banner Associates, 1980
LEE HOLDRIDGE

IF TOMORROW COMES (TF) Aaron Spelling Productions/American Broadcasting Company, 1971
GIL MELLE

IF TOMORROW COMES (TF) CBS Entertainment Productions, 1986
NICK BICAT

IF WINTER COMES MGM, 1948
HERBERT STOTHART†

IF... Paramount, 1969
MARC WILKINSON

IGNATZ& LOTTE Big Stick & Swagger, 1995
WARD SHELLEY

IKE (MS) ABC Circle Films, 1979
FRED KARLIN

IKIRU Brandon, 1952
FUMIO HAYASAKA†

IL BALORDO (TF) 1978
LUIS BACALOV

IL BANAITO DAGLI OCCHI AZZURRI 1980
ENNIO MORRICONE

IL BELL'ANTONIO Cino Del Duca/Arco Film/Lyre Cinematographique, 1960
PIERO PICCIONI

IL BIDONE Astor, 1955
NINO ROTA†

IL BILVIO 1951
CARLO RUSTICHELLI

IL BIRICHINO DI PAPA 1942
NINO ROTA†

IL BOIA DI VENEZIA 1963
CARLO RUSTICHELLI

IL BOSS 1973
LUIS BACALOV

IL BRIGANTE 1961
NINO ROTA†

IL BRIGANTE DI TACCA DEL LUPO 1951
CARLO RUSTICHELLI

IL CAMINO DELLA SPERANZA 1950
CARLO RUSTICHELLI

IL CAPITANO 1991
LARA ACKERLUND
SEBASTIAN OBERG

IL CAPPOTTO DI ASTRAKAN 1980
BRUNO NICOLAI

IL CARRO ARMATO DELL' 8 SETTEMBRE 1959
ARMANDO TROVAJOLI

IL CASANOVA DI FEDERICO FELLINI Universal, 1976
NINO ROTA†

IL CASO RAOUL Iskra Cinematografica, 1975
MANUEL DE SICA

IL CASTELLO DEI MORTI VIVI 1965
ANGELO FRANCESCO LAVAGNINO†

IL CIELO BRUCIA 1957
ANGELO FRANCESCO LAVAGNINO†

IL CINICO, L'INFAME, IL VIOLENTO 1976
FRANCO MICALIZZI

IL COCCO DI MAMMA 1957
ARMANDO TROVAJOLI

IL COLPO SEGRETO DI D'ARTAGNAN 1961
CARLO RUSTICHELLI

IL COMMISSARIO 1962
CARLO RUSTICHELLI

IL COMMISSARIO PEPE Dean Film, 1969
ARMANDO TROVAJOLI

IL COMPAGNO DON CAMILLO Rizzoli Film/Francoriz/Omnia Film, 1965
ALESSANDRO CICOGNINI†

IL COMUNE SENSO DEL PUDORE Rizzoli Film, 1976
PIERO PICCIONI

IL CONTE TACCHIA Gaumont, 1983
ARMANDO TROVAJOLI

IL CONTO E CHIUSO *THE LAST ROUND* 1976
LUIS BACALOV

IL CORAZZIERE 1960
ARMANDO TROVAJOLI

IL CRIMINALE 1963
CARLO RUSTICHELLI

IL DECAMERONE 1971
ENNIO MORRICONE

IL DELITTO DEL DIAVOLO 1971
ANGELO FRANCESCO LAVAGNINO†

IL DELITTO DI GIOVANNI EPISCOPO 1947
NINO ROTA†

IL DESIERTO DEI TARTARI Gaumont, 1977
ENNIO MORRICONE

IL DIAVOLO A SETTE FACCIE 1971
STELVIO CIPRIANI

IL DIAVOLO NEL CERVELLO 1971
ENNIO MORRICONE

IL DIO SOTTO LA PELLE 1974
PIERO PICCIONI

IL DOMINATORE DEI SETTE MARI MGM, 1962
FRANCO MANNINO

IL DOMINATORE DEL DESERTO 1964
CARLO RUSTICHELLI

IL DUE NEMICI Columbia, 1962
NINO ROTA†

IL FALCO E LA COLOMBA 1981
STELVIO CIPRIANI

IL FAUT VIVRE DANGEREUSEMENT *ONE MUST LIVE DANGEROUSLY* 1975
CLAUDE BOLLING

IL FERROVIERE Continental, 1956
CARLO RUSTICHELLI

IL FIGLIO DEL CORSARO NERO 1941
CARLO RUSTICHELLI

IL FIGLIO DI CLEOPATRA 1965
CARLO RUSTICHELLI

IL FIGLIO DI SPARTACUS 1962
PIERO PICCIONI

IL FIGLIOCCIO DEL PADRINO 1973
CARLO RUSTICHELLI

IL FIUME DEL GRANDE CAIMANO *THE GREAT ALLIGATOR* 1979
STELVIO CIPRIANI

IL FOGLIO DELLA SEPOLTA VIVA 1974
FRANCO MICALIZZI

IL FORNARETTO DI VENEZIA 1963
ARMANDO TROVAJOLI

IL GABBIANO (TF) RAI, 1976
NICOLA PIOVANI

IL GATTO 1977
ENNIO MORRICONE

IL GATTO MAMMONE 1975
CARLO RUSTICHELLI

IL GAUCHO Fair Film/Clemente Lococo, 1964
ARMANDO TROVAJOLI

IL GIARDINO DELL'EDEN 1980
STELVIO CIPRIANI

IL GIOVANE NORMALE Dean Film/Italnoleggio, 1969
ARMANDO TROVAJOLI

IL GIOVEDI 1962
ARMANDO TROVAJOLI

IL GIUDIZIO UNIVERSALE 1960
ALESSANDRO CICOGNINI†

IL GIUSTIZIERE SFIDA LA CITTA 1975
FRANCO MICALIZZI

IL GOBBO Dino De Laurentiis Cinematografica, 1960
PIERO PICCIONI

IL GRANDE DUELLO *THE GRAND DUEL* 1972
LUIS BACALOV

IL GRANDE SILENZIO 1968
ENNIO MORRICONE

IL LADRO DI BAGDAD 1960
CARLO RUSTICHELLI

IL LADRO DI BAMBINI *THE STOLEN CHILDREN* 1992
FRANCO PIERSANTI

IL LEONE DI AMALFI 1950
CARLO RUSTICHELLI

IL LEONE DI SAN MARCO 1964
CARLO RUSTICHELLI

IL LEONE DI TEBE 1964
FRANCESCO DE MASI

IL LUNGO SILENZIO *THE LONG SILENCE* 1993
ENNIO MORRICONE

IL LUNGO VIAGGIO (TF) 1975
LUIS BACALOV

IL MAESTRO DI VIGEVANO 1963
NINO ROTA†

IL MAESTRO DI VIOLINO 1976
BRUNO NICOLAI

IL MAESTRO E MARGHERITA 1972
ENNIO MORRICONE

IL MALATO IMMAGINARIO 1980
PIERO PICCIONI

IL MANTENUTO *HIS WOMEN* 1961
ARMANDO TROVAJOLI

IL MARCHESE DEL GRILLO 1981
NICOLA PIOVANI

IL MARITO IN COLLEGIO 1976
ARMANDO TROVAJOLI

IL MATRIMONIO DI CATERINA (TF) 1982
MANUEL DE SICA

IL MEDAGLIONE INSANGUINATO 1975
STELVIO CIPRIANI

IL MEDICO DELLA MUTUA 1968
PIERO PICCIONI

IL MEDICO E LO STREGONE 1957
NINO ROTA†

IL MERLO MASCHIO 1971
RIZ ORTOLANI

IL MINESTRONE 1981
NICOLA PIOVANI

IL MIO AMICO BENITO 1962
ARMANDO TROVAJOLI

IL MIO CORPO CON RABBIA 1972
STELVIO CIPRIANI

IL MIO NOME E SHANGHAI JOE 1973
BRUNO NICOLAI

IL MISTERO DELL'ISOLA MALEDETTA 1965
ANGELO FRANCESCO LAVAGNINO†

IL MOMENTO DELL'AVVENTURA SACIS, 1983
MANUEL DE SICA

IL MONACA DI MONZA 1963
ARMANDO TROVAJOLI

IL MONDO LE CONDANNA 1952
PIERO PICCIONI

IL MONDO NUOVO 1982
ARMANDO TROVAJOLI

IL MONELLO DELLA STRADA *STREET URCHIN* 1951
NINO ROTA†

IL MORALISTA 1959
CARLO SAVINA

IL MOSTRO 1977
ENNIO MORRICONE

IL PADRE DI FAMIGLIA 1967
CARLO RUSTICHELLI

IL PANE AMARO 1966
ARMANDO TROVAJOLI

IL PARAMEDICO 1982
ARMANDO TROVAJOLI

IL PELO NEL MONDO 1963
BRUNO NICOLAI

IL PIATTO PIANGE 1974
FRANCO MICALIZZI

IL PISTOLERO SEGNATO DA DIO 1969
CARLO RUSTICHELLI

IL POLIZIOTTO E MARCIO 1974
LUIS BACALOV

IL POSTINO Miramax, 1995
LUIS BACALOV ★★

IL PRATO 1979
ENNIO MORRICONE

IL PREFETTO DI FERRO 1977
ENNIO MORRICONE

IL PRETE SPOSATO 1970
ARMANDO TROVAJOLI

IL PREZZO DEL POTERE *THE PRICE OF POWER* 1969
LUIS BACALOV

IL PRINCIPE FUSTO 1960
CARLO SAVINA

IL PROFETA *MR. KINKY* 1967
ARMANDO TROVAJOLI

IL PROFUMO DELLA SIGNORA IN NERO 1974
NICOLA PIOVANI

IL RAGAZZO CHE SORRIDE 1969
CARLO RUSTICHELLI

IL RATTO DELLE SABINE 1961
CARLO RUSTICHELLI

IL RITORNO DI RINGO 1965
ENNIO MORRICONE

IL RITORNO DI ZANNA BIANCA 1974
CARLO RUSTICHELLI

IL SEGRETO DEL BOSCH VECCHIO *THE SECRET OF THE OLD WOODS* 1993
FRANCO PIERSANTI

IL SEGRETO DELLA SIERRA DORADA 1957
PIERO PICCIONI

IL SERGENTE KLEMS 1971
CARLO RUSTICHELLI

IL SOLE NEGLI OCCHI 1953
FRANCO MANNINO

IL SOLE SOTTO TERRA 1971
BRUNO NICOLAI

IL SOMMERGIBILE PIU PAZZO DEL MONDO 1983
STELVIO CIPRIANI

IL SORPASSO Embassy, 1962
RIZ ORTOLANI

IL SORRISO DEL GRANDE TENTATORE 1975
ENNIO MORRICONE

IL SUCCESSO 1963
ENNIO MORRICONE

IL TERRIBILE ISPETTORE 1969
CARLO RUSTICHELLI

IL TERRORE DEI MANTELLI ROSSI 1963
CARLO RUSTICHELLI

IL TERRORISTA 22 Dicembre/Galatea, 1964
PIERO PICCIONI

IL TESORO DI ROMMEL 1956
CARLO RUSTICHELLI

IL TETTO Trans-Lux, 1956
ALESSANDRO CICOGNINI†

IL TORO 1994
IVANO FOSSATI

IL TRIONFO DI MACISTE 1963
CARLO RUSTICHELLI

IL TUFFO *THE DIVE* 1993
PETER D'ARGENZIO
MARIO TRONCO

IL TUO VIZIO E UNA STANZA CHIUSA E SOLO IO NE HO LA CHIAVE *EXCITE ME* 1972
BRUNO NICOLAI

IL VEDOVO 1959
ARMANDO TROVAJOLI

IL VIAGGIO *THE VOYAGE* United Artists, 1974
MANUEL DE SICA

IL VICHINGO VENUTO DAL SUD 1971
ARMANDO TROVAJOLI

IL VIZIO HA LE CALZE NERE 1975
CARLO SAVINA

IL VOLCO DI PESCA 1976
TEO USUELLI

IL VUOTO 1963
ARMANDO TROVAJOLI

IL WEST TI VA STRETTO AMICO...E ARRIVATO ALLEJUA 1972
STELVIO CIPRIANI

I'LL BE HOME FOR CHRISTMAS (TF)   NBC Productions, 1988
JORGE CALANDRELLI

I'LL BE SEEING YOU   RKO Radio, 1944
DANIELE AMFITHEATROF†

I'LL BE YOURS   Universal, 1947
FRANK SKINNER†

I'LL CRY TOMORROW   MGM, 1956
ALEX NORTH†

I'LL DO ANYTHING   Columbia, 1994
HANS ZIMMER

I'LL FLY AWAY - THEN AND NOW (TF)   Brand-Falsey/Lorimar TV, 1993
BENNETT SALVAY
W.G. SNUFFY WALDEN

I'LL FLY AWAY (TF)   Falakey/Austin Street/Lorimar TV, 1991
W.G. SNUFFY WALDEN

I'LL GET BY   20th Century-Fox, 1950
LIONEL NEWMAN† ★

I'LL LOVE YOU FOREVER...TONIGHT   Headliner, 1993
ROBERT CAIRNS

ILL MET BY MOONLIGHT   Rank, 1957
MIKIS THEODORAKIS

I'LL NEVER FORGET WHAT'S 'IS NAME   Regional, 1968
FRANCIS LAI

I'LL NEVER FORGET YOU   THE HOUSE IN THE SQUARE   20th Century-Fox, 1951
WILLIAM ALWYN†

I'LL TAKE MANHATTAN (MS)   Steve Krantz Productions, 1987
LEE HOLDRIDGE

I'LL TAKE SWEDEN   United Artists, 1965
JIMMIE HASKELL

I'LL TELL THE WORLD   Universal, 1945
HANS J. SALTER†

I'LL WAIT FOR YOU   MGM, 1941
BRONISLAU KAPER†

ILLEGAL   Warner Bros., 1955
MAX STEINER†

ILLEGAL IN BLUE   Stu Segall Productions, 1994
STEVE EDWARDS

ILLEGALLY YOURS   MGM/UA, 1988
PHIL MARSHALL

ILLICIT BEHAVIOR (CTF)   Prism/Promark/Asok Amritraj Prods., 1992
MICHAEL J. LINN†

ILLICIT DREAMS   Midnight Kiss Prods., 1994
CLAUDE GAUDETTE

ILLICIT INTERLUDE   SOMMARLEK   Janus, 1951
ERIC NORDGREN

ILLUMINATIONS (FD)   1963
MICHEL LEGRAND

ILLUSION ISLAND   1965
TORU TAKEMITSU†

ILLUSIONS (TF)   CBS Entertainment, 1983
ROBERT DRASNIN

ILLUSIONS OF A LADY   1974
ARLON OBER

THE ILLUSTRATED MAN   Warner Bros., 1969
JERRY GOLDSMITH

ILLUSTRIOUS ENERGY   Mirage Entertainment, 1988
JAN PRESTON

ILS ALLAIENT DANS LES CHAMPS   1968
VLADIMIR COSMA

ILS ETAIENT TOUS DES VOLONTAIRES (FD)   1954
DARIUS MILHAUD†

ILS ONT TUE JAURES   1962
JEAN WIENER†

ILS SONT FOUS CES SORCIERS!   1978
PHILIPPE SARDE

ILS SONT GRANDS CES PETITS!   1978
VLADIMIR COSMA

I'M ALL RIGHT JACK   Columbia, 1960
RON GOODWIN

I'M DANCING AS FAST AS I CAN   Paramount, 1982
STANLEY SILVERMAN

I'M FROM THE CITY   RKO Radio, 1938
ROY WEBB†

I'M GONNA GET YOU SUCKA   MGM/UA, 1988
DAVID MICHAEL FRANK

I'M NOBODY'S SWEETHEART NOW   Universal, 1940
HANS J. SALTER†

I'M NOT RAPPAPORT   1996
GERRY MULLIGAN

I'M STILL ALIVE   RKO Radio, 1940
ROY WEBB†

THE IMAGE (CTF)   Citadel Entertainment/HBO, 1990
JAMES NEWTON HOWARD

THE IMAGEMAKER   Castle Hill Prods., 1986
FRED KARNS

IMAGES   Columbia, 1972
JOHN WILLIAMS ★

IMAGINARY CRIMES   Warner Bros., 1994
STEPHEN ENDELMAN

IMAGO   Emerson, 1970
LALO SCHIFRIN

I-MAN (TF)   Mark H. Ovitz Productions/Walt Disney TV, 1986
CRAIG SAFAN

IMITATION OF LIFE   Universal, 1934
HEINZ ROEMHELD†

IMITATION OF LIFE   Universal, 1959
FRANK SKINNER†

IMMEDIATE FAMILY   Columbia, 1989
BRAD FIEDEL

THE IMMIGRANTS (TF)   Universal TV, 1978
GERALD FRIED

THE IMMORTAL (TF)   Paramount TV, 1969
DOMINIC FRONTIERE

THE IMMORTAL BATTALION   20th Century-Fox, 1944
WILLIAM ALWYN†

THE IMMORTAL SERGEANT   20th Century-Fox, 1943
DAVID BUTTOLPH†

THE IMMORTALIZER   Filmwest Productions, 1989
BARRY FASMAN
DANA WALDEN

THE IMMORTALS   End Prods., 1995
CLAUDE GAUDETTE

IMPACT   United Artists, 1949
MICHEL MICHELET†

THE IMPATIENT HEART (TF)   Universal TV, 1971
DAVID SHIRE

IMPERATIVE   Telefilm Saar, 1982
WOJCIECH KILAR

THE IMPERFECT LADY   Paramount, 1947
VICTOR YOUNG†

THE IMPORTANCE OF BEING EARNEST   Eclectic Concepts/Paco Global, 1991
ROGER HAMILTON SPOTTS

THE IMPORTANCE OF BEING ERNEST   Universal, 1952
BENJAMIN FRANKEL†

THE IMPOSSIBLE OBJECT   Valoria, 1973
MICHEL LEGRAND

THE IMPOSSIBLE SPY (CTF)   HBO Showcase/BBC/Quartet International/IMGC, 1987
RICHARD HARTLEY

THE IMPOSSIBLE YEARS   MGM, 1968
DON COSTA

THE IMPOSTER   Universal, 1944
DIMITRI TIOMKIN†

THE IMPOSTER (TF)   Gloria Monty Productions/Comworld Productions, 1984
CRAIG SAFAN

THE IMPOSTER (TF)   Warner Bros. TV, 1975
GIL MELLE

IMPRESSIONS OF MONET   Zeitlos Films, 1983
CARL DANTE

IMPROMPTU   Hemdale, 1991
JOHN STRAUSS

IMPROPER CONDUCT   Everest Pictures, 1994
ALAN DERMARDEROSIAN

IMPROVVISO   1979
LUIS BACALOV

IMPULSE   20th Century Fox, 1984
PAUL CHIHARA

IMPULSE   Warner Bros., 1990
MICHEL COLOMBIER

IMPURE THOUGHTS   ASA Communications, 1986
DAVID KURTZ

IMPUTAZIONE DI OMICIDIO PER UNO STUDENTE   1971
ENNIO MORRICONE

IN A CHILD'S NAME (TF)   New World TV, 1991
RICHARD STONE

IN A LONELY PLACE   Columbia, 1950
GEORGE ANTHEIL†

IN A SHALLOW GRAVE   Skouras Pictures, 1988
JONATHAN SHEFFER

IN AND OUT   1997
MARC SHAIMAN

IN BROAD DAYLIGHT (TF)   Aaron Spelling Productions, 1971
LEONARD ROSENMAN

IN BROAD DAYLIGHT (TF)   Force Ten/New World TV, 1991
PATRICK WILLIAMS

IN CAPO AL MONDO   Zebra Film/Franco London Film, 1963
PIERO PICCIONI

IN COLD BLOOD   Columbia, 1967
QUINCY JONES

IN COLD BLOOD (TF)   Hallmark, 1996
HUMMIE MANN

IN COUNTRY   Warner Bros., 1989
JAMES HORNER

IN CUSTODY   Merchant Ivory, 1993
ZAKIR HUSSAIN
USTAD SULTAN KAHN

IN DANGEROUS COMPANY   Manson International, 1988
EMILIO KAUDERER
BERINGTON VAN CAMPEN

IN DARKNESS WAITING   Universal, 1969
LYN MURRAY†

IN DEFENSE OF KIDS (TF)   MTM Enterprises, 1983
FRED KARLIN

IN ENEMY COUNTRY   Universal, 1968
WILLIAM LAVA†

IN GAY MADRID   MGM, 1930
HERBERT STOTHART†

IN GINOCCHIO DA TE   1964
ENNIO MORRICONE

IN GOD WE TRUST   Universal, 1980
JOHN MORRIS

IN GOLD WE TRUST   Little Bear Films, 1990
HUMMIE MANN

IN HARM'S WAY   Paramount, 1964
JERRY GOLDSMITH

IN ITALIA SI CHIAMA AMORE   1963
ARMANDO TROVAJOLI

IN LIKE FLINT   20th Century-Fox, 1967
JERRY GOLDSMITH

IN LIKE FLYNN (TF)   Glen A. Larson Productions/20th Century-Fox TV, 1985
STU PHILLIPS

IN LOVE AND WAR   20th Century-Fox, 1958
HUGO FRIEDHOFER†

IN LOVE AND WAR   New Line, 1996
GEORGE FENTON

IN LOVE AND WAR (TF)   Carol Schreder Productions/Tisch-Avnet Productions, 1987
CHARLES GROSS

IN LOVE WITH AN OLDER WOMAN (TF)   Pound Ridge Productions/Charles Fries Productions, 1982
LEE HOLDRIDGE

IN LOVE WITH SEX   EFC, 1973
LUIS BACALOV

IN MacARTHUR PARK   Bruce R. Schwartz, 1977
ROCKY DAVIS

IN MY DAUGHTER'S NAME (TF)   Cates-Doty Prods., 1992
CHARLES FOX

IN NAME ONLY   RKO Radio, 1939
ROY WEBB†

IN NOME DEL PAPA RE   1977
ARMANDO TROVAJOLI

IN NOME DEL POPOLO ITALIANO   Apollo International Films, 1971
CARLO RUSTICHELLI

IN NOME DELLA LEGGE   1948
CARLO RUSTICHELLI

IN OLD CALIFORNIA   Republic, 1942
DAVID BUTTOLPH†

IN OLD CHICAGO   20th Century-Fox, 1938
LOUIS SILVERS† ★

IN OLD OKLAHOMA   Republic, 1943
WALTER SCHARF ★

IN OUR TIME   Warner Bros., 1944
FRANZ WAXMAN†

IN PRAISE OF OLDER WOMEN   Avco Embassy, 1978
TIBAR POLGAR

IN PURSUIT OF HONOR (CTF)   Marian Rees Associates/Village Roadshow/HBO Pictures, 1995
JOHN DEBNEY

IN SEARCH OF AMERICA (TF)   Four Star International, 1971
FRED MYROW

IN SEARCH OF DR. SEUSS (CTF)   Point Blank, 1994
STEVEN GOLDSTEIN

IN SEARCH OF GREGORY   Universal, 1970
RON GRAINER†

IN SEARCH OF HISTORIC JESUS   Sunn Classic, 1980
ROBERT SUMMERS

IN SEARCH OF OUR FATHERS (FD)   Conjure Films, 1992
BILLY CHILDS

IN SEARCH OF THE CASTAWAYS   Buena Vista, 1962
WILLIAM ALWYN†

IN SELF DEFENSE (TF)   Leonard Hill Films, 1987
PATRICK GLEESON

IN SICKNESS AND IN HEALTH (TF)   Konigsberg-Sanitsky Prods., 1992
WILLIAM OLVIS

IN TANDEM (TF)   D'Antoni-Weitz TV Productions, 1974
DON ELLIS†

IN THE ARMS OF A KILLER (TF)   RLC/Monarch, 1992
LEE HOLDRIDGE

IN THE ARMY NOW   Buena Vista, 1994
ROBERT FOLK

IN THE BEST INTEREST OF THE CHILD (TF)   Papazian-Hirsch Entertainment, 1990
PETER MANNING ROBINSON

IN THE BEST INTEREST OF THE CHILDREN (TF)   NBC Prods., 1992
JAMES DIPASQUALLE

IN THE BEST OF FAMILIES: MARRIAGE, PRIDE AND MADNESS (TF)   Ambroco Media/Dan Wigutow Prods., 1994
DON DAVIS

IN THE COMPANY OF DARKNESS (TF)   Windy City, 1992
TIM TRUMAN

IN THE CUSTODY OF STRANGERS (TF)   Moonlight Productions/Filmways, 1982
MATTHEW MCCAULEY

IN THE DEEP WOODS (TF)   Frederic Golchan Prods./Leonard Hill Films, 1992
SYLVESTER LEVAY

IN THE DEVIL'S GARDEN   ASSAULT   Hemisphere, 1971
ERIC ROGERS†

IN THE EYES OF A STRANGER (TF)   Power Pictures/Avenue Entertainment/Hearst Entertainment, 1992
TOM BAHLER

IN THE FRENCH STYLE   Columbia, 1963
JOSEPH KOSMA†

IN THE GLITTER PALACE (TF)   The Writer's Company/Columbia TV, 1977
JOHN PARKER

IN THE HEAT OF PASSION   Concorde, 1992
KEN RARICK
ART WOOD

IN THE HEAT OF THE NIGHT   United Artists, 1967
QUINCY JONES

IN THE HEAT OF THE NIGHT (TF)   The Fred Silverman Company/Jadda Productions/MGM/UA TV, 1988
DICK DEBENEDICTIS

IN THE KINGDOM OF THE BLIND, THE MAN WITH ONE EYE IS KING   1995
JAN HAMMER

IN THE LINE OF DUTY: KIDNAPPED (TF)   Patchett-Kaufman/WIN, 1995
CHRISTOPHER FRANKE

IN THE LINE OF DUTY: AMBUSH IN WACO (TF)   Patchett-Kaufman/World Intl Network, 1993
MARK SNOW

IN THE LINE OF DUTY: MANHUNT IN THE DAKOTAS (TF)   Patchett-Kaufman, 1991
MARK SNOW

IN THE LINE OF DUTY: SIEGE AT MARION (TF)   Patchett Kaufman Entertainment, 1992
GARY CHANG

IN THE LINE OF DUTY: STREET WAR (TF)   Patchett-Kaufman, 1992
MARK SNOW

IN THE LINE OF DUTY: THE FBI MURDERS (TF)   Telecom Entertainment/World International Network, 1988
LAURENCE ROSENTHAL

IN THE LINE OF FIRE   Columbia, 1993
ENNIO MORRICONE

IN THE MATTER OF KAREN ANN QUINLAN (TF)   Warren V. Bush Productions, 1977
BILL CONTI

IN THE MEANTIME, DARLING   20th Century-Fox, 1944
DAVID BUTTOLPH†

IN THE MOOD   Lorimar, 1987
RALPH BURNS

IN THE MOUTH OF MADNESS   New Line, 1995
JOHN CARPENTER
JIM LANG

IN THE NAME OF CHRIST   1993
MOHAMMED SOUDANI

IN THE NAME OF LOVE: A TEXAS TRAGEDY (TF)   1995
DENNIS MCCARTHY

IN THE NICK   Columbia, 1960
RON GOODWIN

IN THE NICK OF TIME (TF)   Spectacor/Walt Disney Television, 1991
STEVE DORFF

IN THE SHADOW OF A KILLER (TF)   NBC Prods., 1992
CHARLES GROSS

IN THE SHADOW OF EVIL (TF)   D.W. Prods./CBS Entertainment, 1995
NICHOLAS PIKE

IN THE SHADOW OF KILIMANJARO   Scotti Brothers, 1986
ARLON OBER

IN THE SHADOWS, SOMEONE IS WATCHING (TF)   Arvin Kaufman/Saban, 1993
SHUKI LEVY

IN THE SOUP   Jim Stark, 1992
MADER

IN THE SPIRIT   Castle Hill, 1990
PATRICK WILLIAMS

IN THE WAKE OF A STRANGER   1958
EDWIN ASTLEY

IN THEE I TRUST   1993
VALERY MIAGKIH

IN THIS CORNER   Eagle Lion, 1948
ALBERT GLASSER

IN THIS HOUSE OF BREDE (TF)   Tomorrow Entertainment, 1975
PETER MATZ

INVASION OF THE SAUCER-MEN American International, 1957
RONALD STEIN†

INVASION QUARTET MGM, 1961
RON GOODWIN

INVASION U.S.A. Columbia, 1952
ALBERT GLASSER

INVASION, U.S.A. Cannon, 1985
JAY CHATTAWAY

INVENTING THE ABBOTTS 20th Century Fox, 1997
MICHAEL KAMEN

INVESTIGATION OF A CITIZEN ABOVE SUSPICION Columbia, 1970
ENNIO MORRICONE

THE INVINCIBLE THREE 1964
ANGELO FRANCESCO LAVAGNINO†

THE INVISIBLE AGENT Universal, 1942
HANS J. SALTER†

THE INVISIBLE BOY MGM, 1957
LES BAXTER†

THE INVISIBLE KID Taurus Entertainment, 1988
STEVE HUNTER

THE INVISIBLE MAN Universal, 1933
HEINZ ROEMHELD†

THE INVISIBLE MAN (TF) Universal TV, 1975
RICHARD CLEMENTS

THE INVISIBLE MAN RETURNS Universal, 1940
HANS J. SALTER†
FRANK SKINNER†

THE INVISIBLE MAN'S REVENGE Universal, 1944
WILLIAM LAVA†
HANS J. SALTER†

THE INVISIBLE MENACE Warner Bros., 1937
BERNHARD KAUN†

THE INVISIBLE RAY Universal, 1936
FRANZ WAXMAN†

THE INVISIBLE WOMAN Universal, 1940
CHARLES PREVIN†

THE INVISIBLE WOMAN (TF) Universal TV, 1983
DAVID MICHAEL FRANK

INVISIBLE AGENT Universal, 1942
CHARLES PREVIN†

INVISIBLE STRANGLER Seymour Borde & Associates, 1984
RICHARD HIERONYMOUS
ALAN OLDFIELD

INVISIBLE STRIPES Warner Bros., 1939
HEINZ ROEMHELD†

INVITATION MGM, 1952
BRONISLAU KAPER†

INVITATION AU VOYAGE Mel Difussion/Filmalpha, 1982
GABRIEL YARED

INVITATION TO A GUNFIGHTER United Artists, 1964
DAVID RAKSIN

INVITATION TO HAPPINESS Paramount, 1939
FREDERICK HOLLANDER†

INVITATION TO HELL (TF) Moonlight Productions II, 1984
SYLVESTER LEVAY

INVITATION TO THE WEDDING New Realm, 1983
JOSEPH BROOKS

IO E DIO 1970
MANUEL DE SICA

IO NON VEDO, TU NON PARLI, LUI NON SENTE Italian, 1971
MANUEL DE SICA

IO SPERIAMO CHE ME LA CAVO ME LET'S HOPE I MAKE IT Miramax, 1993
D'ANGIO GRECO

IO, IO, IO E GLI ALTRI 1966
CARLO RUSTICHELLI

I.P.5: L'ILE AUX PACHIDERMES I.P.5: THE ISLAND OF PACHYDERMS 1992
GABRIEL YARED

I.P.5: THE ISLAND OF PACHYDERMS 1992
GABRIEL YARED

THE IPCRESS FILE Universal, 1965
JOHN BARRY

IPHIGENIA Cinema 5, 1977
MIKIS THEODORAKIS

I.Q. Paramount, 1994
JERRY GOLDSMITH

IRENE RKO Radio, 1940
ANTHONY COLLINS† ★

IREZUMI: SPIRIT OF TATTOO Daiei, 1983
MASARU SATO

IRMA LA DOUCE United Artists, 1963
ANDRE PREVIN ★★

IRON AND SILK Prestige, 1991
MICHAEL GIBBS

IRON EAGLE Tri-Star, 1986
BASIL POLEDOURIS

IRON EAGLE II Tri-Star, 1988
AMIN BHATIA

THE IRON GLOVE Columbia, 1954
MISCHA BAKALEINIKOFF†

THE IRON MAIDEN Columbia, 1962
ERIC ROGERS†

THE IRON MAJOR RKO Radio, 1943
ROY WEBB†

IRON MAZE Edward R. Pressman/Oliver Stone, 1991
STANLEY MYERS†

THE IRON MISTRESS Warner Bros., 1952
MAX STEINER†

THE IRON PETTICOAT MGM, 1956
BENJAMIN FRANKEL†

THE IRON SHERIFF United Artists, 1957
EMIL NEWMAN†

IRON WILL Buena Vista, 1994
JOEL MCNEELY

IRONCLADS (CTF) Rosemont, 1991
ALLYN FERGUSON

IRONSIDE (TF) Harbour Productions/Universal TV, 1967
QUINCY JONES

IRONWEED Tri-Star, 1987
JOHN MORRIS

IRRECONCILABLE DIFFERENCES Warner Bros., 1984
PAUL DE SENNEVILLE
OLIVER TOUSSAINT

IRRESISTIBLE IMPULSE Everest Pictures, 1995
ALAN DERMARDEROSIAN

IS MY FACE RED? RKO Radio, 1932
MAX STEINER†

IS PARIS BURNING? Paramount, 1966
MAURICE JARRE

IS THERE LIFE OUT THERE? (TF) Marian Rees Associates/Starstruck Ent., 1994
J.A.C. REDFORD

ISAAC LITTLEFEATHERS Lauron Productions, 1985
PAUL J. ZAZA

ISABEL'S CHOICE (TF) Stuart Miller Productions/Pantheon Television, 1981
GLENN PAXTON

ISADORA THE LOVES OF ISADORA Universal, 1968
MAURICE JARRE

ISHI: THE LAST OF HIS TRIBE (TF) Edward & Mildred Lewis Productions, 1978
MAURICE JARRE

ISHTAR Columbia, 1987
DAVE GRUSIN

THE ISLAND 1966
ERIC NORDGREN

THE ISLAND Universal, 1980
ENNIO MORRICONE

THE ISLAND AT THE TOP OF THE WORLD Buena Vista, 1974
MAURICE JARRE

ISLAND CITY (TF) Lee Rich Co./MDT Prods., 1994
PETER BERNSTEIN

ISLAND IN THE SKY Warner Bros., 1953
HUGO FRIEDHOFER†
EMIL NEWMAN†

ISLAND IN THE SUN 20th Century-Fox, 1957
MALCOLM ARNOLD

ISLAND INVADERS: OTHER WORLDS (TD) WNET/BBC TV, 1993
NIGEL BEAHAM-POWELL
BELLA RUSSELL

THE ISLAND OF APHRODITE 1966
MIKIS THEODORAKIS

THE ISLAND OF DOCTOR MOREAU New Line, 1996
GARY CHANG

THE ISLAND OF DR. MOREAU American International, 1977
LAURENCE ROSENTHAL

ISLAND OF TERROR Universal, 1966
MALCOM LOCKYER

ISLAND OF THE BLUE DOLPHINS Universal, 1964
PAUL SAWTELL†

ISLAND OF THE EVIL SPIRITS Kadokawa/Toei, 1981
NORIO YUASA

ISLAND OF THE LOST 1967
GEORGE BRUNS

ISLAND RESCUE APPOINTMENT WITH VENUS Universal, 1951
BENJAMIN FRANKEL†

ISLAND SONS (TF) Universal TV, 1987
BASIL POLEDOURIS

THE ISLANDER (TF) Glen A. Larson Productions/Universal TV, 1978
JOHN ANDREW TARTAGLIA

THE ISLANDERS 1939
DARIUS MILHAUD†

ISLANDS IN THE STREAM Paramount, 1977
JERRY GOLDSMITH

ISLE OF FORGOTTEN SINS MONSOON Producers Releasing Corp., 1943
LEO ERDODY†

ISLE OF LESBOS Duce Films, 1997
JEFF B. HARMON

ISLE OF THE DEAD RKO Radio, 1945
LEIGH HARLINE†

ISN'T IT SHOCKING? (TF) ABC Circle Films, 1973
DAVID SHIRE

ISN'T LIFE WONDERFUL? United Artists, 1924
LOUIS SILVERS†

ISTANBUL Universal, 1957
HERMAN STEIN

ISTANBUL EXPRESS (TF) Universal TV, 1968
OLIVER NELSON†

IT ALWAYS RAINS ON SUNDAY General Film Distributors, 1947
GEORGES AURIC†

IT BEGAN IN BRIGHTON 1966
GEORGES DELERUE†

IT CAME FROM BENEATH THE SEA Columbia, 1955
MISCHA BAKALEINIKOFF†

IT CAME FROM OUTER SPACE Universal, 1953
IRVING GERTZ
HENRY MANCINI†
HERMAN STEIN

IT CAME UPON THE MIDNIGHT CLEAR (TF) Schenck-Cardea Productions/Columbia TV/LBS Communications, 1984
ARTHUR B. RUBINSTEIN

IT CONQUERED THE WORLD American International, 1956
RONALD STEIN†

IT COULD HAPPEN TO YOU TriStar, 1994
CARTER BURWELL

IT COULDN'T HAPPEN TO A NICER GUY (TF) The Jozak Company, 1974
FRED KARLIN

IT GROWS ON TREES Universal, 1952
FRANK SKINNER†

IT HAD TO BE YOU Columbia, 1947
ARTHUR MORTON
HEINZ ROEMHELD†

IT HAD TO BE YOU Panther Filmworks, 1988
CHARLES FOX

IT HAPPENED AT LAKEWOOD MANOR (TF) Alan Landsburg Productions, 1977
KEN RICHMOND

IT HAPPENED AT THE WORLD'S FAIR MGM, 1963
LEITH STEVENS†

IT HAPPENED IN ATHENS 20th Century-Fox, 1962
MANOS HADJIDAKIS†

IT HAPPENED IN BROOKLYN MGM, 1947
JOHN GREEN†

IT HAPPENED ON FIFTH AVENUE Allied Artists, 1947
EDWARD WARD†

IT HAPPENED ONE CHRISTMAS (TF) Daisy Productions/Universal TV, 1977
STEPHEN LAWRENCE

IT HAPPENS EVERY SPRING 20th Century-Fox, 1949
LEIGH HARLINE†

IT HAPPENS EVERY THURSDAY Universal, 1953
HENRY MANCINI†

IT LIVES AGAIN IT'S ALIVE II Warner Bros., 1978
LAURIE JOHNSON

IT LIVES BY NIGHT American International, 1974
ARTIE KANE

IT SHOULD HAPPEN TO YOU Columbia, 1954
FREDERICK HOLLANDER†

IT SHOULDN'T HAPPEN TO A DOG 20th Century-Fox, 1946
DAVID BUTTOLPH†

IT SHOULDN'T HAPPEN TO A VET EMI, 1976
LAURIE JOHNSON

IT STARTED IN NAPLES Paramount, 1960
ALESSANDRO CICOGNINI†

IT STARTED IN PARADISE Astor, 1952
MALCOLM ARNOLD

IT STARTED WITH A KISS MGM, 1959
JEFF ALEXANDER†

IT STARTED WITH EVE Universal, 1941
HANS J. SALTER†

IT TAKES TWO MGM/UA, 1988
CARTER BURWELL

IT WAS A WONDERFUL LIFE (FD) Cinewomen, 1993
MELISSA ETHERIDGE

IT WAS HIM OR US (TF) 1995
JOHN FRIZZELL

IT! THE TERROR FROM BEYOND SPACE United Artists, 1958
PAUL SAWTELL†
BERT A. SHEFTER

IT'S A BIG COUNTRY MGM, 1952
BRONISLAU KAPER†

IT'S A BIG COUNTRY MGM, 1952
DAVID RAKSIN

IT'S A DATE Universal, 1940
CHARLES PREVIN†

IT'S A DOG'S LIFE MGM, 1955
ELMER BERNSTEIN

IT'S A LONG TIME THAT I'VE LOVED YOU SOUPCON Durham/Pike, 1979
GERARD ANFOSSO

IT'S A MAD, MAD, MAD, MAD WORLD United Artists, 1963
ERNEST GOLD ★

IT'S A SMALL WORLD Eagle Lion, 1950
KARL HAJOS†

IT'S A WONDERFUL LIFE RKO Radio, 1946
DIMITRI TIOMKIN†

IT'S A WONDERFUL WORLD MGM, 1939
EDWARD WARD†

IT'S ALIVE Warner Bros., 1974
BERNARD HERRMANN†

IT'S ALIVE II Warner Bros., 1978
LAURIE JOHNSON

IT'S ALL TRUE (FD) Paramount, 1993
JORGE ARRIAGADA

IT'S ALWAYS FAIR WEATHER MGM, 1955
ANDRE PREVIN

IT'S GOOD TO BE ALIVE (TF) Metromedia Producers Corporation/Larry Harmon Pictures Corporation, 1974
MICHEL LEGRAND

IT'S HARD TO BE GOOD 1946
ANTONY HOPKINS

IT'S IN THE AIR MGM, 1935
WILLIAM AXT†

IT'S IN THE BAG United Artists, 1945
WERNER R. HEYMANN†

IT'S LOVE AGAIN 1936
LOUIS LEVY†

IT'S MY PARTY 1996
BASIL POLEDOURIS

IT'S MY TURN Columbia, 1980
PATRICK WILLIAMS

IT'S NOT THE SIZE THAT COUNTS PERCY'S PROGRESS Joseph Brenner Associates, 1974
TONY MACAULEY

IT'S NOTHING PERSONAL (TF) Lee Rich/Bruce Sallan/Papazian-Hirsch, 1993
TOM SCOTT

IT'S ONLY MONEY Paramount, 1962
WALTER SCHARF

IT'S PAT Buena Vista, 1994
MARK MOTHERSBAUGH

IT'S SHOWTIME United Artists, 1976
ARTIE BUTLER

ITALIA A MANO ARMATA 1976
FRANCO MICALIZZI

ITALIA K2 1955
TEO USUELLI

ITALIA PICCOLA 1957
NINO ROTA†

ITALIAN BRIGANDS IL BRIGANTE 1961
NINO ROTA†

THE ITALIAN CONNECTION LA MALA ORDINA 1972
ARMANDO TROVAJOLI

THE ITALIAN JOB Paramount, 1969
QUINCY JONES

ITALIAN SECRET SERVICE 1968
FIORENZO CARPI

THE ITALIAN STRAW HAT 1927
JACQUES IBERT†

ITALIANI BRAVA GENTE 1963
ARMANDO TROVAJOLI

ITINERAIRE BIS SIDEROADS 1983
JEAN MUSY

ITINERAIRE D'UN ENFANT GATE Films 13/Cerito Films/TFI Films, 1989
FRANCIS LAI

IVAN PAVLOV 1950
DMITRI KABALEVSKY†

IVAN THE TERRIBLE, PART I Artkino, 1945
SERGEI PROKOFIEV†

IVAN THE TERRIBLE, PART II Artkino, 1946
SERGEI PROKOFIEV†

IVANHOE MGM, 1952
MIKLOS ROZSA† ★

IVANHOE (TF) Rosemont Productions, 1982
ALLYN FERGUSON ☆

I'VE ALWAYS LOVED YOU Republic, 1946
WALTER SCHARF

I'VE GOT YOU, YOU'VE GOT ME BY THE HAIRS OF MY CHINNY CHIN CHIN 1979
JACQUES MORALI

I'VE HEARD THE MERMAIDS SINGING Miramax, 1987
MARK KORVEN

I'VE LIVED BEFORE Universal, 1956
HERMAN STEIN

THE IVORY APE (TF) Rankin-Bass Productions, 1980
BERNARD HOFFER
MAURY LAWS

IVORY HUNTER WHERE NO VULTURES FLY 1951
ALAN RAWSTHORNE†

IVY Universal, 1947
DANIELE AMFITHEATROF†

IZU DANCER 1967
TORU TAKEMITSU

J

IZZY AND MOE (TF) Robert Halmi, Inc., 1985
JACKIE GLEASON†
CHARLES GROSS

J. EDGAR HOOVER (CTF) RLC Productions/
Finnegan Co., 1987
J. PETER ROBINSON

JABBERWOCKY Cinema 5, 1977
DE WOLFE

JACARE United Artists, 1942
MIKLOS ROZSA†

JACK Buena Vista, 1996
MICHAEL KAMEN

JACK (TD) CBS Entertainment Prods., 1993
ADAM GYETTEL

JACK AND SARAH 1995
SIMON BOSWELL.

JACK AND THE BEANSTALK Warner Bros., 1952
HEINZ ROEMHELD†

JACK BE NIMBLE 1993
CHRIS NEAL

JACK OF DIAMONDS MGM, 1967
PETER THOMAS

JACK REED: A SEARCH FOR JUSTICE (TF)
Kushner-Locke/Steve Krantz Prods., 1994
LEE HOLDRIDGE

JACK REED: BADGE OF HONOR (TF) Steve Krantz
Prods/Multimedia, 1993
LEE HOLDRIDGE

JACK SLADE Allied Artists, 1953
PAUL DUNLAP

JACK THE BEAR 20th Century-Fox, 1993
JAMES HORNER

JACK THE GIANT KILLER United Artists, 1962
PAUL SAWTELL†
BERT A. SHEFTER

JACK THE RIPPER Paramount, 1960
STANLEY BLACK
PETE RUGOLO

JACK THE RIPPER (TF) Euston Films/Thames TV/
Hill-O'Connor Entertainment/Lorimar TV, 1988
JOHN CAMERON

JACK'S BACK Palisades Entertainment, 1988
DAN DIPAOLA

JACKALS *AMERICAN JUSTICE* The Movie Store,
1986
PAUL CHIHARA

JACKIE CHAN'S FIRST STRIKE New Line, 1997
J. PETER ROBINSON

JACKIE COLLINS' LADY BOSS (TF) Puma/von
Zerneck-Sertner, 1992
DANA KAPROFF

THE JACKIE ROBINSON STORY Eagle Lion, 1950
HERSCHEL BURKE GILBERT

JACKNIFE Kings Road, 1989
BRUCE BROUGHTON

THE JACKPOT 20th Century-Fox, 1950
LIONEL NEWMAN†

THE JACKSONS - AN AMERICAN DREAM (MS)
Stan Margulies/de passe/Motown/Polygram/KJ
Films, 1992
HAROLD WHEELER

JACOB (CTF) LUBE Prods./LUX/Betafilm/RAI Uno/
Turner Pictures, 1995
MARCO FRISENA

JACOB'S LADDER Tri-Star, 1990
MAURICE JARRE

**JACOBO TIMERMAN: PRISONER WITHOUT A
NAME, CELL WITHOUT A NUMBER**
Chrysalis-Yellen Productions, 1983
BRAD FIEDEL

JACQUELINE BOUVIER KENNEDY (TF) ABC Circle
Films, 1981
BILLY GOLDENBERG ☆

JACQUELINE SUSANN'S ONCE IS NOT ENOUGH
ONCE IS NOT ENOUGH Paramount, 1975
HENRY MANCINI†

**JACQUELINE SUSANN'S VALLEY OF THE DOLLS
1981 (MS)** 20th Century-Fox TV, 1981
FRED KARLIN

JACQUOT DE NANTES (DF) 1991
JOANNE BRUZDOWICZ

JAG (TF) Belisarius Prods./Paramount/NBC, 1995
BRUCE BROUGHTON

JAGGED EDGE Columbia, 1985
JOHN BARRY

JAGUAR Republic, 1956
VAN ALEXANDER

JAGUAR LIVES! American International, 1979
ROBERT O. RAGLAND

JAGUAS (D) Viking Fund, 1942
KAROL RATHAUS†

J'AI ESPOUSE UN OMBRE AMLF, 1983
PHILIPPE SARDE

J'AI MON VOYAGE 1973
CLAUDE BOLLING

J'AI RECONTRE LE PERE NOEL New World, 1985
FRANCIS LAI

JAIL HOUSE BLUES Universal, 1942
FRANK SKINNER†

JAILBIRDS (TF) Spelling, 1991
KEN HARRISON

JAILHOUSE ROCK MGM, 1957
JEFF ALEXANDER†

JAKARTA! Troma, 1988
JAY CHATTAWAY

JAKE AND THE FATMAN (TF) The Fred Silverman
Company/Dean Hargrove Productions/Viacom, 1989
DICK DEBENEDICTIS

JAKE LASSITER: JUSTICE ON THE BAYOU (TF)
Ron Gilbert Associates/Big Prods./Spanish Trail, 1995
MIKE POST

JAKE SPANNER, PRIVATE EYE (TF) Andrew J.
Fenady Productions/Scotti-Vinnedge TV, 1989
JIMMIE HASKELL

JAKE SPEED New World, 1986
MARK SNOW

JAMAICA INN Paramount, 1939
ERIC FENBY

JAMAIS PLUS TOUJOURS 1975
GEORGES DELERUE†

JAMES A. MICHENER'S TEXAS (MS) Spelling TV,
1994
LEE HOLDRIDGE

JAMES AND THE GIANT PEACH (AF) Buena Vista,
1996
RANDY NEWMAN ★

JAMES AT 15 (TF) 20th Century-Fox TV, 1977
RICHARD BASKIN

JAMES CLAVELL'S NOBLE HOUSE *NOBLE
HOUSE* (MS) Noble House Productions Ltd./De
Laurentiis Entertainment Group, 1988
PAUL CHIHARA

THE JAMES DEAN STORY Warner Bros., 1957
LEITH STEVENS†

JAMES DEAN (TF) The Jozak Company, 1976
BILLY GOLDENBERG

JAMES MICHENER'S DYNASTY (TF) David
Paradine TV, 1976
GIL MELLE

JANE AUSTEN IN MANHATTAN Contemporary,
1980
RICHARD ROBBINS

JANE DOE (TF) ITC, 1983
PAUL CHIHARA

JANE EYRE 20th Century-Fox, 1943
BERNARD HERRMANN†

JANE EYRE (TF) Omnibus Productions/Sagittarius
Productions, 1971
JOHN WILLIAMS ☆☆

JANE'S HOUSE (TF) Michael Phillips Prods./Spelling
TV, 1993
DAVID SHIRE

JANICE MEREDITH MGM, 1924
DEEMS TAYLOR†

JANIE Warner Bros., 1944
HEINZ ROEMHELD†

JANIE GETS MARRIED Warner Bros., 1946
FREDERICK HOLLANDER†

THE JANUARY MAN MGM/UA, 1989
MARVIN HAMLISCH

JAPAN AND THE WORLD TODAY (FD) U.S.
Government, 1950
GEORGE BASSMAN

JAPANESE WAR BRIDE 20th Century-Fox, 1952
EMIL NEWMAN†

JARDINES COLGANTES *HANGING GARDENS*
1993
SAIMON SIMONET

JARRETT (TF) Screen Gems/Columbia TV, 1973
ALLYN FERGUSON
JACK ELLIOTT

JASON AND THE ARGONAUTS Columbia, 1963
BERNARD HERRMANN†

JASON GOES TO HELL: THE FINAL FRIDAY New
Line, 1993
HARRY MANFREDINI

JASON'S LYRIC Gramercy, 1994
AFRICA
QUINCY JONES III
THEODOR MILLER
MATT NOBLE

JAWS Universal, 1975
JOHN WILLIAMS ★★

JAWS 2 Universal, 1978
JOHN WILLIAMS

JAWS 3-D Universal, 1983
ALAN PARKER

JAWS THE REVENGE Universal 1987
MICHAEL SMALL

THE JAYHAWKERS Paramount, 1959
JEROME MOROSS†

THE JAYNE MANSFIELD STORY (TF) Alan
Landsburg Productions, 1980
JIMMIE HASKELL

JAZZ BOAT Columbia, 1960
KENNETH V. JONES

THE JAZZ SINGER AFD, 1980
NEIL DIAMOND
LEONARD ROSENMAN

THE JAZZ SINGER Warner Bros., 1927
LOUIS SILVERS†

THE JAZZ SINGER Warner Bros., 1953
MAX STEINER† ★

J.D.'S REVENGE American International, 1976
ROBERT PRINCE

JE REVIENDRAI A KANDARA 1956
JOSEPH KOSMA†

JE SUIS TIMIDE...MAIS JE ME SOIGNE 1978
VLADIMIR COSMA

JE T'AIME MOI NON PLUS 1975
SERGE GAINSBOURG†

JE T'ATTENDRAI 1939
ARTHUR HONEGGER†

JEALOUSY Republic, 1945
HANNS EISLER†

JEALOUSY (TF) Charles Fries Productions/Alan Sacks
Productions, 1984
JIMMIE HASKELL
GIL MELLE

JEAN DE FLORETTE Orion Classics, 1987
JEAN-CLAUDE PETIT

JEAN DE LA LUNE 1948
GEORGES VAN PARYS†

JEANNE LA PUCELLE *JOAN THE MAID* 1994
JORDI SAVALL

JEANNE, LA PUTAIN DU ROI J&M Entertainment,
1990
GABRIEL YARED

JEFFERSON IN PARIS Buena Vista, 1995
RICHARD ROBBINS

JEKYLL & HYDE (TF) David Wickes TV/LWT/King
Phoenix Entertainment, 1990
JOHN CAMERON

JEKYLL AND HYDE...TOGETHER AGAIN
Paramount, 1982
BARRY DEVORZON

J'EMBRASSE PAS *I DON'T KISS* 1991
PHILIPPE SARDE

JENNIFER Allied Artists, 1953
ERNEST GOLD

JENNIFER American International, 1978
JERRY STYNE

JENNIFER EIGHT Paramount, 1992
CHRISTOPHER YOUNG

JENNIFER ON MY MIND United Artists, 1971
STEPHEN LAWRENCE

JENNIFER: A WOMAN'S STORY (TF) Marble Arch
Productions, 1979
WILLIAM GOLDSTEIN

JENNY 1936
JOSEPH KOSMA†

JENNY Cinerama Releasing Corporation, 1970
MICHAEL SMALL

JENNY'S SONG (TF) Westinghouse Broadcasting,
1988
MASON DARING

JENNY'S WAR (TF) Louis Rudolph Productions/
HTV/Columbia TV, 1985
JOHN CACAVAS

JEOPARDY MGM, 1953
DIMITRI TIOMKIN†

JEREMY United Artists, 1973
LEE HOLDRIDGE

JERICHO FEVER (CTF) Sankan Prods./Wilshire
Court, 1993
CAMERON ALLAN

THE JERICHO MILE (TF) ABC Circle Films, 1979
JIMMIE HASKELL
JAMES DIPASQUALLE

JERICO 1991
FREDERICO GAITORNO

THE JERK Universal, 1979
JACK ELLIOTT

THE JERK, TOO (TF) Share Productions/Universal
IV, 1984
PHIL GALSTON
JOHN SEBASTIAN

THE JERKY BOYS Buena Vista, 1995
IRA NEWBORN

JERRY MAGUIRE TriStar, 1996
NANCY WILSON

JERSEY GIRL (TF) Electric Pictures/Interscope, 1993
STEPHEN BEDELL
MISHA SEGAL

THE JERUSALEM FILE MGM, 1972
JOHN SCOTT

JESSE (TF) Turman-Foster Company/Jordan
Productions/Republic Pictures, 1988
DAVID SHIRE

**JESSE E LESTER DUE FRATELLI IN UN POSTO
CHIAMOTO TRINITA** 1972
CARLO SAVINA

JESSE HAWKS (TF) A. Shane Co., 1989
ROBERT FOLK

**JESSE JAMES MEETS FRANKENSTEIN'S
DAUGHTER** 1966
RAOUL KRAUSHAAR

THE JESSE OWENS STORY (TF) Harve Bennett
Productions/Paramount TV, 1984
MICHEL LEGRAND

JESSIE (TF) Lindsay Wagner Productions/MGM-UA TV,
1984
JOHN CACAVAS

JESUS OF MONTREAL Max Films International,
1989
YVES LAFERRIERE

JESUS OF MONTREAL *JESUS OF MONTREAL*
Max Films International, 1989
YVES LAFERRIERE

JESUS OF NAZARETH (MS) Sir Lew Grade
Productions/ITC, 1977
MAURICE JARRE

THE JESUS TRIP EMCO, 1971
BERNARDO SEGALL

JET ATTACK American International, 1958
RONALD STEIN†

JET PILOT RKO Radio, 1957
BRONISLAU KAPER†

J'ETAIS UNE AVENTURIERE 1938
PAUL MISRAKI

JETLAG Wieland Schulz-Keil/Figaro Films, 1981
CARLOS SANTOS

JETSONS: THE MOVIE (AF) Universal, 1990
JOHN DEBNEY

JEUDI ON CHANTERA COMME DIMANCHE 1966
GEORGES DELERUE†

JEUNESSE 1934
GEORGES VAN PARYS†

THE JEWEL IN THE CROWN (MS) Granada TV,
1984
GEORGE FENTON

JEWEL OF THE NILE 20th Century-Fox, 1985
JACK NITZCHE

JEZEBEL Warner Bros., 1938
MAX STEINER† ★

JEZEBEL'S KISS Shapiro-Glickenhaus, 1990
MITCHEL FORMAN

THE JEZEBELS/PLAYGIRL GANG Centaur, 1975
LES BAXTER†

JFK Warner Bros., 1991
JOHN WILLIAMS ★

JFK: RECKLESS YOUTH (TF) Polone Co./Hearst,
1993
CAMERON ALLAN

JIANG-HU 1993
RICHARD YUEN

JIGSAW 1980
CLAUDE BOLLING

JIGSAW *MAN ON THE MOVE (TF)* Universal TV,
1972
ROBERT DRASNIN

THE JIGSAW MAN United Film Distribution, 1984
JOHN CAMERON

THE JILTING OF GRANNY WEATHERALL (TF)
Learning in Focus/American Short Story, 1980
JONATHAN TUNICK

JIM THORPE—ALL AMERICAN Warner Bros.,
1951
MAX STEINER†

JIM, THE WORLD'S GREATEST Universal, 1976
FRED MYROW

JIMMY B. & ANDRE (TF) Georgian Bay
Productions, 1980
BRUCE LANGHORNE

JIMMY HOLLYWOOD Paramount, 1994
ROBBIE ROBERTSON

JINGLE ALL THE WAY 20th Century Fox, 1996
DAVID NEWMAN

JINXED MGM/UA, 1982
MILES GOODMAN†
BRUCE ROBERTS

J'IRAI CRACHER SUR VOS TOMBES 1959
ALAIN GORRAGUER

J.J. STARBUCK (TF) Stephen J. Cannell Productions,
1987
MIKE POST

JO JO DANCER, YOUR LIFE IS CALLING
Columbia, 1986
HERBIE HANCOCK

JOAN OF ARC 1995
RICHARD EINHORN

JOAN OF ARC RKO Radio, 1948
HUGO FRIEDHOFER† ★

JOAN OF ARC AT THE STAKE 1954
ARTHUR HONEGGER†

JOAN OF PARIS RKO Radio, 1942
ROY WEBB† ★

JOAN THE MAID 1994
JORDI SAVALL

JOANNA 20th Century-Fox, 1968
ROD MCKUEN

JOAO 1972
HEITOR VILLA-LOBOS†

JOBMAN Blue Rock Films, 1990
JOEL GOLDSMITH

JOCKS Crown International, 1987
DAVID MCHUGH

**JOE AND ETHEL TURP CALL ON THE
PRESIDENT** MGM, 1939
EDWARD WARD†

'97-'98
FILM
COMPOSERS
INDEX

F
I
L
M

T
I
T
L
E
S

JOE DAKOTA Universal, 1957
HENRY MANCINI†
HANS J. SALTER†
HERMAN STEIN

JOE KIDD Universal, 1972
LALO SCHIFRIN

JOE L'IMPLACABILE Seven/Hispamer, 1967
CARLO SAVINA

THE JOE LOUIS STORY United Artists, 1953
GEORGE BASSMAN

JOE PANTHER Artists Creation & Associates, 1976
FRED KARLIN

JOE SMITH, AMERICAN MGM, 1942
DANIELE AMFITHEATROF†

JOE VILACHI: I SEGRETI DI COSA NOSTRA
Columbia, 1972
RIZ ORTOLANI

JOE VS. THE VOLCANO Warner Bros., 1990
GEORGES DELERUE†

JOE'S APARTMENT Warner Bros., 1996
CARTER BURWELL

**JOE'S BED-STUY BARBERSHOP: WE CUT
HEADS** First Run Features, 1983
BILL LEE

JOERG RATGEB, PAINTER 1978
ANDRZEJ KORZYNSKI

JOEY Satori Entertainment, 1985
JIM ROBERGE

JOEY BREAKER Skouras, 1993
PAUL ASTON

JOHN AND MARY 20th Century-Fox, 1969
QUINCY JONES

JOHN GOLDFARB, PLEASE COME HOME 20th
Century-Fox, 1965
JOHN WILLIAMS

JOHN GRISHAM'S THE CLIENT (TF) Michael
Filerman Prods./Judith Paige Mitchell Prods./New
Regency/Warner Bros. TV, 1995
STEPHEN GRAZIANO

**JOHN JAKES' HEAVEN AND HELL: NORTH AND
SOUTH PART 3 (MS)** Wolper Organization/ABC
Prods., 1994
DAVID BELL

JOHN LOVES MARY Warner Bros., 1949
DAVID BUTTOLPH†

JOHN MEADE'S WOMAN Paramount, 1937
FREDERICK HOLLANDER†

JOHN PAUL JONES Warner Bros., 1959
MAX STEINER†

JOHN STEINBECK'S EAST OF EDEN *EAST OF
EDEN* **(MS)** Mace Neufeld Productions, 1981
LEE HOLDRIDGE

JOHN'S WIFE 1973
GEORGES DELERUE†

JOHNNIE MAE GIBSON: FBI (TF) Fool's Cap
Productions, 1986
BILLY GOLDENBERG

JOHNNY ALLEGRO Columbia, 1949
GEORGE DUNING

JOHNNY AND CLYDE MPCA/Viacom, 1995
KEVIN KINER

JOHNNY ANGEL RKO Radio, 1945
LEIGH HARLINE†

JOHNNY BE GOOD Orion, 1988
JAY FERGUSON

JOHNNY BELINDA Warner Bros., 1948
MAX STEINER† ★

JOHNNY BELINDA (TF) Dick Berg/Stonehenge
Productions/Lorimar Productions, 1982
JOHN RUBINSTEIN

JOHNNY BULL (TF) Titus Productions/Eugene
O'Neill Memorial Theatre Center, 1986
DICK HYMAN

JOHNNY COME LATELY United Artists, 1943
LEIGH HARLINE† ★

JOHNNY COMES FLYING HOME 20th
Century-Fox, 1946
DAVID BUTTOLPH†

JOHNNY CONCHO United Artists, 1956
NELSON RIDDLE†

JOHNNY COOL United Artists, 1963
BILLY MAY

JOHNNY DANGEROUSLY 20th Century Fox, 1984
JOHN MORRIS

JOHNNY DARK Universal, 1954
HENRY MANCINI†
HANS J. SALTER†
HERMAN STEIN

JOHNNY DOESN'T LIVE HERE ANYMORE King
Bros./Mon., 1944
W. FRANKE HARLING†

JOHNNY DOUGHBOY Republic, 1942
WALTER SCHARF ★

JOHNNY EAGER MGM, 1941
BRONISLAU KAPER†

JOHNNY GOT HIS GUN Cinemation, 1971
JERRY FIELDING†

JOHNNY GUITAR Republic, 1954
VICTOR YOUNG†

JOHNNY HANDSOME Tri-Star, 1989
RY COODER

JOHNNY HOLIDAY United Artists, 1949
FRANZ WAXMAN†

JOHNNY IN THE CLOUDS United Artists, 1945
NICHOLAS BRODZSKY†

JOHNNY MNEMONIC TriStar, 1995
BRAD FIEDEL

JOHNNY NOBODY Victory-Medallion, 1965
RON GOODWIN

JOHNNY O'CLOCK Columbia, 1947
GEORGE DUNING

JOHNNY ON THE RUN Associated British Film
Distributors/Children's Film Foundation, 1953
ANTONY HOPKINS

JOHNNY ORO 1966
CARLO SAVINA

JOHNNY RENO Paramount, 1966
JIMMIE HASKELL

JOHNNY RYAN (TF) Dan Curtis TV Productions/
MGM/UA/NBC Productions, 1990
CHRIS BOARDMAN ☆

JOHNNY STECCHINO 1991
EVAN LURIE

JOHNNY SUEDE Mainstream, 1991
JIM FARMER
LINK WRAY

JOHNNY TIGER Universal, 1966
JOHN GREEN†

JOHNNY TREMAIN Buena Vista, 1957
GEORGE BRUNS

JOHNNY TROUBLE Warner Bros., 1957
FRANK DEVOL

JOHNNY VIK 1973
BILL MARX

JOHNNY WEST IL MANCINO 1965
ANGELO FRANCESCO LAVAGNINO†

JOHNNY, WE HARDLY KNEW YE (TF) Talent
Associates/Jamel Productions, 1977
GARRY SHERMAN

JOHNS First Look, 1997
CHARLES BROWN
DANNY CARON

THE JOHNSTOWN MONSTER Sebastian Films,
Ltd., 1971
HARRY ROBERTSON

JO-JO AT THE GATE OF LIONS Nana Films, 1992
JONATHAN SAMPSON

THE JOKER Lopert, 1961
GEORGES DELERUE†

THE JOKER IS WILD *ALL THE WAY* Paramount,
1957
WALTER SCHARF

JOKO INVOCA DIO E MUORI 1968
CARLO SAVINA

JOLANDA, LA FIGLIA DEL CORSARO NERO
1952
NINO ROTA† ★

A JOLLY BAD FELLOW Continental, 1963
JOHN BARRY

JOLSON SINGS AGAIN Columbia, 1949·
GEORGE DUNING

JONAS 1957
DUKE ELLINGTON†

JONATHAN LIVINGSTON SEAGULL Paramount,
1973
LEE HOLDRIDGE
NEIL DIAMOND

JONI World Wide Pictures, 1980
RALPH CARMICHAEL

JONNY'S GOLDEN QUEST (ATF) Hanna-Barbera/
USA/Fil-Cartoons, 1993
JOSEPH BARBERA
HOYT CURTIN
JOHN DEBNEY
WILLIAM HANNA

THE JORDAN CHANCE (TF) Universal TV, 1978
PETE RUGOLO

JOSE TORRES (FD) 1959
TORU TAKEMITSU†

JOSEPH ANDREWS Paramount, 1977
JOHN ADDISON

**JOSEPH WAMBAUGH'S ECHOES IN THE
DARKNESS** *ECHOES IN THE DARKNESS*
(MS) Litke-Grossbart Productions/New World TV,
1987
DAVID SHIRE

THE JOSEPHINE BAKER STORY (CTF) HBO
Pictures/Anglia TV/John Kemeny/RH Entertainment,
1991
RALPH BURNS
GEORGES DELERUE†

JOSETTE 20th Century-Fox, 1938
DAVID BUTTOLPH†

JOSH AND S.A.M. 1993
THOMAS NEWMAN

JOSHUA, THEN AND NOW 20th Century Fox,
1985
PHILIPPE SARDE

JOURNAL D'UNE MAISON DE CORRECTION
1980
STELVIO CIPRIANI

THE JOURNALIST 1979
ALFI KABILJO

THE JOURNEY MGM, 1959
GEORGES AURIC†

JOURNEY (TF) Hallmark Hall of Fame Prods., 1995
PATRICK WILLIAMS

JOURNEY BENEATH THE DESERT *ANTINEA -
L'AMANTE DELLA CITTA SEPOLTA* Embassy,
1961
CARLO RUSTICHELLI

JOURNEY FOR MARGARET MGM, 1942
FRANZ WAXMAN†

JOURNEY FROM DARKNESS (TF) Bob Banner
Associates, 1975
KEN LAUBER

JOURNEY INTO FEAR RKO Radio, 1943
ROY WEBB†

JOURNEY INTO FEAR Stirling Gold, 1975
ALEX NORTH†

JOURNEY INTO HISTORY (D) British Transport
Films, 1951
SIR ARNOLD BAX†

JOURNEY INTO LIGHT 20th Century-Fox, 1951
PAUL DUNLAP

THE JOURNEY OF NATTY GANN Buena Vista,
1985
JAMES HORNER

JOURNEY OF LOVE *VIAGGIO D'AMORE*
Centaur, 1991
ANDREA GUERRA

JOURNEY THROUGH ROSEBUD GSF, 1972
JOHNNY MANDEL

JOURNEY THROUGH THE PAST 1973
NEIL YOUNG

JOURNEY TO SPIRIT ISLAND Pal Prods.-Seven
Wonders Entertainment, 1988
FRED MYROW

JOURNEY TO THE CENTER OF THE EARTH 20th
Century-Fox, 1959
BERNARD HERRMANN†

JOURNEY TO THE CENTER OF THE EARTH (TF)
High Prods., 1993
DAVID KURTZ

JOURNEY TO THE FAR SIDE OF THE SUN
DOPPLEGANGER Universal, 1969
BARRY GRAY†

JOURNEY TO THE LOST CITY American
International, 1959
MICHEL MICHELET†.

JOY HOUSE *LES FELINS* MGM, 1964
LALO SCHIFRIN

JOY IN THE MORNING MGM, 1965
BERNARD HERRMANN†

THE JOY LUCK CLUB Buena Vista, 1993
RACHEL PORTMAN

THE JOY OF ACHIEVEMENT Dana Productions
ANDREA SAPAROFF

JOYRIDE American International, 1977
JIMMIE HASKELL

JOYRIDERS Granada Film Prods., 1989
TONY BRITTEN
HAL LINDES

THE JOYS OF COMMUNICATION Dana
Productions
ANDREA SAPAROFF

JUAREZ Warner Bros., 1939
ERICH WOLFGANG KORNGOLD†

JUBAL Columbia, 1956
DAVID RAKSIN

JUBILEE TRAIL Republic, 1954
VICTOR YOUNG†

JUD Duque Films, 1971
STU PHILLIPS

THE JUDAS PROJECT RS Entertainment, 1993
JAMES H. BARDEN

JUDE 1996
ADRIAN JOHNSTON

JUDEX 1963
MAURICE JARRE

THE JUDGE AND JAKE WYLER (TF) Universal TV,
1972
GIL MELLE

THE JUDGE AND THE ASSASSIN Libra, 1976
PHILIPPE SARDE

**JUDGE DEE AND THE MONASTERY MURDERS
(TF)** ABC Circle Films, 1974
LEONARD ROSENMAN

JUDGE DREDD Buena Vista, 1995
ALAN SILVESTRI

THE JUDGE STEPS OUT RKO Radio, 1949
LEIGH HARLINE†

JUDGEMENT DAY: THE JOHN LIST STORY (TF)
Republic, 1993
CRAIG SAFAN

JUDGMENT Juvie Productions, 1989
GARRY SCHYMAN

JUDGMENT AT NUREMBERG United Artists, 1961
ERNEST GOLD

JUDGMENT IN BERLIN New Line Cinema, 1988
PETER GOLDFOOT

JUDGMENT NIGHT Universal, 1993
ALAN SILVESTRI

JUDICIAL CONSENT (CTF) Rysher/Prelude, 1995
CHRISTOPHER YOUNG

JUDITH Paramount, 1965
SOL KAPLAN

JUDITH KRANTZ'S TILL WE MEET AGAIN (MS)
Steve Krantz Productions/Yorkshire TV, 1989
VLADIMIR COSMA

JUDITH KRANTZ'S TORCH SONG (TF) Steve
Krantz Prods., 1993
LEE HOLDRIDGE

JUGGERNAUT United Artists, 1974
KEN THORNE

THE JUGGLER Columbia, 1953
GEORGE ANTHEIL†

JUICE Paramount, 1992
S Q U A

JUKE GIRL Warner Bros., 1942
ADOLPH DEUTSCH†

JULES AND JIM Janus, 1961
GEORGES DELERUE†

JULIA 20th Century-Fox, 1977
GEORGES DELERUE† ★

JULIA AND JULIA Cinecom, 1987
MAURICE JARRE

JULIA HAS TWO LOVERS South Gate, 1991
EMILIO KAUDERER

JULIA MISBEHAVES MGM, 1948
ADOLPH DEUTSCH†

JULIE MGM, 1956
LEITH STEVENS†

JULIE-POT-DE-COLLE Prodis, 1977
GEORGES DELERUE†

JULIET OF THE SPIRITS Rizzoli, 1965
NINO ROTA†

JULIETTE DE SADE *MADEMOISELLE DE SADE E I
SUOVI VIZI* 1967
BILL CONTI

JULIETTE ET JULIETTE 1973
PAUL MISRAKI

JULIETTE OU LA CLE DES SONGES 1951
JOSEPH KOSMA†

JULIUS CAESAR MGM, 1953
MIKLOS ROZSA† ★

JUMANJI TriStar, 1995
JAMES HORNER

JUMP INTO HELL Warner Bros., 1955
DAVID BUTTOLPH†

JUMPIN' AT THE BONEYARD 20th Century Fox,
1991
STEVE POSTEL

JUMPIN' JACK FLASH 20th Century Fox, 1986
THOMAS NEWMAN

JUMPING OVER PUDDLES AGAIN 1971
ZDENEK LISKA

JUNE BRIDE Warner Bros., 1948
DAVID BUTTOLPH†

THE JUNGLE BOOK *RUDYARD KIPLING'S
JUNGLE BOOK* Buena Vista, 1994
BASIL POLEDOURIS

THE JUNGLE BOOK (AF) Buena Vista, 1967
GEORGE BRUNS

JUNGLE BOOK United Artists, 1942
MIKLOS ROZSA† ★

JUNGLE CAPTIVE Universal, 1944
WILLIAM LAVA†
CHARLES PREVIN†
HANS J. SALTER†
PAUL SAWTELL†

JUNGLE CAT Buena Vista, 1960
OLIVER WALLACE†

JUNGLE FEVER Universal, 1991
TERENCE BLANCHARD

JUNGLE GODDESS Screen Guild, 1948
IRVING GERTZ

JUNGLE HEAT United Artists, 1957
LES BAXTER†

JUNGLE SPELL *MAGIA VERDE (FD)* 1953
ANGELO FRANCESCO LAVAGNINO†

JUNGLE WOMAN Universal, 1944
HANS J. SALTER†
PAUL SAWTELL†

JUNGLE2JUNGLE Buena Vista, 1997
MICHAEL CONVERTINO

JUNIOR Universal, 1994
JAMES NEWTON HOWARD

JUNIOR BONNER Cinerama Releasing Corporation,
1973
JERRY FIELDING†

JUNIOR MISS 20th Century-Fox, 1945
DAVID BUTTOLPH†

THE JUNIPER TREE Keene/Moyroud, 1991
LARRY LIPKIS

JUPITER MENACE 1982
LARRY FAST

JUPITER'S DARLING MGM, 1955
DAVID ROSE†

JUPITER'S THIGH *ON A VOLE LA CRUISSE DE
JUPITER* Quartet/Films Inc., 1980
GEORGE HATZINASSIOS

JURASSIC PARK Universal, 1993
JOHN WILLIAMS

THE JUROR Columbia, 1996
JAMES NEWTON HOWARD

JURY DUTY TriStar, 1995
DAVID KITAY

JURY DUTY (TF) Steve White Productions/Spectacor, 1990
RAY COLCORD

JURY OF ONE 1974
MORTON STEVENS†

JUSQU'AU BOUT DU MONDE 1962
GEORGES DELERUE†

JUST A GIGOLO United Artists Classics, 1979
GUENTHER FISCHER

JUST A LITTLE INCONVENIENCE (TF) Universal TV, 1977
JIMMIE HASKELL

JUST ACROSS THE STREET Universal, 1952
HERMAN STEIN

JUST AN OLD SWEET SONG (TF) MTM Enterprises, 1976
PETER MATZ

JUST ANOTHER MIRACLE Skouras Pictures, 1986
B.A. ROBERTSON

JUST ASK FOR DIAMOND Kings Road, 1988
TREVOR JONES

JUST BEFORE DAWN Picturmedia Limited, 1981
BRAD FIEDEL

JUST BEFORE NIGHTFALL *JUSTE AVANT LA NUIT* Libra, 1971
PIERRE JANSEN

JUST BETWEEN FRIENDS Orion, 1986
PATRICK WILLIAMS

JUST BETWEEN US 1961
RONALD STEIN†

JUST CAUSE Warner Bros., 1995
JAMES NEWTON HOWARD

JUST CRAZY ABOUT HORSES (FD) Fred Baker Films, 1979
SAM WAYMON

JUST FOR YOU Paramount, 1952
HUGO FRIEDHOFER†
EMIL NEWMAN†

JUST IMAGINE Fox, 1930
HUGO FRIEDHOFER†

JUST ME & YOU (TF) Roger Gimbel Productions/EMI, 1978
FRED KARLIN

JUST MY IMAGINATION (TF) Andrea Baynes Prods./Lorimar TV, 1992
DAVID MCHUGH

JUST OFF BROADWAY 20th Century-Fox, 1942
DAVID RAKSIN

JUST ONE OF THE GIRLS (TF) Entertainment Securities/Saban Neal and Gary Prods., 1993
AMIN BHATIA
VINCENT MAI

JUST ONE OF THE GUYS Columbia, 1985
TOM SCOTT

JUST TELL ME WHAT YOU WANT Columbia, 1980
CHARLES STROUSE

JUST THE WAY YOU ARE MGM/UA, 1984
VLADIMIR COSMA

JUST THIS ONCE MGM, 1952
DAVID ROSE†

A JUST WAR? (FD) 1992
ANDERS KOPPEL

JUST WILLIAM'S LUCK United Artists, 1947
ROBERT FARNON

JUST WRITE Curb, 1997
LELAND BOND

JUST YOU AND ME, KID Columbia, 1979
JACK ELLIOTT

JUSTE AVANT LA NUIT Libra, 1971
PIERRE JANSEN

JUSTICE 1993
FRANK LOEF

JUSTICE IN A SMALL TOWN (TF) Hill-Field Prods., 1994
DAVID MCHUGH

JUSTIN CASE (TF) The Blake Edwards Company/Walt Disney TV, 1988
HENRY MANCINI†

JUSTIN DE MARSEILLES 1935
JACQUES IBERT†

JUSTINE 20th Century-Fox, 1969
JERRY GOLDSMITH

JUSTINE OVVERO LE DISAVVENTURE DELLA VIRTU 1968
BRUNO NICOLAI

JUSTINIEN TROUVE, OR GOD'S BASTARD Gaumont Buena Vista International, 1993
GERMINAL TENAS

JUSTINIEN TROUVE, OU LE BATARD DE DIEU *JUSTINIEN TROUVE, OR GOD'S BASTARD* Gaumont Buena Vista International, 1993
GERMINAL TENAS

JUSTIZ *JUSTICE* 1993
FRANK LOEF

JUVENILE PASSIONS 1956
MASARU SATO
TORU TAKEMITSU†

K

K2 British, 1992
HANS ZIMMER

K2 Miramax, 1992
CHAZ JANKEL

K-9 Universal, 1989
MILES GOODMAN†

K-9000 (TF) De Souza Prods./Fries Ent., 1991
JAN HAMMER

KADISBELLAN *THE SLINGSHOT* 1993
BJORN ISFALT

KAERLIGHEDENS SMERTE *PAIN OF LOVE* 1993
GUNNAR MOLLER PEDERSEN

KAFKA Miramax, 1991
CLIFF MARTINEZ

KAGEMUSHA: THE SHADOW WARRIOR 20th Century-Fox, 1980
SHINCHIRO IKEBE

KAIDEN YUKUJORO *SNOW GHOST* 1968
AKIRA IFUKUBE

KALEIDOSCOPE Warner Bros., 1966
STANLEY MYERS†

KALIFORNIA Gramercy, 1993
CARTER BURWELL

KALTE HEIMAT *COLD HOMELAND* Triangel Film, 1979
JURGEN KNIEPER

KAMA SUTRA Rasa Films, 1997
MYCHAEL DANNA

KAMIKAZE Gaumont, 1987
TANGERINE DREAM

KAMIKAZE 1989 1982
FABIO FRIZZI

KAMIN OUNAYNOUTIAN 1992
AVET TERTERIAN

KANCHENJUNGHA Harrison, 1962
SATYAJIT RAY†

KANDYLAND New World, 1988
GEORGE MICHALSKI

KANE & ABEL (MS) Schrekinger Communications/Embassy TV, 1985
BILLY GOLDENBERG

KANEHSATAKE: 270 YEARS OF RESISTANCE (FD) National Film Board of Canada, 1993
FRANCIS GRANDMONT
CLAUDE VENDETTE

KANGAROO 20th Century-Fox, 1952
SOL KAPLAN

KANSAS Trans World Entertainment, 1988
PINO DONAGGIO

THE KANSAS CITY MASSACRE (TF) ABC Circle Films, 1975
BOB COBERT

KANSAS CITY BOMBER MGM, 1972
DON ELLIS†

THE KANSAS TERRORS Republic, 1939
WILLIAM LAVA†

KAPO 1959
CARLO RUSTICHELLI

KARAMOJA (FD) Hallmark, 1954
ERNEST GOLD

THE KARATE KID Columbia, 1984
BILL CONTI

THE KARATE KID II Columbia, 1986
BILL CONTI

KARATE KID III Columbia, 1989
BILL CONTI

THE KAREN CARPENTER STORY (TF) Weintraub Entertainment Group, 1989
DAVID KOLE

KASEKI Haiyuza Films, 1975
TORU TAKEMITSU†

KASPAR HAUSER 1993
NIKOS MAMANGAKIS

KATE BLISS AND THE TICKER TAPE KID (TF) Aaron Spelling Productions, 1978
JEFF ALEXANDER†

KATE McSHANE (TF) Paramount TV, 1975
JOHN CACAVAS

KATE'S SECRET (TF) Andrea Baynes Productions/Columbia TV, 1986
J. PETER ROBINSON

KATHLEEN MGM, 1941
FRANZ WAXMAN†

KATHY O' Universal, 1958
FRANK SKINNER†

KATIE DID IT Universal, 1951
FRANK SKINNER†

KATIE: PORTRAIT OF A CENTERFOLD (TF) Moonlight Productions/Warner Bros. TV, 1978
CHARLES BERNSTEIN

KATSU TAIHEIKI 1974
ISAO TOMITA

KATTORNA 1964
CHRISTOPHER KOMEDA†

KAUBERGERG West German
JURGEN KNIEPER

KAZAAM Buena Vista, 1996
CHRISTOPHER TYNG

KAZABLAN MGM, 1973
DOV SELTZER

KAZOKU 1971
MASARU SATO

KEEFER (TF) David Gerber Productions/Columbia Pictures TV, 1978
DUANE TATRO

THE KEEGANS (TF) Universal TV, 1976
PAUL CHIHARA

THE KEEP Paramount, 1983
CHRISTOPHER FRANKE

THE KEEP Paramount, 1983
TANGERINE DREAM

KEEP 'EM FLYING Universal, 1941
FRANK SKINNER†

KEEP 'EM ROLLING RKO Radio, 1934
MAX STEINER†

KEEP 'EM SLUGGING Universal, 1943
HANS J. SALTER†

KEEP OFF MY GRASS Alan Yasni, 1971
JIM HELMS

KEEP THE CHANGE (CTF) Steve Tisch Co./High Horse Films, 1992
JOHN E. KEANE

KEEPER OF THE CITY (CTF) Viacom, 1992
LEONARD ROSENMAN

KEEPER OF THE FLAME MGM, 1942
BRONISLAU KAPER†

KEEPING COMPANY MGM, 1940
DANIELE AMFITHEATROF†

KEEPING SECRETS (TF) Freyda Rothstein/Hamel-Somers/Finnegan-Pinchuk, 1991
PATRICK WILLIAMS

KEEPING THE PROMISE (TF) Marion Rees/Atlantis, 1996
PETER MANNING ROBINSON

KEETJE TIPPEL 1975
ROGIER VAN OTTERLOO†

KEINER LIEBT MICH German, 1995
NIKI REISER

KELLY THE SECOND MGM, 1936
T. MARVIN HATLEY†

KELLY'S HEROES MGM, 1970
LALO SCHIFRIN

KEN MURRAY SHOOTING STARS Royal Oak, 1979
RICHARD LASALLE

KENNEDY (MS) Central Independent Television Productions/Alan Landsburg Productions, 1983
RICHARD HARTLEY

THE KENNEDYS (TD) WGBH/Thames TV, 1992
MICHAEL BACON

THE KENNEDYS OF MASSACHUSETTS (MS) Edgar J. Scherick Associates/Orion TV, 1990
DAVID SHIRE ☆

KENNY & COMPANY 20th Century-Fox, 1976
FRED MYROW

KENNY ROGERS AS THE GAMBLER - THE ADVENTURE CONTINUES (TF) Lion Share Productions, 1983
LARRY CANSLER

KENNY ROGERS AS THE GAMBLER (TF) Kragen & Co., 1980
LARRY CANSLER

KENNY ROGERS AS THE GAMBLER III: THE LEGEND CONTINUES (TF) Lion Share Productions, 1987
LARRY CANSLER

KENT STATE (TF) Inter Planetary Productions/Osmond TV Productions, 1981
KEN LAUBER

THE KENTUCKIAN Paramount, 1955
BERNARD HERRMANN†

KENTUCKY 20th Century-Fox, 1938
LOUIS SILVERS†

KENTUCKY KERNELS RKO Radio, 1934
MAX STEINER†
ROY WEBB†

KENTUCKY MOONSHINE 20th Century-Fox, 1938
LOUIS SILVERS†

KENTUCKY WOMAN (TF) Walter Doniger Productions/20th Century-Fox TV, 1983
GEORGE ROMANIS

KEPT HUSBANDS RKO Radio, 1931
MAX STEINER†

KES United Artists, 1970
JOHN CAMERON

THE KETTLES IN THE OZARKS Universal, 1956
HERMAN STEIN

THE KETTLES ON OLD MACDONALD'S FARM Universal, 1957
HENRY MANCINI†

THE KEY Columbia, 1958
MALCOLM ARNOLD

THE KEY San Francisco Films, 1983
ENNIO MORRICONE

KEY EXCHANGE TLC Films/20th Century Fox, 1985
MASON DARING
JONATHAN ELIAS

THE KEY IS IN THE DOOR 1978
PHILIPPE SARDE

KEY LARGO Warner Bros., 1948
MAX STEINER†

THE KEY MAN United Artists, 1955
LES BAXTER†

THE KEY TO REBECCA (TF) Taft Entertainment TV/Castle Combe Productions, 1985
J.A.C. REDFORD

KEY TO THE CITY MGM, 1950
BRONISLAU KAPER†

KEY WEST (TF) Warner Bros. TV, 1973
FRANK DEVOL

THE KEYS (TF) Riven Rock Prods./Universal TV, 1992
DALE MENTEN

KEYS (TF) ABC Prods., 1995
JOHN FRIZZELL

THE KEYS OF THE KINGDOM 20th Century-Fox, 1944
ALFRED NEWMAN† ★

KEYS TO FREEDOM RPB Pictures/Queen's Cross Productions, 1989
FRANCIS LAI

KGB—THE SECRET WAR Cinema Group, 1985
MISHA SEGAL

KHARTOUM United Artists, 1966
FRANK CORDELL†

KHOVANSHCHINA Artkino, 1961
DMITRI SHOSTAKOVITCH† ★

KICKBOXER Kings Road, 1989
PAUL HERTZOG

KICKBOXER Pathe Entertainment, 1989
PAUL HARTZOP

KICKBOXER II: THE ROAD BACK KINGS ROAD, 1991
TONY RIPPARETTI

KICKBOXER IV: THE AGRESSOR Kings Road, 1994
TONY RIPPARETTI

KICKING & SCREAMING Trimark, 1995
PHIL MARSHALL

KICKS 1985
PETER BERNSTEIN

THE KID United Artists, 1921
CHARLES CHAPLIN†

KID BLUE 20th Century-Fox, 1973
JOHN RUBINSTEIN

THE KID COMES BACK Warner Bros., 1938
DAVID RAKSIN

A KID FOR TWO FARTHINGS Lopert, 1956
BENJAMIN FRANKEL†

THE KID FROM KOKOMO Warner Bros., 1939
ADOLPH DEUTSCH†

THE KID FROM LEFT FIELD 20th Century-Fox, 1953
LIONEL NEWMAN†

THE KID FROM LEFT FIELD (TF) Gary Coleman Productions/Deena Silver-Kramer's Movie Company, 1979
DAVID MICHAEL FRANK

THE KID FROM NOT-SO-BIG William Crain Productions, 1982
RON GRANT

THE KID FROM NOWHERE (TF) Cates-Bridges Company, 1982
GARRY SHERMAN

THE KID FROM TEXAS MGM, 1939
WILLIAM AXT†

KID GALAHAD United Artists, 1962
JEFF ALEXANDER†

KID GALAHAD Warner Bros., 1937
MAX STEINER†

KID MONK BARONI Realart, 1952
HERSCHEL BURKE GILBERT

KID NINJAS Reel Movies
DAN SLIDER

THE KID SISTER Producers Releasing Corp., 1945
ALBERT GLASSER

THE KID WHO LOVED CHRISTMAS (TF) Eddie Murphy TV/Paramount TV, 1990
STANLEY CLARKE

THE KID WITH THE 200 I.Q. (TF) Guillaume-Margo Productions/Zephyr Productions, 1983
DENNIS MCCARTHY

THE KID WITH THE BROKEN HALO (TF) Satellite Productions, 1982
TOMMY VIG

KIDCO 20th Century-Fox, 1984
MICHAEL SMALL

KIDNAPPED American International, 1971
ROY BUDD†

KIDNAPPED Virgin Vision, 1987
RON JONES

THE KIDNAPPING OF THE PRESIDENT Crown International, 1980
PAUL J. ZAZA

KIDS DON'T TELL (TF) Chris-Rose Productions/Viacom Productions, 1985
FRED KARLIN

KIDS IN THE HALL: BRAIN CANDY 1996
CRAIG NORTHEY

KIDS LIKE THESE (TF) Taft Entertainment TV/Nexus
Productions, 1987
MARK SNOW

KIDS OF THE ROUND TABLE Malofilm, 1995
NORMAND CORBEIL

KIDZ IN THE WOOD (TF) Green-Epstein, 1995
RICHARD BELLIS

KIEZ United Artists, 1983
CARL DANTE

KIGANJO NO BOKEN *ADVENTURES OF TAKLA MAKAN* 1965
AKIRA IFUKUBE

THE KII RIVER 1966
TORU TAKEMITSU†

KIKI United Artists, 1931
ALFRED NEWMAN†

KILL AND GO HIDE *THE CHILD* Boxoffice
International, 1977
ROB WALLACE

KILL HER GENTLY 1957
EDWIN ASTLEY

KILL ME AGAIN MGM/UA, 1990
WILLIAM OLVIS

KILL ME IF YOU CAN (TF) Columbia TV, 1977
BILL CONTI

KILL OR BE KILLED Eagle Lion, 1950
KARL HAJOS†

KILL OR BE KILLED *UCCIDI E MUORI* 1966
CARLO RUSTICHELLI

KILL OR CURE MGM, 1962
RON GOODWIN

KILL SQUAD Summa Vista Pictures, 1982
JOSEPH CONLAN

KILL THE UMPIRE Columbia, 1950
HEINZ ROEMHELD†

KILL! 1968
MASARU SATO

KILL, BABY, KILL *OPERAZIONE PAURA* 1966
CARLO RUSTICHELLI

KILLDOZER (TF) Universal TV, 1974
GIL MELLE

KILLER Keystone/Worldvision, 1994
GRAEME COLEMAN

A KILLER AMONG FRIENDS (TF) Green-Epstein,
1992
RICHARD BELLIS

KILLER APE Columbia, 1953
MISCHA BAKALEINIKOFF†

KILLER AT LARGE Producers Releasing Corp., 1947
ALBERT GLASSER

KILLER BEES (TF) RSO Films, 1974
DAVID SHIRE

KILLER BY NIGHT (TF) Cinema Center 100, 1972
QUINCY JONES

THE KILLER ELITE United Artists, 1975
JERRY FIELDING†

KILLER FISH Associated Film Distribution, 1979
GUIDO DE ANGELIS
MAURIZIO DE ANGELIS

KILLER FORCE American International, 1975
GEORGES GARVARENTZ†

KILLER IN THE FAMILY (TF) Stan Margulies
Productions/Sunn Classic Pictures, 1983
GERALD FRIED

KILLER IN THE MIRROR (TF) Litke-Grossbart
Productions/Warner Bros. TV, 1986
GIL MELLE

THE KILLER INSIDE ME Warner Bros., 1976
JOHN RUBINSTEIN

KILLER INSTINCT Concorde-New Horizons, 1992
NIGEL HOLTON

KILLER INSTINCT (TF) Millar-Bromberg
Productions/ITC, 1988
PAUL CHIHARA

THE KILLER IS LOOSE United Artists, 1956
LIONEL NEWMAN†

KILLER KLOWNS FROM OUTER SPACE Trans
World Entertainment, 1988
JOHN MASSARI

KILLER ON BOARD (TF) Lorimar Productions, 1977
EARLE HAGEN

KILLER PARTY MGM/UA, 1986
JOHN BEAL

KILLER RULES (TF) Lee Rich Co./Warner Bros. TV,
1993
LEE HOLDRIDGE

KILLER SPY 1965
GEORGES DELERUE†

THE KILLER THAT STALKED NEW YORK
Universal, 1950
HANS J. SALTER†

THE KILLER WHO WOULDN'T DIE (TF)
Paramount Pictures TV, 1976
GEORGES GARVARENTZ†

KILLER'S KISS United Artists, 1955
GERALD FRIED

KILLER: A JOURNAL OF MURDER 1996
GRAEME REVELL

THE KILLERS Universal, 1946
MIKLOS ROZSA† ★

THE KILLERS Universal, 1964
JOHN WILLIAMS

THE KILLING United Artists, 1956
GERALD FRIED

A KILLING AFFAIR Hemdale, 1988
JOHN BARRY

A KILLING AFFAIR (TF) David Gerber Productions/
Columbia Pictures TV, 1977
RICHARD SHORES

KILLING AT HELL'S GATE (TF) CBS Entertainment,
1981
DAVID BELL

KILLING DAD (TF) 1989
CHAZ JANKEL

THE KILLING FIELDS Warner Bros., 1984
MIKE OLDFIELD

KILLING GRANDDAD 1993
LITTO NEBBIA

KILLING IN A SMALL TOWN (TF) The IndieProd
Co./Hearst Entertainment Productions, 1990
RICHARD GIBBS

THE KILLING KIND Media Trend, 1974
ANDREW BELLING

THE KILLING MIND (CTF) Hearst, 1991
JAMES DIPASQUALLE ☆

THE KILLING OF A CHINESE BOOKIE Faces
International, 1976
ANTHONY HARRIS
BO HARWOOD

THE KILLING OF AMERICA Toho, 1982
LAURIN RINDER

THE KILLING OF AMERICA (FD) Filmlink Corp.,
1982
W. MICHAEL LEWIS
MARK LINDSAY

THE KILLING OF ANGEL STREET Forest Home
Films, 1981
BRIAN MAY†

THE KILLING OF RANDY WEBSTER (TF) Roger
Gimbel Productions/EMI TV, 1981
PETER MATZ

THE KILLING OF SISTER GEORGE Cinerama
Releasing Corporation, 1968
GERALD FRIED

KILLING STONE (TF) Universal TV, 1978
DAVID ROSE†

THE KILLING TIME New World, 1987
PAUL CHIHARA

THE KILLING ZONE PM, 1991
JEFF LASS

KILLING ZOE Samuel Hadida, 1994
TOMANDANDI

KILLJOY (TF) Lorimar Productions, 1981
BRUCE BROUGHTON ★

KILLPOINT Crown International, 1984
HERMAN JEFFREYS
DARYL STEVENETT

KILRONAN TriStar, 1997
CHRISTOPHER YOUNG

KIM MGM, 1950
ANDRE PREVIN

KIM (TF) London Films, 1984
MARC WILKINSON

KIND LADY MGM, 1935
EDWARD WARD†

KIND LADY MGM, 1951
DAVID RAKSIN

A KIND OF LOVING Continental, 1962
RON GRAINER†

KINDERGARTEN COP Universal, 1990
RANDY EDELMAN

THE KINDRED FM Entertainment, 1987
DAVID NEWMAN

KING (MS) Abby Mann Productions/Filmways, 1978
BILLY GOLDENBERG ☆☆

KING AND COUNTRY Allied Artists, 1965
LARRY ADLER

THE KING AND FOUR QUEENS United Artists,
1956
ALEX NORTH†

THE KING AND THE CHORUS GIRL Warner Bros.,
1937
WERNER R. HEYMANN†

THE KING AND THE MOCKINGBIRD Gaumont,
1980
WOJCIECH KILAR

KING CRAB (TF) Titus Productions, 1980
DICK HYMAN

KING CREOLE Paramount, 1958
WALTER SCHARF

KING DAVID Paramount, 1985
CARL DAVIS

KING ELEPHANT (FD) 1972
LAURENCE ROSENTHAL

A KING IN NEW YORK Archway, 1957
CHARLES CHAPLIN†

KING JAMES VERSION Joseph E. Taylor/Vitascope
Inc., 1988
WENDY BLACKSTONE

KING KONG Paramount, 1976
JOHN BARRY

KING KONG RKO Radio, 1933
MAX STEINER†

KING KONG ESCAPES Universal, 1968
AKIRA IFUKUBE

KING KONG LIVES DEG, 1986
JOHN SCOTT

KING KONG VS. GODZILLA Universal, 1963
AKIRA IFUKUBE

KING LEAR Artkino, 1971
DMITRI SHOSTAKOVITCH†

THE KING OF COMEDY 20th Century-Fox, 1983
ROBBIE ROBERTSON

THE KING OF HEARTS Lopert, 1967
GEORGES DELERUE†

KING OF JAZZ Universal, 1930
FERDE GROFE†

KING OF KINGS MGM, 1961
MIKLOS ROZSA†

THE KING OF LOVE (TF) Sarabande Productions/
MGM-UA TV, 1987
PAUL CHIHARA

KING OF NEW YORK Reteitalia/Scena Films, 1990
JOE DELIA

KING OF PARIS *LE ROI DE PARIS* 1995
QUENTIN DAMAMME

KING OF THE AIRWAVES *LOUIS 19, LE ROI
DES ONDES* 1994
JEAN-MARIE BENOIT

KING OF THE GYPSIES Paramount, 1978
DAVID GRISMAN

KING OF THE HILL Gramercy, 1993
CLIFF MARTINEZ

KING OF THE KHYBER RIFLES 20th Century-Fox,
1954
BERNARD HERRMANN†

KING OF THE MOUNTAIN Universal, 1981
MICHAEL MELVOIN

KING OF THE OLYMPICS (TF) Harmony Gold/Rete
Europa/SFP Productions, 1988
PAUL CHIHARA

**KING OF THE ROARING '20's—THE STORY OF
ARNOLD ROTHSTEIN** Allied Artists, 1961
FRANZ WAXMAN†

KING RALPH Universal, 1991
JAMES NEWTON HOWARD

KING RAT Columbia, 1965
JOHN BARRY

KING RICHARD AND THE CRUSADERS Warner
Bros., 1954
MAX STEINER†

KING SOLOMON'S MINES Cannon, 1985
JERRY GOLDSMITH

THE KING'S THIEF MGM, 1955
MIKLOS ROZSA†

THE KING'S WHORE *JEANNE, LA PUTAIN DU
ROI* J&M Entertainment, 1990
GABRIEL YARED

KING, QUEEN, KNAVE Avco Embassy, 1972
STANLEY MYERS†

KINGFISH: A STORY OF HUEY P. LONG (CTF)
Chris-Rose Prods., 1995
PATRICK WILLIAMS

KINGPIN MGM-UA, 1996
FREDDY JOHNSTON

KINGS GO FORTH United Artists, 1958
ELMER BERNSTEIN

KINGS OF THE SUN United Artists, 1963
ELMER BERNSTEIN

KINGS ROW Warner Bros., 1942
ERICH WOLFGANG KORNGOLD†

KINGSTON: THE POWER PLAY (TF) Groverton
Productions/Universal TV, 1976
LEONARD ROSENMAN

KINJITE *FORBIDDEN GAMES* Cannon, 1989
GREG DE BELLES

KIPPERBANG *P'TANG YANG, KIPPERBANG*
MGM/UA Classics, 1983
DAVID EARL

KIPPS 20th Century-Fox, 1941
WILLIAM ALWYN†

THE KIRLIAN WITNESS 1978
HARRY MANFREDINI

KISMET MGM, 1944
HERBERT STOTHART† ★

KISMET MGM, 1955
ANDRE PREVIN

KISMET Warner Bros., 1931
EDWARD WARD†

THE KISS MGM, 1929
WILLIAM AXT†

THE KISS Tri-Star, 1988
TOM CANNING
J. PETER ROBINSON

THE KISS Universal, 1998
MERVYN WARREN

KISS AND BE KILLED Monarch, 1991
KEVIN KINER

KISS AND TELL Columbia, 1945
WERNER R. HEYMANN†

KISS AND TELL (TF) LWT, 1996
HAL LINDES

A KISS BEFORE DYING Universal, 1991
HOWARD SHORE

A KISS BEFORE THE MIRROR Universal, 1933
W. FRANKE HARLING†

A KISS FOR CORLISS United Artists, 1949
WERNER R. HEYMANN†

A KISS IN THE DARK Warner Bros., 1949
MAX STEINER†

KISS KISS BANG BANG 1966
BRUNO NICOLAI

KISS ME A KILLER Califilm, 1991
NIGEL HOLTON

KISS ME DEADLY United Artists, 1955
FRANK DEVOL

KISS ME GOODBYE 20th Century Fox, 1982
RALPH BURNS

KISS ME KATE MGM, 1953
ANDRE PREVIN ★

KISS ME, STUPID Lopert, 1964
ANDRE PREVIN

KISS ME...KILL ME (TF) The Writers Company/
Columbia Pictures TV, 1976
RICHARD MARKOWITZ†

KISS MEETS THE PHANTOM OF THE PARK (TF)
Hanna-Barbera Productions/KISS Productions, 1978
HOYT CURTIN
FRED KARLIN

KISS OF A KILLER (TF) Andrew Adelson Co./John
Conboy Prods./ABC Prods., 1993
J.A.C. REDFORD

KISS OF DEATH 20th Century Fox, 1995
TREVOR JONES

KISS OF DEATH 20th Century-Fox, 1947
DAVID BUTTOLPH†

KISS OF FIRE Universal, 1955
HERMAN STEIN

THE KISS OF THE VAMPIRE Universal, 1963
JAMES BERNARD

KISS OF THE SPIDER WOMAN Island Alive/Film
Dallas, 1985
JOHN NESCHLING

KISS SHOT (TF) Lonson Productions/Whoop Inc.,
1989
STEVE DORFF

KISS THE BLOOD OFF MY HANDS Universal,
1948
MIKLOS ROZSA†

KISS THE OTHER SHEIK *OGGI, DOMANI E
DOPODAMANI* 1968
NINO ROTA†

KISS THEM FOR ME 20th Century-Fox, 1957
LIONEL NEWMAN†

A KISS TO DIE FOR (TF) Polone Co./Hearst, 1993
GEORGE S. CLINTON

KISS TOMORROW GOODBYE Warner Bros., 1950
CARMEN DRAGON†

KISSES FOR BREAKFAST Warner Bros., 1941
ADOLPH DEUTSCH†

KISSES FOR MY PRESIDENT Warner Bros., 1964
BRONISLAU KAPER†

THE KISSING PLACE (CTF) Cynthia A. Cherbak
Production/Wilshire Court Productions, 1990
LAURENCE ROSENTHAL

KISSINGER AND NIXON (CTF) Paragon, 1995
JONATHAN GOLDSMITH

KIT CARSON United Artists, 1940
EDWARD WARD†

THE KITCHEN TOTO Cannon, 1988
JOHN E. KEANE

KITTY British International, 1929
HUBERT BATH†

KITTY Paramount, 1945
VICTOR YOUNG†

KITTY & THE BAGMAN Quartet/Films Incorporated,
1982
BRIAN MAY†

KITTY FOYLE RKO Radio, 1941
ROY WEBB†

THE KLANSMAN Paramount, 1974
STU GARDNER
DALE O. WARREN

KLIOU *THE TIGER* RKO Radio, 1935
HEINZ ROEMHELD†

KLONDIKE FEVER 1980
HAGOOD HARDY

KLUTE Warner Bros., 1971
MICHAEL SMALL

THE KNACK...AND HOW TO GET IT Lopert, 1965
JOHN BARRY

KNEUSS 1978
TANGERINE DREAM

KNICKERBOCKER HOLIDAY United Artists, 1944
WERNER R. HEYMANN† ★

KNIFE IN THE WATER Kanawha, 1962
CHRISTOPHER KOMEDA†

KN - LA

'97-'98
FILM
COMPOSERS
INDEX

F I L M   T I T L E S

KNIGHT RIDER 2000 (TF) Desperado Films, 1991
JAN HAMMER

KNIGHT WITHOUT ARMOUR United Artists, 1937
MIKLOS ROZSA†

KNIGHTRIDERS United Film Distribution, 1981
DONALD RUBINSTEIN

KNIGHTS Kings Road, 1993
TONY RIPPARETTI

KNIGHTS AND EMERALDS Warner Bros., 1986
COLIN TOWNS

KNIGHTS OF THE CITY New World, 1986
MISHA SEGAL

KNIGHTS OF THE ROUND TABLE MGM, 1953
MIKLOS ROZSA†

KNOCK 1932
JEAN WIENER†

KNOCK 1950
PAUL MISRAKI

KNOCK ON ANY DOOR Columbia, 1949
GEORGE ANTHEIL†

KNOWING LISA Imagining Things Enterprises, 1992
STEPHEN WEBBER

KNUCKLEBALL 1995
MIKE HEWER

KOENIGSMARK 1935
JACQUES IBERT†

KOI TO TASOGARE BREAKABLE 1994
SHINSUKE HONDA

KOJAK (TF) Universal TV, 1989
CAMERON ALLAN

KOJAK: THE BELARUS FILE (TF) Universal TV, 1985
BARRY DEVORZON
JOSEPH CONLAN

KOJAK: THE PRICE OF JUSTICE (TF) Universal TV, 1987
PATRICK WILLIAMS

KOLEJNOSC UCZUC SEQUENCES OF FEELING 1993
JERZY SATANOWSKI

KOLYA Miramax, 1997
ONDREJ SOUKUP

KOMMISSAR X, DREI GRUNE HUNDE 1967
FRANCESCO DE MASI

KONA COAST Warner Bros., 1968
JACK MARSHALL

KONGA American International, 1961
GERARD SCHURMANN

KORCZAK Filmstudio Perspektywa, 1990
WOJCIECH KILAR

KOREA 1995
STEPHEN MCKEON

KORSVATS DRAKHT THE LOST PARADISE 1992
STEPAN LOUSIKYAN

KOSH BA KOSH ODDS AND EVENS 1993
ACHMAD BAKAEV

KOTCH Cinerama Releasing Corporation, 1971
MARVIN HAMLISCH

KOTOVSKY 1943
SERGEI PROKOFIEV†

KOUROTCHKA RIABA/RIABA MA POULE 1994
BORIS BASOUROV

KOYAANISQATSI Island Alive/New Cinema, 1983
PHILIP GLASS

KRAKATOA, EAST OF JAVA Cinerama Releasing Corporation, 1969
FRANK DEVOL

KRAMER VS. KRAMER Columbia, 1979
JOHN KANDER

THE KRAYS Rank, 1990
MICHAEL KAMEN

THE KREMLIN LETTER 20th Century-Fox, 1970
ROBERT DRASNIN

KRONOS 20th Century-Fox, 1957
PAUL SAWTELL†
BERT A. SHEFTER

KRULL Columbia, 1983
JAMES HORNER

KUFFS Universal, 1992
HAROLD FALTERMEYER

KUHLE WAMPE 1931
HANNS EISLER†

THE KULIES Global
W. MICHAEL LEWIS
LAURIN RINDER

KULL THE CONQUEROR Universal, 1997
JOEL GOLDSMITH

KUNG FU (TF) Warner Bros. TV, 1972
JIM HELMS

KUNG FU: THE MOVIE (TF) Lou-Step Productions/Warner Bros. TV, 1986
LALO SCHIFRIN

KUNI LEMI IN TEL AVIV 1978
DOV SELTZER

KVINNA UTAN ANSIKTE 1947
ERIC NORDGREN

KWAIDAN Continental, 1964
TORU TAKEMITSU†

KYO (FD) 1968
TORU TAKEMITSU†

KYOSO TANJO MANY HAPPY RETURNS 1993
NAOYUKI FUJII

L

THE L-SHAPED ROOM Columbia, 1963
JOHN BARRY

LA 317 ÈME SECTION 1965
PIERRE JANSEN

L.627 1992
PHILIPPE SARDE

LA BABY-SITTER Titanus, 1975
FRANCIS LAI

LA BALANCE 1982
ROLAND BOCQUET

LA BALLADE DE MAMLOUK 1982
ARMANDO TROVAJOLI

LA BALLADE DES DALTON THE BALLAD OF THE DALTONS 1978
CLAUDE BOLLING

LA BALLERINA ED IL BUON DIO 1958
PIERO PICCIONI

LA BAMBA Columbia, 1987
MILES GOODMAN†
CURT SOBEL

LA BAMBOLONA BABY DOLL 1968
LUIS BACALOV

LA BANCA DI MONATE 1976
ARMANDO TROVAJOLI

LA BANDA DEL BUCO 1960
LUIS BACALOV

LA BANDA J & S: CRONACA CRIMINALE DEL FAR WEST SONNY AND JED 1972
ENNIO MORRICONE

LA BANDERA 1935
JEAN WIENER†

LA BANQUIERE 1980
ENNIO MORRICONE

LA BARRICADE DU POINT DU JOUR 1977
ANTOINE DUHAMEL

LA BATTAGLIA DEL DESERTO 1968
BRUNO NICOLAI

LA BATTAGLIA DI EL ALAMEIN 1968
CARLO RUSTICHELLI

LA BAULE-LES PINS UGC, 1990
PHILIPPE SARDE

LA BELLA DI ROMA Lux Film, 1955
NINO ROTA†

LA BELLA MUGNAIA 1955
ANGELO FRANCESCO LAVAGNINO†

LA BELLE AVENTURE TWILIGHT 1945
GEORGES AURIC†

LA BELLE FAMIGLIE 1964
ARMANDO TROVAJOLI

LA BELLE HISTOIRE THE BEAUTIFUL STORY 1992
FRANCIS LAI
PHILIPPE SERVAIN

LA BELLE QUE VOILA 1949
JOSEPH KOSMA†

LA BELLE VIE 1963
HENRI LANOE

LA BELLE VIE (TF) 1979
VLADIMIR COSMA

LA BELLEZZA D'IPPOLITA 1962
CARLO RUSTICHELLI

LA BELVA 1970
STELVIO CIPRIANI

LA BERGERE ET LE RAMONEUR 1952
JOSEPH KOSMA†

LA BETE A L'AFFUT 1958
MAURICE JARRE

LA BETE HUMAINE THE HUMAN BEAST 1938
JOSEPH KOSMA†

LA BETIA, OVVERO IN AMORE PER OGNI GAUDENZA 1971
CARLO RUSTICHELLI

LA BOLOGNESE 1975
CARLO SAVINA

LA BONNE ANNEE Avco Embassy, 1973
FRANCIS LAI

LA BOUM 1980
VLADIMIR COSMA

LA BOUM II Gaumont, 1983
VLADIMIR COSMA

LA CAGE 1975
PHILIPPE SARDE

LA CAGE AUX FOLLES 1978
ENNIO MORRICONE

LA CAGE AUX FOLLES 3 Warner Bros./Columbia, 1985
ENNIO MORRICONE

LA CAGE AUX FOLLES II United Artists, 1981
ENNIO MORRICONE

LA CALDA VITA 1964
CARLO RUSTICHELLI

LA CALIFFA 1970
ENNIO MORRICONE

LA CARCASSE ET LE TORD-COU 1947
JEAN WIENER†

LA CARICA DEL 7 CAVALLEGGERI 1964
CARLO RUSTICHELLI

LA CASA DEL TAPPETO GIALLO Gaumont, 1983
STELVIO CIPRIANI

LA CATHEDRALE DES MORTES 1935
JEAN WIENER†

LA CATTURA 1969
RIZ ORTOLANI

LA CAVALE DES FOUS LOONIES AT LARGE 1993
OLIVIER DEFAYS

LA CAVALE DES FOUS LOONIES AT LARGE 1993, French
CHRISTOPHE DEFAYS

LA CECILIA 1974
MICHEL PORTAL

LA CENA DELLA BEFFE 1941
GIUSEPPE BECCE†

LA CENTO CHILOMETRI 1960
ARMANDO TROVAJOLI

LA CEREMONIE 1996
MATTHIEU CHABROL

LA CHAIR DE L'ORCHIDEE 1974
FIORENZO CARPI

LA CHAMBRE ARDENTE THE BURNING COURT 1962
GEORGES AURIC†

LA CHANSON DE ROLAND 1978
ANTOINE DUHAMEL

LA CHARRETTE FANTOME 1939
JACQUES IBERT†

LA CHATELAINE DU LIBAN 1956
PAUL MISRAKI

LA CHEVRE 1982
VLADIMIR COSMA

LA CHIAVE THE KEY San Francisco Films, 1983
ENNIO MORRICONE

LA CIECA DI SORRENTO 1952
CARLO RUSTICHELLI

LA CIGALE ET LA FOURMI 1949
JOSEPH KOSMA†

LA CINE E VICINA 1967
ENNIO MORRICONE

LA CIOCIARA TWO WOMEN 1960
ARMANDO TROVAJOLI

LA CITADELLE DU SILENCE 1937
ARTHUR HONEGGER†
DARIUS MILHAUD†

LA CITE DES ENFANTS PERDUS Sony Classics, 1995
ANGELO BADALAMENTI

LA CITTA SCONVOLTA: CACCIA SPIETATA AI RAPITORI 1975
LUIS BACALOV

LA CITTA SI DIFENDE FOUR WAYS OUT 1951
CARLO RUSTICHELLI

LA CIUDAD SAGRADA 1959
LES BAXTER†

LA CLASE OPERAIA VA IN PARADISO LULU THE TOOL 1971
ENNIO MORRICONE

LA CLASSE 1984
STELVIO CIPRIANI

LA CLE SUR LA PORTE THE KEY IS IN THE DOOR 1978
PHILIPPE SARDE

LA CODA DELLO SCORPIONE 1971
BRUNO NICOLAI

LA COLINA DEI COMALI 1979
ANGELA MORLEY

LA COLLINA DEGLI STIVALI 1970
CARLO RUSTICHELLI

L.A. CONFIDENTIAL 1997
JERRY GOLDSMITH

LA CONGIUNTURA 1965
ARMANDO TROVAJOLI

LA CONGIUNTURA Fair Film/Les Films Concordia, 1965
LUIS BACALOV

A LA CONQUETE DU CIEL 1937
DARIUS MILHAUD†

LA CONTESTAZIONE GENERALE 1970
PIERO PICCIONI

LA CONTROFIGURA 1971
ARMANDO TROVAJOLI

LA CORDE RAIDE 1959
MAURICE JARRE

LA CORONDA DI FERRO 1941
ALESSANDRO CICOGNINI†

LA CORTA NOTTE DELLE BAMBOLE DI VETRO 1971
ENNIO MORRICONE

LA COSA BUFFA 1972
ENNIO MORRICONE

LA COUPE A DIX FRANCS THE TWO DOLLAR HAIRCUT 1974
ANTOINE DUHAMEL

LA COURSE DU LIEVRE A TRAVERS LES CHAMPS 20th Century-Fox, 1972
FRANCIS LAI

LA COURSE A L'ECHALOTE WILD GOOSE CHASE 1975
VLADIMIR COSMA

LA CRISE CRISIS-GO-'ROUND 1992
SONIA WIEDER-ATHERTON

LA CROISIERE DU NAVIGATOR 1969
CLAUDE BOLLING

LA CUCCAGNA A GIRL...AND A MILLION 1963
ENNIO MORRICONE

LA CUGINA 1974
ENNIO MORRICONE

LA CUREE Royal Films International, 1966
JEAN BOUCHETY

LA DAMA ROSSA UCCIDE SETTE VOLTE 1972
BRUNO NICOLAI

LA DAME AUX CAMELIAS 1980
ENNIO MORRICONE

LA DAME D'ONZE HEURES 1947
JOSEPH KOSMA†

LA DECADE PRODIGIEUSE Levitt-Pickman, 1971
PIERRE JANSEN

LA DENTELLIERE THE LACEMAKER New Yorker, 1977
PIERRE JANSEN

LA DERNIERE BOURREE A PARIS 1973
VLADIMIR COSMA

LA DEROBADE THE GETAWAY 1979
VLADIMIR COSMA

LA DESCENTE AUX ENFERS 1986
GEORGES DELERUE†

LA DIAGONALE DU FOU Arthur Cohn Productions, 1984
GABRIEL YARED

LA DISCOTECA DEL AMOR Aries Films, 1980
EMILIO KAUDERER

LA DOLCE VITA Astor, 1960
NINO ROTA†

LA DOMENICA DELLA BUONA GENTE 1954
NINO ROTA†

LA DOMENICA SPECIALMENTE ESPECIALLY ON SUNDAY 1991
ENNIO MORRICONE

LA DONNA CHE VENNE DEL MARE 1956
PIERO PICCIONI

LA DONNA DEL FIUME THE WOMAN OF THE RIVER 1954
ANGELO FRANCESCO LAVAGNINO†
ARMANDO TROVAJOLI

LA DONNA DELLA DOMENICA 1975
ENNIO MORRICONE

LA DONNA DELLA MONTAGNA 1943
NINO ROTA†

LA DONNA E UNA COSA MERAVIGLIOSA 1964
CARLO RUSTICHELLI

LA DONNA NEL MONDO 1963
RIZ ORTOLANI

LA DOUBLE VIE DE THEOPHRASTE LONGUET (TF) 1981
VLADIMIR COSMA

LA DOUBLE VIE DE VERONIQUE THE DOUBLE LIFE OF VERONIKA Miramax, 1991
ZBIGNIEW PREISNER

LA DOUCEUR DU VILLAGE (FD) 1964
MICHEL LEGRAND

LA DOVE NON BATTE IL SOLE 1975
CARLO SAVINA

LA FACCIA VIOLENTA DI NEW YORK 1975
RIZ ORTOLANI

LA FAILLE 1974
ENNIO MORRICONE

LA FAMIGLIA BENVENUTI (TF) 1969
ARMANDO TROVAJOLI

LA FASDIZIOSA 1963
CARLO RUSTICHELLI

LA FAUTE DE L'ABBE MOURET 1970
JEAN WIENER†

LA FEMME-ENFANT 1980
VLADIMIR COSMA

LA FEMME-FLIC 1980
PHILIPPE SARDE

LA FEMME DE JEAN JOHN'S WIFE 1973
GEORGES DELERUE†

LA FEMME ET LE PANTIN 1929
GEORGES VAN PARYS†

LA FEMME INFIDELE Allied Artists, 1968
PIERRE JANSEN

LA FEMME NIKITA 1990
ERIC SERRA

LA FETE A HENRIETTE HOLIDAY FOR HENRIETTE 1953
GEORGES AURIC†

LA FIGLIA DEL DIAVOLO 1953
CARLO RUSTICHELLI

LA FILLE AUX YEUX GRIS 1945
JEAN WIENER†

LA FILLE DE D'ARTAGNAN 1994
PHILIPPE SARDE

LA FILLE DE L'AIR 1992
GABRIEL YARED
LA FINESTRA SUL LUNA PARK Noria Film, 1957
PIERO PICCIONI
LA FLUTE A SIX SCHTROUMPFS 1976
MICHEL LEGRAND
LA FOIRE AUX CHIMERES 1946
PAUL MISRAKI
LA FOLLE DE CHAILLOT (TF) 1980
GEORGES DELERUE†
LA FRANCAISE ET L'AMOUR 1960
GEORGES DELERUE†
LA FRECCIA NEL FIANCO 1943
NINO ROTA†
LA FUGA 1964
PIERO PICCIONI
LA FURIE DU DESIR 1975
BRUNO NICOLAI
LA GABBIA 1985
ENNIO MORRICONE
LA GARCONNE 1956
JEAN WIENER†
LA GENERATION DU DESERT 1957
MAURICE JARRE
LA GIFLE 1974
GEORGES DELERUE†
*LA GIORNATA BALORDA/LOVE IS A DAY'S
WORK/PICKUP IN ROME* Continental, 1960
PIERO PICCIONI
LA GLOIRE DE MON PERE *MY FATHER'S
GLORY* 1991
VLADIMIR COSMA
LA GRAND RENDEZ-VOUS 1949
JOSEPH KOSMA†
LA GRANDE BOUFFE ABKCO, 1973
PHILIPPE SARDE
LA GRANDE BOURGEOISE 1974
ENNIO MORRICONE
LA GRANDE DUNE (TF) 1990
JEAN-CLAUDE PETIT
LA GRANDE NOTTE DI RINGO 1966
CARLO RUSTICHELLI
LA GRANDE SCROFA NERA 1971
LUIS BACALOV
LA GRANDE SPERANZA 1954
NINO ROTA†
LA GRANDE VADROUILLE Cinepix, 1966
GEORGES AURIC†
LA GUERRA CONTINUA 1962
ARMANDO TROVAJOLI
LA GUEULE DE L'EMPLOI 1973
VLADIMIR COSMA
LA HORSE 1969
SERGE GAINSBOURG†
LA JAVA DES OMBRES *SHADOW DANCE* 1983
GABRIEL YARED
LA JEUNE FOLLE 1952
PAUL MISRAKI
LA LAMA NEL CORPO 1966
FRANCESCO DE MASI
L.A. LAW (TF) 20th Century Fox TV, 1986
MIKE POST
LA LECON PARTICULIERE French
FRANCIS LAI
LA LETTRE 1938
JEAN WIENER†
LA LIBERTE EN CROUPE 1970
PHILIPPE SARDE
LA LIGNE DE DEMARCATION CCFC, 1966
PIERRE JANSEN
LA LOI C'EST LA LOI 1958
NINO ROTA†
LA LONGUE MARCHE 1966
ANTOINE DUHAMEL
LA LOUVE SOLITAIRE French
FRANCIS LAI
LA LUMIERE DES JUSTES 1979
GEORGES GARVARENTZ†
LA LUNE DANS LE CANIVEAU Triumph/Columbia,
1983
GABRIEL YARED
LA LUNGA NOTTE DEL '43 1960
CARLO RUSTICHELLI
LA MADAMA 1975
MANUEL DE SICA
LA MADRE MUERTA *THE DEAD MOTHER* 1993
BINGEN MENDIZABAL
LA MAESTRA DI SCI 1981
STELVIO CIPRIANI
LA MAIN A COUPER 1974
PAUL MISRAKI
LA MAISON BONNADIEU 1951
GEORGES VAN PARYS†
LA MAISON DES SEPT JEUNES FILLES 1941
GEORGES VAN PARYS†
LA MAISON DU MALTAIS 1937
JACQUES IBERT†
LA MALA ORDINA 1972
ARMANDO TROVAJOLI

LA MALADIE DE HAMBOURG 1978
JEAN-MICHEL JARRE
LA MANDARINE 1971
CLAUDE BOLLING
LA MANE SUL FUCILE 1963
CARLO RUSTICHELLI
LA MANI SPORCHE 1979
ENNIO MORRICONE
LA MANI SULLA CITTA Galatea Film, 1963
PIERO PICCIONI
LA MANO DEL STRANIERO 1952
NINO ROTA†
LA MANO NERA 1973
CARLO RUSTICHELLI
LA MANO SPIETATA DELLA LEGGE 1974
STELVIO CIPRIANI
LA MARIE DU PORT 1949
JOSEPH KOSMA†
LA MARJOLAINE 1965
PAUL MISRAKI
LA MARQUISE DES ANGES 1963
MICHEL MAGNE†
LA MARSEILLAISE 1938
JOSEPH KOSMA†
LA MATRIARCA 1968
ARMANDO TROVAJOLI
LA MEILLEURE FACON DE MARCHER 1975
ALAIN JOMY
LA MEILLEURE PART 1955
PAUL MISRAKI
LA MIA SIGNORA 1964
ARMANDO TROVAJOLI
LA MINA 1957
CARLO RUSTICHELLI
LA MOGLIE PIU BELLA 1970
ENNIO MORRICONE
LA MOGLIE VERGINE 1975
ARMANDO TROVAJOLI
LA MOINE ET LA SORCIERE European Classics,
1987
MICHEL PORTAL
LA MONJA ALFEREZ 1992
ANTTON LARRAURI
LA MORT DE BELLE Trans-Lux, 1961
GEORGES DELERUE†
LA MORT EN DIRECT Quartet, 1980
ANTOINE DUHAMEL
LA MORTE CAMMINA CON I TACCHI ALTI 1971
STELVIO CIPRIANI
LA MORTE SAISON DES AMOUR 1960
GEORGES DELERUE†
LA MORTE SULL' ALTA COLLINA 1969
LUIS BACALOV
LA MORTE VIENE DALLO SPAZIO 1958
CARLO RUSTICHELLI
LA MORTE VIENE DA MANILA 1966
FRANCESCO DE MASI
LA MOUTARDE ME MONTE AU NEZ 1974
VLADIMIR COSMA
LA MURAGLIA CINESE (FD) 1958
ANGELO FRANCESCO LAVAGNINO†
LA NEMICA 1953
CARLO RUSTICHELLI
LA NIPOTE 1975
CARLO SAVINA
LA NIPOTE DEL PRETE 1975
CARLO SAVINA
LA NOIA Embassy, 1964
LUIS BACALOV
LA NOTTE BRAVA *ON ANY STREET/BAD GIRLS
DON'T CRY* Ajace Film/Franco London Film,
1959
PIERO PICCIONI
LA NOTTE DI SAN LORENZO United Artists Classics,
1981
NICOLA PIOVANI
LA NOTTE DEI SERPENTI 1969
ENNIO MORRICONE
LA NOTTE DEI TEDDY-BOYS 1959
ARMANDO TROVAJOLI
LA NOTTE DEL GRANDE ASSALTO 1959
CARLO RUSTICHELLI
LA NOTTE DELL'ULTIMO GIORNO 1973
STELVIO CIPRIANI
LA NOTTE E IL MOMENTO 1995
ENNIO MORRICONE
LA NUIT AMERICAINE Warner Bros., 1973
GEORGES DELERUE†
LA NUIT SACREE *THE SACRED NIGHT* 1993
GORAN BREGOVIC
LA NUORA GIOVANE 1975
CARLO SAVINA
LA ORGIA DE LOS MUERTOS 1971
FRANCESCO DE MASI
LA PACHA 1968
SERGE GAINSBOURG†
LA PALOMA BLANCA *THE WHITE DOVE* 1991
LOUIS BAGUE

LA PALOMBIERE *THE BIRD WATCH* Gaumont,
1983
JEAN MUSY
LA PARMIGIANA 1963
PIERO PICCIONI
LA PART DE L'OMBRE 1945
GEORGES AURIC†
LA PART DU FEU 1977
PAUL MISRAKI
LA PASSANTE 1981
GEORGES DELERUE†
LA PASSION BEATRICE Samuel Goldwyn Co., 1987
LILI BOULANGER
RON CARTER
LA PASTORELLA (TF) Richard Soto Prods./El Teatro
Campasino/WNET/Channel Four, 1991
JOSEPH JULIAN GONZALES
LA PECORA NERA *THE BLACK SHEEP* 1968
LUIS BACALOV
LA PELLE 1981
LALO SCHIFRIN
LA PETITE APOCALYPSE *THE LITTLE
APOCALYPSE* 1993
PHILIPPE SARDE
LA PETITE FEMME DU MOULIN ROUGE 1943
PAUL MISRAKI
LA PETITE FILLE EN VELOURS BLEU 1977
GEORGES DELERUE†
LA PETITE LILI 1929
DARIUS MILHAUD†
LA PETITE SAUVAGE 1933
WERNER R. HEYMANN†
LA PETITE VERTU 1967
GEORGES DELERUE†
LA PIOVRA 5 (TF) 1990
ENNIO MORRICONE
LA PISCINE 1968
MICHEL LEGRAND
LA PIU BELLA SERATA DELLA MIA VITA 1977
ARMANDO TROVAJOLI
LA PLANETE SAUVAGE 1972
ALAIN GORRAGUER
LA POLIZIA E AL SERVIZIO DEL CITTADINO?
1973
LUIS BACALOV
LA POLIZIA RINGRAZIA 1972
STELVIO CIPRIANI
LA PORTA DEL CANNONE 1969
CARLO RUSTICHELLI
LA PREDA E L'AVVOLTOIO 1972
BRUNO NICOLAI
LA PRESIDENTESSA 1952
CARLO RUSTICHELLI
LA PRIMA NOTTE DEL DOTTOR DANIELI,
INDUSTRIALE, COL COMPLESSO
DEL...GIOCATTOLO 1970
RIZ ORTOLANI
LA PROFANAZIONE 1974
CARLO SAVINA
LA PROPRIETA NON PIU UN FURTO 1973
ENNIO MORRICONE
LA PROVINCIALE 1953
FRANCO MANNINO
LA PUPEE 1962
JOSEPH KOSMA†
LA PUTAIN RESPECTUEUSE *THE RESPECTFUL
PROSTITUTE* 1952
GEORGES AURIC†
LA QUESTION 1977
ANTOINE DUHAMEL
LA RACE DES SEIGNEURS 1974
PHILIPPE SARDE
LA RAFLE EST POUR CE SOIR 1953
JEAN WIENER†
LA RAGAZZA E IL GENERALE 1967
ENNIO MORRICONE
LA RAGAZZA IN PRESTITO 1964
ARMANDO TROVAJOLI
LA RAGAZZA CHE SAPEVE TROPPO American
International, 1963
LES BAXTER†
LA RAGAZZA DI MILLE MESI 1961
ARMANDO TROVAJOLI
LA RAGAZZA DI TRIESTE 1983
RIZ ORTOLANI
LA RAGAZZA DI VIA MILLE LIRE 1980
LUIS BACALOV
LA RAGAZZA SOTTO IL LENZUOLO 1961
CARLO SAVINA
LA RAISON DU PLUS FOU 1972
VLADIMIR COSMA
LA RAISON D'ETAT *STATE REASONS* 1978
VLADIMIR COSMA
LA REGAZZA DI LATTA 1970
NICOLA PIOVANI
LA REGINA DI SABA 1952
NINO ROTA†
LA REINE MARGOT 1954
PAUL MISRAKI
LA REINE MARGOT Miramax, 1994
GORAN BREGOVIC

LA RENDEZ-VOUS DE MINUIT 1962
GEORGES AURIC†
LA RESA DEI CONTI 1966
ENNIO MORRICONE
LA REVOLUTION D'OCTOBRE 1968
JEAN WIENER†
LA RIBELLE *THE REBEL* 1993
CARLO CRIVELLI
LA RISAIA 1955
ANGELO FRANCESCO LAVAGNINO†
LA RIVALE *MY HUSBAND, HIS MISTRESS AND
I* 1974
VLADIMIR COSMA
LA RIVIERE DU HIBOU 1961
HENRI LANOE
LA ROMANA 1988
GABRIEL YARED
LA RONDE Continental, 1964
FRANCIS LAI
MICHEL MAGNE†
LA ROSA ROSSA *THE RED ROSE* 1973
LUIS BACALOV
LA ROUE 1922
ARTHUR HONEGGER†
LA ROUTE DE CORINTHE CCFC, 1967
PIERRE JANSEN
LA ROUTE DE SALINA 1970
MICHEL MAGNE†
LA ROUTE HEUREUSE 1935
GEORGES VAN PARYS†
LA ROUTE NAPOLEON 1953
PAUL MISRAKI
LA RUMBA Hachette Premiere/UIP, 1987
CLAUDE BOLLING
LA RUPTURE New Line Cinema, 1970
PIERRE JANSEN
LA SCARLATINE UGC, 1984
GABRIEL YARED
LA SCHIAVA DI ROMA 1960
ARMANDO TROVAJOLI
LA SCORTA *THE BODYGUARDS* 1993
ENNIO MORRICONE
LA SEDUZIONE *SEDUCTION* Gemini, 1973
LUIS BACALOV
LA SERVANTE (TF) 1978
VLADIMIR COSMA
LA SFIDA DI MACKENNA 1969
BRUNO NICOLAI
LA SIGNORA DI TUTTI 1934
DANIELE AMFITHEATROF†
LA SMANIA ADOSSO 1962
CARLO RUSTICHELLI
LA SOIF DE L'OR *THE THIRST FOR GOLD* 1993
VLADIMIR COSMA
LA SPIAGGIA 1954
PIERO PICCIONI
LA STAGIONE DEI SENSI 1969
ENNIO MORRICONE
LA STORIA DEL TERZO REICH (TD) 1971
DANIELE PARIS
L.A. STORY Tri-Star, 1991
PETER RODGERS MELNICK
LA STRADA Trans-Lux, 1954
NINO ROTA†
LA STREGA IN AMORE Arco Film, 1966
LUIS BACALOV
LA SUPERTESTIMONE 1971
LUIS BACALOV
LA SUPPLENTE VA IN CITTA 1979
STELVIO CIPRIANI
LA SURPRISE DU CHEF 1975
VLADIMIR COSMA
LA SYMPHONIE PASTORALE 1948
GEORGES AURIC†
L.A. TAKEDOWN (TF) AJAR/Mories Film
Productions, 1989
BASIL POLEDOURIS
TIM TRUMAN
LA TARANTOLA DAL VENTRO NERO *THE BLACK
BELLY OF THE TARANTULA* 1971
ENNIO MORRICONE
LA TECNICA E IL RITO 1975
FRANCESCO DE MASI
LA TERRAZZA United Artists, 1980
ARMANDO TROVAJOLI
LA TETE CONTRE LES MURS 1958
MAURICE JARRE
LA TIGRE DEI SETTE MARI 1962
CARLO RUSTICHELLI
LA TOTALE! *THE JACKPOT!* 1992
VLADIMIR COSMA
LA TRACE Fox-Hachette, 1984
MARC PERRONE
NICOLA PIOVANI
LA TRAGEDIE IMPERIALE 1938
DARIUS MILHAUD†
LA TRATTA DELLE BIANCHE *GIRLS MARKED
FOR DANGER* 1952
ARMANDO TROVAJOLI

LA TRUITE *THE TROUT* Gaumont, 1982
RICHARD HARTLEY

LA VACANZA Lion Film, 1972
FIORENZO CARPI

LA VALISE 1973
PHILIPPE SARDE

LA VALLE DELL'ECO TONANTE 1964
CARLO RUSTICHELLI

LA VEDOVA DEL TRULLO 1979
STELVIO CIPRIANI

LA VELA INCANTATA 1982
NICOLA PIOVANI

LA VENA D'ORO Athena Cinematografica, 1955
CARLO RUSTICHELLI

LA VENDETTA DEL CORSARO 1951
CARLO RUSTICHELLI

LA VENERE DEI PIRATI 1960
CARLO RUSTICHELLI

LA VENERE DI CHERONEA 1957
MICHEL MICHELET†

LA VERGINE MODERNA 1954
NINO ROTA†

LA VEUVE COUDERC 1972
PHILIPPE SARDE

LA VIA DEI BABBUINI 1974
ARMANDO TROVAJOLI

LA VIA LACTEA *THE MILKY WAY* 1993
MARIO DE BENITO

LA VIACCIA Embassy, 1960
PIERO PICCIONI

LA VICTOIRE EN CHANTANT Allied Artists, 1978
PIERRE BACHELET

LA VIDA Jeffrey Penichet, 1976
ROCKY DAVIS

LA VIE COMMENCE DEMAIN 1950
DARIUS MILHAUD†

LA VIE CONTINUE Triumph/Columbia, 1982
GEORGES DELERUE†

LA VIE DE CHATEAU 1965
MICHEL LEGRAND

LA VIE DEVANT SOI Atlantic Releasing Corporation, 1978
PHILIPPE SARDE

LA VIE DRAMATIQUE DE MAURICE UTRILLO 1950
GEORGES VAN PARYS†

LA VIE EN ROSE 1947
GEORGES VAN PARYS†

LA VIE EST BELLE 1956
JEAN WIENER†

LA VIE ET RIEN D'AUTRE UGC, 1989
OSWALD D'ANDREA

LA VIEREE SUPERBE 1973
VLADIMIR COSMA

LA VIOLENZA: QUINTO POTERE 1971
ENNIO MORRICONE

LA VISITA 1963
ARMANDO TROVAJOLI

LA VITA, A VOLTE, E MOLTO DURO NEL WEST, VERO PROVVIDENZA? 1972
ENNIO MORRICONE

LA VITA E BELLA 1980
ARMANDO TROVAJOLI

LA VITA IN GIOCO 1973
NICOLA PIOVANI

LA VITA INTERIORE 1980
PINO DONAGGIO

LA VITTIMA DESIGNATA 1971
LUIS BACALOV

LA VOCE 1982
STELVIO CIPRIANI

LA VOGLIE MATTA 1962
ENNIO MORRICONE

LA VOIX *THE VOICE* 1992
PHILIPPE SARDE

LA VOYAGEUR DE LA TOUSSAINT 1942
JEAN WIENER†

L.A. WARS American Cinema, 1993
LOUIS FEBRE

LA ZIZANIE 1978
VLADIMIR COSMA

LAAT DE DOCKTER MAAR SCHUIVEN! 1980
VLADIMIR COSMA

LABBRA DI LURIDO BLU 1975
ENNIO MORRICONE

L'ABOMINABLE GOMME DES DOUANES 1962
GEORGES DELERUE†

LABOR OF LOVE: THE ARLETTE SCHWEITZER STORY (TF) Lauren Film/KLM, 1993
FRED KARLIN

LABYRINTH 1992
LUBOS FISER

LABYRINTH Tri-Star, 1986
TREVOR JONES

LAC AUX DAMES 1934
GEORGES AURIC†

LACE (MS) Lorimar Productions, 1984
NICK BICAT

LACE II (TF) Lorimar Productions, 1985
NICK BICAT

THE LACEMAKER New Yorker, 1977
PIERRE JANSEN

L'ACROBATE 1975
ANTOINE DUHAMEL

LACY AND THE MISSISSIPPI QUEEN (TF) Lawrence Gordon Productions/Paramount Pictures TV, 1978
BARRY DEVORZON

LAD: A DOG Warner Bros., 1961
HEINZ ROEMHELD†

LADDER OF SWORDS Film Four International, 1989
STANLEY MYERS†

LADDIE RKO Radio, 1935
MAX STEINER†
ROY WEBB†

L'ADDITION *THE CAGED HEART* New World, 1985
JEAN-CLAUDE PETIT

LADIES COURAGEOUS Universal, 1944
DIMITRI TIOMKIN†

LADIES' DAY RKO Radio, 1943
ROY WEBB†

LADIES IN LOVE 20th Century-Fox, 1936
LOUIS SILVERS†

LADIES IN RETIREMENT Columbia, 1941
ERNST TOCH ★

LADIES OF THE JURY RKO Radio, 1932
MAX STEINER†

LADIES OF WASHINGTON 20th Century-Fox, 1944
CYRIL J. MOCKRIDGE†

THE LADIES (TF) NBC, 1987
MORTON STEVENS†

THE LADIES CLUB New Line Cinema, 1986
LALO SCHIFRIN

THE LADIES' MAN Paramount, 1961
WALTER SCHARF

LADIES WHO DO Fanfare/Continental, 1963
RON GOODWIN

L'ADOLESCENTE 1978
PHILIPPE SARDE

LADRI DI BICICLETTE Mayer-Burstyn, 1949
ALESSANDRO CICOGNINI†

LADY AGAINST THE ODDS (TF) Robert Greenwald Prods., 1992
JOEL MCNEELY

LADY AND THE TRAMP (AF) Buena Vista, 1955
OLIVER WALLACE†

LADY AT MIDNIGHT Eagle Lion, 1948
LEO ERDODY†

THE LADY AND THE BANDIT Columbia, 1951
GEORGE DUNING

THE LADY AND THE HIGHWAYMAN (TF) Lord Grade Productions/Gainsborough Pictures, 1989
LAURIE JOHNSON

THE LADY AND THE MONSTER Republic, 1944
WALTER SCHARF

LADY AVENGER Marco Colombo, 1989
JAY LEVY

LADY BE GOOD MGM, 1941
GEORGE BASSMAN

LADY BEWARE Scotti Brothers, 1987
CRAIG SAFAN

LADY BLUE (TF) David Gerber Productions Productions/MGM-UA TV, 1985
JOHN CACAVAS

LADY CAROLINE LAMB United Artists, 1973
RICHARD RODNEY BENNETT

LADY CHATTERLEY Global Arts/London Films/BBC, 1993
JEAN-CLAUDE PETIT

LADY CHATTERLEY'S LOVER Cannon, 1982
STANLEY MYERS†

THE LADY CONSENTS RKO Radio, 1936
ROY WEBB†

THE LADY EVE Paramount, 1941
LEO SHUKEN†

LADY FOR A NIGHT Republic, 1942
DAVID BUTTOLPH†

THE LADY FORGETS (TF) Leonard Hill Films, 1989
WALTER MURPHY

THE LADY FROM CHEYENNE Universal, 1941
FRANK SKINNER†

THE LADY FROM KENTUCKY United Artists, 1939
LEO SHUKEN†

THE LADY FROM SHANGHAI Columbia, 1948
HEINZ ROEMHELD†

THE LADY FROM YESTERDAY (TF) Barry Weitz Films/Comworld Productions, 1985
MARK SNOW

LADY GODIVA Universal, 1956
HANS J. SALTER†

LADY GREY Maverick Pictures, 1980
ARTHUR SMITH
CLAY SMITH

THE LADY GAMBLES Universal, 1949
FRANK SKINNER†

LADY HAMILTON United Artists, 1941
MIKLOS ROZSA†

THE LADY HAS PLANS Paramount, 1942
LEIGH HARLINE†
LEO SHUKEN†

LADY ICE National General, 1973
PERRY BOTKIN

LADY IN A CAGE United Artists, 1964
PAUL GLASS

LADY IN A CORNER (TF) Fries Entertainment, 1989
DAVID RAKSIN

LADY IN A JAM Universal, 1942
FRANK SKINNER†

LADY IN THE DARK Paramount, 1944
ROBERT EMMETT DOLAN† ★

LADY IN THE IRON MASK 20th Century-Fox, 1952
DIMITRI TIOMKIN†

THE LADY IN QUESTION Columbia, 1940
LUCIEN MORAWECK†

THE LADY IN RED New World, 1979
JAMES HORNER

THE LADY IN THE CAR WITH GLASSES AND A GUN Columbia, 1970
MICHEL LEGRAND

THE LADY IN WHITE New Century Vista, 1988
FRANK LALOGGIA

THE LADY IS WILLING Columbia, 1942
W. FRANKE HARLING†

LADY JANE Paramount, 1986
STEPHEN OLIVER

LADY KILLER (TF) Kushner-Locke/CBS Entertainment, 1995
MICKEY ERBE
MARYBETH SOLOMON

THE LADY KILLER OF ROME Manson, 1961
PIERO PICCIONI

LADY L MGM, 1965
JEAN WIENER†

LADY LUCK RKO Radio, 1946
LEIGH HARLINE†

LADY MOBSTER (TF) Danjul Films/Frank von Zerneck Productions, 1988
FRED KARLIN

LADY OF SECRETS Columbia, 1936
WILLIAM GRANT STILL†

LADY OF THE HOUSE (TF) Metromedia Productions, 1978
FRED KARLIN

LADY OF THE TROPICS MGM, 1939
FRANZ WAXMAN†

LADY ON A TRAIN Universal, 1945
MIKLOS ROZSA†

THE LADY OBJECTS Columbia, 1938
SIDNEY CUTNER†

LADY PANAME 1949
GEORGES VAN PARYS†

THE LADY PAYS OFF Universal, 1951
FRANK SKINNER†

LADY SINGS THE BLUES Paramount, 1972
MICHEL LEGRAND

THE LADY SAYS NO United Artists, 1951
EMIL NEWMAN†

A LADY TAKES A CHANCE RKO Radio, 1943
ROY WEBB†

THE LADY TAKES A FLYER Universal, 1958
HERMAN STEIN

THE LADY TAKES A SAILOR Warner Bros., 1949
MAX STEINER†

THE LADY VANISHES Rank, 1979
RICHARD HARTLEY

A LADY WITHOUT PASSPORT MGM, 1950
DAVID RAKSIN

LADY WITH RED HAIR Warner Bros., 1940
HEINZ ROEMHELD†

THE LADY WITH THE LAMP British Lion, 1951
ANTHONY COLLINS†

LADYBIRD LADYBIRD 1994
GEORGE FENTON

LADYBIRD LADYBIRD British, 1994
MAURICIO VENEGAS

LADYBUG, LADYBUG United Artists, 1963
BOB COBERT

LADYBUGS Paramount, 1992
RICHARD GIBBS

LADYHAWKE Warner Bros., 1985
ANDREW POWELL

LADYKILLER (TF) MTE, 1992
PHILIP GIFFIN

THE LADYKILLERS Continental, 1956
TRISTRAM CARY

A LADY'S MORALS MGM, 1930
HERBERT STOTHART†

LAFAYETTE ESCADRILLE Warner Bros., 1958
LEONARD ROSENMAN

L'AFFAIRE CRAZY CAPO 1973
VLADIMIR COSMA

L'AFFAIRE DOMINICI 1972
ALAIN GORRAGUER

L'AFFAIRE LAFARGE 1936
GEORGES AURIC†

L'AFFAIRE MANET 1951
GEORGES VAN PARYS†

L'AFFAIRE MAURIZIUS New Realm, 1953
GEORGES VAN PARYS†

L'AFFAIRE NINA B 1962
GEORGES DELERUE†

L'AFRICAIN Renn Productions, 1982
GEORGES DELERUE†

L'AGE INGRAT 1964
GEORGES DELERUE†

L'AGNESE VA A MORIRE 1976
ENNIO MORRICONE

LAGUNA HEAT (CTF) HBO Pictures/Jay Weston Productions, 1987
PATRICK WILLIAMS

L'AIGLE A DEUX TETES *EAGLE WITH TWO HEADS* 1948
GEORGES AURIC†

L'AILE OU LA CUISSE 1976
VLADIMIR COSMA

L'AINE DES FERCHAUX 1962
GEORGES DELERUE†

THE LAIR OF THE WHITE WORM Vestron, 1988
STANISLAS SYREWICZ

LAKE CONSEQUENCE (CTF) 10dB, 1993
GEORGE S. CLINTON

LAKE PLACID SERENADE Republic, 1944
WALTER SCHARF

THE LAKER GIRLS (TF) Viacom Productions/Finnegan-Pinchuk Co./Valente-Hamilton Productions, 1990
SYLVESTER LEVAY

LAKOTA WOMAN: SIEGE AT WOUNDED KNEE (CTF) Fonda Films, 1994
RICHARD HOROWITZ

L'ALBERO DALLE FOGLIE ROSA 1974
FRANCO MICALIZZI

L'ALIBI 1938
GEORGES AURIC†

L'ALPAGUEUR 1975
MICHEL COLOMBIER

L'ALPIN L'E SEMPRE QUEL 1972
BRUNO NICOLAI

L'AMANT MGM, 1992
GABRIEL YARED

L'AMANT DE LADY CHATTERLEY 1955
JOSEPH KOSMA†

LAMB Limehouse/Flickers/Channel Four, 1985
VAN MORRISON

LAMBADA Warner Bros., 1990
GREG DE BELLES

LAMBADA, THE FORBIDDEN DANCE Columbia, 1990
BOB MITHOFF

LAMERICA 1994
FRANCO PIERSANTI

L'AMERICAIN SE DETEND (TF) 1958
MICHEL LEGRAND

L'AMERIQUE INSOLITE (FD) 1960
MICHEL LEGRAND

L'AMERIQUE LUNAIRE (FD) 1962
MICHEL LEGRAND

L'AMICA Fair Film, 1969
LUIS BACALOV

L'AMOUR A LA CHAINE 1964
GEORGES DELERUE†

L'AMOUR A MORT Roissy Film, 1984
HANS WERNER HENZE

L'AMOUR AUTOUR DE LA MAISON 1946
JOSEPH KOSMA†

L'AMOUR BRAQUE 1985
STANISLAS SYREWICZ

THE LAMP TMS Pictures, 1987
JOEL ROSENBAUM

L'AN 2000 1966
MICHEL LEGRAND

LANCELOT AND GUINEVERE Universal, 1963
RON GOODWIN

LANCELOT OF THE LAKE New Yorker, 1975
PHILIPPE SARDE

LAND AND FREEDOM 1995
GEORGE FENTON

THE LAND BEFORE TIME (AF) Universal, 1988
JAMES HORNER

LAND OF DOOM Manson/Maris, 1985
MARK GOVERNOR

LAND OF FURY 1955
WILLIAM ALWYN†

LAND OF MILK & HONEY 1995
CHRISTOPHER HEDGE

LAND OF PROMISE 1975
WOJCIECH KILAR

LAND OF THE MINOTAUR *THE DEVIL'S MEN* 1976
BRIAN ENO

LAND OF THE PHARAOHS Warner Bros., 1955
DIMITRI TIOMKIN†

THE LAND OF NO RETURN International Picture Show, 1981
RALPH GEDDES

LAND RAIDERS 1969
BRUNO NICOLAI

THE LAND THAT TIME FORGOT American International, 1975
DOUGLAS GAMLEY

THE LAND UNKNOWN Universal, 1957
HENRY MANCINI†
HEINZ ROEMHELD†
HANS J. SALTER†
HERMAN STEIN

LANDRU Embassy, 1963
PIERRE JANSEN

LANDSLIDE HBO, 1992
BOB MITHOFF

LANGER GANG *PASSAGES* Wild Okapi Film, 1993 German
RALPH GRAF

THE LANGOLIERS (TF) Laurel-King Prods., 1995
VLADIMIR HORUNZHY

LANGUAGE OF THE HEART (CTF) Showtime, 1995
HUMMIE MANN

LANIGAN'S RABBI (TF) Hayday Productions/Universal TV, 1976
LEONARD ROSENMAN

L'ANIMAL *THE ANIMAL* 1977
VLADIMIR COSMA

L'ANNEE PROCHAINE, SI TOUT VA BIEN 1981
VLADIMIR COSMA

L'ANNEE SAINTE *SAINT ANNE* 1976
CLAUDE BOLLING

LANTERN HILL (TF) Lantern Hill/Disney Channel/CBC/WonderWorks/CPB/Telefilm Canada, 1991
JOHN WELSMAN

L'ANTICRISTO 1974
ENNIO MORRICONE

L'ANTICRISTO *ANTICHRIST/THE TEMPTER* 1974
BRUNO NICOLAI

L'ANTIMIRACOLO 1964
CARLO RUSTICHELLI

L'APOCALYPSE DES ANIMAUX 1970
VANGELIS

L'APPAT *FRESH BAIT* 1995
PHILIPPE HAIM

A LAPSE OF MEMORY 1991
ALEXANDRE DESPLAT

L'ARBRE, LE MAIRE ET LA MEDIATHEQUE *THE TREE, THE MAYOR AND THE MEDIATHEQUE* 1993
SEBASTIEN ERMS

LARCENY Universal, 1948
LEITH STEVENS†

LARCENY, INC. Warner Bros., 1942
ADOLPH DEUTSCH†

LARCENY IN HER HEART Producers Releasing Corp., 1946
LEO ERDODY†

L'ARCHE DE NOE 1946
JOSEPH KOSMA†

L'ARCHE ET LES DELUGES 1992
GABRIEL YARED

L'ARCHITECTE MAUDIT 1955
GEORGES VAN PARYS†

L'ARCODIAVOLO 1966
ARMANDO TROVAJOLI

LARGER THAN LIFE MGM-UA, 1996
MILES GOODMAN†

L'ARMATA BRANCALEONE Fair Film, 1966
CARLO RUSTICHELLI

L'ARME A GAUCHE 1965
MICHEL COLOMBIER

L'ARMOIRE VOLANTE 1948
GEORGES VAN PARYS†

LARRY (TF) Tomorrow Entertainment, 1974
PETER MATZ

L'ART D'AIMER Parafrance, 1983
LUIS BACALOV

L'AS DES AS *ACE OF ACES* Gaumont/Cerito Rene Chateau, 1982
VLADIMIR COSMA

LAS VEGAS LADY Crown International, 1976
ALAN SILVESTRI

THE LAS VEGAS STORY RKO Radio, 1952
LEIGH HARLINE†

LAS VIERNES DE LA ETERNIDAD 1982
LALO SCHIFRIN

LASERBLAST Irwin Yablans, 1978
RICHARD H. BAND
JOEL GOLDSMITH

THE LASERMAN Peter Wang Films/Hong Kong Film Workshop, 1988
MASON DARING

L'ASSASSIN CONNAIT LA MUSIQUE 1963
PAUL MISRAKI

L'ASSASSINO *THE LADY KILLER OF ROME* Manson, 1961
PIERO PICCIONI

L'ASSASSINO E AL TELEFONO 1972
STELVIO CIPRIANI

L'ASSASSINO HA RISERVATO 9 POLTRONE 1974
CARLO SAVINA

LASSIE Paramount, 1994
BASIL POLEDOURIS

LASSIE COME HOME MGM, 1943
DANIELE AMFITHEATROF†

LASSITER Warner Bros., 1984
KEN THORNE

L'ASSOLUTO NATURALE *SHE AND HE* 1969
ENNIO MORRICONE

THE LAST ACTION HERO Columbia, 1993
MICHAEL KAMEN

THE LAST AMERICAN HERO 20th Century Fox, 1973
CHARLES FOX

THE LAST ANGRY MAN (TF) The Jozak Company/Screen Gems/Columbia Pictures TV, 1974
GIL MELLE

THE LAST BORDER 1993
ANSSI TIKANMAKI

THE LAST BOY SCOUT Warner Bros., 1991
MICHAEL KAMEN

THE LAST BULLET (TF) 1995, Japanese, Australian
NERIDA TYSON-CHEW

THE LAST BUTTERFLY 1990
ALEX NORTH†

LAST CALL AT MAUD'S (FD) The Maud's Project, 1993
TIM HORRIGAN

A LAST CRY FOR HELP (TF) Myrt-Hal Productions/Viacom Productions, 1979
MILES GOODMAN†

THE LAST CHALLENGE MGM, 1967
RICHARD SHORES

THE LAST CHASE Crown International, 1981
GIL MELLE

THE LAST CHILD (TF) Aaron Spelling Productions, 1971
LAURENCE ROSENTHAL

THE LAST COMMAND Republic, 1955
MAX STEINER†

THE LAST CONVERTIBLE (MS) Roy Huggins Productions/Universal TV, 1979
PETE RUGOLO ☆

LAST DANCE Buena Vista, 1996
MARK ISHAM

THE LAST DANCE *DAIBYONIN* 1995
TOSHIYUKI HONDA

THE LAST DAY (TF) C Lyles Productions/Paramount Pictures TV, 1975
CARMINE COPPOLA†

THE LAST DAYS OF CHEZ NOUS 1992
PAUL GRABOWSKY

THE LAST DAYS OF DOLWYN *WOMAN OF DOLWYN* 1948
JOHN GREENWOOD†

THE LAST DAYS OF FRANK AND JESSE JAMES (TF) Joseph Cates Productions, 1986
PAUL CHIHARA

THE LAST DAYS OF FRANKIE THE FLY Millenium Pictures, 1997
GEORGE S. CLINTON

THE LAST DAYS OF MUSSOLINI *MUSSOLINI: ULTIMO ATTO* Paramount, 1974
ENNIO MORRICONE

THE LAST DAYS OF PATTON (TF) Entertainment Partners, 1986
ALLYN FERGUSON☆

THE LAST DAYS OF POMPEII RKO Radio, 1935
ROY WEBB†

THE LAST DAYS OF POMPEII United Artists, 1960
ANGELO FRANCESCO LAVAGNINO†

THE LAST DAYS OF POMPEII (MS) David Gerber Company/Columbia TV/Centerpoint Films/RAI, 1984
TREVOR JONES

THE LAST DETAIL Columbia, 1973
JOHNNY MANDEL

THE LAST DINOSAUR (TF) Rankin-Bass Productions, 1977
MAURY LAWS

THE LAST DRAGON Tri-Star, 1985
MISHA SEGAL

LAST EMBRACE United Artists, 1979
MIKLOS ROZSA†

THE LAST ELECTRIC KNIGHT (TF) Walt Disney Productions, 1986
DAVID KURTZ

THE LAST ELEPHANT (TF) RHI/Qunitex, 1990
CHARLES BERNSTEIN

THE LAST EMPEROR Columbia, 1987
DAVID BYRNE ★★
RYUICHI SAKAMOTO ★★
CONG SU ★★

LAST EXIT TO BROOKLYN Cinecom, 1990
MARK KNOPFLER

LAST FLIGHT OUT (TF) The Mannheim Co./Co-Star Entertainment/NBC Productions, 1990
CHRISTOPHER YOUNG ☆

THE LAST FIGHT Marvin Films, 1983
JAY CHATTAWAY

THE LAST FIVE DAYS OF PEACE 1969
ENNIO MORRICONE

THE LAST FLIGHT OF NOAH'S ARK Buena Vista, 1980
MAURICE JARRE

THE LAST FLING (TF) Leonard Hill Films, 1987
CHARLES BERNSTEIN

THE LAST FRONTIER Columbia, 1956
LEIGH HARLINE†

THE LAST FRONTIER (TF) McElroy & McElroy Productions, 1986
BRIAN MAY†

THE LAST GANGSTER MGM, 1937
EDWARD WARD†

THE LAST GENTLEMAN United Artists, 1934
ALFRED NEWMAN†

THE LAST GIRAFFE Westfall Productions, 1979
FRED KARLIN

THE LAST GOOD TIME Samuel Goldwyn, 1995
JONATHAN TUNICK

THE LAST GRENADE Cinerama Releasing Corporation, 1970
JOHN DANKWORTH

LAST HOLIDAY 1950
FRANCES CHAGRIN†

LAST HOURS BEFORE MORNING (TF) Charles Fries Productions/MGM Television, 1975
PETE RUGOLO

LAST HOUSE ON THE LEFT Hallmark Releasing Corporation, 1973
DAVID ALEX HESS

THE LAST HARD MEN 20th Century-Fox, 1976
JERRY GOLDSMITH

THE LAST HIT (CTF) Garson Studios/MTE, 1993
GARY CHANG

THE LAST HORROR FILM Shere Productions, 1984
UDI HARPAZ

THE LAST HORROR FILM *FANATIC* Twin Continental, 1982
UDI HARPAZ

THE LAST HUNT MGM, 1956
DANIELE AMFITHEATROF†

THE LAST HUNTER *HUNTER OF THE APOCALYPSE* World Northal, 1980
FRANCO MICALIZZI

THE LAST HURRAH (TF) O'Connor-Becker Productions/Columbia TV, 1977
PETER MATZ

LAST IMAGES OF THE SHIPWRECK Enrique Marti, Films Cinequanon SRL, 1989
PEDRO AZNAR

THE LAST INNOCENT MAN (CTF) HBO Pictures/Maurice Singer Productions, 1987
BRAD FIEDEL

THE LAST JOB Northern Drive PRods., 1995
ALEX SHAPIRO

LAST JUDGEMENT 1965
TORU TAKEMITSU†

LAST LIGHT (CTF) 1993
JUDD COLE

LAST LIVES Promark, 1997
GREG EDMONSON

LAST MAN STANDING New Line, 1996
RY COODER

LAST MAN STANDING PM Entertainment, 1995
LOUIS FEBRE

THE LAST MAN ON EARTH 1964
PAUL SAWTELL†
BERT A. SHEFTER

THE LAST MARRIED COUPLE IN AMERICA Universal, 1980
CHARLES FOX

THE LAST MERCENARY 1969
BRUNO NICOLAI

THE LAST METRO United Artists Classics, 1980
GEORGES DELERUE†

LAST NIGHT AT THE ALAMO Alamo Films, 1983
WAYNE BELL
CHUCK PINNELL

THE LAST NINJA (TF) Paramount TV, 1983
BOB COBERT

LAST OF THE BUCCANEERS Columbia, 1950
MISCHA BAKALEINIKOFF†

LAST OF THE COMANCHES Columbia, 1953
GEORGE DUNING

LAST OF THE DOGMEN Savoy, 1995
DAVID ARNOLD

LAST OF THE FAST GUNS *THE WESTERN STORY* Universal, 1958
HERMAN STEIN

LAST OF THE GREAT SURVIVORS (TF) CBS Entertainment, 1984
ARTIE BUTLER

LAST OF THE MOBILE HOT-SHOTS Warner Bros., 1970
QUINCY JONES

LAST OF THE RED HOT LOVERS Paramount, 1972
NEAL HEFTI

LAST OF THE WILD HORSES Lippert, 1948
ALBERT GLASSER

THE LAST OF HIS TRIBE (CTF) River City Prods., 1992
JOHN E. KEANE

THE LAST OF MRS. CHEYNEY MGM, 1937
WILLIAM AXT†

THE LAST OF PHILIP BANTER Tesauro, 1986
PHIL MARSHALL

THE LAST OF SHEILA Warner Bros., 1973
BILLY GOLDENBERG

THE LAST OF THE COWBOYS Dimension, 1976
CRAIG SAFAN

THE LAST OF THE FINEST Orion, 1990
JACK NITZCHE

THE LAST OF THE GOOD GUYS (TF) Columbia TV, 1978
DANA KAPROFF

THE LAST OF THE KNUCKLEMEN Hexagon, 1978
BRUCE SMEATON

THE LAST OF THE MOHICANS 1965
PETER THOMAS

THE LAST OF THE MOHICANS 20th Century Fox, 1992
TREVOR JONES
RANDY EDELMAN

THE LAST OF THE MOHICANS United Artists, 1936
NATHANIEL SHILKRET†
ROY WEBB†

THE LAST OF THE MOHICANS (TF) Schick Sunn Classics Productions, 1977
ROBERT SUMMERS

THE LAST OF THE PAGANS MGM, 1935
WILLIAM AXT†
MILAN RODER†

THE LAST OUTLAW (CTF) Davis Entertainment, 1993
MASON DARING

THE LAST OUTLAW (MS) Network Seven/Pegasus Productions, 1980
BRIAN MAY†

THE LAST OUTPOST Paramount, 1935
MILAN RODER†

THE LAST P.O.W.?: THE BOBBY GARWOOD STORY (TF) EMR Prods./Nexus/Fries, 1993
MARK SNOW

LAST PAIR OUT 1956
ERIC NORDGREN

THE LAST PARADISE (FD) 1957
ANGELO FRANCESCO LAVAGNINO†

THE LAST PICNIC 1983
HARRY MANFREDINI

THE LAST PLACE ON EARTH (MS) Central Productions/Renegade Films, 1985
TREVOR JONES

THE LAST PRECINCT (TF) Stephen J. Cannell Productions, 1986
PETE CARPENTER†
MIKE POST

THE LAST PROSTITUTE (CTF) Wilshire Court/BBK Productions/Carmen Culver Films, 1991
FRED KARLIN

LAST RESORT Concorde, 1986
STEVE NELSON
THOM SHARP

LAST RITES MGM/UA, 1988
BRUCE BROUGHTON

LAST RITES *DRACULA'S LAST RITES* Cannon, 1980
PAUL JOST
GEORGE SMALL

THE LAST REMAKE OF BEAU GESTE Universal, 1977
JOHN MORRIS

THE LAST RESORT Dayton Productions, 1997
RICHARD MARVIN

THE LAST RIDE (CTF) Fitzgerald/Hartley Films, 1988
JAMES WESLEY STEMPLE

THE LAST RIDE OF THE DALTON GANG (TF) NBC Productions/Dan Curtis Productions, 1979
BOB COBERT

THE LAST RIDERS PM, 1991
JOHN GONZALEZ

THE LAST ROUND 1976
LUIS BACALOV

THE LAST RUN MGM, 1971
JERRY GOLDSMITH

LAST SONG 1993
NICKY HOPKINS

THE LAST SAFARI Paramount, 1967
JOHN DANKWORTH

THE LAST SEDUCTION (CTF) also released theatrically, ITC, 1994
JOSEPH VITARELLI

THE LAST SHOT YOU HEAR 20th Century-Fox, 1969
BERT A. SHEFTER

THE LAST SONG (TF) Ron Samuels Productions/Motown Productions, 1980
JOHNNY HARRIS

THE LAST STARFIGHTER Universal, 1984
CRAIG SAFAN

LA - LE

'97-'98
FILM
COMPOSERS
INDEX

FILM TITLES

323

THE LAST SUNSET Universal, 1961
ERNEST GOLD

THE LAST SUPPER Sony Classics, 1996
MARK MOTHERSBAUGH

THE LAST SURVIVORS (TF) Bob Banner Associates, 1975
MICHAEL MELVOIN

LAST STOP ON THE NIGHT TRAIN L'ULTIMO TRENO DELLA NOTTE 1974
ENNIO MORRICONE

LAST TANGO IN PARIS United Artists, 1973
GATO BARBIERI
OLIVER NELSON†

THE LAST HALLOWEEN (TF) Hanna-Barbera Prods., 1991
BRUCE BROUGHTON

LAST TRAIN FROM GUN HILL Paramount, 1959
DIMITRI TIOMKIN†

LAST TRAIN HOME (CTF) Atlantis Films/Great North Productions/CBC, 1990
LOUIS NATALE

LAST TRAIN OUT Renegade, 1992
FRANK KAVELIN
DANIEL O'BRIEN

THE LAST TEMPTATION OF CHRIST Universal, 1988
PETER GABRIEL

THE LAST TENANT (TF) Titus Productions, 1978
DICK HYMAN

THE LAST TIME I SAW ARCHIE United Artists, 1961
FRANK COMSTOCK

THE LAST TIME I SAW PARIS MGM, 1954
CONRAD SALINGER†

THE LAST TO GO (TF) Freyda Rothstein/Interscope, 1991
JOHN MORRIS

THE LAST TYCOON Paramount, 1976
MAURICE JARRE

THE LAST UNICORN (AF) Jensen Farley Pictures, 1982
MATTHEW MCCAULEY
JIMMY WEBB

THE LAST VALLEY Cinerama Releasing Corporation, 1971
JOHN BARRY

LAST WISH (TF) Grossbart-Barnett, 1992
DAVID SHIRE

THE LAST WAGON 20th Century-Fox, 1956
LIONEL NEWMAN†

THE LAST WARRIOR Warner Bros., 1970
MARVIN HAMLISCH

THE LAST WOMAN Columbia, 1976
PHILIPPE SARDE

THE LAST WOMAN ON EARTH Filmgroup, 1960
RONALD STEIN†

THE LAST WORD Samuel Goldwyn Company, 1979
CAROL LEES

THE LAST WORD Universal, 1995
PAUL BUCKMASTER

LAST YEAR AT MARIENBAD Astor, 1961
FRANCIS SEYRIG

THE LAST YEAR OF CHILDHOOD 1979
MARKUS URCHS

LATE FOR DINNER Columbia, 1991
DAVID MANSFIELD

THE LATE GEORGE APLEY 20th Century-Fox, 1947
CYRIL J. MOCKRIDGE†

THE LATE GREAT PLANET EARTH (FD) Robert Amram Productions, 1979
DANA KAPROFF

THE LATE SHIFT (CTF) HBO/Northern Lights, 1996
IRA NEWBORN

THE LATE SHOW Warner Bros., 1977
KEN WANNBERG

THE LATHE OF HEAVEN (TF) 1980
MICHAEL SMALL

LATINO Cinecom, 1985
DIANE LOUIE

LATITUDE ZERO National General, 1970
AKIRA IFUKUBE

L'ATLANTIDE 1992
RICHARD HOROWITZ

L'ATLANTIDE LOST ATLANTIS 1932
WOLFGANG ZELLER†

L'ATTENTAT THE FRENCH CONSPIRACY 1972
ENNIO MORRICONE

L'ATTICO 1963
PIERO PICCIONI

LAUGHING ANNE Republic, 1953
ANTHONY COLLINS†

LAUGHING BOY MGM, 1934
HERBERT STOTHART†

THE LAUGHING POLICEMAN 20th Century Fox, 1973
CHARLES FOX

LAUGHTER HOUSE (TF) Film Four International, 1984
DOMINIC MULDOWNEY

LAURA 20th Century-Fox, 1944
DAVID RAKSIN

LAURA LANSING SLEPT HERE (TF) Schaefer-Karpf-Eckstein Productions/Gaylord Production Company, 1988
PETER MATZ

LAURE 1975
FRANCO MICALIZZI

THE LAUREATE Robert Jacobson Films, 1990
NEIL ARGO

LAUREL AND HARDY'S LAUGHING '20s MGM, 1965
JOHN PARKER

LAUREL AVENUE (CTF) HBO Independent Prods., 1993
HAROLD WHEELER

L'AUTRE FEMME 1963
GEORGES DELERUE†

THE LAVENDER HILL MOB Universal, 1951
GEORGES AURIC†

L'AVENTURE C'EST L'AVENTURE GSF, 1972
FRANCIS LAI

L'AVENTURIER 1934
JEAN WIENER†

L'AVVENTURIERO 1967
ENNIO MORRICONE

L'AVVENTURIERO DELLA TORTUGA 1965
CARLO RUSTICHELLI

THE LAW & HARRY MCGRAW (TF) Universal TV, 1987
RICHARD MARKOWITZ†

LAW AND DISORDER Columbia, 1974
ANGELO BADALAMENTI

LAW AND DISORDER Continental, 1958
HUMPHREY SEARLE†

LAW AND ORDER Universal, 1940
HANS J. SALTER†

LAW AND ORDER Universal, 1953
HENRY MANCINI†

LAW AND ORDER (TF) P A Productions/Paramount Pictures TV, 1976
RICHARD HAZARD

THE LAW AND THE LADY MGM, 1951
CARMEN DRAGON†

THE LAW IS THE LAW LA LOI C'EST LA LOI 1958
NINO ROTA†

LAW OF THE LAND (TF) QM Productions, 1976
JOHN PARKER

LAW OF THE LASH Producers Releasing Corp., 1947
ALBERT GLASSER

THE LAW WEST OF TOMBSTONE RKO Radio, 1938
ROY WEBB†

LAWLESS BREED Universal, 1946
MILTON ROSEN†

LAWLESS VALLEY RKO Radio, 1938
ROY WEBB†

THE LAWLESS BREED Universal, 1952
HERMAN STEIN

LAWMAN United Artists, 1971
JERRY FIELDING†

LAWMOWER MAN 2: BEYOND CYBERSPACE New Line, 1996
ROBERT FOLK

LAWN DOGS Rank, 1997
TREVOR JONES

THE LAWNMOWER MAN New Line, 1992
DAN WYMAN

LAWRENCE OF ARABIA Columbia, 1962
MAURICE JARRE ★★

LAYIN' LOW Curb, 1997
EVAN LURIE

LAZY RIVER MGM, 1934
WILLIAM AXT†

LAZZARELLA 1957
CARLO RUSTICHELLI

LBJ (TD) KERA/David Grubin Prods., 1991
MICHAEL BACON

LBJ: THE EARLY YEARS (TF) Louis Rudolph Films/Fries Entertainment, 1987
JOHNNY MANDEL ☆

LE 84 PREND DES VACANCES 1949
GEORGES VAN PARYS†

LE AVVENTURE DI PINNOCHIO RAI/ORTF/Bavaria Film, 1972
FIORENZO CARPI

LE BAISER AU LEPREUX (TF) 1978
VLADIMIR COSMA

LE BAL Almi Classics, 1983
VLADIMIR COSMA

LE BAL DES CASSE-PIEDS 1992
VLADIMIR COSMA
MARIE-CLAUDE HERRY

LE BAMBOLE 1964
ARMANDO TROVAJOLI

LE BAR DU TELEPHONE 1980
VLADIMIR COSMA

LE BARON DE L'ECLUSE 1959
JEAN PRODROMIDES

LE BEAUJOLAIS NOUVEAU EST ARRIVE 1978
CARLO RUSTICHELLI

LE BEL AGE 1958
GEORGES DELERUE†
ALAIN GORRAGUER

LE BEL INDIFFERENT 1958
MAURICE JARRE

LE BESTIAIRE D'AMOUR (FD) 1965
GEORGES DELERUE†

LE BIENFAITEUR 1942
GEORGES VAN PARYS†

LE BON PLAISIR MK2, 1984
GEORGES DELERUE†

LE BONHEUR EST POUR DEMAIN 1962
GEORGES DELERUE†

LE BOSSU 1944
GEORGES AURIC†

LE BOUCHER Cinerama Releasing Corporation, 1969
PIERRE JANSEN

LE BRACONNIER DE DIEU Les Artistes Associes, 1983
CLAUDE BOLLING

LE BRASIER 1990
FREDERIC TALGORN

LE CADRAN SOLAIRE (TF) 1979
GEORGES DELERUE†

LE CAID 1960
PAUL MISRAKI

LE CALDE NOTTE DI DON GIOVANNI 1971
CARLO SAVINA

LE CAPITAINE FRACASSE 1942
ARTHUR HONEGGER†

LE CAPITAN 1945
JEAN WIENER†

LE CAPORAL EPINGLE Pathe Contemporary, 1962
JOSEPH KOSMA†

LE CASSE THE BURGLARS 1971
ENNIO MORRICONE

LE CASTAGNE SONO BUONO 1970
CARLO RUSTICHELLI

LE CAVALEUR 1978
GEORGES DELERUE†

LE CAVIAR ROUGE 1986
JEAN-CLAUDE PETIT

LE CHANTEUR DE MINUIT 1938
PAUL MISRAKI

LE CHAPEAU DE PAILLE D'ITALIE 1952
GEORGES DELERUE†

LE CHASSEUR DE CHEZ MAXIM 1975
PAUL MISRAKI

LE CHAT 1971
PHILIPPE SARDE

LE CHATEAU DE MA MERE MY MOTHER'S CASTLE 1991
VLADIMIR COSMA

LE CHATEAU DES OLIVIERS (TF) 1993
JEAN-CLAUDE PETIT

LE CHAUD LAPIN 1974
VLADIMIR COSMA

LE CHEMIN DE l'ETOILE 1953
JEAN WIENER†

LE CHEMIN SOLITAIRE 1973
BRUNO NICOLAI

LE CHEMINS DES ECOLIERS 1959
PAUL MISRAKI

LE CHEVAL D'ORGUEIL Planfilm, 1980
PIERRE JANSEN

LE CHEVALIER DE PARDAILLAN 1962
PAUL MISRAKI

LE CLOWN BUX 1935
JEAN WIENER†

LE COEUR BATTANT 1960
MICHEL LEGRAND

LE COLLIER PERDU DE LA COLOMBE 1991
JEAN-CLAUDE PETIT

LE COMEDIE DU BONHEUR 1939
JACQUES IBERT†

LE COMPLOT CIC, 1975
MICHEL MAGNE†

LE COMTE DE MONTE-CRISTO 1953
JEAN WIENER†

LE CONFESSIONAL 1995
SACHA PUTTNAM

LE CONNETABLE DE BOURBON (TF) 1978
VLADIMIR COSMA

LE COPPIE
LE CORBUSIER 1956
ALAIN GORRAGUER

LE CORPS DE MON ENNEMI AMLF, 1976
FRANCIS LAI

LE COUP DE SIROCCO 1979
SERGE FRANKLIN

LE COUP DU PARAPLUIE 1980
VLADIMIR COSMA

LE COUPABLE 1936
JACQUES IBERT†

LE COUPLE IDEAL 1945
GEORGES VAN PARYS†

LE COUTURIER DE CES DAMES 1956
PAUL MISRAKI

LE CRABE-TAMBOUR 1977
PHILIPPE SARDE

LE CRI DU LEZARD 1991
GABOR KRISTOF

LE DENONCIATION 1961
GEORGES DELERUE†

LE DEPART Pathe Contemporary, 1966
CHRISTOPHER KOMEDA†

LE DERNIER COMBAT Gaumont/Les Films du Loup/Constantin Alexandrof Productions, 1983
ERIC SERRA

LE DERNIER MATIN DE... (MS) 1964
MAURICE JARRE

LE DERNIER TOURNANT 1939
MICHEL MICHELET†

LE DESERTEUR (TF) 1988
JEAN-CLAUDE PETIT

LE DIABLE PROBABLEMENT Gaumont, 1977
PHILIPPE SARDE

LE DIABLE SOUFFLE 1947
JEAN WIENER†

LE DICIOTENNI 1956
ARMANDO TROVAJOLI

LE DIMANCHE DE LA VIE 1967
GEORGES DELERUE†

LE DINGUE 1972
VLADIMIR COSMA

LE DISTRAIT THE DAYDREAMER 1970
VLADIMIR COSMA

LE DOLCE SIGNORE 1967
ARMANDO TROVAJOLI

LE DOULOUS 1962
PAUL MISRAKI

LE DROIT D'AIMER 1972
PHILIPPE SARDE

LE DUE ORFANELLE 1954
NINO ROTA†

LE FATE Royal Films International, 1966
ARMANDO TROVAJOLI

LE FIL A LA PATTE 1954
PAUL MISRAKI

LE FILS 1972
PHILIPPE SARDE

LE FILS CARDINAUD (TF) 1987
JEAN-CLAUDE PETIT

LE FILS DU REQUIN THE SON OF THE SHARK 1993
BRUNO COULAIS

LE FOTO PROIBITE DI UNA SIGNORA PER BENE 1970
ENNIO MORRICONE

LE FRANCISCAIN DE BOURGES 1967
ANTOINE DUHAMEL

LE FUHRER EN FOLIE 1973
CARLO RUSTICHELLI

LE GANG Warner-Columbia, 1977
CARLO RUSTICHELLI

LE GANG DES OTAGES Gaumont, 1973
MICHEL LEGRAND

LE GANTELET VERT United Artists, 1952
JOSEPH KOSMA†

LE GARCON SAUVAGE 1951
PAUL MISRAKI

LE GITAN 1975
CLAUDE BOLLING

LE GORILLE VOUS SALUE BIEN 1958
GEORGES VAN PARYS†

LE GRAIN DE SABLE 1964
ANTOINE DUHAMEL

LE GRAND CARNAVAL Gaumont, 1983
SERGE FRANKLIN

LE GRAND DADAIS 1966
ANTOINE DUHAMEL
GEORGES GARVARENTZ†

LE GRAND ESCOGRIFFE 1976
GEORGES DELERUE†

LE GRAND ESCROC 1963
MICHEL LEGRAND

LE GRAND JEU 1934
HANNS EISLER†

LE GRAND JEU Dominant Pictures, 1954
GEORGES VAN PARYS†

LE GRAND MELIES THE GREAT MELIES 1952
GEORGES VAN PARYS†

LE GRAND OEUVRE 1958
MAURICE JARRE

LE GRAND SILENCE 1956
MAURICE JARRE

LE GROS COUP 1964
GEORGES DELERUE†

LE GUIGNOLO 1980
PHILIPPE SARDE

LE HASARD ET LA VIOLENCE CHANCE AND VIOLENCE 1974
MICHEL COLOMBIER

LE HEROS DE LA MARNE 1938
JACQUES IBERT†

LE HUITIEME JOUR 1959
JOSEPH KOSMA†

LE HUSSARD SUR LE TOIT 1995
JEAN-CLAUDE PETIT

LE INFIDELI 1952
ARMANDO TROVAJOLI

LE JARDINIER D'ARGENTEUIL 1967
SERGE GAINSBOURG†

LE JEU DE LA PUCE 1969
GEORGES DELERUE†

LE JEU DU SOLITAIRE 1976
GEORGES DELERUE†

LE JEUNE MARIE AMLF, 1982
LUIS BACALOV

LE JOUET Show Biz Company, 1976
VLADIMIR COSMA

LE JOURNAL DE LADY M THE DIARY OF LADY M 1993
ARIE DZIERLATKA

LE JOURNAL D'UN FOU 1963
GEORGES DELERUE†

LE JOURNAL D'UNE FEMME EN BLANC 1965
MICHEL MAGNE†

LE JOURNAL INTIME D'UNE NYMPHOMANE 1974
VLADIMIR COSMA

LE JUGE 1983
LUIS BACALOV

LE JUGE FAYARD DIT LE SHERIFF CCFC, 1977
PHILIPPE SARDE

LE JUMEAU THE TWIN AAA, 1984
VLADIMIR COSMA

LE LEOPARD 1983
CLAUDE BOLLING

LE LONG DES TROTTOIRS 1956
JOSEPH KOSMA†

LE LOUP ET L'AGNEAU 1949
JOSEPH KOSMA†

LE MAESTRO 1975
PAUL MISRAKI

LE MAESTRO (TF) 1979
LUIS BACALOV

LE MAGNIFIQUE THE MAGNIFICENT ONE Cine III, 1973
CLAUDE BOLLING

LE MAIN CHAUDE 1959
MAURICE JARRE

LE MANS National General, 1970
MICHEL LEGRAND

LE MARGINAL THE OUTSIDER Gaumont, 1983
ENNIO MORRICONE

LE MARIAGE A LA MODE 1973
PHILIPPE SARDE

LE MATAF 1973
RIZ ORTOLANI

LE MECREANT (TF) 1979
GEORGES DELERUE†

LE MENSONGE DE NINA PETROVNA 1937
MICHEL MICHELET†

LE MEPRIS Embassy, 1964
GEORGES DELERUE†

LE MERAVIGLIOSE AVVENTURE DI GUERRIN MESCHINO 1952
NINO ROTA†

LE MILLE-PATTES FAIT DES CLAQUETTES 1977
CLAUDE BOLLING

LE MILLION 1931
GEORGES VAN PARYS†

LE MISERIE DEL SIGNOR TRAVET 1945
NINO ROTA†

LE MISTRAL 1972
ANTOINE DUHAMEL

LE MOINE THE MONK Rank, 1972
PIERO PICCIONI

LE MONACHE DI SANT' ARCANGELO Miracle, 1973
PIERO PICCIONI

LE MONASCHINE THE LITTLE NUNS 1963
ENNIO MORRICONE

LE MONOCLE RIT JAUNE 1963
MICHEL MAGNE†

LE MONT SAINT-MICHEL 1934
MICHEL MICHELET†

LE MONTE-CHARGE 1962
GEORGES DELERUE†

LE MUR DE L'ATLANTIQUE 1969
CLAUDE BOLLING

LE NAUFRAGE DE MONTE CRISTO (TF) 1977
GEORGES DELERUE†

LE NOTTE DEL DESPERADO 1965
CARLO RUSTICHELLI

LE NOTTI BIANCHE United Motion Picture Organization, 1957
NINO ROTA†

LE NOUVEAU JOURNAL D'UNE FEMME EN BLANC 1966
MICHEL MAGNE†

LE ORE DELL'AMORE 1963
ENNIO MORRICONE

LE ORE NUDE 1964
RIZ ORTOLANI

LE ORME 1975
NICOLA PIOVANI

LE PAIN VIVANT 1954
MICHEL MAGNE†

LE PALANQUIN DES LARMES 1988
MAURICE JARRE

LE PARADIS DES PILOTES PERDUS 1947
JOSEPH KOSMA†

LE PARFUM DE LA DAME EN NOIR 1949
JEAN WIENER†

LE PART DU CHOSE 1983
STANISLAS SYREWICZ

LE PASSE-MURAILLE 1950
GEORGES VAN PARYS†

LE PATRIOTE 1938
JACQUES IBERT†

LE PAVE DE PARIS 1961
JOSEPH KOSMA†

LE PAYS BLEU Quartet, 1977
GERARD ANFOSSO

LE PERE GORIOT 1944
JEAN WIENER†

LE PERE LEBONNARD 1937
JACQUES IBERT†

LE PERE SERGE 1945
JACQUES IBERT†

LE PETIT GARCON DE L'ASCENSEUR 1961
GEORGES DELERUE†

LE PETIT MATIN 1970
FRANCIS LAI

LE PETIT POUCET TOM THUMB 1972
FRANCIS LAI

LE PETIT SOLDAT 1947
JOSEPH KOSMA†

LE PIEGE 1957
ALAIN GORRAGUER

LE PILLOLE DI ERCOLE THE HERCULES PILLS 1960
ARMANDO TROVAJOLI

LE PISTOLE NON DISCUTUNO 1964
ENNIO MORRICONE

LE POINT DE MIRE Warner-Columbia, 1977
GEORGES DELERUE†

LE POINT DU JOUR 1948
JEAN WIENER†

LE PORT DU DESIR 1954
JOSEPH KOSMA†

LE POUVOIR DU MAL Films Moliere, 1985
WOJCIECH KILAR

LE PRESIDENT 1961
MAURICE JARRE

LE PRIX DU DANGER UGC, 1983
VLADIMIR COSMA

LE PUITS AUX TROIS VERITES 1961
MAURICE JARRE

LE PUITS ET LE PENDULE 1963
ANTOINE DUHAMEL

LE QUATTRE GIORNATE DI NAPOLI 1962
CARLO RUSTICHELLI

LE RAT D'AMERIQUE 1964
GEORGES GARVARENTZ†

LE RAYON VERT Orion Classics, 1986
JEAN-LOUIS VALERO

LE RECREATION PLAYTIME 1960
GEORGES DELERUE†

LE RENDEZ-VOUS 1961
PAUL MISRAKI

LE REPOS DU GUERRIER Royal Films International, 1962
MICHEL MAGNE†

LE REVANCHE DES HUMANOIDES (AF) Planfilm, 1983
MICHEL LEGRAND

LE RIDEAU ROUGE 1952
JOSEPH KOSMA†

LE ROI DE PARIS 1995
QUENTIN DAMAMME

LE ROSE DI DANZICA 1979
LUIS BACALOV

LE ROSIER DE MADAME HUSSON 1950
PAUL MISRAKI

LE RUFFIAN AMLF, 1983
ENNIO MORRICONE

LE SANG DES BETES 1948
JOSEPH KOSMA†

LE SAUVAGE 1975
MICHEL LEGRAND

LE SAUVEUR 1969
PIERRE JANSEN

LE SCANDALE Universal, 1967
PIERRE JANSEN

LE SECRET 1974
ENNIO MORRICONE

LE SECRET DE SOEUR ANGELE 1955
MICHEL MICHELET†

LE SECRET DE WILHELM STORITZ (TF) 1967
GEORGES DELERUE†

LE SECRET DES SELENITES (AF) 1983
SHUKI LEVY

LE SECRET DU CHEVALIER D'EON 1959
CARLO RUSTICHELLI

LE SEX SHOP Peppercorn-Wormser, 1973
SERGE GAINSBOURG†

LE SEXE DES ETOILES THE SEX OF THE STARS 1993
YVES LAFERRIERE

LE SOLEIL DES VOYOUS H.K. Film Distribution, 1967
FRANCIS LAI

LE SOLEIL DANS L'OEIL 1961
MAURICE JARRE

LE SOLITAIRE THE LONER 1973
CLAUDE BOLLING

LE SPIE AMANO I FIORI 1966
ARMANDO TROVAJOLI

LE SPIE UCCIDONO A BEIRUT 1965
CARLO SAVINA

LE SPIE VENGONO DAL SEMIFREDDO American International, 1966
LES BAXTER†

LE STAGIONI DEL NOSTRO AMORE 1965
CARLO RUSTICHELLI

LE SUCRE 1978
PHILIPPE SARDE

LE TAPIS VOLANT 1959
MAURICE JARRE

LE TATOUE 1969
GEORGES GARVARENTZ†

LE TELEPHONE SONNE TOUJOURS DEUX FOIS 1985
GABRIEL YARED

LE TELEPHONE ROSE SJ International, 1975
VLADIMIR COSMA

LE TEMPS DES LOUPS 1969
GEORGES GARVARENTZ†

LE TEMPS DU GHETTO 1961
MAURICE JARRE

LE TEMPS DU GHETTO (FD) 1961
MAURICE JARRE

LE TEMPS REDONNE 1966
GEORGES DELERUE†

LE TESTAMENT DU DR. CORDELIER (TF) 1961
JOSEPH KOSMA†

LE TESTAMENT D'ORPHEE 1960
GEORGES AURIC†

LE TESTAMENT D'UN POETE JUIF ASSASSINE 1988
GABRIEL YARED

LE THEATRE NATIONAL POPULAIRE (DF) 1956
MAURICE JARRE

LE TIGRE AIME LA CHAIR FRAICHE Gaumont, 1964
PIERRE JANSEN

LE TOUBIB 1979
PHILIPPE SARDE

LE TRAIN 1973
PHILIPPE SARDE

LE TRANSFUGE 1985
LUIS BACALOV

LE TRIO INFERNAL 1974
ENNIO MORRICONE

LE TRONC 1993
ALEXANDRE DESPLAT

LE TROU NORMAND 1952
PAUL MISRAKI

LE VEL'-D'HIV (FD) 1959
MAURICE JARRE

LE VERGINE DI NUREMBERG Atlantica Cinematografica, 1964
RIZ ORTOLANI

LE VICE ET LA VERTU 1962
MICHEL MAGNE†

LE VIEL HOMME ET L'ENFANT Cinema 5, 1968
GEORGES DELERUE†

LE VILLAGE AU MILIEU DES BRUMES 1960
GEORGES DELERUE†

LE VILLAGE MAGIQUE 1954
JOSEPH KOSMA†

LE VIOL A QUESTION OF RAPE 1967
MICHEL PORTAL

LE VOLEUR Lopert, 1967
HENRI LANOE

LE VOLEUR DE PARATONNERRES 1944
JEAN WIENER†

LE VOLEUR DE TIBIDABO 1964
ANTOINE DUHAMEL

LE VOYAGE EN GRANDE TARTARIE New Line Cinema, 1973
GERARD ANFOSSO

LE VOYAGE DE NOCES 1976
MICHEL LEGRAND

LE VOYAGE D'ABDALLAH 1952
MAURICE JARRE

LE VOYAGE EN BALLON 1958
JEAN PRODROMIDES

LE ZEBRE 1992
JEAN-CLAUDE PETIT

LEADBELLY Paramount, 1976
FRED KARLIN

LEADER OF THE BAND New Century/Vista, 1987
DICK HYMAN

A LEAGUE OF THEIR OWN Columbia, 1992
HANS ZIMMER

LEAN ON ME Warner Bros., 1989
BILL CONTI

LEAP OF FAITH Paramount, 1992
CLIFF EIDELMAN

LEAP OF FAITH (TF) Hart, Thomas & Berlin Productions, 1988
CHARLES GROSS

LEASE OF LIFE 1954
ALAN RAWSTHORNE†

LEATHERFACE: THE TEXAS CHAINSAW MASSACRE III New Line Cinema, 1990
JIM MANZIE
PATRICK C. REGAN

THE LEATHER PUSHERS Universal, 1940
HANS J. SALTER†

L'EAU A LA BOUCHE 1960
SERGE GAINSBOURG†

L'EAU ET LES HOMMES (FD) 1986
GABRIEL YARED

LEAVE 'EM LAUGHING (TF) Julian Fowles Productions/Charles Fries Productions, 1981
JIMMIE HASKELL

LEAVE HER TO HEAVEN 20th Century-Fox, 1945
ALFRED NEWMAN†

LEAVE IT TO THE MARINES Lippert, 1951
BERT A. SHEFTER

LEAVE OF ABSENCE (TF) Grossbart-Barnett/NBC, 1994
DON DAVIS

LEAVE YESTERDAY BEHIND (TF) ABC Circle Films, 1978
FRED KARLIN

LEAVING LAS VEGAS MGM-UA, 1995
MIKE FIGGIS

LEAVING NORMAL Universal, 1992
W.G. SNUFFY WALDEN

L'ECOLE BUISSONNIERE 1947
JOSEPH KOSMA†

A LECTURE ON MAN 1962
TRISTRAM CARY

LEDA WEB OF PASSION/A DOUBLE TOUR Times, 1959
PAUL MISRAKI

THE LEECH WOMAN Universal, 1960
IRVING GERTZ

L'EFFRONTEE THE HUSSY UGC, 1985
ALAIN JOMY

THE LEFT-HANDED GUN Warner Bros., 1958
ALEXANDER COURAGE

THE LEFT HAND OF GOD 20th Century-Fox, 1955
VICTOR YOUNG†

LEFT, RIGHT AND CENTER 1961
HUMPHREY SEARLE†

THE LEFTOVERS (TF) Walt Disney TV, 1986
TOM SCOTT

LEGACY Kino International, 1976
ROGER KELLAWAY

LEGACY OF LIES (CTF) BAL/MTE, 1992
PATRICK WILLIAMS

THE LEGACY Universal, 1979
MICHAEL J. LEWIS

LEGAL EAGLES Universal, 1986
ELMER BERNSTEIN

LEGEND Universal, 1986
TANGERINE DREAM
CHRISTOPHER FRANKE
JERRY GOLDSMITH

LEGEND (TF) Gekko Film Corp./Mike & Bill Prods./UPN, 1995
KEN HARRISON

LEGEND IN LEOTARDS New World, 1983
WILLIAM MOTZIG

LEGEND OF THE LOST United Artists, 1957
ANGELO FRANCESCO LAVAGNINO†

LEGEND OF THE WEREWOLF Tyburn, 1975
HARRY ROBERTSON

THE LEGEND OF BIGFOOT Palladium Productions, 1975
DON PEAKE

THE LEGEND OF BILLIE JEAN Tri-Star, 1985
CRAIG SAFAN

THE LEGEND OF HELL HOUSE 20th Century-Fox, 1973
DELIA DERBYSHIRE
BRIAN HODGSON

THE LEGEND OF HILLBILLY JOHN Jack H. Harris Enterprises, 1974
ROGER KELLAWAY

THE LEGEND OF LIZZIE BORDEN (TF) Paramount TV, 1975
BILLY GOLDENBERG

THE LEGEND OF LOBO Buena Vista, 1962
OLIVER WALLACE†

THE LEGEND OF LYLAH CLARE MGM, 1968
FRANK DEVOL

THE LEGEND OF RUBY SILVER (TF) Green-Epstein, 1996
RICHARD BELLIS

LES YEUX SANS VISAGE Lopert, 1960
MAURICE JARRE

LES ZOZOS 1972
VLADIMIR COSMA

L'ESCADRON BLANC 1948
JEAN WIENER†

L'ESCLAVE 1953
GEORGES AURIC†

L'ESPOIR 1939
DARIUS MILHAUD†

LESS THAN ZERO 20th Century Fox, 1987
THOMAS NEWMAN

LET HIM HAVE IT 1991
MICHAEL KAMEN
EDWARD SHEARMUR

LET IT BE ME Rysher, 1997
JIM ERVIN

LET IT RIDE Paramount, 1989
GIORGIO MORODER

LET JOY REIGN SUPREME *QUE LA FETE COMMENCE...* SJ International, 1975
ANTOINE DUHAMEL

LET THE BALOON GO 1976
GEORGE DREYFUS

LET THEM LIVE 1937
DAVID RAKSIN

LET US LIVE Columbia, 1939
KAROL RATHAUS†

L'ETA DI COSIMO (TF) 1973
MANUEL DE SICA

L'ETAT SAUVAGE 1978
PIERRE JANSEN

L'ETE MEURTRIER *ONE DEADLY SUMMER* SNV, 1983
GEORGES DELERUE†

L'ETERNEL RETOUR *THE ETERNAL RETURN* 1943
GEORGES AURIC†

LETHAL *KGB—THE SECRET WAR* Cinema Group, 1985
MISHA SEGAL

LETHAL EXPOSURE (TF) Allan B. Schwartz/Papazian-Hirsch/Ellipse, 1993
KEN THORNE

LETHAL INNOCENCE (TF) Entertainment Group/Turtleback, 1991
CHARLES GROSS

LETHAL WEAPON Warner Bros., 1987
ERIC CLAPTON
MICHAEL KAMEN
DAVID SANBORN

LETHAL WEAPON 2 Warner Bros., 1989
ERIC CLAPTON
MICHAEL KAMEN
DAVID SANBORN

LETHAL WEAPON 3 Warner Bros., 1992
ERIC CLAPTON
MICHAEL KAMEN
DAVID SANBORN

L'ETINCELLE 1983
VLADIMIR COSMA

L'ETOILE DU NORD *THE NORTH STAR* Parafrance, 1982
PHILIPPE SARDE

LET'S BE HAPPY Allied Artists, 1957
NICHOLAS BRODZSKY†

LET'S DANCE supervision, Paramount, 1950
ROBERT EMMETT DOLAN†

LET'S DO IT AGAIN Warner Bros., 1975
CURTIS MAYFIELD

LET'S GET HARRY Tri-Star, 1986
BRAD FIEDEL

LET'S KILL ALL THE LAWYERS Lighten Up Films, 1992
MARTIN LIEBMAN

LET'S LIVE A LITTLE Eagle Lion, 1948
WERNER R. HEYMANN†

LET'S MAKE IT LEGAL 20th Century-Fox, 1951
CYRIL J. MOCKRIDGE†

LET'S MAKE LOVE 20th Century-Fox, 1960
LIONEL NEWMAN† ★

LET'S MAKE MUSIC RKO Radio, 1941
ROY WEBB†

LET'S MAKE UP *LILACS IN THE SPRING* Republic, 1954
ROBERT FARNON

LET'S SWITCH (TF) Universal TV, 1975
HARRY GELLER

LET'S TALK ABOUT MEN *QUESTA VOLTA PARLIAMO DI UOMINI* Allied Artists, 1965
LUIS BACALOV

LET'S TRY AGAIN RKO Radio, 1934
MAX STEINER†

A LETTER FOR EVIE MGM, 1946
GEORGE BASSMAN

LETTER FROM AN UNKNOWN WOMAN Universal, 1948
DANIELE AMFITHEATROF†

A LETTER TO THREE WIVES 20th Century-Fox, 1949
ALFRED NEWMAN†

A LETTER TO THREE WIVES (TF) 20th Century Fox TV, 1985
JOHNNY MANDEL ☆

THE LETTER Warner Bros., 1940
MAX STEINER† ★

THE LETTER (TF) Hajeno Productions/Warner Bros. TV, 1982
LAURENCE ROSENTHAL ☆

LETTERS FROM A KILLER Columbia, 1998
DENNIS MCCARTHY

LETTERS FROM FRANK (TF) Paramount Pictures Television, 1979
ERNEST GOLD

LETTERS FROM MARUSIA Azteca Films, 1975
MIKIS THEODORAKIS

LETTERS FROM THREE LOVERS Spelling-Goldberg Productions, 1973
PETE RUGOLO

THE LETTERS Spelling-Goldberg Productions/ABC Circle Films, 1973
PETE RUGOLO

LETTI SBAGLIATI 1965
CARLO RUSTICHELLI

LETTING GO (CTF) Maysles Film, 1996
MADER

LETTING GO (TF) Adam Productions/ITC Productions, 1985
LEE HOLDRIDGE

LETTO A TRE PIAZZE 1960
CARLO RUSTICHELLI

LETTRE POUR L... *LETTER FOR L...* 1993
PHILIPPE HERSANT

LEVA LO DIAVOLO TUO DAL CONVENTO 1973
STELVIO CIPRIANI

L'EVENEMENT LE PLUS IMPORTANT DEPUIS QUE L'HOMME A MARCHE SUR LA LUNE Lira Films/Roas Productions, 1973
MICHEL LEGRAND

LEVIATHAN MGM/UA, 1989
JERRY GOLDSMITH

LEY LINES (FD) Noema Prods., 1993
MARTIN GOTFRIT

LEZIONI DI VIOLONCELLO 1976
BRUNO NICOLAI

LEZIONI PRIVATE 1975
FRANCO MICALIZZI

L'HERITIER *THE INHERITOR* EMI, 1973
MICHEL COLOMBIER

L'HIPPOCAMPE 1934
DARIUS MILHAUD†

L'HOMME 1945
JOSEPH KOSMA†

L'HOMME A FEMMES *MEN AND WOMEN* 1960
CLAUDE BOLLING

L'HOMME A L'HISPANO *THE MAN FROM SPAIN* 1932
JEAN WIENER†

L'HOMME AU CRANE RASE 1966
FREDERIC DEVREESE

L'HOMME DANS LA MUIERE 1952
JEAN PRODROMIDES

L'HOMME DE LONDRES 1943
GEORGES VAN PARYS†

L'HOMME DE NULLE PART 1936
JACQUES IBERT†

L'HOMME DE RIO Lopert, 1964
GEORGES DELERUE†

L'HOMME DES BATEAUX SUR LA VILLE 1985
JEAN-CLAUDE PETIT

L'HOMME DU JOUR 1936
JEAN WIENER†

L'HOMME PRESSE AMLF, 1977
CARLO RUSTICHELLI

L'HOMME QUI A PERDU SON OMBRE *THE MAN WHO LOST HIS SHADOW* 1991
ARIE DZIERLATKA

L'HOMME QUI VALAIT DES MILLIARDS 1967
GEORGES GARVARENTZ†

L'HOMME VOILE 1988
GABRIEL YARED

L'HONNEUR DE LA TRIBU *THE HONOR OF THE TRIBE* 1993
JEAN-MARIE SENIA

L'HONORABLE STANISLAS, AGENT SECRET 1963
GEORGES DELERUE†

L'HORIZON 1967
SERGE GAINSBOURG†

L'HOROSCOPE 1978
CLAUDE BOLLING

LIANNA United Artists Classics, 1983
MASON DARING

LIAR, LIAR (TF) CBC Prods., 1993
FRED MOLLIN

LIAR'S EDGE (CTF) Showtime/New Line/Peter Simpson/Norstar, 1992
PAUL J. ZAZA

LIBEL MGM, 1959
BENJAMIN FRANKEL†

LIBELED LADY MGM, 1936
WILLIAM AXT†

LIBERA, AMORE MIO *LIBERA, MY LOVE* Italnoleggio, 1975
ENNIO MORRICONE

LIBERA, MY LOVE Italnoleggio, 1975
ENNIO MORRICONE

LIBERACE (TF) The Liberace Foundation for the Performing and Creative Arts/Dick Clark Productions/Republic Pictures, 1988
GARY WILLIAM FRIEDMAN

LIBERACE: BEHIND THE MUSIC (TF) Canadian International Studios/Kushner-Locke Productions, 1988
HAGOOD HARDY

THE LIBERATION OF L.B. JONES Columbia, 1970
ELMER BERNSTEIN

THE LIBERATORS (TF) Kenneth Johnson Productions/Walt Disney TV, 1987
JOE HARNELL

LIBERI, ARMATI, PERICOLOSI 1976
GIANFRANCO PLENIZIO

LIBERTE DE LA NUIT 1962
ANTOINE DUHAMEL

THE LIBERTINE *LA MATRIARCA* 1968
ARMANDO TROVAJOLI

LIBERTY (TF) Robert Greenwald Productions, 1986
WILLIAM GOLDSTEIN

LIBERTY BELLE Gaumont, 1983
GEORGES DELERUE†

LIBIDINE 1979
STELVIO CIPRIANI

LIBIDO 1965
CARLO RUSTICHELLI

LICENSE TO DRIVE 20th Century Fox, 1988
JAY FERGUSON

LICENSE TO KILL MGM/UA, 1989
MICHAEL KAMEN

LICENSE TO KILL (TF) Marian Rees Associates/D. Petrie Productions, 1984
LAURENCE ROSENTHAL

L'IDEE 1926
ARTHUR HONEGGER†

LIEB VATTERLAND MAGS West German
JURGEN KNIEPER

LIEBESBRIEFE AUS DEM ENGADIN 1938
GIUSEPPE BECCE†

LIEBESTRAUM MGM-UA, 1991
MIKE FIGGIS

LIEBESWALZER 1929
WERNER R. HEYMANN†

LIES AND LULLABIES (TF) Susan Dey Prods./Alexander-Enright/Hearst. 1993
JOHNNY HARRIS

LIES BEFORE KISSES (TF) Grossbart-Barnett/Spectacor, 1991
DON DAVIS ☆

LIES MY FATHER TOLD ME Columbia, 1975
SOL KAPLAN

LIES OF THE HEART: THE STORY OF LAURIE KELLOGG (TF) MDT Prods./Daniel H. Blatt Prods/Warner Bros. TV, 1994
WALTER SCHARF

LIES OF THE TWINS (CTF) Ricochet Prods., 1991
DAVID MCHUGH

LIEUTENANT KIJE 1934
SERGEI PROKOFIEV†

LIEUTENANT SCHUSTER'S WIFE (TF) Universal TV, 1972
GIL MELLE

THE LIEUTENANT WORE SKIRTS 20th Century-Fox, 1956
CYRIL J. MOCKRIDGE†

LIFE AMONG THE CANNIBALS Trident, 1997
MARK HART

LIFE AT THE TOP Columbia, 1965
RICHARD ADDINSELL†

THE LIFE AND DEATH OF COLONEL BLIMP *COLONEL BLIMP* GFD, 1943
ALLAN GRAY†

THE LIFE AND TIMES OF ALLEN GINSBERG (FD) Cannon, 1993
TOM CAPEK

THE LIFE AND TIMES OF JUDGE ROY BEAN National General, 1972
MAURICE JARRE

LIFE BEGINS AT EIGHT-THIRTY 20th Century-Fox, 1942
ALFRED NEWMAN†

LIFE BEGINS TOMORROW *LA VIE COMMENCE DEMAIN* 1950
DARIUS MILHAUD†

LIFE FOR RUTH Continental, 1962
WILLIAM ALWYN†

LIFE IN THE FOOD CHAIN Katzfilms, 1992
GLEN ROVEN

LIFE IS CHEAP Far East Stars, 1989
MARK ADLER

LIFE IS NICE AFI USA Independent Showcase, 1991
JESSE LOYA

LIFE IS SWEET 1991
RACHEL PORTMAN

LIFE LOVE DEATH Lopert, 1969
FRANCIS LAI

A LIFE OF HER OWN MGM, 1950
BRONISLAU KAPER†

LIFE OF BRIAN Orion, 1979
GEOFFREY BURGON

LIFE OF THE PARTY: THE STORY OF BEATRICE (TF) Welch-Welch Productions/Columbia Pictures TV, 1982
IAN FRASER

LIFE ON A STRING Serene, 1991
QU XIAOSONG

LIFE ON THE EDGE Festival Entertainment, 1992
MIKE GARSON

THE LIFE OF EMILE ZOLA Warner Bros., 1937
MAX STEINER† ★

THE LIFE OF RILEY Universal, 1949
FRANK SKINNER†

THE LIFE OF THE PARTY RKO Radio, 1937
ROY WEBB†

THE LIFE OF VERGIE MINTERS RKO Radio, 1934
MAX STEINER†

LIFE SIZE *GRANDEUR NATURE* 1974
MAURICE JARRE

LIFE STINKS MGM, 1991
JOHN MORRIS

A LIFE TO REMEMBER: ROSE KENNEDY (TD) American Film Foundation, 1990
CHARLES BERNSTEIN

LIFE WITH FATHER Warner Bros., 1947
MAX STEINER† ★

LIFE WITH FATHER (TF) CBS TV, 1954
DAVID RAKSIN

LIFE WITH HENRY Paramount, 1941
FREDERICK HOLLANDER†

LIFE WITH MICKEY Buena Vista, 1993
ALAN MENKEN

LIFEBOAT 20th Century-Fox, 1944
HUGO FRIEDHOFER†

LIFEFORCE Tri-Star, 1985
MICHAEL KAMEN
HENRY MANCINI†

THE LIFEFORCE EXPERIMENT (CTF) Filmline International/Screen Partners/USA Pictures, 1994
OSVALDO MONTES

LIFEGUARD Paramount, 1976
DALE MENTEN

LIFEPOD (TF) RHI/Trilogy, 1993
MARK MANCINA
HANS ZIMMER

LIGHT OF DAY Tri-Star, 1987
THOMAS NEWMAN

LIGHT SLEEPER Seven Arts, 1992
MICHAEL BEEN

THE LIGHT AT THE EDGE OF THE WORLD National General, 1971
PIERO PICCIONI

THE LIGHT THAT FAILED Paramount, 1939
VICTOR YOUNG†

THE LIGHT TOUCH MGM, 1951
JOHN ADDISON
MIKLOS ROZSA†

LIGHT TRAP 1993
WAGNER TISO

LIGHTHOUSE Producers Releasing Corp., 1947
ERNEST GOLD

THE LIGHTHORSEMAN Cinecom International, 1988
MARIO MILLO

LIGHTNING (CTF) Showtime, 1995
HUMMIE MANN

LIGHTNING FIELD (CTF) Mark Gordon Co./Christopher Meledandri, 1991
J. PETER ROBINSON

LIGHTNING JACK Savoy, 1994
BRUCE ROWLAND

LIGHTNING OVER WATER *NICK'S MOVIE* Pari Films, 1980
RONNIE BLAKLEY

LIGHTNING STRIKES TWICE RKO Radio, 1934
ROY WEBB†

LIGHTNING STRIKES TWICE Warner Bros., 1951
MAX STEINER†

LIGHTS OUT IN EUROPE (FD) 1939
WERNER JANSSEN

THE LIGHTSHIP Castle Hill Productions, 1985
STANLEY MYERS†
HANS ZIMMER

L'IGUANA DALLA LINGUA DI FUOCO 1971
STELVIO CIPRIANI

LIKE FATHER AND SON 20th Century-Fox International Classics, 1983
PATRICK WILLIAMS

LIKE FATHER LIKE SON Tri-Star, 1987
MILES GOODMAN†

LIKE IT NEVER WAS BEFORE *PENSIONAT OSKAR* 1995
JOHAN SODERQVIST

LIKE MOM, LIKE ME (TF) CBS Entertainment, 1978
LEE HOLDRIDGE

LIKE NORMAL PEOPLE (TF) Christiana Productions, 20th Century Fox TV, 1979
JOHN ADDISON

A LIKELY STORY RKO Radio, 1947
LEIGH HARLINE†

LIKEWISE Cinema Group, 1988
JONATHAN SHEFFER

LI'L ABNER Paramount, 1959
NELSON RIDDLE† ★

LILAC TIME First National, 1928
NATHANIEL SHILKRET†

LILACS IN THE SPRING Republic, 1954
ROBERT FARNON

L'ILE (TF) 1987
JEAN-CLAUDE PETIT

LILI MGM, 1953
BRONISLAU KAPER† ★★

LILI MARLEEN Luggi Waldleitner, 1981
PEER RABEN

LILIES Triptych Media, 1997
MYCHAEL DANNA

LILIES OF THE FIELD United Artists, 1963
JERRY GOLDSMITH

LILITH Columbia, 1964
KENYON HOPKINS

LILLIAN 1993
H. SHEP WILLIAMS

LILLIOM Fox-Europa, 1934
FRANZ WAXMAN†

THE LILY AND THE ROSE 1915
JOSEPH CARL BREIL†

LILY IN WINTER (CTF) Walter Mirisch Prods./MTE/USA, 1994
DAVID SHIRE

THE LIMBIC REGION (CTF) MGM TV, 1996
GARY CHANG

LIMELIGHT United Artists, 1952
CHARLES CHAPLIN† ★★

LIMIT UP MCEG, 1990
JOHN TESH

L'IMMORALE Lopert, 1967
CARLO RUSTICHELLI

L'IMMORALISTA 1978
ENNIO MORRICONE

L'IMMORTELLE 1962
GEORGES DELERUE†

L'IMPIEGATO 1959
PIERO PICCIONI

L'IMPORTANT C'EST D'AIMER 1974
GEORGES DELERUE†

L'IMPRECATEUR THE ACCUSER Parafrance, 1977
RICHARD RODNEY BENNETT

LINCOLN (TF) Kunhardt Prods., 1992
WALTER LEVINSKY
RICHARD LIEB
ALAN MENKEN

THE LINCOLN CONSPIRACY Sunn Classic, 1977
ROBERT SUMMERS

L'INCONNU DE SHANDIGOR 1967
SERGE GAINSBOURG†

L'INCONNUE DE VIENNE 1986
JEAN-CLAUDE PETIT

LINDA (CTF) Linda Prods./Wilshire Court, 1993
DAVID MICHAEL FRANK

LINDA (TF) Universal TV, 1973
JOHN CACAVAS

THE LINDBERGH KIDNAPPING CASE (TF) Columbia TV, 1976
BILLY GOLDENBERG

L'INDIC THE INFORMER GEF/CCFC, 1983
MICHEL MAGNE†

LINE OF FIRE: THE MORRIS DEES STORY (TF) RoJames Entertainment/Papazian Hirsch, 1991
ARTHUR B. RUBINSTEIN

LINE TO THE TSCHIERVA HUT 1937
BENJAMIN BRITTEN†

L'INGENU 1971
GEORGES DELERUE†

L'INGENUA 1975
CARLO SAVINA

THE LINGUINI INCIDENT Academy Entertainment, 1992
MARK LUNDQUIST
THOMAS NEWMAN

L'INHUMAINE 1925
DARIUS MILHAUD†

LINK Thorn EMI/Cannon, 1986
JERRY GOLDSMITH

THE LINK 1982
ENNIO MORRICONE

L'INSOUMIS 1964
GEORGES DELERUE†

L'INSPECTEUR AIME LA BAGARRE 1956
JOSEPH KOSMA†

L'INSTINCT DE L'ANGE 1993
GABRIEL YARED

L'INTRIGO 1964
ANGELO FRANCESCO LAVAGNINO†

L'INTRUS 1971
GEORGES GARVARENTZ†

L'INVASION 1970
RIZ ORTOLANI

L'INVENZIONE DI MOREL 1974
NICOLA PIOVANI

L'INVINCIBILE CAVALIERE MASCHERATO 1964
ANGELO FRANCESCO LAVAGNINO†

L'INVITEE 1969
GEORGES GARVARENTZ†

LIOLA 1964
CARLO SAVINA

THE LION 20th Century-Fox, 1962
MALCOLM ARNOLD

THE LION AND THE HORSE Warner Bros., 1952
MAX STEINER†

THE LION HAS WINGS United Artists, 1939
RICHARD ADDINSELL†

A LION IS IN THE STREETS Warner Bros., 1953
FRANZ WAXMAN†

THE LION IN WINTER Avco Embassy, 1968
JOHN BARRY ★★

THE LION KING (AF) Buena Vista, 1994
HANS ZIMMER ★★

LION OF THE DESERT United Film Distribution, 1980
MAURICE JARRE

THE LION OF AFRICA (CTF) HBO Pictures/Lois Luger Productions, 1987
GEORGE S. CLINTON

LIONHEART Orion, 1987
JERRY GOLDSMITH

LIPSTICK Paramount, 1976
JIMMIE HASKELL

LIQUID DREAMS Fox/Elwes, 1991
ED TOMNEY

LIQUID SKY Cinevista, 1982
BRENDA HUTCHINSON
CLIVE SMITH
SLAVA TSUKERMAN

LIQUID SUBWAY 1972
BILL CONTI

THE LIQUIDATOR MGM, 1966
LALO SCHIFRIN

L'IRA DI ACHILLE 1962
CARLO SAVINA

LISA United Artists, 1989
JOE RENZETTI

LISA *THE INSPECTOR* 20th Century-Fox, 1962
MALCOLM ARNOLD

LISA, BRIGHT AND DARK (TF) Bob Banner Associates, 1973
ROD MCKUEN

THE LISA THEORY Farallon Pictures/Colossal Pictures, 1994
JIM MATISON

LISBON Republic, 1956
NELSON RIDDLE†

LISBON STORY 1995
JURGEN KNIEPER
MADREDEUS

LISETTE 1961
LES BAXTER†

L'ISOLA 1968
CARLO RUSTICHELLI

THE LIST OF ADRIAN MESSENGER Universal, 1963
JERRY GOLDSMITH

LISTEN, DARLING MGM, 1938
WILLIAM AXT†

LISTEN, LET'S MAKE LOVE 1968
ENNIO MORRICONE

LISTEN TO ME Columbia, 1989
DAVID FOSTER

LISTEN TO YOUR HEART (TF) CBS Entertainment, 1983
JAMES DIPASQUALLE

L'ISTRUTTORIA E' CHIUSA: DIMENTICHI 1971
ENNIO MORRICONE

LISZTOMANIA Warner Bros., 1975
RICK WAKEMAN

L'ITALIA IN PIGIAMA 1976
ANGELO FRANCESCO LAVAGNINO†

LITTLE BIG HORN Lippert, 1951
PAUL DUNLAP

LITTLE BIG LEAGUE Columbia, 1994
JEFF BECK
STANLEY CLARKE

LITTLE BLOND DEATH *DE KLEINE BLONDE DOOD* 1994
JURRE HAANSTRA
TOOTS THIELEMANS

LITTLE BOY BLUE 1997
STEWART COPELAND

LITTLE BOY LOST Paramount, 1953
VICTOR YOUNG†

LITTLE BUDDHA Miramax, 1993
RYUICHI SAKAMOTO

LITTLE CIGARS American International, 1973
HARRY BETTS

LITTLE DARLINGS Paramount, 1980
CHARLES FOX

LITTLE DEVILS AIP, 1991
CHUCK CIRINO

LITTLE FRIEND Gaumont-British, 1934
ERNST TOCH†

A LITTLE GAME (TF) Universal TV, 1971
ROBERT PRINCE

LITTLE GIANTS Warner Bros., 1994
JOHN DEBNEY

LITTLE GIRL LOST (TF) Marian Rees Associates, 1988
BILLY GOLDENBERG

LITTLE GLORIA...HAPPY AT LAST (TF) Edgar J. Scherick Associates/Metromedia Producers Corporation, 1982
BERTHOLD CARRIERE

LITTLE HOUSE ON THE PRAIRIE (TF) NBC Entertainment, 1974
DAVID ROSE†

LITTLE HOUSE: BLESS ALL THE DEAR CHILDREN (TF) NBC Productions/Ed Friendly Productions, 1984
DAVID ROSE†

LITTLE HOUSE: LOOK BACK TO YESTERDAY (TF) NBC Productions/Ed Friendly Productions, 1983
DAVID ROSE†

LITTLE HOUSE: THE LAST FAREWELL (TF) Ed Friendly Productions/NBC Entertainment, 1984
DAVID ROSE†

LITTLE JERK Gaumont, 1984
VLADIMIR COSMA

LITTLE JOE, THE WRANGLER Universal, 1942
HANS J. SALTER†

LITTLE LADIES OF THE NIGHT (TF) Spelling-Goldberg Productions, 1977
JERRY FIELDING†

LITTLE LORD FAUNTLEROY United Artists, 1936
MAX STEINER†

LITTLE LORD FAUNTLEROY (CTF) BBC, 1995
MICHAEL OMER

LITTLE LORD FAUNTLEROY (TF) Norman Rosemont Productions, 1980
ALLYN FERGUSON

LITTLE MALCOLM AND HIS STRUGGLE AGAINST THE EUNUCHS Multicetera Investments, 1974
STANLEY MYERS†

LITTLE MAN TATE Orion, 1991
MARK ISHAM

LITTLE MEN RKO Radio, 1941
ROY WEBB†

LITTLE MISS BIG Universal, 1946
HANS J. SALTER†

LITTLE MISS MARKER Universal, 1980
HENRY MANCINI†

LITTLE MISTER JIM MGM, 1947
GEORGE BASSMAN

LITTLE MO (TF) Mark VII Ltd./Worldvision Enterprises, 1978
CARL BRANDT
BILLY MAY

LITTLE MONSTERS Vestron, 1989
DAVID NEWMAN

LITTLE MURDERS 20th Century-Fox, 1970
FRED KAZ

A LITTLE NIGHT MUSIC New World, 1978
JONATHAN TUNICK ★★

LITTLE NEMO: ADVENTURES IN SLUMBERLAND (AF) Hemdale, 1992
TOM CHASE
STEVE RUCKER

LITTLE NIKITA Columbia, 1988
MARVIN HAMLISCH

LITTLE NINJAS AND THE SACRED TREASURE Comet, 1991
DAN SLIDER

LITTLE NOISES Monument, 1991
KURT HOFFMAN
FRITZ VAN ORDEN

LITTLE OLD NEW YORK 20th Century-Fox, 1940
ALFRED NEWMAN†

LITTLE ORPHAN ANNIE RKO Radio, 1932
MAX STEINER†

A LITTLE PIECE OF HEAVEN (TF) Grossbart-Barnett, 1991
DON DAVIS ☆

A LITTLE PRINCESS Warner Bros., 1995
PATRICK DOYLE ★

A LITTLE ROMANCE Orion/Warner Bros., 1979
GEORGES DELERUE† ★★

LITTLE RASCALS Universal, 1994
WILLIAM ROSS

A LITTLE SEX Universal, 1982
GEORGES DELERUE†

A LITTLE STIFF Just Above The Ground, 1991
KATH BLOOM

LITTLE SECRETS Cinecam, 1991
GENE HOBSON

LITTLE SHOP OF HORRORS The Geffen Company/Warner Bros., 1986
MILES GOODMAN†

LITTLE SISTER InterStar Releasing, 1992
GREG DE BELLES

LITTLE SPIES (TF) Walt Disney TV, 1986
PETER BERNSTEIN

LITTLE SWEETHEART Columbia, 1988
LALO SCHIFRIN

THE LITTLE APOCALYPSE 1993
PHILIPPE SARDE

THE LITTLE ARK National General, 1972
FRED KARLIN

THE LITTLE BROTHER 1983
JURGEN KNIEPER

THE LITTLE DRAGONS Aurora, 1980
KEN LAUBER

THE LITTLE DRUMMER GIRL Warner Bros., 1984
DAVE GRUSIN

THE LITTLE FOXES RKO Radio, 1941
MEREDITH WILLSON† ★

THE LITTLE FUGITIVE 1953
EDDIE LAWRENCE MANSON

THE LITTLE GIRL WHO LIVES DOWN THE LANE American International, 1977
CHRISTIAN GAUBERT

THE LITTLE HUT MGM, 1957
ROBERT FARNON

THE LITTLE MATCH GIRL (TF) NBC Productions, 1987
JOHN MORRIS

THE LITTLE MERMAID 1977
ZDENEK LISKA

THE LITTLE MERMAID (AF) Buena Vista, 1989
ALAN MENKEN† ★★

THE LITTLE MERMAID (AF) Readers Digest, 1973
RON GOODWIN

THE LITTLE MINISTER RKO Radio, 1934
MAX STEINER†

THE LITTLE NUNS 1963
ENNIO MORRICONE

THE LITTLE ONE *MALA* 1992
GORAN BREGOVIC

THE LITTLE ONES Columbia, 1965
MALCOM LOCKYER

THE LITTLE PRINCE Paramount, 1974
ANGELA MORLEY

THE LITTLE PRINCE AND THE EIGHT-HEADED DRAGON (AF) 1963
AKIRA IFUKUBE

THE LITTLE THEATRE OF JEAN RENOIR (TF) Phoenix Films, 1969
JOSEPH KOSMA†

THE LITTLE THIEF AMLF, 1989
ALAIN JOMY

THE LITTLE WORLD OF DON CAMILLO Italian Films Export, 1951
ALESSANDRO CICOGNINI†

LITTLE TREASURE Tri-Star, 1985
LEO KOTTKE

LITTLE VEGAS I.R.S., 1990
MASON DARING

LITTLE WARS LES PETITES GUERRES 1983
GABRIEL YARED

LITTLE WHITE LIES (TF) Larry A. Thompson Organization/New World TV, 1989
LALO SCHIFRIN

LITTLE WOMEN Columbia, 1994
THOMAS NEWMAN ★

LITTLE WOMEN MGM, 1949
ADOLPH DEUTSCH†

LITTLE WOMEN RKO Radio, 1933
MAX STEINER†

LITTLE WOMEN (TF) Universal TV, 1978
ELMER BERNSTEIN

THE LITTLEST HOBO Allied Artists, 1958
RONALD STEIN†

THE LITTLEST HORSE THIEVES *ESCAPE FROM THE DARK* Buena Vista, 1977
RON GOODWIN

THE LITTLEST OUTLAW Buena Vista, 1955
WILLIAM LAVA†

LIVE A LITTLE, STEAL A LOT *MURPH THE SURF/YOU CAN'T STEAL LOVE* American International, 1975
PHILLIP LAMBRO

LIVE AGAIN, DIE AGAIN (TF) Universal TV, 1974
GEORGE ROMANIS

LIVE AND LET DIE United Artists, 1973
GEORGE MARTIN
LINDA MCCARTNEY
PAUL MCCARTNEY

LIVE FOR LIFE United Artists, 1967
FRANCIS LAI

LIVE, LOVE AND LEARN MGM, 1937
EDWARD WARD†

LIVE NUDE GIRLS Republic, 1995
MALCOLM MCLAREN
ANTON SANKO

LIVE: FROM DEATH ROW (TF) D.R. Prods./Charles Mopic Co., 1992
DONN SCHIFF

THE LIVER EATERS/CANNIBAL ORGY 1965
RONALD STEIN†

LOVERS AND OTHER STRANGERS Cinerama Releasing Corporation, 1970
FRED KARLIN

LOVER'S KNOT Two Pauls Prods., 1996
LAURA KARPMAN

THE LOVERS British Lion, 1972
CARL DAVIS

THE LOVERS OF TERUEL 1962
MIKIS THEODORAKIS

LOVE'S DARK RIDE (TF) Mark VII Ltd./Worldvision Enterprises, 1978
JOHN D'ANDREA
MICHAEL LLOYD

LOVE'S DEADLY TRIANGLE: THE TEXAS CADET MURDER (TF) Steve White Prods., 1996
DENNIS MCCARTHY

LOVES OF AN ACTRESS Paramount, 1928
KARL HAJOS†

LOVES OF THREE QUEENS *HELEN OF TROY— THE FACE THAT LAUNCHED A THOUSAND SHIPS* 1954
NINO ROTA†

LOVE'S SAVAGE FURY (TF) Aaron Spelling Productions, 1979
JOHN ADDISON

THE LOVES OF CARMEN Columbia, 1948
MARIO †

THE LOVES OF EDGAR ALLAN POE 20th Century-Fox, 1942
EMIL NEWMAN†

THE LOVES OF ISADORA Universal, 1968
MAURICE JARRE

THE LOVES OF JOANNA GODDEN 1946
RALPH VAUGHAN WILLIAMS†

LOVESICK The Ladd Company/Warner Bros., 1983
PHILIPPE SARDE

LOVEY: A CIRCLE OF CHILDREN, PART II (TF) Time-Life Productions, 1978
JERRY FIELDING

LOVIN' MOLLY Columbia, 1974
FRED HELLERMAN

LOVING Columbia, 1970
BERNARDO SEGALL

LOVING COUPLES 20th Century-Fox, 1980
FRED KARLIN

THE LOVING TOUCH Wakeford/Orloff, 1969
JIM HELMS

LOVING WALTER (TF) Central TV Productions, 1986
GEORGE FENTON

LOVING YOU Paramount, 1957
WALTER SCHARF

A LOW DOWN DIRTY SHAME Buena Vista, 1994
MARCUS MILLER

THE LOW LIFE Zuckerman/Heminway, 1995
BILL BOLL

THE LOW PRICE OF FAME Carvell Productions, 1970
JIM HELMS

THE LOWER DEPTHS 1936
JEAN WIENER†

THE LOWER DEPTHS Brandon, 1957
MASARU SATO

LOYALTIES Norstar Releasing, 1986
MICHAEL CONWAY BAKER

LOYALTY AND BETRAYAL: THE STORY OF THE AMERICAN MOB (TD) Pilleggi-Couturie Prods./ Quest Prods., 1994
TODD BOEKELHEIDE

LT. ROBIN CRUSOE, U.S.N. Buena Vista, 1966
ROBERT F. BRUNNER

LUANA LA FIGLIA DELLA FORESTA VERGINE 1968
STELVIO CIPRIANI

LUCA, BAMBINO MIO 1977
BRUNO NICOLAI

LUCAN (TF) MGM TV, 1977
FRED KARLIN

LUCANTROPUS 1961
ARMANDO TROVAJOLI

LUCAS 20th Century Fox, 1986
DAVE GRUSIN

LUCAS TANNER (TF) Universal TV, 1974
DAVID SHIRE

L'UCCELLO MIGRATORE 1972
ARMANDO TROVAJOLI

LUCIE SUR SEINE Nicole Jouve Interama, 1983
GABRIEL YARED

THE LUCIFER PROJECT 1978
KLAUS SCHULZE

LUCIO FLAVIO Unifilm/Embrafilme, 1978
JOHN NESCHLING

LUCK OF THE IRISH 20th Century-Fox, 1948
CYRIL J. MOCKRIDGE†

THE LUCK OF GINGER COFFEY Continental, 1964
BERNARDO SEGALL

THE LUCKIEST MAN IN THE WORLD Co-Star Entertainment, 1989
JACK GALE
WARREN VACHE

LUCKY DAY (TF) Hearst, 1991
DAVID BELL

LUCKY DEVILS RKO Radio, 1933
MAX STEINER†

LUCKY DEVILS Universal, 1941
HANS J. SALTER†

LUCKY EL INTREPIDO 1967
BRUNO NICOLAI

LUCKY JIM Kingsley International, 1957
JOHN ADDISON

LUCKY JO 1964
GEORGES DELERUE†

LUCKY JORDAN Paramount, 1942
ADOLPH DEUTSCH†

LUCKY LADY 20th Century Fox, 1977
RALPH BURNS

LUCKY LUCIANO Avco Embassy, 1974
PIERO PICCIONI

LUCKY LUKE 1971
CLAUDE BOLLING

LUCKY NICK CAIN 20th Century-Fox, 1951
WALTER GOEHR†

LUCKY PARTNERS RKO Radio, 1940
DIMITRI TIOMKIN†

LUCKY PIERRE *LA MOUTARDE ME MONTE AU NEZ* 1974
VLADIMIR COSMA

LUCKY PUNCH 1996
ALEXANDRE DESPLAT

LUCKY STIFF New Line, 1988
MICHAEL TAVERA

THE LUCKY STAR Pickman Films, 1980
ART PHILIPPS

THE LUCKY STIFF United Artists, 1949
HEINZ ROEMHELD†

LUCY & DESI: BEFORE THE LAUGHTER (TF) Larry Thompson Entertainment, 1991
LEE HOLDRIDGE

LUCY GALLANT Paramount, 1955
NATHAN VAN CLEAVE†

L'UDIENZA Vides, 1971
TEO USUELLI

LUDWIG MGM, 1972
FRANCO MANNINO

LUDWIG 1881 1993
HEINER GOEBBELS

LUDWIG ON THE LOOKOUT FOR A WIFE 1970
ROLF WILHELM

LUI E PEGGIO DI ME 1975
MANUEL DE SICA

LUI PER LEI 1970
ENNIO MORRICONE

LUKAS' CHILD DB USA, 1992
DEAN WALRAFF

L'ULTIMA CHANCE 1973
LUIS BACALOV

L'ULTIMA NEVE DI PRIMAVERA 1974
FRANCO MICALIZZI

L'ULTIMA VOLTA INSIEME 1981
STELVIO CIPRIANI

L'ULTIMO HAREM 1981
STELVIO CIPRIANI

L'ULTIMO TRENO DELLA NOTTE 1974
ENNIO MORRICONE

L'ULTIMO UOMO DI SARA 1973
ENNIO MORRICONE

L'ULTIMO ZAR 1960
ANGELO FRANCESCO LAVAGNINO†

LULU THE TOOL 1971
ENNIO MORRICONE

LUNA 20th Century-Fox, 1979
ENNIO MORRICONE

LUNA DI MIELE IN TRE 1976
ARMANDO TROVAJOLI

LUNATICS: A LOVE STORY Renaissance II, 1991
JOSEPH LO DUCA

THE LUNATIC Triton, 1992
WALLY BADAROU

LUNCH WAGON *LUNCH WAGON GRILS/COME 'N GET IT* Seymour Borde & Associates, 1980
FRED MOLLIN

LUNCH WAGON GRILS/COME 'N GET IT Seymour Borde & Associates, 1980
FRED MOLLIN

LUNDI (TF) 1979
GEORGES DELERUE†

LUNE FROIDE *COLD MOON* 1991
DIDIER LOCKWOOD

L'UNIVERS DU TRIO 1954
MAURICE JARRE

L'UOME CHE RIDE 1966
CARLO SAVINA

L'UOMO CHE SFIDO L'ORGANIZZAZIONE 1975
LUIS BACALOV

L'UOMO DAI CALZONI CORTI 1960
CARLO RUSTICHELLI

L'UOMO DELLA STRADA FA GIUSTIZIA 1975
BRUNO NICOLAI

L'UOMO DI PAGLIA 1957
CARLO RUSTICHELLI

L'UOMO E LA MAGIA (TF) 1976
ENNIO MORRICONE

L'UOMO, L'ORGOGLIO, LA VENDETTA 1967
CARLO RUSTICHELLI

LURE OF THE SWAMP 20th Century-Fox, 1957
PAUL DUNLAP

LURE OF THE WILDERNESS 20th Century-Fox, 1952
FRANZ WAXMAN†

LURED *PERSONAL COLUMN* Universal, 1947
MICHEL MICHELET†

LURKERS Concorde, 1988
WALTER SEAR

L'URLO DEI GIGANTI 1968
ARMANDO TROVAJOLI

LUSH LIFE (CTF) Showtime, 1993
LENNIE NIEHAUS ☆☆

LUST FOR A VAMPIRE American Continental, 1971
HARRY ROBERTSON

LUST FOR GOLD Columbia, 1949
GEORGE DUNING

LUST FOR LIFE MGM, 1956
MIKLOS ROZSA†

LUST IN THE DUST New World, 1985
PETER MATZ

THE LUSTY MEN RKO Radio, 1952
ROY WEBB†

LUTHER American Film Theatre, 1974
JOHN ADDISON

LUXURY GIRLS *FANCIULLE DI LUSSO* 1953
NINO ROTA†

LYCISTRATA 1972
STAVROS XARCHAKOS

LYDIA United Artists, 1941
MIKLOS ROZSA† ★

LYDIA BAILEY 20th Century-Fox, 1952
HUGO FRIEDHOFER†
LIONEL NEWMAN†

M

M Columbia, 1951
MICHEL MICHELET†

M STATION: HAWAII (TF) Lord and Lady Enterprises, 1980
MORTON STEVENS†

M TUTTI W NOI 1975
CARLO RUSTICHELLI

M. BUTTERFLY Warner Bros., 1993
HOWARD SHORE

M. COMME MATHIEU 1973
ANTOINE DUHAMEL

MA AND PA KETTLE AT HOME Universal, 1954
HENRY MANCINI†
HERMAN STEIN

MA AND PA KETTLE AT WAIKIKI Universal, 1955
HERMAN STEIN

MA CHI T'HA DATE LA PATENTE? 1970
CARLO RUSTICHELLI

MA JEANNETTE ET MES COPAINS 1955
JOSEPH KOSMA†

MA SAISON PREFEREE 1993
PHILIPPE SARDE

MA SAISON PREFEREE 1996
PHILIPPE SARDE

MAC Tenenbaum/Goodman, 1992
RICHARD TERMINI
VIN TESE

MAC AND ME Orion, 1988
ALAN SILVESTRI

MAC SHAYNE: WINNER TAKES ALL (TF) Larry Levinson Prods./Kenny Rogers Prods., 1994
KENNY ROGERS,
EDGAR STRUBLE

MACABRE Allied Artists, 1958
LES BAXTER†

MACADAM 1946
JEAN WIENER†

THE MACAHANS (TF) Albert S. Ruddy Productions/ MGM TV, 1976
JERROLD IMMEL

MACAO RKO Radio, 1952
ANTHONY COLLINS†

MACARONI Paramount, 1985
ARMANDO TROVAJOLI

MacARTHUR Universal, 1977
JERRY GOLDSMITH

MacARTHUR'S CHILDREN (FD) Orion Classics, 1985
SHINCHIRO IKEBE

MACBETH British Lion, 1961
RICHARD ADDINSELL†

MACBETH Columbia, 1971
THE THIRD EAR BAND

MACBETH Republic, 1948
JACQUES IBERT†

MACCIE SOLARI 1974
ENNIO MORRICONE

MACGRUDER AND LOUD (TF) Aaron Spelling Productions, 1985
PAUL CHIHARA

MacGYVER: LOST TREASURE OF ATLANTIS (TF) Gekko Films/Winkler-Rich Prods./Paramount Network TV, 1994
KEN HARRISON

MacGYVER: TRAIL TO DOOMSDAY (TF) Gekkofilm/Winkler-Rich Prods./Paramount Network TV, 1994
KEN HARRISON

MACHETE United Artists, 1958
BERT A. SHEFTER

MACHINE GUN KELLY American International, 1958
GERALD FRIED

MACHINE GUN McCAIN *GLI INTOCCABILI* 1968
ENNIO MORRICONE

MACHO CALLAHAN Avco Embassy, 1970
PATRICK WILLIAMS

MACISTE ALLA CORTE DELLO ZAR 1963
CARLO RUSTICHELLI

MACISTE IL GLADIATORE PIU FORTE DEL MONDO 1962
FRANCESCO DE MASI

MACISTE L'EROE PIU GRANDE DEL MONDO 1963
FRANCESCO DE MASI

THE MACK Cinema Releasing Corporation, 1973
ALAN SILVESTRI

MACKENNA'S GOLD Columbia, 1969
QUINCY JONES

THE MACKINTOSH MAN Warner Bros., 1973
MAURICE JARRE

MACKINTOSH & T.J. Penland Productions, 1975
WAYLON JENNINGS

THE MACOMBER AFFAIR United Artists, 1947
MIKLOS ROZSA†

MACON COUNTY LINE American International, 1974
STU PHILLIPS

MACSHAYNE: WINNER TAKES ALL (TF) Larry Levinson Prods./Kenny Rogers Prods., 1994
LARRY BROWN
BOB DE MARCO

MAD ABOUT MEN General Film Distributors, 1954
BENJAMIN FRANKEL†

MAD ABOUT MUSIC Universal, 1938
CHARLES PREVIN† ★
FRANK SKINNER† ★

THE MAD ADVENTURES OF 'RABBI' JACOB 20th Century-Fox, 1974
VLADIMIR COSMA

MAD AT THE MOON (CTF) Michael Jaffe/ Spectacor/Elwes-Kastenbaum, 1992
GERALD GOURIET

MAD AT THE WORLD Filmmakers, 1955
LEITH STEVENS†

MAD BULL (TF) Steckler Productions/Filmways, 1977
AL DELORY

THE MAD DOCTOR Paramount, 1940
VICTOR YOUNG†

THE MAD DOCTOR OF MARKET STREET Universal, 1942
HANS J. SALTER†

MAD DOG AND GLORY Universal, 1993
ELMER BERNSTEIN

MAD DOG COLL 21st Century, 1992
TERRY PLUMERI

MAD DOG COLL Columbia, 1961
STU PHILLIPS

MAD DOG TIME 1996
EARL ROSE

THE MAD GHOUL Universal, 1943
CHARLES HENDERSON†
CHARLES PREVIN†
HANS J. SALTER†
FRANK SKINNER†

MAD HOLIDAY MGM, 1936
WILLIAM AXT†

MAD LOVE Buena Vista, 1995
ANDY ROBERTS

MAD LOVE MGM, 1935
DIMITRI TIOMKIN†

THE MAD MAGICIAN Columbia, 1954
EMIL NEWMAN†

MAD MAX American International, 1979
BRIAN MAY†

MAD MAX BEYOND THUNDERDOME Warner Bros., 1985
MAURICE JARRE

MAD MAX II Warner Bros., 1982
BRIAN MAY†

THE MAD MISS MANTON RKO Radio, 1938
ROY WEBB†

MAD MONSTER PARTY (AF) Embassy, 1967
MAURY LAWS

THE MAD ROOM Columbia, 1969
DAVE GRUSIN

MAD WEDNESDAY RKO Radio, 1947
WERNER R. HEYMANN†

MADADAYO *NOT YET* 1993
SHINCHIRO IKEBE

MADAM SATAN MGM, 1930
HERBERT STOTHART†

MADAME 1962
ANGELO FRANCESCO LAVAGNINO†

MADAME BOVARY 1937
GIUSEPPE BECCE†

MADAME BOVARY C.I.D., 1934
DARIUS MILHAUD†

MADAME BOVARY MGM, 1949
MIKLOS ROZSA†

MADAME BUTTERFLY Paramount, 1932
W. FRANKE HARLING†

MADAME CLAUDE Monarch, 1979
SERGE GAINSBOURG†

MADAME CLAUDE 2 1985
FRANCIS LAI

MADAME CURIE MGM, 1944 ★
HERBERT STOTHART† ★

MADAME DU BARRY 1954
GEORGES VAN PARYS†

MADAME ROSA LA VIE DEVANT SOI Atlantic
Releasing Corporation, 1978
PHILIPPE SARDE

MADAME SIN (TF) ITC, 1972
MICHAEL GIBBS

MADAME SOUSATZKA Universal, 1988
GERALD GOURIET

MADAME SPY Universal, 1942
HANS J. SALTER†

MADAME WUNSCHT KEINE KINDER 1933
BRONISLAU KAPER†

MADAME X Universal, 1966
FRANK SKINNER†

MADAME X (TF) Levenback-Riche Productions/
Universal TV, 1981
ANGELA MORLEY

MADDALENA 1971
ENNIO MORRICONE

M.A.D.D.: MOTHERS AGAINST DRUNK DRIVERS
(TF) Universal TV, 1983
BRUCE BROUGHTON

THE MADDENING IRS Media, 1995
PETER MANNING ROBINSON

MADE International Co-Productions, 1975
JOHN CAMERON

MADE FOR EACH OTHER United Artists, 1939
OSCAR LEVANT†

MADE IN AMERICA Warner Bros., 1993
MARK ISHAM

MADE IN HEAVEN Lorimar, 1987
MARK ISHAM

MADE IN ITALY 1965
CARLO RUSTICHELLI

MADELINE Universal, 1950
WILLIAM ALWYN†

MADEMOISELLE DE MAUPIN Jolly Film/
Consortium Pathe/Tecisa, 1965
FRANCO MANNINO

MADEMOISELLE DE SADE E I SUOVI VIZI 1967
BILL CONTI

MADEMOISELLE DOCTEUR 1935
ARTHUR HONEGGER†

MADEMOISELLE FIFI RKO Radio, 1944
WERNER R. HEYMANN†

MADEMOISELLE JOSETTE MA FEMME 1933
GEORGES VAN PARYS†

MADEMOISELLE S'AMUSE 1948
PAUL MISRAKI

MADHOUSE American International, 1974
DOUGLAS GAMLEY

MADHOUSE Orion, 1990
DAVID NEWMAN

MADIGAN Universal, 1968
DON COSTA

MADISON AVENUE 20th Century-Fox, 1962
HARRY SUKMAN†

MADMAN Jensen Farley Pictures, 1982
STEPHEN HORELICK
GARY SALES

THE MADNESS OF KING GEORGE Samuel
Goldwyn, 1994
GEORGE FENTON

MADNESS OF THE HEART 1949
ALLAN GRAY†

MADO Joseph Green Pictures, 1976
PHILIPPE SARDE

MADREGILDA 1993
JURGEN KNIEPER

MADRI PERICOLOSE 1960
TEO USUELLI

MAE WEST (TF) Hill-Mandelker Productions, 1982
BRAD FIEDEL

MAEDCHEN IN UNIFORM 1965
PETER SANDLOFF

MAERKISCHE FORSCHUNGEN DEFA, 1983
GUENTHER FISCHER

MAFIA PRINCESS (TF) Jack Farren Productions/
Group W Productions, 1985
LEE HOLDRIDGE

MAFIA, UNA LEGGE CHE NON PERDONA 1981
STELVIO CIPRIANI

MAFIOSO 1962
NINO ROTA†

THE MAFU CAGE Clouds Production, 1979
ROGER KELLAWAY

MAGIA VERDE (FD) 1953
ANGELO FRANCESCO LAVAGNINO†

MAGIC 20th Century-Fox, 1978
JERRY GOLDSMITH

THE MAGIC BOX Rank, 1951
WILLIAM ALWYN†

THE MAGIC CANVAS (AF) 1949
MATYAS SEIBER

THE MAGIC CARPET Columbia, 1951
MISCHA BAKALEINIKOFF†

MAGIC CARPET (TF) Westwood Productions/
Universal TV, 1972
LYN MURRAY†

THE MAGIC CHRISTIAN Commonwealth United,
1970
KEN THORNE

THE MAGIC FACE Columbia, 1951
HERSCHEL BURKE GILBERT

MAGIC FIRE Republic, 1956
ERICH WOLFGANG KORNGOLD†

THE MAGIC GARDEN OF STANLEY
SWEETHEART MGM, 1970
MICHEL LEGRAND
JERRY STYNE

MAGIC IN THE WATER TriStar, 1995
DAVID SCHWARTZ

MAGIC KID 2 PM, 1993
JIM HALFPENNY

MAGIC MOMENTS (CTF) Arena Films/Atlantic
Videoventures/Yorkshire TV, 1989
ALAN HAWKSHAW

THE MAGIC SWORD United Artists, 1962
RICHARD MARKOWITZ†

MAGIC TOWN RKO Radio, 1947
ROY WEBB†

THE MAGIC WORLD OF TOPO GIGIO (AF) 1961
ARMANDO TROVAJOLI

THE MAGICAL WORLD OF CHUCK JONES (FD)
Warner Bros., 1992
CAMERON PATRICK

THE MAGICIAN Janus, 1958
ERIC NORDGREN

THE MAGICIAN (TF) B&B Productions/Paramount
Pictures TV, 1973
PATRICK WILLIAMS

THE MAGICIAN OF LUBLIN Cannon, 1978
MAURICE JARRE

THE MAGNET 1951
WILLIAM ALWYN†

THE MAGNICIENT DOPE 20th Century-Fox, 1942
DAVID RAKSIN

MAGNIFICAT 1993
RIZ ORTOLANI

THE MAGNIFICENT AMBERSONS RKO Radio,
1942
BERNARD HERRMANN†
ROY WEBB†

THE MAGNIFICENT BRUTE Universal, 1936
CHARLES PREVIN†

THE MAGNIFICENT CUCKOLD 1964
ARMANDO TROVAJOLI

THE MAGNIFICENT DOLL Universal, 1946
HANS J. SALTER†

THE MAGNIFICENT DOPE 20th Century-Fox, 1942
EMIL NEWMAN†

THE MAGNIFICENT MAGICAL MAGNET OF
SANTA MESA (TF) David Gerber Productions/
Columbia Pictures TV, 1977
ALLYN FERGUSON
JACK ELLIOTT

THE MAGNIFICENT ONE Cine III, 1973
CLAUDE BOLLING

THE MAGNIFICENT SEVEN United Artists, 1960
ELMER BERNSTEIN

THE MAGNIFICENT SEVEN DEADLY SINS 1971
ROY BUDD†

THE MAGNIFICENT SEVEN RIDE! United Artists,
1972
ELMER BERNSTEIN

THE MAGNIFICENT SUMMER 1963
JOSEPH KOSMA†

THE MAGNIFICENT YANKEE MGM, 1950
DAVID RAKSIN

MAGNIFICENT OBSESSION Universal, 1935
FRANZ WAXMAN†

MAGNIFICENT OBSESSION Universal, 1954
FRANK SKINNER†

MAGNIFICENT ROUGHNECKS Allied Artists, 1956
PAUL DUNLAP

MAGNUM FORCE Warner Bros., 1973
LALO SCHIFRIN

MAGNUM, pi (TF) Glen Larson/Bellisarius/Universal
TV, 1980
IAN FREEBAIRN-SMITH

THE MAGUS 20th Century-Fox, 1968
JOHN DANKWORTH

THE MAHABHARATA (MS) 1991
TOSHI TSUCHITORI

MAHOGANY Paramount, 1975
LEE HOLDRIDGE
MICHAEL MASSER

MAID FOR EACH OTHER (TF) Alexander-Enright &
Associates/Hearst, 1992
JOHNNY HARRIS

MAID FOR PLEASURE 1974
OLIVER TOUISSANT

MAID IN AMERICA (TF) Georgian Boy Productions/
CBS Entertainment, 1982
DAVID MICHAEL FRANK

MAID OF SALEM Paramount, 1937
VICTOR YOUNG†

MAID TO ORDER New Century/Vista, 1987
GEORGES DELERUE†

THE MAIDS American Film Theatre, 1975
LAURIE JOHNSON

MAIGRET A PIGALLE 1966
ARMANDO TROVAJOLI

MAIGRET ET L'AFFAIRE SAINT-FIACRE 1959
JEAN PRODROMIDES

MAIGRET TEND UN PIEGE Lopert, 1958
PAUL MISRAKI

MAIL ORDER BRIDE MGM, 1963
GEORGE BASSMAN

THE MAIN EVENT Warner Bros., 1979
MICHAEL MELVOIN

MAIN STREET AFTER DARK MGM, 1945
GEORGE BASSMAN

MAIS OU ET DONC ORNICAR 1979
ANTOINE DUHAMEL

MAISIE MGM, 1939
EDWARD WARD†

MAITRE APRES DIEU 1950
JEAN WIENER†

MAITRE PUNTILA ET SON VALET MATTI 1956
HANNS EISLER†

MAJIN STRIKES AGAIN 1967
AKIRA IFUKUBE

MAJIN, THE HIDEOUS IDOL 1966
AKIRA IFUKUBE

THE MAJOR AND THE MINOR Paramount, 1942
ROBERT EMMETT DOLAN†

MAJOR BARBARA United Artists, 1941
SIR WILLIAM WALTON†

MAJOR DUNDEE Columbia, 1965
DANIELE AMFITHEATROF†

MAJOR LEAGUE Paramount, 1989
JAMES NEWTON HOWARD

MAJOR LEAGUE II Warner Bros., 1994
MICHEL COLOMBIER
JAMES NEWTON HOWARD

MAJOR PAYNE Universal, 1995
CRAIG SAFAN

A MAJORITY OF ONE Warner Bros., 1961
MAX STEINER†

MAJORITY RULE (CTF) Ultra/Citadel, 1992
SHIRLEY WALKER

MAKE HASTE TO LIVE Republic, 1954
ELMER BERNSTEIN

MAKE ME AN OFFER (TF) ABC Circle Films, 1980
RALPH BURNS

MAKE WAY FOR TOMORROW Paramount, 1937
GEORGE ANTHEIL†

MAKE YOUR OWN BED Warner Bros., 1944
HEINZ ROEMHELD†

THE MAKER Mad Chance Prods., 1997
PAUL BUCKMASTER

MAKING LOVE 20th Century-Fox, 1981
LEONARD ROSENMAN

MAKING MR. RIGHT Orion, 1987
CHAZ JANKEL

THE MAKING OF A MALE MODEL (TF) Aaron
Spelling Productions, 1983
ARTIE BUTLER

THE MAKING OF THE PRESIDENT (TD) David
Wolper Productions, 1960
ELMER BERNSTEIN ☆☆

THE MAKING OF...AND GOD SPOKE Brookwood,
1993
JOHN MASSARI

MAKING THE GRADE MGM/UA/Cannon, 1984
BASIL POLEDOURIS

THE MAKIOKA SISTERS RS/58, 1983
SHINNOSUKA OKAWA

MALA 1992
GORAN BREGOVIC

MALAGA MOMENT OF DANGER Warner Bros.,
1959
MATYAS SEIBER

MALAYA MGM, 1949
BRONISLAU KAPER†

MALCOLM Vestron, 1986
THE PENGUIN CAFE ORCHESTRA

MALCOLM X Warner Bros., 1992
TERENCE BLANCHARD

MALDONNE 1968
VLADIMIR COSMA

THE MALE ANIMAL Warner Bros., 1942
HEINZ ROEMHELD†

MALE COMPANION International Classics, 1966
GEORGES DELERUE†

MALEDICTION Henry Plott Productions, 1989
NORMAN MAMEY

MALEVIL UGC, 1981
GABRIEL YARED

MALIBU (TF) Hamner Productions/Columbia TV,
1983
MARK SNOW

THE MALIBU BIKINI SHOP International Film
Marketing, 1986
ROBERT SUMMERS

MALICE Columbia, 1993
JERRY GOLDSMITH

MALICE IN WONDERLAND (TF) ITC Productions,
1985
CHARLES BERNSTEIN

MALLORY: CIRCUMSTANTIAL EVIDENCE (TF)
Universal TV/Crescendo Productions/R.B. Productions,
1976
JAMES DIPASQUALLE

MALLRATS Gramercy, 1995
IRA NEWBORN

Malofilm, 1993
JOHN SEREDA

MALONE Orion, 1987
DAVID NEWMAN

THE MALPAS MYSTERY Anglo-Amalgamated,
1960
ELISABETH LUYTENS†

MALPERTUIS: HISTOIRE D'UNE MAISON
MAUDITE 1971
GEORGES DELERUE†

MALRIF, AIGLE ROYAL 1959
MAURICE JARRE

THE MALTA STORY Universal, 1953
WILLIAM ALWYN†

MALTA, G.C. (D) 1942
SIR ARNOLD BAX†

THE MALTESE BIPPY MGM, 1969
NELSON RIDDLE†

THE MALTESE FALCON Warner Bros., 1941
ADOLPH DEUTSCH†

MAMA LOVES PAPA RKO Radio, 1945
LEIGH HARLINE†

MAMA STEPS OUT MGM, 1937
EDWARD WARD†

MAMA'S DIRTY GIRLS 1974
DON BAGLEY

MAMBA Eidoscope/Reteitalia, 1988
ENNIO MORRICONE

MAMBO Paramount, 1954
ANGELO FRANCESCO LAVAGNINO†
NINO ROTA†

THE MAMBO KINGS Warner Bros., 1992
CARLOS FRANZETTI
ROBERT KRAFT

MAMMA DRACULA 1980
ROY BUDD†

MAMMA ROMA 1962
CARLO RUSTICHELLI

MAMMALS 1962
CHRISTOPHER KOMEDA†

THE MAN Paramount, 1972
JERRY GOLDSMITH

A MAN ABOUT THE HOUSE 1947
NICHOLAS BRODZSKY†

MAN ABOUT THE HOUSE EMI, 1974
CHRISTOPHER GUNNING

MAN AFRAID Universal, 1957
HENRY MANCINI†

MAN AGAINST THE MOB: THE CHINATOWN
MURDERS (TF) von Zerneck-Sertner Productions,
1989
ARTIE KANE

MAN ALIVE RKO Radio, 1945
LEIGH HARLINE†

A MAN ALONE Republic, 1955
VICTOR YOUNG†

A MAN AND A WOMAN UN HOMME ET UNE
FEMME Allied Artists, 1966
FRANCIS LAI ★★

A MAN AND A WOMAN: 20 YEARS LATER
Warner Bros., 1986
FRANCIS LAI

MAN AND BOY Levitt-Pickman, 1972
J.J. JOHNSON
QUINCY JONES

THE MAN AND THE SNAKE 1972
MARC WILKINSON

MAN AND WAR, PART III 1974
MASARU SATO

THE MAN AT THE CARLTON TOWER
Anglo-Amalgam., 1961
RON GOODWIN

THE MAN BEHIND THE GUN Warner Bros., 1953
DAVID BUTTOLPH†

THE MAN BETWEEN   United Artists, 1953
JOHN ADDISON

MAN BITES DOG   1992
VLADIMIR CHEKASSINE

A MAN CALLED ADAM   Embassy, 1966
BENNY CARTER

A MAN CALLED HORSE   National General, 1970
LEONARD ROSENMAN

A MAN CALLED INTREPID (MS)   Lorimar
Productions/Astral Bellevue Pathe/CTV Network,
1979
ROBERT FARNON

A MAN CALLED PETER   20th Century-Fox, 1955
ALFRED NEWMAN†

A MAN CALLED SARGE   Cannon, 1989
CHUCK CIRINO

THE MAN CALLED NOON   1972
LUIS BACALOV

MAN CRAZY   20th Century-Fox, 1953
ERNEST GOLD

MAN FACING SOUTHEAST   FilmDallas, 1987
PEDRO AZNAR

A MAN FOR ALL SEASONS   Columbia, 1966
GEORGES DELERUE†

A MAN FOR ALL SEASONS (CTF)   Agamemnon
Films, 1988
JULIA DOWNES

MAN FRIDAY   Avco Embassy, 1975
CARL DAVIS

THE MAN FROM ATLANTIS (TF)   Solow Production
Company, 1977
FRED KARLIN

THE MAN FROM ATLANTIS IV (TF)   Solow
Production Company, 1977
FRED KARLIN

THE MAN FROM ATLANTIS: DEATH SCOUTS
(TF)   Solow Production Company, 1977
FRED KARLIN

THE MAN FROM ATLANTIS: KILLER SPORES
(TF)   Solow Production Company, 1977
FRED KARLIN

THE MAN FROM BUTTON WILLOW (AF)   1965
GEORGE BRUNS

THE MAN FROM COLORADO   Columbia, 1948
GEORGE DUNING

THE MAN FROM DAKOTA   MGM, 1940
DANIELE AMFITHEATROF†

MAN FROM DEL RIO   United Artists, 1956
FRED STEINER

THE MAN FROM GALVESTON   Warner Bros.,
1964
DAVID BUTTOLPH†

THE MAN FROM LEFT FIELD (TF)   Burt Reynolds
Prods., 1993
BOBBY GOLDSBORO

THE MAN FROM SNOWY RIVER   20th
Century-Fox, 1982
BRUCE ROWLAND

THE MAN FROM SPAIN   1932
JEAN WIENER†

THE MAN FROM THE ALAMO   Universal, 1953
FRANK SKINNER†

THE MAN FROM THE DINER'S CLUB   Columbia,
1963
STU PHILLIPS

THE MAN FROM THE PRU (TF)   1991
CHARLES GUARD

THE MAN I LOVE   Warner Bros., 1947
MAX STEINER†

THE MAN I MARRIED   20th Century-Fox, 1940
DAVID BUTTOLPH†

MAN IN A BAR   Plummer Prods., 1997
NEIL ARGO

MAN IN A COCKED HAT   *CARLTON BROWN OF
THE F.O.*   Show Corporation, 1960
JOHN ADDISON

MAN IN A UNIFORM   IRS, 1994
THE TRAGICALLY HIP
RON SURES

THE MAN IN HALF MOON STREET   Paramount,
1944
MIKLOS ROZSA†

A MAN IN LOVE   Cinecom, 1987
GEORGES DELERUE†

THE MAN IN THE GRAY FLANNEL SUIT   20th
Century-Fox, 1956
BERNARD HERRMANN†

THE MAN IN THE IRON MASK   United Artists,
1939
LUD GLUSKIN† ★
LUCIEN MORAWECK† ★

THE MAN IN THE IRON MASK (TF)   Norman
Rosemont Productions/ITC, 1977
ALLYN FERGUSON

THE MAN IN THE MOON   MGM, 1991
JAMES NEWTON HOWARD

THE MAN IN THE RAINCOAT   Kingsley
International, 1956
GEORGES VAN PARYS†

THE MAN IN THE SANTA CLAUS SUIT (TF)   Dick
Clark Productions, 1979
PETER MATZ

THE MAN IN THE SHADOW   Universal, 1957
HANS J. SALTER†

THE MAN IN THE SKY   MGM, 1956
GERARD SCHURMANN

THE MAN IN THE TRUNK   20th Century-Fox, 1942
CYRIL J. MOCKRIDGE†

THE MAN IN THE WHITE SUIT   Rank, 1952
BENJAMIN FRANKEL†

MAN IN THE MIDDLE   20th Century-Fox, 1964
JOHN BARRY

MAN IN THE NET   Universal, 1959
HANS J. SALTER†

MAN IN THE SADDLE   Columbia, 1951
GEORGE DUNING

MAN IN THE SHADOW   Universal, 1957
HERMAN STEIN

THE MAN IN THE WILDERNESS   Warner Bros., 1971
JOHNNY HARRIS

THE MAN INSIDE   Columbia, 1958
RICHARD RODNEY BENNETT

MAN OF A THOUSAND FACES   Universal, 1957
FRANK SKINNER†

MAN OF AFFAIRS   1937
LOUIS LEVY†

MAN OF AFRICA   Group 3/Eden, 1956
MALCOLM ARNOLD

MAN OF ARAN (FD)   Gaumont-British, 1934
JOHN GREENWOOD†

MAN OF CONFLICT   Atlas, 1953
ALBERT GLASSER

MAN OF CONQUEST   Republic, 1939
VICTOR YOUNG† ★

MAN OF IRON   United Artists Classics, 1981
ANDRZEJ KORZYNSKI

MAN OF LA MANCHA   United Artists, 1972
LAURENCE ROSENTHAL ★

MAN OF MARBLE   New Yorker, 1977
ANDRZEJ KORZYNSKI

A MAN OF NO IMPORTANCE   Sony Classics, 1994
JULIAN NOTT

A MAN OF PASSION   Noble Entertainment, 1988
VLADIMIR HORUNZNY

MAN OF THE HOUSE   Buena Vista, 1995
MARK MANCINA
JOHN VAN TONGEREN

MAN OF THE PEOPLE   MGM, 1937
EDWARD WARD†

MAN OF THE WEST   United Artists, 1958
LEIGH HARLINE†

MAN OF TWO WORLDS   RKO Radio, 1934
MAX STEINER†

MAN ON A SWING   Paramount, 1974
LALO SCHIFRIN

MAN ON A TIGHTROPE   20th Century-Fox, 1953
FRANZ WAXMAN†

MAN ON FIRE   MGM, 1957
DAVID RAKSIN

MAN ON FIRE   Tri-Star, 1987
JOHN SCOTT

THE MAN ON THE EIFFEL TOWER   RKO Radio,
1949
MICHEL MICHELET†

MAN ON THE MOVE (TF)   Universal TV, 1972
ROBERT DRASNIN

MAN ON THE OUTSIDE (TF)   Universal TV, 1975
ELLIOT KAPLAN†

MAN ON THE PROWL   United Artists, 1957
ERNEST GOLD

MAN OUTSIDE   Virgin Vision, 1988
JOHN MCEUEN

A MAN TO REMEMBER   RKO Radio, 1938
ROY WEBB†

MAN TRAP   Paramount, 1961
LEITH STEVENS†

MAN TROUBLE   20th Century Fox, 1992
GEORGES DELERUE†

THE MAN UPSTAIRS (TF)   Burt Reynolds Prods.,
1992
BILLY GOLDENBERG

THE MAN WHO BROKE 1,000 CHAINS (CTF)
HBO Pictures/Journey Entertainment, 1987
CHARLES BERNSTEIN

THE MAN WHO CAME TO DINNER   Warner Bros.,
1942
FREDERICK HOLLANDER†

THE MAN WHO COULD CHEAT DEATH
Paramount, 1959
RICHARD RODNEY BENNETT

THE MAN WHO COULD TALK TO KIDS (TF)
Tomorrow Entertainment, 1973
FRED KARLIN

THE MAN WHO COULD WORK MIRACLES   1937
MISCHA SPOLIANSKY†

THE MAN WHO DIED TWICE (TF)   Cinema Center,
1973
JOHN PARKER

THE MAN WHO FELL TO EARTH   Cinema 5, 1976
JOHN PHILLIPS
STOMU YAMASHITA

THE MAN WHO FELL TO EARTH (TF)   David
Gerber Productions/MGM TV, 1987
DOUG TIMM†

THE MAN WHO HAD POWER OVER WOMEN
Avco Embassy, 1971
JOHNNY MANDEL

THE MAN WHO HAUNTED HIMSELF
Levitt-Pickman, 1970
MICHAEL J. LEWIS

THE MAN WHO KNEW TOO MUCH
Gaumont-British, 1934
ARTHUR BENJAMIN†

THE MAN WHO KNEW TOO MUCH   Paramount,
1956
ARTHUR BENJAMIN†
BERNARD HERRMANN†

THE MAN WHO LOST HIMSELF   Universal, 1941
HANS J. SALTER†

THE MAN WHO LOST HIS SHADOW   1991
ARIE DZIERLATKA

THE MAN WHO LOVED CAT DANCING   MGM,
1973
JOHN WILLIAMS

THE MAN WHO LOVED REDHEADS   United Artists,
1955
BENJAMIN FRANKEL†

THE MAN WHO LOVED WOMEN   Columbia, 1983
HENRY MANCINI†

THE MAN WHO NEVER WAS   20th Century-Fox,
1956
ALAN RAWSTHORNE†

THE MAN WHO RECLAIMED HIS HEAD
Universal, 1934
HEINZ ROEMHELD†

THE MAN WHO SAW TOMORROW   Warner Bros.,
1981
WILLIAM LOOS
WILLIAM LOOSE†
JACK TILLAR

THE MAN WHO SHOT LIBERTY VALANCE
Paramount, 1962
CYRIL J. MOCKRIDGE†

THE MAN WHO TALKED TOO MUCH   Warner
Bros., 1940
HEINZ ROEMHELD†

THE MAN WHO UNDERSTOOD WOMEN   20th
Century-Fox, 1959
ROBERT EMMETT DOLAN†

THE MAN WHO WALKED ALONE   Producers
Releasing Corp., 1945
KARL HAJOS† ★

THE MAN WHO WASN'T THERE   Paramount,
1983
MILES GOODMAN†
UDI HARPAZ

THE MAN WHO WOULD BE KING   Allied Artists,
1975
MAURICE JARRE

THE MAN WHO WOULDN'T DIE   20th
Century-Fox, 1942
EMIL NEWMAN†

THE MAN WHO WOULDN'T DIE   20th
Century-Fox, 1942
DAVID RAKSIN

THE MAN WHO WOULDN'T DIE (TF)   Alan
Barnette Prods./Universal TV, 1995
DAVID SHIRE

THE MAN WITH A CLOAK   MGM, 1951
DAVID RAKSIN

THE MAN WITH A GUN   1938
DMITRI SHOSTAKOVITCH†

MAN WITH A GUN   October Films, 1996
STEVE EDWARDS

MAN WITH A MILLION   *THE MILLION POUND
NOTE*   United Artists, 1954
WILLIAM ALWYN†

THE MAN WITH BOGART'S FACE   20th Century
Fox, 1980
JOHN BEAL

THE MAN WITH BOGART'S FACE   20th
Century-Fox, 1980
GEORGE DUNING

THE MAN WITH ONE RED SHOE   20th Century
Fox, 1985
THOMAS NEWMAN

THE MAN WITH THE BALLOONS   Sigma III, 1968
TEO USUELLI

THE MAN WITH THE GOLDEN ARM   United
Artists, 1955
ELMER BERNSTEIN ★

THE MAN WITH THE GOLDEN GUN   United Artists,
1974
JOHN BARRY

THE MAN WITH THE GREEN CARNATION
Warwick-Viceroy/Kingsley, 1960
RON GOODWIN

THE MAN WITH THE PERFECT SWING   Hovis
Films, 1995
PAUL ENGLISH

THE MAN WITH THE POWER (TF)   Universal TV,
1977
PATRICK WILLIAMS

THE MAN WITH THREE WIVES (TF)   CBS
Entertainment/Arnold Shapiro Prods., 1993
MARK SNOW

THE MAN WITH TWO BRAINS   Warner Bros.,
1983
JOEL GOLDSMITH

MAN WITH THE GUN   United Artists, 1955
ALEX NORTH†

THE MAN WITHOUT A COUNTRY (TF)   Norman
Rosemont Productions, 1973
ALLYN FERGUSON
JACK ELLIOTT

THE MAN WITHOUT A FACE   Warner Bros., 1993
JAMES HORNER

THE MAN WITHOUT A WORLD   Milestone, 1992
LEE ERWIN
CHARLES MORROW

MAN WITHOUT A STAR   Universal, 1955
HANS J. SALTER†
HERMAN STEIN

MAN'S BEST FRIEND   New Line, 1993
JOEL GOLDSMITH

A MAN'S CASTLE   Columbia, 1933
W. FRANKE HARLING†

MAN'S FAVORITE SPORT?   Universal, 1964
HENRY MANCINI†

A MAN, A WOMAN, AND A BANK   Avco Embassy,
1979
BILL CONTI

MAN, WOMAN AND CHILD   Paramount, 1983
GEORGES DELERUE†

MANAGUA   Everest Entertainment, 1997
JOHN LISSAUER

MANBEAST (TF)   Alan Landsburg Productions, 1981
WILLIAM GOLDSTEIN

THE MANCHU EAGLE MURDER CAPER
MYSTERY   United Artists, 1975
DICK DEBENEDICTIS

THE MANCHURIAN CANDIDATE   United Artists,
1962
DAVID AMRAM

MANDELA (CTF)   Titus Productions/Polymuse Inc./
TVS Ltd., 1987
RICHARD HARTLEY

MANDELA AND DE KLERK (CTF)   Showtime/
Hallmark, 1997
CEDRIC GRADUS-SAMSON

MANDINGO   Paramount, 1974
MAURICE JARRE

MANDRAKE (TF)   Universal TV, 1979
MORTON STEVENS†

MANDY   Universal, 1952
WILLIAM ALWYN†

MANEATER (TF)   Universal TV, 1973
GEORGE ROMANIS

MAN-EATER OF KUMAON   Universal, 1948
HANS J. SALTER†

MANEATERS ARE LOOSE! (TF)   Mona Productions/
Finnegan Associates, 1978
GERALD FRIED

MANEGES   1949
PAUL MISRAKI

MANEUVERS   Helma Sanders-Brahms/Metropolis
Films, 1988
JURGEN KNIEPER

MANGIALA   1968
ENNIO MORRICONE

THE MANGLER   New Line, 1995
BARRINGTON PHELOUNG

THE MANGO TREE   1977
MARC WILKINSON

THE MANHATTAN PROJECT   20th Century Fox,
1986
PHILIPPE SARDE

MANHATTAN BABY   Fulvia Film, 1982
FABIO FRIZZI

MANHATTAN MELODRAMA   MGM, 1934
WILLIAM AXT†

MANHATTAN MOON   Universal, 1935
KARL HAJOS†

THE MANHUNT   Samuel Goldwyn Company, 1985
FRANCESCO DE MASI

MANHUNT FOR CLAUDE DALLAS (TF)   London
Films, Inc., 1986
STEVE DORFF

MANHUNT: SEARCH FOR THE NIGHT STALKER
(TF)   Leonard Hill Films, 1989
SYLVESTER LEVAY

MANHUNTER   DEG, 1986
MICHEL RUBINI

MANHUNTER (TF)   QM Productions, 1974
BENNY CARTER

MANIA   *THE FIENDISH GHOULS*   1960
STANLEY BLACK

MANIAC   Analysis, 1981
JAY CHATTAWAY

MANIAC   Columbia, 1963
STANLEY BLACK

MANIAC COP   Shapiro Entertainment, 1987
JAY CHATTAWAY

MANIAC COP 2   Movie House/Fadd, 1990
JAY CHATTAWAY

MANIFESTO Cannon, 1989
NICOLA PIOVANI

MANILA CALLING 20th Century-Fox, 1942
DAVID BUTTOLPH†
CYRIL J. MOCKRIDGE†
DAVID RAKSIN

MANILA PALOMA BLANCA 1993
GIUSEPPE NAPOLI

MANIMAL (TF) Glen A. Larson Productions/20th
Century-Fox TV, 1983
PAUL CHIHARA

THE MANIONS OF AMERICA (MS) Roger Gimbel
Productions/EMI TV/Argonaut Films Ltd., 1981
MORTON STEVENS†

THE MANITOU Avco Embassy, 1978
LALO SCHIFRIN

MAN-MADE MONSTER Universal, 1941
CHARLES PREVIN†
HANS J. SALTER†
FRANK SKINNER†

MANNEQUIN 20th Century Fox, 1987
SYLVESTER LEVAY

MANNEQUIN MGM, 1938
EDWARD WARD†

MANNEQUIN TWO: ON THE MOVE 20th Century
Fox, 1991
DAVID MCHUGH

MANNY AND LO Miramax, 1996
JOHN LURIE

MANON 1949
PAUL MISRAKI

MANON 70 1966
SERGE GAINSBOURG†

MANON 70 1970
MICHEL MAGNE†

MANON DES SOURCES Orion Classics, 1987
JEAN-CLAUDE PETIT

MANON OF THE SPRING *MANON DES
SOURCES* Orion Classics, 1987
JEAN-CLAUDE PETIT

MANONE IL LADRONE Laser Film, 1974
CARLO SAVINA

MANOUSHE: THE LEGEND OF GYPSY LOVE
1993, Brazilian
PACO DE LUCIA

MANPOWER Warner Bros., 1941
ADOLPH DEUTSCH†

MANPOWER (FD) O.W.I., 1942
GAIL KUBIK†

MAN-PROOF MGM, 1938
FRANZ WAXMAN†

MANSION OF THE DOOMED 1977
ROBERT O. RAGLAND

M.A.N.T.I.S. (TF) Universal TV, 1994
CHRISTOPHER FRANKE

MANUELA Paramount, 1957
WILLIAM ALWYN†

MANURA CHUGIGI Morning Calm, 1995
KYUNG-SUK CHONG

MANY CLASSIC MOMENTS Da Capo Films
DAVID WHEATLEY

MANY HAPPY RETURNS 1993
NAOYUKI FUJII

MANY HAPPY RETURNS (TF) Alan M. Levin &
Steven H. Stern Films, 1986
MATTHEW MCCAULEY

MAP OF THE HUMAN HEART Miramax, 1992
GABRIEL YARED

MARA MARU Warner Bros., 1952
MAX STEINER†

MARATHON (TF) Alan Landsburg Productions, 1980
JOE RENZETTI

MARATHON MAN Paramount, 1976
MICHAEL SMALL

MARCEDES *MERCEDES* 1993
MOHAMED NOUH

THE MARCH (CTF) BBC TV/One World, 1991
RICHARD HARVEY

MARCH OR DIE Columbia, 1977
MAURICE JARRE

MARCHE FRANCAISE 1956
GEORGES DELERUE†

MARCHE OU CREVE 1959
GEORGES DELERUE†

MARCIA O CREPA 1963
ANGELO FRANCESCO LAVAGNINO†

MARCIANO (TF) ABC Circle Films, 1979
ERNEST GOLD

MARCO POLO 1962
ANGELO FRANCESCO LAVAGNINO†

MARCO POLO American International, 1961
LES BAXTER†

MARCO POLO (MS) RAI/Franco Cristaldi
Productions/Vincenzo Labella Productions, 1982
ENNIO MORRICONE

MARCUS WELBY, M.D. (TF) Universal TV, 1969
LEONARD ROSENMAN

MARDI GRAS 20th Century-Fox, 1958
LIONEL NEWMAN†

MARDI GRAS FOR THE DEVIL Pyramid, 1993
CHRISTOPHER FARRELL

MARE MATTO 1963
CARLO RUSTICHELLI

MARE NOSTRUM MGM, 1926
WILLIAM AXT†

MARGARET'S MUSEUM 1995
MILAN KYMLICKA

MARGARET-BOURKE WHITE (CTF) TNT Inc./
Projcet VII/Central TV, 1989
JOHN CACAVAS

MARGIE 20th Century-Fox, 1946
ALFRED NEWMAN†

MARGIE Universal, 1940
HANS J. SALTER†

MARGIN FOR ERROR 20th Century-Fox, 1943
LEIGH HARLINE†

MARIA CHAPDELAINE 1934
JEAN WIENER†

MARIA D'ORO UND BELLO BLUE (AF) G.G.
Communications, 1976
PETER THOMAS

MARIA'S LOVERS MGM/UA/Cannon, 1984
GARY REMAL-MALKIN

MARIAGE 1975
FRANCIS LAI

MARIANNE OF MY YOUTH United Motion Picture
Organization, 1955
JACQUES IBERT†

MARIE MGM/UA, 1985
FRANCIS LAI

MARIE ANTOINETTE MGM, 1938
HERBERT STOTHART† ★

MARIE POUPEE 1976
PHILIPPE SARDE

MARIE SOLEIL 1964
FRANCIS SEYRIG

MARIE-CHANTAL CONTRE LE DOCTEUR KHA
SNC, 1965
PIERRE JANSEN

MARIE-LOUISE OU LA PERMISSION 1995
ALEXANDRE DESPLAT

MARIE-MARTINE 1943
GEORGES VAN PARYS†

MARIETTE IN ECSTASY Savoy, 1995
GEORGE FENTON

MARILYN & ME (TF) World International Network/
Samuels Film, 1991
GEORGE BLONDHEIM

MARILYN MONROE: LIFE AFTER DEATH (FD)
Freedman/Greene, 1994
PETER CARL GANDERUP

MARILYN: THE UNTOLD STORY (TF) Lawrence
Schiller Productions, 1980
WILLIAM GOLDSTEIN

MARINE RAIDERS RKO Radio, 1944
ROY WEBB†

THE MARINES FLY HIGH RKO Radio, 1940
ROY WEBB†

MARIO AND THE MAGICIAN *MARIO UND DER
ZAUBERER* Miramax, 1994
CHRISTIAN BRANDAUER

**MARIO PUZO'S THE FORTUNATE PILGRIM
(MS)** Carlo & Alex Ponti Productions/Reteitalia
S.P.A., 1988
MAURO MALAVASI

MARIO PUZO'S THE FORTUNE PILGRIM (MS)
Carlo & Alex Ponti Productions/Reteitalia S.P.A.,
1988
LUCIO DALLA

MARIO UND DER ZAUBERER Miramax, 1994
CHRISTIAN BRANDAUER

MARION ROSE WHITE (TF) Gerald Abram
Productions/Cypress Point Productions, 1982
BILLY GOLDENBERG

MARISA LA CIVETTA Ponti/Balcazar, 1957
CARLO RUSTICHELLI

MARITO E MOGLIE 1952
NINO ROTA†

MARJORIE MORNINGSTAR Warner Bros., 1958
MAX STEINER†

THE MARK Continental, 1961
RICHARD RODNEY BENNETT

MARK COLPISCE ANCORA 1976
STELVIO CIPRIANI

MARK DI SUVERO, SCULPTOR (FD) 1977
PHILIP GLASS

MARK IL POLIZIOTTO 1975
STELVIO CIPRIANI

THE MARK OF THE HAWK 1958
MATYAS SEIBER

MARK OF THE RENEGADE Universal, 1951
FRANK SKINNER†

MARK OF THE VAMPIRE United Artists, 1957
GERALD FRIED

THE MARK OF ZORRO 20th Century-Fox, 1940
ALFRED NEWMAN† ★

THE MARK OF ZORRO (TF) Thompson-Paul
Productions/20th Century-Fox TV, 1974
DOMINIC FRONTIERE

MARK TWAIN (AF) Atlantic Releasing Corporation,
1985
BILLY SCREAM

MARK, I LOVE YOU (TF) The Aubrey Company,
1980
JIMMIE HASKELL

MARKED FOR DEATH 20th Century Fox, 1990
JAMES NEWTON HOWARD

MARKED WOMAN Warner Bros., 1937
DAVID RAKSIN

MARKETA LAZAROVA 1969
ZDENEK LISKA

THE MARLA HANSON STORY (TF) Citadel, 1991
MARK SNOW

THE MARLET'S TALE 1970
MANOS HADJIDAKIS†

MARLOWE MGM, 1969
PETER MATZ

MARNIE Universal, 1964
BERNARD HERRMANN†

MAROC 7
KENNETH V. JONES

MARQUIS DE SADE 1969
BRUNO NICOLAI

A MARRIAGE Cinecom, 1983
JACK WALDMAN

MARRIAGE IN THE SHADOWS 1947
WOLFGANG ZELLER†

MARRIAGE IS A PRIVATE AFFAIR MGM, 1944
BRONISLAU KAPER†

MARRIAGE IS ALIVE AND WELL (TF) Lorimar
Productions, 1980
FRED KARLIN

MARRIAGE ITALIAN STYLE Embassy, 1964
ARMANDO TROVAJOLI

MARRIAGE OF A YOUNG STOCKBROKER 20th
Century-Fox, 1971
FRED KARLIN

MARRIAGE ON THE ROCKS Warner Bros., 1965
NELSON RIDDLE†

MARRIAGE: YEAR ONE (TF) Universal TV, 1971
DAVID SHIRE

MARRIED AND IN LOVE RKO Radio, 1940
ROY WEBB†

A MARRIED MAN (TF) London Weekend TV
Productions/Lionhearted Productions, 1984
WILFRED JOSEPHS
ELLIOT KAPLAN†

MARRIED PEOPLE, SINGLE SEX Miklen
Entertainment, 1993
MIRIAM CUTLER

MARRIED TO IT Orion, 1991
HENRY MANCINI†

MARRY THE GIRL Warner Bros., 1937
DAVID RAKSIN

THE MARRYING KIND Columbia, 1952
HUGO FRIEDHOFER†

THE MARRYING MAN Buena Vista, 1991
DAVID NEWMAN

MARS ATTACKS! 1996
DANNY ELFMAN

THE MARSEILLES CONTRACT American
International, 1974
ROY BUDD†

MARSHAL OF GUNSMOKE Universal, 1944
HANS J. SALTER†

THE MARSUPIALS: THE HOWLING III Square
Pictures, 1987
ALLAN ZAVOD

MARTIAL MARSHALL The Landmark Organization,
1989
SCOTT SMALLEY

THE MARTIAN CHRONICLES (TF) Charles Fries
Productions/Stonehenge Productions, 1980
RICHARD HARVEY
STANLEY MYERS†

MARTIANS GO HOME Orion, 1989
FRANK FITZPATRICK

MARTIANS GO HOME Taurus Entertainment Co.,
1989
ALLAN ZAVOD

MARTIN Libra, 1978
DONALD RUBINSTEIN

MARTIN CHUZZLEWIT (MS) BBC/Pebble Mill/
WGBH Boston, 1995
GEOFFREY BURGON

MARTIN'S DAY MGM/UA, 1985
WILFRED JOSEPHS

MARTY United Artists, 1955
ROY WEBB†

THE MARTYRS OF THE ALAMO 1915
JOSEPH CARL BREIL†

THE MARVA COLLINS STORY (TF) NRW
Productions, 1981
FRED KARLIN

MARVEILLEUSE ANGELIQUE 1964
MICHEL MAGNE†

A MARVELOUS KID 1963
TORU TAKEMITSU†

MARVIN AND TIGE *LIKE FATHER AND SON*
20th Century-Fox International Classics, 1983
PATRICK WILLIAMS

MARVIN'S ROOM Miramax, 1996
RACHEL PORTMAN

MARY AND JOSEPH: A STORY OF FAITH (TF)
Astral Films/Lorimar Productions, 1979
ROBERT FARNON

MARY AND TIM (TF) Hallmark Entertainment,
1996
MICHEL COLOMBIER

MARY BURNS, FUGITIVE Paramount, 1935
HEINZ ROEMHELD†

MARY JANE HARPER CRIED LAST NIGHT (TF)
Paramount TV, 1977
BILLY GOLDENBERG

MARY OF SCOTLAND RKO Radio, 1936
NATHANIEL SHILKRET†

MARY POPPINS Buena Vista, 1964
IRWIN KOSTAL† ★

MARY REILLY TriStar, 1996
GEORGE FENTON

MARY SHELLEY'S FRANKENSTEIN TriStar, 1994
PATRICK DOYLE

MARY WARD 1985
ELMER BERNSTEIN

MARY WHITE (TF) Radnitz-Mattel Productions,
1977
LEONARD ROSENMAN

MARY, MARY, BLOODY MARY 1975
TOM BAHLER

MARY, QUEEN OF SCOTS Universal, 1971
JOHN BARRY ★

MARYLIN & BOBBY: HER FINAL AFFAIR (CTF)
Barry Weitz Films/Auerbach Co./Reitalia Prods.,
1993
JOSEPH CONLAN

MASADA (MS) Arnon Milchan Productions/Universal
TV, 1981
JERRY GOLDSMITH ☆☆
MORTON STEVENS† ☆

MASALA Strand, 1993
LESLIE WINSTON

MASH 20th Century-Fox, 1970
JOHNNY MANDEL

THE MASK New Line, 1994
DAVID MICHAEL FRANK
RANDY EDELMAN

THE MASK OF DIIJON Producers Releasing Corp.,
1946
KARL HAJOS†

THE MASK OF DIMITRIOS Warner Bros., 1944
ADOLPH DEUTSCH†

THE MASK OF SHEBA (TF) MGM TV, 1970
LALO SCHIFRIN

MASK OF THE AVENGER Columbia, 1951
MARIO †

MASOCH Difilm, 1980
GIANFRANCO PLENIZIO

THE MASQUE OF THE RED DEATH American
International, 1964
DAVID LEE

MASQUE OF THE RED DEATH Concorde, 1989
MARK GOVERNOR

THE MASQUERADER United Artists, 1933
ALFRED NEWMAN†

MASQUERADE MGM/UA, 1988
JOHN BARRY

MASQUERADE IN MEXICO Paramount, 1945
VICTOR YOUNG†

MASS APPEAL Universal, 1984
BILL CONTI

MASSACRE IN ROME 1973
ENNIO MORRICONE

MASSACRE RIVER Allied Artists, 1949
LUD GLUSKIN†
LUCIEN MORAWECK†

MASSARATI AND THE BRAIN (TF) Aaron Spelling
Productions, 1982
BILLY GOLDENBERG

THE MASTER GUNFIGHTER Taylor-Laughlin, 1975
LALO SCHIFRIN

MASTER LEON 1985
DOV SELTZER

THE MASTER OF BALLANTRAE Warner Bros.,
1953
WILLIAM ALWYN†

THE MASTER OF BALLANTRAE (TF) Larry
White-Hugh Benson Productions/HTV/Columbia TV,
1984
BRUCE BROUGHTON

MASTER OF THE GAME (MS) Rosemont
Productions, 1984
ALLYN FERGUSON ☆

MASTER OF THE WORLD American International,
1961
LES BAXTER†

THE MASTER RACE RKO Radio, 1944
ROY WEBB†

THE MASTER TOUCH Warner Bros., 1974
ENNIO MORRICONE

*THE MASTER TOUCH/HEARTS AND MINDS/A
MAN TO RESPECT* 1972
ENNIO MORRICONE

MASTERGATE (CTF) Showtime, 1992
BILL MCRAE

MEN WITH WINGS Paramount, 1938
W. FRANKE HARLING†

THE MEN'S CLUB Atlantic Releasing Corporation, 1986
LEE HOLDRIDGE

MENACE IN THE NIGHT United Artists, 1958
RICHARD RODNEY BENNETT

MENACE II SOCIETY NewLine, 1993
RICHARD RODNEY BENNETT
THEODOR MILLER

MENAGE *TENUE DE SOIREE* Cinecom, 1986
SERGE GAINSBOURG†

MENAGE ALL'ITALIANA 1965
ENNIO MORRICONE

MENENDEZ: A KILLING IN BEVERLY HILLS (TF) Frederick S. Pierce Co., 1994
JOSEPH CONLAN

MENSCHEN AUS GLASS West German
JURGEN KNIEPER

THE MEPHISTO WALTZ 20th Century-Fox, 1971
JERRY GOLDSMITH

MERCEDES 1993
MOHAMED NOUH

THE MERCENARY 1969
ENNIO MORRICONE
BRUNO NICOLAI

MERCENARY Mahogany Pictures, 1996
ROGER NEILL

MERCENARY FIGHTERS Cannon, 1988
HOWARD MORGAN

MERCI NATERCIA 1959
GEORGES DELERUE†

MERCY Propaganda, 1996
ROLFE KENT

MERCY ISLAND Republic, 1941
WALTER SCHARF ★

MERCY MISSION: THE RESCUE OF FLIGHT 771 (TF) RHI/Anasazi Prods., 1993
PATRICK WILLIAMS

MERCY OR MURDER? (TF) John J. McMahon Productions/MGM-UA TV, 1987
PETER MATZ

MERIDIAN Full Moon Entertainment, 1990
PINO DONAGGIO

MERMAIDS Orion, 1990
JACK NITZCHE

MERMOZ 1955
JOSEPH KOSMA†

MERRILY WE LIVE MGM, 1938
T. MARVIN HATLEY†

MERRY CHRISTMAS, MR. LAWRENCE Universal, 1983
RYUICHI SAKAMOTO

THE MERRY MONAHANS Universal, 1944
HANS J. SALTER† ★

THE MERRY WIDOW MGM, 1934
HERBERT STOTHART†

THE MESA OF LOST WOMEN 1952
HOYT CURTIN

MESMER Mayfair, 1994
MICHAEL NYMAN

THE MESSAGE Tarik Ben Amar, 1976
MAURICE JARRE ★

A MESSAGE FROM HOLLY (TF) Corapeake/Polson/Procter & Gamble, 1992
STEWART LEVIN

MESSAGE FROM SPACE (AF) United Artists, 1978
KEN-ICHIRO MORIOKA

A MESSAGE TO GARCIA 20th Century-Fox, 1936
LOUIS SILVERS†

MESSAGE TO MY DAUGHTER (TF) Charles Fries Productions/Metromedia Producers Corporation, 1973
FRED MYROW

MESSALINA 1959
ANGELO FRANCESCO LAVAGNINO†

MESSENGER OF DEATH Cannon, 1988
ROBERT O. RAGLAND

MESSIEURS DE VOUOUS: LE CONCIERGE REVIENT DE SUITE (TF) 1980
GEORGES DELERUE†

METAL SKIN 1994
JOHN CLIFFORD WHITE

METALSTORM: THE DESTRUCTION OF JARED SYN Universal, 1983
RICHARD H. BAND

METAMORPHOSIS: THE ALIEN FACTOR International, 1991
JOHN GRAY

METELLO 1970
ENNIO MORRICONE

METEOR American International, 1979
LAURENCE ROSENTHAL

THE METEOR MAN MGM, 1993
CLIFF EIDELMAN

METRALLETA STEIN 1975
CARLO RUSTICHELLI

METRO Buena Vista, 1997
STEVE PORCARO

METROPOLIS 1983
GIORGIO MORODER

METROPOLIS UFA, 1926
GOTTFRIED HUPPERTZ†

METROPOLITAN New Line, 1990
TOM JUDSON
MARK SUOZZO

METTI LO DIAVOLO TUO NE LO MIO INFERNO 1972
STELVIO CIPRIANI

METTI UNA SERA A CENA *LOVE CIRCLE* 1969
ENNIO MORRICONE

MEXICAN SPITFIRE RKO Radio, 1940
PAUL SAWTELL†

MEXICAN SPITFIRE OUT WEST RKO Radio, 1940
ROY WEBB†

MEXICAN SPITFIRE SEES A GHOST RKO Radio, 1942
ROY WEBB†

MEXICAN SPITFIRE'S ELEPHANT RKO Radio, 1942
ROY WEBB†

MGM'S BIG PARADE OF COMEDY MGM, 1964
BERNARD GREEN

MGM: WHEN THE LION ROARS (TD) Joni Levin Point Blank Prods., 1992
STEVEN GOLDSTEIN

MI FAMILIA New Line, 1995
PEPE AVILA
MARK MCKENZIE

MI HERMANO DEL ALMA *MY SOUL BROTHER* 1993
BINGEN MENDIZABAL

MI VEDRAI TORNARE 1966
LUIS BACALOV
ENNIO MORRICONE

MI VIDA LOCA Sony Classics, 1993
JOHN TAYLOR

MIAMI BLUES Orion, 1989
GARY CHANG

MIAMI RHAPSODY Buena Vista, 1995
MARK ISHAM

MIAMI VICE (TF) The Michael Mann Company/Universal TV, 1984
JAN HAMMER

MICHAEL New Line, 1996
RANDY NEWMAN

MICHAEL COLLINS Warner Bros., 1996
ELLIOT GOLDENTHAL ★

MICHAEL KOHLHAAS Horst Film, 1979
PETER SANDLOFF

MICHAEL O'HALLORAN Monogram, 1948
LUD GLUSKIN†

MICHELE STROGOFF 1956
TEO USUELLI

THE MICHIGAN KID Universal, 1947
HANS J. SALTER†

MICHURIN 1947
DMITRI SHOSTAKOVITCH†

MICKEY ONE Columbia, 1965
EDDIE SAUTER

MICKEY SPILLANE'S MARGIN FOR MURDER (TF) Hamner Productions, 1981
NELSON RIDDLE†

MICKEY SPILLANE'S MIKE HAMMER: MORE THAN MURDER (TF) Jay Bernstein/Columbia, 1984
EARLE HAGEN

MICKEY SPILLANE'S MIKE HAMMER: MURDER ME, MURDER YOU (TF) Jay Bernstein Productions/Columbia Pictures Television, 1983
FARI E HAGEN

MICKEY SPILLANE'S MIKE HAMMER: MURDER TAKES ALL (TF) Jay Bernstein Productions/Columbia Pictures TV, 1989
RON RAMIN

MICKI & MAUDE Columbia, 1984
LEE HOLDRIDGE

MICROCOSMOS (FD) 1996
BRUNO COULAIS

MIDAS RUN Cinerama Releasing Corporation, 1969
ELMER BERNSTEIN

MIDAS VALLEY (TF) Edward S. Feldman Productions/Warner Bros. TV, 1985
JERROLD IMMEL

MIDDLE AGE CRAZY 20th Century-Fox, 1980
TONY MACAULAY
MATTHEW MCCAULEY

MIDDLE AGES (TF) Stan Rogow Prods./Paramount TV, 1992
JACK NITZCHE

MIDDLE OF THE NIGHT Columbia, 1959
GEORGE BASSMAN

MIDNIGHT Paramount, 1939
FREDERICK HOLLANDER†

MIDNIGHT SVS, 1989
MICHAEL WETHERWAX

A MIDNIGHT CLEAR InterStar, 1992
MARK ISHAM

MIDNIGHT CABARET 1987
MICHEL COLOMBIER

MIDNIGHT CALLER: LIFE WITHOUT POSSIBILITY (TF) Lorimar TV, 1991
ROSS LEVINSON

MIDNIGHT CONFESSIONS Kravis-Shustak, 1993
SCOTT SINGER

MIDNIGHT COURT Warner Bros., 1937
DAVID RAKSIN

MIDNIGHT COWBOY United Artists, 1969
JOHN BARRY

MIDNIGHT CROSSING Vestron, 1988
STEVE TYRELL

MIDNIGHT DREAMS Filminvest, 1986
CARL DANTE

MIDNIGHT EDITION Shapiro Glickenhaus, 1994
MURRAY ATTAWAY

MIDNIGHT EXPRESS Columbia, 1978
GIORGIO MORODER ★★

MIDNIGHT FEAR New World, 1991
STEVE EDWARDS

THE MIDNIGHT HOUR (TF) ABC Circle Films, 1985
BRAD FIEDEL

MIDNIGHT INTRUDER Universal, 1938
CHARLES PREVIN†

MIDNIGHT LACE Universal, 1960
FRANK SKINNER†

MIDNIGHT LACE (TF) Four R. Productions/Universal TV, 1981
STU PHILLIPS

THE MIDNIGHT MAN Universal, 1974
DAVE GRUSIN

MIDNIGHT MADNESS Buena Vista, 1980
JULIUS WECHTER

MIDNIGHT MARY MGM, 1933
WILLIAM AXT†

MIDNIGHT OFFERINGS (TF) Stephen J. Cannell Productions, 1981
WALTER SCHARF

MIDNIGHT RUN Universal, 1988
DANNY ELFMAN

MIDNIGHT RUN-AROUND (TF) Toto Prods./Viacom, 1994
BENNIE WALLACE

THE MIDNIGHT STORY Universal, 1957
HANS J. SALTER†

MIDNITE SPARES Roadshow Australia, 1983
CAMERON ALLAN

MIDSHIPMAN JACK RKO Radio, 1933
MAX STEINER†

A MIDSUMMER NIGHT'S DREAM Warner Bros., 1935
ERICH WOLFGANG KORNGOLD†

MIDWAY Universal, 1976
JOHN WILLIAMS

A MIDWINTER'S TALE Sony Classics, 1996
JIMMY YUILL

MIGHT MAKES RIGHT 1975
PEER RABEN

THE MIGHTY BARNUM United Artists, 1935
ALFRED NEWMAN†

THE MIGHTY DUCKS Buena Vista, 1992
DAVID NEWMAN

MIGHTY JOE YOUNG RKO Radio, 1949
ROY WEBB†

MIGHTY MORPHIN POWER RANGERS THE MOVIE 20th Century Fox, 1995
GRAEME REVELL

THE MIGHTY QUINN MGM/UA, 1989
ANNE DUDLEY

THE MIGHTY TREVE Universal, 1937
DAVID RAKSIN

THE MIGRANTS (TF) CBS, Inc., 1974
BILLY GOLDENBERG ☆

MIJN HACHTEN MET SUSAN OLGA ALBERT JULIE PIET & SANDRA 1975
ELISABETH LUYTENS†

MIJN VRIENDE 1979
GEORGES DELERUE†

MIKE'S MURDER The Ladd Company/Warner Bros., 1984
JOE JACKSON

MIKE'S MURDER Universal, 1984
JOHN BARRY

MIKEY AND NICKY Paramount, 1976
JOHN STRAUSS

MILADY (TF) 1975
GEORGES DELERUE†

MILADY'S REVENGE 20th Century-Fox, 1975
LALO SCHIFRIN

THE MILAGRO BEANFIELD WAR Universal, 1988
DAVE GRUSIN ★★

MILANO CALIBRO 9 1972
LUIS BACALOV

MILANO ODIA: LA POLIZIA NON PUO SPARARE 1974
ENNIO MORRICONE

MILANO ODIA: LA POLIZIA NON PUO' SPARARE Joseph Brenner, 1980
ENNIO MORRICONE

MILANO ROVENTE 1973
CARLO RUSTICHELLI

MILAREPA Lotar Film, 1974
DANIELE PARIS

MILDRED PIERCE Warner Bros., 1945
MAX STEINER†

MILES FROM HOME Cinecom, 1988
ROBERT FOLK

MILES FROM NOWHERE (TF) Sokolow Co./New World Television, 1992
BILLY GOLDENBERG

MILES TO GO BEFORE I SLEEP (TF) Roger Gimbel Productions/Tomorrow Entertainment, 1975
WLADIMIR SELINSKY

MILES TO GO... (TF) Keating-Shostak Productions, 1986
KEN WANNBERG

MILK MONEY Paramount, 1994
MICHAEL CONVERTINO

THE MILKMAN Universal, 1950
MILTON ROSEN†

THE MILKY WAY 1993
MARIO DE BENITO

MILLE BOLLE BLU 1993
FRANCO PIERSANTI

MILLENIUM (MS) Biniman Prods./Adrian Malone Prods./KCET/BBC, 1992
HANS ZIMMER

MILLENNIUM 20th Century Fox, 1989
ERIC N. ROBERTSON

THE MILLER'S BEAUTIFUL WIFE *LA BELLA MUGNAIA* 1955
ANGELO FRANCESCO LAVAGNINO†

MILLER'S CROSSING 1990
CARTER BURWELL

MILLIE'S DAUGHTER Columbia, 1947
ARTHUR MORTON

THE MILLION DOLLAR FACE (TF) Nephi-Hamner Productions, 1981
MORTON STEVENS†

THE MILLION DOLLAR RIP-OFF (TF) Charles Fries Productions/Montagne Productions, 1976
VIC MIZZY

MILLION DOLLAR BABIES (TF) Bernard Zuckerman Prods./Cinar/CBC/CBS Ent./Telefilm Canada/Ontario Film Development Corp., 1994
CHRISTOPHER DEDRICK

MILLION DOLLAR BABY Warner Bros., 1941
FREDERICK HOLLANDER†

MILLION DOLLAR DUCK Buena Vista, 1971
BUDDY BAKER

MILLION DOLLAR INFIELD (TF) CBS Entertainment, 1982
ARTIE KANE

THE MILLION POUND NOTE United Artists, 1954
WILLIAM ALWYN†

A MILLION TO JUAN Samuel Goldwyn, 1994
JEFFREY JOHNSON
STEVEN JOHNSON
SAMM PENA

A MILLIONAIRE FOR CHRISTY 20th Century-Fox, 1951
VICTOR YOUNG†

THE MILLIONAIRE (TF) Don Fedderson Productions, 1978
FRANK DEVOL

THE MILLIONAIRESS 20th Century-Fox, 1960
GEORGES VAN PARYS†

MILLIONAIRE IN TROUBLE 1978
DOV SELTZER

MILLIONAIRES IN PRISON RKO Radio, 1940
ROY WEBB†

MILLIONS LIKE US 1943
HUBERT BATH†

MIMI 1979
RIZ ORTOLANI

MIMI METALLURGICO FERITO NELL'ONORE New Line Cinema, 1972
PIERO PICCIONI

MINATOMO YOSHITSUNE 1966
TORU TAKEMITSU†

THE MIND BENDERS American International, 1963
GEORGES AURIC†

THE MIND OF MR. SOAMES Columbia, 1970
MICHAEL DRESS

MIND OVER MURDER (TF) Paramount TV, 1979
PAUL CHIHARA

MINDWARP: AN INFINITY OF TERROR/PLANET OF HORRORS New World, 1981
BARRY SCHRADER

MINE OWN EXECUTIONER 1947
BENJAMIN FRANKEL†

THE MINER'S DAUGHTER (AS) Columbia, 1950
GAIL KUBIK†

MING, RAGAZZI! 1973
CARLO RUSTICHELLI
CARLO SAVINA

THE MINI-SKIRT MOB American International, 1968
LES BAXTER†

THE MINISTER'S WIFE Homesick Pictures, 1992
STEVE EDWARDS

MINISTRY OF FEAR Paramount, 1944
VICTOR YOUNG†

MINISTRY OF VENGEANCE Concorde, 1989
SCOTT ROEWE

THE MINIVER STORY MGM, 1950
MIKLOS ROZSA†

MONEY TO BURN (TF) Silverton Productions/
Universal TV, 1973
OLIVER NELSON†

MONEY TRAIN Columbia, 1995
MARK MANCINA
JOHN VAN TONGEREN

MONEY, POWER, MURDER (TF) Skids
Productions/CBS Entertainment, 1989
MILES GOODMAN†

MONEY, WOMEN & GUNS Universal, 1958
HERMAN STEIN

MONGO'S BACK IN TOWN (TF) Bob Banner
Associates, 1971
MICHAEL MELVOIN

MONIKA Janus, 1953
ERIC NORDGREN

MONIKA re-scoring of 1953 Ingmar Bergman film,
1959
LES BAXTER†

THE MONITORS Commonwealth United, 1969
FRED KAZ

THE MONK Rank, 1972
PIERO PICCIONI

THE MONK (TF) Thomas-Spelling Productions, 1969
EARLE HAGEN

MONKEY BUSINESS 20th Century-Fox, 1952
LEIGH HARLINE†
LIONEL NEWMAN†

THE MONKEY MISSION (TF) Mickey Productions/
Filmways, 1981
GEORGE ROMANIS

MONKEY ON MY BACK United Artists, 1957
BERT A. SHEFTER

MONKEY SHINES Orion, 1988
DAVID SHIRE

MONKEY TROUBLE New Line, 1994
MARK MANCINA

THE MONKEY'S PAW RKO Radio, 1932
MAX STEINER†

THE MONKEY'S UNCLE Buena Vista, 1964
BUDDY BAKER

MONKEYS, GO HOME! Buena Vista, 1967
ROBERT F. BRUNNER

MONNAIRE DE SINGE 1965
MICHEL LEGRAND

THE MONOLITH MONSTER Universal, 1957
IRVING GERTZ
HENRY MANCINI†

THE MONOLITH MOSTERS Universal, 1957
HERMAN STEIN

MONSEIGNEUR 1949
GEORGES VAN PARYS†

MONSIEUR BEAUCAIRE Paramount, 1946
ROBERT EMMETT DOLAN†

MONSIEUR LA CAILLE 1955
JOSEPH KOSMA†

MONSIEUR LUDOVIC 1946
JOSEPH KOSMA†

MONSIEUR ROBERT HOUDIN (TF) 1966
GEORGES DELERUE†

MONSIEUR VERDOUX United Artists, 1947
CHARLES CHAPLIN†

MONSIGNOR 20th Century-Fox, 1982
JOHN WILLIAMS

MONSOON Producers Releasing Corp., 1943
LEO ERDODY†

THE MONSTER 1996
EVAN LURIE

THE MONSTER CLUB ITC, 1981
DOUGLAS GAMLEY

MONSTER FROM GREEN HELL DCA, 1957
ALBERT GLASSER

MONSTER ISLAND Fort Films, 1981
ALFONSO AGULLO

THE MONSTER MAKER Producers Releasing Corp.,
1944
ALBERT GLASSER

THE MONSTER OF HIGHGATE PONDS 1966
FRANCES CHAGRIN†

THE MONSTER SQUAD Tri-Star, 1987
BRUCE BROUGHTON

**THE MONSTER THAT CHALLENGED THE
WORLD** United Artists, 1957
HEINZ ROEMHELD†

MONSTER ZERO 1966
AKIRA IFUKUBE

MONTA IN SELLA, FIGLIO DI...! 1972
LUIS BACALOV

MONTANA Warner Bros., 1950
DAVID BUTTOLPH†

MONTANA (CTF) HBO Productions/Zoetrope
Studios/Roger Gimbel Productions, 1990
DAVID MCHUGH

MONTANA MOON MGM, 1930
HERBERT STOTHART†

MONTE CARLO Paramount, 1930
W. FRANKE HARLING†

MONTE CARLO (TF) New World TV/Phoenix
Entertainment Group/Collins-Holm Productions/
Highgate Pictures, 1986
STANLEY MYERS†

MONTE WALSH National General, 1970
JOHN BARRY

A MONTH BY THE LAKE Miramax, 1995
NICOLA PIOVANI

A MONTH IN THE COUNTRY Orion Classics, 1987
HOWARD BLAKE

A MONTH OF SUNDAYS (CTF) HBO Showcase,
1989
STANLEY MYERS†

MONTPARNASSE 19 1958
PAUL MISRAKI

MONTY PYTHON AND THE HOLY GRAIL Cinema
5, 1974
DE WOLFE
NEIL INNES

MONTY PYTHON AT THE HOLLYWOOD BOWL
Columbia, 1982
JOHN DUPREZ

MONTY PYTHON'S THE MEANING OF LIFE
Universal, 1983
JOHN DUPREZ

THE MOON AND SIXPENCE United Artists, 1942
DIMITRI TIOMKIN† ★

THE MOON AND THE GUTTER LA LUNE DANS LE
CANIVEAU Triumph/Columbia, 1983
GABRIEL YARED

THE MOON IS BLUE United Artists, 1953
HERSCHEL BURKE GILBERT

THE MOON IS DOWN 20th Century-Fox, 1943
ALFRED NEWMAN†

MOON OF THE WOLF (TF) Filmways, 1972
BERNARDO SEGALL

MOON OVER BURMA Paramount, 1940
VICTOR YOUNG†

MOON OVER PARADOR Universal, 1988
MAURICE JARRE

MOON PILOT Buena Vista, 1962
PAUL J. SMITH†

MOON SHOT (CTD) TBS Prods., 1994
MALCOLM BROOKS
RUSHMORE DE NOOYER
ED VAN FLEET

MOON ZERO TWO Warner Bros., 1970
DON ELLIS†

MOONCHILD Filmmakers Ltd./American Films Ltd.,
1974
BILLY BYERS
PATRICK WILLIAMS

MOONDANCE 1996
FIACHRA TRENCH

MOONDANCE Mozumdar, 1992
MICHAEL R. SMITH

MOONFLEET MGM, 1955
MIKLOS ROZSA†

MOONLIGHT & VALENTINO Gramercy, 1995
HOWARD SHORE

MOONLIGHT (TF) Universal TV, 1982
PATRICK WILLIAMS

MOONLIGHT IN VERMONT Universal, 1943
EDWARD WARD†

MOONLIGHT MURDER MGM, 1936
HERBERT STOTHART†
EDWARD WARD†

THE MOONLIGHTER Warner Bros., 1953
HEINZ ROEMHELD†

MOONLIGHTING Universal Classics, 1982
STANLEY MYERS†
HANS ZIMMER

MOONLIGHTING (TF) Picturemaker Productions/
ABC Circle Films, 1985
LEE HOLDRIDGE

MOONRAKER United Artists, 1979
JOHN BARRY

MOONRISE Republic, 1948
WILLIAM LAVA†

MOONSHINE COUNTY EXPRESS New World,
1977
FRED WERNER

THE MOONSPINNERS Buena Vista, 1964
RON GRAINER†

MOONSTRUCK MGM/UA, 1987
DICK HYMAN

MOONTIDE 20th Century-Fox, 1942
DAVID BUTTOLPH†
CYRIL J. MOCKRIDGE†

MOONTRAP Shapiro Glickenhaus, 1989
JOSEPH LO DUCA

MOONWALKER Warner Bros., 1988
BRUCE BROUGHTON

MORDI E FUGGE C.C. Champion/Les Films
Concordia, 1973
CARLO RUSTICHELLI

MORE THAN FRIENDS (TF) Reiner-Mishkin
Productions/Columbia TV, 1978
FRED KARLIN

THE MORE THE MERRIER Columbia, 1943
LEIGH HARLINE†

THE MORE THINGS CHANGE Hoyts, 1986
PETER BEST

MORE WILD WILD WEST (TF) CBS Entertainment,
1980
JEFF ALEXANDER†

MORGAN STEWART'S COMING HOME New
Century/Vista, 1987
PETER BERNSTEIN

MORGAN THE PIRATE MGM, 1961
FRANCO MANNINO

MORGAN! MORGAN: A SUITABLE CASE FOR
TREATMENT Cinema 5, 1966
JOHN DANKWORTH

MORIRE A ROMA 1976
NICOLA PIOVANI

MORITURI THE SABOTEUR, CODE NAME

THE MORNING AFTER 20th Century Fox, 1986
PAUL CHIHARA

THE MORNING AFTER (TF) David L. Wolper
Productions, 1974
PETE CARPENTER†
MIKE POST

MORNING BECOMES ELECTRA (MS) 1978
MAURICE JARRE

MORNING DEPARTURE Universal, 1950
WILLIAM ALWYN†

MORNING GLORY Academy, 1993
JONATHAN ELIAS

MORNING GLORY RKO Radio, 1933
MAX STEINER†

MOROCCO Paramount, 1930
KARL HAJOS†

MORONS FROM OUTER SPACE Thorn/EMI, 1985
PETER BREWIS

MORT, OU EST TA VICTOIRE? 1963
MAURICE JARRE

MORTAL KOMBAT New Line, 1995
GEORGE S. CLINTON

MORTAL PASSIONS Gibraltar Releasing
Organization, 1989
PARMER FULLER

MORTAL SINS Silver Chariots, 1991
SIMON BOSWELL

MORTAL SINS (CTF) Blake Edwards TV/Barry Weitz
Films, 1992
JOSEPH CONLAN ☆

THE MORTAL STORM MGM, 1940
BRONISLAU KAPER†

MORTAL THOUGHTS Columbia, 1991
MARK ISHAM

MORTE IN VATICANO 1982
PINO DONAGGIO

MORTUARY Artists Releasing Corporation/Film
Ventures International, 1983
JOHN CACAVAS

MORTUARY ACADEMY Landmark Releasing, 1987
DAVID SPEAR

MOSCA ADDIO Istituto Luce/Italnoleggio, 1987
ENNIO MORRICONE

MOSCOW ON THE HUDSON Columbia, 1984
DAVID MCHUGH

MOSES (MS) ITC/RAI, 1975
ENNIO MORRICONE
DOV SELTZER

THE MOSQUITO COAST Warner Bros., 1986
MAURICE JARRE

MOSQUITO SQUADRON United Artists, 1970
FRANK CORDELL†

MOSS ROSE 20th Century-Fox, 1947
DAVID BUTTOLPH†

THE MOST DANGEROUS GAME RKO Radio, 1932
MAX STEINER†

**THE MOST DANGEROUS MAN IN THE WORLD
(TF)** BBC/Iberoamericana/Celtic Films, 1988
STANLEY MYERS†

MOST WANTED New Line, 1997
PAUL BUCKMASTER

MOST WANTED (TF) QM Productions, 1976
PATRICK WILLIAMS

THE MOST WONDERFUL MOMENT 1956
NINO ROTA†

MOTEL HELL United Artists, 1980
LANCE RUBIN

MOTHER Paramount, 1996
MARC SHAIMAN

**MOTHER AND DAUGHTER - THE LOVING WAR
(TF)** Edgar J. Scherick Associates, 1980
LEE HOLDRIDGE

MOTHER DIDN'T TELL ME 20th Century-Fox,
1950
CYRIL J. MOCKRIDGE†
LIONEL NEWMAN†

MOTHER IS A FRESHMAN 20th Century-Fox,
1949
ALFRED NEWMAN†

MOTHER LODE Agamemnon Films, 1982
KEN WANNBERG

MOTHER NIGHT Fine Line, 1996
MICHAEL CONVERTINO

MOTHER OF THE BRIDE (TF) Baby/Leonard Hill,
1993
BRUCE MILLER

MOTHER TERESA (FD) Petrie Productions, 1986
SUZANNE E. CIANI

MOTHER WORE TIGHTS 20th Century-Fox, 1947
ALFRED NEWMAN† ★★

MOTHER'S BOY Miramax-Dimension, 1994
GEORGE S. CLINTON

**A MOTHER'S COURAGE: THE MARY THOMAS
STORY (TF)** Interscope Communications/Chet
Walker Enterprises/Walt Disney TV, 1989
LEE HOLDRIDGE

MOTHER'S DAY United Film Distribution, 1980
PHILO GALLO
CLEM VICARI

**MOTHER'S DAY ON WALTONS MOUNTAIN
(TF)** Amanda Productions/Lorimar, 1982
ALEXANDER COURAGE

A MOTHER'S GIFT (TF) RHI/TeleVest, 1995
LEE HOLDRIDGE

MOTHER'S HEART CUORE DI MAMMA 1968
ENNIO MORRICONE

A MOTHER'S JUSTICE (TF) Green/Epstein/
Longbow Prods./Lorimar TV, 1991
RICHARD BELLIS

A MOTHER'S REVENGE (TF) Carla Singer/World
Intl. Pictures, 1993
LAURA KARPMAN

**A MOTHER'S RIGHT: THE ELIZABETH MORGAN
STORY (TF)** Landsburg, 1992
JAMES MCVAY

THE MOTIVE WAS JEALOUSY 1970
ARMANDO TROVAJOLI

MOTOR PSYCHO Eve, 1965
PAUL SAWTELL†
BERT A. SHEFTER

MOTORAMA Planet Productions, 1993
ANDY SUMMERS

MOTORCYCLE GANG American International, 1957
ALBERT GLASSER

MOTRE-DAME, CATHEDRALE DE PARIS 1957
JEAN WIENER†

MOUCHETTE 1967
JEAN WIENER†

MOULIN ROUGE United Artists, 1952
GEORGES AURIC†

THE MOUNTAIN Paramount, 1956
DANIELE AMFITHEATROF†

MOUNTAIN FAMILY ROBINSON Pacific
International, 1979
ROBERT O. RAGLAND

MOUNTAIN JUSTICE Warner Bros., 1937
W. FRANKE HARLING†

THE MOUNTAIN MEN Columbia, 1980
MICHEL LEGRAND

THE MOUNTAIN ROAD Columbia, 1960
JEROME MOROSS†

MOUNTAINS OF THE MOON Tri-Star, 1990
MICHAEL SMALL

MOUNTBATTEN: THE LAST VICEROY (MS)
George Walker TV Productions, 1986
JOHN SCOTT

MOURIR A MADRID TO DIE IN MADRID (FD)
1963
MAURICE JARRE

MOURNING BECOMES ELECTRA RKO Radio,
1947
RICHARD HAGEMAN†

THE MOUSE AND HIS CHILD (AF) Sanrio, 1977
ROGER KELLAWAY

THE MOUSE ON THE MOON United Artists, 1963
RON GRAINER†

THE MOUSE THAT ROARED Columbia, 1959
EDWIN ASTLEY

MOUSEY CAT AND MOUSE (TF) Universal TV/
Associated British Films, 1974
RON GRAINER†

MOUVEMENTS DU DESIR DESIRE IN MOTION
Alliance-Vivafilm, 1994
ZBIGNIEW PREISNER

MOVE 20th Century-Fox, 1970
MARVIN HAMLISCH

MOVE OVER, DARLING 20th Century-Fox, 1963
LIONEL NEWMAN†

MOVERS & SHAKERS MGM/UA, 1985
KEN WELCH
MITZIE WELCH

MOVIE MOVIE Warner Brothers, 1978
RALPH BURNS

THE MOVIE TELLER 1993
GUENTHER FISCHER

MOVING Warner Bros., 1988
HOWARD SHORE

MOVING TARGET (TF) Lewis B. Chesler
Productions/Bateman Company Productions/
Finnegan-Pinchuk Company/MGM-UA TV, 1988
FRED KARLIN
MICHEL RUBINI

MOVING THE MOUNTAIN 1994
LOU SOLA

MOVING VIOLATION 20th Century-Fox, 1976
DON PEAKE

MOVING VIOLATIONS 20th Century-Fox, 1985
RALPH BURNS

MOVIOLA: THE SCARLETT O'HARA WAR (TF)
David Wolper-Stan Margulies Productions/Warner
Bros. TV, 1980
WALTER SCHARF

MOVIOLA: THE SILENT LOVERS (MS)   David L. Wolper-Stan Margulies Productions/Warner Bros. TV, 1980
GERALD FRIED ☆

MOVIOLA: THIS YEAR'S BLONDE (MS)   David S. Wolper-Stan Margulies Productions/Warner Bros. TV, 1980
ELMER BERNSTEIN

THE MOZART BIRD   Spellbound, 1993
ROSALIND GEORGE

MR. & MRS. BO JO JONES (TF)   20th Century-Fox TV, 1971
FRED KARLIN

MR. ACE   United Artists, 1947
HEINZ ROEMHELD†

MR. AND MRS. BRIDGE   Miramax, 1990
RICHARD ROBBINS

MR. AND MRS. SMITH   RKO Radio, 1941
EDWARD WARD†

MR. ARKADIN   *CONFIDENTIAL REPORT*   Warner Bros., 1955
PAUL MISRAKI

Mr. BASEBALL   Universal, 1992
JERRY GOLDSMITH

MR. BELVEDERE GOES TO COLLEGE   20th Century-Fox, 1949
ALFRED NEWMAN†

MR. BELVEDERE RINGS THE BELL   20th Century-Fox, 1951
CYRIL J. MOCKRIDGE†

MR. BILLION   20th Century-Fox, 1976
DAVE GRUSIN

MR. BLANDINGS BUILDS HIS DREAM HOUSE   RKO Radio, 1948
LEIGH HARLINE†

MR. BUG GOES TO TOWN   *HOPPITY GOES TO TOWN* (AF)   Paramount, 1941
LEIGH HARLINE†

MR. DEEDS GOES TO TOWN   Columbia, 1936
DIMITRI TIOMKIN†

MR. DESTINY   Buena Vista, 1990
DAVID NEWMAN

MR. DISTRICT ATTORNEY   Columbia, 1947
HERSCHEL BURKE GILBERT

MR. DODD TAKES THE AIR   Warner Bros., 1937
ADOLPH DEUTSCH†

MR. DOODLE KICKS OFF   RKO Radio, 1938
ROY WEBB†

MR. DYNAMITE   Universal, 1941
HANS J. SALTER†

MR. FORBUSH AND THE PENGUINS   EMI, 1971
JOHN ADDISON

MR. HERCULES AGAINST KARATE   *MR. HERCULES AGAINST KUNG FU*   United Artists, 1973
CARLO SAVINA

MR. HERCULES AGAINST KUNG FU   United Artists, 1973
CARLO SAVINA

MR. HOBBS TAKES A VACATION   20th Century-Fox, 1962
HENRY MANCINI†

MR. HOBO   1935
LOUIS LEVY†

MR. HOLLAND'S OPUS   Buena Vista, 1995
MICHAEL KAMEN

MR. HORN (TF)   Lorimar Productions, 1979
JERRY FIELDING†

MR. HULOT'S HOLIDAY   *LES VACANCES DE MR. HULOT*   G-B-D International, 1953
ALAIN ROMANS

MR. IMPERIUM   MGM, 1951
BRONISLAU KAPER†

MR. JERICHO (TF)   ITC, 1970
LAURIE JOHNSON

Mr. JONES   Columbia, 1993
MAURICE JARRE

MR. KINKY   1967
ARMANDO TROVAJOLI

MR. LOVE (TF)   Enigma/Goldcrest Films & TV, 1986
WILLY RUSSELL

MR. LUCKY   RKO Radio, 1943
ROY WEBB†

MR. MAGOO   Buena Vista, 1997
MARK MOTHERSBAUGH

MR. MAJESTYK   United Artists, 1974
CHARLES BERNSTEIN

MR. MOM   20th Century-Fox, 1983
LEE HOLDRIDGE

MR. MOTO'S LAST WARNING   20th Century-Fox, 1939
DAVID RAKSIN

MR. NANNY   New Line, 1993
DAVID JOHANSEN
BRIAN KOONIN

MR. NORTH   Heritage Entertainment, 1988
DAVID MCHUGH

MR. PATMAN   Film Consortium, 1980
PAUL HOFFERT

MR. PEABODY AND THE MERMAID   Universal, 1948
ROBERT EMMETT DOLAN†

MR. PERRIN AND MR. TRAILL   1948
ALLAN GRAY†

MR. QUILP   Avco Embassy, 1975
ELMER BERNSTEIN

MR. RICCO   United Artists, 1975
CHICO HAMILTON

MR. ROBINSON CRUSOE   United Artists, 1932
ALFRED NEWMAN†

MR. SARDONICUS   Columbia, 1961
VON DEXTER

Mr. SATURDAY NIGHT   Universal, 1992
MARC SHAIMAN

MR. SKEFFINGTON   Warner Bros., 1944
FRANZ WAXMAN†

MR. SMITH GOES TO WASHINGTON   Columbia, 1939
DIMITRI TIOMKIN† ★

MR. SOFT TOUCH   Columbia, 1949
HEINZ ROEMHELD†

MR. SYCAMORE   Film Venture, 1975
MAURICE JARRE

MR. UNIVERSE   United Artists, 1951
DIMITRI TIOMKIN†

MR. WINKLE GOES TO WAR   Columbia, 1944
CARMEN DRAGON†
PAUL SAWTELL†

MR. WONDERFUL   Warner Bros., 1993
MICHAEL GORE

MR. WRITE   Shapiro Glickenhaus, 1994
MILES ROSTON

MR. WRONG   Buena Vista, 1996
CRAIG SAFAN

MRS. 'ARRIS GOES TO PARIS (TF)   Accent Films/Novo Films/Corymore Prods., 1992
STANLEY MYERS†

MRS. BROWN, YOU'VE GOT A LOVELY DAUGHTER   MGM, 1968
RON GOODWIN

MRS. DELAFIELD WANTS TO MARRY (TF)   Schaefer-Karpf Productions/Gaylord Production Company, 1986
PETER MATZ

MRS. DOUBTFIRE   20th Century Fox, 1993
HOWARD SHORE

MRS. LAMBERT REMEMBERS LOVE (TF)   RHI, 1991
LEE HOLDRIDGE

MRS. MIKE   United Artists, 1949
MAX STEINER†

MRS. MINIVER   MGM, 1942
HERBERT STOTHART†

MRS. O'MALLEY AND MR. MALONE   MGM, 1950
ADOLPH DEUTSCH†

MRS. PARKER AND THE VICIOUS CIRCLE   Fine Line/Miramax, 1994
MARK ISHAM

MRS. PARKINGTON   MGM, 1945
BRONISLAU KAPER†

MRS. POLIFAX - SPY   United Artists, 1971
LALO SCHIFRIN

MRS. R'S DAUGHTER (TF)   NBC Productions/Dan Curtis Productions, 1979
BOB COBERT

MRS. SOFFEL   MGM/UA, 1984
MARK ISHAM

MRS. SUNDANCE (TF)   20th Century-Fox TV, 1974
PATRICK WILLIAMS

MRS. WIGGS OF THE CABBAGE PATCH   Paramount, 1942
VICTOR YOUNG†

MRS. WINTERBOURNE   TriStar, 1996
PATRICK DOYLE

MS. DON JUAN   *DON JUAN ETAIT UNE FEMME*   Scotia American, 1973
MICHEL MAGNE†

MUCH ADO ABOUT NOTHING   Samuel Goldwyn, 1993
PATRICK DOYLE

MUD   Trident-Barber, 1978
MICHAEL J. LEWIS

MUDDY RIVER   Japan Film Center, 1981
KUROUDO MORI

MUDER IN MY MIND (TF)   CBS TV, 1997
MICHEL COLOMBIER

THE MUDLARK   20th Century-Fox, 1950
WILLIAM ALWYN†

MUG TOWN   Universal, 1943
HANS J. SALTER†

MUGGABLE MARY: STREET COP (TF)   CBS Entertainment, 1982
EARLE HAGEN

THE MUGGER   United Artists, 1958
ALBERT GLASSER

MUI DU DU XANH   *THE SCENT OF THE GREEN PAPAYA*   1993
TON THAT TIET

MULHOLLAND FALLS   MGM-UA, 1995
DAVE GRUSIN

MULLIGAN'S STEW (TF)   Christiana Productions/Paramount Pictures TV, 1977
GEORGE ALICESON TIPTON

MULTIPLICITY   Columbia, 1996
GEORGE FENTON

MUMMY   1993
DOV SELTZER

THE MUMMY   Universal, 1959
FRANZ REIZENSTEIN†

MUMMY'S BOYS   RKO Radio, 1936
ROY WEBB†

THE MUMMY'S CURSE   Universal, 1945
PAUL SAWTELL†

THE MUMMY'S GHOST   Universal, 1944
CHARLES PREVIN†
FRANK SKINNER†

THE MUMMY'S GHOST   Universal, 1944
HANS J. SALTER†

THE MUMMY'S HAND   Universal, 1940
FRANK SKINNER†

THE MUMMY'S HAND   Universal, 1940
HANS J. SALTER†

THE MUMMY'S SHROUD   20th Century-Fox, 1967
DON BANKS

THE MUMMY'S TOMB   Universal, 1942
CHARLES PREVIN†
HEINZ ROEMHELD†

THE MUMMY'S TOMB   Universal, 1942
HANS J. SALTER†

MUMSY, NANNY, SONNY AND GIRLY   *GIRLY*   Cinerama Releasing Corporation, 1970
BERNARD EBBINGHOUSE

MUNCHIE   New Horizon/Concorde, 1991
CHUCK CIRINO

MUNCHIE II   Concorde/New Horizons, 1993
CHUCK CIRINO

MUNCHIES   Concorde, 1987
ERNEST TROOST

MUNSTER, GO HOME   Universal, 1966
JACK MARSHALL

THE MUNSTERS' REVENGE (TF)   Universal TV, 1981
VIC MIZZY

THE MUPPET CHRISTMAS CAROL   Buena Vista, 1992
MILES GOODMAN†

THE MUPPET MOVIE   AFD, 1979
PAUL WILLIAMS ★

MUPPET TREASURE ISLAND   Buena Vista, 1996
HANS ZIMMER

THE MUPPETS TAKE MANHATTAN   Tri-Star, 1984
RALPH BURNS

MURDER 1, DANCER 0 (TF)   Mickey Productions/Filmways, 1983
GEORGE ROMANIS

MURDER 101 (CTF)   Alan Barnette Prods./MCA TV, 1991
PHILIP GIFFIN

MURDER AHOY!   MGM, 1964
RON GOODWIN

MURDER AT 1600   Warner Bros., 1997
CHRISTOPHER YOUNG

MURDER AT THE GALLOP   MGM, 1963
RON GOODWIN

MURDER AT THE WORLD SERIES (TF)   ABC Circle Films, 1977
JOHN CACAVAS

MURDER BETWEEN FRIENDS (TF)   Gimbel-Adelson Co./Anaid Films/ABC Prods., 1994
MARK SNOW

MURDER BY DEATH   Columbia, 1976
DAVE GRUSIN

MURDER BY DECREE   Avco Embassy, 1979
PAUL J. ZAZA
CARL ZITTRER

MURDER BY MAIL   Cannon, 1980
CRAIG HUNDLEY

MURDER BY MOONLIGHT (TF)   Tamara Asseyev Productions/London Weekend TV/Viacom, 1989
TREVOR JONES

MURDER BY NATURAL CAUSES (TF)   Levinson-Link Productions, 1979
DICK DEBENEDICTIS

MURDER BY NUMBERS   Burnhill, 1990
ROBERT SUMMERS

MURDER BY PHONE   *BELLS*   New World, 1980
JOHN BARRY

MURDER BY TELEVISION   1935
OLIVER WALLACE†

MURDER BY THE BOOK (TF)   TVS Ltd./Benton Evans Productions, 1986
MARK SNOW

MURDER C.O.D. (TF)   Kushner-Locke/NBC, 1990
FRED KARLIN

MURDER CAN HURT YOU! (TF)   Aaron Spelling Productions, 1980
ARTIE KANE

MURDER IN COWETA COUNTY (TF)   Telecom Entertainment/International Picture Show Company, 1983
BRAD FIEDEL

MURDER IN MIND   Lakeshore Entertainment, 1997
PAUL BUCKMASTER

MURDER IN MISSISSIPPI (TF)   David L. Wolper Productions, 1990
MASON DARING

MURDER IN MUSIC CITY (TF)   Frankel Films/Gank Inc., 1979
EARLE HAGEN

MURDER IN NEW HAMPSHIRE: THE PAMELA SMART STORY (TF)   New Hampshire Prods./Robert Greenwald, 1992
GARY CHANG

MURDER IN PARADISE (TF)   Bill McCutchen Productions/Columbia Pictures TV, 1990
JOHN CACAVAS

MURDER IN PEYTON PLACE (TF)   20th Century-Fox TV, 1977
LAURENCE ROSENTHAL

MURDER IN SPACE (CTF)   Robert Cooper/Zenith Productions, 1985
ARTHUR B. RUBINSTEIN

MURDER IN TEXAS (TF)   Dick Clark Productions/Billy Hale Films, 1981
LEONARD ROSENMAN

MURDER IN THE FIRST   Warner Bros., 1994
CHRISTOPHER YOUNG

MURDER IN THE HEARTLAND (TF)   O'Hara-Horowitz Prods., 1993
PATRICK WILLIAMS

A MURDER IS A MURDER   1972
PAUL MISRAKI

MURDER IS EASY (TF)   David L. Wolper-Stan Margulies Productions/Warner Bros. TV, 1982
GERALD FRIED

MURDER IS MY BEAT   Allied Artists, 1955
ALBERT GLASSER

MURDER IS MY BUSINESS   Producers Releasing Corp., 1946
LEO ERDODY†

MURDER LIVE ! (TF)   Von Zerneck-Sertner, 1997
GARY CHANG

THE MURDER MAN   MGM, 1935
WILLIAM AXT†

MURDER MOST FOUL   MGM, 1965
RON GOODWIN

THE MURDER OF MARY PHAGAN (MS)   George Stevens Jr. Productions/Century Tower Productions, 1988
MAURICE JARRE

MURDER OF INNOCENCE (TF)   Samuels Film/Polone/Hearst, 1993
DON DAVIS

MURDER ON A BRIDLE PATH   RKO Radio, 1936
ROY WEBB†

MURDER ON DIAMOND ROAD   United Artists, 1937
MIKLOS ROZSA†

MURDER ON MONDAY   1952
MALCOLM ARNOLD

MURDER ON THE BLACKBOARD   RKO Radio, 1934
MAX STEINER†

MURDER ON THE ORIENT EXPRESS   Paramount, 1974
RICHARD RODNEY BENNETT ★

MURDER ONCE REMOVED (TF)   Metromedia Productions, 1971
ROBERT DRASNIN

MURDER ONE: FINAL VERDICT (TF)   Steven Bochco Prods., 1997
MIKE POST

MURDER OR MERCY (TF)   QM Productions, 1974
PATRICK WILLIAMS

MURDER ORDAINED (MS)   Zev Braun Productions/Interscope Communications, 1987
MARK SNOW

THE MURDER THAT WOULDN'T DIE (TF)   Glen A. Larson Productions/Universal TV, 1980
JOE HARNELL
GLEN A. LARSON

MURDER WITHOUT MOTIVE: THE EDMUND PERRY STORY (TF)   Leonard Hill Films, 1992
ROSS LEVINSON

MURDER, CZECH STYLE   1966
ZDENEK LISKA

MURDER, HE SAYS   Paramount, 1945
ROBERT EMMETT DOLAN†

MURDER, INC.   20th Century-Fox, 1960
FRANK DEVOL

MURDER, MY SWEET   RKO Radio, 1944
ROY WEBB†

MURDER, SHE SAID   MGM, 1962
RON GOODWIN

MURDERERS AMONG US: THE SIMON WISENTHAL STORY (CTF)   HBO Pictures/Robert Cooper Productions/TVS Films, 1989
BILL CONTI

MURDERERS' ROW   Columbia, 1967
LALO SCHIFRIN

MURDEROCK, UCCIDE A PASSO DI DANZA   Scena Film, 1984
KEITH EMERSON

F
I
L
M

T
I
T
L
E
S

N

**F
I
L
M

T
I
T
L
E
S**

THE NEVERENDING STORY Warner Bros., 1984
KLAUS DOLDINGER
GIORGIO MORODER
THE NEVERENDING STORY III Warner Bros., 1994
PETER WOLF
THE NEVERENDING STORY II: THE NEXT CHAPTER Warner Bros., 1990
ROBERT FOLK
THE NEW ADVENTURES OF HEIDI (TF) Pierre Cossette Enterprises, 1978
BUZ KOHAN
THE NEW ADVENTURES OF PIPPI LONGSTALKING Columbia, 1988
MISHA SEGAL
THE NEW AGE Warner Bros., 1994
MARK MOTHERSBAUGH
THE NEW BABYLON 1929
DMITRI SHOSTAKOVITCH†
THE NEW CENTURIONS Columbia, 1972
QUINCY JONES
NEW CLOTHES 1963
CHRISTOPHER KOMEDA†
THE NEW DAUGHTERS OF JOSHUA CABE (TF) Spelling-Goldberg Productions, 1976
JEFF ALEXANDER†
NEW EARTH 1934
HANNS EISLER†
NEW EDEN (CTF) Davis Ent./MTE, 1995
BLAKE LEYH
NEW FACES OF 1937 RKO Radio, 1937
ROY WEBB†
NEW FRONTIER Republic, 1939
WILLIAM LAVA†
NEW JACK CITY Warner Bros., 1991
MICHEL COLOMBIER
THE NEW KIDS Columbia, 1985
MICHEL RUBINI
LALO SCHIFRIN
A NEW KIND OF LOVE Paramount, 1963
LEITH STEVENS† ★
A NEW LEAF Paramount, 1971
JOHNNY MANDEL
A NEW LIFE Paramount, 1988
JONATHAN TURRIN
New Line Cinema, 1988
PETER GOLDFOOT
THE NEW LOT 1943
RICHARD ADDINSELL†
THE NEW LOVE BOAT (TF) Aaron Spelling Productions, 1977
ARTIE KANE
THE NEW MAVERICK (TF) Cherokee Productions/ Warner Bros. TV, 1978
JOHN RUBINSTEIN
NEW MEXICO United Artists, 1951
LUCIEN MORAWECK†
NEW MOON MGM, 1931
HERBERT STOTHART†
NEW MOON MGM, 1940
HERBERT STOTHART†
New Star Entertainment, 1989
JULIAN LAXTON
NEW WINE United Artists, 1941
MIKLOS ROZSA†
A NEW WORLD 1966
MICHEL COLOMBIER
NEW YEAR'S EVIL Cannon, 1981
W. MICHAEL LEWIS
LAURIN RINDER
NEW YORK CITY—THE MOST 1968
SOL KAPLAN
NEW YORK COPA Columbia TriStar, 1996
BOB MITHOFF
NEW YORK STORIES Buena Vista, 1989
CARMINE COPPOLA†
NEW YORK TOWN Paramount, 1941
LEO SHUKEN†
NEW YORK, NEW YORK United Artists, 1977
RALPH BURNS
NEWMAN'S LAW Universal, 1974
ROBERT PRINCE
NEWS AT ELEVEN (TF) Turman-Foster Productions/ Finnegan Associates, 1986
MARK SNOW
NEWSFRONT 1978
WILLIAM MOTZIG
NEWSIES Buena Vista, 1992
J.A.C. REDFORD
NEXT DOOR (CTF) Nederlander Television & Film Prods./Tudor Ent./TriStar TV, 1994
VAN DYKE PARKS
THE NEXT KARATE KID Columbia, 1994
BILL CONTI
THE NEXT MAN Allied Artists, 1976
MICHAEL KAMEN
NEXT OF KIN 1942
SIR WILLIAM WALTON†
NEXT OF KIN Warner Bros., 1989
TODD HAYEN
JACK NITZCHE

NEXT STOP, GREENWICH VILLAGE 20th Century Fox, 1976
BILL CONTI
NEXT TIME I MARRY RKO Radio, 1938
ROY WEBB†
NEXT TIME WE LOVE Universal, 1936
FRANZ WAXMAN†
NEXT TO NO TIME! 1958
GEORGES AURIC†
THE NEXT VOICE YOU HEAR MGM, 1950
DAVID RAKSIN
NEZ DE CUIR 1951
GEORGES AURIC†
NIAGRA 20th Century-Fox, 1953
SOL KAPLAN
NIAGRA FALLS United Artists, 1941
EDWARD WARD†
A NICE GIRL LIKE ME Avco Embassy, 1969
PATRICK WILLIAMS
NICE GIRL? Universal, 1941
CHARLES PREVIN†
NICE GIRLS DON'T EXPLODE New World, 1987
BRIAN BANKS
ANTHONY MARINELLI
NICHOLAS AND ALEXANDRA Columbia, 1971
RICHARD RODNEY BENNETT ★
NICHOLAS NICKLEBY 1946
LORD BERNERS†
NICK CARTER, MASTER DETECTIVE MGM, 1939
EDWARD WARD†
NICK KNIGHT (TF) Barry Weitz Films/Robirdle Pictures/New World TV, 1989
JOSEPH CONLAN
NICK'S MOVIE Pari Films, 1980
RONNIE BLAKLEY
NICKEL & DIME August Entertainment, 1992
STEPHEN COHN
NICKEL MOUNTAIN Ziv International, 1985
LINCOLN MAYORGA
THE NICKEL RIDE 20th Century-Fox, 1974
DAVE GRUSIN
NICKELODEON Columbia, 1976
RICHARD HAZARD
NICKY'S WORLD (TF) Tomorrow Entertainment, 1974
CHARLES GROSS
NIGHT AFTER DEATH 1983
ALFI KABILJO
NIGHT AMBUSH ILL MET BY MOONLIGHT Rank, 1957
MIKIS THEODORAKIS
NIGHT AND DAY Warner Bros., 1946
MAX STEINER† ★
NIGHT AND FOG 1955
HANNS EISLER†
NIGHT AND THE CITY 20th Century Fox, 1992
JAMES NEWTON HOWARD
NIGHT AND THE CITY 20th Century-Fox, 1950
FRANZ WAXMAN†
NIGHT ANGEL Fries Entertainment, 1990
CORY LERIOS
A NIGHT AT THE OPERA MGM, 1935
HERBERT STOTHART†
THE NIGHT CALLER PEUR SUR LA VILLE 1975
ENNIO MORRICONE
NIGHT CHASE (TF) Cinema Center 100, 1970
LAURENCE ROSENTHAL
NIGHT CLUB Crown International, 1990
BARRY FASMAN
DANA WALDEN
NIGHT CREATURE Dimension Pictures, 1979
JIM HELMS
NIGHT CREATURES CAPTAIN CLEGG 1962
DON BANKS
NIGHT CRIES (TF) Charles Fries Productions, 1978
PAUL CHIHARA
NIGHT CROSSING Buena Vista, 1982
JERRY GOLDSMITH
THE NIGHT DIGGER MGM, 1971
BERNARD HERRMANN†
NIGHT EDITOR Columbia, 1946
MARIO†
THE NIGHT EVELYN CAME OUT OF THE GRAVE 1973
BRUNO NICOLAI
NIGHT FALLS ON MANHATTAN Paramount, 1997
MARK ISHAM
NIGHT FLIGHT MGM, 1933
HERBERT STOTHART†
NIGHT FLIGHT TO MOSCOW Avco Embassy, 1973
ENNIO MORRICONE
NIGHT FLOWERS Willow Production Co., 1979
HARRY MANFREDINI
NIGHT GALLERY (TF) Universal TV, 1969
BILLY GOLDENBERG
NIGHT GAME Trans World Entertainment, 1989
PINO DONAGGIO
NIGHT GAMES Avco Embassy, 1980
JOHN BARRY

NIGHT GAMES (TF) Paramount TV, 1974
LALO SCHIFRIN
THE NIGHT HAS A THOUSAND EYES Paramount, 1948
VICTOR YOUNG†
THE NIGHT HEAVEN FELL LES BIJOUTIERS DU CLAIR DE LUNE Kingsley International, 1957
GEORGES AURIC†
A NIGHT IN CASABLANCA United Artists, 1946
WERNER JANSSEN†
A NIGHT IN HEAVEN 20th Century-Fox, 1983
JAN HAMMER
NIGHT IN PARADISE Universal, 1946
FRANK SKINNER†
A NIGHT IN THE LIFE OF JIMMY REARDON Island Pictures/20th Century Fox, 1988
ELMER BERNSTEIN
BILL CONTI
NIGHT INTO MORNING MGM, 1951
CARMEN DRAGON†
THE NIGHT IS YOUNG MGM, 1935
HERBERT STOTHART†
NIGHT LIFE Wild Night Productions, 1989
ROGER BOURLAND
NIGHT LIFE OF THE GODS Universal, 1935
ARTHUR MORTON
NIGHT MAIL 1936
BENJAMIN BRITTEN†
NIGHT MONSTER Universal, 1942
HANS J. SALTER†
NIGHT MOVES Warner Bros., 1975
MICHAEL SMALL
NIGHT MUST FALL Embassy, 1964
RON GRAINER†
NIGHT MUST FALL MGM, 1937
EDWARD WARD†
THE NIGHT MY NUMBER CAME UP General Film Distributors, 1955
MALCOLM ARNOLD
THE NIGHT MY PARENTS RAN AWAY (TF) Fox West Pictures/New Line TV/Chanticleer, 1993
J. PETER ROBINSON
A NIGHT OF ADVENTURE RKO Radio, 1944
LEIGH HARLINE†
NIGHT OF COURAGE (TF) Titus Productions/The Eugene O'Neill Memorial Theater Center, 1987
GARY WILLIAM FRIEDMAN
NIGHT OF DARK SHADOWS MGM, 1971
BOB COBERT
THE NIGHT OF NIGHTS Paramount, 1939
VICTOR YOUNG†
THE NIGHT OF THE GENERALS Columbia, 1966
MAURICE JARRE
THE NIGHT OF THE GRIZZLY Paramount, 1966
LEITH STEVENS†
THE NIGHT OF THE HUNTER United Artists, 1955
WALTER SCHUMANN†
THE NIGHT OF THE SEAGULL 1970
CHUMEI WATANABE
THE NIGHT OF THE SHOOTING STARS LA NOTTE DI SAN LORENZO United Artists Classics, 1981
NICOLA PIOVANI
NIGHT OF TERROR (TF) Paramount TV, 1972
ROBERT DRASNIN
NIGHT OF THE BLOOD MONSTER THRONE OF FIRE 1972
BRUNO NICOLAI
NIGHT OF THE COMET Atlantic Releasing Corporation, 1984
DAVID CAMPBELL
NIGHT OF THE CREEPS Tri-Star, 1986
BARRY DEVORZON
NIGHT OF THE DEMON Columbia, 1957
CLIFTON PARKER†
NIGHT OF THE DEMONS International Film Marketing, 1988
DENNIS TENNEY
NIGHT OF THE DEMONS 2 Republic, 1994
JIM MANZIE
NIGHT OF THE EAGLE American International, 1962
WILLIAM ALWYN†
NIGHT OF THE HUNTER (TF) Diana Keren Prods./ Konigsberg-Sanitsky, 1991
PETER MANNING ROBINSON
NIGHT OF THE IGUANA MGM, 1964
BENJAMIN FRANKEL†
NIGHT OF THE JUGGLER Columbia, 1980
ARTIE KANE
NIGHT OF THE LEPUS MGM, 1972
JIMMIE HASKELL
NIGHT OF THE LIVING DEAD Columbia, 1990
PAUL McCOLLOUGH
NIGHT OF THE QUARTER MOON FLESH AND FLAME MGM, 1959
ALBERT GLASSER
NIGHT OF THE RUNNING MAN American World Pictures, 1995
CHRISTOPHER FRANKE
NIGHT OF THE WARRIOR Trimark, 1991
ED TOMNEY

NIGHT OF THE ZOMBIES Motion Picture Marketing, 1980
GOBLIN
NIGHT ON EARTH JVC, 1991
TOM WAITS
NIGHT OWL (CTF) Morgan Hill Films and Hearst Entertainment Inc., 1993
GIL MELLE
NIGHT PARTNERS (TF) Moonlight Productions II, 1983
FRED KARLIN
NIGHT PASSAGE Universal, 1957
DIMITRI TIOMKIN†
NIGHT PATROL New World, 1984
DON PRESTON
NIGHT PEOPLE 20th Century-Fox, 1954
CYRIL J. MOCKRIDGE†
THE NIGHT PORTER Avco Embassy, 1974
DANIELE PARIS
THE NIGHT RAIDERS Republic, 1939
WILLIAM LAVA†
THE NIGHT RIDER (TF) Stephen J. Cannell Productions/Universal TV, 1979
PETE CARPENTER†
MIKE POST
THE NIGHT RUNNER Universal, 1957
HENRY MANCINI†
HERMAN STEIN
NIGHT SCHOOL TERROR EYES Paramount, 1981
BRAD FIEDEL
NIGHT SHADOWS Artists Releasing Corporation/ Film Ventures International, 1984
RICHARD H. BAND
NIGHT SHIFT O.W.I., 1942
MARC BLITZSTEIN†
NIGHT SHIFT The Ladd Company/Warner Bros., 1982
BURT BACHARACH
NIGHT SINS (TF) Michele Brustin Prods./ Scripps-Howard Entertainment, 1997
MARK SNOW
NIGHT SLAVES (TF) Bing Crosby Productions, 1970
BERNARDO SEGALL
NIGHT SONG RKO Radio, 1947
LEITH STEVENS†
NIGHT SPOT RKO Radio, 1938
ROY WEBB†
THE NIGHT STRANGLER (TF) ABC Circle Films, 1973
BOB COBERT
NIGHT TERROR (TF) Charles Fries Productions, 1977
FRED STEINER
THE NIGHT THAT PANICKED AMERICA (TF) The Culzean Corporation/Paramount Pictures TV, 1975
FRANK COMSTOCK
THE NIGHT THE BRIDGE FELL DOWN (TF) Irwin Allen Productions/Warner Bros. Television, 1983
RICHARD LASALLE
THE NIGHT THE LIGHTS WENT OUT IN GEORGIA Avco Embassy, 1981
DAVID SHIRE
THE NIGHT THE PROWLER International Harmony, 1978
CAMERON ALLAN
THE NIGHT THEY KILLED RASPUTIN L'ULTIMO ZAR 1960
ANGELO FRANCESCO LAVAGNINO†
THE NIGHT THEY RAIDED MINSKY'S United Artists, 1968
CHARLES STROUSE
THE NIGHT THEY SAVED CHRISTMAS (TF) Robert Halmi, Inc., 1984
CHARLES GROSS
THE NIGHT THEY TOOK MISS BEAUTIFUL (TF) Don Kirshner Productions/LaRose Productions, 1977
WALTER MURPHY
NIGHT TIDE Universal, 1963
DAVID RAKSIN
A NIGHT TO REMEMBER Columbia, 1942
WERNER R. HEYMANN†
A NIGHT TO REMEMBER Rank, 1958
WILLIAM ALWYN†
NIGHT TRAIN NIGHT TRAIN TO MUNICH MGM, 1940
LOUIS LEVY†
NIGHT TRAIN TO MUNICH MGM, 1940
LOUIS LEVY†
NIGHT TRAIN TO VENICE 1993
ALEXANDER BUBENHEIM
NIGHT UNTO NIGHT Warner Bros., 1949
FRANZ WAXMAN†
THE NIGHT VISITOR UMC, 1971
HENRY MANCINI†
NIGHT VISITOR NEVER CRY DEVIL MGM/UA, 1989
PARMER FULLER
NIGHT VISITORS Continental, 1988
ERNEST TROOST
THE NIGHT WALKER Universal, 1965
VIC MIZZY

NIGHT WARNING Comworld, 1983
BRUCE LANGHORNE

NIGHT WATCH Avco Embassy, 1973
JOHN CAMERON

THE NIGHT WE NEVER MET Miramax, 1993
EVAN LURIE

NIGHT WITHOUT SLEEP 20th Century-Fox, 1952
CYRIL J. MOCKRIDGE†

'NIGHT, MOTHER Universal, 1986
DAVID SHIRE

NIGHTBEAST 1982
ARLON OBER

NIGHTBREAKER (CTF) Turner Network TV, 1989
PETER BERNSTEIN

NIGHTBREED 20th Century Fox, 1990
DANNY ELFMAN
SHIRLEY WALKER

THE NIGHTCOMERS Avco Embassy, 1972
JERRY FIELDING†

NIGHTFALL Concorde, 1988
FRANK SERAFINE

NIGHTFIRE Miklen Entertainment, 1994
MIRIAM CUTLER

NIGHTFLYERS New Century/Vista, 1987
DOUG TIMM†

NIGHTHAWKS Universal, 1981
KEITH EMERSON

NIGHTIE NIGHTMARE New Horizon/Concorde,
1990
CHUCK CIRINO

NIGHTINGALES (TF) Aaron Spelling Productions,
1988
WILLIAM OLVIS

THE NIGHTMAN (TF) Avnet-Kerner Prods., 1992
GARY CHANG

A NIGHTMARE ON ELM STREET New Line Cinema,
1984
CHARLES BERNSTEIN

A NIGHTMARE ON ELM STREET 5: THE DREAM
CHILD New Line Cinema, 1989
JAY FERGUSON

A NIGHTMARE ON ELM STREET III: DREAM
WARRIORS New Line, 1987
KEN HARRISON

THE NIGHTMARE BEFORE CHRISTMAS (AF)
Buena Vista, 1993
DANNY ELFMAN

THE NIGHTMARE YEARS (CMS) Consolidated
Productions, 1989
VLADIMIR COSMA

NIGHTMARE 21st Century, 1981
JACK ERIC WILLIAMS

NIGHTMARE Cannon, 1993
DOV SELTZER

NIGHTMARE United Artists, 1956
HERSCHEL BURKE GILBERT

NIGHTMARE Universal, 1964
DON BANKS

NIGHTMARE (TF) Mark Carliner Productions/CBS
Entertainment, 1974
PETER LINK

NIGHTMARE ALLEY 20th Century-Fox, 1947
CYRIL J. MOCKRIDGE†

NIGHTMARE AT BITTER CREEK (TF) Swanton
Films/Guber-Peters Entertainment/Phoenix
Entertainment Group, 1988
ARTHUR B. RUBINSTEIN

NIGHTMARE AT SHADOW WOODS FCG, 1987
RICHARD EINHORN

NIGHTMARE CASTLE AMANTI D'OLTRE
TOMBA 1965
ENNIO MORRICONE

NIGHTMARE CITY 21st Century, 1980
STELVIO CIPRIANI

NIGHTMARE HONEYMOON MGM, 1974
ELMER BERNSTEIN

NIGHTMARE IN BADHAM COUNTY (TF) ABC
Circle Films, 1976
CHARLES BERNSTEIN

NIGHTMARE IN COLUMBIA COUNTY (TF)
Landsburg Co., 1991
RICHARD BELLIS

NIGHTMARE IN THE DAYLIGHT (TF)
Smith-Richmond/Saban-Sherick, 1992
DAVID SHIRE

NIGHTMARE ON ELM STREET III: DREAM
WARRIORS New Line Cinema, 1987
ANGELO BADALAMENTI

NIGHTMARE ON ELM STREET PART 4: THE
DREAM MASTER New Line Cinema, 1988
CRAIG SAFAN

NIGHTMARE ON ELM STREET, PART 2:
FREDDY'S REVENGE New Line Cinema, 1985
CHRISTOPHER YOUNG

NIGHTMARES Australian
BRIAN MAY†

NIGHTMARES Universal, 1983
CRAIG SAFAN

NIGHTS OF CABIRIA Lopert, 1957
NINO ROTA†

NIGHTS OF DRACULA 1970
BRUNO NICOLAI

NIGHTSTICK Production Distribution Co., 1987
ROBERT O. RAGLAND

NIGHTWATCH Miramax, 1997
JOAKIM HOLBECK

NIGHTWING Columbia, 1979
HENRY MANCINI†

NIJINSKY Paramount, 1980
JOHN LANCHBERY

NIKKI, WILD DOG OF THE NORTH Buena Vista,
1961
OLIVER WALLACE†

NINA 1958
GEORGES VAN PARYS†

NINA TAKES A LOVER Sharona Prods., 1994
TODD BOEKELHEIDE

NINE DAYS A QUEEN TUDOR ROSE Gaumont,
1936
HUBERT BATH†
LOUIS LEVY†

NINE GIRLS Columbia, 1944
JOHN LEIPOLD†

NINE HOURS TO RAMA 20th Century-Fox, 1963
MALCOLM ARNOLD

THE NINE LIVES OF FRITZ THE CAT (AF)
American International, 1974
TOM SCOTT

NINE MEN 1943
JOHN GREENWOOD†

NINE MONTHS 20th Century Fox, 1995
HANS ZIMMER

NINE TO FIVE 20th Century Fox, 1980
CHARLES FOX

NINI TIRABUSCIO, LA DONNA CHE INVENTO LA
MOSSA 1970
CARLO RUSTICHELLI

NINJA III—THE DOMINATION Cannon, 1984
UDI HARPAZ
W. MICHAEL LEWIS
LAURIN RINDER

NINJA TURF Ascot Entertainment Group, 1986
GARY FALCONE
CHARLES PAVLOSKY
CHRISTOPHER L. STONE

NINOTCHKA MGM, 1939
WERNER R. HEYMANN†

THE NINTH CONFIGURATION Warner Bros., 1980
BARRY DEVORZON

THE NINTH HEART Ceskoslovensky Filmexport,
1980
PETR HAPKA

NITCHEVO 1936
ARTHUR HONEGGER†

THE NITWITS RKO Radio, 1935
ROY WEBB†

NIXON Buena Vista, 1995
JOHN WILLIAMS ★

NO BEST MAN 1997
MARK MOTHERSBAUGH

NO CHILD OF MINE (TF) Green-Epstein/Warner
Bros. TV, 1993
RICHARD BELLIS

NO DEPOSIT, NO RETURN Buena Vista, 1976
BUDDY BAKER

NO DOWN PAYMENT 20th Century-Fox, 1957
LEIGH HARLINE†

NO ESCAPE Savoy, 1994
GRAEME REVELL

NO ESCAPE United Artists, 1953
BERT A. SHEFTER

NO GOODBYES Sam Yeung Prods., 1995
BRUNO LOUCHOUARN

NO HANDS ON THE CLOCK Paramount, 1941
PAUL SAWTELL†

NO HIGHWAY 20th Century-Fox, 1951
MALCOLM ARNOLD

NO HIGHWAY IN THE SKY NO HIGHWAY
20th Century-Fox, 1951
MALCOLM ARNOLD

NO HOLDS BARRED New Line Cinema, 1989
JIM JOHNSTON

NO LIFE KING New Century, 1991
SAEKO SUZUKI

NO LOVE FOR JOHNNIE Embassy, 1961
MALCOLM ARNOLD

NO MAN IS AN ISLAND Dana Productions
ANDREA SAPAROFF

NO MAN OF HER OWN Paramount, 1950
HUGO FRIEDHOFER†

NO MAN'S LAND 1930
HANNS EISLER†

NO MAN'S LAND Orion, 1987
BASIL POLEDOURIS

NO MAN'S LAND (TF) JADDA Productions/Warner
Bros. TV, 1984
STEPHEN GEYER

NO MAN'S LAND (TF) JADDA Productions/Warner
Bros. TV, 1984
PETE CARPENTER†

NO MAN'S LAND (TF) JADDA Productions/Warner
Bros. TV, 1984
MIKE POST

NO MARRIAGE TIES RKO Radio, 1933
MAX STEINER†

NO MERCY Tri-Star, 1987
ALAN SILVESTRI

NO MINOR VICES MGM, 1948
FRANZ WAXMAN†

NO MORE LADIES MGM, 1935
EDWARD WARD†

NO NAME ON THE BULLET Universal, 1959
HERMAN STEIN

NO OTHER LOVE (TF) Tisch-Avnet Productions,
1979
CHARLES GROSS

NO OTHER WOMAN RKO Radio, 1933
MAX STEINER†

NO PLACE FOR JENNIFER 1951
ALLAN GRAY†

NO PLACE LIKE HOME (TF) Feury-Grant
Productions/Orion TV, 1989
CHARLES GROSS

NO PLACE TO HIDE Allied Artists, 1956
HERSCHEL BURKE GILBERT

NO PLACE TO HIDE (TF) Metromedia Producers
Corporation, 1981
JOHN CACAVAS

NO PLACE TO RUN (TF) Spelling-Goldberg
Productions/ABC Circle Films, 1972
GEORGE ALICESON TIPTON

NO PROBLEM 1975
PHILIPPE SARDE

NO QUESTIONS ASKED MGM, 1951
LEITH STEVENS†

NO RESTING PLACE 1952
WILLIAM ALWYN†

NO RETREAT, NO SURRENDER New World, 1986
PAUL GILREATH
DAVID SPEAR

NO RETREAT, NO SURRENDER II Shapiro
Glickenhaus Entertainment, 1989
DAVID SPEAR

NO ROOM FOR THE GROOM Universal, 1952
FRANK SKINNER†

NO ROOM TO RUN (TF) Australian Broadcasting
Commission/Trans-Atlantic Enterprises, 1977
BRIAN MAY† ★

NO SAD SONGS FOR ME Columbia, 1950
GEORGE DUNING

NO SAFE HAVEN Overseas Filmgroup, 1989
JOEL GOLDSMITH

NO SECRETS I.R.S., 1991
VINNY GOLIA

NO SMALL AFFAIR Columbia, 1984
RUPERT HOLMES

NO TIME FOR COMEDY Warner Bros., 1940
HEINZ ROEMHELD†

NO TIME FOR FLOWERS RKO Radio, 1952
HERSCHEL BURKE GILBERT

NO TIME FOR LOVE Paramount, 1943
VICTOR YOUNG†

NO TIME TO BE YOUNG Columbia, 1957
MISCHA BAKALEINIKOFF†

NO TIME TO DIE (TF) Universal TV, 1992
PATRICK WILLIAMS

NO WAY OUT 20th Century-Fox, 1950
ALFRED NEWMAN†

NO WAY OUT Orion, 1987
MAURICE JARRE

NO WAY TO TREAT A LADY Paramount, 1968
STANLEY MYERS†

NO, NO, NANETTE RKO Radio, 1940
ANTHONY COLLINS†

NO...SONO VERGINE 1973
GIANFRANCO PLENIZIO

NOAH'S ARK Warner Bros., 1929
LOUIS SILVERS†

NOB HILL 20th Century-Fox, 1945
DAVID BUTTOLPH†
EMIL NEWMAN†

NOBLE HOUSE (MS) Noble House Productions Ltd./
De Laurentiis Entertainment Group, 1988
PAUL CHIHARA

NOBODY LIVES FOREVER Warner Bros., 1945
ADOLPH DEUTSCH†

NOBODY LOVES ME KEINER LIEBT MICH
German, 1995
NIKI REISER

NOBODY RUNS FOREVER Cinerama Releasing
Corporation, 1968
GEORGES DELERUE†

NOBODY'S BABY MGM, 1937
T. MARVIN HATLEY†

NOBODY'S CHILD (TF) Joseph Feury Productions/
Gaylord Production Company, 1986
MICHAEL SMALL

NOBODY'S CHILDREN (CTF) Winkler-Daniel
Prods./Quinta, 1994
JEAN-CLAUDE PETIT

NOBODY'S DARLING Republic, 1943
WALTER SCHARF

NOBODY'S FOOL Island Pictures, 1986
JAMES NEWTON HOWARD

NOBODY'S FOOL Paramount, 1994
HOWARD SHORE

NOBODY'S GIRLS (TF) Maryland Public Television,
1995
RICHARD EINHORN

NOBODY'S PERFECT Moviestore Entertainment,
1989
ROBERT RANDLES

NOBODY'S PERFEKT Columbia, 1981
DAVID MCHUGH

NOCTURNE RKO Radio, 1946
LEIGH HARLINE†

NOH MASK MURDERS 1991
FUMIO MIYASHITA

NOI DONNE SIAMO FATTI COSI Apollo
International Film, 1971
ARMANDO TROVAJOLI

NOI DUE SOLI 1953
NINO ROTA†

A NOI PIACE FREDDO 1960
CARLO RUSTICHELLI

NOISES OFF Buena Vista, 1992
PHIL MARSHALL

NOMAD RIDERS Windjammer Productions, 1982
ROBERT J. WALSH

NOMADS Atlantic Releasing Corporation, 1985
BILL CONTI

NON SI SCRIVE SUI MURI A MILANO 1975
FIORENZO CARPI

NON SIAMO DUE EVASI 1959
CARLO RUSTICHELLI

NON SON DEGNO DI TE 1965
ENNIO MORRICONE

NONE BUT THE BRAVE Warner Bros., 1964
JOHN WILLIAMS

NONE BUT THE LONELY HEART RKO Radio, 1944
HANNS EISLER† ★

NONE SHALL ESCAPE Columbia, 1944
ERNST TOCH†

NOON WINE (TF) Noon Wine Company, 1985
PAUL CHIHARA

NORA PRENTISS Warner Bros., 1947
FRANZ WAXMAN†

NORD NORTH 1991
PHILIPPE CHATILIEZ

THE NORLISS TAPES (TF) Metromedia Producers
Corporation, 1973
BOB COBERT

NORMA JEAN AND MARILYN (CTF) HBO, 1996
CHRISTOPHER YOUNG

NORMA RAE 20th Century-Fox, 1979
DAVID SHIRE

THE NORMAL LIFE 1996
KEN HALE
BOB MCNAUGHTON

NORMAN ROCKWELL'S BREAKING HOME TIES
(TF) John Wilder Productions/Telecom
Entertainment, 1987
JERROLD IMMEL

NORMAN...IS THAT YOU? MGM/United Artists,
1976
WILLIAM GOLDSTEIN

THE NORSEMAN American International, 1978
JAIME MENDOZA-NAVA

NORTH 1991
PHILIPPE CHATILIEZ

NORTH Columbia, 1994
MARC SHAIMAN

NORTH AND SOUTH (MS) Wolper Productions/
Warner Bros. TV, 1985
BILL CONTI ☆

NORTH AND SOUTH, BOOK II (MS) Wolper
Productions/Robert A. Papazian Productions/Warner
Bros. TV, 1986
BILL CONTI

THE NORTH AVENUE IRREGULARS Buena Vista,
1979
ROBERT F. BRUNNER

NORTH BEACH AND RAWHIDE (TF) CBS
Entertainment Productions, 1985
EARLE HAGEN

NORTH BY NORTHWEST MGM, 1959
BERNARD HERRMANN†

NORTH DALLAS FORTY Paramount, 1979
JOHN SCOTT

NORTH OF PITTSBURGH Cinephile, 1992
GRAEME COLEMAN

NORTH SEAS HIJACK Universal, 1980
MICHAEL J. LEWIS

NORTH SHORE Universal, 1987
RICHARD STONE

THE NORTH STAR Parafrance, 1982
PHILIPPE SARDE

THE NORTH STAR Warner Bros., 1996
BRUCE ROWLAND

THE NORTH STAR ARMORED ATTACK RKO
Radio, 1943
AARON COPLAND† ★

NORTH TO ALASKA 20th Century-Fox, 1960
LIONEL NEWMAN†

F
I
L
M

T
I
T
L
E
S

OKINAWA Columbia, 1952
MISCHA BAKALEINIKOFF†

OKINAWAN BOYS 1983
SHINCHIRO IKEBE

THE OKLAHOMA CITY DOLLS (TF) IKE
Productions/Columbia Pictures TV, 1981
JERROLD IMMEL

OKLAHOMA CRUDE Columbia, 1973
HENRY MANCINI†

THE OKLAHOMA KID Warner Bros., 1939
MAX STEINER†

OKLAHOMA TERRITORY United Artists, 1960
ALBERT GLASSER

OKLAHOMA TERRITORY United Artists, 1951
ALBERT GLASSER

THE OKLAHOMA WOMAN American International,
1956
RONALD STEIN†

OKLAHOMA! 20th Century-Fox, 1955
ADOLPH DEUTSCH† ★★

THE OKLAHOMAN Universal, 1957
HANS J. SALTER†

OKNO V PARIZH *WINDOW TO PARIS* Sony
Classics, 1994
YURI MIAMIN
ALEKSEI ZALIVALOV

OLD ACQUAINTANCE Warner Bros., 1943
FRANZ WAXMAN†

OLD BOYFRIENDS Avco Embassy, 1979
DAVID SHIRE

THE OLD CHISHOLM TRAIL Universal, 1942
HANS J. SALTER†

THE OLD CURIOSITY SHOP (CTF) Curiosity Prods.,
1995
MASON DARING

THE OLD DARK HOUSE Columbia, 1963
BENJAMIN FRANKEL†

THE OLD DARK HOUSE Universal, 1932
DAVID BROEKMAN†

OLD DRACULA *VAMPIRA* American International,
1975
DAVID WHITAKER

OLD ENOUGH Orion Classics, 1984
JULIAN MARSHALL

OLD GRINGO Columbia, 1989
LEE HOLDRIDGE

OLD HUTCH MGM, 1936
WILLIAM AXT†

OLD IRONSIDES Paramount, 1926
JOHN S. ZAMECNIK†

OLD LOS ANGELES Republic, 1948
ERNEST GOLD

THE OLD MAID Warner Bros., 1939
MAX STEINER†

THE OLD MAN AND THE SEA Warner Bros., 1958
DIMITRI TIOMKIN† ★★

OLD MAN GE 1993
MO FAN

OLD MAN RHYTHM RKO Radio, 1935
ROY WEBB†

THE OLD MAN WHO CRIED WOLF (TF) Aaron
Spelling Productions, 1970
ROBERT DRASNIN

OLD YELLER Buena Vista, 1957
OLIVER WALLACE†

**OLDEST LIVING CONFEDERATE WIDOW TELLS
ALL (TF)** Konigsberg-Sanitsky/RHI, 1994
MARK SNOW ☆

AN OLD-FASHIONED GIRL Eagle Lion, 1948
HERSCHEL BURKE GILBERT

THE OLD-FASHIONED WAY Paramount, 1934
ANDREA SETARO†

OLEANNA Samuel Goldwyn, 1994
REBECCA PIDGEON

OLIMPIADI DEI MARITI 1960
CARLO RUSTICHELLI

THE OLIVE TREES OF JUSTICE *LES OLIVIERS DE
LA JUSTICE* 1961
MAURICE JARRE

OLIVER & CO. (AF) Buena Vista, 1988
J.A.C. REDFORD

OLIVER TWIST United Artists, 1948
SIR ARNOLD BAX†

OLIVER TWIST (TF) Claridge Group Ltd./Grafton,
1982
NICK BICAT

OLIVER! Columbia, 1968
JOHN GREEN† ★★

OLIVER'S STORY Paramount, 1979
LEE HOLDRIDGE
FRANCIS LAI

OLIVIER, OLIVIER Sony Classics, 1992
ZBIGNIEW PREISNER

OLLY, OLLY, OXEN FREE Sanrio, 1978
BOB ALCIVAR

OLTRE LA NOTTE 1977
BRUNO NICOLAI

THE OLYMPIC ELK RKO Radio, 1952
PAUL J. SMITH†

THE OLYMPIC SUMMER (FD) 1993
HEIDI AYDT
FRANK WILL

OMAR KHAYYAM Paramount, 1957
VICTOR YOUNG†

OMBRE ET LUMIERE 1950
JOSEPH KOSMA†

OMEGA DOOM Filmwerks, 1996
TONY RIPPARETTI

THE OMEGA MAN Warner Bros., 1971
RON GRAINER†

OMEGA SYNDROME New World, 1987
NICHOLAS CARRAS
JACK COOKERLY

THE OMEN 20th Century-Fox, 1976
JERRY GOLDSMITH ★★

OMEN IV: THE AWAKENING (TF) FNM Films,
1991
JONATHAN SHEFFER

OMICIDIO PER APPUNTAMENTO 1967
ARMANDO TROVAJOLI

OMOO-OMOO, THE SHARK GOD Screen Guild,
1949
ALBERT GLASSER

ON A VOLE LA CRUISSE DE JUPITER Quartet/
Films Inc., 1980
GEORGE HATZINASSIOS

ON A VOLE LA JOCONDE 1965
CARLO RUSTICHELLI

ON AGAIN—OFF AGAIN RKO Radio, 1937
ROY WEBB†

ON ANY STREET/BAD GIRLS DON'T CRY Ajace
Film/Franco London Film, 1959
PIERO PICCIONI

ON ANY SUNDAY (FD) Tigon, 1971
DOMINIC FRONTIERE

ON ANY SUNDAY II (FD) International Film
Marketing, 1981
ALLAN ALPER

ON AURA TOUT VU 1976
PHILIPPE SARDE

ON BORROWED TIME MGM, 1939
FRANZ WAXMAN†

ON DANGEROUS GROUND RKO Radio, 1952
BERNARD HERRMANN†

ON DEADLY GROUND Warner Bros., 1994
BASIL POLEDOURIS

ON FIRE (TF) Robert Greenwald Productions, 1987
WILLIAM GOLDSTEIN

ON FRIDAY AT ELEVEN British Lion, 1961
CLAUDE BOLLING

ON GOLDEN POND Universal/AFD, 1981
DAVE GRUSIN ★

ON HER MAJESTY'S SECRET SERVICE United
Artists, 1969
JOHN BARRY

ON MOONLIGHT BAY Warner Bros., 1951
MAX STEINER†

ON MY OWN 1992
FRANCO PIERSANTI

ON NE MEURT QUE DEUX FOIS UGC, 1985
CLAUDE BOLLING

ON OUR MERRY WAY United Artists, 1948
HEINZ ROEMHELD†

ON PROMISED LAND (CTF) Anasazi Prods./Walt
Disney Co., 1994
MASON DARING

ON STAGE EVERYBODY Universal, 1945
MILTON ROSEN†

ON SUCH A NIGHT Paramount, 1937
ERNST TOCH†

ON THE BEACH United Artists, 1959
ERNEST GOLD ★

ON THE DOUBLE Paramount, 1961
LEITH STEVENS†

ON THE EDGE Skouras Pictures, 1985
HERB PHILHOFER

ON THE GAME Eagle, 1973
DE WOLFE

ON THE LOOSE RKO Radio, 1951
LEIGH HARLINE†

ON THE NICKEL Rose's Park, 1980
FRED MYROW

ON THE RIGHT TRACK 20th Century-Fox, 1981
ARTHUR B. RUBINSTEIN

ON THE RIVIERA 20th Century-Fox, 1951
ALFRED NEWMAN† ★

ON THE THRESHHOLD OF SPACE 20th
Century-Fox, 1956
LYN MURRAY†

ON THE TIP OF THE TONGUE Elan Films, 1976
FREDERIC DEVREESE

ON THE WATERFRONT Columbia, 1954
LEONARD BERNSTEIN† ★

ON TRIAL *L'AFFAIRE MAURIZIUS* New Realm,
1953
GEORGES VAN PARYS†

ON VALENTINE'S DAY Angelika Films, 1986
JONATHAN SHEFFER

ON WINGS OF EAGLES (MS) Edgar J. Scherick
Productions/Taft Entertainment TV, 1986
LAURENCE ROSENTHAL

ONCE A THIEF MGM, 1965
LALO SCHIFRIN

ONCE A THIEF United Artists, 1950
MICHEL MICHELET†

ONCE AN EAGLE (MS) Universal TV, 1976
DANA KAPROFF

ONCE AROUND Universal, 1991
JAMES HORNER

ONCE BITTEN Samuel Goldwyn Company, 1985
JOHN DUPREZ

ONCE IN A BLUE MOON Paramount, 1935
GEORGE ANTHEIL†

ONCE IN PARIS... Atlantic Releasing Corporation,
1978
MITCH LEIGH

ONCE IS NOT ENOUGH Paramount, 1975
HENRY MANCINI†

ONCE UPON A CRIME MGM, 1992
RICHARD GIBBS

ONCE UPON A DEAD MAN (TF) Universal TV,
1971
JERRY FIELDING†

ONCE UPON A FAMILY (TF) Universal TV, 1980
FRED KARLIN

ONCE UPON A FOREST (AF) 20th Century Fox,
1993
JAMES HORNER

ONCE UPON A HONEYMOON Paramount, 1942
ROBERT EMMETT DOLAN†

ONCE UPON A SCOUNDREL Image International,
1974
ALEX NORTH†

ONCE UPON A SPY (TF) David Gerber Company/
Columbia TV, 1980
JOHN CACAVAS

ONCE UPON A TEXAS TRAIN (TF) CBS
Entertainment, 1988
ARTHUR B. RUBINSTEIN

ONCE UPON A TIME Columbia, 1944
FREDERICK HOLLANDER†

ONCE UPON A TIME *MARIA D'ORO UND BELLO
BLUE (AF)* G.G. Communications, 1976
PETER THOMAS

ONCE UPON A TIME IN AMERICA The Ladd
Company/Warner Bros., 1984
ENNIO MORRICONE

ONCE UPON A TIME IN THE WEST Paramount,
1969
ENNIO MORRICONE

**ONCE UPON A TIME WHEN WE WERE
COLORED** 1996
PAUL BUCKMASTER
LIONEL COLE

ONCE WE WERE DREAMERS Hemdale, 1987
MISHA SEGAL

ONCE YOU MEET A STRANGER (TF) Warner Bros.
TV, 1996
PETER MANNING ROBINSON

ONE AGAINST THE WIND (TF) Karen Mack/
Republic, 1991
LEE HOLDRIDGE

THE ONE AND ONLY Paramount, 1978
PATRICK WILLIAMS

ONE BY ONE *EAST WIND* 1974
STOMU YAMASHTA

ONE CHRISTMAS (TF) Davis Entertainment, 1994
VAN DYKE PARKS

ONE COOKS, THE OTHER DOESN'T (TF)
Kaleidoscope Films Ltd./Lorimar Productions, 1983
FRED KARLIN

ONE CRAZY SUMMER Warner Bros., 1986
JAMES DIPASQUALLE
CORY LERIOS

ONE CROWDED NIGHT RKO Radio, 1940
ROY WEBB†

ONE CUP OF COFFEE Bullpen/Open Road, 1991
LEE HOLDRIDGE

ONE DARK NIGHT Comworld, 1983
ROBERT SUMMERS

ONE DEADLY SUMMER SNV, 1983
GEORGES DELERUE†

ONE DESIRE Universal, 1955
FRANK SKINNER†

ONE FALSE MOVE I.R.S., 1991
PETER HAYCOCK
DEREK HOLT

ONE FINE DAY 20th Century Fox, 1996
JAMES NEWTON HOWARD

ONE FLEW OVER THE CUCKOO'S NEST United
Artists, 1976
JACK NITZCHE ★

ONE FOOT IN HEAVEN Warner Bros., 1941
MAX STEINER†

ONE FOOT IN HELL 20th Century-Fox, 1960
DOMINIC FRONTIERE

**ONE FOOT ON A BANANA PEEL, THE OTHER
FOOT IN THE GRAVE: SECRETS FROM THE
DOLLY MADISON ROOM (FD)** Clinica Estetico/
Joanne Howard, 1994
ANTON SANKO

ONE FROM THE HEART Columbia, 1982
BOB ALCIVAR
TOM WAITS ★

ONE GOOD COP Hollywood, 1991
DAVID FOSTER
WILLIAM ROSS

ONE GOOD TURN Zeta Entertainment, 1995
JOEL GOLDSMITH

ONE HOUR WITH YOU Paramount, 1932
W. FRANKE HARLING†

ONE HUNDRED AND ONE DALMATIONS (AF)
Buena Vista, 1960
GEORGE BRUNS

**ONE IN A MILLION: THE RON LeFLORE STORY
(TF)** Roger Gimbel Productions/EMI TV, 1978
PETER MATZ

ONE IS A LONELY NUMBER MGM, 1972
MICHEL LEGRAND

ONE LAST FLING Warner Bros., 1949
DAVID BUTTOLPH†

ONE LITTLE INDIAN Buena Vista, 1973
JERRY GOLDSMITH

ONE MAGIC CHRISTMAS Buena Vista, 1985
MICHAEL CONWAY BAKER

ONE MAN FORCE Shaprio Glickenhaus, 1989
DAVID MICHAEL FRANK

ONE MAN'S JOURNEY RKO Radio, 1933
MAX STEINER†

ONE MAN'S WAY Columbia, 1964
RICHARD MARKOWITZ†

ONE MILLION B.C. United Artists, 1940
WERNER R. HEYMANN† ★

ONE MINUTE TO ZERO RKO Radio, 1952
VICTOR YOUNG†

ONE MORE MOUNTAIN (TF) Marian Rees
Associates/Walt Disney TV, 1994
J.A.C. REDFORD

ONE MORE RIVER Universal, 1933
W. FRANKE HARLING†

ONE MORE SATURDAY NIGHT Columbia, 1986
DAVID MCHUGH

ONE MORE TIME United Artists, 1970
LES REED

ONE MORE TOMORROW Warner Bros., 1946
MAX STEINER†

ONE MORE TRAIN TO ROB Universal, 1971
DAVID SHIRE

ONE MUST LIVE DANGEROUSLY 1975
CLAUDE BOLLING

ONE NATION UNDER GOD (FD) 3Z/Hourglass,
1993
ROBERT MITCHELL

ONE NIGHT OF LOVE Columbia, 1934
VICTOR SCHERTZINGER† ★
LOUIS SILVERS†

ONE NIGHT ONLY RSL, Canadian
LAWRENCE SHRAGGE

ONE OF A KIND (TF) 1978
MAURICE JARRE

ONE OF HER OWN (TF) Grossbart-Barnett Prods./
ABC TV, 1994
GEORGE S. CLINTON

ONE OF OUR DINOSAURS IS MISSING Buena
Vista, 1975
RON GOODWIN

ONE OF OUR OWN (TF) Universal TV, 1975
JERRY FIELDING†

ONE ON ONE Warner Bros., 1977
CHARLES FOX

ONE POLICE PLAZA (TF) CBS Entertainment, 1986
MARK SNOW

ONE POTATO, TWO POTATO Cinema 5, 1964
GERALD FRIED

ONE SHOE MAKES IT MURDER (TF)
Fellows-Keegan Company/Lorimar Productions, 1982
BRUCE BROUGHTON

ONE SPECIAL VICTORY (TF) Port Street Films/NBC
Prods., 1991
BILLY GOLDENBERG

ONE SPY TOO MANY MGM, 1966
GERALD FRIED
NELSON RIDDLE†

ONE SUNDAY AFTERNOON Warner Bros., 1948
DAVID BUTTOLPH†

ONE SURVIVOR REMEMBERS (TD) HBO, 1995
RICHARD FIOCCA

ONE TERRIFIC GUY (TF) CBS Entertainment, 1986
MARK SNOW

...ONE THIRD OF A NATION... Paramount, 1939
NATHANIEL SHILKRET†

ONE TOO MANY 1950
BERT A. SHEFTER

ONE TRICK PONY Warner Bros., 1980
PAUL SIMON

ONE WAY PASSAGE Warner Bros., 1932
W. FRANKE HARLING†
BERNHARD KAUN†

THE OUTLAW United Artists, 1943
VICTOR YOUNG†

OUTLAW BLUES Warner Bros., 1977
CHARLES BERNSTEIN
BRUCE LANGHORNE

THE OUTLAW JOSEY WALES Warner Bros., 1976
JERRY FIELDING† ★

OUTLAW'S SON United Artists, 1957
LES BAXTER†

OUTLAWS 1970
MASARU SATO

THE OUTLAWS (TF) Limekiln and Templar
Productions/Universal TV, 1984
JERROLD IMMEL

THE OUTLAWS IS COMING! Columbia, 1965
PAUL DUNLAP

OUTOMLIONNYE SOLNTSEM Studio Trite/Camera
One, 1994
EDUARD ARTEMYEV

OUTPOST IN MALAYA *THE PLANTER'S WIFE*
United Artists, 1952
ALLAN GRAY†

OUTPOST IN MOROCCO United Artists, 1949
MICHEL MICHELET†

OUTPUT West German
JURGEN KNIEPER

THE OUTRAGE MGM, 1964
ALEX NORTH†

OUTRAGE! (TF) ABC Circle Films, 1973
JIMMIE HASKELL

OUTRAGE! (TF) Irwin Allen Productions/Columbia TV,
1986
MORTON STEVENS†

OUTRAGEOUS FORTUNE Buena Vista, 1987
ALAN SILVESTRI

OUTRAGEOUS! Cinema 5, 1977
PAUL HOFFERT

THE OUTRIDERS MGM, 1950
ANDRE PREVIN

OUTSIDE CHANCE (TF) New World Productions/
Miller-Begun Productions, 1978
LOU LEVY
MURPHY DUNNE

OUTSIDE IN Harold Robbins International, 1972
RANDY EDELMAN

THE OUTSIDE MAN *UN HOMME EST MORT*
United Artists, 1973
MICHEL LEGRAND

OUTSIDE THE LAW Universal, 1930
DAVID BROEKMAN†

OUTSIDE THE LAW Universal, 1956
MILTON ROSEN†

THE OUTSIDER *THE GUINEA PIG* Pathe, 1948
JOHN ADDISON

THE OUTSIDER Gaumont, 1983
ENNIO MORRICONE

THE OUTSIDER Mahogany Pictures, 1996
ROGER NEILL

THE OUTSIDER Paramount, 1980
KEN THORNE

THE OUTSIDER Universal, 1961
LEONARD ROSENMAN

THE OUTSIDER (TF) Public Arts Productions/
Universal TV, 1967
PETE RUGOLO

THE OUTSIDERS Warner Bros., 1983
CARMINE COPPOLA†

OVER MY DEAD BODY 20th Century-Fox, 1943
CYRIL J. MOCKRIDGE†

OVER THE BROOKLYN BRIDGE *MY DARLING
SHIKSA* MGM/UA/Cannon, 1984
PINO DONAGGIO

OVER THE EDGE Orion/Warner Bros., 1979
SOL KAPLAN

OVER THE HILL 1992
DAVID MCHUGH

OVER THE OCEAN 1992
SHLOMO GRONICH

OVER THE TOP Cannon, 1987
GIORGIO MORODER

OVERBOARD MGM/UA, 1987
ALAN SILVESTRI

OVERBOARD (TF) Factor-Newland Production
Corporation, 1978
MARK SNOW

OVEREXPOSED Concorde, 1990
MARK GOVERNOR

OVEREXPOSED (TF) LOMO Prods., 1992
GERALD GOURIET

OVERKILL Manson International, 1987
ROBERT J. WALSH

OVERKILL: THE AILEEN WUORNOS STORY (TF)
Republic/C.M. Two, 1992
DENNIS MCCARTHY

THE OVERLANDERS 1946
JOHN IRELAND†

OVERLORD 1975
PAUL GLASS

OVERNIGHT Lauron Productions, 1986
MICHAEL CONWAY BAKER

OVERNIGHT DELIVERY New Line, 1997
ANDREW GROSS

THE OVER-THE-HILL GANG (TF) Thomas-Spelling
Productions, 1969
HUGO FRIEDHOFER†

THE OVER-THE-HILL GANG RIDES AGAIN (TF)
Thomas-Spelling Productions, 1970
DAVID RAKSIN

OVIRI International Film Marketing, 1986
ROGER BOURLAND

OVOCE STROMJ RAJSHYCH JIME 1970
ZDENEK LISKA

OWEN MARSHALL, COUNSELOR AT LAW (TF)
Universal TV, 1971
ELMER BERNSTEIN

THE OWL AND THE PUSSYCAT Columbia, 1970
DICK HALLIGAN

THE OWL AND THE PUSSYCAT (FD) 1954
MATYAS SEIBER

THE OX-BOW INCIDENT 20th Century-Fox, 1943
CYRIL J. MOCKRIDGE†

OXFORD BLUES MGM/UA, 1984
JOHN DUPREZ

P

PACIFIC 231 1931
ARTHUR HONEGGER†

PACIFIC CHALLENGE (FD) Concord Films, 1975
BILL CONTI

PACIFIC HEIGHTS 20th Century-Fox, 1990
HANS ZIMMER

PACIFIC LINER RKO Radio, 1938
ROBERT RUSSELL BENNETT† ★

THE PACK Warner Bros., 1977
LEE HOLDRIDGE

PACK OF LIES (TF) Robert Halmi Inc., 1987
STANLEY MYERS†

THE PACKAGE Orion, 1989
JAMES NEWTON HOWARD

PACKIN' IT IN (TF) Roger Gimbel Productions/Thorn
EMI TV/Jones-Reiker Ink Corporation, 1983
MARK SNOW

THE PAD (AND HOW TO USE IT) Universal, 1966
RUSSELL GARCIA

PADRI E FIGLI Trans-Lux, 1957
CARLO RUSTICHELLI

PAGE BLANCHE 1991
DAM LINH

THE PAGEMASTER Turner Pictures, 1994
JAMES HORNER

THE PAGEMASTER (AF) 20th Century Fox, 1994
JAMES HORNER

PAID IN FULL Paramount, 1950
VICTOR YOUNG†

PAIN OF LOVE 1993
GUNNAR MOLLER PEDERSEN

PAINT IT BLACK Vestron, 1989
JURGEN KNIEPER
SHIRLEY WALKER

THE PAINT JOB Second Son, 1992
JOHN WESLEY HARDING

PAINT YOUR WAGON Paramount, 1969
NELSON RIDDLE† ★

THE PAINTED DESERT Kazuyoshi Okuyama, 1993
MASHAHIRO KAWASAKI

PAINTED DESERT RKO Radio, 1938
ROY WEBB†

THE PAINTED HILLS MGM, 1951
DANIELE AMFITHEATROF†

THE PAINTED VEIL MGM, 1934
HERBERT STOTHART†

PAINTING THE TOWN (FD) Padded Cell, 1992
PETER FISH

PAIR OF ACES (TF) Pedernales Films/Once Upon a
Time Films Ltd., 1990
WILLIAM OLVIS

PAJAMA PARTY American International, 1964
LES BAXTER†

PALACE GUARD (TF) Stephen J. Cannell, 1991
VELTON RAY BUNCH
MIKE POST

PALAIS ROYALE Metaphor, 1989
LAWRENCE SHRAGGE

PALAIS ROYALE Spectrafilm, 1988
JONATHAN GOLDSMITH

PALE FLOWER Shochiku, 1963
TORU TAKEMITSU†

PALE RIDER Warner Bros., 1985
LENNIE NIEHAUS

THE PALEFACE Paramount, 1948
VICTOR YOUNG†

THE PALLBEARER Miramax, 1996
STEWART COPELAND

THE PALM BEACH STORY Paramount, 1942
VICTOR YOUNG†

PALOOKAVILLE 1996
RACHEL PORTMAN

PALS (TF) Robert Halmi, Inc., 1987
MARK SNOW

PAN PROKOUK PRITEL ZVIRATEK (AF) 1953
ZDENEK LISKA

PANACHE (TF) Warner Bros. TV, 1976
FRANK DEVOL

THE PANAMA DECEPTION (FD) Empowerment
Project, 1992
CHUCK WILDE

PANAMA HATTIE MGM, 1942
GEORGE BASSMAN

PANAMA LADY RKO Radio, 1939
ROY WEBB†

PANCHO BARNES (TF) Blue Andre Productions/
Orion TV, 1988
ALLYN FERGUSON ☆

PANCHO VILLA Scotia, 1972
JOHN CACAVAS

PANDEMONIUM MGM/UA, 1982
DANA KAPROFF

PANDORA AND THE FLYING DUTCHMAN MGM,
1951
ALAN RAWSTHORNE†

PANE, AMORE E FANTASIA Italian Film Export,
1953
ALESSANDRO CICOGNINI†

PANE, AMORE E GELOSIA DCA, 1954
ALESSANDRO CICOGNINI†

PANE, AMORE E... DCA, 1955
ALESSANDRO CICOGNINI†

PANIC Tricolore, 1946
JACQUES IBERT†

PANIC IN ECHO PARK (TF) Edgar J. Scherick
Associates, 1977
JOHN SPENCE

PANIC IN THE CITY United Pictures, 1967
PAUL DUNLAP

PANIC IN THE STREETS 20th Century-Fox, 1950
ALFRED NEWMAN†

PANIC IN THE YEAR ZERO American International,
1962
LES BAXTER†

PANIC ON THE 5:22 (TF) QM Productions, 1974
RICHARD MARKOWITZ†

PANO KATO KE PLAGIOS *UP, DOWN AND
SIDEWAYS* 1993
STEFANOS KORKOLIS

PANTALASKAS 1959
JEAN WIENER†

PANTHER Gramercy, 1995
STANLEY CLARKE

PANTHER PANCHALI 1956
RAVI SHANKAR

PAODA SHUANG DENG *RED FIRECRACKER,
GREEN FIRECRACKER* 1994
ZHAO JIPING

PAOLO E FRANCESCA 1970
BRUNO NICOLAI

PAOLO IL CALDO 1973
ARMANDO TROVAJOLI

PAPA, MAMA, THE MAID AND I 1954
GEORGES VAN PARYS†

PAPAKOLEA-A STORY OF HAWAIIAN LAND
1993
JOSEPH VITARELLI

THE PAPER Universal, 1994
RANDY NEWMAN

THE PAPER BRIGADE (TF) Leucadia Films, 1995
RAY COLCORD

THE PAPER CHASE 20th Century-Fox, 1973
JOHN WILLIAMS

PAPER DOLLS (TF) Leonard Goldberg Productions,
1982
MARK SNOW

PAPER LION United Artists, 1968
ROGER KELLAWAY

PAPER TIGER Joseph E. Levine Presents, 1976
ROY BUDD†

PAPERHOUSE Vestron, 1988
HANS ZIMMER

PAPILLON Allied Artists, 1973
JERRY GOLDSMITH ★

PAR LE SANG DES AUTRES 1973
FRANCIS LAI

PAR OU TES RENTRE...ON TA PAS VU SORTIR
Carthago Films, 1984
ALAN SILVESTRI

PAR UN BEAU MATIN D'ETE 1964
MICHEL MAGNE†

PARACHUTE BATTALION RKO Radio, 1941
ROY WEBB†

THE PARADE (TF) Hill-Mandelker Productions, 1984
ARTHUR B. RUBINSTEIN

PARADES Cinerama Releasing Corporation, 1972
GARRY SHERMAN

THE PARADINE CASE Selznick Releasing, 1947
FRANZ WAXMAN†

PARADISE Buena Vista, 1991
DAVID NEWMAN

PARADISE Embassy, 1982
PAUL HOFFERT

PARADISE (TF) Roundelay Productions/Lorimar TV,
1988
JERROLD IMMEL

PARADISE ALLEY Universal, 1978
BILL CONTI

PARADISE CONNECTION (TF) Woodruff
Productions/QM Productions, 1979
BRUCE BROUGHTON

PARADISE FOR THREE MGM, 1938
EDWARD WARD†

PARADISE LAGOON Columbia, 1957
DOUGLAS GAMLEY

PARADISE MOTEL Saturn, 1984
MARK GOVERNOR

THE PARALLAX VIEW Paramount, 1974
MICHAEL SMALL

PARALLEL LIVES (CTF) Showtime Ent., 1994
PATRICK SEYMOUR

PARALLEL SONS Black Brook Films, 1995
E. D. MENASCHE

PARANOIA 1966
TEO USUELLI

PARANOIA L.E.D. Pictures & Dan Purjes, 1997
MARTIN TRUM

PARANOIAC Universal, 1964
ELISABETH LUYTENS†

PARASITE Embassy, 1982
RICHARD H. BAND

PARATROOP COMMAND American International,
1959
RONALD STEIN†

PARATROOPS (FD) O.W.I., 1942
GAIL KUBIK†

PAR-DESSUS LE MUR 1960
GEORGES DELERUE†

PARDNERS Paramount, 1956
FRANK DEVOL

PARDON MON AFFAIRE *AN ELEPHANT CA
TROMPE ENORMEMENT* First Artists, 1976
VLADIMIR COSMA

PARDON MON AFFAIRE, TOO! *NOUS IRONS
TOUS AU PARADIS* First Artists, 1977
VLADIMIR COSMA

PARDON MY PAST Columbia, 1945
DIMITRI TIOMKIN†

PARDON MY RHYTHM Universal, 1944
HANS J. SALTER†

PARENT TRAP II (TF) The Landsburg Company/
Walt Disney TV, 1987
CHARLES FOX

PARENTHOOD Universal, 1989
RANDY NEWMAN

PARENTS Vestron, 1989
JONATHAN ELIAS

PARIGI O CARA 1962
FIORENZO CARPI

PARIS 1936
JACQUES IBERT†

PARIS Warner Bros., 1929
EDWARD WARD†

PARIS AFTER DARK 20th Century-Fox, 1943
HUGO FRIEDHOFER†

PARIS AU MOIS D'AOUT 1966
GEORGES GARVARENTZ†

PARIS AU PRINTEMPS 1948
GEORGES VAN PARYS†

PARIS BLUES United Artists, 1961
DUKE ELLINGTON† ★

PARIS BY NIGHT Cineplex Odeon, 1988
GEORGES DELERUE†

PARIS CALLING Universal, 1942
RICHARD HAGEMAN†

PARIS DOES STRANGE THINGS *ELENA ET LES
HOMMES* Warner Bros., 1956
JOSEPH KOSMA†

PARIS FOLLIES OF 1956 *FRESH FROM PARIS*
Allied Artists, 1955
FRANK DEVOL

PARIS HONEYMOON Paramount, 1939
LEO SHUKEN†

PARIS IN SPRING Paramount, 1935
SIGMUND KRUMGOLD†

PARIS LA NUIT 1955
GEORGES VAN PARYS†

PARIS MODEL Columbia, 1953
ALBERT GLASSER

PARIS N'EXISTE PAS 1968
SERGE GAINSBOURG†

PARIS TROUT (CTF) Viacom/Konigsberg-Sanitsky,
1991
DAVID SHIRE

PARIS WHEN IT SIZZLES Paramount, 1964
NELSON RIDDLE†

PARIS, FRANCE Alliance, 1993
JOHN MCCARTHY

PARIS, TEXAS TLC Films/20th Century Fox, 1984
RY COODER

PARIS-SECRET 1965
ALAIN GORRAGUER

PARIS—UNDERGROUND United Artists, 1945
ALEXANDRE TANSMAN† ★

THE PARK IS MINE (CTF) Astral Film Enterprises/
HBO Premiere Films, 1985
TANGERINE DREAM
CHRISTOPHER FRANKE
PARK ROW United Artists, 1952
PAUL DUNLAP
PARKER Virgin Films, 1985
RICHARD HARTLEY
PARKER KANE (TF) Orion TV, 1990
JAY FERGUSON
PARKING A.M. Films, 1985
MICHEL LEGRAND
PARNELL MGM, 1937
WILLIAM AXT†
PAROLE (TF) Parole Production Company/Robert
Stigwood Organization, 1982
GEORGE FENTON
PAROLES ET MUSIQUES A.A.A., 1984
MICHEL LEGRAND
PARRISH Warner Bros., 1961
MAX STEINER†
THE PARSON OF PANAMINT Paramount, 1941
JOHN LEIPOLD†
PART 2, SOUNDER Gamma III, 1976
TAJ MAHAL
PART 2, WALKING TALL American International,
1975
WALTER SCHARF
A PART OF THE FAMILY (CTF) Interscope
Communications, 1994
WILLIAM OLVIS
PARTIR REVENIR UGC, 1985
MICHEL LEGRAND
PARTIRONO PRETI, TORNARONO...CURATI
1973
LUIS BACALOV
PARTISANS 1974
MIKIS THEODORAKIS
PARTNER 1968
ENNIO MORRICONE
PARTNER 1977
ENNIO MORRICONE
PARTNERS Paramount, 1982
GEORGES DELERUE†
PARTNERS 'N LOVE (CTF) Atlantis/Barry Jossen
Prods./Family Channel, 1992
LOUIS NATALE
PARTNERS IN CRIME Allied Artists, 1961
RON GOODWIN
PARTNERS IN CRIME (TF) Fairmont/Foxcroft
Productions/Universal TV, 1973
GIL MELLE
THE PARTY United Artists, 1968
HENRY MANCINI†
PARTY GIRL First Look, 1995
ANTON SANKO
PARTY GIRL MGM, 1958
JEFF ALEXANDER†
PARTY LINE SVS Films, 1988
SAM WINANS
PAS DE PROBLEME NO PROBLEM 1975
PHILIPPE SARDE
PAS DE ROSES POUR OSS 117 1968
PIERO PICCIONI
PAS DE VIEUX OS (TF) 1984
JEAN-CLAUDE PETIT
PASCALI'S ISLAND Avenue Pictures, 1988
LOEK DIKKER
PASCUAL DUARTE 1976
LUIS DE PABLO
PASQUALINO SETTEBELLEZZE Cinema 5, 1976
ENZO JANNACCI
PASS THE AMMO New Century/Vista Films, 1988
CARTER BURWELL
DAVID NEWMAN
THE PASSAGE Manson International, 1988
PAUL LOOMIS
THE PASSAGE United Artists, 1979
MICHAEL J. LEWIS
A PASSAGE TO INDIA Columbia, 1984
MAURICE JARRE ★★
PASSAGE TO MARSEILLE Warner Bros., 1944
MAX STEINER†
PASSAGES Wild Okapi Film, 1993 German
RALPH GRAF
PASSE MONTAGNE 1978
PHILIPPE SARDE
PASSED AWAY Buena Vista, 1992
RICHARD GIBBS
PASSENGER 57 Warner Bros., 1992
STANLEY CLARKE
PASSEPORT POUR RIO 1944
PAUL MISRAKI
PASSI DI MORTE PERDUTI NEL BUIO 1976
RIZ ORTOLANI
THE PASSING OF THE THIRD FLOOR BACK 1936
LOUIS LEVY†
PASSION AND PARADISE (TF) Picturebase
International/Primedia Productions/Leonard Hill
Films, 1989
HAGOOD HARDY

PASSION FISH Atchafalaya, 1992
MASON DARING
PASSION FLOWER (TF) Doris Keating Productions/
Columbia Pictures TV, 1986
MILES GOODMAN†
PASSION FLOWER HOTEL 1978
FRANCIS LAI
A PASSION FOR JUSTICE: THE HAZEL BRANNON
SMITH STORY (TF) David Brooks Prods./Catfish/
Saban-Sherick/Procter & Gamble Prods., 1994
DAVID MCHUGH
THE PASSION OF DARKLY NOON 1995
NICK BICAT
THE PASSION OF JOAN OF ARC M.J. Gourland,
1928
VICTOR ALLIX†
THE PASSION OF SLOW FIRE LA MORT DE
BELLE Trans-Lux, 1961
GEORGES DELERUE†
A PASSION TO KILL A-Pix, 1994
ROBERT SPRAYBERRY
THE PASSIONATE FRIENDS Universal, 1949
RICHARD ADDINSELL†
PASSIONE D'AMORE 1980
ARMANDO TROVAJOLI
PASSIONS (TF) Carson Production Group/Wizan TV
Enterprises, 1984
BRUCE BROUGHTON
THE PASSOVER PLOT Atlas, 1976
ALEX NORTH†
PASSPORT TO CHINA VISA TO CANTON
Columbia, 1961
EDWIN ASTLEY
PASSPORT TO DESTINY RKO Radio, 1944
ROY WEBB†
PASSPORT TO MURDER (TF) FTM Prods., 1993
CHARLES GROSS
PASSPORT TO PIMLICO 1949
GEORGES AURIC†
PAST MIDNIGHT (CTF) Cinetel, 1992
STEVE BARTEK
PAST TENSE (CTF) Arnold Kopelson Prods./
Showtime Ent., 1994
STEPHEN GRAZIANO
PAST THE BLEACHERS (TF) Signboard Hill, 1995
STEWART LEVIN
PASTACIATTA NEL DESERTO 1962
CARLO RUSTICHELLI
PASTIME ONE CUP OF COFFEE Bullpen/Open
Road, 1991
LEE HOLDRIDGE
PAT AND MIKE MGM, 1952
DAVID RAKSIN
PAT GARRETT AND BILLY THE KID MGM, 1973
BOB DYLAN
A PATCH OF BLUE MGM, 1965
JERRY GOLDSMITH ★
PATERNITY Paramount, 1981
DAVID SHIRE
THE PATHFINDER Columbia, 1952
MISCHA BAKALEINIKOFF†
PATHS OF GLORY United Artists, 1957
GERALD FRIED
PATRICK Cinema Shares International, 1979
GOBLIN
BRIAN MAY†
PATRICK THE GREAT Universal, 1945
HANS J. SALTER†
PATRIE 1946
JEAN WIENER†
THE PATRIOT Crown International, 1986
JAY FERGUSON
PATRIOT GAMES Paramount, 1992
JAMES HORNER
THE PATRIOTS LES PATRIOTES 1994
GERARD TORIKIAN
THE PATSY Paramount, 1964
DAVID RAKSIN
PATTI ROCKS FilmDallas, 1987
DOUG MAYNARD†
PATTON 20th Century-Fox, 1970
JERRY GOLDSMITH ★
PATTY HEARST Zenith Group/Atlantic
Entertainment, 1988
SCOTT JOHNSON
PAUL AND MICHELLE Paramount, 1974
MICHEL COLOMBIER
THE PAUL FLEISS STORY (TF) 1996
CHRIS BOARDMAN
PAULA Columbia, 1952
GEORGE DUNING
PAULINE AT THE BEACH Orion Classics, 1983
JEAN-LOUIS VALERO
PAURA NELLA CITTA' DEI MORTI VIVENTI
Dania Film/Medusa Distribuzione/National
Cinematografica, 1980
FABIO FRIZZI
PAVLINKA 1974
ZDENEK LISKA
THE PAWNBROKER Landau/Allied Artists, 1965
QUINCY JONES

PAY OR DIE Allied Artists, 1960
DAVID RAKSIN
PAYBACK TIME UNINHIBITED Antigua Films,
1993
ROCKY DAVIS
JOEL C. PESKIN
PAYMENT ON DEMAND RKO Radio, 1951
VICTOR YOUNG†
PAYOFF (CTF) Viacom Pictures/Aurora, 1991
CHARLES BERNSTEIN
PAYROLL 1961
GERARD SCHURMANN
PCU 20th Century Fox, 1994
STEVE VAI
THE PEACE KILLERS 1971
KEN WANNBERG
THE PEACEMAKER DreamWorks SKG, 1997
HANS ZIMMER
THE PEANUT BUTTER SOLUTION New World,
1985
LEWIS FUREY
PEARL (TF) Silliphant-Konigsberg Productions/
Warner Bros. TV, 1978
JOHN ADDISON
PEARL HARBOR - SURPRISE AND
REMEMBERANCE (TD) Tom Johnson, Lance Bird
and John Crowley, 1991
ROBERT FITZSIMMONS
PEARL IN THE CROWN 1972
WOJCIECH KILAR
THE PEARL OF DEATH Universal, 1944
HANS J. SALTER†
PAUL SAWTELL†
THE PEASANT UPRISING Yugoslavian
ALFI KABILJO
THE PEBBLE AND THE PENGUIN (AF) MGM-UA,
1995
MARK WATTERS
PEBBLES OF ETRETAT 1972
GEORGES GARVARENTZ†
PECCATO SENZA MALIZIA 1975
STELVIO CIPRIANI
PECK'S BAD BOY WITH THE CIRCUS RKO Radio,
1938
VICTOR YOUNG†
THE PEDESTRIAN Cinerama Releasing Corporation,
1974
MANOS HADJIDAKIS†
PEDRO PERAMO 1977
ENNIO MORRICONE
PEE WEE'S BIG ADVENTURE Warner Bros., 1985
DANNY ELFMAN
PEEPER 20th Century-Fox, 1975
RICHARD CLEMENTS
PEEPING TOM Astor, 1960
BRIAN EASDALE
PEER GYNT 1933
GIUSEPPE BECCE†
PEG O' MY HEART MGM, 1933
HERBERT STOTHART†
PEGGY Triangle, 1916
VICTOR SCHERTZINGER†
PEGGY SUE GOT MARRIED Tri-Star, 1986
JOHN BARRY
PEKING EXPRESS Paramount, 1951
DIMITRI TIOMKIN†
THE PELICAN BRIEF Warner Bros., 1993
JAMES HORNER
PELLA VIVA 1962
CARLO RUSTICHELLI
PELLE THE CONQUEROR Miramax Films, 1988
STEFAN NILSSON
PENALTY PHASE (TF) Tamara Asseyev Productions/
New World TV, 1986
RALPH BURNS
RAYMOND LEPPARD
PENDULUM Columbia, 1969
WALTER SCHARF
PENELOPE MGM, 1966
JOHN WILLIAMS
THE PENGUIN 1965
CHRISTOPHER KOMEDA†
PENGUIN POOL MURDER RKO Radio, 1932
MAX STEINER†
THE PENITENT New Century Vista, 1988
ALEX NORTH†
PENITENTIARY Jerry Gross Organization, 1979
FRANKIE GAYE
PENITENTIARY II MGM/UA, 1982
JACK W. WHEATON
PENITENTIARY III Cannon, 1987
GARRY SCHYMAN
PENN AND TELLER GET KILLED Warner Bros.,
1989
PAUL CHIHARA
PENNIES FROM HEAVEN Columbia, 1936
WILLIAM GRANT STILL†
PENNIES FROM HEAVEN MGM/United Artists,
1981
RALPH BURNS
MARVIN HAMLISCH

PENNY SERENADE Columbia, 1941
W. FRANKE HARLING†
PENSIONAT OSKAR 1995
JOHAN SODERQVIST
PENSIONE AMORE SERVIZIO COMPLETE DER
SEXBOMBER 1979
STELVIO CIPRIANI
THE PENTHOUSE (TF) Greene-White Productions/
Spectacor Films, 1989
PETER MANNING ROBINSON
PENTHOUSE MGM, 1933
WILLIAM AXT†
THE PEOPLE (TF) Metromedia Productions/American
Zoetrope, 1972
CARMINE COPPOLA†
THE PEOPLE ACROSS THE LAKE (TF) Bill
McCutchen Productions/Columbia TV, 1988
DANA KAPROFF
THE PEOPLE AGAINST O'HARA MGM, 1951
CARMEN DRAGON†
PEOPLE LIKE US (TF) CM Two Productions/ITC,
1990
BILLY GOLDENBERG ☆
PEOPLE MEET AND SWEET MUSIC FILLS THE
AIR 1967
CHRISTOPHER KOMEDA†
THE PEOPLE NEXT DOOR (TF) 1961
JERRY GOLDSMITH
THE PEOPLE THAT TIME FORGOT American
International, 1977
JOHN SCOTT
PEOPLE TOYS/THE HORRIBLE HOUSE ON THE
HILL 1974
WILLIAM LOOSE†
THE PEOPLE UNDER THE STAIRS Universal, 1991
DON PEAKE
THE PEOPLE VS. LARRY FLYNT Columbia, 1996
THOMAS NEWMAN
PEOPLE VS. JEAN HARRIS (TF) PKO TV Ltd.,
1981
BRAD FIEDEL
THE PEOPLE'S LAND 1942
RALPH VAUGHAN WILLIAMS†
PEPE Columbia, 1960
JOHN GREEN† ★
PEPO 1935
ARAM KHACHATURIAN†
PEPPINO E VIOLETTA 1951
NINO ROTA†
PER AMORE...PER MAGIA 1967
LUIS BACALOV
PER LE ANTICHE SCALE 1975
ENNIO MORRICONE
PER UN PUGNO DI DIAMANTI 1969
CARLO RUSTICHELLI
PERCEVAL LE GALLOIS Gaumont, 1978
GUY ROBERT
PERCHE QUELLE STRANE GOCCI DE SANGUE SIL
CORPE DE JENNIFER? WHAT ARE THOSE
STRANGE DROPS OF BLOOD ON THE BODY
OF JENNIFER? 1972
BRUNO NICOLAI
PERCY MGM, 1971
RAY DAVIES
PERCY AND THUNDER (CTF) TNT/Amblin TV/
Brandman Prod., 1993
TOM SCOTT
GROVER WASHINGTON, JR
PERCY'S PROGRESS Joseph Brenner Associates,
1974
TONY MACAULEY
PERDONAMI! 1952
CARLO RUSTICHELLI
THE PEREZ FAMILY 1995
ARTURO SANDOVAL
THE PEREZ FAMILY Samuel Goldwyn, 1995
ALAN SILVESTRI
PERFECT Columbia, 1985
RALPH BURNS
THE PERFECT BRIDE (CTF) Perfect Bride Inc., 1991
RICHARD BRONSKILL
PERFECT FRIDAY Chevron, 1970
JOHN DANKWORTH
THE PERFECT FURLOUGH Universal, 1959
FRANK SKINNER†
THE PERFECT GENTLEMAN MGM, 1935
WILLIAM AXT†
PERFECT GENTLEMEN (TF) Paramount TV, 1978
DOMINIC FRONTIERE
A PERFECT HERO (MS) ITV, 1992
RICHARD HOLMES
A PERFECT MATCH (TF) Lorimar Productions, 1980
BILLY GOLDENBERG
THE PERFECT MARRIAGE Paramount, 1947
FREDERICK HOLLANDER†
THE PERFECT MURDER Merchant Ivory Productions,
1988
RICHARD ROBBINS
PERFECT PEOPLE (TF) Robert Greenwald
Productions, 1988
PATRICK GLEESON

A PIED A CHEVAL ET EN VOITURE 1957
PAUL MISRAKI

THE PIED PIPER 20th Century-Fox, 1942
ALFRED NEWMAN†

THE PIED PIPER Paramount, 1972
DONOVAN

A PIEDI NUDI NEL PARCO 1981
ARMANDO TROVAJOLI

PIER 23 Lippert, 1951
BERT A. SHEFTER

PIERINO IL FICHISSIMO 1981
STELVIO CIPRIANI

PIERROT LE FOU Pathe Contemporary, 1965
ANTOINE DUHAMEL

PIERROT MON AMI (TF) 1978
GEORGES DELERUE

PIETA PER CHI CADE 1955
CARLO RUSTICHELLI

THE PIG'S WAR 1975
GATO BARBIERI

PIGALLE SAINT-GERMAIN-DES-PRES 1950
PAUL MISRAKI

THE PIGEON (TF) Thomas-Spelling Productions, 1969
BILLY MAY

THE PIGEON THAT TOOK ROME Paramount, 1962
ALESSANDRO CICOGNINI†

PIGEONS THE SIDELONG GLANCES OF A PIGEON KICKER MGM, 1970
PATRICK WILLIAMS

THE PIGS/DADDY'S GIRL Aquarius, 1984
CHARLES BERNSTEIN

THE PILGRIM United Artists, 1923
CHARLES CHAPLIN†

PILLOW OF DEATH Universal, 1945
FRANK SKINNER† ★

PILLOW TALK Universal, 1959
FRANK DEVOL

PILLOW TO POST Warner Bros., 1945
FREDERICK HOLLANDER†

THE PILOT Summit Features, 1981
JOHN ADDISON

PIMPERNEL SMITH MISTER V Anglo-American, 1941
JOHN GREENWOOD†

PIN New World, 1989
PETE ROBINSON

PINE CANYON IS BURNING (TF) Universal TV, 1977
LEE HOLDRIDGE

PING PONG Samuel Goldwyn Company, 1985
RICHARD HARVEY

PINK CADILLAC Warner Bros., 1989
STEVE DORFF

THE PINK CHIQUITAS Shapiro Entertainment, 1986
PAUL J. ZAZA

PINK FLOYD - THE WALL MGM/UA, 1982
MICHAEL KAMEN

PINK LIGHTNING (TF) FNM Films, 1991
STEVE TYRELL

THE PINK PANTHER United Artists, 1964
HENRY MANCINI† ★

THE PINK PANTHER STRIKES AGAIN United Artists, 1976
HENRY MANCINI†

THE PINK TELEPHONE LE TELEPHONE ROSE SJ International, 1975
VLADIMIR COSMA

PINKY 20th Century-Fox, 1949
ALFRED NEWMAN†

PINOCCHIO EUE, 1971
JOHN BARBER

PINOCCHIO (AF) RKO Radio, 1940
LEIGH HARLINE† ★★
PAUL J. SMITH† ★★

PINOCCHIO AND THE EMPEROR OF THE NIGHT (AF) New World, 1987
BRIAN BANKS
ANTHONY MARINELLI

PIN-UP GIRL 20th Century-Fox, 1944
EMIL NEWMAN†

PIONEER WOMAN (TF) Filmways, 1973
AL DELORY

PIPE DREAMS Avco Embassy, 1976
DOMINIC FRONTIERE

PIRANHA New World, 1978
PINO DONAGGIO

PIRANHA II - THE SPAWNING Saturn International, 1983
STELVIO CIPRIANI

THE PIRATE MOVIE 1982
TONY BRITTEN

PIRATES Cannon, 1986
PHILIPPE SARDE

THE PIRATES OF CAPRI CAPTAIN SIROCCO Film Classics, 1949
NINO ROTA†

PIRATES OF MONTEREY Universal, 1947
MILTON ROSEN†

PIRATES OF TORTUGA 20th Century-Fox, 1961
BERT A. SHEFTER

PIROGOV 1947
DMITRI SHOSTAKOVICH†

THE PISTOL: THE BIRTH OF A LEGEND Premier, 1991
BRENT HAVENS

THE PIT AND THE PENDULUM American International, 1961
LES BAXTER†

THE PIT AND THE PENDULUM Full Moon, 1991
RICHARD H. BAND

THE PITFALL 1962
TORU TAKEMITSU†

PITTSBURGH Universal, 1942
HANS J. SALTER†
FRANK SKINNER†

PIZZA MAN Megalomania, 1991
DANIEL MAY

P.J. Universal, 1968
NEAL HEFTI

P.K. AND THE KID Castle Hill Productions, 1987
JAMES HORNER

A PLACE FOR ANNIE (TF) Gross-Weston Prods./Signboard Hill/Cannell Entertainment, 1994
MARK SNOW

A PLACE FOR LOVERS AMANTI MGM, 1968
MANUEL DE SICA

A PLACE IN THE SUN Paramount, 1951
FRANZ WAXMAN† ★★

A PLACE TO BE LOVED (TF) Polson Co./Corapeake Prods./Procter & Gamble Prods., 1993
W.G. SNUFFY WALDEN

A PLACE TO CALL HOME (TF) Big Deal Productions/Crawford Productions/Embassy TV, 1987
FRED KARLIN

A PLACE TO LIVE (D) Philadelphia Housing Association, 1941
DAVID DIAMOND

PLACES IN THE HEART Tri-Star, 1984
HOWARD SHORE

THE PLAGUE 1992
VANGELIS

THE PLAGUE DOGS (AF) Nepenthe Productions, 1982
PATRICK GLEESON

THE PLAGUE OF THE ZOMBIES Warner/Pathe, 1966
JAMES BERNARD

PLAIN CLOTHES Paramount, 1988
SCOTT WILK

PLAIN PEOPLE 1945
DMITRI SHOSTAKOVICH†

THE PLAINSMAN Paramount, 1937
GEORGE ANTHEIL†

THE PLAINSMAN Universal, 1966
JOHN WILLIAMS

PLAINSMAN AND THE LADY Republic, 1946
GEORGE ANTHEIL†

PLAN B Curb, 1997
ANDREW ROSE

PLANES, TRAINS AND AUTOMOBILES Paramount, 1987
IRA NEWBORN

PLANET EARTH (TF) Warner Bros. TV, 1974
HARRY SUKMAN†

PLANET OF THE APES 20th Century-Fox, 1968
JERRY GOLDSMITH ★

THE PLANETS AGAINST US I PIANETI CONTRO DI NOI 1961
ARMANDO TROVAJOLI

THE PLANTER'S WIFE United Artists, 1952
ALLAN GRAY†

PLATANOV 1977
EDUARD ARTEMYEV

PLATINUM HIGH SCHOOL TROUBLE AT 16 MGM, 1960
VAN ALEXANDER

PLATOON Hemdale, 1986
GEORGES DELERUE†

PLATOON LEADER Cannon, 1988
GEORGE S. CLINTON

PLAY DIRTY United Artists, 1968
MICHEL LEGRAND

PLAY GIRL Warner Bros., 1932
W. FRANKE HARLING†

PLAY IT AGAIN, SAM Paramount, 1972
BILLY GOLDENBERG

PLAY MISTY FOR ME Universal, 1971
DEE BARTON

THE PLAYBOYS Samuel Goldwyn, 1992
JEAN-CLAUDE PETIT

THE PLAYER Fine Line, 1992
THOMAS NEWMAN

PLAYERS Paramount, 1979
JERRY GOLDSMITH

PLAYGIRL Universal, 1954
HERMAN STEIN

THE PLAYGROUND General, 1965
ELLIOT KAPLAN†

PLAYING FOR TIME (TF) Syzygy Productions, 1980
BRAD FIEDEL

PLAYING WITH FIRE (TF) Zephyr Productions/New World Pictures, 1985
DENNIS MCCARTHY

PLAYMAKER Odyssey, 1994
MARK SNOW

PLAYMATES RKO Radio, 1941
ROY WEBB†

PLAYMATES (TF) ABC Circle Films, 1972
ALLYN FERGUSON
JACK ELLIOTT

PLAYTIME 1960
GEORGES DELERUE†

PLAZA SUITE Paramount, 1970
MAURICE JARRE

PLEASE BELIEVE ME Universal, 1950
HANS J. SALTER†

PLEASE DON'T EAT THE DAISIES MGM, 1960
DAVID ROSE†

PLEASE MURDER ME DCA, 1956
ALBERT GLASSER

PLEASURE COVE (TF) Lou Shaw Productions/David Gerber Productions/Columbia Pictures TV, 1979
PERRY BOTKIN

PLEASURE GARDEN 1961
ERIC NORDGREN

THE PLEASURE OF HIS COMPANY Paramount, 1961
ALFRED NEWMAN†

THE PLEASURE PRINCIPLE 1991
SONNY SOUTHON

PLEASURE PALACE (TF) Norman Rosemont Productions/Marble Arch Productions, 1980
ALLYN FERGUSON

PLEASURE PLANET Empire Films, 1988
TONY RIPPARETTI

THE PLEASURE SEEKERS 20th Century-Fox, 1964
BILLY MAY
LIONEL NEWMAN† ★

PLEASURES (TF) Catalina Productions Group/Columbia TV, 1986
LEE HOLDRIDGE

PLEINS FEUX SUR L'ASSASSIN 1961
MAURICE JARRE

PLEINS FEUX SUR STANISLAS 1965
GEORGES DELERUE†

PLENTY 20th Century-Fox, 1985
BRUCE SMEATON

PLEURE PAS LA BOUCHE PLEINE DON'T CRY WITH YOUR MOUTH FULL 1973
VLADIMIR COSMA

THE PLOUGH AND THE STARS RKO Radio, 1937
ROY WEBB†

THE PLOUGHMAN'S LUNCH Samuel Goldwyn Company, 1983
DOMINIC MULDOWNEY

THE PLOW THAT BROKE THE PLAINS (D) U.S. Government; 1936
VIRGIL THOMSON†

THE PLUMBER Barbary Coast, 1978
GERRY TOLAND

THE PLUNDERERS Allied Artists, 1960
LEONARD ROSENMAN

PLUS AMER QUE LA MORT (TF) 1974
GEORGES DELERUE†

PLUS BEAU QUE MOI TU MEURS 1983
ARMANDO TROVAJOLI

THE PLUTONIUM INCIDENT (TF) Time-Life Productions, 1980
FRED KARLIN

PLYMOUTH (TF) Touchstone TV/RAI-Uno/Zlotoff Inc., 1991
BRAD FIEDEL

PLYMOUTH ADVENTURE MGM, 1952
MIKLOS ROZSA†

POCAHONTAS (AF) Buena Vista, 1995
ALAN MENKEN ★★

POCKET MONEY National General, 1972
ALEX NORTH†

POCKETFUL OF MIRACLES United Artists, 1961
WALTER SCHARF

POETIC JUSTICE Columbia, 1993
STANLEY CLARKE

POIL DE CAROTTE 1932
ALEXANDRE TANSMAN†

POINT BLANK MGM, 1967
JOHNNY MANDEL

POINT BREAK 20th Century Fox, 1991
MARK ISHAM

POINT OF NO RETURN Warner Bros., 1993
NICK GLENNIE-SMITH
HANS ZIMMER

POISON 1993
DAVIDE MASARATI

POISON Zeitgeist, 1991
JAMES BENNETT

POISON IVY New Line, 1992
AARON DAVIS
DAVID MICHAEL FRANK

POISON IVY (TF) NBC Entertainment, 1985
MILES GOODMAN†

POISONED BY LOVE: THE KERN COUNTY MURDERS (TF) Morgan Hill/Hearst, 1993
STEVE DORFF

POKLAD NA PTACIM OSTROVE THE TREASURE OF BIRD ISLAND (AF) 1952
ZDENEK LISKA

POLICARPO 1959
ANGELO FRANCESCO LAVAGNINO†

POLICE ACADEMY The Ladd Company/Warner Bros., 1984
ROBERT FOLK

POLICE ACADEMY 2: THEIR FIRST ASSIGNMENT Warner Bros., 1985
ROBERT FOLK

POLICE ACADEMY 3: BACK IN TRAINING Warner Bros., 1986
ROBERT FOLK

POLICE ACADEMY 4: CITIZENS ON PATROL Warner Bros., 1987
ROBERT FOLK

POLICE ACADEMY 5: ASSIGNMENT MIAMI BEACH Warner Bros., 1988
ROBERT FOLK

POLICE ACADEMY 6: CITY UNDER SIEGE Warner Bros., 1989
ROBERT FOLK

POLICE ACADEMY: MISSION TO MOSCOW Warner Bros., 1994
ROBERT FOLK

POLICE NURSE 20th Century-Fox, 1963
RICHARD LASALLE

POLICE PYTHON 357 1976
GEORGES DELERUE†

POLICE STORY (TF) Screen Gems/Columbia TV, 1973
JERRY GOLDSMITH

POLICE STORY II: THE FREEWAY KILLINGS (TF) David Gerber Productions/MGM-UA TV/Columbia TV, 1987
JOHN CACAVAS

POLICE STORY: GLADIATOR SCHOOL (TF) Columbia Pictures TV, 1988
SYLVESTER LEVAY

POLICE STORY: MONSTER MANOR (TF) Columbia Pictures TV, 1988
JOHN LURIE

POLICE STORY: WATCH COMMANDER (TF) Columbia Pictures TV, 1988
ALF CLAUSEN

POLICEWOMAN CENTERFOLD (TF) Moonlight Productions, 1983
FRED KARLIN

POLISH WEDDING 1997
LUIS BACALOV

POLIZIOTTO SOLITUDINE E RABBIA 1980
STELVIO CIPRIANI

POLLY OF THE CIRCUS MGM, 1932
WILLIAM AXT†

POLTERGEIST MGM/UA, 1982
JERRY GOLDSMITH ★

POLTERGEIST 3 MGM/UA, 1988
JOE RENZETTI

POLTERGEIST II: THE OTHER SIDE MGM/UA, 1986
JERRY GOLDSMITH

POLVERE DI STELLE Capitolina Produzioni Cinematografiche, 1973
PIERO PICCIONI

POLYESTER New Line Cinema, 1981
MICHAEL KAMEN
CHRIS STEIN

THE POM POM GIRLS Crown International, 1976
MICHAEL LLOYD

THE POMPATUS OF LOVE 1996
JOHN HILL

PONTIAC MOON Paramount, 1994
RANDY EDELMAN

PONY SOLDIER 20th Century-Fox, 1952
ALEX NORTH†

POOL OF LONDON Universal, 1951
JOHN ADDISON

POOR ALBERT AND LITTLE ANNIE Valiant International, 1972
HERSCHEL BURKE GILBERT

POOR BUT BEAUTIFUL Trans-Lux, 1956
PIERO PICCIONI

POOR DEVIL (TF) Paramount TV, 1973
MORTON STEVENS†

POOR LITTLE RICH GIRL 20th Century-Fox, 1936
LOUIS SILVERS†

POOR LITTLE RICH GIRL: THE BARBARA HUTTON STORY (MS) Lester Persky Productions/ITC Productions, 1987
RICHARD RODNEY BENNETT

POPCORN Studio Three, 1991
PAUL J. ZAZA

POPE JOAN Columbia, 1972
MAURICE JARRE

POPE JOHN PAUL II (TF) Cooperman-DePaul Productions/Taft International Pictures, 1984
WILFRED JOSEPHS

POPE JOHN PAUL II (TF) Trans World Film/ITC/RAI/Film Polski, 1981
WOJCIECH KILAR

THE POPE OF GREENWICH VILLAGE MGM/UA, 1984
DAVE GRUSIN

POPEYE Paramount, 1980
VAN DYKE PARKS

POPEYE DOYLE (TF) December 3rd Productions/20th Century-Fox TV, 1986
BRAD FIEDEL

POPI United Artists, 1969
DOMINIC FRONTIERE

THE POPPY IS ALSO A FLOWER Comet, 1966
GEORGES AURIC†

PORGY AND BESS Columbia, 1959
ANDRE PREVIN ★★

PORK CHOP HILL United Artists, 1959
LEONARD ROSENMAN

PORKY'S 20th Century-Fox, 1981
PAUL J. ZAZA
CARL ZITTRER

PORKY'S II: THE NEXT DAY 20th Century-Fox, 1983
CARL ZITTRER

PORKY'S REVENGE 20th Century Fox, 1985
DAVE EDMONDS

PORNO, SITUACION LIMITE 1980
STELVIO CIPRIANI

THE PORNOGRAPHER Charlie MoPic, 1994
DONN SCHIFF

PORQUE NO HACEMOS EL AMOR 1981
ARMANDO TROVAJOLI

PORT AFRIQUE Columbia, 1956
MALCOLM ARNOLD

PORT OF NEW YORK Eagle Lion, 1949
SOL KAPLAN

PORT OF SEVEN SEAS MGM, 1938
FRANZ WAXMAN†

PORT SINISTER RKO Radio, 1953
ALBERT GLASSER

A PORTE CHIUSE Fair Film/Cinematografica Rire/Societe Generale de Cinematographie/Ultra Film/Lyre Film/Roxy Film, 1960
ARMANDO TROVAJOLI

PORTLAND EXPOSE Allied Artists, 1957
PAUL DUNLAP

PORTNOY'S COMPLAINT Warner Bros., 1972
MICHEL LEGRAND

THE PORTRAIT Raincoast, 1992
MICHAEL CONWAY BAKER

THE PORTRAIT (CTF) Atticus/Robert Greenwald, 1993
CYNTHIA MILLAR

PORTRAIT FROM LIFE *THE GIRL IN THE PAINTING* Universal, 1948
BENJAMIN FRANKEL†

PORTRAIT IN BLACK Universal, 1960
FRANK SKINNER†

PORTRAIT IN SMOKE Columbia, 1956
MALCOLM ARNOLD

PORTRAIT IN TERROR American International, 1966
RONALD STEIN†

A PORTRAIT OF SHUNKIN 1977
MASARU SATO

A PORTRAIT OF THE ARTIST AS A YOUNG MAN Howard Mahler Films, 1979
STANLEY MYERS†

PORTRAIT OF A LADY Gramercy, 1996
WOJCIECH KILAR

PORTRAIT OF A MARRIAGE (MS) 1992
BARRINGTON PHELOUNG

PORTRAIT OF A MOBSTER Warner Bros., 1961
MAX STEINER†

PORTRAIT OF A REBEL: MARGARET SANGER (TF) Marvin Minoff Productions/David Paradine TV, 1980
ARTHUR B. RUBINSTEIN

PORTRAIT OF A SHOWGIRL (TF) Hamner Productions, 1982
JIMMIE HASKELL

PORTRAIT OF A STRIPPER (TF) Moonlight Productions/Filmways, 1979
ARTHUR B. RUBINSTEIN

PORTRAIT OF AN ESCORT (TF) Moonlight Productions/Filmways, 1980
HAGOOD HARDY

PORTRAIT OF CHICKO 1968
MASARU SATO

PORTRAIT OF JENNIE Selznick, 1948
BERNARD HERRMANN†
DIMITRI TIOMKIN†

THE POSEIDON ADVENTURE 20th Century-Fox, 1972
JOHN WILLIAMS ★

THE POSITIVELY TRUE ADVENTURES OF THE ALLEGED TEXAS CHEERLEADER-MURDERING MOM (CTF) Frederick S. Pierce Co./Sudden Entertainment, 1993
LUCY SIMON

POSSE Gramercy, 1993
MICHEL COLOMBIER

POSSE Paramount, 1975
MAURICE JARRE

THE POSSESSED (TF) Warner Bros. TV, 1977
LEONARD ROSENMAN

POSSESSED Warner Bros., 1947
FRANZ WAXMAN†

POSSESSED BY THE NIGHT Vision International, 1993
CHUCK CIRINO

THE POSSESSION OF JOEL DELANEY Paramount, 1972
JOE RAPOSO†

THE POSSESSION OF MICHAEL D. (TF) Atlantis/Flashner-Gernon/CTV, 1995
JOHN MCCARTHY

POSSESSION Gaumont, 1981
ANDRZEJ KORZYNSKI

POSTCARDS FROM AMERICA Islet/Channel Four, 1994
STEPHEN ENDELMAN

POSTCARDS FROM THE EDGE 1990
CARLY SIMON

THE POSTMAN *IL POSTINO* Miramax, 1995
LUIS BACALOV ★★

POSTMAN *YOUCHAI* 1995
CHEN XIANGYU

THE POSTMAN ALWAYS RINGS TWICE MGM, 1946
GEORGE BASSMAN

THE POSTMAN ALWAYS RINGS TWICE Paramount, 1981
MICHAEL SMALL

POSTMAN'S KNOCK MGM, 1962
RON GOODWIN

POT-BOUILLE *THE HOUSE OF LOVERS* Continental, 1957
JEAN WIENER†

POTEMKIN Amkino, 1925
EDMUND MEISEL†

POULET AU VINAIGRE MK2 Diffusion, 1985
MATTHIEU CHABROL

POUND PUPPIES AND THE LEGEND OF BIG PAW (AF) Tri-Star, 1988
STEVE TYRELL

POUR L'ESPAGNE (FD) 1963
MAURICE JARRE

POUR LE MISTRAL 1966
ANTOINE DUHAMEL

POUR UNE NUIT D'AMOUR 1946
JEAN WIENER†

POURQUOI PATRICIA (TF) 1978
GEORGES DELERUE†

POVERI MILIONARI 1958
ARMANDO TROVAJOLI

P.O.W. THE ESCAPE Cannon, 1986
DAVID STORRS

POWAQQATSI Cannon, 1988
PHILIP GLASS

POWDER 1995
JERRY GOLDSMITH

POWDER TOWN RKO Radio, 1942
ROY WEBB†

POWDERKEG (TF) Filmways/Rodphi Productions, 1971
JOHN ANDREW TARTAGLIA

POWER 20th Century Fox, 1986
CY COLEMAN

THE POWER Artists Releasing Corporation/Film Ventures International, 1983
CHRISTOPHER YOUNG

THE POWER MGM, 1968
MIKLOS ROZSA†

POWER (TF) David Gerber Productions/Columbia Pictures TV, 1980
JERROLD IMMEL

POWER AMONG MEN (D) United Nations, 1959
VIRGIL THOMSON†

THE POWER AND THE PRIZE MGM, 1956
BRONISLAU KAPER†

THE POWER OF ONE Warner Bros., 1992
HANS ZIMMER

THE POWER OF THE IMAGE: LENI RIEFENSTAHL (FD) 1993
ULRICH BASSENGE
WOLFGANG NEUMANN

THE POWER OF THE WHISTLER Columbia, 1945
PAUL SAWTELL†

POWER PLAY Magnum International Pictures/Cowry Film Productions, 1978
KEN THORNE

POWER PLAYS (TF) Oxford TV/KCET/ITEL/Channel 4, 1994
BARRINGTON PHELOUNG

THE POWER WITHIN PM Entertainment, 1995
JIM HALFPENNY

POWWOW HIGHWAY Warner Bros., 1989
BARRY GOLDBERG

PRACTICALLY YOURS Paramount, 1944
VICTOR YOUNG†

PRAIRIE CHICKENS United Artists, 1943
EDWARD WARD†

PRAISE MARX AND PASS THE AMMUNITION 1970
CARL DAVIS

PRANCER Orion, 1989
MAURICE JARRE

PRAY FOR THE WILDCATS (TF) ABC Circle Films, 1974
FRED MYROW

PRAY TV (TF) ABC Circle Films, 1982
DENNIS MCCARTHY

A PRAYER FOR THE DYING Samuel Goldwyn Company, 1987
BILL CONTI

PRAYER OF THE ROLLERBOYS Gaga, 1991
STACY WIDELITZ

PRAYING MANTIS Portman Productions/Channel Four, 1982
CARL DAVIS

PRAYING WITH ANGER Crescent Moon, 1992
EDMUND K. CHOI

THE PREACHER'S WIFE Buena Vista, 1996
HANS ZIMMER ★

PRECIOUS VICTIMS (TF) Laurel Prods., 1993
MARK SNOW

THE PREDATOR 1976
MICHEL COLOMBIER

PREDATOR 20th Century-Fox, 1987
ALAN SILVESTRI

PREDATOR 2 20th Century Fox, 1990
ALAN SILVESTRI

PREFONTAINE Buena Vista, 1997
MASON DARING

PREHISTORIC WOMEN United Artists, 1950
MORT GLICKMAN†
RAOUL KRAUSHAAR

PREJUDICE New World/MPSC, 1949
IRVING GERTZ

PRELUDE TO A KISS 20th Century Fox, 1992
HOWARD SHORE

THE PREMATURE BURIAL American International, 1962
RONALD STEIN†

PREMIER BAL 1941
GEORGES VAN PARYS†

PREMIER VOYAGE 1979
GEORGES DELERUE†

PRENDS LA ROUTE 1936
GEORGES VAN PARYS†

PRENDS TON PASSE-MONTAGNE ON VA A LA PLAGE! UGC, 1983
JEAN MUSY

PRESCRIPTION: MURDER (TF) Universal, 1968
DAVE GRUSIN

PRESENCE D'ALBERT CAMUS (FD) 1963
MAURICE JARRE

THE PRESIDENT'S LADY 20th Century-Fox, 1953
ALFRED NEWMAN†

THE PRESIDENT'S ANALYST Paramount, 1967
LALO SCHIFRIN

THE PRESIDENT'S CHILD (TF) Lauren Films, 1992
J. PETER ROBINSON

THE PRESIDENT'S MISTRESS (TF) Stephen Friedman/Kings Road Productions, 1978
LALO SCHIFRIN

THE PRESIDENT'S PLANE IS MISSING (TF) ABC Circle Films, 1973
GIL MELLE

THE PRESIDIO Paramount, 1988
BRUCE BROUGHTON

PRESSURE POINT United Artists, 1962
ERNEST GOLD

PRESUMED INNOCENT Warner Bros., 1990
JOHN WILLIAMS

PRET-A-PORTER Miramax, 1994
MICHEL LEGRAND

PRETTY BABY Warner Bros., 1950
DAVID BUTTOLPH†

PRETTY BOY 1993
JOAKIM HOLBECK

PRETTY IN PINK Paramount, 1986
MICHAEL GORE

PRETTY MAIDS ALL IN A ROW MGM, 1971
LALO SCHIFRIN

PRETTY POISON 20th Century-Fox, 1968
JOHNNY MANDEL

PRETTY POLLY Universal, 1968
MICHEL LEGRAND

PRETTY SMART New World, 1987
EDDIE ARKIN
JAY LEVY

PRETTY WOMAN Buena Vista, 1990
JAMES NEWTON HOWARD

PRETTYKILL Spectrafilm, 1987
ROBERT O. RAGLAND

PREY OF THE CHAMELEON (TF) Saban/Prism, 1992
SHUKI LEVY

PREYING MANTIS (CTF) Fast Track Films/Wilshire Court Prods., 1993
JOHN DEBNEY

THE PRICE OF POWER 1969
LUIS BACALOV

THE PRICE SHE PAID (TF) Producers Entertainment Group/Sandy Hook/World International Network, 1992
GEOFF LEVIN
CHRIS MANY

PRICK UP YOUR EARS Samuel Goldwyn Company, 1987
STANLEY MYERS†

THE PRIDE AND THE PASSION United Artists, 1957
GEORGE ANTHEIL†

PRIDE AND PREJUDICE MGM, 1940
HERBERT STOTHART†

THE PRIDE OF JESSE HALLAM (TF) The Konigsberg Company, 1981
JOHNNY CASH

THE PRIDE OF THE YANKEES RKO Radio, 1942
LEIGH HARLINE† ★

PRIDE OF THE MARINES Warner Bros., 1945
FRANZ WAXMAN†

PRIEST 1994
ANDY ROBERTS

THE PRIEST KILLER (TF) Universal TV, 1971
DAVID SHIRE

THE PRIEST'S WIFE Warner Bros., 1970
ARMANDO TROVAJOLI

PRIGIONIERA DELLA TORRE DI FUOCO 1952
CARLO RUSTICHELLI

PRIMA COMMUNIONE 1949
ALESSANDRO CICOGNINI†

PRIMA NOTTE DI NOZZE 1976
ARMANDO TROVAJOLI

PRIMAL FEAR Paramount, 1996
JAMES NEWTON HOWARD

PRIMARY MOTIVE Blossom Pictures, 1992
JOHN CALE

PRIME CUT National General, 1972
LALO SCHIFRIN

THE PRIME OF MISS JEAN BRODIE 20th Century-Fox, 1969
ROD MCKUEN

PRIME RISK Almi Pictures, 1985
PHIL MARSHALL

PRIME SUSPECT S.V.S., 1989
BRUCE KIMMEL

PRIME SUSPECT (TF) 1992
STEPHEN WARBECK

PRIME SUSPECT (TF) Tisch-Avnet Television, 1982
CHARLES GROSS

PRIME TARGET Hero, 1991
ROBERT GARRETT

PRIME TARGET (TF) MGM TV, 1991
CHRIS BOARDMAN

PRIMO AMORE 1941
ALESSANDRO CICOGNINI†

PRIMROSE PATH RKO Radio, 1940
WERNER R. HEYMANN†

THE PRINCE AND THE PAUPER Warner Bros., 1937
ERICH WOLFGANG KORNGOLD†

THE PRINCE AND THE PAUPER Warner Bros., 1977
MAURICE JARRE

THE PRINCE AND THE SHOWGIRL Warner Bros., 1957
RICHARD ADDINSELL†

PRINCE BOUBOULE 1938
PAUL MISRAKI

PRINCE JACK Castle Hill Productions, 1984
ELMER BERNSTEIN

THE PRINCE OF CENTRAL PARK (TF) Lorimar Productions, 1977
ARTHUR B. RUBINSTEIN

THE PRINCE OF PENNSYLVANIA New Line Cinema, 1988
THOMAS NEWMAN

THE PRINCE OF TIDES Columbia, 1991
JAMES NEWTON HOWARD ★

PRINCE OF BEL-AIR (TF) Leonard Hill Films, 1986
ROBERT FOLK

PRINCE OF DARKNESS Universal, 1987
JOHN CARPENTER
ALAN HOWARTH

PRINCE OF FOXES 20th Century-Fox, 1949
ALFRED NEWMAN†

PRINCE OF JUTLAND 1994
PER NORGAARD

PRINCE OF PIRATES Columbia, 1953
MISCHA BAKALEINIKOFF†

PRINCE OF PLAYERS 20th Century-Fox, 1954
BERNARD HERRMANN†

PRINCE OF THE CITY Orion/Warner Bros., 1981
PAUL CHIHARA

PRINCE VALIANT 20th Century-Fox, 1954
FRANZ WAXMAN†

PRINCE VALIANT   Paramount, 1997
DAVID BERGEAUD

THE PRINCE WHO WAS A THIEF   Universal, 1951
HANS J. SALTER†

PRINCES IN EXILE (TF)   Cinepix/Canada National
Film Board/CBC, 1991
NORMAND CORBEIL

THE PRINCESS ACADEMY   Empire Pictures, 1987
ROGER BELLON

THE PRINCESS AND THE CABBIE (TF)   Freyda
Rothstein Productions/Time-Life Productions, 1981
PATRICK WILLIAMS ☆☆

THE PRINCESS AND THE PIRATE   RKO Radio,
1944
DAVID ROSE† ★

PRINCESS ACADEMY   Weintraub Productions, 1987
PAUL ANTONELLI
DAVID WHEATLEY

THE PRINCESS BRIDE   20th Century Fox, 1987
MARK KNOPFLER

PRINCESS CARABOO   TriStar, 1994
RICHARD HARTLEY

PRINCESS DAISY (TF)   Steve Krantz Productions/
NBC Entertainment, 1983
LALO SCHIFRIN

PRINCESS IN LOVE (TF)   Kushner-Locke, 1996
PETER MANNING ROBINSON

THE PRINCESS OF THE DARK   Ince, 1917
VICTOR SCHERTZINGER†

PRINCESS O'HARA   Universal, 1935
ARTHUR MORTON

PRINCESS O'ROURKE   Warner Bros., 1943
FREDERICK HOLLANDER†

THE PRINCESS STALLION (TF)   1997
ARTHUR B. RUBINSTEIN

THE PRINCIPAL   Tri-Star, 1987
JAY GRUSKA

PRIPAD PRO ZACINAJICHO KATA   A CASE FOR
A YOUNG HANGMAN   1970
ZDENEK LISKA

PRISON   Empire Pictures, 1988
RICHARD H. BAND
CHRISTOPHER L. STONE

PRISON SHIP   Columbia, 1945
MARIO †

THE PRISONER   1973
RONALD STEIN†

THE PRISONER   Columbia, 1955
BENJAMIN FRANKEL†

THE PRISONER OF RIO   Multi Media AG/Samba
Corporation, 1988
HANS ZIMMER

THE PRISONER OF SECOND AVENUE   Warner
Bros., 1975
MARVIN HAMLISCH

THE PRISONER OF SHARK ISLAND   20th
Century-Fox, 1936
R. H. BASSETT†

THE PRISONER OF ZENDA   1913
JOSEPH CARL BREIL†

THE PRISONER OF ZENDA   MGM, 1952
CONRAD SALINGER†

THE PRISONER OF ZENDA   United Artists, 1937
ALFRED NEWMAN† ★

THE PRISONER OF ZENDA   Universal, 1979
HENRY MANCINI†

PRISONER OF HONOR (CTF)   HBO, 1991
BARRY KIRSCH

PRISONER OF JAPAN   Producers Releasing Corp.,
1942
LEO ERDODY†

PRISONER OF THE LOST UNIVERSE (CTF)
Marcel-Robertson Productions/United Media Finance,
1983
HARRY ROBERTSON

PRISONER OF THE MOUNTAINS   Orion Classics,
1997
LEONID DESYATNIKOV

PRISONER OF WAR   MGM, 1954
JEFF ALEXANDER†

THE PRIVATE AFFAIRS OF BEL AMI   United Artists,
1947
DARIUS MILHAUD†

PRIVATE AFFAIRS   Universal, 1940
HANS J. SALTER†

A PRIVATE BATTLE (TF)   Procter & Gamble
Productions Robert Halmi, Inc., 1980
CHARLES GROSS

PRIVATE BENJAMIN   Warner Bros., 1980
BILL CONTI

THE PRIVATE EYES   New World, 1980
PETER MATZ

PRIVATE EYE (TF)   Yerkovich Productions/Universal
TV, 1987
JOE JACKSON

A PRIVATE FUNCTION   Island Alive, 1984
JOHN DUPREZ

PRIVATE HELL 36   RKO Radio, 1954
LEITH STEVENS†

PRIVATE INVESTIGATIONS   MGM/UA, 1987
MURRAY MUNRO

THE PRIVATE LIFE OF DON JUAN   United Artists,
1934
ERNST TOCH†

THE PRIVATE LIFE OF SHERLOCK HOLMES   also
cameo as ballet conductor, United Artists, 1970
MIKLOS ROZSA†

THE PRIVATE LIVES OF ADAM AND EVE
Universal, 1960
VAN ALEXANDER

THE PRIVATE LIVES OF ELIZABETH AND ESSEX
Warner Bros., 1939
ERICH WOLFGANG KORNGOLD† ★

A PRIVATE MATTER (CTF)   HBO Pictures/Longbow/
Mirage, 1992
JAMES NEWTON HOWARD

THE PRIVATE NAVY OF SGT. O'FARRELL   United
Artists, 1968
HARRY SUKMAN†

PRIVATE NUMBER   20th Century-Fox, 1936
LOUIS SILVERS†

PRIVATE PARTS   MGM, 1972
HUGO FRIEDHOFER†

PRIVATE PARTS   Paramount, 1997
VAN DYKE PARKS

PRIVATE ROAD   NO TRESPASSING   Trans
World Entertainment, 1987   NO
TRESPASSING   Trans World Entertainment, 1987
GREG EVIGAN

PRIVATE SESSIONS (TF)   Raven's Claw Productions/
Seltzer-Gimbel Productions/Comworld Productions,
1985
LALO SCHIFRIN

PRIVATE VICES, PUBLIC VIRTUES   1976
FRANCESCO DE MASI

THE PRIVATE WAR OF MAJOR BENSON
Universal, 1955
HENRY MANCINI†
HERMAN STEIN

A PRIVATE'S AFFAIR   20th Century-Fox, 1959
CYRIL J. MOCKRIDGE†

PRIVATE'S PROGRESS   DCA, 1956
JOHN ADDISON

PRIVATES ON PARADE   Orion Classics, 1983
DENIS KING

THE PRIZE   MGM, 1963
JERRY GOLDSMITH

THE PRIZE FIGHTER   New World, 1979
PETER MATZ

A PRIZE OF GOLD   Columbia, 1954
MALCOLM ARNOLD

PRIZZI'S HONOR   20th Century Fox, 1985
ALEX NORTH†

PROBABILITA ZERO   1969
CARLO RUSTICHELLI

PROBABLE CAUSE (CTF)   Wilmont Prods., 1994
GEORGE BLONDHEIM

PROBE (TF)   MCA TV Ltd., 1988
SYLVESTER LEVAY

PROBLEM CHILD   Universal, 1990
MILES GOODMAN†

PROBLEM CHILD 2   Universal Pictures, 1991
DAVID KITAY

PROBLEM CHILD 3: JUNIOR IN LOVE (TF)
Telven Prods./Robert Simonds Co., 1995
DAVID MICHAEL FRANK

PROBLEM GIRLS   Columbia, 1953
ALBERT GLASSER

PROCESSO A STALIN...?   1967
CARLO SAVINA

PROCESSO PER DIRETTISSIMA   1974
STELVIO CIPRIANI

THE PRODIGAL   MGM, 1931
HERBERT STOTHART†

THE PRODIGAL   MGM, 1955
BRONISLAU KAPER†

THE PRODIGAL   World Wide, 1984
BRUCE BROUGHTON

THE PRODIGAL SON   1993
MAURI SUMEN

THE PRODUCERS   Avco Embassy, 1968
JOHN MORRIS

THE PROFESSIONAL   LEON   Columbia, 1994
ERIC SERRA

THE PROFESSIONALS   Columbia, 1966
MAURICE JARRE

PROFESSIONAL SOLDIER   20th Century-Fox, 1936
LOUIS SILVERS†

PROFESSIONAL SWEETHEART   RKO Radio, 1933
MAX STEINER†
ROY WEBB†

PROFESSIONE FIGLIO   1980
ENNIO MORRICONE

PROFESSOR POPPER'S PROBLEMS   1974
KENNETH V. JONES

PROFIL BAS   1993
GABRIEL YARED

PROFONDO ROSSO   Howard Mahler Films, 1976
GOBLIN

THE PROGRAM   Buena Vista, 1993
MICHEL COLOMBIER

PROGRAMMED TO KILL   Trans World
Entertainment, 1987
CRAIG HUNDLEY
JERROLD IMMEL

PROIBITO   Documento Film/UGC/Cormoran Film,
1954
NINO ROTA†

PROIBITO RUBARE   Lux Film, 1948
NINO ROTA†

PROJECT ELIMINATOR   South Gate, 1991
JON MCCALLUM

PROJECT M-7   THE NET   Universal, 1953
BENJAMIN FRANKEL†

PROJECT SHADOWCHASER II   EGM Films, 1994
STEVE EDWARDS

PROJECT SHADOWCHASER III   Escee Films, 1995
STEVE EDWARDS

PROJECT X   20th Century Fox, 1987
JAMES HORNER

PROJECT X   Paramount, 1968
NATHAN VAN CLEAVE†

PROJECT: GENESIS   Prism, 1993
ANDY MCNEILL

THE PROJECTED MAN   1967
KENNETH V. JONES

THE PROJECTIONIST   Maron Films Limited, 1971
IGO KANTOR

PROJECTION PRIVEE   1972
SERGE GAINSBOURG†

PROM NIGHT   Avco Embassy, 1980
PAUL J. ZAZA
CARL ZITTRER

THE PROMISE   DAS VERSPRECHEN   Fine Line,
1995
JURGEN KNIEPER

THE PROMISE   Universal, 1979
DAVID SHIRE

PROMISE (TF)   Garner-Duchow Productions/Warner
Bros. TV, 1986
DAVID SHIRE

PROMISE AT DAWN   Avco Embassy, 1970
GEORGES DELERUE†

PROMISE HER ANYTHING   Paramount, 1966
LYN MURRAY†

PROMISE HIM ANYTHING... (TF)   ABC Circle Films,
1975
NELSON RIDDLE†

THE PROMISE OF LOVE (TF)   Pierre Cossette
Productions, 1980
PAUL CHIHARA

A PROMISE TO CAROLINE (TF)   The Kaufman
Company/Citadel, 1996
LAURA KARPMAN

PROMISED A MIRACLE (TF)   Dick Clark
Productions/Republic Pictures Roni Weisberg
Productions, 1988
LEONARD ROSENMAN

THE PROMISED LAND (TD)   Discovery Prods./
BBC-TV, 1995
TERENCE BLANCHARD

PROMISED LAND   Vestron, 1987
JAMES NEWTON HOWARD

PROMISED LAND   Yugoslavian
ALFI KABILJO

PROMISES IN THE DARK   Orion, 1979
LEONARD ROSENMAN

PROMISES TO KEEP (TF)   Sandra Harmon
Productions/Green-Epstein Productions/Telepictures,
1985
MICHEL LEGRAND

THE PROMOTER   THE CARD   Universal, 1952
WILLIAM ALWYN†

THE PROMPTER   1993
MARGO KOLAR

PRONTO (CTF)   Stonehedge Films, 1997
JOHN ALTMAN

THE PROPHECY   Dimension, 1995
DAVID C. WILLIAMS

PROPHECY   Paramount, 1979
LEONARD ROSENMAN

PROPHET OF EVIL: THE ERVIL LeBARON STORY
(TF)   Dream City Films/Hearst, 1993
CRAIG HUNDLEY

THE PROPRIETOR   1996
RICHARD ROBBINS

PROSPERO'S BOOKS   Miramax, 1991
MICHAEL NYMAN

THE PROTECTOR   Warner Bros., 1985
KEN THORNE

PROTOCOL   Warner Bros., 1984
BASIL POLEDOURIS

PROTOTYPE (TF)   Levinson-Link Productions/Robert
Papazian Productions, 1983
BILLY GOLDENBERG

THE PROUD AND PROFANE   Paramount, 1956
VICTOR YOUNG†

PROUD MEN (TF)   Cowboy Productions/Agamemnon
Films Productions/von Zerneck-Samuels Productions,
1987
LAURENCE ROSENTHAL

THE PROUD ONES   20th Century-Fox, 1956
LIONEL NEWMAN†

THE PROUD REBEL   Buena Vista, 1958
JEROME MOROSS†

PROVIDENCE   Cinema 5, 1977
MIKLOS ROZSA†

PROVINZIA VIOLENTA   1978
STELVIO CIPRIANI

PROVOCATEUR   Capella, 1997
MARK NAKAMURA
RICHARD UGLOW

THE PROWLER   Sandhurst Corporation, 1981
RICHARD EINHORN

THE PROWLER   United Artists, 1951
LYN MURRAY†

PROWLER (TF)   Bakula Prods./Warner Bros. TV,
1995
VELTON RAY BUNCH

PRUDENCE AND THE PILL   20th Century-Fox, 1968
BERNARD EBBINGHOUSE

THE PSYCHIATRIST: GOD BLESS THE CHILDREN
(TF)   Universal TV/Arena Productions, 1970
ROGER KELLAWAY

P.S.I. LUV U (TF)   CBS Entertainment/Glen Larson
Prods., 1991
MATTHEW DELGADO
GLEN A. LARSON

PSYCHIC   Trimark, 1992
MILAN KYMLICKA

PSYCHIC KILLER   Avco Embassy, 1975
WILLIAM KRAFT

PSYCHO   Paramount, 1960
BERNARD HERRMANN†

PSYCHO FROM TEXAS   New American Films, 1974
JAIME MENDOZA-NAVA

PSYCHO GIRLS   Cannon, 1985
JOEL ROSENBAUM

PSYCHO II   Universal, 1983
JERRY GOLDSMITH

PSYCHO III   Universal, 1986
CARTER BURWELL

PSYCHO SUSHI   Nath Productions, 1996
DAVID BERGEAUD

PSYCHOMANIA   Scotia International, 1971
DAVID WHITAKER

THE PSYCHOPATH   Paramount, 1966
ELISABETH LUYTENS†

PSYCH-OUT   American International, 1968
RONALD STEIN†

PSYCOSISSIMO   1961
CARLO RUSTICHELLI

P.T. RAIDERS   Continental, 1955
WILLIAM ALWYN†

PT-109   Warner Bros., 1963
DAVID BUTTOLPH†
WILLIAM LAVA†

P'TANG YANG, KIPPERBANG   MGM/UA Classics,
1983
DAVID EARL

P'TIT CON   LITTLE JERK   Gaumont, 1984
VLADIMIR COSMA

PUBERTY BLUES   Universal Classics, 1982
JIM MANZIE

PUBLIC ACCESS   Cinemabeam, 1993
JOHN OTTMAN

THE PUBLIC DEFENDER   RKO Radio, 1931
MAX STEINER†

THE PUBLIC EYE   Universal, 1972
JOHN BARRY

THE PUBLIC EYE   Universal, 1992
MARK ISHAM

PUBLIC HERO NO. 1   MGM, 1935
EDWARD WARD†

PUBLIC PIGEON NO. ONE   Universal, 1957
DAVID ROSE†

PUCCINI   1952
CARLO RUSTICHELLI

PUDDING CHOMEUR   Aska Film, 1997
JEAN DELORME

PUFNSTUFF   Universal, 1970
CHARLES FOX

PUGNI, PUPE E MARINAI   1961
ARMANDO TROVAJOLI

PULL MY DAISY   G-String Productions, 1959
DAVID AMRAM

PULP   United Artists, 1972
GEORGE MARTIN

PULSE   Columbia, 1988
JAY FERGUSON

PUMP UP THE VOLUME   New Line, 1990
CLIFF MARTINEZ

PUMPING IRON (FD)   Cinema 5. 1977
MICHAEL SMALL

PUMPING IRON II: THE WOMEN (FD)   Cinecom,
1985
DAVID MCHUGH

THE PUMPKIN EATER   Royal International, 1964
GEORGES DELERUE†

PUMPKINHEAD   MGM/UA, 1988
RICHARD STONE

PUNCH AND JODY (TF)   Metromedia Producers
Corporation/Stonehenge Productions, 1974
FRED KARLIN

RADIO FLYER Columbia, 1992
HANS ZIMMER
RADIO INSIDE (CTF) MGM-UA/Showtime
Entertainment, 1994
GIL GOLDSTEIN
RADIOACTIVE DREAMS DEG, 1986
TONY RIPPARETTI
PETE ROBINSON
THE RADIOLAND MURDERS Universal, 1994
JOEL MCNEELY
RAFFERTY AND THE GOLD DUST TWINS Warner
Bros., 1975
ARTIE BUTLER
RAFFLES United Artists, 1940
VICTOR YOUNG†
RAFTER ROMANCE RKO Radio, 1933
MAX STEINER†
RAGA 1971
RAVI SHANKAR
RAGAZZO DI BORGATA Italneggio, 1976
NINO ROTA†
RAGE Tiber International, 1984
STELVIO CIPRIANI
RAGE Warner Bros., 1972
LALO SCHIFRIN
RAGE (TF) Diane Silver Productions/Charles Fries
Productions, 1980
LAURENCE ROSENTHAL
A RAGE IN HARLEM Miramax, 1991
ELMER BERNSTEIN
RAGE IN HEAVEN MGM, 1941
BRONISLAU KAPER†
RAGE OF ANGELS (TF) Furia-Oringer Productions/
NBC Productions, 1983
BILLY GOLDENBERG ☆☆
RAGE OF ANGELS: THE STORY CONTINUES
(MS) NBC Productions, 1986
BILLY GOLDENBERG
RAGE OF HONOR Trans World Entertainment, 1987
STELVIO CIPRIANI
A RAGE TO LIVE United Artists, 1965
NELSON RIDDLE†
RAGGEDY ANN AND ANDY (AF) 20th
Century-Fox, 1977
JOE RAPOSO†
RAGGEDY MAN Universal, 1981
JERRY GOLDSMITH
THE RAGGEDY RAWNEY HandMade Films, 1988
MICHAEL KAMEN
THE RAGING MOON Cinema 5, 1971
STANLEY MYERS†
THE RAGING TIDE Universal, 1951
FRANK SKINNER†
RAGTIME Paramount, 1981
RANDY NEWMAN ★
RAID ON ENTEBBE (TF) Edgar J. Scherick
Associates/20th Century-Fox TV, 1977
DAVID SHIRE ☆
THE RAIDERS Universal, 1952
HENRY MANCINI†
HERMAN STEIN
THE RAIDERS OF THE GOLDEN COBRA World
Northal, 1982
CARLO SAVINA
RAIDERS OF SAN JOAQUIN Universal, 1943
HANS J. SALTER†
RAIDERS OF THE DESERT Universal, 1941
HANS J. SALTER†
RAIDERS OF THE LOST ARK Paramount, 1981
JOHN WILLIAMS ★
THE RAILROAD MAN IL FERROVIERE
Continental, 1956
CARLO RUSTICHELLI
RAILS INTO LARAMIE Universal, 1954
HERMAN STEIN
RAIN Joris Ivens, 1940
HANNS EISLER†
RAIN United Artists, 1932
ALFRED NEWMAN†
THE RAIN KILLER Concorde, 1990
TERRY PLUMERI
RAIN MAN MGM/UA, 1988
HANS ZIMMER ★
THE RAIN PEOPLE Warner Bros., 1969
RONALD STEIN†
THE RAINBOW Vestron, 1989
CARL DAVIS
RAINBOW ITC, 1990
TANGERINE DREAM
RAINBOW (TF) Ten-Four Productions, 1978
CHARLES FOX
THE RAINBOW BOYS 1973
HOWARD BLAKE
RAINBOW BRITE AND THE STAR STEALER (AF)
Warner Bros., 1985
SHUKI LEVY
HAIM SABAN
RAINBOW ISLAND Paramount, 1944
ROY WEBB†
RAINING STONES 1993
STEWART COPELAND

THE RAINMAKER Paramount, 1956
ALEX NORTH† ★
THE RAINMAKERS RKO Radio, 1935
ROY WEBB†
THE RAINS CAME 20th Century-Fox, 1939
ALFRED NEWMAN† ★
THE RAINS OF RANCHIPUR 20th Century-Fox,
1955
HUGO FRIEDHOFER†
RAINTREE COUNTY MGM, 1957
JOHN GREEN† ★
RAINY DAY WOMEN (TF) BBC, 1986
STANLEY MYERS†
RAISE THE RED LANTERN DAHONG DENGLONG
GAOGAO GUA Orion Classics, 1991
ZHAO JIPING
RAISE THE TITANIC AFD, 1980
JOHN BARRY
A RAISIN IN THE SUN Columbia, 1961
LAURENCE ROSENTHAL
RAISING ARIZONA 20th Century Fox, 1987
CARTER BURWELL
RAISING CAIN Universal, 1992
PINO DONAGGIO
RAISING DAISY ROTHCHILD THE LAST
GIRAFFE Westfall Productions, 1979
FRED KARLIN
THE RAISING OF LAZARUS Churchcraft, 1948
MILTON ROSEN†
THE RAKE'S PROGRESS 1945
WILLIAM ALWYN†
RALLY 'ROUND THE FLAG, BOYS! 20th
Century-Fox, 1958
CYRIL J. MOCKRIDGE†
RAMBLING ROSE Seven Arts, 1991
ELMER BERNSTEIN
RAMBO III Tri-Star, 1988
JERRY GOLDSMITH
RAMBO: FIRST BLOOD PART II Tri-Star, 1985
JERRY GOLDSMITH
RAMONA 20th Century-Fox, 1936
ALFRED NEWMAN†
RAMPAGE DEG, 1987
ENNIO MORRICONE
RAMPAGE Warner Bros., 1963
ELMER BERNSTEIN
RAMROD United Artists, 1947
ADOLPH DEUTSCH†
RAN Orion Classics, 1985
TORU TAKEMITSU†
RANCHO DELUXE United Artists, 1975
JIMMY BUFFETT
RANCHO NOTORIOUS RKO Radio, 1952
HUGO FRIEDHOFER†
EMIL NEWMAN†
RANDOM HARVEST MGM, 1942
HERBERT STOTHART† ★
RANGE WAR Paramount, 1939
VICTOR YOUNG†
THE RANGER, THE COOK AND A HOLE IN THE
SKY (TF) Signboard Hill, 1995
LAWRENCE SHRAGGE
RANGERS OF FORTUNE Paramount, 1940
FREDERICK HOLLANDER†
RANGO Paramount, 1931
W. FRANKE HARLING†
RANSOM Buena Vista, 1996
JAMES HORNER
RANSOM MGM, 1956
JEFF ALEXANDER†
RANSOM FOR ALICE! (TF) Universal TV, 1977
DAVID ROSE†
RAPA NUI Warner Bros., 1994
STEWART COPELAND
RAPE AND MARRIAGE—THE RIDEOUT CASE
(TF) Dick Berg/Stonehenge Productions/Lorimar
Productions, 1980
GIL MELLE
THE RAPE OF DR. WILLIS (TF) Interprod, 1991
MARK SNOW
RAPE OF INNOCENCE 1974
VLADIMIR COSMA
RAPE OF MALAYA 1956
MATYAS SEIBER
THE RAPE OF RICHARD BECK (TF) Robert
Papazian Productions/Henerson-Hirsch Productions,
1985
PETER BERNSTEIN
RAPID FIRE 20th Century Fox, 1992
CHRISTOPHER YOUNG
RAPPIN' Cannon, 1985
MICHAEL J. LINN†
RAPPORTE FULLER BASE STOCCOLMA 1967
ARMANDO TROVAJOLI
THE RAPTURE Fine Line, 1991
THOMAS NEWMAN
RAPTURE International Classics, 1965
GEORGES DELERUE†

THE RARE BREED Universal, 1966
JOHN WILLIAMS
RASCAL DAZZLE 1985
RONALD STEIN†
RASCALS AND ROBBERS—THE SECRET
ADVENTURES OF TOM SAWYER AND HUCK
FINN (TF) CBS Entertainment, 1982
JAMES HORNER
RASHOMON RKO Radio, 1950
FUMIO HAYASAKA†
RASPUTIN - THE MAD MONK I KILLED
RASPUTIN 20th Century-Fox, 1966
DON BANKS
RASPUTIN AND THE EMPRESS MGM, 1932
HERBERT STOTHART†
THE RAT RKO Radio, 1938
ANTHONY COLLINS†
RAT DER GOTTER 1951
HANNS EISLER†
RAT FINK/WILD AND WILLING Genesis, 1964
RONALD STEIN†
THE RAT RACE Paramount, 1960
ELMER BERNSTEIN
RATBOY Warner Bros., 1986
LENNIE NIEHAUS
THE RATINGS GAME (CTF) Imagination-New Street
Productions, 1984
BRUCE KIMMEL
DAVID SPEAR
RATON PASS Warner Bros., 1951
MAX STEINER†
RAV'E' - DANCING TO A DIFFERENT BEAT
Smart Egg, 1993
STEVE DEUTSCH
RAVAGER Republic, 1997
JOHN E. NORDSTROM, II
RAVAGERS Columbia, 1979
FRED KARLIN
RAVE REVIEW Wildebeest Co., 1994
AMOTZ PLESSNER
THE RAVEN American International, 1963
LES BAXTER†
THE RAVEN Universal, 1935
CLIFFORD VAUGHAN†
RAVEN (TF) Invader Prods./Columbia TV, 1992
CHRISTOPHER FRANKE
RAVEN DANCE Orphan, 1993
JIMMY LIFTON
RAW DEAL DEG, 1986
CINEMASCORE
CLAUDE GAUDETTE
THE RAW EDGE Universal, 1956
HANS J. SALTER†
RAW FORCE American Panorama, 1982
WALTER MURPHY
RAW NERVE Pyramid/AIP, 1991
GREGG TURNER
RAW WIND IN EDEN Universal, 1958
HANS J. SALTER†
RAWHEAD REX Empire Pictures, 1987
COLIN TOWNS
RAWHIDE 20th Century-Fox, 1951
SOL KAPLAN
THE RAWHIDE YEARS Universal, 1956
HANS J. SALTER†
FRANK SKINNER†
RAY ALEXANDER: A TASTE FOR JUSTICE (TF)
Logo Entertainment/Viacom, 1994
DICK DEBENEDICTIS
RAYMIE Allied Artists, 1960
RONALD STEIN†
THE RAZOR'S EDGE 20th Century-Fox, 1946
ALFRED NEWMAN†
THE RAZOR'S EDGE Columbia, 1984
JACK NITZCHE
REACH FOR THE SKY Rank, 1956
JOHN ADDISON
REACHING FOR THE MOON United Artists, 1931
ALFRED NEWMAN†
REACHING FOR THE SUN Paramount, 1941
VICTOR YOUNG†
READY TO WEAR PRET-A-PORTER Miramax,
1994
MICHEL LEGRAND
A REAL AMERICAN HERO (TF) Bing Crosby
Productions, 1978
WALTER SCHARF
REAL GENIUS Tri-Star, 1985
THOMAS NEWMAN
THE REAL GLORY United Artists, 1939
ALFRED NEWMAN†
REAL LIFE Bedford, 1984
DAVID MINDEL
REAL LIFE Paramount, 1979
MORT LINDSEY
THE REAL McCOY Universal, 1993
BRAD FIEDEL
REAL MEN MGM/UA, 1987
MILES GOODMAN†
THE REAL THING L.A.C.L.P., 1997
PETER LEINHEISER

REAL TIME 1991
ADI RENNERT
REALITY BITES Universal, 1994
GREG O'CONNOR
KARL WALLINGER
REANIMATOR Empire Pictures, 1985
RICHARD H. BAND
REAP THE WILD WIND Paramount, 1942
VICTOR YOUNG†
REAR WINDOW Paramount, 1954
FRANZ WAXMAN†
REARVIEW MIRROR (TF) Simon-Asher
Entertainment/Sunn Classic Pictures, 1984
WILLIAM GOLDSTEIN
A REASON TO LIVE (TF) Rastar Productions/Robert
Papazian Productions, 1985
MILES GOODMAN†
REASONABLE DOUBTS: FOREVER MY LOVE
(TF) Lorimar, 1992
BRAD FIEDEL
ROSS LEVINSON
REBECCA United Artists, 1940
FRANZ WAXMAN† ★
REBECCA'S DAUGHTERS 1992
RACHEL PORTMAN
THE REBEL 1993
CARLO CRIVELLI
REBEL Vestron, 1985
CHRIS NEAL
BRUCE ROWLAND
REBEL HIGHWAY: CONFESSIONS OF A
SORORITY GIRL (CTF) Drive-In Classics, 1994
HUMMIE MANN
REBEL HIGHWAY: COOL AND THE CRAZY
(CTF) Drive-In Classics, 1994
HUMMIE MANN
REBEL HIGHWAY: DRAGSTRIP GIRL (CTF)
Drive-In Classics, 1994
HUMMIE MANN
REBEL HIGHWAY: GIRLS IN PRISON (CTF)
Drive-In Classics, 1994
HUMMIE MANN
REBEL HIGHWAY: JAILBREAKERS (CTF) Drive-In
Classics, 1994
HUMMIE MANN
REBEL HIGHWAY: MOTORCYCLE GANG (CTF)
Drive-In Classics, 1994
HUMMIE MANN
REBEL HIGHWAY: REFORM SCHOOL GIRLS
(CTF) Drive-In Classics, 1994
HUMMIE MANN
REBEL HIGHWAY: ROADRACERS (CTF) Drive-In
Classics, 1994
PAUL BOLL
JOHNNY RENO
REBEL HIGHWAY: RUNAWAY DAUGHTERS
(CTF) Drive-In Classics, 1994
HUMMIE MANN
REBEL HIGHWAY: SHAKE, RATTLE AND ROCK
(CTF) Drive-In Classics, 1994
JOEY ALTRUDA
REBEL IN TOWN United Artists, 1956
LES BAXTER†
REBEL JESUS 1972
ALEX NORTH†
THE REBEL NUN FLAVIA LA MONACA
MUSULMANA 1974
NICOLA PIOVANI
THE REBEL SET Allied Artists, 1959
PAUL DUNLAP
REBEL WITHOUT A CAUSE Warner Bros., 1955
LEONARD ROSENMAN
REBELLION SAMURAI REBELLION Toho, 1967
TORU TAKEMITSU†
THE REBELS (MS) Universal TV, 1979
GERALD FRIED
REBETICO 1983
STAVROS XARCHAKOS
REBUS Luis Bacalov, 1968
LUIS BACALOV
REBUS 1969
BRUNO NICOLAI
RECKLESS MGM, 1935
EDWARD WARD†
RECKLESS MGM/UA, 1984
THOMAS NEWMAN
RECKLESS DISREGARD (CTF) Telecom
Entertainment/Polar Film Corporation/Fremantle of
Canada Ltd., 1985
GIL GOLDSTEIN
RECKLESS KELLY Warner Bros., 1993
TOMMY TYCHO
THE RECKLESS MOMENT Universal, 1949
HANS J. SALTER†
THE RECKONING Columbia, 1969
MALCOLM ARNOLD
RECONTRES SUR LE RHIN 1952
GEORGES VAN PARYS†
RECORD OF A LIVING BEING 1956
MASARU SATO
RECOURS EN GRACE 1960
MAURICE JARRE

RECRUITS Concorde, 1986
STEPHEN PARSONS

RECRUITS IN INGOLSTADT 1971
PEER RABEN

THE RECTOR'S WIFE (TF) Talisman Films, 1994
RICHARD HARTLEY

RED ALERT (TF) The Jozak Company/Paramount
Pictures TV, 1977
GEORGE ALICESON TIPTON

THE RED BADGE OF COURAGE MGM, 1951
BRONISLAU KAPER†

THE RED BADGE OF COURAGE (TF) Norman
Rosemont Productions/20th Century-Fox TV, 1974
JACK ELLIOTT

RED BEARD Toho, 1965
MASARU SATO

RED CANYON United Artists, 1949
WALTER SCHARF

THE RED DANUBE MGM, 1949
MIKLOS ROZSA†

RED DAWN MGM/UA, 1984
BASIL POLEDOURIS

RED EARTH, WHITE EARTH (TF) Chris/Rose
Productions, 1989
RALPH GRIERSON

RED FIRECRACKER, GREEN FIRECRACKER 1994
ZHAO JIPING

THE RED FLAG: THE ULTIMATE GAME (TF)
Marble Arch Productions, 1981
ALLYN FERGUSON

RED FLAG: THE ULTIMATE GAME (TF) Marble
Arch Productions, 1974
ALLYN FERGUSON

RED HEAT Tri-Star, 1988
JAMES HORNER

THE RED HOUSE United Artists, 1947
MIKLOS ROZSA†

RED KING, WHITE KNIGHT (CTF) John Kemeny
Citdale Entertainment/Zenith, 1989
JOHN SCOTT

RED LANTERNS 1964
STAVROS XARCHAKOS

RED LIGHT United Artists, 1949
DIMITRI TIOMKIN†

RED LINE 7000 Paramount, 1965
NELSON RIDDLE†

RED LION 1969
MASARU SATO

THE RED MANTLE 1973
MARC FREDERICKS

RED MEAT Treehouse Films, 1997
THE BLUE HAWAIIANS

RED MOUNTAIN Paramount, 1951
FRANZ WAXMAN†

THE RED PONY Republic, 1949
AARON COPLAND†

THE RED PONY (TF) Universal TV/Omnibus
Productions, 1973
JERRY GOLDSMITH ☆

RED RIBBON BLUES Red Ribbon Prods., 1995
JOHN FRIZZELL

RED RIVER United Artists, 1948
DIMITRI TIOMKIN†

RED RIVER (TF) Catalina Production Group/MGM-UA
TV, 1988
KEN WANNBERG

RED RIVER RANGE Republic, 1938
WILLIAM LAVA†

RED RIVER RIDING HOOD RKO Radio, 1942
PAUL SAWTELL†

RED ROCK WEST Polygram, 1993
WILLIAM OLVIS

THE RED ROSE 1973
LUIS BACALOV

RED ROSE WHITE ROSE *HONG MEIGUI BAI
MEGUI* 1995
JOHNNY CHEN

RED SCORPION Shapiro Glinkenhaus Entertainment,
1989
JAY CHATTAWAY

RED SHOE DIARIES (CTF) Saunders-King, 1992
GEORGE S. CLINTON

THE RED SHOES Eagle-Lion, 1948
BRIAN EASDALE ★★

RED SKIES OF MONTANA 20th Century-Fox, 1952
SOL KAPLAN
LIONEL NEWMAN†

RED SKY AT MORNING Universal, 1971
BILLY GOLDENBERG

RED SONJA MGM/UA, 1985
ENNIO MORRICONE

THE RED SPIDER (TF) CBS Entertainment, 1988
ARTIE KANE

THE RED STALLION Eagle Lion, 1947
FREDERICK HOLLANDER†

RED SUN National General, 1971
MAURICE JARRE

RED SUN RISING 1993
JOHN CODA

RED SUNDOWN Universal, 1956
HANS J. SALTER†

RED SURF Arrowhead Entertainment, 1990
SASHA MATSON

THE RED TENT Paramount, 1971
ENNIO MORRICONE

RED TOMAHAWK Paramount, 1967
JIMMIE HASKELL

RED WAGON American Film Center, 1945
W. FRANKE HARLING†

RED WIND (CTF) Alan Barnette Prods., 1991
PHILIP GIFFIN

RED ZONE AAA/Revcom Films, 1986
GABRIEL YARED

THE REDEEMER Empire, 1966
DAVID RAKSIN

THE REDEEMER...SON OF SATAN! 1978
PHILO GALLO
CLEM VICARI

THE REDHEAD AND THE COWBOY Paramount,
1951
DAVID BUTTOLPH†

THE REDHEAD FROM WYOMING Universal,
1952
HERMAN STEIN

THE RED-LIGHT STING (TF) J.E. Productions/
Universal TV, 1984
JAMES DIPASQUALLE

REDNECK International Amusements, 1975
JOHN CACAVAS

REDS Paramount, 1981
DAVE GRUSIN
STEPHEN SONDHEIM

REDSKIN Paramount, 1929
JOHN S. ZAMECNIK†

REDWOOD CURTAIN (TF) Hallmark Hall of Fame,
1995
LAWRENCE SHRAGGE

THE REF Buena Vista, 1994
DAVID A. STEWART

A REFLECTION OF FEAR Columbia, 1973
FRED MYROW

REFLECTIONS OF MURDER (TF) ABC Circle Films,
1974
BILLY GOLDENBERG

REFORM SCHOOL GIRL American International,
1957
RONALD STEIN†

REFORM SCHOOL GIRLS New World, 1986
TEDRA GABRIEL

THE REFORMER AND THE REDHEAD MGM, 1950
DAVID RAKSIN

THE REFRIGERATOR 1989
WENDY BLACKSTONE

REGAIN 1937
ARTHUR HONEGGER†

REGARDE LES HOMMES TOMBER 1994
ALEXANDRE DESPLAT

REGARDING HENRY Paramount, 1991
HANS ZIMMER

REHEARSAL FOR MURDER (TF) Levinson-Link
Productions/Robert Papazian Productions, 1982
BILLY GOLDENBERG

REIGN OF TERROR Eagle Lion, 1949
SOL KAPLAN

REILLY - ACE OF SPIES (MS) Euston Films Ltd.,
1984
HARRY RABINOWITZ

THE REINCARNATION OF PETER PROUD
American International, 1975
JERRY GOLDSMITH

THE REIVERS National General, 1969
JOHN WILLIAMS ★

THE REJUVENATOR SVS Films, 1988
LARRY JURIS

RELENTLESS New Line Cinema, 1989
JAY CHATTAWAY

RELENTLESS (TF) CBS, Inc., 1977
JOHN CACAVAS

RELENTLESS: MIND OF A KILLER (TF) Universal
TV, 1993
STANLEY CLARKE

THE RELIC Paramount, 1997
JOHN DEBNEY

THE RELUCTANT ASTRONAUT Universal, 1967
VIC MIZZY

THE RELUCTANT DRAGON (AF) RKO Radio, 1941
FRANK CHURCHILL†

THE RELUCTANT HEROES (TF) Aaron Spelling
Productions, 1971
FRANK DEVOL

THE RELUCTANT SAINT Davis-Royal, 1962
NINO ROTA†

THE RELUCTANT VAMPIRE Waymar, 1992
MARK KOVAL

THE RELUCTANT WIDOW 1951
ALLAN GRAY†

RELUCTANT ANGEL Blackwatch Communications,
1997
JOHN McCARTHY

THE REMAINS OF THE DAY Columbia, 1993
RICHARD ROBBINS ★

REMAINS TO BE SEEN MGM, 1953
JEFF ALEXANDER†

REMAKE 1950
GEORGES VAN PARYS†

THE REMARKABLE ANDREW Paramount, 1942
VICTOR YOUNG†

THE REMARKABLE MR. KIPPS *KIPPS* 20th
Century-Fox, 1941
WILLIAM ALWYN†

THE REMARKABLE MR. PENNYPACKER 20th
Century-Fox, 1958
LEIGH HARLINE†

REMBRANDT: FECIT 1668 1978
LAURENS VAN ROOYEN

REMEMBER LAST NIGHT? Universal, 1935
FRANZ WAXMAN†

REMEMBER MY NAME Columbia/Lagoon
Associates, 1979
ALBERTA HUNTER

REMEMBER THE NIGHT Paramount, 1940
FREDERICK HOLLANDER†

REMEMBER WHEN (TF) Danny Thomas
Productions/The Raisin Company, 1974
GEORGE ALICESON TIPTON

REMEMBER? MGM, 1939
EDWARD WARD†

REMEMBRANCE OF LOVE (TF) Doris Quinlan
Productions/Comworld Productions, 1982
WILLIAM GOLDSTEIN

REMO WILLIAMS: THE ADVENTURE BEGINS...
Orion, 1985
CRAIG SAFAN

REMOTE CONTROL Vista Organization, 1988
PETER BERNSTEIN

RENAISSANCE MAN Buena Vista, 1994
HANS ZIMMER

RENATA 1977
ARMANDO TROVAJOLI

RENDEZVOUS MGM, 1935
WILLIAM AXT†

RENDEZVOUS UGC, 1985
PHILIPPE SARDE

RENDEZVOUS 24 20th Century-Fox, 1946
EMIL NEWMAN†

RENDEZ-VOUS A BRAY 1971
FREDERIC DEVREESE

RENDEZ-VOUS DE JUILLET 1949
JEAN WIENER†

RENDEZVOUS HOTEL (TF) Mark Carliner
Productions, 1979
JONATHAN TUNICK

RENE LA CANNE *RENE THE CANE* AMLF, 1977
ENNIO MORRICONE

RENE THE CANE AMLF, 1977
ENNIO MORRICONE

THE RENEGADE RANGER RKO Radio, 1938
ROY WEBB†

THE RENEGADES (TF) Lawrence Gordon
Productions/Paramount Pictures TV, 1982
BARRY DEVORZON
JOSEPH CONLAN

RENEGADES Universal, 1989
MICHAEL KAMEN

RENEGADES OF THE WEST RKO Radio, 1932
MAX STEINER†

RENO RKO Radio, 1939
ROY WEBB†

RENT-A-COP Kings Road Productions, 1988
JERRY GOLDSMITH

RENTADICK 1972
CARL DAVIS

RENTED LIPS New Century Vista, 1988
VAN DYKE PARKS

REPEAT PERFORMANCE Eagle Lion, 1947
GEORGE ANTHEIL†

REPENTANCE Cannon, 1984
NANA DJANELIDZ

REPO MAN Universal, 1984
STEVEN HUFSTETER
TITO LARRIVA

REPORT TO THE COMMISSIONER United Artists,
1975
ELMER BERNSTEIN

THE REPTILE 1966
DON BANKS

REPTILICUS American International, 1961
LES BAXTER†

REPULSION Royal Films International, 1965
CHICO HAMILTON

REQUIEM FOR A GUNFIGHTER Embassy, 1965
RONALD STEIN†

REQUIEM FOR A HEAVYWEIGHT Columbia, 1962
LAURENCE ROSENTHAL

REQUIEM FOR A VILLAGE (FD) British Film
Institute, 1976
DAVID FANSHAWE

REQUIEM PER UN GRINGO 1968
ANGELO FRANCESCO LAVAGNINO†

REQUIESCANT Castoro Film, 1967
RIZ ORTOLANI

THE RESCUE Buena Vista, 1988
BRUCE BROUGHTON

RESCUE FROM GILLIGAN'S ISLAND (TF)
Sherwood Schwartz, 1978
GERALD FRIED

RESCUE ME Cannon, 1993
JOEL HIRSCHHORN
AL KASHA
DAVID WATERS

RESCUE ME Warner Bros., 1997
GEORGE S. CLINTON

THE RESCUERS (CTF) Paramount TV, 1997
HUMMIE MANN

THE RESCUERS DOWN UNDER (AF) Buena Vista,
1990
BRUCE BROUGHTON

THE RESCUERS (AF) Buena Vista, 1978
ARTIE BUTLER

THE RESPECTFUL PROSTITUTE 1952
GEORGES AURIC†

RESTING PLACE (TF) Marian Rees Associates, 1986
PAUL CHIHARA

RESTLESS Endeavour Productions, 1986
GIL MELLE

RESTLESS NATIVES Thorn/EMI, 1985
STUART ADAMSON

RESTORATION Miramax, 1996
JAMES NEWTON HOWARD

THE RESURRECTED Scotti Bros., 1992
RICHARD H. BAND

RESURRECTION Universal, 1931
DIMITRI TIOMKIN†

RESURRECTION Universal, 1980
MAURICE JARRE

RETENEZ MOIL...OU JE FAIS UN MALHEUR *TO
CATCH A COP* Gaumont, 1984
VLADIMIR COSMA

RETOUR A L'AUBE 1939
PAUL MISRAKI

RETOUR A NEW YORK (FD) 1962
MICHEL LEGRAND

RETREAT, HELL! Warner Bros., 1952
WILLIAM LAVA†

RETRIBUTION United Film Distribution, 1987
ALAN HOWARTH

RETROACTIVE Orion, 1997
TIM TRUMAN

THE RETURN 1973
MARC WILKINSON

THE RETURN *THE ALIEN'S RETURN* 1981
DAN WYMAN

THE RETURN (TF) Spectre Productions, 1988
DONAL LUNNY

RETURN FROM THE ASHES United Artists, 1965
JOHN DANKWORTH

RETURN FROM THE SEA Allied Artists, 1954
PAUL DUNLAP

RETURN FROM WITCH MOUNTAIN Buena Vista,
1978
LALO SCHIFRIN

THE RETURN OF A MAN CALLED HORSE United
Artists, 1976
LAURENCE ROSENTHAL

THE RETURN OF CAPTAIN INVINCIBLE *LEGEND
IN LEOTARDS* New World, 1983
WILLIAM MOTZIG

THE RETURN OF CASANOVA 1978
RIZ ORTOLANI

THE RETURN OF CHARLIE CHAN (TF) Charlie
Chan Company/Universal TV, 1979
ROBERT PRINCE

THE RETURN OF COUNT YORGA American
International, 1971
BILL MARX

THE RETURN OF DESPERADO (TF) Walter Mirisch
Productions/Universal TV, 1988
MICHEL COLOMBIER

THE RETURN OF DON CAMILLO 1953
ALESSANDRO CICOGNINI†

THE RETURN OF DR. X Warner Bros., 1939
BERNHARD KAUN†

THE RETURN OF DRACULA *THE CURSE OF
DRACULA* United Artists, 1958
GERALD FRIED

THE RETURN OF ELIOT NESS (TF) Michael
Filerman Prods., 1991
LEE HOLDRIDGE

THE RETURN OF FRANK CANNON (TF) QM
Productions, 1980
BRUCE BROUGHTON

THE RETURN OF FRANK JAMES 20th
Century-Fox, 1940
DAVID BUTTOLPH†

THE RETURN OF GILBERT & SULLIVAN United
Artists, 1951
LYN MURRAY†

THE RETURN OF IRONSIDE (TF) Riven Rock
Prods./Windy City Prods., 1993
JOHN CACAVAS
QUINCY JONES

THE RETURN OF JACK SLADE Allied Artists, 1955
PAUL DUNLAP

THE RETURN OF JAFAR (AF) Buena Vista, 1994
MARK WATTERS

THE RETURN OF JESSE JAMES Lippert, 1950
ALBERT GLASSER

THE RETURN OF JOE FORRESTER (TF) David Gerber Productions/Columbia Pictures TV, 1975
RICHARD MARKOWITZ†

THE RETURN OF MARCUS WELBY, M.D. (TF) Marstar Productions/Universal TV, 1984
LEONARD ROSENMAN

THE RETURN OF MAXIM GORKY 1936
DMITRI SHOSTAKOVITCH†

THE RETURN OF MICKEY SPILLANE'S MIKE HAMMER (TF) Columbia Pictures TV/Jay Bernstein Productions, 1986
EARLE HAGEN

THE RETURN OF MONTE CRISTO Small/Col., 1946
LUCIEN MORAWECK†

THE RETURN OF MR. MOTO 20th Century-Fox, 1965
DOUGLAS GAMLEY

THE RETURN OF OCTOBER Columbia, 1948
GEORGE DUNING

THE RETURN OF RIN TIN TIN Eagle Lion, 1947
LEO ERDODY†

THE RETURN OF SAM McCLOUD (TF) Michael Sloan Productions/Universal TV, 1989
STEVE DORFF

THE RETURN OF SHERLOCK HOLMES (TF) CBS Entertainment, 1987
KEN THORNE

THE RETURN OF SUPERFLY Triton, 1990
CURTIS MAYFIELD

THE RETURN OF SWAMP THING Lightyear Entertainment, 1989
CHUCK CIRINO

THE RETURN OF THE INCREDIBLE HULK (TF) Universal TV, 1977
JOE HARNELL

THE RETURN OF THE JEDI 20th Century-Fox, 1983
JOHN WILLIAMS ★

THE RETURN OF THE KING (ATF) Rankin-Bass Productions, 1979
MAURY LAWS

THE RETURN OF THE LIVING DEAD Orion, 1985
MATT CLIFFORD

THE RETURN OF THE MAN FROM U.N.C.L.E. (TF) Martin Sloan Productions/Viacom Productions, 1983
GERALD FRIED
JERRY GOLDSMITH

THE RETURN OF THE MOD SQUAD (TF) Thomas-Spelling Productions, 1979
SHORTY ROGERS†
MARK SNOW

THE RETURN OF THE MUSKETEERS Universal, 1989
JEAN-CLAUDE PETIT

THE RETURN OF THE NATIVE (TF) Craig Anderson Prods./Signboard Hill, 1994
CARL DAVIS

THE RETURN OF THE SCARLET PIMPERNEL 1938
ARTHUR BENJAMIN†

THE RETURN OF THE SHAGGY DOG (TF) Walt Disney TV, 1987
DAVID BELL

THE RETURN OF THE VAMPIRE Columbia, 1943
MARIO †

THE RETURN OF THE WORLD'S GREATEST DETECTIVE (TF) Universal TV, 1976
DICK DEBENEDICTIS

THE RETURN OF WILDFIRE Lippert, 1948
ALBERT GLASSER

RETURN OF GIANT MAJIN 1967
AKIRA IFUKUBE

RETURN OF THE BEVERLY HILLBILLIES (TF) The Energy Venture, 1981
BILLY MAY

RETURN OF THE FLY 20th Century-Fox, 1959
PAUL SAWTELL†
BERT A. SHEFTER

RETURN OF THE FRONTIERSMAN Warner Bros., 1950
DAVID BUTTOLPH†

RETURN OF THE GUNFIGHTER (TF) King Brothers/MGM TV, 1967
HANS J. SALTER†

RETURN OF THE LIVING DEAD Trimark, 1993
BARRY GOLDBERG

RETURN OF THE LIVING DEAD PART II Lorimar, 1988
J. PETER ROBINSON

RETURN OF THE PINK PANTHER United Artists, 1975
HENRY MANCINI†

RETURN OF THE REBELS (TF) Moonlight Productions/Filmways, 1981
MICHAEL MELVOIN

RETURN OF THE SECAUCUS SEVEN Libra/ Specialty Films, 1980
MASON DARING

RETURN OF THE SEVEN United Artists, 1966
ELMER BERNSTEIN ★

RETURN OF THE SIX MILLION DOLLAR MAN & THE BIONIC WOMAN (TF) Michael Sloan Productions/Universal TV, 1987
MARVIN HAMLISCH

RETURN OF THE SOLDIER European Classics, 1982
RICHARD RODNEY BENNETT

RETURN OF THE TALL BLONDE MAN WITH ONE BLACK SHOE Lanir Releasing, 1974
VLADIMIR COSMA

RETURN OF THE TERROR Warner Bros., 1934
BERNHARD KAUN†

RETURN OF THE TEXAN 20th Century-Fox, 1952
SOL KAPLAN
LIONEL NEWMAN†

RETURN TO BOGGY CREEK 777 Distributors, 1977
DARRELL DECK

RETURN TO EDEN (MS) McElroy & McElroy/ Hanna-Barbera Australia Productions, 1983
BRIAN MAY†

RETURN TO GREEN ACRES (TF) Jaygoe Productions/Orion TV, 1990
DAN FOLIART

RETURN TO HORROR HIGH New World, 1987
STACY WIDELITZ

RETURN TO LONESOME DOVE (MS) RHI/de Passe Entertainment/Nightwatch Prods., 1993
KEN THORNE

RETURN TO MACON COUNTY American International, 1975
ROBERT O. RAGLAND

RETURN TO MAYBERRY (TF) Viacom Productions/ Strathmore Productions, 1986
EARLE HAGEN

RETURN TO OZ Buena Vista, 1985
DAVID SHIRE

RETURN TO PARADISE United Artists, 1953
DIMITRI TIOMKIN†

RETURN TO PEYTON PLACE 20th Century-Fox, 1961
FRANZ WAXMAN†

RETURN TO SNOWY RIVER Buena Vista, 1988
BRUCE ROWLAND

RETURN TO THE BELOVED 1979
ANTOINE DUHAMEL

RETURN TO THE BLUE LAGOON Columbia, 1991
BASIL POLEDOURIS

RETURN TO THE PROMISED LAND *VERATARTS AVEDYATS YERGIR* 1992
AVET TERTERIAN

RETURN TO TREASURE ISLAND United Artists, 1954
PAUL SAWTELL†

RETURN TO TWO MOON JUNCTION Trimark, 1993
JOSEPH CONLAN

THE RETURNING Willow Films, 1983
HARRY MANFREDINI

RETURNING HOME (TF) Samuel Goldwyn Productions/Lorimar Productions, 1975
KEN LAUBER

REUBEN, REUBEN 20th Century-Fox International Classics, 1983
BILLY GOLDENBERG

REUNION Les Films Ariane-FR3 Films, 1989
PHILIPPE SARDE

REUNION MGM, 1936
EMIL NEWMAN†

REUNION (TF) Barry Weitz Films, 1980
GEORGE ROMANIS

REUNION (TF) Hart, Thomas & Berlin Prods./RHI, 1994
DAVID SHIRE

REUNION AT FAIRBOROUGH (CTF) HBO Premiere Films/Alan Wagner Productions/Alan King Productions/Columbia TV, 1985
NIGEL HESS

REUNION IN FRANCE MGM, 1942
FRANZ WAXMAN†

REUNION IN VIENNA MGM, 1933
WILLIAM AXT†

REVEALING EVIDENCE (TF) T.W.S. Productions/ Universal TV, 1991
JAMES NEWTON HOWARD

REVEILLON CHEZ BOB 1984
MICHEL MAGNE†

REVENGE Columbia, 1990
JACK NITZCHE.

REVENGE (TF) Mark Carliner Productions, 1972
DOMINIC FRONTIERE

REVENGE FOR A RAPE (TF) Albert S. Ruddy Productions, 1976
JERROLD IMMEL

THE REVENGE OF AL CAPONE (TF) Unity Productions/River City, 1989
CRAIG SAFAN

THE REVENGE OF FRANKENSTEIN Columbia, 1958
LEONARD SALZEDO

REVENGE OF MECHA-GODZILLA *TERROR OF MECHA-GODZILLA/TERROR OF GODZILLA* 1977
AKIRA IFUKUBE

REVENGE OF THE CALENDAR GIRLS HMS Partnership, 1995
MIRIAM CUTLER

REVENGE OF THE CREATURE Universal, 1955
WILLIAM LAVA†
HERMAN STEIN

REVENGE OF THE MYSTERIONS FROM MARS 1981
BARRY GRAY†

REVENGE OF THE NERDS 20th Century Fox, 1984
THOMAS NEWMAN

REVENGE OF THE NERDS III: THE NEXT GENERATION (TF) FNM Films/Zacharias and Buhai, 1992
GARRY SCHYMAN

REVENGE OF THE NERDS IV: NERDS IN LOVE (TF) Zacharial-Buhai Prods./Fox West Pictures, 1994
GARRY SCHYMAN

REVENGE OF THE NINJA MGM/UA/Cannon, 1983
W. MICHAEL LEWIS
LAURIN RINDER
ROBERT J. WALSH

REVENGE OF THE PINK PANTHER United Artists, 1978
HENRY MANCINI†

REVENGE OF THE PIRATES *LA VENDETTA DEL CORSARO* 1951
CARLO RUSTICHELLI

REVENGE OF THE SHOGUN WOMEN 21st Century, 1982
ROBERT J. WALSH

REVENGE OF THE STEPFORD WIVES (TF) Edgar J. Scherick Productions, 1980
LAURENCE ROSENTHAL

REVENGE ON THE HIGHWAY (TF) Arvin Kaufman Prods./Saban, 1992
SHUKI LEVY

REVERSAL OF FORTUNE Warner Bros., 1990
MARK ISHAM

THE REVOLT AT FORT LARAMIE United Artists, 1957
LES BAXTER†

THE REVOLT OF GUNNER ASCH 1955
ROLF WILHELM

THE REVOLT OF MAMIE STOVER 20th Century-Fox, 1956
HUGO FRIEDHOFER†

THE REVOLT OF THE SLAVES 1961
ANGELO FRANCESCO LAVAGNINO†

THE REVOLUTIONARY United Artists, 1970
MICHAEL SMALL

REVOLUTION Warner Bros., 1985
JOHN CORIGLIANO

REVOLUTION! Dream Bird, 1991
TOM JUDSON

REVOLVER *BLOOD IN THE STREETS* 1973
ENNIO MORRICONE

REVOLVER (TF) Victoria Prods./Noel Films/ Catalunya Prods./Columbia, 1992
PHIL MARSHALL

THE REWARD 20th Century-Fox, 1965
ELMER BERNSTEIN

REWARD (TF) Jerry Adler Productions/Espirit Enterprises/Lorimar Productions, 1980
BARRY DEVORZON

REX STOUT'S NERO WOLFE (TF) Emmett Lavery, Jr. Productions/Paramount TV, 1979
JOHN ADDISON

RHAPSODY MGM, 1954
JOHN GREEN†

RHAPSODY IN AUGUST Orion Classics, 1991
SHINCHIRO IKEBE

RHAPSODY IN BLUE Warner Bros., 1945
MAX STEINER† ★

THE RHINEMANN EXCHANGE (MS) Universal TV, 1977
MICHEL COLOMBIER

RHINESTONE 20th Century Fox, 1984
MIKE POST

RHINO! MGM, 1964
LALO SCHIFRIN

RHINOSKIN: THE MAKING OF A MOVIE STAR (FD) Hapwood, 1994
THOMAS MORSE
IAN CHRISTIAN NICKUS

RHODES OF AFRICA 1936
HUBERT BATH†

RHOSYN A RHITH Red Rooster, 1986
MICHAEL STOREY

RHUBARB Paramount, 1951
NATHAN VAN CLEAVE†

RHYME & REASON Miramax, 1997
BENEDIKT BRYDERN

RHYTHM COUNTRY & BLUES (TD) Thirteen-WNET/Perery Films/MCA Music Ent. Group, 1994
DON WAS

RICE GIRL *LA RISAIA* 1955
ANGELO FRANCESCO LAVAGNINO†

RICH AND FAMOUS MGM/United Artists, 1981
GEORGES DELERUE†

THE RICH ARE ALWAYS WITH US Warner Bros., 1932
W. FRANKE HARLING†

RICH GIRL Filmwest Productions, 1989
BARRY FASMAN
DANA WALDEN

RICH GIRL Studio Three, 1991
JOSEPH SMITH

RICH GIRL Studio Three/Film West, 1991
JAY CHATTAWAY

RICH IN LOVE MGM, 1992
GEORGES DELERUE†

RICH KIDS United Artists, 1979
CRAIG DOERGE

THE RICH MAN'S WIFE Buena Vista, 1996
JOHN FRIZZELL
JAMES NEWTON HOWARD

RICH MAN, POOR GIRL MGM, 1938
WILLIAM AXT†

RICH MAN, POOR MAN (MS) Universal TV, 1976
ALEX NORTH† ☆☆

RICH MEN, SINGLE WOMEN (TF) Aaron Spelling Productions, 1990
CHARLES FOX

RICH, YOUNG AND PRETTY MGM, 1951
NICHOLAS BRODZSKY†
DAVID ROSE†

RICHARD III Lopert, 1956
SIR WILLIAM WALTON†

RICHARD III MGM-UA, 1996
TREVOR JONES

RICHARD PRYOR LIVE ON THE SUNSET STRIP Columbia, 1982
HARRY BETTS

RICHARD'S THINGS New World, 1981
GEORGES DELERUE†

THE RICHEST CAT IN THE WORLD (TF) Les Alexander Productions/Walt Disney TV, 1986
PETER BERNSTEIN

THE RICHEST GIRL IN THE WORLD RKO Radio, 1934
MAX STEINER†

THE RICHEST MAN IN THE WORLD: THE ARISTOTLE ONASSIS STORY (TF) The Konigsberg-Sanitsky Company, 1988
BILLY GOLDENBERG

RICHIE BROCKELMAN: MISSING 24 HOURS (TF) Universal TV, 1976
PETE CARPENTER†
MIKE POST

RICHIE RICH Warner Bros., 1994
ALAN SILVESTRI

RICKY I Tapeworm, 1988
JOEL GOLDSMITH

RICOCHET Warner Bros., 1991
ALAN SILVESTRI

THE RIDDLE OF THE SANDS Satori, 1979
HOWARD BLAKE

RIDE 'EM COWBOY Universal, 1942
FRANK SKINNER†

RIDE A WILD PONY Walt Disney Productions, 1976
JOHN ADDISON

RIDE A WILD PONY *BORN TO RUN* Buena Vista, 1976
RON GOODWIN

THE RIDE BACK United Artists, 1957
FRANK DEVOL

RIDE BEYOND VENGEANCE Columbia, 1966
RICHARD MARKOWITZ†

RIDE CLEAR OF DIABLO Universal, 1954
HERMAN STEIN

RIDE IN THE WHIRLWIND American International, 1966
ROBERT DRASNIN

RIDE LONESOME Columbia, 1959
HEINZ ROEMHELD†

RIDE ON, VAQUERO 20th Century-Fox, 1941
DAVID RAKSIN

RIDE OUT FOR REVENGE United Artists, 1957
LEITH STEVENS†

RIDE THE HIGH COUNTRY MGM, 1962
GEORGE BASSMAN

RIDE THE PINK HORSE Universal, 1947
FRANK SKINNER†

RIDE THE WILD SURF Columbia, 1964
STU PHILLIPS

RIDE TO HANGMAN'S TREE Universal, 1967
FRANK SKINNER†

RIDE WITH THE WIND (TF) Family Tree Prods./ Peter Frankovich Prods./Hearst, 1994
MICHEL RUBINI

RIDE, VAQUERO! MGM, 1953
BRONISLAU KAPER†

RIDER IN THE RAIN Avco Embassy, 1970
FRANCIS LAI

RIDERS IN THE STORM Filmhaus, 1995
KENNY ROGERS
BOB DE MARCO

RIDERS TO THE STARS United Artists, 1954
HARRY SUKMAN†

RIDICULE 1996
ANTOINE DUHAMEL

RIDING ON AIR RKO Radio, 1937
ARTHUR MORTON

RIDING SHOTGUN Warner Bros., 1954
DAVID BUTTOLPH†

RIDING THE EDGE Kodiak Films
MICHAEL GIBBS

RIDING THE EDGE Trans World Entertainment, 1989
MICHAEL GIBBS

RIEL CBC/Green River Productions, 1979
MATTHEW MCCAULEY

RIFF RAFF 1991
STEWART COPELAND

RIFF RAFF MGM, 1936
EDWARD WARD†

RIFFRAFF RKO Radio, 1947
ROY WEBB†

RIFIFI Pathe, 1954
GEORGES AURIC†

RIFIFI IM BEIRUT 1966
ENNIO MORRICONE

RIFIFI IN TOKYO MGM, 1961
GEORGES DELERUE†

RIFT Off-Screen Prods., 1993
TRYAN GEORGE
ERIC MASUNAGA

RIGGED CineStar, 1985
BRIAN BANKS
ANTHONY MARINELLI

RIGHT CROSS MGM, 1950
DAVID RAKSIN

THE RIGHT HAND MAN FilmDallas, 1987
ALLAN ZAVOD

THE RIGHT OF THE PEOPLE (TF) Big Name Films/
Fries Entertainment, 1986
BILLY GOLDENBERG

RIGHT OF WAY (CTF) HBO Premiere Films,
Schaefer-Karpf Productions/Post-Newsweek Video,
1983
BRAD FIEDEL

THE RIGHT STUFF The Ladd Company/Warner Bros.,
1983
BILL CONTI ★★

RIGHT TO DIE (TF) Ohlmeyer Communications,
1987
BRAD FIEDEL

RIGHT TO KILL? (TV) Wrye-Konigsberg
Productions/Taper Media Enterprises/Telepictures
Productions, 1985
PAUL CHIHARA

THE RIGHT TO LOVE Paramount, 1930
W. FRANKE HARLING†

THE RIGHT TO ROMANCE RKO Radio, 1933
MAX STEINER†

THE RIGHT WAY 1996
MARK HOLDEN
JAY OLIVER

RIKKY AND PETE MGM/UA, 1988
PHILIP JUDD
EDDIE RAYNOR

RIKYU 1989
TORU TAKEMITSU†

THE RING United Artists, 1952
HERSCHEL BURKE GILBERT

RING AROUND THE MOON 1950
RICHARD ADDINSELL†

RING OF BRIGHT WATER Cinerama Releasing
Corporation, 1969
FRANK CORDELL†

RING OF FEAR Warner Bros., 1954
EMIL NEWMAN†

RING OF PASSION (TF) 20th Century Fox, 1978
BILL CONTI

RING OF STEEL Shapiro Glickenhaus, 1993
WILLIAM KIDD

THE RINGER British Lion, 1952
MALCOLM ARNOLD

RINGO IL VOLTO DELLA VENDETTA 1966
FRANCESCO DE MASI

RINGO, DOVE VAI? 1968
BRUNO NICOLAI

RIO Universal, 1939
CHARLES PREVIN†

RIO BRAVO Warner Bros., 1959
DIMITRI TIOMKIN†

RIO CONCHOS 20th Century-Fox, 1964
JERRY GOLDSMITH

RIO DIABLO (TF) Kenny Rogers Prods./RHI/World
Intl. Network, 1993
LARRY BROWN

RIO GRANDE Republic, 1950
VICTOR YOUNG†

RIO LOBO National General, 1970
JERRY GOLDSMITH

RIO RITA MGM, 1942
HERBERT STOTHART†

RIO RITA RKO Radio, 1929
MAX STEINER†

RIO SHANNON (TF) Sacret Inc./Warner Bros. TV,
1993
CRAIG SAFAN

RIOT Paramount, 1969
CHRISTOPHER KOMEDA†

RIOT IN CELL BLOCK 11 Allied Artists, 1954
HERSCHEL BURKE GILBERT

RIOT IN JUVENILE PRISON United Artists, 1959
EMIL NEWMAN†

THE RIP-OFF Maverick International, 1976
PAOLO VASILE

RIPTIDE MGM, 1934
HERBERT STOTHART†

RIPTIDE (TF) Stephen J. Cannell Prods., 1984
PETE CARPENTER†
MIKE POST

RISCATTO 1953
NINO ROTA†

THE RISE AND FALL OF LEGS DIAMOND Warner
Bros., 1960
LEONARD ROSENMAN

THE RISE AND RISE OF MICHAEL RIMMER
Warner Bros., 1970
JOHN CAMERON

RISE AND SHINE 20th Century-Fox, 1941
EMIL NEWMAN†

**RISE AND WALK: THE DENNIS BYRD STORY
(TF)** Fox West Pictures, 1994
W.G. SNUFFY WALDEN

RISING STORM Gibraltar Releasing, 1989
JULIAN LAXTON

RISING SUN 20th Century Fox, 1993
TORU TAKEMITSU†

RISK Northern Arts, 1994
JOHN PAUL JONES

RISKY BUSINESS The Geffen Company/Warner
Bros., 1983
TANGERINE DREAM
CHRISTOPHER FRANKE

RITA HAYWORTH: THE LOVE GODDESS (TF)
The Susskind Company, 1983
LALO SCHIFRIN

RITA, SUE AND BOB, TOO Orion Classics, 1987
MICHAEL KAMEN

THE RITZ Warner Bros., 1976
KEN THORNE

**RIUSCIRANNO I NOSTRI EROI A TROVARE
L'AMICO MISTERIOSAMENTE SCOMPARSO IN
AFRICA?** Documento Film, 1968
ARMANDO TROVAJOLI

RIVALS *SINGLE PARENT* Avco Embassy, 1972
PETER MATZ

THE RIVER Universal, 1984
JOHN WILLIAMS ★

THE RIVER (D) U.S. Government, 1937
VIRGIL THOMSON†

THE RIVER BIGER Cine Artists Pictures, 1976
WAR

THE RIVER CHANGES Warner Bros., 1956
ROY WEBB†

THE RIVER GANG Universal, 1945
HANS J. SALTER†

RIVER OF GOLD (TF) Aaron Spelling Productions,
1971
FRED STEINER

RIVER OF NO RETURN 20th Century-Fox, 1954
CYRIL J. MOCKRIDGE†

**RIVER OF RAGE: THE TAKING OF MAGGIE KEENE
(TF)** David C. Thomas, 1993
JOSEPH LO DUCA

THE RIVER RAT Paramount, 1984
MIKE POST

A RIVER RUNS THROUGH IT Columbia, 1992
MARK ISHAM ★

THE RIVER WILD Universal, 1994
JERRY GOLDSMITH

THE RIVER'S EDGE Island Pictures, 1986
JURGEN KNIEPER

RIVERBEND Intercontinental Releasing, 1989
PAUL LOOMIS

RIVKIN, BOUNTY HUNTER (TF) Chiarascurio
Productions/Ten-Four Productions, 1981
ARTHUR B. RUBINSTEIN

RNAISSANCE MAN Buena Vista, 1994
JOHN VAN TONGEREN

ROAD AGENT Universal, 1941
HANS J. SALTER†

THE ROAD BACK Universal, 1937
DIMITRI TIOMKIN†

ROAD GAMES Avco Embassy, 1981
BRIAN MAY†

ROAD HOUSE 20th Century-Fox, 1948
CYRIL J. MOCKRIDGE†

ROAD RACERS American International, 1960
RICHARD MARKOWITZ†

THE ROAD RAIDERS (TF) New East Entertainment/
Universal TV, 1989
STU PHILLIPS

ROAD TO GALVESTON (CTF) Wilshire Court, 1995
STANLEY CLARKE

ROAD TO GLORY 20th Century-Fox, 1936
LOUIS SILVERS†

THE ROAD TO HONG KONG United Artists, 1962
ROBERT FARNON

THE ROAD TO MECCA Distant Horizon/Videovision,
1992
FERDI BRENGEN
NIK PICKARD

THE ROAD TO RIO supervision, Paramount, 1947
ROBERT EMMETT DOLAN† ★

ROAD TO UTOPIA Paramount, 1946
LEIGH HARLINE†

ROAD TO VICTORY Mosfilm, 1978
VLADIMIR HORUNZHY

THE ROAD TO WELLVILLE Columbia, 1994
RACHEL PORTMAN

THE ROAD WARRIOR *MAD MAX II* Warner
Bros., 1982
BRIAN MAY†

ROADHOUSE MGM/UA, 1989
MICHAEL KAMEN

ROADHOUSE 66 Atlantic Releasing, 1984
GARY SCOTT

ROADIE United Artists, 1980
CRAIG HUNDLEY

ROADSIDE PROPHETS Fine Line, 1992
PRAY FOR RAIN

ROANOAK (TF) South Carolina ETV Network/First
Contact Films/National Video Corporation, 1986
PAUL CHIHARA

ROAR Filmways Australasian, 1981
JOHN BEAL
DOMINIC FRONTIERE

ROAR OF THE DRAGON RKO Radio, 1932
MAX STEINER†

ROARING CITY Lippert, 1951
BERT A. SHEFTER

ROB ROY MGM/UA, 1995
CARTER BURWELL

ROBBER'S ROOST United Artists, 1955
PAUL DUNLAP

ROBBERY UNDER ARMS 1958
MATYAS SEIBER

ROBBIE Award Films, 1982
CHRISTOPHER YOUNG

THE ROBE 20th Century-Fox, 1953
ALFRED NEWMAN†

ROBERT ET ROBERT Quartet, 1978
FRANCIS LAI

ROBERT KENNEDY AND HIS TIMES (MS)
Chris-Rose Productions/Columbia TV, 1985
FRED KARLIN

ROBERTA RKO Radio, 1935
MAX STEINER†

ROBIN AND MARIAN Columbia, 1976
JOHN BARRY

ROBIN AND THE SEVEN HOODS Warner Bros.,
1964
NELSON RIDDLE† ★

ROBIN COOK'S HARMFUL INTENT (TF)
Rosemont Productions, 1993
LEE HOLDRIDGE

ROBIN COOK'S VIRUS (TF) Von Zerneck-Sertner,
1995
GARRY SCHYMAN

ROBIN COOKS 'MORTAL FEAR' (TF) Von
Zerneck-Sertner Films, 1994
GARRY SCHYMAN

THE ROBIN HOOD OF EL DORADO MGM, 1936
HERBERT STOTHART†

ROBIN HOOD United Artists, 1922
VICTOR SCHERTZINGER†

ROBIN HOOD (AF) Buena Vista, 1973
GEORGE BRUNS

ROBIN HOOD (TF) 20th Century Fox/Working Title,
1991
GEOFFREY BURGON

ROBIN HOOD AND THE PIRATES 1960
CARLO RUSTICHELLI

ROBIN HOOD AND THE SORCEROR (CTF)
Goldcrest/HTV, 1984
CLANNAD

ROBIN HOOD, L'INVINCIBILE ARCIERE 1970
BRUNO NICOLAI

ROBIN HOOD: MEN IN TIGHTS 20th Century Fox,
1993
HUMMIE MANN

ROBIN HOOD: PRINCE OF THIEVES Warner Bros.,
1991
MICHAEL KAMEN

ROBINSON CRUSOE (TF) BBC/NBC TV, 1974
WILFRED JOSEPHS

ROBINSON CRUSOE ON MARS Paramount, 1964
FRED STEINER
NATHAN VAN CLEAVE†

ROBINSON UND SEINE WILDEN SKLAVINNEN
1971
BRUNO NICOLAI

ROBOCOP Orion, 1987
BASIL POLEDOURIS

ROBOCOP 2 Orion, 1990
LEONARD ROSENMAN

ROBOCOP 3 Orion, 1993
BASIL POLEDOURIS

ROBOCOP: THE SERIES (TF) Skyvision Ent./
RoBoCop Prods./Rysher, 1994
KEVIN GILLIS
BASIL POLEDOURIS
JOHN STROLL

ROBOT MONSTER Astor, 1953
ELMER BERNSTEIN

ROBOTJOX Trans World Entertainment, 1990
FREDERIC TALGORN

ROCCO AND HIS BROTHERS Astor, 1960
NINO ROTA†

THE ROCK Buena Vista, 1996
NICK GLENNIE-SMITH
HARRY GREGSON-WILLIAMS
HANS ZIMMER

ROCK & RULE (AF) MGM/UA, 1983
PATRICIA CULLEN

ROCK ALL NIGHT American International, 1957
RONALD STEIN†

ROCK HUDSON (TF) Konigsberg-Sanitsky Co.,
1990
PAUL CHIHARA

ROCK PRETTY BABY Universal, 1956
HENRY MANCINI†

ROCK'N'ROLL MOM (TF) Walt Disney TV, 1988
LEE RITENOUR

ROCKABILLY BABY 20th Century-Fox, 1957
PAUL DUNLAP

ROCKABYE RKO Radio, 1932
MAX STEINER†

ROCKABYE (TF) Roger Gimbel Productions/
Peregrine Entertainment/Bertinelli Poructions, 1986
CHARLES BERNSTEIN

ROCK-A-BYE BABY Paramount, 1958
WALTER SCHARF

ROCK-A-DOODLE (AF) Samuel Golwyn, 1992
ROBERT FOLK

ROCKET GIBRALTAR Columbia, 1988
ANDREW POWELL

THE ROCKET MAN 20th Century-Fox, 1954
LIONEL NEWMAN†

THE ROCKETEER Buena Vista, 1991
JAMES HORNER

ROCKETSHIP X-M Lippert, 1950
FERDE GROFE†

THE ROCKFORD FILES (TF) Cherokee Productions/
Roy Huggins Productions/Universal TV, 1974
PETE CARPENTER†
MIKE POST

THE ROCKFORD FILES: I STILL LOVE L.A. (TF)
MGB Prods./Universal TV, 1994
MIKE POST

THE ROCKING HORSE WINNER 1950
WILLIAM ALWYN†

ROCKY United Artists, 1976
BILL CONTI

THE ROCKY HORROR PICTURE SHOW 20th
Century-Fox, 1975
RICHARD HARTLEY

ROCKY II United Artists, 1979
BILL CONTI

ROCKY III MGM/UA, 1982
BILL CONTI

ROCKY IV MGM/UA, 1985
VINCE DICOLA

ROCKY MOUNTAIN Warner Bros., 1950
MAX STEINER†

ROCKY V MGM/UA, 1990
BILL CONTI

RODAN DCA, 1957
AKIRA IFUKUBE

RODEO GIRL (TF) Steckler Productions/Marble Arch
Productions, 1980
AL DELORY

ROE VS. WADE (TF) The Manheim Co./NBC
Productions, 1989
W.G. SNUFFY WALDEN

ROGER LA HONTE 1966
ANTOINE DUHAMEL

ROGER TOUHY, GANGSTER 20th Century-Fox,
1944
HUGO FRIEDHOFER†

ROGOPAG 1962
CARLO RUSTICHELLI

ROGUE COP MGM, 1954
JEFF ALEXANDER†

THE ROGUE SONG MGM, 1930
HERBERT STOTHART†
DIMITRI TIOMKIN†

ROGUE'S REGIMENT Universal, 1948
DANIELE AMFITHEATROF†

ROGUES OF SHERWOOD FOREST Columbia,
1950
ARTHUR MORTON
HEINZ ROEMHELD†

ROLL OF THUNDER, HEAR MY CRY (TF)
Tomorrow Entertainment, 1978
FRED KARLIN

ROLL, FREDDY, ROLL! (TF) ABC Circle Films, 1974
ALLYN FERGUSON
JACK ELLIOTT

THE ROLLER AND THE VIOLIN Mosfilm, 1961
VYECHESLAV OVCHINNIKOV

ROLLER BOOGIE United Artists, 1979
CRAIG SAFAN

ROLLER BOOGIE United Artists, 1980
BOB ESTY

ROLLERBALL United Artists, 1975
ANDRE PREVIN

ROLLERCOASTER Universal, 1977
LALO SCHIFRIN

ROLLING THUNDER American International, 1977
BARRY DEVORZON

ROLLOVER Orion/Warner Bros., 1981
MICHAEL SMALL

ROMA BENE 1971
LUIS BACALOV

ROMA, CITTA LIBERA 1946
NINO ROTA†

ROMAN HOLIDAY Paramount, 1953
GEORGES AURIC†

ROMAN HOLIDAY (TF) Jerry Ludwig Enterprises/
Paramount TV, 1987
MARK SNOW

THE ROMAN SPRING OF MRS. STONE Warner
Bros., 1961
RICHARD ADDINSELL†

ROMANCE IN MANHATTAN RKO Radio, 1935
MAX STEINER†

ROMANCE IN THE RAIN Universal, 1934
EDWARD WARD†

THE ROMANCE OF ROSY RIDGE MGM, 1947
GEORGE BASSMAN

ROMANCE ON THE ORIENT EXPRESS (TF) Frank
von Zerneck Productions/Yorkshire TV, 1985
ALLYN FERGUSON

ROMANCING THE STONE 20th Century Fox, 1984
ALAN SILVESTRI

THE ROMANTIC AGONY 1974
ENNIO MORRICONE

ROMANTIC COMEDY MGM/UA, 1983
MARVIN HAMLISCH

THE ROMANTIC ENGLISHWOMAN New World,
1975
RICHARD HARTLEY

ROME ADVENTURE Warner Bros., 1962
MAX STEINER†

ROME LIKE CHICAGO 1968
ENNIO MORRICONE
BRUNO NICOLAI

ROME-O AND JULIE 8 IN OUTER SPACE (ATF)
Canadian
PATRICIA CULLEN

ROMEO AND JULIET 1966
BRUNO NICOLAI

ROMEO AND JULIET MGM, 1936
HERBERT STOTHART†

ROMEO AND JULIET Paramount, 1968
NINO ROTA†

ROMEO IS BLEEDING Gramercy, 1994
MARK ISHAM

ROMERO Four Seasons Entertainment, 1989
GABRIEL YARED

ROMULUS AND THE SABINES *IL RATTO DELLE
SABINE* 1961
CARLO RUSTICHELLI

RONA JAFFE'S MAZES AND MONSTERS (TF)
McDermott Productions/Procter & Gamble
Productions, 1982
HAGOOD HARDY

THE ROOF *IL TETTO* Trans-Lux, 1956
ALESSANDRO CICOGNINI†

ROOFTOPS New Century/Vista, 1989
MICHAEL KAMEN
DAVID A. STEWART

ROOGIE'S RUMP 1954
LEHMAN ENGEL†

THE ROOKIE 20th Century-Fox, 1959
PAUL DUNLAP

THE ROOKIE Warner Bros., 1990
LENNIE NIEHAUS

THE ROOKIE COP RKO Radio, 1939
ROY WEBB†

ROOKIE OF THE YEAR 20th Century Fox, 1993
BILL CONTI

THE ROOKIES (TF) Aaron Spelling Productions/ABC
Circle Films, 1972
ELMER BERNSTEIN

ROOM 43 1958
KENNETH V. JONES

ROOM FOR ONE MORE Warner Bros., 1952
MAX STEINER†

ROOM SERVICE RKO Radio, 1938
ROY WEBB†

THE ROOM UPSTAIRS (TF) Marian Rees
Associates/The Alexander Group Productions, 1987
ROBERT FOLK

A ROOM WITH A VIEW Cinecom, 1986
RICHARD ROBBINS

ROOMMATES Buena Vista, 1995
ELMER BERNSTEIN

ROOMMATES Platinum Pictures, 1982
JONATHAN HANNAH

ROOMMATES (TF) Pacific Motion Pictures/Michael
Filerman Prods., 1994
LEE HOLDRIDGE

ROOSTER (TF) Glen A. Larson Productions/Tugboat
Productions/20th Century-Fox TV, 1982
STU PHILLIPS

ROOSTER COGBURN Universal, 1975
LAURENCE ROSENTHAL

ROOSTERS (TF) released theatrically in 1995 by IRS,
KCET/WMG, 1993
DAVID KITAY

ROOTS (MS) Wolper Productions, 1977
GERALD FRIED ☆☆
QUINCY JONES ☆☆

ROOTS IN THE EARTH (FD) Department of
Agriculture, 1940
PAUL BOWLES

THE ROOTS OF HEAVEN 20th Century-Fox, 1958
MALCOLM ARNOLD

ROOTS: THE GIFT (TF) Wolper Productions/Warner
Bros. TV, 1988
GERALD FRIED

ROOTS: THE NEXT GENERATION (MS) Wolper
Productions, 1979
GERALD FRIED.

ROPE Warner Bros., 1948
DAVID BUTTOLPH†

ROPE OF SAND Paramount, 1949
FRANZ WAXMAN†

ROSA LUXEMBOURG New Yorker, 1986
NICOLAS ECONOMOU

ROSALIE MGM, 1937
HERBERT STOTHART†

ROSALIE GOES SHOPPING Futura Filmverlag/
Pelemele Film, 1989
BOB TELSON

THE ROSARY MURDERS Samuel Goldwyn
Company, 1987
BOBBY LAUREL
DON SEBESKY

ROSE 1936
JEAN WIENER†

THE ROSE AND THE JACKAL (CTF) Steve White
Productions/PWD Productions/Spectator Films/TNT,
1990
MICHAEL J. LEWIS

THE ROSE GARDEN 21st Century, 1989
EGISTO MACCHI

ROSE MARIE MGM, 1936
HERBERT STOTHART†

THE ROSE TATTOO Paramount, 1955
ALEX NORTH† ★

ROSEANNA McCOY RKO Radio, 1949
DAVID BUTTOLPH†
HUGO FRIEDHOFER†

**ROSEANNE AND TOM: BEHIND THE SCENES
(TF)** Brian Pike Prods./NBC Prods., 1994
CRAIG SAFAN

**ROSEANNE: AN UNAUTHORIZED BIOGRAPHY
(TF)** DDF Films, 1994
SCOTT HARPER

ROSEBUD United Artists, 1975
LAURENT PETITGIRARD

THE ROSEBUD BEACH HOTEL Almi Pictures, 1985
JAY CHATTAWAY

ROSELAND Cinema Shares, 1977
MICHAEL GIBSON

ROSEMARY'S BABY Paramount, 1968
CHRISTOPHER KOMEDA†

ROSES ARE FOR THE RICH (TF) Phoenix
Entertainment Group, 1987
ARTHUR B. RUBINSTEIN

ROSEWOOD Warner Bros., 1997
JOHN WILLIAMS

ROSIE! Universal, 1967
LYN MURRAY†

ROSIE: THE ROSEMARY CLOONEY STORY (TF)
Charles Fries Productions/Alan Sacks Productions,
1982
FRANK ORTEGA

ROSMUNDA E ALBOINO 1961
CARLO RUSTICHELLI

ROSOLINO PATERNO, SOLDATO 1970
CARLO RUSTICHELLI

ROSWELL (CTF) Citadel/Viacom/Showtime
Entertainment, 1994
ELLIOT GOLDENTHAL

ROUGH CUT Paramount, 1980
NELSON RIDDLE†

ROUGH MAGIC Savoy, 1995
RICHARD HARTLEY

ROUGH NIGHT IN JERICHO Universal, 1967
DON COSTA

ROUGH SKETCH OF A SPIRAL (FD) 1991
JUN KAMIYAMA
YOSHIKAZU YANO

ROUGHLY SPEAKING Warner Bros., 1945
MAX STEINER†

ROUGHNECKS (TF) Metromedia Producers
Corporation/Rattlesnake Productions, 1980
JERROLD IMMEL

ROUGHSHOD RKO Radio, 1949
ROY WEBB†

ROUND MIDNIGHT Warner Bros., 1986
HERBIE HANCOCK ★★

ROUND NUMBERS Filmthropix, 1992
NORMAN MAMEY

THE ROUND TABLE (TF) Spelling TV, 1992
TIM TRUMAN

ROUND TRIP TO HEAVEN Saban/Prism, 1991
NOAM KANIEL
SHUKI LEVY

THE ROUNDERS MGM, 1965
JEFF ALEXANDER†

THE ROUSTERS (TF) Stephen J. Cannell Productions,
1983
PETE CARPENTER†

THE ROVER *L'AVVENTURIERO* 1967
ENNIO MORRICONE

ROVER DANGERFIELD (AF) Warner Bros., 1991
DAVID NEWMAN

A ROW OF CROWS Propaganda, 1991
ROBERT FOLK

ROXANNE Columbia, 1987
PETER RODGERS MELNICK
BRUCE SMEATON

ROXANNE: THE PRIZE PULITZER (TF) Qintex
Entertainment, 1989
BOB ALCIVAR

ROXIE HART 20th Century-Fox, 1942
ALFRED NEWMAN†

ROY COHN/JACK SMITH Icon & Idiom Prods.,
1994
MICHAEL SAHL

THE ROYAL AFRICAN RIFLES Allied Artists, 1953
PAUL DUNLAP

A ROYAL DIVORCE Paramount, 1938
ANTHONY COLLINS†

ROYAL FLASH 20th Century-Fox, 1976
KEN THORNE

THE ROYAL HUNT OF THE SUN National General,
1969
MARC WILKINSON

ROYAL REGATTA Dovzsenco Films, 1976
VLADIMIR HORUNZHY

**THE ROYAL ROMANCE OF CHARLES AND DIANA
(TF)** Chrysalis-Yellen Productions, 1982
DAVID PALMER

A ROYAL SCANDAL 20th Century-Fox, 1945
ALFRED NEWMAN†

ROYAL WEDDING MGM, 1951
JOHN GREEN†

THE ROYALE (CTF) A&E, 1996
ROLFE KENT

ROYCE (CTF) Gerber/ITC Prods./Showtime, 1994
STANLEY CLARKE

R.P.M. Columbia, 1970
PERRY BOTKIN

R.S.I.: LA REPUBBLICA DI MUSSOLINI (FD)
1976
TEO USUELLI

RUBA AL PROSSIMO TUO 1968
ENNIO MORRICONE

RUBDOWN (CTF) Wilshire Court/Fast Track Films,
1993
GERALD GOURIET

RUBIN AND ED Working Title, 1991
FRED MYROW

RUBY Dimension, 1977
DON ELLIS†

RUBY Triumph, 1992
JOHN SCOTT

RUBY CAIRO Miramax, 1993
JOHN BARRY
ROBERT RANDLES

RUBY GENTRY 20th Century-Fox, 1953
HEINZ ROEMHELD†

RUBY IN PARADISE 1993
CHARLES ENGSTROM

RUBY JEAN & JOE 1996
STEPHEN GRAZIANO

RUBY RING (TF) 1997
ARTHUR B. RUBINSTEIN

RUDE AWAKENING Orion, 1989
JONATHAN ELIAS

RUDE BOY Atlantic Releasing Corporation, 1980
MICK JONES
JOE STRUMMER

RUDY TriStar, 1993
JERRY GOLDSMITH

RUDYARD KIPLING'S JUNGLE BOOK Buena
Vista, 1994
BASIL POLEDOURIS

RUE DES PRAIRIES 1959
GEORGES VAN PARYS†

RUE DU BAC 1991
JEAN-CLAUDE PETIT

RUGANTINO 1962
ARMANDO TROVAJOLI

RUGGED GOLD (CTF) Alliance/Gibson Group/
Family Channel, 1994
DICK LE FORT
ERIC N. ROBERTSON

RUINED MAP 1968
TORU TAKEMITSU†

RULERS OF THE SEA Paramount, 1939
RICHARD HAGEMAN†

RULES OF ENGAGEMENT Mahogany Pictures,
1997
ROGER NEILL

THE RULES OF MARRIAGE (TF) Entheos Unlimited
Productions/Brownstone Productions/20th Century
Fox TV, 1982
PAUL CHIHARA

THE RULES OF THE GAME Janus, 1939
JOSEPH KOSMA†

THE RULING CLASS Avco Embassy, 1972
JOHN CAMERON

RUMBLE FISH Universal, 1983
STEWART COPELAND

RUMBLE IN THE BRONX New Line, 1996
J. PETER ROBINSON

A RUMOR OF WAR (TF) Charles Fries Productions,
1980
CHARLES GROSS

RUMPELSTILTSKIN Cannon, 1987
MAX ROBERT

RUMPELSTILTSKIN Spelling, 1996
CHARLES BERNSTEIN

RUN Hollywood, 1991
PHIL MARSHALL

RUN FOR THE SUN United Artists, 1956
FRED STEINER

RUN MAN RUN! 1968
BRUNO NICOLAI

THE RUN OF THE COUNTRY Columbia, 1995
CYNTHIA MILLAR

RUN OF THE ARROW RKO Radio, 1957
VICTOR YOUNG†

RUN OF THE HOUSE Zoo, 1992
RUSSELL YOUNG

RUN RUN JOE 1974
GUIDO DE ANGELIS
MAURIZIO DE ANGELIS

RUN SILENT, RUN DEEP United Artists, 1958
FRANZ WAXMAN†

RUN TILL YOU FALL (TF) CBS Entertainment, 1988
TOM SCOTT

RUN WILD, RUN FREE Columbia, 1969
DAVID WHITAKER

RUN WITH THE DEVIL *VIA MARGUTTA* 1959
PIERO PICCIONI

RUN, ANGEL, RUN! Fanfare, 1969
STU PHILLIPS

THE RUNAROUND RKO Radio, 1931
MAX STEINER†

THE RUNAROUND Universal, 1946
FRANK SKINNER†

RUNAWAY Tri-Star, 1984
JERRY GOLDSMITH

THE RUNAWAY BARGE (TF) Lorimar Productions,
1975
NELSON RIDDLE†

RUNAWAY DAUGHTERS American International,
1957
RONALD STEIN†

RUNAWAY FATHER (TF) Polone Co./Bonaparte
Prods./Lee Levinson Prods./Hearst, 1991
JAMES DIPASQUALLE

RUNAWAY TRAIN Cannon, 1985
TREVOR JONES

RUNAWAY! (TF) Universal TV, 1973
HAL MOONEY

THE RUNESTONE Hyperion/Signature, 1992
DAVID NEWMAN

THE RUNNER STUMBLES 20th Century-Fox, 1979
ERNEST GOLD

RUNNERS Goldcrest Films & TV, 1983
GEORGE FENTON

RUNNING Columbia, 1979
ANDRE GAGNON

RUNNING AGAINST TIME (CTF) Finnegan-Pinchuk
Prods., 1990
DON DAVIS

RUNNING BRAVE Buena Vista, 1983
MIKE POST

RUNNING FROM THE GUNS 1987
JIM MANZIE
BRUCE ROWLAND

RUNNING HOT New Line Cinema, 1984
AL CAPPS

THE RUNNING MAN Columbia, 1963
WILLIAM ALWYN†

THE RUNNING MAN Tri-Star, 1987
HAROLD FALTERMEYER

RUNNING MATES (CTF) Marvin Worth Prods.,
1992
PETER RODGERS MELNICK

RUNNING ON EMPTY Warner Bros., 1988
TONY MOTTOLA

RUNNING OUT (TF) CBS Entertainment, 1983
LEE HOLDRIDGE

RUNNING SCARED MGM/UA, 1986
UDI HARPAZ
ROD TEMPERTON

RUNNING TARGET United Artists, 1956
ERNEST GOLD

RUSH Cinema Shares International, 1984
FRANCESCO DE MASI

RUSH MGM, 1991
ERIC CLAPTON

RUSH WEEK Noble, 1991
THE HAMILTONS

RUSS MEYER'S UP! RM Films, 1976
WILLIAM LOOSE†

RUSS MEYER'S VIXEN Eve, 1968
IGO KANTOR

THE RUSSIA HOUSE Pathe, 1990
JERRY GOLDSMITH

THE RUSSIAN QUESTION 1948
ARAM KHACHATURIAN†

RUSSIAN ROULETTE Avco Embassy, 1975
MICHAEL J. LEWIS

THE RUSSIAN SOLDIER (TF) BBC, 1985
STANLEY MYERS†

RUSSIAN TERMINATOR Kimmy Christensen and
Finn Madsen, 1991
DANNY YOUNG

**THE RUSSIANS ARE COMING THE RUSSIANS ARE
COMING** United Artists, 1966
JOHNNY MANDEL

RUSSKIES New Century/Vista, 1987
JAMES NEWTON HOWARD

RUSTLER'S ROUND-UP Universal, 1946
MILTON ROSEN†

RUSTLERS' RHAPSODY Paramount, 1985
STEVE DORFF

RUTHLESS Eagle Lion, 1948
WERNER JANSSEN

THE RUTHLESS FOUR *EVERY MAN FOR
HIMSELF/SAM COOPER'S GOLD* 1968
CARLO RUSTICHELLI

THE RUTHLESS ONE 1957
GERARD SCHURMANN

RUTHLESS PEOPLE Buena Vista, 1986
MICHEL COLOMBIER

RUY BLAS 1947
GEORGES AURIC†

RYABA, MY CHICKEN *KOUROTCHKA RIABA/
RIABA MA POULE* 1994
BORIS BASOUROV

THE RYAN WHITE STORY (TF) The Landsburg Co.,
1989
MIKE POST

RYAN'S DAUGHTER MGM, 1970
MAURICE JARRE

RYAN'S FOUR (TF) Fair Dinkum Inc./Groverton
Productions/Paramount TV, 1983
RANDY EDELMAN

S

SAADIA MGM, 1953
BRONISLAU KAPER†

SABOTAGE *A WOMAN ALONE* Gaumont-British,
1936
LOUIS LEVY†

SABOTEUR Universal, 1942
FRANK SKINNER†

SABRE JET United Artists, 1953
HERSCHEL BURKE GILBERT

SABRINA Paramount, 1954
FREDERICK HOLLANDER†

SABRINA Paramount, 1995
JOHN WILLIAMS ★

SABU AND THE MAGIC RING Allied Artists, 1957
HARRY SUKMAN†

SACCO AND VANZETTI 1971
ENNIO MORRICONE

THE SACKETTS (TF) Douglas Netter Enterprises/M.B.
Scott Productions/Shalako Enterprises, 1979
JERROLD IMMEL

THE SACRED NIGHT 1993
GORAN BREGOVIC

SACRED SEX (FD) 1992
NICK PALMER

THE SACRIFICE Orion Classics, 1986
WATAZUMIDO SHUOO

THE SAD HORSE 20th Century-Fox, 1959
BERT A. SHEFTER

THE SAD SACK Paramount, 1957
WALTER SCHARF

SADAT (MS) Blatt-Singer Productions/Columbia TV,
1983
CHARLES BERNSTEIN

SADDLE THE WIND MGM, 1957
ELMER BERNSTEIN

SADIE AND SON (TF) Norton Wright Productions/
Kenny Rogers Organization/ITC Productions, 1987
BILLY GOLDENBERG

SADIE McKEE MGM, 1934
WILLIAM AXT†

SADISMO American International, 1967
LES BAXTER†

SAFARI Columbia, 1956
WILLIAM ALWYN†

SAFARI Paramount, 1940
FREDERICK HOLLANDER†

SAFARI 3000 United Artists, 1982
ERNEST GOLD

SAFE 1993
BILLY BRAGG

SAFE Sony Classics, 1995
ED TOMNEY

SAFE AT HOME! Columbia, 1962
VAN ALEXANDER

SAFE HOUSE Viacom, 1997
KEVIN KINER

SAFE PASSAGE New Line, 1994
MARK ISHAM

THE SAFECRACKER MGM, 1958
RICHARD RODNEY BENNETT

THE SAGA OF ANATAHAN *ANA-TA-HAN* 1953
AKIRA IFUKUBE

THE SAGA OF HEMP BROWN Universal, 1958
HERMAN STEIN

**THE SAGA OF THE VIKING WOMEN AND THEIR
VOYAGE TO THE WATERS OF THE GREAT SEA
SERPENT** American International, 1957
ALBERT GLASSER

SAHARA Columbia, 1943
MIKLOS ROZSA†

SAHARA MGM/UA, 1983
ENNIO MORRICONE

SAI COSA FACEVA STALIN ALLE DONNE? 1969
ENNIO MORRICONE

SAIGON Paramount, 1948
ROBERT EMMETT DOLAN†

SAIGON - YEAR OF THE CAT (TF) Thames TV,
1983
GEORGE FENTON

THE SAILOR TAKES A WIFE MGM, 1945
JOHN GREEN†

**THE SAILOR WHO FELL FROM GRACE WITH THE
SEA** Avco Embassy, 1976
JOHNNY MANDEL

THE SAILOR'S RETURN Euston Films Ltd., 1978
CARL DAVIS

THE SAINT Paramount, 1997
GRAEME REVELL

THE SAINT IN PALM SPRINGS RKO Radio, 1941
ROY WEBB†

THE SAINT OF FORT WASHINGTON Warner
Bros., 1993
JAMES NEWTON HOWARD

SAINT PHANOURIOS' PIE 1993
NIKOS MAMANGAKIS

THE SAINT STRIKES BACK RKO Radio, 1939
ROY WEBB†

THE SAINT TAKES OVER RKO Radio, 1940
ROY WEBB†

THE SAINT'S DOUBLE TROUBLE RKO Radio, 1940
ROY WEBB†

THE SAINT: THE BRAZILIAN CONNECTION (TF)
Saint Productions/London Weekend Television, 1989
SERGE FRANKLIN

THE SAINTED SISTERS Paramount, 1948
NATHAN VAN CLEAVE†

SAINTLY SINNERS United Artists, 1962
RICHARD LASALLE

SAKHAROV (CTF) HBO Premiere Films/Titus
Productions, 1984
CARL DAVIS

SALADINO 1966
ANGELO FRANCESCO LAVAGNINO†

THE SALAMANDER ITC, 1981
JERRY GOLDSMITH

SALAVAT YULAYEV 1941
ARAM KHACHATURIAN†

SALEM'S GHOST Vista Street Entertainment, 1995
MIRIAM CUTLER

SALEM'S LOT (TF) Warner Bros. TV, 1979
HARRY SUKMAN† ☆

SALLY AND SAINT ANNE Universal, 1952
FRANK SKINNER†

SALMONBERRIES 1991
BOB TELSON

SALO OR THE 120 DAYS OF SODOM United
Artists, 1975
ENNIO MORRICONE

SALOME Columbia, 1953
DANIELE AMFITHEATROF†
GEORGE DUNING

SALOME, WHERE SHE DANCED Universal, 1945
EDWARD WARD†

SALOMONICO 1972
DOV SELTZER

SALON KITTY American International, 1976
FIORENZO CARPI

SALT AND PEPPER United Artists, 1968
JOHN DANKWORTH

SALT OF THE EARTH Independent Productions,
1954
SOL KAPLAN

SALT ON OUR SKIN 1993
KLAUS DOLDINGER

SALT TO THE DEVIL 1949
BENJAMIN FRANKEL†

SALTANAT 1955
ARAM KHACHATURIAN†

SALTO NEL VUOTO 1980
NICOLA PIOVANI

SALTY O'ROURKE Paramount, 1945
ROBERT EMMETT DOLAN†

SALUDOS AMIGOS RKO Radio, 1943
EDWARD PLUMB† ★
PAUL J. SMITH† ★

SALUT L'ARTISTE Exxel, 1973
VLADIMIR COSMA

SALUT LA PUCE Naja Film, 1983
FRANCIS LAI

SALVADOR Hemdale, 1986
GEORGES DELERUE†

SALVAGE (TF) Bennett-Katleman Productions/
Columbia Pictures TV, 1979
WALTER SCHARF

SALVATION 1973
ANDRZEJ KORZYNSKI

SALVATORE GIULIANO CCM Films, 1962
PIERO PICCIONI

SALVO D'ACQUISTO 1975
CARLO RUSTICHELLI

THE SALZBURG CONNECTION 20th Century-Fox,
1972
LIONEL NEWMAN†

SAM & ME Sunrise, 1991
MARK KORVEN

**SAM HILL: WHO KILLED THE MYSTERIOUS MR.
FOSTER? (TF)** Public Arts Productions/Universal
TV, 1971
PETE RUGOLO

SAM WHISKEY United Artists, 1969
HERSCHEL BURKE GILBERT

SAM'S ROSE Invictus Entertainment, 1984
DAVID ROSE†

SAMANTHA 1991
JOEL MCNEELY

SAMARITAN (TF) Levine-Robins Productions/Fries
Entertainment, 1986
CRAIG SAFAN

SAME TIME NEXT YEAR Universal, 1979
MARVIN HAMLISCH

SAMIR E IL MARE 1958
CARLO RUSTICHELLI

SAMMIE & ROSIE GET LAID Cinecom, 1987
STANLEY MYERS†

SAMMY GOING SOUTH Paramount, 1963
TRISTRAM CARY

SAMOA Buena Vista, 1956
OLIVER WALLACE†

SAMPAN BOY 1950
PIERO PICCIONI

SAMSON & THE SLAVE QUEEN 1963
ANGELO FRANCESCO LAVAGNINO†

SAMSON AND DELILAH Paramount, 1949
VICTOR YOUNG† ★

SAMSON AND DELILAH (TF) Catalina Production
Group/Comworld Productions, 1983
MAURICE JARRE

**SAMSON AND THE 7 MIRACLES OF THE
WORLD** American International, 1961
LES BAXTER†

**SAMSON AND THE SEVEN MIRACLES OF THE
WORLD** American International, 1962
LES BAXTER†

SAMSON AND THE SLAVE QUEEN American
International, 1962
LES BAXTER†

SAMSON CONTRO I PARATI *SAMSON VS. THE
PIRATES* 1963
ANGELO FRANCESCO LAVAGNINO†

SAMSON VS. THE PIRATES 1963
ANGELO FRANCESCO LAVAGNINO†

SAMUEL LOUNT Moonshine Prods., 1985
KITARO

SAMURAI (TF) Danny Thomas Productions/Universal
TV, 1979
FRED KARLIN

SAMURAI BANNERS 1969
MASARU SATO

SAMURAI REBELLION Toho, 1967
TORU TAKEMITSU†

SAMURAI SPY 1965
TORU TAKEMITSU†

SAN ANTONIO Warner Bros., 1946
MAX STEINER†

SAN BABILA ORE 20: UN DELITTO INUTILE
1976
ENNIO MORRICONE

SAN DIEGO, I LOVE YOU Universal, 1944
HANS J. SALTER†

THE SAN FRANCISCO STORY Warner Bros., 1952
EMIL NEWMAN†
PAUL DUNLAP

SAN FRANCISCO MGM, 1936
HERBERT STOTHART†

SAN FRANCISCO DOCKS Universal, 1941
HANS J. SALTER†

SAN FRANCISCO INTERNATIONAL (TF) Universal
TV, 1970
PATRICK WILLIAMS

THE SAN PEDRO BUMS (TF) Aaron Spelling
Productions, 1977
PETE RUGOLO

SAN QUENTIN Warner Bros., 1937
DAVID RAKSIN

SANCTUARY 20th Century Fox, 1961
ALEX NORTH†

SANCTUARY OF FEAR (TF) Marble Arch
Productions, 1979
ALLYN FERGUSON
JACK ELLIOTT

SAND 20th Century-Fox, 1949
DANIELE AMFITHEATROF†

THE SAND PEBBLES 20th Century-Fox, 1966
JERRY GOLDSMITH ★

SANDCASTLES (TF) Metromedia Productions, 1972
PAUL GLASS

THE SANDLOT 20th Century Fox, 1993
DAVID NEWMAN

THE SANDMAN (TF) Finnegan-Pinchuk/NBC Prods.,
1993
ANTHONY MARINELLI

**SANDOKAN CONTRO IL LEOPARDO DI
SARAWAK** 1964
CARLO RUSTICHELLI

SANDOKAN FIGHTS BACK 1964
CARLO RUSTICHELLI

THE SANDPIPER MGM, 1965
JOHNNY MANDEL

SANDS OF IWO JIMA Republic, 1949
VICTOR YOUNG†

SANDS OF THE KALAHARI Paramount, 1965
JOHN DANKWORTH

SANDSTONE Henderson Films, 1977
DARRYL DRAGON
DENNIS DRAGON

SANDTRAP PM Entertainment, 1997
BENNETT SALVAY

SANDY GETS HER MAN Universal, 1940
HANS J. SALTER†

SANJURO Toho, 1962
MASARU SATO

SANS FAMILE 1958
PAUL MISRAKI

SANS LAISSER D'ADRESSE 1950
JOSEPH KOSMA†

SANS LENDEMAIN 1939
ALLAN GRAY†

SANS MOBILE APPARENT 1971
ENNIO MORRICONE

SANSHO THE BAILIFF 1954
FUMIO HAYASAKA†

THE SANTA CLAUSE Buena Vista, 1994
MICHAEL CONVERTINO

SANTA CLAUS CONQUERS THE MARTIANS
Embassy, 1964
MILTON DELUGG

SANTA CLAUS: THE MOVIE Tri-Star, 1985
HENRY MANCINI†

SANTA FE STAMPEDE Republic, 1938
WILLIAM LAVA†

SANTA FE TRAIL Warner Bros., 1940
MAX STEINER†

SANTA SANGRE Expanded Entertainment, 1990
SIMON BOSWELL

SANTIAGO Warner Bros., 1956
DAVID BUTTOLPH†

SAPPORO WINTER OLYMPICS 1972
MASARU SATO

SAPS AT SEA United Artists, 1940
T. MARVIN HATLEY†

SARABAND *SARABAND FOR DEAD LOVERS*
Eagle Lion, 1948
ALAN RAWSTHORNE†

SARABAND FOR DEAD LOVERS Eagle Lion, 1948
ALAN RAWSTHORNE†

SARAFINA! Miramax, 1992
STANLEY MYERS†

SARAH UGC, 1983
GABRIEL YARED

SARAH PLAIN AND TALL (TF) Self Help Prods./
Trillium, 1991
DAVID SHIRE

**SARAH T. - PORTRAIT OF A TEENAGE
ALCOHOLIC (TF)** Universal TV, 1975
JAMES DIPASQUALLE

SA - SC

'97-'98
FILM
COMPOSERS
INDEX

F I L M   T I T L E S

SARATOGA MGM, 1937
EDWARD WARD†

SARATOGA TRUNK Warner Bros., 1946
MAX STEINER†

SARGE: THE BADGE OR THE CROSS (TF)
Universal TV, 1971
DAVE GRUSIN

SARTANA 1968
PIERO PICCIONI

S.A.S. A SAN SALVADOR S.A.S. - TERMINATE
WITH EXTREME PREJUDICE UGC, 1983
MICHEL MAGNE†

S.A.S. - TERMINATE WITH EXTREME
PREJUDICE UGC, 1983
MICHEL MAGNE†

SASKATCHEWAN Universal, 1954
HANS J. SALTER†
HERMAN STEIN

THE SATAN BUG United Artists, 1965
JERRY GOLDSMITH

SATAN NEVER SLEEPS 20th Century Fox, 1962
RICHARD RODNEY BENNETT

SATAN'S BREW New Yorker, 1976
PEER RABEN

SATAN'S CHEERLEADERS World Amusement,
1977
GERALD LEE

SATAN'S CRADLE United Artists, 1949
ALBERT GLASSER

SATAN'S MISTRESS MPM, 1982
ROGER KELLAWAY

SATAN'S PRINCESS Sun Heat, 1991
NORMAN MAMEY

SATAN'S SCHOOL FOR GIRLS (TF)
Spelling-Goldberg Productions, 1973
LAURENCE ROSENTHAL

SATAN'S SKIN Cannon, 1971
MARC WILKINSON

SATAN'S SLAVE 1976
JOHN SCOTT

SATAN'S TRIANGLE (TF) Danny Thomas
Productions, 1975
JOHNNY PATE

SATANIC RITES OF DRACULA Warner Bros., 1973
JOHN CACAVAS

SATISFACTION 20th Century Fox, 1988
MICHEL COLOMBIER

SATSUJINYO JUDAI THE AGE OF ASSASSINS
1967
MASARU SATO

SATURDAY NIGHT AND SUNDAY MORNING
Continental, 1961
JOHN DANKWORTH

SATURDAY NIGHT FEVER Paramount, 1977
DAVID SHIRE

SATURDAY THE 14TH New World, 1981
PARMER FULLER

SATURDAY THE 14TH STRIKES BACK Concorde,
1988
PARMER FULLER

SATURDAY'S CHILDREN Warner Bros., 1940
ADOLPH DEUTSCH†

SATURDAY'S HERO Columbia, 1951
ELMER BERNSTEIN

SATURN 3 AFD, 1980
ELMER BERNSTEIN

SATYRICON 1969
CARLO RUSTICHELLI

SATYRICOSISSIMO 1970
CARLO RUSTICHELLI

SAUL E DAVID 1965
TEO USUELLI

SAUVE QUI PEUT LA VIE New Yorker/Zoetrope,
1980
GABRIEL YARED

SAVAGE Mahogany Pictures, 1995
ROGER NEILL

SAVAGE (TF) Universal TV, 1973
GIL MELLE

SAVAGE BEACH (TF) Malibu Bay Films, 1989
GARY STOCKDALE

THE SAVAGE BEES (TF) Landsburg-Kirshner
Productions/NBC, 1976
WALTER MURPHY

THE SAVAGE EYE Trans-Lux, 1959
LEONARD ROSENMAN

SAVAGE HARVEST 20th Century-Fox, 1981
ROBERT FOLK

SAVAGE HUNGER OASIS Shapiro Entertainment,
1984
CHRISTOPHER YOUNG

THE SAVAGE INNOCENTS Paramount, 1960
ANGELO FRANCESCO LAVAGNINO†

THE SAVAGE IS LOOSE Campbell Devon, 1974
GIL MELLE

SAVAGE ISLANDS Paramount, 1983
TREVOR JONES

SAVAGE SAM Buena Vista, 1963
OLIVER WALLACE†

SAVAGE SISTERS American International, 1974
LES BAXTER†

SAVAGE STREETS MPM, 1984
JOHN D'ANDREA
MICHAEL LLOYD

SAVAGES Angelika, 1972
JOE RAPOSO†

SAVANNAH 1988
JEAN-CLAUDE PETIT

SAVANNAH (TF) Spelling TV, 1996
GARY STEVAN SCOTT

SAVANNAH SMILES Embassy, 1982
KEN SUTHERLAND

SAVATE MDP Worldwide, 1994
KEVIN KINER

SAVE THE DOG (CTF) The Disney Channel, 1988
J.A.C. REDFORD

SAVE THE TIGER Paramount, 1973
MARVIN HAMLISCH

SAVED Lionheart Films, 1993
STEVE EDWARDS

SAVED BY THE BELL - HAWAIIAN STYLE (TF)
Peter Engel Prods./NBC, 1992
SCOTT GALE
RICH EAMES

SAVED BY THE BELL (TF) Peter Engel Prods./NBC
Prods., 1994
JAY GRUSKA

SAVING GRACE Columbia, 1986
WILLIAM GOLDSTEIN

THE SAVING OF BILL BLEWETT 1936
BENJAMIN BRITTEN†

SAXAPHONE 1978
ENZO JANNACCI

THE SAXON CHARM United Artists, 1948
WALTER SCHARF

SAY ANYTHING 20th Century-Fox, 1989
ANNE DUDLEY
RICHARD GIBBS

SAY IT WITH FLOWERS 1974
CLAUDE BOLLING

SAY ONE FOR ME 20th Century-Fox, 1959
LIONEL NEWMAN† ★

SAY YES Cinetel Films, 1987
TONY RIPPARETTI

SAYONARA Warner Bros., 1957
FRANZ WAXMAN†

SBATTI IL MOSTRO IN PRIMA PAGINA 1972
ENNIO MORRICONE
NICOLA PIOVANI

SBIRRO, LA TUA LEGGE E LENTA...LA MIA NO!
1979
STELVIO CIPRIANI

SCACCO INTERNAZIONALE 1969
CARLO RUSTICHELLI

SCALAWAG Paramount, 1973
JOHN CAMERON

SCALPEL FALSE FACE United International, 1976
BOB COBERT

THE SCALPHUNTERS United Artists, 1968
ELMER BERNSTEIN

SCALPLOCK (TF) Columbia Pictures TV, 1966
RICHARD MARKOWITZ†

SCAM (CTF) Viacom, 1993
STEPHEN GRAZIANO

SCAMPOLO 53' 1953
NINO ROTA†

SCANDAL Miramax Films, 1989
CARL DAVIS

SCANDAL AT SCOURIE MGM, 1953
DANIELE AMFITHEATROF†

A SCANDAL IN PARIS United Artists, 1946
HANNS EISLER†

SCANDAL IN A SMALL TOWN (TF)
Carliner-Rappoport Productions, 1988
MARK SNOW

SCANDAL IN SORRENTO PANE, AMORE E...
DCA, 1955
ALESSANDRO CICOGNINI†

SCANDAL SHEET Columbia, 1952
GEORGE DUNING

SCANDAL SHEET (TF) Fair Dinkum Productions,
1985
RANDY EDELMAN

SCANDAL, INC. Republic, 1956
PAUL SAWTELL†
BERT A. SHEFTER

SCANDALO Joseph Brenner Associates, 1977
RIZ ORTOLANI

SCANDALOUS Orion, 1984
DAVE GRUSIN

SCANDALOUS JOHN Buena Vista, 1971
ROD McKUEN

SCANNERS Avco Embassy, 1981
HOWARD SHORE

SCANNERS II: THE NEW WORLD ORDER Triton,
1991
MARTY SIMON

SCANNERS III: THE TAKEOVER 1992
MARTY SIMON

THE SCAPEGOAT MGM, 1958
BRONISLAU KAPER†

SCARAMOUCHE MGM, 1952
VICTOR YOUNG†

SCARECROW Warner Bros., 1973
FRED MYROW

SCARED STIFF Paramount, 1953
LEITH STEVENS†

SCARED STRAIGHT! ANOTHER STORY (TF)
Golden West TV, 1980
DANA KAPROFF

SCARED TO DEATH Lone Star Pictures, 1982
TOM CHASE
ARDELL HAKE

THE SCARF United Artists, 1951
HERSCHEL BURKE GILBERT

SCARFACE Universal, 1983
GIORGIO MORODER

THE SCARLET AND THE BLACK (TF) Bill
McCutchen Productions/ITC Productions/RAI, 1983
ENNIO MORRICONE

SCARLET AND BLACK originally filmed for
television, Miramax, 1993
JEAN-CLAUDE PETIT

THE SCARLET CLAW Universal, 1944
HANS J. SALTER†
PAUL SAWTELL†

THE SCARLET COAT MGM, 1955
CONRAD SALINGER†

THE SCARLET HOUR Paramount, 1956
LEITH STEVENS†

THE SCARLET LETTER Bauer International, 1973
JURGEN KNIEPER

THE SCARLET LETTER Buena Vista, 1995
JOHN BARRY

THE SCARLET LETTER MGM, 1926
WILLIAM AXT†

THE SCARLET PIMPERNEL 1934
ARTHUR BENJAMIN†

THE SCARLET PIMPERNEL (TF) London Films Ltd.,
1982
NICK BICAT
BOB COBERT

SCARLET STREET Universal, 1945
HANS J. SALTER†

SCARLETT (TF) RHI/Beta Film/Silvio Berlusconi
Comm./TF1, 1994
JOHN MORRIS

THE SCARLETT EMPRESS Paramount, 1934
W. FRANKE HARLING†

THE SCARS OF DRACULA American Continental,
1971
JAMES BERNARD

SCATTERED DREAMS: THE KATHRYN
MESSENGER STORY (TF) Robert Greenwald
Prods., 1993
MARK SNOW

SCATTERGOOD MEETS BROADWAY RKO Radio,
1941
DIMITRI TIOMKIN†

SCAVENGER HUNT 20th Century-Fox, 1979
BILLY GOLDENBERG

THE SCENE OF THE CRIME AMLF, 1986
PHILIPPE SARDE

SCENE OF THE CRIME MGM, 1949
ANDRE PREVIN

SCENES FROM A MALL Touchstone, 1991
MARC SHAIMAN

SCENES FROM THE CLASS STRUGGLE IN
BEVERLY HILLS Cinecom, 1989
STANLEY MYERS†

SCENT OF A WOMAN 20th Century-Fox, 1976
ARMANDO TROVAJOLI

SCENT OF A WOMAN Universal, 1992
THOMAS NEWMAN

THE SCENT OF THE GREEN PAPAYA 1993
TON THAT TIET

THE SCENT OF YVONNE LE PARFUM
D'YVONNE 1994
PASCAL ESTEVE

SCHICKSAL AM LENKRAD 1956
HANNS EISLER†

SCHINDLER'S LIST Universal, 1993
JOHN WILLIAMS ★★

SCHIZOID MURDER BY MAIL Cannon, 1980
CRAIG HUNDLEY

SCHIZOPOLIS 1997
CLIFF MARTINEZ

SCHLOCK Jack H. Harris Enterprises, 1973
DAVID GIBSON

SCHOOL DAZE Columbia, 1988
BILL LEE

SCHOOL FOR SCOUNDRELS Warner Bros., 1960
JOHN ADDISON

A SCHOOL OUTING 1983
RIZ ORTOLANI

SCHOOL SPIRIT Concorde/Cinema Group, 1985
TOM BRUNER

SCHOOL TIES Paramount, 1992
MAURICE JARRE

SCHTONK 1992
KONSTANTIN WECKER

SCHWEITZER Sugar Entertainment, 1990
ZANE KRONJE

SCIENCE-FICTION: A JOURNEY INTO THE
UNKNOWN (TD) Museum of Television & Radio/
SGP, 1994
GREG EDMONSON

SCOOP (TF) London Weekend TV, 1987
STANLEY MYERS†

SCORCHERS Nova, 1991
CARTER BURWELL

SCORCHY American International, 1976
IGO KANTOR

SCORNED AND SWINDLED (TF) Cypress Point
Productions, 1984
BILLY GOLDENBERG

SCORPIO United Artists, 1973
JERRY FIELDING†

THE SCORPIO LETTERS (TF) MGM TV, 1967
DAVE GRUSIN

SCORPION Crown International, 1986
SEAN MURRAY

SCORTICATELI VIVI 1978
STELVIO CIPRIANI

SCOTT FREE (TF) Cherokee Productions/Universal
TV, 1976
PETE CARPENTER†
MIKE POST

SCOTT JOPLIN Universal, 1977
DICK HYMAN

SCOTT OF THE ANTARCTIC 1948
RALPH VAUGHAN WILLIAMS†

THE SCOUNDREL Paramount, 1935
GEORGE ANTHEIL†

THE SCOUT 20th Century Fox, 1994
BILL CONTI

SCOUT TOUJOURS 1985
GABRIEL YARED

SCOUT'S HONOR (TF) Zephyr Productions, 1980
MIKE POST

SCRATCH HARRY 1969
KEN LAUBER

SCREAM Miramax-Dimension, 1996
MARCO BELTRAMI

SCREAM THE OUTING Cal-Com Releasing, 1983
JOSEPH CONLAN

SCREAM AND SCREAM AGAIN American
International, 1970
DAVID WHITAKER

SCREAM FOR HELP Lorimar, 1984
JOHN PAUL JONES

SCREAM OF FEAR TASTE OF FEAR Columbia,
1961
CLIFTON PARKER†

SCREAM OF STONE Saxer/Lange/Sadler, 1991
SARAH HOPKINS
ALAN LAMB
INGRAM MARSHALL
ATUHALPA YUPANQUI

SCREAM OF THE WOLF (TF) Metromedia Producers
Corporation, 1974
BOB COBERT

SCREAM, BLACULA, SCREAM American
International, 1973
BILL MARX

SCREAM, PRETTY PEGGY (TF) Universal TV, 1973
ROBERT PRINCE

SCREAMERS Triumph, 1996
NORMAND CORBEIL

THE SCREAMING SKULL American International,
1958
ERNEST GOLD

THE SCREAMING WOMAN (TF) Universal TV,
1972
JOHN WILLIAMS

SCREAMING EAGLES Allied Artists, 1956
HARRY SUKMAN†

SCREAMS OF A WINTER NIGHT Dimension
Pictures, 1979
DON ZIMMERS

SCREWBALL HOTEL Maurice Smith Productions/
Avatar Film, 1988
NATHAN WANG

SCREWBALLS New World, 1983
TIM McCAULEY

SCROOGE National General, 1970
LESLIE BRICUSSE ★

SCROOGE United Artists, 1951
RICHARD ADDINSELL†

SCROOGED Paramount, 1988
DANNY ELFMAN

SCRUBBERS Orion Classics, 1983
RAY COOPER
MICHAEL HURD

SCRUPLES (MS) Lou-Step Productions/Warner Bros.
TV, 1981
CHARLES BERNSTEIN

SCUDDA HOO! SCUDDA HAY! 20th Century-Fox,
1948
CYRIL J. MOCKRIDGE†

SCUSI, LEI CONOSCE IL SESSO? 1968
ANGELO FRANCESCO LAVAGNINO†

SE NON AVESSI PIU TE 1966
LUIS BACALOV
ENNIO MORRICONE

SE TI INCONTRO TI AMMAZZO 1971
STELVIO CIPRIANI

THE SEA CHASE Warner Bros., 1955
ROY WEBB†

SEA DEVILS RKO Radio, 1937
ROY WEBB†

SEA DEVILS RKO Radio, 1953
RICHARD ADDINSELL†

THE SEA GYPSIES Warner Bros., 1978
FRED STEINER

THE SEA HAWK Warner Bros., 1940
ERICH WOLFGANG KORNGOLD† ★

THE SEA HORSE 1934
DARIUS MILHAUD†

SEA KILLER Italian
FRANCIS LAI

THE SEA OF GRASS MGM, 1947
HERBERT STOTHART†

SEA OF LOVE Universal, 1989
TREVOR JONES

SEA QUEST: DSV (TF) Amblin TV, 1993
JOHN DEBNEY

THE SEA SHALL NOT HAVE THEM United Artists, 1954
MALCOLM ARNOLD

SEA SPIDERS MGM, 1932
WILLIAM AXT†

SEA WIFE 20th Century-Fox, 1957
WILLIAM ALWYN†

THE SEA WOLF Concorde, 1997
ROGER NEILL

THE SEA WOLF Warner Bros., 1941
ERICH WOLFGANG KORNGOLD†

THE SEA WOLF (CTF) Bob Banner/Primedia/Andrew J. Fenady, 1993
CHARLES BERNSTEIN ☆

THE SEA WOLVES Paramount, 1981
ROY BUDD†

SEABO 1977
CLAY SMITH

SEAL ISLAND RKO Radio, 1950
OLIVER WALLACE†

SEALED CARGO RKO Radio, 1951
ROY WEBB†

SEALED LIPS Universal, 1941
HANS J. SALTER†

SEALED VERDICT Paramount, 1948
HUGO FRIEDHOFER†

SEANCE ON A WET AFTERNOON Artixo, 1964
JOHN BARRY

SEAQUEST DSV: 2ND SEASON PREMIERE (TF) Amblin TV/Universal TV, 1994
DON DAVIS

SEARCH AND DESTROY October Films, 1995
ELMER BERNSTEIN

SEARCH AND RESCUE (TF) Black Sheep Prods./NBC, 1994
ROBERT FOLK

THE SEARCH FOR ONE-EYE JIMMY 1996
WILLIAM BLOOM

THE SEARCH FOR SIGNS OF INTELLIGENT LIFE IN THE UNIVERSE Orion Classics, 1991
JERRY GOODMAN

THE SEARCH FOR SOLUTIONS (FD) Playback Associates, 1979
LYLE MAYS
PAT METHENY

SEARCH FOR DANGER Film Classics, 1949
KARL HAJOS†

SEARCH FOR GRACE (TF) CBS Entertainment Prods., 1994
MICHAEL HOENIG

SEARCH FOR PARADISE Cinerama Releasing Corporation, 1957
DIMITRI TIOMKIN†

SEARCH FOR THE LOST DIAMOND Microfon, Argentine
EMILIO KAUDERER

THE SEARCHERS Warner Bros., 1956
MAX STEINER†

THE SEARCHING WIND Paramount, 1946
VICTOR YOUNG†

SEARCHING FOR BOBBY FISHER Paramount, 1993
JAMES HORNER

SEASON CHANGE Jaguar Pictures, 1994
ALBY POTTS

A SEASON IN HELL 1971
MAURICE JARRE

A SEASON IN PURGATORY (TF) Spelling TV, 1996
PETER MANNING ROBINSON

A SEASON OF GIANTS (CTF) TNT/RAI-1/Tiber, 1991
RIZ ORTOLANI

A SEASON OF HOPE (TF) Getting Out Prods./Signboard Hill, 1995
KEN THORNE

SEASON OF FEAR MGM/UA, 1989
DAVID WOLINSKI

SEASON OF PASSION United Artists, 1961
BENJAMIN FRANKEL†

SEASONS OF THE HEART (TF) Joseph Feury Prods./RHI, 1994
MARVIN HAMLISCH

SEBASTIAN Paramount, 1968
JERRY GOLDSMITH

SEBASTIAN AND THE SPARROW Kino Films, 1988
ALLAN ZAVOD

SECOND BEST Warner Bros., 1994
SIMON BOSWELL

SECOND CHANCE RKO Radio, 1953
ROY WEBB†

SECOND CHANCE SI C'ETAIT A REFAIRE United Artists Classics, 1976
FRANCIS LAI

SECOND CHANCE (TF)
RIK HOWARD

SECOND CHANCES (TF) Latham-Lechowick Prods., 1993
MARK MOTHERSBAUGH

THE SECOND CIVIL WAR (CTF) HBO Pictures, 1997
HUMMIE MANN

SECOND FIDDLE 20th Century-Fox, 1939
LOUIS SILVERS†

THE SECOND GREATEST SEX Universal, 1955
HENRY MANCINI†

SECOND HONEYMOON 20th Century-Fox, 1937
DAVID BUTTOLPH†

THE SECOND LIEUTENANT 1993
RANDALL MEYERS

SECOND SERVE (TF) Linda Yellen Productions/Lorimar-Telepictures, 1986
BRAD FIEDEL

SECOND SIGHT Warner Bros., 1989
JOHN MORRIS

SECOND SIGHT: A LOVE STORY (TF) Entheos Unlimited Productions/T.T.C. Enterprises, 1984
DANA KAPROFF

SECOND THOUGHTS Universal, 1983
HENRY MANCINI†

THE SECOND TIME AROUND 20th Century Fox, 1961
GERALD FRIED

THE SECOND VICTORY Filmworld Distributors, 1987
STANLEY MYERS†

SECOND WIFE RKO Radio, 1936
ROY WEBB†

SECOND WIND Health and Entertainment Corporation of America, 1976
HAGOOD HARDY

THE SECOND WIFE 1997
CLIFF MARTINEZ

SECOND-HAND HEARTS Lorimar, 1980
WILLIS ALAN RAMSEY

SECONDLOJTNANTEN THE SECOND LIEUTENANT 1993
RANDALL MEYERS

SECONDS Paramount, 1966
JERRY GOLDSMITH

THE SECRET (TF) RHI Entertainment, 1992
FRED KARLIN

SECRET ADMIRER Orion, 1985
JAN HAMMER

THE SECRET AGENT 1996
PHILIP GLASS

THE SECRET AGENT Gaumont-British, 1936
LOUIS LEVY†

THE SECRET BEYOND THE DOOR Gaumont, 1982
PINO DONAGGIO

SECRET BEYOND THE DOOR Universal, 1948
MIKLOS ROZSA†

SECRET CEREMONY Universal, 1968
RICHARD RODNEY BENNETT

THE SECRET FILES OF J. EDGAR HOOVER American International, 1978
MIKLOS ROZSA†

SECRET FRIENDS 1991
NICHOLAS RUSSELL-PAVIER

THE SECRET FURY RKO Radio, 1950
ROY WEBB†

THE SECRET GARDEN MGM, 1949
BRONISLAU KAPER†

THE SECRET GARDEN Warner Bros., 1993
ZBIGNIEW PREISNER

THE SECRET GARDEN (TF) Norman Rosemont Productions, 1987
JOHN CAMERON

THE SECRET HEART MGM, 1946
BRONISLAU KAPER†

SECRET HONOR Sandcastle 5, 1984
GEORGE BURT

THE SECRET INVASION United Artists, 1964
HUGO FRIEDHOFER†

THE SECRET LAND (FD) MGM, 1948
BRONISLAU KAPER†

THE SECRET LIFE OF AN AMERICAN WIFE 20th Century-Fox, 1968
BILLY MAY

THE SECRET LIFE OF IAN FLEMING (CTF) Saban/Scherick Productions, 1990
CARL DAVIS

THE SECRET LIFE OF JOHN CHAPMAN (TF) The Jozak Company, 1976
FRED MYROW

THE SECRET LIFE OF PLANTS (FD) Paramount, 1978
STEVIE WONDER

THE SECRET LIFE OF WALTER MITTY RKO Radio, 1947
DAVID RAKSIN

THE SECRET NIGHT CALLER (TF) Charles Fries Productions/Penthouse Productions, 1975
JOHN PARKER

THE SECRET OF CONVICT LAKE 20th Century-Fox, 1951
SOL KAPLAN

THE SECRET OF DR. ALUCARD Creative Film Enterprises, 1967
LARRY WELLINGTON

THE SECRET OF LIFE (TD) WGBH/BBC, 1993
JOHN KUSIAC
CALEB SAMPSON

THE SECRET OF MADAME BLANCHE MGM, 1933
WILLIAM AXT†

THE SECRET OF MY SUCCESS MGM, 1965
CHRISTOPHER L. STONE

THE SECRET OF MY SUCCESS Universal, 1987
DAVID FOSTER

THE SECRET OF NIMH (AF) MGM/UA, 1982
JERRY GOLDSMITH

THE SECRET OF ROAN INISH Jones Entertainment Group, 1994
MASON DARING

THE SECRET OF SANTA VITTORIA United Artists, 1969
ERNEST GOLD ★

THE SECRET OF THE LENS Harmony Gold Prods., 1989
PETER DAVISON

SECRET OF DEEP HARBOR United Artists, 1961
RICHARD LASALLE

SECRET OF THE INCAS Warner Bros., 1954
DAVID BUTTOLPH†

SECRET OF THE SAHARA 1987
ENNIO MORRICONE

THE SECRET PASSION OF ROBERT CLAYTON (CTF) Producers Entertainment Group/Wilshire Court Prods., 1992
NICHOLAS PIKE

SECRET PLACES TLC Films/20th Century-Fox, 1984
MICHEL LEGRAND

THE SECRET RAPTURE 1993
RICHARD HARTLEY

SECRET SCROLLS Toho, 1957
AKIRA IFUKUBE

SECRET SERVICE RKO Radio, 1931
MAX STEINER†

SECRET SINS OF THE FATHER (TF) Ultra Ent./Dick Clark Film Group, 1994
JON GILUTIN
KENNY EDWARDS

THE SECRET WAR OF HARRY FRIGG Universal, 1968
CARLO RUSTICHELLI

THE SECRET WAR OF JACKIE'S GIRLS (TF) Public Arts Productions/Penthouse Productions/Universal TV, 1980
FRED KARLIN

THE SECRET WAYS Universal, 1961
JOHN WILLIAMS

SECRET WEAPONS (TF) Goodman-Rosen Productions/ITC Productions, 1985
CHARLES BERNSTEIN

SECRET WITNESS (TF) Just Greene Productions/CBS Entertainment Productions, 1988
ROBERT DRASNIN

THE SECRET WORLD OF DREAMS (TD) Nash Prods./DBA Ent., 1995
SCOOTER PIETSCH

SECRETS 1942
ARTHUR HONEGGER†

SECRETS Lone Star, 1971
MICHAEL GIBBS

SECRETS Samuel Goldwyn Company, 1983
GUY WOOLFENDEN

SECRETS United Artists, 1933
ALFRED NEWMAN†

SECRETS (TF) Dorothea G. Petrie Prods./Signboard Hill/Robert Halmi Ent., 1995
LAWRENCE SHRAGGE

SECRETS (TF) The Jozak Company, 1977
GEORGE ALICESON TIPTON

SECRETS AND LIES 1996
ANDREW DICKSON

SECRETS D'ALCOVE 1954
GEORGES VAN PARYS†

THE SECRETS OF LAKE SUCCESS (MS) Cramer Co./NBC Prods., 1993
HAL LINDES

SECRETS OF A MARRIED MAN (TF) ITC Productions, 1984
MARK SNOW

SECRETS OF A MOTHER AND DAUGHTER (TF) The Shpetner Company/Sunrise Productions, 1983
JOHN RUBINSTEIN

SECRETS OF A SECRETARY Paramount, 1931
JOHN GREEN†

SECRETS OF A SORORITY GIRL Producers Releasing Corp., 1946
KARL HAJOS†

SECRETS OF THE FRENCH POLICE RKO Radio, 1932
MAX STEINER†

SECRETS OF THE UNDERGROUND Republic, 1943
WALTER SCHARF

SECRETS OF THREE HUNGRY WIVES (TF) Penthouse Productions, 1978
JOHN PARKER

SECRETS OF WOMEN Janus, 1952
ERIC NORDGREN

SEDDOK, L'EREDE DI SATANA 1961
ARMANDO TROVAJOLI

SEDOTTI E BIDONATI 1964
CARLO RUSTICHELLI

SEDUCE AND DESTROY 1973
NICHOLAS CARRAS

SEDUCED (TF) Catalina Production Group/Comworld Productions, 1985
PATRICK WILLIAMS ☆

SEDUCED AND ABANDONED Continental, 1964
CARLO RUSTICHELLI

SEDUCED AND BETRAYED (TF) von Zerneck-Sertner, 1995
MARK SNOW

SEDUCED BY EVIL (CTF) CNM Entertainment/Cinestage Prods./Wilshire Court, 1994
GEORGE S. CLINTON

A SEDUCTION IN TRAVIS COUNTY (TF) David Braun Productions/Co-Star Entertainment/Zev Braun Pictures/New World TV, 1991
JOHN DEBNEY

THE SEDUCTION OF GINA (TF) Bertinelli-Jaffee Productions, 1984
THOMAS NEWMAN

THE SEDUCTION OF JOE TYNAN Universal, 1979
BILL CONTI

THE SEDUCTION OF MIMI MIMI METALLURGICO FERITO NELL'ONORE New Line Cinema, 1972
PIERO PICCIONI

THE SEDUCTION OF MISS LEONA (TF) Edgar J. Scherick Associates, 1980
ROBERT PRINCE

THE SEDUCTION Avco Embassy, 1981
LALO SCHIFRIN

SEDUCTION Gemini, 1973
LUIS BACALOV

SEDUCTION: THREE TALES FROM THE INNER SANCTUM (TF) Carroll Newman Prods./Victoria Principal Prods./Polone Co./Hearst Entertainment, 1992
JAMES DIPASQUALLE

SEE HOW SHE RUNS (TF) CLN Productions, 1978
JIMMIE HASKELL ☆☆

SEE HOW THEY RUN (TF) Universal TV, 1964
LALO SCHIFRIN

SEE JANE RUN (TF) Avenue Pictures/Hearst, 1995
JAMES DIPASQUALLE

SEE MY LAWYER Universal, 1945
HANS J. SALTER†

SEE NO EVIL Columbia, 1971
ELMER BERNSTEIN

SEE NO EVIL, HEAR NO EVIL Tri-Star, 1989
STEWART COPELAND

SEE THE MAN RUN (TF) Universal TV, 1971
DAVID SHIRE

SEE YOU IN THE MORNING Warner Bros., 1989
MICHAEL SMALL

SEE YOU TOMORROW 1960
CHRISTOPHER KOMEDA†

THE SEED OF MAN SRL, 1970
TEO USUELLI

THE SEEDING OF SARAH BURNS (TF) Michael Klein Productions/Papazian Productions, 1979
JIMMIE HASKELL

SEEDS OF EVIL THE GARDENER KKI Films, 1981
MARC FREDERICKS

SEEDS OF TRAGEDY (TF) Sanford-Pillsbury Prods./FNM Films, 1991
GERALD GOURIET

SEEING THE WORLD: A VISIT TO NEW YORK Rudolph Burckhardt, 1936
PAUL BOWLES

THE SEEKERS Universal TV, 1978
GERALD FRIED

SEEMS LIKE OLD TIMES Columbia, 1980
MARVIN HAMLISCH

SEI DONNE PER L'ASSASSINO 1964
CARLO RUSTICHELLI

SEIZE THE DAY (TF) Learning in Focus, 1986
ELIZABETH SWADOS

SEIZURE: THE STORY OF KATHY MORRIS (TF)
The Jozak Company, 1980
GEORGE ALICESON TIPTON

SELECTED EXITS (TF) 1993
JOHN ALTMAN

SELENA Warner Bros., 1997
RANDY EDELMAN
DAVE GRUSIN

THE SELFISH GIANT (AF) Readers Digest, 1971
RON GOODWIN

THE SELLOUT MGM, 1951
DAVID BUTTOLPH†

SEMI-TOUGH United Artists, 1978
JERRY FIELDING†

THE SENATOR WAS INDISCREET Universal, 1947
DANIELE AMFITHEATROF†

THE SENATOR'S SNAILS *SENATORUL MELCILOR* 1995
PETRE MARGINEANU

SENATORUL MELCILOR 1995
PETRE MARGINEANU

SEND ME NO FLOWERS Universal, 1964
FRANK DEVOL

THE SENDER Paramount, 1982
TREVOR JONES

SENGOKU JIEITAL *TIME SLIP* Toei, 1981
KENTARO HANEDA

SENILITA Zebra Film/Aera Film, 1961
PIERO PICCIONI

SENIOR TRIP (TF) Kenneth Johnson Productions, 1981
JOE HARNELL

SENIOR YEAR (TF) Universal TV, 1974
JAMES DIPASQUALLE

SENKIFOLDJE *WHY WASN'T HE THERE?* 1993
LASZLO MELIS

SENSATION MDP, 1994
ARTHUR KEMPEL

SENSEI *THE TEACHER* Daiei, 1983
MASARU SATO

A SENSITIVE, PASSIONATE MAN (TF)
Factor-Newland Production Corporation, 1977
BILL CONTI

THE SENSUOUS SICILIAN *PAOLO IL CALDO* 1973
ARMANDO TROVAJOLI

SENTIMENTAL JOURNEY 20th Century-Fox, 1946
CYRIL J. MOCKRIDGE†

SENTIMENTAL JOURNEY (TF) Lucille Ball
Productions/Smith-Richmond Productions/20th
Century Fox TV, 1984
BILLY GOLDENBERG
JACK ELLIOTT

THE SENTINEL Universal, 1977
GIL MELLE

SENZA BUCCIA *WITHOUT SKIN* 1979
PINO DONAGGIO

SENZA PIETA 1948
NINO ROTA†

SENZA SAPERE NIENTE DI LEI 1968
ENNIO MORRICONE

SEPARATE BUT EQUAL (TF) New Liberty Prods./
Republic, 1991
CARL DAVIS

A SEPARATE PEACE Paramount, 1972
CHARLES FOX

SEPARATE TABLES United Artists, 1958
DAVID RAKSIN ★

SEPARATE VACATIONS RSL Entertainment, 1986
STANLEY MYERS†

SEPARATE WAYS Crown International, 1981
JOHN CACAVAS

SEPARATED BY MURDER (TF) Larry Thompson
Ent./CBS, 1994
RICHARD MARVIN

SEPOLTA VIVA 1973
ENNIO MORRICONE

SEPPUKU Shochiku, 1963
TORU TAKEMITSU†

SEPT MORTS SUR ORDONNANCE 1976
PHILIPPE SARDE

SEPTEMBER AFFAIR Paramount, 1950
VICTOR YOUNG†

SEPTEMBER GUN (TF) QM Productions, 1983
LARRY CANSLER

SEQUENCES OF FEELING 1993
JERZY SATANOWSKI

SEQUESTRO DI PERSONA 1968
RIZ ORTOLANI

SEQUOIA MGM, 1935
HERBERT STOTHART†

SERAFINO Royal Films International, 1968
CARLO RUSTICHELLI

SERAIL 1975
MICHEL PORTAL

SERENGETI SHALL NOT DIE 1960
WOLFGANG ZELLER†

SERGEANT DEADHEAD *SERGEANT DEADHEAD, THE ASTRONAUT* American International, 1965
LES BAXTER†

SERGEANT DEADHEAD, THE ASTRONAUT
American International, 1965
LES BAXTER†

SERGEANT MADDEN MGM, 1939
WILLIAM AXT†

SERGEANT MATLOVICH VS. THE U.S. AIR FORCE (TF) Tomorrow Entertainment, 1978
TEO MACERO

SERGEANT RYKER *THE CASE AGAINST PAUL RYKER* Universal, 1968
JOHN WILLIAMS

SERGEANT STEINER Maverick Pictures International, 1978
PETER THOMAS

SERGEANT YORK Warner Bros., 1941
MAX STEINER† ★

SERGEANTS 3 United Artists, 1962
BILLY MAY

SERGIO LEONE'S COLT (MS) 1993
ENNIO MORRICONE

SERIAL Paramount, 1980
LALO SCHIFRIN

SERIAL MOM Savoy, 1994
BASIL POLEDOURIS

THE SERPENT *NIGHT FLIGHT TO MOSCOW*
Avco Embassy, 1973
ENNIO MORRICONE

THE SERPENT AND THE RAINBOW Universal, 1988
BRAD FIEDEL

THE SERPENT'S EGG Paramount, 1978
ROLF WILHELM

THE SERPENT'S TALE 1993
BLAKE LEYH

SERPICO Paramount, 1973
MIKIS THEODORAKIS

SERPICO: THE DEADLY GAME (TF) Dino De
Laurentiis Productions/Paramount TV, 1976
ELMER BERNSTEIN

THE SERVANT Landau, 1964
JOHN DANKWORTH

THE SERVANTS OF TWILIGHT *DEAN R. KOONTZ'S SERVANTS OF TWILIGHT (CTF)*
Trimark/Gibraltar, 1991
JIM MANZIE

SERVING IN SILENCE: THE MARGARETHE CAMMERMEYER STORY (TF) Barwood Films/
Storyline Prods./Trillium Prods./TriStar, 1995
DAVID SHIRE

SESAME STREET PRESENTS: FOLLOW THAT BIRD Warner Bros., 1985
LENNIE NIEHAUS
VAN DYKE PARKS

SESSIONS (TF) Roger Gimbel Productions/EMI TV/
Sarabande Productions, 1983
CHARLES GROSS

SESSO IN CONFESSIONALE 1973
ENNIO MORRICONE

SESSO MATTO 1974
ARMANDO TROVAJOLI

SET IT OFF New Line, 1996
CHRISTOPHER YOUNG

SET THIS TOWN ON FIRE (TF) Public Arts
Productions/Universal TV, 1973
PETE RUGOLO

SETTE CONTRO LA MORTE 1964
CARLO RUSTICHELLI

SETTE CONTRO TUTTI 1966
FRANCESCO DE MASI

SETTE DOLLARI SUL ROSSO 1966
FRANCESCO DE MASI

SETTE DONNE PER I MACGREGOR 1967
ENNIO MORRICONE

SETTE PISTOLE PER I MACGREGOR 1965
ENNIO MORRICONE

SETTE SCIALLI DI SETA GIALLA Italian
MANUEL DE SICA

SETTE UOMINI D'ORO 1965
ARMANDO TROVAJOLI

THE SETTING SUN *TOKYO BLACKOUT* 1991
MAURICE JARRE

SETTLE THE SCORE (TF) Steve Sohmer Productions/
ITC, 1989
MARK SNOW

SEVEN New Line, 1995
HOWARD SHORE

SEVEN ALONE Doty-Dayton, 1975
ROBERT O. RAGLAND

SEVEN BEAUTIES *PASQUALINO SETTEBELLEZZE* Cinema 5, 1976
ENZO JANNACCI

SEVEN BRIDES FOR SEVEN BROTHERS MGM, 1954
ADOLPH DEUTSCH† ★★

SEVEN CAPITAL SINS Embassy, 1962
MICHEL LEGRAND

SEVEN CITIES OF GOLD 20th Century-Fox, 1955
HUGO FRIEDHOFER†

SEVEN DAYS IN MAY Paramount, 1964
JERRY GOLDSMITH

SEVEN DAYS TO NOON Mayer-Kingsley, 1950
JOHN ADDISON

SEVEN DAYS' LEAVE RKO Radio, 1942
ROY WEBB†

SEVEN DEADLY SINS Embassy, 1962
PIERRE JANSEN

THE SEVEN FACES OF DR. LAO MGM, 1964
LEIGH HARLINE†

SEVEN GOLDEN MEN *SETTE UOMINI D'ORO*
1965
ARMANDO TROVAJOLI

SEVEN GRAVES FOR ROGAN Almi Films, 1983
ENNIO MORRICONE
ROBERT O. RAGLAND

SEVEN GUNS TO MESA Allied Artists, 1958
LEITH STEVENS†

SEVEN HOMMES ET UNE GARCE 1966
PAUL MISRAKI

SEVEN HORSE OF THE SUN 1994
VANRAJ BHATIA

SEVEN HOURS OF GUNFIRE 1965
ANGELO FRANCESCO LAVAGNINO†

SEVEN HOURS TO JUDGMENT Trans World
Entertainment, 1988
JOHN DEBNEY

SEVEN MILES FROM ALCATRAZ RKO Radio, 1943
ROY WEBB†

THE SEVEN MINUTES 20th Century-Fox, 1971
STU PHILLIPS

SEVEN MINUTES IN HEAVEN Warner Bros., 1986
ROBERT KRAFT

SEVEN NIGHTS IN JAPAN Paramount, 1976
DAVID HENTSCHEL

THE SEVEN PER CENT SOLUTION Universal, 1976
JOHN ADDISON

SEVEN SAMURAI Landmark Releasing, 1954
FUMIO HAYASAKA†

SEVEN SEAS TO CALAIS *IL DOMINATORE DEI SETTE MARI* MGM, 1962
FRANCO MANNINO

SEVEN SINNERS 1936
LOUIS LEVY†

SEVEN SINNERS Universal, 1940
CHARLES PREVIN†
HANS J. SALTER†.
FRANK SKINNER†

SEVEN SWEETHEARTS MGM, 1942
FRANZ WAXMAN†

SEVEN THIEVES 20th Century-Fox, 1960
DOMINIC FRONTIERE

THE SEVEN UPS 20th Century-Fox, 1973
DON ELLIS†

SEVEN WAYS FROM SUNDOWN Universal, 1960
WILLIAM LAVA†

SEVEN WOMEN MGM, 1965
ELMER BERNSTEIN

SEVEN WOMEN FROM HELL 20th Century-Fox, 1961
PAUL DUNLAP

SEVEN WONDERS OF THE WORLD Stanley
Warner Cinema Corporation, 1956
JEROME MOROSS†
DAVID RAKSIN

THE SEVEN YEAR ITCH 20th Century-Fox, 1955
ALFRED NEWMAN†

SEVENTH AVENUE (MS) Universal TV, 1977
NELSON RIDDLE†

SEVENTH CAVALRY Columbia, 1956
MISCHA BAKALEINIKOFF†

THE SEVENTH CROSS MGM, 1944
ROY WEBB†

THE SEVENTH DAWN United Artists, 1964
RIZ ORTOLANI

SEVENTH HEAVEN 20th Century-Fox, 1937
LOUIS SILVERS†

SEVENTH HEAVEN Fox, 1927
R. H. BASSETT†

THE SEVENTH SEAL Janus, 1957
ERIC NORDGREN

THE SEVENTH SIGN Tri-Star, 1988
JACK NITZCHE

THE SEVENTH SIN MGM, 1957
MIKLOS ROZSA†

THE SEVENTH VEIL Universal, 1945
BENJAMIN FRANKEL†

THE SEVENTH VICTIM RKO Radio, 1943
ROY WEBB†

THE SEVENTH VOYAGE OF SINBAD Columbia, 1958
BERNARD HERRMANN†

SEVERANCE Fox/Lorber Films, 1989
DANIEL MAY

A SEVERED HEAD Columbia, 1971
STANLEY MYERS†

SEX AND THE MARRIED WOMAN (TF) Universal
TV, 1977
GERALD FRIED

SEX AND THE SILVER SCREEN (CMS) ZM Prods., 1995
LAURA KARPMAN

SEX AND THE SINGLE GIRL Warner Bros., 1965
NEAL HEFTI

SEX AND THE SINGLE PARENT (TF) Time-Life
Productions, 1979
FRED KARLIN

SEX CHARADE 1970
BRUNO NICOLAI

THE SEX LIFE OF THE COMMON FILM Rudolph
Burckhardt, 1938
PAUL BOWLES

SEX PLAY 1974
JOHN CAMERON

THE SEX SYMBOL (TF) The Douglas Cramer
Company/Columbia Pictures TV, 1974
JEFF ALEXANDER†

THE SEX THIEF 1974
MICHAEL VICKERS

SEX, LIES AND VIDEOTAPE Outlaw Productions, 1989
CLIFF MARTINEZ

SEX, LOVE AND COLD HARD CASH (CTF)
Citadel/MTE, 1993
JOHN E. KEANE

SEXE FAIBLE 1992
ALEXANDRE DESPLAT

SEXTETTE Crown International, 1978
ARTIE BUTLER

SFIDA AL RE DI CASTIGLIA 1964
CARLO SAVINA

S.F.W. Gramercy, 1994
GRAEME REVELL

SGT. BILKO Universal, 1996
ALAN SILVESTRI

SHACK OUT ON 101 Allied Artists, 1955
PAUL DUNLAP

SHADEY Skouras Pictures, 1986
COLIN TOWNS

THE SHADOW Universal, 1994
JERRY GOLDSMITH

THE SHADOW BOX (TF) The Shadow Box Film
Company, 1980
HENRY MANCINI†

THE SHADOW CONSPIRACY Buena Vista, 1997
BRUCE BROUGHTON

SHADOW DANCE 1983
GABRIEL YARED

SHADOW DANCING Shapiro Glickenhaus
Entertainment, 1988
JAY GRUSKA

SHADOW HUNTER (CTF) Republic/Sandstorm, 1993
ROBERT FOLK

A SHADOW IN THE STREETS (TF) Playboy
Productions, 1975
CHARLES BERNSTEIN

SHADOW IN THE SKY MGM, 1951
BRONISLAU KAPER†

THE SHADOW OF THE CAT 1961
MIKIS THEODORAKIS

SHADOW OF A DOUBT Universal, 1943
DIMITRI TIOMKIN†

SHADOW OF A DOUBT (TF) Rosemont, 1991
ALLYN FERGUSON

SHADOW OF A STRANGER (TF) Doris Keating
Prods./NBC Prods., 1992
GARY CHANG

SHADOW OF A WOMAN Warner Bros., 1946
ADOLPH DEUTSCH†

SHADOW OF CHINA New Line, 1991
YASHUAKI SHIMIZU

SHADOW OF FEAR *BEFORE I WAKE* 1956
LEONARD SALZEDO

SHADOW OF OBSESSION (TF) Saban, 1994
UDI HARPAZ

SHADOW OF TERROR Producers Releasing Corp., 1945
KARL HAJOS†

SHADOW OF THE DRAGON Hatch Entertainment, 1994
JOHN AUTHOR
MICHAEL BENGHIAT

SHADOW OF THE PAST 1950
STANLEY BLACK

SHADOW OF THE WOLF Triumph, 1993
MAURICE JARRE

SHADOW ON THE LAND (TF) Screen Gems/
Columbia Pictures TV, 1968
SOL KAPLAN

SHADOW ON THE WALL MGM, 1950
ANDRE PREVIN

SHADOW OVER ELVERON (TF) Universal TV, 1968
LEONARD ROSENMAN

THE SHADOW RIDERS (TF) Pegasus Group Ltd./
Columbia Pictures TV, 1982
JERROLD IMMEL

SHADOWBUILDER Imperial, 1997
GUY ZERAFA

SHADOWLANDS Savoy, 1993
GEORGE FENTON

SHADOWS OF A HOT SUMMER 1978
ZDENEK LISKA

SHADOWS OF DESIRE (TF) Konigsberg Co., 1994
MARK SNOW

SHADOWS OF THE PEACOCK Castle Hill
Productions/Quartet Films, 1987
WILLIAM MOTZIG

SHADY LADY Universal, 1945
MILTON ROSEN†

SHAFT IN AFRICA MGM, 1973
JOHNNY PATE

SHAFT'S BIG SCORE MGM, 1972
ISAAC HAYES

SHAFTH MGM, 1971
ISAAC HAYES

THE SHAGGY D.A. Buena Vista, 1976
BUDDY BAKER

THE SHAGGY DOG Buena Vista, 1959
PAUL J. SMITH†

SHAKE HANDS WITH THE DEVIL United Artists,
1959
WILLIAM ALWYN†

SHAKEDOWN Universal, 1988
JONATHAN ELIAS

SHAKEDOWN ON THE SUNSET STRIP (TF) CBS
Entertainment, 1988
LALO SCHIFRIN

SHAKER RUN Challenge Film Corporation, 1985
STEPHEN MCCURDY

SHAKESPEARE IN THE PARK SIP Productions,
1994
GREG O'CONNOR

SHAKESPEARE WALLAH Continental, 1966
SATYAJIT RAY†

THE SHAKIEST GUN IN THE WEST Universal,
1968
VIC MIZZY

SHALAKO Dimitri De Grunwald, 1968
ROBERT FARNON

SHALLOW GRAVE Gramercy, 1994
SIMON BOSWELL

SHAME (CTF) Dalrymple Prods./Steinhardt Baer
Pictures/Viacom, 1992
DAVID MCHUGH

SHAME II: THE SECRET (CTF) Viacom/Lifetime TV,
1995
JEFF FAIR
STARR PARODI

SHAMEFUL SECRETS (TF) Steve White Films/ABC,
1993
ALLAN K. ROSEN

THE SHAMROCK CONSPIRACY (TF) Crescendo
Prods./Michael Gleason Prods./Paramount TV, 1995
KEN HARRISON

SHAMROCK HILL Eagle Lion, 1949
HERSCHEL BURKE GILBERT

SHAMUS Columbia, 1973
JERRY GOLDSMITH

SHANE Paramount, 1953
VICTOR YOUNG†

SHANGHAI Paramount, 1935
FREDERICK HOLLANDER†

SHANGHAI EXPRESS Paramount, 1932
W. FRANKE HARLING†

THE SHANGHAI GESTURE United Artists, 1942
RICHARD HAGEMAN† ★

SHANGHAI SURPRISE MGM/UA, 1986
GEORGE HARRISON
MICHAEL KAMEN

SHANGHAI TRIAD *YAO A YAO YAO DAO
WAIPO QIAO* Sony Classics, 1995
ZHANG GUANGTIAN

SHANKS Paramount, 1974
ALEX NORTH† ★

SHANNON'S DEAL (TF) Stan Rogaw Productions/
NBC Productions, 1989
WYNTON MARSALIS

SHANTYTOWN Republic, 1943
WALTER SCHARF

THE SHAPE OF THE WORLD (TD) Grenada/WNET,
1991
RICHARD HARVEY

THE SHAPE OF THINGS TO COME Film Ventures
International, 1979
PAUL HOFFERT

SHARAKU 1995
TORU TAKEMITSU†

SHARING RICHARD (TF) Houston Motion Picture
Entertainment/CBS Entertainment, 1988
MICHAEL MELVOIN

SHARK KILL (TF) D'Antoni-Weitz Productions, 1976
GEORGE ROMANIS

SHARK'S TREASURE United Artists, 1975
ROBERT O. RAGLAND

THE SHARKFIGHTERS United Artists, 1956
JEROME MOROSS†

SHARMA AND BEYOND Cinecom International,
1986
RACHEL PORTMAN

SHARON: PORTRAIT OF A MISTRESS (TF)
Moonlight Productions/Paramount Pictures TV, 1977
ROGER KELLAWAY

SHATTERED 1972
ROY BUDD†

SHATTERED MGM-Pathe, 1991
ALAN SILVESTRI

SHATTERED (TF) 1995
JOHN FRIZZELL

SHATTERED DREAMS (TF) Roger Gimbel
Productions/Carolco TV, 1990
MICHAEL CONVERTINO

SHATTERED IMAGE Arjay Productions, 1994
STEVE EDWARDS

SHATTERED INNOCENCE (TF) Green-Epstein
Productions/Lorimar TV, 1987
RICHARD BELLIS

SHATTERED SPIRITS (TF) Sheen-Greenblatt
Productions/Robert Greenwald Productions, 1986
MICHAEL HOENIG

**SHATTERED TRUST: THE SHARI KARNEY STORY
(TF)** Heartstar Prods./Spectacor/Michael Jaffe
Films, 1993
MICKEY ERBE
MARYBETH SOLOMON

SHATTERED VOWS (TF) Bertinelli-Pequod
Productions, 1984
LEE HOLDRIDGE

THE SHAWSHANK REDEMPTION Columbia, 1994
THOMAS NEWMAN ★

SHE American National Enterprises, 1983
RICK WAKEMAN

SHE MGM, 1965
JAMES BERNARD

SHE RKO Radio, 1935
MAX STEINER†

SHE (TF) Martin Bregman Productions, 1980
MICHAEL KAMEN

SHE AND HE 1969
ENNIO MORRICONE

SHE COULDN'T SAY NO RKO Radio, 1953
ROY WEBB†

THE SHE CREATURE American International, 1956
RONALD STEIN†

SHE DEVIL 20th Century-Fox, 1957
PAUL SAWTELL†
BERT A. SHEFTER

SHE DEVIL Orion, 1989
HOWARD SHORE

SHE GODS OF SHARK REEF American
International, 1957
RONALD STEIN†

SHE KNOWS TOO MUCH (TF) The Fred Silverman
Company/Finnegan-Pinchuk Productions/MGM TV,
1989
ALF CLAUSEN

SHE LOVES ME NOT Paramount, 1934
SIGMUND KRUMGOLD†

SHE PLAYED WITH FIRE Columbia, 1958
WILLIAM ALWYN†

SHE SAID NO (TF) Steve White, 1990
CHARLES BERNSTEIN

SHE SAYS SHE'S INNOCENT (TF) Robert
Greenwald Prods., 1991
GREG DE BELLES

SHE STOOD ALONE (TF) Mighty Fortress Prods./
Walt Disney TV, 1991
MICHAEL J. LEWIS

**SHE STOOD ALONE: THE TAILHOOK SCANDAL
(TF)** Harry Winer Prods./Symphony Prods./ABC,
1995
PETER BERNSTEIN

SHE WAITS (TF) Metromedia Productions, 1972
MORTON STEVENS†

SHE WAS MARKED FOR MURDER (TF) Jack
Grossbart Productions, 1988
NAN SCHWARTZ-MISHKIN

SHE WENT TO THE RACES MGM, 1945
NATHANIEL SHILKRET†

SHE WOKE UP (TF) Empty Chair AProductions,
1992
CHRISTOPHER FRANKE

SHE WORE A YELLOW RIBBON RKO Radio, 1949
RICHARD HAGEMAN†

SHE'LL BE WEARING PINK PAJAMAS Film Four
International, 1985
JOHN DUPREZ

SHE'S A SOLDIER, TOO Columbia, 1944
MARIO †

SHE'S BACK Vestron, 1989
JIMMIE HASKELL

SHE'S BEEN AWAY BBC Films, 1989
RICHARD HARTLEY

SHE'S DANGEROUS Universal, 1937
DAVID RAKSIN

SHE'S DRESSED TO KILL (TF) Grant-Case-McGrath
Enterprises/Barry Weitz Films, 1979
GEORGE ROMANIS

SHE'S GOTTA HAVE IT Island Pictures, 1986
BILL LEE

SHE'S HAVING A BABY Paramount, 1988
STEWART COPELAND
NICKY HOLLAND

SHE'S IN THE ARMY NOW (TF) ABC Circle Films,
1981
ARTIE BUTLER

SHE'S OUT OF CONTROL Columbia/WEG, 1989
ALAN SILVESTRI

SHE'S THE ONE 20th Century Fox, 1996
TOM PETTY

SHE-DEVILS ON WHEELS 1968
HERSCHELL GORDON LEWIS

SHEENA Columbia, 1984
RICHARD HARTLEY

THE SHEEP HAS FIVE LEGS United Motion Picture
Organization, 1954
GEORGES VAN PARYS†

THE SHEEPMAN MGM, 1958
JEFF ALEXANDER†

**SHEILA LEVINE IS DEAD AND LIVING IN NEW
YORK** Paramount, 1975
MICHEL LEGRAND

SHELF LIFE 1993
ANDY PALEY

THE SHELL SEEKERS (TF) Marian Rees Associates/
Central TV, 1989
JAMES DIPASQUALLE ☆

**SHELLEY DUVALL'S FAERIE TALE THEATRE
(CTF)** Platypus Prods./Think Prods., 1984
PETER DAVISON

THE SHELTERING SKY Warner Bros., 1990
RICHARD HOROWITZ
RYUICHI SAKAMOTO

SHENANDOAH Universal, 1965
FRANK SKINNER†

SHENANIGANS Warner Bros., 1978
ARTHUR B. RUBINSTEIN

THE SHERIFF (TF) Screen Gems/Columbia Pictures
TV, 1971
DOMINIC FRONTIERE

THE SHERIFF OF FRACTURED JAW 20th
Century-Fox, 1959
ROBERT FARNON

SHERLOCK HOLMES Fox, 1932
R. H. BASSETT†
HUGO FRIEDHOFER†

**SHERLOCK HOLMES AND THE SECRET
WEAPON** Universal, 1943
HANS J. SALTER†
FRANK SKINNER†

SHERLOCK HOLMES AND THE SPIDER WOMAN
Universal, 1944
HANS J. SALTER†

**SHERLOCK HOLMES AND THE VOICE OF
TERROR** Universal
FRANK SKINNER†

SHERLOCK HOLMES FACES DEATH Universal,
1943
HANS J. SALTER†

SHERLOCK HOLMES IN NEW YORK (TF) 20th
Century-Fox TV, 1976
RICHARD RODNEY BENNETT

SHERLOCK HOLMES IN WASHINGTON Universal,
1943
FRANK SKINNER†

SHE-WOLF OF LONDON Universal, 1946
WILLIAM LAVA†

SHIAWASE 1975
TORU TAKEMITSU†

THE SHIEK
ROGER BELLON

SHIELD FOR MURDER United Artists, 1954
PAUL DUNLAP

**THE SHILLINGBURY BLOWERS ...AND THE
BAND PLAYED ON** Inner Circle, 1980
ED WELCH

SHILOH Overseas Film Group, 1997
JOEL GOLDSMITH

SHIMMER American Playhouse, 1993
TODD BOEKELHEIDE

SHINE Fine Line, 1996
DAVID HIRSHFELDER ★

SHINE ON, HARVEST MOON Warner Bros., 1944
HEINZ ROEMHELD†

THE SHINING Warner Bros., 1980
WENDY CARLOS

THE SHINING (TF) Warner Bros. TV, 1997
NICHOLAS PIKE

THE SHINING HOUR MGM, 1938
FRANZ WAXMAN†

A SHINING SEASON (TF) Green-Epstein
Productions/T-M Productions/Columbia TV, 1979
RICHARD BELLIS

SHINING THROUGH 20th Century Fox, 1992
MICHAEL KAMEN

SHINING VICTORY Warner Bros., 1941
MAX STEINER†

SHIP OF FOOLS Columbia, 1965
ERNEST GOLD

THE SHIP THAT DIED OF SHAME *P.T.
RAIDERS* Continental, 1955
WILLIAM ALWYN†

THE SHIRALEE 1956
MATYAS SEIBER

THE SHIRALEE MGM, 1957
JOHN ADDISON

THE SHIRALEE (MS) SAFC Productions, 1988
CHRIS NEAL

SHIRLEY VALENTINE Paramount, 1989
GEORGE HATZINASSIOS
WILLY RUSSELL

SHIRTLESS SOUL Bergersen Films, 1992
PETER HOWARD FOSSO

SHIRTS/SKINS (TF) MGM TV, 1973
JERRY FIELDING

SHOCK 20th Century-Fox, 1946
DAVID BUTTOLPH†

SHOCK CORRIDOR Allied Artists, 1963
PAUL DUNLAP

SHOCK TO THE SYSTEM Corsair, 1990
GARY CHANG

SHOCK TREATMENT 20th Century-Fox, 1964
JERRY GOLDSMITH

SHOCK TREATMENT 20th Century-Fox, 1981
RICHARD HARTLEY

SHOCK WAVES *DEATH CORPS.* Joseph Brenner
Associates, 1977
RICHARD EINHORN

SHOCK'EM DEAD Noma, 1991
ROBERT DECKER

SHOCKER Universal, 1989
WILLIAM GOLDSTEIN

SHOCKING CANNIBALS Fury Films, 1974
ANGELO FRANCESCO LAVAGNINO†

THE SHOCKING MISS PILGRIM 20th Century-Fox,
1947
DAVID RAKSIN

SHOCKPROOF Columbia, 1949
GEORGE DUNING

THE SHOES OF THE FISHERMAN MGM, 1968
ALEX NORTH† ★

SHOGUN (MS) Paramount TV/NBC Entertainment,
1980
MAURICE JARRE

SHOGUN ASSASSIN New World, 1981
W. MICHAEL LEWIS
LAURIN RINDER

SHOGUN'S SHADOW Toei, 1989
MASARU SATO

SHOOT FIRST: A COP'S VENGEANCE (TF)
Harvey Khan Prods./Interscope, 1991
W.G. SNUFFY WALDEN

SHOOT FOR THE SUN (TF) BBC-TV, 1986
RAY COOPER
MICHAEL KAMEN

**SHOOT LOUD...LOUDER, I DON'T
UNDERSTAND** 1966
NINO ROTA†

SHOOT THE PIANO PLAYER *TIREZ SUR LE
PIANISTE* Astor, 1960
GEORGES DELERUE†

SHOOT TO KILL Buena Vista, 1988
JOHN SCOTT

SHOOTDOWN (TF) Leonard Hill Films, 1988
CRAIG SAFAN

SHOOTER (TF) UBU Productions/Paramount TV,
1988
PAUL CHIHARA

THE SHOOTERS Action International Pictures, 1990
TODD HAYEN

THE SHOOTING American International, 1966
RICHARD MARKOWITZ†

THE SHOOTING PARTY European Classics, 1984
JOHN SCOTT

SHOOTING STARS (TF) Aaron Spelling Productions,
1983
DOMINIC FRONTIERE

THE SHOOTIST Paramount, 1976
ELMER BERNSTEIN

SHOOT-OUT AT MEDICINE BEND Warner Bros.,
1957
ROY WEBB†

SHOOTOUT IN A ONE-DOG TOWN (TF)
Hanna-Barbera Productions, 1974
HOYT CURTIN

THE SHOP AROUND THE CORNER MGM, 1940
WERNER R. HEYMANN†

THE SHOP ON HIGH STREET 1965
ZDENEK LISKA

THE SHOP ON MAIN STREET *THE SHOP ON
HIGH STREET* 1965
ZDENEK LISKA

SHOPPING 1996
BARRINGTON PHELOUNG

SHOPPING Film Four International, 1994
BARRINGTON PHELOUNG

THE SHOPWORN ANGEL MGM, 1938
EDWARD WARD†

SHORS 1939
DMITRI KABALEVSKY†

SHORT CHANGED Greater Union, 1986
CHRIS NEAL

**F
I
L
M**

**T
I
T
L
E
S**

SINGLES Warner Bros., 1992
PAUL WESTERBERG

SINK THE BISMARK! 20th Century Fox, 1960
CLIFTON PARKER†

SINNER TAKE ALL MGM, 1936
EDWARD WARD†

SINS (MS) New World TV/The Greif-Dore Company/
Collins-Holm Productions, 1986
FRANCIS LAI
MICHEL LEGRAND

SINS OF CASANOVA 1954
ANGELO FRANCESCO LAVAGNINO†

SINS OF DESIRE Cinetel, 1992
CHUCK CIRINO

THE SINS OF DORIAN GRAY (TF) Rankin-Bass
Productions, 1983
BERNARD HOFFER

THE SINS OF LOLA MONTES Brandon, 1955
GEORGES AURIC†

SINS OF MAN 20th Century-Fox, 1936
R. H. BASSETT†

THE SINS OF RACHEL CADE Warner Bros., 1961
MAX STEINER†

SINS OF THE FATHER (TF) Fries Entertainment,
1985
SYLVESTER LEVAY

SINS OF THE FATHERS (CTF) Bavaria Atelier
GmbH/Taurus-Film/RAI/RETE, 1988
PEER RABEN

SINS OF THE PAST (TF) Sinpast Entertainment
Company Productions, 1984
ARTHUR B. RUBINSTEIN

SIR HENRY AT RAWLINSON END Charisma Films,
1980
VIVIAN STANSHALL

SIREN OF ATLANTIS United Artists, 1948
MICHEL MICHELET†

SIRENS Miramax, 1994
RACHEL PORTMAN

SIRGA 1993
SALIF KEITA

SIROCCO Columbia, 1951
GEORGE ANTHEIL†

THE SIROCCO BLOW *LE COUP DE SIROCCO*
1979
SERGE FRANKLIN

SISTEMO L'AMERICA E TORNO *I FIX AMERICA
AND RETURN* 1974
LUIS BACALOV

SISTER ACT Buena Vista, 1992
MARC SHAIMAN

SISTER ACT 2: BACK IN THE HABIT Buena Vista,
1993
MILES GOODMAN†
MARC SHAIMAN
MERVYN WARREN

SISTER KENNY RKO Radio, 1946
ALEXANDRE TANSMAN†

SISTER, SISTER New World, 1987
RICHARD EINHORN

SISTER, SISTER (TF) 20th Century-Fox TV, 1982
ALEX NORTH†

THE SISTER-IN-LAW (CTF) CNM Entertainment/
Wilshire Court, 1995
RICHARD BELLIS

THE SISTERS 1957
DMITRI KABALEVSKY†

THE SISTERS Warner Bros., 1938
MAX STEINER†

SISTERS American International, 1973
BERNARD HERRMANN†

THE SITTER (TF) FNM Films, 1991
LAURA KARPMAN

SITTING DUCKS Speciality Films, 1980
RICHARD ROMANUS

SITTING PRETTY 20th Century-Fox, 1948
ALFRED NEWMAN†

SITTING TARGET MGM, 1972
STANLEY MYERS†

SIVA Central Films, 1933
PAUL BOWLES

SIX AGAINST THE ROCK (TF)
Schaefer-Karpf-Epstein Productions/Gaylord
Production Company, 1987
WILLIAM GOLDSTEIN

SIX BRIDGES TO CROSS Universal, 1955
HERMAN STEIN

**SIX CHARACTERS IN SEARCH OF AN AUTHOR
(TF)** 1977
JERRY GOLDSMITH

SIX DEGREES OF SEPARATION MGM, 1993
JERRY GOLDSMITH

SIX PACK 20th Century Fox, 1982
CHARLES FOX

SIX WEEKS Universal, 1982
DUDLEY MOORE

THE SIX-MILLION DOLLAR MAN (TF) Universal
TV, 1973
GIL MELLE

SIXTEEN CANDLES Universal, 1984
IRA NEWBORN

SIXTH AND MAIN National Cinema, 1977
ROBERT SUMMERS

SIXTY GLORIOUS YEARS RKO Radio, 1938
ANTHONY COLLINS†

SIZZLE (TF) Aaron Spelling Productions, 1981
ARTIE BUTLER

THE SKATEBOARD KID II Amritraj Entertainment,
1994
CLAUDE GAUDETTE

SKATETOWN U.S.A. Rastar, 1978
JOHN BEAL

SKATETOWN, U.S.A. Columbia, 1979
MILES GOODMAN†

SKEEZER (TF) Margie-Lee Enterprises/The Blue
Marble Company/Marble Arch Productions, 1982
ARTHUR B. RUBINSTEIN

SKETCH ARTIST (CTF) Motion Picture Corp. of
America, 1992
MARK ISHAM

SKETCH ARTIST II: HANDS THAT SEE (CTF)
Motion Picture Corporation of America, 1995
TIM TRUMAN

SKETCHES MCEG, 1990
DAVID KITAY

SKI FEVER Allied Artists, 1969
JERRY STYNE

SKI LIFT TO DEATH (TF) The Jozak Company/
Paramount Pictures TV, 1978
BARRY DEVORZON

SKI PATROL Universal, 1940
HANS J. SALTER†

SKIN ART ITC, 1993
JAMES LEGG

SKIN DEEP 20th Century Fox, 1989
HENRY MANCINI†

SKIN GAME Warner Bros., 1971
DAVID SHIRE

SKINHEADS Amazing Movies, 1989
DAN SLIDER

SKINLESS NIGHT 1991
AKIRA KOBAYACHI

SKIPALONG ROSENBLOOM United Artists, 1951
IRVING GERTZ

SKIPPER National General, 1971
LEONARD ROSENMAN

THE SKIPPER SURPRISED HIS WIFE MGM, 1950
BRONISLAU KAPER†

THE SKULL Paramount, 1965
ELISABETH LUYTENS†

SKULLDUGGERY Universal, 1970
OLIVER NELSON†

SKY BANDITS Galaxy International, 1986
ALFI KABILJO

SKY DEVILS United Artists, 1932
ALFRED NEWMAN†

SKY GIANT RKO Radio, 1938
ROY WEBB†

SKY HEIST (TF) A J Fenady Associates/Warner Bros.
TV, 1975
LEONARD ROSENMAN

SKY HIGH Lippert, 1951
BERT A. SHEFTER

SKY PIRATES John Lamond Motion Pictures, 1986
BRIAN MAY†

SKY RIDERS 20th Century-Fox, 1976
LALO SCHIFRIN

SKY WEST AND CROOKED Rank/Continental,
1966
MALCOLM ARNOLD

THE SKY'S NO LIMIT (TF) Palance-Levy
Productions, 1983
MAURICE JARRE

THE SKY'S THE LIMIT RKO Radio, 1943
LEIGH HARLINE† ★

SKYJACKED MGM, 1972
PERRY BOTKIN

SKYLARK Paramount, 1941
VICTOR YOUNG†

SKYLARK (TF) Self/Trillium, 1993
DAVID SHIRE

SKYWARD (TF) Major H-Anson Productions, 1980
LEE HOLDRIDGE

SKYWAY TO DEATH (TF) Universal TV, 1974
LEE HOLDRIDGE

SLALOM 1965
ENNIO MORRICONE

SLAM DANCE Island Pictures, 1987
MITCHELL FROOM

SLAM DUNK ERNEST Buena Vista, 1996
MITCHELL FROOM

SLAMMER The Film League, 1977
CURTIS MAYFIELD

SLANDER MGM, 1956
JEFF ALEXANDER†

THE SLAP *LA GIFLE* 1974
GEORGES DELERUE†

SLAP SHOT Universal, 1977
ELMER BERNSTEIN

SLAPSTICK Entertainment Releasing Corporation/
International Film Marketing, 1983
MORTON STEVENS†

SLAPSTICK OF ANOTHER KIND *SLAPSTICK*
Entertainment Releasing Corporation/International
Film Marketing, 1983
MORTON STEVENS†

SLASH DANCE Glencoe Entertainment, 1989
EMILIO KAUDERER

SLATTERY'S HURRICANE 20th Century-Fox, 1949
CYRIL J. MOCKRIDGE†

SLAUGHTER ON TENTH AVENUE Universal, 1957
HERSCHEL BURKE GILBERT

THE SLAVE *IL FIGLIO DI SPARTACUS* 1962
PIERO PICCIONI

SLAVE GIRL Universal, 1947
MILTON ROSEN†

SLAVE GIRLS FROM BEYOND INFINITY Urban
Classics, 1987
CARL DANTE

A SLAVE OF LOVE Cinema 5, 1976
EDUARD ARTEMYEV

SLAVE SHIP 20th Century-Fox, 1937
ALFRED NEWMAN†

SLAVES OF NEW YORK Tri-Star, 1989
RICHARD ROBBINS

THE SLAYER 21st Century Distribution, 1982
ROBERT FOLK

SLAYGROUND Universal/AFD, 1983
COLIN TOWNS

SLEEP WELL, MY LOVE Planbourg Films, 1987
ALFI KABILJO

SLEEP WITH ME MGM, 1994
DAVID LAWRENCE

SLEEPER United Artists, 1973
WOODY ALLEN

SLEEPERS Warner Bros., 1996
JOHN WILLIAMS ★

SLEEPERS (MS) Cinema Verity, 1991
DAVID DUNDAS
RICK WENTWORTH

SLEEPING BEAUTY (AF) Buena Vista, 1959
GEORGE BRUNS ★

THE SLEEPING CAR MURDERS 7 Arts, 1966
MICHEL MAGNE†

THE SLEEPING CITY Universal, 1950
FRANK SKINNER†

SLEEPING CAR TO TRIESTE 1948
BENJAMIN FRANKEL†

THE SLEEPING TIGER Astor, 1954
MALCOLM ARNOLD

SLEEPING WITH THE ENEMY 20th Century Fox,
1991
JERRY GOLDSMITH

SLEEPLESS IN SEATTLE TriStar, 1993
MARC SHAIMAN

SLEEPWALKERS Columbia, 1992
NICHOLAS PIKE

SLEEPY LAGOON Republic, 1943
WALTER SCHARF

THE SLENDER THREAD Paramount, 1965
QUINCY JONES

SLEUTH 20th Century Fox, 1972
JOHN ADDISON ★

A SLICE OF LIFE Australian
BRIAN MAY†

SLIDE, KELLY SLIDE MGM, 1927
WILLIAM AXT†

SLIDERS (TF) Cinevu Films/St. Clare Ent./MCA TV/
Fox, 1995
DENNIS MCCARTHY

SLIGHTLY DANGEROUS MGM, 1943
BRONISLAU KAPER†

SLIGHTLY FRENCH Columbia, 1949
GEORGE DUNING

SLIGHTLY HONORABLE United Artists, 1940
WERNER JANSSEN

SLIGHTLY SCANDALOUS Universal, 1946
MILTON ROSEN†

SLIGHTLY TEMPTED Universal, 1940
HANS J. SALTER†

SLIM Warner Bros., 1937
MAX STEINER†

SLIM CARTER Universal, 1957
HERMAN STEIN

SLING BLADE Miramax, 1996
BRIAN ENO
DANIEL LANOIS

THE SLINGSHOT 1993
BJORN ISFALT

**THE SLIPPER AND THE ROSE: THE STORY OF
CINDERELLA** Universal, 1976
ANGELA MORLEY ★

SLIPSTREAM 1974
VAN MORRISON

SLIPSTREAM Entertainment Film, 1989
ELMER BERNSTEIN

SLITHER MGM, 1973
TOM MCINTOSH

SLIVER Paramount, 1993
HOWARD SHORE
CHRISTOPHER YOUNG

SLOW BURN (CTF) Joel Schumacher Prods./
Universal Pay TV, 1986
LOEK DIKKER

SLOW DANCING IN THE BIG CITY United Artists,
1978
BILL CONTI

SLOW MOTION 1979
ALFI KABILJO

THE SLUGGER'S WIFE Columbia, 1985
PATRICK WILLIAMS

THE SLUMBER PARTY MASSACRE Santa Fe,
1982
RALPH JONES

SLUMBER PARTY '57 Cannon, 1976
MILES GOODMAN†

SLUMBER PARTY MASSACRE 3 Concorde, 1991
JAMIE SHERIFF

SLUMBER PARTY MASSACRE II Concorde/New
Horizons, 1987
RICHARD COX

THE SMALL BACK ROOM *HOUR OF GLORY*
Snader Productions, 1948
BRIAN EASDALE

A SMALL CIRCLE OF FRIENDS United Artists, 1980
JIM STEINMAN

A SMALL DANCE (TF) 1991
RICHARD HARVEY

SMALL FACES 1996
JOHN KEANE
JOHN ZEANE

A SMALL KILLING (TF) Orgolini-Nelson
Productions/Motown Productions, 1981
FRED WERNER

SMALL KILL Rayfield Co. II, 1992
MARK LEGGETT

THE SMALL MIRACLE (TF) FCB Productions/Alan
Landsburg Productions, 1973
ERNEST GOLD

SMALL PLEASURES Wondrous Light, 1993
AN-LU HUANG
KIRK ELLIOT

SMALL SACRIFICES (TF) Louis Rudolph Silms/
Motown/Allarcom Ltd./Fries Entertainment, 1989
PETER MANNING ROBINSON

A SMALL TOWN IN TEXAS American International,
1976
CHARLES BERNSTEIN

SMALL TOWN GIRL MGM, 1936
HERBERT STOTHART†
EDWARD WARD†

SMALL TOWN GIRL MGM, 1953
ANDRE PREVIN

THE SMALLEST SHOW ON EARTH Times Film
Corporation, 1957
WILLIAM ALWYN†

SMART GIRLS DON'T TALK Warner Bros., 1948
DAVID BUTTOLPH†

SMART WOMAN Allied Artists, 1948
LOUIS GRUENBERG†

THE SMARTEST GIRL IN TOWN RKO Radio, 1936
NATHANIEL SHILKRET†

SMASHING TIME Paramount, 1967
JOHN ADDISON

SMASH-UP ON INTERSTATE 5 (TF) Filmways,
1976
BILL CONTI

SMASH-UP, THE STORY OF A WOMAN
Universal, 1947
FRANK SKINNER†

SMIC, SMAC, SMOC GSF, 1971
FRANCIS LAI

SMILE United Artists, 1975
DANIEL OSBORN

A SMILE LIKE YOURS Paramount, 1997
WILLIAM ROSS

SMILES OF A SUMMER NIGHT Janus, 1955
ERIC NORDGREN

SMILEY 1957
WILLIAM ALWYN†

SMILEY'S PEOPLE (MS) BBC/Paramount TV, 1982
PATRICK GOWERS

SMILIN' THROUGH MGM, 1932
WILLIAM AXT†

SMILIN' THROUGH MGM, 1941
HERBERT STOTHART†

THE SMILING GHOST 1941
BERNHARD KAUN†
WILLIAM LAVA†

SMILLA'S SENSE OF SNOW 20th Century Fox,
1997
HANS ZIMMER

SMITH! Buena Vista, 1969
ROBERT F. BRUNNER

SMOKE 1993
ARNIE BIEBER

SMOKE Miramax, 1995
RACHEL PORTMAN

SMOKE IN THE POTATO FIELDS 1977
ZDENEK LISKA

SMOKEY & THE BANDIT - PART 3 Universal,
1983
LARRY CANSLER

SM - SO

'97-'98
FILM
COMPOSERS
INDEX

FILM

TITLES

SMOKEY AND THE BANDIT Universal, 1977
BILL JUSTIS
JERRY REED

SMOKEY AND THE BANDIT II Universal, 1980
SNUFF GARRETT

SMOKING/NO SMOKING 1993
JOHN PATTISON

SMOKY 20th Century-Fox, 1946
DAVID RAKSIN

SMOKY 20th Century-Fox, 1966
LEITH STEVENS†

A SMOKY MOUNTAIN CHRISTMAS (TF)
Sandollar Productions, 1986
DANA KAPROFF

SMOOTH AS SILK Universal, 1946
ERNEST GOLD

SMOOTH TALK Spectrafilm, 1985
RUSS KUNKEL
GEORGE MASSENBURG
BILL PAYNE

SMORGASBORD Warner Bros., 1983
MORTON STEVENS†

SMUGGLER'S GOLD Columbia, 1951
MISCHA BAKALEINIKOFF†

THE SMUGGLERS (TF) Universal TV, 1968
LYN MURRAY†

SMUKKE DRENG PRETTY BOY 1993
JOAKIM HOLBECK

THE SMURFS AND THE MAGIC FLUTE (AF)
Atlantic Releasing, 1984
MICHEL LEGRAND

SNAKE EATER III ...HIS LAW Cinepix, 1992
JOHN MASSARI

SNAKE EYES Mario & Vittorio Cecchi Gori, 1993
JOE DELIA

THE SNAKE PIT 20th Century-Fox, 1948
ALFRED NEWMAN†

THE SNAKE PIT AND THE PENDULUM 1967
PETER THOMAS

SNAPDRAGON Prism, 1993
MICHAEL J. LINN†

SNAPSHOT Group 1, 1979
BRIAN MAY†

SNATCHED (TF) Spelling-Goldberg Productions/ABC
Circle Films, 1973
RANDY EDELMAN

SNEAKERS Universal, 1992
JAMES HORNER

THE SNIPER Columbia, 1952
GEORGE ANTHEIL†

SNIPER TriStar, 1993
GARY CHANG
HANS ZIMMER

SNIPER'S RIDGE 20th Century-Fox, 1961
RICHARD LASALLE

THE SNOOP SISTERS FEMALE INSTINCT (TF)
Universal TV, 1972
JERRY FIELDING†

SNOW DEVILS 1965
ANGELO FRANCESCO LAVAGNINO†

SNOW GHOST 1968
AKIRA IFUKUBE

THE SNOW GOOSE (TF) NBC, 1971
CARL DAVIS ☆

SNOW KILL (CTF) Wilshire Court Productions, 1990
SYLVESTER LEVAY

THE SNOW QUEEN (AF) Universal, 1959
FRANK SKINNER†

SNOW WHITE AND THE SEVEN DWARFS (AF)
RKO Radio, 1938
FRANK CHURCHILL† ★
LEIGH HARLINE† ★
PAUL J. SMITH† ★

SNOW WHITE AND THE THREE STOOGES
Columbia, 1961
LYN MURRAY†

SNOW WHITE IN THE DARK FOREST 1997
JOHN OTTMAN

THE SNOWBALL EXPRESS Buena Vista, 1972
ROBERT F. BRUNNER

SNOWBEAST (TF) Douglas Cramer Productions,
1977
ROBERT PRINCE

SNOWBOUND: THE JIM AND JENNIFER STOLPA
STORY (TF) Pacific Motion Pictures (Stolpa)
Prods./Jaffe-Braunstein Films, 1994
LOUIS NATALE

SNOWFIRE Allied Artists, 1958
ALBERT GLASSER

THE SNOWS OF KILIMANJARO 20th Century-Fox,
1952
BERNARD HERRMANN†

SO BIG Warner Bros., 1953
MAX STEINER†

SO DARK THE NIGHT Columbia, 1946
HUGO FRIEDHOFER†

SO DEAR TO MY HEART RKO Radio, 1948
PAUL J. SMITH†

SO ENDS OUR NIGHT United Artists, 1941
LOUIS GRUENBERG† ★

SO EVIL MY LOVE Paramount, 1948
WILLIAM ALWYN†
VICTOR YOUNG†

SO FINE Warner Bros., 1981
ENNIO MORRICONE

SO GOES MY LOVE Universal, 1946
HANS J. SALTER†

SO I MARRIED AN AXE MURDERER TriStar,
1993
BRUCE BROUGHTON

SO LONG AT THE FAIR GFD, 1950
BENJAMIN FRANKEL†

SO PROUDLY WE HAIL (TF) Lionel Chetwynd
Productions/CBS Entertainment, 1990
GIL MELLE

SO PROUDLY WE HAIL! Paramount, 1943
MIKLOS ROZSA†

SO RED THE ROSE Paramount, 1935
W. FRANKE HARLING†

SO THIS IS LOVE Warner Bros., 1953
MAX STEINER†

SO THIS IS NEW YORK United Artists, 1948
DIMITRI TIOMKIN†

SO THIS IS PARIS Universal, 1954
HENRY MANCINI†
HERMAN STEIN

SO WELL REMEMBERED RKO Radio, 1948
HANNS EISLER†

SO YOU WON'T TALK Columbia, 1940
LEIGH HARLINE†

SOAPDISH Paramount, 1991
ALAN SILVESTRI

S.O.B. Paramount, 1981
HENRY MANCINI†

SOCCER SHOOTOUT (FD) Overseas, 1991
STEPHEN PARSONS

SOCIAL SUICIDE Star, 1991
ROGER BELLON

SOCIETY LAWYER MGM, 1939
EDWARD WARD†

SODBUSTERS (CTF) Atlantis Films/Bond Street
Prods., 1994
BILL GODDARD

SODOM AND GOMORRAH 20th Century-Fox,
1962
MIKLOS ROZSA†

THE SOFT SKIN Cinema 5, 1964
GEORGES DELERUE†

SOHO GORILLA 1972
PETER THOMAS

SOIL (FD) Department of Agriculture, 1939
HANNS EISLER†

SOIR BLEU (CTF) Showtime, 1995
HUMMIE MANN

SOL MADRID MGM, 1968
LALO SCHIFRIN

SOLA 1976
JORGE CALANDRELLI

SOLAMENTE NERO 1978
STELVIO CIPRIANI

SOLANG 'ES HUBSCHE MADCHEN GIBT 1955
ALLAN GRAY†

SOLAR CRISIS 1991
MICHAEL BODDICKER

SOLAR CRISIS STARFIRE 1991
MAURICE JARRE

SOLARBABIES MGM/UA, 1986
MAURICE JARRE

SOLARIS Mosfilm, 1972
EDUARD ARTEMYEV

THE SOLDIER Embassy, 1982
TANGERINE DREAM
CHRISTOPHER FRANKE

THE SOLDIER AND THE LADY RKO Radio, 1937
NATHANIEL SHILKRET†

SOLDIER BLUE Avco Embassy, 1970
ROY BUDD†

SOLDIER IN THE RAIN Allied Artists, 1963
HENRY MANCINI†

SOLDIER OF FORTUNE 20th Century-Fox, 1955
HUGO FRIEDHOFER†

SOLDIER OF ORANGE Rank, 1979
ROGIER VAN OTTERLOO†

A SOLDIER'S STORY Columbia, 1984
HERBIE HANCOCK

A SOLDIER'S TALE Atlantic Releasing Corporation,
1988
JOHN CHARLES

SOLDIER'S FORTUNE Republic, 1989
CHUCK CIRINO

SOLDIERS OF THE SOIL Du Pont, 1943
W. FRANKE HARLING†

SOLDIERS THREE MGM, 1951
ADOLPH DEUTSCH†

SOLE SURVIVOR (TF) Cinema Center 100, 1970
PAUL GLASS

SOLEIL DE PIERRE 1967
MICHEL PORTAL

SOLITAIRE Highway One, 1992
MICHAEL BECKER

THE SOLITARY MAN (TF) John Conboy Productions,
1979
JACK ELLIOTT

SOLO Triumph, 1996
CHRISTOPHER FRANKE

SOLO CONTRO ROMA 1962
ARMANDO TROVAJOLI

SOLOMON & SHEBA (CTF) Dino De Laurentiis
Communications, 1995
DAVID KITAY

SOLOMON AND SHEBA United Artists, 1959
MALCOLM ARNOLD

SOME CALL IT LOVING Cine Globe, 1973
RICHARD HAZARD

SOME CAME RUNNING MGM, 1959
ELMER BERNSTEIN

SOME GIRLS MGM/UA, 1988
JAMES NEWTON HOWARD

SOME KIND OF A NUT United Artists, 1969
JOHNNY MANDEL

SOME KIND OF HERO Paramount, 1982
PATRICK WILLIAMS

SOME KIND OF WONDERFUL Paramount, 1987
STEPHEN HAGUE
JOHN MUSSER

SOME LIKE IT HOT United Artists, 1959
ADOLPH DEUTSCH†

SOME MOTHER'S SON 1996
BILL WHELEN

SOMEBODY HAS TO SHOOT THE PICTURE
(CTF) HBO, 1990
JAMES NEWTON HOWARD

SOMEBODY IS WAITING 1997
ELIA CMIRAL

SOMEBODY KILLED HER HUSBAND Columbia,
1978
ALEX NORTH†

SOMEBODY TO LOVE Lumiere Pictures, 1994
MADER

SOMEBODY UP THERE LIKES ME MGM, 1956
BRONISLAU KAPER†

SOMEBODY'S DAUGHTER (TF) Karen
Danaher-dorr Prods./Republic Pictures TV, 1992
CHARLES BERNSTEIN

SOMEONE ELSE'S AMERICA 1995
ANDREW DICKSON

SOMEONE ELSE'S CHILD (TF) Greengrass Prods./
de Passe Ent., 1994
BILLY GOLDENBERG

SOMEONE I TOUCHED (TF) Charles Fries
Productions/Stonehenge Productions, 1975
AL KASHA

SOMEONE IS WATCHING ME (TF) Warner Bros.
TV, 1978
HARRY SUKMAN†

SOMEONE SHE KNOWS (TF) Thomas Carter Co./
Warner Bros. TV, 1994
WENDY BLACKSTONE

SOMEONE TO REMEMBER Republic, 1943
WALTER SCHARF

SOMEONE TO WATCH OVER ME Columbia, 1987
MICHAEL KAMEN

SOMETHING ABOUT AMELIA (TF) Leonard
Goldberg Productions, 1984
MARK SNOW ☆

SOMETHING BIG National General, 1971
MARVIN HAMLISCH

SOMETHING EVIL (TF) Belford Productions/CBS
International, 1972
WLADIMIR SELINSKY

SOMETHING FOR A LONELY MAN (TF) Universal
TV, 1968
JACK MARSHALL

SOMETHING FOR EVERYONE National General,
1970
JOHN KANDER

SOMETHING FOR JOEY (TF) MTM Productions,
1977
DAVID SHIRE

SOMETHING FOR THE BIRDS 20th Century-Fox,
1952
SOL KAPLAN

SOMETHING IN COMMON (TF) New World TV/
Freyda Rothstein Productions/Littke-Grossbart
Productions, 1986
JOHN ADDISON

SOMETHING IN THE WIND Universal, 1947
JOHN GREEN†

SOMETHING IS CREEPING IN THE DARK 1970
ANGELO FRANCESCO LAVAGNINO†

SOMETHING IS OUT THERE (TF) Columbia TV,
1988
SYLVESTER LEVAY

SOMETHING MONEY CAN'T BUY 1952
NINO ROTA†

SOMETHING OF VALUE MGM, 1957
MIKLOS ROZSA†

SOMETHING SHORT OF PARADISE American
International, 1979
MARK SNOW

SOMETHING SO RIGHT (TF) List-Estrin
Productions/Tisch-Avnet Television, 1982
CHARLES GROSS

SOMETHING SPECIAL WILLY MILLY/I WAS A
TEENAGE BOY Cinema Group, 1986
DAVID MCHUGH

SOMETHING TO HIDE SHATTERED 1972
ROY BUDD†

SOMETHING TO LIVE FOR Paramount, 1952
VICTOR YOUNG†

SOMETHING TO LIVE FOR: THE ALISON GERTZ
STORY (TF) Grossbart-Barnett, 1992
DAVID SHIRE

SOMETHING TO SHOUT ABOUT Columbia, 1943
DAVID RAKSIN

SOMETHING TO SING ABOUT Grand National,
1937
VICTOR SCHERTZINGER† ★

SOMETHING TO TALK ABOUT Warner Bros.,
1995
GRAHAM PRESKETT
HANS ZIMMER

SOMETHING WICKED THIS WAY COMES Buena
Vista, 1983
JAMES HORNER

SOMETHING WILD Orion, 1986
LAURIE ANDERSON
JOHN CALE

SOMETHING WILD United Artists, 1961
AARON COPLAND†

SOMETIMES A GREAT NOTION NEVER GIVE AN
INCH Universal, 1971
HENRY MANCINI†

SOMETIMES THEY COME BACK...AGAIN
Trimark, 1996
PETER MANNING ROBINSON

SOMEWHERE I'LL FIND YOU MGM, 1942
BRONISLAU KAPER†

SOMEWHERE IN THE NIGHT 20th Century-Fox,
1946
DAVID BUTTOLPH†

SOMEWHERE IN TIME Universal, 1980
JOHN BARRY

SOMEWHERE, SOMEONE QUELQUE PART,
QUELQU'UN 1971
GEORGES DELERUE†

SOMMARLEK Janus, 1951
ERIC NORDGREN

SOMMERSBY Warner Bros., 1993
DANNY ELFMAN

SON OF A WITCH 1934
WOLFGANG ZELLER†

SON OF ALI BABA Universal, 1952
MILTON ROSEN†
HERMAN STEIN

SON OF BLOB Jack H. Harris Enterprises, 1972
MORT GARSON

SON OF DARKNESS: TO DIE FOR II Trimark,
1991
CLIFF EIDELMAN
MARK MCKENZIE

THE SON OF DR. JEKYLL Columbia, 1951
PAUL SAWTELL†

SON OF DRACULA Universal, 1943
CHARLES PREVIN†
HANS J. SALTER†
FRANK SKINNER†

SON OF FLUBBER Buena Vista, 1963
GEORGE BRUNS

SON OF FRANKENSTEIN Universal, 1939
FRANK SKINNER†

SON OF FURY 20th Century-Fox, 1942
ALFRED NEWMAN†

SON OF GODZILLA 1969
MASARU SATO

THE SON OF KONG RKO Radio, 1933
MAX STEINER†

SON OF LASSIE MGM, 1945
HERBERT STOTHART†

THE SON OF MONTE CRISTO United Artists, 1941
EDWARD WARD†

SON OF PALEFACE Paramount, 1952
LYN MURRAY†

THE SON OF ROBIN HOOD 20th Century-Fox,
1959
LEIGHTON LUCAS†

SON OF SINBAD RKO Radio, 1955
VICTOR YOUNG†

THE SON OF THE SHARK 1993
BRUNO COULAIS

SON OF THE BORDER RKO Radio, 1933
MAX STEINER†

SON OF THE MORNING STAR (TF) Republic,
1991
CRAIG SAFAN

SON OF THE PINK PANTHER MGM, 1993
HENRY MANCINI†

SON RISE: A MIRACLE OF LOVE (TF)
Rothman-Wohl Productions/Filmways, 1979
GERALD FRIED

A SON'S PROMISE (TF) Marian Rees Associates, 1990
J.A.C. REDFORD

THE SON-DAUGHTER MGM, 1932
HERBERT STOTHART†

A SONG ABOUT HEROES 1932
HANNS EISLER†

A SONG IS BORN RKO Radio, 1948
HUGO FRIEDHOFER†

THE SONG OF BERNADETTE 20th Century-Fox, 1943
ALFRED NEWMAN† ★★

SONG OF LOVE MGM, 1947
BRONISLAU KAPER†

SONG OF RUSSIA MGM, 1944
HERBERT STOTHART†

SONG OF SCHEHERAZADE Universal, 1947
MIKLOS ROZSA†

SONG OF SURRENDER Paramount, 1949
VICTOR YOUNG†

SONG OF THE CITY MGM, 1937
WILLIAM AXT†

SONG OF THE FLAME Warner Bros., 1930
EDWARD WARD†

SONG OF THE OPEN ROAD Universal, 1944
CHARLES PREVIN† ★

SONG OF THE SARONG Universal, 1945
EDWARD WARD†

SONG OF THE SOUTH RKO Radio, 1946
DANIELE AMFITHEATROF† ★
PAUL J. SMITH† ★

A SONG TO REMEMBER Columbia, 1945
MIKLOS ROZSA† ★

SONG WITHOUT END Columbia, 1960
HARRY SUKMAN†

SONGWRITER Tri-Star, 1984
LARRY CANSLER

SON-IN-LAW Hollywood, 1993
RICHARD GIBBS

SONNY AND JED 1972
ENNIO MORRICONE

SONNY BOY Triumph, 1990
CARLO MARIO CORDIO

SONO FOTOGENICO Dean Film/Marceau Cocinor, 1980
MANUEL DE SICA

SONO STATO IO 1973
ARMANDO TROVAJOLI

THE SONS OF KATIE ELDER Paramount, 1965
ELMER BERNSTEIN

SOONER OR LATER (TF) Laughing Willow Company, 1979
STEPHEN LAWRENCE

SOPHIE AND THE MOONHANGER (CTF) Lifetime, 1995
CHARLES BERNSTEIN

SOPHIE'S CHOICE Universal/AFD, 1982
MARVIN HAMLISCH ★

SOPHIE'S PLACE CROOKS AND CORONETS Warner Bros., 1969
JOHN SCOTT

THE SOPHISTICATED GENTS (TF) Daniel Wilson Productions, 1981
BENNY GOLSON

SORCERER Universal/Paramount, 1977
TANGERINE DREAM
CHRISTOPHER FRANKE
KEITH JARRETT

THE SORCERERS 1967
PAUL FERRIS

SORCERESS LA MOINE ET LA SORCIERE European Classics, 1987
MICHEL PORTAL

SORORITY GIRL American International, 1957
RONALD STEIN†

SORORITY HOUSE RKO Radio, 1939
ROY WEBB†

SORORITY HOUSE MASSACRE III Concorde/New Horizons, 1991
CHUCK CIRINO

SORRELL AND SON (TF) Yorkshire Television, 1986
PATRICK GOWERS

SORROWFUL JONES Paramount, 1949
ROBERT EMMETT DOLAN†

SORRY, WRONG NUMBER Paramount, 1948
FRANZ WAXMAN†

SORRY, WRONG NUMBER (CTF) 1989
BRUCE BROUGHTON

SORTIE DE SECOURS 1970
PHILIPPE SARDE

S.O.S. FOCH 1931
JACQUES IBERT†

S.O.S. PACIFIC Universal, 1960
GEORGES AURIC†

S.O.S. TITANIC (TF) Roger Gimbel Productions/EMI TV/Argonaut Films Ltd., 1979
HOWARD BLAKE

SOTTO DIECI BANDIERE 1960
NINO ROTA†

SOTTO IL SOLE DI ROMA 1948
NINO ROTA†

SOTTO...SOTTO Triumph/Columbia, 1984
PAOLO CONTE

SOUL MAN New World, 1986
TOM SCOTT

THE SOUL OF NIGGER CHARLEY Paramount, 1973
DON COSTA

A SOUL SPLIT IN TWO 1993
GIOVANNI VENOSTA

SOUL SURVIVOR 1995
JOHN MCCARTHY

THE SOULER OPPOSITE Buffalo Jump Productions, 1997
PETER HIMMELMAN

SOULMATES Curb, 1997
DAVID RUSSO

SOULS AT SEA Paramount, 1937
W. FRANKE HARLING† ★
MILAN RODER† ★

SOULS FOR SALE/EVILS OF CHINATOWN Allied Artists, 1962
ALBERT GLASSER

THE SOUND AND THE FURY 20th Century Fox, 1959
ALEX NORTH†

THE SOUND AND THE SILENCE (CTF) Screen Star/Atlantis/South Pacific/Kelcom, 1993
JOHN CHARLES

THE SOUND BARRIER United Artists, 1952
MALCOLM ARNOLD

THE SOUND OF ANGER (TF) Public Arts Productions/Universal TV, 1968
PETE RUGOLO

THE SOUND OF FURY United Artists, 1951
HUGO FRIEDHOFER†

THE SOUND OF MUSIC 20th Century-Fox, 1965
IRWIN KOSTAL† ★★

SOUND OFF Columbia, 1952
GEORGE DUNING

SOUNDER 20th Century-Fox, 1972
TAJ MAHAL

SOUNDS OF SILENCE Artist's View, 1992
DEAN WALRAFF

SOUP FOR ONE Warner Bros., 1982
BERNARD EDWARDS
JOHNNY MANDEL
NILE RODGERS

SOUPCON Durham/Pike, 1979
GERARD ANFOSSO

SOURDOUGH Film Saturation Inc., 1977
JERROLD IMMEL

SOURSWEET Skouras Pictures, 1988
RICHARD HARTLEY

SOUS LA TERREUR 1935
MICHEL MICHELET†

SOUS LE CIEL DE PARIS UNDER THE PARIS SKY Discina International, 1951
JEAN WIENER†

SOUS LE CIEL DE PROVENCE 1956
PAUL MISRAKI

SOUS LE SIGNE DU TAUREAU 1968
JEAN PRODROMIDES

SOUS LES YEUX D'OCCIDENT 1936
GEORGES AURIC†

SOUTH 1993
FREDERICO DE ROBERTIS

SOUTH BEACH (TF) Wolf Films/Universal, 1993
MARK MOTHERSBAUGH

SOUTH BRONX HEROES Continental, 1985
AL ZIMA

SOUTH CENTRAL Warner Bros., 1992
TIM TRUMAN

SOUTH OF PAGO PAGO United Artists, 1940
EDWARD WARD†

SOUTH OF RENO Open Road Productions/Pendulum Productions, 1987
NIGEL HOLTON

SOUTH OF ST. LOUIS Warner Bros., 1949
MAX STEINER†

SOUTH OF SUEZ Warner Bros., 1940
FREDERICK HOLLANDER†

SOUTH RIDING 1938
RICHARD ADDINSELL†

SOUTH SEA SINNER Universal, 1950
WALTER SCHARF

SOUTH SEA WOMAN Warner Bros., 1953
DAVID BUTTOLPH†

SOUTH SEAS ADVENTURE Cinerama Releasing Corporation, 1958
ALEX NORTH†

SOUTH TO KARANGA Universal, 1940
HANS J. SALTER†

SOUTH TO RENO Open Road Productions/Pendulum Productions, 1987
CLIVE WRIGHT

SOUTHERN COMFORT 20th Century Fox, 1981
RY COODER

THE SOUTHERN STAR Columbia, 1969
GEORGES GARVARENTZ†

THE SOUTHERNER United Artists, 1945
WERNER JANSSEN ★

SOUTHWEST PASSAGE United Artists, 1954
EMIL NEWMAN†

SOUVENIRS D'EN FRANCE 1974
PHILIPPE SARDE

SOUVENIRS PERDUS 1950
JOSEPH KOSMA†

SOYLENT GREEN MGM, 1972
FRED MYROW

SPACE (MS) Stonehenge Productions/Paramount Pictures TV, 1985
TONY BERG
MILES GOODMAN†

SPACE CASE Lunar Bynne, 1990
PARMER FULLER

THE SPACE CHILDREN Paramount, 1958
NATHAN VAN CLEAVE†

SPACE JAM Warner Bros., 1996
JAMES NEWTON HOWARD

THE SPACE MOVIE (FD) International Harmony, 1980
MIKE OLDFIELD

SPACE: ABOVE AND BEYOND (TF) 20th Century Fox TV/Hard Eight Pictures/Village Roadshow, 1995
SHIRLEY WALKER

SPACEBALLS MGM/UA, 1987
JOHN MORRIS

SPACEBOY 1972
BEBE BARRON
LOUIS BARRON

SPACECAMP 20th Century Fox, 1986
JOHN WILLIAMS

SPACED INVADERS Buena Vista, 1990
DAVID RUSSO

SPACEFLIGHT IC-1 United Artists, 1965
ELISABETH LUTYENS†

SPACEHUNTER: ADVENTURES IN THE FORBIDDEN ZONE Columbia, 1983
ELMER BERNSTEIN

SPACESHIP THE CREATURE WASN'T NICE Almi Cinema 5, 1982
DAVID SPEAR

SPALDING GRAY'S MONSTER IN A BOX Fine Line, 1991
LAURIE ANDERSON

SPANISH AFFAIR Paramount, 1958
DANIELE AMFITHEATROF†

THE SPANISH EARTH (D) Contemporary Historians, 1937
MARC BLITZSTEIN†
VIRGIL THOMSON†

SPANISH FLY EMI, 1975
RON GOODWIN

THE SPANISH MAIN RKO Radio, 1945
HANNS EISLER†

SPANISH ROSE Trimark, 1993
VLADIMIR HORUNZHY

SPANKING THE MONKEY Fine Line, 1994
MARK SANDMAN

SPARE ME Film Crash, 1993
DANNY BRENNER

SPARKLE Warner Bros., 1976
CURTIS MAYFIELD

SPARKS: THE PRICE OF PASSION (TF) Shadowplay Films/Victoria Principal Productions/King Phoenix Entertainment, 1990
BOB ALCIVAR

SPARROW 1993
CLAUDIO CAPPANI
ALESSIO VLAD

SPARTACUS Universal, 1960
ALEX NORTH† ★

SPASMO 1974
ENNIO MORRICONE

SPASMS Producers Distribution Company, 1983
ERIC N. ROBERTSON

SPAWN 1997
GRAEME REVELL

SPAWN OF THE NORTH Paramount, 1938
DIMITRI TIOMKIN†

SPEARFIELD'S DAUGHTER (MS) Robert Halmi, Inc/Channel Seven, 1986
IRWIN FISCH

A SPECIAL DAY Cinema 5, 1977
ARMANDO TROVAJOLI

SPECIAL DELIVERY American International, 1976
LALO SCHIFRIN

SPECIAL DELIVERY VON HIMMEL GEFALLEN Columbia, 1955
BERNHARD KAUN†

SPECIAL DISPATCH 1940
RICHARD ADDINSELL†

SPECIAL EFFECTS New Line Cinema, 1985
MICHAEL MINARD

A SPECIAL FRIENDSHIP (TF) Entertainment Partners, 1987
TEO MACERO

SPECIAL INVESTIGATOR RKO Radio, 1936
ROY WEBB†

SPECIAL OLYMPICS (TF) Roger Gimbel Productions/EMI TV, 1978
PETER MATZ

SPECIAL PEOPLE (TF) Joe Cates Productions, 1986
ERIC N. ROBERTSON

THE SPECIALIST Warner Bros., 1994
JOHN BARRY

THE SPECIALISTS (TF) Mark VII Ltd./Universal TV, 1975
BILLY MAY

SPECIES MGM-UA, 1995
CHRISTOPHER YOUNG

SPECTER OF THE ROSE Republic, 1946
GEORGE ANTHEIL†

SPECTRE (TF) Norway Productions/20th Century-Fox TV, 1977
JOHN CAMERON

SPEECHLESS MGM, 1994
MARC SHAIMAN

SPEED MGM, 1936
EDWARD WARD†

SPEED 20th Century Fox, 1994
MARK MANCINA
JOHN VAN TONGEREN

SPEED 2 20th Century Fox, 1997
MARK MANCINA

SPEED CRAZY Allied Artists, 1959
RICHARD LASALLE

SPEED ZONE Orion, 1989
DAVID WHEATLEY

SPEEDWAY MGM, 1929
WILLIAM AXT†

SPEEDWAY MGM, 1968
JEFF ALEXANDER†

THE SPELL (TF) Charles Fries Productions, 1977
GERALD FRIED

SPELLBINDER WITCHING HOUR MGM/UA, 1988
BASIL POLEDOURIS

SPELLBOUND United Artists, 1945
MIKLOS ROZSA† ★★

SPELLCASTER Empire Pictures, 1987
NATHAN WANG

SPENCER'S MOUNTAIN Warner Bros., 1963
MAX STEINER†

SPENSER: CEREMONY (CTF) Norstar/Boardwalk/Ultra/ABC Video, 1993
PAUL J. ZAZA

SPENSES: PALE KINGS AND PRINCES (CTF) Norstar/Boardwalk/Ultra/ABC Video, 1994
PAUL J. ZAZA

SPETTERS Samuel Goldwyn Company, 1980
ANTON SCHERPENZEEL

SPHINX Orion/Warner Bros., 1981
MICHAEL J. LEWIS

THE SPIDER 20th Century-Fox, 1945
DAVID BUTTOLPH†

THE SPIDER American International, 1958
ALBERT GLASSER

THE SPIDER AND THE FLY General Film Distributors, 1949
GEORGES AURIC†

THE SPIDER AND THE FLY (CTF) Haft-Nasatir Co./Heartstar/Wilshire Court, 1994
RICHARD BELLIS

SPIDER BABY THE LIVER EATERS/CANNIBAL ORGY 1965
RONALD STEIN†

THE SPIDER WOMAN STRIKES BACK Universal, 1946
MILTON ROSEN†

SPIDER-MAN (TF) Charles Fries Productions, 1977
DANA KAPROFF

SPIES LIKE US Warner Bros., 1985
ELMER BERNSTEIN

SPIES, LIES AND NAKED THIES (TF) Robert Halmi Productions, 1988
JACK ELLIOTT

SPIKE OF BENSONHURST FilmDallas, 1988
COATI MUNDI

SPIKER Seymour Borde & Associates, 1986
JEFF BARRY

THE SPIKES GANG United Artists, 1974
FRED KARLIN

THE SPIRAL 1978
WOJCIECH KILAR

THE SPIRAL ROAD Universal, 1962
JERRY GOLDSMITH

THE SPIRAL STAIRCASE RKO Radio, 1945
ROY WEBB†

THE SPIRAL STAIRCASE Warner Bros., 1975
DAVID LINDUP

THE SPIRIT (TF) von Zerneck-Samuels Productions/Warner Bros. TV, 1987
BARRY GOLDBERG

THE SPIRIT IS WILLING Paramount, 1967
VIC MIZZY

THE SPIRIT OF '76 Columbia, 1990
DAVID NICHTERN

THE SPIRIT OF ST. LOUIS Warner Bros., 1957
FRANZ WAXMAN†

THE SPIRIT OF THE BEEHIVE   Janus, 1973
LUIS DE PABLO

SPIRIT OF THE EAGLE   Queen's Cross Productions, 1989
PARMER FULLER

SPIRITS OF THE DEAD   American International, 1967
JEAN PRODROMIDES

SPIRITS OF THE DEAD   HISTOIRES EXTRAORDINAIRES   American International, 1969
NINO ROTA†

SPIRITS OF THE RAINFOREST (TD)   Discovery Prods., 1993
JENNIE MUSKETT

SPIT FIRE   Trimark, 1994
TONY RIPPARETTI

SPITFIRE   RKO Radio, 1934
MAX STEINER†

SPITFIRE   THE FIRST OF THE FEW   RKO Radio, 1942
SIR WILLIAM WALTON†

THE SPITFIRE GRILL   Columbia, 1996
JAMES HORNER

SPLASH   Buena Vista, 1984
LEE HOLDRIDGE

SPLASH, TOO (TF)   Mark H. Ovitz Productions/Walt Disney TV, 1988
JOEL MCNEELY

SPLATTER UNIVERSITY   Troma, 1984
CHRIS BURKE

SPLENDOR   United Artists, 1935
ALFRED NEWMAN†

SPLENDOR IN THE GRASS   Warner Bros., 1961
DAVID AMRAM

SPLENDOR IN THE GRASS (TF)   Katz-Gallin Productions/Half-Pint Productions/Warner Bros. TV, 1981
JOHN MORRIS

THE SPLIT   MGM, 1968
QUINCY JONES

SPLIT DECISIONS   New Century/Vista, 1988
BASIL POLEDOURIS

SPLIT IMAGE   Orion, 1982
BILL CONTI

SPLIT SECOND   InterStar, 1992
FRANCIS HAINES
STEPHEN PARSONS

SPLIT SECOND TO AN EPITAPH (TF)   Universal TV, 1968
QUINCY JONES

SPLITTING HEIRS   Universal, 1993
MICHAEL KAMEN

SPOGLIATI, PROTESTA, UCCIDI   1973
ENNIO MORRICONE

S.P.O.O.K.S.   Vestron, 1989
HANS ZIMMER

S.P.Q.R. 2.000 E 1/2 ANNI FA   1995
FREDERICO DE ROBERTIS

S.P.Q.R.: 2,000 AND A HALF YEARS AGO   S.P.Q.R. 2.000 E 1/2 ANNI FA   1995
FREDERICO DE ROBERTIS

S.P.Y.S.   20th Century-Fox, 1974
JERRY GOLDSMITH

SPOILED CHILDREN   Gaumont, 1977
PHILIPPE SARDE

THE SPOILERS   Universal, 1942
HANS J. SALTER†

THE SPOILERS   Universal, 1955
HENRY MANCINI†
HERMAN STEIN

SPOILS OF WAR (TF)   Evolution Entertainment/Signboard Hill/RHI, 1994
LAWRENCE SHRAGGE

SPONTANEOUS COMBUSTION   Taurus Entertainment, 1990
GRAEME REVELL

THE SPOOK CASTLE IN SPESSART   1960
FREDERICK HOLLANDER†

THE SPOOK WHO SAT BY THE DOOR   United Artists, 1973
HERBIE HANCOCK

SPOONER (TF)   Walt Disney Productions, 1989
BRIAN BANKS
ANTHONY MARINELLI

THE SPORT PARADE   RKO Radio, 1932
MAX STEINER†

SPORTING BLOOD   MGM, 1940
FRANZ WAXMAN†

THE SPORTING CLUB   Avco Embassy, 1971
MICHAEL SMALL

SPRAGUE (TF)   MG Productions/Lorimar Productions, 1984
LALO SCHIFRIN

SPREE (CTF)   MGM-TV, 1997
PETER MANNING ROBINSON

SPRING AND PORT WINE   EMI, 1970
DOUGLAS GAMLEY

SPRING BREAK   Columbia, 1983
HARRY MANFREDINI

SPRING FEVER   Comworld, 1983
FRED MOLLIN

SPRING MADNESS   MGM, 1938
WILLIAM AXT†

SPRING OFFENSIVE   1940
BRIAN EASDALE

SPRING PARADE   Universal, 1940
HANS J. SALTER†

SPRINGFIELD RIFLE   Warner Bros., 1952
MAX STEINER†

SPRINGTIME IN ITALY   E PRIMAVERA   1947
NINO ROTA†

THE SPY   1927
WERNER R. HEYMANN†

SPY HARD   Buena Vista, 1996
BILL CONTI

SPY HUNT   Universal, 1950
WALTER SCHARF

THE SPY IN BLACK   U BOAT 29   Columbia, 1939
MIKLOS ROZSA†

THE SPY WHO CAME IN FROM THE COLD   Paramount, 1965
SOL KAPLAN

THE SPY WHO LOVED ME   United Artists, 1977
PAUL BUCKMASTER
MARVIN HAMLISCH ★

SPYS   20th Century-Fox, 1974
JOHN SCOTT

SQUANTO: A WARRIOR'S TALE   Buena Vista, 1994
JOEL MCNEELY

SQUARE DANCE   Island Pictures, 1986
BRUCE BROUGHTON

THE SQUARE JUNGLE   Universal, 1956
HEINZ ROEMHELD†

THE SQUARE ROOT OF ZERO   1965
ELLIOT KAPLAN†

THE SQUAW MAN   MGM, 1931
HERBERT STOTHART†

THE SQUEAKER   MURDER ON DIAMOND ROAD   United Artists, 1937
MIKLOS ROZSA†

THE SQUEEZE   THE RIP-OFF   Maverick International, 1976
PAOLO VASILE

THE SQUEEZE   Tri-Star, 1987
MILES GOODMAN†

THE SQUEEZE   Warner Bros., 1977
DAVID HENTSCHEL

SQUIRM   American International, 1976
ROBERT PRINCE

SSSSSSS   Universal, 1973
PATRICK WILLIAMS

SST - DEATH FLIGHT (TF)   ABC Circle Films, 1977
JOHN CACAVAS

ST. ELMO'S FIRE   Columbia, 1985
DAVID FOSTER

ST. IVES   Warner Bros., 1976
LALO SCHIFRIN

THE ST. VALENTINE'S DAY MASSACRE   20th Century-Fox, 1967
FRED STEINER

STABLEMATES   MGM, 1938
EDWARD WARD†

STACKING   Spectrafilm, 1987
PATRICK GLEESON

STAG   Cinepix, 1997
PAUL J. ZAZA

STAGE DOOR   RKO Radio, 1937
ROY WEBB†

STAGE FRIGHT   Warner Bros., 1950
LEIGHTON LUCAS†

STAGE STRUCK   RKO Radio, 1958
ALEX NORTH†

STAGE TO THUNDER ROCK   Paramount, 1964
PAUL DUNLAP

STAGECOACH   20th Century-Fox, 1966
JERRY GOLDSMITH

STAGECOACH   United Artists, 1939
RICHARD HAGEMAN† ★★
W. FRANKE HARLING† ★★
JOHN LEIPOLD† ★★
LEO SHUKEN† ★★

STAGECOACH (TF)   Raymond Katz Productions/Heritage Entertainment, 1986
DAVID ALLAN COE
WILLIE NELSON

STAGECOACH BUCKAROO   Universal, 1942
HANS J. SALTER†

STAGECOACH TO FURY   20th Century-Fox, 1956
PAUL DUNLAP

STAIRCASE   20th Century-Fox, 1969
DUDLEY MOORE

STAIRWAY TO HEAVEN   A MATTER OF LIFE AND DEATH   Universal, 1946
ALLAN GRAY†

STAKEOUT   1960
RONALD STEIN†

STAKEOUT   Buena Vista, 1987
ARTHUR B. RUBINSTEIN

STAKE-OUT ON DOPE STREET   Warner Bros., 1958
RICHARD MARKOWITZ†

STALAG 17   Paramount, 1953
FRANZ WAXMAN†

STALIN (CTF)   HBO, 1992
STANISLAS SYREWICZ

STALINGRAD   1992
NORBERT J. SCHNEIDER

STALK THE WILD CHILD (TF)   Charles Fries Productions, 1976
JOHN RUBINSTEIN

STALKER   New Yorker/Media Transactions Corporation, 1979
EDUARD ARTEMYEV

THE STALKING MOON   National General, 1969
FRED KARLIN

STALLION ROAD   Warner Bros., 1947
FREDERICK HOLLANDER†

THE STAND (MS)   Laurel/Greengrass Prods., 1994
W.G. SNUFFY WALDEN ☆

STAND AND DELIVER   Warner Bros., 1988
CRAIG SAFAN

STAND BY ME   Columbia, 1986
JACK NITZCHE

STAND BY YOUR MAN (TF)   Robert Papazian Productions/Guber-Peters Productions, 1981
EARLE HAGEN

STAND UP AND FIGHT   MGM, 1939
WILLIAM AXT†

STAND UP, VIRGIN SOLDIERS   Warner Bros., 1977
ED WELCH

STAND-IN   United Artists, 1937
HEINZ ROEMHELD†

STANDING ROOM ONLY   Paramount, 1944
ROBERT EMMETT DOLAN†

STANDING TALL (TF)   QM Productions, 1978
RICHARD MARKOWITZ†

STANLEY AND IRIS   MGM/UA, 1990
JOHN WILLIAMS

STANLEY AND LIVINGSTONE   20th Century-Fox, 1939
DAVID BUTTOLPH†
DAVID RAKSIN†

STANZA 17-17: PALAZZO DEL TASSE-UFFICIO DELLA IMPOSTE   1971
ARMANDO TROVAJOLI

THE STAR   20th Century-Fox, 1952
VICTOR YOUNG†

STAR 80   The Ladd Company/Warner Bros., 1983
RALPH BURNS

THE STAR CHAMBER   20th Century-Fox, 1983
MICHAEL SMALL

STAR DUST   20th Century-Fox, 1940
DAVID BUTTOLPH†

STAR IN THE DUST   Universal, 1956
FRANK SKINNER†

A STAR IS BORN   United Artists, 1937
MAX STEINER†

A STAR IS BORN   Warner Bros., 1976
RUPERT HOLMES
PAUL WILLIAMS

THE STAR MAKER   1996
ENNIO MORRICONE

THE STAR MAKER (TF)   The Channing-Debin-Locke Company/Carson Productions, 1981
JIMMIE HASKELL

STAR OF INDIA   1953
NINO ROTA†

STAR OF MIDNIGHT   RKO Radio, 1935
MAX STEINER†

THE STAR OF THE SEASON   1971
WOJCIECH KILAR

STAR SPANGLED RHYTHM   Paramount, 1943
ROBERT EMMETT DOLAN† ★

STAR TIME   Alexander Cassini, 1992
BLAKE LEYH

STAR TREK II: THE WRATH OF KHAN   Paramount, 1982
JAMES HORNER

STAR TREK III: THE SEARCH FOR SPOCK   Paramount, 1984
JAMES HORNER

STAR TREK IV: THE VOYAGE HOME   Paramount, 1986
LEONARD ROSENMAN ★

STAR TREK V: THE FINAL FRONTIER   Paramount, 1989
JERRY GOLDSMITH

STAR TREK VI: THE UNDISCOVERED COUNTRY   Paramount, 1992
CLIFF EIDELMAN

STAR TREK: FIRST CONTACT   Paramount, 1996
JERRY GOLDSMITH
JOEL GOLDSMITH

STAR TREK: GENERATIONS   Paramount, 1994
DENNIS MCCARTHY

STAR TREK: THE NEXT GENERATION: ALL GOOD THINGS (TF)   Paramount TV, 1994
DENNIS MCCARTHY ☆

STAR TREK: VOYAGER: THE CARETAKER (TF)   Paramount TV, 1995
JAY CHATTAWAY
JERRY GOLDSMITH ☆☆

STAR TREK: DEEP SPACE NINE: EMISSARY (TF)   Paramount TV, 1993
DENNIS MCCARTHY

STAR TREK: THE MOTION PICTURE   Paramount, 1979
JERRY GOLDSMITH ★

STAR TREK: THE NEXT GENERATION: ENCOUNTER AT FAR POINT (TF)   Paramount TV, 1987
DENNIS MCCARTHY

STAR WARS   20th Century-Fox, 1977
JOHN WILLIAMS ★★

STARCHASER: THE LEGEND OF ORIN (AF)   Atlantic Releasing Corporation, 1985
ANDREW BELLING

STARCRASH   New World, 1979
JOHN BARRY

STARCROSSED (TF)   Fries Entertainment, 1985
GIL MELLE

STARFIRE   1991
MAURICE JARRE

STARFIRE   SOLAR CRISIS   1991
MICHAEL BODDICKER

STARFLIGHT: THE PLANE THAT COULDN'T LAND (TF)   Orgolini-Nelson Productions, 1983
LALO SCHIFRIN

STARGATE   MGM, 1994
DAVID ARNOLD

STARK (TF)   CBS Entertainment, 1985
PETER MYERS

STARK SYSTEM   1980
ENNIO MORRICONE

STARK: MIRROR IMAGE (TF)   CBS Entertainment, 1986
PETER MYERS

STARMAN   Columbia, 1984
JACK NITZCHE

STARS AND BARS   Columbia, 1988
STANLEY MYERS†

STARS AND STRIPES FOREVER   20th Century-Fox, 1952
ALFRED NEWMAN†

THE STARS FELL ON HENRIETTA   Warner Bros., 1995
DAVID BENOIT

STARS IN MY CROWN   MGM, 1950
ADOLPH DEUTSCH†

STARS OVER TEXAS   Producers Releasing Corp., 1946
KARL HAJOS†

STARSHIP INVASIONS   Warner Bros., 1977
GIL MELLE

STARSHIP TROOPERS   1997
BASIL POLEDOURIS

STARSKY AND HUTCH (TF)   Spelling-Goldberg Productions, 1975
LALO SCHIFRIN

STAR-SPANGLED GIRL   Paramount, 1971
CHARLES FOX

START THE REVOLUTION WITHOUT ME   Warner Bros., 1970
JOHN ADDISON

STARTING OVER   Paramount, 1979
MARVIN HAMLISCH

STATE FAIR   20th Century-Fox, 1945
CHARLES HENDERSON† ★
ALFRED NEWMAN† ★

A STATE OF EMERGENCY   Norkat Co., 1986
GEORGES GARVARENTZ†

STATE OF EMERGENCY (CTF)   Chestnut Hill Prods., 1994
ROBERT FOLK

STATE OF GRACE   1990
ENNIO MORRICONE

STATE OF SIEGE   Cinema 6, 1973
MIKIS THEODORAKIS

THE STATE OF THINGS   Gray City, 1982
JURGEN KNIEPER

STATE OF THE UNION   MGM, 1948
VICTOR YOUNG†

STATE PARK   ITC, 1987
MATTHEW MCCAULEY

STATE REASONS   1978
VLADIMIR COSMA

STATE SECRET   1950
WILLIAM ALWYN†

STATE'S ATTORNEY   RKO Radio, 1932
MAX STEINER†

STATION SIX-SAHARA   Allied Artists, 1963
RON GRAINER†

STATION WEST   RKO Radio, 1948
HEINZ ROEMHELD†

THE STATUE   Cinerama Releasing Corporation, 1971
RIZ ORTOLANI

STAVISKY   Cinemation, 1974
STEPHEN SONDHEIM

STAY AWAY, JOE   MGM, 1968
JACK MARSHALL

STAY HUNGRY   United Artists, 1976
BRUCE LANGHORNE

STAY THE NIGHT (TF) New World TV/Stan Margulies, 1992
STEWART LEVIN

STAY TUNED Warner Bros., 1992
BRUCE BROUGHTON

STAYIN' ALIVE Paramount, 1983
VINCE DICOLA

STAYING AFLOAT (TF) Ruddy Morgan Organization/TriStar TV, 1993
DENNIS MCCARTHY

STAYING ALIVE Paramount, 1983
JOHNNY MANDEL

STAYING TOGETHER Hemdale, 1989
MILES GOODMAN†

STAZIONE TERMINI Columbia, 1953
ALESSANDRO CICOGNINI†

THE STEAGLE Avco Embassy, 1971
FRED MYROW

STEAL OF THE SKY (CTF) Yorma Ben-Ami/Paramount, 1988
YANNI

STEALING BEAUTY 1996
RICHARD HARTLEY

STEALING HEAVEN FilmDallas, 1988
NICK BICAT

STEALING HOME Warner Bros., 1988
DAVID FOSTER

STEAMING New World, 1984
RICHARD HARVEY

STEEL Warner Bros., 1997
MERVYN WARREN

STEEL LOOK DOWN AND DIE World Northal, 1980
MICHEL COLOMBIER

STEEL & LACE Fries, 1990
JOHN MASSARI

THE STEEL BAYONET United Artists, 1958
LEONARD SALZEDO

STEEL COWBOY (TF) Roger Gimbel Productions/EMI TV, 1978
CHARLES BERNSTEIN

STEEL DAWN Vestron, 1987
BRIAN MAY†

THE STEEL HELMET Lippert, 1950
PAUL DUNLAP

THE STEEL JUNGLE Warner Bros., 1956
DAVID BUTTOLPH†

THE STEEL LADY United Artists, 1953
EMIL NEWMAN†

STEEL MAGNOLIAS Columbia/Tri-Star, 1989
GEORGES DELERUE†

THE STEEL TRAP 20th Century-Fox, 1952
DIMITRI TIOMKIN†

STEELYARD BLUES Warner Bros., 1973
DAVID SHIRE

STEFANO QUANTESTORIE 1993
SERGIO CONFORTI

STELLA 1943
PAUL MISRAKI

STELLA 20th Century-Fox, 1950
CYRIL J. MOCKRIDGE†

STELLA Buena Vista, 1990
JOHN MORRIS

STELLA Fox-Hachette, 1983
PHILIPPE SARDE

STELLA Milas Films, 1955
MANOS HADJIDAKIS†

STELLA DALLAS United Artists, 1937
ALFRED NEWMAN†

STELLA POLARIS 1993
ARNE NORDHEIM

THE STEPFATHER New Century/Vista, 1987
PATRICK MORAZ

STEPFATHER II Millimeter Films, 1989
JIM MANZIE
PATRICK C. REGAN

STEPFATHER III (CTF) ITC Entertainment Group, 1992
PATRICK C. REGAN

THE STEPFORD CHILDREN (TF) Edgar Scherick, 1987
JOSEPH CONLAN

THE STEPFORD HUSBANDS (TF) Edgar Scherick Associates, 1996
DANA KAPROFF

THE STEPFORD WIVES Columbia, 1975
MICHAEL SMALL

STEPHEN KING'S

STEPHEN KING'S 'GOLDEN YEARS' (TF) Laurel, 1991
JOE TAYLOR

STEPHEN KING'S 'SOMETIME THEY COME BACK' (TF) Come Back Films, 1991
TERRY PLUMERI

STEPHEN KING'S CAT'S EYE CAT'S EYE MGM/UA, 1985
ALAN SILVESTRI

STEPHEN KING'S SILVER BULLET Paramount, 1985
JAY CHATTAWAY

STEPHEN KING'S THE LANGOLIERS THE LANGOLIERS (TF) Laurel-King Prods., 1995
VLADIMIR HORUNZHY

STEPHEN KING'S THINNER Paramount, 1996
DANIEL LICHT

THE STEPPE IFEX Film/Sovexport film, 1977
VYECHESLAV OVCHINNIKOV

STEPPING OUT Paramount, 1991
PETER MATZ

STEPS OF THE BALLET 1948
ARTHUR BENJAMIN†

THE STEPSISTER (CTF) Wilshire Court, 1997
PETER MANNING ROBINSON

THE STERILE CUCKOO Paramount, 1969
FRED KARLIN

STEVIE First Artists, 1978
PATRICK GOWERS
PATRICK YOUNG

STEWARDESS SCHOOL Columbia, 1986
ROBERT FOLK

THE STICK Distant Horizon International, 1987
DANA KAPROFF

STICK Universal, 1985
BARRY DEVORZON
JOSEPH CONLAN
STEVE DORFF

THE STICK UP MUD Trident-Barber, 1978
MICHAEL J. LEWIS

STICKING TOGETHER (TF) Blinn-Thorpe Productions/Viacom Productions, 1978
JOHN RUBINSTEIN

STICKS AND STONES Goldbar, 1995
HUMMIE MANN

STICKY FINGERS Spectrafilm, 1988
GARY CHANG

STILL CRAZY LIKE A FOX (TF) Schenck-Cardea Productions/Columbia TV, 1987
MARK SNOW

STILL NOT QUITE HUMAN (CTF) Resnick-Margellos Prods., 1992
JOHN DEBNEY

STILL OF THE NIGHT MGM/UA, 1982
JOHN KANDER

STILL THE BEAVER Bud Austin Productions/Universal TV, 1983
JOHN CACAVAS

STILLWATCH (TF) Zev Braun Pictures/Potomac Productions/Interscope Communications, 1987
GIL MELLE

THE STING partial Universal, 1973
MARVIN HAMLISCH ★★

THE STING II Universal, 1983
LALO SCHIFRIN ★

STINGAREE RKO Radio, 1934
MAX STEINER†

STINGRAY Avco Embassy, 1978
J.A.C. REDFORD

STINGRAY (TF) Stephen J. Cannell Productions, 1985
PETE CARPENTER†
MIKE POST

STIR Hoyts Distribution, 1980
CAMERON ALLAN

STIR CRAZY Columbia, 1980
TOM SCOTT

A STITCH FOR TIME (FD) 1987
WENDY BLACKSTONE

STITCHES International Film Marketing, 1985
BOB FLOKE

STOLEN BABIES (CTF) ABC Video Enterprises/Sanders-Moses Prods., 1993
MASON DARING

THE STOLEN CHILDREN 1992
FRANCO PIERSANTI

STOLEN FACE Exclusive Films, 1952
MALCOLM ARNOLD

STOLEN HARMONY Paramount, 1935
SIGMUND KRUMGOLD†

STOLEN HOURS United Artists, 1963
MORT LINDSEY

STOLEN KISSES Lopert, 1969
ANTOINE DUHAMEL

A STOLEN LIFE Warner Bros., 1946
MAX STEINER†

STOLEN LIFE Paramount, 1939
SIR WILLIAM WALTON†

STOLEN PARADISE RKO Radio, 1941
NATHANIEL SHILKRET†

THE STOLEN SPRING 1993
JAN GLAESEL

STOLEN WOMEN (TF) CBS Prods., 1996
DANA KAPROFF

STOLEN: ONE HUSBAND (TF) King Phoenix Entertainment, 1990
JAMES DIPASQUALLE

STOMPIN' AT THE SAVOY (TF) Richard Maynard Prods./Gallant Entertainment/Universal TV, 1992
HAROLD WHEELER

THE STONE 1965
STAVROS XARCHAKOS

STONE (TF) Stephen J. Cannell/Universal TV, 1979
PETE CARPENTER†

THE STONE BOY 20th Century Fox, 1984
JOHN BEAL

THE STONE BOY TLC Films/20th Century Fox, 1984
JAMES HORNER

STONE COLD Columbia, 1991
SYLVESTER LEVAY

STONE FOX (TF) Hanna-Barbera Productions/Allarcom Ltd./Taft Entertainment TV, 1987
ALLYN FERGUSON
PETER MATZ

THE STONE KILLER Columbia, 1973
ROY BUDD†

STONE PILLOW (TF) Schaefer-Karpf Productions/Gaylord Productions, 1985
GEORGES DELERUE†

THE STONE RIVER 1983
GUENTHER FISCHER

THE STONED AGE Trimark, 1995
DAVID KITAY

STONES FOR IBARRA (TF) Titus Productions, 1988
STANLEY MYERS†

STONESTREET: WHO KILLED THE CENTERFOLD MODEL? (TF) Universal TV, 1977
PATRICK WILLIAMS

A STONING AT FULHAM COUNTY (TF) The Landsburg Company, 1988
DON DAVIS

STONY ISLAND World-Northal, 1978
DAVID M. MATTHEWS

STOOD UP (TF) ABC-TV, 1990
WENDY BLACKSTONE

STOOGEMANIA Atlantic Releasing Corporation, 1985
HUMMIE MANN

THE STOOLIE Jama, 1972
WILLIAM GOLDSTEIN

STOP AT NOTHING (CTF) Chair/ABC, 1991
J.A.C. REDFORD

STOP PRESS GIRL 1949
WALTER GOEHR†

STOP TRAIN 349 1964
PETER THOMAS

STOP! OR MY MOM WILL SHOOT Universal, 1992
ALAN SILVESTRI

STORIA DELLA BOMBA ATOMICA (TD) 1971
DANIELE PARIS

STORIE DI VITA E MALAVITA 1975
ENNIO MORRICONE

STORIES FROM LOBOS CREEK Home Vision, 1988
CARL DANTE

THE STORK CLUB Paramount, 1945
ROBERT EMMETT DOLAN†

STORM Cannon, 1986
AMIN BHATIA

STORM AT DAYBREAK MGM, 1933
WILLIAM AXT†

STORM BOY South Australian Film Corp., 1976
MICHAEL CARLOS

STORM FEAR United Artists, 1956
ELMER BERNSTEIN

STORM OVER LISBON Republic, 1944
WALTER SCHARF

STORM OVER THE NILE Columbia, 1956
BENJAMIN FRANKEL†

STORM OVER TIBET Columbia, 1951
ARTHUR HONEGGER†
LEITH STEVENS†

THE STORM RIDER 20th Century-Fox, 1957
LES BAXTER†

STORM WARNING 1940
DAVID RAKSIN

STORM WARNING Warner Bros., 1951
DANIELE AMFITHEATROF†

STORMIN' HOME (TF) CBS Entertainment, 1985
BRUCE BROUGHTON

STORMTROOPERS 1977
ENZO JANNACCI

STORMY MONDAY Atlantic Releasing Corporation, 1988
MIKE FIGGIS

STORMY WEATHERS (TF) Haft-Nasatir/River Siren/Tri-Star TV, 1992
DAVID BELL

THE STORY LADY (TF) Michael Filerman Prods./NBC Prods., 1991
LEE HOLDRIDGE

THE STORY OF A WOMAN 1970
JOHN WILLIAMS

STORY OF A GIRL ALONE 1969
ANGELO FRANCESCO LAVAGNINO†

THE STORY OF DR. WASSELL Paramount, 1944
VICTOR YOUNG†

THE STORY OF ESTHER COSTELLO Columbia, 1957
GEORGES AURIC†

THE STORY OF JACOB AND JOSEPH (TF) Milberg Theatrical Productions/Columbia Pictures TV, 1974
MIKIS THEODORAKIS

THE STORY OF LOUIS PASTEUR Warner Bros., 1936
BERNHARD KAUN†

THE STORY OF MONTY THE MAD RAT (AF) Warner Bros., 1997
FREDERIC TALGORN

THE STORY OF PRETTY BOY FLOYD (TF) Public Arts Productions/Universal TV, 1974
PETE RUGOLO

THE STORY OF QIU JU QIU JU DA GUANSI 1992
ZHAO JIPING

THE STORY OF RUTH 20th Century-Fox, 1960
FRANZ WAXMAN†

THE STORY OF SEABISCUIT Warner Bros., 1949
DAVID BUTTOLPH†

THE STORY OF THE TAIRA FAMILY 1972
ISAO TOMITA

THE STORY OF THREE LOVES MGM, 1953
MIKLOS ROZSA†

THE STORY OF WILL ROGERS Warner Bros., 1952
VICTOR YOUNG†

THE STORY ON PAGE ONE 20th Century Fox, 1959
ELMER BERNSTEIN

THE STORYTELLER (TF) Fairmount/Foxcroft Productions/Universal TV, 1977
HAL MOONEY
DAVID SHIRE

STORYVILLE 20th Century Fox, 1992
CARTER BURWELL

STOWAWAY 20th Century-Fox, 1937
LOUIS SILVERS†

STOWAWAY GIRL MANUELA Paramount, 1957
WILLIAM ALWYN†

STOWAWAY TO THE MOON (TF) 20th Century-Fox TV, 1975
PATRICK WILLIAMS

STRAIGHT IS THE WAY MGM, 1934
WILLIAM AXT†

STRAIGHT OUT OF BROOKLYN American Playhouse, 1991
HAROLD WHEELER

STRAIGHT TALK Buena Vista, 1992
BRAD FIEDEL

STRAIGHT TIME Warner Bros., 1978
DAVID SHIRE

STRAIGHT TO HELL 1987
PRAY FOR RAIN

STRAIT-JACKET Columbia, 1964
VAN ALEXANDER

A STRAITLACED GIRL Parafrance, 1977
OLIVER DASSAULT

STRANDED New Line Cinema, 1987
STACY WIDELITZ

STRANDED (TF) Tim Flack Productions/Columbia TV, 1986
ALF CLAUSEN

A STRANGE AFFAIR Parafrance, 1982
PHILIPPE SARDE

THE STRANGE AFFAIR Paramount, 1968
BASIL KIRCHIN

THE STRANGE AFFAIR OF UNCLE HARRY Universal, 1945
HANS J. SALTER†

THE STRANGE AND DEADLU OCCURRENCE (TF) Metromedia Producers Corporation/Alpine Productions, 1974
ROBERT PRINCE.

STRANGE APPOINTMENT 1950
ANGELO FRANCESCO LAVAGNINO†

STRANGE BARGAIN RKO Radio, 1949
FREDERICK HOLLANDER†

STRANGE BEDFELLOWS Universal, 1965
LEIGH HARLINE†

STRANGE BREW MGM/UA, 1983
CHARLES FOX

THE STRANGE CASE OF DR. RX Universal, 1942
HANS J. SALTER†

STRANGE CARGO MGM, 1940
FRANZ WAXMAN†

STRANGE CONFESSION Universal, 1945
FRANK SKINNER†

STRANGE DAYS 20th Century Fox, 1995
GRAEME REVELL

THE STRANGE DEATH OF ADOLPH HITLER Universal, 1943
HANS J. SALTER†

STRANGE EVENTS 1977
PIERO PICCIONI

STRANGE FRUIT 1995
ALEX SHAPIRO

STRANGE HOLIDAY Producers Releasing Corporation, 1946
GORDON JENKINS†

SUEZ 20th Century-Fox, 1939
DAVID RAKSIN

SUFFERING BASTARDS AIP, 1990
DAN DIPAOLA

SUFLOOR *THE PROMPTER* 1993
MARGO KOLAR

SUGAR COLT 1966
LUIS BACALOV

SUGAR HILL 20th Century Fox, 1993
TERENCE BLANCHARD

SUGARFOOT Warner Bros., 1950
MAX STEINER†

THE SUGARLAND EXPRESS Universal, 1974
JOHN WILLIAMS

SUICIDE BATTALION American International, 1958
RONALD STEIN†

SUICIDE SQUADRON *DANGEROUS MOONLIGHT* RKO Radio, 1941
RICHARD ADDINSELL†

THE SUICIDE'S WIFE (TF) Factor-Newland Production Corporation, 1979
DAVID RAKSIN

SUITE FRANCAISE 1943
JEAN WIENER†

SULLIVAN'S EMPIRE Universal, 1967
LALO SCHIFRIN

SULLIVAN'S TRAVELS Paramount, 1941
LEO SHUKEN†

THE SULLIVANS 20th Century-Fox, 1944
CYRIL J. MOCKRIDGE†

SULTAN A VENDRE 1970
GEORGES DELERUE†

SULTAN AND THE ROCK STAR (TF) Walt Disney Productions, 1978
ARTIE BUTLER

THE SULTAN'S DAUGHTER Monogram, 1943
KARL HAJOS†

SUMMER *LE RAYON VERT* Orion Classics, 1986
JEAN-LOUIS VALERO

SUMMER AND SMOKE Paramount, 1961
ELMER BERNSTEIN ★

SUMMER CAMP Filminvest, 1986
CARL DANTE

SUMMER FANTASY (TF) Moonlight Productions II, 1984
PETER BERNSTEIN

SUMMER GIRL (TF) Bruce Lansbury Productions/ Roberta Haynes Productions/Finnegan Associates, 1983
ANGELA MORLEY

SUMMER HEAT Atlantic Releasing Corporation, 1987
RICHARD STONE

THE SUMMER HOUSE Samuel Goldwyn, 1993
STANLEY MYERS†

SUMMER LIGHTNING 1972
STANLEY MYERS†

SUMMER LOVE Universal, 1958
HENRY MANCINI†
HANS J. SALTER†

SUMMER LOVERS Filmways, 1982
BASIL POLEDOURIS

SUMMER MADNESS United Artists, 1955
ALESSANDRO CICOGNINI†

SUMMER MAGIC Buena Vista, 1963
BUDDY BAKER

THE SUMMER MY FATHER GREW UP (TF) Robert Shapiro Productions, 1991
LEE HOLDRIDGE

THE SUMMER OF BEN TYLER (TF) Hallmark Hall of Fame, 1996
VAN DYKE PARKS

SUMMER OF '42 Warner Bros., 1971
MICHEL LEGRAND ★★

SUMMER OF MY GERMAN SOLDIER (TF) Highgate Productions, 1978
STANLEY MYERS†

SUMMER OF SECRETS Greater Union Film Distribution, 1976
CAMERON ALLAN

A SUMMER PLACE Warner Bros., 1959
MAX STEINER†

SUMMER RENTAL Paramount, 1985
ALAN SILVESTRI

SUMMER SCHOOL Paramount, 1987
DANNY ELFMAN

SUMMER SOLDIERS 1972
TORU TAKEMITSU†

A SUMMER STORY Atlantic Releasing Corporation, 1988
GEORGES DELERUE†

SUMMER STOCK MGM, 1950
JOHN GREEN†

SUMMER STORM United Artists, 1944
KARL HAJOS† ★

A SUMMER TO REMEMBER (TF) Inter Planetary Productions, 1985
CHARLES FOX

SUMMER VACATION: 1999 New Yorker, 1989
YURIKO NAKAMURA

SUMMER WISHES, WINTER DREAMS Columbia, 1973
JOHNNY MANDEL

A SUMMER WITHOUT BOYS (TF) Playboy Productions, 1973
ANDREW BELLING

SUMMER'S LEASE (TF) 1991
NIGEL HESS

SUMMERFIELD 1977
BRUCE SMEATON

THE SUMMERTIME KILLER 1971
LUIS BACALOV

SUMMERTIME *SUMMER MADNESS* United Artists, 1955
ALESSANDRO CICOGNINI†

SUMMERTIME SWITCH (TF) Louis Randolph Family Films/Victor TV, 1994
BRADLEY SMITH

SUMMERTREE Columbia, 1971
DAVID SHIRE

Summit Associates Ltd., 1975
FRANCO MICALIZZI

THE SUN ALSO RISES 20th Century-Fox, 1957
HUGO FRIEDHOFER†

THE SUN ALSO RISES (TF) Furia-Oringer Productions/20th Century Fox TV, 1984
BILLY GOLDENBERG

THE SUN COMES UP MGM, 1949
ANDRE PREVIN

THE SUN GODDESS 1993
CHICO HAMILTON

THE SUN NEVER SETS Universal, 1939
FRANK SKINNER†

THE SUN SETS AT DAWN Eagle Lion, 1951
LEITH STEVENS†

THE SUN SHINES BRIGHT Republic, 1953
VICTOR YOUNG†

SUN VALLEY SERENADE 20th Century-Fox, 1941
EMIL NEWMAN† ★

SUN'S HUNTER 1970
TORU TAKEMITSU†

SUNBURN Paramount, 1979
JOHN CAMERON

SUNCHASER Warner Bros., 1996
MAURICE JARRE

SUNDAY DINNER FOR A SOLDIER 20th Century-Fox, 1944
ALFRED NEWMAN†

SUNDAY DRIVE (TF) Wizan TV Enterprises/Walt Disney TV, 1986
BRAD FIEDEL

SUNDAY IN THE COUNTRY American International, 1973
PAUL HOFFERT

SUNDAY IN THE COUNTRY MGM/UA Classics, 1984
PHILIPPE SARDE

SUNDAY LOVERS MGM/United Artists, 1980
MANUEL DE SICA

SUNDAY WOMAN 20th Century-Fox, 1976
ENNIO MORRICONE

SUNDAYS AND CYBELE *CYBELE OU LES DIMANCHES DE VILLE d'AVRAY* Davis-Royal, 1962
MAURICE JARRE ★

SUNDOWN United Artists, 1941
MIKLOS ROZSA† ★

SUNDOWN Vestron, 1989
RICHARD STONE

THE SUNDOWNERS Warner Bros., 1960
DIMITRI TIOMKIN†

SUNFLOWER Avco Embassy, 1969
HENRY MANCINI† ★

SUNNY RKO Radio, 1941
ANTHONY COLLINS† ★

SUNRISE AT CAMPOBELLO Warner Bros., 1960
FRANZ WAXMAN†

SUNSET Tri-Star, 1988
HENRY MANCINI†

SUNSET BOULEVARD Paramount, 1950
FRANZ WAXMAN† ★★

SUNSET LIMOUSINE (TF) Witzend Productions/ITC Productions, 1983
FRANK DENSON

SUNSET PARK TriStar, 1996
KAY GEE
MILES GOODMAN†

SUNSET, SUNRISE 1973
NINO ROTA†

SUNSHINE CHRISTMAS (TF) Universal TV, 1977
LEE HOLDRIDGE

SUNSTROKE (CTF) Wilshire Court, 1992
JOHN DEBNEY

THE SUPER 20th Century Fox, 1991
MILES GOODMAN†

SUPER CHIEF (FD) Direct Cinema Limited, 1990
MARK ADLER

THE SUPER COPS MGM, 1974
JERRY FIELDING†

SUPER MARIO BROS. Buena Vista, 1993
ALAN SILVESTRI

SUPERBEAST United Artists, 1972
RICHARD LASALLE

SUPERCARRIER (TF) Fries Entertainment/Richard Hayward-Real Tinsel Productions, 1988
JACK ESKEW
CRAIG SAFAN

SUPERCOP Dimension, 1996
JOEL McNEELY

SUPERDAD Buena Vista, 1974
BUDDY BAKER

SUPERDOME (TF) ABC Circle Films, 1978
JOHN CACAVAS

SUPERFANTAGENIO *ALADDIN* Cannon, 1987
FABIO FRIZZI

SUPERFLY Warner Bros., 1972
CURTIS MAYFIELD

SUPER-GIANT 2 *SPACEMEN AGAINST THE VAMPIRES FROM SPACE* 1956
CHUMEI WATANABE

SUPERGIRL Warner Bros., 1984
JERRY GOLDSMITH

THE SUPERGRASS Hemdale, 1985
KEITH TIPPET

SUPERMAN Warner Bros., 1978
JOHN WILLIAMS ★

SUPERMAN II Warner Bros., 1981
KEN THORNE

SUPERMAN III Warner Bros., 1983
KEN THORNE

SUPERMAN IV: THE QUEST FOR PEACE Warner Bros., 1987
ALEXANDER COURAGE

THE SUPERNATURALS Republic Entertainment/ Sandy Howard Productions, 1985
ROBERT O. RAGLAND

SUPERNATURAL Paramount, 1933
KARL HAJOS†
MILAN RODER†

SUPERSTITION *THE WITCH* Almi Pictures, 1985
DAVID GIBNEY

SUPPORT YOUR LOCAL GUNFIGHTER United Artists, 1971
ALLYN FERGUSON

SUPPORT YOUR LOCAL SHERIFF! MGM, 1969
JEFF ALEXANDER†

SUPPOSE THEY GAVE A WAR AND NOBODY CAME? Cinerama Releasing Corporation, 1970
JERRY FIELDING†

SUR 1986
ASTOR PIAZZOLA

SUR LE PONT D'AVIGNON (FD) 1956
MAURICE JARRE

SUR UN ARBRE PERCHE 1971
ALAIN GORRAGUER

SURAJ KA SATVAN GHODA *SEVEN HORSE OF THE SUN* 1994
VANRAJ BHATIA

THE SURE THING Embassy, 1985
TOM SCOTT

SURF AND SEAWEED Ralph Steiner, 1931
MARC BLITZSTEIN†

SURF II Arista, 1983
PETER BERNSTEIN
MARK GOVERNOR

SURF NINJAS New Line, 1993
DAVID KITAY

SURPRISE PACKAGE Columbia, 1960
BENJAMIN FRANKEL†

SURPRISE PARTY Uranium Films, 1982
MICHEL MAGNE†

SURRENDER Warner Bros., 1987
MICHEL COLOMBIER

THE SURROGATE (TF) Moore-Weiss Prods./Stephen J. Cannell Prods., 1995
NICHOLAS PIKE

SURVIVAL GAME Trans World Entertainment, 1987
MICHAEL J. LINN†

THE SURVIVAL OF DANA (TF) Roger Gimbel Productions/Marc Trabulus Enterprises/EMI TV, 1979
CRAIG SAFAN

SURVIVAL RUN Spiegel-Bergman, 1980
GARY WILLIAM FRIEDMAN

SURVIVE THE NIGHT (CTF) Heartstar/Once Upon A Time/USA/RAI/Spector, 1993
FRED MOLLIN

SURVIVE THE SAVAGE SEA (TF) von Zerneck-Sertner Films, 1992
FRED KARLIN ☆

SURVIVE! Paramount, 1975
GERALD FRIED

SURVIVING (TF) Telepictures Corporation, 1985
JAMES HORNER

SURVIVING PICASSO Warner Bros., 1996
RICHARD ROBBINS

SURVIVING THE GAME New Line, 1994
STEWART COPELAND

THE SURVIVOR Hemdale, 1981
BRIAN MAY†

THE SURVIVORS Columbia, 1983
PAUL CHIHARA

SUSAN AND GOD MGM, 1940
HERBERT STOTHART†

SUSAN SLADE Warner Bros., 1961
MAX STEINER†

SUSAN SLEPT HERE RKO Radio, 1954
LEIGH HARLINE†

SUSANNAH OF THE MOUNTIES 20th Century-Fox, 1939
LOUIS SILVERS†

THE SUSPECT Universal, 1945
FRANK SKINNER†

SUSPECT Tri-Star, 1987
MICHAEL KAMEN

SUSPECT DEVICE (CTF) New Horizons-Hillwood Entertainment, 1995
CHRISTOPHER LENNERTZ

THE SUSPENDED STEP OF THE STORK 1991
HELENA KARAINDROU

SUSPENSE Monogram, 1946
DANIELE AMFITHEATROF†

SUSPICION RKO Radio, 1941
FRANZ WAXMAN† ★

SUSPICION (TF) Hemisphere Productions/HTV, 1988
LARRY GROSSMAN

SUSPIRIA International Classics, 1977
GOBLIN

SUTJESKA 1973
MIKIS THEODORAKIS

SUTTER'S GOLD Universal, 1936
FRANZ WAXMAN†

SUTURE Kino-Korsakoff, 1993
CARY BERGER

SUZY MGM, 1936
WILLIAM AXT†

SVEGLIATI E UCCIDI 1966
ENNIO MORRICONE

SVENGALI MGM, 1955
WILLIAM ALWYN†

SVENGALI (TF) Robert Halmi Productions, 1983
JOHN BARRY

SWALLOWS AND AMAZONS LDS, 1974
WILFRED JOSEPHS

SWAMP THING Avco Embassy, 1982
HARRY MANFREDINI

SWAMP WATER 20th Century-Fox, 1941
DAVID BUTTOLPH†

THE SWAN MGM, 1956
BRONISLAU KAPER†

THE SWAN PRINCESS (AF) New Line, 1994
LEX DE AZEVEDO

SWAN SONG (TF) Renee Valente Productions/ Topanga Services Ltd./20th Century-Fox, 1980
JONATHAN TUNICK

SWANEE RIVER 20th Century-Fox, 1939
LOUIS SILVERS† ★

SWANN IN LOVE Orion Classics, 1984
HANS WERNER HENZE

THE SWARM Warner Bros., 1978
JERRY GOLDSMITH

SWASHBUCKLER Universal, 1976
JOHN ADDISON

SWEEPINGS RKO Radio, 1933
MAX STEINER†

SWEET BIRD OF YOUTH (TF) 1989
RALPH BURNS

SWEET BUNCH *GLYKIA SYMMORIA* 1983
GEORGE HATZINASSIOS

SWEET CHARITY Universal, 1969
CY COLEMAN ★

SWEET COUNTRY Cinema Group, 1987
STAVROS XARCHAKOS

THE SWEET CREEK COUNTY WAR Key International, 1979
RICHARD BOWDEN

SWEET DREAMS Tri-Star, 1985
CHARLES GROSS

SWEET EMMA, DEAR BOBE - SKETCHES, NUDES 1992
RICHARD SCHUMANN

SWEET HEART'S DANCE Tri-Star, 1988
RICHARD GIBBS

SWEET HOSTAGE (TF) Brut Productions, 1975
LUCHI DEJESUS

SWEET LIBERTY Universal, 1986
BRUCE BROUGHTON

SWEET LIES Island Pictures, 1988
TREVOR JONES

SWEET LORRAINE Angelika Films, 1987
RICHARD ROBBINS

SWEET MONEY Aries Films, Argentine
EMILIO KAUDERER

SWEET MOVIE Biograph, 1975
MANOS HADJIDAKIS†

SWEET NOTHING Concrete Films, 1995
STEVEN M. STERN

SWEET NOVEMBER Warner Bros., 1967
MICHEL LEGRAND

SWEET POISON (CTF) Smart Money Prods./MTE, 1991
JIM MANZIE

SWEET REVENGE Concorde, 1987
ERNEST TROOST

SWEET REVENGE The Movie Group, 1990
HUBERT BOUGIS

SWEET REVENGE *DANDY, THE ALL AMERICAN GIRL* MGM/United Artists, 1976
PAUL CHIHARA

SWEET REVENGE (CTF) Turner Pictures/Chrysalide Films/Canal/The Movie Group, 1990
DIDIER VASSEUR

SWEET REVENGE (TF) David Greene Productions/Robert Papazian Productions, 1984
GIL MELLE

THE SWEET RIDE 20th Century-Fox, 1968
PETE RUGOLO

SWEET SINS *BONA COME IL PANO* 1981
STELVIO CIPRIANI

SWEET SIXTEEN CI Films, 1981
TOMMY VIG

SWEET SMELL OF SUCCESS United Artists, 1957
ELMER BERNSTEIN

SWEET SUZY! *BLACKSNAKE* Signal 166, 1975
WILLIAM LOOSE†

SWEETHEARTS MGM, 1938
HERBERT STOTHART† ★

SWEETIE Avenue Pictures, 1990
MARTIN ARMIGER

SWELL GUY Universal, 1947
FRANK SKINNER†

SWEPT AWAY BY AN UNUSUAL DESTINY IN THE BLUE SEA OF AUGUST Cinema 5, 1974
PIERO PICCIONI

THE SWIMMER Columbia, 1968
MARVIN HAMLISCH

SWIMMING TO CAMBODIA Cinecom, 1987
LAURIE ANDERSON

SWIMSUIT (TF) Musifilm Productions/American First Run Studios, 1989
JOHN D'ANDREA
MICHAEL LLOYD

THE SWINDLE *IL BIDONE* Astor, 1955
NINO ROTA†

THE SWING 1983
PEER RABEN

SWING HIGH, SWING LOW Paramount, 1937
VICTOR YOUNG†

SWING KIDS Hollywood, 1993
JAMES HORNER

SWING OUT, SISTER Universal, 1945
MILTON ROSEN†

SWING SHIFT Warner Bros., 1983
PATRICK WILLIAMS

SWING YOUR LADY Warner Bros., 1938
ADOLPH DEUTSCH†

THE SWINGER Paramount, 1966
MARTY PAICH†

SWINGERS 1996
JULIANNE KELLEY
JUSTIN REINHARDT

THE SWINGIN' MAIDEN *THE IRON MAIDEN* Columbia, 1962
ERIC ROGERS†

THE SWINGING CONFESSORS *IL PRETE SPOSATO* 1970
ARMANDO TROVAJOLI

SWISS FAMILY ROBINSON Buena Vista, 1960
WILLIAM ALWYN†

SWISS FAMILY ROBINSON RKO Radio, 1940
ANTHONY COLLINS†

SWISS FAMILY ROBINSON (TF) Irwin Allen Productions/20th Century-Fox TV, 1975
RICHARD LASALLE

SWISS MISS MGM, 1933
T. MARVIN HATLEY†

SWITCH Warner Bros., 1991
HENRY MANCINI†

THE SWITCH (TF) Avnet-Kerner/Companionway, 1993
TANGERINE DREAM

SWITCH (TF) Glen Larson Productions/Universal TV, 1975
STU PHILLIPS

SWITCHBLADE SISTERS *THE JEZEBELS/PLAYGIRL GANG* Centaur, 1975
LES BAXTER†

SWITCHED AT BIRTH (TF) O'Hara-Horowitz Prods./Morrow-Heus Prods./Guber-Peters/Columbia TV, 1991
MARVIN HAMLISCH

SWITCHING CHANNELS Columbia, 1988
MICHEL LEGRAND
NEIL DIAMOND

SWOON Fine Line, 1992
JAMES BENNETT

THE SWORD AND THE SORCERER Group 1, 1982
DAVID WHITAKER

THE SWORD IN THE STONE (AF) Buena Vista, 1963
GEORGE BRUNS ★

SWORD IN THE DESERT Universal, 1949
FRANK SKINNER

THE SWORD OF ALI BABA Universal, 1965
FRANK SKINNER

THE SWORD OF DOOM Toho, 1967
MASARU SATO

SWORD OF GIDEON (CTF) Alliance Entertainment/Les Films Ariane/HBO Premiere Films/CTV/Telefilm Canada/Rogers Cablesystems/Radio-Canada, 1986
GEORGES DELERUE†

SWORD OF HEAVEN Trans World Entertainment, 1985
CHRISTOPHER L. STONE

SWORD OF LANCELOT *LANCELOT AND GUINEVERE* Universal, 1963
RON GOODWIN

SWORD OF THE CONQUEROR *ROSMUNDA E ALBOINO* 1961
CARLO RUSTICHELLI

SWORD OF THE VALIANT Cannon, 1984
RON GEESIN

SWORDKILL Empire Pictures, 1986
RICHARD H. BAND

THE SWORDSMAN IN DOUBLE-FLAG TOWN 1991
TAO LONG

THE SWORDSMAN Columbia, 1947
HUGO FRIEDHOFER†

THE SWORDSMAN SC Entertainment, 1992
DOMENIC TROIANO

SWORDSMAN II 1992
RICHARD YUEN

SWORDSMAN III 1993
WU WAI-LAP

SWORN ENEMY MGM, 1936
EDWARD WARD†

SWORN TO SILENCE (TF) Daniel H. Blatt-Robert Singer Productions, 1987
DENNIS MCCARTHY

SWORN TO VENGEANCE (TF) A. Shane Co./RHI Entertainment, 1993
ROBERT FOLK

SYBIL (TF) Lorimar Productions, 1976
LEONARD ROSENMAN ☆☆

SYLVESTER Columbia, 1985
LEE HOLDRIDGE

SYLVIA MGM/UA Classics, 1985
LEONARD ROSENMAN

SYLVIA Paramount, 1965
DAVID RAKSIN

SYLVIA SCARLETT RKO Radio, 1936
ROY WEBB†

SYMPHONY FOR A MASSACRE 7 Arts, 1965
MICHEL MAGNE†

SYMPHONY OF SIX MILLION RKO Radio, 1932
MAX STEINER†

SYMPTOMS *THE BLOOD VIRGIN* 1974
JOHN SCOTT

SYNANON Columbia, 1965
NEAL HEFTI

SYNCOPATION RKO Radio, 1942
LEITH STEVENS†

SYNDICATE SADISTS Summit Associates Ltd., 1975
FRANCO MICALIZZI

SYNGENOR Syngenor Production Co., 1990
TOM CHASE
STEVE RUCKER

THE SYSTEM Warner Bros., 1953
DAVID BUTTOLPH†

T

T BONE N WEASEL (CTF) TNT, 1992
STEVE TYRELL

TABLE FOR FIVE Warner Bros., 1983
MILES GOODMAN†
JOHN MORRIS

TACK'S CHICKS Trimark, 1993
DAVID KITAY

TACONES LEJANOS *HIGH HEELS* Miramax, 1991
RYUICHI SAKAMOTO

TAD (CTF) Chris-Rose Prods./Family Prods., 1995
GEORGE S. CLINTON

THE TAEBAEK MOUNTAINS *TAEBAEK SANMAEK* 1995
KIM SOO-CHUL

TAEBAEK SANMAEK 1995
KIM SOO-CHUL

TAFELSPITZ 1993
CRISTIAN KOLONOVITS

TAFFIN MGM/UA, 1988
STANLEY MYERS†

T.A.G.: THE ASSASSINATION GAME New World, 1982
CRAIG SAFAN

TAGGET (CTF) Mirisch/Tagget Prods., 1991
MICHEL COLOMBIER

TAIL GUNNER JOE (TF) Universal TV, 1977
BILLY MAY

THE TAILOR'S MAID *PADRI E FIGLI* Trans-Lux, 1957
CARLO RUSTICHELLI

TAILSPIN: BEHIND THE KOREAN AIRLINE TRAGEDY (TF) Darlow Smithson Productions/HBO, 1989
DAVID FERGUSON

TAINTED BLOOD (CTF) Fast Track Films/Wilshire Court, 1993
DANA KAPROFF

TAI-PAN DEG, 1986
MAURICE JARRE

THE TAKE Columbia, 1974
FRED KARLIN

THE TAKE (CTF) Cine-Nevada Inc./MCA TV, 1990
DAVID BEAL

THE TAKE (CTF) Cine-Nevada Inc./MCA-TV, 1990
DAVID BELL
SUSAN MARDER
MICHAEL SHRIEVE

TAKE A GIANT STEP United Artists, 1959
JACK MARSHALL

TAKE A HARD RIDE 20th Century Fox, 1975
JERRY GOLDSMITH

TAKE A HARD RIDE 20th Century-Fox, 1974
JERRY GOLDSMITH

TAKE A LETTER, DARLING Paramount, 1942
VICTOR YOUNG† ★

TAKE ALL OF ME Group 1, 1978
STELVIO CIPRIANI

TAKE CARE OF MY LITTLE GIRL 20th Century-Fox, 1951
ALFRED NEWMAN†

TAKE DOWN Buena Vista, 1979
MERRILL B. JENSEN

TAKE HER, SHE'S MINE 20th Century-Fox, 1963
JERRY GOLDSMITH

TAKE IT EASY 1974
ANDRZEJ KORZYNSKI

TAKE ME HOME AGAIN (TF) Von Zerneck-Sertner/Patricia K. Meyer Prods./ACI, 1994
PATRICK WILLIAMS

TAKE ME OUT TO THE BALL GAME MGM, 1949
ADOLPH DEUTSCH†

TAKE ME TO TOWN Universal, 1953
HENRY MANCINI†
HERMAN STEIN

TAKE MY LIFE Eagle Lion, 1947
WILLIAM ALWYN†

TAKE ONE FALSE STEP Universal, 1949
WALTER SCHARF

TAKE THE HIGH GROUND MGM, 1953
DIMITRI TIOMKIN†

TAKE THE MONEY AND RUN Cinerama Releasing Corporation, 1969
MARVIN HAMLISCH

TAKE YOUR BEST SHOT (TF) Levinson-Link Productions/Robert Papazian Productions, 1982
PETER MATZ

TAKEN AWAY (TF) Hart, Thomas & Berlin Productions, 1989
ROB MOUNSEY

TAKING BACK MY LIFE (TF) Elliot Fredgen/Lyttle-Heshty/Warner Bros. TV, 1992
RANDY EDELMAN

TAKING CARE OF BUSINESS 1990
STEWART COPELAND

THE TAKING OF BEVERLY HILLS Columbia, 1991
JAN HAMMER

THE TAKING OF FLIGHT 847: THE ULI DERICKSON STORY (TF) Columbia TV, 1988
GIL MELLE

THE TAKING OF PELHAM 1-2-3 United Artists, 1974
DAVID SHIRE

TALE OF A VAMPIRE 1992
JULIAN JOSEPH

A TALE OF TWO CITIES MGM, 1935
HERBERT STOTHART†

A TALE OF TWO CITIES Rank, 1958
RICHARD ADDINSELL†

A TALE OF TWO CITIES (TF) Granada TV/Antenne 2, 1989
SERGE FRANKLIN

A TALE OF TWO CITIES (TF) Norman Rosemont Productions/Marble Arch Productions, 1980
ALLYN FERGUSON

A TALENT FOR LOVING The Mirisch Company, 1969
KEN THORNE

TALENT FOR THE GAME Paramount, 1991
DAVID NEWMAN

TALES FROM HOLLYWOOD (TF) BBC-TV/American Playhouse, 1992
DOMINIC MULDOWNEY

TALES FROM THE CRYPT Cinerama Releasing Corporation, 1972
DOUGLAS GAMLEY

TALES FROM THE CRYPT (CTF) Tales from the Crypt Holdings, 1989
RY COODER
NICHOLAS PIKE
ALAN SILVESTRI

TALES FROM THE CRYPT II Cinerama Releasing Corporation, 1973
DOUGLAS GAMLEY

TALES FROM THE CRYPT PRESENTS BORDELLO OF BLOOD Universal, 1996
CHRIS BOARDMAN

TALES FROM THE CRYPT PRESENTS DEMON KNIGHT Universal, 1995
EDWARD SHEARMUR

TALES FROM THE DARKSIDE: THE MOVIE Paramount, 1990
CHAZ JANKEL
JIM MANZIE
PATRICK C. REGAN
DONALD RUBINSTEIN

TALES FROM THE HOOD Savoy, 1995
CHRISTOPHER YOUNG

TALES OF MANHATTAN 20th Century-Fox, 1942
SOL KAPLAN

TALES OF TERROR American International, 1962
LES BAXTER†

TALES OF THE CITY (MS) Working Title/Propaganda, 1994
JOHN E. KEANE

TALES OF THE DARKSIDE: THE MOVIE Paramount, 1990
JOHN HARRISON

TALES OF THE TAIRA CLAN 1955
FUMIO HAYASAKA†

TALES THAT WITNESS MADNESS Paramount, 1973
BERNARD EBBINGHOUSE

TALK 16 (DF) Films Transit, 1991
AARON DAVIS

TALK ABOUT A STRANGER MGM, 1952
DAVID BUTTOLPH†

TALK OF ANGELS Miramax, 1996
TREVOR JONES

TALK OF THE TOWN Columbia, 1942
FREDERICK HOLLANDER† ★

TALK RADIO Universal, 1988
STEWART COPELAND

TALKING WITH (TF) Thirteen-WNET, 1995
DAVID SHIRE

THE TALL BLOND MAN WITH ONE BLACK SHOE Cinema 5, 1972
VLADIMIR COSMA

THE TALL GUY Vestron, 1989
PETER BREWIS

TALL IN THE SADDLE RKO Radio, 1944
ROY WEBB†

THE TALL MEN 20th Century-Fox, 1955
VICTOR YOUNG†

TALL STORY Warner Bros., 1960
CYRIL J. MOCKRIDGE†

THE TALL STRANGER Universal, 1957
HANS J. SALTER†

THE TALL T Columbia, 1957
HEINZ ROEMHELD†

TALL TALE: THE UNBELIEVABLE ADVENTURES OF PECOS BILL Buena Vista, 1995
RANDY EDELMAN

TALL, DARK AND DEADLY (CTF) Fast Track Films/Wilshire Court, 1995
JOSEPH VITARELLI

TALL, DARK AND HANDSOME 20th Century-Fox, 1941
EMIL NEWMAN†

TALLINN PIMEDUSES *DARKNESS IN TALLINN* FilmZolfo, 1993
MADER

TALONS OF THE EAGLE Shapiro Glickenhaus, 1993
VAROUJE

TALVISOTA National-Filmi Oy, 1989
JUHA TIKKA

TAMAHINE MGM, 1964
MALCOLM ARNOLD

TAMANGO Valiant, 1957
JOSEPH KOSMA†

THE TAMARIND SEED Avco Embassy, 1974
JOHN BARRY

THE T.A.M.I. SHOW 1964
JACK NITZCHE

THE TAMING OF THE SHREW Columbia, 1967
NINO ROTA†

TAMMY AND THE DOCTOR Universal, 1963
FRANK SKINNER†

TAMMY AND THE MILLIONAIRE Universal, 1967
JACK MARSHALL

TAMMY AND THE TEENAGE T-REX Imperial Ent., 1994
TONY RIPPARETTI

TAMPICO 20th Century-Fox, 1944
DAVID RAKSIN

TANGA TIKA 1953
LES BAXTER†

F
I
L
M

T
I
T
L
E
S

TERROR AMONG US (TF) David Gerber Productions, 1981
ALLYN FERGUSON

TERROR AT ALCATRAZ (TF) Glen A. Larson Productions/Universal TV, 1982
STU PHILLIPS

TERROR AT LONDON BRIDGE/ARIZONA RIPPER (TF) Fries Entertainment, 1985
LALO SCHIFRIN

TERROR BY NIGHT Universal, 1946
HANS J. SALTER†

TERROR EYES Paramount, 1981
BRAD FIEDEL

TERROR HOUSE Scope III, 1972
BILL MARX

TERROR IN A TEXAS TOWN United Artists, 1958
GERALD FRIED

TERROR IN THE AISLES Universal, 1984
JOHN BEAL
RICHARD JOHNSTON
DOUG TIMM†

TERROR IN THE FOREST Fury Film Distribution Ltd., 1983
RICHARD HIERONYMOUS
ALAN OLDFIELD

TERROR IN THE JUNGLE 1967
LES BAXTER

TERROR IN THE NIGHT (TF) Landsburg Co./Cinematique/CBS Ent. Prods., 1994
DANA KAPROFF

TERROR IN THE SHADOWS (TF) Freyda Rothstein Prods./Lois Luger Prods./Hearst, 1995
CHRIS BOARDMAN

TERROR IN THE SKY (TF) Paramount Pictures TV, 1971
PATRICK WILLIAMS

TERROR IN THE WAX MUSEUM Cinerama Releasing Corporation, 1974
GEORGE DUNING

THE TERROR OF SHEBA *PERSECUTION* Blueberry Hill, 1974
PAUL FERRIS

THE TERROR OF THE TONGS Columbia, 1961
JAMES BERNARD

TERROR OF MECHA-GODZILLA/TERROR OF GODZILLA 1977
AKIRA IFUKUBE

TERROR OF THE STEPPE *I PREDONI DELLA STEPPA* 1963
CARLO RUSTICHELLI

TERROR ON HIGHWAY 91 (TF) Katy Film Productions, 1989
ARTIE KANE

TERROR ON THE 40TH FLOOR (TF) Montagne Productions/Metromedia Producers Corporation, 1974
VIC MIZZY

TERROR ON TRACK 9 (TF) Richard Crenna Prods./Spelling, 1992
CRAIG SAFAN

TERROR OUT OF THE SKY (TF) Alan Landsburg Productions, 1978
WILLIAM GOLDSTEIN

TERROR SQUAD MCEG, 1987
CHUCK CIRINO

TERROR SQUAD The Matterhorn Group, 1987
DAVID C. WILLIAMS

TERROR TRAIN 20th Century-Fox, 1980
JOHN MILLS-COCKELL

THE TERROR WITHIN Concorde, 1989
RICK CONRAD

TERRORIST ON TRIAL: THE UNITED STATES VS. SALIM AJAMI (TF) George Englund Productions/Robert Papazian Productions, 1988
JIMMIE HASKELL

THE TERRORISTS *RANSOM* 20th Century-Fox, 1975
JERRY GOLDSMITH

THE TERRORNAUTS 1967
ELISABETH LUYTENS†

TERRORVISION Empire Pictures, 1986
RICHARD H. BAND
CHRISTOPHER L. STONE

THE TERRY FOX STORY (CTF) HBO Premiere Films/Robert Cooper Films II, 1983
BILL CONTI

TESEO CONTRO IL MINOTAURO
CARLO RUSTICHELLI

TESS Columbia, 1979
PHILIPPE SARDE ★

TESS OF THE STORM COUNTRY 20th Century-Fox, 1960
BERT A. SHEFTER

TEST PILOT MGM, 1938
FRANZ WAXMAN†

TESTA T'AMMAZZO, CROCE...SEI MORTO...MI CHIAMANO ALLELUJA 1971
STELVIO CIPRIANI

THE TESTAMENT DES DR. MABUSE Janus, 1933
HANS ERDMANN†

TESTAMENT Paramount, 1983
JAMES HORNER

TESTIMONY OF TWO MEN (TF) Universal TV/Operation Prime Time, 1977
MICHEL COLOMBIER
GERALD FRIED

TEVIA AND HIS SEVEN DAUGHTERS 1968
DOV SELTZER

TEX Buena Vista, 1982
PINO DONAGGIO

TEXAS Columbia, 1941
SIDNEY CUTNER†

TEXAS ACROSS THE RIVER Universal, 1966
FRANK DEVOL

TEXAS CARNIVAL MGM, 1951
DAVID ROSE†

THE TEXAS CHAINSAW MASSACRE Bryanston, 1974
WAYNE BELL
TOBE HOOPER

THE TEXAS CHAINSAW MASSACRE PART 2 Cannon, 1986
TOBE HOOPER
JERRY LAMBERT

TEXAS JUSTICE (TF) Patchett-Kaufman Ent./WIN/Nancy Hardin, 1995
MARK SNOW

TEXAS, BROOKLYN AND HEAVEN United Artists, 1948
EMIL NEWMAN†

TEXASVILLE Nelson, 1990
PHIL MARSHALL

THADDEUS ROSE AND EDDIE (TF) CBS, Inc., 1978
CHARLES BERNSTEIN

THANK HEAVEN FOR SMALL FAVORS 1965
JOSEPH KOSMA†

THANK YOU AND GOODNIGHT (FD) Aries, 1992
MARK SUOZZO

THE THANKSGIVING PROMISE (TF) Mark H. Ovitz Productions/Walt Disney TV, 1986
BRUCE BROUGHTON

THAT BRENNAN GIRL Republic, 1946
GEORGE ANTHEIL†

THAT CERTAIN WOMAN Warner Bros., 1937
MAX STEINER†

THAT CHAMPIONSHIP SEASON Cannon, 1982
BILL CONTI

THAT COLD DAY IN THE PARK Commonwealth United, 1969
JOHNNY MANDEL

THAT DARN CAT Buena Vista, 1965
ROBERT F. BRUNNER

THAT DARN CAT Buena Vista, 1997
RICHARD GIBBS

THAT FORSYTE WOMAN MGM, 1949
BRONISLAU KAPER†

THAT GIRL FROM PARIS RKO Radio, 1936
NATHANIEL SHILKRET†

THAT HAGEN GIRL Warner Bros., 1947
FRANZ WAXMAN†

THAT HAMILTON WOMAN *LADY HAMILTON* United Artists, 1941
MIKLOS ROZSA†

THAT KIND OF WOMAN Paramount, 1959
NATHAN VAN CLEAVE†

THAT LADY 20th Century Fox, 1954
JOHN ADDISON

THAT LUCKY TOUCH Allied Artists, 1975
JOHN SCOTT

THAT MAN BOLT Universal, 1973
CHARLES BERNSTEIN

THAT MAN FROM RIO *L'HOMME DE RIO* Lopert, 1964
GEORGES DELERUE†

THAT MAN GEORGE! *L'HOMME DE MARRAKECH* Allied Artists, 1966
ALAIN GORRAGUI†FR

THAT NATZY NUISANCE United Artists, 1943
EDWARD WARD†

THAT NIGHT Warner Bros., 1992
DAVID NEWMAN

THAT NIGHT IN RIO 20th Century-Fox, 1941
ALFRED NEWMAN†

THAT NIGHT WITH YOU Universal, 1945
HANS J. SALTER†

THAT RIVIERA TOUCH Continental, 1966
RON GOODWIN

THAT SECRET SUNDAY (TF) CBS Entertainment, 1986
BOB ALCIVAR

THAT SINKING FEELING Samuel Goldwyn Company, 1979
COLIN TULLY

THAT SPLENDID NOVEMBER 1968
ENNIO MORRICONE

THAT SUMMER! Columbia, 1979
RAY RUSSELL

THAT THING YOU DO! 20th Century Fox, 1996
HOWARD SHORE

THAT UNCERTAIN FEELING United Artists, 1941
WERNER R. HEYMANN† ★

THAT WAS THEN...THIS IS NOW Paramount, 1985
BILL CUOMO
KEITH OLSEN

THAT WAY WITH WOMEN Warner Bros., 1947
FREDERICK HOLLANDER†

THAT WONDERFUL URGE 20th Century-Fox, 1949
CYRIL J. MOCKRIDGE†

THAT'S DANCING! (FD) MGM/UA, 1985
HENRY MANCINI†

THAT'S ENTERTAINMENT III MGM, 1994
MARC SHAIMAN

THAT'S ENTERTAINMENT! (FD) MGM/United Artists, 1974
HENRY MANCINI†

THAT'S ENTERTAINMENT, PART 2 MGM/United Artists, 1976
NELSON RIDDLE†

THAT'S LIFE! Columbia, 1986
HENRY MANCINI†

THAT'S MY BOY Paramount, 1951
LEIGH HARLINE†

THAT'S MY MAN Universal, 1947
HANS J. SALTER†

THAT'S THE SPIRIT Universal, 1945
HANS J. SALTER†

THAT'S THE WAY OF THE WORLD United Artists, 1975
MAURICE WHITE

THEATRE OF BLOOD United Artists, 1973
MICHAEL J. LEWIS

THEATRE OF DEATH *BLOOD FIEND* 1967
ELISABETH LUYTENS†

THEIR BIG MOMENT RKO Radio, 1934
MAX STEINER†

THELMA AND LOUISE Pathe, 1991
HANS ZIMMER

THELMA JORDAN Paramount, 1949
VICTOR YOUNG†

THEM! Warner Bros., 1954
BRONISLAU KAPER†

THEN CAME BRONSON (TF) MGM TV, 1969
GEORGE DUNING

THEODORA GOES WILD Columbia, 1936
WILLIAM GRANT STILL†

THEODORE REX New Line, 1996
ROBERT FOLK

THEOREM *TEOREMA* 1968
ENNIO MORRICONE

THERE ARE NO CHILDREN HERE (TF) Do We/Harpo Prods./LOMO Prods., 1993
HAROLD WHEELER

THERE GOES MY HEART United Artists, 1938
T. MARVIN HATLEY† ★

THERE GOES THE BRIDE Vanguard Releasing, 1980
HARRY ROBINSON

THERE GOES THE NEIGHBORHOOD Paramount, 1992
DAVID BELL

THERE IS NO. 13 1974
ARMANDO TROVAJOLI

THERE MUST BE A PONY (TF) R.J. Productions/Columbia TV, 1986
BILLY GOLDENBERG

THERE WAS A CROOKED MAN Warner Bros., 1970
CHARLES STROUSE

THERE WAS A LITTLE BOY (TF) Craig Anderson Prods./Lorimar TV, 1993
ANTHONY MARINELLI

THERE WERE TIMES, DEAR (TF) Lilac Productions, 1987
JAY GRUSKA

THERE WILL BE NO MORE SORROWS NOR OBLIVION Aries, 1983
OSCAR CARDOZO OCAMPO

THERE'S A GIRL IN MY HEART Allied Artists, 1949
HERSCHEL BURKE GILBERT

THERE'S ALWAYS TOMORROW Universal, 1956
HEINZ ROEMHELD†

THERE'S ALWAYS TOMORROW Universal, 1956
HERMAN STEIN

THERE'S MAGIC IN MUSIC Paramount, 1941
FREDERICK HOLLANDER†

THERE'S NO BUSINESS LIKE SHOW BUSINESS 20th Century-Fox, 1954
ALFRED NEWMAN† ★
LIONEL NEWMAN† ★

THERE'S ONE BORN EVERY MINUTE Universal, 1942
HANS J. SALTER†

THEREMIN: AN ELECTRONIC ODYSSEY (FD) Kaga Bay, 1994
HAL WILNER

THERESE AND ISABELLE Audubon, 1968
GEORGES AURIC†

THERESE DESQUEYROUX 1962
MAURICE JARRE

THERESE MARTIN 1938
JACQUES IBERT†

THESE ARE THE DAMNED *THE DAMNED* Columbia, 1961
JAMES BERNARD

THESE GLAMOUR GIRLS MGM, 1939
EDWARD WARD†

THESE THOUSAND HILLS 20th Century-Fox, 1959
LEIGH HARLINE†

THESE THREE United Artists, 1936
ALFRED NEWMAN†

THESE WILDER YEARS MGM, 1956
JEFF ALEXANDER†

THEY (CTF) Bridget Terry Prods./Viacom, 1993
GERALD GOURIET

THEY ALL COME OUT MGM, 1939
EDWARD WARD†

THEY ALL DIED LAUGHING *A JOLLY BAD FELLOW* Continental, 1963
JOHN BARRY

THEY ALL KISSED THE BRIDE Columbia, 1942
WERNER R. HEYMANN†

THEY CALL IT MURDER (TF) 20th Century-Fox TV, 1971
ROBERT DRASNIN

THEY CALL ME BRUCE? *A FISTFUL OF CHOPSTICKS* Artists Releasing Corporation/Film Ventures International, 1982
TOMMY VIG

THEY CALL ME MISTER TIBBS! United Artists, 1970
QUINCY JONES

THEY CAME TO BLOW UP AMERICA 20th Century-Fox, 1943
HUGO FRIEDHOFER†

THEY CAME TO CORDURA Columbia, 1959
ELIE SIEGMEISTER†

THEY CAME TO ROB LAS VEGAS *SUDARIO DI SABBIA* 1968
GEORGES GARVARENTZ†

THEY DIED WITH THEIR BOOTS ON Warner Bros., 1942
MAX STEINER†

THEY DRIVE BY NIGHT Warner Bros., 1940
ADOLPH DEUTSCH†

THEY FOUGHT FOR THEIR MOTHERLAND Mosfilm, 1974
VYECHESLAV OVCHINNIKOV

THEY GOT ME COVERED RKO Radio, 1943
LEIGH HARLINE†

THEY KNEW WHAT THEY WANTED RKO Radio, 1940
ALFRED NEWMAN†

THEY LIVE Universal, 1988
JOHN CARPENTER
ALAN HOWARTH

THEY LIVE BY NIGHT RKO Radio, 1949
LEIGH HARLINE†

THEY MADE HER A SPY RKO Radio, 1939
ROY WEBB†

THEY MADE ME A CRIMINAL Warner Bros., 1939
MAX STEINER†

THEY MET IN BOMBAY MGM, 1941
HERBERT STOTHART†

THEY MIGHT BE GIANTS Universal, 1971
JOHN BARRY

THEY ONLY KILL THEIR MASTERS MGM, 1972
PERRY BOTKIN

THEY SHALL HAVE MUSIC United Artists, 1939
ALFRED NEWMAN† ★

THEY SHOOT HORSES, DON'T THEY? Cinerama Releasing Corporation, 1969
JOHN GREEN† ★

THEY STILL CALL ME BRUCE Shapiro Entertainment, 1987
MORTON STEVENS†

THEY WENT THAT-A-WAY AND THAT-A-WAY International Picture Show Company, 1978
MICHAEL LEONARD

THEY WERE EXPENDABLE MGM, 1945
HERBERT STOTHART†

THEY WON'T BELIEVE ME RKO Radio, 1947
ROY WEBB†

THEY WON'T FORGET Warner Bros., 1937
ADOLPH DEUTSCH†

THEY'RE PLAYING WITH FIRE New World, 1984
JOHN CACAVAS

THEY'VE TAKEN OUR CHILDREN: THE CROWCHILLA KIDNAPPING (TF) Rom Gilbert/Joel Fields/Leonard Hill, 1993
RON RAMIN

THICKER THAN BLOOD: THE LARRY McLINDEN STORY (TF) Alexander-Enright & Associates, 1994
JOHNNY HARRIS

THICKER THAN WATER (TF) BBC/A&E, 1994
DAEMION BARRY
JULIAN WASTALL

THE THIEF United Artists, 1952
HERSCHEL BURKE GILBERT ★

THIEF United Artists, 1981
TANGERINE DREAM
CHRISTOPHER FRANKE
CRAIG SAFAN

THIEF (TF) Stonehenge Productions/Metromedia Producers Corporation, 1971
RON GRAINER†

THE THIEF OF BAGDAD United Artists, 1924
MORTIMER WILSON†

THE THIEF OF BAGHDAD 1985
CARL DAVIS

THE THIEF OF BAGHDAD United Artists, 1940
MIKLOS ROZSA† ★

THE THIEF OF BAGHDAD (TF) Palm Productions, 1978
JOHN CAMERON

THIEF OF HEARTS Paramount, 1984
HAROLD FALTERMEYER

THE THIEF OF PARIS LE VOLEUR Lopert, 1967
HENRI LANOE

THE THIEF OF VENICE 1950
ALESSANDRO CICOGNINI†

THE THIEF WHO CAME TO DINNER Warner Bros., 1972
HENRY MANCINI†

THIEVES Paramount, 1977
JULE STYNE†

THIEVES IN THE NIGHT (MS) 1988
DOV SELTZER

THIEVES QUARTET Headline Entertainment, 1994
JOHN ZORN

THE THIN BLUE LINE (FD) Miramax Films, 1988
PHILIP GLASS

THIN ICE 1995
RICHARD ALLEN
PETE BAIKIE
CLAIRE VAN CAMPEN

THIN ICE (TF) CBS Entertainment, 1981
EARL ROSE

THE THIN MAN MGM, 1934
WILLIAM AXT†

THE THIN RED LINE Allied Artists, 1964
MALCOLM ARNOLD

THE THING RKO Radio, 1951
DIMITRI TIOMKIN†

THE THING Universal, 1982
ENNIO MORRICONE

THE THING THAT COULDN'T DIE Universal, 1958
HENRY MANCINI†

THE THING WITH TWO HEADS American International, 1972
ROBERT O. RAGLAND

THINGS ARE TOUGH ALL OVER Columbia, 1982
GAYE DELORME

THINGS CHANGE Columbia, 1988
ALARIC JANS

THINGS IN THEIR SEASON (TF) Tomorrow Entertainment, 1974
KEN LAUBER

THE THINGS OF LIFE Columbia, 1970
PHILIPPE SARDE

THINGS TO COME United Artists, 1936
SIR ARTHUR BLISS†

THINGS TO DO IN DENVER WHEN YOU'RE DEAD Miramax, 1995
MICHAEL CONVERTINO

THINK DIRTY EVERY HOME SHOULD HAVE ONE 1970
JOHN CAMERON

THIRD DEGREE BURN (CTF) HBO Pictures/MTM Enterprises/Paramount Pictures, 1989
CHARLES GROSS

THE THIRD GENERATION 1979
PEER RABEN

THE THIRD KEY THE LONG ARM Ealing, 1956
GERARD SCHURMANN

THE THIRD MAN Selznick Releasing, 1949
ANTON KARAS†

THIRD MAN ON THE MOUNTAIN Buena Vista, 1959
WILLIAM ALWYN†

THE THIRD PART OF THE NIGHT 1971
ANDRZEJ KORZYNSKI

THE THIRD VOICE 20th Century Fox, 1959
JOHNNY MANDEL

THE THIRD WALKER 1978
PAUL HOFFERT

THIRST 1979
BRIAN MAY†

THIRST Janus, 1949
ERIC NORDGREN

THE THIRST FOR GOLD 1993
VLADIMIR COSMA

THIRTEEN WOMEN RKO Radio, 1932
MAX STEINER†

THE THIRTEENTH HOUR Columbia, 1947
ARTHUR MORTON

THIRTY DANGEROUS SECONDS Independent Productions
ANDREW BELLING

THIRTY SECONDS OVER TOKYO MGM, 1945
HERBERT STOTHART†

THE THIRTY-NINE STEPS Gaumont-British, 1935
HUBERT BATH†

THIS ABOVE ALL 20th Century-Fox, 1942
ALFRED NEWMAN†

THIS ANGRY AGE Columbia, 1958
NINO ROTA†

THIS BOY'S LIFE Warner Bros., 1993
CARTER BURWELL

THIS CAN'T BE LOVE (TF) Davis Ent./Pacific Motion Picture/WIN, 1994
PETER MATZ

THIS CAN'T HAPPEN HERE Svensk Filmindustri, 1951
ERIC NORDGREN

THIS CHILD IS MINE (TF) Beth Polson Productions/Finnegan Associates/Telepictures Productions, 1985
HAGOOD HARDY

THIS EARTH IS MINE Universal, 1959
HUGO FRIEDHOFER†

THIS ENGLAND 1940
RICHARD ADDINSELL†

THIS GIRL FOR HIRE (TF) Barney Rosenzweig Productions/Orion TV, 1983
BRUCE BROUGHTON

THIS GUN FOR HIRE Paramount, 1942
DAVID BUTTOLPH†

THIS HAPPY FEELING Universal, 1958
FRANK SKINNER†

THIS IS CINERAMA Cinerama, 1952
MAX STEINER†

THIS IS ELVIS (FD) Warner Bros., 1981
WALTER SCHARF

THIS IS KATE BENNETT (TF) Lorimar, 1982
LEE HOLDRIDGE

THIS IS MY LIFE 20th Century Fox, 1992
CARLY SIMON

THIS IS MY LOVE RKO Radio, 1954
FRANZ WAXMAN†

THIS IS RUSSIA (FD) Universal, 1958
HERMAN STEIN

THIS IS THE ARMY Warner Bros., 1943
MAX STEINER†

THIS IS THE LIFE 20th Century-Fox, 1935
DAVID BUTTOLPH†

THIS IS THE NIGHT Paramount, 1932
W. FRANKE HARLING†

THIS IS THE WEST THAT WAS (TF) Public Arts Productions/Universal TV, 1974
DICK DEBENEDICTIS

THIS ISLAND EARTH Universal, 1955
HENRY MANCINI†
HANS J. SALTER†
HERMAN STEIN

THIS LAND IS MINE RKO Radio, 1943
LOTHAR PERL†

THIS LOVE OF OURS Universal, 1945
HANS J. SALTER† ★

THIS MAN IS MINE 1946
ALLAN GRAY†

THIS MAN IS MINE RKO Radio, 1934
MAX STEINER†

THIS MAN MUST DIE QUE LA BETE MEURE Allied Artists, 1969
PIERRE JANSEN

THIS MAN STANDS ALONE (TF) Roger Gimbel Productions/EMI TV/Abby Mann Productions, 1979
FRED KARLIN

THIS MAN'S NAVY MGM, 1945
NATHANIEL SHILKRET†

THIS PROPERTY IS CONDEMNED Paramount, 1966
KENYON HOPKINS

THIS REBEL AGE MGM, 1959
ALBERT GLASSER

THIS REBEL BREED Warner Bros., 1960
DAVID ROSE†

THIS SIDE OF HEAVEN MGM, 1934
WILLIAM AXT†

THIS SIDE OF THE LAW Warner Bros., 1950
WILLIAM LAVA†

THIS THING CALLED LOVE Columbia, 1941
WERNER R. HEYMANN†

THIS WOMAN IS DANGEROUS Warner Bros., 1952
DAVID BUTTOLPH†

THIS WOMAN IS MINE Universal, 1941
RICHARD HAGEMAN† ★

THIS WON'T HURT A BIT! Dendy, 1993
MARIO GRIGORIV

THE THOMAS CROWN AFFAIR United Artists, 1968
MICHEL LEGRAND ★

THOMASINE AND BUSHROD Columbia, 1974
COLERIDGE-TAYLOR PERKINSON

THOMPSON'S LAST RUN (TF) Cypress Point Productions, 1986
MILES GOODMAN†

THE THORN BIRDS (MS) David L. Wolper-Stan Margulies Productions/Edward Lewis Productions/Warner Bros. TV, 1983
HENRY MANCINI† ☆

THORNWELL (TF) MTM Enterprises, 1981
FRED KARLIN

THOROUGHBREDS DON'T CRY MGM, 1937
WILLIAM AXT†

THOROUGHLY MODERN MILLIE Universal, 1967
ELMER BERNSTEIN ★★

THOSE CALLOWAYS Buena Vista, 1965
MAX STEINER†

THOSE DARING YOUNG MEN IN THEIR JAUNTY JALOPIES Paramount, 1969
RON GOODWIN

THOSE ENDEARING YOUNG CHARMS RKO Radio, 1945
ROY WEBB†

THOSE FANTASTIC FLYING FOOLS BLAST OFF/JULES VERNE'S ROCKET TO THE MOON American International, 1967
JOHN SCOTT

THOSE GLORY, GLORY DAYS Cinecom, 1983
TREVOR JONES

THOSE LIPS, THOSE EYES United Artists, 1980
MICHAEL SMALL

THOSE MAGNIFICENT MEN IN THEIR FLYING MACHINES 20th Century-Fox, 1965
RON GOODWIN

THOSE REDHEADS FROM SEATTLE Paramount, 1953
LEO SHUKEN†

THOSE SECRETS (TF) Sarabande Prods., 1992
THOMAS NEWMAN

THOSE SHE LEFT BEHIND (TF) NBC Productions, 1989
MARK SNOW

THOU SHALT NOT KILL Troma, 1985
JOSEPH LO DUCA

THOU SHALT NOT KILL (TF) Edgar J. Scherick Associates/Warner Bros. TV, 1982
LEE HOLDRIDGE

THOUSANDS CHEER MGM, 1944
HERBERT STOTHART† ★

THRASHIN' Fries Entertainment, 1986
BARRY GOLDBERG

THE THREAT Warner Bros., 1960
RONALD STEIN†

THREE United Artists, 1969
LAURENCE ROSENTHAL

THREE AMIGOS! Orion, 1986
ELMER BERNSTEIN

THREE BAD MEN IN A HIDDEN FORTRESS Toho, 1958
MASARU SATO

THREE BAD SISTERS United Artists, 1956
PAUL DUNLAP

THREE BITES OF THE APPLE 1967
EDDIE LAWRENCE MANSON

THREE BRAVE MEN Universal, 1957
HANS J. SALTER†

THE THREE CABALLEROS (AF) RKO Radio, 1944
EDWARD PLUMB† ★
PAUL J. SMITH† ★

THREE CAME HOME 20th Century-Fox, 1950
HUGO FRIEDHOFER†

THREE CAME TO KILL United Artists, 1960
BERT A. SHEFTER

THREE CHEERS FOR THE IRISH Warner Bros., 1940
ADOLPH DEUTSCH†

THREE COINS IN THE FOUNTAIN 20th Century-Fox, 1954
VICTOR YOUNG†

THREE COLORS: BLUE Miramax, 1993
ZBIGNIEW PREISNER

THREE COLORS: RED Miramax, 1994
ZBIGNIEW PREISNER

THREE COLORS: WHITE Miramax, 1994
ZBIGNIEW PREISNER

THREE COMRADES MGM, 1938
FRANZ WAXMAN†

THREE DARING DAUGHTERS MGM, 1948
HERBERT STOTHART†

THREE DAYS AND A CHILD 1967
DOV SELTZER

THREE DESPERATE MEN Lippert, 1951
ALBERT GLASSER

THE THREE FACES OF EVE 20th Century-Fox, 1957
ROBERT EMMETT DOLAN†

THREE FACES WEST Republic, 1940
VICTOR YOUNG†

THREE FOR BEDROOM C Warner Bros., 1952
HEINZ ROEMHELD†

THREE FOR JAMIE DAWN Allied Artists, 1956
WALTER SCHARF

THREE FOR THE ROAD New Century/Vista, 1987
BARRY GOLDBERG

THREE FUGITIVES Buena Vista, 1989
DAVID MCHUGH

THE THREE GODFATHERS MGM, 1936
WILLIAM AXT†

THREE GODFATHERS MGM, 1948
RICHARD HAGEMAN†

THREE GUNS FOR TEXAS Universal, 1968
RUSSELL GARCIA

THREE GUYS NAMED MIKE MGM, 1951
BRONISLAU KAPER†

THREE HEARTS FOR JULIA MGM, 1943
HERBERT STOTHART†

THREE HUSBANDS United Artists, 1950
HERSCHEL BURKE GILBERT

THREE INTO TWO WON'T GO Universal, 1969
FRANCIS LAI

THREE IS A FAMILY United Artists, 1944
WERNER R. HEYMANN†

THREE KIDS AND A QUEEN Universal, 1935
FRANZ WAXMAN†

THE THREE KINGS (TF) Aaron Spelling Productions, 1987
WILLIAM GOLDSTEIN

THREE LITTLE WORDS MGM, 1950
ANDRE PREVIN ★

THE THREE LIVES OF THOMASINA Buena Vista, 1963
PAUL J. SMITH†

THREE LIVE GHOSTS MGM, 1936
WILLIAM AXT†

THREE LOVES HAS NANCY MGM, 1938
WILLIAM AXT†

THREE MEN AND A BABY Buena Vista, 1987
MARVIN HAMLISCH

THREE MEN AND A LITTLE LADY Buena Vista, 1990
JAMES NEWTON HOWARD

THREE MEN FROM TEXAS Paramount, 1940
VICTOR YOUNG†

THREE MEN IN A BOAT DCA, 1958
JOHN ADDISON

THREE MEN IN A BOAT (TF) BBC, 1975
DAVID FANSHAWE

THREE MEN IN WHITE MGM, 1944
NATHANIEL SHILKRET†

THE THREE MUSKETEERS 20th Century-Fox, 1939
DAVID BUTTOLPH†

THE THREE MUSKETEERS Buena Vista, 1993
MICHAEL KAMEN

THE THREE MUSKETEERS MGM, 1948
HERBERT STOTHART†

THE THREE MUSKETEERS RKO Radio, 1935
MAX STEINER†

THE THREE MUSKETEERS THE QUEEN'S DIAMONDS 20th Century-Fox, 1974
MICHEL LEGRAND

THREE O'CLOCK HIGH Universal, 1987
TANGERINE DREAM
CHRISTOPHER FRANKE
SYLVESTER LEVAY

THREE OF HEARTS New Line, 1993
RICHARD GIBBS
JOE JACKSON

THREE ON A DATE (TF) ABC Circle Films, 1978
GEORGE ALICESON TIPTON

THREE RING CIRCUS Paramount, 1954
WALTER SCHARF

THREE RUSSIAN GIRLS United Artists, 1944
W. FRANKE HARLING† ★

THREE SECRETS Warner Bros., 1950
DAVID BUTTOLPH†

THREE SISTERS 1967
MASARU SATO

THREE SISTERS American Film Theatre, 1970
SIR WILLIAM WALTON†

THREE SMART GIRLS Universal, 1936
CHARLES PREVIN†
HEINZ ROEMHELD†

THREE SONS RKO Radio, 1939
ROY WEBB†

THREE SOVEREIGNS FOR SARAH (TF) Night Owl Productions, 1985
CHARLES GROSS

THE THREE STOOGES GO ROUND THE WORLD IN A DAZE Columbia, 1963
PAUL DUNLAP

THE THREE STOOGES IN ORBIT Columbia, 1962
PAUL DUNLAP

THE THREE STOOGES MEET HERCULES Columbia, 1962
PAUL DUNLAP

THREE STRANGE LOVES THIRST Janus, 1949
ERIC NORDGREN

THREE STRANGERS Warner Bros., 1946
ADOLPH DEUTSCH†

THREE TEXAS STEERS Republic, 1939
WILLIAM LAVA†

THREE TOUGH GUYS Paramount, 1974
ISAAC HAYES

THE THREE TREASURES 1960
AKIRA IFUKUBE

THREE VIOLENT PEOPLE Paramount, 1957
WALTER SCHARF

THREE WISE FOOLS MGM, 1946
BRONISLAU KAPER†

THREE WISE GUYS MGM, 1936
WILLIAM AXT†

'97-'98
FILM
COMPOSERS
INDEX

F I L M

T I T L E S

THE THREE WISHES OF BILLY GRIER (TF) I&C
Productions, 1984
BRAD FIEDEL

THREE WISHES Savoy, 1995
CYNTHIA MILLAR

THREE WOMEN 20th Century-Fox, 1977
GERALD BUSBY

THE THREE WORLDS OF GULLIVER Columbia,
1960
BERNARD HERRMANN†

THREESOME TriStar, 1994
THOMAS NEWMAN

THREESOME (TF) CBS Entertainment, 1984
ANGELA MORLEY

THE THRILL OF IT ALL Universal, 1963
FRANK DEVOL

THRILLING 1965
LUIS BACALOV

THRONE OF BLOOD THE CASTLE OF THE
SPIDER'S WEB Brandon, 1957
MASARU SATO

THRONE OF FIRE 1972
BRUNO NICOLAI

THROUGH AIR POWER 1943
OLIVER WALLACE† ★

THROUGH NAKED EYES (TF) Charles Fries
Productions, 1983
GIL MELLE

THROUGH THE EYES OF A KILLER (TF) Pacific/
Morgan Hill/Wilshire Court, 1992
GEORGE S. CLINTON

THROUGH THE LOOKING GLASS Mature Pictures,
1976
ARLON OBER

THROUGH THE LOOKING GLASS (AF) Jambre
Productions, 1987
TODD HAYEN

THROUGH THE MAGIC PYRAMID (TF) Major
Productions, 1981
JOE RENZETTI ★

THROW MOMMA FROM THE TRAIN Orion,
1987
DAVID NEWMAN

THE THRUSTER 1976
ENNIO MORRICONE

THUMBS UP Republic, 1943
WALTER SCHARF

THUNDER MGM, 1929
WILLIAM AXT†

THUNDER Trans World Entertainment, 1983
FRANCESCO DE MASI

THUNDER AFLOAT MGM, 1939
EDWARD WARD†

THUNDER ALLEY Cannon, 1985
ROBERT FOLK

THUNDER AND LIGHTNING American
International, 1977
ANDREW STEIN

THUNDER BAY Universal, 1953
FRANK SKINNER†

THUNDER BIRDS 20th Century-Fox, 1942
DAVID BUTTOLPH†

THUNDER IN PARADISE (TF)
Berk-Schwartz-Bonnan Prods./Rysher/Trimark, 1994
JOHN D'ANDREA
MICHAEL LANNING
CORY LERIOS

THUNDER IN THE CITY Columbia, 1937
MIKLOS ROZSA†

THUNDER IN THE EAST Paramount, 1953
HUGO FRIEDHOFER†

THUNDER IN THE SUN Paramount, 1959
CYRIL J. MOCKRIDGE†

THUNDER IN THE VALLEY 20th Century-Fox,
1947
CYRIL J. MOCKRIDGE†

THUNDER ISLAND 20th Century-Fox, 1963
PAUL SAWTELL†
BERT A. SHEFTER

A THUNDER OF DRUMS MGM, 1961
HARRY SUKMAN†

THUNDER ON THE HILL Universal, 1951
HANS J. SALTER†

THUNDER OVER HAWAII NAKED PARADISE
American International, 1957
RONALD STEIN†

THUNDER OVER THE PLAINS Warner Bros., 1953
DAVID BUTTOLPH†

THUNDER RUN Cannon, 1986
JAY LEVY
MATTHEW MCCAULEY

THUNDER WARRIOR THUNDER Trans World
Entertainment, 1983
FRANCESCO DE MASI

THUNDERBALL United Artists, 1965
JOHN BARRY

THUNDERBIRDS Republic, 1952
VICTOR YOUNG†

THUNDERBIRDS ARE GO 1966
BARRY GRAY†

THUNDERBIRDS SIX 1968
BARRY GRAY†

THUNDERBIRDS TO THE RESCUE 1980
BARRY GRAY†

THUNDERBOLT (FD) A.A.F., 1945
GAIL KUBIK†

THUNDERBOLT AND LIGHTFOOT United Artists,
1974
DEE BARTON

THUNDERHEAD—SON OF FLICKA 20th
Century-Fox, 1945
CYRIL J. MOCKRIDGE†

THUNDERHEART TriStar, 1992
JAMES HORNER

THURSDAY'S CHILD (TF) The Catalina Production
Group/Viacom, 1983
LEE HOLDRIDGE

THX-1138 Warner Bros., 1971
LALO SCHIFRIN

TI HO SEMPRE AMATO 1952
CARLO RUSTICHELLI

TI KNIVER I HJERTET 1995
KJETIL BJERKERSTRAND
MAGNE FURUHOLMEN

A TICKET TO TOMAHAWK 20th Century-Fox,
1950
CYRIL J. MOCKRIDGE†

TICKLE ME Allied Artists, 1965
WALTER SCHARF

TIDAL WAVE 1973
MASARU SATO

TIDY ENDINGS (CTF) HBO Showcase/Sandollar
Productions, 1988
STANLEY MYERS†

TIE ME UP! TIE ME DOWN! Miramax, 1990
ENNIO MORRICONE

TIEFLAND 1945
GIUSEPPE BECCE†

TIEMPO DE REVANCHA Aries Films, 1981
EMILIO KAUDERER

TIES THAT BIND: THE WILLIAM COIT STORY
(TF) Citadel, 1995
MARTIN DAVICH

TIFFANY MEMORANDUM 1966
RIZ ORTOLANI

THE TIGER RKO Radio, 1935
HEINZ ROEMHELD†

THE TIGER MAKES OUT Columbia, 1967
RON GRAINER†

TIGER TOWN (CTF) Thompson Street Pictures, 1983
EDDIE LAWRENCE MANSON

A TIGER WALKS Buena Vista, 1964
BUDDY BAKER

TIGER WARSAW Sony Pictures, 1988
ERNEST TROOST

A TIGER'S TALE Atlantic Releasing Corporation,
1987
LEE HOLDRIDGE

TIGERS IN LIPSTICK WILD BEDS/HIJINKS
Castle Hill, 1978
RIZ ORTOLANI

TIGHT SHOES Universal, 1941
HANS J. SALTER†

TIGHTROPE Warner Bros., 1984
LENNIE NIEHAUS

THE TIJUANA STORY Columbia, 1957
MISCHA BAKALEINIKOFF†

TI-KOYO E IL SUO PESCECANE 1962
FRANCESCO DE MASI

TILL DEATH DO US PART (TF) Saban/Scherick,
1992
GEORGE S. CLINTON

TILL DIVORCE DO YOU PART LE CASTAGNE
SONO BUONO 1970
CARLO RUSTICHELLI

TILL THE END OF TIME RKO Radio, 1946
LEIGH HARLINE†

TILL WE MEET AGAIN Paramount, 1936
FREDERICK HOLLANDER†

TILL WE MEET AGAIN Paramount, 1944
DAVID BUTTOLPH†

TILT Warner Bros., 1979
LEE HOLDRIDGE

TIMBER Universal, 1942
HANS J. SALTER†

TIMBER STAMPEDE RKO Radio, 1939
ROY WEBB†

TIMBERJACK Republic, 1955
VICTOR YOUNG†

TIMBUKTU United Artists, 1959
GERALD FRIED

TIME AFTER TIME BBC-TV, 1985
JIM PARKER

TIME AFTER TIME Warner Bros., 1979
MIKLOS ROZSA†

TIME BANDITS Avco Embassy, 1981
MIKE MORAN

TIME BARBARIANS Vista Street Entertainment,
1990
MIRIAM CUTLER

TIME BOMB (TF) Barry Weitz Films/Universal TV,
1984
SYLVESTER LEVAY

TIME BURST Action International Pictures, 1988
TODD HAYEN

TIME FLIES WHEN YOU'RE ALIVE (CTF) HBO
Showcase/Kings Road Entertainment, 1989
MIKE GARSON

TIME FLYER (TF) Three Blind Mice Productions,
1986
DAVID SHIRE

TIME FOR CHEERIES 1991
ADI RENNERT

A TIME FOR DYING Etoile, 1971
HARRY BETTS

A TIME FOR KILLING Columbia, 1967
VAN ALEXANDER

A TIME FOR MIRACLES (TF) ABC Circle Films,
1980
FRED KARLIN

TIME FRAMES Amidei Productions, 1988
HOWARD WARRENMELER

THE TIME GUARDIAN Hemdale, 1987
ALLAN ZAVOD

TIME LIMIT United Artists, 1957
FRED STEINER

TIME LOST AND TIME REMEMBERED I WAS
HAPPY HERE Continental, 1966
JOHN ADDISON

THE TIME MACHINE MGM, 1960
RUSSELL GARCIA

THE TIME MACHINE (TF) Sunn Classic Productions,
1978
JOHN CACAVAS

A TIME OF DESTINY Columbia, 1988
ENNIO MORRICONE

THE TIME OF THEIR LIVES Universal, 1946
MILTON ROSEN†

THE TIME OF YOUR LIFE United Artists, 1948
CARMEN DRAGON†

TIME OUT OF MIND Universal, 1947
MARIO †
MIKLOS ROZSA†

TIME SLIP Toei, 1981
KENTARO HANEDA

A TIME TO DIE Almi Films, 1983
JOHN CACAVAS

A TIME TO DIE PM Entertainment, 1991
LOUIS FEBRE

A TIME TO DIE SEVEN GRAVES FOR ROGAN
Almi Films, 1983
ENNIO MORRICONE
ROBERT O. RAGLAND

A TIME TO HEAL (TF) based on Jay Gruska's life,
Susan Baerwald Prods./NBC Prods., 1994
JAY GRUSKA

A TIME TO KILL Warner Bros., 1996
ELLIOT GOLDENTHAL

TIME TO KILL 20th Century-Fox, 1942
EMIL NEWMAN†

A TIME TO LIVE (TF) Blue Andre Productions/ITC
Productions, 1985
GEORGES DELERUE†

A TIME TO LOVE AND A TIME TO DIE Universal,
1958
MIKLOS ROZSA†

A TIME TO TRIUMPH (TF) Billos-Kauffman
Productions/Phoenix Entertainment Group, 1986
JOHN CACAVAS

THE TIME TRAVELERS American International, 1964
RICHARD LASALLE

THE TIME TRAVELERS (TF) Irwin Allen
Productions/20th Century-Fox TV, 1976
MORTON STEVENS†

TIME TRAX (TF) Gary Nardino Prods./Lorimar TV,
1993
GARRY MCDONALD
LAURIE STONE

TIME WALKER New World, 1983
RICHARD H. BAND

TIME WITHIN MEMORY 1973
TORU TAKEMITSU†

TIME WITHOUT PITY Astor, 1956
TRISTRAM CARY

THE TIME, THE PLACE AND THE GIRL Warner
Bros., 1946
FREDERICK HOLLANDER†

TIMEBOMB MGM/UA, 1992
PATRICK LEONARD

TIMECOP Universal, 1994
MARK ISHAM
GREG O'CONNOR

TIMERIDER Jensen Farley Pictures, 1983
MICHAEL NESMITH

THE TIMES OF HARVEY MILK (FD) Teleculture,
1984
MARK ISHAM

TIMES SQUARE LADY MGM, 1935
EDWARD WARD†

TIMESTALKERS (TF) Fries Entertainment/
Newland-Raynor Productions, 1987
CRAIG SAFAN

TIMETABLE United Artists, 1956
WALTER SCHARF

TIMETRACKERS Concorde, 1989
PARMER FULLER

TIMIDO Y SALVAJE 1980
STELVIO CIPRIANI

TIN CUP Warner Bros., 1996
WILLIAM ROSS

THE TIN DRUM Argos Films, 1979
MAURICE JARRE

TIN MEN Buena Vista, 1987
ANDY COX
DAVID STEELE

THE TIN SOLDIER (CTF) Crystal Sky Comms./
Showtime, 1995
BENEDIKT BRYDERN

THE TIN STAR Paramount, 1957
ELMER BERNSTEIN

THE TINGLER Columbia, 1959
VON DEXTER

TINKER, TAILOR, SOLDIER, SPY (MS) 1980
GEOFFREY BURGON

TINTIN ET LES ORANGES BLEUES 1964
ANTOINE DUHAMEL

TINTORERA - THE SILENT DEATH 1977
BASIL POLEDOURIS

TIP ON A DEAD JOCKEY MGM, 1957
MIKLOS ROZSA†

TIPS Paragon Arts, 1987
DON PRESTON

TIR A VUE 1984
GABRIEL YARED

TIREZ SUR LE PIANISTE Astor, 1960
GEORGES DELERUE†

TIRO AL PICCIONE 1961
CARLO RUSTICHELLI

TITAN FIND Cardinal Releasing, 1985
TOM CHASE
STEVE RUCKER

TITANIC 1997
JAMES HORNER

THE TITFIELD THUNDERBOLT Universal, 1953
GEORGES AURIC†

TITLE SHOT 1979
PAUL J. ZAZA

TNT Interlight Pictures, 1997
STEVE EDWARDS

TO AN UNKNOWN GOD 1977
LUIS DE PABLO

TO BE OR NOT TO BE 20th Century-Fox, 1983
JOHN MORRIS

TO BE OR NOT TO BE United Artists, 1942
WERNER R. HEYMANN† ★

TO BE THE BEST (MS) Gemmy Prods., 1992
ALAN PARKER

TO CATCH A COP Gaumont, 1984
VLADIMIR COSMA

TO CATCH A KILLER (TF) Schrekinger-Kinberg
Prods/Creative Entertainment Group/Tribune
Entertainment, 1992
PAUL J. ZAZA

TO CATCH A KING (CTF) Entertainment Partners/
Gaylord Production Co./HBO Premiere Films, 1984
NICK BICAT

TO CATCH A THIEF Paramount, 1955
LYN MURRAY†

TO CROSS THE RUBICON Lensman, 1991
DAVID LANZ
PAUL SPEER

TO DANCE WITH THE WHITE DOG (TF) Patricia
Clifford Prods./Signboard Hill Prods., 1993
GERALD GOURIET

TO DIE FOR British, 1994
ROGER BOLTON

TO DIE FOR Columbia, 1995
DANNY ELFMAN

TO DIE FOR Skouras Pictures, 1989
CLIFF EIDELMAN

TO EACH HIS OWN Paramount, 1946
VICTOR YOUNG†

TO FACE HER PAST (TF) Citadel, 1996
PETER MANNING ROBINSON

TO FIND A MAN THE BOY NEXT DOOR/SEX
AND THE TEENAGER Columbia, 1972
DAVID SHIRE

TO FIND MY SON (TF) Green-Epstein Productions/
Columbia Pictures TV, 1980
RALPH GRIERSON

TO FORGET PALERMO Penta, 1990
ENNIO MORRICONE

TO GILLIAN ON HER 37TH BIRTHDAY Triumph,
1996
JAMES HORNER

TO GRANDMOTHER'S HOUSE WE GO (TF)
Green-Epstein, 1992
RICHARD BELLIS

TO HAVE AND HAVE NOT Warner Bros., 1944
FRANZ WAXMAN†

TO HEAL A NATION (TF) Lionel Chetwynd
Productions/Orion TV/von Zerneck-Samuels
Productions, 1988
LAURENCE ROSENTHAL

F
I
L
M

T
I
T
L
E
S

TWO MUCH Buena Vista, 1996
MICHEL CAMILO

TWO MULES FOR SISTER SARAH Universal, 1970
ENNIO MORRICONE

TWO NIGHTS WITH CLEOPATRA 1953
ARMANDO TROVAJOLI

TWO NUDES BATHING 1995
JOCELYN WEST

TWO O'CLOCK COURAGE RKO Radio, 1945
ROY WEBB†

TWO OF A KIND Columbia, 1951
GEORGE DUNING

TWO OF A KIND (TF) Lorimar Productions, 1982
JAMES DIPASQUALLE ☆☆

THE TWO OF US *LE VIEL HOMME ET L'ENFANT* Cinema 5, 1968
GEORGES DELERUE†

TWO ON A BENCH (TF) Universal TV, 1971
PETE CARPENTER†
MIKE POST

TWO ON A GUILLOTINE Warner Bros., 1965
MAX STEINER†

TWO PEOPLE Universal, 1973
DAVID SHIRE

TWO SECONDS Warner Bros., 1932
W. FRANKE HARLING†

TWO SMALL BODIES 1993
SWANS

TWO SMART PEOPLE MGM, 1946
GEORGE BASSMAN

TWO SOLITUDES New World-Mutual, 1977
MAURICE JARRE

TWO THOROUGHBREDS RKO Radio, 1939
ROY WEBB†

TWO TICKETS IN LONDON Universal, 1943
FRANK SKINNER†

TWO TICKETS TO BROADWAY RKO Radio, 1951
WALTER SCHARF

TWO WEEKS IN ANOTHER TOWN MGM, 1962
DAVID RAKSIN

TWO WEEKS IN SEPTEMBER *A COEUR JOIE*
Paramount, 1967
MICHEL MAGNE†

TWO WISE MAIDS Republic, 1937
KARL HAJOS†

TWO WOMEN 1960
ARMANDO TROVAJOLI

THE TWO WORLDS OF JENNIE LOGAN (TF) Joe Wizan TV Productions/Charles Fries Productions, 1979
GLENN PAXTON

TWO YANKS IN TRINIDAD Columbia, 1942
JOHN LEIPOLD†

TWO YEARS BEFORE THE MAST Paramount, 1946
VICTOR YOUNG†

TWO-FACED WOMAN MGM, 1942
BRONISLAU KAPER†

THE TWO-FIVE (TF) Universal TV, 1978
GERALD FRIED

TWOGETHER Twogether Limited, 1992
NIGEL HOLTON

THE TWO-HEADED SPY Columbia, 1959
GERARD SCHURMANN

TWO-MAN SUBMARINE Columbia, 1944
MARIO †

TWO-MINUTE WARNING Universal, 1976
CHARLES FOX

TWO-WAY STRETCH Showcorporation, 1960
KENNETH V. JONES

TYCOON RKO Radio, 1947
LEIGH HARLINE†

TYPHOON Paramount, 1940
FREDERICK HOLLANDER†

TYSON (TF) HBO Pictures, 1995
STEWART COPELAND
FRANKIE MILLER
MICHAEL THOMPSON

U

U BOAT 29 Columbia, 1939
MIKLOS ROZSA†

UCCELLACI E UCCELLINI 1966
ENNIO MORRICONE

UCCIDERE IN SILENZIO 1972
STELVIO CIPRIANI

UCCIDETE IL VITELLO GRASSO E ARROSTITELO 1969
ENNIO MORRICONE

UCCIDI E MUORI 1966
CARLO RUSTICHELLI

U.F.O. BLUE CHRISTMAS *BLOOD TYPE BLUE* 1979
MASARU SATO

THE UFO CHRONICLES Ocean Park, 1973
JIM HELMS

THE UFO REPORT: SIGHTINGS (TD)
Winkler-Daniels Prods., 1991
ANDREA SAPAROFF

UFORIA Universal, 1984
RICHARD BASKIN

UGETSU Harrison Pictures, 1953
FUMIO HAYASAKA†

THE UGLY Essential Prods., 1997
VICTORIA KELLY

THE UGLY AMERICAN Universal, 1963
FRANK SKINNER†

U.H.F. Orion, 1989
JOHN DUPREZ

ULISSE *ULYSSES* 1954
ALESSANDRO CICOGNINI†

ULTERIOR MOTIVES DEN Music/Ian-Page, 1990
PARMER FULLER

ULTIMATE BETRAYAL (TF) Polonga Prods./Hearst, 1994
CHRIS BOARDMAN

THE ULTIMATE IMPOSTER (TF) Universal TV, 1979
DANA KAPROFF

THE ULTIMATE WARRIOR Warner Bros., 1976
GIL MELLE

ULTIME GRIDA DALLA SAVANA (FD) 1975
CARLO SAVINA

ULTIMOS DIAS DE LA VICTIMA Aries Films, 1982
EMILIO KAUDERER

ULYSSES 1954
ALESSANDRO CICOGNINI†

ULYSSES Continental, 1967
STANLEY MYERS†

ULYSSES AGAINST THE SONS OF HERCULES 1961
ANGELO FRANCESCO LAVAGNINO†

ULYSSES' GAZE *TO VLEMMA TOU ODYSSEA* 1995
HELENA KARAINDROU

ULZANA'S RAID Universal, 1972
FRANK DEVOL

UMBERTO D. Harrison Pictures, 1952
ALESSANDRO CICOGNINI†

THE UMBRELLAS OF CHERBOURG *LES PARAPLUIES DE CHERBOURG* Landau, 1964
MICHEL LEGRAND ★

UMBRELLAS (FD) Maysles Films, 1994
PHILLIP JOHNSTON

U.M.C. (TF) MGM TV, 1969
GEORGE ROMANIS
LALO SCHIFRIN

UN AMERICANO IN VAZANZA 1946
NINO ROTA†

UN AMI VIENDRA CE SOIR 1945
ARTHUR HONEGGER†

UN AMORE A ROMA CEI Incom/Fair Film/Laetitia Film/Les Films Cocinor/Alpha Film, 1960
CARLO RUSTICHELLI

UN AMORE COMME LE NOTRE 1974
ARMANDO TROVAJOLI

UN AMOUR DE GUERRE 1964
ANTOINE DUHAMEL

UN AMOUR DE PLUIE 1973
FRANCIS LAI

UN AMOUR INTERDIT 1983
LUIS BACALOV

UN ANGE AU PARADIS 1973
MICHEL MAGNE†

UN ANIMAL CHIAMATO UOMO 1972
CARLO SAVINA

UN ANNO DI SCUOLA 1976
LUIS BACALOV

UN BEAU MONSTRE *A LOVELY MONSTER* 1970
GEORGES GARVARENTZ†

UN CAPITAN DE QUINCE ANOS 1972
BRUNO NICOLAI

UN CASO DI INCOSCIENZA (TF) 1983
LUIS BACALOV

UN CERTAIN MONSIEUR 1949
GEORGES VAN PARYS†

UN CHAPEAU DE PAILLE D'ITALIE *THE ITALIAN STRAW HAT* 1927
JACQUES IBERT†

UN CHOIX D'ASSASSINS 1967
ALAIN GORRAGUER

UN COEUR GROS COMME CA (FD) 1961
GEORGES DELERUE†
MICHEL LEGRAND

UN COEUR QUI SE BRISE (TF) 1967
GEORGES DELERUE†

UN CUORE SEMPLICE 1976
FRANCO MANNINO

UN DEUX TROIS SOLEIL *1,2,3, SUN* 1993
KHALED

UN DIVORCE HEUREUX CFDC, 1975
PHILIPPE SARDE

UN DOLLARO A TESTA 1966
ENNIO MORRICONE

UN DRAMMA BORGHESE *MIMI* 1979
RIZ ORTOLANI

UN DROLE DE DIMANCHE 1958
PAUL MISRAKI

UN EROE BORGHESE 1995
PINO DONAGGIO

UN EROE DEI BOSTRI TEMPI 1955
NINO ROTA†

UN ESERCITO DI 5 UOMIN MGM, 1970
ENNIO MORRICONE

UN ESTATE IN QUATTRO 1969
CARLO RUSTICHELLI

UN ETTARO DI CIELO 1959
NINO ROTA†

UN FEMME EN BLANC SE REVOLTE 1970
MICHEL MAGNE†

UN FLIC *DIRTY MONEY* Warner Bros., 1972
MICHEL COLOMBIER

UN GENIO, DUE COMPARI, UN POLLO Titanus, 1976
ENNIO MORRICONE

UN GIORNO DA LEONI 1961
CARLO RUSTICHELLI

UN GIORNO IN EUROPA (FD) 1958
TEO USUELLI

UN GIORNO IN PRETURA *A DAY IN COURT* 1954
ARMANDO TROVAJOLI

UN GRAN PATRON 1951
JOSEPH KOSMA†

UN HEROS 1996
ALEXANDRE DESPLAT

UN HOMME A ABATTRE 1967
ANTOINE DUHAMEL

UN HOMME A MA TAILLE 1983
PIERRE BACHELET

UN HOMME EST MORT United Artists, 1973
MICHEL LEGRAND

UN HOMME ET UNE FEMME Allied Artists, 1966
FRANCIS LAI ★★

UN HOMME LIBRE *A FREE MAN* 1973
FRANCIS LAI

UN HOMME QUI ME PLAIT United Artists, 1970
FRANCIS LAI

UN INDIEN DANS LA VILLE Buena Vista, 1996
TONTON DAVID
MANU KATCKE
GEOFFREY ORYEMA

UN JARDIN PUBLIC 1955
JEAN PRODROMIDES

UN LENTISSIMO DI SECONDO 1980
STELVIO CIPRIANI

UN MALEDETTO IMBROGLIO Seven Arts, 1959
CARLO RUSTICHELLI

UN MAUVAIS GARCON 1936
GEORGES VAN PARYS†

UN MILITARE E MEZZO 1960
ARMANDO TROVAJOLI

UN MILLIARD DANS UN BILLARD 1967
GEORGES GARVARENTZ†

UN MISSIONNAIRE 1955
MICHEL MICHELET†

UN MONDE NOUVEAU *A NEW WORLD* 1966
MICHEL COLOMBIER

UN MONSIEUR DE COMPAGNIE *MALE COMPANION* International Classics, 1966
GEORGES DELERUE†

UN MURO DE SILENCIO - *A WALL OF SILENCE* 1993
NESTOR MARCONI

UN OMBRA NELL'OMBRA 1979
STELVIO CIPRIANI

UN OTAGE (TF) Also cameo as

UN PAPILLON SUR L'EPAULE Action Films, 1978
CLAUDE BOLLING

UN PARTIE DE CAMPAGNE 1936
JOSEPH KOSMA†

UN POLIZIOTTO SCOMODO *CONVOY BUSTERS* 1978
STELVIO CIPRIANI

UN POVERE RICCO 1983
STELVIO CIPRIANI

UN REVENANT 1946
ARTHUR HONEGGER†

UN ROI SANS DIVERTISSEMENT 1963
MAURICE JARRE

UN SAC DE BILLES 1975
PHILIPPE SARDE

UN SEUL AMOUR 1943
ARTHUR HONEGGER†

UN SINGE EN HIVER 1961
MICHEL MAGNE†

UN SOIR DE RAFLE 1931
GEORGES VAN PARYS†

UN SOIR UN TRAIN 1969
FREDERIC DEVREESE

UN SOURIRE DANS LA TEMPETE 1950
JEAN WIENER†

UN SUSURRO NEL BUIO 1976
PINO DONAGGIO

UN TAXI MAUVE *THE PURPLE TAXI* Parafrance Films, 1977
PHILIPPE SARDE

UN TAXI POUR TOBROUK 1961
GEORGES GARVARENTZ†

UN TENERO TRAMONTO 1984
STELVIO CIPRIANI

UN TRENO PER DURANGO 1967
CARLO RUSTICHELLI

UN UOMO A META 1966
ENNIO MORRICONE

UN UOMO CHIAMATO APOCALISSE JOE 1970
BRUNO NICOLAI

UN UOMO DA RISPETTARE *THE MASTER TOUCH/HEARTS AND MINDS/A MAN TO RESPECT* 1970
ENNIO MORRICONE

UN UOMO FACILE 1959
CARLO RUSTICHELLI

UN UOMO, UNA CITTA 1974
CARLO RUSTICHELLI

UN'ANIMA DIVISA IN DUE *A SOUL SPLIT IN TWO* 1993
GIOVANNI VENOSTA

UN'AVVENTURA DI SALVATORE ROSA 1939
ALESSANDRO CICOGNINI†

UNA BREVE STAGIONE 1969
ENNIO MORRICONE

UNA DOMENICA D'ESTATE 1962
ARMANDO TROVAJOLI

UNA GITA SCOLASTICA *A SCHOOL OUTING* 1983
RIZ ORTOLANI

UNA MATTA MATTA CORSA IN RUSSIA 1973
CARLO RUSTICHELLI

UNA NUVOLA DI POLVERE 1970
BRUNO NICOLAI

UNA PISTOLA PER RINGO 1965
ENNIO MORRICONE

UNA PURA FORMALITA Sony Classics, 1994
ENNIO MORRICONE

UNA RAGIONE PER VIVERE E UNA PER MORIRE 1972
RIZ ORTOLANI

UNA ROMANTICA AVVENTURA 1940
ALESSANDRO CICOGNINI†

UNA SPADA PER BRANDO 1970
CARLO RUSTICHELLI

UNA STORIA DI NOTTE 1966
ARMANDO TROVAJOLI

UNA STORIA MODERNA - L'APE REGINA Embassy, 1963
TEO USUELLI

UNA STRANA PASSIONE 1984
LUIS BACALOV

UNA VERGINE IN FAMIGLIA 1975
CARLO SAVINA

UNA VITA VENDUTA 1976
ENNIO MORRICONE

UNBECOMING AGE Ringelvision, 1992
JEFF LASS

THE UNBELIEVABLE 1966
ALBERT GLASSER

THE UNBELIEVABLE TRUTH Action Features, 1989
JIM COLEMAN

THE UNBORN Califilm, 1991
GARY NUMAN
MICHAEL R. SMITH

UNCAGED Califilm, 1991
TERRY PLUMERI

THE UNCANNY 1977
WILFRED JOSEPHS

UNCERTAIN GLORY Warner Bros., 1944
ADOLPH DEUTSCH†

UNCHAINED Warner Bros., 1955
ALEX NORTH†

THE UNCLE Lennart, 1966
JOHN ADDISON

UNCLE BUCK Universal, 1989
IRA NEWBORN

UNCLE JOE SHANNON United Artists, 1979
BILL CONTI

UNCLE SCAM New World, 1981
MICHAEL LEVANIOS, III

UNCLE TOM'S CABIN 1965
PETER THOMAS

UNCLE TOM'S CABIN (CTF) Edgar J. Scherick Productions/Taft Entertainment TV, 1987
UDI HARPAZ
KENNARD RAMSEY

UNCLE VANYA 1958
WERNER JANSSEN

AN UNCOMMON LOVE (TF) Beechwood Productions/Lorimar, 1983
MILES GOODMAN†

UNCOMMON VALOR Paramount, 1983
JAMES HORNER

UNCOMMON VALOR (TF) Brademan-Self Productions/Sunn Classic, 1983
ROBERT SUMMERS

UNCONQUERED Paramount, 1947
VICTOR YOUNG†

UNCONQUERED (TF) Alexandra Film Productions, 1989
ARTHUR B. RUBINSTEIN

VA VOIR MAMAN...PAPA TRAVAILLE 1977
GEORGES DELERUE†

VAARWEL *THE ROMANTIC AGONY* 1974
ENNIO MORRICONE

VACANCES PORTUGAISES 1963
GEORGES DELERUE†

VACANZE A ISCHIA 1958
ALESSANDRO CICOGNINI†

VACANZE D'INVERNO 1959
ARMANDO TROVAJOLI

VACANZE IN AMERICA C.G. Silver Film, 1984
MANUEL DE SICA

VACANZE IN VAL TREBBIA 1980
NICOLA PIOVANI

VACANZE PER UN MASSACRO 1979
LUIS BACALOV

VACATION FROM LOVE MGM, 1938
EDWARD WARD†

VADO A VIVERE DA SOLO Italian
MANUEL DE SICA

VADO, VERO E SPARO 1968
CARLO RUSTICHELLI

THE VAGABOND KING Paramount, 1956
VICTOR YOUNG†

THE VAGRANT MGM/Pathe, 1992
CHRISTOPHER YOUNG

THE VALACHI PAPERS *JOE VILACHI: I SEGRETI DI COSA NOSTRA* Columbia, 1972
RIZ ORTOLANI

VALDEZ IS COMING United Artists, 1971
CHARLES GROSS

VALENTINE (TF) Malloy-Philips Productions/Edward S. Feldman Company, 1979
LEE HOLDRIDGE

VALENTINE MAGIC ON LOVE ISLAND (TF) Dick Clark Productions/PKO Television/Osmond TV Productions, 1980
PETER MATZ

VALENTINO Columbia, 1951
HEINZ ROEMHELD†

VALERIE United Artists, 1957
ALBERT GLASSER

VALHALLA Arclight Film, 1992
DAVID M. MATTHEWS

VALHALLA (AF) Swan Productions, 1985
RON GOODWIN

THE VALIANT HOMBRE United Artists, 1948
ALBERT GLASSER

VALIANT IS THE WORD FOR CARRIE Paramount, 1936
FREDERICK HOLLANDER†

THE VALLEY OF DECISION MGM, 1945
HERBERT STOTHART† ★

THE VALLEY OF THE BEES 1968
ZDENEK LISKA

VALLEY OF THE DOLLS 20th Century-Fox, 1967
JOHN WILLIAMS ★

VALLEY OF THE EAGLES 1951
NINO ROTA†

VALLEY OF THE GIANTS Warner Bros., 1938
ADOLPH DEUTSCH†
HUGO FRIEDHOFER†

VALLEY OF THE GWANGI Warner Bros., 1969
JEROME MOROSS†

VALLEY OF THE KINGS MGM, 1954
MIKLOS ROZSA†

VALLEY TOWN Willard Van Dyke, 1940
MARC BLITZSTEIN†

VALMONT Orion, 1989
CHRISTOPHER PALMER†

VALUE FOR MONEY Rank, 1957
MALCOLM ARNOLD

VAMOS A MATAR, COMPANEROS 1970
ENNIO MORRICONE

VAMP New World, 1986
JONATHAN ELIAS

VAMPIRA American International, 1975
DAVID WHITAKER

THE VAMPIRE *MARK OF THE VAMPIRE* United Artists, 1957
GERALD FRIED

VAMPIRE UPIOR 1968
WOJCIECH KILAR

VAMPIRE (TF) MTM Enterprises, 1979
FRED KARLIN

THE VAMPIRE BEAST CRAVES BLOOD 1969
PAUL FERRIS

VAMPIRE CIRCUS Rank, 1972
DAVID WHITAKER

THE VAMPIRE LOVERS American International, 1970
HARRY ROBERTSON

VAMPIRE'S KISS Hemdale, 1988
COLIN TOWNS

VAMPIRES American International, 1962
LES BAXTER†

VAMPYR VAMPYR OU L'ETRANGE AVENTURE DE DAVID GRAY 1932
WOLFGANG ZELLER†

VAMPYR OU L'ETRANGE AVENTURE DE DAVID GRAY 1932
WOLFGANG ZELLER†

THE VAN 20th Century Fox, 1997
RICHARD HARTLEY

VANESSA, HER LOVE STORY MGM, 1935
HERBERT STOTHART†

VANISHED (TF) Universal TV, 1971
LEONARD ROSENMAN

THE VANISHING 20th Century Fox, 1993
JERRY GOLDSMITH

VANISHING ACT (TF) Robert Cooper Productions/Levinson-Link Productions, 1986
KEN WANNBERG

VANISHING SON (TF) Universal-MCA TV, 1994
DAVID BERGEAUD

VANYA ON 42nd STREET Sony Classics, 1994
JOSHUA REDMAN

VARAN THE UNBELIEVABLE Crown International, 1958
AKIRA IFUKUBE

VARDO Working Title Films, 1988
HANS ZIMMER

VARIETY Horizon Films, 1985
JOHN LURIE

VASECTOMY: A DELICATE MATTER Seymour Borde & Associates, 1986
FRED KARLIN

VATICAN STORY 1968
LUIS BACALOV

THE VAULT OF HORROR *TALES FROM THE CRYPT II* Cinerama Releasing Corporation, 1973
DOUGLAS GAMLEY

VEDO NUDO Dean Film/Jupiter Generale Cinematografica, 1969
ARMANDO TROVAJOLI

VEGAS (TF) Aaron Spelling Productions, 1978
DOMINIC FRONTIERE

VEGAS IN SPACE Philip R. Ford, 1992
BOB DAVIS

THE VEGAS STRIP WARS (TF) George Englund Productions, 1984
JIMMIE HASKELL

VEGAS VACATION Warner Bros., 1997
JOEL McNEELY

THE VEIL Intercontinental, 1977
PINO DONAGGIO

THE VEILS OF BAGDAD Universal, 1953
HENRY MANCINI†
HERMAN STEIN

VELENO *POISON* 1993
DAVIDE MASARATI

VELVET (TF) Aaron Spelling Productions, 1984
DOMINIC FRONTIERE

THE VELVET TOUCH RKO Radio, 1948
LEIGH HARLINE†

VENDETTA Concorde, 1986
DAVID NEWMAN

VENDETTA RKO Radio, 1950
ROY WEBB†

VENDETTA EN CAMARGUE 1949
JOSEPH KOSMA†

VENDETTA II: THE NEW MAFIA (TF) Titanus/Silvio Berlusconi Ent./Tribune, 1993
STEFANO MAINETTI

VENDREDI OU LA VIE SAUVAGE (TF) 1981
MAURICE JARRE

VENERE CREOLA 1962
CARLO RUSTICHELLI

THE VENETIAN AFFAIR MGM, 1967
LALO SCHIFRIN

VENETIAN BIRD 1952
NINO ROTA†

A VENEZIA, CARNEVALE, UN AMORE 1981
PINO DONAGGIO

THE VENGEANCE OF FU-MANCHU Warner Bros., 1968
MALCOM LOCKYER

VENGEANCE Garrick, 1962
KENNETH V. JONES

VENGEANCE IS MINE Shochiku Co. Ltd., 1980
SHINCHIRO IKEBE

VENGEANCE: THE STORY OF TONY CIMO (TF) Nederlander TV and Film Productions/Robirdie Pictures, 1986
CHARLES GROSS

VENICE 1997
RACHEL PORTMAN

VENOM Paramount, 1982
MICHAEL KAMEN

VENT DE PANIQUE 1988
JEAN-CLAUDE PETIT

VENUS AND ADONIS Harry Durham, 1934
PAUL BOWLES

VERA CRUZ United Artists, 1954
HUGO FRIEDHOFER†

VERATARTS AVEDYATS YERGIR 1992
AVET TERTERIAN

VERBOTEN! Columbia, 1958
HARRY SUKMAN†

THE VERDICT 20th Century-Fox, 1982
JOHNNY MANDEL

THE VERDICT Warner Bros., 1946
FREDERICK HOLLANDER†

VERGOGNA SCHIFOSI 1968
ENNIO MORRICONE

VERMISAT 1975
NICOLA PIOVANI

VERMONT IS FOR LOVERS Zeitgeist, 1992
TONY SILBERT

THE VERNON JOHNS STORY (TF) Laurel Ent./Tribune, 1994
BRIAN KEANE

VERONIKA VOSS Laura Film, 1982
PEER RABEN

VERSO SERA *BY NIGHTFALL* 1991
ROBERTO GATTO
BATTISTA LENA

VERTIGO Paramount, 1958
BERNARD HERRMANN†

VERTIGO EN LA PISTA 1980
STELVIO CIPRIANI

VERUSCHKA, POESIA DI UNA DONNA 1970
ENNIO MORRICONE

A VERY BRADY CHRISTMAS (TF) The Sherwood Schwartz Co./Paramount Network TV, 1988
LAURENCE JUBER

A VERY BRADY SEQUEL Paramount, 1996
GUY MOON

A VERY BRITISH COUP (TF) Skreba Films, 1988
JOHN E. KEANE

VERY CLOSE QUARTERS Cable Star Ltd./Viacom, 1986
JAY CHATTAWAY

THE VERY EDGE OF THE NIGHT 1959
BEBE BARRON
LOUIS BARRON

A VERY FAITHFUL WIFE 1993
EDISON DENISOV

VERY HAPPY ALEXANDER *ALEXANDER* Cinema 5, 1968
VLADIMIR COSMA

A VERY MISSING PERSON (TF) Universal TV, 1972
VIC MIZZY

A VERY PRIVATE AFFAIR MGM, 1962
FIORENZO CARPI

A VERY SPECIAL FAVOR Universal, 1965
VIC MIZZY

THE VERY THOUGHT OF YOU Warner Bros., 1944
FRANZ WAXMAN†

VESSEL OF WRATH 1937
RICHARD ADDINSELL†

VESTIRE GLI INUDI 1954
FRANCO MANNINO

V.I. WARSHAWSKI Buena Vista, 1991
RANDY EDELMAN

VIA APPIA Strand, 1992
CHARLY SCHOPPNER

VIA DEGLI SPECCHI *STREET OF MIRRORS* 1983
PINO DONAGGIO

VIA MARGUTTA 1959
PIERO PICCIONI

VIA PADOVA, 46 1954
NINO ROTA†

VIA RASELLA *MASSACRE IN ROME* 1973
ENNIO MORRICONE

VIAGGIO D'AMORE Centaur, 1991
ANDREA GUERRA

VIBES Columbia, 1988
JAMES HORNER

VICE RAID United Artists, 1959
BERT A. SHEFTER

VICE SQUAD Avco Embassy, 1982
KEITH RUBINSTEIN

VICE SQUAD United Artists, 1953
HERSCHEL BURKE GILBERT

VICE VERSA Columbia, 1988
DAVID SHIRE

VICE VERSA General Film Distributors, 1948
ANTONY HOPKINS

THE VICIOUS BREED 1957
LES BAXTER†

VICKI 20th Century-Fox, 1953
LEIGH HARLINE†

THE VICTIM (TF) Universal TV, 1972
GIL MELLE

VICTIM OF LOVE (TF) Nevermore, 1991
RICHARD STONE

VICTIMS (TF) Hajeno Productions/Warner Bros. TV, 1982
LALO SCHIFRIN

VICTIMS FOR VICTIMS (TF) Daniel L. Paulson-Loehr Spivey Productions/Orion TV, 1984
PAUL CHIHARA

VICTOR'S BIG SCORE Mushikuki, 1992
STEPHEN SNYDER

VICTOR/VICTORIA MGM/United Artists, 1982
HENRY MANCINI† ★★

VICTORIA THE GREAT RKO Radio, 1937
ANTHONY COLLINS†

THE VICTORS Columbia, 1963
SOL KAPLAN

VICTORY Paramount, 1941
FREDERICK HOLLANDER†

VICTORY Paramount, 1981
BILL CONTI

VICTORY Miramax, 1996
MARK ADLER

VICTORY *THROUGH AIR POWER* 1943
OLIVER WALLACE† ★

VICTORY MARCH Summit Features, 1976
NICOLA PIOVANI

VICTORY THROUGH AIR POWER United Artists, 1943
EDWARD PLUMB†
PAUL J. SMITH† ★

VIDEODROME Universal, 1983
HOWARD SHORE

VIEILLE CANAILLE 1993
BRUNO COULAIS

VIEL LARM UM NICHTS 1942
GIUSEPPE BECCE†

VIETNAM SCENE DEL DOPOGUERRA 1975
FIORENZO CARPI

VIETNAM TEXAS Trans World Entertainment, 1990
RICHARD STONE

VIETNAM WAR STORIES (CTF) Nexus Productions, 1987
MARK SNOW

VIETNAM WAR STORY (CTF) Nexus Productions, 1987
JONATHAN SHEFFER

THE VIEW FROM POMPEY'S HEAD 20th Century Fox, 1955
ELMER BERNSTEIN

A VIEW TO A KILL MGM/UA, 1985
JOHN BARRY

VIGIL IN THE NIGHT RKO Radio, 1940
ALFRED NEWMAN†

VIGILANTE *STREET GANG* Artists Releasing Corporation/Film Ventures International, 1983
JAY CHATTAWAY

VIGILANTE FORCE United Artists, 1976
GERALD FRIED

VIGYAZAT *THE WATCHERS* 1993
ZOLTAN JENEY

VILLA RIDES! Paramount, 1968
MAURICE JARRE

VILLA! 20th Century-Fox, 1958
BERT A. SHEFTER

VILLAGE HARVEST (FD) 1938
BENJAMIN BRITTEN†

VILLAGE OF DAUGHTERS MGM, 1962
RON GOODWIN

VILLAGE OF THE DAMNED MGM, 1960
RON GOODWIN

VILLAGE OF THE DAMNED Universal, 1995
JOHN CARPENTER
DAVE DAVIES

VILLAGE OF THE GIANTS Embassy, 1965
JACK NITZCHE

THE VILLAIN Columbia, 1979
BILL JUSTIS

VINCENT & THEO Hemdale, 1990
GABRIEL YARED

VINCENT, FRANCOIS, PAUL AND THE OTHERS Joseph Green Pictures, 1974
PHILIPPE SARDE

THE VINDICATOR *FRANKENSTEIN '88* 20th Century Fox, 1985
PAUL J. ZAZA

VINO, WHISKY E ACQUA SALATA 1962
LUIS BACALOV

THE VINTAGE MGM, 1957
DAVID RAKSIN

VIOLANTA 1976
PEER RABEN

THE VIOLATED The Violated Co., 1984
SHIRLEY WALKER

THE VIOLATION OF SARAH McDAVID (TF) CBS Entertainment, 1981
ROBERT PRINCE

THE VIOLENT ENEMY 1969
JOHN SCOTT

THE VIOLENT EVIL 1959
RONALD STEIN†

THE VIOLENT FOUR *BANDITI A MILANO* Paramount, 1968
RIZ ORTOLANI

THE VIOLENT MEN Columbia, 1954
MAX STEINER†

VIOLENT ROAD Warner Bros., 1958
LEITH STEVENS†

VIOLENT SATURDAY 20th Century-Fox, 1955
HUGO FRIEDHOFER†
LIONEL NEWMAN†

VIOLETS ARE BLUE Columbia, 1986
PATRICK WILLIAMS

WAR OF THE BUTTONS Warner Bors., 1995
RACHEL PORTMAN
WAR OF THE COLOSSAL BEAST American
International, 1958
ALBERT GLASSER
WAR OF THE GARGANTUAS 1966
AKIRA IFUKUBE
WAR OF THE WORLDS Paramount, 1953
LEITH STEVENS†
WAR PAINT United Artists, 1953
EMIL NEWMAN†
WAR PARTY 20th Century-Fox, 1965
RICHARD LASALLE
WAR PARTY Hemdale, 1989
CHAZ JANKEL
THE WAR WAGON Universal, 1967
DIMITRI TIOMKIN†
WARGAMES MGM/UA, 1983
ARTHUR B. RUBINSTEIN
WARLOCK 20th Century-Fox, 1959
LEIGH HARLINE†
WARLOCK New World, 1989
JERRY GOLDSMITH
WARLOCK: THE ARMAGEDDON Trimark, 1993
MARK MCKENZIE
WARLORD 3000 Cinema Studio Corporation, 1993
CHRISTOPHER FARRELL
WARLORDS OF THE 21ST CENTURY New World,
1982
KEVIN PEAK
A WARM DECEMBER National General, 1973
COLERIDGE-TAYLOR PERKINSON
WARM HEARTS, COLD FEET (TF) 1987
MARK SNOW
THE WARM LIFE LA CALDA VITA 1964
CARLO RUSTICHELLI
WARM SUMMER RAIN Trans World Entertainment,
1989
ROGER ENO
WARNING SHOT Paramount, 1967
JERRY GOLDSMITH
WARNING SIGN 20th Century Fox, 1985
CRAIG SAFAN
WARPED Kassel Prods., 1990
VLADIMIR HORUNZHY
WARREN OATES: ACROSS THE BORDER (FD)
1993
FRANK SCHAAP
THE WARRIOR EMPRESS 1961
ANGELO FRANCESCO LAVAGNINO†
THE WARRIORS Paramount, 1979
BARRY DEVORZON
WARRIORS FIVE LA GUERRA CONTINUA 1962
LES BAXTER†
ARMANDO TROVAJOLI
WARRIORS OF ATLANTIS EMI, 1978
MICHAEL VICKERS
THE WASH Skouras Pictures, 1988
JOHN MORRIS
WASHINGTON MASQUERADE MGM, 1932
WILLIAM AXT†
WASHINGTON STORY MGM, 1952
CONRAD SALINGER†
WASHINGTON, BEHIND CLOSED DOORS (MS)
Paramount TV, 1977
RICHARD MARKOWITZ†
WASHINGTON: BEHIND CLOSED DOORS (MS)
Paramount TV, 1977
DOMINIC FRONTIERE
THE WASP WOMAN American International, 1959
FRED KATZ
WATCH IT Skouras, 1993
STANLEY CLARKE
WATCH ON THE RHINE Warner Bros., 1943
MAX STEINER†
WATCH THAT MAN Warner Bros., 1997
CHRISTOPHER YOUNG
THE WATCHER IN THE WOODS Buena Vista,
1980
STANLEY MYERS†
THE WATCHERS 1993
ZOLTAN JENEY
WATCHERS Universal, 1988
JOEL GOLDSMITH
WATCHERS II Concorde, 1990
RICK CONRAD
WATER Atlantic Releasing Corporation, 1984
MIKE MORAN
THE WATER BABIES Pethurst International/Film
Polski, 1978
PHIL COULTER
WATER BIRDS RKO Radio, 1952
PAUL J. SMITH†
THE WATER ENGINE (CTF) Brandman Prods./
Amblin, 1992
ALARIC JANS
THE WATERDANCE Samuel Goldwyn, 1992
MICHAEL CONVERTINO
WATERHOLE #3 Paramount, 1967
DAVE GRUSIN

WATERLAND Fine Line, 1992
CARTER BURWELL
WATERLOO Paramount, 1971
NINO ROTA†
WATERLOO BRIDGE MGM, 1940
HERBERT STOTHART† ★
WATERMELON MAN Columbia, 1970
MELVIN VAN PEEBLES
WATERS OF TIME 1951
ALAN RAWSTHORNE†
WATERSHIP DOWN (AF) Avco Embassy, 1978
MIKE BATT
ANGELA MORLEY
MALCOLM WILLIAMSON
WATERWORLD Universal, 1995
JAMES NEWTON HOWARD
THE WATTS MONSTER Dimension, 1979
JOHNNY PATE
WAVELENGTH New World, 1983
TANGERINE DREAM
CHRISTOPHER FRANKE
WAXWORK Vestron, 1988
ROGER BELLON
THE WAY AHEAD THE IMMORTAL
BATTALION 20th Century-Fox, 1944
WILLIAM ALWYN†
WAY BACK HOME RKO Radio, 1931
MAX STEINER†
WAY DOWN EAST United Artists, 1920
LOUIS SILVERS†
WAY DOWN SOUTH RKO Radio, 1939
VICTOR YOUNG† ★
THE WAY OF A GAUCHO 20th Century-Fox, 1952
SOL KAPLAN
THE WAY OF ALL FLESH Paramount, 1940
VICTOR YOUNG†
WAY OUT WEST MGM, 1937
T. MARVIN HATLEY† ★
THE WAY TO THE STARS JOHNNY IN THE
CLOUDS United Artists, 1945
NICHOLAS BRODZSKY†
THE WAY WE WERE Columbia, 1973
MARVIN HAMLISCH ★★
THE WAY WEST United Artists, 1967
BRONISLAU KAPER†
THE WAY WEST (TD) Steeplechase Films/Channel
Four TV, 1995
BRIAN KEANE
WAY...WAY OUT! 20th Century-Fox, 1966
LALO SCHIFRIN
WAYNE'S WORLD Paramount, 1992
J. PETER ROBINSON
WAYNE'S WORLD 2 Paramount, 1993
CARTER BURWELL
WAYWARD Paramount, 1931
JOHN GREEN†
THE WAYWARD BUS 20th Century-Fox, 1957
LEIGH HARLINE†
W.B. BLUE AND THE BEAN Movie Group, 1989
CHUCK CIRINO
W.C. FIELDS AND ME Universal, 1976
HENRY MANCINI†
WE ALL LOVED EACH OTHER SO MUCH Cinema
5, 1975
ARMANDO TROVAJOLI
WE ARE NOT ALONE Warner Bros., 1939
MAX STEINER†
WE ARE THE CHILDREN (TF) Paulist Pictures/Dan
Fauci-Ted Danson Productions/The Furia Organization,
1987
PAUL CHIHARA
WE ARE THE LAMBETH BOYS Rank, 1958
JOHN DANKWORTH
WE ARE YOUNG 1967
DAVID AMRAM
WE CHOP THE TEACHERS INTO MINCE MEAT
1970
ROLF WILHELM
WE LIVE AGAIN United Artists, 1934
ALFRED NEWMAN†
WE SAIL AT MIDNIGHT 1943
RICHARD ADDINSELL†
WE STILL KILL THE OLD WAY 1967
LUIS BACALOV
WE THINK THE WORLD OF YOU Cinecom, 1988
JULIAN JACOBSON
WE WENT TO COLLEGE MGM, 1936
WILLIAM AXT†
WE WERE DANCING MGM, 1942
BRONISLAU KAPER†
WE WERE STRANGERS Columbia, 1949
GEORGE ANTHEIL†
WE WHO ARE YOUNG MGM, 1940
BRONISLAU KAPER†
WE'LL EAT THE FRUIT OF PARADISE 1970
ZDENEK LISKA
WE'RE BACK! A DINOSAUR'S STORY (AF)
Universal, 1993
JAMES HORNER

WE'RE FIGHTING BACK (TF) Highgate Pictures,
1981
FRED KARLIN
WE'RE NO ANGELS Paramount, 1955
FREDERICK HOLLANDER†
WE'RE NO ANGELS Paramount, 1989
GEORGE FENTON
WE'RE NOT DRESSING Paramount, 1934
SIGMUND KRUMGOLD†
WE'RE NOT MARRIED 20th Century-Fox, 1952
CYRIL J. MOCKRIDGE†
LIONEL NEWMAN†
WE'RE ONLY HUMAN RKO Radio, 1935
ROY WEBB†
WE'RE RICH AGAIN RKO Radio, 1934
MAX STEINER†
WE'VE NEVER BEEN LICKED Universal, 1943
FRANK SKINNER†
THE WEAK AND THE WICKED Allied Artists, 1954
LEIGHTON LUCAS†
THE WEATHER IN THE STREETS (TF) Rediffusion
Films/BBC/Britannia TV, 1983
CARL DAVIS
THE WEB Universal, 1947
HANS J. SALTER†
WEB OF DECEPTION (TF) Morgan Hill/Hearst,
1994
BOB ALCIVAR
WEB OF EVIDENCE BEYOND THIS PLACE Allied
Artists, 1959
DOUGLAS GAMLEY
WEB OF PASSION/A DOUBLE TOUR Times, 1959
PAUL MISRAKI
THE WEDDING BANQUET 1993
MADER
WEDDING BELL BLUES Curb, 1997
TAL BERGMAN
PAUL CHRISTIAN GORDON
WEDDING IN BLOOD LES NOCES ROUGES New
Line Cinema, 1973
PIERRE JANSEN
THE WEDDING MARCH Paramount, 1928
JOHN S. ZAMECNIK†
THE WEDDING NIGHT United Artists, 1935
ALFRED NEWMAN†
A WEDDING ON WALTONS MOUNTAIN (TF)
Amanda Productions/Lorimar Productions, 1982
ALEXANDER COURAGE
WEDDING RINGS Warner Bros., 1930
EDWARD WARD†
WEDNESDAY'S CHILD RKO Radio, 1934
MAX STEINER†
WEE WILLIE WINKIE 20th Century-Fox, 1937
ALFRED NEWMAN†
WEEDS DEG, 1987
ANGELO BADALAMENTI
WEEKEND Grove Press, 1968
ANTOINE DUHAMEL
WEEKEND A ZUYDCOOTE 1964
MAURICE JARRE
WEEKEND AT BERNIE'S 20th Century Fox, 1989
ANDY SUMMERS
WEEKEND AT BERNIE'S II Artimm, 1993
PETER WOLF
WEEKEND AT THE WALDORF MGM, 1945
JOHN GREEN†
WEEKEND FOR THREE RKO Radio, 1941
ROY WEBB†
WEEK-END MARRIAGE Warner Bros., 1932
W. FRANKE HARLING†
WEEKEND OF TERROR (TF) Paramount TV, 1970
RICHARD MARKOWITZ†
WEEKEND WAR (TF) Pompian/Columbia Pictures
TV, 1988
BRAD FIEDEL
WEEKEND WARRIORS The Movie Store, 1986
PERRY BOTKIN
WEEKEND WITH FATHER Universal, 1951
FRANK SKINNER†
WEIRD SCIENCE Universal, 1985
ALF CLAUSEN
IRA NEWBORN
WEIRD WOMAN Universal, 1944
HANS J. SALTER†
WELCOME HOME Columbia, 1989
HENRY MANCINI†
WELCOME HOME, BOBBY (TF) Titus Productions,
1986
DAVID MCHUGH
WELCOME HOME, JOHNNY BRISTOL (TF)
Cinema Center, 1972
LALO SCHIFRIN
WELCOME HOME, ROXY CARMICHAEL
Paramount, 1990
THOMAS NEWMAN
WELCOME HOME, SOLDIER BOYS 20th
Century-Fox, 1972
KEN WANNBERG
WELCOME STRANGER Paramount, 1947
ROBERT EMMETT DOLAN†

WELCOME TO 18 American Distribution Group,
1986
TONY BERG
WELCOME TO BLOOD CITY EMI, 1977
ROY BUDD†
WELCOME TO HARD TIMES MGM, 1967
HARRY SUKMAN†
WELCOME TO L.A. United Artists/Lions Gate, 1976
RICHARD BASKIN
WELCOME TO THE DOLLHOUSE Sony Classics,
1996
JILL WISOFF
WELCOME TO THE QUEEN (FD) 1954
SIR ARTHUR BLISS†
WELCOME TO YOUR LIFE MICHAEL ANGELO
Last Laugh, 1990
NIGEL HOLTON
THE WELL United Artists, 1951
DIMITRI TIOMKIN†
THE WELL GROOMED BRIDE Paramount, 1946
ROY WEBB†
WELLS FARGO Paramount, 1937
VICTOR YOUNG†
WELTMELODIE 1929
WOLFGANG ZELLER†
THE WEREWOLF Columbia, 1956
MISCHA BAKALEINIKOFF†
WEREWOLF (TF) Lycanthrope Productions/Tri-Star
TV, 1987
SYLVESTER LEVAY
WEREWOLF IN A GIRLS' DORMITORY
LUCANTROPUS 1961
ARMANDO TROVAJOLI
WEREWOLF OF LONDON Universal, 1935
KARL HAJOS†
WES CRAVEN'S NEW NIGHTMARE New Line,
1994
CHARLES BERNSTEIN
J. PETER ROBINSON
WEST OF ZANZIBAR 1954
ALAN RAWSTHORNE†
WEST POINT WIDOW Paramount, 1941
LEO SHUKEN†
WEST SIDE STORY United Artists, 1961
JOHN GREEN† ★
IRWIN KOSTAL† ★★
WESTBOUND Warner Bros., 1959
DAVID BUTTOLPH†
WESTERN PACIFIC AGENT Lippert, 1950
ALBERT GLASSER
THE WESTERN STORY Universal, 1958
HERMAN STEIN
WESTERN UNION 20th Century-Fox, 1941
DAVID BUTTOLPH†
THE WESTERNER United Artists, 1940
DIMITRI TIOMKIN†
WESTWARD HO, THE WAGONS Buena Vista,
1956
GEORGE BRUNS
WESTWARD PASSAGE RKO Radio, 1932
MAX STEINER†
WESTWARD THE WOMEN MGM, 1952
JEFF ALEXANDER†
WESTWORLD MGM, 1973
FRED KARLIN
WET GOLD (TF) Telepictures Corporation, 1984
JOHN SCOTT
WET GOLD (TF) Telepictures Productions, 1984
SYLVESTER LEVAY
THE WET PARADE MGM, 1932
WILLIAM AXT†
WETBACKS 1955
LES BAXTER†
WETHERBY MGM/UA Classics, 1985
NICK BICAT
A WHALE FOR THE KILLING (TF) Play
Productions/Beowulf Productions, 1981
BASIL POLEDOURIS
THE WHALE GOD 1962
AKIRA IFUKUBE
WHALE MUSIC Alliance, 1994
GEORGE BLONDHEIM
THE WHALES OF AUGUST Alive Films, 1987
ALAN PRICE
THE WHARF RAT (CTF) Showtime, 1995
MERVYN WARREN
WHAT A BLONDE RKO Radio, 1945
LEIGH HARLINE†
WHAT A WAY TO GO! 20th Century-Fox, 1964
NELSON RIDDLE†
WHAT ABOUT BOB? Buena Vista, 1991
MILES GOODMAN†
WHAT ARE BEST FRIENDS FOR? (TF) ABC Circle
Films, 1973
ALLYN FERGUSON
JACK ELLIOTT
WHAT BECAME OF JACK AND JILL? 1972
CARL DAVIS
WHAT DID YOU DO IN THE WAR, DADDY?
United Artists, 1966
HENRY MANCINI†

WHAT EVER HAPPENED TO AUNT ALICE?
Cinerama Releasing Corporation, 1968
GERALD FRIED

WHAT EVER HAPPENED TO BABY JANE? (TF)
Steve White/Aldrich Group/Spectacor, 1991
PETER MANNING ROBINSON

WHAT EVERY WOMAN KNOWS MGM, 1934
HERBERT STOTHART†

WHAT HAPPENED AT CAMPO GRANDE? *THE MAGNIFICENT TWO* Alan Enterprises, 1967
RON GOODWIN

WHAT HAPPENED WAS Good Machine, 1994
LUDOVICO SORRET

WHAT MAX SAID 1978
LUIS DE PABLO

WHAT PRICE GLORY? 20th Century-Fox, 1952
ALFRED NEWMAN†

WHAT PRICE GLORY? Fox, 1926
R. H. BASSETT†

WHAT PRICE HOLLYWOOD RKO Radio, 1932
MAX STEINER†

WHAT PRICE VICTORY (TF) Wolper Productions/
Warner Bros. TV, 1988
FRED KARLIN

WHAT WAITS BELOW Blossom Pictures, 1984
DENNY JAEGER
MICHEL RUBINI

WHAT! *LA FRUSTRA E IL CORPO* 1963
CARLO RUSTICHELLI

WHAT'S A NICE GIRL LIKE YOU...? (TF)
Universal TV, 1971
ROBERT PRINCE

WHAT'S EATING GILBERT GRAPE Paramount,
1993
ALAN PARKER

WHAT'S EATING GILBERT GRAPE Paramount,
1993
BJORN ISFALT

WHAT'S LOVE GOT TO DO WITH IT Buena Vista,
1993
STANLEY CLARKE

WHAT'S NEW PUSSYCAT? United Artists, 1965
BURT BACHARACH

WHAT'S NEXT? Kingsgate Films, 1974
CARL DAVIS

WHAT'S SO BAD ABOUT FEELING GOOD?
Universal, 1968
FRANK DEVOL

WHAT'S THE MATTER WITH HELEN? United
Artists, 1971
DAVID RAKSIN

WHAT'S UP, DOC? Warner Bros., 1972
ARTIE BUTLER

WHAT? Avco Embassy, 1973
CLAUDIO GIZZI

WHATEVER HAPPENED TO BABY JANE? Warner
Bros., 1962
FRANK DEVOL

WHATEVER IT TAKES Aquarius Films, 1986
GARRY SHERMAN

THE WHEELER DEALERS MGM, 1963
FRANK DEVOL

WHEELS OF FIRE *DESERT WARRIOR* Concorde/
New Horizons, 1984
CHRISTOPHER YOUNG

WHEELS OF TERROR (CTF) Once Upon a Time
Productions/Wilshire Court Productions, 1990
JAY GRUSKA

WHEN A MAN LOVES A WOMAN Buena Vista,
1994
DON DAVIS
ZBIGNIEW PREISNER

WHEN A STRANGER CALLS Columbia, 1979
DANA KAPROFF

WHEN A STRANGER CALLS BACK (CTF)
Krost-Chapin/Producers Entertainment Group/MTE,
1993
DANA KAPROFF

WHEN DREAMS COME TRUE (TF) I&C
Productions, 1985
GIL MELLE

WHEN EIGHT BELLS TOLL Cinerama Releasing
Corporation, 1971
ANGELA MORLEY

**WHEN EVERY DAY WAS THE FOURTH OF JULY
(TF)** Dan Curtis Productions, 1978
WALTER SCHARF

WHEN GANGLAND STRIKES Republic, 1956
VAN ALEXANDER

WHEN HARRY MET SALLY... Columbia, 1989
MARC SHAIMAN

WHEN HELL BROKE LOOSE Paramount, 1958
ALBERT GLASSER

WHEN HELL WAS IN SESSION (TF)
Aubrey-Hamner Productions, 1979
JIMMIE HASKELL

WHEN I GROW UP United Artists, 1951
JEROME MOROSS†

WHEN IN ROME MGM, 1952
CARMEN DRAGON†

WHEN LADIES MEET MGM, 1941
BRONISLAU KAPER†

WHEN LOVE IS YOUNG Universal, 1937
CHARLES PREVIN†

**WHEN LOVE KILLS: THE SEDUCTION OF JOHN
HEARN (TF)** Harvey Kahn Prods./Alexander
Enright & Associates/McGillen Entertainment, 1993
RICHARD MARVIN

WHEN MICHAEL CALLS (TF) Palomar Productions/
20th Century-Fox TV, 1972
LIONEL NEWMAN†

WHEN MY BABY SMILES AT ME 20th
Century-Fox, 1948
ALFRED NEWMAN† ★

WHEN NO ONE WOULD LISTEN (TF) Bruce Sallan
Prods., 1992
ARTHUR B. RUBINSTEIN

WHEN PIGS FLY 1993
JOE STRUMMER

WHEN SHE SAYS NO (TF) I&C Productions, 1984
BRAD FIEDEL

WHEN STRANGERS MARRY Monogram, 1944
DIMITRI TIOMKIN†

WHEN SVANTE DISAPPEARED Dagmar
Distribution, 1976
BENNY ANDERSEN

WHEN THE BOUGH BREAKS Prism, 1993
ED TOMNEY

WHEN THE BOUGH BREAKS (TF) Taft
Entertainment TV/TDF Productions, 1986
PAUL CHIHARA

WHEN THE CIRCUS CAME TO TOWN (TF)
Entheos Unlimited Productions/Meteor Films, 1981
CHARLES GROSS

WHEN THE CLOCK STRIKES United Artists, 1961
RICHARD LASALLE

WHEN THE DALTONS RODE Universal, 1940
FRANK SKINNER†

WHEN THE DARK MAN CALLS (CTF) Power
Pictures/Wilshire Court, 1995
DAVID MICHAEL FRANK

WHEN THE LIGHTS GO ON AGAIN Producers
Releasing Corp., 1944
W. FRANKE HARLING†

WHEN THE PARTY'S OVER WPTO, 1992
JOE ROMANO

WHEN THE TIME COMES (TF) Jaffe-Lansing
Productions/Republic Pictures, 1987
MARVIN HAMLISCH

WHEN THE WHALES CAME 20th Century Fox,
1989
CHRISTOPHER GUNNING
RUTH RENNIE

WHEN TIME RAN OUT Warner Bros., 1980
LALO SCHIFRIN

WHEN WE WERE YOUNG (TF) Richard & Esther
Shapiro Entertainment, 1989
PETER MATZ

WHEN WILLIE COMES MARCHING HOME 20th
Century-Fox, 1950
ALFRED NEWMAN†

WHEN WOMEN HAD TAILS 1970
ENNIO MORRICONE

WHEN WOMEN LOST THEIR TAILS 1971
ENNIO MORRICONE

WHEN WORLDS COLLIDE Paramount, 1951
LEITH STEVENS†

WHEN YOU COMIN' BACK, RED RYDER?
Columbia, 1979
JACK NITZCHE

WHEN YOUR LOVER LEAVES (TF) Major H
Productions, 1983
RANDY EDELMAN

WHERE ANGELS FEAR TO TREAD 1991
RACHEL PORTMAN

WHERE ANGELS GO...TROUBLE FOLLOWS!
Columbia, 1968
LALO SCHIFRIN

WHERE ARE MY CHILDREN? (TF) MDT Prods./
Andrea Baynes Prods./Warner Bros. TV, 1994
CRAIG SAFAN

WHERE ARE THE CHILDREN? Columbia, 1986
SYLVESTER LEVAY

**WHERE ARE WE: OUR TRIP THROUGH AMERICA
(FD)** Telling Pictures, 1992
DANIEL LICHT

WHERE ARE YOU GOING ALL NAKED? 1969
ARMANDO TROVAJOLI

WHERE ARE YOU? I AM HERE 1993
PINO DONAGGIO

WHERE DANGER LIVES RKO Radio, 1950
ROY WEBB†

WHERE DID YOU GET THAT GIRL? Universal,
1941
HANS J. SALTER†

WHERE DO WE GO FROM HERE? 20th
Century-Fox, 1945
DAVID RAKSIN

WHERE EAGLES DARE MGM, 1969
RON GOODWIN

WHERE HAVE ALL THE PEOPLE GONE? (TF)
Metromedia Producers Corporation/The Jozak
Company, 1974
ROBERT PRINCE.

WHERE LOVE HAS GONE Paramount, 1964
WALTER SCHARF

WHERE NO VULTURES FLY 1951
ALAN RAWSTHORNE†

WHERE PIGEONS GO TO DIE (TF) Michael Landon
Productions/World International Network, 1990
LEONARD ROSENMAN

WHERE SINNERS MEET RKO Radio, 1934
MAX STEINER†

WHERE SLEEPING DOGS LIE August Entertainment,
1992
MARK MANCINA
HANS ZIMMER

WHERE THE BOYS ARE '84 Tri-Star, 1984
SYLVESTER LEVAY

WHERE THE BUFFALO ROAM Universal, 1980
NEIL YOUNG

WHERE THE DEVIL CANNOT GO 1960
ZDENEK LISKA

WHERE THE HELL'S THAT GOLD?!! (TF) Willie
Nelson Productions/Brigade Productions/
Konigsberg-Sanitsky Company, 1988
ARTHUR B. RUBINSTEIN

WHERE THE LILLIES BLOOM United Artists, 1974
EARL SCRUGGS

WHERE THE NORTH BEGINS Screen Guild, 1947
ALBERT GLASSER

WHERE THE RED FERN GROWS Doty-Dayton,
1974
LEX DE AZEVEDO

WHERE THE RIVER RUNS BLACK MGM/UA,
1986
JAMES HORNER

WHERE THE SIDEWALK ENDS 20th Century-Fox,
1950
CYRIL J. MOCKRIDGE†
LIONEL NEWMAN†

WHERE'S JACK? Paramount, 1969
ELMER BERNSTEIN

WHERE'S POPPA? United Artists, 1970
JACK ELLIOTT

WHERE'S THE MONEY, NOREEN? (CTF) Wilshire
Court, 1996
RICHARD BELLIS

THE WHEREABOUTS OF JENNY (TF) Katie Face
Prods./Columbia TV, 1991
PATRICK WILLIAMS

WHEREVER YOU ARE Mark Forstater Productions/
Gerhard Schmidt Filmproduktion/Film Polski, 1988
WOJCIECH KILAR

WHICH WAY HOME (CTF) McElroy & McElroy/TV
New Zealand, 1991
BRUCE ROWLAND

WHICH WAY IS UP? Universal, 1977
MARK DAVIS
PAUL RISER

WHIFFS 20th Century-Fox, 1975
JOHN CAMERON

WHILE THE CITY SLEEPS RKO Radio, 1956
HERSCHEL BURKE GILBERT

WHILE THE SUN SHINES Pathe, 1947
NICHOLAS BRODZSKY†

WHILE YOU WERE SLEEPING Buena Vista, 1995
RANDY EDELMAN

THE WHIP HAND RKO, 1951
PAUL SAWTELL†

WHIPLASH Warner Bros., 1948
FRANZ WAXMAN†

THE WHIPPED United Artists, 1950
DAVID ROSE†

THE WHIPPING BOY (CTF) Gemini Films/Jones
Ent./Disney Channel, 1994
LEE HOLDRIDGE

WHIPSAW MGM, 1935
WILLIAM AXT†

WHIRLPOOL 20th Century-Fox, 1950
DAVID RAKSIN

WHIRLPOOL Continental, 1959
RON GOODWIN

WHIRLWIND Columbia, 1951
MISCHA BAKALEINIKOFF†

A WHISPER KILLS (TF) Sandy Hook Productions/
Steve Tisch Company/Phoenix Entertainment Group,
1988
CHARLES BERNSTEIN

THE WHISPERERS United Artists, 1967
JOHN BARRY

WHISPERING GHOSTS 20th Century-Fox, 1942
LEIGH HARLINE†
CYRIL J. MOCKRIDGE†
DAVID RAKSIN

WHISPERING SMITH Paramount, 1949
ADOLPH DEUTSCH†

WHISPERS Distant Horizon, 1989
BARRY FASMAN
DANA WALDEN

WHISPERS ITC/Cinepix, 1990
FRED MOLLIN

WHISPERS IN THE DARK Paramount, 1992
THOMAS NEWMAN

WHISPERS OF WHITE Lone Star Pictures, 1992
GEORGES GARVARENTZ†

THE WHISTLE BLOWER Hemdale, 1987
JOHN SCOTT

WHISTLE DOWN THE WIND Pathe-America, 1962
MALCOLM ARNOLD

WHISTLE IF YOU COME BACK 1993
OHNAY OGUZ

WHISTLE STOP United Artists, 1946
DIMITRI TIOMKIN†

WHISTLING IN BROOKLYN MGM, 1943
GEORGE BASSMAN

WHISTLING IN THE DARK MGM, 1941
BRONISLAU KAPER†

WHITE ANGEL 1993
HARRY GREGSON-WILLIAMS

WHITE BADGE Morning Calm, 1994
BYUNG HA SIN

WHITE BANNERS Warner Bros., 1938
MAX STEINER†

WHITE BONDAGE 1937
CLIFFORD VAUGHAN†

THE WHITE BUFFALO United Artists, 1977
JOHN BARRY

WHITE CARGO MGM, 1942
BRONISLAU KAPER†

THE WHITE CLIFFS OF DOVER MGM, 1944
HERBERT STOTHART†

THE WHITE DAWN 1964
TORU TAKEMITSU†

THE WHITE DAWN Paramount, 1974
HENRY MANCINI†

WHITE DOG Paramount, 1982
ENNIO MORRICONE

THE WHITE DOVE 1991
LOUIS BAGUE

WHITE DWARF (TF) RHI Ent./Elemental Films/
American Zoetrope, 1995
STEWART COPELAND

WHITE FANG Buena Vista, 1991
BASIL POLEDOURIS
FIACHRA TRENCH
SHIRLEY WALKER

WHITE FANG 2: MYTH OF THE WHITE WOLF
Buena Vista, 1994
JOHN DEBNEY

WHITE FEATHER 20th Century-Fox, 1955
HUGO FRIEDHOFER†

WHITE FLOOD Frontier Films, 1940
HANNS EISLER†

WHITE GHOST Trans World Entertainment, 1987
PARMER FULLER

THE WHITE GIRL Tony Brown Productions, 1990
GEORGE PORTER MARTIN

WHITE HEAT Warner Bros., 1949
MAX STEINER†

WHITE HOT *CRACK IN THE MIRROR* Triax
Entertainment Group, 1988
NILE RODGERS

**WHITE HOT: THE MYSTERIOUS MURDER OF
THELMA TODD (TF)** Sandy Hook Prods./
Neufeld-Keating Prods./von Zerneck-Sertner, 1991
MARK SNOW

WHITE HUNTER, BLACK HEART Warner Bros.,
1990
LENNIE NIEHAUS

WHITE LIE (CTF) USA, 1991
PHILIP GIFFIN

WHITE LIGHTNING United Artists, 1973
CHARLES BERNSTEIN

THE WHITE LINE *CUORI SENZA FRONTIERE*
1949
CARLO RUSTICHELLI

WHITE LINE FEVER Columbia, 1975
DAVID NICHTERN

THE WHITE LIONS Alan Landsburg Productions,
1979
WILLIAM GOLDSTEIN

WHITE MAMA (TF) Tomorrow Entertainment, 1980
PETER MATZ

WHITE MAN'S BURDEN 1995
STANLEY CLARKE
HOWARD SHORE

WHITE MEN CAN'T JUMP 20th Century Fox, 1992
BENNIE WALLACE

WHITE MILE (CTF) Stonehenge, 1994
PRAY FOR RAIN

WHITE MISCHIEF Columbia, 1987
GEORGE FENTON

WHITE NIGHTS Columbia, 1985
MICHEL COLOMBIER

WHITE NIGHTS *LE NOTTI BIANCHE* United
Motion Picture Organization, 1957
NINO ROTA†

WHITE OF THE EYE Palisades Entertainment, 1988
RICK FENN
GEORGE FENTON
NICK MASON

WHITE PALACE Universal, 1990
GEORGE FENTON

THE WHITE PHANTOM 1948
ALBERT GLASSER

WHITE PONGO   Producers Releasing Corp., 1945
LEO ERDODY†

WHITE ROCK (FD)   Shueisha Publishing Co., 1977
RICK WAKEMAN

THE WHITE ROSE   United Artists, 1923
JOSEPH CARL BREIL

WHITE SANDS   Warner Bros., 1992
PATRICK O'HEARN

WHITE SAVAGE   Universal, 1943
FRANK SKINNER†

WHITE SHADOWS OF THE SOUTH SEAS   MGM, 1928
WILLIAM AXT†

THE WHITE SHEIK   Pathe Contemporary, 1952
NINO ROTA†

THE WHITE SISTER   MGM, 1933
HERBERT STOTHART†

WHITE SLAVE SHIP   American International, 1962
LES BAXTER†

WHITE SQUALL   Buena Vista, 1996
JEFF RONA

WHITE TIE AND TAILS   Universal, 1946
MILTON ROSEN†

THE WHITE TOWER   RKO Radio, 1950
ROY WEBB†

WHITE TRASH   Fred Baker, 1992
FRED BAKER

WHITE WATER REBELS (TF)   CBS Entertainment, 1983
KEN THORNE

WHITE WATER SUMMER   Columbia, 1987
MICHAEL BODDICKER

WHITE WILDERNESS   Buena Vista, 1958
OLIVER WALLACE† ★

WHITE WITCH DOCTOR   20th Century-Fox, 1953
BERNARD HERRMANN†

WHITY   1971
PEER RABEN

WHO ARE THE DE BOLTS? ...AND WHERE DID THEY GET 19 KIDS? (FD)   Pyramid Films, 1977
ED BOGAS

WHO DARES WINS   MGM/UA, 1982
ROY BUDD†

WHO DONE IT?   Universal, 1942
HANS J. SALTER†
FRANK SKINNER†

WHO FEARS THE DEVIL   THE LEGEND OF HILLBILLY JOHN   Jack H. Harris Enterprises, 1974
ROGER KELLAWAY

WHO FRAMED ROGER RABBIT?   Buena Vista, 1988
ALAN SILVESTRI

WHO GETS THE FRIENDS? (TF)   CBS Entertainment, 1988
GARY WILLIAM FRIEDMAN

WHO IS HOPE SCHUYLER?   20th Century-Fox, 1942
DAVID RAKSIN

WHO IS JULIA? (TF)   CBS Entertainment, 1986
ROBERT DRASNIN

WHO IS KILLING THE GREAT CHEFS OF EUROPE?   Warner Bros., 1978
HENRY MANCINI†

WHO IS THE BLACK DAHLIA? (TF)   Douglas S. Cramer Productions, 1975
DOMINIC FRONTIERE

WHO KILLED DOC ROBBIN?   United Artists, 1948
HEINZ ROEMHELD†

WHO KILLED TEDDY BEAR?   Magna, 1965
JOEL HIRSCHHORN
AL KASHA

WHO KILLED THE BABY JESUS   Douglas Broghi, 1992
JOHN CLIFFORD

WHO LEAVES IN THE RAIN   1976
ZDENEK LISKA

WHO SLEW AUNTIE ROO?   American International, 1971
KENNETH V. JONES

WHO WAS THAT LADY?   Columbia, 1960
ANDRE PREVIN

WHO WILL LOVE MY CHILDREN? (TF)   ABC Circle Films, 1983
LAURENCE ROSENTHAL ☆

WHO'LL SAVE OUR CHILDREN? (TF)   Time-Life Productions, 1978
FRED KARLIN

WHO'LL STOP THE RAIN   United Artists, 1978
LAURENCE ROSENTHAL

WHO'S AFRAID OF VIRGINIA WOOLF?   Warner Bros., 1966
ALEX NORTH† ★

WHO'S HARRY CRUMB?   Tri-Star, 1989
MICHEL COLOMBIER

WHO'S MINDING THE MINT?   Columbia, 1967
LALO SCHIFRIN

WHO'S THE MAN   New Line, 1993
NICOLAS TENBROEK
MICHAEL WOLFF

WHO?   Lorimar, 1982
JOHN CAMERON

THE WHOLE WIDE WORLD   1996
HANS ZIMMER

THE WHOLE WORLD IS WATCHING (TF)   Public Arts Productions/Universal TV, 1969
PETE RUGOLO

WHOLLY MOSES   Columbia, 1980
PATRICK WILLIAMS

WHOM THE GODS WISH TO DESTROY/DIE NIBELUNGEN   1967
ROLF WILHELM

THE WHOOPEE BOYS   Paramount, 1986
UDI HARPAZ
JACK NITZCHE

WHOOPS APOCALYPSE   ITC Entertainment, 1986
PATRICK GOWERS

WHORE   Trimark, 1991
MICHAEL GIBBS

WHOSE CHILD IS THIS? THE WAR FOR BABY JESSICA (TF)   Sofronski Productions/ABC, 1993
LAWRENCE SHRAGGE

WHOSE DAUGHTER IS SHE? (TF)   1995
JOHN FRIZZELL

WHOSE LIFE IS IT ANYWAY?   MGM/United Artists, 1981
ARTHUR B. RUBINSTEIN

WHY BOTHER TO KNOCK?   1964
ELISABETH LUYTENS†

WHY ME?   Trans World Entertainment, 1989
BASIL POLEDOURIS

WHY ME? (TF)   Lorimar Productions, 1984
BILLY GOLDENBERG

WHY WASN'T HE THERE?   1993
LASZLO MELIS

WHY WOULD I LIE?   MGM/United Artists, 1980
CHARLES FOX

WICHITA   Universal, 1955
HANS J. SALTER†

WICKED AS THEY COME   Columbia, 1957
MALCOLM ARNOLD

THE WICKED DREAMS OF PAULA SCHULTZ   United Artists, 1968
JIMMIE HASKELL

THE WICKED LADY   MGM/UA/Cannon, 1983
ANTHONY BANKS

WICKED STEPMOTHER   MGM/UA, 1989
ROBERT FOLK

WICKED WIFE   Allied Artists, 1955
JOHN GREENWOOD†

A WICKED WOMAN   MGM, 1934
WILLIAM AXT†

THE WICKER MAN   Warner Bros., 1975
PAUL GIOVANNI†

THE WICKET GATE   1974
WOJCIECH KILAR

WIDE AWAKE   Miramax, 1997
EDMUND.D.CHOI

WIDE SARGASSO SEA   Fine Line, 1993
STEWART COPELAND

WIDOWS PEAK   Fine Line, 1994
CARL DAVIS

WIDOWS' NEST   Navarro Prods., 1977
FRANCIS LAI

THE WIFE   Ciby 2000, 1995
LUDOVICO SORRET

THE WIFE TAKES A FLYER   Columbia, 1942
WERNER R. HEYMANN†

WIFE VS. SECRETARY   MGM, 1936
HERBERT STOTHART†
EDWARD WARD†

WIFE, MOTHER MURDERER (TF)   Wilshire Court, 1991
MARK SNOW

WIFEMISTRESS   MOGLIAMENTE   1977
ARMANDO TROVAJOLI

WIGSTOCK: THE MOVIE (FD)   Samuel Goldwyn, 1995
PETER FISH
ROBERT REALE

THE WILBY CONSPIRACY   United Artists, 1975
STANLEY MYERS†

THE WILD AND THE FREE (TF)   BSR Productions/Marble Arch Productions, 1980
GERALD FRIED

THE WILD AND THE INNOCENT   Universal, 1959
HANS J. SALTER†

WILD AND WONDERFUL   Universal, 1964
MORTON STEVENS†

WILD AND WOOLY (TF)   Aaron Spelling Productions, 1978
CHARLES BERNSTEIN

THE WILD ANGELS   American International, 1966
MIKE CURB

WILD AT HEART   Samuel Goldwyn Co., 1990
ANGELO BADALAMENTI

WILD BEDS/HIJINKS   Castle Hill, 1978
RIZ ORTOLANI

WILD BILL   MGM-UA, 1995
VAN DYKE PARKS

THE WILD BLUE YONDER   Republic, 1951
VICTOR YOUNG†

THE WILD BUNCH   Warner Bros., 1969
JERRY FIELDING† ★

WILD CARD (CTF)   Davis Entertainment/MCA TV, 1992
W.G. SNUFFY WALDEN

THE WILD CHILD   United Artists, 1970
ANTOINE DUHAMEL

THE WILD COUNTRY   Buena Vista, 1971
ROBERT F. BRUNNER

WILD DOG IN AMERICA (TD)   1972
JOHN SCOTT ☆☆

THE WILD DUCK   RKR Releasing, 1983
SIMON WALKER

WILD FOR KICKS   BEAT GIRL   Renown, 1959
JOHN BARRY

THE WILD FRUIT   1958
JOSEPH KOSMA†

THE WILD GEESE   Allied Artists, 1979
ROY BUDD†

WILD GEESE II   Universal, 1985
ROY BUDD†

WILD GOOSE CHASE   1975
VLADIMIR COSMA

WILD HARVEST   Paramount, 1947
HUGO FRIEDHOFER†

THE WILD HEART   GONE TO EARTH   RKO Radio, 1950
BRIAN EASDALE

WILD HEARTS CAN'T BE BROKEN   Buena Vista, 1991
MASON DARING

WILD HORSE HANK   Film Consortium of Canada, 1979
PAUL HOFFERT

WILD HORSE RUSTLERS   Producers Releasing Corp., 1943
LEO ERDODY†

WILD HORSES   Endeavour, 1983
DAVE FRASER

WILD HORSES (TF)   Wild Horses Productions/Telepictures Productions, 1985
STANLEY MYERS†
HANS ZIMMER

WILD IN THE COUNTRY   20th Century-Fox, 1961
KENYON HOPKINS

WILD IN THE SKY   1972
JERRY STYNE

WILD IN THE STREETS   American International, 1968
LES BAXTER†

WILD IS THE WIND   Paramount, 1957
DIMITRI TIOMKIN†

WILD JUSTICE (MS)   Reitalia/Tribune/Taurus, 1993
ALAN PARKER

WILD LOVE   GLI INNAMORATI   Jacovoni, 1955
CARLO RUSTICHELLI

THE WILD McCULLOCHS   American International, 1975
ERNEST GOLD

THE WILD NORTH   MGM, 1952
BRONISLAU KAPER†

WILD ON THE BEACH   20th Century-Fox, 1965
JIMMIE HASKELL

THE WILD ONE   Columbia, 1954
LEITH STEVENS†

WILD ORCHID   Triumph Releasing Corporation, 1990
GEOFF MACCORMACK

WILD ORCHID II: TWO SHADES OF BLUE   Triumph, 1992
GEORGE S. CLINTON

THE WILD PAIR   DEVIL'S ODDS   Trans World Entertainment, 1987
JOHN DEBNEY

WILD PALMS (MS)   Ixtlan/Greengrass, 1993
RYUICHI SAKAMOTO

THE WILD PARTY   American International, 1975
LAURENCE ROSENTHAL

THE WILD PONY (TF)   Sullivan Films, Inc., 1982
HAGOOD HARDY

WILD RIVER   20th Century-Fox, 1960
KENYON HOPKINS

WILD ROVERS   MGM, 1971
JERRY GOLDSMITH

THE WILD SEED   Universal, 1965
RICHARD MARKOWITZ†

THE WILD SIDE   New World, 1983
ALEX GIBSON

WILD STRAWBERRIES   Janus, 1957
ERIC NORDGREN

WILD STYLE   Wild Style, 1983
FRED BRATHWAITE
CHRIS STEIN

WILD TEXAS WIND (TF)   Sandollar, 1991
RAY BENSON

WILD THING   Atlantic Releasing Corp., 1987
GEORGE S. CLINTON

WILD TIMES (TF)   Metromedia Producers Corporation/Rattlesnake Productions, 1980
JERROLD IMMEL

THE WILD WEST   Warner Bros., 1993
JOHN MCEUEN

WILD WEST   1992
DOMINIC MILLER

WILD WEST   Producers Releasing Corp., 1946
KARL HAJOS†

THE WILD WILD WEST REVISITED (TF)   CBS Entertainment, 1979
JEFF ALEXANDER†

WILD WILD PLANET   I CRIMINALI DELLA GELASSIA   MGM, 1966
ANGELO FRANCESCO LAVAGNINO†

THE WILD WOMEN OF CHASTITY GULCH (TF)   Aaron Spelling Productions, 1982
FRANK DEVOL
TOM WORRALL

WILDCATS   Warner Bros., 1986
JAMES NEWTON HOWARD
HAWK WOLINSKI

WILDER NAPALM   TriStar, 1993
MICHAEL KAMEN

WILDFIRE   Zupnick Enterprises/Jody Ann Productions, 1987
MAURICE JARRE

WILDFLOWER (CTF)   Freed-Laufer Prods./Polone Co./Hearst, 1991
JON GILUTIN
KENNY EDWARDS

WILL PENNY   Paramount, 1968
DAVID RAKSIN

WILL SUCCESS SPOIL ROCK HUNTER?   20th Century-Fox, 1957
CYRIL J. MOCKRIDGE†

WILL THERE REALLY BE A MORNING? (TF)   Jaffe-Blakely Films/Sama Productions/Orion TV, 1983
BILLY GOLDENBERG

WILL, G. GORDON LIDDY (TF)   Shayne Company Productions, 1982
PETE CARPENTER†
MIKE POST

WILLA (TF)   GJL Productions/Dove, Inc., 1979
JOHN BARRY

WILLARD   Cinerama Releasing Corporation, 1971
ALEX NORTH†

WILLIAM SHAKESPEARE'S ROMEO + JULIET   1996
NELLEE HOOPER

WILLIAMSBURG: THE STORY OF A PATRIOT   Paramount, 1956
BERNARD HERRMANN†

WILLIE & PHIL   20th Century-Fox, 1980
CLAUDE BOLLING

WILLIE DYNAMITE   Universal, 1974
J.J. JOHNSON

WILLIE WONKA AND THE CHOCOLATE FACTORY   Paramount, 1971
LESLIE BRICCUSE ★

WILLOW   MGM/UA, 1988
JAMES HORNER

WILLY MILLY/I WAS A TEENAGE BOY   Cinema Group, 1986
DAVID MCHUGH

WILMA (TF)   Cappy Productions, 1977
IRWIN BAZELON

WILSON   20th Century-Fox, 1944
ALFRED NEWMAN† ★

WINCHESTER '73 (TF)   Universal TV, 1967
SOL KAPLAN

THE WIND   Omega Pictures, 1987
STANLEY MYERS†
HANS ZIMMER

THE WIND   Carl Davis

WIND   TriStar, 1992
BASIL POLEDOURIS

THE WIND AND THE LION   MGM/United Artists, 1975
JERRY GOLDSMITH ★

THE WIND IN THE WILLOWS   GoodTimes, 1996
COLIN TOWNS

THE WIND OF EMPTINESS   KAMIN OUNAYNOUTIAN   1992
AVET TERTERIAN

WINDJAMMER   1958
MORTON GOULD

WINDMILL OF THE GODS (TF)   Dove Productions/ITC Productions, 1988
PERRY BOTKIN

THE WINDOW   RKO Radio, 1949
ROY WEBB†

WINDOW TO PARIS   Sony Classics, 1994
YURI MIAMIN
ALEKSEI ZALIVALOV

WINDOWS   United Artists, 1980
ENNIO MORRICONE

WINDRIDER   Hoyts, 1986
KEVIN PEAK

WINDS OF GOD   1993
MICHIRU OSHIMA

THE WINDS OF JARRAH   1983
BRUCE SMEATON

THE WINDS OF KITTY HAWK (TF)   Charles Fries Productions, 1978
CHARLES BERNSTEIN

A WOMAN'S DEVOTION   Republic, 1956
LES BAXTER†

A WOMAN'S FACE   MGM, 1941
BRONISLAU KAPER†

A WOMAN'S SECRET   RKO Radio, 1949
FREDERICK HOLLANDER†

A WOMAN'S VENGEANCE   Universal, 1947
MIKLOS ROZSA†

WOMAN'S WORLD   20th Century-Fox, 1954
CYRIL J. MOCKRIDGE†

A WOMAN, HER MEN, AND HER FUTON
Interpersonal, 1992
JOEL GOLDSMITH

WOMBLING FREE   1978
MIKE BATT

THE WOMEN   MGM, 1939
EDWARD WARD†

WOMEN & MEN 2 (CTF)   David Brown/HBO
Showcase, 1991
ANTON SANKO
SUZANNE VEGA

WOMEN & MEN 2 (CTF)   David Brown/HOB
Showcase, 1991
DICK HYMAN

WOMEN ARE TROUBLE   MGM, 1936
EDWARD WARD†

WOMEN AT WEST POINT (TF)   Green-Epstein
Productions/Alan Sacks Productions, 1979
CHARLES BERNSTEIN

THE WOMEN FROM THE LAKE OF SCENTED
SOULS   1993
WANG LIPING

WOMEN IN LOVE   United Artists, 1970
GEORGES DELERUE†

WOMEN IN WHITE (MS)   NBC, 1979
MORTON STEVENS†

THE WOMEN MEN MARRY   MGM, 1937
EDWARD WARD†

THE WOMEN OF BREWSTER PLACE (MS)
Phoenix Entertainment Group, 1989
DAVID SHIRE

THE WOMEN OF SPRING BREAK (TF)   Ron Gilbert
Ass./Hill-Fields Entertainment, 1995
LARRY BROWN

WOMEN OF SAN QUENTIN (TF)   David Gerber
Company/MGM-UA TV, 1983
JOHN CACAVAS

WOMEN OF VALOR (TF)   Inter Planetary
Productions/Jeni Productions, 1986
GEORGES DELERUE†

THE WOMEN OF WINDSOR (TF)   Sharmhill/
Samuels/World International Network, 1992
MICKEY ERBE
MARYBETH SOLOMON

WOMEN ON A HOLIDAY   1993
ALFREDO MUSCHIETTO

WOMEN ON THE VERGE OF A NERVOUS
BREAKDOWN   Orion Classics, 1988
BERNARDO BONAZZI

THE WOMEN'S CLUB   Weintraub-Cloverleaf/
Scorsese Productions, 1987
PAUL ANTONELLI
DAVID WHEATLEY

THE WOMEN'S ROOM (TF)   Philip Mandelker
Productions/Warner Bros. TV, 1980
BILLY GOLDENBERG

WON TON TON, THE DOG WHO SAVED
HOLLYWOOD   Paramount, 1976
NEAL HEFTI

THE WONDER OF IT ALL   1973
WILLIAM LOOSE†

WONDER WOMAN (TF)   Warner Bros. TV, 1974
ARTIE BUTLER

THE WONDERFUL COUNTRY   United Artists, 1959
ALEX NORTH†

THE WONDERFUL WORLD OF THE BROTHERS
GRIMM   MGM/Cinerama, 1962
LEIGH HARLINE† ★

WONDERLAND   THE FRUIT MACHINE   Vestron,
1988
HANS ZIMMER

THE WONDERS OF ALADDIN   MGM, 1961
ANGELO FRANCESCO LAVAGNINO†

THE WOOD NYMPH   1916
JOSEPH CARL BREIL†

THE WOODEN MAN'S BRIDE   1994
ZHANG DALONG

WOODEN NICKELS   1990
WILLIAM T. STROMBERG

THE WORD (MS)   Charles Fries Productions/
Stonehenge Productions, 1978
ALEX NORTH† ☆

WORD OF HONOR (TF)   Georgian Bay Productions,
1981
BRUCE LANGHORNE

WORKING GIRL   20th Century Fox, 1988
ROB MOUNSEY

WORKING GIRLS   Miramax Films, 1987
DAVID VAN TIEGHEM

WORKING STIFFS   1993
VELTON RAY BUNCH

WORKING TRASH (TF)   Fox, 1990
BOB MITHOFF

WORKS OF CALDER   Herbert Matter, 1950
JOHN CAGE†

THE WORLD ACCORDING TO GARP   Warner
Bros., 1982
DAVID SHIRE

WORLD AND TIME ENOUGH   1 in 10 Films, 1994
EUGENE HUDDLESTON

A WORLD APART   Atlantic Releasing Corporation,
1988
HANS ZIMMER

THE WORLD AT WAR (FD)   O.W.I., 1942
GAIL KUBIK†

WORLD FOR RANSOM   Allied Artists, 1954
FRANK DEVOL

WORLD GONE WILD   Lorimar, 1988
LAURENCE JUBER
KEN LUBER

THE WORLD IN HIS ARMS   Universal, 1952
FRANK SKINNER†

THE WORLD OF APU   1959
RAVI SHANKAR

THE WORLD OF HENRY ORIENT   United Artists,
1964
ELMER BERNSTEIN

WORLD WAR II: WHEN LIONS ROARED (TF)
WWII Co./Gideon Prods., 1994
JOHN MORRIS

WORLD WAR III (TF)   Finnegan Associates/David
Greene Productions, 1982
GIL MELLE

WORLD WITHOUT END   1953
ELISABETH LUYTENS†

WORLD WITHOUT END   Allied Artists, 1956
LEITH STEVENS†

THE WORLD'S GREATEST ATHLETE   Buena Vista,
1973
MARVIN HAMLISCH

THE WORLD'S GREATEST LOVER   20th
Century-Fox, 1977
JOHN MORRIS

THE WORLD'S MOST BEAUTIFUL GIRLS
Universal, 1953
HENRY MANCINI†

THE WORLD, THE FLESH AND THE DEVIL   MGM,
1959
MIKLOS ROZSA†

WORTH WINNING   20th Century Fox, 1989
PATRICK WILLIAMS

WOUNDED HEART (CTF)   USA/Boardwalk/
Hallmark/Stu Segall Prods., 1995
JAMES LEGG

THE WRAITH   New Century/Vista, 1986
MICHAEL HOENIG
J. PETER ROBINSON

WRANGLER   Hemdale, 1993
MARIO MILLO

THE WRATH OF GOD   MGM, 1972
LALO SCHIFRIN

WRESTLING ERNEST HEMINGWAY   Warner Bros.,
1993
MICHAEL CONVERTINO

WRITER'S BLOCK (TF)   Talent Court, 1991
NAN SCHWARTZ-MISHKIN

WRITTEN ON THE WIND   Universal, 1957
FRANK SKINNER†

THE WRONG ARM OF THE LAW   Continental,
1963
RICHARD RODNEY BENNETT

THE WRONG BOX   Columbia, 1966
JOHN BARRY

THE WRONG GUY   Handmade, 1997
LAWRENCE SHRAGGE

THE WRONG GUYS   New World, 1988
JOSEPH CONLAN

WRONG IS RIGHT   Columbia, 1982
ARTIE KANE

THE WRONG MAN (CTF)   Beattie-Chesser, 1993
LOS LOBOS

THE WRONG MAN   Warner Bros., 1956
BERNARD HERRMANN†

THE WRONG MOVE   New Yorker, 1975
JURGEN KNIEPER

WU KUI   THE WOODEN MAN'S BRIDE   1994
ZHANG DALONG

WUSA   Paramount, 1970
LALO SCHIFRIN

WUTHERING HEIGHTS   American International,
1971
MICHEL LEGRAND

WUTHERING HEIGHTS   Paramount, 1992
RYUICHI SAKAMOTO

WUTHERING HEIGHTS   United Artists, 1939
ALFRED NEWMAN† ★

W.W. AND THE DIXIE DANCEKINGS   20th
Century-Fox, 1975
DAVE GRUSIN

WYATT EARP   Warner Bros., 1994
JAMES NEWTON HOWARD

WYOMING   Republic, 1947
ERNEST GOLD

WYOMING OUTLAW   Republic, 1939
WILLIAM LAVA†

X

X THE UNKNOWN   Warner Bros., 1956
JAMES BERNARD

X312 FLUG ZUR HOLLE   1970
BRUNO NICOLAI

XANADU   Universal, 1980
BARRY DEVORZON

XIANG HUN NU   THE WOMEN FROM THE LAKE
OF SCENTED SOULS   1993
WANG LIPING

X-RAY   HOSPITAL MASSACRE   Cannon, 1981
ARLON OBER

XTRO II   1991
BRAUN FARNON
ROBERT SMART

XXX'S & OOO'S(TF)   John Wilder-Nightwatch
Prods/Brandon Tartikoff-Moving Target Prods., 1994
HARRY STINSON
BILL WATSON

THE XYZ MURDERS   Embassy International, 1985
JOSEPH LO DUCA

X, Y, ZEE   ZEE & CO.   Columbia, 1972
STANLEY MYERS†

Y

THE YAKUZA   Warner Bros., 1975
DAVE GRUSIN

YANG KWEI FEI   1955
FUMIO HAYASAKA†

A YANK AT EATON   MGM, 1942
BRONISLAU KAPER†

A YANK AT OXFORD   MGM, 1938
HUBERT BATH†
EDWARD WARD†

A YANK IN LONDON   20th Century-Fox, 1946
ANTHONY COLLINS†

A YANK IN THE R.A.F.   20th Century-Fox, 1941
ALFRED NEWMAN†

A YANK IN VIET-NAM   YEAR OF THE TIGER
Allied Artists, 1964
RICHARD LASALLE

YANKEE DOODLE DANDY   Warner Bros., 1942
HEINZ ROEMHELD† ★★

YANKEE PASHA   Universal, 1954
HANS J. SALTER†

YANKS   Universal, 1979
RICHARD RODNEY BENNETT

YANKS AHOY   United Artists, 1943
EDWARD WARD†

YAO A YAO YAO DAO WAIPO QIAO   Sony
Classics, 1995
ZHANG GUANGTIAN

THE YARN PRINCESS (TF)   Konisberg-Sanitsky,
1994
CHRISTOPHER FRANKE

A YEAR IN PROVENCE (MS)   BBC/A&E, 1993
CARL DAVIS

A YEAR IN THE LIFE (MS)   Falsey/Austin Street
Productions/Universal TV, 1986
MIKE GARSON
DAVID MCHUGH
ELIZABETH SWADOS

THE YEAR OF LIVING DANGEROUSLY   MGM/UA,
1982
MAURICE JARRE

THE YEAR OF THE CANNIBALS   I CANNIBALI
American International, 1969
ENNIO MORRICONE

YEAR OF THE COMET   Columbia, 1992
HUMMIE MANN

YEAR OF THE DRAGON   MGM/UA, 1985
LUCIA HWONG
DAVID MANSFIELD

YEAR OF THE GUN   Triumph, 1991
BILL CONTI

YEAR OF THE TIGER   Allied Artists, 1964
RICHARD LASALLE

THE YEARLING   MGM, 1947
HERBERT STOTHART†

THE YELLOW CAB MAN   MGM, 1950
ADOLPH DEUTSCH†

THE YELLOW CANARY   20th Century-Fox, 1963
KENYON HOPKINS

YELLOW CANARY   RKO Radio, 1943
CLIFTON PARKER†

YELLOW DOG   1973
RON GRAINER†

THE YELLOW HANDKERCHIEF OF HAPPINESS
1978
MASARU SATO

YELLOW JACK   MGM, 1938
WILLIAM AXT†

YELLOW MOUNTAIN   Universal, 1954
HENRY MANCINI†
HERMAN STEIN

THE YELLOW ROLLS-ROYCE   MGM, 1965
RIZ ORTOLANI

YELLOW SKY   20th Century-Fox, 1948
ALFRED NEWMAN†

YELLOW SUBMARINE   United Artists, 1968
GEORGE MARTIN

THE YELLOW TOMAHAWK   United Artists, 1954
LES BAXTER†

YELLOWBEARD   Orion, 1983
JOHN MORRIS

YELLOWNECK   Republic, 1955
LAURENCE ROSENTHAL

YENTL   MGM/UA, 1983   ★★
MICHEL LEGRAND

YES SIR, THAT'S MY BABY   Universal, 1949
WALTER SCHARF

YES, GIORGIO   MGM/UA, 1982
MICHAEL J. LEWIS

YES, VIRGINIA, THERE IS A SANTA CLAUS (TF)
Andrew J. Fenady/Quinta/Paradigm, 1991
CHARLES BERNSTEIN

YESTERDAY'S CHILD (TF)   Paramount TV, 1977
DOMINIC FRONTIERE

YESTERDAY'S HERO   EMI, 1979
STANLEY MYERS†

YESTERDAY, TODAY AND TOMORROW
Embassy, 1963
ARMANDO TROVAJOLI

YGALAH   1972
LES BAXTER†

YOG - MONSTER FROM SPACE   American
International, 1971
AKIRA IFUKUBE

YOJIMBO   Seneca International, 1961
MASARU SATO

YOL   Triumph/Columbia, 1982
SEBASTIAN ARGOL

YOR, THE HUNTER FROM THE FUTURE
Columbia, 1983
JOHN SCOTT

YOU AND ME   Paramount, 1938
KURT WEILL†

YOU ARE MY ONE AND ONLY   1993
ALEKSANDR PANTYCHIN

YOU BELONG TO ME   Columbia, 1942
FREDERICK HOLLANDER†

YOU CAME ALONG   Paramount, 1945
VICTOR YOUNG†

YOU CAN NEVER TELL   Universal, 1951
HANS J. SALTER†

YOU CAN'T BUY EVERYTHING   MGM, 1934
WILLIAM AXT†

YOU CAN'T ESCAPE FOREVER   Warner Bros.,
1942
ADOLPH DEUTSCH†

YOU CAN'T FOOL YOUR WIFE   RKO Radio, 1940
ROY WEBB†

YOU CAN'T GET AWAY WITH MURDER   Warner
Bros., 1939
HEINZ ROEMHELD†

YOU CAN'T GO HOME AGAIN (TF)   CBS
Entertainment, 1979
CHARLES GROSS

YOU CAN'T HAVE EVERYTHING   20th
Century-Fox, 1937
DAVID BUTTOLPH†

YOU CAN'T HURRY LOVE   Lightning Pictures,
1988
BOB ESTY

YOU CAN'T TAKE IT WITH YOU   Columbia, 1938
DIMITRI TIOMKIN†

YOU GOTTA STAY HAPPY   Universal, 1948
DANIELE AMFITHEATROF†

YOU HAVE TO RUN FAST   United Artists, 1961
RICHARD LASALLE

YOU KNOW WHAT SAILORS ARE   United Artists,
1954
MALCOLM ARNOLD

YOU LIE SO DEEP, MY LOVE (TF)   Universal TV,
1975
ELLIOT KAPLAN†

YOU LIGHT UP MY LIFE   Columbia, 1977
JOSEPH BROOKS

YOU MUST BE JOKING!   Columbia, 1965
LAURIE JOHNSON

YOU MUST REMEMBER THIS (TF)   Longride/QED
West/Limbo, 1992
HAROLD WHEELER

YOU ONLY LIVE ONCE   United Artists, 1937
ALFRED NEWMAN†

YOU ONLY LIVE TWICE   United Artists, 1967
JOHN BARRY

YOU RUINED MY LIFE (TF)   Lantana-Kosberg
Productions/Mark H. Ovitz Productions/Walt Disney
TV, 1987
JONATHAN TUNICK

YOU SENG   TEMPTATION OF A MONK   1993
TATS LAU

YOU TALKIN' TO ME MGM/UA, 1987
JOEL MCNEELY

YOU WERE NEVER LOVELIER Columbia, 1942
LEIGH HARLINE† ★

YOU'LL FIND OUT RKO Radio, 1940
ROY WEBB†

YOU'LL LIKE MY MOTHER Universal, 1972
GIL MELLE

YOU'LL NEVER SEE ME AGAIN (TF) Universal TV, 1973
RICHARD CLEMENTS

YOU'RE IN EVERYTHING 20th Century-Fox, 1949
ALFRED NEWMAN†

YOU'RE IN THE NAVY NOW 20th Century-Fox, 1951
CYRIL J. MOCKRIDGE†

YOU'RE NEVER TOO YOUNG Paramount, 1955
WALTER SCHARF

YOU'RE NOT SO TOUGH Universal, 1940
HANS J. SALTER†

YOU'RE TELLING ME Universal, 1942
HANS J. SALTER†

YOUCEF, OR THE LEGEND OF THE SEVENTH SLEEPER 1993
KHALED BARKAT

YOUCEF, OU LA LEGENDE DU SEPTIEME DORMANT *YOUCEF, OR THE LEGEND OF THE SEVENTH SLEEPER* 1993
KHALED BARKAT

YOUCHAI 1995
CHEN XIANGYU

YOUNG AGAIN (TF) Sharmhill Productions/Walt Disney Productions, 1986
JAMES DIPASQUALLE

THE YOUNG AMERICANS Gramercy, 1993
DAVID ARNOLD

THE YOUNG AND THE BRAVE MGM, 1963
RONALD STEIN†

YOUNG AND DANGEROUS 20th Century-Fox, 1957
PAUL DUNLAP

YOUNG AND INNOCENT *THE GIRL WAS YOUNG* Gaumont-British, 1937
LOUIS LEVY†

YOUNG AND WILLING United Artists, 1943
VICTOR YOUNG†

THE YOUNG ANIMALS American International, 1968
LES BAXTER†

YOUNG AT HEART (TF) TSProductions/Warner Bros. TV, 1995
MASON DARING

YOUNG BESS MGM, 1953
MIKLOS ROZSA†

YOUNG BRIDE RKO Radio, 1932
MAX STEINER†

THE YOUNG CAPTIVES Paramount, 1959
RICHARD MARKOWITZ†

YOUNG CATHERINE (CTF) Primedia/Lenfilm, 1991
ISAAC SCHWARTS

YOUNG CHARLIE CHAPLIN (TF) Thames TV Productions/WonderWorks, 1989
RACHEL PORTMAN

THE YOUNG COUNTRY (TF) Public Arts Productions/Universal TV, 1970
PETE RUGOLO

THE YOUNG DOCTORS United Artists, 1961
ELMER BERNSTEIN

YOUNG DOCTORS IN LOVE 20th Century-Fox, 1982
MAURICE JARRE

THE YOUNG DON'T CRY Columbia, 1957
GEORGE ANTHEIL†

YOUNG DONOVAN'S KID RKO Radio, 1931
MAX STEINER†

YOUNG EINSTEIN Warner Bros., 1988
MARTIN ARMIGER
WILLIAM MOTZIG
TOMMY TYCHO

YOUNG FRANKENSTEIN 20th Century-Fox, 1974
JOHN MORRIS

YOUNG FUGITIVE Universal, 1938
HANS J. SALTER†

YOUNG FURY Paramount, 1965
PAUL DUNLAP

YOUNG GIANTS Entertainment Enterprises, 1983
RICK PATTERSON

THE YOUNG GIRLS OF ROCHEFORT *LES DEMOISELLES DE ROCHEFORT* Warner Bros., 1968
MICHEL LEGRAND ★

YOUNG GOODMAN BROWN 50th Street, 1993
JON MCCALLUM

YOUNG GUARD 1947
DMITRI SHOSTAKOVITCH†

YOUNG GUNS 20th Century Fox, 1988
BRIAN BANKS
ANTHONY MARINELLI

YOUNG GUNS II 20th Century-Fox, 1990
ALAN SILVESTRI

YOUNG HARRY HOUDINI (TF) Walt Disney TV, 1987
LEE HOLDRIDGE

YOUNG IDEAS MGM, 1943
GEORGE BASSMAN

THE YOUNG IN HEART Selznick International, 1938
FRANZ WAXMAN† ★

THE YOUNG INDIANA JONES CHRONICLES (TF) Lucasfilm/Paramount, 1992
LAURENCE ROSENTHAL

THE YOUNG INDIANA JONES CHRONICLES: INDIANA JONES AND THE MYSTERY OF THE BLUES (TF) Lucasfilm/Paramount TV, 1993
JOEL MCNEELY

YOUNG INDIANA JONES & THE HOLLYWOOD FOLLIES (CTF) Lucasfilm/Amblin/Paramount TV, 1994
LAURENCE ROSENTHAL

YOUNG JOE, THE FORGOTTEN KENNEDY (TF) ABC Circle Films, 1977
JOHN BARRY

YOUNG LADY CHATTERLEY PRO International, 1977
DON BAGLEY

THE YOUNG LAND Columbia, 1959
DIMITRI TIOMKIN†

THE YOUNG LAWYERS (TF) Paramount Pictures TV, 1969
LALO SCHIFRIN

THE YOUNG LIONS 20th Century-Fox, 1958
HUGO FRIEDHOFER† ★

THE YOUNG LOVERS MGM, 1964
SOL KAPLAN

YOUNG LOVE, FIRST LOVE (TF) Lorimar Productions, 1979
ARTIE KANE

YOUNG MAN WITH IDEAS MGM, 1952
DAVID ROSE†

THE YOUNG MR. PITT 20th Century-Fox, 1942
WILLIAM ALWYN†

YOUNG MR. LINCOLN 20th Century-Fox, 1939
ALFRED NEWMAN†

THE YOUNG PHILADELPHIANS Warner Bros., 1959
ERNEST GOLD

YOUNG PIONEERS (TF) ABC Circle Films, 1976
DOMINIC FRONTIERE
LAURENCE ROSENTHAL

YOUNG PIONEERS' CHRISTMAS (TF) ABC Circle Films, 1976
LAURENCE ROSENTHAL

THE YOUNG POISONER'S HANDBOOK Mass-Sam Taylor, 1995
ROBERT LAKE
ROB LANE
FRANK STROBEL
FRANK STRUBEL

THE YOUNG RACERS American International, 1963
LES BAXTER†

THE YOUNG REBEL *CERVANTES* American International, 1968
LES BAXTER†

THE YOUNG SAVAGES United Artists, 1961
DAVID AMRAM

YOUNG SHERLOCK HOLMES Paramount, 1985
BRUCE BROUGHTON

YOUNG SOUL REBELS 1991
SIMON BOSWELL

THE YOUNG STRANGER Universal, 1957
LEONARD ROSENMAN

YOUNG TOM EDISON MGM, 1940
EDWARD WARD†

YOUNG TORLESS Kanawha, 1966
HANS WERNER HENZE

YOUNG WARRIORS Cannon, 1983
ROBERT J. WALSH

YOUNG WIDOW United Artists, 1946
CARMEN DRAGON†

YOUNGBLOOD American International, 1978
WAR

YOUNGBLOOD MGM/UA, 1986
WILLIAM ORBIT

YOUNGBLOOD HAWKE Warner Bros., 1964
MAX STEINER†

YOUNGER & YOUNGER Vine, 1993
BOB TELSON
HANS ZIMMER

THE YOUNGER BROTHERS Warner Bros., 1949
WILLIAM LAVA†

YOUR MONEY OR YOUR WIFE (TF) Brentwood Productions, 1972
ELLIOT LAWRENCE

YOUR MOTHER WEARS COMBAT BOOTS (TF) NBC Productions, 1989
JEFF BARRY
BARRY FASMAN

YOUR PLACE OR MINE (TF) Finnegan Associates/ Poolhouse Productions, 1983
GERALD ALTERS

YOUR THREE MINUTES ARE UP Cinerama Releasing Corporation, 1973
PERRY BOTKIN

YOUR TICKET IS NO LONGER VALID RSL Productions/Ambassador, 1981
MICHEL LEGRAND

YOUR WITNESS Eagle Lion, 1950
MALCOLM ARNOLD

YOURS, MINE AND OURS United Artists, 1968
FRED KARLIN

THE YOUTH OF MAXIM 1934
DMITRI SHOSTAKOVITCH†

YUMA (TF) Aaron Spelling Productions, 1971
GEORGE DUNING

YURI NOSENKO, KGB (CTF) BBC TV/Primetime TV Ltd., 1986
PETER HOWELL

YVETTE 1970
GEORGES DELERUE†

Z

Z Cinema 5, 1969
MIKIS THEODORAKIS

ZA ZUI ZI *CHATTERBOX* 1993
WEN ZHONGJIA

ZACHARIAH Cinerama Releasing Corporation, 1971
JIMMIE HASKELL

ZADAR! COW FROM HELL Stone Peach, 1989
GREG BROWN

ZANDALEE 1991
PRAY FOR RAIN

ZANDY'S BRIDE Warner Bros., 1974
MICHAEL FRANKS

ZANNA BIANCA 1974
CARLO RUSTICHELLI

ZANNA BIANCA ALLA RISCOSSA 1975
CARLO RUSTICHELLI

THE ZANY ADVENTURES OF ROBIN HOOD (TF) Bobka Productions/Charles Fries Entertainment, 1984
STANLEY MYERS†

ZANZABELLE A PARIS 1948
JEAN WIENER†

ZANZIBAR Universal, 1940
HANS J. SALTER†

ZAPPED! Embassy, 1982
CHARLES FOX

ZARAK Columbia, 1956
WILLIAM ALWYN†

ZARDOZ 20th Century Fox, 1974
DAVID MUNROW†

ZAZA 1943
NINO ROTA†

ZAZIE *ZAZIE DANS LE METRO* Astor, 1960
FIORENZO CARPI

ZAZIE DANS LE METRO Astor, 1960
FIORENZO CARPI

ZEBRAHEAD Oliver Stone, 1992
TAJ MAHAL

A ZED AND TWO NOUGHTS Skouras Pictures, 1985
MICHAEL NYMAN

ZEE & CO. Columbia, 1972
STANLEY MYERS†

ZEGEN Toei, 1987
SHINCHIRO IKEBE

ZELDA (CTF) Turner Pictures/ZDF/ORF/SRG, 1993
PATRICK WILLIAMS

ZELIG Orion/Warner Bros., 1983
DICK HYMAN

ZELLY AND ME Columbia, 1988
PINO DONAGGIO

ZENABEL 1969
BRUNO NICOLAI

ZENOBIA United Artists, 1939
T. MARVIN HATLEY†

ZENTROPA 1991
JOAKIM HOLBECK

ZEPPELIN 1971
ROY BUDD†

THE ZERO BOYS Omega Pictures, 1986
STANLEY MYERS†
HANS ZIMMER

ZERO PATIENCE Zero Patience Prods., 1993
GLENN SCHELLENBERG

ZERO TO SIXTY First Artists, 1977
JOHN BEAL

ZEUS AND ROXANNE MGM-UA, 1997
BRUCE ROWLAND

ZHAMGEDEH YOT OR 1992
ARDASHES KARTALIAN

ZIEGFELD GIRL MGM, 1941
HERBERT STOTHART†

ZIGFELD: THE MAN AND HIS WOMEN (TF) Frankovich Productions/Columbia TV, 1978
DICK DEBENEDICTIS ☆

ZIGZAG Universal, 1970
OLIVER NELSON†

ZIKKIMIN KOKU *BULLSHIT* 1993
OHNAY OGUZ

ZOLTAN, HOUND OF DRACULA Crown International, 1978
ANDREW BELLING

ZOMBI 2 *ZOMBIE FLESH EATERS* Variety Film, 1979
FABIO FRIZZI
GIORGIO TUCCI

ZOMBIE HIGH Cinema Group, 1987
DANIEL MAY

ZOMBIES OF MORA-TAU Columbia, 1957
MISCHA BAKALEINIKOFF†

ZOMBIES ON BROADWAY RKO Radio, 1945
ROY WEBB†

ZONE ROUGE *RED ZONE* AAA/Revcom Films, 1986
GABRIEL YARED

ZONE TROOPERS Empire Pictures, 1986
RICHARD H. BAND

THE ZOO GANG New World, 1985
PATRICK GLEESON
RANDY PETERSEN

ZOOMAN (CTF) Manheim/Logo Prods., 1995
DANIEL LICHT

ZORBA THE GREEK International Classics, 1964
MIKIS THEODORAKIS

ZORRO'S FIGHTING LEGION serial, Republic, 1939
WILLIAM LAVA†

ZORRO, MARCHESE DI NAVARRE 1971
ANGELO FRANCESCO LAVAGNINO†

ZORRO, THE GAY BLADE 20th Century-Fox, 1981
IAN FRASER

ZOTZ! Columbia, 1962
BERNARD GREEN

ZOYA 1944
DMITRI SHOSTAKOVITCH†

ZULU Embassy, 1964
JOHN BARRY

ZULU DAWN American Cinema, 1979
ELMER BERNSTEIN

ZUMA BEACH (TF) Edgar J. Scherick Associates/ Bruce Cohn Curtis Films/Warner Bros. TV, 1978
DICK HALLIGAN

★ ★ ★

INDICES

ACADEMY AWARD NOMINEES AND WINNERS
1955-1995

★★ = Winner in category

1955

Best Score (Drama or Comedy)
LOVE IS A MANY
   SPLENDORED THING .... Alfred Newman ★★
BATTLE CRY .... Max Steiner
THE MAN WITH THE GOLDEN ARM .... Elmer Bernstein
PICNIC .... George Duning
THE ROSE TATTOO .... Alex North

Best Score (Musical)
OKLAHOMA! .... Robert Russell Bennett,
      Jay Blackton and Adolph Deutsch (adaptation) ★★
DADDY LONG LEGS .... Alfred Newman (adaptation)
GUYS AND DOLLS .... Jay Blackton and
                        Cyril J. Mockridge (adaptation)
IT'S ALWAYS FAIR WEATHER .... André Previn
LOVE ME OR LEAVE ME .... Percy Faith and
                        George Stoll (adaptation)

1956

Best Score (Drama or Comedy)
AROUND THE WORLD IN 80 DAYS .... Victor Young ★★
ANASTASIA .... Alfred Newman
BETWEEN HEAVEN AND HELL .... Hugo Friedhofer
GIANT .... Dimitri Tiomkin
THE RAINMAKER .... Alex North

Best Score (Musical)
THE KING AND I .... Alfred Newman
                        and Ken Dar (adaptation) ★★
THE BEST THINGS IN
   LIFE ARE FREE .... Lionel Newman (adaptation)
THE EDDY DUCHIN STORY .... Morris Stoloff
                     and George Duning (adaptation)
HIGH SOCIETY .... Johnny Green
                     and Saul Chaplin (adaptation)
MEET ME IN LAS VEGAS .... George Stoll
                     and Johnny Green (adaptation)

1957

Best Score
THE BRIDGE ON THE RIVER KWAI .... Malcolm Arnold ★★
AN AFFAIR TO REMEMBER .... Hugo Friedhofer
BOY ON A DOLPHIN .... Hugo Friedhofer
PERRI .... Paul Smith
RAINTREE COUNTRY .... Johnny Green

1958

Best Score (Drama or Comedy)
THE OLD MAN AND THE SEA .... Dimitri Tiomkin ★★
THE BIG COUNTRY .... Jerome Moross
SEPARATE TABLES .... David Raksin
WHITE WILDERNESS .... Oliver Wallace
THE YOUNG LIONS .... Hugo Friedhofer

Best Score (Musical)
WEST SIDE STORY .... Saul Champlin, Johnny Green,
            Sid Ramin and Irwin Kostal (adaptation) ★★
BABES ON TOYLAND .... George Bruns (adaptation)
FLOWER DRUM SONG .... Alfred Newman
                     and Ken Dar (adaptation)
KHOVANSHCHINA .... Dimitri Shostakovich (adaptation)
PARIS BLUES .... Duke Ellington (adaptation)

1959

Best Score (Drama or Comedy)
BEN HUR .... Miklos Rosza ★★
THE DIARY OF ANNE FRANK .... Alfred Newman
THE NUN'S STORY .... Franz Waxman
ON THE BEACH .... Ernest Gold
PILLOW TALK .... Frank DeVol

Best Score (Musical)
PORGY AND BESS .... André Previn and Ken Dar ★★
THE FIVE PENNIES .... Leith Stevens (adaptation)
LI'L ABNER .... Nelson Riddle and
                     Joseph J. Lilley (adaptation)
SAY ONE FOR ME .... Lionel Newman (adaptation)
SLEEPING BEAUTY .... George Bruns (adaptation)

1960

Best Score (Drama or Comedy)
EXODUS ....Ernest Gold ★★
THE ALAMO .... Dimitri Tiomkin
ELMER GANTRY .... André Previn
THE MAGNIFICENT SEVEN .... Elmer Bernstein
SPARTACUS .... Alex North

Best Score (Musical)
SONG WITHOUT END
   (THE STORY OF FRANZ LISZT) .... Morris Stoloff and
                     Harry Sukman (adaptation) ★★
BELLS ARE RINGING .... André Previn (adaptation)
CAN-CAN .... Nelson Riddle (adaptation)
LET'S MAKE LOVE .... Lionel Newman and
                     Earle H. Hagen (adaptation)
PEPE .... Johnny Green (adaptation)

1961

Best Score (Drama or Comedy)
BREAKFAST AT TIFFANY'S .... ★★ Henry Mancini
EL CID .... Miklos Rosza
FANNY .... Morris Stoloff and Harry Sukman
THE GUNS OF NAVARONE .... Dimitri Tiomkin
SUMMER AND SMOKE .... Elmer Bernstein

Best Score (Musical)
WEST SIDE STORY .... Saul Champlin, Johnny Green,
            Sid Ramin and Irwin Kostal (adaptation) ★★
BABES ON TOYLAND .... George Bruns (adaptation)

A
C
A
D
E
M
Y

A
W
A
R
D
S

FLOWER DRUM SONG .... Alfred Newman and
Ken Dar (adaptation)
KHOVANSHCHINA .... Dimitri Shostakovich (adaptation)
PARIS BLUES .... Duke Ellington (adaptation)

1962

Best Original Score
LAWRENCE OF ARABIA .... Maurice Jarre ★★
FREUD .... Jerry Goldsmith
MUTINY ON THE BOUNTY .... Bronislau Kaper
TARAS BULBA .... Franz Waxman
TO KILL A MOCKINGBIRD .... Elmer Bernstein

Best Score (Adaptation or Treatment)
MEREDITH WILSON'S
THE MUSIC MAN .... Ray Heindorf (adaptation) ★★
BILLY ROSE'S JUMBO .... George Stoll (adaptation)
GIGOT .... Michel Magne (adaptation)
GYPSY .... Frank Perkins (adaptation)
THE WONDERFUL WORLD OF
THE BROTHERS GRIMM .... Leigh Harline (adaptation)

1963

Best Original Score
TOM JONES .... John Addison ★★
CLEOPATRA .... Alex North
55 DAYS AT PEKING .... Dimitri Tiomkin
HOW THE WEST WAS WON .... Alfred Newman
IT'S A MAD, MAD, MAD, MAD WORLD .... Ernest Gold

Best Score (Adaptation or Treatment)
IRMA LA DOUCE .... André Previn (adaptation) ★★
BYE BYE BIRDIE .... John Green (adaptation)
A NEW KIND OF LOVE .... Leith Stevens (adaptation)
SUNDAYS AND CYBELE *LES DIMANCHES DE VILLE
D'AVRAY* .... Maurice Jarre (original and adaptation)
THE SWORD IN THE STONE ..... George Bruns (adaptation)

1964

Best Original Score
MARY POPPINS .... Richard M. Sherman and
Robert B. Sherman ★★
BECKET .... Laurence Rosenthal
THE FALL OF THE ROMAN EMPIRE .... Dimitri Tiomkin
HUSH... HUSH SWEET CHARLOTTE .... Frank DeVol
THE PINK PANTHER .... Henry Mancini

Best Score (Adaptation or Treatment)
MY FAIR LADY .... André Previn (adaptation) ★★
A HARD DAY'S NIGHT .... George Martin (adaptation)
MARY POPPINS .... Irwin Kostal (adaptation)
ROBIN AND THE 7 HOODS .... Nelson Riddle (adaptation)
THE UNSINKABLE MOLLY BROWN ......Robert Armbruster,
Leo Arnaud, Jack Elliott, Jack Hayes,
Calvin Jackson and Leo Shuken (adaptation)

1965

Best Original Score
DOCTOR ZHIVAGO .... Maurice Jarre ★★
THE AGONY AND THE ECSTASY .... Alex North
THE GREATEST STORY EVER TOLD .... Alfred Newman
A PATCH OF BLUE .... Jerry Goldsmith
THE UMBRELLAS OF CHERBOURG *LES PARAPLUIES
DE CHERBOURG* .... Michel Legrand and Jacques Demy

Best Score (Adaptation or Treatment)
THE SOUND OF MUSIC .... Irwin Kostal (adaptation) ★★
CAT BALLOU .... Frank DeVol (adaptation)
THE PLEASURE SEEKERS .... Lionel Newman and
Alexander Courage (adaptation)
A THOUSAND CLOWNS .... Don Walker (adaptation)
THE UMBRELLAS OF CHERBOURG .... Michel Legrand
(original and adaptation)

1967

Best Original Score
THOUROUGHLY MODERN MILLIE ..... Elmer Bernstein ★★
COOL HAND LUKE .... Lalo Schifrin ★★
DOCTOR DOOLITTLE .... Leslie Bricusse
FAR FROM THE MADDING
CROWD .... Richard Rodney Bennett
IN COLD BLOOD .... Quincy Jones

Best Score (Adaptation or Treatment)
CAMELOT ..... Alfred Newman and Ken Dar (adaptation) ★★
DOCTOR DOOLITTLE .... Lionel Newman and
Alexander Courage
GUESS WHO'S COMING
TO DINNER .... Frank DeVol (adaptation)
THOUROUGHLY
MODERN MILLE .... Joseph Gershenson (adaptation)
VALLEY OF THE DOLLS .... John Williams (adaptation)

1968

Best Original Score
THE LION IN WINTER .... John Barry
THE FOX .... Lalo Schifrin
PLANET OF THE APES .... Jerry Goldsmith
THE SHOES OF THE FISHERMAN .... Alex North
THE THOMAS CROWN AFFAIR .... Michel Legrand

*Best Score of a Musical Picture
(Original or Adaptation)*
OLIVER! .... John Green (adaptation)
FINIAN'S RAINBOW .... Ray Heindorf (adaptation)
FUNNY GIRL .... Walter Scharf (adaptation)
STAR! .... Lennie Hayton (adaptation)
THE YOUNG GIRLS OF ROCHEFORT
(LES DEMOISELLES DE ROCHEFORT) ...Michel Legrand
and Jacques Demy

1969

Best Original Score
BUTCH CASSIDY AND THE
SUNDANCE KID .... Burt Bacharach
ANNE OF THE THOUSAND DAYS .... Georges Delerue
THE REIVERS .... John Williams
THE SECRET OF SANTA VITTORIA .... Ernest Gold
THE WILD BUNCH .... Jerry Fielding

*Best Score of a Musical Picture
(Original or Adaptation)*
HELLO DOLLY! .... Lennie Hayton and
Lionel Newman (adaptation)
GOOD BYE, MR. CHIPS ...... Leslie Bricusse (music & lyrics)
John Williams (adaptation)
PAINT YOUR WAGON .... Nelson Riddle (adaptation)
SWEET CHARITY .... Cy Coleman (adaptation)
THEY SHOOT HORSES, DON'T THEY? .... John Green and
Albert Woodbury (adaptation)

1970

Best Score
LOVE STORY .... Francis Lai ★★
AIRPORT .... Alfred Newman
CROMWELL .... Frank Cordell
PATTON .... Jerry Goldsmith
SUNFLOWER .... Henry Mancini

Best Song Score
LET IT BE .... The Beatles★★
THE BABY MAKER .... Fred Karlin & Tylwyth Kymry
A BOY NAMED CHARLIE BROWN .... Rod Mckuen and
John Scott Trotter, Bill Melendez and Al Shean;
Vince Guaraldi (adaptation)
DARLING LILI .... Henry Mancini and Johnny Mercer
SCROOGE .... Leslie Bricusse; Ian Fraser &
Herbert Spencer (adaptation)

Best Song
For All We Know
(LOVERS AND OTHER   Fred Karlin (music);
STRANGERS) ..... Robb Wilson & James Griffin (lyrics) ★★
Pieces Of Dream
(PIECES OF DREAM) .... Michel Legrand (music);
Alan & Marilyn Bergman (lyrics)
Thank You Very Much (SCROOGE) .... Leslie Bricusse
Till Love Touches Your Life
(MADRON) .... Riz Ortolani (music); Arthur Hamilton (lyrics)
Whistling Away The Dark
(DARLING LILI) .... Henry Mancini (music);
Johnny Mercer (lyrics)

1971

Best Score
SUMMER OF 1942 .... Michel Legrand ★★
MARY, QUEEN OF SCOTS .... John Barry
NICHOLAS AND ALEXANDRA ...... Richard Rodney Bennett
SHAFT .... Isaac Hayes
STRAW DOGS .... Jerry Fielding

Best Adaptation and Song Score
FIDDLER ON THE ROOF ..... John Williams (apaptation) ★★
BEDKNOB AND BROOMSTICKS .... Richard & Robert
Sherman; Irwin Kostal (adaptation)
THE BOY FRIEND .... Peter Maxwell Davies &
Peter Greenwell (adaptation)
TCHAIKOVSKY .... Dimitri Tiomkin (adaptation)
WILLY WONKA AND THE
CHOCOLATE FACTORY .... Leslie Bricusse &
Anthony Newley; Walter Scharf (adaptation)

Best Song
The Age Of Not Believing
(BEDKNOBS AND BROOMSTICKS) ... Richard Sherman &
Robert Sherman ★★
Theme From Shaft (SHAFT) .... Isaac Hayes
All His Children (SOMETIMES A
GREAT NOTION) .... Henry Mancini (music);
Alan & Marilyn Bergman (lyrics)
Bless The Beasts (BLESS THE
BEASTS AND CHILDREN) .... Barry Devorzon
& Perry Botkin Jr

Life Is What You Make It
(KOTCH) .... Marvin Hamlisch (music);
Johnny Mercer (lyrics)

1972

Best Score
LIMELIGHT .... Charles Chaplin, Raymond Rasch &
Larry Russell ★★
IMAGES .... John Williams
NAPOLEON AND SAMANTHA .... Buddy Baker
THE POSEIDON ADVENTURE .... John Williams
SLEUTH .... John Addison

Best Adaptation and Song Score
CABARET .... Ralph Burns (adaptation) ★★
LADY SINGS THE BLUES .... Gil Askey (adaptation)
MAN OF LA MANCHA .... Laurence Rosenthal (adaptation)

Best Song
The Morning After
(THE POSEIDON ADVENTURE) .... Al Kasha &
Joel Hirshhorn★★
Ben (BEN) .... Walter Scharf (music); Don Black (lyrics)
Come Follow, Follow Me
(THE LITTLE ARK) .... Fred Karlin (music);
Marsha Karlin (lyrics)
Marmelade, Molasses & Honey (THE LIFE AND
TIMES OF JUDGE ROY BEAN) ..... Maurice Jarre (music);
Marilyn & Alan Bergman (lyrics)
Strange Are The Way Of Love
(THE STEPMOTHER) .... Sammy Fain (music);
Paul Francis Webster (lyrics)

1973

Best Score
THE WAY WE WERE .... Marvin Hamlisch ★★
CINDERELLA LIBERTY .... John Williams
THE DAY OF THE DOLPHIN .... Georges Delerue
PAPILLON .... Jerry Goldsmith
A TOUCH OF CLASS .... John Cameron

Best Adaptation and Song Score
THE STING .... Marvin Hamlisch (adaptation) ★★
JESUS CHRIST
SUPERSTAR .... Andre Previn, Herbert Spencer &
Andrew Lloyd Webber (adaptation)
TOM SAWYER .... Richard Sherman & Robert Sherman;
John Williams (adaptation)

Best Song
The Way We Were
(THE WAY WE WERE) .... Marvin Hamlisch (music);
Alan & Marilyn Bergman (lyrics) ★★
All That Love Went To Waste
(A TOUCH OF CLASS) .... George Barrie (music);
Sammy Cahn (lyrics)
Live And Let Die
(LIVE AND LET DIE) .... Paul & Linda Mccartney
Love (ROBIN HOOD) .... George Burns (music);
Floyd Huddleston (lyrics)
Nice To Be Around
(CINDERELLA LIBERTY) .... John Williams (music);
Paul Williams (lyrics)

1974

Best Score
THE GODFATHER,
    PART 2 .... Nino Rota & Carmine Coppola ★★
CHINATOWN .... Jerry Goldsmith
MURDER ON THE
    ORIENT EXPRESS .... Richard Rodney Bennett
SHANKS .... Alex North
THE TOWERING INFERNO .... John Williams

Best Adaptation or Song Score
THE GREAT GATS .... Nelson Riddle (adaptation) ★★
THE LITTLE PRINCE ... Alan Jay Lerner & Frederick Loewe;
        Angela Morley & Douglas Gamley (adaptation)
PHANTOM OF
    THE PARADISE .... Paul Williams; Paul Williams &
        George Aliceson Tipton (adaptation)

Best Song
We May Never Love Like This Again
    (THE TOWERING INFERNO) .... Al Kasha &
        Joel Hirshhorn ★★
Benji's Theme
    (BENJI) .... Euel Box (music); Betti Box (lyrics)
Little Prince
    (THE LITTLE PRINCE) .... Frederick Loewe (music);
        Alan Jay Lerner (lyrics)
Wherever Love Takes Me
    (GOLD) .... Elmer Bernstein (music); Don Black (lyrics)

1975

Best Score
JAWS .... John Williams ★★
BIRDS DO IT, BEES DO IT .... Gerald Fried
BITE THE BULLET .... Alex North
ONE FLEW OVER THE CUCKOO'S NEST .... Jack Nitzsche
THE WIND AND THE LION .... Jerry Goldsmith

Best Adaptation or Song Score
BARRY LINDON .... Leonard Rosenman (adaptation) ★★
FUNNY LADY .... Peter Matz (adaptation)
TOMMY .... Peter Townshend (adaptation)

Best Song
I'm Easy (NASHVILLE) .... Keith Carradine ★★
How Lucky Can You Get
    (FUNNY LADY) .... Fred Ebb & John Kander
Now That We're In Love
    (WHIFFS) ..... George Barrie (music); Sammy Cahn (lyrics)
Richard's Window (THE OTHER
    SIDE OF THE MOUNTAIN) .... Charles Fox (music);
        Norman Gimbel (lyrics)
Theme From Mahogany
    (MAHOGANY) .... Michael Masser (music);
        Gerry Goffin (lyrics)

1976

Best Score
THE OMEN .... Jerry Goldsmith ★★
OBSESSION .... Bernard Herrmann
THE OUTLAW JOSEY WALES .... Jerry Fielding
TAXI DRIVER .... Bernard Herrmann
VOYAGE OF THE DAMNED .... Lalo Schifrin

Best Adaptation or Song Score
BOUND FOR GLORY .... Leonard Rosenman
        (adaptation) ★★
BUGSY MALONE .... Paul Williams (adaptation)
A STAR IS BORN .... Roger Kellaway (adaptation)

Best Song
Evergreen
    (A STAR IS BORN) .... Barbra Streisand (music);
        Paul Williams (lyrics) ★★
Ave Satani (THE OMEN) .... Jerry Goldsmith
Come To Me (THE PINK
    PANTHER STRIKES AGAIN) .... Henry Mancini (music);
        Don Black (lyrics)
Gonna Fly Now
    (ROCKY) .... Bill Conti (music); Carol Connors &
        Ayn Robbins (lyrics)
A World That Never Was
    (HALF A HOUSE) .... Sammy Fain (music);
        Paul Francis Webster (lyrics)

1977

Best Score
STAR WARS .... John Williams ★★
CLOSE ENCOUNTERS OF THE
    THIRD KIND .... John Williams
JULIA .... Georges Delerue
MOHAMMAD - MESSENGER OF GOD .... Maurice Jarre
THE SPY WHO LOVED ME .... Marvin Hamlisch

Best Adaptation or Song Score
A LITTLE NIGHT MUSIC .... Jonathan Tunick
        (adaptation) ★★
PETE'S DRAGON .... Irwin Kostal (adaptation)
THE SLIPPER AND
    THE ROSE .... Richard Sherman & Robert Sherman;
        Angela Morley (adaptation)

Best Song
You Light Up My Life
    (YOU LIGHT UP MY LIFE) .... Joseph Brooks ★★
Candle On The Waters
    (PETE'S DRAGON) .... Al Kasha & Joel Hirschhorn
Nobody Does It Better
    (THE SPY WHO LOVED ME) ..... Marvin Hamlisch (music);
        Carole Bayer Sager (lyrics)
The Slipper And The Rose Waltz
    (THE SLIPPER AND THE ROSE) .... Richard Sherman &
        Robert Sherman
Someone's Waiting For You
    (THE RESCUERS) .... Sammy Fain (music);
        Carol Connors & Ayn Robbins (lyrics)

1978

Best Score
MIDNIGHT EXPRESS .... Giorgio Moroder ★★
THE BOYS FROM BRAZIL .... Jerry Goldsmith
DAYS OF HEAVEN .... Ennio Morricone
HEAVEN CAN WAIT .... ave Grusin
SUPERMAN .... John Williams

Best Adaptation
THE BUDDY HOLLY
    STORY .... Joe Renzetti (adaptation) ★★
PRETTY BABY .... Jerry Wexler (adaptation)
THE WIZ .... Quincy Jones (adaptation)

Best Song
Last Dance (THANK GOD IT'S FRIDAY) .... Paul Jabara ★★
Hopelessly Devoted To You (GREASE) .... John Farrar
The Last Time I Felt Like This
   (SAME TIME, NEXT YEAR) .... Marvin Hamlisch (music);
                                  Alan & Marilyn Bergman (lyrics)
Ready To Take A Chance Again
   (FOUL PLAY) .... Charles Fox (music);
                                  Norman Gimbel (lyrics)
When You're Loved
   (THE MAGIC OF LASSIE) .... Richard Sherman &
                                  Robert Sherman

1979

Best Score
A LITTLE ROMANCE .... Georges Delerue ★★
THE AMYTIVILLE HORROR .... Lalo Schifrin
THE CHAMP .... Dave Grusin
STAR TREK .... Jerry Goldsmith
10 .... Henry Mancini

Best Adaptation or Song Score
ALL THAT JAZZ .... Ralph Burns (adaptation) ★★
BREAKING AWAY .... Patrick Williams (adaptation)
THE MUPPET
   MOVIE .... Paul Williams & Kenny Asher (adaptation)

Best Song
It Goes Like It Goes
   (NORMA RAE) .... David Shire (music);
                                  Norman Gimbel (lyrics) ★★
The Rainbow Connection
   (THE MUPPET MOVIE) .... Paul Williams & Kenny Asher
It's Easy To Say
   (10) .... Henry Mancini (music); Robert Wells (lyrics)
Through The Eyes Of Love
   (ICE CASTLES) .... Marvin Hamlisch (music);
                                  Carole Bayer Sager (lyrics)
I'll Never Say Goodbye359

   (THE PROMISE) .... David Shire (music);
                                  Alan & Marylin Bergman (lyrics)

1980

Best Score
FAME .... Michael Gore ★★
ALTERED STATES .... John Corigliano
THE ELEPHANT MAN .... John Morris
THE EMPIRE STRIKES BACK .... John Williams
TESS .... Philippe Sarde

Best Song
Fame
   (FAME) .... Michael Gore (music);
                                  Dean Pitchford (lyrics) ★★
Nine To Five (NINE TO FIVE) .... Dolly Parton
On The Road Again
   (HONEYSUCKLE ROSE) .... Willie Nelson
Out There On My Own
   (FAME) .... Michael Gore (music); Leslie Gore (lyrics)
People Alone
   (THE COMPETITION) .... Lalo Schifrin (music);
                                  Will Jennings (lyrics)

1981

Best Score
CHARIOTS OF FIRE ....,,.......... Vangolis ★★
DRAGONSLAYER .... Alex North
ON GOLDEN POND .... Dave Grusin
RAGTIME .... Randy Newman
RAIDERS OF THE LOST ARK .... John Williams

Best Song
Arthur's Theme
   (ARTHUR) .... Burt Bacharach, Carole Bayer Sager,
                              Christopher Cross & Peter Allen ★★
Endless Love (ENDLESS LOVE) .... Lionel Richie
The First Time It Happens
   (THE GREAT MUPPET CAPER) .... Joe Raposo
For Your Eyes Only
   (FOR YOUR EYES ONLY) .... Bill Conti (music);
                                  Mick Leeson (lyrics)
One More Hour (RAGTIME) .... Randy Newman

1982

Best Score
E.T., THE EXTRA-TERRESTRIAL .... John Williams ★★
GANDHI .... Ravi Shankar & George Fenton
AN OFFICER AND A GENTLEMAN .... Jack Nitzsche
POLTERGEIST .... Jerry Goldsmith
SOPHIE'S CHOICE .... Marvin Hamlisch

Best Adaptation or Song Score
VICTOR/VICTORIA .... Henry Mancini & Leslie Bricusse;
                              Henry Mancini (adaptation) ★★
ANNIE .... Ralph Burns (adaptation)
ONE FROM THE HEART .... Tom Waits

Best Song
Up Where We Belong
   (AN OFFICER AND A GENTLEMAN) .... Jack Nitzsche &
                              Buffy Sainte-Marie (music);
                              Will Jennings (lyrics) ★★
Eye Of The Tiger
   (ROCKY III) .... Jim Peterik & Frankie Sullivan III
How Do You Keep The Music Playing?
   (BEST FRIENDS) .... Michel Legrand (music);
                                  Alan & Marylin Bergman (lyrics)
If We Were In Love
   (YES, GIORGIO) .... John Williams (music);
                                  Alan & Marylin Bergman (lyrics)
It Might Be You
   (TOOTSIE) .... Dave Grusin (music);
                                  Alan & Marylin Bergman (lyrics)

1983

Best Score
THE RIGHT STUFF .... Bill Conti ★★
CROSS CREEK .... Leonard Rosenman
RETURN OF THE JEDI .... John Williams
TERMS OF ENDEARMENT .... Michael Gore
UNDER FIRE .... Jerry Goldsmith

Best Adaptation or Song Score
YENTL .... Michel Legrand, Alan & Marilyn Bergman ★★
THE STING 2 .... Lalo Schifrin (adaptation)
TRADING PLACES ....:........ Elmer Bernstein (adaptation)

A
C
A
D
E
M
Y

A
W
A
R
D
S

Best Song
Flashdance...What A Feeling
   (FLASHDANCE) .... Giogio Moroder (music);
                                    Keith Forsey & Irene Cara (lyrics) ★★
Maniac
   (FLASHDANCE) ...... Michael Sembello & Dennis Matkosky
Over You
   (TENDER MERCIES) .... Austin Roberts & Bob Hart
Papa, Can You Hear Me?
   (YENTL) .... Michel Legrand (music);
                                    Alan & Marilyn Bergman (lyrics)
The Way He Makes Me Feel
   (YENTL) .... Michel Legrand (music);
                                    Alan & Marilyn Bergman (lyrics)

1984

Best Score
A PASSAGE TO INDIA .... Maurice Jarre ★★
INDIANA JONES AND THE
   TEMPLE OF DOOM .... John Williams
THE NATURAL .... Randy Newman
THE RIVER .... John Williams
UNDER THE VOLCANO .... Alex North

Best Song Score
PURPLE RAIN .... Prince ★★
THE MUPPETS TAKE MANHATTAN .... Jeff Moss
SONGWRITER .... Kris Kristofferson

Best Song
I Just Called To Say I Love You
   (THE WOMAN IN RED) .... Stevie Wonder ★★
Against All Odds (AGAINST ALL ODDS) .... Phil Collins
Footloose (FOOTLOOSE) .... Kenny Loggins
                                    & Dean Pitchford
Ghostbusters (GHOSTBUSTERS) .... Ray Parker, Jr.
Let's Hear It For The Boy
   (FOOTLOOSE) .... Tom Snow & Dean Pitchford

1985

Best Score
OUT OF AFRICA .... John Barry ★★
AGNES OF GOD .... Georges Delerue
THE COLOR PURPLE .... Quincy Jones, Jeremy Lubbock,
                              Rod Temperton, Caiphus Semenya,
                              Andrae Crouch, Chris Boardman,
                              Jorge Calandrelli, Joel Rosenbaum,
                              Fred Steiner, Jack Hayes, Jerry Hey & Randy Kerber
SILVERADO .... Bruce Broughton
WITNESS .... Maurice Jarre

Best Song
Say You, Say Me (WHITE NIGHTS) .... Lionel Richie ★★
Miss Celie's Blues
   (THE COLOR PURPLE) .... Quincy Jones &
                              Rod Temperton (music); Quincy Jones,
                              Rod Temperton & Lionel Richie (lyrics)
The Power Of Love
   (BACK TO THE FUTURE) .... Chris Hayes &
                              Johnny Cola (music); Huey Lewis (lyrics)
Separate Lives (WHITE NIGHTS) .... Stephen Bishop
Surprise, Surprise
   (A CHORUS LINE) .... Marvin Hamlisch (music);
                                    Edward Kleban (lyrics)

1986

Best Score
ROUND MIDNIGHT .... Herbie Hancock ★★
ALIENS .... James Horner
HOOSIERS .... Jerry Goldsmith
THE MISSION .... Ennio Morricone
STAR TREK 4 .... Leonard Rosenman

Best Song
Take My Breath Away
   (TOP GUN) .... Giorgio Moroder (music);
                                    Tom Whitlock (lyrics) ★★
Glory Of Love
   (THE KARATE KID, PART II) .... Peter Cetera &
                  David Foster (music); Peter Cetera & Diane Nini (lyrics)
Life In A Looking Glass
   (THAT'S LIFE) .... Henry Mancini (music);
                                    Leslie Bricusse (lyrics)
Mean Green Mother From Outer Space
   (LITTLE SHOP OF HORRORS) .... Alan Menken (music);
                                    Howard Ashman (lyrics)
Somewhere Out There (AN
   AMERICAN TAIL) ...... James Horner & Barry Mann (music);
   Cynthia Weil (lyrics)

1987

Best Score
THE LAST EMPEROR .... Ryuichi Sakamoto,
                              David Byrne & Cong Su ★★
CRY FREEDOM .... George Fenton & Jonas Gwangwa
EMPIRE OF THE SUN .... John Williams
THE WITCHES OF EASTWICK .... John Williams
THE UNTOUCHABLES .... Ennio Morricone

Best Song
The Time Of My Life
   (DIRTY DANCING) .... Franke Previte, John Denicola &
                              Donald Markowitz (music);
                              Franke Previte (lyrics) ★★
Cry Freedom
   (CRY FREEDOM) .... George Fenton & Jonas Gwangwa
Nothing's Gonna Stop Us Now
   (MANNEQUIN) .... Albert Hammond & Dianne Warren
Shakedown
   (BEVERLY HILLS COP II) .... Harold Faltermeyer &
                              Keith Forsey (music); Harold Faltermeyer,
                              Keith Forsey & Bob Seger (lyrics)
Storybook Love (THE PRINCESS BRIDE) .... Willy Deville

1988

Best Score
THE MILAGRO BEANFIELD WAR .... Dave Grusin ★★
THE ACCIDENTAL TOURIST .... John Williams
DANGEROUS LIAISONS .... George Fenton
GORILLAS IN THE MIST .... Maurice Jarre
RAIN MAN .... Hans Zimmer

Best Song
Let The River Run (WORKING GIRL) .... Carly Simon ★★
Calling You (BAGDAD CAFE) .... Bob Telson
Two Hearts
   (BUSTER) .... Lamont Dozier (music); Phil Collins (lyrics)

1989

Best Score
THE LITTLE MERMAID .... Alan Menken ★★
BORN ON THE FOURTH OF JULY .... John Williams
THE FABULOUS BAKER BOYS .... Dave Grusin
FIELD OF DREAMS .... James Horner
INDIANA JONES AND THE
  LAST CRUSADE .... John Williams

Best Song
Under The Sea
  (THE LITTLE MERMAID) .... Alan Menken (music);
    Howard Ashman (lyrics) ★★
After All (CHANCES ARE) .... Tom Snow (music);
    Dean Pitchford (lyrics)
The Girl Who Used To Be Me
  (SHIRLEY VALENTINE) .... Marvin Hamlisch (music);
    Alan & Marilyn Bergman (lyrics)
I Love To See You Smile
  (PARENTHOOD) .... Randy Newman
Kiss The Girl
  (THE LITTLE MERMAID) .... Alan Menken (music);
    Howard Ashman (lyrics)

1990

Best Score
DANCES WITH WOLVES .... John Barry ★★
AVALON .... Randy Newman
GHOST .... Maurice Jarre
HAVANA .... Dave Grusin
HOME ALONE .... John Williams

Best Song
Sooner Or Later (DICK TRACY) .... Stephen Sondheim ★★
Blaze Of Glory (YOUNG GUNS II) .... Jon Bon Jovi
I'm Checking Out
  (POSTCARDS FROM THE EDGE) .... Shel Silverstein
Promise Me You'll Remember
  (THE GODFATHER, PART 3) ... Carmine Coppola (music);
    John Bettis (lyrics)
Somewhere In My Memory
  (HOME ALONE) .... John Williams (music);
    Leslie Bricusse (lyrics)

1991

Best Score
BEAUTY AND THE BEAST .... Alan Menken ★★
BUGSY .... Ennio Morricone
THE FISHER KING .... George Fenton
JFK .... John Williams
THE PRINCE OF TIDES .... James Newton Howard

Best Song
Beauty And The Beast
  (BEAUTY AND THE BEAST) .... Alan Menken (music);
    Howard Ashman (lyrics) ★★
Belle
  (BEAUTY AND THE BEAST) .... Alan Menken (music);
    Howard Ashman (lyrics)
Be Our Guest
  (BEAUTY AND THE BEAST) .... Alan Menken (music);
    Howard Ashman (lyrics)

Everything I Do I Do It For You (ROBIN HOOD:
  PRINCE OF THIEVES) .... Michael Kamen (music);
    Bryan Adams & Robert John Lange (lyrics)
When You're Alone
  (HOOK) ...... John Williams (music); Leslie Bricusse (lyrics)

1992

Best Score
ALADDIN .... Alan Menken ★★
BASIC INSTINCT .... Jerry Goldsmith
CHAPLIN .... John Barry
HOWARDS END .... Richard Robbins
A RIVER RUNS THROUGH IT .... Mark Isham

Best Song
Whole New World
  (ALADDIN) ...... Alan Menken (music); Tim Rice (lyrics) ★★
Beautiful Maria Of My Soul
  (THE MAMBO KINGS) .... Robert Kraft (music);
    Arne Glimcher (lyrics)
Friends Like Me (ALADDIN) .... Alan Menken (music);
    Howard Ashman (lyrics)
I Have Nothing
  (THE BODYGUARD) .... David Foster (music);
    Linda Thompson (lyrics)
Run To You
  (THE BODYGUARD) .... Jud Friedman (music);
    Allan Rich (lyrics)

1993

Best Score
SCHINDLER'S LIST .... John Williams ★★
THE AGE OF INNOCENCE .... Elmer Bernstein
THE FIRM .... Dave Grusin
THE FUGITIVE .... James Newton Howard
THE REMAINS OF THE DAY .... Richard Robbins

Best Song
Streets of Philadelphia
  (PHILADELPHIA) .... Bruce Springsteen ★★
Philadelphia (PHILADELPHIA) .... Neil Young
The Day I Fall In Love
  (BEETOVEN'S 2ND) .... Carole Bayer Sager,
    James Ingram & Cliff Magness
Again
  (POETIC JUSTICE) .... Janet Jackson, James Harris III &
    Terry Lewis
A Wink And A Smile
  (SLEEPLESS IN SEATTLE) .... Marc Shaiman (music);
    Ramsey McLean (lyrics)

1994

Best Score
THE LION KING .... Hans Zimmer★★
FORREST GUMP .... Alan Silvestri
INTERVIEW WITH THE VAMPIRE .... Elliot Goldenthal
LITTLE WOMEN .... Thomas Newman
THE SHAWSHANK REDEMPTION .... Thomas Newman

Best Song
Can You Feel The Love Tonight?
  (THE LION KING) .... Elton John (music),
    Tim Rice (lyrics)★★
Hakuna Matata
  (THE LION KING) .... Elton John (music)
    Tim Rice (lyrics)

Circle of Life
  (THE LION KING) .... Elton John (music),
Tim Rice (lyrics)

Look What Love Has Done
  (JUNIOR) .... Carole Bayer Sager,
James Newton Howard, James Ingram
and Patty Smyth (music and lyrics)

Make Up Your Mind
  (THE PAPER) .... Randy Newman (music and lyrics)

1995

Original Musical or Comedy Score
POCAHONTAS .... Alan Menken (music)
Stephen Schwartz (lyrics)
Alan Menken (orchestral score) ★★
THE AMERICAN PRESIDENT .... Marc Shaiman
SABRINA .... John Williams
TOY STORY .... Randy Newman
UNSTRUNG HEROES .... Thomas Newman

Original Dramatic Score
THE POSTMAN (IL POSTINO) .... Patrick Doyle ★★
APOLLO 13 .... James Horner
BRAVEHEART .... James Horner
NIXON .... John Williams

Original Song
Colors of the Wind
  (POCAHONTAS) .... Alan Menken (music)
Stephen Schwartz (lyrics) ★★

Dead Man Walking
  (DEAD MAN WALKING) .... Bruce Springsteen

Have You Ever Really Loved a Woman
  (DON JUAN DeMARCO) .... Michael Kamen,
Bryan Adams and Robert John Lange
(music and lyrics)

Moonlight
  (SABRINA) .... John Williams (music)
Alan and Marilyn Bergman (lyrics)

You've Got a Friend
  (TOY STORY) .... Randy Newman

1996

Original Musical or Comedy Score
EMMA .... Rachel Portman ★★
THE FIRST WIVES CLUB .... Marc Shaiman
THE HUNCHBACK OF NOTRE DAME .... Alan Menken (music)
Stephen Schwartz (lyrics), Alan Menken (orchestral score)
JAMES AND THE GIANT PEACH .... Randy Newman
THE PREACHER'S WIFE .... Hans Zimmer

Original Dramatic Score
THE ENGLISH PATIENT .... Gabriel Yared ★★
HAMLET .... Patrick Doyle
MICHAEL COLLINS .... Elliot Goldenthal
SHINE .... David Hirschfelder
SLEEPERS .... John Williams

Original Song
You Must Love Me
  (EVITA) .... Andrew Lloyd Webber (music)
Tim Rice (lyrics) ★★

Because You Loved Me
  (UP CLOSE AND PERSONAL) ..... Diane Warren (music and lyrics)

For the First Time
  (ONE FINE DAY) .... James Newton Howard,
Jud J. Friedman, Allan Dennis Rich (music and lyrics)

I Finally Found Someone
  (THE MIRROR HAS TWO FACES) .... Barbra Streisand,
Marvin Hamlisch, Bryan Adams,
Robert "Mutt" Lange (lyrics and music)

That Thing You Do!
  (THAT THING YOU DO!) .... Adam Schlesinger (music and lyrics)

★ ★ ★

EMMY AWARD NOMINEES AND WINNERS
1991-1995

☆☆ = Winner in category

1991

Music for a Series
Kansas (THE YOUNG RIDERS) .... John Debney ☆☆
The Collapse Of 98 (MY LIFE AND TIMES) .... Don Davis
The Consulting Detective Mystery
   (FATHER DOWLING MYSTERIES) .... Bruce Babcock
God Bless The Child
   (JAKE AND THE FATMAN) .... Joel Rosenbaum
Half A Life (STAR TREK:
   THE NEXT GENERATION) .... Dennis J. Mccarthy

Music for a Miniseries or Special
STEPHEN KING'S IT, PART 1 .... Richard Bellis ☆☆
DECORATION DAY .... Patrick Williams
JOHNNY RYAN .... Chris Boardman
THE KILLING MIND .... James Dipasquale
LIES BEFORE KISSES .... Don Davis

Main Title Theme *(Nominations only)*
ABC WORLD OF DISCOVERY .... Lee Holdridge
AGAINST THE LAW .... Thomas Newman
DREAM ON .... Michael Skloff
HULL HIGH .... Stanley Clark, Laurence Edwards,
                               Kenny Ortega & Peggy Holmes
SINGER AND SONS .... Ray Colcord

Music and Lyrics
He's Guilty (COP ROCK) .... Randy Newman ☆☆
Bittersweet Waltz
   (LIFE GOES ON) .... Craig Safan & Mark Mueller
I Didn't Hear You
   (THE LOST CAPONE) .... Mark Snow & Glynn Snow
Love And Justice (MATLOCK) .... Dick Debenedictis
Nowhere To Go, Nothing To Do
   (COP ROCK) .... Ron Boustead & Greg Edmonson

1992

Music Composition for a Series (Underscore)
The Strangler (MATLOCK) .... Bruce H. Babcock ☆☆
Unification 1 (STAR TREK:
   THE NEXT GENERATION) .... Dennis McCarthy ☆☆
Family Reunion
   (IN THE HEAT OF THE NIGHT) .... Nan Schwartz
Tree House Of Horrors II
   (THE SIMPSONS) .... Alf Clausen

Music Composition for a Miniseries or Special (Dramatic Underscore)
O PIONEERS .... Bruce Broughton ☆☆
DOUBLECROSSED .... Richard Bellis
FIRE IN THE DARK .... Arthur Kempel
A LITTLE PIECE OF HEAVEN .... Don Davis
SURVIVE THE SAVAGE SEA .... Fred Karlin

Main Title Theme Music *(Nominations only)*
BROOKLYN
   BRIDGE .... Marvin Hamlisch, Alan & Marylin Bergman
I'LL FLY AWAY .... W.G. Snuffy Walden
MAJOR DAD .... Steve Dorff
SILK STALKINGS .... Mike Post
THE YOUNG INDIANA
   JONES CHRONICLES .... Laurence Rosenthal

Music And Lyrics
Why Do I Lie?
   (CAST A DEADLY SPELL) .... Curt Sobel &
                                           Dennis Spiegel ☆☆
Love Without Strings
   (A SALUTE TO AMERICA'S PETS) .... Jimmie Haskell &
                                           Carol Connors
Rock Out Of That Rocking Chair
   (THE CAROL BURNETT SHOW) .... Mitzie Welch &
                                           Ken Welch
We Have Come To Learn (THE AMERICAN
   TEACHERS AWARDS) .... Larry Grossman
                                           & Buz Kohan

1993

Music Composition for a Series (Dramatic Underscore)
Scandal Of 1920 (THE YOUNG
   INDIANA JONES CHRONICLES) .... Joel Mcneely ☆☆
Leaping On A String, Part 1
   (QUANTUM LEAP) .... Velton Ray Bunch
Treehouse Of Horrors III
   (THE SIMPSONS) .... Alf Clausen
Vienna, 1908 (THE YOUNG
   INDIANA JONES CHRONICLES) .... Laurence Rosenthal
Wind Around The Tower
   (MURDER, SHE WROTE) .... Bruce Babcock

Music Composition for a Miniseries or Special (Dramatic Underscore)
DANIELLE STEEL'S JEWELS
   (PART 1) .... Patrick Williams ☆☆
AN AMERICAN STORY .... Mark Snow
CALL OF THE WILD .... Lee Holdridge
MORTAL SINS .... Joseph Conlan
THE SEA WOLF .... Charles Bernstein

Main Title Theme Music
STAR TREK: DEEP SPACE NINE ...... Dennis McCarthy ☆☆
BOB .... Lee Holdridge
BODIES OF EVIDENCE .... Christopher Klatman
COVINGTON CROSS .... Carl Davis
PICKET FENCES .... Stewart Levin

Music And Lyrics
How Do You Talk To An Angel?
   (THE HEIGHTS) .... Steve Tyrell, Barry Coffing &
                                           Stephanie Tyrell ☆☆

Good Things Grow
  (BLIND SPOT) .... Patrick Williams & Arthur Hamilton
Sorry I Asked
  (LIZA MINELLI LIVE FROM
  RADIO CITY MUSIC HALL) ....John Kander & Fred Ebb
Where There's Life, There's Hope
  (BOB HOPE: THE FIRST 90 YEARS) .... Ray Charles &
                                                    Buz Kohan

1994

Music Composition for a Series
  (Dramatic Underscore)
Ireland, 1916
  (THE YOUNG INDIANA JONES
  CHRONICLES) .... Laurence Rosenthal ☆☆
Cape Fear
  (THE SIMPSONS) .... Alf Clausen
Whale Song
  (seaQuest DSV) .... Don Davis
All Good Things
  (STAR TREK:
  THE NEXT GENERATION) .... Dennis McCarthy
Pilot
  (CHRISTY) .... Ron Ramin

Music Composition for a Miniseries or Special
  (Dramatic Underscore)
LUSH LIFE .... Lennie Niehaus ☆☆
DOUBLE, DOUBLE, TOIL AND TROUBLE ..... Richard Bellis
OLDEST LIVING CONFEDERATE
  WIDOW TELLS ALL - Part 2 .... Mark Snow
STEPHEN KING'S THE
  STAND - Part 4 .... W.G. "Snuffy" Walden
GERONIMO .... Patrick Williams

Music and Lyrics
The Song Remembers When
  (TRISHA YEARWOOD: THE SONG
  REMEMBERS WHEN) .... Hugh Prestwood ☆☆

The Game's Not The Same
  (MURDER SHE WROTE) .... Bruce Babcock (music)
                                             and Tom Sawyer (lyrics)
Who Needs the Kwik-E-Mart?
  (THE SIMPSONS) .... Alf Clausen (music)
                                             and Greg Daniels (lyrics)
Celebrate Broadway
  (THE TONY AWARDS) .... Larry Grossman (music)
                                             and Buz Kohan (lyrics)
One Lucky Lady
  (CAROL BURNETT: THE
  SPECIAL YEARS) .... Mitzie Welch and Ken Welch
Something Is Out There
  (THE CORPSE HAD A
  FAMILIAR FACE) .... Patrick Williams (music)
                                             and Arthur Hamilton (lyrics)

Main Title Theme Music
SEAQUEST, DSV .... John Debney ☆☆
LOIS & CLARK: THE NEW ADVENTURES
  OF SUPERMAN .... Jay Gruska
FRASIER .... Bruce Miller (music),
                                             Darryl Phinnessee (lyrics)
NYPD BLUE .... Mike Post
THE X-FILES .... Mark Snow

1995

Music Composition for a Series
  (Dramatic Underscore)
Daggers
  (SEAQUEST DSV) .... Don Davis ☆☆
Murder in High C
  (MURDER SHE WROTE) .... Bruce Babcock
Caretaker
  (STAR TREK: VOYAGER) .... Jay Chattaway
Tree House of Horror V
  (THE SIMPSONS) .... Alf Clausen
Heroes & Demons
  (STAR TREK: VOYAGER) .... Dennis McCarthy

Music Composition for a Miniseries or Special
  (Dramatic Underscore)
YOUNG INDIANA JONES AND THE
  HOLLYWOOD FOLLIES .... Laurence Rosenthal ☆☆
30 YEARS OF NATIONAL
  GEOGRAPHIC SPECIALS .... Jay Chattaway
BUFFALO GIRLS (Part 1) .... Lee Holdridge
CHILDREN OF THE DUST .... Mark Snow
KINGFISH: THE STORY
  OF HUEY P. LONG .... Patrick Williams

Music and Lyrics
Ordinary Miracles (BARBRA STREISAND:
  THE CONCERT) .... Marvin Hamlisch (music),
                                  Alan and Marilyn Bergman (lyrics) ☆☆
All the Days (aka Rooftop Source)
  (CAGNEY & LACEY:
  TOGETHER AGAIN) .... Nan Schwartz-Mishkin
For A Love Like You
  (A SEASON OF HOPE) .... Ken Thorne (music)
                                             and Dennis Spiegel (lyrics)
Pray
  (ROBBIE ROBERTSON:
  GOING HOME) .... Robbie Robertson
We Do (The Stonecutters Song)
  (THE SIMPSONS –
  HOMER THE GREAT) .... Alf Clausen (music)
                                             and John Schwartzwelder (lyrics)

Main Title Theme Music
STAR TREK: VOYAGER .... Jerry Goldsmith ☆☆
ER .... James Newton Howard
CHICAGO HOPE .... Mark Isham
FRIENDS .... Michael Skloff (music)
                                             and Allee Willis (lyrics)
MY SO-CALLED LIFE .... W.G. "Snuffy" Walden

1996

Music Composition for a Series
  (Dramatic Underscore)
Language Of The Heart
  (PICTURE WINDOWS) .... Hummie Mann ☆☆
Mind Over Murder
  (DIAGNOSIS MURDER) .... Dick DeBenedictis
Brave New World
  (SEAQUEST 2032) .... Russ Landau
The River Of Stars
  (SPACE: ABOVE AND BEYOND) .... Shirley Walker
Our Man Bashir
  (STAR TREK: DEEP SPACE NINE) .... Jay Chattaway

Music Composition for a Miniseries or Special
(Dramatic Underscore)
THE CANTERVILLE GHOST .... Ernest Troost ☆☆
ANNIE: A ROYAL ADVENTURE! .... David Michael Frank
LARRY MCMURTRY'S DEAD MAN'S WALK .... David Bell
NORMA JEAN AND MARILYN .... Christopher Young
TUSKEGEE AIRMEN .... Lee Holdridge

Music and Lyrics
Let's Settle Down
  (BYE BYE BIRDIE) .... Lee Adams (lyrics)
              Charles Strouse (composer) ☆☆
The Perfect Tree (MR. WILLOWBY'S
  CHRISTMAS TREE) .... Patty Silversher (composer)
              Michael Silversher (composer)
Children of the World (PEOPLE: A MUSICAL
  CELEBRATION) .... Nona Hendryx (music & lyrics)
              Jason Miles (music & lyrics)
Senor Burns (THE SIMPSONS;
  Who Shot Mr. Burns) .... Alf Clausen (composer)
              Bill Oakley (lyrics), Josh Weinstein (lyrics)
Come On In (THE WALT DISNEY COMPANY AND
  MCDONALDS PRESENTS THE AMERICAN
  TEACHER AWARDS) .... Larry Grossman (composer)
              Buz Kohan (lyricist)

Main Title Theme Music
MURDER ONE .... Mike Post ☆☆
CENTRAL PARK WEST .... Tim Truman
CHICAGO HOPE .... Mark Isham
JAG .... Bruce Broughton
NOWHERE MAN .... Mark Snow

★ ★ ★

'97-'98
FILM
COMPOSERS
GUIDE

AGENTS AND MANAGERS

A G E N T S & M A N A G E R S

A

AIR-EDEL
Scott Edel
11620 Wilshire Blvd., Suite 230
Los Angeles, CA 90025
310-914-5000
Fax: 310-914-5155

THE ARTISTS GROUP
Susan Grant
10100 Santa Monica Boulevard
Suite 2490
Los Angeles, CA 90067
310-552-1100
Fax: 310-277-9513

C

CRAY ARTIST MANAGEMENT
9909 Robbins Drive, Suite G
Beverly Hills, CA 90212
310-788-8484
Fax: 310-788-8455

CREATIVE ARTISTS AGENCY, INC.
Brian Loucks
9830 Wilshire Boulevard
Beverly Hills, CA 90210
310-288-4545
Fax: 310-288-4795

F

CAROL FAITH AGENCY
Carol Faith
Chris Frankfort
Beth Sanders
280 S. Beverly Drive, Suite 411
Beverly Hills, CA 90212
310-274-0776
Fax: 310-274-2670

FILM MUSIC ASSOCIATES
John Tempereau
Michael Horner
6525 Sunset Boulevard, 3rd Floor
Hollywood, CA 90028
213-463-1070
Fax: 213-463-1077

G

GORFAINE-SCHWARTZ AGENCY
Mike Gorfaine
Sam Schwartz
Cheryl Tiano
3301 Barham Boulevard, Suite 201
Los Angeles, CA 90068
213-969-1011
Fax: 213-969-1022

H

HEI
Jay Hooker
1325 El Hito Circle
Pacific Palisades, CA 90272
310-573-1309
Fax: 310-573-1313

HELLER MANAGEMENT
& CONSULTING
5444 Sepulveda, Suite 209
Sherman Oaks, CA 91411-3431
310-288-2536

K

SETH KAPLAN ENTERTAINMENT
106 S. Orange Drive
Los Angeles, CA 90036
213-525-3477

JEFF H. KAUFMAN AGENCY
Jeff H. Kaufman
12007 Laurel Terrace Drive
Studio City, CA 91604
818-506-6013
Fax: 818-506-7270

THE KOHNER AGENCY
Pearl Wexler
9300 Wilshire Boulevard, Suite 555
Beverly Hills. CA 90212
310-550-1060
Fax: 310-276-1083

THE KORDEK AGENCY
Linda Kordek
1117 Isabel Street
Burbank, CA 91506
818-559-4248
Fax: 818-559-2418

THE KRAFT-BENJAMIN AGENCY
Richard Kraft
Lyn Benjamin
Laura Engel
345 North Maple Drive, Suite 385
Beverly Hills, CA 90210
310-247-0123
Fax: 310-247-0066

KUSHNICK MANAGEMENT
Ken Kushnick
1840 Fairburn Ave., Suite 303
Los Angeles, CA 90025
310-470-5909

L

THE ROBERT LIGHT AGENCY
Robert Light
Thomas Lloyd
Steven Cagan
Helga Wild
6404 Wilshire Boulevard, Suite 900
Los Angeles, CA 90048
213-651-1777
Fax: 213-651-4933

LESLEY LOTTO
20917 Gorgonia St.
Woodland Hills, CA 91364
818-884-2209
Fax: 818-884-0403

M

MARKS MANAGEMENT
Larry Marks
20121 Ventura Blvd., Suite 305
Woodland Hills, CA 91364
818-587-5656
Fax: 818-776-9695

MILLER AGENCY
23236 Lyons Avenue, Suite 219
Santa Clarita, CA 91321
805-255-7173
Fax: 805-255-7286

O

OCEAN PARK MUSIC GROUP
Carol Sue Baker
1861 S. Bundy Drive, Suite 109
Los Angeles, CA 90025
310-315-5266
Fax: 310-315-5256

P

DEREK POWER COMPANY
Derek Power
11450 Albata
Los Angeles, CA 90049
310-472-4647

R

RYAN CO.
Charlie Ryan
13801 Ventura Boulevard, Suite 202
Sherman Oaks, CA 91423
818-981-4111

S

CATHY SCHLEUSSNER COMPANY
Cathy Schleussner
15622 Royal Oak Road
Encino, CA 91436
818-905-7475
Fax: 818-905-7473

SHANKMAN/DEBLASIO/MELINA
Alan Melina
Barry Soloman
740 N. La Brea Avenue, 1st Floor
Los Angeles, CA 90038
213-933-9977

THE SHUKAT COMPANY
Scott Shukat
Pat McLaughlin
340 W. 55th Street, Suite 1A
New York, NY 10019
212-582-7614

SMC ARTISTS
Otto Vavrin II
4400 Coldwater Canyon, Suite 127
Studio City, CA 91604-1480
818-505-9600
Fax: 818-505-0909

T

TWIN TOWERS MANAGEMENT
Jerry Ross
8833 Sunset Boulevard, Penthouse West
Los Angeles, CA 90069
310-659-9644

V

VANGELOS MANAGEMENT
Vasi Vangelos
Robert Messinger
Christa Schrott
Jennifer Brown
16030 Ventura Boulevard, Suite 550
Encino, CA 91436
818-380-1919
Fax: 818-380-1915

W

WILLIAM MORRIS AGENCY
Joel Roman
151 El Camino Drive
Beverly Hills, CA 90212
310-859-4000
Fax: 310-859-4462

Z

ZOMBA SCREEN MUSIC
David May
Steven Cagan
John Bowens
9000 Sunset Boulevard, Suite 300
West Hollywood, CA 90069
310-246-1593
Fax: 310-246-9231

MUSIC PUBLISHERS

All Nations Music
John Massa
8857 W. Olympic Blvd.
Suite 200
Beverly Hills, CA 90211
310-657-9814
Fax: 310-657-2331

BMG Music Publishing
Art Ford
8750 Wilshire Blvd.
3rd Floor
Beverly Hills, CA 90211
310-358-4726
Fax: 310-358-4733

Bug Music
Diane Kornarens
6777 Hollywood Blvd.
7th Floor
Hollywood, CA 90028
213-466-4352
Fax: 213-466-2366

Cherry Lane Music
Jerry Horan
10 Midland Ave.
Port Chester, NY 10573
914-935-5200
914-937-0614

EMI Music Publishing
Pat Lucas
Stacey Palm
8730 Sunset Blvd,
Suite 290
Los Angeles, CA 90069
310-289-6423
Fax: (310)289-6495

Famous Music Publishing Company
Bob Knight
10635 Santa Monica Blvd.
Suite 300
Los Angeles, CA 90025
310-441-1300
Fax: 310-441-4722

Jobete Music
Allison O'Donnell – Creative
Lawnie Grant – Licensing
6255 Sunset Blvd.
18Th Floor
Hollywood, CA 90028
213-856-3513
Fax: 213-957-9372

Leeds Entertainment
Leeds Levy
1077 Montana Ave., Suite 341
Santa Monica , CA 90049
310-440-0140
Fax: 310-440-0240

Leiber & Stoller Music Publishing
Helen Mallory
9000 Sunset Blvd.
Suite 1107
Los Angeles, CA 90069
310-273-6401
Fax: 310-273-1591

MCA Music Publishing
Scott James
Kathy Coleman
2440 Sepulveda, Suite 100
Los Angeles, CA 90064
310-235-4720
Fax: 310-235-4905

MGM/UA Music Publishing
Rita Zak
2500 Broadway
5th Floor
Santa Monica, CA 90404
310-449-3810
Fax: 310-449-3091

Musikuser Publishing
15030 Ventura Blvd., Suite 425
Sherman Oaks, CA 91403
310-440-0140
Fax: 310-440-0240

MPL
Peter Silvestri
Lynnae Crawford
39 West 54th Street
New York, NY 10019
212-246-5881
Fax: 212-977-8408

Opryland Music Group
Suzanne M. Proskasy
65 Music Square West
Nashville, TN 37203
615-321-5000

Original Sound Entertainment
Paul Politi
7120 Sunset Blvd.
Hollywood, CA 90046
213-851-2500
Fax: 213-851-8162

Peer Music
Brady Benton
8159 Hollywood Blvd.
Los Angeles, CA 90069
213-656-0364
Fax: 213-656-3298

Polygram Music Publishing
Danny Benair
Joan Schulman
1416 N. La Brea
Hollywood, CA 90028
213-856-2776
Fax: 213-856-2664

Rondor Music International
Derek Alpert
360 N. La Cienega
Los Angeles, CA 90048
310-289-3500
Fax: 310-289-4000

Sony/ATV Music Publishing
Jennifer Pyken
2100 Colorado Ave
Santa Monica, CA 90404
310-449-2552
Fax: 310-449-2544

Warner/Chappell
Brad Rosenberger – V.P. Film Music
Matthew Downs – Mgr. of Film Music
Pat Woods – Licensing
Paulette Hawkins – Licensing
10585 Santa Monica Blvd.
Los Angeles, CA 90025
310-441-8600
Fax: 310-470-3232

Windswept Pacific Entertainment
Lisa Grande
9320 Wilshire Blvd.
Suite 200
Beverly Hills, CA 90212
310-550-1500
Fax: 310-247-0195

Zomba Music Services
Neil Portnow
Michael Babcock
9000 Sunset Blvd.
Suite 300
W. Hollywood, CA 90069
310-247-8300
Fax: 310-247-8366

STUDIO CONTACTS

20th Century Fox
10201 W. Pico Blvd.
Los Angeles, CA 90035
310-369-1000
Robert Kraft – Executive VP Music
Matthew Walden – Senior VP Music

MGM/UA
2500 Broadway
4th Floor
Santa Monica, CA 90404
310-449-3635
Fax: 310-449-8819
Michael Sandoval – Exec.VP, Music

Miramax Films
375 Greenwich Street
New York, NY 10013
212-941-2446
212-941-2029 Fax:
Jeffrey Kimball – VP Music
Beth Rosenblatt - Senior Director, Music

New Line Cinema
888 7th Ave.
New York, NY 10106
Toby Emmerich – President, Music
212-649-4900

116 N. Robertson Bl., Suite 709
Los Angeles, CA 90048
Dana Sano - VP Music 310-967-6925
Paul Broucek - VP Music 310-967-6930
Jon McHugh - VP Soundtracks
310-967-6927

Polygram Film Entertainment
9348 Civic Center Drive, Suite 300
Beverly Hills, CA 90210
310-777-3135
Dawn Soler - Sr. VP Music

Paramount Pictures
5555 Melrose Ave.
Los Angeles, CA 90038
213-956-5222
Harlan Goodman - Sr. VP Music
Linda Springer - VP Music

Rysher Entertainment
2401 Colorado Ave., Suite 200
Santa Monica, CA 90404
Randy Gerston - Senior V.P. Music
310-309-5383

Sony Pictures - Columbia, Tri-Star
10202 W. Washington Blvd.
Culver City, CA 90232
310-280-8000
Burt Berman - Executive VP, Music
Bob Holmes - Executive VP,
SPE Music Group

Universal Pictures
100 Universal City Plaza
Universal City, CA 91508
818-777-1000
Harry Garfield - Sr. VP, Music

Walt Disney Studios
500 So. Buena Vista St.
Burbank, CA 91521
818-560-1000
Kathy Nelson - President, Music
Bill Green - Sr. V.P., Music
Matt Walker - Sr. V.P., Music
Chris Montan - Executive Music
Producer, Feature Animation

Warner Bros. Inc.
4000 Warner Blvd.
Burbank, CA 91522
818-954-6000
Gary LeMel - President, Music
Doug Frank - Exec. V.P., Music
Tom Bocci - V.P. Television Music

MUSIC CLEARANCE COMPANIES

Arlene Fishbach Enterprises
420 California Ave., Suite 14
Santa Monica, CA 90403
310-451-5916

BZ / Rights and Permissions
Barbara Zimmerman
125 W. 72nd
New York, NY 10023
212-580-0615

Clear Music
Barry Cole
145 Ave. of the Americas, 7th Floor
New York, NY 10013
212-243-3042

Clearing House Ltd.
Lu Kunene
405 Riverside Drive
Burbank, CA 91506
213-469-3186

Copyright Clearinghouse, Inc.
Anita Hunsaker
405 Riverside Drive
Burbank, CA 91506
818-558-3480

Evan Greenspan
11846 Ventura Blvd.
Suite 140
Studio City, CA 91604
818-762-9656

Jill Meyers Music Consultants
10669 Santa Monica Bl.
Los Angeles, CA 90025
310-441-2604

Media Rights Inc.
Melody Siroty
6100 Wilshire Blvd.
Suite 1500
Los Angeles, CA 90048
213-954-0181

Reel Music Ltd.
Robin Urdang
8733 Sunset Blvd., Suite 102
Los Angeles, CA 90069
310-360-0244

Suzy Vaughan Associates Inc.
Suzy Vaughan
Ron McGowan
2029 Century Park East, Suite 450
Los Angeles, CA 90067
310-556-1409

MASTER USE LICENSING CONTACTS

M
A
S
T
E
R

U
S
E

L
I
C
E
N
S
I
N
G

C
O
N
T
A
C
T
S

ARISTA SOUNDTRACKS
(Arista, La Face, Rowdy, Bad Boy,
Reunion, Time Bomb)
Joei Alvarez
9975 Santa Monica Blvd.
3rd Floor
Beverly Hills, CA 90212
310-789-3900
Fax: 310-789-3944

CELEBRITY LICENSING INC.
(Barnaby, Bellamy Brothers,
Cadence, Castle Copyrights Ltd.,
Chrysalis Copyrights Ltd.,
Chancellor, Charger, Class, Coed,
Crusader, Dave Clark London Ltd.,
Eldo, Fraternity, GRT, Janus,
Midland, Monogram, Parlo,
Tony Orlando, Reader's Digest,
Rendezvous and more)
Nola Leone
6711 Forest Lawn Drive, Suite 100
Los Angeles, CA 90048
213-876-9615
Fax: 213-876-1810

CEMA SPECIAL MARKETS
(Capitol, EMI, SBK, Chrysalis,
Sparrow, Hi, Virgin Classics,
Starsong, Blue Note,
Liberty, Angel)
Eddie Lambert
1750 N. Vine
Hollwood, CA 90028
213-960-4651
Fax: 213- 960-4666

DOMINION / K-TEL
Mary Kuehn
2605 Fernbrook Lane North
Minneapolis, MN 55447
612-559-6800
Fax: 612-559-6815

MCA SPECIAL MARKETS
& PRODUCTS
(MCA, Geffen, Decca, Uptown,
DreamWorks SKG, Hippo,
Silas, GRP, Radioactive,
Margaritaville, Gasoline Alley)
Tom Rowland
70 Universal City Plaza
Universal City, CA 91608
818-777-4148
Fax: 818-733-1598

OCEAN PARK MUSIC GROUP
(GNP/Crescendo, Bar None,
American Gramaphone, Rounder,
Promusic, Roadrunner, Frontier,
Ryko)
Carol Sue Baker
1861 S. Bundy Drive
Suite 109
Los Angeles, CA 90025
310-315-5266
Fax: 310- 315-5256

POLYGRAM MUSIC LICENSING
(Island, A&M, Polydor, Polygram,
Motown, Mercury, London, Verve,
Def Jam)
Robin Kaye
1416 N. La Brea
Hollywood, CA 90028
213-856-6634
213-856-6639

RCA RECORDS
(RCA, Zoo Entertainment,
RCA Victor)
Marty Olnick
8750 Wilshire Blvd.
Beverly Hills, Ca 90211
310-358-4016
Fax: 310-358-4168

RHINO RECORDS
Sara Diamond
10635 Santa Monica Blvd.
Los Angeles, CA 90025
310-474-4778

SONY MUSIC LICENSING
(Columbia, Epic, Work, Okeh, 550,
Sony Classical, Relativity)
Kathy Malta
Paula Erickson
2100 Colorado Ave.
Santa Monica, CA 90404
310-449-2555
Fax: 310-449-2570

WARNER SPECIAL PRODUCTS
(Warner, Sire, Mavrick, Reprise,
Elektra, Atlantic)
Bill Bishop
3500 W. Olive, Suite 800
Burbank, CA 91505
818-953-7900
Fax: 818-953-7955

SOUNDTRACK ALBUM COMPANIES

A&M Records
1416 N. La Brea
Hollywood, CA 90028
213-856-7165
Fax: 213-856-2659

Arista Soundtracks
Maureen Crowe
9975 Santa Monica Blvd.
3rd Floor
Beverly Hills, CA 90212
310-789-3900
Fax: 310-789-3944

Atlantic Records
Darren Higman
1290 Ave of Americas 25th Floor
New York, NY 10104
212-508-5480

Capitol Records
Karyn Rachtman
1750 N. Vine Street
Hollywood, CA 90028
213-871-5215
Fax: 213-871-5387

Elektra Entertainment
345 N. Maple Dr.
Suite 123
Beverly Hills, CA 90210
310-288-3826
Fax: 310-657-0277

Epic Soundtrax
Glen Brunman
2100 Colorado Blvd.
Santa Monica, CA 90404
310-449-2249
Fax: 310-449-2879

GNP-Crescendo Records
Mark Banning
8400 Sunset Blvd.
Hollywood, CA 90069
213-656-2614
Fax: 213-656-0693

Hollywood Records
Mitchell Leib
500 So. Buena Vista
Burbank, CA 91521
818-560-5124
Fax: 818-563-1227

Interscope Records
Ronnie Vance
10900 Wilshire Blvd., Suite 1230
Los Angeles, CA 90024
310-209-7689
310-824-3578

Intrada
Doug Fake
1488 Vallejo St.
San Francisco, CA 94109
415-776-1333
Fax: 415-776-2666

Koch International
2700 Shame Dr.
Westbury, NY 11590

MCA Records
Deana Cohen
70 Universal City Plaza
Universal City, CA 91608
818-777-4000
Fax: 818-777-6435

Mammoth Records
Michael Mosier
101 B Street
Carrboro, NC 27510
919-932-1882
Fax: 919-932-1885

Milan Records
Toby Pieniek
1540 Broadway
28th Floor
New York, NY 10036
212-782-1086

Polygram Soundtracks
Jacquie Perryman
1416 N. La Brea
Hollywood, CA 90028
213-856-6631
Fax: 213-856-6639

Rhino Movie Music
Julie D'Angelo
10635 Santa Monica Blvd.
Los Angeles, CA 90025
310-474-4778
Fax: 310-441-6575

Silva Screen
1600 Broadway
Suite 910
New York, NY 10019
212-757-1616
Fax: 212-757-2374

The Track Factory
Tim Sexton
8840 Wilshire Blvd.
Beverly Hills, CA 90211
310-358-3250
Fax: 310-358-3258

TVT Records
Patricia Joseph
23 E. 4th Street
3rd Floor
New York, NY 10003
212-979-6410
Fax: 212-979-6489

Cherry Entertainment Group
(through Universal Records)
Jolene Cherry
100 Wilshire Blvd., Suite1460
Santa Monica, CA 90401
310-899-0088
Fax: 310-899-0190

Varese Sarabande
Robert Townson
11846 Ventura Blvd.
Suite 130
Studio City, CA 91604
818-753-4143
Fax: 818-753-7596

Virgin Records
George Maloian
338 N. Foothill Rd.
Beverly Hills, CA 90210
310-278-1181
Fax: 310-288-2477

Warner Bros.
Danny Bramson
3300 Warner Blvd.
Burbank, CA 91505
818-846-9090
Fax: 818-953-3529

PERFORMING RIGHTS SOCIETIES

Argentina

SADAIC
Lavalle 1547, Buenos Aires, Argentina
011-54-1-40-4867/8
011-54-1-46-2533
Fax: 011-54-1-11-1985

Australia

APRA
P.O. Box 567
Crows Nest, N.S.W. 2065, Australia
011-61-2-922-6422
Fax: 011-61-2-925-0314

Austria

AKM
Baumannstrasse 10, 1031 Vienna,
Austria
011-43-222-717-14
Fax: 011-43-222-717-14210

Belgium

SABAM
Rue d'Arlon 75-77, B-1040
Brussels, Belgium
011-32-2-230-2660
Fax: 011-32-2-231-1800

Brazil

AMAR
Praia de Botafogo 462/Casa 1
CEO 22250, Rio de Janeiro, RJ, Brazil
011-5-21-286-4017

UBC
Rua Visconde de Inhauma 107
CEP 20091 Rio de Janeiro, Brazil
011-55-21-223-3233
Fax: 011-55-21-263-2884

Canada

SOCAN
41 Valleybrook Drive
Don Mills, Ontario M3B 2S6
416-445-8700
Fax: 416-445-7108

Caracas

SACVEN
Av. Andres Bello,Edif. VAM
Torre Oeste, 9 piso, Caracas, Venezuela
011-58-2-573-2389
Fax: 011-58-2-573-6187

Chile

S C D
San Antonio 427, 2 piso
Santiago, Chile
011-56-2-639-3326
011-56-2-638-4694
Fax: 011-56-2-639-7868

Colombia

SAYCO
Carrera 19 No. 40-72
Bogota, Colombia
011-57-1-287-0801
Fax: 011-57-1-287-4657

Costa Rica

ACAM
Avenida 10, C 11 y 13 - No. 1129
San Jose, Costa Rica
011-506-23-4218
Fax: 011-506-23-1684

Czech

OSA
Tr. Cs. Armady 20
160-56 Prague 6-Bubene
Czech Republic
011-42-2-312-12-41-8
Fax: 011-42-2-312-30 73

Denmark

KODA
Maltegardsvej 24
DK-2820 Gentofte, Denmark
011-45-31-68-38-00
Fax: 011-45-31-68-38-13

England

PRS
29/33 Berners Street
London, WIP 4AA, England
011-44-171-580-5544
Fax: 011-44-171-631-4138

France

SACEM
225 Avenue Charles de Gaulle
92521 Neuilly sur Seine
France
011-33-1-47-15-4715
Fax: 011-33-1-47-45-1294

Finland

TEOSTO
Lauttasaarentie 1
00200 Helsinki, Finland
358-0-692-2511
Fax: 358-0-677-134

Germany

GEMA
Rosenheimer Str. 11
D-8000 Munchen 80, Germany
011-49-89-480-03610
011-49-89-480-03000
Fax: 011-49-89-480-03969
Fax: 011-49-89-480-03620

Bayreyther Str. 37/38
1000 Berlin 30, Germany
011-49-30-214 54 000
Fax: 011-49-30-214 54 347

Greece

AEPI
14 Delighianni Street
GR. 106 83 Athens, Greece
011-30-1-821-3917
Fax: 011-30-1-821-9512

Holland

BUMA
Prof. E.M. Meijerslaan 3
1183 AV Amstelveen, Holland
011-31-20-540-7911
Fax: 011-31-20-540-7496

Hungary

ARTISJUS
P.O. Box 67
H-1364 Budapest, Hungary
011-36-1-176-222
Fax: 011-36-1-118-5597

Iceland

STEF
Laufasvegi 40, 101 Reykjavik, Iceland
011-354-2-92-26273

Israel

ACUM
P.O. Box 14.220, Tel Aviv, 61140, Israel
011-972-3-562 0115
Fax: 011-972-3-562 0119

Italy

SIAE
Vialle della Letteratura
No. 30 (EUR), 00100 Rome, Italy
011-39-6-59-901
Fax: 011-39-6-592-3351

Japan

JASRAC
7-13, 1-chome Nishishimbashi
Minato-ku, Tokyo 105, Japan
011-81-3-502-6551
Fax: 011-81-3-503-3444

Korea

KOMKA
Samjeon Bldg., 236-3 Nonhyeon-Dong
Kangnam-gu, Seoul, Korea
011-82-2-547-7080
Fax: 011-82-2-547-8909

Kowloon

CASH
Room 304, 3rd Floor, Tower I
South soas Centre, 75 Mody Road
Tsimshatsui East, Kowloon
011-852-3-722-5225
Fax: 011-852-3-699-625

Manila

FILSCAP
N I D C Building, 6th Floor
259-263 Sen. Gil J. Puyat Avenue
Near Corner Pasong Tamo Street
Makati, Metro Manila, Philippines
011-63-2-818-2699

Mexico

SACM
San Felipe No. 143, Col, Xoco
03330 Mexico D.F., Mexico
011-525-660-2285
011-525-604-7733
Fax: 011-525-524-0564

Norway

TONO
Galleri Oslo
Toyenbekken 21, Oslo 1, Norway
011-47-2-17-0500
Fax: 011-47-2-17-0550

Peru

APDAYC
Jiron Ica 559, Lima, Peru
011-51-14-32-9265
Fax: 011-51-14-3205367

Poland

ZAIKS
UL. Hipoteczna 2
00-092 Warsaw, Poland
011-48-22-2 75 77

Portugal

SPA
Ave. Duque de Louie 31
1098 Lisbon, Portugal
011-351-1-57-8320
Fax: 011-351-1-53-0257

Russia

RAIS
Copywright Agency
B. Bronnaja 6A
103670 Moscow, Russia
011-7-95-203-3260
Fax: 011-7-95-200-1263

Slovakia

SOZA
Kollarovo nam. 20
813 27 Bratislava, Slovakia
011-42-7-541-41

South Africa

SAMRO
P.O. Box 9292
Johannesburg 2000, South Africa
011-27-11-403-6635
Fax: 011-27-11-403-1934

Spain

SGAE
Fernando VI, 4
Madrid 28080, Spain
011-34-1-319-2100
Fax: 011-34-1-310-2569

Sweden

STIM
P.O. Box 27327
S-10254 Stockholm, Sweden
011-46-8-783-8800
Fax: 011-46-8-662-6275

Switzerland

SUISA
Bellariastrasse 82
CH-8032 Zurich, Switzerland
011-41-1-485-6666
Fax: 011-41-1-482-4333

Taiwan

CHA
Copyrights Holders Association
2nd Floor, No. 7
Ching Dao East Road
Taipei, Taiwan, R.O.C.
011-886-2-396-1882
Fax: 011-886-2-392-3248

United States

ASCAP
Nancy Knutsen
7920 Sunset Blvd., Suite 300
Los Angeles, CA 90046
213-883-1000

1 Lincoln Plaza
New York, NY 10023
212-621-6000

BMI
Doreen Ringer-Ross
Linda Livingston
8730 Sunset Boulevard
Third Floor West
Los Angeles, CA 90069-2211
310-659-9109
Fax: 310-657-6947

320 W. 57th Street
New York, NY 10019
212-586-2000

SESAC
421 W. 54th St.
New York, NY 10019
212-586-3450
55 Music Square East
Nashville, TN 37203
615-320-0055

Uruguay

AGADU
Canelones 1130
Montevideo, Uruguay
011-598-2-90-3188
Fax: 011-598-2-91-3951

Yugoslavia

SOKOJ
Misarka 12 - 14
11000 Belgrade
Yugoslavia
011-38-11-334-771/2
Fax: 011-38-11-336-168

Zaire

SONECA
Boite Postale 460
Kinshasa 1, Zaire

MUSIC SUPERVISORS

M
U
S
I
C

S
U
P
E
R
V
I
S
O
R
S

GEORGE ACOGNY
THE SAINT
JUNGLE 2 JUNGLE

PETER AFTERMAN
Agent: CAA – Beverly Hills – 310-288-4545
Contact: Inaudible Productions –
    Los Angeles – 213-653-3728

FATHERS DAY
APOSTLE
THE 6TH MAN
PRIVATE PARTS
SLING BLADE
ONE FINE DAY
ACE VENTURA: PET DETECTIVE
THINGS TO DO IN DENVER WHEN YOUR
    DEAD
HEAVEN'S PRISONERS
STEALING BEAUTY
FRENCH KISS
IT COULD HAPPEN TO YOU
WILD AT HEART
HONEYMOON IN VEGAS
GHOSTBUSTERS II
TWINS
THE BIG EASY

BROOKS ARTHUR
A CHORUS LINE
ALL THE RIGHT MOVES
THE KARATE KID
LEAN ON ME

CAROL SUE BAKER
Contact: Ocean Park Music Group –
    Los Angeles – 310-315-5256

LORD OF ILLUSIONS
THE HIDEAWAY
HELLRAISER III
DREAM LOVER

JELLYBEAN BENITEZ
Contact: Jellybean Productions –
    New York – 212/-777-5678
Agent: William Morris -
    Beverly Hills – 310-859-4000

CARLITO'S WAY
SPECIES
MI VIDA LOCA
THE SHADOW
THE REAL MCCOY
THE PEREZ FAMILY

KEVIN BENSON
MI FAMILIA
HOUSE PARTY

STUART BOROS
BOUND

SHARON BOYLE
Agent: Cathy Schleussner -
    Encino, 818-905-7475
Contact: Sharon Boyle & Associates –
    Los Angeles – 310-358-1890

DOUBLE TEAM
THE FAN
TRESPASS
MORTAL KOMBAT
MR. HOLLAND'S OPUS
SFW
THE AIR UP THERE
GROUNDHOG DAY
TERMINAL VELOCITY
ROMEO IS BLEEDING
POINT BREAK
DEEP COVER
THE SILENCE OF THE LAMBS
UNTIL THE END OF THE WORLD
THE WATERDANCE
QUEEN'S LOGIC
REVERSAL OF FORTUNE
MIAMI BLUES
COLORS
MARRIED TO THE MOB
SOMETHING WILD

DANNY BRAMSON
Exclusive To Warner Bros.
Contact: 818-953-3529

BATMAN & ROBIN
JERRY McGUIRE
NUTTY PROFESSOR
THE COWBOY WAY
WITH HONORS
SINGLES
BULL DURHAM
SAY ANYTHING
THE GETAWAY
NOTHING IN COMMON
TEQUILA SUNRISE

CHRIS BROOKS
INVENTING THE ABBOTTS

DAVID BYRNE
BLUE IN THE FACE

FRANK CALLARI
Agent: CAA – Beverly Hills – 310-288-4545

ANITA CAMARATA
Agent: CAA – Beverly Hills – 310-288-4545

THE FIFTH ELEMENT
BLACK SHEEP
DESTINY TURNS ON THE RADIO
THE JERKY BOYS
JOHNNY MNEMONIC
ABOVE THE RIM
LIGHT OF DAY

JOHN CAPER, JR.
THE A-TEAM
ONE AGAINST THE WIND
ALIEN NATION: MILLENIUM

BUDD CARR
Contact: Windswept Entertainment –
    Beverly Hills – 310-550-1500
Agent: Gorfaine-Schwartz –
    Los Angeles – 213-969-1011

DONNIE BRASCO
TWISTER
NATURAL BORN KILLERS
HEAT
NIXON
COPYCAT
AT CLOSE RANGE
THE DOORS
THE PATRIOT
PLATOON
TALK RADIO

PETER COQUILLARD
Agent: Air-Edel - Los Angeles, 310-914-5000

APOLLO 13
STRIPTEASE
WITH HONORS
FORREST GUMP

MICHAEL DILBECK
BULLETPROOF
BAD BOYS
BATMAN
OVER THE TOP

CHRIS DOURIDAS
Agent: Gorfaine-Schwartz –
    Los Angeles – 213-969-1011

GROSSE POINTE BLANK
GRACE OF MY HEART
HEAT
THE NEW AGE
NORTHERN EXPOSURE

DAVID FRANCO
Contact: David Franco International
    Productions – 310-823-5547

SELENA
I'LL TAKE MANHATTAN
DEATH OF A POET
SURVIVORS OF THE SHOAH
PLATOON

RANDY GERSTON
Exclusive to Rysher Entertainment
Contact: 310-309-5383

TITANIC
A SMILE LIKE YOURS
STRANGE DAYS
TRUE LIES
SLEEP WITH ME
TOMBSTONE
RENAISSANCE MAN

DAVID GOLDBERG
DESPERATELY SEEKING SUSAN
DIRTY DANCING
THE LIGHT OF DAY

**M
U
S
I
C

S
U
P
E
R
V
I
S
O
R
S**

STEPHAN R. GOLDMAN
Agent: The Kordek Agency -
    Burbank, 818-559-4248

THE BRAVE
LOLITA
BOGUS
THE JOY LUCK CLUB
THE MISSION
THE GODFATHER: PART III

BONNIE GREENBERG
Contact: B Sharp Group –
    Los Angeles – 310-275-6646

MY BEST FRIEND'S WEDDING
THE LONG KISS GOODNIGHT
THE TRUTH ABOUT CATS & DOGS
NAKED IN NEW YORK
MENACE TO SOCIETY
DEAD PRESIDENTS
TANK GIRL
BEYOND THERAPY
BLIND FEAR
THE MASK
HAIRSPRAY
JUDY COLLINS, GIRL FROM THE WEST

EVAN GREENSPAN
Contact: EMG 818-762-9656

CARRIED AWAY
AMELIA EARHART: THE FINAL FLIGHT

BARKLIE K. GRIGGS
Agent: Vangelos Management -
    Encino, 818-380-1919

STILL BREATHING
THE ASSOCIATE
BARB WIRE
THE LAST WORD

TIM HAUSER
Contact: 818-508-7791

THE MARRYING MAN

ANDY HILL
Agent: Air-Edel - Los Angeles, 310-914-5000

HOODLUMS
WASHINGTON SQUARE
ANASTASIA

BONES HOWE
Agent: Cathy Schleusner –
    Encino – 818-905-7475

NATIONAL LAMPOON'S VEGAS VACATION
ZEUS AND ROXANNE
BACK TO THE FUTURE
CIRCLE OF FRIENDS
THE PRINCE OF TIDES
BOYZ 'N THE HOOD
RADIO INSIDE
SERIAL MOM

JULIANNE KELLEY
Agent: CAA – Beverly Hills – 310-288-4545

SWINGERS
LUCIA
LAUGHING OUT LOUD

EVYEN KLEAN
Agent: Vangelos Management -
    Encino, 818-380-1919
Contact: Neophonic, Inc. - 213-466-8776

A SMILE LIKE YOURS
JOYRIDE
MEET WALLY SPARKS
MIGHTY DUCKS 2
BYE BYE LOVE

JACKIE KROST
Agent: Air-Edel - Los Angeles, 310-914-5000

LOVE! VALOUR! COMPASSION!
BENNY AND JOON
UNDERCOVER BLUES
DANGEROUS LIAISONS
UNTAMED HEART

KEN KUSHNICK
Contact: 310-470-5909

THE BEAUTICIAN AND THE BEAST
THE NEXT KARATE KID
BEVERLY HILLS COP 3
LOOK WHO'S TALKING NOW
LOOK WHO'S TALKING
NECESSARY ROUGHNESS
BUTCHER'S WIFE
MANNEQUIN ON THE MOVE
SLAVES OF NEW YORK
NO MAN'S LAND
LIKE FATHER LIKE SON
MIAMI VICE (1986-1987)

ANDREW LEARY
2 DAYS IN THE VALLEY

ELLIOT LURIE
Agent: Vangelos Management -
    Encino, 818-380-1919

FIRST STRIKE
LARGER THAN LIFE
DEAR GOD
RUMBLE IN THE BRONX

ALLAN MASON
Agent: Film Music Associates –
    North Hollywood – 818-761-4040

DONNIE BRASCO
LARGER THAN LIFE
SLEEPERS
FATHER OF THE BRIDE II
BENNY & JOON
BUGSY
GOOD MORNING, VIETNAM
RAIN MAN

PILAR McCURRY
Agent: CAA – Beverly Hills – 310-288-4545

B.A.P.S.
LOVE JONES
GRIDLOCK'D
WHITE MAN'S BURDEN
SET IT OFF
KINGPIN
TO WONG FOO

BENNIE MEDINA
BOOTY CALL

JEFF MOST
THE CROW: CITY OF ANGELS

RANDALL POSTER
Contact: 212-603-3920

KISS ME GUIDO
SUBURBIA
I SHOT ANDY WARHOL
KIDS
RECKLESS

DEREK POWER
Contact: 310-472-4647

CAT CHASER
THE EQUALIZER
HIGHLANDER
YOUNGBLOOD

SPENCER PROFFER
Agent: Film Music Associates –
    North Hollywood – 818-761-4040

ANDRE
PHENOMENON
PINOCCHIO
UP THE CREEK

JEFF RABHAN
SCREAM

KARYN RACHTMAN
c/o Capitol Records
213-462-6252

FEELING MINNESOTA
GRACE OF MY HEART
BASKETBALL DIARIES
CLUELESS
GET SHORTY
FRESH
GUNMAN
PULP FICTION
REALITY BITES
RESERVOIR DOGS
THE LAST SEDUCTION

PHIL RAMONE
Agent: Gorfaine-Schwartz –
    Los Angeles – 213-969-1011

EXTREME
A STAR IS BORN
GHOSTBUSTERS
WHITE NIGHTS
LIKEWISE

**MARY RAMOS & MICHELLE
KUZNETSKY (TRI TONE MUSIC)**
Agent: CAA – Beverly Hills – 310-288-4545

DANGEROUS GROUND (Coordinators)
PREFONTAINE
BEVERLY HILLS NINJA
FROM DUSK 'TIL DAWN
HAPPY GILMORE
REBEL HIGHWAY
AMERICAN STRAYS
COPLAND

G. MARQ ROSWELL
Contact: C/O BEACON ENTERTAINMENT
213-850-2500

THE THING CALLED LOVE
THREE OF HEARTS
GUN IN BETTY LOU'S HANDBAG
CAREER OPPORTUNIITES
THE COMMITMENTS
SLEEPING WITH THE ENEMY
THE BLUE IGUANA
CROSS MY HEART
TIN MEN

DICK RUDOLPH
Contact: Douglas-Reuther Prods –
    Los Angeles – 213-956-5700

THE PEST
BAJA OKLAHOMA
DEAD SOLID PERFECT
FLATLINERS
NO MERCY
RUNNING SCARED

RALPH SALL
Contact: Bulletproof Recording
Los Angeles - 213-656-8278

GOING WEST IN AMERICA
OVERNIGHT DELIVERY
BIO-DOME
BILLY MADISON
SPEED
ADAMS FAMILY VALUES
ENCINO MAN
THE CRAFT
BUFFY THE VAMPIRE SLAYER
TREMORS

AMANDA SCHEER-DEMME
FOXFIRE
ALBINO ALLIGATOR
BEAUTIFUL GIRLS

BEN SIDRAN
Agent: Gorfaine-Schwartz –
    Los Angeles – 213-969-1011

HOOP DREAMS

GREG SILL
Agent: The Kordek Agency -
    Burbank, 818-559-4248

FRIENDS
ER
LIVING SINGLE
SISTERS

JOEL SILL
Contact: Windswept Pacific Entertainment –
    310-550-1500
Agent: Gorfaine-Schwartz –
    Los Angeles – 213-969-1011

STRIPTEASE
TWISTER
FORREST GUMP
BRIGHT LIGHTS, BIG CITY
THE FABULOUS BAKER BOYS
MY COUSIN VINNY
COUP DE VILLE
FLASHDANCE
LA BAMBA
PURPLE RAIN

DAWN SOLER
Agent: CAA – Beverly Hills – 310-288-4545

THE GAME
GRIDLOCK'D
PORTRAIT OF A LADY
DEAD MAN WALKING
DON JUAN DEMARCO
DUMB AND DUMBER
NEW JERSEY DRIVE
NOW AND THEN

STEVEN SOLES
Agent: Seth Kaplan 213-525-3477

GEORGIA
THE THING CALLED LOVE (Musical Director)

BILL STEPHNEY
212-366-7200

THE GREAT WHITE HYPE
BEBE'S KIDS

ALEX STEYERMARK
Agent: Vangelos Management –
    Encino – 818-380-1919

ARRESTING GINA
TOUCH
ULEE'S GOLD
GET ON THE BUS
THE ICE STORM
GIRL 6
CROOKLYN
CLOCKERS
FOR LOVE OR MONEY
MALCOLM X

STEVE TYRELL
Contact: Tyrell Music Group –
    8295 Sunset Blvd.,
    Los Angeles, CA 90046

THE HEIGHTS
BABY BOOM
FRANK'S PLACE
GLORY GLORY
MYSTIC PIZZA

ROBIN D. URDANG
Contact: Reel Music – 310-360-0244

THE REAL BLONDE
OUT TO SEA
BASTARD OUT OF CAROLINA
EDIE & PEN
EDEN
LIVE NUDE GIRLS
GEORGIA

KENNY VANCE
EDDIE AND THE CRUISERS
HEART OF DIXIE
LONG GONE
STREETS OF FIRE 1

CHRIS VIOLETTE
Agent: CAA – Beverly Hills – 310-288-4545

EVERY DOG HAS ITS DAY
THE LAST TIME I COMMITED SUICIDE
THE PRICE OF KISSING
SHOOTING LILY

HAPPY WALTERS
Agent: Steve Crawford, ICM 310-550-4000

8 HEADS IN A DUFFEL BAG
RHYME & REASON
TO GILLIAN ON HER 37TH BIRTHDAY
BAD BOYS
THE SCARLET LETTER
WHITE MAN'S BURDEN
BLANKMAN
JUDGEMENT NIGHT

DIANE WESSEL
Contact: Ruby Beat, 213-650-2116

THE SECOND WIFE
STRAWBERRY FIELDS
HYSTERIA
ROWING THROUGH
NABITAT
WILD SIDE
THE GRASS HARP
THE WILD SIDE
HARLEY DAVIDSON & THE MARLBORO
    MAN
SIBLING RIVALRY

Get listed in our new ON-LINE SERVICE and future CD-ROM and DIRECTORY
FILM COMPOSERS GUIDE – 5th Edition
Alllistingsarefree.

INSTRUCTIONS: Qualified composers (or their agents) should fill out information and mail or fax immediately to Lone Eagle (see phone/fax below.) Photocopy this form as necessary.
Please include proof of film credit such as reviews, advertisements, copy of video box, one sheets, etc.

PLEASE PRINT OR TYPE

PERSONAL INFORMATION

Name (as you prefer to be listed)

Company

Address

City/State/Zip

Area Code/Telephone

Birth Date & Place

e-mail address

❏ Home   ❏ Business
❏ Please list my home address and phone number in your directory.

REPRESENTATIVE'S INFORMATION

(List as many representatives as you would like.)
❏ Agent   ❏ Personal Mgr.   ❏ Atty.   ❏ Business Mgr.

Name (as you prefer to be listed)

Company

Address

City/State/Zip

Area Code/Telephone

e-mail address

AFFILIATIONS Please list all Guild, Union and Society memberships:

CREDITS (*Attach a separate sheet, if necessary*) List your credits as follows, noting title, type of work, distribution company, year of release, alternate titles in parentheses, Academy and Emmy nominations/awards for your work, co-composers and adaptations. Please include any additional nominations and awards. Please note the following samples:

DANCES WITH WOLVES ★★   Orion, 1990
STEPHEN KING'S "IT" (MS) ☆   Green-Epstein, 1990
GHANDI ★   co-composer with George Fenton, Colubmia, 1982, British-Indian

---

INDEX OF ADVERTISERS

A
D
V
E
R
T
I
S
E
R
S

ABOUT THE AUTHOR

Vincent J. Francillon has published many interviews with film composers, notably Maurice Jarre, Hans Zimmer, Jerry Goldsmith, Basil Poledouris and Alf Clausen. He currently serves on the Board of Trustees of the Society for the Preservation of Film Music, was a graduate student at the USC School of Cinema-Television where he wrote the music for numerous student films, and is currently producing an upcoming soundtrack album.

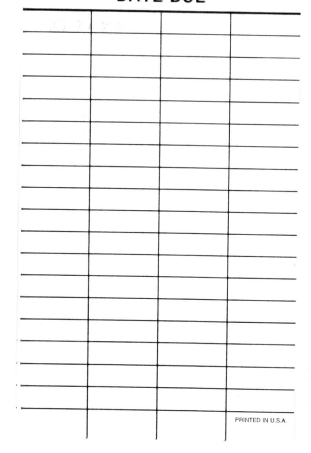

DATE DUE

PRINTED IN U.S.A.